D1414362

Presented to

Julisa Louann Skeens

by _Mom_

on _July 26th_ 19 _85_

_I love you - May you
learn to love + grow
through God's Word._

Youth Bible

An Illustrated Edition
for Youth with
Special Helps for Discipleship,
Evangelism, and Bible Study

New American Standard

Holman Bible Publishers
Nashville

Printed in the United States of America
1 2 3 4 5 6 7 8 9 89 88 87 86 85

Contents

Acknowledgments

The editors of DiscipleYouth Bible express their gratitude to the following authors, editors, and publishers for permission to use materials in DiscipleYouth Bible.

The Eternal Life Birth Certificate, is adapted from *Welcome to God's Family,* Nashville: Convention Press.

Material in "How to Read the Bible Through" is adapted from *Master Study Bible,* Nashville: Holman Bible Publishers, 1981, and from Howard P. Colson, *I Recommend the Bible,* Nashville: Broadman Press, 1976.

"Bible Reading Record" is adapted from R. Clyde Hall, Jr., and Joe L. Ford, compilers, *Disicple Youth Notebook.*

"How to Study the Bible" is adapted from Michael Fink, *equipping youth,* April-June 1985.

"How to Memorize Scripture" is adapted from *DiscipleHelps: a DiscipleYouth Daily Quiet Time Guide* compiled by R. Clyde Hall, Jr., 1984, and from Rollin Delap, "A Plan to Memorize Scripture," *equipping youth,* April-June 1984.

"Using the Roman Road to Share the Gospel," is adapted from Howard Ramsey, *equipping youth,* April-June, 1985.

"Where to Find Help" is adapted from *Truths That Make a Difference* by Lavonn D. Brown, Nashville, Convention Press, 1980.

Study Helps Design Team

R. Clyde Hall, Jr., chairman
Martha Jo Glazner, design editor
Trent Butler
Dean Finley
Johnnie Godwin

Louis Hanks
Samuel J. House, Jr.
Don Mattingly
W. Don Rogers
Terry York

Contributors

Lavonn D. Brown
Martha Jo Glazner
Joe L. Ford
R. Clyde Hall, Jr.
Howard P. Colson
Rollin DeLap
Richard Barnes
Tim Sledge

Louis Hanks
Avery Willis
George E. Worrell
Michael Fink
John Hendrix
Howard Ramsey
Dean Finley

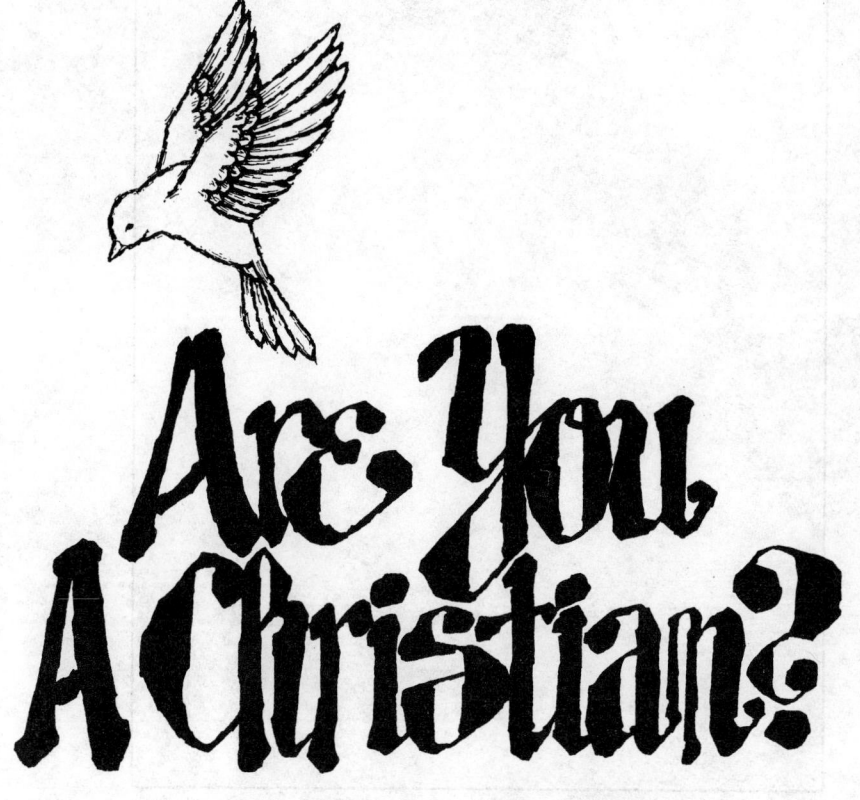

Are You A Christian?

Are You a Christian?

The Bible records God's redemptive message to all people in all places. Study aids in this Bible are especially designed to help you meet God, get right with Him, and then grow in that relationship. If you have never talked with God and confessed your sin, this section will help you. In the Bible you will find actions that God has already taken to make right your relationship with Him. The Bible will show you how you should respond to God's actions.

If you have already accepted God's invitation to be rightly related to Him, the following plan can help you in two ways: (1) You can study the Bible to be sure you have followed God's plan of salvation. (2) You can learn to show someone who is not a Christian how to respond to God's redemptive love.

The Plan of Salvation

You are important to God. Before God created the world, He worked out a plan to set you in right relation with Him. Why did He do this? Because He loves you and wants you to enjoy the best life possible. How can you enjoy God's good life for you? One way to find out is to follow what is called the Roman Road. The Roman Road is a group of verses found in the book of Romans. By following the Roman Road, you learn about God's plan of salvation. You can also use the Roman Road to show someone you know how to accept Jesus as Lord and Savior. You will want to read the Roman Road several times. You will want to be ready to show it to your friends. To make this easier, mark the verses in your *Disciple Youth Bible*.

Mark Your Bible

The first step is to find the Scripture verses in this Bible on the suggested pages and mark them as directed. When you are marking in this Bible, you will need a red ballpoint pen to do the printing at the top and bottom of each page and a soft, red-lead pencil or solid Bible highlighter to underline (or shade) the verses in the biblical text. The following directions are *guidelines for marking a plan of salvation in this Bible*.

1. On the first page of this Bible, print *Turn to page* 1119.

2. On top of page 1119, print *We are all sinners*. Read and underline Romans 3:10-12,23. On the bottom of the page, print *Turn to page* 1122.

3. On top of page 1122, print *The penalty for sin*. Read and underline Romans 6:23. On the bottom of the page, print *Turn to page* 1121.

4. On top of page 1121, print *The payment God made for our sin*. Read and underline Romans 5:8-9. On the bottom of the page, print *Turn to page* 1126.

5. On top of page 1126, print *Confess Jesus as Lord. Ask God to save you*. Read and underline Romans 10:9-10,13. On the bottom of the page, print *Turn to page* 5a and read the following prayer:

How to Ask God to Save You

Dear God: *I know you love me. I realize I am a sinner.* I have not lived as You have wanted me to live. I believe Your Son, Jesus, died for me on the cross and was raised from the death to provide forgiveness and eternal life. Please save me as I turn from my sins, place my faith in Jesus and receive Him as Lord and Savior. I will no longer live according to my selfish desires and plans but will follow Your desires and plans for my life. *Thank You for saving me and giving me eternal life. I pray this prayer in Jesus' name,* **Amen.**

Follow up This Experience

Welcome to God's Family! If you have just declared your faith in Christ for the first time, you are now part of the family of God. God has taken away all your guilt. You are ready for the excitement of real life with Jesus. If you became a Christian earlier, you are already a member of the family of God. In either case, you will want something to help you remember the excitement and meaning of this experience. Here is your spiritual birth certificate. Complete it and turn to it often as a reminder of what God has done in your life.

Eternal Life Birth Certificate

And the witness is this, that God has given us eternal life, and this life is in His Son. He who has the Son has life; he who does not have the Son of God does not have life. These things I have written to you who believe in the name of the Son of God, in order that you may know you have eternal life! (Read 1 John 5:11-13.)

I have accepted Jesus as my Lord and Savior and have eternal life with God.

_____   July 29, 1985
        signed   date

❧❧❧

Turn to page 1211 in your *Disciple Youth Bible* and underline 1 John 5:11-13. To understand even better what salvation means to you, you will want to read John 5:24. Turn to page 1056 and underline John 5:24. Rejoice in the fact that you are now one of God's children.

First Steps as God's Child

You have accepted Christ and become a member of God's family. Now what do you do? Just as a new member of a human family, you want to grow. A baby's first steps are exciting. Your first steps as a Christian will be exciting, too. You will want to take these four steps as soon as you can.

1. Read your Bible each day. God's Word is essential for spiritual growth just as food is for physical growth. Turn to page 1202 in your *Disciple Youth Bible*. Read and underline 1 Peter 2:2-3.

- God's Word will help you grow . . . read it daily.
- God's Word will help guide you . . . listen as it is taught.
- God's Word will help keep you from sin . . . memorize it.
- God's Word will teach you how to live . . . study it.
- God's Word will inspire you . . . meditate on it.
- God's Word will work . . . try it.

My best time to read God's Word each day is _____

2. Pray at the start and close of each day. Prayer is essential to spiritual growth just as breath is to physical growth. Turn in your *Disciple Youth Bible* to page 1208 and underline 1 John 1:9. Praying is like breathing . . .

- As you exhale . . . talk to God.
- As you inhale . . . listen to God.
- Talk to God anytime . . . to worship Him.
- Talk to God anytime . . . you need help.
- Talk to God anytime . . . you are lonely.
- Talk to God anytime . . . you need strength.
- Talk to God anytime . . . you want guidance.
- Talk to God anytime . . . you are tempted.
- Talk to God anytime . . . you sin or fail.

3. Be baptized and join God's church. The church is essential to spiritual growth just as the home is to the baby's growth. What a good home and family are to a baby, the church is to a new Christian. The church is God's people.

- God's people will . . . rejoice in your new birth
  as a Christian,
  accept you in love,
  encourage and support you,
  teach and train you to live
  as a Christian,
  worship God with you.

An important step in identifying with Jesus and your new church family is to be baptized. Turn to page 1081 in your *Disciple Youth Bible* and underline Acts 2:41-47. When you are baptized, you show your friends, family, and church your faith in the death, burial, and resurrection of Jesus Christ. Baptism does not save you, but it shows your obedience to the example and teachings of Jesus. Jesus walked sixty miles to be baptized. Turn to page 988 and read about Jesus' baptism in Mark 1:9-11. Because he placed that much importance on it, you also need to follow his example and be baptized. Baptism is the first act that shows your gratefulness and obedience to God for saving you.

4. Share your faith. Learning to communicate your faith to others is just as important as a baby's learning to talk. As they try to communicate, babies learn and grow. You will grow as you share your new life with others. Turn to page 988 in your *Disciple Youth Bible* and underline Matthew 28:18-20. Who would be the happiest person to know God has saved you? Write that persons's name here: *Mother (Lisa Dundon)* Whom do you know who needs to know about Jesus? You can share your experience with this person. Write that person's name here: _____
Date I shared my salvation experience with this person: _____.
Summary: To grow spiritually . . .

1. Read and think about God's Word daily.
2. Pray regularly.
3. Be baptized and join a church in your community.
4. Share your faith with other people.

These are the first steps you need to take. You will find in this Bible additional helps for studying the Bible, growing as a disciple of Christ, and sharing your faith.

Growing As A Christian

Read the Bible Throughout Your Life

The reading and studying of God's Word is a life-long endeavor that never grows old. Once you have read the Bible through, read it again—in a different translation. Choose different reading plans and schedules. Every time you read through God's Word, you will discover new and meaningful truths.

The Bible holds the answer to humanity's past, present, and future. It is a wellspring of wisdom and divine instruction that never runs dry. Draw from this spring daily and find direction and purpose for your life.

52-Week Bible Reading Plan

1—Genesis 1—26
2—Genesis 27—50
3—Matthew
4—Mark
5—Exodus 1—21
6—Exodus 22—40
7—Luke
8—John
9—Leviticus
10—Acts
11—Numbers 1—18
12—Numbers 19—36
13—Romans; Galatians
14—1 & 2 Corinthians
15—Deuteronomy 1—17
16—Deuteronomy 18—34
17—Ephesians; Philippians; Colossians; 1 & 2 Thessalonians; 1 & 2 Timothy; Titus; Philemon
18—Hebrews; James; 1 & 2 Peter
19—Joshua
20—1, 2, & 3 John; Jude; Revelation
21—Judges; Ruth
22—Job 1—31
23—Job 32—42; Ecclesiastes; Song of Solomon
24—1 Samuel
25—2 Samuel
26—Psalms 1—50

27—1 Kings
28—2 Kings
29—Psalms 51—100
30—1 Chronicles
31—2 Chronicles
32—Psalms 101—150
33—Ezra; Nehemiah; Esther
34—Proverbs
35—Matthew
36—Isaiah 1—35
37—Isaiah 36—66
38—Mark
39—Luke
40—Jeremiah 1—29
41—Jeremiah 30—52; Lamentations
42—John
43—Acts
44—Ezekiel 1—24
45—Ezekiel 25—48
46—Romans; Galatians
47—1 & 2 Corinthians
48—Daniel; Hosea; Joel; Amos
49—Ephesians; Philippians; Colossians; 1 & 2 Thessalonians; 1 & 2 Timothy; Titus; Philemon
50—Obadiah; Jonah; Micah; Nahum; Habakkuk; Zephaniah; Haggai; Zechariah; Malachi
51—Hebrews; James; 1 & 2 Peter
52—1, 2, & 3 John; Jude; Revelation

Growing as a Christian

Discipleship Helps

How to Have a Quiet Time

When you commit your life to God, you begin a new relationship with Him. You become one of His children. You enter into a permanent relationship with God. This relationship with God enables you to have fellowship with Him. You will naturally ask, how do I have fellowship with God. The same way you have fellowship with a person. You enter into conversation. The Bible calls this conversation prayer. You need to find a quiet time each day when you talk to and listen to God.

A quiet time is a way of maintaining fellowship with God and evaluating your life-style. A quiet time is a way of building spiritual strength, becoming more sensitive to God's leadership, and applying His Word to your actions.

Two Essential Steps for Getting Started

STEP 1: Make a commitment to observe a daily quiet time.

Decide that your quiet time will be your first priority each day. Decide that each morning or evening you will devote at least 15 minutes for quiet time with God. Avoid thoughts like *After a while, I will have my quiet time. First, I must . . .*

STEP 2: Develop a plan for observing your daily quiet time.

Establish a regular schedule for your quiet time. Mark the time you will begin each day on the clock.

Decide where you will have your quiet time. You may choose a particular place in your room. When weather permits, you may want to go outdoors for your quiet time. Your quiet time place should be as free from distractions as possible. Choose a place where you can read your Bible and make notes.

My quiet time place will be

_____

If you miss lunch, do you quit eating altogether? Of course not! If you miss your quiet time one day, start again the next day.

Realize that some quiet times will be more meaningful than others. Don't expect every quiet time to be an emotional high.

*One Thing You Must Do If
Your Quiet Time Is to Succeed*

KEEP ON KEEPING ON

If possible, enlist one or two other Christians as prayer partners to encourage you. Be honest with one another. Confess to one another when you miss a day. Support one another in prayer, and discuss ways you can each be more consistent in having a quiet time.

Jesus spent time with His Heavenly Father, seeking fellowship, strength, and guidance. If God's Son needed to spend time with Him, how much more do you need to spend time with Him? Having a quiet time, you will become more like Christ as you follow His example and as you receive His power through prayer and the Word.

What do I do in my quiet time? This is a natural question for a new Christian. You will want to read and study your Bible, memorize parts of your Bible, and talk to God about the joys and sorrows, hopes and fears, fun and frustrations of your life. Information on the following pages will help you learn to do each of these.

How to Read the Bible Through

Your quiet time will usually begin with listening to God's Word. You do this by reading the Bible. But where do I begin, you may ask.

Reading the Bible through from *Genesis 1* to *Revelation 22* is not necessarily the best way to read this unique library. You would be a long time getting to the life and ministry of Jesus Christ as revealed in the Gospels. You will want to balance your Bible reading by alternating between the Old and New Testaments. Here are five approaches for reading through the Bible. Choose one and start reading.

1. Place a bookmark in the Bible at three places: Genesis, Job, and Matthew. By reading one chapter from each of these sections every day, you will read the Old Testament once and the New Testament twice in about eighteen months.

2. Read one Bible chapter a day, and you will read the entire Bible in three years and three months.

3. Read three Bible chapters every weekday and five chapters on Sundays, and you will read the entire Bible in less than a year.

4. In January and February, read Genesis through Deuteronomy. In March and April, read all of the New Testament. In May and June, read Joshua through Esther. In July and August, read Job through Song of Solomon. In September and October, reread all of the New Testament. In November and December, read Isaiah through Malachi.

5. The weekly Bible reading plan on page 10a will guide you in reading through the Old Testament once and the New Testament twice in one year.

The Bible Reading Record on pages 13a-15a will help you chart your progress in reading through the Bible. Always keep a Bible reading notebook or journal so you can compare your notes and observations each time you read particular Bible books.

BIBLE READING RECORD

When you have read a chapter, mark a slash through the square. Beside each book write the date and year you finish reading it. You might keep a separate record of each translation you are reading. Use a different color for marking a slash when you have read the chapter a second time. As you finish each book, ask God, *"What do you want me to do with what I have read?"*

Old Testament

Genesis	1	2	3	4	5	6	7	8	9	10	11	12	13	14	15	16	17	18	19	20
	21	22	23	24	25	26	27	28	29	30	31	32	33	34	35	36	37	38	39	40
	41	42	43	44	45	46	47	48	49	50										
Exodus	1	2	3	4	5	6	7	8	9	10	11	12	13	14	15	16	17	18	19	20
	21	22	23	24	25	26	27	28	29	30	31	32	33	34	35	36	37	38	39	40
Leviticus	1	2	3	4	5	6	7	8	9	10	11	12	13	14	15	16	17	18	19	20
	21	22	23	24	25	26	27													
Numbers	1	2	3	4	5	6	7	8	9	10	11	12	13	14	15	16	17	18	19	20
	21	22	23	24	25	26	27	28	29	30	31	32	33	34	35	36				
Deuteronomy	1	2	3	4	5	6	7	8	9	10	11	12	13	14	15	16	17	18	19	20
	21	22	23	24	25	26	27	28	29	30	31	32	33	34						
Joshua	1	2	3	4	5	6	7	8	9	10	11	12	13	14	15	16	17	18	19	20
	21	22	23	24																
Judges	1	2	3	4	5	6	7	8	9	10	11	12	13	14	15	16	17	18	19	20
	21																			
Ruth	1	2	3	4																
1 Samuel	1	2	3	4	5	6	7	8	9	10	11	12	13	14	15	16	17	18	19	20
	21	22	23	24	25	26	27	28	29	30	31									
2 Samuel	1	2	3	4	5	6	7	8	9	10	11	12	13	14	15	16	17	18	19	20
	21	22	23	24																
1 Kings	1	2	3	4	5	6	7	8	9	10	11	12	13	14	15	16	17	18	19	20
	21	22																		
2 Kings	1	2	3	4	5	6	7	8	9	10	11	12	13	14	15	16	17	18	19	20
	21	22	23	24	25															
1 Chronicles	1	2	3	4	5	6	7	8	9	10	11	12	13	14	15	16	17	18	19	20
	21	22	23	24	25	26	27	28	29											

2 Chronicles	1	2	3	4	5	6	7	8	9	10	11	12	13	14	15	16	17	18	19	20
	21	22	23	24	25	26	27	28	29	30	31	32	33	34	35	36				
Ezra	1	2	3	4	5	6	7	8	9	10										
Nehemiah	1	2	3	4	5	6	7	8	9	10	11	12	13							
Esther	1	2	3	4	5	6	7	8	9	10										
Job	1	2	3	4	5	6	7	8	9	10	11	12	13	14	15	16	17	18	19	20
	21	22	23	24	25	26	27	28	29	30	31	32	33	34	35	36	37	38	39	40
	41	42																		
Psalms	1	2	3	4	5	6	7	8	9	10	11	12	13	14	15	16	17	18	19	20
	21	22	23	24	25	26	27	28	29	30	31	32	33	34	35	36	37	38	39	40
	41	42	43	44	45	46	47	48	49	50	51	52	53	54	55	56	57	58	59	60
	61	62	63	64	65	66	67	68	69	70	71	72	73	74	75	76	77	78	79	80
	81	82	83	84	85	86	87	88	89	90	91	92	93	94	95	96	97	98	99	100
	101	102	103	104	105	106	107	108	109	110	111	112	113	114	115	116	117	118	119	120
	121	122	123	124	125	126	127	128	129	130	131	132	133	134	135	136	137	138	139	140
	141	142	143	144	145	146	147	148	149	150										
Proverbs	1	2	3	4	5	6	7	8	9	10	11	12	13	14	15	16	17	18	19	20
	21	22	23	24	25	26	27	28	29	30	31									
Ecclesiastes	1	2	3	4	5	6	7	8	9	10	11	12								
Song of Solomon	1	2	3	4	5	6	7	8												

Isaiah	1	2	3	4	5	6	7	8	9	10	11	12	13	14	15	16	17	18	19	20
	21	22	23	24	25	26	27	28	29	30	31	32	33	34	35	36	37	38	39	40
	41	42	43	44	45	46	47	48	49	50	51	52	53	54	55	56	57	58	59	60
	61	62	63	64	65	66														
Jeremiah	1	2	3	4	5	6	7	8	9	10	11	12	13	14	15	16	17	18	19	20
	21	22	23	24	25	26	27	28	29	30	31	32	33	34	35	36	37	38	39	40
	41	42	43	44	45	46	47	48	49	50	51	52								
Lamentations	1	2	3	4	5															
Ezekiel	1	2	3	4	5	6	7	8	9	10	11	12	13	14	15	16	17	18	19	20
	21	22	23	24	25	26	27	28	29	30	31	32	33	34	35	36	37	38	39	40
	41	42	43	44	45	46	47	48												
Daniel	1	2	3	4	5	6	7	8	9	10	11	12								
Hosea	1	2	3	4	5	6	7	8	9	10	11	12	13	14						
Joel	1	2	3																	
Amos	1	2	3	4	5	6	7	8	9											
Obadiah	1																			
Jonah	1	2	3	4																
Micah	1	2	3	4	5	6	7													

Nahum	1	2	3																
Habakkuk	1	2	3																
Zephaniah	1	2	3																
Haggai	1	2																	
Zechariah	1	2	3	4	5	6	7	8	9	10	11	12	13	14					
Malachi	1	2	3	4															

New Testament

Matthew	1	2	3	4	5	6	7	8	9	10	11	12	13	14	15	16	17	18	19	20
	21	22	23	24	25	26	27	28												
Mark	1	2	3	4	5	6	7	8	9	10	11	12	13	14	15	16				
Luke	1	2	3	4	5	6	7	8	9	10	11	12	13	14	15	16	17	18	19	20
	21	22	23	24																
John	1	2	3	4	5	6	7	8	9	10	11	12	13	14	15	16	17	18	19	20
	21																			
Acts	1	2	3	4	5	6	7	8	9	10	11	12	13	14	15	16	17	18	19	20
	21	22	23	24	25	26	27	28												
Romans	1	2	3	4	5	6	7	8	9	10	11	12	13	14	15	16				
1 Corinthians	1	2	3	4	5	6	7	8	9	10	11	12	13	14	15	16				
2 Corinthians	1	2	3	4	5	6	7	8	9	10	11	12	13							
Galatians	1	2	3	4	5	6														
Ephesians	1	2	3	4	5	6														
Philippians	1	2	3	4																
Colossians	1	2	3	4																
1 Thessalonians	1	2	3	4	5															
2 Thessalonians	1	2	3																	
1 Timothy	1	2	3	4	5	6														
2 Timothy	1	2	3	4																
Titus	1	2	3																	
Philemon	1																			
Hebrews	1	2	3	4	5	6	7	8	9	10	11	12	13							
James	1	2	3	4	5															
1 Peter	1	2	3	4	5															
2 Peter	1	2	3																	
1 John	1	2	3	4	5															
2 John	1																			
3 John	1																			
Jude	1																			
Revelation	1	2	3	4	5	6	7	8	9	10	11	12	13	14	15	16	17	18	19	20
	21	22																		

How to Study the Bible

Reading the Bible will whet your appetite and arouse your mental curiosity. You will ask, how can I find answers to my questions? How can I learn more about the Bible? Thus you will want to do more than read. You will want to study the Bible.

Bible study can become a means of communication with God. Through Bible study God can reveal Himself to us. He can show us what he wants us to be as His people. Through the study of God's Word we can begin to dialogue with God about our lives and His will.

We should not allow our study of God's Word to become a monologue. If the Bible is to be an instrument through which we dialogue with God, we must be able to distinguish our thoughts from God's thoughts and our conclusions from God's conclusions. This need prompts the following suggestions on how to study the Bible.

Step 1: **Daily Study**
No plan of Bible study will guarantee an instant sense of successful communication with God. As with an infant, we first must learn to sense, hear, understand, imitate, and finally speak before meaningful dialogue can occur. The principles of dialogue are learned in daily Bible study. A few minutes each day spent studying the Bible begins to develop the discipline needed to dialogue with God through His Word.

Step 2: **Extended Study**
Once daily Bible reading has become a major part of our lives, we will begin to long for deeper involvement in God's Word. This longing may not come early in our experience of daily Bible study. At first we may have to discipline ourselves and struggle to spend five or ten minutes each day reading the Bible. Like a child beginning to walk, we will keep losing

our balance and toppling over. However, keeping at it will pay off. Soon we will long for more.

The first symptom we are ready for Step 2 is a dissatisfaction with merely reading eight or ten verses of Scripture each day. We begin to want more. Gradually we begin to expand our Bible reading—more time spent in Bible study each day and more verses read.

As we extend our Bible study, we begin to look for a plan to make our study systematic. This is the time to develop and carry out a plan to read the Bible through. As you carry out this plan, you will discover one or more books that speak to particular needs and questions in your life. You will want to concentrate on these books, reading a chapter or two of a favorite book each day and learning how to study the book in depth.

At this stage of development you may begin to feel the need to record some of your impressions growing out of Bible study. Underline passages in your Bible, write notes in the margin, even make extensive notes on separate sheets of paper or in a notebook. These impressions become a record of your understanding of God's Word. A large, loose-leaf Bible with wide margins is helpful for recording impressions growing out of Bible study. Pages of notes can be inserted where needed. This becomes a valuable record of dialogue with God.

Step 3: **Deepened Study**
As you read more and more of the Bible, you begin to develop some sensitivities to God's Word for you. Because some passages strike you so forcefully, you begin to use those passages to speak to God about your life, your goals, your values, your problems. At this stage the dialogue is beginning, but we still focus on our own needs as we relate to God's Word and talk with God.

The greatest challenge in Bible study comes at the point of allowing God's Word to come alive—finding it truly to be God's Word *for you.* This also is the point of greatest danger, for a living Word can easily be confused with human thought. The need to distinguish our thoughts from God's thoughts is never greater than when we begin to deepen Bible study. Some people have their prejudices strengthened and their Christian freedom stifled because they read their thoughts into the Bible instead of letting God's Word speak and change their opinions.

How can we guard against such distortions as we deepen our Bible study? The following Guide for In-depth Bible Study outlines a four-step approach. If you spend about thirty minutes each day in Bible study, four or five days may be required to study a chapter in the Bible. The guide should be followed in order. The sequence will help protect you from jumping too quickly to your own conclusions. Overview the major steps in the guide. You may want to adapt or add some questions to make the guide more appropriate for your concerns.

1. *Preparing for God's Word.*—The first step in in-depth Bible study is designed to ensure that we are dealing with what God is saying through the Scriptures, not with what we want Him to say. This step focuses on the content of the passage. We seek to understand the original setting and the message God had for the original audience. By identifying the primary focus in the original setting, we avoid majoring on our agenda or on minor issues. We see how God tried to change the thinking of His people the first time these words were read or spoken.

2. *Seeking the Word from God.*—The second step is to ask questions of the text. We begin to discover the intention of God by searching for the abiding truth in the passage. At this point we let God speak to us through His Word. As we listen, however, we should avoid giving in to our desire to personalize the message. We must seek to understand how the original intention of the Word from God can be generalized so that it has meaning for everybody in every generation. At this point we still have not asked what this Word from God seeks to say to our own personal setting.

3. *Seeking God's Word for Me.*— Once we have focused on the true intention of the passage, we are ready to personalize it. We still ask questions of the text, but now we are beginning to dialogue with God based on our own situations. As we engage in this dialogue, God's Word for us begins to become clear. At this stage we should always seek to find how God's Word wants to change my life. Only after we have asked this question should we seek what the Word wants to affirm in our lives. We must not assume we are always wrong and need to change everything about ourselves. But we must never assume we are always right. We must let the Bible change us where it will.

4. *Keeping God's Word.*—To have heard God speak through his Word and then to fail to keep it is a greater sin than not to have heard at all. The fourth step is designed to help us respond with our lives to the truth of God's message for us. Memorization and paraphrasing help us hide God's Word in our hearts so that we can draw upon its guidance as we walk day by day.

The Bible is a book with untold treasures addressed to you. Through daily, disciplined, and deepened study of it, you can learn to converse with the living God. The four step process just summarized will lead you deeper into God's Word. The following outline will show you how to carry out each step.

Guide for In-depth Bible Study

1. Preparing for God's Word
   a. Pray for God's direction as you study His Word.
   b. Read the passage from King James, New American Standard, and Good News translations.
   c. Outline the entire passage.
   d. Describe the original audience.

e. In two or three sentences, summarize what the author was trying to say to the original readers.

f. State the major theme of the passage in one sentence.

2. Seeking the Word from God

a. What doctrines are taught in this passage?

b. What does the passage say about God? Jesus? the Holy Spirit?

c. What commands are given that apply to all of God's people?

d. What promises are given that apply to all of God's people?

e. What conditions must God's people meet to receive these promises?

f. What does the passage say that God's people should be?

g. What does the passage say that God's people should do?

h. What are the results if God's people disobey?

i. What other Bible passages balance or complement the teachings in this passage?

3. Seeking God's Word for Me

a. In what way am I like the original audience?

b. What does this passage imply that I should believe?

c. What does the passage say about God (Jesus, the Holy Spirit) and the way He relates to me?

d. Which command in the passage seems directed most to me?

e. Which promise seems directed most to me?

f. What must I do to claim that promise?

g. What changes do I need to make? What sins do I need to confess? What areas of my life do I need to trust more fully to God?

h. In what ways does this passage affirm God's love for me and His acceptance of my discipleship?

4. Keeping God's Word

a. Identify one verse that best states the message of this passage for me.

b. Memorize that verse.

c. What one thing can I do this week to live out better the message this passage has for me?

d. State the key verse in my own words, reflecting the message of the passage for me.

e. Write a prayer based on the passage. Include in the prayer my commitments to live by the truth of the passage.

How to Memorize Scripture

Memorizing God's Word is a major part of Bible study, as we have seen. No one can take from you the part of God's Word you have memorized. When you memorize God's Word, it stands ready to help you in time of temptation and trouble. God promises some exciting things for those disciples who memorize His Word! The guidelines that follow are designed to help you in Scripture memory.

STEP 1: PRAY ABOUT
          MEMORIZING
          GOD'S WORD!

Commit your will to his will! God's will for all disciples is to remember his Word (Deut. 6:6,7; Ps. 119:11,16,73). The Lord gives you a tremendous promise in Philippians 4:13—I can do all things through Him who strengthens me (NASB). Does the *all things* in this verse include Scripture memory? _____
If you believe it does and you believe it is God's will for you to memorize Scripture, why not right now surrender your mind and will to God? Will you write out a prayer of commitment to ask for God's strength to memorize Scripture? If you will, write your prayer here:

My Prayer Commitment to Remember the Word

My name _____ **Today's date** _____

My prayer _____

_____

_____

_____

_____

Trust the Lord to enable you to remember his Word!

STEP 2: FOLLOW A SCRIPTURE MEMORY PLAN!

Set your own goal: either one or two verses per week. Set your own times each day to work on Scripture memory. Write the verses on cards so you can use every spare moment of the day to work on Scripture memory. Always say the verses out loud so your mouth and ears can join your eyes in helping you memorize Scripture.

STEP 3: CHOOSE VERSES TO MEMORIZE

Here are some different ways to select verses to memorize:

1. You will want to join a Sunday School class in your church to study God's Word with other Christians. Choose at least one verse from your Sunday School lesson each week to memorize. Create a memory card for each verse.

2. As you have your quiet time, you will discover verses you will want to memorize. Create memory cards for these meaningful verses.

3. Ask your Youth leader, Youth minister, or pastor to help you find verses to memorize.

4. As you worship with your church family, listen to the sermon. Find at least one verse to memorize from each worship service.

These verses should be placed on your future memory sheet as described below.

STEP 4: CONSIDER A FEW PRACTICAL SUGGESTIONS

1. Use the awesome power of your SUBCONSCIOUS mind! Sounds scary, right! Try this: Quote your verse (with its topic and reference, of course) the last thing before you go to sleep at night. Then, quote your verse again when you wake up in the morning. Literally sleep on it! Make God's Word your first word in the morning and your last word at night. You will be surprised how easy memory work becomes.

2. As you memorize verses, try to associate the words with VISUAL objects. Get pictures of the verse in your mind.

3. As you review your verses, try to WRITE them down.

4. If you like MUSIC, why not create a tune to help you remember verses.

5. Always speak the verses loudly and distinctly as you work on them. Catch the sound as well as the sight of the verses.

6. Get a family member or friend to be your memory partner. Encourage and challenge one another to memorize God's Word.

7. Finally, RELAX. If you fall behind in Scripture memory, don't quit altogether. Pick up where you left off, review, and start all over again.

Spend time, work, and review. Follow the practical suggestions on this chart:

KEY WORDS FOR SCRIPTURE MEMORY

Time

1. Use three minutes of your daily quiet time Bible study each morning for Scripture memorization.
2. Spend five minutes working on verses just before bedtime.
3. Use spare time for Scripture memorization.

Work

1. Study the context.
2. Think through the verse.
3. Read it aloud several times.
4. Memorize the topic and quote the Scripture reference before and after the verse.
5. Memorize bits and phrases.
6. Connect clauses as you go.
7. Learn the verse word perfect.
8. Meditate on the verse all day.
9. Apply the verse as you go.

Review

1. Review the verses learned each day for thirty days.
2. After you review a verse thirty times, review it once or twice a month.

Review System

As you memorize God's Word, you will want a system to help you review and preserve what you have memorized. You will want to develop a future memory sheet, memory cards, a memory notebook, a memory verse packet, and a review box.

Future Memory Sheet

Develop a Future Memory Sheet in your Bible study notebook so you will have an organized supply of verses each week. The page for future memory should contain the subject and reference of the verse as diagrammed below.

Future Memory Sheet	
Subject	**Reference**
The Word	Job 23:12
Prayer	Jeremiah 33:3
Witnessing	1 Peter 3:15

Memory Cards

Place each verse you want to memorize on a card with the reference in the upper left-hand corner as shown in the diagram. (Use the translation of Scriptures which means the most to you.) Place the date of memorization on the back of your card.

Philippians 4:13

   I can do all things through Him who strengthens me.

FRONT ↵   ↶ BACK

Month	Day	Year

Memory Notebook

You will want to develop a notebook to record and classify verses you have memorized. Divide your pages into three sections as indicated below:

Record of Scripture Memory

Subject	Reference	Date
Grace	Ephesians 2:8-9	6/9/83
Love	1 John 4:18	8/19/83
Peace	John 14:27	8/21/83

Your notebook serves as a backup in case you lose your verse packet. Also, as you continue to memorize Scripture, you will be able to build quite a collection of various biblical subjects to help you in your study, discipling, witnessing, and speaking.

Memory Verse Packet

You can purchase various memory verse card holders. A vinyl or leather packet a little larger than your cards will protect them.

One side of the verse packet is for the new verses you memorize each week. The other side of your pouch is for the review verses.

Review Box

For Scripture memory to become a consistent, daily part of your life, you must review, review, review! You must not only review but have a system of review.

1. *Goal.*—Set a goal of the number of *new* verses you want to review. Three verses a week is a good goal. As you continue to memorize, the new side of your verse packet will fill up (twenty-four verses). Then you will begin placing cards into the *review* side of your packet.

After reaching twenty-four verses, transfer the three oldest verses from the *new* side of your packet to the *review* side each week. Also add three *new* verses in the *new* side weekly.

2. *"Big Review."*—As your system grows, set a goal for the number of verses you want to review each day (suggestion—twenty to thirty). Keep this number of cards in the review side of your packet. Place other cards in a Review Box.

You can get a small box to store and protect your verses. Place a card which stands a little taller than your other cards (labeled "Big Review") at the back of your box.

3. *Rotating system.*—Transfer verses from your review box to the review side of your verse packet each morning. Take the cards from the verse packet review and place them behind the Big Review card in your review box. Your "Big Review" card will gradually move toward the front. When it reaches the front, move it to the back and let it rotate through again.

When you come to your designated day for adding new verses, add three new verses to your system. Put the three *new* cards in on the new side of your packet. Take the three oldest cards out and place them in front of the "Big Review" card in your box. The three oldest verses will come up for review as they rotate through the review system.

Memorizing and reviewing the Word of God consistently through the months and years will help you to experience fantastic growth and blessings in your life as God gives you a spirit of thirst for his righteousness!

Evangelism Helps

Using the Roman Road to Share the Gospel

You have become a member of God's family. How! Because Jesus loved you and gave his life for you, you dedicated your life to Him. That is not the whole story. You became a member of God's family because another member of God's family cared for you and introduced you to Jesus. That loving friend probably opened the Bible to the Book of Romans and pointed you down the Roman Road to Jesus. Now it is your turn to care enough for other people to point them down the Roman Road to Jesus. How do you do this? These evangelistic helps are written to show you how.

To be able to share Jesus with other people, you must develop three characteristics. You must care for people. You must be a person of prayer. You must be a person of the Book.

Do you want to care for people? Spend time with them. Listen to them. Understand where they hurt and what they want. You will develop a loving sensitive heart.

Your loving heart will lead you to pray for the people you love. Ask God to heal their hurts, to use you to help them, and most of all to save them.

Caring and praying, you will be ready to point the people along the Roman Road to Jesus. To use the Roman Road effectively, you need to learn how to get into a discussion that will lead to an opportunity to share the gospel. A careful study of how Jesus went about starting conversations and sharing God's plan of salvation will be our perfect example to follow.

As you present the Roman Road Plan of Salvation, remember that lost persons must recognize their need for salvation. Such understanding will lead the lost person along a four-step path.

1. The person senses that a need or void exists.

2. The person recognizes his or her lost condition.

3. The person wants to be saved.

4. The person willingly repents of sin and places his or her faith in Jesus by receiving Him as Lord and Savior.

The Roman Road Plan of Salvation is designed to lead the lost person step-by-step. Most times, however, more than one visit or discussion is required to bring the person to faith in Christ. When people begin to admit their need, you will want to share the Roman Road with them.

Share the Roman Road with some of your Christian friends before attempting to share it with a lost person. This will help you become familiar with it. Pray to God for the confidence and love to share His Word with lost people. Once you feel comfortable sharing with your friends, God will have many rich blessings in store for you as you begin to share with lost persons.

Any person who accepts Jesus as Lord and Savior needs to receive immediate assurance of salvation and instruction in how to grow as a Christian. You will want to show that person the material at the front of this Bible that welcomes him or her to God's family (see p. 6a.).

You need to be certain that both you and the lost person you are talking to understand the plan of salvation as outlined in Romans (Roman Road). The following notes should help you understand what the Bible means so you can explain it to others.

Romans 3:23

Sin: to miss the mark, to rebel, to live independently of God, to fail to receive Jesus Christ as Lord and Savior.

Fall short of the glory of God: to fail to glorify God by refusing to live the Christlike life He created us to live. People can do the best they can and still miss the mark, or they may simply refuse to aim for the mark.

Romans 6:23
Wages: what we have earned and deserve because of the way we live.
Gift: what God offers freely, but a person must be willing to receive.
Eternal life: the quality of life only God can give which begins when we accept Christ and continues in heaven with Christ after death.

Romans 5:8
Christ died: the death of Jesus on the cross is the act of God which makes available to us the free gift He offers us because He loves us. Jesus sacrificed His earthly life that we might have eternal life.

Romans 10:9-10
Confess Jesus as Lord: to express publicly that Jesus is all the Bible says about Him and that you have decided to let Him control your life.
Believe: putting our complete trust in Jesus as the One God raised from the dead, and living out that belief by living as Jesus lived, following His example.
Be saved: To be delivered from the death sentence our sins deserve and to be admitted to the blessings of God's family forever.

Romans 10:13
Call on the Lord: Persons who truly want to be saved will pray and ask God to save them.

Learning from Jesus . . .
His Witnessing Encounters
A careful study of how Jesus met and talked to people will help us as His disciples know how to meet people and talk to them. Read each of the Scripture passages listed below. Use a blank sheet of paper and answer the questions about each passage.

1. What is the name of the person with whom Jesus was primarily concerned?
2. How did Jesus meet this person and why?
3. What does the Bible tell us about the person?
4. What was this person concerned with as Jesus talked, or what was of primary importance in the person's life?
5. What did Jesus talk to this person about and why?
6. What did Jesus want this person to do?
7. Write the name of a person you know who is like the person to whom Jesus talked. Pray that God will give you an opportunity to talk to that person so you can show how the person's needs, hopes, and opportunities are similar to those of the Bible character.

Jesus' Witnessing Encounters
The calling of disciples—
John 1:35-51, *page 1051*
Nicodemus—John 3:1-21,
pages 1052-53
Leper—Mark 1:40-45, *pages 989-90*
Lawyer—Luke 10:25-37, *pages 1028-29*
Blind man—John 9:1-41, *pages 1062-63*
Sick woman—Mark 5:25-34, *page 994*
Jairus—Mark 5:21-43, *page 994*
Paralytic—Mark 2:1-12, *page 990*
Samaritan woman—John 4:1-42,
pages 1053-55
Demoniac—Mark 5:1-20, *pages 993-94*
Blind man—Mark 8:22-26,
pages 998-99
Widow—Luke 7:11-17, *page 1022*
Ruler—Matthew 19:16-22, *page 974*
Zaccheus—Luke 19:1-10, *page 1040*
Pilate—Luke 23:1-5,13-25,
pages 1046-47
Herod—Luke 23:7-12, *page 1047*
Thieves—Luke 23:32-43, *pages 1047-48*
Prostitute—John 8:1-11, *pages 1060-61*
Young boy—Mark 9:14-29,
pages 999-1000
Centurion—Luke 7:1-10, *pages 1021-22*

Learning from Jesus . . .
His Parables

Jesus always tried to tell those around him about God's plan to bring meaning and hope into their lives. A careful study of Jesus' teachings will help us know how to communicate the gospel better. Jesus had a unique way of teaching. He told brief stories from everyday life. The Bible calls these stories parables. Each parable taught a major truth about human life and our relationship to God. Begin a long-range Bible study project to study Jesus' parables. They are listed below. Read the parable. Then write out in your notebooks answers to the following questions.

1. What is the name of the person(s) Jesus was primarily addressing?
2. What was the person's major problem?
3. How can this parable be outlined?
4. What spiritual truth was Jesus trying to communicate?
5. What does this parable say about God's plan of salvation?
6. What would be a modern-day version of this parable?
7. Write the name of one non-Christian who would benefit from hearing this parable.

Learning from Jesus . . .
His Prayers

Jesus' main concern was to carry out God's plan for His life. That plan led Jesus to the cross where He died so we could be saved. How could Jesus carry out God's plan so perfectly? He continually sought instructions and directions from God in prayer. A careful study of the prayer life of Jesus will aid you in knowing how to find God's plan for your life. Following his example in prayer will give you strength to follow God's plan for your life. Because you are Jesus' follower, you will want to learn to pray. As you study each of the following prayers, write answers in your Bible study notebook to these questions about prayer.

1. Who was praying? When? Where?
2. Why was he praying?
3. How can this prayer be outlined?
4. Is this a prayer I need to be praying?
5. How did God answer this prayer?
6. Whom do I know who needs this prayer? How can I share the prayer with that person?

You will find Jesus' prayers in the following Scripture passages:

To complete your study of the prayer life of Jesus, you will also want to look at:

Do you want to learn more about prayer? Study the following New Testament passages with the questions given above in mind:

The Old Testament can also help you learn to pray. You will want to read the following prayers:

The Book of Psalms is a collection of the prayers of God's people. You will want to study them the rest of your life. You may decide to read a Psalm each day. You will notice the Psalms show us different types of prayers:

Prayers of complaint:
Psalms 3,5,6,28,137
Prayers of thanksgiving:
Psalms 9,75,92,105,106,138
Prayers of praise:
Psalms 47,48,66,67,81,96,100,148
Prayers of Instruction:
Psalms 1,37,49,53
Prayers of confidence:
Psalm 23.

Scripture Songs
The Bible includes a book of Psalms. These are songs God's people used for prayer and praise. God's people use the Psalms to remember God's truth. The following Scripture Songs will help you learn key Scripture passages from God's Word.

32.   Romans 3:23

NASB

STAN PETHEL

For all_ have sinned   and fall short of the glo-ry of God.

For all_ have sinned   and fall short of the glo-ry of God.

33.   Romans 5:8

NASB

KATHIE HILL

But God dem-on-strates his own love toward us, _____ in that

while we were yet sin-ners, Christ died for us._____ But

NASB

34. Romans 6:23

JANET McMAHAN
KATHIE HILL

God dem-on-strates his own love toward us, _____ in that

while we were yet sin-ners, Christ died ___ for ___ us.

For the wa - ges of sin is death, but the

free gift of God is e - ter - nal life in

Christ Je - sus our Lord. _____

* This song may be sung as a round. Each group will enter at the numbers indicated.

35. Romans 10:9-10

NASB

KATHIE HILL

(2)

If you con-fess with your mouth Je - sus as Lord, and be-

lieve in your heart that God raised him from the dead, you shall__ be

saved,_____ you shall__ be saved;_____ For

with the heart man be-lieves,__ re-sult-ing in righ-teous-ness,__ and

with the mouth he con-fess-es, re-sult-ing in sal-va - tion._____

36. Romans 10:13

NASB

GARY LANIER

(4)

For who-ev-er will call up-on the name of the Lord will be saved,

will be saved.___ For who-ev-er will call up-on the

name of the Lord will be saved, will be saved.___

54.   Matthew 28:18-20

NASB

JANET McMAHAN
and GERALD MOORE

Je - sus came up and spoke to them, say - ing, "All au - thor - i-

ty has__ been giv - en to me__ in heav - en

and__ on__ earth. Go there-fore and

make dis - ci - ples of all the na - tions,

31a

baptizing them in the name of the Father, the Son and the Holy Spirit, Teaching them to observe all that I commanded you; and lo, I am with you always, even to the end of the age."

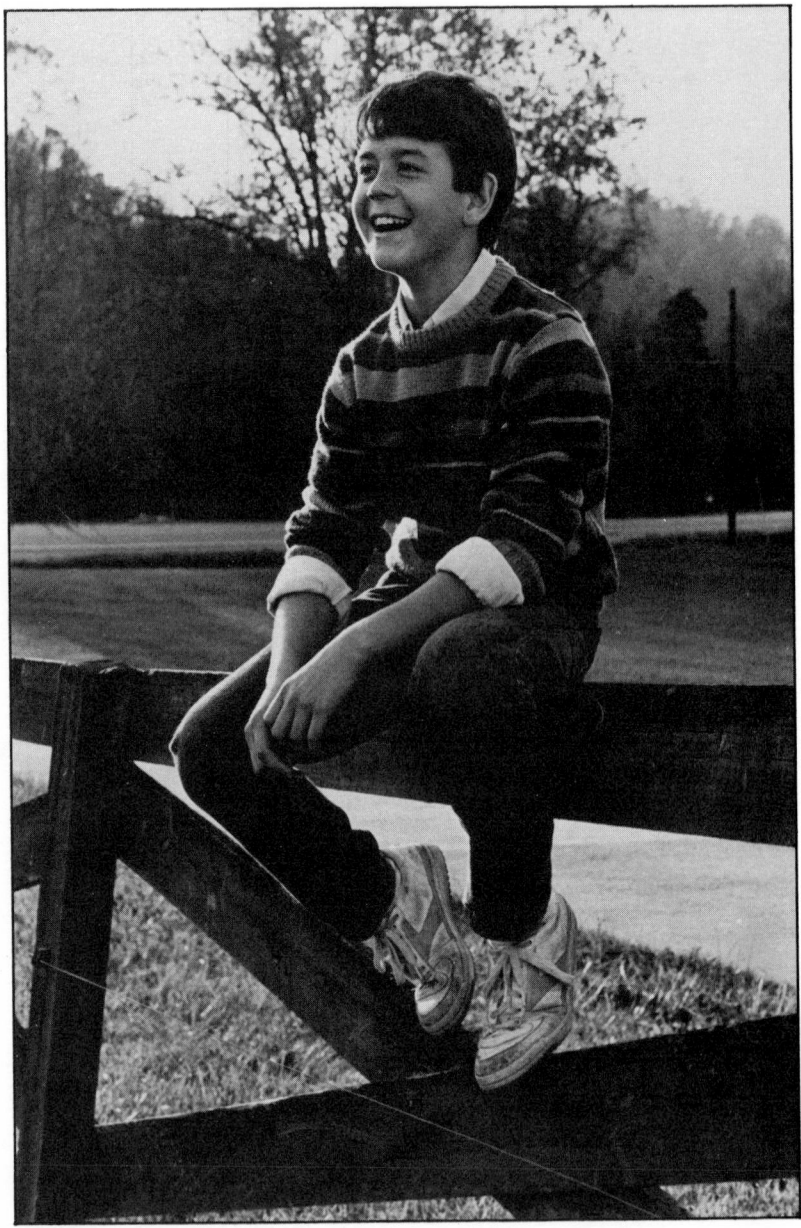

HOLY BIBLE

New
American Standard

HOLY BIBLE

New
American Standard

Text Edition

Holman Bible Publishers
Nashville

Published by
Holman Bible Publishers
Nashville, Tennesse 37234

2 3 4 5 6 7 8 9 10 11 12/87 86 85 84

SCRIPTURAL PROMISE

"The grass withers, the flower fades, but the word of our God stands forever."
Isaiah 40:8

FOREWORD

The New American Standard Bible has been produced with the conviction
that the words of Scripture as originally penned in the Hebrew, Aramaic, and
Greek were inspired by God. Since they are the eternal Word of God, the Holy
Scriptures speak with fresh power to each generation, to give wisdom that leads
to salvation, that men may serve Christ to the glory of God.

The Editorial Board had a twofold purpose in making this translation: to
adhere as closely as possible to the original languages of the Holy Scriptures,
and to make the translation in a fluent and readable style according to current
English usage.

THE FOURFOLD AIM
OF
THE LOCKMAN FOUNDATION

1. These publications shall be true to the original Hebrew, Aramaic, and
   Greek.
2. They shall be grammatically correct.
3. They shall be understandable to the masses.
4. They shall give the Lord Jesus Christ His proper place, the place which
   the Word gives Him; therefore, no work will ever be personalized.

PREFACE TO THE
NEW AMERICAN STANDARD BIBLE

In the history of English Bible translations, the King James Version is the most prestigious. This time-honored version of 1611, itself a revision of the Bishops' Bible of 1568, became the basis for the English Revised Version appearing in 1881 (New Testament) and 1885 (Old Testament). The American counterpart of this last work was published in 1901 as the American Standard Version. Recognizing the values of the American Standard Version, the Lockman Foundation felt an urgency to update it by incorporating recent discoveries of Hebrew and Greek textual sources and by rendering it into more current English. Therefore, in 1959 a new translation project was launched, based on the ASV. The result is the New American Standard Bible.

The American Standard Version (1901) has been highly regarded for its scholarship and accuracy. A product of both British and American scholarship, it has frequently been used as a standard for other translations. It is still recognized as a valuable tool for study of the Scriptures. The New American Standard Bible has sought to preserve these and other lasting values of the ASV.

Furthermore, in the preparation of this work numerous other translations have been consulted along with the linguistic tools and literature of biblical scholarship. Decisions about English renderings were made by consensus of a team composed of educators and pastors. Subsequently, review and evaluation by other Hebrew and Greek scholars outside the Editorial Board were sought and carefully considered.

The Editorial Board has continued to function since publication of the complete Bible in 1971. Minor revisions and refinements, recommended over the last several years, are presented in this edition.

PRINCIPLES OF TRANSLATION

MODERN ENGLISH USAGE: The attempt has been made to render the grammar and terminology in contemporary English. When it was felt that the word-for-word literalness was unacceptable to the modern reader, a change was made in the direction of a more current English idiom. In the instances where this has been done, the more literal rendering has been indicated in the notes.

ALTERNATIVE READINGS: In addition to the more literal renderings, notations have been made to include alternate translations, readings of variant manuscripts and explanatory equivalents of the text. Only such notations have been used as have been felt justified in assisting the reader's comprehension of the terms used by the original author.

HEBREW TEXT: In the present translation the latest edition of Rudolf Kittel's BIBLIA HEBRAICA has been employed together with the most recent light from lexicography, cognate languages, and the Dead Sea Scrolls.

HEBREW TENSES: Consecution of tenses in Hebrew remains a puzzling factor in translation. The translators have been guided by the requirements of a literal translation, the sequence of tenses, and the immediate and broad contexts.

THE PROPER NAME OF GOD IN THE OLD TESTAMENT: In the Scriptures, the name of God is most significant and understandably so. It is inconceivable to think of spiritual matters without a proper designation for the Supreme Deity. Thus the most common name for the Deity is God, a translation of the original Elohim. One of the titles for God is Lord, a translation of Adonai. There is yet another name which is particularly assigned to God as His special or proper name, that is, the four letters YHWH (Exodus 3:14 and Isaiah 42:8). This name has not been pronounced by the Jews because of reverence for the great sacredness of the divine name. Therefore, it has been consistently translated LORD. The only exception to this translation of YHWH is when it occurs in immediate proximity to the word Lord, that is, Adonai. In that case it is regularly translated GOD in order to avoid confusion. It is known that for many years YHWH has been transliterated as Yahweh, however no complete certainty attaches to this pronunciation.

GREEK TEXT: Consideration was given to the latest available manuscripts with a view to determining the best Greek text. In most instances the 23rd edition of Eberhard Nestle's NOVUM TESTAMENTUM GRAECE was followed.

GREEK TENSES: A careful distinction has been made in the treatment of the Greek aorist tense (usually translated as the English past, "He did") and the Greek imperfect tense (rendered either as English past progressive, "He was doing"; or, if inceptive, as "He *began* to do" or "He started to do"; or else if customary past, as "He used to do"). "Began" is italicized if it renders an imperfect tense, in order to distinguish it from the Greek verb for "begin."
    On the other hand, not all aorists have been rendered as English pasts ("He did"), for some of them are clearly to be rendered as English perfects ("He has done"), or even as past perfects ("He had done"), judging from the context in which they occur. Such aorists have been rendered as perfects or past perfects in this translation.
    As for the distinction between aorist and present imperatives, the translators have usually rendered these imperatives in the customary manner, rather than

attempting any such fine distinction as "Begin to do!" (for the aorist imperative), or, "Continually do!" (for the present imperative).

As for sequence of tenses, the translators took care to follow English rules
rather than Greek in translating Greek presents, imperfects and aorists. Thus,
where English says, "We knew that he was doing," Greek puts it, "We knew
that he does"; similarly, "We knew that he had done" is the Greek, "We knew
that he did." Likewise, the English, "When he had come, they met him," is
represented in Greek by: "When he came, they met him." In all cases a
consistent transfer has been made from the Greek tense in the subordinate
clause to the appropriate tense in English.

In the rendering of negative questions introduced by the particle **mē** (which
always expects the answer, "No") the wording has been altered from a mere,
"Will he not do this?" to a more accurate, "He will not do this, will he?"

Editorial Board, THE LOCKMAN FOUNDATION

Explanation of
GENERAL FORMAT

FOOTNOTES are used only where the text especially requires them for clarification. Marginal notes and cross references have been deleted from this edition.

PARAGRAPHS are designated by a paragraph mark with bold face numbers or letters.

QUOTATION MARKS are used in the text in accordance with modern English usage.

"THOU," "THEE" AND "THY" are not used in this translation except in the language of prayer when addressing Deity.

PERSONAL PRONOUNS are capitalized when pertaining to Deity.

ITALICS are used in the text to indicate words which are not found in the original Hebrew, Aramaic, or Greek but implied by it. Italics are used in the footnotes to signify alternate readings for the text.

SMALL CAPS in the New Testament are used in the text to indicate Old Testament quotations or obvious allusions to Old Testament texts. Variations of Old Testament wording are found in New Testament citations depending on whether the New Testament writer translated from a Hebrew text, used existing Greek or Aramaic translations, or paraphrased the material. It should be noted that modern rules for the indication of direct quotation were not used in biblical times thus allowing freedom for omissions or insertions without specific indication of these.

ASTERISKS are used to mark verbs that are historical presents in the Greek which have been translated with an English past tense in order to conform to modern usage. The translators recognized that in some contexts the present tense seems more unexpected and unjustified to the English reader than a past tense would have been. But Greek authors frequently used the present tense for the sake of heightened vividness, thereby transporting their readers in imagination to the actual scene at the time of occurrence. However, the translators felt that it would be wise to change these historical presents to English past tenses.

ABBREVIATIONS AND SPECIAL MARKINGS:

Aram.	=	Aramaic
Gr.	=	Greek translation of O.T. (Septuagint or LXX) or Greek text of N.T.
Heb.	=	Hebrew text, usually Masoretic
M.T.	=	Masoretic text
Syr.	=	Syriac
Lit.	=	A literal translation
Or	=	An alternate translation justified by the Hebrew, Aramaic, or Greek
[ ]	=	In text, brackets indicate words probably not in the original writings
cf.	=	compare
ms., mss.	=	manuscript, manuscripts
v., vv.	=	verse, verses

BOOKS OF
THE OLD TESTAMENT

BOOKS OF
THE NEW TESTAMENT

OLD TESTAMENT

**New American
Standard**

GENESIS

In the beginning God created the heavens and the earth.

2 And the earth was [1]formless and void, and darkness was over the surface of the deep; and the Spirit of God was [2]moving over the surface of the waters.

3 Then God said, "Let there be light"; and there was light.

4 And God saw that the light was good; and God separated the light from the darkness.

5 And God called the light day, and the darkness He called night. And there was evening and there was morning, one day.

6 ¶ Then God said, "Let there be an expanse in the midst of the waters, and let it separate the waters from the waters."

7 And God made the [3]expanse, and separated the waters which were below the expanse from the waters which were above the expanse; and it was so.

8 And God called the expanse heaven. And there was evening and there was morning, a second day.

9 ¶ Then God said, "Let the waters below the heavens be gathered into one place, and let the dry land appear"; and it was so.

10 And God called the dry land earth, and the gathering of the waters He called seas; and God saw that it was good.

11 Then God said, "Let the earth sprout vegetation, plants yielding seed, and fruit trees bearing fruit after their kind, with seed in them, on the earth"; and it was so.

12 And the earth brought forth vegetation, plants yielding seed after their kind, and trees bearing fruit, with seed in them, after their kind; and God saw that it was good.

13 And there was evening and there was morning, a third day.

14 ¶ Then God said, "Let there be lights in the expanse of the heavens to separate the day from the night, and let them be for signs, and for seasons, and for days and years;

15 and let them be for lights in the expanse of the heavens to give light on the earth"; and it was so.

16 And God made the two great lights, the greater light to govern the day, and the lesser light to govern the night; He made the stars also.

17 And God placed them in the expanse of the heavens to give light on the earth,

18 and to govern the day and the night, and to separate the light from the darkness; and God saw that it was good.

19 And there was evening and there was morning, a fourth day.

20 ¶ Then God said, "Let the waters teem with swarms of living creatures, and let birds fly above the earth in the open expanse of the heavens."

21 And God created the great sea monsters, and every living creature that moves, with which the waters swarmed after their kind, and every winged bird after its kind; and God saw that it was good.

22 And God blessed them, saying, "Be fruitful and multiply, and fill the waters in the seas, and let birds multiply on the earth."

23 And there was evening and there was morning, a fifth day.

24 ¶ Then God said, "Let the earth bring forth living creatures after their kind: cattle and creeping things and beasts of the earth after their kind"; and it was so.

25 And God made the beasts of the earth after their kind, and the cattle after their kind, and everything that creeps on the ground after its kind; and God saw that it was good.

26 Then God said, "Let Us make man in Our image, according to Our likeness; and let them rule over the fish of the sea and over the birds of the sky and over the cattle and over all the earth, and over every creeping thing that creeps on the earth."

27 And God created man in His own image, in the image of God He created him; male and female He created them.

28 And God blessed them; and God said to them, "Be fruitful and multiply, and fill the earth, and subdue it; and rule over the fish of the sea and over the birds of the sky, and over every living thing that moves on the earth."

[1] Or, a waste and emptiness [2] Or, hovering
[3] Or, firmament

Turn to page 1119

29 Then God said, "Behold, I have given you every plant yielding seed that is on the surface of all the earth, and every tree which has fruit yielding seed; it shall be food for you;

30 and to every beast of the earth and to every bird of the sky and to every thing that moves on the earth which has life, *I have given* every green plant for food"; and it was so.

31 And God saw all that He had made, and behold, it was very good. And there was evening and there was morning, the sixth day.

CHAPTER 2

THUS the heavens and the earth were completed, and all their hosts.

2 And by the seventh day God completed His work which He had done; and He rested on the seventh day from all His work which He had done.

3 Then God blessed the seventh day and sanctified it, because in it He rested from all His work which God had created and made.

4 ¶ This is the account of the heavens and the earth when they were created, in the day that the LORD God made earth and heaven.

5 Now no shrub of the field was yet in the earth, and no plant of the field had yet sprouted, for the LORD God had not sent rain upon the earth; and there was no man to cultivate the ground.

6 But a mist used to rise from the earth and water the whole surface of the ground.

7 Then the LORD God formed man of dust from the ground, and breathed into his nostrils the breath of life; and man became a living being.

8 And the LORD God planted a garden toward the east, in Eden; and there He placed the man whom He had formed.

9 And out of the ground the LORD God caused to grow every tree that is pleasing to the sight and good for food; the tree of life also in the midst of the garden, and the tree of the knowledge of good and evil.

10 ¶ Now a river flowed out of Eden to water the garden; and from there it divided and became four rivers.

11 The name of the first is Pishon; it flows around the whole land of Havilah, where there is gold.

12 And the gold of that land is good; the bdellium and the onyx stone are there.

13 And the name of the second river is Gihon; it flows around the whole land of Cush.

14 And the name of the third river is Tigris; it flows east of Assyria. And the fourth river is the Euphrates.

15 Then the LORD God took the man and put him into the garden of Eden to cultivate it and keep it.

16 And the LORD God commanded the man, saying, "From any tree of the garden you may eat freely;

17 but from the tree of the knowledge of good and evil you shall not eat, for in the day that you eat from it you shall surely die."

18 ¶ Then the LORD God said, "It is not good for the man to be alone; I will make him a helper [4]suitable for him."

19 And out of the ground the LORD God formed every beast of the field and every bird of the sky, and brought *them* to the man to see what he would call them; and whatever the man called a living creature, that was its name.

20 And the man gave names to all the cattle, and to the birds of the sky, and to every beast of the field, but for [5]Adam there was not found a helper suitable for him.

21 So the LORD God caused a deep sleep to fall upon the man, and he slept; then He took one of his ribs, and closed up the flesh at that place.

22 And the LORD God [6]fashioned into a woman the rib which He had taken from the man, and brought her to the man.

23 And the man said,
"This is now bone of my bones,
    And flesh of my flesh;
    She shall be called Woman,
    Because she was taken out of
        Man."

24 For this cause a man shall leave his father and his mother, and shall cleave to his wife; and they shall become one flesh.

25 And the man and his wife were both naked and were not ashamed.

[4] Lit., *corresponding to*   [5] Or, *man*   [6] Lit., *built*

CHAPTER 3

Now the serpent was more crafty than any beast of the field which the Lord God had made. And he said to the woman, "Indeed, has God said, 'You shall not eat from any tree of the garden'?"

2 And the woman said to the serpent, "From the fruit of the trees of the garden we may eat;

3 but from the fruit of the tree which is in the middle of the garden, God has said, 'You shall not eat from it or touch it, lest you die.'"

4 And the serpent said to the woman, "You surely shall not die!

5 "For God knows that in the day you eat from it your eyes will be opened, and you will be like God, knowing good and evil."

6 When the woman saw that the tree was good for food, and that it was a delight to the eyes, and that the tree was desirable to make *one* wise, she took from its fruit and ate; and she gave also to her husband with her, and he ate.

7 Then the eyes of both of them were opened, and they knew that they were naked; and they sewed fig leaves together and made themselves loin coverings.

8 ¶ And they heard the sound of the Lord God walking in the garden in the cool of the day, and the man and his wife hid themselves from the presence of the Lord God among the trees of the garden.

9 Then the Lord God called to the man, and said to him, "Where are you?"

10 And he said, "I heard the sound of Thee in the garden, and I was afraid because I was naked; so I hid myself."

11 And He said, "Who told you that you were naked? Have you eaten from the tree of which I commanded you not to eat?"

12 And the man said, "The woman whom Thou gavest *to be* with me, she gave me from the tree, and I ate."

13 Then the Lord God said to the woman, "What is this you have done?" And the woman said, "The serpent deceived me, and I ate."

14 And the Lord God said to the serpent,

"Because you have done this,
Cursed are you more than all cattle,
And more than every beast of the field;
On your belly shall you go,
And dust shall you eat
All the days of your life;
15 And I will put enmity
Between you and the woman,
And between your seed and her seed;
He shall bruise you on the head,
And you shall bruise him on the heel."
16 To the woman He said,
"I will greatly multiply
Your pain in childbirth,
In pain you shall bring forth children;
Yet your desire shall be for your husband,
And he shall rule over you."

17 Then to Adam He said, "Because you have listened to the voice of your wife, and have eaten from the tree about which I commanded you, saying, 'You shall not eat from it';

Cursed is the ground because of you;
In toil you shall eat of it
All the days of your life.
18 "Both thorns and thistles it shall grow for you;
And you shall eat the plants of the field;
19 By the sweat of your face
You shall eat bread,
Till you return to the ground,
Because from it you were taken;
For you are dust,
And to dust you shall return."

20 Now the man called his wife's name [7]Eve, because she was the mother of all *the* living.

21 And the Lord God made garments of skin for Adam and his wife, and clothed them.

22 ¶ Then the Lord God said, "Behold, the man has become like one of Us, knowing good and evil; and now, lest he stretch out his hand, and take also from the tree of life, and eat, and live forever"—

23 therefore the Lord God sent him

---

[7] I.e., living or life

out from the garden of Eden, to cultivate the ground from which he was taken.

24 So He drove the man out; and at the east of the garden of Eden He stationed the cherubim, and the flaming sword which turned every direction, to guard the way to the tree of life.

CHAPTER 4

Now the man had relations with his wife Eve, and she conceived and gave birth to Cain, and she said, "I have gotten a manchild with *the help of* the LORD."

2 And again, she gave birth to his brother Abel. And Abel was a keeper of flocks, but Cain was a tiller of the ground.

3 So it came about in the course of time that Cain brought an offering to the LORD of the fruit of the ground.

4 And Abel, on his part also brought of the firstlings of his flock and of their fat portions. And the LORD had regard for Abel and for his offering;

5 but for Cain and for his offering He had no regard. So Cain became very angry and his countenance fell.

6 Then the LORD said to Cain, "Why are you angry? And why has your countenance fallen?

7"If you do well, will not *your countenance* be lifted up? And if you do not do well, sin is crouching at the door; and its desire is for you, but you must master it."

8 And Cain told Abel his brother. And it came about when they were in the field, that Cain rose up against Abel his brother and killed him.

9 ¶ Then the LORD said to Cain, "Where is Abel your brother?" And he said, "I do not know. Am I my brother's keeper?"

10 And He said, "What have you done? The voice of your brother's blood is crying to Me from the ground.

11"And now you are cursed from the ground, which has opened its mouth to receive your brother's blood from your hand.

12"When you cultivate the ground, it shall no longer yield its strength to you; you shall be a vagrant and a wanderer on the earth."

13 And Cain said to the LORD, "My punishment is too great to bear!

14"Behold, Thou hast driven me this day from the face of the ground; and from Thy face I shall be hidden, and I shall be a vagrant and a wanderer on the earth, and it will come about that whoever finds me will kill me."

15 So the LORD said to him, "Therefore whoever kills Cain, vengeance will be taken on him sevenfold." And the LORD appointed a sign for Cain, lest anyone finding him should slay him.

16 ¶ Then Cain went out from the presence of the LORD, and settled in the land of Nod, east of Eden.

17 And Cain had relations with his wife and she conceived, and gave birth to Enoch; and he built a city, and called the name of the city Enoch, after the name of his son.

18 Now to Enoch was born Irad; and Irad became the father of Mehujael; and Mehujael became the father of Methushael; and Methushael became the father of Lamech.

19 And Lamech took to himself two wives: the name of the one was Adah, and the name of the other, Zillah.

20 And Adah gave birth to Jabal; he was the father of those who dwell in tents and *have* livestock.

21 And his brother's name was Jubal; he was the father of all those who play the lyre and pipe.

22 As for Zillah, she also gave birth to Tubal-cain, the forger of all implements of bronze and iron; and the sister of Tubal-cain was Naamah.

23 And Lamech said to his wives,

"Adah and Zillah,
Listen to my voice,
You wives of Lamech,
Give heed to my speech,
For I have killed a man for wounding me;
And a boy for striking me;

24 If Cain is avenged sevenfold,
Then Lamech seventy-sevenfold."

25 ¶ And Adam had relations with his wife again; and she gave birth to a son, and named him Seth, for, *she said*, "God has appointed me another offspring in place of Abel; for Cain killed him."

26 And to Seth, to him also a son was born; and he called his name Enosh. Then *men* began to call upon the name of the Lord.

CHAPTER 5

THIS is the book of the generations of Adam. In the day when God created man, He made him in the likeness of God.

2 He created them male and female, and He blessed them and named them [8]Man in the day when they were created.

3 When Adam had lived one hundred and thirty years, he [9]became the father of *a son* in his own likeness, according to his image, and named him Seth.

4 Then the days of Adam after he became the father of Seth were eight hundred years, and he had *other* sons and daughters.

5 So all the days that Adam lived were nine hundred and thirty years, and he died.

6 ¶ And Seth lived one hundred and five years, and became the father of Enosh.

7 Then Seth lived eight hundred and seven years after he became the father of Enosh, and he had *other* sons and daughters.

8 So all the days of Seth were nine hundred and twelve years, and he died.

9 ¶ And Enosh lived ninety years, and became the father of Kenan.

10 Then Enosh lived eight hundred and fifteen years after he became the father of Kenan, and he had *other* sons and daughters.

11 So all the days of Enosh were nine hundred and five years, and he died.

12 ¶ And Kenan lived seventy years, and became the father of Mahalalel.

13 Then Kenan lived eight hundred and forty years after he became the father of Mahalalel, and he had *other* sons and daughters.

14 So all the days of Kenan were nine hundred and ten years, and he died.

15 ¶ And Mahalalel lived sixty-five years, and became the father of Jared.

16 Then Mahalalel lived eight hundred and thirty years after he became the father of Jared, and he had *other* sons and daughters.

17 So all the days of Mahalalel were eight hundred and ninety-five years, and he died.

18 ¶ And Jared lived one hundred and sixty-two years, and became the father of Enoch.

19 Then Jared lived eight hundred years after he became the father of Enoch, and he had *other* sons and daughters.

20 So all the days of Jared were nine hundred and sixty-two years, and he died.

21 ¶ And Enoch lived sixty-five years, and became the father of Methuselah.

22 Then Enoch walked with God three hundred years after he became the father of Methuselah, and he had *other* sons and daughters.

23 So all the days of Enoch were three hundred and sixty-five years.

24 And Enoch walked with God; and he was not, for God took him.

25 ¶ And Methuselah lived one hundred and eighty-seven years, and became the father of Lamech.

26 Then Methuselah lived seven hundred and eighty-two years after he became the father of Lamech, and he had *other* sons and daughters.

27 So all the days of Methuselah were nine hundred and sixty-nine years, and he died.

28 ¶ And Lamech lived one hundred and eighty-two years, and became the father of a son.

29 Now he called his name Noah, saying, "This one shall give us rest from our work and from the toil of our hands *arising* from the ground which the Lord has cursed."

30 Then Lamech lived five hundred and ninety-five years after he became the father of Noah, and he had *other* sons and daughters.

31 So all the days of Lamech were seven hundred and seventy-seven years, and he died.

32 ¶ And Noah was five hundred years old, and Noah became the father of Shem, Ham, and Japheth.

[8] Lit., *Adam*   [9] Lit., *begot*, and so throughout this context

CHAPTER 6

NOW it came about, when men began to multiply on the face of the land, and daughters were born to them,

2 that the sons of God saw that the daughters of men were beautiful; and they took wives for themselves, whomever they chose.

3 Then the LORD said, "My Spirit shall not strive with man forever, because he also is flesh; nevertheless his days shall be one hundred and twenty years."

4 The [10]Nephilim were on the earth in those days, and also afterward, when the sons of God came in to the daughters of men, and they bore *children* to them. Those were the mighty men who *were* of old, men of renown.

5 ¶ Then the LORD saw that the wickedness of man was great on the earth, and that every intent of the thoughts of his heart was only evil continually.

6 And the LORD was sorry that He had made man on the earth, and He was grieved in His heart.

7 And the LORD said, "I will blot out man whom I have created from the face of the land, from man to animals to creeping things and to birds of the sky; for I am sorry that I have made them."

8 But Noah found favor in the eyes of the LORD.

9 ¶ These are *the records of* the generations of Noah. Noah was a righteous man, blameless in his time; Noah walked with God.

10 And Noah became the father of three sons: Shem, Ham, and Japheth.

11 Now the earth was corrupt in the sight of God, and the earth was filled with violence.

12 And God looked on the earth, and behold, it was corrupt; for all flesh had corrupted their way upon the earth.

13 ¶ Then God said to Noah, "The end of all flesh has come before Me; for the earth is filled with violence because of them; and behold, I am about to destroy them with the earth.

14"Make for yourself an ark of gopher wood; you shall make the ark with rooms, and shall cover it inside and out with pitch.

15"And this is how you shall make it: the length of the ark three hundred [11]cubits, its breadth fifty cubits, and its height thirty cubits.

16"You shall make a window for the ark, and finish it to a cubit from the top; and set the door of the ark in the side of it; you shall make it with lower, second, and third decks.

17"And behold, I, even I am bringing the flood of water upon the earth, to destroy all flesh in which is the breath of life, from under heaven; everything that is on the earth shall perish.

18"But I will establish My covenant with you; and you shall enter the ark—you and your sons and your wife, and your sons' wives with you.

19"And of every living thing of all flesh, you shall bring two of every *kind* into the ark, to keep *them* alive with you; they shall be male and female.

20"Of the birds after their kind, and of the animals after their kind, of every creeping thing of the ground after its kind, two of every *kind* shall come to you to keep *them* alive.

21"And as for you, take for yourself some of all food which is edible, and gather *it* to yourself; and it shall be for food for you and for them."

22 Thus Noah did; according to all that God had commanded him, so he did.

CHAPTER 7

THEN the LORD said to Noah, "Enter the ark, you and all your household; for you *alone* I have seen *to be* righteous before Me in this time.

2"You shall take with you of every clean animal by sevens, a male and his female; and of the animals that are not clean two, a male and his female;

3 also of the birds of the sky, by sevens, male and female, to keep offspring alive on the face of all the earth.

4"For after seven more days, I will send rain on the earth forty days and forty nights; and I will blot out from the face of the land every living thing that I have made."

5 And Noah did according to all that the LORD had commanded him.

---

[10] Or, *giants*   [11] I.e., One cubit equals approx. 18 in.

6 ¶ Now Noah was six hundred years old when the flood of water came upon the earth.

7 Then Noah and his sons and his wife and his sons' wives with him entered the ark because of the water of the flood.

8 Of clean animals and animals that are not clean and birds and everything that creeps on the ground,

9 there went into the ark to Noah by twos, male and female, as God had commanded Noah.

10 And it came about after the seven days, that the water of the flood came upon the earth.

11 In the six hundredth year of Noah's life, in the second month, on the seventeenth day of the month, on the same day all the fountains of the great deep burst open, and the floodgates of the sky were opened.

12 And the rain fell upon the earth for forty days and forty nights.

13 ¶ On the very same day Noah and Shem and Ham and Japheth, the sons of Noah, and Noah's wife and the three wives of his sons with them, entered the ark,

14 they and every beast after its kind, and all the cattle after their kind, and every creeping thing that creeps on the earth after its kind, and every bird after its kind, all sorts of birds.

15 So they went into the ark to Noah, by twos of all flesh in which was the breath of life.

16 And those that entered, male and female of all flesh, entered as God had commanded him; and the LORD closed it behind him.

17 Then the flood came upon the earth for forty days; and the water increased and lifted up the ark, so that it rose above the earth.

18 And the water prevailed and increased greatly upon the earth; and the ark floated on the surface of the water.

19 And the water prevailed more and more upon the earth, so that all the high mountains everywhere under the heavens were covered.

20 The water prevailed fifteen cubits higher, and the mountains were covered.

21 And all flesh that moved on the earth perished, birds and cattle and beasts and every swarming thing that swarms upon the earth, and all mankind;

22 of all that was on the dry land, all in whose nostrils was the breath of the spirit of life, died.

23 Thus He blotted out every living thing that was upon the face of the land, from man to animals to creeping things and to birds of the sky, and they were blotted out from the earth; and only Noah was left, together with those that were with him in the ark.

24 And the water prevailed upon the earth one hundred and fifty days.

CHAPTER 8

BUT God remembered Noah and all the beasts and all the cattle that were with him in the ark; and God caused a wind to pass over the earth, and the water subsided.

2 Also the fountains of the deep and the floodgates of the sky were closed, and the rain from the sky was restrained;

3 and the water receded steadily from the earth, and at the end of one hundred and fifty days the water decreased.

4 And in the seventh month, on the seventeenth day of the month, the ark rested upon the mountains of Ararat.

5 And the water decreased steadily until the tenth month; in the tenth month, on the first day of the month, the tops of the mountains became visible.

6 ¶ Then it came about at the end of forty days, that Noah opened the window of the ark which he had made;

7 and he sent out a raven, and it flew here and there until the water was dried up from the earth.

8 Then he sent out a dove from him, to see if the water was abated from the face of the land;

9 but the dove found no resting place for the sole of her foot, so she returned to him into the ark; for the water was on the surface of all the earth. Then he put out his hand and took her, and brought her into the ark to himself.

10 So he waited yet another seven days; and again he sent out the dove from the ark.

11 And the dove came to him toward evening; and behold, in her beak was a freshly picked olive leaf. So Noah knew that the water was abated from the earth.

12 Then he waited yet another seven days, and sent out the dove; but she did not return to him again.

13 ¶ Now it came about in the six hundred and first year, in the first *month*, on the first of the month, the water was dried up from the earth. Then Noah removed the covering of the ark, and looked, and behold, the surface of the ground was dried up.

14 And in the second month, on the twenty-seventh day of the month, the earth was dry.

15 Then God spoke to Noah, saying,

16"Go out of the ark, you and your wife and your sons and your sons' wives with you.

17"Bring out with you every living thing of all flesh that is with you, birds and animals and every creeping thing that creeps on the earth, that they may breed abundantly on the earth, and be fruitful and multiply on the earth."

18 So Noah went out, and his sons and his wife and his sons' wives with him.

19 Every beast, every creeping thing, and every bird, everything that moves on the earth, went out by their families from the ark.

20 ¶ Then Noah built an altar to the LORD, and took of every clean animal and of every clean bird and offered burnt offerings on the altar.

21 And the LORD smelled the soothing aroma; and the LORD said to Himself, "I will never again curse the ground on account of man, for the intent of man's heart is evil from his youth; and I will never again destroy every living thing, as I have done.

22 "While the earth remains,
Seedtime and harvest,
And cold and heat,
And summer and winter,
And day and night
Shall not cease."

CHAPTER 9

AND God blessed Noah and his sons and said to them, "Be fruitful and multiply, and fill the earth.

2"And the fear of you and the terror of you shall be on every beast of the earth and on every bird of the sky; with everything that creeps on the ground, and all the fish of the sea, into your hand they are given.

3"Every moving thing that is alive shall be food for you; I give all to you, as I *gave* the green plant.

4"Only you shall not eat flesh with its life, *that is*, its blood.

5"And surely I will require your lifeblood; from every beast I will require it. And from *every* man, from every man's brother I will require the life of man.

6 "Whoever sheds man's blood,
By man his blood shall be shed,
For in the image of God
He made man.

7 "And as for you, be fruitful and multiply;
Populate the earth abundantly and multiply in it."

8 ¶ Then God spoke to Noah and to his sons with him, saying,

9"Now behold, I Myself do establish My covenant with you, and with your descendants after you;

10 and with every living creature that is with you, the birds, the cattle, and every beast of the earth with you; of all that comes out of the ark, even every beast of the earth.

11"And I establish My covenant with you; and all flesh shall never again be cut off by the water of the flood, neither shall there again be a flood to destroy the earth."

12 And God said, "This is the sign of the covenant which I am making between Me and you and every living creature that is with you, for all successive generations;

13 I set My bow in the cloud, and it shall be for a sign of a covenant between Me and the earth.

14"And it shall come about, when I bring a cloud over the earth, that the bow shall be seen in the cloud,

15 and I will remember My covenant, which is between Me and you and every living creature of all flesh; and never again shall the water become a flood to destroy all flesh.

16"When the bow is in the cloud, then I will look upon it, to remember the everlasting covenant between God and every living creature of all flesh that is on the earth."

17 And God said to Noah, "This is the sign of the covenant which I have established between Me and all flesh that is on the earth."

18 ¶ Now the sons of Noah who came out of the ark were Shem and Ham and Japheth; and Ham was the father of Canaan.

19 These three *were* the sons of Noah; and from these the whole earth was populated.

20 ¶ Then Noah began farming and planted a vineyard.

21 And he drank of the wine and became drunk, and uncovered himself inside his tent.

22 And Ham, the father of Canaan, saw the nakedness of his father, and told his two brothers outside.

23 But Shem and Japheth took a garment and laid it upon both their shoulders and walked backward and covered the nakedness of their father; and their faces were turned away, so that they did not see their father's nakedness.

24 When Noah awoke from his wine, he knew what his youngest son had done to him.

25 So he said,
"Cursed be Canaan;
[12]A servant of servants
He shall be to his brothers."

26 He also said,
"Blessed be the LORD,
The God of Shem;
And let Canaan be his servant.

27 "May God enlarge Japheth,
And let him dwell in the tents of Shem;
And let Canaan be his servant."

28 ¶ And Noah lived three hundred and fifty years after the flood.

29 So all the days of Noah were nine hundred and fifty years, and he died.

CHAPTER 10

NOW these are *the records of* the generations of Shem, Ham, and Japheth, the sons of Noah; and sons were born to them after the flood.

2 ¶ The sons of Japheth *were* Gomer and Magog and Madai and Javan and Tubal and Meshech and Tiras.

3 And the sons of Gomer *were* Ashkenaz and Riphath and Togarmah.

4 And the sons of Javan *were* Elishah and Tarshish, Kittim and Dodanim.

5 From these the coastlands of the nations were separated into their lands, every one according to his language, according to their families, into their nations.

6 ¶ And the sons of Ham *were* Cush and Mizraim and Put and Canaan.

7 And the sons of Cush *were* Seba and Havilah and Sabtah and Raamah and Sabteca; and the sons of Raamah *were* Sheba and Dedan.

8 Now Cush became the father of Nimrod; he became a mighty one on the earth.

9 He was a mighty hunter before the LORD; therefore it is said, "Like Nimrod a mighty hunter before the LORD."

10 And the beginning of his kingdom was [13]Babel and Erech and Accad and Calneh, in the land of Shinar.

11 From that land he went forth into Assyria, and built Nineveh and Rehoboth-Ir and Calah,

12 and Resen between Nineveh and Calah; that is the great city.

13 And Mizraim became the father of Ludim and Anamim and Lehabim and Naphtuhim

14 and Pathrusim and Casluhim (from which came the Philistines) and Caphtorim.

15 ¶ And Canaan became the father of Sidon, his first-born, and Heth

16 and the Jebusite and the Amorite and the Girgashite

17 and the Hivite and the Arkite and the Sinite

18 and the Arvadite and the Zemarite and the Hamathite; and afterward the families of the Canaanite were spread abroad.

19 And the territory of the Canaanite extended from Sidon as you go toward Gerar, as far as Gaza; as you go toward Sodom and Gomorrah and Admah and Zeboiim, as far as Lasha.

20 These are the sons of Ham, according to their families, according to their languages, by their lands, by their nations.

[12] I.e., The lowest of servants

[13] Or, *Babylon*

21 ¶ And also to Shem, the father of all the children of Eber, *and* the older brother of Japheth, children were born.

22 The sons of Shem *were* Elam and Asshur and Arpachshad and Lud and Aram.

23 And the sons of Aram *were* Uz and Hul and Gether and Mash.

24 And Arpachshad became the father of Shelah; and Shelah became the father of Eber.

25 And two sons were born to Eber; the name of the one *was* Peleg, for in his days the earth was divided; and his brother's name *was* Joktan.

26 And Joktan became the father of Almodad and Sheleph and Hazarmaveth and Jerah

27 and Hadoram and Uzal and Diklah

28 and Obal and Abimael and Sheba

29 and Ophir and Havilah and Jobab; all these were the sons of Joktan.

30 Now their settlement extended from Mesha as you go toward Sephar, the hill country of the east.

31 These are the sons of Shem, according to their families, according to their languages, by their lands, according to their nations.

32 ¶ These are the families of the sons of Noah, according to their genealogies, by their nations; and out of these the nations were separated on the earth after the flood.

CHAPTER 11

Now the whole earth used the same language and the same words.

2 And it came about as they journeyed east, that they found a plain in the land of Shinar and settled there.

3 And they said to one another, "Come, let us make bricks and burn *them* thoroughly." And they used brick for stone, and they used tar for mortar.

4 And they said, "Come, let us build for ourselves a city, and a tower whose top *will reach* into heaven, and let us make for ourselves a name; lest we be scattered abroad over the face of the whole earth."

5 And the Lord came down to see the city and the tower which the sons of men had built.

6 And the Lord said, "Behold, they are one people, and they all have the same language. And this is what they began to do, and now nothing which they purpose to do will be impossible for them.

7 "Come, let Us go down and there confuse their language, that they may not understand one another's speech."

8 So the Lord scattered them abroad from there over the face of the whole earth; and they stopped building the city.

9 Therefore its name was called [14]Babel, because there the Lord confused the language of the whole earth; and from there the Lord scattered them abroad over the face of the whole earth.

10 ¶ These are *the records of* the generations of Shem. Shem was one hundred years old, and became the father of Arpachshad two years after the flood;

11 and Shem lived five hundred years after he became the father of Arpachshad, and he had *other* sons and daughters.

12 ¶ And Arpachshad lived thirty-five years, and became the father of Shelah;

13 and Arpachshad lived four hundred and three years after he became the father of Shelah, and he had *other* sons and daughters.

14 ¶ And Shelah lived thirty years, and became the father of Eber;

15 and Shelah lived four hundred and three years after he became the father of Eber, and he had *other* sons and daughters.

16 ¶ And Eber lived thirty-four years, and became the father of Peleg;

17 and Eber lived four hundred and thirty years after he became the father of Peleg, and he had *other* sons and daughters.

18 ¶ And Peleg lived thirty years, and became the father of Reu;

19 and Peleg lived two hundred and nine years after he became the father of Reu, and he had *other* sons and daughters.

20 ¶ And Reu lived thirty-two years, and became the father of Serug;

21 and Reu lived two hundred and seven years after he became the father

[14] Or, *Babylon*

of Serug, and he had *other* sons and daughters.

22 ¶ And Serug lived thirty years, and became the father of Nahor;

23 and Serug lived two hundred years after he became the father of Nahor, and he had *other* sons and daughters.

24 ¶ And Nahor lived twenty-nine years, and became the father of Terah;

25 and Nahor lived one hundred and nineteen years after he became the father of Terah, and he had *other* sons and daughters.

26 ¶ And Terah lived seventy years, and became the father of Abram, Nahor and Haran.

27 ¶ Now these are *the records of* the generations of Terah. Terah became the father of Abram, Nahor and Haran; and Haran became the father of Lot.

28 And Haran died in the presence of his father Terah in the land of his birth, in Ur of the Chaldeans.

29 And Abram and Nahor took wives for themselves. The name of Abram's wife was Sarai; and the name of Nahor's wife was Milcah, the daughter of Haran, the father of Milcah and Iscah.

30 And Sarai was barren; she had no child.

31 And Terah took Abram his son, and Lot the son of Haran, his grandson, and Sarai his daughter-in-law, his son Abram's wife; and they went out together from Ur of the Chaldeans in order to enter the land of Canaan; and they went as far as Haran, and settled there.

32 And the days of Terah were two hundred and five years; and Terah died in Haran.

CHAPTER 12

NOW the LORD said to Abram,
  "Go forth from your country,
  And from your relatives
  And from your father's house,
  To the land which I will show
    you;
2 And I will make you a great
    nation,
  And I will bless you,
  And make your name great;
  And so you shall be a blessing;
3 And I will bless those who bless
    you,

And the one who curses you I
    will curse.
  And in you all the families of the
    earth shall be blessed."

4 So Abram went forth as the LORD had spoken to him; and Lot went with him. Now Abram was seventy-five years old when he departed from Haran.

5 And Abram took Sarai his wife and Lot his nephew, and all their possessions which they had accumulated, and the persons which they had acquired in Haran, and they set out for the land of Canaan; thus they came to the land of Canaan.

6 And Abram passed through the land as far as the site of Shechem, to the oak of Moreh. Now the Canaanite *was* then in the land.

7 And the LORD appeared to Abram and said, "To your descendants I will give this land." So he built an altar there to the LORD who had appeared to him.

8 Then he proceeded from there to the mountain on the east of Bethel, and pitched his tent, with Bethel on the west and Ai on the east; and there he built an altar to the LORD and called upon the name of the LORD.

9 And Abram journeyed on, continuing toward the [15]Negev.

10 ¶ Now there was a famine in the land; so Abram went down to Egypt to sojourn there, for the famine was severe in the land.

11 And it came about when he came near to Egypt, that he said to Sarai his wife, "See now, I know that you are a beautiful woman;

12 and it will come about when the Egyptians see you, that they will say, 'This is his wife'; and they will kill me, but they will let you live.

13 "Please say that you are my sister so that it may go well with me because of you, and that I may live on account of you."

14 And it came about when Abram came into Egypt, the Egyptians saw that the woman was very beautiful.

15 And Pharaoh's officials saw her and praised her to Pharaoh; and the woman was taken into Pharaoh's house.

[15] I.e., South country

16 Therefore he treated Abram well for her sake; and gave him sheep and oxen and donkeys and male and female servants and female donkeys and camels.

17 But the LORD struck Pharaoh and his house with great plagues because of Sarai, Abram's wife.

18 Then Pharaoh called Abram and said, "What is this you have done to me? Why did you not tell me that she was your wife?

19"Why did you say, 'She is my sister,' so that I took her for my wife? Now then, here is your wife, take her and go."

20 And Pharaoh commanded *his* men concerning him; and they escorted him away, with his wife and all that belonged to him.

CHAPTER 13

So Abram went up from Egypt to the [15]Negev, he and his wife and all that belonged to him; and Lot with him.

2 Now Abram was very rich in livestock, in silver and in gold.

3 And he went on his journeys from the [16]Negev as far as Bethel, to the place where his tent had been at the beginning, between Bethel and Ai,

4 to the place of the altar, which he had made there formerly; and there Abram called on the name of the LORD.

5 Now Lot, who went with Abram, also had flocks and herds and tents.

6 And the land could not sustain them while dwelling together; for their possessions were so great that they were not able to remain together.

7 And there was strife between the herdsmen of Abram's livestock and the herdsmen of Lot's livestock. Now the Canaanite and the Perizzite were dwelling then in the land.

8 Then Abram said to Lot, "Please let there be no strife between you and me, nor between my herdsmen and your herdsmen, for we are brothers.

9"Is not the whole land before you? Please separate from me: if *to* the left, then I will go to the right; or if *to* the right, then I will go to the left."

10 And Lot lifted up his eyes and saw all the valley of the Jordan, that it was well watered everywhere—*this was*

before the LORD destroyed Sodom and Gomorrah—like the garden of the LORD, like the land of Egypt as you go to Zoar.

11 So Lot chose for himself all the valley of the Jordan; and Lot journeyed eastward. Thus they separated from each other.

12 Abram settled in the land of Canaan, while Lot settled in the cities of the valley, and moved his tents as far as Sodom.

13 Now the men of Sodom were wicked exceedingly and sinners against the LORD.

14 ¶ And the LORD said to Abram, after Lot had separated from him, "Now lift up your eyes and look from the place where you are, northward and southward and eastward and westward;

15 for all the land which you see, I will give it to you and to your descendants forever.

16"And I will make your descendants as the dust of the earth; so that if anyone can number the dust of the earth, then your descendants can also be numbered.

17"Arise, walk about the land through its length and breadth; for I will give it to you."

18 Then Abram moved his tent and came and dwelt by the oaks of Mamre, which are in Hebron, and there he built an altar to the LORD.

CHAPTER 14

And it came about in the days of Amraphel king of Shinar, Arioch king of Ellasar, Chedorlaomer king of Elam, and Tidal king of Goiim,

2 *that* they made war with Bera king of Sodom, and with Birsha king of Gomorrah, Shinab king of Admah, and Shemeber king of Zeboiim, and the king of Bela (that is, Zoar).

3 All these came as allies to the valley of Siddim (that is, the Salt Sea).

4 Twelve years they had served Chedorlaomer, but the thirteenth year they rebelled.

5 And in the fourteenth year Chedorlaomer and the kings that were with him, came and defeated the Rephaim in Ashteroth-karnaim and the Zuzim in Ham and the Emim in Shaveh-kiriathaim,

[15] I.e., South country   [16] I.e., South country

6 and the Horites in their Mount Seir, as far as El-paran, which is by the wilderness.

7 Then they turned back and came to En-mishpat (that is, Kadesh), and conquered all the country of the Amalekites, and also the Amorites, who lived in Hazazon-tamar.

8 And the king of Sodom and the king of Gomorrah and the king of Admah and the king of Zeboiim and the king of Bela (that is, Zoar) came out; and they arrayed for battle against them in the valley of Siddim,

9 against Chedorlaomer king of Elam and Tidal king of Goiim and Amraphel king of Shinar and Arioch king of Ellasar—four kings against five.

10 Now the valley of Siddim was full of tar pits; and the kings of Sodom and Gomorrah fled, and they fell into them. But those who survived fled to the hill country.

11 Then they took all the goods of Sodom and Gomorrah and all their food supply, and departed.

12 And they also took Lot, Abram's nephew, and his possessions and departed, for he was living in Sodom.

13 ¶ Then a fugitive came and told Abram the Hebrew. Now he was living by the oaks of Mamre the Amorite, brother of Eshcol and brother of Aner, and these were allies with Abram.

14 And when Abram heard that his relative had been taken captive, he led out his trained men, born in his house, three hundred and eighteen, and went in pursuit as far as Dan.

15 And he divided his forces against them by night, he and his servants, and defeated them, and pursued them as far as Hobah, which is north of Damascus.

16 And he brought back all the goods, and also brought back his relative Lot with his possessions, and also the women, and the people.

17 ¶ Then after his return from the defeat of Chedorlaomer and the kings who were with him, the king of Sodom went out to meet him at the valley of Shaveh (that is, the King's Valley).

18 And Melchizedek king of Salem brought out bread and wine; now he was a priest of God Most High.

19 And he blessed him and said,

"Blessed be Abram of God Most
    High,
  Possessor of heaven and earth;
20 And blessed be God Most High,
    Who has delivered your enemies
    into your hand."

And he gave him a tenth of all.

21 And the king of Sodom said to Abram, "Give the people to me and take the goods for yourself."

22 And Abram said to the king of Sodom, "I have sworn to the LORD God Most High, possessor of heaven and earth,

23 that I will not take a thread or a sandal thong or anything that is yours, lest you should say, 'I have made Abram rich.'

24 "I will take nothing except what the young men have eaten, and the share of the men who went with me, Aner, Eshcol, and Mamre; let them take their share."

CHAPTER 15

AFTER these things the word of the LORD came to Abram in a vision, saying,

  "Do not fear, Abram,
    I am a shield to you;
    Your reward shall be very great."

2 And Abram said, "O Lord GOD, what wilt Thou give me, since I am childless, and the heir of my house is Eliezer of Damascus?"

3 And Abram said, "Since Thou hast given no offspring to me, one born in my house is my heir."

4 Then behold, the word of the LORD came to him, saying, "This man will not be your heir; but one who shall come forth from your own body, he shall be your heir."

5 And He took him outside and said, "Now look toward the heavens, and count the stars, if you are able to count them." And He said to him, "So shall your descendants be."

6 Then he believed in the LORD; and He reckoned it to him as righteousness.

7 And He said to him, "I am the LORD who brought you out of Ur of the Chaldeans, to give you this land to possess it."

8 And he said, "O Lord GOD, how may I know that I shall possess it?"

9 So He said to him, "Bring Me a three year old heifer, and a three year old female goat, and a three year old ram, and a turtledove, and a young pigeon."

10 Then he brought all these to Him and cut them in two, and laid each half opposite the other; but he did not cut the birds.

11 And the birds of prey came down upon the carcasses, and Abram drove them away.

12 ¶ Now when the sun was going down, a deep sleep fell upon Abram; and behold, terror *and* great darkness fell upon him.

13 And *God* said to Abram, "Know for certain that your descendants will be strangers in a land that is not theirs, where they will be enslaved and oppressed four hundred years.

14"But I will also judge the nation whom they will serve; and afterward they will come out with many possessions.

15"And as for you, you shall go to your fathers in peace; you shall be buried at a good old age.

16"Then in the fourth generation they shall return here, for the iniquity of the Amorite is not yet complete."

17 And it came about when the sun had set, that it was very dark, and behold, *there appeared* a smoking oven and a flaming torch which passed between these pieces.

18 On that day the LORD made a covenant with Abram, saying,

> "To your descendants I have
> given this land,
> From the river of Egypt as far as
> the great river, the river Eu-
> phrates:

19 the Kenite and the Kenizzite and the Kadmonite

20 and the Hittite and the Perizzite and the Rephaim

21 and the Amorite and the Canaanite and the Girgashite and the Jebusite."

CHAPTER 16

Now Sarai, Abram's wife had borne him no *children,* and she had an Egyptian maid whose name was Hagar.

2 So Sarai said to Abram, "Now behold, the LORD has prevented me from bearing *children.* Please go in to my maid; perhaps I shall obtain children through her." And Abram listened to the voice of Sarai.

3 And after Abram had lived ten years in the land of Canaan, Abram's wife Sarai took Hagar the Egyptian, her maid, and gave her to her husband Abram as his wife.

4 And he went in to Hagar, and she conceived; and when she saw that she had conceived, her mistress was despised in her sight.

5 And Sarai said to Abram, "May the wrong done me be upon you. I gave my maid into your arms; but when she saw that she had conceived, I was despised in her sight. May the LORD judge between you and me."

6 But Abram said to Sarai, "Behold, your maid is in your power; do to her what is good in your sight." So Sarai treated her harshly, and she fled from her presence.

7 ¶ Now the angel of the LORD found her by a spring of water in the wilderness, by the spring on the way to Shur.

8 And he said, "Hagar, Sarai's maid, where have you come from and where are you going?" And she said, "I am fleeing from the presence of my mistress Sarai."

9 Then the angel of the LORD said to her, "Return to your mistress, and submit yourself to her authority."

10 Moreover, the angel of the LORD said to her, "I will greatly multiply your descendants so that they shall be too many to count."

11 The angel of the LORD said to her further,

> "Behold, you are with child,
> And you shall bear a son;
> And you shall call his name [17]Ish-
> mael,
> Because the LORD has given heed
> to your affliction.

12 "And he will be a wild donkey of a
> man,
> His hand *will be* against every-
> one,
> And everyone's hand *will be*
> against him;
> And he will live to the east of all
> his brothers."

13 Then she called the name of the LORD who spoke to her, "Thou art a

[17] I.e., God hears

God who sees"; for she said, "Have I even remained alive here after seeing Him?"

14 Therefore the well was called [18]Beer-lahai-roi; behold, it is between Kadesh and Bered.

15 ¶ So Hagar bore Abram a son; and Abram called the name of his son, whom Hagar bore, Ishmael.

16 And Abram was eighty-six years old when Hagar bore Ishmael to him.

CHAPTER 17

NOW when Abram was ninety-nine years old, the LORD appeared to Abram and said to him,

"I am God Almighty;
　Walk before Me, and be blameless.

2 "And I will establish My covenant between Me and you,
　And I will multiply you exceedingly."

3 And Abram fell on his face, and God talked with him, saying,

4 "As for Me, behold, My covenant is with you,
　And you shall be the father of a multitude of nations.

5 "No longer shall your name be called [19]Abram,
　But your name shall be [20]Abraham;
　For I will make you the father of a multitude of nations.

6"And I will make you exceedingly fruitful, and I will make nations of you, and kings shall come forth from you.

7"And I will establish My covenant between Me and you and your descendants after you throughout their generations for an everlasting covenant, to be God to you and to your descendants after you.

8"And I will give to you and to your descendants after you, the land of your sojournings, all the land of Canaan, for an everlasting possession; and I will be their God."

9 ¶ God said further to Abraham, "Now as for you, you shall keep My covenant, you and your descendants after you throughout their generations.

10"This is My covenant, which you shall keep, between Me and you and your descendants after you: every male among you shall be circumcised.

11"And you shall be circumcised in the flesh of your foreskin; and it shall be the sign of the covenant between Me and you.

12"And every male among you who is eight days old shall be circumcised throughout your generations, a *servant* who is born in the house or who is bought with money from any foreigner, who is not of your descendants.

13"A *servant* who is born in your house or who is bought with your money shall surely be circumcised; thus shall My covenant be in your flesh for an everlasting covenant.

14"But an uncircumcised male who is not circumcised in the flesh of his foreskin, that person shall be cut off from his people; he has broken My covenant."

15 ¶ Then God said to Abraham, "As for Sarai your wife, you shall not call her name Sarai, but [21]Sarah *shall be* her name.

16"And I will bless her, and indeed I will give you a son by her. Then I will bless her, and she shall be *a mother of* nations; kings of peoples shall come from her."

17 Then Abraham fell on his face and laughed, and said in his heart, "Will a child be born to a man one hundred years old? And will Sarah, who is ninety years old, bear *a child?*"

18 And Abraham said to God, "Oh that Ishmael might live before Thee!"

19 But God said, "No, but Sarah your wife shall bear you a son, and you shall call his name [22]Isaac; and I will establish My covenant with him for an everlasting covenant for his descendants after him.

20"And as for Ishmael, I have heard you; behold, I will bless him, and will make him fruitful, and will multiply him exceedingly. He shall become the father of twelve princes, and I will make him a great nation.

21"But My covenant I will establish with Isaac, whom Sarah will bear to you at this season next year."

22 ¶ And when He finished talking with him, God went up from Abraham.

---

[18] I.e., the well of the living one who sees me
[19] I.e., exalted father　　[20] I.e., father of a multitude
[21] I.e., princess　　[22] I.e., he laughs

23 Then Abraham took Ishmael his son, and all *the servants* who were born in his house and all who were bought with his money, every male among the men of Abraham's household, and circumcised the flesh of their foreskin in the very same day, as God had said to him.

24 Now Abraham was ninety-nine years old when he was circumcised in the flesh of his foreskin.

25 And Ishmael his son was thirteen years old when he was circumcised in the flesh of his foreskin.

26 In the very same day Abraham was circumcised, and Ishmael his son.

27 And all the men of his household, who were born in the house or bought with money from a foreigner, were circumcised with him.

CHAPTER 18

NOW the LORD appeared to him by the oaks of Mamre, while he was sitting at the tent door in the heat of the day.

2 And when he lifted up his eyes and looked, behold, three men were standing opposite him; and when he saw *them,* he ran from the tent door to meet them, and bowed himself to the earth,

3 and said, "My lord, if now I have found favor in your sight, please do not pass your servant by.

4"Please let a little water be brought and wash your feet, and rest yourselves under the tree;

5 and I will bring a piece of bread, that you may refresh yourselves; after that you may go on, since you have visited your servant." And they said, "So do, as you have said."

6 So Abraham hurried into the tent to Sarah, and said, "Quickly, prepare three measures of fine flour, knead *it,* and make bread cakes."

7 Abraham also ran to the herd, and took a tender and choice calf, and gave *it* to the servant; and he hurried to prepare it.

8 And he took curds and milk and the calf which he had prepared, and placed *it* before them; and he was standing by them under the tree as they ate.

9 ¶ Then they said to him, "Where is Sarah your wife?" And he said, "Behold, in the tent."

10 And he said, "I will surely return to you at this time next year; and behold, Sarah your wife shall have a son." And Sarah was listening at the tent door, which was behind him.

11 Now Abraham and Sarah were old, advanced in age; Sarah was past childbearing.

12 And Sarah laughed to herself, saying, "After I have become old, shall I have pleasure, my lord being old also?"

13 And the LORD said to Abraham, "Why did Sarah laugh, saying, 'Shall I indeed bear *a child,* when I am *so* old?'

14"Is anything too difficult for the LORD? At the appointed time I will return to you, at this time next year, and Sarah shall have a son."

15 Sarah denied *it* however, saying, "I did not laugh"; for she was afraid. And He said, "No, but you did laugh."

16 ¶ Then the men rose up from there, and looked down toward Sodom; and Abraham was walking with them to send them off.

17 And the LORD said, "Shall I hide from Abraham what I am about to do,

18 since Abraham will surely become a great and mighty nation, and in him all the nations of the earth will be blessed?

19"For I have chosen him, in order that he may command his children and his household after him to keep the way of the LORD by doing righteousness and justice; in order that the LORD may bring upon Abraham what He has spoken about him."

20 And the LORD said, "The outcry of Sodom and Gomorrah is indeed great, and their sin is exceedingly grave.

21"I will go down now, and see if they have done entirely according to its outcry, which has come to Me; and if not, I will know."

22 ¶ Then the men turned away from there and went toward Sodom, while Abraham was still standing before the LORD.

23 And Abraham came near and said, "Wilt Thou indeed sweep away the righteous with the wicked?

24"Suppose there are fifty righteous within the city; wilt Thou indeed sweep *it* away and not spare the place for the sake of the fifty righteous who are in it?

25"Far be it from Thee to do such a thing, to slay the righteous with the wicked, so that the righteous and the wicked are *treated* alike. Far be it from Thee! Shall not the Judge of all the earth deal justly?"

26 So the LORD said, "If I find in Sodom fifty righteous within the city, then I will spare the whole place on their account."

27 And Abraham answered and said, "Now behold, I have ventured to speak to the Lord, although I am *but* dust and ashes.

28"Suppose the fifty righteous are lacking five, wilt Thou destroy the whole city because of five?" And He said, "I will not destroy *it* if I find forty-five there."

29 And he spoke to Him yet again and said, "Suppose forty are found there?" And He said, "I will not do *it* on account of the forty."

30 Then he said, "Oh may the Lord not be angry, and I shall speak; suppose thirty are found there?" And He said, "I will not do *it* if I find thirty there."

31 And he said, "Now behold, I have ventured to speak to the Lord; suppose twenty are found there?" And He said, "I will not destroy *it* on account of the twenty."

32 Then he said, "Oh may the Lord not be angry, and I shall speak only this once; suppose ten are found there?" And He said, "I will not destroy *it* on account of the ten."

33 And as soon as He had finished speaking to Abraham the LORD departed; and Abraham returned to his place.

CHAPTER 19

Now the two angels came to Sodom in the evening as Lot was sitting in the gate of Sodom. When Lot saw *them,* he rose to meet them and bowed down *with his* face to the ground.

2 And he said, "Now behold, my lords, please turn aside into your servant's house, and spend the night, and wash your feet; then you may rise early and go on your way." They said however, "No, but we shall spend the night in the square."

3 Yet he urged them strongly, so they turned aside to him and entered his house; and he prepared a feast for them, and baked unleavened bread, and they ate.

4 Before they lay down, the men of the city, the men of Sodom, surrounded the house, both young and old, all the people from every quarter;

5 and they called to Lot and said to him, "Where are the men who came to you tonight? Bring them out to us that we may have relations with them."

6 But Lot went out to them at the doorway, and shut the door behind him,

7 and said, "Please, my brothers, do not act wickedly.

8"Now behold, I have two daughters who have not had relations with man; please let me bring them out to you, and do to them whatever you like; only do nothing to these men, inasmuch as they have come under the shelter of my roof."

9 But they said, "Stand aside." Furthermore, they said, "This one came in as an alien, and already he is acting like a judge; now we will treat you worse than them." So they pressed hard against Lot and came near to break the door.

10 But the men reached out their hands and brought Lot into the house with them, and shut the door.

11 And they struck the men who were at the doorway of the house with blindness, both small and great, so that they wearied *themselves trying* to find the doorway.

12 ¶ Then the men said to Lot, "Whom else have you here? A son-in-law, and your sons, and your daughters, and whomever you have in the city, bring *them* out of the place;

13 for we are about to destroy this place, because their outcry has become so great before the LORD that the LORD has sent us to destroy it."

14 And Lot went out and spoke to his sons-in-law, who were to marry his daughters, and said, "Up, get out of this place, for the LORD will destroy the city." But he appeared to his sons-in-law to be jesting.

15 And when morning dawned, the angels urged Lot, saying, "Up, take your wife and your two daughters,

who are here, lest you be swept away in the punishment of the city."

16 But he hesitated. So the men seized his hand and the hand of his wife and the hands of his two daughters, for the compassion of the LORD *was* upon him; and they brought him out, and put him outside the city.

17 And it came about when they had brought them outside, that one said, "Escape for your life! Do not look behind you, and do not stay anywhere in the valley; escape to the mountains, lest you be swept away."

18 But Lot said to them, "Oh no, my lords!

19"Now behold, your servant has found favor in your sight, and you have magnified your lovingkindness, which you have shown me by saving my life; but I cannot escape to the mountains, lest the disaster overtake me and I die;

20 now behold, this town is near *enough* to flee to, and it is small. Please, let me escape there (is it not small?) that my life may be saved."

21 And he said to him, "Behold, I grant you this request also, not to overthrow the town of which you have spoken.

22"Hurry, escape there, for I cannot do anything until you arrive there." Therefore the name of the town was called [23]Zoar.

23 ¶ The sun had risen over the earth when Lot came to Zoar.

24 Then the LORD rained on Sodom and Gomorrah brimstone and fire from the LORD out of heaven,

25 and He overthrew those cities, and all the valley, and all the inhabitants of the cities, and what grew on the ground.

26 But his wife, from behind him, looked *back;* and she became a pillar of salt.

27 ¶ Now Abraham arose early in the morning *and went* to the place where he had stood before the LORD;

28 and he looked down toward Sodom and Gomorrah, and toward all the land of the valley, and he saw, and behold, the smoke of the land ascended like the smoke of a furnace.

29 Thus it came about, when God destroyed the cities of the valley, that God remembered Abraham, and sent Lot out of the midst of the overthrow, when He overthrew the cities in which Lot lived.

30 ¶ And Lot went up from Zoar, and stayed in the mountains, and his two daughters with him; for he was afraid to stay in Zoar; and he stayed in a cave, he and his two daughters.

31 Then the first-born said to the younger, "Our father is old, and there is not a man on earth to come in to us after the manner of the earth.

32"Come, let us make our father drink wine, and let us lie with him, that we may preserve our family through our father."

33 So they made their father drink wine that night, and the first-born went in and lay with her father; and he did not know when she lay down or when she arose.

34 And it came about on the morrow, that the first-born said to the younger, "Behold, I lay last night with my father; let us make him drink wine tonight also; then you go in and lie with him, that we may preserve our family through our father."

35 So they made their father drink wine that night also, and the younger arose and lay with him; and he did not know when she lay down or when she arose.

36 Thus both the daughters of Lot were with child by their father.

37 And the first-born bore a son, and called his name Moab; he is the father of the Moabites to this day.

38 And as for the younger, she also bore a son, and called his name Benammi; he is the father of the sons of Ammon to this day.

CHAPTER 20

Now Abraham journeyed from there toward the land of the [24]Negev, and settled between Kadesh and Shur; then he sojourned in Gerar.

2 And Abraham said of Sarah his wife, "She is my sister." So Abimelech king of Gerar sent and took Sarah.

3 But God came to Abimelech in a dream of the night, and said to him, "Behold, you are a dead man because of the woman whom you have taken, for she is married."

---

[23] I.e., small   [24] I.e., South country

4 Now Abimelech had not come near her; and he said, "Lord, wilt Thou slay a nation, even *though* blameless?

5"Did he not himself say to me, 'She is my sister'? And she herself said, 'He is my brother.' In the integrity of my heart and the innocence of my hands I have done this."

6 Then God said to him in the dream, "Yes, I know that in the integrity of your heart you have done this, and I also kept you from sinning against Me; therefore I did not let you touch her.

7"Now therefore, restore the man's wife, for he is a prophet, and he will pray for you, and you will live. But if you do not restore *her,* know that you shall surely die, you and all who are yours."

8 ¶ So Abimelech arose early in the morning and called all his servants and told all these things in their hearing; and the men were greatly frightened.

9 Then Abimelech called Abraham and said to him, "What have you done to us? And how have I sinned against you, that you have brought on me and on my kingdom a great sin? You have done to me things that ought not to be done."

10 And Abimelech said to Abraham, "What have you encountered, that you have done this thing?"

11 And Abraham said, "Because I thought, surely there is no fear of God in this place; and they will kill me because of my wife.

12"Besides, she actually is my sister, the daughter of my father, but not the daughter of my mother, and she became my wife;

13 and it came about, when God caused me to wander from my father's house, that I said to her, 'This is the kindness which you will show to me: everywhere we go, say of me, "He is my brother." ' "

14 Abimelech then took sheep and oxen and male and female servants, and gave them to Abraham, and restored his wife Sarah to him.

15 And Abimelech said, "Behold, my land is before you; settle wherever you please."

16 And to Sarah he said, "Behold, I have given your brother a thousand pieces of silver; behold, it is your vindication before all who are with you, and before all men you are cleared."

17 And Abraham prayed to God; and God healed Abimelech and his wife and his maids, so that they bore *children.*

18 For the LORD had closed fast all the wombs of the household of Abimelech because of Sarah, Abraham's wife.

CHAPTER 21

THEN the LORD took note of Sarah as He had said, and the LORD did for Sarah as He had promised.

2 So Sarah conceived and bore a son to Abraham in his old age, at the appointed time of which God had spoken to him.

3 And Abraham called the name of his son who was born to him, whom Sarah bore to him, Isaac.

4 Then Abraham circumcised his son Isaac when he was eight days old, as God had commanded him.

5 Now Abraham was one hundred years old when his son Isaac was born to him.

6 And Sarah said, "God has made laughter for me; everyone who hears will laugh with me."

7 And she said, "Who would have said to Abraham that Sarah would nurse children? Yet I have borne him a son in his old age."

8 ¶ And the child grew and was weaned, and Abraham made a great feast on the day that Isaac was weaned.

9 Now Sarah saw the son of Hagar the Egyptian, whom she had borne to Abraham, mocking.

10 Therefore she said to Abraham, "Drive out this maid and her son, for the son of this maid shall not be an heir with my son Isaac."

11 And the matter distressed Abraham greatly because of his son.

12 But God said to Abraham, "Do not be distressed because of the lad and your maid; whatever Sarah tells you, listen to her, for through Isaac your descendants shall be named.

13"And of the son of the maid I will make a nation also, because he is your descendant."

14 So Abraham rose early in the morning, and took bread and a skin of water, and gave *them* to Hagar, putting *them* on her shoulder, and *gave her* the boy, and sent her away. And she departed, and wandered about in the wilderness of Beersheba.

15 And the water in the skin was used up, and she left the boy under one of the bushes.

16 Then she went and sat down opposite him, about a bowshot away, for she said, "Do not let me see the boy die." And she sat opposite him, and lifted up her voice and wept.

17 And God heard the lad crying; and the angel of God called to Hagar from heaven, and said to her, "What is the matter with you, Hagar? Do not fear, for God has heard the voice of the lad where he is.

18 "Arise, lift up the lad, and hold him by the hand; for I will make a great nation of him."

19 Then God opened her eyes and she saw a well of water; and she went and filled the skin with water, and gave the lad a drink.

20 And God was with the lad, and he grew; and he lived in the wilderness, and became an archer.

21 And he lived in the wilderness of Paran; and his mother took a wife for him from the land of Egypt.

22 ¶ Now it came about at that time, that Abimelech and Phicol, the commander of his army, spoke to Abraham, saying, "God is with you in all that you do;

23 now therefore, swear to me here by God that you will not deal falsely with me, or with my offspring, or with my posterity; but according to the kindness that I have shown to you, you shall show to me, and to the land in which you have sojourned."

24 And Abraham said, "I swear it."

25 But Abraham complained to Abimelech because of the well of water which the servants of Abimelech had seized.

26 And Abimelech said, "I do not know who has done this thing; neither did you tell me, nor did I hear of it until today."

27 And Abraham took sheep and oxen, and gave them to Abimelech; and the two of them made a covenant.

28 Then Abraham set seven ewe lambs of the flock by themselves.

29 And Abimelech said to Abraham, "What do these seven ewe lambs mean, which you have set by themselves?"

30 And he said, "You shall take these seven ewe lambs from my hand in order that it may be a witness to me, that I dug this well."

31 Therefore he called that place Beersheba; because there the two of them took an oath.

32 So they made a covenant at Beersheba; and Abimelech and Phicol, the commander of his army, arose and returned to the land of the Philistines.

33 And *Abraham* planted a tamarisk tree at Beersheba, and there he called on the name of the Lord, the Everlasting God.

34 And Abraham sojourned in the land of the Philistines for many days.

CHAPTER 22

Now it came about after these things, that God tested Abraham, and said to him, "Abraham!" And he said, "Here I am."

2 And He said, "Take now your son, your only son, whom you love, Isaac, and go to the land of Moriah; and offer him there as a burnt offering on one of the mountains of which I will tell you."

3 So Abraham rose early in the morning and saddled his donkey, and took two of his young men with him and Isaac his son; and he split wood for the burnt offering, and arose and went to the place of which God had told him.

4 On the third day Abraham raised his eyes and saw the place from a distance.

5 And Abraham said to his young men, "Stay here with the donkey, and I and the lad will go yonder; and we will worship and return to you."

6 And Abraham took the wood of the burnt offering and laid it on Isaac his son, and he took in his hand the fire and the knife. So the two of them walked on together.

7 And Isaac spoke to Abraham his father and said, "My father!" And he said, "Here I am, my son." And he said, "Behold, the fire and the wood,

but where is the lamb for the burnt offering?"

8 And Abraham said, "God will provide for Himself the lamb for the burnt offering, my son." So the two of them walked on together.

9 ¶ Then they came to the place of which God had told him; and Abraham built the altar there, and arranged the wood, and bound his son Isaac, and laid him on the altar on top of the wood.

10 And Abraham stretched out his hand, and took the knife to slay his son.

11 But the angel of the LORD called to him from heaven, and said, "Abraham, Abraham!" And he said, "Here I am."

12 And he said, "Do not stretch out your hand against the lad, and do nothing to him; for now I know that you fear God, since you have not withheld your son, your only son, from Me."

13 Then Abraham raised his eyes and looked, and behold, behind *him* a ram caught in the thicket by his horns; and Abraham went and took the ram, and offered him up for a burnt offering in the place of his son.

14 And Abraham called the name of that place The LORD Will Provide, as it is said to this day, "In the mount of the LORD it will be provided."

15 Then the angel of the LORD called to Abraham a second time from heaven,

16 and said, "By Myself I have sworn, declares the LORD, because you have done this thing, and have not withheld your son, your only son,

17 indeed I will greatly bless you, and I will greatly multiply your seed as the stars of the heavens, and as the sand which is on the seashore; and your seed shall possess the gate of their enemies.

18 "And in your seed all the nations of the earth shall be blessed, because you have obeyed My voice."

19 So Abraham returned to his young men, and they arose and went together to Beersheba; and Abraham lived at Beersheba.

20 ¶ Now it came about after these things, that it was told Abraham, say-ing, "Behold, Milcah also has borne children to your brother Nahor:

21 Uz his first-born and Buz his brother and Kemuel the father of Aram

22 and Chesed and Hazo and Pildash and Jidlaph and Bethuel."

23 And Bethuel became the father of Rebekah: these eight Milcah bore to Nahor, Abraham's brother.

24 And his concubine, whose name was Reumah, also bore Tebah and Gaham and Tahash and Maacah.

CHAPTER 23

NOW Sarah lived one hundred and twenty-seven years; *these were* the years of the life of Sarah.

2 And Sarah died in Kiriath-arba (that is, Hebron) in the land of Canaan; and Abraham went in to mourn for Sarah and to weep for her.

3 Then Abraham rose from before his dead, and spoke to the sons of Heth, saying,

4 "I am a stranger and a sojourner among you; give me a burial site among you, that I may bury my dead out of my sight."

5 And the sons of Heth answered Abraham, saying to him,

6 "Hear us, my lord, you are a mighty prince among us; bury your dead in the choicest of our graves; none of us will refuse you his grave for burying your dead."

7 So Abraham rose and bowed to the people of the land, the sons of Heth.

8 And he spoke with them, saying, "If it is your wish *for me* to bury my dead out of my sight, hear me, and approach Ephron the son of Zohar for me,

9 that he may give me the cave of Machpelah which he owns, which is at the end of his field; for the full price let him give it to me in your presence for a burial site."

10 Now Ephron was sitting among the sons of Heth; and Ephron the Hittite answered Abraham in the hearing of the sons of Heth; *even* of all who went in at the gate of his city, saying,

11 "No, my lord, hear me; I give you the field, and I give you the cave that is in it. In the presence of the sons of

my people I give it to you; bury your dead."

12 And Abraham bowed before the people of the land.

13 And he spoke to Ephron in the hearing of the people of the land, saying, "If you will only please listen to me; I will give the price of the field, accept *it* from me, that I may bury my dead there."

14 Then Ephron answered Abraham, saying to him,

15"My lord, listen to me; a piece of land worth four hundred shekels of silver, what is that between me and you? So bury your dead."

16 And Abraham listened to Ephron; and Abraham weighed out for Ephron the silver which he had named in the hearing of the sons of Heth, four hundred shekels of silver, commercial standard.

17 ¶ So Ephron's field, which was in Machpelah, which faced Mamre, the field and cave which was in it, and all the trees which were in the field, that were within all the confines of its border, were deeded over

18 to Abraham for a possession in the presence of the sons of Heth, before all who went in at the gate of his city.

19 And after this, Abraham buried Sarah his wife in the cave of the field at Machpelah facing Mamre (that is, Hebron) in the land of Canaan.

20 So the field, and the cave that is in it, were deeded over to Abraham for a burial site by the sons of Heth.

CHAPTER 24

NOW Abraham was old, advanced in age; and the LORD had blessed Abraham in every way.

2 And Abraham said to his servant, the oldest of his household, who had charge of all that he owned, "Please place your hand under my thigh,

3 and I will make you swear by the LORD, the God of heaven and the God of earth, that you shall not take a wife for my son from the daughters of the Canaanites, among whom I live,

4 but you shall go to my country and to my relatives, and take a wife for my son Isaac."

5 And the servant said to him,

"Suppose the woman will not be willing to follow me to this land; should I take your son back to the land from where you came?"

6 Then Abraham said to him, "Beware lest you take my son back there!

7"The LORD, the God of heaven, who took me from my father's house and from the land of my birth, and who spoke to me, and who swore to me, saying, 'To your descendants I will give this land,' He will send His angel before you, and you will take a wife for my son from there.

8"But if the woman is not willing to follow you, then you will be free from this my oath; only do not take my son back there."

9 So the servant placed his hand under the thigh of Abraham his master, and swore to him concerning this matter.

10 ¶ Then the servant took ten camels from the camels of his master, and set out with a variety of good things of his master's in his hand; and he arose, and went to Mesopotamia, to the city of Nahor.

11 And he made the camels kneel down outside the city by the well of water at evening time, the time when women go out to draw water.

12 And he said, "O LORD, the God of my master Abraham, please grant me success today, and show lovingkindness to my master Abraham.

13"Behold, I am standing by the spring, and the daughters of the men of the city are coming out to draw water;

14 now may it be that the girl to whom I say, 'Please let down your jar so that I may drink,' and who answers, 'Drink, and I will water your camels also';—*may* she *be the one* whom Thou hast appointed for Thy servant Isaac; and by this I shall know that Thou hast shown lovingkindness to my master."

15 And it came about before he had finished speaking, that behold, Rebekah who was born to Bethuel the son of Milcah, the wife of Abraham's brother Nahor, came out with her jar on her shoulder.

16 And the girl was very beautiful, a virgin, and no man had had relations

with her; and she went down to the spring and filled her jar, and came up.

17 Then the servant ran to meet her, and said, "Please let me drink a little water from your jar."

18 And she said, "Drink, my lord"; and she quickly lowered her jar to her hand, and gave him a drink.

19 Now when she had finished giving him a drink, she said, "I will draw also for your camels until they have finished drinking."

20 So she quickly emptied her jar into the trough, and ran back to the well to draw, and she drew for all his camels.

21 Meanwhile, the man was gazing at her in silence, to know whether the LORD had made his journey successful or not.

22 Then it came about, when the camels had finished drinking, that the man took a gold ring weighing a half-shekel and two bracelets for her wrists weighing ten shekels in gold,

23 and said, "Whose daughter are you? Please tell me, is there room for us to lodge in your father's house?"

24 And she said to him, "I am the daughter of Bethuel, the son of Milcah, whom she bore to Nahor."

25 Again she said to him, "We have plenty of both straw and feed, and room to lodge in."

26 Then the man bowed low and worshiped the LORD.

27 And he said, "Blessed be the LORD, the God of my master Abraham, who has not forsaken His lovingkindness and His truth toward my master; as for me, the LORD has guided me in the way to the house of my master's brothers."

28 ¶ Then the girl ran and told her mother's household about these things.

29 Now Rebekah had a brother whose name was Laban; and Laban ran outside to the man at the spring.

30 And it came about that when he saw the ring, and the bracelets on his sister's wrists, and when he heard the words of Rebekah his sister, saying, "This is what the man said to me," he went to the man; and behold, he was standing by the camels at the spring.

31 And he said, "Come in, blessed of the LORD! Why do you stand outside

since I have prepared the house, and a place for the camels?"

32 So the man entered the house. Then Laban unloaded the camels, and he gave straw and feed to the camels, and water to wash his feet and the feet of the men who were with him.

33 But when *food* was set before him to eat, he said, "I will not eat until I have told my business." And he said, "Speak on."

34 So he said, "I am Abraham's servant.

35 "And the LORD has greatly blessed my master, so that he has become rich; and He has given him flocks and herds, and silver and gold, and servants and maids, and camels and donkeys.

36 "Now Sarah my master's wife bore a son to my master in her old age; and he has given him all that he has.

37 "And my master made me swear, saying, 'You shall not take a wife for my son from the daughters of the Canaanites, in whose land I live;

38 but you shall go to my father's house, and to my relatives, and take a wife for my son.'

39 "And I said to my master, 'Suppose the woman does not follow me.'

40 "And he said to me, 'The LORD, before whom I have walked, will send His angel with you to make your journey successful, and you will take a wife for my son from my relatives, and from my father's house;

41 then you will be free from my oath, when you come to my relatives; and if they do not give her to you, you will be free from my oath.'

42 "So I came today to the spring, and said, 'O LORD, the God of my master Abraham, if now Thou wilt make my journey on which I go successful;

43 behold, I am standing by the spring, and may it be that the maiden who comes out to draw, and to whom I say, "Please let me drink a little water from your jar";

44 and she will say to me, "You drink, and I will draw for your camels also"; let her be the woman whom the LORD has appointed for my master's son.'

45 "Before I had finished speaking in my heart, behold, Rebekah came out with her jar on her shoulder, and went

down to the spring and drew; and I said to her, 'Please let me drink.'

46"And she quickly lowered her jar from her *shoulder*, and said, 'Drink, and I will water your camels also'; so I drank, and she watered the camels also.

47"Then I asked her, and said, 'Whose daughter are you?' And she said, 'The daughter of Bethuel, Nahor's son, whom Milcah bore to him'; and I put the ring on her nose, and the bracelets on her wrists.

48"And I bowed low and worshiped the LORD, and blessed the LORD, the God of my master Abraham, who had guided me in the right way to take the daughter of my master's kinsman for his son.

49"So now if you are going to ²⁵deal kindly and truly with my master, tell me; and if not, let me know, that I may turn to the right hand or the left."

50 ¶ Then Laban and Bethuel answered and said, "The matter comes from the LORD; *so* we cannot speak to you bad or good.

51"Behold, Rebekah is before you, take *her* and go, and let her be the wife of your master's son, as the LORD has spoken."

52 And it came about when Abraham's servant heard their words, that he bowed himself to the ground before the LORD.

53 And the servant brought out articles of silver and articles of gold, and garments, and gave them to Rebekah; he also gave precious things to her brother and to her mother.

54 Then he and the men who were with him ate and drank and spent the night. When they arose in the morning, he said, "Send me away to my master."

55 But her brother and her mother said, "Let the girl stay with us *a few* days, say ten; afterward she may go."

56 And he said to them, "Do not delay me, since the LORD has prospered my way. Send me away that I may go to my master."

57 And they said, "We will call the girl and consult her wishes."

58 Then they called Rebekah and said to her, "Will you go with this man?" And she said, "I will go."

59 Thus they sent away their sister Rebekah and her nurse with Abraham's servant and his men.

60 And they blessed Rebekah and said to her,
"May you, our sister,
Become thousands of ten thousands,
And may your descendants possess
The gate of those who hate them."

61 ¶ Then Rebekah arose with her maids, and they mounted the camels and followed the man. So the servant took Rebekah and departed.

62 Now Isaac had come from going to Beer-lahai-roi; for he was living in the Negev.

63 And Isaac went out to meditate in the field toward evening; and he lifted up his eyes and looked, and behold, camels were coming.

64 And Rebekah lifted up her eyes, and when she saw Isaac she dismounted from the camel.

65 And she said to the servant, "Who is that man walking in the field to meet us?" And the servant said, "He is my master." Then she took her veil and covered herself.

66 And the servant told Isaac all the things that he had done.

67 Then Isaac brought her into his mother Sarah's tent, and he took Rebekah, and she became his wife; and he loved her; thus Isaac was comforted after his mother's death.

CHAPTER 25

NOW Abraham took another wife, whose name was Keturah.

2 And she bore to him Zimran and Jokshan and Medan and Midian and Ishbak and Shuah.

3 And Jokshan became the father of Sheba and Dedan. And the sons of Dedan were Asshurim and Letushim and Leummim.

4 And the sons of Midian *were* Ephah and Epher and Hanoch and Abida and Eldaah. All these *were* the sons of Keturah.

5 Now Abraham gave all that he had to Isaac;

6 but to the sons of his concubines, Abraham gave gifts while he was still living, and sent them away from his

²⁵ Lit., *show lovingkindness and truth*

son Isaac eastward, to the land of the east.

7 And these are all the years of Abraham's life that he lived, one hundred and seventy-five years.

8 And Abraham breathed his last and died in a ripe old age, an old man and satisfied *with life;* and he was gathered to his people.

9 Then his sons Isaac and Ishmael buried him in the cave of Machpelah, in the field of Ephron the son of Zohar the Hittite, facing Mamre,

10 the field which Abraham purchased from the sons of Heth; there Abraham was buried with Sarah his wife.

11 And it came about after the death of Abraham, that God blessed his son Isaac; and Isaac lived by Beer-lahai-roi.

12 ¶ Now these are *the records of* the generations of Ishmael, Abraham's son, whom Hagar the Egyptian, Sarah's maid, bore to Abraham;

13 and these are the names of the sons of Ishmael, by their names, in the order of their birth: Nebaioth, the first-born of Ishmael, and Kedar and Adbeel and Mibsam

14 and Mishma and Dumah and Massa,

15 Hadad and Tema, Jetur, Naphish and Kedemah.

16 These are the sons of Ishmael and these are their names, by their villages, and by their camps; twelve princes according to their tribes.

17 And these are the years of the life of Ishmael, one hundred and thirty-seven years; and he breathed his last and died, and was gathered to his people.

18 And they settled from Havilah to Shur which is east of Egypt as one goes toward Assyria; he settled in defiance of all his relatives.

19 ¶ Now these are *the records of* the generations of Isaac, Abraham's son: Abraham became the father of Isaac;

20 and Isaac was forty years old when he took Rebekah, the daughter of Bethuel the Aramean of Paddan-aram, the sister of Laban the Aramean, to be his wife.

21 And Isaac prayed to the LORD on behalf of his wife, because she was barren; and the LORD answered him and Rebekah his wife conceived.

22 But the children struggled together within her; and she said, "If it is so, why then am I *this way?*" So she went to inquire of the LORD.

23 And the LORD said to her,

"Two nations are in your womb;
   And two peoples shall be separated from your body;
   And one people shall be stronger than the other;
   And the older shall serve the younger."

24 When her days to be delivered were fulfilled, behold, there were twins in her womb.

25 Now the first came forth red, all over like a hairy garment; and they named him Esau.

26 And afterward his brother came forth with his hand holding on to Esau's heel, so his name was called [26]Jacob; and Isaac was sixty years old when she gave birth to them.

27 ¶ When the boys grew up, Esau became a skillful hunter, a man of the field; but Jacob was a peaceful man, living in tents.

28 Now Isaac loved Esau, because he had a taste for game; but Rebekah loved Jacob.

29 And when Jacob had cooked stew, Esau came in from the field and he was famished;

30 and Esau said to Jacob, "Please let me have a swallow of that red stuff there, for I am famished." Therefore his name was called [27]Edom.

31 But Jacob said, "First sell me your birthright."

32 And Esau said, "Behold, I am about to die; so of what *use* then is the birthright to me?"

33 And Jacob said, "First swear to me"; so he swore to him, and sold his birthright to Jacob.

34 Then Jacob gave Esau bread and lentil stew; and he ate and drank, and rose and went on his way. Thus Esau despised his birthright.

CHAPTER 26

Now there was a famine in the land, besides the previous famine that had occurred in the days of Abraham. So

---

[26] I.e., one who takes by the heel, or supplants   [27] I.e., red

Isaac went to Gerar, to Abimelech king of the Philistines.

2 And the LORD appeared to him and said, "Do not go down to Egypt; stay in the land of which I shall tell you.

3 "Sojourn in this land and I will be with you and bless you, for to you and to your descendants I will give all these lands, and I will establish the oath which I swore to your father Abraham.

4 "And I will multiply your descendants as the stars of heaven, and will give your descendants all these lands; and by your descendants all the nations of the earth shall be blessed;

5 because Abraham obeyed Me and kept My charge, My commandments, My statutes and My laws."

6 So Isaac lived in Gerar.

7 When the men of the place asked about his wife, he said, "She is my sister," for he was afraid to say, "my wife," *thinking*, "the men of the place might kill me on account of Rebekah, for she is beautiful."

8 And it came about, when he had been there a long time, that Abimelech king of the Philistines looked out through a window, and saw, and behold, Isaac was caressing his wife Rebekah.

9 Then Abimelech called Isaac and said, "Behold, certainly she is your wife! How then did you say, 'She is my sister'?" And Isaac said to him, "Because I said, 'Lest I die on account of her.'"

10 And Abimelech said, "What is this you have done to us? One of the people might easily have lain with your wife, and you would have brought guilt upon us."

11 So Abimelech charged all the people, saying, "He who touches this man or his wife shall surely be put to death."

12 ¶ Now Isaac sowed in that land, and reaped in the same year a hundredfold. And the LORD blessed him,

13 and the man became rich, and continued to grow richer until he became very wealthy;

14 for he had possessions of flocks and herds and a great household, so that the Philistines envied him.

15 Now all the wells which his father's servants had dug in the days of Abraham his father, the Philistines stopped up by filling them with earth.

16 Then Abimelech said to Isaac, "Go away from us, for you are too powerful for us."

17 And Isaac departed from there and camped in the valley of Gerar, and settled there.

18 ¶ Then Isaac dug again the wells of water which had been dug in the days of his father Abraham, for the Philistines had stopped them up after the death of Abraham; and he gave them the same names which his father had given them.

19 But when Isaac's servants dug in the valley and found there a well of flowing water,

20 the herdsmen of Gerar quarreled with the herdsmen of Isaac, saying, "The water is ours!" So he named the well Esek, because they contended with him.

21 Then they dug another well, and they quarreled over it too, so he named it Sitnah.

22 And he moved away from there and dug another well, and they did not quarrel over it; so he named it Rehoboth, for he said, "At last the LORD has made room for us, and we shall be fruitful in the land."

23 ¶ Then he went up from there to Beersheba.

24 And the LORD appeared to him the same night and said,

"I am the God of your father Abraham;
Do not fear, for I am with you.
I will bless you, and multiply your descendants,
For the sake of My servant Abraham."

25 So he built an altar there, and called upon the name of the LORD, and pitched his tent there; and there Isaac's servants dug a well.

26 ¶ Then Abimelech came to him from Gerar with his adviser Ahuzzath, and Phicol the commander of his army.

27 And Isaac said to them, "Why have you come to me, since you hate me, and have sent me away from you?"

28 And they said, "We see plainly that the LORD has been with you; so we said, 'Let there now be an oath between us, *even* between you and us, and let us make a covenant with you,

29 that you will do us no harm, just as we have not touched you and have done to you nothing but good, and have sent you away in peace. You are now the blessed of the LORD.' "

30 Then he made them a feast, and they ate and drank.

31 And in the morning they arose early and exchanged oaths; then Isaac sent them away and they departed from him in peace.

32 Now it came about on the same day, that Isaac's servants came in and told him about the well which they had dug, and said to him, "We have found water."

33 So he called it Shibah; therefore the name of the city is Beersheba to this day.

34 ¶ And when Esau was forty years old he married Judith the daughter of Beeri the Hittite, and Basemath the daughter of Elon the Hittite;

35 and they [28]brought grief to Isaac and Rebekah.

CHAPTER 27

Now it came about, when Isaac was old, and his eyes were too dim to see, that he called his older son Esau and said to him, "My son." And he said to him, "Here I am."

2 And Isaac said, "Behold now, I am old *and* I do not know the day of my death.

3"Now then, please take your gear, your quiver and your bow, and go out to the field and hunt game for me;

4 and prepare a savory dish for me such as I love, and bring it to me that I may eat, so that my soul may bless you before I die."

5 ¶ And Rebekah was listening while Isaac spoke to his son Esau. So when Esau went to the field to hunt for game to bring *home,*

6 Rebekah said to her son Jacob, "Behold, I heard your father speak to your brother Esau, saying,

7 'Bring me *some* game and prepare a savory dish for me, that I may eat,

and bless you in the presence of the LORD before my death.'

8"Now therefore, my son, listen to me as I command you.

9"Go now to the flock and bring me two choice kids from there, that I may prepare them *as* a savory dish for your father, such as he loves.

10"Then you shall bring *it* to your father, that he may eat, so that he may bless you before his death."

11 And Jacob answered his mother Rebekah, "Behold, Esau my brother is a hairy man and I am a smooth man.

12"Perhaps my father will feel me, then I shall be as a deceiver in his sight; and I shall bring upon myself a curse and not a blessing."

13 But his mother said to him, "Your curse be on me, my son; only obey my voice, and go, get *them* for me."

14 So he went and got *them,* and brought *them* to his mother; and his mother made savory food such as his father loved.

15 Then Rebekah took the best garments of Esau her elder son, which were with her in the house, and put them on Jacob her younger son.

16 And she put the skins of the kids on his hands and on the smooth part of his neck.

17 She also gave the savory food and the bread, which she had made, to her son Jacob.

18 ¶ Then he came to his father and said, "My father." And he said, "Here I am. Who are you, my son?"

19 And Jacob said to his father, "I am Esau your first-born; I have done as you told me. Get up, please, sit and eat of my game, that you may bless me."

20 And Isaac said to his son, "How is it that you have *it* so quickly, my son?" And he said, "Because the LORD your God caused *it* to happen to me."

21 Then Isaac said to Jacob, "Please come close, that I may feel you, my son, whether you are really my son Esau or not."

22 So Jacob came close to Isaac his father, and he felt him and said, "The voice is the voice of Jacob, but the hands are the hands of Esau."

23 And he did not recognize him, because his hands were hairy like his

---

[28] Lit., *were a bitterness of spirit to*

brother Esau's hands; so he blessed him.

24 And he said, "Are you really my son Esau?" And he said, "I am."

25 So he said, "Bring it to me, and I will eat of my son's game, that I may bless you." And he brought it to him, and he ate; he also brought him wine and he drank.

26 Then his father Isaac said to him, "Please come close and kiss me, my son."

27 So he came close and kissed him; and when he smelled the smell of his garments, he blessed him and said,

"See, the smell of my son
Is like the smell of a field which
   the LORD has blessed;
28 Now may God give you of the
      dew of heaven,
   And of the fatness of the earth,
   And an abundance of grain and
      new wine;
29 May peoples serve you,
   And nations bow down to you;
   Be master of your brothers,
   And may your mother's sons
      bow down to you.
   Cursed be those who curse you,
   And blessed be those who bless
      you."

30 ¶ Now it came about, as soon as Isaac had finished blessing Jacob, and Jacob had hardly gone out from the presence of Isaac his father, that Esau his brother came in from his hunting.

31 Then he also made savory food, and brought it to his father; and he said to his father, "Let my father arise, and eat of his son's game, that you may bless me."

32 And Isaac his father said to him, "Who are you?" And he said, "I am your son, your first-born, Esau."

33 Then Isaac trembled violently, and said, "Who was he then that hunted game and brought it to me, so that I ate of all of it before you came, and blessed him? Yes, and he shall be blessed."

34 When Esau heard the words of his father, he cried out with an exceedingly great and bitter cry, and said to his father, "Bless me, even me also, O my father!"

35 And he said, "Your brother came deceitfully, and has taken away your blessing."

36 Then he said, "Is he not rightly named Jacob, for he has supplanted me these two times? He took away my birthright, and behold, now he has taken away my blessing." And he said, "Have you not reserved a blessing for me?"

37 But Isaac answered and said to Esau, "Behold, I have made him your master, and all his relatives I have given to him as servants; and with grain and new wine I have sustained him. Now as for you then, what can I do, my son?"

38 And Esau said to his father, "Do you have only one blessing, my father? Bless me, even me also, O my father." So Esau lifted his voice and wept.

39 Then Isaac his father answered and said to him,

"Behold, away from the fertility of
   the earth shall be your dwelling,
   And away from the dew of
   heaven from above.
40 "And by your sword you shall live,
   And your brother you shall
      serve;
   But it shall come about when
      you become restless,
   That you shall break his yoke
      from your neck."

41 So Esau bore a grudge against Jacob because of the blessing with which his father had blessed him; and Esau said to himself, "The days of mourning for my father are near; then I will kill my brother Jacob."

42 Now when the words of her elder son Esau were reported to Rebekah, she sent and called her younger son Jacob, and said to him, "Behold your brother Esau is consoling himself concerning you, by planning to kill you.

43 "Now therefore, my son, obey my voice, and arise, flee to Haran, to my brother Laban!

44 "And stay with him a few days, until your brother's fury subsides,

45 until your brother's anger against you subsides, and he forgets what you did to him. Then I shall send and get you from there. Why should I be bereaved of you both in one day?"

46 ¶ And Rebekah said to Isaac, "I am tired of living because of the daughters of Heth; if Jacob takes a wife from the daughters of Heth, like

these, from the daughters of the land, what good will my life be to me?"

CHAPTER 28

So Isaac called Jacob and blessed him and charged him, and said to him, "You shall not take a wife from the daughters of Canaan.

2 "Arise, go to Paddan-aram, to the house of Bethuel your mother's father; and from there take to yourself a wife from the daughters of Laban your mother's brother.

3 "And may God Almighty bless you and make you fruitful and multiply you, that you may become a company of peoples.

4 "May He also give you the blessing of Abraham, to you and to your descendants with you; that you may possess the land of your sojournings, which God gave to Abraham."

5 Then Isaac sent Jacob away, and he went to Paddan-aram to Laban, son of Bethuel the Aramean, the brother of Rebekah, the mother of Jacob and Esau.

6 Now Esau saw that Isaac had blessed Jacob and sent him away to Paddan-aram, to take to himself a wife from there, *and that* when he blessed him he charged him, saying, "You shall not take a wife from the daughters of Canaan,"

7 and that Jacob had obeyed his father and his mother and had gone to Paddan-aram.

8 So Esau saw that the daughters of Canaan displeased his father Isaac;

9 and Esau went to Ishmael, and married, besides the wives that he had, Mahalath the daughter of Ishmael, Abraham's son, the sister of Nebaioth.

10 ¶ Then Jacob departed from Beersheba and went toward Haran.

11 And he came to a certain place and spent the night there, because the sun had set; and he took one of the stones of the place and put it under his head, and lay down in that place.

12 And he had a dream, and behold, a ladder was set on the earth with its top reaching to heaven; and behold, the angels of God were ascending and descending on it.

13 And behold, the LORD stood above it and said, "I am the LORD, the God of your father Abraham and the God of

Isaac; the land on which you lie, I will give it to you and to your descendants.

14 "Your descendants shall also be like the dust of the earth, and you shall spread out to the west and to the east and to the north and to the south; and in you and in your descendants shall all the families of the earth be blessed.

15 "And behold, I am with you, and will keep you wherever you go, and will bring you back to this land; for I will not leave you until I have done what I have promised you."

16 Then Jacob awoke from his sleep and said, "Surely the LORD is in this place, and I did not know it."

17 And he was afraid and said, "How awesome is this place! This is none other than the house of God, and this is the gate of heaven."

18 ¶ So Jacob rose early in the morning, and took the stone that he had put under his head and set it up as a pillar, and poured oil on its top.

19 And he called the name of that place [29]Bethel; however, previously the name of the city had been Luz.

20 Then Jacob made a vow, saying, "If God will be with me and will keep me on this journey that I take, and will give me food to eat and garments to wear,

21 and I return to my father's house in safety, then the LORD will be my God.

22 "And this stone, which I have set up as a pillar, will be God's house; and of all that Thou dost give me I will surely give a tenth to Thee."

CHAPTER 29

Then Jacob [30]went on his journey, and came to the land of the sons of the east.

2 And he looked, and saw a well in the field, and behold, three flocks of sheep were lying there beside it, for from that well they watered the flocks. Now the stone on the mouth of the well was large.

3 When all the flocks were gathered there, they would then roll the stone from the mouth of the well, and water the sheep, and put the stone back in its place on the mouth of the well.

[29] I.e., the house of God   [30] Lit., *lifted up his feet*

4 And Jacob said to them, "My brothers, where are you from?" And they said, "We are from Haran."

5 And he said to them, "Do you know Laban the son of Nahor?" And they said, "We know *him*."

6 And he said to them, "Is it well with him?" And they said, "It is well, and behold, Rachel his daughter is coming with the sheep."

7 And he said, "Behold, it is still high day; it is not time for the livestock to be gathered. Water the sheep, and go, pasture them."

8 But they said, "We cannot, until all the flocks are gathered, and they roll the stone from the mouth of the well; then we water the sheep."

9 While he was still speaking with them, Rachel came with her father's sheep, for she was a shepherdess.

10 And it came about, when Jacob saw Rachel the daughter of Laban his mother's brother, and the sheep of Laban his mother's brother, that Jacob went up, and rolled the stone from the mouth of the well, and watered the flock of Laban his mother's brother.

11 Then Jacob kissed Rachel, and lifted his voice and wept.

12 And Jacob told Rachel that he was a relative of her father and that he was Rebekah's son, and she ran and told her father.

13 ¶ So it came about, when Laban heard the news of Jacob his sister's son, that he ran to meet him, and embraced him and kissed him, and brought him to his house. Then he related to Laban all these things.

14 And Laban said to him, "Surely you are my bone and my flesh." And he stayed with him a month.

15 Then Laban said to Jacob, "Because you are my relative, should you therefore serve me for nothing? Tell me, what shall your wages be?"

16 Now Laban had two daughters; the name of the older was Leah, and the name of the younger was Rachel.

17 And Leah's eyes were weak, but Rachel was beautiful of form and face.

18 Now Jacob loved Rachel, so he said, "I will serve you seven years for your younger daughter Rachel."

19 And Laban said, "It is better that I give her to you than that I should give her to another man; stay with me."

20 So Jacob served seven years for Rachel and they seemed to him but a few days because of his love for her.

21 ¶ Then Jacob said to Laban, "Give *me* my wife, for my time is completed, that I may go in to her."

22 And Laban gathered all the men of the place, and made a feast.

23 Now it came about in the evening that he took his daughter Leah, and brought her to him; and *Jacob* went in to her.

24 Laban also gave his maid Zilpah to his daughter Leah as a maid.

25 So it came about in the morning that, behold, it was Leah! And he said to Laban, "What is this you have done to me? Was it not for Rachel that I served with you? Why then have you deceived me?"

26 But Laban said, "It is not the practice in our place, to marry off the younger before the first-born.

27 "Complete the week of this one, and we will give you the other also for the service which you shall serve with me for another seven years."

28 And Jacob did so and completed her week, and he gave him his daughter Rachel as his wife.

29 Laban also gave his maid Bilhah to his daughter Rachel as her maid.

30 So *Jacob* went in to Rachel also, and indeed he loved Rachel more than Leah, and he served with Laban for another seven years.

31 ¶ Now the LORD saw that Leah was unloved, and He opened her womb, but Rachel was barren.

32 And Leah conceived and bore a son and named him Reuben, for she said, "Because the LORD has seen my affliction; surely now my husband will love me."

33 Then she conceived again and bore a son and said, "Because the LORD has heard that I am unloved, He has therefore given me this *son* also." So she named him Simeon.

34 And she conceived again and bore a son and said, "Now this time my husband will become attached to me, because I have borne him three sons." Therefore he was named Levi.

35 And she conceived again and bore a son and said, "This time I will praise the LORD." Therefore she named him Judah. Then she stopped bearing.

CHAPTER 30

NOW when Rachel saw that she bore Jacob no children, she became jealous of her sister; and she said to Jacob, "Give me children, or else I die."

2 Then Jacob's anger burned against Rachel, and he said, "Am I in the place of God, who has withheld from you the fruit of the womb?"

3 And she said, "Here is my maid Bilhah, go in to her, that she may bear on my knees, that through her I too may have children."

4 So she gave him her maid Bilhah as a wife, and Jacob went in to her.

5 And Bilhah conceived and bore Jacob a son.

6 Then Rachel said, "God has vindicated me, and has indeed heard my voice and has given me a son." Therefore she named him Dan.

7 And Rachel's maid Bilhah conceived again and bore Jacob a second son.

8 So Rachel said, "With mighty wrestlings I have wrestled with my sister, *and* I have indeed prevailed." And she named him Naphtali.

9 ¶ When Leah saw that she had stopped bearing, she took her maid Zilpah and gave her to Jacob as a wife.

10 And Leah's maid Zilpah bore Jacob a son.

11 Then Leah said, "How fortunate!" So she named him Gad.

12 And Leah's maid Zilpah bore Jacob a second son.

13 Then Leah said, "Happy am I! For women will call me happy." So she named him Asher.

14 ¶ Now in the days of wheat harvest Reuben went and found mandrakes in the field, and brought them to his mother Leah. Then Rachel said to Leah, "Please give me some of your son's mandrakes."

15 But she said to her, "Is it a small matter for you to take my husband? And would you take my son's mandrakes also?" So Rachel said, "Therefore he may lie with you tonight in return for your son's mandrakes."

16 When Jacob came in from the field in the evening, then Leah went out to meet him and said, "You must come in to me, for I have surely hired you with my son's mandrakes." So he lay with her that night.

17 And God gave heed to Leah, and she conceived and bore Jacob a fifth son.

18 Then Leah said, "God has given me my wages, because I gave my maid to my husband." So she named him Issachar.

19 And Leah conceived again and bore a sixth son to Jacob.

20 Then Leah said, "God has endowed me with a good gift; now my husband will dwell with me, because I have borne him six sons." So she named him Zebulun.

21 And afterward she bore a daughter and named her Dinah.

22 Then God remembered Rachel, and God gave heed to her and opened her womb.

23 So she conceived and bore a son and said, "God has taken away my reproach."

24 And she named him Joseph, saying, "May the LORD give me another son."

25 ¶ Now it came about when Rachel had borne Joseph, that Jacob said to Laban, "Send me away, that I may go to my own place and to my own country.

26 "Give *me* my wives and my children for whom I have served you, and let me depart; for you yourself know my service which I have rendered you."

27 But Laban said to him, "If now [31]it pleases you, *stay with me;* I have divined that the LORD has blessed me on your account."

28 And he continued, "Name me your wages, and I will give it."

29 But he said to him, "You yourself know how I have served you and how your cattle have fared with me.

30 "For you had little before I came, and it has increased to a multitude; and the LORD has blessed you wherever I turned. But now, when shall I provide for my own household also?"

31 So he said, "What shall I give you?" And Jacob said, "You shall not give me anything. If you will do this one thing for me, I will again pasture *and* keep your flock:

32 let me pass through your entire flock today, removing from there every speckled and spotted sheep, and

[31] Lit., *I have found favor in your eyes*

every black one among the lambs, and the spotted and speckled among the goats; and *such* shall be my wages.

33"So my honesty will answer for me later, when you come concerning my wages. Every one that is not speckled and spotted among the goats and black among the lambs, *if found* with me, will be considered stolen."

34 And Laban said, "Good, let it be according to your word."

35 So he removed on that day the striped and spotted male goats and all the speckled and spotted female goats, every one with white in it, and all the black ones among the sheep, and gave them into the care of his sons.

36 And he put *a distance of* three days' journey between himself and Jacob, and Jacob fed the rest of Laban's flocks.

37 ¶ Then Jacob took fresh rods of poplar and almond and plane trees, and peeled white stripes in them, exposing the white which *was* in the rods.

38 And he set the rods which he had peeled in front of the flocks in the gutters, *even* in the watering troughs, where the flocks came to drink; and they mated when they came to drink.

39 So the flocks mated by the rods, and the flocks brought forth striped, speckled, and spotted.

40 And Jacob separated the lambs, and made the flocks face toward the striped and all the black in the flock of Laban; and he put his own herds apart, and did not put them with Laban's flock.

41 Moreover, it came about whenever the stronger of the flock were mating, that Jacob would place the rods in the sight of the flock in the gutters, so that they might mate by the rods;

42 but when the flock was feeble, he did not put *them* in; so the feebler were Laban's and the stronger Jacob's.

43 So the man became exceedingly prosperous, and had large flocks and female and male servants and camels and donkeys.

CHAPTER 31

Now Jacob heard the words of Laban's sons, saying, "Jacob has taken away all that was our father's, and

from what belonged to our father he has made all this wealth."

2 And Jacob saw the [32]attitude of Laban, and behold, it was not *friendly* toward him as formerly.

3 Then the LORD said to Jacob, "Return to the land of your fathers and to your relatives, and I will be with you."

4 So Jacob sent and called Rachel and Leah to his flock in the field,

5 and said to them, "I see your father's attitude, that it is not *friendly* toward me as formerly, but the God of my father has been with me.

6"And you know that I have served your father with all my strength.

7"Yet your father has cheated me and changed my wages ten times; however, God did not allow him to hurt me.

8"If he spoke thus, 'The speckled shall be your wages,' then all the flock brought forth speckled; and if he spoke thus, 'The striped shall be your wages,' then all the flock brought forth striped.

9"Thus God has taken away your father's livestock and given *them* to me.

10"And it came about at the time when the flock were mating that I lifted up my eyes and saw in a dream, and behold, the male goats which were mating *were* striped, speckled, and mottled.

11"Then the angel of God said to me in the dream, 'Jacob,' and I said, 'Here I am.'

12"And he said, 'Lift up, now, your eyes and see *that* all the male goats which are mating are striped, speckled, and mottled; for I have seen all that Laban has been doing to you.

13 'I am the God *of* Bethel, where you anointed a pillar, where you made a vow to Me; now arise, leave this land, and return to the land of your birth.' "

14 And Rachel and Leah answered and said to him, "Do we still have any portion or inheritance in our father's house?

15"Are we not reckoned by him as foreigners? For he has sold us, and has also entirely consumed our purchase price.

16"Surely all the wealth which God

[32] Lit., *face*

has taken away from our father belongs to us and our children; now then, do whatever God has said to you."

17 ¶ Then Jacob arose and put his children and his wives upon camels;

18 and he drove away all his livestock and all his property which he had gathered, his acquired livestock which he had gathered in Paddan-aram, to go to the land of Canaan to his father Isaac.

19 When Laban had gone to shear his flock, then Rachel stole the household idols that were her father's.

20 And Jacob deceived Laban the Aramean, by not telling him that he was fleeing.

21 So he fled with all that he had; and he arose and crossed the *Euphrates* River, and set his face toward the hill country of Gilead.

22 ¶ When it was told Laban on the third day that Jacob had fled,

23 then he took his kinsmen with him, and pursued him *a distance of* seven days' journey; and he overtook him in the hill country of Gilead.

24 And God came to Laban the Aramean in a dream of the night, and said to him, "Be careful that you do not speak to Jacob either good or bad."

25 And Laban caught up with Jacob. Now Jacob had pitched his tent in the hill country, and Laban with his kinsmen camped in the hill country of Gilead.

26 Then Laban said to Jacob, "What have you done by deceiving me and carrying away my daughters like captives of the sword?

27"Why did you flee secretly and deceive me, and did not tell me, so that I might have sent you away with joy and with songs, with timbrel and with lyre;

28 and did not allow me to kiss my sons and my daughters? Now you have done foolishly.

29"It is in my power to do you harm, but the God of your father spoke to me last night, saying, 'Be careful not to speak either good or bad to Jacob.'

30"And now you have indeed gone away because you longed greatly for your father's house; *but* why did you steal my gods?"

31 Then Jacob answered and said to Laban, "Because I was afraid, for I said, 'Lest you would take your daughters from me by force.'

32"The one with whom you find your gods shall not live; in the presence of our kinsmen point out what is yours among my belongings and take *it* for yourself." For Jacob did not know that Rachel had stolen them.

33 ¶ So Laban went into Jacob's tent, and into Leah's tent, and into the tent of the two maids, but he did not find *them*. Then he went out of Leah's tent and entered Rachel's tent.

34 Now Rachel had taken the household idols and put them in the camel's saddle, and she sat on them. And Laban felt through all the tent, but did not find *them*.

35 And she said to her father, "Let not my lord be angry that I cannot rise before you, for the manner of women is upon me." So he searched, but did not find the household idols.

36 ¶ Then Jacob became angry and contended with Laban; and Jacob answered and said to Laban, "What is my transgression? What is my sin, that you have hotly pursued me?

37"Though you have felt through all my goods, what have you found of all your household goods? Set *it* here before my kinsmen and your kinsmen, that they may decide between us two.

38"These twenty years I *have been* with you; your ewes and your female goats have not miscarried, nor have I eaten the rams of your flocks.

39"That which was torn *of beasts* I did not bring to you; I bore the loss of it myself. You required it of my hand *whether* stolen by day or stolen by night.

40"*Thus* I was: by day the heat consumed me, and the frost by night, and my sleep fled from my eyes.

41"These twenty years I have been in your house; I served you fourteen years for your two daughters, and six years for your flock, and you changed my wages ten times.

42"If the God of my father, the God of Abraham, and the fear of Isaac, had not been for me, surely now you would have sent me away empty-handed. God has seen my affliction and the toil of my hands, so He rendered judgment last night."

43 ¶ Then Laban answered and said to Jacob, "The daughters are my daughters, and the children are my children, and the flocks are my flocks, and all that you see is mine. But what can I do this day to these my daughters or to their children whom they have borne?

44"So now come, let us make a covenant, you and I, and let it be a witness between you and me."

45 Then Jacob took a stone and set it up *as* a pillar.

46 And Jacob said to his kinsmen, "Gather stones." So they took stones and made a heap, and they ate there by the heap.

47 Now Laban called it ³³Jegar-saha-dutha, but Jacob called it ³⁴Galeed.

48 And Laban said, "This heap is a witness between you and me this day." Therefore it was named Galeed;

49 and ³⁵Mizpah, for he said, "May the LORD watch between you and me when we are absent one from the other.

50"If you mistreat my daughters, or if you take wives besides my daughters, *although* no man is with us, see, God is witness between you and me."

51 And Laban said to Jacob, "Behold this heap and behold the pillar which I have set between you and me.

52"This heap is a witness, and the pillar is a witness, that I will not pass by this heap to you for harm, and you will not pass by this heap and this pillar to me, for harm.

53"The God of Abraham and the God of Nahor, the God of their father, judge between us." So Jacob swore by the fear of his father Isaac.

54 Then Jacob offered a sacrifice on the mountain, and called his kinsmen to the meal; and they ate the meal and spent the night on the mountain.

55 And early in the morning Laban arose, and kissed his sons and his daughters and blessed them. Then Laban departed and returned to his place.

CHAPTER 32

Now as Jacob went on his way, the angels of God met him.

2 And Jacob said when he saw them, "This is God's ³⁶camp." So he named that place ³⁷Mahanaim.

3 ¶ Then Jacob sent messengers before him to his brother Esau in the land of Seir, the country of Edom.

4 He also commanded them saying, "Thus you shall say to my lord Esau: 'Thus says your servant Jacob, "I have sojourned with Laban, and stayed until now;

5 and I have oxen and donkeys *and* flocks and male and female servants; and I have sent to tell my lord, that I may find favor in your sight." ' "

6 And the messengers returned to Jacob, saying, "We came to your brother Esau, and furthermore he is coming to meet you, and four hundred men are with him."

7 Then Jacob was greatly afraid and distressed; and he divided the people who were with him, and the flocks and the herds and the camels, into two companies;

8 for he said, "If Esau comes to the one company and attacks it, then the company which is left will escape."

9 And Jacob said, "O God of my father Abraham and God of my father Isaac, O LORD, who didst say to me, 'Return to your country and to your relatives, and I will prosper you,'

10 I am unworthy of all the loving-kindness and of all the faithfulness which Thou hast shown to Thy servant; for with my staff *only* I crossed this Jordan, and now I have become two companies.

11"Deliver me, I pray, from the hand of my brother, from the hand of Esau; for I fear him, lest he come and attack me, the mothers with the children.

12"For Thou didst say, 'I will surely prosper you, and make your descendants as the sand of the sea, which cannot be numbered for multitude.' "

13 ¶ So he spent the night there. Then he selected from what he had with him a present for his brother Esau:

14 two hundred female goats and twenty male goats, two hundred ewes and twenty rams,

15 thirty milking camels and their colts, forty cows and ten bulls, twenty female donkeys and ten male donkeys.

16 And he delivered *them* into the

---

³³ I.e., the heap of witness, in Aramaic
³⁴ I.e., the heap of witness, in Hebrew
³⁵ I.e., the watchtower

³⁶ Or, *company*   ³⁷ I.e., Two Camps, or, Two Companies

for he said, "I have seen God face to face, yet my life has been preserved." 31 Now the sun rose upon him just as he crossed over Penuel, and he was ~ing on his thigh. ~refore, to this day the sons of ~ eat the sinew of the hip ~ the socket of the thigh, ~ the socket of the hip.

drove by "Pass

sent to my lord Esau. And behold, he also is behind us.'"

19 Then he commanded also the second and the third, and all those who followed the droves, saying, "After this manner you shall speak to Esau when you find him;

20 and you shall say, 'Behold, your servant Jacob also is behind us.'" For he said, "I will appease him with the present that goes before me. Then afterward I will see his face; perhaps he will accept me."

21 So the present passed on before him, while he himself spent that night in the camp.

22 ¶ Now he arose that same night and took his two wives and his two maids and his eleven children, and crossed the ford of the Jabbok.

23 And he took them and sent them across the stream. And he sent across whatever he had.

24 Then Jacob was left alone, and a man wrestled with him until daybreak.

25 And when he saw that he had not prevailed against him, he touched the socket of his thigh; so the socket of Jacob's thigh was dislocated while he wrestled with him.

26 Then he said, "Let me go, for the dawn is breaking." But he said, "I will not let you go unless you bless me."

27 So he said to him, "What is your name?" And he said, "Jacob."

28 And he said, "Your name shall no longer be Jacob, but [38]Israel; for you have striven with God and with men and have prevailed."

29 Then Jacob asked him and said, "Please tell me your name." But he said, "Why is it that you ask my name?" And he blessed him there.

30 So Jacob named the place [39]Peniel,

THEN Jacob lifted his eyes and looked, and behold, Esau was coming, and four hundred men with him. So he divided the children among Leah and Rachel and the two maids.

2 And he put the maids and their children in front, and Leah and her children next, and Rachel and Joseph last.

3 But he himself passed on ahead of them and bowed down to the ground seven times, until he came near to his brother.

4 Then Esau ran to meet him and embraced him, and fell on his neck and kissed him, and they wept.

5 And he lifted his eyes and saw the women and the children, and said, "Who are these with you?" So he said, "The children whom God has graciously given your servant."

6 Then the maids came near with their children, and they bowed down.

7 And Leah likewise came near with her children, and they bowed down; and afterward Joseph came near with Rachel, and they bowed down.

8 And he said, "What do you mean by all this company which I have met?" And he said, "To find favor in the sight of my lord."

9 But Esau said, "I have plenty, my brother; let what you have be your own."

10 And Jacob said, "No, please, if now I have found favor in your sight, then take my present from my hand, for I see your face as one sees the face of God, and you have received me favorably.

11 "Please take my gift which has been brought to you, because God has dealt graciously with me, and because I have plenty." Thus he urged him and he took it.

[38] I.e., he who strives with God, or, God strives
[39] I.e., the face of God

12 Then Esau said, "Let us take our journey and go, and I will go before you."

13 But he said to him, "My lord knows that the children are frail and that the flocks and herds which are nursing are a care to me. And if they are driven hard one day, all the flocks will die.

14 "Please let my lord proceed ahead of his servant, and I will proceed at my leisure, according to the pace of the cattle that are before me and according to the pace of the children, until I come to my lord at Seir."

15 And Esau said, "Please let me leave with you some of the people who are with me." But he said, "[40]What need is there? Let me find favor in the sight of my lord."

16 So Esau returned that day on his way to Seir.

17 And Jacob journeyed to [41]Succoth; and built for himself a house, and made booths for his livestock, therefore the place is named Succoth.

18 ¶ Now Jacob came safely to the city of Shechem, which is in the land of Canaan, when he came from Paddan-aram, and camped before the city.

19 And he bought the piece of land where he had pitched his tent from the hand of the sons of Hamor, Shechem's father, for one hundred pieces of money.

20 Then he erected there an altar, and called it [42]El-Elohe-Israel.

CHAPTER 34

Now Dinah the daughter of Leah, whom she had borne to Jacob, went out to visit the daughters of the land.

2 And when Shechem the son of Hamor the Hivite, the prince of the land, saw her, he took her and lay with her by force.

3 And he was deeply attracted to Dinah the daughter of Jacob, and he loved the girl and spoke tenderly to her.

4 So Shechem spoke to his father Hamor, saying, "Get me this young girl for a wife."

5 Now Jacob heard that he had defiled Dinah his daughter; but his sons

***

Jacob came in ... when they heard it; and ...en were grieved, and they were very angry because he had done a disgraceful thing in Israel by lying with Jacob's daughter, for such a thing ought not to be done.

8 But Hamor spoke with them, saying, "The soul of my son Shechem longs for your daughter; please give her to him in marriage.

9 "And intermarry with us; give your daughters to us, and take our daughters for yourselves.

10 "Thus you shall live with us, and the land shall be open before you; live and trade in it, and acquire property in it."

11 Shechem also said to her father and to her brothers, "If I find favor in your sight, then I will give whatever you say to me.

12 "Ask me ever so much bridal payment and gift, and I will give according as you say to me; but give me the girl in marriage."

13 But Jacob's sons answered Shechem and his father Hamor, with deceit, and spoke to them, because he had defiled Dinah their sister.

14 And they said to them, "We cannot do this thing, to give our sister to one who is uncircumcised, for that would be a disgrace to us.

15 "Only on this condition will we consent to you: if you will become like us, in that every male of you be circumcised,

16 then we will give our daughters to you, and we will take your daughters for ourselves, and we will live with you and become one people.

17 "But if you will not listen to us to be circumcised, then we will take our daughter and go."

18 ¶ Now their words seemed reasonable to Hamor and Shechem, Hamor's son.

19 And the young man did not delay to do the thing, because he was delighted with Jacob's daughter. Now he was more respected than all the household of his father.

20 So Hamor and his son Shechem

---

[40] Lit., "Why this?"   [41] I.e., booths
[42] I.e., God, the God of Israel

came to the gate of their city, and spoke to the men of their city, saying,

21"These men are friendly with us; therefore let them live in the land and trade in it, for behold, the land is large enough for them. Let us take their daughters in marriage, and give our daughters to them.

22"Only on this *condition* will the men consent to us to live with us, to become one people: that every male among us be circumcised as they are circumcised.

23"Will not their livestock and their property and all their animals be ours? Only let us consent to them, and they will live with us."

24 And all who went out of the gate of his city listened to Hamor and to his son Shechem, and every male was circumcised, all who went out of the gate of his city.

25 Now it came about on the third day, when they were in pain, that two of Jacob's sons, Simeon and Levi, Dinah's brothers, each took his sword and came upon the city unawares, and killed every male.

26 And they killed Hamor and his son Shechem with the edge of the sword, and took Dinah from Shechem's house, and went forth.

27 Jacob's sons came upon the slain and looted the city, because they had defiled their sister.

28 They took their flocks and their herds and their donkeys, and that which was in the city and that which was in the field;

29 and they captured and looted all their wealth and all their little ones and their wives, even all that *was* in the houses.

30 Then Jacob said to Simeon and Levi, "You have brought trouble on me, by making me odious among the inhabitants of the land, among the Canaanites and the Perizzites; and my men being few in number, they will gather together against me and attack me and I shall be destroyed, I and my household."

31 But they said, "Should he treat our sister as a harlot?"

CHAPTER 35

THEN God said to Jacob, "Arise, go up to Bethel, and live there; and make an altar there to God, who appeared to you when you fled from your brother Esau."

2 So Jacob said to his household and to all who were with him, "Put away the foreign gods which are among you, and purify yourselves, and change your garments;

3 and let us arise and go up to Bethel; and I will make an altar there to God, who answered me in the day of my distress, and has been with me wherever I have gone."

4 So they gave to Jacob all the foreign gods which they had, and the rings which were in their ears; and Jacob hid them under the oak which was near Shechem.

5 ¶ As they journeyed, there was a great terror upon the cities which were around them, and they did not pursue the sons of Jacob.

6 So Jacob came to Luz (that is, Bethel), which is in the land of Canaan, he and all the people who were with him.

7 And he built an altar there, and called the place El-bethel, because there God had revealed Himself to him, when he fled from his brother.

8 Now Deborah, Rebekah's nurse, died, and she was buried below Bethel under the oak; it was named [43]Allon-bacuth.

9 ¶ Then God appeared to Jacob again when he came from Paddan-aram, and He blessed him.

10 And God said to him,
"Your name is Jacob;
You shall no longer be called Jacob,
But Israel shall be your name."
Thus He called him Israel.

11 God also said to him,
"I am God Almighty;
Be fruitful and multiply;
A nation and a company of nations shall come from you,
And kings shall come forth from you.

12 "And the land which I gave to Abraham and Isaac,
I will give it to you,
And I will give the land to your descendants after you."

13 Then God went up from him in the place where He had spoken with him.

[43] I.e., oak of weeping

14 And Jacob set up a pillar in the place where He had spoken with him, a pillar of stone, and he poured out a libation on it; he also poured oil on it.

15 So Jacob named the place where God had spoken with him, [44]Bethel.

16 ¶ Then they journeyed from Bethel; and when there was still some distance to go to Ephrath, Rachel began to give birth and she suffered severe labor.

17 And it came about when she was in severe labor that the midwife said to her, "Do not fear, for now you have *another* son."

18 And it came about as her soul was departing (for she died), that she named him [45]Ben-oni; but his father called him [46]Benjamin.

19 So Rachel died and was buried on the way to Ephrath (that is, Bethlehem).

20 And Jacob set up a pillar over her grave; that is the pillar of Rachel's grave to this day.

21 Then Israel journeyed on and pitched his tent beyond the tower of Eder.

22 And it came about while Israel was dwelling in that land, that Reuben went and lay with Bilhah his father's concubine; and Israel heard *of it*.

¶ Now there were twelve sons of Jacob—

23 the sons of Leah: Reuben, Jacob's first-born, then Simeon and Levi and Judah and Issachar and Zebulun;

24 the sons of Rachel: Joseph and Benjamin;

25 and the sons of Bilhah, Rachel's maid: Dan and Naphtali;

26 and the sons of Zilpah, Leah's maid: Gad and Asher. These are the sons of Jacob who were born to him in Paddan-aram.

27 And Jacob came to his father Isaac at Mamre of Kiriath-arba (that is, Hebron), where Abraham and Isaac had sojourned.

28 ¶ Now the days of Isaac were one hundred and eighty years.

29 And Isaac breathed his last and died, and was gathered to his people, an old man of ripe age; and his sons Esau and Jacob buried him.

[44] I.e., the house of God   [45] I.e., the son of my sorrow
[46] I.e., the son of the right hand

CHAPTER 36

NOW these are *the records of* the generations of Esau (that is, Edom).

2 ¶ Esau took his wives from the daughters of Canaan: Adah the daughter of Elon the Hittite, and Oholibamah the daughter of Anah and the granddaughter of Zibeon the Hivite;

3 also Basemath, Ishmael's daughter, the sister of Nebaioth.

4 And Adah bore Eliphaz to Esau, and Basemath bore Reuel,

5 and Oholibamah bore Jeush and Jalam and Korah. These are the sons of Esau who were born to him in the land of Canaan.

6 Then Esau took his wives and his sons and his daughters and all his household, and his livestock and all his cattle and all his goods which he had acquired in the land of Canaan, and went to *another* land away from his brother Jacob.

7 For their property had become too great for them to live together, and the land where they sojourned could not sustain them because of their livestock.

8 So Esau lived in the hill country of Seir; Esau is Edom.

9 These then are *the records of* the generations of Esau the father of the Edomites in the hill country of Seir.

10 ¶ These are the names of Esau's sons: Eliphaz the son of Esau's wife Adah, Reuel the son of Esau's wife Basemath.

11 And the sons of Eliphaz were Teman, Omar, Zepho and Gatam and Kenaz.

12 And Timna was a concubine of Esau's son Eliphaz and she bore Amalek to Eliphaz. These are the sons of Esau's wife Adah.

13 And these are the sons of Reuel: Nahath and Zerah, Shammah and Mizzah. These were the sons of Esau's wife Basemath.

14 And these were the sons of Esau's wife Oholibamah, the daughter of Anah and the granddaughter of Zibeon: she bore to Esau, Jeush and Jalam and Korah.

15 ¶ These are the chiefs of the sons of Esau. The sons of Eliphaz, the firstborn of Esau, are chief Teman, chief Omar, chief Zepho, chief Kenaz,

16 chief Korah, chief Gatam, chief Amalek. These are the chiefs descended from Eliphaz in the land of Edom; these are the sons of Adah.

17 And these are the sons of Reuel, Esau's son: chief Nahath, chief Zerah, chief Shammah, chief Mizzah. These are the chiefs descended from Reuel in the land of Edom; these are the sons of Esau's wife Basemath.

18 And these are the sons of Esau's wife Oholibamah: chief Jeush, chief Jalam, chief Korah. These are the chiefs descended from Esau's wife Oholibamah, the daughter of Anah.

19 These are the sons of Esau (that is, Edom), and these are their chiefs.

20 ¶ These are the sons of Seir the Horite, the inhabitants of the land: Lotan and Shobal and Zibeon and Anah,

21 and Dishon and Ezer and Dishan. These are the chiefs descended from the Horites, the sons of Seir in the land of Edom.

22 And the sons of Lotan were Hori and Hemam; and Lotan's sister was Timna.

23 And these are the sons of Shobal: Alvan and Manahath and Ebal, Shepho and Onam.

24 And these are the sons of Zibeon: Aiah and Anah—he is the Anah who found the hot springs in the wilderness when he was pasturing the donkeys of his father Zibeon.

25 And these are the children of Anah: Dishon, and Oholibamah, the daughter of Anah.

26 And these are the sons of Dishon: Hemdan and Eshban and Ithran and Cheran.

27 These are the sons of Ezer: Bilhan and Zaavan and Akan.

28 These are the sons of Dishan: Uz and Aran.

29 These are the chiefs descended from the Horites: chief Lotan, chief Shobal, chief Zibeon, chief Anah,

30 chief Dishon, chief Ezer, chief Dishan. These are the chiefs descended from the Horites, according to their *various* chiefs in the land of Seir.

31 ¶ Now these are the kings who reigned in the land of Edom before any king reigned over the sons of Israel.

32 Bela the son of Beor reigned in Edom, and the name of his city was Dinhabah.

33 Then Bela died, and Jobab the son of Zerah of Bozrah became king in his place.

34 Then Jobab died, and Husham of the land of the Temanites became king in his place.

35 Then Husham died, and Hadad the son of Bedad, who defeated Midian in the field of Moab, became king in his place; and the name of his city was Avith.

36 Then Hadad died, and Samlah of Masrekah became king in his place.

37 Then Samlah died, and Shaul of Rehoboth on the *Euphrates* River became king in his place.

38 Then Shaul died, and Baal-hanan the son of Achbor became king in his place.

39 Then Baal-hanan the son of Achbor died, and Hadar became king in his place; and the name of his city was Pau; and his wife's name was Mehetabel, the daughter of Matred, daughter of Mezahab.

40 ¶ Now these are the names of the chiefs descended from Esau, according to their families *and* their localities, by their names: chief Timna, chief Alvah, chief Jetheth,

41 chief Oholibamah, chief Elah, chief Pinon,

42 chief Kenaz, chief Teman, chief Mibzar,

43 chief Magdiel, chief Iram. These are the chiefs of Edom (that is, Esau, the father of the Edomites), according to their habitations in the land of their possession.

CHAPTER 37

Now Jacob lived in the land where his father had sojourned, in the land of Canaan.

2 These are *the records of* the generations of Jacob.

¶ Joseph, when seventeen years of age, was pasturing the flock with his brothers while he was *still* a youth, along with the sons of Bilhah and the sons of Zilpah, his father's wives. And Joseph brought back a bad report about them to their father.

3 Now Israel loved Joseph more than all his sons, because he was the

son of his old age; and he made him a [47]varicolored tunic.

4 And his brothers saw that their father loved him more than all his brothers; and so they hated him and could not speak to him [48]on friendly terms.

5 ¶ Then Joseph had a dream, and when he told it to his brothers, they hated him even more.

6 And he said to them, "Please listen to this dream which I have had;

7 for behold, we were binding sheaves in the field, and lo, my sheaf rose up and also stood erect; and behold, your sheaves gathered around and bowed down to my sheaf."

8 Then his brothers said to him, "Are you actually going to reign over us? Or are you really going to rule over us?" So they hated him even more for his dreams and for his words.

9 Now he had still another dream, and related it to his brothers, and said, "Lo, I have had still another dream; and behold, the sun and the moon and eleven stars were bowing down to me."

10 And he related it to his father and to his brothers; and his father rebuked him and said to him, "What is this dream that you have had? Shall I and your mother and your brothers actually come to bow ourselves down before you to the ground?"

11 And his brothers were jealous of him, but his father kept the saying in mind.

12 ¶ Then his brothers went to pasture their father's flock in Shechem.

13 And Israel said to Joseph, "Are not your brothers pasturing the flock in Shechem? Come, and I will send you to them." And he said to him, "I will go."

14 Then he said to him, "Go now and see about the welfare of your brothers and the welfare of the flock; and bring word back to me." So he sent him from the valley of Hebron, and he came to Shechem.

15 And a man found him, and behold, he was wandering in the field; and the man asked him, "What are you looking for?"

16 And he said, "I am looking for my brothers; please tell me where they are pasturing the flock."

17 Then the man said, "They have moved from here; for I heard them say, 'Let us go to Dothan.'" So Joseph went after his brothers and found them at Dothan.

18 ¶ When they saw him from a distance and before he came close to them, they plotted against him to put him to death.

19 And they said to one another, "Here comes this dreamer!

20 "Now then, come and let us kill him and throw him into one of the pits; and we will say, 'A wild beast devoured him.' Then let us see what will become of his dreams!"

21 But Reuben heard this and rescued him out of their hands and said, "Let us not take his life."

22 Reuben further said to them, "Shed no blood. Throw him into this pit that is in the wilderness, but do not lay hands on him"—that he might rescue him out of their hands, to restore him to his father.

23 So it came about, when Joseph reached his brothers, that they stripped Joseph of his tunic, the varicolored tunic that was on him;

24 and they took him and threw him into the pit. Now the pit was empty, without any water in it.

25 ¶ Then they sat down to eat a meal. And as they raised their eyes and looked, behold, a caravan of Ishmaelites was coming from Gilead, with their camels bearing aromatic gum and balm and myrrh, on their way to bring them down to Egypt.

26 And Judah said to his brothers, "What profit is it for us to kill our brother and cover up his blood?

27 "Come and let us sell him to the Ishmaelites and not lay our hands on him; for he is our brother, our own flesh." And his brothers listened to him.

28 Then some Midianite traders passed by, so they pulled him up and lifted Joseph out of the pit, and sold him to the Ishmaelites for twenty shekels of silver. Thus they brought Joseph into Egypt.

29 ¶ Now Reuben returned to the pit, and behold, Joseph was not in the pit; so he tore his garments.

---

[47] Or, full-length robe   [48] Lit., in peace

30 And he returned to his brothers and said, "The boy is not *there;* as for me, where am I to go?"

31 So they took Joseph's tunic, and slaughtered a male goat, and dipped the tunic in the blood;

32 and they sent the varicolored tunic and brought it to their father and said, "We found this; please examine *it* to *see* whether it is your son's tunic or not."

33 Then he examined it and said, "It is my son's tunic. A wild beast has devoured him; Joseph has surely been torn to pieces!"

34 So Jacob tore his clothes, and put sackcloth on his loins, and mourned for his son many days.

35 Then all his sons and all his daughters arose to comfort him, but he refused to be comforted. And he said, "Surely I will go down to Sheol in mourning for my son." So his father wept for him.

36 Meanwhile, the Midianites sold him in Egypt to Potiphar, Pharaoh's officer, the captain of the bodyguard.

CHAPTER 38

AND it came about at that time, that Judah departed from his brothers, and visited a certain Adullamite, whose name was Hirah.

2 And Judah saw there a daughter of a certain Canaanite whose name was Shua; and he took her and went in to her.

3 So she conceived and bore a son and he named him Er.

4 Then she conceived again and bore a son and named him Onan.

5 And she bore still another son and named him Shelah; and it was at Chezib that she bore him.

6 ¶ Now Judah took a wife for Er his first-born, and her name *was* Tamar.

7 But Er, Judah's first-born, was evil in the sight of the LORD, so the LORD took his life.

8 Then Judah said to Onan, "Go in to your brother's wife, and perform your duty as a brother-in-law to her, and raise up offspring for your brother."

9 And Onan knew that the offspring would not be his; so it came about that when he went in to his brother's wife, he wasted his seed on the ground, in order not to give offspring to his brother.

10 But what he did was displeasing in the sight of the LORD; so He took his life also.

11 Then Judah said to his daughter-in-law Tamar, "Remain a widow in your father's house until my son Shelah grows up"; for he thought, "*I am afraid* that he too may die like his brothers." So Tamar went and lived in her father's house.

12 ¶ Now after a considerable time Shua's daughter, the wife of Judah, died; and when the time of mourning was ended, Judah went up to his sheepshearers at Timnah, he and his friend Hirah the Adullamite.

13 And it was told to Tamar, "Behold, your father-in-law is going up to Timnah to shear his sheep."

14 So she removed her widow's garments and covered *herself* with a [49]veil, and wrapped herself, and sat in the gateway of Enaim, which is on the road to Timnah; for she saw that Shelah had grown up, and she had not been given to him as a wife.

15 When Judah saw her, he thought she *was* a harlot, for she had covered her face.

16 So he turned aside to her by the road, and said, "Here now, let me come in to you"; for he did not know that she was his daughter-in-law. And she said, "What will you give me, that you may come in to me?"

17 He said, therefore, "I will send you a kid from the flock." She said, moreover, "Will you give a pledge until you send *it?*"

18 And he said, "What pledge shall I give you?" And she said, "Your seal and your cord, and your staff that is in your hand." So he gave *them* to her, and went in to her, and she conceived by him.

19 Then she arose and departed, and removed her veil and put on her widow's garments.

20 ¶ When Judah sent the kid by his friend the Adullamite, to receive the pledge from the woman's hand, he did not find her.

21 And he asked the men of her place, saying, "Where is the temple prostitute who was by the road at

[49] Or, *shawl*

Enaim?" But they said, "There has been no temple prostitute here."

22 So he returned to Judah, and said, "I did not find her; and furthermore, the men of the place said, 'There has been no temple prostitute here.'"

23 Then Judah said, "Let her keep them, lest we become a laughingstock. After all, I sent this kid, but you did not find her."

24 ¶ Now it was about three months later that Judah was informed, "Your daughter-in-law Tamar has played the harlot, and behold, she is also with child by harlotry." Then Judah said, "Bring her out and let her be burned!"

25 It was while she was being brought out that she sent to her father-in-law, saying, "I am with child by the man to whom these things belong." And she said, "Please examine and see, whose signet ring and cords and staff are these?"

26 And Judah recognized *them,* and said, "She is more righteous than I, inasmuch as I did not give her to my son Shelah." And he did not have relations with her again.

27 ¶ And it came about at the time she was giving birth, that behold, there were twins in her womb.

28 Moreover, it took place while she was giving birth, one put out a hand, and the midwife took and tied a scarlet *thread* on his hand, saying, "This one came out first."

29 But it came about as he drew back his hand, that behold, his brother came out. Then she said, "What a breach you have made for yourself!" So he was named [50]Perez.

30 And afterward his brother came out who had the scarlet *thread* on his hand; and he was named [51]Zerah.

CHAPTER 39

NOW Joseph had been taken down to Egypt; and Potiphar, an Egyptian officer of Pharaoh, the captain of the bodyguard, bought him from the Ishmaelites, who had taken him down there.

2 And the LORD was with Joseph, so he became a successful man. And he was in the house of his master, the Egyptian.

3 Now his master saw that the LORD was with him and *how* the LORD caused all that he did to prosper in his hand.

4 So Joseph found favor in his sight, and became his personal servant; and he made him overseer over his house, and all that he owned he put in his charge.

5 And it came about that from the time he made him overseer in his house, and over all that he owned, the LORD blessed the Egyptian's house on account of Joseph; thus the LORD's blessing was upon all that he owned, in the house and in the field.

6 So he left everything he owned in Joseph's charge; and with him *there* he did not concern himself with anything except the food which he ate. Now Joseph was handsome in form and appearance.

7 ¶ And it came about after these events that his master's wife looked with desire at Joseph, and she said, "Lie with me."

8 But he refused and said to his master's wife, "Behold, with me *here,* my master does not concern himself with anything in the house, and he has put all that he owns in my charge.

9"There is no one greater in this house than I, and he has withheld nothing from me except you, because you are his wife. How then could I do this great evil, and sin against God?"

10 And it came about as she spoke to Joseph day after day, that he did not listen to her to lie beside her, *or* be with her.

11 Now it happened one day that he went into the house to do his work, and none of the men of the household was there inside.

12 And she caught him by his garment, saying, "Lie with me!" And he left his garment in her hand and fled, and went outside.

13 When she saw that he had left his garment in her hand, and had fled outside,

14 she called to the men of her household, and said to them, "See, he has brought in a Hebrew to us to make sport of us; he came in to me to lie with me, and I screamed.

15"And it came about when he heard

50 I.e., a breach   51 I.e., a dawning or brightness

that I raised my voice and [52]screamed, that he left his garment beside me and fled, and went outside."

16 So she left his garment beside her until his master came home.

17 Then she spoke to him with these words, "The Hebrew slave, whom you brought to us, came in to me to make sport of me;

18 and it happened as I raised my voice and screamed, that he left his garment beside me and fled outside."

19 ¶ Now it came about when his master heard the words of his wife, which she spoke to him, saying, "This is what your slave did to me," that his anger burned.

20 So Joseph's master took him and put him into the jail, the place where the king's prisoners were confined; and he was there in the jail.

21 But the LORD was with Joseph and extended kindness to him, and gave him favor in the sight of the chief jailer.

22 And the chief jailer committed to Joseph's charge all the prisoners who were in the jail; so that whatever was done there, he was responsible for it.

23 The chief jailer did not supervise anything under Joseph's charge because the LORD was with him; and whatever he did, the LORD made to prosper.

CHAPTER 40

THEN it came about after these things the cupbearer and the baker for the king of Egypt offended their lord, the king of Egypt.

2 And Pharaoh was furious with his two officials, the chief cupbearer and the chief baker.

3 So he put them in confinement in the house of the captain of the bodyguard, in the jail, the same place where Joseph was imprisoned.

4 And the captain of the bodyguard put Joseph in charge of them, and he took care of them; and they were in confinement for some time.

5 Then the cupbearer and the baker for the king of Egypt, who were confined in jail, both had a dream the same night, each man with his own dream and each dream with its own interpretation.

6 When Joseph came to them in the morning and observed them, behold, they were dejected.

7 And he asked Pharaoh's officials who were with him in confinement in his master's house, "Why are your faces so sad today?"

8 Then they said to him, "We have had a dream and there is no one to interpret it." Then Joseph said to them, "Do not interpretations belong to God? Tell it to me, please."

9 ¶ So the chief cupbearer told his dream to Joseph, and said to him, "In my dream, behold, there was a vine in front of me;

10 and on the vine were three branches. And as it was budding, its blossoms came out, and its clusters produced ripe grapes.

11 "Now Pharaoh's cup was in my hand; so I took the grapes and squeezed them into Pharaoh's cup, and I put the cup into Pharaoh's hand."

12 Then Joseph said to him, "This is the interpretation of it: the three branches are three days;

13 within three more days Pharaoh will [53]lift up your head and restore you to your office; and you will put Pharaoh's cup into his hand according to your former custom when you were his cupbearer.

14 "Only keep me in mind when it goes well with you, and please do me a kindness by mentioning me to Pharaoh, and get me out of this house.

15 "For I was in fact kidnapped from the land of the Hebrews, and even here I have done nothing that they should have put me into the dungeon."

16 ¶ When the chief baker saw that he had interpreted favorably, he said to Joseph, "I also saw in my dream, and behold, there were three baskets of white bread on my head;

17 and in the top basket there were some of all sorts of baked food for Pharaoh, and the birds were eating them out of the basket on my head."

18 Then Joseph answered and said, "This is its interpretation: the three baskets are three days;

19 within three more days Pharaoh will lift up your head from you and

[52] Lit., called out

[53] Or possibly, forgive you

will hang you on a tree; and the birds will eat your flesh off you."

20 ¶ Thus it came about on the third day, *which was* Pharaoh's birthday, that he made a feast for all his servants; and he lifted up the head of the chief cupbearer and the head of the chief baker among his servants.

21 And he restored the chief cupbearer to his office, and he put the cup into Pharaoh's hand;

22 but he hanged the chief baker, just as Joseph had interpreted to them.

23 Yet the chief cupbearer did not remember Joseph, but forgot him.

CHAPTER 41

NOW it happened at the end of two full years that Pharaoh had a dream, and behold, he was standing by the Nile.

2 And lo, from the Nile there came up seven cows, sleek and fat; and they grazed in the marsh grass.

3 Then behold, seven other cows came up after them from the Nile, ugly and gaunt, and they stood by the *other* cows on the bank of the Nile.

4 And the ugly and gaunt cows ate up the seven sleek and fat cows. Then Pharaoh awoke.

5 And he fell asleep and dreamed a second time; and behold, seven ears of grain came up on a single stalk, plump and good.

6 Then behold, seven ears, thin and scorched by the east wind, sprouted up after them.

7 And the thin ears swallowed up the seven plump and full ears. Then Pharaoh awoke, and behold, *it was* a dream.

8 Now it came about in the morning that his spirit was troubled, so he sent and called for all the magicians of Egypt, and all its wise men. And Pharaoh told them his dreams, but there was no one who could interpret them to Pharaoh.

9 ¶ Then the chief cupbearer spoke to Pharaoh, saying, "I would make mention today of my *own* offenses.

10 "Pharaoh was furious with his servants, and he put me in confinement in the house of the captain of the bodyguard, *both* me and the chief baker.

11 "And we had a dream on the same night, he and I; each of us dreamed according to the interpretation of his *own* dream.

12 "Now a Hebrew youth *was* with us there, a servant of the captain of the bodyguard, and we related *them* to him, and he interpreted our dreams for us. To each one he interpreted according to his *own* dream.

13 "And it came about that just as he interpreted for us, so it happened; he restored me in my office, but he hanged him."

14 ¶ Then Pharaoh sent and called for Joseph, and they hurriedly brought him out of the dungeon; and when he had shaved himself and changed his clothes, he came to Pharaoh.

15 And Pharaoh said to Joseph, "I have had a dream, but no one can interpret it; and I have heard it said about you, that when you hear a dream you can interpret it."

16 Joseph then answered Pharaoh, saying, "It is not in me; God will give Pharaoh a favorable answer."

17 So Pharaoh spoke to Joseph, "In my dream, behold, I was standing on the bank of the Nile;

18 and behold, seven cows, fat and sleek came up out of the Nile; and they grazed in the marsh grass.

19 "And lo, seven other cows came up after them, poor and very ugly and gaunt, such as I had never seen for ugliness in all the land of Egypt;

20 and the lean and ugly cows ate up the first seven fat cows.

21 "Yet when they had devoured them, it could not be detected that they had devoured them; for they were just as ugly as before. Then I awoke.

22 "I saw also in my dream, and behold, seven ears, full and good, came up on a single stalk;

23 and lo, seven ears, withered, thin, *and* scorched by the east wind, sprouted up after them;

24 and the thin ears swallowed the seven good ears. Then I told it to the magicians, but there was no one who could explain it to me."

25 ¶ Now Joseph said to Pharaoh, "Pharaoh's dreams are one *and the same;* God has told to Pharaoh what He is about to do.

26"The seven good cows are seven years; and the seven good ears are seven years; the dreams are one *and the same.*

27"And the seven lean and ugly cows that came up after them are seven years, and the seven thin ears scorched by the east wind shall be seven years of famine.

28"It is as I have spoken to Pharaoh: God has shown to Pharaoh what He is about to do.

29"Behold, seven years of great abundance are coming in all the land of Egypt;

30 and after them seven years of famine will come, and all the abundance will be forgotten in the land of Egypt; and the famine will ravage the land.

31"So the abundance will be unknown in the land because of that subsequent famine; for it *will be* very severe.

32"Now as for the repeating of the dream to Pharaoh twice, *it means* that the matter is determined by God, and God will quickly bring it about.

33"And now let Pharaoh look for a man discerning and wise, and set him over the land of Egypt.

34"Let Pharaoh take action to appoint overseers in charge of the land, and let him exact a fifth *of the produce* of the land of Egypt in the seven years of abundance.

35"Then let them gather all the food of these good years that are coming, and store up the grain for food in the cities under Pharaoh's authority, and let them guard *it.*

36"And let the food become as a reserve for the land for the seven years of famine which will occur in the land of Egypt, so that the land may not perish during the famine."

37 ¶ Now the proposal seemed good to Pharaoh and to all his servants.

38 Then Pharaoh said to his servants, "Can we find a man like this, in whom is a divine spirit?"

39 So Pharaoh said to Joseph, "Since God has informed you of all this, there is no one so discerning and wise as you are.

40"You shall be over my house, and according to your command all my people shall do homage; only in the throne I will be greater than you."

41 And Pharaoh said to Joseph, "See I have set you over all the land of Egypt."

42 Then Pharaoh took off his signet ring from his hand, and put it on Joseph's hand, and clothed him in garments of fine linen, and put the gold necklace around his neck.

43 And he had him ride in his second chariot; and they proclaimed before him, "Bow the knee!" And he set him over all the land of Egypt.

44 Moreover, Pharaoh said to Joseph, "*Though* I am Pharaoh, yet without your permission no one shall raise his hand or foot in all the land of Egypt."

45 Then Pharaoh named Joseph [54]Zaphenath-paneah; and he gave him Asenath, the daughter of Potiphera priest of On, as his wife. And Joseph went forth over the land of Egypt.

46 ¶ Now Joseph was thirty years old when he [55]stood before Pharaoh, king of Egypt. And Joseph went out from the presence of Pharaoh, and went through all the land of Egypt.

47 And during the seven years of plenty the land brought forth abundantly.

48 So he gathered all the food of *these* seven years which occurred in the land of Egypt, and placed the food in the cities; he placed in every city the food from its own surrounding fields.

49 Thus Joseph stored up grain in great abundance like the sand of the sea, until he stopped measuring *it,* for it was beyond measure.

50 ¶ Now before the year of famine came, two sons were born to Joseph, whom Asenath, the daughter of Potiphera priest of [56]On, bore to him.

51 And Joseph named the first-born [57]Manasseh, "For," *he said,* "God has made me forget all my trouble and all my father's household."

52 And he named the second [58]Ephraim, "For," *he said,* "God has made me fruitful in the land of my affliction."

53 ¶ When the seven years of plenty

[54] Probably Egyptian for "God speaks; he lives"
[55] Or, *entered the service of*   [56] Or, *Heliopolis*
[57] I.e., *making to forget*   [58] I.e., *fruitfulness*

which had been in the land of Egypt came to an end,

54 and the seven years of famine began to come, just as Joseph had said, then there was famine in all the lands; but in all the land of Egypt there was bread.

55 So when all the land of Egypt was famished, the people cried out to Pharaoh for bread; and Pharaoh said to all the Egyptians, "Go to Joseph; whatever he says to you, you shall do."

56 When the famine was *spread* over all the face of the earth, then Joseph opened all the storehouses, and sold to the Egyptians; and the famine was severe in the land of Egypt.

57 And *the people of* all the earth came to Egypt to buy grain from Joseph, because the famine was severe in all the earth.

CHAPTER 42

Now Jacob saw that there was grain in Egypt, and Jacob said to his sons, "Why are you staring at one another?"

2 And he said, "Behold, I have heard that there is grain in Egypt; go down there and buy *some* for us from that place, so that we may live and not die."

3 Then ten brothers of Joseph went down to buy grain from Egypt.

4 But Jacob did not send Joseph's brother Benjamin with his brothers, for he said, "I am afraid that harm may befall him."

5 So the sons of Israel came to buy grain among those who were coming, for the famine was in the land of Canaan *also.*

6 Now Joseph was the ruler over the land; he was the one who sold to all the people of the land. And Joseph's brothers came and bowed down to him with *their* faces to the ground.

7 When Joseph saw his brothers he recognized them, but he disguised himself to them and spoke to them harshly. And he said to them, "Where have you come from?" And they said, "From the land of Canaan, to buy food."

8 ¶ But Joseph had recognized his brothers, although they did not recognize him.

9 And Joseph remembered the dreams which he had about them, and said to them, "You are spies; you have come to look at the undefended parts of our land."

10 Then they said to him, "No, my lord, but your servants have come to buy food.

11 "We are all sons of one man; we are honest men, your servants are not spies."

12 Yet he said to them, "No, but you have come to look at the undefended parts of our land!"

13 But they said, "Your servants are twelve brothers *in all,* the sons of one man in the land of Canaan; and behold, the youngest is with our father today, and one is no more."

14 And Joseph said to them, "It is as I said to you, you are spies;

15 by this you will be tested: by the life of Pharaoh, you shall not go from this place unless your youngest brother comes here!

16 "Send one of you that he may get your brother, while you remain confined, that your words may be tested, whether there is truth in you. But if not, by the life of Pharaoh, surely you are spies."

17 So he put them all together in prison for three days.

18 ¶ Now Joseph said to them on the third day, "Do this and live, for I fear God:

19 if you are honest men, let one of your brothers be confined in your prison; but as for *the rest of* you, go, carry grain for the famine of your households,

20 and bring your youngest brother to me, so your words may be verified, and you will not die." And they did so.

21 Then they said to one another, "Truly we are guilty concerning our brother, because we saw the distress of his soul when he pleaded with us, yet we would not listen; therefore this distress has come upon us."

22 And Reuben answered them, saying, "Did I not tell you, 'Do not sin against the boy'; and you would not listen? Now comes the reckoning for his blood."

23 They did not know, however, that Joseph understood, for there was an interpreter between them.

24 And he turned away from them and wept. But when he returned to

them and spoke to them, he took Simeon from them and bound him before their eyes.

25 ¶ Then Joseph gave orders to fill their bags with grain and to restore every man's money in his sack, and to give them provisions for the journey. And thus it was done for them.

26 So they loaded their donkeys with their grain, and departed from there.

27 And as one *of them* opened his sack to give his donkey fodder at the lodging place, he saw his money; and behold, it was in the mouth of his sack.

28 Then he said to his brothers, "My money has been returned, and behold, it is even in my sack." And their hearts sank, and they *turned* trembling to one another, saying, "What is this that God has done to us?"

29 ¶ When they came to their father Jacob in the land of Canaan, they told him all that had happened to them, saying,

30"The man, the lord of the land, spoke harshly with us, and took us for spies of the country.

31"But we said to him, 'We are honest men; we are not spies.

32 'We are twelve brothers, sons of our father; one is no more, and the youngest is with our father today in the land of Canaan.'

33"And the man, the lord of the land, said to us, 'By this I shall know that you are honest men: leave one of your brothers with me and take *grain for* the famine of your households, and go.

34 'But bring your youngest brother to me that I may know that you are not spies, but honest men. I will give your brother to you, and you may trade in the land.' "

35 ¶ Now it came about as they were emptying their sacks, that behold, every man's bundle of money *was* in his sack; and when they and their father saw their bundles of money, they were dismayed.

36 And their father Jacob said to them, "You have bereaved me of my children: Joseph is no more, and Simeon is no more, and you would take Benjamin; all these things are against me."

37 Then Reuben spoke to his father, saying, "You may put my two sons to death if I do not bring him *back* to you; put him in my care, and I will return him to you."

38 But Jacob said, "My son shall not go down with you; for his brother is dead, and he alone is left. If harm should befall him on the journey you are taking, then you will bring my gray hair down to Sheol in sorrow."

CHAPTER 43

Now the famine was severe in the land.

2 So it came about when they had finished eating the grain which they had brought from Egypt, that their father said to them, "Go back, buy us a little food."

3 Judah spoke to him, however, saying, "The man solemnly warned us, 'You shall not see my face unless your brother is with you.'

4"If you send our brother with us, we will go down and buy you food.

5"But if you do not send *him*, we will not go down; for the man said to us, 'You shall not see my face unless your brother is with you.' "

6 Then Israel said, "Why did you treat me so badly by telling the man whether you still had *another* brother?"

7 But they said, "The man questioned particularly about us and our relatives, saying, 'Is your father still alive? Have you *another* brother?' So we answered his questions. Could we possibly know that he would say, 'Bring your brother down'?"

8 And Judah said to his father Israel, "Send the lad with me, and we will arise and go, that we may live and not die, we as well as you and our little ones.

9"I myself will be surety for him; you may hold me responsible for him. If I do not bring him *back* to you and set him before you, then let me bear the blame before you forever.

10"For if we had not delayed, surely by now we could have returned twice."

11 ¶ Then their father Israel said to them, "If *it must be* so, then do this: take some of the best products of the land in your bags, and carry down to the man as a present, a little balm and

a little honey, aromatic gum and myrrh, pistachio nuts and almonds.

12"And take double *the* money in your hand, and take back in your hand the money that was returned in the mouth of your sacks; perhaps it was a mistake.

13"Take your brother also, and arise, return to the man;

14 and may God Almighty grant you compassion in the sight of the man, that he may release to you your other brother and Benjamin. And as for me, if I am bereaved of my children, I am bereaved."

15 So the men took this present, and they took double *the* money in their hand, and Benjamin; then they arose and went down to Egypt and stood before Joseph.

16 ¶ When Joseph saw Benjamin with them, he said to his house steward, "Bring the men into the house, and slay *an animal* and make ready; for the men are to dine with me at noon."

17 So the man did as Joseph said, and brought the men to Joseph's house.

18 Now the men were afraid, because they were brought to Joseph's house; and they said, "*It is* because of the money that was returned in our sacks the first time that we are being brought in, that he may seek occasion against us and fall upon us, and take us for slaves with our donkeys."

19 So they came near to Joseph's house steward, and spoke to him at the entrance of the house,

20 and said, "Oh, my lord, we indeed came down the first time to buy food,

21 and it came about when we came to the lodging place, that we opened our sacks, and behold, each man's money was in the mouth of his sack, our money in full. So we have brought it back in our hand.

22"We have also brought down other money in our hand to buy food; we do not know who put our money in our sacks."

23 And he said, "⁵⁹Be at ease, do not be afraid. Your God and the God of your father has given you treasure in your sacks; I had your money." Then he brought Simeon out to them.

24 Then the man brought the men into Joseph's house and gave them water, and they washed their feet; and he gave their donkeys fodder.

25 So they prepared the present for Joseph's coming at noon; for they had heard that they were to eat a meal there.

26 ¶ When Joseph came home, they brought into the house to him the present which was in their hand and bowed to the ground before him.

27 Then he asked them about their welfare, and said, "Is your old father well, of whom you spoke? Is he still alive?"

28 And they said, "Your servant our father is well; he is still alive." And they bowed down in homage.

29 As he lifted his eyes and saw his brother Benjamin, his mother's son, he said, "Is this your youngest brother, of whom you spoke to me?" And he said, "May God be gracious to you, my son."

30 And Joseph hurried *out* for he was deeply stirred over his brother, and he sought *a place* to weep; and he entered his chamber and wept there.

31 Then he washed his face, and came out; and he controlled himself and said, "Serve the meal."

32 So they served him by himself, and them by themselves, and the Egyptians, who ate with him, by themselves; because the Egyptians could not eat bread with the Hebrews, for that is loathsome to the Egyptians.

33 Now they were seated before him, the first-born according to his birthright and the youngest according to his youth, and the men looked at one another in astonishment.

34 And he took portions to them from his own table; but Benjamin's portion was five times as much as any of theirs. So they feasted and drank freely with him.

CHAPTER 44

THEN he commanded his house steward, saying, "Fill the men's sacks with food, as much as they can carry, and put each man's money in the mouth of his sack.

2"And put my cup, the silver cup, in the mouth of the sack of the youngest,

⁵⁹ Lit., *Peace be to you*

and his money for the grain." And he did as Joseph had told *him*.

3 As soon as it was light, the men were sent away, they with their donkeys.

4 They had *just* gone out of the city, *and* were not far off, when Joseph said to his house steward, "Up, follow the men; and when you overtake them, say to them, 'Why have you repaid evil for good?

5 'Is not this the one from which my lord drinks, and which he indeed uses for divination? You have done wrong in doing this.' "

6 ¶ So he overtook them and spoke these words to them.

7 And they said to him, "Why does my lord speak such words as these? Far be it from your servants to do such a thing.

8 "Behold, the money which we found in the mouth of our sacks we have brought back to you from the land of Canaan. How then could we steal silver or gold from your lord's house?

9 "With whomever of your servants it is found, let him die, and we also will be my lord's slaves."

10 So he said, "Now let it also be according to your words; he with whom it is found shall be my slave, and *the rest of* you shall be innocent."

11 Then they hurried, each man lowered his sack to the ground, and each man opened his sack.

12 And he searched, beginning with the oldest and ending with the youngest, and the cup was found in Benjamin's sack.

13 Then they tore their clothes, and when each man loaded his donkey, they returned to the city.

14 ¶ When Judah and his brothers came to Joseph's house, he was still there, and they fell to the ground before him.

15 And Joseph said to them, "What is this deed that you have done? Do you not know that such a man as I can indeed practice divination?"

16 So Judah said, "What can we say to my lord? What can we speak? And how can we justify ourselves? God has found out the iniquity of your servants; behold, we are my lord's slaves,

both we and the one in whose possession the cup has been found."

17 But he said, "Far be it from me to do this. The man in whose possession the cup has been found, he shall be my slave; but as for you, go up in peace to your father."

18 ¶ Then Judah approached him, and said, "Oh my lord, may your servant please speak a word in my lord's ears, and do not be angry with your servant; for you are equal to Pharaoh.

19 "My lord asked his servants, saying, 'Have you a father or a brother?'

20 "And we said to my lord, 'We have an old father and a little child of *his* old age. Now his brother is dead, so he alone is left of his mother, and his father loves him.'

21 "Then you said to your servants, 'Bring him down to me, that I may set my eyes on him.'

22 "But we said to my lord, 'The lad cannot leave his father, for if he should leave his father, his father would die.'

23 "You said to your servants, however, 'Unless your youngest brother comes down with you, you shall not see my face again.'

24 "Thus it came about when we went up to your servant my father, we told him the words of my lord.

25 "And our father said, 'Go back, buy us a little food.'

26 "But we said, 'We cannot go down. If our youngest brother is with us, then we will go down; for we cannot see the man's face unless our youngest brother is with us.'

27 "And your servant my father said to us, 'You know that my wife bore me two sons;

28 and the one went out from me, and I said, "Surely he is torn in pieces," and I have not seen him since.

29 'And if you take this one also from me, and harm befalls him, you will bring my gray hair down to Sheol in sorrow.'

30 "Now, therefore, when I come to your servant my father, and the lad is not with us, since his life is bound up in the lad's life,

31 it will come about when he sees that the lad is not *with us*, that he will die. Thus your servants will bring the

gray hair of your servant our father down to Sheol in sorrow.

32"For your servant became surety for the lad to my father, saying, 'If I do not bring him *back* to you, then let me bear the blame before my father forever.'

33"Now, therefore, please let your servant remain instead of the lad a slave to my lord, and let the lad go up with his brothers.

34"For how shall I go up to my father if the lad is not with me, lest I see the evil that would overtake my father?"

CHAPTER 45

THEN Joseph could not control himself before all those who stood by him, and he cried, "Have everyone go out from me." So there was no man with him when Joseph made himself known to his brothers.

2 And he wept so loudly that the Egyptians heard *it*, and the household of Pharaoh heard *of it*.

3 Then Joseph said to his brothers, "I am Joseph! Is my father still alive?" But his brothers could not answer him, for they were dismayed at his presence.

4 Then Joseph said to his brothers, "Please come closer to me." And they came closer. And he said, "I am your brother Joseph, whom you sold into Egypt.

5"And now do not be grieved or angry with yourselves, because you sold me here; for God sent me before you to preserve life.

6"For the famine *has been* in the land these two years, and there are still five years in which there will be neither plowing nor harvesting.

7"And God sent me before you to preserve for you a remnant in the earth, and to keep you alive by a great deliverance.

8"Now, therefore, it was not you who sent me here, but God; and He has made me a father to Pharaoh and lord of all his household and ruler over all the land of Egypt.

9"Hurry and go up to my father, and say to him, 'Thus says your son Joseph, "God has made me lord of all Egypt; come down to me, do not delay.

10"And you shall live in the land of Goshen, and you shall be near me, you and your children and your children's children and your flocks and your herds and all that you have.

11"There I will also provide for you, for there are still five years of famine *to come*, lest you and your household and all that you have be impoverished." '

12"And behold, your eyes see, and the eyes of my brother Benjamin *see*, that it is my mouth which is speaking to you.

13"Now you must tell my father of all my splendor in Egypt, and all that you have seen; and you must hurry and bring my father down here."

14 Then he fell on his brother Benjamin's neck and wept; and Benjamin wept on his neck.

15 And he kissed all his brothers and wept on them, and afterward his brothers talked with him.

16 ¶ Now when the news was heard in Pharaoh's house that Joseph's brothers had come, it pleased Pharaoh and his servants.

17 Then Pharaoh said to Joseph, "Say to your brothers, 'Do this: load your beasts and go to the land of Canaan,

18 and take your father and your households and come to me, and I will give you the best of the land of Egypt and you shall eat the fat of the land.'

19"Now you are ordered, 'Do this: take wagons from the land of Egypt for your little ones and for your wives, and bring your father and come.

20 'And do not concern yourselves with your goods, for the best of all the land of Egypt is yours.' "

21 ¶ Then the sons of Israel did so; and Joseph gave them wagons according to the command of Pharaoh, and gave them provisions for the journey.

22 To each of them he gave changes of garments, but to Benjamin he gave three hundred *pieces of* silver and five changes of garments.

23 And to his father he sent as follows: ten donkeys loaded with the best things of Egypt, and ten female donkeys loaded with grain and bread and sustenance for his father on the journey.

24 So he sent his brothers away, and as they departed, he said to them, "Do not quarrel on the journey."

25 Then they went up from Egypt, and came to the land of Canaan to their father Jacob.

26 And they told him, saying, "Joseph is still alive, and indeed he is ruler over all the land of Egypt." But he was stunned, for he did not believe them.

27 When they told him all the words of Joseph that he had spoken to them, and when he saw the wagons that Joseph had sent to carry him, the spirit of their father Jacob revived.

28 Then Israel said, "It is enough; my son Joseph is still alive. I will go and see him before I die."

CHAPTER 46

So Israel set out with all that he had, and came to Beersheba, and offered sacrifices to the God of his father Isaac.

2 And God spoke to Israel in visions of the night and said, "Jacob, Jacob." And he said, "Here I am."

3 And He said, "I am God, the God of your father; do not be afraid to go down to Egypt, for I will make you a great nation there.

4 "I will go down with you to Egypt, and I will also surely bring you up again; and Joseph will close your eyes."

5 Then Jacob arose from Beersheba; and the sons of Israel carried their father Jacob and their little ones and their wives, in the wagons which Pharaoh had sent to carry him.

6 And they took their livestock and their property, which they had acquired in the land of Canaan, and came to Egypt, Jacob and all his descendants with him:

7 his sons and his grandsons with him, his daughters and his granddaughters, and all his descendants he brought with him to Egypt.

8 ¶ Now these are the names of the sons of Israel, Jacob and his sons, who went to Egypt: Reuben, Jacob's firstborn.

9 And the sons of Reuben: Hanoch and Pallu and Hezron and Carmi.

10 And the sons of Simeon: Jemuel and Jamin and Ohad and Jachin and Zohar and Shaul the son of a Canaanite woman.

11 And the sons of Levi: Gershon, Kohath, and Merari.

12 And the sons of Judah: Er and Onan and Shelah and Perez and Zerah (but Er and Onan died in the land of Canaan). And the sons of Perez were Hezron and Hamul.

13 And the sons of Issachar: Tola and Puvvah and Iob and Shimron.

14 And the sons of Zebulun: Sered and Elon and Jahleel.

15 These are the sons of Leah, whom she bore to Jacob in Paddan-aram, with his daughter Dinah; all his sons and his daughters *numbered* thirty-three.

16 And the sons of Gad: Ziphion and Haggi, Shuni and Ezbon, Eri and Arodi and Areli.

17 And the sons of Asher: Imnah and Ishvah and Ishvi and Beriah and their sister Serah. And the sons of Beriah: Heber and Malchiel.

18 These are the sons of Zilpah, whom Laban gave to his daughter Leah; and she bore to Jacob these sixteen persons.

19 The sons of Jacob's wife Rachel: Joseph and Benjamin.

20 Now to Joseph in the land of Egypt were born Manasseh and Ephraim, whom Asenath, the daughter of Potiphera, priest of On, bore to him.

21 And the sons of Benjamin: Bela and Becher and Ashbel, Gera and Naaman, Ehi and Rosh, Muppim and Huppim and Ard.

22 These are the sons of Rachel, who were born to Jacob; *there were* fourteen persons in all.

23 And the sons of Dan: Hushim.

24 And the sons of Naphtali: Jahzeel and Guni and Jezer and Shillem.

25 These are the sons of Bilhah, whom Laban gave to his daughter Rachel, and she bore these to Jacob; *there were* seven persons in all.

26 All the persons belonging to Jacob, who came to Egypt, his direct descendants, not including the wives of Jacob's sons, *were* sixty-six persons in all,

27 and the sons of Joseph, who were born to him in Egypt were two; all the persons of the house of Jacob, who came to Egypt, *were* seventy.

28 ¶ Now he sent Judah before him to Joseph, to point out *the way* before

him to Goshen; and they came into the land of Goshen.

29 And Joseph prepared his chariot and went up to Goshen to meet his father Israel; as soon as he appeared before him, he fell on his neck and wept on his neck a long time.

30 Then Israel said to Joseph, "Now let me die, since I have seen your face, that you are still alive."

31 And Joseph said to his brothers and to his father's household, "I will go up and tell Pharaoh, and will say to him, 'My brothers and my father's household, who *were* in the land of Canaan, have come to me;

32 and the men are shepherds, for they have been keepers of livestock; and they have brought their flocks and their herds and all that they have.'

33 "And it shall come about when Pharaoh calls you and says, 'What is your occupation?'

34 that you shall say, 'Your servants have been keepers of livestock from our youth even until now, both we and our fathers,' that you may live in the land of Goshen; for every shepherd is loathsome to the Egyptians."

CHAPTER 47

THEN Joseph went in and told Pharaoh, and said, "My father and my brothers and their flocks and their herds and all that they have, have come out of the land of Canaan; and behold, they are in the land of Goshen."

2 And he took five men from among his brothers, and presented them to Pharaoh.

3 Then Pharaoh said to his brothers, "What is your occupation?" So they said to Pharaoh, "Your servants are shepherds, both we and our fathers."

4 And they said to Pharaoh, "We have come to sojourn in the land, for there is no pasture for your servants' flocks, for the famine is severe in the land of Canaan. Now, therefore, please let your servants live in the land of Goshen."

5 Then Pharaoh said to Joseph, "Your father and your brothers have come to you.

6 "The land of Egypt is [60]at your disposal; settle your father and your

brothers in the best of the land, let them live in the land of Goshen; and if you know any capable men among them, then put them in charge of my livestock."

7 Then Joseph brought his father Jacob and presented him to Pharaoh; and Jacob blessed Pharaoh.

8 And Pharaoh said to Jacob, "How many years have you lived?"

9 So Jacob said to Pharaoh, "The years of my sojourning are one hundred and thirty; few and unpleasant have been the years of my life, nor have they attained the years that my fathers lived during the days of their sojourning."

10 And Jacob blessed Pharaoh, and went out from his presence.

11 So Joseph settled his father and his brothers, and gave them a possession in the land of Egypt, in the best of the land, in the land of Rameses, as Pharaoh had ordered.

12 And Joseph provided his father and his brothers and all his father's household with food, according to their little ones.

13 ¶ Now there was no food in all the land, because the famine was very severe, so that the land of Egypt and the land of Canaan languished because of the famine.

14 And Joseph gathered all the money that was found in the land of Egypt and in the land of Canaan for the grain which they bought, and Joseph brought the money into Pharaoh's house.

15 And when the money was all spent in the land of Egypt and in the land of Canaan, all the Egyptians came to Joseph and said, "Give us food, for why should we die in your presence? For *our* money is gone."

16 Then Joseph said, "Give up your livestock, and I will give you *food* for your livestock, since *your* money is gone."

17 So they brought their livestock to Joseph, and Joseph gave them food in exchange for the horses and the flocks and the herds and the donkeys; and he fed them with food in exchange for all their livestock that year.

18 And when that year was ended, they came to him the next year and said to him, "We will not hide from my

60 Lit., *before you*

lord that our money is all spent, and the cattle are my lord's. There is nothing left for my lord except our bodies and our lands.

19"Why should we die before your eyes, both we and our land? Buy us and our land for food, and we and our land will be slaves to Pharaoh. So give us seed, that we may live and not die, and that the land may not be desolate."

20 ¶ So Joseph bought all the land of Egypt for Pharaoh, for every Egyptian sold his field, because the famine was severe upon them. Thus the land became Pharaoh's.

21 And as for the people, he removed them to the cities from one end of Egypt's border to the other.

22 Only the land of the priests he did not buy, for the priests had an allotment from Pharaoh, and they lived off the allotment which Pharaoh gave them. Therefore, they did not sell their land.

23 Then Joseph said to the people, "Behold, I have today bought you and your land for Pharaoh; now, *here* is seed for you, and you may sow the land.

24"And at the harvest you shall give a fifth to Pharaoh, and four-fifths shall be your own for seed of the field and for your food and for those of your households and as food for your little ones."

25 So they said, "You have saved our lives! Let us find favor in the sight of my lord, and we will be Pharaoh's slaves."

26 And Joseph made it a statute concerning the land of Egypt *valid* to this day, that Pharaoh should have the fifth; only the land of the priests did not become Pharaoh's.

27 ¶ Now Israel lived in the land of Egypt, in Goshen, and they acquired property in it and were fruitful and became very numerous.

28 And Jacob lived in the land of Egypt seventeen years; so the length of Jacob's life was one hundred and forty-seven years.

29 When the time for Israel to die drew near, he called his son Joseph and said to him, "Please, if I have found favor in your sight, place now your hand under my thigh and deal

with me in kindness and [61]faithfulness. Please do not bury me in Egypt,

30 but when I lie down with my fathers, you shall carry me out of Egypt and bury me in their burial place." And he said, "I will do as you have said."

31 And he said, "Swear to me." So he swore to him. Then Israel bowed *in worship* at the head of the bed.

CHAPTER 48

NOW it came about after these things that Joseph was told, "Behold, your father is sick." So he took his two sons Manasseh and Ephraim with him.

2 When it was told to Jacob, "Behold, your son Joseph has come to you," Israel collected his strength and sat up in the bed.

3 Then Jacob said to Joseph, "God Almighty appeared to me at Luz in the land of Canaan and blessed me,

4 and He said to me, 'Behold, I will make you fruitful and numerous, and I will make you a company of peoples, and will give this land to your descendants after you for an everlasting possession.'

5"And now your two sons, who were born to you in the land of Egypt before I came to you in Egypt, are mine; Ephraim and Manasseh shall be mine, as Reuben and Simeon are.

6"But your offspring that have been born after them shall be yours; they shall be called by the names of their brothers in their inheritance.

7"Now as for me, when I came from Paddan, Rachel died, to my sorrow, in the land of Canaan on the journey, when there was still some distance to go to Ephrath; and I buried her there on the way to Ephrath (that is, Bethlehem)."

8 ¶ When Israel saw Joseph's sons, he said, "Who are these?"

9 And Joseph said to his father, "They are my sons, whom God has given me here." So he said, "Bring them to me, please, that I may bless them."

10 Now the eyes of Israel were *so* dim from age *that* he could not see. Then Joseph brought them close to him, and he kissed them and embraced them.

[61] Lit., *truth*

11 And Israel said to Joseph, "I never expected to see your face, and behold, God has let me see your children as well."

12 Then Joseph took them from his knees, and bowed with his face to the ground.

13 And Joseph took them both, Ephraim with his right hand toward Israel's left, and Manasseh with his left hand toward Israel's right, and brought them close to him.

14 But Israel stretched out his right hand and laid it on the head of Ephraim, who was the younger, and his left hand on Manasseh's head, crossing his hands, although Manasseh was the first-born.

15 And he blessed Joseph, and said,
"The God before whom my fathers Abraham and Isaac walked,
The God who has been my shepherd all my life to this day,

16 The angel who has redeemed me from all evil,
Bless the lads;
And may my name live on in them,
And the names of my fathers Abraham and Isaac;
And may they grow into a multitude in the midst of the earth."

17 When Joseph saw that his father laid his right hand on Ephraim's head, it displeased him; and he grasped his father's hand to remove it from Ephraim's head to Manasseh's head.

18 And Joseph said to his father, "Not so, my father, for this one is the first-born. Place your right hand on his head."

19 But his father refused and said, "I know, my son, I know; he also shall become a people and he also shall be great. However, his younger brother shall be greater than he, and his descendants shall become a multitude of nations."

20 And he blessed them that day, saying,
"By you Israel shall pronounce blessing, saying,
'May God make you like Ephraim and Manasseh!'"
Thus he put Ephraim before Manasseh.

21 Then Israel said to Joseph, "Behold, I am about to die, but God will be with you, and bring you back to the land of your fathers.

22 "And I give you one portion more than your brothers, which I took from the hand of the Amorite with my sword and my bow."

CHAPTER 49

THEN Jacob summoned his sons and said, "Assemble yourselves that I may tell you what shall befall you in the days to come.

2 "Gather together and hear, O sons of Jacob;
And listen to Israel your father.

3 ¶ "Reuben, you are my first-born;
My might and the beginning of my strength,
Preeminent in dignity and preeminent in power.

4 "Uncontrolled as water, you shall not have preeminence,
Because you went up to your father's bed;
Then you defiled *it*—he went up to my couch.

5 ¶ "Simeon and Levi are brothers;
Their swords are implements of violence.

6 "Let my soul not enter into their council;
Let not my glory be united with their assembly;
Because in their anger they slew men,
And in their self-will they lamed oxen.

7 "Cursed be their anger, for it is fierce;
And their wrath, for it is cruel.
I will disperse them in Jacob,
And scatter them in Israel.

8 ¶ "Judah, your brothers shall praise you;
Your hand shall be on the neck of your enemies;
Your father's sons shall bow down to you.

9 "Judah is a lion's whelp;
From the prey, my son, you have gone up.
He couches, he lies down as a lion,
And as a lion, who dares rouse him up?

10 "The scepter shall not depart from Judah,

Nor the ruler's staff from between his feet,
[62]Until Shiloh comes,
And to him *shall be* the obedience of the peoples.
11 "He ties *his* foal to the vine,
And his donkey's colt to the
choice vine;
He washes his garments in wine,
And his robes in the blood of
grapes.
12 "His eyes are [63]dull from wine,
And his teeth [64]white from milk.

13 ¶ "Zebulun shall dwell at the sea-
shore;
And he *shall be* a haven for
ships,
And his flank *shall be* toward
Sidon.

14 ¶ "Issachar is a strong donkey,
Lying down between the sheepfolds.
15 "When he saw that a resting place
was good
And that the land was pleasant,
He bowed his shoulder to bear
burdens,
And became a slave at forced
labor.

16 ¶ "Dan shall judge his people,
As one of the tribes of Israel.
17 "Dan shall be a serpent in the
way,
A horned snake in the path,
That bites the horse's heels,
So that his rider falls backward.
18 "For Thy salvation I wait, O Lord.

19 ¶ "As for Gad, raiders shall raid
him,
But he shall raid *at* their heels.

20 ¶ "As for Asher, his food shall be
rich,
And he shall yield royal dainties.

21 ¶ "Naphtali is a doe let loose,
He gives beautiful words.

22 ¶ "Joseph is a fruitful [65]bough,
A fruitful bough by a spring;
Its [66]branches run over a wall.

23 "The archers bitterly attacked
him,
And shot *at him* and harassed
him;
24 But his bow remained firm,
And his arms were agile,
From the hands of the Mighty
One of Jacob
(From there is the Shepherd, the
Stone of Israel),
25 From the God of your father who
helps you,
And by the Almighty who
blesses you
With blessings of heaven above,
Blessings of the deep that lies
beneath,
Blessings of the breasts and of
the womb.
26 "The blessings of your father
Have surpassed the blessings of
my ancestors
Up to the utmost bound of the
everlasting hills;
May they be on the head of
Joseph,
And on the crown of the head of
the one distinguished among
his brothers.

27 ¶ "Benjamin is a ravenous wolf;
In the morning he devours the
prey,
And in the evening he divides the
spoil."

28 ¶ All these are the twelve tribes
of Israel, and this is what their father
said to them when he blessed them. He
blessed them, every one with the
blessing appropriate to him.
29 Then he charged them and said to
them, "I am about to be gathered to
my people; bury me with my fathers in
the cave that is in the field of Ephron
the Hittite,
30 in the cave that is in the field of
Machpelah, which is before Mamre, in
the land of Canaan, which Abraham
bought along with the field from
Ephron the Hittite for a burial site.
31 "There they buried Abraham and
his wife Sarah, there they buried Isaac
and his wife Rebekah, and there I
buried Leah—
32 the field and the cave that is in it,
purchased from the sons of Heth."
33 When Jacob finished charging his
sons, he drew his feet into the bed and

breathed his last, and was gathered to his people.

CHAPTER 50

THEN Joseph fell on his father's face, and wept over him and kissed him.

2 And Joseph commanded his servants the physicians to embalm his father. So the physicians embalmed Israel.

3 Now forty days were required for it, for such is the period required for embalming. And the Egyptians wept for him seventy days.

4 ¶ And when the days of mourning for him were past, Joseph spoke to the household of Pharaoh, saying, "If now I have found favor in your sight, please speak to Pharaoh, saying,

5 'My father made me swear, saying, "Behold, I am about to die; in my grave which I dug for myself in the land of Canaan, there you shall bury me." Now therefore, please let me go up and bury my father; then I will return.' "

6 And Pharaoh said, "Go up and bury your father, as he made you swear."

7 So Joseph went up to bury his father, and with him went up all the servants of Pharaoh, the elders of his household and all the elders of the land of Egypt,

8 and all the household of Joseph and his brothers and his father's household; they left only their little ones and their flocks and their herds in the land of Goshen.

9 There also went up with him both chariots and horsemen; and it was a very great company.

10 When they came to the threshing floor of Atad, which is beyond the Jordan, they lamented there with a very great and sorrowful lamentation; and he observed seven days mourning for his father.

11 Now when the inhabitants of the land, the Canaanites, saw the mourning at the threshing floor of Atad, they said, "This is a grievous mourning for the Egyptians." Therefore it was named Abel-mizraim, which is beyond the Jordan.

12 And thus his sons did for him as he had charged them;

13 for his sons carried him to the land of Canaan, and buried him in the cave of the field of Machpelah before Mamre, which Abraham had bought along with the field for a burial site from Ephron the Hittite.

14 And after he had buried his father, Joseph returned to Egypt, he and his brothers, and all who had gone up with him to bury his father.

15 ¶ When Joseph's brothers saw that their father was dead, they said, "What if Joseph should bear a grudge against us and pay us back in full for all the wrong which we did to him!"

16 So they sent a message to Joseph, saying, "Your father charged before he died, saying,

17 'Thus you shall say to Joseph, "Please forgive, I beg you, the transgression of your brothers and their sin, for they did you wrong." ' And now, please forgive the transgression of the servants of the God of your father." And Joseph wept when they spoke to him.

18 Then his brothers also came and fell down before him and said, "Behold, we are your servants."

19 But Joseph said to them, "Do not be afraid, for am I in God's place?

20 "And as for you, you meant evil against me, but God meant it for good in order to bring about this present result, to preserve many people alive.

21 "So therefore, do not be afraid; I will provide for you and your little ones." So he comforted them and spoke kindly to them.

22 ¶ Now Joseph stayed in Egypt, he and his father's household, and Joseph lived one hundred and ten years.

23 And Joseph saw the third generation of Ephraim's sons; also the sons of Machir, the son of Manasseh, were born on Joseph's knees.

24 And Joseph said to his brothers, "I am about to die, but God will surely take care of you, and bring you up from this land to the land which He promised on oath to Abraham, to Isaac and to Jacob."

25 Then Joseph made the sons of Israel swear, saying, "God will surely take care of you, and you shall carry my bones up from here."

26 So Joseph died at the age of one hundred and ten years; and he was embalmed and placed in a coffin in Egypt.

NOW these are the names of the sons of Israel who came to Egypt with Jacob; they came each one with his household:

2 Reuben, Simeon, Levi and Judah;

3 Issachar, Zebulun and Benjamin;

4 Dan and Naphtali, Gad and Asher.

5 And all the persons who came from the loins of Jacob were seventy in number, but Joseph was *already* in Egypt.

6 And Joseph died, and all his brothers and all that generation.

7 But the sons of Israel were fruitful and increased greatly, and multiplied, and became exceedingly mighty, so that the land was filled with them.

8 ¶ Now a new king arose over Egypt, who did not know Joseph.

9 And he said to his people, "Behold, the people of the sons of Israel are more and mightier than we.

10 "Come, let us deal wisely with them, lest they multiply and in the event of war, they also join themselves to those who hate us, and fight against us, and depart from the land."

11 So they appointed taskmasters over them to afflict them with hard labor. And they built for Pharaoh storage cities, Pithom and Raamses.

12 But the more they afflicted them, the more they multiplied and the more they spread out, so that they were in dread of the sons of Israel.

13 And the Egyptians compelled the sons of Israel to labor rigorously;

14 and they made their lives bitter with hard labor in mortar and bricks and at all *kinds* of labor in the field, all their labors which they rigorously imposed on them.

15 ¶ Then the king of Egypt spoke to the Hebrew midwives, one of whom was named Shiphrah, and the other was named Puah;

16 and he said, "When you are helping the Hebrew women to give birth and see *them* upon the birthstool, if it is a son, then you shall put him to death; but if it is a daughter, then she shall live."

17 But the midwives feared God, and did not do as the king of Egypt had commanded them, but let the boys live.

18 So the king of Egypt called for the midwives, and said to them, "Why have you done this thing, and let the boys live?"

19 And the midwives said to Pharaoh, "Because the Hebrew women are not as the Egyptian women; for they are vigorous, and they give birth before the midwife can get to them."

20 So God was good to the midwives, and the people multiplied, and became very mighty.

21 And it came about because the midwives feared God, that He established households for them.

22 Then Pharaoh commanded all his people, saying, "Every son who is born [1]you are to cast into the Nile, and every daughter you are to keep alive."

CHAPTER 2

NOW a man from the house of Levi went and married a daughter of Levi.

2 And the woman conceived and bore a son; and when she saw that he was beautiful, she hid him for three months.

3 But when she could hide him no longer, she got him a [2]wicker basket and covered it over with tar and pitch. Then she put the child into it, and set *it* among the reeds by the bank of the Nile.

4 And his sister stood at a distance to find out what would happen to him.

5 Then the daughter of Pharaoh came down to bathe at the Nile, with her maidens walking alongside the Nile; and she saw the basket among the reeds and sent her maid, and she brought it *to her.*

6 ¶ When she opened *it,* she saw the child, and behold, *the* boy was crying. And she had pity on him and said, "This is one of the Hebrews' children."

7 Then his sister said to Pharaoh's daughter, "Shall I go and call a nurse for you from the Hebrew women, that she may nurse the child for you?"

8 And Pharaoh's daughter said to her, "Go *ahead.*" So the girl went and called the child's mother.

9 Then Pharaoh's daughter said to her, "Take this child away and nurse him for me and I shall give *you* your

[1] Some versions insert, *to the Hebrews*   [2] I.e., papyrus reeds

wages." So the woman took the child and nursed him.

10 And the child grew, and she brought him to Pharaoh's daughter, and he became her son. And she named him Moses, and said, "Because I drew him out of the water."

11 ¶ Now it came about in those days, when Moses had grown up, that he went out to his brethren and looked on their hard labors; and he saw an Egyptian beating a Hebrew, one of his brethren.

12 So he looked this way and that, and when he saw there was no one *around,* he struck down the Egyptian and hid him in the sand.

13 And he went out the next day, and behold, two Hebrews were fighting with each other; and he said to the offender, "Why are you striking your companion?"

14 But he said, "Who made you a prince or a judge over us? Are you intending to kill me, as you killed the Egyptian?" Then Moses was afraid, and said, "Surely the matter has become known."

15 When Pharaoh heard of this matter, he tried to kill Moses. But Moses fled from the presence of Pharaoh and settled in the land of Midian; and he sat down by a well.

16 ¶ Now the priest of Midian had seven daughters; and they came to draw water, and filled the troughs to water their father's flock.

17 Then the shepherds came and drove them away, but Moses stood up and helped them, and watered their flock.

18 When they came to Reuel their father, he said, "Why have you come *back* so soon today?"

19 So they said, "An Egyptian delivered us from the hand of the shepherds; and what is more, he even drew the water for us and watered the flock."

20 And he said to his daughters, "Where is he then? Why is it that you have left the man behind? Invite him to have something to eat."

21 And Moses was willing to dwell with the man, and he gave his daughter Zipporah to Moses.

22 Then she gave birth to a son, and he named him Gershom, for he said, "I have been a sojourner in a foreign land."

23 ¶ Now it came about in *the course of* those many days that the king of Egypt died. And the sons of Israel sighed because of the bondage, and they cried out; and their cry for help because of *their* bondage rose up to God.

24 So God heard their groaning; and God remembered His covenant with Abraham, Isaac, and Jacob.

25 And God saw the sons of Israel, and God took notice *of them.*

CHAPTER 3

NOW Moses was pasturing the flock of Jethro his father-in-law, the priest of Midian; and he led the flock to the west side of the wilderness, and came to Horeb, the mountain of God.

2 And the angel of the LORD appeared to him in a blazing fire from the midst of a bush; and he looked, and behold, the bush was burning with fire, yet the bush was not consumed.

3 So Moses said, "I must turn aside now, and see this marvelous sight, why the bush is not burned up."

4 When the LORD saw that he turned aside to look, God called to him from the midst of the bush, and said, "Moses, Moses!" And he said, "Here I am."

5 Then He said, "Do not come near here; remove your sandals from your feet, for the place on which you are standing is holy ground."

6 He said also, "I am the God of your father, the God of Abraham, the God of Isaac, and the God of Jacob." Then Moses hid his face, for he was afraid to look at God.

7 And the LORD said, "I have surely seen the affliction of My people who are in Egypt, and have given heed to their cry because of their taskmasters, for I am aware of their sufferings.

8 "So I have come down to deliver them from the power of the Egyptians, and to bring them up from that land to a good and spacious land, to a land flowing with milk and honey, to the place of the Canaanite and the Hittite and the Amorite and the Perizzite and the Hivite and the Jebusite.

9"And now, behold, the cry of the sons of Israel has come to Me; furthermore, I have seen the oppression with which the Egyptians are oppressing them.

10"Therefore, come now, and I will send you to Pharaoh, so that you may bring My people, the sons of Israel, out of Egypt."

11 But Moses said to God, "Who am I, that I should go to Pharaoh, and that I should bring the sons of Israel out of Egypt?"

12 And He said, "Certainly I will be with you, and this shall be the sign to you that it is I who have sent you: when you have brought the people out of Egypt, you shall worship God at this mountain."

13 ¶ Then Moses said to God, "Behold, I am going to the sons of Israel, and I shall say to them, 'The God of your fathers has sent me to you.' Now they may say to me, 'What is His name?' What shall I say to them?"

14 And God said to Moses, "[3]I AM WHO [3]I AM"; and He said, "Thus you shall say to the sons of Israel, '[3]I AM has sent me to you.'"

15 And God, furthermore, said to Moses, "Thus you shall say to the sons of Israel, 'The LORD, the God of your fathers, the God of Abraham, the God of Isaac, and the God of Jacob, has sent me to you.' This is My name forever, and this is My memorial-name to all generations.

16"Go and gather the elders of Israel together, and say to them, 'The LORD, the God of your fathers, the God of Abraham, Isaac and Jacob, has appeared to me, saying, "I am indeed concerned about you and what has been done to you in Egypt.

17"So I said, I will bring you up out of the affliction of Egypt to the land of the Canaanite and the Hittite and the Amorite and the Perizzite and the Hivite and the Jebusite, to a land flowing with milk and honey."'

18"And they will pay heed to what you say; and you with the elders of Israel will come to the king of Egypt, and you will say to him, 'The LORD, the God of the Hebrews, has met with us. So now, please, let us go a three

days' journey into the wilderness, that we may sacrifice to the LORD our God.'

19"But I know that the king of Egypt will not permit you to go, except under compulsion.

20"So I will stretch out My hand, and strike Egypt with all My miracles which I shall do in the midst of it; and after that he will let you go.

21"And I will grant this people favor in the sight of the Egyptians; and it shall be that when you go, you will not go empty-handed.

22"But every woman shall ask of her neighbor and the woman who lives in her house, articles of silver and articles of gold, and clothing; and you will put them on your sons and daughters. Thus you will plunder the Egyptians."

CHAPTER 4

THEN Moses answered and said, "What if they will not believe me, or listen to what I say? For they may say, 'The LORD has not appeared to you.'"

2 And the LORD said to him, "What is that in your hand?" And he said, "A staff."

3 Then He said, "Throw it on the ground." So he threw it on the ground, and it became a serpent; and Moses fled from it.

4 But the LORD said to Moses, "Stretch out your hand and grasp it by its tail"—so he stretched out his hand and caught it, and it became a staff in his hand—

5"that they may believe that the LORD, the God of their fathers, the God of Abraham, the God of Isaac, and the God of Jacob, has appeared to you."

6 And the LORD furthermore said to him, "Now put your hand into your bosom." So he put his hand into his bosom, and when he took it out, behold, his hand was leprous like snow.

7 Then He said, "Put your hand into your bosom again." So he put his hand into his bosom again; and when he took it out of his bosom, behold, it was restored like *the rest of* his flesh.

8"And it shall come about that if they will not believe you or heed the witness of the first sign, they may believe the witness of the last sign.

9"But it shall be that if they will not believe even these two signs or heed

[3] Related to the name of God, YHWH, rendered LORD, which is derived from the verb HAYAH, to be

what you say, then you shall take some water from the Nile and pour it on the dry ground; and the water which you take from the Nile will become blood on the dry ground."

10 ¶ Then Moses said to the LORD, "Please, Lord, I have never been eloquent, neither recently nor in time past, nor since Thou hast spoken to Thy servant; for I am slow of speech and slow of tongue."

11 And the LORD said to him, "Who has made man's mouth? Or who makes *him* dumb or deaf, or seeing or blind? Is it not I, the LORD?

12 "Now then go, and I, even I, will be with your mouth, and teach you what you are to say."

13 But he said, "Please, Lord, now send *the message* by whomever Thou wilt."

14 Then the anger of the LORD burned against Moses, and He said, "Is there not your brother Aaron the Levite? I know that he speaks fluently. And moreover, behold, he is coming out to meet you; when he sees you, he will be glad in his heart.

15 "And you are to speak to him and put the words in his mouth; and I, even I, will be with your mouth and his mouth, and I will teach you what you are to do.

16 "Moreover, he shall speak for you to the people; and it shall come about that he shall be as a mouth for you, and you shall be as God to him.

17 "And you shall take in your hand this staff, with which you shall perform the signs."

18 ¶ Then Moses departed and returned to Jethro his father-in-law, and said to him, "Please, let me go, that I may return to my brethren who are in Egypt, and see if they are still alive." And Jethro said to Moses, "Go in peace."

19 Now the LORD said to Moses in Midian, "Go back to Egypt, for all the men who were seeking your life are dead."

20 So Moses took his wife and his sons and mounted them on a donkey, and he returned to the land of Egypt. Moses also took the staff of God in his hand.

21 And the LORD said to Moses, "When you go back to Egypt see that you perform before Pharaoh all the wonders which I have put in your power; but I will harden his heart so that he will not let the people go.

22 "Then you shall say to Pharaoh, 'Thus says the LORD, "Israel is My son, My first-born.

23 "So I said to you, 'Let My son go, that he may serve Me'; but you have refused to let him go. Behold, I will kill your son, your first-born." ' "

24 ¶ Now it came about at the lodging place on the way that the LORD met him and sought to put him to death.

25 Then Zipporah took a flint and cut off her son's foreskin and threw *it* at Moses' feet, and she said, "You are indeed a bridegroom of blood to me."

26 So He let him alone. At that time she said, "*You are* a bridegroom of blood"—because of the circumcision.

27 ¶ Now the LORD said to Aaron, "Go to meet Moses in the wilderness." So he went and met him at the mountain of God, and he kissed him.

28 And Moses told Aaron all the words of the LORD with which He had sent him, and all the signs that He had commanded him *to do*.

29 Then Moses and Aaron went and assembled all the elders of the sons of Israel;

30 and Aaron spoke all the words which the LORD had spoken to Moses. He then performed the signs in the sight of the people.

31 So the people believed; and when they heard that the LORD was concerned about the sons of Israel and that He had seen their affliction, then they bowed low and worshiped.

CHAPTER 5

AND afterward Moses and Aaron came and said to Pharaoh, "Thus says the LORD, the God of Israel, 'Let My people go that they may celebrate a feast to Me in the wilderness.' "

2 But Pharaoh said, "Who is the LORD that I should obey His voice to let Israel go? I do not know the LORD, and besides, I will not let Israel go."

3 Then they said, "The God of the Hebrews has met with us. Please, let us go a three days' journey into the wilderness that we may sacrifice to the LORD our God, lest He fall upon us with pestilence or with the sword."

4 But the king of Egypt said to them, "Moses and Aaron, why do you draw the people away from their work? Get *back* to your labors!"

5 Again Pharaoh said, "Look, the people of the land are now many, and you would have them cease from their labors!"

6 So the same day Pharaoh commanded the taskmasters over the people and their foremen, saying,

7"You are no longer to give the people straw to make brick as previously; let them go and gather straw for themselves.

8"But the quota of bricks which they were making previously, you shall impose on them; you are not to reduce any of it. Because they are lazy, therefore they cry out, 'Let us go and sacrifice to our God.'

9"Let the labor be heavier on the men, and let them work at it that they may pay no attention to false words."

10 ¶ So the taskmasters of the people and their foremen went out and spoke to the people, saying, "Thus says Pharaoh, 'I am not going to give you *any* straw.

11 'You go *and* get straw for yourselves wherever you can find *it;* but none of your labor will be reduced.' "

12 So the people scattered through all the land of Egypt to gather stubble for straw.

13 And the taskmasters pressed them, saying, "Complete your work quota, *your* daily amount, just as when you had straw."

14 Moreover, the foremen of the sons of Israel, whom Pharaoh's taskmasters had set over them, were beaten and were asked, "Why have you not completed your required amount either yesterday or today in making brick as previously?"

15 ¶ Then the foremen of the sons of Israel came and cried out to Pharaoh, saying, "Why do you deal this way with your servants?

16"There is no straw given to your servants, yet they keep saying to us, 'Make bricks!' And behold, your servants are being beaten; but it is the fault of your *own* people."

17 But he said, "You are lazy, *very* lazy; therefore you say, 'Let us go *and* sacrifice to the LORD.'

18"So go now *and* work; for you shall be given no straw, yet you must deliver the quota of bricks."

19 And the foremen of the sons of Israel saw that they were in trouble because they were told, "You must not reduce *your* daily amount of bricks."

20 When they left Pharaoh's presence, they met Moses and Aaron as they were waiting for them.

21 And they said to them, "May the LORD look upon you and judge *you,* for you have made [4]us odious in Pharaoh's sight and in the sight of his servants, to put a sword in their hand to kill us."

22 ¶ Then Moses returned to the LORD and said, "O Lord, why hast Thou brought harm to this people? Why didst Thou ever send me?

23"Ever since I came to Pharaoh to speak in Thy name, he has done harm to this people; and Thou hast not delivered Thy people at all."

CHAPTER 6

THEN the LORD said to Moses, "Now you shall see what I will do to Pharaoh; for under compulsion he shall let them go, and under compulsion he shall drive them out of his land."

2 ¶ God spoke further to Moses and said to him, "I am the LORD;

3 and I appeared to Abraham, Isaac, and Jacob, as God Almighty, but *by* My name, [5]LORD, I did not make Myself known to them.

4"And I also established My covenant with them, to give them the land of Canaan, the land in which they sojourned.

5"And furthermore I have heard the groaning of the sons of Israel, because the Egyptians are holding them in bondage; and I have remembered My covenant.

6"Say, therefore, to the sons of Israel, 'I am the LORD, and I will bring you out from under the burdens of the Egyptians, and I will deliver you from their bondage. I will also redeem you with an outstretched arm and with great judgments.

7 'Then I will take you for My people, and I will be your God; and you

[4] Lit., *our savor to stink*
[5] Heb., *YHWH,* usually rendered LORD

shall know that I am the LORD your God, who brought you out from under the burdens of the Egyptians.

8 'And I will bring you to the land which I swore to give to Abraham, Isaac, and Jacob, and I will give it to you *for* a possession; I am the LORD.'"

9 So Moses spoke thus to the sons of Israel, but they did not listen to Moses on account of *their* despondency and cruel bondage.

10 ¶ Now the LORD spoke to Moses, saying,

11 "Go, tell Pharaoh king of Egypt to let the sons of Israel go out of his land."

12 But Moses spoke before the LORD, saying, "Behold, the sons of Israel have not listened to me; how then will Pharaoh listen to me, for I am unskilled in speech?"

13 Then the LORD spoke to Moses and to Aaron, and gave them a charge to the sons of Israel and to Pharaoh king of Egypt, to bring the sons of Israel out of the land of Egypt.

14 ¶ These are the heads of their fathers' households. The sons of Reuben, Israel's first-born: Hanoch and Pallu, Hezron and Carmi; these are the families of Reuben.

15 And the sons of Simeon: Jemuel and Jamin and Ohad and Jachin and Zohar and Shaul the son of a Canaanite woman; these are the families of Simeon.

16 And these are the names of the sons of Levi according to their generations: Gershon and Kohath and Merari; and the length of Levi's life was one hundred and thirty-seven years.

17 The sons of Gershon: Libni and Shimei, according to their families.

18 And the sons of Kohath: Amram and Izhar and Hebron and Uzziel; and the length of Kohath's life was one hundred and thirty-three years.

19 And the sons of Merari: Mahli and Mushi. These are the families of the Levites according to their generations.

20 And Amram married his father's sister Jochebed, and she bore him Aaron and Moses; and the length of Amram's life was one hundred and thirty-seven years.

21 And the sons of Izhar: Korah and Nepheg and Zichri.

22 And the sons of Uzziel: Mishael and Elzaphan and Sithri.

23 And Aaron married Elisheba, the daughter of Amminadab, the sister of Nahshon, and she bore him Nadab and Abihu, Eleazar and Ithamar.

24 And the sons of Korah: Assir and Elkanah and Abiasaph; these are the families of the Korahites.

25 And Aaron's son Eleazar married one of the daughters of Putiel, and she bore him Phinehas. These are the heads of the fathers' *households* of the Levites according to their families.

26 It was *the same* Aaron and Moses to whom the LORD said, "Bring out the sons of Israel from the land of Egypt according to their hosts."

27 They were the ones who spoke to Pharaoh king of Egypt about bringing out the sons of Israel from Egypt; it was *the same* Moses and Aaron.

28 ¶ Now it came about on the day when the LORD spoke to Moses in the land of Egypt,

29 that the LORD spoke to Moses, saying, "I am the LORD; speak to Pharaoh king of Egypt all that I speak to you."

30 But Moses said before the LORD, "Behold, I am unskilled in speech; how then will Pharaoh listen to me?"

CHAPTER 7

THEN the LORD said to Moses, "See, I make you *as* God to Pharaoh, and your brother Aaron shall be your prophet.

2 "You shall speak all that I command you, and your brother Aaron shall speak to Pharaoh that he let the sons of Israel go out of his land.

3 "But I will harden Pharaoh's heart that I may multiply My signs and My wonders in the land of Egypt.

4 "When Pharaoh will not listen to you, then I will lay My hand on Egypt, and bring out My hosts, My people the sons of Israel, from the land of Egypt by great judgments.

5 "And the Egyptians shall know that I am the LORD, when I stretch out My hand on Egypt and bring out the sons of Israel from their midst."

6 So Moses and Aaron did *it;* as the LORD commanded them, thus they did.

7 And Moses was eighty years old and Aaron eighty-three, when they spoke to Pharaoh.

8 ¶ Now the LORD spoke to Moses and Aaron, saying,

9"When Pharaoh speaks to you, saying, 'Work a miracle,' then you shall say to Aaron, 'Take your staff and throw *it* down before Pharaoh, *that* it may become a serpent.'"

10 So Moses and Aaron came to Pharaoh, and thus they did just as the LORD had commanded; and Aaron threw his staff down before Pharaoh and his servants, and it became a serpent.

11 Then Pharaoh also called for *the* wise men and *the* sorcerers, and they also, the magicians of Egypt, did the same with their secret arts.

12 For each one threw down his staff and they turned into serpents. But Aaron's staff swallowed up their staffs.

13 Yet Pharaoh's heart was hardened, and he did not listen to them, as the LORD had said.

14 ¶ Then the LORD said to Moses, "Pharaoh's heart is stubborn; he refuses to let the people go.

15"Go to Pharaoh in the morning as he is going out to the water, and station yourself to meet him on the bank of the Nile; and you shall take in your hand the staff that was turned into a serpent.

16"And you will say to him, 'The LORD, the God of the Hebrews, sent me to you, saying, "Let My people go, that they may serve Me in the wilderness. But behold, you have not listened until now."

17 'Thus says the LORD, "By this you shall know that I am the LORD: behold, I will strike the water that is in the Nile with the staff that is in my hand, and it shall be turned to blood.

18"And the fish that are in the Nile will die, and the Nile will become foul; and the Egyptians will find difficulty in drinking water from the Nile."'"

19 Then the LORD said to Moses, "Say to Aaron, 'Take your staff and stretch out your hand over the waters of Egypt, over their rivers, over their streams, and over their pools, and over all their reservoirs of water, that they may become blood; and there shall be blood throughout all the land of Egypt, both in *vessels of* wood and in *vessels of* stone.'"

20 ¶ So Moses and Aaron did even as the LORD had commanded. And he lifted up the staff and struck the water that *was* in the Nile, in the sight of Pharaoh and in the sight of his servants, and all the water that *was* in the Nile was turned to blood.

21 And the fish that *were* in the Nile died, and the Nile became foul, so that the Egyptians could not drink water from the Nile. And the blood was through all the land of Egypt.

22 But the magicians of Egypt did the same with their secret arts; and Pharaoh's heart was hardened, and he did not listen to them, as the LORD had said.

23 Then Pharaoh turned and went into his house with no concern even for this.

24 So all the Egyptians dug around the Nile for water to drink, for they could not drink of the water of the Nile.

25 And seven days passed after the LORD had struck the Nile.

CHAPTER 8

THEN the LORD said to Moses, "Go to Pharaoh and say to him, 'Thus says the LORD, "Let My people go, that they may serve Me.

2"But if you refuse to let *them* go, behold, I will smite your whole territory with frogs.

3"And the Nile will swarm with frogs, which will come up and go into your house and into your bedroom and on your bed, and into the houses of your servants and on your people, and into your ovens and into your kneading bowls.

4"So the frogs will come up on you and your people and all your servants."'"

5 Then the LORD said to Moses, "Say to Aaron, 'Stretch out your hand with your staff over the rivers, over the streams and over the pools, and make frogs come up on the land of Egypt.'"

6 So Aaron stretched out his hand over the waters of Egypt, and the frogs came up and covered the land of Egypt.

7 And the magicians did the same with their secret arts, making frogs come up on the land of Egypt.

8 ¶ Then Pharaoh called for Moses and Aaron and said, "Entreat the LORD that He remove the frogs from me and from my people; and I will let the

people go, that they may sacrifice to the LORD."

9 And Moses said to Pharaoh, "The honor is yours to tell me: when shall I entreat for you and your servants and your people, that the frogs be destroyed from you and your houses, *that* they may be left only in the Nile?"

10 ¶ Then he said, "Tomorrow." So he said, "*May it be* according to your word, that you may know that there is no one like the LORD our God.

11"And the frogs will depart from you and your houses and your servants and your people; they will be left only in the Nile."

12 Then Moses and Aaron went out from Pharaoh, and Moses cried to the LORD concerning the frogs which He had inflicted upon Pharaoh.

13 And the LORD did according to the word of Moses, and the frogs died out of the houses, the courts, and the fields.

14 So they piled them in heaps, and the land became foul.

15 But when Pharaoh saw that there was relief, he hardened his heart and did not listen to them, as the LORD had said.

16 ¶ Then the LORD said to Moses, "Say to Aaron, 'Stretch out your staff and strike the dust of the earth, that it may become [6]gnats through all the land of Egypt.'"

17 And they did so; and Aaron stretched out his hand with his staff, and struck the dust of the earth, and there were gnats on man and beast. All the dust of the earth became gnats through all the land of Egypt.

18 And the magicians tried with their secret arts to bring forth gnats, but they could not; so there were gnats on man and beast.

19 Then the magicians said to Pharaoh, "This is the finger of God." But Pharaoh's heart was hardened, and he did not listen to them, as the LORD had said.

20 ¶ Now the LORD said to Moses, "Rise early in the morning and present yourself before Pharaoh, as he comes out to the water, and say to him, 'Thus says the LORD, "Let My people go, that they may serve Me.

21"For if you will not let My people go, behold, I will send swarms of insects on you and on your servants and on your people and into your houses; and the houses of the Egyptians shall be full of swarms of insects, and also the ground on which they *dwell*.

22"But on that day I will set apart the land of Goshen, where My people are living, so that no swarms of insects will be there, in order that you may know that I, the LORD, am in the midst of the land.

23"And I will [7]put a division between My people and your people. Tomorrow this sign shall occur." ' "

24 Then the LORD did so. And there came great swarms of insects into the house of Pharaoh and the houses of his servants and the land was laid waste because of the swarms of insects in all the land of Egypt.

25 ¶ And Pharaoh called for Moses and Aaron and said, "Go, sacrifice to your God within the land."

26 But Moses said, "It is not right to do so, for we shall sacrifice to the LORD our God what is an abomination to the Egyptians. If we sacrifice what is an abomination to the Egyptians before their eyes, will they not then stone us?

27"We must go a three days' journey into the wilderness and sacrifice to the LORD our God as He commands us."

28 And Pharaoh said, "I will let you go, that you may sacrifice to the LORD your God in the wilderness; only you shall not go very far away. Make supplication for me."

29 Then Moses said, "Behold, I am going out from you, and I shall make supplication to the LORD that the swarms of insects may depart from Pharaoh, from his servants, and from his people tomorrow; only do not let Pharaoh deal deceitfully again in not letting the people go to sacrifice to the LORD."

30 So Moses went out from Pharaoh and made supplication to the LORD.

31 And the LORD did as Moses asked, and removed the swarms of insects from Pharaoh, from his servants and from his people; not one remained.

32 But Pharaoh hardened his heart this time also, and he did not let the people go.

[6] Or, *lice*   [7] Lit., *set a ransom*

CHAPTER 9

THEN the LORD said to Moses, "Go to Pharaoh and speak to him, 'Thus says the LORD, the God of the Hebrews, "Let My people go, that they may serve Me.

2"For if you refuse to let *them* go, and continue to hold them,

3 behold, the hand of the LORD will come *with* a very severe pestilence on your livestock which are in the field, on the horses, on the donkeys, on the camels, on the herds, and on the flocks.

4"But the LORD will make a distinction between the livestock of Israel and the livestock of Egypt, so that nothing will die of all that belongs to the sons of Israel." ' "

5 And the LORD set a definite time, saying, "Tomorrow the LORD will do this thing in the land."

6 So the LORD did this thing on the morrow, and all the livestock of Egypt died; but of the livestock of the sons of Israel, not one died.

7 And Pharaoh sent, and behold, there was not even one of the livestock of Israel dead. But the heart of Pharaoh was hardened, and he did not let the people go.

8 ¶ Then the LORD said to Moses and Aaron, "Take for yourselves handfuls of soot from a kiln, and let Moses throw it toward the sky in the sight of Pharaoh.

9"And it will become fine dust over all the land of Egypt, and will become boils breaking out with sores on man and beast through all the land of Egypt."

10 So they took soot from a kiln, and stood before Pharaoh; and Moses threw it toward the sky, and it became boils breaking out with sores on man and beast.

11 And the magicians could not stand before Moses because of the boils, for the boils were on the magicians as well as on all the Egyptians.

12 And the LORD hardened Pharaoh's heart, and he did not listen to them, just as the LORD had spoken to Moses.

13 ¶ Then the LORD said to Moses, "Rise up early in the morning and stand before Pharaoh and say to him, 'Thus says the LORD, the God of the Hebrews, "Let My people go, that they may serve Me.

14"For this time I will send all My plagues on you and your servants and your people, so that you may know that there is no one like Me in all the earth.

15"For *if by* now I had put forth My hand and struck you and your people with pestilence, you would then have been cut off from the earth.

16"But, indeed, for this cause I have allowed you to remain, in order to show you My power, and in order to proclaim My name through all the earth.

17"Still you exalt yourself against My people by not letting them go.

18"Behold, about this time tomorrow, I will send a very heavy hail, such as has not been *seen* in Egypt from the day it was founded until now.

19"Now therefore send, bring your livestock and whatever you have in the field to safety. Every man and beast that is found in the field and is not brought home, when the hail comes down on them, will die." ' "

20 The one among the servants of Pharaoh who feared the word of the LORD made his servants and his livestock flee into the houses;

21 but he who paid no regard to the word of the LORD left his servants and his livestock in the field.

22 ¶ Now the LORD said to Moses, "Stretch out your hand toward the sky, that hail may fall on all the land of Egypt, on man and on beast and on every plant of the field, throughout the land of Egypt."

23 And Moses stretched out his staff toward the sky, and the LORD sent thunder and hail, and fire ran down to the earth. And the LORD rained hail on the land of Egypt.

24 So there was hail, and fire flashing continually in the midst of the hail, very severe, such as had not been in all the land of Egypt since it became a nation.

25 And the hail struck all that was in the field through all the land of Egypt, both man and beast; the hail also struck every plant of the field and shattered every tree of the field.

26 Only in the land of Goshen, where the sons of Israel *were,* there was no hail.

27 ¶ Then Pharaoh sent for Moses and Aaron, and said to them, "I have sinned this time; the LORD is the righteous one, and I and my people are the wicked ones.

28 "Make supplication to the LORD, for there has been enough of God's thunder and hail; and I will let you go, and you shall stay no longer."

29 And Moses said to him, "As soon as I go out of the city, I will spread out my hands to the LORD; the thunder will cease, and there will be hail no longer, that you may know that the earth is the LORD'S.

30 "But as for you and your servants, I know that you do not yet fear the LORD God."

31 (Now the flax and the barley were ruined, for the barley was in the ear and the flax was in bud.

32 But the wheat and the spelt were not ruined, for they *ripen* late.)

33 So Moses went out of the city from Pharaoh, and spread out his hands to the LORD; and the thunder and the hail ceased, and rain no longer poured on the earth.

34 But when Pharaoh saw that the rain and the hail and the thunder had ceased, he sinned again and hardened his heart, he and his servants.

35 And Pharaoh's heart was hardened, and he did not let the sons of Israel go, just as the LORD had spoken through Moses.

CHAPTER 10

THEN the LORD said to Moses, "Go to Pharaoh, for I have [8]hardened his heart and the heart of his servants, that I may perform these signs of Mine among them,

2 and that you may tell in the hearing of your son, and of your grandson, how I made a mockery of the Egyptians, and how I performed My signs among them; that you may know that I am the LORD."

3 And Moses and Aaron went to Pharaoh and said to him, "Thus says the LORD, the God of the Hebrews, 'How long will you refuse to humble yourself before Me? Let My people go, that they may serve Me.

4 'For if you refuse to let My people go, behold, tomorrow I will bring locusts into your territory.

5 'And they shall cover the surface of the land, so that no one shall be able to see the land. They shall also eat the rest of what has escaped—what is left to you from the hail—and they shall eat every tree which sprouts for you out of the field.

6 'Then your houses shall be filled, and the houses of all your servants and the houses of all the Egyptians, *something* which neither your fathers nor your grandfathers have seen, from the day that they came upon the earth until this day.' " And he turned and went out from Pharaoh.

7 And Pharaoh's servants said to him, "How long will this man be a snare to us? Let the men go, that they may serve the LORD their God. Do you not realize that Egypt is destroyed?"

8 So Moses and Aaron were brought back to Pharaoh, and he said to them, "Go, serve the LORD your God! Who are the ones that are going?"

9 And Moses said, "We shall go with our young and our old; with our sons and our daughters, with our flocks and our herds we will go, for we must hold a feast to the LORD."

10 Then he said to them, "Thus may the LORD be with you, if ever I let you and your little ones go! Take heed, for evil is in your mind.

11 "Not so! Go now, the men *among you,* and serve the LORD, for that is what you desire." So they were driven out from Pharaoh's presence.

12 ¶ Then the LORD said to Moses, "Stretch out your hand over the land of Egypt for the locusts, that they may come up on the land of Egypt, and eat every plant of the land, *even* all that the hail has left."

13 So Moses stretched out his staff over the land of Egypt, and the LORD directed an east wind on the land all that day and all that night; and when it was morning, the east wind brought the locusts.

14 And the locusts came up over all the land of Egypt and settled in all the territory of Egypt; *they were* very numerous. There had never been so *many* locusts, nor would there be so *many* again.

[8] Lit., *made heavy*

15 For they covered the surface of the whole land, so that the land was darkened; and they ate every plant of the land and all the fruit of the trees that the hail had left. Thus nothing green was left on tree or plant of the field through all the land of Egypt.

16 Then Pharaoh hurriedly called for Moses and Aaron, and he said, "I have sinned against the LORD your God and against you.

17"Now therefore, please forgive my sin only this once, and make supplication to the LORD your God, that He would only remove this death from me."

18 And he went out from Pharaoh and made supplication to the LORD.

19 So the LORD shifted *the wind* to a very strong west wind which took up the locusts and drove them into the [9]Red Sea; not one locust was left in all the territory of Egypt.

20 But the LORD hardened Pharaoh's heart, and he did not let the sons of Israel go.

21 ¶ Then the LORD said to Moses, "Stretch out your hand toward the sky, that there may be darkness over the land of Egypt, even a darkness which may be felt."

22 So Moses stretched out his hand toward the sky, and there was thick darkness in all the land of Egypt for three days.

23 They did not see one another, nor did anyone rise from his place for three days, but all the sons of Israel had light in their dwellings.

24 Then Pharaoh called to Moses, and said, "Go, serve the LORD; only let your flocks and your herds be detained. Even your little ones may go with you."

25 But Moses said, "You must also let us have sacrifices and burnt offerings, that we may sacrifice *them* to the LORD our God.

26"Therefore, our livestock, too, will go with us; not a hoof will be left behind, for we shall take some of them to serve the LORD our God. And until we arrive there, we ourselves do not know with what we shall serve the LORD."

27 But the LORD hardened Pharaoh's heart, and he was not willing to let them go.

28 Then Pharaoh said to him, "Get away from me! Beware, do not see my face again, for in the day you see my face you shall die!"

29 And Moses said, "You are right; I shall never see your face again!"

CHAPTER 11

NOW the LORD said to Moses, "One more plague I will bring on Pharaoh and on Egypt; after that he will let you go from here. When he lets you go, he will surely drive you out from here completely.

2"Speak now in the hearing of the people that each man ask from his neighbor and each woman from her neighbor for articles of silver and articles of gold."

3 And the LORD gave the people favor in the sight of the Egyptians. Furthermore, the man Moses *himself* was greatly esteemed in the land of Egypt, *both* in the sight of Pharaoh's servants and in the sight of the people.

4 And Moses said, "Thus says the LORD, 'About midnight I am going out into the midst of Egypt,

5 and all the first-born in the land of Egypt shall die, from the first-born of the Pharaoh who sits on his throne, even to the first-born of the slave girl who is behind the millstones; all the first-born of the cattle as well.

6 'Moreover, there shall be a great cry in all the land of Egypt, such as there has not been *before* and such as shall never be again.

7 'But against any of the sons of Israel a dog shall not *even* bark, whether against man or beast, that you may understand how the LORD makes a distinction between Egypt and Israel.'

8"And all these your servants will come down to me and bow themselves before me, saying, 'Go out, you and all the people who follow you,' and after that I will go out." And he went out from Pharaoh in hot anger.

9 ¶ Then the LORD said to Moses, "Pharaoh will not listen to you, so that My wonders will be multiplied in the land of Egypt."

10 And Moses and Aaron performed all these wonders before Pharaoh; yet

[9] Lit., *Sea of Reeds*

the LORD hardened Pharaoh's heart, and he did not let the sons of Israel go out of his land.

CHAPTER 12

NOW the LORD said to Moses and Aaron in the land of Egypt,

2 "This month shall be the beginning of months for you; it is to be the first month of the year to you.

3 "Speak to all the congregation of Israel, saying, 'On the tenth of this month they are each one to take a lamb for themselves, according to their fathers' households, a lamb for each household.

4 'Now if the household is too small for a lamb, then he and his neighbor nearest to his house are to take one according to the number of persons *in them;* according to what each man should eat, you are to divide the lamb.

5 'Your lamb shall be an unblemished male a year old; you may take it from the sheep or from the goats.

6 'And you shall keep it until the fourteenth day of the same month, then the whole assembly of the congregation of Israel is to kill it at twilight.

7 'Moreover, they shall take some of the blood and put it on the two doorposts and on the lintel of the houses in which they eat it.

8 'And they shall eat the flesh that *same* night, roasted with fire, and they shall eat it with unleavened bread and bitter herbs.

9 'Do not eat any of it raw or boiled at all with water, but rather roasted with fire, *both* its head and its legs along with its entrails.

10 'And you shall not leave any of it over until morning, but whatever is left of it until morning, you shall burn with fire.

11 'Now you shall eat it in this manner: *with* your loins girded, your sandals on your feet, and your staff in your hand; and you shall eat it in haste—it is the LORD's Passover.

12 'For I will go through the land of Egypt on that night, and will strike down all the first-born in the land of Egypt, both man and beast; and against all the gods of Egypt I will execute judgments—I am the LORD.

13 'And the blood shall be a sign for you on the houses where you live; and when I see the blood I will pass over you, and no plague will befall you to destroy *you* when I strike the land of Egypt.

14 'Now this day will be a memorial to you, and you shall celebrate it *as* a feast to the LORD; throughout your generations you are to celebrate it *as* a permanent ordinance.

15 ¶ 'Seven days you shall eat unleavened bread, but on the first day you shall remove leaven from your houses; for whoever eats anything leavened from the first day until the seventh day, that person shall be cut off from Israel.

16 'And on the first day you shall have a holy assembly, and *another* holy assembly on the seventh day; no work at all shall be done on them, except what must be eaten by every person, that alone may be prepared by you.

17 'You shall also observe the *Feast of* Unleavened Bread, for on this very day I brought your hosts out of the land of Egypt; therefore you shall observe this day throughout your generations as a permanent ordinance.

18 'In the first *month,* on the fourteenth day of the month at evening, you shall eat unleavened bread, until the twenty-first day of the month at evening.

19 'Seven days there shall be no leaven found in your houses; for whoever eats what is leavened, that person shall be cut off from the congregation of Israel, whether *he is* an alien or a native of the land.

20 'You shall not eat anything leavened; in all your dwellings you shall eat unleavened bread.' "

21 ¶ Then Moses called for all the elders of Israel, and said to them, "Go and take for yourselves lambs according to your families, and slay the Passover *lamb.*

22 "And you shall take a bunch of hyssop and dip it in the blood which is in the basin, and apply some of the blood that is in the basin to the lintel and the two doorposts; and none of you shall go outside the door of his house until morning.

23 "For the LORD will pass through to smite the Egyptians; and when He sees

the blood on the lintel and on the two doorposts, the LORD will pass over the door and will not allow the destroyer to come in to your houses to smite you.

24"And you shall observe this event as an ordinance for you and your children forever.

25"And it will come about when you enter the land which the LORD will give you, as He has promised, that you shall observe this rite.

26"And it will come about when your children will say to you, 'What does this rite mean to you?'

27 that you shall say, 'It is a Passover sacrifice to the LORD who passed over the houses of the sons of Israel in Egypt when He smote the Egyptians, but spared our homes.'" And the people bowed low and worshiped.

28 Then the sons of Israel went and did so; just as the LORD had commanded Moses and Aaron, so they did.

29 ¶ Now it came about at midnight that the LORD struck all the first-born in the land of Egypt, from the first-born of Pharaoh who sat on his throne to the first-born of the captive who was in the dungeon, and all the first-born of cattle.

30 And Pharaoh arose in the night, he and all his servants and all the Egyptians; and there was a great cry in Egypt, for there was no home where there was not someone dead.

31 Then he called for Moses and Aaron at night and said, "Rise up, get out from among my people, both you and the sons of Israel; and go, worship the LORD, as you have said.

32"Take both your flocks and your herds, as you have said, and go, and bless me also."

33 And the Egyptians urged the people, to send them out of the land in haste, for they said, "We shall all be dead."

34 So the people took their dough before it was leavened, with their kneading bowls bound up in the clothes on their shoulders.

35 Now the sons of Israel had done according to the word of Moses, for they had requested from the Egyptians articles of silver and articles of gold, and clothing;

36 and the LORD had given the people favor in the sight of the Egyptians,

so that they let them have their request. Thus they plundered the Egyptians.

37 ¶ Now the sons of Israel journeyed from Rameses to Succoth, about six hundred thousand men on foot, aside from children.

38 And a mixed multitude also went up with them, along with flocks and herds, a very large number of livestock.

39 And they baked the dough which they had brought out of Egypt into cakes of unleavened bread. For it had not become leavened, since they were driven out of Egypt and could not delay, nor had they prepared any provisions for themselves.

40 ¶ Now the time that the sons of Israel lived in Egypt was four hundred and thirty years.

41 And it came about at the end of four hundred and thirty years, to the very day, that all the hosts of the LORD went out from the land of Egypt.

42 It is a night to be observed for the LORD for having brought them out from the land of Egypt; this night is for the LORD, to be observed by all the sons of Israel throughout their generations.

43 ¶ And the LORD said to Moses and Aaron, "This is the ordinance of the Passover: no [10]foreigner is to eat of it;

44 but every man's slave purchased with money, after you have circumcised him, then he may eat of it.

45"A sojourner or a hired servant shall not eat of it.

46"It is to be eaten in a single house; you are not to bring forth any of the flesh outside of the house, nor are you to break any bone of it.

47"All the congregation of Israel are to celebrate this.

48"But if a stranger sojourns with you, and celebrates the Passover to the LORD, let all his males be circumcised, and then let him come near to celebrate it; and he shall be like a native of the land. But no uncircumcised person may eat of it.

49"The same law shall apply to the native as to the stranger who sojourns among you."

50 Then all the sons of Israel did so;

[10] Lit., son of a stranger

they did just as the LORD had commanded Moses and Aaron.

51 And it came about on that same day that the LORD brought the sons of Israel out of the land of Egypt by their hosts.

CHAPTER 13

THEN the LORD spoke to Moses, saying,

2"Sanctify to Me every first-born, the first offspring of every womb among the sons of Israel, both of man and beast; it belongs to Me."

3 ¶ And Moses said to the people, "Remember this day in which you went out from Egypt, from the house of slavery; for by a powerful hand the LORD brought you out from this place. And nothing leavened shall be eaten.

4"On this day in the month of Abib, you are about to go forth.

5"And it shall be when the LORD brings you to the land of the Canaanite, the Hittite, the Amorite, the Hivite and the Jebusite, which He swore to your fathers to give you, a land flowing with milk and honey, that you shall observe this rite in this month.

6"For seven days you shall eat unleavened bread, and on the seventh day there shall be a feast to the LORD.

7"Unleavened bread shall be eaten throughout the seven days; and nothing leavened shall be seen among you, nor shall any leaven be seen among you in all your borders.

8"And you shall tell your son on that day, saying, 'It is because of what the LORD did for me when I came out of Egypt.'

9"And it shall serve as a sign to you on your hand, and as a reminder on your forehead, that the law of the LORD may be in your mouth; for with a powerful hand the LORD brought you out of Egypt.

10"Therefore, you shall keep this ordinance at its appointed time from year to year.

11 ¶"Now it shall come about when the LORD brings you to the land of the Canaanite, as He swore to you and to your fathers, and gives it to you,

12 that you shall devote to the LORD the first offspring of every womb, and the first offspring of every beast that you own; the males belong to the LORD.

13"But every first offspring of a donkey you shall redeem with a lamb, but if you do not redeem it, then you shall break its neck; and every first-born of man among your sons you shall redeem.

14"And it shall be when your son asks you in time to come, saying, 'What is this?' then you shall say to him, 'With a powerful hand the LORD brought us out of Egypt, from the house of slavery.

15 'And it came about, when Pharaoh was stubborn about letting us go, that the LORD killed every first-born in the land of Egypt, both the first-born of man and the first-born of beast. Therefore, I sacrifice to the LORD the males, the first offspring of every womb, but every first-born of my sons I redeem.'

16"So it shall serve as a sign on your hand, and as phylacteries on your forehead, for with a powerful hand the LORD brought us out of Egypt."

17 ¶ Now it came about when Pharaoh had let the people go, that God did not lead them by the way of the land of the Philistines, even though it was near; for God said, "Lest the people change their minds when they see war, and they return to Egypt."

18 Hence God led the people around by the way of the wilderness to the Red Sea; and the sons of Israel went up in martial array from the land of Egypt.

19 And Moses took the bones of Joseph with him, for he had made the sons of Israel solemnly swear, saying, "God shall surely take care of you; and you shall carry my bones from here with you."

20 Then they set out from Succoth and camped in Etham on the edge of the wilderness.

21 And the LORD was going before them in a pillar of cloud by day to lead them on the way, and in a pillar of fire by night to give them light, that they might travel by day and by night.

22 He did not take away the pillar of cloud by day, nor the pillar of fire by night, from before the people.

CHAPTER 14

NOW the LORD spoke to Moses, saying,

2"Tell the sons of Israel to turn back

and camp before Pi-hahiroth, between Migdol and the sea; you shall camp in front of Baal-zephon, opposite it, by the sea.

3"For Pharaoh will say of the sons of Israel, 'They are wandering aimlessly in the land; the wilderness has shut them in.'

4"Thus I will harden Pharaoh's heart, and he will chase after them; and I will be honored through Pharaoh and all his army, and the Egyptians will know that I am the LORD." And they did so.

5 ¶ When the king of Egypt was told that the people had fled, Pharaoh and his servants had a change of heart toward the people, and they said, "What is this we have done, that we have let Israel go from serving us?"

6 So he made his chariot ready and took his people with him;

7 and he took six hundred select chariots, and all the *other* chariots of Egypt with officers over all of them.

8 And the LORD hardened the heart of Pharaoh, king of Egypt, and he chased after the sons of Israel as the sons of Israel were going out boldly.

9 Then the Egyptians chased after them *with* all the horses *and* chariots of Pharaoh, his horsemen and his army, and they overtook them camping by the sea, beside Pi-hahiroth, in front of Baal-zephon.

10 ¶ And as Pharaoh drew near, the sons of Israel looked, and behold, the Egyptians were marching after them, and they became very frightened; so the sons of Israel cried out to the LORD.

11 Then they said to Moses, "Is it because there were no graves in Egypt that you have taken us away to die in the wilderness? Why have you dealt with us in this way, bringing us out of Egypt?

12"Is this not the word that we spoke to you in Egypt, saying, 'Leave us alone that we may serve the Egyptians'? For it would have been better for us to serve the Egyptians than to die in the wilderness."

13 But Moses said to the people, "Do not fear! Stand by and see the salvation of the LORD which He will accomplish for you today; for the Egyptians whom you have seen today, you will never see them again forever.

14"The LORD will fight for you while you keep silent."

15 ¶ Then the LORD said to Moses, "Why are you crying out to Me? Tell the sons of Israel to go forward.

16"And as for you, lift up your staff and stretch out your hand over the sea and divide it, and the sons of Israel shall go through the midst of the sea on dry land.

17"And as for Me, behold, I will harden the hearts of the Egyptians so that they will go in after them; and I will be honored through Pharaoh and all his army, through his chariots and his horsemen.

18"Then the Egyptians will know that I am the LORD, when I am honored through Pharaoh, through his chariots and his horsemen."

19 And the angel of God, who had been going before the camp of Israel, moved and went behind them; and the pillar of cloud moved from before them and stood behind them.

20 So it came between the camp of Egypt and the camp of Israel; and there was the cloud along with the darkness, yet it gave light at night. Thus the one did not come near the other all night.

21 ¶ Then Moses stretched out his hand over the sea; and the LORD swept the sea *back* by a strong east wind all night, and turned the sea into dry land, so the waters were divided.

22 And the sons of Israel went through the midst of the sea on the dry land, and the waters *were like* a wall to them on their right hand and on their left.

23 Then the Egyptians took up the pursuit, and all Pharaoh's horses, his chariots and his horsemen went in after them into the midst of the sea.

24 And it came about at the morning watch, that the LORD looked down on the army of the Egyptians through the pillar of fire and cloud and brought the army of the Egyptians into confusion.

25 And He caused their chariot wheels to swerve, and He made them drive with difficulty; so the Egyptians said, "Let us flee from Israel, for the LORD is fighting for them against the Egyptians."

26 ¶ Then the LORD said to Moses, "Stretch out your hand over the sea so

that the waters may come back over the Egyptians, over their chariots and their horsemen."

27 So Moses stretched out his hand over the sea, and the sea returned to its normal state at daybreak, while the Egyptians were fleeing right into it; then the LORD overthrew the Egyptians in the midst of the sea.

28 And the waters returned and covered the chariots and the horsemen, even Pharaoh's entire army that had gone into the sea after them; not even one of them remained.

29 But the sons of Israel walked on dry land through the midst of the sea, and the waters *were like* a wall to them on their right hand and on their left.

30 Thus the LORD saved Israel that day from the hand of the Egyptians, and Israel saw the Egyptians dead on the seashore.

31 And when Israel saw the great power which the LORD had used against the Egyptians, the people feared the LORD, and they believed in the LORD and in His servant Moses.

CHAPTER 15

THEN Moses and the sons of Israel sang this song to the LORD, and said,
"I will sing to the LORD, for He is highly exalted;
The horse and its rider He has hurled into the sea.

2 "The LORD is my strength and song,
And He has become my salvation;
This is my God, and I will praise Him;
My father's God, and I will extol Him.

3 "The LORD is a warrior;
The LORD is His name.

4 "Pharaoh's chariots and his army He has cast into the sea;
And the choicest of his officers are drowned in the [11]Red Sea.

5 "The deeps cover them;
They went down into the depths like a stone.

6 "Thy right hand, O LORD, is majestic in power,
Thy right hand, O LORD, shatters the enemy.

7 "And in the greatness of Thine excellence Thou dost overthrow those who rise up against Thee;
Thou dost send forth Thy burning anger, *and* it consumes them as chaff.

8 "And at the blast of Thy nostrils the waters were piled up,
The flowing waters stood up like a heap;
The deeps were congealed in the heart of the sea.

9 "The enemy said, 'I will pursue, I will overtake, I will divide the spoil;
My desire shall be gratified against them;
I will draw out my sword, my hand shall destroy them.'

10 "Thou didst blow with Thy wind, the sea covered them;
They sank like lead in the mighty waters.

11 "Who is like Thee among the gods, O LORD?
Who is like Thee, majestic in holiness,
Awesome in praises, working wonders?

12 "Thou didst stretch out Thy right hand,
The earth swallowed them.

13 "In Thy lovingkindness Thou hast led the people whom Thou hast redeemed;
In Thy strength Thou hast guided *them* to Thy holy habitation.

14 "The peoples have heard, they tremble;
Anguish has gripped the inhabitants of Philistia.

15 "Then the chiefs of Edom were dismayed;
The leaders of Moab, trembling grips them;
All the inhabitants of Canaan have melted away.

16 "Terror and dread fall upon them;
By the greatness of Thine arm they are motionless as stone;
Until Thy people pass over, O LORD,
Until the people pass over whom Thou hast purchased.

17 "Thou wilt bring them and plant them in the mountain of Thine inheritance,

[11] Lit., *Sea of Reeds*

The place, O LORD, which Thou
    hast made for Thy dwelling,
The sanctuary, O Lord, which
    Thy hands have established.
18 "The LORD shall reign forever and
    ever."
19 ¶ For the horses of Pharaoh with
his chariots and his horsemen went
into the sea, and the LORD brought
back the waters of the sea on them;
but the sons of Israel walked on dry
land through the midst of the sea.
20 And Miriam the prophetess, Aaron's sister, took the timbrel in her
hand, and all the women went out
after her with timbrels and with dancing.
21 And Miriam answered them,
    "Sing to the LORD, for He is highly
        exalted;
    The horse and his rider He has
        hurled into the sea."
22 ¶ Then Moses led Israel from the
Red Sea, and they went out into the
wilderness of Shur; and they went
three days in the wilderness and found
no water.
23 And when they came to Marah,
they could not drink the waters of
Marah, for they were bitter; therefore
it was named [12]Marah.
24 So the people grumbled at Moses,
saying, "What shall we drink?"
25 Then he cried out to the LORD,
and the LORD showed him a tree; and
he threw *it* into the waters, and the
waters became sweet. There He made
for them a statute and regulation, and
there He tested them.
26 And He said, "If you will give
earnest heed to the voice of the LORD
your God, and do what is right in His
sight, and give ear to His commandments, and keep all His statutes, I will
put none of the diseases on you which
I have put on the Egyptians; for I, the
LORD, am your healer."
27 ¶ Then they came to Elim where
there *were* twelve springs of water and
seventy date palms, and they camped
there beside the waters.

CHAPTER 16

THEN they set out from Elim, and all
the congregation of the sons of Israel
came to the wilderness of Sin, which is
between Elim and Sinai, on the fifteenth day of the second month after
their departure from the land of Egypt.
2 And the whole congregation of
the sons of Israel grumbled against
Moses and Aaron in the wilderness.
3 And the sons of Israel said to
them, "Would that we had died by the
LORD's hand in the land of Egypt,
when we sat by the pots of meat,
when we ate bread to the full; for you
have brought us out into this wilderness to kill this whole assembly with
hunger."
4 ¶ Then the LORD said to Moses,
"Behold, I will rain bread from heaven
for you; and the people shall go out
and gather a day's portion every day,
that I may test them, whether or not
they will walk in My [13]instruction.
5 "And it will come about on the
sixth day, when they prepare what
they bring in, it will be twice as much
as they gather daily."
6 So Moses and Aaron said to all the
sons of Israel, "At evening you will
know that the LORD has brought you
out of the land of Egypt;
7 and in the morning you will see
the glory of the LORD, for He hears
your grumblings against the LORD;
and what are we, that you grumble
against us?"
8 And Moses said, "*This will happen*
when the LORD gives you meat to eat
in the evening, and bread to the full in
the morning; for the LORD hears your
grumblings which you grumble
against Him. And what are we? Your
grumblings are not against us but
against the LORD."
9 Then Moses said to Aaron, "Say
to all the congregation of the sons of
Israel, 'Come near before the LORD, for
He has heard your grumblings.' "
10 And it came about as Aaron spoke
to the whole congregation of the sons
of Israel, that they looked toward the
wilderness, and behold, the glory of
the LORD appeared in the cloud.
11 And the LORD spoke to Moses,
saying,
12 "I have heard the grumblings of
the sons of Israel; speak to them,
saying, 'At twilight you shall eat meat,
and in the morning you shall be filled

---

[12] I.e., bitterness   [13] Or, *law*

with bread; and you shall know that I am the LORD your God.' "

13 ¶ So it came about at evening that the quails came up and covered the camp, and in the morning there was a layer of dew around the camp.

14 When the layer of dew evaporated, behold, on the surface of the wilderness there was a fine flake-like thing, fine as the frost on the ground.

15 When the sons of Israel saw *it*, they said to one another, "What is it?" For they did not know what it was. And Moses said to them, "It is the bread which the LORD has given you to eat.

16 "This is what the LORD has commanded, 'Gather of it every man as much as he should eat; you shall take an omer apiece according to the number of persons each of you has in his tent.' "

17 And the sons of Israel did so, and *some* gathered much and *some* little.

18 When they measured it with an omer, he who had gathered much had no excess, and he who had gathered little had no lack; every man gathered as much as he should eat.

19 And Moses said to them, "Let no man leave any of it until morning."

20 But they did not listen to Moses, and some left part of it until morning, and it bred worms and became foul; and Moses was angry with them.

21 And they gathered it morning by morning, every man as much as he should eat; but when the sun grew hot, it would melt.

22 ¶ Now it came about on the sixth day they gathered twice as much bread, two omers for each one. When all the leaders of the congregation came and told Moses,

23 then he said to them, "This is what the LORD meant: Tomorrow is a sabbath observance, a holy sabbath to the LORD. Bake what you will bake and boil what you will boil, and all that is left over put aside to be kept until morning."

24 So they put it aside until morning, as Moses had ordered, and it did not become foul, nor was there any worm in it.

25 And Moses said, "Eat it today, for today is a sabbath to the LORD; today you will not find it in the field.

26 "Six days you shall gather it, but on the seventh day, *the* sabbath, there will be none."

27 And it came about on the seventh day that some of the people went out to gather, but they found none.

28 Then the LORD said to Moses, "How long do you refuse to keep My commandments and My [14]instructions?

29 "See, the LORD has given you the sabbath; therefore He gives you bread for two days on the sixth day. Remain every man in his place; let no man go out of his place on the seventh day."

30 So the people rested on the seventh day.

31 ¶ And the house of Israel named it manna, and it was like coriander seed, white; and its taste was like wafers with honey.

32 Then Moses said, "This is what the LORD has commanded, 'Let an omerful of it be kept throughout your generations, that they may see the bread that I fed you in the wilderness, when I brought you out of the land of Egypt.' "

33 And Moses said to Aaron, "Take a jar and put an omerful of manna in it, and place it before the LORD, to be kept throughout your generations."

34 As the LORD commanded Moses, so Aaron placed it before the Testimony, to be kept.

35 And the sons of Israel ate the manna forty years, until they came to an inhabited land; they ate the manna until they came to the border of the land of Canaan.

36 (Now an omer is a tenth of an ephah.)

CHAPTER 17

THEN all the congregation of the sons of Israel journeyed by stages from the wilderness of Sin, according to the command of the LORD, and camped at Rephidim, and there was no water for the people to drink.

2 Therefore the people quarreled with Moses and said, "Give us water that we may drink." And Moses said to them, "Why do you quarrel with me? Why do you test the LORD?"

3 But the people thirsted there for

[14] Or, *laws*

water; and they grumbled against Moses and said, "Why, now, have you brought us up from Egypt, to kill us and our children and our livestock with thirst?"

4 So Moses cried out to the LORD, saying, "What shall I do to this people? A little more and they will stone me."

5 Then the LORD said to Moses, "Pass before the people and take with you some of the elders of Israel; and take in your hand your staff with which you struck the Nile, and go.

6"Behold, I will stand before you there on the rock at Horeb; and you shall strike the rock, and water will come out of it, that the people may drink." And Moses did so in the sight of the elders of Israel.

7 And he named the place [15]Massah and [16]Meribah because of the quarrel of the sons of Israel, and because they tested the LORD, saying, "Is the LORD among us, or not?"

8 ¶ Then Amalek came and fought against Israel at Rephidim.

9 So Moses said to Joshua, "Choose men for us, and go out, fight against Amalek. Tomorrow I will station myself on the top of the hill with the staff of God in my hand."

10 And Joshua did as Moses told him, and fought against Amalek; and Moses, Aaron, and Hur went up to the top of the hill.

11 So it came about when Moses held his hand up, that Israel prevailed, and when he let his hand down, Amalek prevailed.

12 But Moses' hands were heavy. Then they took a stone and put it under him, and he sat on it; and Aaron and Hur supported his hands, one on one side and one on the other. Thus his hands were steady until the sun set.

13 So Joshua overwhelmed Amalek and his people with the edge of the sword.

14 ¶ Then the LORD said to Moses, "Write this in a book as a memorial, and recite it to Joshua, that I will utterly blot out the memory of Amalek from under heaven."

15 And Moses built an altar, and named it The LORD is My Banner;

[15] I.e., test   [16] I.e., quarrel

16 and he said, "The LORD has sworn; the LORD will have war against Amalek from generation to generation."

CHAPTER 18

NOW Jethro, the priest of Midian, Moses' father-in-law, heard of all that God had done for Moses and for Israel His people, how the LORD had brought Israel out of Egypt.

2 And Jethro, Moses' father-in-law, took Moses' wife Zipporah, after he had sent her away,

3 and her two sons, of whom one was named Gershom, for he said, "I have been a sojourner in a foreign land."

4 And the other was named Eliezer, for he said, "The God of my father was my help, and delivered me from the sword of Pharaoh."

5 Then Jethro, Moses' father-in-law, came with his sons and his wife to Moses in the wilderness where he was camped, at the mount of God.

6 And he sent word to Moses, "I, your father-in-law Jethro, am coming to you with your wife and her two sons with her."

7 Then Moses went out to meet his father-in-law, and he bowed down and kissed him; and they asked each other of their welfare, and went into the tent.

8 And Moses told his father-in-law all that the LORD had done to Pharaoh and to the Egyptians for Israel's sake, all the hardship that had befallen them on the journey, and how the LORD had delivered them.

9 And Jethro rejoiced over all the goodness which the LORD had done to Israel, in delivering them from the hand of the Egyptians.

10 So Jethro said, "Blessed be the LORD who delivered you from the hand of the Egyptians and from the hand of Pharaoh, and who delivered the people from under the hand of the Egyptians.

11"Now I know that the LORD is greater than all the gods; indeed, it was proven when they dealt proudly against the people."

12 Then Jethro, Moses' father-in-law, took a burnt offering and sacrifices for God, and Aaron came with all the

elders of Israel to eat a meal with Moses' father-in-law before God.

13 ¶ And it came about the next day that Moses sat to judge the people, and the people stood about Moses from the morning until the evening.

14 Now when Moses' father-in-law saw all that he was doing for the people, he said, "What is this thing that you are doing for the people? Why do you alone sit *as judge* and all the people stand about you from morning until evening?"

15 And Moses said to his father-in-law, "Because the people come to me to inquire of God.

16 "When they have a dispute, it comes to me, and I judge between a man and his neighbor, and make known the statutes of God and His laws."

17 And Moses' father-in-law said to him, "The thing that you are doing is not good.

18 "You will surely wear out, both yourself and these people who are with you, for the task is too heavy for you; you cannot do it alone.

19 "Now listen to me: I shall give you counsel, and God be with you. You be the people's representative before God, and you bring the disputes to God,

20 then teach them the statutes and the laws, and make known to them the way in which they are to walk, and the work they are to do.

21 "Furthermore, you shall select out of all the people able men who fear God, men of truth, those who hate dishonest gain; and you shall place *these* over them, *as* leaders of thousands, of hundreds, of fifties and of tens.

22 "And let them judge the people at all times; and let it be that every major dispute they will bring to you, but every minor dispute they themselves will judge. So it will be easier for you, and they will bear *the burden* with you.

23 "If you do this thing and God *so* commands you, then you will be able to endure, and all these people also will go to their place in peace."

24 ¶ So Moses listened to his father-in-law, and did all that he had said.

25 And Moses chose able men out of all Israel, and made them heads over the people, leaders of thousands, of hundreds, of fifties and of tens.

26 And they judged the people at all times; the difficult dispute they would bring to Moses, but every minor dispute they themselves would judge.

27 Then Moses bade his father-in-law farewell, and he went his way into his own land.

CHAPTER 19

IN the third month after the sons of Israel had gone out of the land of Egypt, on that very day they came into the wilderness of Sinai.

2 When they set out from Rephidim, they came to the wilderness of Sinai, and camped in the wilderness; and there Israel camped in front of the mountain.

3 And Moses went up to God, and the LORD called to him from the mountain, saying, "Thus you shall say to the house of Jacob and tell the sons of Israel:

4 'You yourselves have seen what I did to the Egyptians, and *how* I bore you on eagles' wings, and brought you to Myself.

5 'Now then, if you will indeed obey My voice and keep My covenant, then you shall be My [17]own possession among all the peoples, for all the earth is Mine;

6 and you shall be to Me a kingdom of priests and a holy nation.' These are the words that you shall speak to the sons of Israel."

7 ¶ So Moses came and called the elders of the people, and set before them all these words which the LORD had commanded him.

8 And all the people answered together and said, "All that the LORD has spoken we will do!" And Moses brought back the words of the people to the LORD.

9 And the LORD said to Moses, "Behold, I shall come to you in a thick cloud, in order that the people may hear when I speak with you, and may also believe in you forever." Then Moses told the words of the people to the LORD.

10 The LORD also said to Moses, "Go to the people and consecrate them

[17] Or, *special treasure*

today and tomorrow, and let them wash their garments;

11 and let them be ready for the third day, for on the third day the LORD will come down on Mount Sinai in the sight of all the people.

12 "And you shall set bounds for the people all around, saying, 'Beware that you do not go up on the mountain or touch the border of it; whoever touches the mountain shall surely be put to death.

13 'No hand shall touch him, but he shall surely be stoned or [18]shot through; whether beast or man, he shall not live.' When the ram's horn sounds a long blast, they shall come up to the mountain."

14 So Moses went down from the mountain to the people and consecrated the people, and they washed their garments.

15 And he said to the people, "Be ready for the third day; do not go near a woman."

16 ¶ So it came about on the third day, when it was morning, that there were thunder and lightning flashes and a thick cloud upon the mountain and a very loud trumpet sound, so that all the people who *were* in the camp trembled.

17 And Moses brought the people out of the camp to meet God, and they stood at the foot of the mountain.

18 Now Mount Sinai *was* all in smoke because the LORD descended upon it in fire; and its smoke ascended like the smoke of a furnace, and the whole mountain quaked violently.

19 When the sound of the trumpet grew louder and louder, Moses spoke and God answered him with thunder.

20 And the LORD came down on Mount Sinai, to the top of the mountain; and the LORD called Moses to the top of the mountain, and Moses went up.

21 Then the LORD spoke to Moses, "Go down, warn the people, lest they break through to the LORD to gaze, and many of them perish.

22 "And also let the priests who come near to the LORD consecrate themselves, lest the LORD break out against them."

23 And Moses said to the LORD, "The people cannot come up to Mount Sinai, for Thou didst warn us, saying, 'Set bounds about the mountain and consecrate it.'"

24 Then the LORD said to him, "Go down and come up *again*, you and Aaron with you; but do not let the priests and the people break through to come up to the LORD, lest He break forth upon them."

25 So Moses went down to the people and told them.

CHAPTER 20

THEN God spoke all these words, saying,

2 ¶ "I am the LORD your God, who brought you out of the land of Egypt, out of the house of slavery.

3 ¶ "You shall have no other gods [19]before Me.

4 ¶ "You shall not make for yourself [20]an idol, or any likeness of what is in heaven above or on the earth beneath or in the water under the earth.

5 "You shall not worship them or serve them; for I, the LORD your God, am a jealous God, visiting the iniquity of the fathers on the children, on the third and the fourth generations of those who hate Me,

6 but showing lovingkindness to thousands, to those who love Me and keep My commandments.

7 ¶ "You shall not take the name of the LORD your God in vain, for the LORD will not leave him unpunished who takes His name in vain.

8 ¶ "Remember the sabbath day, to keep it holy.

9 "Six days you shall labor and do all your work,

10 but the seventh day is a sabbath of the LORD your God; *in it* you shall not do any work, you or your son or your daughter, your male or your female servant or your cattle or your sojourner who stays with you.

11 "For in six days the LORD made the heavens and the earth, the sea and all that is in them, and rested on the seventh day; therefore the LORD blessed the sabbath day and made it holy.

12 ¶ "Honor your father and your

---

[18] I.e., with arrows   [19] Or, *besides Me*   [20] Or, *a graven image*

mother, that your days may be prolonged in the land which the LORD your God gives you.

13 ¶"You shall not murder.

14 ¶"You shall not commit adultery.

15 ¶"You shall not steal.

16 ¶"You shall not bear false witness against your neighbor.

17 ¶"You shall not covet your neighbor's house; you shall not covet your neighbor's wife or his male servant or his female servant or his ox or his donkey or anything that belongs to your neighbor."

18 ¶ And all the people perceived the thunder and the lightning flashes and the sound of the trumpet and the mountain smoking; and when the people saw *it,* they trembled and stood at a distance.

19 Then they said to Moses, "Speak to us yourself and we will listen; but let not God speak to us, lest we die."

20 And Moses said to the people, "Do not be afraid; for God has come in order to test you, and in order that the fear of Him may remain with you, so that you may not sin."

21 So the people stood at a distance, while Moses approached the thick cloud where God *was.*

22 ¶ Then the LORD said to Moses, "Thus you shall say to the sons of Israel, 'You yourselves have seen that I have spoken to you from heaven.

23 'You shall not make *other gods* besides Me; gods of silver or gods of gold, you shall not make for yourselves.

24 'You shall make an altar of earth for Me, and you shall sacrifice on it your burnt offerings and your peace offerings, your sheep and your oxen; in every place where I cause My name to be remembered, I will come to you and bless you.

25 'And if you make an altar of stone for Me, you shall not build it of cut stones, for if you wield your tool on it, you will profane it.

26 'And you shall not go up by steps to My altar, that your nakedness may not be exposed on it.'

CHAPTER 21

"Now these are the ordinances which you are to set before them.

2"If you buy a Hebrew slave, he shall serve for six years; but on the seventh he shall go out as a free man without payment.

3"If he comes alone, he shall go out alone; if he is the husband of a wife, then his wife shall go out with him.

4"If his master gives him a wife, and she bears him sons or daughters, the wife and her children shall belong to her master, and he shall go out alone.

5"But if the slave plainly says, 'I love my master, my wife and my children; I will not go out as a free man,'

6 then his master shall bring him to [21]God, then he shall bring him to the door or the doorpost. And his master shall pierce his ear with an awl; and he shall serve him permanently.

7"And if a man sells his daughter as a female slave, she is not to go free as the male slaves do.

8"If she is displeasing in the eyes of her master who designated her for himself, then he shall let her be redeemed. He does not have authority to sell her to a foreign people because of his unfairness to her.

9"And if he designates her for his son, he shall deal with her according to the custom of daughters.

10"If he takes to himself another woman, he may not reduce her food, her clothing, or her conjugal rights.

11"And if he will not do these three *things* for her, then she shall go out for nothing, without *payment of* money.

12 ¶"He who strikes a man so that he dies shall surely be put to death.

13"But if he did not lie in wait *for him,* but God let *him* fall into his hand, then I will appoint you a place to which he may flee.

14"If, however, a man acts presumptuously toward his neighbor, so as to kill him craftily, you are to take him *even* from My altar, that he may die.

15 ¶"And he who strikes his father or his mother shall surely be put to death.

16 ¶"And he who kidnaps a man, whether he sells him or he is found in his possession, shall surely be put to death.

17"And he who curses his father or his mother shall surely be put to death.

18 ¶"And if men have a quarrel and one strikes the other with a stone or

[21] Or, *the judges who acted in God's name*

with *his* fist, and he does not die but remains in bed;

19 if he gets up and walks around outside on his staff, then he who struck him shall go unpunished; he shall only pay for his loss of time, and shall take care of him until he is completely healed.

20 ¶"And if a man strikes his male or female slave with a rod and he dies at his hand, he shall be punished.

21"If, however, he survives a day or two, no vengeance shall be taken; for he is his property.

22 ¶"And *if* men struggle with each other and strike a woman with child so that she has a miscarriage, yet there is no *further* injury, he shall surely be fined as the woman's husband may demand of him; and he shall pay as the judges *decide.*

23"But if there is *any further* injury, then you shall appoint *as a penalty* life for life,

24 eye for eye, tooth for tooth, hand for hand, foot for foot,

25 burn for burn, wound for wound, bruise for bruise.

26 ¶"And if a man strikes the eye of his male or female slave, and destroys it, he shall let him go free on account of his eye.

27"And if he knocks out a tooth of his male or female slave, he shall let him go free on account of his tooth.

28 ¶"And if an ox gores a man or a woman to death, the ox shall surely be stoned and its flesh shall not be eaten; but the owner of the ox shall go unpunished.

29"If, however, an ox was previously in the habit of goring, and its owner has been warned, yet he does not confine it, and it kills a man or a woman, the ox shall be stoned and its owner also shall be put to death.

30"If a ransom is demanded of him, then he shall give for the redemption of his life whatever is demanded of him.

31"Whether it gores a son or a daughter, it shall be done to him according to the same rule.

32"If the ox gores a male or female slave, the owner shall give his *or her* master thirty shekels of silver, and the ox shall be stoned.

33 ¶"And if a man opens a pit, or digs a pit and does not cover it over, and an ox or a donkey falls into it,

34 the owner of the pit shall make restitution; he shall give money to its owner, and the dead *animal* shall become his.

35 ¶"And if one man's ox hurts another's so that it dies, then they shall sell the live ox and divide its price equally; and also they shall divide the dead ox.

36"Or *if* it is known that the ox was previously in the habit of goring, yet its owner has not confined it, he shall surely pay ox for ox, and the dead *animal* shall become his.

CHAPTER 22

"IF a man steals an ox or a sheep, and slaughters it or sells it, he shall pay five oxen for the ox and four sheep for the sheep.

2"If the thief is caught while breaking in, and is struck so that he dies, there will be no bloodguiltiness on his account.

3"*But* if the sun has risen on him, there will be bloodguiltiness on his account. He shall surely make restitution; if he owns nothing, then he shall be sold for his theft.

4"If what he stole is actually found alive in his possession, whether an ox or a donkey or a sheep, he shall pay double.

5"If a man lets a field or vineyard be grazed *bare* and lets his animal loose so that it grazes in another man's field, he shall make restitution from the best of his own field and the best of his own vineyard.

6 ¶"If a fire breaks out and spreads to thorn bushes, so that stacked grain or the standing grain or the field *itself* is consumed, he who started the fire shall surely make restitution.

7 ¶"If a man gives his neighbor money or goods to keep *for him,* and it is stolen from the man's house, if the thief is caught, he shall pay double.

8"If the thief is not caught, then the owner of the house shall appear before the judges, *to* determine whether he laid his hands on his neighbor's property.

9"For every breach of trust, *whether it is* for ox, for donkey, for sheep, for clothing, *or* for any lost thing about which one says, 'This is it,' the case of both parties shall come before the judges; he whom the judges condemn shall pay double to his neighbor.

10 ¶"If a man gives his neighbor a donkey, an ox, a sheep, or any animal to keep *for him,* and it dies or is hurt or is driven away while no one is looking,

11 an oath before the LORD shall be made by the two of them, that he has not laid hands on his neighbor's property; and its owner shall accept *it,* and he shall not make restitution.

12"But if it is actually stolen from him, he shall make restitution to its owner.

13"If it is all torn to pieces, let him bring it as evidence; he shall not make restitution for what has been torn to pieces.

14 ¶"And if a man borrows *anything* from his neighbor, and it is injured or dies while its owner is not with it, he shall make full restitution.

15"If its owner is with it, he shall not make restitution; if it is hired, it came for its hire.

16 ¶"And if a man seduces a virgin who is not engaged, and lies with her, he must pay a dowry for her *to be* his wife.

17"If her father absolutely refuses to give her to him, he shall pay money equal to the dowry for virgins.

18 ¶"You shall not allow a sorceress to live.

19 ¶"Whoever lies with an animal shall surely be put to death.

20 ¶"He who sacrifices to any god, other than to the LORD alone, shall be utterly destroyed.

21"And you shall not wrong a stranger or oppress him, for you were strangers in the land of Egypt.

22"You shall not afflict any widow or orphan.

23"If you afflict him at all, *and* if he does cry out to Me, I will surely hear his cry;

24 and My anger will be kindled, and I will kill you with the sword; and your wives shall become widows and your children fatherless.

25 ¶"If you lend money to My people, to the poor among you, you are not to act as a creditor to him; you shall not charge him interest.

26"If you ever take your neighbor's cloak as a pledge, you are to return it to him before the sun sets,

27 for that is his only covering; it is his cloak for his body. What else shall he sleep in? And it shall come about that when he cries out to Me, I will hear *him,* for I am gracious.

28 ¶"You shall not curse God, nor curse a ruler of your people.

29"You shall not delay *the offering from* your harvest and your vintage. The first-born of your sons you shall give to Me.

30"You shall do the same with your oxen *and* with your sheep. It shall be with its mother seven days; on the eighth day you shall give it to Me.

31"And you shall be holy men to Me, therefore you shall not eat *any* flesh torn to pieces in the field; you shall throw it to the dogs.

CHAPTER 23

"YOU shall not bear a false report; do not join your hand with a wicked man to be a malicious witness.

2"You shall not follow a multitude in doing evil, nor shall you testify in a dispute so as to turn aside after a multitude in order to pervert *justice;*

3 nor shall you be partial to a poor man in his dispute.

4 ¶"If you meet your enemy's ox or his donkey wandering away, you shall surely return it to him.

5"If you see the donkey of one who hates you lying *helpless* under its load, you shall refrain from leaving it to him, you shall surely release *it* with him.

6"You shall not pervert the justice *due* to your needy *brother* in his dispute.

7"Keep far from a false charge, and do not kill the innocent or the righteous, for I will not acquit the guilty.

8"And you shall not take a bribe, for a bribe blinds the clear-sighted and subverts the cause of the just.

9"And you shall not oppress a stranger, since you yourselves know the feelings of a stranger, for you *also* were strangers in the land of Egypt.

10 ¶"And you shall sow your land for six years and gather in its yield,

11 but *on* the seventh year you shall let it rest and lie fallow, so that the

needy of your people may eat; and whatever they leave the beast of the field may eat. You are to do the same with your vineyard *and* your olive grove.

12"Six days you are to do your work, but on the seventh day you shall cease *from labor* in order that your ox and your donkey may rest, and the son of your female slave, as well as your stranger, may refresh themselves.

13"Now concerning everything which I have said to you, be on your guard; and do not mention the name of other gods, nor let *them* be heard from your mouth.

14 ¶"Three times a year you shall celebrate a feast to Me.

15"You shall observe the Feast of Unleavened Bread; for seven days you are to eat unleavened bread, as I commanded you, at the appointed time in the month Abib, for in it you came out of Egypt. And none shall appear before Me empty-handed.

16"Also *you shall observe* the Feast of the Harvest *of* the first fruits of your labors *from* what you sow in the field; also the Feast of the Ingathering at the end of the year when you gather in *the fruit of* your labors from the field.

17"Three times a year all your males shall appear before the Lord GOD.

18 ¶"You shall not offer the blood of My sacrifice with leavened bread; nor is the fat of My feast to remain overnight until morning.

19"You shall bring the choice first fruits of your soil into the house of the LORD your God. You are not to boil a kid in the milk of its mother.

20 ¶"Behold, I am going to send an angel before you to guard you along the way, and to bring you into the place which I have prepared.

21"Be on your guard before him and obey his voice; do not be rebellious toward him, for he will not pardon your transgression, since My name is in him.

22"But if you will truly obey his voice and do all that I say, then I will be an enemy to your enemies and an adversary to your adversaries.

23"For My angel will go before you and bring you in to *the land of* the Amorites, the Hittites, the Perizzites, the Canaanites, the Hivites and the Jebusites; and I will completely destroy them.

24"You shall not worship their gods, nor serve them, nor do according to their deeds; but you shall utterly overthrow them, and break their *sacred* pillars in pieces.

25"But you shall serve the LORD your God, and He will bless your bread and your water; and I will remove sickness from your midst.

26"There shall be no one miscarrying or barren in your land; I will fulfill the number of your days.

27"I will send My terror ahead of you, and throw into confusion all the people among whom you come, and I will make all your enemies turn *their* backs to you.

28"And I will send hornets ahead of you, that they may drive out the Hivites, the Canaanites, and the Hittites before you.

29"I will not drive them out before you in a single year, that the land may not become desolate, and the beasts of the field become too numerous for you.

30"I will drive them out before you little by little, until you become fruitful and take possession of the land.

31"And I will fix your boundary from the Red Sea to the sea of the Philistines, and from the wilderness to the River *Euphrates;* for I will deliver the inhabitants of the land into your hand, and you will drive them out before you.

32"You shall make no covenant with them or with their gods.

33"They shall not live in your land, lest they make you sin against Me; for *if* you serve their gods, it will surely be a snare to you."

CHAPTER 24

THEN He said to Moses, "Come up to the LORD, you and Aaron, Nadab and Abihu and seventy of the elders of Israel, and you shall worship at a distance.

2"Moses alone, however, shall come near to the LORD, but they shall not come near, nor shall the people come up with him."

3 Then Moses came and recounted to the people all the words of the LORD and all the ordinances; and all the

people answered with one voice, and said, "All the words which the LORD has spoken we will do!"

4 And Moses wrote down all the words of the LORD. Then he arose early in the morning, and built an altar at the foot of the mountain with twelve pillars for the twelve tribes of Israel.

5 And he sent young men of the sons of Israel, and they offered burnt offerings and sacrificed young bulls as peace offerings to the LORD.

6 And Moses took half of the blood and put it in basins, and the other half of the blood he sprinkled on the altar.

7 Then he took the book of the covenant and read it in the hearing of the people; and they said, "All that the LORD has spoken we will do, and we will be obedient!"

8 So Moses took the blood and sprinkled it on the people, and said, "Behold the blood of the covenant, which the LORD has made with you in accordance with all these words."

9 ¶ Then Moses went up with Aaron, Nadab and Abihu, and seventy of the elders of Israel,

10 and they saw the God of Israel; and under His feet there appeared to be a pavement of sapphire, as clear as the sky itself.

11 Yet He did not stretch out His hand against the nobles of the sons of Israel; and they beheld God, and they ate and drank.

12 ¶ Now the LORD said to Moses, "Come up to Me on the mountain and remain there, and I will give you the stone tablets with the law and the commandment which I have written for their instruction."

13 So Moses arose with Joshua his servant, and Moses went up to the mountain of God.

14 But to the elders he said, "Wait here for us until we return to you. And behold, Aaron and Hur are with you; whoever has a legal matter, let him approach them."

15 Then Moses went up to the mountain, and the cloud covered the mountain.

16 And the glory of the LORD rested on Mount Sinai, and the cloud covered it for six days; and on the seventh day He called to Moses from the midst of the cloud.

17 And to the eyes of the sons of Israel the appearance of the glory of the LORD was like a consuming fire on the mountain top.

18 And Moses entered the midst of the cloud as he went up to the mountain; and Moses was on the mountain forty days and forty nights.

CHAPTER 25

THEN the LORD spoke to Moses, saying,

2 "Tell the sons of Israel to raise a contribution for Me; from every man whose heart moves him you shall raise My contribution.

3 "And this is the contribution which you are to raise from them: gold, silver and bronze,

4 blue, purple and scarlet material, fine linen, goat hair,

5 rams' skins dyed red, porpoise skins, acacia wood,

6 oil for lighting, spices for the anointing oil and for the fragrant incense,

7 onyx stones and setting stones, for the ephod and for the breastpiece.

8 "And let them construct a sanctuary for Me, that I may dwell among them.

9 "According to all that I am going to show you, as the pattern of the tabernacle and the pattern of all its furniture, just so you shall construct it.

10 ¶ "And they shall construct an ark of acacia wood two and a half cubits long, and one and a half cubits wide, and one and a half cubits high.

11 "And you shall overlay it with pure gold, inside and out you shall overlay it, and you shall make a gold molding around it.

12 "And you shall cast four gold rings for it, and fasten them on its four feet, and two rings shall be on one side of it and two rings on the other side of it.

13 "And you shall make poles of acacia wood and overlay them with gold.

14 "And you shall put the poles into the rings on the sides of the ark, to carry the ark with them.

15 "The poles shall remain in the rings of the ark; they shall not be removed from it.

16"And you shall put into the ark the testimony which I shall give you.

17"And you shall make a [22]mercy seat of pure gold, two and a half cubits long and one and a half cubits wide.

18"And you shall make two cherubim of gold, make them of hammered work at the two ends of the mercy seat.

19"And make one cherub at one end and one cherub at the other end; you shall make the cherubim *of one piece* with the mercy seat at its two ends.

20"And the cherubim shall have *their* wings spread upward, covering the mercy seat with their wings and facing one another; the faces of the cherubim are to be *turned* toward the mercy seat.

21"And you shall put the mercy seat on top of the ark, and in the ark you shall put the testimony which I shall give to you.

22"And there I will meet with you; and from above the mercy seat, from between the two cherubim which are upon the ark of the testimony, I will speak to you about all that I will give you in commandment for the sons of Israel.

23 ¶"And you shall make a table of acacia wood, two cubits long and one cubit wide and one and a half cubits high.

24"And you shall overlay it with pure gold and make a gold border around it.

25"And you shall make for it a rim of a handbreadth around *it;* and you shall make a gold border for the rim around it.

26"And you shall make four gold rings for it and put rings on the four corners which are on its four feet.

27"The rings shall be close to the rim as holders for the poles to carry the table.

28"And you shall make the poles of acacia wood and overlay them with gold, so that with them the table may be carried.

29"And you shall make its dishes and its pans and its jars and its bowls, with which to pour libations; you shall make them of pure gold.

30"And you shall set the bread of the Presence on the table before Me at all times.

31 ¶"Then you shall make a lampstand of pure gold. The lampstand *and* its base and its shaft are to be made of hammered work; its cups, its bulbs and its flowers shall be *of one piece* with it.

32"And six branches shall go out from its sides; three branches of the lampstand from its one side, and three branches of the lampstand from its other side.

33"Three cups *shall be* shaped like almond *blossoms* in the one branch, a [23]bulb and a flower, and three cups shaped like almond *blossoms* in the other branch, a bulb and a flower—so for six branches going out from the lampstand;

34 and in the lampstand four cups shaped like almond *blossoms,* its bulbs and its flowers.

35"And a bulb shall be under the *first* pair of branches *coming* out of it, and a bulb under the *second* pair of branches *coming* out of it, and a bulb under the *third* pair of branches *coming* out of it, for the six branches coming out of the lampstand.

36"Their bulbs and their branches *shall be of one piece* with it; all of it shall be one piece of hammered work of pure gold.

37"Then you shall make its lamps seven *in number;* and they shall mount its lamps so as to shed light on the space in front of it.

38"And its snuffers and their trays *shall be* of pure gold.

39"It shall be made from a talent of pure gold, with all these utensils.

40"And see that you make *them* after the pattern for them, which was shown to you on the mountain.

CHAPTER 26

"MOREOVER you shall make the tabernacle with ten curtains of fine twisted linen and [24]blue and purple and scarlet *material;* you shall make them with cherubim, the work of a skillful workman.

2"The length of each curtain shall be twenty-eight cubits, and the width of each curtain four cubits; all the curtains shall have the same measurements.

---

[22] Lit., *propitiatory;* and so through v. 22   [23] Or, *calyx*   [24] Or, *violet,* and so throughout this context

3"Five curtains shall be joined to one another; and *the other* five curtains *shall be* joined to one another.

4"And you shall make loops of blue on the edge of the outermost curtain in the *first* set, and likewise you shall make *them* on the edge of the curtain that is outermost in the second set.

5"You shall make fifty loops in the one curtain, and you shall make fifty loops on the edge of the curtain that is in the second set; the loops shall be opposite each other.

6"And you shall make fifty clasps of gold, and join the curtains to one another with the clasps, that the [25]tabernacle may be a unit.

7 ¶"Then you shall make curtains of goats' *hair* for a tent over the tabernacle; you shall make eleven curtains in all.

8"The length of each curtain *shall be* thirty cubits, and the width of each curtain four cubits; the eleven curtains shall have the same measurements.

9"And you shall join five curtains by themselves, and the *other* six curtains by themselves, and you shall double over the sixth curtain at the front of the tent.

10"And you shall make fifty loops on the edge of the curtain that is outermost in the *first* set, and fifty loops on the edge of the curtain *that is outermost in* the second set.

11"And you shall make fifty clasps of [26]bronze, and you shall put the clasps into the loops and join the tent together, that it may be a unit.

12"And the overlapping part that is left over in the curtains of the tent, the half curtain that is left over, shall lap over the back of the tabernacle.

13"And the cubit on one side and the cubit on the other, of what is left over in the length of the curtains of the tent, shall lap over the sides of the tabernacle on one side and on the other, to cover it.

14"And you shall make a covering for the tent of rams' skins dyed red, and a covering of porpoise skins above.

15 ¶"Then you shall make the boards for the tabernacle of acacia wood, standing upright.

16"Ten cubits *shall be* the length of each board, and one and a half cubits the width of each board.

17"There *shall be* two tenons for each board, fitted to one another; thus you shall do for all the boards of the tabernacle.

18"And you shall make the boards for the tabernacle: twenty boards for the south side.

19"And you shall make forty [27]sockets of silver under the twenty boards, two sockets under one board for its two tenons and two sockets under another board for its two tenons;

20 and for the second side of the tabernacle, on the north side, twenty boards,

21 and their forty sockets of silver; two sockets under one board and two sockets under another board.

22"And for the rear of the tabernacle, to the west, you shall make six boards.

23"And you shall make two boards for the corners of the tabernacle at the rear.

24"And they shall be double beneath, and together they shall be complete to its top to the first ring; thus it shall be with both of them: they shall form the two corners.

25"And there shall be eight boards with their sockets of silver, sixteen sockets; two sockets under one board and two sockets under another board.

26 ¶"Then you shall make bars of acacia wood, five for the boards of one side of the tabernacle,

27 and five bars for the boards of the other side of the tabernacle, and five bars for the boards of the side of the tabernacle for the rear *side* to the west.

28"And the middle bar in the center of the boards shall pass through from end to end.

29"And you shall overlay the boards with gold and make their rings of gold *as* holders for the bars; and you shall overlay the bars with gold.

30"Then you shall erect the tabernacle according to its plan which you have been shown in the mountain.

31 ¶"And you shall make a veil of blue and purple and scarlet *material* and fine twisted linen; it shall be made

---

[25] Or, *dwelling place*, and so throughout the ch.
[26] Or, *copper*

[27] Or, *bases*, and so throughout this context

with cherubim, the work of a skillful workman.

32"And you shall hang it on four pillars of acacia overlaid with gold, their hooks *also being of* gold, on four sockets of silver.

33"And you shall hang up the veil under the clasps, and shall bring in the ark of the testimony there within the veil; and the veil shall serve for you as a partition between the holy place and the holy of holies.

34"And you shall put the mercy seat on the ark of the testimony in the holy of holies.

35"And you shall set the table outside the veil, and the lampstand opposite the table on the side of the tabernacle toward the south; and you shall put the table on the north side.

36 ¶"And you shall make a screen for the doorway of the tent of blue and purple and scarlet *material* and fine twisted linen, the work of a weaver.

37"And you shall make five pillars of acacia for the screen, and overlay them with gold, their hooks *also being of* gold; and you shall cast five sockets of bronze for them.

CHAPTER 27

"AND you shall make the altar of acacia wood, five cubits long and five cubits wide; the altar shall be square, and its height shall be three cubits.

2"And you shall make its horns on its four corners; its horns shall be of one piece with it, and you shall overlay it with bronze.

3"And you shall make its pails for removing its ashes, and its shovels and its basins and its forks and its firepans; you shall make all its utensils of bronze.

4"And you shall make for it a grating of network of bronze, and on the net you shall make four bronze rings at its four corners.

5"And you shall put it beneath, under the ledge of the altar, that the net may reach halfway up the altar.

6"And you shall make poles for the altar, poles of acacia wood, and overlay them with bronze.

7"And its poles shall be inserted into the rings, so that the poles shall be on the two sides of the altar when it is carried.

8"You shall make it hollow with planks; as it was shown to you in the mountain, so they shall make *it.*

9 ¶"And you shall make the court of the tabernacle. On the south side *there shall be* hangings for the court of fine twisted linen one hundred cubits long for one side;

10 and its pillars *shall be* twenty, with their twenty sockets of bronze; the hooks of the pillars and their bands *shall be* of silver.

11"And likewise for the north side in length *there shall be* hangings one hundred *cubits* long, and its twenty pillars with their twenty sockets of bronze; the hooks of the pillars and their bands *shall be* of silver.

12"And *for* the width of the court on the west side *shall be* hangings of fifty cubits *with* their ten pillars and their ten sockets.

13"And the width of the court on the east side *shall be* fifty cubits.

14"The hangings for the *one* side *of the gate shall be* fifteen cubits *with* their three pillars and their three sockets.

15"And for the other side *shall be* hangings of fifteen cubits *with* their three pillars and their three sockets.

16"And for the gate of the court there *shall be* a screen of twenty cubits, of blue and purple and scarlet *material* and fine twisted linen, the work of a weaver, *with* their four pillars and their four sockets.

17"All the pillars around the court shall be furnished with silver bands *with* their hooks of silver and their sockets of bronze.

18"The length of the court *shall be* one hundred cubits, and the width fifty throughout, and the height five cubits of fine twisted linen, and their sockets of bronze.

19"All the utensils of the tabernacle *used* in all its service, and all its pegs, and all the pegs of the court, *shall be* of bronze.

20 ¶"And you shall charge the sons of Israel, that they bring you clear oil of beaten olives for the light, to make a lamp burn continually.

21"In the tent of meeting, outside the veil which is before the testimony, Aaron and his sons shall keep it in order from evening to morning before

the LORD; *it shall be* a perpetual statute throughout their generations for
the sons of Israel.

CHAPTER 28

"THEN bring near to yourself Aaron
your brother, and his sons with him,
from among the sons of Israel, to
minister as priest to Me—Aaron, Nadab and Abihu, Eleazar and Ithamar,
Aaron's sons.

2"And you shall make holy garments for Aaron your brother, for
glory and for beauty.

3"And you shall speak to all the
skillful persons whom I have endowed
with the spirit of wisdom, that they
make Aaron's garments to consecrate
him, that he may minister as priest to
Me.

4"And these are the garments which
they shall make: a [28]breastpiece and an
ephod and a robe and a tunic of checkered work, a turban and a sash, and
they shall make holy garments for
Aaron your brother and his sons, that
he may minister as priest to Me.

5"And they shall take the gold and
the blue and the purple and the scarlet
material and the fine linen.

6 ¶"They shall also make the ephod
of gold, of blue and purple *and* scarlet
material and fine twisted linen, the
work of the skillful workman.

7"It shall have two shoulder pieces
joined to its two ends, that it may be
joined.

8"And the skillfully woven band,
which is on it, shall be like its workmanship, of the same material: of gold,
of blue and purple and scarlet *material*
and fine twisted linen.

9"And you shall take two onyx
stones and engrave on them the
names of the sons of Israel,

10 six of their names on the one
stone, and the names of the remaining
six on the other stone, according to
their birth.

11"As a jeweler engraves a signet,
you shall engrave the two stones according to the names of the sons of
Israel; you shall set them in filigree
settings of gold.

12"And you shall put the two stones
on the shoulder pieces of the ephod, *as*
stones of memorial for the sons of

[28] Or, *pouch*

Israel, and Aaron shall bear their
names before the LORD on his two
shoulders for a memorial.

13"And you shall make filigree *settings* of gold,

14 and two chains of pure gold; you
shall make them of twisted cordage
work, and you shall put the corded
chains on the filigree *settings.*

15 ¶"And you shall make a breastpiece of judgment, the work of a skillful workman; like the work of the
ephod you shall make it: of gold, of
blue and purple and scarlet *material*
and fine twisted linen you shall make
it.

16"It shall be square *and* folded double, a span in length and a span in
width.

17"And you shall mount on it four
rows of stones; the first row *shall be* a
row of ruby, topaz and emerald;

18 and the second row a turquoise, a
sapphire and a diamond;

19 and the third row a jacinth, an
agate and an amethyst;

20 and the fourth row a beryl and an
onyx and a jasper; they shall be set in
gold filigree.

21"And the stones shall be according
to the names of the sons of Israel:
twelve, according to their names; they
shall be *like* the engravings of a seal,
each according to his name for the
twelve tribes.

22"And you shall make on the breastpiece chains of twisted cordage work
in pure gold.

23"And you shall make on the breastpiece two rings of gold, and shall put
the two rings on the two ends of the
breastpiece.

24"And you shall put the two cords of
gold on the two rings at the ends of
the breastpiece.

25"And you shall put the *other* two
ends of the two cords on the two
filigree *settings,* and put them on the
shoulder pieces of the ephod, at the
front of it.

26"And you shall make two rings of
gold and shall place them on the two
ends of the breastpiece, on the edge of
it, which is toward the inner side of
the ephod.

27"And you shall make two rings of
gold and put them on the bottom of
the two shoulder pieces of the ephod,

on the front of it close to the place where it is joined, above the skillfully woven band of the ephod.

28"And they shall bind the breastpiece by its rings to the rings of the ephod with a blue cord, that it may be on the skillfully woven band of the ephod, and that the breastpiece may not come loose from the ephod.

29"And Aaron shall carry the names of the sons of Israel in the breastpiece of judgment over his heart when he enters the holy place, for a memorial before the LORD continually.

30"And you shall put in the breastpiece of judgment the [29]Urim and the Thummim, and they shall be over Aaron's heart when he goes in before the LORD; and Aaron shall carry the judgment of the sons of Israel over his heart before the LORD continually.

31 ¶"And you shall make the robe of the ephod all of blue.

32"And there shall be an opening at its top in the middle of it; around its opening there shall be a binding of woven work, as *it were* the opening of a coat of mail, that it may not be torn.

33"And you shall make on its hem pomegranates of blue and purple and scarlet *material,* all around on its hem, and bells of gold between them all around:

34 a golden bell and a pomegranate, a golden bell and a pomegranate, all around on the hem of the robe.

35"And it shall be on Aaron when he ministers; and its tinkling may be heard when he enters and leaves the holy place before the LORD, that he may not die.

36 ¶"You shall also make a plate of pure gold and shall engrave on it, like the engravings of a seal, 'Holy to the LORD.'

37"And you shall fasten it on a blue cord, and it shall be on the turban; it shall be at the front of the turban.

38"And it shall be on Aaron's forehead, and Aaron shall take away the iniquity of the holy things which the sons of Israel consecrate, with regard to all their holy gifts; and it shall always be on his forehead, that they may be accepted before the LORD.

39"And you shall weave the tunic of checkered work of fine linen, and shall

[29] I.e., lights and perfections

make a turban of fine linen, and you shall make a sash, the work of a weaver.

40 ¶"And for Aaron's sons you shall make tunics; you shall also make sashes for them, and you shall make caps for them, for glory and for beauty.

41"And you shall put them on Aaron your brother and on his sons with him; and you shall anoint them and ordain them and consecrate them, that they may serve Me as priests.

42"And you shall make for them linen breeches to cover *their* bare flesh; they shall reach from the loins even to the thighs.

43"And they shall be on Aaron and on his sons when they enter the tent of meeting, or when they approach the altar to minister in the holy place, so that they do not incur guilt and die. It *shall be* a statute forever to him and to his descendants after him.

CHAPTER 29

"Now this is what you shall do to them to consecrate them to minister as priests to Me: take one young bull and two rams without blemish,

2 and unleavened bread and unleavened cakes mixed with oil, and unleavened wafers spread with oil; you shall make them of fine wheat flour.

3"And you shall put them in one basket, and present them in the basket along with the bull and the two rams.

4"Then you shall bring Aaron and his sons to the doorway of the tent of meeting, and wash them with water.

5"And you shall take the garments, and put on Aaron the tunic and the robe of the ephod and the ephod and the breastpiece, and gird him with the skillfully woven band of the ephod;

6 and you shall set the turban on his head, and put the holy crown on the turban.

7"Then you shall take the anointing oil, and pour it on his head and anoint him.

8"And you shall bring his sons and put tunics on them.

9"And you shall gird them with sashes, Aaron and his sons, and bind caps on them, and they shall have the priesthood by a perpetual statute. So you shall ordain Aaron and his sons.

10 ¶"Then you shall bring the bull before the tent of meeting, and Aaron and his sons shall lay their hands on the head of the bull.

11"And you shall slaughter the bull before the LORD at the doorway of the tent of meeting.

12"And you shall take some of the blood of the bull and put *it* on the horns of the altar with your finger; and you shall pour out all the blood at the base of the altar.

13"And you shall take all the fat that covers the entrails and the lobe of the liver, and the two kidneys and the fat that is on them, and offer them up in smoke on the altar.

14"But the flesh of the bull and its hide and its refuse, you shall burn with fire outside the camp; it is a sin offering.

15 ¶"You shall also take the one ram, and Aaron and his sons shall lay their hands on the head of the ram;

16 and you shall slaughter the ram and shall take its blood and sprinkle it around on the altar.

17"Then you shall cut the ram into its pieces, and wash its entrails and its legs, and put *them* with its pieces and its head.

18"And you shall offer up in smoke the whole ram on the altar; it is a burnt offering to the LORD: it is a soothing aroma, an offering by fire to the LORD.

19 ¶"Then you shall take the other ram, and Aaron and his sons shall lay their hands on the head of the ram.

20"And you shall slaughter the ram, and take some of its blood and put *it* on the lobe of Aaron's right ear and on the lobes of his sons' right ears and on the thumbs of their right hands and on the big toes of their right feet, and sprinkle the *rest of the* blood around on the altar.

21"Then you shall take some of the blood that is on the altar and some of the anointing oil, and sprinkle *it* on Aaron and on his garments, and on his sons and on his sons' garments with him; so he and his garments shall be consecrated, as well as his sons and his sons' garments with him.

22"You shall also take the fat from the ram and the fat tail, and the fat that covers the entrails and the lobe of the liver, and the two kidneys and the

fat that is on them and the right thigh (for it is a ram of ordination),

23 and one cake of bread and one cake of bread *mixed with* oil and one wafer from the basket of unleavened bread which is *set* before the LORD;

24 and you shall put all these in the hands of Aaron and in the hands of his sons, and shall wave them as a wave offering before the LORD.

25"And you shall take them from their hands, and offer them up in smoke on the altar on the burnt offering for a soothing aroma before the LORD; it is an offering by fire to the LORD.

26 ¶"Then you shall take the breast of Aaron's ram of ordination, and wave it as a wave offering before the LORD; and it shall be your portion.

27"And you shall consecrate the breast of the wave offering and the thigh of the heave offering which was waved and which was offered from the ram of ordination, from the one which was for Aaron and from the one which was for his sons.

28"And it shall be for Aaron and his sons as *their* portion forever from the sons of Israel, for it is a heave offering; and it shall be a heave offering from the sons of Israel from the sacrifices of their peace offerings, *even* their heave offering to the LORD.

29 ¶"And the holy garments of Aaron shall be for his sons after him, that in them they may be anointed and ordained.

30"For seven days the one of his sons who is priest in his stead shall put them on when he enters the tent of meeting to minister in the holy place.

31 ¶"And you shall take the ram of ordination and boil its flesh in a holy place.

32"And Aaron and his sons shall eat the flesh of the ram, and the bread that is in the basket, at the doorway of the tent of meeting.

33"Thus they shall eat those things by which atonement was made at their ordination *and* consecration; but a layman shall not eat *them,* because they are holy.

34"And if any of the flesh of ordination or any of the bread remains until morning, then you shall burn the remainder with fire; it shall not be eaten, because it is holy.

35 ¶"And thus you shall do to Aaron and to his sons, according to all that I have commanded you; you shall ordain them through seven days.

36"And each day you shall offer a bull as a sin offering for atonement, and you shall purify the altar when you make atonement for it; and you shall anoint it to consecrate it.

37"For seven days you shall make atonement for the altar and consecrate it; then the altar shall be most holy, and whatever touches the altar shall be holy.

38 ¶"Now this is what you shall offer on the altar: two one year old lambs each day, continuously.

39"The one lamb you shall offer in the morning, and the other lamb you shall offer at twilight;

40 and there shall be one-tenth of an ephah of fine flour mixed with one-fourth of a hin of beaten oil, and one-fourth of a hin of wine for a libation with one lamb.

41"And the other lamb you shall offer at twilight, and shall offer with it the same grain offering as the morning and the same libation, for a soothing aroma, an offering by fire to the LORD.

42"It shall be a continual burnt offering throughout your generations at the doorway of the tent of meeting before the LORD, where I will meet with you, to speak to you there.

43"And I will meet there with the sons of Israel, and it shall be consecrated by My glory.

44"And I will consecrate the tent of meeting and the altar; I will also consecrate Aaron and his sons to minister as priests to Me.

45"And I will dwell among the sons of Israel and will be their God.

46"And they shall know that I am the LORD their God who brought them out of the land of Egypt, that I might dwell among them; I am the LORD their God.

CHAPTER 30

"MOREOVER, you shall make an altar as a place for burning incense; you shall make it of acacia wood.

2"Its length shall be a cubit, and its width a cubit, it shall be square, and its height shall be two cubits; its horns shall be of one piece with it.

3"And you shall overlay it with pure gold, its top and its sides all around, and its horns; and you shall make a gold molding all around for it.

4"And you shall make two gold rings for it under its molding; you shall make them on its two side walls—on opposite sides—and they shall be holders for poles with which to carry it.

5"And you shall make the poles of acacia wood and overlay them with gold.

6"And you shall put this altar in front of the veil that is near the ark of the testimony, in front of the mercy seat that is over the ark of the testimony, where I will meet with you.

7"And Aaron shall burn fragrant incense on it; he shall burn it every morning when he trims the lamps.

8"And when Aaron trims the lamps at twilight, he shall burn incense. There shall be perpetual incense before the LORD throughout your generations.

9"You shall not offer any strange incense on this altar, or burnt offering or meal offering; and you shall not pour out a libation on it.

10"And Aaron shall make atonement on its horns once a year; he shall make atonement on it with the blood of the sin offering of atonement once a year throughout your generations. It is most holy to the LORD."

11 ¶ The LORD also spoke to Moses, saying,

12"When you take a census of the sons of Israel to number them, then each one of them shall give a ransom for himself to the LORD, when you number them, that there may be no plague among them when you number them.

13"This is what everyone who is numbered shall give: half a shekel according to the shekel of the sanctuary (the shekel is twenty gerahs), half a shekel as a contribution to the LORD.

14"Everyone who is numbered, from twenty years old and over, shall give the contribution to the LORD.

15"The rich shall not pay more, and the poor shall not pay less than the half shekel, when you give the contribution to the LORD to make atonement for yourselves.

16"And you shall take the atonement money from the sons of Israel, and shall give it for the service of the tent of meeting, that it may be a memorial for the sons of Israel before the LORD, to make atonement for yourselves."

17 ¶ And the LORD spoke to Moses, saying,

18 "You shall also make a laver of bronze, with its base of bronze, for washing; and you shall put it between the tent of meeting and the altar, and you shall put water in it.

19 "And Aaron and his sons shall wash their hands and their feet from it;

20 when they enter the tent of meeting, they shall wash with water, that they may not die; or when they approach the altar to minister, by offering up in smoke a fire *sacrifice* to the LORD.

21 "So they shall wash their hands and their feet, that they may not die; and it shall be a perpetual statute for them, for Aaron and his descendants throughout their generations."

22 ¶ Moreover, the LORD spoke to Moses, saying,

23 "Take also for yourself the finest of spices: of flowing myrrh five hundred *shekels*, and of fragrant cinnamon half as much, two hundred and fifty, and of fragrant cane two hundred and fifty,

24 and of cassia five hundred, according to the shekel of the sanctuary, and of olive oil a hin.

25 "And you shall make of these a holy anointing oil, a perfume mixture, the work of a perfumer; it shall be a holy anointing oil.

26 "And with it you shall anoint the tent of meeting and the ark of the testimony,

27 and the table and all its utensils, and the lampstand and its utensils, and the altar of incense,

28 and the altar of burnt offering and all its utensils, and the laver and its stand.

29 "You shall also consecrate them, that they may be most holy; whatever touches them shall be holy.

30 "And you shall anoint Aaron and his sons, and consecrate them, that they may minister as priests to Me.

31 "And you shall speak to the sons of Israel, saying, 'This shall be a holy anointing oil to Me throughout your generations.

32 'It shall not be poured on anyone's body, nor shall you make *any* like it, in the same proportions; it is holy, *and* it shall be holy to you.

33 'Whoever shall mix *any* like it, or whoever puts any of it on a layman, shall be cut off from his people.'"

34 ¶ Then the LORD said to Moses, "Take for yourself spices, stacte and onycha and galbanum, spices with pure frankincense; there shall be an equal part of each.

35 "And with it you shall make incense, a perfume, the work of a perfumer, salted, pure, *and* holy.

36 "And you shall beat some of it very fine, and put part of it before the testimony in the tent of meeting, where I shall meet with you; it shall be most holy to you.

37 "And the incense which you shall make, you shall not make in the same proportions for yourselves; it shall be holy to you for the LORD.

38 "Whoever shall make *any* like it, to use as perfume, shall be cut off from his people."

CHAPTER 31

Now the LORD spoke to Moses, saying,

2 "See, I have called by name Bezalel, the son of Uri, the son of Hur, of the tribe of Judah.

3 "And I have filled him with the Spirit of God in wisdom, in understanding, in knowledge, and in all *kinds of* craftsmanship,

4 to make artistic designs for work in gold, in silver, and in bronze,

5 and in the cutting of stones for settings, and in the carving of wood, that he may work in all *kinds of* craftsmanship.

6 "And behold, I Myself have appointed with him Oholiab, the son of Ahisamach, of the tribe of Dan; and in the hearts of all who are skillful I have put skill, that they may make all that I have commanded you:

7 the tent of meeting, and the ark of testimony, and the mercy seat upon it, and all the furniture of the tent,

8 the table also and its utensils, and the pure *gold* lampstand with all its utensils, and the altar of incense,

9 the altar of burnt offering also with all its utensils, and the laver and its stand,

10 the woven garments as well, and the holy garments for Aaron the priest, and the garments of his sons, *with which* to carry on their priesthood;

11 the anointing oil also, and the fragrant incense for the holy place, they are to make *them* according to all that I have commanded you."

12 ¶ And the LORD spoke to Moses, saying,

13"But as for you, speak to the sons of Israel, saying, 'You shall surely observe My sabbaths; for *this* is a sign between Me and you throughout your generations, that you may know that I am the LORD who sanctifies you.

14 'Therefore you are to observe the sabbath, for it is holy to you. Everyone who profanes it shall surely be put to death; for whoever does any work on it, that person shall be cut off from among his people.

15 'For six days work may be done, but on the seventh day there is a sabbath of complete rest, holy to the LORD; whoever does any work on the sabbath day shall surely be put to death.

16 'So the sons of Israel shall observe the sabbath, to celebrate the sabbath throughout their generations as a perpetual covenant.'

17"It is a sign between Me and the sons of Israel forever; for in six days the LORD made heaven and earth, but on the seventh day He ceased *from labor,* and was refreshed."

18 ¶ And when He had finished speaking with him upon Mount Sinai, He gave Moses the two tablets of the testimony, tablets of stone, written by the finger of God.

CHAPTER 32

NOW when the people saw that Moses delayed to come down from the mountain, the people assembled about Aaron, and said to him, "Come, make us a god who will go before us; as for this Moses, the man who brought us up from the land of Egypt, we do not know what has become of him."

2 And Aaron said to them, "Tear off the gold rings which are in the ears of your wives, your sons, and your daughters, and bring *them* to me."

3 Then all the people tore off the gold rings which were in their ears, and brought *them* to Aaron.

4 And he took *this* from their hand, and fashioned it with a graving tool, and made it into a molten calf; and they said, "This is your god, O Israel, who brought you up from the land of Egypt."

5 Now when Aaron saw *this,* he built an altar before it; and Aaron made a proclamation and said, "Tomorrow *shall be* a feast to the LORD."

6 So the next day they rose early and offered burnt offerings, and brought peace offerings; and the people sat down to eat and to drink, and rose up to play.

7 Then the LORD spoke to Moses, "Go down at once, for your people, whom you brought up from the land of Egypt, have corrupted *themselves.*

8"They have quickly turned aside from the way which I commanded them. They have made for themselves a molten calf, and have worshiped it, and have sacrificed to it, and said, 'This is your god, O Israel, who brought you up from the land of Egypt!' "

9 And the LORD said to Moses, "I have seen this people, and behold, they are an obstinate people.

10"Now then let Me alone, that My anger may burn against them, and that I may destroy them; and I will make of you a great nation."

11 Then Moses entreated the LORD his God, and said, "O LORD, why doth Thine anger burn against Thy people whom Thou hast brought out from the land of Egypt with great power and with a mighty hand?

12"Why should the Egyptians speak, saying, 'With evil *intent* He brought them out to kill them in the mountains and to destroy them from the face of the earth'? Turn from Thy burning anger and change Thy mind about *doing* harm to Thy people.

13"Remember Abraham, Isaac, and Israel, Thy servants to whom Thou didst swear by Thyself, and didst say to them, 'I will multiply your descendants as the stars of the heavens, and all this land of which I have spoken I will give to your descendants, and they shall inherit *it* forever.' "

14 So the LORD changed His mind

about the harm which He said He would do to His people.

15 ¶ Then Moses turned and went down from the mountain with the two tablets of the testimony in his hand, tablets which were written on both sides; they were written on one *side* and the other.

16 And the tablets were God's work, and the writing was God's writing engraved on the tablets.

17 Now when Joshua heard the sound of the people as they shouted, he said to Moses, "There is a sound of war in the camp."

18 But he said,

"It is not the sound of the cry of triumph,
    Nor is it the sound of the cry of defeat;
    But the sound of singing I hear."

19 And it came about, as soon as Moses came near the camp, that he saw the calf and *the* dancing; and Moses' anger burned, and he threw the tablets from his hands and shattered them at the foot of the mountain.

20 And he took the calf which they had made and burned *it* with fire, and ground it to powder, and scattered it over the surface of the water, and made the sons of Israel drink *it.*

21 ¶ Then Moses said to Aaron, "What did this people do to you, that you have brought *such* great sin upon them?"

22 And Aaron said, "Do not let the anger of my lord burn; you know the people yourself, that they are prone to evil.

23 "For they said to me, 'Make a god for us who will go before us; for this Moses, the man who brought us up from the land of Egypt, we do not know what has become of him.'

24 "And I said to them, 'Whoever has any gold, let them tear it off.' So they gave *it* to me, and I threw it into the fire, and out came this calf."

25 ¶ Now when Moses saw that the people were out of control—for Aaron had let them get out of control to be a derision among their enemies—

26 then Moses stood in the gate of the camp, and said, "Whoever is for the LORD, *come* to me!" And all the sons of Levi gathered together to him.

27 And he said to them, "Thus says the LORD, the God of Israel, 'Every man *of you* put his sword upon his thigh, and go back and forth from gate to gate in the camp, and kill every man his brother, and every man his friend, and every man his neighbor.' "

28 So the sons of Levi did as Moses instructed, and about three thousand men of the people fell that day.

29 Then Moses said, "Dedicate yourselves today to the LORD—for every man has been against his son and against his brother—in order that He may bestow a blessing upon you today."

30 ¶ And it came about on the next day that Moses said to the people, "You yourselves have committed a great sin; and now I am going up to the LORD, perhaps I can make atonement for your sin."

31 Then Moses returned to the LORD, and said, "Alas, this people has committed a great sin, and they have made a god of gold for themselves.

32 "But now, if Thou wilt, forgive their sin—and if not, please blot me out from Thy book which Thou hast written!"

33 And the LORD said to Moses, "Whoever has sinned against Me, I will blot him out of My book.

34 "But go now, lead the people where I told you. Behold, My angel shall go before you; nevertheless in the day when I punish, I will punish them for their sin."

35 Then the LORD smote the people, because of what they did with the calf which Aaron had made.

CHAPTER 33

THEN the LORD spoke to Moses, "Depart, go up from here, you and the people whom you have brought up from the land of Egypt, to the land of which I swore to Abraham, Isaac, and Jacob, saying, 'To your descendants I will give it.'

2 "And I will send an angel before you and I will drive out the Canaanite, the Amorite, the Hittite, the Perizzite, the Hivite and the Jebusite.

3 "Go up to a land flowing with milk and honey; for I will not go up in your midst, because you are an obstinate people, lest I destroy you on the way."

4 When the people heard this sad word, they went into mourning, and none of them put on his ornaments.

5 For the LORD had said to Moses, "Say to the sons of Israel, 'You are an obstinate people; should I go up in your midst for one moment, I would destroy you. Now therefore, put off your ornaments from you, that I may know what I will do with you.' "

6 So the sons of Israel stripped themselves of their ornaments from Mount Horeb onward.

7 ¶ Now Moses used to take the tent and pitch it outside the camp, a good distance from the camp, and he called it the tent of meeting. And it came about, that everyone who sought the LORD would go out to the tent of meeting which was outside the camp.

8 And it came about, whenever Moses went out to the tent, that all the people would arise and stand, each at the entrance of his tent, and gaze after Moses until he entered the tent.

9 And it came about, whenever Moses entered the tent, the pillar of cloud would descend and stand at the entrance of the tent; and the LORD would speak with Moses.

10 When all the people saw the pillar of cloud standing at the entrance of the tent, all the people would arise and worship, each at the entrance of his tent.

11 Thus the LORD used to speak to Moses face to face, just as a man speaks to his friend. When Moses returned to the camp, his servant Joshua, the son of Nun, a young man, would not depart from the tent.

12 ¶ Then Moses said to the LORD, "See, Thou dost say to me, 'Bring up this people!' But Thou Thyself hast not let me know whom Thou wilt send with me. Moreover, Thou hast said, 'I have known you by name, and you have also found favor in My sight.'

13 "Now therefore, I pray Thee, if I have found favor in Thy sight, let me know Thy ways, that I may know Thee, so that I may find favor in Thy sight. Consider too, that this nation is Thy people."

14 And He said, "My presence shall go with you, and I will give you rest."

15 Then he said to Him, "If Thy presence does not go with us, do not lead us up from here.

16 "For how then can it be known that I have found favor in Thy sight, I and Thy people? Is it not by Thy going with us, so that we, I and Thy people, may be distinguished from all the other people who are upon the face of the earth?"

17 ¶ And the LORD said to Moses, "I will also do this thing of which you have spoken; for you have found favor in My sight, and I have known you by name."

18 Then Moses said, "I pray Thee, show me Thy glory!"

19 And He said, "I Myself will make all My goodness pass before you, and will proclaim the name of the LORD before you; and I will be gracious to whom I will be gracious, and will show compassion on whom I will show compassion."

20 But He said, "You cannot see My face, for no man can see Me and live!"

21 Then the LORD said, "Behold, there is a place by Me, and you shall stand there on the rock;

22 and it will come about, while My glory is passing by, that I will put you in the cleft of the rock and cover you with My hand until I have passed by.

23 "Then I will take My hand away and you shall see My back, but My face shall not be seen."

CHAPTER 34

NOW the LORD said to Moses, "Cut out for yourself two stone tablets like the former ones, and I will write on the tablets the words that were on the former tablets which you shattered.

2 "So be ready by morning, and come up in the morning to Mount Sinai, and present yourself there to Me on the top of the mountain.

3 "And no man is to come up with you, nor let any man be seen anywhere on the mountain; even the flocks and the herds may not graze in front of that mountain."

4 So he cut out two stone tablets like the former ones, and Moses rose up early in the morning and went up to Mount Sinai, as the LORD had commanded him, and he took two stone tablets in his hand.

5 And the LORD descended in the cloud and stood there with him as he called upon the name of the LORD.

6 Then the LORD passed by in front of him and proclaimed, "The LORD, the LORD God, compassionate and gracious, slow to anger, and abounding in lovingkindness and truth;

7 who keeps lovingkindness for thousands, who forgives iniquity, transgression and sin; yet He will by no means leave *the guilty* unpunished, visiting the iniquity of fathers on the children and on the grandchildren to the third and fourth generations."

8 And Moses made haste to bow low toward the earth and worship.

9 And he said, "If now I have found favor in Thy sight, O Lord, I pray, let the Lord go along in our midst, even though the people are so obstinate; and do Thou pardon our iniquity and our sin, and take us as Thine own possession."

10 ¶ Then God said, "Behold, I am going to make a covenant. Before all your people I will perform miracles which have not been produced in all the earth, nor among any of the nations; and all the people among whom you live will see the working of the LORD, for it is a fearful thing that I am going to perform with you.

11 "Be sure to observe what I am commanding you this day: behold, I am going to drive out the Amorite before you, and the Canaanite, the Hittite, the Perizzite, the Hivite and the Jebusite.

12 "Watch yourself that you make no covenant with the inhabitants of the land into which you are going, lest it become a snare in your midst.

13 "But *rather,* you are to tear down their altars and smash their *sacred* pillars and cut down their [30]Asherim

14 —for you shall not worship any other god, for the LORD, whose name is Jealous, is a jealous God—

15 lest you make a covenant with the inhabitants of the land and they play the harlot with their gods, and sacrifice to their gods, and someone invite you to eat of his sacrifice;

16 and you take some of his daughters for your sons, and his daughters play the harlot with their gods, and

cause your sons *also* to play the harlot with their gods.

17 "You shall make for yourself no molten gods.

18 ¶ "You shall observe the Feast of Unleavened Bread. For seven days you are to eat unleavened bread, as I commanded you, at the appointed time in the month of Abib, for in the month of Abib you came out of Egypt.

19 "The first offspring from every womb belongs to Me, and all your male livestock, the first offspring from cattle and sheep.

20 "And you shall redeem with a lamb the first offspring from a donkey; and if you do not redeem *it,* then you shall break its neck. You shall redeem all the first-born of your sons. And none shall appear before Me empty-handed.

21 ¶ "You shall work six days, but on the seventh day you shall rest; *even* during plowing time and harvest you shall rest.

22 "And you shall celebrate the Feast of Weeks, *that is,* the first fruits of the wheat harvest, and the Feast of Ingathering at the turn of the year.

23 "Three times a year all your males are to appear before the Lord GOD, the God of Israel.

24 "For I will drive out nations before you and enlarge your borders, and no man shall covet your land when you go up three times a year to appear before the LORD your God.

25 ¶ "You shall not offer the blood of My sacrifice with leavened bread, nor is the sacrifice of the Feast of the Passover to be left over until morning.

26 "You shall bring the very first of the first fruits of your soil into the house of the LORD your God. You shall not boil a kid in its mother's milk."

27 ¶ Then the LORD said to Moses, "Write down these words, for in accordance with these words I have made a covenant with you and with Israel."

28 So he was there with the LORD forty days and forty nights; he did not eat bread or drink water. And he wrote on the tablets the words of the covenant, the Ten Commandments.

29 ¶ And it came about when Moses was coming down from Mount Sinai (and the two tablets of the testimony *were* in Moses' hand as he was coming down from the mountain), that Moses

---

[30] I.e., wooden symbols of a female deity

did not know that the skin of his face shone because of his speaking with Him.

30 So when Aaron and all the sons of Israel saw Moses, behold, the skin of his face shone, and they were afraid to come near him.

31 Then Moses called to them, and Aaron and all the rulers in the congregation returned to him; and Moses spoke to them.

32 And afterward all the sons of Israel came near, and he commanded them *to do* everything that the Lord had spoken to him on Mount Sinai.

33 When Moses had finished speaking with them, he put a veil over his face.

34 But whenever Moses went in before the Lord to speak with Him, he would take off the veil until he came out; and whenever he came out and spoke to the sons of Israel what he had been commanded,

35 the sons of Israel would see the face of Moses, that the skin of Moses' face shone. So Moses would replace the veil over his face until he went in to speak with Him.

CHAPTER 35

THEN Moses assembled all the congregation of the sons of Israel, and said to them, "These are the things that the Lord has commanded *you* to do.

2 "For six days work may be done, but on the seventh day you shall have a holy *day,* a sabbath of complete rest to the Lord; whoever does any work on it shall be put to death.

3 "You shall not kindle a fire in any of your dwellings on the sabbath day."

4 ¶ And Moses spoke to all the congregation of the sons of Israel, saying, "This is the thing which the Lord has commanded, saying,

5 'Take from among you a contribution to the Lord; whoever is of a willing heart, let him bring it as the Lord's contribution: gold, silver, and bronze,

6 and blue, purple and scarlet *material,* fine linen, goats' hair,

7 and rams' skins dyed red, and porpoise skins, and acacia wood,

8 and oil for lighting, and spices for the anointing oil, and for the fragrant incense,

9 and onyx stones and setting stones, for the ephod and for the breastpiece.

10 ¶ 'And let every skillful man among you come, and make all that the Lord has commanded:

11 the tabernacle, its tent and its covering, its hooks and its boards, its bars, its pillars, and its sockets;

12 the ark and its poles, the mercy seat, and the curtain of the screen;

13 the table and its poles, and all its utensils, and the bread of the [31]Presence;

14 the lampstand also for the light and its utensils and its lamps and the oil for the light;

15 and the altar of incense and its poles, and the anointing oil and the fragrant incense, and the screen for the doorway at the entrance of the tabernacle;

16 the altar of burnt offering with its bronze grating, its poles, and all its utensils, the basin and its stand;

17 the hangings of the court, its pillars and its sockets, and the screen for the gate of the court;

18 the pegs of the tabernacle and the pegs of the court and their cords;

19 the woven garments, for ministering in the holy place, the holy garments for Aaron the priest, and the garments of his sons, to minister as priests.' "

20 ¶ Then all the congregation of the sons of Israel departed from Moses' presence.

21 And everyone whose heart stirred him and everyone whose spirit moved him came *and* brought the Lord's contribution for the work of the tent of meeting and for all its service and for the holy garments.

22 Then all whose hearts moved them, both men and women, came *and* brought brooches and earrings and signet rings and bracelets, all articles of gold; so *did* every man who presented an offering of gold to the Lord.

23 And every man, who had in his possession blue and purple and scarlet *material* and fine linen and goats' *hair* and rams' skins dyed red and porpoise skins, brought them.

[31] Lit., *Face*

24 Everyone who could make a contribution of silver and bronze brought the LORD's contribution; and every man, who had in his possession acacia wood for any work of the service, brought it.

25 And all the skilled women spun with their hands, and brought what they had spun, *in* blue and purple *and* scarlet *material* and *in* fine linen.

26 And all the women whose heart stirred with a skill spun the goats' hair.

27 And the rulers brought the onyx stones and the stones for setting for the ephod and for the breastpiece;

28 and the spice and the oil for the light and for the anointing oil and for the fragrant incense.

29 The Israelites, all the men and women, whose heart moved them to bring *material* for all the work, which the LORD had commanded through Moses to be done, brought a freewill offering to the LORD.

30 ¶ Then Moses said to the sons of Israel, "See, the LORD has called by name Bezalel the son of Uri, the son of Hur, of the tribe of Judah.

31 "And He has filled him with the Spirit of God, in wisdom, in understanding and in knowledge and in all craftsmanship;

32 to make designs for working in gold and in silver and in bronze,

33 and in the cutting of stones for settings, and in the carving of wood, so as to perform in every inventive work.

34 "He also has put in his heart to teach, both he and Oholiab, the son of Ahisamach, of the tribe of Dan.

35 "He has filled them with skill to perform every work of an engraver and of a designer and of an embroiderer, in blue and in purple *and* in scarlet *material,* and in fine linen, and of a weaver, as performers of every work and makers of designs.

CHAPTER 36

"NOW Bezalel and Oholiab, and every skillful person in whom the LORD has put skill and understanding to know how to perform all the work in the construction of the sanctuary, shall perform in accordance with all that the LORD has commanded."

2 ¶ Then Moses called Bezalel and Oholiab and every skillful person in whom the LORD had put skill, everyone whose heart stirred him, to come to the work to perform it.

3 And they received from Moses all the contributions which the sons of Israel had brought to perform the work in the construction of the sanctuary. And they still *continued* bringing to him freewill offerings every morning.

4 And all the skillful men who were performing all the work of the sanctuary came, each from the work which he was performing,

5 and they said to Moses, "The people are bringing much more than enough for the construction work which the LORD commanded *us* to perform."

6 So Moses issued a command, and a proclamation was circulated throughout the camp, saying, "Let neither man nor woman any longer perform work for the contributions of the sanctuary." Thus the people were restrained from bringing *any more.*

7 For the material they had was sufficient and more than enough for all the work, to perform it.

8 ¶ And all the skillful men among those who were performing the work made the tabernacle with ten curtains; of fine twisted linen and blue and purple and scarlet *material,* with cherubim, the work of a skillful workman, Bezalel made them.

9 The length of each curtain was twenty-eight cubits, and the width of each curtain four cubits; all the curtains had the same measurements.

10 And he joined five curtains to one another, and *the other* five curtains he joined to one another.

11 And he made loops of blue on the edge of the outermost curtain in the first set; he did likewise on the edge of the curtain that was outermost in the second set.

12 He made fifty loops in the one curtain and he made fifty loops on the edge of the curtain that was in the second set; the loops were opposite each other.

13 And he made fifty clasps of gold, and joined the curtains to one another with the clasps, so the tabernacle was a unit.

14 ¶ Then he made curtains of goats' *hair* for a tent over the tabernacle; he made eleven curtains in all.

15 The length of each curtain was thirty cubits, and four cubits the width of each curtain; the eleven curtains had the same measurements.

16 And he joined five curtains by themselves, and *the other* six curtains by themselves.

17 Moreover, he made fifty loops on the edge of the curtain that was outermost in the *first* set, and he made fifty loops on the edge of the curtain *that was outermost in* the second set.

18 And he made fifty clasps of bronze to join the tent together, that it might be a unit.

19 And he made a covering for the tent of rams' skins dyed red, and a covering of porpoise skins above.

20 ¶ Then he made the boards for the tabernacle of acacia wood, standing upright.

21 Ten cubits was the length of each board, and one and a half cubits the width of each board.

22 There were two tenons for each board, fitted to one another; thus he did for all the boards of the tabernacle.

23 And he made the boards for the tabernacle: twenty boards for the south side;

24 and he made forty sockets of silver under the twenty boards; two sockets under one board for its two tenons and two sockets under another board for its two tenons.

25 Then for the second side of the tabernacle, on the north side, he made twenty boards,

26 and their forty sockets of silver; two sockets under one board and two sockets under another board.

27 And for the rear of the tabernacle, to the west, he made six boards.

28 And he made two boards for the corners of the tabernacle at the rear.

29 And they were double beneath, and together they were complete to its top to the first ring; thus he did with both of them for the two corners.

30 And there were eight boards with their sockets of silver, sixteen sockets, two under every board.

31 ¶ Then he made bars of acacia wood, five for the boards of one side of the tabernacle,

32 and five bars for the boards of the other side of the tabernacle, and five bars for the boards of the tabernacle for the rear *side* to the west.

33 And he made the middle bar to pass through in the center of the boards from end to end.

34 And he overlaid the boards with gold and made their rings of gold *as* holders for the bars, and overlaid the bars with gold.

35 ¶ Moreover, he made the veil of blue and purple and scarlet *material*, and fine twisted linen; he made it with cherubim, the work of a skillful workman.

36 And he made four pillars of acacia for it, and overlaid them with gold, with their hooks of gold; and he cast four sockets of silver for them.

37 And he made a screen for the doorway of the tent, of blue and purple and scarlet *material*, and fine twisted linen, the work of a weaver;

38 and *he made* its five pillars with their hooks, and he overlaid their tops and their bands with gold; but their five sockets were of bronze.

CHAPTER 37

Now Bezalel made the ark of acacia wood; its length was two and a half cubits, and its width one and a half cubits, and its height one and a half cubits;

2 and he overlaid it with pure gold inside and out, and made a gold molding for it all around.

3 And he cast four rings of gold for it on its four feet; even two rings on one side of it, and two rings on the other side of it.

4 And he made poles of acacia wood and overlaid them with gold.

5 And he put the poles into the rings on the sides of the ark, to carry it.

6 And he made a mercy seat of pure gold, two and a half cubits long, and one and a half cubits wide.

7 And he made two cherubim of gold; he made them of hammered work, at the two ends of the mercy seat;

8 one cherub at the one end, and one cherub at the other end; he made the cherubim *of one piece* with the mercy seat at the two ends.

9 And the cherubim had *their* wings spread upward, covering the mercy seat with their wings, with their faces toward each other; the faces of the cherubim were toward the mercy seat.

10 ¶ Then he made the table of acacia wood, two cubits long and a cubit wide and one and a half cubits high.

11 And he overlaid it with pure gold, and made a gold molding for it all around.

12 And he made a rim for it of a handbreadth all around, and made a gold molding for its rim all around.

13 And he cast four gold rings for it and put the rings on the four corners that were on its four feet.

14 Close by the rim were the rings, the holders for the poles to carry the table.

15 And he made the poles of acacia wood and overlaid them with gold, to carry the table.

16 And he made the utensils which were on the table, its dishes and its pans and its bowls and its jars, with which to pour out libations, of pure gold.

17 ¶ Then he made the lampstand of pure gold. He made the lampstand of hammered work, its base and its shaft; its cups, its bulbs and its flowers were *of one piece* with it.

18 And there were six branches going out of its sides; three branches of the lampstand from the one side of it, and three branches of the lampstand from the other side of it;

19 three cups shaped like almond *blossoms,* a bulb and a flower in one branch, and three cups shaped like almond *blossoms,* a bulb and a flower in the other branch—so for the six branches going out of the lampstand.

20 And in the lampstand *there were* four cups shaped like almond *blossoms,* its bulbs and its flowers;

21 and a bulb was under the *first* pair of branches *coming* out of it, and a bulb under the *second* pair of branches *coming* out of it, and a bulb under the *third* pair of branches *coming* out of it, for the six branches coming out of the lampstand.

22 Their bulbs and their branches were *of one piece* with it; the whole of it *was* a single hammered work of pure gold.

23 And he made its seven lamps with its snuffers and its trays of pure gold.

24 He made it and all its utensils from a talent of pure gold.

25 ¶ Then he made the altar of incense of acacia wood: a cubit long and a cubit wide, square, and two cubits high; its horns were *of one piece* with it.

26 And he overlaid it with pure gold, its top and its sides all around, and its horns; and he made a gold molding for it all around.

27 And he made two golden rings for it under its molding, on its two sides—on opposite sides—as holders for poles with which to carry it.

28 And he made the poles of acacia wood and overlaid them with gold.

29 And he made the holy anointing oil and the pure, fragrant incense of spices, the work of a perfumer.

CHAPTER 38

THEN he made the altar of burnt offering of acacia wood, five cubits long, and five cubits wide, square, and three cubits high.

2 And he made its horns on its four corners, its horns being *of one piece* with it, and he overlaid it with bronze.

3 And he made all the utensils of the altar, the pails and the shovels and the basins, the flesh hooks and the firepans; he made all its utensils of bronze.

4 And he made for the altar a grating of bronze network beneath, under its ledge, reaching halfway up.

5 And he cast four rings on the four ends of the bronze grating *as* holders for the poles.

6 And he made the poles of acacia wood and overlaid them with bronze.

7 And he inserted the poles into the rings on the sides of the altar, with which to carry it. He made it hollow with planks.

8 ¶ Moreover, he made the laver of bronze with its base of bronze, from the mirrors of the serving women who served at the doorway of the tent of meeting.

9 ¶ Then he made the court: for the south side the hangings of the court were of fine twisted linen, one hundred cubits;

10 their twenty pillars, and their twenty sockets, *made* of bronze; the hooks of the pillars and their bands *were* of silver.

11 And for the north side *there were* one hundred cubits; their twenty pillars and their twenty sockets *were* of bronze, the hooks of the pillars and their bands *were* of silver.

12 And for the west side *there were* hangings of fifty cubits *with* their ten pillars and their ten sockets; the hooks of the pillars and their bands *were* of silver.

13 And for the east side fifty cubits.

14 The hangings for the *one* side *of the gate were* fifteen cubits, *with* their three pillars and their three sockets,

15 and so for the other side. On both sides of the gate of the court *were* hangings of fifteen cubits, *with* their three pillars and their three sockets.

16 All the hangings of the court all around *were* of fine twisted linen.

17 And the sockets for the pillars *were* of bronze, the hooks of the pillars and their bands, of silver; and the overlaying of their tops, of silver, and all the pillars of the court were furnished with silver bands.

18 And the screen of the gate of the court was the work of the weaver, of blue and purple and scarlet *material*, and fine twisted linen. And the length was twenty cubits and the height was five cubits, corresponding to the hangings of the court.

19 And their four pillars and their four sockets *were* of bronze; their hooks *were* of silver, and the overlaying of their tops and their bands *were* of silver.

20 And all the pegs of the tabernacle and of the court all around *were* of bronze.

21 ¶ This is the number of *the things for* the tabernacle, the tabernacle of the testimony, as they were numbered according to the command of Moses, for the service of the Levites, by the hand of Ithamar, the son of Aaron the priest.

22 Now Bezalel, the son of Uri the son of Hur, of the tribe of Judah, made all that the LORD had commanded Moses.

23 And with him was Oholiab, the son of Ahisamach, of the tribe of Dan, an engraver and a skillful workman and a weaver in blue and in purple and in scarlet *material*, and fine linen.

24 ¶ All the gold that was used for the work, in all the work of the sanctuary, even the gold of the wave offering, was 29 talents and 730 shekels, according to the shekel of the sanctuary.

25 And the silver of those of the congregation who were numbered was 100 talents and 1,775 shekels, according to the shekel of the sanctuary;

26 a beka a head (*that is,* half a shekel according to the shekel of the sanctuary), for each one who passed over to those who were numbered, from twenty years old and upward, for 603,550 men.

27 And the hundred talents of silver were for casting the sockets of the sanctuary and the sockets of the veil; one hundred sockets for the hundred talents, a talent for a socket.

28 And of the 1,775 *shekels,* he made hooks for the pillars and overlaid their tops and made bands for them.

29 And the bronze of the wave offering was 70 talents, and 2,400 shekels.

30 And with it he made the sockets to the doorway of the tent of meeting, and the bronze altar and its bronze grating, and all the utensils of the altar,

31 and the sockets of the court all around and the sockets of the gate of the court, and all the pegs of the tabernacle and all the pegs of the court all around.

CHAPTER 39

MOREOVER, from the blue and purple and scarlet *material*, they made finely woven garments for ministering in the holy place, as well as the holy garments which were for Aaron, just as the LORD had commanded Moses.

2 ¶ And he made the ephod of gold, *and* of blue and purple and scarlet *material*, and fine twisted linen.

3 Then they hammered out gold sheets and cut *them* into threads to be woven in *with* the blue and the purple and the scarlet *material*, and the fine linen, the work of a skillful workman.

4 They made attaching shoulder pieces for the ephod; it was attached at its two *upper* ends.

5 And the skillfully woven band which was on it was like its workmanship, of the same material: of gold *and* of blue and purple and scarlet *material*, and fine twisted linen, just as the Lord had commanded Moses.

6 ¶ And they made the onyx stones, set in gold filigree *settings;* they were engraved *like* the engravings of a signet, according to the names of the sons of Israel.

7 And he placed them on the shoulder pieces of the ephod, *as* memorial stones for the sons of Israel, just as the Lord had commanded Moses.

8 ¶ And he made the breastpiece, the work of a skillful workman, like the workmanship of the ephod: of gold *and* of blue and purple and scarlet *material* and fine twisted linen.

9 It was square; they made the breastpiece folded double, a span long and a span wide when folded double.

10 And they mounted four rows of stones on it. The first row *was* a row of ruby, topaz, and emerald;

11 and the second row, a turquoise, a sapphire and a diamond;

12 and the third row, a jacinth, an agate, and an amethyst;

13 and the fourth row, a beryl, an onyx, and a jasper. They were set in gold filigree *settings* when they were mounted.

14 And the stones were corresponding to the names of the sons of Israel; they were twelve, corresponding to their names, *engraved with* the engravings of a signet, each with its name for the twelve tribes.

15 And they made on the breastpiece chains like cords, of twisted cordage work in pure gold.

16 And they made two gold filigree *settings* and two gold rings, and put the two rings on the two ends of the breastpiece.

17 Then they put the two gold cords in the two rings at the ends of the breastpiece.

18 And they put the *other* two ends of the two cords on the two filigree *settings,* and put them on the shoulder pieces of the ephod at the front of it.

19 And they made two gold rings and placed *them* on the two ends of the breastpiece, on its inner edge which was next to the ephod.

20 Furthermore, they made two gold rings and placed them on the bottom of the two shoulder pieces of the ephod, on the front of it, close to the place where it joined, above the woven band of the ephod.

21 And they bound the breastpiece by its rings to the rings of the ephod with a blue cord, that it might be on the woven band of the ephod, and that the breastpiece might not come loose from the ephod, just as the Lord had commanded Moses.

22 ¶ Then he made the robe of the ephod of woven work, all of blue;

23 and the opening of the robe was *at the top* in the center, as the opening of a coat of mail, with a binding all around its opening, that it might not be torn.

24 And they made pomegranates of blue and purple and scarlet *material and* twisted *linen* on the hem of the robe.

25 They also made bells of pure gold, and put the bells between the pomegranates all around on the hem of the robe,

26 alternating a bell and a pomegranate all around on the hem of the robe, for the service, just as the Lord had commanded Moses.

27 ¶ And they made the tunics of finely woven linen for Aaron and his sons,

28 and the turban of fine linen, and the decorated caps of fine linen, and the linen breeches of fine twisted linen,

29 and the sash of fine twisted linen, and blue and purple and scarlet *material,* the work of the weaver, just as the Lord had commanded Moses.

30 ¶ And they made the plate of the holy crown of pure gold, and inscribed it like the engravings of a signet, "Holy to the Lord."

31 And they fastened a blue cord to it, to fasten it on the turban above, just as the Lord had commanded Moses.

32 ¶ Thus all the work of the tabernacle of the tent of meeting was completed; and the sons of Israel did according to all that the Lord had commanded Moses; so they did.

33 And they brought the tabernacle

to Moses, the tent and all its [32]furnishings: its clasps, its boards, its bars, and its pillars and its sockets;

34 and the covering of rams' skins dyed red, and the covering of porpoise skins, and the screening veil;

35 the ark of the testimony and its poles and the mercy seat;

36 the table, all its utensils, and the bread of the Presence;

37 the pure *gold* lampstand, with its arrangement of lamps and all its utensils, and the oil for the light;

38 and the gold altar, and the anointing oil and the fragrant incense, and the veil for the doorway of the tent;

39 the bronze altar and its bronze grating, its poles and all its utensils, the laver and its stand;

40 the hangings for the court, its pillars and its sockets, and the screen for the gate of the court, its cords and its pegs and all the equipment for the service of the tabernacle, for the tent of meeting;

41 the woven garments for ministering in the holy place and the holy garments for Aaron the priest and the garments of his sons, to minister as priests.

42 So the sons of Israel did all the work according to all that the LORD had commanded Moses.

43 And Moses examined all the work and behold, they had done it; just as the LORD had commanded, this they had done. So Moses blessed them.

CHAPTER 40

THEN the LORD spoke to Moses, saying,

2"On the first day of the first month you shall set up the tabernacle of the tent of meeting.

3"And you shall place the ark of the testimony there, and you shall screen the ark with the veil.

4"And you shall bring in the table and arrange what belongs on it; and you shall bring in the lampstand and mount its lamps.

5"Moreover, you shall set the gold altar of incense before the ark of the testimony, and set up the veil for the doorway to the tabernacle.

6"And you shall set the altar of burnt offering in front of the doorway

of the tabernacle of the tent of meeting.

7"And you shall set the laver between the tent of meeting and the altar, and put water in it.

8"And you shall set up the court all around and hang up the veil for the gateway of the court.

9"Then you shall take the anointing oil and anoint the tabernacle and all that is in it, and shall consecrate it and all its furnishings; and it shall be holy.

10"And you shall anoint the altar of burnt offering and all its utensils, and consecrate the altar; and the altar shall be most holy.

11"And you shall anoint the laver and its stand, and consecrate it.

12"Then you shall bring Aaron and his sons to the doorway of the tent of meeting and wash them with water.

13"And you shall put the holy garments on Aaron and anoint him and consecrate him, that he may minister as a priest to Me.

14"And you shall bring his sons and put tunics on them;

15 and you shall anoint them even as you have anointed their father, that they may minister as priests to Me; and their anointing shall qualify them for a perpetual priesthood throughout their generations."

16 Thus Moses did; according to all that the LORD had commanded him, so he did.

17 ¶ Now it came about in the first month of the second year, on the first day of the month, that the tabernacle was erected.

18 And Moses erected the tabernacle and laid its sockets, and set up its boards, and inserted its bars and erected its pillars.

19 And he spread the tent over the tabernacle and put the covering of the tent on top of it, just as the LORD had commanded Moses.

20 Then he took the testimony and put *it* into the ark, and attached the poles to the ark, and put the mercy seat on top of the ark.

21 And he brought the ark into the tabernacle, and set up a veil for the screen, and screened off the ark of the testimony, just as the LORD had commanded Moses.

22 Then he put the table in the tent

[32] Or, *utensils,* and so throughout this context

of meeting, on the north side of the tabernacle, outside the veil.

23 And he set the arrangement of bread in order on it before the LORD, just as the LORD had commanded Moses.

24 Then he placed the lampstand in the tent of meeting, opposite the table, on the south side of the tabernacle.

25 And he lighted the lamps before the LORD, just as the LORD had commanded Moses.

26 Then he placed the gold altar in the tent of meeting in front of the veil;

27 and he burned fragrant incense on it, just as the LORD had commanded Moses.

28 Then he set up the veil for the doorway of the tabernacle.

29 And he set the altar of burnt offering *before* the doorway of the tabernacle of the tent of meeting, and offered on it the burnt offering and the meal offering, just as the LORD had commanded Moses.

30 And he placed the laver between the tent of meeting and the altar, and put water in it for washing.

31 And from it Moses and Aaron and his sons washed their hands and their feet.

32 When they entered the tent of meeting, and when they approached the altar, they washed, just as the LORD had commanded Moses.

33 And he erected the court all around the tabernacle and the altar, and hung up the veil for the gateway of the court. Thus Moses finished the work.

34 ¶ Then the cloud covered the tent of meeting, and the glory of the LORD filled the tabernacle.

35 And Moses was not able to enter the tent of meeting because the cloud had settled on it, and the glory of the LORD filled the tabernacle.

36 And throughout all their journeys whenever the cloud was taken up from over the tabernacle, the sons of Israel would set out;

37 but if the cloud was not taken up, then they did not set out until the day when it was taken up.

38 For throughout all their journeys, the cloud of the LORD was on the tabernacle by day, and there was fire in it by night, in the sight of all the house of Israel.

LEVITICUS

THEN the LORD called to Moses and spoke to him from the tent of meeting, saying,

2 "Speak to the sons of Israel and say to them, 'When any man of you brings an offering to the LORD, you shall bring your offering of animals from the herd or the flock.

3 'If his offering is a burnt offering from the herd, he shall offer it, a male without defect; he shall offer it at the doorway of the tent of meeting, that he may be accepted before the LORD.

4 'And he shall lay his hand on the head of the burnt offering, that it may be accepted for him to make atonement on his behalf.

5 'And he shall slay the young bull before the LORD; and Aaron's sons, the priests, shall offer up the blood and sprinkle the blood around on the altar that is at the doorway of the tent of meeting.

6 'He shall then skin the burnt offering and cut it into its pieces.

7 'And the sons of Aaron the priest shall put fire on the altar and arrange wood on the fire.

8 'Then Aaron's sons, the priests, shall arrange the pieces, the head, and the suet over the wood which is on the fire that is on the altar.

9 'Its entrails, however, and its legs he shall wash with water. And the priest shall offer up in smoke all of it on the altar for a burnt offering, an offering by fire of a soothing aroma to the LORD.

10 ¶ 'But if his offering is from the flock, of the sheep or of the goats, for a burnt offering, he shall offer it a male without defect.

11 'And he shall slay it on the side of the altar northward before the Lord, and Aaron's sons, the priests, shall sprinkle its blood around on the altar.

12 'He shall then cut it into its pieces with its head and its suet, and the priest shall arrange them on the wood which is on the fire that is on the altar.

13 'The entrails, however, and the legs he shall wash with water. And the priest shall offer all of it, and offer it up in smoke on the altar; it is a burnt offering, an offering by fire of a soothing aroma to the Lord.

14 ¶ 'But if his offering to the Lord is a burnt offering of birds, then he shall bring his offering from the turtledoves or from young pigeons.

15 'And the priest shall bring it to the altar and wring off its head, and offer it up in smoke on the altar; and its blood is to be drained out on the side of the altar.

16 'He shall also take away its crop with its feathers, and cast it beside the altar eastward, to the place of the ashes.

17 'Then he shall tear it by its wings, but shall not sever it. And the priest shall offer it up in smoke on the altar on the wood which is on the fire; it is a burnt offering, an offering by fire of a soothing aroma to the Lord.

CHAPTER 2

'Now when anyone presents a grain offering as an offering to the Lord, his offering shall be of fine flour, and he shall pour oil on it and put frankincense on it.

2 'He shall then bring it to Aaron's sons, the priests; and shall take from it his handful of its fine flour and of its oil with all of its frankincense. And the priest shall offer it up in smoke as its memorial portion on the altar, an offering by fire of a soothing aroma to the Lord.

3 'And the remainder of the grain offering belongs to Aaron and his sons: a thing most holy, of the offerings to the Lord by fire.

4 ¶ 'Now when you bring an offering of a grain offering baked in an oven, it shall be unleavened cakes of fine flour mixed with oil, or unleavened wafers spread with oil.

5 'And if your offering is a grain offering made on the griddle, it shall be of fine flour, unleavened, mixed with oil;

6 you shall break it into bits, and pour oil on it; it is a grain offering.

7 'Now if your offering is a grain offering made in a pan, it shall be made of fine flour with oil.

8 'When you bring in the grain offering which is made of these things to the Lord, it shall be presented to the priest and he shall bring it to the altar.

9 'The priest then shall take up from the grain offering its memorial portion, and shall offer it up in smoke on the altar as an offering by fire of a soothing aroma to the Lord.

10 'And the remainder of the grain offering belongs to Aaron and his sons: a thing most holy, of the offerings to the Lord by fire.

11 ¶ 'No grain offering, which you bring to the Lord, shall be made with leaven, for you shall not offer up in smoke any leaven or any honey as an offering by fire to the Lord.

12 'As an offering of first fruits, you shall bring them to the Lord, but they shall not ascend for a soothing aroma on the altar.

13 'Every grain offering of yours, moreover, you shall season with salt, so that the salt of the covenant of your God shall not be lacking from your grain offering; with all your offerings you shall offer salt.

14 ¶ 'Also if you bring a grain offering of early ripened things to the Lord, you shall bring fresh heads of grain roasted in the fire, grits of new growth, for the grain offering of your early ripened things.

15 'You shall then put oil on it and lay incense on it; it is a grain offering.

16 'And the priest shall offer up in smoke its memorial portion, part of its grits and its oil with all its incense as an offering by fire to the Lord.

CHAPTER 3

'Now if his offering is a sacrifice of peace offerings, if he is going to offer out of the herd, whether male or female, he shall offer it without defect before the Lord.

2 'And he shall lay his hand on the head of his offering and slay it at the doorway of the tent of meeting, and

Aaron's sons, the priests, shall sprinkle the blood around on the altar.

3 'And from the sacrifice of the peace offerings, he shall present an offering by fire to the LORD, the fat that covers the entrails and all the fat that is on the entrails,

4 and the two kidneys with the fat that is on them, which is on the loins, and the lobe of the liver, which he shall remove with the kidneys.

5 'And Aaron's sons shall offer *it* up in smoke on the altar on the burnt offering, which is on the wood that is on the fire; it is an offering by fire of a soothing aroma to the LORD.

6 'But if his offering for a sacrifice of peace offerings to the LORD is from the flock, he shall offer it, male or female, without defect.

7 'If he is going to offer a lamb for his offering, then he shall offer it before the LORD,

8 and he shall lay his hand on the head of his offering, and slay it before the tent of meeting; and Aaron's sons shall sprinkle its blood around on the altar.

9 'And from the sacrifice of peace offerings he shall bring as an offering by fire to the LORD, its fat, the entire fat tail which he shall remove close to the backbone, and the fat that covers the entrails and all the fat that is on the entrails,

10 and the two kidneys with the fat that is on them, which is on the loins, and the lobe of the liver, which he shall remove with the kidneys.

11 'Then the priest shall offer *it* up in smoke on the altar, *as* food, an offering by fire to the LORD.

12 ¶ 'Moreover, if his offering is a goat, then he shall offer it before the LORD,

13 and he shall lay his hand on its head and slay it before the tent of meeting; and the sons of Aaron shall sprinkle its blood around on the altar.

14 'And from it he shall present his offering as an offering by fire to the LORD, the fat that covers the entrails and all the fat that is on the entrails,

15 and the two kidneys with the fat that is on them, which is on the loins, and the lobe of the liver, which he shall remove with the kidneys.

16 'And the priest shall offer them up in smoke on the altar *as* food, an offering by fire for a soothing aroma; all fat is the LORD's.

17 'It is a perpetual statute throughout your generations in all your dwellings: you shall not eat any fat or any blood.' "

CHAPTER 4

THEN the LORD spoke to Moses, saying,

2 "Speak to the sons of Israel, saying, 'If a person sins unintentionally in any of the things which the LORD has commanded not to be done, and commits any of them,

3 if the anointed priest sins so as to bring guilt on the people, then let him offer to the LORD a bull without defect as a sin offering for the sin he has committed.

4 'And he shall bring the bull to the doorway of the tent of meeting before the LORD, and he shall lay his hand on the head of the bull, and slay the bull before the LORD.

5 'Then the anointed priest is to take some of the blood of the bull and bring it to the tent of meeting,

6 and the priest shall dip his finger in the blood, and sprinkle some of the blood seven times before the LORD, in front of the veil of the sanctuary.

7 'The priest shall also put some of the blood on the horns of the altar of fragrant incense which is before the LORD in the tent of meeting; and all the blood of the bull he shall pour out at the base of the altar of burnt offering which is at the doorway of the tent of meeting.

8 'And he shall remove from it all the fat of the bull of the sin offering: the fat that covers the entrails, and all the fat which is on the entrails,

9 and the two kidneys with the fat that is on them, which is on the loins, and the lobe of the liver, which he shall remove with the kidneys

10 (just as it is removed from the ox of the sacrifice of peace offerings), and the priest is to offer them up in smoke on the altar of burnt offering.

11 'But the hide of the bull and all its flesh with its head and its legs and its entrails and its refuse,

12 that is, all *the rest of* the bull, he is to bring out to a clean place outside the camp where the ashes are poured out, and burn it on wood with fire;

where the ashes are poured out it shall be burned.

13 ¶ 'Now if the whole congregation of Israel commits error, and the matter escapes the notice of the assembly, and they commit any of the things which the LORD has commanded not to be done, and they become guilty;

14 when the sin which they have committed becomes known, then the assembly shall offer a bull of the herd for a sin offering, and bring it before the tent of meeting.

15 'Then the elders of the congregation shall lay their hands on the head of the bull before the LORD, and the bull shall be slain before the LORD.

16 'Then the anointed priest is to bring some of the blood of the bull to the tent of meeting;

17 and the priest shall dip his finger in the blood, and sprinkle *it* seven times before the LORD, in front of the veil.

18 'And he shall put some of the blood on the horns of the altar which is before the LORD in the tent of meeting; and all the blood he shall pour out at the base of the altar of burnt offering which is at the doorway of the tent of meeting.

19 'And he shall remove all its fat from it and offer it up in smoke on the altar.

20 'He shall also do with the bull just as he did with the bull of the sin offering; thus he shall do with it. So the priest shall make atonement for them, and they shall be forgiven.

21 'Then he is to bring out the bull to *a place* outside the camp, and burn it as he burned the first bull; it is the sin offering for the assembly.

22 ¶ 'When a leader sins and unintentionally does any one of all the things which the LORD God has commanded not to be done, and he becomes guilty,

23 if his sin which he has committed is made known to him, he shall bring for his offering a goat, a male without defect.

24 'And he shall lay his hand on the head of the male goat, and slay it in the place where they slay the burnt offering before the LORD; it is a sin offering.

25 'Then the priest is to take some of the blood of the sin offering with his finger, and put it on the horns of the altar of burnt offering; and *the rest of* its blood he shall pour out at the base of the altar of burnt offering.

26 'And all its fat he shall offer up in smoke on the altar as *in the case of* the fat of the sacrifice of peace offerings. Thus the priest shall make atonement for him in regard to his sin, and he shall be forgiven.

27 ¶ 'Now if anyone of the common people sins unintentionally in doing any of the things which the LORD has commanded not to be done, and becomes guilty,

28 if his sin, which he has committed is made known to him, then he shall bring for his offering a goat, a female without defect, for his sin which he has committed.

29 'And he shall lay his hand on the head of the sin offering, and slay the sin offering at the place of the burnt offering.

30 'And the priest shall take some of its blood with his finger and put it on the horns of the altar of burnt offering; and all *the rest of* its blood he shall pour out at the base of the altar.

31 'Then he shall remove all its fat, just as the fat was removed from the sacrifice of peace offerings; and the priest shall offer it up in smoke on the altar for a soothing aroma to the LORD. Thus the priest shall make atonement for him, and he shall be forgiven.

32 ¶ 'But if he brings a lamb as his offering for a sin offering, he shall bring it, a female without defect.

33 'And he shall lay his hand on the head of the sin offering, and slay it for a sin offering in the place where they slay the burnt offering.

34 'And the priest is to take some of the blood of the sin offering with his finger and put it on the horns of the altar of burnt offering; and all *the rest of* its blood he shall pour out at the base of the altar.

35 'Then he shall remove all its fat, just as the fat of the lamb is removed from the sacrifice of the peace offerings, and the priest shall offer them up in smoke on the altar, on the offerings by fire to the LORD. Thus the priest shall make atonement for him in regard to his sin which he has committed, and he shall be forgiven.

CHAPTER 5

'Now if a person sins, after he hears a public adjuration *to testify,* when he is a witness, whether he has seen or *otherwise* known, if he does not tell *it,* then he will bear his guilt.

2 'Or if a person touches any unclean thing, whether a carcass of an unclean beast, or the carcass of unclean cattle, or a carcass of unclean swarming things, though it is hidden from him, and he is unclean, then he will be guilty.

3 'Or if he touches human uncleanness, of whatever *sort* his uncleanness *may* be with which he becomes unclean, and it is hidden from him, and then he comes to know *it,* he will be guilty.

4 'Or if a person swears thoughtlessly with his lips to do evil or to do good, in whatever matter a man may speak thoughtlessly with an oath, and it is hidden from him, and then he comes to know *it,* he will be guilty in one of these.

5 'So it shall be when he becomes guilty in one of these, that he shall confess that in which he has sinned.

6 'He shall also bring his guilt offering to the LORD for his sin which he has committed, a female from the flock, a lamb or a goat as a sin offering. So the priest shall make atonement on his behalf for his sin.

7 ¶ 'But if he cannot afford a lamb, then he shall bring to the LORD his guilt offering for that in which he has sinned, two turtledoves or two young pigeons, one for a sin offering and the other for a burnt offering.

8 'And he shall bring them to the priest, who shall offer first that which is for the sin offering and shall nip its head at the front of its neck, but he shall not sever *it.*

9 'He shall also sprinkle some of the blood of the sin offering on the side of the altar, while the rest of the blood shall be drained out at the base of the altar: it is a sin offering.

10 'The second he shall then prepare as a burnt offering according to the ordinance. So the priest shall make atonement on his behalf for his sin which he has committed, and it shall be forgiven him.

11 ¶ 'But if his means are insufficient for two turtledoves or two young pigeons, then for his offering for that which he has sinned, he shall bring the tenth of an [1]ephah of fine flour for a sin offering; he shall not put oil on it or place incense on it, for it is a sin offering.

12 'And he shall bring it to the priest, and the priest shall take his handful of it as its memorial portion and offer *it* up in smoke on the altar, with the offerings of the LORD by fire: it is a sin offering.

13 'So the priest shall make atonement for him concerning his sin which he has committed from one of these, and it shall be forgiven him; then *the rest* shall become the priest's, like the grain offering.' "

14 ¶ Then the LORD spoke to Moses, saying,

15 "If a person acts unfaithfully and sins unintentionally against the LORD's holy things, then he shall bring his guilt offering to the LORD: a ram without defect from the flock, according to your valuation in silver by shekels, in *terms of* the shekel of the sanctuary, for a guilt offering.

16 "And he shall make restitution for that which he has sinned against the holy thing, and shall add to it a fifth part of it, and give it to the priest. The priest shall then make atonement for him with the ram of the guilt offering, and it shall be forgiven him.

17 ¶ "Now if a person sins and does any of the things which the LORD has commanded not to be done, though he was unaware, still he is guilty, and shall bear his punishment.

18 "He is then to bring to the priest a ram without defect from the flock, according to your valuation, for a guilt offering. So the priest shall make atonement for him concerning his error in which he sinned unintentionally and did not know *it,* and it shall be forgiven him.

19 "It is a guilt offering; he was certainly guilty before the LORD."

CHAPTER 6

THEN the LORD spoke to Moses, saying,

[1] I.e., Approx. one bushel

2"When a person sins and acts unfaithfully against the LORD, and deceives his companion in regard to a deposit or a security entrusted *to him*, or through robbery, or *if* he has extorted from his companion,

3 or has found what was lost and lied about it and sworn falsely, so that he sins in regard to any one of the things a man may do;

4 then it shall be, when he sins and becomes guilty, that he shall restore what he took by robbery, or what he got by extortion, or the deposit which was entrusted to him, or the lost thing which he found,

5 or anything about which he swore falsely; he shall make restitution for it in full, and add to it one-fifth more. He shall give it to the one to whom it belongs on the day *he presents* his guilt offering.

6"Then he shall bring to the priest his guilt offering to the LORD, a ram without defect from the flock, according to your valuation, for a guilt offering,

7 and the priest shall make atonement for him before the LORD; and he shall be forgiven for any one of the things which he may have done to incur guilt."

8 ¶ Then the LORD spoke to Moses, saying,

9"Command Aaron and his sons, saying, 'This is the law for the burnt offering: the burnt offering itself *shall remain* on the hearth on the altar all night until the morning, and the fire on the altar is to be kept burning on it.

10 'And the priest is to put on his linen robe, and he shall put on undergarments next to his flesh; and he shall take up the ashes *to* which the fire reduces the burnt offering on the altar, and place them beside the altar.

11 'Then he shall take off his garments and put on other garments, and carry the ashes outside the camp to a clean place.

12 'And the fire on the altar shall be kept burning on it. It shall not go out, but the priest shall burn wood on it every morning; and he shall lay out the burnt offering on it, and offer up in smoke the fat portions of the peace offerings on it.

13 'Fire shall be kept burning continually on the altar; it is not to go out.

14 ¶ 'Now this is the law of the grain offering: the sons of Aaron shall present it before the LORD in front of the altar.

15 'Then one *of them* shall lift up from it a handful of the fine flour of the grain offering, with its oil and all the incense that is on the grain offering, and he shall offer *it* up in smoke on the altar, a soothing aroma, as its memorial offering to the LORD.

16 'And what is left of it Aaron and his sons are to eat. It shall be eaten as unleavened cakes in a holy place; they are to eat it in the court of the tent of meeting.

17 'It shall not be baked with leaven. I have given it as their share from My offerings by fire; it is most holy, like the sin offering and the guilt offering.

18 'Every male among the sons of Aaron may eat it; it is a permanent ordinance throughout your generations, from the offerings by fire to the LORD. Whoever touches them shall become consecrated.' "

19 ¶ Then the LORD spoke to Moses, saying,

20"This is the offering which Aaron and his sons are to present to the LORD on the day when he is anointed; the tenth of an ephah of fine flour as a regular grain offering, half of it in the morning and half of it in the evening.

21"It shall be prepared with oil on a griddle. When it is *well* stirred, you shall bring it. You shall present the grain offering in baked pieces as a soothing aroma to the LORD.

22"And the anointed priest who will be in his place among his sons shall offer it. By a permanent ordinance it shall be entirely offered up in smoke to the LORD.

23"So every grain offering of the priest shall be burned entirely. It shall not be eaten."

24 ¶ Then the LORD spoke to Moses, saying,

25"Speak to Aaron and to his sons, saying, 'This is the law of the sin offering: in the place where the burnt offering is slain the sin offering shall be slain before the LORD; it is most holy.

26 'The priest who offers it for sin shall eat it. It shall be eaten in a holy place, in the court of the tent of meeting.

27 'Anyone who touches its flesh shall become consecrated; and when any of its blood splashes on a garment, in a holy place you shall wash what was splashed on.

28 'Also the earthenware vessel in which it was boiled shall be broken; and if it was boiled in a bronze vessel, then it shall be scoured and rinsed in water.

29 'Every male among the priests may eat of it; it is most holy.

30 'But no sin offering of which any of the blood is brought into the tent of meeting to make atonement in the holy place shall be eaten; it shall be burned with fire.

CHAPTER 7

'NOW this is the law of the guilt offering; it is most holy.

2 'In the place where they slay the burnt offering they are to slay the guilt offering, and he shall sprinkle its blood around on the altar.

3 'Then he shall offer from it all its fat: the fat tail and the fat that covers the entrails,

4 and the two kidneys with the fat that is on them, which is on the loins, and the lobe on the liver he shall remove with the kidneys.

5 'And the priest shall offer them up in smoke on the altar as an offering by fire to the LORD; it is a guilt offering.

6 'Every male among the priests may eat of it. It shall be eaten in a holy place; it is most holy.

7 'The guilt offering is like the sin offering, there is one law for them; the priest who makes atonement with it shall have it.

8 'Also the priest who presents any man's burnt offering, that priest shall have for himself the skin of the burnt offering which he has presented.

9 'Likewise, every grain offering that is baked in the oven, and everything prepared in a pan or on a griddle, shall belong to the priest who presents it.

10 'And every grain offering mixed with oil, or dry, shall belong to all the sons of Aaron, to all alike.

11 ¶ 'Now this is the law of the sacrifice of peace offerings which shall be presented to the LORD.

12 'If he offers it by way of thanksgiving, then along with the sacrifice of thanksgiving he shall offer unleavened cakes mixed with oil, and unleavened wafers spread with oil, and cakes of well stirred fine flour mixed with oil.

13 'With the sacrifice of his peace offerings for thanksgiving, he shall present his offering with cakes of leavened bread.

14 'And of this he shall present one of every offering as a contribution to the LORD; it shall belong to the priest who sprinkles the blood of the peace offerings.

15 ¶ 'Now as for the flesh of the sacrifice of his thanksgiving peace offerings, it shall be eaten on the day of his offering; he shall not leave any of it over until morning.

16 'But if the sacrifice of his offering is a votive or a freewill offering, it shall be eaten on the day that he offers his sacrifice; and on the next day what is left of it may be eaten;

17 but what is left over from the flesh of the sacrifice on the third day shall be burned with fire.

18 'So if any of the flesh of the sacrifice of his peace offerings should ever be eaten on the third day, he who offers it shall not be accepted, and it shall not be reckoned to his benefit. It shall be an offensive thing, and the person who eats of it shall bear his own iniquity.

19 ¶ 'Also the flesh that touches anything unclean shall not be eaten; it shall be burned with fire. As for other flesh, anyone who is clean may eat such flesh.

20 'But the person who eats the flesh of the sacrifice of peace offerings which belong to the LORD, in his uncleanness, that person shall be cut off from his people.

21 'And when anyone touches anything unclean, whether human uncleanness, or an unclean animal, or any unclean ²detestable thing, and eats of the flesh of the sacrifice of peace offerings which belong to the LORD, that person shall be cut off from his people.'"

22 ¶ Then the LORD spoke to Moses, saying,

23 "Speak to the sons of Israel, saying, 'You shall not eat any fat from an ox, a sheep, or a goat.

² Some mss. read swarming thing

24 'Also the fat of *an animal* which dies, and the fat of an animal torn *by beasts*, may be put to any other use, but you must certainly not eat it.

25 'For whoever eats the fat of the animal from which an offering by fire is offered to the LORD, even the person who eats shall be cut off from his people.

26 'And you are not to eat any blood, either of bird or animal, in any of your dwellings.

27 'Any person who eats any blood, even that person shall be cut off from his people.' "

28 ¶ Then the LORD spoke to Moses, saying,

29 "Speak to the sons of Israel, saying, 'He who offers the sacrifice of his peace offerings to the LORD shall bring his offering to the LORD from the sacrifice of his peace offerings.

30 'His own hands are to bring offerings by fire to the LORD. He shall bring the fat with the breast, that the breast may be presented as a wave offering before the LORD.

31 'And the priest shall offer up the fat in smoke on the altar; but the breast shall belong to Aaron and his sons.

32 'And you shall give the right thigh to the priest as a contribution from the sacrifices of your peace offerings.

33 'The one among the sons of Aaron who offers the blood of the peace offerings and the fat, the right thigh shall be his as *his* portion.

34 'For I have taken the breast of the wave offering and the thigh of the contribution from the sons of Israel from the sacrifices of their peace offerings, and have given them to Aaron the priest and to his sons as *their* due forever from the sons of Israel.

35 ¶ 'This is that which is consecrated to Aaron and that which is consecrated to his sons from the offerings by fire to the LORD, in that day when he presented them to serve as priests to the LORD.

36 'These the LORD had commanded to be given them from the sons of Israel in the day that He anointed them. It is *their* due forever throughout their generations.' "

37 ¶ This is the law of the burnt offering, the grain offering and the sin offering and the guilt offering and the ordination offering and the sacrifice of peace offerings,

38 which the LORD commanded Moses at Mount Sinai in the day that He commanded the sons of Israel to present their offerings to the LORD in the wilderness of Sinai.

CHAPTER 8

THEN the LORD spoke to Moses, saying,

2 "Take Aaron and his sons with him, and the garments and the anointing oil and the bull of the sin offering, and the two rams and the basket of unleavened bread;

3 and assemble all the congregation at the doorway of the tent of meeting."

4 So Moses did just as the LORD commanded him. When the congregation was assembled at the doorway of the tent of meeting,

5 Moses said to the congregation, "This is the thing which the LORD has commanded to do."

6 ¶ Then Moses had Aaron and his sons come near, and washed them with water.

7 And he put the tunic on him and girded him with the sash, and clothed him with the robe, and put the ephod on him; and he girded him with the artistic band of the ephod, with which he tied *it* to him.

8 He then placed the breastpiece on him, and in the breastpiece he put [3]the Urim and the Thummim.

9 He also placed the turban on his head, and on the turban, at its front, he placed the golden plate, the holy crown, just as the LORD had commanded Moses.

10 ¶ Moses then took the anointing oil and anointed the tabernacle and all that was in it, and consecrated them.

11 And he sprinkled some of it on the altar seven times and anointed the altar and all its utensils, and the basin and its stand, to consecrate them.

12 Then he poured some of the anointing oil on Aaron's head and anointed him, to consecrate him.

13 Next Moses had Aaron's sons come near and clothed them with tunics, and girded them with sashes,

[3] I.e., the lights and perfections

and bound caps on them, just as the Lord had commanded Moses.

14 ¶ Then he brought the bull of the sin offering, and Aaron and his sons laid their hands on the head of the bull of the sin offering.

15 Next Moses slaughtered *it* and took the blood and with his finger put *some of it* around on the horns of the altar, and purified the altar. Then he poured out *the rest of* the blood at the base of the altar and consecrated it, to make atonement for it.

16 He also took all the fat that was on the entrails and the lobe of the liver, and the two kidneys and their fat; and Moses offered it up in smoke on the altar.

17 But the bull and its hide and its flesh and its refuse, he burned in the fire outside the camp, just as the Lord had commanded Moses.

18 ¶ Then he presented the ram of the burnt offering, and Aaron and his sons laid their hands on the head of the ram.

19 And Moses slaughtered *it* and sprinkled the blood around on the altar.

20 When he had cut the ram into its pieces, Moses offered up the head and the pieces and the suet in smoke.

21 After he had washed the entrails and the legs with water, Moses offered up the whole ram in smoke on the altar. It was a burnt offering for a soothing aroma; it was an offering by fire to the Lord, just as the Lord had commanded Moses.

22 ¶ Then he presented the second ram, the ram of ⁴ordination; and Aaron and his sons laid their hands on the head of the ram.

23 And Moses slaughtered *it* and took some of its blood and put it on the lobe of Aaron's right ear, and on the thumb of his right hand, and on the big toe of his right foot.

24 He also had Aaron's sons come near; and Moses put some of the blood on the lobe of their right ear, and on the thumb of their right hand, and on the big toe of their right foot. Moses then sprinkled *the rest of* the blood around on the altar.

25 And he took the fat, and the fat tail, and all the fat that was on the

entrails, and the lobe of the liver and the two kidneys and their fat and the right thigh.

26 And from the basket of unleavened bread that was before the Lord, he took one unleavened cake and one cake of bread *mixed with* oil and one wafer, and placed *them* on the portions of fat and on the right thigh.

27 He then put all *these* on the hands of Aaron and on the hands of his sons, and presented them as a wave offering before the Lord.

28 Then Moses took them from their hands and offered them up in smoke on the altar with the burnt offering. They were an ordination offering for a soothing aroma; it was an offering by fire to the Lord.

29 Moses also took the breast and presented it for a wave offering before the Lord; it was Moses' portion of the ram of ordination, just as the Lord had commanded Moses.

30 ¶ So Moses took some of the anointing oil and some of the blood which was on the altar, and sprinkled it on Aaron, on his garments, on his sons, and on the garments of his sons with him; and he consecrated Aaron, his garments, and his sons, and the garments of his sons with him.

31 ¶ Then Moses said to Aaron and to his sons, "Boil the flesh at the doorway of the tent of meeting, and eat it there together with the bread which is in the basket of the ordination offering, just as I commanded, saying, 'Aaron and his sons shall eat it.'

32"And the remainder of the flesh and of the bread you shall burn in the fire.

33"And you shall not go outside the doorway of the tent of meeting for seven days, until the day that the period of your ordination is fulfilled; for he will ordain you through seven days.

34"The Lord has commanded to do as has been done this day, to make atonement on your behalf.

35"At the doorway of the tent of meeting, moreover, you shall remain day and night for seven days, and keep the charge of the Lord, that you may not die, for so I have been commanded."

36 Thus Aaron and his sons did all

---

⁴ Lit., *filling,* and so throughout this context

the things which the LORD had commanded through Moses.

CHAPTER 9

NOW it came about on the eighth day that Moses called Aaron and his sons and the elders of Israel;

2 and he said to Aaron, "Take for yourself a calf, a bull, for a sin offering and a ram for a burnt offering, *both* without defect, and offer *them* before the LORD.

3"Then to the sons of Israel you shall speak, saying, 'Take a male goat for a sin offering, and a calf and a lamb, both one year old, without defect, for a burnt offering,

4 and an ox and a ram for peace offerings, to sacrifice before the LORD, and a grain offering mixed with oil; for today the LORD shall appear to you.'"

5 So they took what Moses had commanded to the front of the tent of meeting, and the whole congregation came near and stood before the LORD.

6 And Moses said, "This is the thing which the LORD has commanded you to do, that the glory of the LORD may appear to you."

7 Moses then said to Aaron, "Come near to the altar and offer your sin offering and your burnt offering, that you may make atonement for yourself and for the people; then make the offering for the people, that you may make atonement for them, just as the LORD has commanded."

8 ¶ So Aaron came near to the altar and slaughtered the calf of the sin offering which was for himself.

9 And Aaron's sons presented the blood to him; and he dipped his finger in the blood, and put *some* on the horns of the altar, and poured out *the rest of* the blood at the base of the altar.

10 The fat and the kidneys and the lobe of the liver of the sin offering, he then offered up in smoke on the altar just as the LORD had commanded Moses.

11 The flesh and the skin, however, he burned with fire outside the camp.

12 ¶ Then he slaughtered the burnt offering; and Aaron's sons handed the blood to him and he sprinkled it around on the altar.

13 And they handed the burnt offering to him in pieces with the head, and he offered *them* up in smoke on the altar.

14 He also washed the entrails and the legs, and offered *them* up in smoke with the burnt offering on the altar.

15 ¶ Then he presented the people's offering, and took the goat of the sin offering which was for the people, and slaughtered it and offered it for sin, like the first.

16 He also presented the burnt offering, and offered it according to the ordinance.

17 Next he presented the grain offering, and filled his hand with some of it and offered *it* up in smoke on the altar, besides the burnt offering of the morning.

18 ¶ Then he slaughtered the ox and the ram, the sacrifice of peace offerings which was for the people; and Aaron's sons handed the blood to him and he sprinkled it around on the altar.

19 As for the portions of fat from the ox and from the ram, the fat tail, and the *fat* covering, and the kidneys and the lobe of the liver,

20 they now placed the portions of fat on the breasts; and he offered them up in smoke on the altar.

21 But the breasts and the right thigh Aaron presented as a wave offering before the LORD, just as Moses had commanded.

22 ¶ Then Aaron lifted up his hands toward the people and blessed them, and he stepped down after making the sin offering and the burnt offering and the peace offerings.

23 And Moses and Aaron went into the tent of meeting. When they came out and blessed the people, the glory of the LORD appeared to all the people.

24 Then fire came out from before the LORD and consumed the burnt offering and the portions of fat on the altar; and when all the people saw *it*, they shouted and fell on their faces.

CHAPTER 10

NOW Nadab and Abihu, the sons of Aaron, took their respective firepans, and after putting fire in them, placed incense on it and offered strange fire before the LORD, which He had not commanded them.

2 And fire came out from the presence of the LORD and consumed them, and they died before the LORD.

3 Then Moses said to Aaron, "It is what the LORD spoke, saying,

'By those who come near Me I will be treated as holy,
And before all the people I will be honored.'"

So Aaron, therefore, kept silent.

4 Moses called also to Mishael and Elzaphan, the sons of Aaron's uncle Uzziel, and said to them, "Come forward, carry your relatives away from the front of the sanctuary to the outside of the camp."

5 So they came forward and carried them still in their tunics to the outside of the camp, as Moses had said.

6 Then Moses said to Aaron and to his sons Eleazar and Ithamar, "Do not [5]uncover your heads nor tear your clothes, so that you may not die, and that He may not become wrathful against all the congregation. But your kinsmen, the whole house of Israel, shall bewail the burning which the LORD has brought about.

7"You shall not even go out from the doorway of the tent of meeting, lest you die; for the LORD's anointing oil is upon you." So they did according to the word of Moses.

8 ¶ The LORD then spoke to Aaron, saying,

9"Do not drink wine or strong drink, neither you nor your sons with you, when you come into the tent of meeting, so that you may not die—it is a perpetual statute throughout your generations—

10 and so as to make a distinction between the holy and the profane, and between the unclean and the clean,

11 and so as to teach the sons of Israel all the statutes which the LORD has spoken to them through Moses."

12 ¶ Then Moses spoke to Aaron, and to his surviving sons, Eleazar and Ithamar, "Take the grain offering that is left over from the LORD's offerings by fire and eat it unleavened beside the altar, for it is most holy.

13"You shall eat it, moreover, in a holy place, because it is your due and

your sons' due out of the LORD's offerings by fire; for thus I have been commanded.

14"The breast of the wave offering, however, and the thigh of the offering you may eat in a clean place, you and your sons and your daughters with you; for they have been given as your due and your sons' due out of the sacrifices of the peace offerings of the sons of Israel.

15"The thigh offered by lifting up and the breast offered by waving, they shall bring along with the offerings by fire of the portions of fat, to present as a wave offering before the LORD; so it shall be a thing perpetually due you and your sons with you, just as the LORD has commanded."

16 ¶ But Moses searched carefully for the goat of the sin offering, and behold, it had been burned up! So he was angry with Aaron's surviving sons Eleazar and Ithamar, saying,

17"Why did you not eat the sin offering at the holy place? For it is most holy, and He gave it to you to bear away the guilt of the congregation, to make atonement for them before the LORD.

18"Behold, since its blood had not been brought inside, into the sanctuary, you should certainly have eaten it in the sanctuary, just as I commanded."

19 But Aaron spoke to Moses, "Behold, this very day they presented their sin offering and their burnt offering before the LORD. When things like these happened to me, if I had eaten a sin offering today, would it have been good in the sight of the LORD?"

20 And when Moses heard *that*, it seemed good in his sight.

CHAPTER 11

THE LORD spoke again to Moses and to Aaron, saying to them,

2"Speak to the sons of Israel, saying, 'These are the creatures which you may eat from all the animals that are on the earth.

3 'Whatever divides a hoof, thus making split hoofs, *and* chews the cud, among the animals, that you may eat.

4 'Nevertheless, you are not to eat of these, among those which chew the cud, or among those which divide the

[5] Lit., *unbind*

hoof: the camel, for though it chews cud, it does not divide the hoof, it is unclean to you.

5 'Likewise, the rock badger, for though it chews cud, it does not divide the hoof, it is unclean to you;

6 the rabbit also, for though it chews cud, it does not divide the hoof, it is unclean to you;

7 and the pig, for though it divides the hoof, thus making a split hoof, it does not chew cud, it is unclean to you.

8 'You shall not eat of their flesh nor touch their carcasses; they are unclean to you.

9 ¶ 'These you may eat, whatever is in the water: all that have fins and scales, those in the water, in the seas or in the rivers, you may eat.

10 'But whatever is in the seas and in the rivers, that do not have fins and scales among all the teeming life of the water, and among all the living creatures that are in the water, they are detestable things to you,

11 and they shall be [6]abhorrent to you; you may not eat of their flesh, and their carcasses you shall detest.

12 'Whatever in the water does not have fins and scales is abhorrent to you.

13 ¶ 'These, moreover, you shall detest among the birds; they are abhorrent, not to be eaten: the eagle and the vulture and the buzzard,

14 and the kite and the falcon in its kind,

15 every raven in its kind,

16 and the ostrich and the owl and the sea gull and the hawk in its kind,

17 and the little owl and the cormorant and the great owl,

18 and the white owl and the pelican and the carrion vulture,

19 and the stork, the heron in its kinds, and the hoopoe, and the bat.

20 ¶ 'All the winged insects that walk on *all* fours are detestable to you.

21 'Yet these you may eat among all the winged insects which walk on *all* fours: those which have above their feet jointed legs with which to jump on the earth.

22 'These of them you may eat: the locust in its kinds, and the devastating locust in its kinds, and the cricket in

its kinds, and the grasshopper in its kinds.

23 'But all other winged insects which are four-footed are detestable to you.

24 ¶ 'By these, moreover, you will be made unclean: whoever touches their carcasses becomes unclean until evening,

25 and whoever picks up any of their carcasses shall wash his clothes and be unclean until evening.

26 'Concerning all the animals which divide the hoof, but do not make a split *hoof*, or which do not chew cud, they are unclean to you: whoever touches them becomes unclean.

27 'Also whatever walks on its paws, among all the creatures that walk on *all* fours, are unclean to you; whoever touches their carcasses becomes unclean until evening,

28 and the one who picks up their carcasses shall wash his clothes and be unclean until evening; they are unclean to you.

29 ¶ 'Now these are to you the unclean among the swarming things which swarm on the earth: the mole, and the mouse, and the great lizard in its kinds,

30 and the gecko, and the crocodile, and the lizard, and the sand reptile, and the chameleon.

31 'These are to you the unclean among all the swarming things; whoever touches them when they are dead becomes unclean until evening.

32 'Also anything on which one of them may fall when they are dead, becomes unclean, including any wooden article, or clothing, or a skin, or a sack—any article of which use is made—it shall be put in the water and be unclean until evening, then it becomes clean.

33 'As for any earthenware vessel into which one of them may fall, whatever is in it becomes unclean and you shall break the vessel.

34 'Any of the food which may be eaten, on which water comes, shall become unclean; and any liquid which may be drunk in every vessel shall become unclean.

35 'Everything, moreover, on which part of their carcass may fall becomes

[6] Lit., *detestable things*

unclean; an oven or a [7]stove shall be smashed; they are unclean and shall continue as unclean to you.

36 'Nevertheless a spring or a cistern collecting water shall be clean, though the one who touches their carcass shall be unclean.

37 'And if a part of their carcass falls on any seed for sowing which is to be sown, it is clean.

38 'Though if water is put on the seed, and a part of their carcass falls on it, it is unclean to you.

39 ¶ 'Also if one of the animals dies which you have for food, the one who touches its carcass becomes unclean until evening.

40 'He too, who eats some of its carcass shall wash his clothes and be unclean until evening; and the one who picks up its carcass shall wash his clothes and be unclean until evening.

41 ¶ 'Now every swarming thing that swarms on the earth is detestable, not to be eaten.

42 'Whatever crawls on its belly, and whatever walks on *all* fours, whatever has many feet, in respect to every swarming thing that swarms on the earth, you shall not eat them, for they are detestable.

43 'Do not render yourselves detestable through any of the swarming things that swarm; and you shall not make yourselves unclean with them so that you become unclean.

44 'For I am the LORD your God. Consecrate yourselves therefore, and be holy; for I am holy. And you shall not make yourselves unclean with any of the swarming things that swarm on the earth.

45 'For I am the LORD, who brought you up from the land of Egypt, to be your God; thus you shall be holy for I am holy.' "

46 ¶ This is the law regarding the animal, and the bird, and every living thing that moves in the waters, and everything that swarms on the earth,

47 to make a distinction between the unclean and the clean, and between the edible creature and the creature which is not to be eaten.

CHAPTER 12

THEN the LORD spoke to Moses, saying,

2"Speak to the sons of Israel, saying, 'When a woman gives birth and bears a male *child*, then she shall be unclean for seven days, as in the days of her menstruation she shall be unclean.

3 'And on the eighth day the flesh of his foreskin shall be circumcised.

4 'Then she shall remain in the blood of *her* purification for thirty-three days; she shall not touch any consecrated thing, nor enter the sanctuary, until the days of her purification are completed.

5 'But if she bears a female *child*, then she shall be unclean for two weeks, as in her menstruation; and she shall remain in the blood of *her* purification for sixty-six days.

6 ¶ 'And when the days of her purification are completed, for a son or for a daughter, she shall bring to the priest at the doorway of the tent of meeting, a one year old lamb for a burnt offering, and a young pigeon or a turtledove for a sin offering.

7 'Then he shall offer it before the LORD and make atonement for her; and she shall be cleansed from the flow of her blood. This is the law for her who bears *a child, whether* a male or a female.

8 'But if she cannot afford a lamb, then she shall take two turtledoves or two young pigeons, the one for a burnt offering and the other for a sin offering; and the priest shall make atonement for her, and she shall be clean.' "

CHAPTER 13

THEN the LORD spoke to Moses and to Aaron, saying,

2"When a man has on the skin of his body a swelling or a scab or a bright spot, and it becomes [8]an infection of leprosy on the skin of his body, then he shall be brought to Aaron the priest, or to one of his sons the priests.

3"And the priest shall look at the mark on the skin of the body, and if the hair in the infection has turned white and the infection appears to be deeper than the skin of his body, it is an infection of leprosy; when the

---

[7] Lit., *hearth for supporting (two) pots*

[8] Lit., *a mark, stroke*, and so throughout this context

priest has looked at him, he shall pronounce him unclean.

4"But if the bright spot is white on the skin of his body, and it does not appear to be deeper than the skin, and the hair on it has not turned white, then the priest shall isolate *him who has* the infection for seven days.

5"And the priest shall look at him on the seventh day, and if in his eyes the infection has not changed, *and* the infection has not spread on the skin, then the priest shall isolate him for seven more days.

6"And the priest shall look at him again on the seventh day; and if the infection has faded, and the mark has not spread on the skin, then the priest shall pronounce him clean; it is *only* a scab. And he shall wash his clothes and be clean.

7 ¶"But if the scab spreads farther on the skin, after he has shown himself to the priest for his cleansing, he shall appear again to the priest.

8"And the priest shall look, and if the scab has spread on the skin, then the priest shall pronounce him unclean; it is leprosy.

9 ¶"When the infection of leprosy is on a man, then he shall be brought to the priest.

10"The priest shall then look, and if there is a white swelling in the skin, and it has turned the hair white, and there is quick raw flesh in the swelling,

11 it is a chronic leprosy on the skin of his body, and the priest shall pronounce him unclean; he shall not isolate him, for he is unclean.

12"And if the leprosy breaks out farther on the skin, and the leprosy covers all the skin of *him who has* the infection from his head even to his feet, as far as the priest can see,

13 then the priest shall look, and behold, *if* the leprosy has covered all his body, he shall pronounce clean *him who has* the infection; it has all turned white *and* he is clean.

14"But whenever raw flesh appears on him, he shall be unclean.

15"And the priest shall look at the raw flesh, and he shall pronounce him unclean; the raw flesh is unclean, it is leprosy.

16"Or if the raw flesh turns again and is changed to white, then he shall come to the priest,

17 and the priest shall look at him, and behold, *if* the infection has turned to white, then the priest shall pronounce clean *him who has* the infection; he is clean.

18 ¶"And when the body has a boil on its skin, and it is healed,

19 and in the place of the boil there is a white swelling or a reddish-white, bright spot, then it shall be shown to the priest;

20 and the priest shall look, and behold, *if* it appears to be lower than the skin, and the hair on it has turned white, then the priest shall pronounce him unclean; it is the infection of leprosy, it has broken out in the boil.

21"But if the priest looks at it, and behold, there are no white hairs in it and it is not lower than the skin and is faded, then the priest shall isolate him for seven days;

22 and if it spreads farther on the skin, then the priest shall pronounce him unclean; it is an infection.

23"But if the bright spot remains in its place, and does not spread, it is *only* the scar of the boil; and the priest shall pronounce him clean.

24 ¶"Or if the body sustains in its skin a burn by fire, and the raw *flesh* of the burn becomes a bright spot, reddish-white, or white,

25 then the priest shall look at it. And if the hair in the bright spot has turned white, and it appears to be deeper than the skin, it is leprosy; it has broken out in the burn. Therefore, the priest shall pronounce him unclean; it is an infection of leprosy.

26"But if the priest looks at it, and indeed, there is no white hair in the bright spot, and it is no deeper than the skin, but is dim, then the priest shall isolate him for seven days;

27 and the priest shall look at him on the seventh day. If it spreads farther in the skin, then the priest shall pronounce him unclean; it is an infection of leprosy.

28"But if the bright spot remains in its place, and has not spread in the skin, but is dim, it is the swelling from the burn; and the priest shall pronounce him clean, for it is *only* the scar of the burn.

29 ¶"Now if a man or woman has an infection on the head or on the beard,

30 then the priest shall look at the

infection, and if it appears to be deeper than the skin, and there is thin yellowish hair in it, then the priest shall pronounce him unclean; it is a scale, it is leprosy of the head or of the beard.

31"But if the priest looks at the infection of the scale, and indeed, it appears to be no deeper than the skin, and there is no black hair in it, then the priest shall isolate *the person* with the scaly infection for seven days.

32"And on the seventh day the priest shall look at the infection, and if the scale has not spread, and no yellowish hair has grown in it, and the appearance of the scale is no deeper than the skin,

33 then he shall shave himself, but he shall not shave the scale; and the priest shall isolate *the person* with the scale seven more days.

34"Then on the seventh day the priest shall look at the scale, and if the scale has not spread in the skin, and it appears to be no deeper than the skin, the priest shall pronounce him clean; and he shall wash his clothes and be clean.

35"But if the scale spreads farther in the skin after his cleansing,

36 then the priest shall look at him, and if the scale has spread in the skin, the priest need not seek for the yellowish hair; he is unclean.

37"If in his sight the scale has remained, however, and black hair has grown in it, the scale has healed, he is clean; and the priest shall pronounce him clean.

38 ¶"And when a man or a woman has bright spots on the skin of the body, *even* white bright spots,

39 then the priest shall look, and if the bright spots on the skin of their bodies are a faint white, it is eczema that has broken out on the skin; he is clean.

40 ¶"Now if a man loses the hair of his head, he is bald; he is clean.

41"And if his head becomes bald at the front and sides, he is bald on the forehead; he is clean.

42"But if on the bald head or the bald forehead, there occurs a reddish-white infection, it is leprosy breaking out on his bald head or on his bald forehead.

43"Then the priest shall look at him; and if the swelling of the infection is reddish-white on his bald head or on his bald forehead, like the appearance of leprosy in the skin of the body,

44 he is a leprous man, he is unclean. The priest shall surely pronounce him unclean; his infection is on his head.

45 ¶"As for the leper who has the infection, his clothes shall be torn, and the hair of his head shall be uncovered, and he shall cover his mustache and cry, 'Unclean! Unclean!'

46"He shall remain unclean all the days during which he has the infection; he is unclean. He shall live alone; his dwelling shall be outside the camp.

47"When a garment has a mark of leprosy in it, whether it is a wool garment or a linen garment,

48 whether in warp or woof, of linen or of wool, whether in leather or in any article made of leather,

49 if the mark is greenish or reddish in the garment or in the leather, or in the warp or in the woof, or in any article of leather, it is a leprous mark and shall be shown to the priest.

50"Then the priest shall look at the mark, and shall quarantine the article with the mark for seven days.

51"He shall then look at the mark on the seventh day; if the mark has spread in the garment, whether in the warp or in the woof, or in the leather, whatever the purpose for which the leather is used, the mark is a leprous malignancy, it is unclean.

52"So he shall burn the garment, whether the warp or the woof, in wool or in linen, or any article of leather in which the mark occurs, for it is a leprous malignancy; it shall be burned in the fire.

53 ¶"But if the priest shall look, and indeed, the mark has not spread in the garment, either in the warp or in the woof, or in any article of leather,

54 then the priest shall order them to wash the thing in which the mark occurs, and he shall quarantine it for seven more days.

55"After the article with the mark has been washed, the priest shall again look, and if the mark has not changed its appearance, even though the mark has not spread, it is unclean; you shall burn it in the fire, whether an eating away has produced bareness on the top or on the front of it.

56 ¶"Then if the priest shall look, and if the mark has faded after it has been washed, then he shall tear it out of the garment or out of the leather, whether from the warp or from the woof;

57 and if it appears again in the garment, whether in the warp or in the woof, or in any article of leather, it is an outbreak; the article with the mark shall be burned in the fire.

58"And the garment, whether the warp or the woof, or any article of leather from which the mark has departed when you washed it, it shall then be washed a second time and shall be clean."

59 ¶ This is the law for the mark of leprosy in a garment of wool or linen, whether in the warp or in the woof, or in any article of leather, for pronouncing it clean or unclean.

CHAPTER 14

THEN the LORD spoke to Moses, saying,

2 "This shall be the law of the leper in the day of his cleansing. Now he shall be brought to the priest,

3 and the priest shall go out to the outside of the camp. Thus the priest shall look, and if the infection of leprosy has been healed in the leper,

4 then the priest shall give orders to take two live clean birds and cedar wood and a scarlet string and hyssop for the one who is to be cleansed.

5"The priest shall also give orders to slay the one bird in an earthenware vessel over running water.

6"As for the live bird, he shall take it, together with the cedar wood and the scarlet string and the hyssop, and shall dip them and the live bird in the blood of the bird that was slain over the running water.

7"He shall then sprinkle seven times the one who is to be cleansed from the leprosy, and shall pronounce him clean, and shall let the live bird go free over the open field.

8"The one to be cleansed shall then wash his clothes and shave off all his hair, and bathe in water and be clean. Now afterward, he may enter the camp, but he shall stay outside his tent for seven days.

9"And it will be on the seventh day that he shall shave off all his hair: he shall shave his head and his beard and his eyebrows, even all his hair. He shall then wash his clothes and bathe his body in water and be clean.

10 ¶"Now on the eighth day he is to take two male lambs without defect, and a yearling ewe lamb without defect, and three-tenths of an ephah of fine flour mixed with oil for a grain offering, and one ⁹log of oil;

11 and the priest who pronounces him clean shall present the man to be cleansed and the aforesaid before the LORD at the doorway of the tent of meeting.

12"Then the priest shall take the one male lamb and bring it for a guilt offering, with the log of oil, and present them as a wave offering before the LORD.

13"Next he shall slaughter the male lamb in the place where they slaughter the sin offering and the burnt offering, at the place of the sanctuary—for the guilt offering, like the sin offering, belongs to the priest; it is most holy.

14"The priest shall then take some of the blood of the guilt offering, and the priest shall put it on the lobe of the right ear of the one to be cleansed, and on the thumb of his right hand, and on the big toe of his right foot.

15"The priest shall also take some of the log of oil, and pour it into his left palm;

16 the priest shall then dip his right-hand finger into the oil that is in his left palm, and with his finger sprinkle some of the oil seven times before the LORD.

17"And of the remaining oil which is in his palm, the priest shall put some on the right ear lobe of the one to be cleansed, and on the thumb of his right hand, and on the big toe of his right foot, on the blood of the guilt offering;

18 while the rest of the oil that is in the priest's palm, he shall put on the head of the one to be cleansed. So the priest shall make atonement on his behalf before the LORD.

19"The priest shall next offer the sin offering and make atonement for the one to be cleansed from his uncleanness. Then afterward, he shall slaughter the burnt offering.

⁹ I.e., Approx. one pint, and so through v. 24

20"And the priest shall offer up the burnt offering and the grain offering on the altar. Thus the priest shall make atonement for him, and he shall be clean.

21 ¶"But if he is poor, and his means are insufficient, then he is to take one male lamb for a guilt offering as a wave offering to make atonement for him, and one-tenth *of an ephah* of fine flour mixed with oil for a grain offering, and a log of oil,

22 and two turtledoves or two young pigeons which are within his means, the one shall be a sin offering and the other a burnt offering.

23"Then the eighth day he shall bring them for his cleansing to the priest, at the doorway of the tent of meeting, before the LORD.

24"And the priest shall take the lamb of the guilt offering, and the log of oil, and the priest shall offer them for a wave offering before the LORD.

25"Next he shall slaughter the lamb of the guilt offering; and the priest is to take some of the blood of the guilt offering and put *it* on the lobe of the right ear of the one to be cleansed and on the thumb of his right hand, and on the big toe of his right foot.

26"The priest shall also pour some of the oil into his left palm;

27 and with his right-hand finger the priest shall sprinkle some of the oil that is in his left palm seven times before the LORD.

28"The priest shall then put some of the oil that is in his palm on the lobe of the right ear of the one to be cleansed, and on the thumb of his right hand, and on the big toe of his right foot, on the place of the blood of the guilt offering.

29"Moreover, the rest of the oil that is in the priest's palm he shall put on the head of the one to be cleansed, to make atonement on his behalf before the LORD.

30"He shall then offer one of the turtledoves or young pigeons, which are within his means.

31"*He shall offer* what he can afford, the one for a sin offering, and the other for a burnt offering, together with the grain offering. So the priest shall make atonement before the LORD on behalf of the one to be cleansed.

32"This is the law *for him* in whom there is an infection of leprosy, whose means are limited for his cleansing."

33 ¶ The LORD further spoke to Moses and to Aaron, saying,

34"When you enter the land of Canaan, which I give you for a possession, and I put a mark of leprosy on a house in the land of your possession,

35 then the one who owns the house shall come and tell the priest, saying, 'Something like a mark *of leprosy* has become visible to me in the house.'

36"The priest shall then order that they empty the house before the priest goes in to look at the mark, so that everything in the house need not become unclean; and afterward the priest shall go in to look at the house.

37"So he shall look at the mark, and if the mark on the walls of the house has greenish or reddish depressions, and appears deeper than the surface;

38 then the priest shall come out of the house, to the doorway, and quarantine the house for seven days.

39"And the priest shall return on the seventh day and make an inspection. If the mark has indeed spread in the walls of the house,

40 then the priest shall order them to tear out the stones with the mark in them and throw them away at an unclean place outside the city.

41"And he shall have the house scraped all around inside, and they shall dump the plaster that they scrape off at an unclean place outside the city.

42"Then they shall take other stones and replace *those* stones; and he shall take other plaster and replaster the house.

43 ¶"If, however, the mark breaks out again in the house, after he has torn out the stones and scraped the house, and after it has been replastered,

44 then the priest shall come in and make an inspection. If he sees that the mark has indeed spread in the house, it is a malignant mark in the house; it is unclean.

45"He shall therefore tear down the house, its stones, and its timbers, and all the plaster of the house, and he shall take *them* outside the city to an unclean place.

46"Moreover, whoever goes into the house during the time that he has quarantined it, becomes unclean until evening.

47"Likewise, whoever lies down in the house shall wash his clothes, and whoever eats in the house shall wash his clothes.

48 ¶"If, on the other hand, the priest comes in and makes an inspection, and the mark has not indeed spread in the house after the house has been replastered, then the priest shall pronounce the house clean because the mark has not reappeared.

49"To cleanse the house then, he shall take two birds and cedar wood and a scarlet string and hyssop,

50 and he shall slaughter the one bird in an earthenware vessel over running water.

51"Then he shall take the cedar wood and the hyssop and the scarlet string, with the live bird, and dip them in the blood of the slain bird, as well as in the running water, and sprinkle the house seven times.

52"He shall thus cleanse the house with the blood of the bird and with the running water, along with the live bird and with the cedar wood and with the hyssop and with the scarlet string.

53"However, he shall let the live bird go free outside the city into the open field. So he shall make atonement for the house, and it shall be clean."

54 ¶ This is the law for any mark of leprosy—even for a scale,

55 and for the leprous garment or house,

56 and for a swelling, and for a scab, and for a bright spot—

57 to teach when they are unclean, and when they are clean. This is the law of leprosy.

CHAPTER 15

THE LORD also spoke to Moses and to Aaron, saying,

2"Speak to the sons of Israel, and say to them, 'When any man has a discharge from his body, his discharge is unclean.

3 'This, moreover, shall be his uncleanness in his discharge: it is his uncleanness whether his body allows its discharge to flow, or whether his body obstructs its discharge.

4 'Every bed on which the person with the discharge lies becomes unclean, and everything on which he sits becomes unclean.

5 'Anyone, moreover, who touches his bed shall wash his clothes and bathe in water and be unclean until evening;

6 and whoever sits on the thing on which the man with the discharge has been sitting, shall wash his clothes and bathe in water and be unclean until evening.

7 'Also whoever touches the person with the discharge shall wash his clothes and bathe in water and be unclean until evening.

8 'Or if the man with the discharge spits on one who is clean, he too shall wash his clothes and bathe in water and be unclean until evening.

9 'And every saddle on which the person with the discharge rides becomes unclean.

10 'Whoever then touches any of the things which were under him shall be unclean until evening, and he who carries them shall wash his clothes and bathe in water and be unclean until evening.

11 'Likewise, whomever the one with the discharge touches without having rinsed his hands in water shall wash his clothes and bathe in water and be unclean until evening.

12 'However, an earthenware vessel which the person with the discharge touches shall be broken, and every wooden vessel shall be rinsed in water.

13 ¶ 'Now when the man with the discharge becomes cleansed from his discharge, then he shall count off for himself seven days for his cleansing; he shall then wash his clothes and bathe his body in running water and shall become clean.

14 'Then on the eighth day he shall take for himself two turtledoves or two young pigeons, and come before the LORD to the doorway of the tent of meeting, and give them to the priest;

15 and the priest shall offer them, one for a sin offering, and the other for a burnt offering. So the priest shall make atonement on his behalf before the LORD because of his discharge.

16 ¶ 'Now if a man has a seminal emission, he shall bathe all his body in water and be unclean until evening.

17 'As for any garment or any leather on which there is seminal emission, it shall be washed with water and be unclean until evening.

18 'If a man lies with a woman *so that* there is a seminal emission, they shall both bathe in water and be unclean until evening.

19 ¶ 'When a woman has a discharge, *if* her discharge in her body is blood, she shall continue in her menstrual impurity for seven days; and whoever touches her shall be unclean until evening.

20 'Everything also on which she lies during her menstrual impurity shall be unclean, and everything on which she sits shall be unclean.

21 'And anyone who touches her bed shall wash his clothes and bathe in water and be unclean until evening.

22 'And whoever touches any thing on which she sits shall wash his clothes and bathe in water and be unclean until evening.

23 'Whether it be on the bed or on the thing on which she is sitting, when he touches it, he shall be unclean until evening.

24 'And if a man actually lies with her, so that her menstrual impurity is on him, he shall be unclean seven days, and every bed on which he lies shall be unclean.

25 ¶ 'Now if a woman has a discharge of her blood many days, not at the period of her menstrual impurity, or if she has a discharge beyond that period, all the days of her impure discharge she shall continue as though in her menstrual impurity; she is unclean.

26 'Any bed on which she lies all the days of her discharge shall be to her like her bed at menstruation; and every thing on which she sits shall be unclean, like her uncleanness at that time.

27 'Likewise, whoever touches them shall be unclean and shall wash his clothes and bathe in water and be unclean until evening.

28 'When she becomes clean from her discharge, she shall count off for herself seven days; and afterward she shall be clean.

29 'Then on the eighth day she shall take for herself two turtledoves or two young pigeons, and bring them in to the priest, to the doorway of the tent of meeting.

30 'And the priest shall offer the one for a sin offering and the other for a burnt offering. So the priest shall make atonement on her behalf before the LORD because of her impure discharge.'

31 ¶ "Thus you shall keep the sons of Israel separated from their uncleanness, lest they die in their uncleanness by their defiling My tabernacle that is among them."

32 This is the law for the one with a discharge, and for the man who has a seminal emission so that he is unclean by it,

33 and for the woman who is ill because of menstrual impurity, and for the one who has a discharge, whether a male or a female, or a man who lies with an unclean woman.

CHAPTER 16

NOW the LORD spoke to Moses after the death of the two sons of Aaron, when they had approached the presence of the LORD and died.

2 And the LORD said to Moses, "Tell your brother Aaron that he shall not enter at any time into the holy place inside the veil, before the [10]mercy seat which is on the ark, lest he die; for I will appear in the cloud over the mercy seat.

3 "Aaron shall enter the holy place with this: with a bull for a sin offering and a ram for a burnt offering.

4 "He shall put on the holy linen tunic, and the linen undergarments shall be next to his body, and he shall be girded with the linen sash, and attired with the linen turban (these are holy garments). Then he shall bathe his body in water and put them on.

5 "And he shall take from the congregation of the sons of Israel two male goats for a sin offering and one ram for a burnt offering.

6 "Then Aaron shall offer the bull for the sin offering which is for himself, that he may make atonement for himself and for his household.

7 "And he shall take the two goats and present them before the LORD at the doorway of the tent of meeting.

8 "And Aaron shall cast lots for the

[10] Lit., *propitiatory*

two goats, one lot for the LORD and the other lot for the [11]scapegoat.

9"Then Aaron shall offer the goat on which the lot for the LORD fell, and make it a sin offering.

10"But the goat on which the lot for the scapegoat fell, shall be presented alive before the LORD, to make atonement upon it, to send it into the wilderness as the scapegoat.

11 ¶"Then Aaron shall offer the bull of the sin offering which is for himself, and make atonement for himself and for his household, and he shall slaughter the bull of the sin offering which is for himself.

12"And he shall take a firepan full of coals of fire from upon the altar before the LORD, and two handfuls of finely ground sweet incense, and bring it inside the veil.

13"And he shall put the incense on the fire before the LORD, that the cloud of incense may cover the mercy seat that is on the ark of the testimony, lest he die.

14"Moreover, he shall take some of the blood of the bull and sprinkle it with his finger on the mercy seat on the east side; also in front of the mercy seat he shall sprinkle some of the blood with his finger seven times.

15 ¶"Then he shall slaughter the goat of the sin offering which is for the people, and bring its blood inside the veil, and do with its blood as he did with the blood of the bull, and sprinkle it on the mercy seat and in front of the mercy seat.

16"And he shall make atonement for the holy place, because of the impurities of the sons of Israel, and because of their transgressions, in regard to all their sins; and thus he shall do for the tent of meeting which abides with them in the midst of their impurities.

17"When he goes in to make atonement in the holy place, no one shall be in the tent of meeting until he comes out, that he may make atonement for himself and for his household and for all the assembly of Israel.

18"Then he shall go out to the altar that is before the LORD and make atonement for it, and shall take some of the blood of the bull and of the

blood of the goat, and put it on the horns of the altar on all sides.

19"And with his finger he shall sprinkle some of the blood on it seven times, and cleanse it, and from the impurities of the sons of Israel consecrate it.

20 ¶"When he finishes atoning for the holy place, and the tent of meeting and the altar, he shall offer the live goat.

21"Then Aaron shall lay both of his hands on the head of the live goat, and confess over it all the iniquities of the sons of Israel, and all their transgressions in regard to all their sins; and he shall lay them on the head of the goat and send it away into the wilderness by the hand of a man who stands in readiness.

22"And the goat shall bear on itself all their iniquities to a solitary land; and he shall release the goat in the wilderness.

23 ¶"Then Aaron shall come into the tent of meeting, and take off the linen garments which he put on when he went into the holy place, and shall leave them there.

24"And he shall bathe his body with water in a holy place and put on his clothes, and come forth and offer his burnt offering and the burnt offering of the people, and make atonement for himself and for the people.

25"Then he shall offer up in smoke the fat of the sin offering on the altar.

26"And the one who released the goat as the scapegoat shall wash his clothes and bathe his body with water; then afterward he shall come into the camp.

27"But the bull of the sin offering and the goat of the sin offering, whose blood was brought in to make atonement in the holy place, shall be taken outside the camp, and they shall burn their hides, their flesh, and their refuse in the fire.

28"Then the one who burns them shall wash his clothes and bathe his body with water, then afterward he shall come into the camp.

29 ¶"And this shall be a permanent statute for you: in the seventh month, on the tenth day of the month, you shall humble your souls, and not do

[11] Lit., goat of removal, or else a name: Azazel

any work, whether the native, or the alien who sojourns among you;

30 for it is on this day that atonement shall be made for you to cleanse you; you shall be clean from all your sins before the Lord.

31"It is to be a sabbath of solemn rest for you, that you may humble your souls; it is a permanent statute.

32"So the priest who is anointed and ordained to serve as priest in his father's place shall make atonement: he shall thus put on the linen garments, the holy garments,

33 and make atonement for the holy sanctuary; and he shall make atonement for the tent of meeting and for the altar. He shall also make atonement for the priests and for all the people of the assembly.

34"Now you shall have this as a permanent statute, to make atonement for the sons of Israel for all their sins once every year." And just as the Lord had commanded Moses, so he did.

CHAPTER 17

Then the Lord spoke to Moses, saying,

2"Speak to Aaron and to his sons, and to all the sons of Israel, and say to them, 'This is what the Lord has commanded, saying,

3"Any man from the house of Israel who slaughters an ox, or a lamb, or a goat in the camp, or who slaughters it outside the camp,

4 and has not brought it to the doorway of the tent of meeting to present it as an offering to the Lord before the tabernacle of the Lord, bloodguiltiness is to be reckoned to that man. He has shed blood and that man shall be cut off from among his people.

5"The reason is so that the sons of Israel may bring their sacrifices which they were sacrificing in the open field, that they may bring them in to the Lord, at the doorway of the tent of meeting to the priest, and sacrifice them as sacrifices of peace offerings to the Lord.

6"And the priest shall sprinkle the blood on the altar of the Lord at the doorway of the tent of meeting, and offer up the fat in smoke as a soothing aroma to the Lord.

7"And they shall no longer sacrifice their sacrifices to the goat demons with which they play the harlot. This shall be a permanent statute to them throughout their generations."'

8 ¶"Then you shall say to them, 'Any man from the house of Israel, or from the aliens who sojourn among them, who offers a burnt offering or sacrifice,

9 and does not bring it to the doorway of the tent of meeting to offer it to the Lord, that man also shall be cut off from his people.

10 ¶ 'And any man from the house of Israel, or from the aliens who sojourn among them, who eats any blood, I will set My face against that person who eats blood, and will cut him off from among his people.

11 'For the life of the flesh is in the blood, and I have given it to you on the altar to make atonement for your souls; for it is the blood by reason of the life that makes atonement.'

12"Therefore I said to the sons of Israel, 'No person among you may eat blood, nor may any alien who sojourns among you eat blood.'

13"So when any man from the sons of Israel, or from the aliens who sojourn among them, in hunting catches a beast or a bird which may be eaten, he shall pour out its blood and cover it with earth.

14 ¶"For as for the life of all flesh, its blood is identified with its life. Therefore I said to the sons of Israel, 'You are not to eat the blood of any flesh, for the life of all flesh is its blood; whoever eats it shall be cut off.'

15"And when any person eats an animal which dies, or is torn by beasts, whether he is a native or an alien, he shall wash his clothes and bathe in water, and remain unclean until evening; then he will become clean.

16"But if he does not wash them or bathe his body, then he shall bear his guilt."

CHAPTER 18

Then the Lord spoke to Moses, saying,

2"Speak to the sons of Israel and say to them, 'I am the Lord your God.

3 'You shall not do what is done in the land of Egypt where you lived, nor are you to do what is done in the land of Canaan where I am bringing you; you shall not walk in their statutes.

4 'You are to perform My judgments and keep My statutes, to live in accord with them; I am the LORD your God.

5 'So you shall keep My statutes and My judgments, by which a man may live if he does them; I am the LORD.

6 ¶ 'None of you shall approach any blood relative of his to uncover nakedness; I am the LORD.

7 'You shall not uncover the nakedness of your father, that is, the nakedness of your mother. She is your mother; you are not to uncover her nakedness.

8 'You shall not uncover the nakedness of your father's wife; it is your father's nakedness.

9 'The nakedness of your sister, *either* your father's daughter or your mother's daughter, whether born at home or born outside, their nakedness you shall not uncover.

10 'The nakedness of your son's daughter or your daughter's daughter, their nakedness you shall not uncover; for their nakedness is yours.

11 'The nakedness of your father's wife's daughter, born to your father, she is your sister, you shall not uncover her nakedness.

12 'You shall not uncover the nakedness of your father's sister; she is your father's blood relative.

13 'You shall not uncover the nakedness of your mother's sister, for she is your mother's blood relative.

14 'You shall not uncover the nakedness of your father's brother; you shall not approach his wife, she is your aunt.

15 'You shall not uncover the nakedness of your daughter-in-law; she is your son's wife, you shall not uncover her nakedness.

16 'You shall not uncover the nakedness of your brother's wife; it is your brother's nakedness.

17 'You shall not uncover the nakedness of a woman and of her daughter, nor shall you take her son's daughter or her daughter's daughter, to uncover her nakedness; they are blood relatives. It is lewdness.

18 'And you shall not marry a woman in addition to her sister as a rival while she is alive, to uncover her nakedness.

19 ¶ 'Also you shall not approach a woman to uncover her nakedness during her menstrual impurity.

20 'And you shall not have intercourse with your neighbor's wife, to be defiled with her.

21 'Neither shall you give any of your offspring to offer them to Molech, nor shall you profane the name of your God; I am the LORD.

22 'You shall not lie with a male as one lies with a female; it is an abomination.

23 'Also you shall not have intercourse with any animal to be defiled with it, nor shall any woman stand before an animal to mate with it; it is a perversion.

24 ¶ 'Do not defile yourselves by any of these things; for by all these the nations which I am casting out before you have become defiled.

25 'For the land has become defiled, therefore I have visited its punishment upon it, so the land has spewed out its inhabitants.

26 'But as for you, you are to keep My statutes and My judgments, and shall not do any of these abominations, *neither* the native, nor the alien who sojourns among you

27 (for the men of the land who have been before you have done all these abominations, and the land has become defiled);

28 so that the land may not spew you out, should you defile it, as it has spewed out the nation which has been before you.

29 'For whoever does any of these abominations, those persons who do *so* shall be cut off from among their people.

30 'Thus you are to keep My charge, that you do not practice any of the abominable customs which have been practiced before you, so as not to defile yourselves with them; I am the LORD your God.' "

CHAPTER 19

THEN the LORD spoke to Moses, saying,

2 "Speak to all the congregation of the sons of Israel and say to them,

'You shall be holy, for I the LORD your God am holy.

3 'Every one of you shall reverence his mother and his father, and you shall keep My sabbaths; I am the LORD your God.

4 'Do not turn to idols or make for yourselves molten gods; I am the LORD your God.

5 ¶ 'Now when you offer a sacrifice of peace offerings to the LORD, you shall offer it so that you may be accepted.

6 'It shall be eaten the same day you offer it, and the next day; but what remains until the third day shall be burned with fire.

7 'So if it is eaten at all on the third day, it is an offense; it will not be accepted.

8 'And everyone who eats it will bear his iniquity, for he has profaned the holy thing of the LORD; and that person shall be cut off from his people.

9 ¶ 'Now when you reap the harvest of your land, you shall not reap to the very corners of your field, neither shall you gather the gleanings of your harvest.

10 'Nor shall you glean your vineyard, nor shall you gather the fallen fruit of your vineyard; you shall leave them for the needy and for the stranger. I am the LORD your God.

11 ¶ 'You shall not steal, nor deal falsely, nor lie to one another.

12 'And you shall not swear falsely by My name, so as to profane the name of your God; I am the LORD.

13 ¶ 'You shall not oppress your neighbor, nor rob him. The wages of a hired man are not to remain with you all night until morning.

14 'You shall not curse a deaf man, nor place a stumbling block before the blind, but you shall revere your God; I am the LORD.

15 ¶ 'You shall do no injustice in judgment; you shall not be partial to the poor nor defer to the great, but you are to judge your neighbor fairly.

16 'You shall not go about as a slanderer among your people, and you are not to act against the life of your neighbor; I am the LORD.

17 ¶ 'You shall not hate your fellow countryman in your heart; you may surely reprove your neighbor, but shall not incur sin because of him.

18 'You shall not take vengeance, nor bear any grudge against the sons of your people, but you shall love your neighbor as yourself; I am the LORD.

19 ¶ 'You are to keep My statutes. You shall not breed together two kinds of your cattle; you shall not sow your field with two kinds of seed, nor wear a garment upon you of two kinds of material mixed together.

20 'Now if a man lies carnally with a woman who is a slave acquired for another man, but who has in no way been redeemed, nor given her freedom, there shall be punishment; they shall not, however, be put to death, because she was not free.

21 'And he shall bring his guilt offering to the LORD to the doorway of the tent of meeting, a ram for a guilt offering.

22 'The priest shall also make atonement for him with the ram of the guilt offering before the LORD for his sin which he has committed, and the sin which he has committed shall be forgiven him.

23 ¶ 'And when you enter the land and plant all kinds of trees for food, then you shall count their fruit as forbidden. Three years it shall be forbidden to you; it shall not be eaten.

24 'But in the fourth year all its fruit shall be holy, an offering of praise to the LORD.

25 'And in the fifth year you are to eat of its fruit, that its yield may increase for you; I am the LORD your God.

26 ¶ 'You shall not eat anything with the blood, nor practice divination or soothsaying.

27 'You shall not round off the sidegrowth of your heads, nor harm the edges of your beard.

28 'You shall not make any cuts in your body for the dead, nor make any tattoo marks on yourselves: I am the LORD.

29 ¶ 'Do not profane your daughter by making her a harlot, so that the land may not fall to harlotry, and the land become full of lewdness.

30 'You shall keep My sabbaths and revere My sanctuary; I am the LORD.

31 ¶ 'Do not turn to mediums or spiritists; do not seek them out to be defiled by them. I am the LORD your God.

32 ¶ 'You shall rise up before the grayheaded, and honor the aged, and you shall revere your God; I am the LORD.

33 ¶ 'When a stranger resides with you in your land, you shall not do him wrong.

34 'The stranger who resides with you shall be to you as the native among you, and you shall love him as yourself; for you were aliens in the land of Egypt: I am the LORD your God.

35 ¶ 'You shall do no wrong in judgment, in measurement of weight, or capacity.

36 'You shall have just balances, just weights, a just ^{12}ephah, and a just ^{13}hin: I am the LORD your God, who brought you out from the land of Egypt.

37 'You shall thus observe all My statutes, and all My ordinances, and do them: I am the LORD.'"

CHAPTER 20

Then the LORD spoke to Moses, saying,

2 "You shall also say to the sons of Israel, 'Any man from the sons of Israel or from the aliens sojourning in Israel, who gives any of his offspring to Molech, shall surely be put to death; the people of the land shall stone him with stones.

3 'I will also set My face against that man and will cut him off from among his people, because he has given some of his offspring to Molech, so as to defile My sanctuary and to profane My holy name.

4 'If the people of the land, however, should ever disregard that man when he gives any of his offspring to Molech, so as not to put him to death,

5 then I Myself will set My face against that man and against his family; and I will cut off from among their people both him and all those who play the harlot after him, by playing the harlot after Molech.

6 ¶ 'As for the person who turns to mediums and to spiritists, to play the harlot after them, I will also set My face against that person and will cut him off from among his people.

7 'You shall consecrate yourselves therefore and be holy, for I am the LORD your God.

8 'And you shall keep My statutes and practice them; I am the LORD who sanctifies you.

9 ¶ 'If *there is* anyone who curses his father or his mother, he shall surely be put to death; he has cursed his father or his mother, his bloodguiltiness is upon him.

10 ¶ 'If *there is* a man who commits adultery with another man's wife, one who commits adultery with his friend's wife, the adulterer and the adulteress shall surely be put to death.

11 'If *there is* a man who lies with his father's wife, he has uncovered his father's nakedness; both of them shall surely be put to death, their bloodguiltiness is upon them.

12 'If *there is* a man who lies with his daughter-in-law, both of them shall surely be put to death; they have committed incest, their bloodguiltiness is upon them.

13 'If *there is* a man who lies with a male as those who lie with a woman, both of them have committed a detestable act; they shall surely be put to death. Their bloodguiltiness is upon them.

14 'If *there is* a man who marries a woman and her mother, it is immorality; both he and they shall be burned with fire, that there may be no immorality in your midst.

15 'If *there is* a man who lies with an animal, he shall surely be put to death; you shall also kill the animal.

16 'If *there is* a woman who approaches any animal to mate with it, you shall kill the woman and the animal; they shall surely be put to death. Their bloodguiltiness is upon them.

17 ¶ 'If *there is* a man who takes his sister, his father's daughter or his mother's daughter, so that he sees her nakedness and she sees his nakedness, it is a disgrace; and they shall be cut off in the sight of the sons of their people. He has uncovered his sister's nakedness; he bears his guilt.

18 'If *there is* a man who lies with a menstruous woman and uncovers her nakedness, he has laid bare her flow, and she has exposed the flow of her blood; thus both of them shall be cut off from among their people.

^{12} I.e., Approx. one bushel ^{13} I.e., Approx. one gallon

19 'You shall also not uncover the nakedness of your mother's sister or of your father's sister, for such a one has made naked his blood relative; they shall bear their guilt.

20 'If *there is* a man who lies with his uncle's wife he has uncovered his uncle's nakedness; they shall bear their sin. They shall die childless.

21 'If *there is* a man who takes his brother's wife, it is abhorrent; he has uncovered his brother's nakedness. They shall be childless.

22 ¶ 'You are therefore to keep all My statutes and all My ordinances and do them, so that the land to which I am bringing you to live will not spew you out.

23 'Moreover, you shall not follow the customs of the nation which I shall drive out before you, for they did all these things, and therefore I have abhorred them.

24 'Hence I have said to you, "You are to possess their land, and I Myself will give it to you to possess it, a land flowing with milk and honey." I am the LORD your God, who has separated you from the peoples.

25 'You are therefore to make a distinction between the clean animal and the unclean, and between the unclean bird and the clean; and you shall not make yourselves detestable by animal or by bird or by anything that creeps on the ground, which I have separated for you as unclean.

26 'Thus you are to be holy to Me, for I the LORD am holy; and I have set you apart from the peoples to be Mine.

27 ¶ 'Now a man or a woman who is a medium or a spiritist shall surely be put to death. They shall be stoned with stones, their bloodguiltiness is upon them.' "

CHAPTER 21

THEN the LORD said to Moses, "Speak to the priests, the sons of Aaron, and say to them, 'No one shall defile himself for a *dead* person among his people,

2 except for his relatives who are nearest to him, his mother and his father and his son and his daughter and his brother,

3 also for his virgin sister, who is near to him because she has had no husband; for her he may defile himself.

4 'He shall not defile himself as a relative by marriage among his people, and so profane himself.

5 'They shall not make any baldness on their heads, nor shave off the edges of their beards, nor make any cuts in their flesh.

6 'They shall be holy to their God and not profane the name of their God, for they present the offerings by fire to the LORD, the bread of their God; so they shall be holy.

7 'They shall not take a woman who is profaned by harlotry, nor shall they take a woman divorced from her husband; for he is holy to his God.

8 'You shall consecrate him, therefore, for he offers the bread of your God; he shall be holy to you; for I the LORD, who sanctifies you, am holy.

9 'Also the daughter of any priest, if she profanes herself by harlotry, she profanes her father; she shall be burned with fire.

10 ¶ 'And the priest who is the highest among his brothers, on whose head the anointing oil has been poured, and who has been consecrated to wear the garments, shall not uncover his head, nor tear his clothes;

11 nor shall he approach any dead person, nor defile himself *even* for his father or his mother;

12 nor shall he go out of the sanctuary, nor profane the sanctuary of his God; for the consecration of the anointing oil of his God is on him: I am the LORD.

13 'And he shall take a wife in her virginity.

14 'A widow, or a divorced woman, or one who is profaned by harlotry, these he may not take; but rather he is to marry a virgin of his own people;

15 that he may not profane his offspring among his people: for I am the LORD who sanctifies him.' "

16 ¶ Then the LORD spoke to Moses, saying,

17 "Speak to Aaron, saying, 'No man of your offspring throughout their generations who has a defect shall approach to offer the bread of his God.

18 'For no one who has a defect shall approach: a blind man, or a lame man,

or he who has a disfigured *face*, or any deformed *limb*,

19 or a man who has a broken foot or broken hand,

20 or a hunchback or a dwarf, or *one who has* a defect in his eye or eczema or scabs or crushed testicles.

21 'No man among the descendants of Aaron the priest, who has a defect, is to come near to offer the LORD's offerings by fire; *since* he has a defect, he shall not come near to offer the bread of his God.

22 'He may eat the bread of his God, *both* of the most holy and of the holy,

23 only he shall not go in to the veil or come near the altar because he has a defect, that he may not profane My sanctuaries. For I am the LORD who sanctifies them.' "

24 So Moses spoke to Aaron and to his sons and to all the sons of Israel.

CHAPTER 22

THEN the LORD spoke to Moses, saying,

2 "Tell Aaron and his sons to be careful with the holy *gifts* of the sons of Israel, which they dedicate to Me, so as not to profane My holy name; I am the LORD.

3 "Say to them, 'If any man among all your descendants throughout your generations approaches the holy *gifts* which the sons of Israel dedicate to the LORD, while he has an uncleanness, that person shall be cut off from before Me. I am the LORD.

4 'No man, of the descendants of Aaron, who is a leper or who has a discharge, may eat of the holy *gifts* until he is clean. And if one touches anything made unclean by a corpse or if a man has a seminal emission,

5 or if a man touches any teeming things, by which he is made unclean, or any man by whom he is made unclean, whatever his uncleanness;

6 a person who touches any such shall be unclean until evening, and shall not eat of the holy *gifts*, unless he has bathed his body in water.

7 'But when the sun sets, he shall be clean, and afterward he shall eat of the holy *gifts*, for it is his food.

8 'He shall not eat *an animal* which dies or is torn *by beasts*, becoming unclean by it; I am the LORD.

9 'They shall therefore keep My charge, so that they may not bear sin because of it, and die thereby because they profane it; I am the LORD who sanctifies them.

10 ¶ 'No [14]layman, however, is to eat the holy *gift*; a sojourner with the priest or a hired man shall not eat of the holy *gift*.

11 'But if a priest buys a slave as *his* property with his money, that one may eat of it, and those who are born in his house may eat of his food.

12 'And if a priest's daughter is married to a layman, she shall not eat of the offering of the *gifts*.

13 'But if a priest's daughter becomes a widow or divorced, and has no child and returns to her father's house as in her youth, she shall eat of her father's food; but no layman shall eat of it.

14 'But if a man eats a holy *gift* unintentionally, then he shall add to it a fifth of it and shall give the holy *gift* to the priest.

15 'And they shall not profane the holy *gifts* of the sons of Israel which they offer to the LORD,

16 and *so* cause them to bear punishment for guilt by eating their holy *gifts*; for I am the LORD who sanctifies them.' "

17 ¶ Then the LORD spoke to Moses, saying,

18 "Speak to Aaron and to his sons and to all the sons of Israel, and say to them, 'Any man of the house of Israel or of the aliens in Israel who presents his offering, whether it is any of their votive or any of their freewill offerings, which they present to the LORD for a burnt offering—

19 for you to be accepted—*it must be* a male without defect from the cattle, the sheep, or the goats.

20 'Whatever has a defect, you shall not offer, for it will not be accepted for you.

21 'And when a man offers a sacrifice of peace offerings to the LORD to fulfill a special vow, or for a freewill offering, of the herd or of the flock, it must be perfect to be accepted; there shall be no defect in it.

22 'Those *that are* blind or fractured or maimed or having a running sore or eczema or scabs, you shall not offer to

[14] Lit., *stranger*

the Lord, nor make of them an offering by fire on the altar to the Lord.

23 'In respect to an ox or a lamb which has an overgrown or stunted *member*, you may present it for a freewill offering, but for a vow it shall not be accepted.

24 'Also anything *with its testicles* bruised or crushed or torn or cut, you shall not offer to the Lord, or sacrifice in your land,

25 nor shall you accept any such from the hand of a foreigner for offering as the food of your God; for their corruption is in them, they have a defect, they shall not be accepted for you.' "

26 ¶ Then the Lord spoke to Moses, saying,

27"When an ox or a sheep or a goat is born, it shall remain seven days with its mother, and from the eighth day on it shall be accepted as a sacrifice of an offering by fire to the Lord.

28"But, *whether* it is an ox or a sheep, you shall not kill *both* it and its young in one day.

29"And when you sacrifice a sacrifice of thanksgiving to the Lord, you shall sacrifice it so that you may be accepted.

30"It shall be eaten on the same day, you shall leave none of it until morning: I am the Lord.

31"So you shall keep My commandments, and do them: I am the Lord.

32"And you shall not profane My holy name, but I will be sanctified among the sons of Israel: I am the Lord who sanctifies you,

33 who brought you out from the land of Egypt, to be your God: I am the Lord."

CHAPTER 23

THE Lord spoke again to Moses, saying,

2"Speak to the sons of Israel, and say to them, 'The Lord's appointed times which you shall proclaim as holy convocations—My appointed times are these:

3 'For six days work may be done; but on the seventh day there is a sabbath of complete rest, a holy convocation. You shall not do any work; it is a sabbath to the Lord in all your dwellings.

4 ¶ 'These are the appointed times of the Lord, holy convocations which you shall proclaim at the times appointed for them.

5 'In the first month, on the fourteenth day of the month at twilight is the Lord's Passover.

6 'Then on the fifteenth day of the same month there is the Feast of Unleavened Bread to the Lord; for seven days you shall eat unleavened bread.

7 'On the first day you shall have a holy convocation; you shall not do any laborious work.

8 'But for seven days you shall present an offering by fire to the Lord. On the seventh day is a holy convocation; you shall not do any laborious work.' "

9 ¶ Then the Lord spoke to Moses, saying,

10"Speak to the sons of Israel, and say to them, 'When you enter the land which I am going to give to you and reap its harvest, then you shall bring in the sheaf of the first fruits of your harvest to the priest.

11 'And he shall wave the sheaf before the Lord for you to be accepted; on the day after the sabbath the priest shall wave it.

12 'Now on the day when you wave the sheaf, you shall offer a male lamb one year old without defect for a burnt offering to the Lord.

13 'Its grain offering shall then be two-tenths *of an ephah* of fine flour mixed with oil, an offering by fire to the Lord *for* a soothing aroma, with its libation, a fourth of a [15]hin of wine.

14 'Until this same day, until you have brought in the offering of your God, you shall eat neither bread nor roasted grain nor new growth. It is to be a perpetual statute throughout your generations in all your dwelling places.

15 ¶ 'You shall also count for yourselves from the day after the sabbath, from the day when you brought in the sheaf of the wave offering; there shall be seven complete sabbaths.

16 'You shall count fifty days to the day after the seventh sabbath; then you shall present a new grain offering to the Lord.

17 'You shall bring in from your dwelling places two *loaves* of bread for

[15] I.e., Approx. one gallon

a wave offering, made of two-tenths *of an ephah*; they shall be of a fine flour, baked with leaven as first fruits to the LORD.

18 'Along with the bread, you shall present seven one year old male lambs without defect, and a bull of the herd, and two rams; they are to be a burnt offering to the LORD, with their grain offering and their libations, an offering by fire of a soothing aroma to the LORD.

19 'You shall also offer one male goat for a sin offering and two male lambs one year old for a sacrifice of peace offerings.

20 'The priest shall then wave them with the bread of the first fruits for a wave offering with two lambs before the LORD; they are to be holy to the LORD for the priest.

21 'On this same day you shall make a proclamation as well; you are to have a holy convocation. You shall do no laborious work. It is to be a perpetual statute in all your dwelling places throughout your generations.

22 ¶ 'When you reap the harvest of your land, moreover, you shall not reap to the very corners of your field, nor gather the gleaning of your harvest; you are to leave them for the needy and the alien. I am the LORD your God.' "

23 ¶ Again the LORD spoke to Moses, saying,

24 "Speak to the sons of Israel, saying, 'In the seventh month on the first of the month, you shall have a rest, a reminder by blowing *of trumpets*, a holy convocation.

25 'You shall not do any laborious work, but you shall present an offering by fire to the LORD.' "

26 ¶ And the LORD spoke to Moses, saying,

27 "On exactly the tenth day of this seventh month is the day of atonement; it shall be a holy convocation for you, and you shall humble your souls and present an offering by fire to the LORD.

28 "Neither shall you do any work on this same day, for it is a day of atonement, to make atonement on your behalf before the LORD your God.

29 "If there is any person who will not humble himself on this same day, he shall be cut off from his people.

30 "As for any person who does any work on this same day, that person I will destroy from among his people.

31 "You shall do no work at all. It is to be a perpetual statute throughout your generations in all your dwelling places.

32 "It is to be a sabbath of complete rest to you, and you shall humble your souls; on the ninth of the month at evening, from evening until evening you shall keep your sabbath."

33 ¶ Again the LORD spoke to Moses, saying,

34 "Speak to the sons of Israel, saying, 'On the fifteenth of this seventh month is the Feast of Booths for seven days to the LORD.

35 'On the first day is a holy convocation; you shall do no laborious work of any kind.

36 'For seven days you shall present an offering by fire to the LORD. On the eighth day you shall have a holy convocation and present an offering by fire to the LORD; it is an assembly. You shall do no laborious work.

37 ¶ 'These are the appointed times of the LORD which you shall proclaim as holy convocations, to present offerings by fire to the LORD—burnt offerings and grain offerings, sacrifices and libations, *each* day's matter on its own day—

38 besides *those of* the sabbaths of the LORD, and besides your gifts, and besides all your votive and freewill offerings, which you give to the LORD.

39 ¶ 'On exactly the fifteenth day of the seventh month, when you have gathered in the crops of the land, you shall celebrate the feast of the LORD for seven days, with a rest on the first day and a rest on the eighth day.

40 'Now on the first day you shall take for yourselves the foliage of beautiful trees, palm branches and boughs of leafy trees and willows of the brook; and you shall rejoice before the LORD your God for seven days.

41 'You shall thus celebrate it *as* a feast to the LORD for seven days in the year. It *shall be* a perpetual statute throughout your generations; you shall celebrate it in the seventh month.

42 'You shall live in booths for seven days; all the native-born in Israel shall live in booths,

43 so that your generations may know that I had the sons of Israel live in booths when I brought them out from the land of Egypt. I am the LORD your God.' "

44 So Moses declared to the sons of Israel the appointed times of the LORD.

CHAPTER 24

THEN the LORD spoke to Moses, saying,

2"Command the sons of Israel that they bring to you clear oil from beaten olives for the light, to make a lamp burn continually.

3"Outside the veil of testimony in the tent of meeting, Aaron shall keep it in order from evening to morning before the LORD continually; *it shall be* a perpetual statute throughout your generations.

4"He shall keep the lamps in order on the pure *gold* lampstand before the LORD continually.

5 ¶"Then you shall take fine flour and bake twelve cakes with it; two-tenths *of an ephah* shall be *in* each cake.

6"And you shall set them *in* two rows, six *to* a row, on the pure *gold* table before the LORD.

7"And you shall put pure frankincense on each row, that it may be a memorial portion for the bread, *even* an offering by fire to the LORD.

8"Every sabbath day he shall set it in order before the LORD continually; it is an everlasting covenant for the sons of Israel.

9"And it shall be for Aaron and his sons, and they shall eat it in a holy place; for it is most holy to him from the LORD's offerings by fire, *his* portion forever."

10 ¶ Now the son of an Israelite woman, whose father was an Egyptian, went out among the sons of Israel; and the Israelite woman's son and a man of Israel struggled with each other in the camp.

11 And the son of the Israelite woman blasphemed the Name and cursed. So they brought him to Moses. (Now his mother's name was Shelomith, the daughter of Dibri, of the tribe of Dan.)

12 And they put him in custody so that the command of the LORD might be made clear to them.

13 ¶ Then the LORD spoke to Moses, saying,

14"Bring the one who has cursed outside the camp, and let all who heard him lay their hands on his head; then let all the congregation stone him.

15"And you shall speak to the sons of Israel, saying, 'If anyone curses his God, then he shall bear his sin.

16 'Moreover, the one who blasphemes the name of the LORD shall surely be put to death; all the congregation shall certainly stone him. The alien as well as the native, when he blasphemes the Name, shall be put to death.

17 ¶ 'And if a man takes the life of any human being, he shall surely be put to death.

18 'And the one who takes the life of an animal shall make it good, life for life.

19 'And if a man injures his neighbor, just as he has done, so it shall be done to him:

20 fracture for fracture, eye for eye, tooth for tooth; just as he has injured a man, so it shall be inflicted on him.

21 'Thus the one who kills an animal shall make it good, but the one who kills a man shall be put to death.

22 'There shall be one standard for you; it shall be for the stranger as well as the native, for I am the LORD your God.' "

23 Then Moses spoke to the sons of Israel, and they brought the one who had cursed outside the camp and stoned him with stones. Thus the sons of Israel did, just as the LORD had commanded Moses.

CHAPTER 25

THE LORD then spoke to Moses at Mount Sinai, saying,

2"Speak to the sons of Israel, and say to them, 'When you come into the land which I shall give you, then the land shall have a sabbath to the LORD.

3 'Six years you shall sow your field, and six years you shall prune your vineyard and gather in its crop,

4 but during the seventh year the land shall have a sabbath rest, a sabbath to the LORD; you shall not sow your field nor prune your vineyard.

5 'Your harvest's [16]aftergrowth you shall not reap, and your grapes of untrimmed vines you shall not gather; the land shall have a sabbatical year.

6 'And all of you shall have the sabbath *products* of the land for food; yourself, and your male and female slaves, and your hired man and your foreign resident, those who live as aliens with you.

7 'Even your cattle and the animals that are in your land shall have all its crops to eat.

8 ¶ 'You are also to count off seven sabbaths of years for yourself, seven times seven years, so that you have the time of the seven sabbaths of years, *namely,* forty-nine years.

9 'You shall then sound a ram's horn abroad on the tenth day of the seventh month; on the day of atonement you shall sound a horn all through your land.

10 'You shall thus consecrate the fiftieth year and proclaim [17]a release through the land to all its inhabitants. It shall be a jubilee for you, and each of you shall return to his own property, and each of you shall return to his family.

11 'You shall have the fiftieth year as a jubilee; you shall not sow, nor reap its aftergrowth, nor gather in *from* its untrimmed vines.

12 'For it is a jubilee; it shall be holy to you. You shall eat its crops out of the field.

13 ¶ 'On this year of jubilee each of you shall return to his own property.

14 'If you make a sale, moreover, to your friend, or buy from your friend's hand, you shall not wrong one another.

15 'Corresponding to the number of years after the jubilee, you shall buy from your friend; he is to sell to you according to the number of years of crops.

16 'In proportion to the extent of the years you shall increase its price, and in proportion to the fewness of the years, you shall diminish its price; for

it is a number of crops he is selling to you.

17 'So you shall not wrong one another, but you shall fear your God; for I am the LORD your God.

18 ¶ 'You shall thus observe My statutes, and keep My judgments, so as to carry them out, that you may live securely on the land.

19 'Then the land will yield its produce, so that you can eat your fill and live securely on it.

20 'But if you say, "What are we going to eat on the seventh year if we do not sow or gather in our crops?"

21 then I will so order My blessing for you in the sixth year that it will bring forth the crop for three years.

22 'When you are sowing the eighth year, you can still eat old things from the crop, eating *the old* until the ninth year when its crop comes in.

23 ¶ 'The land, moreover, shall not be sold permanently, for the land is Mine; for you are *but* aliens and sojourners with Me.

24 'Thus for every piece of your property, you are to provide for the redemption of the land.

25 'If a fellow countryman of yours becomes so poor he has to sell part of his property, then his nearest kinsman is to come and buy back what his relative has sold.

26 'Or in case a man has no kinsman, but so recovers his means as to find sufficient for its redemption,

27 then he shall calculate the years since its sale and refund the balance to the man to whom he sold it, and so return to his property.

28 'But if he has not found sufficient means to get it back for himself, then what he has sold shall remain in the hands of its purchaser until the year of jubilee; but at the jubilee it shall revert, that he may return to his property.

29 ¶ 'Likewise, if a man sells a dwelling house in a walled city, then his redemption right remains valid until a full year from its sale; his right of redemption lasts a full year.

30 'But if it is not bought back for him within the space of a full year, then the house that is in the walled city passes permanently to its purchaser throughout his generations; it does not revert in the jubilee.

[16] Lit., *growth from spilled kernels*   [17] Or, *liberty*

31 'The houses of the villages, however, which have no surrounding wall shall be considered as open fields; they have redemption rights and revert in the jubilee.

32 'As for cities of the Levites, the Levites have a permanent right of redemption for the houses of the cities which are their possession.

33 'What, therefore, belongs to the Levites may be redeemed and a house sale in the city of this possession reverts in the jubilee, for the houses of the cities of the Levites are their possession among the sons of Israel.

34 'But pasture fields of their cities shall not be sold, for that is their perpetual possession.

35 ¶ 'Now in case a countryman of yours becomes poor and his means with regard to you falter, then you are to sustain him, like a stranger or a sojourner, that he may live with you.

36 'Do not take usurious interest from him, but revere your God, that your countryman may live with you.

37 'You shall not give him your silver at interest, nor your food for gain.

38 'I am the LORD your God, who brought you out of the land of Egypt to give you the land of Canaan *and* to be your God.

39 ¶ 'And if a countryman of yours becomes so poor with regard to you that he sells himself to you, you shall not subject him to a slave's service.

40 'He shall be with you as a hired man, as if he were a sojourner; he shall serve with you until the year of jubilee.

41 'He shall then go out from you, he and his sons with him, and shall go back to his family, that he may return to the property of his forefathers.

42 'For they are My servants whom I brought out from the land of Egypt; they are not to be sold *in* a slave sale.

43 'You shall not rule over him with severity, but are to revere your God.

44 'As for your male and female slaves whom you may have—you may acquire male and female slaves from the pagan nations that are around you.

45 'Then, too, *it is* out of the sons of the sojourners who live as aliens among you that you may gain acquisition, and out of their families who are with you, whom they will have produced in your land; they also may become your possession.

46 'You may even bequeath them to your sons after you, to receive as a possession; you can use them as permanent slaves. But in respect to your countrymen, the sons of Israel, you shall not rule with severity over one another.

47 ¶ 'Now if the means of a stranger or of a sojourner with you becomes sufficient, and a countryman of yours becomes so poor with regard to him as to sell himself to a stranger who is sojourning with you, or to the descendants of a stranger's family,

48 then he shall have redemption right after he has been sold. One of his brothers may redeem him,

49 or his uncle, or his uncle's son, may redeem him, or one of his blood relatives from his family may redeem him; or if he prospers, he may redeem himself.

50 'He then with his purchaser shall calculate from the year when he sold himself to him up to the year of jubilee; and the price of his sale shall correspond to the number of years. *It is* like the days of a hired man *that* he shall be with him.

51 'If there are still many years, he shall refund part of his purchase price in proportion to them for his own redemption;

52 and if few years remain until the year of jubilee, he shall so calculate with him. In proportion to his years he is to refund *the amount for* his redemption.

53 'Like a man hired year by year he shall be with him; he shall not rule over him with severity in your sight.

54 'Even if he is not redeemed by these *means*, he shall still go out in the year of jubilee, he and his sons with him.

55 'For the sons of Israel are My servants; they are My servants whom I brought out from the land of Egypt. I am the LORD your God.

CHAPTER 26

'YOU shall not make for yourselves idols, nor shall you set up for yourselves an image or a *sacred* pillar, nor shall you place a figured stone in your land to bow down to it; for I am the LORD your God.

2 'You shall keep My sabbaths and reverence My sanctuary; I am the LORD.

3 'If you walk in My statutes and keep My commandments so as to carry them out,

4 then I shall give you rains in their season, so that the land will yield its produce and the trees of the field will bear their fruit.

5 'Indeed, your threshing will last for you until grape gathering, and grape gathering will last until sowing time. You will thus eat your food to the full and live securely in your land.

6 'I shall also grant peace in the land, so that you may lie down with no one making *you* tremble. I shall also eliminate harmful beasts from the land, and no sword will pass through your land.

7 'But you will chase your enemies, and they will fall before you by the sword;

8 five of you will chase a hundred, and a hundred of you will chase ten thousand, and your enemies will fall before you by the sword.

9 'So I will turn toward you and make you fruitful and multiply you, and I will confirm My covenant with you.

10 'And you will eat the old supply and clear out the old because of the new.

11 'Moreover, I will make My dwelling among you, and My soul will not reject you.

12 'I will also walk among you and be your God, and you shall be My people.

13 'I am the LORD your God, who brought you out of the land of Egypt so that *you* should not be their slaves, and I broke the bars of your yoke and made you walk erect.

14 ¶ 'But if you do not obey Me and do not carry out all these commandments,

15 if, instead, you reject My statutes, and if your soul abhors My ordinances so as not to carry out all My commandments, *and* so break My covenant,

16 I, in turn, will do this to you: I will appoint over you a sudden terror, consumption and fever that shall waste away the eyes and cause the

soul to pine away; also, you shall sow your seed uselessly, for your enemies shall eat it up.

17 'And I will set My face against you so that you shall be struck down before your enemies; and those who hate you shall rule over you, and you shall flee when no one is pursuing you.

18 'If also after these things, you do not obey Me, then I will punish you seven times more for your sins.

19 'And I will also break down your pride of power; I will also make your sky like iron and your earth like bronze.

20 'And your strength shall be spent uselessly, for your land shall not yield its produce and the trees of the land shall not yield their fruit.

21 ¶ 'If then, you act with hostility against Me and are unwilling to obey Me, I will increase the plague on you seven times according to your sins.

22 'And I will let loose among you the beasts of the field, which shall bereave you of your children and destroy your cattle and reduce your number so that your roads lie deserted.

23 ¶ 'And if by these things you are not turned to Me, but act with hostility against Me,

24 then I will act with hostility against you; and I, even I, will strike you seven times for your sins.

25 'I will also bring upon you a sword which will execute vengeance for the covenant; and when you gather together into your cities, I will send pestilence among you, so that you shall be delivered into enemy hands.

26 'When I break your staff of bread, ten women will bake your bread in one oven, and they will bring back your bread [18]in rationed amounts, so that you will eat and not be satisfied.

27 ¶ 'Yet if in spite of this, you do not obey Me, but act with hostility against Me,

28 then I will act with wrathful hostility against you; and I, even I, will punish you seven times for your sins.

29 'Further, you shall eat the flesh of your sons and the flesh of your daughters you shall eat.

30 'I then will destroy your high places, and cut down your incense altars, and heap your remains on the

[18] Lit., *by weight*

remains of your idols; for My soul shall abhor you.

31 'I will lay waste your cities as well, and will make your sanctuaries desolate; and I will not smell your soothing aromas.

32 'And I will make the land desolate so that your enemies who settle in it shall be appalled over it.

33 'You, however, I will scatter among the nations and will draw out a sword after you, as your land becomes desolate and your cities become waste.

34 ¶ 'Then the land will enjoy its sabbaths all the days of the desolation, while you are in your enemies' land; then the land will rest and enjoy its sabbaths.

35 'All the days of *its* desolation it will observe the rest which it did not observe on your sabbaths, while you were living on it.

36 'As for those of you who may be left, I will also bring weakness into their hearts in the lands of their enemies. And the sound of a driven leaf will chase them and even when no one is pursuing, they will flee as though from the sword, and they will fall.

37 'They will therefore stumble over each other as if *running* from the sword, although no one is pursuing; and you will have *no strength* to stand up before your enemies.

38 'But you will perish among the nations, and your enemies' land will consume you.

39 'So those of you who may be left will rot away because of their iniquity in the lands of your enemies; and also because of the iniquities of their forefathers they will rot away with them.

40 ¶ 'If they confess their iniquity and the iniquity of their forefathers, in their unfaithfulness which they committed against Me, and also in their acting with hostility against Me—

41 I also was acting with hostility against them, to bring them into the land of their enemies—or if their uncircumcised heart becomes humbled so that they then make amends for their iniquity,

42 then I will remember My covenant with Jacob, and I will remember also My covenant with Isaac, and My covenant with Abraham as well, and I will remember the land.

43 'For the land shall be abandoned by them, and shall make up for its sabbaths while it is made desolate without them. They, meanwhile, shall be making amends for their iniquity, because they rejected My ordinances and their soul abhorred My statutes.

44 'Yet in spite of this, when they are in the land of their enemies, I will not reject them, nor will I so abhor them as to destroy them, breaking My covenant with them; for I am the Lord their God.

45 'But I will remember for them the covenant with their ancestors, whom I brought out of the land of Egypt in the sight of the nations, that I might be their God. I am the Lord.' "

46 ¶ These are the statutes and ordinances and laws which the Lord established between Himself and the sons of Israel through Moses at Mount Sinai.

CHAPTER 27

AGAIN, the Lord spoke to Moses, saying,

2"Speak to the sons of Israel, and say to them, 'When a man makes a difficult vow, he *shall be valued* according to your valuation of persons belonging to the Lord.

3 'If your valuation is of the male from twenty years even to sixty years old, then your valuation shall be fifty shekels of silver, after the shekel of the sanctuary.

4 'Or if it is a female, then your valuation shall be thirty shekels.

5 'And if it be from five years even to twenty years old then your valuation for the male shall be twenty shekels, and for the female ten shekels.

6 'But if *they are* from a month even up to five years old, then your valuation shall be five shekels of silver for the male, and for the female your valuation shall be three shekels of silver.

7 'And if *they are* from sixty years old and upward, if it is a male, then your valuation shall be fifteen shekels, and for the female ten shekels.

8 'But if he is poorer than your valuation, then he shall be placed before the priest, and the priest shall value him; according to the means of the

one who vowed, the priest shall value him.

9 'Now if it is an animal of the kind which men can present as an offering to the LORD, any such that one gives to the LORD shall be holy.

10 'He shall not replace it or exchange it, a good for a bad, or a bad for a good; or if he does exchange animal for animal, then both it and its substitute shall become holy.

11 'If, however, it is any unclean animal of the kind which men do not present as an offering to the LORD, then he shall place the animal before the priest.

12 'And the priest shall value it as either good or bad; as you, the priest, value it, so it shall be.

13 'But if he should ever *wish to* redeem it, then he shall add one-fifth of it to your valuation.

14 ¶ 'Now if a man consecrates his house as holy to the LORD, then the priest shall value it as either good or bad; as the priest values it, so it shall stand.

15 'Yet if the one who consecrates it should *wish to* redeem his house, then he shall add one-fifth of your valuation price to it, so that it may be his.

16 ¶ 'Again, if a man consecrates to the LORD part of the fields of his own property, then your valuation shall be proportionate to the seed needed for it: a homer of barley seed at fifty shekels of silver.

17 'If he consecrates his field as of the year of jubilee, according to your valuation it shall stand.

18 'If he consecrates his field after the jubilee, however, then the priest shall calculate the price for him proportionate to the years that are left until the year of jubilee; and it shall be deducted from your valuation.

19 'And if the one who consecrates it should ever wish to redeem the field, then he shall add one-fifth of your valuation price to it, so that it may pass to him.

20 'Yet if he will not redeem the field, but has sold the field to another man, it may no longer be redeemed;

21 and when it reverts in the jubilee, the field shall be holy to the LORD, like a field set apart; it shall be for the priest as his property.

22 'Or if he consecrates to the LORD a field which he has bought, which is not a part of the field of his own property,

23 then the priest shall calculate for him the amount of your valuation up to the year of jubilee; and he shall on that day give your valuation as holy to the LORD.

24 'In the year of jubilee the field shall return to the one from whom he bought it, to whom the possession of the land belongs.

25 'Every valuation of yours, moreover, shall be after the shekel of the sanctuary. The shekel shall be twenty gerahs.

26 ¶ 'However, a first-born among animals, which as a first-born belongs to the LORD, no man may consecrate it; whether ox or sheep, it is the LORD's.

27 'But if *it is* among the unclean animals, then he shall redeem it according to your valuation, and add to it one-fifth of it; and if it is not redeemed, then it shall be sold according to your valuation.

28 ¶ 'Nevertheless, anything which a man [19]sets apart to the LORD out of all that he has, of man or animal or of the fields of his own property, shall not be sold or redeemed. Anything devoted to destruction is most holy to the LORD.

29 'No one who may have been set apart among men shall be ransomed; he shall surely be put to death.

30 ¶ 'Thus all the tithe of the land, of the seed of the land or of the fruit of the tree, is the LORD's; it is holy to the LORD.

31 'If, therefore, a man wishes to redeem part of his tithe, he shall add to it one-fifth of it.

32 'And for every tenth part of herd or flock, whatever passes under the rod, the tenth one shall be holy to the LORD.

33 'He is not to be concerned whether *it is* good or bad, nor shall he exchange it; or if he does exchange it, then both it and its substitute shall become holy. It shall not be redeemed.' "

34 ¶ These are the commandments which the LORD commanded Moses for the sons of Israel at Mount Sinai.

[19] Or, *puts under the ban*

NUMBERS

THEN the LORD spoke to Moses in the wilderness of Sinai, in the tent of meeting, on the first of the second month, in the second year after they had come out of the land of Egypt, saying,

2 "Take a ¹census of all the congregation of the sons of Israel, by their families, by their fathers' households, according to the number of names, every male, head by head

3 from twenty years old and upward, whoever *is able to* go out to war in Israel, you and Aaron shall ²number them by their armies.

4 "With you, moreover, there shall be a man of each tribe, each one head of his father's household.

5 "These then are the names of the men who shall stand with you: of Reuben, Elizur the son of Shedeur;

6 of Simeon, Shelumiel the son of Zurishaddai;

7 of Judah, Nahshon the son of Amminadab;

8 of Issachar, Nethanel the son of Zuar;

9 of Zebulun, Eliab the son of Helon;

10 of the sons of Joseph: of Ephraim, Elishama the son of Ammihud; of Manasseh, Gamaliel the son of Pedahzur;

11 of Benjamin, Abidan the son of Gideoni;

12 of Dan, Ahiezer the son of Ammishaddai;

13 of Asher, Pagiel the son of Ochran;

14 of Gad, Eliasaph the son of Deuel;

15 of Naphtali, Ahira the son of Enan.

16 "These are they who were called of the congregation, the leaders of their fathers' tribes; they were the heads of ³divisions of Israel."

17 So Moses and Aaron took these men who had been designated by name,

18 and they assembled all the congregation together on the first of the second month. Then they registered by ancestry in their families, by their fathers' households, according to the number of names, from twenty years old and upward, head by head,

19 just as the LORD had commanded Moses. So he numbered them in the wilderness of Sinai.

20 ¶ Now the sons of Reuben, Israel's first-born, their genealogical registration by their families, by their fathers' households, according to the number of names, head by head, every male from twenty years old and upward, whoever *was able to* go out to war,

21 their numbered men, of the tribe of Reuben, *were* 46,500.

22 ¶ Of the sons of Simeon, their genealogical registration by their families, by their fathers' households, their numbered men, according to the number of names, head by head, every male from twenty years old and upward, whoever *was able to* go out to war,

23 their numbered men, of the tribe of Simeon, *were* 59,300.

24 ¶ Of the sons of Gad, their genealogical registration by their families, by their fathers' households, according to the number of names, from twenty years old and upward, whoever *was able to* go out to war,

25 their numbered men, of the tribe of Gad, *were* 45,650.

26 ¶ Of the sons of Judah, their genealogical registration by their families, by their fathers' households, according to the number of names, from twenty years old and upward, whoever *was able to* go out to war,

27 their numbered men, of the tribe of Judah, *were* 74,600.

28 ¶ Of the sons of Issachar, their genealogical registration by their families, by their fathers' households, according to the number of names, from twenty years old and upward, whoever *was able to* go out to war,

29 their numbered men, of the tribe of Issachar, *were* 54,400.

30 ¶ Of the sons of Zebulun, their genealogical registration by their families, by their fathers' households, according to the number of names, from twenty years old and upward, whoever *was able to* go out to war,

31 their numbered men, of the tribe of Zebulun, *were* 57,400.

32 ¶ Of the sons of Joseph, *namely,* of the sons of Ephraim, their genealogical registration by their families,

---

¹ Lit., *sum* ² Lit., *muster,* and so throughout this context
³ Lit., *thousands,* or, *clans*

by their fathers' households, according to the number of names, from twenty years old and upward, whoever *was able to* go out to war,

33 their numbered men, of the tribe of Ephraim, *were* 40,500.

34 ¶ Of the sons of Manasseh, their genealogical registration by their families, by their fathers' households, according to the number of names, from twenty years old and upward, whoever *was able to* go out to war,

35 their numbered men, of the tribe of Manasseh, *were* 32,200.

36 ¶ Of the sons of Benjamin, their genealogical registration by their families, by their fathers' households, according to the number of names, from twenty years old and upward, whoever *was able to* go out to war,

37 their numbered men, of the tribe of Benjamin, *were* 35,400.

38 ¶ Of the sons of Dan, their genealogical registration by their families, by their fathers' households, according to the number of names, from twenty years old and upward, whoever *was able to* go out to war,

39 their numbered men, of the tribe of Dan, *were* 62,700.

40 ¶ Of the sons of Asher, their genealogical registration by their families, by their fathers' households, according to the number of names, from twenty years old and upward, whoever *was able to* go out to war,

41 their numbered men, of the tribe of Asher, *were* 41,500.

42 ¶ Of the sons of Naphtali, their genealogical registration by their families, by their fathers' households, according to the number of names, from twenty years old and upward, whoever *was able to* go out to war,

43 their numbered men, of the tribe of Naphtali, *were* 53,400.

44 ¶ These are the ones who were numbered, whom Moses and Aaron numbered, with the leaders of Israel, twelve men, each of whom was of his father's household.

45 So all the numbered men of the sons of Israel by their fathers' households, from twenty years old and upward, whoever *was able to* go out to war in Israel,

46 even all the numbered men were 603,550.

47 ¶ The Levites, however, were not numbered among them by their fathers' tribe.

48 For the LORD had spoken to Moses, saying,

49 "Only the tribe of Levi you shall not number, nor shall you take their census among the sons of Israel.

50 "But you shall appoint the Levites over the [4]tabernacle of the testimony, and over all its furnishings and over all that belongs to it. They shall carry the tabernacle and all its furnishings, and they shall take care of it; they shall also camp around the tabernacle.

51 "So when the tabernacle is to set out, the Levites shall take it down; and when the tabernacle encamps, the Levites shall set it up. But the [5]layman who comes near shall be put to death.

52 "And the sons of Israel shall camp, each man by his own camp, and each man by his own standard, according to their armies.

53 "But the Levites shall camp around the tabernacle of the testimony, that there may be no wrath on the congregation of the sons of Israel. So the Levites shall keep charge of the tabernacle of the testimony."

54 Thus the sons of Israel did; according to all which the LORD had commanded Moses, so they did.

CHAPTER 2

NOW the LORD spoke to Moses and to Aaron, saying,

2 "The sons of Israel shall camp, each by his own standard, with the banners of their fathers' households; they shall camp around the tent of meeting at a distance.

3 "Now those who camp on the east side toward the sunrise *shall be* of the standard of the camp of Judah, by their armies, and the leader of the sons of Judah: Nahshon the son of Amminadab,

4 and his army, even their numbered men, 74,600.

5 "And those who camp next to him *shall be* the tribe of Issachar, and the leader of the sons of Issachar: Nethanel the son of Zuar,

6 and his army, even their numbered men, 54,400.

7 "Then *comes* the tribe of Zebulun,

---

[4] Lit., *dwelling place,* and so throughout this context
[5] Lit., *stranger*

and the leader of the sons of Zebulun: Eliab the son of Helon,

8 and his army, even his numbered men, 57,400.

9"The total of the numbered men of the camp of Judah: 186,400, by their armies. They shall set out first.

10 ¶"On the south side *shall be* the standard of the camp of Reuben by their armies, and the leader of the sons of Reuben: Elizur the son of Shedeur,

11 and his army, even their numbered men, 46,500.

12"And those who camp next to him *shall be* the tribe of Simeon, and the leader of the sons of Simeon: Shelumiel the son of Zurishaddai,

13 and his army, even their numbered men, 59,300.

14"Then *comes* the tribe of Gad, and the leader of the sons of Gad: Eliasaph the son of Deuel,

15 and his army, even their numbered men, 45,650.

16"The total of the numbered men of the camp of Reuben: 151,450 by their armies. And they shall set out second.

17 ¶"Then the tent of meeting shall set out *with* the camp of the Levites in the midst of the camps; just as they camp, so they shall set out, every man in his place, by their standards.

18 ¶"On the west side *shall be* the standard of the camp of Ephraim by their armies, and the leader of the sons of Ephraim *shall be* Elishama the son of Ammihud,

19 and his army, even their numbered men, 40,500.

20"And next to him *shall be* the tribe of Manasseh, and the leader of the sons of Manasseh: Gamaliel the son of Pedahzur,

21 and his army, even their numbered men, 32,200.

22"Then *comes* the tribe of Benjamin, and the leader of the sons of Benjamin: Abidan the son of Gideoni,

23 and his army, even their numbered men, 35,400.

24"The total of the numbered men of the camp of Ephraim: 108,100, by their armies. And they shall set out third.

25 ¶"On the north side *shall be* the standard of the camp of Dan by their armies, and the leader of the sons of Dan: Ahiezer the son of Ammishaddai,

26 and his army, even their numbered men, 62,700.

27"And those who camp next to him *shall be* the tribe of Asher, and the leader of the sons of Asher: Pagiel the son of Ochran,

28 and his army, even their numbered men, 41,500.

29"Then *comes* the tribe of Naphtali, and the leader of the sons of Naphtali: Ahira the son of Enan,

30 and his army, even their numbered men, 53,400.

31"The total of the numbered men of the camp of Dan, *was* 157,600. They shall set out last by their standards."

32 ¶ These are the numbered men of the sons of Israel by their fathers' households; the total of the numbered men of the camps by their armies, 603,550.

33 The Levites, however, were not numbered among the sons of Israel, just as the LORD had commanded Moses.

34 Thus the sons of Israel did; according to all that the LORD commanded Moses, so they camped by their standards, and so they set out, every one by his family, according to his father's household.

CHAPTER 3

NOW these are *the records of* the generations of Aaron and Moses at the time when the LORD spoke with Moses on Mount Sinai.

2 These then are the names of the sons of Aaron: Nadab the first-born, and Abihu, Eleazar and Ithamar.

3 These are the names of the sons of Aaron, the anointed priests, whom he ordained to serve as priests.

4 But Nadab and Abihu died before the LORD when they offered strange fire before the LORD in the wilderness of Sinai; and they had no children. So Eleazar and Ithamar served as priests in the lifetime of their father Aaron.

5 ¶ Then the LORD spoke to Moses, saying,

6"Bring the tribe of Levi near and set them before Aaron the priest, that they may serve him.

7"And they shall perform the duties for him and for the whole congregation before the tent of meeting, to do the service of the tabernacle.

8"They shall also keep all the furnishings of the tent of meeting, along with the duties of the sons of Israel, to do the service of the tabernacle.

9"You shall thus give the Levites to Aaron and to his sons; they are wholly given to him from among the sons of Israel.

10"So you shall appoint Aaron and his sons that they may keep their priesthood, but the layman who comes near shall be put to death."

11 ¶ Again the LORD spoke to Moses, saying,

12"Now, behold, I have taken the Levites from among the sons of Israel instead of every first-born, the first issue of the womb among the sons of Israel. So the Levites shall be Mine.

13"For all the first-born are Mine; on the day that I struck down all the first-born in the land of Egypt, I sanctified to Myself all the first-born in Israel, from man to beast. They shall be Mine; I am the LORD."

14 ¶ Then the LORD spoke to Moses in the wilderness of Sinai, saying,

15"Number the sons of Levi by their fathers' households, by their families; every male from a month old and upward you shall number."

16 So Moses numbered them according to the word of the LORD, just as he had been commanded.

17 These then are the sons of Levi by their names: Gershon and Kohath and Merari.

18 And these are the names of the sons of Gershon by their families: Libni and Shimei;

19 and the sons of Kohath by their families: Amram and Izhar, Hebron and Uzziel;

20 and the sons of Merari by their families: Mahli and Mushi. These are the families of the Levites according to their fathers' households.

21 ¶ Of Gershon was the family of the Libnites and the family of the Shimeites; these were the families of the Gershonites.

22 Their numbered men, in the numbering of every male from a month old and upward, even their numbered men were 7,500.

23 The families of the Gershonites were to camp behind the tabernacle westward,

24 and the leader of the fathers' households of the Gershonites was Eliasaph the son of Lael.

25 Now the duties of the sons of Gershon in the tent of meeting involved the tabernacle and the tent, its covering, and the screen for the doorway of the tent of meeting,

26 and the hangings of the court, and the screen for the doorway of the court, which is around the tabernacle and the altar, and its cords, according to all the service concerning them.

27 ¶ And of Kohath was the family of the Amramites and the family of the Izharites and the family of the Hebronites and the family of the Uzzielites; these were the families of the Kohathites.

28 In the numbering of every male from a month old and upward, there were 8,600, performing the duties of the sanctuary.

29 The families of the sons of Kohath were to camp on the southward side of the tabernacle,

30 and the leader of the fathers' households of the Kohathite families was Elizaphan the son of Uzziel.

31 Now their duties involved the ark, the table, the lampstand, the altars, and the utensils of the sanctuary with which they minister, and the screen, and all the service concerning them;

32 and Eleazar the son of Aaron the priest was the chief of the leaders of Levi, and had the oversight of those who perform the duties of the sanctuary.

33 ¶ Of Merari was the family of the Mahlites and the family of the Mushites; these were the families of Merari.

34 Their numbered men in the numbering of every male from a month old and upward, were 6,200.

35 And the leader of the fathers' households of the families of Merari was Zuriel the son of Abihail. They were to camp on the northward side of the tabernacle.

36 Now the appointed duties of the sons of Merari involved the frames of the tabernacle, its bars, its pillars, its sockets, all its equipment, and the service concerning them,

37 and the pillars around the court with their sockets and their pegs and their cords.

38 ¶ Now those who were to camp before the tabernacle eastward, before the tent of meeting toward the

sunrise, are Moses and Aaron and his sons, performing the duties of the sanctuary for the obligation of the sons of Israel; but the layman coming near was to be put to death.

39 All the numbered men of the Levites, whom Moses and Aaron numbered at the command of the LORD by their families, every male from a month old and upward, were 22,000.

40 ¶ Then the LORD said to Moses, "Number every first-born male of the sons of Israel from a month old and upward, and make a list of their names.

41"And you shall take the Levites for Me, I am the LORD, instead of all the first-born among the sons of Israel, and the cattle of the Levites instead of all the first-born among the cattle of the sons of Israel."

42 So Moses numbered all the first-born among the sons of Israel, just as the LORD had commanded him;

43 and all the first-born males by the number of names from a month old and upward, for their numbered men were 22,273.

44 ¶ Then the LORD spoke to Moses, saying,

45"Take the Levites instead of all the first-born among the sons of Israel and the cattle of the Levites. And the Levites shall be Mine; I am the LORD.

46"And for the ransom of the 273 of the first-born of the sons of Israel who are in excess beyond the Levites,

47 you shall take five shekels apiece, per head; you shall take them in terms of the shekel of the sanctuary (the shekel is twenty [6]gerahs),

48 and give the money, the ransom of those who are in excess among them, to Aaron and to his sons."

49 So Moses took the ransom money from those who were in excess, beyond those ransomed by the Levites;

50 from the first-born of the sons of Israel he took the money in terms of the shekel of the sanctuary, 1,365.

51 Then Moses gave the ransom money to Aaron and to his sons, at the command of the LORD, just as the LORD had commanded Moses.

CHAPTER 4

THEN the LORD spoke to Moses and to Aaron, saying,

[6] I.e., A gerah equals approx. one-fortieth ounce

2"Take a census of the descendants of Kohath from among the sons of Levi, by their families, by their fathers' households,

3 from thirty years and upward, even to fifty years old, all who enter the service to do the work in the tent of meeting.

4"This is the work of the descendants of Kohath in the tent of meeting, concerning the most holy things.

5"When the camp sets out, Aaron and his sons shall go in and they shall take down the veil of the screen and cover the ark of the testimony with it;

6 and they shall lay a covering of porpoise skin on it, and shall spread over it a cloth of pure blue, and shall insert its poles.

7"Over the table of the bread of the Presence they shall also spread a cloth of blue and put on it the dishes and the pans and the sacrificial bowls and the jars for the libation, and the continual bread shall be on it.

8"And they shall spread over them a cloth of scarlet material, and cover the same with a covering of porpoise skin, and they shall insert its poles.

9"Then they shall take a blue cloth and cover the lampstand for the light, along with its lamps and its snuffers, and its trays and all its oil vessels, by which they serve it;

10 and they shall put it and all its utensils in a covering of porpoise skin, and shall put it on the carrying bars.

11"And over the golden altar they shall spread a blue cloth and cover it with a covering of porpoise skin, and shall insert its poles;

12 and they shall take all the utensils of service, with which they serve in the sanctuary, and put them in a blue cloth and cover them with a covering of porpoise skin, and put them on the carrying bars.

13"Then they shall take away the ashes from the altar, and spread a purple cloth over it.

14"They shall also put on it all its utensils by which they serve in connection with it: the firepans, the forks and shovels and the basins, all the utensils of the altar; and they shall spread a cover of porpoise skin over it and insert its poles.

15"And when Aaron and his sons

have finished covering the holy *objects* and all the furnishings of the sanctuary, when the camp is to set out, after that the sons of Kohath shall come to carry *them,* so that they may not touch the holy *objects* and die. These are the things in the tent of meeting which the sons of Kohath are to carry.

16"And the responsibility of Eleazar the son of Aaron the priest is the oil for the light and the fragrant incense and the continual grain offering and the anointing oil—the responsibility of all the tabernacle and of all that is in it, with the sanctuary and its furnishings."

17 ¶ Then the LORD spoke to Moses and to Aaron, saying,

18"Do not let the tribe of the families of the Kohathites be cut off from among the Levites.

19"But do this to them that they may live and not die when they approach the most holy *objects:* Aaron and his sons shall go in and assign each of them to his work and to his load;

20 but they shall not go in to see the holy *objects* even for a moment, lest they die."

21 ¶ Then the LORD spoke to Moses, saying,

22"Take a census of the sons of Gershon also, by their fathers' households, by their families;

23 from thirty years and upward to fifty years old, you shall number them; all who enter to perform the service to do the work in the tent of meeting.

24"This is the service of the families of the Gershonites, in serving and in carrying:

25 they shall carry the curtains of the tabernacle and the tent of meeting *with* its covering and the covering of porpoise skin that is on top of it, and the screen for the doorway of the tent of meeting,

26 and the hangings of the court, and the screen for the doorway of the gate of the court which is around the tabernacle and the altar, and their cords and all the equipment for their service; and all that is to be done, they shall perform.

27"All the service of the sons of the Gershonites, in all their loads and in all their work, shall be *performed* at the command of Aaron and his sons; and

you shall assign to them as a duty all their loads.

28"This is the service of the families of the sons of the Gershonites in the tent of meeting, and their duties *shall be* under the direction of Ithamar the son of Aaron the priest.

29 ¶ "*As for* the sons of Merari, you shall number them by their families, by their fathers' households;

30 from thirty years and upward even to fifty years old, you shall number them, everyone who enters the service to do the work of the tent of meeting.

31"Now this is the duty of their loads, for all their service in the tent of meeting: the boards of the tabernacle and its bars and its pillars and its sockets,

32 and the pillars around the court and their sockets and their pegs and their cords, with all their equipment and with all their service; and you shall assign *each man* by name the items he is to carry.

33"This is the service of the families of the sons of Merari, according to all their service in the tent of meeting, under the direction of Ithamar the son of Aaron the priest."

34 ¶ So Moses and Aaron and the leaders of the congregation numbered the sons of the Kohathites by their families, and by their fathers' households,

35 from thirty years and upward even to fifty years old, everyone who entered the service for work in the tent of meeting.

36 And their numbered men by their families were 2,750.

37 These are the numbered men of the Kohathite families, everyone who was serving in the tent of meeting, whom Moses and Aaron numbered according to the commandment of the LORD through Moses.

38 ¶ And the numbered men of the sons of Gershon by their families, and by their fathers' households,

39 from thirty years and upward even to fifty years old, everyone who entered the service for work in the tent of meeting.

40 And their numbered men by their families, by their fathers' households, were 2,630.

41 These are the numbered men of

the families of the sons of Gershon, everyone who was serving in the tent of meeting, whom Moses and Aaron numbered according to the commandment of the LORD.

42 ¶ And the numbered men of the families of the sons of Merari by their families, by their fathers' households,

43 from thirty years and upward even to fifty years old, everyone who entered the service for work in the tent of meeting.

44 And their numbered men by their families were 3,200.

45 These are the numbered men of the families of the sons of Merari, whom Moses and Aaron numbered according to the commandment of the LORD through Moses.

46 ¶ All the numbered men of the Levites, whom Moses and Aaron and the leaders of Israel numbered, by their families and by their fathers' households,

47 from thirty years and upward even to fifty years old, everyone who could enter to do the work of service and the work of carrying in the tent of meeting.

48 And their numbered men were 8,580.

49 According to the commandment of the LORD through Moses, they were numbered, everyone by his serving or carrying; thus these were his numbered men, just as the LORD had commanded Moses.

CHAPTER 5

THEN the LORD spoke to Moses, saying,

2"Command the sons of Israel that they send away from the camp every leper and everyone having a discharge and everyone who is unclean because of a *dead* person.

3"You shall send away both male and female; you shall send them outside the camp so that they will not defile their camp where I dwell in their midst."

4 And the sons of Israel did so and sent them outside the camp; just as the LORD had spoken to Moses, thus the sons of Israel did.

5 ¶ Then the LORD spoke to Moses, saying,

6"Speak to the sons of Israel, 'When a man or woman commits any of the sins of mankind, acting unfaithfully against the LORD, and that person is guilty,

7 then he shall confess his sins which he has committed, and he shall make restitution in full for his wrong, and add to it one-fifth of it, and give *it* to him whom he has wronged.

8 'But if the man has no [7]relative to whom restitution may be made for the wrong, the restitution which is made for the wrong *must* go to the LORD for the priest, besides the ram of atonement, by which atonement is made for him.

9 'Also every contribution pertaining to all the holy *gifts* of the sons of Israel, which they offer to the priest, shall be his.

10 'So every man's holy *gifts* shall be his; whatever any man gives to the priest, it becomes his.' "

11 ¶ Then the LORD spoke to Moses, saying,

12"Speak to the sons of Israel, and say to them, 'If any man's wife goes astray and is unfaithful to him,

13 and a man has intercourse with her and it is hidden from the eyes of her husband and she is undetected, although she has defiled herself, and there is no witness against her and she has not been caught in the act,

14 if a spirit of jealousy comes over him and he is jealous of his wife when she has defiled herself, or if a spirit of jealousy comes over him and he is jealous of his wife when she has not defiled herself,

15 the man shall then bring his wife to the priest, and shall bring *as* an offering for her one-tenth of an ephah of barley meal; he shall not pour oil on it, nor put frankincense on it, for it is a grain offering of jealousy, a grain offering of memorial, a reminder of iniquity.

16 ¶ 'Then the priest shall bring her near and have her stand before the LORD,

17 and the priest shall take holy water in an earthenware vessel; and he shall take some of the dust that is on the floor of the tabernacle and put *it* into the water.

18 'The priest shall then have the

[7] Lit., *redeemer*

woman stand before the LORD and let *the hair of* the woman's head go loose, and place the grain offering of memorial in her hands, which is the grain offering of jealousy, and in the hand of the priest is to be the water of bitterness that brings a curse.

19 'And the priest shall have her take an oath and shall say to the woman, "If no man has lain with you and if you have not gone astray into uncleanness, *being* under *the authority of* your husband, be immune to this water of bitterness that brings a curse;

20 if you, however, have gone astray, *being* under *the authority of* your husband, and if you have defiled yourself and a man other than your husband has had intercourse with you"

21 (then the priest shall have the woman swear with the oath of the curse, and the priest shall say to the woman), "the LORD make you a curse and an oath among your people by the LORD's making your thigh waste away and your abdomen swell;

22 and this water that brings a curse shall go into your stomach, and make your abdomen swell and your thigh waste away." And the woman shall say, "Amen. Amen."

23 ¶ 'The priest shall then write these curses on a scroll, and he shall wash them off into the water of bitterness.

24 'Then he shall make the woman drink the water of bitterness that brings a curse, so that the water which brings a curse will go into her and *cause* bitterness.

25 'And the priest shall take the grain offering of jealousy from the woman's hand, and he shall wave the grain offering before the LORD and bring it to the altar;

26 and the priest shall take a handful of the grain offering as its memorial offering and offer *it* up in smoke on the altar, and afterward he shall make the woman drink the water.

27 'When he has made her drink the water, then it shall come about, if she has defiled herself and has been unfaithful to her husband, that the water which brings a curse shall go into her and *cause* bitterness, and her abdomen will swell and her thigh will waste away, and the woman will become a curse among her people.

28 'But if the woman has not defiled herself and is clean, she will then be free and conceive children.

29 ¶ 'This is the law of jealousy: when a wife, *being* under *the authority of* her husband, goes astray and defiles herself,

30 or when a spirit of jealousy comes over a man and he is jealous of his wife, he shall then make the woman stand before the LORD, and the priest shall apply all this law to her.

31 'Moreover, the man shall be free from guilt, but that woman shall bear her guilt.' "

CHAPTER 6

AGAIN the LORD spoke to Moses, saying,

2 "Speak to the sons of Israel, and say to them, 'When a man or woman makes a special vow, the vow of a [8]Nazirite, to dedicate himself to the LORD,

3 he shall abstain from wine and strong drink; he shall drink no vinegar, whether made from wine or strong drink, neither shall he drink any grape juice, nor eat fresh or dried grapes.

4 'All the days of his [9]separation he shall not eat anything that is produced by the grape vine, from *the* seeds even to *the* skin.

5 ¶ 'All the days of his vow of separation no razor shall pass over his head. He shall be holy until the days are fulfilled for which he separated himself to the LORD; he shall let the locks of hair on his head grow long.

6 ¶ 'All the days of his separation to the LORD he shall not go near to a dead person.

7 'He shall not make himself unclean for his father or for his mother, for his brother or for his sister, when they die, because his separation to God is on his head.

8 'All the days of his separation he is holy to the LORD.

9 ¶ 'But if a man dies very suddenly beside him and he defiles his dedicated head *of hair,* then he shall shave his head on the day when he becomes clean; he shall shave it on the seventh day.

[8] I.e., one separated
[9] Or, *living as a Nazirite,* and so through v. 21

10 'Then on the eighth day he shall bring two turtledoves or two young pigeons to the priest, to the doorway of the tent of meeting.

11 'And the priest shall offer one for a sin offering and *the* other for a burnt offering, and make atonement for him concerning his sin because of the *dead* person. And that same day he shall consecrate his head,

12 and shall dedicate to the LORD his days as a Nazirite, and shall bring a male lamb a year old for a guilt offering; but the former days shall be void because his separation was defiled.

13 ¶ 'Now this is the law of the Nazirite when the days of his separation are fulfilled, he shall bring the offering to the doorway of the tent of meeting.

14 'And he shall present his offering to the LORD: one male lamb a year old without defect for a burnt offering and one ewe-lamb a year old without defect for a sin offering and one ram without defect for a peace offering,

15 and a basket of unleavened cakes of fine flour mixed with oil and unleavened wafers spread with oil, along with their grain offering and their libations.

16 'Then the priest shall present *them* before the LORD and shall offer his sin offering and his burnt offering.

17 'He shall also offer the ram for a sacrifice of peace offerings to the LORD, together with the basket of unleavened cakes; the priest shall likewise offer its grain offering and its libation.

18 'The Nazirite shall then shave his dedicated head *of hair* at the doorway of the tent of meeting, and take the dedicated hair of his head and put *it* on the fire which is under the sacrifice of peace offerings.

19 'And the priest shall take the ram's shoulder *when it has been* boiled, and one unleavened cake out of the basket, and one unleavened wafer, and shall put *them* on the hands of the Nazirite after he has shaved his dedicated *hair*.

20 'Then the priest shall wave them for a wave offering before the LORD. It is holy for the priest, together with the breast offered by waving and the thigh offered by lifting up; and afterward the Nazirite may drink wine.'

21 ¶ "This is the law of the Nazirite who vows his offering to the LORD according to his separation, in addition to what *else* he can afford; according to his vow which he takes, so he shall do according to the law of his separation."

22 ¶ Then the LORD spoke to Moses, saying,

23 "Speak to Aaron and to his sons, saying, 'Thus you shall bless the sons of Israel. You shall say to them:

24 ¶   The LORD bless you, and keep
         you;

25 ¶   The LORD make His face shine
         on you,
         And be gracious to you;

26 ¶   The LORD lift up His counte-
         nance on you,
         And give you peace.'

27 "So they shall invoke My name on the sons of Israel, and I then will bless them."

CHAPTER 7

NOW it came about on the day that Moses had finished setting up the tabernacle, he anointed it and consecrated it with all its furnishings and the altar and all its utensils; he anointed them and consecrated them also.

2 Then the leaders of Israel, the heads of their fathers' households, made an offering (they were the leaders of the tribes; they were the ones who were over the numbered men).

3 When they brought their offering before the LORD, six covered carts and twelve oxen, a cart for *every* two of the leaders and an ox for each one, then they presented them before the tabernacle.

4 Then the LORD spoke to Moses, saying,

5 "Accept *these things* from them, that they may be used in the service of the tent of meeting, and you shall give them to the Levites, *to* each man according to his service."

6 So Moses took the carts and the oxen, and gave them to the Levites.

7 Two carts and four oxen he gave to the sons of Gershon, according to their service,

8 and four carts and eight oxen he gave to the sons of Merari, according to their service, under the direction of Ithamar the son of Aaron the priest.

9 But he did not give *any* to the sons of Kohath because theirs *was* the service of the holy *objects, which they* carried on the shoulder.

10 And the leaders offered the dedication *offering* for the altar when it was anointed, so the leaders offered their offering before the altar.

11 Then the LORD said to Moses, "Let them present their offering, one leader each day, for the dedication of the altar."

12 ¶ Now the one who presented his offering on the first day *was* Nahshon the son of Amminadab, of the tribe of Judah;

13 and his offering *was* one silver [10]dish whose weight *was* one hundred and thirty *shekels*, one silver bowl of seventy shekels, according to [11]the shekel of the sanctuary, both of them full of fine flour mixed with oil for a grain offering;

14 one gold pan of ten *shekels*, full of incense;

15 one bull, one ram, one male lamb one year old, for a burnt offering;

16 one male goat for a sin offering;

17 and for the sacrifice of peace offerings, two oxen, five rams, five male goats, five male lambs one year old. This *was* the offering of Nahshon the son of Amminadab.

18 ¶ On the second day Nethanel the son of Zuar, leader of Issachar, presented *an offering;*

19 he presented as his offering one silver dish whose weight *was* one hundred and thirty *shekels*, one silver bowl of seventy shekels, according to the shekel of the sanctuary, both of them full of fine flour mixed with oil for a grain offering;

20 one gold pan of ten *shekels*, full of incense;

21 one bull, one ram, one male lamb one year old, for a burnt offering;

22 one male goat for a sin offering;

23 and for the sacrifice of peace offerings, two oxen, five rams, five male goats, five male lambs one year old. This *was* the offering of Nethanel the son of Zuar.

24 ¶ On the third day *it was* Eliab the son of Helon, leader of the sons of Zebulun;

25 his offering *was* one silver dish whose weight *was* one hundred and thirty *shekels*, one silver bowl of seventy shekels, according to the shekel of the sanctuary, both of them full of fine flour mixed with oil for a grain offering;

26 one gold pan of ten *shekels*, full of incense;

27 one young bull, one ram, one male lamb one year old, for a burnt offering;

28 one male goat for a sin offering;

29 and for the sacrifice of peace offerings, two oxen, five rams, five male goats, five male lambs one year old. This *was* the offering of Eliab the son of Helon.

30 ¶ On the fourth day *it was* Elizur the son of Shedeur, leader of the sons of Reuben;

31 his offering *was* one silver dish whose weight *was* one hundred and thirty *shekels*, one silver bowl of seventy shekels, according to the shekel of the sanctuary, both of them full of fine flour mixed with oil for a grain offering;

32 one gold pan of ten *shekels*, full of incense;

33 one bull, one ram, one male lamb one year old, for a burnt offering;

34 one male goat for a sin offering;

35 and for the sacrifice of peace offerings, two oxen, five rams, five male goats, five male lambs one year old. This *was* the offering of Elizur the son of Shedeur.

36 ¶ On the fifth day *it was* Shelumiel the son of Zurishaddai, leader of the children of Simeon;

37 his offering *was* one silver dish whose weight *was* one hundred and thirty *shekels*, one silver bowl of seventy shekels, according to the shekel of the sanctuary, both of them full of fine flour mixed with oil for a grain offering;

38 one gold pan of ten *shekels*, full of incense;

39 one bull, one ram, one male lamb one year old, for a burnt offering;

40 one male goat for a sin offering;

41 and for the sacrifice of peace offerings, two oxen, five rams, five male goats, five male lambs one year old. This *was* the offering of Shelumiel the son of Zurishaddai.

---

[10] Or, *platter*, and so through v. 85
[11] I.e., Approx. one-half ounce, and so through v. 86

42 ¶ On the sixth day *it was* Eliasaph the son of Deuel, leader of the sons of Gad;

43 his offering *was* one silver dish whose weight *was* one hundred and thirty *shekels*, one silver bowl of seventy shekels, according to the shekel of the sanctuary, both of them full of fine flour mixed with oil for a grain offering;

44 one gold pan of ten *shekels*, full of incense;

45 one bull, one ram, one male lamb one year old, for a burnt offering;

46 one male goat for a sin offering;

47 and for the sacrifice of peace offerings, two oxen, five rams, five male goats, five male lambs one year old. This *was* the offering of Eliasaph the son of Deuel.

48 ¶ On the seventh day *it was* Elishama the son of Ammihud, leader of the sons of Ephraim;

49 his offering *was* one silver dish whose weight *was* one hundred and thirty *shekels*, one silver bowl of seventy shekels, according to the shekel of the sanctuary, both of them full of fine flour mixed with oil for a grain offering;

50 one gold pan of ten *shekels*, full of incense;

51 one bull, one ram, one male lamb one year old, for a burnt offering;

52 one male goat for a sin offering;

53 and for the sacrifice of peace offerings, two oxen, five rams, five male goats, five male lambs one year old. This *was* the offering of Elishama the son of Ammihud.

54 ¶ On the eighth day *it was* Gamaliel the son of Pedahzur, leader of the sons of Manasseh;

55 his offering *was* one silver dish whose weight *was* one hundred and thirty *shekels*, one silver bowl of seventy shekels, according to the shekel of the sanctuary, both of them full of fine flour mixed with oil for a grain offering;

56 one gold pan of ten *shekels*, full of incense;

57 one bull, one ram, one male lamb one year old, for a burnt offering;

58 one male goat for a sin offering;

59 and for the sacrifice of peace offerings, two oxen, five rams, five male goats, five male lambs one year old.

This *was* the offering of Gamaliel the son of Pedahzur.

60 ¶ On the ninth day *it was* Abidan the son of Gideoni, leader of the sons of Benjamin;

61 his offering *was* one silver dish whose weight *was* one hundred and thirty *shekels*, one silver bowl of seventy shekels, according to the shekel of the sanctuary, both of them full of fine flour mixed with oil for a grain offering;

62 one gold pan of ten *shekels*, full of incense;

63 one bull, one ram, one male lamb one year old, for a burnt offering;

64 one male goat for a sin offering;

65 and for the sacrifice of peace offerings, two oxen, five rams, five male goats, five male lambs one year old. This *was* the offering of Abidan the son of Gideoni.

66 ¶ On the tenth day *it was* Ahiezer the son of Ammishaddai, leader of the sons of Dan;

67 his offering *was* one silver dish whose weight *was* one hundred and thirty *shekels*, one silver bowl of seventy shekels, according to the shekel of the sanctuary, both of them full of fine flour mixed with oil for a grain offering;

68 one gold pan of ten *shekels*, full of incense;

69 one bull, one ram, one male lamb one year old, for a burnt offering;

70 one male goat for a sin offering;

71 and for the sacrifice of peace offerings, two oxen, five rams, five male goats, five male lambs one year old. This *was* the offering of Ahiezer the son of Ammishaddai.

72 ¶ On the eleventh day *it was* Pagiel the son of Ochran, leader of the sons of Asher;

73 his offering *was* one silver dish whose weight *was* one hundred and thirty *shekels*, one silver bowl of seventy shekels, according to the shekel of the sanctuary, both of them full of fine flour mixed with oil for a grain offering;

74 one gold pan of ten *shekels*, full of incense;

75 one bull, one ram, one male lamb one year old, for a burnt offering;

76 one male goat for a sin offering;

77 and for the sacrifice of peace offerings, two oxen, five rams, five male
goats, five male lambs one year old.
This *was* the offering of Pagiel the son
of Ochran.

78 ¶ On the twelfth day *it was* Ahira
the son of Enan, leader of the sons of
Naphtali;

79 his offering *was* one silver dish
whose weight *was* one hundred and
thirty *shekels,* one silver bowl of seventy shekels, according to the shekel
of the sanctuary, both of them full of
fine flour mixed with oil for a grain
offering;

80 one gold pan of ten *shekels,* full of
incense;

81 one bull, one ram, one male lamb
one year old, for a burnt offering;

82 one male goat for a sin offering;

83 and for the sacrifice of peace offerings, two oxen, five rams, five male
goats, five male lambs one year old.
This *was* the offering of Ahira the son
of Enan.

84 ¶ This *was* the dedication *offering*
for the altar from the leaders of Israel
when it was anointed: twelve silver
dishes, twelve silver bowls, twelve
gold pans,

85 each silver dish *weighing* one
hundred and thirty *shekels* and each
bowl seventy; all the silver of the
utensils *was* 2,400 *shekels,* according
to the shekel of the sanctuary;

86 the twelve gold pans, full of incense, *weighing* ten *shekels* apiece,
according to the shekel of the sanctuary, all the gold of the pans 120 *shekels;*

87 all the oxen for the burnt offering
twelve bulls, *all* the rams twelve, the
male lambs one year old with their
grain offering twelve, and the male
goats for a sin offering twelve;

88 and all the oxen for the sacrifice
of peace offerings 24 bulls, *all* the rams
60, the male goats 60, the male lambs
one year old 60. This *was* the dedication *offering* for the altar after it was
anointed.

89 ¶ Now when Moses went into the
tent of meeting to speak with Him, he
heard the voice speaking to him from
above the mercy seat that was on the
ark of the testimony, from between
the two cherubim, so He spoke to him.

CHAPTER 8

THEN the Lord spoke to Moses, saying,

2"Speak to Aaron and say to him,
'When you mount the lamps, the
seven lamps will give light in the front
of the lampstand.'"

3 Aaron therefore did so; he
mounted its lamps at the front of the
lampstand, just as the Lord had commanded Moses.

4 Now this was the workmanship of
the lampstand, hammered work of
gold; from its base to its flowers, it was
hammered work; according to the pattern which the Lord had showed Moses, so he made the lampstand.

5 ¶ Again the Lord spoke to Moses,
saying,

6"Take the Levites from among the
sons of Israel and cleanse them.

7"And thus you shall do to them, for
their cleansing: *sprinkle* purifying water on them, and let them use a razor
over their whole body, and wash their
clothes, and they shall be clean.

8"Then let them take a bull with its
grain offering, fine flour mixed with
oil; and a second bull you shall take
for a sin offering.

9"So you shall present the Levites
before the tent of meeting. You shall
also assemble the whole congregation
of the sons of Israel,

10 and present the Levites before the
Lord; and the sons of Israel shall lay
their hands on the Levites.

11"Aaron then shall present the Levites before the Lord as a wave offering from the sons of Israel, that they
may qualify to perform the service of
the Lord.

12"Now the Levites shall lay their
hands on the heads of the bulls; then
offer the one for a sin offering and the
other for a burnt offering to the Lord,
to make atonement for the Levites.

13"And you shall have the Levites
stand before Aaron and before his sons
so as to present them as a wave offering to the Lord.

14 ¶"Thus you shall separate the
Levites from among the sons of Israel,
and the Levites shall be Mine.

15"Then after that the Levites may
go in to serve the tent of meeting. But
you shall cleanse them and present
them as a wave offering;

16 for they are wholly given to Me from among the sons of Israel. I have taken them for Myself instead of every first issue of the womb, the first-born of all the sons of Israel.

17"For every first-born among the sons of Israel is Mine, among the men and among the animals; on the day that I struck down all the first-born in the land of Egypt I sanctified them for Myself.

18"But I have taken the Levites instead of every first-born among the sons of Israel.

19"And I have given the Levites as a gift to Aaron and to his sons from among the sons of Israel, to perform the service of the sons of Israel at the tent of meeting, and to make atonement on behalf of the sons of Israel, that there may be no plague among the sons of Israel by their coming near to the sanctuary."

20 ¶ Thus did Moses and Aaron and all the congregation of the sons of Israel to the Levites; according to all that the LORD had commanded Moses concerning the Levites, so the sons of Israel did to them.

21 The Levites, too, purified themselves from sin and washed their clothes; and Aaron presented them as a wave offering before the LORD. Aaron also made atonement for them to cleanse them.

22 Then after that the Levites went in to perform their service in the tent of meeting before Aaron and before his sons; just as the LORD had commanded Moses concerning the Levites, so they did to them.

23 ¶ Now the LORD spoke to Moses, saying,

24"This is what *applies* to the Levites: from twenty-five years old and upward they shall enter to perform service in the work of the tent of meeting.

25"But at the age of fifty years they shall retire from service in the work and not work any more.

26"They may, however, assist their brothers in the tent of meeting, to keep an obligation; but they *themselves* shall do no work. Thus you shall deal with the Levites concerning their obligations."

CHAPTER 9

THUS the LORD spoke to Moses in the wilderness of Sinai, in the first month of the second year after they had come out of the land of Egypt, saying,

2"Now, let the sons of Israel observe the Passover at its appointed time.

3"On the fourteenth day of this month, at twilight, you shall observe it at its appointed time; you shall observe it according to all its statutes and according to all its ordinances."

4 So Moses told the sons of Israel to observe the Passover.

5 And they observed the Passover in the first *month*, on the fourteenth day of the month, at twilight, in the wilderness of Sinai; according to all that the LORD had commanded Moses, so the sons of Israel did.

6 But there were *some* men who were unclean because of *the* dead person, so that they could not observe Passover on that day; so they came before Moses and Aaron on that day.

7 And those men said to him, "*Though* we are unclean because of *the* dead person, why are we restrained from presenting the offering of the LORD at its appointed time among the sons of Israel?"

8 Moses therefore said to them, "Wait, and I will listen to what the LORD will command concerning you."

9 ¶ Then the LORD spoke to Moses, saying,

10"Speak to the sons of Israel, saying, 'If any one of you or of your generations becomes unclean because of a *dead* person, or is on a distant journey, he may, however, observe the Passover to the LORD.

11 'In the second month on the fourteenth day at twilight, they shall observe it; they shall eat it with unleavened bread and bitter herbs.

12 'They shall leave none of it until morning, nor break a bone of it; according to all the statute of the Passover they shall observe it.

13 'But the man who is clean and is not on a journey, and yet neglects to observe the Passover, that person shall then be cut off from his people, for he did not present the offering of the LORD at its appointed time. That man shall bear his sin.

14 'And if an alien sojourns among you and observes the Passover to the LORD, according to the statute of the Passover and according to its ordinance, so he shall do; you shall have one statute, both for the alien and for the native of the land.' "

15 ¶ Now on the day that the tabernacle was erected the cloud covered the tabernacle, the tent of the testimony, and in the evening it was like the appearance of fire over the tabernacle, until morning.

16 So it was continuously; the cloud would cover it *by day,* and the appearance of fire by night.

17 And whenever the cloud was lifted from over the tent, afterward the sons of Israel would then set out; and in the place where the cloud settled down, there the sons of Israel would camp.

18 At the command of the LORD the sons of Israel would set out, and at the command of the LORD they would camp; as long as the cloud settled over the tabernacle, they remained camped.

19 Even when the cloud lingered over the tabernacle for many days, the sons of Israel would keep the LORD's charge and not set out.

20 If sometimes the cloud remained a few days over the tabernacle, according to the command of the LORD they remained camped. Then according to the command of the LORD they set out.

21 If sometimes the cloud remained from evening until morning, when the cloud was lifted in the morning, they would move out; or *if it remained* in the daytime and at night, whenever the cloud was lifted, they would set out.

22 Whether it was two days or a month or a year that the cloud lingered over the tabernacle, staying above it, the sons of Israel remained camped and did not set out; but when it was lifted, they did set out.

23 At the command of the LORD they camped, and at the command of the LORD they set out; they kept the LORD's charge, according to the command of the LORD through Moses.

CHAPTER 10

THE LORD spoke further to Moses, saying,

2 "Make yourself two trumpets of silver, of hammered work you shall make them; and you shall use them for summoning the congregation and for having the camps set out.

3 "And when both are blown, all the congregation shall gather themselves to you at the doorway of the tent of meeting.

4 "Yet if *only* one is blown, then the leaders, the heads of the divisions of Israel, shall assemble before you.

5 "But when you blow an alarm, the camps that are pitched on the east side shall set out.

6 "And when you blow an alarm the second time, the camps that are pitched on the south side shall set out; an alarm is to be blown for them to set out.

7 "When convening the assembly, however, you shall blow without sounding an alarm.

8 "The priestly sons of Aaron, moreover, shall blow the trumpets; and this shall be for you a perpetual statute throughout your generations.

9 "And when you go to war in your land against the adversary who attacks you, then you shall sound an alarm with the trumpets, that you may be remembered before the LORD your God, and be saved from your enemies.

10 "Also in the day of your gladness and in your appointed feasts, and on the first *days* of your months, you shall blow the trumpets over your burnt offerings, and over the sacrifices of your peace offerings; and they shall be as a reminder of you before your God. I am the LORD your God."

11 ¶ Now it came about in the second year, in the second month, on the twentieth of the month, that the cloud was lifted from over the tabernacle of the testimony;

12 and the sons of Israel set out on their journeys from the wilderness of Sinai. Then the cloud settled down in the wilderness of Paran.

13 So they moved out for the first time according to the commandment of the LORD through Moses.

14 And the standard of the camp of the sons of Judah, according to their armies, set out first, with Nahshon the son of Amminadab, over its army,

15 and Nethanel the son of Zuar,

over the tribal army of the sons of
Issachar;

16 and Eliab the son of Helon over
the tribal army of the sons of Zebulun.

17 ¶ Then the tabernacle was taken
down; and the sons of Gershon and
the sons of Merari, who were carrying
the tabernacle, set out.

18 Next the standard of the camp of
Reuben, according to their armies, set
out with Elizur the son of Shedeur,
over its army,

19 and Shelumiel the son of Zurishaddai over the tribal army of the
sons of Simeon,

20 and Eliasaph the son of Deuel was
over the tribal army of the sons of
Gad.

21 ¶ Then the Kohathites set out,
carrying the holy *objects;* and the
tabernacle was set up before their
arrival.

22 Next the standard of the camp of
the sons of Ephraim, according to
their armies, was set out, with Elishama the son of Ammihud over its
army,

23 and Gamaliel the son of Pedahzur
over the tribal army of the sons of
Manasseh;

24 and Abidan the son of Gideoni
over the tribal army of the sons of
Benjamin.

25 ¶ Then the standard of the camp
of the sons of Dan, according to their
armies, *which formed* the rear guard
for all the camps, set out, with Ahiezer
the son of Ammishaddai over its army,

26 and Pagiel the son of Ochran over
the tribal army of the sons of Asher;

27 and Ahira the son of Enan over
the tribal army of the sons of Naphtali.

28 This was the order of march of the
sons of Israel by their armies as they
set out.

29 ¶ Then Moses said to Hobab the
son of Reuel the Midianite, Moses'
father-in-law, "We are setting out to
the place of which the LORD said, 'I
will give it to you'; come with us and
we will do you good, for the LORD has
promised good concerning Israel."

30 But he said to him, "I will not
come, but rather will go to my *own*
land and relatives."

31 Then he said, "Please do not leave
us, inasmuch as you know where we
should camp in the wilderness, and
you will be as eyes for us.

32 "So it will be, if you go with us, it
will come about that whatever good
the LORD does for us, we will do for
you."

33 ¶ Thus they set out from the
mount of the LORD three days' journey, with the ark of the covenant of
the LORD journeying in front of them
for the three days, to seek out a resting place for them.

34 And the cloud of the LORD was
over them by day, when they set out
from the camp.

35 ¶ Then it came about when the
ark set out that Moses said,
   "Rise up, O LORD!
   And let Thine enemies be scat-
      tered,
   And let those who hate Thee flee
      [12]before Thee."

36 And when it came to rest, he said,
   "Return Thou, O LORD,
   To the myriad thousands of Is-
      rael."

CHAPTER 11

Now the people became like those
who complain of adversity in the hearing of the LORD; and when the LORD
heard *it,* His anger was kindled, and
the fire of the LORD burned among
them and consumed *some* of the outskirts of the camp.

2 The people therefore cried out to
Moses, and Moses prayed to the LORD,
and the fire died out.

3 So the name of that place was
called [13]Taberah, because the fire of
the LORD burned among them.

4 ¶ And the rabble who were
among them had greedy desires; and
also the sons of Israel wept again and
said, "Who will give us meat to eat?

5 "We remember the fish which we
used to eat free in Egypt, the cucum-
bers and the melons and the leeks and
the onions and the garlic,

6 but now our [14]appetite is gone.
There is nothing at all to look at except this manna."

7 Now the manna was like coriander seed, and its appearance like that
of bdellium.

8 The people would go about and
gather *it* and grind *it* between two
millstones or beat *it* in the mortar, and

[12] Or, *from Thy presence*   [13] I.e., *burning*
[14] Lit., *soul is dried up*

boil *it* in the pot and make cakes with it; and its taste was as the taste of cakes baked with oil.

9 And when the dew fell on the camp at night, the manna would fall with it.

10 ¶ Now Moses heard the people weeping throughout their families, each man at the doorway of his tent; and the anger of the LORD was kindled greatly, and Moses was displeased.

11 So Moses said to the LORD, "Why hast Thou ¹⁵been so hard on Thy servant? And why have I not found favor in Thy sight, that Thou hast laid the burden of all this people on me?

12"Was it I who conceived all this people? Was it I who brought them forth, that Thou shouldest say to me, 'Carry them in your bosom as a nurse carries a nursing infant, to the land which Thou didst swear to their fathers'?

13"Where am I to get meat to give to all this people? For they weep before me, saying, 'Give us meat that we may eat!'

14"I alone am not able to carry all this people, because it is too burdensome for me.

15"So if Thou art going to deal thus with me, please kill me at once, if I have found favor in Thy sight, and do not let me see my wretchedness."

16 ¶ The LORD therefore said to Moses, "Gather for Me seventy men from the elders of Israel, whom you know to be the elders of the people and their officers and bring them to the tent of meeting, and let them take their stand there with you.

17"Then I will come down and speak with you there, and I will take of the Spirit who is upon you, and will put *Him* upon them; and they shall bear the burden of the people with you, so that you shall not bear *it* all alone.

18"And say to the people, 'Consecrate yourselves for tomorrow, and you shall eat meat; for you have wept in the ears of the LORD, saying, "Oh that someone would give us meat to eat! For we were well-off in Egypt." Therefore the LORD will give you meat and you shall eat.

19 'You shall eat, not one day, nor

¹⁵ Lit., *dealt ill with*

two days, nor five days, nor ten days, nor twenty days,

20 but a whole month, until it comes out of your nostrils and becomes loathsome to you; because you have rejected the LORD who is among you and have wept before Him, saying, "Why did we ever leave Egypt?" ' "

21 But Moses said, "The people, among whom I am, are 600,000 on foot; yet Thou hast said, 'I will give them meat in order that they may eat for a whole month.'

22"Should flocks and herds be slaughtered for them, to be sufficient for them? Or should all the fish of the sea be gathered together for them, to be sufficient for them?"

23 And the LORD said to Moses, "Is the LORD's power limited? Now you shall see whether My word will come true for you or not."

24 ¶ So Moses went out and told the people the words of the LORD. Also, he gathered seventy men of the elders of the people, and stationed them around the tent.

25 Then the LORD came down in the cloud and spoke to him; and He took of the Spirit who was upon him and placed *Him* upon the seventy elders. And it came about that when the Spirit rested upon them, they prophesied. But they did not do *it* again.

26 ¶ But two men had remained in the camp; the name of one was Eldad and the name of the other Medad. And the Spirit rested upon them (now they were among those who had been registered, but had not gone out to the tent), and they prophesied in the camp.

27 So a young man ran and told Moses and said, "Eldad and Medad are prophesying in the camp."

28 Then Joshua the son of Nun, the attendant of Moses from his youth, answered and said, "Moses, my lord, restrain them."

29 But Moses said to him, "Are you jealous for my sake? Would that all the LORD's people were prophets, that the LORD would put His Spirit upon them!"

30 Then Moses returned to the camp, *both* he and the elders of Israel.

31 ¶ Now there went forth a wind from the LORD, and it brought quail from the sea, and let *them* fall beside

the camp, about a day's journey on this side and a day's journey on the other side, all around the camp, and about two cubits *deep* on the surface of the ground.

32 And the people spent all day and all night and all the next day, and gathered the quail (he who gathered least gathered ten homers) and they spread *them* out for themselves all around the camp.

33 While the meat was still between their teeth, before it was chewed, the anger of the LORD was kindled against the people, and the LORD struck the people with a very severe plague.

34 So the name of that place was called [16]Kibroth-hattaavah, because there they buried the people who had been greedy.

35 From Kibroth-hattaavah the people set out for Hazeroth, and they remained at Hazeroth.

CHAPTER 12

THEN Miriam and Aaron spoke against Moses because of the Cushite woman whom he had married (for he had married a Cushite woman);

2 and they said, "Has the LORD indeed spoken only through Moses? Has He not spoken through us as well?" And the LORD heard it.

3 (Now the man Moses was very humble, more than any man who was on the face of the earth.)

4 And suddenly the LORD said to Moses and Aaron and to Miriam, "You three come out to the tent of meeting." So the three of them came out.

5 Then the LORD came down in a pillar of cloud and stood at the doorway of the tent, and He called Aaron and Miriam. When they had both come forward,

6 He said,
"Hear now My words:
If there is a prophet among you,
I, the LORD, shall make Myself
   known to him in a vision.
I shall speak with him in a
   dream.

7 "Not so, with My servant Moses,
He is faithful in all My household;

8 With him I speak mouth to
   mouth,

Even openly, and not in dark
   sayings,
And he beholds the form of the
   LORD.
Why then were you not afraid
To speak against My servant,
   against Moses?"

9 ¶ So the anger of the LORD burned against them and He departed.

10 But when the cloud had withdrawn from over the tent, behold, Miriam *was* leprous, as *white as* snow. As Aaron turned toward Miriam, behold, she *was* leprous.

11 Then Aaron said to Moses, "Oh, my lord, I beg you, do not account *this* sin to us, in which we have acted foolishly and in which we have sinned.

12 "Oh, do not let her be like one dead, whose flesh is half eaten away when he comes from his mother's womb!"

13 And Moses cried out to the LORD, saying, "O God, heal her, I pray!"

14 But the LORD said to Moses, "If her father had but spit in her face, would she not bear her shame for seven days? Let her be shut up for seven days outside the camp, and afterward she may be received again."

15 So Miriam was shut up outside the camp for seven days, and the people did not move on until Miriam was received again.

16 ¶ Afterward, however, the people moved out from Hazeroth and camped in the wilderness of Paran.

CHAPTER 13

THEN the LORD spoke to Moses saying,

2 "Send out for yourself men so that they may spy out the land of Canaan, which I am going to give to the sons of Israel; you shall send a man from each of their fathers' tribes, every one a leader among them."

3 So Moses sent them from the wilderness of Paran at the command of the LORD, all of them men who were heads of the sons of Israel.

4 These then *were* their names: from the tribe of Reuben, Shammua the son of Zaccur;

5 from the tribe of Simeon, Shaphat the son of Hori;

6 from the tribe of Judah, Caleb the son of Jephunneh;

[16] I.e., the graves of greediness

7 from the tribe of Issachar, Igal the son of Joseph;

8 from the tribe of Ephraim, Hoshea the son of Nun;

9 from the tribe of Benjamin, Palti the son of Raphu;

10 from the tribe of Zebulun, Gaddiel the son of Sodi;

11 from the tribe of Joseph, from the tribe of Manasseh, Gaddi the son of Susi;

12 from the tribe of Dan, Ammiel the son of Gemalli;

13 from the tribe of Asher, Sethur the son of Michael;

14 from the tribe of Naphtali, Nahbi the son of Vophsi;

15 from the tribe of Gad, Geuel the son of Machi.

16 These are the names of the men whom Moses sent to spy out the land; but Moses called Hoshea the son of Nun, Joshua.

17 ¶ When Moses sent them to spy out the land of Canaan, he said to them, "Go up there into the [17]Negev; then go up into the hill country.

18"And see what the land is like, and whether the people who live in it are strong or weak, whether they are few or many.

19"And how is the land in which they live, is it good or bad? And how are the cities in which they live, are they like open camps or with fortifications?

20"And how is the land, is it fat or lean? Are there trees in it or not? Make an effort then to get some of the fruit of the land." Now the time was the time of the first ripe grapes.

21 ¶ So they went up and spied out the land from the wilderness of Zin as far as Rehob, at Lebo-hamath.

22 When they had gone up into the Negev, they came to Hebron where Ahiman, Sheshai and Talmai, the descendants of Anak were. (Now Hebron was built seven years before Zoan in Egypt.)

23 ¶ Then they came to the valley of [18]Eshcol and from there cut down a branch with a single cluster of grapes; and they carried it on a pole between two men, with some of the pomegranates and the figs.

24 That place was called the valley of Eshcol, because of the cluster which the sons of Israel cut down from there.

25 ¶ When they returned from spying out the land, at the end of forty days,

26 they proceeded to come to Moses and Aaron and to all the congregation of the sons of Israel in the wilderness of Paran, at Kadesh; and they brought back word to them and to all the congregation and showed them the fruit of the land.

27 Thus they told him, and said, "We went in to the land where you sent us; and it certainly does flow with milk and honey, and this is its fruit.

28"Nevertheless, the people who live in the land are strong, and the cities are fortified and very large; and moreover, we saw the descendants of Anak there.

29"Amalek is living in the land of the Negev and the Hittites and the Jebusites and the Amorites are living in the hill country, and the Canaanites are living by the sea and by the side of the Jordan."

30 ¶ Then Caleb quieted the people before Moses, and said, "We should by all means go up and take possession of it, for we shall surely overcome it."

31 But the men who had gone up with him said, "We are not able to go up against the people, for they are too strong for us."

32 So they gave out to the sons of Israel a bad report of the land which they had spied out, saying, "The land through which we have gone, in spying it out, is a land that devours its inhabitants; and all the people whom we saw in it are men of great size.

33"There also we saw the Nephilim (the sons of Anak are part of the Nephilim); and we became like grasshoppers in our own sight, and so we were in their sight."

CHAPTER 14

THEN all the congregation lifted up their voices and cried, and the people wept that night.

2 And all the sons of Israel grumbled against Moses and Aaron; and the whole congregation said to them, "Would that we had died in the land of Egypt! Or would that we had died in this wilderness!

[17] I.e., South country, and so throughout this context
[18] I.e., cluster

3"And why is the LORD bringing us into this land, to fall by the sword? Our wives and our little ones will become plunder; would it not be better for us to return to Egypt?"

4 So they said to one another, "Let us appoint a leader and return to Egypt."

5 ¶ Then Moses and Aaron fell on their faces in the presence of all the assembly of the congregation of the sons of Israel.

6 And Joshua the son of Nun and Caleb the son of Jephunneh, of those who had spied out the land, tore their clothes;

7 and they spoke to all the congregation of the sons of Israel, saying, "The land which we passed through to spy out is an exceedingly good land.

8"If the LORD is pleased with us, then He will bring us into this land, and give it to us—a land which flows with milk and honey.

9"Only do not rebel against the LORD; and do not fear the people of the land, for they shall be our prey. Their protection has been removed from them, and the LORD is with us; do not fear them."

10 But all the congregation said to stone them with stones. Then the glory of the LORD appeared in the tent of meeting to all the sons of Israel.

11 ¶ And the LORD said to Moses, "How long will this people spurn Me? And how long will they not believe in Me, despite all the signs which I have performed in their midst?

12"I will smite them with pestilence and dispossess them, and I will make you into a nation greater and mightier than they."

13 ¶ But Moses said to the LORD, "Then the Egyptians will hear of it, for by Thy strength Thou didst bring up this people from their midst,

14 and they will tell it to the inhabitants of this land. They have heard that Thou, O LORD, art in the midst of this people, for Thou, O LORD, art seen eye to eye, while Thy cloud stands over them; and Thou dost go before them in a pillar of cloud by day and in a pillar of fire by night.

15"Now if Thou dost slay this people as one man, then the nations who have heard of Thy fame will say,

16 'Because the LORD could not bring this people into the land which He promised them by oath, therefore He slaughtered them in the wilderness.'

17"But now, I pray, let the power of the Lord be great, just as Thou hast declared,

18 'The LORD is slow to anger and abundant in lovingkindness, forgiving iniquity and transgression; but He will by no means clear *the guilty*, visiting the iniquity of the fathers on the children to the third and the fourth *generations*.'

19"Pardon, I pray, the iniquity of this people according to the greatness of Thy lovingkindness, just as Thou also hast forgiven this people, from Egypt even until now."

20 ¶ So the LORD said, "I have pardoned *them* according to your word;

21 but indeed, as I live, all the earth will be filled with the glory of the LORD.

22"Surely all the men who have seen My glory and My signs, which I performed in Egypt and in the wilderness, yet have put Me to the test these ten times and have not listened to My voice,

23 shall by no means see the land which I swore to their fathers, nor shall any of those who spurned Me see it.

24"But My servant Caleb, because he has had a different spirit and has followed Me fully, I will bring into the land which he entered, and his descendants shall take possession of it.

25"Now the Amalekites and the Canaanites live in the valleys; turn tomorrow and set out to the wilderness by the way of the Red Sea."

26 ¶ And the LORD spoke to Moses and Aaron, saying,

27"How long *shall I bear* with this evil congregation who are grumbling against Me? I have heard the complaints of the sons of Israel, which they are making against Me.

28"Say to them, 'As I live,' says the LORD, 'just as you have spoken in My hearing, so I will surely do to you;

29 your corpses shall fall in this wilderness, even all your numbered men, according to your complete number from twenty years old and upward, who have grumbled against Me.

30 'Surely you shall not come into the land in which I swore to settle you, except Caleb the son of Jephunneh and Joshua the son of Nun.

31 'Your children, however, whom you said would become a prey—I will bring them in, and they shall know the land which you have rejected.

32 'But as for you, your corpses shall fall in this wilderness.

33 'And your sons shall be shepherds for forty years in the wilderness, and they shall suffer *for* your unfaithfulness, until your corpses lie in the wilderness.

34 'According to the number of days which you spied out the land, forty days, for every day you shall bear your guilt a year, *even* forty years, and you shall know My opposition.

35 'I, the LORD, have spoken, surely this I will do to all this evil congregation who are gathered together against Me. In this wilderness they shall be destroyed, and there they shall die.' "

36 ¶ As for the men whom Moses sent to spy out the land and who returned and made all the congregation grumble against him by bringing out a bad report concerning the land,

37 even those men who brought out the very bad report of the land died by a plague before the LORD.

38 But Joshua the son of Nun and Caleb the son of Jephunneh remained alive out of those men who went to spy out the land.

39 ¶ And when Moses spoke these words to all the sons of Israel, the people mourned greatly.

40 In the morning, however, they rose up early and went up to the ridge of the hill country, saying, "Here we are; we have indeed sinned, but we will go up to the place which the LORD has promised."

41 But Moses said, "Why then are you transgressing the commandment of the LORD, when it will not succeed?

42 "Do not go up, lest you be struck down before your enemies, for the LORD is not among you.

43 "For the Amalekites and the Canaanites will be there in front of you, and you will fall by the sword, inasmuch as you have turned back from

following the LORD. And the LORD will not be with you."

44 But they went up heedlessly to the ridge of the hill country; neither the ark of the covenant of the LORD nor Moses left the camp.

45 Then the Amalekites and the Canaanites who lived in that hill country came down, and struck them and beat them down as far as Hormah.

CHAPTER 15

Now the LORD spoke to Moses, saying,

2 "Speak to the sons of Israel, and say to them, 'When you enter the land where you are to live, which I am giving you,

3 then make an offering by fire to the LORD, a burnt offering or a sacrifice to fulfill a special vow, or as a freewill offering or in your appointed times, to make a soothing aroma to the LORD, from the herd or from the flock.

4 'And the one who presents his offering shall present to the LORD a grain offering of one-tenth *of an ephah* of fine flour mixed with one-fourth of a [19]hin of oil,

5 and you shall prepare wine for the libation, one-fourth of a hin, with the burnt offering or for the sacrifice, for each lamb.

6 'Or for a ram you shall prepare as a grain offering two-tenths *of an ephah* of fine flour mixed with one-third of a hin of oil;

7 and for the libation you shall offer one-third of a hin of wine as a soothing aroma to the LORD.

8 'And when you prepare a bull as a burnt offering or a sacrifice, to fulfill a special vow, or for peace offerings to the LORD,

9 then you shall offer with the bull a grain offering of three-tenths *of an ephah* of fine flour mixed with one-half a hin of oil;

10 and you shall offer as the libation one-half a hin of wine as an offering by fire, as a soothing aroma to the LORD.

11 ¶ 'Thus it shall be done for each ox, or for each ram, or for each of the male lambs, or of the goats.

12 'According to the number that you

[19] I.e., Approx. one gallon, and so through v. 10

prepare, so you shall do for everyone according to their number.

13 'All who are native shall do these things in this manner, in presenting an offering by fire, as a soothing aroma to the LORD.

14 'And if an alien sojourns with you, or one who may be among you throughout your generations, and he *wishes to* make an offering by fire, as a soothing aroma to the LORD, just as you do, so he shall do.

15 '*As for* the assembly, there shall be one statute for you and for the alien who sojourns *with you,* a perpetual statute throughout your generations; as you are, so shall the alien be before the LORD.

16 'There is to be one law and one ordinance for you and for the alien who sojourns with you.' "

17 ¶ Then the LORD spoke to Moses, saying,

18 "Speak to the sons of Israel, and say to them, 'When you enter the land where I bring you,

19 then it shall be, that when you eat of the food of the land, you shall lift up an offering to the LORD.

20 'Of the first of your [20]dough you shall lift up a cake as an offering; as the offering of the threshing floor, so you shall lift it up.

21 'From the first of your [20]dough you shall give to the LORD an offering throughout your generations.

22 ¶ 'But when you unwittingly fail and do not observe all these commandments, which the LORD has spoken to Moses,

23 *even* all that the LORD has commanded you through Moses, from the day when the LORD gave commandment and onward throughout your generations,

24 then it shall be, if it is done unintentionally, without the knowledge of the congregation, that all the congregation shall offer one bull for a burnt offering, as a soothing aroma to the LORD, with its grain offering, and its libation, according to the ordinance, and one male goat for a sin offering.

25 'Then the priest shall make atonement for all the congregation of the sons of Israel, and they shall be forgiven; for it was an error, and they

have brought their offering, an offering by fire to the LORD, and their sin offering before the LORD, for their error.

26 'So all the congregation of the sons of Israel will be forgiven, with the alien who sojourns among them, for *it happened* to all the people through error.

27 ¶ 'Also if one person sins unintentionally, then he shall offer a one year old female goat for a sin offering.

28 'And the priest shall make atonement before the LORD for the person who goes astray when he sins unintentionally, making atonement for him that he may be forgiven.

29 'You shall have one law for him who does *anything* unintentionally, for him who is native among the sons of Israel and for the alien who sojourns among them.

30 'But the person who does *anything* defiantly, whether he is native or an alien, that one is blaspheming the LORD; and that person shall be cut off from among his people.

31 'Because he has despised the word of the LORD and has broken His commandment, that person shall be completely cut off; his guilt *shall be* on him.' "

32 ¶ Now while the sons of Israel were in the wilderness, they found a man gathering wood on the sabbath day.

33 And those who found him gathering wood brought him to Moses and Aaron, and to all the congregation;

34 and they put him in custody because it had not been declared what should be done to him.

35 Then the LORD said to Moses, "The man shall surely be put to death; all the congregation shall stone him with stones outside the camp."

36 So all the congregation brought him outside the camp, and stoned him to death with stones, just as the LORD had commanded Moses.

37 ¶ The LORD also spoke to Moses, saying,

38 "Speak to the sons of Israel, and tell them that they shall make for themselves tassels on the corners of their garments throughout their generations, and that they shall put on the tassel of each corner a cord of blue.

[20] Or, *coarse meal*

39"And it shall be a tassel for you to look at and remember all the commandments of the LORD, so as to do them and not follow after your own heart and your own eyes, after which you played the harlot,

40 in order that you may remember to do all My commandments, and be holy to your God.

41"I am the LORD your God who brought you out from the land of Egypt to be your God; I am the LORD your God."

CHAPTER 16

NOW Korah the son of Izhar, the son of Kohath, the son of Levi, with Dathan and Abiram, the sons of Eliab, and On the son of Peleth, sons of Reuben, took *action,*

2 and they rose up before Moses, together with some of the sons of Israel, two hundred and fifty leaders of the congregation, chosen in the assembly, men of renown.

3 And they assembled together against Moses and Aaron, and said to them, "You have gone far enough, for all the congregation are holy, every one of them, and the LORD is in their midst; so why do you exalt yourselves above the assembly of the LORD?"

4 ¶ When Moses heard *this,* he fell on his face;

5 and he spoke to Korah and all his company, saying, "Tomorrow morning the LORD will show who is His, and who is holy, and will bring *him* near to Himself; even the one whom He will choose, He will bring near to Himself.

6"Do this: take censers for yourselves, Korah and all your company,

7 and put fire in them, and lay incense upon them in the presence of the LORD tomorrow; and the man whom the LORD chooses *shall be* the one who is holy. You have gone far enough, you sons of Levi!"

8 ¶ Then Moses said to Korah, "Hear now, you sons of Levi,

9 is it not enough for you that the God of Israel has separated you from the *rest of* the congregation of Israel, to bring you near to Himself, to do the service of the tabernacle of the LORD, and to stand before the congregation to minister to them;

10 and that He has brought you near,

Korah, and all your brothers, sons of Levi, with you? And are you seeking for the priesthood also?

11"Therefore you and all your company are gathered together against the LORD; but as for Aaron, who is he that you grumble against him?"

12 ¶ Then Moses sent a summons to Dathan and Abiram, the sons of Eliab; but they said, "We will not come up.

13"Is it not enough that you have brought us up out of a land flowing with milk and honey to have us die in the wilderness, but you would also lord it over us?

14"Indeed, you have not brought us into a land flowing with milk and honey, nor have you given us an inheritance of fields and vineyards. Would you put out the eyes of these men? We will not come up!"

15 ¶ Then Moses became very angry and said to the LORD, "Do not regard their offering! I have not taken a single donkey from them, nor have I done harm to any of them."

16 And Moses said to Korah, "You and all your company be present before the LORD tomorrow, both you and they along with Aaron.

17"And each of you take his firepan and put incense on it, and each of you bring his censer before the LORD, two hundred and fifty firepans; also you and Aaron *shall* each *bring* his firepan."

18 So they each took his *own* censer and put fire on it, and laid incense on it; and they stood at the doorway of the tent of meeting, with Moses and Aaron.

19 Thus Korah assembled all the congregation against them at the doorway of the tent of meeting. And the glory of the LORD appeared to all the congregation.

20 ¶ Then the LORD spoke to Moses and Aaron, saying,

21"Separate yourselves from among this congregation, that I may consume them instantly."

22 But they fell on their faces, and said, "O God, Thou God of the spirits of all flesh, when one man sins, wilt Thou be angry with the entire congregation?"

23 Then the LORD spoke to Moses, saying,

24"Speak to the congregation, saying, 'Get back from around the dwellings of Korah, Dathan and Abiram.'"

25 ¶ Then Moses arose and went to Dathan and Abiram, with the elders of Israel following him,

26 and he spoke to the congregation, saying, "Depart now from the tents of these wicked men, and touch nothing that belongs to them, lest you be swept away in all their sin."

27 So they got back from around the dwellings of Korah, Dathan and Abiram; and Dathan and Abiram came out *and* stood at the doorway of their tents, along with their wives and their sons and their little ones.

28 And Moses said, "By this you shall know that the LORD has sent me to do all these deeds; for this is not my doing.

29"If these men die the death of all men, or if they suffer the fate of all men, *then* the LORD has not sent me.

30"But if the LORD brings about an entirely new thing and the ground opens its mouth and swallows them up with all that is theirs, and they descend alive into Sheol, then you will understand that these men have spurned the LORD."

31 ¶ Then it came about as he finished speaking all these words, that the ground that was under them split open;

32 and the earth opened its mouth and swallowed them up, and their households, and all the men who belonged to Korah, with *their* possessions.

33 So they and all that belonged to them went down alive to Sheol; and the earth closed over them, and they perished from the midst of the assembly.

34 And all Israel who *were* around them fled at their outcry, for they said, "The earth may swallow us up!"

35 Fire also came forth from the LORD and consumed the two hundred and fifty men who were offering the incense.

36 ¶ Then the LORD spoke to Moses, saying,

37"Say to Eleazar, the son of Aaron the priest, that he shall take up the censers out of the midst of the blaze, for they are holy; and you scatter the burning coals abroad.

38"As for the censers of these men who have sinned at the cost of their lives, let them be made into hammered sheets for a plating of the altar, since they did present them before the LORD and they are holy; and they shall be for a sign to the sons of Israel."

39 So Eleazar the priest took the bronze censers which the men who were burned had offered; and they hammered them out as a plating for the altar,

40 as a reminder to the sons of Israel that no layman who is not of the descendants of Aaron should come near to burn incense before the LORD; that he might not become like Korah and his company—just as the LORD had spoken to him through Moses.

41 ¶ But on the next day all the congregation of the sons of Israel grumbled against Moses and Aaron, saying, "You are the ones who have caused the death of the LORD's people."

42 It came about, however, when the congregation had assembled against Moses and Aaron, that they turned toward the tent of meeting, and behold, the cloud covered it and the glory of the LORD appeared.

43 Then Moses and Aaron came to the front of the tent of meeting,

44 and the LORD spoke to Moses, saying,

45"Get away from among this congregation, that I may consume them instantly." Then they fell on their faces.

46 And Moses said to Aaron, "Take your censer and put in it fire from the altar, and lay incense *on it;* then bring it quickly to the congregation and make atonement for them, for wrath has gone forth from the LORD, the plague has begun!"

47 Then Aaron took *it* as Moses had spoken, and ran into the midst of the assembly, for behold, the plague had begun among the people. So he put *on* the incense and made atonement for the people.

48 And he took his stand between the dead and the living, so that the plague was checked.

49 But those who died by the plague were 14,700, besides those who died on account of Korah.

50 Then Aaron returned to Moses at the doorway of the tent of meeting, for the plague had been checked.

CHAPTER 17

THEN the LORD spoke to Moses, saying,

2 "Speak to the sons of Israel, and get from them a rod for each father's household: twelve rods, from all their leaders according to their fathers' households. You shall write each name on his rod,

3 and write Aaron's name on the rod of Levi; for there is one rod for the head *of each* of their fathers' households.

4 "You shall then deposit them in the tent of meeting in front of the testimony, where I meet with you.

5 "And it will come about that the rod of the man whom I choose will sprout. Thus I shall lessen from upon Myself the grumblings of the sons of Israel, who are grumbling against you."

6 Moses therefore spoke to the sons of Israel, and all their leaders gave him a rod apiece, for each leader according to their fathers' households, twelve rods, with the rod of Aaron among their rods.

7 So Moses deposited the rods before the LORD in the tent of the testimony.

8 ¶ Now it came about on the next day that Moses went into the tent of the testimony; and behold, the rod of Aaron for the house of Levi had sprouted and put forth buds and produced blossoms, and it bore ripe almonds.

9 Moses then brought out all the rods from the presence of the LORD to all the sons of Israel; and they looked, and each man took his rod.

10 But the LORD said to Moses, "Put back the rod of Aaron before the testimony to be kept as a sign against the rebels, that you may put an end to their grumblings against Me, so that they should not die."

11 Thus Moses did; just as the LORD had commanded him, so he did.

12 ¶ Then the sons of Israel spoke to Moses, saying, "Behold, we perish, we are dying, we are all dying!

13 "Everyone who comes near, who comes near to the tabernacle of the LORD, must die. Are we to perish completely?"

CHAPTER 18

SO the LORD said to Aaron, "You and your sons and your father's household with you shall bear the guilt in connection with the sanctuary; and you and your sons with you shall bear the guilt in connection with your priesthood.

2 "But bring with you also your brothers, the tribe of Levi, the tribe of your father, that they may be joined with you and serve you, while you and your sons with you are before the tent of the testimony.

3 "And they shall thus attend to your obligation and the obligation of all the tent, but they shall not come near to the furnishings of the sanctuary and the altar, lest both they and you die.

4 "And they shall be joined with you and attend to the obligations of the tent of meeting, for all the service of the tent; but an outsider may not come near you.

5 "So you shall attend to the obligations of the sanctuary and the obligations of the altar, that there may no longer be wrath on the sons of Israel.

6 "And behold, I Myself have taken your fellow Levites from among the sons of Israel; they are a gift to you, dedicated to the LORD, to perform the service for the tent of meeting.

7 "But you and your sons with you shall attend to your priesthood for everything concerning the altar and inside the veil, and you are to perform service. I am giving you the priesthood as a bestowed service, but the outsider who comes near shall be put to death."

8 ¶ Then the LORD spoke to Aaron, "Now behold, I Myself have given you charge of My offerings, even all the holy gifts of the sons of Israel, I have given them to you as a portion, and to your sons as a perpetual allotment.

9 "This shall be yours from the most holy *gifts, reserved* from the fire; every offering of theirs, even every grain offering and every sin offering and every guilt offering, which they shall render to Me, shall be most holy for you and for your sons.

10 "As the most holy *gifts* you shall

eat it; every male shall eat it. It shall be holy to you.

11"This also is yours, the offering of their gift, even all the wave offerings of the sons of Israel; I have given them to you and to your sons and daughters with you, as a perpetual allotment. Everyone of your household who is clean may eat it.

12"All the best of the fresh oil and all the best of the fresh wine and of the grain, the first fruits of those which they give to the LORD, I give them to you.

13"The first ripe fruits of all that is in their land, which they bring to the LORD, shall be yours; everyone of your household who is clean may eat it.

14"Every devoted thing in Israel shall be yours.

15"Every first issue of the womb of all flesh, whether man or animal, which they offer to the LORD, shall be yours; nevertheless the first-born of man you shall surely redeem, and the first-born of unclean animals you shall redeem.

16"And as to their redemption price, from a month old you shall redeem them, by your valuation, five [21]shekels in silver, according to the shekel of the sanctuary, which is twenty gerahs.

17"But the first-born of an ox or the first-born of a sheep or the first-born of a goat, you shall not redeem; they are holy. You shall sprinkle their blood on the altar and shall offer up their fat in smoke *as* an offering by fire, for a soothing aroma to the LORD.

18"And their meat shall be yours; it shall be yours like the breast of a wave offering and like the right thigh.

19"All the offerings of the holy *gifts,* which the sons of Israel offer to the LORD, I have given to you and your sons and your daughters with you, as a perpetual allotment. It is an everlasting covenant of salt before the LORD to you and your descendants with you."

20 Then the LORD said to Aaron, "You shall have no inheritance in their land, nor own any portion among them; I am your portion and your inheritance among the sons of Israel.

21 ¶"And to the sons of Levi, behold,

I have given all the tithe in Israel for an inheritance, in return for their service which they perform, the service of the tent of meeting.

22"And the sons of Israel shall not come near the tent of meeting again, lest they bear sin and die.

23"Only the Levites shall perform the service of the tent of meeting, and they shall bear their iniquity; it shall be a perpetual statute throughout your generations, and among the sons of Israel they shall have no inheritance.

24"For the tithe of the sons of Israel, which they offer as an offering to the LORD, I have given to the Levites for an inheritance; therefore I have said concerning them, 'They shall have no inheritance among the sons of Israel.' "

25 ¶ Then the LORD spoke to Moses, saying,

26"Moreover, you shall speak to the Levites and say to them, 'When you take from the sons of Israel the tithe which I have given you from them for your inheritance, then you shall present an offering from it to the LORD, a tithe of the tithe.

27 'And your offering shall be reckoned to you as the grain from the threshing floor or the full produce from the wine vat.

28 'So you shall also present an offering to the LORD from your tithes, which you receive from the sons of Israel; and from it you shall give the LORD's offering to Aaron the priest.

29 'Out of all your gifts you shall present every offering due to the LORD, from all the best of them, the sacred part from them.'

30"And you shall say to them, 'When you have offered from it the best of it, then *the rest* shall be reckoned to the Levites as the product of the threshing floor, and as the product of the wine vat.

31 'And you may eat it anywhere, you and your households, for it is your compensation in return for your service in the tent of meeting.

32 'And you shall bear no sin by reason of it, when you have offered the best of it. But you shall not profane the sacred gifts of the sons of Israel, lest you die.' "

---

[21] I.e., A shekel equals approx. one-half ounce

CHAPTER 19

THEN the LORD spoke to Moses and Aaron, saying,

2 "This is the statute of the law which the LORD has commanded, saying, 'Speak to the sons of Israel that they bring you an unblemished red heifer in which is no defect, *and* on which a yoke has never been placed.

3 'And you shall give it to Eleazar the priest, and it shall be brought outside the camp and be slaughtered in his presence.

4 'Next Eleazar the priest shall take some of its blood with his finger, and sprinkle some of its blood toward the front of the tent of meeting seven times.

5 'Then the heifer shall be burned in his sight; its hide and its flesh and its blood, with its refuse, shall be burned.

6 'And the priest shall take cedar wood and hyssop and scarlet *material,* and cast it into the midst of the burning heifer.

7 'The priest shall then wash his clothes and bathe his body in water, and afterward come into the camp, but the priest shall be unclean until evening.

8 'The one who burns it shall also wash his clothes in water and bathe his body in water, and shall be unclean until evening.

9 'Now a man who is clean shall gather up the ashes of the heifer and deposit them outside the camp in a clean place, and the congregation of the sons of Israel shall keep it as water to remove impurity; it is purification from sin.

10 'And the one who gathers the ashes of the heifer shall wash his clothes and be unclean until evening; and it shall be a perpetual statute to the sons of Israel and to the alien who sojourns among them.

11 ¶ 'The one who touches the corpse of any person shall be unclean for seven days.

12 'That one shall purify himself from uncleanness with the water on the third day and on the seventh day, *and then* he shall be clean; but if he does not purify himself on the third day and on the seventh day, he shall not be clean.

13 'Anyone who touches a corpse, the body of a man who has died, and does not purify himself, defiles the tabernacle of the LORD; and that person shall be cut off from Israel. Because the water for impurity was not sprinkled on him, he shall be unclean; his uncleanness is still on him.

14 ¶ 'This is the law when a man dies in a tent: everyone who comes into the tent and everyone who is in the tent shall be unclean for seven days.

15 'And every open vessel, which has no covering tied down on it, shall be unclean.

16 'Also, anyone who in the open field touches one who has been slain with a sword or who has died *naturally,* or a human bone or a grave, shall be unclean for seven days.

17 'Then for the unclean *person* they shall take some of the ashes of the burnt purification from sin and flowing water shall be added to them in a vessel.

18 'And a clean person shall take hyssop and dip *it* in the water, and sprinkle *it* on the tent and on all the furnishings and on the persons who were there, and on the one who touched the bone or the one slain or the one dying *naturally* or the grave.

19 'Then the clean *person* shall sprinkle on the unclean on the third day and on the seventh day; and on the seventh day he shall purify him from uncleanness, and he shall wash his clothes and bathe *himself* in water and shall be clean by evening.

20 ¶ 'But the man who is unclean and does not purify himself from uncleanness, that person shall be cut off from the midst of the assembly, because he has defiled the sanctuary of the LORD; the water for impurity has not been sprinkled on him, he is unclean.

21 'So it shall be a perpetual statute for them. And he who sprinkles the water for impurity shall wash his clothes, and he who touches the water for impurity shall be unclean until evening.

22 'Furthermore, anything that the unclean *person* touches shall be unclean; and the person who touches *it* shall be unclean until evening.' "

CHAPTER 20

THEN the sons of Israel, the whole congregation, came to the wilderness of Zin in the first month; and the people stayed at Kadesh. Now Miriam died there and was buried there.

2 ¶ And there was no water for the congregation; and they assembled themselves against Moses and Aaron.

3 The people thus contended with Moses and spoke, saying, "If only we had perished when our brothers perished before the LORD!

4 "Why then have you brought the LORD's assembly into this wilderness, for us and our beasts to die here?

5 "And why have you made us come up from Egypt, to bring us in to this wretched place? It is not a place of grain or figs or vines or pomegranates, nor is there water to drink."

6 Then Moses and Aaron came in from the presence of the assembly to the doorway of the tent of meeting, and fell on their faces. Then the glory of the LORD appeared to them;

7 and the LORD spoke to Moses, saying,

8 "Take the rod; and you and your brother Aaron assemble the congregation and speak to the rock before their eyes, that it may yield its water. You shall thus bring forth water for them out of the rock and let the congregation and their beasts drink."

9 So Moses took the rod from before the LORD, just as He had commanded him;

10 and Moses and Aaron gathered the assembly before the rock. And he said to them, "Listen now, you rebels; shall we bring forth water for you out of this rock?"

11 Then Moses lifted up his hand and struck the rock twice with his rod; and water came forth abundantly, and the congregation and their beasts drank.

12 But the LORD said to Moses and Aaron, "Because you have not believed Me, to treat Me as holy in the sight of the sons of Israel, therefore you shall not bring this assembly into the land which I have given them."

13 Those *were* the waters of ²²Meribah, because the sons of Israel contended with the LORD, and He proved Himself holy among them.

14 ¶ From Kadesh Moses then sent messengers to the king of Edom: "Thus your brother Israel has said,

'You know all the hardship that has befallen us;

15 that our fathers went down to Egypt, and we stayed in Egypt a long time, and the Egyptians treated us and our fathers badly.

16 'But when we cried out to the LORD, He heard our voice and sent an angel and brought us out from Egypt; now behold, we are at Kadesh, a town on the edge of your territory.

17 'Please let us pass through your land. We shall not pass through field or through vineyard; we shall not even drink water from a well. We shall go along the king's highway, not turning to the right or left, until we pass through your territory.' "

18 Edom, however, said to him, "You shall not pass through us, lest I come out with the sword against you."

19 Again, the sons of Israel said to him, "We shall go up by the highway, and if I and my livestock do drink any of your water, then I will pay its price. Let me only pass through on my feet, nothing *else.*"

20 But he said, "You shall not pass through." And Edom came out against him with a heavy force, and with a strong hand.

21 Thus Edom refused to allow Israel to pass through his territory; so Israel turned away from him.

22 ¶ Now when they set out from Kadesh, the sons of Israel, the whole congregation, came to Mount Hor.

23 Then the LORD spoke to Moses and Aaron at Mount Hor by the border of the land of Edom, saying,

24 "Aaron shall be gathered to his people; for he shall not enter the land which I have given to the sons of Israel, because you rebelled against My command at the waters of Meribah.

25 "Take Aaron and his son Eleazar, and bring them up to Mount Hor;

26 and strip Aaron of his garments and put them on his son Eleazar. So Aaron will be gathered *to his people,* and will die there."

27 So Moses did just as the LORD had commanded, and they went up to Mount Hor in the sight of all the congregation.

28 And after Moses had stripped Aaron of his garments and put them

on his son Eleazar, Aaron died there on the mountain top. Then Moses and Eleazar came down from the mountain.

29 And when all the congregation saw that Aaron had died, all the house of Israel wept for Aaron thirty days.

CHAPTER 21

WHEN the Canaanite, the king of Arad, who lived in the [23]Negev, heard that Israel was coming by the way of [24]Atharim, then he fought against Israel, and took some of them captive.

2 So Israel made a vow to the LORD, and said, "If Thou wilt indeed deliver this people into my hand, then I will utterly destroy their cities."

3 And the LORD heard the voice of Israel, and delivered up the Canaanites; then they utterly destroyed them and their cities. Thus the name of the place was called [25]Hormah.

4 ¶ Then they set out from Mount Hor by the way of the Red Sea, to go around the land of Edom; and the people became impatient because of the journey.

5 And the people spoke against God and Moses, "Why have you brought us up out of Egypt to die in the wilderness? For there is no food and no water, and we loathe this miserable food."

6 And the LORD sent fiery serpents among the people and they bit the people, so that many people of Israel died.

7 So the people came to Moses and said, "We have sinned, because we have spoken against the LORD and you; intercede with the LORD, that He may remove the serpents from us." And Moses interceded for the people.

8 Then the LORD said to Moses, "Make a fiery serpent, and set it on a standard; and it shall come about, that everyone who is bitten, when he looks at it, he shall live."

9 And Moses made a bronze serpent and set it on the standard; and it came about, that if a serpent bit any man, when he looked to the bronze serpent, he lived.

10 ¶ Now the sons of Israel moved out and camped in Oboth.

11 And they journeyed from Oboth, and camped at Iyeabarim, in the wilderness which is opposite Moab, to the east.

12 From there they set out and camped in [26]Wadi Zered.

13 From there they journeyed and camped on the other side of the Arnon, which is in the wilderness that comes out of the border of the Amorites, for the Arnon is the border of Moab, between Moab and the Amorites.

14 Therefore it is said in the Book of the Wars of the LORD,

"Waheb in Suphah,
And the wadis of the Arnon,
15   And the slope of the wadis
That extends to the site of Ar,
And leans to the border of Moab."

16 And from there *they continued* to Beer, that is the well where the LORD said to Moses, "Assemble the people, that I may give them water."

17 ¶ Then Israel sang this song:
"Spring up, O well! Sing to it!
18 "The well, which the leaders sank,
Which the nobles of the people dug,
With the scepter *and* with their staffs."

And from the wilderness *they continued* to Mattanah,

19 and from Mattanah to Nahaliel, and from Nahaliel to Bamoth,

20 and from Bamoth to the valley that is in the land of Moab, at the top of Pisgah which overlooks the wasteland.

21 ¶ Then Israel sent messengers to Sihon, king of the Amorites, saying,

22 "Let me pass through your land. We will not turn off into field or vineyard; we will not drink water from wells. We will go by the king's highway until we have passed through your border."

23 But Sihon would not permit Israel to pass through his border. So Sihon gathered all his people and went out against Israel in the wilderness, and came to Jahaz and fought against Israel.

24 Then Israel struck him with the edge of the sword, and took possession of his land from the Arnon to the

---

[23] I.e., South country   [24] Or, *the spies*
[25] I.e., a devoted thing; or, Destruction
[26] I.e., a dry ravine except during rainy season

Jabbok, as far as the sons of Ammon; for the border of the sons of Ammon *was* Jazer.

25 And Israel took all these cities and Israel lived in all the cities of the Amorites, in Heshbon, and in all her villages.

26 For Heshbon was the city of Sihon, king of the Amorites, who had fought against the former king of Moab and had taken all his land out of his hand, as far as the Arnon.

27 Therefore those who use proverbs say,

"Come to Heshbon! Let it be built! So let the city of Sihon be established.

28 "For a fire went forth from Heshbon,
A flame from the town of Sihon;
It devoured Ar of Moab,
The dominant heights of the Arnon.

29 "Woe to you, O Moab!
You are ruined, O people of Chemosh!
He has given his sons as fugitives,
And his daughters into captivity,
To an Amorite king, Sihon.

30 "But we have cast them down,
Heshbon is ruined as far as Dibon,
Then we have laid waste even to Nophah,
Which *reaches* to Medeba."

31 Thus Israel lived in the land of the Amorites.

32 And Moses sent to spy out Jazer, and they captured its villages and dispossessed the Amorites who *were* there.

33 ¶ Then they turned and went up by the way of Bashan, and Og the king of Bashan went out with all his people, for battle at Edrei.

34 But the LORD said to Moses, "Do not fear him, for I have given him into your hand, and all his people and his land; and you shall do to him as you did to Sihon, king of the Amorites, who lived at Heshbon."

35 So they killed him and his sons and all his people, until there was no remnant left him; and they possessed his land.

CHAPTER 22

THEN the sons of Israel journeyed, and camped in the plains of Moab beyond the Jordan *opposite* Jericho.

2 ¶ Now Balak the son of Zippor saw all that Israel had done to the Amorites.

3 So Moab was in great fear because of the people, for they were numerous; and Moab was in dread of the sons of Israel.

4 And Moab said to the elders of Midian, "Now this horde will lick up all that is around us, as the ox licks up the grass of the field." And Balak the son of Zippor was king of Moab at that time.

5 So he sent messengers to Balaam the son of Beor, at Pethor, which is near the [27]River, *in* the land of the sons of his people, to call him, saying, "Behold, a people came out of Egypt; behold, they cover the surface of the land, and they are living opposite me.

6"Now, therefore, please come, curse this people for me since they are too mighty for me; perhaps I may be able to defeat them and drive them out of the land. For I know that he whom you bless is blessed, and he whom you curse is cursed."

7 ¶ So the elders of Moab and the elders of Midian departed with the *fees for* divination in their hand; and they came to Balaam and repeated Balak's words to him.

8 And he said to them, "Spend the night here, and I will bring word back to you as the LORD may speak to me." And the leaders of Moab stayed with Balaam.

9 Then God came to Balaam and said, "Who are these men with you?"

10 And Balaam said to God, "Balak the son of Zippor, king of Moab, has sent *word* to me,

11 'Behold, there is a people who came out of Egypt and they cover the surface of the land; now come, curse them for me; perhaps I may be able to fight against them, and drive them out.' "

12 And God said to Balaam, "Do not go with them; you shall not curse the people; for they are blessed."

13 So Balaam arose in the morning and said to Balak's leaders, "Go back

[27] I.e., Euphrates

to your land, for the LORD has refused to let me go with you."

14 And the leaders of Moab arose and went to Balak, and said, "Balaam refused to come with us."

15 ¶ Then Balak again sent leaders, more numerous and more distinguished than the former.

16 And they came to Balaam and said to him, "Thus says Balak the son of Zippor, 'Let nothing, I beg you, hinder you from coming to me;

17 for I will indeed honor you richly, and I will do whatever you say to me. Please come then, curse this people for me.' "

18 And Balaam answered and said to the servants of Balak, "Though Balak were to give me his house full of silver and gold, I could not do anything, either small or great, contrary to the command of the LORD my God.

19 "And now please, you also stay here tonight, and I will find out what else the LORD will speak to me."

20 And God came to Balaam at night and said to him, "If the men have come to call you, rise up *and* go with them; but only the word which I speak to you shall you do."

21 ¶ So Balaam arose in the morning, and saddled his donkey, and went with the leaders of Moab.

22 But God was angry because he was going, and the angel of the LORD took his stand in the way as an adversary against him. Now he was riding on his donkey and his two servants were with him.

23 When the donkey saw the angel of the LORD standing in the way with his drawn sword in his hand, the donkey turned off from the way and went into the field; but Balaam struck the donkey to turn her back into the way.

24 Then the angel of the LORD stood in a narrow path of the vineyards, *with* a wall on this side and a wall on that side.

25 When the donkey saw the angel of the LORD, she pressed herself to the wall and pressed Balaam's foot against the wall, so he struck her again.

26 And the angel of the LORD went further, and stood in a narrow place where there was no way to turn to the right hand or the left.

27 When the donkey saw the angel

of the LORD, she lay down under Balaam; so Balaam was angry and struck the donkey with his stick.

28 And the LORD opened the mouth of the donkey, and she said to Balaam, "What have I done to you, that you have struck me these three times?"

29 Then Balaam said to the donkey, "Because you have made a mockery of me! If there had been a sword in my hand, I would have killed you by now."

30 And the donkey said to Balaam, "Am I not your donkey on which you have ridden all your life to this day? Have I ever been accustomed to do so to you?" And he said, "No."

31 ¶ Then the LORD opened the eyes of Balaam, and he saw the angel of the LORD standing in the way with his drawn sword in his hand; and he bowed all the way to the ground.

32 And the angel of the LORD said to him, "Why have you struck your donkey these three times? Behold, I have come out as an adversary, because your way was contrary to me.

33 "But the donkey saw me and turned aside from me these three times. If she had not turned aside from me, I would surely have killed you just now, and let her live."

34 And Balaam said to the angel of the LORD, "I have sinned, for I did not know that you were standing in the way against me. Now then, if it is displeasing to you, I will turn back."

35 But the angel of the LORD said to Balaam, "Go with the men, but you shall speak only the word which I shall tell you." So Balaam went along with the leaders of Balak.

36 ¶ When Balak heard that Balaam was coming, he went out to meet him at the city of Moab, which is on the Arnon border, at the extreme end of the border.

37 Then Balak said to Balaam, "Did I not urgently send to you to call you? Why did you not come to me? Am I really unable to honor you?"

38 So Balaam said to Balak, "Behold, I have come now to you! Am I able to speak anything at all? The word that God puts in my mouth, that I shall speak."

39 And Balaam went with Balak, and they came to Kiriath-huzoth.

40 And Balak sacrificed oxen and sheep, and sent *some* to Balaam and the leaders who were with him.

41 ¶ Then it came about in the morning that Balak took Balaam, and brought him up to the high places of Baal; and he saw from there a portion of the people.

CHAPTER 23

THEN Balaam said to Balak, "Build seven altars for me here, and prepare seven bulls and seven rams for me here."

2 And Balak did just as Balaam had spoken, and Balak and Balaam offered up a bull and a ram on each altar.

3 Then Balaam said to Balak, "Stand beside your burnt offering, and I will go; perhaps the LORD will come to meet me, and whatever He shows me I will tell you." So he went to a bare hill.

4 Now God met Balaam, and he said to Him, "I have set up the seven altars, and I have offered up a bull and a ram on each altar."

5 Then the LORD put a word in Balaam's mouth and said, "Return to Balak, and you shall speak thus."

6 So he returned to him, and behold, he was standing beside his burnt offering, he and all the leaders of Moab.

7 And he took up his [28]discourse and said,

"From Aram Balak has brought me,
Moab's king from the mountains of the East,
'Come curse Jacob for me,
And come, denounce Israel!'

8 "How shall I curse, whom God has not cursed?
And how can I denounce, whom the LORD has not denounced?

9 "As I see him from the top of the rocks,
And I look at him from the hills;
Behold, a people *who* dwells apart,
And shall not be reckoned among the nations.

10 "Who can count the dust of Jacob,
Or number the fourth part of Israel?

Let me die the death of the upright,
And let my end be like his!"

11 ¶ Then Balak said to Balaam, "What have you done to me? I took you to curse my enemies, but behold, you have actually blessed them!"

12 And he answered and said, "Must I not be careful to speak what the LORD puts in my mouth?"

13 ¶ Then Balak said to him, "Please come with me to another place from where you may see them, although you will only see the extreme end of them, and will not see all of them; and curse them for me from there."

14 So he took him to the field of Zophim, to the top of Pisgah, and built seven altars and offered a bull and a ram on *each* altar.

15 And he said to Balak, "Stand here beside your burnt offering, while I myself meet *the* LORD yonder."

16 Then the LORD met Balaam and put a word in his mouth and said, "Return to Balak, and thus you shall speak."

17 And he came to him, and behold, he was standing beside his burnt offering, and the leaders of Moab with him. And Balak said to him, "What has the LORD spoken?"

18 Then he took up his [28]discourse and said,

"Arise, O Balak, and hear;
Give ear to me, O son of Zippor!

19 "God is not a man, that He should lie,
Nor a son of man, that He should repent;
Has He said, and will He not do it?
Or has He spoken, and will He not make it good?

20 "Behold, I have received *a command* to bless;
When He has blessed, then I cannot revoke it.

21 "He has not observed misfortune in Jacob;
Nor has He seen trouble in Israel;
The LORD his God is with him,
And the shout of a king is among them.

22 "God brings them out of Egypt,

---

[28] Lit., *parable*, and so throughout this context

[28] Lit., *parable*, and so throughout this context

He is for them like the horns of
the wild ox.
23 "For there is no omen against
Jacob,
Nor is there any divination
against Israel;
At the proper time it shall be said
to Jacob
And to Israel, what God has
done.
24 "Behold, a people rises like a lioness,
And as a lion it lifts itself;
It shall not lie down until it devours the prey,
And drinks the blood of the
slain."

25 Then Balak said to Balaam, "Do
not curse them at all nor bless them at
all!"
26 But Balaam answered and said to
Balak, "Did I not tell you, 'Whatever
the LORD speaks, that I must do'?"
27 ¶ Then Balak said to Balaam,
"Please come, I will take you to another place; perhaps it will be agreeable with God that you curse them for
me from there."
28 So Balak took Balaam to the top
of Peor which overlooks the wasteland.
29 And Balaam said to Balak, "Build
seven altars for me here and prepare
seven bulls and seven rams for me
here."
30 And Balak did just as Balaam had
said, and offered up a bull and a ram
on *each* altar.

CHAPTER 24

WHEN Balaam saw that it pleased
the LORD to bless Israel, he did not go
as at other times to seek omens but he
set his face toward the wilderness.
2 And Balaam lifted up his eyes and
saw Israel camping tribe by tribe; and
the Spirit of God came upon him.
3 And he took up his discourse and
said,
"The oracle of Balaam the son of
Beor,
And the oracle of the man whose
eye is opened;
4 The oracle of him who hears the
words of God,
Who sees the vision of the Almighty,

Falling down, yet having his eyes
uncovered,
5 How fair are your tents, O Jacob,
Your dwellings, O Israel!
6 "Like valleys that stretch out,
Like gardens beside the river,
Like aloes planted by the LORD,
Like cedars beside the waters.
7 "Water shall flow from his buck-
ets,
And his seed *shall be* by many
waters,
And his king shall be higher than
Agag,
And his kingdom shall be exalted.
8 "God brings him out of Egypt,
He is for him like the horns of
the wild ox.
He shall devour the nations *who
are* his adversaries,
And shall crush their bones in
pieces,
And shatter *them* with his arrows.
9 "He couches, he lies down as a
lion,
And as a lion, who dares rouse
him?
Blessed is everyone who blesses
you,
And cursed is everyone who
curses you."

10 ¶ Then Balak's anger burned
against Balaam, and he struck his
hands together; and Balak said to
Balaam, "I called you to curse my
enemies, but behold, you have persisted in blessing them these three
times!
11 "Therefore, flee to your place now.
I said I would honor you greatly, but
behold, the LORD has held you back
from honor."
12 And Balaam said to Balak, "Did I
not tell your messengers whom you
had sent to me, saying,
13 'Though Balak were to give me his
house full of silver and gold, I could
not do anything contrary to the command of the LORD, either good or bad,
of my own accord. What the LORD
speaks, that I will speak'?
14 "And now behold, I am going to
my people; come, *and* I will advise you
what this people will do to your people
in the days to come."
15 And he took up his discourse and
said,

"The oracle of Balaam the son of
Beor,
And the oracle of the man whose
eye is opened,

16 The oracle of him who hears the
words of God,
And knows the knowledge of the
Most High,
Who sees the vision of the Al-
mighty,
Falling down, yet having his eyes
uncovered.

17 "I see him, but not now;
I behold him, but not near;
A star shall come forth from Ja-
cob,
And a scepter shall rise from
Israel,
And shall crush through the
forehead of Moab,
And tear down all the sons of
[29]Sheth.

18 "And Edom shall be a possession,
Seir, its enemies, also shall be a
possession,
While Israel performs valiantly.

19 "One from Jacob shall have dominion,
And shall destroy the remnant
from the city."

20 And he looked at Amalek and
took up his discourse and said,

"Amalek was the first of the nations,
But his end *shall be* destruction."

21 And he looked at the Kenite, and
took up his discourse and said,

"Your dwelling place is enduring,
And your nest is set in the cliff.

22 "Nevertheless Kain shall be consumed;
How long shall Asshur keep you
captive?"

23 And he took up his discourse and
said,

"Alas, who can live except God
has ordained it?

24 "But ships *shall come* from the
coast of Kittim,
And they shall afflict Asshur and
shall afflict Eber;
So they also *shall come* to destruction."

25 Then Balaam arose and departed
and returned to his place, and Balak
also went his way.

[29] I.e., tumult

CHAPTER 25

WHILE Israel remained at Shittim,
the people began to play the harlot
with the daughters of Moab.

2 For they invited the people to the
sacrifices of their gods, and the people
ate and bowed down to their gods.

3 So Israel joined themselves to
Baal of Peor, and the LORD was angry
against Israel.

4 And the LORD said to Moses,
"Take all the leaders of the people and
execute them in broad daylight before
the LORD, so that the fierce anger of
the LORD may turn away from Israel."

5 So Moses said to the judges of
Israel, "Each of you slay his men who
have joined themselves to Baal of
Peor."

6 ¶ Then behold, one of the sons of
Israel came and brought to his relatives a Midianite woman, in the sight
of Moses and in the sight of all the
congregation of the sons of Israel,
while they were weeping at the doorway of the tent of meeting.

7 When Phinehas the son of Eleazar, the son of Aaron the priest, saw it,
he arose from the midst of the congregation, and took a spear in his hand;

8 and he went after the man of
Israel into the tent, and pierced both
of them through, the man of Israel and
the woman, through the body. So the
plague on the sons of Israel was
checked.

9 And those who died by the plague
were 24,000.

10 ¶ Then the LORD spoke to Moses,
saying,

11 "Phinehas the son of Eleazar, the
son of Aaron the priest, has turned
away My wrath from the sons of Israel, in that he was jealous with My
jealousy among them, so that I did not
destroy the sons of Israel in My jealousy.

12 "Therefore say, 'Behold, I give him
My covenant of peace;

13 and it shall be for him and his
descendants after him, a covenant of a
perpetual priesthood, because he was
jealous for his God, and made atonement for the sons of Israel.' "

14 ¶ Now the name of the slain man
of Israel who was slain with the Midianite woman, was Zimri the son of

Salu, a leader of a father's household among the Simeonites.

15 And the name of the Midianite woman who was slain was Cozbi the daughter of Zur, who was head of the people of a father's household in Midian.

16 ¶ Then the LORD spoke to Moses, saying,

17"Be hostile to the Midianites and strike them;

18 for they have been hostile to you with their tricks, with which they have deceived you in the affair of Peor, and in the affair of Cozbi, the daughter of the leader of Midian, their sister who was slain on the day of the plague because of Peor."

CHAPTER 26

THEN it came about after the plague, that the LORD spoke to Moses and to Eleazar the son of Aaron the priest, saying,

2"Take a census of all the congregation of the sons of Israel from twenty years old and upward, by their fathers' households, whoever is able to go out to war in Israel."

3 So Moses and Eleazar the priest spoke with them in the plains of Moab by the Jordan at Jericho, saying,

4"Take a census of the people from twenty years old and upward, as the LORD has commanded Moses."

¶ Now the sons of Israel who came out of the land of Egypt were:

5 Reuben, Israel's first-born, the sons of Reuben: of Hanoch, the family of the Hanochites; of Pallu, the family of the Palluites;

6 of Hezron, the family of the Hezronites; of Carmi, the family of the Carmites.

7 These are the families of the Reubenites, and those who were numbered of them were 43,730.

8 And the son of Pallu: Eliab.

9 And the sons of Eliab: Nemuel and Dathan and Abiram. These are the Dathan and Abiram who were called by the congregation, who contended against Moses and against Aaron in the company of Korah, when they contended against the LORD,

10 and the earth opened its mouth and swallowed them up along with Korah, when that company died, when the fire devoured 250 men, so that they became a warning.

11 The sons of Korah, however, did not die.

12 ¶ The sons of Simeon according to their families: of Nemuel, the family of the Nemuelites; of Jamin, the family of the Jaminites; of Jachin, the family of the Jachinites;

13 of Zerah, the family of the Zerahites; of Shaul, the family of the Shaulites.

14 These are the families of the Simeonites, 22,200.

15 ¶ The sons of Gad according to their families: of Zephon, the family of the Zephonites; of Haggi, the family of the Haggites; of Shuni, the family of the Shunites;

16 of Ozni, the family of the Oznites; of Eri, the family of the Erites;

17 of Arod, the family of the Arodites; of Areli, the family of the Arelites.

18 These are the families of the sons of Gad according to those who were numbered of them, 40,500.

19 ¶ The sons of Judah were Er and Onan, but Er and Onan died in the land of Canaan.

20 And the sons of Judah according to their families were: of Shelah, the family of the Shelanites; of Perez, the family of the Perezites; of Zerah, the family of the Zerahites.

21 And the sons of Perez were: of Hezron, the family of the Hezronites; of Hamul, the family of the Hamulites.

22 These are the families of Judah according to those who were numbered of them, 76,500.

23 ¶ The sons of Issachar according to their families: of Tola, the family of the Tolaites; of Puvah, the family of the Punites;

24 of Jashub, the family of the Jashubites; of Shimron, the family of the Shimronites.

25 These are the families of Issachar according to those who were numbered of them, 64,300.

26 ¶ The sons of Zebulun according to their families: of Sered, the family of the Seredites; of Elon, the family of the Elonites; of Jahleel, the family of the Jahleelites.

27 These are the families of the Zebulunites according to those who were numbered of them, 60,500.

28 ¶ The sons of Joseph according to their families: Manasseh and Ephraim.

29 The sons of Manasseh: of Machir, the family of the Machirites; and Machir became the father of Gilead: of Gilead, the family of the Gileadites.

30 These are the sons of Gilead: of Iezer, the family of the Iezerites; of Helek, the family of the Helekites;

31 and of Asriel, the family of the Asrielites; and of Shechem, the family of the Shechemites;

32 and of Shemida, the family of the Shemidaites; and of Hepher, the family of the Hepherites.

33 Now Zelophehad the son of Hepher had no sons, but only daughters; and the names of the daughters of Zelophehad were Mahlah, Noah, Hoglah, Milcah and Tirzah.

34 These are the families of Manasseh; and those who were numbered of them were 52,700.

35 ¶ These are the sons of Ephraim according to their families: of Shuthelah, the family of the Shuthelahites; of Becher, the family of the Becherites; of Tahan, the family of the Tahanites.

36 And these are the sons of Shuthelah: of Eran, the family of the Eranites.

37 These are the families of the sons of Ephraim according to those who were numbered of them, 32,500. These are the sons of Joseph according to their families.

38 ¶ The sons of Benjamin according to their families: of Bela, the family of the Belaites; of Ashbel, the family of the Ashbelites; of Ahiram, the family of the Ahiramites;

39 of Shephupham, the family of the Shuphamites; of Hupham, the family of the Huphamites.

40 And the sons of Bela were Ard and Naaman: of Ard, the family of the Ardites; of Naaman, the family of the Naamites.

41 These are the sons of Benjamin according to their families; and those who were numbered of them were 45,600.

42 ¶ These are the sons of Dan according to their families: of Shuham, the family of the Shuhamites. These are the families of Dan according to their families.

43 All the families of the Shuhamites, according to those who were numbered of them, were 64,400.

44 ¶ The sons of Asher according to their families: of Imnah, the family of the Imnites; of Ishvi, the family of the Ishvites; of Beriah, the family of the Beriites.

45 Of the sons of Beriah: of Heber, the family of the Heberites; of Malchiel, the family of the Malchielites.

46 And the name of the daughter of Asher was Serah.

47 These are the families of the sons of Asher according to those who were numbered of them, 53,400.

48 ¶ The sons of Naphtali according to their families: of Jahzeel, the family of the Jahzeelites; of Guni, the family of the Gunites;

49 of Jezer, the family of the Jezerites; of Shillem, the family of the Shillemites.

50 These are the families of Naphtali according to their families; and those who were numbered of them were 45,400.

51 ¶ These are those who were numbered of the sons of Israel, 601,730.

52 ¶ Then the LORD spoke to Moses, saying,

53 "Among these the land shall be divided for an inheritance according to the number of names.

54 "To the larger group you shall increase their inheritance, and to the smaller group you shall diminish their inheritance; each shall be given their inheritance according to those who were numbered of them.

55 "But the land shall be divided by lot. They shall receive their inheritance according to the names of the tribes of their fathers.

56 "According to the selection by lot, their inheritance shall be divided between the larger and the smaller groups."

57 ¶ And these are those who were numbered of the Levites according to their families: of Gershon, the family of the Gershonites; of Kohath, the family of the Kohathites; of Merari, the family of the Merarites.

58 These are the families of Levi: the family of the Libnites, the family of the Hebronites, the family of the Mahlites, the family of the Mushites, the family of the Korahites. And Kohath became the father of Amram.

59 And the name of Amram's wife was Jochebed, the daughter of Levi,

who was born to Levi in Egypt; and she bore to Amram: Aaron and Moses and their sister Miriam.

60 And to Aaron were born Nadab and Abihu, Eleazar and Ithamar.

61 But Nadab and Abihu died when they offered strange fire before the LORD.

62 And those who were numbered of them were 23,000, every male from a month old and upward, for they were not numbered among the sons of Israel since no inheritance was given to them among the sons of Israel.

63 ¶ These are those who were numbered by Moses and Eleazar the priest, who numbered the sons of Israel in the plains of Moab by the Jordan at Jericho.

64 But among these there was not a man of those who were numbered by Moses and Aaron the priest, who numbered the sons of Israel in the wilderness of Sinai.

65 For the LORD had said of them, "They shall surely die in the wilderness." And not a man was left of them, except Caleb the son of Jephunneh, and Joshua the son of Nun.

CHAPTER 27

THEN the daughters of Zelophehad, the son of Hepher, the son of Gilead, the son of Machir, the son of Manasseh, of the families of Manasseh the son of Joseph, came near; and these are the names of his daughters: Mahlah, Noah and Hoglah and Milcah and Tirzah.

2 And they stood before Moses and before Eleazar the priest and before the leaders and all the congregation, at the doorway of the tent of meeting, saying,

3"Our father died in the wilderness, yet he was not among the company of those who gathered themselves together against the LORD in the company of Korah; but he died in his own sin, and he had no sons.

4"Why should the name of our father be withdrawn from among his family because he had no son? Give us a possession among our father's brothers."

5 And Moses brought their case before the LORD.

6 ¶ Then the LORD spoke to Moses, saying,

7"The daughters of Zelophehad are right in *their* statements. You shall surely give them a hereditary possession among their father's brothers, and you shall transfer the inheritance of their father to them.

8"Further, you shall speak to the sons of Israel, saying, 'If a man dies and has no son, then you shall transfer his inheritance to his daughter.

9 'And if he has no daughter, then you shall give his inheritance to his brothers.

10 'And if he has no brothers, then you shall give his inheritance to his father's brothers.

11 'And if his father has no brothers, then you shall give his inheritance to his nearest relative in his own family, and he shall possess it; and it shall be a statutory ordinance to the sons of Israel, just as the LORD commanded Moses.' "

12 ¶ Then the LORD said to Moses, "Go up to this mountain of Abarim, and see the land which I have given to the sons of Israel.

13"And when you have seen it, you too shall be gathered to your people, as Aaron your brother was;

14 for in the wilderness of Zin, during the strife of the congregation, you rebelled against My command to treat Me as holy before their eyes at the water." (These are the waters of Meribah of Kadesh in the wilderness of Zin.)

15 ¶ Then Moses spoke to the LORD, saying,

16"May the LORD, the God of the spirits of all flesh, appoint a man over the congregation,

17 who will go out and come in before them, and who will lead them out and bring them in, that the congregation of the LORD may not be like sheep which have no shepherd."

18 So the LORD said to Moses, "Take Joshua the son of Nun, a man in whom is the Spirit, and lay your hand on him;

19 and have him stand before Eleazar the priest and before all the congregation; and commission him in their sight.

20"And you shall put some of your authority on him, in order that all the congregation of the sons of Israel may obey *him*.

21"Moreover, he shall stand before Eleazar the priest, who shall inquire for him by the judgment of the Urim before the LORD. At his command they shall go out and at his command they shall come in, *both* he and the sons of Israel with him, even all the congregation."

22 And Moses did just as the LORD commanded him; and he took Joshua and set him before Eleazar the priest, and before all the congregation.

23 Then he laid his hands on him and commissioned him, just as the LORD had spoken through Moses.

CHAPTER 28

THEN the LORD spoke to Moses, saying,

2"Command the sons of Israel and say to them, 'You shall be careful to present My offering, My food for My offerings by fire, of a soothing aroma to Me, at their appointed time.'

3"And you shall say to them, 'This is the offering by fire which you shall offer to the LORD; two male lambs one year old without defect *as* a continual burnt offering every day.

4 'You shall offer the one lamb in the morning, and the other lamb you shall offer at twilight;

5 also a tenth of an ephah of fine flour for a grain offering, mixed with a fourth of a hin of beaten oil.

6 'It is a continual burnt offering which was ordained in Mount Sinai as a soothing aroma, an offering by fire to the LORD.

7 'Then the libation with it *shall be* a fourth of a hin for each lamb, in the holy place you shall pour out a libation of strong drink to the LORD.

8 'And the other lamb you shall offer at twilight; as the grain offering of the morning and as its libation, you shall offer it, an offering by fire, a soothing aroma to the LORD.

9 ¶ 'Then on the sabbath day two male lambs one year old without defect, and two-tenths *of an ephah* of fine flour mixed with oil as a grain offering, and its libation:

10 'This is the burnt offering of every sabbath in addition to the continual burnt offering and its libation.

11 ¶ 'Then at the beginning of each of your months you shall present a burnt offering to the LORD; two bulls and one ram, seven male lambs one year old without defect,

12 and three-tenths *of an ephah* of fine flour for a grain offering, mixed with oil, for each bull; and two-tenths of fine flour for a grain offering, mixed with oil, for the one ram;

13 and a tenth *of an ephah* of fine flour mixed with oil for a grain offering for each lamb, for a burnt offering of a soothing aroma, an offering by fire to the LORD.

14 'And their libations shall be half a hin of wine for a bull and a third of a hin for the ram and a fourth of a hin for a lamb; this is the burnt offering of each month throughout the months of the year.

15 'And one male goat for a sin offering to the LORD; it shall be offered with its libation in addition to the continual burnt offering.

16 ¶ 'Then on the fourteenth day of the first month shall be the LORD's Passover.

17 'And on the fifteenth day of this month *shall be* a feast, unleavened bread *shall be* eaten for seven days.

18 'On the first day *shall be* a holy convocation; you shall do no laborious work.

19 'And you shall present an offering by fire, a burnt offering to the LORD: two bulls and one ram and seven male lambs one year old, having them without defect.

20 'And for their grain offering, you shall offer fine flour mixed with oil: three-tenths *of an ephah* for a bull and two-tenths for the ram.

21 'A tenth *of an ephah* you shall offer for each of the seven lambs,

22 and one male goat for a sin offering, to make atonement for you.

23 'You shall present these besides the burnt offering of the morning, which is for a continual burnt offering.

24 'After this manner you shall present daily, for seven days, the food of the offering by fire, of a soothing aroma to the LORD; it shall be presented with its libation in addition to the continual burnt offering.

25 'And on the seventh day you shall have a holy convocation; you shall do no laborious work.

26 ¶ 'Also on the day of the first fruits, when you present a new grain offering to the LORD in your *Feast of Weeks*, you shall have a holy convocation; you shall do no laborious work.

27 'And you shall offer a burnt offering for a soothing aroma to the LORD, two young bulls, one ram, seven male lambs one year old,

28 and their grain offering, fine flour mixed with oil, three-tenths *of an ephah* for each bull, two-tenths for the one ram,

29 a tenth for each of the seven lambs,

30 one male goat to make atonement for you.

31 'Besides the continual burnt offering and its grain offering, you shall present *them* with their libations. They shall be without defect.

CHAPTER 29

'NOW in the seventh month, on the first day of the month, you shall also have a holy convocation; you shall do no laborious work. It will be to you a day for blowing trumpets.

2 'And you shall offer a burnt offering as a soothing aroma to the LORD: one bull, one ram, *and* seven male lambs one year old without defect;

3 also their grain offering, fine flour mixed with oil, three-tenths *of an ephah* for the bull, two-tenths for the ram,

4 and one-tenth for each of the seven lambs.

5 'And *offer* one male goat for a sin offering, to make atonement for you,

6 besides the burnt offering of the new moon, and its grain offering, and the continual burnt offering and its grain offering, and their libations, according to their ordinance, for a soothing aroma, an offering by fire to the LORD.

7 ¶ 'Then on the tenth day of this seventh month you shall have a holy convocation, and you shall humble yourselves; you shall not do any work.

8 'And you shall present a burnt offering to the LORD *as* a soothing aroma: one bull, one ram, seven male lambs one year old, having them without defect;

9 and their grain offering, fine flour mixed with oil, three-tenths *of an ephah* for the bull, two-tenths for the one ram,

10 a tenth for each of the seven lambs;

11 one male goat for a sin offering, besides the sin offering of atonement and the continual burnt offering and its grain offering, and their libations.

12 ¶ 'Then on the fifteenth day of the seventh month you shall have a holy convocation; you shall do no laborious work, and you shall observe a feast to the LORD for seven days.

13 'And you shall present a burnt offering, an offering by fire as a soothing aroma to the LORD: thirteen bulls, two rams, fourteen male lambs one year old, which are without defect,

14 and their grain offering, fine flour mixed with oil, three-tenths *of an ephah* for each of the thirteen bulls, two-tenths for each of the two rams,

15 and a tenth for each of the fourteen lambs;

16 and one male goat for a sin offering, besides the continual burnt offering, its grain offering and its libation.

17 ¶ 'Then on the second day: twelve bulls, two rams, fourteen male lambs one year old without defect;

18 and their grain offering and their libations for the bulls, for the rams and for the lambs, by their number according to the ordinance;

19 and one male goat for a sin offering, besides the continual burnt offering and its grain offering, and their libations.

20 ¶ 'Then on the third day: eleven bulls, two rams, fourteen male lambs one year old without defect;

21 and their grain offering and their libations for the bulls, for the rams and for the lambs, by their number according to the ordinance;

22 and one male goat for a sin offering, besides the continual burnt offering and its grain offering and its libation.

23 ¶ 'Then on the fourth day: ten bulls, two rams, fourteen male lambs one year old without defect;

24 their grain offering and their libations for the bulls, for the rams and for the lambs, by their number according to the ordinance;

25 and one male goat for a sin offering, besides the continual burnt offering, its grain offering and its libation.

26 ¶ 'Then on the fifth day: nine bulls, two rams, fourteen male lambs one year old without defect;

27 and their grain offering and their libations for the bulls, for the rams and for the lambs, by their number according to the ordinance;

28 and one male goat for a sin offering, besides the continual burnt offering and its grain offering and its libation.

29 ¶ 'Then on the sixth day: eight bulls, two rams, fourteen male lambs one year old without defect;

30 and their grain offering and their libations for the bulls, for the rams and for the lambs, by their number according to the ordinance;

31 and one male goat for a sin offering, besides the continual burnt offering, its grain offering and its libations.

32 ¶ 'Then on the seventh day: seven bulls, two rams, fourteen male lambs one year old without defect;

33 and their grain offering and their libations for the bulls, for the rams and for the lambs, by their number according to the ordinance;

34 and one male goat for a sin offering, besides the continual burnt offering, its grain offering and its libation.

35 ¶ 'On the eighth day you shall have a solemn assembly; you shall do no laborious work.

36 'But you shall present a burnt offering, an offering by fire, as a soothing aroma to the LORD: one bull, one ram, seven male lambs one year old without defect;

37 their grain offering and their libations for the bull, for the ram and for the lambs, by their number according to the ordinance;

38 and one male goat for a sin offering, besides the continual burnt offering and its grain offering and its libation.

39 ¶ 'You shall present these to the LORD at your appointed times, besides your votive offerings and your freewill offerings, for your burnt offerings and for your grain offerings and for your libations and for your peace offerings.' "

40 And Moses spoke to the sons of Israel in accordance with all that the LORD had commanded Moses.

CHAPTER 30

THEN Moses spoke to the heads of the tribes of the sons of Israel, saying, "This is the word which the LORD has commanded.

2 "If a man makes a vow to the LORD, or takes an oath to bind himself with a binding obligation, he shall not violate his word; he shall do according to all that proceeds out of his mouth.

3 "Also if a woman makes a vow to the LORD, and binds herself by an obligation in her father's house in her youth,

4 and her father hears her vow and her obligation by which she has bound herself, and her father says nothing to her, then all her vows shall stand, and every obligation by which she has bound herself shall stand.

5 "But if her father should forbid her on the day he hears *of it,* none of her vows or her obligations by which she has bound herself shall stand; and the LORD will forgive her because her father had forbidden her.

6 ¶ "However, if she should marry while under her vows or the rash statement of her lips by which she has bound herself,

7 and her husband hears of it and says nothing to her on the day he hears *it,* then her vows shall stand and her obligations by which she has bound herself shall stand.

8 "But if on the day her husband hears *of it,* he forbids her, then he shall annul her vow which she is under and the rash statement of her lips by which she has bound herself; and the LORD will forgive her.

9 ¶ "But the vow of a widow or of a divorced woman, everything by which she has bound herself, shall stand against her.

10 "However, if she vowed in her husband's house, or bound herself by an obligation with an oath,

11 and her husband heard *it,* but said nothing to her *and* did not forbid her, then all her vows shall stand, and every obligation by which she bound herself shall stand.

12 "But if her husband indeed annuls them on the day he hears *them,* then whatever proceeds out of her lips concerning her vows or concerning the obligation of herself, shall not stand;

her husband has annulled them, and the LORD will forgive her.

13 ¶"Every vow and every binding oath to humble herself, her husband may confirm it or her husband may annul it.

14"But if her husband indeed says nothing to her from day to day, then he confirms all her vows or all her obligations which are on her; he has confirmed them, because he said nothing to her on the day he heard them.

15"But if he indeed annuls them after he has heard them, then he shall bear her guilt."

16 ¶ These are the statutes which the LORD commanded Moses, *as* between a man and his wife, *and as* between a father and his daughter, *while she is* in her youth in her father's house.

CHAPTER 31

THEN the LORD spoke to Moses, saying,

2"Take full vengeance for the sons of Israel on the Midianites; afterward you will be gathered to your people."

3 And Moses spoke to the people, saying, "Arm men from among you for the war, that they may go against Midian, to execute the LORD's vengeance on Midian.

4"A thousand from each tribe of all the tribes of Israel you shall send to the war."

5 So there were furnished from the thousands of Israel, a thousand from each tribe, twelve thousand armed for war.

6 And Moses sent them, a thousand from each tribe, to the war, and Phinehas the son of Eleazar the priest, to the war with them, and the holy vessels and the trumpets for the alarm in his hand.

7 So they made war against Midian, just as the LORD had commanded Moses, and they killed every male.

8 And they killed the kings of Midian along with the *rest of* their slain: Evi and Rekem and Zur and Hur and Reba, the five kings of Midian; they also killed Balaam the son of Beor with the sword.

9 And the sons of Israel captured the women of Midian and their little ones; and all their cattle and all their flocks and all their goods, they plundered.

10 Then they burned all their cities where they lived and all their camps with fire.

11 And they took all the spoil and all the prey, both of man and of beast.

12 And they brought the captives and the prey and the spoil to Moses, and to Eleazar the priest and to the congregation of the sons of Israel, to the camp at the plains of Moab, which are by the Jordan opposite Jericho.

13 ¶ And Moses and Eleazar the priest and all the leaders of the congregation went out to meet them outside the camp.

14 And Moses was angry with the officers of the army, the captains of thousands and the captains of hundreds, who had come from service in the war.

15 And Moses said to them, "Have you spared all the women?

16"Behold, these caused the sons of Israel, through the counsel of Balaam, to trespass against the LORD in the matter of Peor, so the plague was among the congregation of the LORD.

17"Now therefore, kill every male among the little ones, and kill every woman who has known man intimately.

18"But all the girls who have not known man intimately, spare for yourselves.

19"And you, camp outside the camp seven days; whoever has killed any person, and whoever has touched any slain, purify yourselves, you and your captives, on the third day and on the seventh day.

20"And you shall purify for yourselves every garment and every article of leather and all the work of goats' *hair*, and all articles of wood."

21 ¶ Then Eleazar the priest said to the men of war who had gone to battle, "This is the statute of the law which the LORD has commanded Moses:

22 only the gold and the silver, the bronze, the iron, the tin and the lead,

23 everything that can stand the fire, you shall pass through the fire, and it shall be clean, but it shall be purified with water for impurity. But whatever cannot stand the fire you shall pass through the water.

24"And you shall wash your clothes on the seventh day and be clean, and afterward you may enter the camp."

25 ¶ Then the LORD spoke to Moses, saying,

26"You and Eleazar the priest and the heads of the fathers' *households* of the congregation, take a count of the booty that was captured, both of man and of animal;

27 and divide the booty between the warriors who went out to battle and all the congregation.

28"And levy a tax for the LORD from the men of war who went out to battle, one in five hundred of the persons and of the cattle and of the donkeys and of the sheep;

29 take it from their half and give it to Eleazar the priest, as an offering to the LORD.

30"And from the sons of Israel's half, you shall take one drawn out of every fifty of the persons, of the cattle, of the donkeys and of the sheep, from all the animals, and give them to the Levites who keep charge of the tabernacle of the LORD."

31 And Moses and Eleazar the priest did just as the LORD had commanded Moses.

32 ¶ Now the booty that remained from the spoil which the men of war had plundered was 675,000 sheep,

33 and 72,000 cattle,

34 and 61,000 donkeys,

35 and of human beings, of the women who had not known man intimately, all the persons were 32,000.

36 And the half, the portion of those who went out to war, was *as follows:* the number of sheep was 337,500,

37 and the LORD's levy of the sheep was 675,

38 and the cattle were 36,000, from which the LORD's levy was 72.

39 And the donkeys were 30,500, from which the LORD's levy was 61.

40 And the human beings were 16,000, from whom the LORD's levy was 32 persons.

41 And Moses gave the levy *which was* the LORD's offering to Eleazar the priest, just as the LORD had commanded Moses.

42 ¶ As for the sons of Israel's half,

which Moses separated from the men who had gone to war—

43 now the congregation's half was 337,500 sheep,

44 and 36,000 cattle,

45 and 30,500 donkeys,

46 and the human beings were 16,000—

47 and from the sons of Israel's half, Moses took one drawn out of every fifty, both of man and of animals, and gave them to the Levites, who kept charge of the tabernacle of the LORD, just as the LORD had commanded Moses.

48 ¶ Then the officers who were over the thousands of the army, the captains of thousands and the captains of hundreds, approached Moses;

49 and they said to Moses, "Your servants have taken a census of men of war who are in our charge, and no man of us is missing.

50"So we have brought as an offering to the LORD what each man found, articles of gold, armlets and bracelets, signet rings, earrings and necklaces, to make atonement for ourselves before the LORD."

51 And Moses and Eleazar the priest took the gold from them, all kinds of wrought articles.

52 And all the gold of the offering which they offered up to the LORD, from the captains of thousands and the captains of hundreds, was 16,750 shekels.

53 The men of war had taken booty, every man for himself.

54 So Moses and Eleazar the priest took the gold from the captains of thousands and of hundreds, and brought it to the tent of meeting as a memorial for the sons of Israel before the LORD.

CHAPTER 32

Now the sons of Reuben and the sons of Gad had an exceedingly large number of livestock. So when they saw the land of Jazer and the land of Gilead, that it was indeed a place suitable for livestock,

2 the sons of Gad and the sons of Reuben came and spoke to Moses and to Eleazar the priest and to the leaders of the congregation, saying,

3"Ataroth, Dibon, Jazer, Nimrah,

Heshbon, Elealeh, Sebam, Nebo and Beon,

4 the land which the LORD conquered before the congregation of Israel, is a land for livestock; and your servants have livestock."

5 And they said, "If we have found favor in your sight, let this land be given to your servants as a possession; do not take us across the Jordan."

6 ¶ But Moses said to the sons of Gad and to the sons of Reuben, "Shall your brothers go to war while you yourselves sit here?

7 "Now why are you discouraging the sons of Israel from crossing over into the land which the LORD has given them?

8 "This is what your fathers did when I sent them from Kadesh-barnea to see the land.

9 "For when they went up to the valley of Eshcol and saw the land, they discouraged the sons of Israel so that they did not go into the land which the LORD had given them.

10 "So the LORD's anger burned in that day, and He swore, saying,

11 'None of the men who came up from Egypt, from twenty years old and upward, shall see the land which I swore to Abraham, to Isaac and to Jacob; for they did not follow Me fully,

12 except Caleb the son of Jephunneh the Kenizzite and Joshua the son of Nun, for they have followed the LORD fully.'

13 "So the LORD's anger burned against Israel, and He made them wander in the wilderness forty years, until the entire generation of those who had done evil in the sight of the LORD was destroyed.

14 "Now behold, you have risen up in your fathers' place, a brood of sinful men, to add still more to the burning anger of the LORD against Israel.

15 "For if you turn away from following Him, He will once more abandon them in the wilderness; and you will destroy all these people."

16 ¶ Then they came near to him and said, "We will build here sheepfolds for our livestock and cities for our little ones;

17 but we ourselves will be armed ready *to go* before the sons of Israel, until we have brought them to their place, while our little ones live in the fortified cities because of the inhabitants of the land.

18 "We will not return to our homes until every one of the sons of Israel has possessed his inheritance.

19 "For we will not have an inheritance with them on the other side of the Jordan and beyond, because our inheritance has fallen to us on this side of the Jordan toward the east."

20 ¶ So Moses said to them, "If you will do this, if you will arm yourselves before the LORD for the war,

21 and all of you armed men cross over the Jordan before the LORD until He has driven His enemies out from before Him,

22 and the land is subdued before the LORD, then afterward you shall return and be free of obligation toward the LORD and toward Israel, and this land shall be yours for a possession before the LORD.

23 "But if you will not do so, behold, you have sinned against the LORD, and be sure your sin will find you out.

24 "Build yourselves cities for your little ones, and sheepfolds for your sheep; and do what you have promised."

25 And the sons of Gad and the sons of Reuben spoke to Moses, saying, "Your servants will do just as my lord commands.

26 "Our little ones, our wives, our livestock and all our cattle shall remain there in the cities of Gilead;

27 while your servants, everyone who is armed for war, will cross over in the presence of the LORD to battle, just as my lord says."

28 ¶ So Moses gave command concerning them to Eleazar the priest, and to Joshua the son of Nun, and to the heads of the fathers' *households* of the tribes of the sons of Israel.

29 And Moses said to them, "If the sons of Gad and the sons of Reuben, everyone who is armed for battle, will cross with you over the Jordan in the presence of the LORD, and the land will be subdued before you, then you shall give them the land of Gilead for a possession;

30 but if they will not cross over with you armed, they shall have possessions among you in the land of Canaan."

31 And the sons of Gad and the sons of Reuben answered, saying, "As the LORD has said to your servants, so we will do.

32 "We ourselves will cross over armed in the presence of the LORD into the land of Canaan, and the possession of our inheritance *shall remain* with us across the Jordan."

33 ¶ So Moses gave to them, to the sons of Gad and to the sons of Reuben and to the half-tribe of Joseph's son Manasseh, the kingdom of Sihon, king of the Amorites and the kingdom of Og, the king of Bashan, the land with its cities with *their* territories, the cities of the surrounding land.

34 And the sons of Gad built Dibon and Ataroth and Aroer,

35 and Atroth-shophan and Jazer and Jogbehah,

36 and Beth-nimrah and Beth-haran as fortified cities, and sheepfolds for sheep.

37 And the sons of Reuben built Heshbon and Elealeh and Kiriathaim,

38 and Nebo and Baal-meon—*their* names being changed—and Sibmah, and they gave *other* names to the cities which they built.

39 And the sons of Machir the son of Manasseh went to Gilead and took it, and dispossessed the Amorites who were in it.

40 So Moses gave Gilead to Machir the son of Manasseh, and he lived in it.

41 And Jair the son of Manasseh went and took its towns, and called them Havvoth-jair.

42 And Nobah went and took Kenath and its villages, and called it Nobah after his own name.

CHAPTER 33

THESE are the journeys of the sons of Israel, by which they came out from the land of Egypt by their armies, under the leadership of Moses and Aaron.

2 And Moses recorded their starting places according to their journeys by the command of the LORD, and these are their journeys according to their starting places.

3 And they journeyed from Rameses in the first month, on the fifteenth day of the first month; on the next day after the Passover the sons of Israel started out boldly in the sight of all the Egyptians,

4 while the Egyptians were burying all their first-born whom the LORD had struck down among them. The LORD had also executed judgments on their gods.

5 ¶ Then the sons of Israel journeyed from Rameses, and camped in Succoth.

6 And they journeyed from Succoth, and camped in Etham, which is on the edge of the wilderness.

7 And they journeyed from Etham, and turned back to Pi-hahiroth, which faces Baal-zephon; and they camped before Migdol.

8 And they journeyed from before Hahiroth, and passed through the midst of the sea into the wilderness; and they went three days' journey in the wilderness of Etham, and camped at Marah.

9 And they journeyed from Marah, and came to Elim; and in Elim there were twelve springs of water and seventy palm trees; and they camped there.

10 And they journeyed from Elim, and camped by the Red Sea.

11 And they journeyed from the Red Sea, and camped in the wilderness of Sin.

12 And they journeyed from the wilderness of Sin, and camped at Dophkah.

13 And they journeyed from Dophkah, and camped at Alush.

14 And they journeyed from Alush, and camped at Rephidim; now it was there that the people had no water to drink.

15 And they journeyed from Rephidim, and camped in the wilderness of Sinai.

16 And they journeyed from the wilderness of Sinai, and camped at Kibroth-hattaavah.

17 ¶ And they journeyed from Kibroth-hattaavah, and camped at Hazeroth.

18 And they journeyed from Hazeroth, and camped at Rithmah.

19 And they journeyed from Rithmah, and camped at Rimmon-perez.

20 And they journeyed from Rimmon-perez, and camped at Libnah.

21 And they journeyed from Libnah, and camped at Rissah.

22 And they journeyed from Rissah, and camped in Kehelathah.

23 And they journeyed from Kehelathah, and camped at Mount Shepher.

24 And they journeyed from Mount Shepher, and camped at Haradah.

25 And they journeyed from Haradah, and camped at Makheloth.

26 And they journeyed from Makheloth, and camped at Tahath.

27 And they journeyed from Tahath, and camped at Terah.

28 And they journeyed from Terah, and camped at Mithkah.

29 And they journeyed from Mithkah, and camped at Hashmonah.

30 And they journeyed from Hashmonah, and camped at Moseroth.

31 And they journeyed from Moseroth, and camped at Bene-jaakan.

32 And they journeyed from Bene-jaakan, and camped at Hor-haggidgad.

33 And they journeyed from Hor-haggidgad, and camped at Jotbathah.

34 And they journeyed from Jotbathah, and camped at Abronah.

35 And they journeyed from Abronah, and camped at Ezion-geber.

36 And they journeyed from Ezion-geber, and camped in the wilderness of Zin, that is, Kadesh.

37 And they journeyed from Kadesh, and camped at Mount Hor, at the edge of the land of Edom.

38 ¶ Then Aaron the priest went up to Mount Hor at the command of the LORD, and died there, in the fortieth year after the sons of Israel had come from the land of Egypt on the first *day* in the fifth month.

39 And Aaron was one hundred twenty-three years old when he died on Mount Hor.

40 ¶ Now the Canaanite, the king of Arad who lived in the Negev in the land of Canaan, heard of the coming of the sons of Israel.

41 ¶ Then they journeyed from Mount Hor, and camped at Zalmonah.

42 And they journeyed from Zalmonah, and camped at Punon.

43 And they journeyed from Punon, and camped at Oboth.

44 And they journeyed from Oboth, and camped at Iye-abarim, at the border of Moab.

45 And they journeyed from Iyim, and camped at Dibon-gad.

46 And they journeyed from Dibon-gad, and camped at Almon-diblathaim.

47 And they journeyed from Almon-diblathaim, and camped in the mountains of Abarim, before Nebo.

48 And they journeyed from the mountains of Abarim, and camped in the plains of Moab by the Jordan *opposite* Jericho.

49 And they camped by the Jordan, from Beth-jeshimoth as far as Abel-shittim in the plains of Moab.

50 ¶ Then the LORD spoke to Moses in the plains of Moab by the Jordan *opposite* Jericho, saying,

51 "Speak to the sons of Israel and say to them, 'When you cross over the Jordan into the land of Canaan,

52 then you shall drive out all the inhabitants of the land from before you, and destroy all their figured stones, and destroy all their molten images and demolish all their high places;

53 and you shall take possession of the land and live in it, for I have given the land to you to possess it.

54 'And you shall inherit the land by lot according to your families; to the larger you shall give more inheritance, and to the smaller you shall give less inheritance. Wherever the lot falls to anyone, that shall be his. You shall inherit according to the tribes of your fathers.

55 'But if you do not drive out the inhabitants of the land from before you, then it shall come about that those whom you let remain of them *will become* as pricks in your eyes and as thorns in your sides, and they shall trouble you in the land in which you live.

56 'And it shall come about that as I plan to do to them, so I will do to you.' "

CHAPTER 34

THEN the LORD spoke to Moses, saying,

2 "Command the sons of Israel and say to them, 'When you enter the land of Canaan, this is the land that shall fall to you as an inheritance, *even the* land of Canaan according to its borders.

3 'Your southern sector shall extend from the wilderness of Zin along the

side of Edom, and your southern border shall extend from the end of the Salt Sea eastward.

4 'Then your border shall turn *direction* from the south to the ascent of Akrabbim, and continue to Zin, and its [30]termination shall be to the south of Kadesh-barnea; and it shall reach Hazaraddar, and continue to Azmon.

5 'And the border shall turn *direction* from Azmon to the brook of Egypt, and its termination shall be at the sea.

6 ¶ 'As for the western border, you shall have the Great Sea, that is, *its* coastline; this shall be your west border.

7 ¶ 'And this shall be your north border: you shall draw your *border* line from the Great Sea to Mount Hor.

8 'You shall draw a line from Mount Hor to the Lebo-hamath, and the termination of the border shall be at Zedad;

9 and the border shall proceed to Ziphron, and its termination shall be at Hazar-enan. This shall be your north border.

10 ¶ 'For your eastern border you shall also draw a line from Hazar-enan to Shepham,

11 and the border shall go down from Shepham to Riblah on the east side of Ain; and the border shall go down and reach to the [31]slope on the east side of the Sea of Chinnereth.

12 'And the border shall go down to the Jordan and its termination shall be at the Salt Sea. This shall be your land according to its borders all around.' "

13 ¶ So Moses commanded the sons of Israel, saying, "This is the land that you are to apportion by lot among you as a possession, which the LORD has commanded to give to the nine and a half tribes.

14"For the tribe of the sons of Reuben have received *theirs* according to their fathers' households, and the tribe of the sons of Gad according to their fathers' households, and the half-tribe of Manasseh have received their possession.

15"The two and a half tribes have received their possession across the Jordan opposite Jericho, eastward toward the sunrising."

16 ¶ Then the LORD spoke to Moses, saying,

17"These are the names of the men who shall apportion the land to you for inheritance: Eleazar the priest and Joshua the son of Nun.

18"And you shall take one leader of every tribe to apportion the land for inheritance.

19"And these are the names of the men: of the tribe of Judah, Caleb the son of Jephunneh.

20"And of the tribe of the sons of Simeon, Samuel the son of Ammihud.

21"Of the tribe of Benjamin, Elidad the son of Chislon.

22"And of the tribe of the sons of Dan a leader, Bukki the son of Jogli.

23"Of the sons of Joseph: of the tribe of the sons of Manasseh a leader, Hanniel the son of Ephod.

24"And of the tribe of the sons of Ephraim a leader, Kemuel the son of Shiphtan.

25"And of the tribe of the sons of Zebulun a leader, Elizaphan the son of Parnach.

26"And of the tribe of the sons of Issachar a leader, Paltiel the son of Azzan.

27"And of the tribe of the sons of Asher a leader, Ahihud the son of Shelomi.

28"And of the tribe of the sons of Naphtali a leader, Pedahel the son of Ammihud."

29 These are those whom the LORD commanded to apportion the inheritance to the sons of Israel in the land of Canaan.

CHAPTER 35

NOW the LORD spoke to Moses in the plains of Moab by the Jordan opposite Jericho, saying,

2"Command the sons of Israel that they give to the Levites from the inheritance of their possession, cities to live in; and you shall give to the Levites pasture lands around the cities.

3"And the cities shall be theirs to live in; and their pasture lands shall be for their cattle and for their herds and for all their beasts.

4 ¶"And the pasture lands of the cities which you shall give to the Levites *shall extend* from the wall of the

---

[30] Lit., *goings out,* and so throughout this context
[31] Lit., *shoulder*

city outward a thousand cubits around.

5"You shall also measure outside the city on the east side two thousand cubits, and on the south side two thousand cubits, and on the west side two thousand cubits, and on the north side two thousand cubits, with the city in the center. This shall become theirs as pasture lands for the cities.

6"And the cities which you shall give to the Levites *shall be* the six cities of refuge, which you shall give for the manslayer to flee to; and in addition to them you shall give forty-two cities.

7"All the cities which you shall give to the Levites *shall be* forty-eight cities, together with their pasture lands.

8"As for the cities which you shall give from the possession of the sons of Israel, you shall take more from the larger and you shall take less from the smaller; each shall give some of his cities to the Levites in proportion to his possession which he inherits."

9 ¶ Then the LORD spoke to Moses, saying,

10"Speak to the sons of Israel and say to them, 'When you cross the Jordan into the land of Canaan,

11 then you shall select for yourselves cities to be your cities of refuge, that the manslayer who has killed any person unintentionally may flee there.

12 'And the cities shall be to you as a refuge from the avenger, so that the manslayer may not die until he stands before the congregation for trial.

13 'And the cities which you are to give shall be your six cities of refuge.

14 'You shall give three cities across the Jordan and three cities in the land of Canaan; they are to be cities of refuge.

15 'These six cities shall be for refuge for the sons of Israel, and for the alien and for the sojourner among them; that anyone who kills a person unintentionally may flee there.

16 ¶ 'But if he struck him down with an iron object, so that he died, he is a murderer; the murderer shall surely be put to death.

17 'And if he struck him down with a stone in the hand, by which he may die, and *as a result* he died, he is a murderer; the murderer shall surely be put to death.

18 'Or if he struck him with a wooden object in the hand, by which he may die, and *as a result* he died, he is a murderer; the murderer shall surely be put to death.

19 'The blood avenger himself shall put the murderer to death; he shall put him to death when he meets him.

20 'And if he pushed him of hatred, or threw something at him lying in wait and *as a result* he died,

21 or if he struck him down with his hand in enmity, and *as a result* he died, the one who struck him shall surely be put to death, he is a murderer; the blood avenger shall put the murderer to death when he meets him.

22 ¶ 'But if he pushed him suddenly without enmity, or threw something at him without lying in wait,

23 or with any deadly object of stone, and without seeing it dropped on him so that he died, while he was not his enemy nor seeking his injury,

24 then the congregation shall judge between the slayer and the blood avenger according to these ordinances.

25 'And the congregation shall deliver the manslayer from the hand of the blood avenger, and the congregation shall restore him to his city of refuge to which he fled; and he shall live in it until the death of the high priest who was anointed with the holy oil.

26 'But if the manslayer shall at any time go beyond the border of his city of refuge to which he may flee,

27 and the blood avenger finds him outside the border of his city of refuge, and the blood avenger kills the manslayer, he shall not be guilty of blood

28 because he should have remained in his city of refuge until the death of the high priest. But after the death of the high priest the manslayer shall return to the land of his possession.

29 ¶ 'And these things shall be for a statutory ordinance to you throughout your generations in all your dwellings.

30 'If anyone kills a person, the murderer shall be put to death at the evidence of witnesses, but no person shall be put to death on the testimony of one witness.

31 'Moreover, you shall not take ransom for the life of a murderer who is

guilty of death, but he shall surely be put to death.

32 'And you shall not take ransom for him who has fled to his city of refuge, that he may return to live in the land before the death of the priest.

33 'So you shall not pollute the land in which you are; for blood pollutes the land and no expiation can be made for the land for the blood that is shed on it, except by the blood of him who shed it.

34 'And you shall not defile the land in which you live, in the midst of which I dwell; for I the LORD am dwelling in the midst of the sons of Israel.' "

CHAPTER 36

AND the heads of the fathers' *households* of the family of the sons of Gilead, the son of Machir, the son of Manasseh, of the families of the sons of Joseph, came near and spoke before Moses and before the leaders, the heads of the fathers' *households* of the sons of Israel,

2 and they said, "The LORD commanded my lord to give the land by lot to the sons of Israel as an inheritance, and my lord was commanded by the LORD to give the inheritance of Zelophehad our brother to his daughters.

3"But if they marry one of the sons of the *other* tribes of the sons of Israel, their inheritance will be withdrawn from the inheritance of our fathers and will be added to the inheritance of the tribe to which they belong; thus it will be withdrawn from our allotted inheritance.

4"And when the jubilee of the sons of Israel comes, then their inheritance will be added to the inheritance of the tribe to which they belong; so their inheritance will be withdrawn from

the inheritance of the tribe of our fathers."

5 ¶ Then Moses commanded the sons of Israel according to the word of the LORD, saying, "The tribe of the sons of Joseph are right in *their* statements.

6"This is what the LORD has commanded concerning the daughters of Zelophehad, saying, 'Let them marry whom they wish; only they must marry within the family of the tribe of their father.'

7"Thus no inheritance of the sons of Israel shall be transferred from tribe to tribe, for the sons of Israel shall each hold to the inheritance of the tribe of his fathers.

8"And every daughter who comes into possession of an inheritance of any tribe of the sons of Israel, shall be wife to one of the family of the tribe of her father, so that the sons of Israel each may possess the inheritance of his fathers.

9"Thus no inheritance shall be transferred from one tribe to another tribe, for the tribes of the sons of Israel shall each hold to his own inheritance."

10 ¶ Just as the LORD had commanded Moses, so the daughters of Zelophehad did:

11 Mahlah, Tirzah, Hoglah, Milcah and Noah, the daughters of Zelophehad married their uncles' sons.

12 They married *those* from the families of the sons of Manasseh the son of Joseph, and their inheritance remained with the tribe of the family of their father.

13 ¶ These are the commandments and the ordinances which the LORD commanded to the sons of Israel through Moses in the plains of Moab by the Jordan *opposite* Jericho.

THESE are the words which Moses spoke to all Israel across the Jordan in the wilderness, in the Arabah opposite Suph, between Paran and Tophel and Laban and Hazeroth and Dizahab.

2 It is eleven days' *journey* from Horeb by the way of Mount Seir to Kadesh-barnea.

3 And it came about in the fortieth year, on the first day of the eleventh month, that Moses spoke to the children of Israel, according to all that the LORD had commanded him *to give* to them,

4 after he had defeated Sihon the king of the Amorites, who lived in Heshbon, and Og the king of Bashan, who lived in Ashtaroth and Edrei.

5 Across the Jordan in the land of Moab, Moses undertook to expound this law, saying,

6 "The LORD our God spoke to us at Horeb, saying, 'You have stayed long enough at this mountain.

7 'Turn and set your journey, and go to the hill country of the Amorites, and to all their neighbors in the Arabah, in the hill country and in the lowland and in the [1]Negev and by the seacoast, the land of the Canaanites, and Lebanon, as far as the great river, the river Euphrates.

8 'See, I have placed the land before you; go in and possess the land which the LORD swore to give to your fathers, to Abraham, to Isaac, and to Jacob, to them and their descendants after them.'

9 ¶ "And I spoke to you at that time, saying, 'I am not able to bear *the burden of* you alone.

10 'The LORD your God has multiplied you, and behold, you are this day as the stars of heaven for multitude.

11 'May the LORD, the God of your fathers, increase you a thousand-fold more than you are, and bless you, just as He has promised you!

12 'How can I alone bear the load and burden of you and your strife?

13 'Choose wise and discerning and experienced men from your tribes, and I will appoint them as your heads.'

14 "And you answered me and said, 'The thing which you have said to do is good.'

[1] I.e., South country

15 "So I took the heads of your tribes, wise and experienced men, and appointed them heads over you, leaders of thousands, and of hundreds, of fifties and of tens, and officers for your tribes.

16 ¶ "Then I charged your judges at that time, saying, 'Hear *the cases* between your fellow countrymen, and judge righteously between a man and his fellow countryman, or the alien who is with him.

17 'You shall not show partiality in judgment; you shall hear the small and the great alike. You shall not fear man, for the judgment is God's. And the case that is too hard for you, you shall bring to me, and I will hear it.'

18 "And I commanded you at that time all the things that you should do.

19 ¶ "Then we set out from Horeb, and went through all that great and terrible wilderness which you saw, on the way to the hill country of the Amorites, just as the LORD our God had commanded us; and we came to Kadesh-barnea.

20 "And I said to you, 'You have come to the hill country of the Amorites which the LORD our God is about to give us.

21 'See, the LORD your God has placed the land before you; go up, take possession, as the LORD, the God of your fathers, has spoken to you. Do not fear or be dismayed.'

22 "Then all of you approached me and said, 'Let us send men before us, that they may search out the land for us, and bring back to us word of the way by which we should go up, and the cities which we shall enter.'

23 "And the thing pleased me and I took twelve of your men, one man for each tribe.

24 "And they turned and went up into the hill country, and came to the valley of Eshcol, and spied it out.

25 "Then they took *some* of the fruit of the land in their hands and brought it down to us; and they brought us back a report and said, 'It is a good land which the LORD our God is about to give us.'

26 ¶ "Yet you were not willing to go up, but rebelled against the command of the LORD your God;

27 and you grumbled in your tents and said, 'Because the LORD hates us, He has brought us out of the land of Egypt to deliver us into the hand of the Amorites to destroy us.

28 'Where can we go up? Our brethren have made our hearts melt, saying, "The people are bigger and taller than we; the cities are large and fortified to heaven. And besides, we saw the sons of the Anakim there." '

29"Then I said to you, 'Do not be shocked, nor fear them.

30 'The LORD your God who goes before you will Himself fight on your behalf, just as He did for you in Egypt before your eyes,

31 and in the wilderness where you saw how the LORD your God carried you, just as a man carries his son, in all the way which you have walked, until you came to this place.'

32"But for all this, you did not trust the LORD your God,

33 who goes before you on *your* way, to seek out a place for you to encamp, in fire by night and cloud by day, to show you the way in which you should go.

34 ¶"Then the LORD heard the sound of your words, and He was angry and took an oath, saying,

35 'Not one of these men, this evil generation, shall see the good land which I swore to give your fathers,

36 except Caleb the son of Jephunneh; he shall see it, and to him and to his sons I will give the land on which he has set foot, because he has followed the LORD fully.'

37"The LORD was angry with me also on your account, saying, 'Not even you shall enter there.

38 'Joshua the son of Nun, who stands before you, he shall enter there; encourage him, for he shall cause Israel to inherit it.

39 'Moreover, your little ones who you said would become a prey, and your sons, who this day have no knowledge of good or evil, shall enter there, and I will give it to them, and they shall possess it.

40 'But as for you, turn around and set out for the wilderness by the way to the Red Sea.'

41 ¶"Then you answered and said to me, 'We have sinned against the LORD; we will indeed go up and fight, just as

the LORD our God commanded us.' And every man of you girded on his weapons of war, and regarded it as easy to go up into the hill country.

42"And the LORD said to me, 'Say to them, "Do not go up, nor fight, for I am not among you; lest you be defeated before your enemies." '

43"So I spoke to you, but you would not listen. Instead you rebelled against the command of the LORD, and acted presumptuously and went up into the hill country.

44"And the Amorites who lived in that hill country came out against you, and chased you as bees do, and crushed you from Seir to Hormah.

45"Then you returned and wept before the LORD; but the LORD did not listen to your voice, nor give ear to you.

46"So you remained in Kadesh many days, the days that you spent *there*.

CHAPTER 2

"THEN we turned and set out for the wilderness by the way to the Red Sea, as the LORD spoke to me, and circled Mount Seir for many days.

2"And the LORD spoke to me, saying,

3 'You have circled this mountain long enough. *Now* turn north,

4 and command the people, saying, "You will pass through the territory of your brothers the sons of Esau who live in Seir; and they will be afraid of you. So be very careful;

5 do not provoke them, for I will not give you any of their land, even *as little as* a footstep because I have given Mount Seir to Esau as a possession.

6"You shall buy food from them with money so that you may eat, and you shall also purchase water from them with money so that you may drink.

7"For the LORD your God has blessed you in all that you have done; He has known your wanderings through this great wilderness. These forty years the LORD your God has been with you; you have not lacked a thing." '

8 ¶"So we passed beyond our brothers the sons of Esau, who live in Seir, away from the Arabah road, away

from Elath and from Ezion-geber. And we turned and passed through by the way of the wilderness of Moab.

9"Then the LORD said to me, 'Do not harass Moab, nor provoke them to war, for I will not give you any of their land as a possession, because I have given Ar to the sons of Lot as a possession.

10 (The Emim lived there formerly, a people as great, numerous, and tall as the Anakim.

11 Like the Anakim, they are also regarded as Rephaim, but the Moabites call them Emim.

12 The Horites formerly lived in Seir, but the sons of Esau dispossessed them and destroyed them from before them and settled in their place, just as Israel did to the land of their possession which the LORD gave to them.)

13 'Now arise and cross over the brook Zered yourselves.' So we crossed over the brook Zered.

14"Now the time that it took for us to come from Kadesh-barnea, until we crossed over the brook Zered, was thirty-eight years; until all the generation of the men of war perished from within the camp, as the LORD had sworn to them.

15"Moreover the hand of the LORD was against them, to destroy them from within the camp, until they all perished.

16 ¶"So it came about when all the men of war had finally perished from among the people,

17 that the LORD spoke to me, saying,

18 'You shall cross over Ar, the border of Moab, today.

19 'And when you come opposite the sons of Ammon, do not harass them nor provoke them, for I will not give you any of the land of the sons of Ammon as a possession, because I have given it to the sons of Lot as a possession.'

20 (It is also regarded as the land of the Rephaim, for Rephaim formerly lived in it, but the Ammonites call them Zamzummin,

21 a people as great, numerous, and tall as the Anakim, but the LORD destroyed them before them. And they dispossessed them and settled in their place,

22 just as He did for the sons of Esau, who live in Seir, when He destroyed the Horites from before them; and they dispossessed them, and settled in their place even to this day.

23 And the Avvim, who lived in villages as far as Gaza, the [2]Caphtorim who came from [3]Caphtor, destroyed them and lived in their place.)

24 'Arise, set out, and pass through the valley of Arnon. Look! I have given Sihon the Amorite, king of Heshbon, and his land into your hand; begin to take possession and contend with him in battle.

25 'This day I will begin to put the dread and fear of you upon the peoples everywhere under the heavens, who, when they hear the report of you, shall tremble and be in anguish because of you.'

26 ¶"So I sent messengers from the wilderness of Kedemoth to Sihon king of Heshbon with words of peace, saying,

27 'Let me pass through your land, I will travel only on the highway; I will not turn aside to the right or to the left.

28 'You will sell me food for money so that I may eat, and give me water for money so that I may drink, only let me pass through on foot,

29 just as the sons of Esau who live in Seir and the Moabites who live in Ar did for me, until I cross over the Jordan into the land which the LORD our God is giving to us.'

30"But Sihon king of Heshbon was not willing for us to pass through his land; for the LORD your God hardened his spirit and made his heart obstinate, in order to deliver him into your hand, as he is today.

31"And the LORD said to me, 'See, I have begun to deliver Sihon and his land over to you. Begin to occupy, that you may possess his land.'

32 ¶"Then Sihon with all his people came out to meet us in battle at Jahaz.

33"And the LORD our God delivered him over to us; and we defeated him with his sons and all his people.

34"So we captured all his cities at that time, and utterly destroyed the men, women and children of every city. We left no survivor.

[2] I.e., Philistines   [3] I.e., Crete

35"We took only the animals as our booty and the spoil of the cities which we had captured.

36"From Aroer which is on the edge of the valley of Arnon, and *from* the city which is in the valley, even to Gilead, there was no city that was too high for us; the LORD our God delivered all over to us.

37"Only you did not go near to the land of the sons of Ammon, all along the river Jabbok and the cities of the hill country, and wherever the LORD our God had commanded us.

CHAPTER 3

"THEN we turned and went up the road to Bashan, and Og, king of Bashan, with all his people came out to meet us in battle at Edrei.

2"But the LORD said to me, 'Do not fear him, for I have delivered him and all his people and his land into your hand; and you shall do to him just as you did to Sihon king of the Amorites, who lived at Heshbon.'

3"So the LORD our God delivered Og also, king of Bashan, with all his people into our hand, and we smote them until no survivor was left.

4"And we captured all his cities at that time; there was not a city which we did not take from them: sixty cities, all the region of Argob, the kingdom of Og in Bashan.

5"All these were cities fortified with high walls, gates and bars, besides a great many unwalled towns.

6"And we utterly destroyed them, as we did to Sihon king of Heshbon, utterly destroying the men, women and children of every city.

7"But all the animals and the spoil of the cities we took as our booty.

8"Thus we took the land at that time from the hand of the two kings of the Amorites who were beyond the Jordan, from the valley of Arnon to Mount Hermon

9 (Sidonians call Hermon Sirion, and the Amorites call it Senir):

10 all the cities of the tableland and all Gilead and all Bashan, as far as Salecah and Edrei, cities of the kingdom of Og in Bashan.

11 (For only Og king of Bashan was left of the remnant of the Rephaim. Behold, his bedstead was an iron bedstead; it is in Rabbah of the sons of Ammon. Its length was nine cubits and its width four cubits by ordinary cubit.)

12 ¶"So we took possession of this land at that time. From Aroer, which is by the valley of Arnon, and half the hill country of Gilead and its cities, I gave to the Reubenites and to the Gadites.

13"And the rest of Gilead, and all Bashan, the kingdom of Og, I gave to the half-tribe of Manasseh, all the region of Argob (concerning all Bashan, it is called the land of Rephaim.

14 Jair the son of Manasseh took all the region of Argob as far as the border of the Geshurites and the Maacathites, and called it, *that is*, Bashan, after his own name, Havvoth-jair, *as it is* to this day.)

15"And to Machir I gave Gilead.

16"And to the Reubenites and to the Gadites, I gave from Gilead even as far as the valley of Arnon, the middle of the valley as a border and as far as the river Jabbok, the border of the sons of Ammon;

17 the Arabah also, with the Jordan as *a* border, from [4]Chinnereth even as far as the sea of the Arabah, the Salt Sea, at the foot of the slopes of Pisgah on the east.

18 ¶"Then I commanded you at that time, saying, 'The LORD your God has given you this land to possess it; all you valiant men shall cross over armed before your brothers, the sons of Israel.

19 'But your wives and your little ones and your livestock (I know that you have much livestock), shall remain in your cities which I have given you,

20 until the LORD gives rest to your fellow countrymen as to you, and they also possess the land which the LORD your God will give them beyond the Jordan. Then you may return every man to his possession, which I have given you.'

21"And I commanded Joshua at that time, saying, 'Your eyes have seen all that the LORD your God has done to these two kings; so the LORD shall do

[4] I.e., the Sea of Galilee

to all the kingdoms into which you are about to cross.

22 'Do not fear them, for the LORD your God is the one fighting for you.'

23 ¶"I also pleaded with the LORD at that time, saying,

24 'O Lord GOD, Thou hast begun to show Thy servant Thy greatness and Thy strong hand; for what god is there in heaven or on earth who can do such works and mighty acts as Thine?

25 'Let me, I pray, cross over and see the fair land that is beyond the Jordan, that good hill country and Lebanon.'

26"But the LORD was angry with me on your account, and would not listen to me; and the LORD said to me, 'Enough! Speak to Me no more of this matter.

27 'Go up to the top of Pisgah and lift up your eyes to the west and north and south and east, and see *it* with your eyes, for you shall not cross over this Jordan.

28 'But charge Joshua and encourage him and strengthen him; for he shall go across at the head of this people, and he shall give them as an inheritance the land which you will see.'

29"So we remained in the valley opposite Beth-peor.

CHAPTER 4

"AND now, O Israel, listen to the statutes and the judgments which I am teaching you to perform, in order that you may live and go in and take possession of the land which the LORD, the God of your fathers, is giving you.

2"You shall not add to the word which I am commanding you, nor take away from it, that you may keep the commandments of the LORD your God which I command you.

3"Your eyes have seen what the LORD has done in the case of Baal-peor, for all the men who followed Baal-peor, the LORD your God has destroyed them from among you.

4"But you who held fast to the LORD your God are alive today, every one of you.

5"See, I have taught you statutes and judgments just as the LORD my God commanded me, that you should do thus in the land where you are entering to possess it.

6"So keep and do *them*, for that is your wisdom and your understanding in the sight of the peoples who will hear all these statutes and say, 'Surely this great nation is a wise and understanding people.'

7"For what great nation is there that has a god so near to it as is the LORD our God whenever we call on Him?

8"Or what great nation is there that has statutes and judgments as righteous as this whole law which I am setting before you today?

9 ¶"Only give heed to yourself and keep your soul diligently, lest you forget the things which your eyes have seen, and lest they depart from your heart all the days of your life; but make them known to your sons and your grandsons.

10"*Remember* the day you stood before the LORD your God at Horeb, when the LORD said to me, 'Assemble the people to Me, that I may let them hear My words so they may learn to ⁵fear Me all the days they live on the earth, and that they may teach their children.'

11"And you came near and stood at the foot of the mountain, and the mountain burned with fire to the *very* heart of the heavens: darkness, cloud and thick gloom.

12"Then the LORD spoke to you from the midst of the fire; you heard the sound of words, but you saw no form—only a voice.

13"So He declared to you His covenant which He commanded you to perform, *that is*, the ten commandments; and He wrote them on two tablets of stone.

14"And the LORD commanded me at that time to teach you statutes and judgments, that you might perform them in the land where you are going over to possess it.

15 ¶"So watch yourselves carefully, since you did not see any form on the day the LORD spoke to you at Horeb from the midst of the fire,

16 lest you act corruptly and make a graven image for yourselves in the form of any figure, the likeness of male or female,

17 the likeness of any animal that is

⁵ Or, *reverence*

on the earth, the likeness of any winged bird that flies in the sky,

18 the likeness of anything that creeps on the ground, the likeness of any fish that is in the water below the earth.

19"And *beware*, lest you lift up your eyes to heaven and see the sun and the moon and the stars, all the host of heaven, and be drawn away and worship them and serve them, those which the LORD your God has allotted to all the peoples under the whole heaven.

20"But the LORD has taken you and brought you out of the iron furnace, from Egypt, to be a people for His own possession, as today.

21"Now the LORD was angry with me on your account, and swore that I should not cross the Jordan, and that I should not enter the good land which the LORD your God is giving you as an inheritance.

22"For I shall die in this land, I shall not cross the Jordan, but you shall cross and take possession of this good land.

23"So watch yourselves, lest you forget the covenant of the LORD your God, which He made with you, and make for yourselves a graven image in the form of anything *against* which the LORD your God has commanded you.

24"For the LORD your God is a consuming fire, a jealous God.

25 ¶"When you become the father of children and children's children and have remained long in the land, and act corruptly, and make an idol in the form of anything, and do that which is evil in the sight of the LORD your God *so as* to provoke Him to anger,

26 I call heaven and earth to witness against you today, that you shall surely perish quickly from the land where you are going over the Jordan to possess it. You shall not live long on it, but shall be utterly destroyed.

27"And the LORD will scatter you among the peoples, and you shall be left few in number among the nations, where the LORD shall drive you.

28"And there you will serve gods, the work of man's hands, wood and stone, which neither see nor hear nor eat nor smell.

29"But from there you will seek the LORD your God, and you will find *Him* if you search for Him with all your heart and all your soul.

30"When you are in distress and all these things have come upon you, in the latter days, you will return to the LORD your God and listen to His voice.

31"For the LORD your God is a compassionate God; He will not fail you nor destroy you nor forget the covenant with your fathers which He swore to them.

32 ¶"Indeed, ask now concerning the former days which were before you, since the day that God created man on the earth, and *inquire* from one end of the heavens to the other. Has *anything* been done like this great thing, or has *anything* been heard like it?

33"Has *any* people heard the voice of God speaking from the midst of the fire, as you have heard *it*, and survived?

34"Or has a god tried to go to take for himself a nation from within *another* nation by trials, by signs and wonders and by war and by a mighty hand and by an outstretched arm and by great terrors, as the LORD your God did for you in Egypt before your eyes?

35"To you it was shown that you might know that the LORD, He is God; there is no other besides Him.

36"Out of the heavens He let you hear His voice to discipline you; and on earth He let you see His great fire, and you heard His words from the midst of the fire.

37"Because He loved your fathers, therefore He chose their descendants after them. And He personally brought you from Egypt by His great power,

38 driving out from before you nations greater and mightier than you, to bring you in *and* to give you their land for an inheritance, as it is today.

39"Know therefore today, and take it to your heart, that the LORD, He is God in heaven above and on the earth below; there is no other.

40"So you shall keep His statutes and His commandments which I am giving you today, that it may go well with you and with your children after you, and that you may live long on the land which the LORD your God is giving you for all time."

41 ¶ Then Moses set apart three cities across the Jordan to the east,

42 that a manslayer might flee there, who unintentionally slew his neighbor without having enmity toward him in time past; and by fleeing to one of these cities he might live:

43 Bezer in the wilderness on the plateau for the Reubenites, and Ramoth in Gilead for the Gadites, and Golan in Bashan for the Manassites.

44 ¶ Now this is the law which Moses set before the sons of Israel;

45 these are the testimonies and the statutes and the ordinances which Moses spoke to the sons of Israel, when they came out from Egypt,

46 across the Jordan, in the valley opposite Beth-peor, in the land of Sihon king of the Amorites who lived at Heshbon, whom Moses and the sons of Israel defeated when they came out from Egypt.

47 And they took possession of his land and the land of Og king of Bashan, the two kings of the Amorites, who were across the Jordan to the east,

48 from Aroer, which is on the edge of the valley of Arnon, even as far as Mount Sion (that is, Hermon),

49 with all the Arabah across the Jordan to the east, even as far as the sea of the Arabah, at the foot of the slopes of Pisgah.

CHAPTER 5

THEN Moses summoned all Israel, and said to them, "Hear, O Israel, the statutes and the ordinances which I am speaking today in your hearing, that you may learn them and observe them carefully.

2"The LORD our God made a covenant with us at Horeb.

3"The LORD did not make this covenant with our fathers, but with us, with all those of us alive here today.

4"The LORD spoke to you face to face at the mountain from the midst of the fire,

5 while I was standing between the LORD and you at that time, to declare to you the word of the LORD; for you were afraid because of the fire and did not go up the mountain. He said,

6 ¶ 'I am the LORD your God, who brought you out of the land of Egypt, out of the house of slavery.

7 ¶ 'You shall have no other gods before Me.

8 ¶ 'You shall not make for yourself an idol, or any likeness of what is in heaven above or on the earth beneath or in the water under the earth.

9 'You shall not worship them or serve them; for I, the LORD your God, am a jealous God, visiting the iniquity of the fathers on the children, and on the third and the fourth generations of those who hate Me,

10 but showing lovingkindness to thousands, to those who love Me and keep My commandments.

11 ¶ 'You shall not take the name of the LORD your God in vain, for the LORD will not leave him unpunished who takes His name in vain.

12 ¶ 'Observe the sabbath day to keep it holy, as the LORD your God commanded you.

13 'Six days you shall labor and do all your work,

14 but the seventh day is a sabbath of the LORD your God; in it you shall not do any work, you or your son or your daughter or your male servant or your female servant or your ox or your donkey or any of your cattle or your sojourner who stays with you, so that your male servant and your female servant may rest as well as you.

15 'And you shall remember that you were a slave in the land of Egypt, and the LORD your God brought you out of there by a mighty hand and by an outstretched arm; therefore the LORD your God commanded you to observe the sabbath day.

16 ¶ 'Honor your father and your mother, as the LORD your God has commanded you, that your days may be prolonged, and that it may go well with you on the land which the LORD your God gives you.

17 ¶ 'You shall not murder.

18 ¶ 'You shall not commit adultery.

19 ¶ 'You shall not steal.

20 ¶ 'You shall not bear false witness against your neighbor.

21 ¶ 'You shall not covet your neighbor's wife, and you shall not desire your neighbor's house, his field or his male servant or his female servant, his ox or his donkey or anything that belongs to your neighbor.'

22 ¶"These words the LORD spoke to all your assembly at the mountain from the midst of the fire, of the cloud and of the thick gloom, with a great voice, and He added no more. And He wrote them on two tablets of stone and gave them to me.

23"And it came about, when you heard the voice from the midst of the darkness, while the mountain was burning with fire, that you came near to me, all the heads of your tribes and your elders.

24"And you said, 'Behold, the LORD our God has shown us His glory and His greatness, and we have heard His voice from the midst of the fire; we have seen today that God speaks with man, yet he lives.

25 'Now then why should we die? For this great fire will consume us; if we hear the voice of the LORD our God any longer, then we shall die.

26 'For who is there of all flesh, who has heard the voice of the living God speaking from the midst of the fire, as we have, and lived?

27 'Go near and hear all that the LORD our God says; then speak to us all that the LORD our God will speak to you, and we will hear and do it.'

28 ¶"And the LORD heard the voice of your words when you spoke to me, and the LORD said to me, 'I have heard the voice of the words of this people which they have spoken to you. They have done well in all that they have spoken.

29 'Oh that they had such a heart in them, that they would fear Me, and keep all My commandments always, that it may be well with them and with their sons forever!

30 'Go, say to them, "Return to your tents."

31 'But as for you, stand here by Me, that I may speak to you all the commandments and the statutes and the judgments which you shall teach them, that they may observe them in the land which I give them to possess.'

32"So you shall observe to do just as the LORD your God has commanded you; you shall not turn aside to the right or to the left.

33"You shall walk in all the way which the LORD your God has commanded you, that you may live, and that it may be well with you, and that

you may prolong your days in the land which you shall possess.

CHAPTER 6

"NOW this is the commandment, the statutes and the judgments which the LORD your God has commanded me to teach you, that you might do them in the land where you are going over to possess it,

2 so that you and your son and your grandson might fear the LORD your God, to keep all His statutes and His commandments, which I command you, all the days of your life, and that your days may be prolonged.

3"O Israel, you should listen and be careful to do it, that it may be well with you and that you may multiply greatly, just as the LORD, the God of your fathers, has promised you, in a land flowing with milk and honey.

4 ¶"Hear, O Israel! The LORD is our God, the LORD is one!

5"And you shall love the LORD your God with all your heart and with all your soul and with all your might.

6"And these words, which I am commanding you today, shall be on your heart;

7 and you shall teach them diligently to your sons and shall talk of them when you sit in your house and when you walk by the way and when you lie down and when you rise up.

8"And you shall bind them as a sign on your hand and they shall be as frontals on your forehead.

9"And you shall write them on the doorposts of your house and on your gates.

10 ¶"Then it shall come about when the LORD your God brings you into the land which He swore to your fathers, Abraham, Isaac and Jacob, to give you, great and splendid cities which you did not build,

11 and houses full of all good things which you did not fill, and hewn cisterns which you did not dig, vineyards and olive trees which you did not plant, and you shall eat and be satisfied,

12 then watch yourself, lest you forget the LORD who brought you from the land of Egypt, out of the house of slavery.

13"You shall [6]fear *only* the LORD your God; and you shall worship Him, and swear by His name.

14"You shall not follow other gods, any of the gods of the peoples who surround you,

15 for the LORD your God in the midst of you is a jealous God; otherwise the anger of the LORD your God will be kindled against you, and He will wipe you off the face of the earth.

16 ¶"You shall not put the LORD your God to the test, as you tested *Him* at Massah.

17"You should diligently keep the commandments of the LORD your God, and His testimonies and His statutes which He has commanded you.

18"And you shall do what is right and good in the sight of the LORD, that it may be well with you and that you may go in and possess the good land which the LORD swore to *give* your fathers,

19 by driving out all your enemies from before you, as the LORD has spoken.

20 ¶"When your son asks you in time to come, saying, 'What *do* the testimonies and the statutes and the judgments *mean* which the LORD our God commanded you?'

21 then you shall say to your son, 'We were slaves to Pharaoh in Egypt; and the LORD brought us from Egypt with a mighty hand.

22 'Moreover, the LORD showed great and distressing signs and wonders before our eyes against Egypt, Pharaoh and all his household;

23 and He brought us out from there in order to bring us in, to give us the land which He had sworn to our fathers.'

24"So the LORD commanded us to observe all these statutes, to fear the LORD our God for our good always and for our survival, as *it is* today.

25"And it will be righteousness for us if we are careful to observe all this commandment before the LORD our God, just as He commanded us.

CHAPTER 7

"WHEN the LORD your God shall bring you into the land where you are entering to possess it, and shall clear away many nations before you, the Hittites and the Girgashites and the Amorites and the Canaanites and the Perizzites and the Hivites and the Jebusites, seven nations greater and stronger than you,

2 and when the LORD your God shall deliver them before you, and you shall defeat them, then you shall utterly destroy them. You shall make no covenant with them and show no favor to them.

3"Furthermore, you shall not intermarry with them; you shall not give your daughters to their sons, nor shall you take their daughters for your sons.

4"For they will turn your sons away from following Me to serve other gods; then the anger of the LORD will be kindled against you, and He will quickly destroy you.

5"But thus you shall do to them: you shall tear down their altars, and smash their *sacred* pillars, and hew down their [7]Asherim, and burn their graven images with fire.

6 ¶"For you are a holy people to the LORD your God; the LORD your God has chosen you to be a people for His own possession out of all the peoples who are on the face of the earth.

7"The LORD did not set His love on you nor choose you because you were more in number than any of the peoples, for you were the fewest of all peoples,

8 but because the LORD loved you and kept the oath which He swore to your forefathers, the LORD brought you out by a mighty hand, and redeemed you from the house of slavery, from the hand of Pharaoh king of Egypt.

9"Know therefore that the LORD your God, He is God, the faithful God, who keeps His covenant and His lovingkindness to a thousandth generation with those who love Him and keep His commandments;

10 but repays those who hate Him to their faces, to destroy them; He will not delay with him who hates Him, He will repay him to his face.

11"Therefore, you shall keep the commandment and the statutes and

[6] Or, *reverence*

[7] I.e., wooden symbols of a female deity

the judgments which I am commanding you today, to do them.

12 ¶"Then it shall come about, because you listen to these judgments and keep and do them, that the LORD your God will keep with you His covenant and His lovingkindness which He swore to your forefathers.

13"And He will love you and bless you and multiply you; He will also bless the fruit of your womb and the fruit of your ground, your grain and your new wine and your oil, the increase of your herd and the young of your flock, in the land which He swore to your forefathers to give you.

14"You shall be blessed above all peoples; there shall be no male or female barren among you or among your cattle.

15"And the LORD will remove from you all sickness; and He will not put on you any of the harmful diseases of Egypt which you have known, but He will lay them on all who hate you.

16"And you shall consume all the peoples whom the LORD your God will deliver to you; your eye shall not pity them, neither shall you serve their gods, for that *would be* a snare to you.

17 ¶"If you should say in your heart, 'These nations are greater than I; how can I dispossess them?'

18 you shall not be afraid of them; you shall well remember what the LORD your God did to Pharaoh and to all Egypt:

19 the great trials which your eyes saw and the signs and the wonders and the mighty hand and the outstretched arm by which the LORD your God brought you out. So shall the LORD your God do to all the peoples of whom you are afraid.

20"Moreover, the LORD your God will send the hornet against them, until those who are left and hide themselves from you perish.

21"You shall not dread them, for the LORD your God is in your midst, a great and awesome God.

22"And the LORD your God will clear away these nations before you little by little; you will not be able to put an end to them quickly, lest the wild beasts grow too numerous for you.

23"But the LORD your God shall deliver them before you, and will throw them into great confusion until they are destroyed.

24"And He will deliver their kings into your hand so that you shall make their name perish from under heaven; no man will be able to stand before you until you have destroyed them.

25"The graven images of their gods you are to burn with fire; you shall not covet the silver or the gold that is on them, nor take it for yourselves, lest you be snared by it, for it is an abomination to the LORD your God.

26"And you shall not bring an abomination into your house, and like it come under the ban; you shall utterly detest it and you shall utterly abhor it, for it is something banned.

CHAPTER 8

"ALL the commandments that I am commanding you today you shall be careful to do, that you may live and multiply, and go in and possess the land which the LORD swore *to give* to your forefathers.

2"And you shall remember all the way which the LORD your God has led you in the wilderness these forty years, that He might humble you, testing you, to know what was in your heart, whether you would keep His commandments or not.

3"And He humbled you and let you be hungry, and fed you with manna which you did not know, nor did your fathers know, that He might make you understand that man does not live by bread alone, but man lives by everything that proceeds out of the mouth of the LORD.

4"Your clothing did not wear out on you, nor did your foot swell these forty years.

5"Thus you are to know in your heart that the LORD your God was disciplining you just as a man disciplines his son.

6"Therefore, you shall keep the commandments of the LORD your God, to walk in His ways and to fear Him.

7"For the LORD your God is bringing you into a good land, a land of brooks of water, of fountains and springs, flowing forth in valleys and hills;

8 a land of wheat and barley, of vines and fig trees and pomegranates, a land of olive oil and honey;

9 a land where you shall eat food without scarcity, in which you shall not lack anything; a land whose stones are iron, and out of whose hills you can dig copper.

10"When you have eaten and are satisfied, you shall bless the LORD your God for the good land which He has given you.

11 ¶"Beware lest you forget the LORD your God by not keeping His commandments and His ordinances and His statutes which I am commanding you today;

12 lest, when you have eaten and are satisfied, and have built good houses and lived in them,

13 and when your herds and your flocks multiply, and your silver and gold multiply, and all that you have multiplies,

14 then your heart becomes proud, and you forget the LORD your God who brought you out from the land of Egypt, out of the house of slavery.

15"He led you through the great and terrible wilderness, with its fiery serpents and scorpions and thirsty ground where there was no water; He brought water for you out of the rock of flint.

16"In the wilderness He fed you manna which your fathers did not know, that He might humble you and that He might test you, to do good for you in the end.

17"Otherwise, you may say in your heart, 'My power and the strength of my hand made me this wealth.'

18"But you shall remember the LORD your God, for it is He who is giving you power to make wealth, that He may confirm His covenant which He swore to your fathers, as it is this day.

19"And it shall come about if you ever forget the LORD your God, and go after other gods and serve them and worship them, I testify against you today that you shall surely perish.

20"Like the nations that the LORD makes to perish before you, so you shall perish; because you would not listen to the voice of the LORD your God.

CHAPTER 9

"HEAR, O Israel! You are crossing over the Jordan today to go in to dispossess nations greater and mightier than you, great cities fortified to heaven,

2 a people great and tall, the sons of the Anakim, whom you know and of whom you have heard it said, 'Who can stand before the sons of Anak?'

3"Know therefore today that it is the LORD your God who is crossing over before you as a consuming fire. He will destroy them and He will subdue them before you, so that you may drive them out and destroy them quickly, just as the LORD has spoken to you.

4"Do not say in your heart when the LORD your God has driven them out before you, 'Because of my righteousness the LORD has brought me in to possess this land,' but it is because of the wickedness of these nations that the LORD is dispossessing them before you.

5"It is not for your righteousness or for the uprightness of your heart that you are going to possess their land, but it is because of the wickedness of these nations that the LORD your God is driving them out before you, in order to confirm the oath which the LORD swore to your fathers, to Abraham, Isaac and Jacob.

6"Know, then, it is not because of your righteousness that the LORD your God is giving you this good land to possess, for you are a stubborn people.

7 ¶"Remember, do not forget how you provoked the LORD your God to wrath in the wilderness; from the day that you left the land of Egypt until you arrived at this place, you have been rebellious against the LORD.

8"Even at Horeb you provoked the LORD to wrath, and the LORD was so angry with you that He would have destroyed you.

9"When I went up to the mountain to receive the tablets of stone, the tablets of the covenant which the LORD had made with you, then I remained on the mountain forty days and nights; I neither ate bread nor drank water.

10"And the LORD gave me the two tablets of stone written by the finger of God; and on them were all the words which the LORD had spoken with you at the mountain from the midst of the fire on the day of the assembly.

11"And it came about at the end of forty days and nights that the Lord gave me the two tablets of stone, the tablets of the covenant.

12"Then the Lord said to me, 'Arise, go down from here quickly, for your people whom you brought out of Egypt have acted corruptly. They have quickly turned aside from the way which I commanded them; they have made a molten image for themselves.'

13"The Lord spoke further to me, saying, 'I have seen this people, and indeed, it is a stubborn people.

14 'Let Me alone, that I may destroy them and blot out their name from under heaven; and I will make of you a nation mightier and greater than they.'

15"So I turned and came down from the mountain while the mountain was burning with fire, and the two tablets of the covenant were in my two hands.

16"And I saw that you had indeed sinned against the Lord your God. You had made for yourselves a molten calf; you had turned aside quickly from the way which the Lord had commanded you.

17"And I took hold of the two tablets and threw them from my hands, and smashed them before your eyes.

18"And I fell down before the Lord, as at the first, forty days and nights; I neither ate bread nor drank water, because of all your sin which you had committed in doing what was evil in the sight of the Lord to provoke Him to anger.

19"For I was afraid of the anger and hot displeasure with which the Lord was wrathful against you in order to destroy you, but the Lord listened to me that time also.

20"And the Lord was angry enough with Aaron to destroy him; so I also prayed for Aaron at the same time.

21"And I took your sinful *thing*, the calf which you had made, and burned it with fire and crushed it, grinding it very small until it was as fine as dust; and I threw its dust into the brook that came down from the mountain.

22 ¶"Again at Taberah and at Massah and at Kibroth-hattaavah you provoked the Lord to wrath.

23"And when the Lord sent you from Kadesh-barnea, saying, 'Go up and possess the land which I have given you,' then you rebelled against the command of the Lord your God; you neither believed Him nor listened to His voice.

24"You have been rebellious against the Lord from the day I knew you.

25 ¶"So I fell down before the Lord the forty days and nights, which I did because the Lord had said He would destroy you.

26"And I prayed to the Lord, and said, 'O Lord God, do not destroy Thy people, even Thine inheritance, whom Thou hast redeemed through Thy greatness, whom Thou hast brought out of Egypt with a mighty hand.

27 'Remember Thy servants, Abraham, Isaac, and Jacob; do not look at the stubbornness of this people or at their wickedness or their sin.

28 'Otherwise the land from which Thou didst bring us may say, "Because the Lord was not able to bring them into the land which He had promised them and because He hated them He has brought them out to slay them in the wilderness."

29 'Yet they are Thy people, even Thine inheritance, whom Thou hast brought out by Thy great power and Thine outstretched arm.'

CHAPTER 10

"At that time the Lord said to me, 'Cut out for yourself two tablets of stone like the former ones, and come up to Me on the mountain, and make an ark of wood for yourself.

2 'And I will write on the tablets the words that were on the former tablets which you shattered, and you shall put them in the ark.'

3"So I made an ark of acacia wood and cut out two tablets of stone like the former ones, and went up on the mountain with the two tablets in my hand.

4"And He wrote on the tablets, like the former writing, the Ten Commandments which the Lord had spoken to you on the mountain from the midst of the fire on the day of the assembly; and the Lord gave them to me.

5"Then I turned and came down

from the mountain, and put the tablets in the ark which I had made; and there they are, as the LORD commanded me."

6 ¶ (Now the sons of Israel set out from Beeroth Bene-jaakan to Moserah. There Aaron died and there he was buried and Eleazar his son ministered as priest in his place.

7 From there they set out to Gudgodah; and from Gudgodah to Jotbathah, a land of brooks of water.

8 At that time the LORD set apart the tribe of Levi to carry the ark of the covenant of the LORD, to stand before the LORD to serve Him and to bless in His name until this day.

9 Therefore, Levi does not have a portion or inheritance with his brothers; the LORD is his inheritance, just as the LORD your God spoke to him.)

10 ¶"I, moreover, stayed on the mountain forty days and forty nights like the first time, and the LORD listened to me that time also; the LORD was not willing to destroy you.

11"Then the LORD said to me, 'Arise, proceed on your journey ahead of the people, that they may go in and possess the land which I swore to their fathers to give them.'

12 ¶"And now, Israel, what does the LORD your God require from you, but to fear the LORD your God, to walk in all His ways and love Him, and to serve the LORD your God with all your heart and with all your soul,

13 and to keep the LORD's commandments and His statutes which I am commanding you today for your good?

14"Behold, to the LORD your God belong heaven and the highest heavens, the earth and all that is in it.

15"Yet on your fathers did the LORD set His affection to love them, and He chose their descendants after them, even you above all peoples, as it is this day.

16"Circumcise then your heart, and stiffen your neck no more.

17"For the LORD your God is the God of gods and the Lord of lords, the great, the mighty, and the awesome God who does not show partiality, nor take a bribe.

18"He executes justice for the orphan and the widow, and shows His love for the alien by giving him food and clothing.

19"So show your love for the alien, for you were aliens in the land of Egypt.

20"You shall fear the LORD your God; you shall serve Him and cling to Him, and you shall swear by His name.

21"He is your praise and He is your God, who has done these great and awesome things for you which your eyes have seen.

22"Your fathers went down to Egypt seventy persons in all, and now the LORD your God has made you as numerous as the stars of heaven.

CHAPTER 11

"YOU shall therefore love the LORD your God, and always keep His charge, His statutes, His ordinances, and His commandments.

2"And know this day that I am not speaking with your sons who have not known and who have not seen the [8]discipline of the LORD your God—His greatness, His mighty hand, and His outstretched arm,

3 and His signs and His works which He did in the midst of Egypt to Pharaoh the king of Egypt and to all his land;

4 and what He did to Egypt's army, to its horses and its chariots, when He made the water of the Red Sea to engulf them while they were pursuing you, and the LORD completely destroyed them;

5 and what He did to you in the wilderness until you came to this place;

6 and what He did to Dathan and Abiram, the sons of Eliab, the son of Reuben, when the earth opened its mouth and swallowed them, their households, their tents, and every living thing that followed them, among all Israel—

7 but your own eyes have seen all the great work of the LORD which He did.

8 ¶"You shall therefore keep every commandment which I am commanding you today, so that you may be strong and go in and possess the land into which you are about to cross to possess it;

9 so that you may prolong your days on the land which the LORD

[8] Or, instruction

swore to your fathers to give to them and to their descendants, a land flowing with milk and honey.

10"For the land, into which you are entering to possess it, is not like the land of Egypt from which you came, where you used to sow your seed and water it with your ⁹foot like a vegetable garden.

11"But the land into which you are about to cross to possess it, a land of hills and valleys, drinks water from the rain of heaven,

12 a land for which the LORD your God cares; the eyes of the LORD your God are always on it, from the beginning even to the end of the year.

13 ¶"And it shall come about, if you listen obediently to my commandments which I am commanding you today, to love the LORD your God and to serve Him with all your heart and all your soul,

14 that He will give the rain for your land in its season, the ¹⁰early and late rain, that you may gather in your grain and your new wine and your oil.

15"And He will give grass in your fields for your cattle, and you shall eat and be satisfied.

16"Beware, lest your hearts be deceived and you turn away and serve other gods and worship them.

17"Or the anger of the LORD will be kindled against you, and He will shut up the heavens so that there will be no rain and the ground will not yield its fruit; and you will perish quickly from the good land which the LORD is giving you.

18 ¶"You shall therefore impress these words of mine on your heart and on your soul; and you shall bind them as a sign on your hand, and they shall be as frontals on your forehead.

19"And you shall teach them to your sons, talking of them when you sit in your house and when you walk along the road and when you lie down and when you rise up.

20"And you shall write them on the doorposts of your house and on your gates,

21 so that your days and the days of your sons may be multiplied on the land which the LORD swore to your

fathers to give them, as long as the heavens *remain* above the earth.

22"For if you are careful to keep all this commandment which I am commanding you, to do it, to love the LORD your God, to walk in all His ways and hold fast to Him;

23 then the LORD will drive out all these nations from before you, and you will dispossess nations greater and mightier than you.

24"Every place on which the sole of your foot shall tread shall be yours; your border shall be from the wilderness to Lebanon, *and* from the river, the river Euphrates, as far as ¹¹the western sea.

25"There shall no man be able to stand before you; the LORD your God shall lay the dread of you and the fear of you on all the land on which you set foot, as He has spoken to you.

26 ¶"See, I am setting before you today a blessing and a curse:

27 the blessing, if you listen to the commandments of the LORD your God, which I am commanding you today;

28 and the curse, if you do not listen to the commandments of the LORD your God, but turn aside from the way which I am commanding you today, by following other gods which you have not known.

29"And it shall come about, when the LORD your God brings you into the land where you are entering to possess it, that you shall place the blessing on Mount Gerizim and the curse on Mount Ebal.

30"Are they not across the Jordan, west of the way toward the sunset, in the land of the Canaanites who live in the Arabah, opposite Gilgal, beside the oaks of Moreh?

31"For you are about to cross the Jordan to go in to possess the land which the LORD your God is giving you, and you shall possess it and live in it,

32 and you shall be careful to do all the statutes and the judgments which I am setting before you today.

CHAPTER 12

"THESE are the statutes and the judgments which you shall carefully observe in the land which the LORD,

⁹ I.e., probably a treadmill   ¹⁰ I.e., autumn and spring rain   ¹¹ I.e., the Mediterranean

the God of your fathers, has given you to possess as long as you live on the earth.

2"You shall utterly destroy all the places where the nations whom you shall dispossess serve their gods, on the high mountains and on the hills and under every green tree.

3"And you shall tear down their altars and smash their *sacred* pillars and burn their [12]Asherim with fire, and you shall cut down the engraved images of their gods, and you shall obliterate their name from that place.

4"You shall not act like this toward the LORD your God.

5"But you shall seek *the* LORD at the place which the LORD your God shall choose from all your tribes, to establish His name there for His dwelling, and there you shall come.

6"And there you shall bring your burnt offerings, your sacrifices, your tithes, the contribution of your hand, your votive offerings, your freewill offerings, and the first-born of your herd and of your flock.

7"There also you and your households shall eat before the LORD your God, and rejoice in all your undertakings in which the LORD your God has blessed you.

8"You shall not do at all what we are doing here today, every man *doing* whatever is right in his own eyes;

9 for you have not as yet come to the resting place and the inheritance which the LORD your God is giving you.

10"When you cross the Jordan and live in the land which the LORD your God is giving you to inherit, and He gives you rest from all your enemies around *you* so that you live in security,

11 then it shall come about that the place in which the LORD your God shall choose for His name to dwell, there you shall bring all that I command you: your burnt offerings and your sacrifices, your tithes and the contribution of your hand, and all your choice votive offerings which you will vow to the LORD.

12"And you shall rejoice before the LORD your God, you and your sons and daughters, your male and female

servants, and the Levite who is within your gates, since he has no portion or inheritance with you.

13"Be careful that you do not offer your burnt offerings in every *cultic* place you see,

14 but in the place which the LORD chooses in one of your tribes, there you shall offer your burnt offerings, and there you shall do all that I command you.

15 ¶"However, you may slaughter and eat meat within any of your gates, whatever you desire, according to the blessing of the LORD your God which He has given you; the unclean and the clean may eat of it, as of the gazelle and the deer.

16"Only you shall not eat the blood; you are to pour it out on the ground like water.

17"You are not allowed to eat within your gates the tithe of your grain, or new wine, or oil, or the first-born of your herd or flock, or any of your votive offerings which you vow, or your freewill offerings, or the contribution of your hand.

18"But you shall eat them before the LORD your God in the place which the LORD your God will choose, you and your son and daughter, and your male and female servants, and the Levite who is within your gates; and you shall rejoice before the LORD your God in all your undertakings.

19"Be careful that you do not forsake the Levite as long as you live in your land.

20 ¶"When the LORD your God extends your border as He has promised you, and you say, 'I will eat meat,' because you desire to eat meat, *then* you may eat meat, whatever you desire.

21"If the place which the LORD your God chooses to put His name is too far from you, then you may slaughter of your herd and flock which the LORD has given you, as I have commanded you; and you may eat within your gates whatever you desire.

22"Just as a gazelle or a deer is eaten, so you shall eat it; the unclean and the clean alike may eat of it.

23"Only be sure not to eat the blood, for the blood is the life, and you shall not eat the life with the flesh.

[12] I.e., wooden symbols of a female deity

24"You shall not eat it; you shall pour it out on the ground like water.

25"You shall not eat it, in order that it may be well with you and your sons after you, for you will be doing what is right in the sight of the LORD.

26"Only your holy things which you may have and your votive offerings, you shall take and go to the place which the LORD chooses.

27"And you shall offer your burnt offerings, the flesh and the blood, on the altar of the LORD your God; and the blood of your sacrifices shall be poured out on the altar of the LORD your God, and you shall eat the flesh.

28"Be careful to listen to all these words which I command you, in order that it may be well with you and your sons after you forever, for you will be doing what is good and right in the sight of the LORD your God.

29 ¶"When the LORD your God cuts off before you the nations which you are going in to dispossess, and you dispossess them and dwell in their land,

30 beware that you are not ensnared to follow them, after they are destroyed before you, and that you do not inquire after their gods, saying, 'How do these nations serve their gods, that I also may do likewise?'

31"You shall not behave thus toward the LORD your God, for every abominable act which the LORD hates they have done for their gods; for they even burn their sons and daughters in the fire to their gods.

32 ¶"Whatever I command you, you shall be careful to do; you shall not add to nor take away from it.

CHAPTER 13

"IF a prophet or a dreamer of dreams arises among you and gives you a sign or a wonder,

2 and the sign or the wonder comes true, concerning which he spoke to you, saying, 'Let us go after other gods (whom you have not known) and let us serve them,'

3 you shall not listen to the words of that prophet or that dreamer of dreams; for the LORD your God is testing you to find out if you love the LORD your God with all your heart and with all your soul.

4"You shall follow the LORD your God and fear Him; and you shall keep His commandments, listen to His voice, serve Him, and cling to Him.

5"But that prophet or that dreamer of dreams shall be put to death, because he has counseled rebellion against the LORD your God who brought you from the land of Egypt and redeemed you from the house of slavery, to seduce you from the way in which the LORD your God commanded you to walk. So you shall purge the evil from among you.

6 ¶"If your brother, your mother's son, or your son or daughter, or the wife you cherish, or your friend who is as your own soul, entice you secretly, saying, 'Let us go and serve other gods' (whom neither you nor your fathers have known,

7 of the gods of the peoples who are around you, near you or far from you, from one end of the earth to the other end),

8 you shall not yield to him or listen to him; and your eye shall not pity him, nor shall you spare or conceal him.

9"But you shall surely kill him; your hand shall be first against him to put him to death, and afterwards the hand of all the people.

10"So you shall stone him to death because he has sought to seduce you from the LORD your God who brought you out from the land of Egypt, out of the house of slavery.

11"Then all Israel will hear and be afraid, and will never again do such a wicked thing among you.

12 ¶"If you hear in one of your cities, which the LORD your God is giving you to live in, *anyone* saying *that*

13 some worthless men have gone out from among you and have seduced the inhabitants of their city, saying, 'Let us go and serve other gods' (whom you have not known),

14 then you shall investigate and search out and inquire thoroughly. And if it is true *and* the matter established that this abomination has been done among you,

15 you shall surely strike the inhabitants of that city with the edge of the sword, utterly destroying it and all that is in it and its cattle with the edge of the sword.

16"Then you shall gather all its booty
into the middle of its open square and
burn the city and all its booty with fire
as a whole burnt offering to the Lord
your God; and it shall be a ruin forever. It shall never be rebuilt.

17"And nothing from that which is
put under the ban shall cling to your
hand, in order that the Lord may turn
from His burning anger and show
mercy to you, and have compassion on
you and make you increase, just as He
has sworn to your fathers,

18 if you will listen to the voice of
the Lord your God, keeping all His
commandments which I am commanding you today, and doing what is
right in the sight of the Lord your
God.

CHAPTER 14

"You are the sons of the Lord your
God; you shall not cut yourselves nor
shave your forehead for the sake of
the dead.

2"For you are a holy people to the
Lord your God; and the Lord has
chosen you to be a people for His own
possession out of all the peoples who
are on the face of the earth.

3 ¶"You shall not eat any detestable
thing.

4"These are the animals which you
may eat: the ox, the sheep, the goat,

5 the deer, the gazelle, the roebuck,
the wild goat, the ibex, the antelope
and the mountain sheep.

6"And any animal that divides the
hoof and has the hoof split in two *and*
chews the cud, among the animals,
that you may eat.

7"Nevertheless, you are not to eat of
these among those which chew the
cud, or among those that divide the
hoof in two: the camel and the rabbit
and the rock-badger, for though they
chew the cud, they do not divide the
hoof; they are unclean for you.

8"And the pig, because it divides the
hoof but *does* not *chew* the cud, it is
unclean for you. You shall not eat any
of their flesh nor touch their carcasses.

9 ¶"These you may eat of all that
are in water: anything that has fins
and scales you may eat,

10 but anything that does not have
fins and scales you shall not eat; it is
unclean for you.

11 ¶"You may eat any clean bird.

12"But these are the ones which you
shall not eat: the eagle and the vulture
and the buzzard,

13 and the red kite, the falcon, and
the kite in their kinds,

14 and every raven in its kind,

15 and the ostrich, the owl, the sea
gull, and the hawk in their kinds,

16 the little owl, the great owl, the
white owl,

17 the pelican, the carrion vulture,
the cormorant,

18 the stork, and the heron in their
kinds, and the hoopoe and the bat.

19"And all the teeming life with
wings are unclean to you; they shall
not be eaten.

20"You may eat any clean bird.

21 ¶"You shall not eat anything
which dies *of itself.* You may give it to
the alien who is in your town, so that
he may eat it, or you may sell it to a
foreigner, for you are a holy people to
the Lord your God. You shall not boil
a kid in its mother's milk.

22 ¶"You shall surely tithe all the
produce from what you sow, which
comes out of the field every year.

23"And you shall eat in the presence
of the Lord your God, at the place
where He chooses to establish His
name, the tithe of your grain, your
new wine, your oil, and the first-born
of your herd and your flock, in order
that you may learn to fear the Lord
your God always.

24"And if the distance is so great for
you that you are not able to bring *the
tithe,* since the place where the Lord
your God chooses to set His name is
too far away from you when the Lord
your God blesses you,

25 then you shall exchange *it* for
money, and bind the money in your
hand and go to the place which the
Lord your God chooses.

26"And you may spend the money
for whatever your heart desires, for
oxen, or sheep, or wine, or strong
drink, or whatever your heart desires;
and there you shall eat in the presence
of the Lord your God and rejoice, you
and your household.

27"Also you shall not neglect the
Levite who is in your town, for he has
no portion or inheritance among you.

28 ¶"At the end of every third year
you shall bring out all the tithe of your

produce in that year, and shall deposit *it* in your town.

29"And the Levite, because he has no portion or inheritance among you, and the alien, the orphan and the widow who are in your town, shall come and eat and be satisfied, in order that the LORD your God may bless you in all the work of your hand which you do.

CHAPTER 15

"AT the end of *every* seven years you shall [13]grant a remission *of debts*.

2"And this is the manner of remission: every creditor shall release what he has loaned to his neighbor; he shall not exact it of his neighbor and his brother, because the LORD's remission has been proclaimed.

3"From a foreigner you may exact *it*, but your hand shall release whatever of yours is with your brother.

4"However, there shall be no poor among you, since the LORD will surely bless you in the land which the LORD your God is giving you as an inheritance to possess,

5 if only you listen obediently to the voice of the LORD your God, to observe carefully all this commandment which I am commanding you today.

6"For the LORD your God shall bless you as He has promised you, and you will lend to many nations, but you will not borrow; and you will rule over many nations, but they will not rule over you.

7 ¶"If there is a poor man with you, one of your brothers, in any of your towns in your land which the LORD your God is giving you, you shall not harden your heart, nor close your hand from your poor brother;

8 but you shall freely open your hand to him, and shall generously lend him sufficient for his need *in* whatever he lacks.

9"Beware, lest there is a base thought in your heart, saying, 'The seventh year, the year of remission, is near,' and your eye is hostile toward your poor brother, and you give him nothing; then he may cry to the LORD against you, and it will be a sin in you.

10"You shall generously give to him, and your heart shall not be grieved when you give to him, because for this

thing the LORD your God will bless you in all your work and in all your undertakings.

11"For the poor will never cease *to be* in the land; therefore I command you, saying, 'You shall freely open your hand to your brother, to your needy and poor in your land.'

12 ¶"If your kinsman, a Hebrew man or woman, is sold to you, then he shall serve you six years, but in the seventh year you shall set him free.

13"And when you set him free, you shall not send him away empty-handed.

14"You shall furnish him liberally from your flock and from your threshing floor and from your wine vat; you shall give to him as the LORD your God has blessed you.

15"And you shall remember that you were a slave in the land of Egypt, and the LORD your God redeemed you; therefore I command you this today.

16"And it shall come about if he says to you, 'I will not go out from you,' because he loves you and your household, since he fares well with you;

17 then you shall take an awl and pierce it through his ear into the door, and he shall be your servant forever. And also you shall do likewise to your maidservant.

18"It shall not seem hard to you when you set him free, for he has given you six years *with* double the service of a hired man; so the LORD your God will bless you in whatever you do.

19 ¶"You shall consecrate to the LORD your God all the first-born males that are born of your herd and of your flock; you shall not work with the first-born of your herd, nor shear the first-born of your flock.

20"You and your household shall eat it every year before the LORD your God in the place which the LORD chooses.

21"But if it has any defect, *such as* lameness or blindness, *or* any serious defect, you shall not sacrifice it to the LORD your God.

22"You shall eat it within your gates; the unclean and the clean alike *may eat it*, as a gazelle or a deer.

23"Only you shall not eat its blood; you are to pour it out on the ground like water.

[13] Lit., *make a release*

CHAPTER 16

"OBSERVE the month of Abib and celebrate the Passover to the LORD your God, for in the month of Abib the LORD your God brought you out of Egypt by night.

2"And you shall sacrifice the Passover to the LORD your God from the flock and the herd, in the place where the LORD chooses to establish His name.

3"You shall not eat leavened bread with it; seven days you shall eat with it unleavened bread, the bread of affliction (for you came out of the land of Egypt in haste), in order that you may remember all the days of your life the day when you came out of the land of Egypt.

4"For seven days no leaven shall be seen with you in all your territory, and none of the flesh which you sacrifice on the evening of the first day shall remain overnight until morning.

5"You are not allowed to sacrifice the Passover in any of your towns which the LORD your God is giving you;

6 but at the place where the LORD your God chooses to establish His name, you shall sacrifice the Passover in the evening at sunset, at the time that you came out of Egypt.

7"And you shall cook and eat *it* in the place which the LORD your God chooses. And in the morning you are to return to your tents.

8"Six days you shall eat unleavened bread, and on the seventh day there shall be a solemn assembly to the LORD your God; you shall do no work *on it.*

9 ¶"You shall count seven weeks for yourself; you shall begin to count seven weeks from the time you begin to put the sickle to the standing grain.

10"Then you shall celebrate the Feast of Weeks to the LORD your God with a tribute of a freewill offering of your hand, which you shall give just as the LORD your God blesses you;

11 and you shall rejoice before the LORD your God, you and your son and your daughter and your male and female servants and the Levite who is in your town, and the stranger and the orphan and the widow who are in your midst, in the place where the LORD your God chooses to establish His name.

12"And you shall remember that you were a slave in Egypt, and you shall be careful to observe these statutes.

13 ¶"You shall celebrate the Feast of Booths seven days after you have gathered in from your threshing floor and your wine vat;

14 and you shall rejoice in your feast, you and your son and your daughter and your male and female servants and the Levite and the stranger and the orphan and the widow who are in your towns.

15"Seven days you shall celebrate a feast to the LORD your God in the place which the LORD chooses, because the LORD your God will bless you in all your produce and in all the work of your hands, so that you shall be altogether joyful.

16"Three times in a year all your males shall appear before the LORD your God in the place which He chooses, at the Feast of Unleavened Bread and at the Feast of Weeks and at the Feast of Booths, and they shall not appear before the LORD empty-handed.

17"Every man shall give as he is able, according to the blessing of the LORD your God which He has given you.

18 ¶"You shall appoint for yourself judges and officers in all your towns which the LORD your God is giving you, according to your tribes, and they shall judge the people with righteous judgment.

19"You shall not distort justice; you shall not be partial, and you shall not take a bribe, for a bribe blinds the eyes of the wise and perverts the words of the righteous.

20"Justice, *and only* justice, you shall pursue, that you may live and possess the land which the LORD your God is giving you.

21 ¶"You shall not plant for yourself an Asherah of any kind of tree beside the altar of the LORD your God, which you shall make for yourself.

22"Neither shall you set up for yourself a *sacred* pillar which the LORD your God hates.

CHAPTER 17

"YOU shall not sacrifice to the LORD your God an ox or a sheep which has a blemish or any defect, for that is a detestable thing to the LORD your God.

2 ¶"If there is found in your midst, in any of your towns, which the LORD your God is giving you, a man or a woman who does what is evil in the sight of the LORD your God, by transgressing His covenant,

3 and has gone and served other gods and worshiped them, or the sun or the moon or any of the heavenly host, which I have not commanded,

4 and if it is told you and you have heard of it, then you shall inquire thoroughly. And behold, if it is true and the thing certain that this detestable thing has been done in Israel,

5 then you shall bring out that man or that woman who has done this evil deed, to your gates, *that is*, the man or the woman, and you shall stone them to death.

6"On the evidence of two witnesses or three witnesses, he who is to die shall be put to death; he shall not be put to death on the evidence of one witness.

7"The hand of the witnesses shall be first against him to put him to death, and afterward the hand of all the people. So you shall purge the evil from your midst.

8 ¶"If any case is too difficult for you to decide, between one kind of homicide or another, between one kind of lawsuit or another, and between one kind of assault or another, being cases of dispute in your courts, then you shall arise and go up to the place which the LORD your God chooses.

9"So you shall come to the Levitical priest or the judge who is *in office* in those days, and you shall inquire *of them*, and they will declare to you the verdict in the case.

10"And you shall do according to the terms of the verdict which they declare to you from that place which the LORD chooses; and you shall be careful to observe according to all that they teach you.

11"According to the terms of the law which they teach you, and according to the verdict which they tell you, you shall do; you shall not turn aside from the word which they declare to you, to the right or the left.

12"And the man who acts presumptuously by not listening to the priest who stands there to serve the LORD your God, nor to the judge, that man shall die; thus you shall purge the evil from Israel.

13"Then all the people will hear and be afraid, and will not act presumptuously again.

14 ¶"When you enter the land which the LORD your God gives you, and you possess it and live in it, and you say, 'I will set a king over me like all the nations who are around me,'

15 you shall surely set a king over you whom the LORD your God chooses, *one* from among your countrymen you shall set as king over yourselves; you may not put a foreigner over yourselves who is not your countryman.

16"Moreover, he shall not multiply horses for himself, nor shall he cause the people to return to Egypt to multiply horses, since the LORD has said to you, 'You shall never again return that way.'

17"Neither shall he multiply wives for himself, lest his heart turn away; nor shall he greatly increase silver and gold for himself.

18 ¶"Now it shall come about when he sits on the throne of his kingdom, he shall write for himself a copy of this law on a scroll in the presence of the Levitical priests.

19"And it shall be with him, and he shall read it all the days of his life, that he may learn to fear the LORD his God, by carefully observing all the words of this law and these statutes,

20 that his heart may not be lifted up above his countrymen and that he may not turn aside from the commandment, to the right or the left; in order that he and his sons may continue long in his kingdom in the midst of Israel.

CHAPTER 18

"THE Levitical priests, the whole tribe of Levi, shall have no portion or inheritance with Israel; they shall eat the LORD's offerings by fire and His portion.

2"And they shall have no inheritance among their countrymen; the LORD is their inheritance, as He promised them.

3 ¶"Now this shall be the priests' due from the people, from those who offer a sacrifice, either an ox or a sheep, of which they shall give to the priest the shoulder and the two cheeks and the stomach.

4"You shall give him the first fruits of your grain, your new wine, and your oil, and the first shearing of your sheep.

5"For the LORD your God has chosen him and his sons from all your tribes, to stand and serve in the name of the LORD forever.

6 ¶"Now if a Levite comes from any of your towns throughout Israel where he resides, and comes whenever he desires to the place which the LORD chooses,

7 then he shall serve in the name of the LORD his God, like all his fellow Levites who stand there before the LORD.

8"They shall eat equal portions, except *what they receive* from the sale of their fathers' *estates.*

9 ¶"When you enter the land which the LORD your God gives you, you shall not learn to imitate the detestable things of those nations.

10"There shall not be found among you anyone who makes his son or his daughter pass through the fire, one who uses divination, one who practices witchcraft, or one who interprets omens, or a sorcerer,

11 or one who casts a spell, or a medium, or a spiritist, or one who calls up the dead.

12"For whoever does these things is detestable to the LORD; and because of these detestable things the LORD your God will drive them out before you.

13"You shall be blameless before the LORD your God.

14 ¶"For those nations, which you shall dispossess, listen to those who practice witchcraft and to diviners, but as for you, the LORD your God has not allowed you *to do* so.

15"The LORD your God will raise up for you a prophet like me from among you, from your countrymen, you shall listen to him.

16"This is according to all that you asked of the LORD your God in Horeb on the day of the assembly, saying, 'Let me not hear again the voice of the LORD my God, let me not see this great fire anymore, lest I die.'

17"And the LORD said to me, 'They have spoken well.

18 'I will raise up a prophet from among their countrymen like you, and I will put My words in his mouth, and he shall speak to them all that I command him.

19 'And it shall come about that whoever will not listen to My words which he shall speak in My name, I Myself will require *it* of him.

20 'But the prophet who shall speak a word presumptuously in My name which I have not commanded him to speak, or which he shall speak in the name of other gods, that prophet shall die.'

21"And you may say in your heart, 'How shall we know the word which the LORD has not spoken?'

22"When a prophet speaks in the name of the LORD, if the thing does not come about or come true, that is the thing which the LORD has not spoken. The prophet has spoken it presumptuously; you shall not be afraid of him.

CHAPTER 19

"WHEN the LORD your God cuts off the nations, whose land the LORD your God gives you, and you dispossess them and settle in their cities and in their houses,

2 you shall set aside three cities for yourself in the midst of your land, which the LORD your God gives you to possess.

3"You shall prepare the roads for yourself, and divide into three parts the territory of your land, which the LORD your God will give you as a possession, so that any manslayer may flee there.

4 ¶"Now this is the case of the manslayer who may flee there and live: when he kills his friend unintentionally, not hating him previously—

5 as when *a man* goes into the forest with his friend to cut wood, and his hand swings the axe to cut down the tree, and the iron *head* slips off the

handle and strikes his friend so that he dies—he may flee to one of these cities and live;

6 lest the avenger of blood pursue the manslayer in the heat of his anger, and overtake him, because the way is long, and take his life, though he was not deserving of death, since he had not hated him previously.

7"Therefore, I command you, saying, 'You shall set aside three cities for yourself.'

8"And if the LORD your God enlarges your territory, just as He has sworn to your fathers, and gives you all the land which He promised to give your fathers—

9 if you carefully observe all this commandment, which I command you today, to love the LORD your God, and to walk in His ways always—then you shall add three more cities for yourself, besides these three.

10"So innocent blood will not be shed in the midst of your land which the LORD your God gives you as an inheritance, and bloodguiltiness be on you.

11 ¶"But if there is a man who hates his neighbor and lies in wait for him and rises up against him and strikes him so that he dies, and he flees to one of these cities,

12 then the elders of his city shall send and take him from there and deliver him into the hand of the avenger of blood, that he may die.

13"You shall not pity him, but you shall purge the blood of the innocent from Israel, that it may go well with you.

14 ¶"You shall not move your neighbor's boundary mark, which the ancestors have set, in your inheritance which you shall inherit in the land that the LORD your God gives you to possess.

15 ¶"A single witness shall not rise up against a man on account of any iniquity or any sin which he has committed; on the evidence of two or three witnesses a matter shall be confirmed.

16"If a malicious witness rises up against a man to accuse him of wrongdoing,

17 then both the men who have the dispute shall stand before the LORD, before the priests and the judges who will be *in office* in those days.

18"And the judges shall investigate thoroughly; and if the witness is a false witness *and* he has accused his brother falsely,

19 then you shall do to him just as he had intended to do to his brother. Thus you shall purge the evil from among you.

20"And the rest will hear and be afraid, and will never again do such an evil thing among you.

21"Thus you shall not show pity: life for life, eye for eye, tooth for tooth, hand for hand, foot for foot.

CHAPTER 20

"WHEN you go out to battle against your enemies and see horses and chariots *and* people more numerous than you, do not be afraid of them; for the LORD your God, who brought you up from the land of Egypt, is with you.

2"Now it shall come about that when you are approaching the battle, the priest shall come near and speak to the people.

3"And he shall say to them, 'Hear, O Israel, you are approaching the battle against your enemies today. Do not be fainthearted. Do not be afraid, or panic, or tremble before them,

4 for the LORD your God is the one who goes with you, to fight for you against your enemies, to save you.'

5"The officers also shall speak to the people, saying, 'Who is the man that has built a new house and has not dedicated it? Let him depart and return to his house, lest he die in the battle and another man dedicate it.

6 'And who is the man that has planted a vineyard and has not begun to use its fruit? Let him depart and return to his house, lest he die in the battle and another man begin to use its fruit.

7 'And who is the man that is engaged to a woman and has not married her? Let him depart and return to his house, lest he die in the battle and another man marry her.'

8"Then the officers shall speak further to the people, and they shall say, 'Who is the man that is afraid and fainthearted? Let him depart and return to his house, so that he might not make his brothers' hearts melt like his heart.'

9"And it shall come about that when the officers have finished speaking to the people, they shall appoint commanders of armies at the head of the people.

10 ¶"When you approach a city to fight against it, you shall offer it terms of peace.

11"And it shall come about, if it agrees to make peace with you and opens to you, then it shall be that all the people who are found in it shall become your forced labor and shall serve you.

12"However, if it does not make peace with you, but makes war against you, then you shall besiege it.

13"When the LORD your God gives it into your hand, you shall strike all the men in it with the edge of the sword.

14"Only the women and the children and the animals and all that is in the city, all its spoil, you shall take as booty for yourself; and you shall use the spoil of your enemies which the LORD your God has given you.

15"Thus you shall do to all the cities that are very far from you, which are not of the cities of these nations nearby.

16"Only in the cities of these peoples that the LORD your God is giving you as an inheritance, you shall not leave alive anything that breathes.

17"But you shall utterly destroy them, the Hittite and the Amorite, the Canaanite and the Perizzite, the Hivite and the Jebusite, as the LORD your God has commanded you,

18 in order that they may not teach you to do according to all their detestable things which they have done for their gods, so that you would sin against the LORD your God.

19 ¶"When you besiege a city a long time, to make war against it in order to capture it, you shall not destroy its trees by swinging an axe against them; for you may eat from them, and you shall not cut them down. For is the tree of the field a man, that it should be besieged by you?

20"Only the trees which you know are not fruit trees you shall destroy and cut down, that you may construct siegeworks against the city that is making war with you until it falls.

CHAPTER 21

"IF a slain person is found lying in the open country in the land which the LORD your God gives you to possess, and it is not known who has struck him,

2 then your elders and your judges shall go out and measure the distance to the cities which are around the slain one.

3"And it shall be that the city which is nearest to the slain man, that is, the elders of that city, shall take a heifer of the herd, which has not been worked and which has not pulled in a yoke;

4 and the elders of that city shall bring the heifer down to a valley with running water, which has not been plowed or sown, and shall break the heifer's neck there in the valley.

5"Then the priests, the sons of Levi, shall come near, for the LORD your God has chosen them to serve Him and to bless in the name of the LORD; and every dispute and every assault shall be settled by them.

6"And all the elders of that city which is nearest to the slain man shall wash their hands over the heifer whose neck was broken in the valley;

7 and they shall answer and say, 'Our hands have not shed this blood, nor did our eyes see it.

8 '14Forgive Thy people Israel whom Thou hast redeemed, O LORD, and do not place the guilt of innocent blood in the midst of Thy people Israel.' And the bloodguiltiness shall be forgiven them.

9"So you shall remove the guilt of innocent blood from your midst, when you do what is right in the eyes of the LORD.

10 ¶"When you go out to battle against your enemies, and the LORD your God delivers them into your hands, and you take them away captive,

11 and see among the captives a beautiful woman, and have a desire for her and would take her as a wife for yourself,

12 then you shall bring her home to your house, and she shall shave her head and trim her nails.

14 Lit., Cover over, atone for

13"She shall also remove the clothes of her captivity and shall remain in your house, and mourn her father and mother a full month; and after that you may go in to her and be her husband and she shall be your wife.

14"And it shall be, if you are not pleased with her, then you shall let her go wherever she wishes; but you shall certainly not sell her for money, you shall not mistreat her, because you have humbled her.

15 ¶"If a man has two wives, the one loved and the other unloved, and *both* the loved and the unloved have borne him sons, if the first-born son belongs to the unloved,

16 then it shall be in the day he wills what he has to his sons, he cannot make the son of the loved the first-born before the son of the unloved, who is the first-born.

17"But he shall acknowledge the first-born, the son of the unloved, by giving him a double portion of all that he has, for he is the beginning of his strength; to him belongs the right of the first-born.

18 ¶"If any man has a stubborn and rebellious son who will not obey his father or his mother, and when they chastise him, he will not even listen to them,

19 then his father and mother shall seize him, and bring him out to the elders of his city at the gateway of his home town.

20"And they shall say to the elders of his city, 'This son of ours is stubborn and rebellious, he will not obey us, he is a glutton and a drunkard.'

21"Then all the men of his city shall stone him to death; so you shall remove the evil from your midst, and all Israel shall hear *of it* and fear.

22 ¶"And if a man has committed a sin worthy of death, and he is put to death, and you hang him on a tree,

23 his corpse shall not hang all night on the tree, but you shall surely bury him on the same day (for he who is hanged is accursed of God), so that you do not defile your land which the LORD your God gives you as an inheritance.

CHAPTER 22

"YOU shall not see your countryman's ox or his sheep straying away, and pay no attention to them; you shall certainly bring them back to your countryman.

2"And if your countryman is not near you, or if you do not know him, then you shall bring it home to your house, and it shall remain with you until your countryman looks for it; then you shall restore it to him.

3"And thus you shall do with his donkey, and you shall do the same with his garment, and you shall do likewise with anything lost by your countryman, which he has lost and you have found. You are not allowed to neglect *them.*

4"You shall not see your countryman's donkey or his ox fallen down on the way, and pay no attention to them; you shall certainly help him to raise *them* up.

5 ¶"A woman shall not wear man's clothing, nor shall a man put on a woman's clothing; for whoever does these things is an abomination to the LORD your God.

6 ¶"If you happen to come upon a bird's nest along the way, in any tree or on the ground, with young ones or eggs, and the mother sitting on the young or on the eggs, you shall not take the mother with the young;

7 you shall certainly let the mother go, but the young you may take for yourself, in order that it may be well with you, and that you may prolong your days.

8 ¶"When you build a new house, you shall make a parapet for your roof, that you may not bring bloodguilt on your house if anyone falls from it.

9 ¶"You shall not sow your vineyard with two kinds of seed, lest all the produce of the seed which you have sown, and the increase of the vineyard become defiled.

10"You shall not plow with an ox and a donkey together.

11"You shall not wear a material mixed of wool and linen together.

12 ¶"You shall make yourself tassels on the four corners of your garment with which you cover yourself.

13 ¶"If any man takes a wife and goes in to her and *then* turns against her,

14 and charges her with shameful deeds and publicly defames her, and

says, 'I took this woman, *but* when I came near her, I did not find her a virgin,'

15 then the girl's father and her mother shall take and bring out the *evidence* of the girl's virginity to the elders of the city at the gate.

16"And the girl's father shall say to the elders, 'I gave my daughter to this man for a wife, but he turned against her;

17 and behold, he has charged her with shameful deeds, saying, "I did not find your daughter a virgin." But this is the *evidence* of my daughter's virginity.' And they shall spread the garment before the elders of the city.

18"So the elders of that city shall take the man and chastise him,

19 and they shall fine him a hundred *shekels* of silver and give it to the girl's father, because he publicly defamed a virgin of Israel. And she shall remain his wife; he cannot divorce her all his days.

20"But if this charge is true, that the girl was not found a virgin,

21 then they shall bring out the girl to the doorway of her father's house, and the men of her city shall stone her to death because she has committed an act of folly in Israel, by playing the harlot in her father's house; thus you shall purge the evil from among you.

22 ¶"If a man is found lying with a married woman, then both of them shall die, the man who lay with the woman, and the woman; thus you shall purge the evil from Israel.

23 ¶"If there is a girl who is a virgin engaged to a man, and *another* man finds her in the city and lies with her,

24 then you shall bring them both out to the gate of that city and you shall stone them to death; the girl, because she did not cry out in the city, and the man, because he has violated his neighbor's wife. Thus you shall purge the evil from among you.

25"But if in the field the man finds the girl who is engaged, and the man forces her and lies with her, then only the man who lies with her shall die.

26"But you shall do nothing to the girl; there is no sin in the girl worthy of death, for just as a man rises against his neighbor and murders him, so is this case.

27"When he found her in the field, the engaged girl cried out, but there was no one to save her.

28 ¶"If a man finds a girl who is a virgin, who is not engaged, and seizes her and lies with her and they are discovered,

29 then the man who lay with her shall give to the girl's father fifty *shekels* of silver, and she shall become his wife because he has violated her; he cannot divorce her all his days.

30 ¶"A man shall not take his father's wife so that he shall not uncover his father's skirt.

CHAPTER 23

"No one who is emasculated, or has his male organ cut off, shall enter the assembly of the LORD.

2"No one of illegitimate birth shall enter the assembly of the LORD; none of his *descendants*, even to the tenth generation, shall enter the assembly of the LORD.

3"No Ammonite or Moabite shall enter the assembly of the LORD; none of their *descendants*, even to the tenth generation, shall ever enter the assembly of the LORD,

4 because they did not meet you with food and water on the way when you came out of Egypt, and because they hired against you Balaam the son of Beor from Pethor of Mesopotamia, to curse you.

5"Nevertheless, the LORD your God was not willing to listen to Balaam, but the LORD your God turned the curse into a blessing for you because the LORD your God loves you.

6"You shall never seek their peace or their prosperity all your days.

7 ¶"You shall not detest an Edomite, for he is your brother; you shall not detest an Egyptian, because you were an alien in his land.

8"The sons of the third generation who are born to them may enter the assembly of the LORD.

9 ¶"When you go out as an army against your enemies, then you shall keep yourself from every evil thing.

10"If there is among you any man who is unclean because of a nocturnal emission, then he must go outside the camp; he may not reenter the camp.

11"But it shall be when evening approaches, he shall bathe himself with water, and at sundown he may reenter the camp.

12"You shall also have a place outside the camp and go out there,

13 and you shall have a spade among your tools, and it shall be when you sit down outside, you shall dig with it and shall turn to cover up your excrement.

14"Since the LORD your God walks in the midst of your camp to deliver you and to defeat your enemies before you, therefore your camp must be holy; and He must not see anything indecent among you lest He turn away from you.

15 ¶"You shall not hand over to his master a slave who has escaped from his master to you.

16"He shall live with you in your midst, in the place which he shall choose in one of your towns where it pleases him; you shall not mistreat him.

17 ¶"None of the daughters of Israel shall be a cult prostitute, nor shall any of the sons of Israel be a cult prostitute.

18"You shall not bring the hire of a harlot or the wages of a [15]dog into the house of the LORD your God for any votive offering, for both of these are an abomination to the LORD your God.

19"You shall not charge interest to your countrymen: interest on money, food, or anything that may be loaned at interest.

20"You may charge interest to a foreigner, but to your countryman you shall not charge interest, so that the LORD your God may bless you in all that you undertake in the land which you are about to enter to possess.

21 ¶"When you make a vow to the LORD your God, you shall not delay to pay it, for it would be sin in you, and the LORD your God will surely require it of you.

22"However, if you refrain from vowing, it would not be sin in you.

23"You shall be careful to perform what goes out from your lips, just as you have voluntarily vowed to the LORD your God, what you have promised.

24 ¶"When you enter your neighbor's vineyard, then you may eat grapes until you are fully satisfied, but you shall not put any in your basket.

25"When you enter your neighbor's standing grain, then you may pluck the heads with your hand, but you shall not wield a sickle in your neighbor's standing grain.

CHAPTER 24

"WHEN a man takes a wife and marries her, and it happens that she finds no favor in his eyes because he has found some indecency in her, and he writes her a certificate of divorce and puts *it* in her hand and sends her out from his house,

2 and she leaves his house and goes and becomes another man's *wife,*

3 and if the latter husband turns against her and writes her a certificate of divorce and puts *it* in her hand and sends her out of his house, or if the latter husband dies who took her to be his wife,

4 *then* her former husband who sent her away is not allowed to take her again to be his wife, since she has been defiled; for that is an abomination before the LORD, and you shall not bring sin on the land which the LORD your God gives you as an inheritance.

5 ¶"When a man takes a new wife, he shall not go out with the army, nor be charged with any duty; he shall be free at home one year and shall give happiness to his wife whom he has taken.

6 ¶"No one shall take a handmill or an upper millstone in pledge, for he would be taking a life in pledge.

7 ¶"If a man is caught kidnapping any of his countrymen of the sons of Israel, and he deals with him violently, or sells him, then that thief shall die; so you shall purge the evil from among you.

8 ¶"Be careful against an infection of leprosy, that you diligently observe and do according to all that the Levitical priests shall teach you; as I have commanded them, so you shall be careful to do.

9"Remember what the LORD your God did to Miriam on the way as you came out of Egypt.

---

[15] I.e., male prostitute, sodomite

10 ¶"When you make your neighbor a loan of any sort, you shall not enter his house to take his pledge.

11"You shall remain outside, and the man to whom you make the loan shall bring the pledge out to you.

12"And if he is a poor man, you shall not sleep with his pledge.

13"When the sun goes down you shall surely return the pledge to him, that he may sleep in his cloak and bless you; and it will be righteousness for you before the LORD your God.

14 ¶"You shall not oppress a hired servant *who is* poor and needy, whether *he is* one of your countrymen or one of your aliens who is in your land in your towns.

15"You shall give him his wages on his day before the sun sets, for he is poor and sets his heart on it; so that he may not cry against you to the LORD and it become sin in you.

16 ¶"Fathers shall not be put to death for *their* sons, nor shall sons be put to death for *their* fathers; everyone shall be put to death for his own sin.

17 ¶"You shall not pervert the justice due an alien *or* [16]an orphan, nor take a widow's garment in pledge.

18"But you shall remember that you were a slave in Egypt, and that the LORD your God redeemed you from there; therefore I am commanding you to do this thing.

19 ¶"When you reap your harvest in your field and have forgotten a sheaf in the field, you shall not go back to get it; it shall be for the alien, for the orphan, and for the widow, in order that the LORD your God may bless you in all the work of your hands.

20"When you beat your olive tree, you shall not go over the boughs again; it shall be for the alien, for the orphan, and for the widow.

21"When you gather the grapes of your vineyard, you shall not go over it again; it shall be for the alien, for the orphan, and for the widow.

22"And you shall remember that you were a slave in the land of Egypt; therefore I am commanding you to do this thing.

[16] Or, *the fatherless*, and so throughout this context

CHAPTER 25

"IF there is a dispute between men and they go to court, and the judges decide their case, and they justify the righteous and condemn the wicked,

2 then it shall be if the wicked man deserves to be beaten, the judge shall then make him lie down and be beaten in his presence with the number of stripes according to his guilt.

3"He may beat him forty times *but* no more, lest he beat him with many more stripes than these, and your brother be degraded in your eyes.

4 ¶"You shall not muzzle the ox while he is threshing.

5 ¶"When brothers live together and one of them dies and has no son, the wife of the deceased shall not be *married* outside *the family* to a strange man. Her husband's brother shall go in to her and take her to himself as wife and perform the duty of a husband's brother to her.

6"And it shall be that the first-born whom she bears shall assume the name of his dead brother, that his name may not be blotted out from Israel.

7"But if the man does not desire to take his brother's wife, then his brother's wife shall go up to the gate to the elders and say, 'My husband's brother refuses to establish a name for his brother in Israel; he is not willing to perform the duty of a husband's brother to me.'

8"Then the elders of his city shall summon him and speak to him. And *if* he persists and says, 'I do not desire to take her,'

9 then his brother's wife shall come to him in the sight of the elders, and pull his sandal off his foot and spit in his face; and she shall declare, 'Thus it is done to the man who does not build up his brother's house.'

10"And in Israel his name shall be called, 'The house of him whose sandal is removed.'

11 ¶"If *two* men, a man and his countryman, are struggling together, and the wife of one comes near to deliver her husband from the hand of the one who is striking him, and puts out her hand and seizes his genitals,

12 then you shall cut off her hand; you shall not show pity.

13 ¶"You shall not have in your bag differing weights, a large and a small.

14"You shall not have in your house differing measures, a large and a small.

15"You shall have a full and just weight; you shall have a full and just measure, that your days may be prolonged in the land which the LORD your God gives you.

16"For everyone who does these things, everyone who acts unjustly is an abomination to the LORD your God.

17 ¶"Remember what Amalek did to you along the way when you came out from Egypt,

18 how he met you along the way and attacked among you all the stragglers at your rear when you were faint and weary; and he did not [17]fear God.

19"Therefore it shall come about when the LORD your God has given you rest from all your surrounding enemies, in the land which the LORD your God gives you as an inheritance to possess, you shall blot out the memory of Amalek from under heaven; you must not forget.

CHAPTER 26

"THEN it shall be, when you enter the land which the LORD your God gives you as an inheritance, and you possess it and live in it,

2 that you shall take some of the first of all the produce of the ground which you shall bring in from your land that the LORD your God gives you, and you shall put it in a basket and go to the place where the LORD your God chooses to establish His name.

3"And you shall go to the priest who is in office at that time, and say to him, 'I declare this day to the LORD my God that I have entered the land which the LORD swore to our fathers to give us.'

4"Then the priest shall take the basket from your hand and set it down before the altar of the LORD your God.

5"And you shall answer and say before the LORD your God, 'My father was a wandering Aramean, and he went down to Egypt and sojourned there, few in number; but there he became a great, mighty and populous nation.

6 'And the Egyptians treated us harshly and afflicted us, and imposed hard labor on us.

7 'Then we cried to the LORD, the God of our fathers, and the LORD heard our voice and saw our affliction and our toil and our oppression;

8 and the LORD brought us out of Egypt with a mighty hand and an outstretched arm and with great terror and with signs and wonders;

9 and He has brought us to this place, and has given us this land, a land flowing with milk and honey.

10 'And now behold, I have brought the first of the produce of the ground which Thou, O LORD hast given me.' And you shall set it down before the LORD your God, and worship before the LORD your God;

11 and you and the Levite and the alien who is among you shall rejoice in all the good which the LORD your God has given you and your household.

12 ¶"When you have finished paying all the tithe of your increase in the third year, the year of tithing, then you shall give it to the Levite, to the stranger, to the orphan and to the widow, that they may eat in your towns, and be satisfied.

13"And you shall say before the LORD your God, 'I have removed the sacred *portion* from *my* house, and also have given it to the Levite and the alien, the orphan and the widow, according to all Thy commandments which Thou hast commanded me; I have not transgressed or forgotten any of Thy commandments.

14 'I have not eaten of it while mourning, nor have I removed any of it while I was unclean, nor offered any of it to the dead. I have listened to the voice of the LORD my God; I have done according to all that Thou hast commanded me.

15 'Look down from Thy holy habitation, from heaven, and bless Thy people Israel, and the ground which Thou hast given us, a land flowing with milk and honey, as Thou didst swear to our fathers.'

16 ¶"This day the LORD your God commands you to do these statutes and ordinances. You shall therefore be careful to do them with all your heart and with all your soul.

[17] Or, *reverence*

17"You have today declared the LORD to be your God, and that you would walk in His ways and keep His statutes, His commandments and His ordinances, and listen to His voice.

18"And the LORD has today declared you to be His people, a treasured possession, as He promised you, and that you should keep all His commandments;

19 and that He shall set you high above all nations which He has made, for praise, fame, and honor; and that you shall be a consecrated people to the LORD your God, as He has spoken."

CHAPTER 27

THEN Moses and the elders of Israel charged the people, saying, "Keep all the commandments which I command you today.

2"So it shall be on the day when you shall cross the Jordan to the land which the LORD your God gives you, that you shall set up for yourself large stones, and coat them with lime

3 and write on them all the words of this law, when you cross over, in order that you may enter the land which the LORD your God gives you, a land flowing with milk and honey, as the LORD, the God of your fathers, promised you.

4"So it shall be when you cross the Jordan, you shall set up on Mount Ebal, these stones, as I am commanding you today, and you shall coat them with lime.

5"Moreover, you shall build there an altar to the LORD your God, an altar of stones; you shall not wield an iron *tool* on them.

6"You shall build the altar of the LORD your God of uncut stones; and you shall offer on it burnt offerings to the LORD your God;

7 and you shall sacrifice peace offerings and eat there, and you shall rejoice before the LORD your God.

8"And you shall write on the stones all the words of this law very distinctly."

9 ¶ Then Moses and the Levitical priests spoke to all Israel, saying, "Be silent and listen, O Israel! This day you have become a people for the LORD your God.

10"You shall therefore obey the LORD your God, and do His commandments and His statutes which I command you today."

11 ¶ Moses also charged the people on that day, saying,

12"When you cross the Jordan, these shall stand on Mount Gerizim to bless the people: Simeon, Levi, Judah, Issachar, Joseph, and Benjamin.

13"And for the curse, these shall stand on Mount Ebal: Reuben, Gad, Asher, Zebulun, Dan, and Naphtali.

14"The Levites shall then answer and say to all the men of Israel with a loud voice,

15 ¶ 'Cursed is the man who makes an idol or a molten image, an abomination to the LORD, the work of the hands of the craftsman, and sets *it* up in secret.' And all the people shall answer and say, 'Amen.'

16 ¶ 'Cursed is he who dishonors his father or mother.' And all the people shall say, 'Amen.'

17 ¶ 'Cursed is he who moves his neighbor's boundary mark.' And all the people shall say, 'Amen.'

18 ¶ 'Cursed is he who misleads a blind *person* on the road.' And all the people shall say, 'Amen.'

19 ¶ 'Cursed is he who distorts the justice due an alien, orphan, and widow.' And all the people shall say, 'Amen.'

20 ¶ 'Cursed is he who lies with his father's wife, because he has uncovered his father's skirt.' And all the people shall say, 'Amen.'

21 ¶ 'Cursed is he who lies with any animal.' And all the people shall say, 'Amen.'

22 ¶ 'Cursed is he who lies with his sister, the daughter of his father or of his mother.' And all the people shall say, 'Amen.'

23 ¶ 'Cursed is he who lies with his mother-in-law.' And all the people shall say, 'Amen.'

24 ¶ 'Cursed is he who strikes his neighbor in secret.' And all the people shall say, 'Amen.'

25 ¶ 'Cursed is he who accepts a bribe to strike down an innocent person.' And all the people shall say, 'Amen.'

26 ¶ 'Cursed is he who does not confirm the words of this law by doing them.' And all the people shall say, 'Amen.'

CHAPTER 28

"Now it shall be, if you will diligently obey the Lord your God, being careful to do all His commandments which I command you today, the Lord your God will set you high above all the nations of the earth.

2"And all these blessings shall come upon you and overtake you, if you will obey the Lord your God.

3"Blessed *shall* you *be* in the city, and blessed *shall* you *be* in the country.

4"Blessed *shall be* the offspring of your body and the produce of your ground and the offspring of your beasts, the increase of your herd and the young of your flock.

5"Blessed *shall be* your basket and your kneading bowl.

6"Blessed *shall* you *be* when you come in, and blessed *shall* you *be* when you go out.

7 ¶"The Lord will cause your enemies who rise up against you to be defeated before you; they shall come out against you one way and shall flee before you seven ways.

8"The Lord will command the blessing upon you in your barns and in all that you put your hand to, and He will bless you in the land which the Lord your God gives you.

9"The Lord will establish you as a holy people to Himself, as He swore to you, if you will keep the commandments of the Lord your God, and walk in His ways.

10"So all the peoples of the earth shall see that you are called by the name of the Lord; and they shall be afraid of you.

11"And the Lord will make you abound in prosperity, in the offspring of your body and in the offspring of your beast and in the produce of your ground, in the land which the Lord swore to your fathers to give you.

12"The Lord will open for you His good storehouse, the heavens, to give rain to your land in its season and to bless all the work of your hand; and you shall lend to many nations, but you shall not borrow.

13"And the Lord shall make you the head and not the tail, and you only shall be above, and you shall not be underneath, if you will listen to the commandments of the Lord your God, which I charge you today, to observe *them* carefully,

14 and do not turn aside from any of the words which I command you today, to the right or to the left, to go after other gods to serve them.

15 ¶"But it shall come about, if you will not obey the Lord your God, to observe to do all His commandments and His statutes with which I charge you today, that all these curses shall come upon you and overtake you.

16"Cursed *shall* you *be* in the city, and cursed *shall* you *be* in the country.

17"Cursed *shall be* your basket and your kneading bowl.

18"Cursed *shall be* the offspring of your body and the produce of your ground, the increase of your herd and the young of your flock.

19"Cursed *shall* you *be* when you come in, and cursed *shall* you *be* when you go out.

20 ¶"The Lord will send upon you curses, confusion, and rebuke, in all you undertake to do, until you are destroyed and until you perish quickly, on account of the evil of your deeds, because you have forsaken Me.

21"The Lord will make the pestilence cling to you until He has consumed you from the land, where you are entering to possess it.

22"The Lord will smite you with consumption and with fever and with inflammation and with fiery heat and with [18]the sword and with blight and with mildew, and they shall pursue you until you perish.

23"And the heaven which is over your head shall be bronze, and the earth which is under you, iron.

24"The Lord will make the rain of your land powder and dust; from heaven it shall come down on you until you are destroyed.

25"The Lord will cause you to be defeated before your enemies; you shall go out one way against them, but you shall flee seven ways before them, and you shall be *an example of* terror to all the kingdoms of the earth.

26"And your carcasses shall be food to all birds of the sky and to the beasts of the earth, and there shall be no one to frighten *them* away.

[18] Another reading is *drought*

27 ¶"The LORD will smite you with the boils of Egypt and with tumors and with the scab and with the itch, from which you cannot be healed.

28"The LORD will smite you with madness and with blindness and with bewilderment of heart;

29 and you shall grope at noon, as the blind man gropes in darkness, and you shall not prosper in your ways; but you shall only be oppressed and robbed continually, with none to save you.

30"You shall betroth a wife, but another man shall violate her; you shall build a house, but you shall not live in it; you shall plant a vineyard, but you shall not use its fruit.

31"Your ox shall be slaughtered before your eyes, but you shall not eat of it; your donkey shall be torn away from you, and shall not be restored to you; your sheep shall be given to your enemies, and you shall have none to save you.

32"Your sons and your daughters shall be given to another people, while your eyes shall look on and yearn for them continually; but there shall be nothing you can do.

33"A people whom you do not know shall eat up the produce of your ground and all your labors, and you shall never be anything but oppressed and crushed continually.

34"And you shall be driven mad by the sight of what you see.

35"The LORD will strike you on the knees and legs with sore boils, from which you cannot be healed, from the sole of your foot to the crown of your head.

36"The LORD will bring you and your king, whom you shall set over you, to a nation which neither you nor your fathers have known, and there you shall serve other gods, wood and stone.

37"And you shall become a horror, a proverb, and a taunt among all the people where the LORD will drive you.

38 ¶"You shall bring out much seed to the field but you shall gather in little, for the locust shall consume it.

39"You shall plant and cultivate vineyards, but you shall neither drink of the wine nor gather *the grapes,* for the worm shall devour them.

40"You shall have olive trees throughout your territory but you shall not anoint yourself with the oil, for your olives shall drop off.

41"You shall have sons and daughters but they shall not be yours, for they shall go into captivity.

42"The cricket shall possess all your trees and the produce of your ground.

43"The alien who is among you shall rise above you higher and higher, but you shall go down lower and lower.

44"He shall lend to you, but you shall not lend to him; he shall be the head, and you shall be the tail.

45"So all these curses shall come on you and pursue you and overtake you until you are destroyed, because you would not obey the LORD your God by keeping His commandments and His statutes which He commanded you.

46"And they shall become a sign and a wonder on you and your descendants forever.

47"Because you did not serve the LORD your God with joy and a glad heart, for the abundance of all things;

48 therefore you shall serve your enemies whom the LORD shall send against you, in hunger, in thirst, in nakedness, and in the lack of all things; and He will put an iron yoke on your neck until He has destroyed you.

49 ¶"The LORD will bring a nation against you from afar, from the end of the earth, as the eagle swoops down, a nation whose language you shall not understand,

50 a nation of fierce countenance who shall have no respect for the old, nor show favor to the young.

51"Moreover, it shall eat the offspring of your herd and the produce of your ground until you are destroyed, who also leaves you no grain, new wine, or oil, nor the increase of your herd or the young of your flock until they have caused you to perish.

52"And it shall besiege you in all your towns until your high and fortified walls in which you trusted come down throughout your land, and it shall besiege you in all your towns throughout your land which the LORD your God has given you.

53"Then you shall eat the offspring of your own body, the flesh of your sons and of your daughters whom the LORD your God has given you, during the siege and the distress by which your enemy shall oppress you.

54"The man who is refined and very delicate among you shall be hostile toward his brother and toward the wife he cherishes and toward the rest of his children who remain,

55 so that he will not give *even* one of them any of the flesh of his children which he shall eat, since he has nothing *else* left, during the siege and the distress by which your enemy shall oppress you in all your towns.

56"The refined and delicate woman among you, who would not venture to set the sole of her foot on the ground for delicateness and refinement, shall be hostile toward the husband she cherishes and toward her son and daughter,

57 and toward her afterbirth which issues from between her legs and toward her children whom she bears; for she shall eat them secretly for lack of anything *else,* during the siege and the distress by which your enemy shall oppress you in your towns.

58 ¶"If you are not careful to observe all the words of this law which are written in this book, to fear this honored and awesome name, the LORD your God,

59 then the LORD will bring extraordinary plagues on you and your descendants, even severe and lasting plagues, and miserable and chronic sicknesses.

60"And He will bring back on you all the diseases of Egypt of which you were afraid, and they shall cling to you.

61"Also every sickness and every plague which, not written in the book of this law, the LORD will bring on you until you are destroyed.

62"Then you shall be left few in number, whereas you were as the stars of heaven for multitude, because you did not obey the LORD your God.

63"And it shall come about that as the LORD delighted over you to prosper you, and multiply you, so the LORD will delight over you to make you perish and destroy you; and you shall be torn from the land where you are entering to possess it.

64"Moreover, the LORD will scatter you among all peoples, from one end of the earth to the other end of the earth; and there you shall serve other gods, wood and stone, which you or your fathers have not known.

65"And among those nations you shall find no rest, and there shall be no resting place for the sole of your foot; but there the LORD will give you a trembling heart, failing of eyes, and despair of soul.

66"So your life shall hang in doubt before you; and you shall be in dread night and day, and shall have no assurance of your life.

67"In the morning you shall say, 'Would that it were evening!' And at evening you shall say, 'Would that it were morning!' because of the dread of your heart which you dread, and for the sight of your eyes which you shall see.

68"And the LORD will bring you back to Egypt in ships, by the way about which I spoke to you, 'You will never see it again!' And there you shall offer yourselves for sale to your enemies as male and female slaves, but there will be no buyer."

CHAPTER 29

THESE are the words of the covenant which the LORD commanded Moses to make with the sons of Israel in the land of Moab, besides the covenant which He had made with them at Horeb.

2 ¶ And Moses summoned all Israel and said to them, "You have seen all that the LORD did before your eyes in the land of Egypt to Pharaoh and all his servants and all his land;

3 the great trials which your eyes have seen, those great signs and wonders.

4"Yet to this day the LORD has not given you a heart to know, nor eyes to see, nor ears to hear.

5"And I have led you forty years in the wilderness; your clothes have not worn out on you, and your sandal has not worn out on your foot.

6"You have not eaten bread, nor have you drunk wine or strong drink, in order that you might know that I am the LORD your God.

7"When you reached this place, Sihon the king of Heshbon and Og the king of Bashan came out to meet us for battle, but we defeated them;

8 and we took their land and gave it as an inheritance to the Reubenites, the Gadites, and the half-tribe of the Manassites.

9"So keep the words of this covenant to do them, that you may prosper in all that you do.

10 ¶"You stand today, all of you, before the LORD your God: your chiefs, your tribes, your elders and your officers, *even* all the men of Israel,

11 your little ones, your wives, and the alien who is within your camps, from the one who chops your wood to the one who draws your water,

12 that you may enter into the covenant with the LORD your God, and into His oath which the LORD your God is making with you today,

13 in order that He may establish you today as His people and that He may be your God, just as He spoke to you and as He swore to your fathers, to Abraham, Isaac, and Jacob.

14 ¶"Now not with you alone am I making this covenant and this oath,

15 but both with those who stand here with us today in the presence of the LORD our God and with those who are not with us here today

16 (for you know how we lived in the land of Egypt, and how we came through the midst of the nations through which you passed.

17"Moreover, you have seen their abominations and their idols *of* wood, stone, silver, and gold, which *they had* with them);

18 lest there shall be among you a man or woman, or family or tribe, whose heart turns away today from the LORD our God, to go and serve the gods of those nations; lest there shall be among you a root bearing poisonous fruit and wormwood.

19"And it shall be when he hears the words of this curse, that he will boast, saying, 'I have peace though I walk in the stubbornness of my heart in order to destroy the watered *land* with the dry.'

20"The LORD shall never be willing to forgive him, but rather the anger of the LORD and His jealousy will burn against that man, and every curse which is written in this book will rest on him, and the LORD will blot out his name from under heaven.

21"Then the LORD will single him out for adversity from all the tribes of Israel, according to all the curses of the covenant which are written in this book of the law.

22 ¶"Now the generation to come, your sons who rise up after you and the foreigner who comes from a distant land, when they see the plagues of the land and the diseases with which the LORD has afflicted it, will say,

23 'All its land is brimstone and salt, a burning waste, unsown and unproductive, and no grass grows in it, like the overthrow of Sodom and Gomorrah, Admah and Zeboiim, which the LORD overthrew in His anger and in His wrath.'

24"And all the nations shall say, 'Why has the LORD done thus to this land? Why this great outburst of anger?'

25"Then *men* shall say, 'Because they forsook the covenant of the LORD, the God of their fathers, which He made with them when He brought them out of the land of Egypt.

26 'And they went and served other gods and worshiped them, gods whom they have not known and whom He had not allotted to them.

27 'Therefore, the anger of the LORD burned against that land, to bring upon it every curse which is written in this book;

28 and the LORD uprooted them from their land in anger and in fury and in great wrath, and cast them into another land, as *it is* this day.'

29 ¶"The secret things belong to the LORD our God, but the things revealed belong to us and to our sons forever, that we may observe all the words of this law.

CHAPTER 30

"So it shall be when all of these things have come upon you, the blessing and the curse which I have set before you, and you call *them* to mind in all nations where the LORD your God has banished you,

2 and you return to the LORD your God and obey Him with all your heart and soul according to all that I command you today, you and your sons,

3 then the LORD your God will restore you from captivity, and have

compassion on you, and will gather you again from all the peoples where the LORD your God has scattered you.

4"If your outcasts are at the ends of the earth, from there the LORD your God will gather you, and from there He will bring you back.

5"And the LORD your God will bring you into the land which your fathers possessed, and you shall possess it; and He will prosper you and multiply you more than your fathers.

6"Moreover the LORD your God will circumcise your heart and the heart of your descendants, to love the LORD your God with all your heart and with all your soul, in order that you may live.

7"And the LORD your God will inflict all these curses on your enemies and on those who hate you, who persecuted you.

8"And you shall again obey the LORD, and observe all His commandments which I command you today.

9"Then the LORD your God will prosper you abundantly in all the work of your hand, in the offspring of your body and in the offspring of your cattle and in the produce of your ground, for the LORD will again rejoice over you for good, just as He rejoiced over your fathers;

10 if you obey the LORD your God to keep His commandments and His statutes which are written in this book of the law, if you turn to the LORD your God with all your heart and soul.

11 ¶"For this commandment which I command you today is not too difficult for you, nor is it out of reach.

12"It is not in heaven, that you should say, 'Who will go up to heaven for us to get it for us and make us hear it, that we may observe it?'

13"Nor is it beyond the sea, that you should say, 'Who will cross the sea for us to get it for us and make us hear it, that we may observe it?'

14"But the word is very near you, in your mouth and in your heart, that you may observe it.

15 ¶"See, I have set before you today life and prosperity, and death and adversity;

16 in that I command you today to love the LORD your God, to walk in His ways and to keep His commandments and His statutes and His judgments,

that you may live and multiply, and that the LORD your God may bless you in the land where you are entering to possess it.

17"But if your heart turns away and you will not obey, but are drawn away and worship other gods and serve them,

18 I declare to you today that you shall surely perish. You shall not prolong *your* days in the land where you are crossing the Jordan to enter and possess it.

19"I call heaven and earth to witness against you today, that I have set before you life and death, the blessing and the curse. So choose life in order that you may live, you and your descendants,

20 by loving the LORD your God, by obeying His voice, and by holding fast to Him; for this is your life and the length of your days, that you may live in the land which the LORD swore to your fathers, to Abraham, Isaac, and Jacob, to give them."

CHAPTER 31

So Moses went and spoke these words to all Israel.

2 And he said to them, "I am a hundred and twenty years old today; I am no longer able to come and go, and the LORD has said to me, 'You shall not cross this Jordan.'

3"It is the LORD your God who will cross ahead of you; He will destroy these nations before you, and you shall dispossess them. Joshua is the one who will cross ahead of you, just as the LORD has spoken.

4"And the LORD will do to them just as He did to Sihon and Og, the kings of the Amorites, and to their land, when He destroyed them.

5"And the LORD will deliver them up before you, and you shall do to them according to all the commandments which I have commanded you.

6"Be strong and courageous, do not be afraid or tremble at them, for the LORD your God is the one who goes with you. He will not fail you or forsake you."

7 Then Moses called to Joshua and said to him in the sight of all Israel, "Be strong and courageous, for you shall go with this people into the land

which the Lord has sworn to their fathers to give them, and you shall give it to them as an inheritance.

8"And the Lord is the one who goes ahead of you; He will be with you. He will not fail you or forsake you. Do not fear, or be dismayed."

9 ¶ So Moses wrote this law and gave it to the priests, the sons of Levi who carried the ark of the covenant of the Lord, and to all the elders of Israel.

10 Then Moses commanded them, saying, "At the end of *every* seven years, at the time of the year of remission of debts, at the Feast of Booths,

11 when all Israel comes to appear before the Lord your God at the place which He will choose, you shall read this law in front of all Israel in their hearing.

12"Assemble the people, the men and the women and children and the alien who is in your town, in order that they may hear and learn and fear the Lord your God, and be careful to observe all the words of this law.

13"And their children, who have not known, will hear and learn to fear the Lord your God, as long as you live on the land which you are about to cross the Jordan to possess."

14 ¶ Then the Lord said to Moses, "Behold, the time for you to die is near; call Joshua, and present yourselves at the tent of meeting, that I may commission him." So Moses and Joshua went and presented themselves at the tent of meeting.

15 And the Lord appeared in the tent in a pillar of cloud, and the pillar of cloud stood at the doorway of the tent.

16 And the Lord said to Moses, "Behold, you are about to lie down with your fathers; and this people will arise and play the harlot with the strange gods of the land, into the midst of which they are going, and will forsake Me and break My covenant which I have made with them.

17"Then My anger will be kindled against them in that day, and I will forsake them and hide My face from them, and they shall be consumed, and many evils and troubles shall come upon them; so that they will say in that day, 'Is it not because our God is not among us that these evils have come upon us?'

18"But I will surely hide My face in that day because of all the evil which they will do, for they will turn to other gods.

19"Now therefore, write this song for yourselves, and teach it to the sons of Israel; put it on their lips, in order that this song may be a witness for Me against the sons of Israel.

20"For when I bring them into the land flowing with milk and honey, which I swore to their fathers, and they have eaten and are satisfied and become prosperous, then they will turn to other gods and serve them, and spurn Me and break My covenant.

21"Then it shall come about, when many evils and troubles have come upon them, that this song will testify before them as a witness (for it shall not be forgotten from the lips of their descendants); for I know their intent which they are developing today, before I have brought them into the land which I swore."

22 So Moses wrote this song the same day, and taught it to the sons of Israel.

23 ¶ Then He commissioned Joshua the son of Nun, and said, "Be strong and courageous, for you shall bring the sons of Israel into the land which I swore to them, and I will be with you."

24 ¶ And it came about, when Moses finished writing the words of this law in a book until they were complete,

25 that Moses commanded the Levites who carried the ark of the covenant of the Lord, saying,

26"Take this book of the law and place it beside the ark of the covenant of the Lord your God, that it may remain there as a witness against you.

27"For I know your rebellion and your stubbornness; behold, while I am still alive with you today, you have been rebellious against the Lord; how much more, then, after my death?

28"Assemble to me all the elders of your tribes and your officers, that I may speak these words in their hearing and call the heavens and the earth to witness against them.

29"For I know that after my death you will act corruptly and turn from the way which I have commanded you; and evil will befall you in the latter days, for you will do that which is evil in the sight of the LORD, provoking Him to anger with the work of your hands."

30 ¶ Then Moses spoke in the hearing of all the assembly of Israel the words of this song, until they were complete:

CHAPTER 32

"GIVE ear, O heavens, and let me speak;
　And let the earth hear the words of my mouth.
2"Let my teaching drop as the rain,
　My speech distill as the dew,
　As the droplets on the fresh grass
　And as the showers on the herb.
3"For I proclaim the name of the LORD;
　Ascribe greatness to our God!
4"The Rock! His work is perfect,
　For all His ways are just;
　A God of faithfulness and without injustice,
　Righteous and upright is He.
5"They have acted corruptly toward Him,
　They are not His children, because of their defect;
　But are a perverse and crooked generation.
6"Do you thus repay the LORD,
　O foolish and unwise people?
　Is not He your Father who has bought you?
　He has made you and established you.
7"Remember the days of old,
　Consider the years of all generations.
　Ask your father, and he will inform you,
　Your elders, and they will tell you.
8"When the Most High gave the nations their inheritance,
　When He separated the sons of man,
　He set the boundaries of the peoples
　According to the number of the sons of Israel.
9"For the LORD's portion is His people;
　Jacob is the allotment of His inheritance.
10"He found him in a desert land,
　And in the howling waste of a wilderness;

He encircled him, He cared for him,
　He guarded him as the pupil of His eye.
11"Like an eagle that stirs up its nest,
　That hovers over its young,
　He spread His wings and caught them,
　He carried them on His pinions.
12"The LORD alone guided him,
　And there was no foreign god with him.
13"He made him ride on the high places of the earth,
　And he ate the produce of the field;
　And He made him suck honey from the rock,
　And oil from the flinty rock,
14 Curds of cows, and milk of the flock,
　With fat of lambs,
　And rams, the breed of Bashan, and goats,
　With the finest of the wheat—
　And of the blood of grapes you drank wine.

15 ¶"But [19]Jeshurun grew fat and kicked—
　You are grown fat, thick, and sleek—
　Then he forsook God who made him,
　And scorned the Rock of his salvation.
16"They made Him jealous with strange *gods;*
　With abominations they provoked Him to anger.
17"They sacrificed to demons who were not God,
　To gods whom they have not known,
　New *gods* who came lately,
　Whom your fathers did not dread.
18"You neglected the Rock who begot you,
　And forgot the God who gave you birth.

19 ¶"And the LORD saw *this,* and spurned *them*
　Because of the provocation of His sons and daughters.
20"Then He said, 'I will hide My face from them,

[19] I.e., Israel

I will see what their end *shall be;*
For they are a perverse generation,
Sons in whom is no faithfulness.
21 'They have made Me jealous with
what is not God;
They have provoked Me to anger
with their idols.
So I will make them jealous with
those who are not a people;
I will provoke them to anger with
a foolish nation,
22 For a fire is kindled in My anger,
And burns to the lowest part of
Sheol,
And consumes the earth with its
yield,
And sets on fire the foundations
of the mountains.

23 ¶ 'I will heap misfortunes on
them;
I will use My arrows on them.
24 '*They shall be* wasted by famine,
and consumed by plague
And bitter destruction;
And the teeth of beasts I will send
upon them,
With the venom of crawling
things of the dust.
25 'Outside the sword shall bereave,
And inside terror—
Both young man and virgin,
The nursling with the man of gray
hair.
26 'I would have said, "I will cut them
to pieces,
I will remove the memory of them
from men,"
27 Had I not feared the provocation
by the enemy,
Lest their adversaries should mis-
judge,
Lest they should say, "Our hand is
triumphant,
And the LORD has not done all
this."'

28 ¶ "For they are a nation lacking in
counsel,
And there is no understanding in
them.
29 "Would that they were wise, that
they understood this,
That they would discern their future!
30 "How could one chase a thousand,
And two put ten thousand to
flight,

Unless their Rock had sold them,
And the LORD had given them up?
31 "Indeed their rock is not like our
Rock,
Even our enemies themselves
judge this.
32 "For their vine is from the vine of
Sodom,
And from the fields of Gomorrah;
Their grapes are grapes of poison,
Their clusters, bitter.
33 "Their wine is the venom of ser-
pents,
And the deadly poison of cobras.

34 ¶ 'Is it not laid up in store with
Me,
Sealed up in My treasuries?
35 'Vengeance is Mine, and retribution,
In due time their foot will slip;
For the day of their calamity is
near,
And the impending things are
hastening upon them.'
36 "For the LORD will vindicate His
people,
And will have compassion on His
servants;
When He sees that *their* strength
is gone,
And there is none *remaining,*
bond or free.
37 "And He will say, 'Where are their
gods,
The rock in which they sought
refuge?
38 'Who ate the fat of their sacrifices,
And drank the wine of their libation?
Let them rise up and help you,
Let them be your hiding place!
39 'See now that I, I am He,
And there is no god besides Me;
It is I who put to death and give
life.
I have wounded, and it is I who
heal;
And there is no one who can deliver from My hand.
40 'Indeed, I lift up My hand to
heaven,
And say, as I live forever,
41 If I sharpen My flashing sword,
And My hand takes hold on justice,

I will render vengeance on My
adversaries,
And I will repay those who hate
Me.
42 'I will make My arrows drunk with
blood,
And My sword shall devour flesh,
With the blood of the slain and
the captives,
From the long-haired leaders of
the enemy.'
43"Rejoice, O nations, *with* His peo-
ple;
For He will avenge the blood of
His servants,
And will render vengeance on His
adversaries,
And will atone for His land *and*
His people."

44 ¶ Then Moses came and spoke all
the words of this song in the hearing
of the people, he, with Joshua the son
of Nun.
45 When Moses had finished speaking all these words to all Israel,
46 he said to them, "Take to your
heart all the words with which I am
warning you today, which you shall
command your sons to observe carefully, *even* all the words of this law.
47"For it is not an idle word for you;
indeed it is your life. And by this word
you shall prolong your days in the
land, which you are about to cross the
Jordan to possess."
48 ¶ And the LORD spoke to Moses
that very same day, saying,
49"Go up to this mountain of the
Abarim, Mount Nebo, which is in the
land of Moab opposite Jericho, and
look at the land of Canaan, which I
am giving to the sons of Israel for a
possession.
50"Then die on the mountain where
you ascend, and be gathered to your
people, as Aaron your brother died on
Mount Hor and was gathered to his
people,
51 because you broke faith with Me
in the midst of the sons of Israel at the
waters of Meribah-kadesh, in the wilderness of Zin, because you did not
treat Me as holy in the midst of the
sons of Israel.
52"For you shall see the land at a
distance, but you shall not go there,
into the land which I am giving the
sons of Israel."

CHAPTER 33

Now this is the blessing with which
Moses the man of God blessed the
sons of Israel before his death.
2 And he said,
"The LORD came from Sinai,
And dawned on them from Seir;
He shone forth from Mount Pa-
ran,
And He came from the midst of
ten thousand holy ones;
At His right hand there was
flashing lightning for them.
3 "Indeed, He loves the people;
All Thy holy ones are in Thy
hand,
And they followed in Thy steps;
Everyone receives of Thy words.
4 "Moses charged us with a law,
A possession for the assembly of
Jacob.
5 "And He was king in Jeshurun,
When the heads of the people
were gathered,
The tribes of Israel together.

6 ¶ "May Reuben live and not die,
Nor his men be few."

7 ¶ And this regarding Judah; so he
said,
"Hear, O LORD, the voice of Judah,
And bring him to his people.
With his hands he contended for
them;
And mayest Thou be a help
against his adversaries."

8 ¶ And of Levi he said,
"*Let* Thy Thummim and Thy
Urim *belong* to Thy godly man,
Whom Thou didst prove at Mas-
sah,
With whom Thou didst contend
at the waters of Meribah;
9 Who said of his father and his
mother,
'I did not consider them';
And he did not acknowledge his
brothers,
Nor did he regard his own sons,
For they observed Thy word,
And kept Thy covenant.
10 "They shall teach Thine ordi-
nances to Jacob,
And Thy law to Israel.
They shall put incense before
Thee,

And whole burnt offerings on Thine altar.

11 "O Lord, bless his substance,
And accept the work of his hands;
Shatter the loins of those who rise up against him,
And those who hate him, so that they may not rise *again*."

12 ¶ Of Benjamin he said,
"May the beloved of the Lord dwell in security by Him,
Who shields him all the day,
And he dwells between His shoulders."

13 ¶ And of Joseph he said,
"Blessed of the Lord *be* his land,
With the choice things of heaven, with the dew,
And from the deep lying beneath,

14 And with the choice yield of the sun,
And with the choice produce of the months,

15 "And with the best things of the ancient mountains,
And with the choice things of the everlasting hills,

16 And with the choice things of the earth and its fulness,
And the favor of Him who dwelt in the bush.
Let it come to the head of Joseph,
And to the crown of the head of the one distinguished among his brothers.

17 "As the first-born of his ox, majesty is his,
And his horns are the horns of the wild ox;
With them he shall push the peoples,
All at once, *to* the ends of the earth.
And those are the ten thousands of Ephraim,
And those are the thousands of Manasseh."

18 ¶ And of Zebulun he said,
"Rejoice, Zebulun, in your going forth,
And, Issachar, in your tents.

19 "They shall call peoples *to* the mountain;

There they shall offer righteous sacrifices;
For they shall draw out the abundance of the seas,
And the hidden treasures of the sand."

20 ¶ And of Gad he said,
"Blessed is the one who enlarges Gad;
He lies down as a lion,
And tears the arm, also the crown of the head.

21 "Then he provided the first *part* for himself,
For there the ruler's portion was reserved;
And he came *with* the leaders of the people;
He executed the justice of the Lord,
And His ordinances with Israel."

22 ¶ And of Dan he said,
"Dan is a lion's whelp,
That leaps forth from Bashan."

23 ¶ And of Naphtali he said,
"O Naphtali, satisfied with favor,
And full of the blessing of the Lord,
Take possession of the sea and the south."

24 ¶ And of Asher he said,
"More blessed than sons is Asher;
May he be favored by his brothers,
And may he dip his foot in oil.

25 "Your locks shall be iron and bronze,
And according to your days, so shall your leisurely walk be.

26 ¶ "There is none like the God of [20]Jeshurun,
Who rides the heavens to your help,
And through the skies in His majesty.

27 "The eternal God is a dwelling place,
And underneath are the everlasting arms;
And He drove out the enemy from before you,
And said, 'Destroy!'

[20] I.e., Israel

28 "So Israel dwells in security,
     The fountain of Jacob secluded,
     In a land of grain and new wine;
     His heavens also drop down dew.
29 "Blessed are you, O Israel;
     Who is like you, a people saved
          by the LORD,
     Who is the shield of your help,
     And the sword of your majesty!
     So your enemies shall cringe be-
          fore you,
     And you shall tread upon their
          high places."

CHAPTER 34

NOW Moses went up from the plains
of Moab to Mount Nebo, to the top of
Pisgah, which is opposite Jericho. And
the LORD showed him all the land,
Gilead as far as Dan,

2 and all Naphtali and the land of
Ephraim and Manasseh, and all the
land of Judah as far as the [21]western
sea,

3 and the Negev and the plain in the
valley of Jericho, the city of palm
trees, as far as Zoar.

4 Then the LORD said to him, "This
is the land which I swore to Abraham,
Isaac, and Jacob, saying, 'I will give it
to your descendants'; I have let you

[21] I.e., Mediterranean Sea

see *it* with your eyes, but you shall not
go over there."

5 So Moses the servant of the LORD
died there in the land of Moab, according to the word of the LORD.

6 And He buried him in the valley in
the land of Moab, opposite Beth-peor;
but no man knows his burial place to
this day.

7 Although Moses was one hundred
and twenty years old when he died, his
eye was not dim, nor his vigor abated.

8 So the sons of Israel wept for
Moses in the plains of Moab thirty
days; then the days of weeping *and*
mourning for Moses came to an end.

9 ¶ Now Joshua the son of Nun was
filled with the spirit of wisdom, for
Moses had laid his hands on him; and
the sons of Israel listened to him and
did as the LORD had commanded Moses.

10 Since then no prophet has risen in
Israel like Moses, whom the LORD
knew face to face,

11 for all the signs and wonders
which the LORD sent him to perform in
the land of Egypt against Pharaoh, all
his servants, and all his land,

12 and for all the mighty power and
for all the great terror which Moses
performed in the sight of all Israel.

THE BOOK OF

JOSHUA

NOW it came about after the death
of Moses the servant of the LORD that
the LORD spoke to Joshua the son of
Nun, Moses' [1]servant, saying,

2"Moses My servant is dead; now
therefore arise, cross this Jordan, you
and all this people, to the land which I
am giving to them, to the sons of
Israel.

3"Every place on which the sole of
your foot treads, I have given it to
you, just as I spoke to Moses.

4"From the wilderness and this
Lebanon, even as far as the great river,
the river Euphrates, all the land of the
Hittites, and as far as the Great Sea

[1] Or, minister

toward the setting of the sun, will be
your territory.

5"No man will *be able to* stand before you all the days of your life. Just
as I have been with Moses, I will be
with you; I will not fail you or forsake
you.

6"Be strong and courageous, for you
shall give this people possession of the
land which I swore to their fathers to
give them.

7"Only be strong and very courageous; be careful to do according to all
the law which Moses My servant commanded you; do not turn from it to the
right or to the left, so that you may
have success wherever you go.

8"This book of the law shall not

depart from your mouth, but you shall meditate on it day and night, so that you may be careful to do according to all that is written in it; for then you will make your way prosperous, and then you will have success.

9"Have I not commanded you? Be strong and courageous! Do not tremble or be dismayed, for the LORD your God is with you wherever you go."

10 ¶ Then Joshua commanded the officers of the people, saying,

11"Pass through the midst of the camp and command the people, saying, 'Prepare provisions for yourselves, for within three days you are to cross this Jordan, to go in to possess the land which the LORD your God is giving you, to possess it.' "

12 ¶ And to the Reubenites and to the Gadites and to the half-tribe of Manasseh, Joshua said,

13"Remember the word which Moses the servant of the LORD commanded you, saying, 'The LORD your God gives you rest, and will give you this land.'

14"Your wives, your little ones, and your cattle shall remain in the land which Moses gave you beyond the Jordan, but you shall cross before your brothers in battle array, all your valiant warriors, and shall help them,

15 until the LORD gives your brothers rest, as *He gives* you, and they also possess the land which the LORD your God is giving them. Then you shall return to your own land, and possess that which Moses the servant of the LORD gave you beyond the Jordan toward the sunrise."

16 And they answered Joshua, saying, "All that you have commanded us we will do, and wherever you send us we will go.

17"Just as we obeyed Moses in all things, so we will obey you; only may the LORD your God be with you, as He was with Moses.

18"Anyone who rebels against your command and does not obey your words in all that you command him, shall be put to death; only be strong and courageous."

CHAPTER 2

THEN Joshua the son of Nun sent two men as spies secretly from Shittim, saying, "Go, view the land, espe-

cially Jericho." So they went and came into the house of a harlot whose name was Rahab, and lodged there.

2 And it was told the king of Jericho, saying, "Behold, men from the sons of Israel have come here tonight to search out the land."

3 And the king of Jericho sent *word* to Rahab, saying, "Bring out the men who have come to you, who have entered your house, for they have come to search out all the land."

4 But the woman had taken the two men and hidden them, and she said, "Yes, the men came to me, but I did not know where they were from.

5"And it came about when *it was time* to shut the gate, at dark, that the men went out; I do not know where the men went. Pursue them quickly, for you will overtake them."

6 But she had brought them up to the roof and hidden them in the stalks of flax which she had laid in order on the roof.

7 So the men pursued them on the road to the Jordan to the fords; and as soon as those who were pursuing them had gone out, they shut the gate.

8 ¶ Now before they lay down, she came up to them on the roof,

9 and said to the men, "I know that the LORD has given you the land, and that the terror of you has fallen on us, and that all the inhabitants of the land have melted away before you.

10"For we have heard how the LORD dried up the water of the Red Sea before you when you came out of Egypt, and what you did to the two kings of the Amorites who were beyond the Jordan, to Sihon and Og, whom you utterly destroyed.

11"And when we heard *it*, our hearts melted and no courage remained in any man any longer because of you; for the LORD your God, He is God in heaven above and on earth beneath.

12"Now therefore, please swear to me by the LORD, since I have dealt kindly with you, that you also will deal kindly with my father's household, and give me a pledge of truth,

13 and spare my father and my mother and my brothers and my sisters, with all who belong to them, and deliver our ²lives from death."

² Lit., *souls*

14 So the men said to her, "Our life for yours if you do not tell this business of ours; and it shall come about when the LORD gives us the land that we will deal kindly and faithfully with you."

15 ¶ Then she let them down by a rope through the window, for her house was on the city wall, so that she was living on the wall.

16 And she said to them, "Go to the hill country, lest the pursuers happen upon you, and hide yourselves there for three days, until the pursuers return. Then afterward you may go on your way."

17 And the men said to her, "We *shall be* free from this oath to you which you have made us swear,

18 unless, when we come into the land, you tie this cord of scarlet thread in the window through which you let us down, and gather to yourself into the house your father and your mother and your brothers and all your father's household.

19 "And it shall come about that anyone who goes out of the doors of your house into the street, his blood *shall be* on his own head, and we *shall be* free; but anyone who is with you in the house, his blood *shall be* on our head, if a hand is *laid* on him.

20 "But if you tell this business of ours, then we shall be free from the oath which you have made us swear."

21 And she said, "According to your words, so be it." So she sent them away, and they departed; and she tied the scarlet cord in the window.

22 ¶ And they departed and came to the hill country, and remained there for three days until the pursuers returned. Now the pursuers had sought *them* all along the road, but had not found *them*.

23 Then the two men returned and came down from the hill country and crossed over and came to Joshua the son of Nun, and they related to him all that had happened to them.

24 And they said to Joshua, "Surely the LORD has given all the land into our hands, and all the inhabitants of the land, moreover, have melted away before us."

CHAPTER 3

THEN Joshua rose early in the morning; and he and all the sons of Israel set out from Shittim and came to the Jordan, and they lodged there before they crossed.

2 And it came about at the end of three days that the officers went through the midst of the camp;

3 and they commanded the people, saying, "When you see the ark of the covenant of the LORD your God with the Levitical priests carrying it, then you shall set out from your place and go after it.

4 "However, there shall be between you and it a distance of about 2,000 cubits by measure. Do not come near it, that you may know the way by which you shall go, for you have not passed this way before."

5 ¶ Then Joshua said to the people, "Consecrate yourselves, for tomorrow the LORD will do wonders among you."

6 And Joshua spoke to the priests, saying, "Take up the ark of the covenant and cross over ahead of the people." So they took up the ark of the covenant and went ahead of the people.

7 ¶ Now the LORD said to Joshua, "This day I will begin to exalt you in the sight of all Israel, that they may know that just as I have been with Moses, I will be with you.

8 "You shall, moreover, command the priests who are carrying the ark of the covenant, saying, 'When you come to the edge of the waters of the Jordan, you shall stand *still* in the Jordan.' "

9 Then Joshua said to the sons of Israel, "Come here, and hear the words of the LORD your God."

10 And Joshua said, "By this you shall know that the living God is among you, and that He will assuredly dispossess from before you the Canaanite, the Hittite, the Hivite, the Perizzite, the Girgashite, the Amorite, and the Jebusite.

11 "Behold, the ark of the covenant of the Lord of all the earth is crossing over ahead of you into the Jordan.

12 "Now then, take for yourselves twelve men from the tribes of Israel, one man for each tribe.

13"And it shall come about when the soles of the feet of the priests who carry the ark of the LORD, the Lord of all the earth, shall rest in the waters of the Jordan, the waters of the Jordan shall be cut off, *and* the waters which are flowing down from above shall stand in one heap."

14 ¶ So it came about when the people set out from their tents to cross the Jordan with the priests carrying the ark of the covenant before the people,

15 and when those who carried the ark came into the Jordan, and the feet of the priests carrying the ark were dipped in the edge of the water (for the Jordan overflows all its banks all the days of harvest),

16 that the waters which were flowing down from above stood *and* rose up in one heap, a great distance away at Adam, the city that is beside Zarethan; and those which were flowing down toward the sea of the Arabah, the Salt Sea, were completely cut off. So the people crossed opposite Jericho.

17 And the priests who carried the ark of the covenant of the LORD stood firm on dry ground in the middle of the Jordan while all Israel crossed on dry ground, until all the nation had finished crossing the Jordan.

CHAPTER 4

NOW it came about when all the nation had finished crossing the Jordan, that the LORD spoke to Joshua, saying,

2"Take for yourselves twelve men from the people, one man from each tribe,

3 and command them, saying, 'Take up for yourselves twelve stones from here out of the middle of the Jordan, from the place where the priests' feet are standing firm, and carry them over with you, and lay them down in the lodging place where you will lodge tonight.' "

4 So Joshua called the twelve men whom he had appointed from the sons of Israel, one man from each tribe;

5 and Joshua said to them, "Cross again to the ark of the LORD your God into the middle of the Jordan, and each of you take up a stone on his shoulder, according to the number of the tribes of the sons of Israel.

6"Let this be a sign among you, so that when your children ask later, saying, 'What do these stones mean to you?'

7 then you shall say to them, 'Because the waters of the Jordan were cut off before the ark of the covenant of the LORD; when it crossed the Jordan, the waters of the Jordan were cut off.' So these stones shall become a memorial to the sons of Israel forever."

8 ¶ And thus the sons of Israel did, as Joshua commanded, and took up twelve stones from the middle of the Jordan, just as the LORD spoke to Joshua, according to the number of the tribes of the sons of Israel; and they carried them over with them to the lodging place, and put them down there.

9 Then Joshua set up twelve stones in the middle of the Jordan at the place where the feet of the priests who carried the ark of the covenant were standing, and they are there to this day.

10 For the priests who carried the ark were standing in the middle of the Jordan until everything was completed that the LORD had commanded Joshua to speak to the people, according to all that Moses had commanded Joshua. And the people hurried and crossed;

11 and it came about when all the people had finished crossing, that the ark of the LORD and the priests crossed before the people.

12 And the sons of Reuben and the sons of Gad and the half-tribe of Manasseh crossed over in battle array before the sons of Israel, just as Moses had spoken to them;

13 about 40,000, equipped for war, crossed for battle before the LORD to the desert plains of Jericho.

14 On that day the LORD exalted Joshua in the sight of all Israel; so that they [3]revered him, just as they had revered Moses all the days of his life.

15 ¶ Now the LORD said to Joshua,

16"Command the priests who carry the ark of the testimony that they come up from the Jordan."

17 So Joshua commanded the

[3] Or, *feared*

priests, saying, "Come up from the Jordan."

18 And it came about when the priests who carried the ark of the covenant of the LORD had come up from the middle of the Jordan, and the soles of the priests' feet were lifted up to the dry ground, that the waters of the Jordan returned to their place, and went over all its banks as before.

19 ¶ Now the people came up from the Jordan on the tenth of the first month and camped at Gilgal on the eastern edge of Jericho.

20 And those twelve stones which they had taken from the Jordan, Joshua set up at Gilgal.

21 And he said to the sons of Israel, "When your children ask their fathers in time to come, saying, 'What are these stones?'

22 then you shall inform your children, saying, 'Israel crossed this Jordan on dry ground.'

23 "For the LORD your God dried up the waters of the Jordan before you until you had crossed, just as the LORD your God had done to the Red Sea, which He dried up before us until we had crossed;

24 that all the peoples of the earth may know that the hand of the LORD is mighty, so that you may fear the LORD your God forever."

CHAPTER 5

NOW it came about when all the kings of the Amorites who *were* beyond the Jordan to the west, and all the kings of the Canaanites who *were* by the sea, heard how the LORD had dried up the waters of the Jordan before the sons of Israel until they had crossed, that their hearts melted, and there was no spirit in them any longer, because of the sons of Israel.

2 ¶ At that time the LORD said to Joshua, "Make for yourself flint knives and circumcise again the sons of Israel the second time."

3 So Joshua made himself flint knives and circumcised the sons of Israel at ⁴Gibeath-haaraloth.

4 And this is the reason why Joshua circumcised them: all the people who came out of Egypt who were males, all the men of war, died in the wilderness

along the way, after they came out of Egypt.

5 For all the people who came out were circumcised, but all the people who were born in the wilderness along the way as they came out of Egypt had not been circumcised.

6 For the sons of Israel walked forty years in the wilderness, until all the nation, *that is,* the men of war who came out of Egypt, perished because they did not listen to the voice of the LORD, to whom the LORD had sworn that He would not let them see the land which the LORD had sworn to their fathers to give us, a land flowing with milk and honey.

7 And their children whom He raised up in their place, Joshua circumcised; for they were uncircumcised, because they had not circumcised them along the way.

8 Now it came about when they had finished circumcising all the nation, that they remained in their places in the camp until they were healed.

9 Then the LORD said to Joshua, "Today I have rolled away the reproach of Egypt from you." So the name of that place is called ⁵Gilgal to this day.

10 While the sons of Israel camped at Gilgal, they observed the Passover on the evening of the fourteenth day of the month on the desert plains of Jericho.

11 And on the day after the Passover, on that very day, they ate some of the produce of the land, unleavened cakes and parched *grain*.

12 And the manna ceased on the day after they had eaten some of the produce of the land, so that the sons of Israel no longer had manna, but they ate some of the yield of the land of Canaan during that year.

13 ¶ Now it came about when Joshua was by Jericho, that he lifted up his eyes and looked, and behold, a man was standing opposite him with his sword drawn in his hand, and Joshua went to him and said to him, "Are you for us or for our adversaries?"

14 And he said, "No, rather I indeed come now *as* captain of the host of the LORD." And Joshua fell on his face to

⁴ I.e., the hill of the foreskins

⁵ I.e., rolling

the earth, and bowed down, and said to him, "What has my lord to say to his servant?"

15 And the captain of the LORD's host said to Joshua, "Remove your sandals from your feet, for the place where you are standing is holy." And Joshua did so.

CHAPTER 6

NOW Jericho was tightly shut because of the sons of Israel; no one went out and no one came in.

2 And the LORD said to Joshua, "See, I have given Jericho into your hand, with its king *and* the valiant warriors.

3"And you shall march around the city, all the men of war circling the city once. You shall do so for six days.

4"Also seven priests shall carry seven trumpets of rams' horns before the ark; then on the seventh day you shall march around the city seven times, and the priests shall blow the trumpets.

5"And it shall be that when they make a long blast with the ram's horn, and when you hear the sound of the trumpet, all the people shall shout with a great shout; and the wall of the city will fall down flat, and the people will go up every man straight ahead."

6 ¶ So Joshua the son of Nun called the priests and said to them, "Take up the ark of the covenant, and let seven priests carry seven trumpets of rams' horns before the ark of the LORD."

7 Then he said to the people, "Go forward, and march around the city, and let the armed men go on before the ark of the LORD."

8 And it was *so*, that when Joshua had spoken to the people, the seven priests carrying the seven trumpets of rams' horns before the LORD went forward and blew the trumpets; and the ark of the covenant of the LORD followed them.

9 And the armed men went before the priests who blew the trumpets, and the rear guard came after the ark, while they continued to blow the trumpets.

10 But Joshua commanded the people, saying, "You shall not shout nor let your voice be heard, nor let a word proceed out of your mouth, until the day I tell you, 'Shout!' Then you shall shout!"

11 So he had the ark of the LORD taken around the city, circling *it* once; then they came into the camp and spent the night in the camp.

12 ¶ Now Joshua rose early in the morning, and the priests took up the ark of the LORD.

13 And the seven priests carrying the seven trumpets of rams' horns before the ark of the LORD went on continually, and blew the trumpets; and the armed men went before them, and the rear guard came after the ark of the LORD, while they continued to blow the trumpets.

14 Thus the second day they marched around the city once and returned to the camp; they did so for six days.

15 ¶ Then it came about on the seventh day that they rose early at the dawning of the day and marched around the city in the same manner seven times; only on that day they marched around the city seven times.

16 And it came about at the seventh time, when the priests blew the trumpets, Joshua said to the people, "Shout! For the LORD has given you the city.

17"And the city shall be under the ban, it and all that is in it belongs to the LORD; only Rahab the harlot and all who are with her in the house shall live, because she hid the messengers whom we sent.

18"But as for you, only keep yourselves from the things under the ban, lest you covet *them* and take some of the things under the ban, so you would make the camp of Israel accursed and bring trouble on it.

19"But all the silver and gold and articles of bronze and iron are holy to the LORD; they shall go into the treasury of the LORD."

20 So the people shouted, and *priests* blew the trumpets; and it came about, when the people heard the sound of the trumpet, that the people shouted with a great shout and the wall fell down flat, so that the people went up into the city, every man straight ahead, and they took the city.

21 And they utterly destroyed everything in the city, both man and

woman, young and old, and ox and sheep and donkey, with the edge of the sword.

22 ¶ And Joshua said to the two men who had spied out the land, "Go into the harlot's house and bring the woman and all she has out of there, as you have sworn to her."

23 So the young men who were spies went in and brought out Rahab and her father and her mother and her brothers and all she had; they also brought out all her relatives, and placed them outside the camp of Israel.

24 And they burned the city with fire, and all that was in it. Only the silver and gold and articles of bronze and iron, they put into the treasury of the [6]house of the LORD.

25 However, Rahab the harlot and her father's household and all she had, Joshua spared; and she has lived in the midst of Israel to this day, for she hid the messengers whom Joshua sent to spy out Jericho.

26 ¶ Then Joshua made them take an oath at that time, saying, "Cursed before the LORD is the man who rises up and builds this city Jericho; with *the loss of* his first-born he shall lay its foundation, and with *the loss of* his youngest son he shall set up its gates."

27 So the LORD was with Joshua, and his fame was in all the land.

CHAPTER 7

BUT the sons of Israel acted unfaithfully in regard to the things under the ban, for Achan, the son of Carmi, the son of Zabdi, the son of Zerah, from the tribe of Judah, took some of the things under the ban, therefore the anger of the LORD burned against the sons of Israel.

2 ¶ Now Joshua sent men from Jericho to Ai, which is near Beth-aven, east of Bethel, and said to them, "Go up and spy out the land." So the men went up and spied out Ai.

3 And they returned to Joshua and said to him, "Do not let all the people go up; *only* about two or three thousand men need go up to Ai; do not make all the people toil up there, for they are few."

4 So about three thousand men from the people went up there, but they fled from the men of Ai.

5 And the men of Ai struck down about thirty-six of their men, and pursued them from the gate as far as Shebarim, and struck them down on the descent, so the hearts of the people melted and became as water.

6 ¶ Then Joshua tore his clothes and fell to the earth on his face before the ark of the LORD until the evening, *both* he and the elders of Israel; and they put dust on their heads.

7 And Joshua said, "Alas, O Lord GOD, why didst Thou ever bring this people over the Jordan, *only* to deliver us into the hand of the Amorites, to destroy us? If only we had been willing to dwell beyond the Jordan!

8"O Lord, what can I say since Israel has turned *their* back before their enemies?

9"For the Canaanites and all the inhabitants of the land will hear of it, and they will surround us and cut off our name from the earth. And what wilt Thou do for Thy great name?"

10 ¶ So the LORD said to Joshua, "Rise up! Why is it that you have fallen on your face?

11"Israel has sinned, and they have also transgressed My covenant which I commanded them. And they have even taken some of the things under the ban and have both stolen and deceived. Moreover, they have also put *them* among their own things.

12"Therefore the sons of Israel cannot stand before their enemies; they turn *their* backs before their enemies, for they have become accursed. I will not be with you anymore unless you destroy the things under the ban from your midst.

13"Rise up! Consecrate the people and say, 'Consecrate yourselves for tomorrow, for thus the LORD, the God of Israel, has said, "There are things under the ban in your midst, O Israel. You cannot stand before your enemies until you have removed the things under the ban from your midst."

14 'In the morning then you shall come near by your tribes. And it shall be that the tribe which the LORD takes *by lot* shall come near by families, and the family which the LORD takes shall come near by households, and the

[6] I.e., tabernacle

household which the LORD takes shall come near man by man.

15 'And it shall be that the one who is taken with the things under the ban shall be burned with fire, he and all that belongs to him, because he has transgressed the covenant of the LORD, and because he has committed a disgraceful thing in Israel.'"

16 ¶ So Joshua arose early in the morning and brought Israel near by tribes, and the tribe of Judah was taken.

17 And he brought the family of Judah near, and he took the family of the Zerahites; and he brought the family of the Zerahites near man by man, and Zabdi was taken.

18 And he brought his household near man by man; and Achan, son of Carmi, son of Zabdi, son of Zerah, from the tribe of Judah, was taken.

19 Then Joshua said to Achan, "My son, I implore you, give glory to the LORD, the God of Israel, and give praise to Him; and tell me now what you have done. Do not hide it from me."

20 So Achan answered Joshua and said, "Truly, I have sinned against the LORD, the God of Israel, and this is what I did:

21 when I saw among the spoil a beautiful mantle from Shinar and two hundred shekels of silver and a bar of gold fifty shekels in weight, then I coveted them and took them; and behold, they are concealed in the earth inside my tent with the silver underneath it."

22 ¶ So Joshua sent messengers, and they ran to the tent; and behold, it was concealed in his tent with the silver underneath it.

23 And they took them from inside the tent and brought them to Joshua and to all the sons of Israel, and they poured them out before the LORD.

24 Then Joshua and all Israel with him, took Achan the son of Zerah, the silver, the mantle, the bar of gold, his sons, his daughters, his oxen, his donkeys, his sheep, his tent and all that belonged to him; and they brought them up to the valley of ⁷Achor.

25 And Joshua said, "Why have you troubled us? The LORD will trouble you

this day." And all Israel stoned them with stones; and they burned them with fire after they had stoned them with stones.

26 And they raised over him a great heap of stones that stands to this day, and the LORD turned from the fierceness of His anger. Therefore the name of that place has been called the valley of ⁷Achor to this day.

CHAPTER 8

NOW the LORD said to Joshua, "Do not fear or be dismayed. Take all the people of war with you and arise, go up to Ai; see, I have given into your hand the king of Ai, his people, his city, and his land.

2"And you shall do to Ai and its king just as you did to Jericho and its king; you shall take only its spoil and its cattle as plunder for yourselves. Set an ambush for the city behind it."

3 ¶ So Joshua rose with all the people of war to go up to Ai; and Joshua chose 30,000 men, valiant warriors, and sent them out at night.

4 And he commanded them, saying, "See, you are going to ambush the city from behind it. Do not go very far from the city, but all of you be ready.

5"Then I and all the people who are with me will approach the city. And it will come about when they come out to meet us as at the first, that we will flee before them.

6"And they will come out after us until we have drawn them away from the city, for they will say, 'They are fleeing before us as at the first.' So we will flee before them.

7"And you shall rise from your ambush and take possession of the city, for the LORD your God will deliver it into your hand.

8"Then it will be when you have seized the city, that you shall set the city on fire. You shall do it according to the word of the LORD. See, I have commanded you."

9 So Joshua sent them away, and they went to the place of ambush and remained between Bethel and Ai, on the west side of Ai; but Joshua spent that night among the people.

10 ¶ Now Joshua rose early in the morning and mustered the people, and

---

⁷ I.e., trouble

⁷ I.e., trouble

he went up with the elders of Israel before the people to Ai.

11 Then all the people of war who *were* with him went up and drew near and arrived in front of the city, and camped on the north side of Ai. Now *there was* a valley between him and Ai.

12 And he took about 5,000 men and set them in ambush between Bethel and Ai, on the west side of the city.

13 So they stationed the people, all the army that was on the north side of the city, and its rear guard on the west side of the city, and Joshua spent that night in the midst of the valley.

14 And it came about when the king of Ai saw *it,* that the men of the city hurried and rose up early and went out to meet Israel in battle, he and all his people at the appointed place before the desert plain. But he did not know that *there was* an ambush against him behind the city.

15 And Joshua and all Israel pretended to be beaten before them, and fled by the way of the wilderness.

16 And all the people who were in the city were called together to pursue them, and they pursued Joshua, and were drawn away from the city.

17 So not a man was left in Ai or Bethel who had not gone out after Israel, and they left the city unguarded and pursued Israel.

18 ¶ Then the LORD said to Joshua, "Stretch out the javelin that is in your hand toward Ai, for I will give it into your hand." So Joshua stretched out the javelin that was in his hand toward the city.

19 And the *men in* ambush rose quickly from their place, and when he had stretched out his hand, they ran and entered the city and captured it; and they quickly set the city on fire.

20 When the men of Ai turned back and looked, behold, the smoke of the city ascended to the sky, and they had no place to flee this way or that, for the people who had been fleeing to the wilderness turned against the pursuers.

21 When Joshua and all Israel saw that the *men in* ambush had captured the city and that the smoke of the city ascended, they turned back and slew the men of Ai.

22 And the others came out from the city to encounter them, so that they were *trapped* in the midst of Israel, some on this side and some on that side; and they slew them until no one was left of those who survived or escaped.

23 But they took alive the king of Ai and brought him to Joshua.

24 ¶ Now it came about when Israel had finished killing all the inhabitants of Ai in the field in the wilderness where they pursued them, and all of them were fallen by the edge of the sword until they were destroyed, then all Israel returned to Ai and struck it with the edge of the sword.

25 And all who fell that day, both men and women, were 12,000—all the people of Ai.

26 For Joshua did not withdraw his hand with which he stretched out the javelin until he had utterly destroyed all the inhabitants of Ai.

27 Israel took only the cattle and the spoil of that city as plunder for themselves, according to the word of the LORD which He had commanded Joshua.

28 So Joshua burned Ai and made it a heap forever, a desolation until this day.

29 And he hanged the king of Ai on a tree until evening; and at sunset Joshua gave command and they took his body down from the tree, and threw it at the entrance of the city gate, and raised over it a great heap of stones *that stands* to this day.

30 ¶ Then Joshua built an altar to the LORD, the God of Israel, in Mount Ebal,

31 just as Moses the servant of the LORD had commanded the sons of Israel, as it is written in the book of the law of Moses, an altar of uncut stones, on which no man had wielded an iron *tool;* and they offered burnt offerings on it to the LORD, and sacrificed peace offerings.

32 And he wrote there on the stones a copy of the law of Moses, which he had written, in the presence of the sons of Israel.

33 And all Israel with their elders and officers and their judges were standing on both sides of the ark before the Levitical priests who carried the ark of the covenant of the LORD, the stranger as well as the native. Half

of them *stood* in front of Mount Gerizim and half of them in front of Mount Ebal, just as Moses the servant of the LORD had given command at first to bless the people of Israel.

34 Then afterward he read all the words of the law, the blessing and the curse, according to all that is written in the book of the law.

35 There was not a word of all that Moses had commanded which Joshua did not read before all the assembly of Israel with the women and the little ones and the strangers who were living among them.

CHAPTER 9

NOW it came about when all the kings who were beyond the Jordan, in the hill country and in the lowland and on all the coast of the Great Sea toward Lebanon, the Hittite and the Amorite, the Canaanite, the Perizzite, the Hivite and the Jebusite, heard of it,

2 that they gathered themselves together with one accord to fight with Joshua and with Israel.

3 ¶ When the inhabitants of Gibeon heard what Joshua had done to Jericho and to Ai,

4 they also acted craftily and set out as envoys, and took worn-out sacks on their donkeys, and wineskins, worn-out and torn and mended,

5 and worn-out and patched sandals on their feet, and worn-out clothes on themselves; and all the bread of their provision was dry *and* had become crumbled.

6 And they went to Joshua to the camp at Gilgal, and said to him and to the men of Israel, "We have come from a far country; now therefore, make a covenant with us."

7 And the men of Israel said to the Hivites, "Perhaps you are living within our land; how then shall we make a covenant with you?"

8 But they said to Joshua, "We are your servants." Then Joshua said to them, "Who are you, and where do you come from?"

9 And they said to him, "Your servants have come from a very far country because of the fame of the LORD your God; for we have heard the report of Him and all that He did in Egypt,

10 and all that He did to the two kings of the Amorites who were beyond the Jordan, to Sihon king of Heshbon and to Og king of Bashan who was at Ashtaroth.

11"So our elders and all the inhabitants of our country spoke to us, saying, 'Take provisions in your hand for the journey, and go to meet them and say to them, "We are your servants; now then, make a covenant with us." '

12"This our bread *was* warm *when* we took it for our provisions out of our houses on the day that we left to come to you; but now behold, it is dry and has become crumbled.

13"And these wineskins which we filled were new, and behold, they are torn; and these our clothes and our sandals are worn out because of the very long journey."

14 So the men *of Israel* took some of their provisions, and did not ask for the counsel of the LORD.

15 And Joshua made peace with them and made a covenant with them, to let them live; and the leaders of the congregation swore *an oath* to them.

16 ¶ And it came about at the end of three days after they had made a covenant with them, that they heard that they were neighbors and that they were living within their land.

17 Then the sons of Israel set out and came to their cities on the third day. Now their cities *were* Gibeon and Chephirah and Beeroth and Kiriath-jearim.

18 And the sons of Israel did not strike them because the leaders of the congregation had sworn to them by the LORD the God of Israel. And the whole congregation grumbled against the leaders.

19 But all the leaders said to the whole congregation, "We have sworn to them by the LORD, the God of Israel, and now we cannot touch them.

20"This we will do to them, even let them live, lest wrath be upon us for the oath which we swore to them."

21 And the leaders said to them, "Let them live." So they became hewers of wood and drawers of water for the whole congregation, just as the leaders had spoken to them.

22 ¶ Then Joshua called for them and spoke to them, saying, "Why have

you deceived us, saying, 'We are very far from you,' when you are living within our land?

23"Now therefore, you are cursed, and you shall never cease being slaves, both hewers of wood and drawers of water for the house of my God."

24 So they answered Joshua and said, "Because it was certainly told your servants that the LORD your God had commanded His servant Moses to give you all the land, and to destroy all the inhabitants of the land before you; therefore we feared greatly for our lives because of you, and have done this thing.

25"And now behold, we are in your hands; do as it seems good and right in your sight to do to us."

26 Thus he did to them, and delivered them from the hands of the sons of Israel, and they did not kill them.

27 But Joshua made them that day hewers of wood and drawers of water for the congregation and for the altar of the LORD, to this day, in the place which He would choose.

CHAPTER 10

Now it came about when Adoni-zedek king of Jerusalem heard that Joshua had captured Ai, and had utterly destroyed it (just as he had done to Jericho and its king, so he had done to Ai and its king), and that the inhabitants of Gibeon had made peace with Israel and were within their land,

2 that he feared greatly, because Gibeon *was* a great city, like one of the royal cities, and because it was greater than Ai, and all its men *were* mighty.

3 Therefore Adoni-zedek king of Jerusalem sent *word* to Hoham king of Hebron and to Piram king of Jarmuth and to Japhia king of Lachish and to Debir king of Eglon, saying,

4"Come up to me and help me, and let us attack Gibeon, for it has made peace with Joshua and with the sons of Israel."

5 So the five kings of the Amorites, the king of Jerusalem, the king of Hebron, the king of Jarmuth, the king of Lachish, *and* the king of Eglon, gathered together and went up, they with all their armies, and camped by Gibeon and fought against it.

6 ¶ Then the men of Gibeon sent *word* to Joshua to the camp at Gilgal, saying, "Do not abandon your servants; come up to us quickly and save us and help us, for all the kings of the Amorites that live in the hill country have assembled against us."

7 So Joshua went up from Gilgal, he and all the people of war with him and all the valiant warriors.

8 And the LORD said to Joshua, "Do not fear them, for I have given them into your hands; not one of them shall stand before you."

9 So Joshua came upon them suddenly by marching all night from Gilgal.

10 And the LORD confounded them before Israel, and He slew them with a great slaughter at Gibeon, and pursued them by the way of the ascent of Beth-horon, and struck them as far as Azekah and Makkedah.

11 And it came about as they fled from before Israel, *while* they were at the descent of Beth-horon, that the LORD threw large stones from heaven on them as far as Azekah, and they died; *there were* more who died from the hailstones than those whom the sons of Israel killed with the sword.

12 ¶ Then Joshua spoke to the LORD in the day when the LORD delivered up the Amorites before the sons of Israel, and he said in the sight of Israel,

"O sun, stand still at Gibeon,
And O moon in the valley of Aijalon."

13 So the sun stood still, and the moon stopped,
Until the nation avenged themselves of their enemies.

Is it not written in the book of Jashar? And the sun stopped in the middle of the sky, and did not hasten to go *down* for about a whole day.

14 And there was no day like that before it or after it, when the LORD listened to the voice of a man; for the LORD fought for Israel.

15 Then Joshua and all Israel with him returned to the camp to Gilgal.

16 ¶ Now these five kings had fled and hidden themselves in the cave at Makkedah.

17 And it was told Joshua, saying, "The five kings have been found hidden in the cave at Makkedah."

18 And Joshua said, "Roll large stones against the mouth of the cave, and assign men by it to guard them,

19 but do not stay *there* yourselves; pursue your enemies and attack them in the rear. Do not allow them to enter their cities, for the LORD your God has delivered them into your hand."

20 And it came about when Joshua and the sons of Israel had finished slaying them with a very great slaughter, until they were destroyed, and the survivors *who* remained of them had entered the fortified cities,

21 that all the people returned to the camp to Joshua at Makkedah in peace. No one uttered a word against any of the sons of Israel.

22 ¶ Then Joshua said, "Open the mouth of the cave and bring these five kings out to me from the cave."

23 And they did so, and brought these five kings out to him from the cave: the king of Jerusalem, the king of Hebron, the king of Jarmuth, the king of Lachish, *and* the king of Eglon.

24 And it came about when they brought these kings out to Joshua, that Joshua called for all the men of Israel, and said to the chiefs of the men of war who had gone with him, "Come near, put your feet on the necks of these kings." So they came near and put their feet on their necks.

25 Joshua then said to them, "Do not fear or be dismayed! Be strong and courageous, for thus the LORD will do to all your enemies with whom you fight."

26 So afterward Joshua struck them and put them to death, and he hanged them on five trees; and they hung on the trees until evening.

27 And it came about at sunset that Joshua commanded, and they took them down from the trees and threw them into the cave where they had hidden themselves, and put large stones over the mouth of the cave, to this very day.

28 ¶ Now Joshua captured Makkedah on that day, and struck it and its king with the edge of the sword; he utterly destroyed it and every [8]person who was in it. He left no survivor. Thus he did to the king of Makkedah

just as he had done to the king of Jericho.

29 ¶ Then Joshua and all Israel with him passed on from Makkedah to Libnah, and fought against Libnah.

30 And the LORD gave it also with its king into the hands of Israel, and he struck it and every person who *was* in it with the edge of the sword. He left no survivor in it. Thus he did to its king just as he had done to the king of Jericho.

31 ¶ And Joshua and all Israel with him passed on from Libnah to Lachish, and they camped by it and fought against it.

32 And the LORD gave Lachish into the hands of Israel; and he captured it on the second day, and struck it and every person who *was* in it with the edge of the sword, according to all that he had done to Libnah.

33 ¶ Then Horam king of Gezer came up to help Lachish, and Joshua defeated him and his people until he had left him no survivor.

34 ¶ And Joshua and all Israel with him passed on from Lachish to Eglon, and they camped by it and fought against it.

35 And they captured it on that day and struck it with the edge of the sword; and he utterly destroyed that day every person who *was* in it, according to all that he had done to Lachish.

36 ¶ Then Joshua and all Israel with him went up from Eglon to Hebron, and they fought against it.

37 And they captured it and struck it and its king and all its cities and all the persons who *were* in it with the edge of the sword. He left no survivor, according to all that he had done to Eglon. And he utterly destroyed it and every person who *was* in it.

38 ¶ Then Joshua and all Israel with him returned to Debir, and they fought against it.

39 And he captured it and its king and all its cities, and they struck them with the edge of the sword, and utterly destroyed every person *who was* in it. He left no survivor. Just as he had done to Hebron, so he did to Debir and its king, as he had also done to Libnah and its king.

40 ¶ Thus Joshua struck all the land,

[8] Lit., *soul*, and so throughout this context

the hill country and the [9]Negev and the lowland and the slopes and all their kings. He left no survivor, but he utterly destroyed all who breathed, just as the LORD, the God of Israel, had commanded.

41 And Joshua struck them from Kadesh-barnea even as far as Gaza, and all the country of Goshen even as far as Gibeon.

42 And Joshua captured all these kings and their lands at one time, because the LORD, the God of Israel, fought for Israel.

43 So Joshua and all Israel with him returned to the camp at Gilgal.

CHAPTER 11

THEN it came about, when Jabin king of Hazor heard *of it,* that he sent to Jobab king of Madon and to the king of Shimron and to the king of Achshaph,

2 and to the kings who were of the north in the hill country, and in the Arabah—south of [10]Chinneroth and in the lowland and on the heights of Dor on the west—

3 to the Canaanite on the east and on the west, and the Amorite and the Hittite and the Perizzite and the Jebusite in the hill country, and the Hivite at the foot of Hermon in the land of Mizpeh.

4 And they came out, they and all their armies with them, *as* many people *as* the sand that is on the seashore, with very many horses and chariots.

5 So all of these kings having agreed to meet, came and encamped together at the waters of Merom, to fight against Israel.

6 ¶ Then the LORD said to Joshua, "Do not be afraid because of them, for tomorrow at this time I will deliver all of them slain before Israel; you shall hamstring their horses and burn their chariots with fire."

7 So Joshua and all the people of war with him came upon them suddenly by the waters of Merom, and attacked them.

8 And the LORD delivered them into the hand of Israel, so that they defeated them, and pursued them as far as Great Sidon and Misrephoth-maim and the valley of Mizpeh to the east;

and they struck them until no survivor was left to them.

9 And Joshua did to them as the LORD had told him; he hamstrung their horses, and burned their chariots with fire.

10 ¶ Then Joshua turned back at that time, and captured Hazor and struck its king with the sword; for Hazor formerly was the head of all these kingdoms.

11 And they struck every person who was in it with the edge of the sword, utterly destroying *them;* there was no one left who breathed. And he burned Hazor with fire.

12 And Joshua captured all the cities of these kings, and all their kings, and he struck them with the edge of the sword, *and* utterly destroyed them; just as Moses the servant of the LORD had commanded.

13 However, Israel did not burn any cities that stood on their mounds, except Hazor alone, *which* Joshua burned.

14 And all the spoil of these cities and the cattle, the sons of Israel took as their plunder; but they struck every man with the edge of the sword, until they had destroyed them. They left no one who breathed.

15 Just as the LORD had commanded Moses his servant, so Moses commanded Joshua, and so Joshua did; he left nothing undone of all that the LORD had commanded Moses.

16 ¶ Thus Joshua took all that land: the hill country and all the Negev, all that land of Goshen, the lowland, the Arabah, the hill country of Israel and its lowland

17 from Mount Halak, that rises toward Seir, even as far as Baal-gad in the valley of Lebanon at the foot of Mount Hermon. And he captured all their kings and struck them down and put them to death.

18 Joshua waged war a long time with all these kings.

19 There was not a city which made peace with the sons of Israel except the Hivites living in Gibeon; they took them all in battle.

20 For it was of the LORD to harden their hearts, to meet Israel in battle in order that he might utterly destroy them, that they might receive no

[9] I.e., South country   [10] I.e., Sea of Galilee

mercy, but that he might destroy
them, just as the LORD had commanded Moses.

21 ¶ Then Joshua came at that time
and cut off the Anakim from the hill
country, from Hebron, from Debir,
from Anab and from all the hill country of Judah and from all the hill
country of Israel. Joshua utterly destroyed them with their cities.

22 There were no Anakim left in the
land of the sons of Israel; only in Gaza,
in Gath, and in Ashdod some remained.

23 So Joshua took the whole land,
according to all that the LORD had
spoken to Moses, and Joshua gave it
for an inheritance to Israel according
to their divisions by their tribes. Thus
the land had rest from war.

CHAPTER 12

NOW these are the kings of the land
whom the sons of Israel defeated, and
whose land they possessed beyond the
Jordan toward the sunrise, from the
valley of the Arnon as far as Mount
Hermon, and all the Arabah to the
east:

2 Sihon king of the Amorites, who
lived in Heshbon, and ruled from
Aroer, which is on the edge of the
valley of the Arnon, both the middle of
the valley and half of Gilead, even as
far as the brook Jabbok, the border of
the sons of Ammon;

3 and the Arabah as far as the Sea
of [11]Chinneroth toward the east, and
as far as the sea of the Arabah, even
the Salt Sea, eastward toward Beth-
jeshimoth, and on the south, at the
foot of the slopes of Pisgah;

4 and the territory of Og king of
Bashan, one of the remnant of
Rephaim, who lived at Ashtaroth and
at Edrei,

5 and ruled over Mount Hermon
and Salecah and all Bashan, as far as
the border of the Geshurites and the
Maacathites, and half of Gilead, as far
as the border of Sihon king of Heshbon.

6 Moses the servant of the LORD
and the sons of Israel defeated them;
and Moses the servant of the LORD
gave it to the Reubenites and the

Gadites, and the half-tribe of Manasseh as a possession.

7 ¶ Now these are the kings of the
land whom Joshua and the sons of
Israel defeated beyond the Jordan
toward the west, from Baal-gad in the
valley of Lebanon even as far as
Mount Halak, which rises toward Seir;
and Joshua gave it to the tribes of
Israel as a possession according to
their divisions,

8 in the hill country, in the lowland,
in the Arabah, on the slopes, and in
the wilderness, and in the Negev; the
Hittite, the Amorite and the Canaanite, the Perizzite, the Hivite and the
Jebusite:

9 the king of Jericho, one; the king
of Ai, which is beside Bethel, one;

10 the king of Jerusalem, one; the
king of Hebron, one;

11 the king of Jarmuth, one; the king
of Lachish, one;

12 the king of Eglon, one; the king of
Gezer, one;

13 the king of Debir, one; the king of
Geder, one;

14 the king of Hormah, one; the king
of Arad, one;

15 the king of Libnah, one; the king
of Adullam, one;

16 the king of Makkedah, one; the
king of Bethel, one;

17 the king of Tappuah, one; the
king of Hepher, one;

18 the king of Aphek, one; the king
of Lasharon, one;

19 the king of Madon, one; the king
of Hazor, one;

20 the king of Shimron-meron, one;
the king of Achshaph, one;

21 the king of Taanach, one; the king
of Megiddo, one;

22 the king of Kedesh, one; the king
of Jokneam in Carmel, one;

23 the king of Dor in the heights of
Dor, one; the king of Goiim in Gilgal,
one;

24 the king of Tirzah, one: in all,
thirty-one kings.

CHAPTER 13

NOW Joshua was old and advanced
in years when the LORD said to him,
"You are old and advanced in years,
and very much of the land remains to
be possessed.

2"This is the land that remains: all

[11] I.e., Galilee

the regions of the Philistines and all *those of* the Geshurites;

3 from the Shihor which is east of Egypt, even as far as the border of Ekron to the north (it is counted as Canaanite); the five lords of the Philistines: the Gazite, the Ashdodite, the Ashkelonite, the Gittite, the Ekronite; and the Avvite

4 to the south, all the land of the Canaanite, and Mearah that belongs to the Sidonians, as far as Aphek, to the border of the Amorite;

5 and the land of the Gebalite, and all of Lebanon, toward the east, from Baal-gad below Mount Hermon as far as Lebo-hamath.

6 "All the inhabitants of the hill country from Lebanon as far as Misrephoth-maim, all the Sidonians, I will drive them out from before the sons of Israel; only allot it to Israel for an inheritance as I have commanded you.

7 "Now therefore, apportion this land for an inheritance to the nine tribes, and the half-tribe of Manasseh."

8 ¶ With the other half-tribe, the Reubenites and the Gadites received their inheritance which Moses gave them beyond the Jordan to the east, just as Moses the servant of the LORD gave to them;

9 from Aroer, which is on the edge of the valley of the Arnon, with the city which is in the middle of the valley, and all the plain of Medeba, as far as Dibon;

10 and all the cities of Sihon king of the Amorites, who reigned in Heshbon, as far as the border of the sons of Ammon;

11 and Gilead, and the territory of the Geshurites and Maacathites, and all Mount Hermon, and all Bashan as far as Salecah;

12 all the kingdom of Og in Bashan, who reigned in Ashtaroth and in Edrei (he alone was left of the remnant of the Rephaim); for Moses struck them and dispossessed them.

13 But the sons of Israel did not dispossess the Geshurites or the Maacathites; for Geshur and Maacath live among Israel until this day.

14 Only to the tribe of Levi he did not give an inheritance; the offerings by fire to the LORD, the God of Israel,

are their inheritance, as He spoke to him.

15 ¶ So Moses gave *an inheritance* to the tribe of the sons of Reuben according to their families.

16 And their territory was from Aroer, which is on the edge of the valley of the Arnon, with the city which is in the middle of the valley and all the plain by Medeba;

17 Heshbon, and all its cities which are on the plain: Dibon and Bamoth-baal and Beth-baal-meon,

18 and Jahaz and Kedemoth and Mephaath,

19 and Kiriathaim and Sibmah and Zereth-shahar on the hill of the valley,

20 and Beth-peor and the slopes of Pisgah and Beth-jeshimoth,

21 even all the cities of the plain and all the kingdom of Sihon king of the Amorites who reigned in Heshbon, whom Moses struck with the chiefs of Midian, Evi and Rekem and Zur and Hur and Reba, the princes of Sihon, who lived in the land.

22 The sons of Israel also killed Balaam the son of Beor, the diviner, with the sword among *the rest of* their slain.

23 And the border of the sons of Reuben was the Jordan. This was the inheritance of the sons of Reuben according to their families, the cities and their villages.

24 ¶ Moses also gave *an inheritance* to the tribe of Gad, to the sons of Gad, according to their families.

25 And their territory was Jazer, and all the cities of Gilead, and half the land of the sons of Ammon, as far as Aroer which is before Rabbah;

26 and from Heshbon as far as Ramath-mizpeh and Betonim, and from Mahanaim as far as the border of Debir;

27 and in the valley, Beth-haram and Beth-nimrah and Succoth and Zaphon, the rest of the kingdom of Sihon king of Heshbon, with the Jordan as a border, as far as the *lower* end of the Sea of Chinnereth beyond the Jordan to the east.

28 This is the inheritance of the sons of Gad according to their families, the cities and their villages.

29 ¶ Moses also gave *an inheritance* to the half-tribe of Manasseh; and it was for the half-tribe of the sons of

Manasseh according to their families.

30 And their territory was from Mahanaim, all Bashan, all the kingdom of Og king of Bashan, and all the towns of Jair, which are in Bashan, sixty cities;

31 also half of Gilead, with Ashtaroth and Edrei, the cities of the kingdom of Og in Bashan, were for the sons of Machir the son of Manasseh, for half of the sons of Machir according to their families.

32 ¶ These are the territories which Moses apportioned for an inheritance in the plains of Moab, beyond the Jordan at Jericho to the east.

33 But to the tribe of Levi, Moses did not give an inheritance; the LORD, the God of Israel, is their inheritance, as He had promised to them.

CHAPTER 14

NOW these are the territories which the sons of Israel inherited in the land of Canaan, which Eleazar the priest, and Joshua the son of Nun, and the heads of the households of the tribes of the sons of Israel apportioned to them for an inheritance,

2 by the lot of their inheritance, as the LORD commanded through Moses, for the nine tribes and the half-tribe.

3 For Moses had given the inheritance of the two tribes and the half-tribe beyond the Jordan; but he did not give an inheritance to the Levites among them.

4 For the sons of Joseph were two tribes, Manasseh and Ephraim, and they did not give a portion to the Levites in the land, except cities to live in, with their pasture lands for their livestock and for their property.

5 Thus the sons of Israel did just as the LORD had commanded Moses, and they divided the land.

6 ¶ Then the sons of Judah drew near to Joshua in Gilgal, and Caleb the son of Jephunneh the Kenizzite said to him, "You know the word which the LORD spoke to Moses the man of God concerning you and me in Kadesh-barnea.

7 "I was forty years old when Moses the servant of the LORD sent me from Kadesh-barnea to spy out the land, and I brought word back to him as it was in my heart.

8 "Nevertheless my brethren who went up with me made the heart of the people melt with fear; but I followed the LORD my God fully.

9 "So Moses swore on that day, saying, 'Surely the land on which your foot has trodden shall be an inheritance to you and to your children forever, because you have followed the LORD my God fully.'

10 "And now behold, the LORD has let me live, just as He spoke, these forty-five years, from the time that the LORD spoke this word to Moses, when Israel walked in the wilderness; and now behold, I am eighty-five years old today.

11 "I am still as strong today as I was in the day Moses sent me; as my strength was then, so my strength is now, for war and for going out and coming in.

12 "Now then, give me this hill country about which the LORD spoke on that day, for you heard on that day that Anakim were there, with great fortified cities; perhaps the LORD will be with me, and I shall drive them out as the LORD has spoken."

13 ¶ So Joshua blessed him, and gave Hebron to Caleb the son of Jephunneh for an inheritance.

14 Therefore, Hebron became the inheritance of Caleb the son of Jephunneh the Kenizzite until this day, because he followed the LORD God of Israel fully.

15 Now the name of Hebron was formerly Kiriath-arba; for Arba was the greatest man among the Anakim. Then the land had rest from war.

CHAPTER 15

NOW the lot for the tribe of the sons of Judah according to their families reached the border of Edom, southward to the wilderness of Zin at the extreme south.

2 And their south border was from the lower end of the Salt Sea, from the bay that turns to the south.

3 Then it proceeded southward to the ascent of Akrabbim and continued to Zin, then went up by the south of Kadesh-barnea and continued to Hezron, and went up to Addar and turned about to Karka.

4 And it continued to Azmon and

proceeded to the brook of Egypt; and the border ended at the sea. This shall be your south border.

5 And the east border *was* the Salt Sea, as far as the mouth of the Jordan. And the border of the north side was from the bay of the sea at the mouth of the Jordan.

6 Then the border went up to Beth-hoglah, and continued on the north of Beth-arabah, and the border went up to the stone of Bohan the son of Reuben.

7 And the border went up to Debir from the valley of Achor, and turned northward toward Gilgal which is opposite the ascent of Adummim, which is on the south of the valley; and the border continued to the waters of En-shemesh, and it ended at En-rogel.

8 Then the border went up the valley of Ben-hinnom to the slope of the Jebusite on the south (that is, Jerusalem); and the border went up to the top of the mountain which is before the valley of Hinnom to the west, which is at the end of the valley of Rephaim toward the north.

9 And from the top of the mountain the border curved to the spring of the waters of Nephtoah and proceeded to the cities of Mount Ephron, then the border curved to Baalah (that is, Kiriath-jearim).

10 And the border turned about from Baalah westward to Mount Seir, and continued to the slope of Mount Jearim on the north (that is, Chesalon), and went down to Beth-shemesh and continued through Timnah.

11 And the border proceeded to the side of Ekron northward. Then the border curved to Shikkeron and continued to Mount Baalah and proceeded to Jabneel, and the border ended at the sea.

12 And the west border *was* at the Great Sea, even *its* coastline. This is the border around the sons of Judah according to their families.

13 ¶ Now he gave to Caleb the son of Jephunneh a portion among the sons of Judah, according to the command of the LORD to Joshua, *namely,* Kiriath-arba, *Arba being* the father of Anak (that is, Hebron).

14 And Caleb drove out from there the three sons of Anak: Sheshai and Ahiman and Talmai, the children of Anak.

15 Then he went up from there against the inhabitants of Debir; now the name of Debir formerly was Kiriath-sepher.

16 And Caleb said, "The one who attacks Kiriath-sepher and captures it, I will give him Achsah my daughter as a wife."

17 And Othniel the son of Kenaz, the brother of Caleb, captured it; so he gave him Achsah his daughter as a wife.

18 And it came about that when she came *to him,* she persuaded him to ask her father for a field. So she alighted from the donkey, and Caleb said to her, "What do you want?"

19 Then she said, "Give me a blessing; since you have given me the land of the Negev, give me also springs of water." So he gave her the upper springs and the lower springs.

20 ¶ This is the inheritance of the tribe of the sons of Judah according to their families.

21 ¶ Now the cities at the extremity of the tribe of the sons of Judah toward the border of Edom in the south were Kabzeel and Eder and Jagur,

22 and Kinah and Dimonah and Adadah,

23 and Kedesh and Hazor and Ithnan,

24 Ziph and Telem and Bealoth,

25 and Hazor-hadattah and Kerioth-hezron (that is, Hazor),

26 Amam and Shema and Moladah,

27 and Hazar-gaddah and Heshmon and Beth-pelet,

28 and Hazar-shual and Beersheba and Biziothiah,

29 Baalah and Iim and Ezem,

30 and Eltolad and Chesil and Hormah,

31 and Ziklag and Madmannah and Sansannah,

32 and Lebaoth and Shilhim and Ain and Rimmon; in all, twenty-nine cities with their villages.

33 ¶ In the lowland: Eshtaol and Zorah and Ashnah,

34 and Zanoah and En-gannim, Tappuah and Enam,

35 Jarmuth and Adullam, Socoh and Azekah,

36 and Shaaraim and Adithaim and Gederah and Gederothaim; fourteen cities with their villages.

37 ¶ Zenan and Hadashah and Migdal-gad,

38 and Dilean and Mizpeh and Joktheel,

39 Lachish and Bozkath and Eglon,

40 and Cabbon and Lahmas and Chitlish,

41 and Gederoth, Beth-dagon and Naamah and Makkedah; sixteen cities with their villages.

42 ¶ Libnah and Ether and Ashan,

43 and Iphtah and Ashnah and Nezib,

44 and Keilah and Achzib and Mareshah; nine cities with their villages.

45 ¶ Ekron, with its towns and its villages;

46 from Ekron even to the sea, all that were by the side of Ashdod, with their villages.

47 ¶ Ashdod, its towns and its villages; Gaza, its towns and its villages; as far as the brook of Egypt and the Great Sea, even *its* coastline.

48 ¶ And in the hill country: Shamir and Jattir and Socoh,

49 and Dannah and Kiriath-sannah (that is, Debir),

50 and Anab and Eshtemoh and Anim,

51 and Goshen and Holon and Giloh; eleven cities with their villages.

52 ¶ Arab and Dumah and Eshan,

53 and Janum and Beth-tappuah and Aphekah,

54 and Humtah and Kiriath-arba (that is, Hebron), and Zior; nine cities with their villages.

55 ¶ Maon, Carmel and Ziph and Juttah,

56 and Jezreel and Jokdeam and Zanoah,

57 Kain, Gibeah and Timnah; ten cities with their villages.

58 ¶ Halhul, Beth-zur and Gedor,

59 and Maarath and Beth-anoth and Eltekon; six cities with their villages.

60 ¶ Kiriath-baal (that is, Kiriath-jearim), and Rabbah; two cities with their villages.

61 ¶ In the wilderness: Beth-arabah, Middin and Secacah,

62 and Nibshan and the City of Salt and Engedi; six cities with their villages.

63 ¶ Now as for the Jebusites, the inhabitants of Jerusalem, the sons of Judah could not drive them out; so the Jebusites live with the sons of Judah at Jerusalem until this day.

CHAPTER 16

THEN the lot for the sons of Joseph went from the Jordan at Jericho to the waters of Jericho on the east into the wilderness, going up from Jericho through the hill country to Bethel.

2 And it went from Bethel to Luz, and continued to the border of the Archites at Ataroth.

3 And it went down westward to the territory of the Japhletites, as far as the territory of lower Beth-horon even to Gezer, and it ended at the sea.

4 ¶ And the sons of Joseph, Manasseh and Ephraim, received their inheritance.

5 Now *this* was the territory of the sons of Ephraim according to their families: the border of their inheritance eastward was Ataroth-addar, as far as upper Beth-horon.

6 Then the border went westward at Michmethath on the north, and the border turned about eastward to Taanath-shiloh, and continued *beyond* it to the east of Janoah.

7 And it went down from Janoah to Ataroth and to Naarah, then reached Jericho and came out at the Jordan.

8 From Tappuah the border continued westward to the brook of Kanah, and it ended at the sea. This is the inheritance of the tribe of the sons of Ephraim according to their families,

9 *together* with the cities which were set apart for the sons of Ephraim in the midst of the inheritance of the sons of Manasseh, all the cities with their villages.

10 But they did not drive out the Canaanites who lived in Gezer, so the Canaanites live in the midst of Ephraim to this day, and they became forced laborers.

CHAPTER 17

NOW *this* was the lot for the tribe of Manasseh, for he was the first-born of Joseph. To Machir the first-born of Manasseh, the father of Gilead, was allotted Gilead and Bashan, because he was a man of war.

2 So *the lot* was *made* for the rest of the sons of Manasseh according to their families: for the sons of Abiezer and for the sons of Helek and for the sons of Asriel and for the sons of Shechem and for the sons of Hepher and for the sons of Shemida; these *were* the male *descendants* of Manasseh the son of Joseph according to their families.

3 However, Zelophehad, the son of Hepher, the son of Gilead, the son of Machir, the son of Manasseh, had no sons, only daughters; and these are the names of his daughters: Mahlah and Noah, Hoglah, Milcah and Tirzah.

4 And they came near before Eleazar the priest and before Joshua the son of Nun and before the leaders, saying, "The LORD commanded Moses to give us an inheritance among our brothers." So according to the command of the LORD he gave them an inheritance among their father's brothers.

5 Thus there fell ten portions to Manasseh, besides the land of Gilead and Bashan, which is beyond the Jordan,

6 because the daughters of Manasseh received an inheritance among his sons. And the land of Gilead belonged to the rest of the sons of Manasseh.

7 ¶ And the border of Manasseh ran from Asher to Michmethath which was east of Shechem; then the border went southward to the inhabitants of En-tappuah.

8 The land of Tappuah belonged to Manasseh, but Tappuah on the border of Manasseh *belonged* to the sons of Ephraim.

9 And the border went down to the brook of Kanah, southward of the brook (these cities *belonged* to Ephraim among the cities of Manasseh), and the border of Manasseh *was* on the north side of the brook, and it ended at the sea.

10 The south side *belonged* to Ephraim and the north side to Manasseh, and the sea was their border; and they reached to Asher on the north and to Issachar on the east.

11 And in Issachar and in Asher, Manasseh had Beth-shean and its towns and Ibleam and its towns, and the inhabitants of Dor and its towns,

and the inhabitants of En-dor and its towns, and the inhabitants of Taanach and its towns, and the inhabitants of Megiddo and its towns, the third is Napheth.

12 But the sons of Manasseh could not take possession of these cities, because the Canaanites persisted in living in that land.

13 And it came about when the sons of Israel became strong, they put the Canaanites to forced labor, but they did not drive them out completely.

14 ¶ Then the sons of Joseph spoke to Joshua, saying, "Why have you given me only one lot and one portion for an inheritance, since I am a numerous people whom the LORD has thus far blessed?"

15 And Joshua said to them, "If you are a numerous people, go up to the forest and clear a place for yourself there in the land of the Perizzites and of the Rephaim, since the hill country of Ephraim is too narrow for you."

16 And the sons of Joseph said, "The hill country is not enough for us, and all the Canaanites who live in the valley land have chariots of iron, both those who are in Beth-shean and its towns, and those who are in the valley of Jezreel."

17 And Joshua spoke to the house of Joseph, to Ephraim and Manasseh, saying, "You are a numerous people and have great power; you shall not have one lot *only,*

18 but the hill country shall be yours. For though it is a forest, you shall clear it, and to its farthest borders it shall be yours; for you shall drive out the Canaanites, even though they have chariots of iron *and* though they are strong."

CHAPTER 18

THEN the whole congregation of the sons of Israel assembled themselves at Shiloh, and set up the tent of meeting there; and the land was subdued before them.

2 And there remained among the sons of Israel seven tribes who had not divided their inheritance.

3 So Joshua said to the sons of Israel, "How long will you put off entering to take possession of the land

which the LORD, the God of your fathers, has given you?

4"Provide for yourselves three men from each tribe that I may send them, and that they may arise and walk through the land and write a description of it according to their inheritance; then they shall return to me.

5"And they shall divide it into seven portions; Judah shall stay in its territory on the south, and the house of Joseph shall stay in their territory on the north.

6"And you shall describe the land in seven divisions, and bring the description here to me. And I will cast lots for you here before the LORD our God.

7"For the Levites have no portion among you, because the priesthood of the LORD is their inheritance. Gad and Reuben and the half-tribe of Manasseh also have received their inheritance eastward beyond the Jordan, which Moses the servant of the LORD gave them."

8 ¶ Then the men arose and went, and Joshua commanded those who went to describe the land, saying, "Go and walk through the land and describe it, and return to me; then I will cast lots for you here before the LORD in Shiloh."

9 So the men went and passed through the land, and described it by cities in seven divisions in a book; and they came to Joshua to the camp at Shiloh.

10 And Joshua cast lots for them in Shiloh before the LORD, and there Joshua divided the land to the sons of Israel according to their divisions.

11 ¶ Now the lot of the tribe of the sons of Benjamin came up according to their families, and the territory of their lot lay between the sons of Judah and the sons of Joseph.

12 And their border on the north side was from the Jordan, then the border went up to the side of Jericho on the north, and went up through the hill country westward; and [12]it ended at the wilderness of Beth-aven.

13 And from there the border continued to Luz, to the side of Luz (that is, Bethel) southward; and the border went down to Ataroth-addar, near the hill which lies on the south of lower Beth-horon.

14 And the border extended from there, and turned round on the west side southward, from the hill which lies before Beth-horon southward; and [12]it ended at Kiriath-baal (that is, Kiriath-jearim), a city of the sons of Judah. This was the west side.

15 Then the south side was from the edge of Kiriath-jearim, and the border went westward and went to the fountain of the waters of Nephtoah.

16 And the border went down to the edge of the hill which is in the valley of Ben-hinnom, which is in the valley of Rephaim northward; and it went down to the valley of Hinnom, to the slope of the Jebusite southward, and went down to En-rogel.

17 And it extended northward and went to En-shemesh and went to Geliloth, which is opposite the ascent of Adummim, and it went down to the stone of Bohan the son of Reuben.

18 And it continued to the side in front of the Arabah northward, and went down to the Arabah.

19 And the border continued to the side of Beth-hoglah northward; and the [12]border ended at the north bay of the Salt Sea, at the south end of the Jordan. This was the south border.

20 Moreover, the Jordan was its border on the east side. This was the inheritance of the sons of Benjamin, according to their families and according to its borders all around.

21 ¶ Now the cities of the tribe of the sons of Benjamin according to their families were Jericho and Beth-hoglah and Emek-keziz,

22 and Beth-arabah and Zemaraim and Bethel,

23 and Avvim and Parah and Ophrah,

24 and Chephar-ammoni and Ophni and Geba; twelve cities with their villages.

25 Gibeon and Ramah and Beeroth,

26 and Mizpeh and Chephirah and Mozah,

27 and Rekem and Irpeel and Taralah,

28 and Zelah, Haeleph and the Jebusite (that is, Jerusalem), Gibeah, Kiriath; fourteen cities with their villages.

---

[12] Lit., goings out of it were

[12] Lit., goings out of it were

This is the inheritance of the sons of Benjamin according to their families.

CHAPTER 19

THEN the second lot fell to Simeon, to the tribe of the sons of Simeon according to their families, and their inheritance was in the midst of the inheritance of the sons of Judah.

2 So they had as their inheritance Beersheba or Sheba and Moladah,

3 and Hazar-shual and Balah and Ezem,

4 and Eltolad and Bethul and Hormah,

5 and Ziklag and Beth-marcaboth and Hazar-susah,

6 and Beth-lebaoth and Sharuhen, thirteen cities with their villages;

7 Ain, Rimmon and Ether and Ashan, four cities with their villages;

8 and all the villages which *were* around these cities as far as Baalath-beer, Ramah of the Negev. This *was* the inheritance of the tribe of the sons of Simeon according to their families.

9 The inheritance of the sons of Simeon *was taken* from the portion of the sons of Judah, for the share of the sons of Judah was too large for them; so the sons of Simeon received *an* inheritance in the midst of Judah's inheritance.

10 ¶ Now the third lot came up for the sons of Zebulun according to their families. And the territory of their inheritance was as far as Sarid.

11 Then their border went up to the west and to Maralah, it then touched Dabbesheth, and reached to the brook that is before Jokneam.

12 Then it turned from Sarid to the east toward the sunrise as far as the border of Chisloth-tabor, and it proceeded to Daberath and up to Japhia.

13 And from there it continued eastward toward the sunrise to Gath-hepher, to Eth-kazin, and it proceeded to Rimmon which stretches to Neah.

14 And the border circled around it on the north to Hannathon, and it ended at the valley of Iphtahel.

15 *Included* also *were* Kattah and Nahalal and Shimron and Idalah and Bethlehem; twelve cities with their villages.

16 This *was* the inheritance of the sons of Zebulun according to their families, these cities with their villages.

17 ¶ The fourth lot fell to Issachar, to the sons of Issachar according to their families.

18 And their territory was to Jezreel and *included* Chesulloth and Shunem,

19 and Hapharaim and Shion and Anaharath,

20 and Rabbith and Kishion and Ebez,

21 and Remeth and En-gannim and En-haddah and Beth-pazzez.

22 And the border reached to Tabor and Shahazumah and Beth-shemesh, and their border ended at the Jordan; sixteen cities with their villages.

23 This *was* the inheritance of the tribe of the sons of Issachar according to their families, the cities with their villages.

24 ¶ Now the fifth lot fell to the tribe of the sons of Asher according to their families.

25 And their territory was Helkath and Hali and Beten and Achshaph,

26 and Allammelech and Amad and Mishal; and it reached to Carmel on the west and to Shihor-libnath.

27 And it turned toward the east to Beth-dagon, and reached to Zebulun, and to the valley of Iphtahel northward to Beth-emek and Neiel; then it proceeded on north to Cabul,

28 and Ebron and Rehob and Hammon and Kanah, as far as Great Sidon.

29 And the border turned to Ramah, and to the fortified city of Tyre; then the border turned to Hosah, and it ended at the sea by the region of Achzib.

30 *Included* also *were* Ummah, and Aphek and Rehob; twenty-two cities with their villages.

31 This *was* the inheritance of the tribe of the sons of Asher according to their families, these cities with their villages.

32 ¶ The sixth lot fell to the sons of Naphtali; to the sons of Naphtali according to their families.

33 And their border was from Heleph, from the oak in Zaanannim and Adami-nekeb and Jabneel, as far as Lakkum; and it ended at the Jordan.

34 Then the border turned westward to Aznoth-tabor, and proceeded from there to Hukkok; and it reached to

Zebulun on the south and touched Asher on the west, and to Judah at the Jordan toward the east.

35 And the fortified cities *were* Ziddim, Zer and Hammath, Rakkath and Chinnereth,

36 and Adamah and Ramah and Hazor,

37 and Kedesh and Edrei and En-hazor,

38 and Yiron and Migdal-el, Horem and Beth-anath and Beth-shemesh; nineteen cities with their villages.

39 This *was* the inheritance of the tribe of the sons of Naphtali according to their families, the cities with their villages.

40 ¶ The seventh lot fell to the tribe of the sons of Dan according to their families.

41 And the territory of their inheritance was Zorah and Eshtaol and Ir-shemesh,

42 and Shaalabbin and Aijalon and Ithlah,

43 and Elon and Timnah and Ekron,

44 and Eltekeh and Gibbethon and Baalath,

45 and Jehud and Bene-berak and Gath-rimmon,

46 and Me-jarkon and Rakkon, with the territory over against Joppa.

47 And the territory of the sons of Dan proceeded beyond them; for the sons of Dan went up and fought with Leshem and captured it. Then they struck it with the edge of the sword and possessed it and settled in it; and they called Leshem Dan after the name of Dan their father.

48 This *was* the inheritance of the tribe of the sons of Dan according to their families, these cities with their villages.

49 ¶ When they finished apportioning the land for inheritance by its borders, the sons of Israel gave an inheritance in their midst to Joshua the son of Nun.

50 In accordance with the command of the LORD they gave him the city for which he asked, Timnath-serah in the hill country of Ephraim. So he built the city and settled in it.

51 ¶ These are the inheritances which Eleazar the priest and Joshua the son of Nun and the heads of the households of the tribes of the sons of Israel distributed by lot in Shiloh before the LORD, at the doorway of the tent of meeting. So they finished dividing the land.

CHAPTER 20

THEN the LORD spoke to Joshua, saying,

2 "Speak to the sons of Israel, saying, 'Designate the cities of refuge, of which I spoke to you through Moses,

3 that the manslayer who kills any person unintentionally, without premeditation, may flee there, and they shall become your refuge from the avenger of blood.

4 'And he shall flee to one of these cities, and shall stand at the entrance of the gate of the city and state his case in the hearing of the elders of that city; and they shall take him into the city to them and give him a place, so that he may dwell among them.

5 'Now if the avenger of blood pursues him, then they shall not deliver the manslayer into his hand, because he struck his neighbor without premeditation and did not hate him beforehand.

6 'And he shall dwell in that city until he stands before the congregation for judgment, until the death of the one who is high priest in those days. Then the manslayer shall return to his own city and to his own house, to the city from which he fled.' "

7 ¶ So they set apart Kedesh in Galilee in the hill country of Naphtali and Shechem in the hill country of Ephraim, and Kiriath-arba (that is, Hebron) in the hill country of Judah.

8 And beyond the Jordan east of Jericho, they designated Bezer in the wilderness on the plain from the tribe of Reuben, and Ramoth in Gilead from the tribe of Gad, and Golan in Bashan from the tribe of Manasseh.

9 These were the appointed cities for all the sons of Israel and for the stranger who sojourns among them, that whoever kills any person unintentionally may flee there, and not die by the hand of the avenger of blood until he stands before the congregation.

CHAPTER 21

THEN the heads of households of the Levites approached Eleazar the priest and Joshua the son of Nun and the heads of households of the tribes of the sons of Israel.

2 And they spoke to them at Shiloh in the land of Canaan, saying, "The LORD commanded through Moses to give us cities to live in, with their pasture lands for our cattle."

3 So the sons of Israel gave the Levites from their inheritance these cities with their pasture lands, according to the command of the LORD.

4 Then the lot came out for the families of the Kohathites. And the sons of Aaron the priest, who were of the Levites, received thirteen cities by lot from the tribe of Judah and from the tribe of the Simeonites and from the tribe of Benjamin.

5 And the rest of the sons of Kohath received ten cities by lot from the families of the tribe of Ephraim and from the tribe of Dan and from the half-tribe of Manasseh.

6 And the sons of Gershon received thirteen cities by lot from the families of the tribe of Issachar and from the tribe of Asher and from the tribe of Naphtali and from the half-tribe of Manasseh in Bashan.

7 The sons of Merari according to their families received twelve cities from the tribe of Reuben and from the tribe of Gad and from the tribe of Zebulun.

8 Now the sons of Israel gave by lot to the Levites these cities with their pasture lands, as the LORD had commanded through Moses.

9 ¶ And they gave these cities which are here mentioned by name from the tribe of the sons of Judah and from the tribe of the sons of Simeon;

10 and they were for the sons of Aaron, one of the families of the Kohathites, of the sons of Levi, for the lot was theirs first.

11 Thus they gave them Kiriath-arba, Arba being the father of Anak (that is, Hebron), in the hill country of Judah, with its surrounding pasture lands.

12 But the fields of the city and its villages, they gave to Caleb the son of Jephunneh as his possession.

13 ¶ So to the sons of Aaron the priest they gave Hebron, the city of refuge for the manslayer, with its pasture lands, and Libnah with its pasture lands,

14 and Jattir with its pasture lands and Eshtemoa with its pasture lands,

15 and Holon with its pasture lands and Debir with its pasture lands,

16 and Ain with its pasture lands and Juttah with its pasture lands and Beth-shemesh with its pasture lands; nine cities from these two tribes.

17 And from the tribe of Benjamin, Gibeon with its pasture lands, Geba with its pasture lands,

18 Anathoth with its pasture lands and Almon with its pasture lands; four cities.

19 All the cities of the sons of Aaron, the priests, were thirteen cities with their pasture lands.

20 ¶ Then the cities from the tribe of Ephraim were allotted to the families of the sons of Kohath, the Levites, even to the rest of the sons of Kohath.

21 And they gave them Shechem, the city of refuge for the manslayer, with its pasture lands, in the hill country of Ephraim, and Gezer with its pasture lands,

22 and Kibzaim with its pasture lands and Beth-horon with its pasture lands; four cities.

23 And from the tribe of Dan, Elteke with its pasture lands, Gibbethon with its pasture lands,

24 Aijalon with its pasture lands, Gath-rimmon with its pasture lands; four cities.

25 And from the half-tribe of Manasseh, they allotted Taanach with its pasture lands and Gath-rimmon with its pasture lands; two cities.

26 All the cities with their pasture lands for the families of the rest of the sons of Kohath were ten.

27 ¶ And to the sons of Gershon, one of the families of the Levites, from the half-tribe of Manasseh, they gave Golan in Bashan, the city of refuge for the manslayer, with its pasture lands, and Be-eshterah with its pasture lands; two cities.

28 And from the tribe of Issachar, they gave Kishion with its pasture lands, Daberath with its pasture lands,

29 Jarmuth with its pasture lands, En-gannim with its pasture lands; four cities.

30 And from the tribe of Asher, they

gave Mishal with its pasture lands, Abdon with its pasture lands,

31 Helkath with its pasture lands and Rehob with its pasture lands; four cities.

32 And from the tribe of Naphtali, *they gave* Kedesh in Galilee, the city of refuge for the manslayer, with its pasture lands and Hammoth-dor with its pasture lands and Kartan with its pasture lands; three cities.

33 All the cities of the Gershonites according to their families were thirteen cities with their pasture lands.

34 ¶ And to the families of the sons of Merari, the rest of the Levites, *they gave* from the tribe of Zebulun, Jokneam with its pasture lands and Kartah with its pasture lands.

35 Dimnah with its pasture lands, Nahalal with its pasture lands; four cities.

36 And from the tribe of Reuben, *they gave* Bezer with its pasture lands and Jahaz with its pasture lands,

37 Kedemoth with its pasture lands and Mephaath with its pasture lands; four cities.

38 And from the tribe of Gad, *they gave* Ramoth in Gilead, the city of refuge for the manslayer, with its pasture lands and Mahanaim with its pasture lands,

39 Heshbon with its pasture lands, Jazer with its pasture lands; four cities in all.

40 All *these were* the cities of the sons of Merari according to their families, the rest of the families of the Levites; and their lot was twelve cities.

41 ¶ All the cities of the Levites in the midst of the possession of the sons of Israel were forty-eight cities with their pasture lands.

42 These cities each had its surrounding pasture lands; thus *it was* with all these cities.

43 ¶ So the LORD gave Israel all the land which He had sworn to give to their fathers, and they possessed it and lived in it.

44 And the LORD gave them rest on every side, according to all that He had sworn to their fathers, and no one of all their enemies stood before them; the LORD gave all their enemies into their hand.

45 Not one of the good promises which the LORD had made to the house of Israel failed; all came to pass.

CHAPTER 22

THEN Joshua summoned the Reubenites and the Gadites and the half-tribe of Manasseh,

2 and said to them, "You have kept all that Moses the servant of the LORD commanded you, and have listened to my voice in all that I commanded you.

3 "You have not forsaken your brothers these many days to this day, but have kept the charge of the commandment of the LORD your God.

4 "And now the LORD your God has given rest to your brothers, as He spoke to them; therefore turn now and go to your tents, to the land of your possession, which Moses the servant of the LORD gave you beyond the Jordan.

5 "Only be very careful to observe the commandment and the law which Moses the servant of the LORD commanded you, to love the LORD your God and walk in all His ways and keep His commandments and hold fast to Him and serve Him with all your heart and with all your soul."

6 So Joshua blessed them and sent them away, and they went to their tents.

7 ¶ Now to the one half-tribe of Manasseh Moses had given *a possession* in Bashan, but to the other half Joshua gave *a possession* among their brothers westward beyond the Jordan. So when Joshua sent them away to their tents, he blessed them,

8 and said to them, "Return to your tents with great riches and with very much livestock, with silver, gold, bronze, iron, and with very many clothes; divide the spoil of your enemies with your brothers."

9 And the sons of Reuben and the sons of Gad and the half-tribe of Manasseh returned *home* and departed from the sons of Israel at Shiloh which is in the land of Canaan, to go to the land of Gilead, to the land of their possession which they had possessed, according to the command of the LORD through Moses.

10 ¶ And when they came to the region of the Jordan which is in the land of Canaan, the sons of Reuben

and the sons of Gad and the half-tribe of Manasseh built an altar there by the Jordan, a large altar in appearance.

11 And the sons of Israel heard *it* said, "Behold, the sons of Reuben and the sons of Gad and the half-tribe of Manasseh have built an altar at the frontier of the land of Canaan, in the region of the Jordan, on the side *belonging to* the sons of Israel."

12 And when the sons of Israel heard *of it*, the whole congregation of the sons of Israel gathered themselves at Shiloh, to go up against them in war.

13 ¶ Then the sons of Israel sent to the sons of Reuben and to the sons of Gad and to the half-tribe of Manasseh, into the land of Gilead, Phinehas the son of Eleazar the priest,

14 and with him ten chiefs, one chief for each father's household from each of the tribes of Israel; and each one of them *was* the head of his father's household among the thousands of Israel.

15 And they came to the sons of Reuben and to the sons of Gad and to the half-tribe of Manasseh, to the land of Gilead, and they spoke with them saying,

16 "Thus says the whole congregation of the LORD, 'What is this unfaithful act which you have committed against the God of Israel, turning away from following the LORD this day, by building yourselves an altar, to rebel against the LORD this day?

17 'Is not the iniquity of Peor enough for us, from which we have not cleansed ourselves to this day, although a plague came on the congregation of the LORD,

18 that you must turn away this day from following the LORD? And it will come about if you rebel against the LORD today, that He will be angry with the whole congregation of Israel tomorrow.

19 'If, however, the land of your possession is unclean, then cross into the land of the possession of the LORD, where the LORD's tabernacle stands, and take possession among us. Only do not rebel against the LORD, or rebel against us by building an altar for yourselves, besides the altar of the LORD our God.

20 'Did not Achan the son of Zerah act unfaithfully in the things under the ban, and wrath fall on all the congregation of Israel? And that man did not perish alone in his iniquity.'"

21 ¶ Then the sons of Reuben and the sons of Gad and the half-tribe of Manasseh answered, and spoke to the heads of the families of Israel.

22 "The Mighty One, God, the LORD, the Mighty One, God, the LORD! He knows, and may Israel itself know. If *it was* in rebellion, or if in an unfaithful act against the LORD do not Thou save us this day!

23 "If we have built us an altar to turn away from following the LORD, or if to offer a burnt offering or grain offering on it, or if to offer sacrifices of peace offerings on it, may the LORD Himself require it.

24 "But truly we have done this out of concern, for a reason, saying, 'In time to come your sons may say to our sons, "What have you to do with the LORD, the God of Israel?

25 "For the LORD has made the Jordan a border between us and you, *you* sons of Reuben and sons of Gad; you have no portion in the LORD." So your sons may make our sons stop fearing the LORD.'

26 ¶ "Therefore we said, 'Let us build an altar, not for burnt offering or for sacrifice;

27 rather it shall be a witness between us and you and between our generations after us, that we are to perform the service of the LORD before Him with our burnt offerings, and with our sacrifices and with our peace offerings, that your sons may not say to our sons in time to come, "You have no portion in the LORD."'

28 "Therefore we said, 'It shall also come about if they say *this* to us or to our generations in time to come, then we shall say, "See the copy of the altar of the LORD which our fathers made, not for burnt offering or for sacrifice; rather it is a witness between us and you."'

29 "Far be it from us that we should rebel against the LORD and turn away from following the LORD this day, by building an altar for burnt offering, for grain offering or for sacrifice, besides the altar of the LORD our God which is before His ¹³tabernacle."

¹³ Lit., *dwelling place*

30 ¶ So when Phinehas the priest and the leaders of the congregation, even the heads of the families of Israel who *were* with him, heard the words which the sons of Reuben and the sons of Gad and the sons of Manasseh spoke, it pleased them.

31 And Phinehas the son of Eleazar the priest said to the sons of Reuben and to the sons of Gad and to the sons of Manasseh, "Today we know that the Lord is in our midst, because you have not committed this unfaithful act against the Lord; now you have delivered the sons of Israel from the hand of the Lord."

32 Then Phinehas the son of Eleazar the priest and the leaders returned from the sons of Reuben and from the sons of Gad, from the land of Gilead, to the land of Canaan, to the sons of Israel, and brought back word to them.

33 And the word pleased the sons of Israel, and the sons of Israel blessed God; and they did not speak of going up against them in war, to destroy the land in which the sons of Reuben and the sons of Gad were living.

34 And the sons of Reuben and the sons of Gad called the altar *Witness;* "For," *they said,* "it is a witness between us that the Lord is God."

CHAPTER 23

Now it came about after many days, when the Lord had given rest to Israel from all their enemies on every side, and Joshua was old, advanced in years,

2 that Joshua called for all Israel, for their elders and their heads and their judges and their officers, and said to them, "I am old, advanced in years.

3 "And you have seen all that the Lord your God has done to all these nations because of you, for the Lord your God is He who has been fighting for you.

4 "See, I have apportioned to you these nations which remain as an inheritance for your tribes, with all the nations which I have cut off, from the Jordan even to the Great Sea toward the setting of the sun.

5 "And the Lord your God, He shall thrust them out from before you and drive them from before you; and you

shall possess their land, just as the Lord your God promised you.

6 "Be very firm, then, to keep and do all that is written in the book of the law of Moses, so that you may not turn aside from it to the right hand or to the left,

7 in order that you may not associate with these nations, these which remain among you, or mention the name of their gods, or make *anyone* swear *by them,* or serve them, or bow down to them.

8 "But you are to cling to the Lord your God, as you have done to this day.

9 "For the Lord has driven out great and strong nations from before you; and as for you, no man has stood before you to this day.

10 "One of your men puts to flight a thousand, for the Lord your God is He who fights for you, just as He promised you.

11 "So take diligent heed to yourselves to love the Lord your God.

12 "For if you ever go back and cling to the rest of these nations, these which remain among you, and intermarry with them, so that you associate with them and they with you,

13 know with certainty that the Lord your God will not continue to drive these nations out from before you; but they shall be a snare and a trap to you, and a whip on your sides and thorns in your eyes, until you perish from off this good land which the Lord your God has given you.

14 ¶ "Now behold, today I am going the way of all the earth, and you know in all your hearts and in all your souls that not one word of all the good words which the Lord your God spoke concerning you has failed; all have been fulfilled for you, not one of them has failed.

15 "And it shall come about that just as all the good words which the Lord your God spoke to you have come upon you, so the Lord will bring upon you all the threats, until He has destroyed you from off this good land which the Lord your God has given you.

16 "When you transgress the covenant of the Lord your God, which He commanded you, and go and serve other gods, and bow down to them,

then the anger of the LORD will burn against you, and you shall perish quickly from off the good land which He has given you."

CHAPTER 24

THEN Joshua gathered all the tribes of Israel to Shechem, and called for the elders of Israel and for their heads and their judges and their officers; and they presented themselves before God.

2 And Joshua said to all the people, "Thus says the LORD, the God of Israel, 'From ancient times your fathers lived beyond the [14]River, *namely*, Terah, the father of Abraham and the father of Nahor, and they served other gods.

3 'Then I took your father Abraham from beyond the [14]River, and led him through all the land of Canaan, and multiplied his descendants and gave him Isaac.

4 'And to Isaac I gave Jacob and Esau, and to Esau I gave Mount Seir, to possess it; but Jacob and his sons went down to Egypt.

5 'Then I sent Moses and Aaron, and I plagued Egypt by what I did in its midst; and afterward I brought you out.

6 'And I brought your fathers out of Egypt, and you came to the sea; and Egypt pursued your fathers with chariots and horsemen to the Red Sea.

7 'But when they cried out to the LORD, He put darkness between you and the Egyptians, and brought the sea upon them and covered them; and your own eyes saw what I did in Egypt. And you lived in the wilderness for a long time.

8 'Then I brought you into the land of the Amorites who lived beyond the Jordan, and they fought with you; and I gave them into your hand, and you took possession of their land when I destroyed them before you.

9 'Then Balak the son of Zippor, king of Moab, arose and fought against Israel, and he sent and summoned Balaam the son of Beor to curse you.

10 'But I was not willing to listen to Balaam. So he had to bless you, and I delivered you from his hand.

11 'And you crossed the Jordan and came to Jericho; and the citizens of Jericho fought against you, *and* the Amorite and the Perizzite and the Canaanite and the Hittite and the Girgashite, the Hivite and the Jebusite. Thus I gave them into your hand.

12 'Then I sent the hornet before you and it drove out the two kings of the Amorites from before you, *but* not by your sword or your bow.

13 'And I gave you a land on which you had not labored, and cities which you had not built, and you have lived in them; you are eating of vineyards and olive groves which you did not plant.'

14 ¶"Now, therefore, fear the LORD and serve Him in sincerity and truth; and put away the gods which your fathers served beyond the River and in Egypt, and serve the LORD.

15"And if it is disagreeable in your sight to serve the LORD, choose for yourselves today whom you will serve: whether the gods which your fathers served which were beyond the River, or the gods of the Amorites in whose land you are living; but as for me and my house, we will serve the LORD."

16 ¶ And the people answered and said, "Far be it from us that we should forsake the LORD to serve other gods;

17 for the LORD our God is He who brought us and our fathers up out of the land of Egypt, from the house of bondage, and who did these great signs in our sight and preserved us through all the way in which we went and among all the peoples through whose midst we passed.

18"And the LORD drove out from before us all the peoples, even the Amorites who lived in the land. We also will serve the LORD, for He is our God."

19 ¶ Then Joshua said to the people, "You will not be able to serve the LORD, for He is a holy God. He is a jealous God; He will not forgive your transgression or your sins.

20"If you forsake the LORD and serve foreign gods, then He will turn and do you harm and consume you after He has done good to you."

21 And the people said to Joshua, "No, but we will serve the LORD."

22 And Joshua said to the people, "You are witnesses against yourselves that you have chosen for yourselves

[14] I.e., Euphrates

the Lord, to serve Him." And they said, "We are witnesses."

23 "Now therefore, put away the foreign gods which are in your midst, and incline your hearts to the Lord, the God of Israel."

24 And the people said to Joshua, "We will serve the Lord our God and we will obey His voice."

25 So Joshua made a covenant with the people that day, and made for them a statute and an ordinance in Shechem.

26 And Joshua wrote these words in the book of the law of God; and he took a large stone and set it up there under the oak that was by the sanctuary of the Lord.

27 And Joshua said to all the people, "Behold, this stone shall be for a witness against us, for it has heard all the words of the Lord which He spoke to us; thus it shall be for a witness against you, lest you deny your God."

28 Then Joshua dismissed the people, each to his inheritance.

29 ¶ And it came about after these things that Joshua the son of Nun, the servant of the Lord, died, being one hundred and ten years old.

30 And they buried him in the territory of his inheritance in Timnath-serah, which is in the hill country of Ephraim, on the north of Mount Gaash.

31 And Israel served the Lord all the days of Joshua and all the days of the elders who survived Joshua, and had known all the deeds of the Lord which He had done for Israel.

32 ¶ Now they buried the bones of Joseph, which the sons of Israel brought up from Egypt, at Shechem, in the piece of ground which Jacob had bought from the sons of Hamor the father of Shechem for one hundred pieces of money; and they became the inheritance of Joseph's sons.

33 And Eleazar the son of Aaron died; and they buried him at Gibeah of Phinehas his son, which was given him in the hill country of Ephraim.

THE BOOK OF

JUDGES

Now it came about after the death of Joshua that the sons of Israel inquired of the Lord, saying, "Who shall go up first for us against the Canaanites, to fight against them?"

2 And the Lord said, "Judah shall go up; behold, I have given the land into his hand."

3 Then Judah said to Simeon his brother, "Come up with me into the territory allotted me, that we may fight against the Canaanites; and I in turn will go with you into the territory allotted you." So Simeon went with him.

4 And Judah went up, and the Lord gave the Canaanites and the Perizzites into their hands; and they defeated ten thousand men at Bezek.

5 And they found Adoni-bezek in Bezek and fought against him and they defeated the Canaanites and the Perizzites.

6 But Adoni-bezek fled; and they pursued him and caught him and cut off his thumbs and big toes.

7 And Adoni-bezek said, "Seventy kings with their thumbs and their big toes cut off used to gather up scraps under my table; as I have done, so God has repaid me." So they brought him to Jerusalem and he died there.

8 ¶ Then the sons of Judah fought against Jerusalem and captured it and struck it with the edge of the sword and set the city on fire.

9 And afterward the sons of Judah went down to fight against the Canaanites living in the hill country and in the ¹Negev and in the lowland.

10 So Judah went against the Canaanites who lived in Hebron (now the name of Hebron formerly was Kiriath-arba); and they struck Sheshai and Ahiman and Talmai.

11 ¶ Then from there he went against the inhabitants of Debir (now

¹ I.e., South country

the name of Debir formerly *was* Kiriath-sepher).

12 And Caleb said, "The one who attacks Kiriath-sepher and captures it, I will even give him my daughter Achsah for a wife."

13 And Othniel the son of Kenaz, Caleb's younger brother, captured it; so he gave him his daughter Achsah for a wife.

14 Then it came about when she came *to him*, that she persuaded him to ask her father for a field. Then she alighted from her donkey, and Caleb said to her, "What do you want?"

15 And she said to him, "Give me a blessing, since you have given me the land of the [1]Negev, give me also springs of water." So Caleb gave her the upper springs and the lower springs.

16 ¶ And the descendants of the Kenite, Moses' father-in-law, went up from the city of palms with the sons of Judah, to the wilderness of Judah which is in the south of Arad; and they went and lived with the people.

17 Then Judah went with Simeon his brother, and they struck the Canaanites living in Zephath, and utterly destroyed it. So the name of the city was called Hormah.

18 And Judah took Gaza with its territory and Ashkelon with its territory and Ekron with its territory.

19 Now the LORD was with Judah, and they took possession of the hill country; but they could not drive out the inhabitants of the valley because they had iron chariots.

20 Then they gave Hebron to Caleb, as Moses had promised; and he drove out from there the three sons of Anak.

21 But the sons of Benjamin did not drive out the Jebusites who lived in Jerusalem; so the Jebusites have lived with the sons of Benjamin in Jerusalem to this day.

22 ¶ Likewise the house of Joseph went up against Bethel, and the LORD was with them.

23 And the house of Joseph spied out Bethel (now the name of the city was formerly Luz).

24 And the spies saw a man coming out of the city, and they said to him, "Please show us the entrance to the city and we will treat you kindly."

25 So he showed them the entrance to the city, and they struck the city with the edge of the sword, but they let the man and all his family go free.

26 And the man went into the land of the Hittites and built a city and named it Luz which is its name to this day.

27 ¶ But Manasseh did not take possession of Beth-shean and its villages, or Taanach and its villages, or the inhabitants of Dor and its villages, or the inhabitants of Ibleam and its villages, or the inhabitants of Megiddo and its villages; so the Canaanites persisted in living in that land.

28 And it came about when Israel became strong, that they put the Canaanites to forced labor, but they did not drive them out completely.

29 ¶ Neither did Ephraim drive out the Canaanites who were living in Gezer; so the Canaanites lived in Gezer among them.

30 ¶ Zebulun did not drive out the inhabitants of Kitron, or the inhabitants of Nahalol; so the Canaanites lived among them and became subject to forced labor.

31 ¶ Asher did not drive out the inhabitants of Acco, or the inhabitants of Sidon, or of Ahlab, or of Achzib, or of Helbah, or of Aphik, or of Rehob.

32 So the Asherites lived among the Canaanites, the inhabitants of the land; for they did not drive them out.

33 ¶ Naphtali did not drive out the inhabitants of Beth-shemesh, or the inhabitants of Beth-anath, but lived among the Canaanites, the inhabitants of the land; and the inhabitants of Beth-shemesh and Beth-anath became forced labor for them.

34 ¶ Then the Amorites forced the sons of Dan into the hill country, for they did not allow them to come down to the valley;

35 yet the Amorites persisted in living in Mount Heres, in Aijalon and in Shaalbim; but when the power of the house of Joseph grew strong, they became forced labor.

36 And the border of the Amorites ran from the ascent of Akrabbim, from Sela and upward.

CHAPTER 2

NOW the angel of the LORD came up from Gilgal to Bochim. And he said, "I brought you up out of Egypt and led

[1] I.e., South country

you into the land which I have sworn to your fathers; and I said, 'I will never break My covenant with you,

2 and as for you, you shall make no covenant with the inhabitants of this land; you shall tear down their altars.' But you have not obeyed Me; what is this you have done?

3 "Therefore I also said, 'I will not drive them out before you; but they shall ²become *as thorns* in your sides, and their gods shall be a snare to you.' "

4 And it came about when the angel of the LORD spoke these words to all the sons of Israel, that the people lifted up their voices and wept.

5 So they named that place ³Bochim; and there they sacrificed to the LORD.

6 ¶ When Joshua had dismissed the people, the sons of Israel went each to his inheritance to possess the land.

7 And the people served the LORD all the days of Joshua, and all the days of the elders who survived Joshua, who had seen all the great work of the LORD which He had done for Israel.

8 Then Joshua the son of Nun, the servant of the LORD, died at the age of one hundred and ten.

9 And they buried him in the territory of his inheritance in Timnathheres, in the hill country of Ephraim, north of Mount Gaash.

10 And all that generation also were gathered to their fathers; and there arose another generation after them who did not know the LORD, nor yet the work which He had done for Israel.

11 ¶ Then the sons of Israel did evil in the sight of the LORD, and ⁴served the Baals,

12 and they forsook the LORD, the God of their fathers, who had brought them out of the land of Egypt, and followed other gods from *among* the gods of the peoples who were around them, and bowed themselves down to them; thus they provoked the LORD to anger.

13 So they forsook the LORD and served Baal and the Ashtaroth.

14 And the anger of the LORD burned against Israel, and He gave them into

the hands of plunderers who plundered them; and He sold them into the hands of their enemies around *them*, so that they could no longer stand before their enemies.

15 Wherever they went, the hand of the LORD was against them for evil, as the LORD had spoken and as the LORD had sworn to them, so that they were severely distressed.

16 Then the LORD raised up judges who delivered them from the hands of those who plundered them.

17 And yet they did not listen to their judges, for they played the harlot after other gods and bowed themselves down to them. They turned aside quickly from the way in which their fathers had walked in obeying the commandments of the LORD; they did not do as *their fathers*.

18 And when the LORD raised up judges for them, the LORD was with the judge and delivered them from the hand of their enemies all the days of the judge; for the LORD was moved to pity by their groaning because of those who oppressed and afflicted them.

19 But it came about when the judge died, that they would turn back and act more corruptly than their fathers, in following other gods to serve them and bow down to them; they did not abandon their practices or their stubborn ways.

20 So the anger of the LORD burned against Israel, and He said, "Because this nation has transgressed My covenant which I commanded their fathers, and has not listened to My voice,

21 I also will no longer drive out before them any of the nations which Joshua left when he died,

22 in order to test Israel by them, whether they will keep the way of the LORD to walk in it as their fathers did, or not."

23 So the LORD allowed those nations to remain, not driving them out quickly; and He did not give them into the hand of Joshua.

CHAPTER 3

Now these are the nations which the LORD left, to test Israel by them

² Some ancient mss. read *be adversaries, and*
³ I.e., *weepers*   ⁴ Or, *worshiped*

(*that is,* all who had not experienced any of the wars of Canaan;

2 only in order that the generations of the sons of Israel might be taught war, those who had not experienced it formerly).

3 *These nations are:* the five lords of the Philistines and all the Canaanites and the Sidonians and the Hivites who lived in Mount Lebanon, from Mount Baal-hermon as far as Lebo-hamath.

4 And they were for testing Israel, to find out if they would obey the commandments of the LORD, which He had commanded their fathers through Moses.

5 And the sons of Israel lived among the Canaanites, the Hittites, the Amorites, the Perizzites, the Hivites, and the Jebusites;

6 and they took their daughters for themselves as wives, and gave their own daughters to their sons, and served their gods.

7 And the sons of Israel did what was evil in the sight of the LORD, and forgot the LORD their God, and served the Baals and the [5]Asheroth.

8 Then the anger of the LORD was kindled against Israel, so that He sold them into the hands of Cushan-rishathaim king of Mesopotamia; and the sons of Israel served Cushan-rishathaim eight years.

9 And when the sons of Israel cried to the LORD, the LORD raised up a deliverer for the sons of Israel to deliver them, Othniel the son of Kenaz, Caleb's younger brother.

10 And the Spirit of the LORD came upon him, and he judged Israel. When he went out to war, the LORD gave Cushan-rishathaim king of Mesopotamia into his hand, so that he prevailed over Cushan-rishathaim.

11 Then the land had rest forty years. And Othniel the son of Kenaz died.

12 ¶ Now the sons of Israel again did evil in the sight of the LORD. So the LORD strengthened Eglon the king of Moab against Israel, because they had done evil in the sight of the LORD.

13 And he gathered to himself the sons of Ammon and Amalek; and he went and defeated Israel, and they possessed the city of the palm trees.

14 And the sons of Israel served Eglon the king of Moab eighteen years.

15 ¶ But when the sons of Israel cried to the LORD, the LORD raised up a deliverer for them, Ehud the son of Gera, the Benjamite, a left-handed man. And the sons of Israel sent tribute by him to Eglon the king of Moab.

16 And Ehud made himself a sword which had two edges, a cubit in length; and he bound it on his right thigh under his cloak.

17 And he presented the tribute to Eglon king of Moab. Now Eglon was a very fat man.

18 And it came about when he had finished presenting the tribute, that he sent away the people who had carried the tribute.

19 But he himself turned back from the idols which were at Gilgal, and said, "I have a secret message for you, O king." And he said, "Keep silence." And all who attended him left him.

20 And Ehud came to him while he was sitting alone in his cool roof chamber. And Ehud said, "I have a message from God for you." And he arose from his seat.

21 And Ehud stretched out his left hand, took the sword from his right thigh and thrust it into his belly.

22 The handle also went in after the blade, and the fat closed over the blade, for he did not draw the sword out of his belly; and the refuse came out.

23 Then Ehud went out into the vestibule and shut the doors of the roof chamber behind him, and locked *them.*

24 ¶ When he had gone out, his servants came and looked, and behold, the doors of the roof chamber were locked; and they said, "He is only relieving himself in the cool room."

25 And they waited until they became anxious; but behold, he did not open the doors of the roof chamber. Therefore they took the key and opened them, and behold, their master had fallen to the floor dead.

26 ¶ Now Ehud escaped while they were delaying, and he passed by the idols and escaped to Seirah.

27 And it came about when he had arrived, that he blew the trumpet in the hill country of Ephraim; and the

[5] I.e., wooden symbol of a female deity

sons of Israel went down with him from the hill country, and he *was* in front of them.

28 And he said to them, "Pursue *them*, for the LORD has given your enemies the Moabites into your hands." So they went down after him and seized the fords of the Jordan opposite Moab, and did not allow anyone to cross.

29 And they struck down at that time about ten thousand Moabites, all robust and valiant men; and no one escaped.

30 So Moab was subdued that day under the hand of Israel. And the land was undisturbed for eighty years.

31 ¶ And after him came Shamgar the son of Anath, who struck down six hundred Philistines with an oxgoad; and he also saved Israel.

CHAPTER 4

THEN the sons of Israel again did evil in the sight of the LORD, after Ehud died.

2 And the LORD sold them into the hand of Jabin king of Canaan, who reigned in Hazor; and the commander of his army was Sisera, who lived in Harosheth-hagoyim.

3 And the sons of Israel cried to the LORD; for he had nine hundred iron chariots, and he oppressed the sons of Israel severely for twenty years.

4 ¶ Now Deborah, a prophetess, the wife of Lappidoth, was judging Israel at that time.

5 And she used to sit under the palm tree of Deborah between Ramah and Bethel in the hill country of Ephraim; and the sons of Israel came up to her for judgment.

6 Now she sent and summoned Barak the son of Abinoam from Kedesh-naphtali, and said to him, "Behold, the LORD, the God of Israel, has commanded, 'Go and march to Mount Tabor, and take with you ten thousand men from the sons of Naphtali and from the sons of Zebulun.

7 'And I will draw out to you Sisera, the commander of Jabin's army, with his chariots and his many *troops* to the river Kishon; and I will give him into your hand.'"

8 Then Barak said to her, "If you will go with me, then I will go; but if you will not go with me, I will not go."

9 And she said, "I will surely go with you; nevertheless, the honor shall not be yours on the journey that you are about to take, for the LORD will sell Sisera into the hands of a woman." Then Deborah arose and went with Barak to Kedesh.

10 And Barak called Zebulun and Naphtali together to Kedesh, and ten thousand men went up with him; Deborah also went up with him.

11 ¶ Now Heber the Kenite had separated himself from the Kenites, from the sons of Hobab the father-in-law of Moses, and had pitched his tent as far away as the oak in Zaanannim, which is near Kedesh.

12 ¶ Then they told Sisera that Barak the son of Abinoam had gone up to Mount Tabor.

13 And Sisera called together all his chariots, nine hundred iron chariots, and all the people who *were* with him, from Harosheth-hagoyim to the river Kishon.

14 And Deborah said to Barak, "Arise! For this is the day in which the LORD has given Sisera into your hands; [6]behold, the LORD has gone out before you." So Barak went down from Mount Tabor with ten thousand men following him.

15 And the LORD routed Sisera and all *his* chariots and all *his* army, with the edge of the sword before Barak; and Sisera alighted from *his* chariot and fled away on foot.

16 But Barak pursued the chariots and the army as far as Harosheth-hagoyim, and all the army of Sisera fell by the edge of the sword; not even one was left.

17 ¶ Now Sisera fled away on foot to the tent of Jael the wife of Heber the Kenite, for *there was* peace between Jabin the king of Hazor and the house of Heber the Kenite.

18 And Jael went out to meet Sisera, and said to him, "Turn aside, my master, turn aside to me! Do not be afraid." And he turned aside to her into the tent, and she covered him with a rug.

19 And he said to her, "Please give me a little water to drink, for I am

[6] Or, has not the LORD gone ...?

thirsty." So she opened a ⁷bottle of milk and gave him a drink; then she covered him.

20 And he said to her, "Stand in the doorway of the tent, and it shall be if anyone comes and inquires of you, and says, 'Is there anyone here?' that you shall say, 'No.'"

21 But Jael, Heber's wife, took a tent peg and seized a hammer in her hand, and went secretly to him and drove the peg into his temple, and it went through into the ground; for he was sound asleep and exhausted. So he died.

22 And behold, as Barak pursued Sisera, Jael came out to meet him and said to him, "Come, and I will show you the man whom you are seeking." And he entered with her, and behold Sisera was lying dead with the tent peg in his temple.

23 ¶ So God subdued on that day Jabin the king of Canaan before the sons of Israel.

24 And the hand of the sons of Israel pressed heavier and heavier upon Jabin the king of Canaan, until they had destroyed Jabin the king of Canaan.

CHAPTER 5

THEN Deborah and Barak the son of Abinoam sang on that day, saying,

2 "That the leaders led in Israel,
That the people volunteered,
Bless the LORD!

3 "Hear, O kings; give ear, O rulers!
I—to the LORD, I will sing,
I will sing praise to the LORD, the God of Israel.

4 "LORD, when Thou didst go out from Seir,
When Thou didst march from the field of Edom,
The earth quaked, the heavens also dripped,
Even the clouds dripped water.

5 "The mountains quaked at the presence of the LORD,
This Sinai, at the presence of the LORD, the God of Israel.

6 ¶ "In the days of Shamgar the son of Anath,
In the days of Jael, the highways were deserted,

And travelers went by round-about ways.

7 "The peasantry ceased, they ceased in Israel,
Until I, Deborah, arose,
Until I arose, a mother in Israel.

8 "New gods were chosen;
Then war *was* in the gates.
Not a shield or a spear was seen Among forty thousand in Israel.

9 "My heart *goes out* to the commanders of Israel,
The volunteers among the people;
Bless the LORD!

10 "You who ride on white donkeys,
You who sit on *rich* carpets,
And you who travel on the road—sing!

11 "At the sound of those who divide *flocks* among the watering places,
There they shall recount the righteous deeds of the LORD,
The righteous deeds for His peasantry in Israel.
Then the people of the LORD went down to the gates.

12 ¶ "Awake, awake, Deborah;
Awake, awake, sing a song!
Arise, Barak, and take away your captives, O son of Abinoam.

13 "Then survivors came down to the nobles;
The people of the LORD came down to me as warriors.

14 "From Ephraim those whose root is in Amalek *came down*,
Following you, Benjamin, with your peoples;
From Machir commanders came down,
And from Zebulun those who wield the staff of office.

15 "And the princes of Issachar *were* with Deborah;
As *was* Issachar, so *was* Barak;
Into the valley they rushed at his heels;
Among the divisions of Reuben *There were* great resolves of heart.

16 "Why did you sit among the ⁸sheepfolds,
To hear the piping for the flocks?
Among the divisions of Reuben

---

⁷ I.e., skin container   ⁸ Or, *saddlebags*

There were great searchings of
heart.
17 "Gilead remained across the Jordan;
And why did Dan stay in ships?
Asher sat at the seashore,
And remained by its landings.
18 "Zebulun *was* a people who despised their lives *even* to death,
And Naphtali also, on the high
places of the field.

19 ¶ "The kings came *and* fought;
Then fought the kings of Canaan
At Taanach near the waters of
Megiddo;
They took no plunder in silver.
20 "The stars fought from heaven,
From their courses they fought
against Sisera.
21 "The torrent of Kishon swept
them away,
The ancient torrent, the torrent
Kishon.
O my soul, march on with
strength.
22 "Then the horses' hoofs beat
From the dashing, the dashing of
his valiant steeds.
23 'Curse Meroz,' said the angel of
the LORD,
'Utterly curse its inhabitants;
Because they did not come to the
help of the LORD,
To the help of the LORD against
the warriors.'

24 ¶ "Most blessed of women is Jael,
The wife of Heber the Kenite;
Most blessed is she of women in
the tent.
25 "He asked for water *and* she gave
him milk;
In a magnificent bowl she
brought him curds.
26 "She reached out her hand for the
tent peg,
And her right hand for the workmen's hammer.
Then she struck Sisera, she
smashed his head;
And she shattered and pierced
his temple.
27 "Between her feet he bowed, he
fell, he lay;
Between her feet he bowed, he
fell;
Where he bowed, there he fell
dead.

28 ¶ "Out of the window she looked
and lamented,
The mother of Sisera through
the lattice,
'Why does his chariot delay in
coming?
Why do the hoofbeats of his
chariots tarry?'
29 "Her wise princesses would answer her,
Indeed she repeats her words to
herself,
30 'Are they not finding, are they
not dividing the spoil?
A maiden, two maidens for every
warrior;
To Sisera a spoil of dyed work,
A spoil of dyed work embroidered,
Dyed work of double embroidery
on the neck of the spoiler?'
31 "Thus let all Thine enemies perish, O LORD;
But let those who love Him be
like the rising of the sun in its
might."

And the land was undisturbed for
forty years.

CHAPTER 6

THEN the sons of Israel did what was
evil in the sight of the LORD; and the
LORD gave them into the hands of
Midian seven years.
2 And the power of Midian prevailed against Israel. Because of Midian the sons of Israel made for themselves the dens which were in the
mountains and the caves and the
strongholds.
3 For it was when Israel had sown,
that the Midianites would come up
with the Amalekites and the sons of
the east and go against them.
4 So they would camp against them
and destroy the produce of the earth
as far as Gaza, and leave no sustenance in Israel as well as no sheep, ox,
or donkey.
5 For they would come up with
their livestock and their tents, they
would come in like locusts for number,
both they and their camels were innumerable; and they came into the land
to devastate it.
6 So Israel was brought very low
because of Midian, and the sons of
Israel cried to the LORD.

7 ¶ Now it came about when the sons of Israel cried to the LORD on account of Midian,

8 that the LORD sent a prophet to the sons of Israel, and he said to them, "Thus says the LORD, the God of Israel, 'It was I who brought you up from Egypt, and brought you out from the house of slavery.

9 'And I delivered you from the hands of the Egyptians and from the hands of all your oppressors, and dispossessed them before you and gave you their land,

10 and I said to you, "I am the LORD your God; you shall not fear the gods of the Amorites in whose land you live. But you have not obeyed Me."'"

11 ¶ Then the angel of the LORD came and sat under the oak that was in Ophrah, which belonged to Joash the Abiezrite as his son Gideon was beating out wheat in the wine press in order to save it from the Midianites.

12 And the angel of the LORD appeared to him and said to him, "The LORD is with you, O valiant warrior."

13 Then Gideon said to him, "O my lord, if the LORD is with us, why then has all this happened to us? And where are all His miracles which our fathers told us about, saying, 'Did not the LORD bring us up from Egypt?' But now the LORD has abandoned us and given us into the hand of Midian."

14 And the LORD looked at him and said, "Go in this your strength and deliver Israel from the hand of Midian. Have I not sent you?"

15 And he said to Him, "O Lord, how shall I deliver Israel? Behold, my family is the least in Manasseh, and I am the youngest in my father's house."

16 But the LORD said to him, "Surely I will be with you, and you shall defeat Midian as one man."

17 So Gideon said to Him, "If now I have found favor in Thy sight, then show me a sign that it is Thou who speakest with me.

18 "Please do not depart from here, until I come back to Thee, and bring out my offering and lay it before Thee." And He said, "I will remain until you return."

19 ¶ Then Gideon went in and prepared a kid and unleavened bread from an [9]ephah of flour; he put the meat in a basket and the broth in a pot, and brought them out to him under the oak, and presented them.

20 And the angel of God said to him, "Take the meat and the unleavened bread and lay them on this rock, and pour out the broth." And he did so.

21 Then the angel of the LORD put out the end of the staff that was in his hand and touched the meat and the unleavened bread; and fire sprang up from the rock and consumed the meat and the unleavened bread. Then the angel of the LORD vanished from his sight.

22 When Gideon saw that he was the angel of the LORD, he said, "Alas, O Lord GOD! For now I have seen the angel of the LORD face to face."

23 And the LORD said to him, "Peace to you, do not fear; you shall not die."

24 Then Gideon built an altar there to the LORD and named it The LORD is Peace. To this day it is still in Ophrah of the Abiezrites.

25 ¶ Now the same night it came about that the LORD said to him, "Take your father's bull and a second bull seven years old, and pull down the altar of Baal which belongs to your father, and cut down the [10]Asherah that is beside it;

26 and build an altar to the LORD your God on the top of this stronghold in an orderly manner, and take a second bull and offer a burnt offering with the wood of the Asherah which you shall cut down."

27 Then Gideon took ten men of his servants and did as the LORD had spoken to him; and it came about, because he was too afraid of his father's household and the men of the city to do it by day, that he did it by night.

28 ¶ When the men of the city arose early in the morning, behold, the altar of Baal was torn down, and the Asherah which was beside it was cut down, and the second bull was offered on the altar which had been built.

29 And they said to one another, "Who did this thing?" And when they searched about and inquired, they said, "Gideon the son of Joash did this thing."

[9] I.e., Approx. one bushel
[10] I.e., wooden symbol of a female deity

30 Then the men of the city said to Joash, "Bring out your son, that he may die, for he has torn down the altar of Baal, and indeed, he has cut down the Asherah which was beside it."

31 But Joash said to all who stood against him, "Will you contend for Baal, or will you deliver him? Whoever will plead for him shall be put to death by morning. If he is a god, let him contend for himself, because someone has torn down his altar."

32 Therefore on that day he named him Jerubbaal, that is to say, "Let Baal contend against him," because he had torn down his altar.

33 ¶ Then all the Midianites and the Amalekites and the sons of the east assembled themselves; and they crossed over and camped in the valley of Jezreel.

34 So the Spirit of the LORD came upon Gideon; and he blew a trumpet, and the Abiezrites were called together to follow him.

35 And he sent messengers throughout Manasseh, and they also were called together to follow him; and he sent messengers to Asher, Zebulun, and Naphtali, and they came up to meet them.

36 ¶ Then Gideon said to God, "If Thou wilt deliver Israel through me, as Thou hast spoken,

37 behold, I will put a fleece of wool on the threshing floor. If there is dew on the fleece only, and it is dry on all the ground, then I will know that Thou wilt deliver Israel through me, as Thou hast spoken."

38 And it was so. When he arose early the next morning and squeezed the fleece, he drained the dew from the fleece, a bowl full of water.

39 Then Gideon said to God, "Do not let Thine anger burn against me that I may speak once more; please let me make a test once more with the fleece, let it now be dry only on the fleece, and let there be dew on all the ground."

40 And God did so that night; for it was dry only on the fleece, and dew was on all the ground.

CHAPTER 7

THEN Jerubbaal (that is, Gideon) and all the people who were with him, rose early and camped beside the spring of Harod; and the camp of Midian was on the north side of them by the hill of Moreh in the valley.

2 ¶ And the LORD said to Gideon, "The people who are with you are too many for Me to give Midian into their hands, lest Israel become boastful, saying, 'My own power has delivered me.'

3 "Now therefore come, proclaim in the hearing of the people, saying, 'Whoever is afraid and trembling, let him return and depart from Mount Gilead.' " So 22,000 people returned, but 10,000 remained.

4 ¶ Then the LORD said to Gideon, "The people are still too many; bring them down to the water and I will test them for you there. Therefore it shall be that he of whom I say to you, 'This one shall go with you,' he shall go with you; but everyone of whom I say to you, 'This one shall not go with you,' he shall not go."

5 So he brought the people down to the water. And the LORD said to Gideon, "You shall separate everyone who laps the water with his tongue, as a dog laps, as well as everyone who kneels to drink."

6 Now the number of those who lapped, putting their hand to their mouth, was 300 men; but all the rest of the people kneeled to drink water.

7 And the LORD said to Gideon, "I will deliver you with the 300 men who lapped and will give the Midianites into your hands; so let all the *other* people go, each man to his home."

8 So the 300 men took the people's provisions and their trumpets into their hands. And Gideon sent all the *other* men of Israel, each to his tent, but retained the 300 men; and the camp of Midian was below him in the valley.

9 ¶ Now the same night it came about that the LORD said to him, "Arise, go down against the camp, for I have given it into your hands.

10 "But if you are afraid to go down, go with Purah your servant down to the camp,

11 and you will hear what they say; and afterward your hands will be strengthened that you may go down

against the camp." So he went with Purah his servant down to the outposts of the army that was in the camp.

12 Now the Midianites and the Amalekites and all the sons of the east were lying in the valley as numerous as locusts; and their camels were without number, as numerous as the sand on the seashore.

13 When Gideon came, behold, a man was relating a dream to his friend. And he said, "Behold, I had a dream; a loaf of barley bread was tumbling into the camp of Midian, and it came to the tent and struck it so that it fell, and turned it upside down so that the tent lay flat."

14 And his friend answered and said, "This is nothing less than the sword of Gideon the son of Joash, a man of Israel; God has given Midian and all the camp into his hand."

15 ¶ And it came about when Gideon heard the account of the dream and its interpretation, that he bowed in worship. He returned to the camp of Israel and said, "Arise, for the LORD has given the camp of Midian into your hands."

16 And he divided the 300 men into three companies, and he put trumpets and empty pitchers into the hands of all of them, with torches inside the pitchers.

17 And he said to them, "Look at me, and do likewise. And behold, when I come to the outskirts of the camp, do as I do.

18 "When I and all who are with me blow the trumpet, then you also blow the trumpets all around the camp, and say, 'For the LORD and for Gideon.'"

19 ¶ So Gideon and the hundred men who were with him came to the outskirts of the camp at the beginning of the middle watch, when they had just posted the watch; and they blew the trumpets and smashed the pitchers that were in their hands.

20 When the three companies blew the trumpets and broke the pitchers, they held the torches in their left hands and the trumpets in their right hands for blowing, and cried, "A sword for the LORD and for Gideon!"

21 And each stood in his place

around the camp; and all the [11]army ran, crying out as they fled.

22 And when they blew 300 trumpets, the LORD set the sword of one against another even throughout the whole army; and the army fled as far as Beth-shittah toward Zererah, as far as the edge of Abel-meholah, by Tabbath.

23 And the men of Israel were summoned from Naphtali and Asher and all Manasseh, and they pursued Midian.

24 ¶ And Gideon sent messengers throughout all the hill country of Ephraim, saying, "Come down against Midian and take the waters before them, as far as Beth-barah and the Jordan." So all the men of Ephraim were summoned, and they took the waters as far as Beth-barah and the Jordan.

25 And they captured the two leaders of Midian, Oreb and Zeeb, and they killed Oreb at the rock of Oreb, and they killed Zeeb at the wine press of Zeeb, while they pursued Midian; and they brought the heads of Oreb and Zeeb to Gideon from across the Jordan.

CHAPTER 8

THEN the men of Ephraim said to him, "What is this thing you have done to us, not calling us when you went to fight against Midian?" And they contended with him vigorously.

2 But he said to them, "What have I done now in comparison with you? Is not the gleaning *of the grapes* of Ephraim better than the vintage of Abiezer?

3 "God has given the leaders of Midian, Oreb and Zeeb into your hands; and what was I able to do in comparison with you?" Then their anger toward him subsided when he said that.

4 ¶ Then Gideon and the 300 men who were with him came to the Jordan *and* crossed over, weary yet pursuing.

5 And he said to the men of Succoth, "Please give loaves of bread to the people who are following me, for they are weary, and I am pursuing

[11] Or, *camp*

Zebah and Zalmunna, the kings of Midian."

6 And the leaders of Succoth said, "Are the hands of Zebah and Zalmunna already in your hands, that we should give bread to your army?"

7 And Gideon said, "All right, when the LORD has given Zebah and Zalmunna into my hand, then I will thrash your bodies with the thorns of the wilderness and with briers."

8 And he went up from there to Penuel, and spoke similarly to them; and the men of Penuel answered him just as the men of Succoth had answered.

9 So he spoke also to the men of Penuel, saying, "When I return safely, I will tear down this tower."

10 Now Zebah and Zalmunna were in Karkor, and their armies with them, about 15,000 men, all who were left of the entire army of the sons of the east; for the fallen were 120,000 swordsmen.

11 And Gideon went up by the way of those who lived in tents on the east of Nobah and Jogbehah, and attacked the camp, when the camp was unsuspecting.

12 When Zebah and Zalmunna fled, he pursued them and captured the two kings of Midian, Zebah and Zalmunna, and routed the whole army.

13 ¶ Then Gideon the son of Joash returned from the battle by the ascent of Heres.

14 And he captured a youth from Succoth and questioned him. Then *the youth* wrote down for him the princes of Succoth and its elders, seventy-seven men.

15 And he came to the men of Succoth and said, "Behold Zebah and Zalmunna, concerning whom you taunted me, saying, 'Are the hands of Zebah and Zalmunna already in your hand, that we should give bread to your men who are weary?' "

16 And he took the elders of the city, and thorns of the wilderness and briers, and he disciplined the men of Succoth with them.

17 And he tore down the tower of Penuel and killed the men of the city.

18 ¶ Then he said to Zebah and Zalmunna, "What kind of men *were* they whom you killed at Tabor?" And they said, "They were like you, each one resembling the son of a king."

19 And he said, "They *were* my brothers, the sons of my mother. *As* the LORD lives, if only you had let them live, I would not kill you."

20 So he said to Jether his first-born, "Rise, kill them." But the youth did not draw his sword, for he was afraid, because he was still a youth.

21 Then Zebah and Zalmunna said, "Rise up yourself, and fall on us; for as the man, so is his strength." So Gideon arose and killed Zebah and Zalmunna, and took the crescent ornaments which were on their camels' necks.

22 ¶ Then the men of Israel said to Gideon, "Rule over us, both you and your son, also your son's son, for you have delivered us from the hand of Midian."

23 But Gideon said to them, "I will not rule over you, nor shall my son rule over you; the LORD shall rule over you."

24 Yet Gideon said to them, "I would request of you, that each of you give me an earring from his spoil." (For they had gold earrings, because they were Ishmaelites.)

25 And they said, "We will surely give *them*." So they spread out a garment, and every one of them threw an earring there from his spoil.

26 And the weight of the gold earrings that he requested was 1,700 *shekels* of gold, besides the crescent ornaments and the pendants and the purple robes which *were* on the kings of Midian, and besides the neck bands that *were* on their camels' necks.

27 And Gideon made it into an ephod, and placed it in his city, Ophrah, and all Israel played the harlot with it there, so that it became a snare to Gideon and his household.

28 So Midian was subdued before the sons of Israel, and they did not lift up their heads anymore. And the land was undisturbed for forty years in the days of Gideon.

29 ¶ Then Jerubbaal the son of Joash went and lived in his own house.

30 Now Gideon had seventy sons who were his direct descendants, for he had many wives.

31 And his concubine who was in Shechem also bore him a son, and he named him Abimelech.

32 And Gideon the son of Joash died at a ripe old age and was buried in the

tomb of his father Joash, in Ophrah of the Abiezrites.

33 ¶ Then it came about, as soon as Gideon was dead, that the sons of Israel again played the harlot with the Baals, and made Baal-berith their god.

34 Thus the sons of Israel did not remember the Lord their God, who had delivered them from the hands of all their enemies on every side;

35 nor did they show kindness to the household of Jerubbaal (*that is*, Gideon), in accord with all the good that he had done to Israel.

CHAPTER 9

AND Abimelech the son of Jerubbaal went to Shechem to his mother's relatives, and spoke to them and to the whole clan of the household of his mother's father, saying,

2 "Speak, now, in the hearing of all the leaders of Shechem, 'Which is better for you, that seventy men, all the sons of Jerubbaal, rule over you, or that one man rule over you?' Also, remember that I am your bone and your flesh."

3 And his mother's relatives spoke all these words on his behalf in the hearing of all the leaders of Shechem; and they were inclined to follow Abimelech, for they said, "He is our relative."

4 And they gave him seventy *pieces* of silver from the house of Baal-berith with which Abimelech hired worthless and reckless fellows, and they followed him.

5 Then he went to his father's house at Ophrah, and killed his brothers the sons of Jerubbaal, seventy men, on one stone. But Jotham the youngest son of Jerubbaal was left, for he hid himself.

6 And all the men of Shechem and all [12]Beth-millo assembled together, and they went and made Abimelech king, by the oak of the pillar which was in Shechem.

7 ¶ Now when they told Jotham, he went and stood on the top of Mount Gerizim, and lifted his voice and called out. Thus he said to them, "Listen to me, O men of Shechem, that God may listen to you.

8 "Once the trees went forth to anoint a king over them, and they said to the olive tree, 'Reign over us!'

9 "But the olive tree said to them, 'Shall I leave my fatness with which God and men are honored, and go to wave over the trees?'

10 "Then the trees said to the fig tree, 'You come, reign over us!'

11 "But the fig tree said to them, 'Shall I leave my sweetness and my good fruit, and go to wave over the trees?'

12 "Then the trees said to the vine, 'You come, reign over us!'

13 "But the vine said to them, 'Shall I leave my new wine, which cheers God and men, and go to wave over the trees?'

14 "Finally all the trees said to the bramble, 'You come, reign over us!'

15 "And the bramble said to the trees, 'If in truth you are anointing me as king over you, come and take refuge in my shade; but if not, may fire come out from the bramble and consume the cedars of Lebanon.'

16 ¶ "Now therefore, if you have dealt in truth and integrity in making Abimelech king, and if you have dealt well with Jerubbaal and his house, and have dealt with him as he deserved—

17 for my father fought for you and risked his life and delivered you from the hand of Midian;

18 but you have risen against my father's house today and have killed his sons, seventy men, on one stone, and have made Abimelech, the son of his maidservant, king over the men of Shechem, because he is your relative—

19 if then you have dealt in truth and integrity with Jerubbaal and his house this day, rejoice in Abimelech, and let him also rejoice in you.

20 "But if not, let fire come out from Abimelech and consume the men of Shechem and Beth-millo; and let fire come out from the men of Shechem and from Beth-millo, and consume Abimelech."

21 Then Jotham escaped and fled, and went to Beer and remained there because of Abimelech his brother.

22 ¶ Now Abimelech ruled over Israel three years.

[12] Or, *the house of Millo*

23 Then God sent an evil spirit between Abimelech and the men of Shechem; and the men of Shechem dealt treacherously with Abimelech,

24 in order that the violence done to the seventy sons of Jerubbaal might come, and their blood might be laid on Abimelech their brother, who killed them, and on the men of Shechem, who strengthened his hands to kill his brothers.

25 And the men of Shechem set men in ambush against him on the tops of the mountains, and they robbed all who might pass by them along the road; and it was told to Abimelech.

26 ¶ Now Gaal the son of Ebed came with his relatives, and crossed over into Shechem; and the men of Shechem put their trust in him.

27 And they went out into the field and gathered *the grapes of* their vineyards and trod *them*, and held a festival; and they went into the house of their god, and ate and drank and cursed Abimelech.

28 Then Gaal the son of Ebed said, "Who is Abimelech, and who is Shechem, that we should serve him? Is he not the son of Jerubbaal, and *is* Zebul *not* his lieutenant? Serve the men of Hamor the father of Shechem; but why should we serve him?

29 "Would, therefore, that this people were under my authority! Then I would remove Abimelech." And he said to Abimelech, "Increase your army, and come out."

30 ¶ And when Zebul the ruler of the city heard the words of Gaal the son of Ebed, his anger burned.

31 And he sent messengers to Abimelech deceitfully, saying, "Behold, Gaal the son of Ebed and his relatives have come to Shechem; and behold, they are stirring up the city against you.

32 "Now therefore, arise by night, you and the people who are with you, and lie in wait in the field.

33 "And it shall come about in the morning, as soon as the sun is up, that you shall rise early and rush upon the city; and behold, when he and the people who are with him come out against you, you shall do to them whatever you can."

34 ¶ So Abimelech and all the people who *were* with him arose by night and lay in wait against Shechem in four companies.

35 Now Gaal the son of Ebed went out and stood in the entrance of the city gate; and Abimelech and the people who *were* with him arose from the ambush.

36 And when Gaal saw the people, he said to Zebul, "Look, people are coming down from the tops of the mountains." But Zebul said to him, "You are seeing the shadow of the mountains as *if they were* men."

37 And Gaal spoke again and said, "Behold, people are coming down from the highest part of the land, and one company comes by the way of the diviners' oak."

38 Then Zebul said to him, "Where is your boasting now with which you said, 'Who is Abimelech that we should serve him?' Is this not the people whom you despised? Go out now and fight with them!"

39 So Gaal went out before the leaders of Shechem and fought with Abimelech.

40 And Abimelech chased him, and he fled before him; and many fell wounded up to the entrance of the gate.

41 Then Abimelech remained at Arumah, but Zebul drove out Gaal and his relatives so that they could not remain in Shechem.

42 ¶ Now it came about the next day, that the people went out to the field, and it was told to Abimelech.

43 So he took his people and divided them into three companies, and lay in wait in the field; when he looked and saw the people coming out from the city, he arose against them and slew them.

44 Then Abimelech and the company who was with him dashed forward and stood in the entrance of the city gate; the other two companies then dashed against all who *were* in the field and slew them.

45 And Abimelech fought against the city all that day, and he captured the city and killed the people who *were* in it; then he razed the city and sowed it with salt.

46 ¶ When all the leaders of the tower of Shechem heard of *it*, they entered the inner chamber of the temple of El-berith.

47 And it was told Abimelech that all the leaders of the tower of Shechem were gathered together.

48 So Abimelech went up to Mount Zalmon, he and all the people who *were* with him; and Abimelech took an axe in his hand and cut down a branch from the trees, and lifted it and laid *it* on his shoulder. Then he said to the people who *were* with him, "What you have seen me do, hurry *and* do likewise."

49 And all the people also cut down each one his branch and followed Abimelech, and put *them* on the inner chamber and set the inner chamber on fire over those *inside,* so that all the men of the tower of Shechem also died, about a thousand men and women.

50 ¶ Then Abimelech went to Thebez, and he camped against Thebez and captured it.

51 But there was a strong tower in the center of the city, and all the men and women with all the leaders of the city fled there and shut themselves in; and they went up on the roof of the tower.

52 So Abimelech came to the tower and fought against it, and approached the entrance of the tower to burn it with fire.

53 But a certain woman threw an upper millstone on Abimelech's head, crushing his skull.

54 Then he called quickly to the young man, his armor bearer, and said to him, "Draw your sword and kill me, lest it be said of me, 'A woman slew him.'" So the young man pierced him through, and he died.

55 And when the men of Israel saw that Abimelech was dead, each departed to his home.

56 Thus God repaid the wickedness of Abimelech, which he had done to his father, in killing his seventy brothers.

57 Also God returned all the wickedness of the men of Shechem on their heads, and the curse of Jotham the son of Jerubbaal came upon them.

CHAPTER 10

NOW after Abimelech died, Tola the son of Puah, the son of Dodo, a man of Issachar, arose to save Israel; and he lived in Shamir in the hill country of Ephraim.

2 And he judged Israel twenty-three years. Then he died and was buried in Shamir.

3 ¶ And after him, Jair the Gileadite arose, and judged Israel twenty-two years.

4 And he had thirty sons who rode on thirty donkeys, and they had thirty cities in the land of Gilead that are called Havvoth-jair to this day.

5 And Jair died and was buried in Kamon.

6 ¶ Then the sons of Israel again did evil in the sight of the LORD, served the Baals and the Ashtaroth, the gods of Aram, the gods of Sidon, the gods of Moab, the gods of the sons of Ammon, and the gods of the Philistines; thus they forsook the LORD and did not serve Him.

7 And the anger of the LORD burned against Israel, and He sold them into the hands of the Philistines, and into the hands of the sons of Ammon.

8 And they afflicted and crushed the sons of Israel that year; for eighteen years they *afflicted* all the sons of Israel who were beyond the Jordan in Gilead in the land of the Amorites.

9 And the sons of Ammon crossed the Jordan to fight also against Judah, Benjamin, and the house of Ephraim, so that Israel was greatly distressed.

10 ¶ Then the sons of Israel cried out to the LORD, saying, "We have sinned against Thee, for indeed, we have forsaken our God and served the Baals."

11 And the LORD said to the sons of Israel, "*Did I* not *deliver you* from the Egyptians, the Amorites, the sons of Ammon, and the Philistines?

12 "Also when the Sidonians, the Amalekites and the Maonites oppressed you, you cried out to Me, and I delivered you from their hands.

13 "Yet you have forsaken Me and served other gods; therefore I will deliver you no more.

14 "Go and cry out to the gods which you have chosen; let them deliver you in the time of your distress."

15 And the sons of Israel said to the LORD, "We have sinned, do to us whatever seems good to Thee; only please deliver us this day."

16 So they put away the foreign gods from among them, and served the LORD; and He could bear the misery of Israel no longer.

17 ¶ Then the sons of Ammon were summoned, and they camped in Gilead. And the sons of Israel gathered together, and camped in Mizpah.

18 And the people, the leaders of Gilead, said to one another, "Who is the man who will begin to fight against the sons of Ammon? He shall become head over all the inhabitants of Gilead."

CHAPTER 11

NOW Jephthah the Gileadite was a valiant warrior, but he was the son of a harlot. And Gilead was the father of Jephthah.

2 And Gilead's wife bore him sons; and when his wife's sons grew up, they drove Jephthah out and said to him, "You shall not have an inheritance in our father's house, for you are the son of another woman."

3 So Jephthah fled from his brothers and lived in the land of Tob; and worthless fellows gathered themselves about Jephthah, and they went out with him.

4 ¶ And it came about after a while that the sons of Ammon fought against Israel.

5 And it happened when the sons of Ammon fought against Israel that the elders of Gilead went to get Jephthah from the land of Tob;

6 and they said to Jephthah, "Come and be our chief that we may fight against the sons of Ammon."

7 Then Jephthah said to the elders of Gilead, "Did you not hate me and drive me from my father's house? So why have you come to me now when you are in trouble?"

8 And the elders of Gilead said to Jephthah, "For this reason we have now returned to you, that you may go with us and fight with the sons of Ammon and become head over all the inhabitants of Gilead."

9 So Jephthah said to the elders of Gilead, "If you take me back to fight against the sons of Ammon and the LORD gives them up to me, will I become your head?"

10 And the elders of Gilead said to Jephthah, "The LORD is witness between us; surely we will do as you have said."

11 Then Jephthah went with the elders of Gilead, and the people made him head and chief over them; and Jephthah spoke all his words before the LORD at Mizpah.

12 ¶ Now Jephthah sent messengers to the king of the sons of Ammon, saying, "What is between you and me, that you have come to me to fight against my land?"

13 And the king of the sons of Ammon said to the messengers of Jephthah, "Because Israel took away my land when they came up from Egypt, from the Arnon as far as the Jabbok and the Jordan; therefore, return them peaceably now."

14 But Jephthah sent messengers again to the king of the sons of Ammon,

15 and they said to him, "Thus says Jephthah, 'Israel did not take away the land of Moab, nor the land of the sons of Ammon.

16 'For when they came up from Egypt, and Israel went through the wilderness to the Red Sea and came to Kadesh,

17 then Israel sent messengers to the king of Edom, saying, "Please let us pass through your land," but the king of Edom would not listen. And they also sent to the king of Moab, but he would not consent. So Israel remained at Kadesh.

18 'Then they went through the wilderness and around the land of Edom and the land of Moab, and came to the east side of the land of Moab, and they camped beyond the Arnon; but they did not enter the territory of Moab, for the Arnon was the border of Moab.

19 'And Israel sent messengers to Sihon king of the Amorites, the king of Heshbon, and Israel said to him, "Please let us pass through your land to our place."

20 'But Sihon did not trust Israel to pass through his territory; so Sihon gathered all his people and camped in Jahaz, and fought with Israel.

21 'And the LORD, the God of Israel, gave Sihon and all his people into the hand of Israel, and they defeated them; so Israel possessed all the land

of the Amorites, the inhabitants of that country.

22 'So they possessed all the territory of the Amorites, from the Arnon as far as the Jabbok, and from the wilderness as far as the Jordan.

23 'Since now the LORD, the God of Israel, drove out the Amorites from before His people Israel, are you then to possess it?

24 'Do you not possess what Chemosh your god gives you to possess? So whatever the LORD our God has driven out before us, we will possess it.

25 'And now are you any better than Balak the son of Zippor, king of Moab? Did he ever strive with Israel, or did he ever fight against them?

26 'While Israel lived in Heshbon and its villages, and in Aroer and its villages, and in all the cities that are on the banks of the Arnon, three hundred years, why did you not recover them within that time?

27 'I therefore have not sinned against you, but you are doing me wrong by making war against me; may the LORD, the Judge, judge today between the sons of Israel and the sons of Ammon.' "

28 But the king of the sons of Ammon disregarded the message which Jephthah sent him.

29 ¶ Now the Spirit of the LORD came upon Jephthah, so that he passed through Gilead and Manasseh; then he passed through Mizpah of Gilead, and from Mizpah of Gilead he went on to the sons of Ammon.

30 And Jephthah made a vow to the LORD and said, "If Thou wilt indeed give the sons of Ammon into my hand,

31 then it shall be that whatever comes out of the doors of my house to meet me when I return in peace from the sons of Ammon, it shall be the LORD's, and I will offer it up as a burnt offering."

32 So Jephthah crossed over to the sons of Ammon to fight against them; and the LORD gave them into his hand.

33 And he struck them with a very great slaughter from Aroer to the entrance of Minnith, twenty cities, and as far as Abel-keramim. So the sons of Ammon were subdued before the sons of Israel.

34 ¶ When Jephthah came to his house at Mizpah, behold, his daughter was coming out to meet him with tambourines and with dancing. Now she was his one *and* only child; besides her he had neither son nor daughter.

35 And it came about when he saw her, that he tore his clothes and said, "Alas, my daughter! You have brought me very low, and you are among those who trouble me; for I have given my word to the LORD, and I cannot take *it* back."

36 So she said to him, "My father, you have given your word to the LORD; do to me as you have said, since the LORD has avenged you of your enemies, the sons of Ammon."

37 And she said to her father, "Let this thing be done for me; let me alone two months, that I may go to the mountains and weep because of my virginity, I and my companions."

38 Then he said, "Go." So he sent her away for two months; and she left with her companions, and wept on the mountains because of her virginity.

39 And it came about at the end of two months that she returned to her father, who did to her according to the vow which he had made; and she had no relations with a man. Thus it became a custom in Israel,

40 that the daughters of Israel went yearly to commemorate the daughter of Jephthah the Gileadite four days in the year.

CHAPTER 12

THEN the men of Ephraim were summoned, and they crossed to Zaphon and said to Jephthah, "Why did you cross over to fight against the sons of Ammon without calling us to go with you? We will burn your house down on you."

2 And Jephthah said to them, "I and my people were at great strife with the sons of Ammon; when I called you, you did not deliver me from their hand.

3 "And when I saw that you would not deliver *me,* I took my life in my hands and crossed over against the sons of Ammon, and the LORD gave them into my hand. Why then have you come up to me this day, to fight against me?"

4 Then Jephthah gathered all the men of Gilead and fought Ephraim;

and the men of Gilead defeated Ephraim, because they said, "You are fugitives of Ephraim, O Gileadites, in the midst of Ephraim *and* in the midst of Manasseh."

5 And the Gileadites captured the fords of the Jordan opposite Ephraim. And it happened when *any of* the fugitives of Ephraim said, "Let me cross over," the men of Gilead would say to him, "Are you an Ephraimite?" If he said, "No,"

6 then they would say to him, "Say now, 'Shibboleth.' " But he said, "Sibboleth," for he could not pronounce it correctly. Then they seized him and slew him at the fords of the Jordan. Thus there fell at that time 42,000 of Ephraim.

7 And Jephthah judged Israel six years. Then Jephthah the Gileadite died and was buried in *one of* the cities of Gilead.

8 ¶ Now Ibzan of Bethlehem judged Israel after him.

9 And he had thirty sons, and thirty daughters *whom* he gave in marriage outside *the family,* and he brought in thirty daughters from outside for his sons. And he judged Israel seven years.

10 Then Ibzan died and was buried in Bethlehem.

11 ¶ Now Elon the Zebulunite judged Israel after him; and he judged Israel ten years.

12 Then Elon the Zebulunite died and was buried at Aijalon in the land of Zebulun.

13 ¶ Now Abdon the son of Hillel the Pirathonite judged Israel after him.

14 And he had forty sons and thirty grandsons who rode on seventy donkeys; and he judged Israel eight years.

15 Then Abdon the son of Hillel the Pirathonite died and was buried at Pirathon in the land of Ephraim, in the hill country of the Amalekites.

CHAPTER 13

Now the sons of Israel again did evil in the sight of the Lord, so that the Lord gave them into the hands of the Philistines forty years.

2 ¶ And there was a certain man of Zorah, of the family of the Danites, whose name was Manoah; and his wife was barren and had borne no *children.*

3 Then the angel of the Lord appeared to the woman, and said to her, "Behold now, you are barren and have borne no *children,* but you shall conceive and give birth to a son.

4"Now therefore, be careful not to drink wine or strong drink, nor eat any unclean thing.

5"For behold, you shall conceive and give birth to a son, and no razor shall come upon his head, for the boy shall be a Nazirite to God from the womb; and he shall begin to deliver Israel from the hands of the Philistines."

6 Then the woman came and told her husband, saying, "A man of God came to me and his appearance was like the appearance of the angel of God, very awesome. And I did not ask him where he *came* from, nor did he tell me his name.

7"But he said to me, 'Behold, you shall conceive and give birth to a son, and now you shall not drink wine or strong drink nor eat any unclean thing, for the boy shall be a Nazirite to God from the womb to the day of his death.' "

8 ¶ Then Manoah entreated the Lord and said, "O Lord, please let the man of God whom Thou hast sent come to us again that he may teach us what to do for the boy who is to be born."

9 And God listened to the voice of Manoah; and the angel of God came again to the woman as she was sitting in the field, but Manoah her husband was not with her.

10 So the woman ran quickly and told her husband, "Behold, the man who came the *other* day has appeared to me."

11 Then Manoah arose and followed his wife, and when he came to the man he said to him, "Are you the man who spoke to the woman?" And he said, "I am."

12 And Manoah said, "Now when your words come *to pass,* what shall be the boy's mode of life and his vocation?"

13 So the angel of the Lord said to

Manoah, "Let the woman pay attention to all that I said.

14 "She should not eat anything that comes from the vine nor drink wine or strong drink, nor eat any unclean thing; let her observe all that I commanded."

15 ¶ Then Manoah said to the angel of the LORD, "Please let us detain you so that we may prepare a kid for you."

16 And the angel of the LORD said to Manoah, "Though you detain me, I will not eat your food, but if you prepare a burnt offering, *then* offer it to the LORD." For Manoah did not know that he was the angel of the LORD.

17 And Manoah said to the angel of the LORD, "What is your name, so that when your words come *to pass*, we may honor you?"

18 But the angel of the LORD said to him, "Why do you ask my name, seeing it is [13]wonderful?"

19 So Manoah took the kid with the grain offering and offered it on the rock to the LORD, and He performed wonders while Manoah and his wife looked on.

20 For it came about when the flame went up from the altar toward heaven, that the angel of the LORD ascended in the flame of the altar. When Manoah and his wife saw *this*, they fell on their faces to the ground.

21 Now the angel of the LORD appeared no more to Manoah or his wife. Then Manoah knew that he was the angel of the LORD.

22 So Manoah said to his wife, "We shall surely die, for we have seen God."

23 But his wife said to him, "If the LORD had desired to kill us, He would not have accepted a burnt offering and a grain offering from our hands, nor would He have shown us all these things, nor would He have let us hear *things* like this at this time."

24 ¶ Then the woman gave birth to a son and named him Samson; and the child grew up and the LORD blessed him.

25 And the Spirit of the LORD began to stir him in [14]Mahaneh-dan, between Zorah and Eshtaol.

CHAPTER 14

THEN Samson went down to Timnah and saw a woman in Timnah, *one* of the daughters of the Philistines.

2 So he came back and told his father and mother, "I saw a woman in Timnah, *one* of the daughters of the Philistines; now therefore, get her for me as a wife."

3 Then his father and his mother said to him, "Is there no woman among the daughters of your relatives, or among all our people, that you go to take a wife from the uncircumcised Philistines?" But Samson said to his father, "Get her for me, for she looks good to me."

4 However, his father and mother did not know that it was of the LORD, for He was seeking an occasion against the Philistines. Now at that time the Philistines were ruling over Israel.

5 ¶ Then Samson went down to Timnah with his father and mother, and came as far as the vineyards of Timnah; and behold, a young lion *came* roaring toward him.

6 And the Spirit of the LORD came upon him mightily, so that he tore him as one tears a kid though he had nothing in his hand; but he did not tell his father or mother what he had done.

7 So he went down and talked to the woman; and she looked good to Samson.

8 When he returned later to take her, he turned aside to look at the carcass of the lion; and behold, a swarm of bees and honey were in the body of the lion.

9 So he scraped the honey into his hands and went on, eating as he went. When he came to his father and mother, he gave *some* to them and they ate *it*; but he did not tell them that he had scraped the honey out of the body of the lion.

10 ¶ Then his father went down to the woman; and Samson made a feast there, for the young men customarily did this.

11 And it came about when they saw him that they brought thirty companions to be with him.

12 Then Samson said to them, "Let me now propound a riddle to you; if

---

[13] I.e., incomprehensible   [14] I.e., the camp of Dan

you will indeed tell it to me within the seven days of the feast, and find it out, then I will give you thirty linen wraps and thirty changes of clothes.

13 "But if you are unable to tell me, then you shall give me thirty linen wraps and thirty changes of clothes." And they said to him, "Propound your riddle, that we may hear it."

14 So he said to them,

"Out of the eater came something to eat,

And out of the strong came something sweet."

But they could not tell the riddle in three days.

15 ¶ Then it came about on the fourth day that they said to Samson's wife, "Entice your husband, that he may tell us the riddle, lest we burn you and your father's house with fire. Have you invited us to impoverish us? Is this not so?"

16 And Samson's wife wept before him and said, "You only hate me, and you do not love me; you have propounded a riddle to the sons of my people, and have not told it to me." And he said to her, "Behold, I have not told it to my father or mother; so should I tell you?"

17 However she wept before him seven days while their feast lasted. And it came about on the seventh day that he told her because she pressed him so hard. She then told the riddle to the sons of her people.

18 So the men of the city said to him on the seventh day before the sun went down,

"What is sweeter than honey?

And what is stronger than a lion?"

And he said to them,

"If you had not plowed with my heifer,

You would not have found out my riddle."

19 Then the Spirit of the LORD came upon him mightily, and he went down to Ashkelon and killed thirty of them and took their spoil, and gave the changes of clothes to those who told the riddle. And his anger burned, and he went up to his father's house.

20 But Samson's wife was given to his companion who had been his friend.

CHAPTER 15

BUT after a while, in the time of wheat harvest, it came about that Samson visited his wife with a young goat, and said, "I will go in to my wife in her room." But her father did not let him enter.

2 And her father said, "I really thought that you hated her intensely; so I gave her to your companion. Is not her younger sister more beautiful than she? Please let her be yours instead."

3 Samson then said to them, "This time I shall be blameless in regard to the Philistines when I do them harm."

4 And Samson went and caught three hundred foxes, and took torches, and turned the foxes tail to tail, and put one torch in the middle between two tails.

5 When he had set fire to the torches, he released the foxes into the standing grain of the Philistines, thus burning up both the shocks and the standing grain, along with the vineyards and groves.

6 Then the Philistines said, "Who did this?" And they said, "Samson, the son-in-law of the Timnite, because he took his wife and gave her to his companion." So the Philistines came up and burned her and her father with fire.

7 And Samson said to them, "Since you act like this, I will surely take revenge on you, but after that I will quit."

8 And he struck them ruthlessly with a great slaughter; and he went down and lived in the cleft of the rock of Etam.

9 ¶ Then the Philistines went up and camped in Judah, and spread out in Lehi.

10 And the men of Judah said, "Why have you come up against us?" And they said, "We have come up to bind Samson in order to do to him as he did to us."

11 Then 3,000 men of Judah went down to the cleft of the rock of Etam and said to Samson, "Do you not know that the Philistines are rulers over us? What then is this that you have done to us?" And he said to them, "As they did to me, so I have done to them."

12 And they said to him, "We have come down to bind you so that we may give you into the hands of the Philistines." And Samson said to them, "Swear to me that you will not kill me."

13 So they said to him, "No, but we will bind you fast and give you into their hands; yet surely we will not kill you." Then they bound him with two new ropes and brought him up from the rock.

14 ¶ When he came to Lehi, the Philistines shouted as they met him. And the Spirit of the LORD came upon him mightily so that the ropes that were on his arms were as flax that is burned with fire, and his bonds dropped from his hands.

15 And he found a fresh jawbone of a donkey, so he reached out and took it and killed a thousand men with it.

16 Then Samson said,

"With the jawbone of a donkey,
    Heaps upon heaps,
With the jawbone of a donkey
    I have killed a thousand men."

17 And it came about when he had finished speaking, that he threw the jawbone from his hand; and he named that place [15]Ramath-lehi.

18 Then he became very thirsty, and he called to the LORD and said, "Thou hast given this great deliverance by the hand of Thy servant, and now shall I die of thirst and fall into the hands of the uncircumcised?"

19 But God split the hollow place that is in Lehi so that water came out of it. When he drank, his strength returned and he revived. Therefore, he named it En-hakkore, which is in Lehi to this day.

20 So he judged Israel twenty years in the days of the Philistines.

CHAPTER 16

NOW Samson went to Gaza and saw a harlot there, and went in to her.

2 *When it was told* to the Gazites, saying, "Samson has come here," they surrounded *the place* and lay in wait for him all night at the gate of the city. And they kept silent all night, saying, "*Let us wait* until the morning light, then we will kill him."

3 Now Samson lay until midnight, and at midnight he arose and took hold of the doors of the city gate and the two posts and pulled them up along with the bars; then he put them on his shoulders and carried them up to the top of the mountain which is opposite Hebron.

4 ¶ After this it came about that he loved a woman in the valley of Sorek, whose name was Delilah.

5 And the lords of the Philistines came up to her, and said to her, "Entice him, and see where his great strength *lies* and how we may overpower him that we may bind him to afflict him. Then we will each give you eleven hundred *pieces* of silver."

6 So Delilah said to Samson, "Please tell me where your great strength is and how you may be bound to afflict you."

7 And Samson said to her, "If they bind me with seven fresh cords that have not been dried, then I shall become weak and be like any *other* man."

8 Then the lords of the Philistines brought up to her seven fresh cords that had not been dried, and she bound him with them.

9 Now she had *men* lying in wait in an inner room. And she said to him, "The Philistines are upon you, Samson!" But he snapped the cords as a string of tow snaps when it touches fire. So his strength was not discovered.

10 ¶ Then Delilah said to Samson, "Behold, you have deceived me and told me lies; now please tell me, how you may be bound."

11 And he said to her, "If they bind me tightly with new ropes which have not been used, then I shall become weak and be like any *other* man."

12 So Delilah took new ropes and bound him with them and said to him, "The Philistines are upon you, Samson!" For the *men* were lying in wait in the inner room. But he snapped the ropes from his arms like a thread.

13 ¶ Then Delilah said to Samson, "Up to now you have deceived me and told me lies; tell me how you may be bound." And he said to her, "If you weave the seven locks of my hair with the web [16][and fasten it with a pin,

---

[15] I.e., the high place of the jawbone

[16] The passage in brackets is found in Gr. but not in any Heb. mss.

then I shall become weak and be like any other man."

14 So while he slept, Delilah took the seven locks of his hair and wove them into the web]. And she fastened *it* with the pin, and said to him, "The Philistines are upon you, Samson!" But he awoke from his sleep and pulled out the pin of the loom and the web.

15 ¶ Then she said to him, "How can you say, 'I love you,' when your heart is not with me? You have deceived me these three times and have not told me where your great strength is."

16 And it came about when she pressed him daily with her words and urged him, that his soul was annoyed to death.

17 So he told her all *that was* in his heart and said to her, "A razor has never come on my head, for I have been a Nazirite to God from my mother's womb. If I am shaved, then my strength will leave me and I shall become weak and be like any *other* man."

18 ¶ When Delilah saw that he had told her all *that was* in his heart, she sent and called the lords of the Philistines, saying, "Come up once more, for he has told me all *that is* in his heart." Then the lords of the Philistines came up to her, and brought the money in their hands.

19 And she made him sleep on her knees, and called for a man and had him shave off the seven locks of his hair. Then she began to afflict him, and his strength left him.

20 And she said, "The Philistines are upon you, Samson!" And he awoke from his sleep and said, "I will go out as at other times and shake myself free." But he did not know that the LORD had departed from him.

21 Then the Philistines seized him and gouged out his eyes; and they brought him down to Gaza and bound him with bronze chains, and he was a grinder in the prison.

22 However, the hair of his head began to grow again after it was shaved off.

23 ¶ Now the lords of the Philistines assembled to offer a great sacrifice to Dagon their god, and to rejoice, for they said,

"Our god has given Samson our
   enemy into our hands."

24 When the people saw him, they praised their god, for they said,

"Our god has given our enemy
   into our hands,
Even the destroyer of our country,
Who has slain many of us."

25 It so happened when they were in high spirits, that they said, "Call for Samson, that he may amuse us." So they called for Samson from the prison, and he entertained them. And they made him stand between the pillars.

26 Then Samson said to the boy who was holding his hand, "Let me feel the pillars on which the house rests, that I may lean against them."

27 Now the house was full of men and women, and all the lords of the Philistines were there. And about 3,000 men and women were on the roof looking on while Samson was amusing *them.*

28 ¶ Then Samson called to the LORD and said, "O Lord GOD, please remember me and please strengthen me just this time, O God, that I may at once be avenged of the Philistines for my two eyes."

29 And Samson grasped the two middle pillars on which the house rested, and braced himself against them, the one with his right hand and the other with his left.

30 And Samson said, "Let me die with the Philistines!" And he bent with all his might so that the house fell on the lords and all the people who were in it. So the dead whom he killed at his death were more than those whom he killed in his life.

31 Then his brothers and all his father's household came down, took him, brought him up, and buried him between Zorah and Eshtaol in the tomb of Manoah his father. Thus he had judged Israel twenty years.

CHAPTER 17

NOW there was a man of the hill country of Ephraim whose name was Micah.

2 And he said to his mother, "The eleven hundred *pieces* of silver which were taken from you, about which you uttered a curse in my hearing, behold, the silver is with me; I took it." And

his mother said, "Blessed be my son by the LORD."

3 He then returned the eleven hundred *pieces* of silver to his mother, and his mother said, "I wholly dedicate the silver from my hand to the LORD for my son to make a graven image and a molten image; now therefore, I will return them to you."

4 So when he returned the silver to his mother, his mother took two hundred *pieces* of silver and gave them to the silversmith who made them into a graven image and a molten image, and they were in the house of Micah.

5 And the man Micah had a [17]shrine and he made an ephod and household idols and consecrated one of his sons, that he might become his priest.

6 In those days there was no king in Israel; every man did what was right in his own eyes.

7 ¶ Now there was a young man from Bethlehem in Judah, of the family of Judah, who was a Levite; and he was staying there.

8 Then the man departed from the city, from Bethlehem in Judah, to stay wherever he might find *a place;* and as he made his journey, he came to the hill country of Ephraim to the house of Micah.

9 And Micah said to him, "Where do you come from?" And he said to him, "I am a Levite from Bethlehem in Judah, and I am going to stay wherever I may find *a place.*"

10 Micah then said to him, "Dwell with me and be a father and a priest to me, and I will give you ten *pieces* of silver a year, a suit of clothes, and your maintenance." So the Levite went *in.*

11 And the Levite agreed to live with the man; and the young man became to him like one of his sons.

12 So Micah consecrated the Levite, and the young man became his priest and lived in the house of Micah.

13 Then Micah said, "Now I know that the LORD will prosper me, seeing I have a Levite as priest."

CHAPTER 18

IN those days there was no king of Israel; and in those days the tribe of

[17] Lit., *house of gods*

the Danites was seeking an inheritance for themselves to live in, for until that day an inheritance had not been allotted to them as a possession among the tribes of Israel.

2 So the sons of Dan sent from their family five men out of their whole number, valiant men from Zorah and Eshtaol, to spy out the land and to search it; and they said to them, "Go, search the land." And they came to the hill country of Ephraim, to the house of Micah, and lodged there.

3 When they were near the house of Micah, they recognized the voice of the young man, the Levite; and they turned aside there, and said to him, "Who brought you here? And what are you doing in this *place?* And what do you have here?"

4 And he said to them, "Thus and so has Micah done to me, and he has hired me, and I have become his priest."

5 And they said to him, "Inquire of God, please, that we may know whether our way on which we are going will be prosperous."

6 And the priest said to them, "Go in peace; your way in which you are going has the LORD's approval."

7 ¶ Then the five men departed and came to Laish and saw the people who were in it living in security, after the manner of the Sidonians, quiet and secure; for there was no ruler humiliating *them* for anything in the land, and they were far from the Sidonians and had no dealings with anyone.

8 When they came back to their brothers at Zorah and Eshtaol, their brothers said to them, "What *do* you *report?* "

9 And they said, "Arise, and let us go up against them; for we have seen the land, and behold, it is very good. And will you sit still? Do not delay to go, to enter, to possess the land.

10 "When you enter, you shall come to a secure people with a spacious land; for God has given it into your hand, a place where there is no lack of anything that is on the earth."

11 ¶ Then from the family of the Danites, from Zorah and from Eshtaol, six hundred men armed with weapons of war set out.

12 And they went up and camped at Kiriath-jearim in Judah. Therefore

they called that place [18]Mahaneh-dan to this day; behold, it is west of Kiriath-jearim.

13 And they passed from there to the hill country of Ephraim and came to the house of Micah.

14 ¶ Then the five men who went to spy out the country of Laish answered and said to their kinsmen, "Do you know that there are in these houses an ephod and [19]household idols and a graven image and a molten image? Now therefore, consider what you should do."

15 And they turned aside there and came to the house of the young man, the Levite, to the house of Micah, and asked him of his welfare.

16 And the six hundred men armed with their weapons of war, who were of the sons of Dan, stood by the entrance of the gate.

17 Now the five men who went to spy out the land went up *and* entered there, *and* took the graven image and the ephod and household idols and the molten image, while the priest stood by the entrance of the gate with the six hundred men armed with weapons of war.

18 And when these went into Micah's house and took the graven image, the ephod and household idols and the molten image, the priest said to them, "What are you doing?"

19 And they said to him, "Be silent, put your hand over your mouth and come with us, and be to us a father and a priest. Is it better for you to be a priest to the house of one man, or to be priest to a tribe and a family in Israel?"

20 And the priest's heart was glad, and he took the ephod and household idols and the graven image, and went among the people.

21 ¶ Then they turned and departed, and put the little ones and the livestock and the valuables in front of them.

22 When they had gone some distance from the house of Micah, the men who *were* in the houses near Micah's house assembled and overtook the sons of Dan.

23 And they cried to the sons of Dan,

who turned around and said to Micah, "What is *the matter* with you, that you have assembled together?"

24 And he said, "You have taken away my gods which I made, and the priest, and have gone away, and what do I have besides? So how can you say to me, 'What is *the matter* with you?' "

25 And the sons of Dan said to him, "Do not let your voice be heard among us, lest fierce men fall upon you and you lose your life, with the lives of your household."

26 So the sons of Dan went on their way; and when Micah saw that they were too strong for him, he turned and went back to his house.

27 ¶ Then they took what Micah had made and the priest who had belonged to him, and came to Laish, to a people quiet and secure, and struck them with the edge of the sword; and they burned the city with fire.

28 And there was no one to deliver *them*, because it was far from Sidon and they had no dealings with anyone, and it was in the valley which is near Beth-rehob. And they rebuilt the city and lived in it.

29 And they called the name of the city Dan, after the name of Dan their father who was born in Israel; however, the name of the city formerly was Laish.

30 And the sons of Dan set up for themselves the graven image; and Jonathan, the son of Gershom, the son of [20]Manasseh, he and his sons were priests to the tribe of the Danites until the day of the captivity of the land.

31 So they set up for themselves Micah's graven image which he had made, all the time that the house of God was at Shiloh.

CHAPTER 19

NOW it came about in those days, when there was no king in Israel, that there was a certain Levite staying in the remote part of the hill country of Ephraim, who took a concubine for himself from Bethlehem in Judah.

2 But his concubine played the harlot against him, and she went away from him to her father's house in Bethlehem in Judah, and was there for a period of four months.

---

[18] I.e., the camp of Dan
[19] Heb., *teraphim,* and so throughout this context
[20] Some ancient versions read *Moses*

3 Then her husband arose and went after her to speak tenderly to her in order to bring her back, taking with him his servant and a pair of donkeys. So she brought him into her father's house, and when the girl's father saw him, he was glad to meet him.

4 And his father-in-law, the girl's father, detained him; and he remained with him three days. So they ate and drank and lodged there.

5 Now it came about on the fourth day that they got up early in the morning, and he prepared to go; and the girl's father said to his son-in-law, "Sustain yourself with a piece of bread, and afterward you may go."

6 So both of them sat down and ate and drank together; and the girl's father said to the man, "Please be willing to spend the night, and let your heart be merry."

7 Then the man arose to go, but his father-in-law urged him so that he spent the night there again.

8 And on the fifth day he arose to go early in the morning, and the girl's father said, "Please sustain yourself, and wait until afternoon"; so both of them ate.

9 When the man arose to go along with his concubine and servant, his father-in-law, the girl's father, said to him, "Behold now, the day has drawn to a close; please spend the night. Lo, the day is coming to an end; spend the night here that your heart may be merry. Then tomorrow you may arise early for your journey so that you may go home."

10 ¶ But the man was not willing to spend the night, so he arose and departed and came to *a place* opposite Jebus (that is, Jerusalem). And there were with him a pair of saddled donkeys; his concubine also was with him.

11 When they *were* near Jebus, the day was almost gone; and the servant said to his master, "Please come, and let us turn aside into this city of the Jebusites and spend the night in it."

12 However, his master said to him, "We will not turn aside into the city of foreigners who are not of the sons of Israel; but we will go on as far as Gibeah."

13 And he said to his servant, "Come and let us approach one of these places; and we will spend the night in Gibeah or Ramah."

14 So they passed along and went their way, and the sun set on them near Gibeah which belongs to Benjamin.

15 And they turned aside there in order to enter *and* lodge in Gibeah. When they entered, they sat down in the open square of the city, for no one took them into *his* house to spend the night.

16 ¶ Then behold, an old man was coming out of the field from his work at evening. Now the man was from the hill country of Ephraim, and he was staying in Gibeah, but the men of the place were Benjamites.

17 And he lifted up his eyes and saw the traveler in the open square of the city; and the old man said, "Where are you going, and where do you come from?"

18 And he said to him, "We are passing from Bethlehem in Judah to the remote part of the hill country of Ephraim, *for* I am from there, and I went to Bethlehem in Judah. But I am *now* going to my house, and no man will take me into his house.

19 "Yet there is both straw and fodder for our donkeys, and also bread and wine for me, your maidservant, and the young man who is with your servants; there is no lack of anything."

20 And the old man said, "Peace to you. Only let me *take care of* all your needs; however, do not spend the night in the open square."

21 So he took him into his house and gave the donkeys fodder, and they washed their feet and ate and drank.

22 ¶ While they were making merry, behold, the men of the city, certain worthless fellows, surrounded the house, pounding the door; and they spoke to the owner of the house, the old man, saying, "Bring out the man who came into your house that we may have relations with him."

23 Then the man, the owner of the house, went out to them and said to them, "No, my fellows, please do not act so wickedly; since this man has come into my house, do not commit this act of folly.

24 "Here is my virgin daughter and his concubine. Please let me bring them out that you may ravish them

and do to them whatever you wish. But do not commit such an act of folly against this man."

25 But the men would not listen to him, so the man seized his concubine and brought *her* out to them. And they raped her and abused her all night until morning, then let her go at the approach of dawn.

26 As the day began to dawn, the woman came and fell down at the doorway of the man's house where her master was, until *full* daylight.

27 ¶ When her master arose in the morning and opened the doors of the house and went out to go on his way, then behold, his concubine was lying at the doorway of the house, with her hands on the threshold.

28 And he said to her, "Get up and let us go," but there was no answer. Then he placed her on the donkey; and the man arose and went to his home.

29 When he entered his house, he took a knife and laid hold of his concubine and cut her in twelve pieces, limb by limb, and sent her throughout the territory of Israel.

30 And it came about that all who saw *it* said, "Nothing like this has *ever* happened or been seen from the day when the sons of Israel came up from the land of Egypt to this day. Consider it, take counsel and speak up!"

CHAPTER 20

THEN all the sons of Israel from Dan to Beersheba, including the land of Gilead, came out, and the congregation assembled as one man to the LORD at Mizpah.

2 And the chiefs of all the people, *even* of all the tribes of Israel, took their stand in the assembly of the people of God, 400,000 foot soldiers who drew the sword.

3 (Now the sons of Benjamin heard that the sons of Israel had gone up to Mizpah.) And the sons of Israel said, "Tell *us,* how did this wickedness take place?"

4 So the Levite, the husband of the woman who was murdered, answered and said, "I came with my concubine to spend the night at Gibeah which belongs to Benjamin.

5"But the men of Gibeah rose up against me and surrounded the house at night because of me. They intended to kill me; instead, they ravished my concubine so that she died.

6"And I took hold of my concubine and cut her in pieces and sent her throughout the land of Israel's inheritance; for they have committed a lewd and disgraceful act in Israel.

7"Behold, all you sons of Israel, give your advice and counsel here."

8 ¶ Then all the people arose as one man, saying, "Not one of us will go to his tent, nor will any of us return to his house.

9"But now this is the thing which we will do to Gibeah; *we will go up* against it by lot.

10"And we will take 10 men out of 100 throughout the tribes of Israel, and 100 out of 1,000, and 1,000 out of 10,000 to supply food for the people, that when they come to Gibeah of Benjamin, they may punish *them* for all the disgraceful acts that they have committed in Israel."

11 Thus all the men of Israel were gathered against the city, united as one man.

12 ¶ Then the tribes of Israel sent men through the entire tribe of Benjamin, saying, "What is this wickedness that has taken place among you?

13"Now then, deliver up the men, the [21]worthless fellows in Gibeah, that we may put them to death and remove *this* wickedness from Israel." But the sons of Benjamin would not listen to the voice of their brothers, the sons of Israel.

14 And the sons of Benjamin gathered from the cities to Gibeah, to go out to battle against the sons of Israel.

15 And from the cities on that day the sons of Benjamin were numbered, 26,000 men who draw the sword, besides the inhabitants of Gibeah who were numbered, 700 choice men.

16 Out of all these people 700 choice men were left-handed; each one could sling a stone at a hair and not miss.

17 ¶ Then the men of Israel besides Benjamin were numbered, 400,000 men who draw the sword; all these were men of war.

18 Now the sons of Israel arose, went up to Bethel, and inquired of God, and said, "Who shall go up first for us to

21 Lit., *sons of Belial*

battle against the sons of Benjamin?" Then the LORD said, "Judah *shall go up* first."

19 ¶ So the sons of Israel arose in the morning and camped against Gibeah.

20 And the men of Israel went out to battle against Benjamin, and the men of Israel arrayed for battle against them at Gibeah.

21 Then the sons of Benjamin came out of Gibeah and felled to the ground on that day 22,000 men of Israel.

22 But the people, the men of Israel, encouraged themselves and arrayed for battle again in the place where they had arrayed themselves the first day.

23 And the sons of Israel went up and wept before the LORD until evening, and inquired of the LORD, saying, "Shall we again draw near for battle against the sons of my brother Benjamin?" And the LORD said, "Go up against him."

24 ¶ Then the sons of Israel came against the sons of Benjamin the second day.

25 And Benjamin went out against them from Gibeah the second day and felled to the ground again 18,000 men of the sons of Israel; all these drew the sword.

26 Then all the sons of Israel and all the people went up and came to Bethel and wept; thus they remained there before the LORD and fasted that day until evening. And they offered burnt offerings and peace offerings before the LORD.

27 And the sons of Israel inquired of the LORD (for the ark of the covenant of God *was* there in those days,

28 and Phinehas the son of Eleazar, Aaron's son, stood before it to *minister* in those days), saying, "Shall I yet again go out to battle against the sons of my brother Benjamin, or shall I cease?" And the LORD said, "Go up, for tomorrow I will deliver them into your hand."

29 ¶ So Israel set men in ambush around Gibeah.

30 And the sons of Israel went up against the sons of Benjamin on the third day and arrayed themselves against Gibeah, as at other times.

31 And the sons of Benjamin went out against the people and were drawn away from the city, and they began to strike and kill some of the people, as at other times, on the highways, one of which goes up to Bethel and the other to Gibeah, *and* in the field, about thirty men of Israel.

32 And the sons of Benjamin said, "They are struck down before us, as at the first." But the sons of Israel said, "Let us flee that we may draw them away from the city to the highways."

33 Then all the men of Israel arose from their place and arrayed themselves at Baal-tamar; and the men of Israel in ambush broke out of their place, even out of Maareh-geba.

34 When ten thousand choice men from all Israel came against Gibeah, the battle became fierce; but Benjamin did not know that disaster was close to them.

35 And the LORD struck Benjamin before Israel, so that the sons of Israel destroyed 25,100 men of Benjamin that day, all who draw the sword.

36 ¶ So the sons of Benjamin saw that they were defeated. When the men of Israel gave ground to Benjamin because they relied on the men in ambush whom they had set against Gibeah,

37 the men in ambush hurried and rushed against Gibeah; the men in ambush also deployed and struck all the city with the edge of the sword.

38 Now the appointed sign between the men of Israel and the men in ambush was that they should make a great cloud of smoke rise from the city.

39 Then the men of Israel turned in the battle, and Benjamin began to strike and kill about thirty men of Israel, for they said, "Surely they are defeated before us, as in the first battle."

40 But when the cloud began to rise from the city in a column of smoke, Benjamin looked behind them; and behold, the whole city was going up *in smoke* to heaven.

41 Then the men of Israel turned, and the men of Benjamin were terrified; for they saw that disaster was close to them.

42 Therefore, they turned their backs before the men of Israel toward the direction of the wilderness, but the battle overtook them while those who

came out of the cities destroyed them in the midst of them.

43 They surrounded Benjamin, pursued them without rest *and* trod them down opposite Gibeah toward the east.

44 Thus 18,000 men of Benjamin fell; all these were valiant warriors.

45 The rest turned and fled toward the wilderness to the rock of Rimmon, but they caught 5,000 of them on the highways and overtook them at Gidom and killed 2,000 of them.

46 So all of Benjamin who fell that day were 25,000 men who draw the sword; all these were valiant warriors.

47 But 600 men turned and fled toward the wilderness to the rock of Rimmon, and they remained at the rock of Rimmon four months.

48 The men of Israel then turned back against the sons of Benjamin and struck them with the edge of the sword, both the entire city with the cattle and all that they found; they also set on fire all the cities which they found.

CHAPTER 21

NOW the men of Israel had sworn in Mizpah, saying, "None of us shall give his daughter to Benjamin in marriage."

2 So the people came to Bethel and sat there before God until evening, and lifted up their voices and wept bitterly.

3 And they said, "Why, O LORD, God of Israel, has this come about in Israel, so that one tribe should be *missing* today in Israel?"

4 And it came about the next day that the people arose early and built an altar there, and offered burnt offerings and peace offerings.

5 ¶ Then the sons of Israel said, "Who is there among all the tribes of Israel who did not come up in the assembly to the LORD?" For they had taken a great oath concerning him who did not come up to the LORD at Mizpah, saying, "He shall surely be put to death."

6 And the sons of Israel were sorry for their brother Benjamin and said, "One tribe is cut off from Israel today.

7 "What shall we do for wives for those who are left, since we have sworn by the LORD not to give them any of our daughters in marriage?"

8 ¶ And they said, "What one is there of the tribes of Israel who did not come up to the LORD at Mizpah?" And behold, no one had come to the camp from Jabesh-gilead to the assembly.

9 For when the people were numbered, behold, not one of the inhabitants of Jabesh-gilead was there.

10 And the congregation sent 12,000 of the valiant warriors there, and commanded them, saying, "Go and strike the inhabitants of Jabesh-gilead with the edge of the sword, with the women and the little ones.

11 "And this is the thing that you shall do: you shall utterly destroy every man and every woman who has lain with a man."

12 And they found among the inhabitants of Jabesh-gilead 400 young virgins who had not known a man by lying with him; and they brought them to the camp at Shiloh, which is in the land of Canaan.

13 ¶ Then the whole congregation sent *word* and spoke to the sons of Benjamin who were at the rock of Rimmon, and proclaimed peace to them.

14 And Benjamin returned at that time, and they gave them the women whom they had kept alive from the women of Jabesh-gilead; yet they were not enough for them.

15 And the people were sorry for Benjamin because the LORD had made a breach in the tribes of Israel.

16 ¶ Then the elders of the congregation said, "What shall we do for wives for those who are left, since the women are destroyed out of Benjamin?"

17 And they said, "*There must be* an inheritance for the survivors of Benjamin, that a tribe may not be blotted out from Israel.

18 "But we cannot give them wives of our daughters." For the sons of Israel had sworn, saying, "Cursed is he who gives a wife to Benjamin."

19 ¶ So they said, "Behold, there is a feast of the LORD from year to year in Shiloh, which is on the north side of Bethel, on the east side of the highway that goes up from Bethel to Shechem, and on the south side of Lebonah."

20 And they commanded the sons of Benjamin, saying, "Go and lie in wait in the vineyards,

21 and watch; and behold, if the daughters of Shiloh come out to take part in the dances, then you shall come out of the vineyards and each of you shall catch his wife from the daughters of Shiloh, and go to the land of Benjamin.

22 "And it shall come about, when their fathers or their brothers come to complain to us, that we shall say to them, 'Give them to us voluntarily, because we did not take for each man *of Benjamin* a wife in battle, nor did you give *them* to them, *else* you would now be guilty.'"

23 And the sons of Benjamin did so, and took wives according to their number from those who danced, whom they carried away. And they went and returned to their inheritance, and rebuilt the cities and lived in them.

24 And the sons of Israel departed from there at that time, every man to his tribe and family, and each one of them went out from there to his inheritance.

25 ¶ In those days there was no king in Israel; everyone did what was right in his own eyes.

THE BOOK OF

RUTH

Now it came about in the days when the judges governed, that there was a famine in the land. And a certain man of Bethlehem in Judah went to sojourn in the land of Moab with his wife and his two sons.

2 And the name of the man *was* Elimelech, and the name of his wife, Naomi; and the names of his two sons *were* Mahlon and Chilion, Ephrathites of Bethlehem in Judah. Now they entered the land of Moab and remained there.

3 Then Elimelech, Naomi's husband, died; and she was left with her two sons.

4 And they took for themselves Moabite women *as* wives; the name of the one was Orpah and the name of the other Ruth. And they lived there about ten years.

5 Then both Mahlon and Chilion also died; and the woman was bereft of her two children and her husband.

6 ¶ Then she arose with her daughters-in-law that she might return from the land of Moab, for she had heard in the land of Moab that the LORD had visited His people in giving them food.

7 So she departed from the place where she was, and her two daughters-in-law with her; and they went on the way to return to the land of Judah.

8 And Naomi said to her two daughters-in-law, "Go, return each of you to her mother's house. May the LORD deal kindly with you as you have dealt with the dead and with me.

9 "May the LORD grant that you may find rest, each in the house of her husband." Then she kissed them, and they lifted up their voices and wept.

10 And they said to her, "*No,* but we will surely return with you to your people."

11 But Naomi said, "Return, my daughters. Why should you go with me? Have I yet sons in my womb, that they may be your husbands?

12 "Return, my daughters! Go, for I am too old to have a husband. If I said I have hope, if I should even have a husband tonight and also bear sons,

13 would you therefore wait until they were grown? Would you therefore refrain from marrying? No, my daughters; for it is harder for me than for you, for the hand of the LORD has gone forth against me."

14 And they lifted up their voices and wept again; and Orpah kissed her mother-in-law, but Ruth clung to her.

15 ¶ Then she said, "Behold, your sister-in-law has gone back to her people and her gods; return after your sister-in-law."

16 But Ruth said, "Do not urge me to leave you or turn back from following you; for where you go, I will go, and where you lodge, I will lodge. Your people *shall be* my people, and your God, my God.

17 "Where you die, I will die, and there I will be buried. Thus may the LORD do to me, and worse, if *anything but* death parts you and me."

18 When she saw that she was determined to go with her, she said no more to her.

19 ¶ So they both went until they came to Bethlehem. And it came about when they had come to Bethlehem, that all the city was stirred because of them, and the women said, "Is this Naomi?"

20 And she said to them, "Do not call me ¹Naomi; call me ²Mara, for the Almighty has dealt very bitterly with me.

21 "I went out full, but the LORD has brought me back empty. Why do you call me Naomi, since the LORD has witnessed against me and the Almighty has afflicted me?"

22 ¶ So Naomi returned, and with her Ruth the Moabitess, her daughter-in-law, who returned from the land of Moab. And they came to Bethlehem at the beginning of barley harvest.

CHAPTER 2

NOW Naomi had a kinsman of her husband, a man of great wealth, of the family of Elimelech, whose name was Boaz.

2 And Ruth the Moabitess said to Naomi, "Please let me go to the field and glean among the ears of grain after one in whose sight I may find favor." And she said to her, "Go, my daughter."

3 So she departed and went and gleaned in the field after the reapers; and she happened to come to the portion of the field belonging to Boaz, who was of the family of Elimelech.

4 Now behold, Boaz came from Bethlehem and said to the reapers, "May the LORD be with you." And they said to him, "May the LORD bless you."

5 Then Boaz said to his servant who was in charge of the reapers, "Whose young woman is this?"

6 And the servant in charge of the reapers answered and said, "She is the young Moabite woman who returned with Naomi from the land of Moab.

7 "And she said, 'Please let me glean and gather after the reapers among the sheaves.' Thus she came and has remained from the morning until now; she has been sitting in the house for a little while."

8 ¶ Then Boaz said to Ruth, "Listen carefully, my daughter. Do not go to glean in another field; furthermore, do not go on from this one, but stay here with my maids.

9 "Let your eyes be on the field which they reap, and go after them. Indeed, I have commanded the servants not to touch you. When you are thirsty, go to the water jars and drink from what the servants draw."

10 Then she fell on her face, bowing to the ground and said to him, "Why have I found favor in your sight that you should take notice of me, since I am a foreigner?"

11 And Boaz answered and said to her, "All that you have done for your mother-in-law after the death of your husband has been fully reported to me, and how you left your father and your mother and the land of your birth, and came to a people that you did not previously know.

12 "May the LORD reward your work, and your wages be full from the LORD, the God of Israel, under whose wings you have come to seek refuge."

13 Then she said, "I have found favor in your sight, my lord, for you have comforted me and indeed have spoken kindly to your maidservant, though I am not like one of your maidservants."

14 ¶ And at mealtime Boaz said to her, "Come here, that you may eat of the bread and dip your piece of bread in the vinegar." So she sat beside the reapers; and he served her roasted grain, and she ate and was satisfied and had some left.

15 When she rose to glean, Boaz commanded his servants, saying, "Let her glean even among the sheaves, and do not insult her.

16 "And also you shall purposely pull

out for her *some grain* from the bundles and leave *it* that she may glean, and do not rebuke her."

17 ¶ So she gleaned in the field until evening. Then she beat out what she had gleaned, and it was about an ephah of barley.

18 And she took *it* up and went into the city, and her mother-in-law saw what she had gleaned. She also took *it* out and gave Naomi what she had left after she was satisfied.

19 Her mother-in-law then said to her, "Where did you glean today and where did you work? May he who took notice of you be blessed." So she told her mother-in-law with whom she had worked and said, "The name of the man with whom I worked today is Boaz."

20 And Naomi said to her daughter-in-law, "May he be blessed of the Lord who has not withdrawn his kindness to the living and to the dead." Again Naomi said to her, "The man is our relative, he is one of our closest relatives."

21 Then Ruth the Moabitess said, "Furthermore, he said to me, 'You should stay close to my servants until they have finished all my harvest.' "

22 And Naomi said to Ruth her daughter-in-law, "It is good, my daughter, that you go out with his maids, lest *others* fall upon you in another field."

23 So she stayed close by the maids of Boaz in order to glean until the end of the barley harvest and the wheat harvest. And she lived with her mother-in-law.

CHAPTER 3

THEN Naomi her mother-in-law said to her, "My daughter, shall I not seek security for you, that it may be well with you?

2"And now is not Boaz our kinsman, with whose maids you were? Behold, he winnows barley at the threshing floor tonight.

3"Wash yourself therefore, and anoint yourself and put on your *best* clothes, and go down to the threshing floor; *but* do not make yourself known to the man until he has finished eating and drinking.

4"And it shall be when he lies down,

that you shall notice the place where he lies, and you shall go and uncover his feet and lie down; then he will tell you what you shall do."

5 And she said to her, "All that you say I will do."

6 ¶ So she went down to the threshing floor and did according to all that her mother-in-law had commanded her.

7 When Boaz had eaten and drunk and his heart was merry, he went to lie down at the end of the heap of grain; and she came secretly, and uncovered his feet and lay down.

8 And it happened in the middle of the night that the man was startled and bent forward; and behold, a woman was lying at his feet.

9 And he said, "Who are you?" And she answered, "I am Ruth your maid. So spread your covering over your maid, for you are a ³close relative."

10 Then he said, "May you be blessed of the Lord, my daughter. You have shown your last kindness to be better than the first by not going after young men, whether poor or rich.

11"And now, my daughter, do not fear. I will do for you whatever you ask, for all my people in the city know that you are a woman of excellence.

12"And now it is true I am a close relative; however, there is a relative closer than I.

13"Remain this night, and when morning comes, if he will redeem you, good; let him redeem you. But if he does not wish to redeem you, then I will redeem you, as the Lord lives. Lie down until morning."

14 ¶ So she lay at his feet until morning and rose before one could recognize another; and he said, "Let it not be known that the woman came to the threshing floor."

15 Again he said, "Give me the cloak that is on you and hold it." So she held it, and he measured six *measures* of barley and laid *it* on her. Then she went into the city.

16 And when she came to her mother-in-law, she said, "How did it go, my daughter?" And she told her all that the man had done for her.

17 And she said, "These six *measures* of barley he gave to me, for he said,

³ Or, *redeemer,* and so throughout this context

'Do not go to your mother-in-law empty-handed.' "

18 Then she said, "Wait, my daughter, until you know how the matter turns out; for the man will not rest until he has settled it today."

CHAPTER 4

Now Boaz went up to the gate and sat down there, and behold, the close relative of whom Boaz spoke was passing by, so he said, "Turn aside, friend, sit down here." And he turned aside and sat down.

2 And he took ten men of the elders of the city and said, "Sit down here." So they sat down.

3 Then he said to the closest relative, "Naomi, who has come back from the land of Moab, has to sell the piece of land which belonged to our brother Elimelech.

4 "So I thought to inform you, saying, 'Buy *it* before those who are sitting *here,* and before the elders of my people. If you will redeem *it,* redeem *it;* but if not, tell me that I may know; for there is no one but you to redeem *it,* and I am after you.' " And he said, "I will redeem *it.*"

5 Then Boaz said, "On the day you buy the field from the hand of Naomi, you must also acquire Ruth the Moabitess, the widow of the deceased, in order to raise up the name of the deceased on his inheritance."

6 And the closest relative said, "I cannot redeem *it* for myself, lest I jeopardize my own inheritance. Redeem *it* for yourself; you *may have* my right of redemption, for I cannot redeem *it.*"

7 ¶ Now this was *the custom* in former times in Israel concerning the redemption and the exchange *of land* to confirm any matter: a man removed his sandal and gave it to another; and this was the *manner of* attestation in Israel.

8 So the closest relative said to Boaz, "Buy *it* for yourself." And he removed his sandal.

9 Then Boaz said to the elders and all the people, "You are witnesses today that I have bought from the hand of Naomi all that belonged to Elimelech and all that belonged to Chilion and Mahlon.

10 "Moreover, I have acquired Ruth the Moabitess, the widow of Mahlon, to be my wife in order to raise up the name of the deceased on his inheritance, so that the name of the deceased may not be cut off from his brothers or from the court of his *birth* place; you are witnesses today."

11 And all the people who were in the court, and the elders, said, "*We are* witnesses. May the LORD make the woman who is coming into your home like Rachel and Leah, both of whom built the house of Israel; and may you achieve wealth in Ephrathah and become famous in Bethlehem.

12 "Moreover, may your house be like the house of Perez whom Tamar bore to Judah, through the offspring which the LORD shall give you by this young woman."

13 ¶ So Boaz took Ruth, and she became his wife, and he went in to her. And the LORD enabled her to conceive, and she gave birth to a son.

14 Then the women said to Naomi, "Blessed is the LORD who has not left you without a redeemer today, and may his name become famous in Israel.

15 "May he also be to you a restorer of life and a sustainer of your old age; for your daughter-in-law, who loves you and is better to you than seven sons, has given birth to him."

16 Then Naomi took the child and laid him in her lap, and became his nurse.

17 And the neighbor women gave him a name, saying, "A son has been born to Naomi!" So they named him Obed. He is the father of Jesse, the father of David.

18 ¶ Now these are the generations of Perez: to Perez was born Hezron,

19 and to Hezron was born Ram, and to Ram, Amminadab,

20 and to Amminadab was born Nahshon, and to Nahshon, Salmon,

21 and to Salmon was born Boaz, and to Boaz, Obed,

22 and to Obed was born Jesse, and to Jesse, David.

SAMUEL

Now there was a certain man from Ramathaim-zophim from the hill country of Ephraim, and his name was Elkanah the son of Jeroham, the son of Elihu, the son of Tohu, the son of Zuph, an Ephraimite.

2 And he had two wives: the name of one was Hannah and the name of the other Peninnah; and Peninnah had children, but Hannah had no children.

3 Now this man would go up from his city yearly to worship and to sacrifice to the LORD of hosts in Shiloh. And the two sons of Eli, Hophni and Phinehas were priests to the LORD there.

4 And when the day came that Elkanah sacrificed, he would give portions to Peninnah his wife and to all her sons and her daughters;

5 but to Hannah he would give a double portion, for he loved Hannah, but the LORD had closed her womb.

6 Her rival, however, would provoke her bitterly to irritate her, because the LORD had closed her womb.

7 And it happened year after year, as often as she went up to the house of the LORD, she would provoke her, so she wept and would not eat.

8 Then Elkanah her husband said to her, "Hannah, why do you weep and why do you not eat and why is your heart sad? Am I not better to you than ten sons?"

9 ¶ Then Hannah rose after eating and drinking in Shiloh. Now Eli the priest was sitting on the seat by the doorpost of the temple of the LORD.

10 And she, greatly distressed, prayed to the LORD and wept bitterly.

11 And she made a vow and said, "O LORD of hosts, if Thou wilt indeed look on the affliction of Thy maidservant and remember me, and not forget Thy maidservant, but wilt give Thy maidservant a son, then I will give him to the LORD all the days of his life, and a razor shall never come on his head."

12 ¶ Now it came about, as she continued praying before the LORD, that Eli was watching her mouth.

13 As for Hannah, she was speaking in her heart, only her lips were moving, but her voice was not heard. So Eli thought she was drunk.

14 Then Eli said to her, "How long will you make yourself drunk? Put away your wine from you."

15 But Hannah answered and said, "No, my lord, I am a woman oppressed in spirit; I have drunk neither wine nor strong drink, but I have poured out my soul before the LORD.

16 "Do not consider your maidservant as a worthless woman; for I have spoken until now out of my great concern and provocation."

17 Then Eli answered and said, "Go in peace; and may the God of Israel grant your petition that you have asked of Him."

18 And she said, "Let your maidservant find favor in your sight." So the woman went her way and ate, and her face was no longer sad.

19 ¶ Then they arose early in the morning and worshiped before the LORD, and returned again to their house in Ramah. And Elkanah had relations with Hannah his wife, and the LORD remembered her.

20 And it came about in due time, after Hannah had conceived, that she gave birth to a son; and she named him Samuel, saying, "Because I have asked him of the LORD."

21 ¶ Then the man Elkanah went up with all his household to offer to the LORD the yearly sacrifice and pay his vow.

22 But Hannah did not go up, for she said to her husband, "I will not go up until the child is weaned; then I will bring him, that he may appear before the LORD and stay there forever."

23 And Elkanah her husband said to her, "Do what seems best to you. Remain until you have weaned him; only may the LORD confirm His word." So the woman remained and nursed her son until she weaned him.

24 Now when she had weaned him, she took him up with her, with a three-year-old bull and one ephah of flour and a jug of wine, and brought him to the house of the LORD in Shiloh, although the child was young.

25 Then they slaughtered the bull, and brought the boy to Eli.

26 And she said, "Oh, my lord! As your soul lives, my lord, I am the

woman who stood here beside you, praying to the Lord.

27"For this boy I prayed, and the Lord has given me my petition which I asked of Him.

28"So I have also ¹dedicated him to the Lord; as long as he lives he is ¹dedicated to the Lord." And he worshiped the Lord there.

CHAPTER 2

THEN Hannah prayed and said,
"My heart exults in the Lord;
My horn is exalted in the Lord,
My mouth speaks boldly against my enemies,
Because I rejoice in Thy salvation.

2 "There is no one holy like the Lord,
Indeed, there is no one besides Thee,
Nor is there any rock like our God.

3 "Boast no more so very proudly,
Do not let arrogance come out of your mouth;
For the Lord is a God of knowledge,
And with Him actions are weighed.

4 "The bows of the mighty are shattered,
But the feeble gird on strength.

5 "Those who were full hire themselves out for bread,
But those who were hungry cease *to hunger.*
Even the barren gives birth to seven,
But she who has many children languishes.

6 "The Lord kills and makes alive;
He brings down to Sheol and raises up.

7 "The Lord makes poor and rich;
He brings low, He also exalts.

8 "He raises the poor from the dust,
He lifts the needy from the ash heap
To make them sit with nobles,
And inherit a seat of honor;
For the pillars of the earth are the Lord's,
And He set the world on them.

9 "He keeps the feet of His godly ones,

But the wicked ones are silenced in darkness;
For not by might shall a man prevail.

10 "Those who contend with the Lord will be shattered;
Against them He will thunder in the heavens,
The Lord will judge the ends of the earth;
And He will give strength to His king,
And will exalt the horn of His anointed."

11 ¶ Then Elkanah went to his home at Ramah. But the boy ministered to the Lord before Eli the priest.

12 ¶ Now the sons of Eli were ²worthless men; they did not know the Lord

13 and the custom of the priests with the people. When any man was offering a sacrifice, the priest's servant would come while the meat was boiling, with a three-pronged fork in his hand.

14 Then he would thrust it into the pan, or kettle, or caldron, or pot; all that the fork brought up the priest would take for himself. Thus they did in Shiloh to all the Israelites who came there.

15 Also, before they burned the fat, the priest's servant would come and say to the man who was sacrificing, "Give the priest meat for roasting, as he will not take boiled meat from you, only raw."

16 And if the man said to him, "They must surely burn the fat first, and then take as much as you desire," then he would say, "No, but you shall give *it to me* now; and if not, I will take it by force."

17 Thus the sin of the young men was very great before the Lord, for the men despised the offering of the Lord.

18 ¶ Now Samuel was ministering before the Lord, *as* a boy wearing a linen ephod.

19 And his mother would make him a little robe and bring it to him from year to year when she would come up with her husband to offer the yearly sacrifice.

20 Then Eli would bless Elkanah and

---

¹ Lit., *lent*   ² Lit., *sons of Belial*

his wife and say, "May the LORD give you children from this woman in place of the one she dedicated to the LORD." And they went to their own home.

21 And the LORD visited Hannah; and she conceived and gave birth to three sons and two daughters. And the boy Samuel grew before the LORD.

22 ¶ Now Eli was very old; and he heard all that his sons were doing to all Israel, and how they lay with the women who served at the doorway of the tent of meeting.

23 And he said to them, "Why do you do such things, the evil things that I hear from all these people?

24 "No, my sons; for the report is not good which I hear the LORD's people circulating.

25 "If one man sins against another, God will mediate for him; but if a man sins against the LORD, who can intercede for him?" But they would not listen to the voice of their father, for the LORD desired to put them to death.

26 Now the boy Samuel was growing in stature and in favor both with the LORD and with men.

27 ¶ Then a man of God came to Eli and said to him, "Thus says the LORD, 'Did I *not* indeed reveal Myself to the house of your father when they were in Egypt *in bondage* to Pharaoh's house?

28 'And did I *not* choose them from all the tribes of Israel to be My priests, to go up to My altar, to burn incense, to carry an ephod before Me; and did I *not* give to the house of your father all the fire *offerings* of the sons of Israel?

29 'Why do you kick at My sacrifice and at My offering which I have commanded *in My* dwelling, and honor your sons above Me, by making yourselves fat with the choicest of every offering of My people Israel?'

30 "Therefore the LORD God of Israel declares, 'I did indeed say that your house and the house of your father should walk before Me forever'; but now the LORD declares, 'Far be it from Me—for those who honor Me I will honor, and those who despise Me will be lightly esteemed.

31 'Behold, the days are coming when I will break your strength and the strength of your father's house so that

there will not be an old man in your house.

32 'And you will see the distress of *My* dwelling, in *spite of* all that I do good for Israel; and an old man will not be in your house forever.

33 'Yet I will not cut off every man of yours from My altar that your eyes may fail *from weeping* and your soul grieve, and all the increase of your house will die in the prime of life.

34 'And this will be the sign to you which shall come concerning your two sons, Hophni and Phinehas: on the same day both of them shall die.

35 'But I will raise up for Myself a faithful priest who will do according to what is in My heart and in My soul; and I will build him an enduring house, and he will walk before My anointed always.

36 'And it shall come about that everyone who is left in your house shall come and bow down to him for a piece of silver or a loaf of bread, and say, "Please assign me to one of the priest's offices so that I may eat a piece of bread." ' "

CHAPTER 3

NOW the boy Samuel was ministering to the LORD before Eli. And word from the LORD was rare in those days, visions were infrequent.

2 And it happened at that time as Eli was lying down in his place (now his eyesight had begun to grow dim *and* he could not see well),

3 and the lamp of God had not yet gone out, and Samuel was lying down in the temple of the LORD where the ark of God *was*,

4 that the LORD called Samuel; and he said, "Here I am."

5 Then he ran to Eli and said, "Here I am, for you called me." But he said, "I did not call, lie down again." So he went and lay down.

6 And the LORD called yet again, "Samuel!" So Samuel arose and went to Eli, and said, "Here I am, for you called me." But he answered, "I did not call, my son, lie down again."

7 Now Samuel did not yet know the LORD, nor had the word of the LORD yet been revealed to him.

8 So the LORD called Samuel again for the third time. And he arose and

went to Eli, and said, "Here I am, for you called me." Then Eli discerned that the LORD was calling the boy.

9 And Eli said to Samuel, "Go lie down, and it shall be if He calls you, that you shall say, 'Speak, LORD, for Thy servant is listening.'" So Samuel went and lay down in his place.

10 ¶ Then the LORD came and stood and called as at other times, "Samuel! Samuel!" And Samuel said, "Speak, for Thy servant is listening."

11 And the LORD said to Samuel, "Behold, I am about to do a thing in Israel at which both ears of everyone who hears it will tingle.

12 "In that day I will carry out against Eli all that I have spoken concerning his house, from beginning to end.

13 "For I have told him that I am about to judge his house forever for the iniquity which he knew, because his sons brought a curse on themselves and he did not rebuke them.

14 "And therefore I have sworn to the house of Eli that the iniquity of Eli's house shall not be atoned for by sacrifice or offering forever."

15 ¶ So Samuel lay down until morning. Then he opened the doors of the house of the LORD. But Samuel was afraid to tell the vision to Eli.

16 Then Eli called Samuel and said, "Samuel, my son." And he said, "Here I am."

17 And he said, "What is the word that He spoke to you? Please do not hide it from me. May God do so to you, and more also, if you hide anything from me of all the words that He spoke to you."

18 So Samuel told him everything and hid nothing from him. And he said, "It is the LORD; let Him do what seems good to Him."

19 ¶ Thus Samuel grew and the LORD was with him and let none of his words fail.

20 And all Israel from Dan even to Beersheba knew that Samuel was confirmed as a prophet of the LORD.

21 And the LORD appeared again at Shiloh, because the LORD revealed Himself to Samuel at Shiloh by the word of the LORD.

CHAPTER 4

THUS the word of Samuel came to all Israel. Now Israel went out to meet the Philistines in battle and camped beside Ebenezer while the Philistines camped in Aphek.

2 And the Philistines drew up in battle array to meet Israel. When the battle spread, Israel was defeated before the Philistines who killed about four thousand men on the battlefield.

3 When the people came into the camp, the elders of Israel said, "Why has the LORD defeated us today before the Philistines? Let us take to ourselves from Shiloh the ark of the covenant of the LORD, that it may come among us and deliver us from the power of our enemies."

4 So the people sent to Shiloh, and from there they carried the ark of the covenant of the LORD of hosts who sits *above* the cherubim; and the two sons of Eli, Hophni and Phinehas, *were* there with the ark of the covenant of God.

5 ¶ And it happened as the ark of the covenant of the LORD came into the camp, that all Israel shouted with a great shout, so that the earth resounded.

6 And when the Philistines heard the noise of the shout, they said, "What *does* the noise of this great shout in the camp of the Hebrews *mean?*" Then they understood that the ark of the LORD had come into the camp.

7 And the Philistines were afraid, for they said, "God has come into the camp." And they said, "Woe to us! For nothing like this has happened before.

8 "Woe to us! Who shall deliver us from the hand of these mighty gods? These are the gods who smote the Egyptians with all *kinds of* plagues in the wilderness.

9 "Take courage and be men, O Philistines, lest you become slaves to the Hebrews, as they have been slaves to you; therefore, be men and fight."

10 So the Philistines fought and Israel was defeated, and every man fled to his tent, and the slaughter was very great; for there fell of Israel thirty thousand foot soldiers.

11 And the ark of God was taken; and the two sons of Eli, Hophni and Phinehas, died.

12 ¶ Now a man of Benjamin ran

from the battle line and came to Shiloh the same day with his clothes torn and dust on his head.

13 When he came, behold, Eli was sitting on *his* seat by the road eagerly watching, because his heart was trembling for the ark of God. So the man came to tell *it* in the city, and all the city cried out.

14 When Eli heard the noise of the outcry, he said, "What *does* the noise of this commotion *mean?*" Then the man came hurriedly and told Eli.

15 Now Eli was ninety-eight years old, and his eyes were set so that he could not see.

16 And the man said to Eli, "I am the one who came from the battle line. Indeed, I escaped from the battle line today." And he said, "How did things go, my son?"

17 Then the one who brought the news answered and said, "Israel has fled before the Philistines and there has also been a great slaughter among the people, and your two sons also, Hophni and Phinehas, are dead, and the ark of God has been taken."

18 And it came about when he mentioned the ark of God that Eli fell off the seat backward beside the gate, and his neck was broken and he died, for he was old and heavy. Thus he judged Israel forty years.

19 ¶ Now his daughter-in-law, Phinehas' wife, was pregnant and about to give birth; and when she heard the news that the ark of God was taken and that her father-in-law and her husband had died, she kneeled down and gave birth, for her pains came upon her.

20 And about the time of her death the women who stood by her said to her, "Do not be afraid, for you have given birth to a son." But she did not answer or pay attention.

21 And she called the boy ³Ichabod, saying, "The glory has departed from Israel," because the ark of God was taken and because of her father-in-law and her husband.

22 And she said, "The glory has departed from Israel, for the ark of God was taken."

³ I.e., no glory

CHAPTER 5

Now the Philistines took the ark of God and brought it from Ebenezer to Ashdod.

2 Then the Philistines took the ark of God and brought it to the house of Dagon, and set it by Dagon.

3 When the Ashdodites arose early the next morning, behold, Dagon had fallen on his face to the ground before the ark of the Lord. So they took Dagon and set him in his place again.

4 But when they arose early the next morning, behold, Dagon had fallen on his face to the ground before the ark of the Lord. And the head of Dagon and both the palms of his hands *were* cut off on the threshold; only the trunk of Dagon was left to him.

5 Therefore neither the priests of Dagon nor all who enter Dagon's house tread on the threshold of Dagon in Ashdod to this day.

6 ¶ Now the hand of the Lord was heavy on the Ashdodites, and He ravaged them and smote them with tumors, both Ashdod and its territories.

7 When the men of Ashdod saw that it was so, they said, "The ark of the God of Israel must not remain with us, for His hand is severe on us and on Dagon our god."

8 So they sent and gathered all the lords of the Philistines to them and said, "What shall we do with the ark of the God of Israel?" And they said, "Let the ark of the God of Israel be brought around to Gath." And they brought the ark of the God of Israel *around.*

9 And it came about that after they had brought it around, the hand of the Lord was against the city with very great confusion; and He smote the men of the city, both young and old, so that tumors broke out on them.

10 So they sent the ark of God to Ekron. And it happened as the ark of God came to Ekron that the Ekronites cried out, saying, "They have brought the ark of the God of Israel around to us, to kill us and our people."

11 They sent therefore and gathered all the lords of the Philistines and said, "Send away the ark of the God of Israel, and let it return to its own place, that it may not kill us and our

people." For there was a deadly confusion throughout the city; the hand of God was very heavy there.

12 And the men who did not die were smitten with tumors and the cry of the city went up to heaven.

CHAPTER 6

Now the ark of the LORD had been in the country of the Philistines seven months.

2 And the Philistines called for the priests and the diviners, saying, "What shall we do with the ark of the LORD? Tell us how we shall send it to its place."

3 And they said, "If you send away the ark of the God of Israel, do not send it empty; but you shall surely return to Him a guilt offering. Then you shall be healed and it shall be known to you why His hand is not removed from you."

4 Then they said, "What shall be the guilt offering which we shall return to Him?" And they said, "Five golden tumors and five golden mice *according to* the number of the lords of the Philistines, for one plague was on all of you and on your lords.

5"So you shall make likenesses of your tumors and likenesses of your mice that ravage the land, and you shall give glory to the God of Israel; perhaps He will ease His hand from you, your gods, and your land.

6"Why then do you harden your hearts as the Egyptians and Pharaoh hardened their hearts? When He had severely dealt with them, did they not allow the people to go, and they departed?

7"Now therefore take and prepare a new cart and two milch cows on which there has never been a yoke; and hitch the cows to the cart and take their calves home, away from them.

8"And take the ark of the LORD and place it on the cart; and put the articles of gold which you return to Him as a guilt offering in a box by its side. Then send it away that it may go.

9"And watch, if it goes up by the way of its own territory to Beth-shemesh, then He has done us this great evil. But if not, then we shall know

that it was not His hand that struck us; it happened to us by chance."

10 ¶ Then the men did so, and took two milch cows and hitched them to the cart, and shut up their calves at home.

11 And they put the ark of the LORD on the cart, and the box with the golden mice and the likenesses of their tumors.

12 And the cows took the straight way in the direction of Beth-shemesh; they went along the highway, lowing as they went, and did not turn aside to the right or to the left. And the lords of the Philistines followed them to the border of Beth-shemesh.

13 Now *the people of* Beth-shemesh were reaping their wheat harvest in the valley, and they raised their eyes and saw the ark and were glad to see *it.*

14 And the cart came into the field of Joshua the Beth-shemite and stood there where there *was* a large stone; and they split the wood of the cart and offered the cows as a burnt offering to the LORD.

15 And the Levites took down the ark of the LORD and the box that was with it, in which were the articles of gold, and put them on the large stone; and the men of Beth-shemesh offered burnt offerings and sacrificed sacrifices that day to the LORD.

16 And when the five lords of the Philistines saw it, they returned to Ekron that day.

17 ¶ And these are the golden tumors which the Philistines returned for a guilt offering to the LORD: one for Ashdod, one for Gaza, one for Ashkelon, one for Gath, one for Ekron;

18 and the golden mice, *according to* the number of all the cities of the Philistines belonging to the five lords, both of fortified cities and of country villages. The large stone on which they set the ark of the LORD *is a witness* to this day in the field of Joshua the Beth-shemite.

19 ¶ And He struck down some of the men of Beth-shemesh because they had looked into the ark of the LORD. He struck down of all the people, 50,070 men, and the people mourned because the LORD had struck the people with a great slaughter.

20 And the men of Beth-shemesh said, "Who is able to stand before the LORD, this holy God? And to whom shall He go up from us?"

21 So they sent messengers to the inhabitants of Kiriath-jearim, saying, "The Philistines have brought back the ark of the LORD; come down and take it up to you."

CHAPTER 7

AND the men of Kiriath-jearim came and took the ark of the LORD and brought it into the house of Abinadab on the hill, and consecrated Eleazar his son to keep the ark of the LORD.

2 And it came about from the day that the ark remained at Kiriath-jearim that the time was long, for it was twenty years; and all the house of Israel lamented after the LORD.

3 ¶ Then Samuel spoke to all the house of Israel, saying, "If you return to the LORD with all your heart, remove the foreign gods and the Ashtaroth from among you and direct your hearts to the LORD and serve Him alone; and He will deliver you from the hand of the Philistines."

4 So the sons of Israel removed the Baals and the Ashtaroth and served the LORD alone.

5 ¶ Then Samuel said, "Gather all Israel to Mizpah, and I will pray to the LORD for you."

6 And they gathered to Mizpah, and drew water and poured it out before the LORD, and fasted on that day, and said there, "We have sinned against the LORD." And Samuel judged the sons of Israel at Mizpah.

7 Now when the Philistines heard that the sons of Israel had gathered to Mizpah, the lords of the Philistines went up against Israel. And when the sons of Israel heard it, they were afraid of the Philistines.

8 Then the sons of Israel said to Samuel, "Do not cease to cry to the LORD our God for us, that He may save us from the hand of the Philistines."

9 And Samuel took a suckling lamb and offered it for a whole burnt offering to the LORD; and Samuel cried to the LORD for Israel and the LORD answered him.

10 Now Samuel was offering up the burnt offering, and the Philistines drew near to battle against Israel. But the LORD thundered with a great thunder on that day against the Philistines and confused them, so that they were routed before Israel.

11 And the men of Israel went out of Mizpah and pursued the Philistines, and struck them down as far as below Beth-car.

12 ¶ Then Samuel took a stone and set it between Mizpah and Shen, and named it [4]Ebenezer, saying, "Thus far the LORD has helped us."

13 So the Philistines were subdued and they did not come anymore within the border of Israel. And the hand of the LORD was against the Philistines all the days of Samuel.

14 And the cities which the Philistines had taken from Israel were restored to Israel, from Ekron even to Gath; and Israel delivered their territory from the hand of the Philistines. So there was peace between Israel and the Amorites.

15 ¶ Now Samuel judged Israel all the days of his life.

16 And he used to go annually on circuit to Bethel and Gilgal and Mizpah, and he judged Israel in all these places.

17 Then his return was to Ramah, for his house was there, and there he judged Israel; and he built there an altar to the LORD.

CHAPTER 8

AND it came about when Samuel was old that he appointed his sons judges over Israel.

2 Now the name of his first-born was Joel, and the name of his second, Abijah; they were judging in Beer-sheba.

3 His sons, however, did not walk in his ways, but turned aside after dishonest gain and took bribes and perverted justice.

4 ¶ Then all the elders of Israel gathered together and came to Samuel at Ramah;

5 and they said to him, "Behold, you have grown old, and your sons do not walk in your ways. Now appoint a king for us to judge us like all the nations."

6 But the thing was displeasing in

4 I.e., the stone of help

the sight of Samuel when they said, "Give us a king to judge us." And Samuel prayed to the LORD.

7 And the LORD said to Samuel, "Listen to the voice of the people in regard to all that they say to you, for they have not rejected you, but they have rejected Me from being king over them.

8"Like all the deeds which they have done since the day that I brought them up from Egypt even to this day— in that they have forsaken Me and served other gods—so they are doing to you also.

9"Now then, listen to their voice; however, you shall solemnly warn them and tell them of the ⁵procedure of the king who will reign over them."

10 ¶ So Samuel spoke all the words of the LORD to the people who had asked of him a king.

11 And he said, "This will be the procedure of the king who will reign over you: he will take your sons and place *them* for himself in his chariots and among his horsemen and they will run before his chariots.

12"And he will appoint for himself commanders of thousands and of fifties, and *some* to do his plowing and to reap his harvest and to make his weapons of war and equipment for his chariots.

13"He will also take your daughters for perfumers and cooks and bakers.

14"And he will take the best of your fields and your vineyards and your olive groves, and give *them* to his servants.

15"And he will take a tenth of your seed and of your vineyards, and give to his officers and to his servants.

16"He will also take your male servants and your female servants and your best young men and your donkeys, and use *them* for his work.

17"He will take a tenth of your flocks, and you yourselves will become his servants.

18"Then you will cry out in that day because of your king whom you have chosen for yourselves, but the LORD will not answer you in that day."

19 ¶ Nevertheless, the people refused to listen to the voice of Samuel, and they said, "No, but there shall be a king over us,

20 that we also may be like all the nations, that our king may judge us and go out before us and fight our battles."

21 Now after Samuel had heard all the words of the people, he repeated them in the LORD'S hearing.

22 And the LORD said to Samuel, "Listen to their voice, and appoint them a king." So Samuel said to the men of Israel, "Go every man to his city."

CHAPTER 9

Now there was a man of Benjamin whose name was Kish the son of Abiel, the son of Zeror, the son of Becorath, the son of Aphiah, the son of a Benjamite, a mighty man of valor.

2 And he had a son whose name was Saul, a choice and handsome *man,* and there was not a more handsome person than he among the sons of Israel; from his shoulders and up he was taller than any of the people.

3 Now the donkeys of Kish, Saul's father, were lost. So Kish said to his son Saul, "Take now with you one of the servants, and arise, go search for the donkeys."

4 And he passed through the hill country of Ephraim and passed through the land of Shalishah, but they did not find *them.* Then they passed through the land of Shaalim, but *they were* not *there.* Then he passed through the land of the Benjamites, but they did not find *them.*

5 ¶ When they came to the land of Zuph, Saul said to his servant who was with him, "Come, and let us return, lest my father cease *to be concerned* about the donkeys and become anxious for us."

6 And he said to him, "Behold now, there is a man of God in this city, and the man is held in honor; all that he says surely comes true. Now let us go there, perhaps he can tell us about our journey on which we have set out."

7 Then Saul said to his servant, "But behold, if we go, what shall we bring the man? For the bread is gone from our sack and there is no present to bring to the man of God. What do we have?"

⁵ Lit., *custom*

8 And the servant answered Saul again and said, "Behold, I have in my hand a fourth of a shekel of silver; I will give *it* to the man of God and he will tell us our way."

9 (Formerly in Israel, when a man went to inquire of God, he used to say, "Come, and let us go to the seer"; for *he who is called* a prophet now was formerly called a seer.)

10 Then Saul said to his servant, "Well said; come, let us go." So they went to the city where the man of God was.

11 ¶ As they went up the slope to the city, they found young women going out to draw water, and said to them, "Is the seer here?"

12 And they answered them and said, "He is; see, *he is* ahead of you. Hurry now, for he has come into the city today, for the people have a sacrifice on the high place today.

13 "As soon as you enter the city you will find him before he goes up to the high place to eat, for the people will not eat until he comes, because he must bless the sacrifice; afterward those who are invited will eat. Now therefore, go up for you will find him at once."

14 So they went up to the city. As they came into the city, behold, Samuel was coming out toward them to go up to the high place.

15 ¶ Now a day before Saul's coming, the LORD had revealed *this* to Samuel saying,

16 "About this time tomorrow I will send you a man from the land of Benjamin, and you shall anoint him to be prince over My people Israel; and he shall deliver My people from the hand of the Philistines. For I have regarded My people, because their cry has come to Me."

17 When Samuel saw Saul, the LORD said to him, "Behold, the man of whom I spoke to you! This one shall rule over My people."

18 Then Saul approached Samuel in the gate, and said, "Please tell me where the seer's house is."

19 And Samuel answered Saul and said, "I am the seer. Go up before me to the high place, for you shall eat with me today; and in the morning I will let you go, and will tell you all that is on your mind.

20 "And as for your donkeys which were lost three days ago, do not set your mind on them, for they have been found. And for whom is all that is desirable in Israel? Is it not for you and for all your father's household?"

21 And Saul answered and said, "Am I not a Benjamite, of the smallest of the tribes of Israel, and my family the least of all the families of the tribe of Benjamin? Why then do you speak to me in this way?"

22 ¶ Then Samuel took Saul and his servant and brought them into the hall, and gave them a place at the head of those who were invited, who were about thirty men.

23 And Samuel said to the cook, "Bring the portion that I gave you, concerning which I said to you, 'Set it aside.' "

24 Then the cook took up the leg with what was on it and set *it* before Saul. And *Samuel* said, "Here is what has been reserved! Set *it* before you *and* eat, because it has been kept for you until the appointed time, since I said I have invited the people." So Saul ate with Samuel that day.

25 ¶ When they came down from the high place into the city, *Samuel* spoke with Saul on the roof.[6]

26 And they arose early; and it came about at daybreak that Samuel called to Saul on the roof, saying, "Get up, that I may send you away." So Saul arose, and both he and Samuel went out into the street.

27 As they were going down to the edge of the city, Samuel said to Saul, "Say to the servant that he might go ahead of us and pass on, but you remain standing now, that I may proclaim the word of God to you."

CHAPTER 10

THEN Samuel took the flask of oil, poured it on his head, kissed him and said, "Has not the LORD anointed you a ruler over His inheritance?

2 "When you go from me today, then you will find two men close to Rachel's tomb in the territory of Benjamin at Zelzah; and they will say to you, 'The donkeys which you went to look for have been found. Now behold, your

---

[6] Gr. adds *and they spread a bed for Saul on the roof and he slept.*

father has ceased to be concerned about the donkeys and is anxious for you, saying, "What shall I do about my son?" '

3"Then you will go on further from there, and you will come as far as the oak of Tabor, and there three men going up to God at Bethel will meet you, one carrying three kids, another carrying three loaves of bread, and another carrying a jug of wine;

4 and they will greet you and give you two *loaves* of bread, which you will accept from their hand.

5"Afterward you will come to the hill of God where the Philistine garrison is; and it shall be as soon as you have come there to the city, that you will meet a group of prophets coming down from the high place with harp, tambourine, flute, and a lyre before them, and they will be prophesying.

6"Then the Spirit of the LORD will come upon you mightily, and you shall prophesy with them and be changed into another man.

7"And it shall be when these signs come to you, do for yourself what the occasion requires; for God is with you.

8"And you shall go down before me to Gilgal; and behold, I will come down to you to offer burnt offerings and sacrifice peace offerings. You shall wait seven days until I come to you and show you what you should do."

9 ¶ Then it happened when he turned his back to leave Samuel, God changed his heart; and all those signs came about on that day.

10 When they came to the hill there, behold, a group of prophets met him; and the Spirit of God came upon him mightily, so that he prophesied among them.

11 And it came about, when all who knew him previously saw that he prophesied now with the prophets, that the people said to one another, "What has happened to the son of Kish? Is Saul also among the prophets?"

12 And a man there answered and said, "Now, who is their father?" Therefore it became a proverb: "Is Saul also among the prophets?"

13 When he had finished prophesying, he came to the high place.

14 ¶ Now Saul's uncle said to him and his servant, "Where did you go?"

And he said, "To look for the donkeys. When we saw that they could not be found, we went to Samuel."

15 And Saul's uncle said, "Please tell me what Samuel said to you."

16 So Saul said to his uncle, "He told us plainly that the donkeys had been found." But he did not tell him about the matter of the kingdom which Samuel had mentioned.

17 ¶ Thereafter Samuel called the people together to the LORD at Mizpah;

18 and he said to the sons of Israel, "Thus says the LORD, the God of Israel, 'I brought Israel up from Egypt, and I delivered you from the hand of the Egyptians, and from the power of all the kingdoms that were oppressing you.'

19"But you today rejected your God, who delivers you from all your calamities and your distresses; yet you have said, 'No, but set a king over us!' Now therefore, present yourselves before the LORD by your tribes and by your clans."

20 Thus Samuel brought all the tribes of Israel near, and the tribe of Benjamin was taken by lot.

21 Then he brought the tribe of Benjamin near by its families, and the Matrite family was taken. And Saul the son of Kish was taken; but when they looked for him, he could not be found.

22 Therefore they inquired further of the LORD, "Has the man come here yet?" So the LORD said, "Behold, he is hiding himself by the baggage."

23 So they ran and took him from there, and when he stood among the people, he was taller than any of the people from his shoulders upward.

24 And Samuel said to all the people, "Do you see him whom the LORD has chosen? Surely there is no one like him among all the people." So all the people shouted and said, "*Long* live the king!"

25 Then Samuel told the people the ordinances of the kingdom, and wrote *them* in the book and placed *it* before the LORD. And Samuel sent all the people away, each one to his house.

26 And Saul also went to his house at Gibeah; and the valiant *men* whose hearts God had touched went with him.

27 But certain worthless men said, "How can this one deliver us?" And they despised him and did not bring him any present. But he kept silent.

CHAPTER 11

NOW Nahash the Ammonite came up and besieged Jabesh-gilead; and all the men of Jabesh said to Nahash, "Make a covenant with us and we will serve you."

2 But Nahash the Ammonite said to them, "I will make *it* with you on this condition, that I will gouge out the right eye of every one of you, thus I will make it a reproach on all Israel."

3 And the elders of Jabesh said to him, "Let us alone for seven days, that we may send messengers throughout the territory of Israel. Then, if there is no one to deliver us, we will come out to you."

4 Then the messengers came to Gibeah of Saul and spoke these words in the hearing of the people, and all the people lifted up their voices and wept.

5 Now behold, Saul was coming from the field behind the oxen; and he said, "What is *the matter* with the people that they weep?" So they related to him the words of the men of Jabesh.

6 ¶ Then the Spirit of God came upon Saul mightily when he heard these words, and he became very angry.

7 And he took a yoke of oxen and cut them in pieces, and sent *them* throughout the territory of Israel by the hand of messengers, saying, "Whoever does not come out after Saul and after Samuel, so shall it be done to his oxen." Then the dread of the LORD fell on the people, and they came out as one man.

8 And he numbered them in Bezek; and the sons of Israel were 300,000, and the men of Judah 30,000.

9 And they said to the messengers who had come, "Thus you shall say to the men of Jabesh-gilead, 'Tomorrow, by the time the sun is hot, you shall have deliverance.'" So the messengers went and told the men of Jabesh; and they were glad.

10 Then the men of Jabesh said, "Tomorrow we will come out to you, and you may do to us whatever seems good to you."

11 And it happened the next morning that Saul put the people in three companies; and they came into the midst of the camp at the morning watch, and struck down the Ammonites until the heat of the day. And it came about that those who survived were scattered, so that no two of them were left together.

12 ¶ Then the people said to Samuel, "Who is he that said, 'Shall Saul reign over us?' Bring the men, that we may put them to death."

13 But Saul said, "Not a man shall be put to death this day, for today the LORD has accomplished deliverance in Israel."

14 ¶ Then Samuel said to the people, "Come and let us go to Gilgal and renew the kingdom there."

15 So all the people went to Gilgal, and there they made Saul king before the LORD in Gilgal. There they also offered sacrifices of peace offerings before the LORD; and there Saul and all the men of Israel rejoiced greatly.

CHAPTER 12

THEN Samuel said to all Israel, "Behold, I have listened to your voice in all that you said to me, and I have appointed a king over you.

2 "And now, here is the king walking before you, but I am old and gray, and behold my sons are with you. And I have walked before you from my youth even to this day.

3 "Here I am; bear witness against me before the LORD and His anointed. Whose ox have I taken, or whose donkey have I taken, or whom have I defrauded? Whom have I oppressed, or from whose hand have I taken a bribe to blind my eyes with it? I will restore *it* to you."

4 And they said, "You have not defrauded us, or oppressed us, or taken anything from any man's hand."

5 And he said to them, "The LORD is witness against you, and His anointed is witness this day that you have found nothing in my hand." And they said, "*He is* witness."

6 ¶ Then Samuel said to the people, "It is the LORD who appointed Moses

and Aaron and who brought your fathers up from the land of Egypt.

7"So now, take your stand, that I may plead with you before the LORD concerning all the righteous acts of the LORD which He did for you and your fathers.

8"When Jacob went into Egypt and your fathers cried out to the LORD, then the LORD sent Moses and Aaron who brought your fathers out of Egypt and settled them in this place.

9"But they forgot the LORD their God, so He sold them into the hand of Sisera, captain of the army of Hazor, and into the hand of the Philistines and into the hand of the king of Moab, and they fought against them.

10"And they cried out to the LORD and said, 'We have sinned because we have forsaken the LORD and have served the Baals and the Ashtaroth; but now deliver us from the hands of our enemies, and we will serve Thee.'

11"Then the LORD sent Jerubbaal and [7]Bedan and Jephthah and Samuel, and delivered you from the hands of your enemies all around, so that you lived in security.

12"When you saw that Nahash the king of the sons of Ammon came against you, you said to me, 'No, but a king shall reign over us,' although the LORD your God *was* your king.

13"Now therefore, here is the king whom you have chosen, whom you have asked for, and behold, the LORD has set a king over you.

14"If you will fear the LORD and serve Him, and listen to His voice and not rebel against the command of the LORD, then both you and also the king who reigns over you will follow the LORD your God.

15"And if you will not listen to the voice of the LORD, but rebel against the command of the LORD, then the hand of the LORD will be against you, *as it was* against your fathers.

16"Even now, take your stand and see this great thing which the LORD will do before your eyes.

17"Is it not the wheat harvest today? I will call to the LORD, that He may send thunder and rain. Then you will know and see that your wickedness is great which you have done in the sight of the LORD by asking for yourselves a king."

18 So Samuel called to the LORD, and the LORD sent thunder and rain that day; and all the people greatly feared the LORD and Samuel.

19 ¶ Then all the people said to Samuel, "Pray for your servants to the LORD your God, so that we may not die, for we have added to all our sins *this* evil by asking for ourselves a king."

20 And Samuel said to the people, "Do not fear. You have committed all this evil, yet do not turn aside from following the LORD, but serve the LORD with all your heart.

21"And you must not turn aside, for *then you would go* after futile things which can not profit or deliver, because they are futile.

22"For the LORD will not abandon His people on account of His great name, because the LORD has been pleased to make you a people for Himself.

23"Moreover, as for me, far be it from me that I should sin against the LORD by ceasing to pray for you; but I will instruct you in the good and right way.

24"Only [8]fear the LORD and serve Him in truth with all your heart; for consider what great things He has done for you.

25"But if you still do wickedly, both you and your king shall be swept away."

CHAPTER 13

Saul was *forty* years old when he began to reign, and he reigned *thirty*-two years over Israel.

2 Now Saul chose for himself 3,000 men of Israel, of which 2,000 were with Saul in Michmash and in the hill country of Bethel, while 1,000 were with Jonathan at Gibeah of Benjamin. But he sent away the rest of the people, each to his tent.

3 And Jonathan smote the garrison of the Philistines that was in Geba, and the Philistines heard of *it*. Then Saul blew the trumpet throughout the land, saying, "Let the Hebrews hear."

4 And all Israel heard the news that Saul had smitten the garrison of the Philistines, and also that Israel had

[7] Gr. and Syr. read *Barak*   [8] Or, *reverence*

become odious to the Philistines. The people were then summoned to Saul at Gilgal.

5 ¶ Now the Philistines assembled to fight with Israel, 30,000 chariots and 6,000 horsemen, and people like the sand which is on the seashore in abundance; and they came up and camped in Michmash, east of Beth-aven.

6 When the men of Israel saw that they were in a strait (for the people were hard-pressed), then the people hid themselves in caves, in thickets, in cliffs, in cellars, and in pits.

7 Also *some of* the Hebrews crossed the Jordan into the land of Gad and Gilead. But as for Saul, he *was* still in Gilgal, and all the people followed him trembling.

8 ¶ Now he waited seven days, according to the appointed time set by Samuel, but Samuel did not come to Gilgal; and the people were scattering from him.

9 So Saul said, "Bring to me the burnt offering and the peace offerings." And he offered the burnt offering.

10 And it came about as soon as he finished offering the burnt offering, that behold, Samuel came; and Saul went out to meet him *and* to greet him.

11 But Samuel said, "What have you done?" And Saul said, "Because I saw that the people were scattering from me, and that you did not come within the appointed days, and that the Philistines were assembling at Michmash,

12 therefore I said, 'Now the Philistines will come down against me at Gilgal, and I have not asked the favor of the LORD.' So I forced myself and offered the burnt offering."

13 And Samuel said to Saul, "You have acted foolishly; you have not kept the commandment of the LORD your God, which He commanded you, for now the LORD would have established your kingdom over Israel forever.

14 "But now your kingdom shall not endure. The LORD has sought out for Himself a man after His own heart, and the LORD has appointed him as ruler over His people, because you have not kept what the LORD commanded you."

15 ¶ Then Samuel arose and went up from Gilgal to Gibeah of Benjamin. And Saul numbered the people who were present with him, about six hundred men.

16 Now Saul and his son Jonathan and the people who were present with them were staying in Geba of Benjamin while the Philistines camped at Michmash.

17 And the raiders came from the camp of the Philistines in three companies: one company turned toward Ophrah, to the land of Shual,

18 and another company turned toward Beth-horon, and another company turned toward the border which overlooks the valley of Zeboim toward the wilderness.

19 ¶ Now no blacksmith could be found in all the land of Israel, for the Philistines said, "Lest the Hebrews make swords or spears."

20 So all Israel went down to the Philistines, each to sharpen his plowshare, his mattock, his axe, and his hoe.

21 And the charge was two-thirds of a shekel for the plowshares, the mattocks, the forks, and the axes, and to fix the hoes.

22 So it came about on the day of battle that neither sword nor spear was found in the hands of any of the people who *were* with Saul and Jonathan, but they were found with Saul and his son Jonathan.

23 And the garrison of the Philistines went out to the pass of Michmash.

CHAPTER 14

NOW the day came that Jonathan, the son of Saul, said to the young man who was carrying his armor, "Come and let us cross over to the Philistines' garrison that is on yonder side." But he did not tell his father.

2 And Saul was staying in the outskirts of Gibeah under the pomegranate tree which is in Migron. And the people who *were* with him *were* about six hundred men,

3 and Ahijah, the son of Ahitub, Ichabod's brother, the son of Phinehas, the son of Eli, the priest of the LORD at Shiloh, was wearing an ephod. And the people did not know that Jonathan had gone.

4 And between the passes by which Jonathan sought to cross over to the Philistines' garrison, there was a sharp crag on the one side, and a sharp crag on the other side, and the name of the one was Bozez, and the name of the other Seneh.

5 The one crag rose on the north opposite Michmash, and the other on the south opposite Geba.

6 ¶ Then Jonathan said to the young man who was carrying his armor, "Come and let us cross over to the garrison of these uncircumcised; perhaps the LORD will work for us, for the LORD is not restrained to save by many or by few."

7 And his armor bearer said to him, "Do all that is in your heart; turn yourself, *and* here I am with you according to your desire."

8 Then Jonathan said, "Behold, we will cross over to the men and reveal ourselves to them.

9 "If they say to us, 'Wait until we come to you'; then we will stand in our place and not go up to them.

10 "But if they say, 'Come up to us,' then we will go up, for the LORD has given them into our hands; and this shall be the sign to us."

11 And when both of them revealed themselves to the garrison of the Philistines, the Philistines said, "Behold, Hebrews are coming out of the holes where they have hidden themselves."

12 So the men of the garrison hailed Jonathan and his armor bearer and said, "Come up to us and we will tell you something." And Jonathan said to his armor bearer, "Come up after me, for the LORD has given them into the hands of Israel."

13 Then Jonathan climbed up on his hands and feet, with his armor bearer behind him; and they fell before Jonathan, and his armor bearer put some to death after him.

14 And that first slaughter which Jonathan and his armor bearer made was about twenty men within about half a furrow in an acre of land.

15 And there was a trembling in the camp, in the field, and among all the people. Even the garrison and the raiders trembled, and the earth quaked so that it became a [9]great trembling.

16 ¶ Now Saul's watchmen in Gibeah of Benjamin looked, and behold, the multitude melted away; and they went here and *there*.

17 And Saul said to the people who *were* with him, "Number now and see who has gone from us." And when they had numbered, behold, Jonathan and his armor bearer were not *there*.

18 Then Saul said to Ahijah, "Bring the ark of God here." For the ark of God was at that time with the sons of Israel.

19 And it happened while Saul talked to the priest, that the commotion in the camp of the Philistines continued and increased; so Saul said to the priest, "Withdraw your hand."

20 Then Saul and all the people who *were* with him rallied and came to the battle; and behold, every man's sword was against his fellow, *and there was* very great confusion.

21 Now the Hebrews *who* were with the Philistines previously, who went up with them all around in the camp, even they also *turned* to be with the Israelites who *were* with Saul and Jonathan.

22 When all the men of Israel who had hidden themselves in the hill country of Ephraim heard that the Philistines had fled, even they also pursued them closely in the battle.

23 So the LORD delivered Israel that day, and the battle spread beyond Beth-aven.

24 ¶ Now the men of Israel were hard-pressed on that day, for Saul had put the people under oath, saying, "Cursed be the man who eats food before evening, and until I have avenged myself on my enemies." So none of the people tasted food.

25 And all *the people of* the land entered the forest, and there was honey on the ground.

26 When the people entered the forest, behold, *there was* a flow of honey; but no man put his hand to his mouth, for the people feared the oath.

27 But Jonathan had not heard when his father put the people under oath; therefore, he put out the end of the staff that *was* in his hand and dipped it in the honeycomb, and put his hand to his mouth, and his eyes brightened.

28 Then one of the people answered and said, "Your father strictly put the

[9] Lit., *trembling of God*

people under oath, saying, 'Cursed be the man who eats food today.' " And the people were weary.

29 Then Jonathan said, "My father has troubled the land. See now, how my eyes have brightened because I tasted a little of this honey.

30 "How much more, if only the people had eaten freely today of the spoil of their enemies which they found! For now the slaughter among the Philistines has not been great."

31 ¶ And they struck among the Philistines that day from Michmash to Aijalon. And the people were very weary.

32 And the people rushed greedily upon the spoil, and took sheep and oxen and calves, and slew *them* on the ground; and the people ate *them* with the blood.

33 Then they told Saul, saying, "Behold, the people are sinning against the Lord by eating with the blood." And he said, "You have acted treacherously; roll a great stone to me today."

34 And Saul said, "Disperse yourselves among the people and say to them, 'Each one of you bring me his ox or his sheep, and slaughter *it* here and eat; and do not sin against the Lord by eating with the blood.' " So all the people that night brought each one his ox with him, and slaughtered *it* there.

35 And Saul built an altar to the Lord; it was the first altar that he built to the Lord.

36 ¶ Then Saul said, "Let us go down after the Philistines by night and take spoil among them until the morning light, and let us not leave a man of them." And they said, "Do whatever seems good to you." So the priest said, "Let us draw near to God here."

37 And Saul inquired of God, "Shall I go down after the Philistines? Wilt Thou give them into the hand of Israel?" But He did not answer him on that day.

38 And Saul said, "Draw near here, all you chiefs of the people, and investigate and see how this sin has happened today.

39 "For as the Lord lives, who delivers Israel, though it is in Jonathan my son, he shall surely die." But not one of all the people answered him.

40 Then he said to all Israel, "You shall be on one side and I and Jonathan my son will be on the other side." And the people said to Saul, "Do what seems good to you."

41 Therefore, Saul said to the Lord, the God of Israel, "Give a perfect *lot.*" And Jonathan and Saul were taken, but the people escaped.

42 And Saul said, "Cast *lots* between me and Jonathan my son." And Jonathan was taken.

43 ¶ Then Saul said to Jonathan, "Tell me what you have done." So Jonathan told him and said, "I indeed tasted a little honey with the end of the staff that was in my hand. Here I am, I must die!"

44 And Saul said, "May God do this *to me* and more also, for you shall surely die, Jonathan."

45 But the people said to Saul, "Must Jonathan die, who has brought about this great deliverance in Israel? Far from it! As the Lord lives, there shall not one hair of his head fall to the ground, for he has worked with God this day." So the people rescued Jonathan and he did not die.

46 Then Saul went up from pursuing the Philistines, and the Philistines went to their own place.

47 ¶ Now when Saul had taken the kingdom over Israel, he fought against all his enemies on every side, against Moab, the sons of Ammon, Edom, the kings of Zobah, and the Philistines; and wherever he turned, he inflicted punishment.

48 And he acted valiantly and defeated the Amalekites, and delivered Israel from the hands of those who plundered them.

49 ¶ Now the sons of Saul were Jonathan and Ishvi and Malchi-shua; and the names of his two daughters *were these:* the name of the first-born Merab and the name of the younger Michal.

50 And the name of Saul's wife was Ahinoam the daughter of Ahimaaz. And the name of the captain of his army was Abner the son of Ner, Saul's uncle.

51 And Kish *was* the father of Saul, and Ner the father of Abner *was* the son of Abiel.

52 ¶ Now the war against the Philistines was severe all the days of Saul;

and when Saul saw any mighty man or any valiant man, he attached him to his staff.

CHAPTER 15

THEN Samuel said to Saul, "The LORD sent me to anoint you as king over His people, over Israel; now therefore, listen to the words of the LORD.

2 "Thus says the LORD of hosts, 'I will punish Amalek *for* what he did to Israel, how he set himself against him on the way while he was coming up from Egypt.

3 'Now go and strike Amalek and utterly destroy all that he has, and do not spare him; but put to death both man and woman, child and infant, ox and sheep, camel and donkey.' "

4 ¶ Then Saul summoned the people and numbered them in Telaim, 200,000 foot soldiers and 10,000 men of Judah.

5 And Saul came to the city of Amalek, and set an ambush in the valley.

6 And Saul said to the Kenites, "Go, depart, go down from among the Amalekites, lest I destroy you with them; for you showed kindness to all the sons of Israel when they came up from Egypt." So the Kenites departed from among the Amalekites.

7 So Saul defeated the Amalekites, from Havilah as you go to Shur, which is east of Egypt.

8 And he captured Agag the king of the Amalekites alive, and utterly destroyed all the people with the edge of the sword.

9 But Saul and the people spared Agag and the best of the sheep, the oxen, the fatlings, the lambs, and all that was good, and were not willing to destroy them utterly; but everything despised and worthless, that they utterly destroyed.

10 ¶ Then the word of the LORD came to Samuel, saying,

11 "I regret that I have made Saul king, for he has turned back from following Me, and has not carried out My commands." And Samuel was distressed and cried out to the LORD all night.

12 And Samuel rose early in the morning to meet Saul; and it was told

Samuel, saying, "Saul came to Carmel, and behold, he set up a monument for himself, then turned and proceeded on down to Gilgal."

13 And Samuel came to Saul, and Saul said to him, "Blessed are you of the LORD! I have carried out the command of the LORD."

14 But Samuel said, "What then is this bleating of the sheep in my ears, and the lowing of the oxen which I hear?"

15 And Saul said, "They have brought them from the Amalekites, for the people spared the best of the sheep and oxen, to sacrifice to the LORD your God; but the rest we have utterly destroyed."

16 Then Samuel said to Saul, "Wait, and let me tell you what the LORD said to me last night." And he said to him, "Speak!"

17 ¶ And Samuel said, "Is it not true, though you were little in your own eyes, you were *made* the head of the tribes of Israel? And the LORD anointed you king over Israel,

18 and the LORD sent you on a mission, and said, 'Go and utterly destroy the sinners, the Amalekites, and fight against them until they are exterminated.'

19 "Why then did you not obey the voice of the LORD, but rushed upon the spoil and did what was evil in the sight of the LORD?"

20 ¶ Then Saul said to Samuel, "I did obey the voice of the LORD, and went on the mission on which the LORD sent me, and have brought back Agag the king of Amalek, and have utterly destroyed the Amalekites.

21 "But the people took *some* of the spoil, sheep and oxen, the choicest of the things devoted to destruction, to sacrifice to the LORD your God at Gilgal."

22 And Samuel said,

"Has the LORD as much delight in
    burnt offerings and sacrifices
As in obeying the voice of the
    LORD?
Behold, to obey is better than
    sacrifice,
And to heed than the fat of rams.

23 "For rebellion is as the sin of
    divination,
And insubordination is as iniq-
    uity and idolatry.

Because you have rejected the
word of the LORD,
He has also rejected you from
being king."
24 ¶ Then Saul said to Samuel, "I
have sinned; I have indeed transgressed the command of the LORD and
your words, because I feared the people and listened to their voice.
25 "Now therefore, please pardon my
sin and return with me, that I may
worship the LORD."
26 But Samuel said to Saul, "I will
not return with you; for you have
rejected the word of the LORD, and the
LORD has rejected you from being king
over Israel."
27 And as Samuel turned to go, *Saul*
seized the edge of his robe, and it tore.
28 So Samuel said to him, "The LORD
has torn the kingdom of Israel from
you today, and has given it to your
neighbor who is better than you.
29 "And also the Glory of Israel will
not lie or change His mind; for He is
not a man that He should change His
mind."
30 Then he said, "I have sinned; *but*
please honor me now before the elders
of my people and before Israel, and go
back with me, that I may worship the
LORD your God."
31 So Samuel went back following
Saul, and Saul worshiped the LORD.
32 ¶ Then Samuel said, "Bring me
Agag, the king of the Amalekites."
And Agag came to him cheerfully.
And Agag said, "Surely the bitterness
of death is past."
33 But Samuel said, "As your sword
has made women childless, so shall
your mother be childless among
women." And Samuel hewed Agag to
pieces before the LORD at Gilgal.
34 ¶ Then Samuel went to Ramah,
but Saul went up to his house at Gibeah of Saul.
35 And Samuel did not see Saul
again until the day of his death; for
Samuel grieved over Saul. And the
LORD regretted that He had made Saul
king over Israel.

CHAPTER 16

NOW the LORD said to Samuel, "How
long will you grieve over Saul, since I
have rejected him from being king
over Israel? Fill your horn with oil,

and go; I will send you to Jesse the
Bethlehemite, for I have selected a
king for Myself among his sons."
2 But Samuel said, "How can I go?
When Saul hears *of it,* he will kill me."
And the LORD said, "Take a heifer with
you, and say, 'I have come to sacrifice
to the LORD.'
3 "And you shall invite Jesse to the
sacrifice, and I will show you what
you shall do; and you shall anoint for
Me the one whom I designate to you."
4 So Samuel did what the LORD
said, and came to Bethlehem. And the
elders of the city came trembling to
meet him and said, "Do you come in
peace?"
5 And he said, "In peace; I have
come to sacrifice to the LORD. Consecrate yourselves and come with me to
the sacrifice." He also consecrated
Jesse and his sons, and invited them to
the sacrifice.
6 ¶ Then it came about when they
entered, that he looked at Eliab and
thought, "Surely the LORD's anointed
is before Him."
7 But the LORD said to Samuel, "Do
not look at his appearance or at the
height of his stature, because I have
rejected him; for God *sees* not as man
sees, for man looks at the outward
appearance, but the LORD looks at the
heart."
8 Then Jesse called Abinadab, and
made him pass before Samuel. And he
said, "Neither has the LORD chosen
this one."
9 Next Jesse made Shammah pass
by. And he said, "Neither has the LORD
chosen this one."
10 Thus Jesse made seven of his sons
pass before Samuel. But Samuel said
to Jesse, "The LORD has not chosen
these."
11 And Samuel said to Jesse, "Are
these all the children?" And he said,
"There remains yet the youngest, and
behold, he is tending the sheep." Then
Samuel said to Jesse, "Send and bring
him; for we will not sit down until he
comes here."
12 So he sent and brought him in.
Now he was ruddy, with beautiful eyes
and a handsome appearance. And the
LORD said, "Arise, anoint him; for this
is he."
13 Then Samuel took the horn of oil
and anointed him in the midst of his

brothers; and the Spirit of the LORD came mightily upon David from that day forward. And Samuel arose and went to Ramah.

14 ¶ Now the Spirit of the LORD departed from Saul, and an evil spirit from the LORD terrorized him.

15 Saul's servants then said to him, "Behold now, an evil spirit from God is terrorizing you.

16 "Let our lord now command your servants who are before you. Let them seek a man who is a skillful player on the harp; and it shall come about when the evil spirit from God is on you, that he shall play *the harp* with his hand, and you will be well."

17 So Saul said to his servants, "Provide for me now a man who can play well, and bring *him* to me."

18 Then one of the young men answered and said, "Behold, I have seen a son of Jesse the Bethlehemite who is a skillful musician, a mighty man of valor, a warrior, one prudent in speech, and a handsome man; and the LORD is with him."

19 So Saul sent messengers to Jesse, and said, "Send me your son David who is with the flock."

20 And Jesse took a donkey *loaded with* bread and a jug of wine and a young goat, and sent *them* to Saul by David his son.

21 Then David came to Saul and attended him, and Saul loved him greatly; and he became his armor bearer.

22 And Saul sent to Jesse, saying, "Let David now stand before me; for he has found favor in my sight."

23 So it came about whenever the *evil* spirit from God came to Saul, David would take the harp and play *it* with his hand; and Saul would be refreshed and be well, and the evil spirit would depart from him.

CHAPTER 17

NOW the Philistines gathered their armies for battle; and they were gathered at Socoh which belongs to Judah, and they camped between Socoh and Azekah, in Ephes-dammim.

2 And Saul and the men of Israel were gathered, and camped in the valley of Elah, and drew up in battle array to encounter the Philistines.

3 And the Philistines stood on the mountain on one side while Israel stood on the mountain on the other side, with the valley between them.

4 Then a champion came out from the armies of the Philistines named Goliath, from Gath, whose height was six [10]cubits and a span.

5 And *he had* a bronze helmet on his head, and he was clothed with scale-armor which weighed five thousand shekels of bronze.

6 *He* also *had* bronze [11]greaves on his legs and a bronze javelin *slung* between his shoulders.

7 And the shaft of his spear was like a weaver's beam, and the head of his spear *weighed* six hundred shekels of iron; his shield-carrier also walked before him.

8 And he stood and shouted to the ranks of Israel, and said to them, "Why do you come out to draw up in battle array? Am I not the Philistine and you servants of Saul? Choose a man for yourselves and let him come down to me.

9 "If he is able to fight with me and kill me, then we will become your servants; but if I prevail against him and kill him, then you shall become our servants and serve us."

10 Again the Philistine said, "I defy the ranks of Israel this day; give me a man that we may fight together."

11 When Saul and all Israel heard these words of the Philistine, they were dismayed and greatly afraid.

12 ¶ Now David was the son of the Ephrathite of Bethlehem in Judah, whose name was Jesse, and he had eight sons. And Jesse was old in the days of Saul, advanced *in years* among men.

13 And the three older sons of Jesse had gone after Saul to the battle. And the names of his three sons who went to the battle were Eliab the first-born, and the second to him Abinadab, and the third Shammah.

14 And David was the youngest. Now the three oldest followed Saul,

15 but David went back and forth from Saul to tend his father's flock at Bethlehem.

16 And the Philistine came forward

[10] I.e., One cubit equals approx. 18 in.   [11] Or, *shin guards*

morning and evening for forty days, and took his stand.

17 ¶ Then Jesse said to David his son, "Take now for your brothers an ephah of this roasted grain and these ten loaves, and run to the camp to your brothers.

18"Bring also these ten cuts of cheese to the commander of their thousand, and look into the welfare of your brothers, and bring back news of them.

19"For Saul and they and all the men of Israel are in the valley of Elah, fighting with the Philistines."

20 ¶ So David arose early in the morning and left the flock with a keeper and took the supplies and went as Jesse had commanded him. And he came to the circle of the camp while the army was going out in battle array shouting the war cry.

21 And Israel and the Philistines drew up in battle array, army against army.

22 Then David left his baggage in the care of the baggage keeper, and ran to the battle line and entered in order to greet his brothers.

23 As he was talking with them, behold, the champion, the Philistine from Gath named Goliath, was coming up from the army of the Philistines, and he spoke these same words; and David heard them.

24 When all the men of Israel saw the man, they fled from him and were greatly afraid.

25 And the men of Israel said, "Have you seen this man who is coming up? Surely he is coming up to defy Israel. And it will be that the king will enrich the man who kills him with great riches and will give him his daughter and make his father's house 12free in Israel."

26 ¶ Then David spoke to the men who were standing by him, saying, "What will be done for the man who kills this Philistine, and takes away the reproach from Israel? For who is this uncircumcised Philistine, that he should taunt the armies of the living God?"

27 And the people answered him in accord with this word, saying, "Thus it

will be done for the man who kills him."

28 ¶ Now Eliab his oldest brother heard when he spoke to the men; and Eliab's anger burned against David and he said, "Why have you come down? And with whom have you left those few sheep in the wilderness? I know your insolence and the wickedness of your heart; for you have come down in order to see the battle."

29 But David said, "What have I done now? Was it not just a question?"

30 Then he turned away from him to another and said the same thing; and the people answered the same thing as before.

31 ¶ When the words which David spoke were heard, they told them to Saul, and he sent for him.

32 And David said to Saul, "Let no man's heart fail on account of him; your servant will go and fight with this Philistine."

33 Then Saul said to David, "You are not able to go against this Philistine to fight with him; for you are but a youth while he has been a warrior from his youth."

34 But David said to Saul, "Your servant was tending his father's sheep. When a lion or a bear came and took a lamb from the flock,

35 I went out after him and attacked him, and rescued it from his mouth; and when he rose up against me, I seized him by his beard and struck him and killed him.

36"Your servant has killed both the lion and the bear; and this uncircumcised Philistine will be like one of them, since he has taunted the armies of the living God."

37 And David said, "The LORD who delivered me from the paw of the lion and from the paw of the bear, He will deliver me from the hand of this Philistine." And Saul said to David, "Go, and may the LORD be with you."

38 Then Saul clothed David with his garments and put a bronze helmet on his head, and he clothed him with armor.

39 And David girded his sword over his armor and tried to walk, for he had not tested them. So David said to Saul, "I cannot go with these, for I have not

12 I.e., free from taxes and public service

tested *them*." And David took them off.

40 And he took his stick in his hand and chose for himself five smooth stones from the brook, and put them in the shepherd's bag which he had, even in *his* pouch, and his sling was in his hand; and he approached the Philistine.

41 ¶ Then the Philistine came on and approached David, with the shield-bearer in front of him.

42 When the Philistine looked and saw David, he disdained him; for he was *but* a youth, and ruddy, with a handsome appearance.

43 And the Philistine said to David, "Am I a dog, that you come to me with sticks?" And the Philistine cursed David by his gods.

44 The Philistine also said to David, "Come to me, and I will give your flesh to the birds of the sky and the beasts of the field."

45 Then David said to the Philistine, "You come to me with a sword, a spear, and a javelin, but I come to you in the name of the LORD of hosts, the God of the armies of Israel, whom you have taunted.

46 "This day the LORD will deliver you up into my hands, and I will strike you down and remove your head from you. And I will give the dead bodies of the army of the Philistines this day to the birds of the sky and the wild beasts of the earth, that all the earth may know that there is a God in Israel,

47 and that all this assembly may know that the LORD does not deliver by sword or by spear; for the battle is the LORD'S and He will give you into our hands."

48 Then it happened when the Philistine rose and came and drew near to meet David, that David ran quickly toward the battle line to meet the Philistine.

49 And David put his hand into his bag and took from it a stone and slung *it*, and struck the Philistine on his forehead. And the stone sank into his forehead, so that he fell on his face to the ground.

50 ¶ Thus David prevailed over the Philistine with a sling and a stone, and he struck the Philistine and killed him; but there was no sword in David's hand.

51 Then David ran and stood over the Philistine and took his sword and drew it out of its sheath and killed him, and cut off his head with it. When the Philistines saw that their champion was dead, they fled.

52 And the men of Israel and Judah arose and shouted and pursued the Philistines as far as the valley, and to the gates of Ekron. And the slain Philistines lay along the way to Shaaraim, even to Gath and Ekron.

53 And the sons of Israel returned from chasing the Philistines and plundered their camps.

54 Then David took the Philistine's head and brought it to Jerusalem, but he put his weapons in his tent.

55 ¶ Now when Saul saw David going out against the Philistine, he said to Abner the commander of the army, "Abner, whose son is this young man?" And Abner said, "By your life, O king, I do not know."

56 And the king said, "You inquire whose son the youth is."

57 So when David returned from killing the Philistine, Abner took him and brought him before Saul with the Philistine's head in his hand.

58 And Saul said to him, "Whose son are you, young man?" And David answered, "*I am* the son of your servant Jesse the Bethlehemite."

CHAPTER 18

NOW it came about when he had finished speaking to Saul, that the soul of Jonathan was knit to the soul of David, and Jonathan loved him as himself.

2 And Saul took him that day and did not let him return to his father's house.

3 Then Jonathan made a covenant with David because he loved him as himself.

4 And Jonathan stripped himself of the robe that was on him and gave it to David, with his armor, including his sword and his bow and his belt.

5 So David went out wherever Saul sent him, *and* prospered; and Saul set him over the men of war. And it was pleasing in the sight of all the people and also in the sight of Saul's servants.

6 ¶ And it happened as they were coming, when David returned from

killing the Philistine, that the women came out of all the cities of Israel, singing and dancing, to meet King Saul, with tambourines, with joy and with [13]musical instruments.

7 And the women sang as they played, and said,

"Saul has slain his thousands,
And David his ten thousands."

8 Then Saul became very angry, for this saying displeased him; and he said, "They have ascribed to David ten thousands, but to me they have ascribed thousands. Now what more can he have but the kingdom?"

9 And Saul looked at David with suspicion from that day on.

10 ¶ Now it came about on the next day that an evil spirit from God came mightily upon Saul, and he raved in the midst of the house, while David was playing *the harp* with his hand, as usual; and a spear *was* in Saul's hand.

11 And Saul hurled the spear for he thought, "I will pin David to the wall." But David escaped from his presence twice.

12 Now Saul was afraid of David, for the LORD was with him but had departed from Saul.

13 Therefore Saul removed him from his presence, and appointed him as his commander of a thousand; and he went out and came in before the people.

14 And David was prospering in all his ways for the LORD *was* with him.

15 When Saul saw that he was prospering greatly, he dreaded him.

16 But all Israel and Judah loved David, and he went out and came in before them.

17 ¶ Then Saul said to David, "Here is my older daughter Merab; I will give her to you as a wife, only be a valiant man for me and fight the LORD's battles." For Saul thought, "My hand shall not be against him, but let the hand of the Philistines be against him."

18 But David said to Saul, "Who am I, and what is my life *or* my father's family in Israel, that I should be the king's son-in-law?"

19 So it came about at the time when Merab, Saul's daughter, should have

been given to David, that she was given to Adriel the Meholathite for a wife.

20 ¶ Now Michal, Saul's daughter, loved David. When they told Saul, the thing was agreeable to him.

21 And Saul thought, "I will give her to him that she may become a snare to him, and that the hand of the Philistines may be against him." Therefore Saul said to David, "For a second time you may be my son-in-law today."

22 Then Saul commanded his servants, "Speak to David secretly, saying, 'Behold, the king delights in you, and all his servants love you; now therefore, become the king's son-in-law.'"

23 So Saul's servants spoke these words to David. But David said, "Is it trivial in your sight to become the king's son-in-law, since I am a poor man and lightly esteemed?"

24 And the servants of Saul reported to him according to these words *which* David spoke.

25 Saul then said, "Thus you shall say to David, 'The king does not desire any dowry except a hundred foreskins of the Philistines, to take vengeance on the king's enemies.'" Now Saul planned to make David fall by the hand of the Philistines.

26 When his servants told David these words, it pleased David to become the king's son-in-law. Before the days had expired

27 David rose up and went, he and his men, and struck down two hundred men among the Philistines. Then David brought their foreskins, and they gave them in full number to the king, that he might become the king's son-in-law. So Saul gave him Michal his daughter for a wife.

28 When Saul saw and knew that the LORD was with David, and *that* Michal, Saul's daughter, loved him,

29 then Saul was even more afraid of David. Thus Saul was David's enemy continually.

30 ¶ Then the commanders of the Philistines went out *to battle*, and it happened as often as they went out, that David behaved himself more wisely than all the servants of Saul. So his name was highly esteemed.

[13] I.e., triangles, or three-stringed instruments

CHAPTER 19

NOW Saul told Jonathan his son and all his servants to put David to death. But Jonathan, Saul's son, greatly delighted in David.

2 So Jonathan told David saying, "Saul my father is seeking to put you to death. Now therefore, please be on guard in the morning, and stay in a secret place and hide yourself.

3 "And I will go out and stand beside my father in the field where you are, and I will speak with my father about you; if I find out anything, then I shall tell you."

4 Then Jonathan spoke well of David to Saul his father, and said to him, "Do not let the king sin against his servant David, since he has not sinned against you, and since his deeds *have been* very beneficial to you.

5 "For he took his life in his hand and struck the Philistine, and the LORD brought about a great deliverance for all Israel; you saw *it* and rejoiced. Why then will you sin against innocent blood, by putting David to death without a cause?"

6 And Saul listened to the voice of Jonathan, and Saul vowed, "As the LORD lives, he shall not be put to death."

7 Then Jonathan called David, and Jonathan told him all these words. And Jonathan brought David to Saul, and he was in his presence as formerly.

8 ¶ When there was war again, David went out and fought with the Philistines, and defeated them with great slaughter, so that they fled before him.

9 Now there was an evil spirit from the LORD on Saul as he was sitting in his house with his spear in his hand, and David was playing *the harp* with *his* hand.

10 And Saul tried to pin David to the wall with the spear, but he slipped away out of Saul's presence, so that he stuck the spear into the wall. And David fled and escaped that night.

11 ¶ Then Saul sent messengers to David's house to watch him, in order to put him to death in the morning. But Michal, David's wife, told him, saying, "If you do not save your life

tonight, tomorrow you will be put to death."

12 So Michal let David down through a window, and he went out and fled and escaped.

13 And Michal took the household idol and laid *it* on the bed, and put a quilt of goats' *hair* at its head, and covered *it* with clothes.

14 When Saul sent messengers to take David, she said, "He is sick."

15 Then Saul sent messengers to see David, saying, "Bring him up to me on his bed, that I may put him to death."

16 When the messengers entered, behold, the household idol *was* on the bed with the quilt of goats' *hair* at its head.

17 So Saul said to Michal, "Why have you deceived me like this and let my enemy go, so that he has escaped?" And Michal said to Saul, "He said to me, 'Let me go! Why should I put you to death?' "

18 ¶ Now David fled and escaped and came to Samuel at Ramah, and told him all that Saul had done to him. And he and Samuel went and stayed in Naioth.

19 And it was told Saul, saying, "Behold, David is at Naioth in Ramah."

20 Then Saul sent messengers to take David, but when they saw the company of the prophets prophesying, with Samuel standing *and* presiding over them, the Spirit of God came upon the messengers of Saul; and they also prophesied.

21 And when it was told Saul, he sent other messengers, and they also prophesied. So Saul sent messengers again the third time, and they also prophesied.

22 Then he himself went to Ramah, and came as far as the large well that is in Secu; and he asked and said, "Where are Samuel and David?" And someone said, "Behold, they are at Naioth in Ramah."

23 And he proceeded there to Naioth in Ramah; and the Spirit of God came upon him also, so that he went along prophesying continually until he came to Naioth in Ramah.

24 And he also stripped off his clothes, and he too prophesied before Samuel and lay down naked all that day and all that night. Therefore they

say, "Is Saul also among the prophets?"

CHAPTER 20

THEN David fled from Naioth in Ramah, and came and said to Jonathan, "What have I done? What is my iniquity? And what is my sin before your father, that he is seeking my life?"

2 And he said to him, "Far from it, you shall not die. Behold, my father does nothing either great or small without disclosing it to me. So why should my father hide this thing from me? It is not so!"

3 Yet David vowed again, saying, "Your father knows well that I have found favor in your sight, and he has said, 'Do not let Jonathan know this, lest he be grieved.' But truly as the LORD lives and as your soul lives, there is hardly a step between me and death."

4 Then Jonathan said to David, "Whatever you say, I will do for you."

5 So David said to Jonathan, "Behold, tomorrow is the new moon, and I ought to sit down to eat with the king. But let me go, that I may hide myself in the field until the third evening.

6 "If your father misses me at all, then say, 'David earnestly asked *leave* of me to run to Bethlehem his city, because it is the yearly sacrifice there for the whole family.'

7 "If he says, 'It is good,' your servant *shall be* safe; but if he is very angry, know that he has decided on evil.

8 "Therefore deal kindly with your servant, for you have brought your servant into a covenant of the LORD with you. But if there is iniquity in me, put me to death yourself; for why then should you bring me to your father?"

9 And Jonathan said, "Far be it from you! For if I should indeed learn that evil has been decided by my father to come upon you, then would I not tell you about it?"

10 Then David said to Jonathan, "Who will tell me if your father answers you harshly?"

11 And Jonathan said to David, "Come, and let us go out into the field." So both of them went out into the field.

12 ¶ Then Jonathan said to David, "The LORD, the God of Israel, *be witness*! When I have sounded out my father about this time tomorrow, *or* the third day, behold, if there is good *feeling* toward David, shall I not then send to you and make it known to you?

13 "If it please my father *to do* you harm, may the LORD do so to Jonathan and more also, if I do not make it known to you and send you away, that you may go in safety. And may the LORD be with you as He has been with my father.

14 "And if I am still alive, will you not show me the lovingkindness of the LORD, that I may not die?

15 "And you shall not cut off your lovingkindness from my house forever, not even when the LORD cuts off every one of the enemies of David from the face of the earth."

16 So Jonathan made a *covenant* with the house of David, *saying*, "May the LORD require *it* at the hands of David's enemies."

17 And Jonathan made David vow again because of his love for him, because he loved him as he loved his own life.

18 ¶ Then Jonathan said to him, "Tomorrow is the new moon, and you will be missed because your seat will be empty.

19 "When you have stayed for three days, you shall go down quickly and come to the place where you hid yourself on that eventful day, and you shall remain by the stone Ezel.

20 "And I will shoot three arrows to the side, as though I shot at a target.

21 "And behold, I will send the lad, *saying*, 'Go, find the arrows.' If I specifically say to the lad, 'Behold, the arrows are on this side of you, get them,' then come; for there is safety for you and no harm, as the LORD lives.

22 "But if I say to the youth, 'Behold, the arrows are beyond you,' go, for the LORD has sent you away.

23 "As for the agreement of which you and I have spoken, behold, the LORD is between you and me forever."

24 ¶ So David hid in the field; and when the new moon came, the king sat down to eat food.

25 And the king sat on his seat as usual, the seat by the wall; then Jonathan rose up and Abner sat down by Saul's side, but David's place was empty.

26 Nevertheless Saul did not speak anything that day, for he thought, "It is an accident, he is not clean, surely *he is* not clean."

27 And it came about the next day, the second *day* of the new moon, that David's place was empty; so Saul said to Jonathan his son, "Why has the son of Jesse not come to the meal, either yesterday or today?"

28 Jonathan then answered Saul, "David earnestly asked leave of me *to go* to Bethlehem,

29 for he said, 'Please let me go, since our family has a sacrifice in the city, and my brother has commanded me to attend. And now, if I have found favor in your sight, please let me get away that I may see my brothers.' For this reason he has not come to the king's table."

30 ¶ Then Saul's anger burned against Jonathan and he said to him, "You son of a perverse, rebellious woman! Do I not know that you are choosing the son of Jesse to your own shame and to the shame of your mother's nakedness?

31 "For as long as the son of Jesse lives on the earth, neither you nor your kingdom will be established. Therefore now, send and bring him to me, for he must surely die."

32 But Jonathan answered Saul his father and said to him, "Why should he be put to death? What has he done?"

33 Then Saul hurled his spear at him to strike him down; so Jonathan knew that his father had decided to put David to death.

34 Then Jonathan arose from the table in fierce anger, and did not eat food on the second day of the new moon, for he was grieved over David because his father had dishonored him.

35 ¶ Now it came about in the morning that Jonathan went out into the field for the appointment with David, and a little lad *was* with him.

36 And he said to his lad, "Run, find now the arrows which I am about to shoot." As the lad was running, he shot an arrow past him.

37 When the lad reached the place of the arrow which Jonathan had shot, Jonathan called after the lad, and said, "Is not the arrow beyond you?"

38 And Jonathan called after the lad, "Hurry, be quick, do not stay!" And Jonathan's lad picked up the arrow and came to his master.

39 But the lad was not aware of anything; only Jonathan and David knew about the matter.

40 Then Jonathan gave his weapons to his lad and said to him, "Go, bring *them* to the city."

41 When the lad was gone, David rose from the south side and fell on his face to the ground, and bowed three times. And they kissed each other and wept together, but David more.

42 And Jonathan said to David, "Go in safety, inasmuch as we have sworn to each other in the name of the LORD, saying, 'The LORD will be between me and you, and between my descendants and your descendants forever.' " Then he rose and departed, while Jonathan went into the city.

CHAPTER 21

THEN David came to Nob to Ahimelech the priest; and Ahimelech came trembling to meet David, and said to him, "Why are you alone and no one with you?"

2 And David said to Ahimelech the priest, "The king has commissioned me with a matter, and has said to me, 'Let no one know anything about the matter on which I am sending you and with which I have commissioned you; and I have directed the young men to a certain place.'

3 "Now therefore, what do you have on hand? Give me five loaves of bread, or whatever can be found."

4 And the priest answered David and said, "There is no ordinary bread on hand, but there is consecrated bread; if only the young men have kept themselves from women."

5 And David answered the priest and said to him, "Surely women have been kept from us as previously when I set out and the vessels of the young men were holy, though it was an ordinary journey; how much more then today will their vessels *be holy*?"

6 So the priest gave him conse-crated *bread*; for there was no bread there but the bread of the Presence which was removed from before the LORD, in order to put hot bread *in its place* when it was taken away.

7 ¶ Now one of the servants of Saul was there that day, detained before the LORD; and his name was Doeg the Edomite, the chief of Saul's shepherds.

8 ¶ And David said to Ahimelech, "Now is there not a spear or a sword on hand? For I brought neither my sword nor my weapons with me, be-cause the king's matter was urgent."

9 Then the priest said, "The sword of Goliath the Philistine, whom you killed in the valley of Elah, behold, it is wrapped in a cloth behind the ephod; if you would take it for yourself, take *it*. For there is no other except it here." And David said, "There is none like it; give it to me."

10 ¶ Then David arose and fled that day from Saul, and went to Achish king of Gath.

11 But the servants of Achish said to him, "Is this not David the king of the land? Did they not sing of this one as they danced, saying,

'Saul has slain his thousands,
And David his ten thousands'?"

12 And David took these words to heart, and greatly feared Achish king of Gath.

13 So he disguised his sanity before them, and acted insanely in their hands, and scribbled on the doors of the gate, and let his saliva run down into his beard.

14 Then Achish said to his servants, "Behold, you see the man behaving as a madman. Why do you bring him to me?

15 "Do I lack madmen, that you have brought this one to act the madman in my presence? Shall this one come into my house?"

CHAPTER 22

So David departed from there and escaped to the cave of Adullam; and when his brothers and all his father's household heard *of it*, they went down there to him.

2 And everyone who was in dis-tress, and everyone who was in debt, and everyone who was discontented, gathered to him; and he became cap-tain over them. Now there were about four hundred men with him.

3 ¶ And David went from there to Mizpah of Moab; and he said to the king of Moab, "Please let my father and my mother come *and stay* with you until I know what God will do for me."

4 Then he left them with the king of Moab; and they stayed with him all the time that David was in the strong-hold.

5 And the prophet Gad said to Da-vid, "Do not stay in the stronghold; depart, and go into the land of Judah." So David departed and went into the forest of Hereth.

6 ¶ Then Saul heard that David and the men who were with him had been discovered. Now Saul was sitting in Gibeah, under the tamarisk tree on the height with his spear in his hand, and all his servants were standing around him.

7 And Saul said to his servants who stood around him, "Hear now, O Ben-jamites! Will the son of Jesse also give to all of you fields and vineyards? Will he make you all commanders of thou-sands and commanders of hundreds?

8 "For all of you have conspired against me so that there is no one who discloses to me when my son makes *a covenant* with the son of Jesse, and there is none of you who is sorry for me or discloses to me that my son has stirred up my servant against me to lie in ambush, as *it is* this day."

9 Then Doeg the Edomite, who was standing by the servants of Saul, an-swered and said, "I saw the son of Jesse coming to Nob, to Ahimelech the son of Ahitub.

10 "And he inquired of the LORD for him, gave him provisions, and gave him the sword of Goliath the Philis-tine."

11 ¶ Then the king sent someone to summon Ahimelech the priest, the son of Ahitub, and all his father's house-hold, the priests who were in Nob; and all of them came to the king.

12 And Saul said, "Listen now, son of Ahitub." And he answered, "Here I am, my lord."

13 Saul then said to him, "Why have you and the son of Jesse conspired against me, in that you have given him

bread and a sword and have inquired of God for him, that he should rise up against me by lying in ambush as *it is* this day?"

14 Then Ahimelech answered the king and said, "And who among all your servants is as faithful as David, even the king's son-in-law, who is captain over your guard, and is honored in your house?

15"Did I *just* begin to inquire of God for him today? Far be it from me! Do not let the king impute anything to his servant *or* to any of the household of my father, for your servant knows nothing at all of this whole affair."

16 But the king said, "You shall surely die, Ahimelech, you and all your father's household!"

17 And the king said to the guards who were attending him, "Turn around and put the priests of the LORD to death, because their hand also is with David and because they knew that he was fleeing and did not reveal it to me." But the servants of the king were not willing to put forth their hands to attack the priests of the LORD.

18 Then the king said to Doeg, "You turn around and attack the priests." And Doeg the Edomite turned around and attacked the priests, and he killed that day eighty-five men who wore the linen ephod.

19 And he struck Nob the city of the priests with the edge of the sword, both men and women, children and infants; also oxen, donkeys, and sheep, *he struck* with the edge of the sword.

20 ¶ But one son of Ahimelech the son of Ahitub, named Abiathar, escaped and fled after David.

21 And Abiathar told David that Saul had killed the priests of the LORD.

22 Then David said to Abiathar, "I knew on that day, when Doeg the Edomite was there, that he would surely tell Saul. I have brought about *the death* of every person in your father's household.

23"Stay with me, do not be afraid, for he who seeks my life seeks your life; for you are safe with me."

CHAPTER 23

THEN they told David, saying, "Behold, the Philistines are fighting against Keilah, and are plundering the threshing floors."

2 So David inquired of the LORD, saying, "Shall I go and attack these Philistines?" And the LORD said to David, "Go and attack the Philistines, and deliver Keilah."

3 But David's men said to him, "Behold, we are afraid here in Judah. How much more then if we go to Keilah against the ranks of the Philistines?"

4 Then David inquired of the LORD once more. And the LORD answered him and said, "Arise, go down to Keilah, for I will give the Philistines into your hand."

5 So David and his men went to Keilah and fought with the Philistines; and he led away their livestock and struck them with a great slaughter. Thus David delivered the inhabitants of Keilah.

6 ¶ Now it came about, when Abiathar the son of Ahimelech fled to David at Keilah, *that* he came down *with* an ephod in his hand.

7 When it was told Saul that David had come to Keilah, Saul said, "God has delivered him into my hand, for he shut himself in by entering a city with double gates and bars."

8 So Saul summoned all the people for war, to go down to Keilah to besiege David and his men.

9 Now David knew that Saul was plotting evil against him; so he said to Abiathar the priest, "Bring the ephod here."

10 Then David said, "O LORD God of Israel, Thy servant has heard for certain that Saul is seeking to come to Keilah to destroy the city on my account.

11"Will the men of Keilah surrender me into his hand? Will Saul come down just as Thy servant has heard? O LORD God of Israel, I pray, tell Thy servant." And the LORD said, "He will come down."

12 Then David said, "Will the men of Keilah surrender me and my men into the hand of Saul?" And the LORD said, "They will surrender you."

13 Then David and his men, about six hundred, arose and departed from Keilah, and they went wherever they could go. When it was told Saul that David had escaped from Keilah, he gave up the pursuit.

14 And David stayed in the wilderness in the strongholds, and remained in the hill country in the wilderness of Ziph. And Saul sought him every day, but God did not deliver him into his hand.

15 ¶ Now David became aware that Saul had come out to seek his life while David was in the wilderness of Ziph at Horesh.

16 And Jonathan, Saul's son, arose and went to David at Horesh, and [14]encouraged him in God.

17 Thus he said to him, "Do not be afraid, because the hand of Saul my father shall not find you, and you will be king over Israel and I will be next to you; and Saul my father knows that also."

18 So the two of them made a covenant before the LORD; and David stayed at Horesh while Jonathan went to his house.

19 ¶ Then Ziphites came up to Saul at Gibeah, saying, "Is David not hiding with us in the strongholds at Horesh, on the hill of Hachilah, which is on the south of [15]Jeshimon?

20 "Now then, O king, come down according to all the desire of your soul to do so; and our part *shall be* to surrender him into the king's hand."

21 And Saul said, "May you be blessed of the LORD; for you have had compassion on me.

22 "Go now, make more sure, and investigate and see his place where his haunt is, *and* who has seen him there; for I am told that he is very cunning.

23 "So look, and learn about all the hiding places where he hides himself, and return to me with certainty, and I will go with you; and it shall come about if he is in the land that I will search him out among all the thousands of Judah."

24 ¶ Then they arose and went to Ziph before Saul. Now David and his men were in the wilderness of Maon, in the Arabah to the south of Jeshimon.

25 When Saul and his men went to seek *him*, they told David, and he came down to the rock and stayed in the wilderness of Maon. And when Saul heard *it*, he pursued David in the wilderness of Maon.

26 And Saul went on one side of the mountain, and David and his men on the other side of the mountain; and David was hurrying to get away from Saul, for Saul and his men were surrounding David and his men to seize them.

27 But a messenger came to Saul, saying, "Hurry and come, for the Philistines have made a raid on the land."

28 So Saul returned from pursuing David, and went to meet the Philistines; therefore they called that place the Rock of Escape.

29 And David went up from there and stayed in the strongholds of Engedi.

CHAPTER 24

NOW it came about when Saul returned from pursuing the Philistines, he was told, saying, "Behold, David is in the wilderness of Engedi."

2 Then Saul took three thousand chosen men from all Israel, and went to seek David and his men in front of the Rocks of the Wild Goats.

3 And he came to the sheepfolds on the way, where there *was* a cave; and Saul went in to relieve himself. Now David and his men were sitting in the inner recesses of the cave.

4 And the men of David said to him, "Behold, *this is* the day of which the LORD said to you, 'Behold; I am about to give your enemy into your hand, and you shall do to him as it seems good to you.'" Then David arose and cut off the edge of Saul's robe secretly.

5 And it came about afterward that David's conscience bothered him because he had cut off the edge of Saul's *robe.*

6 So he said to his men, "Far be it from me because of the LORD that I should do this thing to my lord, the LORD's anointed, to stretch out my hand against him, since he is the LORD's anointed."

7 And David persuaded his men with *these* words and did not allow them to rise up against Saul. And Saul arose, left the cave, and went on *his* way.

8 ¶ Now afterward David arose and went out of the cave and called after Saul, saying, "My lord the king!" And when Saul looked behind him, David

[14] Lit., *strengthened his hand*   [15] Or, *the desert*

bowed with his face to the ground and prostrated himself.

9 And David said to Saul, "Why do you listen to the words of men, saying, 'Behold, David seeks to harm you'?

10"Behold, this day your eyes have seen that the LORD had given you today into my hand in the cave, and some said to kill you, but *my eye* had pity on you; and I said, 'I will not stretch out my hand against my lord, for he is the LORD's anointed.'

11"Now, my father, see! Indeed, see the edge of your robe in my hand! For in that I cut off the edge of your robe and did not kill you, know and perceive that there is no evil or rebellion in my hands, and I have not sinned against you, though you are lying in wait for my life to take it.

12"May the LORD judge between you and me, and may the LORD avenge me on you; but my hand shall not be against you.

13"As the proverb of the ancients says, 'Out of the wicked comes forth wickedness'; but my hand shall not be against you.

14"After whom has the king of Israel come out? Whom are you pursuing? A dead dog, a single flea?

15"The LORD therefore be judge and decide between you and me; and may He see and plead my cause, and deliver me from your hand."

16 ¶ Now it came about when David had finished speaking these words to Saul, that Saul said, "Is this your voice, my son David?" Then Saul lifted up his voice and wept.

17 And he said to David, "You are more righteous than I; for you have dealt well with me, while I have dealt wickedly with you.

18"And you have declared today that you have done good to me, that the LORD delivered me into your hand and *yet* you did not kill me.

19"For if a man finds his enemy, will he let him go away safely? May the LORD therefore reward you with good in return for what you have done to me this day.

20"And now, behold, I know that you shall surely be king, and that the kingdom of Israel shall be established in your hand.

21"So now swear to me by the LORD

that you will not cut off my descendants after me, and that you will not destroy my name from my father's household."

22 And David swore to Saul. And Saul went to his home, but David and his men went up to the stronghold.

CHAPTER 25

THEN Samuel died; and all Israel gathered together and mourned for him, and buried him at his house in Ramah. And David arose and went down to the wilderness of Paran.

2 ¶ Now *there was* a man in Maon whose business was in Carmel; and the man was very rich, and he had three thousand sheep and a thousand goats. And it came about while he was shearing his sheep in Carmel

3 (now the man's name was Nabal, and his wife's name was Abigail. And the woman was intelligent and beautiful in appearance, but the man was harsh and evil in *his* dealings, and he was a Calebite),

4 that David heard in the wilderness that Nabal was shearing his sheep.

5 So David sent ten young men, and David said to the young men, "Go up to Carmel, visit Nabal and greet him in my name;

6 and thus you shall say, 'Have a long life, peace be to you, and peace be to your house, and peace be to all that you have.

7 'And now I have heard that you have shearers; now your shepherds have been with us and we have not insulted them, nor have they missed anything all the days they were in Carmel.

8 'Ask your young men and they will tell you. Therefore let *my* young men find favor in your eyes, for we have come on a festive day. Please give whatever you find at hand to your servants and to your son David.' "

9 ¶ When David's young men came, they spoke to Nabal according to all these words in David's name; then they waited.

10 But Nabal answered David's servants, and said, "Who is David? And who is the son of Jesse? There are many servants today who are each breaking away from his master.

11"Shall I then take my bread and my water and my meat that I have slaughtered for my shearers, and give it to men whose origin I do not know?"

12 So David's young men retraced their way and went back; and they came and told him according to all these words.

13 And David said to his men, "Each of you gird on his sword." So each man girded on his sword. And David also girded on his sword, and about four hundred men went up behind David while two hundred stayed with the baggage.

14 ¶ But one of the young men told Abigail, Nabal's wife, saying, "Behold, David sent messengers from the wilderness to greet our master, and he scorned them.

15"Yet the men were very good to us, and we were not insulted, nor did we miss anything as long as we went about with them, while we were in the fields.

16"They were a wall to us both by night and by day, all the time we were with them tending the sheep.

17"Now therefore, know and consider what you should do, for evil is plotted against our master and against all his household; and he is such a worthless man that no one can speak to him."

18 ¶ Then Abigail hurried and took two hundred *loaves* of bread and two jugs of wine and five sheep already prepared and five measures of roasted grain and a hundred clusters of raisins and two hundred cakes of figs, and loaded *them* on donkeys.

19 And she said to her young men, "Go on before me; behold, I am coming after you." But she did not tell her husband Nabal.

20 And it came about as she was riding on her donkey and coming down by the hidden part of the mountain, that behold, David and his men were coming down toward her; so she met them.

21 Now David had said, "Surely in vain I have guarded all that this *man* has in the wilderness, so that nothing was missed of all that belonged to him; and he has returned me evil for good.

22"May God do so to the enemies of David, and more also, if by morning I leave *as much as* one male of any who belong to him."

23 ¶ When Abigail saw David, she hurried and dismounted from her donkey, and fell on her face before David, and bowed herself to the ground.

24 And she fell at his feet and said, "On me alone, my lord, be the blame. And please let your maidservant speak to you, and listen to the words of your maidservant.

25"Please do not let my lord pay attention to this worthless man, Nabal, for as his name is, so is he. Nabal is his name and folly is with him; but I your maidservant did not see the young men of my lord whom you sent.

26"Now therefore, my lord, as the LORD lives, and as your soul lives, since the LORD has restrained you from shedding blood, and from avenging yourself by your own hand, now then let your enemies, and those who seek evil against my lord, be as Nabal.

27"And now let this gift which your maidservant has brought to my lord be given to the young men who accompany my lord.

28"Please forgive the transgression of your maidservant; for the LORD will certainly make for my lord an enduring house, because my lord is fighting the battles of the LORD, and evil shall not be found in you all your days.

29"And should anyone rise up to pursue you and to seek your life, then the life of my lord shall be bound in the bundle of the living with the LORD your God; but the lives of your enemies He will sling out as from the hollow of a sling.

30"And it shall come about when the LORD shall do for my lord according to all the good that He has spoken concerning you, and shall appoint you ruler over Israel,

31 that this will not cause grief or a troubled heart to my lord, both by having shed blood without cause and by my lord having avenged himself. When the LORD shall deal well with my lord, then remember your maidservant."

32 ¶ Then David said to Abigail, "Blessed be the LORD God of Israel, who sent you this day to meet me,

33 and blessed be your discernment, and blessed be you, who have kept me

this day from bloodshed, and from avenging myself by my own hand.

34"Nevertheless, as the LORD God of Israel lives, who has restrained me from harming you, unless you had come quickly to meet me, surely there would not have been left to Nabal until the morning light *as much as* one male."

35 So David received from her hand what she had brought him, and he said to her, "Go up to your house in peace. See, I have listened to you and granted your request."

36 ¶ Then Abigail came to Nabal, and behold, he was holding a feast in his house, like the feast of a king. And Nabal's heart was merry within him, for he was very drunk; so she did not tell him anything at all until the morning light.

37 But it came about in the morning, when the wine had gone out of Nabal, that his wife told him these things, and his heart died within him so that he became *as* a stone.

38 And about ten days later, it happened that the LORD struck Nabal, and he died.

39 ¶ When David heard that Nabal was dead, he said, "Blessed be the LORD, who has pleaded the cause of my reproach from the hand of Nabal, and has kept back His servant from evil. The LORD has also returned the evildoing of Nabal on his own head." Then David sent a proposal to Abigail, to take her as his wife.

40 When the servants of David came to Abigail at Carmel, they spoke to her, saying, "David has sent us to you, to take you as his wife."

41 And she arose and bowed with her face to the ground and said, "Behold, your maidservant is a maid to wash the feet of my lord's servants."

42 Then Abigail quickly arose, and rode on a donkey, with her five maidens who attended her; and she followed the messengers of David, and became his wife.

43 ¶ David had also taken Ahinoam of Jezreel, and they both became his wives.

44 ¶ Now Saul had given Michal his daughter, David's wife, to Palti the son of Laish, who was from Gallim.

CHAPTER 26

THEN the Ziphites came to Saul at Gibeah, saying, "Is not David hiding on the hill of Hachilah, *which is* before [16]Jeshimon?"

2 So Saul arose and went down to the wilderness of Ziph, having with him three thousand chosen men of Israel, to search for David in the wilderness of Ziph.

3 And Saul camped in the hill of Hachilah, which is before [16]Jeshimon, beside the road, and David was staying in the wilderness. When he saw that Saul came after him into the wilderness,

4 David sent out spies, and he knew that Saul was definitely coming.

5 David then arose and came to the place where Saul had camped. And David saw the place where Saul lay, and Abner the son of Ner, the commander of his army; and Saul was lying in the circle of the camp, and the people were camped around him.

6 ¶ Then David answered and said to Ahimelech the Hittite and to Abishai the son of Zeruiah, Joab's brother, saying, "Who will go down with me to Saul in the camp?" And Abishai said, "I will go down with you."

7 So David and Abishai came to the people by night, and behold, Saul lay sleeping inside the circle of the camp, with his spear stuck in the ground at his head; and Abner and the people were lying around him.

8 Then Abishai said to David, "Today God has delivered your enemy into your hand; now therefore, please let me strike him with the spear to the ground with one stroke, and I will not strike him the second time."

9 But David said to Abishai, "Do not destroy him, for who can stretch out his hand against the LORD's anointed and be without guilt?"

10 David also said, "As the LORD lives, surely the LORD will strike him, or his day will come that he dies, or he will go down into battle and perish.

11"The LORD forbid that I should stretch out my hand against the LORD's anointed; but now please take

[16] Or, *the desert*

the spear that is at his head and the jug of water, and let us go."

12 So David took the spear and the jug of water from *beside* Saul's head, and they went away, but no one saw or knew *it*, nor did any awake, for they were all asleep, because a sound sleep from the LORD had fallen on them.

13 ¶ Then David crossed over to the other side, and stood on top of the mountain at a distance *with* a large area between them.

14 And David called to the people and to Abner the son of Ner, saying, "Will you not answer, Abner?" Then Abner answered and said, "Who are you who calls to the king?"

15 So David said to Abner, "Are you not a man? And who is like you in Israel? Why then have you not guarded your lord the king? For one of the people came to destroy the king your lord.

16"This thing that you have done is not good. As the LORD lives, *all* of you must surely die, because you did not guard your lord, the LORD's anointed. And now, see where the king's spear is, and the jug of water that was at his head."

17 ¶ Then Saul recognized David's voice and said, "Is this your voice, my son David?" And David said, "It is my voice, my lord the king."

18 He also said, "Why then is my lord pursuing his servant? For what have I done? Or what evil is in my hand?

19"Now therefore, please let my lord the king listen to the words of his servant. If the LORD has stirred you up against me, let Him accept an offering; but if it is men, cursed are they before the LORD, for they have driven me out today that I should have no attachment with the inheritance of the LORD, saying, 'Go, serve other gods.'

20"Now then, do not let my blood fall to the ground away from the presence of the LORD; for the king of Israel has come out to search for a single flea, just as one hunts a partridge in the mountains."

21 ¶ Then Saul said, "I have sinned. Return, my son David, for I will not harm you again because my life was precious in your sight this day. Behold, I have played the fool and have committed a serious error."

22 And David answered and said, "Behold the spear of the king! Now let one of the young men come over and take it.

23"And the LORD will repay each man *for* his righteousness and his faithfulness; for the LORD delivered you into *my* hand today, but I refused to stretch out my hand against the LORD's anointed.

24"Now behold, as your life was highly valued in my sight this day, so may my life be highly valued in the sight of the LORD, and may He deliver me from all distress."

25 Then Saul said to David, "Blessed are you, my son David; you will both accomplish much and surely prevail." So David went on his way, and Saul returned to his place.

CHAPTER 27

THEN David said to himself, "Now I will perish one day by the hand of Saul. There is nothing better for me than to escape into the land of the Philistines. Saul then will despair of searching for me anymore in all the territory of Israel, and I will escape from his hand."

2 So David arose and crossed over, he and the six hundred men who were with him, to Achish the son of Maoch, king of Gath.

3 And David lived with Achish at Gath, he and his men, each with his household, *even* David with his two wives, Ahinoam the Jezreelitess, and Abigail the Carmelitess, Nabal's widow.

4 Now it was told Saul that David had fled to Gath, so he no longer searched for him.

5 ¶ Then David said to Achish, "If now I have found favor in your sight, let them give me a place in one of the cities in the country, that I may live there; for why should your servant live in the royal city with you?"

6 So Achish gave him Ziklag that day; therefore Ziklag has belonged to the kings of Judah to this day.

7 And the number of days that David lived in the country of the Philistines was a year and four months.

8 ¶ Now David and his men went up and raided the Geshurites and the Girzites and the Amalekites; for they

were the inhabitants of the land from ancient times, as you come to Shur even as far as the land of Egypt.

9 And David attacked the land and did not leave a man or a woman alive, and he took away the sheep, the cattle, the donkeys, the camels, and the clothing. Then he returned and came to Achish.

10 Now Achish said, "Where have you made a raid today?" And David said, "Against the [17]Negev of Judah and against the Negev of the Jerahmeelites and against the Negev of the Kenites."

11 And David did not leave a man or a woman alive, to bring to Gath, saying, "Lest they should tell about us, saying, 'So has David done and so *has been* his practice all the time he has lived in the country of the Philistines.'"

12 So Achish believed David, saying, "He has surely made himself odious among his people Israel; therefore he will become my servant forever."

CHAPTER 28

Now it came about in those days that the Philistines gathered their armed camps for war, to fight against Israel. And Achish said to David, "Know assuredly that you will go out with me in the camp, you and your men."

2 And David said to Achish, "Very well, you shall know what your servant can do." So Achish said to David, "Very well, I will make you my bodyguard for life."

3 ¶ Now Samuel was dead, and all Israel had lamented him and buried him in Ramah his own city. And Saul had removed from the land those who were mediums and spiritists.

4 So the Philistines gathered together and came and camped in Shunem; and Saul gathered all Israel together and they camped in Gilboa.

5 When Saul saw the camp of the Philistines, he was afraid and his heart trembled greatly.

6 When Saul inquired of the Lord, the Lord did not answer him, either by dreams or by Urim or by prophets.

7 Then Saul said to his servants,

"Seek for me a woman who is a medium, that I may go to her and inquire of her." And his servants said to him, "Behold, there is a woman who is a medium at En-dor."

8 ¶ Then Saul disguised himself by putting on other clothes, and went, he and two men with him, and they came to the woman by night; and he said, "Conjure up for me, please, and bring up for me whom I shall name to you."

9 But the woman said to him, "Behold, you know what Saul has done, how he has cut off those who are mediums and spiritists from the land. Why are you then laying a snare for my life to bring about my death?"

10 And Saul vowed to her by the Lord, saying, "As the Lord lives, there shall no punishment come upon you for this thing."

11 Then the woman said, "Whom shall I bring up for you?" And he said, "Bring up Samuel for me."

12 When the woman saw Samuel, she cried out with a loud voice; and the woman spoke to Saul, saying, "Why have you deceived me? For you are Saul."

13 And the king said to her, "Do not be afraid; but what do you see?" And the woman said to Saul, "I see a divine being coming up out of the earth."

14 And he said to her, "What is his form?" And she said, "An old man is coming up, and he is wrapped with a robe." And Saul knew that it was Samuel, and he bowed with his face to the ground and did homage.

15 ¶ Then Samuel said to Saul, "Why have you disturbed me by bringing me up?" And Saul answered, "I am greatly distressed; for the Philistines are waging war against me, and God has departed from me and answers me no more, either through prophets or by dreams; therefore I have called you, that you may make known to me what I should do."

16 And Samuel said, "Why then do you ask me, since the Lord has departed from you and has become your adversary?

17 "And the Lord has done accordingly as He spoke through me; for the Lord has torn the kingdom out of your hand and given it to your neighbor, to David.

[17] I.e., South country

18"As you did not obey the LORD and did not execute His fierce wrath on Amalek, so the LORD has done this thing to you this day.

19"Moreover the LORD will also give over Israel along with you into the hands of the Philistines, therefore tomorrow you and your sons will be with me. Indeed the LORD will give over the army of Israel into the hands of the Philistines!"

20 ¶ Then Saul immediately fell full length upon the ground and was very afraid because of the words of Samuel; also there was no strength in him, for he had eaten no food all day and all night.

21 And the woman came to Saul and saw that he was terrified, and said to him, "Behold, your maidservant has obeyed you, and I have taken my life in my hand, and have listened to your words which you spoke to me.

22"So now also, please listen to the voice of your maidservant, and let me set a piece of bread before you that you may eat and have strength when you go on your way."

23 But he refused and said, "I will not eat." However, his servants together with the woman urged him, and he listened to them. So he arose from the ground and sat on the bed.

24 And the woman had a fattened calf in the house, and she quickly slaughtered it; and she took flour, kneaded it, and baked unleavened bread from it.

25 And she brought it before Saul and his servants, and they ate. Then they arose and went away that night.

CHAPTER 29

NOW the Philistines gathered together all their armies to Aphek, while the Israelites were camping by the spring which is in Jezreel.

2 And the lords of the Philistines were proceeding on by hundreds and by thousands, and David and his men were proceeding on in the rear with Achish.

3 Then the commanders of the Philistines said, "What are these Hebrews doing here?" And Achish said to the commanders of the Philistines, "Is this not David, the servant of Saul the king of Israel, who has been with me these days, or rather these years, and I have found no fault in him from the day he deserted to me to this day?"

4 But the commanders of the Philistines were angry with him, and the commanders of the Philistines said to him, "Make the man go back, that he may return to his place where you have assigned him, and do not let him go down to battle with us, lest in the battle he become an adversary to us. For with what could this man make himself acceptable to his lord? Would it not be with the heads of these men?

5"Is this not David, of whom they sing in the dances, saying,

    'Saul has slain his thousands,
    And David his ten thousands'?"

6 ¶ Then Achish called David and said to him, "As the LORD lives, you have been upright, and your going out and your coming in with me in the army are pleasing in my sight; for I have not found evil in you from the day of your coming to me to this day. Nevertheless, you are not pleasing in the sight of the lords.

7"Now therefore return, and go in peace, that you may not displease the lords of the Philistines."

8 And David said to Achish, "But what have I done? And what have you found in your servant from the day when I came before you to this day, that I may not go and fight against the enemies of my lord the king?"

9 But Achish answered and said to David, "I know that you are pleasing in my sight, like an angel of God; nevertheless the commanders of the Philistines have said, 'He must not go up with us to the battle.'

10"Now then arise early in the morning with the servants of your lord who have come with you, and as soon as you have arisen early in the morning and have light, depart."

11 So David arose early, he and his men, to depart in the morning, to return to the land of the Philistines. And the Philistines went up to Jezreel.

CHAPTER 30

THEN it happened when David and his men came to Ziklag on the third day, that the Amalekites had made a raid on the Negev and on Ziklag, and had overthrown Ziklag and burned it with fire;

2 and they took captive the women *and all* who were in it, both small and great, without killing anyone, and carried *them* off and went their way.

3 And when David and his men came to the city, behold, it was burned with fire, and their wives and their sons and their daughters had been taken captive.

4 Then David and the people who were with him lifted their voices and wept until there was no strength in them to weep.

5 Now David's two wives had been taken captive, Ahinoam the Jezreelitess and Abigail the widow of Nabal the Carmelite.

6 Moreover David was greatly distressed because the people spoke of stoning him, for all the people were embittered, each one because of his sons and his daughters. But David strengthened himself in the LORD his God.

7 ¶ Then David said to Abiathar the priest, the son of Ahimelech, "Please bring me the ephod." So Abiathar brought the ephod to David.

8 And David inquired of the LORD, saying, "Shall I pursue this band? Shall I overtake them?" And He said to him, "Pursue, for you shall surely overtake them, and you shall surely rescue *all*."

9 So David went, he and the six hundred men who were with him, and came to the brook Besor, *where* those left behind remained.

10 But David pursued, he and four hundred men, for two hundred who were too exhausted to cross the brook Besor, remained *behind*.

11 ¶ Now they found an Egyptian in the field and brought him to David, and gave him bread and he ate, and they provided him water to drink.

12 And they gave him a piece of fig cake and two clusters of raisins, and he ate; then his spirit revived. For he had not eaten bread or drunk water for three days and three nights.

13 And David said to him, "To whom do you belong? And where are you from?" And he said, "I am a young man of Egypt, a servant of an Amalekite; and my master left me behind when I fell sick three days ago.

14 "We made a raid on the Negev of the Cherethites, and on that which belongs to Judah, and on the Negev of Caleb, and we burned Ziklag with fire."

15 Then David said to him, "Will you bring me down to this band?" And he said, "Swear to me by God that you will not kill me or deliver me into the hands of my master, and I will bring you down to this band."

16 ¶ And when he had brought him down, behold, they were spread over all the land, eating and drinking and dancing because of all the great spoil that they had taken from the land of the Philistines and from the land of Judah.

17 And David slaughtered them from the twilight until the evening of the next day; and not a man of them escaped, except four hundred young men who rode on camels and fled.

18 So David recovered all that the Amalekites had taken, and rescued his two wives.

19 But nothing of theirs was missing, whether small or great, sons or daughters, spoil or anything that they had taken for themselves; David brought *it* all back.

20 So David had captured all the sheep and the cattle *which the people* drove ahead of the *other* livestock, and they said, "This is David's spoil."

21 ¶ When David came to the two hundred men who were too exhausted to follow David, who had also been left at the brook Besor, and they went out to meet David and to meet the people who were with him, then David approached the people and greeted them.

22 Then all the wicked and worthless men among those who went with David answered and said, "Because they did not go with us, we will not give them any of the spoil that we have recovered, except to every man his wife and his children, that they may lead *them* away and depart."

23 Then David said, "You must not do so, my brothers, with what the LORD has given us, who has kept us and delivered into our hand the band that came against us.

24 "And who will listen to you in this matter? For as his share is who goes down to the battle, so shall his share

be who stays by the baggage; they shall share alike."

25 And so it has been from that day forward, that he made it a statute and an ordinance for Israel to this day.

26 ¶ Now when David came to Ziklag, he sent *some* of the spoil to the elders of Judah, to his friends, saying, "Behold, a gift for you from the spoil of the enemies of the LORD:

27 to those who were in Bethel, and to those who were in Ramoth of the Negev, and to those who were in Jattir,

28 and to those who were in Aroer, and to those who were in Siphmoth, and to those who were in Eshtemoa,

29 and to those who were in Racal, and to those who were in the cities of the Jerahmeelites, and to those who were in the cities of the Kenites,

30 and to those who were in Hormah, and to those who were in Borashan, and to those who were in Athach,

31 and to those who were in Hebron, and to all the places where David himself and his men were accustomed to go."

CHAPTER 31

Now the Philistines were fighting against Israel, and the men of Israel fled from before the Philistines and fell slain on Mount Gilboa.

2 And the Philistines overtook Saul and his sons; and the Philistines killed Jonathan and Abinadab and Malchishua the sons of Saul.

3 And the battle went heavily against Saul, and the archers hit him; and he was badly wounded by the archers.

4 Then Saul said to his armor bearer, "Draw your sword and pierce me through with it, lest these uncircumcised come and pierce me through and make sport of me." But his armor bearer would not, for he was greatly afraid. So Saul took his sword and fell on it.

5 And when his armor bearer saw that Saul was dead, he also fell on his sword and died with him.

6 Thus Saul died with his three sons, his armor bearer, and all his men on that day together.

7 ¶ And when the men of Israel who were on the other side of the valley, with those who were beyond the Jordan, saw that the men of Israel had fled and that Saul and his sons were dead, they abandoned the cities and fled; then the Philistines came and lived in them.

8 And it came about on the next day when the Philistines came to strip the slain, that they found Saul and his three sons fallen on Mount Gilboa.

9 And they cut off his head, and stripped off his weapons, and sent *them* throughout the land of the Philistines, to carry the good news to the house of their idols and to the people.

10 And they put his weapons in the temple of Ashtaroth, and they fastened his body to the wall of Bethshan.

11 Now when the inhabitants of Jabesh-gilead heard what the Philistines had done to Saul,

12 all the valiant men rose and walked all night, and took the body of Saul and the bodies of his sons from the wall of Beth-shan, and they came to Jabesh, and burned them there.

13 And they took their bones and buried them under the tamarisk tree at Jabesh, and fasted seven days.

SAMUEL

Now it came about after the death of Saul, when David had returned from the slaughter of the Amalekites, that David remained two days in Ziklag.

2 And it happened on the third day, that behold, a man came out of the camp from Saul, with his clothes torn and dust on his head. And it came about when he came to David that he fell to the ground and prostrated himself.

3 Then David said to him, "From where do you come?" And he said to him, "I have escaped from the camp of Israel."

4 And David said to him, "How did things go? Please tell me." And he said, "The people have fled from the battle, and also many of the people have fallen and are dead; and Saul and Jonathan his son are dead also."

5 So David said to the young man who told him, "How do you know that Saul and his son Jonathan are dead?"

6 And the young man who told him said, "By chance I happened to be on Mount Gilboa, and behold, Saul was leaning on his spear. And behold, the chariots and the horsemen pursued him closely.

7 "And when he looked behind him, he saw me and called to me. And I said, 'Here I am.'

8 "And he said to me, 'Who are you?' And I answered him, 'I am an Amalekite.'

9 "Then he said to me, 'Please stand beside me and kill me; for agony has seized me because my life still lingers in me.'

10 "So I stood beside him and killed him, because I knew that he could not live after he had fallen. And I took the crown which was on his head and the bracelet which was on his arm, and I have brought them here to my lord."

11 ¶ Then David took hold of his clothes and tore them, and so also did all the men who were with him.

12 And they mourned and wept and fasted until evening for Saul and his son Jonathan and for the people of the Lord and the house of Israel, because they had fallen by the sword.

13 And David said to the young man who told him, "Where are you from?" And he answered, "I am the son of an alien, an Amalekite."

14 Then David said to him, "How is it you were not afraid to stretch out your hand to destroy the Lord's anointed?"

15 And David called one of the young men and said, "Go, cut him down." So he struck him and he died.

16 And David said to him, "Your blood is on your head, for your mouth has testified against you, saying, 'I have killed the Lord's anointed.'"

17 ¶ Then David chanted with this lament over Saul and Jonathan his son,

18 and he told *them* to teach the sons of Judah *the song of* the bow; behold, it is written in the book of Jashar.

19 "Your beauty, O Israel, is slain on
      your high places!
    How have the mighty fallen!

20 "Tell *it* not in Gath,
    Proclaim it not in the streets of
      Ashkelon;
    Lest the daughters of the Philis-
      tines rejoice,
    Lest the daughters of the uncir-
      cumcised exult.

21 "O mountains of Gilboa,
    Let not dew or rain be on you,
      nor fields of offerings;
    For there the shield of the
      mighty was defiled,
    The shield of Saul, not anointed
      with oil.

22 "From the blood of the slain, from
      the fat of the mighty,
    The bow of Jonathan did not
      turn back,
    And the sword of Saul did not
      return empty.

23 "Saul and Jonathan, beloved and
      pleasant in their life,
    And in their death they were not
      parted;
    They were swifter than eagles,
    They were stronger than lions.

24 "O daughters of Israel, weep over
      Saul,
    Who clothed you luxuriously in
      scarlet,
    Who put ornaments of gold on
      your apparel.

25 "How have the mighty fallen in
the midst of the battle!
Jonathan is slain on your high
places.
26 "I am distressed for you, my
brother Jonathan;
You have been very pleasant to
me.
Your love to me was more wonderful
Than the love of women.
27 "How have the mighty fallen,
And the weapons of war perished!"

CHAPTER 2

THEN it came about afterwards that
David inquired of the LORD, saying,
"Shall I go up to one of the cities of
Judah?" And the LORD said to him,
"Go up." So David said, "Where shall I
go up?" And He said, "To Hebron."

2 So David went up there, and his
two wives also, Ahinoam the Jezreelitess and Abigail the widow of Nabal
the Carmelite.

3 And David brought up his men
who *were* with him, each with his
household; and they lived in the cities
of Hebron.

4 Then the men of Judah came and
there anointed David king over the
house of Judah.

¶ And they told David, saying, "It
was the men of Jabesh-gilead who
buried Saul."

5 And David sent messengers to the
men of Jabesh-gilead, and said to
them, "May you be blessed of the
LORD because you have shown this
kindness to Saul your lord, and have
buried him.

6 "And now may the LORD show
lovingkindness and truth to you; and I
also will show this goodness to you,
because you have done this thing.

7 "Now therefore, let your hands be
strong, and be valiant; for Saul your
lord is dead, and also the house of
Judah has anointed me king over
them."

8 ¶ But Abner the son of Ner, commander of Saul's army, had taken [1]Ish-
bosheth the son of Saul, and brought
him over to Mahanaim.

9 And he made him king over Gilead, over the Ashurites, over Jezreel,
over Ephraim, and over Benjamin,
even over all Israel.

10 Ish-bosheth, Saul's son, was forty
years old when he became king over
Israel, and he was king for two years.
The house of Judah, however, followed David.

11 And the time that David was king
in Hebron over the house of Judah
was seven years and six months.

12 ¶ Now Abner the son of Ner,
went out from Mahanaim to Gibeon
with the servants of Ish-bosheth the
son of Saul.

13 And Joab the son of Zeruiah and
the servants of David went out and
met them by the pool of Gibeon;
and they sat down, one on the one side
of the pool and the other on the other
side of the pool.

14 Then Abner said to Joab, "Now let
the young men arise and [2]hold a con-
test before us." And Joab said, "Let
them arise."

15 So they arose and went over by
count, twelve for Benjamin and Ish-
bosheth the son of Saul, and twelve of
the servants of David.

16 And each one of them seized his
opponent by the head, and *thrust* his
sword in his opponent's side; so they
fell down together. Therefore that
place was called [3]Helkath-hazzurim,
which is in Gibeon.

17 And that day the battle was very
severe, and Abner and the men of
Israel were beaten before the servants
of David.

18 ¶ Now the three sons of Zeruiah
were there, Joab and Abishai and Asahel; and Asahel *was as* swift-footed as
one of the gazelles which is in the
field.

19 And Asahel pursued Abner and
did not turn to the right or to the left
from following Abner.

20 Then Abner looked behind him
and said, "Is that you, Asahel?" And
he answered, "It is I."

21 So Abner said to him, "Turn to
your right or to your left, and take
hold of one of the young men for
yourself, and take for yourself his
spoil." But Asahel was not willing to
turn aside from following him.

22 And Abner repeated again to Asahel, "Turn aside from following me.

---

[1] I.e., man of shame   [2] Lit., *make sport*   [3] I.e., the field of sword-edges

Why should I strike you to the ground? How then could I lift up my face to your brother Joab?"

23 However, he refused to turn aside; therefore Abner struck him in the belly with the butt end of the spear, so that the spear came out at his back. And he fell there and died on the spot. And it came about that all who came to the place where Asahel had fallen and died, stood still.

24 ¶ But Joab and Abishai pursued Abner, and when the sun was going down, they came to the hill of Ammah, which is in front of Giah by the way of the wilderness of Gibeon.

25 And the sons of Benjamin gathered together behind Abner and became one band, and they stood on the top of a certain hill.

26 Then Abner called to Joab and said, "Shall the sword devour forever? Do you not know that it will be bitter in the end? How long will you refrain from telling the people to turn back from following their brothers?"

27 And Joab said, "As God lives, if you had not spoken, surely then the people would have gone away in the morning, each from following his brother."

28 So Joab blew the trumpet; and all the people halted and pursued Israel no longer, nor did they continue to fight anymore.

29 Abner and his men then went through the Arabah all that night; so they crossed the Jordan, walked all morning, and came to Mahanaim.

30 ¶ Then Joab returned from following Abner; when he had gathered all the people together, nineteen of David's servants besides Asahel were missing.

31 But the servants of David had struck down many of Benjamin and Abner's men, so that three hundred and sixty men died.

32 And they took up Asahel and buried him in his father's tomb which was in Bethlehem. Then Joab and his men went all night until the day dawned at Hebron.

CHAPTER 3

Now there was a long war between the house of Saul and the house of David; and David grew steadily stronger, but the house of Saul grew weaker continually.

2 ¶ Sons were born to David at Hebron: his first-born was Amnon, by Ahinoam the Jezreelitess;

3 and his second, Chileab, by Abigail the widow of Nabal the Carmelite; and the third, Absalom the son of Maacah, the daughter of Talmai, king of Geshur;

4 and the fourth, Adonijah the son of Haggith; and the fifth, Shephatiah the son of Abital;

5 and the sixth, Ithream, by David's wife Eglah. These were born to David at Hebron.

6 ¶ And it came about while there was war between the house of Saul and the house of David that Abner was making himself strong in the house of Saul.

7 Now Saul had a concubine whose name was Rizpah, the daughter of Aiah; and Ish-bosheth said to Abner, "Why have you gone in to my father's concubine?"

8 Then Abner was very angry over the words of Ish-bosheth and said, "Am I a dog's head that belongs to Judah? Today I show kindness to the house of Saul your father, to his brothers and to his friends, and have not delivered you into the hands of David; and yet today you charge me with a guilt concerning the woman.

9 "May God do so to Abner, and more also, if as the LORD has sworn to David, I do not accomplish this for him,

10 to transfer the kingdom from the house of Saul, and to establish the throne of David over Israel and over Judah, from Dan even to Beersheba."

11 And he could no longer answer Abner a word, because he was afraid of him.

12 ¶ Then Abner sent messengers to David in his place, saying, "Whose is the land? Make your covenant with me, and behold, my hand shall be with you to bring all Israel over to you."

13 And he said, "Good! I will make a covenant with you, but I demand one thing of you, namely, you shall not see my face unless you first bring Michal, Saul's daughter, when you come to see me."

14 So David sent messengers to Ish-bosheth, Saul's son, saying, "Give me my wife Michal, to whom I was betrothed for a hundred foreskins of the Philistines."

15 And Ish-bosheth sent and took her from her husband, from Paltiel the son of Laish.

16 But her husband went with her, weeping as he went, and followed her as far as Bahurim. Then Abner said to him, "Go, return." So he returned.

17 ¶ Now Abner had consultation with the elders of Israel, saying, "In times past you were seeking for David to be king over you.

18 "Now then, do it! For the LORD has spoken of David, saying, 'By the hand of My servant David I will save My people Israel from the hand of the Philistines and from the hand of all their enemies.' "

19 And Abner also spoke in the hearing of Benjamin; and in addition Abner went to speak in the hearing of David in Hebron all that seemed good to Israel and to the whole house of Benjamin.

20 ¶ Then Abner and twenty men with him came to David at Hebron. And David made a feast for Abner and the men who were with him.

21 And Abner said to David, "Let me arise and go, and gather all Israel to my lord the king that they may make a covenant with you, and that you may be king over all that your soul desires." So David sent Abner away, and he went in peace.

22 ¶ And behold, the servants of David and Joab came from a raid and brought much spoil with them; but Abner was not with David in Hebron, for he had sent him away, and he had gone in peace.

23 When Joab and all the army that was with him arrived, they told Joab, saying, "Abner the son of Ner came to the king, and he has sent him away, and he has gone in peace."

24 Then Joab came to the king and said, "What have you done? Behold, Abner came to you; why then have you sent him away and he is already gone?

25 "You know Abner the son of Ner, that he came to deceive you and to learn of your going out and coming in, and to find out all that you are doing."

26 ¶ When Joab came out from David, he sent messengers after Abner, and they brought him back from the well of Sirah; but David did not know it.

27 So when Abner returned to Hebron, Joab took him aside into the middle of the gate to speak with him privately, and there he struck him in the belly so that he died on account of the blood of Asahel his brother.

28 And afterward when David heard it, he said, "I and my kingdom are innocent before the LORD forever of the blood of Abner the son of Ner.

29 "May it fall on the head of Joab and on all his father's house; and may there not fail from the house of Joab one who has a discharge, or who is a leper, or who takes hold of a distaff, or who falls by the sword, or who lacks bread."

30 So Joab and Abishai his brother killed Abner because he had put their brother Asahel to death in the battle at Gibeon.

31 ¶ Then David said to Joab and to all the people who were with him, "Tear your clothes and gird on sackcloth and lament before Abner." And King David walked behind the bier.

32 Thus they buried Abner in Hebron; and the king lifted up his voice and wept at the grave of Abner, and all the people wept.

33 And the king chanted a lament for Abner and said,

"Should Abner die as a fool dies?
34 "Your hands were not bound, nor
        your feet put in fetters;
    As one falls before the wicked,
        you have fallen."
And all the people wept again over him.

35 Then all the people came to persuade David to eat bread while it was still day; but David vowed, saying, "May God do so to me, and more also, if I taste bread or anything else before the sun goes down."

36 Now all the people took note of it, and it pleased them, just as everything the king did pleased all the people.

37 So all the people and all Israel understood that day that it had not been the will of the king to put Abner the son of Ner to death.

38 Then the king said to his servants, "Do you not know that a prince and a

great man has fallen this day in Israel?

39"And I am weak today, though anointed king; and these men the sons of Zeruiah are too difficult for me. May the LORD repay the evildoer according to his evil."

CHAPTER 4

Now when Ish-bosheth, Saul's son, heard that Abner had died in Hebron, he lost courage, and all Israel was disturbed.

2 And Saul's son *had* two men who were commanders of bands: the name of the one was Baanah and the name of the other Rechab, sons of Rimmon the Beerothite, of the sons of Benjamin (for Beeroth is also considered *part* of Benjamin,

3 and the Beerothites fled to Gittaim, and have been aliens there until this day).

4 ¶ Now Jonathan, Saul's son, had a son crippled in his feet. He was five years old when the report of Saul and Jonathan came from Jezreel, and his nurse took him up and fled. And it happened that in her hurry to flee, he fell and became lame. And his name was Mephibosheth.

5 ¶ So the sons of Rimmon the Beerothite, Rechab and Baanah, departed and came to the house of Ish-bosheth in the heat of the day while he was taking his midday rest.

6 And they came to the middle of the house as if to get wheat, and they struck him in the belly; and Rechab and Baanah his brother escaped.

7 Now when they came into the house, as he was lying on his bed in his bedroom, they struck him and killed him and beheaded him. And they took his head and traveled by way of the Arabah all night.

8 Then they brought the head of Ish-bosheth to David at Hebron, and said to the king, "Behold, the head of Ish-bosheth, the son of Saul, your enemy, who sought your life; thus the LORD has given my lord the king vengeance this day on Saul and his descendants."

9 ¶ And David answered Rechab and Baanah his brother, sons of Rimmon the Beerothite, and said to them, "As the LORD lives, who has redeemed my life from all distress,

10 when one told me, saying, 'Behold, Saul is dead,' and thought he was bringing good news, I seized him and killed him in Ziklag, which was the reward I gave him for *his* news.

11"How much more, when wicked men have killed a righteous man in his own house on his bed, shall I not now require his blood from your hand, and destroy you from the earth?"

12 Then David commanded the young men, and they killed them and cut off their hands and feet, and hung them up beside the pool in Hebron. But they took the head of Ish-bosheth and buried it in the grave of Abner in Hebron.

CHAPTER 5

Then all the tribes of Israel came to David at Hebron and said, "Behold, we are your bone and your flesh.

2"Previously, when Saul was king over us, you were the one who led Israel out and in. And the LORD said to you, 'You will shepherd My people Israel, and you will be a ruler over Israel.' "

3 So all the elders of Israel came to the king at Hebron, and King David made a covenant with them before the LORD at Hebron; then they anointed David king over Israel.

4 David was thirty years old when he became king, *and* he reigned forty years.

5 At Hebron he reigned over Judah seven years and six months, and in Jerusalem he reigned thirty-three years over all Israel and Judah.

6 ¶ Now the king and his men went to Jerusalem against the Jebusites, the inhabitants of the land, and they said to David, "You shall not come in here, but the blind and lame shall turn you away"; thinking, "David cannot enter here."

7 Nevertheless, David captured the stronghold of Zion, that is the city of David.

8 And David said on that day, "Whoever would strike the Jebusites, let him reach the lame and the blind, who are hated by David's soul, through the water tunnel." Therefore they say, "The blind or the lame shall not come into the house."

9 So David lived in the stronghold,

and called it the city of David. And David built all around from the [4]Millo and inward.

10 And David became greater and greater, for the LORD God of hosts was with him.

11 ¶ Then Hiram king of Tyre sent messengers to David with cedar trees and carpenters and stonemasons; and they built a house for David.

12 And David realized that the LORD had established him as king over Israel, and that He had exalted his kingdom for the sake of His people Israel.

13 ¶ Meanwhile David took more concubines and wives from Jerusalem, after he came from Hebron; and more sons and daughters were born to David.

14 Now these are the names of those who were born to him in Jerusalem: Shammua, Shobab, Nathan, Solomon,

15 Ibhar, Elishua, Nepheg, Japhia,

16 Elishama, Eliada and Eliphelet.

17 ¶ When the Philistines heard that they had anointed David king over Israel, all the Philistines went up to seek out David; and when David heard of it, he went down to the stronghold.

18 Now the Philistines came and spread themselves out in the valley of Rephaim.

19 Then David inquired of the LORD, saying, "Shall I go up against the Philistines? Wilt Thou give them into my hand?" And the LORD said to David, "Go up, for I will certainly give the Philistines into your hand."

20 So David came to Baal-perazim, and defeated them there; and he said, "The LORD has broken through my enemies before me like the breakthrough of waters." Therefore he named that place [5]Baal-perazim.

21 And they abandoned their idols there, so David and his men carried them away.

22 ¶ Now the Philistines came up once again and spread themselves out in the valley of Rephaim.

23 And when David inquired of the LORD, He said, "You shall not go directly up; circle around behind them and come at them in front of the [6]balsam trees.

24"And it shall be, when you hear the sound of marching in the tops of the [6]balsam trees, then you shall act promptly, for then the LORD will have gone out before you to strike the army of the Philistines."

25 Then David did so, just as the LORD had commanded him, and struck down the Philistines from Geba as far as Gezer.

CHAPTER 6

NOW David again gathered all the chosen men of Israel, thirty thousand.

2 And David arose and went with all the people who were with him to Baale-judah, to bring up from there the ark of God which is called by the Name, the very name of the LORD of hosts who is enthroned above the cherubim.

3 And they placed the ark of God on a new cart that they might bring it from the house of Abinadab which was on the hill; and Uzzah and Ahio, the sons of Abinadab, were leading the new cart.

4 So they brought it with the ark of God from the house of Abinadab, which was on the hill; and Ahio was walking ahead of the ark.

5 Meanwhile, David and all the house of Israel were celebrating before the LORD with all kinds of instruments made of fir wood, and with lyres, harps, tambourines, castanets and cymbals.

6 ¶ But when they came to the threshing floor of Nacon, Uzzah reached out toward the ark of God and took hold of it, for the oxen nearly upset it.

7 And the anger of the LORD burned against Uzzah, and God struck him down there for his irreverence; and he died there by the ark of God.

8 And David became angry because of the LORD's outburst against Uzzah, and that place is called [7]Perez-uzzah to this day.

9 So David was afraid of the LORD that day; and he said, "How can the ark of the LORD come to me?"

10 And David was unwilling to move the ark of the LORD into the city of David with him; but David took it aside to the house of Obed-edom the Gittite.

---

[4] I.e., citadel   [5] I.e., the master of breakthrough
[6] Or, baka-shrubs

[6] Or, baka-shrubs   [7] I.e., the breakthrough of Uzzah

11 Thus the ark of the LORD remained in the house of Obed-edom the Gittite three months, and the LORD blessed Obed-edom and all his household.

12 ¶ Now it was told King David, saying, "The LORD has blessed the house of Obed-edom and all that belongs to him, on account of the ark of God." And David went and brought up the ark of God from the house of Obed-edom into the city of David with gladness.

13 And so it was, that when the bearers of the ark of the LORD had gone six paces, he sacrificed an ox and a fatling.

14 And David was dancing before the LORD with all *his* might, and David was wearing a linen ephod.

15 So David and all the house of Israel were bringing up the ark of the LORD with shouting and the sound of the trumpet.

16 Then it happened *as* the ark of the LORD came into the city of David that Michal the daughter of Saul looked out of the window and saw King David leaping and dancing before the LORD; and she despised him in her heart.

17 So they brought in the ark of the LORD and set it in its place inside the tent which David had pitched for it; and David offered burnt offerings and peace offerings before the LORD.

18 And when David had finished offering the burnt offering and the peace offering, he blessed the people in the name of the LORD of hosts.

19 Further, he distributed to all the people, to all the multitude of Israel, both to men and women, a cake of bread and one of dates and one of raisins to each one. Then all the people departed each to his house.

20 ¶ But when David returned to bless his household, Michal the daughter of Saul came out to meet David and said, "How the king of Israel distinguished himself today! He uncovered himself today in the eyes of his servants' maids as one of the foolish ones shamelessly uncovers himself!"

21 So David said to Michal, "*It was* before the LORD, who chose me above your father and above all his house, to appoint me ruler over the people of the LORD, over Israel; therefore I will celebrate before the LORD.

22 "And I will be more lightly esteemed than this and will be humble in my own eyes, but with the maids of whom you have spoken, with them I will be distinguished."

23 And Michal the daughter of Saul had no child to the day of her death.

CHAPTER 7

Now it came about when the king lived in his house, and the LORD had given him rest on every side from all his enemies,

2 that the king said to Nathan the prophet, "See now, I dwell in a house of cedar, but the ark of God dwells within tent curtains."

3 And Nathan said to the king, "Go, do all that is in your mind, for the LORD is with you."

4 But it came about in the same night that the word of the LORD came to Nathan, saying,

5 "Go and say to My servant David, 'Thus says the LORD, "Are you the one who should build Me a house to dwell in?

6 "For I have not dwelt in a house since the day I brought up the sons of Israel from Egypt, even to this day; but I have been moving about in a tent, even in a tabernacle.

7 "Wherever I have gone with all the sons of Israel, did I speak a word with one of the tribes of Israel, which I commanded to shepherd My people Israel, saying, 'Why have you not built Me a house of cedar?' " '

8 "Now therefore, thus you shall say to My servant David, 'Thus says the LORD of hosts, "I took you from the pasture, from following the sheep, that you should be ruler over My people Israel.

9 "And I have been with you wherever you have gone and have cut off all your enemies from before you; and I will make you a great name, like the names of the great men who are on the earth.

10 "I will also appoint a place for My people Israel and will plant them, that they may live in their own place and not be disturbed again, nor will the wicked afflict them any more as formerly,

11 even from the day that I commanded judges to be over My people Israel; and I will give you rest from all your enemies. The Lord also declares to you that the Lord will make a house for you.

12"When your days are complete and you lie down with your fathers, I will raise up your descendant after you, who will come forth from you, and I will establish his kingdom.

13"He shall build a house for My name, and I will establish the throne of his kingdom forever.

14"I will be a father to him and he will be a son to Me; when he commits iniquity, I will correct him with the rod of men and the strokes of the sons of men,

15 but My lovingkindness shall not depart from him, as I took it away from Saul, whom I removed from before you.

16"And your house and your kingdom shall endure before Me forever; your throne shall be established forever." ' "

17 In accordance with all these words and all this vision, so Nathan spoke to David.

18 ¶ Then David the king went in and sat before the Lord, and he said, "Who am I, O Lord God, and what is my house, that Thou hast brought me this far?

19"And yet this was insignificant in Thine eyes, O Lord God, for Thou hast spoken also of the house of Thy servant concerning the distant future. And this is the custom of man, O Lord God.

20"And again what more can David say to Thee? For Thou knowest Thy servant, O Lord God!

21"For the sake of Thy word, and according to Thine own heart, Thou hast done all this greatness to let Thy servant know.

22"For this reason Thou art great, O Lord God; for there is none like Thee, and there is no God besides Thee, according to all that we have heard with our ears.

23"And what one nation on the earth is like Thy people Israel, whom God went to redeem for Himself as a people and to make a name for Himself, and to do a great thing for Thee and awesome things for Thy land, before Thy people whom Thou hast redeemed for Thyself from Egypt, from nations and their gods?

24"For Thou hast established for Thyself Thy people Israel as Thine own people forever, and Thou, O Lord, hast become their God.

25"Now therefore, O Lord God, the word that Thou hast spoken concerning Thy servant and his house, confirm it forever, and do as Thou hast spoken,

26 that Thy name may be magnified forever, by saying, 'The Lord of hosts is God over Israel'; and may the house of Thy servant David be established before Thee.

27"For Thou, O Lord of hosts, the God of Israel, hast made a revelation to Thy servant, saying, 'I will build you a house'; therefore Thy servant has found courage to pray this prayer to Thee.

28"And now, O Lord God, Thou art God, and Thy words are truth, and Thou hast promised this good thing to Thy servant.

29"Now therefore, may it please Thee to bless the house of Thy servant, that it may continue forever before Thee. For Thou, O Lord God, hast spoken; and with Thy blessing may the house of Thy servant be blessed forever."

CHAPTER 8

NOW after this it came about that David defeated the Philistines and subdued them; and David took control of the chief city from the hand of the Philistines.

2 And he defeated Moab, and measured them with the line, making them lie down on the ground; and he measured two lines to put to death and one full line to keep alive. And the Moabites became servants to David, bringing tribute.

3 ¶ Then David defeated Hadadezer, the son of Rehob king of Zobah, as he went to restore his rule at the [8]River.

4 And David captured from him 1,700 horsemen and 20,000 foot soldiers; and David hamstrung the chariot horses, but reserved enough of them for 100 chariots.

[8] I.e., Euphrates

5 And when the Arameans of Damascus came to help Hadadezer, king of Zobah, David killed 22,000 Arameans.

6 Then David put garrisons among the Arameans of Damascus, and the Arameans became servants to David, bringing tribute. And the LORD helped David wherever he went.

7 And David took the shields of gold which were carried by the servants of Hadadezer, and brought them to Jerusalem.

8 And from Betah and from Berothai, cities of Hadadezer, King David took a very large amount of bronze.

9 ¶ Now when Toi king of Hamath heard that David had defeated all the army of Hadadezer,

10 Toi sent Joram his son to King David to greet him and bless him, because he had fought against Hadadezer and defeated him; for Hadadezer had been at war with Toi. And *Joram* brought with him articles of silver, of gold and of bronze.

11 King David also dedicated these to the LORD, with the silver and gold that he had dedicated from all the nations which he had subdued:

12 from [9]Aram and Moab and the sons of Ammon and the Philistines and Amalek, and from the spoil of Hadadezer, son of Rehob, king of Zobah.

13 ¶ So David made a name *for himself* when he returned from killing 18,000 [9]Arameans in the Valley of Salt.

14 And he put garrisons in Edom. In all Edom he put garrisons, and all the Edomites became servants to David. And the LORD helped David wherever he went.

15 ¶ So David reigned over all Israel; and David administered justice and righteousness for all his people.

16 And Joab the son of Zeruiah *was* over the army, and Jehoshaphat the son of Ahilud *was* recorder.

17 And Zadok the son of Ahitub and Ahimelech the son of Abiathar *were* priests, and Seraiah *was* secretary.

18 And Benaiah the son of Jehoiada was over the Cherethites and the Pelethites; and David's sons were chief ministers.

[9] Some mss. read *Edom(ites)*

CHAPTER 9

THEN David said, "Is there yet anyone left of the house of Saul, that I may show him kindness for Jonathan's sake?"

2 Now there was a servant of the house of Saul whose name was Ziba, and they called him to David; and the king said to him, "Are you Ziba?" And he said, "*I am* your servant."

3 And the king said, "Is there not yet anyone of the house of Saul to whom I may show the kindness of God?" And Ziba said to the king, "There is still a son of Jonathan who is crippled in both feet."

4 So the king said to him, "Where is he?" And Ziba said to the king, "Behold, he is in the house of Machir the son of Ammiel in Lo-debar."

5 Then King David sent and brought him from the house of Machir the son of Ammiel, from Lo-debar.

6 And Mephibosheth, the son of Jonathan the son of Saul, came to David and fell on his face and prostrated himself. And David said, "Mephibosheth." And he said, "Here is your servant!"

7 And David said to him, "Do not fear, for I will surely show kindness to you for the sake of your father Jonathan, and will restore to you all the land of your grandfather Saul; and you shall eat at my table regularly."

8 Again he prostrated himself and said, "What is your servant, that you should regard a dead dog like me?"

9 ¶ Then the king called Saul's servant Ziba, and said to him, "All that belonged to Saul and to all his house I have given to your master's grandson.

10 "And you and your sons and your servants shall cultivate the land for him, and you shall bring in *the produce* so that your master's grandson may have food; nevertheless Mephibosheth your master's grandson shall eat at my table regularly." Now Ziba had fifteen sons and twenty servants.

11 Then Ziba said to the king, "According to all that my lord the king commands his servant so your servant will do." So Mephibosheth ate at David's table as one of the king's sons.

12 And Mephibosheth had a young son whose name was Mica. And all

who lived in the house of Ziba were servants to Mephibosheth.

13 So Mephibosheth lived in Jerusalem, for he ate at the king's table regularly. Now he was lame in both feet.

CHAPTER 10

Now it happened afterwards that the king of the Ammonites died, and Hanun his son became king in his place.

2 Then David said, "I will show kindness to Hanun the son of Nahash, just as his father showed kindness to me." So David sent some of his servants to console him concerning his father. But when David's servants came to the land of the Ammonites,

3 the princes of the Ammonites said to Hanun their lord, "Do you think that David is honoring your father because he has sent consolers to you? Has David not sent his servants to you in order to search the city, to spy it out and overthrow it?"

4 So Hanun took David's servants and shaved off half of their beards, and cut off their garments in the middle as far as their hips, and sent them away.

5 When they told it to David, he sent to meet them, for the men were greatly humiliated. And the king said, "Stay at Jericho until your beards grow, and then return."

6 ¶ Now when the sons of Ammon saw that they had become odious to David, the sons of Ammon sent and hired the Arameans of Beth-rehob and the Arameans of Zobah, 20,000 foot soldiers, and the king of Maacah with 1,000 men, and the men of Tob with 12,000 men.

7 When David heard of it, he sent Joab and all the army, the mighty men.

8 And the sons of Ammon came out and drew up in battle array at the entrance of the city, while the Arameans of Zobah and of Rehob and the men of Tob and Maacah were by themselves in the field.

9 ¶ Now when Joab saw that the battle was set against him in front and in the rear, he selected from all the choice men of Israel, and arrayed them against the Arameans.

10 But the remainder of the people he placed in the hand of Abishai his brother, and he arrayed them against the sons of Ammon.

11 And he said, "If the Arameans are too strong for me, then you shall help me, but if the sons of Ammon are too strong for you, then I will come to help you.

12 "Be strong, and let us show ourselves courageous for the sake of our people and for the cities of our God; and may the LORD do what is good in His sight."

13 So Joab and the people who were with him drew near to the battle against the Arameans, and they fled before him.

14 When the sons of Ammon saw that the Arameans fled, they also fled before Abishai and entered the city. Then Joab returned from fighting against the sons of Ammon and came to Jerusalem.

15 ¶ When the Arameans saw that they had been defeated by Israel, they gathered themselves together.

16 And Hadadezer sent and brought out the Arameans who were beyond the [10]River, and they came to Helam; and Shobach the commander of the army of Hadadezer led them.

17 Now when it was told David, he gathered all Israel together and crossed the Jordan, and came to Helam. And the Arameans arrayed themselves to meet David and fought against him.

18 But the Arameans fled before Israel, and David killed 700 charioteers of the Arameans and 40,000 horsemen and struck down Shobach the commander of their army, and he died there.

19 When all the kings, servants of Hadadezer, saw that they were defeated by Israel, they made peace with Israel and served them. So the Arameans feared to help the sons of Ammon anymore.

CHAPTER 11

Then it happened in the spring, at the time when kings go out to battle, that David sent Joab and his servants with him and all Israel, and they destroyed the sons of Ammon and besieged Rabbah. But David stayed at Jerusalem.

[10] I.e., Euphrates

2 ¶ Now when evening came David arose from his bed and walked around on the roof of the king's house, and from the roof he saw a woman bathing; and the woman was very beautiful in appearance.

3 So David sent and inquired about the woman. And one said, "Is this not Bathsheba, the daughter of Eliam, the wife of Uriah the Hittite?"

4 And David sent messengers and took her, and when she came to him, he lay with her; and when she had purified herself from her uncleanness, she returned to her house.

5 And the woman conceived; and she sent and told David, and said, "I am pregnant."

6 ¶ Then David sent to Joab, *saying*, "Send me Uriah the Hittite." So Joab sent Uriah to David.

7 When Uriah came to him, David asked concerning the welfare of Joab and the people and the state of the war.

8 Then David said to Uriah, "Go down to your house, and wash your feet." And Uriah went out of the king's house, and a present from the king was sent out after him.

9 But Uriah slept at the door of the king's house with all the servants of his lord, and did not go down to his house.

10 Now when they told David, saying, "Uriah did not go down to his house," David said to Uriah, "Have you not come from a journey? Why did you not go down to your house?"

11 And Uriah said to David, "The ark and Israel and Judah are staying in temporary shelters, and my lord Joab and the servants of my lord are camping in the open field. Shall I then go to my house to eat and to drink and to lie with my wife? By your life and the life of your soul, I will not do this thing."

12 Then David said to Uriah, "Stay here today also, and tomorrow I will let you go." So Uriah remained in Jerusalem that day and the next.

13 Now David called him, and he ate and drank before him, and he made him drunk; and in the evening he went out to lie on his bed with his lord's servants, but he did not go down to his house.

14 ¶ Now it came about in the morning that David wrote a letter to Joab, and sent *it* by the hand of Uriah.

15 And he had written in the letter, saying, "Place Uriah in the front line of the fiercest battle and withdraw from him, so that he may be struck down and die."

16 So it was as Joab kept watch on the city, that he put Uriah at the place where he knew there *were* valiant men.

17 And the men of the city went out and fought against Joab, and some of the people among David's servants fell; and Uriah the Hittite also died.

18 Then Joab sent and reported to David all the events of the war.

19 And he charged the messenger, saying, "When you have finished telling all the events of the war to the king,

20 and if it happens that the king's wrath rises and he says to you, 'Why did you go so near to the city to fight? Did you not know that they would shoot from the wall?

21 'Who struck down Abimelech the son of Jerubbesheth? Did not a woman throw an upper millstone on him from the wall so that he died at Thebez? Why did you go so near the wall?'—then you shall say, 'Your servant Uriah the Hittite is dead also.' "

22 ¶ So the messenger departed and came and reported to David all that Joab had sent him *to tell.*

23 And the messenger said to David, "The men prevailed against us and came out against us in the field, but we pressed them as far as the entrance of the gate.

24 "Moreover, the archers shot at your servants from the wall; so some of the king's servants are dead, and your servant Uriah the Hittite is also dead."

25 Then David said to the messenger, "Thus you shall say to Joab, 'Do not let this thing displease you, for the sword devours one as well as another; make your battle against the city stronger and overthrow it'; and *so* encourage him."

26 ¶ Now when the wife of Uriah heard that Uriah her husband was dead, she mourned for her husband.

27 When the *time of* mourning was over, David sent and brought her to his house and she became his wife; then she bore him a son. But the thing that David had done was evil in the sight of the LORD.

CHAPTER 12

THEN the LORD sent Nathan to David. And he came to him, and said,
"There were two men in one city, the one rich and the other poor.
2 "The rich man had a great many flocks and herds.
3 "But the poor man had nothing except one little ewe lamb
Which he bought and nourished;
And it grew up together with him and his children.
It would eat of his bread and drink of his cup and lie in his bosom,
And was like a daughter to him.
4 "Now a traveler came to the rich man,
And he was unwilling to take from his own flock or his own herd,
To prepare for the wayfarer who had come to him;
Rather he took the poor man's ewe lamb and prepared it for the man who had come to him."
5 Then David's anger burned greatly against the man, and he said to Nathan, "As the LORD lives, surely the man who has done this deserves to die.
6 "And he must make restitution for the lamb fourfold, because he did this thing and had no compassion."
7 ¶ Nathan then said to David, "You are the man! Thus says the LORD God of Israel, 'It is I who anointed you king over Israel and it is I who delivered you from the hand of Saul.
8 'I also gave you your master's house and your master's wives into your care, and I gave you the house of Israel and Judah; and if *that had been* too little, I would have added to you many more things like these!
9 'Why have you despised the word of the LORD by doing evil in His sight? You have struck down Uriah the Hittite with the sword, have taken his wife to be your wife, and have killed him with the sword of the sons of Ammon.

10 'Now therefore, the sword shall never depart from your house, because you have despised Me and have taken the wife of Uriah the Hittite to be your wife.'
11 "Thus says the LORD, 'Behold, I will raise up evil against you from your own household; I will even take your wives before your eyes, and give *them* to your companion, and he shall lie with your wives in broad daylight.
12 'Indeed you did it secretly, but I will do this thing before all Israel, and under the sun.' "
13 Then David said to Nathan, "I have sinned against the LORD." And Nathan said to David, "The LORD also has taken away your sin; you shall not die.
14 "However, because by this deed you have given occasion to the enemies of the LORD to blaspheme, the child also that is born to you shall surely die."
15 So Nathan went to his house.
¶ Then the LORD struck the child that Uriah's widow bore to David, so that he was *very* sick.
16 David therefore inquired of God for the child; and David fasted and went and lay all night on the ground.
17 And the elders of his household stood beside him in order to raise him up from the ground, but he was unwilling and would not eat food with them.
18 Then it happened on the seventh day that the child died. And the servants of David were afraid to tell him that the child was dead, for they said, "Behold, while the child was *still* alive, we spoke to him and he did not listen to our voice. How then can we tell him that the child is dead, since he might do *himself* harm!"
19 But when David saw that his servants were whispering together, David perceived that the child was dead; so David said to his servants, "Is the child dead?" And they said, "He is dead."
20 So David arose from the ground, washed, anointed *himself,* and changed his clothes; and he came into the house of the LORD and worshiped. Then he came to his own house, and when he requested, they set food before him and he ate.

21 Then his servants said to him, "What is this thing that you have done? While the child was alive, you fasted and wept; but when the child died, you arose and ate food."

22 And he said, "While the child was *still* alive, I fasted and wept; for I said, 'Who knows, the LORD may be gracious to me, that the child may live.'

23 "But now he has died; why should I fast? Can I bring him back again? I shall go to him, but he will not return to me."

24 ¶ Then David comforted his wife Bathsheba, and went in to her and lay with her; and she gave birth to a son, and he named him Solomon. Now the LORD loved him

25 and sent *word* through Nathan the prophet, and he named him [11]Jedidiah for the LORD's sake.

26 ¶ Now Joab fought against Rabbah of the sons of Ammon, and captured the royal city.

27 And Joab sent messengers to David and said, "I have fought against Rabbah, I have even captured the city of waters.

28 "Now therefore, gather the rest of the people together and camp against the city and capture it, lest I capture the city myself and it be named after me."

29 So David gathered all the people and went to Rabbah, fought against it, and captured it.

30 Then he took the crown of their king from his head; and its weight *was* a talent of gold, and *in it was* a precious stone; and it was *placed* on David's head. And he brought out the spoil of the city in great amounts.

31 He also brought out the people who were in it, and set *them* under saws, sharp iron instruments, and iron axes, and made them pass through the brickkiln. And thus he did to all the cities of the sons of Ammon. Then David and all the people returned *to* Jerusalem.

CHAPTER 13

NOW it was after this that Absalom the son of David had a beautiful sister whose name was Tamar, and Amnon the son of David loved her.

2 And Amnon was so frustrated

because of his sister Tamar that he made himself ill, for she was a virgin, and it seemed hard to Amnon to do anything to her.

3 But Amnon had a friend whose name was Jonadab, the son of Shimeah, David's brother; and Jonadab was a very shrewd man.

4 And he said to him, "O son of the king, why are you so depressed morning after morning? Will you not tell me?" Then Amnon said to him, "I am in love with Tamar, the sister of my brother Absalom."

5 Jonadab then said to him, "Lie down on your bed and pretend to be ill; when your father comes to see you, say to him, 'Please let my sister Tamar come and give me *some* food to eat, and let her prepare the food in my sight, that I may see *it* and eat from her hand.'"

6 So Amnon lay down and pretended to be ill; when the king came to see him, Amnon said to the king, "Please let my sister Tamar come and make me a couple of cakes in my sight, that I may eat from her hand."

7 ¶ Then David sent to the house for Tamar, saying, "Go now to your brother Amnon's house, and prepare food for him."

8 So Tamar went to her brother Amnon's house, and he was lying down. And she took dough, kneaded *it,* made cakes in his sight, and baked the cakes.

9 And she took the pan and dished *them* out before him, but he refused to eat. And Amnon said, "Have everyone go out from me." So everyone went out from him.

10 Then Amnon said to Tamar, "Bring the food into the bedroom, that I may eat from your hand." So Tamar took the cakes which she had made and brought them into the bedroom to her brother Amnon.

11 When she brought *them* to him to eat, he took hold of her and said to her, "Come, lie with me, my sister."

12 But she answered him, "No, my brother, do not violate me, for such a thing is not done in Israel; do not do this disgraceful thing!

13 "As for me, where could I get rid of my reproach? And as for you, you will be like one of the fools in Israel. Now

therefore, please speak to the king, for he will not withhold me from you."

14 However, he would not listen to her; since he was stronger than she, he violated her and lay with her.

15 ¶ Then Amnon hated her with a very great hatred; for the hatred with which he hated her was greater than the love with which he had loved her. And Amnon said to her, "Get up, go away!"

16 But she said to him, "No, because this wrong in sending me away is greater than the other that you have done to me!" Yet he would not listen to her.

17 Then he called his young man who attended him and said, "Now throw this woman out of my *presence*, and lock the door behind her."

18 Now she had on a long-sleeved garment; for in this manner the virgin daughters of the king dressed themselves in robes. Then his attendant took her out and locked the door behind her.

19 And Tamar put ashes on her head, and tore her long-sleeved garment which *was* on her; and she put her hand on her head and went away, crying aloud as she went.

20 ¶ Then Absalom her brother said to her, "Has Amnon your brother been with you? But now keep silent, my sister, he is your brother; do not take this matter to heart." So Tamar remained and was desolate in her brother Absalom's house.

21 Now when King David heard of all these matters, he was very angry.

22 But Absalom did not speak to Amnon either good or bad; for Absalom hated Amnon because he had violated his sister Tamar.

23 ¶ Now it came about after two full years that Absalom had sheepshearers in Baal-hazor, which is near Ephraim, and Absalom invited all the king's sons.

24 And Absalom came to the king and said, "Behold now, your servant has sheepshearers; please let the king and his servants go with your servant."

25 But the king said to Absalom, "No, my son, we should not all go, lest we be burdensome to you." Although he urged him, he would not go, but blessed him.

26 Then Absalom said, "If not, please let my brother Amnon go with us." And the king said to him, "Why should he go with you?"

27 But when Absalom urged him, he let Amnon and all the king's sons go with him.

28 ¶ And Absalom commanded his servants, saying, "See now, when Amnon's heart is merry with wine, and when I say to you, 'Strike Amnon,' then put him to death. Do not fear; have not I myself commanded you? Be courageous and be valiant."

29 And the servants of Absalom did to Amnon just as Absalom had commanded. Then all the king's sons arose and each mounted his mule and fled.

30 ¶ Now it was while they were on the way that the report came to David, saying, "Absalom has struck down all the king's sons, and not one of them is left."

31 Then the king arose, tore his clothes and lay on the ground; and all his servants were standing by with clothes torn.

32 And Jonadab, the son of Shimeah, David's brother, responded, "Do not let my lord suppose they have put to death all the young men, the king's sons, for Amnon alone is dead; because by the intent of Absalom this has been determined since the day that he violated his sister Tamar.

33 "Now therefore, do not let my lord the king take the report to heart, namely, 'all the king's sons are dead,' for only Amnon is dead."

34 ¶ Now Absalom had fled. And the young man who was the watchman raised his eyes and looked, and behold, many people were coming from the road behind him by the side of the mountain.

35 And Jonadab said to the king, "Behold, the king's sons have come; according to your servant's word, so it happened."

36 And it came about as soon as he had finished speaking, that behold, the king's sons came and lifted their voices and wept; and also the king and all his servants wept very bitterly.

37 ¶ Now Absalom fled and went to Talmai the son of Ammihud, the king of Geshur. And *David* mourned for his son every day.

38 So Absalom had fled and gone to Geshur, and was there three years.

39 And *the heart of* King David longed to go out to Absalom; for he was comforted concerning Amnon, since he was dead.

CHAPTER 14

NOW Joab the son of Zeruiah perceived that the king's heart *was inclined* toward Absalom.

2 So Joab sent to Tekoa and brought a wise woman from there and said to her, "Please pretend to be a mourner, and put on mourning garments now, and do not anoint yourself with oil, but be like a woman who has been mourning for the dead many days;

3 then go to the king and speak to him in this manner." So Joab put the words in her mouth.

4 ¶ Now when the woman of Tekoa [12]spoke to the king, she fell on her face to the ground and prostrated herself and said, "Help, O king."

5 And the king said to her, "What is your trouble?" And she answered, "Truly I am a widow, for my husband is dead.

6 "And your maidservant had two sons, but the two of them struggled together in the field, and there was no [13]one to separate them, so one struck the other and killed him.

7 "Now behold, the whole family has risen against your maidservant, and they say, 'Hand over the one who struck his brother, that we may put him to death for the life of his brother whom he killed, and destroy the heir also.' Thus they will extinguish my coal which is left, so as to leave my husband neither name nor remnant on the face of the earth."

8 ¶ Then the king said to the woman, "Go to your house, and I will give orders concerning you."

9 And the woman of Tekoa said to the king, "O my lord, the king, the iniquity is on me and my father's house, but the king and his throne are guiltless."

10 So the king said, "Whoever speaks to you, bring him to me, and he will not touch you anymore."

11 Then she said, "Please let the king remember the LORD your God, *so that* the avenger of blood may not continue to destroy, lest they destroy my son." And he said, "As the LORD lives, not one hair of your son shall fall to the ground."

12 ¶ Then the woman said, "Please let your maidservant speak a word to my lord the king." And he said, "Speak."

13 And the woman said, "Why then have you planned such a thing against the people of God? For in speaking this word the king is as one who is guilty, *in that* the king does not bring back his banished one.

14 "For we shall surely die and are like water spilled on the ground which cannot be gathered up again. Yet God does not take away life, but plans ways so that the banished one may not be cast out from him.

15 "Now the reason I have come to speak this word to my lord the king is because the people have made me afraid; so your maidservant said, 'Let me now speak to the king, perhaps the king will perform the request of his maidservant.

16 'For the king will hear and deliver his maidservant from the hand of the man who would destroy both me and my son from the inheritance of God.'

17 "Then your maidservant said, 'Please let the word of my lord the king be comforting, for as the angel of God, so is my lord the king to discern good and evil. And may the LORD your God be with you.'"

18 ¶ Then the king answered and said to the woman, "Please do not hide anything from me that I am about to ask you." And the woman said, "Let my lord the king please speak."

19 So the king said, "Is the hand of Joab with you in all this?" And the woman answered and said, "As your soul lives, my lord the king, no one can turn to the right or to the left from anything that my lord the king has spoken. Indeed, it was your servant Joab who commanded me, and it was he who put all these words in the mouth of your maidservant;

20 in order to change the appearance of things your servant Joab has done this thing. But my lord is wise, like the

[12] Many mss. and ancient versions read *came*
[13] Lit., *deliverer between*

wisdom of the angel of God, to know all that is in the earth."

21 ¶ Then the king said to Joab, "Behold now, I will surely do this thing; go therefore, bring back the young man Absalom."

22 And Joab fell on his face to the ground, prostrated himself and blessed the king; then Joab said, "Today your servant knows that I have found favor in your sight, O my lord, the king, in that the king has performed the request of his servant."

23 So Joab arose and went to Geshur, and brought Absalom to Jerusalem.

24 However the king said, "Let him turn to his own house, and let him not see my face." So Absalom turned to his own house and did not see the king's face.

25 ¶ Now in all Israel was no one as handsome as Absalom, so highly praised; from the sole of his foot to the crown of his head there was no defect in him.

26 And when he cut the hair of his head (and it was at the end of every year that he cut *it*, for it was heavy on him so he cut it), he weighed the hair of his head at 200 shekels by the king's weight.

27 And to Absalom there were born three sons, and one daughter whose name was Tamar; she was a woman of beautiful appearance.

28 ¶ Now Absalom lived two full years in Jerusalem, and did not see the king's face.

29 Then Absalom sent for Joab, to send him to the king, but he would not come to him. So he sent again a second time, but he would not come.

30 Therefore he said to his servants, "See, Joab's [14]field is next to mine, and he has barley there; go and set it on fire." So Absalom's servants set the field on fire.

31 Then Joab arose, came to Absalom at his house and said to him, "Why have your servants set my [14]field on fire?"

32 And Absalom answered Joab, "Behold, I sent for you, saying, 'Come here, that I may send you to the king, to say, "Why have I come from Geshur? It would be better for me still to

be there."' Now therefore, let me see the king's face; and if there is iniquity in me, let him put me to death."

33 So when Joab came to the king and told him, he called for Absalom. Thus he came to the king and prostrated himself on his face to the ground before the king, and the king kissed Absalom.

CHAPTER 15

NOW it came about after this that Absalom provided for himself a chariot and horses, and fifty men as runners before him.

2 And Absalom used to rise early and stand beside the way to the gate; and it happened that when any man had a suit to come to the king for judgment, Absalom would call to him and say, "From what city are you?" And he would say, "Your servant is from one of the tribes of Israel."

3 Then Absalom would say to him, "See, your claims are good and right, but no man listens to you on the part of the king."

4 Moreover, Absalom would say, "Oh that one would appoint me judge in the land, then every man who has any suit or cause could come to me, and I would give him justice."

5 And it happened that when a man came near to prostrate himself before him, he would put out his hand and take hold of him and kiss him.

6 And in this manner Absalom dealt with all Israel who came to the king for judgment; so Absalom stole away the hearts of the men of Israel.

7 ¶ Now it came about at the end of [15]forty years that Absalom said to the king, "Please let me go and pay my vow which I have vowed to the LORD, in Hebron.

8"For your servant vowed a vow while I was living at Geshur in Aram, saying, 'If the LORD shall indeed bring me back to Jerusalem, then I will serve the LORD.'"

9 And the king said to him, "Go in peace." So he arose and went to Hebron.

10 But Absalom sent spies throughout all the tribes of Israel, saying, "As soon as you hear the sound of the

---

[14] Lit., *portion*   [15] Some ancient versions render *four*

trumpet, then you shall say, 'Absalom is king in Hebron.' "

11 Then two hundred men went with Absalom from Jerusalem, who were invited and went innocently, and they did not know anything.

12 And Absalom sent for Ahithophel the Gilonite, David's counselor, from his city Giloh, while he was offering the sacrifices. And the conspiracy was strong, for the people increased continually with Absalom.

13 ¶ Then a messenger came to David, saying, "The hearts of the men of Israel are with Absalom."

14 And David said to all his servants who were with him at Jerusalem, "Arise and let us flee, for *otherwise* none of us shall escape from Absalom. Go in haste, lest he overtake us quickly and bring down calamity on us and strike the city with the edge of the sword."

15 Then the king's servants said to the king, "Behold, your servants *are ready to do* whatever my lord the king chooses."

16 So the king went out and all his household with him. But the king left ten concubines to keep the house.

17 And the king went out and all the people with him, and they stopped at the last house.

18 Now all his servants passed on beside him, all the Cherethites, all the Pelethites, and all the Gittites, six hundred men who had come with him from Gath, passed on before the king.

19 ¶ Then the king said to Ittai the Gittite, "Why will you also go with us? Return and remain with the king, for you are a foreigner and also an exile; *return* to your own place.

20 "You came *only* yesterday, and shall I today make you wander with us, while I go where I will? Return and take back your brothers; mercy and truth be with you."

21 But Ittai answered the king and said, "As the LORD lives, and as my lord the king lives, surely wherever my lord the king may be, whether for death or for life, there also your servant will be."

22 Therefore David said to Ittai, "Go and pass over." So Ittai the Gittite passed over with all his men and all the little ones who *were* with him.

23 While all the country was weeping with a loud voice, all the people passed over. The king also passed over the brook Kidron, and all the people passed over toward the way of the wilderness.

24 ¶ Now behold, Zadok also *came*, and all the Levites with him carrying the ark of the covenant of God. And they set down the ark of God, and Abiathar came up until all the people had finished passing from the city.

25 And the king said to Zadok, "Return the ark of God to the city. If I find favor in the sight of the LORD, then He will bring me back again, and show me both it and His habitation.

26 "But if He should say thus, 'I have no delight in you,' behold, here I am, let Him do to me as seems good to Him."

27 The king said also to Zadok the priest, "Are you *not* a seer? Return to the city in peace and your two sons with you, your son Ahimaaz and Jonathan the son of Abiathar.

28 "See, I am going to wait at the fords of the wilderness until word comes from you to inform me."

29 Therefore Zadok and Abiathar returned the ark of God to Jerusalem and remained there.

30 ¶ And David went up the ascent of the *Mount of* Olives, and wept as he went, and his head was covered and he walked barefoot. Then all the people who were with him each covered his head and went up weeping as they went.

31 Now someone told David, saying, "Ahithophel is among the conspirators with Absalom." And David said, "O LORD, I pray, make the counsel of Ahithophel foolishness."

32 It happened as David was coming to the summit, where God was worshiped, that behold, Hushai the Archite met him with his coat torn, and dust on his head.

33 And David said to him, "If you pass over with me, then you will be a burden to me.

34 "But if you return to the city, and say to Absalom, 'I will be your servant, O king; as I have been your father's servant in time past, so I will now be your servant,' then you can thwart the counsel of Ahithophel for me.

35"And are not Zadok and Abiathar the priests with you there? So it shall be that whatever you hear from the king's house, you shall report to Zadok and Abiathar the priests.

36"Behold their two sons are with them there, Ahimaaz, Zadok's son and Jonathan, Abiathar's son; and by them you shall send me everything that you hear."

37 So Hushai, David's friend, came into the city, and Absalom came into Jerusalem.

CHAPTER 16

NOW when David had passed a little beyond the summit, behold, Ziba the servant of Mephibosheth met him with a couple of saddled donkeys, and on them *were* two hundred loaves of bread, a hundred clusters of raisins, a hundred summer fruits, and a jug of wine.

2 And the king said to Ziba, "Why do you have these?" And Ziba said, "The donkeys are for the king's household to ride, and the bread and summer fruit for the young men to eat, and the wine, for whoever is faint in the wilderness to drink."

3 Then the king said, "And where is your master's son?" And Ziba said to the king, "Behold, he is staying in Jerusalem, for he said, 'Today the house of Israel will restore the kingdom of my father to me.'"

4 So the king said to Ziba, "Behold, all that belongs to Mephibosheth is yours." And Ziba said, "I prostrate myself; let me find favor in your sight, O my lord, the king!"

5 ¶ When King David came to Bahurim, behold, there came out from there a man of the family of the house of Saul whose name was Shimei, the son of Gera; he came out cursing continually as he came.

6 And he threw stones at David and at all the servants of King David; and all the people and all the mighty men were at his right hand and at his left.

7 And thus Shimei said when he cursed, "Get out, get out, you man of bloodshed, and worthless fellow!

8"The LORD has returned upon you all the bloodshed of the house of Saul, in whose place you have reigned; and the LORD has given the kingdom into the hand of your son Absalom. And behold, you are *taken* in your own evil, for you are a man of bloodshed!"

9 ¶ Then Abishai the son of Zeruiah said to the king, "Why should this dead dog curse my lord the king? Let me go over now, and cut off his head."

10 But the king said, "What have I to do with you, O sons of Zeruiah? If he curses, and if the LORD has told him, 'Curse David,' then who shall say, 'Why have you done so?'"

11 Then David said to Abishai and to all his servants, "Behold, my son who came out from me seeks my life; how much more now this Benjamite? Let him alone and let him curse, for the LORD has told him.

12"Perhaps the LORD will look on my affliction and return good to me instead of his cursing this day."

13 So David and his men went on the way; and Shimei went along on the hillside parallel with him and as he went he cursed, and cast stones and threw dust at him.

14 And the king and all the people who were with him arrived weary and he refreshed himself there.

15 ¶ Then Absalom and all the people, the men of Israel, entered Jerusalem, and Ahithophel with him.

16 Now it came about when Hushai the Archite, David's friend, came to Absalom, that Hushai said to Absalom, "*Long* live the king! *Long* live the king!"

17 And Absalom said to Hushai, "Is this your loyalty to your friend? Why did you not go with your friend?"

18 Then Hushai said to Absalom, "No! For whom the LORD, this people, and all the men of Israel have chosen, his will I be, and with him I will remain.

19"And besides, whom should I serve? *Should I* not *serve* in the presence of his son? As I have served in your father's presence, so I will be in your presence."

20 ¶ Then Absalom said to Ahithophel, "Give your advice. What shall we do?"

21 And Ahithophel said to Absalom, "Go in to your father's concubines, whom he has left to keep the house; then all Israel will hear that you have made yourself odious to your father.

The hands of all who are with you will also be strengthened."

22 So they pitched a tent for Absalom on the roof, and Absalom went in to his father's concubines in the sight of all Israel.

23 And the advice of Ahithophel, which he gave in those days, *was* as if one inquired of the word of God; so was all the advice of Ahithophel *regarded* by both David and Absalom.

CHAPTER 17

Furthermore, Ahithophel said to Absalom, "Please let me choose 12,000 men that I may arise and pursue David tonight.

2"And I will come upon him while he is weary and exhausted and will terrify him so that all the people who are with him will flee. Then I will strike down the king alone,

3 and I will bring back all the people to you. The return of everyone depends on the man you seek; *then* all the people shall be at peace."

4 So the plan pleased Absalom and all the elders of Israel.

5 ¶ Then Absalom said, "Now call Hushai the Archite also, and let us hear what he has to say."

6 When Hushai had come to Absalom, Absalom said to him, "Ahithophel has spoken thus. Shall we carry out his plan? If not, you speak."

7 So Hushai said to Absalom, "This time the advice that Ahithophel has given is not good."

8 Moreover, Hushai said, "You know your father and his men, that they are mighty men and they are fierce, like a bear robbed of her cubs in the field. And your father is an expert in warfare, and will not spend the night with the people.

9"Behold, he has now hidden himself in one of the caves or in another place; and it will be when he falls on them at the first attack, that whoever hears *it* will say, 'There has been a slaughter among the people who follow Absalom.'

10"And even the one who is valiant, whose heart is like the heart of a lion, will completely lose heart; for all Israel knows that your father is a mighty man and those who are with him are valiant men.

11"But I counsel that all Israel be surely gathered to you, from Dan even to Beersheba, as the sand that is by the sea in abundance, and that you personally go into battle.

12"So we shall come to him in one of the places where he can be found, and we will fall on him as the dew falls on the ground; and of him and of all the men who are with him, not even one will be left.

13"And if he withdraws into a city, then all Israel shall bring ropes to that city, and we will drag it into the valley until not even a small stone is found there."

14 Then Absalom and all the men of Israel said, "The counsel of Hushai the Archite is better than the counsel of Ahithophel." For the LORD had ordained to thwart the good counsel of Ahithophel, in order that the LORD might bring calamity on Absalom.

15 ¶ Then Hushai said to Zadok and to Abiathar the priests, "This is what Ahithophel counseled Absalom and the elders of Israel, and this is what I have counseled.

16"Now therefore, send quickly and tell David, saying, 'Do not spend the night at the fords of the wilderness, but by all means cross over, lest the king and all the people who are with him be destroyed.'"

17 Now Jonathan and Ahimaaz were staying at En-rogel, and a maidservant would go and tell them, and they would go and tell King David, for they could not be seen entering the city.

18 But a lad did see them, and told Absalom; so the two of them departed quickly and came to the house of a man in Bahurim, who had a well in his courtyard, and they went down into it.

19 And the woman took a covering and spread it over the well's mouth and scattered grain on it, so that nothing was known.

20 Then Absalom's servants came to the woman at the house and said, "Where are Ahimaaz and Jonathan?" And the woman said to them, "They have crossed the brook of water." And when they searched and could not find *them,* they returned to Jerusalem.

21 ¶ And it came about after they had departed that they came up out of the well and went and told King David; and they said to David, "Arise and

cross over the water quickly for thus Ahithophel has counseled against you."

22 Then David and all the people who *were* with him arose and crossed the Jordan; and by dawn not even one remained who had not crossed the Jordan.

23 Now when Ahithophel saw that his counsel was not followed, he saddled *his* donkey and arose and went to his home, to his city, and set his house in order, and strangled himself; thus he died and was buried in the grave of his father.

24 ¶ Then David came to Mahanaim. And Absalom crossed the Jordan, he and all the men of Israel with him.

25 And Absalom set Amasa over the army in place of Joab. Now Amasa was the son of a man whose name was Ithra the Israelite, who went in to Abigail the daughter of Nahash, sister of Zeruiah, Joab's mother.

26 And Israel and Absalom camped in the land of Gilead.

27 ¶ Now when David had come to Mahanaim, Shobi the son of Nahash from Rabbah of the sons of Ammon, Machir the son of Ammiel from Lodebar, and Barzillai the Gileadite from Rogelim,

28 brought beds, basins, pottery, wheat, barley, flour, parched *grain*, beans, lentils, parched *seeds,*

29 honey, curds, sheep, and cheese of the herd, for David and for the people who *were* with him, to eat; for they said, "The people are hungry and weary and thirsty in the wilderness."

CHAPTER 18

THEN David numbered the people who were with him and set over them commanders of thousands and commanders of hundreds.

2 And David sent the people out, one third under the command of Joab, one third under the command of Abishai the son of Zeruiah, Joab's brother, and one third under the command of Ittai the Gittite. And the king said to the people, "I myself will surely go out with you also."

3 But the people said, "You should not go out; for if we indeed flee, they will not care about us, even if half of us die, they will not care about us. But you are worth ten thousand of us; therefore now it is better that you *be ready* to help us from the city."

4 Then the king said to them, "Whatever seems best to you I will do." So the king stood beside the gate, and all the people went out by hundreds and thousands.

5 And the king charged Joab and Abishai and Ittai, saying, "*Deal* gently for my sake with the young man Absalom." And all the people heard when the king charged all the commanders concerning Absalom.

6 ¶ Then the people went out into the field against Israel, and the battle took place in the forest of Ephraim.

7 And the people of Israel were defeated there before the servants of David, and the slaughter there that day was great, 20,000 men.

8 For the battle there was spread over the whole countryside, and the forest devoured more people that day than the sword devoured.

9 ¶ Now Absalom happened to meet the servants of David. For Absalom was riding on *his* mule, and the mule went under the thick branches of a great oak. And his head caught fast in the oak, so he was left hanging between heaven and earth, while the mule that was under him kept going.

10 When a certain man saw *it,* he told Joab and said, "Behold, I saw Absalom hanging in an oak."

11 Then Joab said to the man who had told him, "Now behold, you saw *him!* Why then did you not strike him there to the ground? And I would have given you ten *pieces* of silver and a belt."

12 And the man said to Joab, "Even if I should receive a thousand *pieces of* silver in my hand, I would not put out my hand against the king's son; for in our hearing the king charged you and Abishai and Ittai, saying, 'Protect for me the young man Absalom!'

13 "Otherwise, if I had dealt treacherously against his life (and there is nothing hidden from the king), then you yourself would have stood aloof."

14 Then Joab said, "I will not waste time here with you." So he took three spears in his hand and thrust them through the heart of Absalom while he was yet alive in the midst of the oak.

15 And ten young men who carried Joab's armor gathered around and struck Absalom and killed him.

16 ¶ Then Joab blew the trumpet, and the people returned from pursuing Israel, for Joab restrained the people.

17 And they took Absalom and cast him into a deep pit in the forest and erected over him a very great heap of stones. And all Israel fled, each to his tent.

18 Now Absalom in his lifetime had taken and set up for himself a pillar which is in the King's Valley, for he said, "I have no son to preserve my name." So he named the pillar after his own name, and it is called Absalom's monument to this day.

19 ¶ Then Ahimaaz the son of Zadok said, "Please let me run and bring the king news that the LORD has freed him from the hand of his enemies."

20 But Joab said to him, "You are not the man to carry news this day, but you shall carry news another day; however, you shall carry no news today because the king's son is dead."

21 Then Joab said to the Cushite, "Go, tell the king what you have seen." So the Cushite bowed to Joab and ran.

22 Now Ahimaaz the son of Zadok said once more to Joab, "But whatever happens, please let me also run after the Cushite." And Joab said, "Why would you run, my son, since you will have no reward for going?"

23"But whatever happens," he said, "I will run." So he said to him, "Run." Then Ahimaaz ran by way of the plain and passed up the Cushite.

24 ¶ Now David was sitting between the two gates; and the watchman went up to the roof of the gate by the wall, and raised his eyes and looked, and behold, a man running by himself.

25 And the watchman called and told the king. And the king said, "If he is by himself there is good news in his mouth." And he came nearer and nearer.

26 Then the watchman saw another man running; and the watchman called to the gatekeeper and said, "Behold, another man running by himself." And the king said, "This one also is bringing good news."

27 And the watchman said, "I think the running of the first one is like the

running of Ahimaaz the son of Zadok." And the king said, "This is a good man and comes with good news."

28 ¶ And Ahimaaz called and said to the king, "[16]All is well." And he prostrated himself before the king with his face to the ground. And he said, "Blessed is the LORD your God, who has delivered up the men who lifted their hands against my lord the king."

29 And the king said, "Is it well with the young man Absalom?" And Ahimaaz answered, "When Joab sent the king's servant, and your servant, I saw a great tumult, but I did not know what it was."

30 Then the king said, "Turn aside and stand here." So he turned aside and stood still.

31 ¶ And behold, the Cushite arrived, and the Cushite said, "Let my lord the king receive good news, for the LORD has freed you this day from the hand of all those who rose up against you."

32 Then the king said to the Cushite, "Is it well with the young man Absalom?" And the Cushite answered, "Let the enemies of my lord the king, and all who rise up against you for evil, be as that young man!"

33 And the king was deeply moved and went up to the chamber over the gate and wept. And thus he said as he walked, "O my son Absalom, my son, my son Absalom! Would I had died instead of you, O Absalom, my son, my son!"

CHAPTER 19

THEN it was told Joab, "Behold, the king is weeping and mourns for Absalom."

2 And the victory that day was turned to mourning for all the people, for the people heard it said that day, "The king is grieved for his son."

3 So the people went by stealth into the city that day, as people who are humiliated steal away when they flee in battle.

4 And the king covered his face and cried out with a loud voice, "O my son Absalom, O Absalom, my son, my son!"

5 Then Joab came into the house to

[16] Lit., Peace.

the king and said, "Today you have covered with shame the faces of all your servants, who today have saved your life and the lives of your sons and daughters, the lives of your wives, and the lives of your concubines,

6 by loving those who hate you, and by hating those who love you. For you have shown today that princes and servants are nothing to you; for I know this day that if Absalom were alive and all of us were dead today, then you would be pleased.

7 "Now therefore arise, go out and speak kindly to your servants, for I swear by the LORD, if you do not go out, surely not a man will pass the night with you, and this will be worse for you than all the evil that has come upon you from your youth until now."

8 So the king arose and sat in the gate. When they told all the people, saying, "Behold, the king is sitting in the gate," then all the people came before the king.

¶ Now Israel had fled, each to his tent.

9 And all the people were quarreling throughout all the tribes of Israel, saying, "The king delivered us from the hand of our enemies and saved us from the hand of the Philistines, but now he has fled out of the land from Absalom.

10 "However, Absalom, whom we anointed over us, has died in battle. Now then, why are you silent about bringing the king back?"

11 ¶ Then King David sent to Zadok and Abiathar the priests, saying, "Speak to the elders of Judah, saying, 'Why are you the last to bring the king back to his house, since the word of all Israel has come to the king, even to his house?

12 'You are my brothers; you are my bone and my flesh. Why then should you be the last to bring back the king?'

13 "And say to Amasa, 'Are you not my bone and my flesh? May God do so to me, and more also, if you will not be commander of the army before me continually in place of Joab.' "

14 Thus he turned the hearts of all the men of Judah as one man, so that they sent word to the king, saying, "Return, you and all your servants."

15 The king then returned and came as far as the Jordan. And Judah came to Gilgal in order to go to meet the king, to bring the king across the Jordan.

16 ¶ Then Shimei the son of Gera, the Benjamite who was from Bahurim, hurried and came down with the men of Judah to meet King David.

17 And there were a thousand men of Benjamin with him, with Ziba the servant of the house of Saul, and his fifteen sons and his twenty servants with him; and they rushed to the Jordan before the king.

18 Then they kept crossing the ford to bring over the king's household, and to do what was good in his sight. And Shimei the son of Gera fell down before the king as he was about to cross the Jordan.

19 So he said to the king, "Let not my lord consider me guilty, nor remember what your servant did wrong on the day when my lord the king came out from Jerusalem, so that the king should take it to heart.

20 "For your servant knows that I have sinned; therefore behold, I have come today, the first of all the house of Joseph to go down to meet my lord the king."

21 But Abishai the son of Zeruiah answered and said, "Should not Shimei be put to death for this, because he cursed the LORD's anointed?"

22 David then said, "What have I to do with you, O sons of Zeruiah, that you should this day be an adversary to me? Should any man be put to death in Israel today? For do I not know that I am king over Israel today?"

23 And the king said to Shimei, "You shall not die." Thus the king swore to him.

24 ¶ Then Mephibosheth the [17]son of Saul came down to meet the king; and he had neither cared for his feet, nor trimmed his mustache, nor washed his clothes, from the day the king departed until the day he came home in peace.

25 And it was when he came from Jerusalem to meet the king, that the king said to him, "Why did you not go with me, Mephibosheth?"

26 So he answered, "O my lord, the king, my servant deceived me; for

17 I.e., grandson

your servant said, 'I will saddle a donkey for myself that I may ride on it and go with the king,' because your servant is lame.

27"Moreover, he has slandered your servant to my lord the king; but my lord the king is like the angel of God, therefore do what is good in your sight.

28"For all my father's household was nothing but dead men before my lord the king; yet you set your servant among those who ate at your own table. What right do I have yet that I should complain anymore to the king?"

29 So the king said to him, "Why do you still speak of your affairs? I have decided, 'You and Ziba shall divide the land.' "

30 And Mephibosheth said to the king, "Let him even take it all, since my lord the king has come safely to his own house."

31 ¶ Now Barzillai the Gileadite had come down from Rogelim; and he went on to the Jordan with the king to escort him over the Jordan.

32 Now Barzillai was very old, being eighty years old; and he had sustained the king while he stayed at Mahanaim, for he was a very great man.

33 And the king said to Barzillai, "You cross over with me and I will sustain you in Jerusalem with me."

34 But Barzillai said to the king, "How long have I yet to live, that I should go up with the king to Jerusalem?

35"I am now eighty years old. Can I distinguish between good and bad? Or can your servant taste what I eat or what I drink? Or can I hear anymore the voice of singing men and women? Why then should your servant be an added burden to my lord the king?

36"Your servant would merely cross over the Jordan with the king. Why should the king compensate me with this reward?

37"Please let your servant return, that I may die in my own city near the grave of my father and my mother. However, here is your servant Chimham, let him cross over with my lord the king, and do for him what is good in your sight."

38 And the king answered, "Chimham shall cross over with me, and I will do for him what is good in your sight; and whatever you require of me, I will do for you."

39 All the people crossed over the Jordan and the king crossed too. The king then kissed Barzillai and blessed him, and he returned to his place.

40 ¶ Now the king went on to Gilgal, and Chimham went on with him; and all the people of Judah and also half the people of Israel accompanied the king.

41 And behold, all the men of Israel came to the king and said to the king, "Why had our brothers the men of Judah stolen you away, and brought the king and his household and all David's men with him over the Jordan?"

42 Then all the men of Judah answered the men of Israel, "Because the king is a close relative to us. Why then are you angry about this matter? Have we eaten at all at the king's *expense*, or has anything been taken for us?"

43 But the men of Israel answered the men of Judah and said, "We have ten parts in the king, therefore we also have more *claim* on David than you. Why then did you treat us with contempt? Was it not our advice first to bring back our king?" Yet the words of the men of Judah were harsher than the words of the men of Israel.

CHAPTER 20

NOW a worthless fellow happened to be there whose name was Sheba, the son of Bichri, a Benjamite; and he blew the trumpet and said,

"We have no portion in David,
Nor do we have inheritance in the son of Jesse;
Every man to his tents, O Israel!"

2 So all the men of Israel withdrew from following David, *and* followed Sheba the son of Bichri; but the men of Judah remained steadfast to their king, from the Jordan even to Jerusalem.

3 ¶ Then David came to his house at Jerusalem, and the king took the ten women, the concubines whom he had left to keep the house, and placed them under guard and provided them with sustenance, but did not go in to them. So they were shut up until the day of their death, living as widows.

4 ¶ Then the king said to Amasa, "Call out the men of Judah for me within three days, and be present here yourself."

5 So Amasa went to call out *the men of* Judah, but he delayed longer than the set time which he had appointed him.

6 And David said to Abishai, "Now Sheba the son of Bichri will do us more harm than Absalom; take your lord's servants and pursue him, lest he find for himself fortified cities and escape from our sight."

7 So Joab's men went out after him, along with the Cherethites and the Pelethites and all the mighty men; and they went out from Jerusalem to pursue Sheba the son of Bichri.

8 When they were at the large stone which is in Gibeon, Amasa came to meet them. Now Joab was dressed in his military attire, and over it was a belt with a sword in its sheath fastened at his waist; and as he went forward, it fell out.

9 And Joab said to Amasa, "Is it well with you, my brother?" And Joab took Amasa by the beard with his right hand to kiss him.

10 But Amasa was not on guard against the sword which was in Joab's hand so he struck him in the belly with it and poured out his inward parts on the ground, and did not *strike* him again; and he died. Then Joab and Abishai his brother pursued Sheba the son of Bichri.

11 Now there stood by him one of Joab's young men, and said, "Whoever favors Joab and whoever is for David, *let him* follow Joab."

12 But Amasa lay wallowing in *his* blood in the middle of the highway. And when the man saw that all the people stood still, he removed Amasa from the highway into the field and threw a garment over him when he saw that everyone who came by him stood still.

13 As soon as he was removed from the highway, all the men passed on after Joab to pursue Sheba the son of Bichri.

14 Now he went through all the tribes of Israel to Abel even to Beth-maacah and all the Berites; and they were gathered together and also went after him.

15 And they came and besieged him in Abel Beth-maacah, and they cast up a mound against the city, and it stood by the rampart; and all the people who were with Joab were wreaking destruction in order to topple the wall.

16 Then a wise woman called from the city, "Hear, hear! Please tell Joab, 'Come here that I may speak with you.'"

17 So he approached her, and the woman said, "Are you Joab?" And he answered, "I am." Then she said to him, "Listen to the words of your maidservant." And he answered, "I am listening."

18 Then she spoke, saying, "Formerly they used to say, 'They will surely ask *advice* at Abel,' and thus they ended *the* dispute.

19 "I am of those who are peaceable *and* faithful in Israel. You are seeking to destroy a city even a mother in Israel. Why would you swallow up the inheritance of the LORD?"

20 And Joab answered and said, "Far be it, far be it from me that I should swallow up or destroy!

21 "Such is not the case. But a man from the hill country of Ephraim, Sheba the son of Bichri by name, has lifted up his hand against King David. Only hand him over, and I will depart from the city." And the woman said to Joab, "Behold, his head will be thrown to you over the wall."

22 Then the woman wisely came to all the people. And they cut off the head of Sheba the son of Bichri and threw it to Joab. So he blew the trumpet, and they were dispersed from the city, each to his tent. Joab also returned to the king at Jerusalem.

23 ¶ Now Joab was over the whole army of Israel, and Benaiah the son of Jehoiada was over the Cherethites and the Pelethites;

24 and Adoram was over the forced labor, and Jehoshaphat the son of Ahilud was the recorder;

25 and Sheva was scribe, and Zadok and Abiathar were priests;

26 and Ira the Jairite was also a priest to David.

CHAPTER 21

NOW there was a famine in the days of David for three years, year after year; and David sought the presence of the LORD. And the LORD said, "It is for Saul and his bloody house, because he put the Gibeonites to death."

2 So the king called the Gibeonites and spoke to them (now the Gibeonites were not of the sons of Israel but of the remnant of the Amorites, and the sons of Israel made a covenant with them, but Saul had sought to kill them in his zeal for the sons of Israel and Judah).

3 Thus David said to the Gibeonites, "What should I do for you? And how can I make atonement that you may bless the inheritance of the LORD?"

4 Then the Gibeonites said to him, "We have no *concern* of silver or gold with Saul or his house, nor is it for us to put any man to death in Israel." And he said, "I will do for you whatever you say."

5 So they said to the king, "The man who consumed us, and who planned to exterminate us from remaining within any border of Israel,

6 let seven men from his sons be given to us, and we will hang them before the LORD in Gibeah of Saul, the chosen of the LORD." And the king said, "I will give *them.*"

7 ¶ But the king spared Mephibosheth, the son of Jonathan the son of Saul, because of the oath of the LORD which was between them, between David and Saul's son Jonathan.

8 So the king took the two sons of Rizpah the daughter of Aiah, Armoni and Mephibosheth whom she had born to Saul, and the five sons of Merab the daughter of Saul, whom she had born to Adriel the son of Barzillai the Meholathite.

9 Then he gave them into the hands of the Gibeonites, and they hanged them in the mountain before the LORD, so that the seven of them fell together; and they were put to death in the first days of harvest at the beginning of barley harvest.

10 ¶ And Rizpah the daughter of Aiah took sackcloth and spread it for herself on the rock, from the beginning of harvest until it rained on them from the sky; and she allowed neither the birds of the sky to rest on them by day nor the beasts of the field by night.

11 When it was told David what Rizpah the daughter of Aiah, the concubine of Saul, had done,

12 then David went and took the bones of Saul and the bones of Jonathan his son from the men of Jabesh-gilead, who had stolen them from the open square of Beth–shan, where the Philistines had hanged them on the day the Philistines struck down Saul in Gilboa.

13 And he brought up the bones of Saul and the bones of Jonathan his son from there, and they gathered the bones of those who had been hanged.

14 And they buried the bones of Saul and Jonathan his son in the country of Benjamin in Zela, in the grave of Kish his father; thus they did all that the king commanded, and after that God was moved by entreaty for the land.

15 ¶ Now when the Philistines were at war again with Israel, David went down and his servants with him; and as they fought against the Philistines, David became weary.

16 Then Ishbi-benob, who was among the descendants of the giant, the weight of whose spear was three hundred *shekels* of bronze in weight, was girded with a new *sword,* and he intended to kill David.

17 But Abishai the son of Zeruiah helped him, and struck the Philistine and killed him. Then the men of David swore to him, saying, "You shall not go out again with us to battle, that you may not extinguish the lamp of Israel."

18 ¶ Now it came about after this that there was war again with the Philistines at Gob; then Sibbecai the Hushathite struck down Saph, who was among the descendants of the giant.

19 And there was war with the Philistines again at Gob, and Elhanan the son of Jaare-oregim the Bethlehemite killed Goliath the Gittite, the shaft of whose spear was like a weaver's beam.

20 And there was war at Gath again, where there was a man of *great* stature who had six fingers on each hand and six toes on each foot, twenty-four in number; and he also had been born to the giant.

21 And when he defied Israel, Jonathan the son of Shimei, David's brother, struck him down.

22 These four were born to the giant in Gath, and they fell by the hand of David and by the hand of his servants.

CHAPTER 22

AND David spoke the words of this song to the LORD in the day that the LORD delivered him from the hand of all his enemies and from the hand of Saul.

2 And he said,
> "The LORD is my rock and my fortress and my deliverer;

3 My God, my rock, in whom I take refuge;
> My shield and the horn of my salvation, my stronghold and my refuge;
> My savior, Thou dost save me from violence.

4 "I call upon the LORD, who is worthy to be praised;
> And I am saved from my enemies.

5 "For the waves of death encompassed me;
> The torrents of destruction overwhelmed me;

6 The cords of Sheol surrounded me;
> The snares of death confronted me.

7 "In my distress I called upon the LORD,
> Yes, I cried to my God;
> And from His temple He heard my voice,
> And my cry for help *came* into His ears.

8 "Then the earth shook and quaked,
> The foundations of heaven were trembling
> And were shaken, because He was angry.

9 "Smoke went up out of His nostrils,
> And fire from His mouth devoured;
> Coals were kindled by it.

10 "He bowed the heavens also, and came down
> With thick darkness under His feet.

11 "And He rode on a cherub and flew;
> And He appeared on the wings of the wind.

12 "And He made darkness canopies around Him,
> A mass of waters, thick clouds of the sky.

13 "From the brightness before Him Coals of fire were kindled.

14 "The LORD thundered from heaven,
> And the Most High uttered His voice.

15 "And He sent out arrows, and scattered them,
> Lightning, and routed them.

16 "Then the channels of the sea appeared,
> The foundations of the world were laid bare,
> By the rebuke of the LORD,
> At the blast of the breath of His nostrils.

17 "He sent from on high, He took me;
> He drew me out of many waters.

18 "He delivered me from my strong enemy,
> From those who hated me, for they were too strong for me.

19 "They confronted me in the day of my calamity,
> But the LORD was my support.

20 "He also brought me forth into a broad place;
> He rescued me, because He delighted in me.

21 "The LORD has rewarded me according to my righteousness;
> According to the cleanness of my hands He has recompensed me.

22 "For I have kept the ways of the LORD,
> And have not acted wickedly against my God.

23 "For all His ordinances *were* before me;
> And *as for* His statutes, I did not depart from them.

24 "I was also blameless toward Him,
> And I kept myself from my iniquity.

25 "Therefore the LORD has recompensed me according to my righteousness,
> According to my cleanness before His eyes.

26 "With the kind Thou dost show
Thyself kind,
With the blameless Thou dost
show Thyself blameless;

27 With the pure Thou dost show
Thyself pure,
And with the perverted Thou
dost show Thyself astute.

28 "And Thou dost save an afflicted
people;
But Thine eyes are on the
haughty *whom* Thou dost
abase.

29 "For Thou art my lamp, O Lord;
And the Lord illumines my darkness.

30 "For by Thee I can [18]run upon a
troop;
By my God I can leap over a
wall.

31 "As for God, His way is blameless;
The word of the Lord is tested;
He is a shield to all who take
refuge in Him.

32 "For who is God, besides the
Lord?
And who is a rock, besides our
God?

33 "God is my strong fortress;
And He sets the blameless in His
way.

34 "He makes my feet like hinds'
feet,
And sets me on my high places.

35 "He trains my hands for battle,
So that my arms can bend a bow
of bronze.

36 "Thou hast also given me the
shield of Thy salvation,
And Thy help makes me great.

37 "Thou dost enlarge my steps under me,
And my feet have not slipped.

38 "I pursued my enemies and destroyed them,
And I did not turn back until
they were consumed.

39 "And I have devoured them and
shattered them, so that they did
not rise;
And they fell under my feet.

40 "For Thou hast girded me with
strength for battle;
Thou hast subdued under me
those who rose up against me.

41 "Thou hast also made my enemies
turn *their* backs to me,
And I destroyed those who hated
me.

42 "They looked, but there was none
to save;
Even to the Lord, but He did not
answer them.

43 "Then I pulverized them as the
dust of the earth,
I crushed *and* stamped them as
the mire of the streets.

44 "Thou hast also delivered me from
the contentions of my people;
Thou hast kept me as head of the
nations;
A people whom I have not
known serve me.

45 "Foreigners pretend obedience to
me;
As soon as they hear, they obey
me.

46 "Foreigners lose heart,
And come trembling out of their
fortresses.

47 "The Lord lives, and blessed be
my rock;
And exalted be God, the rock of
my salvation,

48 The God who executes vengeance for me,
And brings down peoples under
me,

49 Who also brings me out from my
enemies;
Thou dost even lift me above
those who rise up against me;
Thou dost rescue me from the
violent man.

50 "Therefore I will give thanks to
Thee, O Lord, among the nations,
And I will sing praises to Thy
name.

51 "*He* is a tower of [19]deliverance to
His king,
And shows lovingkindness to His
anointed,
To David and his descendants
forever."

CHAPTER 23

Now these are the last words of
David.
David the son of Jesse declares,
And the man who was raised on
high declares,

---

[18] Or, *crush a troop*   [19] I.e., *victories*

The anointed of the God of Jacob,
And the sweet psalmist of Israel,
2 "The Spirit of the LORD spoke by me,
And His word was on my tongue.
3 "The God of Israel said,
The Rock of Israel spoke to me,
'He who rules over men righteously,
Who rules in the fear of God,
4 Is as the light of the morning *when* the sun rises,
A morning without clouds,
When the tender grass *springs* out of the earth,
Through sunshine after rain.'
5 "Truly is not my house so with God?
For He has made an everlasting covenant with me,
Ordered in all things, and secured;
For all my salvation and all *my* desire,
Will He not indeed make *it* grow?
6 "But the worthless, every one of them will be thrust away like thorns,
Because they cannot be taken in hand;
7 But the man who touches them
Must be armed with iron and the shaft of a spear,
And they will be completely burned with fire in *their* place."

8 ¶ These are the names of the mighty men whom David had: Josheb-basshebeth a Tahchemonite, chief of the captains, he was *called* Adino the Eznite, because of eight hundred slain *by him* at one time;

9 and after him was Eleazar the son of Dodo the Ahohite, one of the three mighty men with David when they defied the Philistines who were gathered there to battle and the men of Israel had withdrawn.

10 He arose and struck the Philistines until his hand was weary and clung to the sword, and the LORD brought about a great victory that day; and the people returned after him only to strip *the slain*.

11 ¶ Now after him was Shammah the son of Agee a Hararite. And the Philistines were gathered into a troop, where there was a plot of ground full of lentils, and the people fled from the Philistines.

12 But he took his stand in the midst of the plot, defended it and struck the Philistines; and the LORD brought about a great victory.

13 ¶ Then three of the thirty chief men went down and came to David in the harvest time to the cave of Adullam, while the troop of the Philistines was camping in the valley of Rephaim.

14 And David was then in the stronghold, while the garrison of the Philistines was then in Bethlehem.

15 And David had a craving and said, "Oh that someone would give me water to drink from the well of Bethlehem which is by the gate!"

16 So the three mighty men broke through the camp of the Philistines, and drew water from the well of Bethlehem which was by the gate, and took *it* and brought *it* to David. Nevertheless he would not drink it, but poured it out to the LORD;

17 and he said, "Be it far from me, O LORD, that I should do this. *Shall I drink* the blood of the men who went in *jeopardy* of their lives?" Therefore he would not drink it. These things the three mighty men did.

18 ¶ And Abishai, the brother of Joab, the son of Zeruiah, was chief of the thirty. And he swung his spear against three hundred and killed *them,* and had a name as well as the three.

19 He was most honored of the thirty, therefore he became their commander; however, he did not attain to the three.

20 ¶ Then Benaiah the son of Jehoiada, the son of a valiant man of Kabzeel, who had done mighty deeds, killed the two *sons of* Ariel of Moab. He also went down and killed a lion in the middle of a pit on a snowy day.

21 And he killed an Egyptian, an impressive man. Now the Egyptian *had* a spear in his hand, but he went down to him with a club and snatched the spear from the Egyptian's hand, and killed him with his own spear.

22 These *things* Benaiah the son of Jehoiada did, and had a name as well as the three mighty men.

23 He was honored among the thirty, but he did not attain to the three. And David appointed him over his guard.

24 ¶ Asahel the brother of Joab was among the thirty; Elhanan the son of Dodo of Bethlehem,

25 Shammah the Harodite, Elika the Harodite,

26 Helez the Paltite, Ira the son of Ikkesh the Tekoite,

27 Abiezer the Anathothite, Mebunnai the Hushathite,

28 Zalmon the Ahohite, Maharai the Netophathite,

29 Heleb the son of Baanah the Netophathite, Ittai the son of Ribai of Gibeah of the sons of Benjamin,

30 Benaiah a Pirathonite, Hiddai of the brooks of Gaash,

31 Abi-albon the Arbathite, Azmaveth the Barhumite,

32 Eliahba the Shaalbonite, the sons of Jashen, Jonathan,

33 Shammah the Hararite, Ahiam the son of Sharar the Ararite,

34 Eliphelet the son of Ahasbai, the son of the Maacathite, Eliam the son of Ahithophel the Gilonite,

35 Hezro the Carmelite, Paarai the Arbite,

36 Igal the son of Nathan of Zobah, Bani the Gadite,

37 Zelek the Ammonite, Naharai the Beerothite, armor bearers of Joab the son of Zeruiah,

38 Ira the Ithrite, Gareb the Ithrite,

39 Uriah the Hittite; thirty-seven in all.

CHAPTER 24

NOW again the anger of the LORD burned against Israel, and it incited David against them to say, "Go, number Israel and Judah."

2 And the king said to Joab the commander of the army who was with him, "Go about now through all the tribes of Israel, from Dan to Beersheba, and register the people, that I may know the number of the people."

3 But Joab said to the king, "Now may the LORD your God add to the people a hundred times as many as they are, while the eyes of my lord the king *still* see; but why does my lord the king delight in this thing?"

4 Nevertheless, the king's word prevailed against Joab and against the commanders of the army. So Joab and the commanders of the army went out

from the presence of the king, to register the people of Israel.

5 And they crossed the Jordan and camped in Aroer, on the right side of the city that is in the middle of the valley of Gad, and toward Jazer.

6 Then they came to Gilead and to [20]the land of Tahtim-hodshi, and they came to Dan-jaan and around to Sidon,

7 and came to the fortress of Tyre and to all the cities of the Hivites and of the Canaanites, and they went out to the south of Judah, *to* Beersheba.

8 So when they had gone about through the whole land, they came to Jerusalem at the end of nine months and twenty days.

9 And Joab gave the number of the registration of the people to the king; and there were in Israel eight hundred thousand valiant men who drew the sword, and the men of Judah were five hundred thousand men.

10 ¶ Now David's heart troubled him after he had numbered the people. So David said to the LORD, "I have sinned greatly in what I have done. But now, O LORD, please take away the iniquity of Thy servant, for I have acted very foolishly."

11 When David arose in the morning, the word of the LORD came to the prophet Gad, David's seer, saying,

12"Go and speak to David, 'Thus the LORD says, "I am offering you three things; choose for yourself one of them, which I may do to you." ' "

13 So Gad came to David and told him, and said to him, "Shall seven years of famine come to you in your land? Or will you flee three months before your foes while they pursue you? Or shall there be three days' pestilence in your land? Now consider and see what answer I shall return to Him who sent me."

14 Then David said to Gad, "I am in great distress. Let us now fall into the hand of the LORD for His mercies are great, but do not let me fall into the hand of man."

15 ¶ So the LORD sent a pestilence upon Israel from the morning until the appointed time; and seventy thousand men of the people from Dan to Beersheba died.

[20] Or, *Kadesh in the land of the Hittite*

16 When the angel stretched out his hand toward Jerusalem to destroy it, the LORD relented from the calamity, and said to the angel who destroyed the people, "It is enough! Now relax your hand!" And the angel of the LORD was by the threshing floor of Araunah the Jebusite.

17 Then David spoke to the LORD when he saw the angel who was striking down the people, and said, "Behold, it is I who have sinned, and it is I who have done wrong; but these sheep, what have they done? Please let Thy hand be against me and against my father's house."

18 ¶ So Gad came to David that day and said to him, "Go up, erect an altar to the LORD on the threshing floor of Araunah the Jebusite."

19 And David went up according to the word of Gad, just as the LORD had commanded.

20 And Araunah looked down and saw the king and his servants crossing over toward him; and Araunah went out and bowed his face to the ground before the king.

21 Then Araunah said, "Why has my lord the king come to his servant?" And David said, "To buy the threshing floor from you, in order to build an altar to the LORD, that the plague may be held back from the people."

22 And Araunah said to David, "Let my lord the king take and offer up what is good in his sight. Look, the oxen for the burnt offering, the threshing sledges and the yokes of the oxen for the wood.

23 "Everything, O king, Araunah gives to the king." And Araunah said to the king, "May the LORD your God accept you."

24 However, the king said to Araunah, "No, but I will surely buy it from you for a price, for I will not offer burnt offerings to the LORD my God which cost me nothing." So David bought the threshing floor and the oxen for fifty shekels of silver.

25 And David built there an altar to the LORD, and offered burnt offerings and peace offerings. Thus the LORD was moved by entreaty for the land, and the plague was held back from Israel.

THE FIRST BOOK OF THE

KINGS

NOW King David was old, advanced in age; and they covered him with clothes, but he could not keep warm.

2 So his servants said to him, "Let them seek a young virgin for my lord the king, and let her attend the king and become his nurse; and let her lie in your bosom, that my lord the king may keep warm."

3 So they searched for a beautiful girl throughout all the territory of Israel, and found Abishag the Shunammite, and brought her to the king.

4 And the girl was very beautiful; and she became the king's nurse and served him, but the king did not cohabit with her.

5 ¶ Now Adonijah the son of Haggith exalted himself, saying, "I will be king." So he prepared for himself chariots and horsemen with fifty men to run before him.

6 And his father had never crossed him at any time by asking, "Why have you done so?" And he was also a very handsome man; and he was born after Absalom.

7 And he had conferred with Joab the son of Zeruiah and with Abiathar the priest; and following Adonijah they helped him.

8 But Zadok the priest, Benaiah the son of Jehoiada, Nathan the prophet, Shimei, Rei, and the mighty men who belonged to David, were not with Adonijah.

9 And Adonijah sacrificed sheep and oxen and fatlings by the ¹stone of Zoheleth, which is beside En-rogel; and he invited all his brothers, the

¹ Or, Gliding or Serpent Stone

king's sons, and all the men of Judah, the king's servants.

10 But he did not invite Nathan the prophet, Benaiah, the mighty men, and Solomon his brother.

11 ¶ Then Nathan spoke to Bathsheba the mother of Solomon, saying, "Have you not heard that Adonijah the son of Haggith has become king, and David our lord does not know *it*?

12 "So now come, please let me give you counsel and save your life and the life of your son Solomon.

13 "Go at once to King David and say to him, 'Have you not, my lord, O king, sworn to your maidservant, saying, "Surely Solomon your son shall be king after me, and he shall sit on my throne"? Why then has Adonijah become king?'

14 "Behold, while you are still there speaking with the king, I will come in after you and confirm your words."

15 ¶ So Bathsheba went in to the king in the bedroom. Now the king was very old, and Abishag the Shunammite was ministering to the king.

16 Then Bathsheba bowed and prostrated herself before the king. And the king said, "What do you wish?"

17 And she said to him, "My lord, you swore to your maidservant by the LORD your God, *saying,* 'Surely your son Solomon shall be king after me and he shall sit on my throne.'

18 "And now, behold, Adonijah is king; and now, my lord the king, you do not know *it.*

19 "And he has sacrificed oxen and fatlings and sheep in abundance, and has invited all the sons of the king and Abiathar the priest and Joab the commander of the army; but he has not invited Solomon your servant.

20 "And as for you now, my lord the king, the eyes of all Israel are on you, to tell them who shall sit on the throne of my lord the king after him.

21 "Otherwise it will come about, as soon as my lord the king sleeps with his fathers, that I and my son Solomon will be considered offenders."

22 ¶ And behold, while she was still speaking with the king, Nathan the prophet came in.

23 And they told the king, saying, "Here is Nathan the prophet." And when he came in before the king, he prostrated himself before the king with his face to the ground.

24 Then Nathan said, "My lord the king, have you said, 'Adonijah shall be king after me, and he shall sit on my throne'?

25 "For he has gone down today and has sacrificed oxen and fatlings and sheep in abundance, and has invited all the king's sons and the commanders of the army and Abiathar the priest, and behold, they are eating and drinking before him; and they say, '*Long* live King Adonijah!'

26 "But me, *even* me your servant, and Zadok the priest and Benaiah the son of Jehoiada and your servant Solomon, he has not invited.

27 "Has this thing been done by my lord the king, and you have not shown to your servants who should sit on the throne of my lord the king after him?"

28 ¶ Then King David answered and said, "Call Bathsheba to me." And she came into the king's presence and stood before the king.

29 And the king vowed and said, "As the LORD lives, who has redeemed my life from all distress,

30 surely as I vowed to you by the LORD the God of Israel, saying, 'Your son Solomon shall be king after me, and he shall sit on my throne in my place'; I will indeed do so this day."

31 Then Bathsheba bowed with her face to the ground, and prostrated herself before the king and said, "May my lord King David live forever."

32 ¶ Then King David said, "Call to me Zadok the priest, Nathan the prophet, and Benaiah the son of Jehoiada." And they came into the king's presence.

33 And the king said to them, "Take with you the servants of your lord, and have my son Solomon ride on my own mule, and bring him down to Gihon.

34 "And let Zadok the priest and Nathan the prophet anoint him there as king over Israel, and blow the trumpet and say, '*Long* live King Solomon!'

35 "Then you shall come up after him, and he shall come and sit on my throne and be king in my place; for I have appointed him to be ruler over Israel and Judah."

36 And Benaiah the son of Jehoiada answered the king and said, "Amen! Thus may the LORD, the God of my lord the king, say.

37 "As the LORD has been with my

lord the king, so may He be with Solomon, and make his throne greater than the throne of my lord King David!"

38 ¶ So Zadok the priest, Nathan the prophet, Benaiah the son of Jehoiada, the Cherethites, and the Pelethites went down and had Solomon ride on King David's mule, and brought him to Gihon.

39 Zadok the priest then took the horn of oil from the tent and anointed Solomon. Then they blew the trumpet, and all the people said, "*Long* live King Solomon!"

40 And all the people went up after him, and the people were playing on flutes and rejoicing with great joy, so that the earth shook at their noise.

41 ¶ Now Adonijah and all the guests who were with him heard *it*, as they finished eating. When Joab heard the sound of the trumpet, he said, "Why is the city making such an uproar?"

42 While he was still speaking, behold, Jonathan the son of Abiathar the priest came. Then Adonijah said, "Come in, for you are a valiant man and bring good news."

43 But Jonathan answered and said to Adonijah, "No! Our lord King David has made Solomon king.

44"The king has also sent with him Zadok the priest, Nathan the prophet, Benaiah the son of Jehoiada, the Cherethites, and the Pelethites; and they have made him ride on the king's mule.

45"And Zadok the priest and Nathan the prophet have anointed him king in Gihon, and they have come up from there rejoicing, so that the city is in an uproar. This is the noise which you have heard.

46"Besides, Solomon has even taken his seat on the throne of the kingdom.

47"And moreover, the king's servants came to bless our lord King David, saying, 'May your God make the name of Solomon better than your name and his throne greater than your throne!' And the king bowed himself on the bed.

48"The king has also said thus, 'Blessed be the LORD, the God of Israel, who has granted one to sit on my throne today while my own eyes see *it*.' "

49 ¶ Then all the guests of Adonijah were terrified; and they arose and each went on his way.

50 And Adonijah was afraid of Solomon, and he arose, went and took hold of the horns of the altar.

51 Now it was told Solomon, saying, "Behold, Adonijah is afraid of King Solomon, for behold, he has taken hold of the horns of the altar, saying, 'Let King Solomon swear to me today that he will not put his servant to death with the sword.' "

52 And Solomon said, "If he will be a worthy man, not one of his hairs will fall to the ground; but if wickedness is found in him, he will die."

53 So King Solomon sent, and they brought him down from the altar. And he came and prostrated himself before King Solomon, and Solomon said to him, "Go to your house."

CHAPTER 2

As David's time to die drew near, he charged Solomon his son, saying,

2"I am going the way of all the earth. Be strong, therefore, and show yourself a man.

3"And keep the charge of the LORD your God, to walk in His ways, to keep His statutes, His commandments, His ordinances, and His testimonies, according to what is written in the law of Moses, that you may succeed in all that you do and wherever you turn,

4 so that the LORD may carry out His promise which He spoke concerning me, saying, 'If your sons are careful of their way, to walk before Me in [2]truth with all their heart and with all their soul, you shall not lack a man on the throne of Israel.'

5"Now you also know what Joab the son of Zeruiah did to me, what he did to the two commanders of the armies of Israel, to Abner the son of Ner, and to Amasa the son of Jether, whom he killed; he also shed the blood of war in peace. And he put the blood of war on his belt about his waist, and on his sandals on his feet.

6"So act according to your wisdom, and do not let his gray hair go down to Sheol in peace.

7"But show kindness to the sons of Barzillai the Gileadite, and let them be

[2] Or, *faithfulness*

among those who eat at your table; for they assisted me when I fled from Absalom your brother.

8"And behold, there is with you Shimei the son of Gera the Benjamite, of Bahurim; now it was he who cursed me with a violent curse on the day I went to Mahanaim. But when he came down to me at the Jordan, I swore to him by the LORD, saying, 'I will not put you to death with the sword.'

9"Now therefore, do not let him go unpunished, for you are a wise man; and you will know what you ought to do to him, and you will bring his gray hair down to Sheol with blood."

10 ¶ Then David slept with his fathers and was buried in the city of David.

11 And the days that David reigned over Israel *were* forty years: seven years he reigned in Hebron, and thirty-three years he reigned in Jerusalem.

12 And Solomon sat on the throne of David his father, and his kingdom was firmly established.

13 ¶ Now Adonijah the son of Haggith came to Bathsheba the mother of Solomon. And she said, "Do you come peacefully?" And he said, "Peacefully."

14 Then he said, "I have something *to say* to you." And she said, "Speak."

15 So he said, "You know that the kingdom was mine and that all Israel expected me to be king; however, the kingdom has turned about and become my brother's, for it was his from the LORD.

16"And now I am making one request of you; do not ³refuse me." And she said to him, "Speak."

17 Then he said, "Please speak to Solomon the king, for he will not refuse you, that he may give me Abishag the Shunammite as a wife."

18 And Bathsheba said, "Very well; I will speak to the king for you."

19 ¶ So Bathsheba went to King Solomon to speak to him for Adonijah. And the king arose to meet her, bowed before her, and sat on his throne; then he had a throne set for the king's mother, and she sat on his right.

20 Then she said, "I am making one small request of you; do not refuse

me." And the king said to her, "Ask, my mother, for I will not refuse you."

21 So she said, "Let Abishag the Shunammite be given to Adonijah your brother as a wife."

22 And King Solomon answered and said to his mother, "And why are you asking Abishag the Shunammite for Adonijah? Ask for him also the kingdom—for he is my older brother—even for him, for Abiathar the priest, and for Joab the son of Zeruiah!"

23 Then King Solomon swore by the LORD, saying, "May God do so to me and more also, if Adonijah has not spoken this word against his own life.

24"Now therefore, as the LORD lives, who has established me and set me on the throne of David my father, and who has made me a house as He promised, surely Adonijah will be put to death today."

25 So King Solomon sent Benaiah the son of Jehoiada; and he fell upon him so that he died.

26 ¶ Then to Abiathar the priest the king said, "Go to Anathoth to your own field, for you deserve to die; but I will not put you to death at this time, because you carried the ark of the Lord GOD before my father David, and because you were afflicted in everything with which my father was afflicted."

27 So Solomon dismissed Abiathar from being priest to the LORD, in order to fulfill the word of the LORD, which He had spoken concerning the house of Eli in Shiloh.

28 ¶ Now the news came to Joab, for Joab had followed Adonijah, although he had not followed Absalom. And Joab fled to the tent of the LORD and took hold of the horns of the altar.

29 And it was told King Solomon that Joab had fled to the tent of the LORD, and behold, he is beside the altar. Then Solomon sent Benaiah the son of Jehoiada, saying, "Go, fall upon him."

30 So Benaiah came to the tent of the LORD, and said to him, "Thus the king has said, 'Come out.'" But he said, "No, for I will die here." And Benaiah brought the king word again, saying, "Thus spoke Joab, and thus he answered me."

31 And the king said to him, "Do as he has spoken and fall upon him and

³ Lit., *turn away my (your) face*, and so in vv. 17, 20

bury him, that you may remove from me and from my father's house the blood which Joab shed without cause.

32"And the LORD will return his blood on his own head, because he fell upon two men more righteous and better than he and killed them with the sword, while my father David did not know it: Abner the son of Ner, commander of the army of Israel, and Amasa the son of Jether, commander of the army of Judah.

33"So shall their blood return on the head of Joab and on the head of his descendants forever; but to David and his descendants and his house and his throne, may there be peace from the LORD forever."

34 Then Benaiah the son of Jehoiada went up and fell upon him and put him to death, and he was buried at his own house in the wilderness.

35 And the king appointed Benaiah the son of Jehoiada over the army in his place, and the king appointed Zadok the priest in the place of Abiathar.

36 ¶ Now the king sent and called for Shimei and said to him, "Build for yourself a house in Jerusalem and live there, and do not go out from there to any place.

37"For it will happen on the day you go out and cross over the brook Kidron, you will know for certain that you shall surely die; your blood shall be on your own head."

38 Shimei then said to the king, "The word is good. As my lord the king has said, so your servant will do." So Shimei lived in Jerusalem many days.

39 ¶ But it came about at the end of three years, that two of the servants of Shimei ran away to Achish son of Maacah, king of Gath. And they told Shimei, saying, "Behold, your servants are in Gath."

40 Then Shimei arose and saddled his donkey, and went to Gath to Achish to look for his servants. And Shimei went and brought his servants from Gath.

41 And it was told Solomon that Shimei had gone from Jerusalem to Gath, and had returned.

42 So the king sent and called for Shimei and said to him, "Did I not make you swear by the LORD and solemnly warn you, saying, 'You will know for certain that on the day you depart and go anywhere, you shall

surely die'? And you said to me, 'The word which I have heard is good.'

43"Why then have you not kept the oath of the LORD, and the command which I have laid on you?"

44 The king also said to Shimei, "You know all the evil which you acknowledge in your heart, which you did to my father David; therefore the LORD shall return your evil on your own head.

45"But King Solomon shall be blessed, and the throne of David shall be established before the LORD forever."

46 So the king commanded Benaiah the son of Jehoiada, and he went out and fell upon him so that he died. Thus the kingdom was established in the hands of Solomon.

CHAPTER 3

THEN Solomon formed a marriage alliance with Pharaoh king of Egypt, and took Pharaoh's daughter and brought her to the city of David, until he had finished building his own house and the house of the LORD and the wall around Jerusalem.

2 The people were still sacrificing on the high places, because there was no house built for the name of the LORD until those days.

3 ¶ Now Solomon loved the LORD, walking in the statutes of his father David, except he sacrificed and burned incense on the high places.

4 And the king went to Gibeon to sacrifice there, for that was the great high place; Solomon offered a thousand burnt offerings on that altar.

5 In Gibeon the LORD appeared to Solomon in a dream at night; and God said, "Ask what you wish me to give you."

6 Then Solomon said, "Thou hast shown great lovingkindness to Thy servant David my father, according as he walked before Thee in ⁴truth and righteousness and uprightness of heart toward Thee; and Thou hast reserved for him this great lovingkindness, that Thou hast given him a son to sit on his throne, as it is this day.

7"And now, O LORD my God, Thou hast made Thy servant king in place of my father David, yet I am but a little

⁴ Or, faithfulness

child; I do not know how to go out or come in.

8"And Thy servant is in the midst of Thy people which Thou hast chosen, a great people who cannot be numbered or counted for multitude.

9"So give Thy servant an understanding heart to judge Thy people to discern between good and evil. For who is able to judge this great people of Thine?"

10 ¶ And it was pleasing in the sight of the Lord that Solomon had asked this thing.

11 And God said to him, "Because you have asked this thing and have not asked for yourself long life, nor have asked riches for yourself, nor have you asked for the life of your enemies, but have asked for yourself discernment to understand justice,

12 behold, I have done according to your words. Behold, I have given you a wise and discerning heart, so that there has been no one like you before you, nor shall one like you arise after you.

13"And I have also given you what you have not asked, both riches and honor, so that there will not be any among the kings like you all your days.

14"And if you walk in My ways, keeping My statutes and commandments, as your father David walked, then I will prolong your days."

15 ¶ Then Solomon awoke, and behold, it was a dream. And he came to Jerusalem and stood before the ark of the covenant of the Lord, and offered burnt offerings and made peace offerings, and made a feast for all his servants.

16 ¶ Then two women who were harlots came to the king and stood before him.

17 And the one woman said, "Oh, my lord, this woman and I live in the same house; and I gave birth to a child while she *was* in the house.

18"And it happened on the third day after I gave birth, that this woman also gave birth to a child, and we were together. There was no stranger with us in the house, only the two of us in the house.

19"And this woman's son died in the night, because she lay on it.

20"So she arose in the middle of the night and took my son from beside me while your maidservant slept, and laid him in her bosom, and laid her dead son in my bosom.

21"And when I rose in the morning to nurse my son, behold, he was dead; but when I looked at him carefully in the morning, behold, he was not my son, whom I had borne."

22 Then the other woman said, "No! For the living one is my son, and the dead one is your son." But the first woman said, "No! For the dead one is your son, and the living one is my son." Thus they spoke before the king.

23 ¶ Then the king said, "The one says, 'This is my son who is living, and your son is the dead one'; and the other says, 'No! For your son is the dead one, and my son is the living one.'"

24 And the king said, "Get me a sword." So they brought a sword before the king.

25 And the king said, "Divide the living child in two, and give half to the one and half to the other."

26 Then the woman whose child *was* the living one spoke to the king, for she was deeply stirred over her son and said, "Oh, my lord, give her the living child, and by no means kill him." But the other said, "He shall be neither mine nor yours; divide *him!*"

27 Then the king answered and said, "Give the first woman the living child, and by no means kill him. She is his mother."

28 When all Israel heard of the judgment which the king had handed down, they feared the king; for they saw that the wisdom of God was in him to administer justice.

CHAPTER 4

NOW King Solomon was king over all Israel.

2 And these were his officials: Azariah the son of Zadok *was* the priest;

3 Elihoreph and Ahijah, the sons of Shisha *were* secretaries; Jehoshaphat the son of Ahilud *was* the recorder;

4 and Benaiah the son of Jehoiada *was* over the army; and Zadok and Abiathar *were* priests;

5 and Azariah the son of Nathan *was* over the deputies; and Zabud the

son of Nathan, a priest, *was* the king's friend;

6 and Ahishar was over the household; and Adoniram the son of Abda *was* over the men subject to forced labor.

7 ¶ And Solomon had twelve deputies over all Israel, who provided for the king and his household; each man had to provide for a month in the year.

8 And these are their names: Ben-hur, in the hill country of Ephraim;

9 Ben-deker in Makaz and Shaalbim and Beth-shemesh and Elonbeth-hanan;

10 Ben-hesed, in Arubboth (Socoh *was* his and all the land of Hepher);

11 Ben-abinadab, *in* all the height of Dor (Taphath the daughter of Solomon was his wife);

12 Baana the son of Ahilud, *in* Taanach and Megiddo, and all Beth-shean which is beside Zarethan below Jezreel, from Beth-shean to Abel-meholah as far as the other side of Jokmeam;

13 Ben-geber, in Ramoth-gilead (the towns of Jair, the son of Manasseh, which are in Gilead were his: the region of Argob, which is in Bashan, sixty great cities with walls and bronze bars *were* his);

14 Ahinadab the son of Iddo, *in* Mahanaim;

15 Ahimaaz, in Naphtali (he also married Basemath the daughter of Solomon);

16 Baana the son of Hushai, in Asher and Bealoth;

17 Jehoshaphat the son of Paruah, in Issachar;

18 Shimei the son of Ela, in Benjamin;

19 Geber the son of Uri, in the land of Gilead, the country of Sihon king of the Amorites and of Og king of Bashan; and *he was* the only deputy who *was* in the land.

20 ¶ Judah and Israel *were* as numerous as the sand that is on the seashore in abundance; *they* were eating and drinking and rejoicing.

21 ¶ Now Solomon ruled over all the kingdoms from the [5]River *to* the land of the Philistines and to the border of Egypt; *they* brought tribute and served Solomon all the days of his life.

22 And Solomon's provision for one day was thirty [6]kors of fine flour and sixty kors of meal,

23 ten fat oxen, twenty pasture-fed oxen, a hundred sheep besides deer, gazelles, roebucks, and fattened fowl.

24 For he had dominion over everything west of the River, from Tiphsah even to Gaza, over all the kings west of the River; and he had peace on all sides around about him.

25 So Judah and Israel lived in safety, every man under his vine and his fig tree, from Dan even to Beersheba, all the days of Solomon.

26 And Solomon had [7]40,000 stalls of horses for his chariots, and 12,000 horsemen.

27 And those deputies provided for King Solomon and all who came to King Solomon's table, each in his month; they left nothing lacking.

28 They also brought barley and straw for the horses and swift steeds to the place where it should be, each according to his charge.

29 ¶ Now God gave Solomon wisdom and very great discernment and breadth of mind, like the sand that is on the seashore.

30 And Solomon's wisdom surpassed the wisdom of all the sons of the east and all the wisdom of Egypt.

31 For he was wiser than all men, than Ethan the Ezrahite, Heman, Calcol and Darda, the sons of Mahol; and his fame was *known* in all the surrounding nations.

32 He also spoke 3,000 proverbs, and his songs were 1,005.

33 And he spoke of trees, from the cedar that is in Lebanon even to the hyssop that grows on the wall; he spoke also of animals and birds and creeping things and fish.

34 And men came from all peoples to hear the wisdom of Solomon, from all the kings of the earth who had heard of his wisdom.

CHAPTER 5

Now Hiram king of Tyre sent his servants to Solomon, when he heard that they had anointed him king in place of his father, for Hiram had always been a friend of David.

---

[5] I.e., Euphrates, and so through v. 24
[6] I.e., One kor equals approx. 10 bushels
[7] One ms. reads 4,000, cf. 2 Chr. 9:25

351

1 KINGS 6

2 Then Solomon sent *word* to Hiram, saying,

3 "You know that David my father was unable to build a house for the name of the LORD his God because of the wars which surrounded him, until the LORD put them under the soles of his feet.

4 "But now the LORD my God has given me rest on every side; there is neither adversary nor misfortune.

5 "And behold, I intend to build a house for the name of the LORD my God, as the LORD spoke to David my father, saying, 'Your son, whom I will set on your throne in your place, he will build the house for My name.'

6 "Now therefore, command that they cut for me cedars from Lebanon, and my servants will be with your servants; and I will give you wages for your servants according to all that you say, for you know that there is no one among us who knows how to cut timber like the Sidonians."

7 ¶ And it came about when Hiram heard the words of Solomon, that he rejoiced greatly and said, "Blessed be the LORD today, who has given to David a wise son over this great people."

8 So Hiram sent *word* to Solomon, saying, "I have heard *the message* which you have sent me; I will do what you desire concerning the cedar and cypress timber.

9 "My servants will bring *them* down from Lebanon to the sea; and I will make them into rafts *to go* by sea to the place where you direct me, and I will have them broken up there, and you shall carry *them* away. Then you shall accomplish my desire by giving food to my household."

10 So Hiram gave Solomon as much as he desired of the cedar and cypress timber.

11 Solomon then gave Hiram 20,000 kors of wheat as food for his household, and twenty kors of beaten oil; thus Solomon would give Hiram year by year.

12 And the LORD gave wisdom to Solomon, just as He promised him; and there was peace between Hiram and Solomon, and the two of them made a covenant.

13 ¶ Now King Solomon levied forced laborers from all Israel; and the forced laborers numbered 30,000 men.

14 And he sent them to Lebanon, 10,000 a month in relays; they were in Lebanon a month *and* two months at home. And Adoniram *was* over the forced laborers.

15 Now Solomon had 70,000 transporters, and 80,000 hewers *of stone* in the mountains,

16 besides Solomon's 3,300 chief deputies who *were* over the project *and* who ruled over the people who were doing the work.

17 Then the king commanded, and they quarried great stones, costly stones, to lay the foundation of the house with cut stones.

18 So Solomon's builders and Hiram's builders and the Gebalites cut them, and prepared the timbers and the stones to build the house.

CHAPTER 6

NOW it came about in the four hundred and eightieth year after the sons of Israel came out of the land of Egypt, in the fourth year of Solomon's reign over Israel, in the month of Ziv which is the second month, that he began to build the house of the LORD.

2 As for the house which King Solomon built for the LORD, its length *was* sixty [8]cubits and its width twenty *cubits* and its height thirty cubits.

3 And the porch in front of the nave of the house *was* twenty cubits in length, corresponding to the width of the house, *and* its depth along the front of the house *was* ten cubits.

4 Also for the house he made windows with *artistic* frames.

5 And against the wall of the house he built stories encompassing the walls of the house around both the nave and the inner sanctuary; thus he made side chambers all around.

6 The lowest story *was* five cubits wide, and the middle *was* six cubits wide, and the third *was* seven cubits wide; for on the outside he made offsets *in the wall* of the house all around in order that *the beams* should not be inserted in the walls of the house.

7 And the house, while it was being built, was built of stone prepared at

[8] I.e., One cubit equals approx. 18 in.

the quarry, and there was neither hammer nor axe nor any iron tool heard in the house while it was being built.

8 The doorway for the [9]lowest side chamber *was* on the right side of the house; and they would go up by winding stairs to the middle *story,* and from the middle to the third.

9 So he built the house and finished it; and he covered the house with beams and planks of cedar.

10 He also built the stories against the whole house, each five cubits high; and they were fastened to the house with timbers of cedar.

11 ¶ Now the word of the LORD came to Solomon saying,

12 "Concerning this house which you are building, if you will walk in My statutes and execute My ordinances and keep all My commandments by walking in them, then I will carry out My word with you which I spoke to David your father.

13 "And I will dwell among the sons of Israel, and will not forsake My people Israel."

14 ¶ So Solomon built the house and finished it.

15 Then he built the walls of the house on the inside with boards of cedar; from the floor of the house to the ceiling he overlaid *the walls* on the inside with wood, and he overlaid the floor of the house with boards of cypress.

16 And he built twenty cubits on the rear part of the house with boards of cedar from the floor to the ceiling; he built *them* for it on the inside as an inner sanctuary, *even* as the most holy place.

17 And the house, that is, the nave in front of *the inner sanctuary,* was forty cubits *long.*

18 And there was cedar on the house within, carved *in the shape* of gourds and open flowers; all was cedar, there was no stone seen.

19 Then he prepared an inner sanctuary within the house in order to place there the ark of the covenant of the LORD.

20 And the inner sanctuary *was* twenty cubits in length, twenty cubits in width, and twenty cubits in height,

and he overlaid it with pure gold. He also overlaid the altar with cedar.

21 So Solomon overlaid the inside of the house with pure gold. And he drew chains of gold across the front of the inner sanctuary; and he overlaid it with gold.

22 And he overlaid the whole house with gold, until all the house was finished. Also the whole altar which was by the inner sanctuary he overlaid with gold.

23 ¶ Also in the inner sanctuary he made two cherubim of olive wood, each ten cubits high.

24 And five cubits *was* the one wing of the cherub and five cubits the other wing of the cherub; from the end of one wing to the end of the other wing *were* ten cubits.

25 And the other cherub *was* ten cubits; both the cherubim were of the same measure and the same form.

26 The height of the one cherub *was* ten cubits, and so *was* the other cherub.

27 And he placed the cherubim in the midst of the inner house, and the wings of the cherubim were spread out, so that the wing of the one was touching the *one* wall, and the wing of the other cherub was touching the other wall. So their wings were touching each other in the center of the house.

28 He also overlaid the cherubim with gold.

29 ¶ Then he carved all the walls of the house round about with carved engravings of cherubim, palm trees, and open flowers, inner and outer *sanctuaries.*

30 And he overlaid the floor of the house with gold, inner and outer *sanctuaries.*

31 And for the entrance of the inner sanctuary he made doors of olive wood, the lintel *and* five-sided doorposts.

32 So *he made* two doors of olive wood, and he carved on them carvings of cherubim, palm trees, and open flowers, and overlaid them with gold; and he spread the gold on the cherubim and on the palm trees.

33 So also he made for the entrance of the nave four-sided doorposts of olive wood

34 and two doors of cypress wood; the two leaves of the one door turned on pivots, and the two leaves of the other door turned on pivots.

35 And he carved *on it* cherubim, palm trees, and open flowers; and he overlaid *them* with gold evenly applied on the engraved work.

36 And he built the inner court with three rows of cut stone and a row of cedar beams.

37 ¶ In the fourth year the foundation of the house of the LORD was laid, in the month of Ziv.

38 And in the eleventh year, in the month of Bul, which is the eighth month, the house was finished throughout all its parts and according to all its plans. So he was seven years in building it.

CHAPTER 7

NOW Solomon was building his own house thirteen years, and he finished all his house.

2 And he built the house of the forest of Lebanon; its length was 100 [10]cubits and its width 50 cubits and its height 30 cubits, on four rows of cedar pillars with cedar beams on the pillars.

3 And it was paneled with cedar above the side chambers which were on the 45 pillars, 15 in each row.

4 And *there were artistic window* frames in three rows, and window was opposite window in three ranks.

5 And all the doorways and doorposts *had* squared *artistic* frames, and window was opposite window in three ranks.

6 Then he made the hall of pillars; its length was 50 cubits and its width 30 cubits, and a porch *was* in front of them and pillars and a threshold in front of them.

7 And he made the hall of the throne where he was to judge, the hall of judgment, and it was paneled with cedar from floor to floor.

8 And his house where he was to live, the other court inward from the hall, was of the same workmanship. He also made a house like this hall for Pharaoh's daughter, whom Solomon had married.

9 ¶ All these were of costly stones, of stone cut according to measure,

sawed with saws, inside and outside; even from the foundation to the coping, and so on the outside to the great court.

10 ¶ And the foundation was of costly stones, *even* large stones, stones of ten cubits and stones of eight cubits.

11 And above were costly stones, stone cut according to measure, and cedar.

12 So the great court all around *had* three rows of cut stone and a row of cedar beams even as the inner court of the house of the LORD, and the porch of the house.

13 ¶ Now King Solomon sent and brought Hiram from Tyre.

14 He was a widow's son from the tribe of Naphtali, and his father was a man of Tyre, a worker in bronze; and he was filled with wisdom and understanding and skill for doing any work in bronze. So he came to King Solomon and performed all his work.

15 ¶ And he fashioned the two pillars of bronze; eighteen cubits was the height of one pillar, and a line of twelve cubits measured the circumference of both.

16 He also made two capitals of molten bronze to set on the tops of the pillars; the height of the one capital was five cubits and the height of the other capital was five cubits.

17 *There were* nets of network and twisted threads of chainwork for the capitals which were on the top of the pillars; seven for the one capital and seven for the other capital.

18 So he made the pillars, and two rows around on the one network to cover the capitals which were on the top of the pomegranates; and so he did for the other capital.

19 And the capitals which *were* on the top of the pillars in the porch were of lily design, four cubits.

20 And *there were* capitals on the two pillars, even above *and* close to the rounded projection which was beside the network; and the pomegranates *numbered* two hundred in rows around both capitals.

21 Thus he set up the pillars at the porch of the nave; and he set up the right pillar and named it [11]Jachin, and

[10] I.e., One cubit equals approx. 18 in.   [11] I.e., he shall establish

he set up the left pillar and named it
[12]Boaz.

22 And on the top of the pillars was
lily design. So the work of the pillars
was finished.

23 ¶ Now he made the sea of cast
metal ten cubits from brim to brim,
circular in form, and its height was
five cubits, and thirty cubits in circumference.

24 And under its brim gourds went
around encircling it ten to a cubit,
completely surrounding the sea; the
gourds were in two rows, cast with the
rest.

25 It stood on twelve oxen, three
facing north, three facing west, three
facing south, and three facing east;
and the sea *was set* on top of them,
and all their rear parts *turned* inward.

26 And it was a handbreadth thick,
and its brim was made like the brim of
a cup, *as* a lily blossom; it could hold
two thousand baths.

27 ¶ Then he made the ten stands of
bronze; the length of each stand was
four cubits and its width four cubits
and its height three cubits.

28 And this was the design of the
stands: they had borders, even borders
between the [13]frames,

29 and on the borders which were
between the [13]frames *were* lions, oxen
and cherubim; and on the [13]frames
there *was* a pedestal above, and beneath the lions and oxen *were* wreaths
of hanging work.

30 Now each stand had four bronze
wheels with bronze axles, and its four
feet had supports; beneath the basin
were cast supports with wreaths at
each side.

31 And its opening inside the crown
at the top *was* a cubit, and its opening
was round like the design of a pedestal, a cubit and a half; and also on its
opening *there were* engravings, and
their borders were square, not round.

32 And the four wheels *were* underneath the borders, and the axles of the
wheels *were* on the stand. And the
height of a wheel *was* a cubit and a
half.

33 And the workmanship of the
wheels *was* like the workmanship of a
chariot wheel. Their axles, their rims,

their spokes, and their hubs *were* all
cast.

34 Now *there were* four supports at
the four corners of each stand; its
supports *were* part of the stand itself.

35 And on the top of the stand *there
was* a circular form half a cubit high,
and on the top of the stand its stays
and its borders *were* part of it.

36 And he engraved on the plates of
its stays and on its borders, cherubim,
lions and palm trees, according to the
clear space on each, with wreaths *all*
around.

37 He made the ten stands like this:
all of them had one casting, one measure and one form.

38 And he made ten basins of bronze,
one basin held forty baths; each basin
was four cubits, *and* on each of the ten
stands *was* one basin.

39 Then he set the stands, five on the
right side of the house and five on the
left side of the house; and he set
the sea *of cast metal* on the right side
of the house eastward toward the
south.

40 ¶ Now Hiram made the basins
and the shovels and the bowls. So
Hiram finished doing all the work
which he performed for King Solomon
in the house of the LORD:

41 the two pillars and the *two* bowls
of the capitals which *were* on the top
of the two pillars, and the two networks to cover the two bowls of the
capitals which *were* on the top of the
pillars;

42 and the four hundred pomegranates for the two networks, two rows of
pomegranates for each network to
cover the two bowls of the capitals
which *were* on the tops of the pillars;

43 and the ten stands with the ten
basins on the stands;

44 and the one sea and the twelve
oxen under the sea;

45 and the pails and the shovels and
the bowls; even all these utensils
which Hiram made for King Solomon
in the house of the LORD *were* of
polished bronze.

46 In the plain of the Jordan the king
cast them, in the clay ground between
Succoth and Zarethan.

47 And Solomon left all the utensils
unweighed, because *they were* too
many; the weight of the bronze could
not be ascertained.

[12] I.e., in it is strength   [13] Or, *crossbars*

48 ¶ And Solomon made all the furniture which *was in* the house of the LORD: the golden altar and the golden table on which *was* the bread of the Presence;

49 and the lampstands, five on the right side and five on the left, in front of the inner sanctuary, of pure gold; and the flowers and the lamps and the tongs, of gold;

50 and the cups and the snuffers and the bowls and the spoons and the firepans, of pure gold; and the hinges both for the doors of the inner house, the most holy place, *and* for the doors of the house, *that is,* of the nave, of gold.

51 ¶ Thus all the work that King Solomon performed *in* the house of the LORD was finished. And Solomon brought in the things dedicated by his father David, the silver and the gold and the utensils, *and* he put them in the treasuries of the house of the LORD.

CHAPTER 8

THEN Solomon assembled the elders of Israel and all the heads of the tribes, the leaders of the fathers' *households* of the sons of Israel, to King Solomon in Jerusalem, to bring up the ark of the covenant of the LORD from the city of David, which is Zion.

2 And all the men of Israel assembled themselves to King Solomon at the feast, in the month Ethanim, which is the seventh month.

3 Then all the elders of Israel came, and the priests took up the ark.

4 And they brought up the ark of the LORD and the tent of meeting and all the holy utensils, which were in the tent, and the priests and the Levites brought them up.

5 And King Solomon and all the congregation of Israel, who were assembled to him, were with him before the ark, sacrificing so many sheep and oxen they could not be counted or numbered.

6 Then the priests brought the ark of the covenant of the LORD to its place, into the inner sanctuary of the house, to the most holy place, under the wings of the cherubim.

7 For the cherubim spread *their* wings over the place of the ark, and the cherubim made a covering over the ark and its poles from above.

8 But the poles were so long that the ends of the poles could be seen from the holy place before the inner sanctuary, but they could not be seen outside; they are there to this day.

9 There was nothing in the ark except the two tablets of stone which Moses put there at Horeb, where the LORD made a covenant with the sons of Israel, when they came out of the land of Egypt.

10 And it came about when the priests came from the holy place, that the cloud filled the house of the LORD,

11 so that the priests could not stand to minister because of the cloud, for the glory of the LORD filled the house of the LORD.

12 ¶ Then Solomon said,
   "The LORD has said that He would
      dwell in the thick cloud.
13 "I have surely built Thee a lofty
      house,
   A place for Thy dwelling for-
      ever."

14 Then the king faced about and blessed all the assembly of Israel, while all the assembly of Israel was standing.

15 And he said, "Blessed be the LORD, the God of Israel, who spoke with His mouth to my father David and has fulfilled *it* with His hand, saying,

16 'Since the day that I brought My people Israel from Egypt, I did not choose a city out of all the tribes of Israel *in which* to build a house that My name might be there, but I chose David to be over My people Israel.'

17 "Now it was in the heart of my father David to build a house for the name of the LORD, the God of Israel.

18 "But the LORD said to my father David, 'Because it was in your heart to build a house for My name, you did well that it was in your heart.

19 'Nevertheless you shall not build the house, but your son who shall be born to you, he shall build the house for My name.'

20 "Now the LORD has fulfilled His word which He spoke; for I have risen in place of my father David and sit on the throne of Israel, as the LORD promised, and have built the house for the name of the LORD, the God of Israel.

21"And there I have set a place for the ark, in which is the covenant of the LORD, which He made with our fathers when He brought them from the land of Egypt."

22 ¶ Then Solomon stood before the altar of the LORD in the presence of all the assembly of Israel and spread out his hands toward heaven.

23 And he said, "O LORD, the God of Israel, there is no God like Thee in heaven above or on earth beneath, who art keeping covenant and *showing* lovingkindness to Thy servants who walk before Thee with all their heart,

24 who hast kept with Thy servant, my father David, that which Thou hast promised him; indeed, Thou hast spoken with Thy mouth and hast fulfilled it with Thy hand as it is this day.

25"Now therefore, O LORD, the God of Israel, keep with Thy servant David my father that which Thou hast promised him, saying, 'You shall not lack a man to sit on the throne of Israel, if only your sons take heed to their way to walk before Me as you have walked.'

26"Now therefore, O God of Israel, let Thy word, I pray Thee, be confirmed which Thou hast spoken to Thy servant, my father David.

27 ¶"But will God indeed dwell on the earth? Behold, heaven and the highest heaven cannot contain Thee, how much less this house which I have built!

28"Yet have regard to the prayer of Thy servant and to his supplication, O LORD my God, to listen to the cry and to the prayer which Thy servant prays before Thee today;

29 that Thine eyes may be open toward this house night and day, toward the place of which Thou hast said, 'My name shall be there,' to listen to the prayer which Thy servant shall pray toward this place.

30"And listen to the supplication of Thy servant and of Thy people Israel, when they pray toward this place; hear Thou in heaven Thy dwelling place; hear and forgive.

31 ¶"If a man sins against his neighbor and is made to take an oath, and he comes *and* takes an oath before Thine altar in this house,

32 then hear Thou in heaven and act and judge Thy servants, condemning the wicked by bringing his way on his own head and justifying the righteous by giving him according to his righteousness.

33 ¶"When Thy people Israel are defeated before an enemy, because they have sinned against Thee, if they turn to Thee again and confess Thy name and pray and make supplication to Thee in this house,

34 then hear Thou in heaven, and forgive the sin of Thy people Israel, and bring them back to the land which Thou didst give to their fathers.

35 ¶"When the heavens are shut up and there is no rain, because they have sinned against Thee, and they pray toward this place and confess Thy name and turn from their sin when Thou dost afflict them,

36 then hear Thou in heaven and forgive the sin of Thy servants and of Thy people Israel, indeed, teach them the good way in which they should walk. And send rain on Thy land, which Thou hast given Thy people for an inheritance.

37 ¶"If there is famine in the land, if there is pestilence, if there is blight *or* mildew, locust *or* grasshopper, if their enemy besieges them in the land of their cities, whatever plague, whatever sickness there is,

38 whatever prayer or supplication is made by any man *or* by all Thy people Israel, each knowing the affliction of his own heart, and spreading his hands toward this house;

39 then hear Thou in heaven Thy dwelling place, and forgive and act and render to each according to all his ways, whose heart Thou knowest, for Thou alone dost know the hearts of all the sons of men,

40 that they may [14]fear Thee all the days that they live in the land which Thou hast given to our fathers.

41 ¶"Also concerning the foreigner who is not of Thy people Israel, when he comes from a far country for Thy name's sake

42 (for they will hear of Thy great name and Thy mighty hand, and of Thine outstretched arm); when he comes and prays toward this house,

[14] Or, *revere*

43 hear Thou in heaven Thy dwelling place, and do according to all for which the foreigner calls to Thee, in order that all the peoples of the earth may know Thy name, to [14]fear Thee, as *do* Thy people Israel, and that they may know that this house which I have built is called by Thy name.

44 ¶ "When Thy people go out to battle against their enemy, by whatever way Thou shalt send them, and they pray to the LORD toward the city which Thou hast chosen and the house which I have built for Thy name,

45 then hear in heaven their prayer and their supplication, and maintain their cause.

46 ¶ "When they sin against Thee (for there is no man who does not sin) and Thou art angry with them and dost deliver them to an enemy, so that they take them away captive to the land of the enemy, far off or near;

47 if they take thought in the land where they have been taken captive, and repent and make supplication to Thee in the land of those who have taken them captive, saying, 'We have sinned and have committed iniquity, we have acted wickedly';

48 if they return to Thee with all their heart and with all their soul in the land of their enemies who have taken them captive, and pray to Thee toward their land which Thou hast given to their fathers, the city which Thou hast chosen, and the house which I have built for Thy name;

49 then hear their prayer and their supplication in heaven Thy dwelling place, and maintain their cause,

50 and forgive Thy people who have sinned against Thee and all their transgressions which they have transgressed against Thee, and make them *objects of* compassion before those who have taken them captive, that they may have compassion on them

51 (for they are Thy people and Thine inheritance which Thou hast brought forth from Egypt, from the midst of the iron furnace),

52 that Thine eyes may be open to the supplication of Thy servant and to the supplication of Thy people Israel,

to listen to them whenever they call to Thee.

53 "For Thou hast separated them from all the peoples of the earth as Thine inheritance, as Thou didst speak through Moses Thy servant, when Thou didst bring our fathers forth from Egypt, O Lord GOD."

54 ¶ And it came about that when Solomon had finished praying this entire prayer and supplication to the LORD, he arose from before the altar of the LORD, from kneeling on his knees with his hands spread toward heaven.

55 And he stood and blessed all the assembly of Israel with a loud voice, saying,

56 "Blessed be the LORD, who has given rest to His people Israel, according to all that He promised; not one word has failed of all His good promise, which He promised through Moses His servant.

57 "May the LORD our God be with us, as He was with our fathers; may He not leave us or forsake us,

58 that He may incline our hearts to Himself, to walk in all His ways and to keep His commandments and His statutes and His ordinances, which He commanded our fathers.

59 "And may these words of mine, with which I have made supplication before the LORD, be near to the LORD our God day and night, that He may maintain the cause of His servant and the cause of His people Israel, as each day requires,

60 so that all the peoples of the earth may know that the LORD is God; there is no one else.

61 "Let your heart therefore be wholly devoted to the LORD our God, to walk in His statutes and to keep His commandments, as at this day."

62 ¶ Now the king and all Israel with him offered sacrifice before the LORD.

63 And Solomon offered for the sacrifice of peace offerings, which he offered to the LORD, 22,000 oxen and 120,000 sheep. So the king and all the sons of Israel dedicated the house of the LORD.

64 On the same day the king consecrated the middle of the court that *was* before the house of the LORD, because there he offered the burnt offering and the grain offering and the fat of the peace offerings; for the

[14] Or, *revere*

bronze altar that *was* before the LORD *was* too small to hold the burnt offering and the grain offering and the fat of the peace offerings.

65 So Solomon observed the feast at that time, and all Israel with him, a great assembly from the entrance of Hamath to the brook of Egypt, before the LORD our God, for seven days and seven *more* days, *even* fourteen days.

66 On the eighth day he sent the people away and they blessed the king. Then they went to their tents joyful and glad of heart for all the goodness that the LORD had shown to David His servant and to Israel His people.

CHAPTER 9

NOW it came about when Solomon had finished building the house of the LORD, and the king's house, and all that Solomon desired to do,

2 that the LORD appeared to Solomon a second time, as He had appeared to him at Gibeon.

3 And the LORD said to him, "I have heard your prayer and your supplication, which you have made before Me; I have consecrated this house which you have built by putting My name there forever, and My eyes and My heart will be there perpetually.

4 "And as for you, if you will walk before Me as your father David walked, in integrity of heart and uprightness, doing according to all that I have commanded you *and* will keep My statutes and My ordinances,

5 then I will establish the throne of your kingdom over Israel forever, just as I promised to your father David, saying, 'You shall not lack a man on the throne of Israel.'

6 "But if you or your sons shall indeed turn away from following Me, and shall not keep My commandments and My statutes which I have set before you and shall go and serve other gods and worship them,

7 then I will cut off Israel from the land which I have given them, and the house which I have consecrated for My name, I will cast out of My sight. So Israel will become a proverb and a byword among all peoples.

8 "And this house will become a heap of ruins; everyone who passes by will be astonished and hiss and say, 'Why has the LORD done thus to this land and to this house?'

9 "And they will say, 'Because they forsook the LORD their God, who brought their fathers out of the land of Egypt, and adopted other gods and worshiped them and served them, therefore the LORD has brought all this adversity on them.' "

10 ¶ And it came about at the end of twenty years in which Solomon had built the two houses, the house of the LORD and the king's house

11 (Hiram king of Tyre had supplied Solomon with cedar and cypress timber and gold according to all his desire), then King Solomon gave Hiram twenty cities in the land of Galilee.

12 So Hiram came out from Tyre to see the cities which Solomon had given him, and they did not please him.

13 And he said, "What are these cities which you have given me, my brother?" So they were called the land of [15]Cabul to this day.

14 And Hiram sent to the king 120 talents of gold.

15 ¶ Now this is the account of the forced labor which King Solomon levied to build the house of the LORD, his own house, the [16]Millo, the wall of Jerusalem, Hazor, Megiddo, and Gezer.

16 *For* Pharaoh king of Egypt had gone up and captured Gezer, and burned it with fire, and killed the Canaanites who lived in the city, and had given it *as* a dowry to his daughter, Solomon's wife.

17 So Solomon rebuilt Gezer and the lower Beth-horon

18 and Baalath and Tamar in the wilderness, in the land *of Judah,*

19 and all the storage cities which Solomon had, even the cities for his chariots and the cities for his horsemen, and all that it pleased Solomon to build in Jerusalem, in Lebanon, and in all the land under his rule.

20 *As for* all the people who were left of the Amorites, the Hittites, the Perizzites, the Hivites and the Jebusites, who were not of the sons of Israel,

21 their descendants who were left after them in the land whom the sons

[15] I.e., as good as nothing   [16] I.e., citadel

of Israel were unable to destroy utterly, from them Solomon levied forced laborers, even to this day.

22 But Solomon did not make slaves of the sons of Israel; for they were men of war, his servants, his princes, his captains, his chariot commanders, and his horsemen.

23 ¶ These *were* the chief officers who were over Solomon's work, five hundred and fifty, who ruled over the people doing the work.

24 ¶ As soon as Pharaoh's daughter came up from the city of David to her house which *Solomon* had built for her, then he built the Millo.

25 ¶ Now three times in a year Solomon offered burnt offerings and peace offerings on the altar which he built to the LORD, burning incense with them *on the altar* which *was* before the LORD. So he finished the house.

26 ¶ King Solomon also built a fleet of ships in Ezion-geber, which is near Eloth on the shore of the Red Sea, in the land of Edom.

27 And Hiram sent his servants with the fleet, sailors who knew the sea, along with the servants of Solomon.

28 And they went to Ophir, and took four hundred and twenty talents of gold from there, and brought *it* to King Solomon.

CHAPTER 10

NOW when the queen of Sheba heard about the fame of Solomon concerning the name of the LORD, she came to test him with difficult questions.

2 So she came to Jerusalem with a very large retinue, with camels carrying spices and very much gold and precious stones. When she came to Solomon, she spoke with him about all that was in her heart.

3 And Solomon answered all her questions; nothing was hidden from the king which he did not explain to her.

4 When the queen of Sheba perceived all the wisdom of Solomon, the house that he had built,

5 the food of his table, the seating of his servants, the attendance of his waiters and their attire, his cupbearers, and his stairway by which he went

up to the house of the LORD, there was no more spirit in her.

6 Then she said to the king, "It was a true report which I heard in my own land about your words and your wisdom.

7"Nevertheless I did not believe the reports, until I came and my eyes had seen it. And behold, the half was not told me. You exceed *in* wisdom and prosperity the report which I heard.

8"How blessed are your men, how blessed are these your servants who stand before you continually *and* hear your wisdom.

9"Blessed be the LORD your God who delighted in you to set you on the throne of Israel; because the LORD loved Israel forever, therefore He made you king, to do justice and righteousness."

10 And she gave the king a hundred and twenty talents of gold, and a very great *amount* of spices and precious stones. Never again did such abundance of spices come in as that which the queen of Sheba gave King Solomon.

11 ¶ And also the ships of Hiram, which brought gold from Ophir, brought in from Ophir a very great *number of* almug trees and precious stones.

12 And the king made of the almug trees supports for the house of the LORD and for the king's house, also lyres and harps for the singers; such almug trees have not come in *again,* nor have they been seen to this day.

13 ¶ And King Solomon gave to the queen of Sheba all her desire which she requested, besides what he gave her according to his royal bounty. Then she turned and went to her own land together with her servants.

14 ¶ Now the weight of gold which came in to Solomon in one year *was* 666 talents of gold,

15 besides *that* from the traders and the [17]wares of the merchants and all the kings of the Arabs and the governors of the country.

16 And King Solomon made 200 large shields of beaten gold, using 600 *shekels of* gold on each large shield;

17 And *he made* 300 shields of beaten gold, using three minas of gold on

[17] Or, *traffic*

each shield, and the king put them in the house of the forest of Lebanon.

18 Moreover, the king made a great throne of ivory and overlaid it with refined gold.

19 There *were* six steps to the throne and a round top to the throne at its rear, and arms on each side of the seat, and two lions standing beside the arms.

20 And twelve lions were standing there on the six steps on the one side and on the other; nothing like *it* was made for any other kingdom.

21 And all King Solomon's drinking vessels *were* of gold, and all the vessels of the house of the forest of Lebanon *were* of pure gold. None was of silver; it was not considered [18]valuable in the days of Solomon.

22 For the king had at sea the ships of Tarshish with the ships of Hiram; once every three years the ships of Tarshish came bringing gold and silver, ivory and apes and peacocks.

23 ¶ So King Solomon became greater than all the kings of the earth in riches and in wisdom.

24 And all the earth was seeking the presence of Solomon, to hear his wisdom which God had put in his heart.

25 And they brought every man his gift, articles of silver and gold, garments, weapons, spices, horses, and mules, so much year by year.

26 ¶ Now Solomon gathered chariots and horsemen; and he had 1,400 chariots and 12,000 horsemen, and he stationed them in the chariot cities and with the king in Jerusalem.

27 And the king made silver *as common* as stones in Jerusalem, and he made cedars as plentiful as sycamore trees that are in the [19]lowland.

28 Also Solomon's import of horses was from Egypt and Kue, and the king's merchants procured *them* from Kue for a price.

29 And a chariot was imported from Egypt for 600 *shekels* of silver, and a horse for 150; and by the same means they exported them to all the kings of the Hittites and to the kings of the Arameans.

CHAPTER 11

Now King Solomon loved many foreign women along with the daughter of Pharaoh: Moabite, Ammonite, Edomite, Sidonian, and Hittite women,

2 from the nations concerning which the LORD had said to the sons of Israel, "You shall not associate with them, neither shall they associate with you, *for* they will surely turn your heart away after their gods." Solomon held fast to these in love.

3 And he had seven hundred wives, princesses, and three hundred concubines, and his wives turned his heart away.

4 For it came about when Solomon was old, his wives turned his heart away after other gods; and his heart was not [20]wholly devoted to the LORD his God, as the heart of David his father *had been.*

5 For Solomon went after Ashtoreth the goddess of the Sidonians and after Milcom the detestable idol of the Ammonites.

6 And Solomon did what was evil in the sight of the LORD, and did not follow the LORD fully, as David his father *had done.*

7 Then Solomon built a high place for Chemosh the detestable idol of Moab, on the mountain which is east of Jerusalem, and for Molech the detestable idol of the sons of Ammon.

8 Thus also he did for all his foreign wives, who burned incense and sacrificed to their gods.

9 ¶ Now the LORD was angry with Solomon because his heart was turned away from the LORD, the God of Israel, who had appeared to him twice,

10 and had commanded him concerning this thing, that he should not go after other gods; but he did not observe what the LORD had commanded.

11 So the LORD said to Solomon, "Because you have done this, and you have not kept My covenant and My statutes, which I have commanded you, I will surely tear the kingdom from you, and will give it to your servant.

12 "Nevertheless I will not do it in your days for the sake of your father David, *but* I will tear it out of the hand of your son.

13 "However, I will not tear away all the kingdom, *but* I will give one tribe

---

[18] Lit., *anything*   [19] Or, *Shephelah*   [20] Lit., *complete with*

to your son for the sake of My servant David and for the sake of Jerusalem which I have chosen."

14 ¶ Then the LORD raised up an adversary to Solomon, Hadad the Edomite; he was of the royal line in Edom.

15 For it came about, when David was in Edom, and Joab the commander of the army had gone up to bury the slain, and had struck down every male in Edom

16 (for Joab and all Israel stayed there six months, until he had cut off every male in Edom),

17 that Hadad fled to Egypt, he and certain Edomites of his father's servants with him, while Hadad *was* a young boy.

18 And they arose from Midian and came to Paran; and they took men with them from Paran and came to Egypt, to Pharaoh king of Egypt, who gave him a house and assigned him food and gave him land.

19 Now Hadad found great favor before Pharaoh, so that he gave him in marriage the sister of his own wife, the sister of Tahpenes the queen.

20 And the sister of Tahpenes bore his son Genubath, whom Tahpenes weaned in Pharaoh's house; and Genubath was in Pharaoh's house among the sons of Pharaoh.

21 But when Hadad heard in Egypt that David slept with his fathers, and that Joab the commander of the army was dead, Hadad said to Pharaoh, "Send me away, that I may go to my own country."

22 Then Pharaoh said to him, "But what have you lacked with me, that behold, you are seeking to go to your own country?" And he answered, "Nothing; nevertheless you must surely let me go."

23 ¶ God also raised up *another* adversary to him, Rezon the son of Eliada, who had fled from his lord Hadadezer king of Zobah.

24 And he gathered men to himself and became leader of a marauding band, after David slew them of *Zobah;* and they went to Damascus and stayed there, and reigned in Damascus.

25 So he was an adversary to Israel all the days of Solomon, along with the evil that Hadad *did;* and he abhorred Israel and reigned over Aram.

26 ¶ Then Jeroboam the son of Nebat, an Ephraimite of Zeredah, Solomon's servant, whose mother's name was Zeruah, a widow, also rebelled against the king.

27 Now this was the reason why he rebelled against the king: Solomon built the Millo, *and* closed up the breach of the city of his father David.

28 Now the man Jeroboam was a valiant warrior, and when Solomon saw that the young man was industrious, he appointed him over all the forced labor of the house of Joseph.

29 And it came about at that time, when Jeroboam went out of Jerusalem, that the prophet Ahijah the Shilonite found him on the road. Now Ahijah had clothed himself with a new cloak; and both of them were alone in the field.

30 Then Ahijah took hold of the new cloak which was on him, and tore it into twelve pieces.

31 And he said to Jeroboam, "Take for yourself ten pieces; for thus says the LORD, the God of Israel, 'Behold, I will tear the kingdom out of the hand of Solomon and give you ten tribes

32 (but he will have one tribe, for the sake of My servant David and for the sake of Jerusalem, the city which I have chosen from all the tribes of Israel),

33 because they have forsaken Me, and have worshiped Ashtoreth the goddess of the Sidonians, Chemosh the god of Moab, and Milcom the god of the sons of Ammon; and they have not walked in My ways, doing what is right in My sight and *observing* My statutes and My ordinances, as his father David *did.*

34 'Nevertheless I will not take the whole kingdom out of his hand, but I will make him ruler all the days of his life, for the sake of My servant David whom I chose, who observed My commandments and My statutes;

35 but I will take the kingdom from his son's hand and give it to you, *even* ten tribes.

36 'But to his son I will give one tribe, that My servant David may have a lamp always before Me in Jerusalem, the city where I have chosen for Myself to put My name.

37 'And I will take you, and you shall reign over whatever you desire, and you shall be king over Israel.

38 'Then it will be, that if you listen to all that I command you and walk in My ways, and do what is right in My sight by observing My statutes and My commandments, as My servant David did, then I will be with you and build you an enduring house as I built for David, and I will give Israel to you.

39 'Thus I will afflict the descendants of David for this, but not always.'"

40 Solomon sought therefore to put Jeroboam to death; but Jeroboam arose and fled to Egypt to Shishak king of Egypt, and he was in Egypt until the death of Solomon.

41 ¶ Now the rest of the acts of Solomon and whatever he did, and his wisdom, are they not written in the book of the acts of Solomon?

42 Thus the time that Solomon reigned in Jerusalem over all Israel was forty years.

43 And Solomon slept with his fathers and was buried in the city of his father David, and his son Rehoboam reigned in his place.

CHAPTER 12

THEN Rehoboam went to Shechem, for all Israel had come to Shechem to make him king.

2 Now it came about when Jeroboam the son of Nebat heard *of it*, that he was living in Egypt (for he was yet in Egypt, where he had fled from the presence of King Solomon).

3 Then they sent and called him, and Jeroboam and all the assembly of Israel came and spoke to Rehoboam, saying,

4 "Your father made our yoke hard; now therefore lighten the hard service of your father and his heavy yoke which he put on us, and we will serve you."

5 Then he said to them, "Depart for three days, then return to me." So the people departed.

6 ¶ And King Rehoboam consulted with the elders who had served his father Solomon while he was still alive, saying, "How do you counsel *me* to answer this people?"

7 Then they spoke to him, saying, "If you will be a servant to this people today, will serve them, grant them their petition, and speak good words to them, then they will be your servants forever."

8 But he forsook the counsel of the elders which they had given him, and consulted with the young men who grew up with him and served him.

9 So he said to them, "What counsel do you give that we may answer this people who have spoken to me, saying, 'Lighten the yoke which your father put on us'?"

10 And the young men who grew up with him spoke to him, saying, "Thus you shall say to this people who spoke to you, saying, 'Your father made our yoke heavy, now you make it lighter for us!' But you shall speak to them, 'My little finger is thicker than my father's loins!

11 'Whereas my father loaded you with a heavy yoke, I will add to your yoke; my father disciplined you with whips, but I will discipline you with scorpions.'"

12 ¶ Then Jeroboam and all the people came to Rehoboam on the third day as the king had directed, saying, "Return to me on the third day."

13 And the king answered the people harshly, for he forsook the advice of the elders which they had given him,

14 and he spoke to them according to the advice of the young men, saying, "My father made your yoke heavy, but I will add to your yoke; my father disciplined you with whips, but I will discipline you with scorpions."

15 So the king did not listen to the people; for it was a turn *of events* from the LORD, that He might establish His word, which the LORD spoke through Ahijah the Shilonite to Jeroboam the son of Nebat.

16 ¶ When all Israel *saw* that the king did not listen to them, the people answered the king, saying,

"What portion do we have in David?
We have no inheritance in the son of Jesse;
To your tents, O Israel!
Now look after your own house, David!"

So Israel departed to their tents.

17 But as for the sons of Israel who lived in the cities of Judah, Rehoboam reigned over them.

18 Then King Rehoboam sent Adoram, who was over the forced labor, and all Israel stoned him to death. And King Rehoboam made haste to mount his chariot to flee to Jerusalem.

19 So Israel has been in rebellion against the house of David to this day.

20 And it came about when all Israel heard that Jeroboam had returned, that they sent and called him to the assembly and made him king over all Israel. None but the tribe of Judah followed the house of David.

21 ¶ Now when Rehoboam had come to Jerusalem, he assembled all the house of Judah and the tribe of Benjamin, 180,000 chosen men who were warriors, to fight against the house of Israel to restore the kingdom to Rehoboam the son of Solomon.

22 But the word of God came to Shemaiah the man of God, saying,

23 "Speak to Rehoboam the son of Solomon, king of Judah, and to all the house of Judah and Benjamin and to the rest of the people, saying,

24 'Thus says the LORD, "You must not go up and fight against your relatives the sons of Israel; return every man to his house, for this thing has come from Me." ' " So they listened to the word of the LORD, and returned and went *their way* according to the word of the LORD.

25 ¶ Then Jeroboam built Shechem in the hill country of Ephraim, and lived there. And he went out from there and built Penuel.

26 And Jeroboam said in his heart, "Now the kingdom will return to the house of David.

27 "If this people go up to offer sacrifices in the house of the LORD at Jerusalem, then the heart of this people will return to their lord, *even* to Rehoboam king of Judah; and they will kill me and return to Rehoboam king of Judah."

28 So the king consulted, and made two golden calves, and he said to them, "It is too much for you to go up to Jerusalem; behold your gods, O Israel, that brought you up from the land of Egypt."

29 And he set one in Bethel, and the other he put in Dan.

30 Now this thing became a sin, for the people went *to worship* before the one as far as Dan.

31 And he made houses on high places, and made priests from among all the people who were not of the sons of Levi.

32 And Jeroboam instituted a feast in the eighth month on the fifteenth day of the month, like the feast which is in Judah, and he went up to the altar; thus he did in Bethel, sacrificing to the calves which he had made. And he stationed in Bethel the priests of the high places which he had made.

33 Then he went up to the altar which he had made in Bethel on the fifteenth day in the eighth month, even in the month which he had devised in his own heart; and he instituted a feast for the sons of Israel, and went up to the altar to burn incense.

CHAPTER 13

Now behold, there came a man of God from Judah to Bethel by the word of the LORD, while Jeroboam was standing by the altar to burn incense.

2 And he cried against the altar by the word of the LORD, and said, "O altar, altar, thus says the LORD, 'Behold, a son shall be born to the house of David, Josiah by name; and on you he shall sacrifice the priests of the high places who burn incense on you, and human bones shall be burned on you.' "

3 Then he gave a sign the same day, saying, "This is the sign which the LORD has spoken, 'Behold, the altar shall be split apart and the ashes which are on it shall be poured out.' "

4 Now it came about when the king heard the saying of the man of God, which he cried against the altar in Bethel, that Jeroboam stretched out his hand from the altar, saying, "Seize him." But his hand which he stretched out against him dried up, so that he could not draw it back to himself.

5 The altar also was split apart and the ashes were poured out from the altar, according to the sign which the man of God had given by the word of the LORD.

6 And the king answered and said to the man of God, "Please [21]entreat the LORD your God, and pray for me,

[21] Lit., *soften(ed) the face of*

that my hand may be restored to me." So the man of God [21]entreated the LORD, and the king's hand was restored to him, and it became as it was before.

7 Then the king said to the man of God, "Come home with me and refresh yourself, and I will give you a reward."

8 But the man of God said to the king, "If you were to give me half your house I would not go with you, nor would I eat bread or drink water in this place.

9 "For so it was commanded me by the word of the LORD, saying, 'You shall eat no bread, nor drink water, nor return by the way which you came.' "

10 So he went another way, and did not return by the way which he came to Bethel.

11 ¶ Now an old prophet was living in Bethel; and his sons came and told him all the deeds which the man of God had done that day in Bethel; the words which he had spoken to the king, these also they related to their father.

12 And their father said to them, "Which way did he go?" Now his sons had seen the way which the man of God who came from Judah had gone.

13 Then he said to his sons, "Saddle the donkey for me." So they saddled the donkey for him and he rode away on it.

14 So he went after the man of God and found him sitting under an oak; and he said to him, "Are you the man of God who came from Judah?" And he said, "I am."

15 Then he said to him, "Come home with me and eat bread."

16 And he said, "I cannot return with you, nor go with you, nor will I eat bread or drink water with you in this place.

17 "For a command *came* to me by the word of the LORD, 'You shall eat no bread, nor drink water there; do not return by going the way which you came.' "

18 And he said to him, "I also am a prophet like you, and an angel spoke to me by the word of the LORD, saying, 'Bring him back with you to your house, that he may eat bread and drink water.' " *But* he lied to him.

19 So he went back with him, and ate bread in his house and drank water.

20 ¶ Now it came about, as they were sitting down at the table, that the word of the LORD came to the prophet who had brought him back;

21 and he cried to the man of God who came from Judah, saying, "Thus says the LORD, 'Because you have disobeyed the command of the LORD, and have not observed the commandment which the LORD your God commanded you,

22 but have returned and eaten bread and drunk water in the place of which He said to you, "Eat no bread and drink no water"; your body shall not come to the grave of your fathers.' "

23 And it came about after he had eaten bread and after he had drunk, that he saddled the donkey for him, for the prophet whom he had brought back.

24 Now when he had gone, a lion met him on the way and killed him, and his body was thrown on the road, with the donkey standing beside it; the lion also was standing beside the body.

25 And behold, men passed by and saw the body thrown on the road, and the lion standing beside the body; so they came and told *it* in the city where the old prophet lived.

26 ¶ Now when the prophet who brought him back from the way heard *it*, he said, "It is the man of God, who disobeyed the command of the LORD; therefore the LORD has given him to the lion, which has torn him and killed him, according to the word of the LORD which He spoke to him."

27 Then he spoke to his sons, saying, "Saddle the donkey for me." And they saddled *it*.

28 And he went and found his body thrown on the road with the donkey and the lion standing beside the body; the lion had not eaten the body nor torn the donkey.

29 So the prophet took up the body of the man of God and laid it on the donkey, and brought it back and he came to the city of the old prophet to mourn and to bury him.

[21] Lit., *soften(ed) the face of*

30 And he laid his body in his own grave, and they mourned over him, *saying,* "Alas, my brother!"

31 And it came about after he had buried him, that he spoke to his sons, saying, "When I die, bury me in the grave in which the man of God is buried; lay my bones beside his bones.

32"For the thing shall surely come to pass which he cried by the word of the LORD against the altar in Bethel and against all the houses of the high places which are in the cities of Samaria."

33 ¶ After this event Jeroboam did not return from his evil way, but again he made priests of the high places from among all the people; any who would, he ordained, to be priests of the high places.

34 And this event became sin to the house of Jeroboam, even to blot *it* out and destroy *it* from off the face of the earth.

CHAPTER 14

A T that time Abijah the son of Jeroboam became sick.

2 And Jeroboam said to his wife, "Arise now, and disguise yourself so that they may not know that you are the wife of Jeroboam, and go to Shiloh; behold, Ahijah the prophet is there, who spoke concerning me *that I would be* king over this people.

3"And take ten loaves with you, *some* cakes and a jar of honey, and go to him. He will tell you what will happen to the boy."

4 And Jeroboam's wife did so, and arose and went to Shiloh, and came to the house of Ahijah. Now Ahijah could not see, for his eyes were dim because of his age.

5 Now the LORD had said to Ahijah, "Behold, the wife of Jeroboam is coming to inquire of you concerning her son, for he is sick. You shall say thus and thus to her, for it will be when she arrives that she will pretend to be another woman."

6 ¶ And it came about when Ahijah heard the sound of her feet coming in the doorway, that he said, "Come in, wife of Jeroboam, why do you pretend to be another woman? For I am sent to you *with* a harsh *message.*

7"Go, say to Jeroboam, 'Thus says the LORD God of Israel, "Because I exalted you from among the people and made you leader over My people Israel,

8 and tore the kingdom away from the house of David and gave it to you—yet you have not been like My servant David, who kept My commandments and who followed Me with all his heart, to do only that which was right in My sight;

9 you also have done more evil than all who were before you, and have gone and made for yourself other gods and molten images to provoke Me to anger, and have cast Me behind your back—

10 therefore behold, I am bringing calamity on the house of Jeroboam, and will cut off from Jeroboam every male person, both bond and free in Israel, and I will make a clean sweep of the house of Jeroboam, as one sweeps away dung until it is all gone.

11"Anyone belonging to Jeroboam who dies in the city the dogs will eat. And he who dies in the field the birds of the heavens will eat; for the LORD has spoken *it.*" '

12"Now you arise, go to your house. When your feet enter the city the child will die.

13"And all Israel shall mourn for him and bury him, for he alone of Jeroboam's *family* shall come to the grave, because in him something good was found toward the LORD God of Israel in the house of Jeroboam.

14"Moreover, the LORD will raise up for Himself a king over Israel who shall cut off the house of Jeroboam this day and from now on.

15"For the LORD will strike Israel, as a reed is shaken in the water; and He will uproot Israel from this good land which He gave to their fathers, and will scatter them beyond the *Euphrates* River, because they have made their [22]Asherim, provoking the LORD to anger.

16"And He will give up Israel on account of the sins of Jeroboam, which he committed and with which he made Israel to sin."

17 ¶ Then Jeroboam's wife arose and departed and came to Tirzah. As she

[22] I.e., wooden symbols of a female deity. Also v. 23

was entering the threshold of the house, the child died.

18 And all Israel buried him and mourned for him, according to the word of the LORD which He spoke through His servant Ahijah the prophet.

19 ¶ Now the rest of the acts of Jeroboam, how he made war and how he reigned, behold, they are written in the Book of the Chronicles of the Kings of Israel.

20 And the time that Jeroboam reigned *was* twenty-two years; and he slept with his fathers, and Nadab his son reigned in his place.

21 ¶ Now Rehoboam the son of Solomon reigned in Judah. Rehoboam was forty-one years old when he became king, and he reigned seventeen years in Jerusalem, the city which the LORD had chosen from all the tribes of Israel to put His name there. And his mother's name was Naamah the Ammonitess.

22 And Judah did evil in the sight of the LORD, and they provoked Him to jealousy more than all that their fathers had done, with the sins which they committed.

23 For they also built for themselves high places and *sacred* pillars and Asherim on every high hill and beneath every luxuriant tree.

24 And there were also male cult prostitutes in the land. They did according to all the abominations of the nations which the LORD dispossessed before the sons of Israel.

25 ¶ Now it came about in the fifth year of King Rehoboam, that Shishak the king of Egypt came up against Jerusalem.

26 And he took away the treasures of the house of the LORD and the treasures of the king's house, and he took everything, even taking all the shields of gold which Solomon had made.

27 So King Rehoboam made shields of bronze in their place, and committed them to the care of the commanders of the 23guard who guarded the doorway of the king's house.

28 Then it happened as often as the king entered the house of the LORD, that the 23guards would carry them

and would bring them back into the guards' room.

29 ¶ Now the rest of the acts of Rehoboam and all that he did, are they not written in the Book of the Chronicles of the Kings of Judah?

30 And there was war between Rehoboam and Jeroboam continually.

31 And Rehoboam slept with his fathers, and was buried with his fathers in the city of David; and his mother's name was Naamah the Ammonitess. And Abijam his son became king in his place.

CHAPTER 15

NOW in the eighteenth year of King Jeroboam, the son of Nebat, Abijam became king over Judah.

2 He reigned three years in Jerusalem; and his mother's name was Maacah the daughter of Abishalom.

3 And he walked in all the sins of his father which he had committed before him; and his heart was not wholly devoted to the LORD his God, like the heart of his father David.

4 But for David's sake the LORD his God gave him a lamp in Jerusalem, to raise up his son after him and to establish Jerusalem;

5 because David did what was right in the sight of the LORD, and had not turned aside from anything that He commanded him all the days of his life, except in the case of Uriah the Hittite.

6 And there was war between Rehoboam and Jeroboam all the days of his life.

7 ¶ Now the rest of the acts of Abijam and all that he did, are they not written in the Book of the Chronicles of the Kings of Judah? And there was war between Abijam and Jeroboam.

8 And Abijam slept with his fathers and they buried him in the city of David; and Asa his son became king in his place.

9 ¶ So in the twentieth year of Jeroboam the king of Israel, Asa began to reign as king of Judah.

10 And he reigned forty-one years in Jerusalem; and his mother's name was Maacah the daughter of Abishalom.

11 And Asa did what was right in the sight of the LORD, like David his father.

12 He also put away the male cult

23 Lit., *runner(s)*

prostitutes from the land, and removed all the idols which his fathers had made.

13 And he also removed Maacah his mother from *being* queen mother, because she had made a horrid image as an Asherah; and Asa cut down her horrid image and burned *it* at the brook Kidron.

14 But the high places were not taken away; nevertheless the heart of Asa was wholly devoted to the LORD all his days.

15 And he brought into the house of the LORD the dedicated things of his father and his own dedicated things: silver and gold and utensils.

16 ¶ Now there was war between Asa and Baasha king of Israel all their days.

17 And Baasha king of Israel went up against Judah and fortified Ramah in order to prevent *anyone* from going out or coming in to Asa king of Judah.

18 Then Asa took all the silver and the gold which were left in the treasuries of the house of the LORD and the treasuries of the king's house, and delivered them into the hand of his servants. And King Asa sent them to Ben-hadad the son of Tabrimmon, the son of Hezion, king of Aram, who lived in Damascus, saying,

19 "*Let there be* a treaty between you and me, *as* between my father and your father. Behold, I have sent you a present of silver and gold; go, break your treaty with Baasha king of Israel so that he will withdraw from me."

20 So Ben-hadad listened to King Asa and sent the commanders of his armies against the cities of Israel, and conquered Ijon, Dan, Abel-beth-maacah and all Chinneroth, besides all the land of Naphtali.

21 And it came about when Baasha heard *of it* that he ceased fortifying Ramah, and remained in Tirzah.

22 Then King Asa made a proclamation to all Judah—none was exempt— and they carried away the stones of Ramah and its timber with which Baasha had built. And King Asa built with them Geba of Benjamin and Mizpah.

23 ¶ Now the rest of all the acts of Asa and all his might and all that he did and the cities which he built, are they not written in the Book of the Chronicles of the Kings of Judah? But in the time of his old age he was diseased in his feet.

24 And Asa slept with his fathers and was buried with his fathers in the city of David his father; and Jehoshaphat his son reigned in his place.

25 Now Nadab the son of Jeroboam became king over Israel in the second year of Asa king of Judah, and he reigned over Israel two years.

26 And he did evil in the sight of the LORD, and walked in the way of his father and in his sin which he made Israel sin.

27 Then Baasha the son of Ahijah of the house of Issachar conspired against him, and Baasha struck him down at Gibbethon, which belonged to the Philistines, while Nadab and all Israel were laying siege to Gibbethon.

28 So Baasha killed him in the third year of Asa king of Judah, and reigned in his place.

29 And it came about, as soon as he was king, he struck down all the household of Jeroboam. He did not leave to Jeroboam any persons alive, until he had destroyed them, according to the word of the LORD, which He spoke by His servant Ahijah the Shilonite,

30 *and* because of the sins of Jeroboam which he sinned, and which he made Israel sin, because of his provocation with which he provoked the LORD God of Israel to anger.

31 ¶ Now the rest of the acts of Nadab and all that he did, are they not written in the Book of the Chronicles of the Kings of Israel?

32 And there was war between Asa and Baasha king of Israel all their days.

33 ¶ In the third year of Asa king of Judah, Baasha the son of Ahijah became king over all Israel at Tirzah, *and reigned* twenty-four years.

34 And he did evil in the sight of the LORD, and walked in the way of Jeroboam and in his sin which he made Israel sin.

CHAPTER 16

NOW the word of the LORD came to Jehu the son of Hanani against Baasha, saying,

2 "Inasmuch as I exalted you from

the dust and made you leader over My people Israel, and you have walked in the way of Jeroboam and have made My people Israel sin, provoking Me to anger with their sins,

3 behold, I will consume Baasha and his house, and I will make your house like the house of Jeroboam the son of Nebat.

4 "Anyone of Baasha who dies in the city the dogs shall eat, and anyone of his who dies in the field the birds of the heavens will eat."

5 ¶ Now the rest of the acts of Baasha and what he did and his might, are they not written in the Book of the Chronicles of the Kings of Israel?

6 And Baasha slept with his fathers and was buried in Tirzah, and Elah his son became king in his place.

7 Moreover, the word of the LORD through the prophet Jehu the son of Hanani also came against Baasha and his household, both because of all the evil which he did in the sight of the LORD, provoking Him to anger with the work of his hands, in being like the house of Jeroboam, and because he struck it.

8 ¶ In the twenty-sixth year of Asa king of Judah, Elah the son of Baasha became king over Israel at Tirzah, *and reigned* two years.

9 And his servant Zimri, commander of half his chariots, conspired against him. Now he *was* at Tirzah drinking himself drunk in the house of Arza, who *was* over the household at Tirzah.

10 Then Zimri went in and struck him and put him to death, in the twenty-seventh year of Asa king of Judah, and became king in his place.

11 And it came about, when he became king, as soon as he sat on his throne, that he killed all the household of Baasha; he did not leave a single male, neither of his relatives nor of his friends.

12 Thus Zimri destroyed all the household of Baasha, according to the word of the LORD, which He spoke against Baasha through Jehu the prophet,

13 for all the sins of Baasha and the sins of Elah his son, which they sinned and which they made Israel sin, provoking the LORD God of Israel to anger with their idols.

14 Now the rest of the acts of Elah and all that he did, are they not written in the Book of the Chronicles of the Kings of Israel?

15 ¶ In the twenty-seventh year of Asa king of Judah, Zimri reigned seven days at Tirzah. Now the people were camped against Gibbethon, which belonged to the Philistines.

16 And the people who were camped heard it said, "Zimri has conspired and has also struck down the king." Therefore all Israel made Omri, the commander of the army, king over Israel that day in the camp.

17 Then Omri and all Israel with him went up from Gibbethon, and they besieged Tirzah.

18 And it came about, when Zimri saw that the city was taken, that he went into the citadel of the king's house and burned the king's house over him with fire, and died,

19 because of his sins which he sinned, doing evil in the sight of the LORD, walking in the way of Jeroboam, and in his sin which he did, making Israel sin.

20 Now the rest of the acts of Zimri and his conspiracy which he carried out, are they not written in the Book of the Chronicles of the Kings of Israel?

21 ¶ Then the people of Israel were divided into two parts: half of the people followed Tibni the son of Ginath, to make him king; the *other* half followed Omri.

22 But the people who followed Omri prevailed over the people who followed Tibni the son of Ginath. And Tibni died and Omri became king.

23 In the thirty-first year of Asa king of Judah, Omri became king over Israel, *and reigned* twelve years; he reigned six years at Tirzah.

24 And he bought the hill Samaria from Shemer for two talents of silver; and he built on the hill, and named the city which he built Samaria, after the name of Shemer, the owner of the hill.

25 And Omri did evil in the sight of the LORD, and acted more wickedly than all who *were* before him.

26 For he walked in all the way of Jeroboam the son of Nebat and in his sins which he made Israel sin, provoking the LORD God of Israel with their idols.

27 Now the rest of the acts of Omri which he did and his might which he showed, are they not written in the Book of the Chronicles of the Kings of Israel?

28 So Omri slept with his fathers, and was buried in Samaria; and Ahab his son became king in his place.

29 ¶ Now Ahab the son of Omri became king over Israel in the thirty-eighth year of Asa king of Judah, and Ahab the son of Omri reigned over Israel in Samaria twenty-two years.

30 And Ahab the son of Omri did evil in the sight of the LORD more than all who were before him.

31 And it came about, as though it had been a trivial thing for him to walk in the sins of Jeroboam the son of Nebat, that he married Jezebel the daughter of Ethbaal king of the Sidonians, and went to serve Baal and worshiped him.

32 So he erected an altar for Baal in the house of Baal, which he built in Samaria.

33 And Ahab also made the [24]Asherah. Thus Ahab did more to provoke the LORD God of Israel than all the kings of Israel who were before him.

34 In his days Hiel the Bethelite built Jericho; he laid its foundations with the *loss of* Abiram his first-born, and set up its gates with the *loss of* his youngest son Segub, according to the word of the LORD, which He spoke by Joshua the son of Nun.

CHAPTER 17

NOW Elijah the Tishbite, who was of the settlers of Gilead, said to Ahab, "As the LORD, the God of Israel lives, before whom I stand, surely there shall be neither dew nor rain these years, except by my word."

2 And the word of the LORD came to him, saying,

3 "Go away from here and turn eastward, and hide yourself by the brook Cherith, which is east of the Jordan.

4 "And it shall be that you shall drink of the brook, and I have commanded the ravens to provide for you there."

5 So he went and did according to the word of the LORD, for he went and lived by the brook Cherith, which is east of the Jordan.

6 And the ravens brought him bread and meat in the morning and bread and meat in the evening, and he would drink from the brook.

7 And it happened after a while, that the brook dried up, because there was no rain in the land.

8 ¶ Then the word of the LORD came to him, saying,

9 "Arise, go to Zarephath, which belongs to Sidon, and stay there; behold, I have commanded a widow there to provide for you."

10 So he arose and went to Zarephath, and when he came to the gate of the city, behold, a widow was there gathering sticks; and he called to her and said, "Please get me a little water in a jar, that I may drink."

11 And as she was going to get *it*, he called to her and said, "Please bring me a piece of bread in your hand."

12 But she said, "As the LORD your God lives, I have no bread, only a handful of flour in the bowl and a little oil in the jar; and behold, I am gathering a few sticks that I may go in and prepare for me and my son, that we may eat it and die."

13 Then Elijah said to her, "Do not fear; go, do as you have said, but make me a little bread cake from it first, and bring *it* out to me, and afterward you may make *one* for yourself and for your son.

14 "For thus says the LORD God of Israel, 'The bowl of flour shall not be exhausted, nor shall the jar of oil be empty, until the day that the LORD sends rain on the face of the earth.' "

15 So she went and did according to the word of Elijah, and she and he and her household ate for *many* days.

16 The bowl of flour was not exhausted nor did the jar of oil become empty, according to the word of the LORD which He spoke through Elijah.

17 ¶ Now it came about after these things, that the son of the woman, the mistress of the house, became sick; and his sickness was so severe, that there was no breath left in him.

18 So she said to Elijah, "What do I have to do with you, O man of God? You have come to me to bring my iniquity to remembrance, and to put my son to death!"

[24] I.e., wooden symbol of a female deity

19 And he said to her, "Give me your son." Then he took him from her bosom and carried him up to the upper room where he was living, and laid him on his own bed.

20 And he called to the LORD and said, "O LORD my God, hast Thou also brought calamity to the widow with whom I am staying, by causing her son to die?"

21 Then he stretched himself upon the child three times, and called to the LORD, and said, "O LORD my God, I pray Thee, let this child's life return to him."

22 And the LORD heard the voice of Elijah, and the life of the child returned to him and he revived.

23 And Elijah took the child, and brought him down from the upper room into the house and gave him to his mother; and Elijah said, "See, your son is alive."

24 Then the woman said to Elijah, "Now I know that you are a man of God, and that the word of the LORD in your mouth is truth."

CHAPTER 18

NOW it came about *after* many days, that the word of the LORD came to Elijah in the third year, saying, "Go, show yourself to Ahab, and I will send rain on the face of the earth."

2 So Elijah went to show himself to Ahab. Now the famine *was* severe in Samaria.

3 And Ahab called Obadiah who *was* over the household. (Now Obadiah [25]feared the LORD greatly;

4 for it came about, when Jezebel destroyed the prophets of the LORD, that Obadiah took a hundred prophets and hid them by fifties in a cave, and provided them with bread and water.)

5 Then Ahab said to Obadiah, "Go through the land to all the springs of water and to all the valleys; perhaps we will find grass and keep the horses and mules alive, and not have to kill some of the cattle."

6 So they divided the land between them to survey it; Ahab went one way by himself and Obadiah went another way by himself.

7 ¶ Now as Obadiah was on the way, behold, Elijah met him, and he recognized him and fell on his face and said, "Is this you, Elijah my master?"

8 And he said to him, "It is I. Go, say to your master, 'Behold, Elijah *is* here.'"

9 And he said, "What sin have I committed, that you are giving your servant into the hand of Ahab, to put me to death?

10 As the LORD your God lives, there is no nation or kingdom where my master has not sent to search for you; and when they said, 'He is not *here*,' he made the kingdom or nation swear that they could not find you.

11 And now you are saying, 'Go, say to your master, "Behold, Elijah *is* here."'

12 And it will come about when I leave you that the Spirit of the LORD will carry you where I do not know; so when I come and tell Ahab and he cannot find you, he will kill me, although *I* your servant have feared the LORD from my youth.

13 Has it not been told to my master what I did when Jezebel killed the prophets of the LORD, that I hid a hundred prophets of the LORD by fifties in a cave, and provided them with bread and water?

14 And now you are saying, 'Go, say to your master, "Behold, Elijah *is* here"'; he will then kill me."

15 And Elijah said, "As the LORD of hosts lives, before whom I stand, I will surely show myself to him today."

16 ¶ So Obadiah went to meet Ahab, and told him; and Ahab went to meet Elijah.

17 And it came about, when Ahab saw Elijah that Ahab said to him, "Is this you, you troubler of Israel?"

18 And he said, "I have not troubled Israel, but you and your father's house *have*, because you have forsaken the commandments of the LORD, and you have followed the Baals.

19 Now then send *and* gather to me all Israel at Mount Carmel, *together* with 450 prophets of Baal and 400 prophets of the Asherah, who eat at Jezebel's table."

20 ¶ So Ahab sent *a message* among all the sons of Israel, and brought the prophets together at Mount Carmel.

21 And Elijah came near to all the people and said, "How long *will* you hesitate between two opinions? If the

25 Or, *revered*

Lord is God, follow Him; but if Baal, follow him." But the people did not answer him a word.

22 Then Elijah said to the people, "I alone am left a prophet of the Lord, but Baal's prophets are 450 men.

23 "Now let them give us two oxen; and let them choose one ox for themselves and cut it up, and place it on the wood, but put no fire *under it*; and I will prepare the other ox, and lay it on the wood, and I will not put a fire *under it*.

24 "Then you call on the name of your god, and I will call on the name of the Lord, and the God who answers by fire, He is God." And all the people answered and said, "[26]That is a good idea."

25 ¶ So Elijah said to the prophets of Baal, "Choose one ox for yourselves and prepare it first for you are many, and call on the name of your god, but put no fire *under it*."

26 Then they took the ox which was given them and they prepared it and called on the name of Baal from morning until noon saying, "O Baal, answer us." But there was no voice and no one answered. And they leaped about the altar which they made.

27 And it came about at noon, that Elijah mocked them and said, "Call out with a loud voice, for he is a god; either he is occupied or gone aside, or is on a journey, or perhaps he is asleep and needs to be awakened."

28 So they cried with a loud voice and cut themselves according to their custom with swords and lances until the blood gushed out on them.

29 And it came about when midday was past, that they raved until the time of the offering of the *evening* sacrifice; but there was no voice, no one answered, and no one paid attention.

30 ¶ Then Elijah said to all the people, "Come near to me." So all the people came near to him. And he repaired the altar of the Lord which had been torn down.

31 And Elijah took twelve stones according to the number of the tribes of the sons of Jacob, to whom the word of the Lord had come, saying, "Israel shall be your name."

32 So with the stones he built an altar in the name of the Lord, and he made a trench around the altar, large enough to hold two measures of seed.

33 Then he arranged the wood and cut the ox in pieces and laid *it* on the wood. And he said, "Fill four pitchers with water and pour *it* on the burnt offering and on the wood."

34 And he said, "Do it a second time," and they did it a second time. And he said, "Do it a third time," and they did it a third time.

35 And the water flowed around the altar, and he also filled the trench with water.

36 Then it came about at the time of the offering of the *evening* sacrifice, that Elijah the prophet came near and said, "O Lord, the God of Abraham, Isaac and Israel, today let it be known that Thou art God in Israel, and that I am Thy servant, and that I have done all these things at Thy word.

37 "Answer me, O Lord, answer me, that this people may know that Thou, O Lord, art God, and *that* Thou hast turned their heart back again."

38 Then the fire of the Lord fell, and consumed the burnt offering and the wood and the stones and the dust, and licked up the water that was in the trench.

39 And when all the people saw it, they fell on their faces; and they said, "The Lord, He is God; the Lord, He is God."

40 Then Elijah said to them, "Seize the prophets of Baal; do not let one of them escape." So they seized them; and Elijah brought them down to the brook Kishon, and slew them there.

41 ¶ Now Elijah said to Ahab, "Go up, eat and drink; for there is the sound of the roar of a *heavy* shower."

42 So Ahab went up to eat and drink. But Elijah went up to the top of Carmel; and he crouched down on the earth, and put his face between his knees.

43 And he said to his servant, "Go up now, look toward the sea." So he went up and looked and said, "There is nothing." And he said, "Go back" seven times.

44 And it came about at the seventh *time*, that he said, "Behold, a cloud as small as a man's hand is coming up from the sea." And he said, "Go up,

[26] Lit., *The matter is good*

say to Ahab, 'Prepare *your chariot* and go down, so that the *heavy* shower does not stop you.' "

45 So it came about in a little while, that the sky grew black with clouds and wind, and there was a heavy shower. And Ahab rode and went to Jezreel.

46 Then the hand of the LORD was on Elijah, and he girded up his loins and outran Ahab to Jezreel.

CHAPTER 19

NOW Ahab told Jezebel all that Elijah had done, and how he had killed all the prophets with the sword.

2 Then Jezebel sent a messenger to Elijah, saying, "So may the gods do to me and even more, if I do not make your [27]life as the life of one of them by tomorrow about this time."

3 And he was afraid and arose and ran for his [27]life and came to Beersheba, which belongs to Judah, and left his servant there.

4 But he himself went a day's journey into the wilderness, and came and sat down under a juniper tree; and he requested for himself that he might die, and said, "It is enough; now, O LORD, take my [27]life, for I am not better than my fathers."

5 And he lay down and slept under a juniper tree; and behold, there was an angel touching him, and he said to him, "Arise, eat."

6 Then he looked and behold, there was at his head a bread cake *baked on* hot stones, and a jar of water. So he ate and drank and lay down again.

7 And the angel of the LORD came again a second time and touched him and said, "Arise, eat, because the journey is too great for you."

8 So he arose and ate and drank, and went in the strength of that food forty days and forty nights to Horeb, the mountain of God.

9 ¶ Then he came there to a cave, and lodged there; and behold, the word of the LORD *came* to him, and He said to him, "What are you doing here, Elijah?"

10 And he said, "I have been very zealous for the LORD, the God of hosts; for the sons of Israel have forsaken Thy covenant, torn down Thine altars

and killed Thy prophets with the sword. And I alone am left; and they seek my life, to take it away."

11 So He said, "Go forth, and stand on the mountain before the LORD." And behold, the LORD was passing by! And a great and strong wind was rending the mountains and breaking in pieces the rocks before the LORD; *but* the LORD *was* not in the wind. And after the wind an earthquake, *but* the LORD *was* not in the earthquake.

12 And after the earthquake a fire, *but* the LORD *was* not in the fire; and after the fire a sound of a gentle blowing.

13 And it came about when Elijah heard *it,* that he wrapped his face in his mantle, and went out and stood in the entrance of the cave. And behold, a voice *came* to him and said, "What are you doing here, Elijah?"

14 Then he said, "I have been very zealous for the LORD, the God of hosts; for the sons of Israel have forsaken Thy covenant, torn down Thine altars and killed Thy prophets with the sword. And I alone am left; and they seek my life, to take it away."

15 ¶ And the LORD said to him, "Go, return on your way to the wilderness of Damascus, and when you have arrived, you shall anoint Hazael king over Aram;

16 and Jehu the son of Nimshi you shall anoint king over Israel; and Elisha the son of Shaphat of Abel-meholah you shall anoint as prophet in your place.

17 "And it shall come about, the one who escapes from the sword of Hazael, Jehu shall put to death, and the one who escapes from the sword of Jehu, Elisha shall put to death.

18 "Yet I will leave 7,000 in Israel, all the knees that have not bowed to Baal and every mouth that has not kissed him."

19 ¶ So he departed from there and found Elisha the son of Shaphat, while he was plowing with twelve pairs *of oxen* before him, and he with the twelfth. And Elijah passed over to him and threw his mantle on him.

20 And he left the oxen and ran after Elijah and said, "Please let me kiss my father and my mother, then I will follow you." And he said to him, "Go

[27] Lit., *soul*

back again, for what have I done to you?"

21 So he returned from following him, and took the pair of oxen and sacrificed them and boiled their flesh with the implements of the oxen, and gave *it* to the people and they ate. Then he arose and followed Elijah and ministered to him.

CHAPTER 20

NOW Ben-hadad king of Aram gathered all his army, and there *were* thirty-two kings with him, and horses and chariots. And he went up and besieged Samaria, and fought against it.

2 Then he sent messengers to the city to Ahab king of Israel, and said to him, "Thus says Ben-hadad,

3 'Your silver and your gold are mine; your most beautiful wives and children are also mine.'"

4 And the king of Israel answered and said, "It is according to your word, my lord, O king; I am yours, and all that I have."

5 Then the messengers returned and said, "Thus says Ben-hadad, 'Surely, I sent to you saying, "You shall give me your silver and your gold and your wives and your children,"

6 but about this time tomorrow I will send my servants to you, and they will search your house and the houses of your servants; and it shall come about, whatever is desirable in your eyes, they will take in their hand and carry away.'"

7 ¶ Then the king of Israel called all the elders of the land and said, "Please observe and see how this man is looking for trouble; for he sent to me for my wives and my children and my silver and my gold, and I did not refuse him."

8 And all the elders and all the people said to him, "Do not listen or consent."

9 So he said to the messengers of Ben-hadad, "Tell my lord the king, 'All that you sent for to your servant at the first I will do, but this thing I cannot do.'" And the messengers departed and brought him word again.

10 And Ben-hadad sent to him and said, "May the gods do so to me and more also, if the dust of Samaria shall suffice for handfuls for all the people who follow me."

11 Then the king of Israel answered and said, "Tell *him*, 'Let not him who girds on *his* armor boast like him who takes *it* off.'"

12 And it came about when Ben-hadad heard this message, as he was drinking with the kings in the temporary shelters, that he said to his servants, "Station *yourselves*." So they stationed *themselves* against the city.

13 ¶ Now behold, a prophet approached Ahab king of Israel and said, "Thus says the LORD, 'Have you seen all this great multitude? Behold, I will deliver them into your hand today, and you shall know that I am the LORD.'"

14 And Ahab said, "By whom?" So he said, "Thus says the LORD, 'By the young men of the rulers of the provinces.'" Then he said, "Who shall begin the battle?" And he answered, "You."

15 Then he mustered the young men of the rulers of the provinces, and there were 232; and after them he mustered all the people, *even* all the sons of Israel, 7,000.

16 ¶ And they went out at noon, while Ben-hadad was drinking himself drunk in the temporary shelters with the thirty-two kings who helped him.

17 And the young men of the rulers of the provinces went out first; and Ben-hadad sent out and they told him, saying, "Men have come out from Samaria."

18 Then he said, "If they have come out for peace, take them alive; or if they have come out for war, take them alive."

19 So these went out from the city, the young men of the rulers of the provinces, and the army which followed them.

20 And they killed each his man; and the Arameans fled, and Israel pursued them, and Ben-hadad king of Aram escaped on a horse with horsemen.

21 And the king of Israel went out and struck the horses and chariots, and killed the Arameans with a great slaughter.

22 ¶ Then the prophet came near to the king of Israel, and said to him, "Go, strengthen yourself and observe and see what you have to do; for at the

turn of the year the king of Aram will come up against you."

23 Now the servants of the king of Aram said to him, "Their gods are gods of the mountains, therefore they were stronger than we; but rather let us fight against them in the plain, *and* surely we shall be stronger than they.

24 "And do this thing: remove the kings, each from his place, and put captains in their place,

25 and muster an army like the army that you have lost, horse for horse, and chariot for chariot. Then we will fight against them in the plain, and surely we shall be stronger than they." And he listened to their voice and did so.

26 ¶ So it came about at the turn of the year, that Ben-hadad mustered the Arameans and went up to Aphek to fight against Israel.

27 And the sons of Israel were mustered and were provisioned and went to meet them; and the sons of Israel camped before them like two little flocks of goats, but the Arameans filled the country.

28 Then a man of God came near and spoke to the king of Israel and said, "Thus says the LORD, 'Because the Arameans have said, "The LORD is a god of *the* mountains, but He is not a god of *the* valleys"; therefore I will give all this great multitude into your hand, and you shall know that I am the LORD.' "

29 So they camped one over against the other seven days. And it came about that on the seventh day, the battle was joined, and the sons of Israel killed *of* the Arameans 100,000 foot soldiers in one day.

30 But the rest fled to Aphek into the city, and the wall fell on 27,000 men who were left. And Ben-hadad fled and came into the city into an inner chamber.

31 ¶ And his servants said to him, "Behold now, we have heard that the kings of the house of Israel are merciful kings, please let us put sackcloth on our loins and ropes on our heads, and go out to the king of Israel; perhaps he will save your life."

32 So they girded sackcloth on their loins and *put* ropes on their heads, and came to the king of Israel and said, "Your servant Ben-hadad says, 'Please

let me live.' " And he said, "Is he still alive? He is my brother."

33 Now the men took this as an omen, and quickly catching his word said, "Your brother Ben-hadad." Then he said, "Go, bring him." Then Ben-hadad came out to him, and he took him up into the chariot.

34 And *Ben-hadad* said to him, "The cities which my father took from your father I will restore, and you shall make streets for yourself in Damascus, as my father made in Samaria." *Ahab said,* "And I will let you go with this covenant." So he made a covenant with him and let him go.

35 ¶ Now a certain man of the sons of the prophets said to another by the word of the LORD, "Please strike me." But the man refused to strike him.

36 Then he said to him, "Because you have not listened to the voice of the LORD, behold, as soon as you have departed from me, a lion will kill you." And as soon as he had departed from him a lion found him, and killed him.

37 Then he found another man and said, "Please strike me." And the man struck him, wounding him.

38 So the prophet departed and waited for the king by the way, and disguised himself with a bandage over his eyes.

39 And as the king passed by, he cried to the king and said, "Your servant went out into the midst of the battle; and behold, a man turned aside and brought a man to me and said, 'Guard this man; if for any reason he is missing, then your life shall be for his life, or else you shall pay a talent of silver.'

40 "And while your servant was busy here and there, he was gone." And the king of Israel said to him, "So shall your judgment be; you yourself have decided *it.*"

41 Then he hastily took the bandage away from his eyes, and the king of Israel recognized him that he was of the prophets.

42 And he said to him, "Thus says the LORD, 'Because you have let go out of *your* hand the man whom I had devoted to destruction, therefore your life shall go for his life, and your people for his people.' "

43 So the king of Israel went to his

house sullen and vexed, and came to Samaria.

CHAPTER 21

Now it came about after these things, that Naboth the Jezreelite had a vineyard which *was* in Jezreel beside the palace of Ahab king of Samaria.

2 And Ahab spoke to Naboth, saying, "Give me your vineyard, that I may have it for a vegetable garden because it is close beside my house, and I will give you a better vineyard than it in its place; if you like, I will give you the price of it in money."

3 But Naboth said to Ahab, "The Lord forbid me that I should give you the inheritance of my fathers."

4 So Ahab came into his house sullen and vexed because of the word which Naboth the Jezreelite had spoken to him; for he said, "I will not give you the inheritance of my fathers." And he lay down on his bed and turned away his face and ate no food.

5 ¶ But Jezebel his wife came to him and said to him, "How is it that your spirit is so sullen that you are not eating food?"

6 So he said to her, "Because I spoke to Naboth the Jezreelite, and said to him, 'Give me your vineyard for money; or else, if it pleases you, I will give you a vineyard in its place.' But he said, 'I will not give you my vineyard.'"

7 And Jezebel his wife said to him, "Do you now reign over Israel? Arise, eat bread, and let your heart be joyful; I will give you the vineyard of Naboth the Jezreelite."

8 So she wrote letters in Ahab's name and sealed them with his seal, and sent letters to the elders and to the nobles who were living with Naboth in his city.

9 Now she wrote in the letters, saying, "Proclaim a fast, and seat Naboth at the head of the people;

10 and seat two worthless men before him, and let them testify against him, saying, 'You cursed God and the king.' Then take him out and stone him to death."

11 ¶ So the men of his city, the elders and the nobles who lived in his city, did as Jezebel had sent *word* to them, just as it was written in the letters which she had sent them.

12 They proclaimed a fast and seated Naboth at the head of the people.

13 Then the two worthless men came in and sat before him; and the worthless men testified against him, even against Naboth, before the people, saying, "Naboth cursed God and the king." So they took him outside the city and stoned him to death with stones.

14 Then they sent *word* to Jezebel, saying, "Naboth has been stoned, and is dead."

15 And it came about when Jezebel heard that Naboth had been stoned and was dead, that Jezebel said to Ahab, "Arise, take possession of the vineyard of Naboth, the Jezreelite, which he refused to give you for money; for Naboth is not alive, but dead."

16 And it came about when Ahab heard that Naboth was dead, that Ahab arose to go down to the vineyard of Naboth the Jezreelite, to take possession of it.

17 ¶ Then the word of the Lord came to Elijah the Tishbite, saying,

18 "Arise, go down to meet Ahab king of Israel, who is in Samaria; behold, he is in the vineyard of Naboth where he has gone down to take possession of it.

19 "And you shall speak to him, saying, 'Thus says the Lord, "Have you murdered, and also taken possession?"' And you shall speak to him, saying, 'Thus says the Lord, "In the place where the dogs licked up the blood of Naboth the dogs shall lick up your blood, even yours."'"

20 And Ahab said to Elijah, "Have you found me, O my enemy?" And he answered, "I have found *you*, because you have sold yourself to do evil in the sight of the Lord.

21 "Behold, I will bring evil upon you, and will utterly sweep you away, and will cut off from Ahab every male, both bond and free in Israel;

22 and I will make your house like the house of Jeroboam the son of Nebat, and like the house of Baasha the son of Ahijah, because of the provocation with which you have provoked *Me* to anger, and *because* you have made Israel sin.

23"And of Jezebel also has the LORD spoken, saying, 'The dogs shall eat Jezebel in the district of Jezreel.'

24"The one belonging to Ahab, who dies in the city, the dogs shall eat, and the one who dies in the field the birds of heaven shall eat."

25 ¶ Surely there was no one like Ahab who sold himself to do evil in the sight of the LORD, because Jezebel his wife incited him.

26 And he acted very abominably in following idols, according to all that the Amorites had done, whom the LORD cast out before the sons of Israel.

27 ¶ And it came about when Ahab heard these words, that he tore his clothes and put on sackcloth and fasted, and he lay in sackcloth and went about despondently.

28 Then the word of the LORD came to Elijah the Tishbite, saying,

29"Do you see how Ahab has humbled himself before Me? Because he has humbled himself before Me, I will not bring the evil in his days, but I will bring the evil upon his house in his son's days."

CHAPTER 22

AND three years passed without war between Aram and Israel.

2 And it came about in the third year, that Jehoshaphat the king of Judah came down to the king of Israel.

3 Now the king of Israel said to his servants, "Do you know that Ramoth-gilead belongs to us, and we are still doing nothing to take it out of the hand of the king of Aram?"

4 And he said to Jehoshaphat, "Will you go with me to battle at Ramoth-gilead?" And Jehoshaphat said to the king of Israel, "I am as you are, my people as your people, my horses as your horses."

5 ¶ Moreover, Jehoshaphat said to the king of Israel, "Please inquire first for the word of the LORD."

6 Then the king of Israel gathered the prophets together, about four hundred men, and said to them, "Shall I go against Ramoth-gilead to battle or shall I refrain?" And they said, "Go up, for the Lord will give it into the hand of the king."

7 But Jehoshaphat said, "Is there not yet a prophet of the LORD here, that we may inquire of him?"

8 And the king of Israel said to Jehoshaphat, "There is yet one man by whom we may inquire of the LORD, but I hate him, because he does not prophesy good concerning me, but evil. He is Micaiah son of Imlah." But Jehoshaphat said, "Let not the king say so."

9 Then the king of Israel called an officer and said, "Bring quickly Micaiah son of Imlah."

10 Now the king of Israel and Jehoshaphat king of Judah were sitting each on his throne, arrayed in their robes, at the threshing floor at the entrance of the gate of Samaria; and all the prophets were prophesying before them.

11 Then Zedekiah the son of Chenaanah made horns of iron for himself and said, "Thus says the LORD, 'With these you shall gore the Arameans until they are consumed.' "

12 And all the prophets were prophesying thus, saying, "Go up to Ramoth-gilead and prosper, for the LORD will give it into the hand of the king."

13 ¶ Then the messenger who went to summon Micaiah spoke to him saying, "Behold now, the words of the prophets are uniformly favorable to the king. Please let your word be like the word of one of them, and speak favorably."

14 But Micaiah said, "As the LORD lives, what the LORD says to me, that I will speak."

15 When he came to the king, the king said to him, "Micaiah, shall we go to Ramoth-gilead to battle, or shall we refrain?" And he answered him, "Go up and succeed, and the LORD will give it into the hand of the king."

16 Then the king said to him, "How many times must I adjure you to speak to me nothing but the truth in the name of the LORD?"

17 So he said,

"I saw all Israel
Scattered on the mountains,
Like sheep which have no shepherd.
And the LORD said, 'These have no master.
Let each of them return to his house in peace.' "

18 Then the king of Israel said to Jehoshaphat, "Did I not tell you that he would not prophesy good concerning me, but evil?"

19 And Micaiah said, "Therefore, hear the word of the LORD. I saw the LORD sitting on His throne, and all the host of heaven standing by Him on His right and on His left.

20 "And the LORD said, 'Who will entice Ahab to go up and fall at Ramoth-gilead?' And one said this while another said that.

21 "Then a spirit came forward and stood before the LORD and said, 'I will entice him.'

22 "And the LORD said to him, 'How?' And he said, 'I will go out and be a deceiving spirit in the mouth of all his prophets.' Then He said, 'You are to entice *him* and also prevail. Go and do so.'

23 "Now therefore, behold, the LORD has put a deceiving spirit in the mouth of all these your prophets; and the LORD has proclaimed disaster against you."

24 ¶ Then Zedekiah the son of Chenaanah came near and struck Micaiah on the cheek and said, "How did the Spirit of the LORD pass from me to speak to you?"

25 And Micaiah said, "Behold, you shall see on that day when you enter an inner room to hide yourself."

26 Then the king of Israel said, "Take Micaiah and return him to Amon the governor of the city and to Joash the king's son;

27 and say, 'Thus says the king, "Put this man in prison, and feed him sparingly with bread and water until I return safely."'"

28 And Micaiah said, "If you indeed return safely the LORD has not spoken by me." And he said, "Listen, all you people."

29 ¶ So the king of Israel and Jehoshaphat king of Judah went up against Ramoth-gilead.

30 And the king of Israel said to Jehoshaphat, "I will disguise myself and go into the battle, but you put on your robes." So the king of Israel disguised himself and went into the battle.

31 Now the king of Aram had commanded the thirty-two captains of his chariots, saying, "Do not fight with small or great, but with the king of Israel alone."

32 So it came about, when the captains of the chariots saw Jehoshaphat, that they said, "Surely it is the king of Israel," and they turned aside to fight against him, and Jehoshaphat cried out.

33 Then it happened, when the captains of the chariots saw that it was not the king of Israel, that they turned back from pursuing him.

34 ¶ Now a certain man drew his bow at random and struck the king of Israel in a joint of the armor. So he said to the driver of his chariot, "Turn around, and take me out of the fight; for I am severely wounded."

35 And the battle raged that day, and the king was propped up in his chariot in front of the Arameans, and died at evening, and the blood from the wound ran into the bottom of the chariot.

36 Then a cry passed throughout the army close to sunset, saying, "Every man to his city and every man to his country."

37 ¶ So the king died and was brought to Samaria, and they buried the king in Samaria.

38 And they washed the chariot by the pool of Samaria, and the dogs licked up his blood (now the harlots bathed themselves *there*), according to the word of the LORD which He spoke.

39 Now the rest of the acts of Ahab and all that he did and the ivory house which he built and all the cities which he built, are they not written in the Book of the Chronicles of the Kings of Israel?

40 So Ahab slept with his fathers, and Ahaziah his son became king in his place.

41 ¶ Now Jehoshaphat the son of Asa became king over Judah in the fourth year of Ahab king of Israel.

42 Jehoshaphat was thirty-five years old when he became king, and he reigned twenty-five years in Jerusalem. And his mother's name was Azubah the daughter of Shilhi.

43 And he walked in all the way of Asa his father; he did not turn aside from it, doing right in the sight of the LORD. However, the high places were

not taken away; the people still sacrificed and burnt incense on the high places.

44 Jehoshaphat also made peace with the king of Israel.

45 ¶ Now the rest of the acts of Jehoshaphat, and his might which he showed and how he warred, are they not written in the Book of the Chronicles of the Kings of Judah?

46 And the remnant of the sodomites who remained in the days of his father Asa, he expelled from the land.

47 Now there was no king in Edom; a deputy was king.

48 Jehoshaphat made ships of Tarshish to go to Ophir for gold, but they did not go for the ships were broken at Ezion-geber.

49 Then Ahaziah the son of Ahab said to Jehoshaphat, "Let my servants go with your servants in the ships." But Jehoshaphat was not willing.

50 And Jehoshaphat slept with his fathers and was buried with his fathers in the city of his father David, and Jehoram his son became king in his place.

51 ¶ Ahaziah the son of Ahab became king over Israel in Samaria in the seventeenth year of Jehoshaphat king of Judah, and he reigned two years over Israel.

52 And he did evil in the sight of the LORD and walked in the way of his father and in the way of his mother and in the way of Jeroboam the son of Nebat, who caused Israel to sin.

53 So he served Baal and worshiped him and provoked the LORD God of Israel to anger according to all that his father had done.

THE SECOND BOOK OF THE

KINGS

NOW Moab rebelled against Israel after the death of Ahab.

2 And Ahaziah fell through the lattice in his upper chamber which *was* in Samaria, and became ill. So he sent messengers and said to them, "Go, inquire of Baal-zebub, the god of Ekron, whether I shall recover from this sickness."

3 But the angel of the LORD said to Elijah the Tishbite, "Arise, go up to meet the messengers of the king of Samaria and say to them, 'Is it because there is no God in Israel *that* you are going to inquire of Baal-zebub, the god of Ekron?'

4 "Now therefore thus says the LORD, 'You shall not come down from the bed where you have gone up, but you shall surely die.' " Then Elijah departed.

5 ¶ When the messengers returned to him he said to them, "Why have you returned?"

6 And they said to him, "A man came up to meet us and said to us, 'Go, return to the king who sent you and say to him, "Thus says the LORD, 'Is it because there is no God in Israel *that* you are sending to inquire of Baal-zebub, the god of Ekron? Therefore you shall not come down from the bed where you have gone up, but shall surely die.' " ' "

7 And he said to them, "What kind of man was he who came up to meet you and spoke these words to you?"

8 And they answered him, "*He was* a hairy man with a leather girdle bound about his loins." And he said, "It is Elijah the Tishbite."

9 ¶ Then *the king* sent to him a captain of fifty with his fifty. And he went up to him, and behold, he was sitting on the top of the hill. And he said to him, "O man of God, the king says, 'Come down.' "

10 And Elijah answered and said to the captain of fifty, "If I am a man of God, let fire come down from heaven and consume you and your fifty." Then fire came down from heaven and consumed him and his fifty.

11 So he again sent to him another captain of fifty with his fifty. And he answered and said to him, "O man of God, thus says the king, 'Come down quickly.' "

12 And Elijah answered and said to

them, "If I am a man of God, let fire come down from heaven and consume you and your fifty." Then the fire of God came down from heaven and consumed him and his fifty.

13 So he again sent the captain of a third fifty with his fifty. When the third captain of fifty went up, he came and bowed down on his knees before Elijah, and begged him and said to him, "O man of God, please let my life and the lives of these fifty servants of yours be precious in your sight.

14 "Behold fire came down from heaven, and consumed the first two captains of fifty with their fifties; but now let my life be precious in your sight."

15 And the angel of the LORD said to Elijah, "Go down with him; do not be afraid of him." So he arose and went down with him to the king.

16 Then he said to him, "Thus says the LORD, 'Because you have sent messengers to inquire of Baal-zebub, the god of Ekron—is it because there is no God in Israel to inquire of His word?— therefore you shall not come down from the bed where you have gone up, but shall surely die.'"

17 ¶ So Ahaziah died according to the word of the LORD which Elijah had spoken. And because he had no son, Jehoram became king in his place in the second year of Jehoram the son of Jehoshaphat, king of Judah.

18 Now the rest of the acts of Ahaziah which he did, are they not written in the Book of the Chronicles of the Kings of Israel?

CHAPTER 2

AND it came about when the LORD was about to take up Elijah by a whirlwind to heaven, that Elijah went with Elisha from Gilgal.

2 And Elijah said to Elisha, "Stay here please, for the LORD has sent me as far as Bethel." But Elisha said, "As the LORD lives and as you yourself live, I will not leave you." So they went down to Bethel.

3 Then the sons of the prophets who were at Bethel came out to Elisha and said to him, "Do you know that the LORD will take away your master from over you today?" And he said, "Yes, I know; be still."

4 And Elijah said to him, "Elisha, please stay here, for the LORD has sent me to Jericho." But he said, "As the LORD lives, and as you yourself live, I will not leave you." So they came to Jericho.

5 And the sons of the prophets who were at Jericho approached Elisha and said to him, "Do you know that the LORD will take away your master from over you today?" And he answered, "Yes, I know; be still."

6 Then Elijah said to him, "Please stay here, for the LORD has sent me to the Jordan." And he said, "As the LORD lives, and as you yourself live, I will not leave you." So the two of them went on.

7 ¶ Now fifty men of the sons of the prophets went and stood opposite them at a distance, while the two of them stood by the Jordan.

8 And Elijah took his mantle and folded it together and struck the waters, and they were divided here and there, so that the two of them crossed over on dry ground.

9 Now it came about when they had crossed over, that Elijah said to Elisha, "Ask what I shall do for you before I am taken from you." And Elisha said, "Please, let a double portion of your spirit be upon me."

10 And he said, "You have asked a hard thing. Nevertheless, if you see me when I am taken from you, it shall be so for you; but if not, it shall not be so."

11 Then it came about as they were going along and talking, that behold, there appeared a chariot of fire and horses of fire which separated the two of them. And Elijah went up by a whirlwind to heaven.

12 And Elisha saw it and cried out, "My father, my father, the chariots of Israel and its horsemen!" And he saw him no more. Then he took hold of his own clothes and tore them in two pieces.

13 He also took up the mantle of Elijah that fell from him, and returned and stood by the bank of the Jordan.

14 And he took the mantle of Elijah that fell from him, and struck the waters and said, "Where is the LORD, the God of Elijah?" And when he also

had struck the waters, they were divided here and there; and Elisha crossed over.

15 ¶ Now when the sons of the prophets who *were* at Jericho opposite *him* saw him, they said, "The spirit of Elijah rests on Elisha." And they came to meet him and bowed themselves to the ground before him.

16 And they said to him, "Behold now, there are with your servants fifty strong men, please let them go and search for your master; perhaps the Spirit of the LORD has taken him up and cast him on some mountain or into some valley." And he said, "You shall not send."

17 But when they urged him until he was ashamed, he said, "Send." They sent therefore fifty men; and they searched three days, but did not find him.

18 And they returned to him while he was staying at Jericho; and he said to them, "Did I not say to you, 'Do not go'?"

19 ¶ Then the men of the city said to Elisha, "Behold now, the situation of this city is pleasant, as my lord sees; but the water is bad, and the land is unfruitful."

20 And he said, "Bring me a new jar, and put salt in it." So they brought *it* to him.

21 And he went out to the spring of water, and threw salt in it and said, "Thus says the LORD, 'I have purified these waters; there shall not be from there death or unfruitfulness any longer.'"

22 So the waters have been purified to this day, according to the word of Elisha which he spoke.

23 ¶ Then he went up from there to Bethel; and as he was going up by the way, young lads came out from the city and mocked him and said to him, "Go up, you baldhead; go up, you baldhead!"

24 When he looked behind him and saw them, he cursed them in the name of the LORD. Then two female bears came out of the woods and tore up forty-two lads of their number.

25 And he went from there to Mount Carmel, and from there he returned to Samaria.

CHAPTER 3

Now Jehoram the son of Ahab became king over Israel at Samaria in the eighteenth year of Jehoshaphat king of Judah, and reigned twelve years.

2 And he did evil in the sight of the LORD, though not like his father and his mother; for he put away the *sacred* pillar of Baal which his father had made.

3 Nevertheless, he clung to the sins of Jeroboam the son of Nebat, which he made Israel sin; he did not depart from them.

4 ¶ Now Mesha king of Moab was a sheep breeder, and used to pay the king of Israel 100,000 lambs and the wool of 100,000 rams.

5 But it came about, when Ahab died, the king of Moab rebelled against the king of Israel.

6 And King Jehoram went out of Samaria at that time and mustered all Israel.

7 Then he went and sent *word* to Jehoshaphat the king of Judah, saying, "The king of Moab has rebelled against me. Will you go with me to fight against Moab?" And he said, "I will go up; I am as you are, my people as your people, my horses as your horses."

8 And he said, "Which way shall we go up?" And he answered, "The way of the wilderness of Edom."

9 So the king of Israel went with the king of Judah and the king of Edom; and they made a circuit of seven days' journey, and there was no water for the army or for the cattle that followed them.

10 Then the king of Israel said, "Alas! For the LORD has called these three kings to give them into the hand of Moab."

11 But Jehoshaphat said, "Is there not a prophet of the LORD here, that we may inquire of the LORD by him?" And one of the king of Israel's servants answered and said, "Elisha the son of Shaphat is here, who used to pour water on the hands of Elijah."

12 And Jehoshaphat said, "The word of the LORD is with him." So the king of Israel and Jehoshaphat and the king of Edom went down to him.

13 ¶ Now Elisha said to the king of

Israel, "What do I have to do with you? Go to the prophets of your father and to the prophets of your mother." And the king of Israel said to him, "No, for the LORD has called these three kings *together* to give them into the hand of Moab."

14 And Elisha said, "As the LORD of hosts lives, before whom I stand, were it not that I regard the presence of Jehoshaphat the king of Judah, I would not look at you nor see you.

15"But now bring me a minstrel." And it came about, when the minstrel played, that the hand of the LORD came upon him.

16 And he said, "Thus says the LORD, 'Make this valley full of trenches.'

17"For thus says the LORD, 'You shall not see wind nor shall you see rain; yet that valley shall be filled with water, so that you shall drink, both you and your cattle and your beasts.

18 'And this is but a slight thing in the sight of the LORD; He shall also give the Moabites into your hand.

19 'Then you shall strike every fortified city and every choice city, and fell every good tree and stop all springs of water, and mar every good piece of land with stones.'"

20 And it happened in the morning about the time of offering the sacrifice, that behold, water came by the way of Edom, and the country was filled with water.

21 ¶ Now all the Moabites heard that the kings had come up to fight against them. And all who were able to put on armor and older were summoned, and stood on the border.

22 And they rose early in the morning, and the sun shone on the water, and the Moabites saw the water opposite *them* as red as blood.

23 Then they said, "This is blood; the kings have surely fought together, and they have slain one another. Now therefore, Moab, to the spoil!"

24 But when they came to the camp of Israel, the Israelites arose and struck the Moabites, so that they fled before them; and they went forward into the land, slaughtering the Moabites.

25 Thus they destroyed the cities; and each one threw a stone on every piece of good land and filled it. So they stopped all the springs of water and

felled all the good trees, until in Kir-hareseth *only* they left its stones; however, the slingers went about *it* and struck it.

26 When the king of Moab saw that the battle was too fierce for him, he took with him 700 men who drew swords, to break through to the king of Edom; but they could not.

27 Then he took his oldest son who was to reign in his place, and offered him as a burnt offering on the wall. And there came great wrath against Israel, and they departed from him and returned to their own land.

CHAPTER 4

Now a certain woman of the wives of the sons of the prophets cried out to Elisha, "Your servant my husband is dead, and you know that your servant feared the LORD; and the creditor has come to take my two children to be his slaves."

2 And Elisha said to her, "What shall I do for you? Tell me, what do you have in the house?" And she said, "Your maidservant has nothing in the house except a jar of oil."

3 Then he said, "Go, borrow vessels at large for yourself from all your neighbors, *even* empty vessels; do not get a few.

4"And you shall go in and shut the door behind you and your sons, and pour out into all these vessels; and you shall set aside what is full."

5 So she went from him and shut the door behind her and her sons; they were bringing *the vessels* to her and she poured.

6 And it came about when the vessels were full, that she said to her son, "Bring me another vessel." And he said to her, "There is not one vessel more." And the oil stopped.

7 Then she came and told the man of God. And he said, "Go, sell the oil and pay your debt, and you *and* your sons can live on the rest."

8 ¶ Now there came a day when Elisha passed over to Shunem, where there was a prominent woman, and she persuaded him to eat food. And so it was, as often as he passed by, he turned in there to eat food.

9 And she said to her husband, "Behold now, I perceive that this is a holy

man of God passing by us continually.

10"Please, let us make a little walled upper chamber and let us set a bed for him there, and a table and a chair and a lampstand; and it shall be, when he comes to us, *that* he can turn in there."

11 One day he came there and turned in to the upper chamber and rested.

12 Then he said to Gehazi his servant, "Call this Shunammite." And when he had called her, she stood before him.

13 And he said to him, "Say now to her, 'Behold, you have been careful for us with all this care; what can I do for you? Would you be spoken for to the king or to the captain of the army?'" And she answered, "I live among my own people."

14 So he said, "What then is to be done for her?" And Gehazi answered, "Truly she has no son and her husband is old."

15 And he said, "Call her." When he had called her, she stood in the doorway.

16 Then he said, "At this season next year you shall embrace a son." And she said, "No, my lord, O man of God, do not lie to your maidservant."

17 And the woman conceived and bore a son at that season the next year, as Elisha had said to her.

18 ¶ When the child was grown, the day came that he went out to his father to the reapers.

19 And he said to his father, "My head, my head." And he said to his servant, "Carry him to his mother."

20 When he had taken him and brought him to his mother, he sat on her lap until noon, and *then* died.

21 And she went up and laid him on the bed of the man of God, and shut *the door* behind him, and went out.

22 Then she called to her husband and said, "Please send me one of the servants and one of the donkeys, that I may run to the man of God and return."

23 And he said, "Why will you go to him today? It is neither new moon nor sabbath." And she said, "*It will be* well."

24 Then she saddled a donkey and said to her servant, "Drive and go

forward; do not slow down the pace for me unless I tell you."

25 So she went and came to the man of God to Mount Carmel. And it came about when the man of God saw her at a distance, that he said to Gehazi his servant, "Behold, yonder is the Shunammite.

26"Please run now to meet her and say to her, 'Is it well with you? Is it well with your husband? Is it well with the child?'" And she answered, "It is well."

27 When she came to the man of God to the hill, she caught hold of his feet. And Gehazi came near to push her away; but the man of God said, "Let her alone, for her soul is troubled within her; and the Lord has hidden it from me and has not told me."

28 Then she said, "Did I ask for a son from my lord? Did I not say, 'Do not deceive me'?"

29 ¶ Then he said to Gehazi, "Gird up your loins and take my staff in your hand, and go your way; if you meet any man, do not salute him, and if anyone salutes you, do not answer him; and lay my staff on the lad's face."

30 And the mother of the lad said, "As the Lord lives and as you yourself live, I will not leave you." And he arose and followed her.

31 Then Gehazi passed on before them and laid the staff on the lad's face, but there was neither sound nor response. So he returned to meet him and told him, "The lad has not awakened."

32 When Elisha came into the house, behold the lad was dead and laid on his bed.

33 So he entered and shut the door behind them both, and prayed to the Lord.

34 And he went up and lay on the child, and put his mouth on his mouth and his eyes on his eyes and his hands on his hands, and he stretched himself on him; and the flesh of the child became warm.

35 Then he returned and walked in the house once back and forth, and went up and stretched himself on him; and the lad sneezed seven times and the lad opened his eyes.

36 And he called Gehazi and said, "Call this Shunammite." So he called

her. And when she came in to him, he said, "Take up your son."

37 Then she went in and fell at his feet and bowed herself to the ground, and she took up her son and went out.

38 ¶ When Elisha returned to Gilgal, *there was* a famine in the land. As the sons of the prophets were sitting before him, he said to his servant, "Put on the large pot and boil stew for the sons of the prophets."

39 Then one went out into the field to gather herbs, and found a wild vine and gathered from it his lap full of wild gourds, and came and sliced them into the pot of stew, for they did not know *what they were.*

40 So they poured *it* out for the men to eat. And it came about as they were eating of the stew, that they cried out and said, "O man of God, there is death in the pot." And they were unable to eat.

41 But he said, "Now bring meal." And he threw it into the pot, and he said, "Pour *it* out for the people that they may eat." Then there was no harm in the pot.

42 ¶ Now a man came from Baal-shalishah, and brought the man of God bread of the first fruits, twenty loaves of barley and fresh ears of grain in his sack. And he said, "Give *them* to the people that they may eat."

43 And his attendant said, "What, shall I set this before a hundred men?" But he said, "Give *them* to the people that they may eat, for thus says the Lord, 'They shall eat and have *some* left over.' "

44 So he set *it* before them, and they ate and had *some* left over, according to the word of the Lord.

CHAPTER 5

NOW Naaman, captain of the army of the king of Aram, was a great man with his master, and highly respected, because by him the Lord had given victory to Aram. The man was also a valiant warrior, *but he was* a leper.

2 Now the Arameans had gone out in bands, and had taken captive a little girl from the land of Israel; and she waited on Naaman's wife.

3 And she said to her mistress, "I wish that my master were with the prophet who is in Samaria! Then he would cure him of his leprosy."

4 And Naaman went in and told his master, saying, "Thus and thus spoke the girl who is from the land of Israel."

5 Then the king of Aram said, "Go now, and I will send a letter to the king of Israel." And he departed and took with him ten talents of silver and six thousand *shekels* of gold and ten changes of clothes.

6 And he brought the letter to the king of Israel, saying, "And now as this letter comes to you, behold, I have sent Naaman my servant to you, that you may cure him of his leprosy."

7 And it came about when the king of Israel read the letter, that he tore his clothes and said, "Am I God, to kill and to make alive, that this man is sending *word* to me to cure a man of his leprosy? But consider now, and see how he is seeking a quarrel against me."

8 ¶ And it happened when Elisha the man of God heard that the king of Israel had torn his clothes, that he sent *word* to the king, saying, "Why have you torn your clothes? Now let him come to me, and he shall know that there is a prophet in Israel."

9 So Naaman came with his horses and his chariots, and stood at the doorway of the house of Elisha.

10 And Elisha sent a messenger to him, saying, "Go and wash in the Jordan seven times, and your flesh shall be restored to you and *you shall* be clean."

11 But Naaman was furious and went away and said, "Behold, I thought, 'He will surely come out to me, and stand and call on the name of the Lord his God, and wave his hand over the place, and cure the leper.'

12 "Are not Abanah and Pharpar, the rivers of Damascus, better than all the waters of Israel? Could I not wash in them and be clean?" So he turned and went away in a rage.

13 Then his servants came near and spoke to him and said, "My father, had the prophet told you *to do some* great thing, would you not have done *it*? How much more *then*, when he says to you, 'Wash, and be clean'?"

14 So he went down and dipped *himself* seven times in the Jordan, according to the word of the man of God; and

his flesh was restored like the flesh of a little child, and he was clean.

15 ¶ When he returned to the man of God with all his company, and came and stood before him, he said, "Behold now, I know that there is no God in all the earth, but in Israel; so please take a present from your servant now."

16 But he said, "As the LORD lives, before whom I stand, I will take nothing." And he urged him to take *it,* but he refused.

17 And Naaman said, "If not, please let your servant at least be given two mules' load of earth; for your servant will no more offer burnt offering nor will he sacrifice to other gods, but to the LORD.

18"In this matter may the LORD pardon your servant: when my master goes into the house of Rimmon to worship there, and he leans on my hand and I bow myself in the house of Rimmon, when I bow myself in the house of Rimmon, the LORD pardon your servant in this matter."

19 And he said to him, "Go in peace." So he departed from him some distance.

20 ¶ But Gehazi, the servant of Elisha the man of God, thought, "Behold, my master has spared this Naaman the Aramean, by not receiving from his hands what he brought. As the LORD lives, I will run after him and take something from him."

21 So Gehazi pursued Naaman. When Naaman saw one running after him, he came down from the chariot to meet him and said, "Is all well?"

22 And he said, "All is well. My master has sent me, saying, 'Behold, just now two young men of the sons of the prophets have come to me from the hill country of Ephraim. Please give them a talent of silver and two changes of clothes.' "

23 And Naaman said, "Be pleased to take two talents." And he urged him, and bound two talents of silver in two bags with two changes of clothes, and gave them to two of his servants; and they carried *them* before him.

24 When he came to the hill, he took them from their hand and deposited them in the house, and he sent the men away, and they departed.

25 But he went in and stood before his master. And Elisha said to him,

"Where have you been, Gehazi?" And he said, "Your servant went nowhere."

26 Then he said to him, "Did not my heart go *with you,* when the man turned from his chariot to meet you? Is it a time to receive money and to receive clothes and olive groves and vineyards and sheep and oxen and male and female servants?

27"Therefore, the leprosy of Naaman shall cleave to you and to your descendants forever." So he went out from his presence a leper *as white* as snow.

CHAPTER 6

NOW the sons of the prophets said to Elisha, "Behold now, the place before you where we are living is too limited for us.

2"Please let us go to the Jordan, and each of us take from there a beam, and let us make a place there for ourselves where we may live." So he said, "Go."

3 Then one said, "Please be willing to go with your servants." And he answered, "I shall go."

4 So he went with them; and when they came to the Jordan, they cut down trees.

5 But as one was felling a beam, the axe head fell into the water; and he cried out and said, "Alas, my master! For it was borrowed."

6 Then the man of God said, "Where did it fall?" And when he showed him the place, he cut off a stick, and threw *it* in there, and made the iron float.

7 And he said, "Take it up for yourself." So he put out his hand and took it.

8 ¶ Now the king of Aram was warring against Israel; and he counseled with his servants saying, "In such and such a place shall be my camp."

9 And the man of God sent *word* to the king of Israel saying, "Beware that you do not pass this place, for the Arameans are coming down there."

10 And the king of Israel sent to the place about which the man of God had told him; thus he warned him, so that he guarded himself there, more than once or twice.

11 Now the heart of the king of Aram was enraged over this thing; and

he called his servants and said to them, "Will you tell me which of us is for the king of Israel?"

12 And one of his servants said, "No, my lord, O king; but Elisha, the prophet who is in Israel, tells the king of Israel the words that you speak in your bedroom."

13 So he said, "Go and see where he is, that I may send and take him." And it was told him, saying, "Behold, he is in Dothan."

14 And he sent horses and chariots and a great army there, and they came by night and surrounded the city.

15 ¶ Now when the attendant of the man of God had risen early and gone out, behold, an army with horses and chariots was circling the city. And his servant said to him, "Alas, my master! What shall we do?"

16 So he answered, "Do not fear, for those who are with us are more than those who are with them."

17 Then Elisha prayed and said, "O LORD, I pray, open his eyes that he may see." And the LORD opened the servant's eyes, and he saw; and behold, the mountain was full of horses and chariots of fire all around Elisha.

18 And when they came down to him, Elisha prayed to the LORD and said, "Strike this people with blindness, I pray." So He struck them with blindness according to the word of Elisha.

19 Then Elisha said to them, "This is not the way, nor is this the city; follow me and I will bring you to the man whom you seek." And he brought them to Samaria.

20 ¶ And it came about when they had come into Samaria, that Elisha said, "O LORD, open the eyes of these *men*, that they may see." So the LORD opened their eyes, and they saw; and behold, they were in the midst of Samaria.

21 Then the king of Israel when he saw them, said to Elisha, "My father, shall I kill them? Shall I kill them?"

22 And he answered, "You shall not kill *them*. Would you kill those you have taken captive with your sword and with your bow? Set bread and water before them, that they may eat and drink and go to their master."

23 So he prepared a great feast for them; and when they had eaten and drunk he sent them away, and they went to their master. And the marauding bands of Arameans did not come again into the land of Israel.

24 ¶ Now it came about after this, that Ben-hadad king of Aram gathered all his army and went up and besieged Samaria.

25 And there was a great famine in Samaria; and behold, they besieged it, until a donkey's head was sold for eighty *shekels* of silver, and a fourth of a ¹kab of dove's dung for five *shekels* of silver.

26 And as the king of Israel was passing by on the wall a woman cried out to him, saying, "Help, my lord, O king!"

27 And he said, "If the LORD does not help you, from where shall I help you? From the threshing floor, or from the wine press?"

28 And the king said to her, "What is the matter with you?" And she answered, "This woman said to me, 'Give your son that we may eat him today, and we will eat my son tomorrow.'

29 "So we boiled my son and ate him; and I said to her on the next day, 'Give your son, that we may eat him'; but she has hidden her son."

30 And it came about when the king heard the words of the woman, that he tore his clothes—now he was passing by on the wall—and the people looked, and behold, he had sackcloth beneath on his body.

31 Then he said, "May God do so to me and more also, if the head of Elisha the son of Shaphat remains on him today."

32 ¶ Now Elisha was sitting in his house, and the elders were sitting with him. And *the king* sent a man from his presence; but before the messenger came to him, he said to the elders, "Do you see how this son of a murderer has sent to take away my head? Look, when the messenger comes, shut the door and hold the door shut against him. Is not the sound of his master's feet behind him?"

33 And while he was still talking with them, behold, the messenger came down to him, and he said, "Behold, this evil is from the LORD; why

¹ I.e., One kab equals approx. 2 quarts

should I wait for the LORD any longer?"

CHAPTER 7

THEN Elisha said, "Listen to the word of the LORD; thus says the LORD, 'Tomorrow about this time a measure of fine flour shall be *sold* for a shekel, and two measures of barley for a shekel, in the gate of Samaria.' "

2 And the royal officer on whose hand the king was leaning answered the man of God and said, "Behold, if the LORD should make windows in heaven, could this thing be?" Then he said, "Behold you shall see it with your own eyes, but you shall not eat of it."

3 ¶ Now there were four leprous men at the entrance of the gate; and they said to one another, "Why do we sit here until we die?

4 "If we say, 'We will enter the city,' then the famine is in the city and we shall die there; and if we sit here, we die also. Now therefore come, and let us go over to the camp of the Arameans. If they spare us, we shall live; and if they kill us, we shall but die."

5 And they arose at twilight to go to the camp of the Arameans; when they came to the outskirts of the camp of the Arameans, behold, there was no one there.

6 For the Lord had caused the army of the Arameans to hear a sound of chariots and a sound of horses, *even* the sound of a great army, so that they said to one another, "Behold, the king of Israel has hired against us the kings of the Hittites and the kings of the Egyptians, to come upon us."

7 Therefore they arose and fled in the twilight, and left their tents and their horses and their donkeys, even the camp just as it was, and fled for their life.

8 When these lepers came to the outskirts of the camp, they entered one tent and ate and drank, and carried from there silver and gold and clothes, and went and hid *them*; and they returned and entered another tent and carried from there *also*, and went and hid *them*.

9 ¶ Then they said to one another, "We are not doing right. This day is a day of good news, but we are keeping silent; if we wait until morning light,

punishment will overtake us. Now therefore come, let us go and tell the king's household."

10 So they came and called to the gatekeepers of the city, and they told them, saying, "We came to the camp of the Arameans, and behold, there was no one there, nor the voice of man, only the horses tied and the donkeys tied, and the tents just as they were."

11 And the gatekeepers called, and told *it* within the king's household.

12 Then the king arose in the night and said to his servants, "I will now tell you what the Arameans have done to us. They know that we are hungry; therefore they have gone from the camp to hide themselves in the field, saying, 'When they come out of the city, we shall capture them alive and get into the city.' "

13 And one of his servants answered and said, "Please, let some *men* take five of the horses which remain, which are left in the city. Behold, they *will be in any case* like all the multitude of Israel who are left in it; behold, they *will be in any case* like all the multitude of Israel who have already perished, so let us send and see."

14 They took therefore two chariots with horses, and the king sent after the army of the Arameans, saying, "Go and see."

15 And they went after them to the Jordan, and behold, all the way was full of clothes and equipment, which the Arameans had thrown away in their haste. Then the messengers returned and told the king.

16 ¶ So the people went out and plundered the camp of the Arameans. Then a measure of fine flour *was sold* for a shekel and two measures of barley for a shekel, according to the word of the LORD.

17 Now the king appointed the royal officer on whose hand he leaned to have charge of the gate; but the people trampled on him at the gate, and he died just as the man of God had said, who spoke when the king came down to him.

18 And it came about just as the man of God had spoken to the king, saying, "Two measures of barley for a shekel and a measure of fine flour for a

shekel, shall be *sold* tomorrow about this time at the gate of Samaria."

19 Then the royal officer answered the man of God and said, "Now behold, if the LORD should make windows in heaven, could such a thing be?" And he said, "Behold, you shall see it with your own eyes, but you shall not eat of it."

20 And so it happened to him, for the people trampled on him at the gate, and he died.

CHAPTER 8

NOW Elisha spoke to the woman whose son he had restored to life, saying, "Arise and go with your household, and sojourn wherever you can sojourn; for the LORD has called for a famine, and it shall even come on the land for seven years."

2 So the woman arose and did according to the word of the man of God, and she went with her household and sojourned in the land of the Philistines seven years.

3 And it came about at the end of seven years, that the woman returned from the land of the Philistines; and she went out to appeal to the king for her house and for her field.

4 Now the king was talking with Gehazi, the servant of the man of God, saying, "Please relate to me all the great things that Elisha has done."

5 And it came about, as he was relating to the king how he had restored to life the one who was dead, that behold, the woman whose son he had restored to life, appealed to the king for her house and for her field. And Gehazi said, "My lord, O king, this is the woman and this is her son, whom Elisha restored to life."

6 When the king asked the woman, she related *it* to him. So the king appointed for her a certain officer, saying, "Restore all that was hers and all the produce of the field from the day that she left the land even until now."

7 ¶ Then Elisha came to Damascus. Now Ben-hadad king of Aram was sick, and it was told him, saying, "The man of God has come here."

8 And the king said to Hazael, "Take a gift in your hand and go to meet the man of God, and inquire of the LORD by him, saying, 'Will I recover from this sickness?' "

9 So Hazael went to meet him and took a gift in his hand, even every kind of good thing of Damascus, forty camels' loads; and he came and stood before him and said, "Your son Ben-hadad king of Aram has sent me to you, saying, 'Will I recover from this sickness?' "

10 Then Elisha said to him, "Go, say to him, 'You shall surely recover,' but the LORD has shown me that he will certainly die."

11 And he fixed his gaze steadily *on him* until he was ashamed, and the man of God wept.

12 And Hazael said, "Why does my lord weep?" Then he answered, "Because I know the evil that you will do to the sons of Israel: their strongholds you will set on fire, and their young men you will kill with the sword, and their little ones you will dash in pieces, and their women with child you will rip up."

13 Then Hazael said, "But what is your servant, *who is but* a dog, that he should do this great thing?" And Elisha answered, "The LORD has shown me that you will be king over Aram."

14 So he departed from Elisha and returned to his master, who said to him, "What did Elisha say to you?" And he answered, "He told me that you would surely recover."

15 And it came about on the morrow, that he took the cover and dipped it in water and spread it on his face, so that he died. And Hazael became king in his place.

16 ¶ Now in the fifth year of Joram the son of Ahab king of Israel, Jehoshaphat being then the king of Judah, Jehoram the son of Jehoshaphat king of Judah became king.

17 He was thirty-two years old when he became king, and he reigned eight years in Jerusalem.

18 And he walked in the way of the kings of Israel, just as the house of Ahab had done, for the daughter of Ahab became his wife; and he did evil in the sight of the LORD.

19 However, the LORD was not willing to destroy Judah, for the sake of David His servant, since He had promised him to give a lamp to him through his sons always.

20 ¶ In his days Edom revolted from under the hand of Judah, and made a king over themselves.

21 Then Joram crossed over to Zair, and all his chariots with him. And it came about that he arose by night and struck the Edomites who had surrounded him and the captains of the chariots; but *his* army fled to their tents.

22 So Edom revolted against Judah to this day. Then Libnah revolted at the same time.

23 And the rest of the acts of Joram and all that he did, are they not written in the Book of the Chronicles of the Kings of Judah?

24 So Joram slept with his fathers, and was buried with his fathers in the city of David; and Ahaziah his son became king in his place.

25 ¶ In the twelfth year of Joram the son of Ahab king of Israel, Ahaziah the son of Jehoram king of Judah began to reign.

26 Ahaziah *was* twenty-two years old when he became king, and he reigned one year in Jerusalem. And his mother's name *was* Athaliah the granddaughter of Omri king of Israel.

27 And he walked in the way of the house of Ahab, and did evil in the sight of the LORD, like the house of Ahab *had done*, because he was a son-in-law of the house of Ahab.

28 Then he went with Joram the son of Ahab to war against Hazael king of Aram at Ramoth-gilead, and the Arameans wounded Joram.

29 So King Joram returned to be healed in Jezreel of the wounds which the Arameans had inflicted on him at Ramah, when he fought against Hazael king of Aram. Then Ahaziah the son of Jehoram king of Judah went down to see Joram the son of Ahab in Jezreel because he was sick.

CHAPTER 9

Now Elisha the prophet called one of the sons of the prophets, and said to him, "Gird up your loins, and take this flask of oil in your hand, and go to Ramoth-gilead.

2"When you arrive there, search out Jehu the son of Jehoshaphat the son of Nimshi, and go in and bid him arise from among his brothers, and bring him to an inner room.

3"Then take the flask of oil and pour it on his head and say, 'Thus says the LORD, "I have anointed you king over Israel."' Then open the door and flee and do not wait."

4 So the young man, the servant of the prophet, went to Ramoth-gilead.

5 When he came, behold, the captains of the army were sitting, and he said, "I have a word for you, O captain." And Jehu said, "For which *one* of us?" And he said, "For you, O captain."

6 And he arose and went into the house, and he poured the oil on his head and said to him, "Thus says the LORD, the God of Israel, 'I have anointed you king over the people of the LORD, *even* over Israel.

7 'And you shall strike the house of Ahab your master, that I may avenge the blood of My servants the prophets, and the blood of all the servants of the LORD, at the hand of Jezebel.

8 'For the whole house of Ahab shall perish, and I will cut off from Ahab every male person both bond and free in Israel.

9 'And I will make the house of Ahab like the house of Jeroboam the son of Nebat, and like the house of Baasha the son of Ahijah.

10 'And the dogs shall eat Jezebel in the territory of Jezreel, and none shall bury *her*.'" Then he opened the door and fled.

11 ¶ Now Jehu came out to the servants of his master, and one said to him, "Is all well? Why did this mad fellow come to you?" And he said to them, "You know *very well* the man and his talk."

12 And they said, "It is a lie, tell us now." And he said, "Thus and thus he said to me, 'Thus says the LORD, "I have anointed you king over Israel."'"

13 Then they hurried and each man took his garment and placed it under him on the bare steps, and blew the trumpet, saying, "Jehu is king!"

14 ¶ So Jehu the son of Jehoshaphat the son of Nimshi conspired against Joram. Now Joram with all Israel was defending Ramoth-gilead against Hazael king of Aram,

15 but King [2]Joram had returned to Jezreel to be healed of the wounds which the Arameans had inflicted on him when he fought with Hazael king of Aram. So Jehu said, "If this is your mind, *then* let no one escape *or* leave the city to go tell *it* in Jezreel."

16 Then Jehu rode in a chariot and went to Jezreel, for Joram was lying there. And Ahaziah king of Judah had come down to see Joram.

17 ¶ Now the watchman was standing on the tower in Jezreel and he saw the company of Jehu as he came, and said, "I see a company." And Joram said, "Take a horseman and send him to meet them and let him say, 'Is it peace?' "

18 So a horseman went to meet him and said, "Thus says the king, 'Is it peace?' " And Jehu said, "What have you to do with peace? Turn behind me." And the watchman reported, "The messenger came to them, but he did not return."

19 Then he sent out a second horseman, who came to them and said, "Thus says the king, 'Is it peace?' " And Jehu answered, "What have you to do with peace? Turn behind me."

20 And the watchman reported, "He came even to them, and he did not return; and the driving is like the driving of Jehu the son of Nimshi, for he drives furiously."

21 ¶ Then Joram said, "Get ready." And they made his chariot ready. And Joram king of Israel and Ahaziah king of Judah went out, each in his chariot, and they went out to meet Jehu and found him in the property of Naboth the Jezreelite.

22 And it came about, when Joram saw Jehu, that he said, "Is it peace, Jehu?" And he answered, "What peace, so long as the harlotries of your mother Jezebel and her witchcrafts are so many?"

23 So Joram reined about and fled and said to Ahaziah, "*There is* treachery, O Ahaziah!"

24 And Jehu drew his bow with his full strength and shot Joram between his arms; and the arrow went through his heart, and he sank in his chariot.

25 Then *Jehu* said to Bidkar his officer, "Take *him* up and cast him into the [3]property of the field of Naboth the Jezreelite, for I remember when you and I were riding together after Ahab his father, that the LORD laid this oracle against him:

26 'Surely I have seen yesterday the blood of Naboth and the blood of his sons,' says the LORD, 'and I will repay you in this [3]property,' says the LORD. Now then, take and cast him into the property, according to the word of the LORD."

27 ¶ When Ahaziah the king of Judah saw *this*, he fled by the way of the garden house. And Jehu pursued him and said, "Shoot him too, in the chariot." *So they shot him* at the ascent of Gur, which is at Ibleam. But he fled to Megiddo and died there.

28 Then his servants carried him in a chariot to Jerusalem, and buried him in his grave with his fathers in the city of David.

29 ¶ Now in the eleventh year of Joram, the son of Ahab, Ahaziah became king over Judah.

30 ¶ When Jehu came to Jezreel, Jezebel heard *of it,* and she painted her eyes and adorned her head, and looked out the window.

31 And as Jehu entered the gate, she said, "Is it well, Zimri, your master's murderer?"

32 Then he lifted up his face to the window and said, "Who is on my side? Who?" And two or three officials looked down at him.

33 And he said, "Throw her down." So they threw her down, and some of her blood was sprinkled on the wall and on the horses, and he trampled her under foot.

34 When he came in, he ate and drank; and he said, "See now to this cursed woman and bury her, for she is a king's daughter."

35 And they went to bury her, but they found no more of her than the skull and the feet and the palms of her hands.

36 Therefore they returned and told him. And he said, "This is the word of the LORD, which He spoke by His servant Elijah the Tishbite, saying, 'In the property of Jezreel the dogs shall eat the flesh of Jezebel;

37 and the corpse of Jezebel shall be

---

[2] Heb., *Jehoram,* and so throughout this context

[3] Lit., *portion,* and so throughout this context

as dung on the face of the field in the property of Jezreel, so they cannot say, "This is Jezebel." ' "

CHAPTER 10

N OW Ahab had seventy sons in Samaria. And Jehu wrote letters and sent *them* to Samaria, to the rulers of Jezreel, the elders, and to the guardians of *the children of* Ahab, saying,

2 "And now, when this letter comes to you, since your master's sons are with you, as well as the chariots and horses and a fortified city and the weapons,

3 select the best and 4fittest of your master's sons, and set *him* on his father's throne, and fight for your master's house."

4 But they feared greatly and said, "Behold, the two kings did not stand before him; how then can we stand?"

5 And the one who *was* over the household, and he who *was* over the city, the elders, and the guardians of *the children*, sent *word* to Jehu, saying, "We are your servants, all that you say to us we will do, we will not make any man king; do what is good in your sight."

6 Then he wrote a letter to them a second time saying, "If you are on my side, and you will listen to my voice, take the heads of the men, your master's sons, and come to me at Jezreel tomorrow about this time." Now the king's sons, seventy persons, *were* with the great men of the city, *who* were rearing them.

7 And it came about when the letter came to them, that they took the king's sons, and slaughtered *them*, seventy persons, and put their heads in baskets, and sent *them* to him at Jezreel.

8 When the messenger came and told him, saying, "They have brought the heads of the king's sons," he said, "Put them in two heaps at the entrance of the gate until morning."

9 Now it came about in the morning, that he went out and stood, and said to all the people, "You are innocent; behold, I conspired against my master and killed him, but who killed all these?

10 "Know then that there shall fall to the earth nothing of the word of the LORD, which the LORD spoke concerning the house of Ahab, for the LORD has done what He spoke through His servant Elijah."

11 So Jehu killed all who remained of the house of Ahab in Jezreel, and all his great men and his acquaintances and his priests, until he left him without a survivor.

12 ¶ Then he arose and departed, and went to Samaria. On the way while he was at 5Beth-eked of the shepherds,

13 Jehu met the relatives of Ahaziah king of Judah and said, "Who are you?" And they answered, "We are the relatives of Ahaziah; and we have come down to greet the sons of the king and the sons of the queen mother."

14 And he said, "Take them alive." So they took them alive, and killed them at the pit of Beth-eked, forty-two men; and he left none of them.

15 ¶ Now when he had departed from there, he met Jehonadab the son of Rechab *coming* to meet him; and he greeted him and said to him, "Is your heart right, as my heart is with your heart?" And Jehonadab answered, "It is." *Jehu said*, "If it is, give *me* your hand." And he gave him his hand, and he took him up to him into the chariot.

16 And he said, "Come with me and see my zeal for the LORD." So he made him ride in his chariot.

17 And when he came to Samaria, he killed all who remained to Ahab in Samaria, until he had destroyed him, according to the word of the LORD, which He spoke to Elijah.

18 ¶ Then Jehu gathered all the people and said to them, "Ahab served Baal a little; Jehu will serve him much.

19 "And now, summon all the prophets of Baal, all his worshipers and all his priests; let no one be missing, for I have a great sacrifice for Baal; whoever is missing shall not live." But Jehu did it in cunning, in order that he might destroy the worshipers of Baal.

20 And Jehu said, "Sanctify a solemn assembly for Baal." And they proclaimed *it*.

21 Then Jehu sent throughout Israel and all the worshipers of Baal came, so

---

4 Lit., *most upright*   5 I.e., *house of binding*

that there was not a man left who did not come. And when they went into the house of Baal, the house of Baal was filled from one end to the other.

22 And he said to the one who *was* in charge of the wardrobe, "Bring out garments for all the worshipers of Baal." So he brought out garments for them.

23 And Jehu went into the house of Baal with Jehonadab the son of Rechab; and he said to the worshipers of Baal, "Search and see that there may be here with you none of the servants of the LORD, but only the worshipers of Baal."

24 Then they went in to offer sacrifices and burnt offerings. Now Jehu had stationed for himself eighty men outside, and he had said, "The one who permits any of the men whom I bring into your hands to escape, shall give up his life in exchange."

25 ¶ Then it came about, as soon as he had finished offering the burnt offering, that Jehu said to the guard and to the royal officers, "Go in, kill them; let none come out." And they killed them with the edge of the sword; and the guard and the royal officers threw *them* out, and went to the inner room of the house of Baal.

26 And they brought out the *sacred* pillars of the house of Baal, and burned them.

27 They also broke down the *sacred* pillar of Baal and broke down the house of Baal, and made it a latrine to this day.

28 Thus Jehu eradicated Baal out of Israel.

29 ¶ However, *as for* the sins of Jeroboam the son of Nebat, which he made Israel sin, from these Jehu did not depart, *even* the golden calves that *were* at Bethel and that *were* at Dan.

30 And the LORD said to Jehu, "Because you have done well in executing what is right in My eyes, *and* have done to the house of Ahab according to all that *was* in My heart, your sons of the fourth generation shall sit on the throne of Israel."

31 But Jehu was not careful to walk in the law of the LORD, the God of Israel, with all his heart; he did not depart from the sins of Jeroboam, which he made Israel sin.

32 ¶ In those days the LORD began to cut off *portions* from Israel; and Hazael defeated them throughout the territory of Israel:

33 from the Jordan eastward, all the land of Gilead, the Gadites and the Reubenites and the Manassites, from Aroer, which is by the valley of the Arnon, even Gilead and Bashan.

34 Now the rest of the acts of Jehu and all that he did and all his might, are they not written in the Book of the Chronicles of the Kings of Israel?

35 And Jehu slept with his fathers, and they buried him in Samaria. And Jehoahaz his son became king in his place.

36 Now the time which Jehu reigned over Israel in Samaria *was* twenty-eight years.

CHAPTER 11

WHEN Athaliah the mother of Ahaziah saw that her son was dead, she rose and destroyed all the royal offspring.

2 But Jehosheba, the daughter of King Joram, sister of Ahaziah, took Joash the son of Ahaziah and stole him from among the king's sons who were being put to death, and placed him and his nurse in the bedroom. So they hid him from Athaliah, and he was not put to death.

3 So he was hidden with her in the house of the LORD six years, while Athaliah was reigning over the land.

4 ¶ Now in the seventh year Jehoiada sent and brought the captains of hundreds of the Carites and of the [6]guard, and brought them to him in the house of the LORD. Then he made a covenant with them and put them under oath in the house of the LORD, and showed them the king's son.

5 And he commanded them, saying, "This is the thing that you shall do: one third of you, who come in on the sabbath and keep watch over the king's house

6 (one third also *shall be* at the gate Sur, and one third at the gate behind the [6]guards), shall keep watch over the house for defense.

7 "And two parts of you, *even* all who go out on the sabbath, shall also keep watch over the house of the LORD for the king.

[6] Lit., *runners*

8"Then you shall surround the king, each with his weapons in his hand; and whoever comes within the ranks shall be put to death. And be with the king when he goes out and when he comes in."

9 ¶ So the captains of hundreds did according to all that Jehoiada the priest commanded. And each one of them took his men who were to come in on the sabbath, with those who were to go out on the sabbath, and came to Jehoiada the priest.

10 And the priest gave to the captains of hundreds the spears and shields that had been King David's, which *were* in the house of the LORD.

11 And the guards stood each with his weapons in his hand, from the right side of the house to the left side of the house, by the altar and by the house, around the king.

12 Then he brought the king's son out and put the crown on him, and *gave him* the testimony; and they made him king and anointed him, and they clapped their hands and said, "*Long* live the king!"

13 ¶ When Athaliah heard the noise of the guard *and of* the people, she came to the people in the house of the LORD.

14 And she looked and behold, the king was standing by the pillar, according to the custom, with the captains and the trumpeters beside the king; and all the people of the land rejoiced and blew trumpets. Then Athaliah tore her clothes and cried, "Treason! Treason!"

15 And Jehoiada the priest commanded the captains of hundreds who were appointed over the army, and said to them, "Bring her out between the ranks, and whoever follows her put to death with the sword." For the priest said, "Let her not be put to death in the house of the LORD."

16 So they seized her, and when she arrived at the horses' entrance of the king's house, she was put to death there.

17 ¶ Then Jehoiada made a covenant between the LORD and the king and the people, that they should be the LORD's people, also between the king and the people.

18 And all the people of the land went to the house of Baal, and tore it down; his altars and his images they broke in pieces thoroughly, and killed Mattan the priest of Baal before the altars. And the priest appointed officers over the house of the LORD.

19 And he took the captains of hundreds and the Carites and the guards and all the people of the land; and they brought the king down from the house of the LORD, and came by the way of the gate of the guards to the king's house. And he sat on the throne of the kings.

20 So all the people of the land rejoiced and the city was quiet. For they had put Athaliah to death with the sword at the king's house.

21 ¶ Jehoash was seven years old when he became king.

CHAPTER 12

IN the seventh year of Jehu, Jehoash became king, and he reigned forty years in Jerusalem; and his mother's name was Zibiah of Beersheba.

2 And Jehoash did right in the sight of the LORD all his days in which Jehoiada the priest instructed him.

3 Only the high places were not taken away; the people still sacrificed and burned incense on the high places.

4 ¶ Then Jehoash said to the priests, "All the money of the sacred things which is brought into the house of the LORD, in current money, *both* the money of each man's assessment *and* all the money which any man's heart prompts him to bring into the house of the LORD,

5 let the priests take it for themselves, each from his acquaintance; and they shall repair the [7]damages of the house wherever any damage may be found.

6 ¶ But it came about that in the twenty-third year of King Jehoash the priests had not repaired the damages of the house.

7 Then King Jehoash called for Jehoiada the priest, and for the *other* priests and said to them, "Why do you not repair the damages of the house? Now therefore take no *more* money from your acquaintances, but pay it for the damages of the house."

8 So the priests agreed that they should take no *more* money from the

---

[7] Lit., *breaches*, and so through v. 12

people, nor repair the damages of the house.

9 ¶ But Jehoiada the priest took a chest and bored a hole in its lid, and put it beside the altar, on the right side as one comes into the house of the LORD; and the priests who guarded the threshold put in it all the money which was brought into the house of the LORD.

10 And when they saw that there was much money in the chest, the king's scribe and the high priest came up and tied *it* in bags and counted the money which was found in the house of the LORD.

11 And they gave the money which was weighed out into the hands of those who did the work, who had the oversight of the house of the LORD; and they paid it out to the carpenters and the builders, who worked on the house of the LORD;

12 and to the masons and the stone-cutters, and for buying timber and hewn stone to repair the damages to the house of the LORD, and for all that was laid out for the house to repair it.

13 But there were not made for the house of the LORD silver cups, snuffers, bowls, trumpets, any vessels of gold, or vessels of silver from the money which was brought into the house of the LORD;

14 for they gave that to those who did the work, and with it they repaired the house of the LORD.

15 Moreover, they did not require an accounting from the men into whose hand they gave the money to pay to those who did the work, for they dealt faithfully.

16 The money from the guilt offerings and the money from the sin offerings, was not brought into the house of the LORD; it was for the priests.

17 ¶ Then Hazael king of Aram went up and fought against Gath and captured it, and Hazael set his face to go up to Jerusalem.

18 And Jehoash king of Judah took all the sacred things that Jehoshaphat and Jehoram and Ahaziah, his fathers, kings of Judah, had dedicated, and his own sacred things and all the gold that was found among the treasuries of the house of the LORD and of the king's house, and sent *them* to Hazael king of Aram. Then he went away from Jerusalem.

19 ¶ Now the rest of the acts of Joash and all that he did, are they not written in the Book of the Chronicles of the Kings of Judah?

20 And his servants arose and made a conspiracy, and struck down Joash at the house of Millo *as he was* going down to Silla.

21 For Jozacar the son of Shimeath, and Jehozabad the son of Shomer, his servants, struck *him*, and he died; and they buried him with his fathers in the city of David, and Amaziah his son became king in his place.

CHAPTER 13

IN the twenty-third year of Joash the son of Ahaziah, king of Judah, Jehoahaz the son of Jehu became king over Israel at Samaria, *and he reigned* seventeen years.

2 And he did evil in the sight of the LORD, and followed the sins of Jeroboam the son of Nebat, with which he made Israel sin; he did not turn from them.

3 So the anger of the LORD was kindled against Israel, and He gave them continually into the hand of Hazael king of Aram, and into the hand of Ben-hadad the son of Hazael.

4 Then Jehoahaz entreated the favor of the LORD, and the LORD listened to him; for He saw the oppression of Israel, how the king of Aram oppressed them.

5 And the LORD gave Israel a [8]deliverer, so that they escaped from under the hand of the Arameans; and the sons of Israel lived in their tents as formerly.

6 Nevertheless they did not turn away from the sins of the house of Jeroboam, with which he made Israel sin, but walked in them; and the Asherah also remained standing in Samaria.

7 For he left to Jehoahaz of the army not more than fifty horsemen and ten chariots and 10,000 footmen, for the king of Aram had destroyed them and made them like the dust at threshing.

8 Now the rest of the acts of Jehoahaz, and all that he did and his might,

[8] Or, *savior*

are they not written in the Book of the Chronicles of the Kings of Israel?

9 And Jehoahaz slept with his fathers, and they buried him in Samaria; and Joash his son became king in his place.

10 ¶ In the thirty-seventh year of Joash king of Judah, Jehoash the son of Jehoahaz, became king over Israel in Samaria, *and reigned* sixteen years.

11 And he did evil in the sight of the LORD; he did not turn away from all the sins of Jeroboam the son of Nebat, with which he made Israel sin, but he walked in them.

12 Now the rest of the acts of Joash and all that he did and his might with which he fought against Amaziah king of Judah, are they not written in the Book of the Chronicles of the Kings of Israel?

13 So Joash slept with his fathers, and Jeroboam sat on his throne; and Joash was buried in Samaria with the kings of Israel.

14 ¶ When Elisha became sick with the illness of which he was to die, Joash the king of Israel came down to him and wept over him and said, "My father, my father, the chariots of Israel and its horsemen!"

15 And Elisha said to him, "Take a bow and arrows." So he took a bow and arrows.

16 Then he said to the king of Israel, "Put your hand on the bow." And he put his hand *on it*, then Elisha laid his hands on the king's hands.

17 And he said, "Open the window toward the east," and he opened *it*. Then Elisha said, "Shoot!" And he shot. And he said, "The LORD's arrow of victory, even the arrow of victory over Aram; for you shall defeat the Arameans at Aphek until you have destroyed *them*."

18 Then he said, "Take the arrows," and he took them. And he said to the king of Israel, "Strike the ground," and he struck *it* three times and stopped.

19 So the man of God was angry with him and said, "You should have struck five or six times, then you would have struck Aram until you would have destroyed *it*. But now you shall strike Aram *only* three times."

20 ¶ And Elisha died, and they buried him. Now the bands of the Moabites would invade the land in the spring of the year.

21 And as they were burying a man, behold, they saw a marauding band; and they cast the man into the grave of Elisha. And when the man touched the bones of Elisha he revived and stood up on his feet.

22 ¶ Now Hazael king of Aram had oppressed Israel all the days of Jehoahaz.

23 But the LORD was gracious to them and had compassion on them and turned to them because of His covenant with Abraham, Isaac, and Jacob, and would not destroy them or cast them from His presence until now.

24 When Hazael king of Aram died, Ben-hadad his son became king in his place.

25 Then Jehoash the son of Jehoahaz took again from the hand of Ben-hadad the son of Hazael the cities which he had taken in war from the hand of Jehoahaz his father. Three times Joash defeated him and recovered the cities of Israel.

CHAPTER 14

IN the second year of Joash son of Joahaz king of Israel, Amaziah the son of Joash king of Judah became king.

2 He was twenty-five years old when he became king, and he reigned twenty-nine years in Jerusalem. And his mother's name was Jehoaddin of Jerusalem.

3 And he did right in the sight of the LORD, yet not like David his father; he did according to all that Joash his father had done.

4 Only the high places were not taken away; the people still sacrificed and burned incense on the high places.

5 Now it came about, as soon as the kingdom was firmly in his hand, that he killed his servants who had slain the king his father.

6 But the sons of the slayers he did not put to death, according to what is written in the book of the law of Moses, as the LORD commanded, saying, "The fathers shall not be put to death for the sons, nor the sons be put

to death for the fathers; but each shall be put to death for his own sin."

7 He killed *of* Edom in the Valley of Salt 10,000 and took Sela by war, and named it Joktheel to this day.

8 Then Amaziah sent messengers to Jehoash, the son of Jehoahaz son of Jehu, king of Israel, saying, "Come, let us face each other."

9 And Jehoash king of Israel sent to Amaziah king of Judah, saying, "The thorn bush which was in Lebanon sent to the cedar which was in Lebanon, saying, 'Give your daughter to my son in marriage.' But there passed by a wild beast that was in Lebanon, and trampled the thorn bush.

10 "You have indeed defeated Edom, and your heart has become proud. Enjoy your glory and stay at home; for why should you provoke trouble so that you, even you, should fall, and Judah with you?"

11 ¶ But Amaziah would not listen. So Jehoash king of Israel went up; and he and Amaziah king of Judah faced each other at Beth-shemesh, which belongs to Judah.

12 And Judah was defeated by Israel, and they fled each to his tent.

13 Then Jehoash king of Israel captured Amaziah king of Judah, the son of Jehoash the son of Ahaziah, at Beth-shemesh, and came to Jerusalem and tore down the wall of Jerusalem from the Gate of Ephraim to the Corner Gate, 400 cubits.

14 And he took all the gold and silver and all the utensils which were found in the house of the LORD, and in the treasuries of the king's house, the hostages also, and returned to Samaria.

15 ¶ Now the rest of the acts of Jehoash which he did, and his might and how he fought with Amaziah king of Judah, are they not written in the Book of the Chronicles of the Kings of Israel?

16 So Jehoash slept with his fathers and was buried in Samaria with the kings of Israel; and Jeroboam his son became king in his place.

17 ¶ And Amaziah the son of Joash king of Judah lived fifteen years after the death of Jehoash son of Jehoahaz king of Israel.

18 Now the rest of the acts of Amaziah, are they not written in the Book

of the Chronicles of the Kings of Judah?

19 And they conspired against him in Jerusalem, and he fled to Lachish; but they sent after him to Lachish and killed him there.

20 Then they brought him on horses and he was buried at Jerusalem with his fathers in the city of David.

21 And all the people of Judah took Azariah, who *was* sixteen years old, and made him king in the place of his father Amaziah.

22 He built Elath and restored it to Judah, after the king slept with his fathers.

23 ¶ In the fifteenth year of Amaziah the son of Joash king of Judah, Jeroboam the son of Joash king of Israel became king in Samaria, *and reigned* forty-one years.

24 And he did evil in the sight of the LORD; he did not depart from all the sins of Jeroboam the son of Nebat, which he made Israel sin.

25 He restored the border of Israel from the entrance of Hamath as far as the Sea of the Arabah, according to the word of the LORD, the God of Israel, which He spoke through His servant Jonah the son of Amittai, the prophet, who was of Gath-hepher.

26 For the LORD saw the affliction of Israel, *which was* very bitter; for there was neither bond nor free, nor was there any helper for Israel.

27 And the LORD did not say that He would blot out the name of Israel from under heaven, but He saved them by the hand of Jeroboam the son of Joash.

28 ¶ Now the rest of the acts of Jeroboam and all that he did and his might, how he fought and how he recovered for Israel, Damascus and Hamath, *which had belonged* to Judah, are they not written in the Book of the Chronicles of the Kings of Israel?

29 And Jeroboam slept with his fathers, even with the kings of Israel, and Zechariah his son became king in his place.

CHAPTER 15

IN the twenty-seventh year of Jeroboam king of Israel, Azariah son of Amaziah king of Judah became king.

2 He was sixteen years old when he became king, and he reigned fifty-two years in Jerusalem; and his mother's name was Jecoliah of Jerusalem.

3 And he did right in the sight of the LORD, according to all that his father Amaziah had done.

4 Only the high places were not taken away; the people still sacrificed and burned incense on the high places.

5 And the LORD struck the king, so that he was a leper to the day of his death. And he lived in a separate house, while Jotham the king's son was over the household, judging the people of the land.

6 Now the rest of the acts of Azariah and all that he did, are they not written in the Book of the Chronicles of the Kings of Judah?

7 And Azariah slept with his fathers, and they buried him with his fathers in the city of David, and Jotham his son became king in his place.

8 ¶ In the thirty-eighth year of Azariah king of Judah, Zechariah the son of Jeroboam became king over Israel in Samaria for six months.

9 And he did evil in the sight of the LORD, as his fathers had done; he did not depart from the sins of Jeroboam the son of Nebat, which he made Israel sin.

10 Then Shallum the son of Jabesh conspired against him and struck him before the people and killed him, and reigned in his place.

11 Now the rest of the acts of Zechariah, behold they are written in the Book of the Chronicles of the Kings of Israel.

12 This is the word of the LORD which He spoke to Jehu, saying, "Your sons to the fourth generation shall sit on the throne of Israel." And so it was.

13 ¶ Shallum son of Jabesh became king in the thirty-ninth year of Uzziah king of Judah, and he reigned one month in Samaria.

14 Then Menahem son of Gadi went up from Tirzah and came to Samaria, and struck Shallum son of Jabesh in Samaria, and killed him and became king in his place.

15 Now the rest of the acts of Shallum and his conspiracy which he made, behold they are written in the Book of the Chronicles of the Kings of Israel.

16 Then Menahem struck Tiphsah and all who were in it and its borders from Tirzah, because they did not open to him, therefore he struck it; and he ripped up all its women who were with child.

17 ¶ In the thirty-ninth year of Azariah king of Judah, Menahem son of Gadi became king over Israel and reigned ten years in Samaria.

18 And he did evil in the sight of the LORD; he did not depart all his days from the sins of Jeroboam the son of Nebat, which he made Israel sin.

19 ¶ Pul, king of Assyria, came against the land, and Menahem gave Pul a thousand talents of silver so that his hand might be with him to strengthen the kingdom under his rule.

20 Then Menahem exacted the money from Israel, even from all the mighty men of wealth, from each man fifty shekels of silver to pay the king of Assyria. So the king of Assyria returned and did not remain there in the land.

21 Now the rest of the acts of Menahem and all that he did, are they not written in the Book of the Chronicles of the Kings of Israel?

22 And Menahem slept with his fathers, and Pekahiah his son became king in his place.

23 ¶ In the fiftieth year of Azariah king of Judah, Pekahiah son of Menahem became king over Israel in Samaria, and reigned two years.

24 And he did evil in the sight of the LORD; he did not depart from the sins of Jeroboam son of Nebat, which he made Israel sin.

25 Then Pekah son of Remaliah, his officer, conspired against him and struck him in Samaria, in the castle of the king's house with Argob and Arieh; and with him were fifty men of the Gileadites, and he killed him and became king in his place.

26 Now the rest of the acts of Pekahiah and all that he did, behold they are written in the Book of the Chronicles of the Kings of Israel.

27 ¶ In the fifty-second year of Azariah king of Judah, Pekah son of Remaliah became king over Israel in Samaria, and reigned twenty years.

28 And he did evil in the sight of the LORD; he did not depart from the sins

of Jeroboam son of Nebat, which he made Israel sin.

29 ¶ In the days of Pekah king of Israel, Tiglath-pileser king of Assyria came and captured Ijon and Abel-beth-maacah and Janoah and Kedesh and Hazor and Gilead and Galilee, all the land of Naphtali; and he carried them captive to Assyria.

30 And Hoshea the son of Elah made a conspiracy against Pekah the son of Remaliah, and struck him and put him to death and became king in his place, in the twentieth year of Jotham the son of Uzziah.

31 Now the rest of the acts of Pekah and all that he did, behold, they are written in the Book of the Chronicles of the Kings of Israel.

32 ¶ In the second year of Pekah the son of Remaliah king of Israel, Jotham the son of Uzziah king of Judah became king.

33 He was twenty-five years old when he became king, and he reigned sixteen years in Jerusalem; and his mother's name *was* Jerusha the daughter of Zadok.

34 And he did what was right in the sight of the LORD; he did according to all that his father Uzziah had done.

35 Only the high places were not taken away; the people still sacrificed and burned incense on the high places. He built the upper gate of the house of the LORD.

36 Now the rest of the acts of Jotham and all that he did, are they not written in the Book of the Chronicles of the Kings of Judah?

37 In those days the LORD began to send Rezin king of Aram and Pekah the son of Remaliah against Judah.

38 And Jotham slept with his fathers, and he was buried with his fathers in the city of David his father; and Ahaz his son became king in his place.

CHAPTER 16

IN the seventeenth year of Pekah the son of Remaliah, Ahaz the son of Jotham, king of Judah, became king.

2 Ahaz *was* twenty years old when he became king, and he reigned sixteen years in Jerusalem; and he did not do what was right in the sight of the LORD his God, as his father David *had done.*

3 But he walked in the way of the kings of Israel, and even made his son pass through the fire, according to the abominations of the nations whom the LORD had driven out from before the sons of Israel.

4 And he sacrificed and burned incense on the high places and on the hills and under every green tree.

5 ¶ Then Rezin king of Aram and Pekah son of Remaliah, king of Israel, came up to Jerusalem to *wage* war; and they besieged Ahaz, but could not overcome him.

6 At that time Rezin king of Aram recovered Elath for Aram, and cleared the Judeans out of Elath entirely; and the Arameans came to Elath, and have lived there to this day.

7 ¶ So Ahaz sent messengers to Tiglath-pileser king of Assyria, saying, "I am your servant and your son; come up and deliver me from the hand of the king of Aram, and from the hand of the king of Israel, who are rising up against me."

8 And Ahaz took the silver and gold that was found in the house of the LORD and in the treasuries of the king's house, and sent a present to the king of Assyria.

9 So the king of Assyria listened to him; and the king of Assyria went up against Damascus and captured it, and carried *the people* of it away into exile to Kir, and put Rezin to death.

10 ¶ Now King Ahaz went to Damascus to meet Tiglath-pileser king of Assyria, and saw the altar which *was* at Damascus; and King Ahaz sent to Urijah the priest the pattern of the altar and its model, according to all its workmanship.

11 So Urijah the priest built an altar; according to all that King Ahaz had sent from Damascus, thus Urijah the priest made *it,* before the coming of King Ahaz from Damascus.

12 And when the king came from Damascus, the king saw the altar; then the king approached the altar and went up to it,

13 and burned his burnt offering and his meal offering, and poured his libation and sprinkled the blood of his peace offerings on the altar.

14 And the bronze altar, which *was* before the LORD, he brought from the front of the house, from between *his*

altar and the house of the LORD, and he put it on the north side of *his* altar.

15 Then King Ahaz commanded Urijah the priest, saying, "Upon the great altar burn the morning burnt offering and the evening meal offering and the king's burnt offering and his meal offering, with the burnt offering of all the people of the land and their meal offering and their libations; and sprinkle on it all the blood of the burnt offering and all the blood of the sacrifice. But the bronze altar shall be for me to inquire *by*."

16 So Urijah the priest did according to all that King Ahaz commanded.

17 ¶ Then King Ahaz cut off the borders of the stands, and removed the laver from them; he also took down the sea from the bronze oxen which were under it, and put it on a pavement of stone.

18 And the covered way for the sabbath which they had built in the house, and the outer entry of the king, he removed from the house of the LORD because of the king of Assyria.

19 Now the rest of the acts of Ahaz which he did, are they not written in the Book of the Chronicles of the Kings of Judah?

20 So Ahaz slept with his fathers, and was buried with his fathers in the city of David; and his son Hezekiah reigned in his place.

CHAPTER 17

IN the twelfth year of Ahaz king of Judah, Hoshea the son of Elah became king over Israel in Samaria, *and reigned* nine years.

2 And he did evil in the sight of the LORD, only not as the kings of Israel who were before him.

3 Shalmaneser king of Assyria came up against him, and Hoshea became his servant and paid him tribute.

4 But the king of Assyria found conspiracy in Hoshea, who had sent messengers to So king of Egypt and had offered no tribute to the king of Assyria, as *he had done* year by year; so the king of Assyria shut him up and bound him in prison.

5 Then the king of Assyria invaded the whole land and went up to Samaria and besieged it three years.

6 In the ninth year of Hoshea, the king of Assyria captured Samaria and carried Israel away into exile to Assyria, and settled them in Halah and Habor, *on* the river of Gozan, and in the cities of the Medes.

7 ¶ Now *this* came about, because the sons of Israel had sinned against the LORD their God, who had brought them up from the land of Egypt from under the hand of Pharaoh, king of Egypt, and they had [9]feared other gods

8 and walked in the customs of the nations whom the LORD had driven out before the sons of Israel, and *in the customs* of the kings of Israel which they had introduced.

9 And the sons of Israel did things secretly which were not right, against the LORD their God. Moreover, they built for themselves high places in all their towns, from watchtower to fortified city.

10 And they set for themselves *sacred* pillars and [10]Asherim on every high hill and under every green tree,

11 and there they burned incense on all the high places as the nations *did* which the LORD had carried away to exile before them; and they did evil things provoking the LORD.

12 And they served idols, concerning which the LORD had said to them, "You shall not do this thing."

13 Yet the LORD warned Israel and Judah, through all His prophets *and* every seer, saying, "Turn from your evil ways and keep My commandments, My statutes according to all the law which I commanded your fathers, and which I sent to you through My servants the prophets."

14 However, they did not listen, but stiffened their neck like their fathers, who did not believe in the LORD their God.

15 And they rejected His statutes and His covenant which He made with their fathers, and His warnings with which He warned them. And they followed vanity and became vain, and *went* after the nations which surrounded them, concerning which the LORD had commanded them not to do like them.

16 And they forsook all the commandments of the LORD their God and made for themselves molten images,

---

[9] Lit., *revered,* and so throughout this context
[10] I.e., wooden symbols of a female deity

even two calves, and made an Asherah and worshiped all the host of heaven and served Baal.

17 Then they made their sons and their daughters pass through the fire, and practiced divination and enchantments, and sold themselves to do evil in the sight of the LORD, provoking Him.

18 So the LORD was very angry with Israel, and removed them from His sight; none was left except the tribe of Judah.

19 ¶ Also Judah did not keep the commandments of the LORD their God, but walked in the customs which Israel had introduced.

20 And the LORD rejected all the descendants of Israel and afflicted them and gave them into the hand of plunderers, until He had cast them out of His sight.

21 When He had torn Israel from the house of David, they made Jeroboam the son of Nebat king. Then Jeroboam drove Israel away from following the LORD, and made them commit a great sin.

22 And the sons of Israel walked in all the sins of Jeroboam which he did; they did not depart from them,

23 until the LORD removed Israel from His sight, as He spoke through all His servants the prophets. So Israel was carried away into exile from their own land to Assyria until this day.

24 ¶ And the king of Assyria brought *men* from Babylon and from Cuthah and from Avva and from Hamath and Sephar-vaim, and settled *them* in the cities of Samaria in place of the sons of Israel. So they possessed Samaria and lived in its cities.

25 And it came about at the beginning of their living there, that they did not fear the LORD; therefore the LORD sent lions among them which killed some of them.

26 So they spoke to the king of Assyria, saying, "The nations whom you have carried away into exile in the cities of Samaria do not know the custom of the god of the land; so he has sent lions among them, and behold, they kill them because they do not know the custom of the god of the land."

27 ¶ Then the king of Assyria commanded, saying, "Take there one of the priests whom you carried away into exile, and let him go and live there; and let him teach them the custom of the god of the land."

28 So one of the priests whom they had carried away into exile from Samaria came and lived at Bethel, and taught them how they should fear the LORD.

29 But every nation still made gods of its own and put them in the houses of the high places which the people of Samaria had made, every nation in their cities in which they lived.

30 And the men of Babylon made Succoth-benoth, the men of Cuth made Nergal, the men of Hamath made Ashima,

31 and the Avvites made Nibhaz and Tartak; and the Sepharvites burned their children in the fire to Adrammelech and Anammelech the gods of Sepharvaim.

32 They also feared the LORD and appointed from among themselves priests of the high places, who acted for them in the houses of the high places.

33 They feared the LORD and served their own gods according to the custom of the nations from among whom they had been carried away into exile.

34 ¶ To this day they do according to the earlier customs: they do not fear the LORD, nor do they follow their statutes or their ordinances or the law, or the commandments which the LORD commanded the sons of Jacob, whom He named Israel;

35 with whom the LORD made a covenant and commanded them, saying, "You shall not fear other gods, nor bow down yourselves to them nor serve them nor sacrifice to them.

36 "But the LORD, who brought you up from the land of Egypt with great power and with an outstretched arm, Him you shall fear, and to Him you shall bow yourselves down, and to Him you shall sacrifice.

37 "And the statutes and the ordinances and the law and the commandment, which He wrote for you, you shall observe to do forever; and you shall not fear other gods.

38 "And the covenant that I have made with you, you shall not forget, nor shall you fear other gods.

39"But the LORD your God you shall fear; and He will deliver you from the hand of all your enemies."

40 However, they did not listen, but they did according to their earlier custom.

41 So while these nations feared the LORD, they also served their idols; their children likewise and their grandchildren, as their fathers did, so they do to this day.

CHAPTER 18

NOW it came about in the third year of Hoshea, the son of Elah king of Israel, that Hezekiah the son of Ahaz king of Judah became king.

2 He was twenty-five years old when he became king, and he reigned twenty-nine years in Jerusalem; and his mother's name was Abi the daughter of Zechariah.

3 And he did right in the sight of the LORD, according to all that his father David had done.

4 He removed the high places and broke down the *sacred* pillars and cut down the [11]Asherah. He also broke in pieces the bronze serpent that Moses had made, for until those days the sons of Israel burned incense to it; and it was called [12]Nehushtan.

5 He trusted in the LORD, the God of Israel; so that after him there was none like him among all the kings of Judah, nor *among those* who were before him.

6 For he clung to the LORD; he did not depart from following Him, but kept His commandments, which the LORD had commanded Moses.

7 And the LORD was with him; wherever he went he prospered. And he rebelled against the king of Assyria and did not serve him.

8 He defeated the Philistines as far as Gaza and its territory, from watchtower to fortified city.

9 ¶ Now it came about in the fourth year of King Hezekiah, which was the seventh year of Hoshea son of Elah king of Israel, that Shalmaneser king of Assyria came up against Samaria and besieged it.

10 And at the end of three years they captured it; in the sixth year of Hezekiah, which was the ninth year of Hoshea king of Israel, Samaria was captured.

11 Then the king of Assyria carried Israel away into exile to Assyria, and put them in Halah and on the Habor, the river of Gozan, and in the cities of the Medes,

12 because they did not obey the voice of the LORD their God, but transgressed His covenant, even all that Moses the servant of the LORD commanded; they would neither listen, nor do *it.*

13 ¶ Now in the fourteenth year of King Hezekiah, Sennacherib king of Assyria came up against all the fortified cities of Judah and seized them.

14 Then Hezekiah king of Judah sent to the king of Assyria at Lachish, saying, "I have done wrong. Withdraw from me; whatever you impose on me I will bear." So the king of Assyria required of Hezekiah king of Judah three hundred talents of silver and thirty talents of gold.

15 And Hezekiah gave *him* all the silver which was found in the house of the LORD, and in the treasuries of the king's house.

16 At that time Hezekiah cut off *the gold from* the doors of the temple of the LORD, and *from* the doorposts which Hezekiah king of Judah had overlaid, and gave it to the king of Assyria.

17 ¶ Then the king of Assyria sent Tartan and Rab-saris and Rabshakeh from Lachish to King Hezekiah with a large army to Jerusalem. So they went up and came to Jerusalem. And when they went up, they came and stood by the conduit of the upper pool, which is on the highway of the [13]fuller's field.

18 When they called to the king, Eliakim the son of Hilkiah, who was over the household, and Shebnah the scribe and Joah the son of Asaph the recorder, came out to them.

19 Then Rabshakeh said to them, "Say now to Hezekiah, 'Thus says the great king, the king of Assyria, "What is this confidence that you have?

20"You say (but *they are* only empty words), '*I have* counsel and strength for the war.' Now on whom do you

[11] I.e., wooden symbol of a female deity
[12] I.e., a piece of bronze
[13] I.e., launderer's

rely, that you have rebelled against me?

21"Now behold, you rely on the staff of this crushed reed, *even* on Egypt; on which if a man leans, it will go into his hand and pierce it. So is Pharaoh king of Egypt to all who rely on him.

22"But if you say to me, 'We trust in the LORD our God,' is it not He whose high places and whose altars Hezekiah has taken away, and has said to Judah and to Jerusalem, 'You shall worship before this altar in Jerusalem'?

23"Now therefore, come, make a bargain with my master the king of Assyria, and I will give you two thousand horses, if you are able on your part to set riders on them.

24"How then can you repulse one official of the least of my master's servants, and rely on Egypt for chariots and for horsemen?

25"Have I now come up without the LORD's approval against this place to destroy it? The LORD said to me, 'Go up against this land and destroy it.' " ' "

26 ¶ Then Eliakim the son of Hilkiah, and Shebnah and Joah, said to Rabshakeh, "Speak now to your servants in Aramaic, for we understand *it;* and do not speak with us in Judean, in the hearing of the people who are on the wall."

27 But Rabshakeh said to them, "Has my master sent me only to your master and to you to speak these words, *and* not to the men who sit on the wall, *doomed* to eat their own dung and drink their own urine with you?"

28 Then Rabshakeh stood and cried with a loud voice in Judean, saying, "Hear the word of the great king, the king of Assyria.

29"Thus says the king, 'Do not let Hezekiah deceive you, for he will not be able to deliver you from my hand;

30 nor let Hezekiah make you trust in the LORD, saying, "The LORD will surely deliver us, and this city shall not be given into the hand of the king of Assyria."

31 'Do not listen to Hezekiah, for thus says the king of Assyria, "Make your peace with me and come out to me, and eat each of his vine and each of his fig tree and drink each of the waters of his own cistern,

32 until I come and take you away to a land like your own land, a land of grain and new wine, a land of bread and vineyards, a land of olive trees and honey, that you may live and not die." But do not listen to Hezekiah, when he misleads you, saying, "The LORD will deliver us."

33 'Has any one of the gods of the nations delivered his land from the hand of the king of Assyria?

34 'Where are the gods of Hamath and Arpad? Where are the gods of Sepharvaim, Hena and Ivvah? Have they delivered Samaria from my hand?

35 'Who among all the gods of the lands have delivered their land from my hand, that the LORD should deliver Jerusalem from my hand?' "

36 But the people were silent and answered him not a word, for the king's commandment was, "Do not answer him."

37 Then Eliakim the son of Hilkiah, who was over the household, and Shebna the scribe and Joah the son of Asaph, the recorder, came to Hezekiah with their clothes torn and told him the words of Rabshakeh.

CHAPTER 19

AND when King Hezekiah heard *it,* he tore his clothes, covered himself with sackcloth and entered the house of the LORD.

2 Then he sent Eliakim who was over the household with Shebna the scribe and the elders of the priests, covered with sackcloth, to Isaiah the prophet the son of Amoz.

3 And they said to him, "Thus says Hezekiah, 'This day is a day of distress, rebuke, and rejection; for children have come to birth, and there is no strength to *deliver.*

4 'Perhaps the LORD your God will hear all the words of Rabshakeh, whom his master the king of Assyria has sent to reproach the living God, and will rebuke the words which the LORD your God has heard. Therefore, offer a prayer for the remnant that is left.' "

5 So the servants of King Hezekiah came to Isaiah.

6 And Isaiah said to them, "Thus you shall say to your master, 'Thus

says the LORD, "Do not be afraid because of the words that you have heard, with which the servants of the king of Assyria have blasphemed Me.

7"Behold, I will put a spirit in him so that he shall hear a rumor and return to his own land. And I will make him fall by the sword in his own land." ' "

8 ¶ Then Rabshakeh returned and found the king of Assyria fighting against Libnah, for he had heard that the king had left Lachish.

9 When he heard *them* say concerning Tirhakah king of Cush, "Behold, he has come out to fight against you," he sent messengers again to Hezekiah saying,

10"Thus you shall say to Hezekiah king of Judah, 'Do not let your God in whom you trust deceive you saying, "Jerusalem shall not be given into the hand of the king of Assyria."

11 'Behold, you have heard what the kings of Assyria have done to all the lands, destroying them completely. So will you be spared?

12 'Did the gods of those nations which my fathers destroyed deliver them, *even* Gozan and Haran and Rezeph and the sons of Eden who *were* in Telassar?

13 'Where is the king of Hamath, the king of Arpad, the king of the city of Sepharvaim, and *of* Hena and Ivvah?' "

14 ¶ Then Hezekiah took the letter from the hand of the messengers and read it, and he went up to the house of the LORD and spread it out before the LORD.

15 And Hezekiah prayed before the LORD and said, "O LORD, the God of Israel, who art enthroned *above* the cherubim, Thou art the God, Thou alone, of all the kingdoms of the earth. Thou hast made heaven and earth.

16"Incline Thine ear, O LORD, and hear; open Thine eyes, O LORD, and see; and listen to the words of Sennacherib, which he has sent to reproach the living God.

17"Truly, O LORD, the kings of Assyria have devastated the nations and their lands

18 and have cast their gods into the fire, for they were not gods but the work of men's hands, wood and stone. So they have destroyed them.

19"And now, O LORD our God, I pray, deliver us from his hand that all the kingdoms of the earth may know that Thou alone, O LORD, art God."

20 ¶ Then Isaiah the son of Amoz sent to Hezekiah saying, "Thus says the LORD, the God of Israel, 'Because you have prayed to Me about Sennacherib king of Assyria, I have heard *you.*'

21"This is the word that the LORD has spoken against him:

'She has despised you and
    mocked you,
The virgin daughter of Zion;
She has shaken *her* head behind
    you,
The daughter of Jerusalem!

22 'Whom have you reproached and
    blasphemed?
And against whom have you
    raised *your* voice,
And haughtily lifted up your
    eyes?
Against the Holy One of Israel!

23 'Through your messengers you
    have reproached the Lord,
And you have said, "With my
    many chariots
I came up to the heights of the
    mountains,
To the remotest parts of Lebanon;
And I cut down its tall cedars
    and its choice cypresses.
And I entered its farthest lodging
    place, its thickest forest.

24 "I dug *wells* and drank foreign
    waters,
And with the sole of my feet I
    dried up
All the rivers of Egypt."

25 ¶ 'Have you not heard?
Long ago I did it;
From ancient times I planned it.
Now I have brought it to pass,
That you should turn fortified
    cities into ruinous heaps.

26 'Therefore their inhabitants were
    short of strength,
They were dismayed and put to
    shame;
They were as the vegetation of
    the field and as the green herb,
As grass on the housetops is
    scorched before it is grown up.

27 'But I know your sitting down,
And your going out and your
coming in,
And your raging against Me.
28 'Because of your raging against
Me,
And because your arrogance has
come up to My ears,
Therefore I will put My hook in
your nose,
And My bridle in your lips,
And I will turn you back by the
way which you came.
29 ¶ 'Then this shall be the sign for
you: you shall eat this year what
grows of itself, in the second year
what springs from the same, and in
the third year sow, reap, plant vineyards, and eat their fruit.
30 'And the surviving remnant of the
house of Judah shall again take root
downward and bear fruit upward.
31 'For out of Jerusalem shall go
forth a remnant, and out of Mount
Zion survivors. The zeal of [14]the LORD
shall perform this.
32 'Therefore thus says the LORD concerning the king of Assyria, "He shall
not come to this city or shoot an
arrow there; neither shall he come
before it with a shield, nor throw up a
mound against it.
33 "By the way that he came, by the
same he shall return, and he shall not
come to this city," ' declares the LORD.
34 'For I will defend this city to save
it for My own sake and for My servant
David's sake.' "
35 ¶ Then it happened that night
that the angel of the LORD went out,
and struck 185,000 in the camp of the
Assyrians; and when men rose early in
the morning, behold, all of them were
dead.
36 So Sennacherib king of Assyria
departed and returned *home*, and lived
at Nineveh.
37 And it came about as he was worshiping in the house of Nisroch his
god, that Adrammelech and Sharezer
killed him with the sword; and they
escaped into the land of Ararat. And
Esarhaddon his son became king in his
place.

CHAPTER 20

IN those days Hezekiah became mortally ill. And Isaiah the prophet the

son of Amoz came to him and said to
him, "Thus says the LORD, 'Set your
house in order, for you shall die and
not live.' "
2 Then he turned his face to the
wall, and prayed to the LORD, saying,
3 "Remember now, O LORD, I beseech Thee, how I have walked before
Thee in truth and with a whole heart,
and have done what is good in Thy
sight." And Hezekiah wept bitterly.
4 And it came about before Isaiah
had gone out of the middle court, that
the word of the LORD came to him,
saying,
5 "Return and say to Hezekiah the
leader of My people, 'Thus says the
LORD, the God of your father David, "I
have heard your prayer, I have seen
your tears; behold, I will heal you. On
the third day you shall go up to the
house of the LORD.
6 "And I will add fifteen years to
your life, and I will deliver you and
this city from the hand of the king of
Assyria; and I will defend this city for
My own sake and for My servant David's sake." ' "
7 Then Isaiah said, "Take a cake of
figs." And they took and laid *it* on the
boil, and he recovered.
8 ¶ Now Hezekiah said to Isaiah,
"What will be the sign that the LORD
will heal me, and that I shall go up to
the house of the LORD the third day?"
9 And Isaiah said, "This shall be the
sign to you from the LORD, that the
LORD will do the thing that He has
spoken: shall the shadow go forward
ten steps or go back ten steps?"
10 So Hezekiah answered, "It is easy
for the shadow to decline ten steps;
no, but let the shadow turn backward
ten steps."
11 And Isaiah the prophet cried to
the LORD, and He brought the shadow
on the stairway back ten steps by
which it had gone down on the stairway of Ahaz.
12 ¶ At that time Berodach-baladan
a son of Baladan, king of Babylon, sent
letters and a present to Hezekiah, for
he heard that Hezekiah had been sick.
13 And Hezekiah listened to them,
and showed them all his treasure
house, the silver and the gold and the
spices and the precious oil and the
house of his armor and all that was
found in his treasuries. There was

[14] Some ancient mss. read the LORD of hosts

nothing in his house, nor in all his dominion, that Hezekiah did not show them.

14 Then Isaiah the prophet came to King Hezekiah and said to him, "What did these men say, and from where have they come to you?" And Hezekiah said, "They have come from a far country, from Babylon."

15 And he said, "What have they seen in your house?" So Hezekiah answered, "They have seen all that is in my house; there is nothing among my treasuries that I have not shown them."

16 ¶ Then Isaiah said to Hezekiah, "Hear the word of the LORD.

17 'Behold, the days are coming when all that is in your house, and all that your fathers have laid up in store to this day shall be carried to Babylon; nothing shall be left,' says the LORD.

18 'And some of your sons who shall issue from you, whom you shall beget, shall be taken away; and they shall become officials in the palace of the king of Babylon.' "

19 Then Hezekiah said to Isaiah, "The word of the LORD which you have spoken is good." For he thought, "Is it not so, if there shall be peace and truth in my days?"

20 Now the rest of the acts of Hezekiah and all his might, and how he made the pool and the conduit, and brought water into the city, are they not written in the Book of the Chronicles of the Kings of Judah?

21 So Hezekiah slept with his fathers, and Manasseh his son became king in his place.

CHAPTER 21

MANASSEH was twelve years old when he became king, and he reigned fifty-five years in Jerusalem; and his mother's name was Hephzibah.

2 And he did evil in the sight of the LORD, according to the abominations of the nations whom the LORD dispossessed before the sons of Israel.

3 For he rebuilt the high places which Hezekiah his father had destroyed; and he erected altars for Baal and made an Asherah, as Ahab king of Israel had done, and worshiped all the host of heaven and served them.

4 And he built altars in the house of the LORD, of which the LORD had said, "In Jerusalem I will put My name."

5 For he built altars for all the host of heaven in the two courts of the house of the LORD.

6 And he made his son pass through the fire, practiced witchcraft and used divination, and dealt with mediums and spiritists. He did much evil in the sight of the LORD provoking *Him to anger.*

7 Then he set the carved image of Asherah that he had made, in the house of which the LORD said to David and to his son Solomon, "In this house and in Jerusalem, which I have chosen from all the tribes of Israel, I will put My name forever.

8 "And I will not make the feet of Israel wander anymore from the land which I gave their fathers, if only they will observe to do according to all that I have commanded them, and according to all the law that My servant Moses commanded them."

9 But they did not listen, and Manasseh seduced them to do evil more than the nations whom the LORD destroyed before the sons of Israel.

10 ¶ Now the LORD spoke through His servants the prophets, saying,

11 "Because Manasseh king of Judah has done these abominations, having done wickedly more than all the Amorites did who *were* before him, and has also made Judah sin with his idols;

12 therefore thus says the LORD, the God of Israel, 'Behold, I am bringing *such* calamity on Jerusalem and Judah, that whoever hears of it, both his ears shall tingle.

13 'And I will stretch over Jerusalem the line of Samaria and the plummet of the house of Ahab, and I will wipe Jerusalem as one wipes a dish, wiping it and turning it upside down.

14 'And I will abandon the remnant of My inheritance and deliver them into the hand of their enemies, and they shall become as plunder and spoil to all their enemies;

15 because they have done evil in My sight, and have been provoking Me to anger, since the day their fathers came from Egypt, even to this day.' "

16 ¶ Moreover, Manasseh shed very much innocent blood until he had filled Jerusalem from one end to another; besides his sin with which he

made Judah sin, in doing evil in the sight of the LORD.

17 Now the rest of the acts of Manasseh and all that he did and his sin which he committed, are they not written in the Book of the Chronicles of the Kings of Judah?

18 And Manasseh slept with his fathers and was buried in the garden of his own house, in the garden of Uzza, and Amon his son became king in his place.

19 ¶ Amon was twenty-two years old when he became king, and he reigned two years in Jerusalem; and his mother's name *was* Meshullemeth the daughter of Haruz of Jotbah.

20 And he did evil in the sight of the LORD, as Manasseh his father had done.

21 For he walked in all the way that his father had walked, and served the idols that his father had served and worshiped them.

22 So he forsook the LORD, the God of his fathers, and did not walk in the way of the LORD.

23 And the servants of Amon conspired against him and killed the king in his own house.

24 Then the people of the land killed all those who had conspired against King Amon, and the people of the land made Josiah his son king in his place.

25 Now the rest of the acts of Amon which he did, are they not written in the Book of the Chronicles of the Kings of Judah?

26 And he was buried in his grave in the garden of Uzza, and Josiah his son became king in his place.

CHAPTER 22

JOSIAH was eight years old when he became king, and he reigned thirty-one years in Jerusalem; and his mother's name *was* Jedidah the daughter of Adaiah of Bozkath.

2 And he did right in the sight of the LORD and walked in all the way of his father David, nor did he turn aside to the right or to the left.

3 ¶ Now it came about in the eighteenth year of King Josiah that the king sent Shaphan, the son of Azaliah the son of Meshullam the scribe, to the house of the LORD saying,

4 "Go up to Hilkiah the high priest that he may count the money brought in to the house of the LORD which the doorkeepers have gathered from the people.

5 "And let them deliver it into the hand of the workmen who have the oversight of the house of the LORD, and let them give it to the workmen who are in the house of the LORD to repair the damages of the house,

6 to the carpenters and the builders and the masons and for buying timber and hewn stone to repair the house.

7 "Only no accounting shall be made with them for the money delivered into their hands, for they deal faithfully."

8 ¶ Then Hilkiah the high priest said to Shaphan the scribe, "I have found the book of the law in the house of the LORD." And Hilkiah gave the book to Shaphan who read it.

9 And Shaphan the scribe came to the king and brought back word to the king and said, "Your servants have emptied out the money that was found in the house, and have delivered it into the hand of the workmen who have the oversight of the house of the LORD."

10 Moreover, Shaphan the scribe told the king saying, "Hilkiah the priest has given me a book." And Shaphan read it in the presence of the king.

11 And it came about when the king heard the words of the book of the law, that he tore his clothes.

12 Then the king commanded Hilkiah the priest, Ahikam the son of Shaphan, Achbor the son of Micaiah, Shaphan the scribe, and Asaiah the king's servant saying,

13 "Go, inquire of the LORD for me and the people and all Judah concerning the words of this book that has been found, for great is the wrath of the LORD that burns against us, because our fathers have not listened to the words of this book, to do according to all that is written concerning us."

14 ¶ So Hilkiah the priest, Ahikam, Achbor, Shaphan, and Asaiah went to Huldah the prophetess, the wife of Shallum the son of Tikvah, the son of Harhas, keeper of the wardrobe (now she lived in Jerusalem in the Second Quarter); and they spoke to her.

15 And she said to them, "Thus says

the LORD God of Israel, 'Tell the man who sent you to me,

16 thus says the LORD, "Behold, I bring evil on this place and on its inhabitants, *even* all the words of the book which the king of Judah has read.

17"Because they have forsaken Me and have burned incense to other gods that they might provoke Me to anger with all the work of their hands, therefore My wrath burns against this place, and it shall not be quenched." '

18"But to the king of Judah who sent you to inquire of the LORD thus shall you say to him, 'Thus says the LORD God of Israel, "*Regarding* the words which you have heard,

19 because your heart was tender and you humbled yourself before the LORD when you heard what I spoke against this place and against its inhabitants that they should become a desolation and a curse, and you have torn your clothes and wept before Me, I truly have heard you," declares the LORD.

20"Therefore, behold, I will gather you to your fathers, and you shall be gathered to your grave in peace, neither shall your eyes see all the evil which I will bring on this place." ' " So they brought back word to the king.

CHAPTER 23

THEN the king sent, and they gathered to him all the elders of Judah and of Jerusalem.

2 And the king went up to the house of the LORD and all the men of Judah and all the inhabitants of Jerusalem with him, and the priests and the prophets and all the people, both small and great; and he read in their hearing all the words of the book of the covenant, which was found in the house of the LORD.

3 And the king stood by the pillar and made a covenant before the LORD, to walk after the LORD, and to keep His commandments and His testimonies and His statutes with all *his* heart and all *his* soul, to carry out the words of this covenant that were written in this book. And all the people entered into the covenant.

4 ¶ Then the king commanded Hilkiah the high priest and the priests of

the second order and the doorkeepers, to bring out of the temple of the LORD all the vessels that were made for Baal, for [15]Asherah, and for all the host of heaven; and he burned them outside Jerusalem in the fields of the Kidron, and carried their ashes to Bethel.

5 And he did away with the idolatrous priests whom the kings of Judah had appointed to burn incense in the high places in the cities of Judah and in the surrounding area of Jerusalem, also those who burned incense to Baal, to the sun and to the moon and to the constellations and to all the host of heaven.

6 And he brought out the Asherah from the house of the LORD outside Jerusalem to the brook Kidron, and burned it at the brook Kidron, and ground *it* to dust, and threw its dust on the graves of the common people.

7 He also broke down the houses of the *male* cult prostitutes which *were* in the house of the LORD, where the women were weaving hangings for the Asherah.

8 Then he brought all the priests from the cities of Judah, and defiled the high places where the priests had burned incense, from Geba to Beersheba; and he broke down the high places of the gates which *were* at the entrance of the gate of Joshua the governor of the city, which *were* on one's left at the city gate.

9 Nevertheless the priests of the high places did not go up to the altar of the LORD in Jerusalem, but they ate unleavened bread among their brothers.

10 He also defiled [16]Topheth, which is in the valley of the son of Hinnom, that no man might make his son or his daughter pass through the fire for Molech.

11 And he did away with the horses which the kings of Judah had given to the sun, at the entrance of the house of the LORD, by the chamber of Nathan-melech the official, which *was* in the precincts; and he burned the chariots of the sun with fire.

12 And the altars which *were* on the roof, the upper chamber of Ahaz, which the kings of Judah had made, and the altars which Manasseh had

15 I.e., wooden symbol of a female deity
16 I.e., place of burning

made in the two courts of the house of the LORD, the king broke down; and he [17]smashed them there, and threw their dust into the brook Kidron.

13 And the high places which *were* before Jerusalem, which *were* on the right of the mount of destruction which Solomon the king of Israel had built for Ashtoreth the abomination of the Sidonians, and for Chemosh the abomination of Moab, and for Milcom the abomination of the sons of Ammon, the king defiled.

14 And he broke in pieces the *sacred* pillars and cut down the Asherim and filled their places with human bones.

15 ¶ Furthermore, the altar that *was* at Bethel *and* the high place which Jeroboam the son of Nebat, who made Israel sin, had made, even that altar and the high place he broke down. Then he demolished its stones, ground them to dust, and burned the Asherah.

16 Now when Josiah turned, he saw the graves that *were* there on the mountain, and he sent and took the bones from the graves and burned *them* on the altar and defiled it according to the word of the LORD which the man of God proclaimed, who proclaimed these things.

17 Then he said, "What is this monument that I see?" And the men of the city told him, "It is the grave of the man of God who came from Judah and proclaimed these things which you have done against the altar of Bethel."

18 And he said, "Let him alone; let no one disturb his bones." So they left his bones undisturbed with the bones of the prophet who came from Samaria.

19 And Josiah also removed all the houses of the high places which *were* in the cities of Samaria, which the kings of Israel had made provoking the LORD; and he did to them just as he had done in Bethel.

20 And all the priests of the high places who *were* there he slaughtered on the altars and burned human bones on them; then he returned to Jerusalem.

21 ¶ Then the king commanded all the people saying, "Celebrate the Passover to the LORD your God as it is written in this book of the covenant."

22 Surely such a Passover had not been celebrated from the days of the judges who judged Israel, nor in all the days of the kings of Israel and of the kings of Judah.

23 But in the eighteenth year of King Josiah, this Passover was observed to the LORD in Jerusalem.

24 ¶ Moreover, Josiah removed the mediums and the spiritists and the teraphim and the idols and all the abominations that were seen in the land of Judah and in Jerusalem, that he might confirm the words of the law which were written in the book that Hilkiah the priest found in the house of the LORD.

25 And before him there was no king like him who turned to the LORD with all his heart and with all his soul and with all his might, according to all the law of Moses; nor did any like him arise after him.

26 ¶ However, the LORD did not turn from the fierceness of His great wrath with which His anger burned against Judah, because of all the provocations with which Manasseh had provoked Him.

27 And the LORD said, "I will remove Judah also from My sight, as I have removed Israel. And I will cast off Jerusalem, this city which I have chosen, and the temple of which I said, 'My name shall be there.'"

28 ¶ Now the rest of the acts of Josiah and all that he did, are they not written in the Book of the Chronicles of the Kings of Judah?

29 In his days Pharaoh Neco king of Egypt went up to the king of Assyria to the river Euphrates. And King Josiah went to meet him, and when *Pharaoh Neco* saw him he killed him at Megiddo.

30 And his servants drove his body in a chariot from Megiddo, and brought him to Jerusalem and buried him in his own tomb. Then the people of the land took Jehoahaz the son of Josiah and anointed him and made him king in place of his father.

31 ¶ Jehoahaz was twenty-three years old when he became king, and he reigned three months in Jerusalem; and his mother's name was Hamutal the daughter of Jeremiah of Libnah.

32 And he did evil in the sight of the

[17] Or, *ran from there*

LORD, according to all that his fathers had done.

33 And Pharaoh Neco imprisoned him at Riblah in the land of Hamath, that he might not reign in Jerusalem; and he imposed on the land a fine of one hundred talents of silver and a talent of gold.

34 And Pharaoh Neco made Eliakim the son of Josiah king in the place of Josiah his father, and changed his name to Jehoiakim. But he took Jehoahaz away and brought *him* to Egypt, and he died there.

35 So Jehoiakim gave the silver and gold to Pharaoh, but he taxed the land in order to give the money at the command of Pharaoh. He exacted the silver and gold from the people of the land, each according to his valuation, to give it to Pharaoh Neco.

36 ¶ Jehoiakim was twenty-five years old when he became king, and he reigned eleven years in Jerusalem; and his mother's name *was* Zebidah the daughter of Pedaiah of Rumah.

37 And he did evil in the sight of the LORD, according to all that his fathers had done.

CHAPTER 24

IN his days Nebuchadnezzar king of Babylon came up, and Jehoiakim became his servant *for* three years; then he turned and rebelled against him.

2 And the LORD sent against him bands of Chaldeans, bands of Arameans, bands of Moabites, and bands of Ammonites. So He sent them against Judah to destroy it, according to the word of the LORD, which He had spoken through His servants the prophets.

3 Surely at the command of the LORD it came upon Judah, to remove *them* from His sight because of the sins of Manasseh, according to all that he had done,

4 and also for the innocent blood which he shed, for he filled Jerusalem with innocent blood; and the LORD would not forgive.

5 Now the rest of the acts of Jehoiakim and all that he did, are they not written in the Book of the Chronicles of the Kings of Judah?

6 So Jehoiakim slept with his fathers, and Jehoiachin his son became king in his place.

7 And the king of Egypt did not come out of his land again, for the king of Babylon had taken all that belonged to the king of Egypt from the brook of Egypt to the river Euphrates.

8 ¶ Jehoiachin was eighteen years old when he became king, and he reigned three months in Jerusalem; and his mother's name *was* Nehushta the daughter of Elnathan of Jerusalem.

9 And he did evil in the sight of the LORD, according to all that his father had done.

10 ¶ At that time the servants of Nebuchadnezzar king of Babylon went up to Jerusalem, and the city came under siege.

11 And Nebuchadnezzar the king of Babylon came to the city, while his servants were besieging it.

12 And Jehoiachin the king of Judah went out to the king of Babylon, he and his mother and his servants and his captains and his officials. So the king of Babylon took him captive in the eighth year of his reign.

13 And he carried out from there all the treasures of the house of the LORD, and the treasures of the king's house, and cut in pieces all the vessels of gold which Solomon king of Israel had made in the temple of the LORD, just as the LORD had said.

14 Then he led away into exile all Jerusalem and all the captains and all the mighty men of valor, ten thousand captives, and all the craftsmen and the smiths. None remained except the poorest people of the land.

15 So he led Jehoiachin away into exile to Babylon; also the king's mother and the king's wives and his officials and the leading men of the land, he led away into exile from Jerusalem to Babylon.

16 And all the men of valor, seven thousand, and the craftsmen and the smiths, one thousand, all strong and fit for war, and these the king of Babylon brought into exile to Babylon.

17 Then the king of Babylon made his uncle Mattaniah, king in his place, and changed his name to Zedekiah.

18 ¶ Zedekiah was twenty-one years old when he became king, and he reigned eleven years in Jerusalem; and his mother's name *was* Hamutal the daughter of Jeremiah of Libnah.

19 And he did evil in the sight of the LORD, according to all that Jehoiakim had done.

20 For through the anger of the LORD *this* came about in Jerusalem and Judah until He cast them out from His presence. And Zedekiah rebelled against the king of Babylon.

CHAPTER 25

NOW it came about in the ninth year of his reign, on the tenth day of the tenth month, that Nebuchadnezzar king of Babylon came, he and all his army, against Jerusalem, camped against it, and built a siege wall all around it.

2 So the city was under siege until the eleventh year of King Zedekiah.

3 On the ninth day of the *fourth* month the famine was so severe in the city that there was no food for the people of the land.

4 Then the city was broken into, and all the men of war *fled* by night by way of the gate between the two walls beside the king's garden, though the Chaldeans were all around the city. And they went by way of the Arabah.

5 But the army of the Chaldeans pursued the king and overtook him in the plains of Jericho and all his army was scattered from him.

6 Then they captured the king and brought him to the king of Babylon at Riblah, and he passed sentence on him.

7 And they slaughtered the sons of Zedekiah before his eyes, then put out the eyes of Zedekiah and bound him with bronze fetters and brought him to Babylon.

8 ¶ Now on the seventh day of the fifth month, which was the nineteenth year of King Nebuchadnezzar, king of Babylon, Nebuzaradan the captain of the guard, a servant of the king of Babylon, came to Jerusalem.

9 And he burned the house of the LORD, the king's house, and all the houses of Jerusalem; even every great house he burned with fire.

10 So all the army of the Chaldeans who *were with* the captain of the guard broke down the walls around Jerusalem.

11 Then the rest of the people who were left in the city and the deserters who had deserted to the king of Babylon and the rest of the multitude, Nebuzaradan the captain of the guard carried away into exile.

12 But the captain of the guard left some of the poorest of the land to be vinedressers and plowmen.

13 ¶ Now the bronze pillars which were in the house of the LORD, and the stands and the bronze sea which were in the house of the LORD, the Chaldeans broke in pieces and carried the bronze to Babylon.

14 And they took away the pots, the shovels, the snuffers, the spoons, and all the bronze vessels which were used in *temple* service.

15 The captain of the guard also took away the firepans and the basins, what was fine gold and what was fine silver.

16 The two pillars, the one sea, and the stands which Solomon had made for the house of the LORD—the bronze of all these vessels was beyond weight.

17 The height of the one pillar was eighteen cubits, and a bronze capital was on it; the height of the capital was three cubits, with a network and pomegranates on the capital all around, all of bronze. And the second pillar was like these with network.

18 ¶ Then the captain of the guard took Seraiah the chief priest and Zephaniah the second priest, with the three officers of the temple.

19 And from the city he took one official who was overseer of the men of war, and five of the king's advisers who were found in the city; and the scribe of the captain of the army, who mustered the people of the land; and sixty men of the people of the land who were found in the city.

20 And Nebuzaradan the captain of the guard took them and brought them to the king of Babylon at Riblah.

21 Then the king of Babylon struck them down and put them to death at Riblah in the land of Hamath. So Judah was led away into exile from its land.

22 ¶ Now *as for* the people who were left in the land of Judah, whom Nebuchadnezzar king of Babylon had left, he appointed Gedaliah the son of Ahikam, the son of Shaphan over them.

23 When all the captains of the forces, they and *their* men, heard that

the king of Babylon had appointed Gedaliah *governor,* they came to Gedaliah to Mizpah, namely, Ishmael the son of Nethaniah, and Johanan the son of Kareah, and Seraiah the son of Tanhumeth the Netophathite, and Jaazaniah the son of the Maacathite, they and their men.

24 And Gedaliah swore to them and their men and said to them, "Do not be afraid of the servants of the Chaldeans; live in the land and serve the king of Babylon, and it will be well with you."

25 ¶ But it came about in the seventh month, that Ishmael the son of Nethaniah, the son of Elishama, of the royal family, came with ten men and struck Gedaliah down so that he died along with the Jews and the Chaldeans who were with him at Mizpah.

26 Then all the people, both small and great, and the captains of the forces arose and went to Egypt; for they were afraid of the Chaldeans.

27 ¶ Now it came about in the thirty-seventh year of the exile of Jehoiachin king of Judah, in the twelfth month, on the twenty-seventh *day* of the month, that Evil-merodach king of Babylon, in the year that he became king, released Jehoiachin king of Judah from prison;

28 and he spoke kindly to him and set his throne above the throne of the kings who *were* with him in Babylon.

29 And Jehoiachin changed his prison clothes, and had his meals in the king's presence regularly all the days of his life;

30 and for his allowance, a regular allowance was given him by the king, a portion for each day, all the days of his life.

THE FIRST BOOK OF THE

CHRONICLES

Adam, Seth, Enosh,

2 Kenan, Mahalalel, Jared,

3 Enoch, Methuselah, Lamech,

4 Noah, Shem, Ham and Japheth.

5 ¶ The sons of Japheth *were* Gomer, Magog, Madai, Javan, Tubal, Meshech, and Tiras.

6 And the sons of Gomer *were* Ashkenaz, Diphath, and Togarmah.

7 And the sons of Javan *were* Elishah, Tarshish, Kittim, and Rodanim.

8 ¶ The sons of Ham *were* Cush, Mizraim, Put, and Canaan.

9 And the sons of Cush *were* Seba, Havilah, Sabta, Raama, and Sabteca; and the sons of Raamah *were* Sheba and Dedan.

10 And Cush became the father of Nimrod; he began to be a mighty one in the earth.

11 And Mizraim became the father of the people of Lud, Anam, Lehab, Naphtuh,

12 Pathrus, Casluh, from which the Philistines came, and Caphtor.

13 ¶ And Canaan became the father of Sidon, his first-born, Heth,

14 and the Jebusites, the Amorites, the Girgashites,

15 the Hivites, the Arkites, the Sinites,

16 the Arvadites, the Zemarites, and the Hamathites.

17 ¶ The sons of Shem *were* Elam, Asshur, Arpachshad, Lud, Aram, Uz, Hul, Gether, and Meshech.

18 And Arpachshad became the father of Shelah and Shelah became the father of Eber.

19 And two sons were born to Eber, the name of the one was Peleg, for in his days the earth was divided, and his brother's name was Joktan.

20 And Joktan became the father of Almodad, Sheleph, Hazarmaveth, Jerah,

21 Hadoram, Uzal, Diklah,

22 Ebal, Abimael, Sheba,

23 Ophir, Havilah, and Jobab; all these *were* the sons of Joktan.

24 ¶ Shem, Arpachshad, Shelah,

25 Eber, Peleg, Reu,

26 Serug, Nahor, Terah,

27 Abram, that is Abraham.

28 ¶ The sons of Abraham *were* Isaac and Ishmael.

29 These are their genealogies: the first-born of Ishmael *was* Nebaioth, then Kedar, Adbeel, Mibsam,

30 Mishma, Dumah, Massa, Hadad, Tema,

31 Jetur, Naphish and Kedemah; these *were* the sons of Ishmael.

32 And the sons of Keturah, Abraham's concubine, *whom* she bore, *were* Zimran, Jokshan, Medan, Midian, Ishbak, and Shuah. And the sons of Jokshan *were* Sheba and Dedan.

33 And the sons of Midian *were* Ephah, Epher, Hanoch, Abida, and Eldaah. All these were the sons of Keturah.

34 And Abraham became the father of Isaac. The sons of Isaac *were* Esau and Israel.

35 The sons of Esau *were* Eliphaz, Reuel, Jeush, Jalam, and Korah.

36 The sons of Eliphaz *were* Teman, Omar, Zephi, Gatam, Kenaz, Timna, and Amalek.

37 The sons of Reuel *were* Nahath, Zerah, Shammah, and Mizzah.

38 And the sons of Seir *were* Lotan, Shobal, Zibeon, Anah, Dishon, Ezer, and Dishan.

39 And the sons of Lotan *were* Hori and Homam; and Lotan's sister *was* Timna.

40 The sons of Shobal *were* Alian, Manahath, Ebal, Shephi, and Onam. And the sons of Zibeon *were* Aiah and Anah.

41 The son of Anah *was* Dishon. And the sons of Dishon *were* Hamran, Eshban, Ithran, and Cheran.

42 The sons of Ezer *were* Bilhan, Zaavan and Jaakan. The sons of Dishan *were* Uz and Aran.

43 ¶ Now these are the kings who reigned in the land of Edom before any king of the sons of Israel reigned. Bela *was* the son of Beor, and the name of his city was Dinhabah.

44 When Bela died, Jobab the son of Zerah of Bozrah became king in his place.

45 When Jobab died, Husham of the land of the Temanites became king in his place.

46 When Husham died, Hadad the son of Bedad, who defeated Midian in the field of Moab, became king in his

place; and the name of his city *was* Avith.

47 When Hadad died, Samlah of Masrekah became king in his place.

48 When Samlah died, Shaul of Rehoboth by the River became king in his place.

49 When Shaul died, Baal-hanan the son of Achbor became king in his place.

50 When Baal-hanan died, Hadad became king in his place; and the name of his city was Pai, and his wife's name was Mehetabel, the daughter of Matred, the daughter of Mezahab.

51 Then Hadad died. Now the chiefs of Edom were: chief Timna, chief Aliah, chief Jetheth,

52 chief Oholibamah, chief Elah, chief Pinon,

53 chief Kenaz, chief Teman, chief Mibzar,

54 chief Magdiel, chief Iram. These *were* the chiefs of Edom.

CHAPTER 2

THESE are the sons of Israel: Reuben, Simeon, Levi, Judah, Issachar, Zebulun,

2 Dan, Joseph, Benjamin, Naphtali, Gad, and Asher.

3 ¶ The sons of Judah *were* Er, Onan, and Shelah; *these* three were born to him by Bath-shua the Canaanitess. And Er, Judah's first-born, was wicked in the sight of the LORD, so He put him to death.

4 And Tamar his daughter-in-law bore him Perez and Zerah. Judah had five sons in all.

5 ¶ The sons of Perez *were* Hezron and Hamul.

6 And the sons of Zerah *were* Zimri, Ethan, Heman, Calcol, and Dara; five of them in all.

7 And the son of Carmi *was* Achar, the troubler of Israel, who violated the ban.

8 And the son of Ethan *was* Azariah.

9 ¶ Now the sons of Hezron, who were born to him *were* Jerahmeel, Ram, and Chelubai.

10 And Ram became the father of Amminadab, and Amminadab became the father of Nahshon, leader of the sons of Judah;

11 Nahshon became the father of

Salma, Salma became the father of Boaz,

12 Boaz became the father of Obed, and Obed became the father of Jesse;

13 and Jesse became the father of Eliab his first-born, then Abinadab the second, Shimea the third,

14 Nethanel the fourth, Raddai the fifth,

15 Ozem the sixth, David the seventh;

16 and their sisters were Zeruiah and Abigail. And the three sons of Zeruiah were Abshai, Joab, and Asahel.

17 And Abigail bore Amasa, and the father of Amasa was Jether the Ishmaelite.

18 ¶ Now Caleb the son of Hezron had sons by Azubah his wife, and by Jerioth; and these were her sons: Jesher, Shobab, and Ardon.

19 When Azubah died, Caleb married Ephrath, who bore him Hur.

20 And Hur became the father of Uri, and Uri became the father of Bezalel.

21 ¶ Afterward Hezron went in to the daughter of Machir the father of Gilead, whom he married when he was sixty years old; and she bore him Segub.

22 And Segub became the father of Jair, who had twenty-three cities in the land of Gilead.

23 But Geshur and Aram took the towns of Jair from them, with Kenath and its villages, even sixty cities. All these were the sons of Machir, the father of Gilead.

24 And after the death of Hezron in Caleb-ephrathah, Abijah, Hezron's wife, bore him Ashhur the father of Tekoa.

25 ¶ Now the sons of Jerahmeel the first-born of Hezron were Ram the first-born, then Bunah, Oren, Ozem, and Ahijah.

26 And Jerahmeel had another wife, whose name was Atarah; she was the mother of Onam.

27 And the sons of Ram, the first-born of Jerahmeel, were Maaz, Jamin, and Eker.

28 And the sons of Onam were Shammai and Jada. And the sons of Shammai were Nadab and Abishur.

29 And the name of Abishur's wife was Abihail, and she bore him Ahban and Molid.

30 And the sons of Nadab were Seled and Appaim, and Seled died without sons.

31 And the son of Appaim was Ishi. And the son of Ishi was Sheshan. And the son of Sheshan was Ahlai.

32 And the sons of Jada the brother of Shammai were Jether and Jonathan, and Jether died without sons.

33 And the sons of Jonathan were Peleth and Zaza. These were the sons of Jerahmeel.

34 Now Sheshan had no sons, only daughters. And Sheshan had an Egyptian servant whose name was Jarha.

35 And Sheshan gave his daughter to Jarha his servant in marriage, and she bore him Attai.

36 And Attai became the father of Nathan, and Nathan became the father of Zabad,

37 and Zabad became the father of Ephlal, and Ephlal became the father of Obed,

38 and Obed became the father of Jehu, and Jehu became the father of Azariah,

39 and Azariah became the father of Helez, and Helez became the father of Eleasah,

40 and Eleasah became the father of Sismai, and Sismai became the father of Shallum,

41 and Shallum became the father of Jekamiah, and Jekamiah became the father of Elishama.

42 ¶ Now the sons of Caleb, the brother of Jerahmeel, were Mesha his first-born, who was the father of Ziph; and his son was Mareshah, the father of Hebron.

43 And the sons of Hebron were Korah and Tappuah and Rekem and Shema.

44 And Shema became the father of Raham, the father of Jorkeam; and Rekem became the father of Shammai.

45 And the son of Shammai was Maon, and Maon was the father of Bethzur.

46 And Ephah, Caleb's concubine, bore Haran, Moza, and Gazez; and Haran became the father of Gazez.

47 And the sons of Jahdai were Regem, Jotham, Geshan, Pelet, Ephah, and Shaaph.

48 Maacah, Caleb's concubine, bore Sheber and Tirhanah.

49 She also bore Shaaph the father of Madmannah, Sheva the father of Machbena and the father of Gibea; and the daughter of Caleb *was* Achsah.

50 These were the sons of Caleb.

¶ The sons of Hur, the first-born of Ephrathah, *were* Shobal the father of Kiriath-jearim,

51 Salma the father of Bethlehem *and* Hareph the father of Beth-gader.

52 And Shobal the father of Kiriath-jearim had sons: Haroeh, half of the Manahathites,

53 and the families of Kiriath-jearim: the Ithrites, the Puthites, the Shumathites, and the Mishraites; from these came the Zorathites and the Eshtaolites.

54 The sons of Salma *were* Bethlehem and the Netophathites, Atroth-beth-joab and half of the Manahathites, the Zorites.

55 And the families of scribes who lived at Jabez *were* the Tirathites, the Shimeathites, *and* the Sucathites. Those are the Kenites who came from Hammath, the father of the house of Rechab.

CHAPTER 3

NOW these were the sons of David who were born to him in Hebron: the first-born *was* Amnon, by Ahinoam the Jezreelitess; the second *was* Daniel, by Abigail the Carmelitess;

2 the third *was* Absalom the son of Maacah, the daughter of Talmai king of Geshur; the fourth *was* Adonijah the son of Haggith;

3 the fifth *was* Shephatiah, by Abital; the sixth *was* Ithream, by his wife Eglah.

4 Six were born to him in Hebron, and there he reigned seven years and six months. And in Jerusalem he reigned thirty-three years.

5 And these were born to him in Jerusalem: Shimea, Shobab, Nathan, and Solomon, four, by Bath-shua the daughter of Ammiel;

6 and Ibhar, Elishama, Eliphelet,

7 Nogah, Nepheg, and Japhia,

8 Elishama, Eliada, and Eliphelet, nine.

9 All *these were* the sons of David, besides the sons of the concubines; and Tamar *was* their sister.

10 ¶ Now Solomon's son *was* Rehoboam, Abijah *was* his son, Asa his son, Jehoshaphat his son,

11 Joram his son, Ahaziah his son, Joash his son,

12 Amaziah his son, Azariah his son, Jotham his son,

13 Ahaz his son, Hezekiah his son, Manasseh his son,

14 Amon his son, Josiah his son.

15 And the sons of Josiah *were* Johanan the first-born, and the second *was* Jehoiakim, the third Zedekiah, the fourth Shallum.

16 And the sons of Jehoiakim *were* Jeconiah his son, Zedekiah his son.

17 And the sons of Jeconiah, the prisoner, *were* Shealtiel his son,

18 and Malchiram, Pedaiah, Shenazzar, Jekamiah, Hoshama, and Nedabiah.

19 And the sons of Pedaiah *were* Zerubbabel and Shimei. And the sons of Zerubbabel *were* Meshullam and Hananiah, and Shelomith *was* their sister;

20 and Hashubah, Ohel, Berechiah, Hasadiah, and Jushab-hesed, five.

21 And the sons of Hananiah *were* Pelatiah and Jeshaiah, the sons of Rephaiah, the sons of Arnan, the sons of Obadiah, the sons of Shecaniah.

22 And the [1]son of Shecaniah *was* Shemaiah, and the sons of Shemaiah *were* Hattush, Igal, Bariah, Neariah, and Shaphat, six.

23 And the sons of Neariah *were* Elioenai, Hizkiah, and Azrikam, three.

24 And the sons of Elioenai *were* Hodaviah, Eliashib, Pelaiah, Akkub, Johanan, Delaiah, and Anani, seven.

CHAPTER 4

THE sons of Judah *were* Perez, Hezron, Carmi, Hur, and Shobal.

2 And Reaiah the son of Shobal became the father of Jahath, and Jahath became the father of Ahumai and Lahad. These *were* the families of the Zorathites.

3 And these *were* the sons of Etam: Jezreel, Ishma, and Idbash; and the name of their sister *was* Hazzelelponi.

4 And Penuel *was* the father of Gedor, and Ezer the father of Hushah.

[1] Lit., *sons*

These *were* the sons of Hur, the first-born of Ephrathah, the father of Beth-lehem.

5 And Ashhur, the father of Tekoa, had two wives, Helah and Naarah.

6 And Naarah bore him Ahuzzam, Hepher, Temeni, and Haahashtari. These were the sons of Naarah.

7 And the sons of Helah *were* Zereth, Izhar and Ethna...

8 And Koz became the father of Anub and Zobebah, and the families of Aharhel the son of Harum.

9 And Jabez was more honorable than his brothers, and his mother named him Jabez saying, "Because I bore *him* with pain."

10 Now Jabez called on the God of Israel, saying, "Oh that Thou wouldst bless me indeed, and enlarge my border, and that Thy hand might be with me, and that Thou wouldst keep *me* from harm, that *it* may not pain me!" And God granted him what he requested.

11 ¶ And Chelub the brother of Shuhah became the father of Mehir, who was the father of Eshton.

12 And Eshton became the father of Beth-rapha and Paseah, and Tehinnah the father of Ir-nahash. These are the men of Recah.

13 ¶ Now the sons of Kenaz *were* Othniel and Seraiah. And the son of Othniel *was* Hathath.

14 And Meonothai became the father of Ophrah, and Seraiah became the father of Joab the father of Ge-harashim, for they were craftsmen.

15 And the sons of Caleb the son of Jephunneh *were* Iru, Elah and Naam; and the son of Elah *was* Kenaz.

16 And the sons of Jehallelel *were* Ziph and Ziphah, Tiria and Asarel.

17 And the sons of Ezrah *were* Jether, Mered, Epher, and Jalon. (And these are the sons of Bithia the daughter of Pharaoh, whom Mered took) and she conceived *and bore* Miriam, Shammai, and Ishbah the father of Eshtemoa.

18 And his Jewish wife bore Jered the father of Gedor, and Heber the father of Soco, and Jekuthiel the father of Zanoah.

19 And the sons of the wife of Hodiah, the sister of Naham, *were* the fathers of Keilah the Garmite and Eshtemoa the Maacathite.

20 And the sons of Shimon *were* Amnon and Rinnah, Benhanan and Tilon. And the sons of Ishi *were* Zoheth and Ben-zoheth.

21 The sons of Shelah the son of Judah *were* Er the father of Lecah and Laadah the father of Mareshah, and the families of the house of the linen workers at Beth-ashbea;

22 and Jokim, the men of Cozeba, Joash, Saraph, who ruled in Moab, and Jashubi-lehem. And the records are ancient.

23 These were the potters and the inhabitants of Netaim and Gederah; they lived there with the king for his work.

24 ¶ The sons of Simeon *were* Nemuel and Jamin, Jarib, Zerah, Shaul;

25 Shallum his son, Mibsam his son, Mishma his son.

26 And the sons of Mishma *were* Hammuel his son, Zaccur his son, Shimei his son.

27 Now Shimei had sixteen sons and six daughters; but his brothers did not have many sons, nor did all their family multiply like the sons of Judah.

28 And they lived at Beersheba, Moladah, and Hazar-shual,

29 at Bilhah, Ezem, Tolad,

30 Bethuel, Hormah, Ziklag,

31 Beth-marcaboth, Hazar-susim, Beth-biri, and Shaaraim. These *were* their cities until the reign of David.

32 And their villages *were* Etam, Ain, Rimmon, Tochen, and Ashan, five cities;

33 and all their villages that *were* around the same cities as far as Baal. These *were* their settlements, and they have their genealogy.

34 And Meshobab and Jamlech and Joshah the son of Amaziah,

35 and Joel and Jehu the son of Joshibiah, the son of Seraiah, the son of Asiel,

36 and Elioenai, Jaakobah, Jeshohaiah, Asaiah, Adiel, Jesimiel, Benaiah,

37 Ziza the son of Shiphi, the son of Allon, the son of Jedaiah, the son of Shimri, the son of Shemaiah;

38 these mentioned by name *were* leaders in their families; and their fathers' houses increased greatly.

39 And they went to the entrance of Gedor, even to the east side of the valley, to seek pasture for their flocks.

40 And they found rich and good pasture, and the land was broad and quiet and peaceful; for those who lived there formerly *were* Hamites.

41 And these, recorded by name, came in the days of Hezekiah king of Judah, and attacked their tents, and the Meunites who were found there, and destroyed them utterly to this day, and lived in their place; because there was pasture there for their flocks.

42 And from them, from the sons of Simeon, five hundred men went to Mount Seir, with Pelatiah, Neariah, Rephaiah, and Uzziel, the sons of Ishi, as their leaders.

43 And they destroyed the remnant of the Amalekites who escaped, and have lived there to this day.

CHAPTER 5

NOW the sons of Reuben the first-born of Israel (for he was the first-born, but because he defiled his father's bed, his birthright was given to the sons of Joseph the son of Israel; so that he is not enrolled in the genealogy according to the birthright.

2 Though Judah prevailed over his brothers, and from him *came* the leader, yet the birthright belonged to Joseph),

3 the sons of Reuben the first-born of Israel *were* Hanoch and Pallu, Hezron and Carmi.

4 The sons of Joel *were* Shemaiah his son, Gog his son, Shimei his son,

5 Micah his son, Reaiah his son, Baal his son,

6 Beerah his son, whom Tilgath-pilneser king of Assyria carried away into exile; he was leader of the Reubenites.

7 And his kinsmen by their families, in the genealogy of their generations, *were* Jeiel the chief, then Zechariah

8 and Bela the son of Azaz, the son of Shema, the son of Joel, who lived in Aroer, even to Nebo and Baal-meon.

9 And to the east he settled as far as the entrance of the wilderness from the river Euphrates, because their cattle had increased in the land of Gilead.

10 And in the days of Saul they made war with the Hagrites, who fell by their hand, so that they occupied their tents throughout all the land east of Gilead.

11 ¶ Now the sons of Gad lived opposite them in the land of Bashan as far as Salecah.

12 Joel *was* the chief, and Shapham the second, then Janai and Shaphat in Bashan.

13 And their kinsmen of their fathers' households *were* Michael, Meshullam, Sheba, Jorai, Jacan, Zia, and Eber, seven.

14 These *were* the sons of Abihail, the son of Huri, the son of Jaroah, the son of Gilead, the son of Michael, the son of Jeshishai, the son of Jahdo, the son of Buz;

15 Ahi the son of Abdiel, the son of Guni, *was* head of their fathers' households.

16 And they lived in Gilead, in Bashan and in its towns, and in all the pasture lands of Sharon, as far as their borders.

17 All of these were enrolled in the genealogies in the days of Jotham king of Judah and in the days of Jeroboam king of Israel.

18 ¶ The sons of Reuben and the Gadites and the half-tribe of Manasseh, *consisting* of valiant men, men who bore shield and sword and shot with bow, and *were* skillful in battle, *were* 44,760, who went to war.

19 And they made war against the Hagrites, Jetur, Naphish, and Nodab.

20 And they were helped against them, and the Hagrites and all who *were* with them were given into their hand; for they cried out to God in the battle, and He was entreated for them, because they trusted in Him.

21 And they took away their cattle: their 50,000 camels, 250,000 sheep, 2,000 donkeys, and 100,000 men.

22 For many fell slain, because the war *was* of God. And they settled in their place until the exile.

23 ¶ Now the sons of the half-tribe of Manasseh lived in the land; from Bashan to Baal-hermon and Senir and Mount Hermon they were numerous.

24 And these were the heads of their fathers' households, even Epher, Ishi, Eliel, Azriel, Jeremiah, Hodaviah, and Jahdiel, mighty men of valor, famous men, heads of their fathers' households.

25 ¶ But they acted treacherously against the God of their fathers, and played the harlot after the gods of the

peoples of the land, whom God had destroyed before them.

26 So the God of Israel stirred up the spirit of Pul, king of Assyria, even the spirit of Tilgath-pilneser king of Assyria, and he carried them away into exile, namely the Reubenites, the Gadites, and the half-tribe of Manasseh, and brought them to Halah, Habor, Hara, and to the river of Gozan, to this day.

CHAPTER 6

THE sons of Levi *were* Gershon, Kohath and Merari.

2 And the sons of Kohath *were* Amram, Izhar, Hebron, and Uzziel.

3 And the children of Amram *were* Aaron, Moses, and Miriam. And the sons of Aaron *were* Nadab, Abihu, Eleazar, and Ithamar.

4 Eleazar became the father of Phinehas, *and* Phinehas became the father of Abishua,

5 and Abishua became the father of Bukki, and Bukki became the father of Uzzi,

6 and Uzzi became the father of Zerahiah, and Zerahiah became the father of Meraioth,

7 Meraioth became the father of Amariah, and Amariah became the father of Ahitub,

8 and Ahitub became the father of Zadok, and Zadok became the father of Ahimaaz,

9 and Ahimaaz became the father of Azariah, and Azariah became the father of Johanan,

10 and Johanan became the father of Azariah (it was he who served as the priest in the house which Solomon built in Jerusalem),

11 and Azariah became the father of Amariah, and Amariah became the father of Ahitub,

12 and Ahitub became the father of Zadok, and Zadok became the father of Shallum,

13 and Shallum became the father of Hilkiah, and Hilkiah became the father of Azariah,

14 and Azariah became the father of Seraiah, and Seraiah became the father of Jehozadak;

15 and Jehozadak went *along* when the LORD carried Judah and Jerusalem away into exile by Nebuchadnezzar.

16 ¶ The sons of Levi *were* Gershom, Kohath, and Merari.

17 And these are the names of the sons of Gershom: Libni and Shimei.

18 And the sons of Kohath *were* Amram, Izhar, Hebron, and Uzziel.

19 The sons of Merari *were* Mahli and Mushi. And these are the families of the Levites according to their fathers' *households*.

20 Of Gershom: Libni his son, Jahath his son, Zimmah his son,

21 Joah his son, Iddo his son, Zerah his son, Jeatherai his son.

22 The sons of Kohath *were* Amminadab his son, Korah his son, Assir his son,

23 Elkanah his son, Ebiasaph his son, and Assir his son,

24 Tahath his son, Uriel his son, Uzziah his son, and Shaul his son.

25 And the sons of Elkanah *were* Amasai and Ahimoth.

26 *As for* Elkanah, the sons of Elkanah *were* Zophai his son and Nahath his son,

27 Eliab his son, Jeroham his son, Elkanah his son.

28 And the sons of Samuel *were* Joel, the first-born and Abijah, the second.

29 The sons of Merari *were* Mahli, Libni his son, Shimei his son, Uzzah his son,

30 Shimea his son, Haggiah his son, Asaiah his son.

31 ¶ Now these are those whom David appointed over the service of song in the house of the LORD, after the ark rested *there*.

32 And they ministered with song before the tabernacle of the tent of meeting, until Solomon had built the house of the LORD in Jerusalem; and they served in their office according to their order.

33 And these are those who served with their sons. From the sons of the Kohathites *were* Heman the singer, the son of Joel, the son of Samuel,

34 the son of Elkanah, the son of Jeroham, the son of Eliel, the son of Toah,

35 the son of Zuph, the son of Elkanah, the son of Mahath, the son of Amasai,

36 the son of Elkanah, the son of Joel, the son of Azariah, the son of Zephaniah,

37 the son of Tahath, the son of Assir, the son of Ebiasaph, the son of Korah,

38 the son of Izhar, the son of Kohath, the son of Levi, the son of Israel.

39 And *Heman's* brother Asaph stood at his right hand, even Asaph the son of Berechiah, the son of Shimea,

40 the son of Michael, the son of Baaseiah, the son of Malchijah,

41 the son of Ethni, the son of Zerah, the son of Adaiah,

42 the son of Ethan, the son of Zimmah, the son of Shimei,

43 the son of Jahath, the son of Gershom, the son of Levi.

44 And on the left hand *were* their kinsmen the sons of Merari: Ethan the son of Kishi, the son of Abdi, the son of Malluch,

45 the son of Hashabiah, the son of Amaziah, the son of Hilkiah,

46 the son of Amzi, the son of Bani, the son of Shemer,

47 the son of Mahli, the son of Mushi, the son of Merari, the son of Levi.

48 And their kinsmen the Levites were appointed for all the service of the tabernacle of the house of God.

49 ¶ But Aaron and his sons offered on the altar of burnt offering and on the altar of incense, for all the work of the most holy place, and to make atonement for Israel, according to all that Moses the servant of God had commanded.

50 And these are the sons of Aaron: Eleazar his son, Phinehas his son, Abishua his son,

51 Bukki his son, Uzzi his son, Zerahiah his son,

52 Meraioth his son, Amariah his son, Ahitub his son,

53 Zadok his son, Ahimaaz his son.

54 ¶ Now these are their settlements according to their camps within their borders. To the sons of Aaron of the families of the Kohathites (for theirs was the *first* lot),

55 to them they gave Hebron in the land of Judah, and its pasture lands around it;

56 but the fields of the city and its villages, they gave to Caleb the son of Jephunneh.

57 And to the sons of Aaron they gave the *following* cities of refuge: Hebron, Libnah also with its pasture lands, Jattir, Eshtemoa with its pasture lands,

58 Hilen with its pasture lands, Debir with its pasture lands,

59 Ashan with its pasture lands, and Beth-shemesh with its pasture lands;

60 and from the tribe of Benjamin: Geba with its pasture lands, Allemeth with its pasture lands, and Anathoth with its pasture lands. All their cities throughout their families were thirteen cities.

61 ¶ Then to the rest of the sons of Kohath *were given* by lot, from the family of the tribe, from the half-tribe, the half of Manasseh, ten cities.

62 And to the sons of Gershom, according to their families, *were given* from the tribe of Issachar and from the tribe of Asher, the tribe of Naphtali, and the tribe of Manasseh, thirteen cities in Bashan.

63 To the sons of Merari *were given* by lot, according to their families, from the tribe of Reuben, the tribe of Gad, and the tribe of Zebulun, twelve cities.

64 So the sons of Israel gave to the Levites the cities with their pasture lands.

65 And they gave by lot from the tribe of the sons of Judah, the tribe of the sons of Simeon, and the tribe of the sons of Benjamin, these cities which are mentioned by name.

66 ¶ Now some of the families of the sons of Kohath had cities of their territory from the tribe of Ephraim.

67 And they gave to them the *following* cities of refuge: Shechem in the hill country of Ephraim with its pasture lands, Gezer also with its pasture lands,

68 Jokmeam with its pasture lands, Beth-horon with its pasture lands,

69 Aijalon with its pasture lands, and Gath-rimmon with its pasture lands;

70 and from the half-tribe of Manasseh: Aner with its pasture lands and Bileam with its pasture lands, for the rest of the family of the sons of Kohath.

71 ¶ To the sons of Gershom *were given*, from the family of the half-tribe of Manasseh: Golan in Bashan with its pasture lands and Ashtaroth with its pasture lands;

72 and from the tribe of Issachar:

Kedesh with its pasture lands, Daberath with its pasture lands,

73 and Ramoth with its pasture lands, Anem with its pasture lands;

74 and from the tribe of Asher: Mashal with its pasture lands, Abdon with its pasture lands,

75 Hukok with its pasture lands, and Rehob with its pasture lands;

76 and from the tribe of Naphtali: Kedesh in Galilee with its pasture lands, Hammon with its pasture lands, and Kiriathaim with its pasture lands.

77 ¶ To the rest of *the Levites,* the sons of Merari, *were given,* from the tribe of Zebulun: Rimmono with its pasture lands, Tabor with its pasture lands;

78 and beyond the Jordan at Jericho, on the east side of the Jordan, *were given them,* from the tribe of Reuben: Bezer in the wilderness with its pasture lands, Jahzah with its pasture lands,

79 Kedemoth with its pasture lands, and Mephaath with its pasture lands;

80 and from the tribe of Gad: Ramoth in Gilead with its pasture lands, Mahanaim with its pasture lands,

81 Heshbon with its pasture lands, and Jazer with its pasture lands.

CHAPTER 7

NOW the sons of Issachar *were* four: Tola, Puah, Jashub, and Shimron.

2 And the sons of Tola *were* Uzzi, Rephaiah, Jeriel, Jahmai, Ibsam, and Samuel, heads of their fathers' households. *The sons* of Tola *were* mighty men of valor in their generations; their number in the days of David was 22,600.

3 And the son of Uzzi *was* Izrahiah. And the sons of Izrahiah *were* Michael, Obadiah, Joel, Isshiah; all five of them *were* chief men.

4 And with them by their generations according to their fathers' households were 36,000 troops of the army for war, for they had many wives and sons.

5 And their relatives among all the families of Issachar *were* mighty men of valor, enrolled by genealogy, in all 87,000.

6 ¶ *The sons* of Benjamin *were* three: Bela and Becher and Jediael.

7 And the sons of Bela were five:

Ezbon, Uzzi, Uzziel, Jerimoth, and Iri. They *were* heads of fathers' households, mighty men of valor, and were 22,034 enrolled by genealogy.

8 And the sons of Becher *were* Zemirah, Joash, Eliezer, Elioenai, Omri, Jeremoth, Abijah, Anathoth, and Alemeth. All these *were* the sons of Becher.

9 And they were enrolled by genealogy, according to their generations, heads of their fathers' households, 20,200 mighty men of valor.

10 And the son of Jediael *was* Bilhan. And the sons of Bilhan *were* Jeush, Benjamin, Ehud, Chenaanah, Zethan, Tarshish, and Ahishahar.

11 All these *were* sons of Jediael, according to the heads of their fathers' households, 17,200 mighty men of valor, who were ready to go out with the army to war.

12 And Shuppim and Huppim *were* the sons of Ir; Hushim *was* the son of Aher.

13 ¶ The sons of Naphtali *were* Jahziel, Guni, Jezer, and Shallum, the sons of Bilhah.

14 ¶ The sons of Manasseh *were* Asriel, whom his Aramean concubine bore; she bore Machir the father of Gilead.

15 And Machir took a wife for Huppim and Shuppim, whose sister's name was Maacah. And the name of the second was Zelophehad, and Zelophehad had daughters.

16 And Maacah the wife of Machir bore a son, and she named him Peresh; and the name of his brother *was* Sheresh, and his sons *were* Ulam and Rakem.

17 And the son of Ulam *was* Bedan. These *were* the sons of Gilead the son of Machir, the son of Manasseh.

18 And his sister Hammolecheth bore Ishhod and Abiezer and Mahlah.

19 And the sons of Shemida were Ahian and Shechem and Likhi and Aniam.

20 ¶ And the sons of Ephraim *were* Shuthelah and Bered his son, Tahath his son, Eleadah his son, Tahath his son,

21 Zabad his son, Shuthelah his son, and Ezer and Elead whom the men of Gath who were born in the land killed, because they came down to take their livestock.

22 And their father Ephraim mourned many days, and his relatives came to comfort him.

23 Then he went in to his wife, and she conceived and bore a son, and he named him Beriah, because misfortune had come upon his house.

24 And his daughter was Sheerah, who built lower and upper Beth-horon, also Uzzen-sheerah.

25 And Rephah was his son *along* with Resheph, Telah his son, Tahan his son,

26 Ladan his son, Ammihud his son, Elishama his son,

27 Non his son, and Joshua his son.

28 ¶ And their possessions and settlements *were* Bethel with its towns, and to the east Naaran, and to the west Gezer with its towns, and Shechem with its towns as far as Ayyah with its towns,

29 and along the borders of the sons of Manasseh, Beth-shean with its towns, Taanach with its towns, Megiddo with its towns, Dor with its towns. In these lived the sons of Joseph the son of Israel.

30 ¶ The sons of Asher *were* Imnah, Ishvah, Ishvi and Beriah, and Serah their sister.

31 And the sons of Beriah *were* Heber and Malchiel, who was the father of Birzaith.

32 And Heber became the father of Japhlet, Shomer and Hotham, and Shua their sister.

33 And the sons of Japhlet *were* Pasach, Bimhal, and Ashvath. These were the sons of Japhlet.

34 And the sons of Shemer *were* Ahi and Rohgah, Jehubbah and Aram.

35 And the sons of his brother Helem *were* Zophah, Imna, Shelesh, and Amal.

36 The sons of Zophah *were* Suah, Harnepher, Shual, Beri, and Imrah,

37 Bezer, Hod, Shamma, Shilshah, Ithran, and Beera.

38 And the sons of Jether *were* Jephunneh, Pispa, and Ara.

39 And the sons of Ulla *were* Arah, Hanniel, and Rizia.

40 All these *were* the sons of Asher, heads of the fathers' houses, choice and mighty men of valor, heads of the princes. And the number of them enrolled by genealogy for service in war was 26,000 men.

CHAPTER 8

AND Benjamin became the father of Bela his first-born, Ashbel the second, Aharah the third,

2 Nohah the fourth, and Rapha the fifth.

3 And Bela had sons: Addar, Gera, Abihud,

4 Abishua, Naaman, Ahoah,

5 Gera, Shephuphan, and Huram.

6 And these are the sons of Ehud: these are the heads of fathers' *households* of the inhabitants of Geba, and they carried them into exile to Manahath,

7 namely, Naaman, Ahijah, and Gera—he carried them into exile; and he became the father of Uzza and Ahihud.

8 And Shaharaim became the father of children in the country of Moab, after he had sent away Hushim and Baara his wives.

9 And by Hodesh his wife he became the father of Jobab, Zibia, Mesha, Malcam,

10 Jeuz, Sachia, Mirmah. These were his sons, heads of fathers' *households*.

11 And by Hushim he became the father of Abitub and Elpaal.

12 And the sons of Elpaal *were* Eber, Misham, and Shemed, who built Ono and Lod, with its towns;

13 and Beriah and Shema, who were heads of fathers' *households* of the inhabitants of Aijalon, who put to flight the inhabitants of Gath;

14 and Ahio, Shashak, and Jeremoth.

15 And Zebadiah, Arad, Eder,

16 Michael, Ishpah, and Joha *were* the sons of Beriah.

17 And Zebadiah, Meshullam, Hizki, Heber,

18 Ishmerai, Izliah, and Jobab *were* the sons of Elpaal.

19 And Jakim, Zichri, Zabdi,

20 Elienai, Zillethai, Eliel,

21 Adaiah, Beraiah, and Shimrath *were* the sons of Shimei.

22 And Ishpan, Eber, Eliel,

23 Abdon, Zichri, Hanan,

24 Hananiah, Elam, Anthothijah,

25 Iphdeiah, and Penuel *were* the sons of Shashak.

26 And Shamsherai, Shehariah, Athaliah,

27 Jaareshiah, Elijah, and Zichri *were* the sons of Jeroham.

28 These were heads of the fathers' *households* according to their generations, chief men, who lived in Jerusalem.

29 ¶ Now in Gibeon, *Jeiel,* the father of Gibeon lived, and his wife's name was Maacah;

30 and his first-born son *was* Abdon, then Zur, Kish, Baal, Nadab,

31 Gedor, Ahio, and Zecher.

32 And Mikloth became the father of Shimeah. And they also lived with their relatives in Jerusalem opposite their *other* relatives.

33 And Ner became the father of Kish, and Kish became the father of Saul, and Saul became the father of Jonathan, Malchi-shua, Abinadab, and Eshbaal.

34 And the son of Jonathan *was* Merib-baal, and Merib-baal became the father of Micah.

35 And the sons of Micah *were* Pithon, Melech, Tarea, and Ahaz.

36 And Ahaz became the father of Jehoaddah, and Jehoaddah became the father of Alemeth, Azmaveth, and Zimri; and Zimri became the father of Moza.

37 And Moza became the father of Binea; Raphah *was* his son, Eleasah his son, Azel his son.

38 And Azel had six sons, and these *were* their names: Azrikam, Bocheru, Ishmael, Sheariah, Obadiah and Hanan. All these *were* the sons of Azel.

39 And the sons of Eshek his brother *were* Ulam his first-born, Jeush the second, and Eliphelet the third.

40 And the sons of Ulam were mighty men of valor, archers, and had many sons and grandsons, 150 *of them.* All these *were* of the sons of Benjamin.

CHAPTER 9

SO all Israel was enrolled by genealogies; and behold, they are written in the Book of the Kings of Israel. And Judah was carried away into exile to Babylon for their unfaithfulness.

2 ¶ Now the first who lived in their possessions in their cities *were* Israel, the priests, the Levites and the temple servants.

3 And some of the sons of Judah, of the sons of Benjamin, and of the sons of Ephraim and Manasseh lived in Jerusalem:

4 Uthai the son of Ammihud, the son of Omri, the son of Imri, the son of Bani, from the sons of Perez the son of Judah.

5 And from the Shilonites *were* Asaiah the first-born and his sons.

6 And from the sons of Zerah *were* Jeuel and their relatives, 690 *of them.*

7 And from the sons of Benjamin *were* Sallu the son of Meshullam, the son of Hodaviah, the son of Hassenuah,

8 and Ibneiah the son of Jeroham, and Elah the son of Uzzi, the son of Michri, and Meshullam the son of Shephatiah, the son of Reuel, the son of Ibnijah;

9 and their relatives according to their generations, 956. All these *were* heads of fathers' *households* according to their fathers' houses.

10 ¶ And from the priests *were* Jedaiah, Jehoiarib, Jachin,

11 and Azariah the son of Hilkiah, the son of Meshullam, the son of Zadok, the son of Meraioth, the son of Ahitub, the chief officer of the house of God;

12 and Adaiah the son of Jeroham, the son of Pashhur, the son of Malchijah, and Maasai the son of Adiel, the son of Jahzerah, the son of Meshullam, the son of Meshillemith, the son of Immer;

13 and their relatives, heads of their fathers' households, 1,760 very able men for the work of the service of the house of God.

14 ¶ And of the Levites *were* Shemaiah the son of Hasshub, the son of Azrikam, the son of Hashabiah, of the sons of Merari;

15 and Bakbakkar, Heresh and Galal and Mattaniah the son of Mica, the son of Zichri, the son of Asaph,

16 and Obadiah the son of Shemaiah, the son of Galal, the son of Jeduthun, and Berechiah the son of Asa, the son of Elkanah, who lived in the villages of the Netophathites.

17 ¶ Now the gatekeepers *were* Shallum and Akkub and Talmon and Ahiman and their relatives (Shallum the chief

18 *being stationed* until now at the king's gate to the east). These *were* the gatekeepers for the camp of the sons of Levi.

19 And Shallum the son of Kore, the son of Ebiasaph, the son of Korah, and his relatives, of his father's house, the Korahites, *were* over the work of the service, keepers of the thresholds of the tent; and their fathers had been over the camp of the LORD, keepers of the entrance.

20 And Phinehas the son of Eleazar was ruler over them previously, *and* the LORD was with him.

21 Zechariah the son of Meshelemiah was gatekeeper of the entrance of the tent of meeting.

22 All these who were chosen to be gatekeepers in the thresholds were 212. These were enrolled by genealogy in their villages, whom David and Samuel the seer appointed in their office of trust.

23 So they and their sons had charge of the gates of the house of the LORD, *even* the house of the tent, as guards.

24 The gatekeepers were on the four sides, to the east, west, north, and south.

25 And their relatives in their villages *were* to come in every seven days from time to time *to be* with them;

26 for the four chief gatekeepers who *were* Levites, were in an office of trust, and were over the chambers and over the treasuries in the house of God.

27 And they spent the night around the house of God, because the watch was committed to them; and they *were* in charge of opening *it* morning by morning.

28 ¶ Now some of them had charge of the utensils of service, for they counted them when they brought them in and when they took them out.

29 Some of them also were appointed over the furniture and over all the utensils of the sanctuary and over the fine flour and the wine and the oil and the frankincense and the spices.

30 And some of the sons of the priests prepared the mixing of the spices.

31 And Mattithiah, one of the Levites, who was the first-born of Shallum the Korahite, had the responsibility over the things which were baked in pans.

32 And some of their relatives of the sons of the Kohathites *were* over the showbread to prepare it every sabbath.

33 ¶ Now these are the singers, heads of fathers' *households* of the Levites, *who lived* in the chambers *of the temple* free *from other service;* for they were engaged in their work day and night.

34 These were heads of fathers' *households* of the Levites according to their generations, chief men, who lived in Jerusalem.

35 ¶ And in Gibeon Jeiel the father of Gibeon lived, and his wife's name was Maacah,

36 and his first-born son *was* Abdon, then Zur, Kish, Baal, Ner, Nadab,

37 Gedor, Ahio, Zechariah, and Mikloth.

38 And Mikloth became the father of Shimeam. And they also lived with their relatives in Jerusalem opposite their *other* relatives.

39 And Ner became the father of Kish, and Kish became the father of Saul, and Saul became the father of Jonathan, Malchi-shua, Abinadab, and Eshbaal.

40 And the son of Jonathan *was* Merib-baal; and Merib-baal became the father of Micah.

41 And the sons of Micah *were* Pithon, Melech, Tahrea, *and Ahaz.*

42 And Ahaz became the father of Jarah, and Jarah became the father of Alemeth, Azmaveth, and Zimri; and Zimri became the father of Moza,

43 and Moza became the father of Binea and Rephaiah his son, Eleasah his son, Azel his son.

44 And Azel had six sons whose names are these: Azrikam, Bocheru and Ishmael and Sheariah and Obadiah and Hanan. These were the sons of Azel.

CHAPTER 10

Now the Philistines fought against Israel; and the men of Israel fled before the Philistines, and fell slain on Mount Gilboa.

2 And the Philistines closely pursued Saul and his sons, and the Philistines struck down Jonathan, Abinadab and Malchi-shua, the sons of Saul.

3 And the battle became heavy against Saul, and the archers overtook him; and he was wounded by the archers.

4 Then Saul said to his armor

bearer, "Draw your sword and thrust me through with it, lest these uncircumcised come and abuse me." But his armor bearer would not, for he was greatly afraid. Therefore Saul took his sword and fell on it.

5 And when his armor bearer saw that Saul was dead, he likewise fell on his sword and died.

6 Thus Saul died with his three sons, and all *those* of his house died together.

7 ¶ When all the men of Israel who were in the valley saw that they had fled, and that Saul and his sons were dead, they forsook their cities and fled; and the Philistines came and lived in them.

8 And it came about the next day, when the Philistines came to strip the slain, that they found Saul and his sons fallen on Mount Gilboa.

9 So they stripped him and took his head and his armor and sent *messengers* around the land of the Philistines, to carry the good news to their idols and to the people.

10 And they put his armor in the house of their gods and fastened his head in the house of Dagon.

11 When all Jabesh-gilead heard all that the Philistines had done to Saul,

12 all the valiant men arose and took away the body of Saul and the bodies of his sons, and brought them to Jabesh and buried their bones under the oak in Jabesh, and fasted seven days.

13 ¶ So Saul died for his trespass which he committed against the LORD, because of the word of the LORD which he did not keep; and also because he asked counsel of a medium, making inquiry *of it,*

14 and did not inquire of the LORD. Therefore He killed him, and turned the kingdom to David the son of Jesse.

CHAPTER 11

THEN all Israel gathered to David at Hebron and said, "Behold, we are your bone and your flesh.

2"In times past, even when Saul was king, you *were* the one who led out and brought in Israel; and the LORD your God said to you, 'You shall shepherd My people Israel, and you shall be prince over My people Israel.' "

3 So all the elders of Israel came to the king at Hebron, and David made a covenant with them in Hebron before the LORD; and they anointed David king over Israel, according to the word of the LORD through Samuel.

4 ¶ Then David and all Israel went to Jerusalem (that is, Jebus); and the Jebusites, the inhabitants of the land, *were* there.

5 And the inhabitants of Jebus said to David, "You shall not enter here." Nevertheless David captured the stronghold of Zion (that is, the city of David).

6 Now David had said, "Whoever strikes down a Jebusite first shall be chief and commander." And Joab the son of Zeruiah went up first, so he became chief.

7 Then David dwelt in the stronghold; therefore it was called the city of David.

8 And he built the city all around, from the ²Millo even to the surrounding area; and Joab repaired the rest of the city.

9 And David became greater and greater, for the LORD of hosts *was* with him.

10 ¶ Now these are the heads of the mighty men whom David had, who gave him strong support in his kingdom, together with all Israel, to make him king, according to the word of the LORD concerning Israel.

11 And these *constitute* the list of the mighty men whom David had: Jashobeam, the son of a Hachmonite, the chief of the thirty; he lifted up his spear against three hundred whom he killed at one time.

12 And after him was Eleazar the son of Dodo, the Ahohite, who *was* one of the three mighty men.

13 He was with David at Pasdammim when the Philistines were gathered together there to battle, and there was a plot of ground full of barley; and the people fled before the Philistines.

14 And they took their stand in the midst of the plot, and defended it, and struck down the Philistines; and the LORD saved them by a great victory.

15 ¶ Now three of the thirty chief men went down to the rock to David, into the cave of Adullam, while the

² I.e., citadel

army of the Philistines was camping in the valley of Rephaim.

16 And David was then in the stronghold, while the garrison of the Philistines *was* then in Bethlehem.

17 And David had a craving and said, "Oh that someone would give me water to drink from the well of Bethlehem, which is by the gate!"

18 So the three broke through the camp of the Philistines, and drew water from the well of Bethlehem which *was* by the gate, and took *it* and brought *it* to David; nevertheless David would not drink it, but poured it out to the LORD;

19 and he said, "Be it far from me before my God that I should do this. Shall I drink the blood of these men *who went* at the risk of their lives? For at the risk of their lives they brought it." Therefore he would not drink it. These things the three mighty men did.

20 ¶ As for Abshai the brother of Joab, he was chief of the thirty, and he swung his spear against three hundred and killed them; and he had a name as well as the thirty.

21 Of the three in the second *rank* he was the most honored, and became their commander; however, he did not attain to the *first* three.

22 ¶ Benaiah the son of Jehoiada, the son of a valiant man of Kabzeel, mighty in deeds, struck down the two *sons of* Ariel of Moab. He also went down and killed a lion inside a pit on a snowy day.

23 And he killed an Egyptian, a man of *great* stature five cubits tall. Now in the Egyptian's hand *was* a spear like a weaver's beam, but he went down to him with a club and snatched the spear from the Egyptian's hand, and killed him with his own spear.

24 These *things* Benaiah the son of Jehoiada did, and had a name as well as the three mighty men.

25 Behold, he was honored among the thirty, but he did not attain to the three; and David appointed him over his guard.

26 ¶ Now the mighty men of the armies *were* Asahel the brother of Joab, Elhanan the son of Dodo of Bethlehem,

27 Shammoth the Harorite, Helez the Pelonite,

28 Ira the son of Ikkesh the Tekoite, Abiezer the Anathothite,

29 Sibbecai the Hushathite, Ilai the Ahohite,

30 Maharai the Netophathite, Heled the son of Baanah the Netophathite,

31 Ithai the son of Ribai of Gibeah of the sons of Benjamin, Benaiah the Pirathonite,

32 Hurai of the brooks of Gaash, Abiel the Arbathite,

33 Azmaveth the Baharumite, Eliahba the Shaalbonite,

34 the sons of Hashem the Gizonite, Jonathan the son of Shagee the Hararite,

35 Ahiam the son of Sacar the Hararite, Eliphal the son of Ur,

36 Hepher the Mecherathite, Ahijah the Pelonite,

37 Hezro the Carmelite, Naarai the son of Ezbai,

38 Joel the brother of Nathan, Mibhar the son of Hagri,

39 Zelek the Ammonite, Naharai the Berothite, the armor bearer of Joab the son of Zeruiah,

40 Ira the Ithrite, Gareb the Ithrite,

41 Uriah the Hittite, Zabad the son of Ahlai,

42 Adina the son of Shiza the Reubenite, a chief of the Reubenites, and thirty with him,

43 Hanan the son of Maacah and Joshaphat the Mithnite,

44 Uzzia the Ashterathite, Shama and Jeiel the sons of Hotham the Aroerite,

45 Jediael the son of Shimri and Joha his brother, the Tizite,

46 Eliel the Mahavite and Jeribai and Joshaviah, the sons of Elnaam, and Ithmah the Moabite,

47 Eliel and Obed and Jaasiel the Mezobaite.

CHAPTER 12

NOW these are the ones who came to David at Ziklag, while he was still restricted because of Saul the son of Kish; and they were among the mighty men who helped *him* in war.

2 They were equipped with bows, using both the right hand and the left *to sling* stones and *to shoot* arrows from the bow; *they were* Saul's kinsmen from Benjamin.

3 The chief was Ahiezer, then Joash, the sons of Shemaah the Gibeathite; and Jeziel and Pelet, the sons of Azmaveth, and Beracah and Jehu the Anathothite,

4 and Ishmaiah the Gibeonite, a mighty man among the thirty, and over the thirty. Then Jeremiah, Jahaziel, Johanan, Jozabad the Gederathite,

5 Eluzai, Jerimoth, Bealiah, Shemariah, Shephatiah the Haruphite,

6 Elkanah, Isshiah, Azarel, Joezer, Jashobeam, the Korahites,

7 and Joelah and Zebadiah, the sons of Jeroham of Gedor.

8 ¶ And from the Gadites there came over to David in the stronghold in the wilderness, mighty men of valor, men trained for war, who could handle shield and spear, and whose faces were like the faces of lions, and *they were* as swift as the gazelles on the mountains.

9 Ezer *was* the first, Obadiah the second, Eliab the third,

10 Mishmannah the fourth, Jeremiah the fifth,

11 Attai the sixth, Eliel the seventh,

12 Johanan the eighth, Elzabad the ninth,

13 Jeremiah the tenth, Machbannai the eleventh.

14 These of the sons of Gad were captains of the army; he who was least was equal to a hundred and the greatest to a thousand.

15 These are the ones who crossed the Jordan in the first month when it was overflowing all its banks and they put to flight all those in the valleys, both to the east and to the west.

16 ¶ Then some of the sons of Benjamin and Judah came to the stronghold to David.

17 And David went out to meet them, and answered and said to them, "If you come peacefully to me to help me, my heart shall be united with you; but if to betray me to my adversaries, since there is no wrong in my hands, may the God of our fathers look on *it* and decide."

18 Then the Spirit came upon Amasai, who was the chief of the thirty, *and he said,*

"*We* are yours, O David,
And with you, O son of Jesse!
Peace, peace to you,
And peace to him who helps you;
Indeed, your God helps you!"

Then David received them and made them captains of the band.

19 ¶ From Manasseh also some defected to David, when he was about to go to battle with the Philistines against Saul. But they did not help them, for the lords of the Philistines after consultation sent him away, saying, "At *the cost of* our heads he may defect to his master Saul."

20 As he went to Ziklag, there defected to him from Manasseh: Adnah, Jozabad, Jediael, Michael, Jozabad, Elihu, and Zillethai, captains of thousands who belonged to Manasseh.

21 And they helped David against the band of raiders, for they were all mighty men of valor, and were captains in the army.

22 For day by day *men* came to David to help him, until there was a great army like the army of God.

23 ¶ Now these are the numbers of the divisions equipped for war, who came to David at Hebron, to turn the kingdom of Saul to him, according to the word of the LORD.

24 The sons of Judah who bore shield and spear *were* 6,800, equipped for war.

25 Of the sons of Simeon, mighty men of valor for war, 7,100.

26 Of the sons of Levi 4,600.

27 Now Jehoiada was the leader of *the house of* Aaron, and with him were 3,700,

28 also Zadok, a young man mighty of valor, and of his father's house twenty-two captains.

29 And of the sons of Benjamin, Saul's kinsmen, 3,000; for until now the greatest part of them had kept their allegiance to the house of Saul.

30 And of the sons of Ephraim 20,800, mighty men of valor, famous men in their fathers' households.

31 And of the half-tribe of Manasseh 18,000, who were designated by name to come and make David king.

32 And of the sons of Issachar, men who understood the times, with knowledge of what Israel should do, their chiefs were two hundred; and all their kinsmen were at their command.

33 Of Zebulun, there were 50,000

who went out in the army, who could draw up in battle formation with all kinds of weapons of war and helped *David* with an undivided heart.

34 And of Naphtali *there were* 1,000 captains, and with them 37,000 with shield and spear.

35 And of the Danites who could draw up in battle formation, *there were* 28,600.

36 And of Asher *there were* 40,000 who went out in the army to draw up in battle formation.

37 And from the other side of the Jordan, of the Reubenites and the Gadites and of the half-tribe of Manasseh, *there were* 120,000 with all *kinds* of weapons of war for the battle.

38 ¶ All these, being men of war, who could draw up in battle formation, came to Hebron with a perfect heart, to make David king over all Israel; and all the rest also of Israel were of one mind to make David king.

39 And they were there with David three days, eating and drinking; for their kinsmen had prepared for them.

40 Moreover those who were near to them, *even* as far as Issachar and Zebulun and Naphtali, brought food on donkeys, camels, mules, and on oxen, great quantities of flour cakes, fig cakes and bunches of raisins, wine, oil, oxen and sheep. There was joy indeed in Israel.

CHAPTER 13

THEN David consulted with the captains of the thousands and the hundreds, even with every leader.

2 And David said to all the assembly of Israel, "If it seems good to you, and if it is from the LORD our God, let us send everywhere to our kinsmen who remain in all the land of Israel, also to the priests and Levites who are with them in their cities with pasture lands, that they may meet with us;

3 and let us bring back the ark of our God to us, for we did not seek it in the days of Saul."

4 Then all the assembly said that they would do so, for the thing was right in the eyes of all the people.

5 So David assembled all Israel together, from the Shihor of Egypt even to the entrance of Hamath, to bring the ark of God from Kiriath-jearim.

6 And David and all Israel went up to Baalah, *that is,* to Kiriath-jearim, which belongs to Judah, to bring up from there the ark of God, the LORD who is enthroned *above* the cherubim, where His name is called.

7 And they carried the ark of God on a new cart from the house of Abinadab, and Uzza and Ahio drove the cart.

8 And David and all Israel were celebrating before God with all *their* might, even with songs and with lyres, harps, tambourines, cymbals, and with trumpets.

9 ¶ When they came to the threshing floor of Chidon, Uzza put out his hand to hold the ark, because the oxen nearly upset *it.*

10 And the anger of the LORD burned against Uzza, so He struck him down because he put out his hand to the ark; and he died there before God.

11 Then David became angry because of the LORD'S outburst against Uzza; and he called that place [3]Perezuzza to this day.

12 And David was afraid of God that day, saying, "How can I bring the ark of God *home* to me?"

13 So David did not take the ark with him to the city of David, but took it aside to the house of Obed-edom the Gittite.

14 Thus the ark of God remained with the family of Obed-edom in his house three months; and the LORD blessed the family of Obed-edom with all that he had.

CHAPTER 14

NOW Hiram king of Tyre sent messengers to David with cedar trees, masons, and carpenters, to build a house for him.

2 And David realized that the LORD had established him as king over Israel, *and* that his kingdom was highly exalted, for the sake of His people Israel.

3 ¶ Then David took more wives at Jerusalem, and David became the father of more sons and daughters.

4 And these are the names of the children born *to him* in Jerusalem: Shammua, Shobab, Nathan, Solomon,

5 Ibhar, Elishua, Elpelet,

[3] I.e., the breakthrough of Uzza

6 Nogah, Nepheg, Japhia,

7 Elishama, Beeliada and Eliphelet.

8 ¶ When the Philistines heard that David had been anointed king over all Israel, all the Philistines went up in search of David; and David heard of it and went out against them.

9 Now the Philistines had come and made a raid in the valley of Rephaim.

10 And David inquired of God, saying, "Shall I go up against the Philistines? And wilt Thou give them into my hand?" Then the LORD said to him, "Go up, for I will give them into your hand."

11 So they came up to Baal-perazim, and David defeated them there; and David said, "God has broken through my enemies by my hand, like the breakthrough of waters." Therefore they named that place ⁴Baal-perazim.

12 And they abandoned their gods there; so David gave the order and they were burned with fire.

13 ¶ And the Philistines made yet another raid in the valley.

14 And David inquired again of God, and God said to him, "You shall not go up after them; circle around behind them, and come at them in front of the balsam trees.

15 "And it shall be when you hear the sound of marching in the tops of the balsam trees, then you shall go out to battle, for God will have gone out before you to strike the army of the Philistines."

16 And David did just as God had commanded him, and they struck down the army of the Philistines from Gibeon even as far as Gezer.

17 Then the fame of David went out into all the lands; and the LORD brought the fear of him on all the nations.

CHAPTER 15

NOW *David* built houses for himself in the city of David; and he prepared a place for the ark of God, and pitched a tent for it.

2 Then David said, "No one is to carry the ark of God but the Levites; for the LORD chose them to carry the ark of God, and to minister to Him forever."

3 And David assembled all Israel at Jerusalem, to bring up the ark of the LORD to its place, which he had prepared for it.

4 And David gathered together the sons of Aaron, and the Levites:

5 of the sons of Kohath, Uriel the chief, and 120 of his relatives;

6 of the sons of Merari, Asaiah the chief, and 220 of his relatives;

7 of the sons of Gershom, Joel the chief, and 130 of his relatives;

8 of the sons of Elizaphan, Shemaiah the chief, and 200 of his relatives;

9 of the sons of Hebron, Eliel the chief, and 80 of his relatives;

10 of the sons of Uzziel, Amminadab the chief, and 112 of his relatives.

11 Then David called for Zadok and Abiathar the priests, and for the Levites, for Uriel, Asaiah, Joel, Shemaiah, Eliel, and Amminadab,

12 and said to them, "You are the heads of the fathers' *households* of the Levites; consecrate yourselves both you and your relatives, that you may bring up the ark of the LORD God of Israel, to *the place* that I have prepared for it.

13 "Because you did not *carry it* at the first, the LORD our God made an outburst on us, for we did not seek Him according to the ordinance."

14 So the priests and the Levites consecrated themselves to bring up the ark of the LORD God of Israel.

15 And the sons of the Levites carried the ark of God on their shoulders, with the poles thereon as Moses had commanded according to the word of the LORD.

16 ¶ Then David spoke to the chiefs of the Levites to appoint their relatives the singers, with instruments of music, harps, lyres, loud-sounding cymbals, to raise sounds of joy.

17 So the Levites appointed Heman the son of Joel, and from his relatives, Asaph the son of Berechiah; and from the sons of Merari their relatives, Ethan the son of Kushaiah,

18 and with them their relatives of the second rank, Zechariah, Ben, Jaaziel, Shemiramoth, Jehiel, Unni, Eliab, Benaiah, Maaseiah, Mattithiah, Eliphelehu, Mikneiah, Obed-edom, and Jeiel, the gatekeepers.

19 So the singers, Heman, Asaph, and Ethan *were appointed* to sound aloud cymbals of bronze;

⁴ I.e., the master of breakthrough

20 and Zechariah, Aziel, Shemiramoth, Jehiel, Unni, Eliab, Maaseiah,
and Benaiah, with harps *tuned* to alamoth;

21 and Mattithiah, Eliphelehu, Mikneiah, Obed-edom, Jeiel, and Azaziah,
to lead with lyres tuned to the shemi-
nith.

22 And Chenaniah, chief of the Levites, was *in charge of* the singing; he
gave instruction in singing because he
was skillful.

23 And Berechiah and Elkanah were
gatekeepers for the ark.

24 And Shebaniah, Joshaphat, Nethanel, Amasai, Zechariah, Benaiah,
and Eliezer, the priests, blew the trumpets before the ark of God. Obed-edom
and Jehiah also *were* gatekeepers for
the ark.

25 ¶ So *it was* David, with the elders
of Israel and the captains over thousands, who went to bring up the ark of
the covenant of the LORD from the
house of Obed-edom with joy.

26 And it came about because God
was helping the Levites who were
carrying the ark of the covenant of the
LORD, that they sacrificed seven bulls
and seven rams.

27 Now David was clothed with a
robe of fine linen with all the Levites
who were carrying the ark, and the
singers and Chenaniah the leader of
the singing *with* the singers. David
also wore an ephod of linen.

28 Thus all Israel brought up the ark
of the covenant of the LORD with
shouting, and with sound of the horn,
with trumpets, with loud-sounding
cymbals, with harps and lyres.

29 ¶ And it happened when the ark
of the covenant of the LORD came to
the city of David, that Michal the
daughter of Saul looked out of the
window, and saw King David leaping
and making merry; and she despised
him in her heart.

CHAPTER 16

AND they brought in the ark of God
and placed it inside the tent which
David had pitched for it, and they
offered burnt offerings and peace offerings before God.

2 When David had finished offering
the burnt offering and the peace offerings, he blessed the people in the name
of the LORD.

3 And he distributed to everyone of
Israel, both man and woman, to everyone a loaf of bread and a portion *of
meat* and a raisin cake.

4 ¶ And he appointed some of the
Levites *as* ministers before the ark of
the LORD, even to celebrate and to
thank and praise the LORD God of
Israel:

5 Asaph the chief, and second to
him Zechariah, *then* Jeiel, Shemiramoth, Jehiel, Mattithiah, Eliab, Benaiah, Obed-edom, and Jeiel, with musical instruments, harps, lyres; also
Asaph *played* loud-sounding cymbals,

6 and Benaiah and Jahaziel the
priests *blew* trumpets continually before the ark of the covenant of God.

7 ¶ Then on that day David first
assigned Asaph and his relatives to
give thanks to the LORD.

8 Oh give thanks to the LORD, call
   upon His name;
   Make known His deeds among
   the peoples.
9 Sing to Him, sing praises to Him;
   [5]Speak of all His wonders.
10 Glory in His holy name;
   Let the heart of those who seek
   the LORD be glad.
11 Seek the LORD and His strength;
   Seek His face continually.
12 Remember His wonderful deeds
   which He has done,
   His marvels and the judgments
   from His mouth,
13 O seed of Israel His servant,
   Sons of Jacob, His chosen ones!
14 He is the LORD our God;
   His judgments are in all the earth.
15 Remember His covenant forever,
   The word which He commanded
   to a thousand generations,
16 *The covenant* which He made
   with Abraham,
   And His oath to Isaac.
17 He also confirmed it to Jacob for a
   statute,
   To Israel as an everlasting covenant,
18 Saying, "To you I will give the
   land of Canaan,
   As the portion of your inheritance."
19 When they were only a few in
   number,
   Very few, and strangers in it,

[5] Or, *Meditate on*

20 And they wandered about from
  nation to nation,
  And from *one* kingdom to another
  people,
21 He permitted no man to oppress
  them,
  And He reproved kings for their
  sakes, *saying,*
22 "Do not touch My anointed ones,
  And do My prophets no harm."
23 Sing to the LORD, all the earth;
  Proclaim good tidings of His salvation from day to day.
24 Tell of His glory among the nations,
  His wonderful deeds among all
  the peoples.
25 For great is the LORD, and greatly
  to be praised;
  He also is to be feared above all
  gods.
26 For all the gods of the peoples are
  idols,
  But the LORD made the heavens.
27 Splendor and majesty are before
  Him,
  Strength and joy are in His place.
28 Ascribe to the LORD, O families of
  the peoples,
  Ascribe to the LORD glory and
  strength.
29 Ascribe to the LORD the glory due
  His name;
  Bring an offering, and come before Him;
  Worship the LORD in holy array.
30 Tremble before Him, all the earth;
  Indeed, the world is firmly established, it will not be moved.
31 Let the heavens be glad, and let
  the earth rejoice;
  And let them say among the nations, "The LORD reigns."
32 Let the sea roar, and all it contains;
  Let the field exult, and all that is
  in it.
33 Then the trees of the forest will
  sing for joy before the LORD;
  For He is coming to judge the
  earth.
34 O give thanks to the LORD, for *He
  is* good;
  For His lovingkindness is everlasting.
35 Then say, "Save us, O God of our
  salvation,
  And gather us and deliver us from
  the nations,

To give thanks to Thy holy name,
  And glory in Thy praise."
36 Blessed be the LORD, the God of
  Israel,
  From everlasting even to everlasting.
Then all the people said, "Amen," and
praised the LORD.
37 ¶ So he left Asaph and his relatives there before the ark of the covenant of the LORD, to minister before
the ark continually, as every day's
work required;
38 and Obed-edom with his 68 relatives; Obed-edom, also the son of Jeduthun, and Hosah as gatekeepers.
39 And *he left* Zadok the priest and
his relatives the priests before the
tabernacle of the LORD in the high
place which *was* at Gibeon,
40 to offer burnt offerings to the
LORD on the altar of burnt offering
continually morning and evening,
even according to all that is written in
the law of the LORD, which He commanded Israel.
41 And with them *were* Heman and
Jeduthun, and the rest who were chosen, who were designated by name, to
give thanks to the LORD, because His
lovingkindness is everlasting.
42 And with them *were* Heman and
Jeduthun *with* trumpets and cymbals
for those who should sound aloud, and
with instruments *for* the songs of God,
and the sons of Jeduthun for the gate.
43 Then all the people departed each
to his house, and David returned to
bless his household.

CHAPTER 17

AND it came about, when David
dwelt in his house, that David said to
Nathan the prophet, "Behold, I am
dwelling in a house of cedar, but the
ark of the covenant of the LORD is
under curtains."
2 Then Nathan said to David, "Do
all that is in your heart, for God is with
you."
3 And it came about the same night,
that the word of God came to Nathan,
saying,
4 "Go and tell David My servant,
'Thus says the LORD, "You shall not
build a house for Me to dwell in;
5 for I have not dwelt in a house
since the day that I brought up Israel

to this day, but I have gone from tent to tent and from *one* dwelling place *to another.*

6"In all places where I have walked with all Israel, have I spoken a word with any of the judges of Israel, whom I commanded to shepherd My people, saying, 'Why have you not built for Me a house of cedar?' " '

7"Now, therefore, thus shall you say to My servant David, 'Thus says the LORD of hosts, "I took you from the pasture, from following the sheep, that you should be leader over My people Israel.

8"And I have been with you wherever you have gone, and have cut off all your enemies from before you; and I will make you a name like the name of the great ones who are in the earth.

9"And I will appoint a place for My people Israel, and will plant them, that they may dwell in their own place and be moved no more; neither shall the wicked waste them anymore as formerly,

10 even from the day that I commanded judges *to be* over My people Israel. And I will subdue all your enemies. Moreover, I tell you that the LORD will build a house for you.

11"And it shall come about when your days are fulfilled that you must go *to be* with your fathers, that I will set up *one of* your descendants after you, who shall be of your sons; and I will establish his kingdom.

12"He shall build for Me a house, and I will establish his throne forever.

13"I will be his father, and he shall be My son; and I will not take My loving-kindness away from him, as I took it from him who was before you.

14"But I will settle him in My house and in My kingdom forever, and his throne shall be established forever." ' "

15 According to all these words and according to all this vision, so Nathan spoke to David.

16 ¶ Then David the king went in and sat before the LORD and said, "Who am I, O LORD God, and what is my house that Thou hast brought me this far?

17"And this was a small thing in Thine eyes, O God; but Thou hast spoken of Thy servant's house for a great while to come, and hast regarded me according to the standard of a man of high degree, O LORD God.

18"What more can David still *say* to Thee concerning the honor *bestowed* on Thy servant? For Thou knowest Thy servant.

19"O LORD, for Thy servant's sake, and according to Thine own heart, Thou hast wrought all this greatness, to make known all these great things.

20"O LORD, there is none like Thee, neither is there any God besides Thee, according to all that we have heard with our ears.

21"And what one nation in the earth is like Thy people Israel, whom God went to redeem for Himself *as* a people, to make Thee a name by great and terrible things, in driving out nations from before Thy people, whom Thou didst redeem out of Egypt?

22"For Thy people Israel Thou didst make Thine own people forever, and Thou, O LORD, didst become their God.

23"And now, O LORD, let the word that Thou hast spoken concerning Thy servant and concerning his house, be established forever, and do as Thou hast spoken.

24"And let Thy name be established and magnified forever, saying, 'The LORD of hosts is the God of Israel, *even* a God to Israel; and the house of David Thy servant is established before Thee.'

25"For Thou, O my God, hast revealed to Thy servant that Thou wilt build for him a house; therefore Thy servant hath found *courage* to pray before Thee.

26"And now, O LORD, Thou art God, and hast promised this good thing to Thy servant.

27"And now it hath pleased Thee to bless the house of Thy servant, that it may continue forever before Thee; for Thou, O LORD, hast blessed, and it is blessed forever."

CHAPTER 18

NOW after this it came about that David defeated the Philistines and subdued them and took Gath and its towns from the hand of the Philistines.

2 And he defeated Moab, and the Moabites became servants to David, bringing tribute.

3 David also defeated Hadadezer

king of Zobah *as far as* Hamath, as he went to establish his rule to the Euphrates River.

4 And David took from him 1,000 chariots and 7,000 horsemen and 20,000 foot soldiers, and David hamstrung all the chariot horses, but reserved *enough* of them for 100 chariots.

5 ¶ When the Arameans of Damascus came to help Hadadezer king of Zobah, David killed 22,000 men of the Arameans.

6 Then David put *garrisons* among the Arameans of Damascus; and the Arameans became servants to David, bringing tribute. And the LORD helped David wherever he went.

7 And David took the shields of gold which were carried by the servants of Hadadezer, and brought them to Jerusalem.

8 Also from Tibhath and from Cun, cities of Hadadezer, David took a very large amount of bronze, with which Solomon made the bronze sea and the pillars and the bronze utensils.

9 ¶ Now when Tou king of Hamath heard that David had defeated all the army of Hadadezer king of Zobah,

10 he sent Hadoram his son to King David, to greet him and to bless him, because he had fought against Hadadezer and had defeated him; for Hadadezer had been at war with Tou. And *Hadoram brought* all kinds of articles of gold and silver and bronze.

11 King David also dedicated these to the LORD with the silver and the gold which he had carried away from all the nations: from Edom, Moab, the sons of Ammon, the Philistines, and from Amalek.

12 ¶ Moreover Abishai the son of Zeruiah defeated 18,000 Edomites in the Valley of Salt.

13 Then he put garrisons in Edom, and all the Edomites became servants to David. And the LORD helped David wherever he went.

14 ¶ So David reigned over all Israel; and he administered justice and righteousness for all his people.

15 And Joab the son of Zeruiah *was* over the army, and Jehoshaphat the son of Ahilud *was* recorder;

16 and Zadok the son of Ahitub and Abimelech the son of Abiathar *were* priests, and Shavsha *was* secretary;

17 and Benaiah the son of Jehoiada *was* over the Cherethites and the Pelethites, and the sons of David *were* chiefs at the king's side.

CHAPTER 19

Now it came about after this, that Nahash the king of the sons of Ammon died, and his son became king in his place.

2 Then David said, "I will show kindness to Hanun the son of Nahash, because his father showed kindness to me." So David sent messengers to console him concerning his father. And David's servants came into the land of the sons of Ammon to Hanun, to console him.

3 But the princes of the sons of Ammon said to Hanun, "Do you think that David is honoring your father, in that he has sent comforters to you? Have not his servants come to you to search and to overthrow and to spy out the land?"

4 So Hanun took David's servants and shaved them, and cut off their garments in the middle as far as their hips, and sent them away.

5 Then *certain persons* went and told David about the men. And he sent to meet them, for the men were greatly humiliated. And the king said, "Stay at Jericho until your beards grow, and *then* return."

6 ¶ When the sons of Ammon saw that they had made themselves odious to David, Hanun and the sons of Ammon sent 1,000 talents of silver to hire for themselves chariots and horsemen from Mesopotamia, from Aram-maacah, and from Zobah.

7 So they hired for themselves 32,000 chariots, and the king of Maacah and his people, who came and camped before Medeba. And the sons of Ammon gathered together from their cities and came to battle.

8 When David heard *of it,* he sent Joab and all the army, the mighty men.

9 And the sons of Ammon came out and drew up in battle array at the entrance of the city, and the kings who had come were by themselves in the field.

10 ¶ Now when Joab saw that the battle was set against him in front and

in the rear, he selected from all the choice men of Israel and they arrayed themselves against the Arameans.

11 But the remainder of the people he placed in the hand of Abshai his brother; and they arrayed themselves against the sons of Ammon.

12 And he said, "If the Arameans are too strong for me, then you shall help me; but if the sons of Ammon are too strong for you, then I will help you.

13 "Be strong, and let us show ourselves courageous for the sake of our people and for the cities of our God; and may the Lord do what is good in His sight."

14 So Joab and the people who were with him drew near to the battle against the Arameans, and they fled before him.

15 When the sons of Ammon saw that the Arameans fled, they also fled before Abshai his brother, and entered the city. Then Joab came to Jerusalem.

16 ¶ When the Arameans saw that they had been defeated by Israel, they sent messengers, and brought out the Arameans who were beyond the [6]River, with Shophach the commander of the army of Hadadezer leading them.

17 When it was told David, he gathered all Israel together and crossed the Jordan, and came upon them and drew up in formation against them. And when David drew up in battle array against the Arameans, they fought against him.

18 And the Arameans fled before Israel, and David killed of the Arameans 7,000 charioteers and 40,000 foot soldiers, and put to death Shophach the commander of the army.

19 So when the servants of Hadadezer saw that they were defeated by Israel, they made peace with David and served him. Thus the Arameans were not willing to help the sons of Ammon anymore.

CHAPTER 20

THEN it happened in the spring, at the time when kings go out to battle, that Joab led out the army and ravaged the land of the sons of Ammon, and came and besieged Rabbah. But

David stayed at Jerusalem. And Joab struck Rabbah and overthrew it.

2 And David took the crown of their king from his head, and he found it to weigh a talent of gold, and there was a precious stone in it; and it was placed on David's head. And he brought out the spoil of the city, a very great amount.

3 And he brought out the people who were in it, and cut them with saws and with sharp instruments and with axes. And thus David did to all the cities of the sons of Ammon. Then David and all the people returned to Jerusalem.

4 ¶ Now it came about after this, that war broke out at Gezer with the Philistines; then Sibbecai the Hushathite killed Sippai, one of the descendants of the giants, and they were subdued.

5 And there was war with the Philistines again, and Elhanan the son of Jair killed Lahmi the brother of Goliath the Gittite, the shaft of whose spear was like a weaver's beam.

6 And again there was war at Gath, where there was a man of great stature who had twenty-four fingers and toes, six fingers on each hand and six toes on each foot; and he also was descended from the giants.

7 And when he taunted Israel, Jonathan the son of Shimea, David's brother, killed him.

8 These were descended from the giants in Gath, and they fell by the hand of David and by the hand of his servants.

CHAPTER 21

THEN Satan stood up against Israel and moved David to number Israel.

2 So David said to Joab and to the princes of the people, "Go, number Israel from Beersheba even to Dan, and bring me word that I may know their number."

3 And Joab said, "May the Lord add to His people a hundred times as many as they are! But, my lord the king, are they not all my lord's servants? Why does my lord seek this thing? Why should he be a cause of guilt to Israel?"

4 Nevertheless, the king's word prevailed against Joab. Therefore, Joab

[6] I.e., Euphrates

departed and went throughout all Israel, and came to Jerusalem.

5 And Joab gave the number of the census of *all* the people to David. And all Israel were 1,100,000 men who drew the sword; and Judah *was* 470,000 men who drew the sword.

6 But he did not number Levi and Benjamin among them, for the king's command was abhorrent to Joab.

7 And God was displeased with this thing, so He struck Israel.

8 And David said to God, "I have sinned greatly, in that I have done this thing. But now, please take away the iniquity of Thy servant, for I have done very foolishly."

9 ¶ And the LORD spoke to Gad, David's seer, saying,

10 "Go and speak to David, saying, 'Thus says the LORD, "I offer you three things; choose for yourself one of them, that I may do *it* to you." ' "

11 So Gad came to David and said to him, "Thus says the LORD, 'Take for yourself

12 either three years of famine, or three months to be swept away before your foes, while the sword of your enemies overtakes *you*, or else three days of the sword of the LORD, even pestilence in the land, and the angel of the LORD destroying throughout all the territory of Israel.' Now, therefore, consider what answer I shall return to Him who sent me."

13 And David said to Gad, "I am in great distress; please let me fall into the hand of the LORD, for His mercies are very great. But do not let me fall into the hand of man."

14 So the LORD sent a pestilence on Israel; 70,000 men of Israel fell.

15 And God sent an angel to Jerusalem to destroy it; but as he was about to destroy *it*, the LORD saw and was sorry over the calamity, and said to the destroying angel, "It is enough; now relax your hand." And the angel of the LORD was standing by the threshing floor of Ornan the Jebusite.

16 Then David lifted up his eyes and saw the angel of the LORD standing between earth and heaven, with his drawn sword in his hand stretched out over Jerusalem. Then David and the elders, covered with sackcloth, fell on their faces.

17 And David said to God, "Is it not I who commanded to count the people? Indeed, I am the one who has sinned and done very wickedly, but these sheep, what have they done? O LORD my God, please let Thy hand be against me and my father's household, but not against Thy people that they should be plagued."

18 ¶ Then the angel of the LORD commanded Gad to say to David, that David should go up and build an altar to the LORD on the threshing floor of Ornan the Jebusite.

19 So David went up at the word of Gad, which he spoke in the name of the LORD.

20 Now Ornan turned back and saw the angel, and his four sons *who were* with him hid themselves. And Ornan was threshing wheat.

21 And as David came to Ornan, Ornan looked and saw David, and went out from the threshing floor, and prostrated himself before David with his face to the ground.

22 Then David said to Ornan, "Give me the site of *this* threshing floor, that I may build on it an altar to the LORD; for the full price you shall give it to me, that the plague may be restrained from the people."

23 And Ornan said to David, "Take *it* for yourself; and let my lord the king do what is good in his sight. See, I will give the oxen for burnt offerings and the threshing sledges for wood and the wheat for the grain offering; I will give *it* all."

24 But King David said to Ornan, "No, but I will surely buy *it* for the full price; for I will not take what is yours for the LORD, or offer a burnt offering which costs me nothing."

25 So David gave Ornan 600 shekels of gold by weight for the site.

26 Then David built an altar to the LORD there, and offered burnt offerings and peace offerings. And he called to the LORD and He answered him with fire from heaven on the altar of burnt offering.

27 And the LORD commanded the angel, and he put his sword back in its sheath.

28 ¶ At that time, when David saw that the LORD had answered him on the threshing floor of Ornan the Jebusite, he offered sacrifice there.

29 For the tabernacle of the LORD,

which Moses had made in the wilderness, and the altar of burnt offering *were* in the high place at Gibeon at that time.

30 But David could not go before it to inquire of God, for he was terrified by the sword of the angel of the LORD.

CHAPTER 22

THEN David said, "This is the house of the LORD God, and this is the altar of burnt offering for Israel."

2 ¶ So David gave orders to gather the foreigners who were in the land of Israel, and he set stonecutters to hew out stones to build the house of God.

3 And David prepared large quantities of iron to make the nails for the doors of the gates and for the clamps, and more bronze than could be weighed;

4 and timbers of cedar logs beyond number, for the Sidonians and Tyrians brought large quantities of cedar timber to David.

5 And David said, "My son Solomon is young and inexperienced, and the house that is to be built for the LORD shall be exceedingly magnificent, famous and glorious throughout all lands. *Therefore* now I will make preparation for it." So David made ample preparations before his death.

6 ¶ Then he called for his son Solomon, and charged him to build a house for the LORD God of Israel.

7 And David said to Solomon, "My son, I had intended to build a house to the name of the LORD my God.

8"But the word of the LORD came to me, saying, 'You have shed much blood, and have waged great wars; you shall not build a house to My name, because you have shed so much blood on the earth before Me.

9 'Behold, a son shall be born to you, who shall be a man of rest; and I will give him rest from all his enemies on every side; for his name shall be [7]Solomon, and I will give peace and quiet to Israel in his days.

10 'He shall build a house for My name, and he shall be My son, and I will be his father; and I will establish the throne of his kingdom over Israel forever.'

11"Now, my son, the LORD be with you that you may be successful, and build the house of the LORD your God just as He has spoken concerning you.

12"Only the LORD give you discretion and understanding, and give you charge over Israel, so that you may keep the law of the LORD your God.

13"Then you shall prosper, if you are careful to observe the statutes and the ordinances which the LORD commanded Moses concerning Israel. Be strong and courageous, do not fear nor be dismayed.

14"Now behold, with great pains I have prepared for the house of the LORD 100,000 talents of gold and 1,000,000 talents of silver, and bronze and iron beyond weight, for they are in great quantity; also timber and stone I have prepared, and you may add to them.

15"Moreover, there are many workmen with you, stonecutters and masons of stone and carpenters, and all men who are skillful in every kind of work.

16"Of the gold, the silver and the bronze and the iron, there is no limit. Arise and work, and may the LORD be with you."

17 ¶ David also commanded all the leaders of Israel to help his son Solomon, *saying,*

18"Is not the LORD your God with you? And has He not given you rest on every side? For He has given the inhabitants of the land into my hand, and the land is subdued before the LORD and before His people.

19"Now set your heart and your soul to seek the LORD your God; arise, therefore, and build the sanctuary of the LORD God, so that you may bring the ark of the covenant of the LORD, and the holy vessels of God into the house that is to be built for the name of the LORD."

CHAPTER 23

NOW when David reached old age, he made his son Solomon king over Israel.

2 And he gathered together all the leaders of Israel with the priests and the Levites.

3 And the Levites were numbered from thirty years old and upward, and

---

[7] I.e., peaceful

their number by census of men was 38,000.

4 Of these, 24,000 were to oversee the work of the house of the LORD; and 6,000 were officers and judges,

5 and 4,000 were gatekeepers, and 4,000 were praising the LORD with the instruments which David made for giving praise.

6 And David divided them into divisions according to the sons of Levi: Gershon, Kohath, and Merari.

7 ¶ Of the Gershonites were Ladan and Shimei.

8 The sons of Ladan were Jehiel the first and Zetham and Joel, three.

9 The sons of Shimei were Shelomoth and Haziel and Haran, three. These were the heads of the fathers' households of Ladan.

10 And the sons of Shimei were Jahath, Zina, Jeush, and Beriah. These four were the sons of Shimei.

11 And Jahath was the first, and Zizah the second; but Jeush and Beriah did not have many sons, so they became a father's household, one class.

12 ¶ The sons of Kohath were four: Amram, Izhar, Hebron and Uzziel.

13 The sons of Amram were Aaron and Moses. And Aaron was set apart to sanctify him as most holy, he and his sons forever, to burn incense before the LORD, to minister to Him and to bless in His name forever.

14 But as for Moses the man of God, his sons were named among the tribe of Levi.

15 The sons of Moses were Gershom and Eliezer.

16 The son of Gershom was Shebuel the chief.

17 And the son of Eliezer was Rehabiah the chief; and Eliezer had no other sons, but the sons of Rehabiah were very many.

18 The son of Izhar was Shelomith the chief.

19 The sons of Hebron were Jeriah the first, Amariah the second, Jahaziel the third and Jekameam the fourth.

20 The sons of Uzziel were Micah the first and Isshiah the second.

21 ¶ The sons of Merari were Mahli and Mushi. The sons of Mahli were Eleazar and Kish.

22 And Eleazar died and had no sons, but daughters only, so their brothers, the sons of Kish, took them as wives.

23 The sons of Mushi were three: Mahli, Eder, and Jeremoth.

24 ¶ These were the sons of Levi according to their fathers' households, even the heads of the fathers' households of those of them who were counted, in the number of names by their census, doing the work for the service of the house of the LORD, from twenty years old and upward.

25 For David said, "The LORD God of Israel has given rest to His people, and He dwells in Jerusalem forever.

26 "And also, the Levites will no longer need to carry the tabernacle and all its utensils for its service."

27 For by the last words of David the sons of Levi were numbered, from twenty years old and upward.

28 For their office is to assist the sons of Aaron with the service of the house of the LORD, in the courts and in the chambers and in the purifying of all holy things, even the work of the service of the house of God,

29 and with the showbread, and the fine flour for a grain offering, and unleavened wafers, or what is baked in the pan, or what is well-mixed, and all measures of volume and size.

30 And they are to stand every morning to thank and to praise the LORD, and likewise at evening,

31 and to offer all burnt offerings to the LORD, on the sabbaths, the new moons and the fixed festivals in the number set by the ordinance concerning them, continually before the LORD.

32 Thus they are to keep charge of the tent of meeting, and charge of the holy place, and charge of the sons of Aaron their relatives, for the service of the house of the LORD.

CHAPTER 24

NOW the divisions of the descendants of Aaron were these: the sons of Aaron were Nadab, Abihu, Eleazar, and Ithamar.

2 But Nadab and Abihu died before their father and had no sons. So Eleazar and Ithamar served as priests.

3 And David, with Zadok of the sons of Eleazar and Ahimelech of the sons of Ithamar, divided them according to their offices for their ministry.

4 Since more chief men were found

from the descendants of Eleazar than the descendants of Ithamar, they divided them thus: *there were* sixteen heads of fathers' households of the descendants of Eleazar, and eight of the descendants of Ithamar according to their fathers' households.

5 Thus they were divided by lot, the one as the other; for they were officers of the sanctuary and officers of God, both from the descendants of Eleazar and the descendants of Ithamar.

6 And Shemaiah, the son of Nethanel the scribe, from the Levites, recorded them in the presence of the king, the princes, Zadok the priest, Ahimelech the son of Abiathar, and the heads of the fathers' *households* of the priests and of the Levites; one father's household taken for Eleazar and one taken for Ithamar.

7 ¶ Now the first lot came out for Jehoiarib, the second for Jedaiah,

8 the third for Harim, the fourth for Seorim,

9 the fifth for Malchijah, the sixth for Mijamin,

10 the seventh for Hakkoz, the eighth for Abijah,

11 the ninth for Jeshua, the tenth for Shecaniah,

12 the eleventh for Eliashib, the twelfth for Jakim,

13 the thirteenth for Huppah, the fourteenth for Jeshebeab,

14 the fifteenth for Bilgah, the sixteenth for Immer,

15 the seventeenth for Hezir, the eighteenth for Happizzez,

16 the nineteenth for Pethahiah, the twentieth for Jehezkel,

17 the twenty-first for Jachin, the twenty-second for Gamul,

18 the twenty-third for Delaiah, the twenty-fourth for Maaziah.

19 These were their offices for their ministry, when *they* came in to the house of the LORD according to the ordinance *given* to them through Aaron their father, just as the LORD God of Israel had commanded him.

20 ¶ Now for the rest of the sons of Levi: of the sons of Amram, Shubael; of the sons of Shubael, Jehdeiah.

21 Of Rehabiah: of the sons of Rehabiah, Isshiah the first.

22 Of the Izharites, Shelomoth; of the sons of Shelomoth, Jahath.

23 And the sons *of Hebron:* Jeriah

the first, Amariah the second, Jahaziel the third, Jekameam the fourth.

24 *Of* the sons of Uzziel, Micah; of the sons of Micah, Shamir.

25 The brother of Micah, Isshiah; of the sons of Isshiah, Zechariah.

26 The sons of Merari, Mahli and Mushi; the sons of Jaaziah, Beno.

27 The sons of Merari: by Jaaziah *were* Beno, Shoham, Zaccur, and Ibri.

28 By Mahli: Eleazar, who had no sons.

29 By Kish: the sons of Kish, Jerahmeel.

30 And the sons of Mushi: Mahli, Eder, and Jerimoth. These *were* the sons of the Levites according to their fathers' households.

31 These also cast lots just as their relatives the sons of Aaron in the presence of David the king, Zadok, Ahimelech, and the heads of the fathers' *households* of the priests and of the Levites—the head of fathers' *households* as well as those of his younger brother.

CHAPTER 25

MOREOVER, David and the commanders of the army set apart for the service *some* of the sons of Asaph and of Heman and of Jeduthun, who *were* to prophesy with lyres, harps, and cymbals; and the number of those who performed their service was:

2 Of the sons of Asaph: Zaccur, Joseph, Nethaniah, and Asharelah; the sons of Asaph *were* under the direction of Asaph, who prophesied under the direction of the king.

3 Of Jeduthun, the sons of Jeduthun: Gedaliah, Zeri, Jeshaiah, Shimei, Hashabiah, and Mattithiah, six, under the direction of their father Jeduthun with the harp, who prophesied in giving thanks and praising the LORD.

4 Of Heman, the sons of Heman: Bukkiah, Mattaniah, Uzziel, Shebuel and Jerimoth, Hananiah, Hanani, Eliathah, Giddalti and Romamti-ezer, Joshbekashah, Mallothi, Hothir, Mahazioth.

5 All these *were* the sons of Heman the king's seer to exalt him according to the words of God, for God gave fourteen sons and three daughters to Heman.

6 All these were under the direction of their father to sing in the house of

the LORD, with cymbals, harps and lyres, for the service of the house of God. Asaph, Jeduthun and Heman *were* under the direction of the king.

7 And their number who were trained in singing to the LORD, with their [8]relatives, all who were skillful, *was* 288.

8 And they cast lots for their duties, all alike, the small as well as the great, the teacher *as well* as the pupil.

9 ¶ Now the first lot came out for Asaph to Joseph, the second for Gedaliah, he with his relatives and sons *were* twelve;

10 the third to Zaccur, his sons and his relatives, twelve;

11 the fourth to Izri, his sons and his relatives, twelve;

12 the fifth to Nethaniah, his sons and his relatives, twelve;

13 the sixth to Bukkiah, his sons and his relatives, twelve;

14 the seventh to Jesharelah, his sons and his relatives, twelve;

15 the eighth to Jeshaiah, his sons and his relatives, twelve;

16 the ninth to Mattaniah, his sons and his relatives, twelve;

17 the tenth to Shimei, his sons and his relatives, twelve;

18 the eleventh to Azarel, his sons and his relatives, twelve;

19 the twelfth to Hashabiah, his sons and his relatives, twelve;

20 for the thirteenth, Shubael, his sons and his relatives, twelve;

21 for the fourteenth, Mattithiah, his sons and his relatives, twelve;

22 for the fifteenth to Jeremoth, his sons and his relatives, twelve;

23 for the sixteenth to Hananiah, his sons and his relatives, twelve;

24 for the seventeenth to Joshbekashah, his sons and his relatives, twelve;

25 for the eighteenth to Hanani, his sons and his relatives, twelve;

26 for the nineteenth to Mallothi, his sons and his relatives, twelve;

27 for the twentieth to Eliathah, his sons and his relatives, twelve;

28 for the twenty-first to Hothir, his sons and his relatives, twelve;

29 for the twenty-second to Giddalti, his sons and his relatives, twelve;

30 for the twenty-third to Mahazioth, his sons and his relatives, twelve;

31 for the twenty-fourth to Romamti-ezer, his sons and his relatives, twelve.

CHAPTER 26

FOR the divisions of the gatekeepers *there were* of the Korahites, Meshelemiah the son of Kore, of the sons of Asaph.

2 And Meshelemiah had sons: Zechariah the first-born, Jediael the second, Zebadiah the third, Jathniel the fourth,

3 Elam the fifth, Johanan the sixth, Eliehoenai the seventh.

4 And Obed-edom had sons: Shemaiah the first-born, Jehozabad the second, Joah the third, Sacar the fourth, Nethanel the fifth,

5 Ammiel the sixth, Issachar the seventh, *and* Peullethai the eighth; God had indeed blessed him.

6 Also to his son Shemaiah sons were born who ruled over the house of their father, for they were mighty men of valor.

7 The sons of Shemaiah *were* Othni, Rephael, Obed, and Elzabad, whose brothers, Elihu and Semachiah, were valiant men.

8 All these *were* of the sons of Obed-edom; they and their sons and their relatives *were* able men with strength for the service, 62 from Obed-edom.

9 And Meshelemiah had sons and relatives, 18 valiant men.

10 Also Hosah, one of the sons of Merari had sons: Shimri the first (although he was not the first-born, his father made him first),

11 Hilkiah the second, Tebaliah the third, Zechariah the fourth; all the sons and relatives of Hosah *were* 13.

12 ¶ To these divisions of the gatekeepers, the chief men, *were given* duties like their relatives to minister in the house of the LORD.

13 And they cast lots, the small and the great alike, according to their fathers' households, for every gate.

14 And the lot to the east fell to Shelemiah. Then they cast lots *for his* son Zechariah, a counselor with insight, and his lot came out to the north.

[8] Lit., *brothers*, and so throughout this context

437

1 CHRONICLES 27

15 For Obed-edom *it fell* to the south, and to his sons went the storehouse.

16 For Shuppim and Hosah *it was* to the west, by the gate of Shallecheth, on the ascending highway. Guard corresponded to guard.

17 On the east there were six Levites, on the north four daily, on the south four daily, and at the storehouse two by two.

18 At the ⁹Parbar on the west *there were* four at the highway and two at the Parbar.

19 These were the divisions of the gatekeepers of the sons of Korah and of the sons of Merari.

20 ¶ ¹⁰And the Levites, their relatives, had charge of the treasures of the house of God, and of the treasures of the dedicated gifts.

21 The sons of Ladan, the sons of the Gershonites belonging to Ladan, *namely,* the Jehielites, *were* the heads of the fathers' *households,* belonging to Ladan the Gershonite.

22 The sons of Jehieli, Zetham and Joel his brother, had charge of the treasures of the house of the LORD.

23 As for the Amramites, the Izharites, the Hebronites, and the Uzzielites,

24 Shebuel the son of Gershom, the son of Moses, was officer over the treasures.

25 And his relatives by Eliezer *were* Rehabiah his son, Jeshaiah his son, Joram his son, Zichri his son, and Shelomoth his son.

26 This Shelomoth and his relatives had charge of all the treasures of the dedicated gifts, which King David and the heads of the fathers' *households,* the commanders of thousands and hundreds, and commanders of the army, had dedicated.

27 They dedicated part of the spoil won in battles to repair the house of the LORD.

28 And all that Samuel the seer had dedicated and Saul the son of Kish, Abner the son of Ner and Joab the son of Zeruiah, everyone who had dedicated *anything, all of this* was in the care of Shelomoth and his relatives.

29 As for the Izharites, Chenaniah and his sons were *assigned* to outside duties for Israel, as officers and judges.

30 As for the Hebronites, Hashabiah and his relatives, 1,700 capable men, had charge of the affairs of Israel west of the Jordan, for all the work of the LORD and the service of the king.

31 As for the Hebronites, Jerijah the chief (these Hebronites were investigated according to their genealogies and fathers' *households,* in the fortieth year of David's reign, and men of outstanding capability were found among them at Jazer of Gilead)

32 and his relatives, capable men, *were* 2,700 in number, heads of fathers' *households.* And King David made them overseers of the Reubenites, the Gadites and the half-tribe of the Manassites concerning all the affairs of God and of the king.

CHAPTER 27

NOW *this is* the enumeration of the sons of Israel, the heads of fathers' *households,* the commanders of thousands and of hundreds, and their officers who served the king in all the affairs of the divisions which came in and went out month by month throughout all the months of the year, each division *numbering* 24,000.

2 Jashobeam the son of Zabdiel ¹¹had charge of the first division for the first month; and in his division *were* 24,000.

3 *He was* from the sons of Perez, *and was* chief of all the commanders of the army for the first month.

4 Dodai the Ahohite and his division had charge of the division for the second month, Mikloth *being* the chief officer; and in his division *were* 24,000.

5 The third commander of the army for the third month *was* Benaiah, the son of Jehoiada the priest, *as* chief; and in his division *were* 24,000.

6 This Benaiah *was* the mighty man of the thirty, and had charge of thirty; and over his division was Ammizabad his son.

7 The fourth for the fourth month *was* Asahel the brother of Joab, and Zebadiah his son after him; and in his division *were* 24,000.

8 The fifth for the fifth month *was*

---

⁹ Possibly *court* or *colonnade*
¹⁰ So Gr.; Heb., *As for the Levites, Ahijah had*

¹¹ Lit., *was over,* and so throughout the ch.

the commander Shamhuth the Izrahite; and in his division were 24,000.

9 The sixth for the sixth month was Ira the son of Ikkesh the Tekoite; and in his division were 24,000.

10 The seventh for the seventh month was Helez the Pelonite of the sons of Ephraim; and in his division were 24,000.

11 The eighth for the eighth month was Sibbecai the Hushathite of the Zerahites; and in his division were 24,000.

12 The ninth for the ninth month was Abiezer the Anathothite of the Benjamites; and in his division were 24,000.

13 The tenth for the tenth month was Maharai the Netophathite of the Zerahites; and in his division were 24,000.

14 The eleventh for the eleventh month was Benaiah the Pirathonite of the sons of Ephraim; and in his division were 24,000.

15 The twelfth for the twelfth month was Heldai the Netophathite of Othniel; and in his division were 24,000.

16 ¶ Now in charge of the tribes of Israel: chief officer for the Reubenites was Eliezer the son of Zichri; for the Simeonites, Shephatiah the son of Maacah;

17 for Levi, Hashabiah the son of Kemuel; for Aaron, Zadok;

18 for Judah, Elihu, one of David's brothers; for Issachar, Omri the son of Michael;

19 for Zebulun, Ishmaiah the son of Obadiah; for Naphtali, Jeremoth the son of Azriel;

20 for the sons of Ephraim, Hoshea the son of Azaziah; for the half-tribe of Manasseh, Joel the son of Pedaiah;

21 for the half-tribe of Manasseh in Gilead, Iddo the son of Zechariah; for Benjamin, Jaasiel the son of Abner;

22 for Dan, Azarel the son of Jeroham. These were the princes of the tribes of Israel.

23 But David did not count those twenty years of age and under, because the LORD had said He would multiply Israel as the stars of heaven.

24 Joab the son of Zeruiah had begun to count them, but did not finish; and because of this, wrath came upon Israel, and the number was not included in the account of the chronicles of King David.

25 ¶ Now Azmaveth the son of Adiel had charge of the king's storehouses. And Jonathan the son of Uzziah had charge of the storehouses in the country, in the cities, in the villages, and in the towers.

26 And Ezri the son of Chelub had charge of the agricultural workers who tilled the soil.

27 And Shimei the Ramathite had charge of the vineyards; and Zabdi the Shiphmite had charge of the produce of the vineyards stored in the wine cellars.

28 And Baal-hanan the Gederite had charge of the olive and sycamore trees in the [12]Shephelah; and Joash had charge of the stores of oil.

29 And Shitrai the Sharonite had charge of the cattle which were grazing in Sharon; and Shaphat the son of Adlai had charge of the cattle in the valleys.

30 And Obil the Ishmaelite had charge of the camels; and Jehdeiah the Meronothite had charge of the donkeys.

31 And Jaziz the Hagrite had charge of the flocks. All these were overseers of the property which belonged to King David.

32 ¶ Also Jonathan, David's uncle, was a counselor, a man of understanding, and a scribe; and Jehiel the son of Hachmoni tutored the king's sons.

33 And Ahithophel was counselor to the king; and Hushai the Archite was the king's friend.

34 And Jehoiada the son of Benaiah, and Abiathar succeeded Ahithophel; and Joab was the commander of the king's army.

CHAPTER 28

NOW David assembled at Jerusalem all the officials of Israel, the princes of the tribes, and the commanders of the divisions that served the king, and the commanders of thousands, and the commanders of hundreds, and the overseers of all the property and livestock belonging to the king and his sons, with the officials and the mighty men, even all the valiant men.

12 Or, lowlands

2 Then King David rose to his feet and said, "Listen to me, my brethren and my people; I *had* [13]intended to build a [14]permanent home for the ark of the covenant of the LORD and for the footstool of our God. So I had made preparations to build *it.*

3"But God said to me, 'You shall not build a house for My name because you are a man of war and have shed blood.'

4"Yet, the LORD, the God of Israel, chose me from all the house of my father to be king over Israel forever. For He has chosen Judah to be a leader; and in the house of Judah, my father's house, and among the sons of my father He took pleasure in me to make *me* king over all Israel.

5"And of all my sons (for the LORD has given me many sons), He has chosen my son Solomon to sit on the throne of the kingdom of the LORD over Israel.

6"And He said to me, 'Your son Solomon is the one who shall build My house and My courts; for I have chosen him to be a son to Me, and I will be a father to him.

7 'And I will establish his kingdom forever, if he resolutely performs My commandments and My ordinances, as is done now.'

8"So now, in the sight of all Israel, the assembly of the LORD, and in the hearing of our God, observe and seek after all the commandments of the LORD your God in order that you may possess the good land and bequeath *it* to your sons after you forever.

9 ¶"As for you, my son Solomon, know the God of your father, and serve Him with a whole heart and a willing mind; for the LORD searches all hearts, and understands every intent of the thoughts. If you seek Him, He will let you find Him; but if you forsake Him, He will reject you forever.

10"Consider now, for the LORD has chosen you to build a house for the sanctuary; be courageous and act."

11 ¶ Then David gave to his son Solomon the plan of the porch of *the temple,* its buildings, its storehouses, its upper rooms, its inner rooms, and the room for the mercy seat;

12 and the plan of all that he had in

mind, for the courts of the house of the LORD, and for all the surrounding rooms, for the storehouses of the house of God, and for the storehouses of the dedicated things;

13 also for the divisions of the priests and the Levites and for all the work of the service of the house of the LORD and for all the utensils of service in the house of the LORD;

14 for the golden *utensils,* the weight of gold for all utensils for every kind of service; for the silver utensils, the weight *of silver* for all utensils for every kind of service;

15 and the weight *of gold* for the golden lampstands and their golden lamps, with the weight of each lampstand and its lamps; and *the weight of silver* for the silver lampstands, with the weight of each lampstand and its lamps according to the use of each lampstand;

16 and the gold by weight for the tables of showbread, for each table; and silver for the silver tables;

17 and the forks, the basins, and the pitchers of pure gold; and for the golden bowls with the weight for each bowl; and for the silver bowls with the weight for each bowl;

18 and for the altar of incense refined gold by weight; and gold for the model of the chariot, *even* the cherubim, that spread out *their wings,* and covered the ark of the covenant of the LORD.

19"All *this,*" said David, "the LORD made me understand in writing by His hand upon me, all the details of this pattern."

20 ¶ Then David said to his son Solomon, "Be strong and courageous, and act; do not fear nor be dismayed, for the LORD God, my God, is with you. He will not fail you nor forsake you until all the work for the service of the house of the LORD is finished.

21"Now behold, *there are* the divisions of the priests and the Levites for all the service of the house of God, and every willing man of any skill will be with you in all the work for all kinds of service. The officials also and all the people will be entirely at your command."

CHAPTER 29

THEN King David said to the entire assembly, "My son Solomon, whom

---

[13] Lit., *in my heart*   [14] Lit., *house of rest*

alone God has chosen, is still young and inexperienced and the work is great; for the temple is not for man, but for the LORD God.

2"Now with all my ability I have provided for the house of my God the gold for the *things of* gold, and the silver for the *things of* silver, and the bronze for the *things of* bronze, the iron for the *things of* iron, and wood for the *things of* wood, onyx stones and inlaid *stones,* stones of antimony, and stones of various colors, and all kinds of precious stones, and alabaster in abundance.

3"And moreover, in my delight in the house of my God, the treasure I have of gold and silver, I give to the house of my God, over and above all that I have already provided for the holy [15]temple,

4 *namely,* 3,000 talents of gold, of the gold of Ophir, and 7,000 talents of refined silver, to overlay the walls of the buildings;

5 of gold for the *things of* gold, and of silver for the *things of* silver, that is, for all the work done by the craftsmen. Who then is willing to consecrate himself this day to the LORD?"

6 ¶ Then the rulers of the fathers' *households,* and the princes of the tribes of Israel, and the commanders of thousands and of hundreds, with the overseers over the king's work, offered willingly;

7 and for the service for the house of God they gave 5,000 talents and 10,000 darics of gold, and 10,000 talents of silver, and 18,000 talents of brass, and 100,000 talents of iron.

8 And whoever possessed *precious* stones gave them to the treasury of the house of the LORD, in care of Jehiel the Gershonite.

9 Then the people rejoiced because they had offered so willingly, for they made their offering to the LORD with a whole heart, and King David also rejoiced greatly.

10 ¶ So David blessed the LORD in the sight of all the assembly; and David said, "Blessed art Thou, O LORD God of Israel our father, forever and ever.

11"Thine, O LORD, is the greatness and the power and the glory and the

victory and the majesty, indeed everything that is in the heavens and the earth; Thine is the dominion, O LORD, and Thou dost exalt Thyself as head over all.

12"Both riches and honor *come* from Thee, and Thou dost rule over all, and in Thy hand is power and might; and it lies in Thy hand to make great, and to strengthen everyone.

13"Now therefore, our God, we thank Thee, and praise Thy glorious name.

14"But who am I and who are my people that we should be able to offer as generously as this? For all things come from Thee, and from Thy hand we have given Thee.

15"For we are sojourners before Thee, and tenants, as all our fathers were; our days on the earth are like a shadow, and there is no hope.

16"O LORD our God, all this abundance that we have provided to build Thee a house for Thy holy name, it is from Thy hand, and all is Thine.

17"Since I know, O my God, that Thou triest the heart and delightest in uprightness, I, in the integrity of my heart, have willingly offered all these *things;* so now with joy I have seen Thy people, who are present here, make *their* offerings willingly to Thee.

18"O LORD, the God of Abraham, Isaac, and Israel, our fathers, preserve this forever in the intentions of the heart of Thy people, and direct their heart to Thee;

19"and give to my son Solomon a perfect heart to keep Thy commandments, Thy testimonies, and Thy statutes, and to do *them* all, and to build the temple, for which I have made provision."

20 Then David said to all the assembly, "Now bless the LORD your God." And all the assembly blessed the LORD, the God of their fathers, and bowed low and did homage to the LORD and to the king.

21 And on the next day they made sacrifices to the LORD and offered burnt offerings to the LORD, 1,000 bulls, 1,000 rams *and* 1,000 lambs, with their libations and sacrifices in abundance for all Israel.

22 So they ate and drank that day before the LORD with great gladness.

¶ And they made Solomon the son of David king a second time, and they

[15] Lit., *house*

anointed *him* as ruler for the LORD and Zadok as priest.

23 Then Solomon sat on the throne of the LORD as king instead of David his father; and he prospered, and all Israel obeyed him.

24 And all the officials, the mighty men, and also all the sons of King David pledged allegiance to King Solomon.

25 And the LORD highly exalted Solomon in the sight of all Israel, and bestowed on him royal majesty which had not been on any king before him in Israel.

26 ¶ Now David the son of Jesse reigned over all Israel.

27 And the period which he reigned over Israel *was* forty years; he reigned in Hebron seven years and in Jerusalem thirty-three *years*.

28 Then he died in a ripe old age, full of days, riches and honor; and his son Solomon reigned in his place.

29 Now the acts of King David, from first to last, are written in the chronicles of Samuel the seer, in the chronicles of Nathan the prophet, and in the chronicles of Gad the seer,

30 with all his reign, his power, and the circumstances which came on him, on Israel, and on all the kingdoms of the lands.

THE SECOND BOOK OF THE

CHRONICLES

NOW Solomon the son of David established himself securely over his kingdom, and the LORD his God *was* with him and exalted him greatly.

2 And Solomon spoke to all Israel, to the commanders of thousands and of hundreds and to the judges and to every leader in all Israel, the heads of the fathers' *households*.

3 Then Solomon, and all the assembly with him, went to the high place which was at Gibeon; for God's tent of meeting was there, which Moses the servant of the LORD had made in the wilderness.

4 However, David had brought up the ark of God from Kiriath-jearim to the place he had prepared for it; for he had pitched a tent for it in Jerusalem.

5 Now the bronze altar, which Bezalel the son of Uri, the son of Hur, had made, was there before the tabernacle of the LORD, and Solomon and the assembly sought it out.

6 And Solomon went up there before the LORD to the bronze altar which *was* at the tent of meeting, and offered a thousand burnt offerings on it.

7 ¶ In that night God appeared to Solomon and said to him, "Ask what I shall give you."

8 And Solomon said to God, "Thou hast dealt with my father David with great lovingkindness, and hast made me king in his place.

9 "Now, O LORD God, Thy promise to my father David is fulfilled; for Thou hast made me king over a people as numerous as the dust of the earth.

10 "Give me now wisdom and knowledge, that I may go out and come in before this people; for who can rule this great people of Thine?"

11 And God said to Solomon, "Because you had this in mind, and did not ask for riches, wealth, or honor, or the life of those who hate you, nor have you even asked for long life, but you have asked for yourself wisdom and knowledge, that you may rule My people, over whom I have made you king,

12 wisdom and knowledge have been granted to you. And I will give you riches and wealth and honor, such as none of the kings who were before you has possessed, nor those who will come after you."

13 So Solomon went from the high place which was at Gibeon, from the tent of meeting, to Jerusalem, and he reigned over Israel.

14 ¶ And Solomon amassed chariots and horsemen. He had 1,400 chariots,

and 12,000 horsemen, and he stationed them in the chariot cities and with the king at Jerusalem.

15 And the king made silver and gold as plentiful in Jerusalem as stones, and he made cedars as plentiful as sycamores in the lowland.

16 And Solomon's horses were imported from Egypt and from Kue; the king's traders procured them from Kue for a price.

17 And they imported chariots from Egypt for 600 *shekels* of silver apiece, and horses for 150 apiece, and by the same means they exported them to all the kings of the Hittites and the kings of Aram.

CHAPTER 2

NOW Solomon decided to build a house for the name of the LORD, and a royal palace for himself.

2 So Solomon assigned 70,000 men to carry loads, and 80,000 men to quarry *stone* in the mountains, and 3,600 to supervise them.

3 Then Solomon sent *word* to Huram the king of Tyre, saying, "As you dealt with David my father, and sent him cedars to build him a house to dwell in, so do for me.

4"Behold, I am about to build a house for the name of the LORD my God, dedicating it to Him, to burn fragrant incense before Him, and *to set out* the showbread continually, and to offer burnt offerings morning and evening, on sabbaths and on new moons and on the appointed feasts of the LORD our God, this *being required* forever in Israel.

5"And the house which I am about to build *will be* great; for greater is our God than all the gods.

6"But who is able to build a house for Him, for the heavens and the highest heavens cannot contain Him? So who am I, that I should build a house for Him, except to [1]burn *incense* before Him?

7"And now send me a skilled man to work in gold, silver, brass and iron, and in purple, crimson and violet *fabrics*, and who knows how to make engravings, to *work* with the skilled men whom I have in Judah and Jerusalem, whom David my father provided.

8"Send me also cedar, cypress and algum timber from Lebanon, for I know that your servants know how to cut timber of Lebanon; and indeed, my servants *will work* with your servants,

9 to prepare timber in abundance for me, for the house which I am about to build *will be* great and wonderful.

10"Now behold, I will give to your servants, the woodsmen who cut the timber, 20,000 [2]kors of crushed wheat, and 20,000 kors of barley, and 20,000 baths of wine, and 20,000 baths of oil."

11 ¶ Then Huram, king of Tyre, answered in a letter sent to Solomon: "Because the LORD loves His people, He has made you king over them."

12 Then Huram continued, "Blessed be the LORD, the God of Israel, who has made heaven and earth, who has given King David a wise son, endowed with discretion and understanding, who will build a house for the LORD and a royal palace for himself.

13"And now I am sending a skilled man, endowed with understanding, Huram-abi,

14 the son of a Danite woman and a Tyrian father, who knows how to work in gold, silver, bronze, iron, stone and wood, *and* in purple, violet, linen and crimson fabrics, and *who knows how* to make all kinds of engravings and to execute any design which may be assigned to him, *to work* with your skilled men, and with those of my lord David your father.

15"Now then, let my lord send to his servants wheat and barley, oil and wine, of which he has spoken.

16"And we will cut whatever timber you need from Lebanon, and bring it to you on rafts by sea to Joppa, so that you may carry it up to Jerusalem."

17 ¶ And Solomon numbered all the aliens who *were* in the land of Israel, following the census which his father David had taken; and 153,600 were found.

18 And he appointed 70,000 of them to carry loads, and 80,000 to quarry *stones* in the mountains, and 3,600 supervisors to make the people work.

---

[1] Lit., *offer up in smoke*   [2] I.e., A kor equals approx. 10 bushels

CHAPTER 3

THEN Solomon began to build the house of the LORD in Jerusalem on Mount Moriah, where *the* LORD had appeared to his father David, at the place that David had prepared, on the threshing floor of Ornan the Jebusite.

2 And he began to build on the second *day* in the second month of the fourth year of his reign.

3 Now these are the foundations which Solomon laid for building the house of God. The length in [3]cubits, according to the old standard *was* sixty cubits, and the width twenty cubits.

4 And the porch which was in front of the house was as long as the width of the house, twenty cubits, and the height 120; and inside he overlaid it with pure gold.

5 And he overlaid the main room with cypress wood and overlaid it with fine gold, and ornamented it with palm trees and chains.

6 Further, he adorned the house with precious stones; and the gold was gold from Parvaim.

7 He also overlaid the house with gold—the beams, the thresholds, and its walls, and its doors; and he carved cherubim on the walls.

8 ¶ Now he made the room of the holy of holies: its length, across the width of the house, *was* twenty cubits, and its width *was* twenty cubits; and he overlaid it with fine gold, *amounting* to 600 talents.

9 And the weight of the nails was fifty shekels of gold. He also overlaid the upper rooms with gold.

10 ¶ Then he made two sculptured cherubim in the room of the holy of holies and overlaid them with gold.

11 And the wingspan of the cherubim *was* twenty cubits; the wing of one, of five cubits, touched the wall of the house, and *its* other wing, of five cubits, touched the wing of the other cherub.

12 And the wing of the other cherub, of five cubits, touched the wall of the house; and *its* other wing of five cubits, was attached to the wing of the first cherub.

[3] I.e., One cubit equals approx. 18 in.

13 The wings of these cherubim extended twenty cubits, and they stood on their feet facing the *main* room.

14 And he made the veil of violet, purple, crimson and fine linen, and he worked cherubim on it.

15 ¶ He also made two pillars for the front of the house, thirty-five cubits high, and the capital on the top of each *was* five cubits.

16 And he made chains in the inner sanctuary, and placed *them* on the tops of the pillars; and he made one hundred pomegranates and placed *them* on the chains.

17 And he erected the pillars in front of the temple, one on the right and the other on the left, and named the one on the right Jachin and the one on the left Boaz.

CHAPTER 4

THEN he made a bronze altar, twenty cubits in length and twenty cubits in width and ten cubits in height.

2 Also he made the cast *metal* sea, ten cubits from brim to brim, circular in form, and its height *was* five cubits and its circumference thirty cubits.

3 Now figures like oxen *were* under it *and* all around it, ten cubits, entirely encircling the sea. The oxen *were* in two rows, cast in one piece.

4 It stood on twelve oxen, three facing the north, three facing west, three facing south, and three facing east; and the sea *was set* on top of them, and all their hindquarters turned inwards.

5 And it was a handbreadth thick, and its brim was made like the brim of a cup, *like* a lily blossom; it could hold 3,000 baths.

6 He also made ten basins in which to wash, and he set five on the right side and five on the left, to rinse things for the burnt offering; but the sea *was* for the priests to wash in.

7 ¶ Then he made the ten golden lampstands in the way prescribed for them, and he set them in the temple, five on the right side and five on the left.

8 He also made ten tables and placed them in the temple, five on the right side and five on the left. And he made one hundred golden bowls.

9 Then he made the court of the priests and the great court and doors for the court, and overlaid their doors with bronze.

10 And he set the sea on the right side *of the house* toward the southeast.

11 ¶ Huram also made the pails, the shovels, and the bowls. So Huram finished doing the work which he performed for King Solomon in the house of God:

12 the two pillars, the bowls and the two capitals on top of the pillars, and the two networks to cover the two bowls of the capitals which were on top of the pillars,

13 and the four hundred pomegranates for the two networks, two rows of pomegranates for each network to cover the two bowls of the capitals which were on the pillars.

14 He also made the stands and he made the basins on the stands,

15 *and* the one sea with the twelve oxen under it.

16 And the pails, the shovels, the forks, and all its utensils, Huram-abi made of polished bronze for King Solomon for the house of the LORD.

17 On the plain of the Jordan the king cast them, in the clay ground between Succoth and Zeredah.

18 Thus Solomon made all these utensils in great quantities, for the weight of the bronze could not be found out.

19 ¶ Solomon also made all the things that *were* in the house of God: even the golden altar, the tables with the bread of the Presence on them,

20 the lampstands with their lamps of pure gold, to burn in front of the inner sanctuary in the way prescribed;

21 the flowers, the lamps, and the tongs of gold, of purest gold;

22 and the snuffers, the bowls, the spoons, and the firepans of pure gold; and the entrance of the house, its inner doors for the holy of holies, and the doors of the house, *that is,* of the nave, of gold.

CHAPTER 5

THUS all the work that Solomon performed for the house of the LORD was finished. And Solomon brought in the things that David his father had dedicated, even the silver and the gold and all the utensils, *and* put *them* in the treasuries of the house of God.

2 ¶ Then Solomon assembled to Jerusalem the elders of Israel and all the heads of the tribes, the leaders of the fathers' *households* of the sons of Israel, to bring up the ark of the covenant of the LORD out of the city of David, which is Zion.

3 And all the men of Israel assembled themselves to the king at the feast, that is *in* the seventh month.

4 Then all the elders of Israel came, and the Levites took up the ark.

5 And they brought up the ark and the tent of meeting and all the holy utensils which *were* in the tent; the Levitical priests brought them up.

6 And King Solomon and all the congregation of Israel who were assembled with him before the ark were sacrificing so many sheep and oxen, that they could not be counted or numbered.

7 Then the priests brought the ark of the covenant of the LORD to its place, into the inner sanctuary of the house, to the holy of holies, under the wings of the cherubim.

8 For the cherubim spread their wings over the place of the ark, so that the cherubim made a covering over the ark and its poles.

9 And the poles were so long that the ends of the poles of the ark could be seen in front of the inner sanctuary, but they could not be seen outside; and they are there to this day.

10 There was nothing in the ark except the two tablets which Moses put *there* at Horeb, where the LORD made a covenant with the sons of Israel, when they came out of Egypt.

11 ¶ And when the priests came forth from the holy place (for all the priests who were present had sanctified themselves, without regard to divisions),

12 and all the Levitical singers, Asaph, Heman, Jeduthun, and their sons and kinsmen, clothed in fine linen, with cymbals, harps, and lyres, standing east of the altar, and with them one hundred and twenty priests blowing trumpets

13 in unison when the trumpeters and the singers were to make themselves heard with one voice to praise

and to glorify the LORD, and when they lifted up their voice accompanied by trumpets and cymbals and instruments of music, and when they praised the LORD *saying,* "He indeed is good for His lovingkindness is everlasting," then the house, the house of the LORD, was filled with a cloud,

14 so that the priests could not stand to minister because of the cloud, for the glory of the LORD filled the house of God.

CHAPTER 6

THEN Solomon said,
"The LORD has said that He would dwell in the thick cloud.

2 "I have built Thee a lofty house,
And a place for Thy dwelling forever."

3 Then the king faced about and blessed all the assembly of Israel, while all the assembly of Israel was standing.

4 ¶ And he said, "Blessed be the LORD, the God of Israel, who spoke with His mouth to my father David and has fulfilled *it* with His hands, saying,

5 'Since the day that I brought My people from the land of Egypt, I did not choose a city out of all the tribes of Israel *in which* to build a house that My name might be there, nor did I choose any man for a leader over My people Israel;

6 but I have chosen Jerusalem that My name might be there, and I have chosen David to be over My people Israel.'

7 "Now it was in the heart of my father David to build a house for the name of the LORD, the God of Israel.

8 "But the LORD said to my father David, 'Because it was in your heart to build a house for My name, you did well that it was in your heart.

9 'Nevertheless you shall not build the house, but your son who shall be born to you, he shall build the house for My name.'

10 "Now the LORD has fulfilled His word which He spoke; for I have risen in the place of my father David and sit on the throne of Israel, as the LORD promised, and have built the house for the name of the LORD, the God of Israel.

11 "And there I have set the ark, in which is the covenant of the LORD, which He made with the sons of Israel."

12 ¶ Then he stood before the altar of the LORD in the presence of all the assembly of Israel and spread out his hands.

13 Now Solomon had made a bronze platform, five cubits long, five cubits wide, and three cubits high, and had set it in the midst of the court; and he stood on it, knelt on his knees in the presence of all the assembly of Israel, and spread out his hands toward heaven.

14 And he said, "O LORD, the God of Israel, there is no god like Thee in heaven or on earth, keeping covenant and *showing* lovingkindness to Thy servants who walk before Thee with all their heart;

15 who has kept with Thy servant David, my father, that which Thou hast promised him; indeed, Thou hast spoken with Thy mouth, and hast fulfilled it with Thy hand, as it is this day.

16 "Now therefore, O LORD, the God of Israel, keep with Thy servant David, my father, that which Thou hast promised him, saying, 'You shall not lack a man to sit on the throne of Israel, if only your sons take heed to their way, to walk in My law as you have walked before Me.'

17 "Now therefore, O LORD, the God of Israel, let Thy word be confirmed which Thou hast spoken to Thy servant David.

18 ¶ "But will God indeed dwell with mankind on the earth? Behold, heaven and the highest heaven cannot contain Thee; how much less this house which I have built.

19 "Yet have regard to the prayer of Thy servant and to his supplication, O LORD my God, to listen to the cry and to the prayer which Thy servant prays before Thee;

20 that Thine eyes may be open toward this house day and night, toward the place of which Thou hast said that *Thou wouldst* put Thy name there, to listen to the prayer which Thy servant shall pray toward this place.

21 "And listen to the supplications of

Thy servant and of Thy people Israel, when they pray toward this place; hear Thou from Thy dwelling place, from heaven; hear Thou and forgive.

22 ¶"If a man sins against his neighbor, and is made to take an oath, and he comes *and* takes an oath before Thine altar in this house,

23 then hear Thou from heaven and act and judge Thy servants, punishing the wicked by bringing his way on his own head and justifying the righteous by giving him according to his righteousness.

24 ¶"And if Thy people Israel are defeated before an enemy, because they have sinned against Thee, and they return *to Thee* and confess Thy name, and pray and make supplication before Thee in this house,

25 then hear Thou from heaven and forgive the sin of Thy people Israel, and bring them back to the land which Thou hast given to them and to their fathers.

26 ¶"When the heavens are shut up and there is no rain because they have sinned against Thee, and they pray toward this place and confess Thy name, and turn from their sin when Thou dost afflict them;

27 then hear Thou in heaven and forgive the sin of Thy servants and Thy people Israel, indeed, teach them the good way in which they should walk. And send rain on Thy land, which Thou hast given to Thy people for an inheritance.

28 ¶"If there is famine in the land, if there is pestilence, if there is blight or mildew, if there is locust or grasshopper, if their enemies besiege them in the land of their cities, whatever plague or whatever sickness *there is,*

29 whatever prayer or supplication is made by any man or by all Thy people Israel, each knowing his own affliction and his own pain, and spreading his hands toward this house,

30 then hear Thou from heaven Thy dwelling place, and forgive, and render to each according to all his ways, whose heart Thou knowest for Thou alone dost know the hearts of the sons of men,

31 that they may ⁴fear Thee, to walk

in Thy ways as long as they live in the land which Thou hast given to our fathers.

32 ¶"Also concerning the foreigner who is not from Thy people Israel, when he comes from a far country for Thy great name's sake and Thy mighty hand and Thine outstretched arm, when they come and pray toward this house,

33 then hear Thou from heaven, from Thy dwelling place, and do according to all for which the foreigner calls to Thee, in order that all the peoples of the earth may know Thy name, and ⁴fear Thee, as *do* Thy people Israel, and that they may know that this house which I have built is called by Thy name.

34 ¶"When Thy people go out to battle against their enemies, by whatever way Thou shalt send them, and they pray to Thee toward this city which Thou hast chosen, and the house which I have built for Thy name,

35 then hear Thou from heaven their prayer and their supplication, and maintain their cause.

36 ¶"When they sin against Thee (for there is no man who does not sin) and Thou art angry with them and dost deliver them to an enemy, so that they take them away captive to a land far off or near,

37 if they take thought in the land where they are taken captive, and repent and make supplication to Thee in the land of their captivity, saying, 'We have sinned, we have committed iniquity, and have acted wickedly';

38 if they return to Thee with all their heart and with all their soul in the land of their captivity, where they have been taken captive, and pray toward their land which Thou hast given to their fathers, and the city which Thou hast chosen, and toward the house which I have built for Thy name,

39 then hear from heaven, from Thy dwelling place, their prayer and supplications, and maintain their cause, and forgive Thy people who have sinned against Thee.

40 ¶"Now, O my God, I pray Thee, let Thine eyes be open, and Thine ears

⁴ Or, *reverence*

attentive to the prayer *offered* in this place.

41"Now therefore arise, O Lord God, to Thy resting place, Thou and the ark of Thy might; let Thy priests, O Lord God, be clothed with salvation, and let Thy godly ones rejoice in what is good.

42"O Lord God, do not turn away the face of Thine anointed; remember *Thy* lovingkindness to Thy servant David."

CHAPTER 7

Now when Solomon had finished praying, fire came down from heaven and consumed the burnt offering and the sacrifices; and the glory of the Lord filled the house.

2 And the priests could not enter into the house of the Lord, because the glory of the Lord filled the Lord's house.

3 And all the sons of Israel, seeing the fire come down and the glory of the Lord upon the house, bowed down on the pavement with their faces to the ground, and they worshiped and gave praise to the Lord, *saying,* "Truly He is good, truly His lovingkindness is everlasting."

4 ¶ Then the king and all the people offered sacrifice before the Lord.

5 And King Solomon offered a sacrifice of 22,000 oxen, and 120,000 sheep. Thus the king and all the people dedicated the house of God.

6 And the priests stood at their posts and the Levites, with the instruments of music to the Lord, which King David had made for giving praise to the Lord—"for His lovingkindness is everlasting"—whenever he gave praise by their means, while the priests on the other side blew trumpets; and all Israel was standing.

7 Then Solomon consecrated the middle of the court that *was* before the house of the Lord, for there he offered the burnt offerings and the fat of the peace offerings, because the bronze altar which Solomon had made was not able to contain the burnt offering, the grain offering, and the fat.

8 ¶ So Solomon observed the feast at that time for seven days, and all Israel with him, a very great assembly, who *came* from the entrance of Hamath to the brook of Egypt.

9 And on the eighth day they held a solemn assembly, for the dedication of the altar they observed seven days, and the feast seven days.

10 Then on the twenty-third day of the seventh month he sent the people to their tents, rejoicing and happy of heart because of the goodness that the Lord had shown to David and to Solomon and to His people Israel.

11 ¶ Thus Solomon finished the house of the Lord and the king's palace, and successfully completed all that he had planned on doing in the house of the Lord and in his palace.

12 Then the Lord appeared to Solomon at night and said to him, "I have heard your prayer, and have chosen this place for Myself as a house of sacrifice.

13"If I shut up the heavens so that there is no rain, or if I command the locust to devour the land, or if I send pestilence among My people,

14 and My people who are called by My name humble themselves and pray, and seek My face and turn from their wicked ways, then I will hear from heaven, will forgive their sin, and will heal their land.

15"Now My eyes shall be open and My ears attentive to the prayer *offered* in this place.

16"For now I have chosen and consecrated this house that My name may be there forever, and My eyes and My heart will be there perpetually.

17"And as for you, if you walk before Me as your father David walked even to do according to all that I have commanded you and will keep My statutes and My ordinances,

18 then I will establish your royal throne as I covenanted with your father David, saying, 'You shall not lack a man *to be* ruler in Israel.'

19 ¶"But if you turn away and forsake My statutes and My commandments which I have set before you and shall go and serve other gods and worship them,

20 then I will uproot you from My land which I have given you, and this house which I have consecrated for My name I will cast out of My sight, and I will make it a proverb and a byword among all peoples.

21"As for this house, which was exalted, everyone who passes by it will be astonished and say, 'Why has the LORD done thus to this land and to this house?'

22"And they will say, 'Because they forsook the LORD, the God of their fathers, who brought them from the land of Egypt, and they adopted other gods and worshiped them and served them, therefore He has brought all this adversity on them.'"

CHAPTER 8

NOW it came about at the end of the twenty years in which Solomon had built the house of the LORD and his own house

2 that he built the cities which Huram had given to him, and settled the sons of Israel there.

3 Then Solomon went to Hamath-zobah and captured it.

4 And he built Tadmor in the wilderness and all the storage cities which he had built in Hamath.

5 He also built upper Beth-horon and lower Beth-horon, fortified cities with walls, gates, and bars;

6 and Baalath and all the storage cities that Solomon had, and all the cities for his chariots and cities for his horsemen, and all that it pleased Solomon to build in Jerusalem, in Lebanon, and in all the land under his rule.

7 ¶ All of the people who were left of the Hittites, the Amorites, the Perizzites, the Hivites, and the Jebusites, who were not of Israel,

8 namely, from their descendants who were left after them in the land whom the sons of Israel had not destroyed, them Solomon raised as forced laborers to this day.

9 But Solomon did not make slaves for his work from the sons of Israel; they were men of war, his chief captains, and commanders of his chariots and his horsemen.

10 And these were the chief officers of King Solomon, two hundred and fifty who ruled over the people.

11 ¶ Then Solomon brought Pharaoh's daughter up from the city of David to the house which he had built for her; for he said, "My wife shall not dwell in the house of David king of Israel, because the places are holy where the ark of the LORD has entered."

12 ¶ Then Solomon offered burnt offerings to the LORD on the altar of the LORD which he had built before the porch;

13 and did so according to the daily rule, offering them up according to the commandment of Moses, for the sabbaths, the new moons, and the three annual feasts—the Feast of Unleavened Bread, the Feast of Weeks, and the Feast of Booths.

14 ¶ Now according to the ordinance of his father David, he appointed the divisions of the priests for their service, and the Levites for their duties of praise and ministering before the priests according to the daily rule, and the gatekeepers by their divisions at every gate; for David the man of God had so commanded.

15 And they did not depart from the commandment of the king to the priests and Levites in any manner or concerning the storehouses.

16 ¶ Thus all the work of Solomon was carried out from the day of the foundation of the house of the LORD, and until it was finished. So the house of the LORD was completed.

17 ¶ Then Solomon went to Ezion-geber and to Eloth on the seashore in the land of Edom.

18 And Huram by his servants sent him ships and servants who knew the sea; and they went with Solomon's servants to Ophir, and took from there four hundred and fifty talents of gold, and brought them to King Solomon.

CHAPTER 9

NOW when the queen of Sheba heard of the fame of Solomon, she came to Jerusalem to test Solomon with difficult questions. She had a very large retinue, with camels carrying spices, and a large amount of gold and precious stones; and when she came to Solomon, she spoke with him about all that was on her heart.

2 And Solomon answered all her questions; nothing was hidden from Solomon which he did not explain to her.

3 And when the queen of Sheba had seen the wisdom of Solomon, the house which he had built,

4 the food at his table, the seating of his servants, the attendance of his ministers and their attire, his cupbearers and their attire, and his stairway by which he went up to the house of the LORD, she was breathless.

5 Then she said to the king, "It was a true report which I heard in my own land about your words and your wisdom.

6 "Nevertheless I did not believe their reports until I came and my eyes had seen it. And behold, the half of the greatness of your wisdom was not told me. You surpass the report that I heard.

7 "How blessed are your men, how blessed are these your servants who stand before you continually and hear your wisdom.

8 "Blessed be the LORD your God who delighted in you, setting you on His throne as king for the LORD your God; because your God loved Israel establishing them forever, therefore He made you king over them, to do justice and righteousness."

9 Then she gave the king one hundred and twenty talents of gold, and a very great *amount of* spices and precious stones; there had never been spice like that which the queen of Sheba gave to King Solomon.

10 And the servants of Huram and the servants of Solomon who brought gold from Ophir, also brought algum trees and precious stones.

11 And from the algum the king made steps for the house of the LORD and for the king's palace, and lyres and harps for the singers; and none like that was seen before in the land of Judah.

12 And King Solomon gave to the queen of Sheba all her desire which she requested besides *a return for* what she had brought to the king. Then she turned and went to her own land with her servants.

13 ¶ Now the weight of gold which came to Solomon in one year was 666 talents of gold,

14 besides that which the traders and merchants brought; and all the kings of Arabia and the governors of the country brought gold and silver to Solomon.

15 And King Solomon made 200 large shields of beaten gold, using 600 *shekels of* beaten gold on each large shield.

16 And *he made* 300 shields of beaten gold, using three hundred shekels of gold on each shield, and the king put them in the house of the forest of Lebanon.

17 ¶ Moreover, the king made a great throne of ivory and overlaid it with pure gold.

18 And *there were* six steps to the throne and a footstool in gold attached to the throne, and arms on each side of the seat, and two lions standing beside the arms.

19 And twelve lions were standing there on the six steps on the one side and on the other; nothing like *it* was made for any *other* kingdom.

20 And all King Solomon's drinking vessels *were* of gold, and all the vessels of the house of the forest of Lebanon *were* of pure gold; silver was not considered valuable in the days of Solomon.

21 For the king had ships which went to Tarshish with the servants of Huram; once every three years the ships of Tarshish came bringing gold and silver, ivory and apes and peacocks.

22 ¶ So King Solomon became greater than all the kings of the earth in riches and wisdom.

23 And all the kings of the earth were seeking the presence of Solomon, to hear his wisdom which God had put in his heart.

24 And they brought every man his gift, articles of silver and gold, garments, weapons, spices, horses, and mules, so much year by year.

25 ¶ Now Solomon had 4,000 stalls for horses and chariots and 12,000 horsemen, and he stationed them in the chariot cities and with the king in Jerusalem.

26 And he was the ruler over all the kings from the Euphrates River even to the land of the Philistines, and as far as the border of Egypt.

27 And the king made silver *as common* as stones in Jerusalem, and he made cedars as plentiful as sycamore trees that are in the lowland.

28 And they were bringing horses for Solomon from Egypt and from all countries.

29 ¶ Now the rest of the acts of

Solomon, from first to last, are they not written in the records of Nathan the prophet, and in the prophecy of Ahijah the Shilonite, and in the visions of Iddo the seer concerning Jeroboam the son of Nebat?

30 And Solomon reigned forty years in Jerusalem over all Israel.

31 And Solomon slept with his fathers and was buried in the city of his father David; and his son Rehoboam reigned in his place.

CHAPTER 10

THEN Rehoboam went to Shechem, for all Israel had come to Shechem to make him king.

2 And it came about when Jeroboam the son of Nebat heard *of it* (for he was in Egypt where he had fled from the presence of King Solomon), that Jeroboam returned from Egypt.

3 So they sent and summoned him. When Jeroboam and all Israel came, they spoke to Rehoboam, saying,

4 "Your father made our yoke hard; now therefore lighten the hard service of your father and his heavy yoke which he put on us, and we will serve you."

5 And he said to them, "Return to me again in three days." So the people departed.

6 ¶ Then King Rehoboam consulted with the elders who had served his father Solomon while he was still alive, saying, "How do you counsel *me* to answer this people?"

7 And they spoke to him, saying, "If you will be kind to this people and please them and speak good words to them, then they will be your servants forever."

8 But he forsook the counsel of the elders which they had given him, and consulted with the young men who grew up with him and served him.

9 So he said to them, "What counsel do you give that we may answer this people, who have spoken to me, saying, 'Lighten the yoke which your father put on us'?"

10 And the young men who grew up with him spoke to him, saying, "Thus you shall say to the people who spoke to you, saying, 'Your father made our yoke heavy, but you make it lighter for us.' Thus you shall say to them,

'My little finger is thicker than my father's loins!

11 'Whereas my father loaded you with a heavy yoke, I will add to your yoke; my father disciplined you with whips, but I *will discipline you* with scorpions.' "

12 ¶ So Jeroboam and all the people came to Rehoboam on the third day as the king had directed, saying, "Return to me on the third day."

13 And the king answered them harshly, and King Rehoboam forsook the counsel of the elders.

14 And he spoke to them according to the advice of the young men, saying, "My father made your yoke heavy, but I will add to it; my father disciplined you with whips, but I *will discipline you* with scorpions."

15 So the king did not listen to the people, for it was a turn *of events* from God that the LORD might establish His word, which He spoke through Ahijah the Shilonite to Jeroboam the son of Nebat.

16 ¶ And when all Israel *saw* that the king did not listen to them the people answered the king, saying,

"What portion do we have in David?
    We have no inheritance in the son of Jesse.
Every man to your tents, O Israel;
Now look after your own house, David."

So all Israel departed to their tents.

17 But as for the sons of Israel who lived in the cities of Judah, Rehoboam reigned over them.

18 Then King Rehoboam sent Hadoram, who was over the forced labor, and the sons of Israel stoned him to death. And King Rehoboam made haste to mount his chariot to flee to Jerusalem.

19 So Israel has been in rebellion against the house of David to this day.

CHAPTER 11

NOW when Rehoboam had come to Jerusalem, he assembled the house of Judah and Benjamin, 180,000 chosen men who were warriors, to fight against Israel to restore the kingdom to Rehoboam.

2 But the word of the LORD came to Shemaiah the man of God, saying,

3"Speak to Rehoboam the son of Solomon, king of Judah, and to all Israel in Judah and Benjamin, saying,

4 'Thus says the LORD, "You shall not go up or fight against your relatives; return every man to his house, for this thing is from Me." ' " So they listened to the words of the LORD and returned from going against Jeroboam.

5 ¶ Rehoboam lived in Jerusalem and built cities for defense in Judah.

6 Thus he built Bethlehem, Etam, Tekoa,

7 Beth-zur, Soco, Adullam,

8 Gath, Mareshah, Ziph,

9 Adoraim, Lachish, Azekah,

10 Zorah, Aijalon, and Hebron, which are fortified cities in Judah and in Benjamin.

11 He also strengthened the fortresses and put officers in them and stores of food, oil and wine.

12 And *he put* shields and spears in every city and strengthened them greatly. So he held Judah and Benjamin.

13 ¶ Moreover, the priests and the Levites who were in all Israel stood with him from all their districts.

14 For the Levites left their pasture lands and their property and came to Judah and Jerusalem, for Jeroboam and his sons had excluded them from serving as priests to the LORD.

15 And he set up priests of his own for the high places, for the satyrs, and for the calves which he had made.

16 And those from all the tribes of Israel who set their hearts on seeking the LORD God of Israel, followed them to Jerusalem to sacrifice to the LORD God of their fathers.

17 And they strengthened the kingdom of Judah and supported Rehoboam the son of Solomon for three years, for they walked in the way of David and Solomon for three years.

18 ¶ Then Rehoboam took as a wife Mahalath the daughter of Jerimoth the son of David *and of* Abihail the daughter of Eliab the son of Jesse,

19 and she bore him sons: Jeush, Shemariah, and Zaham.

20 And after her he took Maacah the daughter of Absalom, and she bore him Abijah, Attai, Ziza, and Shelomith.

21 And Rehoboam loved Maacah the daughter of Absalom more than all his *other* wives and concubines. For he had taken eighteen wives and sixty concubines and fathered twenty-eight sons and sixty daughters.

22 And Rehoboam appointed Abijah the son of Maacah as head and leader among his brothers, for he *intended* to make him king.

23 And he acted wisely and distributed some of his sons through all the territories of Judah and Benjamin to all the fortified cities, and he gave them food in abundance. And he sought many wives *for them.*

CHAPTER 12

IT took place when the kingdom of Rehoboam was established and strong that he and all Israel with him forsook the law of the LORD.

2 And it came about in King Rehoboam's fifth year, because they had been unfaithful to the LORD, that Shishak king of Egypt came up against Jerusalem

3 with 1,200 chariots and 60,000 horsemen. And the people who came with him from Egypt were without number: the Lubim, the Sukkiim, and the Ethiopians.

4 And he captured the fortified cities of Judah and came as far as Jerusalem.

5 Then Shemaiah the prophet came to Rehoboam and the princes of Judah who had gathered at Jerusalem because of Shishak, and he said to them, "Thus says the LORD, 'You have forsaken Me, so I also have forsaken you to Shishak.' "

6 So the princes of Israel and the king humbled themselves and said, "The LORD is righteous."

7 ¶ And when the LORD saw that they humbled themselves, the word of the LORD came to Shemaiah, saying, "They have humbled themselves so I will not destroy them, but I will grant them some *measure* of deliverance, and My wrath shall not be poured out on Jerusalem by means of Shishak.

8 "But they will become his slaves so that they may learn *the difference between* My service and the service of the kingdoms of the countries."

9 ¶ So Shishak king of Egypt came up against Jerusalem, and took the

treasures of the house of the LORD and the treasures of the king's palace. He took everything; he even took the golden shields which Solomon had made.

10 Then King Rehoboam made shields of bronze in their place, and committed them to the care of the commanders of the guard who guarded the door of the king's house.

11 And it happened as often as the king entered the house of the LORD, the guards came and carried them and *then* brought them back into the guards' room.

12 And when he humbled himself, the anger of the LORD turned away from him, so as not to destroy *him* completely; and also conditions were good in Judah.

13 ¶ So King Rehoboam strengthened himself in Jerusalem, and reigned. Now Rehoboam was forty-one years old when he began to reign, and he reigned seventeen years in Jerusalem, the city which the LORD had chosen from all the tribes of Israel, to put His name there. And his mother's name was Naamah the Ammonitess.

14 And he did evil because he did not set his heart to seek the LORD.

15 ¶ Now the acts of Rehoboam, from first to last, are they not written in the records of Shemaiah the prophet and of Iddo the seer, according to genealogical enrollment? And *there were* wars between Rehoboam and Jeroboam continually.

16 And Rehoboam slept with his fathers, and was buried in the city of David; and his son Abijah became king in his place.

CHAPTER 13

IN the eighteenth year of King Jeroboam, Abijah became king over Judah.

2 He reigned three years in Jerusalem; and his mother's name was Micaiah the daughter of Uriel of Gibeah. And there was war between Abijah and Jeroboam.

3 And Abijah began the battle with an army of valiant warriors, 400,000 chosen men, while Jeroboam drew up in battle formation against him with 800,000 chosen men *who were* valiant warriors.

4 ¶ Then Abijah stood on Mount Zemaraim, which is in the hill country of Ephraim, and said, "Listen to me, Jeroboam and all Israel:

5 "Do you not know that the LORD God of Israel gave the rule over Israel forever to David and his sons by a covenant of salt?

6 "Yet Jeroboam the son of Nebat, the servant of Solomon the son of David, rose up and rebelled against his master,

7 and worthless men gathered about him, scoundrels, who proved too strong for Rehoboam, the son of Solomon, when he was young and timid and could not hold his own against them.

8 "So now you intend to resist the kingdom of the LORD through the sons of David, being a great multitude and *having* with you the golden calves which Jeroboam made for gods for you.

9 "Have you not driven out the priests of the LORD, the sons of Aaron and the Levites, and made for yourselves priests like the peoples of *other* lands? Whoever comes to consecrate himself with a young bull and seven rams, even he may become a priest of *what are* no gods.

10 "But as for us, the LORD is our God, and we have not forsaken Him; and the sons of Aaron are ministering to the LORD as priests, and the Levites attend to their work.

11 "And every morning and evening they burn to the LORD burnt offerings and fragrant incense, and the showbread is *set* on the clean table, and the golden lampstand with its lamps is *ready* to light every evening; for we keep the charge of the LORD our God, but you have forsaken Him.

12 "Now behold, God is with us at *our* head and His priests with the signal trumpets to sound the alarm against you. O sons of Israel, do not fight against the LORD God of your fathers, for you will not succeed."

13 ¶ But Jeroboam had set an ambush to come from the rear, so that *Israel* was in front of Judah, and the ambush was behind them.

14 When Judah turned around, behold, they were attacked both front

and rear; so they cried to the LORD, and the priests blew the trumpets.

15 Then the men of Judah raised a war cry, and when the men of Judah raised the war cry, then it was that God routed Jeroboam and all Israel before Abijah and Judah.

16 And when the sons of Israel fled before Judah, God gave them into their hand.

17 And Abijah and his people defeated them with a great slaughter, so that 500,000 chosen men of Israel fell slain.

18 Thus the sons of Israel were subdued at that time, and the sons of Judah conquered because they trusted in the LORD, the God of their fathers.

19 And Abijah pursued Jeroboam, and captured from him *several* cities, Bethel with its villages, Jeshanah with its villages, and Ephron with its villages.

20 And Jeroboam did not again recover strength in the days of Abijah; and the LORD struck him and he died.

21 ¶ But Abijah became powerful, and took fourteen wives to himself; and became the father of twenty-two sons and sixteen daughters.

22 Now the rest of the acts of Abijah, and his ways and his words are written in the treatise of the prophet Iddo.

CHAPTER 14

So Abijah slept with his fathers, and they buried him in the city of David, and his son Asa became king in his place. The land was undisturbed for ten years during his days.

2 ¶ And Asa did good and right in the sight of the LORD his God,

3 for he removed the foreign altars and high places, tore down the *sacred* pillars, cut down the [5]Asherim,

4 and commanded Judah to seek the LORD God of their fathers and to observe the law and the commandment.

5 He also removed the high places and the incense altars from all the cities of Judah. And the kingdom was undisturbed under him.

6 And he built fortified cities in Judah, since the land was undisturbed, and there was no one at war with him

---

[5] I.e., wooden symbols of a female deity

---

during those years, because the LORD had given him rest.

7 For he said to Judah, "Let us build these cities and surround *them* with walls and towers, gates and bars. The land is still ours, because we have sought the LORD our God; we have sought Him, and He has given us rest on every side." So they built and prospered.

8 Now Asa had an army of 300,000 from Judah, bearing large shields and spears, and 280,000 from Benjamin, bearing shields and wielding bows; all of them were valiant warriors.

9 ¶ Now Zerah the Ethiopian came out against them with an army of a million men and 300 chariots, and he came to Mareshah.

10 So Asa went out to meet him, and they drew up in battle formation in the valley of Zephathah at Mareshah.

11 Then Asa called to the LORD his God, and said, "LORD, there is no one besides Thee to help *in the battle* between the powerful and those who have no strength; so help us, O LORD our God, for we trust in Thee, and in Thy name have come against this multitude. O LORD, Thou art our God; let not man prevail against Thee."

12 So the LORD routed the Ethiopians before Asa and before Judah, and the Ethiopians fled.

13 And Asa and the people who *were* with him pursued them as far as Gerar; and so many Ethiopians fell that they could not recover, for they were shattered before the LORD, and before His army. And they carried away very much plunder.

14 And they destroyed all the cities around Gerar, for the dread of the LORD had fallen on them; and they despoiled all the cities, for there was much plunder in them.

15 They also struck down those who owned livestock, and they carried away large numbers of sheep and camels. Then they returned to Jerusalem.

CHAPTER 15

Now the Spirit of God came on Azariah the son of Oded,

2 and he went out to meet Asa and said to him, "Listen to me, Asa, and all Judah and Benjamin: the LORD is with you when you are with Him. And if

you seek Him, He will let you find Him; but if you forsake Him, He will forsake you.

3 "And for many days Israel was without the true God and without a teaching priest and without law.

4 "But in their distress they turned to the LORD God of Israel, and they sought Him, and He let them find Him.

5 "And in those times there was no peace to him who went out or to him who came in, for many disturbances afflicted all the inhabitants of the lands.

6 "And nation was crushed by nation, and city by city, for God troubled them with every kind of distress.

7 "But you, be strong and do not lose courage, for there is reward for your work."

8 ¶ Now when Asa heard these words and the prophecy which Azariah the son of Oded the prophet spoke, he took courage and removed the abominable idols from all the land of Judah and Benjamin and from the cities which he had captured in the hill country of Ephraim. He then restored the altar of the LORD which was in front of the porch of the LORD.

9 And he gathered all Judah and Benjamin and those from Ephraim, Manasseh, and Simeon who resided with them, for many defected to him from Israel when they saw that the LORD his God was with him.

10 So they assembled at Jerusalem in the third month of the fifteenth year of Asa's reign.

11 And they sacrificed to the LORD that day 700 oxen and 7,000 sheep from the spoil they had brought.

12 And they entered into the covenant to seek the LORD God of their fathers with all their heart and soul;

13 and whoever would not seek the LORD God of Israel should be put to death, whether small or great, man or woman.

14 Moreover, they made an oath to the LORD with a loud voice, with shouting, with trumpets, and with horns.

15 And all Judah rejoiced concerning the oath, for they had sworn with their whole heart and had sought Him earnestly, and He let them find Him. So the LORD gave them rest on every side.

16 ¶ And he also removed Maacah, the mother of King Asa, from the *position of* queen mother, because she had made a horrid image as an Asherah, and Asa cut down her horrid image, crushed *it* and burned *it* at the brook Kidron.

17 But the high places were not removed from Israel; nevertheless Asa's heart was blameless all his days.

18 And he brought into the house of God the dedicated things of his father and his own dedicated things: silver and gold and utensils.

19 And there was no more war until the thirty-fifth year of Asa's reign.

CHAPTER 16

IN the thirty-sixth year of Asa's reign Baasha king of Israel came up against Judah and fortified Ramah in order to prevent *anyone* from going out or coming in to Asa king of Judah.

2 Then Asa brought out silver and gold from the treasuries of the house of the LORD and the king's house, and sent them to Ben-hadad king of Aram, who lived in Damascus, saying,

3 "*Let there be* a treaty between you and me, *as* between my father and your father. Behold, I have sent you silver and gold; go, break your treaty with Baasha king of Israel so that he will withdraw from me."

4 So Ben-hadad listened to King Asa and sent the commanders of his armies against the cities of Israel, and they conquered Ijon, Dan, Abel-maim, and all the store cities of Naphtali.

5 And it came about when Baasha heard *of it* that he ceased fortifying Ramah and stopped his work.

6 Then King Asa brought all Judah, and they carried away the stones of Ramah and its timber with which Baasha had been building, and with them he fortified Geba and Mizpah.

7 ¶ At that time Hanani the seer came to Asa king of Judah and said to him, "Because you have relied on the king of Aram and have not relied on the LORD your God, therefore the army of the king of Aram has escaped out of your hand.

8 "Were not the Ethiopians and the Lubim an immense army with very many chariots and horsemen? Yet, because you relied on the LORD, He delivered them into your hand.

9"For the eyes of the LORD move to and fro throughout the earth that He may strongly support those whose heart is completely His. You have acted foolishly in this. Indeed, from now on you will surely have wars."

10 Then Asa was angry with the seer and put him in prison, for he was enraged at him for this. And Asa oppressed some of the people at the same time.

11 ¶ And now, the acts of Asa from first to last, behold, they are written in the Book of the Kings of Judah and Israel.

12 And in the thirty-ninth year of his reign Asa became diseased in his feet. His disease was severe, yet even in his disease he did not seek the LORD, but the physicians.

13 So Asa slept with his fathers, having died in the forty-first year of his reign.

14 And they buried him in his own tomb which he had cut out for himself in the city of David, and they laid him in the resting place which he had filled with spices of various kinds blended by the perfumers' art; and they made a very great fire for him.

CHAPTER 17

JEHOSHAPHAT his son then became king in his place, and made his position over Israel firm.

2 He placed troops in all the fortified cities of Judah, and set garrisons in the land of Judah, and in the cities of Ephraim which Asa his father had captured.

3 And the LORD was with Jehoshaphat because he followed the example of his father David's earlier days and did not seek the Baals,

4 but sought the God of his father, followed His commandments, and did not act as Israel did.

5 So the LORD established the kingdom in his control, and all Judah brought tribute to Jehoshaphat, and he had great riches and honor.

6 And he took great pride in the ways of the LORD and again removed the high places and the Asherim from Judah.

7 ¶ Then in the third year of his reign he sent his officials, Ben-hail, Obadiah, Zechariah, Nethanel, and Micaiah, to teach in the cities of Judah;

8 and with them the Levites, Shemaiah, Nethaniah, Zebadiah, Asahel, Shemiramoth, Jehonathan, Adonijah, Tobijah, and Tobadonijah, the Levites; and with them Elishama and Jehoram, the priests.

9 And they taught in Judah, *having* the book of the law of the LORD with them; and they went throughout all the cities of Judah and taught among the people.

10 ¶ Now the dread of the LORD was on all the kingdoms of the lands which *were* around Judah, so that they did not make war against Jehoshaphat.

11 And some of the Philistines brought gifts and silver as tribute to Jehoshaphat; the Arabians also brought him flocks, 7,700 rams and 7,700 male goats.

12 So Jehoshaphat grew greater and greater, and he built fortresses and store cities in Judah.

13 And he had large supplies in the cities of Judah, and warriors, valiant men, in Jerusalem.

14 And this was their muster according to their fathers' households: of Judah, commanders of thousands, Adnah *was* the commander, and with him 300,000 valiant warriors;

15 and next to him *was* Johanan the commander, and with him 280,000;

16 and next to him Amasiah the son of Zichri, who volunteered for the LORD, and with him 200,000 valiant warriors;

17 and of Benjamin, Eliada a valiant warrior, and with him 200,000 armed with bow and shield;

18 and next to him Jehozabad, and with him 180,000 equipped for war.

19 These are they who served the king, apart from those whom the king put in the fortified cities through all Judah.

CHAPTER 18

NOW Jehoshaphat had great riches and honor; and he allied himself by marriage with Ahab.

2 And some years later he went down to *visit* Ahab at Samaria. And Ahab slaughtered many sheep and oxen for him and the people who were

with him, and induced him to go up against Ramoth-gilead.

3 And Ahab king of Israel said to Jehoshaphat king of Judah, "Will you go with me *against* Ramoth-gilead?" And he said to him, "I am as you are, and my people as your people, and *we will be* with you in the battle."

4 ¶ Moreover, Jehoshaphat said to the king of Israel, "Please inquire first for the word of the LORD."

5 Then the king of Israel assembled the prophets, four hundred men, and said to them, "Shall we go against Ramoth-gilead to battle, or shall I refrain?" And they said, "Go up, for God will give *it* into the hand of the king."

6 But Jehoshaphat said, "Is there not yet a prophet of the LORD here that we may inquire of him?"

7 And the king of Israel said to Jehoshaphat, "There is yet one man by whom we may inquire of the LORD, but I hate him, for he never prophesies good concerning me but always evil. He is Micaiah, son of Imla." But Jehoshaphat said, "Let not the king say so."

8 Then the king of Israel called an officer and said, "Bring quickly Micaiah, Imla's son."

9 Now the king of Israel and Jehoshaphat the king of Judah were sitting each on his throne, arrayed in *their* robes, and *they* were sitting at the threshing floor at the entrance of the gate of Samaria; and all the prophets were prophesying before them.

10 And Zedekiah the son of Chenaanah made horns of iron for himself and said, "Thus says the LORD, 'With these you shall gore the Arameans, until they are consumed.' "

11 And all the prophets were prophesying thus, saying, "Go up to Ramoth-gilead and succeed, for the LORD will give *it* into the hand of the king."

12 ¶ Then the messenger who went to summon Micaiah spoke to him saying, "Behold, the words of the prophets are uniformly favorable to the king. So please let your word be like one of them and speak favorably."

13 But Micaiah said, "As the LORD lives, what my God says, that I will speak."

14 And when he came to the king, the king said to him, "Micaiah, shall we go to Ramoth-gilead to battle, or shall I refrain?" He said, "Go up and succeed, for they will be given into your hand."

15 Then the king said to him, "How many times must I adjure you to speak to me nothing but the truth in the name of the LORD?"

16 So he said,
"I saw all Israel
Scattered on the mountains,
Like sheep which have no shepherd;
And the LORD said,
'These have no master.
Let each of them return to his house in peace.' "

17 Then the king of Israel said to Jehoshaphat, "Did I not tell you that he would not prophesy good concerning me, but evil?"

18 And Micaiah said, "Therefore, hear the word of the LORD. I saw the LORD sitting on His throne, and all the host of heaven standing on His right and on His left.

19 "And the LORD said, 'Who will entice Ahab king of Israel to go up and fall at Ramoth-gilead?' And one said this while another said that.

20 "Then a spirit came forward and stood before the LORD and said, 'I will entice him.' And the LORD said to him, 'How?'

21 "And he said, 'I will go and be a deceiving spirit in the mouth of all his prophets.' Then He said, 'You are to entice *him* and prevail also. Go and do so.'

22 "Now therefore, behold, the LORD has put a deceiving spirit in the mouth of these your prophets; for the LORD has proclaimed disaster against you."

23 ¶ Then Zedekiah the son of Chenaanah came near and struck Micaiah on the cheek and said, "How did the Spirit of the LORD pass from me to speak to you?"

24 And Micaiah said, "Behold, you shall see on that day, when you enter an inner room to hide yourself."

25 Then the king of Israel said, "Take Micaiah and return him to Amon the governor of the city, and to Joash the king's son;

26 and say, 'Thus says the king, "Put this *man* in prison, and feed him sparingly with bread and water until I return safely." ' "

27 And Micaiah said, "If you indeed return safely, the LORD has not spoken by me." And he said, "Listen, all you people."

28 ¶ So the king of Israel and Jehoshaphat king of Judah went up against Ramoth-gilead.

29 And the king of Israel said to Jehoshaphat, "I will disguise myself and go into battle, but you put on your robes." So the king of Israel disguised himself, and they went into battle.

30 Now the king of Aram had commanded the captains of his chariots, saying, "Do not fight with small or great, but with the king of Israel alone."

31 So it came about when the captains of the chariots saw Jehoshaphat, that they said, "It is the king of Israel," and they turned aside to fight against him. But Jehoshaphat cried out, and the LORD helped him, and God diverted them from him.

32 Then it happened when the captains of the chariots saw that it was not the king of Israel, that they turned back from pursuing him.

33 And a certain man drew his bow at random and struck the king of Israel in a joint of the armor. So he said to the driver of the chariot, "Turn around, and take me out of the fight; for I am severely wounded."

34 And the battle raged that day, and the king of Israel propped himself up in his chariot in front of the Arameans until the evening; and at sunset he died.

CHAPTER 19

THEN Jehoshaphat the king of Judah returned in safety to his house in Jerusalem.

2 And Jehu the son of Hanani the seer went out to meet him and said to King Jehoshaphat, "Should you help the wicked and love those who hate the LORD and so *bring* wrath on yourself from the LORD?

3"But there is *some* good in you, for you have removed the Asheroth from the land and you have set your heart to seek God."

4 So Jehoshaphat lived in Jerusalem and went out again among the people from Beersheba to the hill country of Ephraim and brought them back to the LORD, the God of their fathers.

5 And he appointed judges in the land in all the fortified cities of Judah, city by city.

6 And he said to the judges, "Consider what you are doing, for you do not judge for man but for the LORD who is with you when you render judgment.

7"Now then let the fear of the LORD be upon you; be very careful what you do, for the LORD our God will have no part in unrighteousness, or partiality, or the taking of a bribe."

8 ¶ And in Jerusalem also Jehoshaphat appointed some of the Levites and priests, and some of the heads of the fathers' *households* of Israel, for the judgment of the LORD and to judge disputes among the inhabitants of Jerusalem.

9 Then he charged them saying, "Thus you shall do in the fear of the LORD, faithfully and wholeheartedly.

10"And whenever any dispute comes to you from your brethren who live in their cities, between blood and blood, between law and commandment, statutes and ordinances, you shall warn them that they may not be guilty before the LORD, and wrath may *not* come on you and your brethren. Thus you shall do and you will not be guilty.

11"And behold, Amariah the chief priest will be over you in all that pertains to the LORD; and Zebadiah the son of Ishmael, the ruler of the house of Judah, in all that pertains to the king. Also the Levites shall be officers before you. Act resolutely, and the LORD be with the upright."

CHAPTER 20

NOW it came about after this that the sons of Moab and the sons of Ammon, together with some of the Meunites, came to make war against Jehoshaphat.

2 Then some came and reported to Jehoshaphat, saying, "A great multitude is coming against you from beyond the sea, out of Aram and behold, they are in Hazazon-tamar (that is Engedi)."

3 And Jehoshaphat was afraid and turned his attention to seek the LORD;

and proclaimed a fast throughout all Judah.

4 So Judah gathered together to seek help from the LORD; they even came from all the cities of Judah to seek the LORD.

5 ¶ Then Jehoshaphat stood in the assembly of Judah and Jerusalem, in the house of the LORD before the new court,

6 and he said, "O LORD, the God of our fathers, art Thou not God in the heavens? And art Thou not ruler over all the kingdoms of the nations? Power and might are in Thy hand so that no one can stand against Thee.

7 "Didst Thou not, O our God, drive out the inhabitants of this land before Thy people Israel, and give it to the descendants of Abraham Thy friend forever?

8 "And they lived in it, and have built Thee a sanctuary there for Thy name, saying,

9 'Should evil come upon us, the sword, or judgment, or pestilence, or famine, we will stand before this house and before Thee (for Thy name is in this house) and cry to Thee in our distress, and Thou wilt hear and deliver us.'

10 "And now behold, the sons of Ammon and Moab and Mount Seir, whom Thou didst not let Israel invade when they came out of the land of Egypt (they turned aside from them and did not destroy them),

11 behold how they are rewarding us, by coming to drive us out from Thy possession which Thou hast given us as an inheritance.

12 "O our God, wilt Thou not judge them? For we are powerless before this great multitude who are coming against us; nor do we know what to do, but our eyes are on Thee."

13 And all Judah was standing before the LORD, with their infants, their wives, and their children.

14 ¶ Then in the midst of the assembly the Spirit of the LORD came upon Jahaziel the son of Zechariah, the son of Benaiah, the son of Jeiel, the son of Mattaniah, the Levite of the sons of Asaph;

15 and he said, "Listen, all Judah and the inhabitants of Jerusalem and King Jehoshaphat: thus says the LORD to you, 'Do not fear or be dismayed because of this great multitude, for the battle is not yours but God's.

16 'Tomorrow go down against them. Behold, they will come up by the ascent of Ziz, and you will find them at the end of the valley in front of the wilderness of Jeruel.

17 'You need not fight in this battle; station yourselves, stand and see the salvation of the LORD on your behalf, O Judah and Jerusalem.' Do not fear or be dismayed; tomorrow go out to face them, for the LORD is with you."

18 And Jehoshaphat bowed his head with his face to the ground, and all Judah and the inhabitants of Jerusalem fell down before the LORD, worshiping the LORD.

19 And the Levites, from the sons of the Kohathites and of the sons of the Korahites, stood up to praise the LORD God of Israel, with a very loud voice.

20 ¶ And they rose early in the morning and went out to the wilderness of Tekoa; and when they went out, Jehoshaphat stood and said, "Listen to me, O Judah and inhabitants of Jerusalem, put your trust in the LORD your God, and you will be established. Put your trust in His prophets and succeed."

21 And when he had consulted with the people, he appointed those who sang to the LORD and those who praised Him in holy attire, as they went out before the army and said, "Give thanks to the LORD, for His lovingkindness is everlasting."

22 And when they began singing and praising, the LORD set ambushes against the sons of Ammon, Moab, and Mount Seir, who had come against Judah; so they were routed.

23 For the sons of Ammon and Moab rose up against the inhabitants of Mount Seir destroying them completely, and when they had finished with the inhabitants of Seir, they helped to destroy one another.

24 ¶ When Judah came to the lookout of the wilderness, they looked toward the multitude; and behold, they were corpses lying on the ground, and no one had escaped.

25 And when Jehoshaphat and his people came to take their spoil, they found much among them, including goods, garments, and valuable things

which they took for themselves, more than they could carry. And they were three days taking the spoil because there was so much.

26 Then on the fourth day they assembled in the valley of Beracah, for there they blessed the LORD. Therefore they have named that place "The Valley of [6]Beracah" until today.

27 And every man of Judah and Jerusalem returned with Jehoshaphat at their head, returning to Jerusalem with joy, for the LORD had made them to rejoice over their enemies.

28 And they came to Jerusalem with harps, lyres, and trumpets to the house of the LORD.

29 And the dread of God was on all the kingdoms of the lands when they heard that the LORD had fought against the enemies of Israel.

30 So the kingdom of Jehoshaphat was at peace, for his God gave him rest on all sides.

31 ¶ Now Jehoshaphat reigned over Judah. He *was* thirty-five years old when he became king, and he reigned in Jerusalem twenty-five years. And his mother's name *was* Azubah the daughter of Shilhi.

32 And he walked in the way of his father Asa and did not depart from it, doing right in the sight of the LORD.

33 The high places, however, were not removed; the people had not yet directed their hearts to the God of their fathers.

34 Now the rest of the acts of Jehoshaphat, first to last, behold, they are written in the annals of Jehu the son of Hanani, which is recorded in the Book of the Kings of Israel.

35 ¶ And after this Jehoshaphat king of Judah allied himself with Ahaziah king of Israel. He acted wickedly in so doing.

36 So he allied himself with him to make ships to go to Tarshish, and they made the ships in Ezion-geber.

37 Then Eliezer the son of Dodavahu of Mareshah prophesied against Jehoshaphat saying, "Because you have allied yourself with Ahaziah, the LORD has destroyed your works." So the ships were broken and could not go to Tarshish.

CHAPTER 21

THEN Jehoshaphat slept with his fathers and was buried with his fathers in the city of David, and Jehoram his son became king in his place.

2 And he had brothers, the sons of Jehoshaphat: Azariah, Jehiel, Zechariah, Azaryahu, Michael, and Shephatiah. All these *were* the sons of Jehoshaphat king of Israel.

3 And their father gave them many gifts of silver, gold and precious things, with fortified cities in Judah, but he gave the kingdom to Jehoram because he was the first-born.

4 ¶ Now when Jehoram had taken over the kingdom of his father and made himself secure, he killed all his brothers with the sword, and some of the rulers of Israel also.

5 Jehoram *was* thirty-two years old when he became king, and he reigned eight years in Jerusalem.

6 And he walked in the way of the kings of Israel, just as the house of Ahab did (for Ahab's daughter was his wife), and he did evil in the sight of the LORD.

7 Yet the LORD was not willing to destroy the house of David because of the covenant which He had made with David, and since He had promised to give a lamp to him and his sons forever.

8 ¶ In his days Edom revolted [7]against the rule of Judah, and set up a king over themselves.

9 Then Jehoram crossed over with his commanders and all his chariots with him. And it came about that he arose by night and struck down the Edomites who were surrounding him and the commanders of the chariots.

10 So Edom revolted [7]against Judah to this day. Then Libnah revolted at the same time against his rule, because he had forsaken the LORD God of his fathers.

11 Moreover, he made high places in the mountains of Judah, and caused the inhabitants of Jerusalem to play the harlot and led Judah astray.

12 Then a letter came to him from Elijah the prophet saying, "Thus says the LORD God of your father David, 'Because you have not walked in the

---

[6] I.e., blessing

[7] Lit., *from under the hand of*

ways of Jehoshaphat your father and the ways of Asa king of Judah,

13 but have walked in the way of the kings of Israel, and have caused Judah and the inhabitants of Jerusalem to play the harlot as the house of Ahab played the harlot, and you have also killed your brothers, your own family, who were better than you,

14 behold, the LORD is going to strike your people, your sons, your wives, and all your possessions with a great calamity;

15 and you will suffer severe sickness, a disease of your bowels, until your bowels come out because of the sickness, day by day.' "

16 ¶ Then the LORD stirred up against Jehoram the spirit of the Philistines and the Arabs who bordered the Ethiopians;

17 and they came against Judah and invaded it, and carried away all the possessions found in the king's house together with his sons and his wives, so that no son was left to him except Jehoahaz, the youngest of his sons.

18 So after all this the LORD smote him in his bowels with an incurable sickness.

19 Now it came about in the course of time, at the end of two years, that his bowels came out because of his sickness and he died in great pain. And his people made no fire for him like the fire for his fathers.

20 He was thirty-two years old when he became king, and he reigned in Jerusalem eight years; and he departed with no one's regret, and they buried him in the city of David, but not in the tombs of the kings.

CHAPTER 22

THEN the inhabitants of Jerusalem made Ahaziah, his youngest son, king in his place, for the band of men who came with the Arabs to the camp had slain all the older *sons*. So Ahaziah the son of Jehoram king of Judah began to reign.

2 Ahaziah *was* twenty-two years old when he became king, and he reigned one year in Jerusalem. And his mother's name was Athaliah, the granddaughter of Omri.

3 He also walked in the ways of the house of Ahab, for his mother was his counselor to do wickedly.

4 And he did evil in the sight of the LORD like the house of Ahab, for they were his counselors after the death of his father, to his destruction.

5 He also walked according to their counsel, and went with Jehoram the son of Ahab king of Israel to wage war against Hazael king of Aram at Ramoth-gilead. But the Arameans wounded Joram.

6 So he returned to be healed in Jezreel of the wounds which they had inflicted on him at Ramah, when he fought against Hazael king of Aram. And Ahaziah, the son of Jehoram king of Judah, went down to see Jehoram the son of Ahab in Jezreel, because he was sick.

7 ¶ Now the destruction of Ahaziah was from God, in that he went to Joram. For when he came, he went out with Jehoram against Jehu the son of Nimshi, whom the LORD had anointed to cut off the house of Ahab.

8 And it came about when Jehu was executing judgment on the house of Ahab, he found the princes of Judah and the sons of Ahaziah's brothers, ministering to Ahaziah, and slew them.

9 He also sought Ahaziah, and they caught him while he was hiding in Samaria; they brought him to Jehu, put him to death, and buried him. For they said, "He is the son of Jehoshaphat, who sought the LORD with all his heart." So there was no one of the house of Ahaziah to retain the power of the kingdom.

10 ¶ Now when Athaliah the mother of Ahaziah saw that her son was dead, she rose and destroyed all the royal offspring of the house of Judah.

11 But Jehoshabeath the king's daughter took Joash the son of Ahaziah, and stole him from among the king's sons who were being put to death, and placed him and his nurse in the bedroom. So Jehoshabeath, the daughter of King Jehoram, the wife of Jehoiada the priest (for she was the sister of Ahaziah), hid him from Athaliah so that she would not put him to death.

12 And he was hidden with them in the house of God six years while Athaliah reigned over the land.

CHAPTER 23

Now in the seventh year Jehoiada strengthened himself, and took captains of hundreds: Azariah the son of Jeroham, Ishmael the son of Johanan, Azariah the son of Obed, Maaseiah the son of Adaiah, and Elishaphat the son of Zichri, *and they entered* into a covenant with him.

2 And they went throughout Judah and gathered the Levites from all the cities of Judah, and the heads of the fathers' *households* of Israel, and they came to Jerusalem.

3 Then all the assembly made a covenant with the king in the house of God. And Jehoiada said to them, "Behold, the king's son shall reign, as the LORD has spoken concerning the sons of David.

4"This is the thing which you shall do: one third of you, of the priests and Levites who come in on the sabbath, *shall be* gatekeepers,

5 and one third *shall be* at the king's house, and a third at the Gate of the Foundation; and all the people *shall be* in the courts of the house of the LORD.

6"But let no one enter the house of the LORD except the priests and the ministering Levites; they may enter, for they are holy. And let all the people keep the charge of the LORD.

7"And the Levites will surround the king, each man with his weapons in his hand; and whoever enters the house, let him be killed. Thus be with the king when he comes in and when he goes out."

8 So the Levites and all Judah did according to all that Jehoiada the priest commanded. And each one of them took his men who were to come in on the sabbath, with those who were to go out on the sabbath, for Jehoiada the priest did not dismiss *any of* the divisions.

9 Then Jehoiada the priest gave to the captains of hundreds the spears and the large and small shields which had been King David's, which *were* in the house of God.

10 And he stationed all the people, each man with his weapon in his hand, from the right side of the house to the left side of the house, by the altar and by the house, around the king.

11 Then they brought out the king's son and put the crown on him, and *gave him* the testimony, and made him king. And Jehoiada and his sons anointed him and said, "Long live the king!"

12 ¶ When Athaliah heard the noise of the people running and praising the king, she came into the house of the LORD to the people.

13 And she looked, and behold, the king was standing by his pillar at the entrance, and the captains and the trumpeters *were* beside the king. And all the people of the land rejoiced and blew trumpets, the singers with *their* musical instruments leading the praise. Then Athaliah tore her clothes and said, "Treason! Treason!"

14 And Jehoiada the priest brought out the captains of hundreds who were appointed over the army, and said to them, "Bring her out between the ranks; and whoever follows her, put to death with the sword." For the priest said, "Let her not be put to death in the house of the LORD."

15 So they seized her, and when she arrived at the entrance of the Horse Gate of the king's house, they put her to death there.

16 ¶ Then Jehoiada made a covenant between himself and all the people and the king, that they should be the LORD's people.

17 And all the people went to the house of Baal, and tore it down, and they broke in pieces his altars and his images, and killed Mattan the priest of Baal before the altars.

18 Moreover, Jehoiada placed the offices of the house of the LORD under the authority of the Levitical priests, whom David had assigned over the house of the LORD, to offer the burnt offerings of the LORD, as it is written in the law of Moses—with rejoicing and singing according to the order of David.

19 And he stationed the gatekeepers of the house of the LORD, so that no one should enter *who was* in any way unclean.

20 And he took the captains of hundreds, the nobles, the rulers of the people, and all the people of the land, and brought the king down from the house of the LORD, and came through the upper gate to the king's house.

And they placed the king upon the royal throne.

21 So all of the people of the land rejoiced and the city was quiet. For they had put Athaliah to death with the sword.

CHAPTER 24

JOASH *was* seven years old when he became king, and he reigned forty years in Jerusalem; and his mother's name *was* Zibiah from Beersheba.

2 And Joash did what was right in the sight of the LORD all the days of Jehoiada the priest.

3 And Jehoiada took two wives for him, and he became the father of sons and daughters.

4 ¶ Now it came about after this that Joash decided to restore the house of the LORD.

5 And he gathered the priests and Levites, and said to them, "Go out to the cities of Judah, and collect money from all Israel to repair the house of your God annually, and you shall do the matter quickly." But the Levites did not act quickly.

6 So the king summoned Jehoiada the chief *priest* and said to him, "Why have you not required the Levites to bring in from Judah and from Jerusalem the levy *fixed by* Moses the servant of the LORD on the congregation of Israel for the tent of the testimony?"

7 For the sons of the wicked Athaliah had broken into the house of God and even used the holy things of the house of the LORD for the Baals.

8 ¶ So the king commanded, and they made a chest and set it outside by the gate of the house of the LORD.

9 And they made a proclamation in Judah and Jerusalem to bring to the LORD the levy *fixed by* Moses the servant of God on Israel in the wilderness.

10 And all the officers and all the people rejoiced and brought in their levies and dropped *them* into the chest until they had finished.

11 And it came about whenever the chest was brought in to the king's officer by the Levites, and when they saw that there was much money, then the king's scribe and the chief priest's officer would come, empty the chest, take it, and return it to its place. Thus they did daily and collected much money.

12 And the king and Jehoiada gave it to those who did the work of the service of the house of the LORD; and they hired masons and carpenters to restore the house of the LORD, and also workers in iron and bronze to repair the house of the LORD.

13 So the workmen labored, and the repair work progressed in their hands, and they restored the house of God according to its specifications, and strengthened it.

14 And when they had finished, they brought the rest of the money before the king and Jehoiada; and it was made into utensils for the house of the LORD, utensils for the service and the burnt offering, and pans and utensils of gold and silver. And they offered burnt offerings in the house of the LORD continually all the days of Jehoiada.

15 ¶ Now when Jehoiada reached a ripe old age he died; he was one hundred and thirty years old at his death.

16 And they buried him in the city of David among the kings, because he had done well in Israel and to God and His house.

17 But after the death of Jehoiada the officials of Judah came and bowed down to the king, and the king listened to them.

18 And they abandoned the house of the LORD, the God of their fathers, and served the [8]Asherim and the idols; so wrath came upon Judah and Jerusalem for this their guilt.

19 Yet He sent prophets to them to bring them back to the LORD; though they testified against them, they would not listen.

20 Then the Spirit of God came on Zechariah the son of Jehoiada the priest; and he stood above the people and said to them, "Thus God has said, 'Why do you transgress the commandments of the LORD and do not prosper? Because you have forsaken the LORD, He has also forsaken you.'"

21 So they conspired against him and at the command of the king they stoned him to death in the court of the house of the LORD.

[8] I.e., wooden symbols of a female deity

22 Thus Joash the king did not remember the kindness which his father Jehoiada had shown him, but he murdered his son. And as he died he said, "May the Lord see and avenge!"

23 ¶ Now it came about at the turn of the year that the army of the Arameans came up against him; and they came to Judah and Jerusalem, destroyed all the officials of the people from among the people, and sent all their spoil to the king of Damascus.

24 Indeed the army of the Arameans came with a small number of men; yet the Lord delivered a very great army into their hands, because they had forsaken the Lord, the God of their fathers. Thus they executed judgment on Joash.

25 And when they had departed from him (for they left him very sick), his own servants conspired against him because of the blood of the son of Jehoiada the priest, and murdered him on his bed. So he died, and they buried him in the city of David, but they did not bury him in the tombs of the kings.

26 Now these are those who conspired against him: Zabad the son of Shimeath the Ammonitess, and Jehozabad the son of Shimrith the Moabitess.

27 As to his sons and the many oracles against him and the rebuilding of the house of God, behold, they are written in the treatise of the Book of the Kings. Then Amaziah his son became king in his place.

CHAPTER 25

AMAZIAH was twenty-five years old when he became king, and he reigned twenty-nine years in Jerusalem. And his mother's name was Jehoaddan of Jerusalem.

2 And he did right in the sight of the Lord, yet not with a whole heart.

3 Now it came about as soon as the kingdom was firmly in his grasp, that he killed his servants who had slain his father the king.

4 However, he did not put their children to death, but did as it is written in the law in the book of Moses, which the Lord commanded, saying, "Fathers shall not be put to death for sons, nor sons be put to death for fathers, but each shall be put to death for his own sin."

5 ¶ Moreover, Amaziah assembled Judah and appointed them according to their fathers' households under commanders of thousands and commanders of hundreds throughout Judah and Benjamin; and he took a census of those from twenty years old and upward, and found them to be 300,000 choice men, able to go to war and handle spear and shield.

6 He hired also 100,000 valiant warriors out of Israel for one hundred talents of silver.

7 But a man of God came to him saying, "O king, do not let the army of Israel go with you, for the Lord is not with Israel nor with any of the sons of Ephraim.

8 "But if you do go, do it, be strong for the battle; yet God will bring you down before the enemy, for God has power to help and to bring down."

9 And Amaziah said to the man of God, "But what shall we do for the hundred talents which I have given to the troops of Israel?" And the man of God answered, "The Lord has much more to give you than this."

10 Then Amaziah dismissed them, the troops which came to him from Ephraim, to go home; so their anger burned against Judah and they returned home in fierce anger.

11 ¶ Now Amaziah strengthened himself, and led his people forth, and went to the Valley of Salt, and struck down 10,000 of the sons of Seir.

12 The sons of Judah also captured 10,000 alive and brought them to the top of the cliff, and threw them down from the top of the cliff so that they were all dashed to pieces.

13 But the troops whom Amaziah sent back from going with him to battle, raided the cities of Judah, from Samaria to Beth-horon, and struck down 3,000 of them, and plundered much spoil.

14 ¶ Now it came about after Amaziah came from slaughtering the Edomites that he brought the gods of the sons of Seir, set them up as his gods, bowed down before them, and burned incense to them.

15 Then the anger of the Lord burned against Amaziah, and He sent

him a prophet who said to him, "Why
have you sought the gods of the people who have not delivered their own
people from your hand?"

16 And it came about as he was talking with him that the king said to him,
"Have we appointed you a royal counselor? Stop! Why should you be struck
down?" Then the prophet stopped and
said, "I know that God has planned to
destroy you, because you have done
this, and have not listened to my counsel."

17 ¶ Then Amaziah king of Judah
took counsel and sent to Joash the son
of Jehoahaz the son of Jehu, the king
of Israel, saying, "Come, let us face
each other."

18 And Joash the king of Israel sent
to Amaziah king of Judah, saying,
"The thorn bush which was in Lebanon sent to the cedar which was in
Lebanon, saying, 'Give your daughter
to my son in marriage.' But there
passed by a wild beast that was in
Lebanon, and trampled the thorn
bush.

19"You said, 'Behold, you have defeated Edom.' And your heart has
become proud in boasting. Now stay
at home; for why should you provoke
trouble that you, even you, should fall
and Judah with you?"

20 But Amaziah would not listen, for
it was from God, that He might deliver
them into the hand of Joash because
they had sought the gods of Edom.

21 So Joash king of Israel went up,
and he and Amaziah king of Judah
faced each other at Beth-shemesh,
which belonged to Judah.

22 And Judah was defeated by Israel,
and they fled each to his tent.

23 Then Joash king of Israel captured Amaziah king of Judah, the son
of Joash the son of Jehoahaz, at Beth-
shemesh, and brought him to Jerusalem, and tore down the wall of Jerusalem from the Gate of Ephraim to the
Corner Gate, 400 cubits.

24 And he took all the gold and silver, and all the utensils which were
found in the house of God with Obed-
edom, and the treasures of the king's
house, the hostages also, and returned
to Samaria.

25 ¶ And Amaziah, the son of Joash
king of Judah, lived fifteen years after
the death of Joash, son of Jehoahaz,
king of Israel.

26 Now the rest of the acts of Amaziah, from first to last, behold, are they
not written in the Book of the Kings of
Judah and Israel?

27 And from the time that Amaziah
turned away from following the LORD
they conspired against him in Jerusalem, and he fled to Lachish; but they
sent after him to Lachish and killed
him there.

28 Then they brought him on horses
and buried him with his fathers in the
city of Judah.

CHAPTER 26

AND all the people of Judah took
Uzziah, who was sixteen years old,
and made him king in the place of his
father Amaziah.

2 He built Eloth and restored it to
Judah after the king slept with his
fathers.

3 Uzziah was sixteen years old
when he became king, and he reigned
fifty-two years in Jerusalem; and his
mother's name was Jechiliah of Jerusalem.

4 And he did right in the sight of the
LORD according to all that his father
Amaziah had done.

5 And he continued to seek God in
the days of Zechariah, who had understanding through the vision of God;
and as long as he sought the LORD,
God prospered him.

6 ¶ Now he went out and warred
against the Philistines, and broke
down the wall of Gath and the wall of
Jabneh and the wall of Ashdod; and he
built cities in the area of Ashdod and
among the Philistines.

7 And God helped him against the
Philistines, and against the Arabians
who lived in Gur-baal, and the Meunites.

8 The Ammonites also gave tribute
to Uzziah, and his fame extended to
the border of Egypt, for he became
very strong.

9 Moreover, Uzziah built towers in
Jerusalem at the Corner Gate and at
the Valley Gate and at the corner
buttress and fortified them.

10 And he built towers in the wilderness and hewed many cisterns, for he

had much livestock, both in the lowland and in the plain. *He also had* plowmen and vinedressers in the hill country and the fertile fields, for he loved the soil.

11 Moreover, Uzziah had an army ready for battle, which entered combat by divisions, according to the number of their muster, prepared by Jeiel the scribe and Maaseiah the official, under the direction of Hananiah, one of the king's officers.

12 The total number of the heads of the households, of valiant warriors, was 2,600.

13 And under their direction was an elite army of 307,500, who could wage war with great power, to help the king against the enemy.

14 Moreover, Uzziah prepared for all the army shields, spears, helmets, body armor, bows and sling stones.

15 And in Jerusalem he made engines *of war* invented by skillful men to be on the towers and on the corners, for the purpose of shooting arrows and great stones. Hence his fame spread afar, for he was marvelously helped until he *was* strong.

16 ¶ But when he became strong, his heart was so proud that he acted corruptly, and he was unfaithful to the LORD his God, for he entered the temple of the LORD to burn incense on the altar of incense.

17 Then Azariah the priest entered after him and with him eighty priests of the LORD, valiant men.

18 And they opposed Uzziah the king and said to him, "It is not for you, Uzziah, to burn incense to the LORD, but for the priests, the sons of Aaron who are consecrated to burn incense. Get out of the sanctuary, for you have been unfaithful, and will have no honor from the LORD God."

19 But Uzziah, with a censer in his hand for burning incense, was enraged; and while he was enraged with the priests, the leprosy broke out on his forehead before the priests in the house of the LORD, beside the altar of incense.

20 And Azariah the chief priest and all the priests looked at him, and behold, he *was* leprous on his forehead; and they hurried him out of there, and he himself also hastened to get out because the LORD had smitten him.

21 And King Uzziah was a leper to the day of his death; and he lived in a separate house, being a leper, for he was cut off from the house of the LORD. And Jotham his son *was* over the king's house judging the people of the land.

22 Now the rest of the acts of Uzziah, first to last, the prophet Isaiah, the son of Amoz, has written.

23 So Uzziah slept with his fathers, and they buried him with his fathers in the field of the grave which belonged to the kings, for they said, "He is a leper." And Jotham his son became king in his place.

CHAPTER 27

JOTHAM was twenty-five years old when he became king, and he reigned sixteen years in Jerusalem. And his mother's name was Jerushah the daughter of Zadok.

2 And he did right in the sight of the LORD, according to all that his father Uzziah had done; however he did not enter the temple of the LORD. But the people continued acting corruptly.

3 He built the upper gate of the house of the LORD, and he built extensively the wall of Ophel.

4 Moreover, he built cities in the hill country of Judah, and he built fortresses and towers on the wooded *hills*.

5 He fought also with the king of the Ammonites and prevailed over them so that the Ammonites gave him during that year one hundred talents of silver, ten thousand [9]kors of wheat and ten thousand of barley. The Ammonites also paid him this *amount* in the second and in the third year.

6 So Jotham became mighty because he ordered his ways before the LORD his God.

7 Now the rest of the acts of Jotham, even all his wars and his acts, behold, they are written in the Book of the Kings of Israel and Judah.

8 He was twenty-five years old when he became king, and he reigned sixteen years in Jerusalem.

9 And Jotham slept with his fathers, and they buried him in the city of David; and Ahaz his son became king in his place.

[9] I.e., A kor equals approx. 10 bushels

CHAPTER 28

AHAZ *was* twenty years old when he became king, and he reigned sixteen years in Jerusalem; and he did not do right in the sight of the LORD as David his father *had done.*

2 But he walked in the ways of the kings of Israel; he also made molten images for the Baals.

3 Moreover, he burned incense in the valley of Ben-hinnom, and burned his sons in fire, according to the abominations of the nations whom the LORD had driven out before the sons of Israel.

4 And he sacrificed and burned incense on the high places, on the hills, and under every green tree.

5 ¶ Wherefore, the LORD his God delivered him into the hand of the king of Aram; and they defeated him and carried away from him a great number of captives, and brought *them* to Damascus. And he was also delivered into the hand of the king of Israel, who inflicted him with heavy casualties.

6 For Pekah the son of Remaliah slew in Judah 120,000 in one day, all valiant men, because they had forsaken the LORD God of their fathers.

7 And Zichri, a mighty man of Ephraim, slew Maaseiah the king's son, and Azrikam the ruler of the house and Elkanah the second to the king.

8 ¶ And the sons of Israel carried away captive of their brethren 200,000 women, sons, and daughters; and took also a great deal of spoil from them, and they brought the spoil to Samaria.

9 But a prophet of the LORD was there, whose name *was* Oded; and he went out to meet the army which came to Samaria and said to them, "Behold, because the LORD, the God of your fathers, was angry with Judah, He has delivered them into your hand, and you have slain them in a rage *which* has even reached heaven.

10 "And now you are proposing to subjugate for yourselves the people of Judah and Jerusalem for male and female slaves. Surely, *do* you not *have* transgressions of your own against the LORD your God?

11 "Now therefore, listen to me and return the captives whom you captured from your brothers, for the burning anger of the LORD is against you."

12 Then some of the heads of the sons of Ephraim—Azariah the son of Johanan, Berechiah the son of Meshillemoth, Jehizkiah the son of Shallum, and Amasa the son of Hadlai—arose against those who were coming from the battle,

13 and said to them, "You must not bring the captives in here, for you are proposing *to bring* upon us guilt against the LORD adding to our sins and our guilt; for our guilt is great so that *His* burning anger is against Israel."

14 So the armed men left the captives and the spoil before the officers and all the assembly.

15 Then the men who were designated by name arose, took the captives, and they clothed all their naked ones from the spoil; and they gave them clothes and sandals, fed them and gave them drink, anointed them *with oil,* led all their feeble ones on donkeys, and brought them to Jericho, the city of palm trees, to their brothers; then they returned to Samaria.

16 ¶ At that time King Ahaz sent to the [10]kings of Assyria for help.

17 For again the Edomites had come and attacked Judah, and carried away captives.

18 The Philistines also had invaded the cities of the lowland and of the Negev of Judah, and had taken Bethshemesh, Aijalon, Gederoth, and Soco with its villages, Timnah with its villages, and Gimzo with its villages, and they settled there.

19 For the LORD humbled Judah because of Ahaz king of Israel, for he had brought about a lack of restraint in Judah and was very unfaithful to the LORD.

20 So Tilgath-pilneser king of Assyria came against him and afflicted him instead of strengthening him.

21 Although Ahaz took a portion out of the house of the LORD and out of the palace of the king and of the princes, and gave *it* to the king of Assyria, it did not help him.

22 ¶ Now in the time of his distress

[10] Ancient versions read *king*

this same King Ahaz became yet more unfaithful to the LORD.

23 For he sacrificed to the gods of Damascus which had defeated him, and said, "Because the gods of the kings of Aram helped them, I will sacrifice to them that they may help me." But they became the downfall of him and all Israel.

24 Moreover, when Ahaz gathered together the utensils of the house of God, he cut the utensils of the house of God in pieces; and he closed the doors of the house of the LORD, and made altars for himself in every corner of Jerusalem.

25 And in every city of Judah he made high places to burn incense to other gods, and provoked the LORD, the God of his fathers, to anger.

26 Now the rest of his acts and all his ways, from first to last, behold, they are written in the Book of the Kings of Judah and Israel.

27 So Ahaz slept with his fathers, and they buried him in the city, in Jerusalem, for they did not bring him into the tombs of the kings of Israel; and Hezekiah his son reigned in his place.

CHAPTER 29

HEZEKIAH became king *when he was* twenty-five years old; and he reigned twenty-nine years in Jerusalem. And his mother's name *was* Abijah, the daughter of Zechariah.

2 And he did right in the sight of the LORD, according to all that his father David had done.

3 ¶ In the first year of his reign, in the first month, he opened the doors of the house of the LORD and repaired them.

4 And he brought in the priests and the Levites, and gathered them into the square on the east.

5 Then he said to them, "Listen to me, O Levites. Consecrate yourselves now, and consecrate the house of the LORD, the God of your fathers, and carry the uncleanness out from the holy place.

6"For our fathers have been unfaithful and have done evil in the sight of the LORD our God, and have forsaken Him and turned their faces away from the dwelling place of the LORD, and have turned *their* backs.

7"They have also shut the doors of the porch and put out the lamps, and have not burned incense or offered burnt offerings in the holy place to the God of Israel.

8"Therefore the wrath of the LORD was against Judah and Jerusalem, and He has made them an object of terror, of horror, and of hissing, as you see with your own eyes.

9"For behold, our fathers have fallen by the sword, and our sons and our daughters and our wives are in captivity for this.

10"Now it is in my heart to make a covenant with the LORD God of Israel, that His burning anger may turn away from us.

11"My sons, do not be negligent now, for the LORD has chosen you to stand before Him, to minister to Him, and to be His ministers and burn incense."

12 ¶ Then the Levites arose: Mahath, the son of Amasai and Joel the son of Azariah, from the sons of the Kohathites; and from the sons of Merari, Kish the son of Abdi and Azariah the son of Jehallelel; and from the Gershonites, Joah the son of Zimmah and Eden the son of Joah;

13 and from the sons of Elizaphan, Shimri and Jeiel; and from the sons of Asaph, Zechariah and Mattaniah;

14 and from the sons of Heman, Jehiel and Shimei; and from the sons of Jeduthun, Shemaiah and Uzziel.

15 And they assembled their brothers, consecrated themselves, and went in to cleanse the house of the LORD, according to the commandment of the king by the words of the LORD.

16 So the priests went in to the inner part of the house of the LORD to cleanse *it,* and every unclean thing which they found in the temple of the LORD they brought out to the court of the house of the LORD. Then the Levites received *it* to carry out to the Kidron valley.

17 Now they began the consecration on the first *day* of the first month, and on the eighth day of the month they entered the porch of the LORD. Then they consecrated the house of the LORD in eight days, and finished on the sixteenth day of the first month.

18 Then they went in to King Hezekiah and said, "We have cleansed the whole house of the LORD, the altar of

burnt offering with all of its utensils, and the table of showbread with all of its utensils.

19 "Moreover, all the utensils which King Ahaz had discarded during his reign in his unfaithfulness, we have prepared and consecrated; and behold, they are before the altar of the LORD."

20 ¶ Then King Hezekiah arose early and assembled the princes of the city and went up to the house of the LORD.

21 And they brought seven bulls, seven rams, seven lambs, and seven male goats for a sin offering for the kingdom, the sanctuary, and Judah. And he ordered the priests, the sons of Aaron, to offer *them* on the altar of the LORD.

22 So they slaughtered the bulls, and the priests took the blood and sprinkled it on the altar. They also slaughtered the rams and sprinkled the blood on the altar; they slaughtered the lambs also and sprinkled the blood on the altar.

23 Then they brought the male goats of the sin offering before the king and the assembly, and they laid their hands on them.

24 And the priests slaughtered them and purged the altar with their blood to atone for all Israel, for the king ordered the burnt offering and the sin offering for all Israel.

25 ¶ He then stationed the Levites in the house of the LORD with cymbals, with harps, and with lyres, according to the command of David and of Gad the king's seer, and of Nathan the prophet; for the command was from the LORD through His prophets.

26 And the Levites stood with the *musical* instruments of David, and the priests with the trumpets.

27 Then Hezekiah gave the order to offer the burnt offering on the altar. When the burnt offering began, the song to the LORD also began with the trumpets, *accompanied* by the instruments of David, king of Israel.

28 While the whole assembly worshiped, the singers also sang and the trumpets sounded; all this *continued* until the burnt offering was finished.

29 ¶ Now at the completion of the burnt offerings, the king and all who were present with him bowed down and worshiped.

30 Moreover, King Hezekiah and the officials ordered the Levites to sing praises to the LORD with the words of David and Asaph the seer. So they sang praises with joy, and bowed down and worshiped.

31 Then Hezekiah answered and said, "Now *that* you have consecrated yourselves to the LORD, come near and bring sacrifices and thank offerings to the house of the LORD." And the assembly brought sacrifices and thank offerings, and all those who were willing *brought* burnt offerings.

32 And the number of the burnt offerings which the assembly brought was 70 bulls, 100 rams, and 200 lambs; all these were for a burnt offering to the LORD.

33 And the consecrated things were 600 bulls and 3,000 sheep.

34 But the priests were too few, so that they were unable to skin all the burnt offerings; therefore their brothers the Levites helped them until the work was completed, and until the *other* priests had consecrated themselves. For the Levites were more conscientious to consecrate themselves than the priests.

35 And there *were* also many burnt offerings with the fat of the peace offerings and with the libations for the burnt offerings. Thus the service of the house of the LORD was established *again*.

36 Then Hezekiah and all the people rejoiced over what God had prepared for the people, because the thing came about suddenly.

CHAPTER 30

NOW Hezekiah sent to all Israel and Judah and wrote letters also to Ephraim and Manasseh, that they should come to the house of the LORD at Jerusalem to celebrate the Passover to the LORD God of Israel.

2 For the king and his princes and all the assembly in Jerusalem had decided to celebrate the Passover in the second month,

3 since they could not celebrate it at that time, because the priests had not consecrated themselves in sufficient numbers, nor had the people been gathered to Jerusalem.

4 Thus the thing was right in the sight of the king and all the assembly.

5 So they established a decree to circulate a proclamation throughout all Israel from Beersheba even to Dan, that they should come to celebrate the Passover to the LORD God of Israel at Jerusalem. For they had not celebrated *it* in great numbers as it was prescribed.

6 And the couriers went throughout all Israel and Judah with the letters from the hand of the king and his princes, even according to the command of the king, saying, "O sons of Israel, return to the LORD God of Abraham, Isaac, and Israel, that He may return to those of you who escaped *and* are left from the hand of the kings of Assyria.

7 "And do not be like your fathers and your brothers, who were unfaithful to the LORD God of their fathers, so that He made them a horror, as you see.

8 "Now do not stiffen your neck like your fathers, but yield to the LORD and enter His sanctuary which He has consecrated forever, and serve the LORD your God, that His burning anger may turn away from you.

9 "For if you return to the LORD, your brothers and your sons *will find* compassion before those who led them captive, and will return to this land. For the LORD your God is gracious and compassionate, and will not turn *His* face away from you if you return to Him."

10 So the couriers passed from city to city through the country of Ephraim and Manasseh, and as far as Zebulun, but they laughed them to scorn, and mocked them.

11 Nevertheless some men of Asher, Manasseh, and Zebulun humbled themselves and came to Jerusalem.

12 The hand of God was also on Judah to give them one heart to do what the king and the princes commanded by the word of the LORD.

13 ¶ Now many people were gathered at Jerusalem to celebrate the Feast of Unleavened Bread in the second month, a very large assembly.

14 And they arose and removed the altars which *were* in Jerusalem; they also removed all the incense altars and cast *them* into the brook Kidron.

15 Then they slaughtered the Passover *lambs* on the fourteenth of the second month. And the priests and Levites were ashamed of themselves and consecrated themselves, and brought burnt offerings to the house of the LORD.

16 And they stood at their stations after their custom, according to the law of Moses the man of God; the priests sprinkled the blood *which they received* from the hand of the Levites.

17 For *there were* many in the assembly who had not consecrated themselves; therefore, the Levites *were* over the slaughter of the Passover *lambs* for everyone who *was* unclean, in order to consecrate *them* to the LORD.

18 For a multitude of the people, *even* many from Ephraim and Manasseh, Issachar and Zebulun, had not purified themselves, yet they ate the Passover otherwise than prescribed. For Hezekiah prayed for them, saying, "May the good LORD pardon

19 everyone who prepares his heart to seek God, the LORD God of his fathers, though not according to the purification *rules* of the sanctuary."

20 So the LORD heard Hezekiah and healed the people.

21 And the sons of Israel present in Jerusalem celebrated the Feast of Unleavened Bread *for* seven days with great joy, and the Levites and the priests praised the LORD day after day with loud instruments to the LORD.

22 Then Hezekiah spoke encouragingly to all the Levites who showed good insight *in the things* of the LORD. So they ate for the appointed seven days, sacrificing peace offerings and giving thanks to the LORD God of their fathers.

23 ¶ Then the whole assembly decided to celebrate *the feast* another seven days, so they celebrated the seven days with joy.

24 For Hezekiah king of Judah had contributed to the assembly 1,000 bulls and 7,000 sheep, and the princes had contributed to the assembly 1,000 bulls and 10,000 sheep; and a large number of priests consecrated themselves.

25 And all the assembly of Judah rejoiced, with the priests and the Levites, and all the assembly that came from Israel, both the sojourners who came from the land of Israel and those living in Judah.

26 So there was great joy in Jerusalem, because there was nothing like this in Jerusalem since the days of Solomon the son of David, king of Israel.

27 Then the Levitical priests arose and blessed the people; and their voice was heard and their prayer came to His holy dwelling place, to heaven.

CHAPTER 31

Now when all this was finished, all Israel who were present went out to the cities of Judah, broke the pillars in pieces, cut down the [11]Asherim, and pulled down the high places and the altars throughout all Judah and Benjamin, as well as in Ephraim and Manasseh, until they had destroyed them all. Then all the sons of Israel returned to their cities, each to his possession.

2 ¶ And Hezekiah appointed the divisions of the priests and the Levites by their divisions, each according to his service, *both* the priests and the Levites, for burnt offerings and for peace offerings, to minister and to give thanks and to praise in the gates of the camp of the LORD.

3 *He* also *appointed* the king's portion of his goods for the burnt offerings, *namely,* for the morning and evening burnt offerings, and the burnt offerings for the sabbaths and for the new moons and for the fixed festivals, as it is written in the law of the LORD.

4 Also he commanded the people who lived in Jerusalem to give the portion due to the priests and the Levites, that they might devote themselves to the law of the LORD.

5 And as soon as the order spread, the sons of Israel provided in abundance the first fruits of grain, new wine, oil, honey, and of all the produce of the field; and they brought in abundantly the tithe of all.

6 And the sons of Israel and Judah who lived in the cities of Judah, also brought in the tithe of oxen and sheep, and the tithe of sacred gifts which were consecrated to the LORD their God, and placed *them* in heaps.

7 In the third month they began to make the heaps, and finished *them* by the seventh month.

8 And when Hezekiah and the rulers came and saw the heaps, they blessed the LORD and His people Israel.

9 Then Hezekiah questioned the priests and the Levites concerning the heaps.

10 And Azariah the chief priest of the house of Zadok said to him, "Since the contributions began to be brought into the house of the LORD, we have had enough to eat with plenty left over, for the LORD has blessed His people, and this great quantity is left over."

11 ¶ Then Hezekiah commanded *them* to prepare rooms in the house of the LORD, and they prepared *them*.

12 And they faithfully brought in the contributions and the tithes and the consecrated things; and Conaniah the Levite *was* the officer in charge of them and his brother Shimei *was* second.

13 And Jehiel, Azaziah, Nahath, Asahel, Jerimoth, Jozabad, Eliel, Ismachiah, Mahath, and Benaiah *were* overseers under the authority of Conaniah and Shimei his brother by the appointment of King Hezekiah, and Azariah *was* the *chief* officer of the house of God.

14 And Kore the son of Imnah the Levite, the keeper of the eastern *gate,* *was* over the freewill offerings of God, to apportion the contributions for the LORD and the most holy things.

15 And under his authority *were* Eden, Miniamin, Jeshua, Shemaiah, Amariah, and Shecaniah in the cities of the priests, to distribute faithfully *their portions* to their brothers by divisions, whether great or small,

16 without regard to their genealogical enrollment, to the males from thirty years old and upward—everyone who entered the house of the LORD for his daily obligations—for their work in their duties according to their divisions;

17 as well as the priests who were enrolled genealogically according to their fathers' households, and the Levites from twenty years old and upwards, by their duties *and* their divisions.

18 And the genealogical enrollment *included* all their little children, their wives, their sons, and their daughters,

11 I.e., wooden symbols of a female deity

for the whole assembly, for they consecrated themselves faithfully in holiness.

19 Also for the sons of Aaron the priests *who were* in the pasture lands of their cities, or in each and every city, *there were* men who were designated by name to distribute portions to every male among the priests and to everyone genealogically enrolled among the Levites.

20 ¶ And thus Hezekiah did throughout all Judah; and he did what *was* good, right, and true before the LORD his God.

21 And every work which he began in the service of the house of God in law and in commandment, seeking his God, he did with all his heart and prospered.

CHAPTER 32

AFTER these acts of faithfulness Sennacherib king of Assyria came and invaded Judah and besieged the fortified cities, and thought to break into them for himself.

2 Now when Hezekiah saw that Sennacherib had come, and that he intended to make war on Jerusalem,

3 he decided with his officers and his warriors to cut off the *supply of* water from the springs which *were* outside the city, and they helped him.

4 So many people assembled and stopped up all the springs and the stream which flowed through the region, saying, "Why should the kings of Assyria come and find abundant water?"

5 And he took courage and rebuilt all the wall that had been broken down, and erected towers on it, and *built* another outside wall, and strengthened the Millo *in* the city of David, and made weapons and shields in great number.

6 And he appointed military officers over the people, and gathered them to him in the square at the city gate, and spoke encouragingly to them, saying,

7 "Be strong and courageous, do not fear or be dismayed because of the king of Assyria, nor because of all the multitude which is with him; for the one with us is greater than the one with him.

8 "With him is *only* an arm of flesh, but with us is the LORD our God to help us and to fight our battles." And the people relied on the words of Hezekiah king of Judah.

9 ¶ After this Sennacherib king of Assyria sent his servants to Jerusalem while he *was* besieging Lachish with all his forces with him, against Hezekiah king of Judah and against all Judah who *were* at Jerusalem, saying,

10 "Thus says Sennacherib king of Assyria, 'On what are you trusting that you are remaining in Jerusalem under siege?

11 'Is not Hezekiah misleading you to give yourselves over to die by hunger and by thirst, saying, "The LORD our God will deliver us from the hand of the king of Assyria"?

12 'Has not the same Hezekiah taken away His high places and His altars, and said to Judah and Jerusalem, "You shall worship before one altar, and on it you shall burn incense"?

13 'Do you not know what I and my fathers have done to all the peoples of the lands? Were the gods of the nations of the lands able at all to deliver their land from my hand?

14 'Who *was there* among all the gods of those nations which my fathers utterly destroyed who could deliver his people out of my hand, that your God should be able to deliver you from my hand?

15 'Now therefore, do not let Hezekiah deceive you or mislead you like this, and do not believe him, for no god of any nation or kingdom was able to deliver his people from my hand or from the hand of my fathers. How much less shall your God deliver you from my hand?' "

16 ¶ And his servants spoke further against the LORD God and against His servant Hezekiah.

17 He also wrote letters to insult the LORD God of Israel, and to speak against Him, saying, "As the gods of the nations of the lands have not delivered their people from my hand, so the God of Hezekiah shall not deliver His people from my hand."

18 And they called this out with a loud voice in the language of Judah to the people of Jerusalem who were on the wall, to frighten and terrify them, so that they might take the city.

19 And they spoke of the God of Jerusalem as of the gods of the peoples of the earth, the work of men's hands.

20 ¶ But King Hezekiah and Isaiah the prophet, the son of Amoz, prayed about this and cried out to heaven.

21 And the LORD sent an angel who destroyed every mighty warrior, commander and officer in the camp of the king of Assyria. So he returned in shame to his own land. And when he had entered the temple of his god, some of his own children killed him there with the sword.

22 So the LORD saved Hezekiah and the inhabitants of Jerusalem from the hand of Sennacherib the king of Assyria, and from the hand of all *others*, and guided them on every side.

23 And many were bringing gifts to the LORD at Jerusalem and choice presents to Hezekiah king of Judah, so that he was exalted in the sight of all nations thereafter.

24 ¶ In those days Hezekiah became mortally ill; and he prayed to the LORD, and the LORD spoke to him and gave him a sign.

25 But Hezekiah gave no return for the benefit he received, because his heart was proud; therefore wrath came on him and on Judah and Jerusalem.

26 However, Hezekiah humbled the pride of his heart, both he and the inhabitants of Jerusalem, so that the wrath of the LORD did not come on them in the days of Hezekiah.

27 ¶ Now Hezekiah had immense riches and honor; and he made for himself treasuries for silver, gold, precious stones, spices, shields and all kinds of valuable articles,

28 storehouses also for the produce of grain, wine and oil, pens for all kinds of cattle and sheepfolds for the flocks.

29 And he made cities for himself, and acquired flocks and herds in abundance; for God had given him very great wealth.

30 It was Hezekiah who stopped the upper outlet of the waters of Gihon and directed them to the west side of the city of David. And Hezekiah prospered in all that he did.

31 And even *in the matter of* the envoys of the rulers of Babylon, who sent to him to inquire of the wonder that had happened in the land, God left him *alone only* to test him, that He might know all that was in his heart.

32 ¶ Now the rest of the acts of Hezekiah and his deeds of devotion, behold, they are written in the vision of Isaiah the prophet, the son of Amoz, in the Book of the Kings of Judah and Israel.

33 So Hezekiah slept with his fathers, and they buried him in the upper section of the tombs of the sons of David; and all Judah and the inhabitants of Jerusalem honored him at his death. And his son Manasseh became king in his place.

CHAPTER 33

MANASSEH was twelve years old when he became king, and he reigned fifty-five years in Jerusalem.

2 And he did evil in the sight of the LORD according to the abominations of the nations whom the LORD dispossessed before the sons of Israel.

3 For he rebuilt the high places which Hezekiah his father had broken down; he also erected altars for the Baals and made [12]Asherim, and worshiped all the host of heaven and served them.

4 And he built altars in the house of the LORD of which the LORD had said, "My name shall be in Jerusalem forever."

5 For he built altars for all the host of heaven in the two courts of the house of the LORD.

6 And he made his sons pass through the fire in the valley of Benhinnom; and he practiced witchcraft, used divination, practiced sorcery, and dealt with mediums and spiritists. He did much evil in the sight of the LORD, provoking Him *to anger*.

7 Then he put the carved image of the idol which he had made in the house of God, of which God had said to David and to Solomon his son, "In this house and in Jerusalem, which I have chosen from all the tribes of Israel, I will put My name forever;

8 and I will not again remove the foot of Israel from the land which I have appointed for your fathers, if only they will observe to do all that I have commanded them according to

[12] I.e., wooden symbols of a female deity

all the law, the statutes, and the ordinances *given* through Moses."

9 Thus Manasseh misled Judah and the inhabitants of Jerusalem to do more evil than the nations whom the LORD destroyed before the sons of Israel.

10 ¶ And the LORD spoke to Manasseh and his people, but they paid no attention.

11 Therefore the LORD brought the commanders of the army of the king of Assyria against them, and they captured Manasseh with [13]hooks, bound him with bronze *chains,* and took him to Babylon.

12 And when he was in distress, he entreated the LORD his God and humbled himself greatly before the God of his fathers.

13 When he prayed to Him, He was moved by his entreaty and heard his supplication, and brought him again to Jerusalem to his kingdom. Then Manasseh knew that the LORD *was* God.

14 ¶ Now after this he built the outer wall of the city of David on the west side of Gihon, in the valley, even to the entrance of the Fish Gate; and he encircled the Ophel *with it* and made it very high. Then he put army commanders in all the fortified cities of Judah.

15 He also removed the foreign gods and the idol from the house of the LORD, as well as all the altars which he had built on the mountain of the house of the LORD and in Jerusalem, and he threw *them* outside the city.

16 And he set up the altar of the LORD and sacrificed peace offerings and thank offerings on it; and he ordered Judah to serve the LORD God of Israel.

17 Nevertheless the people still sacrificed in the high places, *although* only to the LORD their God.

18 ¶ Now the rest of the acts of Manasseh even his prayer to his God, and the words of the seers who spoke to him in the name of the LORD God of Israel, behold, they are among the records of the kings of Israel.

19 His prayer also and *how God* was entreated by him, and all his sin, his unfaithfulness, and the sites on which he built high places and erected the

Asherim and the carved images, before he humbled himself, behold, they are written in the records of the Hozai.

20 So Manasseh slept with his fathers, and they buried him in his own house. And Amon his son became king in his place.

21 ¶ Amon *was* twenty-two years old when he became king, and he reigned two years in Jerusalem.

22 And he did evil in the sight of the LORD as Manasseh his father had done, and Amon sacrificed to all the carved images which his father Manasseh had made, and he served them.

23 Moreover, he did not humble himself before the LORD as his father Manasseh had done, but Amon multiplied guilt.

24 Finally his servants conspired against him and put him to death in his own house.

25 But the people of the land killed all the conspirators against King Amon, and the people of the land made Josiah his son king in his place.

CHAPTER 34

JOSIAH *was* eight years old when he became king, and he reigned thirty-one years in Jerusalem.

2 And he did right in the sight of the LORD, and walked in the ways of his father David and did not turn aside to the right or to the left.

3 For in the eighth year of his reign while he was still a youth, he began to seek the God of his father David; and in the twelfth year he began to purge Judah and Jerusalem of the high places, the Asherim, the carved images, and the molten images.

4 And they tore down the altars of the Baals in his presence, and the incense altars that were high above them he chopped down; also the Asherim, the carved images, and the molten images he broke in pieces and ground to powder and scattered *it* on the graves of those who had sacrificed to them.

5 Then he burned the bones of the priests on their altars, and purged Judah and Jerusalem.

6 And in the cities of Manasseh, Ephraim, Simeon, even as far as Naphtali, in their surrounding ruins,

7 he also tore down the altars and

---

[13] I.e., thong put through the nose

beat the Asherim and the carved images into powder, and chopped down all the incense altars throughout the land of Israel. Then he returned to Jerusalem.

8 ¶ Now in the eighteenth year of his reign, when he had purged the land and the house, he sent Shaphan the son of Azaliah, and Maaseiah an official of the city, and Joah the son of Joahaz the recorder, to repair the house of the LORD his God.

9 And they came to Hilkiah the high priest and delivered the money that was brought into the house of God, which the Levites, the doorkeepers, had collected from Manasseh and Ephraim, and from all the remnant of Israel, and from all Judah and Benjamin and the inhabitants of Jerusalem.

10 Then they gave *it* into the hands of the workmen who had the oversight of the house of the LORD, and the workmen who were working in the house of the LORD used it to restore and repair the house.

11 They in turn gave *it* to the carpenters and to the builders to buy quarried stone and timber for couplings and to make beams for the houses which the kings of Judah had let go to ruin.

12 And the men did the work faithfully with foremen over them to supervise: Jahath and Obadiah, the Levites of the sons of Merari, Zechariah and Meshullam of the sons of the Kohathites, and the Levites, all who were skillful with musical instruments.

13 *They were* also over the burden bearers, and supervised all the workmen from job to job; and *some* of the Levites *were* scribes and officials and gatekeepers.

14 ¶ When they were bringing out the money which had been brought into the house of the LORD, Hilkiah the priest found the book of the law of the LORD *given* by Moses.

15 And Hilkiah responded and said to Shaphan the scribe, "I have found the book of the law in the house of the LORD." And Hilkiah gave the book to Shaphan.

16 Then Shaphan brought the book to the king and reported further word to the king, saying, "Everything that was entrusted to your servants they are doing.

17 "They have also emptied out the money which was found in the house of the LORD, and have delivered it into the hands of the supervisors and the workmen."

18 Moreover, Shaphan the scribe told the king saying, "Hilkiah the priest gave me a book." And Shaphan read from it in the presence of the king.

19 And it came about when the king heard the words of the law that he tore his clothes.

20 Then the king commanded Hilkiah, Ahikam the son of Shaphan, Abdon the son of Micah, Shaphan the scribe, and Asaiah the king's servant, saying,

21 "Go, inquire of the LORD for me and for those who are left in Israel and in Judah, concerning the words of the book which has been found; for great is the wrath of the LORD which is poured out on us because our fathers have not observed the word of the LORD, to do according to all that is written in this book."

22 ¶ So Hilkiah and *those* whom the king had told went to Huldah the prophetess, the wife of Shallum the son of Tokhath, the son of Hasrah, the keeper of the wardrobe (now she lived in Jerusalem in the Second Quarter); and they spoke to her regarding this.

23 And she said to them, "Thus says the LORD, the God of Israel, 'Tell the man who sent you to Me,

24 thus says the LORD, "Behold, I am bringing evil on this place and on its inhabitants, *even* all the curses written in the book which they have read in the presence of the king of Judah.

25 "Because they have forsaken Me and have burned incense to other gods, that they might provoke Me to anger with all the works of their hands, therefore My wrath will be poured out on this place, and it shall not be quenched." '

26 "But to the king of Judah who sent you to inquire of the LORD, thus you will say to him, 'Thus says the LORD God of Israel *regarding* the words which you have heard,

27 "Because your heart was tender and you humbled yourself before God, when you heard His words against this place and against its inhabitants, and *because* you humbled yourself before

Me, tore your clothes, and wept before Me, I truly have heard you," declares the LORD.

28"Behold, I will gather you to your fathers and you shall be gathered to your grave in peace, so your eyes shall not see all the evil which I will bring on this place and on its inhabitants." ' " And they brought back word to the king.

29 ¶ Then the king sent and gathered all the elders of Judah and Jerusalem.

30 And the king went up to the house of the LORD and all the men of Judah, the inhabitants of Jerusalem, the priests, the Levites, and all the people, from the greatest to the least; and he read in their hearing all the words of the book of the covenant which was found in the house of the LORD.

31 Then the king stood in his place and made a covenant before the LORD to walk after the LORD, and to keep His commandments and His testimonies and His statutes with all his heart and with all his soul, to perform the words of the covenant written in this book.

32 Moreover, he made all who were present in Jerusalem and Benjamin to stand *with him*. So the inhabitants of Jerusalem did according to the covenant of God, the God of their fathers.

33 And Josiah removed all the abominations from all the lands belonging to the sons of Israel, and made all who were present in Israel to serve the LORD their God. Throughout his lifetime they did not turn from following the LORD God of their fathers.

CHAPTER 35

THEN Josiah celebrated the Passover to the LORD in Jerusalem, and they slaughtered the Passover *animals* on the fourteenth *day* of the first month.

2 And he set the priests in their offices and encouraged them in the service of the house of the LORD.

3 He also said to the Levites who taught all Israel *and* who were holy to the LORD, "Put the holy ark in the house which Solomon the son of David king of Israel built; it will be a burden on *your* shoulders no longer. Now serve the LORD your God and His people Israel.

4"And prepare *yourselves* by your fathers' households in your divisions, according to the writing of David king of Israel and according to the writing of his son Solomon.

5"Moreover, stand in the holy place according to the sections of the fathers' households of your brethren the lay people, and according to the Levites, by division of a father's household.

6"Now slaughter the Passover *animals*, sanctify yourselves, and prepare for your brethren to do according to the word of the LORD by Moses."

7 ¶ And Josiah contributed to the lay people, to all who were present, flocks of lambs and kids, all for the Passover offerings, numbering 30,000 plus 3,000 bulls; these were from the king's possessions.

8 His officers also contributed a freewill offering to the people, the priests, and the Levites. Hilkiah and Zechariah and Jehiel, the officials of the house of God, gave to the priests for the Passover offerings 2,600 *from the flocks* and 300 bulls.

9 Conaniah also, and Shemaiah and Nethanel, his brothers, and Hashabiah and Jeiel and Jozabad, the officers of the Levites, contributed to the Levites for the Passover offerings 5,000 *from the flocks* and 500 bulls.

10 ¶ So the service was prepared, and the priests stood at their stations and the Levites by their divisions according to the king's command.

11 And they slaughtered the Passover *animals*, and while the priests sprinkled the blood *received* from their hand, the Levites skinned *them*.

12 Then they removed the burnt offerings that *they* might give them to the sections of the fathers' households of the lay people to present to the LORD, as it is written in the book of Moses. *They did* this also with the bulls.

13 So they roasted the Passover *animals* on the fire according to the ordinance, and they boiled the holy things in pots, in kettles, in pans, and carried *them* speedily to all the lay people.

14 And afterwards they prepared for themselves and for the priests, because the priests, the sons of Aaron, *were* offering the burnt offerings and

the fat until night; therefore the Levites prepared for themselves and for the priests, the sons of Aaron.

15 The singers, the sons of Asaph, *were* also at their stations according to the command of David, Asaph, Heman, and Jeduthun the king's seer; and the gatekeepers at each gate did not have to depart from their service, because the Levites their brethren prepared for them.

16 ¶ So all the service of the LORD was prepared on that day to celebrate the Passover, and to offer burnt offerings on the altar of the LORD according to the command of King Josiah.

17 Thus the sons of Israel who were present celebrated the Passover at that time, and the Feast of Unleavened Bread seven days.

18 And there had not been celebrated a Passover like it in Israel since the days of Samuel the prophet; nor had any of the kings of Israel celebrated such a Passover as Josiah did with the priests, the Levites, all Judah and Israel who were present, and the inhabitants of Jerusalem.

19 In the eighteenth year of Josiah's reign this Passover was celebrated.

20 ¶ After all this, when Josiah had set the temple in order, Neco king of Egypt came up to make war at Carchemish on the Euphrates, and Josiah went out to engage him.

21 But Neco sent messengers to him, saying, "What have we to do with each other, O King of Judah? *I am* not coming against you today but against the house with which I am at war, and God has ordered me to hurry. Stop for your own sake from *interfering with* God who is with me, that He may not destroy you."

22 However, Josiah would not turn away from him, but disguised himself in order to make war with him; nor did he listen to the words of Neco from the mouth of God, but came to make war on the plain of Megiddo.

23 And the archers shot King Josiah, and the king said to his servants, "Take me away, for I am badly wounded."

24 So his servants took him out of the chariot and carried him in the second chariot which he had, and brought him to Jerusalem where he died and was buried in the tombs of his fathers. And all Judah and Jerusalem mourned for Josiah.

25 Then Jeremiah chanted a lament for Josiah. And all the male and female singers speak about Josiah in their lamentations to this day. And they made them an ordinance in Israel; behold, they are also written in the Lamentations.

26 Now the rest of the acts of Josiah and his deeds of devotion as written in the law of the LORD,

27 and his acts, first to last, behold, they are written in the Book of the Kings of Israel and Judah.

CHAPTER 36

THEN the people of the land took [14]Joahaz the son of Josiah, and made him king in place of his father in Jerusalem.

2 Joahaz was twenty-three years old when he became king, and he reigned three months in Jerusalem.

3 Then the king of Egypt deposed him at Jerusalem, and imposed on the land a fine of one hundred talents of silver and one talent of gold.

4 And the king of Egypt made Eliakim his brother king over Judah and Jerusalem, and changed his name to Jehoiakim. But Neco took Joahaz his brother and brought him to Egypt.

5 Jehoiakim was twenty-five years old when he became king, and he reigned eleven years in Jerusalem; and he did evil in the sight of the LORD his God.

6 Nebuchadnezzar king of Babylon came up against him and bound him with bronze *chains* to take him to Babylon.

7 Nebuchadnezzar also brought *some* of the articles of the house of the LORD to Babylon and put them in his temple at Babylon.

8 Now the rest of the acts of Jehoiakim and the abominations which he did, and what was found against him, behold, they are written in the Book of the Kings of Israel and Judah. And Jehoiachin his son became king in his place.

9 ¶ Jehoiachin was eight years old when he became king, and he reigned

[14] I.e., short form of Jehoahaz

three months and ten days in Jerusalem, and he did evil in the sight of the LORD.

10 And at the turn of the year King Nebuchadnezzar sent and brought him to Babylon with the valuable articles of the house of the LORD, and he made his kinsman Zedekiah king over Judah and Jerusalem.

11 Zedekiah was twenty-one years old when he became king, and he reigned eleven years in Jerusalem.

12 And he did evil in the sight of the LORD his God; he did not humble himself before Jeremiah the prophet who spoke for the LORD.

13 And he also rebelled against King Nebuchadnezzar who had made him swear *allegiance* by God. But he stiffened his neck and hardened his heart against turning to the LORD God of Israel.

14 Furthermore, all the officials of the priests and the people were very unfaithful *following* all the abominations of the nations; and they defiled the house of the LORD which He had sanctified in Jerusalem.

15 And the LORD, the God of their fathers, sent *word* to them again and again by His messengers, because He had compassion on His people and on His dwelling place;

16 but they *continually* mocked the messengers of God, despised His words and scoffed at His prophets, until the wrath of the LORD arose against His people, until there was no remedy.

17 Therefore He brought up against them the king of the Chaldeans who slew their young men with the sword in the house of their sanctuary, and had no compassion on young man or virgin, old man or infirm; He gave *them* all into his hand.

18 And all the articles of the house of God, great and small, and the treasures of the house of the LORD, and the treasures of the king and of his officers, he brought *them* all to Babylon.

19 Then they burned the house of God, and broke down the wall of Jerusalem and burned all its fortified buildings with fire, and destroyed all its valuable articles.

20 And those who had escaped from the sword he carried away to Babylon; and they were servants to him and to his sons until the rule of the kingdom of Persia,

21 to fulfill the word of the LORD by the mouth of Jeremiah, until the land had enjoyed its sabbaths. All the days of its desolation it kept sabbath until seventy years were complete.

22 ¶ Now in the first year of Cyrus king of Persia—in order to fulfill the word of the LORD by the mouth of Jeremiah—the LORD stirred up the spirit of Cyrus king of Persia, so that he sent a proclamation throughout his kingdom, and also *put it* in writing, saying,

23 "Thus says Cyrus king of Persia, 'The LORD, the God of heaven, has given me all the kingdoms of the earth, and He has appointed me to build Him a house in Jerusalem, which is in Judah. Whoever there is among you of all His people, may the LORD his God be with him, and let him go up!' "

THE BOOK OF

EZRA

NOW in the first year of Cyrus king of Persia, in order to fulfill the word of the LORD by the mouth of Jeremiah, the LORD stirred up the spirit of Cyrus king of Persia, so that he sent a proclamation throughout all his kingdom, and also *put it* in writing, saying,

2"Thus says Cyrus king of Persia, 'The LORD, the God of heaven, has given me all the kingdoms of the earth, and He has appointed me to build Him a house in Jerusalem, which is in Judah.

3 'Whoever there is among you of all His people, may his God be with him! Let him go up to Jerusalem which is in Judah, and rebuild the house of the LORD, the God of Israel; He is the God who is in Jerusalem.

4 'And every survivor, at whatever place he may live, let the men of that place support him with silver and gold, with goods and cattle, together with a freewill offering for the house of God which is in Jerusalem.' "

5 ¶ Then the heads of fathers' *households* of Judah and Benjamin and the priests and the Levites arose, even everyone whose spirit God had stirred to go up and rebuild the house of the LORD which is in Jerusalem.

6 And all those about them encouraged them with articles of silver, with gold, with goods, with cattle, and with valuables, aside from all that was given as a freewill offering.

7 Also King Cyrus brought out the articles of the house of the LORD, which Nebuchadnezzar had carried away from Jerusalem and put in the house of his gods;

8 and Cyrus, king of Persia, had them brought out by the hand of Mithredath the treasurer, and he counted them out to Sheshbazzar, the prince of Judah.

9 Now this *was* their number: 30 gold dishes, 1,000 silver dishes, 29 duplicates;

10 30 gold bowls, 410 silver bowls of a second *kind, and* 1,000 other articles.

11 All the articles of gold and silver *numbered* 5,400. Sheshbazzar brought them all up with the exiles who went up from Babylon to Jerusalem.

CHAPTER 2

NOW these are the people of the province who came up out of the captivity of the exiles whom Nebuchadnezzar the king of Babylon had carried away to Babylon, and returned to Jerusalem and Judah, each to his city.

2 These came with Zerubbabel, Jeshua, Nehemiah, Seraiah, Reelaiah, Mordecai, Bilshan, Mispar, Bigvai, Rehum, and Baanah.

¶ The number of the men of the people of Israel:

3 the sons of Parosh, 2,172;

4 the sons of Shephatiah, 372;

5 the sons of Arah, 775;

6 the sons of Pahath-moab of the sons of Jeshua *and* Joab, 2,812;

7 the sons of Elam, 1,254;

8 the sons of Zattu, 945;

9 the sons of Zaccai, 760;

10 the sons of Bani, 642;

11 the sons of Bebai, 623;

12 the sons of Azgad, 1,222;

13 the sons of Adonikam, 666;

14 the sons of Bigvai, 2,056;

15 the sons of Adin, 454;

16 the sons of Ater of Hezekiah, 98;

17 the sons of Bezai, 323;

18 the sons of Jorah, 112;

19 the sons of Hashum, 223;

20 the sons of Gibbar, 95;

21 the men of Bethlehem, 123;

22 the men of Netophah, 56;

23 the men of Anathoth, 128;

24 the sons of Azmaveth, 42;

25 the sons of Kiriath-arim, Chephirah, and Beeroth, 743;

26 the sons of Ramah and Geba, 621;

27 the men of Michmas, 122;

28 the men of Bethel and Ai, 223;

29 the sons of Nebo, 52;

30 the sons of Magbish, 156;

31 the sons of the other Elam, 1,254;

32 the sons of Harim, 320;

33 the sons of Lod, Hadid, and Ono, 725;

34 the men of Jericho, 345;

35 the men of Senaah, 3,630.

36 ¶ The priests: the sons of Jedaiah of the house of Jeshua, 973;

37 the sons of Immer, 1,052;

38 the sons of Pashhur, 1,247;

39 the sons of Harim, 1,017.

40 ¶ The Levites: the sons of Jeshua

and Kadmiel, of the sons of Hodaviah, 74.

41 The singers: the sons of Asaph, 128.

42 The sons of the gatekeepers: the sons of Shallum, the sons of Ater, the sons of Talmon, the sons of Akkub, the sons of Hatita, the sons of Shobai, in all 139.

43 ¶ The temple servants: the sons of Ziha, the sons of Hasupha, the sons of Tabbaoth,

44 the sons of Keros, the sons of Siaha, the sons of Padon,

45 the sons of Lebanah, the sons of Hagabah, the sons of Akkub,

46 the sons of Hagab, the sons of Shalmai, the sons of Hanan,

47 the sons of Giddel, the sons of Gahar, the sons of Reaiah,

48 the sons of Rezin, the sons of Nekoda, the sons of Gazzam,

49 the sons of Uzza, the sons of Paseah, the sons of Besai,

50 the sons of Asnah, the sons of Meunim, the sons of Nephisim,

51 the sons of Bakbuk, the sons of Hakupha, the sons of Harhur,

52 the sons of Bazluth, the sons of Mehida, the sons of Harsha,

53 the sons of Barkos, the sons of Sisera, the sons of Temah,

54 the sons of Neziah, the sons of Hatipha.

55 ¶ The sons of Solomon's servants: the sons of Sotai, the sons of Hassophereth, the sons of Peruda,

56 the sons of Jaalah, the sons of Darkon, the sons of Giddel,

57 the sons of Shephatiah, the sons of Hattil, the sons of Pochereth-hazzebaim, the sons of Ami.

58 All the temple servants, and the sons of Solomon's servants, were 392.

59 ¶ Now these are those who came up from Tel-melah, Tel-harsha, Cherub, Addan, *and* Immer, but they were not able to give evidence of their fathers' households, and their descendants, whether they were of Israel:

60 the sons of Delaiah, the sons of Tobiah, the sons of Nekoda, 652.

61 And of the sons of the priests: the sons of Habaiah, the sons of Hakkoz, the sons of Barzillai, who took a wife from the daughters of Barzillai the Gileadite, and he was called by their name.

62 These searched *among* their ancestral registration, but they could not be located; therefore they were considered unclean *and excluded* from the priesthood.

63 And the governor said to them that they should not eat from the most holy things until a priest stood up with Urim and Thummim.

64 ¶ The whole assembly numbered 42,360,

65 besides their male and female servants, who numbered 7,337; and they had 200 singing men and women.

66 Their horses were 736; their mules, 245;

67 their camels, 435; *their* donkeys, 6,720.

68 ¶ And some of the heads of fathers' *households*, when they arrived at the house of the LORD which is in Jerusalem, offered willingly for the house of God to restore it on its foundation.

69 According to their ability they gave to the treasury for the work 61,000 gold drachmas, and 5,000 silver minas, and 100 priestly garments.

70 ¶ Now the priests and the Levites, some of the people, the singers, the gatekeepers, and the temple servants lived in their cities, and all Israel in their cities.

CHAPTER 3

NOW when the seventh month came, and the sons of Israel *were* in the cities, the people gathered together as one man to Jerusalem.

2 Then Jeshua the son of Jozadak and his brothers the priests, and Zerubbabel the son of Shealtiel, and his brothers arose and built the altar of the God of Israel, to offer burnt offerings on it, as it is written in the law of Moses, the man of God.

3 So they set up the altar on its foundation, for they were terrified because of the peoples of the lands; and they offered burnt offerings on it to the LORD, burnt offerings morning and evening.

4 And they celebrated the Feast of [1]Booths, as it is written, and *offered* the fixed number of burnt offerings daily, according to the ordinance, as each day required;

[1] Or, *Tabernacles*

5 and afterward *there was* a continual burnt offering, also for the new moons and for all the fixed festivals of the LORD that were consecrated, and from everyone who offered a freewill offering to the LORD.

6 From the first day of the seventh month they began to offer burnt offerings to the LORD, but the foundation of the temple of the LORD had not been laid.

7 Then they gave money to the masons and carpenters, and food, drink, and oil to the Sidonians and to the Tyrians, to bring cedar wood from Lebanon to the sea at Joppa, according to the permission they had from Cyrus king of Persia.

8 Now in the second year of their coming to the house of God at Jerusalem in the second month, Zerubbabel the son of Shealtiel and Jeshua the son of Jozadak and the rest of their brothers the priests and the Levites, and all who came from the captivity to Jerusalem, began *the work* and appointed the Levites from twenty years and older to oversee the work of the house of the LORD.

9 Then Jeshua *with* his sons and brothers stood united *with* Kadmiel and his sons, the sons of Judah *and* the sons of Henadad *with* their sons and brothers the Levites, to oversee the workmen in the temple of God.

10 Now when the builders had laid the foundation of the temple of the LORD, the priests stood in their apparel with trumpets, and the Levites, the sons of Asaph, with cymbals, to praise the LORD according to the directions of King David of Israel.

11 And they sang, praising and giving thanks to the LORD, *saying*, "For He is good, for His lovingkindness is upon Israel forever." And all the people shouted with a great shout when they praised the LORD because the foundation of the house of the LORD was laid.

12 Yet many of the priests and Levites and heads of fathers' *households*, the old men who had seen the first temple, wept with a loud voice when the foundation of this house was laid before their eyes, while many shouted aloud for joy;

13 so that the people could not distinguish the sound of the shout of joy from the sound of the weeping of the people, for the people shouted with a loud shout, and the sound was heard far away.

CHAPTER 4

NOW when the enemies of Judah and Benjamin heard that the people of the exile were building a temple to the LORD God of Israel,

2 they approached Zerubbabel and the heads of fathers' *households*, and said to them, "Let us build with you, for we, like you, seek your God; and we have been sacrificing to Him since the days of Esarhaddon king of Assyria, who brought us up here."

3 But Zerubbabel and Jeshua and the rest of the heads of fathers' *households* of Israel said to them, "You have nothing in common with us in building a house to our God; but we ourselves will together build to the LORD God of Israel, as King Cyrus, the king of Persia has commanded us."

4 Then the people of the land discouraged the people of Judah, and frightened them from building,

5 and hired counselors against them to frustrate their counsel all the days of Cyrus king of Persia, even until the reign of Darius king of Persia.

6 ¶ Now in the reign of [2]Ahasuerus, in the beginning of his reign, they wrote an accusation against the inhabitants of Judah and Jerusalem.

7 ¶ And in the days of Artaxerxes, Bishlam, Mithredath, Tabeel, and the rest of his colleagues, wrote to Artaxerxes king of Persia; and the text of the letter was written in Aramaic and translated *from* Aramaic.

8 Rehum the commander and Shimshai the scribe wrote a letter against Jerusalem to King Artaxerxes, as follows—

9 then *wrote* Rehum the commander and Shimshai the scribe and the rest of their colleagues, the judges and the lesser governors, the officials, the secretaries, the men of Erech, the Babylonians, the men of Susa, that is, the Elamites,

10 and the rest of the nations which the great and honorable Osnappar deported and settled in the city of

[2] Or, *Xerxes*

Samaria, and in the rest of the region beyond the [3]River. And now

11 this is the copy of the letter which they sent to him: "To King Artaxerxes: Your servants, the men in the region beyond the River, and now

12 let it be known to the king, that the Jews who came up from you have come to us at Jerusalem; they are rebuilding the rebellious and evil city, and are finishing the walls and repairing the foundations.

13"Now let it be known to the king, that if that city is rebuilt and the walls are finished, they will not pay tribute, custom, or toll, and it will damage the revenue of the kings.

14"Now because we are in the service of the palace, and it is not fitting for us to see the king's dishonor, therefore we have sent and informed the king,

15 so that a search may be made in the record books of your fathers. And you will discover in the record books, and learn that that city is a rebellious city and damaging to kings and provinces, and that they have incited revolt within it in past days; therefore that city was laid waste.

16"We inform the king that, if that city is rebuilt and the walls finished, as a result you will have no possession in *the province* beyond the River."

17 ¶ *Then* the king sent an answer to Rehum the commander, to Shimshai the scribe, and to the rest of their colleagues who live in Samaria and in the rest of *the provinces* beyond the River: "Peace. And now

18 the document which you sent to us has been translated and read before me.

19"And a decree has been issued by me, and a search has been made and it has been discovered that that city has risen up against the kings in past days, that rebellion and revolt have been perpetrated in it,

20 that mighty kings have ruled over Jerusalem, governing all *the provinces* beyond the River, and that tribute, custom, and toll were paid to them.

21"So, now issue a decree to make these men stop *work*, that the city may not be rebuilt until a decree is issued by me.

22"And beware of being negligent in carrying out this *matter*; why should damage increase to the detriment of the kings?"

23 ¶ Then as soon as the copy of King Artaxerxes' document was read before Rehum and Shimshai the scribe and their colleagues, they went in haste to Jerusalem to the Jews and stopped them by force of arms.

24 ¶ Then work on the house of God in Jerusalem ceased, and it was stopped until the second year of the reign of Darius king of Persia.

CHAPTER 5

WHEN the prophets, Haggai the prophet and Zechariah the son of Iddo, prophesied to the Jews who were in Judah and Jerusalem, in the name of the God of Israel, who was over them,

2 then Zerubbabel the son of Shealtiel and Jeshua the son of Jozadak arose and began to rebuild the house of God which is in Jerusalem; and the prophets of God were with them supporting them.

3 At that time Tattenai, the governor of *the province* beyond the River, and Shethar-bozenai and their colleagues came to them and spoke to them thus, "Who issued you a decree to rebuild this [4]temple and to finish this structure?"

4 Then we told them accordingly what the names of the men were who were reconstructing this building.

5 But the eye of their God was on the elders of the Jews, and they did not stop them until a report should come to Darius, and then a written reply be returned concerning it.

6 ¶ *This is* the copy of the letter which Tattenai, the governor of *the province* beyond the River, and Shethar-bozenai and his colleagues the officials, who were beyond the River, sent to Darius the king.

7 They sent a report to him in which it was written thus: "To Darius the king, all peace.

8"Let it be known to the king, that we have gone to the province of Judah, to the house of the great God, which is being built with huge stones, and beams are being laid in the walls;

---

[3] I.e., Euphrates, and so throughout this context   [4] Lit., *house*, and so in vv. 9, 11, 12

and this work is going on with great care and is succeeding in their hands.

9"Then we asked those elders and said to them thus, 'Who issued you a decree to rebuild this temple and to finish this structure?'

10"We also asked them their names so as to inform you, and that we might write down the names of the men who were at their head.

11"And thus they answered us, saying, 'We are the servants of the God of heaven and earth and are rebuilding the temple that was built many years ago, which a great king of Israel built and finished.

12 'But because our fathers had provoked the God of heaven to wrath, He gave them into the hand of Nebuchadnezzar king of Babylon, the Chaldean, who destroyed this temple and deported the people to Babylon.

13 'However, in the first year of Cyrus king of Babylon, King Cyrus issued a decree to rebuild this house of God.

14 'And also the gold and silver utensils of the house of God which Nebuchadnezzar had taken from the temple in Jerusalem, and brought them to the temple of Babylon, these King Cyrus took from the temple of Babylon, and they were given to one whose name was Sheshbazzar, whom he had appointed governor.

15 'And he said to him, "Take these utensils, go and deposit them in the temple in Jerusalem, and let the house of God be rebuilt in its place."

16 'Then that Sheshbazzar came and laid the foundations of the house of God in Jerusalem; and from then until now it has been under construction, and it is not yet completed.'

17"And now, if it pleases the king let a search be conducted in the king's treasure house, which is there in Babylon, if it be that a decree was issued by King Cyrus to rebuild this house of God at Jerusalem; and let the king send to us his decision concerning this matter."

CHAPTER 6

THEN King Darius issued a decree, and search was made in the [5]archives, where the treasures were stored in Babylon.

2 And in [6]Ecbatana in the fortress, which is in the province of Media, a scroll was found and there was written in it as follows: "Memorandum—

3"In the first year of King Cyrus, Cyrus the king issued a decree: 'Concerning the house of God at Jerusalem, let the temple, the place where sacrifices are offered, be rebuilt and let its foundations be retained, its height being 60 cubits and its width 60 cubits;

4 with three layers of huge stones, and one layer of timbers. And let the cost be paid from the royal treasury.

5 'And also let the gold and silver utensils of the temple of God, which Nebuchadnezzar took from the temple in Jerusalem and brought to Babylon, be returned and brought to their places in the temple in Jerusalem; and you shall put them in the house of God.'

6 ¶"Now therefore, Tattenai, governor of the province beyond the River, Shethar-bozenai, and your colleagues, the officials of the provinces beyond the River, keep away from there.

7"Leave this work on the house of God alone; let the governor of the Jews and the elders of the Jews rebuild this house of God on its site.

8"Moreover, I issue a decree concerning what you are to do for these elders of Judah in the rebuilding of this house of God: the full cost is to be paid to these people from the royal treasury out of the taxes of the provinces beyond the River, and that without delay.

9"And whatever is needed, both young bulls, rams, and lambs for a burnt offering to the God of heaven, and wheat, salt, wine, and anointing oil, as the priests in Jerusalem request, it is to be given to them daily without fail,

10 that they may offer [7]acceptable sacrifices to the God of heaven and pray for the life of the king and his sons.

11"And I issued a decree that any man who violates this edict, a timber shall be drawn from his house and he shall be impaled on it and his house shall be made a refuse heap on account of this.

12"And may the God who has caused

---

[5] Lit., house of the books
[6] Aram., Achmetha
[7] Lit., pleasing or sweet-smelling sacrifices

His name to dwell there overthrow any king or people who attempts to change *it,* so as to destroy this house of God in Jerusalem. I, Darius, have issued *this* decree, let *it* be carried out with all diligence!"

13 ¶ Then Tattenai, the governor of *the province* beyond the River, She-thar-bozenai, and their colleagues carried out *the decree* with all diligence, just as King Darius had sent.

14 And the elders of the Jews were successful in building through the prophesying of Haggai the prophet and Zechariah the son of Iddo. And they finished building according to the command of the God of Israel and the decree of Cyrus, Darius, and Artaxerxes king of Persia.

15 And this temple was completed on the third day of the month Adar; it was the sixth year of the reign of King Darius.

16 ¶ And the sons of Israel, the priests, the Levites, and the rest of the exiles, celebrated the dedication of this house of God with joy.

17 And they offered for the dedication of this temple of God 100 bulls, 200 rams, 400 lambs, and as a sin offering for all Israel 12 male goats, corresponding to the number of the tribes of Israel.

18 Then they appointed the priests to their divisions and the Levites in their orders for the service of God in Jerusalem, as it is written in the book of Moses.

19 ¶ And the exiles observed the Passover on the fourteenth of the first month.

20 For the priests and the Levites had purified themselves together; all of them were pure. Then they slaughtered the Passover *lamb* for all the exiles, both for their brothers the priests and for themselves.

21 And the sons of Israel who returned from exile and all those who had separated themselves from the impurity of the nations of the land to *join* them, to seek the Lord God of Israel, ate *the Passover.*

22 And they observed the Feast of Unleavened Bread seven days with joy, for the Lord had caused them to rejoice, and had turned the heart of the king of Assyria toward them to

encourage them in the work of the house of God, the God of Israel.

CHAPTER 7

Now after these things, in the reign of Artaxerxes king of Persia, *there went up* Ezra son of Seraiah, son of Azariah, son of Hilkiah,

2 son of Shallum, son of Zadok, son of Ahitub,

3 son of Amariah, son of Azariah, son of Meraioth,

4 son of Zerahiah, son of Uzzi, son of Bukki,

5 son of Abishua, son of Phinehas, son of Eleazar, son of Aaron the chief priest.

6 This Ezra went up from Babylon, and he was a scribe skilled in the law of Moses, which the Lord God of Israel had given; and the king granted him all he requested because the hand of the Lord his God *was* upon him.

7 And some of the sons of Israel and some of the priests, the Levites, the singers, the gatekeepers, and the temple servants went up to Jerusalem in the seventh year of King Artaxerxes.

8 And he came to Jerusalem in the fifth month, which was in the seventh year of the king.

9 For on the first of the first month he began to go up from Babylon; and on the first of the fifth month he came to Jerusalem, because the good hand of his God *was* upon him.

10 For Ezra had set his heart to study the law of the Lord, and to practice *it,* and to teach *His* statutes and ordinances in Israel.

11 ¶ Now this is the copy of the decree which King Artaxerxes gave to Ezra the priest, the scribe, learned in the words of the commandments of the Lord and His statutes to Israel:

12"Artaxerxes, king of kings, to Ezra the priest, the scribe of the law of the God of heaven, perfect *peace.* And now

13 I have issued a decree that any of the people of Israel and their priests and the Levites in my kingdom who are willing to go to Jerusalem, may go with you.

14"Forasmuch as you are sent by the king and his seven counselors to inquire concerning Judah and Jerusalem according to the law of your God which is in your hand,

15 and to bring the silver and gold, which the king and his counselors have freely offered to the God of Israel, whose dwelling is in Jerusalem,

16 with all the silver and gold which you shall find in the whole province of Babylon, along with the freewill offering of the people and of the priests, who offered willingly for the house of their God which is in Jerusalem;

17 with this money, therefore, you shall diligently buy bulls, rams, and lambs, with their grain offerings and their libations and offer them on the altar of the house of your God which is in Jerusalem.

18 "And whatever seems good to you and to your brothers to do with the rest of the silver and gold, you may do according to the will of your God.

19 "Also the utensils which are given to you for the service of the house of your God, deliver in full before the God of Jerusalem.

20 "And the rest of the needs for the house of your God, for which you may have occasion to provide, provide *for it* from the royal treasury.

21 "And I, even I King Artaxerxes, issue a decree to all the treasurers who are *in the provinces* beyond the River, that whatever Ezra the priest, the scribe of the law of the God of heaven, may require of you, it shall be done diligently,

22 *even* up to 100 talents of silver, 100 kors of wheat, 100 baths of wine, 100 baths of oil, and salt as needed.

23 "Whatever is commanded by the God of heaven, let it be done with zeal for the house of the God of heaven, lest there be wrath against the kingdom of the king and his sons.

24 "We also inform you that it is not allowed to impose tax, tribute or toll *on* any of the priests, Levites, singers, doorkeepers, Nethinim, or servants of this house of God.

25 "And you, Ezra, according to the wisdom of your God which is in your hand, appoint magistrates and judges that they may judge all the people who are in *the province* beyond the River, *even* all those who know the laws of your God; and you may teach anyone who is ignorant *of them*.

26 "And whoever will not observe the law of your God and the law of the king, let judgment be executed upon him strictly, whether for death or for banishment or for confiscation of goods or for imprisonment."

27 ¶ Blessed be the LORD, the God of our fathers, who has put *such a thing* as this in the king's heart, to adorn the house of the LORD which is in Jerusalem,

28 and has extended lovingkindness to me before the king and his counselors and before all the king's mighty princes. Thus I was strengthened according to the hand of the LORD my God upon me, and I gathered leading men from Israel to go up with me.

CHAPTER 8

NOW these are the heads of their fathers' *households* and the genealogical enrollment of those who went up with me from Babylon in the reign of King Artaxerxes:

2 of the sons of Phinehas, Gershom; of the sons of Ithamar, Daniel; of the sons of David, Hattush;

3 of the sons of Shecaniah *who was* of the sons of Parosh, Zechariah and with him 150 males *who were in* the genealogical list;

4 of the sons of Pahath-moab, Eliehoenai the son of Zerahiah and 200 males with him;

5 of the sons of Shecaniah, the son of Jahaziel and 300 males with him;

6 and of the sons of Adin, Ebed the son of Jonathan and 50 males with him;

7 and of the sons of Elam, Jeshaiah the son of Athaliah and 70 males with him;

8 and of the sons of Shephatiah, Zebadiah the son of Michael and 80 males with him;

9 of the sons of Joab, Obadiah the son of Jehiel and 218 males with him;

10 and of the sons of Shelomith, the son of Josiphiah and 160 males with him;

11 and of the sons of Bebai, Zechariah the son of Bebai and 28 males with him;

12 and of the sons of Azgad, Johanan the son of Hakkatan and 110 males with him;

13 and of the sons of Adonikam, the last ones, these being their names,

Eliphelet, Jeuel, and Shemaiah and 60 males with them;

14 and of the sons of Bigvai, Uthai and Zabbud and 70 males with them.

15 ¶ Now I assembled them at the river that runs to Ahava, where we camped for three days; and when I observed the people and the priests, I did not find any Levites there.

16 So I sent for Eliezer, Ariel, Shemaiah, Elnathan, Jarib, Elnathan, Nathan, Zechariah, and Meshullam, leading men, and for Joiarib and Elnathan, teachers.

17 And I sent them to Iddo the leading man at the place Casiphia; and I told them what to say to Iddo and his brothers, the temple servants at the place Casiphia, that is, to bring ministers to us for the house of our God.

18 And according to the good hand of our God upon us they brought us a man of insight of the sons of Mahli, the son of Levi, the son of Israel, namely Sherebiah, and his sons and brothers, 18 men;

19 and Hashabiah and Jeshaiah of the sons of Merari, with his brothers and their sons, 20 men;

20 and 220 of the temple servants, whom David and the princes had given for the service of the Levites, all of them designated by name.

21 ¶ Then I proclaimed a fast there at the river of Ahava, that we might humble ourselves before our God to seek from Him a safe journey for us, our little ones, and all our possessions.

22 For I was ashamed to request from the king troops and horsemen to protect us from the enemy on the way, because we had said to the king, "The hand of our God is favorably disposed to all those who seek Him, but His power and His anger are against all those who forsake Him."

23 So we fasted and sought our God concerning this matter, and He listened to our entreaty.

24 ¶ Then I set apart twelve of the leading priests, Sherebiah, Hashabiah, and with them ten of their brothers;

25 and I weighed out to them the silver, the gold, and the utensils, the offering for the house of our God which the king and his counselors and his princes, and all Israel present there, had offered.

26 Thus I weighed into their hands

650 talents of silver, and silver utensils worth 100 talents, and 100 gold talents,

27 and 20 gold bowls, worth 1,000 darics; and two utensils of fine shiny bronze, precious as gold.

28 Then I said to them, "You are holy to the LORD, and the utensils are holy; and the silver and the gold are a freewill offering to the LORD God of your fathers.

29 "Watch and keep them until you weigh them before the leading priests, the Levites, and the heads of the fathers' households of Israel at Jerusalem, in the chambers of the house of the LORD."

30 So the priests and the Levites accepted the weighed out silver and gold and the utensils, to bring them to Jerusalem to the house of our God.

31 ¶ Then we journeyed from the river Ahava on the twelfth of the first month to go to Jerusalem; and the hand of our God was over us, and He delivered us from the hand of the enemy and the ambushes by the way.

32 Thus we came to Jerusalem and remained there three days.

33 And on the fourth day the silver and the gold and the utensils were weighed out in the house of our God into the hand of Meremoth the son of Uriah the priest, and with him was Eleazar the son of Phinehas; and with them were the Levites, Jozabad the son of Jeshua and Noadiah the son of Binnui.

34 Everything was numbered and weighed, and all the weight was recorded at that time.

35 ¶ The exiles who had come from the captivity offered burnt offerings to the God of Israel: 12 bulls for all Israel, 96 rams, 77 lambs, 12 male goats for a sin offering, all as a burnt offering to the LORD.

36 Then they delivered the king's edicts to the king's satraps, and to the governors in the provinces beyond the River, and they supported the people and the house of God.

CHAPTER 9

Now when these things had been completed, the princes approached me, saying, "The people of Israel and the priests and the Levites have not separated themselves from the peoples of the lands, according to their abominations, *those* of the Canaanites, the Hittites, the Perizzites, the Jebusites, the Ammonites, the Moabites, the Egyptians, and the Amorites.

2 "For they have taken some of their daughters *as wives* for themselves and for their sons, so that the holy race has intermingled with the peoples of the lands; indeed, the hands of the princes and the rulers have been foremost in this unfaithfulness."

3 And when I heard about this matter, I tore my garment and my robe, and pulled some of the hair from my head and my beard, and sat down appalled.

4 Then everyone who trembled at the words of the God of Israel on account of the unfaithfulness of the exiles gathered to me, and I sat appalled until the evening offering.

5 ¶ But at the evening offering I arose from my humiliation, even with my garment and my robe torn, and I fell on my knees and stretched out my hands to the LORD my God;

6 and I said, "O my God, I am ashamed and embarrassed to lift up my face to Thee, my God, for our iniquities have risen above our heads, and our guilt has grown even to the heavens.

7 "Since the days of our fathers to this day we *have been* in great guilt, and on account of our iniquities we, our kings *and* our priests have been given into the hand of the kings of the lands, to the sword, to captivity, and to plunder and to open shame, as *it is* this day.

8 "But now for a brief moment grace has been *shown* from the LORD our God, to leave us an escaped remnant and to give us a peg in His holy place, that our God may enlighten our eyes and grant us a little reviving in our bondage.

9 "For we are slaves; yet in our bondage, our God has not forsaken us, but has extended lovingkindness to us in the sight of the kings of Persia, to give us reviving to raise up the house of our God, to restore its ruins, and to give us a wall in Judah and Jerusalem.

10 "And now, our God, what shall we say after this? For we have forsaken Thy commandments,

11 which Thou hast commanded by Thy servants the prophets, saying, 'The land which you are entering to possess is an unclean land with the uncleanness of the peoples of the lands, with their abominations which have filled it from end to end *and* with their impurity.

12 'So now do not give your daughters to their sons nor take their daughters to your sons, and never seek their peace or their prosperity, that you may be strong and eat the good *things* of the land and leave *it* as an inheritance to your sons forever.'

13 "And after all that has come upon us for our evil deeds and our great guilt, since Thou our God hast requited *us* less than our iniquities *deserve*, and hast given us an escaped remnant as this,

14 shall we again break Thy commandments and intermarry with the peoples who commit these abominations? Wouldst Thou not be angry with us to the point of destruction, until there is no remnant nor any who escape?

15 "O LORD God of Israel, Thou art righteous, for we have been left an escaped remnant, as *it is* this day; behold, we are before Thee in our guilt, for no one can stand before Thee because of this."

CHAPTER 10

NOW while Ezra was praying and making confession, weeping and prostrating himself before the house of God, a very large assembly, men, women, and children, gathered to him from Israel; for the people wept bitterly.

2 And Shecaniah the son of Jehiel, one of the sons of Elam, answered and said to Ezra, "We have been unfaithful to our God, and have married foreign women from the peoples of the land; yet now there is hope for Israel in spite of this.

3 "So now let us make a covenant with our God to put away all the wives and their children, according to the counsel of [8]my lord and of those who tremble at the commandment of our God; and let it be done according to the law.

[8] Or, the Lord

4"Arise! For *this* matter is your responsibility, but we will be with you; be courageous and act."

5 ¶ Then Ezra rose and made the leading priests, the Levites, and all Israel, take oath that they would do according to this proposal; so they took the oath.

6 Then Ezra rose from before the house of God and went into the chamber of Jehohanan the son of Eliashib. Although he went there, he did not eat bread, nor drink water, for he was mourning over the unfaithfulness of the exiles.

7 And they made a proclamation throughout Judah and Jerusalem to all the exiles, that they should assemble at Jerusalem,

8 and that whoever would not come within three days, according to the counsel of the leaders and the elders, all his possessions should be forfeited and he himself excluded from the assembly of the exiles.

9 ¶ So all the men of Judah and Benjamin assembled at Jerusalem within the three days. It was the ninth month on the twentieth of the month, and all the people sat in the open square *before* the house of God, trembling because of this matter and the heavy rain.

10 Then Ezra the priest stood up and said to them, "You have been unfaithful and have married foreign wives adding to the guilt of Israel.

11"Now, therefore, make confession to the LORD God of your fathers, and do His will; and separate yourselves from the peoples of the land and from the foreign wives."

12 Then all the assembly answered and said with a loud voice, "That's right! As you have said, so it is our duty to do.

13"But there are many people, it is the rainy season, and we are not able to stand in the open. Nor *can* the task *be done* in one or two days, for we have transgressed greatly in this matter.

14"Let our leaders represent the whole assembly and let all those in our cities who have married foreign wives come at appointed times, together with the elders and judges of each city, until the fierce anger of our God on account of this matter is turned away from us."

15 Only Jonathan the son of Asahel and Jahzeiah the son of Tikvah opposed this, with Meshullam and Shabbethai the Levite supporting them.

16 ¶ But the exiles did so. And Ezra the priest selected men *who were* heads of fathers' *households* for *each* of their father's households, all of them by name. So they convened on the first day of the tenth month to investigate the matter.

17 And they finished *investigating* all the men who had married foreign wives by the first of the first month.

18 ¶ And among the sons of the priests who had married foreign wives were found of the sons of Jeshua the son of Jozadak, and his brothers: Maaseiah, Eliezer, Jarib, and Gedaliah.

19 And they pledged to put away their wives, and being guilty, *they offered* a ram of the flock for their offense.

20 And of the sons of Immer *there were* Hanani and Zebadiah;

21 and of the sons of Harim: Maaseiah, Elijah, Shemaiah, Jehiel, and Uzziah;

22 and of the sons of Pashhur: Elioenai, Maaseiah, Ishmael, Nethanel, Jozabad, and Elasah.

23 ¶ And of Levites *there were* Jozabad, Shimei, Kelaiah (that is, Kelita), Pethahiah, Judah, and Eliezer.

24 ¶ And of the singers *there was* Eliashib; and of the gatekeepers: Shallum, Telem, and Uri.

25 ¶ And of Israel, of the sons of Parosh *there were* Ramiah, Izziah, Malchijah, Mijamin, Eleazar, Malchijah, and Benaiah;

26 and of the sons of Elam: Mattaniah, Zechariah, Jehiel, Abdi, Jeremoth, and Elijah;

27 and of the sons of Zattu: Elioenai, Eliashib, Mattaniah, Jeremoth, Zabad, and Aziza;

28 and of the sons of Bebai: Jehohanan, Hananiah, Zabbai, *and* Athlai;

29 and of the sons of Bani: Meshullam, Malluch, and Adaiah, Jashub, Sheal, *and* Jeremoth;

30 and of the sons of Pahath-moab: Adna, Chelal, Benaiah, Maaseiah, Mattaniah, Bezalel, Binnui, and Manasseh;

31 and *of* the sons of Harim: Eliezer, Isshijah, Malchijah, Shemaiah, Shimeon,

32 Benjamin, Malluch, *and* Shemariah;

33 of the sons of Hashum: Mattenai, Mattattah, Zabad, Eliphelet, Jeremai, Manasseh, *and* Shimei;

34 of the sons of Bani: Maadai, Amram, Uel,

35 Benaiah, Bedeiah, Cheluhi,

36 Vaniah, Meremoth, Eliashib,

37 Mattaniah, Mattenai, Jaasu,

38 Bani, Binnui, Shimei,

39 Shelemiah, Nathan, Adaiah,

40 Machnadebai, Shashai, Sharai,

41 Azarel, Shelemiah, Shemariah,

42 Shallum, Amariah, *and* Joseph.

43 Of the sons of Nebo *there were* Jeiel, Mattithiah, Zabad, Zebina, Jaddai, Joel, *and* Benaiah.

44 All these had married foreign wives, and some of them had wives *by whom* they had children.

THE BOOK OF

NEHEMIAH

THE words of Nehemiah the son of Hacaliah.

¶ Now it happened in the month Chislev, *in* the twentieth year, while I was in Susa the ¹capitol,

2 that Hanani, one of my brothers, and some men from Judah came; and I asked them concerning the Jews who had escaped *and* had survived the captivity, and about Jerusalem.

3 And they said to me, "The remnant there in the province who survived the captivity are in great distress and reproach, and the wall of Jerusalem is broken down and its gates are burned with fire."

4 ¶ Now it came about when I heard these words, I sat down and wept and mourned for days; and I was fasting and praying before the God of heaven.

5 And I said, "I beseech Thee, O Lord God of heaven, the great and awesome God, who preserves the covenant and lovingkindness for those who love Him and keep His commandments,

6 let Thine ear now be attentive and Thine eyes open to hear the prayer of Thy servant which I am praying before Thee now, day and night, on behalf of the sons of Israel Thy servants, confessing the sins of the sons of Israel which we have sinned against Thee; I and my father's house have sinned.

7 "We have acted very corruptly against Thee and have not kept the commandments, nor the statutes, nor the ordinances which Thou didst command Thy servant Moses.

8 "Remember the word which Thou didst command Thy servant Moses, saying, 'If you are unfaithful I will scatter you among the peoples;

9 but if you return to Me and keep My commandments and do them, though those of you who have been scattered were in the most remote part of the heavens, I will gather them from there and will bring them to the place where I have chosen to cause My name to dwell.'

10 "And they are Thy servants and Thy people whom Thou didst redeem by Thy great power and by Thy strong hand.

11 "O Lord, I beseech Thee, may Thine ear be attentive to the prayer of Thy servant and the prayer of Thy servants who delight to revere Thy name, and make Thy servant successful today, and grant him compassion before this man."

¶ Now I was the cupbearer to the king.

CHAPTER 2

AND it came about in the month Nisan, in the twentieth year of King Artaxerxes, that wine *was* before him, and I took up the wine and gave it to the king. Now I had not been sad in his presence.

¹ Or, *palace or citadel*

2 So the king said to me, "Why is your face sad though you are not sick? This is nothing but sadness of heart." Then I was very much afraid.

3 And I said to the king, "Let the king live forever. Why should my face not be sad when the city, the place of my fathers' tombs, lies desolate and its gates have been consumed by fire?"

4 Then the king said to me, "What would you request?" So I prayed to the God of heaven.

5 And I said to the king, "If it please the king, and if your servant has found favor before you, send me to Judah, to the city of my fathers' tombs, that I may rebuild it."

6 Then the king said to me, the queen sitting beside him, "How long will your journey be, and when will you return?" So it pleased the king to send me, and I gave him a definite time.

7 And I said to the king, "If it please the king, let letters be given me for the governors *of the provinces* beyond the River, that they may allow me to pass through until I come to Judah,

8 and a letter to Asaph the keeper of the king's forest, that he may give me timber to make beams for the gates of the fortress which is by the ²temple, for the wall of the city, and for the house to which I will go." And the king granted *them* to me because the good hand of my God *was* on me.

9 ¶ Then I came to the governors *of the provinces* beyond the River and gave them the king's letters. Now the king had sent with me officers of the army and horsemen.

10 And when Sanballat the Horonite and Tobiah the Ammonite official heard *about it,* it was very displeasing to them that someone had come to seek the welfare of the sons of Israel.

11 So I came to Jerusalem and was there three days.

12 And I arose in the night, I and a few men with me. I did not tell anyone what my God was putting into my mind to do for Jerusalem and there was no animal with me except the animal on which I was riding.

13 So I went out at night by the Valley Gate in the direction of the Dragon's Well and *on* to the Refuse Gate, inspecting the walls of Jerusalem which were broken down and its gates which were consumed by fire.

14 Then I passed on to the Fountain Gate and the King's Pool, but there was no place for my mount to pass.

15 So I went up at night by the ravine and inspected the wall. Then I entered the Valley Gate again and returned.

16 And the officials did not know where I had gone or what I had done; nor had I as yet told the Jews, the priests, the nobles, the officials, or the rest who did the work.

17 ¶ Then I said to them, "You see the bad situation we are in, that Jerusalem is desolate and its gates burned by fire. Come, let us rebuild the wall of Jerusalem that we may no longer be a reproach."

18 And I told them how the hand of my God had been favorable to me, and also about the king's words which he had spoken to me. Then they said, "Let us arise and build." So they put their hands to the good *work.*

19 But when Sanballat the Horonite, and Tobiah the Ammonite official, and Geshem the Arab heard *it,* they mocked us and despised us and said, "What is this thing you are doing? Are you rebelling against the king?"

20 So I answered them and said to them, "The God of heaven will give us success; therefore we His servants will arise and build, but you have no portion, right, or memorial in Jerusalem."

CHAPTER 3

THEN Eliashib the high priest arose with his brothers the priests and built the Sheep Gate; they consecrated it and hung its doors. They consecrated the wall to the Tower of the Hundred *and* the Tower of Hananel.

2 And next to him the men of Jericho built, and next to them Zaccur the son of Imri built.

3 ¶ Now the sons of Hassenaah built the Fish Gate; they laid its beams and hung its doors with its bolts and bars.

4 And next to them Meremoth the son of Uriah the son of Hakkoz made repairs. And next to him Meshullam the son of Berechiah the son of Meshezabel made repairs. And next to

² Lit., *house*

him Zadok the son of Baana also made repairs.

5 Moreover, next to him the Tekoites made repairs, but their nobles did not support the work of their masters.

6 ¶ And Joiada the son of Paseah and Meshullam the son of Besodeiah repaired the Old Gate; they laid its beams and hung its doors, with its bolts and its bars.

7 Next to them Melatiah the Gibeonite and Jadon the Meronothite, the men of Gibeon and of Mizpah, also made repairs for the official seat of the governor *of the province* beyond the River.

8 Next to him Uzziel the son of Harhaiah of the goldsmiths made repairs. And next to him Hananiah, one of the perfumers, made repairs, and they restored Jerusalem as far as the Broad Wall.

9 And next to them Rephaiah the son of Hur, the official of half the district of Jerusalem, made repairs.

10 Next to them Jedaiah the son of Harumaph made repairs opposite his house. And next to him Hattush the son of Hashabneiah made repairs.

11 Malchijah the son of Harim and Hasshub the son of Pahath-moab repaired another section and the Tower of Furnaces.

12 And next to him Shallum the son of Hallohesh, the official of half the district of Jerusalem, made repairs, he and his daughters.

13 Hanun and the inhabitants of Zanoah repaired the Valley Gate. They built it and hung its doors with its bolts and its bars, and a thousand cubits of the wall to the Refuse Gate.

14 And Malchijah the son of Rechab, the official of the district of Bethhaccherem repaired the Refuse Gate. He built it and hung its doors with its bolts and its bars.

15 Shallum the son of Col-hozeh, the official of the district of Mizpah, repaired the Fountain Gate. He built it, covered it, and hung its doors with its bolts and its bars, and the wall of the Pool of Shelah at the king's garden as far as the steps that descend from the city of David.

16 After him Nehemiah the son of Azbuk, official of half the district of Beth-zur, made repairs as far as *a point* opposite the tombs of David, and as far as the artificial pool and the house of the mighty men.

17 After him the Levites carried out repairs *under* Rehum the son of Bani. Next to him Hashabiah, the official of half the district of Keilah, carried out repairs for his district.

18 After him their brothers carried out repairs *under* Bavvai the son of Henadad, official of *the other* half of the district of Keilah.

19 And next to him Ezer the son of Jeshua, the official of Mizpah, repaired another section, in front of the ascent of the armory at the Angle.

20 After him Baruch the son of Zabbai zealously repaired another section, from the Angle to the doorway of the house of Eliashib the high priest.

21 After him Meremoth the son of Uriah the son of Hakkoz repaired another section, from the doorway of Eliashib's house even as far as the end of his house.

22 And after him the priests, the men of the [3]valley, carried out repairs.

23 After them Benjamin and Hasshub carried out repairs in front of their house. After them Azariah the son of Maaseiah, son of Ananiah carried out repairs beside his house.

24 After him Binnui the son of Henadad repaired another section, from the house of Azariah as far as the Angle and as far as the corner.

25 Palal the son of Uzai *made repairs* in front of the Angle and the tower projecting from the upper house of the king, which is by the court of the guard. After him Pedaiah the son of Parosh *made repairs*.

26 And the temple servants living in Ophel *made repairs* as far as the front of the Water Gate toward the east and the projecting tower.

27 After him the Tekoites repaired another section in front of the great projecting tower and as far as the wall of Ophel.

28 ¶ Above the Horse Gate the priests carried out repairs, each in front of his house.

29 After them Zadok the son of Immer carried out repairs in front of his house. And after him Shemaiah the son of Shecaniah, the keeper of the East Gate, carried out repairs.

[3] Lit., *circle*; i.e., lower Jordan valley

30 After him Hananiah the son of Shelemiah, and Hanun the sixth son of Zalaph, repaired another section. After him Meshullam the son of Berechiah carried out repairs in front of his own quarters.

31 After him Malchijah one of the goldsmiths, carried out repairs as far as the house of the temple servants and of the merchants, in front of the Inspection Gate and as far as the upper room of the corner.

32 And between the upper room of the corner and the Sheep Gate the goldsmiths and the merchants carried out repairs.

CHAPTER 4

NOW it came about that when Sanballat heard that we were rebuilding the wall, he became furious and very angry and mocked the Jews.

2 And he spoke in the presence of his brothers and the wealthy men of Samaria and said, "What are these feeble Jews doing? Are they going to restore it for themselves? Can they offer sacrifices? Can they finish in a day? Can they revive the stones from the dusty rubble even the burned ones?"

3 Now Tobiah the Ammonite was near him and he said, "Even what they are building—if a fox should jump on it, he would break their stone wall down!"

4 ¶ Hear, O our God, how we are despised! Return their reproach on their own heads and give them up for plunder in a land of captivity.

5 Do not forgive their iniquity and let not their sin be blotted out before Thee, for they have demoralized the builders.

6 So we built the wall and the whole wall was joined together to half its height, for the people had a mind to work.

7 ¶ Now it came about when Sanballat, Tobiah, the Arabs, the Ammonites, and the Ashdodites heard that the repair of the walls of Jerusalem went on, and that the breaches began to be closed, they were very angry.

8 And all of them conspired together to come and fight against Jerusalem and to cause a disturbance in it.

9 But we prayed to our God, and because of them we set up a guard against them day and night.

10 Thus in Judah it was said,
"The strength of the burden bearers is failing,
Yet there is much rubbish;
And we ourselves are unable
To rebuild the wall."

11 And our enemies said, "They will not know or see until we come among them, kill them, and put a stop to the work."

12 And it came about when the Jews who lived near them came and told us ten times, "They will come up against us from every place where you may turn,"

13 then I stationed men in the lowest parts of the space behind the wall, the exposed places, and I stationed the people in families with their swords, spears, and bows.

14 When I saw their fear, I rose and spoke to the nobles, the officials, and the rest of the people: "Do not be afraid of them; remember the Lord who is great and awesome, and fight for your brothers, your sons, your daughters, your wives, and your houses."

15 ¶ And it happened when our enemies heard that it was known to us, and that God had frustrated their plan, then all of us returned to the wall, each one to his work.

16 And it came about from that day on, that half of my servants carried on the work while half of them held the spears, the shields, the bows, and the breastplates; and the captains were behind the whole house of Judah.

17 Those who were rebuilding the wall and those who carried burdens took their load with one hand doing the work and the other holding a weapon.

18 As for the builders, each wore his sword girded at his side as he built, while the trumpeter stood near me.

19 And I said to the nobles, the officials, and the rest of the people, "The work is great and extensive, and we are separated on the wall far from one another.

20 "At whatever place you hear the sound of the trumpet, rally to us there. Our God will fight for us."

21 ¶ So we carried on the work with half of them holding spears from dawn until the stars appeared.

22 At that time I also said to the people, "Let each man with his servant spend the night within Jerusalem so that they may be a guard for us by night and a laborer by day."

23 So neither I, my brothers, my servants, nor the men of the guard who followed me, none of us removed our clothes, each *took* his weapon *even to* the water.

CHAPTER 5

NOW there was a great outcry of the people and of their wives against their Jewish brothers.

2 For there were those who said, "We, our sons and our daughters, are many; therefore let us get grain that we may eat and live."

3 And there were others who said, "We are mortgaging our fields, our vineyards, and our houses that we might get grain because of the famine."

4 Also there were those who said, "We have borrowed money for the king's tax *on* our fields and our vineyards.

5"And now our flesh is like the flesh of our brothers, our children like their children. Yet behold, we are forcing our sons and our daughters to be slaves, and some of our daughters are forced into bondage *already*, and we are helpless because our fields and vineyards belong to others."

6 ¶ Then I was very angry when I had heard their outcry and these words.

7 And I consulted with myself, and contended with the nobles and the rulers and said to them, "You are exacting usury, each from his brother!" Therefore, I held a great assembly against them.

8 And I said to them, "We according to our ability have redeemed our Jewish brothers who were sold to the nations; now would you even sell your brothers that they may be sold to us?" Then they were silent and could not find a word *to* say.

9 Again I said, "The thing which you are doing is not good; should you not walk in the fear of our God because of the reproach of the nations, our enemies?

10"And likewise I, my brothers and my servants, are lending them money and grain. Please, let us leave off this usury.

11"Please, give back to them this very day their fields, their vineyards, their olive groves, and their houses, also the hundredth *part* of the money and of the grain, the new wine, and the oil that you are exacting from them."

12 Then they said, "We will give *it* back and will require nothing from them; we will do exactly as you say." So I called the priests and took an oath from them that they would do according to this promise.

13 I also shook out the front of my garment and said, "Thus may God shake out every man from his house and from his possessions who does not fulfill this promise; even thus may he be shaken out and emptied." And all the assembly said, "Amen!" And they praised the LORD. Then the people did according to this promise.

14 ¶ Moreover, from the day that I was appointed to be their governor in the land of Judah, from the twentieth year to the thirty-second year of King Artaxerxes, *for* twelve years, neither I nor my kinsmen have eaten the governor's food *allowance*.

15 But the former governors who were before me laid burdens on the people and took from them bread and wine besides forty shekels of silver; even their servants domineered the people. But I did not do so because of the fear of God.

16 And I also ⁴applied myself to the work on this wall; we did not buy any land, and all my servants were gathered there for the work.

17 Moreover, *there were* at my table one hundred and fifty Jews and officials, besides those who came to us from the nations that were around us.

18 Now that which was prepared for each day was one ox *and* six choice sheep, also birds were prepared for me; and once in ten days all sorts of wine *were furnished* in abundance. Yet for

4 Or, *held fast*

all this I did not demand the governor's food *allowance,* because the servitude was heavy on this people.

19 Remember me, O my God, for good, *according to* all that I have done for this people.

CHAPTER 6

Now it came about when it was reported to Sanballat, Tobiah, to Geshem the Arab, and to the rest of our enemies that I had rebuilt the wall, and *that* no breach remained in it, although at that time I had not set up the doors at the gates,

2 that Sanballat and Geshem sent *a message* to me, saying, "Come, let us meet together at ⁵Chephirim in the plain of Ono." But they were planning to harm me.

3 So I sent messengers to them, saying, "I am doing a great work and I cannot come down. Why should the work stop while I leave it and come down to you?"

4 And they sent *messages* to me four times in this manner, and I answered them in the same way.

5 Then Sanballat sent his servant to me in the same manner a fifth time with an open letter in his hand.

6 In it was written, "It is reported among the nations, and Gashmu says, that you and the Jews are planning to rebel; therefore you are rebuilding the wall. And you are to be their king, according to these reports.

7 "And you have also appointed prophets to proclaim in Jerusalem concerning you, 'A king is in Judah!' And now it will be reported to the king according to these reports. So come now, let us take counsel together."

8 Then I sent *a message* to him saying, "Such things as you are saying have not been done, but you are inventing them in your own mind."

9 For all of them were *trying* to frighten us, thinking, "They will become discouraged with the work and it will not be done." But now, O God, strengthen my hands.

10 ¶ And when I entered the house of Shemaiah the son of Delaiah, son of Mehetabel, who was confined at home, he said, "Let us meet together in the house of God, within the temple,

⁵ Another reading is, one of *the villages*

and let us close the doors of the temple, for they are coming to kill you, and they are coming to kill you at night."

11 But I said, "Should a man like me flee? And could one such as I go into the temple to save his life? I will not go in."

12 Then I perceived that surely God had not sent him, but he uttered *his* prophecy against me because Tobiah and Sanballat had hired him.

13 He was hired for this reason, that I might become frightened and act accordingly and sin, so that they might have an evil report in order that they could reproach me.

14 Remember, O my God, Tobiah and Sanballat according to these works of theirs, and also Noadiah the prophetess and the rest of the prophets who were *trying* to frighten me.

15 ¶ So the wall was completed on the twenty-fifth of *the month* Elul, in fifty-two days.

16 And it came about when all our enemies heard *of it,* and all the nations surrounding us saw *it,* they lost their confidence; for they recognized that this work had been accomplished with the help of our God.

17 Also in those days many letters went from the nobles of Judah to Tobiah, and Tobiah's *letters* came to them.

18 For many in Judah were bound by oath to him because he was the son-in-law of Shecaniah the son of Arah, and his son Jehohanan had married the daughter of Meshullam the son of Berechiah.

19 Moreover, they were speaking about his good deeds in my presence and reported my words to him. Then Tobiah sent letters to frighten me.

CHAPTER 7

Now it came about when the wall was rebuilt and I had set up the doors, and the gatekeepers and the singers and the Levites were appointed,

2 that I put Hanani my brother, and Hananiah the commander of the fortress, in charge of Jerusalem, for he was a faithful man and feared God more than many.

3 Then I said to them, "Do not let the gates of Jerusalem be opened until

the sun is hot, and while they are standing *guard*, let them shut and bolt the doors. Also appoint guards from the inhabitants of Jerusalem, each at his post, and each in front of his own house."

4 Now the city was large and spacious, but the people in it were few and the houses were not built.

5 ¶ Then my God put it into my heart to assemble the nobles, the officials, and the people to be enrolled by genealogies. Then I found the book of the genealogy of those who came up first in which I found the following record:

6 These are the people of the province who came up from the captivity of the exiles whom Nebuchadnezzar the king of Babylon had carried away, and who returned to Jerusalem and Judah, each to his city,

7 who came with Zerubbabel, Jeshua, Nehemiah, Azariah, Raamiah, Nahamani, Mordecai, Bilshan, Mispereth, Bigvai, Nehum, Baanah.

¶ The number of men of the people of Israel:

8 the sons of Parosh, 2,172;
9 the sons of Shephatiah, 372;
10 the sons of Arah, 652;
11 the sons of Pahath-moab of the sons of Jeshua and Joab, 2,818;
12 the sons of Elam, 1,254;
13 the sons of Zattu, 845;
14 the sons of Zaccai, 760;
15 the sons of Binnui, 648;
16 the sons of Bebai, 628;
17 the sons of Azgad, 2,322;
18 the sons of Adonikam, 667;
19 the sons of Bigvai, 2,067;
20 the sons of Adin, 655;
21 the sons of Ater, of Hezekiah, 98;
22 the sons of Hashum, 328;
23 the sons of Bezai, 324;
24 the sons of Hariph, 112;
25 the sons of Gibeon, 95;
26 the men of Bethlehem and Netophah, 188;
27 the men of Anathoth, 128;
28 the men of Beth-azmaveth, 42;
29 the men of Kiriath-jearim, Chephirah, and Beeroth, 743;
30 the men of Ramah and Geba, 621;
31 the men of Michmas, 122;
32 the men of Bethel and Ai, 123;
33 the men of the other Nebo, 52;
34 the sons of the other Elam, 1,254;
35 the sons of Harim, 320;

36 the men of Jericho, 345;
37 the sons of Lod, Hadid, and Ono, 721;
38 the sons of Senaah, 3,930.

39 ¶ The priests: the sons of Jedaiah of the house of Jeshua, 973;
40 the sons of Immer, 1,052;
41 the sons of Pashhur, 1,247;
42 the sons of Harim, 1,017.

43 ¶ The Levites: the sons of Jeshua, of Kadmiel, of the sons of Hodevah, 74.

44 The singers: the sons of Asaph, 148.

45 The gatekeepers: the sons of Shallum, the sons of Ater, the sons of Talmon, the sons of Akkub, the sons of Hatita, the sons of Shobai, 138.

46 ¶ The temple servants: the sons of Ziha, the sons of Hasupha, the sons of Tabbaoth,
47 the sons of Keros, the sons of Sia, the sons of Padon,
48 the sons of Lebana, the sons of Hagaba, the sons of Shalmai,
49 the sons of Hanan, the sons of Giddel, the sons of Gahar,
50 the sons of Reaiah, the sons of Rezin, the sons of Nekoda,
51 the sons of Gazzam, the sons of Uzza, the sons of Paseah,
52 the sons of Besai, the sons of Meunim, the sons of Nephushesim,
53 the sons of Bakbuk, the sons of Hakupha, the sons of Harhur,
54 the sons of Bazlith, the sons of Mehida, the sons of Harsha,
55 the sons of Barkos, the sons of Sisera, the sons of Temah,
56 the sons of Neziah, the sons of Hatipha.

57 ¶ The sons of Solomon's servants: the sons of Sotai, the sons of Sophereth, the sons of Perida,
58 the sons of Jaala, the sons of Darkon, the sons of Giddel,
59 the sons of Shephatiah, the sons of Hattil, the sons of Pochereth-hazzebaim, the sons of Amon.

60 All the temple servants and the sons of Solomon's servants *were* 392.

61 ¶ And these *were* they who came up from Tel-melah, Tel-harsha, Cherub, Addon, and Immer; but they could not show their fathers' houses or their descendants, whether they were of Israel:

62 the sons of Delaiah, the sons of Tobiah, the sons of Nekoda, 642.

63 And of the priests: the sons of Hobaiah, the sons of Hakkoz, the sons of Barzillai, who took a wife of the daughters of Barzillai, the Gileadite, and was named after them.

64 These searched *among* their ancestral registration, but it could not be located; therefore they were considered unclean *and excluded* from the priesthood.

65 And the governor said to them that they should not eat from the most holy things until a priest arose with Urim and Thummim.

66 ¶ The whole assembly together *was* 42,360,

67 besides their male and their female servants, of whom *there were* 7,337; and they had 245 male and female singers.

68 Their horses were 736; their mules, 245;

69 *their* camels, 435; *their* donkeys, 6,720.

70 ¶ And some from among the heads of fathers' *households* gave to the work. The governor gave to the treasury 1,000 gold drachmas, 50 basins, 530 priests' garments.

71 And some of the heads of fathers' *households* gave into the treasury of the work 20,000 gold drachmas, and 2,200 silver minas.

72 And that which the rest of the people gave was 20,000 gold drachmas and 2,000 silver minas, and 67 priests' garments.

73 ¶ Now the priests, the Levites, the gatekeepers, the singers, some of the people, the temple servants, and all Israel, lived in their cities.

¶ And when the seventh month came, the sons of Israel *were* in their cities.

CHAPTER 8

AND all the people gathered as one man at the square which was in front of the Water Gate, and they asked Ezra the scribe to bring the book of the law of Moses which the LORD had given to Israel.

2 Then Ezra the priest brought the law before the assembly of men, women, and all who *could* listen with understanding, on the first day of the seventh month.

3 And he read from it before the square which was in front of the Water Gate from early morning until midday, in the presence of men and women, those who could understand; and all the people were attentive to the book of the law.

4 And Ezra the scribe stood at a wooden podium which they had made for the purpose. And beside him stood Mattithiah, Shema, Anaiah, Uriah, Hilkiah, and Maaseiah on his right hand; and Pedaiah, Mishael, Malchijah, Hashum, Hashbaddanah, Zechariah, *and* Meshullam on his left hand.

5 And Ezra opened the book in the sight of all the people for he was standing above all the people; and when he opened it, all the people stood up.

6 Then Ezra blessed the LORD the great God. And all the people answered, "Amen, Amen!" while lifting up their hands; then they bowed low and worshiped the LORD with *their* faces to the ground.

7 Also Jeshua, Bani, Sherebiah, Jamin, Akkub, Shabbethai, Hodiah, Maaseiah, Kelita, Azariah, Jozabad, Hanan, Pelaiah, and the Levites, explained the law to the people while the people *remained* in their place.

8 And they read from the book, from the law of God, translating to give the sense so that they understood the reading.

9 ¶ Then Nehemiah, who was the governor, and Ezra the priest *and* scribe, and the Levites who taught the people said to all the people, "This day is holy to the LORD your God; do not mourn or weep." For all the people were weeping when they heard the words of the law.

10 Then he said to them, "Go, eat of the fat, drink of the sweet, and send portions to him who has nothing prepared; for this day is holy to our Lord. Do not be grieved, for the joy of the LORD is your strength."

11 So the Levites calmed all the people, saying, "Be still, for the day is holy; do not be grieved."

12 And all the people went away to eat, to drink, to send portions and to celebrate a great festival, because they understood the words which had been made known to them.

13 ¶ Then on the second day the heads of fathers' *households* of all the

people, the priests, and the Levites were gathered to Ezra the scribe that they might gain insight into the words of the law.

14 And they found written in the law how the Lord had commanded through Moses that the sons of Israel should live in booths during the feast of the seventh month.

15 So they proclaimed and circulated a proclamation in all their cities and in Jerusalem, saying, "Go out to the hills, and bring olive branches, and wild olive branches, myrtle branches, palm branches, and branches of *other* leafy trees, to make booths, as it is written."

16 So the people went out and brought *them* and made booths for themselves, each on his roof, and in their courts, and in the courts of the house of God, and in the square at the Water Gate, and in the square at the Gate of Ephraim.

17 And the entire assembly of those who had returned from the captivity made booths and lived in them. The sons of Israel had indeed not done so from the days of Joshua the son of Nun to that day. And there was great rejoicing.

18 And he read from the book of the law of God daily, from the first day to the last day. And they celebrated the feast seven days, and on the eighth day *there was* a solemn assembly according to the ordinance.

CHAPTER 9

Now on the twenty-fourth day of this month the sons of Israel assembled with fasting, in sackcloth, and with dirt upon them.

2 And the descendants of Israel separated themselves from all foreigners, and stood and confessed their sins and the iniquities of their fathers.

3 While they stood in their place, they read from the book of the law of the Lord their God for a fourth of the day; and for *another* fourth they confessed and worshiped the Lord their God.

4 Now on the Levites' platform stood Jeshua, Bani, Kadmiel, Shebaniah, Bunni, Sherebiah, Bani, *and* Chenani, and they cried with a loud voice to the Lord their God.

5 ¶ Then the Levites, Jeshua, Kadmiel, Bani, Hashabneiah, Sherebiah, Hodiah, Shebaniah, *and* Pethahiah, said, "Arise, bless the Lord your God forever and ever!
O may Thy glorious name be blessed
And exalted above all blessing and praise!
6"Thou alone art the Lord.
Thou hast made the heavens,
The heaven of heavens with all their host,
The earth and all that is on it,
The seas and all that is in them.
Thou dost give life to all of them
And the heavenly host bows down before Thee.
7"Thou art the Lord God,
Who chose Abram
And brought him out from Ur of the Chaldees,
And gave him the name Abraham.
8"And Thou didst find his heart faithful before Thee,
And didst make a covenant with him
To give *him* the land of the Canaanite,
Of the Hittite and the Amorite,
Of the Perizzite, the Jebusite, and the Girgashite—
To give *it* to his descendants.
And Thou hast fulfilled Thy promise,
For Thou art righteous.

9 ¶"Thou didst see the affliction of our fathers in Egypt,
And didst hear their cry by the Red Sea.
10"Then Thou didst perform signs and wonders against Pharaoh,
Against all his servants and all the people of his land;
For Thou didst know that they acted arrogantly toward them,
And didst make a name for Thyself as *it is* this day.
11"And Thou didst divide the sea before them,
So they passed through the midst of the sea on dry ground;
And their pursuers Thou didst hurl into the depths,
Like a stone into raging waters.
12"And with a pillar of cloud Thou didst lead them by day,
And with a pillar of fire by night

To light for them the way
In which they were to go.
13"Then Thou didst come down on
Mount Sinai,
And didst speak with them from
heaven;
Thou didst give to them just ordinances and true laws,
Good statutes and commandments.
14"So Thou didst make known to
them Thy holy sabbath,
And didst lay down for them commandments, statutes, and law,
Through Thy servant Moses.
15"Thou didst provide bread from
heaven for them for their hunger,
Thou didst bring forth water from
a rock for them for their thirst,
And Thou didst tell them to enter
in order to possess
The land which Thou didst swear
to give them.

16 ¶"But they, our fathers, acted
arrogantly;
They [6]became stubborn and
would not listen to Thy commandments.
17"And they refused to listen,
And did not remember Thy wondrous deeds which Thou hadst
performed among them;
So they [6]became stubborn and
appointed a leader to return to
their slavery in Egypt.
But Thou art a God of forgiveness,
Gracious and compassionate,
Slow to anger, and abounding in
lovingkindness;
And Thou didst not forsake them.
18"Even when they made for themselves
A calf of molten metal
And said, 'This is your God
Who brought you up from Egypt,'
And committed great [7]blasphe-
mies,
19 Thou, in Thy great compassion,
Didst not forsake them in the
wilderness;
The pillar of cloud did not leave
them by day,
To guide them on their way,
Nor the pillar of fire by night, to
light for them the way in which
they were to go.

20"And Thou didst give Thy good
Spirit to instruct them,
Thy manna Thou didst not withhold from their mouth,
And Thou didst give them water
for their thirst.
21"Indeed, forty years Thou didst
provide for them in the wilderness *and* they were not in want;
Their clothes did not wear out,
nor did their feet swell.
22"Thou didst also give them kingdoms and peoples,
And Thou didst allot *them* to
them as a boundary.
And they took possession of the
land of Sihon the king of Heshbon,
And the land of Og the king of
Bashan.
23"And Thou didst make their sons
numerous as the stars of
heaven,
And Thou didst bring them into
the land
Which Thou hadst told their fathers to enter and possess.
24"So their sons entered and possessed the land.
And Thou didst subdue before
them the inhabitants of the
land, the Canaanites,
And Thou didst give them into
their hand, with their kings, and
the peoples of the land,
To do with them as they desired.
25"And they captured fortified cities
and a fertile land.
They took possession of houses
full of every good thing,
Hewn cisterns, vineyards, olive
groves,
Fruit trees in abundance.
So they ate, were filled, and grew
fat,
And reveled in Thy great goodness.

26 ¶"But they became disobedient
and rebelled against Thee,
And cast Thy law behind their
backs
And killed Thy prophets who had
admonished them
So that they might return to Thee,
And they committed great [7]blas-
phemies.

[6] Lit., *stiffened their neck*   [7] Lit., *acts of contempt*

27"Therefore Thou didst deliver them
into the hand of their oppressors who oppressed them,
But when they cried to Thee in
the time of their distress,
Thou didst hear from heaven, and
according to Thy great compassion
Thou didst give them deliverers
who delivered them from the
hand of their oppressors.

28"But as soon as they had rest, they
did evil again before Thee;
Therefore Thou didst abandon
them to the hand of their enemies, so that they ruled over
them.
When they cried again to Thee,
Thou didst hear from heaven,
And many times Thou didst rescue them according to Thy
compassion,

29 And admonished them in order to
turn them back to Thy law.
Yet they acted arrogantly and did
not listen to Thy commandments but sinned against Thine
ordinances,
By which if a man observes them
he shall live.
And they turned a stubborn
shoulder and stiffened their
neck, and would not listen.

30"However, Thou didst bear with
them for many years,
And admonished them by Thy
Spirit through Thy prophets,
Yet they would not give ear.
Therefore Thou didst give them
into the hand of the peoples of
the lands.

31"Nevertheless, in Thy great compassion Thou didst not make an
end of them or forsake them,
For Thou art a gracious and compassionate God.

32 ¶"Now therefore, our God, the
great, the mighty, and the awesome God, who dost keep covenant and lovingkindness,
Do not let all the hardship seem
insignificant before Thee,
Which has come upon us, our
kings, our princes, our priests,
our prophets, our fathers, and
on all Thy people,
From the days of the kings of
Assyria to this day.

33"However, Thou art just in all that
has come upon us;
For Thou hast dealt faithfully, but
we have acted wickedly.

34"For our kings, our leaders, our
priests, and our fathers have
not kept Thy law
Or paid attention to Thy commandments and Thine admoni-
tions with which Thou hast admonished them.

35"But they, in their own kingdom,
With Thy great goodness which
Thou didst give them,
With the broad and rich land
which Thou didst set before
them,
Did not serve Thee or turn from
their evil deeds.

36"Behold, we are slaves today,
And as to the land which Thou
didst give to our fathers to eat
of its fruit and its bounty,
Behold, we are slaves on it.

37"And its abundant produce is for
the kings
Whom Thou hast set over us be-
cause of our sins;
They also rule over our bodies
And over our cattle as they please,
So we are in great distress.

38"Now because of all this
We are making an agreement in
writing;
And on the sealed document *are
the names of* our leaders, our
Levites *and* our priests."

CHAPTER 10

N OW on the sealed document *were
the names of:* Nehemiah the governor,
the son of Hacaliah, and Zedekiah,

2 Seraiah, Azariah, Jeremiah,

3 Pashhur, Amariah, Malchijah,

4 Hattush, Shebaniah, Malluch,

5 Harim, Meremoth, Obadiah,

6 Daniel, Ginnethon, Baruch,

7 Meshullam, Abijah, Mijamin,

8 Maaziah, Bilgai, Shemaiah. These
were the priests.

9 And the Levites: Jeshua the son of
Azaniah, Binnui of the sons of Henadad, Kadmiel;

10 also their brothers Shebaniah, Hodiah, Kelita, Pelaiah, Hanan,

11 Mica, Rehob, Hashabiah,

12 Zaccur, Sherebiah, Shebaniah,

13 Hodiah, Bani, Beninu.

14 The leaders of the people: Parosh, Pahath-moab, Elam, Zattu, Bani,

15 Bunni, Azgad, Bebai,

16 Adonijah, Bigvai, Adin,

17 Ater, Hezekiah, Azzur,

18 Hodiah, Hashum, Bezai,

19 Hariph, Anathoth, Nebai,

20 Magpiash, Meshullam, Hezir,

21 Meshezabel, Zadok, Jaddua,

22 Pelatiah, Hanan, Anaiah,

23 Hoshea, Hananiah, Hasshub,

24 Hallohesh, Pilha, Shobek,

25 Rehum, Hashabnah, Maaseiah,

26 Ahiah, Hanan, Anan,

27 Malluch, Harim, Baanah.

28 ¶ Now the rest of the people, the priests, the Levites, the gatekeepers, the singers, the temple servants, and all those who had separated themselves from the peoples of the lands to the law of God, their wives, their sons and their daughters, all those who had knowledge and understanding,

29 are joining with their kinsmen, their nobles, and are taking on themselves a curse and an oath to walk in God's law, which was given through Moses, God's servant, and to keep and to observe all the commandments of GOD our Lord, and His ordinances and His statutes;

30 and that we will not give our daughters to the peoples of the land or take their daughters for our sons.

31 As for the peoples of the land who bring wares or any grain on the sabbath day to sell, we will not buy from them on the sabbath or a holy day; and we will forego *the crops* the seventh year and the exaction of every debt.

32 ¶ We also placed ourselves under obligation to contribute yearly one third of a shekel for the service of the house of our God:

33 for the showbread, for the continual grain offering, for the continual burnt offering, the sabbaths, the new moon, for the appointed times, for the holy things and for the sin offerings to make atonement for Israel, and all the work of the house of our God.

34 ¶ Likewise we cast lots for the supply of wood *among* the priests, the Levites, and the people in order that they might bring it to the house of our God, according to our fathers' households, at fixed times annually, to burn

on the altar of the LORD our God as it is written in the law;

35 and in order that they might bring the first fruits of our ground and the first fruits of all the fruit of every tree to the house of the LORD annually,

36 and bring to the house of our God the first-born of our sons and of our cattle, and the first-born of our herds and our flocks as it is written in the law, for the priests who are ministering in the house of our God.

37 We will also bring the first of our dough, our contributions, the fruit of every tree, the new wine and the oil to the priests at the chambers of the house of our God, and the tithe of our ground to the Levites, for the Levites are they who receive the tithes in all the rural towns.

38 And the priest, the son of Aaron, shall be with the Levites when the Levites receive tithes, and the Levites shall bring up the tenth of the tithes to the house of our God, to the chambers of the storehouse.

39 For the sons of Israel and the sons of Levi shall bring the contribution of the grain, the new wine and the oil, to the chambers; there are the utensils of the sanctuary, the priests who are ministering, the gatekeepers, and the singers. Thus we will not neglect the house of our God.

CHAPTER 11

NOW the leaders of the people lived in Jerusalem, but the rest of the people cast lots to bring one out of ten to live in Jerusalem, the holy city, while nine-tenths *remained* in the *other* cities.

2 And the people blessed all the men who volunteered to live in Jerusalem.

3 ¶ Now these are the heads of the provinces who lived in Jerusalem, but in the cities of Judah each lived on his own property in their cities—the Israelites, the priests, the Levites, the temple servants and the descendants of Solomon's servants.

4 And some of the sons of Judah and some of the sons of Benjamin lived in Jerusalem. From the sons of Judah: Athaiah the son of Uzziah, the son of Zechariah, the son of Amariah, the son of Shephatiah, the son of Mahalalel, of the sons of Perez;

5 and Maaseiah the son of Baruch, the son of Col-hozeh, the son of Hazaiah, the son of Adaiah, the son of Joiarib, the son of Zechariah, the son of the Shilonite.

6 All the sons of Perez who lived in Jerusalem were 468 able men.

7 ¶ Now these are the sons of Benjamin: Sallu the son of Meshullam, the son of Joed, the son of Pedaiah, the son of Kolaiah, the son of Maaseiah, the son of Ithiel, the son of Jeshaiah;

8 and after him Gabbai *and* Sallai, 928.

9 And Joel the son of Zichri was their overseer, and Judah the son of Hassenuah was second in command of the city.

10 ¶ From the priests: Jedaiah the son of Joiarib, Jachin,

11 Seraiah the son of Hilkiah, the son of Meshullam, the son of Zadok, the son of Meraioth, the son of Ahitub, the leader of the house of God,

12 and their [8]kinsmen who performed the work of the temple, 822; and Adaiah the son of Jeroham, the son of Pelaliah, the son of Amzi, the son of Zechariah, the son of Pashhur, the son of Malchijah,

13 and his kinsmen, heads of fathers' *households,* 242; and Amashsai the son of Azarel, the son of Ahzai, the son of Meshillemoth, the son of Immer,

14 and their brothers, valiant warriors, 128. And their overseer was Zabdiel, the son of Haggedolim.

15 ¶ Now from the Levites: Shemaiah the son of Hasshub, the son of Azrikam, the son of Hashabiah, the son of Bunni;

16 and Shabbethai and Jozabad, from the leaders of the Levites, who were in charge of the outside work of the house of God;

17 and Mattaniah the son of Mica, the son of Zabdi, the son of Asaph, who was the leader in beginning the thanksgiving at prayer, and Bakbukiah, the second among his brethren; and Abda the son of Shammua, the son of Galal, the son of Jeduthun.

18 All the Levites in the holy city were 284.

19 ¶ Also the gatekeepers, Akkub, Talmon, and their brethren, who kept watch at the gates, were 172.

20 And the rest of Israel, of the priests, *and* of the Levites, *were* in all the cities of Judah, each on his own inheritance.

21 But the temple servants were living in Ophel, and Ziha and Gishpa were in charge of the temple servants.

22 ¶ Now the overseer of the Levites in Jerusalem was Uzzi the son of Bani, the son of Hashabiah, the son of Mattaniah, the son of Mica, from the sons of Asaph, who were the singers for the service of the house of God.

23 For *there was* a commandment from the king concerning them and a firm regulation for the song leaders day by day.

24 And Pethahiah the son of Meshezabel, of the sons of Zerah the son of Judah, was the king's representative in all matters concerning the people.

25 ¶ Now as for the villages with their fields, some of the sons of Judah lived in Kiriath-arba and its [9]towns, in Dibon and its towns, and in Jekabzeel and its villages,

26 and in Jeshua, in Moladah and Beth-pelet,

27 and in Hazar-shual, in Beersheba and its towns,

28 and in Ziklag, in Meconah and in its towns,

29 and in En-rimmon, in Zorah and in Jarmuth,

30 Zanoah, Adullam, and their villages, Lachish and its fields, Azekah and its towns. So they encamped from Beersheba as far as the valley of Hinnom.

31 The sons of Benjamin also *lived* from Geba *onward,* at Michmash and Aija, at Bethel and its towns,

32 at Anathoth, Nob, Ananiah,

33 Hazor, Ramah, Gittaim,

34 Hadid, Zeboim, Neballat,

35 Lod and Ono, the valley of craftsmen.

36 And from the Levites, *some* divisions in Judah belonged to Benjamin.

CHAPTER 12

NOW these are the priests and the Levites who came up with Zerubbabel the son of Shealtiel, and Jeshua: Seraiah, Jeremiah, Ezra,

2 Amariah, Malluch, Hattush,

3 Shecaniah, Rehum, Meremoth,

---

[8] Lit., *brothers,* and so throughout this context   [9] Lit., *daughters,* and so through this ch.

4 Iddo, Ginnethoi, Abijah,

5 Mijamin, Maadiah, Bilgah,

6 Shemaiah and Joiarib, Jedaiah,

7 Sallu, Amok, Hilkiah, and Jedaiah. These were the heads of the priests and their kinsmen in the days of Jeshua.

8 ¶ And the Levites were Jeshua, Binnui, Kadmiel, Sherebiah, Judah, and Mattaniah who was in charge of the songs of thanksgiving, he and his brothers.

9 Also Bakbukiah and Unni, their brothers, stood opposite them in their service divisions.

10 And Jeshua became the father of Joiakim, and Joiakim became the father of Eliashib, and Eliashib became the father of Joiada,

11 and Joiada became the father of Jonathan, and Jonathan became the father of Jaddua.

12 ¶ Now in the days of Joiakim the priests, the heads of fathers' households were: of Seraiah, Meraiah; of Jeremiah, Hananiah;

13 of Ezra, Meshullam; of Amariah, Jehohanan;

14 of Malluchi, Jonathan; of Shebaniah, Joseph;

15 of Harim, Adna; of Meraioth, Helkai;

16 of Iddo, Zechariah; of Ginnethon, Meshullam;

17 of Abijah, Zichri; of Miniamin, of Moadiah, Piltai;

18 of Bilgah, Shammua; of Shemaiah, Jehonathan;

19 of Joiarib, Mattenai; of Jedaiah, Uzzi;

20 of Sallai, Kallai; of Amok, Eber;

21 of Hilkiah, Hashabiah; of Jedaiah, Nethanel.

22 ¶ As for the Levites, the heads of fathers' households were registered in the days of Eliashib, Joiada, and Johanan, and Jaddua; so were the priests in the reign of Darius the Persian.

23 The sons of Levi, the heads of fathers' households, were registered in the Book of the Chronicles up to the days of Johanan the son of Eliashib.

24 And the heads of the Levites were Hashabiah, Sherebiah, and Jeshua the son of Kadmiel, with their brothers opposite them, to praise and give thanks, as prescribed by David the man of God, division corresponding to division.

25 Mattaniah, and Bakbukiah, Obadiah, Meshullam, Talmon, and Akkub were gatekeepers keeping watch at the storehouses of the gates.

26 These served in the days of Joiakim the son of Jeshua, the son of Jozadak, and in the days of Nehemiah the governor and of Ezra the priest and scribe.

27 ¶ Now at the dedication of the wall of Jerusalem they sought out the Levites from all their places, to bring them to Jerusalem so that they might celebrate the dedication with gladness, with hymns of thanksgiving and with songs to the accompaniment of cymbals, harps, and lyres.

28 So the sons of the singers were assembled from the district around Jerusalem, and from the villages of the Netophathites,

29 from Beth-gilgal, and from their fields in Geba and Azmaveth, for the singers had built themselves villages around Jerusalem.

30 And the priests and the Levites purified themselves; they also purified the people, the gates, and the wall.

31 ¶ Then I had the leaders of Judah come up on top of the wall, and I appointed two great choirs, the first proceeding to the right on top of the wall toward the Refuse Gate.

32 Hoshaiah and half of the leaders of Judah followed them,

33 with Azariah, Ezra, Meshullam,

34 Judah, Benjamin, Shemaiah, Jeremiah,

35 and some of the sons of the priests with trumpets; and Zechariah the son of Jonathan, the son of Shemaiah, the son of Mattaniah, the son of Micaiah, the son of Zaccur, the son of Asaph,

36 and his kinsmen, Shemaiah, Azarel, Milalai, Gilalai, Maai, Nethanel, Judah and Hanani, with the musical instruments of David the man of God. And Ezra the scribe went before them.

37 And at the Fountain Gate they went directly up the steps of the city of David by the stairway of the wall above the house of David to the Water Gate on the east.

38 ¶ The second choir proceeded to the left, while I followed them with half of the people on the wall, above the Tower of Furnaces, to the Broad Wall,

39 and above the Gate of Ephraim, by the Old Gate, by the Fish Gate, the Tower of Hananel, and the Tower of the Hundred, as far as the Sheep Gate, and they stopped at the Gate of the Guard.

40 Then the two choirs took their stand in the house of God. So did I and half of the officials with me;

41 and the priests, Eliakim, Maaseiah, Miniamin, Micaiah, Elioenai, Zechariah, and Hananiah, with the trumpets;

42 and Maaseiah, Shemaiah, Eleazar, Uzzi, Jehohanan, Malchijah, Elam, and Ezer. And the singers sang, with Jezrahiah *their* leader,

43 and on that day they offered great sacrifices and rejoiced because God had given them great joy, even the women and children rejoiced, so that the joy of Jerusalem was heard from afar.

44 ¶ On that day men were also appointed over the chambers for the stores, the contributions, the first fruits, and the tithes, to gather into them from the fields of the cities the portions required by the law for the priests and Levites; for Judah rejoiced over the priests and Levites who served.

45 For they performed the worship of their God and the service of purification, together with the singers and the gatekeepers in accordance with the command of David *and* of his son Solomon.

46 For in the days of David and Asaph, in ancient times, *there were* leaders of the singers, songs of praise and hymns of thanksgiving to God.

47 And so all Israel in the days of Zerubbabel and Nehemiah gave the portions due the singers and the gatekeepers as each day required, and set apart the consecrated *portion* for the Levites, and the Levites set apart the consecrated *portion* for the sons of Aaron.

CHAPTER 13

ON that day they read aloud from the book of Moses in the hearing of the people; and there was found written in it that no Ammonite or Moabite should ever enter the assembly of God,

2 because they did not meet the sons of Israel with bread and water, but hired Balaam against them to curse them. However, our God turned the curse into a blessing.

3 So it came about, that when they heard the law, they excluded all foreigners from Israel.

4 ¶ Now prior to this, Eliashib the priest, who was appointed over the chambers of the house of our God, being related to Tobiah,

5 had prepared a large room for him, where formerly they put the grain offerings, the frankincense, the utensils, and the tithes of grain, wine and oil prescribed for the Levites, the singers and the gatekeepers, and the contributions for the priests.

6 But during all this *time* I was not in Jerusalem, for in the thirty-second year of Artaxerxes king of Babylon I had gone to the king. After some time, however, I asked leave from the king,

7 and I came to Jerusalem and learned about the evil that Eliashib had done for Tobiah, by preparing a room for him in the courts of the house of God.

8 And it was very displeasing to me, so I threw all of Tobiah's household goods out of the room.

9 Then I gave an order and they cleansed the rooms; and I returned there the utensils of the house of God with the grain offerings and the frankincense.

10 ¶ I also discovered that the portions of the Levites had not been given *them*, so that the Levites and the singers who performed the service had gone away, each to his own field.

11 So I reprimanded the officials and said, "Why is the house of God forsaken?" Then I gathered them together and restored them to their posts.

12 All Judah then brought the tithe of the grain, wine, and oil into the storehouses.

13 And in charge of the storehouses I appointed Shelemiah the priest, Zadok the scribe, and Pedaiah of the Levites, and in addition to them was Hanan the son of Zaccur, the son of Mattaniah; for they were considered reliable, and it was their task to distribute to their kinsmen.

14 Remember me for this, O my God, and do not blot out my loyal deeds

which I have performed for the house of my God and its services.

15 ¶ In those days I saw in Judah some who were treading wine presses on the sabbath, and bringing in sacks of grain and loading *them* on donkeys, as well as wine, grapes, figs, and all kinds of loads, and they brought *them* into Jerusalem on the sabbath day. So I admonished *them* on the day they sold food.

16 Also men of Tyre were living there *who* imported fish and all kinds of merchandise, and sold *them* to the sons of Judah on the sabbath, even in Jerusalem.

17 Then I reprimanded the nobles of Judah and said to them, "What is this evil thing you are doing, by profaning the sabbath day?

18 "Did not your fathers do the same so that our God brought on us, and on this city, all this trouble? Yet you are adding to the wrath on Israel by profaning the sabbath."

19 ¶ And it came about that just as it grew dark at the gates of Jerusalem before the sabbath, I commanded that the doors should be shut and that they should not open them until after the sabbath. Then I stationed some of my servants at the gates *that* no load should enter on the sabbath day.

20 Once or twice the traders and merchants of every kind of merchandise spent the night outside Jerusalem.

21 Then I warned them and said to them, "Why do you spend the night in front of the wall? If you do so again, I will use force against you." From that time on they did not come on the sabbath.

22 And I commanded the Levites that they should purify themselves and come as gatekeepers to sanctify the sabbath day. *For* this also remember me, O my God, and have compassion on me according to the greatness of Thy lovingkindness.

23 ¶ In those days I also saw that the Jews had married women from Ashdod, Ammon, and Moab.

24 As for their children, half spoke in the language of Ashdod, and none of them was able to speak the language of Judah, but the language of his own people.

25 So I contended with them and cursed them and struck some of them and pulled out their hair, and made them swear by God, "You shall not give your daughters to their sons, nor take of their daughters for your sons or for yourselves.

26 "Did not Solomon king of Israel sin regarding these things? Yet among the many nations there was no king like him, and he was loved by his God, and God made him king over all Israel; nevertheless the foreign women caused even him to sin.

27 "Do we then hear about you that you have committed all this great evil by acting unfaithfully against our God by marrying foreign women?"

28 Even one of the sons of Joiada, the son of Eliashib the high priest, was a son-in-law of Sanballat the Horonite, so I drove him away from me.

29 Remember them, O my God, because they have defiled the priesthood and the covenant of the priesthood and the Levites.

30 ¶ Thus I purified them from everything foreign and appointed duties for the priests and the Levites, each in his task,

31 and *I arranged* for the supply of wood at appointed times and for the first fruits. Remember me, O my God, for good.

Now it took place in the days of Ahasuerus, the Ahasuerus who reigned from India to Ethiopia over 127 provinces,

2 in those days as King Ahasuerus sat on his royal throne which *was* in Susa the capital,

3 in the third year of his reign, he gave a banquet for all his princes and attendants, the army *officers* of Persia and Media, the nobles, and the princes of his provinces being in his presence.

4 And he displayed the riches of his royal glory and the splendor of his great majesty for many days, 180 days.

5 And when these days were completed, the king gave a banquet lasting seven days for all the people who were present in Susa the capital, from the greatest to the least, in the court of the garden of the king's palace.

6 *There were hangings of* fine white and violet linen held by cords of fine purple linen on silver rings and marble columns, *and* couches of gold and silver on a mosaic pavement of porphyry, marble, mother-of-pearl, and precious stones.

7 Drinks were served in golden vessels of various kinds, and the royal wine was plentiful according to the king's bounty.

8 And the drinking was *done* according to the law, there was no compulsion, for so the king had given orders to each official of his household that he should do according to the desires of each person.

9 Queen Vashti also gave a banquet for the women in the palace which belonged to King Ahasuerus.

10 ¶ On the seventh day, when the heart of the king was merry with wine, he commanded Mehuman, Biztha, Harbona, Bigtha, Abagtha, Zethar, and Carkas, the seven eunuchs who served in the presence of King Ahasuerus,

11 to bring Queen Vashti before the king with *her* royal crown in order to display her beauty to the people and the princes, for she was beautiful.

12 But Queen Vashti refused to come at the king's command delivered by the eunuchs. Then the king became very angry and his wrath burned within him.

13 Then the king said to the wise men who understood the times—for it was the custom of the king so *to speak* before all who knew law and justice,

14 and were close to him: Carshena, Shethar, Admatha, Tarshish, Meres, Marsena, and Memucan, the seven princes of Persia and Media who had access to the king's presence and sat in the first place in the kingdom—

15 "According to law, what is to be done with Queen Vashti, because she did not obey the command of King Ahasuerus *delivered* by the eunuchs?"

16 And in the presence of the king and the princes, Memucan said, "Queen Vashti has wronged not only the king but *also* all the princes, and all the peoples who are in all the provinces of King Ahasuerus.

17 "For the queen's conduct will become known to all the women causing them to look with contempt on their husbands by saying, 'King Ahasuerus commanded Queen Vashti to be brought in to his presence, but she did not come.'

18 "And this day the ladies of Persia and Media who have heard of the queen's conduct will speak in *the same way* to all the king's princes, and there will be plenty of contempt and anger.

19 "If it pleases the king, let a royal edict be issued by him and let it be written in the laws of Persia and Media so that it cannot be repealed, that Vashti should come no more into the presence of King Ahasuerus, and let the king give her royal position to another who is more worthy than she.

20 "And when the king's edict which he shall make is heard throughout all his kingdom, great as it is, then all women will give honor to their husbands, great and small."

21 And *this* word pleased the king and the princes, and the king did as Memucan proposed.

22 So he sent letters to all the king's provinces, to each province according to its script and to every people according to their language, that every man should be the master in his own house and the one who speaks in the language of his own people.

CHAPTER 2

AFTER these things when the anger of King Ahasuerus had subsided, he remembered Vashti and what she had done and what had been decreed against her.

2 Then the king's attendants, who served him, said, "Let beautiful young virgins be sought for the king.

3 "And let the king appoint overseers in all the provinces of his kingdom that they may gather every beautiful young virgin to Susa the capital, to the harem, into the custody of Hegai, the king's eunuch, who is in charge of the women; and let their cosmetics be given *them*.

4 "Then let the young lady who pleases the king be queen in place of Vashti." And the matter pleased the king, and he did accordingly.

5 ¶ *Now* there was a Jew in Susa the capital whose name was Mordecai, the son of Jair, the son of Shimei, the son of Kish, a Benjamite,

6 who had been taken into exile from Jerusalem with the captives who had been exiled with Jeconiah king of Judah, whom Nebuchadnezzar the king of Babylon had exiled.

7 And he was bringing up Hadassah, that is Esther, his uncle's daughter, for she had neither father nor mother. Now the young lady was beautiful of form and face, and when her father and her mother died, Mordecai took her as his own daughter.

8 ¶ So it came about when the command and decree of the king were heard and many young ladies were gathered to Susa the capital into the custody of Hegai, that Esther was taken to the king's palace into the custody of Hegai, who was in charge of the women.

9 Now the young lady pleased him and found favor with him. So he quickly provided her with her cosmetics and food, gave her seven choice maids from the king's palace, and transferred her and her maids to the best place in the harem.

10 Esther did not make known her people or her kindred, for Mordecai had instructed her that she should not make *them* known.

11 And every day Mordecai walked back and forth in front of the court of the harem to learn how Esther was and how she fared.

12 ¶ Now when the turn of each young lady came to go in to King Ahasuerus, after the end of her twelve months under the regulations for the women—for the days of their beautification were completed as follows: six months with oil of myrrh and six months with spices and the cosmetics for women—

13 the young lady would go in to the king in this way: anything that she desired was given her to take with her from the harem to the king's palace.

14 In the evening she would go in and in the morning she would return to the second harem, to the custody of Shaashgaz, the king's eunuch who was in charge of the concubines. She would not again go in to the king unless the king delighted in her and she was summoned by name.

15 Now when the turn of Esther, the daughter of Abihail the uncle of Mordecai who had taken her as his daughter, came to go in to the king, she did not request anything except what Hegai, the king's eunuch who was in charge of the women, advised. And Esther found favor in the eyes of all who saw her.

16 ¶ So Esther was taken to King Ahasuerus to his royal palace in the tenth month which is the month Tebeth, in the seventh year of his reign.

17 And the king loved Esther more than all the women, and she found favor and kindness with him more than all the virgins, so that he set the royal crown on her head and made her queen instead of Vashti.

18 Then the king gave a great banquet, Esther's banquet, for all his princes and his servants; he also made a holiday for the provinces and gave gifts according to the king's bounty.

19 ¶ And when the virgins were gathered together the second time, then Mordecai was sitting at the king's gate.

20 Esther had not yet made known her kindred or her people, even as Mordecai had commanded her, for Esther did what Mordecai told her as she had done when under his care.

21 In those days, while Mordecai was sitting at the king's gate, Bigthan and Teresh, two of the king's officials from

those who guarded the door, became angry and sought to lay hands on King Ahasuerus.

22 But the plot became known to Mordecai, and he told Queen Esther, and Esther informed the king in Mordecai's name.

23 Now when the plot was investigated and found *to be so,* they were both hanged on a ¹gallows; and it was written in the Book of the Chronicles in the king's presence.

CHAPTER 3

AFTER these events King Ahasuerus promoted Haman, the son of Hammedatha the Agagite, and advanced him and established his authority over all the princes who *were* with him.

2 And all the king's servants who were at the king's gate bowed down and paid homage to Haman; for so the king had commanded concerning him. But Mordecai neither bowed down nor paid homage.

3 Then the king's servants who were at the king's gate said to Mordecai, "Why are you transgressing the king's command?"

4 Now it was when they had spoken daily to him and he would not listen to them, that they told Haman to see whether Mordecai's reason would stand; for he had told them that he was a Jew.

5 When Haman saw that Mordecai neither bowed down nor paid homage to him, Haman was filled with rage.

6 But he disdained to lay hands on Mordecai alone, for they had told him *who* the people of Mordecai *were;* therefore Haman sought to destroy all the Jews, the people of Mordecai, who *were* throughout the whole kingdom of Ahasuerus.

7 ¶ In the first month, which is the month Nisan, in the twelfth year of King Ahasuerus, Pur, that is the lot, was cast before Haman from day to day and from month *to month,* until the twelfth month, that is the month Adar.

8 Then Haman said to King Ahasuerus, "There is a certain people scattered and dispersed among the peoples in all the provinces of your kingdom; their laws are different from *those* of

all *other* people, and they do not observe the king's laws, so it is not in the king's interest to let them remain.

9 "If it is pleasing to the king, let it be decreed that they be destroyed, and I will pay ten thousand talents of silver into the hands of those who carry on the *king's* business, to put into the king's treasuries."

10 Then the king took his signet ring from his hand and gave it to Haman, the son of Hammedatha the Agagite, the enemy of the Jews.

11 And the king said to Haman, "The silver is yours, and the people *also,* to do with them as you please."

12 Then the king's scribes were summoned on the thirteenth day of the first month, and it was written just as Haman commanded to the king's satraps, to the governors who were over each province, and to the princes of each people, each province according to its script, each people according to its language, being written in the name of King Ahasuerus and sealed with the king's signet ring.

13 And letters were sent by couriers to all the king's provinces to destroy, to kill, and to annihilate all the Jews, both young and old, women and children, in one day, the thirteenth *day* of the twelfth month, which is the month Adar, and to seize their possessions as plunder.

14 A copy of the edict to be issued as law in every province was published to all the peoples so that they should be ready for this day.

15 The couriers went out impelled by the king's command while the decree was issued in Susa the capital; and while the king and Haman sat down to drink, the city of Susa was in confusion.

CHAPTER 4

WHEN Mordecai learned all that had been done, he tore his clothes, put on sackcloth and ashes, and went out into the midst of the city and wailed loudly and bitterly.

2 And he went as far as the king's gate, for no one was to enter the king's gate clothed in sackcloth.

3 And in each and every province where the command and decree of the king came, there was great mourning

¹ Lit., *tree*

among the Jews, with fasting, weeping, and wailing; and many lay on sackcloth and ashes.

4 ¶ Then Esther's maidens and her eunuchs came and told her, and the queen writhed in great anguish. And she sent garments to clothe Mordecai that he might remove his sackcloth from him, but he did not accept *them*.

5 Then Esther summoned Hathach from the king's eunuchs, whom the king had appointed to attend her, and ordered him *to go* to Mordecai to learn what this *was* and why it *was*.

6 So Hathach went out to Mordecai to the city square in front of the king's gate.

7 And Mordecai told him all that had happened to him, and the exact amount of money that Haman had promised to pay to the king's treasuries for the destruction of the Jews.

8 He also gave him a copy of the text of the edict which had been issued in Susa for their destruction, that he might show Esther and inform her, and to order her to go in to the king to implore his favor and to plead with him for her people.

9 ¶ And Hathach came back and related Mordecai's words to Esther.

10 Then Esther spoke to Hathach and ordered him *to reply* to Mordecai:

11 "All the king's servants and the people of the king's provinces know that for any man or woman who comes to the king to the inner court who is not summoned, he has but one law, that he be put to death, unless the king holds out to him the golden scepter so that he may live. And I have not been summoned to come to the king for these thirty days."

12 And they related Esther's words to Mordecai.

13 ¶ Then Mordecai told *them* to reply to Esther, "Do not imagine that you in the king's palace can escape any more than all the Jews.

14 "For if you remain silent at this time, relief and deliverance will arise for the Jews from another place and you and your father's house will perish. And who knows whether you have not attained royalty for such a time as this?"

15 Then Esther told *them* to reply to Mordecai,

16 "Go, assemble all the Jews who are found in Susa, and fast for me; do not eat or drink for three days, night or day. I and my maidens also will fast in the same way. And thus I will go in to the king, which is not according to the law; and if I perish, I perish."

17 So Mordecai went away and did just as Esther had commanded him.

CHAPTER 5

Now it came about on the third day that Esther put on her royal robes and stood in the inner court of the king's palace in front of the king's rooms, and the king was sitting on his royal throne in the throne room, opposite the entrance to the palace.

2 And it happened when the king saw Esther the queen standing in the court, she obtained favor in his sight; and the king extended to Esther the golden scepter which was in his hand. So Esther came near and touched the top of the scepter.

3 Then the king said to her, "What is *troubling* you, Queen Esther? And what is your request? Even to half of the kingdom it will be given to you."

4 And Esther said, "If it please the king, may the king and Haman come this day to the banquet that I have prepared for him."

5 ¶ Then the king said, "Bring Haman quickly that we may do as Esther desires." So the king and Haman came to the banquet which Esther had prepared.

6 And, as they drank their wine at the banquet, the king said to Esther, "What is your petition, for it shall be granted to you. And what is your request? Even to half of the kingdom it shall be done."

7 So Esther answered and said, "My petition and my request is:

8 if I have found favor in the sight of the king, and if it please the king to grant my petition and do what I request, may the king and Haman come to the banquet which I shall prepare for them, and tomorrow I will do as the king says."

9 ¶ Then Haman went out that day glad and pleased of heart; but when Haman saw Mordecai in the king's gate, and that he did not stand up or tremble before him, Haman was filled with anger against Mordecai.

10 Haman controlled himself, however, went to his house, and sent for his friends and his wife Zeresh.

11 Then Haman recounted to them the glory of his riches, and the number of his sons, and every *instance* where the king had magnified him, and how he had promoted him above the princes and servants of the king.

12 Haman also said, "Even Esther the queen let no one but me come with the king to the banquet which she had prepared; and tomorrow also I am invited by her with the king.

13 "Yet all of this does not satisfy me every time I see Mordecai the Jew sitting at the king's gate."

14 Then Zeresh his wife and all his friends said to him, "Have a gallows fifty cubits high made and in the morning ask the king to have Mordecai hanged on it, then go joyfully with the king to the banquet." And the advice pleased Haman, so he had the gallows made.

CHAPTER 6

DURING that night the king could not sleep so he gave an order to bring the book of records, the chronicles, and they were read before the king.

2 And it was found written what Mordecai had reported concerning Bigthana and Teresh, two of the king's eunuchs who were doorkeepers, that they had sought to lay hands on King Ahasuerus.

3 And the king said, "What honor or dignity has been bestowed on Mordecai for this?" Then the king's servants who attended him said, "Nothing has been done for him."

4 So the king said, "Who is in the court?" Now Haman had just entered the outer court of the king's palace in order to speak to the king about hanging Mordecai on the gallows which he had prepared for him.

5 And the king's servants said to him, "Behold, Haman is standing in the court." And the king said, "Let him come in."

6 So Haman came in and the king said to him, "What is to be done for the man whom the king desires to honor?" And Haman said to himself, "Whom would the king desire to honor more than me?"

7 Then Haman said to the king, "For the man whom the king desires to honor,

8 let them bring a royal robe which the king has worn, and the horse on which the king has ridden, and on whose head a royal crown has been placed;

9 and let the robe and the horse be handed over to one of the king's most noble princes and let them array the man whom the king desires to honor and lead him on horseback through the city square, and proclaim before him, 'Thus it shall be done to the man whom the king desires to honor.' "

10 ¶ Then the king said to Haman, "Take quickly the robes and the horse as you have said, and do so for Mordecai the Jew, who is sitting at the king's gate; do not fall short in anything of all that you have said."

11 So Haman took the robe and the horse, and arrayed Mordecai, and led him *on horseback* through the city square, and proclaimed before him, "Thus it shall be done to the man whom the king desires to honor."

12 Then Mordecai returned to the king's gate. But Haman hurried home, mourning, with *his* head covered.

13 And Haman recounted to Zeresh his wife and all his friends everything that had happened to him. Then his wise men and Zeresh his wife said to him, "If Mordecai, before whom you have begun to fall, is of Jewish origin, you will not overcome him, but will surely fall before him."

14 While they were still talking with him, the king's eunuchs arrived and hastily brought Haman to the banquet which Esther had prepared.

CHAPTER 7

NOW the king and Haman came to drink *wine* with Esther the queen.

2 And the king said to Esther on the second day also as they drank their wine at the banquet, "What is your petition, Queen Esther? It shall be granted you. And what is your request? Even to half of the kingdom it shall be done."

3 Then Queen Esther answered and said, "If I have found favor in your sight, O king, and if it please the king,

let my life be given me as my petition, and my people as my request;

4 for we have been sold, I and my people, to be destroyed, to be killed and to be annihilated. Now if we had only been sold as slaves, men and women, I would have remained silent, for the trouble would not be commensurate with the annoyance to the king."

5 Then King Ahasuerus asked Queen Esther, "Who is he, and where is he, who would presume to do thus?"

6 And Esther said, "A foe and an enemy, is this wicked Haman!" Then Haman became terrified before the king and queen.

7 And the king arose in his anger from drinking wine *and went* into the palace garden; but Haman stayed to beg for his life from Queen Esther, for he saw that harm had been determined against him by the king.

8 Now when the king returned from the palace garden into the place where they were drinking wine, Haman was falling on the couch where Esther was. Then the king said, "Will he even assault the queen with me in the house?" As the word went out of the king's mouth, they covered Haman's face.

9 Then Harbonah, one of the eunuchs who *were* before the king said, "Behold indeed, the gallows standing at Haman's house fifty cubits high, which Haman made for Mordecai who spoke good on behalf of the king!" And the king said, "Hang him on it."

10 So they hanged Haman on the gallows which he had prepared for Mordecai, and the king's anger subsided.

CHAPTER 8

ON that day King Ahasuerus gave the house of Haman, the enemy of the Jews, to Queen Esther; and Mordecai came before the king, for Esther had disclosed what he was to her.

2 And the king took off his signet ring which he had taken away from Haman, and gave it to Mordecai. And Esther set Mordecai over the house of Haman.

3 ¶ Then Esther spoke again to the king, fell at his feet, wept, and implored him to avert the evil *scheme* of Haman the Agagite and his plot which he had devised against the Jews.

4 And the king extended the golden scepter to Esther. So Esther arose and stood before the king.

5 Then she said, "If it pleases the king and if I have found favor before him and the matter *seems* proper to the king and I am pleasing in his sight, let it be written to revoke the letters devised by Haman, the son of Hammedatha the Agagite, which he wrote to destroy the Jews who are in all the king's provinces.

6 "For how can I endure to see the calamity which shall befall my people, and how can I endure to see the destruction of my kindred?"

7 So King Ahasuerus said to Queen Esther and to Mordecai the Jew, "Behold, I have given the house of Haman to Esther, and him they have hanged on the gallows because he had stretched out his hands against the Jews.

8 "Now you write to the Jews as you see fit, in the king's name, and seal *it* with the king's signet ring; for a decree which is written in the name of the king and sealed with the king's signet ring may not be revoked."

9 ¶ So the king's scribes were called at that time in the third month (that is, the month Sivan), on the twenty-third day; and it was written according to all that Mordecai commanded to the Jews, the satraps, the governors, and the princes of the provinces which *extended* from India to Ethiopia, 127 provinces, to every province according to its script, and to every people according to their language, as well as to the Jews according to their script and their language.

10 And he wrote in the name of King Ahasuerus, and sealed it with the king's signet ring, and sent letters by couriers on horses, riding on steeds sired by the royal stud.

11 In them the king granted the Jews who were in each and every city *the right* to assemble and to defend their lives, to destroy, to kill, and to annihilate the entire army of any people or province which might attack them, including children and women, and to plunder their spoil,

12 on one day in all the provinces of King Ahasuerus, the thirteenth *day* of

the twelfth month (that is, the month Adar).

13 A copy of the edict to be issued as law in each and every province, was published to all the peoples, so that the Jews should be ready for this day to avenge themselves on their enemies.

14 The couriers, hastened and impelled by the king's command, went out, riding on the royal steeds; and the decree was given out in Susa the capital.

15 ¶ Then Mordecai went out from the presence of the king in royal robes of blue and white, with a large crown of gold and a garment of fine linen and purple; and the city of Susa shouted and rejoiced.

16 For the Jews there was light and gladness and joy and honor.

17 And in each and every province, and in each and every city, wherever the king's commandment and his decree arrived, there was gladness and joy for the Jews, a feast and a holiday. And many among the peoples of the land became Jews, for the dread of the Jews had fallen on them.

CHAPTER 9

NOW in the twelfth month (that is, the month Adar), on the thirteenth day when the king's command and edict were about to be executed, on the day when the enemies of the Jews hoped to gain the mastery over them, it was turned to the contrary so that the Jews themselves gained the mastery over those who hated them.

2 The Jews assembled in their cities throughout all the provinces of King Ahasuerus to lay hands on those who sought their harm; and no one could stand before them, for the dread of them had fallen on all the peoples.

3 Even all the princes of the provinces, the satraps, the governors, and those who were doing the king's business assisted the Jews, because the dread of Mordecai had fallen on them.

4 Indeed, Mordecai was great in the king's house, and his fame spread throughout all the provinces; for the man Mordecai became greater and greater.

5 Thus the Jews struck all their enemies with the sword, killing and destroying; and they did what they pleased to those who hated them.

6 And in Susa the capital the Jews killed and destroyed five hundred men,

7 and Parshandatha, Dalphon, Aspatha,

8 Poratha, Adalia, Aridatha,

9 Parmashta, Arisai, Aridai, and Vaizatha,

10 the ten sons of Haman the son of Hammedatha, the Jews' enemy; but they did not lay their hands on the plunder.

11 ¶ On that day the number of those who were killed in Susa the capital was reported to the king.

12 And the king said to Queen Esther, "The Jews have killed and destroyed five hundred men and the ten sons of Haman in Susa the capital. What have they done in the rest of the king's provinces! Now what is your petition? It shall even be granted you. And what is your further request? It shall also be done."

13 Then said Esther, "If it pleases the king, let tomorrow also be granted to the Jews who are in Susa to do according to the edict of today; and let Haman's ten sons be hanged on the gallows."

14 So the king commanded that it should be done so; and an edict was issued in Susa, and Haman's ten sons were hanged.

15 And the Jews who were in Susa assembled also on the fourteenth day of the month Adar and killed three hundred men in Susa, but they did not lay their hands on the plunder.

16 ¶ Now the rest of the Jews who *were* in the king's provinces assembled, to defend their lives and rid themselves of their enemies, and kill 75,000 of those who hated them; but they did not lay their hands on the plunder.

17 *This was done* on the thirteenth day of the month Adar, and on the fourteenth day they rested and made it a day of feasting and rejoicing.

18 But the Jews who were in Susa assembled on the thirteenth and the fourteenth of the same month, and they rested on the fifteenth day and made it a day of feasting and rejoicing.

19 Therefore the Jews of the rural areas, who live in the rural towns, make the fourteenth day of the month

Adar *a* holiday for rejoicing and feasting and sending portions *of food* to one another.

20 ¶ Then Mordecai recorded these events, and he sent letters to all the Jews who were in all the provinces of King Ahasuerus, both near and far,

21 obliging them to celebrate the fourteenth day of the month Adar, and the fifteenth day of the same month, annually,

22 because on those days the Jews rid themselves of their enemies, and *it was a* month which was turned for them from sorrow into gladness and from mourning into a holiday; that they should make them days of feasting and rejoicing and sending portions *of food* to one another and gifts to the poor.

23 Thus the Jews undertook what they had started to do, and what Mordecai had written to them.

24 For Haman the son of Hammedatha, the Agagite, the adversary of all the Jews, had schemed against the Jews to destroy them, and had cast Pur, that is the lot, to disturb them and destroy them.

25 But when it came to the king's attention, he commanded by letter that his wicked scheme which he had devised against the Jews, should return on his own head, and that he and his sons should be hanged on the gallows.

26 Therefore they called these days Purim after the name of Pur. And because of the instructions in this letter, both what they had seen in this regard and what had happened to them,

27 the Jews established and made a custom for themselves, and for their descendants, and for all those who allied themselves with them, so that they should not fail to celebrate these two days according to their regulation, and according to their appointed time annually.

28 So these days were to be remembered and celebrated throughout every generation, every family, every province, and every city; and these days of Purim were not to fail from among the Jews, or their memory fade from their descendants.

29 ¶ Then Queen Esther, daughter of Abihail, with Mordecai the Jew, wrote with full authority to confirm this second letter about Purim.

30 And he sent letters to all the Jews, to the 127 provinces of the kingdom of Ahasuerus, namely, words of peace and truth,

31 to establish these days of Purim at their appointed times, just as Mordecai the Jew and Queen Esther had established for them, and just as they had established for themselves and for their descendants with instructions for their times of fasting and their lamentations.

32 And the command of Esther established these customs for Purim, and it was written in the book.

CHAPTER 10

Now King Ahasuerus laid a tribute on the land and on the coastlands of the sea.

2 And all the accomplishments of his authority and strength, and the full account of the greatness of Mordecai, to which the king advanced him, are they not written in the Book of the Chronicles of the Kings of Media and Persia?

3 For Mordecai the Jew was second *only* to King Ahasuerus and great among the Jews, and in favor with the multitude of his kinsmen, one who sought the good of his people and one who spoke for the welfare of his whole nation.

THE BOOK OF

JOB

THERE was a man in the land of Uz, whose name was Job, and that man was blameless, upright, fearing God, and turning away from evil.

2 And seven sons and three daughters were born to him.

3 His possessions also were 7,000 sheep, 3,000 camels, 500 yoke of oxen, 500 female donkeys, and very many servants; and that man was the greatest of all the men of the east.

4 And his sons used to go and hold a feast in the house of each one on his day, and they would send and invite their three sisters to eat and drink with them.

5 And it came about, when the days of feasting had completed their cycle, that Job would send and consecrate them, rising up early in the morning and offering burnt offerings *according to* the number of them all; for Job said, "Perhaps my sons have sinned and cursed God in their hearts." Thus Job did continually.

6 Now there was a day when the sons of God came to present themselves before the Lord, and ¹Satan also came among them.

7 And the Lord said to Satan, "From where do you come?" Then Satan answered the Lord and said, "From roaming about on the earth and walking around on it."

8 And the Lord said to Satan, "Have you considered My servant Job? For there is no one like him on the earth, a blameless and upright man, fearing God and turning away from evil."

9 Then Satan answered the Lord, "Does Job fear God for nothing?

10 "Hast Thou not made a hedge about him and his house and all that he has, on every side? Thou hast blessed the work of his hands, and his possessions have increased in the land.

11 "But put forth Thy hand now and touch all that he has; he will surely curse Thee to Thy face."

12 Then the Lord said to Satan, "Behold, all that he has is in your power, only do not put forth your hand on him." So Satan departed from the presence of the Lord.

13 ¶ Now it happened on the day when his sons and his daughters were eating and drinking wine in their oldest brother's house,

14 that a messenger came to Job and said, "The oxen were plowing and the donkeys feeding beside them,

15 and the Sabeans attacked and took them. They also slew the servants with the edge of the sword, and I alone have escaped to tell you."

16 While he was still speaking, another also came and said, "The fire of God fell from heaven and burned up the sheep and the servants and consumed them, and I alone have escaped to tell you."

17 While he was still speaking, another also came and said, "The Chaldeans formed three bands and made a raid on the camels and took them and slew the servants with the edge of the sword; and I alone have escaped to tell you."

18 While he was still speaking, another also came and said, "Your sons and your daughters were eating and drinking wine in their oldest brother's house,

19 and behold, a great wind came from across the wilderness and struck the four corners of the house, and it fell on the young people and they died; and I alone have escaped to tell you."

20 ¶ Then Job arose and tore his robe and shaved his head, and he fell to the ground and worshiped.

21 And he said,

"Naked I came from my mother's womb,
And naked I shall return there.
The Lord gave and the Lord has taken away.
Blessed be the name of the Lord."

22 Through all this Job did not sin nor did he blame God.

CHAPTER 2

AGAIN there was a day when the sons of God came to present themselves before the Lord, and Satan also came among them to present himself before the Lord.

2 And the Lord said to Satan, "Where have you come from?" Then

---

¹ I.e., the adversary; so through chs. 1 and 2

Satan answered the LORD and said, "From roaming about on the earth, and walking around on it."

3 And the LORD said to Satan, "Have you considered My servant Job? For there is no one like him on the earth, a blameless and upright man fearing God and turning away from evil. And he still holds fast his integrity, although you incited Me against him, to ruin him without cause."

4 And Satan answered the LORD and said, "Skin for skin! Yes, all that a man has he will give for his life.

5 "However, put forth Thy hand, now, and touch his bone and his flesh; he will curse Thee to Thy face."

6 So the LORD said to Satan, "Behold, he is in your power, only spare his life."

7 ¶ Then Satan went out from the presence of the LORD, and smote Job with sore boils from the sole of his foot to the crown of his head.

8 And he took a potsherd to scrape himself while he was sitting among the ashes.

9 Then his wife said to him, "Do you still hold fast your integrity? Curse God and die!"

10 But he said to her, "You speak as one of the foolish women speaks. Shall we indeed accept good from God and not accept adversity?" In all this Job did not sin with his lips.

11 ¶ Now when Job's three friends heard of all this adversity that had come upon him, they came each one from his own place, Eliphaz the Temanite, Bildad the Shuhite, and Zophar the Naamathite; and they made an appointment together to come to sympathize with him and comfort him.

12 And when they lifted up their eyes at a distance, and did not recognize him, they raised their voices and wept. And each of them tore his robe, and they threw dust over their heads toward the sky.

13 Then they sat down on the ground with him for seven days and seven nights with no one speaking a word to him, for they saw that *his* pain was very great.

CHAPTER 3

AFTERWARD Job opened his mouth and cursed the day of his *birth*.

2 And Job said,
3 "Let the day perish on which I was
   to be born,
   And the night *which* said, 'A boy
   is conceived.'
4 "May that day be darkness;
   Let not God above care for it,
   Nor light shine on it.
5 "Let darkness and black gloom
   claim it;
   Let a cloud settle on it;
   Let the blackness of the day terrify it.
6 "*As for* that night, let darkness
   seize it;
   Let it not rejoice among the days
   of the year;
   Let it not come into the number
   of the months.
7 "Behold, let that night be barren;
   Let no joyful shout enter it.
8 "Let those curse it who curse the
   day,
   Who are prepared to rouse Leviathan.
9 "Let the stars of its twilight be
   darkened;
   Let it wait for light but have none,
   Neither let it see the breaking
   dawn;
10 Because it did not shut the opening of my *mother's* womb,
   Or hide trouble from my eyes.

11 ¶ "Why did I not die at birth,
   Come forth from the womb and
   expire?
12 "Why did the knees receive me,
   And why the breasts, that I
   should suck?
13 "For now I would have lain down
   and been quiet;
   I would have slept then, I would
   have been at rest,
14 With kings and *with* counselors of
   the earth,
   Who rebuilt ruins for themselves;
15 Or with princes who had gold,
   Who were filling their houses *with*
   silver.
16 "Or like a miscarriage which is
   discarded, I would not be,
   As infants that never saw light.
17 "There the wicked cease from raging,
   And there the weary are at rest.
18 "The prisoners are at ease together;

They do not hear the voice of the taskmaster.
19"The small and the great are there, And the slave is free from his master.

20 ¶"Why is light given to him who suffers, And life to the bitter of soul;
21 Who long for death, but there is none, And dig for it more than for hidden treasures;
22 Who rejoice greatly, They exult when they find the grave?
23"Why is light given to a man whose way is hidden, And whom God has hedged in?
24"For my groaning comes at the sight of my food, And my cries pour out like water.
25"For what I fear comes upon me, And what I dread befalls me.
26"I am not at ease, nor am I quiet, And I am not at rest, but turmoil comes."

CHAPTER 4

THEN Eliphaz the Temanite answered,
2"If one ventures a word with you, will you become impatient? But who can refrain from speaking?
3"Behold you have admonished many, And you have strengthened weak hands.
4"Your words have helped the tottering to stand, And you have strengthened feeble knees.
5"But now it has come to you, and you are impatient; It touches you, and you are dismayed.
6"Is not your ²fear of God your confidence, And the integrity of your ways your hope?

7 ¶"Remember now, who ever perished being innocent? Or where were the upright destroyed?

8"According to what I have seen, those who plow iniquity And those who sow trouble harvest it.
9"By the breath of God they perish, And by the blast of His anger they come to an end.
10"The roaring of the lion and the voice of the fierce lion, And the teeth of the young lions are broken.
11"The lion perishes for lack of prey, And the whelps of the lioness are scattered.

12 ¶"Now a word was brought to me stealthily, And my ear received a whisper of it.
13"Amid disquieting thoughts from the visions of the night, When deep sleep falls on men,
14 Dread came upon me, and trembling, And made all my bones shake.
15"Then a ³spirit passed by my face; The hair of my flesh bristled up.
16"It stood still, but I could not discern its appearance; A form was before my eyes; There was silence, then I heard a voice:
17 'Can mankind be just before God? Can a man be pure before his Maker?
18 'He puts no trust even in His servants; And against His angels He charges error.
19 'How much more those who dwell in houses of clay, Whose foundation is in the dust, Who are crushed before the moth!
20 'Between morning and evening they are broken in pieces; Unobserved, they perish forever.
21 'Is not their tent-cord plucked up within them? They die, yet without wisdom.'

CHAPTER 5

"CALL now, is there anyone who will answer you? And to which of the holy ones will you turn?
2"For vexation slays the foolish man,

---

² Or, reverence

³ Or, breath passed over

And anger kills the simple.
3"I have seen the foolish taking
  root,
  And I cursed his abode immediately.
4"His sons are far from safety,
  They are even ⁴oppressed in the
  gate,
  Neither is there a deliverer.
5"His harvest the hungry devour,
  And take it to a *place of* thorns;
  And the schemer is eager for their
  wealth.
6"For affliction does not come from
  the dust,
  Neither does trouble sprout from
  the ground,
7 For man is born for trouble,
  As sparks fly upward.

8 ¶"But as for me, I would seek
  God,
  And I would place my cause before God;
9 Who does great and unsearchable
  things,
  Wonders without number.
10"He gives rain on the earth,
  And sends water on the fields,
11 So that He sets on high those who
  are lowly,
  And those who mourn are lifted to
  safety.
12"He frustrates the plotting of the
  shrewd,
  So that their hands cannot attain
  success.
13"He captures the wise by their own
  shrewdness
  And the advice of the cunning is
  quickly thwarted.
14"By day they meet with darkness,
  And grope at noon as in the night.
15"But He saves from the sword of
  their mouth,
  And the poor from the hand of the
  mighty.
16"So the helpless has hope,
  And unrighteousness must shut
  its mouth.

17 ¶"Behold, how happy is the man
  whom God reproves,
  So do not despise the discipline of
  the Almighty.
18"For He inflicts pain, and gives
  relief;

He wounds, and His hands *also*
  heal.
19"From six troubles He will deliver
  you,
  Even in seven evil will not touch
  you.
20"In famine He will redeem you
  from death,
  And in war from the power of the
  sword.
21"You will be hidden from the
  scourge of the tongue,
  Neither will you be afraid of violence when it comes.
22"You will laugh at violence and
  famine,
  Neither will you be afraid of wild
  beasts.
23"For you will be in league with the
  stones of the field;
  And the beasts of the field will be
  at peace with you.
24"And you will know that your tent
  is secure,
  For you will visit your abode and
  fear no loss.
25"You will know also that your
  descendants will be many,
  And your offspring as the grass of
  the earth.
26"You will come to the grave in full
  vigor,
  Like the stacking of grain in its
  season.
27"Behold this, we have investigated
  it, thus it is;
  Hear it, and know for yourself."

CHAPTER 6

THEN Job answered,
2"Oh that my vexation were actually weighed,
  And laid in the balances together
  with my iniquity!
3"For then it would be heavier than
  the sand of the seas,
  Therefore my words have been
  rash.
4"For the arrows of the Almighty
  are within me;
  Their poison my spirit drinks;
  The terrors of God are arrayed
  against me.
5"Does the wild donkey bray over
  his grass,
  Or does the ox low over his fodder?

---

⁴ Lit., *crushed*

6"Can something tasteless be eaten
without salt,
Or is there any taste in the white
of an egg?
7"My soul refuses to touch *them;*
They are like loathsome food to
me.

8 ¶"Oh that my request might come
to pass,
And that God would grant my
longing!
9"Would that God were willing to
crush me;
That He would loose His hand and
cut me off!
10"But it is still my consolation,
And I rejoice in unsparing pain,
That I have not denied the words
of the Holy One.
11"What is my strength, that I should
wait?
And what is my end, that I should
endure?
12"Is my strength the strength of
stones,
Or is my flesh bronze?
13"Is it that my help is not within me,
And that deliverance is driven
from me?

14 ¶"For the despairing man *there
should be* kindness from his
friend;
Lest he forsake the fear of the
Almighty.
15"My brothers have acted deceitfully like a wadi,
Like the torrents of wadis which
vanish,
16 Which are turbid because of ice,
And into which the snow melts.
17"When they become waterless,
they are silent,
When it is hot, they vanish from
their place.
18"The paths of their course wind
along,
They go up into nothing and perish.
19"The caravans of Tema looked,
The travelers of Sheba hoped for
them.
20"They were disappointed for they
had trusted,
They came there and were confounded.

21"Indeed, you have now become
such,
You see a terror and are afraid.
22"Have I said, 'Give me *something,'*
Or, 'Offer a bribe for me from your
wealth,'
23 Or, 'Deliver me from the hand of
the adversary,'
Or, 'Redeem me from the hand of
the tyrants'?

24 ¶"Teach me, and I will be silent;
And show me how I have erred.
25"How painful are honest words!
But what does your argument
prove?
26"Do you intend to reprove *my*
words,
When the words of one in despair
belong to the wind?
27"You would even cast *lots* for the
orphans,
And barter over your friend.
28"And now please look at me,
And *see* if I lie to your face.
29"Desist now, let there be no injustice;
Even desist, my righteousness is
yet in it.
30"Is there injustice on my tongue?
Cannot my palate discern calamities?

CHAPTER 7

"IS not man forced to labor on earth,
And *are not* his days like the days
of a hired man?
2"As a slave who pants for the
shade,
And as a hired man who eagerly
waits for his wages,
3 So am I allotted months of vanity,
And nights of trouble are appointed me.
4"When I lie down I say,
'When shall I arise?'
But the night continues,
And I am continually tossing until
dawn.
5"My flesh is clothed with worms
and a crust of dirt;
My skin hardens and runs.
6"My days are swifter than a weaver's shuttle,
And come to an end without
hope.

7 ¶"Remember that my life is *but*
breath,
My eye will not again see good.

8"The eye of him who sees me will
   behold me no more;
   Thine eyes *will be* on me, but I
   will not be.
9"When a cloud vanishes, it is gone,
   So he who goes down to Sheol
   does not come up.
10"He will not return again to his
   house,
   Nor will his place know him anymore.

11 ¶"Therefore, I will not restrain my
   mouth;
   I will speak in the anguish of my
   spirit,
   I will complain in the bitterness of
   my soul.
12"Am I the sea, or the sea monster,
   That Thou dost set a guard over
   me?
13"If I say, 'My bed will comfort me,
   My couch will ease my complaint,'
14 Then Thou dost frighten me with
   dreams
   And terrify me by visions;
15 So that my soul would choose
   suffocation,
   Death rather than my pains.
16"I waste away; I will not live forever.
   Leave me alone, for my days are
   but a breath.
17"What is man that Thou dost magnify him,
   And that Thou art concerned
   about him,
18 That Thou dost examine him every morning,
   And try him every moment?
19"Wilt Thou never turn Thy gaze
   away from me,
   Nor let me alone until I swallow
   my spittle?
20"Have I sinned? What have I done
   to Thee,
   O watcher of men?
   Why hast Thou set me as Thy
   target,
   So that I am a burden to myself?
21"Why then dost Thou not pardon
   my transgression
   And take away my iniquity?
   For now I will lie down in the
   dust;
   And Thou wilt seek me, but I will
   not be."

CHAPTER 8

THEN Bildad the Shuhite answered,
   2"How long will you say these
   things,
   And the words of your mouth be a
   mighty wind?
3"Does God pervert justice
   Or does the Almighty pervert
   what is right?
4"If your sons sinned against Him,
   Then He delivered them into the
   power of their transgression.
5"If you would seek God
   And implore the compassion of
   the Almighty,
6 If you are pure and upright,
   Surely now He would rouse Himself for you
   And restore your righteous estate.
7"Though your beginning was insignificant,
   Yet your end will increase greatly.

8 ¶"Please inquire of past generations,
   And consider the things searched
   out by their fathers.
9"For we are *only* of yesterday and
   know nothing,
   Because our days on earth are as a
   shadow.
10"Will they not teach you *and* tell
   you,
   And bring forth words from their
   minds?

11 ¶"Can the papyrus grow up without marsh?
   Can the rushes grow without water?
12"While it is still green *and* not cut
   down,
   Yet it withers before any *other*
   plant.
13"So are the paths of all who forget
   God,
   And the hope of the godless will
   perish,
14 Whose confidence is fragile,
   And whose trust a spider's web.
15"He trusts in his house, but it does
   not stand;
   He holds fast to it, but it does not
   endure.
16"He thrives before the sun,
   And his shoots spread out over his
   garden.

17"His roots wrap around a rock pile,
He grasps a house of stones.
18"If he is removed from his place,
Then it will deny him, *saying,* 'I
never saw you.'
19"Behold, this is the joy of His way;
And out of the dust others will
spring.
20"Lo, God will not reject *a man of
integrity,*
Nor will He support the evildoers.
21"He will yet fill your mouth with
laughter,
And your lips with shouting.
22"Those who hate you will be
clothed with shame;
And the tent of the wicked will be
no more."

CHAPTER 9

THEN Job answered,
2"In truth I know that this is so,
But how can a man be in the right
before God?
3"If one wished to dispute with Him,
He could not answer Him once in
a thousand *times.*
4"Wise in heart and mighty in
strength,
Who has defied Him without
harm?
5"*It is God* who removes the mountains, they know not *how,*
When He overturns them in His
anger;
6 Who shakes the earth out of its
place,
And its pillars tremble;
7 Who commands the sun not to
shine,
And sets a seal upon the stars;
8 Who alone stretches out the heavens,
And tramples down the waves of
the sea;
9 Who makes the Bear, Orion, and
the Pleiades,
And the chambers of the south;
10 Who does great things, unfathomable,
And wondrous works without
number.
11"Were He to pass by me, I would
not see Him;
Were He to move past *me,* I
would not perceive Him.
12"Were He to snatch away, who
could restrain Him?

Who could say to Him, 'What art
Thou doing?'

13 ¶"God will not turn back His anger;
Beneath Him crouch the helpers
of Rahab.
14"How then can I answer Him,
And choose my words before
Him?
15"For though I were right, I could
not answer;
I would have to implore the
mercy of my judge.
16"If I called and He answered me,
I could not believe that He was
listening to my voice.
17"For He bruises me with a tempest,
And multiplies my wounds without cause.
18"He will not allow me to get my
breath,
But saturates me with bitterness.
19"If *it is a matter* of power, behold,
He is the strong one!
And if *it is a matter* of justice,
who can summon Him?
20"Though I am righteous, my
mouth will condemn me;
Though I am guiltless, He will
declare me guilty.
21"I am guiltless;
I do not take notice of myself;
I despise my life.
22"It is *all* one; therefore I say,
'He destroys the guiltless and the
wicked.'
23"If the scourge kills suddenly,
He mocks the despair of the innocent.
24"The earth is given into the hand of
the wicked;
He covers the faces of its judges.
If *it is* not He, then who is it?

25 ¶"Now my days are swifter than a
runner;
They flee away, they see no good.
26"They slip by like reed boats,
Like an eagle that swoops on its
prey.
27"Though I say, 'I will forget my
complaint,
I will leave off my *sad* countenance and be cheerful,'
28 I am afraid of all my pains,
I know that Thou wilt not acquit
me.

29"I am accounted wicked,
 Why then should I toil in vain?
30"If I should wash myself with snow
 And cleanse my hands with lye,
31 Yet Thou wouldst plunge me into
 the pit,
 And my own clothes would abhor
 me.
32"For *He is* not a man as I am that I
 may answer Him,
 That we may go to court together.
33"There is no umpire between us,
 Who may lay his hand upon us
 both.
34"Let Him remove His rod from me,
 And let not dread of Him terrify
 me.
35"*Then* I would speak and not fear
 Him;
 But I am not like that in myself.

CHAPTER 10

"I LOATHE my own life;
 I will give full vent to my complaint;
 I will speak in the bitterness of my
 soul.
2"I will say to God, 'Do not condemn me;
 Let me know why Thou dost contend with me.
3 'Is it right for Thee indeed to oppress,
 To reject the labor of Thy hands,
 And to look favorably on the
 schemes of the wicked?
4 'Hast Thou eyes of flesh?
 Or dost Thou see as a man sees?
5 'Are Thy days as the days of a
 mortal,
 Or Thy years as man's years,
6 That Thou shouldst seek for my
 guilt,
 And search after my sin?
7 'According to Thy knowledge I am
 indeed not guilty;
 Yet there is no deliverance from
 Thy hand.

8 ¶ 'Thy hands fashioned and made
 me altogether,
 And wouldst Thou destroy me?
9 'Remember now, that Thou hast
 made me as clay;
 And wouldst Thou turn me into
 dust again?
10 'Didst Thou not pour me out like
 milk,

And curdle me like cheese;
11 Clothe me with skin and flesh,
 And knit me together with bones
 and sinews?
12 'Thou hast granted me life and
 lovingkindness;
 And Thy care has preserved my
 spirit.
13 'Yet these things Thou hast concealed in Thy heart;
 I know that this is within Thee:
14 If I sin, then Thou wouldst take
 note of me,
 And wouldst not acquit me of my
 guilt.
15 'If I am wicked, woe to me!
 And if I am righteous, I dare not
 lift up my head.
 I am sated with disgrace and conscious of my misery.
16 'And should *my head* be lifted up,
 Thou wouldst hunt me like a
 lion;
 And again Thou wouldst show
 Thy power against me.
17 'Thou dost renew Thy witnesses
 against me,
 And increase Thine anger toward
 me,
 Hardship after hardship is with
 me.

18 ¶ 'Why then hast Thou brought
 me out of the womb?
 Would that I had died and no eye
 had seen me!
19 'I should have been as though I
 had not been,
 Carried from womb to tomb.'
20"Would He not let my few days
 alone?
 Withdraw from me that I may
 have a little cheer
21 Before I go—and I shall not return—
 To the land of darkness and deep
 shadow;
22 The land of utter gloom as darkness *itself*,
 Of deep shadow without order,
 And which shines as the darkness."

CHAPTER 11

THEN Zophar the Naamathite answered,
2"Shall a multitude of words go
 unanswered,

And a talkative man be acquitted?
3"Shall your boasts silence men?
And shall you scoff and none rebuke?
4"For you have said, 'My teaching is pure,
And I am innocent in your eyes.'
5"But would that God might speak,
And open His lips against you,
6 And show you the secrets of wisdom!
For sound wisdom has two sides.
Know then that God forgets a part of your iniquity.

7 ¶"Can you discover the depths of God?
Can you discover the limits of the Almighty?
8"*They are* high as the heavens, what can you do?
Deeper than Sheol, what can you know?
9"Its measure is longer than the earth,
And broader than the sea.
10"If He passes by or shuts up,
Or calls an assembly, who can restrain Him?
11"For He knows false men,
And He sees iniquity without investigating.
12"And an idiot will become intelligent
When the foal of a wild donkey is born a man.

13 ¶"If you would direct your heart right,
And spread out your hand to Him;
14 If iniquity is in your hand, put it far away,
And do not let wickedness dwell in your tents.
15"Then, indeed, you could lift up your face without *moral* defect,
And you would be steadfast and not fear.
16"For you would forget *your* trouble,
As waters that have passed by, you would remember *it*.
17"And your life would be brighter than noonday;
Darkness would be like the morning.
18"Then you would trust, because there is hope;

And you would look around and rest securely.
19"You would lie down and none would disturb *you*,
And many would entreat your favor.
20"But the eyes of the wicked will fail,
And there will be no escape for them;
And their hope is to breathe their last."

CHAPTER 12

THEN Job responded,
2"Truly then you are the people,
And with you wisdom will die!
3"But I have intelligence as well as you;
I am not inferior to you.
And who does not know such things as these?
4"I am a joke to my friends.
The one who called on God, and He answered him;
The just *and* blameless *man* is a joke.
5"He who is at ease holds calamity in contempt,
As prepared for those whose feet slip.
6"The tents of the destroyers prosper,
And those who provoke God are secure,
Whom God brings into ⁵their power.

7 ¶"But now ask the beasts, and let them teach you;
And the birds of the heavens, and let them tell you.
8"Or speak to the earth, and let it teach you;
And let the fish of the sea declare to you.
9"Who among all these does not know
That the hand of the LORD has done this,
10 In whose hand is the life of every living thing,
And the breath of all mankind?
11"Does not the ear test words,
As the palate tastes its food?
12"Wisdom is with aged men,
With long life is understanding.

⁵ Lit., *his*

13 ¶"With Him are wisdom and
      might;
   To Him belong counsel and un-
      derstanding.
14"Behold, He tears down, and it
      cannot be rebuilt;
   He imprisons a man, and there
      can be no release.
15"Behold, He restrains the waters,
      and they dry up;
   And He sends them out, and they
      inundate the earth.
16"With Him are strength and sound
      wisdom,
   The misled and the misleader be-
      long to Him.
17"He makes counselors walk bare-
      foot,
   And makes fools of judges.
18"He loosens the bond of kings,
   And binds their loins with a girdle.
19"He makes priests walk barefoot,
   And overthrows the secure ones.
20"He deprives the trusted ones of
      speech,
   And takes away the discernment
      of the elders.
21"He pours contempt on nobles,
   And loosens the belt of the strong.
22"He reveals mysteries from the
      darkness,
   And brings the deep darkness into
      light.
23"He makes the nations great, then
      destroys them;
   He enlarges the nations, then
      leads them away.
24"He deprives of intelligence the
      chiefs of the earth's people,
   And makes them wander in a
      pathless waste.
25"They grope in darkness with no
      light,
   And He makes them stagger like a
      drunken man.

CHAPTER 13

"BEHOLD, my eye has seen all *this*,
   My ear has heard and understood
      it.
2"What you know I also know.
   I am not inferior to you.

3 ¶"But I would speak to the Al-
      mighty,
   And I desire to argue with God.
4"But you smear with lies;
   You are all worthless physicians.

5"O that you would be completely
      silent,
   And that it would become your
      wisdom!
6"Please hear my argument,
   And listen to the contentions of
      my lips.
7"Will you speak what is unjust for
      God,
   And speak what is deceitful for
      Him?
8"Will you show partiality for Him?
   Will you contend for God?
9"Will it be well when He examines
      you?
   Or will you deceive Him as one
      deceives a man?
10"He will surely reprove you,
   If you secretly show partiality.
11"Will not His majesty terrify you,
   And the dread of Him fall on you?
12"Your memorable sayings are
      proverbs of ashes,
   Your defenses are defenses of
      clay.

13 ¶"Be silent before me so that I
      may speak;
   Then let come on me what may.
14"Why should I take my flesh in my
      teeth,
   And put my life in my hands?
15"Though He slay me,
   I will hope in Him.
   Nevertheless I will argue my ways
      before Him.
16"This also will be my salvation,
   For a godless man may not come
      before His presence.
17"Listen carefully to my speech,
   And let my declaration *fill* your
      ears.
18"Behold now, I have prepared my
      case;
   I know that I will be vindicated.
19"Who will contend with me?
   For then I would be silent and die.

20 ¶"Only two things do not do to
      me,
   Then I will not hide from Thy
      face:
21 Remove Thy hand from me,
   And let not the dread of Thee
      terrify me.
22"Then call, and I will answer;
   Or let me speak, then reply to me.
23"How many are my iniquities and
      sins?

Make known to me my rebellion
and my sin.
24"Why dost Thou hide Thy face,
And consider me Thine enemy?
25"Wilt Thou cause a driven leaf to
tremble?
Or wilt Thou pursue the dry
chaff?
26"For Thou dost write bitter things
against me,
And dost make me to inherit the
iniquities of my youth.
27"Thou dost put my feet in the
stocks,
And dost watch all my paths;
Thou dost set a limit for the soles
of my feet,
28 While I am decaying like a rotten
thing,
Like a garment that is moth-
eaten.

CHAPTER 14

"MAN, who is born of woman,
Is short-lived and full of turmoil.
2"Like a flower he comes forth and
withers.
He also flees like a shadow and
does not remain.
3"Thou also dost open Thine eyes
on him,
And bring him into judgment with
Thyself.
4"Who can make the clean out of
the unclean?
No one!
5"Since his days are determined,
The number of his months is with
Thee,
And his limits Thou hast set so
that he cannot pass.
6"Turn Thy gaze from him that he
may rest,
Until he fulfills his day like a hired
man.

7 ¶"For there is hope for a tree,
When it is cut down, that it will
sprout again,
And its shoots will not fail.
8"Though its roots grow old in the
ground,
And its stump dies in the dry soil,
9 At the scent of water it will flourish
And put forth sprigs like a plant.
10"But man dies and lies prostrate.
Man expires, and where is he?

11"As water evaporates from the sea,
And a river becomes parched and
dried up,
12 So man lies down and does not
rise.
Until the heavens be no more,
He will not awake nor be aroused
out of his sleep.

13 ¶"Oh that Thou wouldst hide me
in Sheol,
That Thou wouldst conceal me
until Thy wrath returns to
Thee,
That Thou wouldst set a limit for
me and remember me!
14"If a man dies, will he live again?
All the days of my struggle I will
wait,
Until my change comes.
15"Thou wilt call, and I will answer
Thee;
Thou wilt long for the work of
Thy hands.
16"For now Thou dost number my
steps,
Thou dost not observe my sin.
17"My transgression is sealed up in a
bag,
And Thou dost wrap up my iniquity.

18 ¶"But the falling mountain crum-
bles away,
And the rock moves from its
place;
19 Water wears away stones,
Its torrents wash away the dust of
the earth;
So Thou dost destroy man's hope.
20"Thou dost forever overpower him
and he departs;
Thou dost change his appearance
and send him away.
21"His sons achieve honor, but he
does not know it;
Or they become insignificant, but
he does not perceive it.
22"But his body pains him,
And he mourns only for himself."

CHAPTER 15

THEN Eliphaz the Temanite responded,
2"Should a wise man answer with
windy knowledge,
And fill himself with the east
wind?

3"Should he argue with useless talk,
Or with words which are not profitable?
4"Indeed, you do away with reverence,
And hinder meditation before God.
5"For your guilt teaches your mouth,
And you choose the language of the crafty.
6"Your own mouth condemns you, and not I;
And your own lips testify against you.

7 ¶"Were you the first man to be born,
Or were you brought forth before the hills?
8"Do you hear the secret counsel of God,
And limit wisdom to yourself?
9"What do you know that we do not know?
What do you understand that we do not?
10"Both the gray-haired and the aged are among us,
Older than your father.
11"Are the consolations of God too small for you,
Even the word *spoken* gently with you?
12"Why does your heart carry you away?
And why do your eyes flash,
13 That you should turn your spirit against God,
And allow *such* words to go out of your mouth?
14"What is man, that he should be pure,
Or he who is born of a woman, that he should be righteous?
15"Behold, He puts no trust in His holy ones,
And the heavens are not pure in His sight;
16 How much less one who is detestable and corrupt,
Man, who drinks iniquity like water!

17 ¶"I will tell you, listen to me;
And what I have seen I will also declare;
18 What wise men have told,
And have not concealed from their fathers,
19 To whom alone the land was given,
And no alien passed among them.
20"The wicked man writhes in pain all *his* days,
And numbered are the years stored up for the ruthless.
21"Sounds of terror are in his ears,
While at peace the destroyer comes upon him.
22"He does not believe that he will return from darkness,
And he is destined for the sword.
23"He wanders about for food, saying, 'Where is it?'
He knows that a day of darkness is at hand.
24"Distress and anguish terrify him,
They overpower him like a king ready for the attack,
25 Because he has stretched out his hand against God,
And conducts himself arrogantly against the Almighty.
26"He rushes headlong at Him
With his massive shield.
27"For he has covered his face with his fat,
And made his thighs heavy with flesh.
28"And he has lived in desolate cities,
In houses no one would inhabit,
Which are destined to become ruins.
29"He will not become rich, nor will his wealth endure;
And his grain will not bend down to the ground.
30"He will not escape from darkness;
The flame will wither his shoots,
And by the breath of His mouth he will go away.
31"Let him not trust in emptiness, deceiving himself;
For emptiness will be his reward.
32"It will be accomplished before his time,
And his palm branch will not be green.
33"He will drop off his unripe grape like the vine,
And will cast off his flower like the olive tree.
34"For the company of the godless is barren,
And fire consumes the tents of the corrupt.

35"They conceive mischief and bring
   forth iniquity,
   And their mind prepares deception."

CHAPTER 16

THEN Job answered,
2"I have heard many such things;
   Sorry comforters are you all.
3"Is there *no* limit to windy words?
   Or what plagues you that you
   answer?
4"I too could speak like you,
   If I were in your place.
   I could compose words against
   you,
   And shake my head at you.
5"I could strengthen you with my
   mouth,
   And the solace of my lips could
   lessen *your pain.*

6 ¶"If I speak, my pain is not less-
   ened,
   And if I hold back, what has left
   me?
7"But now He has exhausted me;
   Thou hast laid waste all my company.
8"And Thou hast shriveled me up,
   It has become a witness;
   And my leanness rises up against
   me,
   It testifies to my face.
9"His anger has torn me and hunted
   me down,
   He has gnashed at me with His
   teeth;
   My adversary glares at me.
10"They have gaped at me with their
   mouth,
   They have slapped me on the
   cheek with contempt;
   They have massed themselves
   against me.
11"God hands me over to ruffians,
   And tosses me into the hands of
   the wicked.
12"I was at ease, but He shattered
   me,
   And He has grasped me by the
   neck and shaken me to pieces;
   He has also set me up as His target.
13"His arrows surround me.
   Without mercy He splits my kidneys open;

He pours out my gall on the
   ground.
14"He breaks through me with
   breach after breach;
   He runs at me like a warrior.
15"I have sewed sackcloth over my
   skin,
   And thrust my horn in the dust.
16"My face is flushed from weeping,
   And deep darkness is on my eyelids,
17 Although there is no violence in
   my hands,
   And my prayer is pure.

18 ¶"O earth, do not cover my blood,
   And let there be no *resting* place
   for my cry.
19"Even now, behold, my witness is
   in heaven,
   And my advocate is on high.
20"My friends are my scoffers;
   My eye weeps to God.
21"O that a man might plead with
   God
   As a man with his neighbor!
22"For when a few years are past,
   I shall go the way of no return.

CHAPTER 17

"MY spirit is broken, my days are
   extinguished,
   The grave is *ready* for me.
2"Surely mockers are with me,
   And my eye gazes on their provocation.

3 ¶"Lay down, now, a pledge for me
   with Thyself;
   Who is there that will be my guar-
   antor?
4"For Thou hast kept their heart
   from understanding;
   Therefore Thou wilt not exalt
   them.
5"He who informs against friends
   for a share *of the spoil,*
   The eyes of his children also shall
   languish.

6 ¶"But He has made me a byword
   of the people,
   And I am one at whom men spit.
7"My eye has also grown dim because of grief,
   And all my members are as a
   shadow.

8"The upright shall be appalled at
    this,
  And the innocent shall stir up
    himself against the godless.
9"Nevertheless the righteous shall
    hold to his way,
  And he who has clean hands shall
    grow stronger and stronger.
10"But come again all of you now,
  For I do not find a wise man
    among you.
11"My days are past, my plans are
    torn apart,
  Even the wishes of my heart.
12"They make night into day, *saying,*
  'The light is near,' in the presence
    of darkness.
13"If I look for Sheol as my home,
  I make my bed in the darkness;
14 If I call to the pit, 'You are my
    father';
  To the worm, 'my mother and my
    sister';
15 Where now is my hope?
  And who regards my hope?
16"Will it go down with me to Sheol?
  Shall we together go down into
    the dust?"

CHAPTER 18

THEN Bildad the Shuhite responded,
2"How long will you hunt for
    words?
  Show understanding and then we
    can talk.
3"Why are we regarded as beasts,
  As stupid in your eyes?
4"O you who tear yourself in your
    anger—
  For your sake is the earth to be
    abandoned,
  Or the rock to be moved from its
    place?

5 ¶"Indeed, the light of the wicked
    goes out,
  And the flame of his fire gives no
    light.
6"The light in his tent is darkened,
  And his lamp goes out above him.
7"His vigorous stride is shortened,
  And his own scheme brings him
    down.
8"For he is thrown into the net by
    his own feet,
  And he steps on the webbing.
9"A snare seizes *him* by the heel,
  And a trap snaps shut on him.

10"A noose for him is hidden in the
    ground,
  And a trap for him on the path.
11"All around terrors frighten him,
  And harry him at every step.
12"His strength is famished,
  And calamity is ready at his side.
13"His skin is devoured by disease,
  The first-born of death devours
    his limbs.
14"He is torn from the security of his
    tent,
  And they march him before the
    king of terrors.
15"There dwells in his tent nothing of
    his;
  Brimstone is scattered on his habi-
    tation.
16"His roots are dried below,
  And his branch is cut off above.
17"Memory of him perishes from the
    earth,
  And he has no name abroad.
18"He is driven from light into dark-
    ness,
  And chased from the inhabited
    world.
19"He has no offspring or posterity
    among his people,
  Nor any survivor where he so-
    journed.
20"Those in the west are appalled at
    his fate,
  And those in the east are seized
    with horror.
21"Surely such are the dwellings of
    the wicked,
  And this is the place of him who
    does not know God."

CHAPTER 19

THEN Job responded,
2"How long will you torment me,
  And crush me with words?
3"These ten times you have insulted
    me,
  You are not ashamed to wrong
    me.
4"Even if I have truly erred,
  My error lodges with me.
5"If indeed you vaunt yourselves
    against me,
  And prove my disgrace to me,
6 Know then that God has wronged
    me,
  And has closed His net around
    me.

7 ¶"Behold, I cry, 'Violence!' but I get no answer;
I shout for help, but there is no justice.

8"He has walled up my way so that I cannot pass;
And He has put darkness on my paths.

9"He has stripped my honor from me,
And removed the crown from my head.

10"He breaks me down on every side, and I am gone;
And He has uprooted my hope like a tree.

11"He has also kindled His anger against me,
And considered me as His enemy.

12"His troops come together,
And build up their way against me,
And camp around my tent.

13 ¶"He has removed my brothers far from me,
And my acquaintances are completely estranged from me.

14"My relatives have failed,
And my intimate friends have forgotten me.

15"Those who live in my house and my maids consider me a stranger.
I am a foreigner in their sight.

16"I call to my servant, but he does not answer,
I have to implore him with my mouth.

17"My breath is offensive to my wife,
And I am loathsome to my own brothers.

18"Even young children despise me;
I rise up and they speak against me.

19"All my associates abhor me,
And those I love have turned against me.

20"My bone clings to my skin and my flesh,
And I have escaped *only* by the skin of my teeth.

21"Pity me, pity me, O you my friends,
For the hand of God has struck me.

22"Why do you persecute me as God *does*,

And are not satisfied with my flesh?

23 ¶"Oh that my words were written!
Oh that they were inscribed in a book!

24"That with an iron stylus and lead
They were engraved in the rock forever!

25"And as for me, I know that my Redeemer lives,
And at the last He will take His stand on the earth.

26"Even after my skin is destroyed,
Yet from my flesh I shall see God;

27 Whom I myself shall behold,
And whom my eyes shall see and not another.
My heart faints within me.

28"If you say, 'How shall we persecute him?'
And 'What pretext for a case against him can we find?'

29 *Then* be afraid of the sword for yourselves,
For wrath *brings* the punishment of the sword,
So that you may know there is judgment."

CHAPTER 20

THEN Zophar the Naamathite answered,

2"Therefore my disquieting thoughts make me respond,
Even because of my inward agitation.

3"I listened to the reproof which insults me,
And the spirit of my understanding makes me answer.

4"Do you know this from of old,
From the establishment of man on earth,

5 That the triumphing of the wicked is short,
And the joy of the godless momentary?

6"Though his loftiness reaches the heavens,
And his head touches the clouds,

7 He perishes forever like his refuse;
Those who have seen him will say, 'Where is he?'

8"He flies away like a dream, and they cannot find him;
Even like a vision of the night he is chased away.

9"The eye which saw him sees him
no more,
And his place no longer beholds
him.
10"His sons favor the poor,
And his hands give back his
wealth.
11"His bones are full of his youthful
vigor,
But it lies down with him in the
dust.

12 ¶"Though evil is sweet in his
mouth,
And he hides it under his tongue,
13 *Though* he desires it and will not
let it go,
But holds it in his mouth,
14 *Yet* his food in his stomach is
changed
To the venom of cobras within
him.
15"He swallows riches,
But will vomit them up;
God will expel them from his
belly.
16"He sucks the poison of cobras;
The viper's tongue slays him.
17"He does not look at the streams,
The rivers flowing with honey and
curds.
18"He returns what he has attained
And cannot swallow *it;*
As to the riches of his trading,
He cannot even enjoy *them.*
19"For he has oppressed *and* forsaken the poor;
He has seized a house which he
has not built.

20 ¶"Because he knew no quiet
within him
He does not retain anything he
desires.
21"Nothing remains for him to devour,
Therefore his prosperity does not
endure.
22"In the fulness of his plenty he will
be cramped;
The hand of everyone who suffers
will come *against* him.
23"When he fills his belly,
God will send His fierce anger on
him
And will rain *it* on him while he is
eating.
24"He may flee from the iron
weapon,

But the bronze bow will pierce
him.
25"It is drawn forth and comes out of
his back,
Even the glittering point from his
gall.
Terrors come upon him,
26 Complete darkness is held in reserve for his treasures,
And unfanned fire will devour
him;
It will consume the survivor in his
tent.
27"The heavens will reveal his iniquity,
And the earth will rise up against
him.
28"The increase of his house will
depart;
His possessions will flow away in
the day of His anger.
29"This is the wicked man's portion
from God,
Even the heritage decreed to him
by God."

CHAPTER 21

THEN Job answered,
2"Listen carefully to my speech,
And let this be your *way of* consolation.
3"Bear with me that I may speak;
Then after I have spoken, you
may mock.
4"As for me, is my complaint to
man?
And why should I not be impatient?
5"Look at me, and be astonished,
And put *your* hand over *your*
mouth.
6"Even when I remember, I am disturbed,
And horror takes hold of my flesh.
7"Why do the wicked *still* live,
Continue on, also become very
powerful?
8"Their descendants are established
with them in their sight,
And their offspring before their
eyes,
9 Their houses are safe from fear,
Neither is the rod of God on them.
10"His ox mates without fail;
His cow calves and does not abort.
11"They send forth their little ones
like the flock,
And their children skip about.

12"They sing to the timbrel and harp
And rejoice at the sound of the
flute.
13"They spend their days in prosperity,
And suddenly they go down to
Sheol.
14"And they say to God, 'Depart
from us!
We do not even desire the knowledge of Thy ways.
15 'Who is the Almighty, that we
should serve Him,
And what would we gain if we
entreat Him?'
16"Behold, their prosperity is not in
their hand;
The counsel of the wicked is far
from me.

17 ¶"How often is the lamp of the
wicked put out,
Or *does* their calamity fall on
them?
Does God apportion destruction
in His anger?
18"Are they as straw before the wind,
And like chaff which the storm
carries away?
19"*You say*, 'God stores away a
man's iniquity for his sons.'
Let God repay him so that he may
know *it*.
20"Let his own eyes see his decay,
And let him drink of the wrath of
the Almighty.
21"For what does he care for his
household ⁶after him,
When the number of his months
is cut off?
22"Can anyone teach God knowledge,
In that He judges those on high?
23"One dies in his full strength,
Being wholly at ease and satisfied;
24 His sides are filled out with fat,
And the marrow of his bones is
moist,
25 While another dies with a bitter
soul,
Never even tasting *anything*
good.
26"Together they lie down in the
dust,
And worms cover them.

⁶ I.e., after he dies

27 ¶"Behold, I know your thoughts,
And the plans by which you
would wrong me.
28"For you say, 'Where is the house
of the nobleman,
And where is the tent, the dwelling places of the wicked?'
29"Have you not asked wayfaring
men,
And do you not recognize their
witness?
30"For the wicked is reserved for the
day of calamity;
They will be led forth at the day of
fury.
31"Who will confront him with his
actions,
And who will repay him for what
he has done?
32"While he is carried to the grave,
Men will keep watch over *his*
tomb.
33"The clods of the valley will gently
cover him;
Moreover, all men will follow after him,
While countless ones *go* before
him.
34"How then will you vainly comfort
me,
For your answers remain *full of*
falsehood?"

CHAPTER 22

T HEN Eliphaz the Temanite responded,
2"Can a vigorous man be of use to
God,
Or a wise man be useful to himself?
3"Is there any pleasure to the Almighty if you are righteous,
Or profit if you make your ways
perfect?
4"Is it because of your reverence
that He reproves you,
That He enters into judgment
against you?
5"Is not your wickedness great,
And your iniquities without end?
6"For you have taken pledges of
your brothers without cause,
And stripped men naked.
7"To the weary you have given no
water to drink,
And from the hungry you have
withheld bread.

8"But the earth belongs to the mighty man,
And the honorable man dwells in it.

9"You have sent widows away empty,
And the strength of the orphans has been crushed.

10"Therefore snares surround you,
And sudden dread terrifies you,

11 Or darkness, so that you cannot see,
And an abundance of water covers you.

12 ¶"Is not God *in* the height of heaven?
Look also at the distant stars, how high they are!

13"And you say, 'What does God know?
Can He judge through the thick darkness?

14 'Clouds are a hiding place for Him, so that He cannot see;
And He walks on the vault of heaven.'

15"Will you keep to the ancient path
Which wicked men have trod,

16 Who were snatched away before their time,
Whose foundations were washed away by a river?

17"They said to God, 'Depart from us!'
And 'What can the Almighty do to them?'

18"Yet He filled their houses with good *things;*
But the counsel of the wicked is far from me.

19"The righteous see and are glad,
And the innocent mock them,

20 *Saying,* 'Truly our adversaries are cut off,
And their abundance the fire has consumed.'

21 ¶"Yield now and be at peace with Him;
Thereby good will come to you.

22"Please receive instruction from His mouth,
And establish His words in your heart.

23"If you return to the Almighty, you will be restored;
If you remove unrighteousness far from your tent,

24 And place *your* gold in the dust,
And *the gold of* Ophir among the stones of the brooks,

25 Then the Almighty will be your gold
And choice silver to you.

26"For then you will delight in the Almighty,
And lift up your face to God.

27"You will pray to Him, and He will hear you;
And you will pay your vows.

28"You will also decree a thing, and it will be established for you;
And light will shine on your ways.

29"When you are cast down, you will speak with confidence
And the humble person He will save.

30"He will deliver one who is not innocent,
And he will be delivered through the cleanness of your hands."

CHAPTER 23

THEN Job replied,

2"Even today my complaint is rebellion;
His hand is heavy despite my groaning.

3"Oh that I knew where I might find Him,
That I might come to His seat!

4"I would present *my* case before Him
And fill my mouth with arguments.

5"I would learn the words *which* He would answer,
And perceive what He would say to me.

6"Would He contend with me by the greatness of *His* power?
No, surely He would pay attention to me.

7"There the upright would reason with Him;
And I would be delivered forever from my Judge.

8 ¶"Behold, I go forward but He is not *there,*
And backward, but I cannot perceive Him;

9 When He acts on the left, I cannot behold *Him;*

He turns on the right, I cannot see
Him.
10"But He knows the way I take;
When He has tried me, I shall
come forth as gold.
11"My foot has held fast to His path;
I have kept His way and not
turned aside.
12"I have not departed from the command of His lips;
I have treasured the words of His
mouth more than my necessary
food.
13"But He is unique and who can
turn Him?
And *what* His soul desires, that
He does.
14"For He performs what is appointed for me,
And many such *decrees* are with
Him.
15"Therefore, I would be dismayed at
His presence;
When I consider, I am terrified of
Him.
16"*It is* God *who* has made my heart
faint,
And the Almighty *who* has dismayed me,
17 But I am not silenced by the darkness,
Nor deep gloom *which* covers *me*.

CHAPTER 24

" W HY are times not stored up by
the Almighty,
And why do those who know Him
not see His days?
2"Some remove the landmarks;
They seize and devour flocks.
3"They drive away the donkeys of
the orphans;
They take the widow's ox for a
pledge.
4"They push the needy aside from
the road;
The poor of the land are made to
hide themselves altogether.
5"Behold, as wild donkeys in the
wilderness
They go forth seeking food in
their activity,
As bread for *their* children in the
desert.
6"They harvest their fodder in the
field,
And they glean the vineyard of
the wicked.

7"They spend the night naked, without clothing,
And have no covering against the
cold.
8"They are wet with the mountain
rains,
And they hug the rock for want of
a shelter.
9"Others snatch the orphan from
the breast,
And against the poor they take a
pledge.
10"They cause *the poor* to go about
naked without clothing,
And they take away the sheaves
from the hungry.
11"Within the walls they produce oil;
They tread wine presses but
thirst.
12"From the city men groan,
And the souls of the wounded cry
out;
Yet God does not pay attention to
folly.

13 ¶"Others have been with those
who rebel against the light;
They do not want to know its
ways,
Nor abide in its paths.
14"The murderer arises at dawn;
He kills the poor and the needy,
And at night he is as a thief.
15"And the eye of the adulterer waits
for the twilight,
Saying, 'No eye will see me.'
And he disguises his face.
16"In the dark they dig into houses,
They shut themselves up by day;
They do not know the light.
17"For the morning is the same to
him as thick darkness,
For he is familiar with the terrors
of thick darkness.

18 ¶"They are insignificant on the
surface of the water;
Their portion is cursed on the
earth.
They do not turn toward the vineyards.
19"Drought and heat consume the
snow waters,
So does Sheol *those who* have
sinned.
20"A mother will forget him;
The worm feeds sweetly till he is
remembered no more.

And wickedness will be broken
like a tree.

21"He wrongs the barren woman,
And does no good for the widow.

22"But He drags off the valiant by His
power;
He rises, but no one has assurance
of life.

23"He provides them with security,
and they are supported;
And His eyes are on their ways.

24"They are exalted a little while,
then they are gone;
Moreover, they are brought low
and like everything gathered
up;
Even like the heads of grain they
are cut off.

25"Now if it is not so, who can prove
me a liar,
And make my speech worthless?"

CHAPTER 25

THEN Bildad the Shuhite answered,

2"Dominion and awe belong to Him
Who establishes peace in His
heights.

3"Is there any number to His
troops?
And upon whom does His light
not rise?

4"How then can a man be just with
God?
Or how can he be clean who is
born of woman?

5"If even the moon has no brightness
And the stars are not pure in His
sight,

6 How much less man, *that* maggot,
And the son of man, *that* worm!"

CHAPTER 26

THEN Job responded,

2"What a help you are to the weak!
How you have saved the arm
without strength!

3"What counsel you have given to
one without wisdom!
What helpful insight you have
abundantly provided!

4"To whom have you uttered
words?
And whose spirit was expressed
through you?

5 ¶"The departed spirits tremble
Under the waters and their inhabitants.

6"Naked is Sheol before Him
And [7]Abaddon has no covering.

7"He stretches out the north over
empty space,
And hangs the earth on nothing.

8"He wraps up the waters in His
clouds;
And the cloud does not burst under them.

9"He obscures the face of the full
moon,
And spreads His cloud over it.

10"He has inscribed a circle on the
surface of the waters,
At the boundary of light and darkness.

11"The pillars of heaven tremble,
And are amazed at His rebuke.

12"He quieted the sea with His
power,
And by His understanding He
shattered Rahab.

13"By His breath the heavens are
cleared;
His hand has pierced the fleeing
serpent.

14"Behold, these are the fringes of
His ways;
And how faint a word we hear of
Him!
But His mighty thunder, who can
understand?"

CHAPTER 27

THEN Job continued his discourse
and said,

2"As God lives, who has taken away
my right,
And the Almighty, who has embittered my soul,

3 For as long as life is in me,
And the breath of God is in my
nostrils,

4 My lips certainly will not speak
unjustly,
Nor will my tongue mutter deceit.

5"Far be it from me that I should
declare you right;
Till I die I will not put away my
integrity from me.

6"I hold fast my righteousness and
will not let it go.
My heart does not reproach any
of my days.

7 ¶"May my enemy be as the
wicked,

[7] I.e., place of destruction

And my opponent as the unjust.

8"For what is the hope of the godless when he is cut off,
When God requires his life?

9"Will God hear his cry,
When distress comes upon him?

10"Will he take delight in the Almighty,
Will he call on God at all times?

11"I will instruct you in the power of God;
What is with the Almighty I will not conceal.

12"Behold, all of you have seen *it*;
Why then do you act foolishly?

13 ¶"This is the portion of a wicked man from God,
And the inheritance *which* tyrants receive from the Almighty.

14"Though his sons are many, they are destined for the sword;
And his descendants will not be satisfied with bread.

15"His survivors will be buried because of the plague,
And their widows will not be able to weep.

16"Though he piles up silver like dust,
And prepares garments as *plentiful as* the clay;

17 He may prepare *it*, but the just will wear *it*,
And the innocent will divide the silver.

18"He has built his house like the spider's web,
Or as a hut *which* the watchman has made.

19"He lies down rich, but never again;
He opens his eyes, and it is no more.

20"Terrors overtake him like a flood;
A tempest steals him away in the night.

21"The east wind carries him away, and he is gone,
For it whirls him away from his place.

22"For it will hurl at him without sparing;
He will surely try to flee from its power.

23"*Men* will clap their hands at him,
And will hiss him from his place.

CHAPTER 28

"SURELY there is a [8]mine for silver,
And a place where they refine gold.

2"Iron is taken from the dust,
And from rock copper is smelted.

3"*Man* puts an end to darkness,
And to the farthest limit he searches out
The rock in gloom and deep shadow.

4"He sinks a shaft far from habitation,
Forgotten by the foot;
They hang and swing to and fro far from men.

5"The earth, from it comes food,
And underneath it is turned up as fire.

6"Its rocks are the source of sapphires,
And its dust *contains* gold.

7"The path no bird of prey knows,
Nor has the falcon's eye caught sight of it.

8"The proud beasts have not trodden it,
Nor has the *fierce* lion passed over it.

9"He puts his hand on the flint;
He overturns the mountains at the base.

10"He hews out channels through the rocks;
And his eye sees anything precious.

11"He dams up the streams from flowing;
And what is hidden he brings out to the light.

12 ¶"But where can wisdom be found?
And where is the place of understanding?

13"Man does not know its value,
Nor is it found in the land of the living.

14"The deep says, 'It is not in me';
And the sea says, 'It is not with me.'

15"Pure gold cannot be given in exchange for it,
Nor can silver be weighed as its price.

16"It cannot be valued in the gold of Ophir,

[8] Or, *source*

In precious onyx, or sapphire.
17"Gold or glass cannot equal it,
    Nor can it be exchanged for arti-
        cles of fine gold.
18"Coral and crystal are not to be
        mentioned;
    And the acquisition of wisdom is
        above *that of* pearls.
19"The topaz of Ethiopia cannot
        equal it,
    Nor can it be valued in pure gold.
20"Where then does wisdom come
        from?
    And where is the place of under-
        standing?
21"Thus it is hidden from the eyes of
        all living,
    And concealed from the birds of
        the sky.
22"⁹Abaddon and Death say,
    'With our ears we have heard a
        report of it.'

23 ¶"God understands its way;
    And He knows its place.
24"For He looks to the ends of the
        earth,
    And sees everything under the
        heavens.
25"When He imparted weight to the
        wind,
    And meted out the waters by
        measure,
26 When He set a limit for the rain,
    And a course for the thunderbolt,
27 Then He saw it and declared it;
    He established it and also
        searched it out.
28"And to man He said, 'Behold, the
        fear of the Lord, that is wisdom;
    And to depart from evil is under-
        standing.' "

CHAPTER 29

AND Job again took up his discourse
and said,
2"Oh that I were as in months gone
        by,
    As in the days when God watched
        over me;
3 When His lamp shone over my
        head,
    And by His light I walked through
        darkness;
4 As I was in ¹⁰the prime of my
        days,

When the friendship of God *was*
        over my tent;
5 When the Almighty was yet with
        me,
    And my children were around me;
6 When my steps were bathed in
        butter,
    And the rock poured out for me
        streams of oil!
7"When I went out to the gate of
        the city,
    When I took my seat in the
        square;
8 The young men saw me and hid
        themselves,
    And the old men arose *and* stood.
9"The princes stopped talking,
    And put *their* hands on their
        mouths;
10 The voice of the nobles was
        hushed,
    And their tongue stuck to their
        palate.
11"For when the ear heard, it called
        me blessed;
    And when the eye saw, it gave
        witness of me,
12 Because I delivered the poor who
        cried for help,
    And the orphan who had no
        helper.
13"The blessing of the one ready to
        perish came upon me,
    And I made the widow's heart
        sing for joy.
14"I put on righteousness, and it
        clothed me;
    My justice was like a robe and a
        turban.
15"I was eyes to the blind,
    And feet to the lame.
16"I was a father to the needy,
    And I investigated the case which
        I did not know.
17"And I broke the jaws of the
        wicked,
    And snatched the prey from his
        teeth.
18"Then I thought, 'I shall die in my
        nest,
    And I shall multiply *my* days as
        the sand.
19 'My root is spread out to the wa-
        ters,
    And dew lies all night on my
        branch.
20 'My glory is *ever* new with me,

⁹ I.e., Destruction   ¹⁰ Lit., *the days of my autumn*

And my bow is renewed in my hand.'

21 ¶"To me they listened and waited,
And kept silent for my counsel.
22"After my words they did not speak again,
And my speech dropped on them.
23"And they waited for me as for the rain,
And opened their mouth as for the spring rain.
24"I smiled on them when they did not believe,
And the light of my face they did not cast down.
25"I chose a way for them and sat as chief,
And dwelt as a king among the troops,
As one who comforted the mourners.

CHAPTER 30

"BUT now those younger than I mock me,
Whose fathers I disdained to put with the dogs of my flock.
2"Indeed, what *good was* the strength of their hands to me?
Vigor had perished from them.
3"From want and famine they are gaunt
Who gnaw the dry ground by night in waste and desolation,
4 Who pluck [11]mallow by the bushes,
And whose food is the root of the broom shrub.
5"They are driven from the community;
They shout against them as *against* a thief,
6 So that they dwell in dreadful valleys,
In holes of the earth and of the rocks.
7"Among the bushes they cry out;
Under the nettles they are gathered together.
8"Fools, even those without a name,
They were scourged from the land.

9 ¶"And now I have become their taunt,

I have even become a byword to them.
10"They abhor me *and* stand aloof from me,
And they do not refrain from spitting at my face.
11"Because He has loosed His bowstring and afflicted me,
They have cast off the bridle before me.
12"On the right hand their brood arises;
They thrust aside my feet and build up against me their ways of destruction.
13"They break up my path,
They profit from my destruction,
No one restrains them.
14"As *through* a wide breach they come,
Amid the tempest they roll on.
15"Terrors are turned against me,
They pursue my honor as the wind,
And my prosperity has passed away like a cloud.

16 ¶"And now my soul is poured out within me;
Days of affliction have seized me.
17"At night it pierces my bones within me,
And my gnawing *pains* take no rest.
18"By a great force my garment is distorted;
It binds me about as the collar of my coat.
19"He has cast me into the mire,
And I have become like dust and ashes.
20"I cry out to Thee for help, but Thou dost not answer me;
I stand up, and Thou dost turn Thy attention against me.
21"Thou hast become cruel to me;
With the might of Thy hand Thou dost persecute me.
22"Thou dost lift me up to the wind *and* cause me to ride;
And Thou dost dissolve me in a storm.
23"For I know that Thou wilt bring me to death
And to the house of meeting for all living.

[11] I.e., plant of the salt marshes

24 ¶"Yet does not one in a heap of ruins stretch out *his* hand,
   Or in his disaster therefore cry out for help?
25"Have I not wept for the one whose life is hard?
   Was not my soul grieved for the needy?
26"When I expected good, then evil came;
   When I waited for light, then darkness came.
27"I am seething within, and cannot relax;
   Days of affliction confront me.
28"I go about mourning without comfort;
   I stand up in the assembly *and* cry out for help.
29"I have become a brother to jackals,
   And a companion of ostriches.
30"My skin turns black on me,
   And my bones burn with fever.
31"Therefore my harp is turned to mourning,
   And my flute to the sound of those who weep.

CHAPTER 31

"I HAVE made a covenant with my eyes;
   How then could I gaze at a virgin?
2"And what is the portion of God from above
   Or the heritage of the Almighty from on high?
3"Is it not calamity to the unjust,
   And disaster to those who work iniquity?
4"Does He not see my ways,
   And number all my steps?

5 ¶"If I have walked with falsehood,
   And my foot has hastened after deceit,
6 Let Him weigh me with accurate scales,
   And let God know my integrity.
7"If my step has turned from the way,
   Or my heart followed my eyes,
   Or if any spot has stuck to my hands,
8 Let me sow and another eat,
   And let my crops be uprooted.

9 ¶"If my heart has been enticed by a woman,

Or I have lurked at my neighbor's doorway,
10 May my wife grind for another,
   And let others kneel down over her.
11"For that would be a lustful crime;
   Moreover, it would be an iniquity *punishable by* judges.
12"For it would be fire that consumes to Abaddon,
   And would uproot all my increase.

13 ¶"If I have despised the claim of my male or female slaves
   When they filed a complaint against me,
14 What then could I do when God arises,
   And when He calls me to account, what will I answer Him?
15"Did not He who made me in the womb make him,
   And the same one fashion us in the womb?

16 ¶"If I have kept the poor from *their* desire,
   Or have caused the eyes of the widow to fail,
17 Or have eaten my morsel alone,
   And the orphan has not shared it
18 (But from my youth he grew up with me as with a father,
   And from infancy I guided her),
19 If I have seen anyone perish for lack of clothing,
   Or that the needy had no covering,
20 If his loins have not thanked me,
   And if he has not been warmed with the fleece of my sheep,
21 If I have lifted up my hand against the orphan,
   Because I saw I had support in the gate,
22 Let my shoulder fall from the socket,
   And my arm be broken off at the elbow.
23"For calamity from God is a terror to me,
   And because of His majesty I can do nothing.

24 ¶"If I have put my confidence *in* gold,
   And called fine gold my trust,
25 If I have gloated because my wealth was great,

And because my hand had secured *so* much;
26 If I have looked at the sun when it
   shone,
   Or the moon going in splendor,
27 And my heart became secretly
   enticed,
   And my hand threw a kiss from
    my mouth,
28 That too would have been an iniquity *calling for* judgment,
   For I would have denied God
    above.

29 ¶"Have I rejoiced at the extinc-
   tion of my enemy,
   Or exulted when evil befell him?
30 "No, I have not allowed my mouth
   to sin
   By asking for his life in a curse.
31 "Have the men of my tent not said,
   'Who can find one who has not
    been satisfied with his meat'?
32 "The alien has not lodged outside,
   For I have opened my doors to the
    traveler.
33 "Have I covered my transgressions
   like Adam,
   By hiding my iniquity in my
    bosom,
34 Because I feared the great multitude,
   And the contempt of families ter-
    rified me,
   And kept silent and did not go out
    of doors?
35 "Oh that I had one to hear me!
   Behold, here is my signature;
   Let the Almighty answer me!
   And the indictment which my ad-
    versary has written,
36 Surely I would carry it on my
   shoulder;
   I would bind it to myself like a
    crown.
37 "I would declare to Him the number of my steps;
   Like a prince I would approach
    Him.

38 ¶"If my land cries out against me,
   And its furrows weep together;
39 If I have eaten its fruit without
   money,
   Or have caused its owners to lose
    their lives,
40 Let briars grow instead of wheat,
   And stinkweed instead of barley."
The words of Job are ended.

CHAPTER 32

THEN these three men ceased answering Job, because he was righteous
in his own eyes.
2 But the anger of Elihu the son of
Barachel the Buzite, of the family of
Ram burned; against Job his anger
burned, because he justified himself
before God.
3 And his anger burned against his
three friends because they had found
no answer, and yet had condemned
Job.
4 Now Elihu had waited to speak to
Job because they were years older
than he.
5 And when Elihu saw that there
was no answer in the mouth of the
three men his anger burned.
6 So Elihu the son of Barachel the
Buzite spoke out and said,
   "I am young in years and you are
   old;
   Therefore I was shy and afraid to
    tell you what I think.
7 "I thought age should speak,
   And increased years should teach
    wisdom.
8 "But it is a spirit in man,
   And the breath of the Almighty
    gives them understanding.
9 "The abundant *in years* may not be
   wise,
   Nor may elders understand jus-
    tice.
10 "So I say, 'Listen to me,
   I too will tell what I think.'

11 ¶"Behold, I waited for your words,
   I listened to your reasonings,
   While you pondered what to say.
12 "I even paid close attention to you,
   Indeed, there was no one who
    refuted Job,
   Not one of you who answered his
    words.
13 "Do not say,
   'We have found wisdom;
   God will rout him, not man.'
14 "For he has not arranged *his* words
   against me;
   Nor will I reply to him with your
    arguments.

15 ¶"They are dismayed, they answer
   no more;
   Words have failed them.

16"And shall I wait, because they do
  not speak,
  Because they stop *and* answer no
  more?
17"I too will answer my share,
  I also will tell my opinion.
18"For I am full of words;
  The spirit within me constrains
  me.
19"Behold, my belly is like unvented
  wine,
  Like new wineskins it is about to
  burst.
20"Let me speak that I may get relief;
  Let me open my lips and answer.
21"Let me now be partial to no one;
  Nor flatter *any* man.
22"For I do not know how to flatter,
  Else my Maker would soon take
  me away.

CHAPTER 33

"HOWEVER now, Job, please hear
  my speech,
  And listen to all my words.
2"Behold now, I open my mouth,
  My tongue in my mouth speaks.
3"My words are *from* the uprightness of my heart;
  And my lips speak knowledge sincerely.
4"The Spirit of God has made me,
  And the breath of the Almighty
  gives me life.
5"Refute me if you can;
  Array yourselves before me, take
  your stand.
6"Behold, I belong to God like you;
  I too have been formed out of the
  clay.
7"Behold, no fear of me should terrify you,
  Nor should my pressure weigh
  heavily on you.

8 ¶"Surely you have spoken in my
  hearing,
  And I have heard the sound of
  your words:
9 'I am pure, without transgression;
  I am innocent and there is no
  guilt in me.
10 'Behold, He invents pretexts
  against me;
  He counts me as His enemy.
11 'He puts my feet in the stocks;
  He watches all my paths.'

12"Behold, let me tell you, you are
  not right in this,
  For God is greater than man.

13 ¶"Why do you complain against
  Him,
  That He does not give an account
  of all His doings?
14"Indeed God speaks once,
  Or twice, *yet* no one notices it.
15"In a dream, a vision of the night,
  When sound sleep falls on men,
  While they slumber in their beds,
16 Then He opens the ears of men,
  And seals their instruction,
17 That He may turn man aside *from
  his* conduct,
  And keep man from pride;
18 He keeps back his soul from the
  pit,
  And his life from passing over into
  Sheol.

19 ¶"Man is also chastened with pain
  on his bed,
  And with unceasing complaint in
  his bones;
20 So that his life loathes bread,
  And his soul favorite food.
21"His flesh wastes away from sight,
  And his bones which were not
  seen stick out.
22"Then his soul draws near to the
  pit,
  And his life to those who bring
  death.

23 ¶"If there is an angel *as* mediator
  for him,
  One out of a thousand,
  To remind a man what is right for
  him,
24 Then let him be gracious to him,
  and say,
  'Deliver him from going down to
  the pit,
  I have found a ransom';
25 Let his flesh become fresher than
  in youth,
  Let him return to the days of his
  youthful vigor;
26 Then he will pray to God, and He
  will accept him,
  That he may see His face with joy,
  And He may restore His righteousness to man.
27"He will sing to men and say,
  'I have sinned and perverted what
  is right,

And it is not proper for me.

28 'He has redeemed my soul from
going to the pit,
And my life shall see the light.'

29 ¶"Behold, God does all these of-
tentimes with men,
30 To bring back his soul from the
pit,
That he may be enlightened with
the light of life.
31"Pay attention, O Job, listen to me;
Keep silent and let me speak.
32"*Then* if you have anything to say,
answer me;
Speak, for I desire to justify you.
33"If not, listen to me;
Keep silent, and I will teach you
wisdom."

CHAPTER 34

THEN Elihu continued and said,
2"Hear my words, you wise men,
And listen to me, you who know.
3"For the ear tests words,
As the palate tastes food.
4"Let us choose for ourselves what
is right;
Let us know among ourselves
what is good.
5"For Job has said, 'I am righteous,
But God has taken away my right;
6 Should I lie concerning my right?
My wound is incurable, *though I
am* without transgression.'
7"What man is like Job,
Who drinks up derision like water,
8 Who goes in company with the
workers of iniquity,
And walks with wicked men?
9"For he has said, 'It profits a man
nothing
When he is pleased with God.'

10 ¶"Therefore, listen to me, you
men of understanding.
Far be it from God to do wickedness,
And from the Almighty to do
wrong.
11"For He pays a man according to
his work,
And makes him find it according
to his way.
12"Surely, God will not act wickedly,
And the Almighty will not pervert
justice.
13"Who gave Him authority over the
earth?

And who has laid *on Him* the
whole world?
14"If He should determine to do so,
If He should gather to Himself His
spirit and His breath,
15 All flesh would perish together,
And man would return to dust.

16 ¶"But if *you have* understanding,
hear this;
Listen to the sound of my words.
17"Shall one who hates justice rule?
And will you condemn a righteous
mighty one,
18 Who says to a king, 'Worthless
one,'
To nobles, 'Wicked ones';
19 Who shows no partiality to
princes,
Nor regards the rich above the
poor,
For they all are the work of His
hands?
20"In a moment they die, and at
midnight
People are shaken and pass away,
And the mighty are taken away
without a hand.

21 ¶"For His eyes are upon the ways
of a man,
And He sees all his steps.
22"There is no darkness or deep
shadow
Where the workers of iniquity
may hide themselves.
23"For He does not *need to* consider
a man further,
That he should go before God in
judgment.
24"He breaks in pieces mighty men
without inquiry,
And sets others in their place.
25"Therefore He knows their works,
And He overthrows *them* in the
night,
And they are crushed.
26"He strikes them like the wicked
In a public place,
27 Because they turned aside from
following Him,
And had no regard for any of His
ways;
28 So that they caused the cry of the
poor to come to Him,
And that He might hear the cry of
the afflicted—
29 When He keeps quiet, who then
can condemn?

And when He hides His face, who
then can behold Him,
That is, in regard to both nation
and man?—
30 So that godless men should not
rule,
Nor be snares of the people.

31 ¶"For has anyone said to God,
'I have borne *chastisement;*
I will not offend *anymore;*
32 Teach Thou me what I do not see;
If I have done iniquity,
I will do it no more'?
33"Shall He recompense on your
terms, because you have re-
jected *it?*
For you must choose, and not I;
Therefore declare what you know.
34"Men of understanding will say to
me,
And a wise man who hears me,
35 'Job speaks without knowledge,
And his words are without wis-
dom.
36 'Job ought to be tried to the limit,
Because he answers like wicked
men.
37 'For he adds rebellion to his sin;
He claps his hands among us,
And multiplies his words against
God.' "

CHAPTER 35

THEN Elihu continued and said,
2"Do you think this is according to
justice?
Do you say, 'My righteousness is
more than God's'?
3"For you say, 'What advantage will
it be to You?
What profit shall I have, more
than if I had sinned?'
4"I will answer you,
And your friends with you.
5"Look at the heavens and see;
And behold the clouds—they are
higher than you.
6"If you have sinned, what do you
accomplish against Him?
And if your transgressions are
many, what do you do to Him?
7"If you are righteous, what do you
give to Him?
Or what does He receive from
your hand?
8"Your wickedness is for a man like
yourself,

And your righteousness is for a
son of man.

9 ¶"Because of the multitude of
oppressions they cry out;
They cry for help because of the
arm of the mighty.
10"But no one says, 'Where is God
my Maker,
Who gives songs in the night,
11 Who teaches us more than the
beasts of the earth,
And makes us wiser than the
birds of the heavens?'
12"There they cry out, but He does
not answer
Because of the pride of evil men.
13"Surely God will not listen to an
empty *cry,*
Nor will the Almighty regard it.
14"How much less when you say you
do not behold Him,
The case is before Him, and you
must wait for Him!
15"And now, because He has not
visited *in* His anger,
Nor has He acknowledged transgression well,
16 So Job opens his mouth emptily;
He multiplies words without
knowledge."

CHAPTER 36

THEN Elihu continued and said,
2"Wait for me a little, and I will
show you
That there is yet more to be said
in God's behalf.
3"I will fetch my knowledge from
afar,
And I will ascribe righteousness
to my Maker.
4"For truly my words are not false;
One who is perfect in knowledge
is with you.
5"Behold, God is mighty but does
not despise *any;*
He is mighty in strength of understanding.
6"He does not keep the wicked
alive,
But gives justice to the afflicted.
7"He does not withdraw His eyes
from the righteous;
But with kings on the throne
He has seated them forever, and
they are exalted.
8"And if they are bound in fetters,

And are caught in the cords of
affliction,
9 Then he declares to them their
work
And their transgressions, that
they have magnified them-
selves.
10"And He opens their ear to instruction,
And commands that they return
from evil.
11"If they hear and serve *Him*,
They shall end their days in prosperity,
And their years in pleasures.
12"But if they do not hear, they shall
perish by the sword,
And they shall die without knowledge.
13"But the godless in heart lay up
anger;
They do not cry for help when He
binds them.
14"They die in youth,
And their life *perishes* among the
cult prostitutes.
15"He delivers the afflicted in their
affliction,
And opens their ear in *time of*
oppression.
16"Then indeed, He enticed you from
the mouth of distress,
Instead of it, a broad place with
no constraint;
And that which was set on your
table was full of fatness.

17 ¶"But you were full of judgment
on the wicked;
Judgment and justice take hold *of
you*.
18"*Beware* lest wrath entice you to
scoffing;
And do not let the greatness of
the ransom turn you aside.
19"Will your riches keep *you* from
distress,
Or all the forces of *your* strength?
20"Do not long for the night,
When people vanish in their place.
21"Be careful, do not turn to evil;
For you have preferred this to
affliction.
22"Behold, God is exalted in His
power;
Who is a teacher like Him?
23"Who has appointed Him His way,
And who has said, 'Thou hast
done wrong'?

24 ¶"Remember that you should
exalt His work,
Of which men have sung.
25"All men have seen it;
Man beholds from afar.
26"Behold, God is exalted, and we do
not know *Him;*
The number of His years is unsearchable.
27"For He draws up the drops of
water,
They distill rain from the mist,
28 Which the clouds pour down,
They drip upon man abundantly.
29"Can anyone understand the
spreading of the clouds,
The thundering of His pavilion?
30"Behold, He spreads His lightning
about Him,
And He covers the depths of the
sea.
31"For by these He judges peoples;
He gives food in abundance.
32"He covers *His* hands with the
lightning,
And commands it to strike the
mark.
33"Its noise declares His presence;
The cattle also, concerning what
is coming up.

CHAPTER 37

"AT this also my heart trembles,
And leaps from its place.
2"Listen closely to the thunder of
His voice,
And the rumbling that goes out
from His mouth.
3"Under the whole heaven He lets it
loose,
And His lightning to the ends of
the earth.
4"After it, a voice roars;
He thunders with His majestic
voice;
And He does not restrain the
lightnings when His voice is
heard.
5"God thunders with His voice wondrously,
Doing great things which we cannot comprehend.
6"For to the snow He says, 'Fall on
the earth,'
And to the downpour and the
rain, 'Be strong.'
7"He seals the hand of every man,
That all men may know His work.

8"Then the beast goes into its lair,
And remains in its den.
9"Out of the south comes the storm,
And out of the north the cold.
10"From the breath of God ice is made,
And the expanse of the waters is frozen.
11"Also with moisture He loads the thick cloud;
He disperses the cloud of His lightning.
12"And it changes direction, turning around by His guidance,
That it may do whatever He commands it
On the face of the inhabited earth.
13"Whether for correction, or for His world,
Or for lovingkindness, He causes it to happen.

14 ¶"Listen to this, O Job,
Stand and consider the wonders of God.
15"Do you know how God establishes them,
And makes the lightning of His cloud to shine?
16"Do you know about the layers of the thick clouds,
The wonders of one perfect in knowledge,
17 You whose garments are hot,
When the land is still because of the south wind?
18"Can you, with Him, spread out the skies,
Strong as a molten mirror?
19"Teach us what we shall say to Him;
We cannot arrange *our case* because of darkness.
20"Shall it be told Him that I would speak?
Or should a man say that he would be swallowed up?

21 ¶"And now men do not see the light which is bright in the skies;
But the wind has passed and cleared them.
22"Out of the north comes golden *splendor;*
Around God is awesome majesty.
23"The Almighty—we cannot find Him;

He is exalted in power;
And He will not do violence to justice and abundant righteousness.
24"Therefore men fear Him;
He does not regard any who are wise of heart."

CHAPTER 38

THEN the LORD answered Job out of the whirlwind and said,
2"Who is this that darkens counsel By words without knowledge?
3"Now gird up your loins like a man,
And I will ask you, and you instruct Me!
4"Where were you when I laid the foundation of the earth?
Tell *Me*, if you have understanding,
5 Who set its measurements, since you know?
Or who stretched the line on it?
6"On what were its bases sunk?
Or who laid its cornerstone,
7 When the morning stars sang together,
And all the sons of God shouted for joy?

8 ¶"Or *who* enclosed the sea with doors,
When, bursting forth, it went out from the womb;
9 When I made a cloud its garment,
And thick darkness its swaddling band,
10 And I placed boundaries on it,
And I set a bolt and doors,
11 And I said, 'Thus far you shall come, but no farther;
And here shall your proud waves stop'?

12 ¶"Have you ever in your life commanded the morning,
And caused the dawn to know its place;
13 That it might take hold of the ends of the earth,
And the wicked be shaken out of it?
14"It is changed like clay *under* the seal;
And they stand forth like a garment.

15"And from the wicked their light is
    withheld,
    And the uplifted arm is broken.

16 ¶"Have you entered into the
    springs of the sea?
    Or have you walked in the re-
      cesses of the deep?
17"Have the gates of death been re-
    vealed to you?
    Or have you seen the gates of
      deep darkness?
18"Have you understood the expanse
    of the earth?
    Tell *Me*, if you know all this.

19 ¶"Where is the way to the dwell-
    ing of light?
    And darkness, where is its place,
20 That you may take it to its terri-
    tory,
    And that you may discern the
      paths to its home?
21"You know, for you were born
    then,
    And the number of your days is
      great!
22"Have you entered the storehouses
    of the snow,
    Or have you seen the storehouses
      of the hail,
23 Which I have reserved for the
    time of distress,
    For the day of war and battle?
24"Where is the way that the light is
    divided,
    Or the east wind scattered on the
      earth?

25 ¶"Who has cleft a channel for the
    flood,
    Or a way for the thunderbolt;
26 To bring rain on a land without
    people,
    On a desert without a man in it,
27 To satisfy the waste and desolate
    land,
    And to make the seeds of grass to
      sprout?
28"Has the rain a father?
    Or who has begotten the drops of
      dew?
29"From whose womb has come the
    ice?
    And the frost of heaven, who has
      given it birth?
30"Water becomes hard like stone,
    And the surface of the deep is
      imprisoned.

31 ¶"Can you bind the chains of the
    Pleiades,
    Or loose the cords of Orion?
32"Can you lead forth a constellation
    in its season,
    And guide the Bear with her satel-
      lites?
33"Do you know the ordinances of
    the heavens,
    Or fix their rule over the earth?

34 ¶"Can you lift up your voice to
    the clouds,
    So that an abundance of water
      may cover you?
35"Can you send forth lightnings
    that they may go
    And say to you, 'Here we are'?
36"Who has put wisdom in the inner-
    most being,
    Or has given understanding to the
      mind?
37"Who can count the clouds by
    wisdom,
    Or tip the water jars of the heav-
      ens,
38 When the dust hardens into a
    mass,
    And the clods stick together?

39 ¶"Can you hunt the prey for the
    lion,
    Or satisfy the appetite of the
      young lions,
40 When they crouch in *their* dens,
    And lie in wait in *their* lair?
41"Who prepares for the raven its
    nourishment,
    When its young cry to God,
    And wander about without food?

CHAPTER 39

"Do you know the time the moun-
    tain goats give birth?
    Do you observe the calving of the
      deer?
2"Can you count the months they
    fulfill,
    Or do you know the time they
      give birth?
3"They kneel down, they bring forth
    their young,
    They get rid of their labor pains.
4"Their offspring become strong,
    they grow up in the open field;
    They leave and do not return to
      them.

5 ¶"Who sent out the wild donkey
   free?
   And who loosed the bonds of the
      swift donkey,
6 To whom I gave the wilderness
   for a home,
   And the salt land for his dwelling
      place?
7"He scorns the tumult of the city,
   The shoutings of the driver he
      does not hear.
8"He explores the mountains for his
   pasture,
   And he searches after every green
      thing.
9"Will the wild ox consent to serve
   you?
   Or will he spend the night at your
      manger?
10"Can you bind the wild ox in a
   furrow with ropes?
   Or will he harrow the valleys after
      you?
11"Will you trust him because his
   strength is great
   And leave your labor to him?
12"Will you have faith in him that he
   will return your grain,
   And gather *it from* your threshing
      floor?

13 ¶"The ostriches' wings flap joyously
   With the pinion and plumage of
      [12]love,
14 For she abandons her eggs to the
   earth,
   And warms them in the dust,
15 And she forgets that a foot may
   crush them,
   Or that a wild beast may trample
      them.
16"She treats her young cruelly, as if
   they were not hers;
   Though her labor be in vain, *she* is
      unconcerned;
17 Because God has made her forget
   wisdom,
   And has not given her a share of
      understanding.
18"When she lifts herself on high,
   She laughs at the horse and his
      rider.

19 ¶"Do you give the horse *his*
   might?

Do you clothe his neck with a
   mane?
20"Do you make him leap like the
   locust?
   His majestic snorting is terrible.
21"He paws in the valley, and rejoices in *his* strength;
   He goes out to meet the weapons.
22"He laughs at fear and is not dismayed;
   And he does not turn back from
      the sword.
23"The quiver rattles against him,
   The flashing spear and javelin.
24"With shaking and rage he races
   over the ground;
   And he does not stand still at the
      voice of the trumpet.
25"As often as the trumpet *sounds* he
   says, 'Aha!'
   And he scents the battle from
      afar,
   And thunder of the captains, and
      the war cry.

26 ¶"Is it by your understanding that
   the hawk soars,
   Stretching his wings toward the
      south?
27"Is it at your command that the
   eagle mounts up,
   And makes his nest on high?
28"On the cliff he dwells and lodges,
   Upon the rocky crag, an inacces-
      sible place.
29"From there he spies out food;
   His eyes see *it* from afar.
30"His young ones also suck up
   blood;
   And where the slain are, there is
      he."

CHAPTER 40

THEN the LORD said to Job,
2"Will the faultfinder contend with
   the Almighty?
   Let him who reproves God answer
      it."

3 ¶ Then Job answered the LORD
   and said,
4"Behold, I am insignificant; what
   can I reply to Thee?
   I lay my hand on my mouth.
5"Once I have spoken, and I will not
   answer;

[12] Or, *a stork*

Even twice, and I will add no
more."

6 ¶ Then the LORD answered Job
out of the storm, and said,

7"Now gird up your loins like a man;
I will ask you, and you instruct
Me.

8"Will you really annul My judgment?
Will you condemn Me that you
may be justified?

9"Or do you have an arm like God,
And can you thunder with a voice
like His?

10 ¶"Adorn yourself with eminence
and dignity;
And clothe yourself with honor
and majesty.

11"Pour out the overflowings of your
anger;
And look on everyone who is
proud, and make him low.

12"Look on everyone who is proud,
and humble him;
And tread down the wicked where
they stand.

13"Hide them in the dust together;
Bind them in the hidden place.

14"Then I will also confess to you,
That your own right hand can
save you.

15 ¶"Behold now, [13]Behemoth, which
I made as well as you;
He eats grass like an ox.

16"Behold now, his strength in his
loins,
And his power in the muscles of
his belly.

17"He bends his tail like a cedar;
The sinews of his thighs are knit
together.

18"His bones are tubes of bronze;
His limbs are like bars of iron.

19 ¶"He is the first of the ways of
God;
Let his maker bring near his
sword.

20"Surely the mountains bring him
food,
And all the beasts of the field play
there.

21"Under the lotus plants he lies
down,

In the covert of the reeds and the
marsh.

22"The lotus plants cover him with
shade;
The willows of the brook surround him.

23"If a river rages, he is not alarmed;
He is confident, though the Jordan rushes to his mouth.

24"Can anyone capture him when he
is on watch,
With barbs can anyone pierce his
nose?

CHAPTER 41

"CAN you draw out [14]Leviathan
with a fishhook?
Or press down his tongue with a
cord?

2"Can you put a rope in his nose?
Or pierce his jaw with a hook?

3"Will he make many supplications
to you?
Or will he speak to you soft
words?

4"Will he make a covenant with
you?
Will you take him for a servant
forever?

5"Will you play with him as with a
bird?
Or will you bind him for your
maidens?

6"Will the traders bargain over him?
Will they divide him among the
merchants?

7"Can you fill his skin with har-
poons,
Or his head with fishing spears?

8"Lay your hand on him;
Remember the battle; you will not
do it again!

9"Behold, your expectation is false;
Will you be laid low even at the
sight of him?

10"No one is so fierce that he dares to
arouse him;
Who then is he that can stand
before Me?

11"Who has given to Me that I
should repay him?
Whatever is under the whole
heaven is Mine.

12 ¶"I will not keep silence concerning his limbs,

---

[13] Or, the hippopotamus

[14] Or, the crocodile

Or his mighty strength, or his
orderly frame.
13"Who can strip off his outer armor?
Who can come within his double
mail?
14"Who can open the doors of his
face?
Around his teeth there is terror.
15"*His* strong scales are *his* pride,
Shut up *as with* a tight seal.
16"One is so near to another,
That no air can come between
them.
17"They are joined one to another;
They clasp each other and cannot
be separated.
18"His sneezes flash forth light,
And his eyes are like the eyelids of
the morning.
19"Out of his mouth go burning
torches;
Sparks of fire leap forth.
20"Out of his nostrils smoke goes
forth,
As *from* a boiling pot and *burning*
rushes.
21"His breath kindles coals,
And a flame goes forth from his
mouth.
22"In his neck lodges strength,
And dismay leaps before him.
23"The folds of his flesh are joined
together,
Firm on him and immovable.
24"His heart is as hard as a stone;
Even as hard as a lower millstone.
25"When he raises himself up, the
mighty fear;
Because of the crashing they are
bewildered.
26"The sword that reaches him cannot avail;
Nor the spear, the dart, or the
javelin.
27"He regards iron as straw,
Bronze as rotten wood.
28"The arrow cannot make him flee;
Slingstones are turned into stubble for him.
29"Clubs are regarded as stubble;
He laughs at the rattling of the
javelin.
30"His underparts are *like* sharp pot-
sherds;
He spreads out *like* a threshing
sledge on the mire.
31"He makes the depths boil like a
pot;

He makes the sea like a jar of
ointment.
32"Behind him he makes a wake to
shine;
One would think the deep to be
gray-haired.
33"Nothing on earth is like him,
One made without fear.
34"He looks on everything that is
high;
He is king over all the sons of
pride."

CHAPTER 42

THEN Job answered the LORD, and
said,
2"I know that Thou canst do all
things,
And that no purpose of Thine can
be thwarted.
3 'Who is this that hides counsel
without knowledge?'
"Therefore I have declared that
which I did not understand,
Things too wonderful for me,
which I did not know."
4 'Hear, now, and I will speak;
I will ask Thee, and do Thou instruct me.'
5"I have heard of Thee by the hearing of the ear;
But now my eye sees Thee;
6 Therefore I retract,
And I repent in dust and ashes."
7 ¶ And it came about after the
LORD had spoken these words to Job,
that the LORD said to Eliphaz the Temanite, "My wrath is kindled against
you and against your two friends,
because you have not spoken of Me
what is right as My servant Job has.
8"Now therefore, take for yourselves seven bulls and seven rams, and
go to My servant Job, and offer up a
burnt offering for yourselves, and My
servant Job will pray for you. For I will
accept him so that I may not do with
you *according to your* folly, because
you have not spoken of Me what is
right, as My servant Job has."
9 So Eliphaz the Temanite and
Bildad the Shuhite *and* Zophar the
Naamathite went and did as the LORD
told them; and the LORD accepted Job.
10 ¶ And the LORD restored the fortunes of Job when he prayed for his
friends, and the LORD increased all
that Job had twofold.

11 Then all his brothers, and all his sisters, and all who had known him before, came to him, and they ate bread with him in his house; and they consoled him and comforted him for all the evil that the LORD had brought on him. And each one gave him one piece of money, and each a ring of gold.

12 And the LORD blessed the latter *days* of Job more than his beginning, and he had 14,000 sheep, and 6,000 camels, and 1,000 yoke of oxen, and 1,000 female donkeys.

13 And he had seven sons and three daughters.

14 And he named the first Jemimah, and the second Keziah, and the third Keren-happuch.

15 And in all the land no women were found so fair as Job's daughters; and their father gave them inheritance among their brothers.

16 And after this Job lived 140 years, and saw his sons, and his grandsons, four generations.

17 And Job died, an old man and full of days.

THE PSALMS

The following expressions occur often in the Psalms:

Selah   May mean *Pause, Crescendo* or *Musical Interlude*
Maskil   Possibly, *Contemplative,* or *Didactic,* or *Skillful Psalm*
Mikhtam   Possibly, *Epigrammatic Poem,* or *Atonement Psalm*
Sheol   The nether world

BOOK 1

PSALM 1

How blessed is the man who does not walk in the counsel of the wicked,
Nor stand in the path of sinners,
Nor sit in the seat of scoffers!
2 But his delight is in the law of the LORD,
And in His law he meditates day and night.
3 And he will be like a tree *firmly* planted by streams of water,
Which yields its fruit in its season,
And its leaf does not wither;
And in whatever he does, he prospers.

4 ¶ The wicked are not so,
But they are like chaff which the wind drives away.
5 Therefore the wicked will not stand in the judgment,
Nor sinners in the assembly of the righteous.
6 For the LORD knows the way of the righteous,
But the way of the wicked will perish.

PSALM 2

Why are the nations in an uproar,
And the peoples devising a vain thing?
2 The kings of the earth take their stand,
And the rulers take counsel together
Against the LORD and against His [1]Anointed:
3 "Let us tear their fetters apart,
And cast away their cords from us!"

4 ¶ He who [2]sits in the heavens laughs,
The Lord scoffs at them.
5 Then He will speak to them in His anger
And terrify them in His fury:
6 "But as for Me, I have installed My King
Upon Zion, My holy mountain."

7 ¶ "I will surely tell of the decree of the LORD:
He said to Me, 'Thou art My Son,
Today I have begotten Thee.

[1] Or, *Messiah*   [2] Or, *is enthroned*

8 'Ask of Me, and I will surely give
the nations as Thine inheritance,
And the *very* ends of the earth as
Thy possession.
9 'Thou shalt ³break them with a rod
of iron,
Thou shalt shatter them like
earthenware.' "

10 ¶ Now therefore, O kings, show
discernment;
Take warning, O ⁴judges of the
earth.
11 Worship the LORD with reverence,
And rejoice with trembling.
12 Do homage to the Son, lest He
become angry, and you perish
in the way,
For His wrath may ⁵soon be kindled.
How blessed are all who take refuge in Him!

PSALM 3
A Psalm of David, when he fled from
Absalom his son.

O LORD, how my adversaries have
increased!
Many are rising up against me.
2 Many are saying of my soul,
"There is no deliverance for him in
God." [⁶Selah.

3 ¶ But Thou, O LORD, art a shield
about me,
My glory, and the One who lifts
my head.
4 I was crying to the LORD with my
voice,
And He answered me from His
holy mountain. [Selah.
5 I lay down and slept;
I awoke, for the LORD sustains
me.
6 I will not be afraid of ten thousands of people
Who have set themselves against
me round about.

7 ¶ Arise, O LORD; save me, O my
God!
For Thou hast smitten all my en-
emies on the cheek;
Thou hast shattered the teeth of
the wicked.

8 Salvation belongs to the LORD;
Thy blessing *be* upon Thy people! [Selah.

PSALM 4
For the choir director; on stringed instruments.
A Psalm of David.

ANSWER me when I call, O God of
my righteousness!
Thou hast relieved me in my distress;
Be gracious to me and hear my
prayer.

2 ¶ O sons of men, how long will
my honor become a reproach?
How long will you love what is
worthless and aim at deception?
[Selah.
3 But know that the LORD has set
apart the godly man for Himself;
The LORD hears when I call to
Him.

4 ¶ Tremble, and do not sin;
Meditate in your heart upon your
bed, and be still. [Selah.
5 Offer the sacrifices of righteousness,
And trust in the LORD.

6 ¶ Many are saying, "Who will
show us *any* good?"
Lift up the light of Thy countenance upon us, O LORD!
7 Thou hast put gladness in my
heart,
More than when their grain and
new wine abound.
8 In peace I will both lie down and
sleep,
For Thou alone, O LORD, dost
make me to dwell in safety.

PSALM 5
For the choir director; for flute accompaniment.
A Psalm of David.

GIVE ear to my words, O LORD,
Consider my ⁷groaning.
2 Heed the sound of my cry for
help, my King and my God,
For to Thee do I pray.
3 In the morning, O LORD, Thou
wilt hear my voice;
In the morning I will order *my
prayer* to Thee and *eagerly*
watch.

³ Another reading is *rule*   ⁴ Or, *leaders*
⁵ Or, *quickly, suddenly, easily*
⁶ *Selah* may mean: Pause, Crescendo or Musical Interlude

⁷ Or, *meditation*

4 ¶ For Thou art not a God who takes pleasure in wickedness;
No evil dwells with Thee.
5 The boastful shall not stand before Thine eyes;
Thou dost hate all who do iniquity.
6 Thou dost destroy those who speak falsehood;
The LORD abhors the man of bloodshed and deceit.
7 But as for me, by Thine abundant lovingkindness I will enter Thy house,
At Thy holy temple I will bow in reverence for Thee.

8 ¶ O LORD, lead me in Thy righteousness because of my foes;
Make Thy way straight before me.
9 There is nothing reliable in what they say;
Their inward part is destruction *itself*;
Their throat is an open grave;
They flatter with their tongue.
10 Hold them guilty, O God;
By their own devices let them fall!
In the multitude of their transgressions thrust them out,
For they are rebellious against Thee.

11 ¶ But let all who take refuge in Thee be glad,
Let them ever sing for joy;
And mayest Thou shelter them,
That those who love Thy name may exult in Thee.
12 For it is Thou who dost bless the righteous man, O LORD,
Thou dost surround him with favor as with a shield.

PSALM 6

For the choir director; with stringed instruments, upon an eight-stringed lyre.
A Psalm of David.

O LORD, do not rebuke me in Thine anger,
Nor chasten me in Thy wrath.
2 Be gracious to me, O LORD, for I *am* pining away;
Heal me, O LORD, for my bones are dismayed.
3 And my soul is greatly dismayed;
But Thou, O LORD—how long?

4 ¶ Return, O LORD, rescue my [8]soul;
Save me because of Thy lovingkindness.
5 For there is no [9]mention of Thee in death;
In Sheol who will give Thee thanks?

6 ¶ I am weary with my sighing;
Every night I make my bed swim,
I dissolve my couch with my tears.
7 My eye has wasted away with grief;
It has become old because of all my adversaries.

8 ¶ Depart from me, all you who do iniquity,
For the LORD has heard the voice of my weeping.
9 The LORD has heard my supplication,
The LORD receives my prayer.
10 All my enemies shall be ashamed and greatly dismayed;
They shall turn back, they shall suddenly be ashamed.

PSALM 7

A [10]Shiggaion of David, which he sang to the Lord
concerning Cush, a Benjamite.

O LORD my God, in Thee I have taken refuge;
Save me from all those who pursue me, and deliver me,
2 Lest he tear my soul like a lion,
Dragging me away, while there is none to deliver.

3 ¶ O LORD my God, if I have done this,
If there is injustice in my hands,
4 If I have rewarded evil to my friend,
Or have plundered him who without cause was my adversary,
5 Let the enemy pursue my soul and overtake *it*;
And let him trample my life down to the ground,
And lay my glory in the dust.   [Selah.

[8] Or, *life*   [9] Or, *remembrance*
[10] I.e., Dithyrambic rhythm, or, *wild, passionate song*

6 ¶ Arise, O LORD, in Thine anger;
Lift up Thyself against the rage of
my adversaries,
And arouse Thyself for me; Thou
hast appointed judgment.
7 And let the assembly of the peoples encompass Thee;
And over them return Thou on
high.
8 The LORD judges the peoples;
Vindicate me, O LORD, according
to my righteousness and my
integrity that is in me.
9 O let the evil of the wicked come
to an end, but establish the
righteous;
For the righteous God tries the
hearts and [11]minds.
10 My shield is with God,
Who saves the upright in heart.
11 God is a righteous judge,
And a God who has indignation
every day.

12 ¶ If a man does not repent, He
will sharpen His sword;
He has bent His bow and made it
ready.
13 He has also prepared for Himself
deadly weapons;
He makes His arrows fiery shafts.
14 Behold, he travails with wickedness,
And he conceives mischief, and
brings forth falsehood.
15 He has dug a pit and hollowed it
out,
And has fallen into the hole which
he made.
16 His mischief will return upon his
own head,
And his violence will descend
upon [12]his own pate.

17 ¶ I will give thanks to the LORD
according to His righteousness,
And will sing praise to the name
of the LORD Most High.

PSALM 8
For the choir director; on the Gittith.
A Psalm of David.

O LORD, our Lord,
How majestic is Thy name in all
the earth,
Who hast displayed Thy splendor
above the heavens!

2 From the mouth of infants and
nursing babes Thou hast established strength,
Because of Thine adversaries,
To make the enemy and the revengeful cease.

3 ¶ When I consider Thy heavens,
the work of Thy fingers,
The moon and the stars, which
Thou hast ordained;
4 What is man, that Thou dost take
thought of him?
And the son of man, that Thou
dost care for him?
5 Yet Thou hast made him a little
lower than God,
And dost crown him with glory
and majesty!
6 Thou dost make him to rule over
the works of Thy hands;
Thou hast put all things under his
feet,
7 All sheep and oxen,
And also the beasts of the field,
8 The birds of the heavens, and the
fish of the sea,
Whatever passes through the
paths of the seas.

9 ¶ O LORD, our Lord,
How majestic is Thy name in all
the earth!

PSALM 9
For the choir director; on [13]Muth-labben.
A Psalm of David.

I WILL give thanks to the LORD with
all my heart;
I will tell of all Thy wonders.
2 I will be glad and exult in Thee;
I will sing praise to Thy name, O
Most High.

3 ¶ When my enemies turn back,
They stumble and perish before
Thee.
4 For Thou hast maintained my just
cause;
Thou dost sit on the throne judging righteously.
5 Thou hast rebuked the nations;
Thou hast destroyed the
wicked;
Thou hast blotted out their name
forever and ever.

[11] Lit., *kidneys*, figurative for inner man
[12] I.e., the crown of his own head

[13] I.e., "Death to the Son"

6 The enemy has come to an end in
  perpetual ruins,
  And Thou hast uprooted the
  cities;
  The very memory of them has
  perished.

7 ¶ But the LORD [14]abides forever;
  He has established His throne for
  judgment,
8 And He will judge the world in
  righteousness;
  He will execute judgment for the
  peoples with equity.
9 The LORD also will be a stronghold
  for the oppressed,
  A stronghold in times of trouble,
10 And those who know Thy name
  will put their trust in Thee;
  For Thou, O LORD, hast not forsaken those who seek Thee.

11 ¶ Sing praises to the LORD, who
  dwells in Zion;
  Declare among the peoples His
  deeds.
12 For He who [15]requires blood remembers them;
  He does not forget the cry of the
  afflicted.
13 Be gracious to me, O LORD;
  Behold my affliction from those
  who hate me,
  Thou who dost lift me up from the
  gates of death;
14 That I may tell of all Thy praises,
  That in the gates of the daughter
  of Zion
  I may rejoice in Thy salvation.
15 The nations have sunk down in
  the pit which they have made;
  In the net which they hid, their
  own foot has been caught.
16 The LORD has made Himself
  known;
  He has executed judgment.
  In the work of his own hands the
  wicked is snared.
                    [Higgaion Selah.

17 ¶ The wicked will return to Sheol,
  Even all the nations who forget
  God.
18 For the needy will not always be
  forgotten,
  Nor the hope of the afflicted perish forever.

19 Arise, O LORD, do not let man
  prevail;
  Let the nations be judged before
  Thee.
20 Put them in fear, O LORD;
  Let the nations know that they
  are but men.   [Selah.

PSALM 10

WHY dost Thou stand afar off, O
  LORD?
  Why dost Thou hide *Thyself* in
  times of trouble?
2 In pride the wicked hotly pursue
  the afflicted;
  Let them be caught in the plots
  which they have devised.

3 ¶ For the wicked boasts of his
  heart's desire,
  And [16]the greedy man curses *and*
  spurns the LORD.
4 The wicked, in the haughtiness of
  his countenance, does not seek
  Him.
  All his thoughts are, "There is no
  God."

5 ¶ His ways prosper at all times;
  Thy judgments are on high, out of
  his sight;
  As for all his adversaries, he
  snorts at them.
6 He says to himself, "I shall not be
  moved;
  Throughout all generations I shall
  not be in adversity."
7 His mouth is full of curses and
  deceit and oppression;
  Under his tongue is mischief and
  wickedness.
8 He sits in the lurking places of the
  villages;
  In the hiding places he kills the
  innocent;
  His eyes stealthily watch for the
  unfortunate.
9 He lurks in a hiding place as a lion
  in his lair;
  He lurks to catch the afflicted;
  He catches the afflicted when he
  draws him into his net.
10 He crouches, he bows down,
  And the unfortunate fall [17]by his
  mighty ones.
11 He says to himself, "God has forgotten;

[14] Or, *sits as king*   [15] I.e., avenges bloodshed   [16] Or, *blesses the greedy man*   [17] Or, *into his claws*

He has hidden His face; He will
never see it."

12 ¶ Arise, O LORD; O God, lift up
Thy hand.
Do not forget the afflicted.
13 Why has the wicked spurned
God?
He has said to himself, "Thou wilt
not require *it*."
14 Thou hast seen *it*, for Thou hast
beheld mischief and vexation to
take it into Thy hand.
The unfortunate commits *himself*
to Thee;
Thou hast been the helper of the
orphan.
15 Break the arm of the wicked and
the evildoer,
Seek out his wickedness until
Thou dost find none.

16 ¶ The LORD is King forever and
ever;
Nations have perished from His
land.
17 O LORD, Thou hast heard the desire of the [18]humble;
Thou wilt strengthen their heart,
Thou wilt incline Thine ear
18 To [19]vindicate the orphan and the
oppressed,
That man who is of the earth may
cause terror no more.

PSALM 11
For the choir director. *A Psalm* of David.

IN the LORD I take refuge;
How can you say to my soul,
"Flee *as* a bird to your mountain;
2 For, behold, the wicked bend the
bow,
They make ready their arrow
upon the string,
To shoot in darkness at the upright in heart.
3 If the foundations are destroyed,
What can the righteous do?"

4 ¶ The LORD is in His holy temple;
the LORD's throne is in heaven;
His eyes behold, His eyelids test
the sons of men.
5 The LORD tests the righteous and
the wicked,
And the one who loves violence
His soul hates.

6 Upon the wicked He will rain
[20]snares;
Fire and brimstone and burning
wind will be the portion of their
cup.
7 For the LORD is righteous; He
loves righteousness;
The upright will behold His face.

PSALM 12
For the choir director; upon an eight-stringed lyre.
A Psalm of David.

HELP, LORD, for the godly man
ceases to be,
For the faithful disappear from
among the sons of men.
2 They speak falsehood to one another;
With flattering lips and with a
double heart they speak.
3 May the LORD cut off all flattering
lips,
The tongue that speaks great
things;
4 ¶ Who have said, "With our
tongue we will prevail;
Our lips are our own; who is lord
over us?"
5"Because of the devastation of the
afflicted, because of the groaning of the needy,
Now I will arise," says the LORD;
"I will set him in the safety for
which he longs."

6 ¶ The words of the LORD are pure
words;
As silver tried in a furnace on the
earth, refined seven times.
7 Thou, O LORD, wilt keep them;
Thou wilt preserve him from this
generation forever.
8 The wicked strut about on every
side,
When [21]vileness is exalted among
the sons of men.

PSALM 13
For the choir director. A Psalm of David.

HOW long, O LORD? Wilt Thou forget
me forever?
How long wilt Thou hide Thy face
from me?
2 How long shall I take counsel in
my soul,
Having sorrow in my heart all the
day?

---

[18] Or, *afflicted*   [19] Lit., *judge*   [20] Or, *coals of fire*   [21] Or, *worthlessness*

How long will my enemy be exalted over me?

3 ¶ Consider *and* answer me, O
LORD, my God;
Enlighten my eyes, lest I sleep the
sleep of death,
4 Lest my enemy say, "I have over-
come him,"
Lest my adversaries rejoice when
I am shaken.

5 ¶ But I have trusted in Thy
lovingkindness;
My heart shall rejoice in Thy salvation.
6 I will sing to the LORD,
Because He has dealt bountifully
with me.

PSALM 14

For the choir director. *A Psalm of David.*

THE fool has said in his heart, "There
is no God."
They are corrupt, they have committed abominable deeds;
There is no one who does good.
2 The LORD has looked down from
heaven upon the sons of men,
To see if there are any who understand,
Who seek after God.
3 They have all turned aside; together they have become corrupt;
There is no one who does good,
not even one.

4 ¶ Do all the workers of wickedness not know,
Who eat up my people *as* they eat
bread,
And do not call upon the Lord?
5 There they are in great dread,
For God is with the righteous
generation.
6 You would put to shame the
counsel of the afflicted,
But the LORD is his refuge.

7 ¶ Oh, that the salvation of Israel
would come out of Zion!
When the LORD [22]restores His captive people,
Jacob will rejoice, Israel will be
glad.

PSALM 15

A Psalm of David.

O LORD, who may abide in Thy
tent?
Who may dwell on Thy holy hill?
2 He who walks with integrity, and
works righteousness,
And speaks truth in his heart.
3 He does not slander with his
tongue,
Nor does evil to his neighbor,
Nor takes up a reproach against
his friend;
4 In whose eyes a reprobate is despised,
But who honors those who fear
the LORD;
He swears to his own hurt, and
does not change;
5 He does not put out his money [23]at
interest,
Nor does he take a bribe against
the innocent.
He who does these things will
never be shaken.

PSALM 16

A [24]Mikhtam of David.

PRESERVE me, O God, for I take
refuge in Thee.
2 I said to the LORD, "Thou art my
Lord;
I have no good besides Thee."
3 As for the saints who are in the
earth,
They are the majestic ones in
whom is all my delight.
4 The sorrows of those who have
bartered for another *god* will be
multiplied;
I shall not pour out their libations
of blood,
Nor shall I take their names upon
my lips.

5 ¶ The LORD is the portion of my
inheritance and my cup;
Thou dost support my lot.
6 The lines have fallen to me in
pleasant places;
Indeed, my heritage is beautiful to
me.

7 ¶ I will bless the LORD who has
counseled me;

[22] Or, *restores the fortunes of His people*

[23] I.e., to a fellow Israelite
[24] Possibly Epigrammatic Poem, or, Atonement Psalm

Indeed, my mind instructs me in the night.

8 I have set the LORD continually before me;
Because He is at my right hand, I will not be shaken.

9 Therefore my heart is glad, and my glory rejoices;
My flesh also will dwell securely.

10 For Thou wilt not abandon my soul to Sheol;
Neither wilt Thou allow Thy Holy One to ²⁵undergo decay.

11 Thou wilt make known to me the path of life;
In Thy presence is fulness of joy;
In Thy right hand there are pleasures forever.

PSALM 17
A Prayer of David.

HEAR a just cause, O LORD, give heed to my cry;
Give ear to my prayer, which is not from deceitful lips.

2 Let my judgment come forth from Thy presence;
Let Thine eyes look with equity.

3 Thou hast tried my heart;
Thou hast visited *me* by night;
Thou hast tested me and dost find ²⁶nothing;
I have purposed that my mouth will not transgress.

4 As for the deeds of men, by the word of Thy lips
I have kept from the paths of the violent.

5 My steps have held fast to Thy paths.
My feet have not slipped.

6 ¶ I have called upon Thee, for Thou wilt answer me, O God;
Incline Thine ear to me, hear my speech.

7 Wondrously show Thy loving-kindness,
O Savior of those who take refuge at Thy right hand
From those who rise up *against them*.

8 Keep me as ²⁷the apple of the eye;
Hide me in the shadow of Thy wings,

9 From the wicked who despoil me,
My deadly enemies, who surround me.

10 They have closed their unfeeling *heart*;
With their mouth they speak proudly.

11 They have now surrounded us in our steps;
They set their eyes to cast *us* down to the ground.

12 He is like a lion that is eager to tear,
And as a young lion lurking in hiding places.

13 ¶ Arise, O LORD, confront him, bring him low;
Deliver my soul from the wicked with Thy sword,

14 From men with Thy hand, O LORD,
From men of the world, whose portion is in *this* life;
And whose belly Thou dost fill with Thy treasure;
They are satisfied with children,
And leave their abundance to their babes.

15 As for me, I shall behold Thy face in righteousness;
I will be satisfied with Thy likeness when I awake.

PSALM 18
For the choir director. *A Psalm* of David the servant of the LORD, who spoke to the LORD the words of this song in the day that the LORD delivered him from the hand of all his enemies and from the hand of Saul. And he said,

"I LOVE Thee, O LORD, my strength."

2 The LORD is my rock and my fortress and my deliverer,
My God, my rock, in whom I take refuge;
My shield and the horn of my salvation, my stronghold.

3 I call upon the LORD, who is worthy to be praised,
And I am saved from my enemies.

4 ¶ The cords of death encompassed me,
And the torrents of ²⁸ungodliness terrified me.

5 The cords of Sheol surrounded me;

---

²⁵ Or, *see corruption or the pit*   ²⁶ Or, *no evil device in me*
²⁷ Lit., *the pupil, the daughter of the eye*

²⁸ Or, *destruction*

The snares of death confronted me.
6 In my distress I called upon the LORD,
And cried to my God for help;
He heard my voice out of His temple,
And my cry for help before Him came into His ears.

7 ¶ Then the earth shook and quaked;
And the foundations of the mountains were trembling
And were shaken, because He was angry.
8 Smoke went up out of His nostrils,
And fire from His mouth devoured;
Coals were kindled by it.
9 He bowed the heavens also, and came down
With thick darkness under His feet.
10 And He rode upon a cherub and flew;
And He sped upon the wings of the wind.
11 He made darkness His hiding place, His canopy around Him,
Darkness of waters, thick clouds of the skies.
12 From the brightness before Him passed His thick clouds,
Hailstones and coals of fire.
13 The LORD also thundered in the heavens,
And the Most High uttered His voice,
Hailstones and coals of fire.
14 And He sent out His arrows, and scattered them,
And lightning flashes in abundance, and routed them.
15 Then the channels of water appeared,
And the foundations of the world were laid bare
At Thy rebuke, O LORD,
At the blast of the breath of Thy nostrils.

16 ¶ He sent from on high, He took me;
He drew me out of many waters.
17 He delivered me from my strong enemy,
And from those who hated me, for they were too mighty for me.
18 They confronted me in the day of my calamity,
But the LORD was my stay.
19 He brought me forth also into a broad place;
He rescued me, because He delighted in me.

20 ¶ The LORD has rewarded me according to my righteousness;
According to the cleanness of my hands He has recompensed me.
21 For I have kept the ways of the LORD,
And have not wickedly departed from my God.
22 For all His ordinances were before me,
And I did not put away His statutes from me.
23 I was also [29]blameless with Him,
And I kept myself from my iniquity.
24 Therefore the LORD has recompensed me according to my righteousness,
According to the cleanness of my hands in His eyes.

25 ¶ With the kind Thou dost show Thyself kind;
With the blameless Thou dost show Thyself blameless;
26 With the pure Thou dost show Thyself pure;
And with the crooked Thou dost show Thyself [30]astute.
27 For Thou dost save an afflicted people;
But haughty eyes Thou dost abase.
28 For Thou dost light my lamp;
The LORD my God illumines my darkness.
29 For by Thee I can [31]run upon a troop;
And by my God I can leap over a wall.

30 ¶ As for God, His way is blameless;
The word of the LORD is tried;
He is a shield to all who take refuge in Him.
31 For who is God, but the LORD?

[29] Lit., *complete; or, having integrity*   [30] Lit., *twisted*
[31] Or, *crush a troop*

And who is a rock, except our God,

32 The God who girds me with strength,
And makes my way blameless?

33 He makes my feet like hinds' *feet*,
And sets me upon my high places.

34 He trains my hands for battle,
So that my arms can bend a bow of bronze.

35 Thou hast also given me the shield of Thy salvation,
And Thy right hand upholds me;
And Thy gentleness makes me great.

36 Thou dost enlarge my steps under me,
And my feet have not slipped.

37 ¶ I pursued my enemies and overtook them,
And I did not turn back until they were consumed.

38 I shattered them, so that they were not able to rise;
They fell under my feet.

39 For Thou hast girded me with strength for battle;
Thou hast subdued under me those who rose up against me.

40 Thou hast also made my enemies turn their backs to me,
And I [32]destroyed those who hated me.

41 They cried for help, but there was none to save,
Even to the LORD, but He did not answer them.

42 Then I beat them fine as the dust before the wind;
I emptied them out as the mire of the streets.

43 ¶ Thou hast delivered me from the contentions of the people;
Thou hast placed me as head of the nations;
A people whom I have not known serve me.

44 As soon as they hear, they obey me;
Foreigners [33]submit to me.

45 Foreigners fade away,
And come trembling out of their fortresses.

46 ¶ The LORD lives, and blessed be my rock;

And exalted be the God of my salvation,

47 The God who executes vengeance for me,
And subdues peoples under me.

48 He delivers me from my enemies;
Surely Thou dost lift me above those who rise up against me;
Thou dost rescue me from the violent man.

49 Therefore I will give thanks to Thee among the nations, O LORD,
And I will sing praises to Thy name.

50 He gives great [34]deliverance to His king,
And shows lovingkindness to His anointed,
To David and his descendants forever.

PSALM 19

For the choir director. A Psalm of David.

THE heavens are telling of the glory of God;
And their expanse is declaring the work of His hands.

2 Day to day pours forth speech,
And night to night reveals knowledge.

3 There is no speech, nor are there words;
Their voice is not heard.

4 Their [35]line has gone out through all the earth,
And their utterances to the end of the world.
In them He has placed a tent for the sun,

5 Which is as a bridegroom coming out of his chamber;
It rejoices as a strong man to run his course.

6 Its rising is from one end of the heavens,
And its circuit to the other end of them;
And there is nothing hidden from its heat.

7 ¶ The law of the LORD is [36]perfect, restoring the soul;
The testimony of the LORD is sure, making wise the simple.

[32] Or, *silenced*   [33] I.e., give feigned obedience

[34] I.e., victories   [35] Another reading is *sound*
[36] I.e., blameless

8 The precepts of the LORD are
   right, rejoicing the heart;
   The commandment of the LORD is
   pure, enlightening the eyes.
9 The fear of the LORD is clean,
   enduring forever;
   The judgments of the LORD are
   true; they are righteous altogether.
10 They are more desirable than
   gold, yes, than much fine gold;
   Sweeter also than honey and the
   drippings of the honeycomb.
11 Moreover, by them Thy servant is
   warned;
   In keeping them there is great
   reward.
12 Who can discern *his* errors? Acquit me of hidden *faults*.
13 Also keep back Thy servant from
   presumptuous *sins*;
   Let them not rule over me;
   Then I shall be [37]blameless,
   And I shall be acquitted of great
   transgression.
14 Let the words of my mouth and
   the meditation of my heart
   Be acceptable in Thy sight,
   O LORD, my rock and my Redeemer.

PSALM 20

For the choir director. A Psalm of David.

M AY the LORD answer you in the
   day of trouble!
   May the name of the God of Jacob
   set you *securely* on high!
2 May He send you help from the
   sanctuary,
   And support you from Zion!
3 May He remember all your meal
   offerings,
   And find your burnt offering acceptable!   [Selah.

4 ¶ May He grant you your heart's
   desire,
   And fulfill all your [38]counsel!
5 We will sing for joy over your
   victory,
   And in the name of our God we
   will set up our banners.
   May the LORD fulfill all your petitions.

6 ¶ Now I know that the LORD
   saves His anointed;

He will answer him from His holy
   heaven,
   With the saving strength of His
   right hand.
7 Some *boast* in chariots, and some
   in horses;
   But we will boast in the name of
   the LORD, our God.
8 They have bowed down and
   fallen;
   But we have risen and stood upright.
9 Save, O LORD;
   May the King answer us in the
   day we call.

PSALM 21

For the choir director. A Psalm of David.

O LORD, in Thy strength the king
   will be glad,
   And in Thy [39]salvation how
   greatly he will rejoice!
2 Thou hast given him his heart's
   desire,
   And Thou hast not withheld the
   request of his lips.   [Selah.
3 For Thou dost meet him with the
   blessings of good things;
   Thou dost set a crown of fine gold
   on his head.
4 He asked life of Thee,
   Thou didst give it to him,
   Length of days forever and ever.
5 His glory is great through Thy
   [39]salvation,
   Splendor and majesty Thou dost
   place upon him.
6 For Thou dost make him most
   blessed forever;
   Thou dost make him joyful with
   gladness in Thy presence.

7 ¶ For the king trusts in the LORD,
   And through the lovingkindness
   of the Most High he will not be
   shaken.
8 Your hand will find out all your
   enemies;
   Your right hand will find out
   those who hate you.
9 You will make them as a fiery
   oven in the time of your anger;
   The LORD will swallow them up in
   His wrath,
   And fire will devour them.
10 Their [40]offspring Thou wilt destroy from the earth,

[37] Lit., *complete*   [38] Or, *purpose*   [39] Or, *victory*   [40] Lit., *fruit*

And their [41]descendants from among the sons of men.

11 Though they intended evil against Thee,
And devised a plot,
They will not succeed.

12 For Thou wilt make them turn their back;
Thou wilt aim with Thy bowstrings at their faces.

13 Be Thou exalted, O Lord, in Thy strength;
We will sing and praise Thy power.

PSALM 22

For the choir director; upon [42]Aijeleth Hashshahar.
A Psalm of David.

My God, my God, why hast Thou forsaken me?
Far from my deliverance are the words of my groaning.

2 O my God, I cry by day, but Thou dost not answer;
And by night, but I have no rest.

3 Yet Thou art holy,
O Thou who art enthroned upon the praises of Israel.

4 In Thee our fathers trusted;
They trusted, and Thou didst deliver them.

5 To Thee they cried out, and were delivered;
In Thee they trusted, and were not disappointed.

6 ¶ But I am a worm, and not a man,
A reproach of men, and despised by the people.

7 All who see me sneer at me;
They [43]separate with the lip, they wag the head, *saying,*

8 "[44]Commit *yourself* to the Lord; let Him deliver him;
Let Him rescue him, because He delights in him."

9 ¶ Yet Thou art He who didst bring me forth from the womb;
Thou didst make me trust *when* upon my mother's breasts.

10 Upon Thee I was cast from birth;
Thou hast been my God from my mother's womb.

11 ¶ Be not far from me, for trouble is near;
For there is none to help.

12 Many bulls have surrounded me;
Strong *bulls* of Bashan have encircled me.

13 They open wide their mouth at me,
As a ravening and a roaring lion.

14 I am poured out like water,
And all my bones are out of joint;
My heart is like wax;
It is melted within me.

15 My strength is dried up like a potsherd,
And my tongue cleaves to my jaws;
And Thou dost lay me in the dust of death.

16 For dogs have surrounded me;
A band of evildoers has encompassed me;
They pierced my hands and my feet.

17 I can count all my bones.
They look, they stare at me;

18 They divide my garments among them,
And for my clothing they cast lots.

19 ¶ But Thou, O Lord, be not far off;
O Thou my help, hasten to my assistance.

20 Deliver my soul from the sword,
My only *life* from the power of the dog.

21 Save me from the lion's mouth;
And from the horns of the wild oxen Thou dost answer me.

22 ¶ I will tell of Thy name to my brethren;
In the midst of the assembly I will praise Thee.

23 You who fear the Lord, praise Him;
All you descendants of Jacob, glorify Him,
And stand in awe of Him, all you descendants of Israel.

24 For He has not despised nor abhorred the affliction of the afflicted;
Neither has He hidden His face from him;

[41] Lit., *seed*   [42] Lit., *the hind of the morning*
[43] I.e., make mouths at me
[44] Another reading is *He committed* himself

But when he cried to Him for help,
He heard.

25 ¶ From Thee *comes* my praise in
the great assembly;
I shall pay my vows before those
who fear Him.

26 The [45]afflicted shall eat and be
satisfied;
Those who seek Him will praise
the LORD.
Let your heart live forever!

27 All the ends of the earth will remember and turn to the LORD,
And all the families of the nations
will worship before Thee.

28 For the kingdom is the LORD's,
And He rules over the nations.

29 All the prosperous of the earth
will eat and worship,
All those who go down to the dust
will bow before Him,
Even he who cannot keep his soul
alive.

30 Posterity will serve Him;
It will be told of the Lord to the
coming generation.

31 They will come and will declare
His righteousness
To a people who will be born, that
He has performed *it.*

PSALM 23
A Psalm of David.

THE LORD is my shepherd,
I shall not want.

2 He makes me lie down in green
pastures;
He leads me beside quiet waters.

3 He restores my soul;
He guides me in the paths of
righteousness
For His name's sake.

4 ¶ Even though I walk through
the [46]valley of the shadow of
death,
I fear no [47]evil; for Thou art with
me;
Thy rod and Thy staff, they comfort me.

5 Thou dost prepare a table before
me in the presence of my enemies;
Thou hast anointed my head with
oil;
My cup overflows.

6 Surely goodness and lovingkindness will follow me all the days
of my life,
And I will [48]dwell in the house of
the LORD forever.

PSALM 24
A Psalm of David.

THE earth is the LORD's, and [49]all it
contains,
The world, and those who dwell in
it.

2 For He has founded it upon the
seas,
And established it upon the rivers.

3 Who may ascend into the hill of
the LORD?
And who may stand in His holy
place?

4 He who has clean hands and a
pure heart,
Who has not lifted up his soul to
falsehood,
And has not sworn deceitfully.

5 He shall receive a blessing from
the LORD
And righteousness from the God
of his salvation.

6 This is the generation of those
who seek Him,
Who seek Thy face—*even* Jacob.   [Selah.

7 ¶ Lift up your heads, O gates,
And be lifted up, O [50]ancient
doors,
That the King of glory may come
in!

8 Who is the King of glory?
The LORD strong and mighty,
The LORD mighty in battle.

9 Lift up your heads, O gates,
And lift *them* up, O [50]ancient
doors,
That the King of glory may come
in!

10 Who is this King of glory?
The LORD of hosts,
He is the King of glory.   [Selah.

PSALM 25
A Psalm of David.

TO Thee, O LORD, I lift up my soul.

2 O my God, in Thee I trust,
Do not let me be ashamed;

---

[45] Or, *poor* [46] Or, *valley of deep darkness*
[47] Or, *harm*

[48] Another reading is *return to* [49] Lit., *its fulness*
[50] Lit., *everlasting*

Do not let my enemies exult over
me.
3 Indeed, none of those who wait
for Thee will be ashamed;
Those who deal treacherously
without cause will be ashamed.

4 ¶ Make me know Thy ways, O
LORD;
Teach me Thy paths.
5 Lead me in Thy truth and teach
me,
For Thou art the God of my salvation;
For Thee I wait all the day.
6 Remember, O LORD, Thy compassion and Thy lovingkindnesses,
For they have been [50]from of old.
7 Do not remember the sins of my
youth or my transgressions;
According to Thy lovingkindness
remember Thou me,
For Thy goodness' sake, O LORD.

8 ¶ Good and upright is the LORD;
Therefore He instructs sinners in
the way.
9 He leads the humble in justice,
And He teaches the humble His
way.
10 All the paths of the LORD are
lovingkindness and truth
To those who keep His covenant
and His testimonies.
11 For Thy name's sake, O LORD,
Pardon my iniquity, for it is great.

12 ¶ Who is the man who fears the
LORD?
He will instruct him in the way he
should choose.
13 His soul will abide in prosperity,
And his [51]descendants will inherit
the land.
14 The secret of the LORD is for those
who fear Him,
And He will make them know His
covenant.
15 My eyes are continually toward
the LORD,
For He will pluck my feet out of
the net.

16 ¶ Turn to me and be gracious to
me,
For I am lonely and afflicted.

17 The troubles of my heart are enlarged;
Bring me out of my distresses.
18 Look upon my affliction and my
[52]trouble,
And forgive all my sins.
19 Look upon my enemies, for they
are many;
And they hate me with violent
hatred.
20 Guard my soul and deliver me;
Do not let me be ashamed, for I
take refuge in Thee.
21 Let integrity and uprightness preserve me,
For I wait for Thee.
22 Redeem Israel, O God,
Out of all his troubles.

PSALM 26

A Psalm of David.

[53]VINDICATE me, O LORD, for I
have walked in my integrity;
And I have trusted in the LORD
without wavering.
2 Examine me, O LORD, and try me;
Test my [54]mind and my heart.
3 For Thy lovingkindness is before
my eyes,
And I have walked in Thy truth.
4 I do not sit with [55]deceitful men,
Nor will I go with pretenders.
5 I hate the assembly of evildoers,
And I will not sit with the wicked.
6 I shall wash my hands in innocence,
And I will go about Thine altar, O
LORD,
7 That I may proclaim with the
voice of thanksgiving,
And declare all Thy wonders.

8 ¶ O LORD, I love the habitation of
Thy house,
And the place where Thy glory
dwells.
9 Do not take my soul away *along*
with sinners,
Nor my life with men of bloodshed,
10 In whose hands is a wicked
scheme,
And whose right hand is full of
bribes.
11 But as for me, I shall walk in my
integrity;

[50] Lit., *everlasting*   [51] Lit., *seed*

[52] Lit., *toil*   [53] Lit., *Judge*
[54] Lit., *kidneys*, figurative for inner man   [55] Or, *worthless*

Redeem me, and be gracious to
me.
12 My foot stands on a level place;
In the congregations I shall bless
the LORD.

PSALM 27
A Psalm of David.

THE LORD is my light and my salvation;
Whom shall I fear?
The LORD is the defense of my life;
Whom shall I dread?
2 When evildoers came upon me to
devour my flesh,
My adversaries and my enemies,
they stumbled and fell.
3 Though a host encamp against
me,
My heart will not fear;
Though war arise against me,
In *spite of* this I shall be confident.

4 ¶ One thing I have asked from
the LORD, that I shall seek:
That I may dwell in the house of
the LORD all the days of my life,
To behold the [56]beauty of the
LORD,
And to [57]meditate in His temple.
5 For in the day of trouble He will
conceal me in His tabernacle;
In the secret place of His tent He
will hide me;
He will lift me up on a rock.
6 And now my head will be lifted up
above my enemies around me;
And I will offer in His tent sacrifices with shouts of joy;
I will sing, yes, I will sing praises
to the LORD.

7 ¶ Hear, O LORD, when I cry with
my voice,
And be gracious to me and answer
me.
8 *When Thou didst say*, "Seek My
face," my heart said to Thee,
"Thy face, O LORD, I shall seek."
9 Do not hide Thy face from me,
Do not turn Thy servant away in
anger;
Thou hast been my help;
Do not abandon me nor forsake
me,
O God of my salvation!

10 For my father and my mother
have forsaken me,
But the LORD will take me up.

11 ¶ Teach me Thy way, O LORD,
And lead me in a level path,
Because of my foes.
12 Do not deliver me over to the
desire of my adversaries;
For false witnesses have risen
against me,
And such as breathe out violence.
13 *I would have despaired* unless I
had believed that I would see
the goodness of the LORD
In the land of the living.
14 Wait for the LORD;
Be strong, and let your heart take
courage;
Yes, wait for the LORD.

PSALM 28
A Psalm of David.

TO Thee, O LORD, I call;
My rock, do not be deaf to me,
Lest, if Thou be silent to me,
I become like those who go down
to the pit.
2 Hear the voice of my supplications when I cry to Thee for
help,
When I lift up my hands toward
[58]Thy holy sanctuary.
3 Do not drag me away with the
wicked
And with those who work iniquity;
Who speak peace with their
neighbors,
While evil is in their hearts.
4 Requite them according to their
work and according to the evil
of their practices;
Requite them according to the
deeds of their hands;
Repay them their [59]recompense.
5 Because they do not regard the
works of the LORD
Nor the deeds of His hands,
He will tear them down and not
build them up.

6 ¶ Blessed be the LORD,
Because He has heard the voice of
my supplication.

---

[56] Lit., *delightfulness* [57] Lit., *inquire*

[58] Lit., *the innermost place of Thy sanctuary*
[59] Or, *dealings*

7 The Lord is my strength and my
   shield;
   My heart trusts in Him, and I am
      helped;
   Therefore my heart exults,
   And with my song I shall thank
      Him.
8 The Lord is their strength,
   And He is a saving defense to His
      anointed.
9 Save Thy people, and bless Thine
      inheritance;
   Be their shepherd also, and carry
      them forever.

PSALM 29

A Psalm of David.

Ascribe to the Lord, O sons of the
   mighty,
   Ascribe to the Lord glory and
      strength.
2 Ascribe to the Lord the glory due
      to His name;
   Worship the Lord in holy array.

3 ¶ The voice of the Lord is upon
      the waters;
   The God of glory thunders,
   The Lord is over many waters.
4 The voice of the Lord is powerful,
   The voice of the Lord is majestic.
5 The voice of the Lord breaks the
      cedars;
   Yes, the Lord breaks in pieces the
      cedars of Lebanon.
6 And He makes Lebanon skip like
      a calf,
   And Sirion like a young wild ox.
7 The voice of the Lord hews out
      flames of fire.
8 The voice of the Lord shakes the
      wilderness;
   The Lord shakes the wilderness
      of Kadesh.
9 The voice of the Lord makes the
      deer to calve,
   And strips the forests bare,
   And in His temple everything
      says, "Glory!"

10 ¶ The Lord sat as King at the
      flood;
   Yes, the Lord sits as King forever.
11 The Lord will give strength to His
      people;
   The Lord will bless His people
      with peace.

PSALM 30

A Psalm; a Song at the Dedication of the House.
A Psalm of David.

I will extol Thee, O Lord, for Thou
   hast lifted me up,
   And hast not let my enemies re-
      joice over me.
2 O Lord my God,
   I cried to Thee for help, and Thou
      didst heal me.
3 O Lord, Thou hast brought up my
      soul from Sheol;
   Thou hast kept me alive, that I
      should not go down to the pit.
4 Sing praise to the Lord, you His
      godly ones,
   And give thanks to His holy
      name.
5 For His anger is but for a moment,
   His favor is for a lifetime;
   Weeping may last for the night,
   But a shout of joy comes in the
      morning.

6 ¶ Now as for me, I said in my
      prosperity,
   "I will never be moved."
7 O Lord, by Thy favor Thou hast
      made my mountain to stand
      strong;
   Thou didst hide Thy face, I was
      dismayed.
8 To Thee, O Lord, I called,
   And to the Lord I made supplica-
      tion:
9 "What profit is there in my blood, if
      I go down to the pit?
   Will the dust praise Thee? Will it
      declare Thy faithfulness?

10 ¶ "Hear, O Lord, and be gracious
      to me;
   O Lord, be Thou my helper."
11 Thou hast turned for me my
      mourning into dancing;
   Thou hast loosed my sackcloth
      and girded me with gladness;
12 That my soul may sing praise to
      Thee, and not be silent.
   O Lord my God, I will give thanks
      to Thee forever.

PSALM 31

For the choir director. A Psalm of David.

In Thee, O Lord, I have taken refuge;
   Let me never be ashamed;
   In Thy righteousness deliver me.
2 Incline Thine ear to me, rescue
      me quickly;

Be Thou to me a rock of strength,
A stronghold to save me.
3 For Thou art my rock and my
  fortress;
For Thy name's sake Thou wilt
  lead me and guide me.
4 Thou wilt pull me out of the net
  which they have secretly laid
  for me;
For Thou art my strength.
5 Into Thy hand I commit my spirit;
Thou hast ransomed me, O LORD,
  God of truth.

6 ¶ I hate those who regard vain
  idols;
But I trust in the LORD.
7 I will rejoice and be glad in Thy
  lovingkindness,
Because Thou hast seen my affliction;
Thou hast known the troubles of
  my soul,
8 And Thou hast not given me over
  into the hand of the enemy;
Thou hast set my feet in a large
  place.

9 ¶ Be gracious to me, O LORD, for I
  am in distress;
My eye is wasted away from grief,
  my soul and my body *also*.
10 For my life is spent with sorrow,
  And my years with sighing;
My strength has failed because of
  my iniquity,
And my body has wasted away.
11 Because of all my adversaries, I
  have become a reproach,
Especially to my neighbors,
And an object of dread to my
  acquaintances;
Those who see me in the street
  flee from me.
12 I am forgotten as a dead man, out
  of mind,
I am like a broken vessel.
13 For I have heard the slander of
  many,
Terror is on every side;
While they took counsel together
  against me,
They schemed to take away my
  life.

14 ¶ But as for me, I trust in Thee, O
  LORD,
I say, "Thou art my God."

15 My times are in Thy hand;
Deliver me from the hand of my
  enemies, and from those who
  persecute me.
16 Make Thy face to shine upon Thy
  servant;
Save me in Thy lovingkindness.
17 Let me not be put to shame, O
  LORD, for I call upon Thee;
Let the wicked be put to shame,
  let them be silent in Sheol.
18 Let the lying lips be dumb,
Which speak arrogantly against
  the righteous
With pride and contempt.

19 ¶ How great is Thy goodness,
Which Thou hast stored up for
  those who fear Thee,
Which Thou hast wrought for
  those who take refuge in Thee,
Before the sons of men!
20 Thou dost hide them in the secret
  place of Thy presence from the
  conspiracies of man;
Thou dost keep them secretly in a
  shelter from the strife of
  tongues.
21 Blessed be the LORD,
For He has made marvelous His
  lovingkindness to me in a besieged city.
22 As for me, I said in my alarm,
"I am cut off from before Thine
  eyes";
Nevertheless Thou didst hear the
  voice of my supplications
When I cried to Thee.

23 ¶ O love the LORD, all you His
  godly ones!
The LORD preserves the faithful,
And fully recompenses the proud
  doer.
24 Be strong, and let your heart take
  courage,
All you who hope in the LORD.

PSALM 32

A Psalm of David. A [60]Maskil.

HOW blessed is he whose transgression is forgiven,
Whose sin is covered!
2 How blessed is the man to whom
  the LORD does not impute iniquity,

[60] Possibly, *Contemplative* or *Didactic,* or *Skillful Psalm*

And in whose spirit there is no deceit!

3 ¶ When I kept silent *about my sin,* my body wasted away
Through my groaning all day long.
4 For day and night Thy hand was heavy upon me;
My vitality was drained away *as* with the fever heat of summer. [Selah.
5 I acknowledged my sin to Thee,
And my iniquity I did not hide;
I said, "I will confess my transgressions to the Lord";
And Thou didst forgive the guilt of my sin. [Selah.
6 Therefore, let everyone who is godly pray to Thee in a time when Thou mayest be found;
Surely in a flood of great waters they shall not reach him.
7 Thou art my hiding place; Thou dost preserve me from trouble;
Thou dost surround me with songs of deliverance. [Selah.

8 ¶ I will instruct you and teach you in the way which you should go;
I will counsel you with My eye upon you.
9 Do not be as the horse or as the mule which have no understanding,
Whose trappings include bit and bridle to hold them in check,
Otherwise they will not come near to you.
10 Many are the sorrows of the wicked;
But he who trusts in the Lord, lovingkindness shall surround him.
11 Be glad in the Lord and rejoice, you righteous ones,
And shout for joy, all you who are upright in heart.

PSALM 33

Sing for joy in the Lord, O you righteous ones;
Praise is becoming to the upright.
2 Give thanks to the Lord with the lyre;
Sing praises to Him with a harp of ten strings.

3 Sing to Him a new song;
Play skillfully with a shout of joy.
4 For the word of the Lord is upright;
And all His work is *done* in faithfulness.
5 He loves righteousness and justice;
The earth is full of the lovingkindness of the Lord.

6 ¶ By the word of the Lord the heavens were made,
And by the breath of His mouth all their host.
7 He gathers the waters of the sea together as a heap;
He lays up the deeps in storehouses.
8 Let all the earth fear the Lord;
Let all the inhabitants of the world stand in awe of Him.
9 For He spoke, and it was done;
He commanded, and it stood fast.
10 The Lord nullifies the counsel of the nations;
He frustrates the plans of the peoples.
11 The counsel of the Lord stands forever,
The plans of His heart from generation to generation.
12 Blessed is the nation whose God is the Lord,
The people whom He has chosen for His own inheritance.

13 ¶ The Lord looks from heaven;
He sees all the sons of men;
14 From His dwelling place He looks out
On all the inhabitants of the earth,
15 He who fashions the hearts of them all,
He who understands all their works.
16 The king is not saved by a mighty army;
A warrior is not delivered by great strength.
17 A horse is a false hope for victory;
Nor does it deliver anyone by its great strength.

18 ¶ Behold, the eye of the Lord is on those who fear Him,
On those who hope for His lovingkindness,

19 To deliver their soul from death,
And to keep them alive in famine.
20 Our soul waits for the LORD;
He is our help and our shield.
21 For our heart rejoices in Him,
Because we trust in His holy
name.
22 Let Thy lovingkindness, O LORD,
be upon us,
According as we have hoped in
Thee.

PSALM 34

A Psalm of David when he feigned madness
before Abimelech, who drove him away and he
departed.

I WILL bless the LORD at all times;
His praise shall continually be in
my mouth.
2 My soul shall make its boast in
the LORD;
The humble shall hear it and rejoice.
3 O magnify the LORD with me,
And let us exalt His name together.

4 ¶ I sought the LORD, and He answered me,
And delivered me from all my
fears.
5 They looked to Him and were
radiant,
And their faces shall never be
ashamed.
6 This poor man cried and the LORD
heard him,
And saved him out of all his troubles.
7 The angel of the LORD encamps
around those who fear Him,
And rescues them.

8 ¶ O taste and see that the LORD is
good;
How blessed is the man who takes
refuge in Him!
9 O fear the LORD, you His saints;
For to those who fear Him, there
is no want.
10 The young lions do lack and suffer
hunger;
But they who seek the LORD shall
not be in want of any good
thing.
11 Come, you children, listen to me;
I will teach you the fear of the
LORD.

12 Who is the man who desires life,
And loves *length of* days that he
may see good?
13 Keep your tongue from evil,
And your lips from speaking deceit.
14 Depart from evil, and do good;
Seek peace, and pursue it.

15 ¶ The eyes of the LORD are
toward the righteous,
And His ears are *open* to their cry.
16 The face of the LORD is against
evildoers,
To cut off the memory of them
from the earth.
17 *The righteous* cry and the LORD
hears,
And delivers them out of all their
troubles.
18 The LORD is near to the brokenhearted,
And saves those who are
[61]crushed in spirit.

19 ¶ Many are the afflictions of the
righteous;
But the LORD delivers him out of
them all.
20 He keeps all his bones;
Not one of them is broken.
21 Evil shall slay the wicked;
And those who hate the righteous
will be condemned.
22 The LORD redeems the soul of His
servants;
And none of those who take refuge in Him will be condemned.

PSALM 35

A Psalm of David.

CONTEND, O LORD, with those who
contend with me;
Fight against those who fight
against me.
2 Take hold of [62]buckler and shield,
And rise up for my help.
3 Draw also the spear and the bat-
tle-axe to meet those who pursue me;
Say to my soul, "I am your salvation."
4 Let those be ashamed and dishonored who seek my life;
Let those be turned back and humiliated who devise evil against
me.

[61] Or, *contrite*   [62] I.e., small shield

5 Let them be like chaff before the
 wind,
 With the angel of the LORD driving *them* on.
6 Let their way be dark and slippery,
 With the angel of the LORD pursuing them.
7 For without cause they hid their
 net for me;
 Without cause they dug a pit for
 my soul.
8 Let destruction come upon him
 unawares;
 And let the net which he hid catch
 himself;
 Into that very destruction let him
 fall.

9 ¶ And my soul shall rejoice in the
 LORD;
 It shall exult in His salvation.
10 All my bones will say, "LORD, who
 is like Thee,
 Who delivers the afflicted from
 him who is too strong for him,
 And the afflicted and the needy
 from him who robs him?"
11 Malicious witnesses rise up;
 They ask me of things that I do
 not know.
12 They repay me evil for good,
 To the bereavement of my soul.
13 But as for me, when they were
 sick, my clothing was sackcloth;
 I humbled my soul with fasting;
 And my prayer kept returning to
 my bosom.
14 I went about as though it were
 my friend or brother;
 I bowed down mourning, as one
 who sorrows for a mother.
15 But at my [63]stumbling they rejoiced, and gathered themselves
 together;
 The smiters whom I did not know
 gathered together against me,
 They slandered me without ceasing.
16 Like godless jesters at a feast,
 They gnashed at me with their
 teeth.

17 ¶ Lord, how long wilt Thou look
 on?

[63] Or, *limping*

Rescue my soul from their rav-
 ages,
 My only *life* from the lions.
18 I will give Thee thanks in the
 great congregation;
 I will praise Thee among a mighty
 throng.
19 Do not let those who are wrongfully my enemies rejoice over
 me;
 Neither let those who hate me
 without cause wink mali-
 ciously.
20 For they do not speak peace,
 But they devise deceitful words
 against those who are quiet in
 the land.
21 And they opened their mouth
 wide against me;
 They said, "Aha, aha, our eyes
 have seen it!"

22 ¶ Thou hast seen it, O LORD, do
 not keep silent;
 O Lord, do not be far from me.
23 Stir up Thyself, and awake to my
 right,
 And to my cause, my God and my
 Lord.
24 Judge me, O LORD my God, according to Thy righteousness;
 And do not let them rejoice over
 me.
25 Do not let them say in their heart,
 "Aha, our desire!"
 Do not let them say, "We have
 swallowed him up!"
26 Let those be ashamed and humiliated altogether who rejoice at
 my distress;
 Let those be clothed with shame
 and dishonor who magnify
 themselves over me.

27 ¶ Let them shout for joy and re-
 joice, who favor my vindica-
 tion;
 And let them say continually,
 "The LORD be magnified,
 Who delights in the prosperity of
 His servant."
28 And my tongue shall declare Thy
 righteousness
 And Thy praise all day long.

PSALM 36

For the choir director.　*A Psalm* of David the
servant of the LORD.

Transgression speaks to the ungodly within his heart;

There is no fear of God before his
eyes.

2 For it flatters him in his *own* eyes,
Concerning the discovery of his
iniquity *and* the hatred *of it*.

3 The words of his mouth are wickedness and deceit;
He has ceased to be wise *and* to
do good.

4 He plans wickedness upon his
bed;
He sets himself on a path that is
not good;
He does not despise evil.

5 ¶ Thy lovingkindness, O LORD,
extends to the heavens,
Thy faithfulness *reaches* to the
skies.

6 Thy righteousness is like the
mountains of God;
Thy judgments are *like* a great
deep.
O LORD, Thou preservest man and
beast.

7 How precious is Thy lovingkindness, O God!
And the children of men take refuge in the shadow of Thy
wings.

8 They drink their fill of the abundance of Thy house;
And Thou dost give them to drink
of the river of Thy delights.

9 For with Thee is the fountain of
life;
In Thy light we see light.

10 ¶ O continue Thy lovingkindness
to those who know Thee,
And Thy righteousness to the upright in heart.

11 Let not the foot of pride come
upon me,
And let not the hand of the
wicked drive me away.

12 There the doers of iniquity have
fallen;
They have been thrust down and
cannot rise.

PSALM 37
A Psalm of David.

Do not fret because of evildoers,
Be not envious toward wrongdoers.

2 For they will wither quickly like
the grass,
And fade like the green herb.

3 Trust in the LORD, and do good;
Dwell in the land and [64]cultivate
faithfulness.

4 Delight yourself in the LORD;
And He will give you the desires
of your heart.

5 Commit your way to the LORD,
Trust also in Him, and He will do
it.

6 And He will bring forth your
righteousness as the light,
And your judgment as the noonday.

7 ¶ [65]Rest in the LORD and wait
[66]patiently for Him;
Do not fret because of him who
prospers in his way,
Because of the man who carries
out wicked schemes.

8 Cease from anger, and forsake
wrath;
Do not fret, *it leads* only to evildoing.

9 For evildoers will be cut off,
But those who wait for the LORD,
they will inherit the land.

10 Yet a little while and the wicked
man will be no more;
And you will look carefully for his
place, and he will not be *there*.

11 But the humble will inherit the
land,
And will delight themselves in
abundant prosperity.

12 ¶ The wicked plots against the
righteous,
And gnashes at him with his
teeth.

13 The Lord laughs at him;
For He sees his day is coming.

14 The wicked have drawn the sword
and bent their bow,
To cast down the afflicted and the
needy,
To slay those who are upright in
conduct.

15 Their sword will enter their own
heart,
And their bows will be broken.

16 ¶ Better is the little of the righteous
Than the abundance of many
wicked.

64 Or, *feed securely, or, feed on His faithfulness*
65 Or, *Be still*   66 Or, *longingly*

17 For the arms of the wicked will be
broken;
But the LORD sustains the righteous.
18 The LORD knows the days of the
blameless;
And their inheritance will be forever.
19 They will not be ashamed in the
time of evil;
And in the days of famine they
will have abundance.
20 But the wicked will perish;
And the enemies of the LORD will
be like the [67]glory of the pastures,
They vanish—like smoke they
vanish away.
21 The wicked borrows and does not
pay back,
But the righteous is gracious and
gives.
22 For those blessed by Him will
inherit the land;
But those cursed by Him will be
cut off.

23 ¶ The steps of a man are established by the LORD;
And He delights in his way.
24 When he falls, he shall not be
hurled headlong;
Because the LORD is the One who
holds his hand.
25 I have been young, and now I am
old;
Yet I have not seen the righteous
forsaken,
Or his descendants begging bread.
26 All day long he is gracious and
lends;
And his descendants are a blessing.

27 ¶ Depart from evil, and do good,
So you will abide forever.
28 For the LORD loves justice,
And does not forsake His godly
ones;
They are preserved forever;
But the descendants of the wicked
will be cut off.
29 The righteous will inherit the
land,
And dwell in it forever.
30 The mouth of the righteous utters
wisdom,

And his tongue speaks justice.
31 The law of his God is in his heart;
His steps do not slip.
32 The wicked spies upon the righteous,
And seeks to kill him.
33 The LORD will not leave him in his
hand,
Or let him be condemned when he
is judged.
34 Wait for the LORD, and keep His
way,
And He will exalt you to inherit
the land;
When the wicked are cut off, you
will see it.

35 ¶ I have seen a violent, wicked
man
Spreading himself like a luxuriant
tree in its native soil.
36 Then he passed away, and lo, he
was no more;
I sought for him, but he could not
be found.
37 Mark the blameless man, and behold the upright;
For the man of peace will have a
posterity.
38 But transgressors will be altogether destroyed;
The posterity of the wicked will
be cut off.
39 But the salvation of the righteous
is from the LORD;
He is their strength in time of
trouble.
40 And the LORD helps them, and
delivers them;
He delivers them from the wicked,
and saves them,
Because they take refuge in Him.

PSALM 38
A Psalm of David, for a memorial.

O LORD, rebuke me not in Thy
wrath;
And chasten me not in Thy burning anger.
2 For Thine arrows have sunk deep
into me,
And Thy hand has pressed down
on me.
3 There is no soundness in my flesh
because of Thine indignation;
There is no health in my bones
because of my sin.

[67] I.e., flowers

4 For my iniquities are gone over
  my head;
   As a heavy burden they weigh too
   much for me.
5 My wounds grow foul *and* fester.
   Because of my folly,
6 I am bent over and greatly bowed
   down;
   I go mourning all day long.
7 For my loins are filled with burning;
   And there is no soundness in my
   flesh.
8 I am benumbed and badly
   crushed;
   I groan because of the agitation of
   my heart.

9 ¶ Lord, all my desire is before
   Thee;
   And my sighing is not hidden
   from Thee.
10 My heart throbs, my strength fails
   me;
   And the light of my eyes, even
   that has gone from me.
11 My loved ones and my friends
   stand aloof from my plague;
   And my kinsmen stand afar off.
12 Those who seek my life lay snares
   for me;
   And those who seek to injure me
   have threatened destruction,
   And they devise treachery all day
   long.

13 ¶ But I, like a deaf man, do not
   hear;
   And I am like a dumb man who
   does not open his mouth.
14 Yes, I am like a man who does not
   hear,
   And in whose mouth are no arguments.
15 For I hope in Thee, O LORD;
   Thou wilt answer, O Lord my
   God.
16 For I said, "May they not rejoice
   over me,
   Who, when my foot slips, would
   magnify themselves against
   me."
17 For I am ready to fall,
   And my [68]sorrow is continually
   before me.
18 For I confess my iniquity;
   I am full of anxiety because of my
   sin.

19 But my enemies are vigorous *and*
   [69]strong;
   And many are those who hate me
   wrongfully.
20 And those who repay evil for
   good,
   They oppose me, because I follow
   what is good.
21 Do not forsake me, O LORD;
   O my God, do not be far from me!
22 Make haste to help me,
   O Lord, my salvation!

PSALM 39

For the choir director, for Jeduthun.
A Psalm of David.

I SAID, "I will guard my ways,
   That I may not sin with my
   tongue;
   I will guard my mouth as with a
   muzzle,
   While the wicked are in my presence."
2 I was dumb and silent,
   I [70]refrained *even* from good;
   And my [68]sorrow grew worse.
3 My heart was hot within me;
   While I was musing the fire
   burned;
   Then I spoke with my tongue:
4"LORD, make me to know my end,
   And what is the extent of my
   days,
   Let me know how transient I am.
5"Behold, Thou hast made my days
   as handbreadths,
   And my lifetime as nothing in Thy
   sight,
   Surely every man at his best is a
   mere breath.   [Selah.
6"Surely every man walks about as
   [71]a phantom;
   Surely they make an uproar for
   nothing;
   He amasses *riches*, and does not
   know who will gather them.

7 ¶"And now, Lord, for what do I
   wait?
   My hope is in Thee.
8"Deliver me from all my transgressions;
   Make me not the reproach of the
   foolish.
9"I have become dumb, I do not
   open my mouth,

---

[68] Lit., *pain*   [69] Or, *numerous*   [70] Lit., *kept silence*   [71] Lit., *an image*

Because it is Thou who hast done
it.
10"Remove Thy plague from me;
Because of the opposition of Thy
hand, I am perishing.
11"With reproofs Thou dost chasten
a man for iniquity;
Thou dost consume as a moth
what is precious to him;
Surely every man is a mere
breath.   [Selah.

12 ¶"Hear my prayer, O LORD, and
give ear to my cry;
Do not be silent at my tears;
For I am a stranger with Thee,
A sojourner like all my fathers.
13"Turn Thy gaze away from me,
that I may 72smile *again,*
Before I depart and am no more."

PSALM 40

For the choir director. A Psalm of David.

I WAITED 73patiently for the LORD;
And He inclined to me, and heard
my cry.
2 He brought me up out of the pit of
destruction, out of the miry
clay;
And He set my feet upon a rock
making my footsteps firm.
3 And He put a new song in my
mouth, a song of praise to our
God;
Many will see and fear,
And will trust in the LORD.

4 ¶ How blessed is the man who
has made the LORD his trust,
And has not turned to the proud,
nor to those who lapse into
falsehood.
5 Many, O LORD my God, are the
wonders which Thou hast done,
And Thy thoughts toward us;
There is none to compare with
Thee;
If I would declare and speak of
them,
They would be too numerous to
count.

6 ¶ Sacrifice and meal offering
Thou hast not desired;
My ears Thou hast 74opened;

Burnt offering and sin offering
Thou hast not required.
7 Then I said, "Behold, I come;
In the scroll of the book it is
written of me;
8 I delight to do Thy will, O my
God;
Thy Law is within my heart."

9 ¶ I have proclaimed glad tidings
of righteousness in the great
congregation;
Behold, I will not restrain my lips,
O LORD, Thou knowest.
10 I have not hidden Thy righteousness within my heart;
I have spoken of Thy faithfulness
and Thy salvation;
I have not concealed Thy lovingkindness and Thy truth from
the great congregation.

11 ¶ Thou, O LORD, wilt not withhold Thy compassion from me;
Thy lovingkindness and Thy truth
will continually preserve me.
12 For evils beyond number have
surrounded me;
My iniquities have overtaken me,
so that I am not able to see;
They are more numerous than the
hairs of my head;
And my heart has failed me.

13 ¶ Be pleased, O LORD, to deliver
me;
Make haste, O LORD, to help me.
14 Let those be ashamed and humiliated together
Who seek my 75life to destroy it;
Let those be turned back and dishonored
Who delight 76in my hurt.
15 Let those be appalled because of
their shame
Who say to me, "Aha, aha!"
16 Let all who seek Thee rejoice and
be glad in Thee;
Let those who love Thy salvation
say continually,
"The LORD be magnified!"
17 Since I am afflicted and needy,
Let the Lord be mindful of me;
Thou art my help and my deliverer;
Do not delay, O my God.

---

72 Or, *become cheerful*   73 Or, *intently*
74 Lit., *dug,* or possibly, *pierced*
75 Or, *soul*   76 Or, *to injure me*

PSALM 41

For the choir director. A Psalm of David.

How blessed is he who considers the
helpless;
The Lord will deliver him in a day
of trouble.
2 The Lord will protect him, and
keep him alive,
And he shall be called blessed
upon the earth;
And do not give him over to the
desire of his enemies.
3 The Lord will sustain him upon
his sickbed;
In his illness, Thou dost [77]restore
him to health.

4 ¶ As for me, I said, "O Lord, be
gracious to me;
Heal my soul, for I have sinned
against Thee."
5 My enemies speak evil against me,
"When will he die, and his name
perish?"
6 And when he comes to see *me*, he
speaks falsehood;
His heart gathers wickedness to
itself;
When he goes outside, he tells it.
7 All who hate me whisper together
against me;
Against me they devise my hurt,
saying,
8 "A wicked thing is poured out
upon him,
That when he lies down, he will
not rise up again."
9 Even my close friend, in whom I
trusted,
Who ate my bread,
Has lifted up his heel against me.

10 ¶ But Thou, O Lord, be gracious
to me, and raise me up,
That I may repay them.
11 By this I know that Thou art
pleased with me,
Because my enemy does not shout
in triumph over me.
12 As for me, Thou dost uphold me
in my integrity,
And Thou dost set me in Thy
presence forever.

13 ¶ Blessed be the Lord, the God of
Israel,
From everlasting to everlasting.
Amen, and Amen.

BOOK 2

PSALM 42

For the choir director.
A Maskil of the sons of Korah.

As the deer [78]pants for the water
brooks,
So my soul pants for Thee, O God.
2 My soul thirsts for God, for the
living God;
When shall I come and appear
before God?
3 My tears have been my food day
and night,
While *they* say to me all day long,
"Where is your God?"
4 These things I remember, and I
pour out my soul within me.
For I used to go along with the
throng *and* lead them in procession to the house of God,
With the voice of joy and thanksgiving, a multitude keeping festival.

5 ¶ Why are you in despair, O my
soul?
And *why* have you become disturbed within me?
Hope in God, for I shall again
praise Him
For the help of His presence.
6 O my God, my soul is in despair
within me;
Therefore I remember Thee from
the land of the Jordan,
And the peaks of Hermon, from
Mount Mizar.
7 Deep calls to deep at the sound of
Thy waterfalls;
All Thy breakers and Thy waves
have rolled over me.
8 The Lord will command His
lovingkindness in the daytime;
And His song will be with me in
the night,
A prayer to the God of my life.

9 ¶ I will say to God my rock, "Why
hast Thou forgotten me?
Why do I go mourning because of
the oppression of the enemy?"
10 As a shattering of my bones, my
adversaries revile me,
While they say to me all day long,
"Where is your God?"

[77] Lit., *turn all his bed*

[78] Lit., *longs for*

11 Why are you in despair, O my
soul?
And why have you become dis-
turbed within me?
Hope in God, for I shall yet praise
Him,
The help of my countenance, and
my God.

PSALM 43

VINDICATE me, O God, and plead
my case against an ungodly nation;
O deliver me from the deceitful
and unjust man!
2 For Thou art the God of my
strength; why hast Thou rejected me?
Why do I go mourning because of
the oppression of the enemy?

3 ¶ O send out Thy light and Thy
truth, let them lead me;
Let them bring me to Thy holy
hill,
And to Thy dwelling places.
4 Then I will go to the altar of God,
To God my exceeding joy;
And upon the lyre I shall praise
Thee, O God, my God.

5 ¶ Why are you in despair, O my
soul?
And why are you disturbed within
me?
Hope in God, for I shall again
praise Him,
The help of my countenance, and
my God.

PSALM 44

For the choir director.
A Maskil of the sons of Korah.

O GOD, we have heard with our ears,
Our fathers have told us,
The work that Thou didst in their
days,
In the days of old.
2 Thou with Thine own hand didst
drive out the nations;
Then Thou didst plant them;
Thou didst afflict the peoples,
Then Thou didst spread them
abroad.
3 For by their own sword they did
not possess the land;
And their own arm did not save
them;

But Thy right hand, and Thine
arm, and the light of Thy presence,
For Thou didst favor them.

4 ¶ Thou art my King, O God;
Command victories for Jacob.
5 Through Thee we will push back
our adversaries;
Through Thy name we will trample down those who rise up
against us.
6 For I will not trust in my bow,
Nor will my sword save me.
7 But Thou hast saved us from our
adversaries,
And Thou hast put to shame
those who hate us.
8 In God we have boasted all day
long,
And we will give thanks to Thy
name forever.   [Selah.

9 ¶ Yet Thou hast rejected us and
brought us to dishonor,
And dost not go out with our
armies.
10 Thou dost cause us to turn back
from the adversary;
And those who hate us have
taken spoil for themselves.
11 Thou dost give us as sheep to be
eaten,
And hast scattered us among the
nations.
12 Thou dost sell Thy people
cheaply,
And hast not [79]profited by their
sale.
13 Thou dost make us a reproach to
our neighbors,
A scoffing and a derision to those
around us.
14 Thou dost make us a byword
among the nations,
A laughingstock among the peoples.
15 All day long my dishonor is before
me,
And my humiliation has overwhelmed me,
16 Because of the voice of him who
reproaches and reviles,
Because of the presence of the
enemy and the avenger.

[79] Or, set a high price on them

17 ¶ All this has come upon us, but we have not forgotten Thee,
And we have not dealt falsely with Thy covenant.
18 Our heart has not turned back, And our steps have not deviated from Thy way,
19 Yet Thou hast crushed us in a place of jackals,
And covered us with the shadow of death.

20 ¶ If we had forgotten the name of our God,
Or extended our hands to a strange god;
21 Would not God find this out? For He knows the secrets of the heart.
22 But for Thy sake we are killed all day long;
We are considered as sheep to be slaughtered.
23 Arouse Thyself, why dost Thou sleep, O Lord?
Awake, do not reject us forever.
24 Why dost Thou hide Thy face, And forget our affliction and our oppression?
25 For our soul has sunk down into the dust;
Our body cleaves to the earth.
26 Rise up, be our help, And redeem us for the sake of Thy lovingkindness.

PSALM 45

For the choir director; according to the
80Shoshannim. A Maskil of the sons of Korah. A Song of Love.

MY heart 81overflows with a good theme;
I address my verses to the King;
My tongue is the pen of a ready writer.
2 Thou art fairer than the sons of men;
Grace is poured upon Thy lips;
Therefore God has blessed Thee forever.

3 ¶ Gird Thy sword on *Thy* thigh, O Mighty One,
In Thy splendor and Thy majesty!
4 And in Thy majesty ride on victoriously,
For the cause of truth and meekness *and* righteousness;

Let Thy right hand teach Thee awesome things.
5 Thine arrows are sharp;
The peoples fall under Thee;
Thine arrows are in the heart of the King's enemies.

6 ¶ Thy throne, O God, is forever and ever;
A scepter of uprightness is the scepter of Thy kingdom.
7 Thou hast loved righteousness, and hated wickedness;
Therefore God, Thy God, has anointed Thee
With the oil of joy above Thy fellows.
8 All Thy garments are *fragrant with* myrrh and aloes *and* cassia;
Out of ivory palaces stringed instruments have made Thee glad.
9 Kings' daughters are among Thy noble ladies;
At Thy right hand stands the queen in gold from Ophir.

10 ¶ Listen, O daughter, give attention and incline your ear;
Forget your people and your father's house;
11 Then the King will desire your beauty;
Because He is your Lord, bow down to Him.
12 And the daughter of Tyre *will come* with a gift;
The rich among the people will entreat your favor.

13 ¶ The King's daughter is all glorious within;
Her clothing is interwoven with gold.
14 She will be led to the King in embroidered work;
The virgins, her companions who follow her,
Will be brought to Thee.
15 They will be led forth with gladness and rejoicing;
They will enter into the King's palace.

16 ¶ In place of your fathers will be your sons;
You shall make them princes in all the earth.

80 Possibly, *Lilies*   81 Lit., *is astir*

17 I will cause Thy name to be re-
 membered in all generations;
 Therefore the peoples will give
 Thee thanks forever and ever.

PSALM 46

For the choir director. *A Psalm* of the sons of
Korah, [82]set to Alamoth. A Song.

GOD is our refuge and strength,
 [83]A very present help in trouble.
2 Therefore we will not fear, though
 the earth should change,
 And though the mountains slip
 into the heart of the sea;
3 Though its waters roar *and* foam,
 Though the mountains quake at
 its swelling pride.   [Selah.
4 ¶ There is a river whose streams
 make glad the city of God,
 The holy dwelling places of the
 Most High.
5 God is in the midst of her, she will
 not be moved;
 God will help her when morning
 dawns.
6 The nations made an uproar, the
 kingdoms tottered;
 He raised His voice, the earth
 melted.
7 The LORD of hosts is with us;
 The God of Jacob is our stronghold.   [Selah.
8 ¶ Come, behold the works of the
 LORD,
 Who has wrought desolations in
 the earth.
9 He makes wars to cease to the
 end of the earth;
 He breaks the bow and cuts the
 spear in two;
 He burns the chariots with fire.
10 "Cease *striving* and know that I am
 God;
 I will be exalted among the nations, I will be exalted in the
 earth."
11 The LORD of hosts is with us;
 The God of Jacob is our stronghold.   [Selah.

PSALM 47

For the choir director.
A Psalm of the sons of Korah.

O CLAP your hands, all peoples;
 Shout to God with the voice of
 joy.
2 For the LORD Most High is to be
 feared,

A great King over all the earth.
3 He subdues peoples under us,
 And nations under our feet.
4 He chooses our inheritance for us,
 The glory of Jacob whom He
 loves.   [Selah.

5 ¶ God has ascended with a shout,
 The LORD, with the sound of a
 trumpet.
6 Sing praises to God, sing praises;
 Sing praises to our King, sing
 praises.
7 For God is the King of all the
 earth;
 Sing praises with a skillful psalm.
8 God reigns over the nations,
 God sits on His holy throne.
9 The princes of the people have
 assembled themselves *as the*
 people of the God of Abraham;
 For the shields of the earth belong
 to God;
 He is highly exalted.

PSALM 48

A Song; a Psalm of the sons of Korah.

GREAT is the LORD, and greatly to
 be praised,
 In the city of our God, His holy
 mountain.
2 Beautiful in elevation, the joy of
 the whole earth,
 Is Mount Zion *in* the far north,
 The city of the great King.
3 God, in her palaces,
 Has made Himself known as a
 stronghold.

4 ¶ For, lo, the kings assembled
 themselves,
 They passed by together.
5 They saw *it*, then they were
 amazed;
 They were terrified, they fled in
 alarm.
6 Panic seized them there,
 Anguish, as of a woman in childbirth.
7 With the east wind
 Thou dost break the ships of Tarshish.
8 As we have heard, so have we
 seen
 In the city of the LORD of hosts, in
 the city of our God;
 God will establish her forever.
                            [Selah.

9 ¶ We have thought on Thy
lovingkindness, O God,
In the midst of Thy temple.
10 As is Thy name, O God,
So is Thy praise to the ends of the
earth;
Thy right hand is full of righteousness.
11 Let Mount Zion be glad,
Let the daughters of Judah rejoice,
Because of Thy judgments.
12 Walk about Zion, and go around
her;
Count her towers;
13 Consider her ramparts;
Go through her palaces;
That you may tell it to the next
generation.
14 For such is God,
Our God forever and ever;
He will guide us 84until death.

PSALM 49
For the choir director.
A Psalm of the sons of Korah.

HEAR this, all peoples;
Give ear, all inhabitants of the
world,
2 Both low and high,
Rich and poor together.
3 My mouth will speak wisdom;
And the meditation of my heart
will be understanding.
4 I will incline my ear to a proverb;
I will express my riddle on the
harp.

5 ¶ Why should I fear in days of
adversity,
When the iniquity of my foes surrounds me,
6 Even those who trust in their
wealth,
And boast in the abundance of
their riches?
7 No man can by any means redeem
his brother,
Or give to God a ransom for
him—
8 For the redemption of his soul is
costly,
And he should cease trying forever—
9 That he should live on eternally;
That he should not 85undergo decay.

10 ¶ For he sees that even wise men
die;
The stupid and the senseless alike
perish,
And leave their wealth to others.
11 Their 86inner thought is, that their
houses are forever,
And their dwelling places to all
generations;
They have called their lands after
their own names.
12 But man in his pomp will not
endure;
He is like the beasts that perish.

13 ¶ This is the way of those who are
foolish,
And of those after them who approve their words. [Selah.
14 As sheep they are appointed for
Sheol;
Death shall be their shepherd;
And the upright shall rule over
them in the morning;
And their form shall be for Sheol
to consume,
So that they have no habitation.
15 But God will redeem my soul from
the power of Sheol;
For He will receive me. [Selah.

16 ¶ Do not be afraid when a man
becomes rich,
When the 87glory of his house is
increased;
17 For when he dies he will carry
nothing away;
His 87glory will not descend after
him.
18 Though while he lives he con-
gratulates himself—
And though men praise you when
you do well for yourself—
19 He shall go to the generation of
his fathers;
They shall never see the light.
20 Man in his pomp, yet without
understanding,
Is like the beasts that perish.

PSALM 50
A Psalm of Asaph.

THE Mighty One, God, the LORD, has
spoken,
And summoned the earth from

---

84 Some mss. and the Gr. read forever
85 Or, see corruption or the pit

86 Some versions read graves are their houses
87 Or, wealth

the rising of the sun to its setting.
2 Out of Zion, the perfection of
beauty,
God has shone forth.
3 May our God come and not keep
silence;
Fire devours before Him,
And it is very tempestuous around
Him.
4 He summons the heavens above,
And the earth, to judge His people:
5 "Gather My godly ones to Me,
Those who have made a covenant
with Me by sacrifice."
6 And the heavens declare His
righteousness,
For God Himself is judge. [Selah.

7 ¶ "Hear, O My people, and I will
speak;
O Israel, I will testify against you;
I am God, your God.
8 "I do not reprove you for your
sacrifices,
And your burnt offerings are continually before Me.
9 "I shall take no young bull out of
your house,
Nor male goats out of your folds.
10 "For every beast of the forest is
Mine,
The cattle on a thousand hills.
11 "I know every bird of the mountains,
And everything that moves in the
field is [88]Mine.
12 "If I were hungry, I would not tell
you;
For the world is Mine, and all it
contains.
13 "Shall I eat the flesh of bulls,
Or drink the blood of male goats?
14 "Offer to God a sacrifice of thanksgiving,
And pay your vows to the Most
High;
15 And call upon Me in the day of
trouble;
I shall rescue you, and you will
honor Me."

16 ¶ But to the wicked God says,
"What right have you to tell of My
statutes,
And to take My covenant in your
mouth?

17 "For you hate discipline,
And you cast My words behind
you.
18 "When you see a thief, you are
pleased with him,
And you associate with adulterers.
19 "You let your mouth loose in evil,
And your tongue frames deceit.
20 "You sit and speak against your
brother;
You slander your own mother's
son.
21 "These things you have done, and I
kept silence;
You thought that I was just like
you;
I will reprove you, and state *the
case* in order before your eyes.

22 ¶ "Now consider this, you who
forget God,
Lest I tear *you* in pieces, and there
be none to deliver.
23 "He who offers a sacrifice of
thanksgiving honors Me;
And to him who orders *his* way
aright
I shall show the salvation of God."

PSALM 51

For the choir director.   A Psalm of David, when
Nathan the prophet came to him, after he had
gone in to Bathsheba.

BE gracious to me, O God, according
to Thy lovingkindness;
According to the greatness of Thy
compassion blot out my transgressions.
2 Wash me thoroughly from my
iniquity,
And cleanse me from my sin.
3 For I know my transgressions,
And my sin is ever before me.
4 Against Thee, Thee only, I have
sinned,
And done what is evil in Thy
sight,
So that Thou [89]art justified when
Thou dost speak,
And blameless when Thou dost
judge.

5 ¶ Behold, I was brought forth in
iniquity,
And in sin my mother conceived
me.

[88] Or, *in My mind*   [89] Or, *mayest be in the right*

6 Behold, Thou dost desire truth in
the innermost being,
And in the hidden part Thou wilt
make me know wisdom.
7 Purify me with hyssop, and I shall
be clean;
Wash me, and I shall be whiter
than snow.
8 Make me to hear joy and gladness,
Let the bones which Thou hast
broken rejoice.
9 Hide Thy face from my sins,
And blot out all my iniquities.

10 ¶ Create in me a clean heart, O
God,
And renew a steadfast spirit
within me.
11 Do not cast me away from Thy
presence,
And do not take Thy Holy Spirit
from me.
12 Restore to me the joy of Thy salvation,
And sustain me with a willing
spirit.
13 *Then* I will teach transgressors
Thy ways,
And sinners will ⁹⁰be converted to
Thee.

14 ¶ Deliver me from bloodguiltiness, O God, Thou God of my
salvation;
Then my tongue will joyfully sing
of Thy righteousness.
15 O Lord, open my lips,
That my mouth may declare Thy
praise.
16 For Thou dost not delight in sacrifice, otherwise I would give it;
Thou art not pleased with burnt
offering.
17 The sacrifices of God are a broken
spirit;
A broken and a contrite heart, O
God, Thou wilt not despise.

18 ¶ By Thy favor do good to Zion;
Build the walls of Jerusalem.
19 Then Thou wilt delight in righteous sacrifices,
In burnt offering and whole burnt
offering;
Then young bulls will be offered
on Thine altar.

PSALM 52

For the choir director. A Maskil of David, when
Doeg the Edomite came and told Saul, and said to
him, "David has come to the house of Ahimelech."

WHY do you boast in evil, O mighty
man?
The lovingkindness of God *endures* all day long.
2 Your tongue devises destruction,
Like a sharp razor, O worker of
deceit.
3 You love evil more than good,
Falsehood more than speaking
what is right. [Selah.
4 You love all words that devour,
O deceitful tongue.

5 ¶ But God will break you down
forever;
He will snatch you up, and tear
you away from *your* tent,
And uproot you from the land of
the living. [Selah.
6 And the righteous will see and
fear,
And will laugh at him, *saying,*
7"Behold, the man who would not
make God his refuge,
But trusted in the abundance of
his riches,
And was strong in his *evil* desire."

8 ¶ But as for me, I am like a green
olive tree in the house of God;
I trust in the lovingkindness of
God forever and ever.
9 I will give Thee thanks forever,
because Thou hast done *it,*
And I will wait on Thy name, for
it is good, in the presence of
Thy godly ones.

PSALM 53

For the choir director; according to ⁹¹Mahalath. A
Maskil of David.

THE fool has said in his heart, "There
is no God,"
They are corrupt, and have committed abominable injustice;
There is no one who does good.
2 God has looked down from
heaven upon the sons of men,
To see if there is anyone who
understands,
Who seeks after God.
3 Every one of them has turned

⁹⁰ Or, *turn back*   ⁹¹ I.e., *sickness, a sad tone*

aside; together they have become corrupt;
There is no one who does good, not even one.

4 ¶ Have the workers of wickedness no knowledge,
Who eat up My people *as though* they ate bread,
And have not called upon God?
5 There they were in great fear *where* no fear had been;
For God scattered the bones of him who encamped against you;
You put *them* to shame, because God had rejected them.
6 Oh, that the salvation of Israel would come out of Zion!
When God restores His captive people,
Let Jacob rejoice, let Israel be glad.

PSALM 54

For the choir director; on stringed instruments. A Maskil of David, when the Ziphites came and said to Saul, "Is not David hiding himself among us?"

SAVE me, O God, by Thy name,
And [92]vindicate me by Thy power.
2 Hear my prayer, O God;
Give ear to the words of my mouth.
3 For strangers have risen against me,
And violent men have sought my life;
They have not set God before them.   [Selah.

4 ¶ Behold, God is my helper;
The Lord is the sustainer of my soul.
5 [93]He will recompense the evil to my foes;
Destroy them in Thy faithfulness.

6 ¶ Willingly I will sacrifice to Thee;
I will give thanks to Thy name, O LORD, for it is good.
7 For He has delivered me from all trouble;
And my eye has looked *with satisfaction* upon my enemies.

PSALM 55

For the choir director; on stringed instruments.
A Maskil of David.

GIVE ear to my prayer, O God;
And do not hide Thyself from my supplication.
2 Give heed to me, and answer me;
I am restless in my complaint and [94]am surely distracted,
3 Because of the voice of the enemy,
Because of the pressure of the wicked;
For they bring down trouble upon me,
And in anger they bear a grudge against me.

4 ¶ My heart is in anguish within me,
And the terrors of death have fallen upon me.
5 Fear and trembling come upon me;
And horror has overwhelmed me.
6 And I said, "Oh, that I had wings like a dove!
I would fly away and [95]be at rest.
7"Behold, I would wander far away,
I would lodge in the wilderness.
                                        [Selah.
8"I would hasten to my place of refuge
From the stormy wind *and* tempest."

9 ¶ Confuse, O Lord, divide their tongues,
For I have seen violence and strife in the city.
10 Day and night they go around her upon her walls;
And iniquity and mischief are in her midst.
11 Destruction is in her midst;
Oppression and deceit do not depart from her streets.

12 ¶ For it is not an enemy who reproaches me,
Then I could bear *it*;
Nor is it one who hates me who has exalted himself against me,
Then I could hide myself from him.
13 But it is you, a man my equal,
My companion and my familiar friend.

---

[92] Lit., *judge*   [93] Lit., *The evil will return*   [94] Or, *I must moan*   [95] Lit., *settle down*

14 We who had sweet [96]fellowship
    together,
    Walked in the house of God in the
    throng.
15 Let death come deceitfully upon
    them;
    Let them go down alive to Sheol,
    For evil is in their dwelling, in
    their midst.

16 ¶ As for me, I shall call upon God,
    And the LORD will save me.
17 Evening and morning and at
    noon, I will complain and mur-
    mur,
    And He will hear my voice.
18 He will redeem my soul in peace
    from the battle *which is* against
    me,
    For they are many *who strive*
    with me.
19 God will hear and answer them—
    Even the one who sits enthroned
    from of old—   [Selah.
    With whom there is no change,
    And who do not fear God.
20 He has put forth his hands against
    those who were at peace with
    him;
    He has [97]violated his covenant.
21 His speech was smoother than
    butter,
    But his heart was war;
    His words were softer than oil,
    Yet they were drawn swords.

22 ¶ Cast your burden upon the
    LORD, and He will sustain you;
    He will never allow the righteous
    to be shaken.
23 But Thou, O God, wilt bring them
    down to the pit of destruction;
    Men of bloodshed and deceit will
    not live out half their days.
    But I will trust in Thee.

PSALM 56

For the choir director; according to Jonath elem
rehokim.   A Mikhtam of David, when the
Philistines seized him in Gath.

BE gracious, O God, for man has
    trampled upon me;
    Fighting all day long he oppresses
    me.
2 My foes have trampled upon me
    all day long,
    For they are many who fight
    proudly against me.

3 When I am afraid,
    I will put my trust in Thee.
4 In God, whose word I praise,
    In God I have put my trust;
    I shall not be afraid.
    What can *mere* man do to me?
5 All day long they [98]distort my
    words;
    All their thoughts are against me
    for evil.
6 They [99]attack, they lurk,
    They watch my steps,
    As they have waited *to take* my
    life.
7 Because of wickedness, cast them
    forth,
    In anger put down the peoples, O
    God!

8 ¶ Thou hast taken account of my
    wanderings;
    Put my tears in Thy bottle;
    Are *they* not in Thy book?
9 Then my enemies will turn back
    in the day when I call;
    This I know, [100]that God is for me.
10 In God, *whose* word I praise,
    In the LORD, *whose* word I praise,
11 In God I have put my [101]trust, I
    shall not be afraid.
    What can man do to me?
12 Thy vows are *binding* upon me, O
    God;
    I will render thank offerings to
    Thee.
13 For Thou hast delivered my soul
    from death,
    Indeed my feet from stumbling,
    So that I may walk before God
    In the light of the living.

PSALM 57

For the choir director; *set to* [102]Al-tashheth. A
Mikhtam of David, when he fled from Saul, in the
cave.

BE gracious to me, O God, be gra-
    cious to me,
    For my soul takes refuge in Thee;
    And in the shadow of Thy wings I
    will take refuge,
    Until destruction passes by.
2 I will cry to God Most High,
    To God who accomplishes *all
    things* for me.
3 He will send from heaven and
    save me;

96 Lit., *counsel*   97 Lit., *profaned*
98 Or, *trouble my affairs*   99 Or, *stir up strife*
100 Or, *because*   101 Or, *trust without fear*
102 Lit., *Do Not Destroy*

He reproaches him who tramples
  upon me.   [Selah.
God will send forth His lovingkindness and His truth.

4 ¶ My soul is among lions;
  I must lie among those who
    breathe forth fire,
  Even the sons of men, whose
    teeth are spears and arrows,
  And their tongue a sharp sword.
5 Be exalted above the heavens, O
    God;
  Let Thy glory *be* above all the
    earth.
6 They have [103]prepared a net for
    my steps;
  My soul is bowed down;
  They dug a pit before me;
  They *themselves* have fallen into
    the midst of it.   [Selah.

7 ¶ My heart is steadfast, O God,
    my heart is steadfast;
  I will sing, yes, I will sing praises!
8 Awake, my glory;
  Awake, harp and lyre,
  I will awaken the dawn!
9 I will give thanks to Thee, O Lord,
    among the peoples;
  I will sing praises to Thee among
    the nations.
10 For Thy lovingkindness is great to
    the heavens,
  And Thy truth to the clouds.
11 Be exalted above the heavens, O
    God;
  Let Thy glory *be* above all the
    earth.

PSALM 58

For the choir director; *set to* Al-tashheth.
A Mikhtam of David.

Do you indeed speak righteousness,
  O [104]gods?
  Do you judge [105]uprightly, O sons
    of men?
2 No, in heart you work unright-
    eousness;
  On earth you weigh out the vio-
    lence of your hands.
3 The wicked are estranged from
    the womb;
  These who speak lies go astray
    from birth.
4 They have venom like the venom
    of a serpent;

Like a deaf cobra that stops up its
  ear,
5 So that it does not hear the voice
    of charmers,
  Or a skillful caster of spells.

6 ¶ O God, shatter their teeth in
    their mouth;
  Break out the fangs of the young
    lions, O Lord.
7 Let them flow away like water
    that runs off;
  When he aims his arrows, let
    them be as headless shafts.
8 *Let them be* as a snail which melts
    away as it goes along,
  Like the miscarriages of a woman
    which never see the sun.
9 Before your pots can feel *the fire
    of* thorns,
  He will sweep them away with a
    whirlwind, the green and the
    burning alike.

10 ¶ The righteous will rejoice when
    he sees the vengeance;
  He will wash his feet in the blood
    of the wicked.
11 And men will say, "Surely there is
    a reward for the righteous;
  Surely there is a God who judges
    on earth!"

PSALM 59

For the choir director; *set to* Al-tashheth. A
Mikhtam of David, when Saul sent *men,* and they
watched the house in order to kill him.

Deliver me from my enemies, O
  my God;
  Set me *securely* on high away
    from those who rise up against
    me.
2 Deliver me from those who do
    iniquity,
  And save me from men of blood-
    shed.
3 For behold, they have set an am-
    bush for my life;
  Fierce men [106]launch an attack
    against me,
  Not for my transgression nor for
    my sin, O Lord,
4 For no guilt of *mine,* they run and
    set themselves against me.
  Arouse Thyself to help me, and
    see!
5 And Thou, O Lord God of hosts,
    the God of Israel,

---

[103] Or, *spread*   [104] Or, *judges*
[105] Or, *uprightly the sons of men?*   [106] Or, *stir up strife*

Awake to punish all the nations;
Do not be gracious to any *who are*
treacherous in iniquity. [Selah.
6 They return at evening, they howl
like a dog,
And go around the city.
7 Behold, they belch forth with
their mouth;
Swords are in their lips,
For, *they say,* "Who hears?"
8 But Thou, O LORD, dost laugh at
them;
Thou dost scoff at all the nations.

9 ¶ *Because of* [107]his strength I will
watch for Thee,
For God is my stronghold.
10 My God in His lovingkindness will
meet me;
God will let me look *triumphantly*
upon my foes.
11 Do not slay them, lest my people
forget;
Scatter them by Thy power, and
bring them down,
O Lord, our shield.
12 *On account of* the sin of their
mouth *and* the words of their
lips,
Let them even be caught in their
pride,
And on account of curses and lies
which they utter.
13 [108]Destroy *them* in wrath, [108]de-
stroy *them*, that they may be no
more;
That *men* may know that God
rules in Jacob,
To the ends of the earth. [Selah.
14 And they return at evening, they
howl like a dog,
And go around the city.
15 They wander about [109]for food,
And growl if they are not satisfied.

16 ¶ But as for me, I shall sing of
Thy strength;
Yes, I shall joyfully sing of Thy
lovingkindness in the morning,
For Thou hast been my stronghold,
And a refuge in the day of my
distress.
17 O my strength, I will sing praises
to Thee;

For God is my stronghold, the
God who shows me lovingkindness.

PSALM 60

For the choir director; according to
[110]Shushan Eduth. A Mikhtam of David, to teach;
when he struggled with Aram-naharaim and with
Aram-zobah, and Joab returned, and smote twelve
thousand of Edom in the Valley of Salt.

O GOD, Thou hast rejected us. Thou
hast broken us;
Thou hast been angry; O, restore
us.
2 Thou hast made the land quake,
Thou hast split it open;
Heal its breaches, for it totters.
3 Thou hast made Thy people experience hardship;
Thou hast given us wine to drink
that makes us stagger.
4 Thou hast given a banner to those
who fear Thee,
That it may be displayed because
of the truth. [Selah.
5 That Thy beloved may be delivered,
Save with Thy right hand, and
answer us!

6 ¶ God has spoken in His [111]holi-
ness:
"I will exult, I will portion out
Shechem and measure out the
valley of Succoth.
7 "Gilead is Mine, and Manasseh is
Mine;
Ephraim also is the helmet of My
head;
Judah is My [112]scepter.
8 "Moab is My washbowl;
Over Edom I shall throw My shoe;
Shout loud, O Philistia, because of
Me!"

9 ¶ Who will bring me into the besieged city?
Who will lead me to Edom?
10 Hast not Thou Thyself, O God,
rejected us?
And wilt Thou not go forth with
our armies, O God?
11 O give us help against the adversary,
For deliverance by man is in vain.
12 Through God we shall do valiantly,

---

[107] Many mss. and some ancient versions read *My strength*
[108] Lit., *Bring to an end*   [109] Or, *to devour*
[110] Lit., *The lily of testimony*   [111] Or, *sanctuary*
[112] Or, *lawgiver*

And it is He who will tread down
our adversaries.

PSALM 61

For the choir director; on a stringed instrument.
A Psalm of David.

HEAR my cry, O God;
Give heed to my prayer.
2 From the end of the earth I call to
Thee, when my heart is faint;
Lead me to the rock that is higher
than I.
3 For Thou hast been a refuge for
me,
A tower of strength against the
enemy.
4 Let me dwell in Thy tent forever;
Let me take refuge in the shelter
of Thy wings.   [Selah.

5 ¶ For Thou hast heard my vows,
O God;
Thou hast given *me* the inheritance of those who fear Thy
name.
6 Thou wilt prolong the king's life;
His years will be as many generations.
7 He will abide before God forever;
Appoint lovingkindness and truth,
that they may preserve him.
8 So I will sing praise to Thy name
forever,
That I may pay my vows day by
day.

PSALM 62

For the choir director; according to Jeduthun.
A Psalm of David.

MY soul *waits* in silence for God
only;
From Him is my salvation.
2 He only is my rock and my salvation,
My stronghold; I shall not be
greatly shaken.

3 ¶ How long will you assail a man,
That you may murder *him,* all of
you,
Like a leaning wall, like a tottering fence?
4 They have counseled only to
thrust him down from his high
position;
They delight in falsehood;
They bless with their mouth,
But inwardly they curse. [Selah.

5 ¶ My soul, wait in silence for God
only,
For my hope is from Him.
6 He only is my rock and my salvation,
My stronghold; I shall not be
shaken.
7 On God my salvation and my
glory *rest;*
The rock of my strength, my refuge is in God.
8 Trust in Him at all times, O people;
Pour out your heart before Him;
God is a refuge for us.   [Selah.

9 ¶ Men of low degree are only
vanity, and men of rank are a
lie;
In the balances they go up;
They are together lighter than
breath.
10 Do not trust in oppression,
And do not vainly hope in robbery;
If riches increase, do not set *your*
heart *upon them.*

11 ¶ [113]Once God has spoken;
[114]Twice I have heard this:
That power belongs to God;
12 And lovingkindness is Thine, O
Lord,
For Thou dost recompense a man
according to his work.

PSALM 63

A Psalm of David, when he was in the wilderness
of Judah.

O GOD, Thou art my God; I shall
seek Thee [115]earnestly;
My soul thirsts for Thee, my flesh
yearns for Thee,
In a dry and weary land where
there is no water.
2 Thus I have beheld Thee in the
sanctuary,
To see Thy power and Thy glory.
3 Because Thy lovingkindness is
better than life,
My lips will praise Thee.
4 So I will bless Thee as long as I
live;
I will lift up my hands in Thy
name.

[113] Or, *One thing*   [114] Or, *These two things I have heard*
[115] Lit., *early*

5 My soul is satisfied as with [116]marrow and fatness,
   And my mouth offers praises with joyful lips.

6 ¶ When I remember Thee on my bed,
   I meditate on Thee in the night watches,
7 For Thou hast been my help,
   And in the shadow of Thy wings I sing for joy.
8 My soul clings to Thee;
   Thy right hand upholds me.

9 ¶ But those who seek my life, to destroy it,
   Will go into the depths of the earth.
10 They will be delivered over to the power of the sword;
   They will be a prey for foxes.
11 But the king will rejoice in God;
   Everyone who swears by Him will glory,
   For the mouths of those who speak lies will be stopped.

PSALM 64

For the choir director. A Psalm of David.

HEAR my voice, O God, in my [117]complaint;
   Preserve my life from dread of the enemy.
2 Hide me from the secret counsel of evildoers,
   From the tumult of those who do iniquity,
3 Who have sharpened their tongue like a sword.
   They aimed bitter speech *as* their arrow,
4 To shoot from concealment at the blameless;
   Suddenly they shoot at him, and do not fear.
5 They hold fast to themselves an evil purpose;
   They talk of laying snares secretly;
   They say, "Who can see them?"
6 They [118]devise injustices, *saying,*
   "We are ready with a well-conceived plot";
   For the inward thought and the heart of a man are [119]deep.

7 ¶ But God will shoot at them with an arrow;
   Suddenly they will be wounded.
8 So they will make him stumble;
   Their own tongue is against them;
   All who see them will shake the head.
9 Then all men will fear,
   And will declare the work of God,
   And will consider what He has done.
10 The righteous man will be glad in the LORD, and will take refuge in Him;
   And all the upright in heart will glory.

PSALM 65

For the choir director. A Psalm of David. A Song.

THERE will be silence before Thee, *and* praise in Zion, O God;
   And to Thee the vow will be performed.
2 O Thou who dost hear prayer,
   To Thee all men come.
3 Iniquities prevail against me;
   As for our transgressions, Thou dost forgive them.
4 How blessed is the one whom Thou dost choose, and bring near *to Thee,*
   To dwell in Thy courts.
   We will be satisfied with the goodness of Thy house,
   Thy holy temple.

5 ¶ By awesome *deeds* Thou dost answer us in righteousness, O God of our salvation,
   Thou who art the trust of all the ends of the earth and of the farthest sea;
6 Who dost establish the mountains by His strength,
   Being girded with might;
7 Who dost still the roaring of the seas,
   The roaring of their waves,
   And the tumult of the peoples.
8 And they who dwell in the ends *of the earth* stand in awe of Thy signs;
   Thou dost make the dawn and the sunset shout for joy.

9 ¶ Thou dost visit the earth, and cause it to overflow;
   Thou dost greatly enrich it;

---

[116] Lit., *fat*   [117] Or, *concern*   [118] Or, *search out*
[119] Or, *unsearchable*

The stream of God is full of water;
Thou dost prepare their grain, for thus Thou dost prepare the earth.
10 Thou dost water its furrows abundantly;
Thou dost settle its ridges;
Thou dost soften it with showers;
Thou dost bless its growth.
11 Thou hast crowned the year with Thy bounty,
And Thy paths drip *with* fatness.
12 The pastures of the wilderness drip,
And the hills gird themselves with rejoicing.
13 The meadows are clothed with flocks,
And the valleys are covered with grain;
They shout for joy, yes, they sing.

PSALM 66
For the choir director. A Song. A Psalm.

SHOUT joyfully to God, all the earth;
2 Sing the glory of His name;
Make His praise glorious;
3 Say to God, "How awesome are Thy works!
Because of the greatness of Thy power Thine enemies will give feigned obedience to Thee.
4 "All the earth will worship Thee,
And will sing praises to Thee;
They will sing praises to Thy name."   [Selah.

5 ¶ Come and see the works of God,
Who is awesome in *His* deeds toward the sons of men.
6 He turned the sea into dry land;
They passed through the river on foot;
There let us rejoice in Him!
7 He rules by His might forever;
His eyes keep watch on the nations;
Let not the rebellious exalt themselves.   [Selah.

8 ¶ Bless our God, O peoples,
And sound His praise abroad,
9 Who keeps us in life,
And does not allow our feet to slip.
10 For Thou hast tried us, O God;
Thou hast refined us as silver is refined.

11 Thou didst bring us into the net;
Thou didst lay an oppressive burden upon our loins.
12 Thou didst make men ride over our heads;
We went through fire and through water;
Yet Thou didst bring us out into *a place of* abundance.
13 I shall come into Thy house with burnt offerings;
I shall pay Thee my vows,
14 Which my lips uttered
And my mouth spoke when I was in distress.
15 I shall offer to Thee burnt offerings of fat beasts,
With the smoke of rams;
I shall make *an offering of* bulls with male goats.   [Selah.

16 ¶ Come *and* hear, all who [120]fear God,
And I will tell of what He has done for my soul.
17 I cried to Him with my mouth,
And He was extolled with my tongue.
18 If I [121]regard wickedness in my heart,
The Lord will not hear;
19 But certainly God has heard;
He has given heed to the voice of my prayer.
20 Blessed be God,
Who has not turned away my prayer,
Nor His lovingkindness from me.

PSALM 67
For the choir director; with stringed instruments.
A Psalm. A Song.

GOD be gracious to us and bless us,
And cause His face to shine upon us—   [Selah.
2 That Thy way may be known on the earth,
Thy salvation among all nations.
3 Let the peoples praise Thee, O God;
Let all the peoples praise Thee.
4 Let the nations be glad and sing for joy;
For Thou wilt judge the peoples with uprightness,
And guide the nations on the earth.   [Selah.

[120] Or, *revere*
[121] Or, *had regarded ... would not have heard*

5 Let the peoples praise Thee, O
   God;
   Let all the peoples praise Thee.
6 The earth has yielded its produce;
   God, our God, blesses us.
7 God blesses us,
   [122]That all the ends of the earth
   may fear Him.

PSALM 68

For the choir director. A Psalm of David. A
Song.

LET God arise, let His enemies be
   scattered;
   And let those who hate Him flee
   before Him.
2 As smoke is driven away, *so* drive
   them away;
   As wax melts before the fire,
   So let the wicked perish before
   God.
3 But let the righteous be glad; let
   them exult before God;
   Yes, let them rejoice with gladness.
4 Sing to God, sing praises to His
   name;
   Lift up *a song* for Him who rides
   through the deserts,
   Whose name is the Lord, and
   exult before Him.

5 ¶ A father of the fatherless and a
   judge [123]for the widows,
   Is God in His holy habitation.
6 God makes a home for the lonely;
   He leads out the prisoners into
   prosperity,
   Only the rebellious dwell in a
   parched land.

7 ¶ O God, when Thou didst go
   forth before Thy people,
   When Thou didst march through
   the wilderness,   [Selah.
8 The earth quaked;
   The heavens also dropped *rain* at
   the presence of God;
   Sinai itself *quaked* at the presence
   of God, the God of Israel.
9 Thou didst shed abroad a plentiful
   rain, O God;
   Thou didst confirm Thine inheritance, when it was parched.
10 Thy creatures settled in it;
   Thou didst provide in Thy goodness for the poor, O God.

11 ¶ The Lord gives the command;
   The women who proclaim the
   good tidings are a great host:
12 "Kings of armies flee, they flee,
   And she who remains at home
   will divide the spoil!"
13 [124]When you lie down among the
   [125]sheepfolds,
   You are like the wings of a dove
   covered with silver,
   And its pinions with glistening
   gold.
14 When the Almighty scattered the
   kings there,
   It was snowing in Zalmon.

15 ¶ A mountain of God is the
   mountain of Bashan;
   A mountain *of many* peaks is the
   mountain of Bashan.
16 Why do you look with envy, O
   mountains with *many* peaks,
   At the mountain which God has
   desired for His abode?
   Surely, the Lord will dwell *there*
   forever.
17 The chariots of God are [126]myr-
   iads, thousands upon thousands;
   The Lord is among them *as at*
   Sinai, in holiness.
18 Thou hast ascended on high,
   Thou hast led captive *Thy* captives;
   Thou hast received gifts among
   men,
   Even *among* the rebellious also,
   that the Lord God may dwell
   there.

19 ¶ Blessed be the Lord, who daily
   bears our burden,
   The God *who* is our salvation.
                                   [Selah.
20 God is to us a God of deliverances;
   And to God the Lord belong escapes from death.
21 Surely God will shatter the head
   of His enemies,
   The hairy crown of him who goes
   on in his guilty deeds.
22 The Lord said, "I will bring *them*
   back from Bashan.
   I will bring *them* back from the
   depths of the sea;

[122] Or, *And let all . . . earth fear Him*   [123] Lit., *of*
[124] Lit., *If*   [125] Or, *cooking stones, or, saddle bags*
[126] Lit., *twice ten thousand*

23 That your foot may shatter *them*
    in blood,
    The tongue of your dogs *may
    have* its portion from *your* en-
    emies."

24 ¶ They have seen Thy procession,
    O God,
    The procession of my God, my
    King, into the sanctuary.
25 The singers went on, the musi-
    cians after *them,*
    In the midst of the maidens beat-
    ing tambourines.
26 Bless God in the congregations,
    Even the LORD, *you who are* of
    the fountain of Israel.
27 There is Benjamin, the youngest,
    ruling them,
    The princes of Judah *in their*
    throng,
    The princes of Zebulun, the
    princes of Naphtali.

28 ¶ Your God has commanded your
    strength;
    Show Thyself strong, O God, who
    hast acted on our behalf.
29 Because of Thy temple at Jerusa-
    lem
    Kings will bring gifts to Thee.
30 Rebuke the beasts in the reeds,
    The herd of bulls with the calves
    of the peoples,
    Trampling under foot the pieces
    of silver;
    He has scattered the peoples who
    delight in war.
31 Envoys will come out of Egypt;
    Ethiopia will quickly stretch out
    her hands to God.

32 ¶ Sing to God, O kingdoms of the
    earth;
    Sing praises to the Lord,   [Selah.
33 To Him who rides upon the high-
    est heavens, which are from
    ancient times;
    Behold, He speaks forth with His
    voice, a mighty voice.
34 Ascribe strength to God;
    His majesty is over Israel,
    And His strength is in the skies.
35 O God, *Thou art* awesome from
    Thy sanctuary.
    The God of Israel Himself gives
    strength and power to the peo-
    ple.
    Blessed be God!

PSALM 69

For the choir director; according to
[127]Shoshannim.   *A Psalm* of David.

SAVE me, O God,
    For the waters have threatened
    my life.
2 I have sunk in deep mire, and
    there is no foothold;
    I have come into deep waters, and
    a flood overflows me.
3 I am weary with my crying; my
    throat is parched;
    My eyes fail while I wait for my
    God.
4 Those who hate me without a
    cause are more than the hairs of
    my head;
    Those who would destroy me are
    powerful, being wrongfully my
    enemies,
    What I did not steal, I then have
    to restore.

5 ¶ O God, it is Thou who dost
    know my folly,
    And my wrongs are not hidden
    from Thee.
6 May those who wait for Thee not
    be ashamed through me, O Lord
    GOD of hosts;
    May those who seek Thee not be
    dishonored through me, O God
    of Israel,
7 Because for Thy sake I have
    borne reproach;
    Dishonor has covered my face.
8 I have become estranged from my
    brothers,
    And an alien to my mother's sons.
9 For zeal for Thy house has con-
    sumed me,
    And the reproaches of those who
    reproach Thee have fallen on
    me.
10 When I wept in my soul with
    fasting,
    It became my reproach.
11 When I made sackcloth my cloth-
    ing,
    I became a byword to them.
12 Those who sit in the gate talk
    about me,
    And I *am* the song of the drunk-
    ards.

[127] Or possibly, *Lilies*

13 ¶ But as for me, my prayer is to
Thee, O LORD, at an acceptable
time;
O God, in the greatness of Thy
lovingkindness,
Answer me with Thy saving truth.

14 Deliver me from the mire, and do
not let me sink;
May I be delivered from my foes,
and from the deep waters.

15 May the flood of water not overflow me,
And may the deep not swallow me
up,
And may the pit not shut its
mouth on me.

16 ¶ Answer me, O LORD, for Thy
lovingkindness is good;
According to the greatness of Thy
compassion, turn to me,

17 And do not hide Thy face from
Thy servant,
For I am in distress; answer me
quickly.

18 Oh draw near to my soul *and*
redeem it;
Ransom me because of my enemies!

19 Thou dost know my reproach and
my shame and my dishonor;
All my adversaries are [128]before
Thee.

20 ¶ Reproach has broken my heart,
and I am so sick.
And I looked for sympathy, but
there was none,
And for comforters, but I found
none.

21 They also gave me [129]gall for my
food,
And for my thirst they gave me
vinegar to drink.

22 ¶ May their table before them
become a snare;
And when they are in peace, *may
it become* a trap.

23 May their eyes grow dim so that
they cannot see,
And make their loins shake continually.

24 Pour out Thine indignation on
them,
And may Thy burning anger overtake them.

25 May their camp be desolate;
May none dwell in their tents.

26 For they have persecuted him
whom Thou Thyself hast smitten,
And they tell of the pain of those
whom Thou hast wounded.

27 Do Thou add iniquity to their
iniquity,
And may they not come into Thy
righteousness.

28 May they be blotted out of the
book of life,
And may they not be recorded
with the righteous.

29 ¶ But I am afflicted and in pain;
May Thy salvation, O God, set me
securely on high.

30 I will praise the name of God with
song,
And shall magnify Him with
thanksgiving.

31 And it will please the LORD better
than an ox
Or a young bull with horns and
hoofs.

32 The humble have seen *it and* are
glad;
You who seek God, let your heart
revive.

33 For the LORD hears the needy,
And does not despise His *who are*
prisoners.

34 ¶ Let heaven and earth praise
Him,
The seas and everything that
moves in them.

35 For God will save Zion and build
the cities of Judah,
That they may dwell there and
possess it.

36 And the descendants of His servants will inherit it,
And those who love His name will
dwell in it.

PSALM 70

For the choir director. *A Psalm* of David; for a
memorial.

O GOD, *hasten* to deliver me;
O LORD, hasten to my help!

2 Let those be ashamed and humil-
iated
Who seek my life;
Let those be turned back and dis-
honored
Who delight in my hurt.

128 Or, known *to Thee*   129 Or, *poison*

3 Let those be turned back because
of their shame
Who say, "Aha, aha!"

4 ¶ Let all who seek Thee rejoice
and be glad in Thee;
And let those who love Thy salva-
tion say continually,
"Let God be magnified."
5 But I am afflicted and needy;
Hasten to me, O God!
Thou art my help and my deliv-
erer;
O LORD, do not delay.

PSALM 71

IN Thee, O LORD, I have taken refuge;
Let me never be ashamed.
2 In Thy righteousness deliver me,
and rescue me;
Incline Thine ear to me, and save
me.
3 Be Thou to me a rock of habitation, to which I may continually
come;
Thou hast given commandment
to save me,
For Thou art my rock and my
fortress.
4 Rescue me, O my God, out of the
hand of the wicked,
Out of the grasp of the wrongdoer
and ruthless man,
5 For Thou art my hope;
O Lord GOD, *Thou art* my confidence from my youth.
6 By Thee I have been sustained
from *my* birth;
Thou art He who took me from
my mother's womb;
My praise is continually of Thee.

7 ¶ I have become a marvel to
many;
For Thou art my strong refuge.
8 My mouth is filled with Thy
praise,
And with Thy glory all day long.
9 Do not cast me off in the time of
old age;
Do not forsake me when my
strength fails.
10 For my enemies have spoken
against me;
And those who watch for my life
have consulted together,
11 Saying, "God has forsaken him;
Pursue and seize him, for there is
no one to deliver."

12 ¶ O God, do not be far from me;
O my God, hasten to my help!
13 Let those who are adversaries of
my soul be ashamed *and* consumed;
Let them be covered with reproach and dishonor, who seek
to injure me.
14 But as for me, I will hope continually,
And will praise Thee yet more and
more.
15 My mouth shall tell of Thy righteousness,
And of Thy salvation all day long;
For I do not know the sum *of
them.*
16 I will come with the mighty deeds
of the Lord GOD;
I will make mention of Thy righteousness, Thine alone.

17 ¶ O God, Thou hast taught me
from my youth;
And I still declare Thy wondrous
deeds.
18 And even when *I am* old and gray,
O God, do not forsake me,
Until I declare Thy strength to
this generation,
Thy power to all who are to come.
19 For Thy righteousness, O God,
reaches to the heavens,
Thou who hast done great things;
O God, who is like Thee?
20 Thou, who hast shown [130]me
many troubles and distresses,
Wilt revive [130]me again,
And wilt bring [130]me up again
from the depths of the earth.
21 Mayest Thou increase my greatness,
And turn *to* comfort me.

22 ¶ I will also praise Thee with a
harp,
Even Thy truth, O my God;
To Thee I will sing praises with
the lyre,
O Thou Holy One of Israel.
23 My lips will shout for joy when I
sing praises to Thee;
And my soul, which Thou hast
redeemed.
24 My tongue also will utter Thy
righteousness all day long;

[130] Another reading is *us*

For they are ashamed, for they
are humiliated who seek my
hurt.

PSALM 72
A Psalm of Solomon.

GIVE the king Thy judgments, O
God,
And Thy righteousness to the
king's son.
2 May he judge Thy people with
righteousness,
And [131]Thine afflicted with justice.
3 Let the mountains bring peace to
the people,
And the hills in righteousness.
4 May he vindicate the afflicted of
the people,
Save the children of the needy,
And crush the oppressor.

5 ¶ Let them fear Thee while the
sun endures,
And as long as the moon,
throughout all generations.
6 May he come down like rain upon
the mown grass,
Like showers that water the
earth.
7 In his days may the righteous
flourish,
And abundance of peace till the
moon is no more.

8 ¶ May he also rule from sea to
sea,
And from the River to the ends of
the earth.
9 Let the nomads of the desert bow
before him;
And his enemies lick the dust.
10 Let the kings of Tarshish and of
the islands bring presents;
The kings of Sheba and Seba offer
gifts.
11 And let all kings bow down before
him,
All nations serve him.

12 ¶ For he will deliver the needy
when he cries for help,
The afflicted also, and him who
has no helper.
13 He will have compassion on the
poor and needy,
And the lives of the needy he will
save.

[131] Or, *Thy humble*

14 He will rescue their life from oppression and violence;
And their blood will be precious in
his sight;
15 So may he live; and may the gold
of Sheba be given to him;
And let them pray for him continually;
Let them bless him all day long.

16 ¶ May there be abundance of
grain in the earth on top of the
mountains;
Its fruit will wave like *the cedars
of* Lebanon;
And may those from the city
flourish like vegetation of the
earth.
17 May his name endure forever;
May his name increase as long as
the sun *shines*;
And let *men* bless themselves by
him;
Let all nations call him blessed.

18 ¶ Blessed be the LORD God, the
God of Israel,
Who alone works wonders.
19 And blessed be His glorious name
forever;
And may the whole earth be filled
with His glory.
Amen, and Amen.

20 ¶ The prayers of David the son of
Jesse are ended.

BOOK 3

PSALM 73
A Psalm of Asaph.

SURELY God is good to Israel,
To those who are pure in heart!
2 But as for me, my feet came close
to stumbling;
My steps had almost slipped.
3 For I was envious of the arrogant,
As I saw the prosperity of the
wicked.
4 For there are no pains in their
death;
And their body is fat.
5 They are not in trouble *as other*
men;
Nor are they plagued like mankind.
6 Therefore pride is their necklace;

The garment of violence covers them.

7 Their eye bulges from fatness;
The imaginations of *their* heart run riot.

8 They mock, and wickedly speak of oppression;
They speak from on high.

9 They have set their mouth against the heavens,
And their tongue parades through the earth.

10 ¶ Therefore his people return to this place;
And waters of abundance are drunk by them.

11 And they say, "How does God know?
And is there knowledge with the Most High?"

12 Behold, these are the wicked;
And always at ease, they have increased *in* wealth.

13 Surely in vain I have kept my heart pure,
And washed my hands in innocence;

14 For I have been stricken all day long,
And chastened every morning.

15 ¶ If I had said, "I will speak thus,"
Behold, I should have betrayed the generation of Thy children.

16 When I pondered to understand this,
It was troublesome in my sight

17 Until I came into the sanctuary of God;
Then I perceived their end.

18 Surely Thou dost set them in slippery places;
Thou dost cast them down to destruction.

19 How they are destroyed in a moment!
They are utterly swept away by sudden terrors!

20 Like a dream when one awakes,
O Lord, when aroused, Thou wilt despise their form.

21 ¶ When my heart was embittered,
And I was pierced within,

22 Then I was senseless and ignorant;
I was *like* a beast before Thee.

23 Nevertheless I am continually with Thee;
Thou hast taken hold of my right hand.

24 With Thy counsel Thou wilt guide me,
And afterward receive me to glory.

25 ¶ Whom have I in heaven *but* Thee?
And besides Thee, I desire nothing on earth.

26 My flesh and my heart may fail,
But God is the strength of my heart and my portion forever.

27 For, behold, those who are far from Thee will perish;
Thou hast destroyed all those who are unfaithful to Thee.

28 But as for me, the nearness of God is my good;
I have made the Lord GOD my refuge,
That I may tell of all Thy works.

PSALM 74
A Maskil of Asaph.

O GOD, why hast Thou rejected *us* forever?
Why does Thine anger smoke against the sheep of Thy pasture?

2 Remember Thy congregation, which Thou hast purchased of old,
Which Thou hast redeemed to be the tribe of Thine inheritance;
And this Mount Zion, where Thou hast dwelt.

3 Turn Thy footsteps toward the perpetual ruins;
The enemy has damaged everything within the sanctuary.

4 Thine adversaries have roared in the midst of Thy meeting place;
They have set up their own standards for signs.

5 It seems as if one had lifted up
His axe in a forest of trees.

6 And now all its carved work
They smash with hatchet and hammers.

7 They have burned Thy sanctuary to the ground;
They have defiled the dwelling place of Thy name.

8 They said in their heart, "Let us completely subdue them."

They have burned all the meeting places of God in the land.
9 We do not see our signs;
There is no longer any prophet,
Nor is there any among us who knows how long.
10 How long, O God, will the adversary revile,
And the enemy spurn Thy name forever?
11 Why dost Thou withdraw Thy hand, even Thy right hand?
From within Thy bosom, destroy *them*!

12 ¶ Yet God is my king from of old,
Who works deeds of deliverance in the midst of the earth.
13 [132]Thou didst divide the sea by Thy strength;
Thou didst break the heads of the sea monsters in the waters.
14 Thou didst crush the heads of Leviathan;
Thou didst give him as food for the creatures of the wilderness.
15 Thou didst break open springs and torrents;
Thou didst dry up ever-flowing streams.
16 Thine is the day, Thine also is the night;
Thou hast prepared the light and the sun.
17 Thou hast established all the boundaries of the earth;
Thou hast made summer and winter.

18 ¶ Remember this, O LORD, that the enemy has reviled;
And a foolish people has spurned Thy name.
19 Do not deliver the soul of Thy turtledove to the wild beast;
Do not forget the life of Thine afflicted forever.
20 Consider the covenant;
For the dark places of the land are full of the habitations of violence.
21 Let not the oppressed return dishonored;
Let the afflicted and needy praise Thy name.

22 ¶ Do arise, O God, *and* plead Thine own cause;

Remember how the foolish man reproaches Thee all day long.
23 Do not forget the voice of Thine adversaries,
The uproar of those who rise against Thee which ascends continually.

PSALM 75
For the choir director; *set to* Al-tashheth.
A Psalm of Asaph, a Song.

WE give thanks to Thee, O God, we give thanks,
For Thy name is near;
Men declare Thy wondrous works.
2 "When I select an appointed time,
It is I who judge with equity.
3 "The earth and all who dwell in it [133]melt;
It is I who have firmly set its pillars. [Selah.
4 "I said to the boastful, 'Do not boast,'
And to the wicked, 'Do not lift up the horn;
5 Do not lift up your horn on high,
Do not speak with insolent pride.'"

6 ¶ For not from the east, nor from the west,
Nor from the desert *comes* exaltation;
7 But God is the Judge;
He puts down one, and exalts another.
8 For a cup is in the hand of the LORD, and the wine foams;
It is well mixed, and He pours out of this;
Surely all the wicked of the earth must drain *and* drink down its dregs.

9 ¶ But as for me, I will declare *it* forever;
I will sing praises to the God of Jacob.
10 And all the horns of the wicked He will cut off,
But the horns of the righteous will be lifted up.

PSALM 76
For the choir director; on stringed instruments.
A Psalm of Asaph, a Song.

GOD is known in Judah;
His name is great in Israel.

132 Or, *Thou Thyself,* and so through v. 17   133 Or, *totter*

2 And His tabernacle is in Salem;
   His dwelling place also is in Zion.
3 There He broke the flaming arrows,
   The shield, and the sword, and the
   weapons of war.   [Selah.

4 ¶ Thou art resplendent,
   More majestic than the mountains of prey.
5 The stouthearted were plundered;
   They sank into sleep;
   And none of the warriors could
   use his hands.
6 At Thy rebuke, O God of Jacob,
   Both rider and horse were cast
   into a dead sleep.
7 Thou, even Thou, art to be feared;
   And who may stand in Thy presence when once Thou art angry?

8 ¶ Thou didst cause judgment to
   be heard from heaven;
   The earth feared, and was still,
9 When God arose to judgment,
   To save all the humble of the
   earth.   [Selah.
10 For the wrath of man shall praise
   Thee;
   With a remnant of wrath Thou
   shalt gird Thyself.

11 ¶ Make vows to the LORD your
   God and fulfill *them*;
   Let all who are around Him bring
   gifts to Him who is to be feared.
12 He will cut off the spirit of
   princes;
   He is feared by the kings of the
   earth.

PSALM 77

For the choir director; according to Jeduthun.
A Psalm of Asaph.

MY voice *rises* to God, and I will cry
   aloud;
   My voice *rises* to God, and He will
   hear me.
2 In the day of my trouble I sought
   the Lord;
   In the night my hand was
   stretched out [134]without weariness;
   My soul refused to be comforted.
3 *When* I remember God, then I
   am disturbed;

When I sigh, then my spirit grows
   faint.   [Selah.
4 Thou hast held my eyelids *open*;
   I am so troubled that I cannot
   speak.
5 I have considered the days of old,
   The years of long ago.
6 I will remember my song in the
   night;
   I will meditate with my heart;
   And my spirit ponders.

7 ¶ Will the Lord reject forever?
   And will He never be favorable
   again?
8 Has His lovingkindness ceased
   forever?
   Has *His* promise come to an end
   forever?
9 Has God forgotten to be gracious?
   Or has He in anger withdrawn His
   compassion?   [Selah.
10 Then I said, "It is my grief,
   That the right hand of the Most
   High has changed."

11 ¶ I shall remember the deeds of
   the LORD;
   Surely I will remember Thy wonders of old.
12 I will meditate on all Thy work,
   And muse on Thy deeds.
13 Thy way, O God, is holy;
   What god is great like our God?
14 Thou art the God who workest
   wonders;
   Thou hast made known Thy
   strength among the peoples.
15 Thou hast by Thy power redeemed Thy people,
   The sons of Jacob and
   Joseph.   [Selah.

16 ¶ The waters saw Thee, O God;
   The waters saw Thee, they were
   in anguish;
   The deeps also trembled.
17 The clouds poured out water;
   The skies gave forth a sound;
   Thy arrows flashed here and
   there.
18 The sound of Thy thunder was in
   the whirlwind;
   The lightnings lit up the world;
   The earth trembled and shook.
19 Thy way was in the sea,
   And Thy paths in the mighty waters,

[134] Lit., *and did not grow numb*

And Thy footprints may not be known.

20 Thou didst lead Thy people like a flock,
By the hand of Moses and Aaron.

PSALM 78
A Maskil of Asaph.

LISTEN, O my people, to my instruction;
Incline your ears to the words of my mouth.
2 I will open my mouth in a parable;
I will utter dark sayings of old,
3 Which we have heard and known,
And our fathers have told us.
4 We will not conceal them from their children,
But tell to the generation to come the praises of the LORD,
And His strength and His wondrous works that He has done.

5 ¶ For He established a testimony in Jacob,
And appointed a law in Israel,
Which He commanded our fathers,
That they should teach them to their children,
6 That the generation to come might know, *even* the children *yet* to be born,
That they may arise and tell *them* to their children,
7 That they should put their confidence in God,
And not forget the works of God,
But keep His commandments,
8 And not be like their fathers,
A stubborn and rebellious generation,
A generation that did not [135]prepare its heart,
And whose spirit was not faithful to God.

9 ¶ The sons of Ephraim were archers equipped with bows,
Yet they turned back in the day of battle.
10 They did not keep the covenant of God,
And refused to walk in His law;
11 And they forgot His deeds,
And His miracles that He had shown them.

[135] Or, *put right*

12 He wrought wonders before their fathers,
In the land of Egypt, in the field of Zoan.
13 He divided the sea, and caused them to pass through;
And He made the waters stand up like a heap.
14 Then He led them with the cloud by day,
And all the night with a light of fire.
15 He split the rocks in the wilderness,
And gave *them* abundant drink like the ocean depths.
16 He brought forth streams also from the rock,
And caused waters to run down like rivers.

17 ¶ Yet they still continued to sin against Him,
To rebel against the Most High in the desert.
18 And in their heart they put God to the test
By asking food according to their desire.
19 Then they spoke against God;
They said, "Can God prepare a table in the wilderness?
20 "Behold, He struck the rock, so that waters gushed out,
And streams were overflowing;
Can He give bread also?
Will He provide meat for His people?"

21 ¶ Therefore the LORD heard and was full of wrath,
And a fire was kindled against Jacob,
And anger also mounted against Israel;
22 Because they did not believe in God,
And did not trust in His salvation.
23 Yet He commanded the clouds above,
And opened the doors of heaven;
24 And He rained down manna upon them to eat,
And gave them food from heaven.
25 Man did eat the bread of angels;
He sent them food in abundance.
26 He caused the east wind to blow in the heavens;

And by His power He directed the south wind.

27 When He rained meat upon them like the dust,
Even winged fowl like the sand of the seas,

28 Then He let *them* fall in the midst of their camp,
Round about their dwellings.

29 So they ate and were well filled;
And their desire He gave to them.

30 Before they had satisfied their desire,
While their food was in their mouths,

31 The anger of God rose against them,
And killed some of their stoutest ones,
And subdued the choice men of Israel.

32 In spite of all this they still sinned,
And did not believe in His wonderful works.

33 So He brought their days to an end in futility,
And their years in sudden terror.

34 ¶ When He killed them, then they sought Him,
And returned and searched diligently for God;

35 And they remembered that God was their rock,
And the Most High God their Redeemer.

36 But they deceived Him with their mouth,
And lied to Him with their tongue.

37 For their heart was not steadfast toward Him,
Nor were they faithful in His covenant.

38 But He, being compassionate, forgave *their* iniquity, and did not destroy *them*;
And often He restrained His anger,
And did not arouse all His wrath.

39 Thus He remembered that they were but flesh,
A wind that passes and does not return.

40 ¶ How often they rebelled against Him in the wilderness,
And grieved Him in the desert!

41 And again and again they [136]tempted God,
And pained the Holy One of Israel.

42 They did not remember His power,
The day when He redeemed them from the adversary,

43 When He performed His signs in Egypt,
And His marvels in the field of Zoan,

44 And turned their rivers to blood,
And their streams, they could not drink.

45 He sent among them swarms of flies, which devoured them,
And frogs which destroyed them.

46 He gave also their crops to the grasshopper,
And the product of their labor to the locust.

47 He destroyed their vines with hailstones,
And their sycamore trees with frost.

48 He gave over their cattle also to the hailstones,
And their herds to bolts of lightning.

49 He sent upon them His burning anger,
Fury, and indignation, and trouble,
A band of destroying angels.

50 He leveled a path for His anger;
He did not spare their soul from death,
But gave over their life to the plague,

51 And smote all the first-born in Egypt,
The first *issue* of their virility in the tents of Ham.

52 But He led forth His own people like sheep,
And guided them in the wilderness like a flock;

53 And He led them safely, so that they did not fear;
But the sea engulfed their enemies.

54 ¶ So He brought them to His holy land,
To this hill country which His right hand had gained.

[136] Or, *put to the test*

55 He also drove out the nations
before them,
And He apportioned them for an
inheritance by measurement,
And made the tribes of Israel
dwell in their tents.
56 Yet they [136]tempted and rebelled
against the Most High God,
And did not keep His testimonies,
57 But turned back and acted treacherously like their fathers;
They turned aside like a treacherous bow.
58 For they provoked Him with their
high places,
And aroused His jealousy with
their graven images.
59 When God heard, He was filled
with wrath,
And greatly abhorred Israel;
60 So that He abandoned the dwelling place at Shiloh,
The tent which He had pitched
among men,
61 And gave up His strength to captivity,
And His glory into the hand of the
adversary.
62 He also delivered His people to the
sword,
And was filled with wrath at His
inheritance.
63 Fire devoured His young men;
And His virgins had no wedding
songs.
64 His priests fell by the sword;
And His widows could not weep.

65 ¶ Then the Lord awoke as *if from*
sleep,
Like a warrior overcome by wine.
66 And He drove His adversaries
backward;
He put on them an everlasting
reproach.
67 He also rejected the tent of
Joseph,
And did not choose the tribe of
Ephraim,
68 But chose the tribe of Judah,
Mount Zion which He loved.
69 And He built His sanctuary like
the heights,
Like the earth which He has
founded forever.
70 He also chose David His servant,

And took him from the sheepfolds;
71 From the care of the ewes with
suckling lambs He brought him,
To shepherd Jacob His people,
And Israel His inheritance.
72 So he shepherded them according
to the integrity of his heart,
And guided them with his skillful
hands.

PSALM 79
A Psalm of Asaph.

O GOD, the nations have invaded
Thine inheritance;
They have defiled Thy holy temple;
They have laid Jerusalem in ruins.
2 They have given the dead bodies
of Thy servants for food to the
birds of the heavens,
The flesh of Thy godly ones to the
beasts of the earth.
3 They have poured out their blood
like water round about Jerusalem;
And there was no one to bury
them.
4 We have become a reproach to
our neighbors,
A scoffing and derision to those
around us.
5 How long, O LORD? Wilt Thou be
angry forever?
Will Thy jealousy burn like fire?
6 Pour out Thy wrath upon the nations which do not know Thee,
And upon the kingdoms which do
not call upon Thy name.
7 For they have devoured Jacob,
And laid waste his habitation.

8 ¶ Do not remember the iniquities
of *our* forefathers against us;
Let Thy compassion come quickly
to meet us;
For we are brought very low.
9 Help us, O God of our salvation,
for the glory of Thy name;
And deliver us, and forgive our
sins, for Thy name's sake.
10 Why should the nations say,
"Where is their God?"
Let there be known among the
nations in our sight,
Vengeance for the blood of Thy
servants, which has been shed.
11 Let the groaning of the prisoner
come before Thee;

[136] Or, *put to the test*

According to the greatness of Thy
power preserve those who are
doomed to die.

12 And return to our neighbors
sevenfold into their bosom
The reproach with which they
have reproached Thee, O Lord.

13 So we Thy people and the sheep
of Thy pasture
Will give thanks to Thee forever;
To all generations we will tell of
Thy praise.

PSALM 80

For the choir director; *set to* El Shoshannim;
Eduth. A Psalm of Asaph.

OH, give ear, Shepherd of Israel,
Thou who dost lead Joseph like a
flock;
Thou who art enthroned *above*
the cherubim, shine forth!

2 Before Ephraim and Benjamin
and Manasseh, stir up Thy
power,
And come to save us!

3 O God, restore us,
And cause Thy face to shine *upon
us*, and we will be saved.

4 ¶ O LORD God *of* hosts,
How long wilt Thou be angry with
the prayer of Thy people?

5 Thou hast fed them with the
bread of tears,
And Thou hast made them to
drink tears in large measure.

6 Thou dost make us [137]an object of
contention to our neighbors;
And our enemies laugh among
themselves.

7 O God *of* hosts, restore us,
And cause Thy face to shine *upon
us*, [138]and we will be saved.

8 ¶ Thou didst remove a vine from
Egypt;
Thou didst drive out the nations,
and didst plant it.

9 Thou didst clear *the ground* before it,
And it took deep root and filled
the land.

10 The mountains were covered with
its shadow;
And the cedars of God with its
boughs.

11 It was sending out its branches to
the sea,
And its shoots to the River.

12 Why hast Thou broken down its
hedges,
So that all who pass *that* way pick
its *fruit*?

13 A boar from the forest eats it
away,
And whatever moves in the field
feeds on it.

14 ¶ O God *of* hosts, turn again now,
we beseech Thee;
Look down from heaven and see,
and take care of this vine,

15 Even the shoot which Thy right
hand has planted,
And on the son whom Thou hast
strengthened for Thyself.

16 It is burned with fire, it is cut
down;
They perish at the rebuke of Thy
countenance.

17 Let Thy hand be upon the man of
Thy right hand,
Upon the son of man whom Thou
didst make strong for Thyself.

18 Then we shall not turn back from
Thee;
Revive us, and we will call upon
Thy name.

19 O LORD God of hosts, restore us;
Cause Thy face to shine *upon us*,
and we will be saved.

PSALM 81

For the choir director; on the Gittith.
A Psalm of Asaph.

SING for joy to God our strength;
Shout joyfully to the God of Jacob.

2 Raise a song, strike the timbrel,
The sweet sounding lyre with the
harp.

3 Blow the trumpet at the new
moon,
At the full moon, on our feast day.

4 For it is a statute for Israel,
An ordinance of the God of Jacob.

5 He established it for a testimony
in Joseph,
When he went throughout the
land of Egypt.
I heard a language that I did not
know:

6 ¶"I relieved his shoulder of the
burden,

---

[137] Lit., *a strife to*   [138] Or, *that we may*

His hands were freed from the
basket.
7"You called in trouble, and I rescued you;
I answered you in the hiding place
of thunder;
I proved you at the waters of
Meribah. [Selah.
8"Hear, O My people, and I will
admonish you;
O Israel, if you would listen to Me!
9"Let there be no strange god
among you;
Nor shall you worship any foreign
god.
10"I, the Lord, am your God,
Who brought you up from the
land of Egypt;
Open your mouth wide and I will
fill it.

11 ¶"But My people did not listen to
My voice;
And Israel did not obey Me.
12"So I gave them over to the stubbornness of their heart,
To walk in their own devices.
13"Oh that My people would listen to
Me,
That Israel would walk in My
ways!
14"I would quickly subdue their enemies,
And turn My hand against their
adversaries.
15"Those who hate the Lord would
pretend obedience to Him;
And their time *of punishment*
would be forever.
16"But I would feed you with the
finest of the wheat;
And with honey from the rock I
would satisfy you."

PSALM 82

A Psalm of Asaph.

GOD takes His stand in His own
congregation;
He judges in the midst of the
rulers.
2 How long will you judge unjustly,
And show partiality to the
wicked? [Selah.
3 Vindicate the weak and fatherless;
Do justice to the afflicted and
destitute.
4 Rescue the weak and needy;

Deliver *them* out of the hand of
the wicked.

5 ¶ They do not know nor do they
understand;
They walk about in darkness;
All the foundations of the earth
are shaken.
6 I said, "You are gods,
And all of you are sons of the
Most High.
7"Nevertheless you will die like
men,
And fall like *any* one of the
princes."
8 Arise, O God, judge the earth!
For it is Thou who dost possess all
the nations.

PSALM 83

A Song, a Psalm of Asaph.

O GOD, do not remain quiet;
Do not be silent and, O God, do
not be still.
2 For, behold, Thine enemies make
an uproar;
And those who hate Thee have
exalted themselves.
3 They make shrewd plans against
Thy people,
And conspire together against
Thy treasured ones.
4 They have said, "Come, and let us
wipe them out as a nation,
That the name of Israel be remembered no more."
5 For they have conspired together
with one mind;
Against Thee do they make a covenant:
6 The tents of Edom and the Ishmaelites;
Moab, and the Hagrites;
7 Gebal, and Ammon, and Amalek;
Philistia with the inhabitants of
Tyre;
8 Assyria also has joined with them;
They have become a help to the
children of Lot. [Selah.

9 ¶ Deal with them as with Midian,
As with Sisera *and* Jabin, at the
torrent of Kishon,
10 Who were destroyed at En-dor,
Who became as dung for the
ground.
11 Make their nobles like Oreb and
Zeeb,

And all their princes like Zebah
and Zalmunna,
12 Who said, "Let us possess for
ourselves
The pastures of God."

13 ¶ O my God, make them like the
[139]whirling dust;
Like chaff before the wind.
14 Like fire that burns the forest,
And like a flame that sets the
mountains on fire,
15 So pursue them with Thy tempest,
And terrify them with Thy storm.
16 Fill their faces with dishonor,
That they may seek Thy name, O
LORD.
17 Let them be ashamed and dismayed forever;
And let them be humiliated and
perish,
18 That they may know that Thou
alone, whose name is the LORD,
Art the Most High over all the
earth.

PSALM 84

For the choir director; on the Gittith.
A Psalm of the sons of Korah.

How lovely are Thy dwelling places,
O LORD of hosts!
2 My soul longed and even yearned
for the courts of the LORD;
My heart and my flesh sing for joy
to the living God.
3 The bird also has found a house,
And the swallow a nest for herself, where she may lay her
young,
Even Thine altars, O LORD of
hosts,
My King and my God.
4 How blessed are those who dwell
in Thy house!
They are ever praising Thee.
[Selah.

5 ¶ How blessed is the man whose
strength is in Thee;
In whose heart are the highways
to Zion!
6 Passing through the valley of
[140]Baca, they make it a spring,
The early rain also covers it with
blessings.
7 They go from strength to
strength,

Every one of them appears before
God in Zion.

8 ¶ O LORD God of hosts, hear my
prayer;
Give ear, O God of Jacob! [Selah.
9 Behold our shield, O God,
And look upon the face of Thine
anointed.
10 For a day in Thy courts is better
than a thousand outside.
I would rather stand at the
threshold of the house of my
God,
Than dwell in the tents of wickedness.
11 For the LORD God is a sun and
shield;
The LORD gives grace and glory;
No good thing does He withhold
from those who walk uprightly.
12 O LORD of hosts,
How blessed is the man who
trusts in Thee!

PSALM 85

For the choir director.
A Psalm of the sons of Korah.

O LORD, Thou didst show favor to
Thy land;
Thou didst [141]restore the captivity
of Jacob.
2 Thou didst forgive the iniquity of
Thy people;
Thou didst cover all their
sin.   [Selah.
3 Thou didst withdraw all Thy fury;
Thou didst turn away from Thy
burning anger.

4 ¶ Restore us, O God of our salvation,
And cause Thine indignation
toward us to cease.
5 Wilt Thou be angry with us forever?
Wilt Thou prolong Thine anger to
all generations?
6 Wilt Thou not Thyself revive us
again,
That Thy people may rejoice in
Thee?
7 Show us Thy lovingkindness, O
LORD,
And grant us Thy salvation.

8 ¶ I will hear what God the LORD
will say;

[139] Or, tumbleweed   [140] Probably, Weeping or Balsam trees   [141] Or, restore the fortunes

For He will speak peace to His
people, to His godly ones;
But let them not turn back to
folly.
9 Surely His salvation is near to
those who [142]fear Him,
That glory may dwell in our land.
10 Lovingkindness and truth have
met together;
Righteousness and peace have
kissed each other.
11 Truth springs from the earth;
And righteousness looks down
from heaven.
12 Indeed, the LORD will give what is
good;
And our land will yield its produce.
13 Righteousness will go before Him,
And will make His footsteps into a
way.

PSALM 86
A Prayer of David.

INCLINE Thine ear, O LORD, *and*
answer me;
For I am afflicted and needy.
2 Do preserve my soul, for I am a
godly man;
O Thou my God, save Thy servant
who trusts in Thee.
3 Be gracious to me, O Lord,
For to Thee I cry all day long.
4 Make glad the soul of Thy servant,
For to Thee, O Lord, I lift up my
soul.
5 For Thou, Lord, art good, and
ready to forgive,
And abundant in lovingkindness
to all who call upon Thee.
6 Give ear, O LORD, to my prayer;
And give heed to the voice of my
supplications!
7 In the day of my trouble I shall
call upon Thee,
For Thou wilt answer me.
8 There is no one like Thee among
the gods, O Lord;
Nor are there any works like
Thine.
9 All nations whom Thou hast made
shall come and worship before
Thee, O Lord;
And they shall glorify Thy name.

10 For Thou art great and doest wondrous deeds;
Thou alone art God.

11 ¶ Teach me Thy way, O LORD;
I will walk in Thy truth;
Unite my heart to fear Thy name.
12 I will give thanks to Thee, O Lord
my God, with all my heart,
And will glorify Thy name forever.
13 For Thy lovingkindness toward
me is great,
And Thou hast delivered my soul
from the depths of Sheol.

14 ¶ O God, arrogant men have risen
up against me,
And a band of violent men have
sought my life,
And they have not set Thee before
them.
15 But Thou, O Lord, art a God merciful and gracious,
Slow to anger and abundant in
lovingkindness and truth.
16 Turn to me, and be gracious to
me;
Oh grant Thy strength to Thy
servant,
And save the son of Thy handmaid.
17 Show me a sign for good,
That those who hate me may see
it, and be ashamed,
Because Thou, O LORD, hast
helped me and comforted me.

PSALM 87
A Psalm of the sons of Korah. A Song.

HIS foundation is in the holy mountains.
2 The LORD loves the gates of Zion
More than all the *other* dwelling
places of Jacob.
3 Glorious things are spoken of you,
O city of God.   [Selah.
4 "I shall mention [143]Rahab and
Babylon among those who
know Me;
Behold, Philistia and Tyre with
Ethiopia:
'This one was born there.' "
5 But of Zion it shall be said, "This
one and that one were born in
her";

---

[142] Or, *reverence*   [143] I.e., Egypt

And the Most High Himself will establish her.

6 The LORD shall count when He registers the peoples,
"This one was born there." [Selah.

7 Then those who sing as well as those who play the flutes *shall say,*
"All my springs *of joy* are in you."

PSALM 88

A Song. A Psalm of the sons of Korah. For the choir director; according to Mahalath Leannoth. A Maskil of Heman the Ezrahite.

O LORD, the God of my salvation,
I have cried out by day and in the night before Thee.

2 Let my prayer come before Thee;
Incline Thine ear to my cry!

3 For my soul has had enough troubles,
And my life has drawn near to Sheol.

4 I am reckoned among those who go down to the pit;
I have become like a man without strength,

5 Forsaken among the dead,
Like the slain who lie in the grave,
Whom Thou dost remember no more,
And they are cut off from Thy hand.

6 Thou hast put me in the lowest pit,
In dark places, in the depths.

7 Thy wrath has rested upon me,
And Thou hast afflicted me with all Thy waves.   [Selah.

8 Thou hast removed my acquaintances far from me;
Thou hast made me an [144]object of loathing to them;
I am shut up and cannot go out.

9 My eye has wasted away because of affliction;
I have called upon Thee every day, O LORD;
I have spread out my hands to Thee.

10 ¶ Wilt Thou perform wonders for the dead?
Will the departed spirits rise *and* praise Thee?   [Selah.

11 Will Thy lovingkindness be declared in the grave,
Thy faithfulness in Abaddon?

[144] Lit., *abomination to them*

12 Will Thy wonders be made known in the darkness?
And Thy righteousness in the land of forgetfulness?

13 ¶ But I, O LORD, have cried out to Thee for help,
And in the morning my prayer comes before Thee.

14 O LORD, why dost Thou reject my soul?
Why dost Thou hide Thy face from me?

15 I was afflicted and about to die from my youth on;
I suffer Thy terrors; I am overcome.

16 Thy burning anger has passed over me;
Thy terrors have destroyed me.

17 They have surrounded me like water all day long;
They have encompassed me altogether.

18 Thou hast removed lover and friend far from me;
My acquaintances are *in* darkness.

PSALM 89

A Maskil of Ethan the Ezrahite.

I WILL sing of the lovingkindness of the LORD forever;
To all generations I will make known Thy faithfulness with my mouth.

2 For I have said, "Lovingkindness will be built up forever;
In the heavens Thou wilt establish Thy faithfulness."

3 "I have made a covenant with My chosen;
I have sworn to David My servant,

4 I will establish your seed forever,
And build up your throne to all generations."   [Selah.

5 ¶ And the heavens will praise Thy wonders, O LORD;
Thy faithfulness also in the assembly of the holy ones.

6 For who in the skies is comparable to the LORD?
Who among the sons of the mighty is like the LORD,

7 A God greatly feared in the council of the holy ones,

And awesome above all those who
are around Him?

8 O Lord God of hosts, who is like
Thee, O mighty Lord?
Thy faithfulness also surrounds
Thee.

9 Thou dost rule the swelling of the
sea;
When its waves rise, Thou dost
still them.

10 Thou Thyself didst crush Rahab
like one who is slain;
Thou didst scatter Thine enemies
with Thy mighty arm.

11 ¶ The heavens are Thine, the
earth also is Thine;
The world and [145]all it contains,
Thou hast founded them.

12 The north and the south, Thou
hast created them;
Tabor and Hermon shout for joy
at Thy name.

13 Thou hast a strong arm;
Thy hand is mighty, Thy right
hand is exalted.

14 Righteousness and justice are the
foundation of Thy throne;
Lovingkindness and truth go before Thee.

15 How blessed are the people who
know the [146]joyful sound!
O Lord, they walk in the light of
Thy countenance.

16 In Thy name they rejoice all the
day,
And by Thy righteousness they
are exalted.

17 For Thou art the glory of their
strength,
And by Thy favor our horn is
exalted.

18 For our shield belongs to the
Lord,
[147]And our king to the Holy One of
Israel.

19 ¶ Once Thou didst speak in vision
to Thy godly ones,
And didst say, "I have given help
to one who is mighty;
I have exalted one chosen from
the people.

20 "I have found David My servant;
With My holy oil I have anointed
him,

21 With whom My hand will be established;
My arm also will strengthen him.

22 "The enemy will not [148]deceive him,
Nor the son of wickedness afflict
him.

23 "But I shall crush his adversaries
before him,
And strike those who hate him.

24 "And My faithfulness and My
lovingkindness will be with him,
And in My name his horn will be
exalted.

25 "I shall also set his hand on the sea,
And his right hand on the rivers.

26 "He will cry to Me, 'Thou art my
Father,
My God, and the rock of my sal-
vation.'

27 "I also shall make him My first-
born,
The highest of the kings of the
earth.

28 "My lovingkindness I will keep for
him forever,
And My covenant shall be confirmed to him.

29 "So I will establish his descendants
forever,
And his throne as the days of
heaven.

30 ¶"If his sons forsake My law,
And do not walk in My judgments,

31 If they [149]violate My statutes,
And do not keep My commandments,

32 Then I will visit their transgression with the rod,
And their iniquity with stripes.

33 "But I will not break off My lovingkindness from him,
Nor deal falsely in My faithfulness.

34 "My covenant I will not violate,
Nor will I alter the utterance of
My lips.

35 "[150]Once I have sworn by My holiness;
I will not lie to David.

36 "His descendants shall endure for-
ever,
And his throne as the sun before
Me.

37 "It shall be established forever like
the moon,

---

145 Lit., *its fulness* 146 Or, *blast of the trumpet, shout of joy*
147 Or, *Even to the Holy One of Israel our King*
148 Or, *exact usury from him* 149 Lit., *profane*
150 Or, *One thing*

And the witness in the sky is faithful."   [Selah.

38 ¶ But Thou hast cast off and rejected,
Thou hast been full of wrath against Thine anointed.
39 Thou hast spurned the covenant of Thy servant;
Thou hast profaned his crown in the dust.
40 Thou hast broken down all his walls;
Thou hast brought his strongholds to ruin.
41 All who pass along the way plunder him;
He has become a reproach to his neighbors.
42 Thou hast exalted the right hand of his adversaries;
Thou hast made all his enemies rejoice.
43 Thou dost also turn back the edge of his sword,
And hast not made him stand in battle.
44 Thou hast made his splendor to cease,
And cast his throne to the ground.
45 Thou hast shortened the days of his youth;
Thou hast covered him with shame.   [Selah.

46 ¶ How long, O LORD?
Wilt Thou hide Thyself forever?
Will Thy wrath burn like fire?
47 Remember what my span of life is;
For what vanity Thou hast created all the sons of men!
48 What man can live and not see death?
Can he deliver his soul from the power of Sheol?   [Selah.

49 ¶ Where are Thy former lovingkindnesses, O Lord,
Which Thou didst swear to David in Thy faithfulness?
50 Remember, O Lord, the reproach of Thy servants;
How I do bear in my bosom *the reproach of* all the many peoples,
51 With which Thine enemies have reproached, O LORD,

With which they have reproached the footsteps of Thine anointed.

52 ¶ Blessed be the LORD forever!
Amen and Amen.

BOOK 4

PSALM 90
A Prayer of Moses the man of God.

LORD, Thou hast been our [151]dwelling place in all generations.
2 Before the mountains were born,
Or Thou didst give birth to the earth and the world,
Even from everlasting to everlasting, Thou art God.

3 ¶ Thou dost turn man back into dust,
And dost say, "Return, O children of men."
4 For a thousand years in Thy sight
Are like yesterday when it passes by,
Or *as* a watch in the night.
5 Thou hast swept them away like a flood, they fall asleep;
In the morning they are like grass which sprouts anew.
6 In the morning it flourishes, and sprouts anew;
Toward evening it fades, and withers away.

7 ¶ For we have been consumed by Thine anger,
And by Thy wrath we have been dismayed.
8 Thou hast placed our iniquities before Thee,
Our secret *sins* in the light of Thy presence.
9 For all our days have declined in Thy fury;
We have finished our years like a sigh.
10 As for the days of our life, they contain seventy years,
Or if due to strength, eighty years,
Yet their pride is *but* labor and sorrow;
For soon it is gone and we fly away.
11 Who understands the power of Thine anger,

---

[151] Or, *hiding place; some ancient mss. read place of refuge*

And Thy fury, according to the
fear that is due Thee?
12 So teach us to number our days,
That we may present to Thee a
heart of wisdom.

13 ¶ Do return, O LORD; how long
will it be?
And be sorry for Thy servants.
14 O satisfy us in the morning with
Thy lovingkindness,
That we may sing for joy and be
glad all our days.
15 Make us glad according to the
days Thou hast afflicted us,
And the years we have seen
[152]evil.
16 Let Thy work appear to Thy servants,
And Thy majesty to their children.
17 And let the favor of the Lord our
God be upon us;
And do [153]confirm for us the work
of our hands;
Yes, [153]confirm the work of our
hands.

PSALM 91

HE who dwells in the shelter of the
Most High
Will abide in the shadow of the
Almighty.
2 I will say to the LORD, "My refuge
and my fortress,
My God, in whom I trust!"
3 For it is He who delivers you from
the snare of the trapper,
And from the deadly pestilence.
4 He will cover you with His pinions,
And under His wings you may
seek refuge;
His faithfulness is a shield and
bulwark.

5 ¶ You will not be afraid of the
terror by night,
Or of the arrow that flies by day;
6 Of the pestilence that stalks in
darkness,
Or of the destruction that lays
waste at noon.
7 A thousand may fall at your side,
And ten thousand at your right
hand;
But it shall not approach you.

8 You will only look on with your
eyes,
And see the recompense of the
wicked.
9 For you have made the LORD, my
refuge,
Even the Most High, your dwelling place.
10 No evil will befall you,
Nor will any plague come near
your tent.

11 ¶ For He will give His angels
charge concerning you,
To guard you in all your ways.
12 They will bear you up in their
hands,
Lest you strike your foot against a
stone.
13 You will tread upon the lion and
cobra,
The young lion and the serpent
you will trample down.

14 ¶"Because he has loved Me, therefore I will deliver him;
I will set him *securely* on high,
because he has known My
name.
15"He will call upon Me, and I will
answer him;
I will be with him in trouble;
I will rescue him, and honor him.
16"With a long life I will satisfy him,
And let him behold My salvation."

PSALM 92

A Psalm, a Song for the Sabbath day.

IT is good to give thanks to the LORD,
And to sing praises to Thy name,
O Most High;
2 To declare Thy lovingkindness in
the morning,
And Thy faithfulness by night,
3 With the ten-stringed lute, and
with the harp;
With resounding music upon the
lyre.
4 For Thou, O LORD, hast made me
glad by what Thou hast done,
I will sing for joy at the works of
Thy hands.

5 ¶ How great are Thy works, O
LORD!
Thy thoughts are very deep.
6 A senseless man has no knowledge;

[152] Or, *trouble*   [153] Or, *give permanence to*

Nor does a stupid man understand this:

7 That when the wicked sprouted up like grass,
And all who did iniquity flourished,
It *was only* that they might be destroyed forevermore.

8 But Thou, O LORD, art on high forever.

9 For, behold, Thine enemies, O LORD,
For, behold, Thine enemies will perish;
All who do iniquity will be scattered.

10 ¶ But Thou hast exalted my horn like *that of* the wild ox;
I have been anointed with fresh oil.

11 And my eye has looked *exultantly* upon my foes,
My ears hear of the evildoers who rise up against me.

12 The righteous man will flourish like the palm tree,
He will grow like a cedar in Lebanon.

13 Planted in the house of the LORD,
They will flourish in the courts of our God.

14 They will still yield fruit in old age;
They shall be [154]full of sap and very green,

15 To declare that the LORD is upright;
He is my rock, and there is no unrighteousness in Him.

PSALM 93

THE LORD reigns, He is clothed with majesty;
The LORD has clothed and girded Himself with strength;
Indeed, the world is firmly established, it will not be moved.

2 Thy throne is established from of old;
Thou art from everlasting.

3 ¶ The floods have lifted up, O LORD,
The floods have lifted up their voice;

The floods lift up their pounding waves.

4 More than the sounds of many waters,
Than the mighty breakers of the sea,
The LORD on high is mighty.

5 Thy testimonies are fully confirmed;
Holiness befits Thy house,
O LORD, forevermore.

PSALM 94

O LORD, God of vengeance;
God of vengeance, shine forth!

2 Rise up, O Judge of the earth;
Render recompense to the proud.

3 How long shall the wicked, O LORD,
How long shall the wicked exult?

4 They pour forth *words*, they speak arrogantly;
All who do wickedness vaunt themselves.

5 They crush Thy people, O LORD,
And afflict Thy heritage.

6 They slay the widow and the stranger,
And murder the orphans.

7 And they have said, "The LORD does not see,
Nor does the God of Jacob pay heed."

8 ¶ Pay heed, you senseless among the people;
And when will you understand, stupid ones?

9 He who planted the ear, does He not hear?
He who formed the eye, does He not see?

10 He who chastens the nations, will He not rebuke,
Even He who teaches man knowledge?

11 The LORD knows the thoughts of man,
That they are a *mere* breath.

12 ¶ Blessed is the man whom Thou dost chasten, O LORD,
And dost teach out of Thy law;

13 That Thou mayest grant him relief from the days of adversity,
Until a pit is dug for the wicked.

14 For the LORD will not abandon His people,

[154] Lit., *fat and*

Nor will He forsake His inheritance.

15 For judgment will again be righteous;
And all the upright in heart will follow it.

16 Who will stand up for me against evildoers?
Who will take his stand for me against those who do wickedness?

17 ¶ If the LORD had not been my help,
My soul would soon have dwelt in *the abode of* silence.

18 If I should say, "My foot has slipped,"
Thy lovingkindness, O LORD, will hold me up.

19 When my anxious thoughts multiply within me,
Thy consolations delight my soul.

20 Can a throne of destruction be allied with Thee,
One which devises mischief by decree?

21 They band themselves together against the life of the righteous,
And condemn the innocent to death.

22 But the LORD has been my stronghold,
And my God the rock of my refuge.

23 And He has brought back their wickedness upon them,
And will destroy them in their evil;
The LORD our God will destroy them.

PSALM 95

O COME, let us sing for joy to the LORD;
Let us shout joyfully to the rock of our salvation.

2 Let us come before His presence with thanksgiving;
Let us shout joyfully to Him with psalms.

3 For the LORD is a great God,
And a great King above all gods,

4 In whose hand are the depths of the earth;
The peaks of the mountains are His also.

5 The sea is His, for it was He who made it;
And His hands formed the dry land.

6 ¶ Come, let us worship and bow down;
Let us kneel before the LORD our Maker.

7 For He is our God,
And we are the people of His pasture, and the sheep of His hand.
Today, if you would hear His voice,

8 Do not harden your hearts, as at [155]Meribah,
As in the day of [156]Massah in the wilderness;

9 "When your fathers tested Me,
They tried Me, though they had seen My work.

10 "For forty years I loathed *that* generation,
And said they are a people who err in their heart,
And they do not know My ways.

11 "Therefore I swore in My anger,
Truly they shall not enter into My rest."

PSALM 96

SING to the LORD a new song;
Sing to the LORD, all the earth.

2 Sing to the LORD, bless His name;
Proclaim good tidings of His salvation from day to day.

3 Tell of His glory among the nations,
His wonderful deeds among all the peoples.

4 For great is the LORD, and greatly to be praised;
He is to be feared above all gods.

5 For all the gods of the peoples are idols,
But the LORD made the heavens.

6 Splendor and majesty are before Him,
Strength and beauty are in His sanctuary.

7 ¶ [157]Ascribe to the LORD, O families of the peoples,
[157]Ascribe to the LORD glory and strength.

8 [157]Ascribe to the LORD the glory of His name;

---

[155] Or, *place of strife*   [156] Or, *temptation*   [157] Lit., *Give*

Bring an offering, and come into His courts.

9 Worship the LORD in [158]holy attire;
Tremble before Him, all the earth.

10 Say among the nations, "The LORD reigns;
Indeed, the world is firmly established, it will not be moved;
He will judge the peoples with [159]equity."

11 ¶ Let the heavens be glad, and let the earth rejoice;
Let the sea roar, and all it contains;

12 Let the field exult, and all that is in it.
Then all the trees of the forest will sing for joy

13 Before the LORD, for He is coming;
For He is coming to judge the earth.
He will judge the world in righteousness,
And the peoples in His faithfulness.

PSALM 97

THE LORD reigns; let the earth rejoice;
Let the many [160]islands be glad.

2 Clouds and thick darkness surround Him;
Righteousness and justice are the foundation of His throne.

3 Fire goes before Him,
And burns up His adversaries round about.

4 His lightnings lit up the world;
The earth saw and trembled.

5 The mountains melted like wax at the presence of the LORD,
At the presence of the Lord of the whole earth.

6 The heavens declare His righteousness,
And all the peoples have seen His glory.

7 ¶ Let all those be ashamed who serve graven images,
Who boast themselves of idols;
Worship Him, all you gods.

8 Zion heard *this* and was glad,
And the daughters of Judah have rejoiced

Because of Thy judgments, O LORD.

9 For Thou art the LORD Most High over all the earth;
Thou art exalted far above all gods.

10 ¶ Hate evil, you who love the LORD,
Who preserves the souls of His godly ones;
He delivers them from the hand of the wicked.

11 Light is sown *like seed* for the righteous,
And gladness for the upright in heart.

12 Be glad in the LORD, you righteous ones;
And give thanks to His holy name.

PSALM 98
A Psalm.

O SING to the LORD a new song,
For He has done wonderful things,
His right hand and His holy arm have [161]gained the victory for Him.

2 The LORD has made known His salvation;
He has revealed His righteousness in the sight of the nations.

3 He has remembered His lovingkindness and His faithfulness to the house of Israel;
All the ends of the earth have seen the salvation of our God.

4 ¶ Shout joyfully to the LORD, all the earth;
Break forth and sing for joy and sing praises.

5 Sing praises to the LORD with the lyre;
With the lyre and the sound of melody.

6 With trumpets and the sound of the horn
Shout joyfully before the King, the LORD.

7 ¶ Let the sea roar and all it contains,
The world and those who dwell in it.

[158] Or, *the splendor of holiness*   [159] Or, *uprightness*
[160] Or, *coastlands*   [161] Or, *accomplished salvation*

8 Let the rivers clap their hands;
   Let the mountains sing together
     for joy
9 Before the LORD; for He is coming
   to judge the earth;
   He will judge the world with
    righteousness,
   And the peoples with equity.

PSALM 99

THE LORD reigns, let the peoples
   tremble;
   He is enthroned *above* the cheru-
    bim, let the earth shake!
2 The LORD is great in Zion,
   And He is exalted above all the
    peoples.
3 Let them praise Thy great and
   awesome name;
   Holy is He.
4 And the strength of the King
   loves [162]justice;
   Thou hast established equity;
   Thou hast executed [162]justice and
    righteousness in Jacob.
5 Exalt the LORD our God,
   And worship at His footstool;
   Holy is He.

6 ¶ Moses and Aaron were among
   His priests,
   And Samuel was among those
    who called on His name;
   They called upon the LORD, and
    He answered them.
7 He spoke to them in the pillar of
   cloud;
   They kept His testimonies,
   And the statute that He gave
    them.
8 O LORD our God, Thou didst an-
   swer them;
   Thou wast a forgiving God to
    them,
   And *yet* an avenger of their *evil*
    deeds.
9 Exalt the LORD our God,
   And worship at His holy hill;
   For holy is the LORD our God.

PSALM 100

A Psalm for Thanksgiving.

SHOUT joyfully to the LORD, all the
   earth.
2 Serve the LORD with gladness;

Come before Him with joyful
   singing.
3 Know that the LORD Himself is
   God;
   It is He who has made us, and
    [163]not we ourselves;
   We are His people and the sheep
    of His pasture.

4 ¶ Enter His gates with thanksgiv-
   ing,
   And His courts with praise.
   Give thanks to Him; bless His
    name.
5 For the LORD is good;
   His lovingkindness is everlasting,
   And His faithfulness to all genera-
    tions.

PSALM 101

A Psalm of David.

I WILL sing of lovingkindness and
   justice,
   To Thee, O LORD, I will sing
    praises.
2 I will give heed to the [164]blameless
   way.
   When wilt Thou come to me?
   I will walk within my house in the
    integrity of my heart.
3 I will set no worthless thing before my eyes;
   I hate the work of those who fall
    away;
   It shall not fasten its grip on me.
4 A perverse heart shall depart from
   me;
   I will know no evil.
5 Whoever secretly slanders his
   neighbor, him I will destroy;
   No one who has a haughty look
    and an arrogant heart will I
    endure.

6 ¶ My eyes shall be upon the faithful of the land, that they may
    dwell with me;
   He who walks in a [164]blameless
    way is the one who will minister
    to me.
7 He who practices deceit shall not
   dwell within my house;
   He who speaks falsehood shall not
    maintain his position before me.

[162] Or, *judgment*   [163] Some mss. read *His we are*   [164] Or, *way of integrity*

8 Every morning I will [165]destroy all
the wicked of the land,
So as to cut off from the city of
the LORD all those who do iniquity.

PSALM 102

A Prayer of the Afflicted, when he is faint, and
pours out his complaint before the LORD.

HEAR my prayer, O LORD!
And let my cry for help come to
Thee.
2 Do not hide Thy face from me in
the day of my distress;
Incline Thine ear to me;
In the day when I call answer me
quickly.
3 For my days have been consumed
in smoke,
And my bones have been
scorched like a hearth.
4 My heart has been smitten like
grass and has withered away,
Indeed, I forget to eat my bread.
5 Because of the loudness of my
groaning
My bones cling to my flesh.
6 I resemble a pelican of the wilderness;
I have become like an owl of the
waste places.
7 I lie awake,
I have become like a lonely bird
on a housetop.

8 ¶ My enemies have reproached
me all day long;
Those who deride me have used
my *name* as a curse.
9 For I have eaten ashes like bread,
And mingled my drink with weeping,
10 Because of Thine indignation and
Thy wrath;
For Thou hast lifted me up and
cast me away.
11 My days are like a lengthened
shadow;
And I wither away like grass.

12 ¶ But Thou, O LORD, dost abide
forever;
And Thy name to all generations.
13 Thou wilt arise *and* have compassion on Zion;

For it is time to be gracious to her,
For the appointed time has come.
14 Surely Thy servants find pleasure
in her stones,
And feel pity for her dust.
15 So the nations will fear the name
of the LORD,
And all the kings of the earth Thy
glory.
16 For the LORD has built up Zion;
He has appeared in His glory.
17 He has regarded the prayer of the
destitute,
And has not despised their prayer.

18 ¶ This will be written for the generation to come;
That a people yet to be created
may praise the LORD.
19 For He looked down from His
holy height;
From heaven the LORD gazed
upon the earth,
20 To hear the groaning of the prisoner;
To set free those who were
doomed to death;
21 That *men* may tell of the name of
the LORD in Zion,
And His praise in Jerusalem;
22 When the peoples are gathered
together,
And the kingdoms, to serve the
LORD.

23 ¶ He has weakened my strength
in the way;
He has shortened my days.
24 I say, "O my God, do not take me
away in the midst of my days,
Thy years are throughout all generations.
25 "Of old Thou didst found the earth;
And the heavens are the work of
Thy hands.
26 "Even they will perish, but Thou
dost endure;
And all of them will wear out like
a garment;
Like clothing Thou wilt change
them, and they will be changed.
27 "But Thou art the same,
And Thy years will not come to an
end.
28 "The children of Thy servants will
continue,

[165] Or, *silence*

And their descendants will be established before Thee."

PSALM 103
A Psalm of David.

Bless the Lord, O my soul;
And all that is within me, *bless* His holy name.
2 Bless the Lord, O my soul,
And forget none of His benefits;
3 Who pardons all your iniquities;
Who heals all your diseases;
4 Who redeems your life from the pit;
Who crowns you with lovingkindness and compassion;
5 Who satisfies your [166]years with good things,
So that your youth is renewed like the eagle.

6 ¶ The Lord performs righteous deeds,
And judgments for all who are oppressed.
7 He made known His ways to Moses,
His acts to the sons of Israel.
8 The Lord is compassionate and gracious,
Slow to anger and abounding in lovingkindness.
9 He will not always strive *with us*;
Nor will He keep *His anger* forever.
10 He has not dealt with us according to our sins,
Nor rewarded us according to our iniquities.
11 For as high as the heavens are above the earth,
So great is His lovingkindness toward those who [167]fear Him.
12 As far as the east is from the west,
So far has He removed our transgressions from us.
13 Just as a father has compassion on *his* children,
So the Lord has compassion on those who fear Him.
14 For He Himself knows [168]our frame;
He is mindful that we are *but* dust.

15 ¶ As for man, his days are like grass;

As a flower of the field, so he flourishes.
16 When the wind has passed over it, it is no more;
And its place acknowledges it no longer.
17 But the lovingkindness of the Lord is from everlasting to everlasting on those who [167]fear Him,
And His righteousness to children's children,
18 To those who keep His covenant,
And who remember His precepts to do them.

19 ¶ The Lord has established His throne in the heavens;
And His [169]sovereignty rules over all.
20 Bless the Lord, you His angels,
Mighty in strength, who perform His word,
Obeying the voice of His word!
21 Bless the Lord, all you His hosts,
You who serve Him, doing His will.
22 Bless the Lord, all you works of His,
In all places of His dominion;
Bless the Lord, O my soul!

PSALM 104

Bless the Lord, O my soul!
O Lord my God, Thou art very great;
Thou art clothed with splendor and majesty,
2 Covering Thyself with light as with a cloak,
Stretching out heaven like a *tent* curtain.
3 [170]He lays the beams of His upper chambers in the waters;
He makes the clouds His chariot;
He walks upon the wings of the wind;
4 He makes [171]the winds His messengers,
[172]Flaming fire His ministers.

5 ¶ He established the earth upon its foundations,

---

[166] Or, *desire*   [167] Or, *revere*   [168] I.e., what we are made of
[169] Or, *kingdom*
[170] Lit., *Who, so through v. 4, and vv. 13, 14*
[171] Or, *His angels, spirits*
[172] Or, *His ministers flames of fire*

So that it will not [173]totter forever
and ever.
6 Thou didst cover it with the deep
as with a garment;
The waters were standing above
the mountains.
7 At Thy rebuke they fled;
At the sound of Thy thunder they
hurried away.
8 The mountains rose; the valleys
sank down
To the place which Thou didst
establish for them.
9 Thou didst set a boundary that
they may not pass over;
That they may not return to cover
the earth.

10 ¶ He sends forth springs in the
valleys;
They flow between the mountains;
11 They give drink to every beast of
the field;
The wild donkeys quench their
thirst.
12 Beside them the birds of the heavens dwell;
They lift up *their* voices among
the branches.
13 He waters the mountains from His
upper chambers;
The earth is satisfied with the
fruit of His works.

14 ¶ He causes the grass to grow for
the cattle,
And vegetation for the labor of
man,
So that he may bring forth food
from the earth,
15 And wine which makes man's
heart glad,
So that he may make *his* face
glisten with oil,
And food which sustains man's
heart.
16 The trees of the LORD drink their
fill,
The cedars of Lebanon which He
planted,
17 Where the birds build their nests,
And the stork, whose home is the
fir trees.

18 ¶ The high mountains are for the
wild goats;
The cliffs are a refuge for the rock
badgers.
19 He made the moon for the seasons;
The sun knows the place of its
setting.
20 Thou dost appoint darkness and it
becomes night,
In which all the beasts of the
forest prowl about.
21 The young lions roar after their
prey,
And seek their food from God.
22 *When* the sun rises they withdraw,
And lie down in their dens.
23 Man goes forth to his work
And to his labor until evening.

24 ¶ O LORD, how many are Thy
works!
In wisdom Thou hast made them
all;
The earth is full of Thy [174]posses-
sions.
25 There is the sea, great and broad,
In which are swarms without
number,
Animals both small and great.
26 There the ships move along,
And [175]Leviathan, which Thou
hast formed to sport in it.

27 ¶ They all wait for Thee,
To give them their food in [176]due
season.
28 Thou dost give to them, they
gather *it* up;
Thou dost open Thy hand, they
are satisfied with good.
29 Thou dost hide Thy face, they are
dismayed;
Thou dost take away their
[177]spirit, they expire,
And return to their dust.
30 Thou dost send forth Thy [177]Spirit,
they are created;
And Thou dost renew the face of
the ground.

31 ¶ Let the glory of the LORD endure forever;

[173] Or, *move out of place*

[174] Or, *creatures*   [175] Or, *a sea monster*
[176] Lit., *its appointed time*   [177] Or, *breath*

Let the LORD be glad in His works;

32 He looks at the earth, and it trembles;
He touches the mountains, and
they smoke.

33 I will sing to the LORD as long as I
live;
I will sing praise to my God while
I have my being.

34 Let my meditation be pleasing to
Him;
As for me, I shall be glad in the
LORD.

35 Let sinners be consumed from the
earth,
And let the wicked be no more.
Bless the LORD, O my soul.
Praise the LORD!

PSALM 105

OH give thanks to the LORD, call
upon His name;
Make known His deeds among
the peoples.

2 Sing to Him, sing praises to Him;
[178]Speak of all His wonders.

3 Glory in His holy name;
Let the heart of those who seek
the LORD be glad.

4 Seek the LORD and His strength;
Seek His face continually.

5 Remember His wonders which He
has done,
His marvels, and the judgments
uttered by His mouth,

6 O seed of Abraham, His servant,
O sons of Jacob, His chosen ones!

7 He is the LORD our God;
His judgments are in all the earth.

8 ¶ He has remembered His covenant forever,
The word which He commanded
to a thousand generations,

9 *The covenant* which He made
with Abraham,
And His oath to Isaac.

10 Then He confirmed it to Jacob for
a statute,
To Israel as an everlasting covenant,

11 Saying, "To you I will give the
land of Canaan
As the portion of your inheritance,"

12 When they were only a few men
in number,
Very few, and strangers in it.

13 And they wandered about from
nation to nation,
From *one* kingdom to another
people.

14 He permitted no man to oppress
them,
And He reproved kings for their
sakes:

15 "Do not touch My anointed ones,
And do My prophets no harm."

16 ¶ And He called for a famine
upon the land;
He broke the whole staff of bread.

17 He sent a man before them,
Joseph, *who* was sold as a slave.

18 They afflicted his feet with fetters,
He himself was laid in irons;

19 Until the time that his word came
to pass,
The word of the LORD tested him.

20 The king sent and released him,
The ruler of peoples, and set him
free.

21 He made him lord of his house,
And ruler over all his possessions,

22 To imprison his princes at will,
That he might teach his elders
wisdom.

23 Israel also came into Egypt;
Thus Jacob sojourned in the land
of Ham.

24 And He caused His people to be
very fruitful,
And made them stronger than
their adversaries.

25 ¶ He turned their heart to hate
His people,
To deal craftily with His servants.

26 He sent Moses His servant,
And Aaron whom He had chosen.

27 They performed His wondrous
acts among them,
And miracles in the land of Ham.

28 He sent darkness and made *it*
dark;
And they did not rebel against His
words.

29 He turned their waters into blood,
And caused their fish to die.

30 Their land swarmed with frogs
Even in the chambers of their
kings.

31 He spoke, and there came a
swarm of flies

[178] Or, *Meditate on*

And gnats in all their territory.
32 He gave them hail for rain,
   And flaming fire in their land.
33 He struck down their vines also
     and their fig trees,
   And shattered the trees of their
     territory.
34 He spoke, and locusts came,
   And young locusts, even without
     number,
35 And ate up all vegetation in their
     land,
   And ate up the fruit of their
     ground.
36 He also struck down all the first-
     born in their land,
   The first fruits of all their vigor.

37 ¶ Then He brought them out with
     silver and gold;
   And among His tribes there was
     not one who stumbled.
38 Egypt was glad when they de-
     parted;
   For the dread of them had fallen
     upon them.
39 He spread a cloud for a [179]cover-
     ing,
   And fire to illumine by night.
40 They asked, and He brought quail,
   And satisfied them with the bread
     of heaven.
41 He opened the rock, and water
     flowed out;
   It ran in the dry places *like* a river.
42 For He remembered His holy
     word
   With Abraham His servant;
43 And He brought forth His people
     with joy,
   His chosen ones with a joyful
     shout.
44 He gave them also the lands of the
     nations,
   That they might take possession
     of *the fruit of* the peoples' labor,
45 So that they might keep His stat-
     utes,
   And observe His laws,
   Praise the LORD!

PSALM 106

PRAISE the LORD!
   Oh give thanks to the LORD, for
     He is good;
   For His lovingkindness is ever-
     lasting.

2 Who can speak of the mighty
     deeds of the LORD,
   Or can show forth all His praise?
3 How blessed are those who keep
     justice,
   Who practice righteousness at all
     times!

4 ¶ Remember me, O LORD, in *Thy*
     favor toward Thy people;
   Visit me with Thy salvation,
5 That I may see the prosperity of
     Thy chosen ones,
   That I may rejoice in the gladness
     of Thy nation,
   That I may glory with Thine [180]in-
     heritance.

6 ¶ We have sinned like our fathers,
   We have committed iniquity, we
     have behaved wickedly.
7 Our fathers in Egypt did not un-
     derstand Thy wonders;
   They did not remember Thine
     abundant kindnesses,
   But rebelled by the sea, at the
     [181]Red Sea.
8 Nevertheless He saved them for
     the sake of His name,
   That He might make His power
     known.
9 Thus He rebuked the [181]Red Sea
     and it dried up;
   And He led them through the
     deeps, as through the wilder-
     ness.
10 So He saved them from the hand
     of the one who hated *them,*
   And redeemed them from the
     hand of the enemy.
11 And the waters covered their ad-
     versaries;
   Not one of them was left.
12 Then they believed His words;
   They sang His praise.

13 ¶ They quickly forgot His works;
   They did not wait for His counsel,
14 But craved intensely in the wilder-
     ness,
   And tempted God in the desert.
15 So He gave them their request,
   But sent a wasting disease among
     them.

16 ¶ When they became envious of
     Moses in the camp,

---

[179] Or, *curtain*   [180] I.e., people   [181] Lit., *Sea of Reeds*

And of Aaron, the holy one of the
LORD,

17 The earth opened and swallowed
up Dathan,
And engulfed the company of Abiram.

18 And a fire blazed up in their company;
The flame consumed the wicked.

19 ¶ They made a calf in Horeb,
And worshiped a molten image.

20 Thus they exchanged their glory
For the image of an ox that eats
grass.

21 They forgot God their Savior,
Who had done great things in
Egypt,

22 Wonders in the land of Ham,
And awesome things by the [181]Red
Sea.

23 Therefore He said that He would
destroy them,
Had not Moses His chosen one
stood in the breach before Him,
To turn away His wrath from destroying *them.*

24 Then they despised the pleasant
land;
They did not believe in His word,

25 But grumbled in their tents;
They did not listen to the voice of
the LORD.

26 Therefore He swore to them,
That He would cast them down in
the wilderness,

27 And that He would cast their seed
among the nations,
And scatter them in the lands.

28 ¶ They joined themselves also to
Baal-peor,
And ate sacrifices offered to the
dead.

29 Thus they provoked *Him* to anger
with their deeds;
And the plague broke out among
them.

30 Then Phinehas stood up and interposed;
And so the plague was stayed.

31 And it was reckoned to him for
righteousness,
To all generations forever.

32 ¶ They also provoked *Him* to
wrath at the waters of [182]Meri-
bah,

So that it went hard with Moses
on their account;

33 Because they were rebellious
against His Spirit,
He spoke rashly with his lips.

34 ¶ They did not destroy the peoples,
As the LORD commanded them,

35 But they mingled with the nations,
And learned their practices,

36 And served their idols,
Which became a snare to them.

37 They even sacrificed their sons
and their daughters to the demons,

38 And shed innocent blood,
The blood of their sons and their
daughters,
Whom they sacrificed to the idols
of Canaan;
And the land was polluted with
the blood.

39 Thus they became unclean in
their practices,
And played the harlot in their
deeds.

40 ¶ Therefore the anger of the LORD
was kindled against His people,
And He abhorred His inheritance.

41 Then He gave them into the hand
of the nations;
And those who hated them ruled
over them.

42 Their enemies also oppressed
them,
And they were subdued under
their power.

43 Many times He would deliver
them;
They, however, were rebellious in
their counsel,
And *so* sank down in their iniquity.

44 ¶ Nevertheless He looked upon
their distress,
When He heard their cry;

45 And He remembered His covenant
for their sake,
And relented according to the
greatness of His lovingkindness.

46 He also made them *objects* of
compassion
In the presence of all their captors.

[181] Lit., *Sea of Reeds*   [182] Lit., *strife*

47 ¶ Save us, O LORD our God,
And gather us from among the nations,
To give thanks to Thy holy name,
And glory in Thy praise.
48 Blessed be the LORD, the God of Israel,
From everlasting even to everlasting.
And let all the people say, "Amen."
Praise the LORD!

BOOK 5

PSALM 107

OH give thanks to the LORD, for He is good;
For His lovingkindness is everlasting.
2 Let the redeemed of the LORD say *so,*
Whom He has redeemed from the hand of the adversary,
3 And gathered from the lands,
From the east and from the west,
From the north and from the south.

4 ¶ They wandered in the wilderness in a desert region;
They did not find a way to an inhabited city.
5 *They were* hungry and thirsty;
Their soul fainted within them.
6 Then they cried out to the LORD in their trouble;
He delivered them out of their distresses.
7 He led them also by a straight way,
To go to an inhabited city.
8 Let them give thanks to the LORD for His lovingkindness,
And for His wonders to the sons of men!
9 For He has satisfied the thirsty soul,
And the hungry soul He has filled with what is good.

10 ¶ There were those who dwelt in darkness and in the shadow of death,
Prisoners in misery and chains,
11 Because they had rebelled against the words of God,

And spurned the counsel of the Most High.
12 Therefore He humbled their heart with labor;
They stumbled and there was none to help.
13 Then they cried out to the LORD in their trouble;
He saved them out of their distresses.
14 He brought them out of darkness and the shadow of death,
And broke their bands apart.
15 Let them give thanks to the LORD for His lovingkindness,
And for His wonders to the sons of men!
16 For He has shattered gates of bronze,
And cut bars of iron asunder.

17 ¶ Fools, because of their rebellious way,
And because of their iniquities, were afflicted.
18 Their soul abhorred all kinds of food;
And they drew near to the gates of death.
19 Then they cried out to the LORD in their trouble;
He saved them out of their distresses.
20 He sent His word and healed them,
And delivered *them* from their [183]destructions.
21 Let them give thanks to the LORD for His lovingkindness,
And for His wonders to the sons of men!
22 Let them also offer sacrifices of thanksgiving,
And tell of His works with joyful singing.

23 ¶ Those who go down to the sea in ships,
Who do business on great waters;
24 They have seen the works of the LORD,
And His wonders in the deep.
25 For He spoke and raised up a stormy wind,
Which lifted up the waves of the sea.
26 They rose up to the heavens, they went down to the depths;

[183] Or, *pits*

Their soul melted away in *their*
misery.

27 They reeled and staggered like a
drunken man,
And [184]were at their wits' end.

28 Then they cried to the LORD in
their trouble,
And He brought them out of their
distresses.

29 He caused the storm to be still,
So that the waves of the sea were
hushed.

30 Then they were glad because they
were quiet;
So He guided them to their desired haven.

31 Let them give thanks to the LORD
for His lovingkindness,
And for His wonders to the sons
of men!

32 Let them extol Him also in the
congregation of the people,
And praise Him at the seat of the
elders.

33 ¶ He [185]changes rivers into a wilderness,
And springs of water into a thirsty
ground;

34 A fruitful land into a salt waste,
Because of the wickedness of
those who dwell in it.

35 He changes a wilderness into a
pool of water,
And a dry land into springs of
water;

36 And there He makes the hungry
to dwell,
So that they may establish an
inhabited city,

37 And sow fields, and plant vineyards,
And gather a fruitful harvest.

38 Also He blesses them and they
multiply greatly;
And He does not let their cattle
decrease.

39 ¶ When they are diminished and
bowed down
Through oppression, misery, and
sorrow,

40 He pours contempt upon princes,
And makes them wander in a
pathless waste.

41 But He sets the needy securely on
high away from affliction,
And makes *his* families like a
flock.

42 The upright see it, and are glad;
But all unrighteousness shuts its
mouth.

43 Who is wise? Let him give heed to
these things;
And consider the lovingkindnesses of the LORD.

PSALM 108

A Song, a Psalm of David.

MY heart is steadfast, O God;
I will sing, I will sing praises, even
with my soul.

2 Awake, harp and lyre;
I will awaken the dawn!

3 I will give thanks to Thee, O
LORD, among the peoples;
And I will sing praises to Thee
among the nations.

4 For Thy lovingkindness is great
above the heavens;
And Thy truth *reaches* to the
skies.

5 Be exalted, O God, above the
heavens,
And Thy glory above all the earth.

6 That Thy beloved may be delivered,
Save with Thy right hand, and
answer me!

7 ¶ God has spoken in His [186]holi-
ness:
"I will exult, I will portion out
Shechem,
And measure out the valley of
Succoth.

8 "Gilead is Mine, Manasseh is Mine;
Ephraim also is the helmet of My
head;
Judah is My [187]scepter.

9 "Moab is My washbowl;
Over Edom I shall throw My shoe;
Over Philistia I will shout aloud."

10 ¶ Who will bring me into the besieged city?
Who will lead me to Edom?

11 Hast not Thou Thyself, O God,
rejected us?
And wilt Thou not go forth with
our armies, O God?

---

[184] Lit., *all their wisdom was swallowed up*
[185] Or, *turns rivers into a desert*

[186] Or, *sanctuary*   [187] Or, *lawgiver*

12 Oh give us help against the adversary,
   For deliverance by man is in vain.
13 Through God we shall do valiantly;
   And it is He who will tread down our adversaries.

PSALM 109
For the choir director. A Psalm of David.

O GOD of my praise,
  Do not be silent!
2 For they have opened the wicked and deceitful mouth against me;
  They have spoken against me with a lying tongue.
3 They have also surrounded me with words of hatred,
  And fought against me without cause.
4 In return for my love they act as my accusers;
  But I am *in* prayer.
5 Thus they have repaid me evil for good,
  And hatred for my love.

6 ¶ Appoint a wicked man over him;
  And let an accuser stand at his right hand.
7 When he is judged, let him come forth guilty;
  And let his prayer become sin.
8 Let his days be few;
  Let another take his office.
9 Let his children be fatherless,
  And his wife a widow.
10 Let his children wander about and beg;
  And let them seek *sustenance* far from their ruined homes.
11 Let the creditor seize all that he has;
  And let strangers plunder the product of his labor.
12 Let there be none to extend lovingkindness to him,
  Nor any to be gracious to his fatherless children.
13 Let his posterity be cut off;
  In a following generation let their name be blotted out.

14 ¶ Let the iniquity of his fathers be remembered before the LORD,
  And do not let the sin of his mother be blotted out.

15 Let them be before the LORD continually,
  That He may cut off their memory from the earth;
16 Because he did not remember to show lovingkindness,
  But persecuted the afflicted and needy man,
  And the despondent in heart, to put *them* to death.
17 He also loved cursing, so it came to him;
  And he did not delight in blessing, so it was far from him.
18 But he clothed himself with cursing as with his garment,
  And it entered into his body like water,
  And like oil into his bones.
19 Let it be to him as a garment with which he covers himself,
  And for a belt with which he constantly girds himself.
20 Let this be the reward of my accusers from the LORD,
  And of those who speak evil against my soul.

21 ¶ But Thou, O GOD, the Lord, deal *kindly* with me for Thy name's sake;
  Because Thy lovingkindness is good, deliver me;
22 For I am afflicted and needy,
  And my heart is wounded within me.
23 I am passing like a shadow when it lengthens;
  I am shaken off like the locust.
24 My knees are weak from fasting;
  And my flesh has grown lean, without fatness.
25 I also have become a reproach to them;
  When they see me, they wag their head.

26 ¶ Help me, O LORD my God;
  Save me according to Thy lovingkindness.
27 And let them know that this is Thy hand;
  Thou, LORD, hast done it.
28 Let them curse, but do Thou bless;
  When they arise, they shall be ashamed,
  But Thy servant shall be glad.
29 Let my accusers be clothed with dishonor,

And let them cover themselves
with their own shame as with a
robe.

30 ¶ With my mouth I will give
thanks abundantly to the LORD;
And in the midst of many I will
praise Him.
31 For He stands at the right hand of
the needy,
To save him from those who
judge his soul.

PSALM 110
A Psalm of David.

THE LORD says to my Lord:
"Sit at My right hand,
Until I make Thine enemies a
footstool for Thy feet."
2 The LORD will stretch forth Thy
strong scepter from Zion, *saying,*
"Rule in the midst of Thine enemies."
3 Thy people will volunteer freely in
the day of Thy power;
In holy array, from the womb of
the dawn,
Thy youth are to Thee *as* the dew.

4 ¶ The LORD has sworn and will
not change His mind,
"Thou art a priest forever
According to the order of Melchizedek."
5 The Lord is at Thy right hand;
He will shatter kings in the day of
His wrath.
6 He will judge among the nations,
He will fill *them* with corpses,
He will shatter the chief men over
a broad country.
7 He will drink from the brook by
the wayside;
Therefore He will lift up *His* head.

PSALM 111

PRAISE the LORD!
I will give thanks to the LORD
with all *my* heart,
In the company of the upright
and in the assembly.
2 Great are the works of the LORD;
They are studied by all who delight in them.
3 Splendid and majestic is His work;
And His righteousness endures
forever.

4 He has made His wonders to be
remembered;
The LORD is gracious and compassionate.
5 He has given food to those who
[188]fear Him;
He will remember His covenant
forever.
6 He has made known to His people
the power of His works,
In giving them the heritage of the
nations.

7 ¶ The works of His hands are
truth and justice;
All His precepts are sure.
8 They are upheld forever and ever;
They are performed in truth and
uprightness.
9 He has sent redemption to His
people;
He has ordained His covenant forever;
Holy and awesome is His name.
10 The [189]fear of the LORD is the
beginning of wisdom;
A good understanding have all
those who do *His commandments*;
His praise endures forever.

PSALM 112

PRAISE the LORD!
How blessed is the man who fears
the LORD,
Who greatly delights in His commandments.
2 His [190]descendants will be mighty
on earth;
The generation of the upright will
be blessed.
3 Wealth and riches are in his
house,
And his righteousness endures
forever.
4 Light arises in the darkness for
the upright;
He is gracious and compassionate
and righteous.
5 It is well with the man who is
gracious and lends;
He will maintain his cause in
judgment.
6 For he will never be shaken;
The righteous will be remembered
forever.

---

[188] Or, *revere*   [189] Or, *reverence for*   [190] Lit., *seed*

7 ¶ He will not fear evil tidings;
His heart is steadfast, trusting in
the LORD.
8 His heart is upheld, he will not
fear,
Until he looks *with satisfaction*
on his adversaries.
9 He has given freely to the poor;
His righteousness endures forever;
His horn will be exalted in honor.

10 ¶ The wicked will see it and be
vexed;
He will gnash his teeth and melt
away;
The desire of the wicked will perish.

PSALM 113

PRAISE the LORD!
Praise, O servants of the LORD.
Praise the name of the LORD.
2 Blessed be the name of the LORD
From this time forth and forever.
3 From the rising of the sun to its
setting
The name of the LORD is to be
praised.
4 The LORD is high above all nations;
His glory is above the heavens.

5 ¶ Who is like the LORD our God,
Who is enthroned on high,
6 Who humbles Himself to behold
The things that are in heaven and
in the earth?
7 He raises the poor from the dust,
And lifts the needy from the ash
heap,
8 To make *them* sit with princes,
With the princes of His people.
9 He makes the barren woman
abide in the house
As a joyful mother of children.
Praise the LORD!

PSALM 114

WHEN Israel went forth from Egypt,
The house of Jacob from a people
of strange language,
2 Judah became His sanctuary,
Israel, His dominion.

3 ¶ The sea looked and fled;
The Jordan turned back.

4 The mountains skipped like rams,
The hills, like lambs.
5 What ails you, O sea, that you
flee?
O Jordan, that you turn back?
6 O mountains, that you skip like
rams?
O hills, like lambs?

7 ¶ Tremble, O earth, before the
Lord,
Before the God of Jacob,
8 Who turned the rock into a pool
of water,
The flint into a fountain of water.

PSALM 115

NOT to us, O LORD, not to us,
But to Thy name give glory
Because of Thy lovingkindness,
because of Thy truth.
2 Why should the nations say,
"Where, now, is their God?"
3 But our God is in the heavens;
He does whatever He pleases.
4 Their idols are silver and gold,
The work of man's hands.
5 They have mouths, but they cannot speak;
They have eyes, but they cannot
see;
6 They have ears, but they cannot
hear;
They have noses, but they cannot
smell;
7 They have hands, but they cannot
feel;
They have feet, but they cannot
walk;
They cannot make a sound with
their throat.
8 Those who make them will become like them,
Everyone who trusts in them.

9 ¶ O Israel, trust in the LORD;
He is their help and their shield.
10 O house of Aaron, trust in the
LORD;
He is their help and their shield.
11 You who [191]fear the LORD, trust in
the LORD;
He is their help and their shield.
12 The LORD has been mindful of us;
He will bless *us*;
He will bless the house of Israel;
He will bless the house of Aaron.

[191] Or, *revere*

13 He will bless those who [191]fear the
  LORD,
  The small together with the great.
14 May the LORD give you increase,
  You and your children.
15 May you be blessed of the LORD,
  Maker of heaven and earth.

16 ¶ The heavens are the heavens of
  the LORD;
  But the earth He has given to the
  sons of men.
17 The dead do not praise the LORD,
  Nor *do* any who go down into
  silence;
18 But as for us, we will bless the
  LORD
  From this time forth and forever.
  Praise the LORD!

PSALM 116

I LOVE the LORD, because He hears
  My voice *and* my supplications.
2 Because He has inclined His ear to
  me,
  Therefore I shall call *upon Him* as
  long as I live.
3 The cords of death encompassed
  me,
  And the terrors of Sheol came
  upon me;
  I found distress and sorrow.
4 Then I called upon the name of
  the LORD:
  "O LORD, I beseech Thee, save my
  life!"

5 ¶ Gracious is the LORD, and righteous;
  Yes, our God is compassionate.
6 The LORD preserves the simple;
  I was brought low, and He saved
  me.
7 Return to your rest, O my soul,
  For the LORD has dealt bountifully
  with you.
8 For Thou hast rescued my soul
  from death,
  My eyes from tears,
  My feet from stumbling.
9 I shall walk before the LORD
  In the land of the living.
10 I believed when I said,
  "I am greatly afflicted."
11 I said in my alarm,
  "All men are liars."

12 ¶ What shall I render to the LORD
  For all His benefits toward me?
13 I shall lift up the cup of salvation,
  And call upon the name of the
  LORD.
14 I shall pay my vows to the LORD,
  Oh *may it be* in the presence of all
  His people.
15 Precious in the sight of the LORD
  Is the death of His godly ones.
16 O LORD, surely I am Thy servant,
  I am Thy servant, the son of Thy
  handmaid,
  Thou hast loosed my bonds.
17 To Thee I shall offer a sacrifice of
  thanksgiving,
  And call upon the name of the
  LORD.
18 I shall pay my vows to the LORD,
  Oh *may it be* in the presence of all
  His people,
19 In the courts of the LORD's house,
  In the midst of you, O Jerusalem.
  Praise the LORD!

PSALM 117

PRAISE the LORD, all nations;
  Laud Him, all peoples!
2 For His lovingkindness [192]is great
  toward us,
  And the truth of the LORD is everlasting.
  Praise the LORD!

PSALM 118

GIVE thanks to the LORD, for He is
  good;
  For His lovingkindness is everlasting.
2 Oh let Israel say,
  "His lovingkindness is everlasting."
3 Oh let the house of Aaron say,
  "His lovingkindness is everlasting."
4 Oh let those who [193]fear the LORD
  say,
  "His lovingkindness is everlasting."

5 ¶ From *my* distress I called upon
  the LORD;
  The LORD answered me *and set
  me* in a large place.
6 The LORD is for me; I will not fear;
  What can man do to me?
7 The LORD is for me among those
  who help me;
  Therefore I shall look *with satisfaction* on those who hate me.

[191] Or, *revere*   [192] Lit., *prevails over us*   [193] Or, *revere*

8 It is better to take refuge in the
   LORD
   Than to trust in man.
9 It is better to take refuge in the
   LORD
   Than to trust in princes.

10 ¶ All nations surrounded me;
   In the name of the LORD I will
   surely cut them off.
11 They surrounded me, yes, they
   surrounded me;
   In the name of the LORD I will
   surely cut them off.
12 They surrounded me like bees;
   They were extinguished as a fire
   of thorns;
   In the name of the LORD I will
   surely cut them off.
13 You pushed me violently so that I
   was falling,
   But the LORD helped me.
14 The LORD is my strength and
   song,
   And He has become my salvation.

15 ¶ The sound of joyful shouting
   and salvation is in the tents of
   the righteous;
   The right hand of the LORD does
   valiantly.
16 The right hand of the LORD is
   exalted;
   The right hand of the LORD does
   valiantly.
17 I shall not die, but live,
   And tell of the works of the LORD.
18 The LORD has disciplined me severely,
   But He has not given me over to
   death.

19 ¶ Open to me the gates of righteousness;
   I shall enter through them, I shall
   give thanks to the LORD.
20 This is the gate of the LORD;
   The righteous will enter through
   it.
21 I shall give thanks to Thee, for
   Thou hast answered me;
   And Thou hast become my salvation.

22 ¶ The stone which the builders
   rejected
   Has become the chief corner
   stone.

23 This is [194]the LORD's doing;
   It is marvelous in our eyes.
24 This is the day which the LORD
   has made;
   Let us rejoice and be glad in it.
25 O LORD, do save, we beseech
   Thee;
   O LORD, we beseech Thee, do send
   prosperity!
26 Blessed is the one who comes in
   the name of the LORD;
   We have blessed you from the
   house of the LORD.
27 The LORD is God, and He has
   given us light;
   Bind the festival sacrifice with
   cords to the horns of the altar.
28 Thou art my God, and I give
   thanks to Thee;
   Thou art my God, I extol Thee.
29 Give thanks to the LORD, for He is
   good;
   For His lovingkindness is everlasting.

PSALM 119

א ALEPH.

How blessed are those whose way is
   [195]blameless,
   Who walk in the law of the LORD.
2 How blessed are those who observe His testimonies,
   Who seek Him with all *their*
   heart.
3 They also do no unrighteousness;
   They walk in His ways.
4 Thou hast ordained Thy precepts,
   That we should keep *them* diligently.
5 Oh that my ways may be established
   To keep Thy statutes!
6 Then I shall not be ashamed
   When I look upon all Thy commandments.
7 I shall give thanks to Thee with
   uprightness of heart,
   When I learn Thy righteous judgments.
8 I shall keep Thy statutes;
   Do not forsake me utterly!

ב BETH.

9 ¶ How can a young man keep his
   way pure?

[194] Lit., *from the* LORD
[195] Lit., *complete,* or, *having integrity*

By keeping *it* according to Thy word.

10 With all my heart I have sought Thee;
Do not let me wander from Thy commandments.

11 Thy word I have treasured in my heart,
That I may not sin against Thee.

12 Blessed art Thou, O LORD;
Teach me Thy statutes.

13 With my lips I have told of
All the ordinances of Thy mouth.

14 I have rejoiced in the way of Thy testimonies,
As much as in all riches.

15 I will meditate on Thy precepts,
And regard Thy ways.

16 I shall delight in Thy statutes;
I shall not forget Thy word.

ג GIMEL.

17 ¶ Deal bountifully with Thy servant,
That I may live and keep Thy word.

18 Open my eyes, that I may behold
Wonderful things from Thy law.

19 I am a stranger in the earth;
Do not hide Thy commandments from me.

20 My soul is crushed with longing
After Thine ordinances at all times.

21 Thou dost rebuke the arrogant, the cursed,
Who wander from Thy commandments.

22 Take away reproach and contempt from me,
For I observe Thy testimonies.

23 Even though princes sit and talk against me,
Thy servant meditates on Thy statutes.

24 Thy testimonies also are my delight;
They are my counselors.

ד DALETH.

25 ¶ My soul cleaves to the dust;
Revive me according to Thy word.

26 I have told of my ways, and Thou hast answered me;
Teach me Thy statutes.

27 Make me understand the way of Thy precepts,

So I will meditate on Thy wonders.

28 My soul weeps because of grief;
Strengthen me according to Thy word.

29 Remove the false way from me,
And graciously grant me Thy law.

30 I have chosen the faithful way;
I have placed Thine ordinances *before me.*

31 I cleave to Thy testimonies;
O LORD, do not put me to shame!

32 I shall run the way of Thy commandments,
For Thou wilt enlarge my heart.

ה HE.

33 ¶ Teach me, O LORD, the way of Thy statutes,
And I shall observe it to the end.

34 Give me understanding, that I may observe Thy law,
And keep it with all *my* heart.

35 Make me walk in the path of Thy commandments,
For I delight in it.

36 Incline my heart to Thy testimonies,
And not to *dishonest* gain.

37 Turn away my eyes from looking at vanity,
And revive me in Thy ways.

38 Establish Thy word to Thy servant,
As that which produces reverence for Thee.

39 Turn away my reproach which I dread,
For Thine ordinances are good.

40 Behold, I long for Thy precepts;
Revive me through Thy righteousness.

ו VAV.

41 ¶ May Thy lovingkindnesses also come to me, O LORD,
Thy salvation according to Thy word;

42 So I shall have an answer for him who reproaches me,
For I trust in Thy word.

43 And do not take the word of truth utterly out of my mouth,
For I wait for Thine ordinances.

44 So I will keep Thy law continually,
Forever and ever.

45 And I will walk at liberty,
For I seek Thy precepts.

46 I will also speak of Thy testimonies before kings,
And shall not be ashamed.
47 And I shall delight in Thy commandments,
Which I love.
48 And I shall lift up my hands to
Thy commandments,
Which I love;
And I will meditate on Thy statutes.

ז ZAYIN.

49 ¶ Remember the word to Thy servant,
In which Thou hast made me
hope.
50 This is my comfort in my affliction,
That Thy word has revived me.
51 The arrogant utterly deride me,
Yet I do not turn aside from Thy
law.
52 I have remembered Thine ordinances from [196]of old, O LORD,
And comfort myself.
53 Burning indignation has seized
me because of the wicked,
Who forsake Thy law.
54 Thy statutes are my songs
In the house of my pilgrimage.
55 O LORD, I remember Thy name in
the night,
And keep Thy law.
56 This has become mine,
That I observe Thy precepts.

ח HETH.

57 ¶ The LORD is my portion;
I have promised to keep Thy
words.
58 I entreated Thy favor with all *my*
heart;
Be gracious to me according to
Thy word.
59 I considered my ways,
And turned my feet to Thy testimonies.
60 I hastened and did not delay
To keep Thy commandments.
61 The cords of the wicked have
encircled me,
But I have not forgotten Thy law.
62 At midnight I shall rise to give
thanks to Thee
Because of Thy righteous ordinances.

63 I am a companion of all those who
fear Thee,
And of those who keep Thy precepts.
64 The earth is full of Thy lovingkindness, O LORD;
Teach me Thy statutes.

ט TETH.

65 ¶ Thou hast dealt well with Thy
servant,
O LORD, according to Thy word.
66 Teach me good discernment and
knowledge,
For I believe in Thy commandments.
67 Before I was afflicted I went
astray,
But now I keep Thy word.
68 Thou art good and doest good;
Teach me Thy statutes.
69 The arrogant [197]have forged a lie
against me;
With all *my* heart I will observe
Thy precepts.
70 Their heart is covered with fat,
But I delight in Thy law.
71 It is good for me that I was afflicted,
That I may learn Thy statutes.
72 The law of Thy mouth is better to
me
Than thousands of gold and silver
pieces.

י YODH.

73 ¶ Thy hands made me and [198]fash-
ioned me;
Give me understanding, that I
may learn Thy commandments.
74 May those who fear Thee see me
and be glad,
Because I wait for Thy word.
75 I know, O LORD, that Thy judgments are righteous,
And that in faithfulness Thou hast
afflicted me.
76 O may Thy lovingkindness comfort me,
According to Thy word to Thy
servant.
77 May Thy compassion come to me
that I may live,
For Thy law is my delight.
78 May the arrogant be ashamed, for
they subvert me with a lie;

But I shall meditate on Thy precepts.

79 May those who fear Thee turn to me,
Even those who know Thy testimonies.

80 May my heart be blameless in Thy statutes,
That I may not be ashamed.

⊃ Kaph.

81 ¶ My soul languishes for Thy salvation;
I wait for Thy word.

82 My eyes fail *with longing* for Thy word,
While I say, "When wilt Thou comfort me?"

83 Though I have become like a wineskin in the smoke,
I do not forget Thy statutes.

84 How many are the days of Thy servant?
When wilt Thou execute judgment on those who persecute me?

85 The arrogant have dug pits for me,
Men who are not in accord with Thy law.

86 All Thy commandments are faithful;
They have persecuted me with a lie; help me!

87 They almost destroyed me on earth,
But as for me, I did not forsake Thy precepts.

88 Revive me according to Thy lovingkindness,
So that I may keep the testimony of Thy mouth.

⅃ Lamedh.

89 ¶ Forever, O Lord,
Thy word [199]is settled in heaven.

90 Thy faithfulness *continues* throughout all generations;
Thou didst establish the earth, and it stands.

91 They stand this day according to Thine ordinances,
For all things are Thy servants.

92 If Thy law had not been my delight,
Then I would have perished in my affliction.

93 I will never forget Thy precepts,
For by them Thou hast revived me.

94 I am Thine, save me;
For I have sought Thy precepts.

95 The wicked wait for me to destroy me;
I shall diligently consider Thy testimonies.

96 I have seen a limit to all perfection;
Thy commandment is exceedingly broad.

⍢ Mem.

97 ¶ O how I love Thy law!
It is my meditation all the day.

98 Thy commandments make me wiser than my enemies,
For they are ever mine.

99 I have more insight than all my teachers,
For Thy testimonies are my meditation.

100 I understand more than the aged,
Because I have observed Thy precepts.

101 I have restrained my feet from every evil way,
That I may keep Thy word.

102 I have not turned aside from Thine ordinances,
For Thou Thyself hast taught me.

103 How sweet are Thy words to my taste!
Yes, *sweeter* than honey to my mouth!

104 From Thy precepts I get understanding;
Therefore I hate every false way.

⅃ Nun.

105 ¶ Thy word is a lamp to my feet,
And a light to my path.

106 I have sworn, and I will confirm it,
That I will keep Thy righteous ordinances.

107 I am exceedingly afflicted;
Revive me, O Lord, according to Thy word.

108 O accept the freewill offerings of my mouth, O Lord,
And teach me Thine ordinances.

109 My life is continually [200]in my hand,
Yet I do not forget Thy law.

110 The wicked have laid a snare for me,

---

[199] Lit., *stands firm*

[200] I.e., in danger

Yet I have not gone astray from
Thy precepts.
111 I have inherited Thy testimonies
forever,
For they are the joy of my heart.
112 I have inclined my heart to perform Thy statutes
Forever, *even* to the end.

ס Samekh.

113 ¶ I hate those who are double-
minded,
But I love Thy law.
114 Thou art my hiding place and my
shield;
I wait for Thy word.
115 Depart from me, evildoers,
That I may observe the commandments of my God.
116 Sustain me according to Thy
word, that I may live;
And do not let me be ashamed of
my hope.
117 Uphold me that I may be safe,
That I may have regard for Thy
statutes continually.
118 Thou hast rejected all those who
wander from Thy statutes,
For their deceitfulness is useless.
119 Thou hast removed all the wicked
of the earth *like* dross;
Therefore I love Thy testimonies.
120 My flesh trembles for fear of Thee,
And I am afraid of Thy judgments.

ע Ayin.

121 ¶ I have done justice and righteousness;
Do not leave me to my oppressors.
122 Be surety for Thy servant for
good;
Do not let the arrogant oppress
me.
123 My eyes fail *with longing* for Thy
salvation,
And for Thy righteous word.
124 Deal with Thy servant according
to Thy lovingkindness,
And teach me Thy statutes.
125 I am Thy servant; give me understanding,
That I may know Thy testimonies.
126 It is time for the LORD to act,
For they have broken Thy law.
127 Therefore I love Thy commandments

Above gold, yes, above fine gold.
128 Therefore I esteem right all *Thy*
precepts concerning every-
thing,
I hate every false way.

פ Pe.

129 ¶ Thy testimonies are wonderful;
Therefore my soul observes them.
130 The unfolding of Thy words gives
light;
It gives understanding to the simple.
131 I opened my mouth wide and
panted,
For I longed for Thy commandments.
132 Turn to me and be gracious to me,
After Thy manner with those who
love Thy name.
133 Establish my footsteps in Thy
word,
And do not let any iniquity have
dominion over me.
134 Redeem me from the oppression
of man,
That I may keep Thy precepts.
135 Make Thy face shine upon Thy
servant,
And teach me Thy statutes.
136 My eyes shed streams of water,
Because they do not keep Thy
law.

צ Tsadhe.

137 ¶ Righteous art Thou, O LORD,
And upright are Thy judgments.
138 Thou hast commanded Thy testimonies in righteousness
And exceeding faithfulness.
139 My zeal has consumed me,
Because my adversaries have forgotten Thy words.
140 Thy word is very pure,
Therefore Thy servant loves it.
141 I am small and despised,
Yet I do not forget Thy precepts.
142 Thy righteousness is an everlasting righteousness,
And Thy law is truth.
143 Trouble and anguish have come
upon me;
Yet Thy commandments are my
delight.
144 Thy testimonies are righteous forever;
Give me understanding that I may
live.

ק Qoph.

145 ¶ I cried with all my heart; answer me, O Lord!
I will observe Thy statutes.

146 I cried to Thee; save me,
And I shall keep Thy testimonies.

147 I rise before dawn and cry for help;
I wait for Thy words.

148 My eyes anticipate the night watches,
That I may meditate on Thy word.

149 Hear my voice according to Thy lovingkindness;
Revive me, O Lord, according to Thine ordinances.

150 Those who follow after wickedness draw near;
They are far from Thy law.

151 Thou art near, O Lord,
And all Thy commandments are truth.

152 Of old I have known from Thy testimonies,
That Thou hast founded them forever.

ר Resh.

153 ¶ Look upon my affliction and rescue me,
For I do not forget Thy law.

154 Plead my cause and redeem me;
Revive me according to Thy word.

155 Salvation is far from the wicked,
For they do not seek Thy statutes.

156 Great are Thy mercies, O Lord;
Revive me according to Thine ordinances.

157 Many are my persecutors and my adversaries,
Yet I do not turn aside from Thy testimonies.

158 I behold the treacherous and loathe *them*,
Because they do not keep Thy word.

159 Consider how I love Thy precepts;
Revive me, O Lord, according to Thy lovingkindness.

160 The sum of Thy word is truth,
And every one of Thy righteous ordinances is everlasting.

ש Shin.

161 ¶ Princes persecute me without cause,
But my heart stands in awe of Thy words.

162 I rejoice at Thy word,
As one who finds great spoil.

163 I hate and despise falsehood,
But I love Thy law.

164 Seven times a day I praise Thee,
Because of Thy righteous ordinances.

165 Those who love Thy law have great peace,
And nothing causes them to stumble.

166 I hope for Thy salvation, O Lord,
And do Thy commandments.

167 My soul keeps Thy testimonies,
And I love them exceedingly.

168 I keep Thy precepts and Thy testimonies,
For all my ways are before Thee.

ת Tav.

169 ¶ Let my cry come before Thee, O Lord;
Give me understanding according to Thy word.

170 Let my supplication come before Thee;
Deliver me according to Thy word.

171 Let my lips utter praise,
For Thou dost teach me Thy statutes.

172 Let my tongue sing of Thy word,
For all Thy commandments are righteousness.

173 Let Thy hand be ready to help me,
For I have chosen Thy precepts.

174 I long for Thy salvation, O Lord,
And Thy law is my delight.

175 Let my soul live that it may praise Thee,
And let Thine ordinances help me.

176 I have gone astray like a lost sheep; seek Thy servant,
For I do not forget Thy commandments.

PSALM 120
A Song of Ascents.

In my trouble I cried to the Lord,
And He answered me.

2 Deliver my soul, O Lord, from lying lips,
From a deceitful tongue.

3 What shall be given to you, and what more shall be done to you,
You deceitful tongue?

4 Sharp arrows of the warrior,
With the *burning* coals of the broom tree.

5 ¶ Woe is me, for I sojourn in Meshech,
For I dwell among the tents of Kedar!
6 Too long has my soul had its dwelling
With those who hate peace.
7 I am *for* peace, but when I speak,
They are for war.

PSALM 121
A Song of Ascents.

I WILL lift up my eyes to the mountains;
From whence shall my help come?
2 My help *comes* from the LORD,
Who made heaven and earth.
3 He will not allow your foot to slip;
He who keeps you will not slumber.
4 Behold, He who keeps Israel
Will neither slumber nor sleep.

5 ¶ The LORD is your keeper;
The LORD is your shade on your right hand.
6 The sun will not smite you by day,
Nor the moon by night.
7 The LORD will [201]protect you from all evil;
He will keep your soul.
8 The LORD will [201]guard your going out and your coming in
From this time forth and forever.

PSALM 122
A Song of Ascents, of David.

I WAS glad when they said to me,
"Let us go to the house of the LORD."
2 Our feet are standing
Within your gates, O Jerusalem,
3 Jerusalem, that is built
As a city that is compact together;
4 To which the tribes go up, even the tribes of the LORD—
An ordinance for Israel—
To give thanks to the name of the LORD.
5 For there thrones were set for judgment,
The thrones of the house of David.

6 ¶ Pray for the peace of Jerusalem:
"May they prosper who love you.
7"May peace be within your walls,

And prosperity within your palaces."
8 For the sake of my brothers and my friends,
I will now say, "May peace be within you."
9 For the sake of the house of the LORD our God
I will seek your good.

PSALM 123
A Song of Ascents.

To Thee I lift up my eyes,
O Thou who art enthroned in the heavens!
2 Behold, as the eyes of servants *look* to the hand of their master,
As the eyes of a maid to the hand of her mistress;
So our eyes *look* to the LORD our God,
Until He shall be gracious to us.

3 ¶ Be gracious to us, O LORD, be gracious to us;
For we are greatly filled with contempt.
4 Our soul is greatly filled
With the scoffing of those who are at ease,
And with the contempt of the proud.

PSALM 124
A Song of Ascents, of David.

"HAD it not been the LORD who was on our side,"
Let Israel now say,
2"Had it not been the LORD who was on our side,
When men rose up against us;
3 Then they would have swallowed us alive,
When their anger was kindled against us;
4 Then the waters would have engulfed us,
The stream would have swept over our soul;
5 Then the raging waters would have swept over our soul."

6 ¶ Blessed be the LORD,
Who has not given us to be torn by their teeth.
7 Our soul has escaped as a bird out of the snare of the trapper;
The snare is broken and we have escaped.

8 Our help is in the name of the
LORD,
Who made heaven and earth.

PSALM 125
A Song of Ascents.

THOSE who trust in the LORD
Are as Mount Zion, which cannot
be moved, but abides forever.
2 As the mountains surround Jerusalem,
So the LORD surrounds His people
From this time forth and forever.
3 For the scepter of wickedness
shall not rest upon the land of
the righteous;
That the righteous may not put
forth their hands to do wrong.

4 ¶ Do good, O LORD, to those who
are good,
And to those who are upright in
their hearts.
5 But as for those who turn aside to
their crooked ways,
The LORD will lead them away
with the doers of iniquity.
Peace be upon Israel.

PSALM 126
A Song of Ascents.

WHEN the LORD brought back the
captive ones of Zion,
We were like those who dream.
2 Then our mouth was filled with
laughter,
And our tongue with joyful shouting;
Then they said among the nations,
"The LORD has done great things
for them."
3 The LORD has done great things
for us;
We are glad.

4 ¶ Restore our captivity, O LORD,
As the streams in the South.
5 Those who sow in tears shall reap
with joyful shouting.
6 He who goes to and fro weeping,
carrying *his* bag of seed,
Shall indeed come again with a
shout of joy, bringing his
sheaves *with him.*

PSALM 127
A Song of Ascents, of Solomon.

UNLESS the LORD builds the house,
They labor in vain who build it;
Unless the LORD guards the city,
The watchman keeps awake in
vain.
2 It is vain for you to rise up early,
To retire late,
To eat the bread of painful labors;
For He gives to His beloved *even
in his* sleep.

3 ¶ Behold, children are a gift of the
LORD;
The fruit of the womb is a reward.
4 Like arrows in the hand of a warrior,
So are the children of one's youth.
5 How blessed is the man whose
quiver is full of them;
They shall not be ashamed,
When they speak with their enemies in the gate.

PSALM 128
A Song of Ascents.

HOW blessed is everyone who fears
the LORD,
Who walks in His ways.
2 When you shall eat of the [202]fruit
of your hands,
You will be happy and it will be
well with you.
3 Your wife shall be like a fruitful
vine,
Within your house,
Your children like olive plants
Around your table.
4 Behold, for thus shall the man be
blessed
Who fears the LORD.

5 ¶ The LORD bless you from Zion,
And may you see the prosperity of
Jerusalem all the days of your
life.
6 Indeed, may you see your children's children.
Peace be upon Israel!

PSALM 129
A Song of Ascents.

"MANY times they have persecuted
me from my youth up,"
Let Israel now say,

[202] Lit., *labor*

2"Many times they have persecuted
　　me from my youth up;
　Yet they have not prevailed
　　against me.
3"The plowers plowed upon my
　　back;
　They lengthened their furrows."
4 The LORD is righteous;
　He has cut in two the cords of the
　　wicked.

5 ¶ May all who hate Zion,
　Be put to shame and turned back-
　　ward,
6 Let them be like grass upon the
　　housetops,
　Which withers before it grows up;
7 With which the reaper does not
　　fill his hand,
　Or the binder of sheaves his
　　bosom;
8 Nor do those who pass by say,
　"The blessing of the LORD be upon
　　you;
　We bless you in the name of the
　　LORD."

PSALM 130

A Song of Ascents.

OUT of the depths I have cried to
　Thee, O LORD.
2 Lord, hear my voice!
　Let Thine ears be attentive
　To the voice of my supplications.
3 If Thou, LORD, shouldst mark in-
　　iquities,
　O Lord, who could stand?
4 But there is forgiveness with
　　Thee,
　That Thou mayest be feared.

5 ¶ I wait for the LORD, my soul
　　does wait,
　And in His word do I hope.
6 My soul *waits* for the Lord
　More than the watchmen for the
　　morning;
　Indeed, more than the watchmen
　　for the morning.
7 O Israel, hope in the LORD;
　For with the LORD there is loving-
　　kindness,
　And with Him is abundant re-
　　demption.
8 And He will redeem Israel
　From all his iniquities.

PSALM 131

A Song of Ascents, of David.

O LORD, my heart is not proud, nor
　my eyes haughty;
　Nor do I involve myself in great
　　matters,
　Or in things too difficult for me.
2 Surely I have composed and
　　quieted my soul;
　Like a weaned child *rests* against
　　his mother,
　My soul is like a weaned child
　　within me.
3 O Israel, hope in the LORD
　From this time forth and forever.

PSALM 132

A Song of Ascents.

REMEMBER, O LORD, on David's
　　behalf,
　All his affliction;
2 How he swore to the LORD,
　And vowed to the Mighty One of
　　Jacob,
3"Surely I will not enter my house,
　Nor lie on my bed;
4 I will not give sleep to my eyes,
　Or slumber to my eyelids;
5 Until I find a place for the LORD,
　A dwelling place for the Mighty
　　One of Jacob."

6 ¶ Behold, we heard of it in Ephra-
　　thah;
　We found it in the field of Jaar.
7 Let us go into His dwelling place;
　Let us worship at His footstool.
8 Arise, O LORD, to Thy resting
　　place;
　Thou and the ark of Thy strength.
9 Let Thy priests be clothed with
　　righteousness;
　And let Thy godly ones sing for
　　joy.

10 ¶ For the sake of David Thy ser-
　　vant,
　Do not turn away the face of
　　Thine anointed.
11 The LORD has sworn to David,
　A truth from which He will not
　　turn back;
　"Of the fruit of your body I will set
　　upon your throne.
12"If your sons will keep My cov-
　　enant,
　And My testimony which I will
　　teach them,

Their sons also shall sit upon your
    throne forever."

13 ¶ For the LORD has chosen Zion;
    He has desired it for His habita-
        tion.
14"This is My resting place forever;
    Here I will dwell, for I have de-
        sired it.
15"I will abundantly bless her provi-
        sion;
    I will satisfy her needy with bread.
16"Her priests also I will clothe with
        salvation;
    And her godly ones will sing aloud
        for joy.
17"There I will cause the horn of
        David to spring forth;
    I have prepared a lamp for Mine
        anointed.
18"His enemies I will clothe with
        shame;
    But upon himself his crown shall
        shine."

PSALM 133

A Song of Ascents, of David.

BEHOLD, how good and how pleas-
    ant it is
    For brothers to dwell together in
        unity!
2 It is like the precious oil upon the
        head,
    Coming down upon the beard,
    Even Aaron's beard,
    Coming down upon the edge of
        his robes.
3 It is like the dew of Hermon,
    Coming down upon the moun-
        tains of Zion;
    For there the LORD commanded
        the blessing—life forever.

PSALM 134

A Song of Ascents.

BEHOLD, bless the LORD, all servants
    of the LORD,
    Who serve by night in the house
        of the LORD!
2 Lift up your hands to the sanctu-
        ary,
    And bless the LORD.
3 May the LORD bless you from
        Zion,
    He who made heaven and earth.

PSALM 135

PRAISE the LORD!
    Praise the name of the LORD;
    Praise *Him*, O servants of the
        LORD,
2 You who stand in the house of the
        LORD,
    In the courts of the house of our
        God!
3 Praise the LORD, for the LORD is
        good;
    Sing praises to His name, for it is
        lovely.
4 For the LORD has chosen Jacob
        for Himself,
    Israel for His own possession.

5 ¶ For I know that the LORD is
        great,
    And that our Lord is above all
        gods.
6 Whatever the LORD pleases, He
        does,
    In heaven and in earth, in the seas
        and in all deeps.
7 He causes the vapors to ascend
        from the ends of the earth;
    Who makes lightnings for the
        rain;
    Who brings forth the wind from
        His treasuries.

8 ¶ He smote the first-born of
        Egypt,
    Both of man and beast.
9 He sent signs and wonders into
        your midst, O Egypt,
    Upon Pharaoh and all his ser-
        vants.
10 He smote many nations,
    And slew mighty kings,
11 Sihon, king of the Amorites,
    And Og, king of Bashan,
    And all the kingdoms of Canaan;
12 And He gave their land as a heri-
        tage,
    A heritage to Israel His people.
13 Thy name, O LORD, is everlasting,
    Thy remembrance, O LORD,
        throughout all generations.
14 For the LORD will judge His peo-
        ple,
    And will have compassion on His
        servants.
15 The idols of the nations are *but*
        silver and gold,
    The work of man's hands.

16 They have mouths, but they do
　　not speak;
　　They have eyes, but they do not
　　see;
17 They have ears, but they do not
　　hear;
　　Nor is there any breath at all in
　　their mouths.
18 Those who make them will be like
　　them,
　　Yes, everyone who trusts in them.

19 ¶ O house of Israel, bless the
　　Lord;
　　O house of Aaron, bless the Lord;
20 O house of Levi, bless the Lord;
　　You who [203]revere the Lord, bless
　　the Lord.
21 Blessed be the Lord from Zion,
　　Who dwells in Jerusalem.
　　Praise the Lord!

PSALM 136

Give thanks to the Lord, for He is
　　good;
　　For His lovingkindness is ever-
　　lasting.
2 Give thanks to the God of gods,
　　For His lovingkindness is ever-
　　lasting.
3 Give thanks to the Lord of lords,
　　For His lovingkindness is ever-
　　lasting.
4 To Him who alone does great
　　wonders,
　　For His lovingkindness is ever-
　　lasting;
5 To Him who made the heavens
　　with skill,
　　For His lovingkindness is ever-
　　lasting;
6 To Him who spread out the earth
　　above the waters,
　　For His lovingkindness is ever-
　　lasting;
7 To Him who made *the* great
　　lights,
　　For His lovingkindness is ever-
　　lasting:
8 The sun to rule by day,
　　For His lovingkindness is ever-
　　lasting,
9 The moon and stars to rule by
　　night,
　　For His lovingkindness is ever-
　　lasting.

10 ¶ To Him who smote the Egyp-
　　tians in their first-born,
　　For His lovingkindness is ever-
　　lasting,
11 And brought Israel out from their
　　midst,
　　For His lovingkindness is ever-
　　lasting,
12 With a strong hand and an out-
　　stretched arm,
　　For His lovingkindness is ever-
　　lasting;
13 To Him who divided the Red Sea
　　asunder,
　　For His lovingkindness is ever-
　　lasting,
14 And made Israel pass through the
　　midst of it,
　　For His lovingkindness is ever-
　　lasting;
15 But He overthrew Pharaoh and
　　his army in the Red Sea,
　　For His lovingkindness is ever-
　　lasting.
16 To Him who led His people
　　through the wilderness,
　　For His lovingkindness is ever-
　　lasting;
17 To Him who smote great kings,
　　For His lovingkindness is ever-
　　lasting,
18 And slew mighty kings,
　　For His lovingkindness is ever-
　　lasting;
19 Sihon, king of the Amorites,
　　For His lovingkindness is ever-
　　lasting,
20 And Og, king of Bashan,
　　For His lovingkindness is ever-
　　lasting,
21 And gave their land as a heritage,
　　For His lovingkindness is ever-
　　lasting,
22 Even a heritage to Israel His ser-
　　vant,
　　For His lovingkindness is ever-
　　lasting.

23 ¶ Who remembered us in our low
　　estate,
　　For His lovingkindness is ever-
　　lasting,
24 And has rescued us from our ad-
　　versaries,
　　For His lovingkindness is ever-
　　lasting;
25 Who gives food to all flesh,

[203] Or, *fear*

For His lovingkindness is everlasting.
26 Give thanks to the God of heaven,
For His lovingkindness is everlasting.

PSALM 137

By the rivers of Babylon,
There we sat down and wept,
When we remembered Zion.
2 Upon the willows in the midst of it
We hung our harps.
3 For there our captors demanded
of us songs,
And our tormentors mirth, *saying,*
"Sing us one of the songs of Zion."

4 ¶ How can we sing the LORD's
song
In a foreign land?
5 If I forget you, O Jerusalem,
May my right hand forget *her
skill.*
6 May my tongue cleave to the roof
of my mouth,
If I do not remember you,
If I do not exalt Jerusalem
Above my chief joy.

7 ¶ Remember, O LORD, against the
sons of Edom
The day of Jerusalem,
Who said, "Raze it, raze it,
To its very foundation."
8 O daughter of Babylon, you devastated one,
How blessed will be the one who
repays you
With the recompense with which
you have repaid us.
9 How blessed will be the one who
seizes and dashes your little
ones
Against the rock.

PSALM 138

A Psalm of David.

I WILL give Thee thanks with all my
heart;
I will sing praises to Thee before
the gods.
2 I will bow down toward Thy holy
temple,
And give thanks to Thy name for
Thy lovingkindness and Thy
truth;
For Thou hast magnified Thy

word according to all Thy
name.
3 On the day I called Thou didst
answer me;
Thou didst make me bold with
strength in my soul.

4 ¶ All the kings of the earth will
give thanks to Thee, O LORD,
When they have heard the words
of Thy mouth.
5 And they will sing of the ways of
the LORD.
For great is the glory of the LORD.
6 For though the LORD is exalted,
Yet He regards the lowly;
But the haughty He knows from
afar.

7 ¶ Though I walk in the midst of
trouble, Thou wilt revive me;
Thou wilt stretch forth Thy hand
against the wrath of my enemies,
And Thy right hand will save me.
8 The LORD will accomplish what
concerns me;
Thy lovingkindness, O LORD, is
everlasting;
Do not forsake the works of Thy
hands.

PSALM 139

For the choir director. A Psalm of David.

O LORD, Thou hast searched me and
known *me.*
2 Thou dost know when I sit down
and when I rise up;
Thou dost understand my thought
from afar.
3 Thou dost scrutinize my path and
my lying down,
And art intimately acquainted
with all my ways.
4 Even before there is a word on my
tongue,
Behold, O LORD, Thou dost know
it all.
5 Thou hast enclosed me behind
and before,
And laid Thy hand upon me.
6 *Such* knowledge is too wonderful
for me;
It is *too* high, I cannot attain to it.

7 ¶ Where can I go from Thy
Spirit?
Or where can I flee from Thy
presence?

8 If I ascend to heaven, Thou art
    there;
  If I make my bed in Sheol, behold,
    Thou art there.
9 If I take the wings of the dawn,
  If I dwell in the remotest part of
    the sea,
10 Even there Thy hand will lead me,
  And Thy right hand will lay hold
    of me.
11 If I say, "Surely the darkness will
    overwhelm me,
  And the light around me will be
    night,"
12 Even the darkness is not dark to
    Thee,
  And the night is as bright as the
    day.
  Darkness and light are alike *to
    Thee.*

13 ¶ For Thou didst form my inward
    parts;
  Thou didst weave me in my moth-
    er's womb.
14 I will give thanks to Thee, for [204]I
    am fearfully and wonderfully
    made;
  Wonderful are Thy works,
  And my soul knows it very well.
15 My frame was not hidden from
    Thee,
  When I was made in secret,
  And skillfully wrought in the
    depths of the earth.
16 Thine eyes have seen my un-
    formed substance;
  And in Thy book they were all
    written,
  The days that were ordained *for
    me,*
  When as yet there was not one of
    them.

17 ¶ How precious also are Thy
    thoughts to me, O God!
  How vast is the sum of them!
18 If I should count them, they
    would outnumber the sand.
  When I awake, I am still with
    Thee.

19 ¶ O that Thou wouldst slay the
    wicked, O God;
  Depart from me, therefore, men of
    bloodshed.

20 For they speak against Thee wick-
    edly,
  And Thine enemies take *Thy
    name* in vain.
21 Do I not hate those who hate
    Thee, O LORD?
  And do I not loathe those who
    rise up against Thee?
22 I hate them with the utmost ha-
    tred;
  They have become my enemies.

23 ¶ Search me, O God, and know
    my heart;
  Try me and know my anxious
    thoughts;
24 And see if there be any hurtful
    way in me,
  And lead me in the everlasting
    way.

PSALM 140
For the choir director. A Psalm of David.

RESCUE me, O LORD, from evil men;
  Preserve me from violent men,
2 Who devise evil things in *their*
    hearts;
  They continually stir up wars.
3 They sharpen their tongues as a
    serpent;
  Poison of a viper is under their
    lips.   [Selah.

4 ¶ Keep me, O LORD, from the
    hands of the wicked;
  Preserve me from violent men,
  Who have purposed to [205]trip up
    my feet.
5 The proud have hidden a trap for
    me, and cords;
  They have spread a net by the
    wayside;
  They have set snares for
    me.   [Selah.

6 ¶ I said to the LORD, "Thou art
    my God;
  Give ear, O LORD, to the voice of
    my supplications.
7 "O GOD the Lord, the strength of
    my salvation,
  Thou hast covered my head in the
    day of battle.
8 "Do not grant, O LORD, the desires
    of the wicked;
  Do not promote his *evil* device,
    lest they be exalted. [Selah.

[204] Some ancient versions read *Thou art fearfully wonderful*   [205] Lit., *push violently*

9 ¶"As for the head of those who
surround me,
May the mischief of their lips
cover them.
10"May burning coals fall upon them;
May they be cast into the fire,
Into deep pits from which they
cannot rise.
11"May a slanderer not be established in the earth;
May evil hunt the violent man
[206]speedily."

12 ¶ I know that the LORD will maintain the cause of the afflicted,
And justice for the poor.
13 Surely the righteous will give
thanks to Thy name;
The upright will dwell in Thy
presence.

PSALM 141
A Psalm of David.

O LORD, I call upon Thee; hasten to
me!
Give ear to my voice when I call
to Thee!
2 May my prayer be counted as
incense before Thee;
The lifting up of my hands as the
evening offering.
3 Set a guard, O LORD, over my
mouth;
Keep watch over the door of my
lips.
4 Do not incline my heart to any
evil thing,
To practice deeds of wickedness
With men who do iniquity;
And do not let me eat of their
delicacies.

5 ¶ Let the righteous smite me in
kindness and reprove me;
It is oil upon the head;
Do not let my head refuse it,
For still my prayer is against their
wicked deeds.
6 Their judges are thrown down by
the sides of the rock,
And they hear my words, for they
are pleasant.
7 As when one plows and breaks
open the earth,
Our bones have been scattered at
the mouth of Sheol.

8 ¶ For my eyes are toward Thee, O
GOD, the Lord;
In Thee I take refuge; do not
leave me defenseless.
9 Keep me from the jaws of the trap
which they have set for me,
And from the snares of those who
do iniquity.
10 Let the wicked fall into their own
nets,
While I pass by safely.

PSALM 142
Maskil of David, when he was in the cave. A Prayer.

I CRY aloud with my voice to the
LORD;
I make supplication with my
voice to the LORD.
2 I pour out my complaint before
Him;
I declare my trouble before Him.
3 When my spirit was overwhelmed
within me,
Thou didst know my path.
In the way where I walk
They have hidden a trap for me.
4 Look to the right and see;
For there is no one who regards
me;
There is no escape for me;
No one cares for my soul.

5 ¶ I cried out to Thee, O LORD;
I said, "Thou art my refuge,
My portion in the land of the
living.
6"Give heed to my cry,
For I am brought very low;
Deliver me from my persecutors,
For they are too strong for me.
7"Bring my soul out of prison,
So that I may give thanks to Thy
name;
The righteous will surround me,
For Thou wilt deal bountifully
with me."

PSALM 143
A Psalm of David.

HEAR my prayer, O LORD,
Give ear to my supplications!
Answer me in Thy faithfulness, in
Thy righteousness!
2 And do not enter into judgment
with Thy servant,
For in Thy sight no man living is
righteous.

[206] Lit., *thrust upon thrust*

3 For the enemy has persecuted my
soul;
He has crushed my life to the
ground;
He has made me dwell in dark
places, like those who have long
been dead.
4 Therefore my spirit is overwhelmed within me;
My heart is [207]appalled within me.

5 ¶ I remember the days of old;
I meditate on all Thy doings;
I muse on the work of Thy hands.
6 I stretch out my hands to Thee;
My soul *longs* for Thee, as a
parched land.   [Selah.

7 ¶ Answer me quickly, O LORD, my
spirit fails;
Do not hide Thy face from me,
Lest I become like those who go
down to the pit.
8 Let me hear Thy lovingkindness
in the morning;
For I trust in Thee;
Teach me the way in which I
should walk;
For to Thee I lift up my soul.
9 Deliver me, O LORD, from my enemies;
I take refuge in Thee.

10 ¶ Teach me to do Thy will,
For Thou art my God;
Let Thy good Spirit lead me on
level ground.
11 For the sake of Thy name, O
LORD, revive me.
In Thy righteousness bring my
soul out of trouble.
12 And in Thy lovingkindness cut off
my enemies,
And destroy all those who afflict
my soul;
For I am Thy servant.

PSALM 144
A Psalm of David.

BLESSED be the LORD, my rock,
Who trains my hands for war,
And my fingers for battle;
2 My lovingkindness and my for-
tress,
My stronghold and my deliverer;
My shield and He in whom I take
refuge;

Who subdues my people under
me.
3 O LORD, what is man, that Thou
dost take knowledge of him?
Or the son of man, that Thou dost
think of him?
4 Man is like a mere breath;
His days are like a passing
shadow.

5 ¶ Bow Thy heavens, O LORD, and
come down;
Touch the mountains, that they
may smoke.
6 Flash forth lightning and scatter
them;
Send out Thine arrows and confuse them.
7 Stretch forth Thy hand from on
high;
Rescue me and deliver me out of
great waters,
Out of the hand of aliens
8 Whose mouths speak deceit,
And whose right hand is a right
hand of falsehood.

9 ¶ I will sing a new song to Thee,
O God;
Upon a harp of ten strings I will
sing praises to Thee,
10 Who dost give salvation to kings;
Who dost rescue David His servant from the evil sword.
11 Rescue me, and deliver me out of
the hand of aliens,
Whose mouth speaks deceit,
And whose right hand is a right
hand of falsehood.

12 ¶ Let our sons in their youth be as
grown-up plants,
And our daughters as corner pillars fashioned as for a palace;
13 *Let* our garners be full, furnishing
every kind of produce,
And our flocks bring forth thousands and ten thousands in our
fields;
14 *Let* our cattle bear,
Without mishap and without loss,
Let there be no outcry in our
streets!
15 How blessed are the people who
are so situated;
How blessed are the people whose
God is the LORD!

[207] Or, *desolate*

PSALM 145

A Psalm of Praise, of David.

I WILL extol Thee, my God, O King;
And I will bless Thy name forever
and ever.
2 Every day I will bless Thee,
And I will praise Thy name forever and ever.
3 Great is the LORD, and highly to
be praised;
And His greatness is unsearchable.
4 One generation shall praise Thy
works to another,
And shall declare Thy mighty
acts.
5 On the glorious splendor of Thy
majesty,
And on Thy wonderful works, I
will meditate.
6 And men shall speak of the power
of Thine awesome acts;
And I will tell of Thy greatness.
7 They shall eagerly utter the memory of Thine abundant goodness,
And shall shout joyfully of Thy
righteousness.

8 ¶ The LORD is gracious and merciful;
Slow to anger and great in lovingkindness.
9 The LORD is good to all,
And His mercies are over all His
works.
10 All Thy works shall give thanks to
Thee, O LORD,
And Thy godly ones shall bless
Thee.
11 They shall speak of the glory of
Thy kingdom,
And talk of Thy power;
12 To make known to the sons of
men Thy mighty acts,
And the glory of the majesty of
Thy kingdom.
13 Thy kingdom is an everlasting
kingdom,
And Thy dominion *endures*
throughout all generations.

14 ¶ The LORD sustains all who fall,
And raises up all who are bowed
down.
15 The eyes of all look to Thee,
And Thou dost give them their
food in due time.

16 Thou dost open Thy hand,
And dost satisfy the desire of every living thing.

17 ¶ The LORD is righteous in all His
ways,
And kind in all His deeds.
18 The LORD is near to all who call
upon Him,
To all who call upon Him in truth.
19 He will fulfill the desire of those
who fear Him;
He will also hear their cry and will
save them.
20 The LORD keeps all who love Him;
But all the wicked, He will destroy.
21 My mouth will speak the praise of
the LORD;
And all flesh will bless His holy
name forever and ever.

PSALM 146

PRAISE the LORD!
Praise the LORD, O my soul!
2 I will praise the LORD while I live;
I will sing praises to my God while
I have my being.
3 Do not trust in princes,
In mortal man, in whom there is
no salvation.
4 His spirit departs, he returns to
the earth;
In that very day his thoughts perish.
5 How blessed is he whose help is
the God of Jacob,
Whose hope is in the LORD his
God;
6 Who made heaven and earth,
The sea and all that is in them;
Who keeps faith forever;
7 Who executes justice for the oppressed;
Who gives food to the hungry.
The LORD sets the prisoners free.

8 ¶ The LORD opens *the eyes of* the
blind;
The LORD raises up those who are
bowed down;
The LORD loves the righteous;
9 The LORD protects the strangers;
He supports the fatherless and the
widow;
But He thwarts the way of the
wicked.
10 The LORD will reign forever,

Thy God, O Zion, to all generations.
Praise the LORD!

PSALM 147

PRAISE the LORD!
For it is good to sing praises to
our God;
For [208]it is pleasant *and* praise is
becoming.
2 The LORD builds up Jerusalem;
He gathers the outcasts of Israel.
3 He heals the brokenhearted,
And binds up their [209]wounds.
4 He counts the number of the
stars;
He gives names to all of them.
5 Great is our Lord, and abundant
in strength;
His understanding is infinite.
6 The LORD [210]supports the afflicted;
He brings down the wicked to the
ground.

7 ¶ Sing to the LORD with thanksgiving;
Sing praises to our God on the
lyre,
8 Who covers the heavens with
clouds,
Who provides rain for the earth,
Who makes grass to grow on the
mountains.
9 He gives to the beast its food,
And to the young ravens which
cry.
10 He does not delight in the
strength of the horse;
He does not take pleasure in the
legs of a man.
11 The LORD favors those who fear
Him,
Those who wait for His lovingkindness.

12 ¶ Praise the LORD, O Jerusalem!
Praise your God, O Zion!
13 For He has strengthened the bars
of your gates;
He has blessed your sons within
you.
14 He makes peace in your borders;
He satisfies you with the finest of
the wheat.
15 He sends forth His command to
the earth;

His word runs very swiftly.
16 He gives snow like wool;
He scatters the frost like ashes.
17 He casts forth His ice as fragments;
Who can stand before His cold?
18 He sends forth His word and melts
them;
He causes His wind to blow and
the waters to flow.
19 He declares His words to Jacob,
His statutes and His ordinances to
Israel.
20 He has not dealt thus with any
nation;
And as for His ordinances, they
have not known them.
Praise the LORD!

PSALM 148

PRAISE the LORD!
Praise the LORD from the heavens;
Praise Him in the heights!
2 Praise Him, all His angels;
Praise Him, all His hosts!
3 Praise Him, sun and moon;
Praise Him, all stars of light!
4 Praise Him, highest heavens,
And the waters that are above the
heavens!
5 Let them praise the name of the
LORD,
For He commanded and they
were created.
6 He has also established them forever and ever;
He has made a decree which will
not pass away.

7 ¶ Praise the LORD from the earth,
Sea monsters and all deeps;
8 Fire and hail, snow and clouds;
Stormy wind, fulfilling His word;
9 Mountains and all hills;
Fruit trees and all cedars;
10 Beasts and all cattle;
Creeping things and winged fowl;
11 Kings of the earth and all peoples;
Princes and all judges of the
earth;
12 Both young men and virgins;
Old men and children.

13 ¶ Let them praise the name of the
LORD,
For His name alone is exalted;
His glory is above earth and
heaven.

---

[208] Or, *He is gracious*   [209] Lit., *sorrows*   [210] Or, *relieves*

14 And He has lifted up a horn for
His people,
Praise for all His godly ones;
Even for the sons of Israel, a peo-
ple near to Him.
Praise the LORD!

PSALM 149

PRAISE the LORD!
Sing to the LORD a new song,
And His praise in the congregation of the godly ones.
2 Let Israel be glad in his Maker;
Let the sons of Zion rejoice in
their King.
3 Let them praise His name with
dancing;
Let them sing praises to Him with
timbrel and lyre.
4 For the LORD takes pleasure in His
people;
He will beautify the afflicted ones
with salvation.

5 ¶ Let the godly ones exult in
glory;
Let them sing for joy on their
beds.
6 *Let* the high praises of God *be* in
their mouth,
And a two-edged sword in their
hand,

7 To execute vengeance on the nations,
And punishment on the peoples;
8 To bind their kings with chains,
And their nobles with fetters of
iron;
9 To execute on them the judgment
written;
This is an honor for all His godly
ones.
Praise the LORD!

PSALM 150

PRAISE the LORD!
Praise God in His sanctuary;
Praise Him in His mighty expanse.
2 Praise Him for His mighty deeds;
Praise Him according to His excel-
lent greatness.

3 ¶ Praise Him with trumpet sound;
Praise Him with harp and lyre.
4 Praise Him with timbrel and dancing;
Praise Him with stringed instruments and pipe.
5 Praise Him with loud cymbals;
Praise Him with resounding cymbals.
6 Let everything that has breath
praise the LORD.
Praise the LORD!

THE PROVERBS

THE proverbs of Solomon the son of
David, king of Israel:
2 To know wisdom and instruction,
To discern the sayings of understanding,
3 To receive instruction in wise behavior,
Righteousness, justice and equity;
4 To give prudence to the naive,
To the youth knowledge and discretion,
5 A wise man will hear and increase
in learning,
And a man of understanding will
acquire wise counsel,
6 To understand a proverb and a
figure,
The words of the wise and their
riddles.

7 ¶ The fear of the LORD is the
beginning of knowledge;
Fools despise wisdom and instruction.

8 ¶ Hear, my son, your father's instruction,
And do not forsake your mother's
teaching;
9 Indeed, they are a graceful wreath
to your head,
And ornaments about your neck.
10 My son, if sinners entice you,
Do not consent.
11 If they say, "Come with us,
Let us lie in wait for blood,
Let us ambush the innocent without cause;

12 Let us swallow them alive like
Sheol,
Even whole, as those who go
down to the pit;
13 We shall find all *kinds* of precious
wealth,
We shall fill our houses with spoil;
14 Throw in your lot with us,
We shall all have one purse,"
15 My son, do not walk in the way
with them.
Keep your feet from their path,
16 For their feet run to evil,
And they hasten to shed blood.
17 Indeed, it is useless to spread the
net
In the eyes of any bird;
18 But they lie in wait for their own
blood;
They ambush their own lives.
19 So are the ways of everyone who
gains by violence;
It takes away the life of its possessors.

20 ¶ Wisdom shouts in the street,
She lifts her voice in the square;
21 At the head of the noisy *streets*
she cries out;
At the entrance of the gates in the
city, she utters her sayings:
22"How long, O naive ones, will you
love simplicity?
And scoffers delight themselves in
scoffing,
And fools hate knowledge?
23"Turn to my reproof,
Behold, I will pour out my spirit
on you;
I will make my words known to
you.
24 Because I called, and you refused;
I stretched out my hand, and no
one paid attention;
25 And you neglected all my counsel,
And did not want my reproof;
26 I will even laugh at your calamity;
I will mock when your dread
comes,
27 When your dread comes like a
storm,
And your calamity comes on like
a whirlwind,
When distress *and* anguish come
on you.
28"Then they will call on me, but I
will not answer;
They will seek me diligently, but
they shall not find me,

29 Because they hated knowledge,
And did not choose the fear of the
Lord.
30"They would not accept my counsel,
They spurned all my reproof.
31"So they shall eat of the fruit of
their own way,
And be satiated with their own
devices.
32"For the waywardness of the naive
shall kill them,
And the complacency of fools
shall destroy them.
33"But he who listens to me shall live
securely,
And shall be at ease from the
dread of evil."

CHAPTER 2

My son, if you will receive my sayings,
And treasure my commandments
within you,
2 Make your ear attentive to wisdom,
Incline your heart to understanding;
3 For if you cry for discernment,
Lift your voice for understanding;
4 If you seek her as silver,
And search for her as for hidden
treasures;
5 Then you will discern the fear of
the Lord,
And discover the knowledge of
God.
6 For the Lord gives wisdom;
From His mouth *come* knowledge
and understanding.
7 He stores up sound wisdom for
the upright;
He is a shield to those who walk
in integrity,
8 Guarding the paths of justice,
And He preserves the way of His
godly ones.
9 Then you will discern righteousness and justice
And equity *and* every good
course.
10 For wisdom will enter your heart,
And knowledge will be pleasant to
your soul;
11 Discretion will guard you,
Understanding will watch over
you,

12 To deliver you from the way of
   evil,
   From the man who speaks perverse things;
13 From those who leave the paths
   of uprightness,
   To walk in the ways of darkness;
14 Who delight in doing evil,
   And rejoice in the perversity of
   evil;
15 Whose paths are crooked,
   And who are devious in their
   ways;
16 To deliver you from the strange
   woman,
   From the adulteress who flatters
   with her words;
17 That leaves the companion of her
   youth,
   And forgets the covenant of her
   God;
18 For her house sinks down to
   death,
   And her tracks *lead* to the dead;
19 None who go to her return again,
   Nor do they reach the paths of
   life.
20 So you will walk in the way of
   good men,
   And keep to the paths of the
   righteous.
21 For the upright will live in the
   land,
   And the blameless will remain in
   it;
22 But the wicked will be cut off
   from the land,
   And the treacherous will be uprooted from it.

CHAPTER 3

MY son, do not forget my teaching,
   But let your heart keep my commandments;
2 For length of days and years of
   life,
   And peace they will add to you.
3 Do not let kindness and truth
   leave you;
   Bind them around your neck,
   Write them on the tablet of your
   heart.
4 So you will find favor and good
   repute
   In the sight of God and man.
5 Trust in the Lord with all your
   heart,

And do not lean on your own
   understanding.
6 In all your ways acknowledge
   Him,
   And He will make your paths
   straight.
7 Do not be wise in your own eyes;
   Fear the Lord and turn away
   from evil.
8 It will be healing to your body,
   And refreshment to your bones.
9 Honor the Lord from your
   wealth,
   And from the first of all your produce;
10 So your barns will be filled with
   plenty,
   And your vats will overflow with
   new wine.
11 My son, do not reject the discipline of the Lord,
   Or loathe His reproof,
12 For whom the Lord loves He reproves,
   Even as a father, the son in whom
   he delights.

13 ¶ How blessed is the man who
   finds wisdom,
   And the man who gains understanding.
14 For its profit is better than the
   profit of silver,
   And its gain than fine gold.
15 She is more precious than jewels;
   And nothing you desire compares
   with her.
16 Long life is in her right hand;
   In her left hand are riches and
   honor.
17 Her ways are pleasant ways,
   And all her paths are peace.
18 She is a tree of life to those who
   take hold of her,
   And happy are all who hold her
   fast.
19 The Lord by wisdom founded the
   earth;
   By understanding He established
   the heavens.
20 By His knowledge the deeps were
   broken up,
   And the skies drip with dew.
21 My son, let them not depart from
   your sight;
   Keep sound wisdom and discretion,
22 So they will be life to your soul,
   And adornment to your neck.

23 Then you will walk in your way
securely,
And your foot will not stumble.
24 When you lie down, you will not
be afraid;
When you lie down, your sleep
will be sweet.
25 Do not be afraid of sudden fear,
Nor of the onslaught of the
wicked when it comes;
26 For the LORD will be your confidence,
And will keep your foot from being caught.

27 ¶ Do not withhold good from
those to whom it is due,
When it is in your power to do *it*.
28 Do not say to your neighbor, "Go,
and come back,
And tomorrow I will give *it*,"
When you have it with you.
29 Do not devise harm against your
neighbor,
While he lives in security beside
you.
30 Do not contend with a man without cause,
If he has done you no harm.
31 Do not envy a man of violence,
And do not choose any of his
ways.
32 For the crooked *man* is an abomination to the LORD;
But He is intimate with the upright.
33 The curse of the LORD is on the
house of the wicked,
But He blesses the dwelling of the
righteous.
34 Though He scoffs at the scoffers,
Yet He gives grace to the afflicted.
35 The wise will inherit honor,
But fools display dishonor.

CHAPTER 4

H EAR, O sons, the instruction of a
father,
And give attention that you may
gain understanding,
2 For I give you sound teaching;
Do not abandon my instruction.
3 When I was a son to my father,
Tender and the only son in the
sight of my mother,
4 Then he taught me and said to
me,

"Let your heart hold fast my
words;
Keep my commandments and
live;
5 Acquire wisdom! Acquire understanding!
Do not forget, nor turn away from
the words of my mouth.
6 "Do not forsake her, and she will
guard you;
Love her, and she will watch over
you.
7 "The beginning of wisdom *is:* Acquire wisdom;
And with all your acquiring, get
understanding.
8 "Prize her, and she will exalt you;
She will honor you if you embrace
her.
9 "She will place on your head a
garland of grace;
She will present you with a crown
of beauty."

10 ¶ Hear, my son, and accept my
sayings,
And the years of your life will be
many.
11 I have directed you in the way of
wisdom;
I have led you in upright paths.
12 When you walk, your steps will
not be impeded;
And if you run, you will not stumble.
13 Take hold of instruction; do not
let go.
Guard her, for she is your life.
14 Do not enter the path of the
wicked,
And do not proceed in the way of
evil men.
15 Avoid it, do not pass by it;
Turn away from it and pass on.
16 For they cannot sleep unless they
do evil;
And they are robbed of sleep unless they make *someone* stumble.
17 For they eat the bread of wickedness,
And drink the wine of violence.
18 But the path of the righteous is
like the light of dawn,
That shines brighter and brighter
until the full day.
19 The way of the wicked is like
darkness;

They do not know over what they
stumble.

20 ¶ My son, give attention to my
words;
Incline your ear to my sayings.
21 Do not let them depart from your
sight;
Keep them in the midst of your
heart.
22 For they are life to those who find
them,
And health to all their whole
body.
23 Watch over your heart with all
diligence,
For from it *flow* the springs of life.
24 Put away from you a deceitful
mouth,
And put devious lips far from you.
25 Let your eyes look directly ahead,
And let your gaze be fixed straight
in front of you.
26 Watch the path of your feet,
And all your ways will be established.
27 Do not turn to the right nor to the
left;
Turn your foot from evil.

CHAPTER 5

My son, give attention to my wisdom,
Incline your ear to my understanding;
2 That you may observe discretion,
And your lips may reserve knowledge.
3 For the lips of an adulteress drip
honey,
And smoother than oil is her
speech;
4 But in the end she is bitter as
wormwood,
Sharp as a two-edged sword.
5 Her feet go down to death,
Her steps lay hold of Sheol.
6 She does not ponder the path of
life;
Her ways are unstable, she does
not know *it.*

7 ¶ Now then, *my* sons, listen to
me,
And do not depart from the words
of my mouth.
8 Keep your way far from her,

And do not go near the door of
her house,
9 Lest you give your vigor to others,
And your years to the cruel one;
10 Lest strangers be filled with your
strength,
And your hard-earned goods go to
the house of an alien;
11 And you groan at your latter end,
When your flesh and your body
are consumed;
12 And you say, "How I have hated
instruction!
And my heart spurned reproof!
13 "And I have not listened to the
voice of my teachers,
Nor inclined my ear to my in-
structors!
14 "I was almost in utter ruin
In the midst of the assembly and
congregation."

15 ¶ Drink water from your own
cistern,
And fresh water from your own
well.
16 Should your springs be dispersed
abroad,
Streams of water in the streets?
17 Let them be yours alone,
And not for strangers with you.
18 Let your fountain be blessed,
And rejoice in the wife of your
youth.
19 As a loving hind and a graceful
doe,
Let her breasts satisfy you at all
times;
Be exhilarated always with her
love.
20 For why should you, my son, be
exhilarated with an adulteress,
And embrace the bosom of a foreigner?
21 For the ways of a man are before
the eyes of the LORD,
And He watches all his paths.
22 His own iniquities will capture the
wicked,
And he will be held with the cords
of his sin.
23 He will die for lack of instruction,
And in the greatness of his folly
he will go astray.

CHAPTER 6

My son, if you have become surety
for your neighbor,

Have given a pledge for a stranger,
2 *If* you have been snared with the words of your mouth,
Have been caught with the words of your mouth,
3 Do this then, my son, and deliver yourself;
Since you have come into the hand of your neighbor,
Go, humble yourself, and importune your neighbor.
4 Do not give sleep to your eyes,
Nor slumber to your eyelids;
5 Deliver yourself like a gazelle from *the hunter's* hand,
And like a bird from the hand of the fowler.

6 ¶ Go to the ant, O sluggard,
Observe her ways and be wise,
7 Which, having no chief,
Officer or ruler,
8 Prepares her food in the summer,
And gathers her provision in the harvest.
9 How long will you lie down, O sluggard?
When will you arise from your sleep?
10 "A little sleep, a little slumber,
A little folding of the hands to rest"—
11 And your poverty will come in like a vagabond,
And your need like an armed man.

12 ¶ A worthless person, a wicked man,
Is the one who walks with a false mouth,
13 Who winks with his eyes, who signals with his feet,
Who points with his fingers;
14 Who *with* perversity in his heart devises evil continually,
Who spreads strife.
15 Therefore his calamity will come suddenly;
Instantly he will be broken, and there will be no healing.

16 ¶ There are six things which the LORD hates,
Yes, seven which are an abomination to Him:
17 Haughty eyes, a lying tongue,
And hands that shed innocent blood,

18 A heart that devises wicked plans,
Feet that run rapidly to evil,
19 A false witness *who* utters lies,
And one who spreads strife among brothers.

20 ¶ My son, observe the commandment of your father,
And do not forsake the teaching of your mother;
21 Bind them continually on your heart;
Tie them around your neck.
22 When you walk about, they will guide you;
When you sleep, they will watch over you;
And when you awake, they will talk to you.
23 For the commandment is a lamp, and the teaching is light;
And reproofs for discipline are the way of life,
24 To keep you from the evil woman,
From the smooth tongue of the adulteress.
25 Do not desire her beauty in your heart,
Nor let her catch you with her eyelids.
26 For on account of a harlot *one is reduced* to a loaf of bread,
And an adulteress hunts for the precious life.
27 Can a man take fire in his bosom,
And his clothes not be burned?
28 Or can a man walk on hot coals,
And his feet not be scorched?
29 So is the one who goes in to his neighbor's wife;
Whoever touches her will not go unpunished.
30 Men do not despise a thief if he steals
To satisfy himself when he is hungry;
31 But when he is found, he must repay sevenfold;
He must give all the substance of his house.
32 The one who commits adultery with a woman is lacking sense;
He who would destroy himself does it.
33 Wounds and disgrace he will find,
And his reproach will not be blotted out.
34 For jealousy enrages a man,

And he will not spare in the day of vengeance.

35 He will not accept any ransom,
Nor will he be content though you give many gifts.

CHAPTER 7

MY son, keep my words,
And treasure my commandments within you.

2 Keep my commandments and live,
And my teaching as the apple of your eye.

3 Bind them on your fingers;
Write them on the tablet of your heart.

4 Say to wisdom, "You are my sister,"
And call understanding *your* intimate friend;

5 That they may keep you from an adulteress,
From the foreigner who flatters with her words.

6 ¶ For at the window of my house
I looked out through my lattice,

7 And I saw among the naive,
I discerned among the youths,
A young man lacking sense,

8 Passing through the street near her corner;
And he takes the way to her house,

9 In the twilight, in the evening,
In the middle of the night and *in* the darkness.

10 And behold, a woman *comes* to meet him,
Dressed as a harlot and cunning of heart.

11 She is boisterous and rebellious;
Her feet do not remain at home;

12 *She is* now in the streets, now in the squares,
And lurks by every corner.

13 So she seizes him and kisses him,
And with a brazen face she says to him:

14 "I was due to offer peace offerings;
Today I have paid my vows.

15 "Therefore I have come out to meet you,
To seek your presence earnestly, and I have found you.

16 "I have spread my couch with coverings,

With colored linens of Egypt.

17 "I have sprinkled my bed
With myrrh, aloes and cinnamon.

18 "Come, let us drink our fill of love until morning;
Let us delight ourselves with caresses.

19 "For the man is not at home,
He has gone on a long journey;

20 He has taken a bag of money with him,
At full moon he will come home."

21 With her many persuasions she entices him;
With her flattering lips she seduces him.

22 Suddenly he follows her,
As an ox goes to the slaughter,
Or as *one in* fetters to the discipline of a fool,

23 Until an arrow pierces through his liver;
As a bird hastens to the snare,
So he does not know that it *will cost him* his life.

24 ¶ Now therefore, *my* sons, listen to me,
And pay attention to the words of my mouth.

25 Do not let your heart turn aside to her ways,
Do not stray into her paths.

26 For many are the victims she has cast down,
And numerous are all her slain.

27 Her house is the way to Sheol,
Descending to the chambers of death.

CHAPTER 8

DOES not wisdom call,
And understanding lift up her voice?

2 On top of the heights beside the way,
Where the paths meet, she takes her stand;

3 Beside the gates, at the opening to the city,
At the entrance of the doors, she cries out:

4 "To you, O men, I call,
And my voice is to the sons of men.

5 "O naive ones, discern prudence;
And, O fools, discern wisdom.

6"Listen, for I shall speak noble
things;
And the opening of my lips *will
produce* right things.
7"For my mouth will utter truth;
And wickedness is an abomination to my lips.
8"All the utterances of my mouth
are in righteousness;
There is nothing crooked or perverted in them.
9"They are all straightforward to
him who understands,
And right to those who find
knowledge.
10"Take my instruction, and not silver,
And knowledge rather than choicest gold.
11"For wisdom is better than jewels;
And all desirable things can not
compare with her.

12 ¶"I, wisdom, dwell with prudence,
And I find knowledge *and* discretion.
13"The fear of the LORD is to hate
evil;
Pride and arrogance and the evil
way,
And the perverted mouth, I hate.
14"Counsel is mine and sound wisdom;
I am understanding, power is
mine.
15"By me kings reign,
And rulers decree justice.
16"By me princes rule, and nobles,
All who judge rightly.
17"I love those who love me;
And those who diligently seek me
will find me.
18"Riches and honor are with me,
Enduring wealth and righteousness.
19"My fruit is better than gold, even
pure gold,
And my yield than choicest silver.
20"I walk in the way of righteousness,
In the midst of the paths of justice,
21 To endow those who love me with
wealth,
That I may fill their treasuries.

22 ¶"The LORD possessed me at the
beginning of His way,
Before His works of old.

23"From everlasting I was established,
From the beginning, from the earliest times of the earth.
24"When there were no depths I was
brought forth,
When there were no springs
abounding with water.
25"Before the mountains were settled,
Before the hills I was brought
forth;
26 While He had not yet made the
earth and the fields,
Nor the first dust of the world.
27"When He established the heavens,
I was there,
When He inscribed a circle on the
face of the deep,
28 When He made firm the skies
above,
When the springs of the deep became fixed,
29 When He set for the sea its
boundary,
So that the water should not
transgress His command,
When He marked out the foundations of the earth;
30 Then I was beside Him, *as* a master workman;
And I was daily *His* delight,
Rejoicing always before Him,
31 Rejoicing in the world, His earth,
And *having* my delight in the sons
of men.

32 ¶"Now therefore, O sons, listen to
me,
For blessed are they who keep my
ways.
33"Heed instruction and be wise,
And do not neglect *it.*
34"Blessed is the man who listens to
me,
Watching daily at my gates,
Waiting at my doorposts.
35"For he who finds me finds life,
And obtains favor from the LORD.
36"But he who sins against me injures himself;
All those who hate me love
death."

CHAPTER 9

WISDOM has built her house,
She has hewn out her seven pillars;

2 She has prepared her food, she
 has mixed her wine;
 She has also set her table;
3 She has sent out her maidens, she
 calls
 From the tops of the heights of
 the city:
4"Whoever is naive, let him turn in
 here!"
 To him who lacks understanding
 she says,
5"Come, eat of my food,
 And drink of the wine I have
 mixed.
6"Forsake *your* folly and live,
 And proceed in the way of understanding."

7 ¶ He who corrects a scoffer gets
 dishonor for himself,
 And he who reproves a wicked
 man *gets* insults for himself.
8 Do not reprove a scoffer, lest he
 hate you,
 Reprove a wise man, and he will
 love you.
9 Give *instruction* to a wise man,
 and he will be still wiser,
 Teach a righteous man, and he
 will increase *his* learning.
10 The fear of the LORD is the beginning of wisdom,
 And the knowledge of the Holy
 One is understanding.
11 For by me your days will be multiplied,
 And years of life will be added to
 you.
12 If you are wise, you are wise for
 yourself,
 And if you scoff, you alone will
 bear it.

13 ¶ The woman of folly is boisterous,
 She is naive, and knows nothing.
14 And she sits at the doorway of her
 house,
 On a seat by the high places of the
 city,
15 Calling to those who pass by,
 Who are making their paths
 straight:
16"Whoever is naive, let him turn in
 here,"
 And to him who lacks understanding she says,
17"Stolen water is sweet;

And bread *eaten* in secret is pleasant."
18 But he does not know that the
 dead are there,
 That her guests are in the depths
 of Sheol.

CHAPTER 10

THE proverbs of Solomon.
 A wise son makes a father glad,
 But a foolish son is a grief to his
 mother.
2 Ill-gotten gains do not profit,
 But righteousness delivers from
 death.
3 The LORD will not allow the righteous to hunger,
 But He will thrust *aside* the craving of the wicked.
4 Poor is he who works with a negligent hand,
 But the hand of the diligent
 makes rich.
5 He who gathers in summer is a
 son who acts wisely,
 But he who sleeps in harvest is a
 son who acts shamefully.
6 Blessings are on the head of the
 righteous,
 But the mouth of the wicked conceals violence.
7 The memory of the righteous is
 blessed,
 But the name of the wicked will
 rot.
8 The wise of heart will receive
 commands,
 But a babbling fool will be thrown
 down.
9 He who walks in integrity walks
 securely,
 But he who perverts his ways will
 be found out.
10 He who winks the eye causes
 trouble,
 And a babbling fool will be
 thrown down.
11 The mouth of the righteous is a
 fountain of life,
 But the mouth of the wicked conceals violence.
12 Hatred stirs up strife,
 But love covers all transgressions.
13 On the lips of the discerning, wisdom is found,
 But a rod is for the back of him
 who lacks understanding.
14 Wise men store up knowledge,

But with the mouth of the foolish,
ruin is at hand.
15 The rich man's wealth is his fortress,
The ruin of the poor is their poverty.
16 The wages of the righteous is life,
The income of the wicked, punishment.
17 He is *on* the path of life who heeds
instruction,
But he who forsakes reproof goes
astray.
18 He who conceals hatred *has* lying
lips,
And he who spreads slander is a
fool.
19 When there are many words,
transgression is unavoidable,
But he who restrains his lips is
wise.
20 The tongue of the righteous is *as*
choice silver,
The heart of the wicked is *worth*
little.
21 The lips of the righteous feed
many,
But fools die for lack of understanding.
22 It is the blessing of the LORD that
makes rich,
And He adds no sorrow to it.
23 Doing wickedness is like sport to
a fool;
And *so is* wisdom to a man of
understanding.
24 What the wicked fears will come
upon him,
And the desire of the righteous
will be granted.
25 When the whirlwind passes, the
wicked is no more,
But the righteous *has* an everlasting foundation.
26 Like vinegar to the teeth and
smoke to the eyes,
So is the lazy one to those who
send him.
27 The fear of the LORD prolongs life,
But the years of the wicked will
be shortened.
28 The hope of the righteous is gladness,
But the expectation of the wicked
perishes.
29 The way of the LORD is a stronghold to the upright,
But ruin to the workers of iniquity.

30 The righteous will never be
shaken,
But the wicked will not dwell in
the land.
31 The mouth of the righteous flows
with wisdom,
But the perverted tongue will be
cut out.
32 The lips of the righteous bring
forth what is acceptable,
But the mouth of the wicked,
what is perverted.

CHAPTER 11

A FALSE balance is an abomination
to the LORD,
But a just weight is His delight.
2 When pride comes, then comes
dishonor,
But with the humble is wisdom.
3 The integrity of the upright will
guide them,
But the falseness of the treacherous will destroy them.
4 Riches do not profit in the day of
wrath,
But righteousness delivers from
death.
5 The righteousness of the blameless will smooth his way,
But the wicked will fall by his own
wickedness.
6 The righteousness of the upright
will deliver them,
But the treacherous will be
caught by *their own* greed.
7 When a wicked man dies, *his* expectation will perish,
And the hope of strong men perishes.
8 The righteous is delivered from
trouble,
But the wicked takes his place.
9 With *his* mouth the godless man
destroys his neighbor,
But through knowledge the righteous will be delivered.
10 When it goes well with the righteous, the city rejoices,
And when the wicked perish,
there is glad shouting.
11 By the blessing of the upright a
city is exalted,
But by the mouth of the wicked it
is torn down.
12 He who despises his neighbor
lacks sense,

But a man of understanding keeps silent.

13 He who goes about as a talebearer reveals secrets,
But he who is trustworthy conceals a matter.

14 Where there is no guidance, the people fall,
But in abundance of counselors there is victory.

15 He who is surety for a stranger will surely suffer for it,
But he who hates going surety is safe.

16 A gracious woman attains honor,
And violent men attain riches.

17 The merciful man does himself good,
But the cruel man does himself harm.

18 The wicked earns deceptive wages,
But he who sows righteousness *gets* a true reward.

19 He who is steadfast in righteousness *will attain* to life,
And he who pursues evil *will bring about* his own death.

20 The perverse in heart are an abomination to the LORD,
But the blameless in *their* walk are His delight.

21 Assuredly, the evil man will not go unpunished,
But the descendants of the righteous will be delivered.

22 *As* a ring of gold in a swine's snout,
So is a beautiful woman who lacks ¹discretion.

23 The desire of the righteous is only good,
But the expectation of the wicked is wrath.

24 There is one who scatters, yet increases all the more,
And there is one who withholds what is justly due, but *it results* only in want.

25 The generous man will be prosperous,
And he who waters will himself be watered.

26 He who withholds grain, the people will curse him,
But blessing will be on the head of him who sells *it*.

27 He who diligently seeks good seeks favor,
But he who searches after evil, it will come to him.

28 He who trusts in his riches will fall,
But the righteous will flourish like the *green* leaf.

29 He who troubles his own house will inherit wind,
And the foolish will be servant to the wisehearted.

30 The fruit of the righteous is a tree of life,
And he who is wise wins souls.

31 If the righteous will be rewarded in the earth,
How much more the wicked and the sinner!

CHAPTER 12

WHOEVER loves discipline loves knowledge,
But he who hates reproof is stupid.

2 A good man will obtain favor from the LORD,
But He will condemn a man who devises evil.

3 A man will not be established by wickedness,
But the root of the righteous will not be moved.

4 An excellent wife is the crown of her husband,
But she who shames *him* is as rottenness in his bones.

5 The thoughts of the righteous are just,
But the counsels of the wicked are deceitful.

6 The words of the wicked lie in wait for blood,
But the mouth of the upright will deliver them.

7 The wicked are overthrown and are no more,
But the house of the righteous will stand.

8 A man will be praised according to his insight,
But one of perverse mind will be despised.

9 Better is he who is lightly esteemed and has a servant,
Than he who honors himself and lacks bread.

¹ Lit., *taste*

10 A righteous man has regard for the life of his beast,
But the compassion of the wicked is cruel.

11 He who tills his land will have plenty of bread,
But he who pursues vain *things* lacks sense.

12 The wicked desires the booty of evil men,
But the root of the righteous yields *fruit*.

13 An evil man is ensnared by the transgression of his lips,
But the righteous will escape from trouble.

14 A man will be satisfied with good by the fruit of his words,
And the deeds of a man's hands will return to him.

15 The way of a fool is right in his own eyes,
But a wise man is he who listens to counsel.

16 A fool's vexation is known at once,
But a prudent man conceals dishonor.

17 He who speaks truth tells what is right,
But a false witness, deceit.

18 There is one who speaks rashly like the thrusts of a sword,
But the tongue of the wise brings healing.

19 Truthful lips will be established forever,
But a lying tongue is only for a moment.

20 Deceit is in the heart of those who devise evil,
But counselors of peace have joy.

21 No harm befalls the righteous,
But the wicked are filled with trouble.

22 Lying lips are an abomination to the LORD,
But those who deal faithfully are His delight.

23 A prudent man conceals knowledge,
But the heart of fools proclaims folly.

24 The hand of the diligent will rule,
But the slack *hand* will be put to forced labor.

25 Anxiety in the heart of a man weighs it down,
But a good word makes it glad.

26 The righteous is a guide to his neighbor,
But the way of the wicked leads them astray.

27 A slothful man does not roast his prey,
But the precious possession of a man *is* diligence.

28 In the way of righteousness is life,
And in *its* pathway there is no death.

CHAPTER 13

A WISE son *accepts his* father's discipline,
But a scoffer does not listen to rebuke.

2 From the fruit of a man's mouth he enjoys good,
But the desire of the treacherous is violence.

3 The one who guards his mouth preserves his life;
The one who opens wide his lips comes to ruin.

4 The soul of the sluggard craves and *gets* nothing,
But the soul of the diligent is made fat.

5 A righteous man hates falsehood,
But a wicked man acts disgustingly and shamefully.

6 Righteousness guards the one whose way is blameless,
But wickedness subverts the sinner.

7 There is one who pretends to be rich, but has nothing;
Another pretends to be poor, but has great wealth.

8 The ransom of a man's life is his riches,
But the poor hears no rebuke.

9 The light of the righteous [2]rejoices,
But the lamp of the wicked goes out.

10 Through presumption comes nothing but strife,
But with those who receive counsel is wisdom.

11 Wealth *obtained* by fraud dwindles,
But the one who gathers by labor increases *it*.

12 Hope deferred makes the heart sick,

[2] I.e., shines brightly

But desire fulfilled is a tree of life.

13 The one who despises the word
will be in debt to it,
But the one who fears the commandment will be rewarded.

14 The teaching of the wise is a fountain of life,
To turn aside from the snares of
death.

15 Good understanding produces favor,
But the way of the treacherous is
hard.

16 Every prudent man acts with
knowledge,
But a fool displays folly.

17 A wicked messenger falls into
adversity,
But a faithful envoy *brings* healing.

18 Poverty and shame *will come* to
him who neglects discipline,
But he who regards reproof will
be honored.

19 Desire realized is sweet to the
soul,
But it is an abomination to fools
to depart from evil.

20 He who walks with wise men will
be wise,
But the companion of fools will
suffer harm.

21 Adversity pursues sinners,
But the righteous will be rewarded with prosperity.

22 A good man leaves an inheritance
to his children's children,
And the wealth of the sinner is
stored up for the righteous.

23 Abundant food *is in* the fallow
ground of the poor,
But it is swept away by injustice.

24 He who spares his rod hates his
son,
But he who loves him disciplines
him diligently.

25 The righteous has enough to satisfy his appetite,
But the stomach of the wicked is
in want.

CHAPTER 14

THE wise woman builds her house,
But the foolish tears it down with
her own hands.

2 He who walks in his uprightness
fears the LORD,

But he who is crooked in his ways
despises Him.

3 In the mouth of the foolish is a
rod for *his* back,
But the lips of the wise will preserve them.

4 Where no oxen are, the manger is
clean,
But much increase *comes* by the
strength of the ox.

5 A faithful witness will not lie,
But a false witness speaks lies.

6 A scoffer seeks wisdom, and *finds*
none,
But knowledge is easy to him who
has understanding.

7 Leave the presence of a fool,
Or you will not discern words of
knowledge.

8 The wisdom of the prudent is to
understand his way,
But the folly of fools is deceit.

9 Fools mock at sin,
But among the upright there is
good will.

10 The heart knows its own bitterness,
And a stranger does not share its
joy.

11 The house of the wicked will be
destroyed,
But the tent of the upright will
flourish.

12 There is a way *which seems* right
to a man,
But its end is the way of death.

13 Even in laughter the heart may be
in pain,
And the end of joy may be grief.

14 The backslider in heart will have
his fill of his own ways,
But a good man will *be satisfied*
with his.

15 The naive believes everything,
But the prudent man considers his
steps.

16 A wise man is cautious and turns
away from evil,
But a fool is arrogant and careless.

17 A quick-tempered man acts foolishly,
And a man of evil devices is hated.

18 The naive inherit folly,
But the prudent are crowned with
knowledge.

19 The evil will bow down before the
good,
And the wicked at the gates of the
righteous.

20 The poor is hated even by his neighbor,
But those who love the rich are many.

21 He who despises his neighbor sins,
But happy is he who is gracious to the poor.

22 Will they not go astray who devise evil?
But kindness and truth *will be to* those who devise good.

23 In all labor there is profit,
But mere talk *leads* only to poverty.

24 The crown of the wise is their riches,
But the folly of fools is foolishness.

25 A truthful witness saves lives,
But he who speaks lies is treacherous.

26 In the [3]fear of the LORD there is strong confidence,
And his children will have refuge.

27 The [3]fear of the LORD is a fountain of life,
That one may avoid the snares of death.

28 In a multitude of people is a king's glory,
But in the dearth of people is a prince's ruin.

29 He who is slow to anger has great understanding,
But he who is quick-tempered exalts folly.

30 A tranquil heart is life to the body,
But passion is rottenness to the bones.

31 He who oppresses the poor reproaches his Maker,
But he who is gracious to the needy honors Him.

32 The wicked is thrust down by his wrongdoing,
But the righteous has a refuge when he dies.

33 Wisdom rests in the heart of one who has understanding,
But in the bosom of fools it is made known.

34 Righteousness exalts a nation,
But sin is a disgrace to *any* people.

35 The king's favor is toward a servant who acts wisely,
But his anger is toward him who acts shamefully.

CHAPTER 15

A GENTLE answer turns away wrath,
But a harsh word stirs up anger.

2 The tongue of the wise makes knowledge acceptable,
But the mouth of fools spouts folly.

3 The eyes of the LORD are in every place,
Watching the evil and the good.

4 A soothing tongue is a tree of life,
But perversion in it crushes the spirit.

5 A fool rejects his father's discipline,
But he who regards reproof is prudent.

6 Much wealth is *in* the house of the righteous,
But trouble is in the income of the wicked.

7 The lips of the wise spread knowledge,
But the hearts of fools are not so.

8 The sacrifice of the wicked is an abomination to the LORD,
But the prayer of the upright is His delight.

9 The way of the wicked is an abomination to the LORD,
But He loves him who pursues righteousness.

10 Stern discipline is for him who forsakes the way;
He who hates reproof will die.

11 Sheol and Abaddon *lie open* before the LORD,
How much more the hearts of men!

12 A scoffer does not love one who reproves him,
He will not go to the wise.

13 A joyful heart makes a cheerful face,
But when the heart is sad, the spirit is broken.

14 The mind of the intelligent seeks knowledge,
But the mouth of fools feeds on folly.

15 All the days of the afflicted are bad,
But a cheerful heart *has* a continual feast.

16 Better is a little with the fear of the LORD,

[3] Or, *reverence*

Than great treasure and turmoil
with it.

17 Better is a dish of vegetables
where love is,
Than a fattened ox and hatred
with it.

18 A hot-tempered man stirs up
strife,
But the slow to anger pacifies
contention.

19 The way of the sluggard is as a
hedge of thorns,
But the path of the upright is a
highway.

20 A wise son makes a father glad,
But a foolish man despises his
mother.

21 Folly is joy to him who lacks
sense,
But a man of understanding walks
straight.

22 Without consultation, plans are
frustrated,
But with many counselors they
succeed.

23 A man has joy in an apt answer,
And how delightful is a timely
word!

24 The path of life *leads* upward for
the wise,
That he may keep away from
Sheol below.

25 The LORD will tear down the
house of the proud,
But He will establish the boundary of the widow.

26 Evil plans are an abomination to
the LORD,
But pleasant words are pure.

27 He who profits illicitly troubles his
own house,
But he who hates bribes will live.

28 The heart of the righteous ponders how to answer,
But the mouth of the wicked
pours out evil things.

29 The LORD is far from the wicked,
But He hears the prayer of the
righteous.

30 Bright eyes gladden the heart;
Good news puts fat on the bones.

31 He whose ear listens to the life-
giving reproof
Will dwell among the wise.

32 He who neglects discipline despises himself,
But he who listens to reproof acquires understanding.

33 The fear of the LORD is the instruction for wisdom,
And before honor *comes* humility.

CHAPTER 16

THE plans of the heart belong to
man,
But the answer of the tongue is
from the LORD.

2 All the ways of a man are clean in
his own sight,
But the LORD weighs the motives.

3 Commit your works to the LORD,
And your plans will be established.

4 The LORD has made everything
for its own purpose,
Even the wicked for the day of
evil.

5 Everyone who is proud in heart is
an abomination to the LORD;
Assuredly, he will not be unpunished.

6 By lovingkindness and truth iniquity is atoned for,
And by the fear of the LORD one
keeps away from evil.

7 When a man's ways are pleasing
to the LORD,
He makes even his enemies to be
at peace with him.

8 Better is a little with righteousness
Than great income with injustice.

9 The mind of man plans his way,
But the LORD directs his steps.

10 A divine decision is in the lips of
the king;
His mouth should not err in judgment.

11 A just balance and scales belong
to the LORD;
All the weights of the bag are His
concern.

12 It is an abomination for kings to
commit wickedness,
For a throne is established on
righteousness.

13 Righteous lips are the delight of
kings,
And he who speaks right is loved.

14 The wrath of a king is *as* messengers of death,
But a wise man will appease it.

15 In the light of a king's face is life,
And his favor is like a cloud with
the spring rain.

16 How much better it is to get wisdom than gold!
   And to get understanding is to be
   chosen above silver.
17 The highway of the upright is to
   depart from evil;
   He who watches his way preserves his life.
18 Pride *goes* before destruction,
   And a haughty spirit before stumbling.
19 It is better to be of a humble spirit
   with the lowly,
   Than to divide the spoil with the
   proud.
20 He who gives attention to the
   word shall find good,
   And blessed is he who trusts in
   the LORD.
21 The wise in heart will be called
   discerning,
   And sweetness of speech increases persuasiveness.
22 Understanding is a fountain of life
   to him who has it,
   But the discipline of fools is folly.
23 The heart of the wise teaches his
   mouth,
   And adds persuasiveness to his
   lips.
24 Pleasant words are a honeycomb,
   Sweet to the soul and healing to
   the bones.
25 There is a way *which seems* right
   to a man,
   But its end is the way of death.
26 A worker's appetite works for
   him,
   For his hunger urges him *on.*
27 A worthless man digs up evil,
   While his words are as a scorching fire.
28 A perverse man spreads strife,
   And a slanderer separates intimate friends.
29 A man of violence entices his
   neighbor,
   And leads him in a way that is not
   good.
30 He who winks his eyes *does so* to
   devise perverse things;
   He who compresses his lips brings
   evil to pass.
31 A gray head is a crown of glory;
   It is found in the way of righteousness.
32 He who is slow to anger is better
   than the mighty,

And he who rules his spirit, than
   he who captures a city.
33 The lot is cast into the lap,
   But its every decision is from the
   LORD.

CHAPTER 17

BETTER is a dry morsel and quietness with it
   Than a house full of feasting with
   strife.
2 A servant who acts wisely will
   rule over a son who acts shamefully,
   And will share in the inheritance
   among brothers.
3 The refining pot is for silver and
   the furnace for gold,
   But the LORD tests hearts.
4 An evildoer listens to wicked lips,
   A liar pays attention to a destructive tongue.
5 He who mocks the poor reproaches his Maker;
   He who rejoices at calamity will
   not go unpunished.
6 Grandchildren are the crown of
   old men,
   And the glory of sons is their
   fathers.
7 Excellent speech is not fitting for
   a fool;
   Much less are lying lips to a
   prince.
8 A bribe is a charm in the sight of
   its owner;
   Wherever he turns, he prospers.
9 He who covers a transgression
   seeks love,
   But he who repeats a matter separates intimate friends.
10 A rebuke goes deeper into one
   who has understanding
   Than a hundred blows into a fool.
11 A rebellious man seeks only evil,
   So a cruel messenger will be sent
   against him.
12 Let a man meet a bear robbed of
   her cubs,
   Rather than a fool in his folly.
13 He who returns evil for good,
   Evil will not depart from his
   house.
14 The beginning of strife is *like*
   letting out water,
   So abandon the quarrel before it
   breaks out.
15 He who justifies the wicked, and

he who condemns the righteous,
Both of them alike are an abomination to the LORD.
16 Why is there a price in the hand of
a fool to buy wisdom,
When he has no sense?
17 A friend loves at all times,
And a brother is born for adversity.
18 A man lacking in sense pledges,
And becomes surety in the presence of his neighbor.
19 He who loves transgression loves
strife;
He who raises his door seeks destruction.
20 He who has a crooked mind finds
no good,
And he who is perverted in his
language falls into evil.
21 He who begets a fool *does so* to
his sorrow,
And the father of a fool has no
joy.
22 A joyful heart is good medicine,
But a broken spirit dries up the
bones.
23 A wicked man receives a bribe
from the bosom
To pervert the ways of justice.
24 Wisdom is in the presence of the
one who has understanding,
But the eyes of a fool are on the
ends of the earth.
25 A foolish son is a grief to his
father,
And bitterness to her who bore
him.
26 It is also not good to fine the
righteous,
Nor to strike the noble for *their*
uprightness.
27 He who restrains his words has
knowledge,
And he who has a cool spirit is a
man of understanding.
28 Even a fool, when he keeps silent,
is considered wise;
When he closes his lips, he is
counted prudent.

CHAPTER 18

HE who separates himself seeks *his*
own desire,
He quarrels against all sound wisdom.

2 A fool does not delight in understanding,
But only in revealing his own
mind.
3 When a wicked man comes, contempt also comes,
And with dishonor *comes* reproach.
4 The words of a man's mouth are
deep waters;
The fountain of wisdom is a bub-
bling brook.
5 To show partiality to the wicked
is not good,
Nor to thrust aside the righteous
in judgment.
6 A fool's lips bring strife,
And his mouth calls for blows.
7 A fool's mouth is his ruin,
And his lips are the snare of his
soul.
8 The words of a whisperer are like
dainty morsels,
And they go down into the innermost parts of the body.
9 He also who is slack in his work
Is brother to him who destroys.
10 The name of the LORD is a strong
tower;
The righteous runs into it and is
safe.
11 A rich man's wealth is his strong
city,
And like a high wall in his own
imagination.
12 Before destruction the heart of
man is haughty,
But humility *goes* before honor.
13 He who gives an answer before he
hears,
It is folly and shame to him.
14 The spirit of a man can endure his
sickness,
But a broken spirit who can bear?
15 The mind of the prudent acquires
knowledge,
And the ear of the wise seeks
knowledge.
16 A man's gift makes room for him,
And brings him before great men.
17 The first to plead his case *seems*
just,
Until another comes and examines him.
18 The lot puts an end to contentions,
And decides between the mighty.

19 A brother offended *is harder to be won* than a strong city,
And contentions are like the bars of a castle.

20 With the fruit of a man's mouth his stomach will be satisfied;
He will be satisfied *with* the product of his lips.

21 Death and life are in the power of the tongue,
And those who love it will eat its fruit.

22 He who finds a wife finds a good thing,
And obtains favor from the LORD.

23 The poor man utters supplications,
But the rich man answers roughly.

24 A man of *many* friends *comes* to ruin,
But there is a friend who sticks closer than a brother.

CHAPTER 19

BETTER is a poor man who walks in his integrity
Than he who is perverse in speech and is a fool.

2 Also it is not good for a person to be without knowledge,
And he who makes haste with his feet errs.

3 The foolishness of man subverts his way,
And his heart rages against the LORD.

4 Wealth adds many friends,
But a poor man is separated from his friend.

5 A false witness will not go unpunished,
And he who tells lies will not escape.

6 Many will entreat the favor of a generous man,
And every man is a friend to him who gives gifts.

7 All the brothers of a poor man hate him;
How much more do his friends go far from him!
He pursues *them with* words, *but* they are gone.

8 He who gets wisdom loves his own soul;
He who keeps understanding will find good.

9 A false witness will not go unpunished,
And he who tells lies will perish.

10 Luxury is not fitting for a fool;
Much less for a slave to rule over princes.

11 A man's discretion makes him slow to anger,
And it is his glory to overlook a transgression.

12 The king's wrath is like the roaring of a lion,
But his favor is like dew on the grass.

13 A foolish son is destruction to his father,
And the contentions of a wife are a constant dripping.

14 House and wealth are an inheritance from fathers,
But a prudent wife is from the LORD.

15 Laziness casts into a deep sleep,
And an idle man will suffer hunger.

16 He who keeps the commandment keeps his soul,
But he who is careless of his ways will die.

17 He who is gracious to a poor man lends to the LORD,
And He will repay him for his good deed.

18 Discipline your son while there is hope,
And do not desire his death.

19 *A man of* great anger shall bear the penalty,
For if you rescue *him,* you will only have to do it again.

20 Listen to counsel and accept discipline,
That you may be wise the rest of your days.

21 Many are the plans in a man's heart,
But the counsel of the LORD, it will stand.

22 What is desirable in a man is his [4]kindness,
And *it is* better to be a poor man than a liar.

23 The fear of the LORD *leads* to life,
So that one may sleep satisfied, untouched by evil.

24 The sluggard buries his hand in the dish,

[4] Or, *loyalty*

And will not even bring it back to his mouth.

25 Strike a scoffer and the naive may become shrewd,
But reprove one who has understanding and he will gain knowledge.

26 He who assaults *his* father *and* drives *his* mother away
Is a shameful and disgraceful son.

27 Cease listening, my son, to discipline,
And you will stray from the words of knowledge.

28 A rascally witness makes a mockery of justice,
And the mouth of the wicked spreads iniquity.

29 Judgments are prepared for scoffers,
And blows for the back of fools.

CHAPTER 20

WINE is a mocker, strong drink a brawler,
And whoever is intoxicated by it is not wise.

2 The terror of a king is like the growling of a lion;
He who provokes him to anger forfeits his own life.

3 Keeping away from strife is an honor for a man,
But any fool will quarrel.

4 The sluggard does not plow after the autumn,
So he begs during the harvest and has nothing.

5 A plan in the heart of a man is *like* deep water,
But a man of understanding draws it out.

6 Many a man proclaims his own loyalty,
But who can find a trustworthy man?

7 A righteous man who walks in his integrity—
How blessed are his sons after him.

8 A king who sits on the throne of justice
Disperses all evil with his eyes.

9 Who can say, "I have cleansed my heart,
I am pure from my sin"?

10 Differing weights and differing measures,

Both of them are abominable to the LORD.

11 It is by his deeds that a lad distinguishes himself
If his conduct is pure and right.

12 The hearing ear and the seeing eye,
The LORD has made both of them.

13 Do not love sleep, lest you become poor;
Open your eyes, *and* you will be satisfied with food.

14 "Bad, bad," says the buyer;
But when he goes his way, then he boasts.

15 There is gold, and an abundance of jewels;
But the lips of knowledge are a more precious thing.

16 Take his garment when he becomes surety for a stranger;
And for foreigners, hold him in pledge.

17 Bread obtained by falsehood is sweet to a man,
But afterward his mouth will be filled with gravel.

18 Prepare plans by consultation,
And make war by wise guidance.

19 He who goes about as a slanderer reveals secrets,
Therefore do not associate with a gossip.

20 He who curses his father or his mother,
His lamp will go out in time of darkness.

21 An inheritance gained hurriedly at the beginning,
Will not be blessed in the end.

22 Do not say, "I will repay evil";
Wait for the LORD, and He will save you.

23 Differing weights are an abomination to the LORD,
And a false scale is not good.

24 Man's steps are *ordained* by the LORD,
How then can man understand his way?

25 It is a snare for a man to say rashly, "It is holy!"
And after the vows to make inquiry.

26 A wise king winnows the wicked,
And drives the *threshing* wheel over them.

27 The spirit of man is the lamp of the LORD,

Searching all the innermost parts of his being.
28 Loyalty and truth preserve the king,
And he upholds his throne by righteousness.
29 The glory of young men is their strength,
And the honor of old men is their gray hair.
30 Stripes that wound scour away evil,
And strokes *reach* the innermost parts.

CHAPTER 21

THE king's heart is *like* channels of water in the hand of the LORD; He turns it wherever He wishes.
2 Every man's way is right in his own eyes,
But the LORD weighs the hearts.
3 To do righteousness and justice Is desired by the LORD rather than sacrifice.
4 Haughty eyes and a proud heart, The lamp of the wicked, is sin.
5 The plans of the diligent *lead* surely to advantage,
But everyone who is hasty *comes* surely to poverty.
6 The getting of treasures by a lying tongue
Is a fleeting vapor, the pursuit of death.
7 The violence of th~~~~~~ with ~~~~ked,
But as for the pure, his conduct is upright.
    d guilty man is
9 It is better to live in a corner of a roof,
Than in a house shared with a contentious woman.
10 The soul of the wicked desires evil;
His neighbor finds no favor in his eyes.
11 When the scoffer is punished, the naive becomes wise;
But when the wise is instructed, he receives knowledge.
12 The righteous one considers the house of the wicked,
Turning the wicked to ruin.

13 He who shuts his ear to the cry of the poor
Will also cry himself and not be answered.
14 A gift in secret subdues anger, And a bribe in the bosom, strong wrath.
15 The execution of justice is joy for the righteous,
But is terror to the workers of iniquity.
16 A man who wanders from the way of understanding
Will rest in the assembly of the dead.
17 He who loves pleasure *will become* a poor man;
He who loves wine and oil will not become rich.
18 The wicked is a ransom for the righteous,
And the treacherous is in the place of the upright.
19 It is better to live in a desert land, Than with a contentious and vexing woman.
20 There is precious treasure and oil in the dwelling of the wise,
But a foolish man swallows it up.
21 He who pursues righteousness and loyalty
Finds life, righteousness and honor.
22 A wise man scales th~ ~~y of the might~~ down the stronghold
~~In which they trust.
23 He who guards his mouth and his tongue,
Guards his soul from troubles.
24 "Proud," "Haughty," "Scoffer," are his names,
Who acts with insolent pride.
25 The desire of the sluggard puts him to death,
For his hands refuse to work;
26 All day long he is craving,
While the righteous gives and does not hold back.
27 The sacrifice of the wicked is an abomination,
How much more when he brings it with evil intent!
28 A false witness will perish,
But the man who listens to the truth will speak forever.
29 A wicked man shows a bold face, But as for the upright, he makes his way sure.

30 There is no wisdom and no under-
    standing
    And no counsel against the LORD.
31 The horse is prepared for the day
    of battle,
    But victory belongs to the LORD.

CHAPTER 22

A GOOD name is to be more desired
    than great riches,
    Favor is better than silver and
    gold.
2 The rich and the poor have a com-
    mon bond,
    The LORD is the maker of them all.
3 The prudent sees the evil and
    hides himself,
    But the naive go on, and are pun-
    ished for it.
4 The reward of humility and the
    fear of the LORD
    Are riches, honor and life.
5 Thorns and snares are in the way
    of the perverse;
    He who guards himself will be far
    from them.
6 Train up a child in the way he
    should go,
    Even when he is old he will not
    depart from it.
7 The rich rules over the poor,
    And the borrower becomes the
    lender's slave.
8 He who vanity, sows iniquity will reap
    And the rod of his
9 He who is generous
    blessed,
    For he gives some of his food to
    the poor.
10 Drive out the scoffer, and conten-
    tion will go out,
    Even strife and dishonor will
    cease.
11 He who loves purity of heart
    And whose speech is gracious, the
    king is his friend.
12 The eyes of the LORD preserve
    knowledge,
    But He overthrows the words of
    the treacherous man.
13 The sluggard says, "There is a lion
    outside;
    I shall be slain in the streets!"
14 The mouth of an adulteress is a
    deep pit;
    He who is cursed of the LORD will
    fall into it.

15 Foolishness is bound up in the
    heart of a child;
    The rod of discipline will remove
    it far from him.
16 He who oppresses the poor to
    make much for himself
    Or who gives to the rich, will only
    come to poverty.

17 ¶ Incline your ear and hear the
    words of the wise,
    And apply your mind to my
    knowledge;
18 For it will be pleasant if you keep
    them within you,
    That they may be ready on your
    lips.
19 So that your trust may be in the
    LORD,
    I have taught you today, even
    you.
20 Have I not written to you excel-
    lent things
    Of counsels and knowledge,
21 To make you know the certainty
    of the words of truth
    That you may correctly answer to
    him who sent you?

22 ¶ Do not rob the poor because he
    is poor,
    Or crush the afflicted at the gate;
23 For the LORD will plead their case,
    And take the life of those who rob
    them.

25 ¶ Do not associate with a man
    And fine anger;

26 ¶ Do not be among ered man,
    give pledges,
    Among those who become sure
    ties for debts.
27 If you have nothing with which to
    pay,
    Why should he take your bed
    from under you?

28 ¶ Do not move the ancient
    boundary
    Which your fathers have set.

29 ¶ Do you see a man skilled in his
    work?
    He will stand before kings;

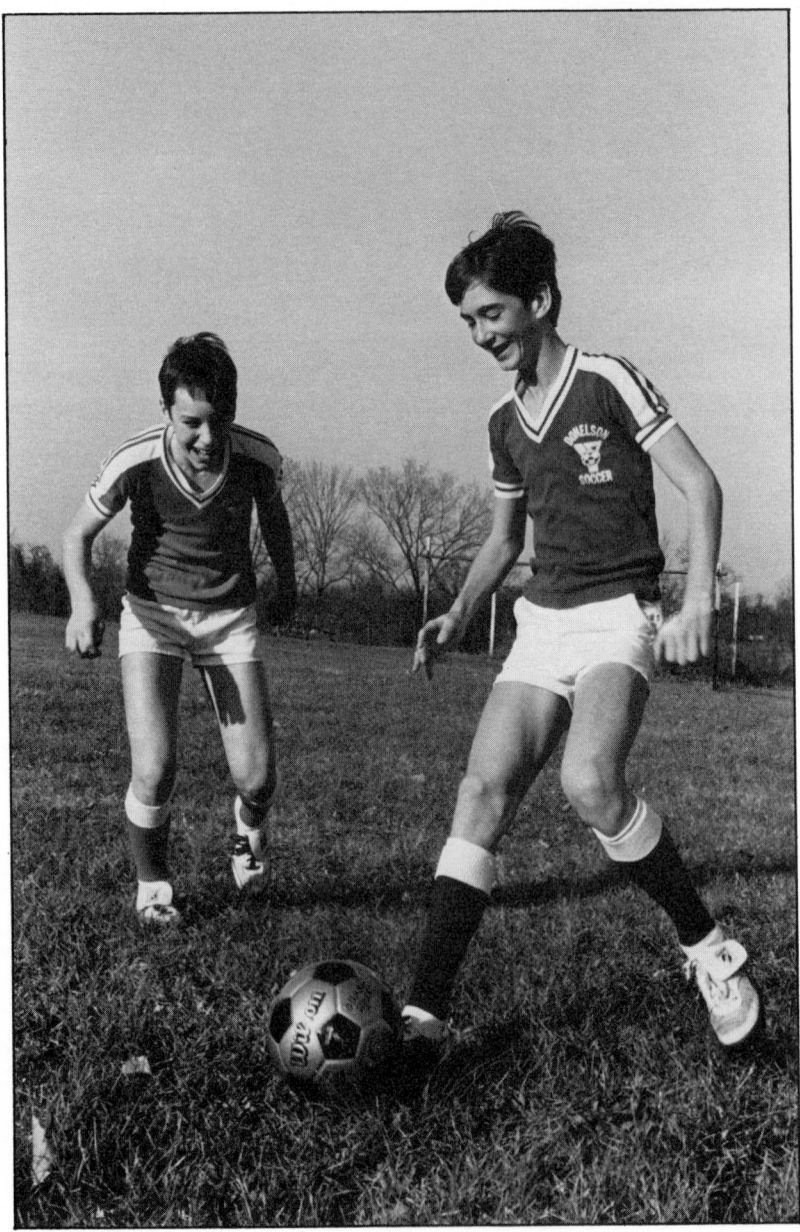

He will not stand before obscure men.

CHAPTER 23

WHEN you sit down to dine with a ruler,
Consider carefully what is before you;
2 And put a knife to your throat,
If you are a man of *great* appetite.
3 Do not desire his delicacies,
For it is deceptive food.

4 ¶ Do not weary yourself to gain wealth,
Cease from your consideration *of it.*
5 When you set your eyes on it, it is gone.
For *wealth* certainly makes itself wings,
Like an eagle that flies *toward* the heavens.

6 ¶ Do not eat the bread of a selfish man,
Or desire his delicacies;
7 For as he thinks within himself, so he is.
He says to you, "Eat and drink!"
But his heart is not with you.
8 You will vomit up the morsel you have eaten,
And waste your compliments.

9 ¶ Do not speak in the hearing of a fool,
For he will despise the wisdom of your words.

10 ¶ Do not move the ancient boundary,
Or go into the fields of the fatherless;
11 For their Redeemer is strong;
He will plead their case against you.
12 Apply your heart to discipline,
And your ears to words of knowledge.

13 ¶ Do not hold back discipline from the child,
Although you beat him with the rod, he will not die.
14 You shall beat him with the rod,
And deliver his soul from Sheol.

15 ¶ My son, if your heart is wise,
My own heart also will be glad;
16 And my inmost being will rejoice,
When your lips speak what is right.

17 ¶ Do not let your heart envy sinners,
But *live* in the fear of the LORD always.
18 Surely there is a future,
And your hope will not be cut off.
19 Listen, my son, and be wise,
And direct your heart in the way.
20 Do not be with heavy drinkers of wine,
Or with gluttonous eaters of meat;
21 For the heavy drinker and the glutton will come to poverty,
And drowsiness will clothe *a man* with rags.

22 ¶ Listen to your father who begot you,
And do not despise your mother when she is old.
23 Buy truth, and do not sell *it,*
Get wisdom and instruction and understanding.
24 ¶ The father of the righteous will greatly rejoice,
And he who begets a wise son will be glad in him.
25 Let your father and your mother be glad,
And let her rejoice who gave birth to you.

26 ¶ Give me your heart, my son,
And let your eyes delight in my ways.
27 For a harlot is a deep pit,
And an adulterous woman is a narrow well.
28 Surely she lurks as a robber,
And increases the faithless among men.

29 ¶ Who has woe? Who has sorrow?
Who has contentions? Who has complaining?
Who has wounds without cause?
Who has redness of eyes?
30 Those who linger long over wine,
Those who go to taste mixed wine.

31 Do not look on the wine when it is
   red,
   When it sparkles in the cup,
   When it goes down smoothly;
32 At the last it bites like a serpent,
   And stings like a viper.
33 Your eyes will see strange things,
   And your mind will utter perverse
   things.
34 And you will be like one who lies
   down in the middle of the sea,
   Or like one who lies down on the
   top of a [5]mast.
35 "They struck me, *but* I did not
   become ill;
   They beat me, *but* I did not know
   it.
   When shall I awake?
   I will seek another drink."

CHAPTER 24

Do not be envious of evil men,
   Nor desire to be with them;
2 For their minds devise violence,
   And their lips talk of trouble.

3 ¶ By wisdom a house is built,
   And by understanding it is established;
4 And by knowledge the rooms are
   filled
   With all precious and pleasant
   riches.

5 ¶ A wise man is strong,
   And a man of knowledge increases power.
6 For by wise guidance you will
   wage war,
   And in abundance of counselors
   there is victory.

7 ¶ Wisdom is too high for a fool,
   He does not open his mouth in the
   gate.

8 ¶ He who plans to do evil,
   Men will call him a schemer.
9 The devising of folly is sin,
   And the scoffer is an abomination
   to men.

10 ¶ If you are slack in the day of
   distress,
   Your strength is limited.

11 ¶ Deliver those who are being
   taken away to death,
   And those who are staggering to
   slaughter, O hold *them* back.
12 If you say, "See, we did not know
   this,"
   Does He not consider *it* who
   weighs the hearts?
   And does He not know *it* who
   keeps your soul?
   And will He not render to man
   according to his work?

13 ¶ My son, eat honey, for it is
   good,
   Yes, the honey from the comb is
   sweet to your taste;
14 Know *that* wisdom is thus for
   your soul;
   If you find *it,* then there will be a
   future,
   And your hope will not be cut off.

15 ¶ Do not lie in wait, O wicked
   man, against the dwelling of the
   righteous;
   Do not destroy his resting place;
16 For a righteous man falls seven
   times, and rises again,
   But the wicked stumble in *time of*
   calamity.

17 ¶ Do not rejoice when your
   enemy falls,
   And do not let your heart be glad
   when he stumbles;
18 Lest the LORD see *it* and be displeased,
   And He turn away His anger from
   him.

19 ¶ Do not fret because of evildoers,
   Or be envious of the wicked;
20 For there will be no future for the
   evil man;
   The lamp of the wicked will be
   put out.

21 ¶ My son, fear the LORD and the
   king;
   Do not associate with those who
   are given to change;
22 For their calamity will rise suddenly,
   And who knows the ruin *that*
   comes from both of them?

23 ¶ These also are sayings of the
   wise.

[5] Or, *lookout*

To show partiality in judgment is not good.

24 He who says to the wicked, "You are righteous,"
Peoples will curse him, nations will abhor him;

25 But to those who rebuke the *wicked* will be delight,
And a good blessing will come upon them.

26 He kisses the lips
Who gives a right answer.

27 ¶ Prepare your work outside,
And make it ready for yourself in the field;
Afterwards, then, build your house.

28 ¶ Do not be a witness against your neighbor without cause,
And do not deceive with your lips.

29 Do not say, "Thus I shall do to him as he has done to me;
I will render to the man according to his work."

30 ¶ I passed by the field of the sluggard,
And by the vineyard of the man lacking sense;

31 And behold, it was completely overgrown with thistles,
Its surface was covered with nettles,
And its stone wall was broken down.

32 When I saw, I reflected upon it;
I looked, *and* received instruction.

33 "A little sleep, a little slumber,
A little folding of the hands to rest,"

34 Then your poverty will come *as* a robber,
And your want like an armed man.

CHAPTER 25

THESE also are proverbs of Solomon which the men of Hezekiah, king of Judah, transcribed.

2 ¶ It is the glory of God to conceal a matter,
But the glory of kings is to search out a matter.

3 *As* the heavens for height and the earth for depth,

So the heart of kings is unsearchable.

4 Take away the dross from the silver,
And there comes out a vessel for the smith;

5 Take away the wicked *from* before the king,
And his throne will be established in righteousness.

6 Do not claim honor in the presence of the king,
And do not stand in the place of great men;

7 For it is better that it be said to you, "Come up here,"
Than that you should be put lower in the presence of the prince,
Whom your eyes have seen.

8 ¶ Do not go out hastily to argue *your case;*
Otherwise, what will you do in the end,
When your neighbor puts you to shame?

9 Argue your case with your neighbor,
And do not reveal the secret of another,

10 Lest he who hears *it* reproach you,
And the evil report about you not pass away.

11 ¶ *Like* apples of gold in settings of silver
Is a word spoken in right circumstances.

12 *Like* an earring of gold and an ornament of fine gold
Is a wise reprover to a listening ear.

13 Like the cold of snow in the time of harvest
Is a faithful messenger to those who send him,
For he refreshes the soul of his masters.

14 *Like* clouds and wind without rain
Is a man who boasts of his gifts falsely.

15 By forbearance a ruler may be persuaded,
And a soft tongue breaks the bone.

16 Have you found honey? Eat *only* what you need,

Lest you have it in excess and vomit it.

17 Let your foot rarely be in your neighbor's house,
Lest he become weary of you and hate you.

18 *Like* a club and a sword and a sharp arrow
Is a man who bears false witness against his neighbor.

19 *Like* a bad tooth and an unsteady foot
Is confidence in a faithless man in time of trouble.

20 *Like* one who takes off a garment on a cold day, *or like* vinegar on soda,
Is he who sings songs to a troubled heart.

21 If your enemy is hungry, give him food to eat;
And if he is thirsty, give him water to drink;

22 For you will heap burning coals on his head,
And the LORD will reward you.

23 The north wind brings forth rain,
And a backbiting tongue, an angry countenance.

24 It is better to live in a corner of the roof
Than in a house shared with a contentious woman.

25 *Like* cold water to a weary soul,
So is good news from a distant land.

26 *Like* a trampled spring and a polluted well
Is a righteous man who gives way before the wicked.

27 It is not good to eat much honey,
Nor is it glory to search out one's own glory.

28 *Like* a city that is broken into *and* without walls
Is a man who has no control over his spirit.

CHAPTER 26

LIKE snow in summer and like rain in harvest,
So honor is not fitting for a fool.

2 Like a sparrow in *its* flitting, like a swallow in *its* flying,
So a curse without cause does not alight.

3 A whip is for the horse, a bridle for the donkey,
And a rod for the back of fools.

4 Do not answer a fool according to his folly,
Lest you also be like him.

5 Answer a fool as his folly *deserves*,
Lest he be wise in his own eyes.

6 He cuts off *his own* feet, *and* drinks violence
Who sends a message by the hand of a fool.

7 *Like* the legs *which* hang down from the lame,
So is a proverb in the mouth of fools.

8 Like one who binds a stone in a sling,
So is he who gives honor to a fool.

9 *Like* a thorn *which* falls into the hand of a drunkard,
So is a proverb in the mouth of fools.

10 *Like* an archer who wounds everyone,
So is he who hires a fool or who hires those who pass by.

11 Like a dog that returns to its vomit
Is a fool who repeats his folly.

12 Do you see a man wise in his own eyes?
There is more hope for a fool than for him.

13 The sluggard says, "There is a lion in the road!
A lion is in the open square!"

14 *As* the door turns on its hinges,
So *does* the sluggard on his bed.

15 The sluggard buries his hand in the dish;
He is weary of bringing it to his mouth again.

16 The sluggard is wiser in his own eyes
Than seven men who can give a discreet answer.

17 *Like* one who takes a dog by the ears
Is he who passes by *and* meddles with strife not belonging to him.

18 Like a madman who throws
Firebrands, arrows and death,

19 So is the man who deceives his neighbor,
And says, "Was I not joking?"

20 For lack of wood the fire goes out,
And where there is no whisperer, contention quiets down.

21 *Like* charcoal to hot embers and wood to fire,
So is a contentious man to kindle strife.
22 The words of a whisperer are like dainty morsels,
And they go down into the innermost parts of the body.
23 *Like* an earthen vessel overlaid with silver dross
Are burning lips and a wicked heart.
24 He who hates disguises *it* with his lips,
But he lays up deceit in his heart.
25 When he speaks graciously, do not believe him,
For there are seven abominations in his heart.
26 *Though his* hatred covers itself with guile,
His wickedness will be revealed before the assembly.
27 He who digs a pit will fall into it,
And he who rolls a stone, it will come back on him.
28 A lying tongue hates those it crushes,
And a flattering mouth works ruin.

CHAPTER 27

Do not boast about tomorrow,
For you do not know what a day may bring forth.
2 Let another praise you, and not your own mouth;
A stranger, and not your own lips.
3 A stone is heavy and the sand weighty,
But the provocation of a fool is heavier than both of them.
4 Wrath is fierce and anger is a flood,
But who can stand before jealousy?
5 Better is open rebuke
Than love that is concealed.
6 Faithful are the wounds of a friend,
But deceitful are the kisses of an enemy.
7 A sated man loathes honey,
But to a famished man any bitter thing is sweet.
8 Like a bird that wanders from her nest,
So is a man who wanders from his home.
9 Oil and perfume make the heart glad,
So a man's counsel is sweet to his friend.
10 Do not forsake your own friend or your father's friend,
And do not go to your brother's house in the day of your calamity;
Better is a neighbor who is near than a brother far away.
11 Be wise, my son, and make my heart glad,
That I may reply to him who reproaches me.
12 A prudent man sees evil *and* hides himself,
The naive proceed *and* pay the penalty.
13 Take his garment when he becomes surety for a stranger;
And for an adulterous woman hold him in pledge.
14 He who blesses his friend with a loud voice early in the morning,
It will be reckoned a curse to him.
15 A constant dripping on a day of steady rain
And a contentious woman are alike;
16 He who would restrain her restrains the wind,
And grasps oil with his right hand.
17 Iron sharpens iron,
So one man sharpens another.
18 He who tends the fig tree will eat its fruit;
And he who cares for his master will be honored.
19 As in water face *reflects* face,
So the heart of man *reflects* man.
20 Sheol and Abaddon are never satisfied,
Nor are the eyes of man ever satisfied.
21 The crucible is for silver and the furnace for gold,
And a man *is tested* by the praise accorded him.
22 Though you pound a fool in a mortar with a pestle along with crushed grain,
Yet his folly will not depart from him.
23 ¶ Know well the condition of your flocks,

And pay attention to your herds;
24 For riches are not forever,
Nor does a crown *endure* to all
generations.
25 *When* the grass disappears, the
new growth is seen,
And the herbs of the mountains
are gathered in,
26 The lambs *will be* for your clothing,
And the goats *will bring* the price
of a field,
27 And *there will be* goats' milk
enough for your food,
For the food of your household,
And sustenance for your maidens.

CHAPTER 28

THE wicked flee when no one is pursuing,
But the righteous are bold as a
lion.
2 By the transgression of a land
many are its princes,
But by a man of understanding
and knowledge, so it endures.
3 A poor man who oppresses the
lowly
Is *like* a driving rain which leaves
no food.
4 Those who forsake the law praise
the wicked,
But those who keep the law strive
with them.
5 Evil men do not understand justice,
But those who seek the LORD understand all things.
6 Better is the poor who walks in
his integrity,
Than he who is crooked though
he be rich.
7 He who keeps the law is a discerning son,
But he who is a companion of
gluttons humiliates his father.
8 He who increases his wealth by
interest and usury,
Gathers it for him who is gracious
to the poor.
9 He who turns away his ear from
listening to the law,
Even his prayer is an abomination.
10 He who leads the upright astray in
an evil way
Will himself fall into his own pit,

But the blameless will inherit
good.
11 The rich man is wise in his own
eyes,
But the poor who has understanding sees through him.
12 When the righteous triumph,
there is great glory,
But when the wicked rise, men
hide themselves.
13 He who conceals his transgressions will not prosper,
But he who confesses and forsakes *them* will find compassion.
14 How blessed is the man who fears
always,
But he who hardens his heart will
fall into calamity.
15 *Like* a roaring lion and a rushing
bear
Is a wicked ruler over a poor people.
16 A leader who is a great oppressor
lacks understanding,
But he who hates unjust gain will
prolong *his* days.
17 A man who is laden with the guilt
of human blood
Will be a fugitive until death; let
no one support him.
18 He who walks blamelessly will be
delivered,
But he who is crooked will fall all
at once.
19 He who tills his land will have
plenty of food,
But he who follows empty *pursuits* will have poverty in
plenty.
20 A faithful man will abound with
blessings,
But he who makes haste to be rich
will not go unpunished.
21 To show partiality is not good,
Because for a piece of bread a
man will transgress.
22 A man with an evil eye hastens
after wealth,
And does not know that want will
come upon him.
23 He who rebukes a man will afterward find *more* favor
Than he who flatters with the
tongue.
24 He who robs his father or his
mother,
And says, "It is not a transgression,"

Is the companion of a man who destroys.

25 An arrogant man stirs up strife,
But he who trusts in the LORD will prosper.

26 He who trusts in his own heart is a fool,
But he who walks wisely will be delivered.

27 He who gives to the poor will never want,
But he who shuts his eyes will have many curses.

28 When the wicked rise, men hide themselves;
But when they perish, the righteous increase.

CHAPTER 29

A MAN who hardens his neck after much reproof
Will suddenly be broken beyond remedy.

2 When the righteous increase, the people rejoice,
But when a wicked man rules, people groan.

3 A man who loves wisdom makes his father glad,
But he who keeps company with harlots wastes his wealth.

4 The king gives stability to the land by justice,
But a man who takes bribes overthrows it.

5 A man who flatters his neighbor
Is spreading a net for his steps.

6 By transgression an evil man is ensnared,
But the righteous sings and rejoices.

7 The righteous is concerned for the rights of the poor,
The wicked does not understand such concern.

8 Scorners set a city aflame,
But wise men turn away anger.

9 When a wise man has a controversy with a foolish man,
The foolish man either rages or laughs, and there is no rest.

10 Men of bloodshed hate the blameless,
But the upright are concerned for his life.

11 A fool always loses his temper,
But a wise man holds it back.

12 If a ruler pays attention to falsehood,
All his ministers become wicked.

13 The poor man and the oppressor have this in common:
The LORD gives light to the eyes of both.

14 If a king judges the poor with truth,
His throne will be established forever.

15 The rod and reproof give wisdom,
But a child who gets his own way brings shame to his mother.

16 When the wicked increase, transgression increases;
But the righteous will see their fall.

17 Correct your son, and he will give you comfort;
He will also delight your soul.

18 Where there is no vision, the people are unrestrained,
But happy is he who keeps the law.

19 A slave will not be instructed by words alone;
For though he understands, there will be no response.

20 Do you see a man who is hasty in his words?
There is more hope for a fool than for him.

21 He who pampers his slave from childhood
Will in the end find him to be a son.

22 An angry man stirs up strife,
And a hot-tempered man abounds in transgression.

23 A man's pride will bring him low,
But a humble spirit will obtain honor.

24 He who is a partner with a thief hates his own life;
He hears the oath but tells nothing.

25 The fear of man brings a snare,
But he who trusts in the LORD will be exalted.

26 Many seek the ruler's favor,
But justice for man comes from the LORD.

27 An unjust man is abominable to the righteous,
And he who is upright in the way is abominable to the wicked.

CHAPTER 30

THE words of Agur the son of Jakeh, the oracle.

¶ The man declares to Ithiel, to Ithiel and Ucal:

2 Surely I am more stupid than any man,
And I do not have the understanding of a man.

3 Neither have I learned wisdom,
Nor do I have the knowledge of the Holy One.

4 Who has ascended into heaven and descended?
Who has gathered the wind in His fists?
Who has wrapped the waters in His garment?
Who has established all the ends of the earth?
What is His name or His son's name?
Surely you know!

5 ¶ Every word of God is tested;
He is a shield to those who take refuge in Him.

6 Do not add to His words
Lest He reprove you, and you be proved a liar.

7 ¶ Two things I asked of Thee,
Do not refuse me before I die:

8 Keep deception and lies far from me,
Give me neither poverty nor riches;
Feed me with the food that is my portion,

9 Lest I be full and deny Thee and say, "Who is the LORD?"
Or lest I be in want and steal,
And profane the name of my God.

10 ¶ Do not slander a slave to his master,
Lest he curse you and you be found guilty.

11 ¶ There is a [6]kind of man who curses his father,
And does not bless his mother.

12 There is a kind who is pure in his own eyes,
Yet is not washed from his filthiness.

13 There is a kind—oh how lofty are his eyes!

And his eyelids are raised in arrogance.

14 There is a kind of man whose teeth are like swords,
And his jaw teeth like knives,
To devour the afflicted from the earth,
And the needy from among men.

15 ¶ The leech has two daughters, "Give," "Give."
There are three things that will not be satisfied,
Four that will not say, "Enough":

16 Sheol, and the barren womb,
Earth that is never satisfied with water,
And fire that never says, "Enough."

17 The eye that mocks a father,
And scorns a mother,
The ravens of the valley will pick it out,
And the young eagles will eat it.

18 ¶ There are three things which are too wonderful for me,
Four which I do not understand:

19 The way of an eagle in the sky,
The way of a serpent on a rock,
The way of a ship in the middle of the sea,
And the way of a man with a maid.

20 This is the way of an adulterous woman:
She eats and wipes her mouth,
And says, "I have done no wrong."

21 ¶ Under three things the earth quakes,
And under four, it cannot bear up:

22 Under a slave when he becomes king,
And a fool when he is satisfied with food,

23 Under an unloved woman when she gets a husband,
And a maidservant when she supplants her mistress.

24 ¶ Four things are small on the earth,
But they are exceedingly wise:

25 The ants are not a strong folk,
But they prepare their food in the summer;

---

[6] Or, generation; so through v. 14

26 The badgers are not mighty folk,
   Yet they make their houses in the
      rocks;
27 The locusts have no king,
   Yet all of them go out in ranks;
28 The lizard you may grasp with the
      hands,
   Yet it is in kings' palaces.

29 ¶ There are three things which
      are stately in *their* march,
   Even four which are stately when
      they walk:
30 The lion *which* is mighty among
      beasts
   And does not retreat before any,
31 The strutting cock, the male goat
      also,
   And a king *when his* army is with
      him.

32 ¶ If you have been foolish in ex-
      alting yourself
   Or if you have plotted *evil, put
      your* hand on your mouth.
33 For the churning of milk produces
      butter,
   And pressing the nose brings forth
      blood;
   So the churning of anger pro-
      duces strife.

CHAPTER 31

THE words of King Lemuel, the ora-
cle which his mother taught him.
2 ¶ What, O my son?
   And what, O son of my womb?
   And what, O son of my vows?
3 Do not give your strength to
      women,
   Or your ways to that which de-
      stroys kings.
4 It is not for kings, O Lemuel,
   It is not for kings to drink wine,
   Or for rulers to desire strong
      drink.
5 Lest they drink and forget what is
      decreed,
   And pervert the rights of all the
      afflicted.
6 Give strong drink to him who is
      perishing,
   And wine to him whose life is
      bitter.
7 Let him drink and forget his pov-
      erty,

And remember his trouble no
      more.
8 Open your mouth for the dumb,
   For the rights of all the unfortu-
      nate.
9 Open your mouth, judge right-
      eously,
   And defend the rights of the af-
      flicted and needy.

10 ¶ An excellent wife, who can
      find?
   For her worth is far above jewels.
11 The heart of her husband trusts in
      her,
   And he will have no lack of gain.
12 She does him good and not evil
   All the days of her life.
13 She looks for wool and flax,
   And works with her hands in de-
      light.
14 She is like merchant ships;
   She brings her food from afar.
15 She rises also while it is still night,
   And gives food to her household,
   And portions to her maidens.
16 She considers a field and buys it;
   From her earnings she plants a
      vineyard.
17 She girds herself with strength,
   And makes her arms strong.
18 She senses that her gain is good;
   Her lamp does not go out at night.
19 She stretches out her hands to the
      distaff,
   And her hands grasp the spindle.
20 She extends her hand to the poor;
   And she stretches out her hands
      to the needy.
21 She is not afraid of the snow for
      her household,
   For all her household are clothed
      with scarlet.
22 She makes coverings for herself;
   Her clothing is fine linen and pur-
      ple.
23 Her husband is known in the
      gates,
   When he sits among the elders of
      the land.
24 She makes linen garments and
      sells *them,*
   And supplies belts to the trades-
      men.
25 Strength and dignity are her
      clothing,
   And she smiles at the future.
26 She opens her mouth in wisdom,

And the teaching of kindness is on
her tongue.
27 She looks well to the ways of her
household,
And does not eat the bread of
idleness.
28 Her children rise up and bless her;
Her husband *also,* and he praises
her, *saying:*

29"Many daughters have done nobly,
But you excel them all."
30 Charm is deceitful and beauty is
vain,
But a woman who fears the Lord,
she shall be praised.
31 Give her the product of her hands,
And let her works praise her in
the gates.

THE BOOK OF

ECCLESIASTES

THE words of the Preacher, the son
of David, king in Jerusalem.
2 "¹Vanity of vanities," says the
Preacher,
"¹Vanity of vanities! All is vanity."

3 ¶ What advantage does man have
in all his work
Which he does under the sun?
4 A generation goes and a generation comes,
But the earth remains forever.
5 Also, the sun rises and the sun
sets;
And hastening to its place it rises
there *again.*
6 Blowing toward the south,
Then turning toward the north,
The wind continues swirling
along;
And on its circular courses the
wind returns.
7 All the rivers flow into the sea,
Yet the sea is not full.
To the place where the rivers
flow,
There they flow again.
8 All things are wearisome;
Man is not able to tell *it.*
The eye is not satisfied with seeing,
Nor is the ear filled with hearing.
9 That which has been is that which
will be,
And that which has been done is
that which will be done.
So, there is nothing new under
the sun.

10 Is there anything of which one
might say,
"See this, it is new"?
Already it has existed for ages
Which were before us.
11 There is no remembrance of earlier things;
And also of the later things which
will occur,
There will be for them no remembrance
Among those who will come later
still.

12 ¶ I, the Preacher, have been king
over Israel in Jerusalem.
13 And I set my mind to seek and
explore by wisdom concerning all that
has been done under heaven. *It* is a
grievous task *which* God has given to
the sons of men to be afflicted with.
14 I have seen all the works which
have been done under the sun, and
behold, all is vanity and striving after
wind.
15 What is crooked cannot be
straightened, and what is lacking cannot be counted.
16 I said to myself, "Behold, I have
magnified and increased wisdom more
than all who were over Jerusalem
before me; and my mind has observed
a wealth of wisdom and knowledge."
17 And I set my mind to know wisdom and to know madness and folly; I
realized that this also is striving after
wind.
18 Because in much wisdom there is
much grief, and increasing knowledge
results in increasing pain.

¹ Or, *Futility of futilities*

CHAPTER 2

I SAID to myself, "Come now, I will test you with pleasure. So enjoy yourself." And behold, it too was futility.

2 I said of laughter, "It is madness," and of pleasure, "What does it accomplish?"

3 I explored with my mind *how* to stimulate my body with wine while my mind was guiding *me* wisely, and how to take hold of folly, until I could see what good there is for the sons of men to do under heaven the few years of their lives.

4 I enlarged my works: I built houses for myself, I planted vineyards for myself;

5 I made gardens and parks for myself, and I planted in them all kinds of fruit trees;

6 I made ponds of water for myself from which to irrigate a forest of growing trees.

7 I bought male and female slaves, and I had homeborn slaves. Also I possessed flocks and herds larger than all who preceded me in Jerusalem.

8 Also, I collected for myself silver and gold, and the treasure of kings and provinces. I provided for myself male and female singers and the pleasures of men—many concubines.

9 Then I became great and increased more than all who preceded me in Jerusalem. My wisdom also stood by me.

10 And all that my eyes desired I did not refuse them. I did not withhold my heart from any pleasure, for my heart was pleased because of all my labor and this was my reward for all my labor.

11 Thus I considered all my activities which my hands had done and the labor which I had exerted, and behold all was ²vanity and striving after wind and there was no profit under the sun.

12 ¶ So I turned to consider wisdom, madness and folly, for what *will* the man *do* who will come after the king *except* what has already been done?

13 And I saw that wisdom excels folly as light excels darkness.

14 The wise man's eyes are in his head, but the fool walks in darkness. And yet I know that one fate befalls them both.

² Or, *futility,* and so throughout this context

15 Then I said to myself, "As is the fate of the fool, it will also befall me. Why then have I been extremely wise?" So I said to myself, "This too is vanity."

16 For there is no lasting remembrance of the wise man *as* with the fool, inasmuch as *in* the coming days all will be forgotten. And how the wise man and the fool alike die!

17 So I hated life, for the work which had been done under the sun was grievous to me; because everything is futility and striving after wind.

18 ¶ Thus I hated all the fruit of my labor for which I had labored under the sun, for I must leave it to the man who will come after me.

19 And who knows whether he will be a wise man or a fool? Yet he will have control over all the fruit of my labor for which I have labored by acting wisely under the sun. This too is vanity.

20 Therefore I completely despaired of all the fruit of my labor for which I had labored under the sun.

21 When there is a man who has labored with wisdom, knowledge and skill, then he gives his legacy to one who has not labored with them. This too is vanity and a great evil.

22 For what does a man get in all his labor and in his striving with which he labors under the sun?

23 Because all his days his task is painful and grievous; even at night his mind does not rest. This too is vanity.

24 ¶ There is nothing better for a man *than* to eat and drink and tell himself that his labor is good. This also I have seen, that it is from the hand of God.

25 For who can eat and who can have enjoyment without Him?

26 For to a person who is good in His sight He has given wisdom and knowledge and joy, while to the sinner He has given the task of gathering and collecting so that he may give to one who is good in God's sight. This too is vanity and striving after wind.

CHAPTER 3

THERE is an appointed time for everything. And there is a time for every event under heaven—

2 A time to give birth, and a time
   to die;
   A time to plant, and a time to
   uproot what is planted.
3 A time to kill, and a time to heal;
   A time to tear down, and a time
   to build up.
4 A time to weep, and a time to
   laugh;
   A time to mourn, and a time to
   dance.
5 A time to throw stones, and a
   time to gather stones;
   A time to embrace, and a time to
   shun embracing.
6 A time to search, and a time to
   give up as lost;
   A time to keep, and a time to
   throw away.
7 A time to tear apart, and a time
   to sew together;
   A time to be silent, and a time to
   speak.
8 A time to love, and a time to
   hate;
   A time for war, and a time for
   peace.

9 ¶ What profit is there to the
worker from that in which he toils?
10 I have seen the task which God
has given the sons of men with which
to occupy themselves.
11 He has made everything ³appro-
priate in its time. He has also set
eternity in their heart, yet so that man
will not find out the work which God
has done from the beginning even to
the end.
12 ¶ I know that there is nothing
better for them than to rejoice and to
do good in one's lifetime;
13 moreover, that every man who
eats and drinks sees good in all his
labor—it is the gift of God.
14 I know that everything God does
will remain forever; there is nothing to
add to it and there is nothing to take
from it, for God has so worked that
men should fear Him.
15 That which is has been already,
and that which will be has already
been, for God seeks what has passed
by.
16 Furthermore, I have seen under
the sun that in the place of justice
there is wickedness, and in the place
of righteousness there is wickedness.

³ Lit., *beautiful*

17 I said to myself, "God will judge
both the righteous man and the
wicked man," for a time for every
matter and for every deed is there.
18 I said to myself concerning the
sons of men, "God has surely tested
them in order for them to see that they
are but beasts."
19 For the fate of the sons of men
and the fate of beasts is the same. As
one dies so dies the other; indeed, they
all have the same breath and there is
no advantage for man over beast, for
all is vanity.
20 All go to the same place. All came
from the dust and all return to the
dust.
21 Who knows that the breath of
man ascends upward and the breath of
the beast descends downward to the
earth?
22 And I have seen that nothing is
better than that man should be happy
in his activities, for that is his lot. For
who will bring him to see what will
occur after him?

CHAPTER 4

THEN I looked again at all the acts of
oppression which were being done
under the sun. And behold I *saw* the
tears of the oppressed and *that* they
had no one to comfort *them;* and on
the side of their oppressors was power,
but they had no one to comfort *them*.
2 So I congratulated the dead who
are already dead more than the living
who are still living.
3 But better *off* than both of them is
the one who has never existed, who
has never seen the evil activity that is
done under the sun.
4 ¶ And I have seen that every labor and every skill which is done is *the
result of* rivalry between a man and
his neighbor. This too is vanity and
striving after wind.
5 The fool folds his hands and consumes his own flesh.
6 One hand full of rest is better than
two fists full of labor and striving after
wind.
7 ¶ Then I looked again at vanity
under the sun.
8 There was a certain man without
a dependent, having neither a son nor
a brother, yet there was no end to all
his labor. Indeed, his eyes were not

satisfied with riches *and he never asked,* "And for whom am I laboring and depriving myself of pleasure?" This too is vanity and it is a grievous task.

9 ¶ Two are better than one because they have a good return for their labor.

10 For if either of them falls, the one will lift up his companion. But woe to the one who falls when there is not another to lift him up.

11 Furthermore, if two lie down together they keep warm, but how can one be warm *alone?*

12 And if one can overpower him who is alone, two can resist him. A cord of three *strands* is not quickly torn apart.

13 ¶ A poor, yet wise lad is better than an old and foolish king who no longer knows *how* to receive instruction.

14 For he has come out of prison to become king, even though he was born poor in his kingdom.

15 I have seen all the living under the sun throng to the side of the second lad who replaces him.

16 There is no end to all the people, to all who were before them, and even the ones who will come later will not be happy with him, for this too is vanity and striving after wind.

CHAPTER 5

GUARD your steps as you go to the house of God, and draw near to listen rather than to offer the sacrifice of fools; for they do not know they are doing evil.

2 Do not be hasty in word or impulsive in thought to bring up a matter in the presence of God. For God is in heaven and you are on the earth; therefore let your words be few.

3 For the dream comes through much effort, and the voice of a fool through many words.

4 When you make a vow to God, do not be late in paying it, for *He takes* no delight in fools. Pay what you vow!

5 It is better that you should not vow than that you should vow and not pay.

6 Do not let your speech cause you to sin and do not say in the presence of the messenger *of* God that it was a mistake. Why should God be angry on account of your voice and destroy the work of your hands?

7 For in many dreams and in many words there is emptiness. Rather, fear God.

8 ¶ If you see oppression of the poor and denial of justice and righteousness in the province, do not be shocked at the sight, for one official watches over another official, and there are higher officials over them.

9 After all, a king who cultivates the field is an advantage to the land.

10 ¶ He who loves money will not be satisfied with money, nor he who loves abundance *with its* income. This too is vanity.

11 When good things increase, those who consume them increase. So what is the advantage to their owners except to look on?

12 The sleep of the working man is pleasant, whether he eats little or much. But the full stomach of the rich man does not allow him to sleep.

13 ¶ There is a grievous evil *which* I have seen under the sun: riches being hoarded by their owner to his hurt.

14 When those riches were lost through a bad investment and he had fathered a son, then there was nothing to support him.

15 As he had come naked from his mother's womb, so will he return as he came. He will take nothing from the fruit of his labor that he can carry in his hand.

16 And this also is a grievous evil— exactly as a man is born, thus will he die. So, what is the advantage to him who toils for the wind?

17 Throughout his life *he* also eats in darkness with great vexation, sickness and anger.

18 ¶ Here is what I have seen to be good and fitting: to eat, to drink and enjoy oneself in all one's labor in which he toils under the sun *during* the few years of his life which God has given him; for this is his reward.

19 Furthermore, as for every man to whom God has given riches and wealth, He has also empowered him to eat from them and to receive his reward and rejoice in his labor; this is the gift of God.

20 For he will not often consider the years of his life, because God keeps

him occupied with the gladness of his heart.

CHAPTER 6

THERE is an evil which I have seen under the sun and it is prevalent among men—

2 a man to whom God has given riches and wealth and honor so that his soul lacks nothing of all that he desires, but God has not empowered him to eat from them, for a foreigner enjoys them. This is vanity and a severe affliction.

3 If a man fathers a hundred *children* and lives many years, however many they be, but his soul is not satisfied with good things, and he does not even have a *proper* burial, *then* I say, "Better the miscarriage than he,

4 for it comes in futility and goes into obscurity; and its name is covered in obscurity.

5 "It never sees the sun and it never knows *anything;* it is better off than he.

6 "Even if the *other* man lives a thousand years twice and does not enjoy good things—do not all go to one place?"

7 ¶ All a man's labor is for his mouth and yet the appetite is not satisfied.

8 For what advantage does the wise man have over the fool? What *advantage* does the poor man have, knowing *how* to walk before the living?

9 What the eyes see is better than what the soul desires. This too is futility and a striving after wind.

10 ¶ Whatever exists has already been named, and it is known what man is; for he cannot dispute with him who is stronger than he is.

11 For there are many words which increase futility. What *then* is the advantage to a man?

12 For who knows what is good for a man during *his* lifetime, *during* the few years of his futile life? He will spend them like a shadow. For who can tell a man what will be after him under the sun?

CHAPTER 7

A GOOD name is better than a good ointment,
And the day of *one's* death is better than the day of one's birth.

2 It is better to go to a house of mourning
Than to go to a house of feasting,
Because that is the end of every man,
And the living takes *it* to heart.

3 Sorrow is better than laughter,
For when a face is sad a heart may be happy.

4 The mind of the wise is in the house of mourning,
While the mind of fools is in the house of pleasure.

5 It is better to listen to the rebuke of a wise man
Than for one to listen to the song of fools.

6 For as the crackling of thorn bushes under a pot,
So is the laughter of the fool,
And this too is futility.

7 For oppression makes a wise man mad,
And a bribe corrupts the heart.

8 The end of a matter is better than its beginning;
Patience of spirit is better than haughtiness of spirit.

9 Do not be eager in your heart to be angry,
For anger resides in the bosom of fools.

10 Do not say, "Why is it that the former days were better than these?"
For it is not from wisdom that you ask about this.

11 Wisdom along with an inheritance is good
And an advantage to those who see the sun.

12 For wisdom is protection *just as* money is protection.
But the advantage of knowledge is that wisdom preserves the lives of its possessors.

13 Consider the work of God,
For who is able to straighten what He has bent?

14 In the day of prosperity be happy,
But in the day of adversity consider—
God has made the one as well as the other

So that man may not discover anything *that will be* after him.

15 ¶ I have seen everything during my lifetime of futility; there is a righteous man who perishes in his righteousness, and there is a wicked man who prolongs *his life* in his wickedness.

16 Do not be excessively righteous, and do not be overly wise. Why should you ruin yourself?

17 Do not be excessively wicked, and do not be a fool. Why should you die before your time?

18 It is good that you grasp one thing, and also not let go of the other; for the one who fears God comes forth with both of them.

19 ¶ Wisdom strengthens a wise man more than ten rulers who are in a city.

20 Indeed, there is not a righteous man on earth who *continually* does good and who never sins.

21 Also, do not take seriously all words which are spoken, lest you hear your servant cursing you.

22 For you also have realized that you likewise have many times cursed others.

23 ¶ I tested all this with wisdom, *and* I said, "I will be wise," but it was far from me.

24 What has been is remote and exceedingly mysterious. Who can discover it?

25 I directed my mind to know, to investigate, and to seek wisdom and an explanation, and to know the evil of folly and the foolishness of madness.

26 And I discovered more bitter than death the woman whose heart is snares and nets, whose hands are chains. One who is pleasing to God will escape from her, but the sinner will be captured by her.

27 ¶"Behold, I have discovered this," says the Preacher, "*adding* one thing to another to find an explanation,

28 which I am still seeking but have not found. I have found one man among a thousand, but I have not found a woman among all these.

29"Behold, I have found only this, that God made men upright, but they have sought out many devices."

CHAPTER 8

WHO is like the wise man and who knows the interpretation of a matter? A man's wisdom illumines him and causes his stern face to beam.

2 ¶ I say, "Keep the command of the king because of the oath before God.

3"Do not be in a hurry to leave him. Do not join in an evil matter, for he will do whatever he pleases."

4 Since the word of the king is authoritative, who will say to him, "What are you doing?"

5 ¶ He who keeps a *royal* command experiences no trouble, for a wise heart knows the proper time and procedure.

6 For there is a proper time and procedure for every delight, when a man's trouble is heavy upon him.

7 If no one knows what will happen, who can tell him when it will happen?

8 No man has authority to restrain the wind with the wind, or authority over the day of death; and there is no discharge in the time of war, and evil will not deliver those who practice it.

9 All this I have seen and applied my mind to every deed that has been done under the sun wherein a man has exercised authority over *another* man to his hurt.

10 ¶ So then, I have seen the wicked buried, those who used to go in and out from the holy place, and they are *soon* forgotten in the city where they did thus. This too is futility.

11 Because the sentence against an evil deed is not executed quickly, therefore the hearts of the sons of men among them are given fully to do evil.

12 Although a sinner does evil a hundred *times* and may lengthen his *life*, still I know that it will be well for those who fear God, who fear Him openly.

13 But it will not be well for the evil man and he will not lengthen his days like a shadow, because he does not fear God.

14 There is futility which is done on the earth, that is, there are righteous men to whom it happens according to the deeds of the wicked. On the other hand, there are evil men to whom it

happens according to the deeds of the righteous. I say that this too is futility.

15 So I commended pleasure, for there is nothing good for a man under the sun except to eat and to drink and to be merry, and this will stand by him in his toils *throughout* the days of his life which God has given him under the sun.

16 ¶ When I gave my heart to know wisdom and to see the task which has been done on the earth (even though one should never sleep day or night),

17 and I saw every work of God, *I concluded* that man cannot discover the work which has been done under the sun. Even though man should seek laboriously, he will not discover; and though the wise man should say, "I know," he cannot discover.

CHAPTER 9

FOR I have taken all this to my heart and explain it that righteous men, wise men, and their deeds are in the hand of God. Man does not know whether *it will be* love or hatred; anything awaits him.

2 ¶ It is the same for all. There is one fate for the righteous and for the wicked; for the good, for the clean, and for the unclean; for the man who offers a sacrifice and for the one who does not sacrifice. As the good man is, so is the sinner; as the swearer is, so is the one who is afraid to swear.

3 This is an evil in all that is done under the sun, that there is one fate for all men. Furthermore, the hearts of the sons of men are full of evil, and insanity is in their hearts throughout their lives. Afterwards they go to the dead.

4 For whoever is joined with all the living, there is hope; surely a live dog is better than a dead lion.

5 For the living know they will die; but the dead do not know anything, nor have they any longer a reward, for their memory is forgotten.

6 Indeed their love, their hate, and their zeal have already perished, and they will no longer have a share in all that is done under the sun.

7 ¶ Go *then*, eat your bread in happiness, and drink your wine with a cheerful heart; for God has already approved your works.

8 Let your clothes be white all the time, and let not oil be lacking on your head.

9 Enjoy life with the woman whom you love all the days of your fleeting life which He has given to you under the sun; for this is your reward in life, and in your toil in which you have labored under the sun.

10 ¶ Whatever your hand finds to do, verily, do *it* with all your might; for there is no activity or planning or wisdom in Sheol where you are going.

11 I again saw under the sun that the race is not to the swift, and the battle is not to the warriors, and neither is bread to the wise, nor wealth to the discerning, nor favor to men of ability; for time and chance overtake them all.

12 Moreover, man does not know his time: like fish caught in a treacherous net, and birds trapped in a snare, so the sons of men are ensnared at an evil time when it suddenly falls on them.

13 ¶ Also this I came to see as wisdom under the sun, and it impressed me.

14 There was a small city with few men in it and a great king came to it, surrounded it, and constructed large siegeworks against it.

15 But there was found in it a poor wise man and he delivered the city by his wisdom. Yet no one remembered that poor man.

16 So I said, "Wisdom is better than strength." But the wisdom of the poor man is despised and his words are not heeded.

17 The words of the wise heard in quietness are *better* than the shouting of a ruler among fools.

18 Wisdom is better than weapons of war, but one sinner destroys much good.

CHAPTER 10

DEAD flies make a perfumer's oil stink, so a little foolishness is weightier than wisdom *and* honor.

2 A wise man's heart *directs him* toward the right, but the foolish man's heart *directs him* toward the left.

3 Even when the fool walks along the road his sense is lacking, and he demonstrates to everyone *that* he is a fool.

4 If the ruler's temper rises against you, do not abandon your position, because composure allays great offenses.

5 ¶ There is an evil I have seen under the sun, like an error which goes forth from the ruler—

6 folly is set in many exalted places while rich men sit in humble places.

7 I have seen slaves *riding* on horses and princes walking like slaves on the land.

8 ¶ He who digs a pit may fall into it, and a serpent may bite him who breaks through a wall.

9 He who quarries stones may be hurt by them, and he who splits logs may be endangered by them.

10 If the axe is dull and he does not sharpen *its* edge, then he must exert more strength. Wisdom has the advantage of giving success.

11 If the serpent bites before being charmed, there is no profit for the charmer.

12 Words from the mouth of a wise man are gracious, while the lips of a fool consume him;

13 the beginning of his talking is folly, and the end of it is wicked madness.

14 Yet the fool multiplies words. No man knows what will happen, and who can tell him what will come after him?

15 The toil of a fool *so* wearies him that he does not *even* know how to go to a city.

16 Woe to you, O land, whose king is a lad and whose princes feast in the morning.

17 Blessed are you, O land, whose king is of nobility and whose princes eat at the appropriate time—for strength, and not for drunkenness.

18 Through indolence the rafters sag, and through slackness the house leaks.

19 *Men* prepare a meal for enjoyment, and wine makes life merry, and money is the answer to everything.

20 Furthermore, in your bedchamber do not curse a king, and in your sleeping rooms do not curse a rich man, for a bird of the heavens will carry the sound, and the winged creature will make the matter known.

CHAPTER 11

CAST your bread on the surface of the waters, for you will find it after many days.

2 Divide your portion to seven, or even to eight, for you do not know what misfortune may occur on the earth.

3 If the clouds are full, they pour out rain upon the earth; and whether a tree falls toward the south or toward the north, wherever the tree falls, there it lies.

4 He who watches the wind will not sow and he who looks at the clouds will not reap.

5 Just as you do not know the path of the wind and how bones *are formed* in the womb of the pregnant woman, so you do not know the activity of God who makes all things.

6 Sow your seed in the morning, and do not be idle in the evening, for you do not know whether morning or evening sowing will succeed, or whether both of them alike will be good.

7 ¶ The light is pleasant, and *it is* good for the eyes to see the sun.

8 Indeed, if a man should live many years, let him rejoice in them all, and let him remember the days of darkness, for they shall be many. Everything that is to come *will be* futility.

9 Rejoice, young man, during your childhood, and let your heart be pleasant during the days of young manhood. And follow the impulses of your heart and the desires of your eyes. Yet know that God will bring you to judgment for all these things.

10 So, remove vexation from your heart and put away pain from your body, because childhood and the prime of life are fleeting.

CHAPTER 12

REMEMBER also your Creator in the days of your youth, before the evil days come and the years draw near when you will say, "I have no delight in them";

2 before the sun, the light, the moon, and the stars are darkened, and clouds return after the rain;

3 in the day that the watchmen of

the house tremble, and mighty men stoop, the grinding ones stand idle because they are few, and those who look through windows grow dim;

4 and the doors on the street are shut as the sound of the grinding mill is low, and one will arise at the sound of the bird, and all the daughters of song will sing softly.

5 Furthermore, men are afraid of a high place and of terrors on the road; the almond tree blossoms, the grasshopper drags himself along, and the caperberry is ineffective. For man goes to his eternal home while mourners go about in the street.

6 *Remember Him* before the silver cord is broken and the golden bowl is crushed, the pitcher by the well is shattered and the wheel at the cistern is crushed;

7 then the dust will return to the earth as it was, and the spirit will return to God who gave it.

8"Vanity of vanities," says the Preacher, "all is vanity!"

9 ¶ In addition to being a wise man, the Preacher also taught the people knowledge; and he pondered, searched out and arranged many proverbs.

10 The Preacher sought to find delightful words and to write words of truth correctly.

11 ¶ The words of wise men are like goads, and masters of *these* collections are like well-driven nails; they are given by one Shepherd.

12 But beyond this, my son, be warned: the writing of many books is endless, and excessive devotion *to books* is wearying to the body.

13 ¶ The conclusion, when all has been heard, *is:* fear God and keep His commandments, because this *applies to* every person.

14 For God will bring every act to judgment, everything which is hidden, whether it is good or evil.

THE SONG OF

SOLOMON

T HE [1]Song of Songs, which is Solomon's.

2 ¶"[2]May he kiss me with the kisses of his mouth!
For your love is better than wine.
3"Your oils have a pleasing fragrance,
Your name is *like* purified oil;
Therefore the maidens love you.
4"Draw me after you *and* let us run *together!*
The king has brought me into his chambers."

¶"[3]We will rejoice in you and be glad;
We will extol your love more than wine.
Rightly do they love you."

5 ¶"[4]I am black but lovely,
O daughters of Jerusalem,

Like the tents of Kedar,
Like the curtains of Solomon.
6"Do not stare at me because I am swarthy,
For the sun has burned me.
My mother's sons were angry with me;
They made me caretaker of the vineyards,
But I have not taken care of my own vineyard.
7"Tell me, O you whom my soul loves,
Where do you pasture *your flock,*
Where do you make *it* lie down at noon?
For why should I be like one who veils herself
Beside the flocks of your companions?"

8 ¶"[5]If you yourself do not know,
Most beautiful among women,
Go forth on the trail of the flock,

[1] Or, *Best of the Songs*   [2] BRIDE   [3] CHORUS
[4] BRIDE   [5] BRIDEGROOM

And pasture your young goats
By the tents of the shepherds.

9 ¶"To me, my darling, you are like
My mare among the chariots of
Pharaoh.

10"Your cheeks are lovely with ornaments,
Your neck with strings of beads."

11 ¶"⁶We will make for you ornaments of gold
With beads of silver."

12 ¶"⁴While the king was at his table,
My perfume gave forth its fragrance.

13"My beloved is to me a pouch of
myrrh
Which lies all night between my
breasts.

14"My beloved is to me a cluster of
henna blossoms
In the vineyards of Engedi."

15 ¶"⁵How beautiful you are, my dar-
ling,
How beautiful you are!
Your eyes are *like* doves."

16 ¶"⁴How handsome you are, my
beloved,
And so pleasant!
Indeed, our couch is luxuriant!

17"The beams of our houses are cedars,
Our rafters, cypresses.

CHAPTER 2

"⁴I AM the rose of Sharon,
The lily of the valleys."

2 ¶"⁵Like a lily among the thorns,
So is my darling among the maidens."

3 ¶"⁷Like an apple tree among the
trees of the forest,
So is my beloved among the
young men.
In his shade I took great delight
and sat down,
And his fruit was sweet to my
taste.

4"He has brought me to *his* banquet
hall,
And his banner over me is love.

5"Sustain me with raisin cakes,
Refresh me with apples,
Because I am lovesick.

6"*Let* his left hand be under my
head
And his right hand embrace me."

7 ¶"⁸I adjure you, O daughters of
Jerusalem,
By the gazelles or by the hinds of
the field,
That you will not arouse or
awaken *my* love,
Until she pleases."

8 ¶"⁷Listen! My beloved!
Behold, he is coming,
Climbing on the mountains,
Leaping on the hills!

9"My beloved is like a gazelle or a
young stag.
Behold, he is standing behind our
wall,
He is looking through the windows,
He is peering through the lattice.

10 ¶"My beloved responded and said
to me,
'Arise, my darling, my beautiful
one,
And come along.

11 'For behold, the winter is past,
The rain is over *and* gone.

12 'The flowers have *already* appeared in the land;
The time has arrived for pruning
the vines,
And the voice of the turtledove
has been heard in our land.

13 'The fig tree has ripened its figs,
And the vines in blossom have
given forth *their* fragrance.
Arise, my darling, my beautiful
one,
And come along!' "

14"O my dove, in the clefts of the
rock,
In the secret place of the steep
pathway,
Let me see your form,
Let me hear your voice;
For your voice is sweet,
And your form is lovely."

15 ¶"Catch the foxes for us,
The little foxes that are ruining
the vineyards,

⁴ BRIDE   ⁵ BRIDEGROOM   ⁶ CHORUS   ⁷ BRIDE   ⁷ BRIDE   ⁸ BRIDEGROOM

While our vineyards are in blossom."

16"My beloved is mine, and I am his;
He pastures *his flock* among the lilies.

17"Until the cool of the day when the shadows flee away,
Turn, my beloved, and be like a gazelle
Or a young stag on the mountains of Bether."

CHAPTER 3

"9On my bed night after night I sought him
Whom my soul loves;
I sought him but did not find him.

2 'I must arise now and go about the city;
In the streets and in the squares
I must seek him whom my soul loves.'
I sought him but did not find him.

3"The watchmen who make the rounds in the city found me,
And I said, 'Have you seen him whom my soul loves?'

4"Scarcely had I left them
When I found him whom my soul loves;
I held on to him and would not let him go,
Until I had brought him to my mother's house,
And into the room of her who conceived me."

5 ¶"10I adjure you, O daughters of Jerusalem,
By the gazelles or by the hinds of the field,
That you will not arouse or awaken *my* love,
Until she pleases."

6 ¶"11What is this coming up from the wilderness
Like columns of smoke,
Perfumed with myrrh and frankincense,
With all scented powders of the merchant?

7"Behold, it is the *traveling* couch of Solomon;
Sixty mighty men around it,
Of the mighty men of Israel.

8"All of them are wielders of the sword,
Expert in war;
Each man has his sword at his side,
Guarding against the terrors of the night.

9"King Solomon has made for himself a sedan chair
From the timber of Lebanon.

10"He made its posts of silver,
Its back of gold
And its seat of purple fabric,
With its interior lovingly fitted out
By the daughters of Jerusalem.

11"Go forth, O daughters of Zion,
And gaze on King Solomon with the crown
With which his mother has crowned him
On the day of his wedding,
And on the day of his gladness of heart."

CHAPTER 4

"10How beautiful you are, my darling,
How beautiful you are!
Your eyes are *like* doves behind your veil;
Your hair is like a flock of goats
That have descended from Mount Gilead.

2"Your teeth are like a flock of *newly* shorn ewes
Which have come up from *their* washing,
All of which bear twins,
And not one among them has lost her young.

3"Your lips are like a scarlet thread,
And your mouth is lovely.
Your temples are like a slice of a pomegranate
Behind your veil.

4"Your neck is like the tower of David
Built with rows of stones,
On which are hung a thousand shields,
All the round shields of the mighty men.

5"Your two breasts are like two fawns,
Twins of a gazelle,
Which feed among the lilies.

⁹ BRIDE   ¹⁰ BRIDEGROOM   ¹¹ CHORUS   ¹⁰ BRIDEGROOM

6"Until the cool of the day
When the shadows flee away,
I will go my way to the mountain
of myrrh
And to the hill of frankincense.

7 ¶"You are altogether beautiful,
my darling,
And there is no blemish in you.
8"*Come* with me from Lebanon, *my*
bride,
May you come with me from
Lebanon.
Journey down from the summit of
Amana,
From the summit of Senir and
Hermon,
From the dens of lions,
From the mountains of leopards.
9"You have made my heart beat
faster, my sister, *my* bride;
You have made my heart beat
faster with a single *glance* of
your eyes,
With a single strand of your necklace.
10"How beautiful is your love, my
sister, *my* bride!
How much better is your love
than wine,
And the fragrance of your oils
Than all *kinds* of spices!
11"Your lips, *my* bride, drip honey;
Honey and milk are under your
tongue,
And the fragrance of your garments is like the fragrance of
Lebanon.
12"A garden locked is my sister, *my*
bride,
A rock garden locked, a spring
sealed up.
13"Your shoots are an orchard of
pomegranates
With choice fruits, henna with
nard plants,
14 Nard and saffron, calamus and
cinnamon,
With all the trees of frankincense,
Myrrh and aloes, along with all
the finest spices.
15"*You are* a garden spring,
A well of fresh water,
And streams *flowing* from Lebanon."

16 ¶"[12]Awake, O north *wind,*
And come, *wind of* the south;

Make my garden breathe out *fra-
grance,*
Let its spices be wafted abroad.
May my beloved come into his
garden
And eat its choice fruits!"

CHAPTER 5

"[13]I HAVE come into my garden, my
sister, *my* bride;
I have gathered my myrrh along
with my balsam.
I have eaten my honeycomb and
my honey;
I have drunk my wine and my
milk.
Eat, friends;
Drink and imbibe deeply, O lovers."

2 ¶"[14]I was asleep, but my heart was
awake.
A voice! My beloved was knock-
ing:
'Open to me, my sister, my darling,
My dove, my perfect one!
For my head is drenched with
dew,
My locks with the damp of the
night.'
3"I have taken off my dress,
How can I put it on *again*?
I have washed my feet,
How can I dirty them *again*?
4"My beloved extended his hand
through the opening,
And my feelings were aroused for
him.
5"I arose to open to my beloved;
And my hands dripped with
myrrh,
And my fingers with liquid myrrh,
On the handles of the bolt.
6"I opened to my beloved,
But my beloved had turned away
and had gone!
My heart went out *to him* as he
spoke.
I searched for him, but I did not
find him;
I called him, but he did not answer me.
7"The watchmen who make the
rounds in the city found me,
They struck me *and* wounded me;
The guardsmen of the walls took
away my shawl from me.

8"I adjure you, O daughters of Jeru-
salem,
If you find my beloved,
As to what you will tell him:
For I am lovesick."

9 ¶"¹⁵What kind of beloved is your
beloved,
O most beautiful among women?
What kind of beloved is your be-
loved,
That thus you adjure us?"

10 ¶"¹⁴My beloved is dazzling and
ruddy,
Outstanding among ten thousand.
11"His head is *like* gold, pure gold;
His locks are *like* clusters of dates,
And black as a raven.
12"His eyes are like doves,
Beside streams of water,
Bathed in milk,
And reposed in *their* setting.
13"His cheeks are like a bed of bal-
sam,
Banks of sweet-scented herbs;
His lips are lilies,
Dripping with liquid myrrh.
14"His hands are rods of gold
Set with beryl;
His abdomen is carved ivory
Inlaid with sapphires.
15"His legs are pillars of alabaster
Set on pedestals of pure gold;
His appearance is like Lebanon,
Choice as the cedars.
16"His mouth is *full of* sweetness.
And he is wholly desirable.
This is my beloved and this is my
friend,
O daughters of Jerusalem."

CHAPTER 6

"¹⁶WHERE has your beloved gone,
O most beautiful among women?
Where has your beloved turned,
That we may seek him with you?"

2 ¶"¹⁷My beloved has gone down to
his garden,
To the beds of balsam,
To pasture *his flock* in the gardens
And gather lilies.
3"I am my beloved's and my beloved
is mine,
He who pastures *his flock* among
the lilies."

4 ¶"¹⁸You are as beautiful as Tirzah,
my darling,
As lovely as Jerusalem,
As awesome as an army with banners.
5"Turn your eyes away from me,
For they have confused me;
Your hair is like a flock of goats
That have descended from Gilead.
6"Your teeth are like a flock of ewes
Which have come up from *their*
washing,
All of which bear twins,
And not one among them has lost
her young.
7"Your temples are like a slice of a
pomegranate
Behind your veil.
8"There are sixty queens and eighty
concubines,
And maidens without number;
9 *But* my dove, my perfect one, is
unique:
She is her mother's only *daughter;*
She is the pure *child* of the one
who bore her.
The maidens saw her and called
her blessed,
The queens and the concubines
also, and they praised her, *saying,*

10 ¶ 'Who is this that grows like the
dawn,
As beautiful as the full moon,
As pure as the sun,
As awesome as an army with banners?'
11"I went down to the orchard of nut
trees
To see the blossoms of the valley,
To see whether the vine had budded
Or the pomegranates had
bloomed.
12"Before I was aware, my soul set
me
Over the chariots of my noble
people."

13 ¶"¹⁹Come back, come back, O
Shulammite;
Come back, come back, that we
may gaze at you!"

¶"²⁰Why should you gaze at the
Shulammite,

¹⁴ BRIDE   ¹⁵ CHORUS   ¹⁶ CHORUS   ¹⁷ BRIDE   ¹⁸ BRIDEGROOM   ¹⁹ CHORUS   ²⁰ BRIDEGROOM

As at the dance of the two companies?

CHAPTER 7

"How beautiful are your feet in
    sandals,
  O prince's daughter!
  The curves of your hips are like
    jewels,
  The work of the hands of an art-
    ist.
2"Your navel is *like* a round goblet
  Which never lacks mixed wine;
  Your belly is like a heap of wheat
  Fenced about with lilies.
3"Your two breasts are like two
    fawns,
  Twins of a gazelle.
4"Your neck is like a tower of ivory,
  Your eyes *like* the pools in Hesh-
    bon
  By the gate of Bath-rabbim;
  Your nose is like the tower of
    Lebanon,
  Which faces toward Damascus.
5"Your head crowns you like Car-
    mel,
  And the flowing locks of your
    head are like purple threads;
  The king is captivated by *your*
    tresses.
6"How beautiful and how delightful
    you are,
  My love, with *all* your charms!
7"Your stature is like a palm tree,
  And your breasts are *like its* clus-
    ters.
8"I said, 'I will climb the palm tree,
  I will take hold of its fruit stalks.'
  Oh, may your breasts be like clus-
    ters of the vine,
  And the fragrance of your breath
    like apples,
9 And your mouth like the best
    wine!"

  ¶"²¹It goes *down* smoothly for my
    beloved,
  Flowing gently *through* the lips of
    those who fall asleep.

10 ¶"I am my beloved's,
  And his desire is for me.
11"Come, my beloved, let us go out
    into the country,
  Let us spend the night in the vil-
    lages.

12"Let us rise early *and go* to the
    vineyards;
  Let us see whether the vine has
    budded
  And its blossoms have opened,
  And whether the pomegranates
    have bloomed.
  There I will give you my love.
13"The mandrakes have given forth
    fragrance;
  And over our doors are all choice
    fruits,
  Both new and old,
  Which I have saved up for you,
    my beloved.

CHAPTER 8

"Oh that you were like a brother to
    me
  Who nursed at my mother's
    breasts.
  If I found you outdoors, I would
    kiss you;
  No one would despise me, either.
2"I would lead you *and* bring you
  Into the house of my mother, who
    used to instruct me;
  I would give you spiced wine to
    drink from the juice of my
    pomegranates.
3"Let his left hand be under my
    head,
  And his right hand embrace me."

4 ¶"²²I want you to swear, O daugh-
    ters of Jerusalem,
  Do not arouse or awaken *my* love,
  Until she pleases."

5 ¶"²³Who is this coming up from
    the wilderness,
  Leaning on her beloved?"

  ¶"²²Beneath the apple tree I awak-
    ened you;
  There your mother was in labor
    with you,
  There she was in labor *and* gave
    you birth.
6"Put me like a ²⁴seal over your
    heart,
  Like a seal on your arm.
  For love is as strong as death,
  Jealousy is as severe as Sheol;
  Its flashes are flashes of fire,
  The *very* flame of the LORD.
7"Many waters cannot quench love,

Nor will rivers overflow it;
If a man were to give all the
riches of his house for love,
It would be utterly despised."

8 ¶"[25]We have a little sister,
And she has no breasts;
What shall we do for our sister
On the day when she is spoken
for?
9"If she is a wall,
We shall build on her a battlement
of silver;
But if she is a door,
We shall barricade her with
planks of cedar."

10 ¶"[26]I was a wall, and my breasts
were like towers;
Then I became in his eyes as one
who finds peace.

[25] CHORUS   [26] BRIDE

11"Solomon had a vineyard at Baal-
hamon;
He entrusted the vineyard to caretakers;
Each one was to bring a thousand
shekels of silver for its fruit.
12"My very own vineyard is at my
disposal;
The thousand *shekels* are for you,
Solomon,
And two hundred are for those
who take care of its fruit."
13"[27]O you who sit in the gardens,
My companions are listening for
your voice—
Let me hear it!"
14"[26]Hurry, my beloved,
And be like a gazelle or a young
stag
On the mountains of spices."

[26] BRIDE   [27] BRIDEGROOM

THE BOOK OF

ISAIAH

THE vision of Isaiah the son of
Amoz, concerning Judah and Jerusa-
lem which he saw during the reigns of
Uzziah, Jotham, Ahaz, *and* Hezekiah,
kings of Judah.
2 Listen, O heavens, and hear, O
earth;
For the Lord speaks,
"Sons I have reared and brought
up,
But they have revolted against
Me.
3"An ox knows its owner,
And a donkey its master's man-
ger,
But Israel does not know,
My people do not understand."

4 ¶ Alas, sinful nation,
People weighed down with iniq-
uity,
Offspring of evildoers,
Sons who act corruptly!
They have abandoned the Lord,
They have despised the Holy One
of Israel,
They have turned away from Him.

5 ¶ Where will you be stricken
again,

As you continue in *your* rebellion?
The whole head is sick,
And the whole heart is faint.
6 From the sole of the foot even to
the head
There is nothing sound in it,
Only bruises, welts, and raw
wounds,
Not pressed out or bandaged,
Nor softened with oil.

7 ¶ Your land is desolate,
Your cities are burned with fire,
Your fields—strangers are devouring them in your presence;
It is desolation, as overthrown by
strangers.
8 And the daughter of Zion is left
like a shelter in a vineyard,
Like a watchman's hut in a cucumber field, like a besieged
city.
9 Unless the Lord of hosts
Had left us a few survivors,
We would be like Sodom,
We would be like Gomorrah.

10 ¶ Hear the word of the Lord,
You rulers of Sodom;
Give ear to the instruction of our
God,

You people of Gomorrah.

11"What are your multiplied sacrifices to Me?"
Says the LORD.
"I have had enough of burnt offerings of rams,
And the fat of fed cattle.
And I take no pleasure in the blood of bulls, lambs, or goats.

12"When you come to appear before Me,
Who requires of you this trampling of My courts?

13"Bring your worthless offerings no longer,
Incense is an abomination to Me.
New moon and sabbath, the calling of assemblies—
I cannot endure iniquity and the solemn assembly.

14"I hate your new moon *festivals* and your appointed feasts,
They have become a burden to Me.
I am weary of bearing *them.*

15"So when you spread out your hands *in prayer,*
I will hide My eyes from you,
Yes, even though you multiply prayers,
I will not listen.
Your hands are covered with blood.

16 ¶"Wash yourselves, make yourselves clean;
Remove the evil of your deeds from My sight.
Cease to do evil,

17 Learn to do good;
Seek justice,
Reprove the ruthless;
Defend the orphan,
Plead for the widow.

18 ¶"Come now, and let us reason together,"
Says the LORD,
"Though your sins are as scarlet,
They will be as white as snow;
Though they are red like crimson,
They will be like wool.

19"If you consent and obey,
You will eat the best of the land;

20"But if you refuse and rebel,
You will be devoured by the sword."
Truly, the mouth of the LORD has spoken.

21 ¶ How the faithful city has become a harlot,
She *who* was full of justice!
Righteousness once lodged in her,
But now murderers.

22 Your silver has become dross,
Your drink diluted with water.

23 Your rulers are rebels,
And companions of thieves;
Everyone loves a bribe,
And chases after rewards.
They do not defend the orphan,
Nor does the widow's plea come before them.

24 ¶ Therefore the Lord GOD of hosts,
The Mighty One of Israel declares,
"Ah, I will be relieved of My adversaries,
And avenge Myself on My foes.

25"I will also turn My hand against you,
And will smelt away your dross as with lye,
And will remove all your alloy.

26"Then I will restore your judges as at the first,
And your counselors as at the beginning;
After that you will be called the city of righteousness,
A faithful city."

27 ¶ Zion will be redeemed with justice,
And her repentant ones with righteousness.

28 But transgressors and sinners will be crushed together,
And those who forsake the LORD shall come to an end.

29 Surely, you will be ashamed of the oaks which you have desired,
And you will be embarrassed at the gardens which you have chosen.

30 For you will be like an oak whose leaf fades away,
Or as a garden that has no water.

31 And the strong man will become tinder,
His work also a spark.
Thus they shall both burn together,
And there will be none to quench *them.*

CHAPTER 2

THE word which Isaiah the son of
Amoz saw concerning Judah and Jerusalem.

2 ¶ Now it will come about that
In the last days,
The mountain of the house of the
LORD
Will be established as the chief of
the mountains,
And will be raised above the hills;
And all the nations will stream to
it.

3 And many peoples will come and
say,
"Come, let us go up to the moun-
tain of the LORD,
To the house of the God of Jacob;
That He may teach us concerning
His ways,
And that we may walk in His
paths."
For the law will go forth from
Zion,
And the word of the LORD from
Jerusalem.

4 And He will judge between the
nations,
And will render decisions for
many peoples;
And they will hammer their
swords into plowshares, and
their spears into pruning hooks.
Nation will not lift up sword
against nation,
And never again will they learn
war.

5 ¶ Come, house of Jacob, and let
us walk in the light of the LORD.

6 For Thou hast abandoned Thy
people, the house of Jacob,
Because they are filled *with influ-
ences* from the east,
And *they are* soothsayers like the
Philistines,
And they strike *bargains* with the
children of foreigners.

7 Their land has also been filled
with silver and gold,
And there is no end to their treasures;
Their land has also been filled
with horses,
And there is no end to their chariots.

8 Their land has also been filled
with idols;

They worship the work of their
hands,
That which their fingers have
made.

9 So the *common* man has been
humbled,
And the man *of importance* has
been abased,
But do not forgive them.

10 Enter the rock and hide in the
dust
From the terror of the LORD and
from the splendor of His majesty.

11 The proud look of man will be
abased,
And the loftiness of man will be
humbled,
And the LORD alone will be exalted in that day.

12 ¶ For the LORD of hosts will have
a day of reckoning
Against everyone who is proud
and lofty,
And against everyone who is
lifted up,
That he may be abased.

13 And *it will be* against all the cedars of Lebanon that are lofty
and lifted up,
Against all the oaks of Bashan,

14 Against all the lofty mountains,
Against all the hills that are
lifted up,

15 Against every high tower,
Against every fortified wall,

16 Against all the ships of Tarshish,
And against all the beautiful craft.

17 And the pride of man will be humbled,
And the loftiness of men will be
abased,
And the LORD alone will be exalted in that day.

18 But the idols will completely vanish.

19 And *men* will go into caves of the
rocks,
And into holes of the ground
Before the terror of the LORD,
And before the splendor of His
majesty,
When He arises to make the earth
tremble.

20 In that day men will cast away to
the moles and the bats
Their idols of silver and their idols
of gold,

Which they made for themselves
to worship,

21 In order to go into the caverns of
the rocks and the clefts of the
cliffs,
Before the terror of the LORD and
the splendor of His majesty,
When He arises to make the earth
tremble.

22 Stop regarding man, whose breath
of life is in his nostrils;
For why should he be esteemed?

CHAPTER 3

FOR behold, the Lord GOD of hosts is
going to remove from Jerusalem and Judah
Both supply and support, the
whole supply of bread,
And the whole supply of water;

2 The mighty man and the warrior,
The judge and the prophet,
The diviner and the elder,

3 The captain of fifty and the honorable man,
The counselor and the expert arti-
san,
And the skillful enchanter.

4 And I will make mere lads their
princes
And capricious children will rule
over them,

5 And the people will be oppressed,
Each one by another, and each
one by his neighbor;
The youth will storm against the
elder,
And the inferior against the honorable.

6 When a man lays hold of his
brother in his father's house,
saying,
"You have a cloak, you shall be our
ruler,
And these ruins will be under
your charge,"

7 On that day will he protest, saying,
"I will not be *your* healer,
For in my house there is neither
bread nor cloak;
You should not appoint me ruler
of the people."

8 For Jerusalem has stumbled, and
Judah has fallen,
Because their speech and their
actions are against the LORD,

To rebel against His glorious presence.

9 The expression of their faces
bears witness against them.
And they display their sin like
Sodom;
They do not *even* conceal *it.*
Woe to them!
For they have brought evil on
themselves.

10 Say to the righteous that *it will go*
well *with them,*
For they will eat the fruit of their
actions.

11 Woe to the wicked! *It will go*
badly *with him,*
For what he deserves will be done
to him.

12 O My people! Their oppressors are
children,
And women rule over them.
O My people! Those who guide
you lead *you* astray,
And confuse the direction of your
paths.

13 ¶ The LORD arises to contend,
And stands to judge the people.

14 The LORD enters into judgment
with the elders and princes of
His people,
"It is you who have devoured the
vineyard;
The plunder of the poor is in your
houses.

15 "What do you mean by crushing
My people,
And grinding the face of the
poor?"
Declares the Lord GOD of hosts.

16 ¶ Moreover, the LORD said, "Because the daughters of Zion are
proud,
And walk with heads held high
and seductive eyes,
And go along with mincing steps,
And tinkle the bangles on their
feet,

17 Therefore the Lord will afflict the
scalp of the daughters of Zion
with scabs,
And the LORD will make their
foreheads bare."

18 In that day the Lord will take
away the beauty of *their* anklets,
headbands, crescent ornaments,

19 dangling earrings, bracelets, veils,

20 headdresses, ankle chains, sashes, perfume boxes, amulets,
21 finger rings, nose rings,
22 festal robes, outer tunics, cloaks, money purses,
23 hand mirrors, undergarments, turbans, and veils.
24 Now it will come about that instead of sweet perfume there will be putrefaction;
Instead of a belt, a rope;
Instead of well-set hair, a plucked-out scalp;
Instead of fine clothes, a donning of sackcloth;
And branding instead of beauty.
25 Your men will fall by the sword, And your mighty ones in battle.
26 And her gates will lament and mourn;
And deserted she will sit on the ground.

CHAPTER 4

FOR seven women will take hold of one man in that day, saying, "We will eat our own bread and wear our own clothes, only let us be called by your name; take away our reproach!"

2 ¶ In that day the Branch of the LORD will be beautiful and glorious, and the fruit of the earth *will* be the pride and the adornment of the survivors of Israel.

3 And it will come about that he who is left in Zion and remains in Jerusalem will be called holy—everyone who is recorded for life in Jerusalem.

4 When the Lord has washed away the filth of the daughters of Zion, and purged the bloodshed of Jerusalem from her midst, by the spirit of judgment and the spirit of burning,

5 then the LORD will create over the whole area of Mount Zion and over her assemblies a cloud by day, even smoke, and the brightness of a flaming fire by night; for over all the glory will be a canopy.

6 And there will be a shelter to *give* shade from the heat by day, and refuge and protection from the storm and the rain.

CHAPTER 5

LET me sing now for my well-beloved
A song of my beloved concerning
His vineyard.

My well-beloved had a vineyard
on a fertile hill.
2 And He dug it all around, removed its stones,
And planted it with the choicest vine.
And He built a tower in the middle of it,
And hewed out a wine vat in it;
Then He expected *it* to produce *good* grapes,
But it produced *only* worthless ones.

3 ¶"And now, O inhabitants of Jerusalem and men of Judah,
Judge between Me and My vineyard.
4"What more was there to do for My vineyard that I have not done in it?
Why, when I expected *it* to produce *good* grapes did it produce worthless ones?
5"So now let Me tell you what I am going to do to My vineyard:
I will remove its hedge and it will be consumed;
I will break down its wall and it will become trampled ground.
6"And I will lay it waste;
It will not be pruned or hoed,
But briars and thorns will come up.
I will also charge the clouds to rain no rain on it."

7 ¶ For the vineyard of the LORD of hosts is the house of Israel,
And the men of Judah His delightful plant.
Thus He looked for justice, but behold, bloodshed;
For righteousness, but behold, a cry of distress.

8 ¶ Woe to those who add house to house *and* join field to field,
Until there is no more room,
So that you have to live alone in the midst of the land!
9 In my ears the LORD of hosts *has* sworn, "Surely, many houses shall become desolate,
Even great and fine ones, without occupants.
10"For ten acres of vineyard will yield *only* one ¹bath *of wine*,

---
¹ I.e., Approx. 10½ gal.

And a homer of seed will yield *but* an ²ephah of grain."

11 Woe to those who rise early in the morning that they may pursue strong drink;
Who stay up late in the evening that wine may inflame them!

12 And their banquets are *accompanied* by lyre and harp, by tambourine and flute, and by wine;
But they do not pay attention to the deeds of the Lord,
Nor do they consider the work of His hands.

13 ¶ Therefore My people go into exile for their lack of knowledge;
And their honorable men are famished,
And their multitude is parched with thirst.

14 Therefore Sheol has enlarged its throat and opened its mouth without measure;
And Jerusalem's splendor, her multitude, her din *of revelry*, and the jubilant within her, descend *into it*.

15 So the *common* man will be humbled, and the man of *importance* abased,
The eyes of the proud also will be abased.

16 But the Lord of hosts will be exalted in judgment,
And the holy God will show Himself holy in righteousness.

17 Then the lambs will graze as in their pasture,
And strangers will eat in the waste places of the wealthy.

18 ¶ Woe to those who drag iniquity with the cords of falsehood,
And sin as if with cart ropes;

19 Who say, "Let Him make speed, let Him hasten His work, that we may see *it*;
And let the purpose of the Holy One of Israel draw near
And come to pass, that we may know *it*!"

20 Woe to those who call evil good, and good evil;
Who substitute darkness for light and light for darkness;

Who substitute bitter for sweet, and sweet for bitter!

21 Woe to those who are wise in their own eyes,
And clever in their own sight!

22 Woe to those who are heroes in drinking wine,
And valiant men in mixing strong drink;

23 Who justify the wicked for a bribe,
And take away the rights of the ones who are in the right!

24 ¶ Therefore, as a tongue of fire consumes stubble,
And dry grass collapses into the flame,
So their root will become like rot and their blossom blow away as dust;
For they have rejected the law of the Lord of hosts,
And despised the word of the Holy One of Israel.

25 On this account the anger of the Lord has burned against His people,
And He has stretched out His hand against them and struck them down,
And the mountains quaked; and their corpses lay like refuse in the middle of the streets.
For all this His anger is not spent,
But His hand is still stretched out.

26 ¶ He will also lift up a standard to the distant nation,
And will whistle for it from the ends of the earth;
And behold, it will come with speed swiftly.

27 No one in it is weary or stumbles, None slumbers or sleeps;
Nor is the belt at its waist undone, Nor its sandal strap broken.

28 Its arrows are sharp, and all its bows are bent;
The hoofs of its horses seem like flint, and its *chariot* wheels like a whirlwind.

29 Its roaring is like a lioness, and it roars like young lions;
It growls as it seizes the prey,
And carries *it* off with no one to deliver *it*.

30 And it shall growl over it in that day like the roaring of the sea.

² I.e., Approx. one bu.

If one looks to the land, behold,
there is darkness *and* distress;
Even the light is darkened by its
clouds.

CHAPTER 6

IN the year of King Uzziah's death, I
saw the Lord sitting on a throne, lofty
and exalted, with the train of His robe
filling the temple.

2 Seraphim stood above Him, each
having six wings; with two he covered
his face, and with two he covered his
feet, and with two he flew.

3 And one called out to another and
said,
"Holy, Holy, Holy, is the LORD of
hosts,
The whole earth is full of His
glory."

4 And the foundations of the
thresholds trembled at the voice of
him who called out, while the temple
was filling with smoke.

5 Then I said,
"Woe is me, for I am ruined!
Because I am a man of unclean
lips,
And I live among a people of un-
clean lips;
For my eyes have seen the King,
the LORD of hosts."

6 ¶ Then one of the seraphim flew
to me, with a burning coal in his hand
which he had taken from the altar
with tongs.

7 And he touched my mouth *with it*
and said, "Behold, this has touched
your lips; and your iniquity is taken
away, and your sin is forgiven."

8 Then I heard the voice of the
Lord, saying, "Whom shall I send, and
who will go for Us?" Then I said,
"Here am I. Send me!"

9 And He said, "Go, and tell this
people:
'Keep on listening, but do not perceive;
Keep on looking, but do not understand.'

10"Render the hearts of this people
insensitive,
Their ears dull,
And their eyes dim,
Lest they see with their eyes,
Hear with their ears,
Understand with their hearts,
And return and be healed."

11 Then I said, "Lord, how long?"
And He answered,
"Until cities are devastated *and*
without inhabitant,
Houses are without people,
And the land is utterly desolate,

12"The LORD has removed men far
away,
And the forsaken places are many
in the midst of the land.

13"Yet there will be a tenth portion
in it,
And it will again be *subject* to
burning,
Like a terebinth or an oak
Whose stump remains when it is
felled.
The holy seed is its stump."

CHAPTER 7

NOW it came about in the days of
Ahaz, the son of Jotham, the son of
Uzziah, king of Judah, that Rezin the
king of Aram and Pekah the son of
Remaliah, king of Israel, went up to
Jerusalem to *wage* war against it, but
could not conquer it.

2 When it was reported to the
house of David, saying, "The Arameans have camped in Ephraim," his
heart and the hearts of his people
shook as the trees of the forest shake
with the wind.

3 ¶ Then the LORD said to Isaiah,
"Go out now to meet Ahaz, you and
your son Shear-jashub, at the end of
the conduit of the upper pool, on the
highway to the fuller's field,

4 and say to him, 'Take care, and be
calm, have no fear and do not be
fainthearted because of these two
stubs of smoldering firebrands, on account of the fierce anger of Rezin and
Aram, and the son of Remaliah.

5 'Because Aram, *with* Ephraim and
the son of Remaliah, has planned evil
against you, saying,

6"Let us go up against Judah and
terrorize it, and make for ourselves a
breach in its walls, and set up the son
of Tabeel as king in the midst of it,"

7 thus says the Lord GOD, "It shall
not stand nor shall it come to pass.

8"For the head of Aram is Damascus and the head of Damascus is Rezin
(now within another 65 years Ephraim
will be shattered, *so that it is* no longer
a people),

9 and the head of Ephraim is Samaria and the head of Samaria is the son of Remaliah. If you will not believe, you surely shall not last." ' "

10 ¶ Then the LORD spoke again to Ahaz, saying,

11"Ask a sign for yourself from the LORD your God; make *it* deep as Sheol or high as heaven."

12 But Ahaz said, "I will not ask, nor will I test the LORD!"

13 Then he said, "Listen now, O house of David! Is it too slight a thing for you to try the patience of men, that you will try the patience of my God as well?

14"Therefore the Lord Himself will give you a sign: Behold, a virgin will be with child and bear a son, and she will call His name [3]Immanuel.

15"He will eat curds and honey at the time He knows *enough* to refuse evil and choose good.

16"For before the boy will know *enough* to refuse evil and choose good, the land whose two kings you dread will be forsaken.

17"The LORD will bring on you, on your people, and on your father's house such days as have never come since the day that Ephraim separated from Judah, the king of Assyria."

18 And it will come about in that day, that the LORD will whistle for the fly that is in the remotest part of the rivers of Egypt, and for the bee that is in the land of Assyria.

19 And they will all come and settle on the steep ravines, on the ledges of the cliffs, on all the thorn bushes, and on all the watering places.

20 ¶ In that day the Lord will shave with a razor, hired from regions beyond the Euphrates (*that is,* with the king of Assyria), the head and the hair of the legs; and it will also remove the beard.

21 ¶ Now it will come about in that day that a man may keep alive a heifer and a pair of sheep;

22 and it will happen that because of the abundance of the milk produced he will eat curds, for everyone that is left within the land will eat curds and honey.

23 And it will come about in that day, that every place where there used

to be a thousand vines, *valued* at a thousand *shekels* of silver, will become briars and thorns.

24 *People* will come there with bows and arrows because all the land will be briars and thorns.

25 And as for all the hills which used to be cultivated with the hoe, you will not go there for fear of briars and thorns; but they will become a place for pasturing oxen and for sheep to trample.

CHAPTER 8

THEN the LORD said to me, "Take for yourself a large tablet and write on it in ordinary letters: Swift is the booty, speedy is the prey.

2"And I will take to Myself faithful witnesses for testimony, Uriah the priest and Zechariah the son of Jeberechiah."

3 So I approached the prophetess, and she conceived and gave birth to a son. Then the LORD said to me, "Name him [4]Maher-shalal-hash-baz;

4 for before the boy knows how to cry out 'My father' or 'My mother,' the wealth of Damascus and the spoil of Samaria will be carried away before the king of Assyria."

5 ¶ And again the LORD spoke to me further, saying,

6 "Inasmuch as these people have
   rejected the gently flowing wa-
    ters of Shiloah,
And rejoice in Rezin and the son
   of Remaliah;

7 "Now therefore, behold, the Lord
   is about to bring on them the
   strong and abundant waters of
   the Euphrates,
Even the king of Assyria and all
   his glory;
And it will rise up over all its
   channels and go over all its
   banks.

8 "Then it will sweep on into Judah,
   it will overflow and pass
   through,
It will reach even to the neck;
And the spread of its wings will
   fill the breadth of your land, O
   Immanuel.

9 ¶ "Be broken, O peoples, and be
   shattered;

[3] I.e., God is with us

[4] I.e., swift is the booty, speedy is the prey

And give ear, all remote places of
the earth.
Gird yourselves, yet be shattered;
Gird yourselves, yet be shattered.

10 "Devise a plan but it will be
thwarted;
State a proposal, but it will not
stand,
For God is with us."

11 For thus the LORD spoke to me
with mighty power and instructed me
not to walk in the way of this people,
saying,

12 "You are not to say, 'It is a conspiracy!'
In regard to all that this people
call a conspiracy,
And you are not to fear what
they fear or be in dread of it.

13 "It is the LORD of hosts whom you
should regard as holy.
And He shall be your fear,
And He shall be your dread.

14 "Then He shall become a sanctuary;
But to both the houses of Israel,
a stone to strike and a rock to
stumble over,
And a snare and a trap for the
inhabitants of Jerusalem.

15 "And many will stumble over
them,
Then they will fall and be broken;
They will even be snared and
caught."

16 ¶ Bind up the testimony, seal the
law among my disciples.

17 And I will wait for the LORD who
is hiding His face from the house of
Jacob; I will even look eagerly for
Him.

18 Behold, I and the children whom
the LORD has given me are for signs
and wonders in Israel from the LORD
of hosts, who dwells on Mount Zion.

19 ¶ And when they say to you,
"Consult the mediums and the spiritists who whisper and mutter," should
not a people consult their God? Should
they consult the dead on behalf of the
living?

20 To the law and to the testimony!
If they do not speak according to this
word, it is because they have no dawn.

21 And they will pass through the
land hard-pressed and famished, and it
will turn out that when they are hungry, they will be enraged and curse
their king and their God as they face
upward.

22 Then they will look to the earth,
and behold, distress and darkness, the
gloom of anguish; and they will be
driven away into darkness.

CHAPTER 9

BUT there will be no more gloom for
her who was in anguish; in earlier
times He treated the land of Zebulun
and the land of Naphtali with contempt, but later on He shall make it
glorious, by the way of the sea, on the
other side of Jordan, Galilee of the
Gentiles.

2 The people who walk in darkness
Will see a great light;
Those who live in a dark land,
The light will shine on them.

3 Thou shalt multiply the nation,
Thou shalt increase their glad-
ness;
They will be glad in Thy presence
As with the gladness of harvest,
As men rejoice when they divide
the spoil.

4 For Thou shalt break the yoke of
their burden and the staff on
their shoulders,
The rod of their oppressor, as at
the battle of Midian.

5 For every boot of the booted warrior in the battle tumult,
And cloak rolled in blood, will be
for burning, fuel for the fire.

6 For a child will be born to us, a
son will be given to us;
And the government will rest on
His shoulders;
And His name will be called Won-
derful Counselor, Mighty God,
Eternal Father, Prince of Peace.

7 There will be no end to the increase of His government or of
peace,
On the throne of David and over
his kingdom,
To establish it and to uphold it
with justice and righteousness
From then on and forevermore.
The zeal of the LORD of hosts will
accomplish this.

8 ¶ The Lord sends a message
against Jacob,

And it falls on Israel.

9 And all the people know *it,*
That is, Ephraim and the inhabitants of Samaria,
Asserting in pride and in arrogance of heart:

10 "The bricks have fallen down,
But we will rebuild with smooth
stones;
The sycamores have been cut
down,
But we will replace *them* with
cedars."

11 Therefore the LORD raises against
them adversaries from Rezin,
And spurs their enemies on,

12 The Arameans on the east and the
Philistines on the west;
And they devour Israel with gap-
ing jaws.
In *spite of* all this His anger does
not turn away,
And His hand is still stretched out.

13 ¶ Yet the people do not turn back
to Him who struck them,
Nor do they seek the LORD of
hosts.

14 So the LORD cuts off head and tail
from Israel,
Both palm branch and bulrush in
a single day.

15 The head is the elder and honorable man,
And the prophet who teaches
falsehood is the tail.

16 For those who guide this people
are leading *them* astray;
And those who are guided by
them are brought to confusion.

17 Therefore the Lord does not take
pleasure in their young men,
Nor does He have pity on their
orphans or their widows;
For every one of them is godless
and an evildoer,
And every mouth is speaking foolishness.
In *spite of* all this His anger does
not turn away,
And His hand is still stretched out.

18 ¶ For wickedness burns like a
fire;
It consumes briars and thorns;
It even sets the thickets of the
forest aflame,
And they roll upward in a column
of smoke.

19 By the fury of the LORD of hosts
the land is burned up,
And the people are like fuel for
the fire;
No man spares his brother.

20 And they slice off *what is* on the
right hand but *still* are hungry,
And they eat *what is* on the left
hand but they are not satisfied;
Each of them eats the flesh of his
own arm.

21 Manasseh *devours* Ephraim, and
Ephraim Manasseh,
And together they are against
Judah.
In *spite of* all this His anger does
not turn away,
And His hand is still stretched out.

CHAPTER 10

WOE to those who enact evil statutes,
And to those who constantly record unjust decisions,

2 So as to deprive the needy of
justice,
And rob the poor of My people of
their rights,
In order that widows may be their
spoil,
And that they may plunder the
orphans.

3 Now what will you do in the day
of punishment,
And in the devastation which will
come from afar?
To whom will you flee for help?
And where will you leave your
wealth?

4 Nothing *remains* but to crouch
among the captives
Or fall among the slain.
In *spite of* all this His anger does
not turn away,
And His hand is still stretched out.

5 ¶ Woe to Assyria, the rod of My
anger
And the staff in whose hands is
My indignation,

6 I send it against a godless nation
And commission it against the
people of My fury
To capture booty and to seize
plunder,
And to trample them down like
mud in the streets.

7 Yet it does not so intend

Nor does it plan so in its heart,
But rather it is its purpose to
destroy,
And to cut off many nations.

8 For it says, "Are not my princes
all kings?

9 "Is not Calno like Carchemish,
Or Hamath like Arpad,
Or Samaria like Damascus?

10 "As my hand has reached to the
kingdoms of the idols,
Whose graven images *were*
greater than those of Jerusalem
and Samaria,

11 Shall I not do to Jerusalem and
her images
Just as I have done to Samaria
and her idols?"

12 ¶ So it will be that when the Lord
has completed all His work on Mount
Zion and on Jerusalem, *He will say*, "I
will punish the fruit of the arrogant
heart of the king of Assyria and the
pomp of his haughtiness."

13 For he has said,
"By the power of my hand and by
my wisdom I did *this*,
For I have understanding;
And I removed the boundaries of
the peoples,
And plundered their treasures,
And like a mighty man I brought
down *their* inhabitants,

14 And my hand reached to the
riches of the peoples like a nest,
And as one gathers abandoned
eggs, I gathered all the earth;
And there was not one that
flapped its wing or opened *its*
beak or chirped."

15 ¶ Is the axe to boast itself over
the one who chops with it?
Is the saw to exalt itself over the
one who wields it?
That would be like a club wielding
those who lift it,
Or like a rod lifting *him who* is not
wood.

16 Therefore the Lord, the GOD of
hosts, will send a wasting disease among his stout warriors;
And under his glory a fire will be
kindled like a burning flame.

17 And the light of Israel will become
a fire and his Holy One a flame,
And it will burn and devour his
thorns and his briars in a single
day.

18 And He will destroy the glory of
his forest and of his fruitful
garden, both soul and body;
And it will be as when a sick man
wastes away.

19 And the rest of the trees of his
forest will be so small in number
That a child could write them
down.

20 ¶ Now it will come about in that
day that the remnant of Israel, and
those of the house of Jacob who have
escaped, will never again rely on the
one who struck them, but will truly
rely on the LORD, the Holy One of
Israel.

21 A remnant will return, the remnant of Jacob, to the mighty
God.

22 For though your people, O Israel,
may be like the sand of the sea,
Only a remnant within them will
return;
A destruction is determined, overflowing with righteousness.

23 For a complete destruction, one
that is decreed, the Lord GOD of hosts
will execute in the midst of the whole
land.

24 ¶ Therefore thus says the Lord
GOD of hosts, "O My people who dwell
in Zion, do not fear the Assyrian who
strikes you with the rod and lifts up
his staff against you, the way Egypt
did.

25 "For in a very little while My indignation *against you* will be spent, and
My anger *will be directed* to their
destruction."

26 And the LORD of hosts will arouse
a scourge against him like the slaughter of Midian at the rock of Oreb; and
His staff will be over the sea, and He
will lift it up the way *He did* in Egypt.

27 So it will be in that day, that his
burden will be removed from your
shoulders and his yoke from your
neck, and the yoke will be broken
because of fatness.

28 ¶ He has come against Aiath,
He has passed through Migron;
At Michmash he deposited his
baggage.

29 They have gone through the pass,
saying,
"Geba will be our lodging place."
Ramah is terrified, and Gibeah of
Saul has fled away.

30 Cry aloud with your voice, O
daughter of Gallim!
Pay attention, Laishah *and*
wretched Anathoth!
31 Madmenah has fled.
The inhabitants of Gebim have
sought refuge.
32 Yet today he will halt at Nob;
He shakes his fist at the mountain
of the daughter of Zion, the hill
of Jerusalem.

33 ¶ Behold, the Lord, the GOD of
hosts, will lop off the boughs
with a terrible crash;
Those also who are tall in stature
will be cut down,
And those who are lofty will be
abased.
34 And He will cut down the thickets
of the forest with an iron *axe*,
And Lebanon will fall by the
Mighty One.

CHAPTER 11

THEN a shoot will spring from the
stem of Jesse,
And a branch from his roots will
bear fruit.
2 And the Spirit of the LORD will
rest on Him,
The spirit of wisdom and understanding,
The spirit of counsel and strength,
The spirit of knowledge and the
fear of the LORD.
3 And He will delight in the fear of
the LORD,
And He will not judge by what His
eyes see,
Nor make a decision by what His
ears hear;
4 But with righteousness He will
judge the poor,
And decide with fairness for the
afflicted of the earth;
And He will strike the earth with
the rod of His mouth,
And with the breath of His lips He
will slay the wicked.
5 Also righteousness will be the belt
about His loins,
And faithfulness the belt about
His waist.

6 ¶ And the wolf will dwell with the
lamb,
And the leopard will lie down with
the kid,

And the calf and the young lion
[5]and the fatling together;
And a little boy will lead them.
7 Also the cow and the bear will
graze;
Their young will lie down together;
And the lion will eat straw like the
ox.
8 And the nursing child will play by
the hole of the cobra,
And the weaned child will put his
hand on the viper's den.
9 They will not hurt or destroy in all
My holy mountain,
For the earth will be full of the
knowledge of the LORD
As the waters cover the sea.

10 ¶ Then it will come about in that
day
That the nations will resort to the
root of Jesse,
Who will stand as a signal for the
peoples;
And His resting place will be glorious.

11 ¶ Then it will happen on that day
that the Lord
Will again recover the second
time with His hand
The remnant of His people, who
will remain,
From Assyria, Egypt, Pathros,
Cush, Elam, Shinar, Hamath,
And from the islands of the sea.
12 And He will lift up a standard for
the nations,
And will assemble the banished
ones of Israel,
And will gather the dispersed of
Judah
From the four corners of the
earth.
13 Then the jealousy of Ephraim will
depart,
And those who harass Judah will
be cut off;
Ephraim will not be jealous of
Judah,
And Judah will not harass
Ephraim.
14 And they will swoop down on the
slopes of the Philistines on the
west;

[5] Some versions read *will feed together*

Together they will plunder the
sons of the east;
They will possess Edom and
Moab;
And the sons of Ammon will be
subject to them.
15 And the LORD will utterly destroy
The tongue of the Sea of Egypt;
And He will wave His hand over
the River
With His scorching wind;
And He will strike it into seven
streams,
And make *men* walk over dry-
shod.
16 And there will be a highway from
Assyria
For the remnant of His people
who will be left,
Just as there was for Israel
In the day that they came up out
of the land of Egypt.

CHAPTER 12

THEN you will say on that day,
"I will give thanks to Thee, O
LORD;
For although Thou wast angry
with me,
Thine anger is turned away,
And Thou dost comfort me.
2"Behold, God is my salvation,
I will trust and not be afraid;
For the LORD GOD is my strength
and song,
And He has become my salva-
tion."
3 Therefore you will joyously draw
water
From the springs of salvation.
4 And in that day you will say,
"Give thanks to the LORD, call on
His name.
Make known His deeds among
the peoples;
Make *them* remember that His
name is exalted."
5 Praise the LORD in song, for He
has done excellent things;
Let this be known throughout the
earth.
6 Cry aloud and shout for joy, O
inhabitant of Zion,
For great in your midst is the Holy
One of Israel.

CHAPTER 13

THE oracle concerning Babylon
which Isaiah the son of Amoz saw.

2 Lift up a standard on the [6]bare
hill,
Raise your voice to them,
Wave the hand that they may
enter the doors of the nobles.
3 I have commanded My consecrated ones,
I have even called My mighty
warriors,
My proudly exulting ones,
To *execute* My anger.
4 A sound of tumult on the mountains,
Like that of many people!
A sound of the uproar of kingdoms,
Of nations gathered together!
The LORD of hosts is mustering
the army for battle.
5 They are coming from a far country
From the farthest horizons,
The LORD and His instruments of
indignation,
To destroy the whole land.
6 Wail, for the day of the LORD is
near!
It will come as destruction from
the Almighty.
7 Therefore all hands will fall limp,
And every man's heart will melt.
8 And they will be terrified,
Pains and anguish will take hold
of *them*;
They will writhe like a woman in
labor,
They will look at one another in
astonishment,
Their faces aflame.
9 Behold, the day of the LORD is
coming,
Cruel, with fury and burning anger,
To make the land a desolation;
And He will exterminate its sinners from it.
10 For the stars of heaven and their
constellations
Will not flash forth their light;
The sun will be dark when it rises,
And the moon will not shed its
light.
11 Thus I will punish the world for
its evil,
And the wicked for their iniquity;
I will also put an end to the arrogance of the proud,

[6] Or, *wind-swept mountain*

And abase the haughtiness of the ruthless.

12 I will make mortal man scarcer than pure gold,
And mankind than the gold of Ophir.

13 Therefore I shall make the heavens tremble,
And the earth will be shaken from its place
At the fury of the LORD of hosts
In the day of His burning anger.

14 And it will be that like a hunted gazelle,
Or like sheep with none to gather *them*,
They will each turn to his own people,
And each one flee to his own land.

15 Anyone who is found will be thrust through,
And anyone who is captured will fall by the sword.

16 Their little ones also will be dashed to pieces
Before their eyes;
Their houses will be plundered
And their wives ravished.

17 ¶ Behold, I am going to stir up the Medes against them,
Who will not value silver or take pleasure in gold,

18 And *their* bows will mow down the young men,
They will not even have compassion on the fruit of the womb,
Nor will their eye pity children.

19 And Babylon, the beauty of kingdoms, the glory of the Chaldeans' pride,
Will be as when God overthrew Sodom and Gomorrah.

20 It will never be inhabited or lived in from generation to generation;
Nor will the Arab pitch *his* tent there,
Nor will shepherds make *their* flocks lie down there.

21 But desert creatures will lie down there,
And their houses will be full of owls,
Ostriches also will live there, and shaggy goats will frolic there.

22 And hyenas will howl in their fortified towers

And jackals in their luxurious palaces.
Her *fateful* time also will soon come
And her days will not be prolonged.

CHAPTER 14

WHEN the LORD will have compassion on Jacob, and again choose Israel, and settle them in their own land, then strangers will join them and attach themselves to the house of Jacob.

2 And the peoples will take them along and bring them to their place, and the house of Israel will possess them as an inheritance in the land of the LORD as male servants and female servants; and they will take their captors captive, and will rule over their oppressors.

3 ¶ And it will be in the day when the LORD gives you rest from your pain and turmoil and harsh service in which you have been enslaved,

4 that you will take up this taunt against the king of Babylon, and say,
"How the oppressor has ceased,
And how fury has ceased!

5 "The LORD has broken the staff of the wicked,
The scepter of rulers

6 Which used to strike the peoples in fury with unceasing strokes,
Which subdued the nations in anger with unrestrained persecution.

7 "The whole earth is at rest *and* is quiet;
They break forth into shouts of joy.

8 "Even the cypress trees rejoice over you, *and* the cedars of Lebanon, *saying,*
'Since you were laid low, no *tree* cutter comes up against us.'

9 "Sheol from beneath is excited over you to meet you when you come;
It arouses for you the spirits of the dead, all the leaders of the earth;
It raises all the kings of the nations from their thrones.

10 "They will all respond and say to you,
'Even you have been made weak as we,

You have become like us.

11 'Your pomp *and* the music of your
harps
Have been brought down to
Sheol;
Maggots are spread out *as your
bed* beneath you,
And worms are your covering.'

12"How you have fallen from heaven,
O star of the morning, son of the
dawn!
You have been cut down to the
earth,
You who have weakened the nations!

13"But you said in your heart,
'I will ascend to heaven;
I will raise my throne above the
stars of God,
And I will sit on the mount of
assembly
In the recesses of the north.

14 'I will ascend above the heights of
the clouds;
I will make myself like the Most
High.'

15"Nevertheless you will be thrust
down to Sheol,
To the recesses of the pit.

16"Those who see you will gaze at
you,
They will ponder over you, *saying,*
'Is this the man who made the
earth tremble,
Who shook kingdoms,

17 Who made the world like a wilderness
And overthrew its cities,
Who did not allow his prisoners to
go home?'

18"All the kings of the nations lie in
glory,
Each in his own tomb.

19"But you have been cast out of
your tomb
Like a rejected branch,
Clothed with the slain who are
pierced with a sword,
Who go down to the stones of the
pit,
Like a trampled corpse.

20"You will not be united with them
in burial,
Because you have ruined your
country,
You have slain your people.
May the offspring of evildoers not
be mentioned forever.

21"Prepare for his sons a place of
slaughter
Because of the iniquity of their
fathers.
They must not arise and take possession of the earth
And fill the face of the world with
cities."

22"And I will rise up against them,"
declares the LORD of hosts, "and will
cut off from Babylon name and survivors, offspring and posterity," declares
the LORD.

23"I will also make it a possession for
the hedgehog, and swamps of water,
and I will sweep it with the broom of
destruction," declares the LORD of
hosts.

24 The LORD of hosts has sworn saying, "Surely, just as I have intended so
it has happened, and just as I have
planned so it will stand,

25 to break Assyria in My land, and I
will trample him on My mountains.
Then his yoke will be removed from
them, and his burden removed from
their shoulder.

26"This is the plan devised against
the whole earth; and this is the hand
that is stretched out against all the
nations.

27"For the LORD of hosts has
planned, and who can frustrate *it*?
And as for His stretched-out hand,
who can turn it back?"

28 In the year that King Ahaz died
this oracle came:

29"Do not rejoice, O Philistia, all of
you,
Because the rod that struck you is
broken;
For from the serpent's root a viper
will come out,
And its fruit will be a flying serpent.

30"And those who are most helpless
will eat,
And the needy will lie down in
security;
I will destroy your root with famine,
And it will kill off your survivors.

31"Wail, O gate; cry, O city;
Melt away, O Philistia, all of you;
For smoke comes from the north,
And there is no straggler in his
ranks.

32"How then will one answer the
messengers of the nation?

That the LORD has founded Zion,
And the afflicted of His people will
seek refuge in it."

CHAPTER 15

THE oracle concerning Moab.
Surely in a night Ar of Moab is
devastated *and* ruined;
Surely in a night Kir of Moab is
devastated *and* ruined.
2 They have gone up to the temple
and *to* Dibon, *even* to the high
places to weep.
Moab wails over Nebo and Medeba;
Everyone's head is bald *and* every
beard is cut off.
3 In their streets they have girded
themselves with sackcloth;
On their housetops and in their
squares
Everyone is wailing, dissolved in
tears.
4 Heshbon and Elealeh also cry out,
Their voice is heard all the way to
Jahaz;
Therefore the armed men of Moab
cry aloud;
His soul trembles within him.
5 My heart cries out for Moab;
His fugitives are as far as Zoar
and Eglath-shelishiyah,
For they go up the ascent of Luhith weeping;
Surely on the road to Horonaim
they raise a cry of distress over
their ruin.
6 For the waters of Nimrim are
desolate.
Surely the grass is withered, the
tender grass died out,
There is no green thing.
7 Therefore the abundance *which*
they have acquired and stored
up
They carry off over the brook of
Arabim.
8 For the cry of distress has gone
around the territory of Moab,
Its wail *goes* as far as Eglaim and
its wailing even to Beer-elim.
9 For the waters of Dimon are full
of blood;
Surely I will bring added *woes*
upon Dimon,
A lion upon the fugitives of Moab
and upon the remnant of the
land.

CHAPTER 16

SEND the *tribute* lamb to the ruler of
the land,
From Sela by way of the wilderness to the mountain of the
daughter of Zion.
2 Then, like fleeing birds *or* scattered nestlings,
The daughters of Moab will be at
the fords of the Arnon.
3"Give *us* advice, make a decision;
Cast your shadow like night at
high noon;
Hide the outcasts, do not betray
the fugitive.
4"Let the outcasts of Moab stay
with you;
Be a hiding place to them from
the destroyer."
For the extortioner has come to
an end, destruction has ceased,
Oppressors have completely *dis-
appeared* from the land.
5 A throne will even be established
in lovingkindness,
And a judge will sit on it in faithfulness in the tent of David;
Moreover, he will seek justice
And be prompt in righteousness.

6 ¶ We have heard of the pride of
Moab, an excessive pride;
Even of his arrogance, pride, and
fury;
His idle boasts are false.
7 Therefore Moab shall wail; everyone of Moab shall wail.
You shall moan for the raisin
cakes of Kir-hareseth
As those who are utterly stricken.
8 For the fields of Heshbon have
withered, the vines of Sibmah
as well;
The lords of the nations have
trampled down its choice clusters
Which reached as far as Jazer *and*
wandered to the deserts;
Its tendrils spread themselves out
and passed over the sea.
9 Therefore I will weep bitterly for
Jazer, for the vine of Sibmah;
I will drench you with my tears, O
Heshbon and Elealeh;
For the shouting over your summer fruits and your harvest has
fallen away.

10 And gladness and joy are taken
away from the fruitful field;
In the vineyards also there will be
no cries of joy or jubilant shouting,
No treader treads out wine in the
presses,
For I have made the shouting to
cease.

11 Therefore my heart intones like a
harp for Moab,
And my inward feelings for Kir-
hareseth.

12 So it will come about when Moab
presents himself,
When he wearies himself upon *his*
high place,
And comes to his sanctuary to
pray,
That he will not prevail.

13 ¶ This is the word which the
LORD spoke earlier concerning Moab.
14 But now the LORD speaks, saying,
"Within three years, as a hired man
would count them, the glory of Moab
will be degraded along with all *his*
great population, and *his* remnant will
be very small *and* impotent."

CHAPTER 17

THE oracle concerning Damascus.
"Behold, Damascus is about to be
removed from being a city,
And it will become a fallen ruin.

2 "The cities of Aroer are forsaken;
They will be for flocks to lie down
in,
And there will be no one to
frighten *them.*

3 "The fortified city will disappear
from Ephraim,
And sovereignty from Damascus
And the remnant of Aram;
They will be like the glory of the
sons of Israel,"
Declares the LORD of hosts.

4 ¶ Now it will come about in that
day that the glory of Jacob will
fade,
And the fatness of his flesh will
become lean.

5 It will be even like the reaper
gathering the standing grain,
As his arm harvests the ears,
Or it will be like one gleaning ears
of grain
In the valley of Rephaim.

6 Yet gleanings will be left in it like
the shaking of an olive tree,
Two *or* three olives on the top-
most bough,
Four *or* five on the branches of a
fruitful tree,
Declares the LORD, the God of
Israel.

7 In that day man will have regard
for his Maker,
And his eyes will look to the Holy
One of Israel.

8 And he will not have regard for
the altars, the work of his
hands,
Nor will he look to that which his
fingers have made,
Even the [7]Asherim and incense
stands.

9 In that day their strong cities will
be like forsaken places in the
forest,
Or like branches which they abandoned before the sons of Israel;
And the land will be a desolation.

10 For you have forgotten the God of
your salvation
And have not remembered the
rock of your refuge.
Therefore you plant delightful
plants
And set them with vine slips of a
strange *god.*

11 In the day that you plant *it* you
carefully fence *it* in,
And in the morning you bring
your seed to blossom;
But the harvest will be a heap
In a day of sickliness and incurable pain.

12 ¶ Alas, the uproar of many peoples
Who roar like the roaring of the
seas,
And the rumbling of nations
Who rush on like the rumbling of
mighty waters!

13 The nations rumble on like the
rumbling of many waters,
But He will rebuke them and they
will flee far away,
And be chased like chaff in the
mountains before the wind,
Or like whirling dust before a gale.

14 At evening time, behold, *there is*
terror!

[7] I.e., wooden symbols of a female deity

Before morning they are no more.
Such *will be* the portion of those
who plunder us,
And the lot of those who pillage
us.

CHAPTER 18

ALAS, oh land of whirring wings
Which lies beyond the rivers of
[8]Cush,

2 Which sends envoys by the sea,
Even in papyrus vessels on the
surface of the waters.
Go, swift messengers, to a nation
tall and smooth,
To a people feared far and wide,
A powerful and oppressive nation
Whose land the rivers divide.

3 All you inhabitants of the world
and dwellers on earth,
As soon as a standard is raised on
the mountains, you will see *it,*
And as soon as the trumpet is
blown, you will hear *it.*

4 For thus the LORD has told me,
"I will look from My dwelling place
quietly
Like dazzling heat in the sunshine,
Like a cloud of dew in the heat of
harvest."

5 For before the harvest, as soon as
the bud blossoms
And the flower becomes a ripen-
ing grape,
Then He will cut off the sprigs
with pruning knives
And remove *and* cut away the
spreading branches

6 They will be left together for
mountain birds of prey,
And for the beasts of the earth;
And the birds of prey will spend
the summer *feeding* on them,
And all the beasts of the earth will
spend harvest time on them.

7 At that time a gift of homage will
be brought to the LORD of hosts
From a people tall and smooth,
Even from a people feared far and
wide,
A powerful and oppressive nation,
Whose land the rivers divide—
To the place of the name of the
LORD of hosts, *even* Mount
Zion.

[8] Or, *Ethiopia*

CHAPTER 19

THE oracle concerning Egypt.
Behold, the LORD is riding on a
swift cloud, and is about to
come to Egypt;
The idols of Egypt will tremble at
His presence,
And the heart of the Egyptians
will melt within them.

2 "So I will incite Egyptians against
Egyptians;
And they will each fight against
his brother, and each against
his neighbor,
City against city, *and* kingdom
against kingdom.

3 "Then the spirit of the Egyptians
will be demoralized within
them;
And I will confound their strat-
egy,
So that they will resort to idols
and ghosts of the dead,
And to mediums and spiritists.

4 "Moreover, I will deliver the Egyptians into the hand of a cruel
master,
And a mighty king will rule over
them," declares the Lord GOD of
hosts.

5 ¶ And the waters from the sea
will dry up,
And the river will be parched and
dry.

6 And the canals will emit a stench,
The streams of Egypt will thin out
and dry up;
The reeds and rushes will rot
away.

7 The bulrushes by the Nile, by the
edge of the Nile
And all the sown fields by the Nile
Will become dry, be driven away,
and be no more.

8 And the fishermen will lament,
And all those who cast a line into
the Nile will mourn,
And those who spread nets on the
waters will pine away.

9 Moreover, the manufacturers of
linen made from combed flax
And the weavers of white cloth
will be utterly dejected.

10 And the pillars *of* Egypt will be
crushed;
All the hired laborers will be
grieved in soul.

11 ¶ The princes of Zoan are mere fools;
The advice of Pharaoh's wisest advisers has become stupid.
How can you *men* say to Pharaoh, "I am a son of the wise, a son of ancient kings"?

12 Well then, where are your wise men?
Please let them tell you,
And let them understand what the LORD of hosts
Has purposed against Egypt.

13 The princes of Zoan have acted foolishly,
The princes of Memphis are deluded;
Those who are the cornerstone of her tribes
Have led Egypt astray.

14 The LORD has mixed within her a spirit of distortion;
They have led Egypt astray in all that it does,
As a drunken man staggers in his vomit.

15 And there will be no work for Egypt
Which *its* head or tail, *its* palm branch or bulrush, may do.

16 ¶ In that day the Egyptians will become like women, and they will tremble and be in dread because of the waving of the hand of the LORD of hosts, which He is going to wave over them.

17 And the land of Judah will become a terror to Egypt; everyone to whom it is mentioned will be in dread of it, because of the purpose of the LORD of hosts which He is purposing against them.

18 ¶ In that day five cities in the land of Egypt will be speaking the language of Canaan and swearing *allegiance* to the LORD of hosts; one will be called the City of ⁹Destruction.

19 ¶ In that day there will be an altar to the LORD in the midst of the land of Egypt, and a pillar to the LORD near its border.

20 And it will become a sign and a witness to the LORD of hosts in the land of Egypt; for they will cry to the LORD because of oppressors, and He will send them a Savior and a Champion, and He will deliver them.

21 Thus the LORD will make Himself known to Egypt, and the Egyptians will know the LORD in that day. They will even worship with sacrifice and offering, and will make a vow to the LORD and perform it.

22 And the LORD will strike Egypt, striking but healing; so they will return to the LORD, and He will respond to them and will heal them.

23 ¶ In that day there will be a highway from Egypt to Assyria, and the Assyrians will come into Egypt and the Egyptians into Assyria, and the Egyptians will worship with the Assyrians.

24 ¶ In that day Israel will be the third *party* with Egypt and Assyria, a blessing in the midst of the earth,

25 whom the LORD of hosts has blessed, saying, "Blessed is Egypt My people, and Assyria the work of My hands, and Israel My inheritance."

CHAPTER 20

IN the year that the commander came to Ashdod, when Sargon the king of Assyria sent him and he fought against Ashdod and captured it,

2 at that time the LORD spoke through Isaiah the son of Amoz, saying, "Go and loosen the sackcloth from your hips, and take your shoes off your feet." And he did so, going naked and barefoot.

3 And the LORD said, "Even as My servant Isaiah has gone naked and barefoot three years as a sign and token against Egypt and Cush,

4 so the king of Assyria will lead away the captives of Egypt and the exiles of Cush, young and old, naked and barefoot with buttocks uncovered, to the shame of Egypt.

5 "Then they shall be dismayed and ashamed because of Cush their hope and Egypt their boast.

6 "So the inhabitants of this coastland will say in that day, 'Behold, such is our hope, where we fled for help to be delivered from the king of Assyria; and we, how shall we escape?' "

CHAPTER 21

THE oracle concerning the ¹⁰wilderness of the sea.

---

⁹ Some ancient mss. and versions read *the Sun*

¹⁰ Or, *sandy wastes, sea country*

As windstorms in the Negev
sweep on,
It comes from the wilderness,
from a terrifying land.
2 A harsh vision has been shown to
me;
The treacherous one still deals
treacherously, *and* the destroyer still destroys.
Go up, Elam, lay siege, Media;
I have made an end of all the
groaning she has caused.
3 For this reason my loins are full of
anguish;
Pains have seized me like the
pains of a woman in labor.
I am so bewildered I cannot hear,
so terrified I cannot see.
4 My mind reels, horror overwhelms me;
The twilight I longed for has been
turned for me into trembling.
5 They set the table, they [11]spread
out the cloth, they eat, they
drink;
"Rise up, captains, oil the shields,"
6 For thus the Lord says to me,
"Go, station the lookout, let him
report what he sees.
7"When he sees riders, horsemen in
pairs,
A train of donkeys, a train of
camels,
Let him pay close attention, very
close attention."
8 Then the lookout called,
"O Lord, I stand continually by day
on the watchtower,
And I am stationed every night at
my guard post.
9"Now behold, here comes a troop
of riders, horsemen in pairs."
And one answered and said,
"Fallen, fallen is Babylon;
And all the images of her gods are
shattered on the ground."
10 O my threshed *people*, and my
afflicted of the threshing floor!
What I have heard from the Lord
of hosts,
The God of Israel, I make known
to you.

11 ¶ The oracle concerning Edom.
One keeps calling to me from Seir,
"Watchman, [12]how far gone is the
night?

Watchman, [12]how far gone is the
night?"
12 The watchman says,
"Morning comes but also night.
If you would inquire, inquire;
Come back again."

13 ¶ The oracle about Arabia.
In the thickets of Arabia you
must spend the night,
O caravans of Dedanites.
14 Bring water for the thirsty,
O inhabitants of the land of Tema,
Meet the fugitive with bread.
15 For they have fled from the
swords,
From the drawn sword, and from
the bent bow,
And from the press of battle.
16 For thus the Lord said to me, "In
a year, as a hired man would count it,
all the splendor of Kedar will termi-
nate;
17 and the remainder of the number
of bowmen, the mighty men of the
sons of Kedar, will be few; for the
Lord God of Israel has spoken."

CHAPTER 22

THE oracle concerning the valley of
vision.
What is the matter with you now,
that you have all gone up to the
housetops?
2 You who were full of noise,
You boisterous town, you exultant city;
Your slain were not slain with the
sword,
Nor did they die in battle.
3 All your rulers have fled together,
And have been captured without
the bow;
All of you who were found eere
taken captive together,
Though they had fled far away.
4 Therefore I say, "Turn your eyes
away from me,
Let me weep bitterly,
Do not try to comfort me concerning the destruction of the
daughter of my people."
5 For the Lord God of hosts has a
day of panic, subjugation, and
confusion
In the valley of vision,
A breaking down of walls

---

[11] Or, *spread out the rugs;* or possibly, *arranged the seating*
[12] Lit., *what is the time of the night?*

[12] Lit., *what is the time of the night?*

And a crying to the mountain.

6 And Elam took up the quiver
   With the chariots, infantry, *and*
     horsemen;
   And Kir uncovered the shield.
7 Then your choicest valleys were
     full of chariots,
   And the horsemen took up fixed
     positions at the gate.
8 And He removed the defense of
   Judah.
   In that day you depended on the
     weapons of the house of the
     forest,
9 And you saw that the breaches
   In the *wall* of the city of David
     were many;
   And you collected the waters of
     the lower pool.
10 Then you counted the houses of
    Jerusalem,
   And you tore down houses to for-
     tify the wall.
11 And you made a reservoir be-
    tween the two walls
   For the waters of the old pool.
   But you did not depend on Him
     who made it,
   Nor did you take into consider-
     ation Him who planned it long
     ago.

12 ¶ Therefore in that day the Lord
    God of hosts, called *you* to
    weeping, to wailing,
   To shaving the head, and to wear-
     ing sackcloth.
13 Instead, there is gaiety and glad-
    ness,
   Killing of cattle and slaughtering
     of sheep,
   Eating of meat and drinking of
     wine:
   "Let us eat and drink, for tomor-
     row we may die."
14 But the LORD of hosts revealed
    Himself to me,
   "Surely this iniquity shall not be
     forgiven you
   Until you die," says the Lord GOD
     of hosts.

15 ¶ Thus says the Lord GOD of
    hosts,
   "Come, go to this steward,
   To Shebna, who is in charge of
     the *royal* household,
16 'What right do you have here,
   And whom do you have here,

That you have hewn a tomb for
   yourself here,
You who hew a tomb on the
   height,
You who carve a resting place for
   yourself in the rock?
17 'Behold, the LORD is about to hurl
   you headlong, O man.
   And He is about to grasp you
    firmly,
18 *And* roll you tightly like a ball,
   To be cast into a vast country;
   There you will die,
   And there your splendid chariots
    will be,
   You shame of your master's
    house.'
19 "And I will depose you from your
   office,
   And I will pull you down from
    your station.
20 "Then it will come about in that
   day,
   That I will summon My servant
    Eliakim the son of Hilkiah
21 And I will clothe him with your
   tunic,
   And tie your sash securely about
    him,
   I will entrust him with your au-
    thority,
   And he will become a father to the
    inhabitants of Jerusalem and to
    the house of Judah.
22 "Then I will set the key of the
   house of David on his shoulder,
   When he opens no one will shut,
   When he shuts no one will open.
23 "And I will drive him *like* a peg in a
   firm place,
   And he will become a throne of
    glory to his father's house.
24 "So they will hang on him all the
glory of his father's house, offspring
and issue, all the least of vessels, from
bowls to all the jars.
25 "In that day," declares the LORD of
hosts, "the peg driven in a firm place
will give way; it will even break off
and fall, and the load hanging on it
will be cut off, for the LORD has spoken."

CHAPTER 23

THE oracle concerning Tyre.
   Wail, O ships of Tarshish,
    For *Tyre* is destroyed, without
     house *or* harbor;

It is reported to them from the land of Cyprus.

2 Be silent, you inhabitants of the coastland,
You merchants of Sidon;
Your messengers crossed the sea

3 And *were* on many waters.
The grain of the Nile, the harvest of the River was her revenue;
And she was the market of nations.

4 Be ashamed, O Sidon;
For the sea speaks, the stronghold of the sea, saying,
"I have neither travailed nor given birth,
I have neither brought up young men *nor* reared virgins."

5 When the report *reaches* Egypt,
They will be in anguish at the report of Tyre.

6 Pass over to Tarshish;
Wail, O inhabitants of the coastland.

7 Is this your jubilant *city,*
Whose origin is from antiquity,
Whose feet used to carry her to colonize distant places?

8 ¶ Who has planned this against Tyre, the bestower of crowns,
Whose merchants were princes, whose traders were the honored of the earth?

9 The LORD of hosts has planned it to defile the pride of all beauty,
To despise all the honored of the earth.

10 Overflow your land like the Nile, O daughter of Tarshish,
There is no more restraint.

11 He has stretched His hand out over the sea,
He has made the kingdoms tremble;
The LORD has given a command concerning Canaan to demolish its strongholds.

12 And He has said, "You shall exult no more, O crushed virgin daughter of Sidon.
Arise, pass over to Cyprus; even there you will find no rest."

13 Behold, the land of the Chaldeans—this is the people *which* was not; Assyria appointed it for desert creatures—they erected their siege towers, they stripped its palaces, they made it a ruin.

14 Wail, O ships of Tarshish,
For your stronghold is destroyed.

15 Now it will come about in that day that Tyre will be forgotten for seventy years like the days of one king. At the end of seventy years it will happen to Tyre as *in* the song of the harlot:

16 Take *your* harp, walk about the city,
O forgotten harlot;
Pluck the strings skillfully, sing many songs,
That you may be remembered.

17 And it will come about at the end of seventy years that the LORD will visit Tyre. Then she will go back to her harlot's wages, and will play the harlot with all the kingdoms on the face of the earth.

18 And her gain and her harlot's wages will be set apart to the LORD; it will not be stored up or hoarded, but her gain will become sufficient food and choice attire for those who dwell in the presence of the LORD.

CHAPTER 24

BEHOLD, the LORD lays the earth waste, devastates it, distorts its surface, and scatters its inhabitants.

2 And the people will be like the priest, the servant like his master, the maid like her mistress, the buyer like the seller, the lender like the borrower, the creditor like the debtor.

3 The earth will be completely laid waste and completely despoiled, for the LORD has spoken this word.

4 The earth mourns *and* withers, the world fades *and* withers, the exalted of the people of the earth fade away.

5 The earth is also polluted by its inhabitants, for they transgressed laws, violated statutes, broke the everlasting covenant.

6 Therefore, a curse devours the earth, and those who live in it are held guilty. Therefore, the inhabitants of the earth are burned, and few men are left.

7 ¶ The new wine mourns,
The vine decays,
All the merry-hearted sigh.

8 The gaiety of tambourines ceases,
The noise of revelers stops,
The gaiety of the harp ceases.

9 They do not drink wine with song;
   Strong drink is bitter to those who
   drink it.
10 The city of chaos is broken down;
   Every house is shut up so that
   none may enter.
11 There is an outcry in the streets
   concerning the wine;
   All joy turns to gloom.
   The gaiety of the earth is banished.
12 Desolation is left in the city,
   And the gate is battered to ruins.
13 For thus it will be in the midst of
   the earth among the peoples,
   As the shaking of an olive tree,
   As the gleanings when the grape
   harvest is over.
14 They raise their voices, they shout
   for joy.
   They cry out from the west concerning the majesty of the
   LORD.
15 Therefore glorify the LORD in the
   east,
   The name of the LORD, the God of
   Israel
   In the coastlands of the sea.
16 From the ends of the earth we
   hear songs, "Glory to the Righteous One,"
   But I say, "Woe to me! Woe to
   me! Alas for me!
   The treacherous deal treacherously,
   And the treacherous deal very
   treacherously."
17 Terror and pit and snare
   Confront you, O inhabitant of the
   earth.
18 Then it will be that he who flees
   the report of disaster will fall
   into the pit,
   And he who climbs out of the pit
   will be caught in the snare;
   For the windows above are
   opened, and the foundations of
   the earth shake.
19 The earth is broken asunder,
   The earth is split through,
   The earth is shaken violently.
20 The earth reels to and fro like a
   drunkard,
   And it totters like a shack,
   For its transgression is heavy
   upon it,
   And it will fall, never to rise again.
21 So it will happen in that day,

That the LORD will punish the
   host of heaven, on high,
And the kings of the earth, on
   earth.
22 And they will be gathered together
   Like prisoners in the dungeon,
   And will be confined in prison;
   And after many days they will be
   punished.
23 Then the moon will be abashed
   and the sun ashamed,
   For the LORD of hosts will reign
   on Mount Zion and in Jerusalem,
   And His glory will be before His
   elders.

CHAPTER 25

O LORD, Thou art my God;
   I will exalt Thee, I will give
   thanks to Thy name;
   For Thou hast worked wonders,
   Plans formed long ago, with perfect faithfulness.
2 For Thou hast made a city into a
   heap,
   A fortified city into a ruin;
   A palace of strangers is a city no
   more,
   It will never be rebuilt.
3 Therefore a strong people will
   glorify Thee;
   Cities of ruthless nations will revere Thee.
4 For Thou hast been a defense for
   the helpless,
   A defense for the needy in his
   distress,
   A refuge from the storm, a shade
   from the heat;
   For the breath of the ruthless
   Is like a rain storm against a wall.
5 Like heat in drought, Thou dost
   subdue the uproar of aliens;
   Like heat by the shadow of a
   cloud, the song of the ruthless is
   silenced.

6 ¶ And the LORD of hosts will prepare a lavish banquet for all
   peoples on this mountain;
   A banquet of aged wine, choice
   pieces with marrow,
   And refined, aged wine.
7 And on this mountain He will
   swallow up the covering which
   is over all peoples,

Even the veil which is stretched
over all nations.

8 He will swallow up death for all
time,
And the Lord GOD will wipe tears
away from all faces,
And He will remove the reproach
of His people from all the earth;
For the LORD has spoken.

9 And it will be said in that day,
"Behold, this is our God for whom
we have waited that He might
save us.
This is the LORD for whom we
have waited;
Let us rejoice and be glad in His
salvation."

10 For the hand of the LORD will rest
on this mountain,
And Moab will be trodden down
in his place
As straw is trodden down in the
water of a manure pile.

11 And he will spread out his hands
in the middle of it
As a swimmer spreads out *his
hands* to swim,
But *the Lord* will lay low his pride
together with the trickery of his
hands.

12 And the unassailable fortifications
of your walls He will bring
down,
Lay low, *and* cast to the ground,
even to the dust.

CHAPTER 26

IN that day this song will be sung in
the land of Judah:
"We have a strong city;
He sets up walls and ramparts for
security.

2 "Open the gates, that the righteous
nation may enter,
The one that remains faithful.

3 "The steadfast of mind Thou wilt
keep in perfect peace,
Because he trusts in Thee.

4 "Trust in the LORD forever,
For in GOD the LORD, *we have* an
everlasting Rock.

5 "For He has brought low those
who dwell on high, the unassailable city;
He lays it low, He lays it low to
the ground, He casts it to the
dust.

6 "The foot will trample it,

The feet of the afflicted, the steps
of the helpless."

7 ¶ The way of the righteous is
smooth;
O Upright One, make the path of
the righteous level.

8 Indeed, *while following* the way
of Thy judgments, O LORD,
We have waited for Thee eagerly;
Thy name, even Thy memory, is
the desire of *our* souls.

9 At night my soul longs for Thee,
Indeed, my spirit within me seeks
Thee diligently;
For when the earth experiences
Thy judgments
The inhabitants of the world learn
righteousness.

10 *Though* the wicked is shown favor,
He does not learn righteousness;
He deals unjustly in the land of
uprightness,
And does not perceive the majesty of the LORD.

11 ¶ O LORD, Thy hand is lifted up
yet they do not see it.
They see *Thy* zeal for the people
and are put to shame;
Indeed, fire will devour Thine enemies.

12 LORD, Thou wilt establish peace
for us,
Since Thou hast also performed
for us all our works.

13 O LORD our God, other masters
besides Thee have ruled us;
But through Thee alone we confess Thy name.

14 The dead will not live, the departed spirits will not rise;
Therefore Thou hast punished
and destroyed them,
And Thou hast wiped out all remembrance of them.

15 Thou hast increased the nation, O
LORD,
Thou hast increased the nation,
Thou art glorified;
Thou hast extended all the bor-
ders of the land.

16 O LORD, they sought Thee in dis-
tress;
They could only whisper a prayer,
Your chastening was upon them.

17 As the pregnant woman approaches *the time* to give birth,

She writhes *and* cries out in her
labor pains,
Thus were we before Thee, O
LORD.
18 We were pregnant, we writhed *in
labor,*
We gave birth, as it were, *only* to
wind.
We could not accomplish deliverance for the earth
Nor were inhabitants of the world
born.
19 Your dead will live;
Their corpses will rise.
You who lie in the dust, awake
and shout for joy,
For your dew is as the dew of the
dawn,
And the earth will give birth to
the departed spirits.

20 ¶ Come, my people, enter into
your rooms,
And close your doors behind you;
Hide for a little while,
Until indignation runs *its* course.
21 For behold, the LORD is about to
come out from His place
To punish the inhabitants of the
earth for their iniquity;
And the earth will reveal her
bloodshed,
And will no longer cover her slain.

CHAPTER 27

IN that day the LORD will punish
Leviathan the fleeing serpent,
With His fierce and great and
mighty sword,
Even Leviathan the twisted ser-
pent;
And He will kill the dragon who
lives in the sea.

2 ¶ In that day,
"A vineyard of wine, sing of it!
3"I, the LORD, am its keeper;
I water it every moment.
Lest anyone damage it,
I guard it night and day.
4"I have no wrath.
Should someone give Me briars
and thorns in battle,
Then I would step on them, I
would burn them completely.
5"Or let him rely on My protection,
Let him make peace with Me,
Let him make peace with Me."

6 In the days to come Jacob will
take root,
Israel will blossom and sprout;
And they will fill the whole world
with fruit.

7 ¶ Like the striking of Him who
has struck them, has He struck
them?
Or like the slaughter of His slain,
have they been slain?
8 Thou didst contend with them by
banishing them, by driving
them away.
With His fierce wind He has expelled *them* on the day of the
east wind.
9 Therefore through this Jacob's
iniquity will be forgiven;
And this will be the full price of
the pardoning of his sin:
When he makes all the altar
stones like pulverized chalk
stones;
When Asherim and incense altars
will not stand.
10 For the fortified city is isolated,
A homestead forlorn and forsaken
like the desert;
There the calf will graze,
And there it will lie down and feed
on its branches.
11 When its limbs are dry, they are
broken off;
Women come *and* make a fire
with them.
For they are not a people of discernment,
Therefore their Maker will not
have compassion on them.
And their Creator will not be gracious to them.
12 And it will come about in that
day, that the LORD will start *His*
threshing from the flowing stream of
the Euphrates to the brook of Egypt;
and you will be gathered up one by
one, O sons of Israel.
13 It will come about also in that day
that a great trumpet will be blown;
and those who were perishing in the
land of Assyria and who were scattered in the land of Egypt will come
and worship the LORD in the holy
mountain at Jerusalem.

CHAPTER 28

WOE to the proud crown of the
drunkards of Ephraim,

And to the fading flower of its
glorious beauty,
Which is at the head of the fertile
valley
Of those who are overcome with
wine!
2 Behold, the Lord has a strong and
mighty *agent;*
As a storm of hail, a tempest of
destruction,
Like a storm of mighty overflowing waters,
He has cast *it* down to the earth
with *His* hand.
3 The proud crown of the drunkards of Ephraim is trodden under foot.
4 And the fading flower of its glorious beauty,
Which is at the head of the fertile
valley,
Will be like the first-ripe fig prior
to summer;
Which one sees,
And as soon as it is in his hand,
He swallows it.
5 In that day the LORD of hosts will
become a beautiful crown
And a glorious diadem to the remnant of His people;
6 A spirit of justice for him who sits
in judgment,
A strength to those who repel the
onslaught at the gate.
7 And these also reel with wine and
stagger from strong drink:
The priest and the prophet reel
with strong drink,
They are confused by wine, they
stagger from strong drink;
They reel while having visions,
They totter *when rendering* judgment.
8 For all the tables are full of filthy
vomit, without a *single clean*
place.

9 ¶"To whom would He teach
knowledge?
And to whom would He interpret
the message?
Those *just* weaned from milk?
Those *just* taken from the breast?
10"For *He says,*
'Order on order, order on order,
Line on line, line on line,
A little here, a little there.' "
11 Indeed, He will speak to this peo-
ple

Through stammering lips and a
foreign tongue,
12 He who said to them, "Here is
rest, give rest to the weary,"
And, "Here is repose," but they
would not listen.
13 So the word of the LORD to them
will be,
"Order on order, order on order,
Line on line, line on line,
A little here, a little there,"
That they may go and stumble
backward, be broken, snared,
and taken captive.
14 Therefore, hear the word of the
LORD, O scoffers,
Who rule this people who are in
Jerusalem,
15 Because you have said, "We have
made a covenant with death,
And with Sheol we have made a
pact.
The overwhelming scourge will
not reach us when it passes by,
For we have made falsehood our
refuge and we have concealed
ourselves with deception."
16 Therefore thus says the Lord GOD,
"Behold, I am laying in Zion a
stone, a tested stone,
A costly cornerstone *for* the foundation, firmly placed.
He who believes *in it* will not be
disturbed.
17"And I will make justice the measuring line,
And righteousness the level;
Then hail shall sweep away the
refuge of lies,
And the waters shall overflow the
secret place.
18"And your covenant with death
shall be canceled,
And your pact with Sheol shall
not stand;
When the overwhelming scourge
passes through,
Then you become its trampling
place.
19"As often as it passes through, it
will seize you.
For morning after morning it will
pass through, *anytime* during
the day or night.
And it will be sheer terror to understand what it means."
20 The bed is too short on which to
stretch out,

And the blanket is too small to
    wrap oneself in.
21 For the LORD will rise up as *at*
    Mount Perazim,
    He will be stirred up as in the
    valley of Gibeon;
    To do His task, His unusual task,
    And to work His work, His
    extraordinary work.
22 And now do not carry on as scoff-
    ers,
    Lest your fetters be made stron-
    ger;
    For I have heard from the Lord
    GOD of hosts,
    Of decisive destruction on all the
    earth.

23 ¶ Give ear and hear my voice,
    Listen and hear my words.
24 Does the farmer plow continually
    to plant seed?
    Does he *continually* turn and har-
    row the ground?
25 Does he not level its surface,
    And sow dill and scatter cummin,
    And plant wheat in rows,
    Barley in its place, and rye within
    its area?
26 For his God instructs and teaches
    him properly.
27 For dill is not threshed with a
    threshing sledge,
    Nor is the cartwheel driven over
    cummin;
    But dill is beaten out with a rod,
    and cummin with a club.
28 *Grain for* bread is crushed,
    Indeed, he does not continue to
    thresh it forever.
    Because the wheel of *his* cart and
    his horses *eventually* damage *it,*
    He does not thresh it longer.
29 This also comes from the LORD of
    hosts,
    Who has made *His* counsel won-
    derful and *His* wisdom great.

CHAPTER 29

WOE, O Ariel, Ariel the city *where*
    David *once* camped!
    Add year to year, observe *your*
    feasts on schedule.
2 And I will bring distress to Ariel,
    And she shall be *a city of* lament-
    ing and mourning;
    And she shall be like an Ariel to
    me.

3 And I will camp against you encir-
    cling *you,*
    And I will set siegeworks against
    you,
    And I will raise up battle towers
    against you.
4 Then you shall be brought low;
    From the earth you shall speak,
    And from the dust *where* you are
    prostrate,
    Your words *shall come.*
    Your voice shall also be like that
    of a spirit from the ground,
    And your speech shall whisper
    from the dust.

5 ¶ But the multitude of your en-
    emies shall become like fine
    dust,
    And the multitude of the ruthless
    ones like the chaff which blows
    away;
    And it shall happen instantly, sud-
    denly.
6 From the LORD of hosts you will
    be punished with thunder and
    earthquake and loud noise,
    With whirlwind and tempest and
    the flame of a consuming fire.
7 And the multitude of all the na-
    tions who wage war against
    Ariel,
    Even all who wage war against
    her and her stronghold, and
    who distress her,
    Shall be like a dream, a vision of
    the night.
8 And it will be as when a hungry
    man dreams—
    And behold, he is eating;
    But when he awakens, his hunger
    is not satisfied,
    Or as when a thirsty man
    dreams—
    And behold, he is drinking,
    But when he awakens, behold, he
    is faint,
    And his thirst is not quenched.
    Thus the multitude of all the na-
    tions shall be,
    Who wage war against Mount
    Zion.

9 ¶ Be delayed and wait.
    Blind yourselves and be blind.
    They become drunk, but not with
    wine;
    They stagger, but not with strong
    drink.

10 For the LORD has poured over you
    a spirit of deep sleep,
    He has shut your eyes, the proph-
      ets;
    And He has covered your heads,
      the seers.

11 And the entire vision shall be to
you like the words of a sealed book,
which when they give it to the one
who is literate, saying, "Please read
this," he will say, "I cannot, for it is
sealed."

12 Then the book will be given to the
one who is illiterate, saying, "Please
read this." And he will say, "I cannot
read."

13 ¶ Then the Lord said,
   "Because this people draw near
    with their words
   And honor Me with their lip ser-
    vice,
   But they remove their hearts far
    from Me,
   And their reverence for Me con-
    sists of tradition learned *by
    rote*,

14 Therefore behold, I will once
    again deal marvelously with
    this people, wondrously marvel-
    ous;
   And the wisdom of their wise men
    shall perish,
   And the discernment of their dis-
    cerning men shall be concealed.

15 ¶ Woe to those who deeply hide
    their plans from the LORD,
   And whose deeds are *done* in a
    dark place,
   And they say, "Who sees us?" or
    "Who knows us?"

16 You turn *things* around!
   Shall the potter be considered as
    equal with the clay,
   That what is made should say to
    its maker, "He did not make
    me";
   Or what is formed say to him who
    formed it, "He has no under-
    standing"?

17 ¶ Is it not yet just a little while
   Before Lebanon will be turned
    into a fertile field,
   And the fertile field will be consid-
    ered as a forest?

18 And on that day the deaf shall
    hear words of a book,

   And out of *their* gloom and dark-
    ness the eyes of the blind shall
    see.

19 The afflicted also shall increase
    their gladness in the LORD,
   And the needy of mankind shall
    rejoice in the Holy One of Is-
    rael.

20 For the ruthless will come to an
    end, and the scorner will be
    finished,
   Indeed all who are intent on doing
    evil will be cut off;

21 Who cause a person to be indicted
    by a word,
   And ensnare him who adjudicates
    at the gate,
   And defraud the one in the right
    with meaningless arguments.

22 ¶ Therefore thus says the LORD,
who redeemed Abraham, concerning
the house of Jacob,
   "Jacob shall not now be ashamed,
    nor shall his face now turn pale;

23 But when he sees his children, the
    work of My hands, in his midst,
   They will sanctify My name;
   Indeed, they will sanctify the Holy
    One of Jacob,
   And will stand in awe of the God
    of Israel.

24 "And those who err in mind will
    know the truth,
   And those who criticize will ac-
    cept instruction.

CHAPTER 30

"WOE to the rebellious children,"
    declares the LORD,
   "Who execute a plan, but not Mine,
   And make an alliance, but not of
    My Spirit,
   In order to add sin to sin;

2 Who proceed down to Egypt,
   Without consulting Me,
   To take refuge in the safety of
    Pharaoh,
   And to seek shelter in the shadow
    of Egypt!

3 "Therefore the safety of Pharaoh
    will be your shame,
   And the shelter in the shadow of
    Egypt, your humiliation.

4 "For their princes are at Zoan,
   And their ambassadors arrive at
    Hanes.

5 "Everyone will be ashamed be-
    cause of a people who cannot
    profit them,

Who are not for help or profit, but
for shame and also for reproach."

6 ¶ The oracle concerning the
beasts of the Negev.
Through a land of distress and
anguish,
From where *come* lioness and
lion, viper and flying serpent,
They carry their riches on the
backs of young donkeys
And their treasures on camels'
humps,
To a people who cannot profit
them;
7 Even Egypt, whose help is vain
and empty.
Therefore, I have called her
"Rahab who has been exterminated."
8 Now go, write it on a tablet before
them
And inscribe it on a scroll,
That it may serve in the time to
come
As a witness forever.
9 For this is a rebellious people,
false sons,
Sons who refuse to listen
To the instruction of the LORD;
10 Who say to the seers, "You must
not see *visions*";
And to the prophets, "You must
not prophesy to us what is
right,
Speak to us pleasant words,
Prophesy illusions.
11 "Get out of the way, turn aside
from the path,
Let us hear no more about the
Holy One of Israel."
12 Therefore thus says the Holy One
of Israel,
"Since you have rejected this word,
And have put your trust in oppression and guile, and have
relied on them,
13 Therefore this iniquity will be to
you
Like a breach about to fall,
A bulge in a high wall,
Whose collapse comes suddenly in
an instant.
14 "And whose collapse is like the
smashing of a potter's jar;
So ruthlessly shattered
That a sherd will not be found
among its pieces

To take fire from a hearth,
Or to scoop water from a cistern."
15 For thus the Lord GOD, the Holy
One of Israel, has said,
"In repentance and rest you shall
be saved,
In quietness and trust is your
strength."
But you were not willing,
16 And you said, "No, for we will flee
on horses,"
Therefore you shall flee!
"And we will ride on swift *horses*,"
Therefore those who pursue you
shall be swift.
17 One thousand *shall flee* at the
threat of one *man*,
You shall flee at the threat of five;
Until you are left as a flag on a
mountain top,
And as a signal on a hill.

18 ¶ Therefore the LORD longs to be
gracious to you,
And therefore He waits on high to
have compassion on you.
For the LORD is a God of justice;
How blessed are all those who
long for Him.
19 O people in Zion, inhabitant in
Jerusalem, you will weep no longer.
He will surely be gracious to you at
the sound of your cry; when He hears
it, He will answer you.
20 Although the Lord has given you
bread of privation and water of oppression, *He*, your Teacher will no
longer hide Himself, but your eyes will
behold your Teacher.
21 And your ears will hear a word
behind you, "This is the way, walk in
it," whenever you turn to the right or
to the left.
22 And you will defile your graven
images, overlaid with silver, and your
molten images plated with gold. You
will scatter them as an impure thing;
and say to them, "Be gone!"
23 ¶ Then He will give *you* rain for
the seed which you will sow in the
ground, and bread *from* the yield of
the ground, and it will be rich and
plenteous; on that day your livestock
will graze in a roomy pasture.
24 Also the oxen and the donkeys
which work the ground will eat salted
fodder, which has been winnowed
with shovel and fork.

25 And on every lofty mountain and on every high hill there will be streams running with water on the day of the great slaughter, when the towers fall.

26 And the light of the moon will be as the light of the sun, and the light of the sun will be seven times *brighter*, like the light of seven days, on the day the Lord binds up the fracture of His people and heals the bruise He has inflicted.

27 ¶ Behold, the name of the Lord
    comes from a remote place;
    Burning is His anger, and dense is
    His smoke;
    His lips are filled with indignation,
    And His tongue is like a consum-
    ing fire;

28 And His breath is like an over-
    flowing torrent,
    Which reaches to the neck,
    To shake the nations back and
    forth in a sieve,
    And to *put* in the jaws of the
    peoples the bridle which leads
    to ruin.

29 You will have songs as in the
    night when you keep the festi-
    val;
    And gladness of heart as when
    one marches to *the sound of* the
    flute,
    To go to the mountain of the
    Lord, to the Rock of Israel.

30 And the Lord will cause His voice
    of authority to be heard.
    And the descending of His arm to
    be seen in fierce anger,
    And *in* the flame of a consuming
    fire,
    In cloudburst, downpour, and
    hailstones.

31 For at the voice of the Lord As-
    syria will be terrified,
    When He strikes with the rod.

32 And every blow of the rod of pun-
    ishment,
    Which the Lord will lay on him,
    Will be with *the music of* tambou-
    rines and lyres;
    And in battles, brandishing weap-
    ons, He will fight them.

33 For [13]Topheth has long been
    ready,
    Indeed, it has been prepared for
    the king.
    He has made it deep and large,

[13] I.e., the place of human sacrifice to Molech

A pyre of fire with plenty of wood;
The breath of the Lord, like a
    torrent of brimstone, sets it
    afire.

CHAPTER 31

WOE to those who go down to
    Egypt for help,
    And rely on horses,
    And trust in chariots because they
    are many,
    And in horsemen because they are
    very strong,
    But they do not look to the Holy
    One of Israel, nor seek the
    Lord!

2 Yet He also is wise and will bring
    disaster,
    And does not retract His words,
    But will arise against the house of
    evildoers,
    And against the help of the work-
    ers of iniquity.

3 Now the Egyptians are men, and
    not God,
    And their horses are flesh and not
    spirit;
    So the Lord will stretch out His
    hand,
    And he who helps will stumble
    And he who is helped will fall,
    And all of them will come to an
    end together.

4 ¶ For thus says the Lord to me,
    "As the lion or the young lion
    growls over his prey,
    Against which a band of shep-
    herds is called out,
    Will not be terrified at their voice,
    nor disturbed at their noise,
    So will the Lord of hosts come
    down to wage war on Mount
    Zion and on its hill."

5 Like flying birds so the Lord of
    hosts will protect Jerusalem.
    He will protect and deliver *it;*
    He will pass over and rescue *it.*

6 Return to Him from whom you
have deeply defected, O sons of Israel.

7 For in that day every man will
cast away his silver idols and his gold
idols, which your hands have made as
a sin.

8 And the Assyrian will fall by a
    sword not of man,
    And a sword not of man will de-
    vour him.
    So he will not escape the sword,

And his young men will become forced laborers.

9 "And his rock will pass away because of panic,
And his princes will be terrified at the standard,"

Declares the LORD, whose fire is in Zion and whose furnace is in Jerusalem.

CHAPTER 32

BEHOLD, a king will reign righteously,
And princes will rule justly.

2 And each will be like a refuge from the wind,
And a shelter from the storm,
Like streams of water in a dry country,
Like the shade of a huge rock in a parched land.

3 Then the eyes of those who see will not be blinded,
And the ears of those who hear will listen.

4 And the mind of the hasty will discern the truth,
And the tongue of the stammerers will hasten to speak clearly.

5 No longer will the fool be called noble,
Or the rogue be spoken of as generous.

6 For a fool speaks nonsense,
And his heart inclines toward wickedness,
To practice ungodliness and to speak error against the LORD,
To keep the hungry person unsatisfied
And to withhold drink from the thirsty.

7 As for a rogue, his weapons are evil;
He devises wicked schemes
To destroy the afflicted with slander,
Even though the needy one speaks what is right.

8 But the noble man devises noble plans;
And by noble plans he stands.

9 ¶ Rise up you women who are at ease,
And hear my voice;
Give ear to my word,
You complacent daughters.

10 Within a year and a few days,
You will be troubled, O complacent daughters;
For the vintage is ended,
And the fruit gathering will not come.

11 Tremble, you women who are at ease;
Be troubled, you complacent daughters;
Strip, undress, and put sackcloth on your waist,

12 Beat your breasts for the pleasant fields, for the fruitful vine,

13 For the land of my people in which thorns and briars shall come up;
Yea, for all the joyful houses, and for the jubilant city.

14 Because the palace has been abandoned, the populated city forsaken.
Hill and watch-tower have become caves forever,
A delight for wild donkeys, a pasture for flocks;

15 Until the Spirit is poured out upon us from on high,
And the wilderness becomes a fertile field
And the fertile field is considered as a forest.

16 Then justice will dwell in the wilderness,
And righteousness will abide in the fertile field.

17 And the work of righteousness will be peace,
And the service of righteousness, quietness and confidence forever.

18 Then my people will live in a peaceful habitation,
And in secure dwellings and in undisturbed resting places;

19 And it will hail when the forest comes down,
And the city will be utterly laid low.

20 How blessed will you be, you who sow beside all waters,
Who let out freely the ox and the donkey.

CHAPTER 33

WOE to you, O destroyer,
While you were not destroyed;
And he who is treacherous, while

others did not deal treacherously with him.
As soon as you shall finish destroying, you shall be destroyed;
As soon as you shall cease to deal treacherously, *others* shall deal treacherously with you.

2 O Lord, be gracious to us; we have waited for Thee.
Be Thou their strength every morning,
Our salvation also in the time of distress.

3 At the sound of the tumult peoples flee;
At the lifting up of Thyself nations disperse.

4 And your spoil is gathered *as* the caterpillar gathers;
As locusts rushing about, men rush about on it.

5 The Lord is exalted, for He dwells on high;
He has filled Zion with justice and righteousness.

6 And He shall be the stability of your times,
A wealth of salvation, wisdom, and knowledge;
The fear of the Lord is his treasure.

7 Behold, their brave men cry in the streets,
The ambassadors of peace weep bitterly.

8 The highways are desolate, the traveler has ceased,
He has broken the covenant, he has despised the cities,
He has no regard for man.

9 The land mourns and pines away,
Lebanon is shamed and withers;
Sharon is like a desert plain,
And Bashan and Carmel lose *their foliage.*

10 "Now I will arise," says the Lord,
"Now I will be exalted, now I will be lifted up.

11 "You have conceived chaff, you will give birth to stubble;
My breath will consume you like a fire.

12 "And the peoples will be burned to lime,
Like cut thorns which are burned in the fire.

13 ¶"You who are far away, hear what I have done;
And you who are near, acknowledge My might."

14 Sinners in Zion are terrified;
Trembling has seized the godless.
"Who among us can live with the consuming fire?
Who among us can live with continual burning?"

15 He who walks righteously, and speaks with sincerity,
He who rejects unjust gain,
And shakes his hands so that they hold no bribe;
He who stops his ears from hearing about bloodshed,
And shuts his eyes from looking upon evil;

16 He will dwell on the heights;
His refuge will be the impregnable rock;
His bread will be given *him;*
His water will be sure.

17 ¶ Your eyes will see the King in His beauty;
They will behold a far-distant land.

18 Your heart will meditate on terror:
"Where is he who counts?
Where is he who weighs?
Where is he who counts the towers?"

19 You will no longer see a fierce people,
A people of unintelligible speech which no one comprehends,
Of a stammering tongue which no one understands.

20 Look upon Zion, the city of our appointed feasts;
Your eyes shall see Jerusalem an undisturbed habitation,
A tent which shall not be folded,
Its stakes shall never be pulled up
Nor any of its cords be torn apart.

21 But there the majestic *One,* the Lord, shall be for us
A place of rivers *and* wide canals,
On which no boat with oars shall go,
And on which no mighty ship shall pass—

22 For the Lord is our judge,
The Lord is our lawgiver,
The Lord is our king;
He will save us—

23 Your tackle hangs slack;
It cannot hold the base of its mast
firmly,
Nor spread out the sail.
Then the prey of an abundant
spoil will be divided;
The lame will take the plunder.
24 And no resident will say, "I am
sick";
The people who dwell there will
be forgiven *their* iniquity.

CHAPTER 34

DRAW near, O nations, to hear; and
listen, O peoples!
Let the earth and all it contains
hear, and the world and all that
springs from it.
2 For the LORD's indignation is
against all the nations,
And *His* wrath against all their
armies;
He has utterly destroyed them,
He has given them over to slaughter.
3 So their slain will be thrown out,
And their corpses will give off
their stench,
And the mountains will be
drenched with their blood.
4 And all the host of heaven will
wear away,
And the sky will be rolled up like a
scroll;
All their hosts will also wither
away
As a leaf withers from the vine,
Or as *one* withers from the fig
tree.
5 For My sword is satiated in
heaven,
Behold it shall descend for judgment upon Edom,
And upon the people whom I have
devoted to destruction.
6 The sword of the LORD is filled
with blood,
It is sated with fat, with the blood
of lambs and goats,
With the fat of the kidneys of
rams.
For the LORD has a sacrifice in
Bozrah,
And a great slaughter in the land
of Edom.
7 Wild oxen shall also fall with
them,
And young bulls with strong ones;

Thus their land shall be soaked
with blood,
And their dust become greasy
with fat.
8 For the LORD has a day of vengeance,
A year of recompense for the
cause of Zion.
9 And its streams shall be turned
into pitch,
And its loose earth into brimstone,
And its land shall become burning
pitch.
10 It shall not be quenched night or
day;
Its smoke shall go up forever;
From generation to generation it
shall be desolate;
None shall pass through it forever
and ever.
11 But pelican and hedgehog shall
possess it,
And owl and raven shall dwell in
it;
And He shall stretch over it the
line of desolation
And the plumb line of emptiness.
12 Its nobles—there is no one there
Whom they may proclaim king—
And all its princes shall be nothing.
13 And thorns shall come up in its
fortified towers,
Nettles and thistles in its fortified
cities;
It shall also be a haunt of jackals
And an abode of ostriches.
14 And the desert creatures shall
meet with the wolves,
The hairy goat also shall cry to its
kind;
Yes, the night monster shall settle
there
And shall find herself a resting
place.
15 The tree snake shall make its nest
and lay *eggs* there,
And it will hatch and gather *them*
under its protection.
Yes, the hawks shall be gathered
there,
Every one with its kind.

16 ¶ Seek from the book of the
LORD, and read:
Not one of these will be missing;
None will lack its mate.

For His mouth has commanded,
And His Spirit has gathered them.
17 And He has cast the lot for them,
And His hand has divided it to
them by line.
They shall possess it forever;
From generation to generation
they shall dwell in it.

CHAPTER 35

THE wilderness and the desert will be
glad,
And the Arabah will rejoice and
blossom;
Like the crocus
2 It will blossom profusely
And rejoice with rejoicing and
shout of joy.
The glory of Lebanon will be
given to it,
The majesty of Carmel and
Sharon.
They will see the glory of the
LORD,
The majesty of our God.
3 Encourage the exhausted, and
strengthen the feeble.
4 Say to those with anxious heart,
"Take courage, fear not.
Behold, your God will come *with*
vengeance;
The recompense of God will come,
But He will save you."
5 Then the eyes of the blind will be
opened,
And the ears of the deaf will be
unstopped.
6 Then the lame will leap like a
deer,
And the tongue of the dumb will
shout for joy.
For waters will break forth in the
wilderness
And streams in the Arabah.
7 And the scorched land will become a pool,
And the thirsty ground springs of
water;
In the haunt of jackals, its resting
place,
Grass *becomes* reeds and rushes.
8 And a highway will be there, a
roadway,
And it will be called the Highway
of Holiness.
The unclean will not travel on it,
But it *will* be for him who walks
that way,

And fools will not wander *on it.*
9 No lion will be there,
Nor will any vicious beast go up
on it;
These will not be found there.
But the redeemed will walk *there,*
10 And the ransomed of the LORD
will return,
And come with joyful shouting to
Zion,
With everlasting joy upon their
heads.
They will find gladness and joy,
And sorrow and sighing will flee
away.

CHAPTER 36

NOW it came about in the fourteenth
year of King Hezekiah, Sennacherib
king of Assyria came up against all the
fortified cities of Judah and seized
them.

2 And the king of Assyria sent Rabshakeh from Lachish to Jerusalem to
King Hezekiah with a large army. And
he stood by the conduit of the upper
pool on the highway of the fuller's
field.

3 Then Eliakim the son of Hilkiah,
who was over the household, and
Shebna the scribe, and Joah the son of
Asaph, the recorder, came out to him.

4 ¶ Then Rabshakeh said to them,
"Say now to Hezekiah, 'Thus says the
great king, the king of Assyria, "What
is this confidence that you have?

5 "I say, 'Your counsel and strength
for the war are only empty words.'
Now on whom do you rely, that you
have rebelled against me?

6 "Behold, you rely on the staff of
this crushed reed, *even* on Egypt; on
which if a man leans, it will go into his
hand and pierce it. So is Pharaoh king
of Egypt to all who rely on him.

7 "But if you say to me, 'We trust in
the LORD our God,' is it not He whose
high places and whose altars Hezekiah
has taken away, and has said to Judah
and to Jerusalem, 'You shall worship
before this altar'?

8 "Now therefore, come make a bargain with my master the king of Assyria, and I will give you two thousand
horses, if you are able on your part to
set riders on them.

9 "How then can you repulse one
official of the least of my master's

servants, and rely on Egypt for chariots and for horsemen?

10 "And have I now come up without the LORD's approval against this land to destroy it? The LORD said to me, 'Go up against this land, and destroy it.' " ' "

11 ¶ Then Eliakim and Shebna and Joah said to Rabshakeh, "Speak now to your servants in Aramaic, for we understand it; and do not speak with us in Judean, in the hearing of the people who are on the wall."

12 But Rabshakeh said, "Has my master sent me only to your master and to you to speak these words, and not to the men who sit on the wall, doomed to eat their own dung and drink their own urine with you?"

13 ¶ Then Rabshakeh stood and cried with a loud voice in Judean, and said, "Hear the words of the great king, the king of Assyria.

14 "Thus says the king, 'Do not let Hezekiah deceive you, for he will not be able to deliver you;

15 nor let Hezekiah make you trust in the LORD, saying, "The LORD will surely deliver us, this city shall not be given into the hand of the king of Assyria."

16 'Do not listen to Hezekiah,' for thus says the king of Assyria, 'Make your peace with me and come out to me, and eat each of his vine and each of his fig tree and drink each of the waters of his own cistern,

17 until I come and take you away to a land like your own land, a land of grain and new wine, a land of bread and vineyards.

18 'Beware lest Hezekiah misleads you, saying, "The LORD will deliver us." Has any one of the gods of the nations delivered his land from the hand of the king of Assyria?

19 'Where are the gods of Hamath and Arpad? Where are the gods of Sepharvaim? And when have they delivered Samaria from my hand?

20 'Who among all the gods of these lands have delivered their land from my hand, that the LORD should deliver Jerusalem from my hand?' "

21 ¶ But they were silent and answered him not a word; for the king's commandment was, "Do not answer him."

22 Then Eliakim the son of Hilkiah, who was over the household, and Shebna the scribe and Joah the son of Asaph, the recorder, came to Hezekiah with their clothes torn and told him the words of Rabshakeh.

CHAPTER 37

AND when King Hezekiah heard it, he tore his clothes, covered himself with sackcloth and entered the house of the LORD.

2 Then he sent Eliakim who was over the household with Shebna the scribe and the elders of the priests, covered with sackcloth, to Isaiah the prophet, the son of Amoz.

3 And they said to him, "Thus says Hezekiah, 'This day is a day of distress, rebuke, and rejection; for children have come to birth, and there is no strength to deliver.

4 'Perhaps the LORD your God will hear the words of Rabshakeh, whom his master the king of Assyria has sent to reproach the living God, and will rebuke the words which the LORD your God has heard. Therefore, offer a prayer for the remnant that is left.' "

5 So the servants of King Hezekiah came to Isaiah.

6 And Isaiah said to them, "Thus you shall say to your master, 'Thus says the LORD, "Do not be afraid because of the words that you have heard, with which the servants of the king of Assyria have blasphemed Me.

7 "Behold, I will put a spirit in him so that he shall hear a rumor and return to his own land. And I will make him fall by the sword in his own land." ' "

8 ¶ Then Rabshakeh returned and found the king of Assyria fighting against Libnah, for he had heard that the king had left Lachish.

9 When he heard them say concerning Tirhakah king of Cush, "He has come out to fight against you," and when he heard it he sent messengers to Hezekiah, saying,

10 "Thus you shall say to Hezekiah king of Judah, 'Do not let your God in whom you trust deceive you, saying, "Jerusalem shall not be given into the hand of the king of Assyria."

11 'Behold, you have heard what the kings of Assyria have done to all the

lands, destroying them completely. So will you be spared?

12 'Did the gods of those nations which my fathers have destroyed deliver them, *even* Gozan and Haran and Rezeph and the sons of Eden who *were* in Telassar?

13 'Where is the king of Hamath, the king of Arpad, the king of the city of Sepharvaim, *and of* Hena and Ivvah?' "

14 ¶ Then Hezekiah took the letter from the hand of the messengers and read it, and he went up to the house of the LORD and spread it out before the LORD.

15 And Hezekiah prayed to the LORD saying,

16 "O LORD of hosts, the God of Israel, who art enthroned *above* the cherubim, Thou art the God, Thou alone, of all the kingdoms of the earth. Thou hast made heaven and earth.

17 "Incline Thine ear, O LORD, and hear; open Thine eyes, O LORD, and see; and listen to all the words of Sennacherib, who sent *them* to reproach the living God.

18 "Truly, O LORD, the kings of Assyria have devastated all the countries and their lands,

19 and have cast their gods into the fire, for they were not gods but the work of men's hands, wood and stone. So they have destroyed them.

20 "And now, O LORD our God, deliver us from his hand that all the kingdoms of the earth may know that Thou alone, LORD, art God."

21 Then Isaiah the son of Amoz sent *word* to Hezekiah, saying, "Thus says the LORD, the God of Israel, 'Because you have prayed to Me about Sennacherib king of Assyria,

22 this is the word that the LORD has spoken against him:

"She has despised you and mocked you,
     The virgin daughter of Zion;
She has shaken *her* head behind you,
     The daughter of Jerusalem!

23 "Whom have you reproached and blasphemed?
     And against whom have you raised *your* voice,
And haughtily lifted up your eyes?
     Against the Holy One of Israel!

24 "Through your servants you have reproached the Lord,
     And you have said, 'With my many chariots I came up to the heights of the mountains,
To the remotest parts of Lebanon;
     And I cut down its tall cedars *and* its choice cypresses.
And I will go to its highest peak, its thickest forest.

25 'I dug *wells* and drank waters,
     And with the sole of my feet I dried up
All the rivers of Egypt.'

26 "Have you not heard?
     Long ago I did it,
From ancient times I planned it.
     Now I have brought it to pass,
That you should turn fortified cities into ruinous heaps.

27 "Therefore their inhabitants were short of strength,
     They were dismayed and put to shame;
They were *as* the vegetation of the field and *as* the green herb,
     As grass on the housetops is scorched before it is grown up.

28 "But I know your sitting down,
     And your going out and your coming in,
And your raging against Me.

29 "Because of your raging against Me,
     And because your arrogance has come up to My ears,
Therefore I will put My hook in your nose,
     And My bridle in your lips,
And I will turn you back by the way which you came.

30 ¶ "Then this shall be the sign for you: you shall eat this year what grows of itself, in the second year what springs from the same, and in the third year sow, reap, plant vineyards, and eat their fruit.

31 "And the surviving remnant of the house of Judah shall again take root downward and bear fruit upward.

32 "For out of Jerusalem shall go forth a remnant, and out of Mount Zion survivors. The zeal of the LORD of hosts shall perform this." '

33 "Therefore, thus says the LORD concerning the king of Assyria, 'He shall not come to this city, or shoot an arrow there; neither shall he come

before it with a shield, nor throw up a mound against it.

34 'By the way that he came, by the same he shall return, and he shall not come to this city,' declares the LORD.

35 'For I will defend this city to save it for My own sake and for My servant David's sake.' "

36 ¶ Then the angel of the LORD went out, and struck 185,000 in the camp of the Assyrians; and when men arose early in the morning, behold, all of these were dead.

37 So Sennacherib, king of Assyria, departed and returned *home*, and lived at Nineveh.

38 And it came about as he was worshiping in the house of Nisroch his god, that Adrammelech and Sharezer his sons killed him with the sword; and they escaped into the land of Ararat. And Esarhaddon his son became king in his place.

CHAPTER 38

IN those days Hezekiah became mortally ill. And Isaiah the prophet the son of Amoz came to him and said to him, "Thus says the LORD, 'Set your house in order, for you shall die and not live.' "

2 Then Hezekiah turned his face to the wall, and prayed to the LORD,

3 and said, "Remember now, O LORD, I beseech Thee, how I have walked before Thee in truth and with a whole heart, and have done what is good in Thy sight." And Hezekiah wept bitterly.

4 Then the word of the LORD came to Isaiah, saying,

5 "Go and say to Hezekiah, 'Thus says the LORD, the God of your father David, "I have heard your prayer, I have seen your tears; behold, I will add fifteen years to your life.

6 "And I will deliver you and this city from the hand of the king of Assyria; and I will defend this city." '

7 "And this shall be the sign to you from the LORD, that the LORD will do this thing that He has spoken:

8 "Behold, I will cause the shadow on the stairway, which has gone down with the sun on the stairway of Ahaz, to go back ten steps." So the sun's *shadow* went back ten steps on the stairway on which it had gone down.

9 ¶ A writing of Hezekiah king of Judah, after his illness and recovery:

10 I said, "In the middle of my life
   I am to enter the gates of Sheol;
   I am to be deprived of the rest of
     my years."

11 I said, "I shall not see the LORD,
   The LORD in the land of the living;
   I shall look on man no more
     among the inhabitants of the
     world.

12 "Like a shepherd's tent my dwelling is pulled up and removed from me;
   As a weaver I rolled up my life.
   He cuts me off from the loom;
   From day until night Thou dost
     make an end of me.

13 "I composed *my soul* until morning.
   Like a lion—so He breaks all my
     bones,
   From day until night Thou dost
     make an end of me.

14 "Like a swallow, *like* a crane, so I twitter;
   I moan like a dove;
   My eyes look wistfully to the
     heights;
   O Lord, I am oppressed, be my
     security.

15 ¶ "What shall I say?
   For He has spoken to me, and He
     Himself has done it;
   I shall wander about all my years
     because of the bitterness of my
     soul.

16 "O Lord, by *these* things *men* live;
   And in all these is the life of my
     spirit;
   O restore me to health, and let me
     live!

17 "Lo, for *my own* welfare I had great bitterness;
   It is Thou who hast kept my soul
     from the pit of nothingness,
   For Thou hast cast all my sins
     behind Thy back.

18 "For Sheol cannot thank Thee,
   Death cannot praise Thee;
   Those who go down to the pit
     cannot hope for Thy faithfulness.

19 "It is the living who give thanks to Thee, as I do today;
   A father tells his sons about Thy
     faithfulness.

20 "The LORD will surely save me;

So we will play my songs on
    stringed instruments
All *the* days of our life at the
    house of the Lord."

21 ¶ Now Isaiah had said, "Let them
take a cake of figs, and apply it to the
boil, that he may recover."

22 Then Hezekiah had said, "What is
the sign that I shall go up to the house
of the Lord?"

CHAPTER 39

AT that time Merodach-baladan son
of Baladan, king of Babylon, sent letters and a present to Hezekiah, for he
heard that he had been sick and had
recovered.

2 And Hezekiah was pleased, and
showed them all his treasure house,
the silver and the gold and the spices
and the precious oil and his whole
armory and all that was found in his
treasuries. There was nothing in his
house, nor in all his dominion, that
Hezekiah did not show them.

3 Then Isaiah the prophet came to
King Hezekiah and said to him, "What
did these men say, and from where
have they come to you?" And Hezekiah said, "They have come to me
from a far country, from Babylon."

4 And he said, "What have they
seen in your house?" So Hezekiah
answered, "They have seen all that is
in my house; there is nothing among
my treasuries that I have not shown
them."

5 Then Isaiah said to Hezekiah,
"Hear the word of the Lord of hosts,

6 'Behold, the days are coming when
all that is in your house, and all that
your fathers have laid up in store to
this day shall be carried to Babylon;
nothing shall be left,' says the Lord.

7 'And *some* of your sons who shall
issue from you, whom you shall beget,
shall be taken away; and they shall
become officials in the palace of the
king of Babylon.' "

8 Then Hezekiah said to Isaiah,
"The word of the Lord which you
have spoken is good." For he thought,
"For there will be peace and truth in
my days."

CHAPTER 40

"COMFORT, O comfort My people,"
    says your God.

2 "Speak kindly to Jerusalem;
  And call out to her, that her war-
    fare has ended,
  That her iniquity has been re-
    moved,
  That she has received of the
    Lord's hand
  Double for all her sins."

3 ¶ A voice is calling,
  "Clear the way for the Lord in the
    wilderness;
  Make smooth in the desert a high-
    way for our God.

4 "Let every valley be lifted up,
  And every mountain and hill be
    made low;
  And let the rough ground become
    a plain,
  And the rugged terrain a broad
    valley;

5 Then the glory of the Lord will be
    revealed,
  And all flesh will see *it* together;
  For the mouth of the Lord has
    spoken."

6 A voice says, "Call out."
  Then he answered, "What shall I
    call out?"
  All flesh is grass, and all its loveli-
    ness is like the flower of the
    field.

7 The grass withers, the flower
    fades,
  When the breath of the Lord
    blows upon it;
  Surely the people are grass.

8 The grass withers, the flower
    fades,
  But the word of our God stands
    forever.

9 ¶ Get yourself up on a high
    mountain,
  O Zion, bearer of good news,
  Lift up your voice mightily,
  O Jerusalem, bearer of good news;
  Lift *it* up, do not fear.
  Say to the cities of Judah,
  "Here is your God!"

10 Behold, the Lord God will come
    with might,
  With His arm ruling for Him.
  Behold, His reward is with Him,
  And His recompense before Him.

11 Like a shepherd He will tend His
    flock,
  In His arm He will gather the
    lambs,

And carry *them* in His bosom;
He will gently lead the nursing
ewes.

12 ¶ Who has measured the waters
in the hollow of His hand,
And marked off the heavens by
the span,
And calculated the dust of the
earth by the measure,
And weighed the mountains in a
balance,
And the hills in a pair of scales?
13 Who has directed the Spirit of the
Lord,
Or as His counselor has informed
Him?
14 With whom did He consult and
who gave Him understanding?
And *who* taught Him in the path
of justice and taught Him
knowledge,
And informed Him of the way of
understanding?
15 Behold, the nations are like a drop
from a bucket,
And are regarded as a speck of
dust on the scales;
Behold, He lifts up the islands like
fine dust.
16 Even Lebanon is not enough to
burn,
Nor its beasts enough for a burnt
offering.
17 All the nations are as nothing
before Him,
They are regarded by Him as less
than nothing and meaningless.

18 ¶ To whom then will you liken
God?
Or what likeness will you compare with Him?
19 *As for* the idol, a craftsman casts
it,
A goldsmith plates it with gold,
And a silversmith *fashions* chains
of silver.
20 He who is too impoverished for
such an offering
Selects a tree that does not rot;
He seeks out for himself a skillful
craftsman
To prepare an idol that will not
totter.

21 ¶ Do you not know? Have you
not heard?

Has it not been declared to you
from the beginning?
Have you not understood from
the foundations of the earth?
22 It is He who [14]sits above the
[15]vault of the earth,
And its inhabitants are like grasshoppers,
Who stretches out the heavens
like a curtain
And spreads them out like a tent
to dwell in.
23 He *it is* who reduces rulers to
nothing,
Who makes the judges of the
earth meaningless.
24 [16]Scarcely have they been planted,
[16]Scarcely have they been sown,
[16]Scarcely has their stock taken
root in the earth,
But He merely blows on them,
and they wither,
And the storm carries them away
like stubble.
25 "To whom then will you liken Me
That I should be *his* equal?" says
the Holy One.
26 Lift up your eyes on high
And see who has created these
stars,
The One who leads forth their
host by number,
He calls them all by name;
Because of the greatness of His
might and the strength of *His*
power
Not one *of them* is missing.

27 ¶ Why do you say, O Jacob, and
assert, O Israel,
"My way is hidden from the Lord,
And the justice due me escapes
the notice of my God"?
28 Do you not know? Have you not
heard?
The Everlasting God, the Lord,
the Creator of the ends of the
earth
Does not become weary or tired.
His understanding is inscrutable.
29 He gives strength to the weary,
And to *him who* lacks might He
increases power.
30 Though youths grow weary and
tired,
And vigorous young men stumble
badly,

---

[14] Or, *is enthroned*   [15] Or, *circle*   [16] Or, *Not even*

31 Yet those who wait for the LORD
Will gain new strength;
They will mount up *with* wings
like eagles,
They will run and not get tired,
They will walk and not become
weary.

CHAPTER 41

"COASTLANDS, listen to Me in silence,
And let the peoples gain new
strength;
Let them come forward, then let
them speak;
Let us come together for judgment.

2 "Who has aroused one from the
east
Whom He calls in righteousness
to His feet?
He delivers up nations before him,
And subdues kings.
He makes them like dust with his
sword,
As the wind-driven chaff with his
bow.

3 "He pursues them, passing on in
safety,
By a way he had not been travers-
ing with his feet.

4 "Who has performed and accomplished *it*,
Calling forth the generations from
the beginning?
'I, the LORD, am the first, and
with the last. I am He.' "

5 ¶ The coastlands have seen and
are afraid;
The ends of the earth tremble;
They have drawn near and have
come.

6 Each one helps his neighbor,
And says to his brother, "Be
strong!"

7 So the craftsman encourages the
smelter,
And he who smooths *metal* with
the hammer *encourages* him
who beats the anvil,
Saying of the soldering, "It is
good";
And he fastens it with nails,
That it should not totter.

8 "But you, Israel, My servant,
Jacob whom I have chosen,
Descendant of Abraham My
friend,

9 "You whom I have taken from the
ends of the earth,
And called from its remotest
parts,
And said to you, 'You are My
servant,
I have chosen you and not rejected you.

10 'Do not fear, for I am with you;
Do not anxiously look about you,
for I am your God.
I will strengthen you, surely I will
help you,
Surely I will uphold you with My
righteous right hand.'

11 "Behold, all those who are angered
at you will be shamed and dishonored;
Those who contend with you will
be as nothing, and will perish.

12 "You will seek those who quarrel
with you, but will not find them,
Those who war with you will be
as nothing, and nonexistent.

13 "For I am the LORD your God, who
upholds your right hand,
Who says to you, 'Do not fear, I
will help you.'

14 "Do not fear, you worm Jacob, you
men of Israel;
I will help you," declares the
LORD, "and your Redeemer is
the Holy One of Israel.

15 "Behold, I have made you a new,
sharp threshing sledge with
double edges;
You will thresh the mountains,
and pulverize *them*,
And will make the hills like chaff.

16 "You will winnow them, and the
wind will carry them away,
And the storm will scatter them;
But you will rejoice in the LORD,
You will glory in the Holy One of
Israel.

17 ¶ "The afflicted and needy are
seeking water, but there is
none,
And their tongue is parched with
thirst;
I, the LORD, will answer them
Myself,
As the God of Israel I will not
forsake them.

18"I will open rivers on the bare
heights,
And springs in the midst of the
valleys;
I will make the wilderness a pool
of water,
And the dry land fountains of
water.

19"I will put the cedar in the wilderness,
The acacia, and the myrtle, and
the olive tree;
I will place the juniper in the
desert,
Together with the box tree and
the cypress,

20 That they may see and recognize,
And consider and gain insight as
well,
That the hand of the LORD has
done this,
And the Holy One of Israel has
created it.

21 ¶"Present your case," the LORD
says.
"Bring forward your strong *arguments*,"
The King of Jacob says.

22 Let them bring forth and declare
to us what is going to take
place;
As for the former *events*, declare
what they *were*,
That we may consider them, and
know their outcome;
Or announce to us what is coming.

23 Declare the things that are going
to come afterward,
That we may know that you are
gods;
Indeed, do good or evil, that we
may anxiously look about us
and fear together.

24 Behold, you are of no account,
And your work amounts to nothing;
He who chooses you is an abomination.

25 ¶"I have aroused one from the
north, and he has come;
From the rising of the sun he will
call on My name;
And he will come upon rulers as
upon mortar,
Even as the potter treads clay."

26 Who has declared *this* from the
beginning, that we might
know?
Or from former times, that we
may say, "*He is* right!"?
Surely there was no one who declared,
Surely there was no one who proclaimed,
Surely there was no one who
heard your words.

27"Formerly *I* said to Zion, 'Behold,
here they are.'
And to Jerusalem, 'I will give a
messenger of good news.'

28"But when I look, there is no one,
And there is no counselor among
them
Who, if I ask, can give an answer.

29"Behold, all of them are [17]false;
Their works are worthless,
Their molten images are wind and
emptiness.

CHAPTER 42

"BEHOLD, My Servant, whom I uphold;
My chosen one *in whom* My soul
delights.
I have put My Spirit upon Him;
He will bring forth justice to the
nations.

2"He will not cry out or raise *His
voice*,
Nor make His voice heard in the
street.

3"A bruised reed He will not break,
And a dimly burning wick He will
not extinguish;
He will faithfully bring forth justice.

4"He will not be disheartened or
crushed,
Until He has established justice in
the earth;
And the coastlands will wait expectantly for His law."

5 ¶ Thus says God the LORD,
Who created the heavens and
stretched them out,
Who spread out the earth and its
offspring,
Who gives breath to the people on
it,
And spirit to those who walk in it,

[17] Another reading is *nothing*

6"I am the LORD, I have called you
in righteousness,
I will also hold you by the hand
and watch over you,
And I will appoint you as a covenant to the people,
As a light to the nations,

7 To open blind eyes,
To bring out prisoners from the
dungeon,
And those who dwell in darkness
from the prison.

8"I am the LORD, that is My name;
I will not give My glory to an-
other,
Nor My praise to graven images.

9"Behold, the former things have
come to pass,
Now I declare new things;
Before they spring forth I proclaim *them* to you."

10 ¶ Sing to the LORD a new song,
Sing His praise from the end of
the earth!
You who go down to the sea, and
all that is in it.
You islands and those who dwell
on them.

11 Let the wilderness and its cities
lift up *their voices,*
The settlements where Kedar inhabits.
Let the inhabitants of Sela sing
aloud,
Let them shout for joy from the
tops of the mountains.

12 Let them give glory to the LORD,
And declare His praise in the
coastlands.

13 The LORD will go forth like a warrior,
He will arouse *His* zeal like a man
of war.
He will utter a shout, yes, He will
raise a war cry.
He will prevail against His enemies.

14 ¶"I have kept silent for a long
time,
I have kept still and restrained
Myself.
Now like a woman in labor I will
groan,
I will both gasp and pant.

15"I will lay waste the mountains and
hills,
And wither all their vegetation;
I will make the rivers into coast-
lands,
And dry up the ponds.

16"And I will lead the blind by a way
they do not know,
In paths they do not know I will
guide them.
I will make darkness into light
before them
And rugged places into plains.
These are the things I will do,
And I will not leave them un-
done."

17 They shall be turned back and be
utterly put to shame,
Who trust in idols,
Who say to molten images,
"You are our gods."

18 ¶ Hear, you deaf!
And look, you blind, that you may
see.

19 Who is blind but My servant,
Or so deaf as My messenger
whom I send?
Who is so blind as he that is at
peace *with Me,*
Or so blind as the servant of the
LORD?

20 You have seen many things, but
you do not observe *them;*
Your ears are open, but none
hears.

21 The LORD was pleased for His
righteousness' sake
To make the law great and glorious.

22 But this is a people plundered and
despoiled;
All of them are trapped in caves,
Or are hidden away in prisons;
They have become a prey with
none to deliver *them,*
And a spoil, with none to say,
"Give *them* back!"

23 ¶ Who among you will give ear to
this?
Who will give heed and listen
hereafter?

24 Who gave Jacob up for spoil, and
Israel to plunderers?
Was it not the LORD, against
whom we have sinned,

And in whose ways they were not
willing to walk,
And whose law they did not obey?
25 So He poured out on him the heat
of His anger
And the fierceness of battle;
And it set him aflame all around,
Yet he did not recognize *it;*
And it burned him, but he paid no
attention.

CHAPTER 43

BUT now, thus says the LORD, your
Creator, O Jacob,
And He who formed you, O Israel,
"Do not fear, for I have redeemed
you;
I have called you by name; you
are Mine!
2"When you pass through the waters, I will be with you;
And through the rivers, they will
not overflow you.
When you walk through the fire,
you will not be scorched,
Nor will the flame burn you.
3"For I am the LORD your God,
The Holy One of Israel, your Savior;
I have given Egypt as your ransom,
Cush and Seba in your place.
4"Since you are precious in My
sight,
Since you are honored and I love
you,
I will give *other* men in your place
and *other* peoples in exchange
for your life.
5"Do not fear, for I am with you;
I will bring your offspring from
the east,
And gather you from the west.
6"I will say to the north, 'Give *them*
up!'
And to the south, 'Do not hold
them back.'
Bring My sons from afar,
And My daughters from the ends
of the earth,
7 Everyone who is called by My
name,
And whom I have created for My
glory,
Whom I have formed, even whom
I have made."

8 ¶ Bring out the people who are
blind, even though they have
eyes,
And the deaf, even though they
have ears.
9 All the nations have gathered together
In order that the peoples may be
assembled.
Who among them can declare this
And proclaim to us the former
things?
Let them present their witnesses
that they may be justified,
Or let them hear and say, "It is
true."
10"You are My witnesses," declares
the LORD,
"And My servant whom I have
chosen,
In order that you may know and
believe Me,
And understand that I am He.
Before Me there was no God
formed,
And there will be none after Me.
11"I, even I, am the LORD;
And there is no savior besides Me.
12"It is I who have declared and
saved and proclaimed,
And there was no strange *god*
among you;
So you are My witnesses," declares the LORD,
"And I am God.
13"Even from eternity I am He;
And there is none who can deliver
out of My hand;
I act and who can reverse it?"

14 ¶ Thus says the LORD your Redeemer, the Holy One of Israel,
"For your sake I have sent to
Babylon,
And will bring them all down as
fugitives,
[18]Even the Chaldeans, into the
ships in which they rejoice.
15"I am the LORD, your Holy One,
The Creator of Israel, your King."
16 Thus says the LORD,
Who makes a way through the
sea
And a path through the mighty
waters,

[18] Another reading is *As for the Chaldeans, their rejoicing is*
turned into lamentations

17 Who brings forth the chariot and
   the horse,
   The army and the mighty man
   (They will lie down together *and*
   not rise again;
   They have been quenched *and*
   extinguished like a wick):
18"Do not call to mind the former
   things,
   Or ponder things of the past.
19"Behold, I will do something new,
   Now it will spring forth;
   Will you not be aware of it?
   I will even make a roadway in the
   wilderness,
   Rivers in the desert.
20"The beasts of the field will glorify
   Me;
   The jackals and the ostriches;
   Because I have given waters in
   the wilderness
   And rivers in the desert,
   To give drink to My chosen peo-
   ple.
21"The people whom I formed for
   Myself,
   Will declare My praise.

22 ¶"Yet you have not called on Me,
   O Jacob;
   But you have become weary of
   Me, O Israel.
23"You have not brought to Me the
   sheep of your burnt offerings;
   Nor have you honored Me with
   your sacrifices.
   I have not burdened you with
   offerings,
   Nor wearied you with incense.
24"You have bought Me no sweet
   cane with money,
   Neither have you filled Me with
   the fat of your sacrifices;
   Rather you have burdened Me
   with your sins,
   You have wearied Me with your
   iniquities.

25 ¶"I, even I, am the one who wipes
   out your transgressions for My
   own sake;
   And I will not remember your
   sins.
26"Put Me in remembrance; let us
   argue our case together,
   State your *cause*, that you may be
   proved right.

27"Your first forefather sinned,
   And your spokesmen have transgressed against Me.
28"So I will pollute the princes of the
   sanctuary;
   And I will consign Jacob to the
   ban, and Israel to revilement.

CHAPTER 44

"BUT now listen, O Jacob, My servant;
   And Israel, whom I have chosen:
2 Thus says the LORD who made
   you
   And formed you from the womb,
   who will help you,
   'Do not fear, O Jacob My servant;
   And you Jeshurun whom I have
   chosen.
3 'For I will pour out water on the
   thirsty *land*
   And streams on the dry ground;
   I will pour out My Spirit on your
   offspring,
   And My blessing on your descendants;
4 And they will spring up among
   the grass
   Like poplars by streams of water.'
5"This one will say, 'I am the
   LORD'S';
   And that one will call on the name
   of Jacob;
   And another will write *on* his
   hand, 'Belonging to the LORD,'
   And will name Israel's name with
   honor.

6 ¶"Thus says the LORD, the King of
   Israel
   And his Redeemer, the LORD of
   hosts:
   'I am the first and I am the last,
   And there is no God besides Me.
7 'And who is like Me? Let him proclaim and declare it;
   Yes, let him recount it to Me in
   order,
   From the time that I established
   the ancient nation.
   And let them declare to them the
   things that are coming
   And the events that are going to
   take place.
8 'Do not tremble and do not be
   afraid;

Have I not long since announced
it to you and declared it?
And you are My witnesses.
Is there any God besides Me,
Or is there any *other* Rock?
I know of none.' "

9 Those who fashion a graven
image are all of them futile, and their
precious things are of no profit; even
their own witnesses fail to see or
know, so that they will be put to
shame.

10 Who has fashioned a god or cast
an idol to no profit?

11 Behold, all his companions will be
put to shame, for the craftsmen themselves are mere men. Let them all
assemble themselves, let them stand
up, let them tremble, let them together
be put to shame.

12 ¶ The man shapes iron into a
cutting tool, and does his work over
the coals, fashioning it with hammers,
and working it with his strong arm. He
also gets hungry and his strength fails;
he drinks no water and becomes
weary.

13 *Another* shapes wood, he extends
a measuring line; he outlines it with
red chalk. He works it with planes, and
outlines it with a compass, and makes
it like the form of a man, like the
beauty of man, so that it may sit in a
house.

14 Surely he cuts cedars for himself,
and takes a cypress or an oak, and
raises *it* for himself among the trees of
the forest. He plants a fir, and the rain
makes it grow.

15 Then it becomes *something* for a
man to burn, so he takes one of them
and warms himself; he also makes a
fire to bake bread. He also makes
a god and worships it; he makes it a
graven image, and falls down before it.

16 Half of it he burns in the fire; over
this half he eats meat as he roasts a
roast, and is satisfied. He also warms
himself and says, "Aha! I am warm, I
have seen the fire."

17 But the rest of it he makes into a
god, his graven image. He falls down
before it and worships; he also prays
to it and says, "Deliver me, for thou
art my god."

18 ¶ They do not know, nor do they
understand, for He has smeared over
their eyes so that they cannot see and
their hearts so that they cannot comprehend.

19 And no one recalls, nor is there
knowledge or understanding to say, "I
have burned half of it in the fire, and
also have baked bread over its coals. I
roast meat and eat *it*. Then I make the
rest of it into an abomination, I fall
down before a block of wood!"

20 He feeds on ashes; a deceived
heart has turned him aside. And he
cannot deliver himself, nor say, "Is
there not a lie in my right hand?"

21 ¶"Remember these things, O Jacob,
And Israel, for you are My servant;
I have formed you, you are My
servant,
O Israel, you will not be forgotten
by Me.

22"I have wiped out your transgressions like a thick cloud,
And your sins like a heavy mist.
Return to Me, for I have redeemed you."

23 Shout for joy, O heavens, for the
LORD has done *it!*
Shout joyfully, you lower parts of
the earth;
Break forth into a shout of joy,
you mountains,
O forest, and every tree in it;
For the LORD has redeemed Jacob
And in Israel He shows forth His
glory.

24 ¶ Thus says the LORD, your Redeemer, and the one who
formed you from the womb,
"I, the LORD, am the maker of all
things,
Stretching out the heavens by
Myself,
And spreading out the earth all
alone,

25 Causing the omens of boasters to
fail,
Making fools out of diviners,
Causing wise men to draw back,
And turning their knowledge into
foolishness,

26 Confirming the word of His ser-
vant,
And performing the purpose of
His messengers.

It is I who says of Jerusalem, 'She shall be inhabited!'
And of the cities of Judah, 'They shall be built.'
And I will raise up her ruins *again.*
27"*It is I* who says to the depth of the sea, 'Be dried up!'
And I will make your rivers dry.
28"*It is I* who says of Cyrus, '*He is* My shepherd!
And he will perform all My desire.'
And he declares of Jerusalem, 'She will be built,'
And of the temple, 'Your foundation will be laid.' "

CHAPTER 45

THUS says the LORD to Cyrus His anointed,
Whom I have taken by the right hand,
To subdue nations before him,
And to loose the loins of kings;
To open doors before him so that gates will not be shut:
2"I will go before you and make the rough places smooth;
I will shatter the doors of bronze, and cut through their iron bars.
3"And I will give you the treasures of darkness,
And hidden wealth of secret places,
In order that you may know that it is I,
The LORD, the God of Israel, who calls you by your name.
4"For the sake of Jacob My servant,
And Israel My chosen *one,*
I have also called you by your name;
I have given you a title of honor
Though you have not known Me.
5"I am the LORD, and there is no other;
Besides Me there is no God.
I will gird you, though you have not known Me;
6 That men may know from the rising to the setting of the sun
That there is no one besides Me.
I am the LORD, and there is no other,
7 The One forming light and creating darkness,

Causing well-being and creating calamity;
I am the LORD who does all these.

8 ¶"Drip down, O heavens, from above,
And let the clouds pour down righteousness;
Let the earth open up and salvation bear fruit,
And righteousness spring up with it.
I, the LORD, have created it.

9 ¶"Woe to *the one* who quarrels with his Maker—
An earthenware vessel among the vessels of earth!
Will the clay say to the potter, 'What are you doing?'
Or the thing you are making *say,* 'He has no hands'?
10"Woe to him who says to a father, 'What are you begetting?'
Or to a woman, 'To what are you giving birth?' "

11 ¶ Thus says the LORD, the Holy One of Israel, and his Maker:
"Ask Me about the things to come concerning My sons,
And you shall commit to Me the work of My hands.
12"It is I who made the earth, and created man upon it.
I stretched out the heavens with My hands,
And I ordained all their host.
13"I have aroused him in righteousness,
And I will make all his ways smooth;
He will build My city, and will let My exiles go free,
Without any payment or reward," says the LORD of hosts.

14 ¶ Thus says the LORD,
"The products of Egypt and the merchandise of Cush
And the Sabeans, men of stature,
Will come over to you and will be yours;
They will walk behind you, they will come over in chains
And will bow down to you;
They will make supplication to you:

'Surely, God is with you, and there
is none else,
No other God.' "
15 Truly, Thou art a God who hides
Himself,
O God of Israel, Savior!
16 They will be put to shame and
even humiliated, all of them;
The manufacturers of idols will go
away together in humiliation.
17 Israel has been saved by the LORD
With an everlasting salvation;
You will not be put to shame or
humiliated
To all eternity.

18 ¶ For thus says the LORD, who
created the heavens
(He is the God who formed the
earth and made it,
He established it and did not cre-
ate it a waste place,
But formed it to be inhabited),
"I am the LORD, and there is none
else.
19"I have not spoken in secret,
In some dark land;
I did not say to the offspring of
Jacob,
'Seek Me in a waste place';
I, the LORD, speak righteousness
Declaring things that are upright.

20 ¶"Gather yourselves and come;
Draw near together, you fugitives
of the nations;
They have no knowledge,
Who carry about their wooden
idol,
And pray to a god who cannot
save.
21"Declare and set forth *your case;*
Indeed, let them consult together.
Who has announced this from of
old?
Who has long since declared it?
Is it not I, the LORD?
And there is no other God besides
Me,
A righteous God and a Savior;
There is none except Me.
22"Turn to Me, and be saved, all the
ends of the earth;
For I am God, and there is no
other.
23"I have sworn by Myself,
The word has gone forth from My
mouth in righteousness

And will not turn back,
That to Me every knee will bow,
every tongue will swear *allegiance.*
24"They will say of Me, 'Only in the
LORD are righteousness and
strength.'
Men will come to Him,
And all who were angry at Him
shall be put to shame.
25"In the LORD all the offspring of
Israel
Will be justified, and will glory."

CHAPTER 46

BEL has bowed down, Nebo stoops
over;
Their images are *consigned* to the
beasts and the cattle.
The things that you carry are
burdensome,
A load for the weary *beast.*
2 They stooped over, they have
bowed down together;
They could not rescue the burden,
But have themselves gone into
captivity.

3 ¶"Listen to Me, O house of Jacob,
And all the remnant of the house
of Israel,
You who have been borne by Me
from birth,
And have been carried from the
womb;
4 Even to your old age, I shall be
the same,
And even to your graying years I
shall bear *you!*
I have done *it,* and I shall carry
you;
And I shall bear *you,* and I shall
deliver *you.*

5 ¶"To whom would you liken Me,
And make Me equal and compare
Me,
That we should be alike?
6"Those who lavish gold from the
purse
And weigh silver on the scale
Hire a goldsmith, and he makes it
into a god;
They bow down, indeed they worship it.
7"They lift it upon the shoulder and
carry it;

They set it in its place and it
stands *there*.
It does not move from its place.
Though one may cry to it, it cannot answer;
It cannot deliver him from his
distress.

8 ¶"Remember this, and be assured;
Recall it to mind, you transgressors.
9"Remember the former things long
past,
For I am God, and there is no
other;
I am God, and there is no one like
Me,
10 Declaring the end from the beginning
And from ancient times things
which have not been done,
Saying, 'My purpose will be established,
And I will accomplish all My good
pleasure';
11 Calling a bird of prey from the
east,
The man of My purpose from a far
country.
Truly I have spoken; truly I will
bring it to pass.
I have planned *it, surely* I will do
it.

12 ¶"Listen to Me, you stubborn-
minded,
Who are far from righteousness.
13"I bring near My righteousness, it
is not far off;
And My salvation will not delay.
And I will grant salvation in Zion,
And My glory for Israel.

CHAPTER 47

"COME down and sit in the dust,
O virgin daughter of Babylon;
Sit on the ground without a
throne,
O daughter of the Chaldeans.
For you shall no longer be called
tender and delicate.
2"Take the millstones and grind
meal.
Remove your veil, strip off the
skirt,
Uncover the leg, cross the rivers.
3"Your nakedness will be uncovered,

Your shame also will be exposed;
I will take vengeance and will not
spare a man."
4 Our Redeemer, the LORD of hosts
is His name,
The Holy One of Israel.
5"Sit silently, and go into darkness,
O daughter of the Chaldeans;
For you will no more be called
The queen of kingdoms.
6"I was angry with My people,
I profaned My heritage,
And gave them into your hand.
You did not show mercy to them,
On the aged you made your yoke
very heavy.
7"Yet you said, 'I shall be a queen
forever.'
These things you did not consider,
Nor remember the outcome of
them.

8 ¶"Now, then, hear this, you sen-
sual one,
Who dwells securely,
Who says in your heart,
'I am, and there is no one besides
me.
I shall not sit as a widow,
Nor shall I know loss of children.'
9"But these two things shall come
on you suddenly in one day:
Loss of children and widowhood.
They shall come on you in full
measure
In spite of your many sorceries,
In spite of the great power of your
spells.
10"And you felt secure in your wick-
edness and said,
'No one sees me,'
Your wisdom and your knowl-
edge, they have deluded you;
For you have said in your heart,
'I am, and there is no one besides
me.'
11"But evil will come on you
Which you will not know how to
charm away;
And disaster will fall on you
For which you cannot atone,
And destruction about which you
do not know
Will come on you suddenly.

12 ¶"Stand *fast* now in your spells
And in your many sorceries

With which you have labored
from your youth;
Perhaps you will be able to profit,
Perhaps you may cause trembling.
13"You are wearied with your many
counsels;
Let now the astrologers,
Those who prophesy by the stars,
Those who predict by the new
moons,
Stand up and save you from what
will come upon you.
14"Behold, they have become like
stubble,
Fire burns them;
They cannot deliver themselves
from the power of the flame;
There will be no coal to warm by,
Nor a fire to sit before!
15"So have those become to you with
whom you have labored,
Who have trafficked with you
from your youth;
Each has wandered in his own
way.
There is none to save you.

CHAPTER 48

"HEAR this, O house of Jacob, who
are named Israel
And who came forth from the
loins of Judah,
Who swear by the name of the
LORD
And invoke the God of Israel,
But not in truth nor in righteousness.
2"For they call themselves after the
holy city,
And lean on the God of Israel;
The LORD of hosts is His name.
3"I declared the former things long
ago
And they went forth from My
mouth, and I proclaimed them.
Suddenly I acted, and they came
to pass.
4"Because I know that you are obstinate,
And your neck is an iron sinew,
And your forehead bronze,
5 Therefore I declared *them* to you
long ago,
Before they took place I proclaimed *them* to you,
Lest you should say, 'My idol has
done them,

And my graven image and my
molten image have commanded
them.'
6"You have heard; look at all this.
And you, will you not declare it?
I proclaim to you new things from
this time,
Even hidden things which you
have not known.
7"They are created now and not
long ago;
And before today you have not
heard them,
Lest you should say, 'Behold, I
knew them.'
8"You have not heard, you have not
known.
Even from long ago your ear has
not been open,
Because I knew that you would
deal very treacherously;
And you have been called a rebel
from birth.
9"For the sake of My name I delay
My wrath,
And *for* My praise I restrain *it* for
you,
In order not to cut you off.
10"Behold, I have refined you, but
not as silver;
I have tested you in the furnace of
affliction.
11"For My own sake, for My own
sake, I will act;
For how can *My name* be profaned?
And My glory I will not give to
another.

12 ¶"Listen to Me, O Jacob, even
Israel whom I called;
I am He, I am the first, I am also
the last.
13"Surely My hand founded the
earth,
And My right hand spread out the
heavens;
When I call to them, they stand
together.
14"Assemble, all of you, and listen!
Who among them has declared
these things?
The LORD loves him; he shall
carry out His good pleasure on
Babylon,
And His arm *shall be against* the
Chaldeans.

15"I, even I, have spoken; indeed I
　　have called him,
　　I have brought him, and He will
　　make his ways successful.
16"Come near to Me, listen to this:
　　From the first I have not spoken
　　in secret,
　　From the time it took place, I was
　　there.
　　And now the Lord God has sent
　　Me, and His Spirit."

17 ¶ Thus says the Lord, your Re-
　　deemer, the Holy One of Israel;
　　"I am the Lord your God, who
　　teaches you to profit,
　　Who leads you in the way you
　　should go.
18"If only you had paid attention to
　　My commandments!
　　Then your well-being would have
　　been like a river,
　　And your righteousness like the
　　waves of the sea.
19"Your descendants would have
　　been like the sand,
　　And your offspring like its grains;
　　Their name would never be cut off
　　or destroyed from My pres-
　　ence."

20 ¶ Go forth from Babylon! Flee
　　from the Chaldeans!
　　Declare with the sound of joyful
　　shouting, proclaim this,
　　Send it out to the end of the earth;
　　Say, "The Lord has redeemed His
　　servant Jacob."
21 And they did not thirst when He
　　led them through the deserts.
　　He made the water flow out of the
　　rock for them;
　　He split the rock, and the water
　　gushed forth.
22"There is no peace for the wicked,"
　　says the Lord.

CHAPTER 49

LISTEN to Me, O islands,
　　And pay attention, you peoples
　　from afar.
　　The Lord called Me from the
　　womb;
　　From the body of My mother He
　　named Me.
2 And He has made My mouth like
　　a sharp sword;

In the shadow of His hand He has
　　concealed Me,
　　And He has also made Me a select
　　arrow;
　　He has hidden Me in His quiver.
3 And He said to Me, "You are My
　　Servant, Israel,
　　In Whom I will show My glory."
4 But I said, "I have toiled in vain,
　　I have spent My strength for
　　nothing and vanity;
　　Yet surely the justice due to Me is
　　with the Lord,
　　And My reward with My God."

5 ¶ And now says the Lord, who
　　formed Me from the womb to
　　be His Servant,
　　To bring Jacob back to Him, in
　　order that Israel might be gath-
　　ered to Him
　　(For I am honored in the sight of
　　the Lord,
　　And My God is My strength),
6 He says, "It is too small a thing
　　that You should be My Servant
　　To raise up the tribes of Jacob,
　　and to restore the preserved
　　ones of Israel;
　　I will also make You a light of the
　　nations
　　So that My salvation may reach to
　　the end of the earth."
7 Thus says the Lord, the Re-
　　deemer of Israel, and its Holy
　　One,
　　To the despised One,
　　To the One abhorred by the na-
　　tion,
　　To the Servant of rulers,
　　"Kings shall see and arise,
　　Princes shall also bow down;
　　Because of the Lord who is faith-
　　ful, the Holy One of Israel who
　　has chosen You."

8 ¶ Thus says the Lord, "In a fa-
　　vorable time I have answered
　　You,
　　And in a day of salvation I have
　　helped You;
　　And I will keep You and give You
　　for a covenant of the people,
　　To restore the land, to make them
　　inherit the desolate heritages;
9 Saying to those who are bound,
　　'Go forth,'

To those who are in darkness,
'Show yourselves.'
Along the roads they will feed,
And their pasture will be on all
bare heights.
10"They will not hunger or thirst,
Neither will the scorching heat or
sun strike them down;
For He who has compassion on
them will lead them,
And will guide them to springs of
water.
11"And I will make all My mountains
a road,
And My highways will be raised
up.
12"Behold, these shall come from
afar;
And lo, these *will come* from the
north and from the west,
And these from the land of Si-
nim."

13 Shout for joy, O heavens! And
rejoice, O earth!
Break forth into joyful shouting,
O mountains!
For the LORD has comforted His
people,
And will have compassion on His
afflicted.

14 ¶ But Zion said, "The LORD has
forsaken me,
And the Lord has forgotten me."
15"Can a woman forget her nursing
child,
And have no compassion on the
son of her womb?
Even these may forget, but I will
not forget you.
16"Behold, I have inscribed you on
the palms *of My hands;*
Your walls are continually before
Me.
17"Your builders hurry;
Your destroyers and devastators
Will depart from you.
18"Lift up your eyes and look around;
All of them gather together, they
come to you.
As I live," declares the LORD,
"You shall surely put on all of them
as jewels, and bind them on as a
bride.
19"For your waste and desolate
places, and your destroyed
land—

Surely now you will be too
cramped for the inhabitants,
And those who swallowed you
will be far away.
20"The children of whom you were
bereaved will yet say in your
ears,
'The place is too cramped for me;
Make room for me that I may live
here.'
21"Then you will say in your heart,
'Who has begotten these for me,
Since I have been bereaved of my
children,
And am barren, an exile and a
wanderer?
And who has reared these?
Behold, I was left alone;
From where did these come?' "

22 ¶ Thus says the Lord GOD,
"Behold, I will lift up My hand to
the nations,
And set up My standard to the
peoples;
And they will bring your sons in
their bosom,
And your daughters will be car-
ried on *their* shoulders.
23"And kings will be your guardians,
And their princesses your nurses.
They will bow down to you with
their faces to the earth,
And lick the dust of your feet;
And *you* will know that I am the
LORD;
Those who hopefully wait for Me
will not be put to shame.

24 ¶"Can the prey be taken from the
mighty man,
Or the captives of a tyrant be
rescued?"
25 Surely, thus says the LORD,
"Even the captives of the mighty
man will be taken away,
And the prey of the tyrant will be
rescued;
For I will contend with the one
who contends with you,
And I will save your sons.
26"And I will feed your oppressors
with their own flesh,
And they will become drunk with
their own blood as with sweet
wine;
And all flesh will know that I, the
LORD, am your Savior,

And your Redeemer, the Mighty
One of Jacob."

CHAPTER 50

THUS says the LORD,
"Where is the certificate of di-
vorce,
By which I have sent your mother
away?
Or to whom of My creditors did I
sell you?
Behold, you were sold for your
iniquities,
And for your transgressions your
mother was sent away.
2 "Why was there no man when I
came?
When I called, *why* was there
none to answer?
Is My hand so short that it cannot
ransom?
Or have I no power to deliver?
Behold, I dry up the sea with My
rebuke,
I make the rivers a wilderness;
Their fish stink for lack of water,
And die of thirst.
3 "I clothe the heavens with blackness,
And I make sackcloth their covering."

4 ¶ The Lord GOD has given Me the
tongue of disciples,
That I may know how to sustain
the weary one with a word.
He awakens *Me* morning by
morning,
He awakens My ear to listen as a
disciple.
5 The Lord GOD has opened My ear;
And I was not disobedient,
Nor did I turn back.
6 I gave My back to those who
strike *Me*,
And My cheeks to those who
pluck out the beard;
I did not cover My face from humiliation and spitting.
7 For the Lord GOD helps Me,
Therefore, I am not disgraced;
Therefore, I have set My face like
flint,
And I know that I shall not be
ashamed.
8 He who vindicates Me is near;
Who will contend with Me?

Let us stand up to each other;
Who has a case against Me?
Let him draw near to Me.
9 Behold, the Lord GOD helps Me;
Who is he who condemns Me?
Behold, they will all wear out like
a garment;
The moth will eat them.
10 Who is among you that fears the
LORD,
That obeys the voice of His ser-
vant,
That walks in darkness and has
no light?
Let him trust in the name of the
LORD and rely on his God.
11 Behold, all you who kindle a fire,
Who encircle yourselves with fire-
brands,
Walk in the light of your fire
And among the brands you have
set ablaze.
This you will have from My hand;
And you will lie down in torment.

CHAPTER 51

"LISTEN to me, you who pursue
righteousness,
Who seek the LORD:
Look to the rock from which you
were hewn,
And to the quarry from which you
were dug.
2 "Look to Abraham your father,
And to Sarah who gave birth to
you in pain;
When *he was* one I called him,
Then I blessed him and multiplied
him."
3 Indeed, the LORD will comfort
Zion;
He will comfort all her waste
places.
And her wilderness He will make
like Eden,
And her desert like the garden of
the LORD;
Joy and gladness will be found in
her,
Thanksgiving and sound of a mel-
ody.

4 ¶ "Pay attention to Me, O My peo-
ple;
And give ear to Me, O My nation;
For a law will go forth from Me,
And I will set My justice for a
light of the peoples.

5"My righteousness is near, My sal-
  vation has gone forth,
  And My arms will judge the peo-
    ples;
  The coastlands will wait for Me,
  And for My arm they will wait
    expectantly.
6"Lift up your eyes to the sky,
  Then look to the earth beneath;
  For the sky will vanish like
    smoke,
  And the earth will wear out like a
    garment,
  And its inhabitants will die in like
    manner,
  But My salvation shall be forever,
  And My righteousness shall not
    wane.
7"Listen to Me, you who know
  righteousness,
  A people in whose heart is My
    law;
  Do not fear the reproach of man,
  Neither be dismayed at their revil-
    ings.
8"For the moth will eat them like a
  garment,
  And the grub will eat them like
    wool.
  But My righteousness shall be
    forever,
  And My salvation to all genera-
    tions."

9 ¶ Awake, awake, put on strength,
  O arm of the LORD;
  Awake as in the days of old, the
    generations of long ago.
  Was it not Thou who cut Rahab in
    pieces,
  Who pierced the dragon?
10 Was it not Thou who dried up the
   sea,
   The waters of the great deep;
   Who made the depths of the sea a
     pathway
   For the redeemed to cross over?
11 So the ransomed of the LORD will
   return,
   And come with joyful shouting to
     Zion;
   And everlasting joy *will be* on
     their heads.
   They will obtain gladness and joy,
   And sorrow and sighing will flee
     away.

12 ¶"I, even I, am He who comforts
   you.
   Who are you that you are afraid
     of man who dies,
   And of the son of man who is
     made like grass;
13 That you have forgotten the LORD
   your Maker,
   Who stretched out the heavens,
   And laid the foundations of the
     earth;
   That you fear continually all day
     long because of the fury of the
     oppressor,
   As he makes ready to destroy?
   But where is the fury of the op-
     pressor?
14"The exile will soon be set free, and
will not die in the dungeon, nor will his
bread be lacking.
15"For I am the LORD your God, who
stirs up the sea and its waves roar (the
LORD of hosts is His name).
16"And I have put My words in your
mouth, and have covered you with the
shadow of My hand, to establish the
heavens, to found the earth, and to say
to Zion, 'You are My people.'"
17 ¶ Rouse yourself! Rouse yourself!
   Arise, O Jerusalem,
   You who have drunk from the
     LORD's hand the cup of His an-
     ger;
   The chalice of reeling you have
     drained to the dregs.
18 There is none to guide her among
   all the sons she has borne;
   Nor is there one to take her by the
     hand among all the sons she has
     reared.
19 These two things have befallen
   you;
   Who will mourn for you?
   The devastation and destruction,
     famine and sword;
   How shall I comfort you?
20 Your sons have fainted,
   They lie *helpless* at the head of
     every street,
   Like an antelope in a net,
   Full of the wrath of the LORD,
   The rebuke of your God.

21 ¶ Therefore, please hear this, you
   afflicted,
   Who are drunk, but not with
     wine:

22 Thus says your Lord, the LORD,
   even your God
   Who contends for His people,
   "Behold, I have taken out of your
      hand the cup of reeling;
   The chalice of My anger,
   You will never drink it again.
23"And I will put it into the hand of
   your tormentors,
   Who have said to you, 'Lie down
      that we may walk over you.'
   You have even made your back
      like the ground,
   And like the street for those who
      walk over it."

CHAPTER 52

AWAKE, awake,
   Clothe yourself in your strength,
      O Zion;
   Clothe yourself in your beautiful
      garments,
   O Jerusalem, the holy city.
   For the uncircumcised and the
      unclean
   Will no more come into you.
2 Shake yourself from the dust, rise
   up,
   O captive Jerusalem;
   Loose yourself from the chains
      around your neck,
   O captive daughter of Zion.
3 For thus says the LORD, "You
   were sold for nothing and you will be
   redeemed without money."
4 For thus says the Lord GOD, "My
   people went down at the first into
   Egypt to reside there, then the Assyrian oppressed them without cause.
5"Now therefore, what do I have
   here," declares the LORD, "seeing that
   My people have been taken away
   without cause?" Again the LORD declares, "Those who rule over them
   howl, and My name is continually
   blasphemed all day long.
6"Therefore My people shall know
   My name; therefore in that day I am
   the one who is speaking, 'Here I am.' "
7 ¶ How lovely on the mountains
   Are the feet of him who brings
      good news,
   Who announces peace
   And brings good news of happi-
      ness,
   Who announces salvation,
   And says to Zion, "Your God
      reigns!"

8 Listen! Your watchmen lift up
   their voices,
   They shout joyfully together;
   For they will see with their own
      eyes
   When the LORD restores Zion.
9 Break forth, shout joyfully to-
   gether,
   You waste places of Jerusalem;
   For the LORD has comforted His
      people,
   He has redeemed Jerusalem.
10 The LORD has bared His holy arm
   In the sight of all the nations,
   That all the ends of the earth may
      see
   The salvation of our God.

11 ¶ Depart, depart, go out from
   there,
   Touch nothing unclean;
   Go out of the midst of her, purify
      yourselves,
   You who carry the vessels of the
      LORD.
12 But you will not go out in haste,
   Nor will you go as fugitives;
   For the LORD will go before you,
   And the God of Israel will be your
      rear guard.

13 ¶ Behold, My servant will prosper,
   He will be high and lifted up, and
      greatly exalted.
14 Just as many were astonished at
   you, My people,
   So His appearance was marred
      more than any man,
   And His form more than the sons
      of men.
15 Thus He will sprinkle many na-
   tions,
   Kings will shut their mouths on
      account of Him;
   For what had not been told them
      they will see,
   And what they had not heard they
      will understand.

CHAPTER 53

WHO has believed our message?
   And to whom has the arm of the
      LORD been revealed?
2 For He grew up before Him like a
   tender shoot,
   And like a root out of parched
      ground;

He has no *stately* form or majesty
That we should look upon Him,
Nor appearance that we should
[19]be attracted to Him.
3 He was despised and forsaken of
men,
A man of sorrows, and acquainted
with grief;
And like one from whom men
hide their face,
He was despised, and we did not
esteem Him.

4 ¶ Surely our [20]griefs He Himself
bore,
And our sorrows He carried;
Yet we ourselves esteemed Him
stricken,
Smitten of God, and afflicted.
5 But He was [21]pierced through for
our transgressions,
He was crushed for our iniquities;
The chastening for our well-being
fell upon Him,
And by His scourging we are
healed.
6 All of us like sheep have gone
astray,
Each of us has turned to his own
way;
But the LORD has caused the iniquity of us all
To fall on Him.

7 ¶ He was oppressed and He was
afflicted,
Yet He did not open His mouth;
Like a lamb that is led to slaughter,
And like a sheep that is silent
before its shearers,
So He did not open His mouth.
8 By oppression and judgment He
was taken away;
And as for His generation, who
considered
That He was cut off out of the
land of the living,
For the transgression of my people to whom the stroke *was
due?*
9 His grave was assigned with
wicked men,
Yet He was with a rich man in His
death,
Because He had done no violence,

Nor was there any deceit in His
mouth.

10 ¶ But the LORD was pleased
To crush Him, putting *Him* to
grief;
If He would render Himself *as* a
guilt offering,
He will see *His* offspring,
He will prolong *His* days,
And the good pleasure of the
LORD will prosper in His hand.
11 As a result of the anguish of His
soul,
He will see *it* and be satisfied;
By His knowledge the Righteous
One,
My Servant, will justify the many,
As He will bear their iniquities.
12 Therefore, I will allot Him a por-
tion with the great,
And He will divide the booty with
the strong;
Because He poured out Himself to
death,
And was numbered with the
transgressors;
Yet He Himself bore the sin of
many,
And interceded for the transgres-
sors.

CHAPTER 54

"SHOUT for joy, O barren one, you
who have borne no *child;*
Break forth into joyful shouting
and cry aloud, you who have
not travailed;
For the sons of the desolate one
will be more numerous
Than the sons of the married
woman," says the LORD.
2 "Enlarge the place of your tent;
Stretch out the curtains of your
dwellings, spare not;
Lengthen your cords,
And strengthen your pegs.
3 "For you will spread abroad to the
right and to the left.
And your descendants will possess
nations,
And they will resettle the desolate
cities.

4 ¶ "Fear not, for you will not be put
to shame;
Neither feel humiliated, for you
will not be disgraced;

[19] Lit., *desire*   [20] Or, *sickness*   [21] Or, *wounded*

But you will forget the shame of
    your youth,
And the reproach of your widow-
    hood you will remember no
    more.
5"For your husband is your Maker,
    Whose name is the Lord of hosts;
And your Redeemer is the Holy
    One of Israel,
Who is called the God of all the
    earth.
6"For the Lord has called you,
    Like a wife forsaken and grieved
    in spirit,
Even like a wife of *one's* youth
    when she is rejected,"
Says your God.
7"For a brief moment I forsook you,
    But with great compassion I will
    gather you.
8"In an outburst of anger
    I hid My face from you for a mo-
    ment;
But with everlasting lovingkind-
    ness I will have compassion on
    you,"
Says the Lord your Redeemer.

9 ¶"For this is like the days of Noah
    to Me;
When I swore that the waters of
    Noah
Should not flood the earth again,
So I have sworn that I will not be
    angry with you,
Nor will I rebuke you.
10"For the mountains may be re-
    moved and the hills may shake,
But My lovingkindness will not be
    removed from you,
And My covenant of peace will
    not be shaken,"
Says the Lord who has compas-
    sion on you.

11 ¶"O afflicted one, storm-tossed,
    and not comforted,
Behold, I will set your stones in
    antimony,
And your foundations I will lay in
    sapphires.
12"Moreover, I will make your battle-
    ments of rubies,
And your gates of crystal,
And your entire wall of precious
    stones.
13"And all your sons will be taught of
    the Lord;

And the well-being of your sons
    will be great.
14"In righteousness you will be es-
    tablished;
You will be far from oppression,
    for you will not fear;
And from terror, for it will not
    come near you.
15"If anyone fiercely assails *you* it
    will not be from Me.
Whoever assails you will fall be-
    cause of you.
16"Behold, I Myself have created the
    smith who blows the fire of
    coals,
And brings out a weapon for its
    work;
And I have created the destroyer
    to ruin.
17"No weapon that is formed against
    you shall prosper;
And every tongue that accuses
    you in judgment you will con-
    demn.
This is the heritage of the ser-
    vants of the Lord,
And their vindication is from Me,"
    declares the Lord.

CHAPTER 55

"Ho! Every one who thirsts, come
    to the waters;
And you who have no money
    come, buy and eat.
Come, buy wine and milk
Without money and without cost.
2"Why do you spend money for
    what is not bread,
And your wages for what does not
    satisfy?
Listen carefully to Me, and eat
    what is good,
And delight yourself in abun-
    dance.
3"Incline your ear and come to Me.
Listen, that you may live;
And I will make an everlasting
    covenant with you,
According to the faithful mercies
    shown to David.
4"Behold, I have made him a wit-
    ness to the peoples,
A leader and commander for the
    peoples.
5"Behold, you will call a nation you
    do not know,
And a nation which knows you
    not will run to you,

Because of the LORD your God,
even the Holy One of Israel;
For He has glorified you."

6 ¶ Seek the LORD while He may be
found;
Call upon Him while He is near.
7 Let the wicked forsake his way,
And the unrighteous man his
thoughts;
And let him return to the LORD,
And He will have compassion on
him;
And to our God,
For He will abundantly pardon.
8"For My thoughts are not your
thoughts,
Neither are your ways My ways,"
declares the LORD.
9"For *as* the heavens are higher
than the earth,
So are My ways higher than your
ways,
And My thoughts than your
thoughts.
10"For as the rain and the snow come
down from heaven,
And do not return there without
watering the earth,
And making it bear and sprout,
And furnishing seed to the sower
and bread to the eater;
11 So shall My word be which goes
forth from My mouth;
It shall not return to Me empty,
Without accomplishing what I
desire,
And without succeeding *in the
matter* for which I sent it.
12"For you will go out with joy,
And be led forth with peace;
The mountains and the hills will
break forth into shouts of joy
before you,
And all the trees of the field will
clap *their* hands.
13"Instead of the thorn bush the
cypress will come up;
And instead of the nettle the myrtle will come up;
And it will be a memorial to the
LORD,
For an everlasting sign which will
not be cut off."

CHAPTER 56

THUS says the LORD,
"Preserve justice, and do righteousness,

For My salvation is about to come
And My righteousness to be revealed.
2"How blessed is the man who does
this,
And the son of man who takes
hold of it;
Who keeps from profaning the
sabbath,
And keeps his hand from doing
any evil."
3 Let not the foreigner who has
joined himself to the LORD say,
"The LORD will surely separate me
from His people."
Neither let the eunuch say, "Behold, I am a dry tree."
4 For thus says the LORD,
"To the eunuchs who keep My
sabbaths,
And choose what pleases Me,
And hold fast My covenant,
5 To them I will give in My house
and within My walls a memorial,
And a name better than that of
sons and daughters;
I will give them an everlasting
name which will not be cut off.

6 ¶"Also the foreigners who join
themselves to the LORD,
To minister to Him, and to love
the name of the LORD,
To be His servants, every one who
keeps from profaning the sabbath,
And holds fast My covenant;
7 Even those I will bring to My holy
mountain,
And make them joyful in My
house of prayer.
Their burnt offerings and their
sacrifices will be acceptable on
My altar;
For My house will be called a
house of prayer for all the peoples."
8 The Lord GOD, who gathers the
dispersed of Israel, declares,
"Yet *others* I will gather to them,
to those *already* gathered."

9 ¶ All you beasts of the field,
All you beasts in the forest,
Come to eat.
10 His watchmen are blind,
All of them know nothing.

All of them are dumb dogs unable
to bark,
Dreamers lying down, who love to
slumber;
11 And the dogs are greedy, they are
not satisfied.
And they are shepherds who have
no understanding;
They have all turned to their own
way,
Each one to his unjust gain, to the
last one.
12"Come," *they say,* "let us get wine,
and let us drink heavily of
strong drink;
And tomorrow will be like today,
only more so."

CHAPTER 57

THE righteous man perishes, and no
man takes it to heart;
And devout men are taken away,
while no one understands.
For the righteous man is taken
away from evil,
2 He enters into peace;
They rest in their beds,
Each one who walked in his upright way.
3"But come here, you sons of a
sorceress,
Offspring of an adulterer and a
prostitute.
4"Against whom do you jest?
Against whom do you open wide
your mouth
And stick out your tongue?
Are you not children of rebellion,
Offspring of deceit,
5 *Who* inflame yourselves among
the oaks,
Under every luxuriant tree,
Who slaughter the children in the
ravines,
Under the clefts of the crags?
6"Among the smooth *stones* of the
ravine
Is your portion, they are your lot;
Even to them you have poured
out a libation,
You have made a grain offering.
Shall I relent concerning these
things?
7"Upon a high and lofty mountain
You have made your bed.
You also went up there to offer
sacrifice.

8"And behind the door and the
doorpost
You have set up your sign;
Indeed, far removed from Me, you
have uncovered yourself;
And have gone up and made your
bed wide.
And you have made an agreement
for yourselves with them,
You have loved their bed,
You have looked on *their* man-
hood.
9"And you have journeyed to the
king with oil
And increased your perfumes;
You have sent your envoys a
great distance,
And made *them* go down to Sheol.
10"You were tired out by the length
of your road,
Yet you did not say, 'It is hope-
less.'
You found renewed strength,
Therefore you did not faint.

11 ¶"Of whom were you worried and
fearful,
When you lied, and did not remember Me,
Nor give *Me* a thought?
Was I not silent even for a long
time
So you do not fear Me?
12"I will declare your righteousness
and your deeds,
But they will not profit you.
13"When you cry out, let your collection *of idols* deliver you.
But the wind will carry all of them
up,
And a breath will take *them*
away.
But he who takes refuge in Me
shall inherit the land,
And shall possess My holy mountain."

14 ¶ And it shall be said,
"Build up, build up, prepare the
way,
Remove *every* obstacle out of the
way of My people."
15 For thus says the high and exalted
One
Who lives forever, whose name is
Holy,
"I dwell *on* a high and holy place,

And *also* with the contrite and
lowly of spirit
In order to revive the spirit of the
lowly
And to revive the heart of the
contrite.

16"For I will not contend forever,
Neither will I always be angry;
For the spirit would grow faint
before Me,
And the breath *of those whom* I
have made.

17"Because of the iniquity of his
unjust gain I was angry and
struck him;
I hid *My face* and was angry,
And he went on turning away, in
the way of his heart.

18"I have seen his ways, but I will
heal him;
I will lead him and restore comfort to him and to his mourners,

19 Creating the praise of the lips.
Peace, peace to him who is far and
to him who is near,"
Says the LORD, "and I will heal
him."

20 But the wicked are like the tossing sea,
For it cannot be quiet,
And its waters toss up refuse and
mud.

21"There is no peace," says my God,
"for the wicked."

CHAPTER 58

"CRY loudly, do not hold back;
Raise your voice like a trumpet,
And declare to My people their
transgression,
And to the house of Jacob their
sins.

2"Yet they seek Me day by day, and
delight to know My ways,
As a nation that has done right-
eousness,
And has not forsaken the ordi-
nance of their God.
They ask Me *for* just decisions,
They delight in the nearness of
God.

3 'Why have we fasted and Thou
dost not see?
Why have we humbled ourselves
and Thou dost not notice?'
Behold, on the day of your fast
you find *your* desire,

And drive hard all your workers.

4"Behold, you fast for contention
and strife and to strike with a
wicked fist.
You do not fast like *you do* today
to make your voice heard on
high.

5"Is it a fast like this which I
choose, a day for a man to humble himself?
Is it for bowing one's head like a
reed,
And for spreading out sackcloth
and ashes as a bed?
Will you call this a fast, even an
acceptable day to the LORD?

6"Is this not the fast which I choose,
To loosen the bonds of wicked-
ness,
To undo the bands of the yoke,
And to let the oppressed go free,
And break every yoke?

7"Is it not to divide your bread with
the hungry,
And bring the homeless poor into
the house;
When you see the naked, to cover
him;
And not to hide yourself from
your own flesh?

8"Then your light will break out like
the dawn,
And your recovery will speedily
spring forth;
And your righteousness will go
before you;
The glory of the LORD will be your
rear guard.

9"Then you will call, and the LORD
will answer;
You will cry, and He will say,
'Here I am.'
If you remove the yoke from your
midst,
The pointing of the finger, and
speaking wickedness,

10 And if you give yourself to the
hungry,
And satisfy the desire of the afflicted,
Then your light will rise in darkness,
And your gloom *will become* like
midday.

11"And the LORD will continually
guide you,

And satisfy your desire in
scorched places,
And give strength to your bones;
And you will be like a watered
garden,
And like a spring of water whose
waters do not fail.

12 "And those from among you will
rebuild the ancient ruins;
You will raise up the age-old
foundations;
And you will be called the repairer
of the breach,
The restorer of the streets in
which to dwell.

13 ¶ "If because of the sabbath, you
turn your foot
From doing your *own* pleasure on
My holy day,
And call the sabbath a delight, the
holy *day* of the LORD honorable,
And shall honor it, desisting from
your *own* ways,
From seeking your *own* pleasure,
And speaking *your own* word,

14 Then you will take delight in the
LORD,
And I will make you ride on the
heights of the earth;
And I will feed you *with* the heri-
tage of Jacob your father,
For the mouth of the LORD has
spoken."

CHAPTER 59

BEHOLD, the LORD's hand is not so
short
That it cannot save;
Neither is His ear so dull
That it cannot hear.

2 But your iniquities have made a
separation between you and
your God,
And your sins have hidden *His*
face from you, so that He does
not hear.

3 For your hands are defiled with
blood,
And your fingers with iniquity;
Your lips have spoken falsehood,
Your tongue mutters wickedness.

4 No one sues righteously and no
one pleads honestly.
They trust in confusion, and
speak lies;
They conceive mischief, and bring
forth iniquity.

5 They hatch adders' eggs and
weave the spider's web;
He who eats of their eggs dies,
And *from* that which is crushed a
snake breaks forth.

6 Their webs will not become clothing,
Nor will they cover themselves
with their works;
Their works are works of iniquity,
And an act of violence is in their
hands.

7 Their feet run to evil,
And they hasten to shed innocent
blood;
Their thoughts are thoughts of
iniquity;
Devastation and destruction are
in their highways.

8 They do not know the way of
peace,
And there is no justice in their
tracks;
They have made their paths
crooked;
Whoever treads on them does not
know peace.

9 ¶ Therefore, justice is far from us,
And righteousness does not overtake us;
We hope for light, but behold,
darkness;
For brightness, but we walk in
gloom.

10 We grope along the wall like blind
men,
We grope like those who have no
eyes;
We stumble at midday as in the
twilight,
Among those who are vigorous
we are like dead men.

11 All of us growl like bears,
And moan sadly like doves;
We hope for justice, but there is
none,
For salvation, *but* it is far from us.

12 For our transgressions are multi-
plied before Thee,
And our sins testify against us;
For our transgressions are with
us,
And we know our iniquities:

13 Transgressing and denying the
LORD,
And turning away from our God,
Speaking oppression and revolt,

Conceiving *in* and uttering from the heart lying words.

14 And justice is turned back,
And righteousness stands far away;
For truth has stumbled in the street,
And uprightness cannot enter.

15 Yes, truth is lacking;
And he who turns aside from evil makes himself a prey.

¶ Now the LORD saw,
And it was displeasing in His sight that there was no justice.

16 And He saw that there was no man,
And was astonished that there was no one to intercede;
Then His own arm brought salvation to Him;
And His righteousness upheld Him.

17 And He put on righteousness like a breastplate,
And a helmet of salvation on His head;
And He put on garments of vengeance for clothing,
And wrapped Himself with zeal as a mantle.

18 According to *their* deeds, so He will repay,
Wrath to His adversaries, recompense to His enemies;
To the coastlands He will make recompense.

19 So they will fear the name of the LORD from the west
And His glory from the rising of the sun,
For He will come like a rushing stream,
Which the wind of the LORD drives.

20 "And a Redeemer will come to Zion,
And to those who turn from transgression in Jacob," declares the LORD.

21 "And as for Me, this is My covenant with them," says the LORD: "My Spirit which is upon you, and My words which I have put in your mouth, shall not depart from your mouth, nor from the mouth of your offspring, nor from the mouth of your offspring's offspring," says the LORD, "from now and forever."

CHAPTER 60

"ARISE, shine; for your light has come,
And the glory of the LORD has risen upon you.

2 "For behold, darkness will cover the earth,
And deep darkness the peoples;
But the LORD will rise upon you,
And His glory will appear upon you.

3 "And nations will come to your light,
And kings to the brightness of your rising.

4 ¶ "Lift up your eyes round about, and see;
They all gather together, they come to you.
Your sons will come from afar,
And your daughters will be carried in the arms.

5 "Then you will see and be radiant,
And your heart will thrill and rejoice;
Because the abundance of the sea will be turned to you,
The wealth of the nations will come to you.

6 "A multitude of camels will cover you,
The young camels of Midian and Ephah;
All those from Sheba will come;
They will bring gold and frankincense,
And will bear good news of the praises of the LORD.

7 "All the flocks of Kedar will be gathered together to you,
The rams of Nebaioth will minister to you;
They will go up with acceptance on My altar,
And I shall glorify My glorious house.

8 "Who are these who fly like a cloud,
And like the doves to their lattices?

9 "Surely the coastlands will wait for Me;

And the ships of Tarshish *will
come* first,
To bring your sons from afar,
Their silver and their gold with
them,
For the name of the LORD your
God,
And for the Holy One of Israel
because He has glorified you.

10 ¶"And foreigners will build up
your walls,
And their kings will minister to
you;
For in My wrath I struck you,
And in My favor I have had compassion on you.
11"And your gates will be open continually;
They will not be closed day or
night,
So that *men* may bring to you the
wealth of the nations,
With their kings led in procession.
12"For the nation and the kingdom
which will not serve you will
perish,
And the nations will be utterly
ruined.
13"The glory of Lebanon will come to
you,
The juniper, the box tree, and the
cypress together,
To beautify the place of My sanctuary;
And I shall make the place of My
feet glorious.
14"And the sons of those who afflicted you will come bowing to
you,
And all those who despised you
will bow themselves at the soles
of your feet;
And they will call you the city of
the LORD,
The Zion of the Holy One of Israel.

15 ¶"Whereas you have been forsaken and hated
With no one passing through,
I will make you an everlasting
pride,
A joy from generation to generation.
16"You will also suck the milk of
nations,

And will suck the breast of kings;
Then you will know that I, the
LORD, am your Savior,
And your Redeemer, the Mighty
One of Jacob.
17"Instead of bronze I will bring gold,
And instead of iron I will bring
silver,
And instead of wood, bronze,
And instead of stones, iron.
And I will make peace your ad-
ministrators,
And righteousness your overseers.
18"Violence will not be heard again
in your land,
Nor devastation or destruction
within your borders;
But you will call your walls salva-
tion, and your gates praise.
19"No longer will you have the sun
for light by day,
Nor for brightness will the moon
give you light;
But you will have the LORD for an
everlasting light,
And your God for your glory.
20"Your sun will set no more,
Neither will your moon wane;
For you will have the LORD for an
everlasting light,
And the days of your mourning
will be finished.
21"Then all your people *will be* righteous;
They will possess the land forever,
The branch of My planting,
The work of My hands,
That I may be glorified.
22"The smallest one will become a
clan,
And the least one a mighty nation.
I, the LORD, will hasten it in its
time."

CHAPTER 61

THE Spirit of the Lord GOD is upon
me,
Because the LORD has anointed
me
To bring good news to the afflicted;
He has sent me to bind up the
brokenhearted,
To proclaim liberty to captives,
And freedom to prisoners;
2 To proclaim the favorable year of
the LORD,

And the day of vengeance of our
God;
To comfort all who mourn,
3 To grant those who mourn *in*
Zion,
Giving them a garland instead of
ashes,
The oil of gladness instead of
mourning,
The mantle of praise instead of a
spirit of fainting.
So they will be called oaks of
righteousness,
The planting of the LORD, that He
may be glorified.

4 ¶ Then they will rebuild the ancient ruins,
They will raise up the former dev-
astations,
And they will repair the ruined
cities,
The desolations of many generations.
5 And strangers will stand and pasture your flocks,
And foreigners will be your farmers and your vinedressers.
6 But you will be called the priests
of the LORD;
You will be spoken of *as* ministers
of our God.
You will eat the wealth of nations,
And in their riches you will boast.
7 Instead of your shame *you will
have a* double *portion,*
And *instead of* humiliation they
will shout for joy over their
portion.
Therefore they will possess a double *portion* in their land,
Everlasting joy will be theirs.
8 For I, the LORD, love justice,
I hate robbery in the burnt offering;
And I will faithfully give them
their recompense,
And I will make an everlasting
covenant with them.
9 Then their offspring will be
known among the nations,
And their descendants in the
midst of the peoples.
All who see them will recognize
them
Because they are the offspring
whom the LORD has blessed.

10 ¶ I will rejoice greatly in the
LORD,
My soul will exult in my God;
For He has clothed me with garments of salvation,
He has wrapped me with a robe of
righteousness,
As a bridegroom decks himself
with a garland,
And as a bride adorns herself with
her jewels.
11 For as the earth brings forth its
sprouts,
And as a garden causes the things
sown in it to spring up,
So the Lord GOD will cause righteousness and praise
To spring up before all the nations.

CHAPTER 62

FOR Zion's sake I will not keep silent,
And for Jerusalem's sake I will
not keep quiet,
Until her righteousness goes forth
like brightness,
And her salvation like a torch that
is burning.
2 And the nations will see your
righteousness,
And all kings your glory;
And you will be called by a new
name,
Which the mouth of the LORD will
designate.
3 You will also be a crown of beauty
in the hand of the LORD,
And a royal diadem in the hand of
your God.
4 It will no longer be said to you,
"Forsaken,"
Nor to your land will it any longer
be said, "Desolate";
But you will be called, "My delight
is in her,"
And your land, "Married";
For the LORD delights in you,
And *to Him* your land will be married.
5 For *as* a young man marries a
virgin,
So your sons will marry you;
And *as* the bridegroom rejoices
over the bride,
So your God will rejoice over you.

6 ¶ On your walls, O Jerusalem, I
  have appointed watchmen;
  All day and all night they will
  never keep silent.
  You who remind the LORD, take
  no rest for yourselves;
7 And give Him no rest until He
  establishes
  And makes Jerusalem a praise in
  the earth.
8 The LORD has sworn by His right
  hand and by His strong arm,
  "I will never again give your grain
  as food for your enemies;
  Nor will foreigners drink your
  new wine, for which you have
  labored."
9 But those who garner it will eat it,
  and praise the LORD;
  And those who gather it will drink
  it in the courts of My sanctuary.

10 ¶ Go through, go through the
   gates;
   Clear the way for the people;
   Build up, build up the highway;
   Remove the stones, lift up a standard over the peoples.
11 Behold, the LORD has proclaimed
   to the end of the earth,
   Say to the daughter of Zion, "Lo,
   your salvation comes;
   Behold His reward is with Him,
   and His recompense before
   Him."
12 And they will call them, "The holy
   people,
   The redeemed of the LORD";
   And you will be called, "Sought
   out, a city not forsaken."

CHAPTER 63

WHO is this who comes from Edom,
  With garments of glowing colors
  from Bozrah,
  This One who is majestic in His
  apparel,
  Marching in the greatness of His
  strength?
  "It is I who speak in righteousness,
  mighty to save."
2 Why is Your apparel red,
  And Your garments like the one
  who treads in the wine press?
3 "I have trodden the wine trough
  alone,
  And from the peoples there was
  no man with Me.
  I also trod them in My anger,
  And trampled them in My wrath;
  And their lifeblood is sprinkled on
  My garments,
  And I stained all My raiment.
4 "For the day of vengeance was in
  My heart,
  And My year of redemption has
  come.
5 "And I looked, and there was no
  one to help,
  And I was astonished and there
  was no one to uphold;
  So My own arm brought salvation
  to Me;
  And My wrath upheld Me.
6 "And I trod down the peoples in
  My anger,
  And made them drunk in My
  wrath,
  And I poured out their lifeblood
  on the earth."

7 ¶ I shall make mention of the
  lovingkindnesses of the LORD,
  the praises of the LORD,
  According to all that the LORD has
  granted us,
  And the great goodness toward
  the house of Israel,
  Which He has granted them according to His compassion,
  And according to the multitude of
  His lovingkindnesses.
8 For He said, "Surely, they are My
  people,
  Sons who will not deal falsely."
  So He became their Savior.
9 In all their affliction He was afflicted,
  And the angel of His presence
  saved them;
  In His love and in His mercy He
  redeemed them;
  And He lifted them and carried
  them all the days of old.
10 But they rebelled
   And grieved His Holy Spirit;
   Therefore, He turned Himself to
   become their enemy,
   He fought against them.
11 Then His people remembered the
   days of old, of Moses.
   Where is He who brought them
   up out of the sea with the shepherds of His flock?
   Where is He who put His Holy
   Spirit in the midst of them,

12 Who caused His glorious arm to
go at the right hand of Moses,
Who divided the waters before
them to make for Himself an
everlasting name,
13 Who led them through the
depths?
Like the horse in the wilderness,
they did not stumble;
14 As the cattle which go down into
the valley,
The Spirit of the LORD gave them
rest.
So didst Thou lead Thy people,
To make for Thyself a glorious
name.

15 ¶ Look down from heaven, and
see from Thy holy and glorious
habitation;
Where are Thy zeal and Thy
mighty deeds?
The stirrings of Thy heart and
Thy compassion are restrained
toward me.
16 For Thou art our Father, though
Abraham does not know us,
And Israel does not recognize us.
Thou, O LORD, art our Father,
Our Redeemer from of old is Thy
name.
17 Why, O LORD, dost Thou cause us
to stray from Thy ways,
And harden our heart from fearing Thee?
Return for the sake of Thy servants, the tribes of Thy heritage.
18 Thy holy people possessed Thy
sanctuary for a little while,
Our adversaries have trodden *it*
down.
19 We have become *like* those over
whom Thou hast never ruled,
Like those who were not called by
Thy name.

CHAPTER 64

OH, that Thou wouldst rend the
heavens *and* come down,
That the mountains might quake
at Thy presence—
2 As fire kindles the brushwood, *as*
fire causes water to boil—
To make Thy name known to
Thine adversaries,
That the nations may tremble at
Thy presence!

3 When Thou didst awesome things
which we did not expect,
Thou didst come down, the mountains quaked at Thy presence.
4 For from of old they have not
heard nor perceived by ear,
Neither has the eye seen a God
besides Thee,
Who acts in behalf of the one who
waits for Him.
5 Thou dost meet him who rejoices
in doing righteousness,
Who remembers Thee in Thy
ways.
Behold, Thou wast angry, for we
sinned,
We continued in them a long
time;
And shall we be saved?
6 For all of us have become like one
who is unclean,
And all our righteous deeds are
like a filthy garment;
And all of us wither like a leaf,
And our iniquities, like the wind,
take us away.
7 And there is no one who calls on
Thy name,
Who arouses himself to take hold
of Thee;
For Thou hast hidden Thy face
from us,
And hast delivered us into the
power of our iniquities.

8 ¶ But now, O LORD, Thou art our
Father,
We are the clay, and Thou our
potter;
And all of us are the work of Thy
hand.
9 Do not be angry beyond measure,
O LORD,
Neither remember iniquity for-
ever;
Behold, look now, all of us are
Thy people.
10 Thy holy cities have become a
wilderness,
Zion has become a wilderness,
Jerusalem a desolation.
11 Our holy and beautiful house,
Where our fathers praised Thee,
Has been burned *by* fire;
And all our precious things have
become a ruin.
12 Wilt Thou restrain Thyself at
these things, O LORD?

Wilt Thou keep silent and afflict us beyond measure?

CHAPTER 65

"I PERMITTED Myself to be sought by those who did not ask *for Me;*
I permitted Myself to be found by those who did not seek Me.
I said, 'Here am I, here am I,'
To a nation which did not call on My name.

2 "I have spread out My hands all day long to a rebellious people,
Who walk *in* the way which is not good, following their own thoughts,

3 A people who continually provoke Me to My face,
Offering sacrifices in gardens and burning incense on bricks;

4 Who sit among graves, and spend the night in secret places;
Who eat swine's flesh,
And the broth of unclean meat is *in* their pots.

5 "Who say, 'Keep to yourself, do not come near me,
For I am holier than you!'
These are smoke in My nostrils,
A fire that burns all the day.

6 "Behold, it is written before Me,
I will not keep silent, but I will repay;
I will even repay into their bosom,

7 Both their own iniquities and the iniquities of their fathers together," says the LORD.
"Because they have burned incense on the mountains,
And scorned Me on the hills,
Therefore I will measure their former work into their bosom."

8 ¶ Thus says the LORD,
"As the new wine is found in the cluster,
And one says, 'Do not destroy it, for there is benefit in it,'
So I will act on behalf of My servants
In order not to destroy all of them.

9 "And I will bring forth offspring from Jacob,
And an heir of My mountains from Judah;
Even My chosen ones shall inherit it,
And My servants shall dwell there.

10 "And Sharon shall be a pasture land for flocks,
And the valley of Achor a resting place for herds,
For My people who seek Me.

11 "But you who forsake the LORD,
Who forget My holy mountain,
Who set a table for Fortune,
And who fill *cups* with mixed wine for Destiny,

12 I will destine you for the sword,
And all of you shall bow down to the slaughter.
Because I called, but you did not answer;
I spoke, but you did not hear.
And you did evil in My sight,
And chose that in which I did not delight."

13 ¶ Therefore, thus says the Lord GOD,
"Behold, My servants shall eat, but you shall be hungry.
Behold, My servants shall drink, but you shall be thirsty.
Behold, My servants shall rejoice, but you shall be put to shame.

14 "Behold, My servants shall shout joyfully with a glad heart,
But you shall cry out with a heavy heart,
And you shall wail with a broken spirit.

15 "And you will leave your name for a curse to My chosen ones,
And the Lord GOD will slay you.
But My servants will be called by another name.

16 "Because he who is blessed in the earth
Shall be blessed by the God of truth;
And he who swears in the earth
Shall swear by the God of truth;
Because the former troubles are forgotten,
And because they are hidden from My sight!

17 ¶ "For behold, I create new heavens and a new earth;
And the former things shall not be remembered or come to mind.

18"But be glad and rejoice forever in
　what I create;
　For behold, I create Jerusalem *for*
　rejoicing,
　And her people *for* gladness.
19"I will also rejoice in Jerusalem,
　and be glad in My people;
　And there will no longer be heard
　in her
　The voice of weeping and the
　sound of crying.
20"No longer will there be in it an
　infant *who lives but a few* days,
　Or an old man who does not live
　out his days;
　For the youth will die at the age
　of one hundred
　And the one who does not reach
　the age of one hundred
　Shall be *thought* accursed.
21"And they shall build houses and
　inhabit *them;*
　They shall also plant vineyards
　and eat their fruit.
22"They shall not build, and another
　inhabit,
　They shall not plant, and another
　eat;
　For as the lifetime of a tree, *so
　shall be* the days of My people,
　And My chosen ones shall wear
　out the work of their hands.
23"They shall not labor in vain,
　Or bear *children* for calamity;
　For they are the offspring of those
　blessed by the LORD,
　And their descendants with them.
24"It will also come to pass that
before they call, I will answer; and
while they are still speaking, I will
hear.
25"The wolf and the lamb shall graze
together, and the lion shall eat straw
like the ox; and dust shall be the
serpent's food. They shall do no evil or
harm in all My holy mountain," says
the LORD.

CHAPTER 66

THUS says the LORD,
　"Heaven is My throne, and the
　earth is My footstool.
　Where then is a house you could
　build for Me?
　And where is a place that I may
　rest?
2"For My hand made all these
　things,

Thus all these things came into
　being," declares the LORD.
"But to this one I will look,
　To him who is humble and con-
　trite of spirit, and who trembles
　at My word.

3 ¶"*But* he who kills an ox is *like*
　one who slays a man;
　He who sacrifices a lamb is *like*
　the one who breaks a dog's
　neck;
　He who offers a grain offering *is
　like one who offers* swine's
　blood;
　He who burns incense is *like* the
　one who blesses an idol.
　As they have chosen their *own*
　ways,
　And their soul delights in their
　abominations,
4 So I will choose their punish-
　ments,
　And I will bring on them what
　they dread.
　Because I called, but no one an-
　swered;
　I spoke, but they did not listen.
　And they did evil in My sight,
　And chose that in which I did not
　delight."
5 Hear the word of the LORD, you
　who tremble at His word:
"Your brothers who hate you, who
　exclude you for My name's
　sake,
　Have said, 'Let the LORD be glori-
　fied, that we may see your joy.'
　But they will be put to shame.
6"A voice of uproar from the city, a
　voice from the temple,
　The voice of the LORD who is
　rendering recompense to His
　enemies.

7 ¶"Before she travailed, she
　brought forth;
　Before her pain came, she gave
　birth to a boy.
8"Who has heard such a thing? Who
　has seen such things?
　Can a land be born in one day?
　Can a nation be brought forth all
　at once?
　As soon as Zion travailed, she also
　brought forth her sons.
9"Shall I bring to the point of birth,

and not give delivery?" says the
Lord.

"Or shall I who gives delivery shut
the womb?" says your God.

10"Be joyful with Jerusalem and rejoice for her, all you who love
her;

Be exceedingly glad with her, all
you who mourn over her,

11 That you may nurse and be satisfied with her comforting
breasts,

That you may suck and be delighted with her bountiful
bosom."

12 For thus says the Lord, "Behold, I
extend peace to her like a river,

And the glory of the nations like
an overflowing stream;

And you shall be nursed, you shall
be carried on the hip and
fondled on the knees.

13"As one whom his mother comforts, so I will comfort you;

And you shall be comforted in
Jerusalem."

14 Then you shall see *this,* and your
heart shall be glad,

And your bones shall flourish like
the new grass;

And the hand of the Lord shall be
made known to His servants,

But He shall be indignant toward
His enemies.

15 For behold, the Lord will come in
fire

And His chariots like the whirlwind,

To render His anger with fury,

And His rebuke with flames of
fire.

16 For the Lord will execute judgment by fire

And by His sword on all flesh,

And those slain by the Lord will
be many.

17"Those who sanctify and purify
themselves *to go* to the gardens,

Following one in the center,

Who eat swine's flesh, detestable
things, and mice,

Shall come to an end altogether,"
declares the Lord.

18"For I know their works and their
thoughts; the time is coming to gather
all nations and tongues. And they shall
come and see My glory.

19"And I will set a sign among them
and will send survivors from them to
the nations: Tarshish, Put, Lud, Meshech, Rosh, Tubal, and Javan, to the
distant coastlands that have neither
heard My fame nor seen My glory.
And they will declare My glory among
the nations.

20"Then they shall bring all your
brethren from all the nations as a
grain offering to the Lord, on horses,
in chariots, in litters, on mules, and on
camels, to My holy mountain Jerusalem," says the Lord, "just as the sons
of Israel bring their grain offering in a
clean vessel to the house of the Lord.

21"I will also take some of them for
priests *and* for Levites," says the Lord.

22"For just as the new heavens and
the new earth

Which I make will endure before
Me," declares the Lord,

"So your offspring and your name
will endure.

23"And it shall be from new moon to
new moon

And from sabbath to sabbath,

All mankind will come to bow
down before Me," says the
Lord.

24"Then they shall go forth and look
On the corpses of the men
Who have transgressed against
Me.

For their worm shall not die,

And their fire shall not be
quenched;

And they shall be an abhorrence
to all mankind."

THE BOOK OF

JEREMIAH

THE words of Jeremiah, the son of Hilkiah, of the priests who were in Anathoth in the land of Benjamin,

2 to whom the word of the LORD came in the days of Josiah, the son of Amon, king of Judah, in the thirteenth year of his reign.

3 It came also in the days of Jehoiakim, the son of Josiah, king of Judah, until the end of the eleventh year of Zedekiah, the son of Josiah, king of Judah, until the exile of Jerusalem in the fifth month.

4 ¶ Now the word of the LORD came to me saying,

5"Before I formed you in the womb
I knew you,
And before you were born I consecrated you;
I have appointed you a prophet to the nations."

6 Then I said, "Alas, Lord GOD!
Behold, I do not know how to speak,
Because I am a youth."

7 But the LORD said to me,
"Do not say, 'I am a youth,'
Because everywhere I send you, you shall go,
And all that I command you, you shall speak.

8"Do not be afraid of them,
For I am with you to deliver you," declares the LORD.

9 Then the LORD stretched out His hand and touched my mouth, and the LORD said to me,
"Behold, I have put My words in your mouth.

10"See, I have appointed you this day over the nations and over the kingdoms,
To pluck up and to break down,
To destroy and to overthrow,
To build and to plant."

11 ¶ And the word of the LORD came to me saying, "What do you see, Jeremiah?" And I said, "I see a rod of an almond tree."

12 Then the LORD said to me, "You have seen well, for I am watching over My word to perform it."

13 ¶ And the word of the LORD came to me a second time saying, "What do you see?" And I said, "I see a boiling pot, facing away from the north."

14 Then the LORD said to me, "Out of the north the evil will break forth on all the inhabitants of the land.

15"For, behold, I am calling all the families of the kingdoms of the north," declares the LORD; "and they will come, and they will set each one his throne at the entrance of the gates of Jerusalem, and against all its walls round about, and against all the cities of Judah.

16"And I will pronounce My judgments on them concerning all their wickedness, whereby they have forsaken Me and have offered sacrifices to other gods, and worshiped the works of their own hands.

17"Now, gird up your loins, and arise, and speak to them all which I command you. Do not be dismayed before them, lest I dismay you before them.

18"Now behold, I have made you today as a fortified city, and as a pillar of iron and as walls of bronze against the whole land, to the kings of Judah, to its princes, to its priests and to the people of the land.

19"And they will fight against you, but they will not overcome you, for I am with you to deliver you," declares the LORD.

CHAPTER 2

NOW the word of the LORD came to me saying,

2"Go and proclaim in the ears of Jerusalem, saying, 'Thus says the LORD,
"I remember concerning you the devotion of your youth,
The love of your betrothals,
Your following after Me in the wilderness,
Through a land not sown.

3"Israel was holy to the LORD,
The first of His harvest;
All who ate of it became guilty;
Evil came upon them," declares the LORD.' "

4 ¶ Hear the word of the LORD, O house of Jacob, and all the families of the house of Israel.

5 Thus says the LORD,
"What injustice did your fathers find in Me,
That they went far from Me
And walked after emptiness and became empty?

6"And they did not say, 'Where is
  the LORD
    Who brought us up out of the
      land of Egypt,
    Who led us through the wilder-
      ness,
    Through a land of deserts and of
      pits,
    Through a land of drought and of
      deep darkness,
    Through a land that no one
      crossed
    And where no man dwelt?'
7"And I brought you into the fruitful land,
    To eat its fruit and its good things.
    But you came and defiled My
      land,
    And My inheritance you made an
      abomination.
8"The priests did not say, 'Where is
  the LORD?'
    And those who handle the law did
      not know Me;
    The rulers also transgressed
      against Me,
    And the prophets prophesied by
      Baal
    And walked after things that did
      not profit.

9 ¶"Therefore I will yet contend
  with you," declares the LORD,
    "And with your sons' sons I will
      contend.
10"For cross to the coastlands of
    Kittim and see,
    And send to Kedar and observe
      closely,
    And see if there has been such a
      thing as this!
11"Has a nation changed gods,
    When they were not gods?
    But My people have changed their
      glory
    For that which does not profit.
12"Be appalled, O heavens, at this,
    And shudder, be very desolate,"
      declares the LORD.
13"For My people have committed
    two evils:
    They have forsaken Me,
    The fountain of living waters,
    To hew for themselves cisterns,
    Broken cisterns,
    That can hold no water.

14 ¶"Is Israel a slave? Or is he a
    homeborn servant?

Why has he become a prey?
15"The young lions have roared at
    him,
    They have roared loudly.
    And they have made his land a
      waste;
    His cities have been destroyed,
      without inhabitant.
16"Also the men of Memphis and
    Tahpanhes
    Have shaved the crown of your
      head.
17"Have you not done this to your-
    self,
    By your forsaking the LORD your
      God,
    When He led you in the way?
18"But now what are you doing on
    the road to Egypt,
    To drink the waters of the Nile?
    Or what are you doing on the road
      to Assyria,
    To drink the waters of the Eu-
      phrates?
19"Your own wickedness will correct
    you,
    And your apostasies will reprove
      you;
    Know therefore and see that it is
      evil and bitter
    For you to forsake the LORD your
      God,
    And the dread of Me is not in
      you," declares the Lord GOD of
      hosts.

20 ¶"For long ago I broke your yoke
    And tore off your bonds;
    But you said, 'I will not serve!'
    For on every high hill
    And under every green tree
    You have lain down as a harlot.
21"Yet I planted you a choice vine,
    A completely faithful seed.
    How then have you turned your-
      self before Me
    Into the degenerate shoots of a
      foreign vine?
22"Although you wash yourself with
    lye
    And use much soap,
    The stain of your iniquity is before
      Me," declares the Lord GOD.
23"How can you say, 'I am not de-
      filed,
    I have not gone after the Baals'?
    Look at your way in the valley!
    Know what you have done!

You are a swift young camel en-
tangling her ways,

24 A wild donkey accustomed to the
wilderness,
That sniffs the wind in her passion.
In *the time of* her heat who can
turn her away?
All who seek her will not become
weary;
In her month they will find her.

25 "Keep your feet from being unshod
And your throat from thirst;
But you said, 'It is hopeless!
No! For I have loved strangers,
And after them I will walk.'

26 ¶ "As the thief is shamed when he
is discovered,
So the house of Israel is shamed;
They, their kings, their princes,
And their priests, and their proph-
ets,

27 Who say to a tree, 'You are my
father,'
And to a stone, 'You gave me
birth.'
For they have turned *their* back
to Me,
And not *their* face;
But in the time of their trouble
they will say,
'Arise and save us.'

28 "But where are your gods
Which you made for yourself?
Let them arise, if they can save
you
In the time of your trouble;
For *according to* the number of
your cities
Are your gods, O Judah.

29 ¶ "Why do you contend with Me?
You have all transgressed against
Me," declares the Lord.

30 "In vain I have struck your sons;
They accepted no chastening.
Your sword has devoured your
prophets
Like a destroying lion.

31 "O generation, heed the word of
the Lord.
Have I been a wilderness to Israel,
Or a land of thick darkness?
Why do My people say, 'We *are
free to* roam;
We will come no more to Thee'?

32 "Can a virgin forget her ornaments,

Or a bride her attire?
Yet My people have forgotten Me
Days without number.

33 "How well you prepare your way
To seek love!
Therefore even the wicked
women
You have taught your ways.

34 "Also on your skirts is found
The lifeblood of the innocent
poor;
You did not find them breaking in.
But in spite of all these things,

35 Yet you said, 'I am innocent;
Surely His anger is turned away
from me.'
Behold, I will enter into judgment
with you
Because you say, 'I have not
sinned.'

36 "Why do you go around so much
Changing your way?
Also, you shall be put to shame by
Egypt
As you were put to shame by
Assyria.

37 "From this *place* also you shall go
out
With your hands on your head;
For the Lord has rejected those in
whom you trust,
And you shall not prosper with
them."

CHAPTER 3

GOD says, "If a husband divorces his
wife,
And she goes from him,
And belongs to another man,
Will he still return to her?
Will not that land be completely
polluted?
But you are a harlot *with* many
lovers;
Yet you turn to Me," declares the
Lord.

2 "Lift up your eyes to the bare
heights and see;
Where have you not been vio-
lated?
By the roads you have sat for
them
Like an Arab in the desert,
And you have polluted a land
With your harlotry and with your
wickedness.

3 "Therefore the showers have been
withheld,

And there has been no spring rain.
Yet you had a harlot's forehead;
You refused to be ashamed.
4"Have you not just now called to
Me,
'My Father, Thou art the friend of
my youth?
5 'Will He be angry forever?
Will He be indignant to the end?'
Behold, you have spoken
And have done evil things,
And you have had your way."

6 ¶ Then the LORD said to me in the days of Josiah the king, "Have you seen what faithless Israel did? She went up on every high hill and under every green tree, and she was a harlot there.

7"And I thought, 'After she has done all these things, she will return to Me'; but she did not return, and her treacherous sister Judah saw it.

8"And I saw that for all the adulteries of faithless Israel, I had sent her away and given her a writ of divorce, yet her treacherous sister Judah did not fear; but she went and was a harlot also.

9"And it came about because of the lightness of her harlotry, that she polluted the land and committed adultery with stones and trees.

10"And yet in spite of all this her treacherous sister Judah did not return to Me with all her heart, but rather in deception," declares the LORD.

11 ¶ And the LORD said to me, "Faithless Israel has proved herself more righteous than treacherous Judah.

12"Go, and proclaim these words toward the north and say,
'Return, faithless Israel,' declares
the LORD;
'I will not look upon you in anger.
For I am gracious,' declares the
LORD;
'I will not be angry forever.
13 'Only acknowledge your iniquity,
That you have transgressed
against the LORD your God
And have scattered your favors to
the strangers under every green
tree,
And you have not obeyed My
voice,' declares the LORD.
14 'Return, O faithless sons,' declares
the LORD;

'For I am a master to you,
And I will take you one from a
city and two from a family,
And I will bring you to Zion.'
15"Then I will give you shepherds after My own heart, who will feed you on knowledge and understanding.

16"And it shall be in those days when you are multiplied and increased in the land," declares the LORD, "they shall say no more, 'The ark of the covenant of the LORD.' And it shall not come to mind, nor shall they remember it, nor shall they miss *it*, nor shall it be made again.

17"At that time they shall call Jerusalem 'The Throne of the LORD,' and all the nations will be gathered to it, to Jerusalem, for the name of the LORD; nor shall they walk anymore after the stubbornness of their evil heart.

18"In those days the house of Judah will walk with the house of Israel, and they will come together from the land of the north to the land that I gave your fathers as an inheritance.

19 ¶"Then I said,
'How I would set you among My
sons,
And give you a pleasant land,
The most beautiful inheritance of
the nations!'
And I said, 'You shall call Me, My
Father,
And not turn away from following
Me.'
20"Surely, as a woman treacherously
departs from her lover,
So you have dealt treacherously
with Me,
O house of Israel," declares the
LORD.

21 ¶ A voice is heard on the bare
heights,
The weeping *and* the supplications of the sons of Israel;
Because they have perverted their
way,
They have forgotten the LORD
their God.
22"Return, O faithless sons,
I will heal your faithlessness."
"Behold, we come to Thee;
For Thou art the LORD our God.
23"Surely, the hills are a deception,
A tumult *on* the mountains.
Surely, in the LORD our God
Is the salvation of Israel.

24"But the shameful thing has consumed the labor of our fathers since our youth, their flocks and their herds, their sons and their daughters.

25"Let us lie down in our shame, and let our humiliation cover us; for we have sinned against the LORD our God, we and our fathers, since our youth even to this day. And we have not obeyed the voice of the LORD our God."

CHAPTER 4

"IF you will return, O Israel," declares the LORD,
"Then you should return to Me.
And if you will put away your detested things from My presence,
And will not waver,
2 And you will swear, 'As the LORD lives,'
In truth, in justice, and in righteousness;
Then the nations will bless themselves in Him,
And in Him they will glory."

3 ¶ For thus says the LORD to the men of Judah and to Jerusalem,
"Break up your fallow ground,
And do not sow among thorns.
4"Circumcise yourselves to the LORD
And remove the foreskins of your heart,
Men of Judah and inhabitants of Jerusalem,
Lest My wrath go forth like fire
And burn with none to quench it,
Because of the evil of your deeds."

5 ¶ Declare in Judah and proclaim in Jerusalem, and say,
"Blow the trumpet in the land;
Cry aloud and say,
'Assemble yourselves, and let us go
Into the fortified cities.'
6"Lift up a standard toward Zion!
Seek refuge, do not stand *still*,
For I am bringing evil from the north,
And great destruction.
7"A lion has gone up from his thicket,
And a destroyer of nations has set out;

He has gone out from his place
To make your land a waste.
Your cities will be ruins
Without inhabitant.
8"For this, put on sackcloth,
Lament and wail;
For the fierce anger of the LORD
Has not turned back from us."

9"And it shall come about in that day," declares the LORD, "that the heart of the king and the heart of the princes will fail; and the priests will be appalled, and the prophets will be astounded."

10 ¶ Then I said, "Ah, Lord GOD! Surely Thou hast utterly deceived this people and Jerusalem, saying, 'You will have peace'; whereas a sword touches the throat."

11 ¶ In that time it will be said to this people and to Jerusalem, "A scorching wind from the bare heights in the wilderness in the direction of the daughter of My people—not to winnow, and not to cleanse,

12 a wind too strong for this—will come at My command; now I will also pronounce judgments against them.

13"Behold, he goes up like clouds,
And his chariots like the whirlwind;
His horses are swifter than eagles.
Woe to us, for we are ruined!"

14 ¶ Wash your heart from evil, O Jerusalem,
That you may be saved.
How long will your wicked thoughts
Lodge within you?
15 For a voice declares from Dan,
And proclaims wickedness from Mount Ephraim.
16"Report *it* to the nations, now!
Proclaim over Jerusalem,
'Besiegers come from a far country,
And lift their voices against the cities of Judah.
17 'Like watchmen of a field they are against her round about,
Because she has rebelled against Me,' declares the LORD.
18"Your ways and your deeds
Have brought these things to you.
This is your evil. How bitter!
How it has touched your heart!"

19 ¶ My soul, my soul! I am in an-
　　guish! Oh, my heart!
My heart is pounding in me;
I cannot be silent,
Because you have heard, O my
　　soul,
The sound of the trumpet,
The alarm of war.
20 Disaster on disaster is proclaimed,
For the whole land is devastated;
Suddenly my tents are devastated,
My curtains in an instant.
21 How long must I see the standard,
And hear the sound of the trum-
　　pet?
22"For My people are foolish,
They know Me not;
They are stupid children,
And they have no understanding.
They are shrewd to do evil,
But to do good they do not
　　know."

23 ¶ I looked on the earth, and be-
　　hold, *it was* formless and void;
And to the heavens, and they had
　　no light.
24 I looked on the mountains, and
　　behold, they were quaking,
And all the hills moved to and fro.
25 I looked, and behold, there was no
　　man,
And all the birds of the heavens
　　had fled.
26 I looked, and behold, the fruitful
　　land was a wilderness,
And all its cities were pulled down
Before the LORD, before His fierce
　　anger.

27 ¶ For thus says the LORD,
"The whole land shall be a desola-
　　tion,
Yet I will not execute a complete
　　destruction.
28"For this the earth shall mourn,
And the heavens above be dark,
Because I have spoken, I have
　　purposed,
And I will not change My mind,
　　nor will I turn from it."
29 At the sound of the horseman and
　　bowman every city flees;
They go into the thickets and
　　climb among the rocks;
Every city is forsaken,
And no man dwells in them.
30 And you, O desolate one, what
　　will you do?

Although you dress in scarlet,
Although you decorate *yourself
　　with* ornaments of gold,
Although you enlarge your eyes
　　with paint,
In vain you make yourself beauti-
　　ful;
Your lovers despise you;
They seek your life.
31 For I heard a cry as of a woman in
　　labor,
The anguish as of one giving birth
　　to her first child,
The cry of the daughter of Zion
　　gasping for breath,
Stretching out her hands, *saying,*
"Ah, woe is me, for I faint before
　　murderers."

CHAPTER 5

"ROAM to and fro through the
　　streets of Jerusalem,
And look now, and take note.
And seek in her open squares,
If you can find a man,
If there is one who does justice,
　　who seeks truth,
Then I will pardon her.
2"And although they say, 'As the
　　LORD lives,'
Surely they swear falsely."
3 O LORD, do not Thine eyes look
　　for truth?
Thou hast smitten them,
But they did not weaken;
Thou hast consumed them,
But they refused to take correc-
　　tion.
They have made their faces
　　harder than rock;
They have refused to repent.

4 ¶ Then I said, "They are only the
　　poor,
They are foolish;
For they do not know the way of
　　the LORD
Or the ordinance of their God.
5"I will go to the great
And will speak to them,
For they know the way of the
　　LORD,
And the ordinance of their God."
But they too, with one accord,
　　have broken the yoke
And burst the bonds.
6 Therefore a lion from the forest
　　shall slay them,

A wolf of the deserts shall destroy
them,
A leopard is watching their cities.
Everyone who goes out of them
shall be torn in pieces,
Because their transgressions are
many,
Their apostasies are numerous.

7 ¶"Why should I pardon you?
Your sons have forsaken Me
And sworn by those who are not
gods.
When I had fed them to the full,
They committed adultery
And trooped to the harlot's house.
8"They were well-fed lusty horses,
Each one neighing after his neigh-
bor's wife.
9"Shall I not punish these *people*,"
declares the LORD,
"And on a nation such as this
Shall I not avenge Myself?

10 ¶"Go up through her vine rows
and destroy,
But do not execute a complete
destruction;
Strip away her branches,
For they are not the LORD'S.
11"For the house of Israel and the
house of Judah
Have dealt very treacherously
with Me," declares the LORD.
12 They have lied about the LORD
And said, "¹Not He;
Misfortune will not come on us;
And we will not see sword or
famine.
13"And the prophets are *as* wind,
And the word is not in them.
Thus it will be done to them!"

14 ¶ Therefore, thus says the LORD,
the God of hosts,
"Because you have spoken this
word,
Behold, I am making My words in
your mouth fire
And this people wood, and it will
consume them.
15"Behold, I am bringing a nation
against you from afar, O house
of Israel," declares the LORD.
"It is an enduring nation,
It is an ancient nation,

A nation whose language you do
not know,
Nor can you understand what
they say.
16"Their quiver is like an open grave,
All of them are mighty men.
17"And they will devour your harvest
and your food;
They will devour your sons and
your daughters;
They will devour your flocks and
your herds;
They will devour your vines and
your fig trees;
They will demolish with the sword
your fortified cities in which
you trust.
18 ¶"Yet even in those days," declares the LORD, "I will not make you a
complete destruction.
19"And it shall come about when
they say, 'Why has the LORD our God
done all these things to us?' then you
shall say to them, 'As you have forsaken Me and served foreign gods in
your land, so you shall serve strangers
in a land that is not yours.'
20 ¶"Declare this in the house of
Jacob
And proclaim it in Judah, saying,
21 'Hear this, O foolish and senseless
people,
Who have eyes, but see not;
Who have ears, but hear not.
22 'Do you not fear Me?' declares the
LORD.
'Do you not tremble in My presence?
For I have placed the sand as a
boundary for the sea,
An eternal decree, so it cannot
cross over it.
Though the waves toss, yet they
cannot prevail;
Though they roar, yet they cannot cross over it.
23 'But this people has a stubborn
and rebellious heart;
They have turned aside and departed.
24 'They do not say in their heart,
"Let us now fear the LORD our God,
Who gives rain in its season,
Both the autumn rain and the
spring rain,
Who keeps for us
The appointed weeks of the harvest."

¹ Lit., *He is not*

25 'Your iniquities have turned these
away,
And your sins have withheld good
from you.
26 'For wicked men are found among
My people,
They watch like fowlers lying in
wait;
They set a trap,
They catch men.
27 'Like a cage full of birds,
So their houses are full of deceit;
Therefore they have become great
and rich.
28 'They are fat, they are sleek,
They also ²excel in deeds of wick-
edness;
They do not plead the cause,
The cause of the orphan, that
they may prosper;
And they do not defend the rights
of the poor.
29 'Shall I not punish these *people?*'
declares the LORD,
'On a nation such as this
Shall I not avenge Myself?'

30 ¶"An appalling and horrible thing
Has happened in the land:
31 The prophets prophesy falsely,
And the priests rule on their *own*
authority;
And My people love it so!
But what will you do at the end of
it?

CHAPTER 6

"FLEE for safety, O sons of Benjamin,
From the midst of Jerusalem!
Now blow a trumpet in Tekoa,
And raise a signal over ³Beth-
haccerem;
For evil looks down from the
north,
And a great destruction.
2"The comely and dainty one, the
daughter of Zion, I will cut off.
3"Shepherds and their flocks will
come to her,
They will pitch *their* tents around
her,
They will pasture each in his
place.
4"Prepare war against her;
Arise, and let us attack at noon.
Woe to us, for the day declines,

For the shadows of the evening
lengthen!
5"Arise, and let us attack by night
And destroy her palaces!"
6 For thus says the LORD of hosts,
"Cut down her trees,
And cast up a siege against Jeru-
salem.
This is the city to be punished,
In whose midst there is only op-
pression.
7"As a well keeps its waters fresh,
So she keeps fresh her wicked-
ness.
Violence and destruction are
heard in her;
Sickness and wounds are ever
before Me.
8"Be warned, O Jerusalem,
Lest I be alienated from you;
Lest I make you a desolation,
A land not inhabited."

9 ¶ Thus says the LORD of hosts,
"They will thoroughly glean as the
vine the remnant of Israel;
Pass your hand again like a grape
gatherer
Over the branches."
10 To whom shall I speak and give
warning,
That they may hear?
Behold, their ears are closed,
And they cannot listen.
Behold, the word of the LORD has
become a reproach to them;
They have no delight in it.
11 But I am full of the wrath of the
LORD:
I am weary with holding *it* in.
"Pour *it* out on the children in the
street,
And on the gathering of young
men together;
For both husband and wife shall
be taken,
The aged and the very old.
12"And their houses shall be turned
over to others,
Their fields and their wives to-
gether;
For I will stretch out My hand
Against the inhabitants of the
land," declares the LORD.
13"For from the least of them even to
the greatest of them,
Everyone is greedy for gain,

---

² Or, *overlook deeds*   ³ I.e., *house of the vineyard*

And from the prophet even to the priest
Everyone deals falsely.
14"And they have healed the brokenness of My people superficially,
Saying, 'Peace, peace,'
But there is no peace.
15"Were they ashamed because of the abomination they have done?
They were not even ashamed at all;
They did not even know how to blush.
Therefore they shall fall among those who fall;
At the time that I punish them,
They shall be cast down," says the LORD.

16 ¶ Thus says the LORD,
"Stand by the ways and see and ask for the ancient paths,
Where the good way is, and walk in it;
And you shall find rest for your souls.
But they said, 'We will not walk in it.'
17"And I set watchmen over you, saying,
'Listen to the sound of the trumpet!'
But they said, 'We will not listen.'
18"Therefore hear, O nations,
And know, O congregation, what is among them.
19"Hear, O earth: behold, I am bringing disaster on this people,
The fruit of their plans,
Because they have not listened to My words,
And as for My law, they have rejected it also.
20"For what purpose does frankincense come to Me from Sheba,
And the sweet cane from a distant land?
Your burnt offerings are not acceptable,
And your sacrifices are not pleasing to Me."
21 Therefore, thus says the LORD,
"Behold, I am laying stumbling blocks before this people.
And they will stumble against them,
Fathers and sons together;
Neighbor and friend will perish."

22 ¶ Thus says the LORD,
"Behold, a people is coming from the north land,
And a great nation will be aroused from the remote parts of the earth.
23"They seize bow and spear;
They are cruel and have no mercy;
Their voice roars like the sea,
And they ride on horses,
Arrayed as a man for the battle
Against you, O daughter of Zion!"
24 We have heard the report of it;
Our hands are limp.
Anguish has seized us,
Pain as of a woman in childbirth.
25 Do not go out into the field,
And do not walk on the road,
For the enemy has a sword,
Terror is on every side.
26 O daughter of my people, put on sackcloth
And roll in ashes;
Mourn as for an only son,
A lamentation most bitter.
For suddenly the destroyer
Will come upon us.

27 ¶"I have made you an assayer and a tester among My people,
That you may know and assay their way."
28 All of them are stubbornly rebellious,
Going about as a talebearer.
They are bronze and iron;
They, all of them, are corrupt.
29 The bellows blow fiercely,
The lead is consumed by the fire;
In vain the refining goes on,
But the wicked are not separated.
30 They call them rejected silver,
Because the LORD has rejected them.

CHAPTER 7

THE word that came to Jeremiah from the LORD, saying,
2"Stand in the gate of the LORD's house and proclaim there this word, and say, 'Hear the word of the LORD, all you of Judah, who enter by these gates to worship the LORD!'"
3 Thus says the LORD of hosts, the God of Israel, "Amend your ways and your deeds, and I will let you dwell in this place.

4"Do not trust in deceptive words, saying, 'This is the temple of the LORD, the temple of the LORD, the temple of the LORD.'

5"For if you truly amend your ways and your deeds, if you truly practice justice between a man and his neighbor,

6 if you do not oppress the alien, the orphan, or the widow, and do not shed innocent blood in this place, nor walk after other gods to your own ruin,

7 then I will let you dwell in this place, in the land that I gave to your fathers forever and ever.

8 ¶"Behold, you are trusting in deceptive words to no avail.

9"Will you steal, murder, and commit adultery, and swear falsely, and offer sacrifices to Baal, and walk after other gods that you have not known,

10 then come and stand before Me in this house, which is called by My name, and say, 'We are delivered!'— that you may do all these abominations?

11"Has this house, which is called by My name, become a den of robbers in your sight? Behold, I, even I, have seen it," declares the LORD.

12 ¶"But go now to My place which was in Shiloh, where I made My name dwell at the first, and see what I did to it because of the wickedness of My people Israel.

13"And now, because you have done all these things," declares the LORD, "and I spoke to you, rising up early and speaking, but you did not hear, and I called you but you did not answer,

14 therefore, I will do to the house which is called by My name, in which you trust, and to the place which I gave you and your fathers, as I did to Shiloh.

15"And I will cast you out of My sight, as I have cast out all your brothers, all the offspring of Ephraim.

16 ¶"As for you, do not pray for this people, and do not lift up cry or prayer for them, and do not intercede with Me; for I do not hear you.

17"Do you not see what they are doing in the cities of Judah and in the streets of Jerusalem?

18"The children gather wood, and the fathers kindle the fire, and the women knead dough to make cakes for the queen of heaven; and they pour out libations to other gods in order to spite Me.

19"Do they spite Me?" declares the LORD. "Is it not themselves they spite, to their own shame?"

20 Therefore thus says the Lord GOD, "Behold, My anger and My wrath will be poured out on this place, on man and on beast and on the trees of the field and on the fruit of the ground; and it will burn and not be quenched."

21 ¶ Thus says the LORD of hosts, the God of Israel, "Add your burnt offerings to your sacrifices and eat flesh.

22"For I did not speak to your fathers, or command them in the day that I brought them out of the land of Egypt, concerning burnt offerings and sacrifices.

23"But this is what I commanded them, saying, 'Obey My voice, and I will be your God, and you will be My people; and you will walk in all the way which I command you, that it may be well with you.'

24"Yet they did not obey or incline their ear, but walked in their own counsels and in the stubbornness of their evil heart, and went backward and not forward.

25"Since the day that your fathers came out of the land of Egypt until this day, I have sent you all My servants the prophets, daily rising early and sending them.

26"Yet they did not listen to Me or incline their ear, but stiffened their neck; they did evil more than their fathers.

27 ¶"And you shall speak all these words to them, but they will not listen to you; and you shall call to them, but they will not answer you.

28"And you shall say to them, 'This is the nation that did not obey the voice of the LORD their God or accept correction; truth has perished and has been cut off from their mouth.

29 'Cut off your hair and cast it away,
   And take up a lamentation on the
      bare heights;
   For the LORD has rejected and
      forsaken
   The generation of His wrath.'

30"For the sons of Judah have done that which is evil in My sight," declares the LORD, "they have set their detestable things in the house which is called by My name, to defile it.

31"And they have built the high places of Topheth, which is in the valley of the son of Hinnom, to burn their sons and their daughters in the fire, which I did not command, and it did not come into My mind.

32"Therefore, behold, days are coming," declares the LORD, "when it will no more be called Topheth, or the valley of the son of Hinnom, but the valley of the Slaughter; for they will bury in Topheth because there is no *other* place.

33"And the dead bodies of this people will be food for the birds of the sky, and for the beasts of the earth; and no one will frighten *them away*.

34"Then I will make to cease from the cities of Judah and from the streets of Jerusalem the voice of joy and the voice of gladness, the voice of the bridegroom and the voice of the bride; for the land will become a ruin.

CHAPTER 8

"AT that time," declares the LORD, "they will bring out the bones of the kings of Judah, and the bones of its princes, and the bones of the priests, and the bones of the prophets, and the bones of the inhabitants of Jerusalem from their graves.

2"And they will spread them out to the sun, the moon, and to all the host of heaven, which they have loved, and which they have served, and which they have gone after, and which they have sought, and which they have worshiped. They will not be gathered or buried; they will be as dung on the face of the ground.

3"And death will be chosen rather than life by all the remnant that remains of this evil family, that remains in all the places to which I have driven them," declares the LORD of hosts.

4"And you shall say to them, 'Thus says the LORD,

"Do *men* fall and not get up again?
Does one turn away and not repent?
5"Why then has this people, Jerusalem,
Turned away in continual apostasy?
They hold fast to deceit,

They refuse to return.
6"I have listened and heard,
They have spoken what is not right;
No man repented of his wickedness,
Saying, 'What have I done?'
Everyone turned to his course,
Like a horse charging into the battle.
7"Even the stork in the sky
Knows her seasons;
And the turtledove and the swift and the thrush
Observe the time of their migration;
But My people do not know
The ordinance of the LORD.

8 ¶"How can you say, 'We are wise,
And the law of the LORD is with us'?
But behold, the lying pen of the scribes
Has made *it* into a lie.
9"The wise men are put to shame,
They are dismayed and caught;
Behold, they have rejected the word of the LORD,
And what kind of wisdom do they have?
10"Therefore I will give their wives to others,
Their fields to new owners;
Because from the least even to the greatest
Everyone is greedy for gain;
From the prophet even to the priest
Everyone practices deceit.
11"And they heal the brokenness of the daughter of My people superficially,
Saying, 'Peace, peace,'
But there is no peace.
12"Were they ashamed because of the abomination they had done?
They certainly were not ashamed,
And they did not know how to blush;
Therefore they shall fall among those who fall;
At the time of their punishment they shall be brought down,"
Declares the LORD.

13 ¶"I will surely snatch them away," declares the LORD;

"There will be no grapes on the
   vine,
And no figs on the fig tree,
And the leaf shall wither;
And what I have given them shall
   pass away." ' "
14 Why are we sitting still?
Assemble yourselves, and let us
   go into the fortified cities,
And let us perish there,
Because the LORD our God has
   doomed us
And given us poisoned water to
   drink,
For we have sinned against the
   LORD.
15 *We* waited for peace, but no good
   came;
For a time of healing, but behold,
   terror!
16 From Dan is heard the snorting of
   his horses;
At the sound of the neighing of
   his stallions
The whole land quakes;
For they come and devour the
   land and its fulness,
The city and its inhabitants.
17"For behold, I am sending serpents
   against you,
Adders, for which there is no
   charm,
And they will bite you," declares
   the LORD.

18 ¶ My sorrow is beyond healing,
My heart is faint *within me!*
19 Behold, listen! The cry of the
   daughter of my people from a
   distant land:
"Is the LORD not in Zion? Is her
   King not within her?"
"Why have they provoked Me with
   their graven images, with foreign idols?"
20"Harvest is past, summer is ended,
And we are not saved."
21 For the brokenness of the daughter of my people I am broken;
I mourn, dismay has taken hold of
   me.
22 Is there no balm in Gilead?
Is there no physician there?
Why then has not the health of
   the daughter of my people been
   restored?

CHAPTER 9

OH, that my head were waters,
   And my eyes a fountain of tears,
   That I might weep day and night
   For the slain of the daughter of
      my people!
2 O that I had in the desert
   A wayfarers' lodging place;
   That I might leave my people,
   And go from them!
   For all of them are adulterers,
   An assembly of treacherous men.
3"And they bend their tongue *like*
      their bow;
   Lies and not truth prevail in the
      land;
   For they proceed from evil to evil,
   And they do not know Me," de-
      clares the LORD.
4"Let everyone be on guard against
      his neighbor,
   And do not trust any brother;
   Because every brother deals craft-
      ily,
   And every neighbor goes about as
      a slanderer.
5"And everyone deceives his neigh-
      bor,
   And does not speak the truth,
   They have taught their tongue to
      speak lies;
   They weary themselves commit-
      ting iniquity.
6"Your dwelling is in the midst of
      deceit;
   Through deceit they refuse to
      know Me," declares the LORD.

7 ¶ Therefore thus says the LORD of
      hosts,
   "Behold, I will refine them and
      assay them;
   For what *else* can I do, because of
      the daughter of My people?
8"Their tongue is a deadly arrow;
   It speaks deceit;
   With his mouth one speaks peace
      to his neighbor,
   But inwardly he sets an ambush
      for him.
9"Shall I not punish them for these
      things?" declares the LORD.
   "On a nation such as this
   Shall I not avenge Myself?

10 ¶"For the mountains I will take
      up a weeping and wailing,
   And for the pastures of the wilder-
      ness a dirge,

Because they are laid waste, so
  that no one passes through,
And the lowing of the cattle is not
  heard;
Both the birds of the sky and the
  beasts have fled; they are gone.
11"And I will make Jerusalem a heap
  of ruins,
  A haunt of jackals;
  And I will make the cities of Judah a desolation, without inhabitant."
12 ¶ Who is the wise man that may
understand this? And *who is* he to
whom the mouth of the LORD has
spoken, that he may declare it? Why is
the land ruined, laid waste like a desert, so that no one passes through?
13 And the LORD said, "Because they
have forsaken My law which I set
before them, and have not obeyed My
voice nor walked according to it,
14 but have walked after the stubbornness of their heart and after the
Baals, as their fathers taught them,"
15 therefore thus says the LORD of
hosts, the God of Israel, "behold, I will
feed them, this people, with wormwood and give them poisoned water to
drink.
16"And I will scatter them among the
nations, whom neither they nor their
fathers have known; and I will send
the sword after them until I have
annihilated them."
17 ¶ Thus says the LORD of hosts,
  "Consider and call for the mourning women, that they may
  come;
  And send for the wailing women,
  that they may come!
18"And let them make haste, and
  take up a wailing for us,
  That our eyes may shed tears,
  And our eyelids flow with water.
19"For a voice of wailing is heard
  from Zion,
  'How are we ruined!
  We are put to great shame,
  For we have left the land,
  Because they have cast down our
  dwellings.' "
20 Now hear the word of the LORD, O
  you women,
  And let your ear receive the word
  of His mouth;
  Teach your daughters wailing,
  And everyone her neighbor a
  dirge.

21 For death has come up through
  our windows;
  It has entered our palaces
  To cut off the children from the
  streets,
  The young men from the town
  squares.
22 Speak, "Thus declares the LORD,
  'The corpses of men will fall like
  dung on the open field,
  And like the sheaf after the
  reaper,
  But no one will gather *them.*' "
23 ¶ Thus says the LORD, "Let not a
wise man boast of his wisdom, and let
not the mighty man boast of his
might, let not a rich man boast of his
riches;
24 but let him who boasts boast of
this, that he understands and knows
Me, that I am the LORD who exercises
lovingkindness, justice, and righteousness on earth; for I delight in these
things," declares the LORD.
25 ¶"Behold, the days are coming,"
declares the LORD, "that I will punish
all who are circumcised and yet uncircumcised—
26 Egypt, and Judah, and Edom, and
the sons of Ammon, and Moab, and all
those inhabiting the desert who clip
the hair on their temples; for all the
nations are uncircumcised, and all the
house of Israel are uncircumcised of
heart."

CHAPTER 10

HEAR the word which the LORD
speaks to you, O house of Israel.
2 Thus says the LORD,
  "Do not learn the way of the nations,
  And do not be terrified by the
  signs of the heavens
  Although the nations are terrified
  by them;
3 For the customs of the peoples are
  delusion;
  Because it is wood cut from the
  forest,
  The work of the hands of a craftsman with a cutting tool.
4"They decorate *it* with silver and
  with gold;
  They fasten it with nails and with
  hammers
  So that it will not totter.

5"Like a scarecrow in a cucumber
   field are they,
And they cannot speak;
They must be carried,
Because they cannot walk!
Do not fear them,
For they can do no harm,
Nor can they do any good."

6 ¶ There is none like Thee, O
   LORD;
Thou art great, and great is Thy
   name in might.
7 Who would not fear Thee, O King
   of the nations?
Indeed it is Thy due!
For among all the wise men of the
   nations,
And in all their kingdoms,
There is none like Thee.
8 But they are altogether stupid and
   foolish
In their discipline of delusion—
   their idol is wood!
9 Beaten silver is brought from Tarshish,
And gold from Uphaz,
The work of a craftsman and of
   the hands of a goldsmith;
Violet and purple are their clothing;
They are all the work of skilled
   men.
10 But the LORD is the true God;
He is the living God and the everlasting King.
At His wrath the earth quakes,
And the nations cannot endure
   His indignation.
11 ¶ Thus you shall say to them,
"The gods that did not make the heavens and the earth shall perish from the
earth and from under the heavens."
12 ¶ *It is* He who made the earth by
   His power,
Who established the world by His
   wisdom;
And by His understanding He has
   stretched out the heavens.
13 When He utters His voice, *there is*
   a tumult of waters in the heavens,
And He causes the clouds to ascend from the end of the earth;
He makes lightning for the rain,
And brings out the wind from His
   storehouses.
14 Every man is stupid, devoid of
   knowledge;

Every goldsmith is put to shame
   by his idols;
For his molten images are deceitful,
And there is no breath in them.
15 They are worthless, a work of
   mockery;
In the time of their punishment
   they will perish.
16 The portion of Jacob is not like
   these;
For the Maker of all is He,
And Israel is the tribe of His inheritance;
The LORD of hosts is His name.

17 ¶ Pick up your bundle from the
   ground,
You who dwell under siege!
18 For thus says the LORD,
"Behold, I am slinging out the in-
   habitants of the land
At this time,
And will cause them distress,
That they may be found."

19 ¶ Woe is me, because of my injury!
My wound is incurable.
But I said, "Truly this is a sick-
   ness,
And I must bear it."
20 My tent is destroyed,
And all my ropes are broken;
My sons have gone from me and
   are no more.
There is no one to stretch out my
   tent again
Or to set up my curtains.
21 For the shepherds have become
   stupid
And have not sought the LORD;
Therefore they have not pros-
   pered,
And all their flock is scattered.
22 The sound of a report! Behold, it
   comes—
A great commotion out of the
   land of the north—
To make the cities of Judah
A desolation, a haunt of jackals.

23 ¶ I know, O LORD, that a man's
   way is not in himself;
Nor is it in a man who walks to
   direct his steps.
24 Correct me, O LORD, but with
   justice;

Not with Thine anger, lest Thou
bring me to nothing.

25 Pour out Thy wrath on the nations that do not know Thee,
And on the families that do not
call Thy name;
For they have devoured Jacob;
They have devoured him and consumed him,
And have laid waste his habitation.

CHAPTER 11

THE word which came to Jeremiah
from the LORD, saying,

2 "Hear the words of this covenant,
and speak to the men of Judah and to
the inhabitants of Jerusalem;

3 and say to them, 'Thus says the
LORD, the God of Israel, "Cursed is the
man who does not heed the words of
this covenant

4 which I commanded your forefathers in the day that I brought them
out of the land of Egypt, from the iron
furnace, saying, 'Listen to My voice,
and do according to all which I command you; so you shall be My people,
and I will be your God,'

5 in order to confirm the oath which
I swore to your forefathers, to give
them a land flowing with milk and
honey, as *it is* this day." ' " Then I
answered and said, "Amen, O LORD."

6 ¶ And the LORD said to me, "Proclaim all these words in the cities of
Judah and in the streets of Jerusalem,
saying, 'Hear the words of this covenant and do them.

7 'For I solemnly warned your fathers in the day that I brought them
up from the land of Egypt, even to this
day, warning persistently, saying, "Listen to My voice."

8 'Yet they did not obey or incline
their ear, but walked, each one, in the
stubbornness of his evil heart; therefore I brought on them all the words
of this covenant, which I commanded
them to do, but they did not.' "

9 ¶ Then the LORD said to me, "A
conspiracy has been found among the
men of Judah and among the inhabitants of Jerusalem.

10 "They have turned back to the
iniquities of their ancestors who refused to hear My words, and they have
gone after other gods to serve them;
the house of Israel and the house of
Judah have broken My covenant
which I made with their fathers."

11 Therefore thus says the LORD,
"Behold I am bringing disaster on
them which they will not be able to
escape; though they will cry to Me, yet
I will not listen to them.

12 "Then the cities of Judah and the
inhabitants of Jerusalem will go and
cry to the gods to whom they burn
incense, but they surely will not save
them in the time of their disaster.

13 "For your gods are as many as your
cities, O Judah; and as many as the
streets of Jerusalem are the altars you
have set up to the shameful thing,
altars to burn incense to Baal.

14 ¶ "Therefore do not pray for this
people, nor lift up a cry or prayer for
them; for I will not listen when they
call to Me because of their disaster.

15 "What right has My beloved in My
house
When she has done many vile
deeds?
Can the sacrificial flesh take away
from you your disaster,
So *that* you can rejoice?"

16 The LORD called your name,
"A green olive tree, beautiful in
fruit and form";
With the noise of a great tumult
He has kindled fire on it,
And its branches are worthless.

17 And the LORD of hosts, who
planted you, has pronounced evil
against you because of the evil of the
house of Israel and of the house of
Judah, which they have done to provoke Me by offering up sacrifices to
Baal.

18 ¶ Moreover, the LORD made it
known to me and I knew it;
Then Thou didst show me their
deeds.

19 But I was like a gentle lamb led to
the slaughter;
And I did not know that they had
devised plots against me, *saying,*
"Let us destroy the tree with its
fruit,
And let us cut him off from the
land of the living,
That his name be remembered no
more."

20 But, O Lord of hosts, who judges
righteously,
Who tries the feelings and the
heart,
Let me see Thy vengeance on
them,
For to Thee have I committed my
cause.
21 ¶ Therefore thus says the Lord
concerning the men of Anathoth, who
seek your life, saying, "Do not prophesy in the name of the Lord, that you
might not die at our hand";
22 therefore, thus says the Lord of
hosts, "Behold, I am about to punish
them! The young men will die by the
sword, their sons and daughters will
die by famine;
23 and a remnant will not be left to
them, for I will bring disaster on the
men of Anathoth—the year of their
punishment."

CHAPTER 12

RIGHTEOUS art Thou, O Lord, that
I would plead *my* case with
Thee;
Indeed I would discuss matters of
justice with Thee:
Why has the way of the wicked
prospered?
Why are all those who deal in
treachery at ease?
2 Thou hast planted them, they
have also taken root;
They grow, they have even pro-
duced fruit.
Thou art near to their lips
But far from their mind.
3 But Thou knowest me, O Lord;
Thou seest me;
And Thou dost examine my
heart's *attitude* toward Thee.
Drag them off like sheep for the
slaughter
And set them apart for a day of
carnage!
4 How long is the land to mourn
And the vegetation of the countryside to wither?
For the wickedness of those who
dwell in it,
Animals and birds have been
snatched away,
Because *men* have said, "He will
not see our latter ending."

5 ¶"If you have run with footmen
and they have tired you out,

Then how can you compete with
horses?
If you fall down in a land of peace,
How will you do in the thicket of
the Jordan?
6"For even your brothers and the
household of your father,
Even they have dealt treacherously with you,
Even they have cried aloud after
you.
Do not believe them, although
they may say nice things to
you."

7 ¶"I have forsaken My house,
I have abandoned My inheritance;
I have given the beloved of My
soul
Into the hand of her enemies.
8"My inheritance has become to Me
Like a lion in the forest;
She has roared against Me;
Therefore I have come to hate
her.
9"Is My inheritance like a speckled
bird of prey to Me?
Are the birds of prey against her
on every side?
Go, gather all the beasts of the
field,
Bring them to devour!
10"Many shepherds have ruined My
vineyard,
They have trampled down My
field;
They have made My pleasant field
A desolate wilderness.
11"It has been made a desolation,
Desolate, it mourns before Me;
The whole land has been made
desolate,
Because no man lays it to heart.
12"On all the bare heights in the
wilderness
Destroyers have come,
For a sword of the Lord is de-
vouring
From one end of the land even to
the other;
There is no peace for anyone.
13"They have sown wheat and have
reaped thorns,
They have strained themselves to
no profit.
But be ashamed of your harvest
Because of the fierce anger of the
Lord."

14 ¶ Thus says the LORD concerning all My wicked neighbors who strike at the inheritance with which I have endowed My people Israel, "Behold I am about to uproot them from their land and will uproot the house of Judah from among them.

15"And it will come about that after I have uprooted them, I will again have compassion on them; and I will bring them back, each one to his inheritance and each one to his land.

16"Then it will come about that if they will really learn the ways of My people, to swear by My name, 'As the LORD lives,' even as they taught My people to swear by Baal, then they will be built up in the midst of My people.

17"But if they will not listen, then I will uproot that nation, uproot and destroy it," declares the LORD.

CHAPTER 13

THUS the LORD said to me, "Go and buy yourself a linen waistband, and put it around your waist, but do not put it in water."

2 So I bought the waistband in accordance with the word of the LORD and put it around my waist.

3 Then the word of the LORD came to me a second time, saying,

4"Take the waistband that you have bought, which is around your waist, and arise, go to the Euphrates and hide it there in a crevice of the rock."

5 So I went and hid it by the Euphrates, as the LORD had commanded me.

6 And it came about after many days that the LORD said to me, "Arise, go to the Euphrates and take from there the waistband which I commanded you to hide there."

7 Then I went to the Euphrates and dug, and I took the waistband from the place where I had hidden it; and lo, the waistband was ruined, it was totally worthless.

8 ¶ Then the word of the LORD came to me, saying,

9"Thus says the LORD, 'Just so will I destroy the pride of Judah and the great pride of Jerusalem.

10 'This wicked people, who refuse to listen to My words, who walk in the stubbornness of their hearts and have gone after other gods to serve them

and to bow down to them, let them be just like this waistband, which is totally worthless.

11 'For as the waistband clings to the waist of a man, so I made the whole household of Israel and the whole household of Judah cling to Me,' declares the LORD, 'that they might be for Me a people, for renown, for praise, and for glory; but they did not listen.'

12 ¶"Therefore you are to speak this word to them, 'Thus says the LORD, the God of Israel, "Every jug is to be filled with wine." ' And when they say to you, 'Do we not very well know that every jug is to be filled with wine?'

13 then say to them, 'Thus says the LORD, "Behold I am about to fill all the inhabitants of this land—the kings that sit for David on his throne, the priests, the prophets and all the inhabitants of Jerusalem—with drunkenness!

14"And I will dash them against each other, both the fathers and the sons together," declares the LORD. "I will not show pity nor be sorry nor have compassion that I should not destroy them." ' "

15 ¶ Listen and give heed, do not be haughty,
　For the LORD has spoken.
16 Give glory to the LORD your God,
　Before He brings darkness
　And before your feet stumble
　On the dusky mountains,
　And while you are hoping for light
　He makes it into deep darkness,
　And turns it into gloom.
17 But if you will not listen to it,
　My soul will sob in secret for such pride;
　And my eyes will bitterly weep
　And flow down with tears,
　Because the flock of the LORD has been taken captive.
18 Say to the king and the queen mother,
　"Take a lowly seat,
　For your beautiful crown
　Has come down from your head."
19 The cities of the Negev have been locked up,
　And there is no one to open them;
　All Judah has been carried into exile,
　Wholly carried into exile.

20 ¶"Lift up your eyes and see
Those coming from the north.
Where is the flock that was given
you,
Your beautiful sheep?
21"What will you say when He ap-
points over you—
And you yourself had taught
them—
Former companions to be head
over you?
Will not pangs take hold of you,
Like a woman in childbirth?
22"And if you say in your heart,
'Why have these things happened
to me?'
Because of the magnitude of your
iniquity
Your skirts have been removed,
And your heels have been ex-
posed.
23"Can the Ethiopian change his skin
Or the leopard his spots?
Then you also can do good
Who are accustomed to do evil.
24"Therefore I will scatter them like
drifting straw
To the desert wind.
25"This is your lot, the portion mea-
sured to you
From Me," declares the LORD,
"Because you have forgotten Me
And trusted in falsehood.
26"So I Myself have also stripped
your skirts off over your face,
That your shame may be seen.
27"As for your adulteries and your
lustful neighings,
The lewdness of your prostitution
On the hills in the field,
I have seen your abominations.
Woe to you, O Jerusalem!
How long will you remain un-
clean?"

CHAPTER 14

THAT which came as the word of the
LORD to Jeremiah in regard to the
drought:
2"Judah mourns,
And her gates languish
They sit on the ground in mourning,
And the cry of Jerusalem has ascended.
3"And their nobles have sent their
servants for water;

They have come to the cisterns
and found no water.
They have returned with their
vessels empty;
They have been put to shame and
humiliated,
And they cover their heads.
4"Because the ground is cracked,
For there has been no rain on the
land;
The farmers have been put to
shame,
They have covered their heads.
5"For even the doe in the field has
given birth only to abandon *her
young,*
Because there is no grass.
6"And the wild donkeys stand on
the bare heights;
They pant for air like jackals,
Their eyes fail
For there is no vegetation.
7"Although our iniquities testify
against us,
O LORD, act for Thy name's sake!
Truly our apostasies have been
many,
We have sinned against Thee.
8"Thou Hope of Israel,
Its Savior in time of distress,
Why art Thou like a stranger in
the land
Or like a traveler who has pitched
his *tent* for the night?
9"Why art Thou like a man dis-
mayed,
Like a mighty man who cannot
save?
Yet Thou art in our midst, O
LORD,
And we are called by Thy name;
Do not forsake us!"

10 ¶ Thus says the LORD to this people, "Even so they have loved to wander; they have not kept their feet in
check. Therefore the LORD does not
accept them; now He will remember
their iniquity and call their sins to
account."
11 So the LORD said to me, "Do not
pray for the welfare of this people.
12"When they fast, I am not going to
listen to their cry; and when they offer
burnt offering and grain offering, I am
not going to accept them. Rather I am
going to make an end of them by the
sword, famine and pestilence."
13 ¶ But, "Ah, Lord GOD!" I said,
"Look, the prophets are telling them,

'You will not see the sword nor will you have famine, but I will give you lasting peace in this place.' "

14 Then the LORD said to me, "The prophets are prophesying falsehood in My name. I have neither sent them nor commanded them nor spoken to them; they are prophesying to you a false vision, divination, futility and the deception of their own minds.

15 "Therefore thus says the LORD concerning the prophets who are prophesying in My name, although it was not I who sent them—yet they keep saying, 'There shall be no sword or famine in this land'—by sword and famine those prophets shall meet their end!

16 "The people also to whom they are prophesying will be thrown out into the streets of Jerusalem because of the famine and the sword; and there will be no one to bury them—neither them, nor their wives, nor their sons, nor their daughters—for I shall pour out their own wickedness on them.

17 "And you will say this word to them,

'Let my eyes flow down with tears night and day,
And let them not cease;
For the virgin daughter of my people has been crushed with a mighty blow,
With a sorely infected wound.

18 'If I go out to the country,
Behold, those slain with the sword!
Or if I enter the city,
Behold, diseases of famine!
For both prophet and priest
Have gone roving about in the land that they do not know.' "

19 ¶ Hast Thou completely rejected Judah?
Or hast Thou loathed Zion?
Why hast Thou stricken us so that we are beyond healing?
We waited for peace, but nothing good came;
And for a time of healing, but behold, terror!

20 We know our wickedness, O LORD,
The iniquity of our fathers, for we have sinned against Thee.

21 Do not despise us, for Thine own name's sake;

Do not disgrace the throne of Thy glory;
Remember and do not annul Thy covenant with us.

22 Are there any among the idols of the nations who give rain?
Or can the heavens grant showers?
Is it not Thou, O LORD our God?
Therefore we hope in Thee,
For Thou art the one who hast done all these things.

CHAPTER 15

THEN the LORD said to me, "Even though Moses and Samuel were to stand before Me, My heart would not be with this people; send them away from My presence and let them go!

2 "And it shall be that when they say to you, 'Where should we go?' then you are to tell them, 'Thus says the LORD:

"Those destined for death, to death;
And those destined for the sword, to the sword;
And those destined for famine, to famine;
And those destined for captivity, to captivity." '

3 "And I shall appoint over them four kinds of doom," declares the LORD: "the sword to slay, the dogs to drag off, and the birds of the sky and the beasts of the earth to devour and destroy.

4 "And I shall make them an object of horror among all the kingdoms of the earth because of Manasseh, the son of Hezekiah, the king of Judah, for what he did in Jerusalem.

5 ¶ "Indeed, who will have pity on you, O Jerusalem,
Or who will mourn for you,
Or who will turn aside to ask about your welfare?

6 "You who have forsaken Me," declares the LORD,
"You keep going backward.
So I will stretch out My hand against you and destroy you;
I am tired of relenting!

7 "And I will winnow them with a winnowing fork
At the gates of the land;
I will bereave them of children, I will destroy My people;

They did not repent of their ways.
8"Their widows will be more numerous before Me
Than the sand of the seas;
I will bring against them, against the mother of a young man,
A destroyer at noonday;
I will suddenly bring down on her
Anguish and dismay.
9"She who bore seven *sons* pines away;
Her breathing is labored.
Her sun has set while it was yet day;
She has been shamed and humiliated.
So I shall give over their survivors to the sword
Before their enemies," declares the LORD.

10 ¶ Woe to me, my mother, that you have borne me
As a man of strife and a man of contention to all the land!
I have neither lent, nor have men lent money to me,
Yet everyone curses me.
11 The LORD said, "Surely I will set you free for *purposes of* good;
Surely I will cause the enemy to make supplication to you
In a time of disaster and a time of distress.

12 ¶"Can anyone smash iron,
Iron from the north, or bronze?
13"Your wealth and your treasures
I will give for booty without cost,
Even for all your sins
And within all your borders.
14"Then I will cause your enemies to bring *it*
Into a land you do not know;
For a fire has been kindled in My anger,
It will burn upon you."

15 ¶ Thou who knowest, O LORD,
Remember me, take notice of me,
And take vengeance for me on my persecutors.
Do *not*, in view of Thy patience, take me away;
Know that for Thy sake I endure reproach.
16 Thy words were found and I ate them,

And Thy words became for me a joy and the delight of my heart;
For I have been called by Thy name,
O LORD God of hosts.
17 I did not sit in the circle of merrymakers,
Nor did I exult.
Because of Thy hand *upon me* I sat alone,
For Thou didst fill me with indignation.
18 Why has my pain been perpetual
And my wound incurable, refusing to be healed?
Wilt Thou indeed be to me like a deceptive *stream*
With water that is unreliable?

19 ¶ Therefore, thus says the LORD,
"If you return, then I will restore you—
Before Me you will stand;
And if you extract the precious from the worthless,
You will become My spokesman.
They for their part may turn to you,
But as for you, you must not turn to them.
20"Then I will make you to this people
A fortified wall of bronze;
And though they fight against you,
They will not prevail over you;
For I am with you to save you
And deliver you," declares the LORD.
21"So I will deliver you from the hand of the wicked,
And I will redeem you from the grasp of the violent."

CHAPTER 16

THE word of the LORD also came to me saying,
2"You shall not take a wife for yourself nor have sons or daughters in this place."
3 For thus says the LORD concerning the sons and daughters born in this place, and concerning their mothers who bear them, and their fathers who beget them in this land:
4"They will die of deadly diseases, they will not be lamented or buried; they will be as dung on the surface of

the ground and come to an end by sword and famine, and their carcasses will become food for the birds of the sky and for the beasts of the earth."

5 ¶ For thus says the LORD, "Do not enter a house of mourning, or go to lament or to console them; for I have withdrawn My peace from this people," declares the LORD, "My lovingkindness and compassion.

6"Both great men and small will die in this land; they will not be buried, they will not be lamented, nor will anyone gash himself or shave his head for them.

7"Neither will men break *bread* in mourning for them, to comfort anyone for the dead, nor give them a cup of consolation to drink for anyone's father or mother.

8"Moreover you shall not go into a house of feasting to sit with them to eat and drink."

9 For thus says the LORD of hosts, the God of Israel: "Behold, I am going to eliminate from this place, before your eyes and in your time, the voice of rejoicing and the voice of gladness, the voice of the groom and the voice of the bride.

10 ¶"Now it will come about when you tell this people all these words that they will say to you, 'For what reason has the LORD declared all this great calamity against us? And what is our iniquity, or what is our sin which we have committed against the LORD our God?'

11"Then you are to say to them, '*It is* because your forefathers have forsaken Me,' declares the LORD, 'and have followed other gods and served them and bowed down to them; but Me they have forsaken and have not kept My law.

12 'You too have done evil, *even* more than your forefathers; for behold, you are each one walking according to the stubbornness of his own evil heart, without listening to Me.

13 'So I will hurl you out of this land into the land which you have not known, neither you nor your fathers; and there you will serve other gods day and night, for I shall grant you no favor.'

14 ¶"Therefore behold, days are coming," declares the LORD, "when it will

no longer be said, 'As the LORD lives, who brought up the sons of Israel out of the land of Egypt,'

15 but, 'As the LORD lives, who brought up the sons of Israel from the land of the north and from all the countries where He had banished them.' For I will restore them to their own land which I gave to their fathers.

16 ¶"Behold, I am going to send for many fishermen," declares the LORD, "and they will fish for them; and afterwards I shall send for many hunters, and they will hunt them from every mountain and every hill, and from the clefts of the rocks.

17"For My eyes are on all their ways; they are not hidden from My face, nor is their iniquity concealed from My eyes.

18"And I will first doubly repay their iniquity and their sin, because they have polluted My land; they have filled My inheritance with the carcasses of their detestable idols and with their abominations."

19 ¶ O LORD, my strength and my
    stronghold,
And my refuge in the day of distress,
To Thee the nations will come
From the ends of the earth and say,
"Our fathers have inherited nothing but falsehood,
Futility and things of no profit."
20 Can man make gods for himself?
Yet they are not gods!

21 ¶"Therefore behold, I am going to
    make them know—
This time I will make them know
My power and My might;
And they shall know that My name is the LORD."

CHAPTER 17

THE sin of Judah is written down
    with an iron stylus;
With a diamond point it is engraved upon the tablet of their heart,
And on the horns of their altars,
2 As they remember their children,
So they *remember* their altars and their Asherim
By green trees on the high hills.

3 O mountain of Mine in the coun-
   tryside,
   I will give over your wealth and
      all your treasures for booty,
   Your high places for sin through-
      out your borders.
4 And you will, even of yourself, let
      go of your inheritance
   That I gave you;
   And I will make you serve your
      enemies
   In the land which you do not
      know;
   For you have kindled a fire in My
      anger
   Which will burn forever.

5 ¶ Thus says the LORD,
   "Cursed is the man who trusts in
      mankind
   And makes flesh his strength,
   And whose heart turns away from
      the LORD.
6"For he will be like a bush in the
      desert
   And will not see when prosperity
      comes,
   But will live in stony wastes in the
      wilderness,
   A land of salt without inhabitant.
7"Blessed is the man who trusts in
      the LORD
   And whose trust is the LORD.
8"For he will be like a tree planted
      by the water,
   That extends its roots by a stream
   And will not fear when the heat
      comes;
   But its leaves will be green,
   And it will not be anxious in a
      year of drought
   Nor cease to yield fruit.

9 ¶"The heart is more deceitful than
      all else
   And is desperately sick;
   Who can understand it?
10"I, the LORD, search the heart,
   I test the mind,
   Even to give to each man accord-
      ing to his ways,
   According to the results of his
      deeds.
11"As a partridge that hatches eggs
      which it has not laid,
   So is he who makes a fortune, but
      unjustly;
   In the midst of his days it will
      forsake him,
   And in the end he will be a fool."

12 ¶ A glorious throne on high from
      the beginning
   Is the place of our sanctuary.
13 O LORD, the hope of Israel,
   All who forsake Thee will be put
      to shame.
   Those who turn away on earth
      will be written down,
   Because they have forsaken the
      fountain of living water, even
      the LORD.
14 Heal me, O LORD, and I will be
      healed;
   Save me and I will be saved,
   For Thou art my praise.
15 Look, they keep saying to me,
   "Where is the word of the LORD?
      Let it come now!"
16 But as for me, I have not hurried
      away from *being* a shepherd
      after Thee,
   Nor have I longed for the woeful
      day;
   Thou Thyself knowest the utter-
      ance of my lips
   Was in Thy presence.
17 Do not be a terror to me;
   Thou art my refuge in the day of
      disaster.
18 Let those who persecute me be
      put to shame, but as for me, let
      me not be put to shame;
   Let them be dismayed, but let me
      not be dismayed.
   Bring on them a day of disaster,
   And crush them with twofold de-
      struction!

19 ¶ Thus the LORD said to me, "Go
and stand in the public gate, through
which the kings of Judah come in and
go out, as well as in all the gates of
Jerusalem;
20 and say to them, 'Listen to the
word of the LORD, kings of Judah, and
all Judah, and all inhabitants of Jerusalem, who come in through these
gates:
21 'Thus says the LORD, "Take heed
for yourselves, and do not carry any
load on the sabbath day or bring anything in through the gates of Jerusalem.
22"And you shall not bring a load out
of your houses on the sabbath day nor
do any work, but keep the sabbath day
holy, as I commanded your forefathers.
23"Yet they did not listen or incline

their ears, but stiffened their necks in order not to listen or take correction.

24 ¶"But it will come about, if you listen attentively to Me," declares the LORD, "to bring no load in through the gates of this city on the sabbath day, but to keep the sabbath day holy by doing no work on it,

25 then there will come in through the gates of this city kings and princes sitting on the throne of David, riding in chariots and on horses, they and their princes, the men of Judah, and the inhabitants of Jerusalem; and this city will be inhabited forever.

26"They will come in from the cities of Judah and from the environs of Jerusalem, from the land of Benjamin, from the lowland, from the hill country, and from the Negev, bringing burnt offerings, sacrifices, grain offerings and incense, and bringing sacrifices of thanksgiving to the house of the LORD.

27"But if you do not listen to Me to keep the sabbath day holy by not carrying a load and coming in through the gates of Jerusalem on the sabbath day, then I shall kindle a fire in its gates, and it will devour the palaces of Jerusalem and not be quenched." ' "

CHAPTER 18

THE word which came to Jeremiah from the LORD saying,

2"Arise and go down to the potter's house, and there I shall announce My words to you."

3 Then I went down to the potter's house, and there he was, making something on the wheel.

4 But the vessel that he was making of clay was spoiled in the hand of the potter; so he remade it into another vessel, as it pleased the potter to make.

5 ¶ Then the word of the LORD came to me saying,

6"Can I not, O house of Israel, deal with you as this potter does?" declares the LORD. "Behold, like the clay in the potter's hand, so are you in My hand, O house of Israel.

7"At one moment I might speak concerning a nation or concerning a kingdom to uproot, to pull down, or to destroy it;

8 if that nation against which I

have spoken turns from its evil, I will [4]relent concerning the calamity I planned to bring on it.

9"Or at another moment I might speak concerning a nation or concerning a kingdom to build up or to plant it;

10 if it does evil in My sight by not obeying My voice, then I will [4]think better of the good with which I had promised to bless it.

11"So now then, speak to the men of Judah and against the inhabitants of Jerusalem saying, 'Thus says the LORD, "Behold, I am fashioning calamity against you and devising a plan against you. Oh turn back, each of you from his evil way, and reform your ways and your deeds." '

12"But they will say, 'It's hopeless! For we are going to follow our own plans, and each of us will act according to the stubbornness of his evil heart.'

13 ¶"Therefore thus says the LORD,
'Ask now among the nations,
Who ever heard the like of this?
The virgin of Israel
Has done a most appalling thing.

14 'Does the snow of Lebanon forsake the rock of the open country?
Or is the cold flowing water *from* a foreign *land* ever snatched away?

15 'For My people have forgotten Me,
They burn incense to worthless gods
And they have stumbled from their ways,
From the ancient paths,
To walk in bypaths,
Not on a highway,

16 To make their land a desolation,
An object of perpetual hissing;
Everyone who passes by it will be astonished
And shake his head.

17 'Like an east wind I will scatter them
Before the enemy;
I will show them My back and not *My* face
In the day of their calamity.' "

18 ¶ Then they said, "Come and let us devise plans against Jeremiah. Surely the law is not going to be lost

---

[4] Lit., *repent (of)*

to the priest, nor counsel to the sage, nor the *divine* word to the prophet! Come on and let us strike at him with *our* tongue, and let us give no heed to any of his words."

19 ¶ Do give heed to me, O LORD,
   And listen to what my opponents
     are saying!
20 Should good be repaid with evil?
   For they have dug a pit for me.
   Remember how I stood before
     Thee
   To speak good on their behalf,
   So as to turn away Thy wrath
     from them.
21 Therefore, give their children over
     to famine,
   And deliver them up to the power
     of the sword;
   And let their wives become child-
     less and widowed.
   Let their men also be smitten to
     death,
   Their young men struck down by
     the sword in battle.
22 May an outcry be heard from
     their houses,
   When Thou suddenly bringest
     raiders upon them;
   For they have dug a pit to capture
     me
   And hidden snares for my feet.
23 Yet Thou, O LORD, knowest
   All their deadly designs against
     me;
   Do not forgive their iniquity
   Or blot out their sin from Thy
     sight.
   But may they be overthrown be-
     fore Thee;
   Deal with them in the time of
     Thine anger!

CHAPTER 19

THUS says the LORD, "Go and buy a potter's earthenware jar, and *take* some of the elders of the people and some of the senior priests.

2"Then go out to the valley of Ben-hinnom, which is by the entrance of the potsherd gate; and proclaim there the words that I shall tell you,

3 and say, 'Hear the word of the LORD, O kings of Judah and inhabitants of Jerusalem: thus says the LORD of hosts, the God of Israel, "Behold I am about to bring a calamity upon this

place, at which the ears of everyone that hears of it will tingle.

4"Because they have forsaken Me and have made this an alien place and have burned sacrifices in it to other gods that neither they nor their forefathers nor the kings of Judah had *ever* known, and *because* they have filled this place with the blood of the innocent

5 and have built the high places of Baal to burn their sons in the fire as burnt offerings to Baal, a thing which I never commanded or spoke of, nor did it *ever* enter My mind;

6 therefore, behold, days are coming," declares the LORD, "when this place will no longer be called Topheth or the valley of Ben-hinnom, but rather the valley of Slaughter.

7"And I shall make void the counsel of Judah and Jerusalem in this place, and I shall cause them to fall by the sword before their enemies and by the hand of those who seek their life; and I shall give over their carcasses as food for the birds of the sky and the beasts of the earth.

8"I shall also make this city a desolation and an *object of* hissing; everyone who passes by it will be astonished and hiss because of all its disasters.

9"And I shall make them eat the flesh of their sons and the flesh of their daughters, and they will eat one another's flesh in the siege and in the distress with which their enemies and those who seek their life will distress them." '

10 ¶ "Then you are to break the jar in the sight of the men who accompany you

11 and say to them, 'Thus says the LORD of hosts, "Just so shall I break this people and this city, even as one breaks a potter's vessel, which cannot again be repaired; and they will bury in Topheth because there is no *other* place for burial.

12"This is how I shall treat this place and its inhabitants," declares the LORD, "so as to make this city like Topheth.

13"And the houses of Jerusalem and the houses of the kings of Judah will be defiled like the place Topheth, because of all the houses on whose rooftops they burned sacrifices to all the heavenly host and poured out libations to other gods." ' "

14 ¶ Then Jeremiah came from Topheth, where the LORD had sent him to prophesy; and he stood in the court of the LORD's house and said to all the people:

15 "Thus says the LORD of hosts, the God of Israel, 'Behold, I am about to bring on this city and all its towns the entire calamity that I have declared against it, because they have stiffened their necks so as not to heed My words.' "

CHAPTER 20

WHEN Pashhur the priest, the son of Immer, who was chief officer in the house of the LORD, heard Jeremiah prophesying these things,

2 Pashhur had Jeremiah the prophet beaten, and put him in the stocks that were at the upper Benjamin Gate, which was by the house of the LORD.

3 Then it came about on the next day, when Pashhur released Jeremiah from the stocks, that Jeremiah said to him, "Pashhur is not the name the LORD has called you, but rather ⁵Magor-missabib.

4 "For thus says the LORD, 'Behold, I am going to make you a terror to yourself and to all your friends; and while your eyes look on, they will fall by the sword of their enemies. So I shall give over all Judah to the hand of the king of Babylon, and he will carry them away as exiles to Babylon and will slay them with the sword.

5 'I shall also give over all the wealth of this city, all its produce, and all its costly things; even all the treasures of the kings of Judah I shall give over to the hand of their enemies, and they will plunder them, take them away, and bring them to Babylon.

6 'And you, Pashhur, and all who live in your house will go into captivity; and you will enter Babylon, and there you will die, and there you will be buried, you and all your friends to whom you have falsely prophesied.' "

7 ¶ O LORD, Thou hast deceived me and I was deceived;
Thou hast overcome me and prevailed.

⁵ I.e., terror on every side

I have become a laughingstock all day long;
Everyone mocks me.
8 For each time I speak, I cry aloud;
I proclaim violence and destruction,
Because for me the word of the LORD has resulted
In reproach and derision all day long.
9 But if I say, "I will not remember Him
Or speak anymore in His name,"
Then in my heart it becomes like a burning fire
Shut up in my bones;
And I am weary of holding it in,
And I cannot endure it.
10 For I have heard the whispering of many,
"Terror on every side!
Denounce him; yes, let us denounce him!"
All my trusted friends,
Watching for my fall, say:
"Perhaps he will be deceived, so that we may prevail against him
And take our revenge on him."
11 But the LORD is with me like a dread champion;
Therefore my persecutors will stumble and not prevail.
They will be utterly ashamed, because they have failed,
With an everlasting disgrace that will not be forgotten.
12 Yet, O LORD of hosts, Thou who dost test the righteous,
Who seest the mind and the heart;
Let me see Thy vengeance on them;
For to Thee I have set forth my cause.
13 Sing to the LORD, praise the LORD!
For He has delivered the soul of the needy one
From the hand of evildoers.

14 ¶ Cursed be the day when I was born;
Let the day not be blessed when my mother bore me!
15 Cursed be the man who brought the news
To my father, saying,
"A baby boy has been born to you!"
And made him very happy.

16 But let that man be like the cities
   Which the LORD overthrew with-
     out [6]relenting,
   And let him hear an outcry in the
     morning
   And a shout of alarm at noon;
17 Because he did not kill me before
     birth,
   So that my mother would have
     been my grave,
   And her womb ever pregnant.
18 Why did I ever come forth from
     the womb
   To look on trouble and sorrow,
   So that my days have been spent
     in shame?

CHAPTER 21

THE word which came to Jeremiah
from the LORD when King Zedekiah
sent to him Pashhur the son of Malchijah, and Zephaniah the priest, the son
of Maaseiah, saying,

2"Please inquire of the LORD on our
behalf, for Nebuchadnezzar king of
Babylon is warring against us; perhaps
the LORD will deal with us according
to all His wonderful acts, that *the
enemy* may withdraw from us."

3 ¶ Then Jeremiah said to them,
"You shall say to Zedekiah as follows:

4 'Thus says the LORD God of Israel,
"Behold, I am about to turn back the
weapons of war which are in your
hands, with which you are warring
against the king of Babylon and the
Chaldeans who are besieging you outside the wall; and I shall gather them
into the center of this city.

5"And I Myself shall war against
you with an outstretched hand and a
mighty arm, even in anger and wrath
and great indignation.

6"I shall also strike down the inhabitants of this city, both man and
beast; they will die of a great pestilence.

7"Then afterwards," declares the
LORD, "I shall give over Zedekiah king
of Judah and his servants and the
people, even those who survive in this
city from the pestilence, the sword,
and the famine, into the hand of Nebuchadnezzar king of Babylon, and into
the hand of their foes, and into the
hand of those who seek their lives; and
he will strike them down with the

edge of the sword. He will not spare
them nor have pity nor compassion." '

8 ¶"You shall also say to this people, 'Thus says the LORD, "Behold, I set
before you the way of life and the way
of death.

9"He who dwells in this city will die
by the sword and by famine and by
pestilence; but he who goes out and
falls away to the Chaldeans who are
besieging you will live, and he will
have his own life as booty.

10"For I have set My face against
this city for harm and not for good,"
declares the LORD. "It will be given
into the hand of the king of Babylon,
and he will burn it with fire." '

11 ¶"Then *say* to the household of
the king of Judah, 'Hear the word of
the LORD,

12 O house of David, thus says the
LORD:
   "Administer justice every morning;
     And deliver the *person* who has
      been robbed from the power of
      his oppressor,
     That My wrath may not go forth
      like fire
     And burn with none to extinguish
      it,
     Because of the evil of their deeds.

13 ¶"Behold, I am against you, O
     valley dweller,
   O rocky plain," declares the LORD,
   "You men who say, 'Who will
     come down against us?
   Or who will enter into our habita-
     tions?'
14"But I shall punish you according
     to the results of your deeds,"
     declares the LORD,
   "And I shall kindle a fire in its
     forest
   That it may devour all its envi-
     rons." ' "

CHAPTER 22

THUS says the LORD, "Go down to
the house of the king of Judah, and
there speak this word,

2 and say, 'Hear the word of the
LORD, O king of Judah, who sits on
David's throne, you and your servants
and your people who enter these
gates.

3 'Thus says the LORD, "Do justice
and righteousness, and deliver the one

[6] Lit., *being sorry*

who has been robbed from the power of *his* oppressor. Also do not mistreat *or* do violence to the stranger, the orphan, or the widow; and do not shed innocent blood in this place.

4"For if you men will indeed perform this thing, then kings will enter the gates of this house, sitting in David's place on his throne, riding in chariots and on horses, *even the king* himself and his servants and his people.

5"But if you will not obey these words, I swear by Myself," declares the LORD, "that this house will become a desolation." ' "

6 For thus says the LORD concerning the house of the king of Judah:

"You are *like* Gilead to Me,
Like the summit of Lebanon;
Yet most assuredly I shall make
you like a wilderness,
Like cities which are not inhabited.

7"For I shall set apart destroyers
against you,
Each with his weapons;
And they will cut down your
choicest cedars
And throw *them* on the fire.

8"And many nations will pass by this city; and they will say to one another, 'Why has the LORD done thus to this great city?'

9"Then they will answer, 'Because they forsook the covenant of the LORD their God and bowed down to other gods and served them.' "

10 ¶ Do not weep for the dead or
mourn for him,
But weep continually for the one
who goes away;
For he will never return
Or see his native land.

11 For thus says the LORD in regard to Shallum the son of Josiah, king of Judah, who became king in the place of Josiah his father, who went forth from this place, "He will never return there;

12 but in the place where they led him captive, there he will die and not see this land again.

13 ¶"Woe to him who builds his
house without righteousness
And his upper rooms without justice,
Who uses his neighbor's services
without pay

And does not give him his wages,
14 Who says, 'I will build myself a
roomy house
With spacious upper rooms,
And cut out its windows,
Paneling *it* with cedar and painting *it* bright red.'

15"Do you become a king because
you are competing in cedar?
Did not your father eat and drink,
And do justice and righteousness?
Then it was well with him.

16"He pled the cause of the afflicted
and needy;
Then it was well.
Is not that what it means to know
Me?"
Declares the LORD.

17"But your eyes and your heart
Are *intent* only upon your own
dishonest gain,
And on shedding innocent blood
And on practicing oppression and
extortion."

18 Therefore thus says the LORD in regard to Jehoiakim the son of Josiah, king of Judah,

"They will not lament for him:
'Alas, my brother!' or, 'Alas, sister!'
They will not lament for him:
'Alas for the master!' or, 'Alas for
his splendor!'

19"He will be buried with a donkey's
burial,
Dragged off and thrown out beyond the gates of Jerusalem.

20"Go up to Lebanon and cry out,
And lift up your voice in Bashan;
Cry out also from Abarim,
For all your lovers have been
crushed.

21"I spoke to you in your prosperity;
But you said, 'I will not listen!'
This has been your practice from
your youth,
That you have not obeyed My
voice.

22"The wind will sweep away all your
shepherds,
And your lovers will go into captivity;
Then you will surely be ashamed
and humiliated
Because of all your wickedness.

23"You who dwell in Lebanon,
Nested in the cedars,
How you will groan when pangs
come upon you,
Pain like a woman in childbirth!

24 ¶"As I live," declares the LORD, "even though [7]Coniah the son of Jehoiakim king of Judah were a signet *ring* on My right hand, yet I would pull you off;

25 and I shall give you over into the hand of those who are seeking your life, yes, into the hand of those whom you dread, even into the hand of Nebuchadnezzar king of Babylon, and into the hand of the Chaldeans.

26"I shall hurl you and your mother who bore you into another country where you were not born, and there you will die.

27"But as for the land to which they desire to return, they will not return to it.

28"Is this man Coniah a despised, shattered jar?
Or is he an undesirable vessel?
Why have he and his descendants been hurled out
And cast into a land that they had not known?

29"O land, land, land,
Hear the word of the LORD!

30"Thus says the LORD,
'Write this man down childless,
A man who will not prosper in his days;
For no man of his descendants will prosper
Sitting on the throne of David
Or ruling again in Judah.' "

CHAPTER 23

"WOE to the shepherds who are destroying and scattering the sheep of My pasture!" declares the LORD.

2 Therefore thus says the LORD God of Israel concerning the shepherds who are tending My people: "You have scattered My flock and driven them away, and have not attended to them; behold, I am about to attend to you for the evil of your deeds," declares the LORD.

3"Then I Myself shall gather the remnant of My flock out of all the countries where I have driven them and shall bring them back to their pasture; and they will be fruitful and multiply.

4"I shall also raise up shepherds over them and they will tend them; and they will not be afraid any longer,

nor be terrified, nor will any be missing," declares the LORD.

5 ¶"Behold, *the* days are coming," declares the LORD,
"When I shall raise up for David a righteous Branch;
And He will reign as king and act wisely
And do justice and righteousness in the land.

6"In His days Judah will be saved,
And Israel will dwell securely;
And this is His name by which He will be called,
'The LORD our righteousness.'

7"Therefore behold, *the* days are coming," declares the LORD, "when they will no longer say, 'As the LORD lives, who brought up the sons of Israel from the land of Egypt,'

8 but, 'As the LORD lives, who brought up and led back the descendants of the household of Israel from *the* north land and from all the countries where I had driven them.' Then they will live on their own soil."

9 As for the prophets:
My heart is broken within me,
All my bones tremble;
I have become like a drunken man,
Even like a man overcome with wine,
Because of the LORD
And because of His holy words.

10 For the land is full of adulterers;
For the land mourns because of the curse.
The pastures of the wilderness have dried up.
Their course also is evil,
And their might is not right.

11"For both prophet and priest are polluted;
Even in My house I have found their wickedness," declares the LORD.

12"Therefore their way will be like slippery paths to them,
They will be driven away into the gloom and fall down in it;
For I shall bring calamity upon them,
The year of their punishment," declares the LORD.

13 ¶"Moreover, among the prophets of Samaria I saw an offensive thing:

They prophesied by Baal and led
My people Israel astray.
14"Also among the prophets of Jerusalem I have seen a horrible
thing:
The committing of adultery and
walking in falsehood;
And they strengthen the hands of
evildoers,
So that no one has turned back
from his wickedness.
All of them have become to Me
like Sodom,
And her inhabitants like Gomorrah.
15"Therefore thus says the LORD of
hosts concerning the prophets,
'Behold, I am going to feed them
wormwood
And make them drink poisonous
water,
For from the prophets of Jerusalem
Pollution has gone forth into all
the land.'"

16 ¶ Thus says the LORD of hosts,
"Do not listen to the words of the
prophets who are prophesying
to you.
They are leading you into futility;
They speak a vision of their own
imagination,
Not from the mouth of the LORD.
17"They keep saying to those who
despise Me,
'The LORD has said, "You will have
peace"';
And as for everyone who walks in
the stubbornness of his own
heart,
They say, 'Calamity will not come
upon you.'
18"But who has stood in the council
of the LORD,
That he should see and hear His
word?
Who has given heed to His word
and listened?
19"Behold, the storm of the LORD has
gone forth in wrath,
Even a whirling tempest;
It will swirl down on the head of
the wicked.
20"The anger of the LORD will not
turn back
Until He has performed and carried out the purposes of His
heart;

In the last days you will clearly
understand it.
21"I did not send these prophets,
But they ran.
I did not speak to them,
But they prophesied.
22"But if they had stood in My coun-
cil,
Then they would have announced
My words to My people,
And would have turned them
back from their evil way
And from the evil of their deeds.

23 ¶"Am I a God who is near," declares the LORD,
"And not a God far off?
24"Can a man hide himself in hiding
places,
So I do not see him?" declares the
LORD.
"Do I not fill the heavens and the
earth?" declares the LORD.
25 ¶"I have heard what the prophets
have said who prophesy falsely in My
name, saying, 'I had a dream, I had a
dream!'
26"How long? Is there anything in
the hearts of the prophets who prophesy falsehood, even these prophets of
the deception of their own heart,
27 who intend to make My people
forget My name by their dreams which
they relate to one another, just as
their fathers forgot My name because
of Baal?
28"The prophet who has a dream
may relate his dream, but let him who
has My word speak My word in truth.
What does straw have in common
with grain?" declares the LORD.
29"Is not My word like fire?" declares
the LORD, "and like a hammer which
shatters a rock?
30"Therefore behold, I am against
the prophets," declares the LORD,
"who steal My words from each other.
31"Behold, I am against the prophets," declares the LORD, "who use their
tongues and declare, 'The Lord declares.'
32"Behold, I am against those who
have prophesied false dreams," declares the LORD, "and related them,
and led My people astray by their
falsehoods and reckless boasting; yet I
did not send them or command them,

nor do they furnish this people the slightest benefit," declares the LORD.

33 ¶"Now when this people or the prophet or a priest asks you saying, 'What is the ⁸oracle of the LORD?' then you shall say to them, 'What oracle?' The LORD declares, 'I shall abandon you.'

34"Then as for the prophet or the priest or the people who say, 'The oracle of the LORD,' I shall bring punishment upon that man and his household.

35"Thus shall each of you say to his neighbor and to his brother, 'What has the LORD answered?' or, 'What has the LORD spoken?'

36"Fcr you will no longer remember the oracle of the LORD, because every man's own word will become the oracle, and you have perverted the words of the living God, the LORD of hosts, our God.

37"Thus you will say to *that* prophet, 'What has the LORD answered you?' and, 'What has the LORD spoken?'

38"For if you say, 'The oracle of the LORD!' surely thus says the LORD, 'Because you said this word, "The oracle of the LORD!" I have also sent to you, saying, "You shall not say, 'The oracle of the LORD!' " ' '

39"Therefore behold, I shall surely forget you and cast you away from My presence, along with the city which I gave you and your fathers.

40"And I will put an everlasting reproach on you and an everlasting humiliation which will not be forgotten."

CHAPTER 24

AFTER Nebuchadnezzar king of Babylon had carried away captive Jeconiah the son of Jehoiakim, king of Judah, and the officials of Judah with the craftsmen and smiths from Jerusalem and had brought them to Babylon, the LORD showed me: behold, two baskets of figs set before the temple of the LORD!

2 One basket had very good figs, like first-ripe figs; and the other basket had very bad figs, which could not be eaten due to rottenness.

3 Then the LORD said to me, "What do you see, Jeremiah?" And I said, "Figs, the good figs, very good; and

⁸ Or, *burden,* and so throughout the ch.

the bad *figs,* very bad, which cannot be eaten due to rottenness."

4 ¶ Then the word of the LORD came to me, saying,

5"Thus says the LORD God of Israel, 'Like these good figs, so I will regard as good the captives of Judah, whom I have sent out of this place *into* the land of the Chaldeans.

6 'For I will set My eyes on them for good, and I will bring them again to this land; and I will build them up and not overthrow them, and I will plant them and not pluck *them* up.

7 'And I will give them a heart to know Me, for I am the LORD; and they will be My people, and I will be their God, for they will return to Me with their whole heart.

8 ¶ 'But like the bad figs which cannot be eaten due to rottenness—indeed, thus says the LORD—so I will abandon Zedekiah king of Judah and his officials, and the remnant of Jerusalem who remain in this land, and the ones who dwell in the land of Egypt.

9 'And I will make them a terror *and an* evil for all the kingdoms of the earth, as a reproach and a proverb, a taunt and a curse in all places where I shall scatter them.

10 'And I will send the sword, the famine, and the pestilence upon them until they are destroyed from the land which I gave to them and their forefathers.' "

CHAPTER 25

THE word that came to Jeremiah concerning all the people of Judah, in the fourth year of Jehoiakim the son of Josiah, king of Judah (that was the first year of Nebuchadnezzar king of Babylon),

2 which Jeremiah the prophet spoke to all the people of Judah and to all the inhabitants of Jerusalem, saying,

3"From the thirteenth year of Josiah the son of Amon, king of Judah, even to this day, these twenty-three years the word of the LORD has come to me, and I have spoken to you again and again, but you have not listened.

4"And the LORD has sent to you all His servants the prophets again and again, but you have not listened nor inclined your ear to hear,

5 saying, 'Turn now everyone from his evil way and from the evil of your deeds, and dwell on the land which the LORD has given to you and your forefathers forever and ever;

6 and do not go after other gods to serve them and to worship them, and do not provoke Me to anger with the work of your hands, and I will do you no harm.'

7"Yet you have not listened to Me," declares the LORD, "in order that you might provoke Me to anger with the work of your hands to your own harm.

8"Therefore thus says the LORD of hosts, 'Because you have not obeyed My words,

9 behold, I will send and take all the families of the north,' declares the LORD, 'and I will send to Nebuchadnezzar king of Babylon, My servant, and will bring them against this land, and against its inhabitants, and against all these nations round about; and I will utterly destroy them, and make them a horror, and a hissing, and an everlasting desolation.

10 'Moreover, I will take from them the voice of joy and the voice of gladness, the voice of the bridegroom and the voice of the bride, the sound of the millstones and the light of the lamp.

11 'And this whole land shall be a desolation and a horror, and these nations shall serve the king of Babylon seventy years.

12 ¶ 'Then it will be when seventy years are completed I will punish the king of Babylon and that nation,' declares the LORD, 'for their iniquity, and the land of the Chaldeans; and I will make it an everlasting desolation.

13 'And I will bring upon that land all My words which I have pronounced against it, all that is written in this book, which Jeremiah has prophesied against all the nations.

14 '(For many nations and great kings shall make slaves of them, even them; and I will recompense them according to their deeds, and according to the work of their hands.)' "

15 ¶ For thus the LORD, the God of Israel, says to me, "Take this cup of the wine of wrath from My hand, and cause all the nations, to whom I send you, to drink it.

16"And they shall drink and stagger and go mad because of the sword that I will send among them."

17 Then I took the cup from the LORD's hand, and made all the nations drink, to whom the LORD sent me:

18 Jerusalem and the cities of Judah, and its kings and its princes, to make them a ruin, a horror, a hissing, and a curse, as it is this day;

19 Pharaoh king of Egypt, his servants, his princes, and all his people;

20 and all the foreign people, all the kings of the land of Uz, all the kings of the land of the Philistines (even Ashkelon, Gaza, Ekron, and the remnant of Ashdod);

21 Edom, Moab, and the sons of Ammon;

22 and all the kings of Tyre, all the kings of Sidon, and the kings of the coastlands which are beyond the sea;

23 and Dedan, Tema, Buz, and all who cut the corners of their hair;

24 and all the kings of Arabia and all the kings of the foreign people who dwell in the desert;

25 and all the kings of Zimri, all the kings of Elam, and all the kings of Media;

26 and all the kings of the north, near and far, one with another; and all the kingdoms of the earth which are upon the face of the ground, and the king of Sheshach shall drink after them.

27 ¶"And you shall say to them, 'Thus says the LORD of hosts, the God of Israel, "Drink, be drunk, vomit, fall, and rise no more because of the sword which I will send among you." '

28"And it will be, if they refuse to take the cup from your hand to drink, then you will say to them, 'Thus says the LORD of hosts: "You shall surely drink!

29"For behold, I am beginning to work calamity in this city which is called by My name, and shall you be completely free from punishment? You will not be free from punishment; for I am summoning a sword against all the inhabitants of the earth," declares the LORD of hosts.'

30 ¶"Therefore you shall prophesy against them all these words, and you shall say to them,

'The LORD will roar from on high,
    And utter His voice from His holy
        habitation;

He will roar mightily against His
    fold.
He will shout like those who tread
    the grapes,
Against all the inhabitants of the
    earth.
31 'A clamor has come to the end of
    the earth,
    Because the LORD has a contro-
       versy with the nations.
    He is entering into judgment with
       all flesh;
    As for the wicked, He has given
       them to the sword,' declares the
       LORD."

32 ¶ Thus says the LORD of hosts,
  "Behold, evil is going forth
    From nation to nation,
    And a great storm is being stirred
      up
    From the remotest parts of the
      earth.
33"And those slain by the LORD on
that day shall be from one end of the
earth to the other. They shall not be
lamented, gathered, or buried; they
shall be like dung on the face of the
ground.
34"Wail, you shepherds, and cry;
    And wallow *in ashes,* you masters
      of the flock;
    For the days of your slaughter
      and your dispersions have
      come,
    And you shall fall like a choice
      vessel.
35"Flight shall perish from the shep-
    herds,
    And escape from the masters of
      the flock.
36"*Hear* the sound of the cry of the
    shepherds,
    And the wailing of the masters of
      the flock!
    For the LORD is destroying their
      pasture,
37"And the peaceful folds are made
    silent
    Because of the fierce anger of the
      LORD.
38"He has left His hiding place like
    the lion;
    For their land has become a hor-
      ror
    Because of the fierceness of the
      oppressing *sword,*
    And because of His fierce anger."

CHAPTER 26

IN the beginning of the reign of Jehoiakim the son of Josiah, king of
Judah, this word came from the LORD,
saying,
2"Thus says the LORD, 'Stand in the
court of the LORD's house, and speak
to all the cities of Judah, who have
come to worship *in* the LORD's house,
all the words that I have commanded
you to speak to them. Do not omit a
word!
3 'Perhaps they will listen and everyone will turn from his evil way, that I
may repent of the calamity which I am
planning to do to them because of the
evil of their deeds.'
4"And you will say to them, 'Thus
says the LORD, "If you will not listen
to Me, to walk in My law, which I
have set before you,
5 to listen to the words of My servants the prophets, whom I have been
sending to you again and again, but
you have not listened;
6 then I will make this house like
Shiloh, and this city I will make a
curse to all the nations of the
earth." ' "
7 ¶ And the priests and the prophets and all the people heard Jeremiah
speaking these words in the house of
the LORD.
8 And when Jeremiah finished
speaking all that the LORD had commanded *him* to speak to all the people,
the priests and the prophets and all the
people seized him, saying, "You must
die!
9"Why have you prophesied in the
name of the LORD saying, 'This house
will be like Shiloh, and this city will be
desolate, without inhabitant'?" And all
the people gathered about Jeremiah in
the house of the LORD.
10 ¶ And when the princes of Judah
heard these things, they came up from
the king's house to the house of the
LORD and sat in the entrance of the
New Gate of the LORD's *house.*
11 Then the priests and the prophets
spoke to the officials and to all the
people, saying, "A death sentence for
this man! For he has prophesied
against this city as you have heard in
your hearing."
12 Then Jeremiah spoke to all the
officials and to all the people, saying,

"The LORD sent me to prophesy against this house and against this city all the words that you have heard.

13"Now therefore amend your ways and your deeds, and obey the voice of the LORD your God; and the LORD will change His mind about the misfortune which He has pronounced against you.

14"But as for me, behold, I am in your hands; do with me as is good and right in your sight.

15"Only know for certain that if you put me to death, you will bring innocent blood on yourselves, and on this city, and on its inhabitants; for truly the LORD has sent me to you to speak all these words in your hearing."

16 ¶ Then the officials and all the people said to the priests and to the prophets, "No death sentence for this man! For he has spoken to us in the name of the LORD our God."

17 Then some of the elders of the land rose up and spoke to all the assembly of the people, saying,

18"Micah of Moresheth prophesied in the days of Hezekiah king of Judah; and he spoke to all the people of Judah, saying, 'Thus the LORD of hosts has said,

"Zion will be plowed as a field,
And Jerusalem will become ruins,
And the mountain of the house as the high places of a forest." '

19"Did Hezekiah king of Judah and all Judah put him to death? Did he not fear the LORD and entreat the favor of the LORD, and the LORD changed His mind about the misfortune which He had pronounced against them? But we are committing a great evil against ourselves."

20 ¶ Indeed, there was also a man who prophesied in the name of the LORD, Uriah the son of Shemaiah from Kiriath-jearim; and he prophesied against this city and against this land words similar to all those of Jeremiah.

21 When King Jehoiakim and all his mighty men and all the officials heard his words, then the king sought to put him to death; but Uriah heard it, and he was afraid and fled, and went to Egypt.

22 Then King Jehoiakim sent men to Egypt: Elnathan the son of Achbor and certain men with him went into Egypt.

23 And they brought Uriah from Egypt and led him to King Jehoiakim, who slew him with a sword, and cast his dead body into the burial place of the common people.

24 ¶ But the hand of Ahikam the son of Shaphan was with Jeremiah, so that he was not given into the hands of the people to put him to death.

CHAPTER 27

IN the beginning of the reign of Zedekiah the son of Josiah, king of Judah, this word came to Jeremiah from the LORD, saying—

2 thus says the LORD to me—"Make for yourself bonds and yokes and put them on your neck,

3 and send word to the king of Edom, to the king of Moab, to the king of the sons of Ammon, to the king of Tyre, and to the king of Sidon by the messengers who come to Jerusalem to Zedekiah king of Judah.

4"And command them to go to their masters, saying, 'Thus says the LORD of hosts, the God of Israel, thus you shall say to your masters,

5"I have made the earth, the men and the beasts which are on the face of the earth by My great power and by My outstretched arm, and I will give it to the one who is pleasing in My sight.

6"And now I have given all these lands into the hand of Nebuchadnezzar king of Babylon, My servant, and I have given him also the wild animals of the field to serve him.

7"And all the nations shall serve him, and his son, and his grandson, until the time of his own land comes; then many nations and great kings will make him their servant.

8"And it will be, that the nation or the kingdom which will not serve him, Nebuchadnezzar king of Babylon, and which will not put its neck under the yoke of the king of Babylon, I will punish that nation with the sword, with famine, and with pestilence," declares the LORD, "until I have destroyed it by his hand.

9"But as for you, do not listen to your prophets, your diviners, your dreamers, your soothsayers, or your sorcerers, who speak to you, saying, 'You shall not serve the king of Babylon.'

10"For they prophesy a lie to you, in

order to remove you far from your land; and I will drive you out, and you will perish.

11"But the nation which will bring its neck under the yoke of the king of Babylon and serve him, I will let remain on its land," declares the LORD, "and they will till it and dwell in it." ' "

12 ¶ And I spoke words like all these to Zedekiah king of Judah, saying, "Bring your necks under the yoke of the king of Babylon, and serve him and his people, and live!

13"Why will you die, you and your people, by the sword, famine, and pestilence, as the LORD has spoken to that nation which will not serve the king of Babylon?

14"So do not listen to the words of the prophets who speak to you, saying, 'You shall not serve the king of Babylon,' for they prophesy a lie to you;

15 for I have not sent them," declares the LORD, "but they prophesy falsely in My name, in order that I may drive you out, and that you may perish, you and the prophets who prophesy to you."

16 ¶ *Then* I spoke to the priests and to all this people, saying, "Thus says the LORD: Do not listen to the words of your prophets who prophesy to you, saying, 'Behold, the vessels of the LORD's house will now shortly be brought again from Babylon'; for they are prophesying a lie to you.

17"Do not listen to them; serve the king of Babylon, and live! Why should this city become a ruin?

18"But if they are prophets, and if the word of the LORD is with them, let them now entreat the LORD of hosts, that the vessels which are left in the house of the LORD, in the house of the king of Judah, and in Jerusalem, may not go to Babylon.

19"For thus says the LORD of hosts concerning the pillars, concerning the sea, concerning the stands, and concerning the rest of the vessels that are left in this city,

20 which Nebuchadnezzar king of Babylon did not take when he carried into exile Jeconiah the son of Jehoiakim, king of Judah, from Jerusalem to Babylon, and all the nobles of Judah and Jerusalem.

21"Yes, thus says the LORD of hosts, the God of Israel, concerning the vessels that are left in the house of the LORD, and in the house of the king of Judah, and in Jerusalem,

22 'They shall be carried to Babylon, and they shall be there until the day I visit them,' declares the LORD. 'Then I will bring them back and restore them to this place.' "

CHAPTER 28

NOW it came about in the same year, in the beginning of the reign of Zedekiah king of Judah, in the fourth year, in the fifth month, that Hananiah the son of Azzur, the prophet, who was from Gibeon, spoke to me in the house of the LORD in the presence of the priests and all the people, saying,

2"Thus says the LORD of hosts, the God of Israel, 'I have broken the yoke of the king of Babylon.

3 'Within two years I am going to bring back to this place all the vessels of the LORD's house, which Nebuchadnezzar king of Babylon took away from this place and carried to Babylon.

4 'I am also going to bring back to this place Jeconiah the son of Jehoiakim, king of Judah, and all the exiles of Judah who went to Babylon,' declares the LORD, 'for I will break the yoke of the king of Babylon.' "

5 ¶ Then the prophet Jeremiah spoke to the prophet Hananiah in the presence of the priests and in the presence of all the people who were standing in the house of the LORD,

6 and the prophet Jeremiah said, "Amen! May the LORD do so; may the LORD confirm your words which you have prophesied to bring back the vessels of the LORD's house and all the exiles, from Babylon to this place.

7"Yet hear now this word which I am about to speak in your hearing and in the hearing of all the people!

8"The prophets who were before me and before you from ancient times prophesied against many lands and against great kingdoms, of war and of calamity and of pestilence.

9"The prophet who prophesies of peace, when the word of the prophet shall come to pass, then that prophet will be known *as* one whom the LORD has truly sent."

10 Then Hananiah the prophet took the yoke from the neck of Jeremiah the prophet and broke it.

11 And Hananiah spoke in the presence of all the people, saying, "Thus says the LORD, 'Even so will I break within two full years, the yoke of Nebuchadnezzar king of Babylon from the neck of all the nations.' " Then the prophet Jeremiah went his way.

12 ¶ And the word of the LORD came to Jeremiah, after Hananiah the prophet had broken the yoke from off the neck of the prophet Jeremiah, saying,

13 "Go and speak to Hananiah, saying, 'Thus says the LORD, "You have broken the yokes of wood, but you have made instead of them yokes of iron."

14 'For thus says the LORD of hosts, the God of Israel, "I have put a yoke of iron on the neck of all these nations, that they may serve Nebuchadnezzar king of Babylon; and they shall serve him. And I have also given him the beasts of the field." ' "

15 Then Jeremiah the prophet said to Hananiah the prophet, "Listen now, Hananiah, the LORD has not sent you, and you have made this people trust in a lie.

16 "Therefore thus says the LORD, 'Behold, I am about to remove you from the face of the earth. This year you are going to die, because you have counseled rebellion against the LORD.' "

17 So Hananiah the prophet died in the same year in the seventh month.

CHAPTER 29

NOW these are the words of the letter which Jeremiah the prophet sent from Jerusalem to the rest of the elders of the exile, the priests, the prophets, and all the people whom Nebuchadnezzar had taken into exile from Jerusalem to Babylon.

2 (This was after King Jeconiah and the queen mother, the court officials, the princes of Judah and Jerusalem, the craftsmen and the smiths had departed from Jerusalem.)

3 *The letter was sent* by the hand of Elasah the son of Shaphan, and Gemariah the son of Hilkiah, whom Zedekiah king of Judah sent to Babylon to Nebuchadnezzar king of Babylon, saying,

4 "Thus says the LORD of hosts, the God of Israel, to all the exiles whom I have sent into exile from Jerusalem to Babylon,

5 'Build houses and live *in them;* and plant gardens, and eat their produce.

6 'Take wives and become the fathers of sons and daughters, and take wives for your sons and give your daughters to husbands, that they may bear sons and daughters; and multiply there and do not decrease.

7 'And seek the welfare of the city where I have sent you into exile, and pray to the LORD on its behalf; for in its welfare you will have welfare.

8 "For thus says the LORD of hosts, the God of Israel, 'Do not let your prophets who are in your midst and your diviners deceive you, and do not listen to the dreams which they dream.

9 'For they prophesy falsely to you in My name; I have not sent them,' declares the LORD.

10 "For thus says the LORD, 'When seventy years have been completed for Babylon, I will visit you and fulfill My good word to you, to bring you back to this place.

11 'For I know the plans that I have for you,' declares the LORD, 'plans for welfare and not for calamity to give you a future and a hope.

12 'Then you will call upon Me and come and pray to Me, and I will listen to you.

13 'And you will seek Me and find *Me,* when you search for Me with all your heart.

14 'And I will be found by you,' declares the LORD, 'and I will restore your fortunes and will gather you from all the nations and from all the places where I have driven you,' declares the LORD, 'and I will bring you back to the place from where I sent you into exile.'

15 ¶ "Because you have said, 'The LORD has raised up prophets for us in Babylon'—

16 for thus says the LORD concerning the king who sits on the throne of David, and concerning all the people who dwell in this city, your brothers who did not go with you into exile—

17 thus says the LORD of hosts, 'Behold, I am sending upon them the sword, famine, and pestilence, and I will make them like split-open figs that cannot be eaten due to rottenness.

18 'And I will pursue them with the sword, with famine and with pestilence; and I will make them a terror to all the kingdoms of the earth, to be a curse, and a horror, and a hissing, and a reproach among all the nations where I have driven them,

19 because they have not listened to My words,' declares the LORD, 'which I sent to them again and again by My servants the prophets; but you did not listen,' declares the LORD.

20"You, therefore, hear the word of the LORD, all you exiles, whom I have sent away from Jerusalem to Babylon.

21 ¶"Thus says the LORD of hosts, the God of Israel, concerning Ahab the son of Kolaiah and concerning Zedekiah the son of Maaseiah, who are prophesying to you falsely in My name, 'Behold, I will deliver them into the hand of Nebuchadnezzar king of Babylon, and he shall slay them before your eyes.

22 'And because of them a curse shall be used by all the exiles from Judah who are in Babylon, saying, "May the LORD make you like Zedekiah and like Ahab, whom the king of Babylon roasted in the fire,

23 because they have acted foolishly in Israel, and have committed adultery with their neighbors' wives, and have spoken words in My name falsely, which I did not command them; and I am He who knows, and am a witness," declares the LORD.' "

24 ¶ And to Shemaiah the Nehelamite you shall speak, saying,

25"Thus says the LORD of hosts, the God of Israel, 'Because you have sent letters in your own name to all the people who are in Jerusalem, and to Zephaniah the son of Maaseiah, the priest, and to all the priests, saying,

26"The LORD has made you priest instead of Jehoiada the priest, to be the overseer in the house of the LORD over every madman who prophesies, to put him in the stocks and in the iron collar,

27 now then, why have you not rebuked Jeremiah of Anathoth who prophesies to you?

28"For he has sent to us in Babylon, saying, 'The exile will be long; build houses and live in them and plant gardens and eat their produce.' " ' "

29 ¶ And Zephaniah the priest read this letter to Jeremiah the prophet.

30 Then came the word of the LORD to Jeremiah, saying,

31"Send to all the exiles, saying, 'Thus says the LORD concerning Shemaiah the Nehelamite, "Because Shemaiah has prophesied to you, although I did not send him, and he has made you trust in a lie,"

32 therefore thus says the LORD, "Behold, I am about to punish Shemaiah the Nehelamite and his descendants; he shall not have anyone living among this people, and he shall not see the good that I am about to do to My people," declares the LORD, "because he has preached rebellion against the LORD." ' "

CHAPTER 30

THE word which came to Jeremiah from the LORD, saying,

2"Thus says the LORD, the God of Israel, 'Write all the words which I have spoken to you in a book.

3 'For, behold, days are coming,' declares the LORD, 'when I will restore the fortunes of My people Israel and Judah.' The LORD says, 'I will also bring them back to the land that I gave to their forefathers, and they shall possess it.' "

4 ¶ Now these are the words which the LORD spoke concerning Israel and concerning Judah,

5"For thus says the LORD,
    'I have heard a sound of terror,
    Of dread, and there is no peace.
6 'Ask now, and see,
    If a male can give birth.
    Why do I see every man
    With his hands on his loins, as a
        woman in childbirth?
    And why have all faces turned
        pale?
7 'Alas! for that day is great,
    There is none like it;
    And it is the time of Jacob's distress,

But he will be saved from it.

8 'And it shall come about on that day,' declares the LORD of hosts, 'that I will break his yoke from off their neck, and will tear off their bonds; and strangers shall no longer make them their slaves.

9 'But they shall serve the LORD their God, and David their king, whom I will raise up for them.

10 'And fear not, O Jacob My servant,' declares the LORD,
'And do not be dismayed, O Israel;
For behold, I will save you from afar,
And your offspring from the land of their captivity.
And Jacob shall return, and shall be quiet and at ease,
And no one shall make him afraid.

11 'For I am with you,' declares the LORD, 'to save you;
For I will destroy completely all the nations where I have scattered you,
Only I will not destroy you completely.
But I will chasten you justly,
And will by no means leave you unpunished.'

12 ¶"For thus says the LORD,
'Your wound is incurable,
And your injury is serious.

13 'There is no one to plead your cause;
No healing for your sore,
No recovery for you.

14 'All your lovers have forgotten you,
They do not seek you;
For I have wounded you with the wound of an enemy,
With the punishment of a cruel one,
Because your iniquity is great
And your sins are numerous.

15 'Why do you cry out over your injury?
Your pain is incurable.
Because your iniquity is great
And your sins are numerous,
I have done these things to you.

16 'Therefore all who devour you shall be devoured;
And all your adversaries, every one of them, shall go into captivity;

And those who plunder you shall be for plunder,
And all who prey upon you I will give for prey.

17 'For I will restore you to health
And I will heal you of your wounds,' declares the LORD,
'Because they have called you an outcast, saying:
"It is Zion; no one cares for her." '

18 ¶"Thus says the LORD,
'Behold, I will restore the fortunes of the tents of Jacob
And have compassion on his dwelling places;
And the city shall be rebuilt on its ruin,
And the palace shall stand on its rightful place.

19 'And from them shall proceed thanksgiving
And the voice of those who make merry;
And I will multiply them, and they shall not be diminished;
I will also honor them, and they shall not be insignificant.

20 'Their children also shall be as formerly,
And their congregation shall be established before Me;
And I will punish all their oppressors.

21 'And their leader shall be one of them,
And their ruler shall come forth from their midst;
And I will bring him near, and he shall approach Me;
For who would dare to risk his life to approach Me?' declares the LORD.

22 'And you shall be My people,
And I will be your God.' "

23 ¶ Behold, the tempest of the LORD!
Wrath has gone forth,
A sweeping tempest;
It will burst on the head of the wicked.

24 The fierce anger of the LORD will not turn back,
Until He has performed, and until He has accomplished
The intent of His heart;
In the latter days you will understand this.

CHAPTER 31

"AT that time," declares the LORD, "I will be the God of all the families of Israel, and they shall be My people."

2 Thus says the LORD,

"The people who survived the sword
Found grace in the wilderness—
Israel, when it went to find its rest."

3 The LORD appeared to him from afar, *saying,*

"I have loved you with an everlasting love;
Therefore I have drawn you with lovingkindness.

4 "Again I will build you, and you shall be rebuilt,
O virgin of Israel!
Again you shall take up your tambourines,
And go forth to the dances of the merrymakers.

5 "Again you shall plant vineyards
On the hills of Samaria;
The planters shall plant
And shall enjoy *them.*

6 "For there shall be a day when watchmen
On the hills of Ephraim shall call out,
'Arise, and let us go up *to* Zion,
To the LORD our God.' "

7 ¶ For thus says the LORD,

"Sing aloud with gladness for Jacob,
And shout among the chiefs of the nations;
Proclaim, give praise, and say,
'O LORD, save Thy people,
The remnant of Israel.'

8 "Behold, I am bringing them from the north country,
And I will gather them from the remote parts of the earth,
Among them the blind and the lame,
The woman with child and she who is in labor with child, together;
A great company, they shall return here.

9 "With weeping they shall come,
And by supplication I will lead them;
I will make them walk by streams of waters,

On a straight path in which they shall not stumble;
For I am a father to Israel,
And Ephraim is My first-born."

10 ¶ Hear the word of the LORD, O nations,
And declare in the coastlands afar off,
And say, "He who scattered Israel will gather him,
And keep him as a shepherd keeps his flock."

11 For the LORD has ransomed Jacob,
And redeemed him from the hand of him who was stronger than he.

12 "And they shall come and shout for joy on the height of Zion,
And they shall be radiant over the bounty of the LORD—
Over the grain, and the new wine, and the oil,
And over the young of the flock and the herd;
And their life shall be like a watered garden,
And they shall never languish again.

13 "Then the virgin shall rejoice in the dance,
And the young men and the old, together,
For I will turn their mourning into joy,
And will comfort them, and give them joy for their sorrow.

14 "And I will fill the soul of the priests with abundance,
And My people shall be satisfied with My goodness," declares the LORD.

15 ¶ Thus says the LORD,

"A voice is heard in Ramah,
Lamentation *and* bitter weeping.
Rachel is weeping for her children;
She refuses to be comforted for her children,
Because they are no more."

16 Thus says the LORD,

"Restrain your voice from weeping,
And your eyes from tears;
For your work shall be rewarded," declares the LORD,
"And they shall return from the land of the enemy.

17"And there is hope for your future," declares the LORD,
"And *your* children shall return to their own territory.
18"I have surely heard Ephraim grieving,
'Thou hast chastised me, and I was chastised,
Like an untrained calf;
Bring me back that I may be restored,
For Thou art the LORD my God.
19 'For after I turned back, I repented;
And after I was instructed, I smote on *my* thigh;
I was ashamed, and also humiliated,
Because I bore the reproach of my youth.'
20"Is Ephraim My dear son?
Is he a delightful child?
Indeed, as often as I have spoken against him,
I certainly *still* remember him;
Therefore My heart yearns for him;
I will surely have mercy on him," declares the LORD.

21 ¶"Set up for yourself roadmarks,
Place for yourself guideposts;
Direct your mind to the highway,
The way by which you went.
Return, O virgin of Israel,
Return to these your cities.
22"How long will you go here and there,
O faithless daughter?
For the LORD has created a new thing in the earth—
A woman will encompass a man."
23 ¶ Thus says the LORD of hosts, the God of Israel, "Once again they will speak this word in the land of Judah and in its cities, when I restore their fortunes,
'The LORD bless you, O abode of righteousness,
O holy hill!'
24"And Judah and all its cities will dwell together in it, the farmer and they who go about with flocks.
25"For I satisfy the weary ones and refresh everyone who languishes."
26 At this I awoke and looked, and my sleep was pleasant to me.
27 ¶"Behold, days are coming," declares the LORD, "when I will sow the

house of Israel and the house of Judah with the seed of man and with the seed of beast.
28"And it will come about that as I have watched over them to pluck up, to break down, to overthrow, to destroy, and to bring disaster, so I will watch over them to build and to plant," declares the LORD.
29"In those days they will not say again,
'The fathers have eaten sour grapes,
And the children's teeth are set on edge.'
30"But everyone will die for his own iniquity; each man who eats the sour grapes, his teeth will be set on edge.
31"Behold, days are coming," declares the LORD, "when I will make a new covenant with the house of Israel and with the house of Judah,
32 not like the covenant which I made with their fathers in the day I took them by the hand to bring them out of the land of Egypt, My covenant which they broke, although I was a husband to them," declares the LORD.
33"But this is the covenant which I will make with the house of Israel after those days," declares the LORD, "I will put My law within them, and on their heart I will write it; and I will be their God, and they shall be My people.
34"And they shall not teach again, each man his neighbor and each man his brother, saying, 'Know the LORD,' for they shall all know Me, from the least of them to the greatest of them," declares the LORD, "for I will forgive their iniquity, and their sin I will remember no more."
35 ¶ Thus says the LORD,
Who gives the sun for light by day,
And the fixed order of the moon and the stars for light by night,
Who stirs up the sea so that its waves roar;
The LORD of hosts is His name:
36"If this fixed order departs
From before Me," declares the LORD,
"Then the offspring of Israel also shall cease
From being a nation before Me forever."
37 Thus says the LORD,

"If the heavens above can be measured,
And the foundations of the earth searched out below,
Then I will also cast off all the offspring of Israel
For all that they have done," declares the LORD.

38 ¶ "Behold, days are coming," declares the LORD, "when the city shall be rebuilt for the LORD from the Tower of Hananel to the Corner Gate.

39 "And the measuring line shall go out farther straight ahead to the hill Gareb; then it will turn to Goah.

40 "And the whole valley of the dead bodies and of the ashes, and all the fields as far as the brook Kidron, to the corner of the Horse Gate toward the east, shall be holy to the LORD; it shall not be plucked up, or overthrown anymore forever."

CHAPTER 32

THE word that came to Jeremiah from the LORD in the tenth year of Zedekiah king of Judah, which was the eighteenth year of Nebuchadnezzar.

2 Now at that time the army of the king of Babylon was besieging Jerusalem, and Jeremiah the prophet was shut up in the court of the guard, which was in the house of the king of Judah,

3 because Zedekiah king of Judah had shut him up, saying, "Why do you prophesy, saying, 'Thus says the LORD, "Behold, I am about to give this city into the hand of the king of Babylon, and he will take it;

4 and Zedekiah king of Judah shall not escape out of the hand of the Chaldeans, but he shall surely be given into the hand of the king of Babylon, and he shall speak with him face to face, and see him eye to eye;

5 and he shall take Zedekiah to Babylon, and he shall be there until I visit him," declares the LORD. "If you fight against the Chaldeans, you shall not succeed" ' ? "

6 ¶ And Jeremiah said, "The word of the LORD came to me, saying,

7 'Behold, Hanamel the son of Shallum your uncle is coming to you, saying, "Buy for yourself my field which is at Anathoth, for you have the right of redemption to buy it." '

8 "Then Hanamel my uncle's son came to me in the court of the guard according to the word of the LORD, and said to me, 'Buy my field, please, that is at Anathoth, which is in the land of Benjamin; for you have the right of possession and the redemption is yours; buy it for yourself.' Then I knew that this was the word of the LORD.

9 "And I bought the field which was at Anathoth from Hanamel my uncle's son, and I weighed out the silver for him, seventeen shekels of silver.

10 "And I signed and sealed the deed, and called in witnesses, and weighed out the silver on the scales.

11 "Then I took the deeds of purchase, both the sealed copy containing the terms and conditions, and the open copy;

12 and I gave the deed of purchase to Baruch the son of Neriah, the son of Mahseiah, in the sight of Hanamel my uncle's son, and in the sight of the witnesses who signed the deed of purchase, before all the Jews who were sitting in the court of the guard.

13 "And I commanded Baruch in their presence, saying,

14 'Thus says the LORD of hosts, the God of Israel, "Take these deeds, this sealed deed of purchase, and this open deed, and put them in an earthenware jar, that they may last a long time."

15 'For thus says the LORD of hosts, the God of Israel, "Houses and fields and vineyards shall again be bought in this land." '

16 ¶ "After I had given the deed of purchase to Baruch the son of Neriah, then I prayed to the LORD, saying,

17 'Ah Lord GOD! Behold, Thou hast made the heavens and the earth by Thy great power and by Thine outstretched arm! Nothing is too difficult for Thee,

18 who showest lovingkindness to thousands, but repayest the iniquity of fathers into the bosom of their children after them, O great and mighty God. The LORD of hosts is His name;

19 great in counsel and mighty in deed, whose eyes are open to all the ways of the sons of men, giving to everyone according to his ways and according to the fruit of his deeds;

20 who hast set signs and wonders in the land of Egypt, *and* even to this day both in Israel and among mankind; and Thou hast made a name for Thyself, as at this day.

21 'And Thou didst bring Thy people Israel out of the land of Egypt with signs and with wonders, and with a strong hand and with an outstretched arm, and with great terror;

22 and gavest them this land, which Thou didst swear to their forefathers to give them, a land flowing with milk and honey.

23 'And they came in and took possession of it, but they did not obey Thy voice or walk in Thy law; they have done nothing of all that Thou commandedst them to do; therefore Thou hast made all this calamity come upon them.

24 'Behold, the siege mounds have reached the city to take it; and the city is given into the hand of the Chaldeans who fight against it, because of the sword, the famine, and the pestilence; and what Thou hast spoken has come to pass; and, behold, Thou seest *it.*

25 'And Thou hast said to me, O Lord GOD, "Buy for yourself the field with money, and call in witnesses"—although the city is given into the hand of the Chaldeans.' "

26 ¶ Then the word of the LORD came to Jeremiah, saying,

27"Behold, I am the LORD, the God of all flesh; is anything too difficult for Me?"

28 Therefore thus says the LORD, "Behold, I am about to give this city into the hand of the Chaldeans and into the hand of Nebuchadnezzar king of Babylon, and he shall take it.

29"And the Chaldeans who are fighting against this city shall enter and set this city on fire and burn it, with the houses where *people* have offered incense to Baal on their roofs and poured out libations to other gods to provoke Me to anger.

30"Indeed the sons of Israel and the sons of Judah have been doing only evil in My sight from their youth; for the sons of Israel have been only provoking Me to anger by the work of their hands," declares the LORD.

31"Indeed this city has been to Me *a provocation of* My anger and My wrath from the day that they built it, even to this day, that it should be removed from before My face,

32 because of all the evil of the sons of Israel and the sons of Judah, which they have done to provoke Me to anger—they, their kings, their leaders, their priests, their prophets, the men of Judah, and the inhabitants of Jerusalem.

33"And they have turned *their* back to Me, and not *their* face; though *I* taught them, teaching again and again, they would not listen and receive instruction.

34"But they put their detestable things in the house which is called by My name, to defile it.

35"And they built the high places of Baal that are in the valley of Ben-hinnom to cause their sons and their daughters to pass through *the fire* to Molech, which I had not commanded them nor had it entered My mind that they should do this abomination, to cause Judah to sin.

36 ¶"Now therefore thus says the LORD God of Israel concerning this city of which you say, 'It is given into the hand of the king of Babylon by sword, by famine, and by pestilence.'

37"Behold, I will gather them out of all the lands to which I have driven them in My anger, in My wrath, and in great indignation; and I will bring them back to this place and make them dwell in safety.

38"And they shall be My people, and I will be their God;

39 and I will give them one heart and one way, that they may fear Me always, for their own good, and for *the good of* their children after them.

40"And I will make an everlasting covenant with them that I will not turn away from them, to do them good; and I will put the fear of Me in their hearts so that they will not turn away from Me.

41"And I will rejoice over them to do them good, and I will faithfully plant them in this land with all My heart and with all My soul.

42"For thus says the LORD, 'Just as I brought all this great disaster on this people, so I am going to bring on them all the good that I am promising them.

43 'And fields shall be bought in this

land of which you say, "It is a desolation, without man or beast; it is given into the hand of the Chaldeans."

44 'Men shall buy fields for money, sign and seal deeds, and call in witnesses in the land of Benjamin, in the environs of Jerusalem, in the cities of Judah, in the cities of the hill country, in the cities of the lowland, and in the cities of the ⁹Negev; for I will restore their fortunes,' declares the Lord."

CHAPTER 33

THEN the word of the Lord came to Jeremiah the second time, while he was still confined in the court of the guard, saying,

2 "Thus says the Lord who made *the earth*, the Lord who formed it to establish it, the Lord is His name,

3 'Call to Me, and I will answer you, and I will tell you great and mighty things, which you do not know.'

4 "For thus says the Lord God of Israel concerning the houses of this city, and concerning the houses of the kings of Judah, which are broken down *to make a defense* against the siege mounds and against the sword,

5 'While *they* are coming to fight with the Chaldeans, and to fill them with the corpses of men whom I have slain in My anger and in My wrath, and I have hidden My face from this city because of all their wickedness:

6 'Behold, I will bring to it health and healing, and I will heal them; and I will reveal to them an abundance of peace and truth.

7 'And I will restore the fortunes of Judah and the fortunes of Israel, and I will rebuild them as they were at first.

8 'And I will cleanse them from all their iniquity by which they have sinned against Me, and I will pardon all their iniquities by which they have sinned against Me, and by which they have transgressed against Me.

9 'And ¹⁰it shall be to Me a name of joy, praise, and glory before all the nations of the earth, which shall hear of all the good that I do for them, and they shall fear and tremble because of all the good and all the peace that I make for it.'

10 ¶"Thus says the Lord, 'Yet again there shall be heard in this place, of

which you say, "It is a waste, without man and without beast," *that is*, in the cities of Judah and in the streets of Jerusalem that are desolate, without man and without inhabitant and without beast,

11 the voice of joy and the voice of gladness, the voice of the bridegroom and the voice of the bride, the voice of those who say,

"Give thanks to the Lord of hosts,
    For the Lord is good,
    For His lovingkindness is everlasting";

and of those who bring a thank offering into the house of the Lord. For I will restore the fortunes of the land as they were at first,' says the Lord.

12 ¶"Thus says the Lord of hosts, 'There shall again be in this place which is waste, without man or beast, and in all its cities, a habitation of shepherds who rest their flocks.

13 'In the cities of the hill country, in the cities of the lowland, in the cities of the Negev, in the land of Benjamin, in the environs of Jerusalem, and in the cities of Judah, the flocks shall again pass under the hands of the one who numbers them,' says the Lord.

14 ¶ 'Behold, days are coming,' declares the Lord, 'when I will fulfill the good word which I have spoken concerning the house of Israel and the house of Judah.

15 'In those days and at that time I will cause a righteous Branch of David to spring forth; and He shall execute justice and righteousness on the earth.

16 'In those days Judah shall be saved, and Jerusalem shall dwell in safety; and this is *the name* by which she shall be called: the Lord is our righteousness.'

17 "For thus says the Lord, 'David shall never lack a man to sit on the throne of the house of Israel;

18 and the Levitical priests shall never lack a man before Me to offer burnt offerings, to burn grain offerings, and to prepare sacrifices continually.' "

19 ¶ And the word of the Lord came to Jeremiah, saying,

20 "Thus says the Lord, 'If you can break My covenant for the day, and My covenant for the night, so that day and night will not be at their appointed time,

---

⁹ I.e., South country   ¹⁰ I.e., this city

21 then My covenant may also be broken with David My servant that he shall not have a son to reign on his throne, and with the Levitical priests, My ministers.

22 'As the host of heaven cannot be counted, and the sand of the sea cannot be measured, so I will multiply the descendants of David My servant and the Levites who minister to Me.' "

23 ¶ And the word of the LORD came to Jeremiah, saying,

24"Have you not observed what this people have spoken, saying, 'The two families which the LORD chose, He has rejected them'? Thus they despise My people, no longer are they as a nation in their sight.

25"Thus says the LORD, 'If My covenant *for* day and night *stand* not, *and* the fixed patterns of heaven and earth I have not established,

26 then I would reject the descendants of Jacob and David My servant, not taking from his descendants rulers over the descendants of Abraham, Isaac, and Jacob. But I will restore their fortunes and will have mercy on them.' "

CHAPTER 34

THE word which came to Jeremiah from the LORD, when Nebuchadnezzar king of Babylon and all his army, with all the kingdoms of the earth that were under his dominion and all the peoples, were fighting against Jerusalem and against all its cities, saying,

2"Thus says the LORD God of Israel, 'Go and speak to Zedekiah king of Judah and say to him: "Thus says the LORD, 'Behold, I am giving this city into the hand of the king of Babylon, and he will burn it with fire.

3 'And you will not escape from his hand, for you will surely be captured and delivered into his hand; and you will see the king of Babylon eye to eye, and he will speak with you face to face, and you will go to Babylon.' " '

4"Yet hear the word of the LORD, O Zedekiah king of Judah! Thus says the LORD concerning you, 'You will not die by the sword.

5 'You will die in peace; and as spices were burned for your fathers, the former kings who were before you, so they will burn spices for you; and

they will lament for you, "Alas, lord!" ' For I have spoken the word," declares the LORD.

6 ¶ Then Jeremiah the prophet spoke all these words to Zedekiah king of Judah in Jerusalem

7 when the army of the king of Babylon was fighting against Jerusalem and against all the remaining cities of Judah, *that is,* Lachish and Azekah, for they *alone* remained as fortified cities among the cities of Judah.

8 ¶ The word which came to Jeremiah from the LORD, after King Zedekiah had made a covenant with all the people who were in Jerusalem to proclaim release to them:

9 that each man should set free his male servant and each man his female servant, a Hebrew man or a Hebrew woman; so that no one should keep them, a Jew his brother, in bondage.

10 And all the officials and all the people obeyed, who had entered into the covenant that each man should set free his male servant and each man his female servant, so that no one should keep them any longer in bondage; they obeyed, and set *them free.*

11 But afterward they turned around and took back the male servants and the female servants, whom they had set free, and brought them into subjection for male servants and for female servants.

12 ¶ Then the word of the LORD came to Jeremiah from the LORD, saying,

13"Thus says the LORD God of Israel, 'I made a covenant with your forefathers in the day that I brought them out of the land of Egypt, from the house of bondage, saying,

14"At the end of seven years each of you shall set free his Hebrew brother, who has been sold to you and has served you six years, you shall send him out free from you; but your forefathers did not obey Me, or incline their ear to Me.

15"Although recently you *had* turned and done what is right in My sight, each man proclaiming release to his neighbor, and you had made a covenant before Me in the house which is called by My name.

16"Yet you turned and profaned My name, and each man took back his male servant and each man his female servant, whom you had set free according to their desire, and you brought them into subjection to be your male servants and female servants.'"

17 ¶"Therefore thus says the LORD, 'You have not obeyed Me in proclaiming release each man to his brother, and each man to his neighbor. Behold, I am proclaiming a release to you,' declares the LORD, 'to the sword, to the pestilence, and to the famine; and I will make you a terror to all the kingdoms of the earth.

18 'And I will give the men who have transgressed My covenant, who have not fulfilled the words of the covenant which they made before Me, *when* they cut the calf in two and passed between its parts—

19 the officials of Judah, and the officials of Jerusalem, the court officers, and the priests, and all the people of the land, who passed between the parts of the calf—

20 and I will give them into the hand of their enemies and into the hand of those who seek their life. And their dead bodies shall be food for the birds of the sky and the beasts of the earth.

21 'And Zedekiah king of Judah and his officials I will give into the hand of their enemies, and into the hand of those who seek their life, and into the hand of the army of the king of Babylon which has gone away from you.

22 'Behold, I am going to command,' declares the LORD, 'and I will bring them back to this city; and they shall fight against it and take it and burn it with fire; and I will make the cities of Judah a desolation without inhabitant.'"

CHAPTER 35

THE word which came to Jeremiah from the LORD in the days of Jehoiakim the son of Josiah, king of Judah, saying,

2 "Go to the house of the Rechabites, and speak to them, and bring them into the house of the LORD, into one of the chambers, and give them wine to drink."

3 Then I took Jaazaniah the son of Jeremiah, son of Habazziniah, and his

brothers, and all his sons, and the whole house of the Rechabites,

4 and I brought them into the house of the LORD, into the chamber of the sons of Hanan the son of Igdaliah, the man of God, which was near the chamber of the officials, which was above the chamber of Maaseiah the son of Shallum, the doorkeeper.

5 Then I set before the men of the house of the Rechabites pitchers full of wine, and cups; and I said to them, "Drink wine!"

6 But they said, "We will not drink wine, for Jonadab the son of Rechab, our father, commanded us, saying, 'You shall not drink wine, you or your sons, forever.

7 'And you shall not build a house, and you shall not sow seed, and you shall not plant a vineyard or own one; but in tents you shall dwell all your days, that you may live many days in the land where you sojourn.'

8"And we have obeyed the voice of Jonadab the son of Rechab, our father, in all that he commanded us, not to drink wine all our days, we, our wives, our sons, or our daughters,

9 nor to build ourselves houses to dwell in; and we do not have vineyard or field or seed.

10"We have only dwelt in tents, and have obeyed, and have done according to all that Jonadab our father commanded us.

11"But it came about, when Nebuchadnezzar king of Babylon came up against the land, that we said, 'Come and let us go to Jerusalem before the army of the Chaldeans and before the army of the Arameans.' So we have dwelt in Jerusalem."

12 ¶ Then the word of the LORD came to Jeremiah, saying,

13"Thus says the LORD of hosts, the God of Israel, 'Go and say to the men of Judah and the inhabitants of Jerusalem, "Will you not receive instruction by listening to My words?" declares the LORD.

14"The words of Jonadab the son of Rechab, which he commanded his sons not to drink wine, are observed. So they do not drink *wine* to this day, for they have obeyed their father's command. But I have spoken to you again and again; yet you have not listened to Me.

15"Also I have sent to you all My servants the prophets, sending *them* again and again, saying: 'Turn now every man from his evil way, and amend your deeds, and do not go after other gods to worship them, then you shall dwell in the land which I have given to you and to your forefathers; but you have not inclined your ear or listened to Me.

16 'Indeed, the sons of Jonadab the son of Rechab have observed the command of their father which he commanded them, but this people has not listened to Me.' " '

17"Therefore thus says the LORD, the God of hosts, the God of Israel, 'Behold, I am bringing on Judah and on all the inhabitants of Jerusalem all the disaster that I have pronounced against them; because I spoke to them but they did not listen, and I have called them but they did not answer.' "

18 ¶ Then Jeremiah said to the house of the Rechabites, "Thus says the LORD of hosts, the God of Israel, 'Because you have obeyed the command of Jonadab your father, kept all his commands, and done according to all that he commanded you;

19 therefore thus says the LORD of hosts, the God of Israel, "Jonadab the son of Rechab shall not lack a man to stand before Me always." ' "

CHAPTER 36

AND it came about in the fourth year of Jehoiakim the son of Josiah, king of Judah, that this word came to Jeremiah from the LORD, saying,

2"Take a scroll and write on it all the words which I have spoken to you concerning Israel, and concerning Judah, and concerning all the nations, from the day I *first* spoke to you, from the days of Josiah, even to this day.

3"Perhaps the house of Judah will hear all the calamity which I plan to bring on them, in order that every man will turn from his evil way; then I will forgive their iniquity and their sin."

4 ¶ Then Jeremiah called Baruch the son of Neriah, and Baruch wrote at the dictation of Jeremiah all the words of the LORD, which He had spoken to him, on a scroll.

5 And Jeremiah commanded Baruch, saying, "I am restricted; I cannot go into the house of the LORD.

6"So you go and read from the scroll which you have written at my dictation the words of the LORD to the people in the LORD's house on a fast day. And also you shall read them to all *the people of* Judah who come from their cities.

7"Perhaps their supplication will come before the LORD, and everyone will turn from his evil way, for great is the anger and the wrath that the LORD has pronounced against this people."

8 And Baruch the son of Neriah did according to all that Jeremiah the prophet commanded him, reading from the book the words of the LORD in the LORD's house.

9 ¶ Now it came about in the fifth year of Jehoiakim the son of Josiah, king of Judah, in the ninth month, that all the people in Jerusalem and all the people who came from the cities of Judah to Jerusalem proclaimed a fast before the LORD.

10 Then Baruch read from the book the words of Jeremiah in the house of the LORD in the chamber of Gemariah the son of Shaphan the scribe, in the upper court, at the entry of the New Gate of the LORD's house, to all the people.

11 ¶ Now when Micaiah the son of Gemariah, the son of Shaphan, had heard all the words of the LORD from the book,

12 he went down to the king's house, into the scribe's chamber. And, behold, all the officials were sitting there— Elishama the scribe, and Delaiah the son of Shemaiah, and Elnathan the son of Achbor, and Gemariah the son of Shaphan, and Zedekiah the son of Hananiah, and all the *other* officials.

13 And Micaiah declared to them all the words that he had heard, when Baruch read from the book to the people.

14 Then all the officials sent Jehudi the son of Nethaniah, the son of Shelemiah, the son of Cushi, to Baruch, saying, "Take in your hand the scroll from which you have read to the people and come." So Baruch the son of Neriah took the scroll in his hand and went to them.

15 And they said to him, "Sit down please, and read it to us." So Baruch read it to them.

16 Now it came about when they had heard all the words, they turned in fear one to another and said to Baruch, "We will surely report all these words to the king."

17 And they asked Baruch, saying, "Tell us please, how did you write all these words? Was it at his dictation?"

18 Then Baruch said to them, "He dictated all these words to me, and I wrote them with ink on the book."

19 Then the officials said to Baruch, "Go, hide yourself, you and Jeremiah, and do not let anyone know where you are."

20 ¶ So they went to the king in the court, but they had deposited the scroll in the chamber of Elishama the scribe, and they reported all the words to the king.

21 Then the king sent Jehudi to get the scroll, and he took it out of the chamber of Elishama the scribe. And Jehudi read it to the king as well as to all the officials who stood beside the king.

22 Now the king was sitting in the winter house in the ninth month, with a fire burning in the brazier before him.

23 And it came about, when Jehudi had read three or four columns, the king cut it with a scribe's knife and threw it into the fire that was in the brazier, until all the scroll was consumed in the fire that was in the brazier.

24 Yet the king and all his servants who heard all these words were not afraid, nor did they rend their garments.

25 Even though Elnathan and Delaiah and Gemariah entreated the king not to burn the scroll, he would not listen to them.

26 And the king commanded Jerahmeel the king's son, Seraiah the son of Azriel, and Shelemiah the son of Abdeel to seize Baruch the scribe and Jeremiah the prophet, but the LORD hid them.

27 ¶ Then the word of the LORD came to Jeremiah after the king had burned the scroll and the words which Baruch had written at the dictation of Jeremiah, saying,

28 "Take again another scroll and write on it all the former words that were on the first scroll which Jehoiakim the king of Judah burned.

29 "And concerning Jehoiakim king of Judah you shall say, 'Thus says the LORD, "You have burned this scroll, saying, 'Why have you written on it that the king of Babylon shall certainly come and destroy this land, and shall make man and beast to cease from it?'"

30 'Therefore thus says the LORD concerning Jehoiakim king of Judah, "He shall have no one to sit on the throne of David, and his dead body shall be cast out to the heat of the day and the frost of the night.

31 "I shall also punish him and his descendants and his servants for their iniquity, and I shall bring on them and the inhabitants of Jerusalem and the men of Judah all the calamity that I have declared to them—but they did not listen." '"

32 Then Jeremiah took another scroll and gave it to Baruch the son of Neraiah, the scribe, and he wrote on it at the dictation of Jeremiah all the words of the book which Jehoiakim king of Judah had burned in the fire; and many similar words were added to them.

CHAPTER 37

NOW Zedekiah the son of Josiah whom Nebuchadnezzar king of Babylon had made king in the land of Judah, reigned as king in place of Coniah the son of Jehoiakim.

2 But neither he nor his servants nor the people of the land listened to the words of the LORD which He spoke through Jeremiah the prophet.

3 ¶ Yet King Zedekiah sent Jehucal the son of Shelemiah, and Zephaniah the son of Maaseiah, the priest, to Jeremiah the prophet, saying, "Please pray to the LORD our God on our behalf."

4 Now Jeremiah was still coming in and going out among the people, for they had not yet put him in the prison.

5 Meanwhile, Pharaoh's army had set out from Egypt; and when the Chaldeans who had been besieging Jerusalem heard the report about

them, they lifted the *siege* from Jerusalem.

6 ¶ Then the word of the LORD came to Jeremiah the prophet, saying,

7"Thus says the LORD God of Israel, 'Thus you are to say to the king of Judah, who sent you to Me to inquire of Me: "Behold, Pharaoh's army which has come out for your assistance is going to return to its own land of Egypt.

8"The Chaldeans will also return and fight against this city, and they will capture it and burn it with fire." '

9"Thus says the LORD, 'Do not deceive yourselves, saying, "The Chaldeans will surely go away from us," for they will not go.

10'For even if you had defeated the entire army of Chaldeans who were fighting against you, and there were *only* wounded men left among them, each man in his tent, they would rise up and burn this city with fire.' "

11 ¶ Now it happened, when the army of the Chaldeans had lifted *the siege* from Jerusalem because of Pharaoh's army,

12 that Jeremiah went out from Jerusalem to go to the land of Benjamin in order to take possession of *some* property there among the people.

13 While he was at the Gate of Benjamin, a captain of the guard whose name was Irijah, the son of Shelemiah the son of Hananiah was there; and he arrested Jeremiah the prophet, saying, "You are going over to the Chaldeans!"

14 But Jeremiah said, "A lie! I am not going over to the Chaldeans"; yet he would not listen to him. So Irijah arrested Jeremiah and brought him to the officials.

15 Then the officials were angry at Jeremiah and beat him, and they put him in jail in the house of Jonathan the scribe, which they had made into the prison.

16 For Jeremiah had come into the dungeon, that is, the vaulted cell; and Jeremiah stayed there many days.

17 ¶ Now King Zedekiah sent and took him *out;* and in his palace the king secretly asked him and said, "Is there a word from the LORD?" And Jeremiah said, "There is!" Then he said, "You will be given into the hand of the king of Babylon!"

18 Moreover Jeremiah said to King Zedekiah, "*In* what *way* have I sinned against you, or against your servants, or against this people, that you have put me in prison?

19"Where then are your prophets who prophesied to you, saying, 'The king of Babylon will not come against you or against this land'?

20"But now, please listen, O my lord the king; please let my petition come before you, and do not make me return to the house of Jonathan the scribe, that I may not die there."

21 Then King Zedekiah gave commandment, and they committed Jeremiah to the court of the guardhouse and gave him a loaf of bread daily from the bakers' street, until all the bread in the city was gone. So Jeremiah remained in the court of the guardhouse.

CHAPTER 38

NOW Shephatiah the son of Mattan, and Gedaliah the son of Pashhur, and Jucal the son of Shelemiah, and Pashhur the son of Malchijah heard the words that Jeremiah was speaking to all the people, saying,

2"Thus says the LORD, 'He who stays in this city will die by the sword and by famine and by pestilence, but he who goes out to the Chaldeans will live and have his *own* life as booty and stay alive.'

3"Thus says the LORD, 'This city will certainly be given into the hand of the army of the king of Babylon, and he will capture it.' "

4 Then the officials said to the king, "Now let this man be put to death, inasmuch as he is discouraging the men of war who are left in this city and all the people, by speaking such words to them; for this man is not seeking the well-being of this people, but rather their harm."

5 So King Zedekiah said, "Behold, he is in your hands; for the king can *do* nothing against you."

6 Then they took Jeremiah and cast him into the cistern *of* Malchijah the king's son, which was in the court of the guardhouse; and they let Jeremiah down with ropes. Now in the cistern there was no water but only mud, and Jeremiah sank into the mud.

7 But Ebed-melech the Ethiopian, a eunuch, while he was in the king's palace, heard that they had put Jeremiah into the cistern. Now the king was sitting in the Gate of Benjamin;

8 and Ebed-melech went out from the king's palace and spoke to the king, saying,

9 "My lord the king, these men have acted wickedly in all that they have done to Jeremiah the prophet whom they have cast into the cistern; and he will die right where he is because of the famine, for there is no more bread in the city."

10 Then the king commanded Ebed-melech the Ethiopian, saying, "Take thirty men from here under your authority, and bring up Jeremiah the prophet from the cistern before he dies."

11 So Ebed-melech took the men under his authority and went into the king's palace to *a place* beneath the storeroom and took from there worn-out clothes and worn-out rags and let them down by ropes into the cistern to Jeremiah.

12 Then Ebed-melech the Ethiopian said to Jeremiah, "Now put these worn-out clothes and rags under your armpits under the ropes"; and Jeremiah did so.

13 So they pulled Jeremiah up with the ropes and lifted him out of the cistern, and Jeremiah stayed in the court of the guardhouse.

14 ¶ Then King Zedekiah sent and had Jeremiah the prophet brought to him at the third entrance that is in the house of the Lord; and the king said to Jeremiah, "I am going to ask you something; do not hide anything from me."

15 Then Jeremiah said to Zedekiah, "If I tell you, will you not certainly put me to death? Besides, if I give you advice, you will not listen to me."

16 But King Zedekiah swore to Jeremiah in secret saying, "As the Lord lives, who made this life for us, surely I will not put you to death nor will I give you over to the hand of these men who are seeking your life."

17 ¶ Then Jeremiah said to Zedekiah, "Thus says the Lord God of hosts, the God of Israel, 'If you will indeed go out to the officers of the king of Babylon, then you will live, this city will not be burned with fire, and you and your household will survive.

18 'But if you will not go out to the officers of the king of Babylon, then this city will be given over to the hand of the Chaldeans; and they will burn it with fire, and you yourself will not escape from their hand.' "

19 Then King Zedekiah said to Jeremiah, "I dread the Jews who have gone over to the Chaldeans, lest they give me over into their hand and they abuse me."

20 But Jeremiah said, "They will not give you over. Please obey the Lord in what I am saying to you, that it may go well with you and you may live.

21 "But if you keep refusing to go out, this is the word which the Lord has shown me:

22 'Then behold, all of the women who have been left in the palace of the king of Judah are going to be brought out to the officers of the king of Babylon; and those women will say,

"Your close friends
Have misled and overpowered you;
While your feet were sunk in the mire,
They turned back."

23 'They will also bring out all your wives and your sons to the Chaldeans, and you yourself will not escape from their hand, but will be seized by the hand of the king of Babylon, and this city will be burned with fire.' "

24 ¶ Then Zedekiah said to Jeremiah, "Let no man know about these words and you will not die.

25 "But if the officials hear that I have talked with you and come to you and say to you, 'Tell us now what you said to the king, and what the king said to you; do not hide *it* from us, and we will not put you to death,'

26 then you are to say to them, 'I was presenting my petition before the king, not to make me return to the house of Jonathan to die there.' "

27 Then all the officials came to Jeremiah and questioned him. So he reported to them in accordance with all these words which the king had commanded; and they ceased speaking with him, since the conversation had not been overheard.

28 So Jeremiah stayed in the court of

the guardhouse until the day that Jerusalem was captured.

CHAPTER 39

Now it came about when Jerusalem was captured in the ninth year of Zedekiah king of Judah, in the tenth month, Nebuchadnezzar king of Babylon and all his army came to Jerusalem and laid siege to it;

2 in the eleventh year of Zedekiah, in the fourth month, in the ninth *day* of the month, the city *wall* was breached.

3 Then all the officials of the king of Babylon came in and sat down at the Middle Gate: Nergal-sar-ezer, Samgarnebu, Sar-sekim the Rab-saris, Nergalsar-ezer *the* Rab-mag, and all the rest of the officials of the king of Babylon.

4 And it came about, when Zedekiah the king of Judah and all the men of war saw them, that they fled and went out of the city at night by way of the king's garden through the gate between the two walls; and he went out toward the [11]Arabah.

5 But the army of the Chaldeans pursued them and overtook Zedekiah in the plains of Jericho; and they seized him and brought him up to Nebuchadnezzar king of Babylon at Riblah in the land of Hamath, and he passed sentence on him.

6 Then the king of Babylon slew the sons of Zedekiah before his eyes at Riblah; the king of Babylon also slew all the nobles of Judah.

7 He then blinded Zedekiah's eyes and bound him in fetters of bronze to bring him to Babylon.

8 The Chaldeans also burned with fire the king's palace and the houses of the people, and they broke down the walls of Jerusalem.

9 And as for the rest of the people who were left in the city, the deserters who had gone over to him and the rest of the people who remained, Nebuzaradan the captain of the bodyguard carried *them* into exile in Babylon.

10 But some of the poorest people who had nothing, Nebuzaradan the captain of the bodyguard left behind in the land of Judah, and gave them vineyards and fields at that time.

11 ¶ Now Nebuchadnezzar king of

[11] I.e., Jordan valley

Babylon gave orders about Jeremiah through Nebuzaradan the captain of the bodyguard, saying,

12"Take him and look after him, and do nothing harmful to him; but rather deal with him just as he tells you."

13 So Nebuzaradan the captain of the bodyguard sent *word*, along with Nebushazban the Rab-saris, and Nergal-sar-ezer the Rab-mag, and all the leading officers of the king of Babylon;

14 they even sent and took Jeremiah out of the court of the guardhouse and entrusted him to Gedaliah, the son of Ahikam, the son of Shaphan, to take him home. So he stayed among the people.

15 ¶ Now the word of the LORD had come to Jeremiah while he was confined in the court of the guardhouse, saying,

16"Go and speak to Ebed-melech the Ethiopian, saying, 'Thus says the LORD of hosts, the God of Israel, "Behold, I am about to bring My words on this city for disaster and not for prosperity; and they will take place before you on that day.

17"But I will deliver you on that day," declares the LORD, "and you shall not be given into the hand of the men whom you dread.

18"For I will certainly rescue you, and you will not fall by the sword; but you will have your *own* life as booty, because you have trusted in Me," declares the LORD.' "

CHAPTER 40

THE word which came to Jeremiah from the LORD after Nebuzaradan captain of the bodyguard had released him from Ramah, when he had taken him bound in chains, among all the exiles of Jerusalem and Judah, who were being exiled to Babylon.

2 Now the captain of the bodyguard had taken Jeremiah and said to him, "The LORD your God promised this calamity against this place;

3 and the LORD has brought *it* on and done just as He promised. Because you *people* sinned against the LORD and did not listen to His voice, therefore this thing has happened to you.

4"But now, behold, I am freeing you today from the chains which are on your hands. If you would prefer to come with me to Babylon, come *along*, and I will look after you; but if you would prefer not to come with me to Babylon, never mind. Look, the whole land is before you; go wherever it seems good and right for you to go."

5 As Jeremiah was still not going back, *he said*, "Go on back then to Gedaliah the son of Ahikam, the son of Shaphan, whom the king of Babylon has appointed over the cities of Judah, and stay with him among the people; or else go anywhere it seems right for you to go." So the captain of the bodyguard gave him a ration and a gift and let him go.

6 Then Jeremiah went to Mizpah to Gedaliah the son of Ahikam and stayed with him among the people who were left in the land.

7 ¶ Now all the commanders of the forces that were in the field, they and their men, heard that the king of Babylon had appointed Gedaliah the son of Ahikam over the land and that he had put him in charge of the men, women and children, those of the poorest of the land who had not been exiled to Babylon.

8 So they came to Gedaliah at Mizpah, along with Ishmael the son of Nethaniah, and Johanan and Jonathan the sons of Kareah, and Seraiah the son of Tanhumeth, and the sons of Ephai the Netophathite, and Jezaniah the son of the Maacathite, *both* they and their men.

9 Then Gedaliah the son of Ahikam, the son of Shaphan, swore to them and to their men, saying, "Do not be afraid of serving the Chaldeans; stay in the land and serve the king of Babylon, that it may go well with you.

10"Now as for me, behold, I am going to stay at Mizpah to stand *for you* before the Chaldeans who come to us; but as for you, gather in wine and summer fruit and oil, and put *them* in your *storage* vessels, and live in your cities that you have taken over."

11 Likewise also all the Jews who were in Moab and among the sons of Ammon and in Edom, and who were in all the *other* countries, heard that the king of Babylon had left a remnant for Judah and that he had appointed over them Gedaliah the son of Ahikam, the son of Shaphan.

12 Then all the Jews returned from all the places to which they had been driven away and came to the land of Judah, to Gedaliah at Mizpah, and gathered in wine and summer fruit in great abundance.

13 ¶ Now Johanan the son of Kareah and all the commanders of the forces that were in the field came to Gedaliah at Mizpah,

14 and said to him, "Are you well aware that Baalis the king of the sons of Ammon has sent Ishmael the son of Nethaniah to take your life?" But Gedaliah the son of Ahikam did not believe them.

15 Then Johanan the son of Kareah spoke secretly to Gedaliah in Mizpah, saying, "Let me go and kill Ishmael the son of Nethaniah, and not a man will know! Why should he take your life, so that all the Jews who are gathered to you should be scattered and the remnant of Judah perish?"

16 But Gedaliah the son of Ahikam said to Johanan the son of Kareah, "Do not do this thing, for you are telling a lie about Ishmael."

CHAPTER 41

Now it came about in the seventh month that Ishmael the son of Nethaniah, the son of Elishama, of the royal family and *one* of the chief officers of the king, along with ten men, came to Mizpah to Gedaliah the son of Ahikam. While they were eating bread together there in Mizpah,

2 Ishmael the son of Nethaniah and the ten men who were with him arose and struck down Gedaliah the son of Ahikam, the son of Shaphan, with the sword and put to death the one whom the king of Babylon had appointed over the land.

3 Ishmael also struck down all the Jews who were with him, *that is* with Gedaliah at Mizpah, and the Chaldeans who were found there, the men of war.

4 ¶ Now it happened on the next day after the killing of Gedaliah, when no one knew about *it*,

5 that eighty men came from Shechem, from Shiloh, and from Samaria with their beards shaved off and their clothes torn and their bodies gashed, having grain offerings and incense in

their hands to bring to the house of the LORD.

6 Then Ishmael the son of Nethaniah went out from Mizpah to meet them, weeping as he went; and it came about as he met them that he said to them, "Come to Gedaliah the son of Ahikam!"

7 Yet it turned out that as soon as they came inside the city, Ishmael the son of Nethaniah and the men that were with him slaughtered them, *and cast them* into the cistern.

8 But ten men who were found among them said to Ishmael, "Do not put us to death; for we have stores of wheat, barley, oil and honey hidden in the field." So he refrained and did not put them to death along with their companions.

9 Now as for the cistern where Ishmael had cast all the corpses of the men whom he had struck down because of Gedaliah, it was the one that King Asa had made on account of Baasha, king of Israel; Ishmael the son of Nethaniah filled it with the slain.

10 Then Ishmael took captive all the remnant of the people who were in Mizpah, the king's daughters and all the people who were left in Mizpah, whom Nebuzaradan the captain of the bodyguard had put under the charge of Gedaliah the son of Ahikam; thus Ishmael the son of Nethaniah took them captive and proceeded to cross over to the sons of Ammon.

11 ¶ But Johanan the son of Kareah and all the commanders of the forces that were with him heard of all the evil that Ishmael the son of Nethaniah had done.

12 So they took all the men and went to fight with Ishmael the son of Nethaniah and they found him by the great pool that is in Gibeon.

13 Now it came about, as soon as all the people who were with Ishmael saw Johanan the son of Kareah and the commanders of the forces that were with him, they were glad.

14 So all the people whom Ishmael had taken captive from Mizpah turned around and came back, and went to Johanan the son of Kareah.

15 But Ishmael the son of Nethaniah escaped from Johanan with eight men and went to the sons of Ammon.

16 Then Johanan the son of Kareah and all the commanders of the forces that were with him took from Mizpah all the remnant of the people whom he had recovered from Ishmael the son of Nethaniah, after he had struck down Gedaliah the son of Ahikam, *that is,* the men who were soldiers, *the* women, *the* children, and *the* eunuchs, whom he had brought back from Gibeon.

17 And they went and stayed in Geruth Chimham, which is beside Bethlehem, in order to proceed into Egypt

18 because of the Chaldeans; for they were afraid of them, since Ishmael the son of Nethaniah had struck down Gedaliah the son of Ahikam, whom the king of Babylon had appointed over the land.

CHAPTER 42

THEN all the commanders of the forces, Johanan the son of Kareah, Jezaniah the son of Hoshaiah, and all the people both small and great approached

2 and said to Jeremiah the prophet, "Please let our petition come before you, and pray for us to the LORD your God, *that is* for all this remnant; because we are left *but* a few out of many, as your own eyes *now* see us,

3 that the LORD your God may tell us the way in which we should walk and the thing that we should do."

4 Then Jeremiah the prophet said to them, "I have heard *you.* Behold, I am going to pray to the LORD your God in accordance with your words; and it will come about that the whole message which the LORD will answer you I will tell you. I will not keep back a word from you."

5 Then they said to Jeremiah, "May the LORD be a true and faithful witness against us, if we do not act in accordance with the whole message with which the LORD your God will send you to us.

6 "Whether *it* is pleasant or unpleasant, we will listen to the voice of the LORD our God to whom we are sending you, in order that it may go well with us when we listen to the voice of the LORD our God."

7 ¶ Now it came about at the end of ten days that the word of the LORD came to Jeremiah.

8 Then he called for Johanan the son of Kareah, and all the commanders of the forces that were with him, and for all the people both small and great,

9 and said to them, "Thus says the LORD the God of Israel, to whom you sent me to present your petition before Him:

10 'If you will indeed stay in this land, then I will build you up and not tear you down, and I will plant you and not uproot you; for I shall relent concerning the calamity that I have inflicted on you.

11 'Do not be afraid of the king of Babylon, whom you are *now* fearing; do not be afraid of him,' declares the LORD, 'for I am with you to save you and deliver you from his hand.

12 'I will also show you compassion, so that he will have compassion on you and restore you to your own soil.

13 'But if you are going to say, "We will not stay in this land," so as not to listen to the voice of the LORD your God,

14 saying, "No, but we will go to the land of Egypt, where we shall not see war or hear the sound of a trumpet or hunger for bread, and we will stay there";

15 then in that case listen to the word of the LORD, O remnant of Judah. Thus says the LORD of hosts, the God of Israel, "If you really set your mind to enter Egypt, and go in to reside there,

16 then it will come about that the sword, which you are afraid of will overtake you there in the land of Egypt; and the famine, about which you are anxious, will follow closely after you there *in* Egypt; and you will die there.

17 "So all the men who set their mind to go to Egypt to reside there will die by the sword, by famine, and by pestilence; and they will have no survivors or refugees from the calamity that I am going to bring on them." ' "

18 ¶ For thus says the LORD of hosts, the God of Israel, "As My anger and wrath have been poured out on the inhabitants of Jerusalem, so My wrath will be poured out on you when you enter Egypt. And you will become a curse, an object of horror, an imprecation, and a reproach; and you will see this place no more."

19 The LORD has spoken to you, O remnant of Judah, "Do not go into Egypt!" You should clearly understand that today I have testified against you.

20 For you have *only* deceived yourselves; for it is you who sent me to the LORD your God, saying, "Pray for us to the LORD our God; and whatever the LORD our God says, tell us so, and we will do it."

21 So, I have told you today, but you have not obeyed the LORD your God, even in whatever He has sent me to *tell* you.

22 Therefore you should now clearly understand that you will die by the sword, by famine, and by pestilence, in the place where you wish to go to reside.

CHAPTER 43

BUT it came about, as soon as Jeremiah whom the LORD their God had sent, had finished telling all the people all the words of the LORD their God— that is, all these words—

2 that Azariah the son of Hoshaiah, and Johanan the son of Kareah, and all the arrogant men said to Jeremiah, "You are telling a lie! The LORD our God has not sent you to say, 'You are not to enter Egypt to reside there';

3 but Baruch the son of Neriah is inciting you against us to give us over into the hand of the Chaldeans, so they may put us to death or exile us to Babylon."

4 So Johanan the son of Kareah and all the commanders of the forces, and all the people, did not obey the voice of the LORD, so as to stay in the land of Judah.

5 But Johanan the son of Kareah and all the commanders of the forces took the entire remnant of Judah who had returned from all the nations to which they had been driven away, in order to reside in the land of Judah—

6 the men, the women, the children, the king's daughters and every person that Nebuzaradan the captain of the bodyguard had left with Gedaliah the son of Ahikam and grandson of Shaphan, together with Jeremiah the

prophet and Baruch the son of Neriah—

7 and they entered the land of Egypt (for they did not obey the voice of the LORD) and went in as far as Tahpanhes.

8 ¶ Then the word of the LORD came to Jeremiah in Tahpanhes, saying,

9"Take *some* large stones in your hands and hide them in the mortar in the brick *terrace* which is at the entrance of Pharaoh's palace in Tahpanhes, in the sight of some *of the* Jews;

10 and say to them, 'Thus says the LORD of hosts, the God of Israel, "Behold, I am going to send and get Nebuchadnezzar the king of Babylon, My servant, and I am going to set his throne *right* over these stones that I have hidden; and he will spread his canopy over them.

11"He will also come and strike the land of Egypt; those who are *meant* for death *will be given over* to death, and those for captivity to captivity, and those for the sword to the sword.

12"And I shall set fire to the temples of the gods of Egypt, and he will burn them and take them captive. So he will wrap himself with the land of Egypt as a shepherd wraps himself with his garment, and he will depart from there safely.

13"He will also shatter the obelisks of Heliopolis, which is in the land of Egypt; and the temples of the gods of Egypt he will burn with fire." ' "

CHAPTER 44

THE word that came to Jeremiah for all the Jews living in the land of Egypt, those who were living in Migdol, Tahpanhes, Memphis, and the land of Pathros, saying,

2"Thus says the LORD of hosts, the God of Israel, 'You yourselves have seen all the calamity that I have brought on Jerusalem and all the cities of Judah; and behold, this day they are in ruins and no one lives in them,

3 because of their wickedness which they committed so as to provoke Me to anger by continuing to burn sacrifices *and* to serve other gods whom they had not known, *neither* they, you, nor your fathers.

4 'Yet I sent you all My servants the prophets, again and again, saying, "Oh, do not do this abominable thing which I hate."

5 'But they did not listen or incline their ears to turn from their wickedness, so as not to burn sacrifices to other gods.

6 'Therefore My wrath and My anger were poured out and burned in the cities of Judah and in the streets of Jerusalem, so they have become a ruin and a desolation as it is this day.

7 'Now then thus says the LORD God of hosts, the God of Israel, "Why are you doing great harm to yourselves, so as to cut off from you man and woman, child and infant, from among Judah, leaving yourselves without remnant,

8 provoking Me to anger with the works of your hands, burning sacrifices to other gods in the land of Egypt, where you are entering to reside, so that you might be cut off and become a curse and a reproach among all the nations of the earth?

9"Have you forgotten the wickedness of your fathers, the wickedness of the kings of Judah, and the wickedness of their wives, your own wickedness, and the wickedness of your wives, which they committed in the land of Judah and in the streets of Jerusalem?

10"But they have not become contrite even to this day, nor have they feared nor walked in My law or My statutes, which I have set before you and before your fathers." '

11 ¶ "Therefore thus says the LORD of hosts, the God of Israel, 'Behold, I am going to set My face against you for woe, even to cut off all Judah.

12 'And I will take away the remnant of Judah who have set their mind on entering the land of Egypt to reside there, and they will all meet their end in the land of Egypt; they will fall by the sword *and* meet their end by famine. Both small and great will die by the sword and famine; and they will become a curse, an object of horror, an imprecation and a reproach.

13 'And I will punish those who live in the land of Egypt, as I have punished Jerusalem, with the sword, with famine, and with pestilence.

14 'So there will be no refugees or survivors for the remnant of Judah

who have entered the land of Egypt to reside there and then to return to the land of Judah, to which they are longing to return and live; for none will return except *a few* refugees.' "

15 ¶ Then all the men who were aware that their wives were burning sacrifices to other gods, along with all the women who were standing by, *as* a large assembly, including all the people who were living in Pathros in the land of Egypt, responded to Jeremiah, saying,

16"As for the message that you have spoken to us in the name of the LORD, we are not going to listen to you!

17"But rather we will certainly carry out every word that has proceeded from our mouths, by burning sacrifices to the queen of heaven and pouring out libations to her, just as we ourselves, our forefathers, our kings and our princes did in the cities of Judah and in the streets of Jerusalem; for *then* we had plenty of food, and were well off, and saw no misfortune.

18"But since we stopped burning sacrifices to the queen of heaven and pouring out libations to her, we have lacked everything and have met our end by the sword and by famine."

19"And," *said the women,* "when we were burning sacrifices to the queen of heaven, and were pouring out libations to her, was it without our husbands that we made for her *sacrificial* cakes in her image and poured out libations to her?"

20 ¶ Then Jeremiah said to all the people, to the men and women—even to all the people who were giving him *such* an answer—saying,

21"As for the smoking sacrifices that you burned in the cities of Judah and in the streets of Jerusalem, you and your forefathers, your kings and your princes, and the people of the land, did not the LORD remember them, and did not *all this* come into His mind?

22"So the LORD was no longer able to endure *it,* because of the evil of your deeds, because of the abominations which you have committed; thus your land has become a ruin, an object of horror and a curse, without an inhabitant, as *it is* this day.

23"Because you have burned sacrifices and have sinned against the LORD and not obeyed the voice of the LORD

or walked in His law, His statutes or His testimonies, therefore this calamity has befallen you, as *it has* this day."

24 Then Jeremiah said to all the people, including all the women, "Hear the word of the LORD, all Judah who are in the land of Egypt,

25 thus says the LORD of hosts, the God of Israel, as follows: 'As for you and your wives, you have spoken with your mouths and fulfilled *it* with your hands, saying, "We will certainly perform our vows that we have vowed, to burn sacrifices to the queen of heaven and pour out libations to her." Go ahead and confirm your vows, and certainly perform your vows!'

26"Nevertheless hear the word of the LORD, all Judah who are living in the land of Egypt, 'Behold, I have sworn by My great name,' says the LORD, 'never shall My name be invoked again by the mouth of any man of Judah in all the land of Egypt, saying, "As the Lord GOD lives."

27 'Behold, I am watching over them for harm and not for good, and all the men of Judah who are in the land of Egypt will meet their end by the sword and by famine until they are completely gone.

28 'And those who escape the sword will return out of the land of Egypt to the land of Judah few in number. Then all the remnant of Judah who have gone to the land of Egypt to reside there will know whose word will stand, Mine or theirs.

29 'And this will be the sign to you,' declares the LORD, 'that I am going to punish you in this place, so that you may know that My words will surely stand against you for harm.'

30"Thus says the LORD, 'Behold, I am going to give over Pharaoh Hophra king of Egypt to the hand of his enemies, to the hand of those who seek his life, just as I gave over Zedekiah king of Judah to the hand of Nebuchadnezzar king of Babylon, *who was* his enemy and was seeking his life.' "

CHAPTER 45

*T*HIS is the message which Jeremiah the prophet spoke to Baruch the son of Neriah, when he had written down these words in a book at Jeremiah's dictation, in the fourth year of Jehoiakim the son of Josiah, king of Judah, saying:

2 "Thus says the LORD the God of Israel to you, O Baruch:

3 'You said, "Ah, woe is me! For the LORD has added sorrow to my pain; I am weary with my groaning and have found no rest." '

4 "Thus you are to say to him, 'Thus says the LORD, "Behold, what I have built I am about to tear down, and what I have planted I am about to uproot, that is, the whole land."

5 'But you, are you seeking great things for yourself? Do not seek *them;* for behold, I am going to bring disaster on all flesh,' declares the LORD, 'but I will give your life to you as booty in all the places where you may go.' "

CHAPTER 46

THAT which came as the word of the LORD to Jeremiah the prophet concerning the nations.

2 To Egypt, concerning the army of Pharaoh Neco king of Egypt, which was by the Euphrates River at Carchemish, which Nebuchadnezzar king of Babylon defeated in the fourth year of Jehoiakim the son of Josiah, king of Judah:

3 "Line up the shield and buckler,
    And draw near for the battle!
4 "Harness the horses,
    And mount the steeds,
    And take your stand with helmets *on!*
    Polish the spears,
    Put on the scale-armor!
5 "Why have I seen *it?*
    They are terrified,
    They are drawing back,
    And their mighty men are defeated
    And have taken refuge in flight,
    Without facing back;
    Terror is on every side!"
    Declares the LORD.
6 Let not the swift man flee,
    Nor the mighty man escape;
    In the north beside the river Euphrates
    They have stumbled and fallen.
7 Who is this that rises like the Nile,
    Like the rivers whose waters surge about?
8 Egypt rises like the Nile,

Even like the rivers whose waters surge about;
    And He has said, "I will rise and cover *that* land;
    I will surely destroy the city and its inhabitants."
9 Go up, you horses, and drive madly, you chariots,
    That the mighty men may march forward:
    Ethiopia and Put, that handle the shield,
    And the Lydians, that handle *and* bend the bow.
10 For that day belongs to the Lord GOD of hosts,
    A day of vengeance, so as to avenge Himself on His foes;
    And the sword will devour and be satiated
    And drink its fill of their blood;
    For there will be a slaughter for the Lord GOD of hosts,
    In the land of the north by the river Euphrates.
11 Go up to Gilead and obtain balm,
    O virgin daughter of Egypt!
    In vain have you multiplied remedies;
    There is no healing for you.
12 The nations have heard of your shame,
    And the earth is full of your cry *of distress;*
    For one warrior has stumbled over another,
    And both of them have fallen down together.

13 ¶ *This is* the message which the LORD spoke to Jeremiah the prophet about the coming of Nebuchadnezzar king of Babylon to smite the land of Egypt:

14 "Declare in Egypt and proclaim in Migdol,
    Proclaim also in Memphis and Tahpanhes;
    Say, 'Take your stand and get yourself ready,
    For the sword has devoured those around you.'
15 "Why have your mighty ones become prostrate?
    They do not stand because the LORD has thrust them down.
16 "They have repeatedly stumbled;
    Indeed, they have fallen one against another.

Then they said, 'Get up! And let
us go back
To our own people and our native
land
Away from the sword of the oppressor.'
17"They cried there, 'Pharaoh king of
Egypt *is but* a big noise;
He has let the appointed time pass
by!'
18"As I live," declares the King
Whose name is the LORD of hosts,
"Surely one shall come *who looms
up* like Tabor among the mountains,
Or like Carmel by the sea.
19"Make your baggage ready for exile,
O daughter dwelling in Egypt,
For Memphis will become a desolation;
It will even be burned down *and*
bereft of inhabitants.
20"Egypt is a pretty heifer,
But a horsefly is coming from the
north—it is coming!
21"Also her mercenaries in her midst
Are like fattened calves,
For even they too have turned
back *and* have fled away together;
They did not stand *their ground.*
For the day of their calamity has
come upon them,
The time of their punishment.
22"Its sound moves along like a serpent;
For they move on like an army
And come to her as woodcutters
with axes.
23"They have cut down her forest,"
declares the LORD;
"Surely it will no *more* be found,
Even though they are *now* more
numerous than locusts
And are without number.
24"The daughter of Egypt has been
put to shame,
Given over to the power of the
people of the north."
25 The LORD of hosts, the God of
Israel, says, "Behold, I am going to
punish Amon of Thebes, and Pharaoh,
and Egypt along with her gods and her
kings, even Pharaoh and those who
trust in him.
26"And I shall give them over to the
power of those who are seeking their

lives, even into the hand of Nebuchadnezzar king of Babylon and into the
hand of his officers. Afterwards, however, it will be inhabited as in the days
of old," declares the LORD.
27 ¶"But as for you, O Jacob My
servant, do not fear,
Nor be dismayed, O Israel!
For, see, I am going to save you
from afar,
And your descendants from the
land of their captivity;
And Jacob shall return and be
undisturbed
And secure, with no one making
him tremble.
28"O Jacob My servant, do not fear,"
declares the LORD,
"For I am with you.
For I shall make a full end of all
the nations
Where I have driven you,
Yet I shall not make a full end of
you;
But I shall correct you properly
And by no means leave you un-
punished."

CHAPTER 47

THAT which came as the word of the
LORD to Jeremiah the prophet concerning the Philistines, before Pharaoh
conquered Gaza.
2 Thus says the LORD:
"Behold, waters are going to rise
from the north
And become an overflowing torrent,
And overflow the land and all its
fulness,
The city and those who live in it;
And the men will cry out,
And every inhabitant of the land
will wail.
3"Because of the noise of the galloping hoofs of his stallions,
The tumult of his chariots, *and*
the rumbling of his wheels,
The fathers have not turned back
for *their* children,
Because of the limpness of *their*
hands,
4 On account of the day that is
coming
To destroy all the Philistines,
To cut off from Tyre and Sidon
Every ally that is left;

For the Lord is going to destroy
the Philistines,
The remnant of the coastland of
Caphtor.
5"Baldness has come upon Gaza;
Ashkelon has been ruined.
O remnant of their valley,
How long will you gash yourself?
6"Ah, sword of the Lord,
How long will you not be quiet?
Withdraw into your sheath;
Be at rest and stay still.
7"How can it be quiet,
When the Lord has given it an
order?
Against Ashkelon and against the
seacoast—
There He has assigned it."

CHAPTER 48

Concerning Moab.
Thus says the Lord of hosts, the
God of Israel,
"Woe to Nebo, for it has been destroyed;
Kiriathaim has been put to shame,
it has been captured;
The lofty stronghold has been put
to shame and shattered.
2"There is praise for Moab no
longer;
In Heshbon they have devised
calamity against her:
'Come and let us cut her off from
being a nation!'
You too, [12]Madmen, will be silenced;
The sword will follow after you.
3"The sound of an outcry from
Horonaim,
'Devastation and great destruction!'
4"Moab is broken,
Her little ones have sounded out a
cry of distress.
5"For by the ascent of Luhith
They will ascend with continual
weeping;
For at the descent of Horonaim
They have heard the anguished
cry of destruction.
6"Flee, save your lives,
That you may be like a juniper in
the wilderness.
7"For because of your trust in your
own achievements and treasures,

Even you yourself will be cap-
tured;
And Chemosh will go off into exile
Together with his priests and his
princes.
8"And a destroyer will come to ev-
ery city,
So that no city will escape;
The valley also will be ruined,
And the plateau will be destroyed,
As the Lord has said.
9"Give wings to Moab,
For she will flee away;
And her cities will become a deso-
lation,
Without inhabitants in them.
10"Cursed be the one who does the
Lord's work negligently,
And cursed be the one who re-
strains his sword from blood.

11 ¶"Moab has been at ease since his
youth;
He has also been undisturbed on
his lees,
Neither has he been emptied from
vessel to vessel,
Nor has he gone into exile.
Therefore he retains his flavor,
And his aroma has not changed.
12"Therefore behold, the days are
coming," declares the Lord, "when I
shall send to him those who tip vessels, and they will tip him over, and
they will empty his vessels and shatter
his jars.
13"And Moab will be ashamed of
Chemosh, as the house of Israel was
ashamed of Bethel, their confidence.
14"How can you say, 'We are mighty
warriors,
And men valiant for battle'?
15"Moab has been destroyed, and
men have gone up to his cities;
His choicest young men have also
gone down to the slaughter,"
Declares the King, whose name is
the Lord of hosts.
16"The disaster of Moab will soon
come,
And his calamity has swiftly hastened.
17"Mourn for him, all you who live
around him,
Even all of you who know his
name;
Say, 'How has the mighty scepter
been broken,
A staff of splendor!'

12 I.e., a city of Moab

18"Come down from your glory
    And sit on the parched ground,
    O daughter dwelling in Dibon,
    For the destroyer of Moab has
        come up against you,
    He has ruined your strongholds.
19"Stand by the road and keep
        watch,
    O inhabitant of Aroer;
    Ask him who flees and her who
        escapes
    And say, 'What has happened?'
20"Moab has been put to shame, for
        it has been shattered.
    Wail and cry out;
    Declare by the Arnon
    That Moab has been destroyed.
21"Judgment has also come upon the
plain, upon Holon, Jahzah, and against
Mephaath,
22 against Dibon, Nebo, and Beth-
diblathaim,
23 against Kiriathaim, Beth-gamul,
and Beth-meon,
24 against Kerioth, Bozrah, and all
the cities of the land of Moab, far and
near.
25"The horn of Moab has been cut
off, and his arm broken," declares the
LORD.
26"Make him drunk, for he has become arrogant toward the LORD; so
Moab will wallow in his vomit, and he
also will become a laughingstock.
27"Now was not Israel a laughingstock to you? Or was he caught among
thieves? For each time you speak
about him you shake *your head in
scorn.*
28"Leave the cities and dwell among
        the crags,
    O inhabitants of Moab,
    And be like a dove that nests
    Beyond the mouth of the chasm.
29"We have heard of the pride of
        Moab—he *is* very proud—
    Of his haughtiness, his pride, his
        arrogance and his self-exalta-
        tion.
30"I know his fury," declares the
        LORD,
    "But it is futile;
    His idle boasts have accomplished
        nothing.
31"Therefore I shall wail for Moab,
    Even for all Moab shall I cry out;
    I will moan for the men of Kir-
        heres.

32"More than the weeping for Jazer
    I shall weep for you, O vine of
        Sibmah!
    Your tendrils stretched across the
        sea,
    They reached to the sea of Jazer;
    Upon your summer fruits and
        your grape harvest
    The destroyer has fallen.
33"So gladness and joy are taken
        away
    From the fruitful field, even from
        the land of Moab.
    And I have made the wine to
        cease from the wine presses;
    No one will tread *them* with
        shouting,
    The shouting will not be shouts *of
    joy.*
34"From the outcry at Heshbon even
to Elealeh, even to Jahaz they have
raised their voice, from Zoar even to
Horonaim *and to* Eglath-shelishiyah;
for even the waters of Nimrim will
become desolate.
35"And I shall make an end of
Moab," declares the LORD, "the one
who offers *sacrifice* on the high place
and the one who burns incense to his
gods.
36 ¶"Therefore My heart wails for
Moab like flutes; My heart also wails
like flutes for the men of Kir-heres.
Therefore they have lost the abundance it produced.
37"For every head is bald and every
beard cut short; there are gashes on all
the hands and sackcloth on the loins.
38"On all the housetops of Moab and
in its streets there is lamentation
everywhere; for I have broken Moab
like an undesirable vessel," declares
the LORD.
39"How shattered it is! *How* they
have wailed! How Moab has turned his
back—he is ashamed! So Moab will
become a laughingstock and an object
of terror to all around him."
40 For thus says the LORD,
    "Behold, one will fly swiftly like an
        eagle,
    And spread out his wings against
        Moab.
41"Kerioth has been captured
    And the strongholds have been
        seized,
    So the hearts of the mighty men
        of Moab in that day

Will be like the heart of a woman
in labor.

42"And Moab will be destroyed from
being a people
Because he has become arrogant
toward the LORD.

43"Terror, pit, and snare are *coming*
upon you,
O inhabitant of Moab," declares
the LORD.

44"The one who flees from the terror
Will fall into the pit,
And the one who climbs up out of
the pit
Will be caught in the snare;
For I shall bring upon her, *even*
upon Moab,
The year of their punishment,"
declares the LORD.

45 ¶"In the shadow of Heshbon
The fugitives stand without
strength;
For a fire has gone forth from
Heshbon,
And a flame from the midst of
Sihon,
And it has devoured the forehead
of Moab
And the scalps of the riotous rev-
elers.

46"Woe to you, Moab!
The people of Chemosh have perished;
For your sons have been taken
away captive,
And your daughters into captivity.

47"Yet I will restore the fortunes of
Moab
In the latter days," declares the
LORD.
Thus far the judgment on Moab.

CHAPTER 49

CONCERNING the sons of Ammon.
Thus says the LORD:
"Does Israel have no sons?
Or has he no heirs?
Why then has Malcam taken pos-
session of Gad
And his people settled in its cities?

2"Therefore behold, the days are
coming," declares the LORD,
"That I shall cause a trumpet blast
of war to be heard
Against Rabbah of the sons of
Ammon;

And it will become a desolate
heap,
And her towns will be set on fire.
Then Israel will take possession of
his possessors,"
Says the LORD.

3"Wail, O Heshbon, for Ai has been
destroyed!
Cry out, O daughters of Rabbah,
Gird yourselves with sackcloth
and lament,
And rush back and forth inside
the walls;
For Malcam will go into exile
Together with his priests and his
princes.

4"How boastful you are about the
valleys!
Your valley is flowing *away*,
O backsliding daughter
Who trusts in her treasures, *say-
ing*,
'Who will come against me?'

5"Behold, I am going to bring terror
upon you,"
Declares the Lord GOD of hosts,
"From all *directions* around you;
And each of you will be driven out
headlong,
With no one to gather the fugi-
tives together.

6"But afterward I will restore
The fortunes of the sons of Am-
mon,"
Declares the LORD.

7 ¶ Concerning Edom.
Thus says the LORD of hosts,
"Is there no longer any wisdom in
Teman?
Has good counsel been lost to the
prudent?
Has their wisdom decayed?

8"Flee away, turn back, dwell in the
depths,
O inhabitants of Dedan,
For I will bring the disaster of
Esau upon him
At the time I punish him.

9"If grape gatherers came to you,
Would they not leave gleanings?
If thieves *came* by night,
They would destroy *only* until
they had enough.

10"But I have stripped Esau bare,
I have uncovered his hiding
places
So that he will not be able to
conceal himself;

His offspring has been destroyed
along with his relatives
And his neighbors, and he is no
more.
11"Leave your orphans behind, I will
keep *them* alive;
And let your widows trust in Me."
12 For thus says the LORD, "Behold,
those who were not sentenced to
drink the cup will certainly drink *it*,
and are you the one who will be completely acquitted? You will not be
acquitted, but you will certainly drink
it.
13"For I have sworn by Myself,"
declares the LORD, "that Bozrah will
become an object of horror, a reproach, a ruin and a curse; and all its
cities will become perpetual ruins."
14 ¶ I have heard a message from
the LORD,
And an envoy is sent among the
nations, *saying*,
"Gather yourselves together and
come against her,
And rise up for battle!"
15"For behold, I have made you small
among the nations,
Despised among men.
16"As for the terror of you,
The arrogance of your heart has
deceived you,
O you who live in the clefts of the
rock,
Who occupy the height of the hill.
Though you make your nest as
high as an eagle's,
I will bring you down from there,"
declares the LORD.
17"And Edom will become an object
of horror; everyone who passes by it
will be horrified and will hiss at all its
wounds.
18"Like the overthrow of Sodom and
Gomorrah with its neighbors," says
the LORD, "no one will live there, nor
will a son of man reside in it.
19"Behold, one will come up like a
lion from the thickets of the Jordan
against a perennially watered pasture;
for in an instant I shall make him run
away from it, and whoever is chosen I
shall appoint over it. For who is like
Me, and who will summon Me *into
court*? And who then is the shepherd
who can stand against Me?"
20 ¶ Therefore hear the plan of the
LORD which He has planned against
Edom, and His purposes which He has

purposed against the inhabitants of
Teman: surely they will drag them off,
even the little ones of the flock; surely
He will make their pasture desolate
because of them.
21 The earth has quaked at the noise
of their downfall. There is an outcry!
The noise of it has been heard at the
Red Sea.
22 Behold, He will mount up and
swoop like an eagle, and spread out
His wings against Bozrah; and the
hearts of the mighty men of Edom in
that day will be like the heart of a
woman in labor.
23 ¶ Concerning Damascus.
"Hamath and Arpad are put to
shame,
For they have heard bad news;
They are disheartened.
There is anxiety by the sea,
It cannot be calmed.
24"Damascus has become helpless;
She has turned away to flee,
And panic has gripped her;
Distress and pangs have taken
hold of her
Like a woman in childbirth.
25"How the city of praise has not
been deserted,
The town of My joy!
26"Therefore, her young men will fall
in her streets,
And all the men of war will be
silenced in that day," declares
the LORD of hosts.
27"And I shall set fire to the wall of
Damascus,
And it will devour the fortified
towers of Ben-hadad."
28 ¶ Concerning Kedar and the
kingdoms of Hazor, which Nebuchadnezzar king of Babylon defeated. Thus
says the LORD,
"Arise, go up to Kedar
And devastate the men of the
east.
29"They will take away their tents
and their flocks;
They will carry off for themselves
Their tent curtains, all their
goods, and their camels,
And they will call out to one another, 'Terror on every side!'
30"Run away, flee! Dwell in the
depths,
O inhabitants of Hazor," declares
the LORD;

"For Nebuchadnezzar king of
Babylon has formed a plan
against you
And devised a scheme against
you.
31"Arise, go up against a nation
which is at ease,
Which lives securely," declares
the LORD.
"It has no gates or bars;
They dwell alone.
32"And their camels will become
plunder,
And the multitude of their cattle
for booty,
And I shall scatter to all the winds
those who cut the corners *of
their hair;*
And I shall bring their disaster
from every side," declares the
LORD.
33"And Hazor will become a haunt of
jackals,
A desolation forever;
No one will live there,
Nor will a son of man reside in it."
34 ¶ That which came as the word of
the LORD to Jeremiah the prophet
concerning Elam, at the beginning of
the reign of Zedekiah king of Judah,
saying,
35"Thus says the LORD of hosts,
'Behold, I am going to break the
bow of Elam,
The finest of their might.
36 'And I shall bring upon Elam the
four winds
From the four ends of heaven,
And shall scatter them to all these
winds;
And there will be no nation
To which the outcasts of Elam
will not go.
37 'So I shall shatter Elam before
their enemies
And before those who seek their
lives;
And I shall bring calamity upon
them,
Even My fierce anger,' declares
the LORD.
'And I shall send out the sword
after them
Until I have consumed them.
38 'Then I shall set My throne in
Elam,
And I shall destroy out of it king
and princes,'
Declares the LORD.

39 'But it will come about in the last
days
That I shall restore the fortunes of
Elam,' "
Declares the LORD.

CHAPTER 50

THE word which the LORD spoke
concerning Babylon, the land of the
Chaldeans, through Jeremiah the
prophet:
2"Declare and proclaim among the
nations.
Proclaim it and lift up a standard.
Do not conceal *it but* say,
'Babylon has been captured,
Bel has been put to shame, Mar-
duk has been shattered;
Her images have been put to
shame, her idols have been
shattered.'
3"For a nation has come up against
her out of the north; it will make her
land an object of horror, and there will
be no inhabitant in it. Both man and
beast have wandered off, they have
gone away!
4"In those days and at that time,"
declares the LORD, "the sons of Israel
will come, *both* they and the sons of
Judah as well; they will go along
weeping as they go, and it will be the
LORD their God they will seek.
5"They will ask for the way to Zion,
turning their faces in its direction;
they will come that they may join
themselves to the LORD *in* an everlasting covenant that will not be forgotten.
6"My people have become lost
sheep;
Their shepherds have led them
astray.
They have made them turn aside
on the mountains;
They have gone along from
mountain to hill
And have forgotten their resting
place.
7"All who came upon them have
devoured them;
And their adversaries have said,
'We are not guilty,
Inasmuch as they have sinned
against the LORD *who is* the
habitation of righteousness,
Even the LORD, the hope of their
fathers.'

8"Wander away from the midst of
Babylon,
And go forth from the land of the
Chaldeans;
Be also like male goats at the head
of the flock.
9"For behold, I am going to arouse
and bring up against Babylon
A horde of great nations from the
land of the north,
And they will draw up *their* battle
lines against her;
From there she will be taken captive.
Their arrows will be like an expert
warrior
Who does not return empty-
handed.
10"And Chaldea will become plunder;
All who plunder her will have
enough," declares the LORD.

11 ¶"Because you are glad, because
you are jubilant,
O you who pillage My heritage,
Because you skip about like a
threshing heifer
And neigh like stallions,
12 Your mother will be greatly
ashamed,
She who gave you birth will be
humiliated.
Behold, *she will be* the least of the
nations,
A wilderness, a parched land, and
a desert.
13"Because of the indignation of the
LORD she will not be inhabited,
But she will be completely deso-
late;
Everyone who passes by Babylon
will be horrified
And will hiss because of all her
wounds.
14"Draw up your battle lines against
Babylon on every side,
All you who bend the bow;
Shoot at her, do not be sparing
with *your* arrows,
For she has sinned against the
LORD.
15"Raise your battle cry against her
on every side!
She has given herself up, her pil-
lars have fallen,
Her walls have been torn down.
For this is the vengeance of the
LORD:
Take vengeance on her;

As she has done *to others*, *so* do to
her.
16"Cut off the sower from Babylon,
And the one who wields the sickle
at the time of harvest;
From before the sword of the oppressor
They will each turn back to his
own people,
And they will each flee to his own
land.
17 ¶"Israel is a scattered flock, the
lions have driven *them* away. The first
one *who* devoured him was the king of
Assyria, and this last one *who* has
broken his bones is Nebuchadnezzar
king of Babylon.
18"Therefore thus says the LORD of
hosts, the God of Israel: 'Behold, I am
going to punish the king of Babylon
and his land, just as I punished the
king of Assyria.
19 'And I shall bring Israel back to his
pasture, and he will graze on Carmel
and Bashan, and his desire will be
satisfied in the hill country of Ephraim
and Gilead.
20 'In those days and at that time,'
declares the LORD, 'search will be
made for the iniquity of Israel, but
there will be none; and for the sins of
Judah, but they will not be found; for I
shall pardon those whom I leave as a
remnant.'
21 ¶"Against the land of [13]Mera-
thaim, go up against it,
And against the inhabitants of
[14]Pekod.
Slay and utterly destroy them,"
declares the LORD,
"And do according to all that I
have commanded you.
22"The noise of battle is in the land,
And great destruction.
23"How the hammer of the whole
earth
Has been cut off and broken!
How Babylon has become
An object of horror among the
nations!
24"I set a snare for you, and you
were also caught, O Babylon,
While you yourself were not
aware;
You have been found and also
seized

[13] Or, *Double Rebellion*   [14] Or, *Punishment*

Because you have engaged in conflict with the Lord."

25 The Lord has opened His armory
And has brought forth the weapons of His indignation,
For it is a work of the Lord God of hosts
In the land of the Chaldeans.
26 Come to her from the farthest border;
Open up her barns,
Pile her up like heaps
And utterly destroy her,
Let nothing be left to her.
27 Put all her young bulls to the sword;
Let them go down to the slaughter!
Woe be upon them, for their day has come,
The time of their punishment.
28 There is a sound of fugitives and refugees from the land of Babylon,
To declare in Zion the vengeance of the Lord our God,
Vengeance for His temple.

29 ¶"Summon [15]many against Babylon,
All those who bend the bow:
Encamp against her on every side,
Let there be no escape.
Repay her according to her work;
According to all that she has done, so do to her;
For she has become arrogant against the Lord,
Against the Holy One of Israel.
30"Therefore her young men will fall in her streets,
And all her men of war will be silenced in that day," declares the Lord.
31"Behold, I am against you, O arrogant one,"
Declares the Lord God of hosts,
"For your day has come,
The time when I shall punish you.
32"And the arrogant one will stumble and fall
With no one to raise him up;
And I shall set fire to his cities,
And it will devour all his environs."

33 ¶ Thus says the Lord of hosts,
"The sons of Israel are oppressed,
And the sons of Judah as well;
And all who took them captive have held them fast,
They have refused to let them go.
34"Their Redeemer is strong, the Lord of hosts is His name;
He will vigorously plead their case,
So that He may bring rest to the earth,
But turmoil to the inhabitants of Babylon.
35"A sword against the Chaldeans," declares the Lord,
"And against the inhabitants of Babylon,
And against her officials and her wise men!
36"A sword against the oracle priests, and they will become fools!
A sword against her mighty men, and they will be shattered!
37"A sword against their horses and against their chariots,
And against all the foreigners who are in the midst of her,
And they will become women!
A sword against her treasures, and they will be plundered!
38"A drought on her waters, and they will be dried up!
For it is a land of idols,
And they are mad over fearsome idols.
39"Therefore the desert creatures will live there along with the jackals;
The ostriches also will live in it,
And it will never again be inhabited
Or dwelt in from generation to generation.
40"As when God overthrew Sodom
And Gomorrah with its neighbors," declares the Lord,
"No man will live there,
Nor will any son of man reside in it.

41 ¶"Behold, a people is coming from the north,
And a great nation and many kings
Will be aroused from the remote parts of the earth.
42"They seize their bow and javelin;

15 Another reading is archers

They are cruel and have no
  mercy.
Their voice roars like the sea,
And they ride on horses,
Marshalled like a man for the
  battle
Against you, O daughter of Babylon.
43"The king of Babylon has heard the
  report about them,
And his hands hang limp;
Distress has gripped him,
Agony like a woman in childbirth.
44"Behold, one will come up like a
lion from the thicket of the Jordan to a
perennially watered pasture; for in an
instant I shall make them run away
from it, and whoever is chosen I shall
appoint over it. For who is like Me,
and who will summon Me *into court?*
And who then is the shepherd who
can stand before Me?"

45 Therefore hear the plan of the
LORD which He has planned against
Babylon, and His purposes which He
has purposed against the land of the
Chaldeans: surely they will drag them
off, *even* the little ones of the flock;
surely He will make their pasture
desolate because of them.

46 At the shout, "Babylon has been
seized!" the earth is shaken, and an
outcry is heard among the nations.

CHAPTER 51

THUS says the LORD:
  "Behold, I am going to arouse
    against Babylon
  And against the inhabitants of
    [16]Leb-kamai
  The spirit of a destroyer.
2"And I shall dispatch foreigners to
    Babylon that they may winnow
    her
  And may devastate her land;
  For on every side they will be
    opposed to her
  In the day of *her* calamity.
3"Let not him who bends his bow
    bend *it*,
  Nor let him rise up in his scale-
    armor;
  So do not spare her young men;
  Devote all her army to destruc-
    tion.
4"And they will fall down slain in
    the land of the Chaldeans,

[16] Cryptic name for Chaldea

And pierced through in their
  streets."

5 ¶ For neither Israel nor Judah has
    been forsaken
By his God, the LORD of hosts,
Although their land is full of guilt
Before the Holy One of Israel.
6 Flee from the midst of Babylon,
And each of you save his life!
Do not be destroyed in her pun-
  ishment,
For this is the LORD's time of
  vengeance;
He is going to render recompense
  to her.
7 Babylon has been a golden cup in
    the hand of the LORD,
Intoxicating all the earth.
The nations have drunk of her
  wine;
Therefore the nations are going
  mad.
8 Suddenly Babylon has fallen and
    been broken;
Wail over her!
Bring balm for her pain;
Perhaps she may be healed.
9 We applied healing to Babylon,
    but she was not healed;
Forsake her and let us each go to
  his own country,
For her judgment has reached to
  heaven
And towers up to the very skies.
10 The LORD has brought about our
    vindication;
Come and let us recount in Zion
The work of the LORD our God!

11 ¶ Sharpen the arrows, fill the
    quivers!
The LORD has aroused the spirit of
  the kings of the Medes,
Because His purpose is against
  Babylon to destroy it;
For it is the vengeance of the
  LORD, vengeance for His tem-
  ple.
12 Lift up a signal against the walls
    of Babylon;
Post a strong guard,
Station sentries,
Place men in ambush!
For the LORD has both purposed
  and performed
What He spoke concerning the
  inhabitants of Babylon.

13 O you who dwell by many waters,
   Abundant in treasures,
   Your end has come,
   The measure of your end.
14 The Lord of hosts has sworn by
   Himself:
   "Surely I will fill you with a popu-
      lation like locusts,
   And they will cry out with shouts
      of victory over you."

15 ¶ *It is* He who made the earth by
      His power,
   Who established the world by His
      wisdom,
   And by His understanding He
      stretched out the heavens.
16 When He utters His voice, *there is*
      a tumult of waters in the heav-
      ens,
   And He causes the clouds to as-
      cend from the end of the earth;
   He makes lightning for the rain,
   And brings forth the wind from
      His storehouses.
17 All mankind is stupid, devoid of
      knowledge;
   Every goldsmith is put to shame
      by his idols,
   For his molten images are deceit-
      ful,
   And there is no breath in them.
18 They are worthless, a work of
      mockery;
   In the time of their punishment
      they will perish.
19 The portion of Jacob is not like
      these;
   For the Maker of all is He,
   And of the tribe of His inheri-
      tance;
   The Lord of hosts is His name.
20 *He says,* "You are My war-club,
      My weapon of war;
   And with you I shatter nations,
   And with you I destroy kingdoms.
21 "And with you I shatter the horse
      and his rider,
22 And with you I shatter the chariot
      and its rider,
   And with you I shatter man and
      woman,
   And with you I shatter old man
      and youth,
   And with you I shatter young
      man and virgin,
23 And with you I shatter the shep-
      herd and his flock,

And with you I shatter the farmer
   and his team,
And with you I shatter governors
   and prefects.
24 ¶ "But I will repay Babylon and all
   the inhabitants of Chaldea for all their
   evil that they have done in Zion before
   your eyes," declares the Lord.
25 "Behold, I am against you, O de-
      stroying mountain,
   Who destroy the whole earth,"
      declares the Lord,
   "And I will stretch out My hand
      against you,
   And roll you down from the crags
   And I will make you a burnt out
      mountain.
26 "And they will not take from you
      even a stone for a corner
   Nor a stone for foundations,
   But you will be desolate forever,"
      declares the Lord.

27 ¶ Lift up a signal in the land,
   Blow a trumpet among the na-
      tions!
   Consecrate the nations against
      her,
   Summon against her the king-
      doms of Ararat, Minni and Ash-
      kenaz;
   Appoint a marshal against her,
   Bring up the horses like bristly
      locusts.
28 Consecrate the nations against
      her,
   The kings of the Medes,
   Their governors and all their pre-
      fects,
   And every land of their dominion.
29 So the land quakes and writhes,
   For the purposes of the Lord
      against Babylon stand,
   To make the land of Babylon
   A desolation without inhabitants.
30 The mighty men of Babylon have
      ceased fighting,
   They stay in the strongholds;
   Their strength is exhausted,
   They are becoming *like* women;
   Their dwelling places are set on
      fire,
   The bars of her *gates* are broken.
31 One courier runs to meet another,
   And one messenger to meet an-
      other,
   To tell the king of Babylon
   That his city has been captured
      from end *to end;*

32 The fords also have been seized,
And they have burned the
marshes with fire,
And the men of war are terrified.

33 ¶ For thus says the LORD of hosts,
the God of Israel:
"The daughter of Babylon is like a
threshing floor
At the time it is stamped firm;
Yet in a little while the time of
harvest will come for her."

34 ¶"Nebuchadnezzar king of Baby-
lon has devoured me *and*
crushed me,
He has set me down *like* an empty
vessel;
He has swallowed me like a monster,
He has filled his stomach with my
delicacies;
He has washed me away.
35"May the violence *done* to me and
to my flesh be upon Babylon,"
The inhabitant of Zion will say;
And, "May my blood be upon the
inhabitants of Chaldea,"
Jerusalem will say.
36 Therefore thus says the LORD,
"Behold, I am going to plead your
case
And exact full vengeance for you;
And I shall dry up her sea
And make her fountain dry.
37"And Babylon will become a heap
of ruins, a haunt of jackals,
An object of horror and hissing,
without inhabitants.
38"They will roar together like young
lions,
They will growl like lions' cubs.
39"When they become heated up, I
shall serve *them* their banquet
And make them drunk, that they
may become jubilant
And may sleep a perpetual sleep
And not wake up," declares the
LORD.
40"I shall bring them down like
lambs to the slaughter,
Like rams together with male
goats.

41 ¶"How [17]Sheshak has been captured,

And the praise of the whole earth
been seized!
How Babylon has become an object of horror among the nations!
42"The sea has come up over Babylon;
She has been engulfed with its
tumultuous waves.
43"Her cities have become an object
of horror,
A parched land and a desert,
A land in which no man lives,
And through which no son of man
passes.
44"And I shall punish Bel in Babylon,
And I shall make what he has
swallowed come out of his
mouth;
And the nations will no longer
stream to him.
Even the wall of Babylon has
fallen down!

45 ¶"Come forth from her midst, My
people,
And each of you save yourselves
From the fierce anger of the LORD.
46"Now lest your heart grow faint,
And you be afraid at the report
that *will be* heard in the land—
For the report will come one year,
And after that another report in
another year,
And violence *will be* in the land
With ruler against ruler—
47 Therefore behold, days are com-
ing
When I shall punish the idols of
Babylon;
And her whole land will be put to
shame,
And all her slain will fall in her
midst.
48"Then heaven and earth and all
that is in them
Will shout for joy over Babylon,
For the destroyers will come to
her from the north,"
Declares the LORD.

49 ¶ Indeed Babylon is to fall *for* the
slain of Israel,
As also for Babylon the slain of all
the earth have fallen.
50 You who have escaped the sword,
Depart! Do not stay!

[17] Cryptic name for Babylon

Remember the LORD from afar,
And let Jerusalem come to your
mind.

51 We are ashamed because we have
heard reproach;
Disgrace has covered our faces,
For aliens have entered
The holy places of the LORD's
house.

52 ¶"Therefore behold, the days are
coming," declares the LORD,
"When I shall punish her idols,
And the mortally wounded will
groan throughout her land.

53"Though Babylon should ascend to
the heavens,
And though she should fortify her
lofty stronghold,
From Me destroyers will come to
her," declares the LORD.

54 ¶ The sound of an outcry from
Babylon,
And of great destruction from the
land of the Chaldeans!

55 For the LORD is going to destroy
Babylon,
And He will make *her* loud noise
vanish from her.
And their waves will roar like
many waters;
The tumult of their voices sounds
forth.

56 For the destroyer is coming
against her, against Babylon,
And her mighty men will be cap-
tured,
Their bows are shattered;
For the LORD is a God of recom-
pense,
He will fully repay.

57"And I shall make her princes and
her wise men drunk,
Her governors, her prefects, and
her mighty men,
That they may sleep a perpetual
sleep and not wake up,"
Declares the King, whose name is
the LORD of hosts.

58 Thus says the LORD of hosts,
"The broad wall of Babylon will be
completely razed,
And her high gates will be set on
fire;
So the peoples will toil for nothing,
And the nations become exhausted *only* for fire."

59 ¶ The message which Jeremiah
the prophet commanded Seraiah the
son of Neriah, the grandson of Mahseiah, when he went with Zedekiah the
king of Judah to Babylon in the fourth
year of his reign. (Now Seraiah was
quartermaster.)

60 So Jeremiah wrote in a single
scroll all the calamity which would
come upon Babylon, *that is,* all these
words which have been written concerning Babylon.

61 Then Jeremiah said to Seraiah,
"As soon as you come to Babylon,
then see that you read all these words
aloud,

62 and say, 'Thou, O LORD, hast
promised concerning this place to cut
it off, so that there will be nothing
dwelling in it, whether man or beast,
but it will be a perpetual desolation.'

63"And it will come about as soon as
you finish reading this scroll, you will
tie a stone to it and throw it into the
middle of the Euphrates,

64 and say, 'Just so shall Babylon
sink down and not rise again, because
of the calamity that I am going to
bring upon her; and they will become
exhausted.'" Thus far are the words of
Jeremiah.

CHAPTER 52

ZEDEKIAH was twenty-one years
old when he became king, and he
reigned eleven years in Jerusalem; and
his mother's name was Hamutal the
daughter of Jeremiah of Libnah.

2 And he did evil in the sight of the
LORD like all that Jehoiakim had done.

3 For through the anger of the
LORD *this* came about in Jerusalem
and Judah until He cast them out from
His presence. And Zedekiah rebelled
against the king of Babylon.

4 Now it came about in the ninth
year of his reign, on the tenth day of
the tenth month, that Nebuchadnezzar king of Babylon came, he and all
his army, against Jerusalem, camped
against it, and built a siege wall all
around it.

5 So the city was under siege until
the eleventh year of King Zedekiah.

6 On the ninth day of the fourth
month the famine was so severe in the
city that there was no food for the
people of the land.

7 Then the city was broken into, and all the men of war fled and went forth from the city at night by way of the gate between the two walls which *was* by the king's garden, though the Chaldeans were all around the city. And they went by way of the Arabah.

8 But the army of the Chaldeans pursued the king and overtook Zedekiah in the plains of Jericho, and all his army was scattered from him.

9 Then they captured the king and brought him up to the king of Babylon at Riblah in the land of Hamath; and he passed sentence on him.

10 And the king of Babylon slaughtered the sons of Zedekiah before his eyes, and he also slaughtered all the princes of Judah in Riblah.

11 Then he blinded the eyes of Zedekiah; and the king of Babylon bound him with bronze fetters and brought him to Babylon, and put him in prison until the day of his death.

12 ¶ Now on the tenth day of the fifth month, which was the nineteenth year of King Nebuchadnezzar, king of Babylon, Nebuzaradan the captain of the bodyguard, who was in the service of the king of Babylon, came to Jerusalem.

13 And he burned the house of the LORD, the king's house, and all the houses of Jerusalem; even every large house he burned with fire.

14 So all the army of the Chaldeans who *were* with the captain of the guard broke down all the walls around Jerusalem.

15 Then Nebuzaradan the captain of the guard carried away into exile some of the poorest of the people, the rest of the people who were left in the city, the deserters who had deserted to the king of Babylon, and the rest of the artisans.

16 But Nebuzaradan the captain of the guard left some of the poorest of the land to be vinedressers and plowmen.

17 ¶ Now the bronze pillars which belonged to the house of the LORD and the stands and the bronze sea, which were in the house of the LORD, the Chaldeans broke in pieces and carried all their bronze to Babylon.

18 And they also took away the pots, the shovels, the snuffers, the basins,

the pans, and all the bronze vessels which were used in *temple* service.

19 The captain of the guard also took away the bowls, the firepans, the basins, the pots, the lampstands, the pans and the libation bowls, what was fine gold and what was fine silver.

20 The two pillars, the one sea, and the twelve bronze bulls that were under the sea, *and* the stands, which King Solomon had made for the house of the LORD—the bronze of all these vessels was beyond weight.

21 As for the pillars, the height of each pillar was eighteen cubits, and it was twelve cubits in circumference and four fingers in thickness, *and* hollow.

22 Now a capital of bronze was on it; and the height of each capital was five cubits, with network and pomegranates upon the capital all around, all of bronze. And the second pillar was like these, including pomegranates.

23 And there were ninety-six exposed pomegranates; all the pomegranates *numbered* a hundred on the network all around.

24 ¶ Then the captain of the guard took Seraiah the chief priest and Zephaniah the second priest, with the three officers of the temple.

25 He also took from the city one official who was overseer of the men of war, and seven of the king's advisers who were found in the city, and the scribe of the commander of the army who mustered the people of the land, and sixty men of the people of the land who were found in the midst of the city.

26 And Nebuzaradan the captain of the guard took them and brought them to the king of Babylon at Riblah.

27 Then the king of Babylon struck them down and put them to death at Riblah in the land of Hamath. So Judah was led away into exile from its land.

28 ¶ These are the people whom Nebuchadnezzar carried away into exile: in the seventh year 3,023 Jews;

29 in the eighteenth year of Nebuchadnezzar 832 persons from Jerusalem;

30 in the twenty-third year of Nebuchadnezzar, Nebuzaradan the captain

of the guard carried into exile 745
Jewish people; there were 4,600 persons in all.

31 ¶ Now it came about in the
thirty-seventh year of the exile of
Jehoiachin king of Judah, in the
twelfth month, on the twenty-fifth of
the month, that Evil-merodach king of
Babylon, in the *first* year of his reign,
showed favor to Jehoiachin king of
Judah and brought him out of prison.

32 Then he spoke kindly to him and
set his throne above the thrones of the
kings who *were* with him in Babylon.

33 So Jehoiachin changed his prison
clothes, and had his meals in the
king's presence regularly all the days
of his life.

34 And for his allowance, a regular
allowance was given him by the king
of Babylon, a daily portion all the days
of his life until the day of his death.

THE LAMENTATIONS

OF JEREMIAH

HOW lonely sits the city
　　That was full of people!
　　She has become like a widow
　　Who was *once* great among the
　　　nations!
　　She who was a princess among
　　　the provinces
　　Has become a forced laborer!

2　She weeps bitterly in the night,
　　And her tears are on her cheeks;
　　She has none to comfort her
　　Among all her lovers.
　　All her friends have dealt treach-
　　　erously with her;
　　They have become her enemies.

3　Judah has gone into exile under
　　　affliction,
　　And under harsh servitude;
　　She dwells among the nations,
　　But she has found no rest;
　　All her pursuers have overtaken
　　　her
　　In the midst of distress.

4　The roads of Zion are in mourning
　　Because no one comes to the ap-
　　　pointed feasts.
　　All her gates are desolate;
　　Her priests are groaning,
　　Her virgins are afflicted,
　　And she herself is bitter.

5　Her adversaries have become her
　　　masters,
　　Her enemies prosper;
　　For the LORD has caused her grief
　　Because of the multitude of her
　　　transgressions;
　　Her little ones have gone away
　　As captives before the adversary.

6　And all her majesty
　　Has departed from the daughter
　　　of Zion;
　　Her princes have become like
　　　bucks
　　That have found no pasture;
　　And they have fled without
　　　strength
　　Before the pursuer.

7　In the days of her affliction and
　　　homelessness
　　Jerusalem remembers all her pre-
　　　cious things
　　That were from the days of old
　　When her people fell into the
　　　hand of the adversary,
　　And no one helped her.
　　The adversaries saw her,
　　They mocked at her ruin.

8　Jerusalem sinned greatly,
　　Therefore she has become an un-
　　　clean thing.
　　All who honored her despise her
　　Because they have seen her na-
　　　kedness;
　　Even she herself groans and turns
　　　away.

9　Her uncleanness was in her skirts;
　　She did not consider her future;
　　Therefore she has fallen astonish-
　　　ingly;
　　She has no comforter.
　　"See, O LORD, my affliction,
　　For the enemy has magnified him-
　　　self!"

10　The adversary has stretched out
　　　his hand
　　Over all her precious things,

For she has seen the nations enter her sanctuary,
The ones whom Thou didst command
That they should not enter into Thy congregation.

11 All her people groan seeking bread;
They have given their precious things for food
To restore their lives themselves.
"See, O LORD, and look,
For I am despised."

12"Is it nothing to all you who pass this way?
Look and see if there is any pain like my pain
Which was severely dealt out to me,
Which the LORD inflicted on the day of His fierce anger.

13"From on high He sent fire into my bones,
And it prevailed *over them;*
He has spread a net for my feet;
He has turned me back;
He has made me desolate,
Faint all day long.

14"The yoke of my transgressions is bound;
By His hand they are knit together;
They have come upon my neck;
He has made my strength fail;
The Lord has given me into the hands
Of *those against whom* I am not able to stand.

15"The Lord has rejected all my strong men
In my midst;
He has called an appointed time against me
To crush my young men;
The Lord has trodden *as in* a wine press
The virgin daughter of Judah.

16"For these things I weep;
My eyes run down with water;
Because far from me is a comforter,
One who restores my soul;
My children are desolate
Because the enemy has prevailed."

17 Zion stretches out her hands;
There is no one to comfort her;
The LORD has commanded concerning Jacob

That the ones round about him should be his adversaries;
Jerusalem has become an unclean thing among them.

18"The LORD is righteous;
For I have rebelled against His command;
Hear now, all peoples,
And behold my pain;
My virgins and my young men
Have gone into captivity.

19"I called to my lovers, *but* they deceived me;
My priests and my elders perished in the city,
While they sought food to restore their strength themselves.

20"See, O LORD, for I am in distress;
My spirit is greatly troubled;
My heart is overturned within me,
For I have been very rebellious.
In the street the sword slays;
In the house it is like death.

21"They have heard that I groan;
There is no one to comfort me;
All my enemies have heard of my calamity;
They are glad that Thou hast done *it.*
Oh, that Thou wouldst bring the day which Thou hast proclaimed,
That they may become like me.

22"Let all their wickedness come before Thee;
And deal with them as Thou hast dealt with me
For all my transgressions;
For my groans are many, and my heart is faint."

CHAPTER 2

How the Lord has covered the daughter of Zion
With a cloud in His anger!
He has cast from heaven to earth
The glory of Israel,
And has not remembered His footstool
In the day of His anger.

2 The Lord has swallowed up; He has not spared
All the habitations of Jacob.
In His wrath He has thrown down
The strongholds of the daughter of Judah;
He has brought *them* down to the ground;

He has profaned the kingdom and
its princes.

3 In fierce anger He has cut off
All the strength of Israel;
He has drawn back His right hand
From before the enemy.
And He has burned in Jacob like a
flaming fire
Consuming round about.

4 He has bent His bow like an
enemy,
He has set His right hand like an
adversary
And slain all that were pleasant to
the eye;
In the tent of the daughter of
Zion
He has poured out His wrath like
fire.

5 The Lord has become like an
enemy.
He has swallowed up Israel;
He has swallowed up all its pal-
aces;
He has destroyed its strongholds
And multiplied in the daughter of
Judah
Mourning and moaning.

6 And He has violently treated His
tabernacle like a garden *booth;*
He has destroyed His appointed
meeting place;
The LORD has caused to be forgotten
The appointed feast and sabbath
in Zion,
And He has despised king and
priest
In the indignation of His anger.

7 The Lord has rejected His altar,
He has abandoned His sanctuary;
He has delivered into the hand of
the enemy
The walls of her palaces.
They have made a noise in the
house of the LORD
As in the day of an appointed
feast.

8 The LORD determined to destroy
The wall of the daughter of Zion.
He has stretched out a line,
He has not restrained His hand
from destroying;
And He has caused rampart and
wall to lament;
They have languished together.

9 Her gates have sunk into the
ground,

He has destroyed and broken her
bars.
Her king and her princes are
among the nations;
The law is no more;
Also, her prophets find
No vision from the LORD.

10 The elders of the daughter of Zion
Sit on the ground, they are silent.
They have thrown dust on their
heads;
They have girded themselves with
sackcloth.
The virgins of Jerusalem
Have bowed their heads to the
ground.

11 My eyes fail because of tears,
My spirit is greatly troubled;
My heart is poured out on the
earth,
Because of the destruction of the
daughter of my people,
When little ones and infants faint
In the streets of the city.

12 They say to their mothers,
"Where is grain and wine?"
As they faint like a wounded man
In the streets of the city,
As their life is poured out
On their mothers' bosom.

13 How shall I admonish you?
To what shall I compare you,
O daughter of Jerusalem?
To what shall I liken you as I
comfort you,
O virgin daughter of Zion?
For your ruin is as vast as the sea;
Who can heal you?

14 Your prophets have seen for you
False and foolish *visions;*
And they have not exposed your
iniquity
So as to restore you from captiv-
ity,
But they have seen for you false
and misleading oracles.

15 All who pass along the way
Clap their hands *in derision* at
you;
They hiss and shake their heads
At the daughter of Jerusalem,
"Is this the city of which they said,
'The perfection of beauty,
A joy to all the earth'?"

16 All your enemies
Have opened their mouths wide
against you;

They hiss and gnash *their* teeth.
They say, "We have swallowed
  her up!
Surely this is the day for which
  we waited;
We have reached *it,* we have seen
  it."

17 The LORD has done what He purposed;
He has accomplished His word
Which He commanded from days
  of old.
He has thrown down without
  sparing,
And He has caused the enemy to
  rejoice over you;
He has exalted the might of your
  adversaries.

18 Their heart cried out to the Lord,
"O wall of the daughter of Zion,
Let *your* tears run down like a
  river day and night;
Give yourself no relief;
Let your eyes have no rest.

19 "Arise, cry aloud in the night
At the beginning of the night
  watches;
Pour out your heart like water
Before the presence of the Lord;
Lift up your hands to Him
For the life of your little ones
Who are faint because of hunger
At the head of every street."

20 See, O LORD, and look!
With whom hast Thou dealt thus?
Should women eat their offspring,
The little ones who were born
  healthy?
Should priest and prophet be slain
In the sanctuary of the Lord?

21 On the ground in the streets
Lie young and old,
My virgins and my young men
Have fallen by the sword.
Thou hast slain *them* in the day of
  Thine anger,
Thou hast slaughtered, not spar-
  ing.

22 Thou didst call as in the day of an
  appointed feast
My terrors on every side;
And there was no one who es-
  caped or survived
In the day of the LORD's anger.
Those whom I bore and reared,
My enemy annihilated them.

CHAPTER 3

I AM the man who has seen affliction
Because of the rod of His wrath.

2 He has driven me and made me
  walk
In darkness and not in light.

3 Surely against me He has turned
  His hand
Repeatedly all the day.

4 He has caused my flesh and my
  skin to waste away,
He has broken my bones.

5 He has besieged and encompassed
  me with bitterness and hardship.

6 In dark places He has made me
  dwell,
Like those who have long been
  dead.

7 He has walled *me* in so that I
  cannot go out;
He has made my chain heavy.

8 Even when I cry out and call for
  help,
He shuts out my prayer.

9 He has blocked my ways with
  hewn stone;
He has made my paths crooked.

10 He is to me like a bear lying in
  wait,
Like a lion in secret places.

11 He has turned aside my ways and
  torn me to pieces;
He has made me desolate.

12 He bent His bow
And set me as a target for the
  arrow.

13 He made the arrows of His quiver
To enter into my inward parts.

14 I have become a laughingstock to
  all my people,
Their *mocking* song all the day.

15 He has filled me with bitterness,
He has made me drunk with
  wormwood.

16 And He has broken my teeth with
  gravel;
He has made me cower in the
  dust.

17 And my soul has been rejected
  from peace;
I have forgotten happiness.

18 So I say, "My strength has per-
  ished,
And *so has* my hope from the
  LORD."

19 ¶ Remember my affliction and my wandering, the wormwood and bitterness.

20 Surely my soul remembers
And is bowed down within me.

21 This I recall to my mind,
Therefore I have hope.

22 The LORD's lovingkindnesses indeed never cease,
For His compassions never fail.

23 *They* are new every morning;
Great is Thy faithfulness.

24 "The LORD is my portion," says my soul,
"Therefore I have hope in Him."

25 The LORD is good to those who wait for Him,
To the person who seeks Him.

26 *It is* good that he waits silently
For the salvation of the LORD.

27 *It is* good for a man that he should bear
The yoke in his youth.

28 Let him sit alone and be silent
Since He has laid *it* on him.

29 Let him put his mouth in the dust,
Perhaps there is hope.

30 Let him give his cheek to the smiter;
Let him be filled with reproach.

31 For the Lord will not reject forever,

32 For if He causes grief,
Then He will have compassion
According to His abundant lovingkindness.

33 For He does not afflict willingly,
Or grieve the sons of men.

34 To crush under His feet
All the prisoners of the land,

35 To deprive a man of justice
In the presence of the Most High,

36 To defraud a man in his lawsuit—
Of these things the Lord does not approve.

37 Who is there who speaks and it comes to pass,
Unless the Lord has commanded *it*?

38 *Is it* not from the mouth of the Most High
That both good and ill go forth?

39 ¶ Why should *any* living mortal, or *any* man,
Offer complaint in view of his sins?

40 Let us examine and probe our ways,

And let us return to the LORD.

41 We lift up our heart and hands
Toward God in heaven;

42 We have transgressed and rebelled,
Thou hast not pardoned.

43 Thou hast covered *Thyself* with anger
And pursued us;
Thou hast slain *and* hast not spared.

44 Thou hast covered Thyself with a cloud
So that no prayer can pass through.

45 *Mere* offscouring and refuse Thou hast made us
In the midst of the peoples.

46 All our enemies have opened their mouths against us.

47 Panic and pitfall have befallen us,
Devastation and destruction;

48 My eyes run down with streams of water
Because of the destruction of the daughter of my people.

49 My eyes pour down unceasingly,
Without stopping,

50 Until the LORD looks down
And sees from heaven.

51 My eyes bring pain to my soul
Because of all the daughters of my city.

52 My enemies without cause
Hunted me down like a bird;

53 They have silenced me in the pit
And have placed a stone on me.

54 Waters flowed over my head;
I said, "I am cut off!"

55 I called on Thy name, O LORD,
Out of the lowest pit.

56 Thou hast heard my voice,
"Do not hide Thine ear from my *prayer for* relief,
From my cry for help."

57 Thou didst draw near when I called on Thee;
Thou didst say, "Do not fear!"

58 O Lord, Thou didst plead my soul's cause;
Thou hast redeemed my life.

59 O LORD, Thou hast seen my oppression;
Judge my case.

60 Thou hast seen all their vengeance,
All their schemes against me.

61 Thou hast heard their reproach, O LORD,

All their schemes against me.
62 The lips of my assailants and their
   whispering
   Are against me all day long.
63 Look on their sitting and their
   rising;
   I am their mocking song.
64 Thou wilt recompense them, O
   LORD,
   According to the work of their
   hands.
65 Thou wilt give them hardness of
   heart,
   Thy curse will be on them.
66 Thou wilt pursue them in anger
   and destroy them
   From under the heavens of the
   LORD!

CHAPTER 4

How dark the gold has become,
   How the pure gold has changed!
   The sacred stones are poured out
   At the corner of every street.
2 The precious sons of Zion,
   Weighed against fine gold,
   How they are regarded as earthen
   jars,
   The work of a potter's hands!
3 Even jackals offer the breast,
   They nurse their young;
   But the daughter of my people has
   become cruel
   Like ostriches in the wilderness.
4 The tongue of the infant cleaves
   To the roof of its mouth because
   of thirst;
   The little ones ask for bread,
   But no one breaks *it* for them.
5 Those who ate delicacies
   Are desolate in the streets;
   Those reared in purple
   Embrace ash pits.
6 For the iniquity of the daughter of
   my people
   Is greater than the sin of Sodom,
   Which was overthrown as in a
   moment,
   And no hands were turned toward
   her.
7 Her consecrated ones were purer
   than snow,
   They were whiter than milk;
   They were more ruddy *in* body
   than corals,
   Their polishing *was* like lapis la-
   zuli.

8 Their appearance is blacker than
   soot,
   They are not recognized in the
   streets;
   Their skin is shriveled on their
   bones,
   It is withered, it has become like
   wood.
9 Better are those slain with the
   sword
   Than those slain with hunger;
   For they pine away, being
   stricken
   For lack of the fruits of the field.
10 The hands of compassionate
   women
   Boiled their own children;
   They became food for them
   Because of the destruction of the
   daughter of my people.
11 The LORD has accomplished His
   wrath,
   He has poured out His fierce anger;
   And He has kindled a fire in Zion
   Which has consumed its foundations.
12 The kings of the earth did not
   believe,
   Nor *did* any of the inhabitants of
   the world,
   That the adversary and the enemy
   Could enter the gates of Jerusalem.
13 Because of the sins of her prophets
   And the iniquities of her priests,
   Who have shed in her midst
   The blood of the righteous,
14 They wandered, blind, in the
   streets;
   They were defiled with blood
   So that no one could touch their
   garments.
15 "Depart! Unclean!" they cried of
   themselves.
   "Depart, depart, do not touch!"
   So they fled and wandered;
   Men among the nations said,
   "They shall not continue to dwell
   with us."
16 The presence of the LORD has
   scattered them;
   He will not continue to regard
   them.
   They did not honor the priests,
   They did not favor the elders.
17 Yet our eyes failed;
   Looking for help was useless.

In our watching we have watched
For a nation that could not save.
18 They hunted our steps
So that we could not walk in our
streets;
Our end drew near,
Our days were finished
For our end had come.
19 Our pursuers were swifter
Than the eagles of the sky.
They chased us on the mountains;
They waited in ambush for us in
the wilderness.
20 The breath of our nostrils, the
LORD's anointed,
Was captured in their pits,
Of whom we had said, "Under his
shadow
We shall live among the nations."
21 Rejoice and be glad, O daughter
of Edom,
Who dwells in the land of Uz;
But the cup will come around to
you as well,
You will become drunk and make
yourself naked.
22 *The punishment* of your iniquity
has been completed, O daughter
of Zion;
He will exile you no longer.
But He will punish your iniquity,
O daughter of Edom;
He will expose your sins!

CHAPTER 5

REMEMBER, O LORD, what has befallen us;
Look, and see our reproach!
2 Our inheritance has been turned
over to strangers,
Our houses to aliens.
3 We have become orphans without
a father,
Our mothers are like widows.
4 We have to pay for our drinking
water,
Our wood comes *to us* at a price.
5 Our pursuers are at our necks;
We are worn out, there is no rest
for us.
6 We have submitted to Egypt *and*
Assyria to get enough bread.

7 Our fathers sinned, *and* are no
more;
It is we who have borne their
iniquities.
8 Slaves rule over us;
There is no one to deliver us from
their hand.
9 We get our bread at the risk of
our lives
Because of the sword in the wilderness.
10 Our skin has become as hot as an
oven,
Because of the burning heat of
famine.
11 They ravished the women in Zion,
The virgins in the cities of Judah.
12 Princes were hung by their hands;
Elders were not respected.
13 Young men worked at the grinding mill;
And youths stumbled under *loads*
of wood.
14 Elders are gone from the gate,
Young men from their music.
15 The joy of our hearts has ceased;
Our dancing has been turned into
mourning.
16 The crown has fallen from our
head;
Woe to us, for we have sinned!
17 Because of this our heart is faint;
Because of these things our eyes
are dim;
18 Because of Mount Zion which lies
desolate,
Foxes prowl in it.

19 ¶ Thou, O LORD, dost rule forever;
Thy throne is from generation to
generation.
20 Why dost Thou forget us forever;
Why dost Thou forsake us so
long?
21 Restore us to Thee, O LORD, that
we may be restored;
Renew our days as of old,
22 Unless Thou hast utterly rejected
us,
And art exceedingly angry with
us.

EZEKIEL

NOW it came about in the thirtieth year, on the fifth *day* of the fourth month, while I was by the river Chebar among the exiles, the heavens were opened and I saw visions of God.

2 (On the fifth of the month in the fifth year of King Jehoiachin's exile,

3 the word of the LORD came expressly to Ezekiel the priest, son of Buzi, in the land of the Chaldeans by the river Chebar; and there the hand of the LORD came upon him.)

4 ¶ And as I looked, behold, a storm wind was coming from the north, a great cloud with fire flashing forth continually and a bright light around it, and in its midst something like glowing metal in the midst of the fire.

5 And within it there were figures resembling four living beings. And this was their appearance: they had human form.

6 Each of them had four faces and four wings.

7 And their legs were straight and their feet were like a calf's hoof, and they gleamed like burnished bronze.

8 Under their wings on their four sides *were* human hands. As for the faces and wings of the four of them,

9 their wings touched one another; their *faces* did not turn when they moved, each went straight forward.

10 As for the form of their faces, *each* had the face of a man, all four had the face of a lion on the right and the face of a bull on the left, and all four had the face of an eagle.

11 Such were their faces. Their wings were spread out above; each had two touching another *being*, and two covering their bodies.

12 And each went straight forward; wherever the spirit was about to go, they would go, without turning as they went.

13 In the midst of the living beings there was something that looked like burning coals of fire, like torches darting back and forth among the living beings. The fire was bright, and lightning was flashing from the fire.

14 And the living beings ran to and fro like bolts of lightning.

15 ¶ Now as I looked at the living beings, behold, there was one wheel on the earth beside the living beings, for *each of* the four of them.

16 The appearance of the wheels and their workmanship *was* like sparkling beryl, and all four of them had the same form, their appearance and workmanship *being* as if one wheel were within another.

17 Whenever they moved, they moved in any of their four directions, without turning as they moved.

18 As for their rims they were lofty and awesome, and the rims of all four of them were full of eyes round about.

19 And whenever the living beings moved, the wheels moved with them. And whenever the living beings rose from the earth, the wheels rose *also*.

20 Wherever the spirit was about to go, they would go in that direction. And the wheels rose close beside them; for the spirit of the living beings *was* in the wheels.

21 Whenever those went, these went; and whenever those stood still, these stood still. And whenever those rose from the earth, the wheels rose close beside them; for the spirit of the living beings *was* in the wheels.

22 ¶ Now over the heads of the living beings *there was* something like an expanse, like the awesome gleam of crystal, extended over their heads.

23 And under the expanse their wings *were stretched out* straight, one toward the other; each one also had two wings covering their bodies on the one side and on the other.

24 I also heard the sound of their wings like the sound of abundant waters as they went, like the voice of the Almighty, a sound of tumult like the sound of an army camp; whenever they stood still, they dropped their wings.

25 And there came a voice from above the expanse that was over their heads; whenever they stood still, they dropped their wings.

26 ¶ Now above the expanse that was over their heads there was something resembling a throne, like lapis lazuli in appearance; and on that which resembled a throne, high up, *was* a figure with the appearance of a man.

27 Then I noticed from the appearance of His loins and upward something like glowing metal that looked like fire all around within it, and from the appearance of His loins and downward I saw something like fire; and *there was* a radiance around Him.

28 As the appearance of the rainbow in the clouds on a rainy day, so *was* the appearance of the surrounding radiance. Such *was* the appearance of the likeness of the glory of the LORD. And when I saw *it,* I fell on my face and heard a voice speaking.

CHAPTER 2

THEN He said to me, "Son of man, stand on your feet that I may speak with you!"

2 And as He spoke to me the Spirit entered me and set me on my feet; and I heard *Him* speaking to me.

3 Then He said to me, "Son of man, I am sending you to the sons of Israel, to a rebellious people who have rebelled against Me; they and their fathers have transgressed against Me to this very day.

4"And I am sending you to them who are stubborn and obstinate children; and you shall say to them, 'Thus says the Lord GOD.'

5"As for them, whether they listen or not—for they are a rebellious house—they will know that a prophet has been among them.

6"And you, son of man, neither fear them nor fear their words, though thistles and thorns are with you and you sit on scorpions; neither fear their words nor be dismayed at their presence, for they are a rebellious house.

7"But you shall speak My words to them whether they listen or not, for they are rebellious.

8 ¶"Now you, son of man, listen to what I am speaking to you; do not be rebellious like that rebellious house. Open your mouth and eat what I am giving you."

9 Then I looked, behold, a hand was extended to me; and lo, a scroll *was* in it.

10 When He spread it out before me, it was written on the front and back; and written on it were lamentations, mourning and woe.

CHAPTER 3

THEN He said to me, "Son of man, eat what you find; eat this scroll, and go, speak to the house of Israel."

2 So I opened my mouth, and He fed me this scroll.

3 And He said to me, "Son of man, feed your stomach, and fill your body with this scroll which I am giving you." Then I ate it, and it was sweet as honey in my mouth.

4 ¶ Then He said to me, "Son of man, go to the house of Israel and speak with My words to them.

5"For you are not being sent to a people of unintelligible speech or difficult language, *but* to the house of Israel,

6 nor to many peoples of unintelligible speech or difficult language, whose words you cannot understand. But I have sent you to them who should listen to you;

7 yet the house of Israel will not be willing to listen to you, since they are not willing to listen to Me. Surely the whole house of Israel is stubborn and obstinate.

8"Behold, I have made your face as hard as their faces, and your forehead as hard as their foreheads.

9"Like emery harder than flint I have made your forehead. Do not be afraid of them or be dismayed before them, though they are a rebellious house."

10 Moreover, He said to me, "Son of man, take into your heart all My words which I shall speak to you, and listen closely.

11"And go to the exiles, to the sons of your people, and speak to them and tell them, whether they listen or not, 'Thus says the Lord GOD.' "

12 ¶ Then the Spirit lifted me up, and I heard a great rumbling sound behind me, "Blessed be the glory of the LORD in His place."

13 And I *heard* the sound of the wings of the living beings touching one another, and the sound of the wheels beside them, even a great rumbling sound.

14 So the Spirit lifted me up and took me away; and I went embittered in the rage of my spirit, and the hand of the LORD was strong on me.

15 Then I came to the exiles who

lived beside the river Chebar at Tel–abib, and I sat there seven days where they were living, causing consternation among them.

16 ¶ Now it came about at the end of seven days that the word of the LORD came to me, saying,

17"Son of man, I have appointed you a watchman to the house of Israel; whenever you hear a word from My mouth, warn them from Me.

18"When I say to the wicked, 'You shall surely die'; and you do not warn him or speak out to warn the wicked from his wicked way that he may live, that wicked man shall die in his iniquity, but his blood I will require at your hand.

19"Yet if you have warned the wicked, and he does not turn from his wickedness or from his wicked way, he shall die in his iniquity; but you have delivered yourself.

20"Again, when a righteous man turns away from his righteousness and commits iniquity, and I place an obstacle before him, he shall die; since you have not warned him, he shall die in his sin, and his righteous deeds which he has done shall not be remembered; but his blood I will require at your hand.

21"However, if you have warned the righteous man that the righteous should not sin, and he does not sin, he shall surely live because he took warning; and you have delivered yourself."

22 ¶ And the hand of the LORD was on me there, and He said to me, "Get up, go out to the plain, and there I will speak to you."

23 So I got up and went out to the plain; and behold, the glory of the LORD was standing there, like the glory which I saw by the river Chebar, and I fell on my face.

24 The Spirit then entered me and made me stand on my feet, and He spoke with me and said to me, "Go, shut yourself up in your house.

25"As for you, son of man, they will put ropes on you and bind you with them, so that you cannot go out among them.

26"Moreover, I will make your tongue stick to the roof of your mouth so that you will be dumb, and cannot be a man who rebukes them, for they are a rebellious house.

27"But when I speak to you, I will open your mouth, and you will say to them, 'Thus says the Lord GOD.' He who hears, let him hear; and he who refuses, let him refuse; for they are a rebellious house.

CHAPTER 4

"NOW you son of man, get yourself a brick, place it before you, and inscribe a city on it, Jerusalem.

2"Then lay siege against it, build a siege wall, raise up a ramp, pitch camps, and place battering rams against it all around.

3"Then get yourself an iron plate and set it up as an iron wall between you and the city, and set your face toward it so that it is under siege, and besiege it. This is a sign to the house of Israel.

4 ¶"As for you, lie down on your left side, and lay the iniquity of the house of Israel on it; you shall bear their iniquity for the number of days that you lie on it.

5"For I have assigned you a number of days corresponding to the years of their iniquity, three hundred and ninety days; thus you shall bear the iniquity of the house of Israel.

6"When you have completed these, you shall lie down a second time, but on your right side, and bear the iniquity of the house of Judah; I have assigned it to you for forty days, a day for each year.

7"Then you shall set your face toward the siege of Jerusalem with your arm bared, and prophesy against it.

8"Now behold, I will put ropes on you so that you cannot turn from one side to the other, until you have completed the days of your siege.

9 ¶"But as for you, take wheat, barley, beans, lentils, millet and spelt, put them in one vessel and make them into bread for yourself; you shall eat it according to the number of the days that you lie on your side, three hundred and ninety days.

10"And your food which you eat shall be twenty shekels a day by weight; you shall eat it from time to time.

11"And the water you drink will be

the sixth part of a hin by measure; you shall drink it from time to time.

12"And you shall eat it as a barley cake, having baked *it* in their sight over human dung."

13 Then the LORD said, "Thus shall the sons of Israel eat their bread unclean among the nations where I shall banish them."

14 But I said, "Ah, Lord GOD! Behold, I have never been defiled; for from my youth until now I have never eaten what died of itself or was torn by beasts, nor has any unclean meat ever entered my mouth."

15 Then He said to me, "See, I shall give you cow's dung in place of human dung over which you will prepare your bread."

16 Moreover, He said to me, "Son of man, behold, I am going to break the staff of bread in Jerusalem, and they will eat bread by weight and with anxiety, and drink water by measure and in horror,

17 because bread and water will be scarce; and they will be appalled with one another and waste away in their iniquity.

CHAPTER 5

"As for you, son of man, take a sharp sword; take and use it *as* a barber's razor on your head and beard. Then take scales for weighing and divide the hair.

2"One third you shall burn in the fire at the center of the city, when the days of the siege are completed. Then you shall take one third and strike *it* with the sword all around the city, and one third you shall scatter to the wind; and I will unsheathe a sword behind them.

3"Take also a few in number from them and bind them in the edges of your *robes*.

4"And take again some of them and throw them into the fire, and burn them in the fire; from it a fire will spread to all the house of Israel.

5"Thus says the Lord GOD, 'This is Jerusalem; I have set her at the center of the nations, with lands around her.

6 'But she has rebelled against My ordinances more wickedly than the nations and against My statutes more than the lands which surround her; for

they have rejected My ordinances and have not walked in My statutes.'

7"Therefore, thus says the Lord GOD, 'Because you have more turmoil than the nations which surround you, and have not walked in My statutes, nor observed My ordinances, nor observed the ordinances of the nations which surround you,'

8 therefore, thus says the Lord GOD, 'Behold, I, even I, am against you, and I will execute judgments among you in the sight of the nations.

9 'And because of all your abominations, I will do among you what I have not done, and the like of which I will never do again.

10 'Therefore, fathers will eat *their* sons among you, and sons will eat their fathers; for I will execute judgments on you, and scatter all your remnant to every wind.

11 'So as I live,' declares the Lord GOD, 'surely, because you have defiled My sanctuary with all your detestable idols and with all your abominations, therefore I will also withdraw, and My eye shall have no pity and I will not spare.

12 'One third of you will die by plague or be consumed by famine among you, one third will fall by the sword around you, and one third I will scatter to every wind, and I will unsheathe a sword behind them.

13 ¶ 'Thus My anger will be spent, and I will satisfy My wrath on them, and I shall be appeased; then they will know that I, the LORD, have spoken in My zeal when I have spent My wrath upon them.

14 'Moreover, I will make you a desolation and a reproach among the nations which surround you, in the sight of all who pass by.

15 'So it will be a reproach, a reviling, a warning and an object of horror to the nations who surround you, when I execute judgments against you in anger, wrath, and raging rebukes. I, the LORD, have spoken.

16 'When I send against them the deadly arrows of famine which were for the destruction of those whom I shall send to destroy you, then I shall also intensify the famine upon you, and break the staff of bread.

17 'Moreover, I will send on you famine and wild beasts, and they will

bereave you of children; plague and bloodshed also will pass through you, and I will bring the sword on you. I, the LORD, have spoken.' "

CHAPTER 6

AND the word of the LORD came to me saying,

2"Son of man, set your face toward the mountains of Israel, and prophesy against them,

3 and say, 'Mountains of Israel, listen to the word of the Lord GOD! Thus says the Lord GOD to the mountains, the hills, the ravines and the valleys: "Behold, I Myself am going to bring a sword on you, and I will destroy your high places.

4"So your altars will become desolate, and your incense altars will be smashed; and I shall make your slain fall in front of your idols.

5"I shall also lay the dead bodies of the sons of Israel in front of their idols; and I shall scatter your bones around your altars.

6"In all your dwellings, cities will become waste and the high places will be desolate, that your altars may become waste and desolate, your idols may be broken and brought to an end, your incense altars may be cut down, and your works may be blotted out.

7"And the slain will fall among you, and you will know that I am the LORD.

8 ¶"However, I shall leave a remnant, for you will have those who escaped the sword among the nations when you are scattered among the countries.

9"Then those of you who escape will remember Me among the nations to which they will be carried captive, how I have been hurt by their adulterous hearts which turned away from Me, and by their eyes, which played the harlot after their idols; and they will loathe themselves in their own sight for the evils which they have committed, for all their abominations.

10"Then they will know that I am the LORD; I have not said in vain that I would inflict this disaster on them." '

11 ¶"Thus says the Lord GOD, 'Clap your hand, stamp your foot, and say, "Alas, because of all the evil abominations of the house of Israel, which will fall by sword, famine, and plague!

12"He who is far off will die by the plague, and he who is near will fall by the sword, and he who remains and is besieged will die by the famine. Thus shall I spend My wrath on them.

13"Then you will know that I am the LORD, when their slain are among their idols around their altars, on every high hill, on all the tops of the mountains, under every green tree, and under every leafy oak—the places where they offered soothing aroma to all their idols.

14"So throughout all their habitations I shall stretch out My hand against them and make the land more desolate and waste than the wilderness toward Diblah; thus they will know that I am the LORD." ' "

CHAPTER 7

MOREOVER, the word of the LORD came to me saying,

2"And you, son of man, thus says the Lord GOD to the land of Israel, 'An end! The end is coming on the four corners of the land.

3 'Now the end is upon you, and I shall send My anger against you; I shall judge you according to your ways, and I shall bring all your abominations upon you.

4 'For My eye will have no pity on you, nor shall I spare you, but I shall bring your ways upon you, and your abominations will be among you; then you will know that I am the LORD!

5 ¶"Thus says the Lord GOD, 'A disaster, unique disaster, behold it is coming!

6 'An end is coming; the end has come! It has awakened against you; behold, it has come!

7 'Your doom has come to you, O inhabitant of the land. The time has come, the day is near—tumult rather than joyful shouting on the mountains.

8 'Now I will shortly pour out My wrath on you, and spend My anger against you, judge you according to your ways, and bring on you all your abominations.

9 'And My eye will show no pity, nor will I spare. I will repay you according to your ways, while your abominations are in your midst; then you will know that I, the LORD, do the smiting.

10 ¶ 'Behold, the day! Behold, it is coming! *Your* doom has gone forth; the rod has budded, arrogance has blossomed.

11 'Violence has grown into a rod of wickedness. None of them *shall remain*, none of their multitude, none of their wealth, nor anything eminent among them.

12 'The time has come, the day has arrived. Let not the buyer rejoice nor the seller mourn; for wrath is against all their multitude.

13 'Indeed, the seller will not regain what he sold as long as they *both* live; for the vision regarding all their multitude will not be averted, nor will any of them maintain his life by his iniquity.

14 ¶ 'They have blown the trumpet and made everything ready, but no one is going to the battle; for My wrath is against all their multitude.

15 'The sword is outside, and the plague and the famine are within. He who is in the field will die by the sword; famine and the plague will also consume those in the city.

16 'Even when their survivors escape, they will be on the mountains like doves of the valleys, all of them mourning, each over his own iniquity.

17 'All hands will hang limp, and all knees will become like water.

18 'And they will gird themselves with sackcloth, and shuddering will overwhelm them; and shame *will be* on all faces, and baldness on all their heads.

19 'They shall fling their silver into the streets, and their gold shall become an abhorrent thing; their silver and their gold shall not be able to deliver them in the day of the wrath of the LORD. They cannot satisfy their appetite, nor can they fill their stomachs, for their iniquity has become an occasion of stumbling.

20 'And they transformed the beauty of His ornaments into pride, and they made the images of their abominations *and* their detestable things with it; therefore I will make it an abhorrent thing to them.

21 'And I shall give it into the hands of the foreigners as plunder and to the wicked of the earth as spoil, and they will profane it.

22 'I shall also turn My face from them, and they will profane My secret place; then robbers will enter and profane it.

23 ¶ 'Make the chain, for the land is full of bloody crimes, and the city is full of violence.

24 'Therefore, I shall bring the worst of the nations, and they will possess their houses. I shall also make the pride of the strong ones cease, and their holy places will be profaned.

25 'When anguish comes, they will seek peace, but there will be none.

26 'Disaster will come upon disaster, and rumor will be *added* to rumor; then they will seek a vision from a prophet, but the law will be lost from the priest and counsel from the elders.

27 'The king will mourn, the prince will be clothed with horror, and the hands of the people of the land will tremble. According to their conduct I shall deal with them, and by their judgments I shall judge them. And they will know that I am the LORD.' "

CHAPTER 8

AND it came about in the sixth year, on the fifth *day* of the sixth month, as I was sitting in my house with the elders of Judah sitting before me, that the hand of the Lord GOD fell on me there.

2 Then I looked, and behold, a likeness as the appearance of a man; from His loins and downward *there was* the appearance of fire, and from His loins and upward the appearance of brightness, like the appearance of glowing metal.

3 And He stretched out the form of a hand and caught me by a lock of my head; and the Spirit lifted me up between earth and heaven and brought me in the visions of God to Jerusalem, to the entrance of the north gate of the inner *court*, where the seat of the idol of jealousy, which provokes to jealousy, was *located*.

4 And behold, the glory of the God of Israel *was* there, like the appearance which I saw in the plain.

5 ¶ Then He said to me, "Son of man, raise your eyes, now, toward the north." So I raised my eyes toward the north, and behold, to the north of

the altar gate *was* this idol of jealousy at the entrance.

6 And He said to me, "Son of man, do you see what they are doing, the great abominations which the house of Israel are committing here, that I should be far from My sanctuary? But yet you will see still greater abominations."

7 ¶ Then He brought me to the entrance of the court, and when I looked, behold, a hole in the wall.

8 And He said to me, "Son of man, now dig through the wall." So I dug through the wall, and behold, an entrance.

9 And He said to me, "Go in and see the wicked abominations that they are committing here."

10 So I entered and looked, and behold, every form of creeping things and beasts *and* detestable things, with all the idols of the house of Israel, were carved on the wall all around.

11 And standing in front of them were seventy elders of the house of Israel, with Jaazaniah the son of Shaphan standing among them, each man with his censer in his hand, and the fragrance of the cloud of incense rising.

12 Then He said to me, "Son of man, do you see what the elders of the house of Israel are committing in the dark, each man in the room of his carved images? For they say, 'The LORD does not see us; the LORD has forsaken the land.' "

13 And He said to me, "Yet you will see still greater abominations which they are committing."

14 ¶ Then He brought me to the entrance of the gate of the LORD's house which *was* toward the north; and behold, women were sitting there weeping for Tammuz.

15 And He said to me, "Do you see *this,* son of man? Yet you will see still greater abominations than these."

16 ¶ Then He brought me into the inner court of the LORD's house. And behold, at the entrance to the temple of the LORD, between the porch and the altar, *were* about twenty-five men with their backs to the temple of the LORD and their faces toward the east; and they were prostrating themselves eastward toward the sun.

17 And He said to me, "Do you see *this,* son of man? Is it too light a thing for the house of Judah to commit the abominations which they have committed here, that they have filled the land with violence and provoked Me repeatedly? For behold, they are putting the twig to their nose.

18"Therefore, I indeed shall deal in wrath. My eye will have no pity nor shall I spare; and though they cry in My ears with a loud voice, yet I shall not listen to them."

CHAPTER 9

THEN He cried out in my hearing with a loud voice saying, "Draw near, O executioners of the city, each with his destroying weapon in his hand."

2 And behold, six men came from the direction of the upper gate which faces north, each with his shattering weapon in his hand; and among them was a certain man clothed in linen with a writing case at his loins. And they went in and stood beside the bronze altar.

3 ¶ Then the glory of the God of Israel went up from the cherub on which it had been, to the threshold of the temple. And He called to the man clothed in linen at whose loins was the writing case.

4 And the LORD said to him, "Go through the midst of the city, *even* through the midst of Jerusalem, and put a mark on the foreheads of the men who sigh and groan over all the abominations which are being committed in its midst."

5 But to the others He said in my hearing, "Go through the city after him and strike; do not let your eye have pity, and do not spare.

6"Utterly slay old men, young men, maidens, little children, and women, but do not touch any man on whom is the mark; and you shall start from My sanctuary." So they started with the elders who *were* before the temple.

7 And He said to them, "Defile the temple and fill the courts with the slain. Go out!" Thus they went out and struck down *the people* in the city.

8 Then it came about as they were striking and I *alone* was left, that I fell on my face and cried out saying, "Alas, Lord GOD! Art Thou destroying

the whole remnant of Israel by pouring out Thy wrath on Jerusalem?"

9 ¶ Then He said to me, "The iniquity of the house of Israel and Judah is very, very great, and the land is filled with blood, and the city is full of perversion; for they say, 'The LORD has forsaken the land, and the LORD does not see!'

10"But as for Me, My eye will have no pity nor shall I spare, but I shall bring their conduct upon their heads."

11 ¶ Then behold, the man clothed in linen at whose loins was the writing case reported, saying, "I have done just as Thou hast commanded me."

CHAPTER 10

THEN I looked, and behold, in the expanse that was over the heads of the cherubim something like a sapphire stone, in appearance resembling a throne, appeared above them.

2 And He spoke to the man clothed in linen and said, "Enter between the whirling wheels under the cherubim, and fill your hands with coals of fire from between the cherubim, and scatter *them* over the city." And he entered in my sight.

3 ¶ Now the cherubim were standing on the right side of the temple when the man entered, and the cloud filled the inner court.

4 Then the glory of the LORD went up from the cherub to the threshold of the temple, and the temple was filled with the cloud, and the court was filled with the brightness of the glory of the LORD.

5 Moreover, the sound of the wings of the cherubim was heard as far as the outer court, like the voice of God Almighty when He speaks.

6 ¶ And it came about when He commanded the man clothed in linen, saying, "Take fire from between the whirling wheels, from between the cherubim," he entered and stood beside a wheel.

7 Then the cherub stretched out his hand from between the cherubim to the fire which *was* between the cherubim, took some and put it into the hands of the one clothed in linen, who took *it* and went out.

8 And the cherubim appeared to have the form of a man's hand under their wings.

9 ¶ Then I looked, and behold, four wheels beside the cherubim, one wheel beside each cherub; and the appearance of the wheels *was* like the gleam of a Tarshish stone.

10 And as for their appearance, all four of them had the same likeness, as if one wheel were within another wheel.

11 When they moved, they went in *any of* their four directions without turning as they went; but they followed in the direction which they faced, without turning as they went.

12 And their whole body, their backs, their hands, their wings, and the wheels were full of eyes all around, the wheels belonging to all four of them.

13 The wheels were called in my hearing, the whirling wheels.

14 And each one had four faces. The first face *was* the face of a cherub, the second face *was* the face of a man, the third the face of a lion, and the fourth the face of an eagle.

15 ¶ Then the cherubim rose up. They are the living beings that I saw by the river Chebar.

16 Now when the cherubim moved, the wheels would go beside them; also when the cherubim lifted up their wings to rise from the ground, the wheels would not turn from beside them.

17 When the cherubim stood still, the wheels would stand still; and when they rose up, the wheels would rise with them; for the spirit of the living beings *was* in them.

18 ¶ Then the glory of the LORD departed from the threshold of the temple and stood over the cherubim.

19 When the cherubim departed, they lifted their wings and rose up from the earth in my sight with the wheels beside them; and they stood still at the entrance of the east gate of the LORD's house. And the glory of the God of Israel hovered over them.

20 ¶ These are the living beings that I saw beneath the God of Israel by the river Chebar; so I knew that they *were* cherubim.

21 Each one had four faces and each one four wings, and beneath their wings *was* the form of human hands.

22 As for the likeness of their

faces, they were the same faces whose appearance I had seen by the river Chebar. Each one went straight ahead.

CHAPTER 11

MOREOVER, the Spirit lifted me up and brought me to the east gate of the LORD's house which faced eastward. And behold, *there were* twenty-five men at the entrance of the gate, and among them I saw Jaazaniah son of Azzur and Pelatiah son of Benaiah, leaders of the people.

2 And He said to me, "Son of man, these are the men who devise iniquity and give evil advice in this city,

3 who say, 'Is not *the time* near to build houses? This *city* is the pot and we are the flesh.'

4"Therefore, prophesy against them, son of man, prophesy!"

5 ¶ Then the Spirit of the LORD fell upon me, and He said to me, "Say, 'Thus says the LORD, "So you think, house of Israel, for I know your thoughts.

6"You have multiplied your slain in this city, filling its streets with them."

7 'Therefore, thus says the Lord GOD, "Your slain whom you have laid in the midst of the city are the flesh, and this *city* is the pot; but I shall bring you out of it.

8"You have feared a sword; so I will bring a sword upon you," the Lord GOD declares.

9"And I shall bring you out of the midst of the city, and I shall deliver you into the hands of strangers and execute judgments against you.

10"You will fall by the sword. I shall judge you to the border of Israel; so you shall know that I am the LORD.

11"This *city* will not be a pot for you, nor will you be flesh in the midst of it, *but* I shall judge you to the border of Israel.

12"Thus you will know that I am the LORD; for you have not walked in My statutes nor have you executed My ordinances, but have acted according to the ordinances of the nations around you."' "

13 ¶ Now it came about as I prophesied, that Pelatiah son of Benaiah died. Then I fell on my face and cried out with a loud voice and said, "Alas, Lord GOD! Wilt Thou bring the remnant of Israel to a complete end?"

14 ¶ Then the word of the LORD came to me, saying,

15"Son of man, your brothers, your relatives, your fellow exiles, and the whole house of Israel, all of them, *are those* to whom the inhabitants of Jerusalem have said, 'Go far from the LORD; this land has been given us as a possession.'

16"Therefore say, 'Thus says the Lord GOD, "Though I had removed them far away among the nations, and though I had scattered them among the countries, yet I was a sanctuary for them a little while in the countries where they had gone." '

17"Therefore say, 'Thus says the Lord GOD, "I shall gather you from the peoples and assemble you out of the countries among which you have been scattered, and I shall give you the land of Israel." '

18"When they come there, they will remove all its detestable things and all its abominations from it.

19"And I shall give them one heart, and shall put a new spirit within them. And I shall take the heart of stone out of their flesh and give them a heart of flesh,

20 that they may walk in My statutes and keep My ordinances, and do them. Then they will be My people, and I shall be their God.

21"But as for those whose hearts go after their detestable things and abominations, I shall bring their conduct down on their heads," declares the Lord GOD.

22 ¶ Then the cherubim lifted up their wings with the wheels beside them, and the glory of the God of Israel hovered over them.

23 And the glory of the LORD went up from the midst of the city, and stood over the mountain which is east of the city.

24 And the Spirit lifted me up and brought me in a vision by the Spirit of God to the exiles in Chaldea. So the vision that I had seen left me.

25 Then I told the exiles all the things that the LORD had shown me.

CHAPTER 12

THEN the word of the LORD came to me saying,

2"Son of man, you live in the midst

of the rebellious house, who have eyes to see but do not see, ears to hear but do not hear; for they are a rebellious house.

3"Therefore, son of man, prepare for yourself baggage for exile and go into exile by day in their sight; even go into exile from your place to another place in their sight. Perhaps they will understand though they are a rebellious house.

4"And bring your baggage out by day in their sight, as baggage for exile. Then you will go out at evening in their sight, as those going into exile.

5"Dig a hole through the wall in their sight and go out through it.

6"Load the baggage on your shoulder in their sight, and carry it out in the dark. You shall cover your face so that you can not see the land, for I have set you as a sign to the house of Israel."

7 ¶ And I did so, as I had been commanded. By day I brought out my baggage like the baggage of an exile. Then in the evening I dug through the wall with my hands; I went out in the dark and carried the baggage on my shoulder in their sight.

8 ¶ And in the morning the word of the LORD came to me, saying,

9"Son of man, has not the house of Israel, the rebellious house, said to you, 'What are you doing?'

10"Say to them, 'Thus says the Lord GOD, "This burden concerns the prince in Jerusalem, as well as all the house of Israel who are in it." '

11"Say, 'I am a sign to you. As I have done, so it will be done to them; they will go into exile, into captivity.'

12"And the prince who is among them will load his baggage on his shoulder in the dark and go out. They will dig a hole through the wall to bring it out. He will cover his face so that he can not see the land with his eyes.

13"I shall also spread My net over him, and he will be caught in My snare. And I shall bring him to Babylon in the land of the Chaldeans; yet he will not see it, though he will die there.

14"And I shall scatter to every wind all who are around him, his helpers and all his troops; and I shall draw out a sword after them.

15"So they will know that I am the LORD when I scatter them among the nations, and spread them among the countries.

16"But I shall spare a few of them from the sword, the famine, and the pestilence that they may tell all their abominations among the nations where they go, and may know that I am the LORD."

17 ¶ Moreover, the word of the LORD came to me, saying,

18"Son of man, eat your bread with trembling, and drink your water with quivering and anxiety.

19"Then say to the people of the land, 'Thus says the Lord GOD concerning the inhabitants of Jerusalem in the land of Israel, "They will eat their bread with anxiety and drink their water with horror, because their land will be stripped of its fulness on account of the violence of all who live in it.

20"And the inhabited cities will be laid waste, and the land will be a desolation. So you will know that I am the LORD." ' "

21 ¶ Then the word of the LORD came to me, saying,

22"Son of man, what is this proverb you people have concerning the land of Israel, saying, 'The days are long and every vision fails'?

23"Therefore say to them, 'Thus says the Lord GOD, "I will make this proverb cease so that they will no longer use it as a proverb in Israel." But tell them, "The days draw near as well as the fulfillment of every vision.

24"For there will no longer be any false vision or flattering divination within the house of Israel.

25"For I the LORD shall speak, and whatever word I speak will be performed. It will no longer be delayed, for in your days, O rebellious house, I shall speak the word and perform it," declares the Lord GOD.' "

26 ¶ Furthermore, the word of the LORD came to me, saying,

27"Son of man, behold, the house of Israel is saying, 'The vision that he sees is for many years from now, and he prophesies of times far off.'

28"Therefore say to them, 'Thus says the Lord GOD, "None of My words will be delayed any longer. Whatever word

I speak will be performed,' ' " declares the Lord GOD.

CHAPTER 13

THEN the word of the LORD came to me saying,

2"Son of man, prophesy against the prophets of Israel who prophesy, and say to those who prophesy from their own inspiration, 'Listen to the word of the LORD!

3 'Thus says the Lord GOD, "Woe to the foolish prophets who are following their own spirit and have seen nothing.

4"O Israel, your prophets have been like foxes among ruins.

5"You have not gone up into the breaches, nor did you build the wall around the house of Israel to stand in the battle on the day of the LORD.

6"They see falsehood and lying divination who are saying, 'The LORD declares,' when the LORD has not sent them; yet they hope for the fulfillment of their word.

7"Did you not see a false vision and speak a lying divination when you said, 'The LORD declares,' but it is not I who have spoken?" ' "

8 ¶ Therefore, thus says the Lord GOD, "Because you have spoken falsehood and seen a lie, therefore behold, I am against you," declares the Lord GOD.

9"So My hand will be against the prophets who see false visions and utter lying divinations. They will have no place in the council of My people, nor will they be written down in the register of the house of Israel, nor will they enter the land of Israel, that you may know that I am the Lord GOD.

10"It is definitely because they have misled My people by saying, 'Peace!' when there is no peace. And when anyone builds a wall, behold, they plaster it over with whitewash;

11 so tell those who plaster it over with whitewash, that it will fall. A flooding rain will come, and you, O hailstones, will fall; and a violent wind will break out.

12"Behold, when the wall has fallen, will you not be asked, 'Where is the plaster with which you plastered it?' "

13 Therefore, thus says the Lord

GOD, "I will make a violent wind break out in My wrath. There will also be in My anger a flooding rain and hailstones to consume it in wrath.

14"So I shall tear down the wall which you plastered over with whitewash and bring it down to the ground, so that its foundation is laid bare; and when it falls, you will be consumed in its midst. And you will know that I am the LORD.

15"Thus I shall spend My wrath on the wall and on those who have plastered it over with whitewash; and I shall say to you, 'The wall is gone and its plasterers are gone,

16 along with the prophets of Israel who prophesy to Jerusalem, and who see visions of peace for her when there is no peace,' declares the Lord GOD.

17 ¶"Now you, son of man, set your face against the daughters of your people who are prophesying from their own inspiration. Prophesy against them,

18 and say, 'Thus says the Lord GOD, "Woe to the women who sew magic bands on all wrists, and make veils for the heads of persons of every stature to hunt down lives! Will you hunt down the lives of My people, but preserve the lives of others for yourselves?

19"And for handfuls of barley and fragments of bread, you have profaned Me to My people to put to death some who should not die and to keep others alive who should not live, by your lying to My people who listen to lies." ' "

20 ¶ Therefore, thus says the Lord GOD, "Behold, I am against your magic bands by which you hunt lives there as birds, and I will tear them off your arms; and I will let them go, even those lives whom you hunt as birds.

21"I will also tear off your veils and deliver My people from your hands, and they will no longer be in your hands to be hunted; and you will know that I am the LORD.

22"Because you disheartened the righteous with falsehood when I did not cause him grief, but have encouraged the wicked not to turn from his wicked way and preserve his life,

23 therefore, you women will no longer see false visions or practice

divination, and I will deliver My people out of your hand. Thus you will know that I am the LORD."

CHAPTER 14

THEN some elders of Israel came to me and sat down before me.

2 And the word of the LORD came to me saying,

3"Son of man, these men have set up their idols in their hearts, and have put right before their faces the stumbling block of their iniquity. Should I be consulted by them at all?

4"Therefore speak to them and tell them, 'Thus says the Lord GOD, "Any man of the house of Israel who sets up his idols in his heart, puts right before his face the stumbling block of his iniquity, and then comes to the prophet, I the LORD will be brought to give him an answer in the matter in view of the multitude of his idols,

5 in order to lay hold of the hearts of the house of Israel who are estranged from Me through all their idols.' "

6 ¶"Therefore say to the house of Israel, 'Thus says the Lord GOD, "Repent and turn away from your idols, and turn your faces away from all your abominations.

7"For anyone of the house of Israel or of the immigrants who stay in Israel who separates himself from Me, sets up his idols in his heart, puts right before his face the stumbling block of his iniquity, and then comes to the prophet to inquire of Me for himself, I the LORD will be brought to answer him in My own person.

8"And I shall set My face against that man and make him a sign and a proverb, and I shall cut him off from among My people. So you will know that I am the LORD.

9"But if the prophet is prevailed upon to speak a word, it is I, the LORD, who have prevailed upon that prophet, and I will stretch out My hand against him and destroy him from among My people Israel.

10"And they will bear the punishment of their iniquity; as the iniquity of the inquirer is, so the iniquity of the prophet will be,

11 in order that the house of Israel may no longer stray from Me and no longer defile themselves with all their transgressions. Thus they will be My people, and I shall be their God,"' declares the Lord GOD."

12 ¶ Then the word of the LORD came to me saying,

13"Son of man, if a country sins against Me by committing unfaithfulness, and I stretch out My hand against it, destroy its supply of bread, send famine against it, and cut off from it both man and beast,

14 even though these three men, Noah, Daniel, and Job were in its midst, by their own righteousness they could only deliver themselves," declares the Lord GOD.

15"If I were to cause wild beasts to pass through the land, and they depopulated it, and it became desolate so that no one would pass through it because of the beasts,

16 though these three men were in its midst, as I live," declares the Lord GOD, "they could not deliver either their sons or their daughters. They alone would be delivered, but the country would be desolate.

17"Or if I should bring a sword on that country and say, 'Let the sword pass through the country and cut off man and beast from it,'

18 even though these three men were in its midst, as I live," declares the Lord GOD, "they could not deliver either their sons or their daughters, but they alone would be delivered.

19"Or if I should send a plague against that country and pour out My wrath in blood on it, to cut off man and beast from it,

20 even though Noah, Daniel, and Job were in its midst, as I live," declares the Lord GOD, "they could not deliver either their son or their daughter. They would deliver only themselves by their righteousness."

21 ¶ For thus says the Lord GOD, "How much more when I send My four severe judgments against Jerusalem: sword, famine, wild beasts, and plague to cut off man and beast from it!

22"Yet, behold, survivors will be left in it who will be brought out, both sons and daughters. Behold, they are going to come forth to you and you will see their conduct and actions; then you will be comforted for the calamity which I have brought against Jerusalem for everything which I have brought upon it.

23"Then they will comfort you when you see their conduct and actions, for you will know that I have not done in vain whatever I did to it," declares the Lord GOD.

CHAPTER 15

THEN the word of the LORD came to me saying,

2"Son of man, how is the wood of the vine *better* than any wood of a branch which is among the trees of the forest?

3"Can wood be taken from it to make anything, or can *men* take a peg from it on which to hang any vessel?

4"If it has been put into the fire for fuel, *and* the fire has consumed both of its ends, and its middle part has been charred, is it *then* useful for anything?

5"Behold, while it is intact, it is not made into anything. How much less, when the fire has consumed it and it is charred, can it still be made into anything!

6"Therefore, thus says the Lord GOD, 'As the wood of the vine among the trees of the forest, which I have given to the fire for fuel, so have I given up the inhabitants of Jerusalem;

7 and I set My face against them. *Though* they have come out of the fire, yet the fire will consume them. Then you will know that I am the LORD, when I set My face against them.

8 'Thus I will make the land desolate, because they have acted unfaithfully,'" declares the Lord GOD.

CHAPTER 16

THEN the word of the LORD came to me saying,

2"Son of man, make known to Jerusalem her abominations,

3 and say, 'Thus says the Lord GOD to Jerusalem, "Your origin and your birth are from the land of the Canaanite, your father was an Amorite and your mother a Hittite.

4"As for your birth, on the day you were born your navel cord was not cut, nor were you washed with water for cleansing; you were not rubbed with salt or even wrapped in cloths.

5"No eye looked with pity on you to do any of these things for you, to have compassion on you. Rather you were thrown out into the open field, for you were abhorred on the day you were born.

6 ¶"When I passed by you and saw you squirming in your blood, I said to you *while you were* in your blood, 'Live!' I said to you while you were in your blood, 'Live!'

7"I made you numerous like plants of the field. Then you grew up, became tall, and reached the age for fine ornaments; *your* breasts were formed and your hair had grown. Yet you were naked and bare.

8"Then I passed by you and saw you, and behold, you were at the time for love; so I spread My skirt over you and covered your nakedness. I also swore to you and entered into a covenant with you so that you became Mine," declares the Lord GOD.

9"Then I bathed you with water, washed off your blood from you, and anointed you with oil.

10"I also clothed you with embroidered cloth, and put sandals of porpoise skin on your feet; and I wrapped you with fine linen and covered you with silk.

11"And I adorned you with ornaments, put bracelets on your hands, and a necklace around your neck.

12"I also put a ring in your nostril, earrings in your ears, and a beautiful crown on your head.

13"Thus you were adorned with gold and silver, and your dress was of fine linen, silk, and embroidered cloth. You ate fine flour, honey, and oil; so you were exceedingly beautiful and advanced to royalty.

14"Then your fame went forth among the nations on account of your beauty, for it was perfect because of My splendor which I bestowed on you," declares the Lord GOD.

15 ¶"But you trusted in your beauty and played the harlot because of your fame, and you poured out your harlotries on every passer-by who might be *willing.*

16"And you took some of your clothes, made for yourself high places of various colors, and played the harlot on them, which should never come about nor happen.

17"You also took your beautiful jewels *made* of My gold and of My silver, which I had given you, and made for yourself male images that you might play the harlot with them.

18"Then you took your embroidered cloth and covered them, and offered My oil and My incense before them.

19"Also My bread which I gave you, fine flour, oil, and honey with which I fed you, you would offer before them for a soothing aroma; so it happened," declares the Lord GOD.

20"Moreover, you took your sons and daughters whom you had borne to Me, and you sacrificed them to idols to be devoured. Were your harlotries so small a matter?

21"You slaughtered My children, and offered them up to idols by causing them to pass through *the fire.*

22"And besides all your abominations and harlotries you did not remember the days of your youth, when you were naked and bare and squirming in your blood.

23 ¶"Then it came about after all your wickedness ('Woe, woe to you!' declares the Lord GOD),

24 that you built yourself a shrine and made yourself a high place in every square.

25"You built yourself a high place at the top of every street, and made your beauty abominable; and you spread your legs to every passer-by to multiply your harlotry.

26"You also played the harlot with the Egyptians, your lustful neighbors, and multiplied your harlotry to make Me angry.

27"Behold now, I have stretched out My hand against you and diminished your rations. And I delivered you up to the desire of those who hate you, the daughters of the Philistines, who are ashamed of your lewd conduct.

28"Moreover, you played the harlot with the Assyrians because you were not satisfied; you even played the harlot with them and still were not satisfied.

29"You also multiplied your harlotry with the land of merchants, Chaldea, yet even with this you were not satisfied." '

30 ¶"How languishing is your heart," declares the Lord GOD, "while you do all these things, the actions of a bold-faced harlot.

31"When you built your shrine at the beginning of every street and made your high place in every square, in disdaining money, you were not like a harlot.

32"You adulteress wife, who takes strangers instead of her husband!

33"Men give gifts to all harlots, but you give your gifts to all your lovers to bribe them to come to you from every direction for your harlotries.

34"Thus you are different from those women in your harlotries, in that no one plays the harlot as you do, because you give money and no money is given you; thus you are different."

35 ¶ Therefore, O harlot, hear the word of the LORD.

36 Thus says the Lord GOD, "Because your lewdness was poured out and your nakedness uncovered through your harlotries with your lovers and with all your detestable idols, and because of the blood of your sons which you gave to idols,

37 therefore, behold, I shall gather all your lovers with whom you took pleasure, even all those whom you loved *and* all those whom you hated. So I shall gather them against you from every direction and expose your nakedness to them that they may see all your nakedness.

38"Thus I shall judge you, like women who commit adultery or shed blood are judged; and I shall bring on you the blood of wrath and jealousy.

39"I shall also give you into the hands of your lovers, and they will tear down your shrines, demolish your high places, strip you of your clothing, take away your jewels, and will leave you naked and bare.

40"They will incite a crowd against you, and they will stone you and cut you to pieces with their swords.

41"And they will burn your houses with fire and execute judgments on you in the sight of many women. Then I shall stop you from playing the harlot, and you will also no longer pay your lovers.

42"So I shall calm My fury against you, and My jealousy will depart from you, and I shall be pacified and angry no more.

43"Because you have not remembered the days of your youth but have enraged Me by all these things, behold, I in turn will bring your conduct down on your own head," declares the Lord GOD, "so that you will not commit this lewdness on top of all your *other* abominations.

44 ¶"Behold, everyone who quotes proverbs will quote *this* proverb concerning you, saying, 'Like mother, like daughter.'

45"You are the daughter of your mother, who loathed her husband and children. You are also the sister of your sisters, who loathed their husbands and children. Your mother was a Hittite and your father an Amorite.

46"Now your older sister is Samaria, who lives north of you with her daughters; and your younger sister, who lives south of you, is Sodom with her daughters.

47"Yet you have not merely walked in their ways or done according to their abominations; but, as if that were too little, you acted more corruptly in all your conduct than they.

48"As I live," declares the Lord GOD, "Sodom, your sister, and her daughters, have not done as you and your daughters have done.

49"Behold, this was the guilt of your sister Sodom: she and her daughters had arrogance, abundant food, and careless ease, but she did not help the poor and needy.

50"Thus they were haughty and committed abominations before Me. Therefore I removed them when I saw *it*.

51"Furthermore, Samaria did not commit half of your sins, for you have multiplied your abominations more than they. Thus you have made your sisters appear righteous by all your abominations which you have committed.

52"Also bear your disgrace in that you have made judgment favorable for your sisters. Because of your sins in which you acted more abominably than they, they are more in the right than you. Yes, be also ashamed and bear your disgrace, in that you made your sisters appear righteous.

53 ¶"Nevertheless, I will restore their captivity, the captivity of Sodom and her daughters, the captivity of Samaria and her daughters, and along with them your own captivity,

54 in order that you may bear your humiliation, and feel ashamed for all that you have done when you become a consolation to them.

55"And your sisters, Sodom with her daughters and Samaria with her daughters, will return to their former state, and you with your daughters will *also* return to your former state.

56"As *the name of* your sister Sodom was not heard from your lips in your day of pride,

57 before your wickedness was uncovered, so now you have become the reproach of the daughters of Edom, and of all who are around her, of the daughters of the Philistines—those surrounding *you* who despise you.

58"You have borne *the penalty of* your lewdness and abominations," the LORD declares.

59 For thus says the Lord GOD, "I will also do with you as you have done, you who have despised the oath by breaking the covenant.

60 ¶"Nevertheless, I will remember My covenant with you in the days of your youth, and I will establish an everlasting covenant with you.

61"Then you will remember your ways and be ashamed when you receive your sisters, *both* your older and your younger; and I will give them to you as daughters, but not because of your covenant.

62"Thus I will establish My covenant with you, and you shall know that I am the LORD,

63 in order that you may remember and be ashamed, and never open your mouth anymore because of your humiliation, when I have forgiven you for all that you have done," the Lord GOD declares.

CHAPTER 17

NOW the word of the LORD came to me saying,

2"Son of man, propound a riddle, and speak a parable to the house of Israel,

3 saying, 'Thus says the Lord GOD, "A great eagle with great wings, long pinions and a full plumage of many

colors, came to Lebanon and took away the top of the cedar.

4"He plucked off the topmost of its young twigs and brought it to a land of merchants; he set it in a city of traders.

5"He also took some of the seed of the land and planted it in fertile soil. He placed it beside abundant waters; he set it like a willow.

6"Then it sprouted and became a low, spreading vine with its branches turned toward him, but its roots remained under it. So it became a vine, and yielded shoots and sent out branches.

7 ¶"But there was another great eagle with great wings and much plumage; and behold, this vine bent its roots toward him and sent out its branches toward him from the beds where it was planted, that he might water it.

8"It was planted in good soil beside abundant waters, that it might yield branches and bear fruit, and become a splendid vine." '

9"Say, 'Thus says the Lord GOD, "Will it thrive? Will he not pull up its roots and cut off its fruit, so that it withers—so that all its sprouting leaves wither? And neither by great strength nor by many people can it be raised from its roots again.

10"Behold, though it is planted, will it thrive? Will it not completely wither as soon as the east wind strikes it— wither on the beds where it grew?" ' "

11 ¶ Moreover, the word of the LORD came to me saying,

12"Say now to the rebellious house, 'Do you not know what these things mean?' Say, 'Behold, the king of Babylon came to Jerusalem, took its king and princes, and brought them to him in Babylon.

13 'And he took one of the royal family and made a covenant with him, putting him under oath. He also took away the mighty of the land,

14 that the kingdom might be in subjection, not exalting itself, but keeping his covenant, that it might continue.

15 'But he rebelled against him by sending his envoys to Egypt that they might give him horses and many troops. Will he succeed? Will he who

does such things escape? Can he indeed break the covenant and escape?

16 'As I live,' declares the Lord GOD, 'Surely in the country of the king who put him on the throne, whose oath he despised, and whose covenant he broke, in Babylon he shall die.

17 'And Pharaoh with his mighty army and great company will not help him in the war, when they cast up mounds and build siege walls to cut off many lives.

18 'Now he despised the oath by breaking the covenant, and behold, he pledged his allegiance, yet did all these things; he shall not escape.' "

19 Therefore, thus says the Lord GOD, "As I live, surely My oath which he despised and My covenant which he broke, I will inflict on his head.

20"And I will spread My net over him, and he will be caught in My snare. Then I will bring him to Babylon and enter into judgment with him there regarding the unfaithful act which he has committed against Me.

21"And all the choice men in all his troops will fall by the sword, and the survivors will be scattered to every wind; and you will know that I, the LORD, have spoken."

22 ¶ Thus says the Lord GOD, "I shall also take a sprig from the lofty top of the cedar and set it out; I shall pluck from the topmost of its young twigs a tender one, and I shall plant it on a high and lofty mountain.

23"On the high mountain of Israel I shall plant it, that it may bring forth boughs and bear fruit, and become a stately cedar. And birds of every kind will nest under it; they will nest in the shade of its branches.

24"And all the trees of the field will know that I am the LORD; I bring down the high tree, exalt the low tree, dry up the green tree, and make the dry tree flourish. I am the LORD; I have spoken, and I will perform it."

CHAPTER 18

THEN the word of the LORD came to me saying,

2"What do you mean by using this proverb concerning the land of Israel saying,

'The fathers eat the sour grapes,

But the children's teeth are set on edge'?

3"As I live," declares the Lord God, "you are surely not going to use this proverb in Israel anymore.

4"Behold, all souls are Mine; the soul of the father as well as the soul of the son is Mine. The soul who sins will die.

5"But if a man is righteous, and practices justice and righteousness,

6 and does not eat at the mountain *shrines* or lift up his eyes to the idols of the house of Israel, or defile his neighbor's wife, or approach a woman during her menstrual period—

7 if a man does not oppress anyone, but restores to the debtor his pledge, does not commit robbery, *but* gives his bread to the hungry, and covers the naked with clothing,

8 if he does not lend *money* on interest or take increase, *if* he keeps his hand from iniquity, *and* executes true justice between man and man,

9 *if* he walks in My statutes and My ordinances so as to deal faithfully—he is righteous *and* will surely live," declares the Lord God.

10 ¶"Then he may have a violent son who sheds blood, and who does any of these things to a brother

11 (though he himself did not do any of these things), that is, he even eats at the mountain *shrines,* and defiles his neighbor's wife,

12 oppresses the poor and needy, commits robbery, does not restore a pledge, but lifts up his eyes to the idols, *and* commits abomination,

13 he lends *money* on interest and takes increase; will he live? He will not live! He has committed all these abominations, he will surely be put to death; his blood will be on his own head.

14 ¶"Now behold, he has a son who has observed all his father's sins which he committed, and observing does not do likewise.

15"He does not eat at the mountain *shrines* or lift up his eyes to the idols of the house of Israel, or defile his neighbor's wife,

16 or oppress anyone, or retain a pledge, or commit robbery, *but* he gives his bread to the hungry, and covers the naked with clothing,

17 he keeps his hand from the poor,

does not take interest or increase, *but* executes My ordinances, and walks in My statutes; he will not die for his father's iniquity, he will surely live.

18"As for his father, because he practiced extortion, robbed *his* brother, and did what was not good among his people, behold, he will die for his iniquity.

19 ¶"Yet you say, 'Why should the son not bear the punishment for the father's iniquity?' When the son has practiced justice and righteousness, and has observed all My statutes and done them, he shall surely live.

20"The person who sins will die. The son will not bear the punishment for the father's iniquity, nor will the father bear the punishment for the son's iniquity; the righteousness of the righteous will be upon himself, and the wickedness of the wicked will be upon himself.

21 ¶"But if the wicked man turns from all his sins which he has committed and observes all My statutes and practices justice and righteousness, he shall surely live; he shall not die.

22"All his transgressions which he has committed will not be remembered against him; because of his righteousness which he has practiced, he will live.

23"Do I have any pleasure in the death of the wicked," declares the Lord God, "rather than that he should turn from his ways and live?

24 ¶"But when a righteous man turns away from his righteousness, commits iniquity, and does according to all the abominations that a wicked man does, will he live? All his righteous deeds which he has done will not be remembered for his treachery which he has committed and his sin which he has committed; for them he will die.

25"Yet you say, 'The way of the Lord is not right.' Hear now, O house of Israel! Is My way not right? Is it not your ways that are not right?

26"When a righteous man turns away from his righteousness, commits iniquity, and dies because of it, for his iniquity which he has committed he will die.

27"Again, when a wicked man turns away from his wickedness which he has committed and practices justice and righteousness, he will save his life.

28"Because he considered and turned away from all his transgressions which he had committed, he shall surely live; he shall not die.

29"But the house of Israel says, 'The way of the Lord is not right.' Are My ways not right, O house of Israel? Is it not your ways that are not right?

30 ¶"Therefore I will judge you, O house of Israel, each according to his conduct," declares the Lord GOD. "Repent and turn away from all your transgressions, so that iniquity may not become a stumbling block to you.

31"Cast away from you all your transgressions which you have committed, and make yourselves a new heart and a new spirit! For why will you die, O house of Israel?

32"For I have no pleasure in the death of anyone who dies," declares the Lord GOD. "Therefore, repent and live."

CHAPTER 19

"AS for you, take up a lamentation for the princes of Israel,

  2 and say,
    'What was your mother?
    A lioness among lions!
    She lay down among young lions,
    She reared her cubs.
  3 'When she brought up one of her cubs,
    He became a lion,
    And he learned to tear *his* prey;
    He devoured men.
  4 'Then nations heard about him;
    He was captured in their pit,
    And they brought him with hooks
    To the land of Egypt.
  5 'When she saw, as she waited,
    That her hope was lost,
    She took another of her cubs
    And made him a young lion.
  6 'And he walked about among the lions;
    He became a young lion,
    He learned to tear *his* prey;
    He devoured men.
  7 'And he destroyed their fortified towers
    And laid waste their cities;
    And the land and its fulness were appalled

    Because of the sound of his roaring.
  8 'Then nations set against him
    On every side from *their* provinces,
    And they spread their net over him;
    He was captured in their pit.
  9 'And they put him in a cage with hooks
    And brought him to the king of Babylon;
    They brought him in hunting nets
    So that his voice should be heard no more
    On the mountains of Israel.
  10 'Your mother was like a vine in your vineyard,
    Planted by the waters;
    It was fruitful and full of branches
    Because of abundant waters.
  11 'And it had strong branches *fit* for scepters of rulers,
    And its height was raised above the clouds
    So that it was seen in its height with the mass of its branches.
  12 'But it was plucked up in fury;
    It was cast down to the ground;
    And the east wind dried up its fruit.
    Its strong branch was torn off
    So that it withered;
    The fire consumed it.
  13 'And now it is planted in the wilderness,
    In a dry and thirsty land.
  14 'And fire has gone out from *its* branch;
    It has consumed its shoots *and* fruit,
    So that there is not in it a strong branch,
    A scepter to rule.' "
This is a lamentation, and has become a lamentation.

CHAPTER 20

NOW it came about in the seventh year, in the fifth *month,* on the tenth of the month, that certain of the elders of Israel came to inquire of the LORD, and sat before me.

2 And the word of the LORD came to me saying,

  3"Son of man, speak to the elders of

Israel, and say to them, 'Thus says the Lord God, "Do you come to inquire of Me? As I live," declares the Lord God, "I will not be inquired of by you." '

4"Will you judge them, will you judge them, son of man? Make them know the abominations of their fathers;

5 and say to them, 'Thus says the Lord God, "On the day when I chose Israel and swore to the descendants of the house of Jacob and made Myself known to them in the land of Egypt, when I swore to them, saying, I am the Lord your God,

6 on that day I swore to them, to bring them out from the land of Egypt into a land that I had selected for them, flowing with milk and honey, which is the glory of all lands.

7"And I said to them, 'Cast away, each of you, the detestable things of his eyes, and do not defile yourselves with the idols of Egypt; I am the Lord your God.'

8"But they rebelled against Me and were not willing to listen to Me; they did not cast away the detestable things of their eyes, nor did they forsake the idols of Egypt.

¶ Then I resolved to pour out My wrath on them, to accomplish My anger against them in the midst of the land of Egypt.

9"But I acted for the sake of My name, that it should not be profaned in the sight of the nations among whom they *lived*, in whose sight I made Myself known to them by bringing them out of the land of Egypt.

10"So I took them out of the land of Egypt and brought them into the wilderness.

11"And I gave them My statutes and informed them of My ordinances, by which, if a man observes them, he will live.

12"And also I gave them My sabbaths to be a sign between Me and them, that they might know that I am the Lord who sanctifies them.

13"But the house of Israel rebelled against Me in the wilderness. They did not walk in My statutes, and they rejected My ordinances, by which, if a man observes them, he will live; and My sabbaths they greatly profaned. Then I resolved to pour out My wrath

on them in the wilderness, to annihilate them.

14"But I acted for the sake of My name, that it should not be profaned in the sight of the nations, before whose sight I had brought them out.

15"And also I swore to them in the wilderness that I would not bring them into the land which I had given them, flowing with milk and honey, which is the glory of all lands,

16 because they rejected My ordinances, and as for My statutes, they did not walk in them; they even profaned My sabbaths, for their heart continually went after their idols.

17"Yet My eye spared them rather than destroying them, and I did not cause their annihilation in the wilderness.

18 ¶"And I said to their children in the wilderness, 'Do not walk in the statutes of your fathers, or keep their ordinances, or defile yourselves with their idols.

19 'I am the Lord your God; walk in My statutes, and keep My ordinances, and observe them.

20 'And sanctify My sabbaths; and they shall be a sign between Me and you, that you may know that I am the Lord your God.'

21"But the children rebelled against Me; they did not walk in My statutes, nor were they careful to observe My ordinances, by which, *if* a man observes them, he will live; they profaned My sabbaths. So I resolved to pour out My wrath on them, to accomplish My anger against them in the wilderness.

22"But I withdrew My hand and acted for the sake of My name, that it should not be profaned in the sight of the nations in whose sight I had brought them out.

23"Also I swore to them in the wilderness that I would scatter them among the nations and disperse them among the lands,

24 because they had not observed My ordinances, but had rejected My statutes, and had profaned My sabbaths, and their eyes were on the idols of their fathers.

25"And I also gave them statutes that were not good and ordinances by which they could not live;

26 and I pronounced them unclean

because of their gifts, in that they caused all their first-born to pass through *the fire* so that I might make them desolate, in order that they might know that I am the LORD." '

27 ¶"Therefore, son of man, speak to the house of Israel, and say to them, 'Thus says the Lord GOD, "Yet in this your fathers have blasphemed Me by acting treacherously against Me.

28"When I had brought them into the land which I swore to give to them, then they saw every high hill and every leafy tree, and they offered there their sacrifices, and there they presented the provocation of their offering. There also they made their soothing aroma, and there they poured out their libations.

29"Then I said to them, 'What is the high place to which you go?' So its name is called ¹Bamah to this day." '

30"Therefore, say to the house of Israel, 'Thus says the Lord GOD, "Will you defile yourselves after the manner of your fathers and play the harlot after their detestable things?

31"And when you offer your gifts, when you cause your sons to pass through the fire, you are defiling yourselves with all your idols to this day. And shall I be inquired of by you, O house of Israel? As I live," declares the Lord GOD, "I will not be inquired of by you.

32"And what comes into your mind will not come about, when you say: 'We will be like the nations, like the tribes of the lands, serving wood and stone.'

33"As I live," declares the Lord GOD, "surely with a mighty hand and with an outstretched arm and with wrath poured out, I shall be king over you.

34"And I shall bring you out from the peoples and gather you from the lands where you are scattered, with a mighty hand and with an outstretched arm and with wrath poured out;

35 and I shall bring you into the wilderness of the peoples, and there I shall enter into judgment with you face to face.

36"As I entered into judgment with your fathers in the wilderness of the land of Egypt, so I will enter into judgment with you," declares the Lord GOD.

37"And I shall make you pass under the rod, and I shall bring you into the bond of the covenant;

38 and I shall purge from you the rebels and those who transgress against Me; I shall bring them out of the land where they sojourn, but they will not enter the land of Israel. Thus you will know that I am the LORD.

39"As for you, O house of Israel," thus says the Lord GOD, "Go, serve everyone his idols; but later, you will surely listen to Me, and My holy name you will profane no longer with your gifts and with your idols.

40"For on My holy mountain, on the high mountain of Israel," declares the Lord GOD, "there the whole house of Israel, all of them, will serve Me in the land; there I shall accept them, and there I shall seek your contributions and the choicest of your gifts, with all your holy things.

41"As a soothing aroma I shall accept you, when I bring you out from the peoples and gather you from the lands where you are scattered; and I shall prove Myself holy among you in the sight of the nations.

42"And you will know that I am the LORD, when I bring you into the land of Israel, into the land which I swore to give to your forefathers.

43"And there you will remember your ways and all your deeds, with which you have defiled yourselves; and you will loathe yourselves in your own sight for all the evil things that you have done.

44"Then you will know that I am the LORD when I have dealt with you for My name's sake, not according to your evil ways or according to your corrupt deeds, O house of Israel," declares the Lord GOD.' "

45 Now the word of the LORD came to me saying,

46"Son of man, set your face toward Teman, and speak out against the south, and prophesy against the forest land of the Negev,

47 and say to the forest of the Negev, 'Hear the word of the LORD: thus says the Lord GOD, "Behold, I am about to kindle a fire in you, and it shall consume every green tree in you, as well as every dry tree; the blazing flame

---

¹ Or, *High Place*

will not be quenched, and the whole surface from south to north will be burned by it.

48"And all flesh will see that I, the LORD, have kindled it; it shall not be quenched." ' "

49 Then I said, "Ah Lord GOD! They are saying of me, 'Is he not *just* speaking parables?' "

CHAPTER 21

AND the word of the LORD came to me saying,

2"Son of man, set your face toward Jerusalem, and speak against the sanctuaries, and prophesy against the land of Israel;

3 and say to the land of Israel, 'Thus says the LORD, "Behold, I am against you; and I shall draw My sword out of its sheath and cut off from you the righteous and the wicked.

4"Because I shall cut off from you the righteous and the wicked, therefore My sword shall go forth from its sheath against all flesh from south *to* north.

5"Thus all flesh will know that I, the LORD, have drawn My sword out of its sheath. It will not return *to its sheath* again." '

6"As for you, son of man, groan with breaking heart and bitter grief, groan in their sight.

7"And it will come about when they say to you, 'Why do you groan?' that you will say, 'Because of the news that is coming; and every heart will melt, all hands will be feeble, every spirit will faint, and all knees will be weak as water. Behold, it comes and it will happen,' declares the Lord GOD."

8 Again the word of the LORD came to me saying,

9"Son of man, prophesy and say, 'Thus says the LORD.' Say,

'A sword, a sword sharpened
And also polished!

10 'Sharpened to make a slaughter,
Polished to flash like lightning!'
Or shall we rejoice, the rod of My son despising every tree?

11"And it is given to be polished, that it may be handled; the sword is sharpened and polished, to give it into the hand of the slayer.

12"Cry out and wail, son of man; for it is against My people, it is against all

the officials of Israel. They are delivered over to the sword with My people, therefore strike *your* thigh.

13"For *there is* a testing; and what if even the rod which despises will be no more?" declares the Lord GOD.

14 ¶"You therefore, son of man, prophesy, and clap *your* hands together; and let the sword be doubled the third time, the sword for the slain. It is the sword for the great one slain, which surrounds them,

15 that *their* hearts may melt, and many fall at all their gates. I have given the glittering sword. Ah! It is made *for striking* like lightning, it is wrapped up *in readiness* for slaughter.

16"Show yourself sharp, go to the right; set yourself; go to the left, wherever your edge is appointed.

17"I shall also clap My hands together, and I shall appease My wrath; I, the LORD, have spoken."

18 ¶ And the word of the LORD came to me saying,

19"As for you, son of man, make two ways for the sword of the king of Babylon to come; both of them will go out of one land. And make a signpost; make it at the head of the way to the city.

20"You shall mark a way for the sword to come to Rabbah of the sons of Ammon, and to Judah into fortified Jerusalem.

21"For the king of Babylon stands at the parting of the way, at the head of the two ways, to use divination; he shakes the arrows, he consults the household idols, he looks at the liver.

22"Into his right hand came the divination, 'Jerusalem,' to set battering rams, to open the mouth for slaughter, to lift up the voice with a battle cry, to set battering rams against the gates, to cast up mounds, to build a siege wall.

23"And it will be to them like a false divination in their eyes; they have *sworn* solemn oaths. But he brings iniquity to remembrance, that they may be seized.

24"Therefore, thus says the Lord GOD, 'Because you have made your iniquity to be remembered, in that your transgressions are uncovered, so that in all your deeds your sins appear—because you have come to remembrance, you will be seized with the hand.

25 'And you, O slain, wicked one, the prince of Israel, whose day has come, in the time of the punishment of the end,'

26 thus says the Lord GOD, 'Remove the turban, and take off the crown; this will be no more the same. Exalt that which is low, and abase that which is high.

27 'A ruin, a ruin, a ruin, I shall make it. This also will be no more, until He comes whose right it is; and I shall give it to Him.'

28 ¶"And you, son of man, prophesy and say, 'Thus says the Lord GOD concerning the sons of Ammon and concerning their reproach,' and say: 'A sword, a sword is drawn, polished for the slaughter, to cause it to consume, that it may be like lightning—

29 while they see for you false visions, while they divine lies for you—to place you on the necks of the wicked who are slain, whose day has come, in the time of the punishment of the end.

30 'Return it to its sheath. In the place where you were created, in the land of your origin, I shall judge you.

31 'And I shall pour out My indignation on you; I shall blow on you with the fire of My wrath, and I shall give you into the hand of brutal men, skilled in destruction.

32 'You will be fuel for the fire; your blood will be in the midst of the land. You will not be remembered, for I, the LORD, have spoken.' "

CHAPTER 22

THEN the word of the LORD came to me saying,

2 "And you, son of man, will you judge, will you judge the bloody city? Then cause her to know all her abominations.

3 "And you shall say, 'Thus says the Lord GOD, "A city shedding blood in her midst, so that her time will come, and that makes idols, contrary to her interest, for defilement!

4 "You have become guilty by the blood which you have shed, and defiled by your idols which you have made. Thus you have brought your day near and have come to your years; therefore I have made you a reproach to the nations, and a mocking to all the lands.

5 "Those who are near and those who are far from you will mock you, you of ill repute, full of turmoil.

6 "Behold, the rulers of Israel, each according to his power, have been in you for the purpose of shedding blood.

7 "They have treated father and mother lightly within you. The alien they have oppressed in your midst; the fatherless and the widow they have wronged in you.

8 "You have despised My holy things and profaned My sabbaths.

9 "Slanderous men have been in you for the purpose of shedding blood, and in you they have eaten at the mountain shrines. In your midst they have committed acts of lewdness.

10 "In you they have uncovered their fathers' nakedness; in you they have humbled her who was unclean in her menstrual impurity.

11 "And one has committed abomination with his neighbor's wife, and another has lewdly defiled his daughter-in-law. And another in you has humbled his sister, his father's daughter.

12 "In you they have taken bribes to shed blood; you have taken interest and profits, and you have injured your neighbors for gain by oppression, and you have forgotten Me," declares the Lord GOD.

13 ¶"Behold, then, I smite My hand at your dishonest gain which you have acquired and at the bloodshed which is among you.

14 "Can your heart endure, or can your hands be strong, in the days that I shall deal with you? I, the LORD, have spoken and shall act.

15 "And I shall scatter you among the nations, and I shall disperse you through the lands, and I shall consume your uncleanness from you.

16 "And you will profane yourself in the sight of the nations, and you will know that I am the LORD." ' "

17 ¶ And the word of the LORD came to me saying,

18 "Son of man, the house of Israel has become dross to Me; all of them are bronze and tin and iron and lead in the furnace; they are the dross of silver.

19 "Therefore, thus says the Lord GOD, 'Because all of you have become

dross, therefore, behold, I am going to gather you into the midst of Jerusalem.

20 'As they gather silver and bronze and iron and lead and tin into the furnace to blow fire on it in order to melt *it,* so I shall gather *you* in My anger and in My wrath, and I shall lay you *there* and melt you.

21 'And I shall gather you and blow on you with the fire of My wrath, and you will be melted in the midst of it.

22 'As silver is melted in the furnace, so you will be melted in the midst of it; and you will know that I, the LORD, have poured out My wrath on you.' "

23 ¶ And the word of the LORD came to me saying,

24"Son of man, say to her, 'You are a land that is not cleansed or rained on in the day of indignation.'

25"There is a conspiracy of her prophets in her midst, like a roaring lion tearing the prey. They have devoured lives; they have taken treasure and precious things; they have made many widows in the midst of her.

26"Her priests have done violence to My law and have profaned My holy things; they have made no distinction between the holy and the profane, and they have not taught the difference between the unclean and the clean; and they hide their eyes from My sabbaths, and I am profaned among them.

27"Her princes within her are like wolves tearing the prey, by shedding blood *and* destroying lives in order to get dishonest gain.

28"And her prophets have smeared whitewash for them, seeing false visions and divining lies for them, saying, 'Thus says the Lord GOD,' when the LORD has not spoken.

29"The people of the land have practiced oppression and committed robbery, and they have wronged the poor and needy and have oppressed the sojourner without justice.

30"And I searched for a man among them who should build up the wall and stand in the gap before Me for the land, that I should not destroy it; but I found no one.

31"Thus I have poured out My indignation on them; I have consumed them with the fire of My wrath; their way I have brought upon their heads," declares the Lord GOD.

CHAPTER 23

THE word of the LORD came to me again saying,

2"Son of man, there were two women, the daughters of one mother;

3 and they played the harlot in Egypt. They played the harlot in their youth; there their breasts were pressed, and there their virgin bosom was handled.

4"And their names were Oholah the elder and Oholibah her sister. And they became Mine, and they bore sons and daughters. And *as for* their names, Samaria is Oholah, and Jerusalem is Oholibah.

5 ¶"And Oholah played the harlot while she was Mine; and she lusted after her lovers, after the Assyrians, *her* neighbors,

6 who were clothed in purple, governors and officials, all of them desirable young men, horsemen riding on horses.

7"And she bestowed her harlotries on them, all of whom *were* the choicest men of Assyria; and with all whom she lusted after, with all their idols she defiled herself.

8"And she did not forsake her harlotries from *the time in* Egypt; for in her youth men had lain with her, and they handled her virgin bosom and poured out their lust on her.

9"Therefore, I gave her into the hand of her lovers, into the hand of the Assyrians, after whom she lusted.

10"They uncovered her nakedness; they took her sons and her daughters, but they slew her with the sword. Thus she became a byword among women, and they executed judgments on her.

11 ¶"Now her sister Oholibah saw *this,* yet she was more corrupt in her lust than she, and her harlotries were more than the harlotries of her sister.

12"She lusted after the Assyrians, governors and officials, the ones near, magnificently dressed, horsemen riding on horses, all of them desirable young men.

13"And I saw that she had defiled herself; they both took the same way.

14"So she increased her harlotries.

And she saw men portrayed on the wall, images of the Chaldeans portrayed with vermilion,

15 girded with belts on their loins, with flowing turbans on their heads, all of them looking like officers, like the Babylonians in Chaldea, the land of their birth.

16"And when she saw them she lusted after them and sent messengers to them in Chaldea.

17"And the Babylonians came to her to the bed of love, and they defiled her with their harlotry. And when she had been defiled by them, she became disgusted with them.

18"And she uncovered her harlotries and uncovered her nakedness; then I became disgusted with her, as I had become disgusted with her sister.

19"Yet she multiplied her harlotries, remembering the days of her youth, when she played the harlot in the land of Egypt.

20"And she lusted after their paramours, whose flesh is like the flesh of donkeys and whose issue is like the issue of horses.

21"Thus you longed for the lewdness of your youth, when the Egyptians handled your bosom because of the breasts of your youth.

22 ¶"Therefore, O Oholibah, thus says the Lord GOD, 'Behold I will arouse your lovers against you, from whom you were alienated, and I will bring them against you from every side:

23 the Babylonians and all the Chaldeans, Pekod and Shoa and Koa, and all the Assyrians with them; desirable young men, governors and officials all of them, officers and men of renown, all of them riding on horses.

24 'And they will come against you with weapons, chariots, and wagons, and with a company of peoples. They will set themselves against you on every side with buckler and shield and helmet; and I shall commit the judgment to them, and they will judge you according to their customs.

25 'And I will set My jealousy against you, that they may deal with you in wrath. They will remove your nose and your ears; and your survivors will fall by the sword. They will take your sons and your daughters; and your survivors will be consumed by the fire.

26 'They will also strip you of your clothes and take away your beautiful jewels.

27 'Thus I shall make your lewdness and your harlotry brought from the land of Egypt to cease from you, so that you will not lift up your eyes to them or remember Egypt anymore.'

28"For thus says the Lord GOD, 'Behold, I will give you into the hand of those whom you hate, into the hand of those from whom you were alienated.

29 'And they will deal with you in hatred, take all your property, and leave you naked and bare. And the nakedness of your harlotries shall be uncovered, both your lewdness and your harlotries.

30 'These things will be done to you because you have played the harlot with the nations, because you have defiled yourself with their idols.

31 'You have walked in the way of your sister; therefore I will give her cup into your hand.'

32"Thus says the Lord GOD,
'You will drink your sister's cup,
Which is deep and wide.
You will be laughed at and held
    in derision;
It contains much.

33 'You will be filled with drunkenness and sorrow,
The cup of horror and desolation,
The cup of your sister Samaria.

34 'And you will drink it and drain it.
Then you will gnaw its fragments
And tear your breasts;
for I have spoken,' declares the Lord GOD.

35"Therefore, thus says the Lord GOD, 'Because you have forgotten Me and cast Me behind your back, bear now the punishment of your lewdness and your harlotries.' "

36 ¶ Moreover, the LORD said to me, "Son of man, will you judge Oholah and Oholibah? Then declare to them their abominations.

37"For they have committed adultery, and blood is on their hands. Thus they have committed adultery with their idols and even caused their sons, whom they bore to Me, to pass through the fire to them as food.

38"Again, they have done this to Me:

they have defiled My sanctuary on the same day and have profaned My sabbaths.

39"For when they had slaughtered their children for their idols, they entered My sanctuary on the same day to profane it; and lo, thus they did within My house.

40"Furthermore, they have even sent for men who come from afar, to whom a messenger was sent; and lo, they came—for whom you bathed, painted your eyes, and decorated yourselves with ornaments;

41 and you sat on a splendid couch with a table arranged before it, on which you had set My incense and My oil.

42"And the sound of a carefree multitude was with her; and drunkards were brought from the wilderness with men of the common sort. And they put bracelets on the hands of the women and beautiful crowns on their heads.

43"Then I said concerning her who was worn out by adulteries, 'Will they now commit adultery with her when she is *thus*?'

44"But they went in to her as they would go in to a harlot. Thus they went in to Oholah and to Oholibah, the lewd women.

45"But they, righteous men, will judge them with the judgment of adulteresses, and with the judgment of women who shed blood, because they are adulteresses and blood is on their hands.

46 ¶"For thus says the Lord GOD, 'Bring up a company against them, and give them over to terror and plunder.

47 'And the company will stone them with stones and cut them down with their swords; they will slay their sons and their daughters and burn their houses with fire.

48 'Thus I shall make lewdness cease from the land, that all women may be admonished and not commit lewdness as you have done.

49 'And your lewdness will be requited upon you, and you will bear the penalty of *worshiping* your idols; thus you will know that I am the Lord GOD.'"

CHAPTER 24

AND the word of the LORD came to me in the ninth year, in the tenth month, on the tenth of the month, saying,

2"Son of man, write the name of the day, this very day. The king of Babylon has laid siege to Jerusalem this very day.

3"And speak a parable to the rebellious house, and say to them, 'Thus says the Lord GOD,

"Put on the pot, put *it* on, and also pour water in it;
4   Put in it the pieces,
    Every good piece, the thigh, and the shoulder;
    Fill *it* with choice bones.
5   "Take the choicest of the flock,
    And also pile wood under the pot.
    Make it boil vigorously.
    Also seethe its bones in it."

6 ¶   'Therefore, thus says the Lord GOD,
    "Woe to the bloody city,
    To the pot in which there is rust
    And whose rust has not gone out of it!
    Take out of it piece after piece,
    Without making a choice.
7   "For her blood is in her midst;
    She placed it on the bare rock;
    She did not pour it on the ground
    To cover it with dust.
8   "That it may cause wrath to come up to take vengeance,
    I have put her blood on the bare rock,
    That it may not be covered."
9   'Therefore, thus says the Lord GOD,
    "Woe to the bloody city!
    I also shall make the pile great.
10 "Heap on the wood, kindle the fire,
    Boil the flesh well,
    And mix in the spices,
    And let the bones be burned.
11 "Then set it empty on its coals,
    So that it may be hot,
    And its bronze may glow,
    And its filthiness may be melted in it,
    Its rust consumed.
12 "She has wearied *Me* with toil,
    Yet her great rust has not gone from her;

Let her rust *be* in the fire!

13 "In your filthiness is lewdness.

Because I *would* have cleansed
you,

Yet you are not clean,

You will not be cleansed from
your filthiness again,

Until I have spent My wrath on
you.

14"I, the LORD, have spoken; it is
coming and I shall act. I shall not
relent, and I shall not pity, and I shall
not be sorry; according to your ways
and according to your deeds I shall
judge you," declares the Lord GOD.'"

15 ¶ And the word of the LORD came
to me saying,

16"Son of man, behold, I am about to
take from you the desire of your eyes
with a blow; but you shall not mourn,
and you shall not weep, and your tears
shall not come.

17"Groan silently; make no mourning
for the dead. Bind on your turban, and
put your shoes on your feet, and do
not cover *your* mustache, and do not
eat the bread of men."

18 So I spoke to the people in the
morning, and in the evening my wife
died. And in the morning I did as I was
commanded.

19 And the people said to me, "Will
you not tell us what these things that
you are doing mean for us?"

20 Then I said to them, "The word of
the LORD came to me saying,

21 'Speak to the house of Israel,
"Thus says the Lord GOD, 'Behold, I
am about to profane My sanctuary,
the pride of your power, the desire of
your eyes, and the delight of your soul;
and your sons and your daughters
whom you have left behind will fall by
the sword.

22 'And you will do as I have done;
you will not cover *your* mustache, and
you will not eat the bread of men.

23 'And your turbans will be on your
heads and your shoes on your feet.
You will not mourn, and you will not
weep; but you will rot away in your
iniquities, and you will groan to one
another.

24 'Thus Ezekiel will be a sign to you;
according to all that he has done you
will do; when it comes, then you will
know that I am the Lord GOD.'"

25 ¶ 'As for you, son of man, will *it*
not be on the day when I take from

them their stronghold, the joy of their
pride, the desire of their eyes, and
their heart's delight, their sons and
their daughters,

26 that on that day he who escapes
will come to you with information for
your ears?

27 'On that day your mouth will be
opened to him who escaped, and you
will speak and be dumb no longer.
Thus you will be a sign to them, and
they will know that I am the LORD.'"

CHAPTER 25

AND the word of the LORD came to
me saying,

2"Son of man, set your face toward
the sons of Ammon, and prophesy
against them,

3 and say to the sons of Ammon,
'Hear the word of the Lord GOD! Thus
says the Lord GOD, "Because you said,
'Aha!' against My sanctuary when it
was profaned, and against the land of
Israel when it was made desolate, and
against the house of Judah when they
went into exile,

4 therefore, behold, I am going to
give you to the sons of the east for a
possession, and they will set their
encampments among you and make
their dwellings among you; they will
eat your fruit and drink your milk.

5"And I shall make Rabbah a pasture for camels and the sons of Ammon a resting place for flocks. Thus
you will know that I am the LORD."

6 'For thus says the Lord GOD, "Because you have clapped your hands
and stamped your feet and rejoiced
with all the scorn of your soul against
the land of Israel,

7 therefore, behold, I have stretched
out My hand against you, and I shall
give you for spoil to the nations. And I
shall cut you off from the peoples and
make you perish from the lands; I
shall destroy you. Thus you will know
that I am the LORD."

8 ¶ Thus says the Lord GOD, "Because Moab and Seir say, 'Behold, the
house of Judah is like all the nations,'

9 therefore, behold, I am going to
deprive the flank of Moab of *its* cities,
of its cities which are on its frontiers,
the glory of the land, Beth-jeshimoth,
Baal-meon, and Kiriathaim,

10 and I will give it for a possession,

along with the sons of Ammon, to the sons of the east, that the sons of Ammon may not be remembered among the nations.

11"Thus I will execute judgments on Moab, and they will know that I am the LORD."

12 ¶ 'Thus says the Lord GOD, "Because Edom has acted against the house of Judah by taking vengeance, and has incurred grievous guilt, and avenged themselves upon them,"

13 therefore, thus says the Lord GOD, "I will also stretch out My hand against Edom and cut off man and beast from it. And I will lay it waste; from Teman even to Dedan they will fall by the sword.

14"And I will lay My vengeance on Edom by the hand of My people Israel. Therefore, they will act in Edom according to My anger and according to My wrath; thus they will know My vengeance," declares the Lord GOD.

15 ¶ 'Thus says the Lord GOD, "Because the Philistines have acted in revenge and have taken vengeance with scorn of soul to destroy with everlasting enmity,"

16 therefore, thus says the Lord GOD, "Behold, I will stretch out My hand against the Philistines, even cut off the Cherethites and destroy the remnant of the seacoast.

17"And I will execute great vengeance on them with wrathful rebukes; and they will know that I am the LORD when I lay My vengeance on them." ' "

CHAPTER 26

Now it came about in the eleventh year, on the first of the month, that the word of the LORD came to me saying,

2"Son of man, because Tyre has said concerning Jerusalem, 'Aha, the gateway of the peoples is broken; it has opened to me. I shall be filled, *now that* she is laid waste,'

3 therefore, thus says the Lord GOD, 'Behold, I am against you, O Tyre, and I will bring up many nations against you, as the sea brings up its waves.

4 'And they will destroy the walls of Tyre and break down her towers; and I will scrape her debris from her and make her a bare rock.

5 'She will be a place for the spreading of nets in the midst of the sea, for I have spoken,' declares the Lord GOD, 'and she will become spoil for the nations.

6 'Also her daughters who are on the mainland will be slain by the sword, and they will know that I am the LORD.' "

7 ¶ For thus says the Lord GOD, "Behold, I will bring upon Tyre from the north Nebuchadnezzar king of Babylon, king of kings, with horses, chariots, cavalry, and a great army.

8"He will slay your daughters on the mainland with the sword; and he will make siege walls against you, cast up a mound against you, and raise up a large shield against you.

9"And the blow of his battering rams he will direct against your walls, and with his axes he will break down your towers.

10"Because of the multitude of his horses, the dust *raised by* them will cover you; your walls will shake at the noise of cavalry and wagons and chariots, when he enters your gates as men enter a city that is breached.

11"With the hoofs of his horses he will trample all your streets. He will slay your people with the sword; and your strong pillars will come down to the ground.

12"Also they will make a spoil of your riches and a prey of your merchandise, break down your walls and destroy your pleasant houses, and throw your stones and your timbers and your debris into the water.

13"So I will silence the sound of your songs, and the sound of your harps will be heard no more.

14"And I will make you a bare rock; you will be a place for the spreading of nets. You will be built no more, for I the LORD have spoken," declares the Lord GOD.

15 ¶ Thus says the Lord GOD to Tyre, "Shall not the coastlands shake at the sound of your fall when the wounded groan, when the slaughter occurs in your midst?

16"Then all the princes of the sea will go down from their thrones, remove their robes, and strip off their embroidered garments. They will clothe themselves with trembling; they will sit on the ground, tremble every moment, and be appalled at you.

17"And they will take up a lamentation over you and say to you,

'How you have perished, O inhabited one,
From the seas, O renowned city,
Which was mighty on the sea,
She and her inhabitants,
Who imposed her terror
On all her inhabitants!

18 'Now the coastlands will tremble
On the day of your fall;
Yes, the coastlands which are by the sea
Will be terrified at your passing.' "

19 For thus says the Lord GOD, "When I shall make you a desolate city, like the cities which are not inhabited, when I shall bring up the deep over you, and the great waters will cover you,

20 then I shall bring you down with those who go down to the pit, to the people of old, and I shall make you dwell in the lower parts of the earth, like the ancient waste places, with those who go down to the pit, so that you will not be inhabited; but I shall set glory in the land of the living.

21"I shall bring terrors on you, and you will be no more; though you will be sought, you will never be found again," declares the Lord GOD.

CHAPTER 27

MOREOVER, the word of the LORD came to me saying,

2"And you, son of man, take up a lamentation over Tyre;

3 and say to Tyre, who dwells at the entrance to the sea, merchant of the peoples to many coastlands, 'Thus says the Lord GOD,

"O Tyre, you have said, 'I am perfect in beauty.'

4 "Your borders are in the heart of the seas;
Your builders have perfected your beauty.

5 "They have made all your planks of fir trees from Senir;
They have taken a cedar from Lebanon to make a mast for you.

6 "Of oaks from Bashan they have made your oars;

With ivory they have inlaid your deck of boxwood from the coastlands of Cyprus.

7 "Your sail was of fine embroidered linen from Egypt
So that it became your distinguishing mark;
Your awning was blue and purple from the coastlands of Elishah.

8 "The inhabitants of Sidon and Arvad were your rowers;
Your wise men, O Tyre, were aboard; they were your pilots.

9 "The elders of Gebal and her wise men were with you repairing your seams;
All the ships of the sea and their sailors were with you in order to deal in your merchandise.

10 ¶"Persia and Lud and Put were in your army, your men of war. They hung shield and helmet in you; they set forth your splendor.

11"The sons of Arvad and your army were on your walls, all around, and the Gammadim were in your towers. They hung their shields on your walls, all around; they perfected your beauty.

12 ¶"Tarshish was your customer because of the abundance of all kinds of wealth; with silver, iron, tin, and lead, they paid for your wares.

13"Javan, Tubal, and Meshech, they were your traders; with the lives of men and vessels of bronze they paid for your merchandise.

14"Those from Beth-togarmah gave horses and war horses and mules for your wares.

15"The sons of Dedan were your traders. Many coastlands were your market; ivory tusks and ebony they brought as your payment.

16"Aram was your customer because of the abundance of your goods; they paid for your wares with emeralds, purple, embroidered work, fine linen, coral, and rubies.

17"Judah and the land of Israel, they were your traders; with the wheat of Minnith, cakes, honey, oil, and balm they paid for your merchandise.

18"Damascus was your customer because of the abundance of your goods, because of the abundance of all kinds of wealth, because of the wine of Helbon and white wool.

19"Vedan and Javan paid for your wares from Uzal; wrought iron, cassia, and sweet cane were among your merchandise.

20"Dedan traded with you in saddlecloths for riding.

21"Arabia and all the princes of Kedar, they were your customers for lambs, rams, and goats; for these they were your customers.

22"The traders of Sheba and Raamah, they traded with you; they paid for your wares with the best of all *kinds* of spices, and with all *kinds* of precious stones, and gold.

23"Haran, Canneh, Eden, the traders of Sheba, Asshur, *and* Chilmad traded with you.

24"They traded with you in choice garments, in clothes of blue and embroidered work, and in carpets of many colors, *and* tightly wound cords, *which were* among your merchandise.

25"The ships of Tarshish were the carriers for your merchandise.

And you were filled and were very
    glorious
In the heart of the seas.

26 ¶"Your rowers have brought you
Into great waters;
The east wind has broken you
In the heart of the seas.

27"Your wealth, your wares, your
    merchandise,
Your sailors, and your pilots,
Your repairers of seams, your
    dealers in merchandise,
And all your men of war who are
    in you,
With all your company that is in
    your midst,
Will fall into the heart of the seas
On the day of your overthrow.

28"At the sound of the cry of your
    pilots
The pasture lands will shake.

29"And all who handle the oar,
The sailors, *and* all the pilots of
    the sea
Will come down from their ships;
They will stand on the land,

30 And they will make their voice
    heard over you
And will cry bitterly.
They will cast dust on their heads,
They will wallow in ashes.

31"Also they will make themselves
    bald for you

And gird themselves with sackcloth;
And they will weep for you in
    bitterness of soul
With bitter mourning.

32"Moreover, in their wailing they
    will take up a lamentation for
    you
And lament over you:
'Who is like Tyre,
Like her who is silent in the midst
    of the sea?

33 'When your wares went out from
    the seas,
You satisfied many peoples;
With the abundance of your
    wealth and your merchandise
You enriched the kings of earth.

34 'Now that you are broken by the
    seas
In the depths of the waters,
Your merchandise and all your
    company
Have fallen in the midst of you.

35 'All the inhabitants of the coastlands
Are appalled at you,
And their kings are horribly
    afraid;
They are troubled in countenance.

36 'The merchants among the peoples
    hiss at you;
You have become terrified,
And you will be no more.' " ' "

CHAPTER 28

T HE word of the LORD came again to me saying,

2"Son of man, say to the leader of
    Tyre, 'Thus says the Lord GOD,
"Because your heart is lifted up
And you have said, 'I am a god,
I sit in the seat of gods,
In the heart of the seas';
Yet you are a man and not God,
Although you make your heart
    like the heart of God—

3 Behold, you are wiser than Daniel;
There is no secret that is a match
    for you.

4"By your wisdom and understanding
You have acquired riches for
    yourself,
And have acquired gold and silver
    for your treasuries.

5"By your great wisdom, by your
    trade

You have increased your riches,
And your heart is lifted up be-
cause of your riches—
6 Therefore, thus says the Lord
God,
'Because you have made your
heart
Like the heart of God,
7 Therefore, behold, I will bring
strangers upon you,
The most ruthless of the nations.
And they will draw their swords
Against the beauty of your wis-
dom
And defile your splendor.
8 'They will bring you down to the
pit,
And you will die the death of
those who are slain
In the heart of the seas.
9 'Will you still say, "I am a god,"
In the presence of your slayer,
Although you are a man and not
God,
In the hands of those who wound
you?
10 'You will die the death of the un-
circumcised
By the hand of strangers,
For I have spoken!' declares the
Lord God!" ' "

11 ¶ Again the word of the Lord
came to me saying,
12"Son of man, take up a lamentation over the king of Tyre, and say to
him, 'Thus says the Lord God,
"You had the seal of perfection,
Full of wisdom and perfect in
beauty.
13"You were in Eden, the garden of
God;
Every precious stone was your
covering:
The ruby, the topaz, and the dia-
mond;
The beryl, the onyx, and the jas-
per;
The lapis lazuli, the turquoise, and
the emerald;
And the gold, the workmanship of
your settings and sockets,
Was in you.
On the day that you were created
They were prepared.
14"You were the anointed cherub
who covers,
And I placed you there.
You were on the holy mountain of
God;

You walked in the midst of the
stones of fire.
15"You were blameless in your ways
From the day you were created,
Until unrighteousness was found
in you.
16"By the abundance of your trade
You were internally filled with
violence,
And you sinned;
Therefore I have cast you as pro-
fane
From the mountain of God.
And I have destroyed you, O cov-
ering cherub,
From the midst of the stones of
fire.
17"Your heart was lifted up because
of your beauty;
You corrupted your wisdom by
reason of your splendor.
I cast you to the ground;
I put you before kings,
That they may see you.
18"By the multitude of your iniqui-
ties,
In the unrighteousness of your
trade,
You profaned your sanctuaries.
Therefore I have brought fire
from the midst of you;
It has consumed you,
And I have turned you to ashes on
the earth
In the eyes of all who see you.
19"All who know you among the
peoples
Are appalled at you;
You have become terrified,
And you will be no more." ' "

20 ¶ And the word of the Lord came
to me saying,
21"Son of man, set your face toward
Sidon, prophesy against her,
22 and say, 'Thus says the Lord God,
"Behold, I am against you, O Sidon,
And I shall be glorified in your
midst.
Then they will know that I am the
Lord, when I execute judgments in her,
And I shall manifest My holiness
in her.
23"For I shall send pestilence to her
And blood to her streets,
And the wounded will fall in her
midst
By the sword upon her on every
side;

Then they will know that I am the
LORD.

24"And there will be no more for the
house of Israel a prickling brier or a
painful thorn from any round about
them who scorned them; then they
will know that I am the Lord GOD."

25 ¶ 'Thus says the Lord GOD, "When
I gather the house of Israel from the
peoples among whom they are scattered, and shall manifest My holiness
in them in the sight of the nations,
then they will live in their land which I
gave to My servant Jacob.

26"And they will live in it securely;
and they will build houses, plant vineyards, and live securely, when I execute judgments upon all who scorn
them round about them. Then they
will know that I am the LORD their
God." ' "

CHAPTER 29

IN the tenth year, in the tenth *month,*
on the twelfth of the month, the word
of the LORD came to me saying,

2"Son of man, set your face against
Pharaoh, king of Egypt, and prophesy
against him and against all Egypt.

3"Speak and say, 'Thus says the
Lord GOD,

"Behold, I am against you, Pharaoh, king of Egypt,
The great monster that lies in the
midst of his rivers,
That has said, 'My Nile is mine,
and I myself have made it.'
4"And I shall put hooks in your
jaws,
And I shall make the fish of your
rivers cling to your scales.
And I shall bring you up out of
the midst of your rivers,
And all the fish of your rivers will
cling to your scales.
5"And I shall abandon you to the
wilderness, you and all the fish
of your rivers;
You will fall on the open field; you
will not be brought together or
gathered.
I have given you for food to the
beasts of the earth and to the
birds of the sky.
6"Then all the inhabitants of Egypt
will know that I am the LORD,
Because they have been *only* a

staff *made* of reed to the house
of Israel.
7"When they took hold of you with
the hand,
You broke and tore all their
hands;
And when they leaned on you,
You broke and made all their loins
quake."

8 'Therefore, thus says the Lord
GOD, "Behold, I shall bring upon you a
sword, and I shall cut off from you
man and beast.

9"And the land of Egypt will become
a desolation and waste. Then they will
know that I am the LORD.

¶ Because you said, 'The Nile is
mine, and I have made *it,*'

10 therefore, behold, I am against
you and against your rivers, and I will
make the land of Egypt an utter waste
and desolation, from Migdol *to* Syene
and even to the border of Ethiopia.

11"A man's foot will not pass through
it, and the foot of a beast will not pass
through it, and it will not be inhabited
for forty years.

12"So I shall make the land of Egypt
a desolation in the midst of desolated
lands. And her cities, in the midst of
cities that are laid waste, will be desolate forty years; and I shall scatter the
Egyptians among the nations and disperse them among the lands."

13 ¶ 'For thus says the Lord GOD, "At
the end of forty years I shall gather
the Egyptians from the peoples among
whom they were scattered.

14"And I shall turn the fortunes of
Egypt and shall make them return to
the land of Pathros, to the land of their
origin; and there they will be a lowly
kingdom.

15"It will be the lowest of the kingdoms; and it will never again lift itself
up above the nations. And I shall
make them so small that they will not
rule over the nations.

16"And it will never again be the
confidence of the house of Israel,
bringing to mind the iniquity of their
having turned to Egypt. Then they will
know that I am the Lord GOD." ' "

17 ¶ Now in the twenty-seventh
year, in the first *month,* on the first of
the month, the word of the LORD came
to me saying,

18"Son of man, Nebuchadnezzar
king of Babylon made his army labor

hard against Tyre; every head was made bald, and every shoulder was rubbed bare. But he and his army had no wages from Tyre for the labor that he had performed against it."

19 Therefore, thus says the Lord GOD, "Behold, I shall give the land of Egypt to Nebuchadnezzar king of Babylon. And he will carry off her wealth, and capture her spoil and seize her plunder; and it will be wages for his army.

20"I have given him the land of Egypt *for* his labor which he performed, because they acted for Me," declares the Lord GOD.

21 ¶"On that day I shall make a horn sprout for the house of Israel, and I shall open your mouth in their midst. Then they will know that I am the LORD."

CHAPTER 30

THE word of the LORD came again to me saying,

2"Son of man, prophesy and say, 'Thus says the Lord GOD,

"Wail, 'Alas for the day!'

3 "For the day is near,
Even the day of the LORD is near;
It will be a day of clouds,
A time *of doom* for the nations.

4 "And a sword will come upon Egypt,
And anguish will be in Ethiopia,
When the slain fall in Egypt,
They take away her wealth,
And her foundations are torn down.

5"Ethiopia, Put, Lud, all Arabia, Libya, and the people of the land that is in league will fall with them by the sword."

6 ¶ 'Thus says the LORD,
"Indeed, those who support Egypt will fall,
And the pride of her power will come down;
From Migdol *to* Syene
They will fall within her by the sword,"
Declares the Lord GOD.

7 "And they will be desolate
In the midst of the desolated lands;
And her cities will be
In the midst of the devastated cities.

8 "And they will know that I am the LORD,
When I set a fire in Egypt
And all her helpers are broken.

9"On that day messengers will go forth from Me in ships to frighten secure Ethiopia; and anguish will be on them as on the day of Egypt; for, behold, it comes!"

10 'Thus says the Lord GOD,
"I will also make the multitude of Egypt cease
By the hand of Nebuchadnezzar king of Babylon.

11 "He and his people with him,
The most ruthless of the nations,
Will be brought in to destroy the land;
And they will draw their swords against Egypt
And fill the land with the slain.

12 "Moreover, I will make the Nile canals dry
And sell the land into the hands of evil men.
And I will make the land desolate,
And all that is in it,
By the hand of strangers; I, the LORD, have spoken."

13 ¶ 'Thus says the Lord GOD,
"I will also destroy the idols
And make the images cease from Memphis.
And there will no longer be a prince in the land of Egypt;
And I will put fear in the land of Egypt.

14 "And I will make Pathros desolate,
Set a fire in Zoan,
And execute judgments on ²Thebes.

15 "And I will pour out My wrath on ³Sin,
The stronghold of Egypt;
I will also cut off the multitude of Thebes.

16 "And I will set a fire in Egypt;
Sin will writhe in anguish,
Thebes will be breached,
And ⁴Memphis *will have* distresses daily.

17 "The young men of ⁵On and of Pi-beseth

---

² Or, *No*   ³ Or, *Pelusium*   ⁴ Or, *Noph*   ⁵ Or, *Aven*

Will fall by the sword,
And the women will go into captivity.

18 "And in Tehaphnehes the day will
be dark
When I break there the yoke
bars of Egypt.
Then the pride of her power will
cease in her;
A cloud will cover her,
And her daughters will go into
captivity.

19 "Thus I will execute judgments
on Egypt,
And they will know that I am the
LORD." ' "

20 ¶ And it came about in the eleventh year, in the first *month,* on the
seventh of the month, that the word of
the LORD came to me saying,

21 "Son of man, I have broken the
arm of Pharaoh king of Egypt; and,
behold, it has not been bound up for
healing or wrapped with a bandage,
that it may be strong to hold the
sword.

22 "Therefore, thus says the Lord
GOD, 'Behold, I am against Pharaoh
king of Egypt and will break his arms,
both the strong and the broken; and I
will make the sword fall from his hand.

23 'And I will scatter the Egyptians
among the nations and disperse them
among the lands.

24 'For I will strengthen the arms of
the king of Babylon and put My sword
in his hand; and I will break the arms
of Pharaoh, so that he will groan before him with the groanings of a
wounded man.

25 'Thus I will strengthen the arms of
the king of Babylon, but the arms of
Pharaoh will fall. Then they will know
that I am the LORD, when I put My
sword into the hand of the king of
Babylon and he stretches it out
against the land of Egypt.

26 'When I scatter the Egyptians
among the nations and disperse them
among the lands, then they will know
that I am the LORD.' "

CHAPTER 31

AND it came about in the eleventh
year, in the third *month,* on the first of
the month, that the word of the LORD
came to me saying,

2 "Son of man, say to Pharaoh king
of Egypt, and to his multitude,
'Whom are you like in your greatness?

3 'Behold, Assyria *was* a cedar in
Lebanon
With beautiful branches and for-
est shade,
And very high;
And its top was among the
clouds.

4 'The waters made it grow, the
deep made it high.
With its rivers it continually extended all around its planting
place,
And it sent out its channels to all
the trees of the field.

5 'Therefore its height was loftier
than all the trees of the field
And its boughs became many
and its branches long
Because of many waters as it
spread them out.

6 'All the birds of the heavens
nested in its boughs,
And under its branches all the
beasts of the field gave birth,
And all great nations lived under
its shade.

7 'So it was beautiful in its greatness, in the length of its
branches;
For its roots extended to many
waters.

8 'The cedars in God's garden could
not match it;
The cypresses could not compare
with its boughs,
And the plane trees could not
match its branches.
No tree in God's garden could
compare with it in its beauty.

9 'I made it beautiful with the multitude of its branches,
And all the trees of Eden, which
were in the garden of God, were
jealous of it.

10 ¶ 'Therefore, thus says the Lord
GOD, "Because it is high in stature,
and it has set its top among the clouds,
and its heart is haughty in its loftiness,

11 therefore, I will give it into the
hand of a despot of the nations; he will
thoroughly deal with it. According to
its wickedness I have driven it away.

12 "And alien tyrants of the nations
have cut it down and left it; on the
mountains and in all the valleys its

branches have fallen, and its boughs have been broken in all the ravines of the land. And all the peoples of the earth have gone down from its shade and left it.

13"On its ruin all the birds of the heavens will dwell. And all the beasts of the field will be on its *fallen* branches

14 in order that all the trees by the waters may not be exalted in their stature, nor set their top among the clouds, nor their well-watered mighty ones stand *erect* in their height. For they have all been given over to death, to the earth beneath, among the sons of men, with those who go down to the pit."

15 ¶ Thus says the Lord GOD, "On the day when it went down to Sheol I caused lamentations; I closed the deep over it and held back its rivers. And *its* many waters were stopped up, and I made Lebanon mourn for it, and all the trees of the field wilted away on account of it.

16"I made the nations quake at the sound of its fall when I made it go down to Sheol with those who go down to the pit; and all the well-watered trees of Eden, the choicest and best of Lebanon, were comforted in the earth beneath.

17"They also went down with it to Sheol to those who were slain by the sword; and those who were its strength lived under its shade among the nations.

18"To which among the trees of Eden are you thus equal in glory and greatness? Yet you will be brought down with the trees of Eden to the earth beneath; you will lie in the midst of the uncircumcised, with those who were slain by the sword. So is Pharaoh and all his multitude!"' declares the Lord GOD."

CHAPTER 32

AND it came about in the twelfth year, in the twelfth *month*, on the first of the month, that the word of the LORD came to me saying,

2"Son of man, take up a lamentation over Pharaoh king of Egypt, and say to him,

'You compared yourself to a young lion of the nations,

Yet you are like the monster in the seas;
And you burst forth in your rivers,
And muddied the waters with your feet,
And fouled their rivers.' "

3 Thus says the Lord GOD,
"Now I will spread My net over you
With a company of many peoples,
And they shall lift you up in My net.

4 "And I will leave you on the land;
I will cast you on the open field.
And I will cause all the birds of the heavens to dwell on you,
And I will satisfy the beasts of the whole earth with you.

5 "And I will lay your flesh on the mountains,
And fill the valleys with your refuse.

6 "I will also make the land drink the discharge of your blood,
As far as the mountains,
And the ravines shall be full of you.

7 "And when I extinguish you,
I will cover the heavens, and darken their stars;
I will cover the sun with a cloud,
And the moon shall not give its light.

8 "All the shining lights in the heavens
I will darken over you
And will set darkness on your land,"
Declares the Lord GOD.

9"I will also trouble the hearts of many peoples, when I bring your destruction among the nations, into lands which you have not known.

10"And I will make many peoples appalled at you, and their kings shall be horribly afraid of you when I brandish My sword before them; and they shall tremble every moment, every man for his own life, on the day of your fall."

11 ¶ For thus says the Lord GOD, "The sword of the king of Babylon shall come upon you.

12"By the swords of the mighty ones I will cause your multitude to fall; all of them are tyrants of the nations,

And they shall devastate the
pride of Egypt,
And all its multitude shall be
destroyed.
13 "I will also destroy all its cattle
from beside many waters;
And the foot of man shall not
muddy them anymore,
And the hoofs of beasts shall not
muddy them.
14 "Then I will make their waters
settle,
And will cause their rivers to run
like oil,"
Declares the Lord GOD.
15 "When I make the land of Egypt a
desolation,
And the land is destitute of that
which filled it,
When I smite all those who live
in it,
Then they shall know that I am
the LORD.
16"This is a lamentation and they
shall chant it. The daughters of the
nations shall chant it. Over Egypt and
over all her multitude they shall chant
it," declares the Lord GOD.
17 ¶ And it came about in the
twelfth year, on the fifteenth of the
month, that the word of the LORD
came to me saying,
18"Son of man, wail for the multitude
of Egypt, and bring it down, her and
the daughters of the powerful nations,
to the nether world, with those who go
down to the pit;
19 'Whom do you surpass in beauty?
Go down and make your bed
with the uncircumcised.'
20"They shall fall in the midst of
those who are slain by the sword. She
is given over to the sword; they have
drawn her and all her multitudes
away.
21"The strong among the mighty
ones shall speak of him and his helpers
from the midst of Sheol, 'They have
gone down, they lie still, the uncircumcised, slain by the sword.'
22 ¶"Assyria is there and all her company; her graves are round about her.
All of them are slain, fallen by the
sword,
23 whose graves are set in the remotest parts of the pit, and her company is
round about her grave. All of them are
slain, fallen by the sword, who spread
terror in the land of the living.

24 ¶"Elam is there and all her multitude around her grave; all of them
slain, fallen by the sword, who went
down uncircumcised to the lower
parts of the earth, who instilled their
terror in the land of the living, and
bore their disgrace with those who
went down to the pit.
25"They have made a bed for her
among the slain with all her multitude.
Her graves are around it, they are all
uncircumcised, slain by the sword (although their terror was instilled in the
land of the living), and they bore their
disgrace with those who go down to
the pit; they were put in the midst of
the slain.
26 ¶"Meshech, Tubal and all their
multitude are there; their graves surround them. All of them were slain by
the sword uncircumcised, though they
instilled their terror in the land of the
living.
27"Nor do they lie beside the fallen
heroes of the uncircumcised, who
went down to Sheol with their weapons of war, and whose swords were
laid under their heads; but the punishment for their iniquity rested on their
bones, though the terror of these heroes was once in the land of the living.
28"But in the midst of the uncircumcised you will be broken and lie with
those slain by the sword.
29 ¶"There also is Edom, its kings,
and all its princes, who for all their
might are laid with those slain by the
sword; they will lie with the uncircumcised, and with those who go down to
the pit.
30 ¶"There also are the chiefs of the
north, all of them, and all the Sidonians, who in spite of the terror resulting
from their might, in shame went down
with the slain. So they lay down uncircumcised with those slain by the
sword, and bore their disgrace with
those who go down to the pit.
31 ¶"These Pharaoh will see, and he
will be comforted for all his multitude
slain by the sword, even Pharaoh and
all his army," declares the Lord GOD.
32"Though I instilled a terror of him
in the land of the living, yet he will be
made to lie down among the uncircumcised along with those slain by the
sword, even Pharaoh and all his multitude," declares the Lord GOD.

CHAPTER 33

AND the word of the LORD came to me saying,

2"Son of man, speak to the sons of your people, and say to them, 'If I bring a sword upon a land, and the people of the land take one man from among them and make him their watchman;

3 and he sees the sword coming upon the land, and he blows on the trumpet and warns the people,

4 then he who hears the sound of the trumpet and does not take warning, and a sword comes and takes him away, his blood will be on his *own* head.

5 'He heard the sound of the trumpet, but did not take warning; his blood will be on himself. But had he taken warning, he would have delivered his life.

6 'But if the watchman sees the sword coming and does not blow the trumpet, and the people are not warned, and a sword comes and takes a person from them, he is taken away in his iniquity; but his blood I will require from the watchman's hand.'

7 ¶"Now as for you, son of man, I have appointed you a watchman for the house of Israel; so you will hear a message from My mouth, and give them warning from Me.

8"When I say to the wicked, 'O wicked man, you shall surely die,' and you do not speak to warn the wicked from his way, that wicked man shall die in his iniquity, but his blood I will require from your hand.

9"But if you on your part warn a wicked man to turn from his way, and he does not turn from his way, he will die in his iniquity; but you have delivered your life.

10 ¶"Now as for you, son of man, say to the house of Israel, 'Thus you have spoken, saying, "Surely our transgressions and our sins are upon us, and we are rotting away in them; how then can we survive?"'

11"Say to them, 'As I live!' declares the Lord GOD, 'I take no pleasure in the death of the wicked, but rather that the wicked turn from his way and live. Turn back, turn back from your evil ways! Why then will you die, O house of Israel?'

12"And you, son of man, say to your fellow citizens, 'The righteousness of a righteous man will not deliver him in the day of his transgression, and as for the wickedness of the wicked, he will not stumble because of it in the day when he turns from his wickedness; whereas a righteous man will not be able to live by his righteousness on the day when he commits sin.'

13"When I say to the righteous he will surely live, and he *so* trusts in his righteousness that he commits iniquity, none of his righteous deeds will be remembered; but in that same iniquity of his which he has committed he will die.

14"But when I say to the wicked, 'You will surely die,' and he turns from his sin and practices justice and righteousness,

15 *if a* wicked man restores a pledge, pays back what he has taken by robbery, walks by the statutes which ensure life without committing iniquity, he will surely live; he shall not die.

16"None of his sins that he has committed will be remembered against him. He has practiced justice and righteousness; he will surely live.

17 ¶"Yet your fellow citizens say, 'The way of the Lord is not right,' when it is their own way that is not right.

18"When the righteous turns from his righteousness and commits iniquity, then he shall die in it.

19"But when the wicked turns from his wickedness and practices justice and righteousness, he will live by them.

20"Yet you say, 'The way of the Lord is not right.' O house of Israel, I will judge each of you according to his ways."

21 ¶ Now it came about in the twelfth year of our exile, on the fifth of the tenth month, that the refugees from Jerusalem came to me, saying, "The city has been taken."

22 Now the hand of the LORD had been upon me in the evening, before the refugees came. And He opened my mouth at the time *they* came to me in the morning; so my mouth was opened, and I was no longer speechless.

23 ¶ Then the word of the LORD came to me saying,

24"Son of man, they who live in these waste places in the land of Israel are saying, 'Abraham was *only* one, yet he possessed the land; so to us who are many the land has been given as a possession.'

25"Therefore, say to them, 'Thus says the Lord GOD, "You eat *meat* with the blood *in it*, lift up your eyes to your idols as you shed blood. Should you then possess the land?

26"You rely on your sword, you commit abominations, and each of you defiles his neighbor's wife. Should you then possess the land?"'

27"Thus you shall say to them, 'Thus says the Lord GOD, "As I live, surely those who are in the waste places will fall by the sword, and whoever is in the open field I will give to the beasts to be devoured, and those who are in the strongholds and in the caves will die of pestilence.

28"And I shall make the land a desolation and a waste, and the pride of her power will cease; and the mountains of Israel will be desolate, so that no one will pass through.

29"Then they will know that I am the LORD, when I make the land a desolation and a waste because of all their abominations which they have committed."'

30 ¶"But as for you, son of man, your fellow citizens who talk about you by the walls and in the doorways of the houses, speak to one another, each to his brother, saying, 'Come now, and hear what the message is which comes forth from the LORD.'

31"And they come to you as people come, and sit before you *as* My people, and hear your words, but they do not do them, for they do the lustful desires *expressed* by their mouth, *and* their heart goes after their gain.

32"And behold, you are to them like a sensual song by one who has a beautiful voice and plays well on an instrument; for they hear your words, but they do not practice them.

33"So when it comes to pass—as surely it will—then they will know that a prophet has been in their midst."

CHAPTER 34

THEN the word of the LORD came to me saying,

2"Son of man, prophesy against the shepherds of Israel. Prophesy and say to those shepherds, 'Thus says the Lord GOD, "Woe, shepherds of Israel who have been feeding themselves! Should not the shepherds feed the flock?

3"You eat the fat and clothe yourselves with the wool, you slaughter the fat *sheep* without feeding the flock.

4"Those who are sickly you have not strengthened, the diseased you have not healed, the broken you have not bound up, the scattered you have not brought back, nor have you sought for the lost; but with force and with severity you have dominated them.

5"And they were scattered for lack of a shepherd, and they became food for every beast of the field and were scattered.

6"My flock wandered through all the mountains and on every high hill, and My flock was scattered over all the surface of the earth; and there was no one to search or seek *for them.*"'

7 ¶ Therefore, you shepherds, hear the word of the LORD:

8"As I live," declares the Lord GOD, "surely because My flock has become a prey, My flock has even become food for all the beasts of the field for lack of a shepherd, and My shepherds did not search for My flock, but *rather* the shepherds fed themselves and did not feed My flock;

9 therefore, you shepherds, hear the word of the LORD:

10 'Thus says the Lord GOD, "Behold, I am against the shepherds, and I shall demand My sheep from them and make them cease from feeding sheep. So the shepherds will not feed themselves anymore, but I shall deliver My flock from their mouth, that they may not be food for them."'"

11 ¶ For thus says the Lord GOD, "Behold, I Myself will search for My sheep and seek them out.

12"As a shepherd cares for his herd in the day when he is among his scattered sheep, so I will care for My sheep and will deliver them from all the places to which they were scattered on a cloudy and gloomy day.

13"And I will bring them out from the peoples and gather them from the countries and bring them to their own land; and I will feed them on the mountains of Israel, by the streams, and in all the inhabited places of the land.

14"I will feed them in a good pasture, and their grazing ground will be on the mountain heights of Israel. There they will lie down in good grazing ground, and they will feed in rich pasture on the mountains of Israel.

15"I will feed My flock and I will lead them to rest," declares the Lord GOD.

16"I will seek the lost, bring back the scattered, bind up the broken, and strengthen the sick; but the fat and the strong I will destroy. I will feed them with judgment.

17 ¶"And as for you, My flock, thus says the Lord GOD, 'Behold, I will judge between one sheep and another, between the rams and the male goats.

18 'Is it too slight a thing for you that you should feed in the good pasture, that you must tread down with your feet the rest of your pastures? Or that you should drink of the clear waters, that you must foul the rest with your feet?

19 'And as for My flock, they must eat what you tread down with your feet, and they must drink what you foul with your feet!' "

20 ¶ Therefore, thus says the Lord GOD to them, "Behold, I, even I, will judge between the fat sheep and the lean sheep.

21"Because you push with side and with shoulder, and thrust at all the weak with your horns, until you have scattered them abroad,

22 therefore, I will deliver My flock, and they will no longer be a prey; and I will judge between one sheep and another.

23"Then I will set over them one shepherd, My servant David, and he will feed them; he will feed them himself and be their shepherd.

24"And I, the LORD, will be their God, and My servant David will be prince among them; I, the LORD, have spoken.

25 ¶"And I will make a covenant of peace with them and eliminate harmful beasts from the land, so that they may live securely in the wilderness and sleep in the woods.

26"And I will make them and the places around My hill a blessing. And I will cause showers to come down in their season; they will be showers of blessing.

27"Also the tree of the field will yield its fruit, and the earth will yield its increase, and they will be secure on their land. Then they will know that I am the LORD, when I have broken the bars of their yoke and have delivered them from the hand of those who enslaved them.

28"And they will no longer be a prey to the nations, and the beasts of the earth will not devour them; but they will live securely, and no one will make *them* afraid.

29"And I will establish for them a renowned planting place, and they will not again be victims of famine in the land, and they will not endure the insults of the nations anymore.

30"Then they will know that I, the LORD their God, am with them, and that they, the house of Israel, are My people," declares the Lord GOD.

31"As for you, My sheep, the sheep of My pasture, you are men, and I am your God," declares the Lord GOD.

CHAPTER 35

MOREOVER, the word of the LORD came to me saying,

2"Son of man, set your face against Mount Seir, and prophesy against it,

3 and say to it, 'Thus says the Lord GOD,

"Behold, I am against you, Mount Seir,
And I will stretch out My hand against you,
And I will make you a desolation and a waste.

4 "I will lay waste your cities,
And you will become a desolation.
Then you will know that I am the LORD.

5"Because you have had everlasting enmity and have delivered the sons of Israel to the power of the sword at the time of their calamity, at the time of the punishment of the end,

6 therefore, as I live," declares the Lord GOD, "I will give you over to bloodshed, and bloodshed will pursue you; since you have not hated bloodshed, therefore bloodshed will pursue you.

7"And I will make Mount Seir a waste and a desolation, and I will cut off from it the one who passes through and returns.

8"And I will fill its mountains with its slain; on your hills and in your valleys and in all your ravines those slain by the sword will fall.

9"I will make you an everlasting desolation, and your cities will not be inhabited. Then you will know that I am the LORD.

10 ¶"Because you have said, 'These two nations and these two lands will be mine, and we will possess them,' although the LORD was there,

11 therefore, as I live," declares the Lord GOD, "I will deal *with you* according to your anger and according to your envy which you showed because of your hatred against them; so I will make Myself known among them when I judge you.

12"Then you will know that I, the LORD, have heard all your revilings which you have spoken against the mountains of Israel saying, 'They are laid desolate; they are given to us for food.'

13"And you have spoken arrogantly against Me and have multiplied your words against Me; I have heard."

14 'Thus says the Lord GOD, "As all the earth rejoices, I will make you a desolation.

15"As you rejoiced over the inheritance of the house of Israel because it was desolate, so I will do to you. You will be a desolation, O Mount Seir, and all Edom, all of it. Then they will know that I am the LORD."'

CHAPTER 36

"AND you, son of man, prophesy to the mountains of Israel and say, 'O mountains of Israel, hear the word of the LORD.

2 'Thus says the Lord GOD, "Because the enemy has spoken against you, 'Aha!' and, 'The everlasting heights have become our possession,'

3 therefore, prophesy and say, 'Thus says the Lord GOD, "For good cause they have made you desolate and crushed you from every side, that you should become a possession of the rest of the nations, and you have been taken up in the talk and the whispering of the people."'"

4 'Therefore, O mountains of Israel, hear the word of the Lord GOD. Thus says the Lord GOD to the mountains and to the hills, to the ravines and to the valleys, to the desolate wastes and to the forsaken cities, which have become a prey and a derision to the rest of the nations which are round about,

5 therefore, thus says the Lord GOD, "Surely in the fire of My jealousy I have spoken against the rest of the nations, and against all Edom, who appropriated My land for themselves as a possession with wholehearted joy *and* with scorn of soul, to drive it out for a prey."

6 'Therefore, prophesy concerning the land of Israel, and say to the mountains and to the hills, to the ravines and to the valleys, "Thus says the Lord GOD, 'Behold, I have spoken in My jealousy and in My wrath because you have endured the insults of the nations.'

7"Therefore, thus says the Lord GOD, 'I have sworn that surely the nations which are around you will themselves endure their insults.

8 'But you, O mountains of Israel, you will put forth your branches and bear your fruit for My people Israel; for they will soon come.

9 'For, behold, I am for you, and I will turn to you, and you shall be cultivated and sown.

10 'And I will multiply men on you, all the house of Israel, all of it; and the cities will be inhabited, and the waste places will be rebuilt.

11 'And I will multiply on you man and beast; and they will increase and be fruitful; and I will cause you to be inhabited as you were formerly and will treat you better than at the first. Thus you will know that I am the LORD.

12 'Yes, I will cause men—My people Israel—to walk on you and possess you, so that you will become their inheritance and never again bereave them of children.'

13"Thus says the Lord God, 'Because they say to you, "You are a devourer of men and have bereaved your nation of children,"

14 therefore, you will no longer devour men, and no longer bereave your nation of children,' declares the Lord God.

15"And I will not let you hear insults from the nations anymore, nor will you bear disgrace from the peoples any longer, nor will you cause your nation to stumble any longer," declares the Lord God.' "

16 ¶ Then the word of the Lord came to me saying,

17"Son of man, when the house of Israel was living in their own land, they defiled it by their ways and their deeds; their way before Me was like the uncleanness of a woman in her impurity.

18"Therefore, I poured out My wrath on them for the blood which they had shed on the land, because they had defiled it with their idols.

19"Also I scattered them among the nations, and they were dispersed throughout the lands. According to their ways and their deeds I judged them.

20"When they came to the nations where they went, they profaned My holy name, because it was said of them, 'These are the people of the Lord; yet they have come out of His land.'

21"But I had concern for My holy name, which the house of Israel had profaned among the nations where they went.

22 ¶"Therefore, say to the house of Israel, 'Thus says the Lord God, "It is not for your sake, O house of Israel, that I am about to act, but for My holy name, which you have profaned among the nations where you went.

23"And I will vindicate the holiness of My great name which has been profaned among the nations, which you have profaned in their midst. Then the nations will know that I am the Lord," declares the Lord God, "when I prove Myself holy among you in their sight.

24"For I will take you from the nations, gather you from all the lands, and bring you into your own land.

25"Then I will sprinkle clean water on you, and you will be clean; I will cleanse you from all your filthiness and from all your idols.

26"Moreover, I will give you a new heart and put a new spirit within you; and I will remove the heart of stone from your flesh and give you a heart of flesh.

27"And I will put My Spirit within you and cause you to walk in My statutes, and you will be careful to observe My ordinances.

28"And you will live in the land that I gave to your forefathers; so you will be My people, and I will be your God.

29"Moreover, I will save you from all your uncleanness; and I will call for the grain and multiply it, and I will not bring a famine on you.

30"And I will multiply the fruit of the tree and the produce of the field, that you may not receive again the disgrace of famine among the nations.

31"Then you will remember your evil ways and your deeds that were not good, and you will loathe yourselves in your own sight for your iniquities and your abominations.

32"I am not doing *this* for your sake," declares the Lord God, "let it be known to you. Be ashamed and confounded for your ways, O house of Israel!"

33 ¶ 'Thus says the Lord God, "On the day that I cleanse you from all your iniquities, I will cause the cities to be inhabited, and the waste places will be rebuilt.

34"And the desolate land will be cultivated instead of being a desolation in the sight of everyone who passed by.

35"And they will say, 'This desolate land has become like the garden of Eden; and the waste, desolate, and ruined cities are fortified *and* inhabited.'

36"Then the nations that are left round about you will know that I, the Lord, have rebuilt the ruined places *and* planted that which was desolate; I, the Lord, have spoken and will do it."

37 ¶ 'Thus says the Lord God, "This also I will let the house of Israel ask Me to do for them: I will increase their men like a flock.

38"Like the flock for sacrifices, like

the flock at Jerusalem during her appointed feasts, so will the waste cities be filled with flocks of men. Then they will know that I am the Lord.'"'"

CHAPTER 37

THE hand of the Lord was upon me, and He brought me out by the Spirit of the Lord and set me down in the middle of the valley; and it was full of bones.

2 And He caused me to pass among them round about, and behold, *there were* very many on the surface of the valley; and lo, *they were* very dry.

3 And He said to me, "Son of man, can these bones live?" And I answered, "O Lord God, Thou knowest."

4 Again He said to me, "Prophesy over these bones, and say to them, 'O dry bones, hear the word of the Lord.'

5 "Thus says the Lord God to these bones, 'Behold, I will cause [6]breath to enter you that you may come to life.

6 'And I will put sinews on you, make flesh grow back on you, cover you with skin, and put breath in you that you may come alive; and you will know that I am the Lord.'"

7 ¶ So I prophesied as I was commanded; and as I prophesied, there was a noise, and behold, a rattling; and the bones came together, bone to its bone.

8 And I looked, and behold, sinews were on them, and flesh grew, and skin covered them; but there was no breath in them.

9 Then He said to me, "Prophesy to the breath, prophesy, son of man, and say to the breath, 'Thus says the Lord God, "Come from the four winds, O breath, and breathe on these slain, that they come to life."'"

10 So I prophesied as He commanded me, and the breath came into them, and they came to life, and stood on their feet, an exceedingly great army.

11 ¶ Then He said to me, "Son of man, these bones are the whole house of Israel; behold, they say, 'Our bones are dried up, and our hope has perished. We are completely cut off.'

12 "Therefore prophesy, and say to them, 'Thus says the Lord God, "Behold, I will open your graves and cause you to come up out of your graves, My people; and I will bring you into the land of Israel.

13 "Then you will know that I am the Lord, when I have opened your graves and caused you to come up out of your graves, My people.

14 "And I will put My [7]Spirit within you, and you will come to life, and I will place you on your own land. Then you will know that I, the Lord, have spoken and done it," declares the Lord.'"

15 ¶ The word of the Lord came again to me saying,

16 "And you, son of man, take for yourself one stick and write on it, 'For Judah and for the sons of Israel, his companions'; then take another stick and write on it, 'For Joseph, the stick of Ephraim and all the house of Israel, his companions.'

17 "Then join them for yourself one to another into one stick, that they may become one in your hand.

18 "And when the sons of your people speak to you saying, 'Will you not declare to us what you mean by these?'

19 say to them, 'Thus says the Lord God, "Behold, I will take the stick of Joseph, which is in the hand of Ephraim, and the tribes of Israel, his companions; and I will put them with it, with the stick of Judah, and make them one stick, and they will be one in My hand."'

20 "And the sticks on which you write will be in your hand before their eyes.

21 "And say to them, 'Thus says the Lord God, "Behold, I will take the sons of Israel from among the nations where they have gone, and I will gather them from every side and bring them into their own land;

22 and I will make them one nation in the land, on the mountains of Israel; and one king will be king for all of them; and they will no longer be two nations, and they will no longer be divided into two kingdoms.

23 "And they will no longer defile themselves with their idols, or with their detestable things, or with any of their transgressions; but I will deliver them from all their [8]dwelling places in which they have sinned, and will

---

[6] Or, *spirit,* and so throughout this context

[7] Or, *breath*   [8] Another reading is *backslidings*

cleanse them. And they will be My people, and I will be their God.

24 ¶"And My servant David will be king over them, and they will all have one shepherd; and they will walk in My ordinances, and keep My statutes, and observe them.

25"And they shall live on the land that I gave to Jacob My servant, in which your fathers lived; and they will live on it, they, and their sons, and their sons' sons, forever; and David My servant shall be their prince forever.

26"And I will make a covenant of peace with them; it will be an everlasting covenant with them. And I will place them and multiply them, and will set My sanctuary in their midst forever.

27"My dwelling place also will be with them; and I will be their God, and they will be My people.

28"And the nations will know that I am the LORD who sanctifies Israel, when My sanctuary is in their midst forever."' "

CHAPTER 38

A_ND the word of the LORD came to me saying,

2"Son of man, set your face toward Gog of the land of Magog, the prince of Rosh, Meshech, and Tubal, and prophesy against him,

3 and say, 'Thus says the Lord GOD, "Behold, I am against you, O Gog, prince of Rosh, Meshech, and Tubal.

4"And I will turn you about, and put hooks into your jaws, and I will bring you out, and all your army, horses and horsemen, all of them splendidly attired, a great company *with* buckler and shield, all of them wielding swords;

5 Persia, Ethiopia, and Put with them, all of them *with* shield and helmet;

6 Gomer with all its troops; Bethtogarmah *from* the remote parts of the north with all its troops—many peoples with you.

7 ¶"Be prepared, and prepare yourself, you and all your companies that are assembled about you, and be a guard for them.

8"After many days you will be summoned; in the latter years you will come into the land that is restored from the sword, *whose inhabitants* have been gathered from many nations to the mountains of Israel which had been a continual waste; but its people were brought out from the nations, and they are living securely, all of them.

9"And you will go up, you will come like a storm; you will be like a cloud covering the land, you and all your troops, and many peoples with you."

10 ¶ 'Thus says the Lord GOD, "It will come about on that day, that thoughts will come into your mind, and you will devise an evil plan,

11 and you will say, 'I will go up against the land of [9]unwalled villages. I will go against those who are at rest, that live securely, all of them living without walls, and having no bars or gates,

12 to capture spoil and to seize plunder, to turn your hand against the waste places which are *now* inhabited, and against the people who are gathered from the nations, who have acquired cattle and goods, who live at the center of the world.'

13"Sheba, and Dedan, and the merchants of Tarshish, with all its villages, will say to you, 'Have you come to capture spoil? Have you assembled your company to seize plunder, to carry away silver and gold, to take away cattle and goods, to capture great spoil?' " '

14 ¶"Therefore, prophesy, son of man, and say to Gog, 'Thus says the Lord GOD, "On that day when My people Israel are living securely, will you not know *it*?

15"And you will come from your place out of the remote parts of the north, you and many peoples with you, all of them riding on horses, a great assembly and a mighty army;

16 and you will come up against My people Israel like a cloud to cover the land. It will come about in the last days that I shall bring you against My land, in order that the nations may know Me when I shall be sanctified through you before their eyes, O Gog."

17 ¶ 'Thus says the Lord GOD, "Are you the one of whom I spoke in former days through My servants the

[9] Or, *open country*

prophets of Israel, who prophesied in those days for *many* years that I would bring you against them?

18"And it will come about on that day, when Gog comes against the land of Israel," declares the Lord GOD, "that My fury will mount up in My anger.

19"And in My zeal and in My blazing wrath I declare *that* on that day there will surely be a great earthquake in the land of Israel.

20"And the fish of the sea, the birds of the heavens, the beasts of the field, all the creeping things that creep on the earth, and all the men who are on the face of the earth will shake at My presence; the mountains also will be thrown down, the steep pathways will collapse, and every wall will fall to the ground.

21"And I shall call for a sword against him on all My mountains," declares the Lord GOD. "Every man's sword will be against his brother.

22"And with pestilence and with blood I shall enter into judgment with him; and I shall rain on him, and on his troops, and on the many peoples who are with him, a torrential rain, with hailstones, fire, and brimstone.

23"And I shall magnify Myself, sanctify Myself, and make Myself known in the sight of many nations; and they will know that I am the LORD."'

CHAPTER 39

"AND you, son of man, prophesy against Gog, and say, 'Thus says the Lord GOD, "Behold, I am against you, O Gog, prince of Rosh, Meshech, and Tubal;

2 and I shall turn you around, drive you on, take you up from the remotest parts of the north, and bring you against the mountains of Israel.

3"And I shall strike your bow from your left hand, and dash down your arrows from your right hand.

4"You shall fall on the mountains of Israel, you and all your troops, and the peoples who are with you; I shall give you as food to every kind of predatory bird and beast of the field.

5"You will fall on the open field; for it is I who have spoken," declares the Lord GOD.

6"And I shall send fire upon Magog and those who inhabit the coastlands in safety; and they will know that I am the LORD.

7 ¶"And My holy name I shall make known in the midst of My people Israel; and I shall not let My holy name be profaned anymore. And the nations will know that I am the LORD, the Holy One in Israel.

8"Behold, it is coming and it shall be done," declares the Lord GOD. "That is the day of which I have spoken.

9 ¶"Then those who inhabit the cities of Israel will go out, and make fires with the weapons and burn *them,* both shields and bucklers, bows and arrows, war clubs and spears and for seven years they will make fires of them.

10"And they will not take wood from the field or gather firewood from the forests, for they will make fires with the weapons; and they will take the spoil of those who despoiled them, and seize the plunder of those who plundered them," declares the Lord GOD.

11 ¶"And it will come about on that day that I shall give Gog a burial ground there in Israel, the valley of those who pass by east of the sea, and it will block off the passers-by. So they will bury Gog there with all his multitude, and they will call *it* the valley of Hamon-gog.

12"For seven months the house of Israel will be burying them in order to cleanse the land.

13"Even all the people of the land will bury *them;* and it will be to their renown *on* the day that I glorify Myself," declares the Lord GOD.

14"And they will set apart men who will constantly pass through the land, burying those who were passing through, even those left on the surface of the ground, in order to cleanse it. At the end of seven months they will make a search.

15"And as those who pass through the land pass through and anyone sees a man's bone, then he will set up a marker by it until the buriers have buried it in the valley of Hamon-gog.

16"And even *the* name of *the* city will be Hamonah. So they will cleanse the land."'

17 ¶"And as for you, son of man, thus says the Lord GOD, 'Speak to every kind of bird and to every beast

of the field, "Assemble and come, gather from every side to My sacrifice which I am going to sacrifice for you, as a great sacrifice on the mountains of Israel, that you may eat flesh and drink blood.

18"You shall eat the flesh of mighty men, and drink the blood of the princes of the earth, as *though they were* rams, lambs, goats, and bulls, all of them fatlings of Bashan.

19"So you will eat fat until you are glutted, and drink blood until you are drunk, from My sacrifice which I have sacrificed for you.

20"And you will be glutted at My table with horses and charioteers, with mighty men and all the men of war," declares the Lord GOD.

21 ¶"And I shall set My glory among the nations; and all the nations will see My judgment which I have executed, and My hand which I have laid on them.

22"And the house of Israel will know that I am the LORD their God from that day onward.

23"And the nations will know that the house of Israel went into exile for their iniquity because they acted treacherously against Me, and I hid My face from them; so I gave them into the hand of their adversaries, and all of them fell by the sword.

24"According to their uncleanness and according to their transgressions I dealt with them, and I hid My face from them." ' "

25 ¶ Therefore thus says the Lord GOD, "Now I shall restore the fortunes of Jacob, and have mercy on the whole house of Israel; and I shall be jealous for My holy name.

26"And they shall [10]forget their disgrace and all their treachery which they [11]perpetrated against Me, when they live securely on their *own* land with no one to make them afraid.

27"When I bring them back from the peoples and gather them from the lands of their enemies, then I shall be sanctified through them in the sight of the many nations.

28"Then they will know that I am the LORD their God because I made them go into exile among the nations, and then gathered them *again* to their own

land; and I will leave none of them there any longer.

29"And I will not hide My face from them any longer, for I shall have poured out My Spirit on the house of Israel," declares the Lord GOD.

CHAPTER 40

IN the twenty-fifth year of our exile, at the beginning of the year, on the tenth of the month, in the fourteenth year after the city was taken, on that same day the hand of the LORD was upon me and He brought me there.

2 In the visions of God He brought me into the land of Israel, and set me on a very high mountain; and on it to the south *there was* a structure like a city.

3 So He brought me there; and behold, there was a man whose appearance was like the appearance of bronze, with a line of flax and a measuring rod in his hand; and he was standing in the gateway.

4 And the man said to me, "Son of man, see with your eyes, hear with your ears, and give attention to all that I am going to show you; for you have been brought here in order to show *it* to you. Declare to the house of Israel all that you see."

5 ¶ And behold, there was a wall on the outside of the temple all around, and in the man's hand was a measuring rod of six cubits, *each of which was* a cubit and a handbreadth. So he measured the thickness of the wall, one rod; and the height, one rod.

6 Then he went to the gate which faced east, went up its steps, and measured the threshold of the gate, one rod in width; and the other threshold *was* one rod in width.

7 And the guardroom *was* one rod long and one rod wide; and *there were* five cubits between the guardrooms. And the threshold of the gate by the porch of the gate facing inward *was* one rod.

8 Then he measured the porch of the gate facing inward, one rod.

9 And he measured the porch of the gate, eight cubits; and its side pillars, two cubits. And the porch of the gate was faced inward.

10 And the guardrooms of the gate toward the east *numbered* three on

[10] Another reading is *bear*   [11] Lit., *did treacherously*

each side; the three of them had the same measurement. The side pillars also had the same measurement on each side.

11 And he measured the width of the gateway, ten cubits, and the length of the gate, thirteen cubits.

12 And *there was* a barrier *wall* one cubit *wide* in front of the guardrooms on each side; and the guardrooms *were* six cubits *square* on each side.

13 And he measured the gate from the roof of the one guardroom to the roof of the other, a width of twenty-five cubits from *one* door to *the* door opposite.

14 And he made the side pillars sixty cubits *high;* the gate *extended* round about to the side pillar of the courtyard.

15 And *from* the front of the entrance gate to the front of the inner porch of the gate *was* fifty cubits.

16 And *there were* shuttered windows *looking* toward the guardrooms, and toward their side pillars within the gate all around, and likewise for the porches. And *there were* windows all around inside; and on *each* side pillar *were* palm tree ornaments.

17 ¶ Then he brought me into the outer court, and behold, *there were* chambers and a pavement, made for the court all around; thirty chambers faced the pavement.

18 And the pavement (*that is,* the lower pavement) *was* by the side of the gates, corresponding to the length of the gates.

19 Then he measured the width from the front of the lower gate to the front of the exterior of the inner court, a hundred cubits on the east and on the north.

20 ¶ And *as for* the gate of the outer court which faced the north, he measured its length and its width.

21 And it had three guardrooms on each side; and its side pillars and its porches had the same measurement as the first gate. Its length *was* fifty cubits, and the width twenty-five cubits.

22 And its windows, and its porches, and its palm tree ornaments *had* the same measurements as the gate which faced toward the east; and it was reached by seven steps, and its porch *was* in front of them.

23 And the inner court had a gate opposite the gate on the north as well as *the gate* on the east; and he measured a hundred cubits from gate to gate.

24 ¶ Then he led me toward the south, and behold, there was a gate toward the south; and he measured its side pillars and its porches according to those same measurements.

25 And the gate and its porches had windows all around like those other windows; the length *was* fifty cubits and the width twenty-five cubits.

26 And *there were* seven steps going up to it, and its porches *were* in front of them; and it had palm tree ornaments on its side pillars, one on each side.

27 And the inner court had a gate toward the south; and he measured from gate to gate toward the south, a hundred cubits.

28 ¶ Then he brought me to the inner court by the south gate; and he measured the south gate according to those same measurements.

29 Its guardrooms also, its side pillars, and its porches *were* according to those same measurements. And the gate and its porches had windows all around; it *was* fifty cubits long and twenty-five cubits wide.

30 And *there were* porches all around, twenty-five cubits long and five cubits wide.

31 And its porches *were* toward the outer court; and palm tree ornaments *were* on its side pillars, and its stairway had eight steps.

32 ¶ And he brought me into the inner court toward the east. And he measured the gate according to those same measurements.

33 Its guardrooms also, its side pillars, and its porches *were* according to those same measurements. And the gate and its porches had windows all around; it *was* fifty cubits long and twenty-five cubits wide.

34 And its porches *were* toward the outer court; and palm tree ornaments *were* on its side pillars, on each side, and its stairway had eight steps.

35 ¶ Then he brought me to the north gate; and he measured *it* according to those same measurements,

36 *with* its guardrooms, its side pillars, and its porches. And the gate had

windows all around; the length *was* fifty cubits and the width twenty-five cubits.

37 And its side pillars *were* toward the outer court; and palm tree ornaments *were* on its side pillars on each side, and its stairway had eight steps.

38 ¶ And a chamber with its doorway was by the side pillars at the gates; there they rinse the burnt offering.

39 And in the porch of the gate *were* two tables on each side, on which to slaughter the burnt offering, the sin offering, and the guilt offering.

40 And on the outer side, as one went up to the gateway toward the north, were two tables; and on the other side of the porch of the gate *were* two tables.

41 Four tables *were* on each side next to the gate; *or,* eight tables on which they slaughter *sacrifices.*

42 And for the burnt offering *there were* four tables of hewn stone, a cubit and a half long, a cubit and a half wide, and one cubit high, on which they lay the instruments with which they slaughter the burnt offering and the sacrifice.

43 And the double hooks, one handbreadth in length, were installed in the house all around; and on the tables *was* the flesh of the offering.

44 ¶ And from the outside to the inner gate were chambers for the singers in the inner court, *one of* which was at the side of the north gate, with its front toward the south, and one at the side of the east gate facing toward the north.

45 And he said to me, "This is the chamber which faces toward the south, *intended* for the priests who keep charge of the temple;

46 but the chamber which faces toward the north is for the priests who keep charge of the altar. These are the sons of Zadok, who from the sons of Levi come near to the LORD to minister to Him."

47 And he measured the court, a *perfect* square, a hundred cubits long and a hundred cubits wide; and the altar was in front of the temple.

48 ¶ Then he brought me to the porch of the temple and measured *each* side pillar of the porch, five cubits on each side; and the width of the gate was three cubits on each side.

49 The length of the porch was twenty cubits, and the width eleven cubits; and at the stairway by which it was ascended *were* columns belonging to the side pillars, one on each side.

CHAPTER 41

THEN he brought me to the nave and measured the side pillars; six cubits wide on each side *was* the width of the side pillar.

2 And the width of the entrance *was* ten cubits, and the sides of the entrance were five cubits on each side. And he measured the length of the nave, forty cubits, and the width, twenty cubits.

3 Then he went inside and measured each side pillar of the doorway, two cubits, and the doorway, six cubits *high;* and the width of the doorway, seven cubits.

4 And he measured its length, twenty cubits, and the width, twenty cubits, before the nave; and he said to me, "This is the most holy *place.*"

5 ¶ Then he measured the wall of the temple, six cubits; and the width of the side chambers, four cubits, all around about the house on every side.

6 And the side chambers were in three stories, one above another, and thirty in each story; and the side chambers extended to the wall which *stood* on their inward side all around, that they might be fastened, and not be fastened into the wall of the temple *itself.*

7 And the side chambers surrounding the temple were wider at each successive story. Because the structure surrounding the temple went upward by stages on all sides of the temple, therefore the width of the temple *increased* as it went higher; and thus one went up from the lowest *story* to the highest by way of the second *story.*

8 I saw also that the house had a raised platform all around; the foundations of the side chambers were a full rod of six long cubits *in height.*

9 The thickness of the outer wall of the side chambers was five cubits. But

the free space between the side chambers belonging to the temple

10 and the *outer* chambers *was* twenty cubits in width all around the temple on every side.

11 And the doorways of the side chambers toward the free space *consisted of* one doorway toward the north and another doorway toward the south; and the width of the free space was five cubits all around.

12 ¶ And the building that *was* in front of the separate area at the side toward the west *was* seventy cubits wide; and the wall of the building was five cubits thick all around, and its length *was* ninety cubits.

13 Then he measured the temple, a hundred cubits long; the separate area with the building and its walls *were* also a hundred cubits long.

14 Also the width of the front of the temple and *that of* the separate areas along the east *side totaled* a hundred cubits.

15 ¶ And he measured the length of the building along the front of the separate area behind it, with a gallery on each side, a hundred cubits; *he* also *measured* the inner nave and the porches of the court.

16 The thresholds, the latticed windows, and the galleries round about their three stories, opposite the threshold, were paneled with wood all around, and *from* the ground to the windows (but the windows were covered),

17 over the entrance, and to the inner house, and on the outside, and on all the wall all around inside and outside, by measurement.

18 And it was carved with cherubim and palm trees; and a palm tree was between cherub and cherub, and every cherub had two faces,

19 a man's face toward the palm tree on one side, and a young lion's face toward the palm tree on the other side; they were carved on all the house all around.

20 From the ground to above the entrance cherubim and palm trees were carved, as well as *on* the wall of the nave.

21 ¶ The doorposts of the nave were square; as for the front of the sanctuary, the appearance of one doorpost was like that of the other.

22 The altar *was* of wood, three cubits high, and its length two cubits; its corners, its base, and its sides *were* of wood. And he said to me, "This is the table that is before the LORD."

23 And the nave and the sanctuary each had a double door.

24 And each of the doors had two leaves, two swinging leaves; two *leaves* for one door and two leaves for the other.

25 Also there were carved on them, on the doors of the nave, cherubim and palm trees like those carved on the walls; and *there was* a threshold of wood on the front of the porch outside.

26 And *there were* latticed windows and palm trees on one side and on the other, on the sides of the porch; thus *were* the side chambers of the house and the thresholds.

CHAPTER 42

THEN he brought me out into the outer court, the way toward the north; and he brought me to the chamber which *was* opposite the separate area and opposite the building toward the north.

2 Along the length, *which was* a hundred cubits, *was* the north door; the width *was* fifty cubits.

3 Opposite the twenty *cubits* which belonged to the inner court, and opposite the pavement which belonged to the outer court, *was* gallery corresponding to gallery in three stories.

4 And before the chambers *was* an inner walk ten cubits wide, a way of one *hundred* cubits; and their openings *were* on the north.

5 Now the upper chambers *were* smaller because the galleries took more *space* away from them than from the lower and middle ones in the building.

6 For they *were* in three stories and had no pillars like the pillars of the courts; therefore *the upper chambers* were set back from the ground upward, more than the lower and middle ones.

7 As for the outer wall by the side of the chambers, toward the outer court facing the chambers, its length *was* fifty cubits.

8 For the length of the chambers

which *were* in the outer court *was* fifty cubits; and behold, *the length of those* facing the temple *was* a hundred cubits.

9 And below these chambers *was* the entrance on the east side, as one enters them from the outer court.

10 ¶ In the thickness of the wall of the court toward the east, facing the separate area and facing the building, *there were* chambers.

11 And the way in front of them *was* like the appearance of the chambers which *were* on the north, according to their length so was their width; and all their exits *were* both according to their arrangements and openings.

12 And corresponding to the openings of the chambers which were toward the south was an opening at the head of the way, the way in front of the wall toward the east, as one enters them.

13 ¶ Then he said to me, "The north chambers *and* the south chambers, which are opposite the separate area, they are the holy chambers where the priests who are near to the Lord shall eat the most holy things. There they shall lay the most holy things, the grain offering, the sin offering, and the guilt offering; for the place is holy.

14"When the priests enter, then they shall not go out into the outer court from the sanctuary without laying there their garments in which they minister, for they are holy. They shall put on other garments; then they shall approach that which is for the people."

15 ¶ Now when he had finished measuring the inner house, he brought me out by the way of the gate which faced toward the east, and measured it all around.

16 He measured on the east side with the measuring reed five hundred reeds, by the measuring reed.

17 He measured on the north side five hundred reeds by the measuring reed.

18 On the south side he measured five hundred reeds with the measuring reed.

19 He turned to the west side, *and* measured five hundred reeds with the measuring reed.

20 He measured it on the four sides; it had a wall all around, the length five hundred and the width five hundred,

to divide between the holy and the profane.

CHAPTER 43

THEN he led me to the gate, the gate facing toward the east;

2 and behold, the glory of the God of Israel was coming from the way of the east. And His voice was like the sound of many waters; and the earth shone with His glory.

3 And *it was* like the appearance of the vision which I saw, like the vision which I saw when He came to destroy the city. And the visions *were* like the vision which I saw by the river Chebar; and I fell on my face.

4 And the glory of the Lord came into the house by the way of the gate facing toward the east.

5 And the Spirit lifted me up and brought me into the inner court; and behold, the glory of the Lord filled the house.

6 ¶ Then I heard one speaking to me from the house, while a man was standing beside me.

7 And He said to me, "Son of man, *this is* the place of My throne and the place of the soles of My feet, where I will dwell among the sons of Israel forever. And the house of Israel will not again defile My holy name, neither they nor their kings, by their harlotry and by the [12]corpses of their kings [13]when they die,

8 by setting their threshold by My threshold, and their door post beside My door post, with *only* the wall between Me and them. And they have defiled My holy name by their abominations which they have committed. So I have consumed them in My anger.

9"Now let them put away their harlotry and the [12]corpses of their kings far from Me; and I will dwell among them forever.

10 ¶"As for you, son of man, describe the temple to the house of Israel, that they may be ashamed of their iniquities; and let them measure the plan.

11"And if they are ashamed of all that they have done, make known to them the design of the house, its structure, its exits, its entrances, all its designs, all its statutes, and all its laws.

[12] Or, *monuments*   [13] Or, *in their high places*

And write *it* in their sight, so that they may observe its whole design and all its statutes, and do them.

12"This is the law of the house: its entire area on the top of the mountain all around *shall be* most holy. Behold, this is the law of the house.

13 ¶"And these are the measurements of the altar by cubits (the cubit being a cubit and a handbreadth): the base *shall be* a cubit, and the width a cubit, and its border on its edge round about one span; and this *shall be* the *height of* the base of the altar.

14"And from the base on the ground to the lower ledge *shall be* two cubits, and the width one cubit; and from the smaller ledge to the larger ledge *shall be* four cubits, and the width one cubit.

15"And the altar hearth *shall be* four cubits; and from the altar hearth shall extend upwards four horns.

16"Now the altar hearth *shall be* twelve *cubits* long by twelve wide, square in its four sides.

17"And the ledge *shall be* fourteen *cubits* long by fourteen wide in its four sides, the border around it *shall be* half a cubit, and its base *shall be* a cubit round about; and its steps shall face the east."

18 ¶ And He said to me, "Son of man, thus says the Lord God, 'These are the statutes for the altar on the day it is built, to offer burnt offerings on it and to sprinkle blood on it.

19 'And you shall give to the Levitical priests who are from the offspring of Zadok, who draw near to Me to minister to Me,' declares the Lord God, 'a young bull for a sin offering.

20 'And you shall take some of its blood, and put it on its four horns, and on the four corners of the ledge, and on the border round about; thus you shall cleanse it and make atonement for it.

21 'You shall also take the bull for the sin offering; and it *shall be* burned in the appointed place of the house, outside the sanctuary.

22 'And on the second day you shall offer a male goat without blemish for a sin offering; and they shall cleanse the altar, as they cleansed *it* with the bull.

23 'When you have finished cleansing

it, you shall present a young bull without blemish and a ram without blemish from the flock.

24 'And you shall present them before the Lord, and the priests shall throw salt on them, and they shall offer them up as a burnt offering to the Lord.

25 'For seven days you shall prepare daily a goat for a sin offering; also a young bull and a ram from the flock, without blemish, shall be prepared.

26 'For seven days they shall make atonement for the altar and purify it; so shall they consecrate it.

27 'And when they have completed the days, it shall be that on the eighth day and onward, the priests shall offer your burnt offerings on the altar, and your peace offerings; and I will accept you,' declares the Lord God."

CHAPTER 44

THEN He brought me back by the way of the outer gate of the sanctuary, which faces the east; and it was shut.

2 And the Lord said to me, "This gate shall be shut; it shall not be opened, and no one shall enter by it, for the Lord God of Israel has entered by it; therefore it shall be shut.

3"As for the prince, he shall sit in it as prince to eat bread before the Lord; he shall enter by way of the porch of the gate, and shall go out by the same way."

4 ¶ Then He brought me by way of the north gate to the front of the house; and I looked, and behold, the glory of the Lord filled the house of the Lord, and I fell on my face.

5 And the Lord said to me, "Son of man, mark well, see with your eyes, and hear with your ears all that I say to you concerning all the statutes of the house of the Lord and concerning all its laws; and mark well the entrance of the house, with all exits of the sanctuary.

6"And you shall say to the rebellious ones, to the house of Israel, 'Thus says the Lord God, "Enough of all your abominations, O house of Israel,

7 when you brought in foreigners, uncircumcised in heart and uncircumcised in flesh, to be in My sanctuary to profane it, *even* My house, when you offered My food, the fat and the blood;

for they made My covenant void—*this* in addition to all your abominations.

8"And you have not kept charge of My holy things yourselves, but you have set *foreigners* to keep charge of My sanctuary."

9 ¶ 'Thus says the Lord GOD, "No foreigner, uncircumcised in heart and uncircumcised in flesh, of all the foreigners who are among the sons of Israel, shall enter My sanctuary.

10"But the Levites who went far from Me, when Israel went astray, who went astray from Me after their idols, shall bear the punishment for their iniquity.

11"Yet they shall be ministers in My sanctuary, having oversight at the gates of the house and ministering in the house; they shall slaughter the burnt offering and the sacrifice for the people, and they shall stand before them to minister to them.

12"Because they ministered to them before their idols and became a stumbling block of iniquity to the house of Israel, therefore I have sworn against them," declares the Lord GOD, "that they shall bear the punishment for their iniquity.

13"And they shall not come near to Me to serve as a priest to Me, nor come near to any of My holy things, to the things that are most holy; but they shall bear their shame and their abominations which they have committed.

14"Yet I will appoint them to keep charge of the house, of all its service, and of all that shall be done in it.

15 ¶ "But the Levitical priests, the sons of Zadok, who kept charge of My sanctuary when the sons of Israel went astray from Me, shall come near to Me to minister to Me; and they shall stand before Me to offer Me the fat and the blood," declares the Lord GOD.

16"They shall enter My sanctuary; they shall come near to My table to minister to Me and keep My charge.

17"And it shall be that when they enter at the gates of the inner court, they shall be clothed with linen garments; and wool shall not be on them while they are ministering in the gates of the inner court and in the house.

18"Linen turbans shall be on their heads, and linen undergarments shall be on their loins; they shall not gird themselves with *anything which makes them* sweat.

19"And when they go out into the outer court, into the outer court to the people, they shall put off their garments in which they have been ministering and lay them in the holy chambers; then they shall put on other garments that they may not transmit holiness to the people with their garments.

20"Also they shall not shave their heads, yet they shall not let their locks grow long; they shall only trim *the hair of* their heads.

21"Nor shall any of the priests drink wine when they enter the inner court.

22"And they shall not marry a widow or a divorced woman but shall take virgins from the offspring of the house of Israel, or a widow who is the widow of a priest.

23"Moreover, they shall teach My people *the difference* between the holy and the profane, and cause them to discern between the unclean and the clean.

24"And in a dispute they shall take their stand to judge; they shall judge it according to My ordinances. They shall also keep My laws and My statutes in all My appointed feasts, and sanctify My sabbaths.

25"And they shall not go to a dead person to defile *themselves;* however, for father, for mother, for son, for daughter, for brother, or for a sister who has not had a husband, they may defile themselves.

26"And after he is cleansed, seven days shall [14]elapse for him.

27"And on the day that he goes into the sanctuary, into the inner court to minister in the sanctuary, he shall offer his sin offering," declares the Lord GOD.

28 ¶ "And it shall be with regard to an inheritance for them, *that* I am their inheritance; and you shall give them no possession in Israel—I am their possession.

29"They shall eat the grain offering, the sin offering, and the guilt offering; and every devoted thing in Israel shall be theirs.

30"And the first of all the first fruits of every kind and every contribution

---

[14] Lit., *be counted*

of every kind, from all your contributions, shall be for the priests; you shall also give to the priest the first of your dough to cause a blessing to rest on your house.

31"The priests shall not eat any bird or beast that has died a natural death or has been torn to pieces.

CHAPTER 45

"AND when you shall divide by lot the land for inheritance, you shall offer an allotment to the LORD, a holy portion of the land; the length shall be the length of 25,000 *cubits*, and the width shall be 10,000. It shall be holy within all its boundary round about.

2"Out of this there shall be for the holy place a square round about five hundred by five hundred *cubits*, and fifty cubits for its open space round about.

3"And from this area you shall measure a length of 25,000 *cubits*, and a width of 10,000 *cubits;* and in it shall be the sanctuary, the most holy place.

4"It shall be the holy portion of the land; it shall be for the priests, the ministers of the sanctuary, who come near to minister to the LORD, and it shall be a place for their houses and a holy place for the sanctuary.

5"And *an area* 25,000 *cubits* in length and 10,000 in width shall be for the Levites, the ministers of the house, *and* for their possession cities to dwell in.

6"And you shall give the city possession of *an area* 5,000 *cubits* wide and 25,000 *cubits* long, alongside the [15]allotment of the holy portion; it shall be for the whole house of Israel.

7"And the prince shall have *land* on either side of the holy [15]allotment and the property of the city, adjacent to the holy [15]allotment and the property of the city, on the west side toward the west and on the east side toward the east, and in length comparable to one of the portions, from the west border to the east border.

8"This shall be his land for a possession in Israel; so My princes shall no longer oppress My people, but they shall give *the rest of* the land to the house of Israel according to their tribes."

9 ¶ 'Thus says the Lord GOD, "Enough, you princes of Israel; put away violence and destruction, and practice justice and righteousness. Stop your expropriations from My people," declares the Lord GOD.

10"You shall have just balances, a just ephah, and a just bath.

11"The ephah and the bath shall be the same quantity, so that the bath may contain a tenth of a homer, and the ephah a tenth of a homer; their standard shall be according to the homer.

12"And the shekel shall be twenty gerahs; twenty shekels, twenty-five shekels, *and* fifteen shekels shall be your maneh.

13 ¶ "This is the offering that you shall offer: a sixth of an ephah from a homer of wheat; a sixth of an ephah from a homer of barley;

14 and the prescribed portion of oil (*namely,* the bath of oil), a tenth of a bath from *each* kor (*which is* ten baths *or* a homer, for ten baths are a homer);

15 and one sheep from *each* flock of two hundred from the watering places of Israel—for a grain offering, for a burnt offering, and for peace offerings, to make atonement for them," declares the Lord GOD.

16"All the people of the land shall give to this offering for the prince in Israel.

17"And it shall be the prince's part *to provide* the burnt offerings, the grain offerings, and the libations, at the feasts, on the new moons, and on the sabbaths, at all the appointed feasts of the house of Israel; he shall provide the sin offering, the grain offering, the burnt offering, and the peace offerings, to make atonement for the house of Israel."

18 ¶ 'Thus says the Lord GOD, "In the first *month,* on the first of the month, you shall take a young bull without blemish and cleanse the sanctuary.

19"And the priest shall take some of the blood from the sin offering and put *it* on the door posts of the house, on the four corners of the ledge of the altar, and on the posts of the gate of the inner court.

20"And thus you shall do on the seventh *day* of the month for everyone who goes astray or is naive; so you shall make atonement for the house.

21 ¶"In the first *month,* on the fourteenth day of the month, you shall have the Passover, a feast of seven days; unleavened bread shall be eaten.

22"And on that day the prince shall provide for himself and all the people of the land a bull for a sin offering.

23"And *during* the seven days of the feast he shall provide as a burnt offering to the LORD seven bulls and seven rams without blemish on every day of the seven days, and a male goat daily for a sin offering.

24"And he shall provide as a grain offering an ephah with a bull, an ephah with a ram, and a hin of oil with an ephah.

25"In the seventh *month,* on the fifteenth day of the month, at the feast, he shall provide like this, seven days for the sin offering, the burnt offering, the grain offering, and the oil."

CHAPTER 46

'THUS says the Lord GOD, "The gate of the inner court facing east shall be shut the six working days; but it shall be opened on the sabbath day, and opened on the day of the new moon.

2"And the prince shall enter by way of the porch of the gate from outside and stand by the post of the gate. Then the priests shall provide his burnt offering and his peace offerings, and he shall worship at the threshold of the gate and then go out; but the gate shall not be shut until the evening.

3"The people of the land shall also worship at the doorway of that gate before the LORD on the sabbaths and on the new moons.

4"And the burnt offering which the prince shall offer to the LORD on the sabbath day shall be six lambs without blemish and a ram without blemish;

5 and the grain offering shall be an ephah with the ram, and the grain offering with the lambs as much as he is able to give, and a hin of oil with an ephah.

6"And on the day of the new moon *he shall offer* a young bull without blemish, also six lambs and a ram, *which* shall be without blemish.

7"And he shall provide a grain offering, an ephah with the bull, and an ephah with the ram, and with the lambs as much as he is able, and a hin of oil with an ephah.

8"And when the prince enters, he shall go in by way of the porch of the gate and go out by the same way.

9"But when the people of the land come before the LORD at the appointed feasts, he who enters by way of the north gate to worship shall go out by way of the south gate. And he who enters by way of the south gate shall go out by way of the north gate. No one shall return by way of the gate by which he entered but shall go straight out.

10"And when they go in, the prince shall go in among them; and when they go out, he shall go out.

11"And at the festivals and the appointed feasts the grain offering shall be an ephah with a bull and an ephah with a ram, and with the lambs as much as one is able to give, and a hin of oil with an ephah.

12"And when the prince provides a freewill offering, a burnt offering, or peace offerings *as* a freewill offering to the LORD, the gate facing east shall be opened for him. And he shall provide his burnt offering and his peace offerings as he does on the sabbath day. Then he shall go out, and the gate shall be shut after he goes out.

13 ¶"And you shall provide a lamb a year old without blemish for a burnt offering to the LORD daily; morning by morning you shall provide it.

14"Also you shall provide a grain offering with it morning by morning, a sixth of an ephah, and a third of a hin of oil to moisten the fine flour, a grain offering to the LORD continually by a perpetual ordinance.

15"Thus they shall provide the lamb, the grain offering, and the oil, morning by morning, for a continual burnt offering.

16 ¶ Thus says the Lord GOD, "If the prince gives a gift *out of* his inheritance to any of his sons, it shall belong to his sons; it is their possession by inheritance.

17"But if he gives a gift from his inheritance to one of his servants, it shall be his until the year of liberty; then it shall return to the prince. His inheritance *shall be* only his sons'; it shall belong to them.

18"And the prince shall not take from the people's inheritance, thrusting them out of their possession; he shall give his sons inheritance from his own possession so that My people shall not be scattered, anyone from his possession." ' "

19 ¶ Then he brought me through the entrance, which *was* at the side of the gate, into the holy chambers for the priests, which faced north; and behold, there *was* a place at the extreme rear toward the west.

20 And he said to me, "This is the place where the priests shall boil the guilt offering and the sin offering, *and* where they shall bake the grain offering, in order that they may not bring *them* out into the outer court to transmit holiness to the people."

21 Then he brought me out into the outer court and led me across to the four corners of the court; and behold, in every corner of the court *there was* a *small* court.

22 In the four corners of the court *there were* enclosed courts, forty *cubits* long and thirty wide; these four in the corners *were* the same size.

23 And *there was* a row *of masonry* round about in them, around the four of them, and boiling places were made under the rows round about.

24 Then he said to me, "These are the boiling places where the ministers of the house shall boil the sacrifices of the people."

CHAPTER 47

THEN he brought me back to the door of the house; and behold, water was flowing from under the threshold of the house toward the east, for the house faced east. And the water was flowing down from under, from the right side of the house, from south of the altar.

2 And he brought me out by way of the north gate and led me around on the outside to the outer gate by way of *the gate* that faces east. And behold, water was trickling from the south side.

3 ¶ When the man went out toward the east with a line in his hand, he measured a thousand cubits, and he led me through the water, water *reaching* the ankles.

4 Again he measured a thousand and led me through the water, water *reaching* the knees. Again he measured a thousand and led me through *the water,* water *reaching* the loins.

5 Again he measured a thousand; *and it was* a river that I could not ford, for the water had risen, *enough* water to swim in, a river that could not be forded.

6 And he said to me, "Son of man, have you seen *this*?" Then he brought me back to the bank of the river.

7 Now when I had returned, behold, on the bank of the river there *were* very many trees on the one side and on the other.

8 Then he said to me, "These waters go out toward the eastern region and go down into the Arabah; then they go toward the sea, being made to flow into the sea, and the waters *of the sea* become fresh.

9"And it will come about that every living creature which swarms in every place where the river goes, will live. And there will be very many fish, for these waters go there, and *the others* become fresh; so everything will live where the river goes.

10"And it will come about that fishermen will stand beside it; from Engedi to Eneglaim there will be a place for the spreading of nets. Their fish will be according to their kinds, like the fish of the Great Sea, very many.

11"But its swamps and marshes will not become fresh; they will be left for salt.

12"And by the river on its bank, on one side and on the other, will grow all *kinds of* trees for food. Their leaves will not wither, and their fruit will not fail. They will bear every month because their water flows from the sanctuary, and their fruit will be for food and their leaves for healing."

13 ¶ Thus says the Lord GOD, "This *shall be* the boundary by which you shall divide the land for an inheritance among the twelve tribes of Israel; Joseph *shall have two* portions.

14"And you shall divide it for an inheritance, each one equally with the other; for I swore to give it to your forefathers, and this land shall fall to you as an inheritance.

15 ¶"And this *shall be* the boundary of the land: on the north side, from the Great Sea *by* the way of Hethlon, to the entrance of Zedad;
16 Hamath, Berothah, Sibraim, which is between the border of Damascus and the border of Hamath; Hazer-hatticon, which is by the border of Hauran.
17"And the boundary shall extend from the sea *to* Hazar-enan *at* the border of Damascus, and on the north toward the north is the border of Hamath. This is the north side.
18"And the east side, from between Hauran, Damascus, Gilead, and the land of Israel, *shall be* the Jordan; from the *north* border to the eastern sea you shall measure. This is the east side.
19"And the south side toward the south *shall extend* from Tamar as far as the waters of Meribath-kadesh, to the brook *of Egypt, and* to the Great Sea. This is the south side toward the south.
20"And the west side *shall be* the Great Sea, from the *south* border to a point opposite Lebo-hamath. This is the west side.
21 ¶"So you shall divide this land among yourselves according to the tribes of Israel.
22"And it will come about that you shall divide it by lot for an inheritance among yourselves and among the aliens who stay in your midst, who bring forth sons in your midst. And they shall be to you as the native-born among the sons of Israel; they shall be allotted an inheritance with you among the tribes of Israel.
23"And it will come about that in the tribe with which the alien stays, there you shall give *him* his inheritance," declares the Lord GOD.

CHAPTER 48

"NOW these are the names of the tribes: from the northern extremity, beside the way of Hethlon to Lebo-hamath, *as far as* Hazar-enan *at* the border of Damascus, toward the north beside Hamath, running from east to west, Dan, one *portion.*
2"And beside the border of Dan, from the east side to the west side, Asher, one *portion.*

3"And beside the border of Asher, from the east side to the west side, Naphtali, one *portion.*
4"And beside the border of Naphtali, from the east side to the west side, Manasseh, one *portion.*
5"And beside the border of Manasseh, from the east side to the west side, Ephraim, one *portion.*
6"And beside the border of Ephraim, from the east side to the west side, Reuben, one *portion.*
7"And beside the border of Reuben, from the east side to the west side, Judah, one *portion.*
8 ¶"And beside the border of Judah, from the east side to the west side, shall be the [16]allotment which you shall set apart, 25,000 *cubits* in width, and in length like one of the portions, from the east side to the west side; and the sanctuary shall be in the middle of it.
9"The allotment that you shall set apart to the LORD *shall be* 25,000 *cubits* in length, and 10,000 in width.
10"And the holy allotment shall be for these, *namely* for the priests, toward the north 25,000 *cubits in length,* toward the west 10,000 in width, toward the east 10,000 in width, and toward the south 25,000 in length; and the sanctuary of the LORD shall be in its midst.
11"*It shall be* for the priests who are sanctified of the sons of Zadok, who have kept My charge, who did not go astray when the sons of Israel went astray, as the Levites went astray.
12"And it shall be an allotment to them from the allotment of the land, a most holy place, by the border of the Levites.
13"And alongside the border of the priests the Levites *shall have* 25,000 *cubits* in length and 10,000 in width. The whole length *shall be* 25,000 *cubits* and the width 10,000.
14"Moreover, they shall not sell or exchange any of it, or alienate this choice *portion* of land; for it is holy to the LORD.
15 ¶"And the remainder, 5,000 *cubits* in width and 25,000 in length, shall be for common use for the city, for dwellings and for open spaces; and the city shall be in its midst.

[16]Or, *contribution,* and so throughout this context

16"And these *shall be* its measurements: the north side 4,500 *cubits,* the south side 4,500 *cubits,* the east side 4,500 *cubits,* and the west side 4,500 *cubits.*

17"And the city shall have open spaces: on the north 250 *cubits,* on the south 250 *cubits,* on the east 250 *cubits,* and on the west 250 *cubits.*

18"And the remainder of the length alongside the holy allotment shall be 10,000 *cubits* toward the east, and 10,000 toward the west; and it shall be alongside the holy allotment. And its produce shall be food for the workers of the city.

19"And the workers of the city, out of all the tribes of Israel, shall cultivate it.

20"The whole allotment *shall be* 25,000 by 25,000 *cubits;* you shall set apart the holy allotment, a square, with the property of the city.

21 ¶"And the remainder *shall be* for the prince, on the one side and on the other of the holy allotment and of the property of the city; in front of the 25,000 *cubits* of the allotment toward the east border and westward in front of the 25,000 toward the west border, alongside the portions, *it shall be* for the prince. And the holy allotment and the sanctuary of the house shall be in the middle of it.

22"And exclusive of the property of the Levites and the property of the city, *which* are in the middle of that which belongs to the prince, *every-thing* between the border of Judah and the border of Benjamin shall be for the prince.

23 ¶"As for the rest of the tribes: from the east side to the west side, Benjamin, one *portion.*

24"And beside the border of Benjamin, from the east side to the west side, Simeon, one *portion.*

25"And beside the border of Simeon, from the east side to the west side, Issachar, one *portion.*

26"And beside the border of Issachar, from the east side to the west side, Zebulun, one *portion.*

27"And beside the border of Zebulun, from the east side to the west side, Gad, one *portion.*

28"And beside the border of Gad, at the south side toward the south, the border shall be from Tamar to the waters of Meribath-kadesh, to the brook *of Egypt,* to the Great Sea.

29"This is the land which you shall divide by lot to the tribes of Israel for an inheritance, and these are their *several* portions," declares the Lord GOD.

30 ¶"And these are the exits of the city: on the north side, 4,500 *cubits* by measurement,

31 shall be the gates of the city, named for the tribes of Israel, three gates toward the north: the gate of Reuben, one; the gate of Judah, one; the gate of Levi, one.

32"And on the east side, 4,500 *cubits,* shall be three gates: the gate of Joseph, one; the gate of Benjamin, one; the gate of Dan, one.

33"And on the south side, 4,500 *cubits* by measurement, shall be three gates: the gate of Simeon, one; the gate of Issachar, one; the gate of Zebulun, one.

34"On the west side, 4,500 *cubits,* shall be three gates: the gate of Gad, one; the gate of Asher, one; the gate of Naphtali, one.

35"*The city shall be* 18,000 *cubits* round about; and the name of the city from *that* day *shall be,* 'The LORD is there.' "

THE BOOK OF

DANIEL

IN the third year of the reign of Jehoiakim king of Judah, Nebuchadnezzar king of Babylon came to Jerusalem and besieged it.

2 And the Lord gave Jehoiakim king of Judah into his hand, along with some of the vessels of the house of God; and he brought them to the land of Shinar, to the house of his [1]god, and he brought the vessels into the treasury of his [1]god.

3 Then the king ordered Ashpenaz, the chief of his [2]officials, to bring in some of the sons of Israel, including some of the royal family and of the nobles,

4 youths in whom was no defect, who were good-looking, showing intelligence in every *branch of* wisdom, endowed with understanding, and discerning knowledge, and who had ability for serving in the king's court; and *he ordered him* to teach them the [3]literature and language of the Chaldeans.

5 And the king appointed for them a daily ration from the king's choice food and from the wine which he drank, and *appointed* that they should be educated three years, at the end of which they were to enter the king's personal service.

6 Now among them from the sons of Judah were Daniel, Hananiah, Mishael and Azariah.

7 Then the commander of the officials assigned *new* names to them; and to Daniel he assigned *the name* Belteshazzar, to Hananiah Shadrach, to Mishael Meshach, and to Azariah Abed-nego.

8 ¶ But Daniel made up his mind that he would not defile himself with the king's choice food or with the wine which he drank; so he sought *permission* from the commander of the officials that he might not defile himself.

9 Now God granted Daniel favor and compassion in the sight of the commander of the officials,

10 and the commander of the officials said to Daniel, "I am afraid of my lord the king, who has appointed your food and your drink; for why should he see your faces looking more haggard than the youths who are your own age? Then you would make me forfeit my head to the king."

11 But Daniel said to the overseer whom the commander of the officials had appointed over Daniel, Hananiah, Mishael and Azariah,

12 "Please test your servants for ten days, and let us be given some vegetables to eat and water to drink.

13 "Then let our appearance be observed in your presence, and the appearance of the youths who are eating the king's choice food; and deal with your servants according to what you see."

14 ¶ So he listened to them in this matter and tested them for ten days.

15 And at the end of ten days their appearance seemed better and they were fatter than all the youths who had been eating the king's choice food.

16 So the overseer continued to withhold their choice food and the wine they were to drink, and kept giving them vegetables.

17 ¶ And as for these four youths, God gave them knowledge and intelligence in every *branch of* literature and wisdom; Daniel even understood all *kinds of* visions and dreams.

18 Then at the end of the days which the king had specified for presenting them, the commander of the officials presented them before Nebuchadnezzar.

19 And the king talked with them, and out of them all not one was found like Daniel, Hananiah, Mishael and Azariah; so they entered the king's personal service.

20 And as for every matter of wisdom and understanding about which the king consulted them, he found them ten times better than all the magicians *and* conjurers who *were* in all his realm.

21 And Daniel continued until the first year of Cyrus the king.

CHAPTER 2

NOW in the second year of the reign of Nebuchadnezzar, Nebuchadnezzar had dreams; and his spirit was troubled and his sleep left him.

2 Then the king gave orders to call

[1] Or, *gods*   [2] Or, *eunuchs,* and so throughout the ch.
[3] Or, *writing*

in the [4]magicians, the conjurers, the sorcerers and the [5]Chaldeans, to tell the king his dreams. So they came in and stood before the king.

3 And the king said to them, "I had a dream, and my spirit is anxious to understand the dream."

4 ¶ Then the Chaldeans spoke to the king in Aramaic: "O king, live forever! Tell the dream to your servants, and we will declare the interpretation."

5 The king answered and said to the Chaldeans, "The command from me is firm: if you do not make known to me the dream and its interpretation, you will be torn limb from limb, and your houses will be made a rubbish heap.

6 "But if you declare the dream and its interpretation, you will receive from me gifts and a reward and great honor; therefore declare to me the dream and its interpretation."

7 They answered a second time and said, "Let the king tell the dream to his servants, and we will declare the interpretation."

8 The king answered and said, "I know for certain that you are bargaining for time, inasmuch as you have seen that the command from me is firm,

9 that if you do not make the dream known to me, there is only one decree for you. For you have agreed together to speak lying and corrupt words before me until the situation is changed; therefore tell me the dream, that I may know that you can declare to me its interpretation."

10 The Chaldeans answered the king and said, "There is not a man on earth who could declare the matter for the king, inasmuch as no great king or ruler has ever asked anything like this of any magician, conjurer or Chaldean.

11 "Moreover, the thing which the king demands is difficult, and there is no one else who could declare it to the king except gods, whose dwelling place is not with mortal flesh."

12 Because of this the king became indignant and very furious, and gave orders to destroy all the wise men of Babylon.

13 So the decree went forth that the wise men should be slain; and they looked for Daniel and his friends to kill them.

14 ¶ Then Daniel replied with discretion and discernment to Arioch, the captain of the king's bodyguard, who had gone forth to slay the wise men of Babylon;

15 he answered and said to Arioch, the king's commander, "For what reason is the decree from the king so urgent?" Then Arioch informed Daniel about the matter.

16 So Daniel went in and requested of the king that he would give him time, in order that he might declare the interpretation to the king.

17 ¶ Then Daniel went to his house and informed his friends, Hananiah, Mishael and Azariah, about the matter,

18 in order that they might request compassion from the God of heaven concerning this mystery, so that Daniel and his friends might not be destroyed with the rest of the wise men of Babylon.

19 Then the mystery was revealed to Daniel in a night vision. Then Daniel blessed the God of heaven;

20 Daniel answered and said,
"Let the name of God be blessed
    forever and ever,
  For wisdom and power belong to
    Him.
21 "And it is He who changes the
    times and the epochs;
  He removes kings and estab-
    lishes kings;
  He gives wisdom to wise men,
  And knowledge to men of under-
    standing.
22 "It is He who reveals the pro-
    found and hidden things;
  He knows what is in the dark-
    ness,
  And the light dwells with Him.
23 "To Thee, O God of my fathers, I
    give thanks and praise,
  For Thou hast given me wisdom
    and power;
  Even now Thou hast made
    known to me what we re-
    quested of Thee,
  For Thou hast made known to us
    the king's matter."

24 Therefore, Daniel went in to Arioch, whom the king had appointed to destroy the wise men of Babylon; he

---

[4] Or, soothsayer priests
[5] Or, master astrologers, and so throughout this context

went and spoke to him as follows: "Do not destroy the wise men of Babylon! Take me into the king's presence, and I will declare the interpretation to the king."

25 ¶ Then Arioch hurriedly brought Daniel into the king's presence and spoke to him as follows: "I have found a man among the exiles from Judah who can make the interpretation known to the king!"

26 The king answered and said to Daniel, whose name was Belteshazzar, "Are you able to make known to me the dream which I have seen and its interpretation?"

27 Daniel answered before the king and said, "As for the mystery about which the king has inquired, neither wise men, conjurers, magicians, nor diviners are able to declare it to the king.

28"However, there is a God in heaven who reveals mysteries, and He has made known to King Nebuchadnezzar what will take place in the latter days. This was your dream and the visions in your mind while on your bed.

29"As for you, O king, while on your bed your thoughts turned to what would take place in the future; and He who reveals mysteries has made known to you what will take place.

30"But as for me, this mystery has not been revealed to me for any wisdom residing in me more than in any other living man, but for the purpose of making the interpretation known to the king, and that you may understand the thoughts of your mind.

31 ¶"You, O king, were looking and behold, there was a single great statue; that statue, which was large and of extraordinary splendor, was standing in front of you, and its appearance was awesome.

32"The head of that statue was made of fine gold, its breast and its arms of silver, its belly and its thighs of bronze,

33 its legs of iron, its feet partly of iron and partly of clay.

34"You continued looking until a stone was cut out without hands, and it struck the statue on its feet of iron and clay, and crushed them.

35"Then the iron, the clay, the bronze, the silver and the gold were crushed all at the same time, and became like chaff from the summer threshing floors; and the wind carried them away so that not a trace of them was found. But the stone that struck the statue became a great mountain and filled the whole earth.

36 ¶"This was the dream; now we shall tell its interpretation before the king.

37"You, O king, are the king of kings, to whom the God of heaven has given the kingdom, the power, the strength, and the glory;

38 and wherever the sons of men dwell, or the beasts of the field, or the birds of the sky, He has given them into your hand and has caused you to rule over them all. You are the head of gold.

39"And after you there will arise another kingdom inferior to you, then another third kingdom of bronze, which will rule over all the earth.

40"Then there will be a fourth kingdom as strong as iron; inasmuch as iron crushes and shatters all things, so, like iron that breaks in pieces, it will crush and break all these in pieces.

41"And in that you saw the feet and toes, partly of potter's clay and partly of iron, it will be a divided kingdom; but it will have in it the toughness of iron, inasmuch as you saw the iron mixed with common clay.

42"And as the toes of the feet were partly of iron and partly of pottery, so some of the kingdom will be strong and part of it will be brittle.

43"And in that you saw the iron mixed with common clay, they will combine with one another in the seed of men; but they will not adhere to one another, even as iron does not combine with pottery.

44"And in the days of those kings the God of heaven will set up a kingdom which will never be destroyed, and that kingdom will not be left for another people; it will crush and put an end to all these kingdoms, but it will itself endure forever.

45"Inasmuch as you saw that a stone was cut out of the mountain without hands and that it crushed the iron, the bronze, the clay, the silver, and the gold, the great God has made known to the king what will take place in the future; so the dream is true, and its interpretation is trustworthy."

46 ¶ Then King Nebuchadnezzar fell on his face and did homage to Daniel, and gave orders to present to him an offering and fragrant incense.

47 The king answered Daniel and said, "Surely your God is a God of gods and a Lord of kings and a revealer of mysteries, since you have been able to reveal this mystery."

48 Then the king promoted Daniel and gave him many great gifts, and he made him ruler over the whole province of Babylon and chief prefect over all the wise men of Babylon.

49 And Daniel made request of the king, and he appointed Shadrach, Meshach and Abed-nego over the administration of the province of Babylon, while Daniel *was* at the king's court.

CHAPTER 3

NEBUCHADNEZZAR the king made an image of gold, the height of which *was* sixty cubits *and* its width six cubits; he set it up on the plain of Dura in the province of Babylon.

2 Then Nebuchadnezzar the king sent *word* to assemble the satraps, the prefects and the governors, the counselors, the treasurers, the judges, the magistrates and all the rulers of the provinces to come to the dedication of the image that Nebuchadnezzar the king had set up.

3 Then the satraps, the prefects and the governors, the counselors, the treasurers, the judges, the magistrates and all the rulers of the provinces were assembled for the dedication of the image that Nebuchadnezzar the king had set up; and they stood before the image that Nebuchadnezzar had set up.

4 Then the herald loudly proclaimed: "To you the command is given, O peoples, nations and *men of every* language,

5 that at the moment you hear the sound of the horn, flute, lyre, trigon, psaltery, bagpipe, and all kinds of music, you are to fall down and worship the golden image that Nebuchadnezzar the king has set up.

6 "But whoever does not fall down and worship shall immediately be cast into the midst of a furnace of blazing fire."

7 Therefore at that time, when all the peoples heard the sound of the horn, flute, lyre, trigon, psaltery, bagpipe, and all kinds of music, all the peoples, nations and *men of every* language fell down *and* worshiped the golden image that Nebuchadnezzar the king had set up.

8 ¶ For this reason at that time certain Chaldeans came forward and brought charges against the Jews.

9 They responded and said to Nebuchadnezzar the king: "O king, live forever!

10 "You yourself, O king, have made a decree that every man who hears the sound of the horn, flute, lyre, trigon, psaltery, and bagpipe, and all kinds of music, is to fall down and worship the golden image.

11 "But whoever does not fall down and worship shall be cast into the midst of a furnace of blazing fire.

12 "There are certain Jews whom you have appointed over the administration of the province of Babylon, *namely* Shadrach, Meshach and Abed-nego. These men, O king, have disregarded you; they do not serve your gods or worship the golden image which you have set up."

13 ¶ Then Nebuchadnezzar in rage and anger gave orders to bring Shadrach, Meshach and Abed-nego; then these men were brought before the king.

14 Nebuchadnezzar responded and said to them, "Is it true, Shadrach, Meshach and Abed-nego, that you do not serve my gods or worship the golden image that I have set up?

15 "Now if you are ready, at the moment you hear the sound of the horn, flute, lyre, trigon, psaltery, and bagpipe, and all kinds of music, to fall down and worship the image that I have made, *very well.* But if you will not worship, you will immediately be cast into the midst of a furnace of blazing fire; and what god is there who can deliver you out of my hands?"

16 Shadrach, Meshach and Abed-nego answered and said to the king, "O Nebuchadnezzar, we do not need to give you an answer concerning this matter.

17 "If it be *so,* our God whom we serve is able to deliver us from the furnace of blazing fire; and He will

deliver us out of your hand, O king.

18"But *even* if He *does* not, let it be known to you, O king, that we are not going to serve your gods or worship the golden image that you have set up."

19 ¶ Then Nebuchadnezzar was filled with wrath, and his facial expression was altered toward Shadrach, Meshach and Abed-nego. He answered by giving orders to heat the furnace seven times more than it was usually heated.

20 And he commanded certain valiant warriors who *were* in his army to tie up Shadrach, Meshach and Abed-nego, in order to cast *them* into the furnace of blazing fire.

21 Then these men were tied up in their trousers, their coats, their caps and their *other* clothes, and were cast into the midst of the furnace of blazing fire.

22 For this reason, because the king's command *was* urgent and the furnace had been made extremely hot, the flame of the fire slew those men who carried up Shadrach, Meshach and Abed-nego.

23 But these three men, Shadrach, Meshach and Abed-nego, fell into the midst of the furnace of blazing fire *still* tied up.

24 ¶ Then Nebuchadnezzar the king was astounded and stood up in haste; he responded and said to his high officials, "Was it not three men we cast bound into the midst of the fire?" They answered and said to the king, "Certainly, O king."

25 He answered and said, "Look! I see four men loosed *and* walking *about* in the midst of the fire without harm, and the appearance of the fourth is like a son of *the* gods!"

26 Then Nebuchadnezzar came near to the door of the furnace of blazing fire; he responded and said, "Shadrach, Meshach and Abed-nego, come out, you servants of the Most High God, and come here!" Then Shadrach, Meshach and Abed-nego came out of the midst of the fire.

27 And the satraps, the prefects, the governors and the king's high officials gathered around *and* saw in regard to these men that the fire had no effect on the bodies of these men nor was the hair of their head singed, nor were

their trousers damaged, nor had the smell of fire *even* come upon them.

28 ¶ Nebuchadnezzar responded and said, "Blessed be the God of Shadrach, Meshach and Abed-nego, who has sent His angel and delivered His servants who put their trust in Him, violating the king's command, and yielded up their bodies so as not to serve or worship any god except their own God.

29"Therefore, I make a decree that any people, nation or tongue that speaks anything offensive against the God of Shadrach, Meshach and Abed-nego shall be torn limb from limb and their houses reduced to a rubbish heap, inasmuch as there is no other god who is able to deliver in this way."

30 Then the king caused Shadrach, Meshach and Abed-nego to prosper in the province of Babylon.

CHAPTER 4

NEBUCHADNEZZAR the king to all the peoples, nations, and *men of every* language that live in all the earth: "May your peace abound!

2"It has seemed good to me to declare the signs and wonders which the Most High God has done for me.

3 "How great are His signs,
And how mighty are His wonders!
His kingdom is an everlasting kingdom,
And His dominion is from generation to generation.

4 ¶"I, Nebuchadnezzar, was at ease in my house and flourishing in my palace.

5"I saw a dream and it made me fearful; and *these* fantasies *as I lay* on my bed and the visions in my mind kept alarming me.

6"So I gave orders to bring into my presence all the wise men of Babylon, that they might make known to me the interpretation of the dream.

7"Then the magicians, the conjurers, the Chaldeans, and the diviners came in, and I related the dream to them; but they could not make its interpretation known to me.

8"But finally Daniel came in before me, whose name is Belteshazzar according to the name of my god, and in whom is ⁶a spirit of the holy gods; and I related the dream to him, *saying,*

9 'O Belteshazzar, chief of the magicians, since I know that a spirit of the holy gods is in you and no mystery baffles you, tell *me* the visions of my dream which I have seen, along with its interpretation.

10 'Now *these were* the visions in my mind *as I lay* on my bed: I was looking, and behold, *there was* a tree in the midst of the earth, and its height *was* great.

11 'The tree grew large and became strong,
And its height reached to the sky,
And it *was* visible to the end of the whole earth.

12 'Its foliage *was* beautiful and its fruit abundant,
And in it *was* food for all.
The beasts of the field found shade under it,
And the birds of the sky dwelt in its branches,
And all living creatures fed themselves from it.

13 ¶ 'I was looking in the visions in my mind *as I lay* on my bed, and behold, an *angelic* watcher, a holy one, descended from heaven.

14 'He shouted out and spoke as follows:
"Chop down the tree and cut off its branches,
Strip off its foliage and scatter its fruit;
Let the beasts flee from under it,
And the birds from its branches.

15 "Yet leave the stump with its roots in the ground,
But with a band of iron and bronze *around it*
In the new grass of the field;
And let him be drenched with the dew of heaven,
And let him share with the beasts in the grass of the earth.

16 "Let his mind be changed from *that of* a man,
And let a beast's mind be given to him,
And let seven periods of time pass over him.

17 "This sentence is by the decree of the *angelic* watchers,

⁶ Or possibly, *the Spirit of the holy God,* and so throughout this context

And the decision is a command of the holy ones,
In order that the living may know
That the Most High is ruler over the realm of mankind,
And bestows it on whom He wishes,
And sets over it the lowliest of men."

18 'This is the dream *which* I, King Nebuchadnezzar, have seen. Now you, Belteshazzar, tell *me* its interpretation, inasmuch as none of the wise men of my kingdom is able to make known to me the interpretation; but you are able, for a spirit of the holy gods is in you.'

19 ¶ "Then Daniel, whose name is Belteshazzar, was appalled for a while as his thoughts alarmed him. The king responded and said, 'Belteshazzar, do not let the dream or its interpretation alarm you.' Belteshazzar answered and said, 'My lord, *if only* the dream applied to those who hate you, and its interpretation to your adversaries!

20 'The tree that you saw, which became large and grew strong, whose height reached to the sky and was visible to all the earth,

21 and whose foliage *was* beautiful and its fruit abundant, and in which *was* food for all, under which the beasts of the field dwelt and in whose branches the birds of the sky lodged—

22 it is you, O king; for you have become great and grown strong, and your majesty has become great and reached to the sky and your dominion to the end of the earth.

23 'And in that the king saw an *angelic* watcher, a holy one, descending from heaven and saying, "Chop down the tree and destroy it; yet leave the stump with its roots in the ground, but with a band of iron and bronze *around it* in the new grass of the field, and let him be drenched with the dew of heaven, and let him share with the beasts of the field until seven periods of time pass over him";

24 this is the interpretation, O king, and this is the decree of the Most High, which has come upon my lord the king:

25 that you be driven away from mankind, and your dwelling place be with the beasts of the field, and you

be given grass to eat like cattle and be drenched with the dew of heaven; and seven periods of time will pass over you, until you recognize that the Most High is ruler over the realm of mankind, and bestows it on whomever He wishes.

26 'And in that it was commanded to leave the stump with the roots of the tree, your kingdom will be assured to you after you recognize that *it is* Heaven *that* rules.

27 'Therefore, O king, may my advice be pleasing to you: break away now from your sins by *doing* righteousness, and from your iniquities by showing mercy to *the* poor, in case there may be a prolonging of your prosperity.'

28 ¶"All *this* happened to Nebuchadnezzar the king.

29"Twelve months later he was walking on the *roof of* the royal palace of Babylon.

30"The king reflected and said, 'Is this not Babylon the great, which I myself have built as a royal residence by the might of my power and for the glory of my majesty?'

31"While the word *was* in the king's mouth, a voice came from heaven, *saying,* 'King Nebuchadnezzar, to you it is declared: sovereignty has been removed from you,

32 and you will be driven away from mankind, and your dwelling place *will be* with the beasts of the field. You will be given grass to eat like cattle, and seven periods of time will pass over you, until you recognize that the Most High is ruler over the realm of mankind, and bestows it on whomever He wishes.'

33"Immediately the word concerning Nebuchadnezzar was fulfilled; and he was driven away from mankind and began eating grass like cattle, and his body was drenched with the dew of heaven, until his hair had grown like eagles' *feathers* and his nails like birds' *claws.*

34 ¶"But at the end of that period I, Nebuchadnezzar, raised my eyes toward heaven, and my reason returned to me, and I blessed the Most High and praised and honored Him who lives forever;

For His dominion is an ever-lasting dominion,

And His kingdom *endures* from generation to generation.

35 "And all the inhabitants of the earth are accounted as nothing,
But He does according to His will in the host of heaven
And *among* the inhabitants of earth;
And no one can ward off His hand
Or say to Him, 'What hast Thou done?'

36"At that time my reason returned to me. And my majesty and splendor were restored to me for the glory of my kingdom, and my counselors and my nobles began seeking me out; so I was reestablished in my sovereignty, and surpassing greatness was added to me.

37"Now I Nebuchadnezzar praise, exalt, and honor the King of heaven, for all His works are true and His ways just, and He is able to humble those who walk in pride."

CHAPTER 5

BELSHAZZAR the king held a great feast for a thousand of his nobles, and he was drinking wine in the presence of the thousand.

2 When Belshazzar tasted the wine, he gave orders to bring the gold and silver vessels which Nebuchadnezzar his father had taken out of the temple which *was* in Jerusalem, in order that the king and his nobles, his wives, and his concubines might drink from them.

3 Then they brought the gold vessels that had been taken out of the temple, the house of God which *was* in Jerusalem; and the king and his nobles, his wives, and his concubines drank from them.

4 They drank the wine and praised the gods of gold and silver, of bronze, iron, wood, and stone.

5 ¶ Suddenly the fingers of a man's hand emerged and began writing opposite the lampstand on the plaster of the wall of the king's palace, and the king saw the back of the hand that did the writing.

6 Then the king's face grew pale, and his thoughts alarmed him; and his hip joints went slack, and his knees began knocking together.

7 The king called aloud to bring in

the conjurers, the Chaldeans and the diviners. The king spoke and said to the wise men of Babylon, "Any man who can read this inscription and explain its interpretation to me will be clothed with purple, and *have* a necklace of gold around his neck, and have authority as third *ruler* in the kingdom."

8 Then all the king's wise men came in, but they could not read the inscription or make known its interpretation to the king.

9 Then King Belshazzar was greatly alarmed, his face grew *even* paler, and his nobles were perplexed.

10 ¶ The queen entered the banquet hall because of the words of the king and his nobles; the queen spoke and said, "O king, live forever! Do not let your thoughts alarm you or your face be pale.

11"There is a man in your kingdom in whom is a spirit of the holy gods; and in the days of your father, illumination, insight, and wisdom like the wisdom of the gods were found in him. And King Nebuchadnezzar, your father, your father the king, appointed him chief of the magicians, conjurers, Chaldeans, *and* diviners.

12"*This was* because an extraordinary spirit, knowledge and insight, interpretation of dreams, explanation of enigmas, and solving of difficult problems were found in this Daniel, whom the king named Belteshazzar. Let Daniel now be summoned, and he will declare the interpretation."

13 ¶ Then Daniel was brought in before the king. The king spoke and said to Daniel, "Are you that Daniel who is one of the exiles from Judah, whom my father the king brought from Judah?

14"Now I have heard about you that a spirit of the gods is in you, and that illumination, insight, and extraordinary wisdom have been found in you.

15"Just now the wise men *and* the conjurers were brought in before me that they might read this inscription and make its interpretation known to me, but they could not declare the interpretation of the message.

16"But I personally have heard about you, that you are able to give interpretations and solve difficult problems. Now if you are able to read the inscription and make its interpretation known to me, you will be clothed with purple and *wear* a necklace of gold around your neck, and you will have authority as the third *ruler* in the kingdom."

17 ¶ Then Daniel answered and said before the king, "Keep your gifts for yourself, or give your rewards to someone else; however, I will read the inscription to the king and make the interpretation known to him.

18"O king, the Most High God granted sovereignty, grandeur, glory, and majesty to Nebuchadnezzar your father.

19"And because of the grandeur which He bestowed on him, all the peoples, nations, and *men of every* language feared and trembled before him; whomever he wished he killed, and whomever he wished he spared alive; and whomever he wished he elevated, and whomever he wished he humbled.

20"But when his heart was lifted up and his spirit became so proud that he behaved arrogantly, he was deposed from his royal throne, and *his* glory was taken away from him.

21"He was also driven away from mankind, and his heart was made like *that of* beasts, and his dwelling place *was* with the wild donkeys. He was given grass to eat like cattle, and his body was drenched with the dew of heaven, until he recognized that the Most High God is ruler over the realm of mankind, and *that* He sets over it whomever He wishes.

22"Yet you, his son, Belshazzar, have not humbled your heart, even though you knew all this,

23 but you have exalted yourself against the Lord of heaven; and they have brought the vessels of His house before you, and you and your nobles, your wives and your concubines have been drinking wine from them; and you have praised the gods of silver and gold, of bronze, iron, wood and stone, which do not see, hear or understand. But the God in whose hand are your life-breath and your ways, you have not glorified.

24"Then the hand was sent from

Him, and this inscription was written out.

25 ¶"Now this is the inscription that was written out: 'MENĒ, MENĒ, TEKĒL, UPHARSIN.'

26"This is the interpretation of the message: 'MENĒ'—God has numbered your kingdom and put an end to it.

27" 'TEKĒL'—you have been weighed on the scales and found deficient.

28" 'PERĒS'—your kingdom has been divided and given over to the Medes and Persians."

29 ¶ Then Belshazzar gave orders, and they clothed Daniel with purple and *put* a necklace of gold around his neck, and issued a proclamation concerning him that he *now* had authority as the third *ruler* in the kingdom.

30 ¶ That same night Belshazzar the Chaldean king was slain.

31 So Darius the Mede received the kingdom at about the age of sixty-two.

CHAPTER 6

IT seemed good to Darius to appoint 120 satraps over the kingdom, that they should be in charge of the whole kingdom,

2 and over them three commissioners (of whom Daniel was one), that these satraps might be accountable to them, and that the king might not suffer loss.

3 Then this Daniel began distinguishing himself among the commissioners and satraps because he possessed an extraordinary spirit, and the king planned to appoint him over the entire kingdom.

4 Then the commissioners and satraps began trying to find a ground of accusation against Daniel in regard to government affairs; but they could find no ground of accusation or *evidence of* corruption, inasmuch as he was faithful, and no negligence or corruption was *to be* found in him.

5 Then these men said, "We shall not find any ground of accusation against this Daniel unless we find *it* against him with regard to the law of his God."

6 Then these commissioners and satraps came by agreement to the king and spoke to him as follows: "King Darius, live forever!

7"All the commissioners of the kingdom, the prefects and the satraps, the high officials and the governors have consulted together that the king should establish a statute and enforce an injunction that anyone who makes a petition to any god or man besides you, O king, for thirty days, shall be cast into the lions' den.

8"Now, O king, establish the injunction and sign the document so that it may not be changed, according to the law of the Medes and Persians, which may not be revoked."

9 Therefore King Darius signed the document, that is, the injunction.

10 ¶ Now when Daniel knew that the document was signed, he entered his house (now in his roof chamber he had windows open toward Jerusalem); and he continued kneeling on his knees three times a day, praying and giving thanks before his God, as he had been doing previously.

11 Then these men came by agreement and found Daniel making petition and supplication before his God.

12 Then they approached and spoke before the king about the king's injunction, "Did you not sign an injunction that any man who makes a petition to any god or man besides you, O king, for thirty days, is to be cast into the lions' den?" The king answered and said, "The statement is true, according to the law of the Medes and Persians, which may not be revoked."

13 Then they answered and spoke before the king, "Daniel, who is one of the exiles from Judah, pays no attention to you, O king, or to the injunction which you signed, but keeps making his petition three times a day."

14 Then, as soon as the king heard this statement, he was deeply distressed and set *his* mind on delivering Daniel; and even until sunset he kept exerting himself to rescue him.

15 Then these men came by agreement to the king and said to the king, "Recognize, O king, that it is a law of the Medes and Persians that no injunction or statute which the king establishes may be changed."

16 ¶ Then the king gave orders, and Daniel was brought in and cast into the lions' den. The king spoke and said to Daniel, "Your God whom you constantly serve will Himself deliver you."

17 And a stone was brought and laid over the mouth of the den; and the king sealed it with his own signet ring and with the signet rings of his nobles, so that nothing might be changed in regard to Daniel.

18 Then the king went off to his palace and spent the night fasting, and no entertainment was brought before him; and his sleep fled from him.

19 ¶ Then the king arose with the dawn, at the break of day, and went in haste to the lions' den.

20 And when he had come near the den to Daniel, he cried out with a troubled voice. The king spoke and said to Daniel, "Daniel, servant of the living God, has your God, whom you constantly serve, been able to deliver you from the lions?"

21 Then Daniel spoke to the king, "O king, live forever!

22 "My God sent His angel and shut the lions' mouths, and they have not harmed me, inasmuch as I was found innocent before Him; and also toward you, O king, I have committed no crime."

23 Then the king was very pleased and gave orders for Daniel to be taken up out of the den. So Daniel was taken up out of the den, and no injury whatever was found on him, because he had trusted in his God.

24 The king then gave orders, and they brought those men who had maliciously accused Daniel, and they cast them, their children, and their wives into the lions' den; and they had not reached the bottom of the den before the lions overpowered them and crushed all their bones.

25 ¶ Then Darius the king wrote to all the peoples, nations, and men of every language who were living in all the land: "May your peace abound!

26 "I make a decree that in all the dominion of my kingdom men are to fear and tremble before the God of Daniel;

For He is the living God and
enduring forever,
And His kingdom is one which
will not be destroyed,
And His dominion will be forever.

27 "He delivers and rescues and performs signs and wonders

In heaven and on earth,
Who has also delivered Daniel
from the power of the lions."

28 ¶ So this Daniel enjoyed success in the reign of Darius and in the reign of Cyrus the Persian.

CHAPTER 7

IN the first year of Belshazzar king of Babylon Daniel saw a dream and visions in his mind as he lay on his bed; then he wrote the dream down and related the following summary of it.

2 Daniel said, "I was looking in my vision by night, and behold, the four winds of heaven were stirring up the great sea.

3 "And four great beasts were coming up from the sea, different from one another.

4 "The first was like a lion and had the wings of an eagle. I kept looking until its wings were plucked, and it was lifted up from the ground and made to stand on two feet like a man; a human mind also was given to it.

5 "And behold, another beast, a second one, resembling a bear. And it was raised up on one side, and three ribs were in its mouth between its teeth; and thus they said to it, 'Arise, devour much meat!'

6 "After this I kept looking, and behold, another one, like a leopard, which had on its back four wings of a bird; the beast also had four heads, and dominion was given to it.

7 "After this I kept looking in the night visions, and behold, a fourth beast, dreadful and terrifying and extremely strong; and it had large iron teeth. It devoured and crushed, and trampled down the remainder with its feet; and it was different from all the beasts that were before it, and it had ten horns.

8 "While I was contemplating the horns, behold, another horn, a little one, came up among them, and three of the first horns were pulled out by the roots before it; and behold, this horn possessed eyes like the eyes of a man, and a mouth uttering great boasts.

9 ¶ "I kept looking
Until thrones were set up,
And the Ancient of Days took
His seat;

His vesture *was* like white snow,
And the hair of His head like
pure wool.
His throne *was* ablaze with
flames,
Its wheels *were* a burning fire.
10 "A river of fire was flowing
And coming out from before
Him;
Thousands upon thousands were
attending Him,
And myriads upon myriads were
standing before Him;
The court sat,
And the books were opened.
11"Then I kept looking because of
the sound of the boastful words which
the horn was speaking; I kept looking
until the beast was slain, and its body
was destroyed and given to the burning fire.
12"As for the rest of the beasts, their
dominion was taken away, but an
extension of life was granted to them
for an appointed period of time.
13 ¶ "I kept looking in the night
visions,
And behold, with the clouds of
heaven
One like a Son of Man was coming,
And He came up to the Ancient
of Days
And was presented before Him.
14 "And to Him was given dominion,
Glory and a kingdom,
That all the peoples, nations, and
men of every language
Might serve Him.
His dominion is an everlasting
dominion
Which will not pass away;
And His kingdom is one
Which will not be destroyed.
15"As for me, Daniel, my spirit was
distressed within me, and the visions
in my mind kept alarming me.
16"I approached one of those who
were standing by and began asking
him the exact meaning of all this. So
he told me and made known to me the
interpretation of these things:
17 'These great beasts, which are four
in number, are four kings *who* will
arise from the earth.
18 'But the saints of the Highest One
will receive the kingdom and possess

the kingdom forever, for all ages to
come.'
19"Then I desired to know the exact
meaning of the fourth beast, which
was different from all the others, exceedingly dreadful, with its teeth of
iron and its claws of bronze, *and
which* devoured, crushed, and trampled down the remainder with its feet,
20 and *the meaning* of the ten horns
that *were* on its head, and the other
horn which came up, and before which
three *of them* fell, namely, that horn
which had eyes and a mouth uttering
great *boasts,* and which was larger in
appearance than its associates.
21"I kept looking, and that horn was
waging war with the saints and over-
powering them
22 until the Ancient of Days came,
and judgment was passed in favor of
the saints of the Highest One, and the
time arrived when the saints took
possession of the kingdom.
23 ¶ "Thus he said: 'The fourth beast
will be a fourth kingdom on the earth,
which will be different from all the
other kingdoms, and it will devour the
whole earth and tread it down and
crush it.
24 'As for the ten horns, out of this
kingdom ten kings will arise; and another will arise after them, and he will
be different from the previous ones
and will subdue three kings.
25 'And he will speak out against the
Most High and wear down the saints
of the Highest One, and he will intend
to make alterations in times and in
law; and they will be given into his
hand for a time, times, and half a time.
26 'But the court will sit *for judgment,* and his dominion will be taken
away, annihilated and destroyed forever.
27 'Then the sovereignty, the dominion, and the greatness of *all* the kingdoms under the whole heaven will be
given to the people of the saints of the
Highest One; His kingdom *will be* an
everlasting kingdom, and all the dominions will serve and obey Him.'
28"At this point the revelation ended.
As for me, Daniel, my thoughts were
greatly alarming me and my face grew
pale, but I kept the matter to myself."

the reign of Bel-
a vision appeared to
ubsequent to the one
ared to me previously.

looked in the vision, and it
about while I was looking, that I
s in the citadel of Susa, which is in
the province of Elam; and I looked in
the vision, and I myself was beside the
Ulai Canal.

3 Then I lifted my gaze and looked,
and behold, a ram which had two
horns was standing in front of the
canal. Now the two horns *were* long,
but one *was* longer than the other,
with the longer one coming up last.

4 I saw the ram butting westward,
northward, and southward, and no
other beasts could stand before him,
nor was there anyone to rescue from
his power; but he did as he pleased and
magnified *himself*.

5 ¶ While I was observing, behold,
a male goat was coming from the west
over the surface of the whole earth
without touching the ground; and the
goat *had* a conspicuous horn between
his eyes.

6 And he came up to the ram that
had the two horns, which I had seen
standing in front of the canal, and
rushed at him in his mighty wrath.

7 And I saw him come beside the
ram, and he was enraged at him; and
he struck the ram and shattered his
two horns, and the ram had no
strength to withstand him. So he
hurled him to the ground and trampled on him, and there was none to
rescue the ram from his power.

8 Then the male goat magnified
himself exceedingly. But as soon as he
was mighty, the large horn was broken; and in its place there came up
four conspicuous *horns* toward the
four winds of heaven.

9 ¶ And out of one of them came
forth a rather small horn which grew
exceedingly great toward the south,
toward the east, and toward the
[7]Beautiful *Land.*

10 And it grew up to the host of
heaven and caused some of the host
and some of the stars to fall to the
earth, and it trampled them down.

11 It even magnified *itself* to be

[7] I.e., Palestine

equal with the Commander of the
host; and it removed the regular sacrifice from Him, and the place of His
sanctuary was thrown down.

12 And on account of transgression
the host will be given over *to the horn*
along with the regular sacrifice; and it
will fling truth to the ground and
perform *its will* and prosper.

13 Then I heard a holy one speaking,
and another holy one said to that
particular one who was speaking,
"How long will the vision *about* the
regular sacrifice apply, while the
transgression causes horror, so as to
allow both the holy place and the host
to be trampled?"

14 And he said to me, "For 2,300
evenings *and* mornings; then the holy
place will be properly restored."

15 ¶ And it came about when I, Daniel, had seen the vision, that I sought
to understand it; and behold, standing
before me was one who looked like a
man.

16 And I heard the voice of a man
between *the banks of* Ulai, and he
called out and said, "Gabriel, give this
man an understanding of the vision."

17 So he came near to where I was
standing, and when he came I was
frightened and fell on my face; but he
said to me, "Son of man, understand
that the vision pertains to the time of
the end."

18 Now while he was talking with
me, I sank into a deep sleep with my
face to the ground; but he touched me
and made me stand upright.

19 And he said, "Behold, I am going
to let you know what will occur at the
final period of the indignation, for *it*
pertains to the appointed time of the
end.

20 "The ram which you saw with the
two horns represents the kings of
Media and Persia.

21 "And the shaggy goat *represents*
the kingdom of Greece, and the large
horn that is between his eyes is the
first king.

22 "And the broken *horn* and the four
horns that arose in its place *represent*
four kingdoms *which* will arise from
his nation, although not with his
power.

23 "And in the latter period of their
rule,

When the transgressors have run
their course,
A king will arise
Insolent and skilled in intrigue.
24 "And his power will be mighty,
but not by his own power,
And he will destroy to an
extraordinary degree
And prosper and perform his
will;
He will destroy mighty men and
the holy people.
25 "And through his shrewdness
He will cause deceit to succeed
by his influence;
And he will magnify himself in
his heart,
And he will destroy many while
they are at ease.
He will even oppose the Prince of
princes,
But he will be broken without
human agency.
26 "And the vision of the evenings
and mornings
Which has been told is true;
But keep the vision secret,
For it pertains to many days in
the future."
27 Then I, Daniel, was exhausted and
sick for days. Then I got up again and
carried on the king's business; but I
was astounded at the vision, and there
was none to explain it.

CHAPTER 9

IN the first year of Darius the son of
Ahasuerus, of Median descent, who
was made king over the kingdom of
the Chaldeans—
2 in the first year of his reign I,
Daniel, observed in the books the
number of the years which was revealed as the word of the LORD to
Jeremiah the prophet for the completion of the desolations of Jerusalem,
namely, seventy years.
3 So I gave my attention to the
Lord God to seek Him by prayer and
supplications, with fasting, sackcloth,
and ashes.
4 And I prayed to the LORD my God
and confessed and said, "Alas, O Lord,
the great and awesome God, who
keeps His covenant and lovingkindness for those who love Him and keep
His commandments,

5 we have sinned, committed iniquity, acted wickedly, and rebelled,
even turning aside from Thy commandments and ordinances.
6"Moreover, we have not listened to
Thy servants the prophets, who spoke
in Thy name to our kings, our princes,
our fathers, and all the people of the
land.
7"Righteousness belongs to Thee, O
Lord, but to us open shame, as it is this
day—to the men of Judah, the inhabitants of Jerusalem, and all Israel,
those who are nearby and those who
are far away in all the countries to
which Thou hast driven them, because
of their unfaithful deeds which they
have committed against Thee.
8"Open shame belongs to us, O
Lord, to our kings, our princes, and
our fathers, because we have sinned
against Thee.
9"To the Lord our God belong compassion and forgiveness, for we have
rebelled against Him;
10 nor have we obeyed the voice of
the LORD our God, to walk in His
teachings which He set before us
through His servants the prophets.
11"Indeed all Israel has transgressed
Thy law and turned aside, not obeying
Thy voice; so the curse has been
poured out on us, along with the oath
which is written in the law of Moses
the servant of God, for we have sinned
against Him.
12"Thus He has confirmed His words
which He had spoken against us and
against our rulers who ruled us, to
bring on us great calamity; for under
the whole heaven there has not been
done anything like what was done to
Jerusalem.
13"As it is written in the law of Moses, all this calamity has come on us;
yet we have not sought the favor of
the LORD our God by turning from our
iniquity and giving attention to Thy
truth.
14"Therefore, the LORD has kept the
calamity in store and brought it on us;
for the LORD our God is righteous with
respect to all His deeds which He has
done, but we have not obeyed His
voice.
15"And now, O Lord our God, who
hast brought Thy people out of the
land of Egypt with a mighty hand and
hast made a name for Thyself, as it is

this day—we have sinned, we have been wicked.

16"O Lord, in accordance with all Thy righteous acts, let now Thine anger and Thy wrath turn away from Thy city Jerusalem, Thy holy mountain; for because of our sins and the iniquities of our fathers, Jerusalem and Thy people *have become* a reproach to all those around us.

17"So now, our God, listen to the prayer of Thy servant and to his supplications, and for Thy sake, O Lord, let Thy face shine on Thy desolate sanctuary.

18"O my God, incline Thine ear and hear! Open Thine eyes and see our desolations and the city which is called by Thy name; for we are not presenting our supplications before Thee on account of any merits of our own, but on account of Thy great compassion.

19"O Lord, hear! O Lord, forgive! O Lord, listen and take action! For Thine own sake, O my God, do not delay, because Thy city and Thy people are called by Thy name."

20 ¶ Now while I was speaking and praying, and confessing my sin and the sin of my people Israel, and presenting my supplication before the LORD my God in behalf of the holy mountain of my God,

21 while I was still speaking in prayer, then the man Gabriel, whom I had seen in the vision previously, came to me in *my* extreme weariness about the time of the evening offering.

22 And he gave *me* instruction and talked with me, and said, "O Daniel, I have now come forth to give you insight with understanding.

23"At the beginning of your supplications the command was issued, and I have come to tell *you*, for you are highly esteemed; so give heed to the message and gain understanding of the vision.

24 ¶"Seventy weeks have been decreed for your people and your holy city, to finish the transgression, to make an end of sin, to make atonement for iniquity, to bring in everlasting righteousness, to seal up vision and prophecy, and to anoint the most holy *place*.

25"So you are to know and discern *that* from the issuing of a decree to restore and rebuild Jerusalem until Messiah the Prince *there will be* seven weeks and sixty-two weeks; it will be built again, with plaza and moat, even in times of distress.

26"Then after the sixty-two weeks the Messiah will be cut off and have nothing, and the people of the prince who is to come will destroy the city and the sanctuary. And its end *will come* with a flood; even to the end there will be war; desolations are determined.

27"And he will make a firm covenant with the many for one week, but in the middle of the week he will put a stop to sacrifice and grain offering; and on the wing of abominations *will come* one who makes desolate, even until a complete destruction, one that is decreed, is poured out on the one who makes desolate."

CHAPTER 10

IN the third year of Cyrus king of Persia a message was revealed to Daniel, who was named Belteshazzar; and the message was true and *one of* great conflict, but he understood the message and had an understanding of the vision.

2 In those days I, Daniel, had been mourning for three entire weeks.

3 I did not eat any tasty food, nor did meat or wine enter my mouth, nor did I use any ointment at all, until the entire three weeks were completed.

4 And on the twenty-fourth day of the first month, while I was by the bank of the great river, that is, the Tigris,

5 I lifted my eyes and looked, and behold, there was a certain man dressed in linen, whose waist was girded with *a belt of* pure gold of Uphaz.

6 His body also was like beryl, his face had the appearance of lightning, his eyes were like flaming torches, his arms and feet like the gleam of polished bronze, and the sound of his words like the sound of a tumult.

7 Now I, Daniel, alone saw the vision, while the men who were with me did not see the vision; nevertheless, a great dread fell on them, and they ran away to hide themselves.

8 So I was left alone and saw this

great vision; yet no strength was left in me, for my natural color turned to a deathly pallor, and I retained no strength.

9 But I heard the sound of his words; and as soon as I heard the sound of his words, I fell into a deep sleep on my face, with my face to the ground.

10 ¶ Then behold, a hand touched me and set me trembling on my hands and knees.

11 And he said to me, "O Daniel, man of high esteem, understand the words that I am about to tell you and stand upright, for I have now been sent to you." And when he had spoken this word to me, I stood up trembling.

12 Then he said to me, "Do not be afraid, Daniel, for from the first day that you set your heart on understanding *this* and on humbling yourself before your God, your words were heard, and I have come in response to your words.

13"But the prince of the kingdom of Persia was withstanding me for twenty-one days; then behold, Michael, one of the chief princes, came to help me, for I had been left there with the kings of Persia.

14"Now I have come to give you an understanding of what will happen to your people in the latter days, for the vision pertains to the days yet *future.*"

15 And when he had spoken to me according to these words, I turned my face toward the ground and became speechless.

16 And behold, one who resembled a human being was touching my lips; then I opened my mouth and spoke, and said to him who was standing before me, "O my lord, as a result of the vision anguish has come upon me, and I have retained no strength.

17"For how can such a servant of my lord talk with such as my lord? As for me, there remains just now no strength in me, nor has any breath been left in me."

18 ¶ Then *this* one with human appearance touched me again and strengthened me.

19 And he said, "O man of high esteem, do not be afraid. Peace be with you; take courage and be courageous!" Now as soon as he spoke to me, I received strength and said,

"May my lord speak, for you have strengthened me."

20 Then he said, "Do you understand why I came to you? But I shall now return to fight against the prince of Persia; so I am going forth, and behold, the prince of Greece is about to come.

21"However, I will tell you what is inscribed in the writing of truth. Yet there is no one who stands firmly with me against these *forces* except Michael your prince.

CHAPTER 11

"AND in the first year of Darius the Mede, I arose to be an encouragement and a protection for him.

2"And now I will tell you the truth. Behold, three more kings are going to arise in Persia. Then a fourth will gain far more riches than all *of them;* as soon as he becomes strong through his riches, he will arouse the whole *empire* against the realm of Greece.

3"And a mighty king will arise, and he will rule with great authority and do as he pleases.

4"But as soon as he has arisen, his kingdom will be broken up and parceled out toward the four points of the compass, though not to his *own* descendants, nor according to his authority which he wielded; for his sovereignty will be uprooted and *given* to others besides them.

5 ¶"Then the king of the South will grow strong, along with *one* of his princes who will gain ascendancy over him and obtain dominion; his domain *will be* a great dominion *indeed.*

6"And after some years they will form an alliance, and the daughter of the king of the South will come to the king of the North to carry out a peaceful arrangement. But she will not retain her position of power, nor will he remain with his power, but she will be given up, along with those who brought her in, and the one who sired her, as well as he who supported her in *those* times.

7"But one of the descendants of her line will arise in his place, and he will come against *their* army and enter the fortress of the king of the North, and he will deal with them and display *great* strength.

8"And also their gods with their metal images *and* their precious vessels of silver and gold he will take into captivity to Egypt, and he on his part will refrain from *attacking* the king of the North for *some* years.

9"Then the latter will enter the realm of the king of the South, but will return to his *own* land.

10 ¶"And his sons will mobilize and assemble a multitude of great forces; and one of them will keep on coming and overflow and pass through, that he may again wage war up to his *very* fortress.

11"And the king of the South will be enraged and go forth and fight with the king of the North. Then the latter will raise a great multitude, but *that* multitude will be given into the hand of the *former.*

12"When the multitude is carried away, his heart will be lifted up, and he will cause tens of thousands to fall; yet he will not prevail.

13"For the king of the North will again raise a greater multitude than the former, and after an interval of some years he will press on with a great army and much equipment.

14 ¶"Now in those times many will rise up against the king of the South; the violent ones among your people will also lift themselves up in order to fulfill the vision, but they will fall down.

15"Then the king of the North will come, cast up a siege mound, and capture a well-fortified city; and the forces of the South will not stand *their ground,* not even their choicest troops, for there will be no strength to make a stand.

16"But he who comes against him will do as he pleases, and no one will *be able to* withstand him; he will also stay *for a time* in the Beautiful Land, with destruction in his hand.

17"And he will set his face to come with the power of his whole kingdom, bringing with him a proposal of peace which he will put into effect; he will also give him the daughter of women to ruin it. But she will not take a stand *for him* or be on his side.

18"Then he will turn his face to the coastlands and capture many. But a commander will put a stop to his scorn against him; moreover, he will repay him for his scorn.

19"So he will turn his face toward the fortresses of his own land, but he will stumble and fall and be found no more.

20 ¶"Then in his place one will arise who will send an oppressor through the [8]Jewel of *his* kingdom; yet within a few days he will be shattered, though neither in anger nor in battle.

21"And in his place a despicable person will arise, on whom the honor of kingship has not been conferred, but he will come in a time of tranquility and seize the kingdom by intrigue.

22"And the overflowing forces will be flooded away before him and shattered, and also the prince of the covenant.

23"And after an alliance is made with him he will practice deception, and he will go up and gain power with a small *force of* people.

24"In a time of tranquility he will enter the richest *parts* of the realm, and he will accomplish what his fathers never did, nor his ancestors; he will distribute plunder, booty, and possessions among them, and he will devise his schemes against strongholds, but *only* for a time.

25"And he will stir up his strength and courage against the king of the South with a large army; so the king of the South will mobilize an extremely large and mighty army for war; but he will not stand, for schemes will be devised against him.

26"And those who eat his choice food will destroy him, and his army will overflow, but many will fall down slain.

27"As for both kings, their hearts will be *intent* on evil, and they will speak lies *to each other* at the same table; but it will not succeed, for the end is still *to come* at the appointed time.

28"Then he will return to his land with much plunder; but his heart will be *set* against the holy covenant, and he will take action and *then* return to his *own* land.

29 ¶"At the appointed time he will return and come into the South, but this last time it will not turn out the way it did before.

---

[8] Lit., *adornment;* i.e., probably Jerusalem and its temple

30"For ships of Kittim will come against him; therefore he will be disheartened, and will return and become enraged at the holy covenant and take action; so he will come back and show regard for those who forsake the holy covenant.

31"And forces from him will arise, desecrate the sanctuary fortress, and do away with the regular sacrifice. And they will set up the abomination of desolation.

32"And by smooth *words* he will turn to godlessness those who act wickedly toward the covenant, but the people who know their God will display strength and take action.

33"And those who have insight among the people will give understanding to the many; yet they will fall by sword and by flame, by captivity and by plunder, for *many* days.

34"Now when they fall they will be granted a little help, and many will join with them in hypocrisy.

35"And some of those who have insight will fall, in order to refine, purge, and make them pure, until the end time; because *it is* still *to come* at the appointed time.

36 ¶"Then the king will do as he pleases, and he will exalt and magnify himself above every god, and will speak monstrous things against the God of gods; and he will prosper until the indignation is finished, for that which is decreed will be done.

37"And he will show no regard for the gods of his fathers or for the desire of women, nor will he show regard for any *other* god; for he will magnify himself above *them* all.

38"But instead he will honor a god of fortresses, a god whom his fathers did not know; he will honor *him* with gold, silver, costly stones, and treasures.

39"And he will take action against the strongest of fortresses with *the help of* a foreign god; he will give great honor to those who acknowledge *him*, and he will cause them to rule over the many, and will parcel out land for a price.

40 ¶"And at the end time the king of the South will collide with him, and the king of the North will storm against him with chariots, with horsemen, and with many ships; and he will

enter countries, overflow *them,* and pass through.

41"He will also enter the Beautiful Land, and many *countries* will fall; but these will be rescued out of his hand: Edom, Moab and the foremost of the sons of Ammon.

42"Then he will stretch out his hand against *other* countries, and the land of Egypt will not escape.

43"But he will gain control over the hidden treasures of gold and silver, and over all the precious things of Egypt; and Libyans and Ethiopians *will follow* at his heels.

44"But rumors from the East and from the North will disturb him, and he will go forth with great wrath to destroy and annihilate many.

45"And he will pitch the tents of his royal pavilion between the seas and the beautiful Holy Mountain; yet he will come to his end, and no one will help him.

CHAPTER 12

"Now at that time Michael, the great prince who stands *guard* over the sons of your people, will arise. And there will be a time of distress such as never occurred since there was a nation until that time; and at that time your people, everyone who is found written in the book, will be rescued.

2"And many of those who sleep in the dust of the ground will awake, these to everlasting life, but the others to disgrace *and* everlasting contempt.

3"And those who have insight will shine brightly like the brightness of the expanse of heaven, and those who lead the many to righteousness, like the stars forever and ever.

4"But as for you, Daniel, conceal these words and seal up the book until the end of time; many will go back and forth, and knowledge will increase."

5 ¶ Then I, Daniel, looked and behold, two others were standing, one on this bank of the river, and the other on that bank of the river.

6 And one said to the man dressed in linen, who was above the waters of the river, "How long *will it be* until the end of *these* wonders?"

7 And I heard the man dressed in linen, who was above the waters of the

river, as he raised his right hand and his left toward heaven, and swore by Him who lives forever that it would be for a time, times, and half *a time;* and as soon as they finish shattering the power of the holy people, all these *events* will be completed.

8 As for me, I heard but could not understand; so I said, "My lord, what *will be* the outcome of these *events?"*

9 And he said, "Go *your way,* Daniel, for *these* words are concealed and sealed up until the end time.

10"Many will be purged, purified and refined; but the wicked will act wickedly, and none of the wicked will understand, but those who have insight will understand.

11"And from the time that the regular sacrifice is abolished, and the abomination of desolation is set up, *there will be* 1,290 days.

12"How blessed is he who keeps waiting and attains to the 1,335 days!

13"But as for you, go *your way* to the end; then you will enter into rest and rise *again* for your allotted portion at the end of the age."

THE BOOK OF

HOSEA

THE word of the LORD which came to Hosea the son of Beeri, during the days of Uzziah, Jotham, Ahaz, *and* Hezekiah, kings of Judah, and during the days of Jeroboam the son of Joash, king of Israel.

2 ¶ When the LORD first spoke through Hosea, the LORD said to Hosea, "Go, take to yourself a wife of harlotry, and *have* children of harlotry; for the land commits flagrant harlotry, forsaking the LORD."

3 So he went and took Gomer the daughter of Diblaim, and she conceived and bore him a son.

4 And the LORD said to him, "Name him Jezreel; for yet a little while, and I will punish the house of Jehu for the bloodshed of Jezreel, and I will put an end to the kingdom of the house of Israel.

5"And it will come about on that day, that I will break the bow of Israel in the valley of Jezreel."

6 Then she conceived again and gave birth to a daughter. And the LORD said to him, "Name her [1]Loruhamah, for I will no longer have compassion on the house of Israel, that I should ever forgive them.

7"But I will have compassion on the house of Judah and deliver them by the LORD their God, and will not deliver them by bow, sword, battle, horses, or horsemen."

8 When she had weaned Lo-ruhamah, she conceived and gave birth to a son.

9 And the LORD said, "Name him [2]Lo-ammi, for you are not My people and I am not your God."

10 ¶ Yet the number of the sons of Israel
Will be like the sand of the sea,
Which cannot be measured or numbered;
And it will come about that, in the place
Where it is said to them,
"You are not My people,"
It will be said to them,
"You are the sons of the living God."

11 And the sons of Judah and the sons of Israel will be gathered together,
And they will appoint for themselves one leader,
And they will go up from the land,
For great will be the day of Jezreel.

CHAPTER 2

SAY to your brothers, "[3]Ammi," and to your sisters, "[4]Ruhamah."

---

[1] I.e., she has not obtained compassion

[2] I.e., not my people   [3] I.e., my people
[4] I.e., she has obtained compassion

2"Contend with your mother, contend,
   For she is not my wife, and I am not her husband;
   And let her put away her harlotry from her face,
   And her adultery from between her breasts,
3 Lest I strip her naked
   And expose her as on the day when she was born.
   I will also make her like a wilderness,
   Make her like desert land,
   And slay her with thirst.
4"Also, I will have no compassion on her children,
   Because they are children of harlotry.
5"For their mother has played the harlot;
   She who conceived them has acted shamefully.
   For she said, 'I will go after my lovers,
   Who give *me* my bread and my water,
   My wool and my flax, my oil and my drink.'
6"Therefore, behold, I will hedge up her way with thorns,
   And I will build a wall against her so that she cannot find her paths.
7"And she will pursue her lovers, but she will not overtake them;
   And she will seek them, but will not find *them*.
   Then she will say, 'I will go back to my first husband,
   For it was better for me then than now!'

8 ¶"For she does not know that it was I who gave her the grain, the new wine, and the oil,
   And lavished on her silver and gold,
   Which they used for Baal.
9"Therefore, I will take back My grain at harvest time
   And My new wine in its season.
   I will also take away My wool and My flax
   Given to cover her nakedness.
10"And then I will uncover her lewdness
   In the sight of her lovers,

And no one will rescue her out of My hand.
11"I will also put an end to all her gaiety,
   Her feasts, her new moons, her sabbaths,
   And all her festal assemblies.
12"And I will destroy her vines and fig trees,
   Of which she said, 'These are my wages
   Which my lovers have given me.'
   And I will make them a forest,
   And the beasts of the field will devour them.
13"And I will punish her for the days of the Baals
   When she used to offer sacrifices to them
   And adorn herself with her earrings and jewelry,
   And follow her lovers, so that she forgot Me," declares the LORD.

14 ¶"Therefore, behold, I will allure her,
   Bring her into the wilderness,
   And speak kindly to her.
15"Then I will give her her vineyards from there,
   And the valley of Achor as a door of hope.
   And she will sing there as in the days of her youth,
   As in the day when she came up from the land of Egypt.
16"And it will come about in that day," declares the LORD,
   "That you will call Me [5]Ishi
   And will no longer call Me [6]Baali.
17"For I will remove the names of the Baals from her mouth,
   So that they will be mentioned by their names no more.
18"In that day I will also make a covenant for them
   With the beasts of the field,
   The birds of the sky,
   And the creeping things of the ground.
   And I will abolish the bow, the sword, and war from the land,
   And will make them lie down in safety.
19"And I will betroth you to Me forever;

[5] I.e., my Husband   [6] I.e., my Master, or, my Baal

Yes, I will betroth you to Me in
  righteousness and in justice,
In lovingkindness and in compassion,
20 And I will betroth you to Me in
  faithfulness.
Then you will know the LORD.

21 ¶"And it will come about in that
  day that I will respond," declares the LORD.
"I will respond to the heavens, and
  they will respond to the earth,
22 And the earth will respond to the
  grain, to the new wine, and to
  the oil,
And they will respond to [7]Jezreel.
23"And I will sow her for Myself in
  the land.
I will also have compassion on her
  who had not obtained compassion,
And I will say to those who were
  not My people,
'You are My people!'
And they will say, '*Thou art* my
  God!' "

CHAPTER 3

THEN the LORD said to me, "Go
again, love a woman *who* is loved by
her husband, yet an adulteress, even
as the LORD loves the sons of Israel,
though they turn to other gods and
love raisin cakes."

2 So I bought her for myself for
fifteen *shekels* of silver and a homer
and a half of barley.

3 Then I said to her, "You shall stay
with me for many days. You shall not
play the harlot, nor shall you have a
man; so I will also be toward you."

4 For the sons of Israel will remain
for many days without king or prince,
without sacrifice or *sacred* pillar, and
without ephod or household idols.

5 Afterward the sons of Israel will
return and seek the LORD their God
and David their king; and they will
come trembling to the LORD and to His
goodness in the last days.

CHAPTER 4

LISTEN to the word of the LORD, O
  sons of Israel,
For the LORD has a case against
  the inhabitants of the land,

Because there is no faithfulness or
  kindness
Or knowledge of God in the land.
2 *There is* swearing, deception,
  murder, stealing, and adultery.
They employ violence, so that
  bloodshed follows bloodshed.
3 Therefore the land mourns,
And everyone who lives in it languishes
Along with the beasts of the field
  and the birds of the sky;
And also the fish of the sea disappear.

4 ¶ Yet let no one find fault, and let
  none offer reproof;
For your people are like those
  who contend with the priest.
5 So you will stumble by day,
And the prophet also will stumble
  with you by night;
And I will destroy your mother.
6 My people are destroyed for lack
  of knowledge.
Because you have rejected knowledge,
I also will reject you from being
  My priest.
Since you have forgotten the law
  of your God,
I also will forget your children.

7 ¶ The more they multiplied, the
  more they sinned against Me;
I will change their glory into
  shame.
8 They feed on the sin of My people,
And direct their desire toward
  their iniquity.
9 And it will be, like people, like
  priest;
So I will punish them for their
  ways,
And repay them for their deeds.
10 And they will eat, but not have
  enough;
They will play the harlot, but not
  increase,
Because they have stopped giving
  heed to the LORD.

11 ¶ Harlotry, wine, and new wine
  take away the understanding.
12 My people consult their wooden
  idol, and their *diviner's* wand
  informs them;
For a spirit of harlotry has led
  them astray,

---

[7] I.e., God sows

And they have played the harlot,
departing from their God.
13 They offer sacrifices on the tops of
the mountains
And burn incense on the hills,
Under oak, poplar, and terebinth,
Because their shade is pleasant.
Therefore your daughters play the
harlot,
And your brides commit adultery.
14 I will not punish your daughters
when they play the harlot
Or your brides when they commit
adultery,
For *the men* themselves go apart
with harlots
And offer sacrifices with temple
prostitutes;
So the people without understanding are ruined.

15 ¶ Though you, Israel, play the
harlot,
Do not let Judah become guilty;
Also do not go to Gilgal,
Or go up to Beth-aven,
And take the oath:
"As the LORD lives!"
16 Since Israel is stubborn
Like a stubborn heifer,
Can the LORD now pasture them
Like a lamb in a large field?
17 Ephraim is joined to idols;
Let him alone.
18 Their liquor gone,
They play the harlot continually;
Their rulers dearly love shame.
19 The wind wraps them in its wings,
And they will be ashamed because
of their sacrifices.

CHAPTER 5

HEAR this, O priests!
Give heed, O house of Israel!
Listen, O house of the king!
For the judgment applies to you,
For you have been a snare at
Mizpah,
And a net spread out on Tabor.
2 And the revolters have gone deep
in depravity,
But I will chastise all of them.
3 I know Ephraim, and Israel is not
hidden from Me;
For now, O Ephraim, you have
played the harlot,
Israel has defiled itself.
4 Their deeds will not allow them

To return to their God.
For a spirit of harlotry is within
them,
And they do not know the LORD.
5 Moreover, the pride of Israel testifies against him,
And Israel and Ephraim stumble
in their iniquity;
Judah also has stumbled with
them.
6 They will go with their flocks and
herds
To seek the LORD, but they will
not find *Him*;
He has withdrawn from them.
7 They have dealt treacherously
against the LORD,
For they have borne illegitimate
children.
Now the new moon will devour
them with their land.

8 ¶ Blow the horn in Gibeah,
The trumpet in Ramah.
Sound an alarm at Beth-aven:
"Behind you, Benjamin!"
9 Ephraim will become a desolation
in the day of rebuke;
Among the tribes of Israel I declare what is sure.
10 The princes of Judah have be-
come like those who move a
boundary;
On them I will pour out My wrath
like water.
11 Ephraim is oppressed, crushed in
judgment,
Because he was determined to
follow *man's* command.
12 Therefore I am like a moth to
Ephraim,
And like rottenness to the house
of Judah.
13 When Ephraim saw his sickness,
And Judah his wound,
Then Ephraim went to Assyria
And sent to King Jareb.
But he is unable to heal you,
Or to cure you of your wound.
14 For I *will be* like a lion to
Ephraim,
And like a young lion to the house
of Judah.
I, even I, will tear to pieces and go
away,
I will carry away, and there will
be none to deliver.
15 I will go away *and* return to My
place

Until they acknowledge their guilt
  and seek My face;
In their affliction they will earnestly seek Me.

CHAPTER 6

"COME, let us return to the LORD.
  For He has torn *us*, but He will
    heal us;
  He has wounded *us*, but He will
    bandage us.
2"He will revive us after two days;
  He will raise us up on the third
    day
  That we may live before Him.
3"So let us know, let us press on to
    know the LORD.
  His going forth is as certain as the
    dawn;
  And He will come to us like the
    rain,
  Like the spring rain watering the
    earth."

4 ¶ What shall I do with you, O
    Ephraim?
  What shall I do with you, O Ju-
    dah?
  For your loyalty is like a morning
    cloud,
  And like the dew which goes
    away early.
5 Therefore I have hewn *them* in
    pieces by the prophets;
  I have slain them by the words of
    My mouth;
  And the judgments on you are
    like the light that goes forth.
6 For I delight in loyalty rather than
    sacrifice,
  And in the knowledge of God
    rather than burnt offerings.
7 But like Adam they have trans-
    gressed the covenant;
  There they have dealt treacher-
    ously against Me.
8 Gilead is a city of wrongdoers,
  Tracked with bloody *footprints*.
9 And as raiders wait for a man,
  So a band of priests murder on the
    way to Shechem;
  Surely they have committed
    crime.
10 In the house of Israel I have seen
    a horrible thing;
  Ephraim's harlotry is there, Israel
    has defiled itself.

11 Also, O Judah, there is a harvest
    appointed for you,
  When I restore the fortunes of My
    people.

CHAPTER 7

WHEN I would heal Israel, The iniq-
    uity of Ephraim is uncovered,
  And the evil deeds of Samaria,
  For they deal falsely;
  The thief enters in,
  Bandits raid outside,
2 And they do not consider in their
    hearts
  That I remember all their wicked-
    ness.
  Now their deeds are all around
    them;
  They are before My face.
3 With their wickedness they make
    the king glad,
  And the princes with their lies.
4 They are all adulterers
  Like an oven heated by the baker,
  Who ceases to stir up *the fire*
  From the kneading of the dough
    until it is leavened.
5 On the day of our king, the
    princes became sick with the
    heat of wine;
  He stretched out his hand with
    scoffers,
6 For their hearts are like an oven
  As they approach their plotting;
  Their anger smolders all night,
  In the morning it burns like a
    flaming fire.
7 All of them are hot like an oven,
  And they consume their rulers;
  All their kings have fallen.
  None of them calls on Me.

8 ¶ Ephraim mixes himself with the
    nations;
  Ephraim has become a cake not
    turned.
9 Strangers devour his strength,
  Yet he does not know *it*;
  Gray hairs also are sprinkled on
    him,
  Yet he does not know *it*.
10 Though the pride of Israel testifies
    against him,
  Yet they have neither returned to
    the LORD their God,
  Nor have they sought Him, for all
    this.

11 So Ephraim has become like a
   silly dove, without sense;
   They call to Egypt, they go to
   Assyria.
12 When they go, I will spread My
   net over them;
   I will bring them down like the
   birds of the sky.
   I will chastise them in accordance
   with the proclamation to their
   assembly.
13 Woe to them, for they have
   strayed from Me!
   Destruction is theirs, for they
   have rebelled against Me!
   I would redeem them, but they
   speak lies against Me.
14 And they do not cry to Me from
   their heart
   When they wail on their beds;
   For the sake of grain and new
   wine they assemble themselves,
   They turn away from Me.
15 Although I trained *and*
   strengthened their arms,
   Yet they devise evil against Me.
16 They turn, *but* not upward,
   They are like a deceitful bow;
   Their princes will fall by the
   sword
   Because of the insolence of their
   tongue.
   This *will be* their derision in the
   land of Egypt.

CHAPTER 8

PUT the trumpet to your lips!
   Like an eagle *the enemy comes*
   against the house of the LORD,
   Because they have transgressed
   My covenant,
   And rebelled against My law.
2 They cry out to Me,
   "My God, we of Israel know Thee!"
3 Israel has rejected the good;
   The enemy will pursue him.
4 They have set up kings, but not
   by Me;
   They have appointed princes, but
   I did not know *it.*
   With their silver and gold they
   have made idols for themselves,
   That they might be cut off.
5 He has rejected your calf, O Sa-
   maria, saying,
   "My anger burns against them!"
   How long will they be incapable
   of innocence?

6 For from Israel is even this!
   A craftsman made it, so it is not
   God;
   Surely the calf of Samaria will be
   broken to pieces.
7 For they sow the wind,
   And they reap the whirlwind.
   The standing grain has no heads;
   It yields no grain.
   Should it yield, strangers would
   swallow it up.

8 ¶ Israel is swallowed up;
   They are now among the nations
   Like a vessel in which no one
   delights.
9 For they have gone up to Assyria,
   Like a wild donkey all alone;
   Ephraim has hired lovers.
10 Even though they hire *allies*
   among the nations,
   Now I will gather them up;
   And they will begin to diminish
   Because of the burden of the king
   of princes.

11 ¶ Since Ephraim has multiplied
   altars for sin,
   They have become altars of sinning for him.
12 Though I wrote for him ten thousand *precepts* of My law,
   They are regarded as a strange
   thing.
13 As for My sacrificial gifts,
   They sacrifice the flesh and eat *it,*
   But the LORD has taken no delight
   in them.
   Now He will remember their iniquity,
   And punish *them* for their sins;
   They will return to Egypt.
14 For Israel has forgotten his Maker
   and built palaces;
   And Judah has multiplied fortified
   cities,
   But I will send a fire on its cities
   that it may consume its palatial
   dwellings.

CHAPTER 9

DO not rejoice, O Israel, with exultation like the nations!
   For you have played the harlot,
   forsaking your God.
   You have loved *harlots'* earnings
   on every threshing floor.

2 Threshing floor and wine press
   will not feed them,
And the new wine will fail them.
3 They will not remain in the
   LORD's land,
But Ephraim will return to Egypt,
And in Assyria they will eat un-
   clean *food.*
4 They will not pour out libations of
   wine to the LORD,
Their sacrifices will not please
   Him.
Their bread will be like mourners'
   bread;
All who eat of it will be defiled,
For their bread will be for them-
   selves *alone*;
It will not enter the house of the
   LORD.
5 What will you do on the day of
   the appointed festival
And on the day of the feast of the
   LORD?
6 For behold, they will go because
   of destruction;
Egypt will gather them up, Mem-
   phis will bury them.
Weeds will take over their trea-
   sures of silver;
Thorns *will be* in their tents.

7 ¶ The days of punishment have
   come,
The days of retribution have
   come;
Let Israel know *this*!
The prophet is a fool,
The inspired man is demented,
Because of the grossness of your
   iniquity,
And *because* your hostility is *so*
   great.
8 Ephraim *was* a watchman with
   my God, a prophet;
Yet the snare of a bird catcher is
   in all his ways,
And there is *only* hostility in the
   house of his God.
9 They have gone deep in depravity
As in the days of Gibeah;
He will remember their iniquity,
He will punish their sins.

10 ¶ I found Israel like grapes in the
   wilderness;
I saw your forefathers as the earliest fruit on the fig tree in its
   first *season.*

But they came to Baal–peor and
   devoted themselves to [8]shame,
And they became as detestable as
   that which they loved.
11 As for Ephraim, their glory will fly
   away like a bird—
No birth, no pregnancy, and no
   conception!
12 Though they bring up their children,
Yet I will bereave them until not a
   man is left.
Yes, woe to them indeed when I
   depart from them!
13 Ephraim, as I have seen,
Is planted in a pleasant meadow
   like Tyre;
But Ephraim will bring out his
   children for slaughter.
14 Give them, O LORD—what wilt
   Thou give?
Give them a miscarrying womb
   and dry breasts.

15 ¶ All their evil is at Gilgal;
Indeed, I came to hate them
   there!
Because of the wickedness of
   their deeds
I will drive them out of My house!
I will love them no more;
All their princes are rebels.
16 Ephraim is stricken, their root is
   dried up,
They will bear no fruit.
Even though they bear children,
I will slay the precious ones of
   their womb.
17 My God will cast them away
Because they have not listened to
   Him;
And they will be wanderers
   among the nations.

CHAPTER 10

ISRAEL is a luxuriant vine;
He produces fruit for himself.
The more his fruit,
The more altars he made;
The richer his land,
The better he made the *sacred*
   pillars.
2 Their heart is faithless;
Now they must bear their guilt.
The LORD will break down their
   altars
And destroy their *sacred* pillars.

[8] I.e., Baal

3 ¶ Surely now they will say, "We have no king,
For we do not revere the LORD.
As for the king, what can he do for us?"
4 They speak *mere* words,
With worthless oaths they make covenants;
And judgment sprouts like poisonous weeds in the furrows of the field.
5 The inhabitants of Samaria will fear
For the calf of Beth-aven.
Indeed, its people will mourn for it,
And its idolatrous priests will cry out over it,
Over its glory, since it has departed from it.
6 The thing itself will be carried to Assyria
As tribute to King Jareb;
Ephraim will be seized with shame,
And Israel will be ashamed of its own counsel.
7 Samaria will be cut off *with* her king,
Like a stick on the surface of the water.
8 Also the high places of Aven, the sin of Israel, will be destroyed;
Thorn and thistle will grow on their altars,
Then they will say to the mountains,
"Cover us!" And to the hills, "Fall on us!"
9 From the days of Gibeah you have sinned, O Israel;
There they stand!
Will not the battle against the sons of iniquity overtake them in Gibeah?
10 When it is My desire, I will chastise them;
And the peoples will be gathered against them
When they are bound for their double guilt.

11 ¶ And Ephraim is a trained heifer that loves to thresh,
But I will come over her fair neck *with a yoke*;
I will harness Ephraim,
Judah will plow, Jacob will harrow for himself.

12 Sow with a view to righteousness,
Reap in accordance with kindness;
Break up your fallow ground,
For it is time to seek the LORD
Until He comes to rain righteousness on you.
13 You have plowed wickedness, you have reaped injustice,
You have eaten the fruit of lies.
Because you have trusted in your way, in your numerous warriors,
14 Therefore, a tumult will arise among your people,
And all your fortresses will be destroyed,
As Shalman destroyed Beth-arbel on the day of battle,
When mothers were dashed in pieces with *their* children.
15 Thus it will be done to you at Bethel because of your great wickedness.
At dawn the king of Israel will be completely cut off.

CHAPTER 11

WHEN Israel *was* a youth I loved him,
And out of Egypt I called My son.
2 The more they called them,
The more they went from them;
They kept sacrificing to the Baals
And burning incense to idols.
3 Yet it is I who taught Ephraim to walk,
I took them in My arms;
But they did not know that I healed them.
4 I led them with cords of a man, with bonds of love,
And I became to them as one who lifts the yoke from their jaws;
And I bent down *and* fed them.

5 ¶ They will not return to the land of Egypt;
But Assyria—he will be their king,
Because they refused to return *to Me.*
6 And the sword will whirl against their cities,
And will demolish their gate bars
And consume *them* because of their counsels.
7 So My people are bent on turning from Me.

Though they call them to *the One*
on high,
None at all exalts *Him*.

8 ¶ How can I give you up, O
Ephraim?
How can I surrender you, O Is-
rael?
How can I make you like Admah?
How can I treat you like Zeboiim?
My heart is turned over within
Me,
All my compassions are kindled.
9 I will not execute My fierce anger;
I will not destroy Ephraim again.
For I am God and not man, the
Holy One in your midst,
And I will not come in wrath.
10 They will walk after the LORD,
He will roar like a lion;
Indeed He will roar,
And *His* sons will come trembling
from the west.
11 They will come trembling like
birds from Egypt,
And like doves from the land of
Assyria;
And I will settle them in their
houses, declares the LORD.

12 ¶ Ephraim surrounds Me with
lies,
And the house of Israel with deceit;
Judah is also unruly against God,
Even against the Holy One who is
faithful.

CHAPTER 12

EPHRAIM feeds on wind,
And pursues the east wind continually;
He multiplies lies and violence.
Moreover, he makes a covenant
with Assyria,
And oil is carried to Egypt.
2 The LORD also has a dispute with
Judah,
And will punish Jacob according
to his ways;
He will repay him according to his
deeds.
3 In the womb he took his brother
by the heel,
And in his maturity he contended
with God.
4 Yes, he wrestled with the angel
and prevailed;

He wept and sought His favor.
He found Him at Bethel,
And there He spoke with us,
5 Even the LORD, the God of hosts;
The LORD is His name.
6 Therefore, return to your God,
Observe kindness and justice,
And wait for your God continually.
7 A merchant, in whose hands are
false balances,
He loves to oppress.
8 And Ephraim said, "Surely I have
become rich,
I have found wealth for myself;
In all my labors they will find in
me
No iniquity, which *would be* sin."
9 But I *have been* the LORD your
God since the land of Egypt;
I will make you live in tents again,
As in the days of the appointed
festival.
10 I have also spoken to the proph-
ets,
And I gave numerous visions;
And through the prophets I gave
parables.
11 Is there iniquity *in* Gilead?
Surely they are worthless.
In Gilgal they sacrifice bulls,
Yes, their altars are like the stone
heaps
Beside the furrows of the field.

12 ¶ Now Jacob fled to the land of
Aram,
And Israel worked for a wife,
And for a wife he kept *sheep*.
13 But by a prophet the LORD
brought Israel from Egypt,
And by a prophet he was kept.
14 Ephraim has provoked to bitter
anger;
So his Lord will leave his bloodguilt on him,
And bring back his reproach to
him.

CHAPTER 13

WHEN Ephraim spoke, *there was*
trembling.
He exalted himself in Israel,
But through Baal he did wrong
and died.
2 And now they sin more and more,
And make for themselves molten
images,

Idols skillfully made from their
   silver,
All of them the work of craftsmen.
They say of them, "Let the men
   who sacrifice kiss the calves!"
3 Therefore, they will be like the
   morning cloud,
And like dew which soon disappears,
Like chaff which is blown away
   from the threshing floor,
And like smoke from a chimney.

4 ¶ Yet I *have been* the LORD your
   God
Since the land of Egypt;
And you were not to know any
   god except Me,
For there is no savior besides Me.
5 I cared for you in the wilderness,
   In the land of drought.
6 As *they had* their pasture, they
   became satisfied,
And being satisfied, their heart
   became proud;
Therefore, they forgot Me.
7 So I will be like a lion to them;
Like a leopard I will lie in wait by
   the wayside.
8 I will encounter them like a bear
   robbed of her cubs,
And I will tear open their chests;
There I will also devour them like
   a lioness,
As a wild beast would tear them.

9 ¶ *It is* your destruction, O Israel,
That *you are* against Me, against
   your help.
10 Where now is your king
That he may save you in all your
   cities,
And your judges of whom you
   requested,
"Give me a king and princes"?
11 I gave you a king in My anger,
   And took him away in My wrath.

12 ¶ The iniquity of Ephraim is
   bound up;
His sin is stored up.
13 The pains of childbirth come upon
   him;
He is not a wise son,
For it is not the time that he
   should delay at the opening of
   the womb.

14 Shall I ransom them from the
   power of Sheol?
Shall I redeem them from death?
O Death, where are your thorns?
O Sheol, where is your sting?
Compassion will be hidden from
   My sight.

15 ¶ Though he flourishes among
   the reeds,
An east wind will come,
The wind of the LORD coming up
   from the wilderness;
And his fountain will become dry,
And his spring will be dried up;
It will plunder *his* treasury of
   every precious article.
16 Samaria will be held guilty,
For she has rebelled against her
   God.
They will fall by the sword,
Their little ones will be dashed in
   pieces,
And their pregnant women will be
   ripped open.

CHAPTER 14

RETURN, O Israel, to the LORD your
   God,
For you have stumbled because of
   your iniquity.
2 Take words with you and return
   to the LORD.
Say to Him, "Take away all iniq-
   uity,
And receive *us* graciously,
That we may present the fruit of
   our lips.
3 "Assyria will not save us,
We will not ride on horses;
Nor will we say again, 'Our god,'
To the work of our hands;
For in Thee the orphan finds
   mercy."

4 ¶ I will heal their apostasy,
I will love them freely,
For My anger has turned away
   from them.
5 I will be like the dew to Israel;
He will blossom like the lily,
And he will take root like *the
   cedars of* Lebanon.
6 His shoots will sprout,
And his beauty will be like the
   olive tree,
And his fragrance like *the cedars
of* Lebanon.

7 Those who live in his shadow
Will again raise grain,
And they will blossom like the
vine.
His renown *will be* like the wine
of Lebanon.

8 ¶ O Ephraim, what more have I to
do with idols?
It is I who answer and look after
you.

I am like a luxuriant cypress;
From Me comes your fruit.

9 ¶ Whoever is wise, let him understand these things;
Whoever is discerning, let him
know them.
For the ways of the LORD are
right,
And the righteous will walk in
them,
But transgressors will stumble in
them.

THE BOOK OF

JOEL

THE word of the LORD that came to
Joel, the son of Pethuel.
2 Hear this, O elders,
And listen, all inhabitants of the
land.
Has *anything like* this happened
in your days
Or in your fathers' days?
3 Tell your sons about it,
And *let* your sons *tell* their sons,
And their sons the next genera-
tion.

4 ¶ What the gnawing locust has
left, the swarming locust has
eaten;
And what the swarming locust
has left, the creeping locust has
eaten;
And what the creeping locust has
left, the stripping locust has
eaten.
5 Awake, drunkards, and weep;
And wail, all you wine drinkers,
On account of the sweet wine
That is cut off from your mouth.
6 For a nation has invaded my land,
Mighty and without number;
Its teeth are the teeth of a lion,
And it has the fangs of a lioness.
7 It has made my vine a waste,
And my fig tree splinters.
It has stripped them bare and cast
them away;
Their branches have become
white.

8 ¶ Wail like a virgin girded with
sackcloth
For the bridegroom of her youth.
9 The grain offering and the libation
are cut off
From the house of the LORD.
The priests mourn,
The ministers of the LORD.
10 The field is ruined,
The land mourns,
For the grain is ruined,
The new wine dries up,
Fresh oil fails.
11 Be ashamed, O farmers,
Wail, O vinedressers,
For the wheat and the barley;
Because the harvest of the field is
destroyed.
12 The vine dries up,
And the fig tree fails;
The pomegranate, the palm also,
and the apple tree,
All the trees of the field dry up.
Indeed, rejoicing dries up
From the sons of men.

13 ¶ Gird yourselves *with sackcloth*,
And lament, O priests;
Wail, O ministers of the altar!
Come, spend the night in sack-
cloth,
O ministers of my God,
For the grain offering and the
libation
Are withheld from the house of
your God.
14 Consecrate a fast,

Proclaim a solemn assembly;
Gather the elders
And all the inhabitants of the land
To the house of the LORD your
God,
And cry out to the LORD.
15 Alas for the day!
For the day of the LORD is near,
And it will come as destruction
from the Almighty.
16 Has not food been cut off before
our eyes,
Gladness and joy from the house
of our God?
17 The seeds shrivel under their
clods;
The storehouses are desolate,
The barns are torn down,
For the grain is dried up.
18 How the beasts groan!
The herds of cattle wander aim-
lessly
Because there is no pasture for
them;
Even the flocks of sheep suffer.
19 To Thee, O LORD, I cry;
For fire has devoured the pastures
of the wilderness,
And the flame has burned up all
the trees of the field.
20 Even the beasts of the field pant
for Thee;
For the water brooks are dried up,
And fire has devoured the pastures of the wilderness.

CHAPTER 2

BLOW a trumpet in Zion,
And sound an alarm on My holy
mountain!
Let all the inhabitants of the land
tremble,
For the day of the LORD is coming;
Surely it is near,
2 A day of darkness and gloom,
A day of clouds and thick dark-
ness.
As the dawn is spread over the
mountains,
So there is a great and mighty
people;
There has never been *anything*
like it,
Nor will there be again after it
To the years of many generations.
3 A fire consumes before them,
And behind them a flame burns.

The land is like the garden of
Eden before them,
But a desolate wilderness behind
them,
And nothing at all escapes them.
4 Their appearance is like the ap-
pearance of horses;
And like war horses, so they run.
5 With a noise as of chariots
They leap on the tops of the
mountains,
Like the crackling of a flame of
fire consuming the stubble,
Like a mighty people arranged for
battle.
6 Before them the people are in
anguish;
All faces turn pale.
7 They run like mighty men;
They climb the wall like soldiers;
And they each march in line,
Nor do they deviate from their
paths.
8 They do not crowd each other;
They march everyone in his path.
When they burst through the de-
fenses,
They do not break ranks.
9 They rush on the city,
They run on the wall;
They climb into the houses,
They enter through the windows
like a thief.
10 Before them the earth quakes,
The heavens tremble,
The sun and the moon grow dark,
And the stars lose their bright-
ness.
11 And the LORD utters His voice
before His army;
Surely His camp is very great,
For strong is he who carries out
His word.
The day of the LORD is indeed
great and very awesome,
And who can endure it?
12 "Yet even now," declares the LORD,
"Return to Me with all your heart,
And with fasting, weeping, and
mourning;
13 And rend your heart and not your
garments."
Now return to the LORD your God,
For He is gracious and compas-
sionate,
Slow to anger, abounding in
lovingkindness,
And relenting of evil.

14 Who knows whether He will *not*
  turn and relent,
  And leave a blessing behind Him,
  Even a grain offering and a libation
  For the Lord your God?
15 Blow a trumpet in Zion,
  Consecrate a fast, proclaim a solemn assembly,
16 Gather the people, sanctify the
  congregation,
  Assemble the elders,
  Gather the children and the nursing infants.
  Let the bridegroom come out of
  his room
  And the bride out of her *bridal*
  chamber.
17 Let the priests, the Lord's ministers,
  Weep between the porch and the
  altar,
  And let them say, "Spare Thy
  people, O Lord,
  And do not make Thine inheritance a reproach,
  A byword among the nations.
  Why should they among the peoples say,
  'Where is their God?' "

18 ¶ Then the Lord will be zealous
  for His land,
  And will have pity on His people.
19 And the Lord will answer and say
  to His people,
  "Behold, I am going to send you
  grain, new wine, and oil,
  And you will be satisfied *in full*
  with them;
  And I will never again make you a
  reproach among the nations.
20 "But I will remove the northern
  army far from you,
  And I will drive it into a parched
  and desolate land,
  And its vanguard into the eastern
  sea,
  And its rear guard into the western sea.
  And its stench will arise and its
  foul smell will come up,
  For it has done great things."

21 ¶ Do not fear, O land, rejoice and
  be glad,
  For the Lord has done great
  things.
22 Do not fear, beasts of the field,

For the pastures of the wilderness
  have turned green,
For the tree has borne its fruit,
The fig tree and the vine have
  yielded in full.
23 So rejoice, O sons of Zion,
  And be glad in the Lord your
  God;
  For He has given you the [1]early
  rain for *your* vindication.
  And He has poured down for you
  the rain,
  The [1]early and [2]latter rain as before.
24 And the threshing floors will be
  full of grain,
  And the vats will overflow with
  the new wine and oil.
25 "Then I will make up to you for the
  years
  That the swarming locust has
  eaten,
  The creeping locust, the stripping
  locust, and the gnawing locust,
  My great army which I sent
  among you.
26 "And you shall have plenty to eat
  and be satisfied,
  And praise the name of the Lord
  your God,
  Who has dealt wondrously with
  you;
  Then My people will never be put
  to shame.
27 "Thus you will know that I am in
  the midst of Israel,
  And that I am the Lord your God
  And there is no other;
  And My people will never be put
  to shame.

28 ¶ "And it will come about after
  this
  That I will pour out My Spirit on
  all mankind;
  And your sons and daughters will
  prophesy,
  Your old men will dream dreams,
  Your young men will see visions.
29 "And even on the male and female
  servants
  I will pour out My Spirit in those
  days.
30 "And I will display wonders in the
  sky and on the earth,
  Blood, fire, and columns of smoke.

[1] I.e., autumn [2] I.e., spring

31"The sun will be turned into darkness,
  And the moon into blood,
  Before the great and awesome day
    of the LORD comes.
32"And it will come about that whoever calls on the name of the
    LORD
  Will be delivered;
  For on Mount Zion and in Jerusalem
  There will be those who escape,
  As the LORD has said,
  Even among the survivors whom
    the LORD calls.

CHAPTER 3

"FOR behold, in those days and at
    that time,
  When I restore the fortunes of
    Judah and Jerusalem,
2 I will gather all the nations,
  And bring them down to the valley of Jehoshaphat.
  Then I will enter into judgment
    with them there
  On behalf of My people and My
    inheritance, Israel,
  Whom they have scattered among
    the nations;
  And they have divided up My
    land.
3"They have also cast lots for My
    people,
  Traded a boy for a harlot,
  And sold a girl for wine that they
    may drink.
4"Moreover, what are you to Me, O
Tyre, Sidon, and all the regions of
Philistia? Are you rendering Me a recompense? But if you do recompense
Me, swiftly and speedily I will return
your recompense on your head.
5"Since you have taken My silver
and My gold, brought My precious
treasures to your temples,
6 and sold the sons of Judah and
Jerusalem to the Greeks in order to
remove them far from their territory,
7 behold, I am going to arouse them
from the place where you have sold
them, and return your recompense on
your head.
8"Also I will sell your sons and your
daughters into the hand of the sons of
Judah, and they will sell them to the
Sabeans, to a distant nation," for the
LORD has spoken.

9 ¶ Proclaim this among the nations:
  Prepare a war; rouse the mighty
    men!
  Let all the soldiers draw near, let
    them come up!
10 Beat your plowshares into swords,
  And your pruning hooks into
    spears;
  Let the weak say, "I am a mighty
    man."
11 Hasten and come, all you surrounding nations,
  And gather yourselves there.
  Bring down, O LORD, Thy mighty
    ones.
12 Let the nations be aroused
  And come up to the valley of Jehoshaphat,
  For there I will sit to judge
  All the surrounding nations.
13 Put in the sickle, for the harvest is
    ripe.
  Come, tread, for the wine press is
    full;
  The vats overflow, for their wickedness is great.
14 Multitudes, multitudes in the valley of decision!
  For the day of the LORD is near in
    the valley of decision.
15 The sun and moon grow dark,
  And the stars lose their brightness.
16 And the LORD roars from Zion
  And utters His voice from Jerusalem,
  And the heavens and the earth
    tremble.
  But the LORD is a refuge for His
    people
  And a stronghold to the sons of
    Israel.
17 Then you will know that I am the
    LORD your God,
  Dwelling in Zion My holy mountain.
  So Jerusalem will be holy,
  And strangers will pass through it
    no more.

18 ¶ And it will come about in that
    day
  That the mountains will drip with
    sweet wine,
  And the hills will flow with milk,
  And all the brooks of Judah will
    flow with water;

And a spring will go out from the
house of the LORD,
To water the valley of Shittim.
19 Egypt will become a waste,
And Edom will become a desolate
wilderness,
Because of the violence done to
the sons of Judah,
In whose land they have shed
innocent blood.
20 But Judah will be inhabited forever,
And Jerusalem for all generations.
21 And I will avenge their blood
which I have not avenged,
For the LORD dwells in Zion.

THE BOOK OF

AMOS

THE words of Amos, who was among
the sheepherders from Tekoa, which
he envisioned in visions concerning
Israel in the days of Uzziah king of
Judah, and in the days of Jeroboam
son of Joash, king of Israel, two years
before the earthquake.
2 And he said,
"The LORD roars from Zion,
And from Jerusalem He utters His
voice;
And the shepherds' pasture
grounds mourn,
And the summit of Carmel dries
up."

3 ¶ Thus says the LORD,
"For three transgressions of Damascus and for four
I will not revoke its *punishment*,
Because they threshed Gilead
with *implements* of sharp iron.
4"So I will send fire upon the house
of Hazael,
And it will consume the citadels
of Ben-hadad.
5"I will also break the *gate* bar of
Damascus,
And cut off the inhabitant from
the valley of Aven,
And him who holds the scepter,
from Beth-eden;
So the people of Aram will go
exiled to Kir,"
Says the LORD.

6 ¶ Thus says the LORD,
"For three transgressions of Gaza
and for four
I will not revoke its *punishment*,
Because they deported an entire
population
To deliver *it* up to Edom.

7"So I will send fire upon the wall of
Gaza,
And it will consume her citadels.
8"I will also cut off the inhabitant
from Ashdod,
And him who holds the scepter,
from Ashkelon;
I will even unleash My power
upon Ekron,
And the remnant of the Philistines
will perish,"
Says the Lord GOD.

9 ¶ Thus says the LORD,
"For three transgressions of Tyre
and for four
I will not revoke its *punishment*,
Because they delivered up an en-
tire population to Edom
And did not remember *the* cov-
enant of brotherhood.
10"So I will send fire upon the wall of
Tyre,
And it will consume her citadels."

11 ¶ Thus says the LORD,
"For three transgressions of Edom
and for four
I will not revoke its *punishment*,
Because he pursued his brother
with the sword,
While he stifled his compassion;
His anger also tore continually,
And he maintained his fury for-
ever.
12"So I will send fire upon Teman,
And it will consume the citadels
of Bozrah."

13 ¶ Thus says the LORD,
"For three transgressions of the
sons of Ammon and for four
I will not revoke its *punishment*,

Because they ripped open the
  pregnant women of Gilead
In order to enlarge their borders.
14"So I will kindle a fire on the wall
  of Rabbah,
  And it will consume her citadels
  Amid war cries on the day of battle
  And a storm on the day of tempest.
15"Their king will go into exile,
  He and his princes together," says
  the Lord.

CHAPTER 2

THUS says the Lord,
  "For three transgressions of Moab
  and for four
  I will not revoke its *punishment,*
  Because he burned the bones of
  the king of Edom to lime.
2"So I will send fire upon Moab,
  And it will consume the citadels
  of Kerioth;
  And Moab will die amid tumult,
  With war cries and the sound of a
  trumpet.
3"I will also cut off the judge from
  her midst,
  And slay all her princes with
  him," says the Lord.

4 ¶ Thus says the Lord,
  "For three transgressions of Judah
  and for four
  I will not revoke its *punishment,*
  Because they rejected the law of
  the Lord
  And have not kept His statutes;
  Their lies also have led them
  astray,
  Those after which their fathers
  walked.
5"So I will send fire upon Judah,
  And it will consume the citadels
  of Jerusalem."

6 ¶ Thus says the Lord,
  "For three transgressions of Israel
  and for four
  I will not revoke its *punishment,*
  Because they sell the righteous for
  money
  And the needy for a pair of sandals.
7"These who pant after the *very*
  dust of the earth on the head of
  the helpless

Also turn aside the way of the
  humble;
  And a man and his father resort to
  the same girl
  In order to profane My holy
  name.
8"And on garments taken as pledges
  they stretch out beside every
  altar,
  And in the house of their God
  they drink the wine of those
  who have been fined.

9 ¶ "Yet it was I who destroyed the
  Amorite before them,
  Though his height *was* like the
  height of cedars
  And he *was* strong as the oaks;
  I even destroyed his fruit above
  and his root below.
10"And it was I who brought you up
  from the land of Egypt,
  And I led you in the wilderness
  forty years
  That you might take possession of
  the land of the Amorite.
11"Then I raised up some of your
  sons to be prophets
  And some of your young men to
  be Nazirites.
  Is this not so, O sons of Israel?"
  declares the Lord.
12"But you made the Nazirites drink
  wine,
  And you commanded the prophets saying, 'You shall not prophesy!'
13"Behold, I am weighted down beneath you
  As a wagon is weighted down
  when filled with sheaves.
14"Flight will perish from the swift,
  And the stalwart will not
  strengthen his power,
  Nor the mighty man save his life.
15"He who grasps the bow will not
  stand *his* ground,
  The swift of foot will not escape,
  Nor will he who rides the horse
  save his life.
16"Even the bravest among the warriors will flee naked in that
  day," declares the Lord.

CHAPTER 3

HEAR this word which the Lord has
spoken against you, sons of Israel,

against the entire family which He
brought up from the land of Egypt,

2"You only have I chosen among all
the families of the earth;

Therefore, I will punish you for all
your iniquities."

3 Do two men walk together unless
they have made an appointment?

4 Does a lion roar in the forest
when he has no prey?

Does a young lion growl from his
den unless he has captured
something?

5 Does a bird fall into a trap on the
ground when there is no bait in
it?

Does a trap spring up from the
earth when it captures nothing
at all?

6 If a trumpet is blown in a city will
not the people tremble?

If a calamity occurs in a city has
not the LORD done it?

7 Surely the Lord GOD does nothing
Unless He reveals His secret counsel

To His servants the prophets.

8 A lion has roared! Who will not
fear?

The Lord GOD has spoken! Who
can but prophesy?

9 ¶ Proclaim on the citadels in Ashdod and on the citadels in the land of
Egypt and say, "Assemble yourselves
on the mountains of Samaria and see
the great tumults within her and *the*
oppressions in her midst.

10"But they do not know how to do
what is right," declares the LORD,
"these who hoard up violence and
devastation in their citadels."

11 ¶ Therefore, thus says the Lord
GOD,

"An enemy, even one surrounding
the land,

Will pull down your strength from
you

And your citadels will be looted."

12 Thus says the LORD,

"Just as the shepherd snatches
from the lion's mouth a couple
of legs or a piece of an ear,

So will the sons of Israel dwelling
in Samaria be snatched away—

With the corner of a bed and *the*
cover of a couch!

13"Hear and testify against the house
of Jacob,"

Declares the Lord GOD, the God of
hosts.

14"For on the day that I punish Israel's transgressions,

I will also punish the altars of
Bethel;

The horns of the altar will be cut
off,

And they will fall to the ground.

15"I will also smite the winter house
together with the summer
house;

The houses of ivory will also perish

And the great houses will come to
an end,"

Declares the LORD.

CHAPTER 4

HEAR this word, you cows of Bashan
who are on the mountain of
Samaria,

Who oppress the poor, who crush
the needy,

Who say to your husbands, "Bring
now, that we may drink!"

2 The Lord GOD has sworn by His
holiness,

"Behold, the days are coming upon
you

When they will take you away
with meat hooks,

And the last of you with fish
hooks.

3"You will go out *through* breaches
in the walls,

Each one straight before her,

And you will be cast to Harmon,"
declares the LORD.

4 ¶"Enter Bethel and transgress;

In Gilgal multiply transgression!

Bring your sacrifices every morning,

Your tithes every three days.

5"Offer a thank offering also from
that which is leavened,

And proclaim freewill offerings,
make them known.

For so you love *to do*, you sons of
Israel,"

Declares the Lord GOD.

6 ¶"But I gave you also cleanness of
teeth in all your cities

And lack of bread in all your
places,

Yet you have not returned to Me," declares the Lord.

7"And furthermore, I withheld the rain from you
While *there were* still three months until harvest.
Then I would send rain on one city
And on another city I would not send rain;
One part would be rained on,
While the part not rained on would dry up.

8"So two or three cities would stagger to another city to drink water,
But would not be satisfied;
Yet you have not returned to Me," declares the Lord.

9"I smote you with scorching *wind* and mildew;
And the caterpillar was devouring Your many gardens and vineyards, fig trees and olive trees;
Yet you have not returned to Me," declares the Lord.

10"I sent a plague among you after the manner of Egypt;
I slew your young men by the sword along with your captured horses,
And I made the stench of your camp rise up in your nostrils;
Yet you have not returned to Me," declares the Lord.

11"I overthrew you as God overthrew Sodom and Gomorrah,
And you were like a firebrand snatched from a blaze;
Yet you have not returned to Me," declares the Lord.

12"Therefore, thus I will do to you, O Israel;
Because I shall do this to you,
Prepare to meet your God, O Israel."

13 For behold, He who forms mountains and creates the wind
And declares to man what are His thoughts,
He who makes dawn into darkness
And treads on the high places of the earth,
The Lord God of hosts is His name.

CHAPTER 5

HEAR this word which I take up for you as a dirge, O house of Israel.

2 She has fallen, she will not rise again—
The virgin Israel.
She *lies* neglected on her land;
There is none to raise her up.

3 For thus says the Lord GOD,
"The city which goes forth a thousand *strong*
Will have a hundred left,
And the one which goes forth a hundred *strong*
Will have ten left to the house of Israel."

4 ¶ For thus says the Lord to the house of Israel,
"Seek Me that you may live.

5"But do not resort to Bethel,
And do not come to Gilgal,
Nor cross over to Beersheba;
For Gilgal will certainly go into captivity,
And Bethel will come to trouble.

6"Seek the Lord that you may live,
Lest He break forth like a fire, O house of Joseph,
And it consume with none to quench *it* for Bethel,

7 *For* those who turn justice into wormwood
And cast righteousness down to the earth."

8 ¶ He who made the Pleiades and Orion
And changes deep darkness into morning,
Who also darkens day *into* night,
Who calls for the waters of the sea
And pours them out on the surface of the earth,
The Lord is His name.

9 It is He who flashes forth *with* destruction upon the strong,
So that destruction comes upon the fortress.

10 ¶ They hate him who reproves in the gate,
And they abhor him who speaks *with* integrity.

11 Therefore, because you impose heavy rent on the poor

And exact a tribute of grain from
them,
Though you have built houses of
well-hewn stone,
Yet you will not live in them;
You have planted pleasant vineyards, yet you will not drink
their wine.
12 For I know your transgressions
are many and your sins are
great,
You who distress the righteous
and accept bribes,
And turn aside the poor in the
gate.
13 Therefore, at such a time the prudent person keeps silent, for it is
an evil time.

14 ¶ Seek good and not evil, that
you may live;
And thus may the LORD God of
hosts be with you,
Just as you have said!
15 Hate evil, love good,
And establish justice in the gate!
Perhaps the LORD God of hosts
May be gracious to the remnant
of Joseph.

16 ¶ Therefore, thus says the LORD
God of hosts, the Lord,
"There is wailing in all the plazas,
And in all the streets they say,
'Alas! Alas!'
They also call the farmer to
mourning
And professional mourners to
lamentation.
17"And in all the vineyards *there is*
wailing,
Because I shall pass through the
midst of you," says the LORD.

18 ¶ Alas, you who are longing for
the day of the LORD,
For what purpose *will* the day of
the LORD *be* to you?
It *will be* darkness and not light;
19 As when a man flees from a lion,
And a bear meets him,
Or goes home, leans his hand
against the wall,
And a snake bites him.
20 *Will* not the day of the LORD *be*
darkness instead of light,

Even gloom with no brightness in
it?

21 ¶"I hate, I reject your festivals,
Nor do I delight in your solemn
assemblies.
22"Even though you offer up to Me
burnt offerings and your grain
offerings,
I will not accept *them*;
And I will not *even* look at the
peace offerings of your fatlings.
23"Take away from Me the noise of
your songs;
I will not even listen to the sound
of your harps.
24"But let justice roll down like waters
And righteousness like an ever-
flowing stream.

25 ¶"Did you present Me with sacrifices and grain offerings in the wilderness for forty years, O house of Israel?
26"You also carried along Sikkuth
your king and Kiyyun, your images,
the star of your gods which you made
for yourselves.
27"Therefore, I will make you go into
exile beyond Damascus," says the
LORD, whose name is the God of hosts.

CHAPTER 6

Woe to those who are at ease in
Zion,
And to those who *feel* secure in
the mountain of Samaria,
The distinguished men of the foremost of nations,
To whom the house of Israel
comes.
2 Go over to Calneh and look,
And go from there to Hamath the
great,
Then go down to Gath of the
Philistines.
Are they better than these kingdoms,
Or is their territory greater than
yours?
3 Do you put off the day of calamity,
And would you bring near the
seat of violence?

4 ¶ Those who recline on beds of
ivory
And sprawl on their couches,
And eat lambs from the flock

And calves from the midst of the stall,

5 Who improvise to the sound of the harp,
And like David have composed songs for themselves,

6 Who drink wine from sacrificial bowls
While they anoint themselves with the finest of oils,
Yet they have not grieved over the ruin of Joseph.

7 Therefore, they will now go into exile at the head of the exiles,
And the sprawlers' banqueting will pass away.

8 ¶ The Lord GOD has sworn by Himself, the LORD God of hosts has declared:
"I loathe the arrogance of Jacob,
And I detest his citadels;
Therefore, I will deliver up *the* city and all it contains."

9 And it will be, if ten men are left in one house, they will die.

10 Then one's uncle, or his undertaker, will lift him up to carry out *his* bones from the house, and he will say to the one who is in the innermost part of the house, "Is anyone else with you?" And that one will say, "No one." Then he will answer, "Keep quiet. For the name of the LORD is not to be mentioned."

11 For behold, the LORD is going to command that the great house be smashed to pieces and the small house to fragments.

12 ¶ Do horses run on rocks?
Or does one plow them with oxen?
Yet you have turned justice into poison,
And the fruit of righteousness into [1]wormwood.

13 You who rejoice in [2]Lo–debar,
And say, "Have we not by our *own* strength taken [3]Karnaim for ourselves?"

14"For behold, I am going to raise up a nation against you,
O house of Israel," declares the LORD God of hosts,
"And they will afflict you from the entrance of Hamath
To the brook of the Arabah."

[1] I.e., bitterness   [2] Lit., *a thing of nothing*
[3] Lit., *a pair of horns*

CHAPTER 7

THUS the Lord GOD showed me, and behold, He was forming a locust-swarm when the spring crop began to sprout. And behold, the spring crop *was* after the king's mowing.

2 And it came about, when it had finished eating the vegetation of the land, that I said,
"Lord GOD, please pardon!
How can Jacob stand,
For he is small?"

3 The LORD changed His mind about this.
"It shall not be," said the LORD.

4 ¶ Thus the Lord GOD showed me, and behold, the Lord GOD was calling to contend *with them* by fire, and it consumed the great deep and began to consume the farm land.

5 Then I said,
"Lord GOD, please stop!
How can Jacob stand, for he is small?"

6 The LORD changed His mind about this.
"This too shall not be," said the Lord GOD.

7 ¶ Thus He showed me, and behold, the Lord was standing by a vertical wall, with a plumb line in His hand.

8 And the LORD said to me, "What do you see, Amos?" And I said, "A plumb line." Then the Lord said,
"Behold I am about to put a plumb line
In the midst of My people Israel.
I will spare them no longer.

9"The high places of Isaac will be desolated
And the sanctuaries of Israel laid waste.
Then shall I rise up against the house of Jeroboam with the sword."

10 ¶ Then Amaziah, the priest of Bethel, sent *word* to Jeroboam, king of Israel, saying, "Amos has conspired against you in the midst of the house of Israel; the land is unable to endure all his words.

11"For thus Amos says, 'Jeroboam will die by the sword and Israel will certainly go from its land into exile.'"

12 Then Amaziah said to Amos, "Go, you seer, flee away to the land of Judah, and there eat bread and there do your prophesying!

13"But no longer prophesy at Bethel, for it is a sanctuary of the king and a royal residence."

14 ¶ Then Amos answered and said to Amaziah, "I am not a prophet, nor am I the son of a prophet; for I am a herdsman and a grower of sycamore figs.

15"But the LORD took me from following the flock and the LORD said to me, 'Go prophesy to My people Israel.'

16"And now hear the word of the LORD: you are saying, 'You shall not prophesy against Israel nor shall you speak against the house of Isaac.'

17"Therefore, thus says the LORD, 'Your wife will become a harlot in the city, your sons and your daughters will fall by the sword, your land will be parceled up by a *measuring* line, and you yourself will die upon unclean soil. Moreover, Israel will certainly go from its land into exile.' "

CHAPTER 8

THUS the Lord GOD showed me, and behold, *there was* a basket of summer fruit.

2 And He said, "What do you see, Amos?" And I said, "A basket of summer fruit." Then the LORD said to me, "The end has come for My people Israel. I will spare them no longer.

3"The songs of the palace will turn to wailing in that day," declares the Lord GOD. "Many *will be* the corpses; in every place they will cast them forth in silence."

4 ¶ Hear this, you who trample the needy, to do away with the humble of the land,

5 saying,
"When will the new moon be over,
So that we may sell grain,
And the sabbath, that we may open the wheat *market*,
To make the bushel smaller and the shekel bigger,
And to cheat with dishonest scales,

6 So as to buy the helpless for money
And the needy for a pair of sandals,
And *that* we may sell the refuse of the wheat?"

7 ¶ The LORD has sworn by the pride of Jacob,

"Indeed, I will never forget any of their deeds.

8"Because of this will not the land quake
And everyone who dwells in it mourn?
Indeed, all of it will rise up like the Nile,
And it will be tossed about,
And subside like the Nile of Egypt.

9"And it will come about in that day," declares the Lord GOD,
"That I shall make the sun go down at noon
And make the earth dark in broad daylight.

10"Then I shall turn your festivals into mourning
And all your songs into lamentation;
And I will bring sackcloth on everyone's loins
And baldness on every head.
And I will make it like *a time of* mourning for an only son,
And the end of it will be like a bitter day.

11 ¶"Behold, days are coming," declares the Lord GOD,
"When I will send a famine on the land,
Not a famine for bread or a thirst for water,
But rather for hearing the words of the LORD.

12"And people will stagger from sea to sea,
And from the north even to the east;
They will go to and fro to seek the word of the LORD,
But they will not find *it*.

13"In that day the beautiful virgins
And the young men will faint from thirst.

14"*As for* those who swear by the guilt of Samaria,
Who say, 'As your god lives, O Dan,'
And, 'As the way of Beersheba lives,'
They will fall and not rise again."

CHAPTER 9

I SAW the Lord standing beside the altar, and He said,
"Smite the capitals so that the thresholds will shake,

And break them on the heads of
　them all!
Then I will slay the rest of them
　with the sword;
They will not have a fugitive who
　will flee,
Or a refugee who will escape.
2 "Though they dig into Sheol,
　From there shall My hand take
　　them;
　And though they ascend to
　　heaven,
　From there will I bring them
　　down.
3 "And though they hide on the sum-
　mit of Carmel,
　I will search them out and take
　　them from there;
　And though they conceal them-
　　selves from My sight on the
　　floor of the sea,
　From there I will command the
　　serpent and it will bite them.
4 "And though they go into captivity
　before their enemies,
　From there I will command the
　　sword that it slay them,
　And I will set My eyes against
　　them for evil and not for good."

5 ¶ And the Lord God of hosts,
　The One who touches the land so
　　that it melts,
　And all those who dwell in it
　　mourn,
　And all of it rises up like the Nile
　And subsides like the Nile of
　　Egypt;
6 The One who builds His upper
　chambers in the heavens,
　And has founded His vaulted
　　dome over the earth,
　He who calls for the waters of the
　　sea
　And pours them out on the face of
　　the earth,
　The Lord is His name.

7 ¶ "Are you not as the sons of Ethi-
　opia to Me,
　O sons of Israel?" declares the
　　Lord.
　"Have I not brought up Israel from
　　the land of Egypt,

And the Philistines from Caphtor
　and the Arameans from Kir?
8 "Behold, the eyes of the Lord God
　are on the sinful kingdom,
　And I will destroy it from the face
　　of the earth;
　Nevertheless, I will not totally
　　destroy the house of Jacob,"
　Declares the Lord.
9 "For behold, I am commanding,
　And I will shake the house of
　　Israel among all nations
　As *grain* is shaken in a sieve,
　But not a kernel will fall to the
　　ground.
10 "All the sinners of My people will
　die by the sword,
　Those who say, 'The calamity will
　　not overtake or confront us.'
11 "In that day I will raise up the
　fallen booth of David,
　And wall up its breaches;
　I will also raise up its ruins,
　And rebuild it as in the days of
　　old;
12 That they may possess the rem-
　nant of Edom
　And all the nations who are called
　　by My name,"
　Declares the Lord who does this.

13 ¶ "Behold, days are coming," de-
　clares the Lord,
　"When the plowman will overtake
　　the reaper
　And the treader of grapes him
　　who sows seed;
　When the mountains will drip
　　sweet wine,
　And all the hills will be dissolved.
14 "Also I will restore the captivity of
　My people Israel,
　And they will rebuild the ruined
　　cities and live *in them*,
　They will also plant vineyards and
　　drink their wine,
　And make gardens and eat their
　　fruit.
15 "I will also plant them on their
　land,
　And they will not again be rooted
　　out from their land
　Which I have given them,"
　Says the Lord your God.

THE BOOK OF

OBADIAH

THE vision of Obadiah.
Thus says the Lord GOD concerning Edom—
We have heard a report from the LORD,
And an envoy has been sent among the nations saying,
"Arise and let us go against her for battle"—
2"Behold, I will make you small among the nations;
You are greatly despised.
3"The arrogance of your heart has deceived you,
You who live in the clefts of the rock,
In the loftiness of your dwelling place,
Who say in your heart,
'Who will bring me down to earth?'
4"Though you build high like the eagle,
Though you set your nest among the stars,
From there I will bring you down," declares the LORD.
5"If thieves came to you,
If robbers by night—
O how you will be ruined!—
Would they not steal *only* until they had enough?
If grape gatherers came to you,
Would they not leave *some* gleanings?
6"O how Esau will be ransacked,
And his hidden treasures searched out!
7"All the men allied with you
Will send you forth to the border,
And the men at peace with you
Will deceive you and overpower you.
They who eat your bread
Will set an ambush for you.
(There is no understanding in him.)
8"Will I not on that day," declares the LORD,
"Destroy wise men from Edom
And understanding from the mountain of Esau?
9"Then your mighty men will be dismayed, O Teman,
In order that everyone may be cut off from the mountain of Esau by slaughter.

10 ¶"Because of violence to your brother Jacob,
You will be covered *with* shame,
And you will be cut off forever.
11"On the day that you stood aloof,
On the day that strangers carried off his wealth,
And foreigners entered his gate
And cast lots for Jerusalem—
You too were as one of them.
12"Do not gloat over your brother's day,
The day of his misfortune.
And do not rejoice over the sons of Judah
In the day of their destruction;
Yes, do not boast
In the day of *their* distress.
13"Do not enter the gate of My people
In the day of their disaster.
Yes, you, do not gloat over their calamity
In the day of their disaster.
And do not loot their wealth
In the day of their disaster.
14"And do not stand at the fork of the road
To cut down their fugitives;
And do not imprison their survivors
In the day of their distress.

15 ¶"For the day of the LORD draws near on all the nations.
As you have done, it will be done to you.
Your dealings will return on your own head.
16"Because just as you drank on My holy mountain,
All the nations will drink continually.
They will drink and swallow,
And become as if they had never existed.
17"But on Mount Zion there will be those who escape,
And it will be holy.
And the house of Jacob will possess their possessions.
18"Then the house of Jacob will be a fire
And the house of Joseph a flame;
But the house of Esau *will be* as stubble.
And they will set them on fire and consume them,

So that there will be no survivor
of the house of Esau,"
For the LORD has spoken.
19 Then *those of* the ¹Negev will
possess the mountain of Esau,
And *those of* the ²Shephelah the
Philistine *plain*;
Also, they will possess the territory of Ephraim and the territory of Samaria,
And Benjamin *will possess* Gilead.

¹ I.e., South country   ² I.e., the foothills

20 And the exiles of this host of the
sons of Israel,
Who are *among* the Canaanites as
far as Zarephath,
And the exiles of Jerusalem who
are in Sepharad
Will possess the cities of the
Negev.
21 The deliverers will ascend Mount
Zion
To judge the mountain of Esau,
And the kingdom will be the
LORD's.

THE BOOK OF

JONAH

THE word of the LORD came to Jonah
the son of Amittai saying,
2 "Arise, go to Nineveh the great
city, and cry against it, for their wickedness has come up before Me."
3 But Jonah rose up to flee to Tarshish from the presence of the LORD.
So he went down to Joppa, found a
ship which was going to Tarshish, paid
the fare, and went down into it to go
with them to Tarshish from the presence of the LORD.
4 ¶ And the LORD hurled a great
wind on the sea and there was a great
storm on the sea so that the ship was
about to break up.
5 Then the sailors became afraid,
and every man cried to his god, and
they threw the cargo which was in the
ship into the sea to lighten *it* for them.
But Jonah had gone below into the
hold of the ship, lain down, and fallen
sound asleep.
6 So the captain approached him
and said, "How is it that you are sleeping? Get up, call on your god. Perhaps
your god will be concerned about us so
that we will not perish."
7 And each man said to his mate,
"Come, let us cast lots so we may
learn on whose account this calamity
has struck us." So they cast lots and
the lot fell on Jonah.
8 Then they said to him, "Tell us,
now! On whose account *has* this calamity *struck* us? What is your occu-

pation? And where do you come from?
What is your country? From what
people are you?"
9 And he said to them, "I am a
Hebrew, and I fear the LORD God of
heaven who made the sea and the dry
land."
10 ¶ Then the men became extremely frightened and they said to
him, "How could you do this?" For the
men knew that he was fleeing from
the presence of the LORD, because he
had told them.
11 So they said to him, "What should
we do to you that the sea may become
calm for us?"—for the sea was becoming increasingly stormy.
12 And he said to them, "Pick me up
and throw me into the sea. Then the
sea will become calm for you, for I
know that on account of me this great
storm *has come* upon you."
13 However, the men rowed *desperately* to return to land but they could
not, for the sea was becoming *even*
stormier against them.
14 Then they called on the LORD and
said, "We earnestly pray, O LORD, do
not let us perish on account of this
man's life and do not put innocent
blood on us; for Thou, O LORD, hast
done as Thou hast pleased."
15 ¶ So they picked up Jonah, threw
him into the sea, and the sea stopped
its raging.
16 Then the men feared the LORD

greatly, and they offered a sacrifice to the LORD and made vows.

17 ¶ And the LORD appointed a great fish to swallow Jonah, and Jonah was in the stomach of the fish three days and three nights.

CHAPTER 2

THEN Jonah prayed to the LORD his God from the stomach of the fish,

2 and he said,

"I called out of my distress to the LORD,
And He answered me.
I cried for help from the depth of Sheol;
Thou didst hear my voice.

3"For Thou hadst cast me into the deep,
Into the heart of the seas,
And the current engulfed me.
All Thy breakers and billows passed over me.

4"So I said, 'I have been expelled from Thy sight.
Nevertheless I will look again toward Thy holy temple.'

5"Water encompassed me to the point of death.
The great deep engulfed me,
Weeds were wrapped around my head.

6"I descended to the roots of the mountains.
The earth with its bars *was* around me forever,
But Thou hast brought up my life from the pit, O LORD my God.

7"While I was fainting away,
I remembered the LORD;
And my prayer came to Thee,
Into Thy holy temple.

8"Those who regard vain idols
Forsake their faithfulness,

9 But I will sacrifice to Thee
With the voice of thanksgiving.
That which I have vowed I will pay.
Salvation is from the LORD."

10 ¶ Then the LORD commanded the fish, and it vomited Jonah up onto the dry land.

CHAPTER 3

NOW the word of the LORD came to Jonah the second time, saying,

2"Arise, go to Nineveh the great city

and proclaim to it the proclamation which I am going to tell you."

3 So Jonah arose and went to Nineveh according to the word of the LORD. Now Nineveh was [1]an exceedingly great city, a three days' walk.

4 Then Jonah began to go through the city one day's walk; and he cried out and said, "Yet forty days and Nineveh will be overthrown."

5 ¶ Then the people of Nineveh believed in God; and they called a fast and put on sackcloth from the greatest to the least of them.

6 When the word reached the king of Nineveh, he arose from his throne, laid aside his robe from him, covered *himself* with sackcloth, and sat on the ashes.

7 And he issued a proclamation and it said, "In Nineveh by the decree of the king and his nobles: Do not let man, beast, herd, or flock taste a thing. Do not let them eat or drink water.

8"But both man and beast must be covered with sackcloth; and let men call on God earnestly that each may turn from his wicked way and from the violence which is in his hands.

9"Who knows, God may turn and relent, and withdraw His burning anger so that we shall not perish?"

10 ¶ When God saw their deeds, that they turned from their wicked way, then God relented concerning the calamity which He had declared He would bring upon them. And He did not do *it*.

CHAPTER 4

BUT it greatly displeased Jonah, and he became angry.

2 And he prayed to the LORD and said, "Please LORD, was not this what I said while I was still in my *own* country? Therefore, in order to forestall this I fled to Tarshish, for I knew that Thou art a gracious and compassionate God, slow to anger and abundant in lovingkindness, and one who relents concerning calamity.

3"Therefore now, O LORD, please take my life from me, for death is better to me than life."

4 And the LORD said, "Do you have good reason to be angry?"

[1] Lit., *a great city to God*

5 ¶ Then Jonah went out from the city and sat east of it. There he made a shelter for himself and sat under it in the shade until he could see what would happen in the city.

6 So the LORD God appointed a plant and it grew up over Jonah to be a shade over his head to deliver him from his discomfort. And Jonah was extremely happy about the plant.

7 But God appointed a worm when dawn came the next day, and it attacked the plant and it withered.

8 And it came about when the sun came up that God appointed a scorching east wind, and the sun beat down on Jonah's head so that he became faint and begged with *all* his soul to die, saying, "Death is better to me than life."

9 ¶ Then God said to Jonah, "Do you have good reason to be angry about the plant?" And he said, "I have good reason to be angry, even to death."

10 Then the LORD said, "You had compassion on the plant for which you did not work, and *which* you did not cause to grow, which came up overnight and perished overnight.

11 "And should I not have compassion on Nineveh, the great city in which there are more than 120,000 persons who do not know *the difference* between their right and left hand, as well as many animals?"

THE BOOK OF

MICAH

THE word of the LORD which came *to* Micah of Moresheth in the days of Jotham, Ahaz, *and* Hezekiah, kings of Judah, which he saw concerning Samaria and Jerusalem.

2 Hear, O peoples, all of you;
   Listen, O earth and all it contains,
   And let the Lord GOD be a witness against you,
   The Lord from His holy temple.

3 For behold, the LORD is coming forth from His place.
   He will come down and tread on the high places of the earth.

4 The mountains will melt under Him,
   And the valleys will be split,
   Like wax before the fire,
   Like water poured down a steep place.

5 All this is for the rebellion of Jacob
   And for the sins of the house of Israel.
   What is the rebellion of Jacob?
   Is it not Samaria?
   What is the high place of Judah?
   Is it not Jerusalem?

6 For I will make Samaria a heap of ruins in the open country,
   Planting places for a vineyard.
   I will pour her stones down into the valley,
   And will lay bare her foundations.

7 All of her idols will be smashed,
   All of her earnings will be burned with fire,
   And all of her images I will make desolate,
   For she collected *them* from a harlot's earnings,
   And to the earnings of a harlot they will return.

8 ¶ Because of this I must lament and wail,
   I must go barefoot and naked;
   I must make a lament like the jackals
   And a mourning like the ostriches.

9 For her wound is incurable,
   For it has come to Judah;
   It has reached the gate of my people,
   Even to Jerusalem.

10 Tell it not in Gath,
   Weep not at all.
   At ¹Beth-le-aphrah roll yourself in the dust.

11 Go on your way, inhabitant of ²Shaphir, in shameful nakedness.
   The inhabitant of ³Zaanan does not escape.

¹ I.e., house of dust   ² I.e., pleasantness   ³ I.e., going out

The lamentation of [4]Beth–ezel:
"He will take from you its support."

12 For the inhabitant of [5]Maroth
Becomes weak waiting for good,
Because a calamity has come
down from the LORD
To the gate of Jerusalem.

13 Harness the chariot to the team of
horses,
O inhabitant of Lachish—
She was the beginning of sin
To the daughter of Zion—
Because in you were found
The rebellious acts of Israel.

14 Therefore, you will give parting
gifts
On behalf of Moresheth–gath;
The houses of Achzib *will* become
a deception
To the kings of Israel.

15 Moreover, I will bring on you
The one who takes possession,
O inhabitant of [6]Mareshah.
The glory of Israel will enter
Adullam.

16 Make yourself bald and cut off
your hair,
Because of the children of your
delight;
Extend your baldness like the
eagle,
For they will go from you into
exile.

CHAPTER 2

WOE to those who scheme iniquity,
Who work out evil on their beds!
When morning comes, they do it,
For it is in the power of their
hands.

2 They covet fields and then seize
them,
And houses, and take *them* away.
They rob a man and his house,
A man and his inheritance.

3 Therefore, thus says the LORD,
"Behold, I am planning against this
family a calamity
From which you cannot remove
your necks;
And you will not walk haughtily,
For it will be an evil time.

4"On that day they will take up
against you a taunt

And utter a bitter lamentation
and say,
'We are completely destroyed!
He exchanges the portion of my
people;
How He removes it from me!
To the apostate He apportions our
fields.'

5"Therefore, you will have no one
stretching a measuring line
For you by lot in the assembly of
the LORD.

6 ¶ 'Do not speak out,' so they
speak out.
But if they do not speak out concerning these things,
Reproaches will not be turned
back.

7"Is it being said, O house of Jacob:
'Is the Spirit of the LORD impatient?
Are these His doings?'
Do not My words do good
To the one walking uprightly?

8"Recently My people have arisen
as an enemy—
You strip the robe off the garment,
From unsuspecting passers-by,
From those returned from war.

9"The women of My people you
evict,
Each *one* from her pleasant house.
From her children you take My
splendor forever.

10"Arise and go,
For this is no place of rest
Because of the uncleanness that
brings on destruction,
A painful destruction.

11"If a man walking after wind and
falsehood
Had told lies *and said,*
'I will speak out to you concerning
wine and liquor,'
He would be spokesman to this
people.

12 ¶"I will surely assemble all of you,
Jacob,
I will surely gather the remnant of
Israel.
I will put them together like sheep
in the fold;
Like a flock in the midst of its
pasture
They will be noisy with men.

[4] I.e., house of removal   [5] I.e., bitterness
[6] I.e., possession

13"The breaker goes up before them;
They break out, pass through the
gate, and go out by it.
So their king goes on before them,
And the Lord at their head."

CHAPTER 3

And I said,
"Hear now, heads of Jacob
And rulers of the house of Israel.
Is it not for you to know justice?
2"You who hate good and love evil,
Who tear off their skin from them
And their flesh from their bones,
3 And who eat the flesh of my peo-
ple,
Strip off their skin from them,
Break their bones,
And chop *them* up as for the pot
And as meat in a kettle."
4 Then they will cry out to the
Lord,
But He will not answer them.
Instead, He will hide His face from
them at that time,
Because they have practiced evil
deeds.

5 ¶ Thus says the Lord concerning
the prophets
Who lead my people astray;
When they have *something* to bite
with their teeth,
They cry, "Peace,"
But against him who puts nothing
in their mouths,
They declare holy war.
6 Therefore *it will be* night for
you—without vision,
And darkness for you—without
divination.
The sun will go down on the
prophets,
And the day will become dark
over them.
7 The seers will be ashamed
And the diviners will be embar-
rassed.
Indeed, they will all cover *their*
mouths
Because there is no answer from
God.
8 On the other hand I am filled with
power—
With the Spirit of the Lord—
And with justice and courage
To make known to Jacob his rebellious act,

Even to Israel his sin.
9 Now hear this, heads of the house
of Jacob
And rulers of the house of Israel,
Who abhor justice
And twist everything that is
straight,
10 Who build Zion with bloodshed
And Jerusalem with violent injustice.
11 Her leaders pronounce judgment
for a bribe,
Her priests instruct for a price,
And her prophets divine for
money.
Yet they lean on the Lord saying,
"Is not the Lord in our midst?
Calamity will not come upon us."
12 Therefore, on account of you,
Zion will be plowed as a field,
Jerusalem will become a heap of
ruins,
And the mountain of the temple
will become high places of a
forest.

CHAPTER 4

And it will come about in the last
days
That the mountain of the house of
the Lord
Will be established as the chief of
the mountains.
It will be raised above the hills,
And the peoples will stream to it.
2 And many nations will come and
say,
"Come and let us go up to the
mountain of the Lord
And to the house of the God of
Jacob,
That He may teach us about His
ways
And that we may walk in His
paths."
For from Zion will go forth the
law,
Even the word of the Lord from
Jerusalem.
3 And He will judge between many
peoples
And render decisions for mighty,
distant nations.
Then they will hammer their
swords into plowshares
And their spears into pruning
hooks;

Nation will not lift up sword
against nation,
And never again will they train
for war.
4 And each of them will sit under
his vine
And under his fig tree,
With no one to make *them* afraid,
For the mouth of the LORD of
hosts has spoken.
5 Though all the peoples walk
Each in the name of his god,
As for us, we will walk
In the name of the LORD our God
forever and ever.

6 ¶"In that day," declares the LORD,
"I will assemble the lame,
And gather the outcasts,
Even those whom I have afflicted.
7"I will make the lame a remnant,
And the outcasts a strong nation,
And the LORD will reign over
them in Mount Zion
From now on and forever.
8"And as for you, tower of the flock,
Hill of the daughter of Zion,
To you it will come—
Even the former dominion will
come,
The kingdom of the daughter of
Jerusalem.

9 ¶"Now, why do you cry out
loudly?
Is there no king among you,
Or has your counselor perished,
That agony has gripped you like a
woman in childbirth?
10"Writhe and labor to give birth,
Daughter of Zion,
Like a woman in childbirth,
For now you will go out of the
city,
Dwell in the field,
And go to Babylon.
There you will be rescued;
There the LORD will redeem you
From the hand of your enemies.
11"And now many nations have been
assembled against you
Who say, 'Let her be polluted,
And let our eyes gloat over Zion.'
12"But they do not know the
thoughts of the LORD,
And they do not understand His
purpose;
For He has gathered them like
sheaves to the threshing floor.

13"Arise and thresh, daughter of
Zion,
For your horn I will make iron
And your hoofs I will make
bronze,
That you may pulverize many
peoples,
That you may devote to the LORD
their unjust gain
And their wealth to the Lord of all
the earth.

CHAPTER 5

"NOW muster yourselves in troops,
daughter of troops;
They have laid siege against us;
With a rod they will smite the
judge of Israel on the cheek.
2"But as for you, Bethlehem Ephra-
thah,
Too little to be among the clans of
Judah,
From you One will go forth for Me
to be ruler in Israel.
His goings forth are from long
ago,
From the days of eternity."
3 Therefore, He will give them *up*
until the time
When she who is in labor has
borne a child.
Then the remainder of His breth-
ren
Will return to the sons of Israel.
4 And He will arise and shepherd
His flock
In the strength of the LORD,
In the majesty of the name of the
LORD His God.
And they will remain,
Because at that time He will be
great
To the ends of the earth.
5 And this One will be *our* peace.

¶ When the Assyrian invades our
land,
When he tramples on our citadels,
Then we will raise against him
Seven shepherds and eight leaders
of men.
6 And they will shepherd the land of
Assyria with the sword,
The land of Nimrod at its en-
trances;
And He will deliver *us* from the
Assyrian
When he attacks our land

And when he tramples our territory.

7 ¶ Then the remnant of Jacob
Will be among many peoples
Like dew from the LORD,
Like showers on vegetation
Which do not wait for man
Or delay for the sons of men.
8 And the remnant of Jacob
Will be among the nations,
Among many peoples
Like a lion among the beasts of
the forest,
Like a young lion among flocks of
sheep,
Which, if he passes through,
Tramples down and tears,
And there is none to rescue.
9 Your hand will be lifted up against
your adversaries,
And all your enemies will be cut
off.

10 ¶"And it will be in that day,"
declares the LORD,
"That I will cut off your horses
from among you
And destroy your chariots.
11"I will also cut off the cities of your
land
And tear down all your fortifications.
12"I will cut off sorceries from your
hand,
And you will have fortunetellers
no more.
13"I will cut off your carved images
And your *sacred* pillars from
among you,
So that you will no longer bow
down
To the work of your hands.
14"I will root out your Asherim from
among you
And destroy your cities.
15"And I will execute vengeance in
anger and wrath
On the nations which have not
obeyed."

CHAPTER 6

HEAR now what the LORD is saying,
"Arise, plead your case before the
mountains,
And let the hills hear your voice.
2"Listen, you mountains, to the indictment of the LORD,

And you enduring foundations of
the earth,
Because the LORD has a case
against His people;
Even with Israel He will dispute.
3"My people, what have I done to
you,
And how have I wearied you?
Answer Me.
4"Indeed, I brought you up from the
land of Egypt
And ransomed you from the
house of slavery,
And I sent before you Moses,
Aaron, and Miriam.
5"My people, remember now
What Balak king of Moab counseled
And what Balaam son of Beor
answered him,
And from Shittim to Gilgal,
In order that you might know the
righteous acts of the LORD."

6 ¶ With what shall I come to the
LORD
And bow myself before the God
on high?
Shall I come to Him with burnt
offerings,
With yearling calves?
7 Does the LORD take delight in
thousands of rams,
In ten thousand rivers of oil?
Shall I present my first-born *for*
my rebellious acts,
The fruit of my body for the sin of
my soul?
8 He has told you, O man, what is
good;
And what does the LORD require
of you
But to do justice, to love kindness,
And to walk humbly with your
God?

9 ¶ The voice of the LORD will call
to the city—
And it is sound wisdom to fear
Thy name:
"Hear, O tribe. Who has appointed
its time?
10"Is there yet a man in the wicked
house,
Along with treasures of wickedness,
And a short measure *that is*
cursed?

11"Can I justify wicked scales
    And a bag of deceptive weights?
12"For the rich men of *the* city are
    full of violence,
    Her residents speak lies,
    And their tongue is deceitful in
    their mouth.
13"So also I will make *you* sick, strik-
    ing you down,
    Desolating *you* because of your
    sins.
14"You will eat, but you will not be
    satisfied,
    And your [7]vileness will be in your
    midst.
    You will *try to* remove *for safe-*
    keeping,
    But you will not preserve *any-*
    thing,
    And what you do preserve I will
    give to the sword.
15"You will sow but you will not
    reap.
    You will tread the olive but will
    not anoint yourself with oil;
    And the grapes, but you will not
    drink wine.
16"The statutes of Omri
    And all the works of the house of
    Ahab are observed;
    And in their devices you walk.
    Therefore, I will give you up for
    destruction
    And your inhabitants for derision,
    And you will bear the reproach of
    My people."

CHAPTER 7

WOE is me! For I am
    Like the fruit pickers and the
    grape gatherers.
    There is not a cluster of grapes to
    eat,
    Or a first-ripe fig *which* I crave.
2 The godly person has perished
    from the land,
    And there is no upright *person*
    among men.
    All of them lie in wait for blood-
    shed;
    Each of them hunts the other
    with a net.
3 Concerning evil, both hands do it
    well.
    The prince asks, also the judge,
    for a bribe,

[7] Or possibly, *garbage* or *excreta*

And a great man speaks the desire
    of his soul;
    So they weave it together.
4 The best of them is like a briar,
    The most upright like a thorn
    hedge.
    The day when you post a watch-
    man,
    Your punishment will come.
    Then their confusion will occur.
5 Do not trust in a neighbor;
    Do not have confidence in a
    friend.
    From her who lies in your bosom
    Guard your lips.
6 For son treats father contemptu-
    ously,
    Daughter rises up against her
    mother,
    Daughter-in-law against her
    mother-in-law;
    A man's enemies are the men of
    his own household.

7 ¶ But as for me, I will watch ex-
    pectantly for the LORD;
    I will wait for the God of my
    salvation.
    My God will hear me.
8 Do not rejoice over me, O my
    enemy.
    Though I fall I will rise;
    Though I dwell in darkness, the
    LORD is a light for me.

9 ¶ I will bear the indignation of
    the LORD
    Because I have sinned against
    Him,
    Until He pleads my case and ex-
    ecutes justice for me.
    He will bring me out to the light,
    And I will see His righteousness.
10 Then my enemy will see,
    And shame will cover her who
    said to me,
   "Where is the LORD your God?"
    My eyes will look on her;
    At that time she will be trampled
    down,
    Like mire of the streets.
11 *It will be* a day for building your
    walls.
    On that day will your boundary be
    extended.
12 It *will be* a day when they will
    come to you
    From Assyria and the cities of
    Egypt,

From Egypt even to the Euphrates,
Even from sea to sea and mountain to mountain.
13 And the earth will become desolate because of her inhabitants,
On account of the fruit of their
deeds.

14 ¶ Shepherd Thy people with Thy
scepter,
The flock of Thy possession
Which dwells by itself in the
woodland,
In the midst of a fruitful field.
Let them feed in Bashan and Gilead
As in the days of old.
15 "As in the days when you came out
from the land of Egypt,
I will show you miracles."
16 Nations will see and be ashamed
Of all their might.
They will put *their* hand on *their*
mouth,
Their ears will be deaf.
17 They will lick the dust like a serpent,

Like reptiles of the earth.
They will come trembling out of
their fortresses;
To the LORD our God they will
come in dread,
And they will be afraid before
Thee.
18 Who is a God like Thee, who pardons iniquity
And passes over the rebellious act
of the remnant of His possession?
He does not retain His anger forever,
Because He delights in unchanging love.
19 He will again have compassion on
us;
He will tread our iniquities under
foot.
Yes, Thou wilt cast all their sins
Into the depths of the sea.
20 Thou wilt give truth to Jacob
And unchanging love to Abraham,
Which Thou didst swear to our
forefathers
From the days of old.

THE BOOK OF

NAHUM

THE ¹oracle of Nineveh. The book of
the vision of Nahum the Elkoshite.
2 ¶ A jealous and avenging God is
the LORD;
The LORD is avenging and wrathful.
The LORD takes vengeance on His
adversaries,
And He reserves wrath for His
enemies.
3 The LORD is slow to anger and
great in power,
And the LORD will by no means
leave *the guilty* unpunished.
In whirlwind and storm is His
way,
And clouds are the dust beneath
His feet.
4 He rebukes the sea and makes it
dry;

He dries up all the rivers.
Bashan and Carmel wither;
The blossoms of Lebanon wither.
5 Mountains quake because of Him,
And the hills dissolve;
Indeed the earth is upheaved by
His presence,
The world and all the inhabitants
in it.
6 Who can stand before His indig-
nation?
Who can endure the burning of
His anger?
His wrath is poured out like fire,
And the rocks are broken up by
Him.
7 The LORD is good,
A stronghold in the day of trouble,
And He knows those who take
refuge in Him.
8 But with an overflowing flood

¹ Or, *burden*

He will make a complete end of its
site,
And will pursue His enemies into
darkness.

9 ¶ Whatever you devise against
the LORD,
He will make a complete end of it.
Distress will not rise up twice.
10 Like tangled thorns,
And like those who are drunken
with their drink,
They are consumed
As stubble completely withered.
11 From you has gone forth
One who plotted evil against the
LORD,
A wicked counselor.
12 Thus says the LORD,
"Though they are at full *strength*
and likewise many,
Even so, they will be cut off and
pass away.
Though I have afflicted you,
I will afflict you no longer.
13 "So now, I will break his yoke bar
from upon you,
And I will tear off your shackles."

14 ¶ The LORD has issued a com-
mand concerning you:
"Your name will no longer be per-
petuated.
I will cut off idol and image
From the house of your gods.
I will prepare your grave,
For you are contemptible."

15 ¶ Behold, on the mountains the
feet of him who brings good
news,
Who announces peace!
Celebrate your feasts, O Judah;
Pay your vows.
For never again will the wicked
one pass through you;
He is cut off completely.

CHAPTER 2

THE one who scatters has come up
against you.
Man the fortress, watch the road;
Strengthen your back, summon
all *your* strength.
2 For the LORD will restore the
splendor of Jacob

Like the splendor of Israel,
Even though devastators have
devastated them
And destroyed their vine
branches.

3 ¶ The shields of his mighty men
are *colored* red,
The warriors are dressed in scar-
let,
The chariots are *enveloped* in
flashing steel
When he is prepared *to march*,
And the cypress *spears* are bran-
dished.
4 The chariots race madly in the
streets,
They rush wildly in the squares,
Their appearance is like torches,
They dash to and fro like light-
ning flashes.
5 He remembers his nobles;
They stumble in their march,
They hurry to her wall,
And the mantelet is set up.
6 The gates of the rivers are opened,
And the palace is dissolved.
7 And it is fixed:
She is stripped, she is carried
away,
And her handmaids are moaning
like the sound of doves,
Beating on their breasts.

8 ¶ Though Nineveh *was* like a pool
of water throughout her days,
Now they are fleeing;
"Stop, stop,"
But no one turns back.
9 Plunder the silver!
Plunder the gold!
For there is no limit to the trea-
sure—
Wealth from every kind of desir-
able object.
10 She is emptied! Yes, she is deso-
late and waste!
Hearts are melting and knees
knocking!
Also anguish is in the whole body,
And all their faces are grown pale!
11 Where is the den of the lions
And the feeding place of the
young lions,
Where the lion, lioness, and lion's
cub prowled,
With nothing to disturb *them*?

12 The lion tore enough for his cubs,
     Killed *enough* for his lionesses,
     And filled his lairs with prey
     And his dens with torn flesh.
13 "Behold, I am against you," declares the LORD of hosts. "I will burn
up her chariots in smoke, a sword will
devour your young lions, I will cut off
your prey from the land, and no longer
will the voice of your messengers be
heard."

CHAPTER 3

WOE to the bloody city, completely
     full of lies *and* pillage;
     Her prey never departs.
 2 The noise of the whip,
     The noise of the rattling of the
         wheel,
     Galloping horses,
     And bounding chariots!
 3 Horsemen charging,
     Swords flashing, spears gleaming,
     Many slain, a mass of corpses,
     And countless dead bodies—
     They stumble over the dead bod-
         ies!
 4 *All* because of the many harlotries
         of the harlot,
     The charming one, the mistress of
         sorceries,
     Who sells nations by her harlot-
         ries
     And families by her sorceries.
 5 "Behold, I am against you," de-
     clares the LORD of hosts;
     "And I will lift up your skirts over
         your face,
     And show to the nations your
         nakedness
     And to the kingdoms your dis-
         grace.
 6 "I will throw filth on you
     And make you vile,
     And set you up as a spectacle.
 7 "And it will come about that all
         who see you
     Will shrink from you and say,
     'Nineveh is devastated!
     Who will grieve for her?'
     Where will I seek comforters for
         you?"

 8 ¶ Are you better than ²No-amon,
     Which was situated by the waters
         of the Nile,

With water surrounding her,
     Whose rampart *was* the sea,
     Whose wall *consisted* of the sea?
 9 Ethiopia was *her* might,
     And Egypt too, without limits.
     Put and Lubim were among her
         helpers.
10 Yet she became an exile,
     She went into captivity;
     Also her small children were
         dashed to pieces
     At the head of every street;
     They cast lots for her honorable
         men,
     And all her great men were bound
         with fetters.
11 You too will become drunk,
     You will be hidden.
     You too will search for a refuge
         from the enemy.
12 All your fortifications are fig trees
         with ripe fruit—
     When shaken, they fall into the
         eater's mouth.
13 Behold, your people are women in
         your midst!
     The gates of your land are opened
         wide to your enemies;
     Fire consumes your gate bars.
14 Draw for yourself water for the
         siege!
     Strengthen your fortifications!
     Go into the clay and tread the
         mortar!
     Take hold of the brick mold!
15 There fire will consume you,
     The sword will cut you down;
     It will consume you as the locust
         does.

 ¶ Multiply yourself like the creeping
         locust,
     Multiply yourself like the swarm-
         ing locust.
16 You have increased your traders
         more than the stars of heaven—
     The creeping locust strips and
         flies away.
17 Your guardsmen are like the
         swarming locust.
     Your marshals are like hordes of
         grasshoppers
     Settling in the stone walls on a
         cold day.
     The sun rises and they flee,
     And the place where they are is
         not known.

² I.e., the city of Amon: Thebes

18 Your shepherds are sleeping, O
    king of Assyria;
Your nobles are lying down.
Your people are scattered on the
    mountains,
And there is no one to regather
    them.

19 There is no relief for your break-
    down,
Your wound is incurable.
All who hear about you
Will clap *their* hands over you,
For on whom has not your evil
    passed continually?

THE BOOK OF

HABAKKUK

THE ¹oracle which Habakkuk the
prophet saw.
2 ¶ How long, O LORD, will I call for
    help,
And Thou wilt not hear?
I cry out to Thee, "Violence!"
Yet Thou dost not save.
3 Why dost Thou make me see iniq-
    uity,
And cause *me* to look on wicked-
    ness?
Yes, destruction and violence are
    before me;
Strife exists and contention arises.
4 Therefore, the law is ignored
And justice is never upheld.
For the wicked surround the
    righteous;
Therefore, justice comes out per-
    verted.

5 ¶"Look among the nations! Ob-
    serve!
Be astonished! Wonder!
Because *I* am doing something in
    your days—
You would not believe if you were
    told.
6"For behold, I am raising up the
    Chaldeans,
That fierce and impetuous people
Who march throughout the earth
To seize dwelling places which are
    not theirs.
7"They are dreaded and feared.
Their justice and authority origi-
    nate with themselves.
8"Their horses are swifter than leop-
    ards
And keener than wolves in the
    evening.

Their horsemen come galloping,
Their horsemen come from afar;
They fly like an eagle swooping
    down to devour.
9"All of them come for violence.
Their horde of faces *moves* for-
    ward.
They collect captives like sand.
10"They mock at kings,
And rulers are a laughing matter
    to them.
They laugh at every fortress,
And heap up rubble to capture it.
11"Then they will sweep through *like*
    the wind and pass on.
But they will be held guilty,
They whose strength is their god."

12 ¶ Art Thou not from everlasting,
O LORD, my God, my Holy One?
We will not die.
Thou, O LORD, hast appointed
    them to judge;
And Thou, O Rock, hast estab-
    lished them to correct.
13 *Thine* eyes are too pure to ap-
    prove evil,
And Thou canst not look on wick-
    edness *with favor.*
Why dost Thou look with favor
On those who deal treacherously?
Why art Thou silent when the
    wicked swallow up
Those more righteous than they?
14 *Why* hast Thou made men like
    the fish of the sea,
Like creeping things without a
    ruler over them?
15 *The Chaldeans* bring all of them
    up with a hook,
Drag them away with their net,
And gather them together in their
    fishing net.

¹ Or, *burden*

Therefore, they rejoice and are glad.

16 Therefore, they offer a sacrifice to their net.
And burn incense to their fishing net;
Because through these things their catch is large,
And their food is plentiful.

17 Will they therefore empty their net
And continually slay nations without sparing?

CHAPTER 2

I WILL stand on my guard post
And station myself on the rampart;
And I will keep watch to see what He will speak to me,
And how I may reply when I am reproved.

2 Then the LORD answered me and said,
"Record the vision
And inscribe it on tablets,
That the one who reads it may run.

3"For the vision is yet for the appointed time;
It hastens toward the goal, and it will not fail.
Though it tarries, wait for it;
For it will certainly come, it will not delay.

4 ¶"Behold, as for the proud one,
His soul is not right within him;
But the righteous will live by his faith.

5"Furthermore, wine betrays the haughty man,
So that he does not stay at home.
He enlarges his appetite like Sheol,
And he is like death, never satisfied.
He also gathers to himself all nations
And collects to himself all peoples.

6 ¶"Will not all of these take up a taunt-song against him,
Even mockery and insinuations against him,
And say, 'Woe to him who increases what is not his—
For how long—

And makes himself rich with loans?'

7"Will not your creditors rise up suddenly,
And those who collect from you awaken?
Indeed, you will become plunder for them.

8"Because you have looted many nations,
All the remainder of the peoples will loot you—
Because of human bloodshed and violence done to the land,
To the town and all its inhabitants.

9 ¶"Woe to him who gets evil gain for his house
To put his nest on high
To be delivered from the hand of calamity!

10"You have devised a shameful thing for your house
By cutting off many peoples;
So you are sinning against yourself.

11"Surely the stone will cry out from the wall,
And the rafter will answer it from the framework.

12 ¶"Woe to him who builds a city with bloodshed
And founds a town with violence!

13"Is it not indeed from the LORD of hosts
That peoples toil for fire,
And nations grow weary for nothing?

14"For the earth will be filled
With the knowledge of the glory of the LORD,
As the waters cover the sea.

15 ¶"Woe to you who make your neighbors drink,
Who mix in your venom even to make them drunk
So as to look on their nakedness!

16"You will be filled with disgrace rather than honor.
Now you yourself drink and expose your own nakedness.
The cup in the LORD's right hand will come around to you,
And utter disgrace will come upon your glory.

17"For the violence done to Lebanon will overwhelm you,

And the devastation of *its* beasts
by which you terrified them,
Because of human bloodshed and
violence done to the land,
To the town and all its inhabitants.

18 ¶"What profit is the idol when its
maker has carved it,
Or an image, a teacher of falsehood?
For *its* maker trusts in his *own*
handiwork
When he fashions speechless
idols.
19"Woe to him who says to a *piece of*
wood, 'Awake!'
To a dumb stone, 'Arise!'
And that is *your* teacher?
Behold, it is overlaid with gold
and silver,
And there is no breath at all inside
it.
20"But the Lord is in His holy temple.
Let all the earth be silent before
Him."

CHAPTER 3

A PRAYER of Habakkuk the
prophet, according to ²Shigionoth.
2 ¶ Lord, I have heard the report
about Thee *and* I fear.
O Lord, revive Thy work in the
midst of the years,
In the midst of the years make it
known;
In wrath remember mercy.

3 ¶ God comes from Teman,
And the Holy One from Mount
Paran.   [Selah.
His splendor covers the heavens,
And the earth is full of His praise.
4 *His* radiance is like the sunlight;
He has rays *flashing* from His
hand,
And there is the hiding of His
power.
5 Before Him goes pestilence,
And plague comes after Him.
6 He stood and surveyed the earth;
He looked and startled the na-
tions.
Yes, the perpetual mountains
were shattered,
The ancient hills collapsed.
His ways are everlasting.

² I.e., A highly emotional poetic form

7 I saw the tents of Cushan under
distress,
The tent curtains of the land of
Midian were trembling.

8 ¶ Did the Lord rage against the
rivers,
Or *was* Thine anger against the
rivers,
Or *was* Thy wrath against the sea,
That Thou didst ride on Thy
horses,
On Thy chariots of salvation?
9 Thy bow was made bare,
The rods of chastisement were
sworn.   [Selah.
Thou didst cleave the earth with
rivers.
10 The mountains saw Thee *and*
quaked;
The downpour of waters swept
by.
The deep uttered forth its voice,
It lifted high its hands.
11 Sun *and* moon stood in their
places;
They went away at the light of
Thine arrows,
At the radiance of Thy gleaming
spear.
12 In indignation Thou didst march
through the earth;
In anger Thou didst trample the
nations.
13 Thou didst go forth for the salvation of Thy people,
For the salvation of Thine
anointed.
Thou didst strike the head of the
house of the evil
To lay him open from thigh to
neck.   [Selah.
14 Thou didst pierce with his own
spears
The head of his throngs.
They stormed in to scatter us;
Their exultation *was* like those
Who devour the oppressed in secret.
15 Thou didst tread on the sea with
Thy horses,
On the surge of many waters.

16 ¶ I heard and my inward parts
trembled,
At the sound my lips quivered.
Decay enters my bones,

And in my place I tremble.
Because I must wait quietly for
the day of distress,
For the people to arise *who* will
invade us.

17 Though the fig tree should not
blossom,
And there be no fruit on the vines,
Though the yield of the olive
should fail,
And the fields produce no food,
Though the flock should be cut off
from the fold,

And there be no cattle in the
stalls,

18 Yet I will exult in the LORD,
I will rejoice in the God of my
salvation.

19 The Lord GOD is my strength,
And He has made my feet like
hinds' *feet,*
And makes me walk on my high
places.

For the choir director, on my stringed
instruments.

THE BOOK OF

ZEPHANIAH

THE word of the LORD which came to
Zephaniah son of Cushi, son of Gedaliah, son of Amariah, son of Hezekiah,
in the days of Josiah son of Amon,
king of Judah,

2 ¶"I will completely remove all
things
From the face of the earth," declares the LORD.

3 "I will remove man and beast;
I will remove the birds of the sky
And the fish of the sea,
And the ruins along with the
wicked;
And I will cut off man from the
face of the earth," declares the
LORD.

4 "So I will stretch out My hand
against Judah
And against all the inhabitants of
Jerusalem.
And I will cut off the remnant of
Baal from this place,
And the names of the idolatrous
priests along with the priests.

5 "And those who bow down on the
housetops to the host of
heaven,
And those who bow down *and*
swear to the LORD and *yet*
swear by Milcom,

6 And those who have turned back
from following the LORD,
And those who have not sought
the LORD or inquired of Him."

7 ¶ Be silent before the Lord GOD!
For the day of the LORD is near,
For the LORD has prepared a sacri-
fice,
He has consecrated His guests.

8 "Then it will come about on the
day of the LORD's sacrifice,
That I will punish the princes, the
king's sons,
And all who clothe themselves
with foreign garments.

9 "And I will punish on that day all
who leap on the *temple* threshold,
Who fill the house of their lord
with violence and deceit.

10 "And on that day," declares the
LORD,
"There will be the sound of a cry
from the Fish Gate,
A wail from the [1]Second Quarter,
And a loud crash from the hills.

11 "Wail, O inhabitants of the [1]Mor-
tar,
For all the people of Canaan will
be silenced;
All who weigh out silver will be
cut off.

12 "And it will come about at that
time
That I will search Jerusalem with
lamps,
And I will punish the men
Who are stagnant in spirit,
Who say in their hearts,

[1] I.e., a district of Jerusalem

'The LORD will not do good or evil!'
13"Moreover, their wealth will become plunder,
And their houses desolate;
Yes, they will build houses but not inhabit *them*,
And plant vineyards but not drink their wine."

14 ¶ Near is the great day of the LORD,
Near and coming very quickly;
Listen, the day of the LORD!
In it the warrior cries out bitterly.
15 A day of wrath is that day,
A day of trouble and distress,
A day of destruction and desolation,
A day of darkness and gloom,
A day of clouds and thick darkness,
16 A day of trumpet and battle cry,
Against the fortified cities
And the high corner towers.
17 And I will bring distress on men,
So that they will walk like the blind,
Because they have sinned against the LORD;
And their blood will be poured out like dust,
And their flesh like dung.
18 Neither their silver nor their gold
Will be able to deliver them
On the day of the LORD's wrath;
And all the earth will be devoured
In the fire of His jealousy,
For He will make a complete end,
Indeed a terrifying one,
Of all the inhabitants of the earth.

CHAPTER 2

GATHER yourselves together, yes, gather,
O nation without shame,
2 Before the decree takes effect—
The day passes like the chaff—
Before the burning anger of the LORD comes upon you,
Before the day of the LORD's anger comes upon you.
3 Seek the LORD,
All you humble of the earth
Who have carried out His ordinances;
Seek righteousness, seek humility.
Perhaps you will be hidden
In the day of the LORD's anger.

4 ¶ For Gaza will be abandoned,
And Ashkelon a desolation;
Ashdod will be driven out at noon,
And Ekron will be uprooted.
5 Woe to the inhabitants of the seacoast,
The nation of the ²Cherethites!
The word of the LORD is against you,
O Canaan, land of the Philistines;
And I will destroy you,
So that there will be no inhabitant.
6 So the seacoast will be pastures,
With caves for shepherds and folds for flocks.
7 And the coast will be
For the remnant of the house of Judah,
They will pasture on it.
In the houses of Ashkelon they will lie down at evening;
For the LORD their God will care for them
And restore their fortune.

8 ¶"I have heard the taunting of Moab
And the revilings of the sons of Ammon,
With which they have taunted My people
And become arrogant against their territory.
9"Therefore, as I live," declares the LORD of hosts,
The God of Israel,
"Surely Moab will be like Sodom,
And the sons of Ammon like Gomorrah—
A place possessed by nettles and salt pits,
And a perpetual desolation.
The remnant of My people will plunder them,
And the remainder of My nation will inherit them."
10 This they will have in return for their pride, because they have taunted and become arrogant against the people of the LORD of hosts.
11 The LORD will be terrifying to them, for He will starve all the gods of the earth; and all the coastlands of the nations will bow down to Him, everyone from his *own* place.

² I.e., a segment of the Philistines with roots in Crete

12 ¶"You also, O Ethiopians, will be slain by My sword."
13 And He will stretch out His hand against the north
And destroy Assyria,
And He will make Nineveh a desolation,
Parched like the wilderness.
14 And flocks will lie down in her midst,
All beasts which range in herds;
Both the pelican and the hedgehog
Will lodge in the tops of her pillars;
Birds will sing in the window,
Desolation *will be* on the threshold;
For He has laid bare the cedar work.
15 This is the exultant city
Which dwells securely,
Who says in her heart,
"I am, and there is no one besides me."
How she has become a desolation,
A resting place for beasts!
Everyone who passes by her will hiss
And wave his hand *in contempt.*

CHAPTER 3

WOE to her who is rebellious and defiled,
The tyrannical city!
2 She heeded no voice;
She accepted no instruction.
She did not trust in the LORD;
She did not draw near to her God.
3 Her princes within her are roaring lions,
Her judges are wolves at evening;
They leave nothing for the morning.
4 Her prophets are reckless, treacherous men;
Her priests have profaned the sanctuary.
They have done violence to the law.
5 The LORD is righteous within her;
He will do no injustice.
Every morning He brings His justice to light;
He does not fail.
But the unjust knows no shame.
6 "I have cut off nations;
Their corner towers are in ruins.

I have made their streets desolate,
With no one passing by;
Their cities are laid waste,
Without a man, without an inhabitant.
7 "I said, 'Surely you will revere Me,
Accept instruction.'
So her dwelling will not be cut off
According to all that I have appointed concerning her.
But they were eager to corrupt all their deeds.

8 ¶"Therefore, wait for Me," declares the LORD,
"For the day when I rise up to the prey.
Indeed, My decision is to gather nations,
To assemble kingdoms,
To pour out on them My indignation,
All My burning anger;
For all the earth will be devoured
By the fire of My zeal.
9 "For then I will give to the peoples purified lips,
That all of them may call on the name of the LORD,
To serve Him shoulder to shoulder.
10 "From beyond the rivers of Ethiopia
My worshipers, My dispersed ones,
Will bring My offerings.
11 "In that day you will feel no shame
Because of all your deeds
By which you have rebelled against Me;
For then I will remove from your midst
Your proud, exulting ones,
And you will never again be haughty
On My holy mountain.
12 "But I will leave among you
A humble and lowly people,
And they will take refuge in the name of the LORD.
13 "The remnant of Israel will do no wrong
And tell no lies,
Nor will a deceitful tongue
Be found in their mouths;
For they shall feed and lie down
With no one to make them tremble."

14 ¶ Shout for joy, O daughter of
Zion!
Shout *in triumph,* O Israel!
Rejoice and exult with all *your*
heart,
O daughter of Jerusalem!
15 The Lord has taken away *His*
judgments against you,
He has cleared away your en-
emies.
The King of Israel, the Lord, is in
your midst;
You will fear disaster no more.
16 In that day it will be said to Jeru-
salem:
"Do not be afraid, O Zion;
Do not let your hands fall limp.
17"The Lord your God is in your
midst,
A victorious warrior.
He will exult over you with joy,
He will be quiet in His love,
He will rejoice over you with
shouts of joy.

18"I will gather those who grieve
about the appointed feasts—
They came from you, O *Zion;*
The reproach *of exile* is a burden
on them.
19"Behold, I am going to deal at that
time
With all your oppressors,
I will save the lame
And gather the outcast,
And I will turn their shame into
praise and renown
In all the earth.
20"At that time I will bring you in,
Even at the time when I gather
you together;
Indeed, I will give you renown
and praise
Among all the peoples of the
earth,
When I restore your fortunes be-
fore your eyes,"
Says the Lord.

THE BOOK OF

HAGGAI

IN the second year of Darius the king,
on the first day of the sixth month, the
word of the Lord came by the prophet
Haggai to Zerubbabel the son of
Shealtiel, governor of Judah, and to
Joshua the son of Jehozadak, the high
priest saying,

2"Thus says the Lord of hosts, 'This
people says, "The time has not come,
even the time for the house of the
Lord to be rebuilt." ' "

3 Then the word of the Lord came
by Haggai the prophet saying,

4"Is it time for you yourselves to
dwell in your paneled houses while
this house *lies* desolate?"

5 Now therefore, thus says the
Lord of hosts, "Consider your ways!

6"You have sown much, but harvest
little; *you* eat, but *there is* not *enough*
to be satisfied; *you* drink, but *there is*
not *enough* to become drunk; *you* put
on clothing, but no one is warm
enough; and he who earns, earns
wages *to put* into a purse with holes."

7 ¶ Thus says the Lord of hosts,
"Consider your ways!

8"Go up to the mountains, bring
wood and rebuild the temple, that I
may be pleased with it and be glorified," says the Lord.

9"*You* look for much, but behold, *it*
comes to little; when you bring *it*
home, I blow it *away.* Why?" declares
the Lord of hosts, "Because of My
house which *lies* desolate, while each
of you runs to his own house.

10"Therefore, because of you the sky
has withheld its dew, and the earth
has withheld its produce.

11"And I called for a drought on the
land, on the mountains, on the grain,
on the new wine, on the oil, on what
the ground produces, on men, on cattle, and on all the labor of your
hands."

12 ¶ Then Zerubbabel the son of
Shealtiel, and Joshua the son of Jehozadak, the high priest, with all the
remnant of the people, obeyed
the voice of the Lord their God and

the words of Haggai the prophet, as the LORD their God had sent him. And the people showed reverence for the LORD.

13 Then Haggai, the messenger of the LORD, spoke by the commission of the LORD to the people saying, " 'I am with you,' declares the LORD."

14 So the LORD stirred up the spirit of Zerubbabel the son of Shealtiel, governor of Judah, and the spirit of Joshua the son of Jehozadak, the high priest, and the spirit of all the remnant of the people; and they came and worked on the house of the LORD of hosts, their God,

15 on the twenty-fourth day of the sixth month in the second year of Darius the king.

CHAPTER 2

ON the twenty-first of the seventh month, the word of the LORD came by Haggai the prophet saying,

2"Speak now to Zerubbabel the son of Shealtiel, governor of Judah, and to Joshua the son of Jehozadak, the high priest, and to the remnant of the people saying,

3 'Who is left among you who saw this temple in its former glory? And how do you see it now? Does it not seem to you like nothing in comparison?

4 'But now take courage, Zerubbabel,' declares the LORD, 'take courage also, Joshua son of Jehozadak, the high priest, and all you people of the land take courage,' declares the LORD, 'and work; for I am with you,' says the LORD of hosts.

5 'As for the promise which I made you when you came out of Egypt, My Spirit is abiding in your midst; do not fear!'

6"For thus says the LORD of hosts, 'Once more in a little while, I am going to shake the heavens and the earth, the sea also and the dry land.

7 'And I will shake all the nations; and they will come with the wealth of all nations; and I will fill this house with glory,' says the LORD of hosts.

8 'The silver is Mine, and the gold is Mine,' declares the LORD of hosts.

9 'The latter glory of this house will be greater than the former,' says the LORD of hosts, 'and in this place I shall give peace,' declares the LORD of hosts."

10 ¶ On the twenty-fourth of the ninth *month,* in the second year of Darius, the word of the LORD came to Haggai the prophet saying,

11"Thus says the LORD of hosts, 'Ask now the priests *for* a ruling:

12 'If a man carries holy meat in the fold of his garment, and touches bread with this fold, or cooked food, wine, oil, or any *other* food, will it become holy?' " And the priests answered and said, "No."

13 Then Haggai said, "If one who is unclean from a corpse touches any of these, will *the latter* become unclean?" And the priests answered and said, "It will become unclean."

14 Then Haggai answered and said, " 'So is this people. And so is this nation before Me,' declares the LORD, 'and so is every work of their hands; and what they offer there is unclean.

15 'But now, do consider from this day onward: before one stone was placed on another in the temple of the LORD,

16 from that time *when* one came to a *grain* heap of twenty *measures,* there would be only ten; and *when* one came to the wine vat to draw fifty measures, there would be *only* twenty.

17 'I smote you *and* every work of your hands with blasting wind, mildew, and hail; yet you *did* not *come back* to Me,' declares the LORD.

18 'Do consider from this day onward, from the twenty-fourth day of the ninth *month;* from the day when the temple of the LORD was founded, consider:

19 'Is the seed still in the barn? Even including the vine, the fig tree, the pomegranate, and the olive tree, it has not borne *fruit.* Yet from this day on I will bless *you.*' "

20 ¶ Then the word of the LORD came a second time to Haggai on the twenty-fourth *day* of the month saying,

21"Speak to Zerubbabel governor of Judah saying, 'I am going to shake the heavens and the earth.

22 'And I will overthrow the thrones of kingdoms and destroy the power of the kingdoms of the nations; and I will

overthrow the chariots and their riders, and the horses and their riders will go down, everyone by the sword of another.'

23 'On that day,' declares the LORD of hosts, 'I will take you, Zerubbabel, son of Shealtiel, my servant,' declares the LORD, 'and I will make you like a signet *ring*, for I have chosen you,'" declares the LORD of hosts.

THE BOOK OF

ZECHARIAH

IN the eighth month of the second year of Darius, the word of the LORD came to Zechariah the prophet, the son of Berechiah, the son of Iddo saying,

2"The LORD was very angry with your fathers.

3"Therefore say to them, 'Thus says the LORD of hosts, "Return to Me," declares the LORD of hosts, "that I may return to you," says the LORD of hosts.

4"Do not be like your fathers, to whom the former prophets proclaimed, saying, 'Thus says the LORD of hosts, "Return now from your evil ways and from your evil deeds."' But they did not listen or give heed to Me," declares the LORD.

5"Your fathers, where are they? And the prophets, do they live forever?

6"But did not My words and My statutes, which I commanded My servants the prophets, overtake your fathers? Then they repented and said, 'As the LORD of hosts purposed to do to us in accordance with our ways and our deeds, so He has dealt with us.'"'"

7 ¶ On the twenty-fourth day of the eleventh month, which is the month Shebat, in the second year of Darius, the word of the LORD came to Zechariah the prophet, the son of Berechiah, the son of Iddo, as follows:

8 I saw at night, and behold, a man was riding on a red horse, and he was standing among the myrtle trees which were in the ravine, with red, sorrel, and white horses behind him.

9 Then I said, "My lord, what are these?" And the angel who was speaking with me said to me, "I will show you what these are."

10 And the man who was standing among the myrtle trees answered and said, "These are those whom the LORD has sent to patrol the earth."

11 So they answered the angel of the LORD who was standing among the myrtle trees, and said, "We have patrolled the earth, and behold, all the earth is peaceful and quiet."

12 ¶ Then the angel of the LORD answered and said, "O LORD of hosts, how long wilt Thou have no compassion for Jerusalem and the cities of Judah, with which Thou hast been indignant these seventy years?"

13 And the LORD answered the angel who was speaking with me with gracious words, comforting words.

14 So the angel who was speaking with me said to me, "Proclaim, saying, 'Thus says the LORD of hosts, "I am exceedingly jealous for Jerusalem and Zion.

15"But I am very angry with the nations who are at ease; for while I was only a little angry, they furthered the disaster."

16"Therefore, thus says the LORD, "I will return to Jerusalem with compassion; My house will be built in it," declares the LORD of hosts, "and a measuring line will be stretched over Jerusalem."'

17"Again, proclaim, saying, 'Thus says the LORD of hosts, "My cities will again overflow with prosperity, and the LORD will again comfort Zion and again choose Jerusalem."'"

18 ¶ Then I lifted up my eyes and looked, and behold, *there were* four horns.

19 So I said to the angel who was speaking with me, "What are these?" And he answered me, "These are the

horns which have scattered Judah, Israel, and Jerusalem."

20 Then the LORD showed me four craftsmen.

21 And I said, "What are these coming to do?" And he said, "These are the horns which have scattered Judah, so that no man lifts up his head; but these *craftsmen* have come to terrify them, to throw down the horns of the nations who have lifted up *their* horns against the land of Judah in order to scatter it."

CHAPTER 2

THEN I lifted up my eyes and looked, and behold, *there was* a man with a measuring line in his hand.

2 So I said, "Where are you going?" And he said to me, "To measure Jerusalem, to see how wide it is and how long it is."

3 And behold, the angel who was speaking with me was going out, and another angel was coming out to meet him,

4 and said to him, "Run, speak to that young man, saying, 'Jerusalem will be inhabited without walls, because of the multitude of men and cattle within it.

5 'For I,' declares the LORD, 'will be a wall of fire around her, and I will be the glory in her midst.' "

6 ¶"Ho there! Flee from the land of the north," declares the LORD, "for I have dispersed you as the four winds of the heavens," declares the LORD.

7 "Ho, Zion! Escape, you who are living with the daughter of Babylon."

8 For thus says the LORD of hosts, "After glory He has sent me against the nations which plunder you, for he who touches you, touches the apple of His eye.

9 "For behold, I will wave My hand over them, so that they will be plunder for their slaves. Then you will know that the LORD of hosts has sent Me.

10 "Sing for joy and be glad, O daughter of Zion; for behold I am coming and I will dwell in your midst," declares the LORD.

11 "And many nations will join themselves to the LORD in that day and will become My people. Then I will dwell in your midst, and you will know that the LORD of hosts has sent Me to you.

12 "And the LORD will possess Judah as His portion in the holy land, and will again choose Jerusalem.

13 "Be silent, all flesh, before the LORD; for He is aroused from His holy habitation."

CHAPTER 3

THEN he showed me Joshua the high priest standing before the angel of the LORD, and Satan standing at his right hand to accuse him.

2 And the LORD said to Satan, "The LORD rebuke you, Satan! Indeed, the LORD who has chosen Jerusalem rebuke you! Is this not a brand plucked from the fire?"

3 Now Joshua was clothed with filthy garments and standing before the angel.

4 And he spoke and said to those who were standing before him saying, "Remove the filthy garments from him." Again he said to him, "See, I have taken your iniquity away from you and will clothe you with festal robes."

5 Then I said, "Let them put a clean turban on his head." So they put a clean turban on his head and clothed him with garments, while the angel of the LORD was standing by.

6 ¶ And the angel of the LORD admonished Joshua saying,

7 "Thus says the LORD of hosts, 'If you will walk in My ways, and if you will perform My service, then you will also govern My house and also have charge of My courts, and I will grant you free access among these who are standing *here*.

8 'Now listen, Joshua the high priest, you and your friends who are sitting in front of you—indeed they are men who are a symbol, for behold, I am going to bring in My servant the Branch.

9 'For behold, the stone that I have set before Joshua; on one stone are seven eyes. Behold, I will engrave an inscription on it,' declares the LORD of hosts, 'and I will remove the iniquity of that land in one day.

10 'In that day,' declares the LORD of hosts, 'every one of you will invite his neighbor to *sit* under *his* vine and under *his* fig tree.' "

CHAPTER 4

THEN the angel who was speaking with me returned, and roused me as a man who is awakened from his sleep.

2 And he said to me, "What do you see?" And I said, "I see, and behold, a lampstand all of gold with its bowl on the top of it, and its seven lamps on it with seven spouts belonging to each of the lamps which are on the top of it;

3 also two olive trees by it, one on the right side of the bowl and the other on its left side."

4 Then I answered and said to the angel who was speaking with me saying, "What are these, my lord?"

5 So the angel who was speaking with me answered and said to me, "Do you not know what these are?" And I said, "No, my lord."

6 Then he answered and said to me, "This is the word of the LORD to Zerubbabel saying, 'Not by might nor by power, but by My Spirit,' says the LORD of hosts.

7 'What are you, O great mountain? Before Zerubbabel *you will become* a plain; and he will bring forth the top stone with shouts of "Grace, grace to it!"'"

8 Also the word of the LORD came to me saying,

9 "The hands of Zerubbabel have laid the foundation of this house, and his hands will finish *it*. Then you will know that the LORD of hosts has sent me to you.

10 "For who has despised the day of small things? But these seven will be glad when they see the plumb line in the hand of Zerubbabel—*these are* the eyes of the LORD which range to and fro throughout the earth."

11 ¶ Then I answered and said to him, "What are these two olive trees on the right of the lampstand and on its left?"

12 And I answered the second time and said to him, "What are the two olive branches which are beside the two golden pipes, which empty the golden *oil* from themselves?"

13 So he answered me saying, "Do you not know what these are?" And I said, "No, my lord."

14 Then he said, "These are the two anointed ones, who are standing by the Lord of the whole earth."

CHAPTER 5

THEN I lifted up my eyes again and looked, and behold, *there was* a flying scroll.

2 And he said to me, "What do you see?" And I answered, "I see a flying scroll; its length is twenty cubits and its width ten cubits."

3 Then he said to me, "This is the curse that is going forth over the face of the whole land; surely everyone who steals will be purged away according to the writing on one side, and everyone who swears will be purged away according to the writing on the other side.

4 "I will make it go forth," declares the LORD of hosts, "and it will enter the house of the thief and the house of the one who swears falsely by My name; and it will spend the night within that house and consume it with its timber and stones."

5 ¶ Then the angel who was speaking with me went out, and said to me, "Lift up now your eyes, and see what this is, going forth."

6 And I said, "What is it?" And he said, "This is the ephah going forth." Again he said, "This is their appearance in all the land

7 (and behold, a lead cover was lifted up); and this is a woman sitting inside the ephah."

8 Then he said, "This is Wickedness!" And he threw her down into the middle of the ephah and cast the lead weight on its opening.

9 Then I lifted up my eyes and looked, and there two women were coming out with the wind in their wings; and they had wings like the wings of a stork, and they lifted up the ephah between the earth and the heavens.

10 And I said to the angel who was speaking with me, "Where are they taking the ephah?"

11 Then he said to me, "To build a temple for her in the land of Shinar; and when it is prepared, she will be set there on her own pedestal."

CHAPTER 6

NOW I lifted up my eyes again and looked, and behold, four chariots were coming forth from between the two mountains; and the mountains *were* bronze mountains.

2 With the first chariot *were* red horses, with the second chariot black horses,

3 with the third chariot white horses, and with the fourth chariot strong dappled horses.

4 Then I spoke and said to the angel who was speaking with me, "What are these, my lord?"

5 And the angel answered and said to me, "These are the four spirits of heaven, going forth after standing before the Lord of all the earth,

6 with one of which the black horses are going forth to the north country; and the white ones go forth after them, while the dappled ones go forth to the south country.

7"When the strong ones went out, they were eager to go to patrol the earth." And He said, "Go, patrol the earth." So they patrolled the earth.

8 Then He cried out to me and spoke to me saying, "See, those who are going to the land of the north have appeased My wrath in the land of the north."

9 ¶ The word of the LORD also came to me saying,

10"Take *an offering* from the exiles, from Heldai, Tobijah, and Jedaiah; and you go the same day and enter the house of Josiah the son of Zephaniah, where they have arrived from Babylon.

11"And take silver and gold, make an *ornate* crown, and set *it* on the head of Joshua the son of Jehozadak, the high priest.

12"Then say to him, 'Thus says the LORD of hosts, "Behold, a man whose name is Branch, for He will branch out from where He is; and He will build the temple of the LORD.

13"Yes, it is He who will build the temple of the LORD, and He who will bear the honor and sit and rule on His throne. Thus, He will be a priest on His throne, and the counsel of peace will be between the two offices." '

14"Now the crown will become a reminder in the temple of the LORD to Helem, Tobijah, Jedaiah, and Hen the son of Zephaniah.

15"And those who are far off will come and build the temple of the

LORD." Then you will know that the LORD of hosts has sent me to you. And it will take place, if you completely obey the LORD your God.

CHAPTER 7

THEN it came about in the fourth year of King Darius, that the word of the LORD came to Zechariah on the fourth *day* of the ninth month, *which is* Chislev.

2 Now *the town of* Bethel had sent Sharezer and Regemmelech and their men to seek the favor of the LORD,

3 speaking to the priests who belong to the house of the LORD of hosts, and to the prophets saying, "Shall I weep in the fifth month and abstain, as I have done these many years?"

4 Then the word of the LORD of hosts came to me saying,

5"Say to all the people of the land and to the priests, 'When you fasted and mourned in the fifth and seventh months these seventy years, was it actually for Me that you fasted?

6 'And when you eat and drink, do you not eat for yourselves and do you not drink for yourselves?

7 'Are not *these* the words which the LORD proclaimed by the former prophets, when Jerusalem was inhabited and prosperous with its cities around it, and the Negev and the foothills were inhabited?' "

8 ¶ Then the word of the LORD came to Zechariah saying,

9"Thus has the LORD of hosts said, 'Dispense true justice, and practice kindness and compassion each to his brother;

10 and do not oppress the widow or the orphan, the stranger or the poor; and do not devise evil in your hearts against one another.'

11"But they refused to pay attention, and turned a stubborn shoulder and stopped their ears from hearing.

12"And they made their hearts *like* flint so that they could not hear the law and the words which the LORD of hosts had sent by His Spirit through the former prophets; therefore great wrath came from the LORD of hosts.

13"And it came about that just as He called and they would not listen, so they called and I would not listen," says the LORD of hosts;

14"but I scattered them with a storm wind among all the nations whom they have not known. Thus the land is desolated behind them, so that no one went back and forth, for they made the pleasant land desolate."

CHAPTER 8

THEN the word of the LORD of hosts came saying,

2"Thus says the LORD of hosts, 'I am exceedingly jealous for Zion, yes, with great wrath I am jealous for her.'

3"Thus says the LORD, 'I will return to Zion and will dwell in the midst of Jerusalem. Then Jerusalem will be called the City of Truth, and the mountain of the LORD of hosts *will be called* the Holy Mountain.'

4"Thus says the LORD of hosts, 'Old men and old women will again sit in the ¹streets of Jerusalem, each man with his staff in his hand because of age.

5 'And the ¹streets of the city will be filled with boys and girls playing in its ¹streets.'

6"Thus says the LORD of hosts, 'If it is too difficult in the sight of the remnant of this people in those days, will it also be too difficult in My sight?' declares the LORD of hosts.

7"Thus says the LORD of hosts, 'Behold, I am going to save My people from the land of the east and from the land of the west;

8 and I will bring them *back,* and they will live in the midst of Jerusalem, and they will be My people and I will be their God in truth and righteousness.'

9 ¶"Thus says the LORD of hosts, 'Let your hands be strong, you who are listening in these days to these words from the mouth of the prophets, *those* who *spoke* in the day that the foundation of the house of the LORD of hosts was laid, to the end that the temple might be built.

10 'For before those days there was no wage for man or any wage for animal; and for him who went out or came in there was no peace because of his enemies, and I set all men one against another.

11 'But now I will not treat the remnant of this people as in the former days,' declares the LORD of hosts.

12 'For *there will be* peace for the seed: the vine will yield its fruit, the land will yield its produce, and the heavens will give their dew; and I will cause the remnant of this people to inherit all these *things.*

13 'And it will come about that just as you were a curse among the nations, O house of Judah and house of Israel, so I will save you that you may become a blessing. Do not fear; let your hands be strong.'

14 ¶"For thus says the LORD of hosts, 'Just as I purposed to do harm to you when your fathers provoked Me to wrath,' says the LORD of hosts, 'and I have not relented,

15 so I have again purposed in these days to do good to Jerusalem and to the house of Judah. Do not fear!

16 'These are the things which you should do: speak the truth to one another; judge with truth and judgment for peace in your ²gates.

17 'Also, let none of you devise evil in your heart against another, and do not love perjury; for all these are what I hate,' declares the LORD."

18 ¶ Then the word of the LORD of hosts came to me saying,

19"Thus says the LORD of hosts, 'The fast of the fourth, the fast of the fifth, the fast of the seventh, and the fast of the tenth *months* will become joy, gladness, and cheerful feasts for the house of Judah; so love truth and peace.'

20"Thus says the LORD of hosts, '*It will* yet *be* that peoples will come, even the inhabitants of many cities.

21 'And the inhabitants of one will go to another saying, "Let us go at once to entreat the favor of the LORD, and to seek the LORD of hosts; I will also go."

22 'So many peoples and mighty nations will come to seek the LORD of hosts in Jerusalem and to entreat the favor of the LORD.'

23"Thus says the LORD of hosts, 'In those days ten men from all the nations will grasp the garment of a Jew saying, "Let us go with you, for we have heard that God is with you." ' "

¹ Or, *squares*   ² I.e., the place where court was held

CHAPTER 9

THE burden of the word of the LORD is against the land of Hadrach, with Damascus as its resting place (for the eyes of men, especially of all the tribes of Israel, are toward the LORD),

2 And Hamath also, which borders on it;
Tyre and Sidon, though they are very wise.

3 For Tyre built herself a fortress
And piled up silver like dust,
And gold like the mire of the streets.

4 Behold, the Lord will dispossess her
And cast her wealth into the sea;
And she will be consumed with fire.

5 Ashkelon will see *it* and be afraid.
Gaza too will writhe in great pain;
Also Ekron, for her expectation has been confounded.
Moreover, the king will perish from Gaza,
And Ashkelon will not be inhabited.

6 And a mongrel race will dwell in Ashdod,
And I will cut off the pride of the Philistines.

7 And I will remove their blood from their mouth,
And their detestable things from between their teeth.
Then they also will be a remnant for our God,
And be like a clan in Judah,
And Ekron like a Jebusite.

8 But I will camp around My house because of an army,
Because of him who passes by and returns;
And no oppressor will pass over them anymore,
For now I have seen with My eyes.

9 Rejoice greatly, O daughter of Zion!
Shout *in triumph*, O daughter of Jerusalem!
Behold, your king is coming to you;
He is just and endowed with salvation,
Humble, and mounted on a donkey,
Even on a colt, the foal of a donkey.

10 And I will cut off the chariot from Ephraim,
And the horse from Jerusalem;
And the bow of war will be cut off.
And He will speak peace to the nations;
And His dominion will be from sea to sea,
And from the [3]River to the ends of the earth.

11 ¶ As for you also, because of the blood of *My* covenant with you,
I have set your prisoners free from the waterless pit.

12 Return to the stronghold, O prisoners who have the hope;
This very day I am declaring that I will restore double to you.

13 For I will bend Judah as My bow,
I will fill the bow with Ephraim.
And I will stir up your sons, O Zion, against your sons, O Greece;
And I will make you like a warrior's sword.

14 Then the LORD will appear over them,
And His arrow will go forth like lightning;
And the Lord GOD will blow the trumpet,
And will march in the storm winds of the south.

15 The LORD of hosts will defend them.
And they will devour, and trample on the sling stones;
And they will drink, *and* be boisterous as with wine;
And they will be filled like a *sacrificial* basin,
Drenched like the corners of the altar.

16 And the LORD their God will save them in that day
As the flock of His people;
For *they are as* the stones of a crown,
Sparkling in His land.

17 For what comeliness and beauty *will be* theirs!

[3] I.e., Euphrates

Grain will make the young men flourish, and new wine the virgins.

CHAPTER 10

Ask rain from the Lord at the time of the spring rain—
The Lord who makes the storm clouds;
And He will give them showers of rain, vegetation in the field to *each* man.

2 For the teraphim speak iniquity,
And the diviners see lying visions,
And tell false dreams;
They comfort in vain.
Therefore *the people* wander like sheep,
They are afflicted, because there is no shepherd.

3 "My anger is kindled against the shepherds,
And I will punish the male goats;
For the Lord of hosts has visited His flock, the house of Judah,
And will make them like His majestic horse in battle.

4 "From them will come the cornerstone,
From them the tent peg,
From them the bow of battle,
From them every ruler, *all* of them together.

5 "And they will be as mighty men,
Treading down *the enemy* in the mire of the streets in battle;
And they will fight, for the Lord *will be* with them;
And the riders on horses will be put to shame.

6 "And I shall strengthen the house of Judah,
And I shall save the house of Joseph,
And I shall bring them back,
Because I have had compassion on them;
And they will be as though I had not rejected them,
For I am the Lord their God, and I will answer them.

7 "And Ephraim will be like a mighty man,
And their heart will be glad as if *from* wine;
Indeed, their children will see *it* and be glad,

Their heart will rejoice in the Lord.

8 "I will whistle for them to gather them together,
For I have redeemed them;
And they will be as numerous as they were before.

9 "When I scatter them among the peoples,
They will remember Me in far countries,
And they with their children will live and come back.

10 "I will bring them back from the land of Egypt,
And gather them from Assyria;
And I will bring them into the land of Gilead and Lebanon,
Until no *room* can be found for them.

11 "And He will pass through the sea *of* distress,
And strike the waves in the sea,
So that all the depths of the Nile will dry up;
And the pride of Assyria will be brought down,
And the scepter of Egypt will depart.

12 "And I shall strengthen them in the Lord,
And in His name they will walk,"
declares the Lord.

CHAPTER 11

Open your doors, O Lebanon,
That a fire may feed on your cedars.

2 Wail, O cypress, for the cedar has fallen,
Because the glorious *trees* have been destroyed;
Wail, O oaks of Bashan,
For the impenetrable forest has come down.

3 There is a sound of the shepherds' wail,
For their glory is ruined;
There is a sound of the young lions' roar,
For the pride of the Jordan is ruined.

4 ¶ Thus says the Lord my God, "Pasture the flock *doomed* to slaughter.

5 "Those who buy them slay them and go unpunished, and *each of* those who sell them says, 'Blessed be the

LORD, for I have become rich!' And their own shepherds have no pity on them.

6"For I shall no longer have pity on the inhabitants of the land," declares the LORD; "but behold, I shall cause the men to fall, each into another's power and into the power of his king; and they will strike the land, and I shall not deliver *them* from their power."

7 So I pastured the flock *doomed* to slaughter, hence the afflicted of the flock. And I took for myself two staffs: the one I called Favor, and the other I called Union; so I pastured the flock.

8 Then I annihilated the three shepherds in one month, for my soul was impatient with them, and their soul also was weary of me.

9 Then I said, "I will not pasture you. What is to die, let it die, and what is to be annihilated, let it be annihilated; and let those who are left eat one another's flesh."

10 And I took my staff, Favor, and cut it in pieces, to break my covenant which I had made with all the peoples.

11 So it was broken on that day, and ⁴thus the afflicted of the flock who were watching me realized that it was the word of the LORD.

12 And I said to them, "If it is good in your sight, give *me* my wages; but if not, never mind!" So they weighed out thirty *shekels* of silver as my wages.

13 Then the LORD said to me, "Throw it to the potter, *that* magnificent price at which I was valued by them." So I took the thirty *shekels* of silver and threw them to the potter in the house of the LORD.

14 Then I cut my second staff, Union, in pieces, to break the brotherhood between Judah and Israel.

15 ¶ And the LORD said to me, "Take again for yourself the equipment of a foolish shepherd.

16"For behold, I am going to raise up a shepherd in the land who will not care for the perishing, seek the scattered, heal the broken, or sustain the one standing, but will devour the flesh of the fat *sheep* and tear off their hoofs.

17 "Woe to the worthless shepherd Who leaves the flock!

⁴ Another reading is *the sheep dealers who*

A sword will be on his arm
And on his right eye!
His arm will be totally withered,
And his right eye will be blind."

CHAPTER 12

THE ⁵burden of the word of the LORD concerning Israel.

¶ *Thus* declares the LORD who stretches out the heavens, lays the foundation of the earth, and forms the spirit of man within him,

2"Behold, I am going to make Jerusalem a cup that causes reeling to all the peoples around; and when the siege is against Jerusalem, it will also be against Judah.

3"And it will come about in that day that I will make Jerusalem a heavy stone for all the peoples; all who lift it will be severely injured. And all the nations of the earth will be gathered against it.

4"In that day," declares the LORD, "I will strike every horse with bewilderment, and his rider with madness. But I will watch over the house of Judah, while I strike every horse of the peoples with blindness.

5"Then the clans of Judah will say in their hearts, 'A strong support for us are the inhabitants of Jerusalem through the LORD of hosts, their God.'

6"In that day I will make the clans of Judah like a firepot among pieces of wood and a flaming torch among sheaves, so they will consume on the right hand and on the left all the surrounding peoples, while the inhabitants of Jerusalem again dwell on their own sites in Jerusalem.

7"The LORD also will save the tents of Judah first in order that the glory of the house of David and the glory of the inhabitants of Jerusalem may not be magnified above Judah.

8"In that day the LORD will defend the inhabitants of Jerusalem, and the one who is feeble among them in that day will be like David, and the house of David *will be* like God, like the angel of the LORD before them.

9"And it will come about in that day that I will set about to destroy all the nations that come against Jerusalem.

10 ¶"And I will pour out on the house of David and on the inhabitants

⁵ Or, *oracle*

of Jerusalem, the Spirit of grace and of supplication, so that they will look on Me whom they have pierced; and they will mourn for Him, as one mourns for an only son, and they will weep bitterly over Him, like the bitter weeping over a first-born.

11"In that day there will be great mourning in Jerusalem, like the mourning of Hadadrimmon in the plain of Megiddo.

12"And the land will mourn, every family by itself; the family of the house of David by itself, and their wives by themselves; the family of the house of Nathan by itself, and their wives by themselves;

13 the family of the house of Levi by itself, and their wives by themselves; the family of the Shimeites by itself, and their wives by themselves;

14 all the families that remain, every family by itself, and their wives by themselves.

CHAPTER 13

"IN that day a fountain will be opened for the house of David and for the inhabitants of Jerusalem, for sin and for impurity.

2 ¶"And it will come about in that day," declares the LORD of hosts, "that I will cut off the names of the idols from the land, and they will no longer be remembered; and I will also remove the prophets and the unclean spirit from the land.

3"And it will come about that if anyone still prophesies, then his father and mother who gave birth to him will say to him, 'You shall not live, for you have spoken falsely in the name of the LORD'; and his father and mother who gave birth to him will pierce him through when he prophesies.

4"Also it will come about in that day that the prophets will each be ashamed of his vision when he prophesies, and they will not put on a hairy robe in order to deceive;

5 but he will say, 'I am not a prophet; I am a tiller of the ground, for a man sold me as a slave in my youth.'

6"And one will say to him, 'What are these wounds between your arms?' Then he will say, '*Those* with which I was wounded in the house of my friends.'

7 ¶ "Awake, O sword, against My Shepherd,
And against the man, My Associate,"
Declares the LORD of hosts.
"Strike the Shepherd that the sheep may be scattered;
And I will turn My hand against the little ones.

8 "And it will come about in all the land,"
Declares the LORD,
"That two parts in it will be cut off *and* perish;
But the third will be left in it.

9 "And I will bring the third part through the fire,
Refine them as silver is refined,
And test them as gold is tested.
They will call on My name,
And I will answer them;
I will say, 'They are My people,'
And they will say, 'The LORD is my God.' "

CHAPTER 14

BEHOLD, a day is coming for the LORD when the spoil taken from you will be divided among you.

2 For I will gather all the nations against Jerusalem to battle, and the city will be captured, the houses plundered, the women ravished, and half of the city exiled, but the rest of the people will not be cut off from the city.

3 Then the LORD will go forth and fight against those nations, as when He fights on a day of battle.

4 And in that day His feet will stand on the Mount of Olives, which is in front of Jerusalem on the east; and the Mount of Olives will be split in its middle from east to west by a very large valley, so that half of the mountain will move toward the north and the other half toward the south.

5 And you will flee by the valley of My mountains, for the valley of the mountains will reach to Azel; yes, you will flee just as you fled before the earthquake in the days of Uzziah king of Judah. Then the LORD, my God, will come, *and* all the holy ones with Him!

6 And it will come about in that day that there will be no light; the luminaries will dwindle.

7 For it will be a unique day which is known to the LORD, neither day nor

night, but it will come about that at evening time there will be light.

8 And it will come about in that day that living waters will flow out of Jerusalem, half of them toward the eastern sea and the other half toward the western sea; it will be in summer as well as in winter.

9 ¶ And the LORD will be king over all the earth; in that day the LORD will be *the only* one, and His name *the only* one.

10 All the land will be changed into a plain from Geba to Rimmon south of Jerusalem; but Jerusalem will rise and remain on its site from Benjamin's Gate as far as the place of the First Gate to the Corner Gate, and from the Tower of Hananel to the king's wine presses.

11 And people will live in it, and there will be no more curse, for Jerusalem will dwell in security.

12 ¶ Now this will be the plague with which the LORD will strike all the peoples who have gone to war against Jerusalem; their flesh will rot while they stand on their feet, and their eyes will rot in their sockets, and their tongue will rot in their mouth.

13 And it will come about in that day that a great panic from the LORD will fall on them; and they will seize one another's hand, and the hand of one will be lifted against the hand of another.

14 And Judah also will fight at Jerusalem; and the wealth of all the surrounding nations will be gathered, gold and silver and garments in great abundance.

15 So also like this plague, will be the plague on the horse, the mule, the camel, the donkey, and all the cattle that will be in those camps.

16 ¶ Then it will come about that any who are left of all the nations that went against Jerusalem will go up from year to year to worship the King, the LORD of hosts, and to celebrate the Feast of Booths.

17 And it will be that whichever of the families of the earth does not go up to Jerusalem to worship the King, the LORD of hosts, there will be no rain on them.

18 And if the family of Egypt does not go up or enter, then no *rain will fall* on them; it will be the plague with which the LORD smites the nations who do not go up to celebrate the Feast of Booths.

19 This will be the punishment of Egypt, and the punishment of all the nations who do not go up to celebrate the Feast of Booths.

20 In that day there will *be inscribed* on the bells of the horses, "HOLY TO THE LORD." And the cooking pots in the LORD's house will be like the bowls before the altar.

21 And every cooking pot in Jerusalem and in Judah will be holy to the LORD of hosts; and all who sacrifice will come and take of them and boil in them. And there will no longer be a Canaanite in the house of the LORD of hosts in that day.

MALACHI

THE oracle of the word of the LORD to Israel through Malachi.

2 ¶"I have loved you," says the LORD. But you say, "How hast Thou loved us?" "Was not Esau Jacob's brother?" declares the LORD. "Yet I have loved Jacob;

3 but I have hated Esau, and I have made his mountains a desolation, and appointed his inheritance for the jackals of the wilderness."

4 Though Edom says, "We have been beaten down, but we will return and build up the ruins"; thus says the LORD of hosts, "They may build, but I will tear down; and men will call them the wicked territory, and the people toward whom the LORD is indignant forever."

5 And your eyes will see this and you will say, "The LORD be magnified beyond the border of Israel!"

6 ¶"A son honors his father, and a servant his master. Then if I am a father, where is My honor? And if I am a master, where is My respect?' says the LORD of hosts to you, O priests who despise My name. But you say, 'How have we despised Thy name?'

7"You are presenting defiled food upon My altar. But you say, 'How have we defiled Thee?' In that you say, 'The table of the LORD is to be despised.'

8"But when you present the blind for sacrifice, is it not evil? And when you present the lame and sick, is it not evil? Why not offer it to your governor? Would he be pleased with you? Or would he receive you kindly?" says the LORD of hosts.

9"But now will you not entreat God's favor, that He may be gracious to us? With such an offering on your part, will He receive any of you kindly?" says the LORD of hosts.

10"Oh that there were one among you who would shut the gates, that you might not uselessly kindle fire on My altar! I am not pleased with you," says the LORD of hosts, "nor will I accept an offering from you.

11"For from the rising of the sun, even to its setting, My name will be great among the nations, and in every place incense is going to be offered to My name, and a grain offering that is pure; for My name will be great among the nations," says the LORD of hosts.

12"But you are profaning it, in that you say, 'The table of the Lord is defiled, and as for its fruit, its food is to be despised.'

13"You also say, 'My, how tiresome it is!' And you disdainfully sniff at it," says the LORD of hosts, "and you bring what was taken by robbery, and what is lame or sick; so you bring the offering! Should I receive that from your hand?" says the LORD.

14"But cursed be the swindler who has a male in his flock, and vows it, but sacrifices a blemished animal to the Lord, for I am a great King," says the LORD of hosts, "and My name is feared among the nations."

CHAPTER 2

"AND now, this commandment is for you, O priests.

2"If you do not listen, and if you do not take it to heart to give honor to My name," says the LORD of hosts, "then I will send the curse upon you, and I will curse your blessings; and indeed, I have cursed them already, because you are not taking it to heart.

3"Behold, I am going to rebuke your offspring, and I will spread refuse on your faces, the refuse of your feasts; and you will be taken away with it.

4"Then you will know that I have sent this commandment to you, that My covenant may continue with Levi," says the LORD of hosts.

5"My covenant with him was one of life and peace, and I gave them to him as an object of reverence; so he revered Me, and stood in awe of My name.

6"True instruction was in his mouth, and unrighteousness was not found on his lips; he walked with Me in peace and uprightness, and he turned many back from iniquity.

7"For the lips of a priest should preserve knowledge, and men should seek instruction from his mouth; for he is the messenger of the LORD of hosts.

8"But as for you, you have turned aside from the way; you have caused many to stumble by the instruction; you have corrupted the covenant of Levi," says the LORD of hosts.

9"So I also have made you despised and abased before all the people, just as you are not keeping My ways, but are showing partiality in the instruction.

10 ¶"Do we not all have one father? Has not one God created us? Why do we deal treacherously each against his brother so as to profane the covenant of our fathers?

11"Judah has dealt treacherously, and an abomination has been committed in Israel and in Jerusalem; for Judah has profaned the sanctuary of the LORD which He loves, and has married the daughter of a foreign god.

12"As for the man who does this, may the LORD cut off from the tents of Jacob *everyone* who awakes and answers, or who presents an offering to the LORD of hosts.

13"And this is another thing you do: you cover the altar of the LORD with tears, with weeping and with groaning, because He no longer regards the offering or accepts *it with* favor from your hand.

14"Yet you say, 'For what reason?' Because the LORD has been a witness between you and the wife of your youth, against whom you have dealt treacherously, though she is your companion and your wife by covenant.

15"But not one has done *so* who has a remnant of the Spirit. And what did *that* one *do* while he was seeking a godly offspring? Take heed then, to your spirit, and let no one deal treacherously against the wife of your youth.

16"For I hate divorce," says the LORD, the God of Israel, "and him who covers his garment with wrong," says the LORD of hosts. "So take heed to your spirit, that you do not deal treacherously."

17 ¶ You have wearied the LORD with your words. Yet you say, "How have we wearied *Him*?" In that you say, "Everyone who does evil is good in the sight of the LORD, and He delights in them," or, "Where is the God of justice?"

CHAPTER 3

"BEHOLD, I am going to send My messenger, and he will clear the way before Me. And the Lord, whom you seek, will suddenly come to His temple; and the messenger of the covenant, in whom you delight, behold, He is coming," says the LORD of hosts.

2"But who can endure the day of His coming? And who can stand when He appears? For He is like a refiner's fire and like fullers' soap.

3"And He will sit as a smelter and purifier of silver, and He will purify the sons of Levi and refine them like gold and silver, so that they may present to the LORD offerings in righteousness.

4"Then the offering of Judah and Jerusalem will be pleasing to the LORD, as in the days of old and as in former years.

5"Then I will draw near to you for judgment; and I will be a swift witness against the sorcerers and against the adulterers and against those who swear falsely, and against those who oppress the wage earner in his wages, the widow and the orphan, and those who turn aside the alien, and do not fear Me," says the LORD of hosts.

6"For I, the LORD, do not change; therefore you, O sons of Jacob, are not consumed.

7 ¶"From the days of your fathers you have turned aside from My statutes, and have not kept *them*. Return to Me, and I will return to you," says the LORD of hosts. "But you say, 'How shall we return?'

8"Will a man ¹rob God? Yet you are robbing Me! But you say, 'How have we robbed Thee?' In tithes and offerings.

9"You are cursed with a curse, for you are ¹robbing Me, the whole nation of *you!*

10"Bring the whole tithe into the storehouse, so that there may be food in My house, and test Me now in this," says the LORD of hosts, "if I will not open for you the windows of heaven, and pour out for you a blessing until ²it overflows.

11"Then I will rebuke the devourer for you, so that it may not destroy the fruits of the ground; nor will your vine

---

¹ Or, *defraud(ing)*   ² Or, *there is not room enough*

in the field cast *its grapes*," says the Lord of hosts.

12"And all the nations will call you blessed, for you shall be a delightful land," says the Lord of hosts.

13 ¶"Your words have been arrogant against Me," says the Lord. "Yet you say, 'What have we spoken against Thee?'

14"You have said, 'It is vain to serve God; and what profit is it that we have kept His charge, and that we have walked in mourning before the Lord of hosts?

15 'So now we call the arrogant blessed; not only are the doers of wickedness built up, but they also test God and escape.'"

16 ¶ Then those who [3]feared the Lord spoke to one another, and the Lord gave attention and heard *it,* and a book of remembrance was written before Him for those who [3]fear the Lord and who esteem His name.

17"And they will be Mine," says the Lord of hosts, "on the day that I prepare *My* own possession, and I will spare them as a man spares his own son who serves him."

18 So you will again distinguish between the righteous and the wicked, between one who serves God and one who does not serve Him.

[3] Or, *revere(d)*

CHAPTER 4

"FOR behold, the day is coming, burning like a furnace; and all the arrogant and every evildoer will be chaff; and the day that is coming will set them ablaze," says the Lord of hosts, "so that it will leave them neither root nor branch."

2"But for you who [3]fear My name the sun of righteousness will rise with healing in its wings; and you will go forth and skip about like calves from the stall.

3"And you will tread down the wicked, for they shall be ashes under the soles of your feet on the day which I am preparing," says the Lord of hosts.

4 ¶"Remember the law of Moses My servant, *even the* statutes and ordinances which I commanded him in Horeb for all Israel.

5"Behold, I am going to send you Elijah the prophet before the coming of the great and terrible day of the Lord.

6"And he will restore the hearts of the fathers to *their* children, and the hearts of the children to their fathers, lest I come and smite the land with a curse."

[3] Or, *revere(d)*

NEW TESTAMENT

New American
Standard

MATTHEW

THE book of the genealogy of Jesus Christ, the son of David, the son of Abraham.

2 ¶ To Abraham was born Isaac; and to Isaac, Jacob; and to Jacob, [1]Judah and his brothers;

3 and to Judah were born Perez and Zerah by Tamar; and to Perez was born Hezron; and to Hezron, Ram;

4 and to Ram was born Amminadab; and to Amminadab, Nahshon; and to Nahshon, Salmon;

5 and to Salmon was born Boaz by Rahab; and to Boaz was born Obed by Ruth; and to Obed, Jesse;

6 and to Jesse was born David the king.

¶ And to David was born Solomon by her *who had been the wife* of Uriah;

7 and to Solomon was born Rehoboam; and to Rehoboam, Abijah; and to Abijah, Asa;

8 and to Asa was born Jehoshaphat; and to Jehoshaphat, Joram; and to Joram, Uzziah;

9 and to Uzziah was born Jotham; and to Jotham, Ahaz; and to Ahaz, Hezekiah;

10 and to Hezekiah was born Manasseh; and to Manasseh, Amon; and to Amon, Josiah;

11 and to Josiah were born Jeconiah and his brothers, at the time of the deportation to Babylon.

12 ¶ And after the deportation to Babylon, to Jeconiah was born Shealtiel; and to Shealtiel, Zerubbabel;

13 and to Zerubbabel was born Abiud; and to Abiud, Eliakim; and to Eliakim, Azor;

14 and to Azor was born Zadok; and to Zadok, Achim; and to Achim, Eliud;

15 and to Eliud was born Eleazar; and to Eleazar, Matthan; and to Matthan, Jacob;

16 and to Jacob was born Joseph the husband of Mary, by whom was born Jesus, who is called Christ.

17 ¶ Therefore all the generations from Abraham to David are fourteen generations; and from David to the deportation to Babylon fourteen generations; and from the deportation to Babylon to *the time of* Christ fourteen generations.

18 ¶ Now the birth of Jesus Christ was as follows. When His mother Mary had been betrothed to Joseph, before they came together she was found to be with child by the Holy Spirit.

19 And Joseph her husband, being a righteous man, and not wanting to disgrace her, desired [2]to put her away secretly.

20 But when he had considered this, behold, an angel of the Lord appeared to him in a dream, saying, "Joseph, son of David, do not be afraid to take Mary as your wife; for that which has been [3]conceived in her is of the Holy Spirit.

21 "And she will bear a Son; and you shall call His name Jesus, for it is He who will save His people from their sins."

22 Now all this took place that what was spoken by the Lord through the prophet might be fulfilled, saying,

23 "BEHOLD, THE VIRGIN SHALL BE WITH CHILD, AND SHALL BEAR A SON, AND THEY SHALL CALL HIS NAME IMMANUEL," which translated means, "GOD WITH US."

24 And Joseph arose from his sleep, and did as the angel of the Lord commanded him, and took *her* as his wife,

25 and [4]kept her a virgin until she gave birth to a Son; and he called His name Jesus.

CHAPTER 2

NOW after Jesus was born in Bethlehem of Judea in the days of Herod the king, behold, [5]magi from the east arrived in Jerusalem, saying,

2 "Where is He who has been born King of the Jews? For we saw His star in the east, and have come to worship Him."

3 And when Herod the king heard it, he was troubled, and all Jerusalem with him.

4 And gathering together all the chief priests and scribes of the people,

---

[1] Gr., *Judas.* Names of Old Testament characters will be given in their Old Testament form.
[2] Or, *to divorce her*   [3] Lit., *begotten*
[4] Lit., *was not knowing her*
[5] Pronounced may-ji, a caste of wise men specializing in astrology, medicine and natural science

he *began* to inquire of them where the Christ was to be born.

5 And they said to him, "In Bethlehem of Judea, for so it has been written by the prophet,

6 'AND YOU, BETHLEHEM, LAND OF
  JUDAH,
  ARE BY NO MEANS LEAST AMONG
  THE LEADERS OF JUDAH;
  FOR OUT OF YOU SHALL COME
  FORTH A RULER,
  WHO WILL SHEPHERD MY PEOPLE
  ISRAEL.' "

7 ¶ Then Herod secretly called the magi, and ascertained from them the time the star appeared.

8 And he sent them to Bethlehem, and said, "Go and make careful search for the Child; and when you have found *Him,* report to me, that I too may come and worship Him."

9 And having heard the king, they went their way; and lo, the star, which they had seen in the east, went on before them, until it came and stood over where the Child was.

10 And when they saw the star, they rejoiced exceedingly with great joy.

11 And they came into the house and saw the Child with Mary His mother; and they fell down and worshiped Him; and opening their treasures they presented to Him gifts of gold and frankincense and myrrh.

12 And having been warned *by God* in a dream not to return to Herod, they departed for their own country by another way.

13 ¶ Now when they had departed, behold, an angel of the Lord *appeared to Joseph in a dream, saying, "Arise and take the Child and His mother, and flee to Egypt, and remain there until I tell you; for Herod is going to search for the Child to destroy Him."

14 And he arose and took the Child and His mother by night, and departed for Egypt;

15 and was there until the death of Herod, that what was spoken by the Lord through the prophet might be fulfilled, saying, "OUT OF EGYPT DID I CALL MY SON."

16 ¶ Then when Herod saw that he had been tricked by the magi, he became very enraged, and sent and slew all the male children who were in Bethlehem and in all its environs, from two years old and under, according to

the time which he had ascertained from the magi.

17 Then that which was spoken through Jeremiah the prophet was fulfilled, saying,

18 "A VOICE WAS HEARD IN RAMAH,
  WEEPING AND GREAT MOURNING,
  RACHEL WEEPING FOR HER CHIL-
  DREN;
  AND SHE REFUSED TO BE COM-
  FORTED,
  BECAUSE THEY WERE NO MORE."

19 ¶ But when Herod was dead, behold, an angel of the Lord *appeared in a dream to Joseph in Egypt, saying,

20 "Arise and take the Child and His mother, and go into the land of Israel; for those who sought the Child's life are dead."

21 And he arose and took the Child and His mother, and came into the land of Israel.

22 But when he heard that Archelaus was reigning over Judea in place of his father Herod, he was afraid to go there. And being warned *by God* in a dream, he departed for the regions of Galilee,

23 and came and resided in a city called Nazareth, that what was spoken through the prophets might be fulfilled, "He shall be called a Nazarene."

CHAPTER 3

NOW in those days John the Baptist *came, preaching in the wilderness of Judea, saying,

2 "Repent, for the kingdom of heaven is at hand."

3 For this is the one referred to by Isaiah the prophet, saying,

  "THE VOICE OF ONE CRYING IN THE
  WILDERNESS,
  'MAKE READY THE WAY OF THE
  LORD,
  MAKE HIS PATHS STRAIGHT!' "

4 Now John himself had a garment of camel's hair, and a leather belt about his waist; and his food was locusts and wild honey.

5 Then Jerusalem was going out to him, and all Judea, and all the district around the Jordan;

6 and they were being baptized by him in the Jordan River, as they confessed their sins.

7 But when he saw many of the Pharisees and Sadducees coming for baptism, he said to them, "You brood

of vipers, who warned you to flee from the wrath to come?

8"Therefore bring forth fruit in keeping with repentance;

9 and do not suppose that you can say to yourselves, 'We have Abraham for our father'; for I say to you, that God is able from these stones to raise up children to Abraham.

10"And the axe is already laid at the root of the trees; every tree therefore that does not bear good fruit is cut down and thrown into the fire.

11"As for me, I baptize you ⁶with water for repentance, but He who is coming after me is mightier than I, and I am not fit to remove His sandals; He will baptize you with the Holy Spirit and fire.

12"And His winnowing fork is in His hand, and He will thoroughly clear His threshing floor; and He will gather His wheat into the barn, but He will burn up the chaff with unquenchable fire."

13 ¶ Then Jesus *arrived from Galilee at the Jordan *coming* to John, to be baptized by him.

14 But John tried to prevent Him, saying, "I have need to be baptized by You, and do You come to me?"

15 But Jesus answering said to him, "Permit *it* at this time; for in this way it is fitting for us to fulfill all righteousness." Then he *permitted Him.

16 And after being baptized, Jesus went up immediately from the water; and behold, the heavens were opened, and he saw the Spirit of God descending as a dove, *and* coming upon Him,

17 and behold, a voice out of the heavens, saying, "This is ⁷My beloved Son, in whom I am well-pleased."

CHAPTER 4

THEN Jesus was led up by the Spirit into the wilderness to be tempted by the devil.

2 And after He had fasted forty days and forty nights, He ⁸then became hungry.

3 And the tempter came and said to Him, "If You are the Son of God, command that these stones become bread."

4 But He answered and said, "It is written, 'MAN SHALL NOT LIVE ON BREAD ALONE, BUT ON EVERY WORD THAT PROCEEDS OUT OF THE MOUTH OF GOD.'"

5 Then the devil *took Him into the holy city; and he had Him stand on the pinnacle of the temple,

6 and *said to Him, "If You are the Son of God throw Yourself down; for it is written,

'HE WILL GIVE HIS ANGELS CHARGE
    CONCERNING YOU';
and
'ON *their* HANDS THEY WILL BEAR
    YOU UP,
LEST YOU STRIKE YOUR FOOT
    AGAINST A STONE.'"

7 Jesus said to him, "On the other hand, it is written, 'YOU SHALL NOT ⁹PUT THE LORD YOUR GOD TO THE TEST.'"

8 Again, the devil *took Him to a very high mountain, and *showed Him all the kingdoms of the world, and their glory;

9 and he said to Him, "All these things will I give You, if You fall down and worship me."

10 Then Jesus *said to him, "Begone, Satan! For it is written, 'YOU SHALL WORSHIP THE LORD YOUR GOD, AND SERVE HIM ONLY.'"

11 Then the devil *left Him; and behold, angels came and *began* to minister to Him.

12 ¶ Now when He heard that John had been taken into custody, He withdrew into Galilee;

13 and leaving Nazareth, He came and settled in Capernaum, which is by the sea, in the region of Zebulun and Naphtali.

14 *This was* to fulfill what was spoken through Isaiah the prophet, saying,

15 "THE LAND OF ZEBULUN AND THE
    LAND OF NAPHTALI,
BY THE WAY OF THE SEA, BEYOND
    THE JORDAN, GALILEE OF THE
    ¹⁰GENTILES—

16 "THE PEOPLE WHO WERE SITTING
    IN DARKNESS SAW A GREAT
    LIGHT,
AND TO THOSE WHO WERE SIT-
    TING IN THE LAND AND SHADOW
    OF DEATH,
UPON THEM A LIGHT DAWNED."

---

⁶ The Gr. here can be translated *in*, *with* or *by*
⁷ Lit., *My Son, the Beloved*   ⁸ Lit., *later, afterward*
⁹ Or, *tempt . . . God*   ¹⁰ Or, *nations*

17 ¶ From that time Jesus began to preach and say, "Repent, for the kingdom of heaven is at hand."

18 ¶ And walking by the Sea of Galilee, He saw two brothers, Simon who was called Peter, and Andrew his brother, casting a net into the sea; for they were fishermen.

19 And He *said to them, "Follow Me, and I will make you fishers of men."

20 And they immediately left the nets, and followed Him.

21 And going on from there He saw two other brothers, James the *son* of Zebedee, and John his brother, in the boat with Zebedee their father, mending their nets; and He called them.

22 And they immediately left the boat and their father, and followed Him.

23 ¶ And *Jesus* was going about in all Galilee, teaching in their synagogues, and proclaiming the gospel of the kingdom, and healing every kind of disease and every kind of sickness among the people.

24 And the news about Him went out into all Syria; and they brought to Him all who were ill, taken with various diseases and pains, demoniacs, epileptics, paralytics; and He healed them.

25 And great multitudes followed Him from Galilee and Decapolis and Jerusalem and Judea and *from* beyond the Jordan.

CHAPTER 5

AND when He saw the multitudes, He went up on the mountain; and after He sat down, His disciples came to Him.

2 And opening His mouth He *began* to teach them, saying,

3 ¶'Blessed are the poor in spirit, for theirs is the kingdom of heaven.

4 ¶'Blessed are those who mourn, for they shall be comforted.

5 ¶'Blessed are the [11]gentle, for they shall inherit the earth.

6 ¶'Blessed are those who hunger and thirst for righteousness, for they shall be satisfied.

7 ¶'Blessed are the merciful, for they shall receive mercy.

8 ¶'Blessed are the pure in heart, for they shall see God.

9 ¶'Blessed are the peacemakers, for they shall be called sons of God.

10 ¶'Blessed are those who have been persecuted for the sake of righteousness, for theirs is the kingdom of heaven.

11'Blessed are you when *men* cast insults at you, and persecute you, and say all kinds of evil against you falsely, on account of Me.

12'Rejoice, and be glad, for your reward in heaven is great, for so they persecuted the prophets who were before you.

13'You are the salt of the earth; but if the salt has become tasteless, how will it be made salty *again*? It is good for nothing anymore, except to be thrown out and trampled under foot by men.

14'You are the light of the world. A city set on a hill cannot be hidden.

15'Nor do *men* light a lamp, and put it under the peck-measure, but on the lampstand; and it gives light to all who are in the house.

16'Let your light shine before men in such a way that they may see your good works, and glorify your Father who is in heaven.

17 ¶'Do not think that I came to abolish the Law or the Prophets; I did not come to abolish, but to fulfill.

18'For truly I say to you, until heaven and earth pass away, not the smallest letter or stroke shall pass away from the Law, until all is accomplished.

19'Whoever then annuls one of the least of these commandments, and so teaches others, shall be called least in the kingdom of heaven; but whoever keeps and teaches *them*, he shall be called great in the kingdom of heaven.

20'For I say to you, that unless your righteousness surpasses *that* of the scribes and Pharisees, you shall not enter the kingdom of heaven.

21 ¶'You have heard that the ancients were told, 'YOU SHALL NOT COMMIT MURDER' and 'Whoever commits murder shall be [12]liable to the court.'

22'But I say to you that everyone who is angry with his brother[13] shall be guilty before the court; and whoever shall say to his brother, '[14]Raca,'

---

[11] Or, *humble, meek*

[12] Or, *guilty before*
[13] Some mss. insert here: *without cause*
[14] Aramaic for *empty-head* or, *good for nothing*

shall be guilty before [15]the supreme court; and whoever shall say, 'You fool,' shall be guilty *enough to go* into the [16]fiery hell.

23 "If therefore you are presenting your offering at the altar, and there remember that your brother has something against you,

24 leave your offering there before the altar, and go your way; first be reconciled to your brother, and then come and present your offering.

25 "Make friends quickly with your opponent at law while you are with him on the way, in order that your opponent may not deliver you to the judge, and the judge to the officer, and you be thrown into prison.

26 "Truly I say to you, you shall not come out of there, until you have paid up the last [17]cent.

27 ¶ "You have heard that it was said, 'YOU SHALL NOT COMMIT ADULTERY';

28 but I say to you, that everyone who looks on a woman to lust for her has committed adultery with her already in his heart.

29 "And if your right eye makes you stumble, tear it out, and throw it from you; for it is better for you that one of the parts of your body perish, than for your whole body to be thrown into hell.

30 "And if your right hand makes you stumble, cut it off, and throw it from you; for it is better for you that one of the parts of your body perish, than for your whole body to go into hell.

31 "And it was said, 'WHOEVER SENDS HIS WIFE AWAY, LET HIM GIVE HER A CERTIFICATE OF DIVORCE';

32 but I say to you that everyone who divorces his wife, except for *the* cause of unchastity, makes her commit adultery; and whoever marries a divorced woman commits adultery.

33 ¶ "Again, you have heard that the ancients were told, 'YOU SHALL NOT MAKE FALSE VOWS, BUT SHALL FULFILL YOUR VOWS TO THE LORD.'

34 "But I say to you, make no oath at all, either by heaven, for it is the throne of God,

35 or by the earth, for it is the footstool of His feet, or by Jerusalem, for it is THE CITY OF THE GREAT KING.

36 "Nor shall you make an oath by your head, for you cannot make one hair white or black.

37 "But let your statement be, 'Yes, yes' *or* 'No, no'; and anything beyond these is of evil.

38 ¶ "You have heard that it was said, 'AN EYE FOR AN EYE, AND A TOOTH FOR A TOOTH.'

39 "But I say to you, do not resist him who is evil; but whoever slaps you on your right cheek, turn to him the other also.

40 "And if anyone wants to sue you, and take your [18]shirt, let him have your [19]coat also.

41 "And whoever shall force you to go one mile, go with him two.

42 "Give to him who asks of you, and do not turn away from him who wants to borrow from you.

43 ¶ "You have heard that it was said, 'YOU SHALL LOVE YOUR NEIGHBOR, and hate your enemy.'

44 "But I say to you, love your enemies, and pray for those who persecute you

45 in order that you may be sons of your Father who is in heaven; for He causes His sun to rise on *the* evil and *the* good, and sends rain on *the* righteous and *the* unrighteous.

46 "For if you love those who love you, what reward have you? Do not even the tax-gatherers do the same?

47 "And if you greet your brothers only, what do you do more *than others*? Do not even the Gentiles do the same?

48 "Therefore you are to be perfect, as your heavenly Father is perfect.

CHAPTER 6

"BEWARE of practicing your righteousness before men to be noticed by them; otherwise you have no reward with your Father who is in heaven.

2 ¶ "When therefore you give alms, do not sound a trumpet before you, as the hypocrites do in the synagogues and in the streets, that they may be honored by men. Truly I say to you, they have their reward in full.

3 "But when you give alms, do not let your left hand know what your right hand is doing

[15] Lit., *the Sanhedrin*　[16] Lit., *Gehenna of fire*
[17] Lit., *quadrans* (equaling two lepta or mites), i.e., 1/64 of a denarius

[18] Or, *tunic*; i.e., garment worn next to the body
[19] Or, *cloak*; i.e., outer garment

4 that your alms may be in secret; and your Father who sees in secret will repay you.

5 ¶'And when you pray, you are not to be as the hypocrites; for they love to stand and pray in the synagogues and on the street corners, in order to be seen by men. Truly I say to you, they have their reward in full.

6'But you, when you pray, go into your inner room, and when you have shut your door, pray to your Father who is in secret, and your Father who sees in secret will repay you.

7'And when you are praying, do not use meaningless repetition, as the Gentiles do, for they suppose that they will be heard for their many words.

8'Therefore do not be like them; for your Father knows what you need, before you ask Him.

9'Pray, then, in this way:
'Our Father who art in heaven,
Hallowed be Thy name.
10 'Thy kingdom come.
Thy will be done,
On earth as it is in heaven.
11 'Give us this day our daily bread.
12 'And forgive us our debts, as we also have forgiven our debtors.
13 'And do not lead us into temptation, but deliver us from evil.
[For Thine is the kingdom, and the power, and the glory, forever. Amen.]

14'For if you forgive men for their transgressions, your heavenly Father will also forgive you.

15'But if you do not forgive men, then your Father will not forgive your transgressions.

16 ¶'And whenever you fast, do not put on a gloomy face as the hypocrites do, for they neglect their appearance in order to be seen fasting by men. Truly I say to you, they have their reward in full.

17'But you, when you fast, anoint your head, and wash your face

18 so that you may not be seen fasting by men, but by your Father who is in secret; and your Father who sees in secret will repay you.

19 ¶'Do not lay up for yourselves treasures upon earth, where moth and rust destroy, and where thieves break in and steal.

20'But lay up for yourselves treasures in heaven, where neither moth nor rust destroys, and where thieves do not break in or steal;

21 for where your treasure is, there will your heart be also.

22'The lamp of the body is the eye; if therefore your eye is clear, your whole body will be full of light.

23'But if your eye is bad, your whole body will be full of darkness. If therefore the light that is in you is darkness, how great is the darkness!

24'No one can serve two masters; for either he will hate the one and love the other, or he will hold to one and despise the other. You cannot serve God and 20mammon.

25'For this reason I say to you, do not be anxious for your life, *as to* what you shall eat, or what you shall drink; nor for your body, *as to* what you shall put on. Is not life more than food, and the body than clothing?

26'Look at the birds of the air, that they do not sow, neither do they reap, nor gather into barns, and *yet* your heavenly Father feeds them. Are you not worth much more than they?

27'And which of you by being anxious can add a *single* cubit to his life's span?

28'And why are you anxious about clothing? Observe how the lilies of the field grow; they do not toil nor do they spin,

29 yet I say to you that even Solomon in all his glory did not clothe himself like one of these.

30'But if God so arrays the grass of the field, which is *alive* today and tomorrow is thrown into the furnace, *will He* not much more *do so for* you, O men of little faith?

31'Do not be anxious then, saying, 'What shall we eat?' or 'What shall we drink?' or 'With what shall we clothe ourselves?'

32'For all these things the Gentiles eagerly seek; for your heavenly Father knows that you need all these things.

33'But seek first His kingdom and His righteousness; and all these things shall be added to you.

34'Therefore do not be anxious for tomorrow; for tomorrow will care for itself. *Each* day has enough trouble of its own.

20 Or, *riches*

CHAPTER 7

"Do not judge lest you be judged.

2"For in the way you judge, you will be judged; and by your standard of measure, it will be measured to you.

3"And why do you look at the speck that is in your brother's eye, but do not notice the log that is in your own eye?

4"Or how can you say to your brother, 'Let me take the speck out of your eye,' and behold, the log is in your own eye?

5"You hypocrite, first take the log out of your own eye, and then you will see clearly to take the speck out of your brother's eye.

6 ¶"Do not give what is holy to dogs, and do not throw your pearls before swine, lest they trample them under their feet, and turn and tear you to pieces.

7 ¶"Ask, and it shall be given to you; seek, and you shall find; knock, and it shall be opened to you.

8"For everyone who asks receives, and he who seeks finds, and to him who knocks it shall be opened.

9"Or what man is there among you, when his son shall ask him for a loaf, will give him a stone?

10"Or if he shall ask for a fish, he will not give him a snake, will he?

11"If you then, being evil, know how to give good gifts to your children, how much more shall your Father who is in heaven give what is good to those who ask Him!

12"Therefore, however you want people to treat you, so treat them, for this is the Law and the Prophets.

13 ¶"Enter by the narrow gate; for the gate is wide, and the way is broad that leads to destruction, and many are those who enter by it.

14"For the gate is small, and the way is narrow that leads to life, and few are those who find it.

15 ¶"Beware of the false prophets, who come to you in sheep's clothing, but inwardly are ravenous wolves.

16"You will know them by their fruits. Grapes are not gathered from thorn *bushes*, nor figs from thistles, are they?

17"Even so, every good tree bears good fruit; but the bad tree bears bad fruit.

18"A good tree cannot produce bad fruit, nor can a bad tree produce good fruit.

19"Every tree that does not bear good fruit is cut down and thrown into the fire.

20"So then, you will know them by their fruits.

21"Not everyone who says to Me, 'Lord, Lord,' will enter the kingdom of heaven; but he who does the will of My Father who is in heaven.

22"Many will say to Me on that day, 'Lord, Lord, did we not prophesy in Your name, and in Your name cast out demons, and in Your name perform many miracles?'

23"And then I will declare to them, 'I never knew you; DEPART FROM ME, YOU WHO PRACTICE LAWLESSNESS.'

24 ¶"Therefore everyone who hears these words of Mine, and acts upon them, may be compared to a wise man, who built his house upon the rock.

25"And the rain descended, and the floods came, and the winds blew, and burst against that house; and *yet* it did not fall, for it had been founded upon the rock.

26"And everyone who hears these words of Mine, and does not act upon them, will be like a foolish man, who built his house upon the sand.

27"And the rain descended, and the floods came, and the winds blew, and burst against that house; and it fell, and great was its fall."

28 ¶ The result was that when Jesus had finished these words, the multitudes were amazed at His teaching;

29 for He was teaching them as *one* having authority, and not as their scribes.

CHAPTER 8

And when He had come down from the mountain, great multitudes followed Him.

2 And behold, a leper came to Him, and bowed down to Him, saying, "Lord, if You are willing, You can make me clean."

3 And He stretched out His hand and touched him, saying, "I am willing; be cleansed." And immediately his leprosy was cleansed.

4 And Jesus *said to him, "See that you tell no one; but go, show yourself

to the priest, and present the offering that Moses commanded, for a testimony to them."

5 ¶ And when He had entered Capernaum, a centurion came to Him, entreating Him,

6 and saying, "Lord, my servant is lying paralyzed at home, suffering great pain."

7 And He *said to him, "I will come and heal him."

8 But the centurion answered and said, "Lord, I am not worthy for You to come under my roof, but just say the word, and my servant will be healed.

9 "For I, too, am a man under authority, with soldiers under me; and I say to this one, 'Go!' and he goes, and to another, 'Come!' and he comes, and to my slave, 'Do this!' and he does it."

10 Now when Jesus heard this, He marveled, and said to those who were following, "Truly I say to you, I have not found such great faith with anyone in Israel.

11 "And I say to you, that many shall come from east and west, and ²¹recline at the table with Abraham, and Isaac, and Jacob, in the kingdom of heaven;

12 but the sons of the kingdom shall be cast out into the outer darkness; in that place there shall be weeping and gnashing of teeth."

13 And Jesus said to the centurion, "Go your way; let it be done to you as you have believed." And the servant was healed that very hour.

14 ¶ And when Jesus had come to Peter's home, He saw his mother-in-law lying sick in bed with a fever.

15 And He touched her hand, and the fever left her; and she arose, and waited on Him.

16 And when evening had come, they brought to Him many who were demon-possessed; and He cast out the spirits with a word, and healed all who were ill

17 in order that what was spoken through Isaiah the prophet might be fulfilled, saying, "HE HIMSELF TOOK OUR INFIRMITIES, AND CARRIED AWAY OUR DISEASES."

18 ¶ Now when Jesus saw a crowd around Him, He gave orders to depart to the other side.

19 And a certain scribe came and said to Him, "Teacher, I will follow You wherever You go."

20 And Jesus *said to him, "The foxes have holes, and the birds of the air have nests; but the Son of Man has nowhere to lay His head."

21 And another of the disciples said to Him, "Lord, permit me first to go and bury my father."

22 But Jesus *said to him, "Follow Me; and allow the dead to bury their own dead."

23 ¶ And when He got into the boat, His disciples followed Him.

24 And behold, there arose a great storm in the sea, so that the boat was covered with the waves; but He Himself was asleep.

25 And they came to Him, and awoke Him, saying, "Save us, Lord; we are perishing!"

26 And He *said to them, "Why are you timid, you men of little faith?" Then He arose, and rebuked the winds and the sea; and it became perfectly calm.

27 And the men marveled, saying, "What kind of a man is this, that even the winds and the sea obey Him?"

28 ¶ And when He had come to the other side into the country of the Gadarenes, two men who were demon-possessed met Him as they were coming out of the tombs; they were so exceedingly violent that no one could pass by that road.

29 And behold, they cried out, saying, "What do we have to do with You, Son of God? Have You come here to torment us before the time?"

30 Now there was at a distance from them a herd of many swine feeding.

31 And the demons began to entreat Him, saying, "If You are going to cast us out, send us into the herd of swine."

32 And He said to them, "Begone!" And they came out, and went into the swine, and behold, the whole herd rushed down the steep bank into the sea and perished in the waters.

33 And the herdsmen ran away, and went to the city, and reported everything, including the incident of the demoniacs.

34 And behold, the whole city came out to meet Jesus; and when they saw Him, they entreated Him to depart from their region.

²¹ Or, dine

CHAPTER 9

AND getting into a boat, He crossed over, and came to His own city.

2 And behold, they were bringing to Him a paralytic, lying on a bed; and Jesus seeing their faith said to the paralytic, "Take courage, My son, your sins are forgiven."

3 And behold, some of the scribes said to themselves, "This *fellow* blasphemes."

4 And Jesus knowing their thoughts said, "Why are you thinking evil in your hearts?

5"For which is easier, to say, 'Your sins are forgiven,' or to say, 'Rise, and walk'?

6"But in order that you may know that the Son of Man has authority on earth to forgive sins"—then He *said to the paralytic—"Rise, take up your bed, and go home."

7 And he rose, and went home.

8 But when the multitudes saw *this,* they were filled with awe, and glorified God, who had given such authority to men.

9 ¶ And as Jesus passed on from there, He saw a man, called Matthew, sitting in the tax office; and He *said to him, "Follow Me!" And he rose, and followed Him.

10 ¶ And it happened that as He was reclining *at the table* in the house, behold many tax-gatherers and sinners came and were dining with Jesus and His disciples.

11 And when the Pharisees saw *this,* they said to His disciples, "Why is your Teacher eating with the tax-gatherers and sinners?"

12 But when He heard this, He said, "*It is* not those who are healthy who need a physician, but those who are sick.

13"But go and learn what *this* means, 'I DESIRE COMPASSION, [22]AND NOT SACRIFICE,' for I did not come to call the righteous, but sinners."

14 ¶ Then the disciples of John *came to Him, saying, "Why do we and the Pharisees fast, but Your disciples do not fast?"

15 And Jesus said to them, "The attendants of the bridegroom cannot mourn as long as the bridegroom is with them, can they? But the days will come when the bridegroom is taken away from them, and then they will fast.

16"But no one puts a patch of unshrunk cloth on an old garment; for the patch pulls away from the garment, and a worse tear results.

17"Nor do *men* put new wine into old wineskins; otherwise the wineskins burst, and the wine pours out, and the wineskins are ruined; but they put new wine into fresh wineskins, and both are preserved."

18 ¶ While He was saying these things to them, behold, there came a *synagogue* official, and bowed down before Him, saying, "My daughter has just died; but come and lay Your hand on her, and she will live."

19 And Jesus rose and *began* to follow him, and so *did* His disciples.

20 And behold, a woman who had been suffering from a hemorrhage for twelve years, came up behind Him and touched the fringe of His cloak;

21 for she was saying to herself, "If I only touch His garment, I shall get well."

22 But Jesus turning and seeing her said, "Daughter, take courage; your faith has made you well." And at once the woman was made well.

23 And when Jesus came into the official's house, and saw the flute-players, and the crowd in noisy disorder,

24 He *began* to say, "Depart; for the girl has not died, but is asleep." And they *began* laughing at Him.

25 But when the crowd had been put out, He entered and took her by the hand; and the girl arose.

26 And this news went out into all that land.

27 ¶ And as Jesus passed on from there, two blind men followed Him, crying out, and saying, "Have mercy on us, Son of David!"

28 And after He had come into the house, the blind men came up to Him, and Jesus *said to them, "Do you believe that I am able to do this?" They *said to Him, "Yes, Lord."

29 Then He touched their eyes, saying, "Be it done to you according to your faith."

30 And their eyes were opened. And Jesus sternly warned them, saying,

[22] I.e., more than

"See *here*, let no one know *about this!*"

31 But they went out, and spread the news about Him in all that land.

32 ¶ And as they were going out, behold, a dumb man, demon-possessed, was brought to Him.

33 And after the demon was cast out, the dumb man spoke; and the multitudes marveled, saying, "Nothing like this was ever seen in Israel."

34 But the Pharisees were saying, "He casts out the demons by the ruler of the demons."

35 ¶ And Jesus was going about all the cities and the villages, teaching in their synagogues, and proclaiming the gospel of the kingdom, and healing every kind of disease and every kind of sickness.

36 And seeing the multitudes, He felt compassion for them, because they were distressed and downcast like sheep without a shepherd.

37 Then He *said to His disciples, "The harvest is plentiful, but the workers are few.

38 "Therefore beseech the Lord of the harvest to send out workers into His harvest."

CHAPTER 10

AND having summoned His twelve disciples, He gave them authority over unclean spirits, to cast them out, and to heal every kind of disease and every kind of sickness.

2 ¶ Now the names of the twelve apostles are these: The first, Simon, who is called Peter, and Andrew his brother; and James the *son* of Zebedee, and John his brother;

3 Philip and Bartholomew; Thomas and Matthew the tax-gatherer; James the *son* of Alphaeus, and Thaddaeus;

4 Simon the Zealot, and Judas Iscariot, the one who betrayed Him.

5 ¶ These twelve Jesus sent out after instructing them, saying, "Do not go in *the* way of *the* Gentiles, and do not enter *any* city of the Samaritans;

6 but rather go to the lost sheep of the house of Israel.

7 "And as you go, preach, saying, 'The kingdom of heaven is at hand.'

8 "Heal *the* sick, raise *the* dead, cleanse *the* lepers, cast out demons; freely you received, freely give.

9 "Do not acquire gold, or silver, or copper for your money belts,

10 or a bag for *your* journey, or even two tunics, or sandals, or a staff; for the worker is worthy of his support.

11 "And into whatever city or village you enter, inquire who is worthy in it; and abide there until you go away.

12 "And as you enter the house, give it your greeting.

13 "And if the house is worthy, let your *greeting of* peace come upon it; but if it is not worthy, let your *greeting of* peace return to you.

14 "And whoever does not receive you, nor heed your words, as you go out of that house or that city, shake off the dust of your feet.

15 "Truly I say to you, it will be more tolerable for *the* land of Sodom and Gomorrah in the day of judgment, than for that city.

16 ¶ "Behold, I send you out as sheep in the midst of wolves; therefore be shrewd as serpents, and innocent as doves.

17 "But beware of men; for they will deliver you up to *the* courts, and scourge you in their synagogues;

18 and you shall even be brought before governors and kings for My sake, as a testimony to them and to the Gentiles.

19 "But when they deliver you up, do not become anxious about how or what you will speak; for it shall be given you in that hour what you are to speak.

20 "For it is not you who speak, but *it is* the Spirit of your Father who speaks in you.

21 "And brother will deliver up brother to death, and a father *his* child; and children will rise up against parents, and cause them to be put to death.

22 "And you will be hated by all on account of My name, but it is the one who has endured to the end who will be saved.

23 "But whenever they persecute you in this city, flee to the next; for truly I say to you, you shall not finish *going through* the cities of Israel, until the Son of Man comes.

24 ¶ "A disciple is not above his teacher, nor a slave above his master.

25 "It is enough for the disciple that he become as his teacher, and the

slave as his master. If they have called the head of the house Beelzebul, how much more the members of his household!

26‘Therefore do not fear them, for there is nothing covered that will not be revealed, and hidden that will not be known.

27‘What I tell you in the darkness, speak in the light; and what you hear *whispered* in *your* ear, proclaim upon the housetops.

28‘And do not fear those who kill the body, but are unable to kill the soul; but rather fear Him who is able to destroy both soul and body in hell.

29‘Are not two sparrows sold for a 23cent? And *yet* not one of them will fall to the ground apart from your Father.

30‘But the very hairs of your head are all numbered.

31‘Therefore do not fear; you are of more value than many sparrows.

32‘Everyone therefore who shall confess Me before men, I will also confess him before My Father who is in heaven.

33‘But whoever shall deny Me before men, I will also deny him before My Father who is in heaven.

34 ¶‘Do not think that I came to bring peace on the earth; I did not come to bring peace, but a sword.

35‘For I came to SET A MAN AGAINST HIS FATHER, AND A DAUGHTER AGAINST HER MOTHER, AND A DAUGHTER-IN-LAW AGAINST HER MOTHER-IN-LAW;

36 and A MAN'S ENEMIES WILL BE THE MEMBERS OF HIS HOUSEHOLD.

37‘He who loves father or mother more than Me is not worthy of Me; and he who loves son or daughter more than Me is not worthy of Me.

38‘And he who does not take his cross and follow after Me is not worthy of Me.

39‘He who has found his life shall lose it, and he who has lost his life for My sake shall find it.

40 ¶‘He who receives you receives Me, and he who receives Me receives Him who sent Me.

41‘He who receives a prophet in *the* name of a prophet shall receive a prophet's reward; and he who receives a righteous man in the name of a

23 Gr., *assarion*, the smallest copper coin

righteous man shall receive a righteous man's reward.

42‘And whoever in the name of a disciple gives to one of these little ones even a cup of cold water to drink, truly I say to you he shall not lose his reward.”

CHAPTER 11

AND it came about that when Jesus had finished giving instructions to His twelve disciples, He departed from there to teach and preach in their cities.

2 ¶ Now when John in prison heard of the works of Christ, he sent *word* by his disciples,

3 and said to Him, “Are You the Expected One, or shall we look for someone else?”

4 And Jesus answered and said to them, “Go and report to John what you hear and see:

5 *the* BLIND RECEIVE SIGHT and *the* lame walk, *the* lepers are cleansed and *the* deaf hear, and *the* dead are raised up, and *the* POOR HAVE THE GOSPEL PREACHED TO THEM.

6‘And blessed is he who keeps from stumbling over Me.”

7 ¶ And as these were going *away,* Jesus began to speak to the multitudes about John,“What did you go out into the wilderness to look at? A reed shaken by the wind?

8‘But what did you go out to see? A man dressed in soft *clothing*? Behold, those who wear soft *clothing* are in kings' palaces.

9‘But why did you go out? To see a prophet? Yes, I say to you, and one who is more than a prophet.

10‘This is the one about whom it is written,

    ‘BEHOLD, I SEND MY MESSENGER
      BEFORE YOUR FACE,
    WHO WILL PREPARE YOUR WAY
      BEFORE YOU.’

11‘Truly, I say to you, among those born of women there has not arisen *anyone* greater than John the Baptist; yet he who is least in the kingdom of heaven is greater than he.

12‘And from the days of John the Baptist until now the kingdom of heaven suffers violence, and violent men take it by force.

13 "For all the prophets and the Law prophesied until John.

14 "And if you care to accept *it*, he himself is Elijah, who was to come.

15 "He who has ears to hear, let him hear.

16 "But to what shall I compare this generation? It is like children sitting in the market places, who call out to the other *children,*

17 and say, 'We played the flute for you, and you did not dance; we sang a dirge, and you did not mourn.'

18 "For John came neither eating nor drinking, and they say, 'He has a demon!'

19 "The Son of Man came eating and drinking, and they say, 'Behold, a gluttonous man and a drunkard, a friend of tax-gatherers and sinners!' Yet wisdom is vindicated by her deeds."

20 ¶ Then He began to reproach the cities in which most of His miracles were done, because they did not repent.

21 "Woe to you, Chorazin! Woe to you, Bethsaida! For if the miracles had occurred in Tyre and Sidon which occurred in you, they would have repented long ago in sackcloth and ashes.

22 "Nevertheless I say to you, it shall be more tolerable for Tyre and Sidon in *the* day of judgment, than for you.

23 "And you, Capernaum, will not be exalted to heaven, will you? You shall descend to Hades; for if the miracles had occurred in Sodom which occurred in you, it would have remained to this day.

24 "Nevertheless I say to you that it shall be more tolerable for the land of Sodom in *the* day of judgment, than for you."

25 ¶ At that time Jesus answered and said, "I praise Thee, O Father, Lord of heaven and earth, that Thou didst hide these things from *the* wise and intelligent and didst reveal them to babes.

26 "Yes, Father, for thus it was well-pleasing in Thy sight.

27 "All things have been handed over to Me by My Father; and no one knows the Son, except the Father; nor does anyone know the Father, except the Son, and anyone to whom the Son wills to reveal *Him.*

28 "Come to Me, all who are weary and heavy-laden, and I will give you rest.

29 "Take My yoke upon you, and learn from Me, for I am gentle and humble in heart; and YOU SHALL FIND REST FOR YOUR SOULS.

30 "For My yoke is easy, and My load is light."

CHAPTER 12

At that time Jesus went on the Sabbath through the grainfields, and His disciples became hungry and began to pick the heads *of grain* and eat.

2 But when the Pharisees saw it, they said to Him, "Behold, Your disciples do what is not lawful to do on a Sabbath."

3 But He said to them, "Have you not read what David did, when he became hungry, he and his companions;

4 how he entered the house of God, and they ate the consecrated bread, which was not lawful for him to eat, nor for those with him, but for the priests alone?

5 "Or have you not read in the Law, that on the Sabbath the priests in the temple break the Sabbath, and are innocent?

6 "But I say to you, that something greater than the temple is here.

7 "But if you had known what this means, 'I DESIRE COMPASSION, AND NOT A SACRIFICE,' you would not have condemned the innocent.

8 "For the Son of Man is Lord of the Sabbath."

9 ¶ And departing from there, He went into their synagogue.

10 And behold, *there was* a man with a withered hand. And they questioned Him, saying, "Is it lawful to heal on the Sabbath?"—in order that they might accuse Him.

11 And He said to them, "What man shall there be among you, who shall have one sheep, and if it falls into a pit on the Sabbath, will he not take hold of it, and lift it out?

12 "Of how much more value then is a man than a sheep? So then, it is lawful to do good on the Sabbath."

13 Then He *said to the man, "Stretch out your hand!" And he

stretched it out, and it was restored to normal, like the other.

14 But the Pharisees went out, and counseled together against Him, *as to* how they might destroy Him.

15 ¶ But Jesus, aware of *this,* withdrew from there. And many followed Him, and He healed them all,

16 and warned them not to make Him known,

17 in order that what was spoken through Isaiah the prophet, might be fulfilled, saying,

18 "BEHOLD, MY SERVANT WHOM I
   HAVE CHOSEN;
   MY BELOVED IN WHOM MY SOUL
   IS WELL-PLEASED;
   I WILL PUT MY SPIRIT UPON HIM,
   AND HE SHALL PROCLAIM JUSTICE
   TO THE GENTILES.

19 "HE WILL NOT QUARREL, NOR CRY
   OUT;
   NOR WILL ANYONE HEAR HIS
   VOICE IN THE STREETS.

20 "A BATTERED REED HE WILL NOT
   BREAK OFF,
   AND A SMOLDERING WICK HE
   WILL NOT PUT OUT,
   UNTIL HE LEADS JUSTICE TO VIC-
   TORY.

21 "AND IN HIS NAME THE GENTILES
   WILL HOPE."

22 ¶ Then there was brought to Him a demon-possessed man *who was* blind and dumb, and He healed him, so that the dumb man spoke and saw.

23 And all the multitudes were amazed, and *began* to say, "This *man* cannot be the Son of David, can he?"

24 But when the Pharisees heard it, they said, "This man casts out demons only by Beelzebul the ruler of the demons."

25 And knowing their thoughts He said to them, "Any kingdom divided against itself is laid waste; and any city or house divided against itself shall not stand.

26 'And if Satan casts out Satan, he is divided against himself; how then shall his kingdom stand?

27 'And if I by Beelzebul cast out demons, by whom do your sons cast them out? Consequently they shall be your judges.

28 'But if I cast out demons by the Spirit of God, then the kingdom of God has come upon you.

29 'Or how can anyone enter the strong man's house and carry off his property, unless he first binds the strong *man?* And then he will plunder his house.

30 'He who is not with Me is against Me; and he who does not gather with Me scatters.

31 "Therefore I say to you, any sin and blasphemy shall be forgiven men, but blasphemy against the Spirit shall not be forgiven.

32 'And whoever shall speak a word against the Son of Man, it shall be forgiven him; but whoever shall speak against the Holy Spirit, it shall not be forgiven him, either in this age, or in the *age* to come.

33 'Either make the tree good, and its fruit good; or make the tree bad, and its fruit bad; for the tree is known by its fruit.

34 'You brood of vipers, how can you, being evil, speak what is good? For the mouth speaks out of that which fills the heart.

35 'The good man out of *his* good treasure brings forth what is good; and the evil man out of *his* evil treasure brings forth what is evil.

36 'And I say to you, that every careless word that men shall speak, they shall render account for it in the day of judgment.

37 'For by your words you shall be justified, and by your words you shall be condemned."

38 ¶ Then some of the scribes and Pharisees answered Him, saying, "Teacher, we want to see a sign from You."

39 But He answered and said to them, "An evil and adulterous generation craves for a sign; and *yet* no sign shall be given to it but the sign of Jonah the prophet;

40 for just as JONAH WAS THREE DAYS AND THREE NIGHTS IN THE BELLY OF THE SEA MONSTER, so shall the Son of Man be three days and three nights in the heart of the earth.

41 "The men of Nineveh shall stand up with this generation at the judgment, and shall condemn it because they repented at the preaching of Jonah; and behold, something greater than Jonah is here.

42 'The Queen of *the* South shall rise

up with this generation at the judgment and shall condemn it, because she came from the ends of the earth to hear the wisdom of Solomon; and behold, something greater than Solomon is here.

43 "Now when the unclean spirit goes out of a man, it passes through waterless places, seeking rest, and does not find *it*.

44 "Then it says, 'I will return to my house from which I came'; and when it comes, it finds it unoccupied, swept, and put in order.

45 "Then it goes, and takes along with it seven other spirits more wicked than itself, and they go in and live there; and the last state of that man becomes worse than the first. That is the way it will also be with this evil generation."

46 ¶ While He was still speaking to the multitudes, behold, His mother and brothers were standing outside, seeking to speak to Him.

47 And someone said to Him, "Behold, Your mother and Your brothers are standing outside seeking to speak to You."

48 But He answered the one who was telling Him and said, "Who is My mother and who are My brothers?"

49 And stretching out His hand toward His disciples, He said, "Behold, My mother and My brothers!

50 "For whoever does the will of My Father who is in heaven, he is My brother and sister and mother."

CHAPTER 13

ON that day Jesus went out of the house, and was sitting by the sea.

2 And great multitudes gathered to Him, so that He got into a boat and sat down, and the whole multitude was standing on the beach.

3 And He spoke many things to them in parables, saying, "Behold, the sower went out to sow;

4 and as he sowed, some *seeds* fell beside the road, and the birds came and ate them up.

5 "And others fell upon the rocky places, where they did not have much soil; and immediately they sprang up, because they had no depth of soil.

6 "But when the sun had risen, they were scorched; and because they had no root, they withered away.

7 "And others fell among the thorns, and the thorns came up and choked them out.

8 "And others fell on the good soil, and *yielded a crop, some a hundredfold, some sixty, and some thirty.

9 "He who has ears, let him hear."

10 ¶ And the disciples came and said to Him, "Why do You speak to them in parables?"

11 And He answered and said to them, "To you it has been granted to know the mysteries of the kingdom of heaven, but to them it has not been granted.

12 "For whoever has, to him shall *more* be given, and he shall have an abundance; but whoever does not have, even what he has shall be taken away from him.

13 "Therefore I speak to them in parables; because while seeing they do not see, and while hearing they do not hear, nor do they understand.

14 "And in their case the prophecy of Isaiah is being fulfilled, which says,

'YOU WILL KEEP ON HEARING, BUT
    WILL NOT UNDERSTAND;
AND YOU WILL KEEP ON SEEING,
    BUT WILL NOT PERCEIVE;
15 FOR THE HEART OF THIS PEOPLE
    HAS BECOME DULL,
AND WITH THEIR EARS THEY
    SCARCELY HEAR,
AND THEY HAVE CLOSED THEIR
    EYES
LEST THEY SHOULD SEE WITH
    THEIR EYES,
AND HEAR WITH THEIR EARS,
AND UNDERSTAND WITH THEIR
    HEART AND RETURN,
AND I SHOULD HEAL THEM.'

16 "But blessed are your eyes, because they see; and your ears, because they hear.

17 "For truly I say to you, that many prophets and righteous men desired to see what you see, and did not see *it*; and to hear what you hear, and did not hear *it*.

18 "Hear then the parable of the sower.

19 "When anyone hears the word of the kingdom, and does not understand it, the evil *one* comes and snatches away what has been sown in his heart.

This is the one on whom seed was sown beside the road.

20 'And the one on whom seed was sown on the rocky places, this is the man who hears the word, and immediately receives it with joy;

21 yet he has no *firm* root in himself, but is *only* temporary, and when affliction or persecution arises because of the word, immediately he falls away.

22 'And the one on whom seed was sown among the thorns, this is the man who hears the word, and the worry of the world, and the deceitfulness of riches choke the word, and it becomes unfruitful.

23 'And the one on whom seed was sown on the good soil, this is the man who hears the word and understands it; who indeed bears fruit, and brings forth, some a hundredfold, some sixty, and some thirty.''

24 ¶ He presented another parable to them, saying, ''The kingdom of heaven may be compared to a man who sowed good seed in his field.

25 'But while men were sleeping, his enemy came and sowed 24tares also among the wheat, and went away.

26 'But when the wheat sprang up and bore grain, then the tares became evident also.

27 'And the slaves of the landowner came and said to him, 'Sir, did you not sow good seed in your field? How then does it have tares?'

28 'And he said to them, 'An enemy has done this!' And the slaves *said to him, 'Do you want us, then, to go and gather them up?'

29 'But he *said, 'No; lest while you are gathering up the tares, you may root up the wheat with them.

30 'Allow both to grow together until the harvest; and in the time of the harvest I will say to the reapers, ''First gather up the tares and bind them in bundles to burn them up; but gather the wheat into my barn.'' ' ''

31 ¶ He presented another parable to them, saying, ''The kingdom of heaven is like a mustard seed, which a man took and sowed in his field;

32 and this is smaller than all *other* seeds; but when it is full grown, it is larger than the garden plants, and becomes a tree, so that THE BIRDS OF

24 Or, *darnel,* a weed resembling wheat

THE AIR come and NEST IN ITS BRANCHES.''

33 ¶ He spoke another parable to them, ''The kingdom of heaven is like leaven, which a woman took and hid in three pecks of meal, until it was all leavened.''

34 ¶ All these things Jesus spoke to the multitudes in parables, and He did not speak to them without a parable,

35 so that what was spoken through the prophet might be fulfilled, saying,

''I WILL OPEN MY MOUTH IN PARABLES;

I WILL UTTER THINGS HIDDEN SINCE THE FOUNDATION OF THE WORLD.''

36 ¶ Then He left the multitudes, and went into the house. And His disciples came to Him, saying, ''Explain to us the parable of the tares of the field.''

37 And He answered and said, ''The one who sows the good seed is the Son of Man,

38 and the field is the world; and *as for* the good seed, these are the sons of the kingdom; and the tares are the sons of the evil *one;*

39 and the enemy who sowed them is the devil, and the harvest is the end of the age; and the reapers are angels.

40 'Therefore just as the tares are gathered up and burned with fire, so shall it be at the end of the age.

41 'The Son of Man will send forth His angels, and they will gather out of His kingdom all stumbling blocks, and those who commit lawlessness,

42 and will cast them into the furnace of fire; in that place there shall be weeping and gnashing of teeth.

43 'Then THE RIGHTEOUS WILL SHINE FORTH AS THE SUN in the kingdom of their Father. He who has ears, let him hear.

44 ¶'The kingdom of heaven is like a treasure hidden in the field, which a man found and hid; and from joy over it he goes and sells all that he has, and buys that field.

45 ¶'Again, the kingdom of heaven is like a merchant seeking fine pearls,

46 and upon finding one pearl of great value, he went and sold all that he had, and bought it.

47 ¶'Again, the kingdom of heaven is like a dragnet cast into the sea, and gathering *fish* of every kind;

48 and when it was filled, they drew it up on the beach; and they sat down, and gathered the good *fish* into containers, but the bad they threw away.

49 "So it will be at the end of the age; the angels shall come forth, and take out the wicked from among the righteous,

50 and will cast them into the furnace of fire; there shall be weeping and gnashing of teeth.

51 ¶ "Have you understood all these things?" They *said to Him, "Yes."

52 And He said to them, "Therefore every scribe who has become a disciple of the kingdom of heaven is like a head of a household, who brings forth out of his treasure things new and old."

53 ¶ And it came about that when Jesus had finished these parables, He departed from there.

54 And coming to His home town He *began* teaching them in their synagogue, so that they became astonished, and said, "Where *did* this man *get* this wisdom, and *these* miraculous powers?

55 "Is not this the carpenter's son? Is not His mother called Mary, and His brothers, James and Joseph and Simon and Judas?

56 "And His sisters, are they not all with us? Where then *did* this man *get* all these things?"

57 And they took offense at Him. But Jesus said to them, "A prophet is not without honor except in his home town, and in his *own* household."

58 And He did not do many miracles there because of their unbelief.

CHAPTER 14

At that time Herod the tetrarch heard the news about Jesus,

2 and said to his servants, "This is John the Baptist; he has risen from the dead; and that is why miraculous powers are at work in him."

3 For when Herod had John arrested, he bound him, and put him in prison on account of Herodias, the wife of his brother Philip.

4 For John had been saying to him, "It is not lawful for you to have her."

5 And although he wanted to put him to death, he feared the multitude, because they regarded him as a prophet.

6 But when Herod's birthday came, the daughter of Herodias danced before *them* and pleased Herod.

7 Thereupon he promised with an oath to give her whatever she asked.

8 And having been prompted by her mother, she *said, "Give me here on a platter the head of John the Baptist."

9 And although he was grieved, the king commanded *it* to be given because of his oaths, and because of his dinner guests.

10 And he sent and had John beheaded in the prison.

11 And his head was brought on a platter and given to the girl; and she brought *it* to her mother.

12 And his disciples came and took away the body and buried it; and they went and reported to Jesus.

13 ¶ Now when Jesus heard *it,* He withdrew from there in a boat, to a lonely place by Himself; and when the multitudes heard *of this,* they followed Him on foot from the cities.

14 And when He went ashore, He saw a great multitude, and felt compassion for them, and healed their sick.

15 And when it was evening, the disciples came to Him, saying, "The place is desolate, and the time is already past; so send the multitudes away, that they may go into the villages and buy food for themselves."

16 But Jesus said to them, "They do not need to go away; you give them *something* to eat!"

17 And they *said to Him, "We have here only five loaves and two fish."

18 And He said, "Bring them here to Me."

19 And ordering the multitudes to recline on the grass, He took the five loaves and the two fish, and looking up toward heaven, He blessed *the food,* and breaking the loaves He gave them to the disciples, and the disciples *gave* to the multitudes,

20 and they all ate, and were satisfied. And they picked up what was left over of the broken pieces, twelve full baskets.

21 And there were about five thousand men who ate, aside from women and children.

22 ¶ And immediately He made the disciples get into the boat, and go ahead of Him to the other side, while He sent the multitudes away.

23 And after He had sent the multitudes away, He went up to the mountain by Himself to pray; and when it was evening, He was there alone.

24 But the boat was already many 25stadia away from the land, battered by the waves; for the wind was contrary.

25 And in the 26fourth watch of the night He came to them, walking on the sea.

26 And when the disciples saw Him walking on the sea, they were frightened, saying, "It is a ghost!" And they cried out for fear.

27 But immediately Jesus spoke to them, saying, "Take courage, it is I; do not be afraid."

28 And Peter answered Him and said, "Lord, if it is You, command me to come to You on the water."

29 And He said, "Come!" And Peter got out of the boat, and walked on the water and came toward Jesus.

30 But seeing the wind, he became afraid, and beginning to sink, he cried out, saying, "Lord, save me!"

31 And immediately Jesus stretched out His hand and took hold of him, and *said to him, "O you of little faith, why did you doubt?"

32 And when they got into the boat, the wind stopped.

33 And those who were in the boat worshiped Him, saying, "You are certainly God's Son!"

34 ¶ And when they had crossed over, they came to land at Gennesaret.

35 And when the men of that place recognized Him, they sent into all that surrounding district and brought to Him all who were sick;

36 and they *began* to entreat Him that they might just touch the fringe of His cloak; and as many as touched *it* were cured.

CHAPTER 15

THEN some Pharisees and scribes *came to Jesus from Jerusalem, saying,

2 "Why do Your disciples transgress the tradition of the elders? For they do not wash their hands when they eat bread."

3 And He answered and said to them, "And why do you yourselves transgress the commandment of God for the sake of your tradition?

4 'For God said, 'HONOR YOUR FATHER AND MOTHER,' and, 'HE WHO SPEAKS EVIL OF FATHER OR MOTHER, LET HIM BE PUT TO DEATH.'

5 'But you say, 'Whoever shall say to *his* father or mother, "Anything of mine you might have been helped by has been given *to God*,"

6 he is not to honor his father 27or his mother28.' And *thus* you invalidated the word of God for the sake of your tradition.

7 'You hypocrites, rightly did Isaiah prophesy of you, saying,

8   'THIS PEOPLE HONORS ME WITH
        THEIR LIPS,
     BUT THEIR HEART IS FAR AWAY
        FROM ME.

9   'BUT IN VAIN DO THEY WORSHIP
        ME,
     TEACHING AS DOCTRINES THE PRE-
        CEPTS OF MEN.' "

10 And after He called the multitude to Him, He said to them, "Hear, and understand.

11 "Not what enters into the mouth defiles the man, but what proceeds out of the mouth, this defiles the man."

12 Then the disciples *came and *said to Him, "Do You know that the Pharisees were offended when they heard this statement?"

13 But He answered and said, "Every plant which My heavenly Father did not plant shall be rooted up.

14 'Let them alone; they are blind guides 29of the blind. And if a blind man guides a blind man, both will fall into a pit.'

15 And Peter answered and said to Him, "Explain the parable to us."

16 And He said, "Are you still lacking in understanding also?

17 "Do you not understand that everything that goes into the mouth passes into the stomach, and is eliminated?

18 'But the things that proceed out of the mouth come from the heart, and those defile the man.

---

25 A stadion was about 600 feet   26 I.e., 3–6 a.m.

27 Many mss. do not contain *or his mother*
28 I.e., by supporting them with it
29 Some mss. do not contain *of the blind*

19 "For out of the heart come evil thoughts, murders, adulteries, fornications, thefts, false witness, slanders.

20 "These are the things which defile the man; but to eat with unwashed hands does not defile the man."

21 ¶ And Jesus went away from there, and withdrew into the district of Tyre and Sidon.

22 And behold, a Canaanite woman came out from that region, and *began* to cry out, saying, "Have mercy on me, O Lord, Son of David; my daughter is cruelly demon-possessed."

23 But He did not answer her a word. And His disciples came to *Him* and kept asking Him, saying, "Send her away, for she is shouting out after us."

24 But He answered and said, "I was sent only to the lost sheep of the house of Israel."

25 But she came and *began* to bow down before Him, saying, "Lord, help me!"

26 And He answered and said, "It is not good to take the children's bread and throw it to the dogs."

27 But she said, "Yes, Lord; but even the dogs feed on the crumbs which fall from their masters' table."

28 Then Jesus answered and said to her, "O woman, your faith is great; be it done for you as you wish." And her daughter was healed at once.

29 ¶ And departing from there, Jesus went along by the Sea of Galilee, and having gone up to the mountain, He was sitting there.

30 And great multitudes came to Him, bringing with them *those who were* lame, crippled, blind, dumb, and many others, and they laid them down at His feet; and He healed them,

31 so that the multitude marveled as they saw the dumb speaking, the crippled restored, and the lame walking, and the blind seeing; and they glorified the God of Israel.

32 ¶ And Jesus called His disciples to Him, and said, "I feel compassion for the multitude, because they have remained with Me now three days and have nothing to eat; and I do not wish to send them away hungry, lest they faint on the way."

33 And the disciples *said to Him, "Where would we get so many loaves in a desolate place to satisfy such a great multitude?"

34 And Jesus *said to them, "How many loaves do you have?" And they said, "Seven, and a few small fish."

35 And He directed the multitude to sit down on the ground;

36 and He took the seven loaves and the fish; and giving thanks, He broke them and started giving them to the disciples, and the disciples *in turn,* to the multitudes.

37 And they all ate, and were satisfied, and they picked up what was left over of the broken pieces, seven large baskets full.

38 And those who ate were four thousand men, besides women and children.

39 And sending away the multitudes, He got into the boat, and came to the region of Magadan.

CHAPTER 16

AND the Pharisees and Sadducees came up, and testing Him asked Him to show them a sign from heaven.

2 But He answered and said to them, "When it is evening, you say, '*It will be* fair weather, for the sky is red.'

3 "And in the morning, '*There will be* a storm today, for the sky is red and threatening.' Do you know how to discern the appearance of the sky, but cannot *discern* the signs of the times?

4 "An evil and adulterous generation seeks after a sign; and a sign will not be given it, except the sign of Jonah." And He left them, and went away.

5 ¶ And the disciples came to the other side and had forgotten to take bread.

6 And Jesus said to them, "Watch out and beware of the leaven of the Pharisees and Sadducees."

7 And they began to discuss among themselves, saying, "*It is* because we took no bread."

8 But Jesus, aware of this, said, "You men of little faith, why do you discuss among yourselves that you have no bread?

9 "Do you not yet understand or remember the five loaves of the five thousand, and how many baskets you took up?

10 "Or the seven loaves of the four thousand, and how many large baskets you took up?

11"How is it that you do not understand that I did not speak to you concerning bread? But beware of the leaven of the Pharisees and Sadducees."

12 Then they understood that He did not say to beware of the leaven of bread, but of the teaching of the Pharisees and Sadducees.

13 ¶ Now when Jesus came into the district of Caesarea Philippi, He *began* asking His disciples, saying, "Who do people say that the Son of Man is?"

14 And they said, "Some *say* John the Baptist; and others, Elijah; but still others, Jeremiah, or one of the prophets."

15 He *said to them, "But who do you say that I am?"

16 And Simon Peter answered and said, "Thou art the Christ, the Son of the living God."

17 And Jesus answered and said to him, "Blessed are you, Simon Barjona, because flesh and blood did not reveal *this* to you, but My Father who is in heaven.

18'And I also say to you that you are Peter, and upon this rock I will build My church; and the gates of Hades shall not overpower it.

19'I will give you the keys of the kingdom of heaven; and whatever you shall bind on earth shall be bound in heaven, and whatever you shall loose on earth shall be loosed in heaven."

20 Then He warned the disciples that they should tell no one that He was the Christ.

21 ¶ From that time Jesus Christ began to show His disciples that He must go to Jerusalem, and suffer many things from the elders and chief priests and scribes, and be killed, and be raised up on the third day.

22 And Peter took Him aside and began to rebuke Him, saying, "God forbid *it,* Lord! This shall never happen to You."

23 But He turned and said to Peter, "Get behind Me, Satan! You are a stumbling block to Me; for you are not setting your mind on God's interests, but man's."

24 Then Jesus said to His disciples, "If anyone wishes to come after Me, let him deny himself, and take up his cross, and follow Me.

25'For whoever wishes to save his life shall lose it; but whoever loses his life for My sake shall find it.

26'For what will a man be profited, if he gains the whole world, and forfeits his soul? Or what will a man give in exchange for his soul?

27'For the Son of Man is going to come in the glory of His Father with His angels; and WILL THEN RECOMPENSE EVERY MAN ACCORDING TO HIS DEEDS.

28'Truly I say to you, there are some of those who are standing here who shall not taste death until they see the Son of Man coming in His kingdom."

CHAPTER 17

AND six days later Jesus *took with Him Peter and James and John his brother, and *brought them up to a high mountain by themselves.

2 And He was transfigured before them; and His face shone like the sun, and His garments became as white as light.

3 And behold, Moses and Elijah appeared to them, talking with Him.

4 And Peter answered and said to Jesus, "Lord, it is good for us to be here; if You wish, I will make three tabernacles here, one for You, and one for Moses, and one for Elijah."

5 While he was still speaking, behold, a bright cloud overshadowed them; and behold, a voice out of the cloud, saying, "This is My beloved Son, with whom I am well-pleased; listen to Him!"

6 And when the disciples heard *this,* they fell on their faces and were much afraid.

7 And Jesus came to *them* and touched them and said, "Arise, and do not be afraid."

8 And lifting up their eyes, they saw no one, except Jesus Himself alone.

9 ¶ And as they were coming down from the mountain, Jesus commanded them, saying, "Tell the vision to no one until the Son of Man has risen from the dead."

10 And His disciples asked Him, saying, "Why then do the scribes say that Elijah must come first?"

11 And He answered and said, "Elijah is coming and will restore all things;

12 but I say to you, that Elijah already came, and they did not recognize him, but did to him whatever they wished. So also the Son of Man is going to suffer at their hands."

13 Then the disciples understood that He had spoken to them about John the Baptist.

14 ¶ And when they came to the multitude, a man came up to Him, falling on his knees before Him, and saying,

15 "Lord, have mercy on my son, for he is a lunatic, and is very ill; for he often falls into the fire, and often into the water.

16 "And I brought him to Your disciples, and they could not cure him."

17 And Jesus answered and said, "O unbelieving and perverted generation, how long shall I be with you? How long shall I put up with you? Bring him here to Me."

18 And Jesus rebuked him, and the demon came out of him, and the boy was cured at once.

19 ¶ Then the disciples came to Jesus privately and said, "Why could we not cast it out?"

20 And He *said to them, "Because of the littleness of your faith; for truly I say to you, if you have faith as a mustard seed, you shall say to this mountain, 'Move from here to there,' and it shall move; and nothing shall be impossible to you.

21 ["30But this kind does not go out except by prayer and fasting."]

22 ¶ And while they were gathering together in Galilee, Jesus said to them, "The Son of Man is going to be delivered into the hands of men;

23 and they will kill Him, and He will be raised on the third day." And they were deeply grieved.

24 ¶ And when they had come to Capernaum, those who collected the 31two-drachma *tax* came to Peter, and said, "Does your teacher not pay the 31two-drachma *tax*?"

25 He *said, "Yes." And when he came into the house, Jesus spoke to him first, saying, "What do you think, Simon? From whom do the kings of the earth collect customs or poll-tax, from their sons or from strangers?"

26 And upon his saying, "From strangers," Jesus said to him, "Consequently the sons are exempt.

27 "But, lest we give them offense, go to the sea, and throw in a hook, and take the first fish that comes up; and when you open its mouth, you will find a 32stater. Take that and give it to them for you and Me."

CHAPTER 18

AT that time the disciples came to Jesus, saying, "Who then is greatest in the kingdom of heaven?"

2 And He called a child to Himself and set him before them,

3 and said, "Truly I say to you, unless you are converted and become like children, you shall not enter the kingdom of heaven.

4 "Whoever then humbles himself as this child, he is the greatest in the kingdom of heaven.

5 "And whoever receives one such child in My name receives Me;

6 but whoever causes one of these little ones who believe in Me to stumble, it is better for him that a heavy millstone be hung around his neck, and that he be drowned in the depth of the sea.

7 ¶ "Woe to the world because of *its* stumbling blocks! For it is inevitable that stumbling blocks come; but woe to that man through whom the stumbling block comes!

8 "And if your hand or your foot causes you to stumble, cut it off and throw it from you; it is better for you to enter life crippled or lame, than having two hands or two feet, to be cast into the eternal fire.

9 "And if your eye causes you to stumble, pluck it out, and throw it from you. It is better for you to enter life with one eye, than having two eyes, to be cast into the fiery hell.

10 "See that you do not despise one of these little ones, for I say to you, that their angels in heaven continually behold the face of My Father who is in heaven.

11 ["33For the Son of Man has come to save that which was lost.]

12 "What do you think? If any man has a hundred sheep, and one of them

---

30 Many mss. do not contain this verse
31 Equivalent to two denarii or two days' wages paid as a temple tax

32 Or, *shekel*, worth four drachmas
33 Most ancient mss. do not contain this verse

has gone astray, does he not leave the ninety-nine on the mountains and go and search for the one that is straying?

13'And if it turns out that he finds it, truly I say to you, he rejoices over it more than over the ninety-nine which have not gone astray.

14'Thus it is not *the* will of your Father who is in heaven that one of these little ones perish.

15 ¶'And if your brother sins[34], go and reprove him in private; if he listens to you, you have won your brother.

16'But if he does not listen *to you,* take one or two more with you, so that BY THE MOUTH OF TWO OR THREE WITNESSES EVERY FACT MAY BE CONFIRMED.

17'And if he refuses to listen to them, tell it to the church; and if he refuses to listen even to the church, let him be to you as a Gentile and a tax-gatherer.

18'Truly I say to you, whatever you shall bind on earth shall be bound in heaven; and whatever you loose on earth shall be loosed in heaven.

19'Again I say to you, that if two of you agree on earth about anything that they may ask, it shall be done for them by My Father who is in heaven.

20'For where two or three have gathered together in My name, there I am in their midst."

21 ¶ Then Peter came and said to Him, "Lord, how often shall my brother sin against me and I forgive him? Up to seven times?"

22 Jesus *said to him, "I do not say to you, up to seven times, but up to seventy times seven.

23'For this reason the kingdom of heaven may be compared to a certain king who wished to settle accounts with his slaves.

24'And when he had begun to settle *them,* there was brought to him one who owed him [35]ten thousand talents.

25'But since he did not have *the means* to repay, his lord commanded him to be sold, along with his wife and children and all that he had, and repayment to be made.

26'The slave therefore falling down, prostrated himself before him, saying,

'Have patience with me, and I will repay you everything.'

27'And the lord of that slave felt compassion and released him and forgave him the debt.

28'But that slave went out and found one of his fellow slaves who owed him a hundred [36]denarii; and he seized him and *began* to choke *him,* saying, 'Pay back what you owe.'

29'So his fellow slave fell down and *began* to entreat him, saying, 'Have patience with me and I will repay you.'

30'He was unwilling however, but went and threw him in prison until he should pay back what was owed.

31'So when his fellow slaves saw what had happened, they were deeply grieved and came and reported to their lord all that had happened.

32'Then summoning him, his lord *said to him, 'You wicked slave, I forgave you all that debt because you entreated me.

33'Should you not also have had mercy on your fellow slave, even as I had mercy on you?'

34'And his lord, moved with anger, handed him over to the torturers until he should repay all that was owed him.

35'So shall My heavenly Father also do to you, if each of you does not forgive his brother from your heart."

CHAPTER 19

AND it came about that when Jesus had finished these words, He departed from Galilee, and came into the region of Judea beyond the Jordan;

2 and great multitudes followed Him, and He healed them there.

3 ¶ And *some* Pharisees came to Him, testing Him, and saying, "Is it lawful *for a man* to divorce his wife for any cause at all?"

4 And He answered and said, "Have you not read, that He who created *them* from the beginning MADE THEM MALE AND FEMALE,

5 and said, 'FOR THIS CAUSE A MAN SHALL LEAVE HIS FATHER AND MOTHER, AND SHALL CLEAVE TO HIS WIFE; AND THE TWO SHALL BECOME ONE FLESH'?

6'Consequently they are no longer two, but one flesh. What therefore God has joined together, let no man separate."

---

[34] Many mss. add here: *against you*
[35] About $10,000,000 in silver content but worth much more in buying power
[36] The denarius was equivalent to one day's wage

7 They *said to Him, "Why then did Moses command to GIVE HER A CERTIFICATE OF DIVORCE AND SEND *her* AWAY?"

8 He *said to them, "Because of your hardness of heart, Moses permitted you to divorce your wives; but from the beginning it has not been this way.

9 "And I say to you, whoever divorces his wife, except for immorality, and marries another woman commits adultery."

10 The disciples *said to Him, "If the relationship of the man with his wife is like this, it is better not to marry."

11 But He said to them, "Not all men *can* accept this statement, but *only* those to whom it has been given.

12 "For there are eunuchs who were born that way from their mother's womb; and there are eunuchs who were made eunuchs by men; and there are *also* eunuchs who made themselves eunuchs for the sake of the kingdom of heaven. He who is able to accept *this*, let him accept *it*."

13 ¶ Then *some* children were brought to Him so that He might lay His hands on them and pray; and the disciples rebuked them.

14 But Jesus said, "Let the children alone, and do not hinder them from coming to Me; for the kingdom of heaven belongs to such as these."

15 And after laying His hands on them, He departed from there.

16 ¶ And behold, one came to Him and said, "Teacher, what good thing shall I do that I may obtain eternal life?"

17 And He said to him, "Why are you asking Me about what is good? There is *only* One who is good; but if you wish to enter into life, keep the commandments."

18 He *said to Him, "Which ones?" And Jesus said, "YOU SHALL NOT COMMIT MURDER; YOU SHALL NOT COMMIT ADULTERY; YOU SHALL NOT STEAL; YOU SHALL NOT BEAR FALSE WITNESS;

19 HONOR YOUR FATHER AND MOTHER; and YOU SHALL LOVE YOUR NEIGHBOR AS YOURSELF."

20 The young man *said to Him, "All these things I have kept; what am I still lacking?"

21 Jesus said to him, "If you wish to be complete, go *and* sell your possessions and give to *the* poor, and you shall have treasure in heaven; and come, follow Me."

22 But when the young man heard this statement, he went away grieved; for he was one who owned much property.

23 ¶ And Jesus said to His disciples, "Truly I say to you, it is hard for a rich man to enter the kingdom of heaven.

24 "And again I say to you, it is easier for a camel to go through the eye of a needle, than for a rich man to enter the kingdom of God."

25 And when the disciples heard *this*, they were very astonished and said, "Then who can be saved?"

26 And looking upon *them* Jesus said to them, "With men this is impossible, but with God all things are possible."

27 Then Peter answered and said to Him, "Behold, we have left everything and followed You; what then will there be for us?"

28 And Jesus said to them, "Truly I say to you, that you who have followed Me, in the regeneration when the Son of Man will sit on His glorious throne, you also shall sit upon twelve thrones, judging the twelve tribes of Israel.

29 "And everyone who has left houses or brothers or sisters or father or mother[37] or children or farms for My name's sake, shall receive many times as much, and shall inherit eternal life.

30 "But many *who are* first will be last; and *the* last, first.

CHAPTER 20

"FOR the kingdom of heaven is like a landowner who went out early in the morning to hire laborers for his vineyard.

2 "And when he had agreed with the laborers for a [38]denarius for the day, he sent them into his vineyard.

3 "And he went out about the [39]third hour and saw others standing idle in the market place;

4 and to those he said, 'You too go into the vineyard, and whatever is right I will give you.' And *so* they went.

---

37 Many mss. add here, *or wife*
38 The denarius was equivalent to one day's wage
39 I.e., 9 a.m.

5 'Again he went out about the ⁴⁰sixth and the ninth hour, and did the same thing.

6 'And about the ⁴¹eleventh *hour* he went out, and found others standing; and he *said to them, 'Why have you been standing here idle all day long?'

7 "They *said to him, 'Because no one hired us.' He *said to them, 'You too go into the vineyard.'

8 'And when evening had come, the owner of the vineyard *said to his foreman, 'Call the laborers and pay them their wages, beginning with the last *group* to the first.'

9 'And when those *hired* about the eleventh hour came, each one received a ³⁸denarius.

10 'And when those *hired* first came, they thought that they would receive more; and they also received each one a ³⁸denarius.

11 'And when they received it, they grumbled at the landowner,

12 saying, 'These last men have worked *only* one hour, and you have made them equal to us who have borne the burden and the scorching heat of the day.'

13 'But he answered and said to one of them, 'Friend, I am doing you no wrong; did you not agree with me for a ³⁸denarius?

14 'Take what is yours and go your way, but I wish to give to this last man the same as to you.

15 'Is it not lawful for me to do what I wish with what is my own? Or is your eye envious because I am generous?'

16 'Thus the last shall be first, and the first last."

17 ¶ And as Jesus was about to go up to Jerusalem, He took the twelve *disciples* aside by themselves, and on the way He said to them,

18 'Behold, we are going up to Jerusalem; and the Son of Man will be delivered to the chief priests and scribes, and they will condemn Him to death,

19 and will deliver Him to the Gentiles to mock and scourge and crucify *Him*, and on the third day He will be raised up."

20 ¶ Then the mother of the sons of Zebedee came to Him with her sons,

bowing down, and making a request of Him.

21 And He said to her, "What do you wish?" She *said to Him, "Command that in Your kingdom these two sons of mine may sit, one on Your right and one on Your left."

22 But Jesus answered and said, "You do not know what you are asking for. Are you able to drink the cup that I am about to drink?" They *said to Him, "We are able."

23 He *said to them, "My cup you shall drink; but to sit on My right and on *My* left, this is not Mine to give, but it is for those for whom it has been prepared by My Father."

24 And hearing *this,* the ten became indignant with the two brothers.

25 But Jesus called them to Himself, and said, "You know that the rulers of the Gentiles lord it over them, and *their* great men exercise authority over them.

26 'It is not so among you, but whoever wishes to become great among you shall be your servant,

27 and whoever wishes to be first among you shall be your slave;

28 just as the Son of Man did not come to be served, but to serve, and to give His life a ransom for many."

29 ¶ And as they were going out from Jericho, a great multitude followed Him.

30 And behold, two blind men sitting by the road, hearing that Jesus was passing by, cried out, saying, "Lord, have mercy on us, Son of David!"

31 And the multitude sternly told them to be quiet; but they cried out all the more, saying, "Lord, have mercy on us, Son of David!"

32 And Jesus stopped and called them, and said, "What do you want Me to do for you?"

33 They *said to Him, "Lord, *we want* our eyes to be opened."

34 And moved with compassion, Jesus touched their eyes; and immediately they regained their sight and followed Him.

CHAPTER 21

AND when they had approached Jerusalem and had come to Bethphage, to the Mount of Olives, then Jesus sent two disciples,

---

³⁸ The denarius was equivalent to one day's wage
⁴⁰ I.e., Noon and 3 p.m.   ⁴¹ I.e., 5 p.m.

2 saying to them, "Go into the village opposite you, and immediately you will find a donkey tied *there* and a colt with her; untie *them*, and bring *them* to Me.

3 "And if anyone says something to you, you shall say, 'The Lord has need of them,' and immediately he will send them."

4 Now this took place that what was spoken through the prophet might be fulfilled, saying,

5 "SAY TO THE DAUGHTER OF ZION,
'BEHOLD YOUR KING IS COMING TO YOU,
GENTLE, AND MOUNTED ON A DONKEY,
EVEN ON A COLT, THE FOAL OF A BEAST OF BURDEN.' "

6 And the disciples went and did just as Jesus had directed them,

7 and brought the donkey and the colt, and laid on them their garments, on which He sat.

8 And most of the multitude spread their garments in the road, and others were cutting branches from the trees, and spreading them in the road.

9 And the multitudes going before Him, and those who followed after were crying out, saying,

"Hosanna to the Son of David;
BLESSED IS HE WHO COMES IN THE NAME OF THE LORD;
Hosanna in the highest!"

10 And when He had entered Jerusalem, all the city was stirred, saying, "Who is this?"

11 And the multitudes were saying, "This is the prophet Jesus, from Nazareth in Galilee."

12 ¶ And Jesus entered the temple and cast out all those who were buying and selling in the temple, and overturned the tables of the moneychangers and the seats of those who were selling doves.

13 And He *said to them, "It is written, 'MY HOUSE SHALL BE CALLED A HOUSE OF PRAYER'; but you are making it a ROBBERS' DEN."

14 And *the* blind and *the* lame came to Him in the temple, and He healed them.

15 But when the chief priests and the scribes saw the wonderful things that He had done, and the children who were crying out in the temple and saying, "Hosanna to the Son of David," they became indignant,

16 and said to Him, "Do You hear what these are saying?" And Jesus *said to them, "Yes; have you never read, 'OUT OF THE MOUTH OF INFANTS AND NURSING BABES THOU HAST PREPARED PRAISE FOR THYSELF'?"

17 And He left them and went out of the city to Bethany, and lodged there.

18 ¶ Now in the morning, when He returned to the city, He became hungry.

19 And seeing a lone fig tree by the road, He came to it, and found nothing on it except leaves only; and He *said to it, "No longer shall there ever be *any* fruit from you." And at once the fig tree withered.

20 And seeing *this*, the disciples marveled, saying, "How did the fig tree wither at once?"

21 And Jesus answered and said to them, "Truly I say to you, if you have faith, and do not doubt, you shall not only do what was done to the fig tree, but even if you say to this mountain, 'Be taken up and cast into the sea,' it shall happen.

22 "And all things you ask in prayer, believing, you shall receive."

23 ¶ And when He had come into the temple, the chief priests and the elders of the people came to Him as He was teaching, and said, "By what authority are You doing these things, and who gave You this authority?"

24 And Jesus answered and said to them, "I will ask you one thing too, which if you tell Me, I will also tell you by what authority I do these things.

25 "The baptism of John was from what *source*, from heaven or from men?" And they *began* reasoning among themselves, saying, "If we say, 'From heaven,' He will say to us, 'Then why did you not believe him?'

26 "But if we say, 'From men,' we fear the multitude; for they all hold John to be a prophet."

27 And answering Jesus, they said, "We do not know." He also said to them, "Neither will I tell you by what authority I do these things.

28 "But what do you think? A man had two sons, and he came to the first and said, 'Son, go work today in the vineyard.'

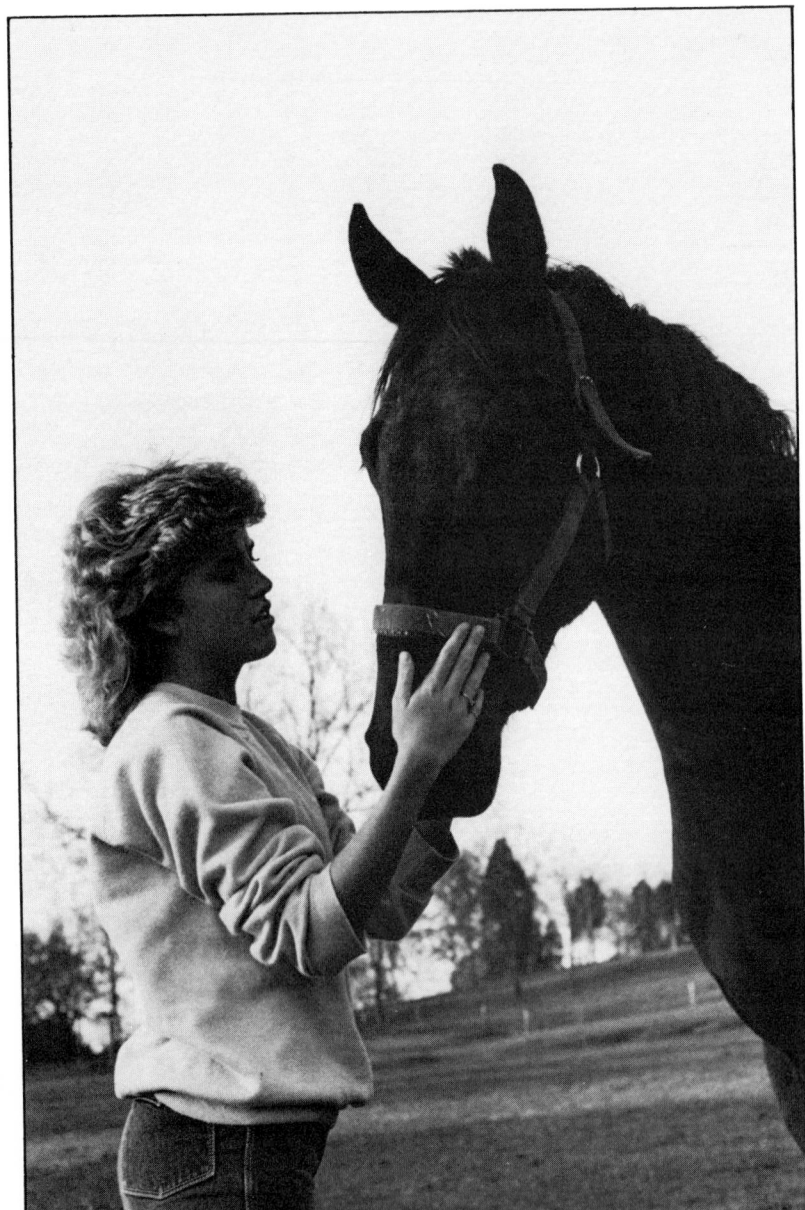

29 "And he answered and said, 'I will, sir'; and he did not go.

30 "And he came to the second and said the same thing. But he answered and said, 'I will not'; *yet* he afterward regretted *it* and went.

31 "Which of the two did the will of his father?" They *said, "The latter." Jesus *said to them, "Truly I say to you that the tax-gatherers and harlots will get into the kingdom of God before you.

32 "For John came to you in the way of righteousness and you did not believe him; but the tax-gatherers and harlots did believe him; and you, seeing this, did not even feel remorse afterward so as to believe him.

33 ¶ "Listen to another parable. There was a landowner who PLANTED A VINE-YARD AND PUT A WALL AROUND IT AND DUG A WINE PRESS IN IT, AND BUILT A TOWER, and rented it out to vine-growers, and went on a journey.

34 "And when the harvest time approached, he sent his slaves to the vine-growers to receive his produce.

35 "And the vine-growers took his slaves and beat one, and killed another, and stoned a third.

36 "Again he sent another group of slaves larger than the first; and they did the same thing to them.

37 "But afterward he sent his son to them, saying, 'They will respect my son.'

38 "But when the vine-growers saw the son, they said among themselves, 'This is the heir; come, let us kill him, and seize his inheritance.'

39 "And they took him, and threw him out of the vineyard, and killed him.

40 "Therefore when the owner of the vineyard comes, what will he do to those vine-growers?"

41 They *said to Him, "He will bring those wretches to a wretched end, and will rent out the vineyard to other vine-growers, who will pay him the proceeds at the *proper* seasons."

42 Jesus *said to them, "Did you never read in the Scriptures,

'THE STONE WHICH THE BUILDERS REJECTED,

THIS BECAME THE CHIEF CORNER stone;

THIS CAME ABOUT FROM THE LORD,

AND IT IS MARVELOUS IN OUR EYES'?

43 "Therefore I say to you, the kingdom of God will be taken away from you, and be given to a nation producing the fruit of it.

44 "And he who falls on this stone will be broken to pieces; but on whomever it falls, it will scatter him like dust."

45 And when the chief priests and the Pharisees heard His parables, they understood that He was speaking about them.

46 And when they sought to seize Him, they feared the multitudes, because they held Him to be a prophet.

CHAPTER 22

AND Jesus answered and spoke to them again in parables, saying,

2 "The kingdom of heaven may be compared to a king, who gave a wedding feast for his son.

3 "And he sent out his slaves to call those who had been invited to the wedding feast, and they were unwilling to come.

4 "Again he sent out other slaves saying, 'Tell those who have been invited, 'Behold, I have prepared my dinner; my oxen and my fattened livestock are *all* butchered and everything is ready; come to the wedding feast." '

5 "But they paid no attention and went their way, one to his own farm, another to his business,

6 and the rest seized his slaves and mistreated them and killed them.

7 "But the king was enraged and sent his armies, and destroyed those murderers, and set their city on fire.

8 "Then he *said to his slaves, 'The wedding is ready, but those who were invited were not worthy.

9 'Go therefore to the main highways, and as many as you find *there,* invite to the wedding feast.'

10 "And those slaves went out into the streets, and gathered together all they found, both evil and good; and the wedding hall was filled with dinner guests.

11 "But when the king came in to look over the dinner guests, he saw there a man not dressed in wedding clothes,

12 and he *said to him, 'Friend, how

did you come in here without wedding clothes?' And he was speechless.

13"Then the king said to the servants, 'Bind him hand and foot, and cast him into the outer darkness; in that place there shall be weeping and gnashing of teeth.'

14"For many are called, but few *are* chosen."

15 ¶ Then the Pharisees went and counseled together how they might trap Him in what He said.

16 And they *sent their disciples to Him, along with the Herodians, saying, "Teacher, we know that You are truthful and teach the way of God in truth, and defer to no one; for You are not partial to any.

17"Tell us therefore, what do You think? Is it lawful to give a poll-tax to Caesar, or not?"

18 But Jesus perceived their malice, and said, "Why are you testing Me, you hypocrites?

19"Show Me the coin *used* for the poll-tax." And they brought Him a denarius.

20 And He *said to them, "Whose likeness and inscription is this?"

21 They *said to Him, "Caesar's." Then He *said to them, "Then render to Caesar the things that are Caesar's; and to God the things that are God's."

22 And hearing *this*, they marveled, and leaving Him, they went away.

23 ¶ On that day *some* Sadducees (who say there is no resurrection) came to Him and questioned Him,

24 saying, "Teacher, Moses said, 'IF A MAN DIES, HAVING NO CHILDREN, HIS BROTHER AS NEXT OF KIN SHALL MARRY HIS WIFE, AND RAISE UP AN OFFSPRING TO HIS BROTHER.'

25"Now there were seven brothers with us; and the first married and died, and having no offspring left his wife to his brother;

26 so also the second, and the third, down to the seventh.

27"And last of all, the woman died.

28"In the resurrection therefore whose wife of the seven shall she be? For they all had her."

29 But Jesus answered and said to them, "You are mistaken, not understanding the Scriptures, or the power of God.

30"For in the resurrection they neither marry, nor are given in marriage, but are like angels in heaven.

31"But regarding the resurrection of the dead, have you not read that which was spoken to you by God, saying,

32 'I AM THE GOD OF ABRAHAM, AND THE GOD OF ISAAC, AND THE GOD OF JACOB'? He is not the God of the dead but of the living."

33 And when the multitudes heard *this*, they were astonished at His teaching.

34 ¶ But when the Pharisees heard that He had put the Sadducees to silence, they gathered themselves together.

35 And one of them, [42]a lawyer, asked Him *a question*, testing Him,

36"Teacher, which is the great commandment in the Law?"

37 And He said to him, " 'YOU SHALL LOVE THE LORD YOUR GOD WITH ALL YOUR HEART, AND WITH ALL YOUR SOUL, AND WITH ALL YOUR MIND.'

38"This is the great and foremost commandment.

39"The second is like it, 'YOU SHALL LOVE YOUR NEIGHBOR AS YOURSELF.'

40"On these two commandments depend the whole Law and the Prophets."

41 ¶ Now while the Pharisees were gathered together, Jesus asked them a question,

42 saying, "What do you think about the Christ, whose son is He?" They *said to Him, "*The son* of David."

43 He *said to them, "Then how does David in the Spirit call Him 'Lord,' saying,

44 'THE LORD SAID TO MY LORD,
   "SIT AT MY RIGHT HAND,
      UNTIL I PUT THINE ENEMIES BENEATH THY FEET" '?

45"If David then calls Him 'Lord,' how is He his son?"

46 And no one was able to answer Him a word, nor did anyone dare from that day on to ask Him another question.

CHAPTER 23

THEN Jesus spoke to the multitudes and to His disciples,

2 saying, "The scribes and the

---

42 I.e., an expert in the Mosaic law

Pharisees have seated themselves in the chair of Moses;

3 therefore all that they tell you, do and observe, but do not do according to their deeds; for they say *things*, and do not do *them*.

4 "And they tie up heavy loads, and lay them on men's shoulders; but they themselves are unwilling to move them with *so much as* a finger.

5 "But they do all their deeds to be noticed by men; for they broaden their [43]phylacteries, and lengthen the tassels *of their garments.*

6 "And they love the place of honor at banquets, and the chief seats in the synagogues,

7 and respectful greetings in the market places, and being called by men, Rabbi.

8 "But do not be called Rabbi; for One is your Teacher, and you are all brothers.

9 "And do not call *anyone* on earth your father; for One is your Father, He who is in heaven.

10 "And do not be called leaders; for One is your Leader, *that is,* Christ.

11 "But the greatest among you shall be your servant.

12 "And whoever exalts himself shall be humbled; and whoever humbles himself shall be exalted.

13 ¶ "But woe to you, scribes and Pharisees, hypocrites, because you shut off the kingdom of heaven from men; for you do not enter in yourselves, nor do you allow those who are entering to go in.

14 [[44]Woe to you, scribes and Pharisees, hypocrites, because you devour widows' houses, even while for a pretense you make long prayers; therefore you shall receive greater condemnation.]

15 ¶ "Woe to you, scribes and Pharisees, hypocrites, because you travel about on sea and land to make one proselyte; and when he becomes one, you make him twice as much a son of hell as yourselves.

16 ¶ "Woe to you, blind guides, who say, 'Whoever swears by the temple, that is nothing; but whoever swears by the gold of the temple, he is obligated.'

17 "You fools and blind men; which is more important, the gold, or the temple that sanctified the gold?

18 "And, 'Whoever swears by the altar, *that* is nothing, but whoever swears by the offering upon it, he is obligated.'

19 "You blind men, which is more important, the offering or the altar that sanctifies the offering?

20 "Therefore he who swears, swears *both* by the altar and by everything on it.

21 "And he who swears by the temple, swears *both* by the temple and by Him who dwells within it.

22 "And he who swears by heaven, swears *both* by the throne of God and by Him who sits upon it.

23 ¶ "Woe to you, scribes and Pharisees, hypocrites! For you tithe mint and dill and cummin, and have neglected the weightier provisions of the law: justice and mercy and faithfulness; but these are the things you should have done without neglecting the others.

24 "You blind guides, who strain out a gnat and swallow a camel!

25 ¶ "Woe to you, scribes and Pharisees, hypocrites! For you clean the outside of the cup and of the dish, but inside they are full of robbery and self-indulgence.

26 "You blind Pharisee, first clean the inside of the cup and of the dish, so that the outside of it may become clean also.

27 ¶ "Woe to you, scribes and Pharisees, hypocrites! For you are like whitewashed tombs which on the outside appear beautiful, but inside they are full of dead men's bones and all uncleanness.

28 "Even so you too outwardly appear righteous to men, but inwardly you are full of hypocrisy and lawlessness.

29 ¶ "Woe to you, scribes and Pharisees, hypocrites! For you build the tombs of the prophets and adorn the monuments of the righteous,

30 and say, 'If we had been *living* in the days of our fathers, we would not have been partners with them in *shedding* the blood of the prophets.'

31 "Consequently you bear witness against yourselves, that you are sons of those who murdered the prophets.

32"Fill up then the measure *of the guilt* of your fathers.

33"You serpents, you brood of vipers, how shall you escape the sentence of hell?

34"Therefore, behold, I am sending you prophets and wise men and scribes; some of them you will kill and crucify, and some of them you will scourge in your synagogues, and persecute from city to city,

35 that upon you may fall *the guilt of* all the righteous blood shed on earth, from the blood of righteous Abel to the blood of Zechariah, the son of Berechiah, whom you murdered between the temple and the altar.

36"Truly I say to you, all these things shall come upon this generation.

37 ¶"O Jerusalem, Jerusalem, who kills the prophets and stones those who are sent to her! How often I wanted to gather your children together, the way a hen gathers her chicks under her wings, and you were unwilling.

38"Behold, your house is being left to you desolate!

39"For I say to you, from now on you shall not see Me until you say, 'BLESSED IS HE WHO COMES IN THE NAME OF THE LORD!' "

CHAPTER 24

AND Jesus came out from the temple and was going away when His disciples came up to point out the temple buildings to Him.

2 And He answered and said to them, "Do you not see all these things? Truly I say to you, not one stone here shall be left upon another, which will not be torn down."

3 ¶ And as He was sitting on the Mount of Olives, the disciples came to Him privately, saying, "Tell us, when will these things be, and what *will be* the sign of Your coming, and of the end of the age?"

4 And Jesus answered and said to them, "See to it that no one misleads you.

5"For many will come in My name, saying, 'I am the Christ,' and will mislead many.

6"And you will be hearing of wars and rumors of wars; see that you are not frightened, for *those things* must take place, but *that* is not yet the end.

7"For nation will rise against nation, and kingdom against kingdom, and in various places there will be famines and earthquakes.

8"But all these things are *merely* the beginning of birth pangs.

9"Then they will deliver you to tribulation, and will kill you, and you will be hated by all nations on account of My name.

10"And at that time many will fall away and will deliver up one another and hate one another.

11"And many false prophets will arise, and will mislead many.

12"And because lawlessness is increased, most people's love will grow cold.

13"But the one who endures to the end, he shall be saved.

14"And this gospel of the kingdom shall be preached in the whole world for a witness to all the nations, and then the end shall come.

15 ¶"Therefore when you see the ABOMINATION OF DESOLATION which was spoken of through Daniel the prophet, standing in the holy place (let the reader understand),

16 then let those who are in Judea flee to the mountains;

17 let him who is on the housetop not go down to get the things out that are in his house;

18 and let him who is in the field not turn back to get his cloak.

19"But woe to those who are with child and to those who nurse babes in those days!

20"But pray that your flight may not be in the winter, or on a Sabbath;

21 for then there will be a great tribulation, such as has not occurred since the beginning of the world until now, nor ever shall.

22"And unless those days had been cut short, no life would have been saved; but for the sake of the elect those days shall be cut short.

23"Then if anyone says to you, 'Behold, here is the Christ,' or 'There *He is*,' do not believe *him.*

24"For false Christs and false prophets will arise and will show great signs and wonders, so as to mislead, if possible, even the elect.

25 "Behold, I have told you in advance.

26 "If therefore they say to you, 'Behold, He is in the wilderness,' do not go forth, or, 'Behold, He is in the inner rooms,' do not believe them.

27 "For just as the lightning comes from the east, and flashes even to the west, so shall the coming of the Son of Man be.

28 "Wherever the corpse is, there the vultures will gather.

29 ¶ "But immediately after the tribulation of those days THE SUN WILL BE DARKENED, AND THE MOON WILL NOT GIVE ITS LIGHT, AND THE STARS WILL FALL from the sky, and the powers of the heavens will be shaken,

30 and then the sign of the Son of Man will appear in the sky, and then all the tribes of the earth will mourn, and they will see the SON OF MAN COMING ON THE CLOUDS OF THE SKY with power and great glory.

31 "And He will send forth His angels with A GREAT TRUMPET and THEY WILL GATHER TOGETHER His elect from the four winds, from one end of the sky to the other.

32 ¶ "Now learn the parable from the fig tree: when its branch has already become tender, and puts forth its leaves, you know that summer is near;

33 even so you too, when you see all these things, recognize that He is near, right at the door.

34 "Truly I say to you, this generation will not pass away until all these things take place.

35 "Heaven and earth will pass away, but My words shall not pass away.

36 "But of that day and hour no one knows, not even the angels of heaven, nor the Son, but the Father alone.

37 "For the coming of the Son of Man will be just like the days of Noah.

38 "For as in those days which were before the flood they were eating and drinking, they were marrying and giving in marriage, until the day that Noah entered the ark,

39 and they did not understand until the flood came and took them all away; so shall the coming of the Son of Man be.

40 "Then there shall be two men in the field; one will be taken, and one will be left.

41 "Two women will be grinding at the mill; one will be taken, and one will be left.

42 "Therefore be on the alert, for you do not know which day your Lord is coming.

43 "But be sure of this, that if the head of the house had known at what time of the night the thief was coming, he would have been on the alert and would not have allowed his house to be broken into.

44 "For this reason you be ready too; for the Son of Man is coming at an hour when you do not think He will.

45 ¶ "Who then is the faithful and sensible slave whom his master put in charge of his household to give them their food at the proper time?

46 "Blessed is that slave whom his master finds so doing when he comes.

47 "Truly I say to you, that he will put him in charge of all his possessions.

48 "But if that evil slave says in his heart, 'My master is not coming for a long time,'

49 and shall begin to beat his fellow slaves and eat and drink with drunkards;

50 the master of that slave will come on a day when he does not expect him and at an hour which he does not know,

51 and shall cut him in pieces and assign him a place with the hypocrites; weeping shall be there and the gnashing of teeth.

CHAPTER 25

"THEN the kingdom of heaven will be comparable to ten virgins, who took their lamps, and went out to meet the bridegroom.

2 "And five of them were foolish, and five were prudent.

3 "For when the foolish took their lamps, they took no oil with them,

4 but the prudent took oil in flasks along with their lamps.

5 "Now while the bridegroom was delaying, they all got drowsy and began to sleep.

6 "But at midnight there was a shout, 'Behold, the bridegroom! Come out to meet him.'

7 "Then all those virgins rose, and trimmed their lamps.

8"And the foolish said to the prudent, 'Give us some of your oil, for our lamps are going out.'

9"But the prudent answered, saying, 'No, there will not be enough for us and you *too;* go instead to the dealers and buy *some* for yourselves.'

10"And while they were going away to make the purchase, the bridegroom came, and those who were ready went in with him to the wedding feast; and the door was shut.

11"And later the other virgins also came, saying, 'Lord, lord, open up for us.'

12"But he answered and said, 'Truly I say to you, I do not know you.'

13"Be on the alert then, for you do not know the day nor the hour.

14 ¶ "For *it is* just like a man *about* to go on a journey, who called his own slaves, and entrusted his possessions to them.

15"And to one he gave five talents, to another, two, and to another, one, each according to his own ability; and he went on his journey.

16"Immediately the one who had received the five talents went and traded with them, and gained five more talents.

17"In the same manner the one who *had received* the two *talents* gained two more.

18"But he who received the one *talent* went away and dug in the ground, and hid his master's money.

19"Now after a long time the master of those slaves *came and *settled accounts with them.

20"And the one who had received the five talents came up and brought five more talents, saying, 'Master, you entrusted five talents to me; see, I have gained five more talents.'

21"His master said to him, 'Well done, good and faithful slave; you were faithful with a few things, I will put you in charge of many things, enter into the joy of your master.'

22"The one also who *had received* the two talents came up and said, 'Master, you entrusted to me two talents; see, I have gained two more talents.'

23"His master said to him, 'Well done, good and faithful slave; you were faithful with a few things, I will

put you in charge of many things; enter into the joy of your master.'

24"And the one also who had received the one talent came up and said, 'Master, I knew you to be a hard man, reaping where you did not sow, and gathering where you scattered no *seed.*

25 'And I was afraid, and went away and hid your talent in the ground; see, you have what is yours.'

26"But his master answered and said to him, 'You wicked, lazy slave, you knew that I reap where I did not sow, and gather where I scattered no *seed.*

27 'Then you ought to have put my money in the bank, and on my arrival I would have received my *money* back with interest.

28 'Therefore take away the talent from him, and give it to the one who has the ten talents.'

29"For to everyone who has shall *more* be given, and he shall have an abundance; but from the one who does not have, even what he does have shall be taken away.

30"And cast out the worthless slave into the outer darkness; in that place there shall be weeping and gnashing of teeth.

31 ¶ "But when the Son of Man comes in His glory, and all the angels with Him, then He will sit on His glorious throne.

32"And all the nations will be gathered before Him; and He will separate them from one another, as the shepherd separates the sheep from the goats;

33 and He will put the sheep on His right, and the goats on the left.

34"Then the King will say to those on His right, 'Come, you who are blessed of My Father, inherit the kingdom prepared for you from the foundation of the world.

35 'For I was hungry, and you gave Me *something* to eat; I was thirsty, and you gave Me drink; I was a stranger, and you invited Me in;

36 naked, and you clothed Me; I was sick, and you visited Me; I was in prison, and you came to Me.'

37"Then the righteous will answer Him, saying, 'Lord, when did we see You hungry, and feed You, or thirsty, and give You drink?

38 'And when did we see You a stranger, and invite You in, or naked, and clothe You?

39 'And when did we see You sick, or in prison, and come to You?'

40 "And the King will answer and say to them, 'Truly I say to you, to the extent that you did it to one of these brothers of Mine, *even* the least *of them,* you did it to Me.'

41 "Then He will also say to those on His left, 'Depart from Me, accursed ones, into the eternal fire which has been prepared for the devil and his angels;

42 for I was hungry, and you gave Me *nothing* to eat; I was thirsty, and you gave Me nothing to drink;

43 I was a stranger, and you did not invite Me in; naked, and you did not clothe Me; sick, and in prison, and you did not visit Me.'

44 "Then they themselves also will answer, saying, 'Lord, when did we see You hungry, or thirsty, or a stranger, or naked, or sick, or in prison, and did not take care of You?'

45 "Then He will answer them, saying, 'Truly I say to you, to the extent that you did not do it to one of the least of these, you did not do it to Me.'

46 "And these will go away into eternal punishment, but the righteous into eternal life."

CHAPTER 26

AND it came about that when Jesus had finished all these words, He said to His disciples,

2 "You know that after two days the Passover is coming, and the Son of Man is *to be* delivered up for crucifixion."

3 Then the chief priests and the elders of the people were gathered together in the court of the high priest, named Caiaphas;

4 and they plotted together to seize Jesus by stealth, and kill *Him.*

5 But they were saying, "Not during the festival, lest a riot occur among the people."

6 ¶ Now when Jesus was in Bethany, at the home of Simon the leper,

7 a woman came to Him with an alabaster vial of very costly perfume, and she poured it upon His head as He reclined *at the table.*

8 But the disciples were indignant when they saw *this,* and said, "Why this waste?

9 "For this *perfume* might have been sold for a high price and *the money* given to the poor."

10 But Jesus, aware of this, said to them, "Why do you bother the woman? For she has done a good deed to Me.

11 "For the poor you have with you always; but you do not always have Me.

12 "For when she poured this perfume upon My body, she did it to prepare Me for burial.

13 "Truly I say to you, wherever this gospel is preached in the whole world, what this woman has done shall also be spoken of in memory of her."

14 ¶ Then one of the twelve, named Judas Iscariot, went to the chief priests,

15 and said, "What are you willing to give me to deliver Him up to you?" And they weighed out to him thirty pieces of silver.

16 And from then on he *began* looking for a good opportunity to betray Him.

17 ¶ Now on the first *day* of Unleavened Bread the disciples came to Jesus, saying, "Where do You want us to prepare for You to eat the Passover?"

18 And He said, "Go into the city to a certain man, and say to him, 'The Teacher says, "My time is at hand; I *am* to keep the Passover at your house with My disciples." ' "

19 And the disciples did as Jesus had directed them; and they prepared the Passover.

20 ¶ Now when evening had come, He was reclining *at the table* with the twelve disciples.

21 And as they were eating, He said, "Truly I say to you that one of you will betray Me."

22 And being deeply grieved, they each one began to say to Him, "Surely not I, Lord?"

23 And He answered and said, "He who dipped his hand with Me in the bowl is the one who will betray Me.

24 "The Son of Man *is to* go, just as it is written of Him; but woe to that man by whom the Son of Man is betrayed!

It would have been good for that man if he had not been born."

25 And Judas, who was betraying Him, answered and said, "Surely it is not I, Rabbi?" He *said to him, "You have said it yourself."

26 ¶ And while they were eating, Jesus took some bread, and after a blessing, He broke it and gave it to the disciples, and said, "Take, eat; this is My body."

27 And when He had taken a cup and given thanks, He gave it to them, saying, "Drink from it, all of you;

28 for this is My blood of the covenant, which is poured out for many for forgiveness of sins.

29"But I say to you, I will not drink of this fruit of the vine from now on until that day when I drink it new with you in My Father's kingdom."

30 ¶ And after singing a hymn, they went out to the Mount of Olives.

31 ¶ Then Jesus *said to them, "You will all fall away because of Me this night, for it is written, 'I WILL STRIKE DOWN THE SHEPHERD, AND THE SHEEP OF THE FLOCK SHALL BE SCATTERED.'

32"But after I have been raised, I will go before you to Galilee."

33 But Peter answered and said to Him, "Even though all may fall away because of You, I will never fall away."

34 Jesus said to him, "Truly I say to you that this very night, before a cock crows, you shall deny Me three times."

35 Peter *said to Him, "Even if I have to die with You, I will not deny You." All the disciples said the same thing too.

36 ¶ Then Jesus *came with them to a place called Gethsemane, and *said to His disciples, "Sit here while I go over there and pray."

37 And He took with Him Peter and the two sons of Zebedee, and began to be grieved and distressed.

38 Then He *said to them, "My soul is deeply grieved, to the point of death; remain here and keep watch with Me."

39 And He went a little beyond them, and fell on His face and prayed, saying, "My Father, if it is possible, let this cup pass from Me; yet not as I will, but as Thou wilt."

40 And He *came to the disciples and *found them sleeping, and *said to Peter, "So, you men could not keep watch with Me for one hour?

41"Keep watching and praying, that you may not enter into temptation; the spirit is willing, but the flesh is weak."

42 He went away again a second time and prayed, saying, "My Father, if this cannot pass away unless I drink it, Thy will be done."

43 And again He came and found them sleeping, for their eyes were heavy.

44 And He left them again, and went away and prayed a third time, saying the same thing once more.

45 Then He *came to the disciples, and *said to them, "Are you still sleeping and taking your rest? Behold, the hour is at hand and the Son of Man is being betrayed into the hands of sinners.

46"Arise, let us be going; behold, the one who betrays Me is at hand!"

47 ¶ And while He was still speaking, behold, Judas, one of the twelve, came up, accompanied by a great multitude with swords and clubs, from the chief priests and elders of the people.

48 Now he who was betraying Him gave them a sign, saying, "Whomever I shall kiss, He is the one; seize Him."

49 And immediately he went to Jesus and said, "Hail, Rabbi!" and kissed Him.

50 And Jesus said to him, "Friend, do what you have come for." Then they came and laid hands on Jesus and seized Him.

51 And behold, one of those who were with Jesus reached and drew out his sword, and struck the slave of the high priest, and cut off his ear.

52 Then Jesus *said to him, "Put your sword back into its place; for all those who take up the sword shall perish by the sword.

53"Or do you think that I cannot appeal to My Father, and He will at once put at My disposal more than twelve [45]legions of angels?

54"How then shall the Scriptures be fulfilled, that it must happen this way?"

55 At that time Jesus said to the multitudes, "Have you come out with swords and clubs to arrest Me as

[45] A legion equaled 6,000 troops

against a robber? Every day I used to sit in the temple teaching and you did not seize Me.

56 "But all this has taken place that the Scriptures of the prophets may be fulfilled." Then all the disciples left Him and fled.

57 ¶ And those who had seized Jesus led Him away to Caiaphas, the high priest, where the scribes and the elders were gathered together.

58 But Peter also was following Him at a distance as far as the courtyard of the high priest, and entered in, and sat down with the officers to see the outcome.

59 Now the chief priests and the whole Council kept trying to obtain false testimony against Jesus, in order that they might put Him to death;

60 and they did not find any, even though many false witnesses came forward. But later on two came forward,

61 and said, "This man stated, 'I am able to destroy the temple of God and to rebuild it in three days.'"

62 And the high priest stood up and said to Him, "Do You make no answer? What is it that these men are testifying against You?"

63 But Jesus kept silent. And the high priest said to Him, "I adjure You by the living God, that You tell us whether You are the Christ, the Son of God."

64 Jesus *said to him, "You have said it yourself; nevertheless I tell you, hereafter you shall see THE SON OF MAN SITTING AT THE RIGHT HAND OF POWER, and COMING ON THE CLOUDS OF HEAVEN."

65 Then the high priest tore his robes, saying, "He has blasphemed! What further need do we have of witnesses? Behold, you have now heard the blasphemy;

66 what do you think?" They answered and said, "He is deserving of death!"

67 Then they spat in His face and beat Him with their fists; and others slapped Him,

68 and said, "Prophesy to us, You Christ; who is the one who hit You?"

69 ¶ Now Peter was sitting outside in the courtyard, and a certain servant-girl came to him and said, "You too were with Jesus the Galilean."

70 But he denied it before them all, saying, "I do not know what you are talking about."

71 And when he had gone out to the gateway, another servant-girl saw him and *said to those who were there, "This man was with Jesus of Nazareth."

72 And again he denied it with an oath, "I do not know the man."

73 And a little later the bystanders came up and said to Peter, "Surely you too are one of them; for the way you talk gives you away."

74 Then he began to curse and swear, "I do not know the man!" And immediately a cock crowed.

75 And Peter remembered the word which Jesus had said, "Before a cock crows, you will deny Me three times." And he went out and wept bitterly.

CHAPTER 27

NOW when morning had come, all the chief priests and the elders of the people took counsel against Jesus to put Him to death;

2 and they bound Him, and led Him away, and delivered Him up to Pilate the governor.

3 ¶ Then when Judas, who had betrayed Him, saw that He had been condemned, he felt remorse and returned the thirty pieces of silver to the chief priests and elders,

4 saying, "I have sinned by betraying innocent blood." But they said, "What is that to us? See to that yourself!"

5 And he threw the pieces of silver into the sanctuary and departed; and he went away and hanged himself.

6 And the chief priests took the pieces of silver and said, "It is not lawful to put them into the temple treasury, since it is the price of blood."

7 And they counseled together and with the money bought the Potter's Field as a burial place for strangers.

8 For this reason that field has been called the Field of Blood to this day.

9 Then that which was spoken through Jeremiah the prophet was fulfilled, saying, "AND THEY TOOK THE THIRTY PIECES OF SILVER, THE PRICE OF THE ONE WHOSE PRICE HAD BEEN SET by the sons of Israel;

10 AND THEY GAVE THEM FOR THE

POTTER'S FIELD, AS THE LORD DIRECTED ME."

11 ¶ Now Jesus stood before the governor, and the governor questioned Him, saying, "Are You the King of the Jews?" And Jesus said to him, "*It is as* you say."

12 And while He was being accused by the chief priests and elders, He made no answer.

13 Then Pilate *said to Him, "Do You not hear how many things they testify against You?"

14 And He did not answer him with regard to even a *single* charge, so that the governor was quite amazed.

15 Now at *the* feast the governor was accustomed to release for the multitude *any* one prisoner whom they wanted.

16 And they were holding at that time a notorious prisoner, called Barabbas.

17 When therefore they were gathered together, Pilate said to them, "Whom do you want me to release for you? Barabbas, or Jesus who is called Christ?"

18 For he knew that because of envy they had delivered Him up.

19 And while he was sitting on the judgment seat, his wife sent to him, saying, "Have nothing to do with that righteous Man; for last night I suffered greatly in a dream because of Him."

20 But the chief priests and the elders persuaded the multitudes to ask for Barabbas, and to put Jesus to death.

21 But the governor answered and said to them, "Which of the two do you want me to release for you?" And they said, "Barabbas."

22 Pilate *said to them, "Then what shall I do with Jesus who is called Christ?" They all *said, "Let Him be crucified!"

23 And he said, "Why, what evil has He done?" But they kept shouting all the more, saying, "Let Him be crucified!"

24 And when Pilate saw that he was accomplishing nothing, but rather that a riot was starting, he took water and washed his hands in front of the multitude, saying, "I am innocent of this Man's blood; see *to that* yourselves."

25 And all the people answered and said, "His blood *be* on us and on our children!"

26 Then he released Barabbas for them; but after having Jesus scourged, he delivered Him to be crucified.

27 ¶ Then the soldiers of the governor took Jesus into the Praetorium and gathered the whole *Roman* cohort around Him.

28 And they stripped Him, and put a scarlet robe on Him.

29 And after weaving a crown of thorns, they put it on His head, and a reed in His right hand; and they kneeled down before Him and mocked Him, saying, "Hail, King of the Jews!"

30 And they spat on Him, and took the reed and *began* to beat Him on the head.

31 And after they had mocked Him, they took His robe off and put His garments on Him, and led Him away to crucify *Him.*

32 ¶ And as they were coming out, they found a man of Cyrene named Simon, whom they pressed into service to bear His cross.

33 ¶ And when they had come to a place called Golgotha, which means Place of a Skull,

34 they gave Him wine to drink mingled with gall; and after tasting *it*, He was unwilling to drink.

35 And when they had crucified Him, they divided up His garments among themselves, casting lots;

36 and sitting down, they *began* to keep watch over Him there.

37 And they put up above His head the charge against Him which read, "THIS IS JESUS THE KING OF THE JEWS."

38 At that time two robbers *were crucified with Him, one on the right and one on the left.

39 And those passing by were hurling abuse at Him, wagging their heads,

40 and saying, "You who *are going to* destroy the temple and rebuild it in three days, save Yourself! If You are the Son of God, come down from the cross."

41 In the same way the chief priests also, along with the scribes and elders, were mocking *Him*, and saying,

42 "He saved others; He cannot save Himself. He is the King of Israel; let Him now come down from the cross, and we shall believe in Him.

43"HE TRUSTS IN GOD; LET HIM DELIVER *Him* now, IF HE TAKES PLEASURE IN HIM; for He said, 'I am the Son of God.' "

44 And the robbers also who had been crucified with Him were casting the same insult at Him.

45 ¶ Now from the [46]sixth hour darkness fell upon all the land until the [47]ninth hour.

46 And about the ninth hour Jesus cried out with a loud voice, saying, "ELI, ELI, LAMA SABACHTHANI?" that is, "MY GOD, MY GOD, WHY HAST THOU FORSAKEN ME?"

47 And some of those who were standing there, when they heard it, *began* saying, "This man is calling for Elijah."

48 And immediately one of them ran, and taking a sponge, he filled it with sour wine, and put it on a reed, and gave Him a drink.

49 But the rest *of them* said, "Let us see whether Elijah will come to save Him."[48]

50 And Jesus cried out again with a loud voice, and yielded up *His* spirit.

51 And behold, the veil of the temple was torn in two from top to bottom, and the earth shook; and the rocks were split,

52 and the tombs were opened; and many bodies of the saints who had fallen asleep were raised;

53 and coming out of the tombs after His resurrection they entered the holy city and appeared to many.

54 Now the centurion, and those who were with him keeping guard over Jesus, when they saw the earthquake and the things that were happening, became very frightened and said, "Truly this was the Son of God!"

55 And many women were there looking on from a distance, who had followed Jesus from Galilee, ministering to Him,

56 among whom was Mary Magdalene, *along with* Mary the mother of James and Joseph, and the mother of the sons of Zebedee.

57 ¶ And when it was evening, there came a rich man from Arimathea, named Joseph, who himself had also become a disciple of Jesus.

58 This man went to Pilate and asked for the body of Jesus. Then Pilate ordered *it* to be given over *to him.*

59 And Joseph took the body and wrapped it in a clean linen cloth,

60 and laid it in his own new tomb, which he had hewn out in the rock; and he rolled a large stone against the entrance of the tomb and went away.

61 And Mary Magdalene was there, and the other Mary, sitting opposite the grave.

62 ¶ Now on the next day, which is *the one* after the preparation, the chief priests and the Pharisees gathered together with Pilate,

63 and said, "Sir, we remember that when He was still alive that deceiver said, 'After three days I *am to* rise again.'

64"Therefore, give orders for the grave to be made secure until the third day, lest the disciples come and steal Him away and say to the people, 'He has risen from the dead,' and the last deception will be worse than the first."

65 Pilate said to them, "You have a guard; go, make it *as* secure as you know how."

66 And they went and made the grave secure, and along with the guard they set a seal on the stone.

CHAPTER 28

NOW after the Sabbath, as it began to dawn toward the first *day* of the week, Mary Magdalene and the other Mary came to look at the grave.

2 And behold, a severe earthquake had occurred, for an angel of the Lord descended from heaven and came and rolled away the stone and sat upon it.

3 And his appearance was like lightning, and his garment as white as snow;

4 and the guards shook for fear of him, and became like dead men.

5 And the angel answered and said to the women, "Do not be afraid; for I know that you are looking for Jesus who has been crucified.

6"He is not here, for He has risen, just as He said. Come, see the place where He was lying.

7"And go quickly and tell His disciples that He has risen from the dead; and behold, He is going before you

---

[46] I.e., noon   [47] I.e., 3 p.m.
[48] Some early mss. add: *And another took a spear and pierced His side, and there came out water and blood.* (cf. John 19:34)

into Galilee, there you will see Him; behold, I have told you."

8 And they departed quickly from the tomb with fear and great joy and ran to report it to His disciples.

9 And behold, Jesus met them and greeted them. And they came up and took hold of His feet and worshiped Him.

10 Then Jesus *said to them, "Do not be afraid; go and take word to My brethren to leave for Galilee, and there they shall see Me."

11 ¶ Now while they were on their way, behold, some of the guard came into the city and reported to the chief priests all that had happened.

12 And when they had assembled with the elders and counseled together, they gave a large sum of money to the soldiers,

13 and said, "You are to say, 'His disciples came by night and stole Him away while we were asleep.'

14"And if this should come to the governor's ears, we will win him over and keep you out of trouble."

15 And they took the money and did as they had been instructed; and this story was widely spread among the Jews, *and is* to this day.

16 ¶ But the eleven disciples proceeded to Galilee, to the mountain which Jesus had designated.

17 And when they saw Him, they worshiped *Him*; but some were doubtful.

18 And Jesus came up and spoke to them, saying, "All authority has been given to Me in heaven and on earth.

19"Go therefore and make disciples of all the nations, baptizing them in the name of the Father and the Son and the Holy Spirit,

20 teaching them to observe all that I commanded you; and lo, I am with you always, even to the end of the age."

THE GOSPEL ACCORDING TO

MARK

T HE beginning of the gospel of Jesus Christ, [1]the Son of God.

2 ¶ As it is written in Isaiah the prophet,

"BEHOLD, I SEND MY MESSENGER
   BEFORE YOUR FACE,
WHO WILL PREPARE YOUR WAY;

3 THE VOICE OF ONE CRYING IN THE
      WILDERNESS,
'MAKE READY THE WAY OF THE
   LORD,
MAKE HIS PATHS STRAIGHT.' "

4 John the Baptist appeared in the wilderness [2]preaching a baptism of repentance for the forgiveness of sins.

5 And all the country of Judea was going out to him, and all the people of Jerusalem; and they were being baptized by him in the Jordan River, confessing their sins.

6 And John was clothed with camel's hair and *wore* a leather belt

around his waist, and his diet was locusts and wild honey.

7 And he was preaching, and saying, "After me One is coming who is mightier than I, and I am not fit to stoop down and untie the thong of His sandals.

8"I baptized you [3]with water; but He will baptize you [3]with the Holy Spirit."

9 ¶ And it came about in those days that Jesus came from Nazareth in Galilee, and was baptized by John in the Jordan.

10 And immediately coming up out of the water, He saw the heavens opening, and the Spirit like a dove descending upon Him;

11 and a voice came out of the heavens: "Thou art My beloved Son, in Thee I am well-pleased."

12 ¶ And immediately the Spirit *impelled Him *to go* out into the wilderness.

13 And He was in the wilderness

---

[1] Many mss. do not contain *the Son of God*
[2] Or, *proclaiming*
[3] The Gr. here can be translated *in, with* or *by*

forty days being tempted by Satan; and He was with the wild beasts, and the angels were ministering to Him.

14 ¶ And after John had been taken into custody, Jesus came into Galilee, preaching the gospel of God,

15 and saying, "The time is fulfilled, and the kingdom of God is at hand; repent and believe in the gospel."

16 ¶ And as He was going along by the Sea of Galilee, He saw Simon and Andrew, the brother of Simon, casting a net in the sea; for they were fishermen.

17 And Jesus said to them, "Follow Me, and I will make you become fishers of men."

18 And they immediately left the nets and followed Him.

19 And going on a little farther, He saw James the *son* of Zebedee, and John his brother, who were also in the boat mending the nets.

20 And immediately He called them; and they left their father Zebedee in the boat with the hired servants, and went away to follow Him.

21 ¶ And they *went into Capernaum; and immediately on the Sabbath He entered the synagogue and *began* to teach.

22 And they were amazed at His teaching; for He was teaching them as *one* having authority, and not as the scribes.

23 And just then there was in their synagogue a man with an unclean spirit; and he cried out,

24 saying, "What do we have to do with You, Jesus [4]of Nazareth? Have You come to destroy us? I know who You are—the Holy One of God!"

25 And Jesus rebuked him, saying, "Be quiet, and come out of him!"

26 And throwing him into convulsions, the unclean spirit cried out with a loud voice, and came out of him.

27 And they were all amazed, so that they debated among themselves, saying, "What is this? A new teaching with authority! He commands even the unclean spirits, and they obey Him."

28 And immediately the news about Him went out everywhere into all the surrounding district of Galilee.

29 ¶ And immediately after they had come out of the synagogue, they came into the house of Simon and Andrew, with James and John.

30 Now Simon's mother-in-law was lying sick with a fever; and immediately they *spoke to Him about her.

31 And He came to her and raised her up, taking her by the hand, and the fever left her, and she [5]waited on them.

32 ¶ And when evening had come, after the sun had set, they *began* bringing to Him all who were ill and those who were demon-possessed.

33 And the whole city had gathered at the door.

34 And He healed many who were ill with various diseases, and cast out many demons; and He was not permitting the demons to speak, because they [6]knew who He was.

35 ¶ And in the early morning, while it was still dark, He arose and went out and departed to a lonely place, and was praying there.

36 And Simon and his companions hunted for Him;

37 and they found Him, and *said to Him, "Everyone is looking for You."

38 And He *said to them, "Let us go somewhere else to the towns nearby, in order that I may preach there also; for that is what I came out for."

39 And He went into their synagogues throughout all Galilee, preaching and casting out the demons.

40 ¶ And a leper *came to Him, beseeching Him and falling on his knees before Him, and saying to Him, "If You are willing, You can make me clean."

41 And moved with compassion, He stretched out His hand, and touched him, and *said to him, "I am willing; be cleansed."

42 And immediately the leprosy left him and he was cleansed.

43 And He sternly warned him and immediately sent him away,

44 and He *said to him, "See that you say nothing to anyone; but go, show yourself to the priest and offer for your cleansing what Moses commanded, for a testimony to them."

45 But he went out and began to proclaim it freely and to spread the

---

[4] Lit., *the Nazarene*   [5] Or, *served*   [6] Some mss. read: *knew Him to be Christ*

news about, to such an extent that Jesus could no longer publicly enter a city, but [7]stayed out in unpopulated areas; and they were coming to Him from everywhere.

CHAPTER 2

AND when He had come back to Capernaum several days afterward, it was heard that He was at home.

2 And many were gathered together, so that there was no longer room, even near the door; and He was speaking the word to them.

3 And they *came, bringing to Him a paralytic, carried by four men.

4 And being unable to get to Him because of the crowd, they removed the roof above Him; and when they had dug an opening, they let down the pallet on which the paralytic was lying.

5 And Jesus seeing their faith *said to the paralytic, "My [8]son, your sins are forgiven."

6 But there were some of the scribes sitting there and reasoning in their hearts,

7"Why does this man speak that way? He is blaspheming; who can forgive sins but God alone?"

8 And immediately Jesus, aware in His spirit that they were reasoning that way within themselves, *said to them, "Why are you reasoning about these things in your hearts?

9"Which is easier, to say to the paralytic, 'Your sins are forgiven'; or to say, 'Arise, and take up your pallet and walk'?

10"But in order that you may know that the Son of Man has authority on earth to forgive sins"—He *said to the paralytic—

11"I say to you, rise, take up your pallet and go home."

12 And he rose and immediately took up the pallet and went out in the sight of all; so that they were all amazed and were glorifying God, saying, "We have never seen anything like this."

13 ¶ And He went out again by the seashore; and all the multitude were coming to Him, and He was teaching them.

14 And as He passed by, He saw Levi the *son* of Alphaeus sitting in the tax office, and He *said to him, "Follow Me!" And he rose and followed Him.

15 ¶ And it came about that He was reclining *at the table* in his house, and many tax-gatherers and sinners were dining with Jesus and His disciples; for there were many of them, and they were following Him.

16 And when the scribes of the Pharisees saw that He was eating with the sinners and tax-gatherers, they *began* saying to His disciples, "Why is He eating and drinking with tax-gatherers and sinners?"

17 And hearing this, Jesus *said to them, "*It is* not those who are healthy who need a physician, but those who are sick; I did not come to call the righteous, but sinners."

18 ¶ And John's disciples and the Pharisees were fasting; and they *came and *said to Him, "Why do John's disciples and the disciples of the Pharisees fast, but Your disciples do not fast?"

19 And Jesus said to them, "While the bridegroom is with them, the attendants of the bridegroom do not fast, do they? So long as they have the bridegroom with them, they cannot fast.

20"But the days will come when the bridegroom is taken away from them, and then they will fast in that day.

21"No one sews a patch of unshrunk cloth on an old garment; otherwise the patch pulls away from it, the new from the old, and a worse tear results.

22"And no one puts new wine into old wineskins; otherwise the wine will burst the skins, and the wine is lost, and the skins *as well;* but *one puts* new wine into fresh wineskins."

23 ¶ And it came about that He was passing through the grainfields on the Sabbath, and His disciples began to make their way along while picking the heads *of grain.*

24 And the Pharisees were saying to Him, "See here, why are they doing what is not lawful on the Sabbath?"

25 And He *said to them, "Have you never read what David did when he was in need and became hungry, he and his companions:

26 how he entered the house of God in the time of Abiathar *the* high priest, and ate the consecrated bread, which is not lawful for *anyone* to eat except

[7] Lit., *was*   [8] Lit., *child*

the priests, and he gave *it* also to those who were with him?"

27 And He was saying to them, "The Sabbath was made for man, and not man for the Sabbath.

28 "Consequently, the Son of Man is Lord even of the Sabbath."

CHAPTER 3

AND He entered again into a synagogue; and a man was there with a withered hand.

2 And they were watching Him *to see* if He would heal him on the Sabbath, in order that they might accuse Him.

3 And He *said to the man with the withered hand, "Rise and *come* forward!"

4 And He *said to them, "Is it lawful on the Sabbath to do good or to do harm, to save a life or to kill?" But they kept silent.

5 And after looking around at them with anger, grieved at their hardness of heart, He *said to the man, "Stretch out your hand." And he stretched it out, and his hand was restored.

6 And the Pharisees went out and immediately *began* taking counsel with the Herodians against Him, *as to* how they might destroy Him.

7 ¶ And Jesus withdrew to the sea with His disciples; and a great multitude from Galilee followed; and *also* from Judea,

8 and from Jerusalem, and from Idumea, and beyond the Jordan, and the vicinity of Tyre and Sidon, a great multitude heard of all that He was doing and came to Him.

9 And He told His disciples that a boat should stand ready for Him because of the multitude, in order that they might not crowd Him;

10 for He had healed many, with the result that all those who had afflictions pressed about Him in order to touch Him.

11 And whenever the unclean spirits beheld Him, they would fall down before Him and cry out, saying, "You are the Son of God!"

12 And He earnestly warned them not to make Him known.

13 ¶ And He *went up to the mountain and *summoned those whom He

Himself wanted, and they came to Him.

14 And He appointed twelve[9], that they might be with Him, and that He might send them out to preach,

15 and to have authority to cast out the demons.

16 And He appointed the twelve: Simon (to whom He gave the name Peter),

17 and James, the *son* of Zebedee, and John the brother of James (to them He gave the name Boanerges, which means, "Sons of Thunder");

18 and Andrew, and Philip, and Bartholomew, and Matthew, and Thomas, and James the *son* of Alphaeus, and Thaddaeus, and Simon the Zealot;

19 and Judas Iscariot, who also betrayed Him.

20 ¶ And He *came [10]home, and the multitude *gathered again, to such an extent that they could not even eat a meal.

21 And when His own [11]people heard *of this,* they went out to take custody of Him; for they were saying, "He has lost His senses."

22 And the scribes who came down from Jerusalem were saying, "He is possessed by Beelzebul," and "He casts out the demons by the ruler of the demons."

23 And He called them to Himself and began speaking to them in parables, "How can Satan cast out Satan?

24 "And if a kingdom is divided against itself, that kingdom cannot stand.

25 "And if a house is divided against itself, that house will not be able to stand.

26 "And if Satan has risen up against himself and is divided, he cannot stand, but he is finished!

27 "But no one can enter the strong man's house and plunder his property unless he first binds the strong man, and then he will plunder his house.

28 "Truly I say to you, all sins shall be forgiven the sons of men, and whatever blasphemies they utter;

29 but whoever blasphemes against the Holy Spirit never has forgiveness, but is guilty of an eternal sin"—

---

[9] Some early mss. add: *whom He named apostles*
[10] Lit., *into a house*   [11] Or, *kinsmen*

30 because they were saying, "He has an unclean spirit."

31 ¶ And His mother and His brothers *arrived, and standing outside they sent *word* to Him, and called Him.

32 And a multitude was sitting around Him, and they *said to Him, "Behold, Your mother and Your brothers[12] are outside looking for You."

33 And answering them, He *said, "Who are My mother and My brothers?"

34 And looking about on those who were sitting around Him, He *said, "Behold, My mother and My brothers!

35"For whoever does the will of God, he is My brother and sister and mother."

CHAPTER 4

AND He began to teach again by the sea. And such a very great multitude gathered to Him that He got into a boat in the sea and sat down; and the whole multitude was by the sea on the land.

2 And He was teaching them many things in parables, and was saying to them in His teaching,

3"Listen *to this*! Behold, the sower went out to sow;

4 and it came about that as he was sowing, some *seed* fell beside the road, and the birds came and ate it up.

5"And other *seed* fell on the rocky *ground* where it did not have much soil; and immediately it sprang up because it had no depth of soil.

6"And after the sun had risen, it was scorched; and because it had no root, it withered away.

7"And other *seed* fell among the thorns, and the thorns came up and choked it, and it yielded no crop.

8"And other *seeds* fell into the good soil and as they grew up and increased, they yielded a crop and produced thirty, sixty, and a hundred-fold."

9 And He was saying, "He who has ears to hear, let him hear."

10 ¶ And as soon as He was alone, His followers, along with the twelve, *began* asking Him *about* the parables.

11 And He was saying to them, "To you has been given the mystery of the kingdom of God; but those who are outside get everything in parables,

12 in order that WHILE SEEING, THEY MAY SEE AND NOT PERCEIVE; AND WHILE HEARING, THEY MAY HEAR AND NOT UNDERSTAND LEST THEY RETURN AND BE FORGIVEN."

13 And He *said to them, "Do you not understand this parable? And how will you understand all the parables?

14"The sower sows the word.

15"And these are the ones who are beside the road where the word is sown; and when they hear, immediately Satan comes and takes away the word which has been sown in them.

16"And in a similar way these are the ones on whom seed was sown on the rocky *places*, who, when they hear the word, immediately receive it with joy;

17 and they have no *firm* root in themselves, but are *only* temporary; then, when affliction or persecution arises because of the word, immediately they fall away.

18"And others are the ones on whom seed was sown among the thorns; these are the ones who have heard the word,

19 and the worries of the [13]world, and the deceitfulness of riches, and the desires for other things enter in and choke the word, and it becomes unfruitful.

20"And those are the ones on whom seed was sown on the good soil; and they hear the word and accept it, and bear fruit, thirty, sixty, and a hundredfold."

21 ¶ And He was saying to them, "A lamp is not brought to be put under a peck-measure, is it, or under a bed? Is it not *brought* to be put on the lampstand?

22"For nothing is hidden, except to be revealed; nor has *anything* been secret, but that it should come to light.

23"If any man has ears to hear, let him hear."

24 And He was saying to them, "Take care what you listen to. By your standard of measure it shall be measured to you; and more shall be given you besides.

25"For whoever has, to him shall *more* be given; and whoever does not

12 Later mss. add: *and Your sisters*   13 Or, *age*

have, even what he has shall be taken away from him."

26 ¶ And He was saying, "The kingdom of God is like a man who casts seed upon the soil;

27 and goes to bed at night and gets up by day, and the seed sprouts up and grows—how, he himself does not know.

28"The soil produces crops by itself; first the blade, then the head, then the mature grain in the head.

29"But when the crop permits, he immediately puts in the sickle, because the harvest has come."

30 ¶ And He said, "How shall we [14]picture the kingdom of God, or by what parable shall we present it?

31"*It is* like a mustard seed, which, when sown upon the soil, though it is smaller than all the seeds that are upon the soil,

32 yet when it is sown, grows up and becomes larger than all the garden plants and forms large branches; so that THE BIRDS OF THE [15]AIR can NEST UNDER ITS SHADE."

33 ¶ And with many such parables He was speaking the word to them as they were able to hear it;

34 and He did not speak to them without a parable; but He was explaining everything privately to His own disciples.

35 ¶ And on that day, when evening had come, He *said to them, "Let us go over to the other side."

36 And leaving the multitude, they *took Him along with them, just as He was, in the boat; and other boats were with Him.

37 And there *arose a fierce gale of wind, and the waves were breaking over the boat so much that the boat was already filling up.

38 And He Himself was in the stern, asleep on the cushion; and they *awoke Him and *said to Him, "Teacher, do You not care that we are perishing?"

39 And being aroused, He rebuked the wind and said to the sea, "Hush, be still." And the wind died down and it became perfectly calm.

40 And He said to them, "Why are you so timid? How is it that you have no faith?"

41 And they became very much afraid and said to one another, "Who then is this, that even the wind and the sea obey Him?"

CHAPTER 5

AND they came to the other side of the sea, into the country of the Gerasenes.

2 And when He had come out of the boat, immediately a man from the tombs with an unclean spirit met Him,

3 and he had his dwelling among the tombs. And no one was able to bind him anymore, even with a chain;

4 because he had often been bound with shackles and chains, and the chains had been torn apart by him, and the shackles broken in pieces, and no one was strong enough to subdue him.

5 And constantly night and day, among the tombs and in the mountains, he was crying out and gashing himself with stones.

6 And seeing Jesus from a distance, he ran up and bowed down before Him;

7 and crying out with a loud voice, he *said, "What do I have to do with You, Jesus, Son of the Most High God? I implore You by God, do not torment me!"

8 For He had been saying to him, "Come out of the man, you unclean spirit!"

9 And He was asking him, "What is your name?" And he *said to Him, "My name is Legion; for we are many."

10 And he *began to entreat Him earnestly not to send them out of the country.

11 Now there was a big herd of swine feeding there on the mountain.

12 And *the demons* entreated Him, saying, "Send us into the swine so that we may enter them."

13 And He gave them permission. And coming out, the unclean spirits entered the swine; and the herd rushed down the steep bank into the sea, about two thousand *of them;* and they were drowned in the sea.

14 And their herdsmen ran away and reported it in the city and *out* in the

[14] Lit., *compare*   [15] Or, *sky*

country. And *the people* came to see what it was that had happened.

15 And they *came to Jesus and *observed the man who had been demon-possessed sitting down, clothed and in his right mind, the very man who had had the "legion"; and they became frightened.

16 And those who had seen it described to them how it had happened to the demon-possessed man, and *all* about the swine.

17 And they began to entreat Him to depart from their region.

18 And as He was getting into the boat, the man who had been demon-possessed was entreating Him that he might accompany Him.

19 And He did not let him, but He *said to him, "Go home to your people and report to them [16]what great things the Lord has done for you, and *how* He had mercy on you."

20 And he went away and began to proclaim in Decapolis what great things Jesus had done for him; and everyone marveled.

21 ¶ And when Jesus had crossed over again in the boat to the other side, a great multitude gathered about Him; and He stayed by the seashore.

22 And one of the synagogue officials named Jairus *came up, and upon seeing Him, *fell at His feet,

23 and *entreated Him earnestly, saying, "My little daughter is at the point of death; *please* come and lay Your hands on her, that she may get well and live."

24 And He went off with him; and a great multitude was following Him and pressing in on Him.

25 ¶ And a woman who had had a hemorrhage for twelve years,

26 and had endured much at the hands of many physicians, and had spent all that she had and was not helped at all, but rather had grown worse,

27 after hearing about Jesus, came up in the crowd behind *Him*, and touched His cloak.

28 For she thought, "If I just touch His garments, I shall get well."

29 And immediately the flow of her blood was dried up; and she felt in her body that she was healed of her affliction.

30 And immediately Jesus, perceiving in Himself that the power *proceeding* from Him had gone forth, turned around in the crowd and said, "Who touched My garments?"

31 And His disciples said to Him, "You see the multitude pressing in on You, and You say, 'Who touched Me?'"

32 And He looked around to see the woman who had done this.

33 But the woman fearing and trembling, aware of what had happened to her, came and fell down before Him, and told Him the whole truth.

34 And He said to her, "Daughter, your faith has made you well; go in peace, and be healed of your affliction."

35 ¶ While He was still speaking, they *came from the *house of* the synagogue official, saying, "Your daughter has died; why trouble the Teacher anymore?"

36 But Jesus, overhearing what was being spoken, *said to the synagogue official, "Do not be afraid *any longer*, only believe."

37 And He allowed no one to follow with Him, except Peter and James and John the brother of James.

38 And they *came to the house of the synagogue official; and He *beheld a commotion, and *people* loudly weeping and wailing.

39 And entering in, He *said to them, "Why make a commotion and weep? The child has not died, but is asleep."

40 And they *began* laughing at Him. But putting them all out, He *took along the child's father and mother and His own companions, and *entered *the room* where the child was.

41 And taking the child by the hand, He *said to her, "Talitha kum!"(which translated means, "Little girl, I say to you, arise!").

42 And immediately the girl rose and *began* to walk; for she was twelve years old. And immediately they were completely astounded.

43 And He gave them strict orders that no one should know about this; and He said that *something* should be given her to eat.

[16] Or, *everything that*

CHAPTER 6

A ND He went out from there, and He *came into His home town; and His disciples *followed Him.

2 And when the Sabbath had come, He began to teach in the synagogue; and the many listeners were astonished, saying, "Where did this man *get* these things, and what is *this* wisdom given to Him, and such miracles as these performed by His hands?

3"Is not this the carpenter, the son of Mary, and brother of James, and Joses, and Judas, and Simon? Are not His sisters here with us?" And they took offense at Him.

4 And Jesus said to them, "A prophet is not without honor except in his home town and among his *own* relatives and in his *own* household."

5 And He could do no miracle there except that He laid His hands upon a few sick people and healed them.

6 And He wondered at their unbelief.

¶ And He was going around the villages teaching.

7 ¶ And He *summoned the twelve and began to send them out in pairs; and He was giving them authority over the unclean spirits;

8 and He instructed them that they should take nothing for *their* journey, except a mere staff; no bread, no bag, no money in their belt;

9 but *to* wear sandals; and *He* added, "Do not put on two [17]tunics."

10 And He said to them, "Wherever you enter a house, stay there until you leave town.

11"And any place that does not receive you or listen to you, as you go out from there, shake off the dust from the soles of your feet for a testimony against them."

12 And they went out and preached that *men* should repent.

13 And they were casting out many demons and were anointing with oil many sick people and healing them.

14 ¶ And King Herod heard *of it,* for His name had become well known; and *people* were saying, "John the Baptist has risen from the dead, and that is why these miraculous powers are at work in Him."

15 But others were saying, "He is Elijah." And others were saying, "He is a prophet, like one of the prophets *of old.*"

16 But when Herod heard *of it,* he kept saying, "John, whom I beheaded, has risen!"

17 For Herod himself had sent and had John arrested and bound in prison on account of Herodias, the wife of his brother Philip, because he had married her.

18 For John had been saying to Herod, "It is not lawful for you to have your brother's wife."

19 And Herodias had a grudge against him and wanted to put him to death and could not *do so;*

20 for Herod was afraid of John, knowing that he was a righteous and holy man, and kept him safe. And when he heard him, he was very perplexed; but he used to enjoy listening to him.

21 And a strategic day came when Herod on his birthday gave a banquet for his lords and military commanders and the leading men of Galilee;

22 and when the daughter of Herodias herself came in and danced, she pleased Herod and his dinner guests; and the king said to the girl, "Ask me for whatever you want and I will give it to you."

23 And he swore to her, "Whatever you ask of me, I will give it to you; up to half of my kingdom."

24 And she went out and said to her mother, "What shall I ask for?" And she said, "The head of John the Baptist."

25 And immediately she came in haste before the king and asked, saying, "I want you to give me right away the head of John the Baptist on a platter."

26 And although the king was very sorry, *yet* because of his oaths and because of his dinner guests, he was unwilling to refuse her.

27 And immediately the king sent an executioner and commanded *him* to bring *back* his head. And he went and had him beheaded in the prison,

28 and brought his head on a platter, and gave it to the girl; and the girl gave it to her mother.

29 And when his disciples heard

[17] Or, *inner garments*

about this, they came and took away his body and laid it in a tomb.

30 ¶ And the apostles *gathered together with Jesus; and they reported to Him all that they had done and taught.

31 And He *said to them, "Come away by yourselves to a lonely place and rest a while." (For there were many *people* coming and going, and they did not even have time to eat.)

32 And they went away in the boat to a lonely place by themselves.

33 And *the people* saw them going, and many recognized *them*, and they ran there together on foot from all the cities, and got there ahead of them.

34 And when He went ashore, He saw a great multitude, and He felt compassion for them because they were like sheep without a shepherd; and He began to teach them many things.

35 And when it was already quite late, His disciples came up to Him and *began* saying, "The place is desolate and it is already quite late;

36 send them away so that they may go into the surrounding countryside and villages and buy themselves something to eat."

37 But He answered and said to them, "You give them *something* to eat!" And they *said to Him, "Shall we go and spend two hundred [18]denarii on bread and give them *something* to eat?"

38 And He *said to them, "How many loaves do you have? Go look!" And when they found out, they *said, "Five and two fish."

39 And He commanded them all to recline by groups on the green grass.

40 And they reclined in companies of hundreds and of fifties.

41 And He took the five loaves and the two fish, and looking up toward heaven, He blessed *the food* and broke the loaves and He kept giving *them* to the disciples to set before them; and He divided up the two fish among them all.

42 And they all ate and were satisfied.

43 And they picked up twelve full baskets of the broken pieces, and also of the fish.

44 And there were five thousand men who ate the loaves.

45 ¶ And immediately He made His disciples get into the boat and go ahead of *Him* to the other side to Bethsaida, while He Himself was sending the multitude away.

46 And after bidding them farewell, He departed to the mountain to pray.

47 And when it was evening, the boat was in the midst of the sea, and He *was* alone on the land.

48 And seeing them straining at the oars, for the wind was against them, at about the fourth watch of the night, He *came to them, walking on the sea; and He intended to pass by them.

49 But when they saw Him walking on the sea, they supposed that it was a ghost, and cried out;

50 for they all saw Him and were frightened. But immediately He spoke with them and *said to them, "Take courage; it is I, do not be afraid."

51 And He got into the boat with them, and the wind stopped; and they were greatly astonished,

52 for they had not gained any insight from the *incident of* the loaves, but their heart was hardened.

53 ¶ And when they had crossed over they came to land at Gennesaret, and moored to the shore.

54 And when they had come out of the boat, immediately *the people* recognized Him,

55 and ran about that whole country and began to carry about on their pallets those who were sick, to the place they heard He was.

56 And wherever He entered villages, or cities, or countryside, they were laying the sick in the market places, and entreating Him that they might just touch the fringe of His cloak; and as many as touched it were being cured.

CHAPTER 7

AND the Pharisees and some of the scribes gathered together around Him when they had come from Jerusalem,

2 and had seen that some of His disciples were eating their bread with impure hands, that is, unwashed.

3 (For the Pharisees and all the Jews do not eat unless they carefully

---

[18] The denarius was equivalent to one day's wage

wash their hands, *thus* observing the traditions of the elders;

4 and *when they come* from the market place, they do not eat unless they cleanse themselves; and there are many other things which they have received in order to observe, such as the washing of cups and pitchers and copper pots.)

5 And the Pharisees and the scribes *asked Him, "Why do Your disciples not walk according to the tradition of the elders, but eat their bread with impure hands?"

6 And He said to them, "Rightly did Isaiah prophesy of you hypocrites, as it is written,

> 'THIS PEOPLE HONORS ME WITH
> THEIR LIPS,
> BUT THEIR HEART IS FAR AWAY
> FROM ME.

7 'BUT IN VAIN DO THEY WORSHIP
> ME,
> TEACHING AS DOCTRINES THE PRE-
> CEPTS OF MEN.'

8"Neglecting the commandment of God, you hold to the tradition of men."

9 He was also saying to them, "You nicely set aside the commandment of God in order to keep your tradition.

10"For Moses said, 'HONOR YOUR FA-THER AND YOUR MOTHER'; and, 'HE WHO SPEAKS EVIL OF FATHER OR MOTHER, LET HIM BE PUT TO DEATH';

11 but you say, 'If a man says to *his* father or *his* mother, anything of mine you might have been helped by is Corban (that is to say, [19]given *to God*),'

12 you no longer permit him to do anything for *his* father or *his* mother;

13 *thus* invalidating the word of God by your tradition which you have handed down; and you do many things such as that."

14 And after He called the multitude to Him again, He *began* saying to them, "Listen to Me, all of you, and understand:

15 there is nothing outside the man which going into him can defile him; but the things which proceed out of the man are what defile the man.

16 ["[20]If any man has ears to hear, let him hear."]

17 And when leaving the multitude, He had entered the house, His disciples questioned Him about the parable.

18 And He *said to them, "Are you so lacking in understanding also? Do you not understand that whatever goes into the man from outside cannot defile him;

19 because it does not go into his heart, but into his stomach, and is eliminated?" (*Thus He* declared all foods clean.)

20 And He was saying, "That which proceeds out of the man, that is what defiles the man.

21"For from within, out of the heart of men, proceed the evil thoughts, fornications, thefts, murders, adulteries,

22 deeds of coveting *and* wickedness, *as well as* deceit, sensuality, envy, slander, pride *and* foolishness.

23"All these evil things proceed from within and defile the man."

24 ¶ And from there He arose and went away to the region of Tyre[21]. And when He had entered a house, He wanted no one to know *of it;* yet He could not escape notice.

25 But after hearing of Him, a woman whose little daughter had an unclean spirit, immediately came and fell at His feet.

26 Now the woman was a [22]Gentile, of the Syrophoenician race. And she kept asking Him to cast the demon out of her daughter.

27 And He was saying to her, "Let the children be satisfied first, for it is not good to take the children's bread and throw it to the dogs."

28 But she answered and *said to Him, "Yes, Lord, *but* even the dogs under the table feed on the children's crumbs."

29 And He said to her, "Because of this answer go your way; the demon has gone out of your daughter."

30 And going back to her home, she found the child lying on the bed, the demon having departed.

31 ¶ And again He went out from the region of Tyre, and came through Sidon to the Sea of Galilee, within the region of Decapolis.

32 And they *brought to Him one

---

[19] Or, *a gift, an offering*
[20] Many mss. do not contain this verse
[21] Some early mss. add: *and Sidon* [22] Lit., *Greek*

who was deaf and spoke with difficulty, and they *entreated Him to lay His hand upon him.

33 And He took him aside from the multitude by himself, and put His fingers into his ears, and after spitting, He touched his tongue *with the saliva;*

34 and looking up to heaven with a deep sigh, He *said to him, "Ephphatha!" that is, "Be opened!"

35 And his ears were opened, and the impediment of his tongue was removed, and he *began* speaking plainly.

36 And He gave them orders not to tell anyone; but the more He ordered them, the more widely they continued to proclaim it.

37 And they were utterly astonished, saying, "He has done all things well; He makes even the deaf to hear, and the dumb to speak."

CHAPTER 8

IN those days again, when there was a great multitude and they had nothing to eat, He called His disciples and *said to them,

2 "I feel compassion for the multitude because they have remained with Me now three days, and have nothing to eat;

3 and if I send them away hungry to their home, they will faint on the way; and some of them have come from a distance."

4 And His disciples answered Him, "Where will anyone be able to *find enough to* satisfy these men with bread here in a desolate place?"

5 And He was asking them, "How many loaves do you have?" And they said, "Seven."

6 And He *directed the multitude to sit down on the ground; and taking the seven loaves, He gave thanks and broke them, and started giving them to His disciples to serve to them, and they served them to the multitude.

7 They also had a few small fish; and after He had blessed them, He ordered these to be served as well.

8 And they ate and were satisfied; and they picked up seven large baskets full of what was left over of the broken pieces.

9 And about four thousand were *there;* and He sent them away.

10 And immediately He entered the boat with His disciples, and came to the district of Dalmanutha.

11 ¶ And the Pharisees came out and began to argue with Him, seeking from Him a sign from heaven, to test Him.

12 And sighing deeply in His spirit, He *said, "Why does this generation seek for a sign? Truly I say to you, no sign shall be given to this generation."

13 And leaving them, He again embarked and went away to the other side.

14 ¶ And they had forgotten to take bread; and did not have more than one loaf in the boat with them.

15 And He was giving orders to them, saying, "Watch out! Beware of the leaven of the Pharisees and the leaven of Herod."

16 And they *began* to discuss with one another *the fact* that they had no bread.

17 And Jesus, aware of this, *said to them, "Why do you discuss *the fact* that you have no bread? Do you not yet see or understand? Do you have a hardened heart?

18 "HAVING EYES, DO YOU NOT SEE? AND HAVING EARS, DO YOU NOT HEAR? And do you not remember,

19 when I broke the five loaves for the five thousand, how many baskets full of broken pieces you picked up?" They *said to Him, "Twelve."

20 "And when *I broke* the seven for the four thousand, how many large baskets full of broken pieces did you pick up?" And they *said to Him, "Seven."

21 And He was saying to them, "Do you not yet understand?"

22 ¶ And they *came to Bethsaida. And they *brought a blind man to Him, and *entreated Him to touch him.

23 And taking the blind man by the hand, He brought him out of the village; and after spitting on his eyes, and laying His hands upon him, He asked him, "Do you see anything?"

24 And he looked up and said, "I see men, for I am seeing *them* like trees, walking about."

25 Then again He laid His hands upon his eyes; and he looked intently and was restored, and *began* to see everything clearly.

26 And He sent him to his home,

saying, "Do not even enter the village."

27 ¶ And Jesus went out, along with His disciples, to the villages of Caesarea Philippi; and on the way He questioned His disciples, saying to them, "Who do people say that I am?"

28 And they told Him, saying, "John the Baptist; and others say Elijah; but others, one of the prophets."

29 And He continued by questioning them, "But who do you say that I am?" Peter *answered and *said to Him, "Thou art the Christ."

30 And He warned them to tell no one about Him.

31 ¶ And He began to teach them that the Son of Man must suffer many things and be rejected by the elders and the chief priests and the scribes, and be killed, and after three days rise again.

32 And He was stating the matter plainly. And Peter took Him aside and began to rebuke Him.

33 But turning around and seeing His disciples, He rebuked Peter, and *said, "Get behind Me, Satan; for you are not setting your mind on ²³God's interests, but man's."

34 And He summoned the multitude with His disciples, and said to them, "If anyone wishes to come after Me, let him deny himself, and take up his cross, and follow Me.

35 "For whoever wishes to save his life shall lose it; but whoever loses his life for My sake and the gospel's shall save it.

36 "For what does it profit a man to gain the whole world, and forfeit his soul?

37 "For what shall a man give in exchange for his soul?

38 "For whoever is ashamed of Me and My words in this adulterous and sinful generation, the Son of Man will also be ashamed of him when He comes in the glory of His Father with the holy angels."

CHAPTER 9

AND He was saying to them, "Truly I say to you, there are some of those who are standing here who shall not taste death until they see the kingdom of God after it has come with power."

²³ Lit., the things of God

2 ¶ And six days later, Jesus *took with Him Peter and James and John, and *brought them up to a high mountain by themselves. And He was transfigured before them;

3 and His garments became radiant and exceedingly white, as no launderer on earth can whiten them.

4 And Elijah appeared to them along with Moses; and they were talking with Jesus.

5 And Peter answered and *said to Jesus, "Rabbi, it is good for us to be here; and let us make three tabernacles, one for You, and one for Moses, and one for Elijah."

6 For he did not know what to answer; for they became terrified.

7 Then a cloud formed, overshadowing them, and a voice came out of the cloud, "This is My beloved Son, listen to Him!"

8 And all at once they looked around and saw no one with them anymore, except Jesus alone.

9 ¶ And as they were coming down from the mountain, He gave them orders not to relate to anyone what they had seen, until the Son of Man should rise from the dead.

10 And they seized upon that statement, discussing with one another what rising from the dead might mean.

11 And they asked Him, saying, "Why is it that the scribes say that Elijah must come first?"

12 And He said to them, "Elijah does first come and restore all things. And yet how is it written of the Son of Man that He should suffer many things and be treated with contempt?

13 "But I say to you, that Elijah has indeed come, and they did to him whatever they wished, just as it is written of him."

14 ¶ And when they came back to the disciples, they saw a large crowd around them, and some scribes arguing with them.

15 And immediately, when the entire crowd saw Him, they were amazed, and began running up to greet Him.

16 And He asked them, "What are you discussing with them?"

17 And one of the crowd answered Him, "Teacher, I brought You my son,

possessed with a spirit which makes him mute;

18 and whenever it seizes him, it dashes him *to the ground* and he foams *at the mouth*, and grinds his teeth, and stiffens out. And I told Your disciples to cast it out, and they could not *do it.*"

19 And He *answered them and *said, "O unbelieving generation, how long shall I be with you? How long shall I put up with you? Bring him to Me!"

20 And they brought the boy to Him. And when he saw Him, immediately the spirit threw him into a convulsion, and falling to the ground, he *began* rolling about and foaming *at the mouth.*

21 And He asked his father, "How long has this been happening to him?" And he said, "From childhood.

22 "And it has often thrown him both into the fire and into the water to destroy him. But if You can do anything, take pity on us and help us!"

23 And Jesus said to him, " 'If You can!' All things are possible to him who believes."

24 Immediately the boy's father cried out and *began* saying, "I do believe; help my unbelief."

25 And when Jesus saw that a crowd was rapidly gathering, He rebuked the unclean spirit, saying to it, "You deaf and dumb spirit, I command you, come out of him and do not enter him again."

26 And after crying out and throwing him into terrible convulsions, it came out; and *the boy* became so much like a corpse that most *of them* said, "He is dead!"

27 But Jesus took him by the hand and raised him; and he got up.

28 And when He had come into *the* house, His disciples *began* questioning Him privately, "Why could we not cast it out?"

29 And He said to them, "This kind cannot come out by anything but prayer²⁴."

30 ¶ And from there they went out and *began* to go through Galilee, and He was unwilling for anyone to know *about it.*

31 For He was teaching His disciples

and telling them, "The Son of Man is to be ²⁵delivered into the hands of men, and they will kill Him; and when He has been killed, He will rise three days later."

32 But they did not understand *this* statement, and they were afraid to ask Him.

33 ¶ And they came to Capernaum; and when He was in the house, He *began* to question them, "What were you discussing on the way?"

34 But they kept silent, for on the way they had discussed with one another which *of them was* the greatest.

35 And sitting down, He called the twelve and *said to them, "If anyone wants to be first, he shall be last of all, and servant of all."

36 And taking a child, He set him before them, and taking him in His arms, He said to them,

37 "Whoever receives one child like this in My name receives Me; and whoever receives Me does not receive Me, but Him who sent Me."

38 ¶ John said to Him, "Teacher, we saw someone casting out demons in Your name, and we tried to hinder him because he was not following us."

39 But Jesus said, "Do not hinder him, for there is no one who shall perform a miracle in My name, and be able soon afterward to speak evil of Me.

40 "For he who is not against us is ²⁶for us.

41 "For whoever gives you a cup of water to drink because of your name as *followers* of Christ, truly I say to you, he shall not lose his reward.

42 "And whoever causes one of these little ones who believe to stumble, it would be better for him if, with a heavy millstone hung around his neck, he had been cast into the sea.

43 "And if your hand causes you to stumble, cut it off; it is better for you to enter life crippled, than having your two hands, to go into hell, into the unquenchable fire,

44 [²⁷where THEIR WORM DOES NOT DIE, AND THE FIRE IS NOT QUENCHED.]

45 "And if your foot causes you to stumble, cut it off; it is better for you

---

²⁴ Many mss. add: *and fasting*

²⁵ Or, *betrayed*   ²⁶ Or, *on our side*
²⁷ Vv. 44 and 46, which are identical with v. 48, are not found in the best ancient mss.

to enter life lame, than having your two feet, to be cast into hell,

46 [²⁷where THEIR WORM DOES NOT DIE, AND THE FIRE IS NOT QUENCHED.]

47 "And if your eye causes you to stumble, cast it out; it is better for you to enter the kingdom of God with one eye, than having two eyes, to be cast into hell,

48 where THEIR WORM DOES NOT DIE, AND THE FIRE IS NOT QUENCHED.

49 "For everyone will be salted with fire.

50 "Salt is good; but if the salt becomes unsalty, with what will you make it salty again? Have salt in yourselves, and be at peace with one another."

CHAPTER 10

AND rising up, He *went from there to the region of Judea, and beyond the Jordan; and crowds *gathered around Him again, and, according to His custom, He once more began to teach them.

2 ¶ And some Pharisees came up to Him, testing Him, and began to question Him whether it was lawful for a man to divorce a wife.

3 And He answered and said to them, "What did Moses command you?"

4 And they said, "Moses permitted a man TO WRITE A CERTIFICATE OF DIVORCE AND SEND her AWAY."

5 But Jesus said to them, "Because of your hardness of heart he wrote you this commandment.

6 "But from the beginning of creation, God MADE THEM MALE AND FEMALE.

7 "FOR THIS CAUSE A MAN SHALL LEAVE HIS FATHER AND MOTHER,²⁸

8 AND THE TWO SHALL BECOME ONE FLESH; consequently they are no longer two, but one flesh.

9 "What therefore God has joined together, let no man separate."

10 And in the house the disciples began questioning Him about this again.

11 And He *said to them, "Whoever divorces his wife and marries another woman commits adultery against her;

12 and if she herself divorces her

husband and marries another man, she is committing adultery."

13 ¶ And they were bringing children to Him so that He might touch them; and the disciples rebuked them.

14 But when Jesus saw this, He was indignant and said to them, "Permit the children to come to Me; do not hinder them; for the kingdom of God belongs to such as these.

15 "Truly I say to you, whoever does not receive the kingdom of God like a child shall not enter it at all."

16 And He took them in His arms and began blessing them, laying His hands upon them.

17 ¶ And as He was setting out on a journey, a man ran up to Him and knelt before Him, and began asking Him, "Good Teacher, what shall I do to inherit eternal life?"

18 And Jesus said to him, "Why do you call Me good? No one is good except God alone.

19 "You know the commandments, 'DO NOT MURDER, DO NOT COMMIT ADULTERY, DO NOT STEAL, DO NOT BEAR FALSE WITNESS, Do not defraud, HONOR YOUR FATHER AND MOTHER.' "

20 And he said to Him, "Teacher, I have kept all these things from my youth up."

21 And looking at him, Jesus felt a love for him, and said to him, "One thing you lack: go and sell all you possess, and give to the poor, and you shall have treasure in heaven; and come, follow Me."

22 But at these words his face fell, and he went away grieved, for he was one who owned much property.

23 ¶ And Jesus, looking around, *said to His disciples, "How hard it will be for those who are wealthy to enter the kingdom of God!"

24 And the disciples were amazed at His words. But Jesus *answered again and *said to them, "Children, how hard it is ²⁹to enter the kingdom of God!

25 'It is easier for a camel to go through the eye of a needle than for a rich man to enter the kingdom of God."

26 And they were even more astonished and said to Him, "Then who can be saved?"

---

²⁷ Vv. 44 and 46, which are identical with v. 48, are not found in the best ancient mss.
²⁸ Some mss. add: and shall cleave to his wife

²⁹ Later mss. insert: for those who trust in wealth

27 Looking upon them, Jesus *said, "With men it is impossible, but not with God; for all things are possible with God."

28 Peter began to say to Him, "Behold, we have left everything and followed You."

29 Jesus said, "Truly I say to you, there is no one who has left house or brothers or sisters or mother or father or children or farms, for My sake and for the gospel's sake,

30 but that he shall receive a hundred times as much now in the present age, houses and brothers and sisters and mothers and children and farms, along with persecutions; and in the age to come, eternal life.

31 "But many who are first, will be last; and the last, first."

32 ¶ And they were on the road, going up to Jerusalem, and Jesus was walking on ahead of them; and they were amazed, and those who followed were fearful. And again He took the twelve aside and began to tell them what was going to happen to Him,

33 saying, "Behold, we are going up to Jerusalem, and the Son of Man will be ³⁰delivered to the chief priests and the scribes; and they will condemn Him to death, and will deliver Him to the Gentiles.

34 "And they will mock Him and spit upon Him, and scourge Him, and kill Him, and three days later He will rise again."

35 ¶ And James and John, the two sons of Zebedee, *came up to Him, saying to Him, "Teacher, we want You to do for us whatever we ask of You."

36 And He said to them, "What do you want Me to do for you?"

37 And they said to Him, "Grant that we may sit in Your glory, one on Your right, and one on Your left."

38 But Jesus said to them, "You do not know what you are asking for. Are you able to drink the cup that I drink, or to be baptized with the baptism with which I am baptized?"

39 And they said to Him, "We are able." And Jesus said to them, "The cup that I drink you shall drink; and you shall be baptized with the baptism with which I am baptized.

40 "But to sit on My right or on My left, this is not Mine to give; but it is for those for whom it has been prepared."

41 And hearing this, the ten began to feel indignant with James and John.

42 And calling them to Himself, Jesus *said to them, "You know that those who are recognized as rulers of the Gentiles lord it over them; and their great men exercise authority over them.

43 "But it is not so among you, but whoever wishes to become great among you shall be your servant;

44 and whoever wishes to be first among you shall be slave of all.

45 "For even the Son of Man did not come to be served, but to serve, and to give His life a ransom for many."

46 ¶ And they *came to Jericho. And as He was going out from Jericho with His disciples and a great multitude, a blind beggar named Bartimaeus, the son of Timaeus, was sitting by the road.

47 And when he heard that it was Jesus the Nazarene, he began to cry out and say, "Jesus, Son of David, have mercy on me!"

48 And many were sternly telling him to be quiet, but he kept crying out all the more, "Son of David, have mercy on me!"

49 And Jesus stopped and said, "Call him here." And they *called the blind man, saying to him, "Take courage, arise! He is calling for you."

50 And casting aside his cloak, he jumped up, and came to Jesus.

51 And answering him, Jesus said, "What do you want Me to do for you?" And the blind man said to Him, "³¹Rabboni, I want to regain my sight!"

52 And Jesus said to him, "Go your way; your faith has made you well." And immediately he regained his sight and began following Him on the road.

CHAPTER 11

AND as they *approached Jerusalem, at Bethphage and Bethany, near the Mount of Olives, He *sent two of His disciples,

2 and *said to them, "Go into the village opposite you, and immediately as you enter it, you will find a colt tied

³⁰ Or, betrayed   ³¹ I.e., My Master

there, on which no one yet has ever sat; untie it and bring it *here.*

3 "And if anyone says to you, 'Why are you doing this?' you say, 'The Lord has need of it'; and immediately he will send it back here.''

4 And they went away and found a colt tied at the door outside in the street; and they *untied it.

5 And some of the bystanders were saying to them, "What are you doing, untying the colt?"

6 And they spoke to them just as Jesus had told *them,* and they gave them permission.

7 And they *brought the colt to Jesus and put their garments on it; and He sat upon it.

8 And many spread their garments in the road, and others *spread* leafy branches which they had cut from the fields.

9 And those who went before, and those who followed after, were crying out,

"Hosanna!
BLESSED IS HE WHO COMES IN THE
NAME OF THE LORD;
10 Blessed *is* the coming kingdom
of our father David;
Hosanna in the highest!"

11 ¶ And He entered Jerusalem *and came* into the temple; and after looking all around, He departed for Bethany with the twelve, since it was already late.

12 ¶ And on the next day, when they had departed from Bethany, He became hungry.

13 And seeing at a distance a fig tree in leaf, He went *to see* if perhaps He would find anything on it; and when He came to it, He found nothing but leaves, for it was not the season for figs.

14 And He answered and said to it, "May no one ever eat fruit from you again!" And His disciples were listening.

15 ¶ And they *came to Jerusalem. And He entered the temple and began to cast out those who were buying and selling in the temple, and overturned the tables of the moneychangers and the seats of those who were selling doves;

16 and He would not permit anyone to carry goods through the temple.

17 And He *began* to teach and say to them, "Is it not written, 'MY HOUSE SHALL BE CALLED A HOUSE OF PRAYER FOR ALL THE NATIONS'? But you have made it a ROBBERS' DEN."

18 And the chief priests and the scribes heard *this,* and *began* seeking how to destroy Him; for they were afraid of Him, for all the multitude was astonished at His teaching.

19 ¶ And whenever evening came, they would go out of the city.

20 ¶ And as they were passing by in the morning, they saw the fig tree withered from the roots *up.*

21 And being reminded, Peter *said to Him, "Rabbi, behold, the fig tree which You cursed has withered.''

22 And Jesus *answered saying to them, "Have faith in God.

23 "Truly I say to you, whoever says to this mountain, 'Be taken up and cast into the sea,' and does not doubt in his heart, but believes that what he says is going to happen, it shall be *granted* him.

24 "Therefore I say to you, all things for which you pray and ask, believe that you have received them, and they shall be *granted* you.

25 "And whenever you stand praying, forgive, if you have anything against anyone; so that your Father also who is in heaven may forgive you your transgressions.

26 ["[32]But if you do not forgive, neither will your Father who is in heaven forgive your transgressions."]

27 ¶ And they *came again to Jerusalem. And as He was walking in the temple, the chief priests, and scribes, and elders *came to Him,

28 and *began* saying to Him, "By what authority are You doing these things, or who gave You this authority to do these things?"

29 And Jesus said to them, "I will ask you one question, and you answer Me, and *then* I will tell you by what authority I do these things.

30 "Was the baptism of John from heaven, or from men? Answer Me."

31 And they *began* reasoning among themselves, saying, "If we say, 'From heaven,' He will say, 'Then why did you not believe him?'

32 "But shall we say, 'From men'?"—

[32] Many mss. do not contain this verse

they were afraid of the multitude, for all considered John to have been a prophet indeed.

33 And answering Jesus, they *said, "We do not know." And Jesus *said to them, "Neither will I tell you by what authority I do these things."

CHAPTER 12

AND He began to speak to them in parables: "A man PLANTED A VINE-YARD, AND PUT A WALL AROUND IT, AND DUG A VAT UNDER THE WINE PRESS, AND BUILT A TOWER, and rented it out to [33]vine-growers and went on a journey.

2 "And at the *harvest* time he sent a slave to the vine-growers, in order to receive *some* of the produce of the vineyard from the vine-growers.

3 "And they took him, and beat him, and sent him away empty-handed.

4 "And again he sent them another slave, and they wounded him in the head, and treated him shamefully.

5 "And he sent another, and that one they killed; and *so with* many others, beating some, and killing others.

6 "He had one more *to send*, a beloved son; he sent him last *of all* to them, saying, 'They will respect my son.'

7 "But those vine-growers said to one another, 'This is the heir; come, let us kill him, and the inheritance will be ours!'

8 "And they took him, and killed him, and threw him out of the vineyard.

9 "What will the owner of the vineyard do? He will come and destroy the vine-growers, and will give the vineyard to others.

10 "Have you not even read this Scripture:

'THE STONE WHICH THE BUILDERS REJECTED,
THIS BECAME THE CHIEF CORNER *stone*;

11 THIS CAME ABOUT FROM THE LORD,
AND IT IS MARVELOUS IN OUR EYES'?"

12 And they were seeking to seize Him; and *yet* they feared the multitude; for they understood that He spoke the parable against them. And *so* they left Him, and went away.

13 ¶ And they *sent some of the Pharisees and Herodians to Him, in order to trap Him in a statement.

14 And they *came and *said to Him, "Teacher, we know that You are truthful, and defer to no one; for You are not partial to any, but teach the way of God in truth. Is it lawful to pay a poll-tax to Caesar, or not?

15 "Shall we pay, or shall we not pay?" But He, knowing their hypocrisy, said to them, "Why are you testing Me? Bring Me a [34]denarius to look at."

16 And they brought *one*. And He *said to them, "Whose likeness and inscription is this?" And they said to Him, "Caesar's."

17 And Jesus said to them, "Render to Caesar the things that are Caesar's, and to God the things that are God's." And they were amazed at Him.

18 ¶ And *some* Sadducees (who say that there is no resurrection) *came to Him, and *began* questioning Him, saying,

19 "Teacher, Moses wrote for us that IF A MAN'S BROTHER DIES, and leaves behind a wife, AND LEAVES NO CHILD, HIS BROTHER SHOULD TAKE THE WIFE, AND RAISE UP OFFSPRING TO HIS BROTHER.

20 "There were seven brothers; and the first took a wife, and died, leaving no offspring.

21 "And the second one took her, and died, leaving behind no offspring; and the third likewise;

22 and *so* all seven left no offspring. Last of all the woman died also.

23 "In the resurrection, [35]when they rise again, which one's wife will she be? For all seven had her as wife."

24 Jesus said to them, "Is this not the reason you are mistaken, that you do not understand the Scriptures, or the power of God?

25 "For when they rise from the dead, they neither marry, nor are given in marriage, but are like angels in heaven.

26 "But regarding the fact that the dead rise again, have you not read in the book of Moses, in the *passage about the burning* bush, how God spoke to him, saying, 'I AM THE GOD OF

---

[33] Or, *tenant farmers*, also vv. 2, 7, 9
[34] The denarius was equivalent to one day's wage
[35] Most ancient mss. do not contain *when they rise again*

ABRAHAM, AND THE GOD OF ISAAC, AND THE GOD OF JACOB'?

27 "He is not the God of the dead, but of the living; you are greatly mistaken."

28 ¶ And one of the scribes came and heard them arguing, and recognizing that He had answered them well, asked Him, "What commandment is the foremost of all?"

29 Jesus answered, "The foremost is, 'HEAR, O ISRAEL! THE LORD OUR GOD IS ONE LORD;

30 AND YOU SHALL LOVE THE LORD YOUR GOD WITH ALL YOUR HEART, AND WITH ALL YOUR SOUL, AND WITH ALL YOUR MIND, AND WITH ALL YOUR STRENGTH.'

31 "The second is this, 'YOU SHALL LOVE YOUR NEIGHBOR AS YOURSELF.' There is no other commandment greater than these."

32 And the scribe said to Him, "Right, Teacher, You have truly stated that HE IS ONE; AND THERE IS NO ONE ELSE BESIDES HIM;

33 AND TO LOVE HIM WITH ALL THE HEART AND WITH ALL THE UNDERSTANDING AND WITH ALL THE STRENGTH, AND TO LOVE ONE'S NEIGHBOR AS HIMSELF, is much more than all burnt offerings and sacrifices."

34 And when Jesus saw that he had answered intelligently, He said to him, "You are not far from the kingdom of God." And after that, no one would venture to ask Him any more questions.

35 ¶ And Jesus answering *began* to say, as He taught in the temple, "How *is it that* the scribes say that the Christ is the son of David?

36 "David himself said in the Holy Spirit,

'THE LORD SAID TO MY LORD,
"SIT AT MY RIGHT HAND,
UNTIL I PUT THINE ENEMIES BENEATH THY FEET." '

37 "David himself calls Him 'Lord'; and *so* in what sense is He his son?" And the great crowd enjoyed listening to Him.

38 ¶ And in His teaching He was saying: "Beware of the scribes who like to walk around in long robes, and *like* respectful greetings in the market places,

39 and chief seats in the synagogues, and places of honor at banquets,

40 who devour widows' houses, and for appearance's sake offer long prayers; these will receive greater condemnation."

41 ¶ And He sat down opposite the treasury, and *began* observing how the multitude were putting money into the treasury; and many rich people were putting in large sums.

42 And a poor widow came and put in two small copper coins, which amount to a cent.

43 And calling His disciples to Him, He said to them, "Truly I say to you, this poor widow put in more than all the contributors to the treasury;

44 for they all put in out of their surplus, but she, out of her poverty, put in all she owned, all she had to live on."

CHAPTER 13

AND as He was going out of the temple, one of His disciples *said to Him, "Teacher, behold [36]what wonderful stones and what wonderful buildings!"

2 And Jesus said to him, "Do you see these great buildings? Not one stone shall be left upon another which will not be torn down."

3 ¶ And as He was sitting on the Mount of Olives opposite the temple, Peter and James and John and Andrew were questioning Him privately,

4 "Tell us, when will these things be, and what *will be* the sign when all these things are going to be fulfilled?"

5 And Jesus began to say to them, "See to it that no one misleads you.

6 "Many will come in My name, saying, 'I am *He!*' and will mislead many.

7 "And when you hear of wars and rumors of wars, do not be frightened; *those things* must take place; but *that is* not yet the end.

8 "For nation will arise against nation, and kingdom against kingdom; there will be earthquakes in various places; there will *also* be famines. These things are *merely* the beginning of birth pangs.

9 ¶ "But be on your guard; for they will deliver you to *the* courts, and you will be flogged in *the* synagogues, and you will stand before governors and

[36] Lit., *how great*

kings for My sake, as a testimony to them.

10 "And the gospel must first be preached to all the nations.

11 "And when they arrest you and deliver you up, do not be anxious beforehand about what you are to say, but say whatever is given you in that hour; for it is not you who speak, but *it is* the Holy Spirit.

12 "And brother will deliver brother to death, and a father *his* child; and children will rise up against parents and have them put to death.

13 "And you will be hated by all on account of My name, but the one who endures to the end, he shall be saved.

14 ¶ "But when you see the ABOMINATION OF DESOLATION standing where it should not be (let the reader understand), then let those who are in Judea flee to the mountains.

15 "And let him who is on the housetop not go down, or enter in, to get anything out of his house;

16 and let him who is in the field not turn back to get his cloak.

17 "But woe to those who are with child and to those who nurse babes in those days!

18 "But pray that it may not happen in the winter.

19 "For those days will be a *time of* tribulation such as has not occurred since the beginning of the creation which God created, until now, and never shall.

20 "And unless the Lord had shortened *those* days, no life would have been saved; but for the sake of the elect whom He chose, He shortened the days.

21 "And then if anyone says to you, 'Behold, here is the Christ'; or, 'Behold, *He is* there'; do not believe *him;*

22 for false Christs and false prophets will arise, and will show signs and wonders, in order, if possible, to lead the elect astray.

23 "But take heed; behold, I have told you everything in advance.

24 ¶ "But in those days, after that tribulation, THE SUN WILL BE DARKENED, AND THE MOON WILL NOT GIVE ITS LIGHT,

25 AND THE STARS WILL BE FALLING from heaven, and the powers that are in the heavens will be shaken.

26 "And then they will see THE SON OF

MAN COMING IN CLOUDS with great power and glory.

27 "And then He will send forth the angels, and will gather together His elect from the four winds, from the farthest end of the earth, to the farthest end of heaven.

28 ¶ "Now learn the parable from the fig tree: when its branch has already become tender, and puts forth its leaves, you know that summer is near.

29 "Even so, you too, when you see these things happening, recognize that He is near, *right* at the door.

30 "Truly I say to you, this [37]generation will not pass away until all these things take place.

31 "Heaven and earth will pass away, but My words will not pass away.

32 "But of that day or hour no one knows, not even the angels in heaven, nor the Son, but the Father *alone.*

33 ¶ "Take heed, keep on the alert; for you do not know when the *appointed* time is.

34 "*It is* like a man, away on a journey, *who* upon leaving his house and putting his slaves in charge, *assigning* to each one his task, also commanded the doorkeeper to stay on the alert.

35 "Therefore, be on the alert—for you do not know when the master of the house is coming, whether in the evening, at midnight, at cockcrowing, or in the morning—

36 lest he come suddenly and find you asleep.

37 "And what I say to you I say to all, 'Be on the alert!' "

CHAPTER 14

NOW the Passover and Unleavened Bread was two days off; and the chief priests and the scribes were seeking how to seize Him by stealth, and kill Him;

2 for they were saying, "Not during the festival, lest there be a riot of the people."

3 ¶ And while He was in Bethany at the home of Simon the leper, and reclining *at the table,* there came a woman with an alabaster vial of very costly perfume of pure nard; *and* she broke the vial and poured it over His head.

[37] Or, *race*

4 But some were indignantly *remarking* to one another, "Why has this perfume been wasted?

5"For this perfume might have been sold for over three hundred [38]denarii, and *the money* given to the poor." And they were scolding her.

6 But Jesus said, "Let her alone; why do you bother her? She has done a good deed to Me.

7"For the poor you always have with you, and whenever you wish, you can do them good; but you do not always have Me.

8"She has done what she could; she has anointed My body beforehand for the burial.

9"And truly I say to you, wherever the gospel is preached in the whole world, that also which this woman has done shall be spoken of in memory of her."

10 ¶ And Judas Iscariot, who was one of the twelve, went off to the chief priests, in order to betray Him to them.

11 And they were glad when they heard *this*, and promised to give him money. And he *began* seeking how to betray Him at an opportune time.

12 ¶ And on the first day of Unleavened Bread, when the Passover *lamb* was being sacrificed, His disciples *said to Him, "Where do You want us to go and prepare for You to eat the Passover?"

13 And He *sent two of His disciples, and *said to them, "Go into the city, and a man will meet you carrying a pitcher of water; follow him;

14 and wherever he enters, say to the owner of the house, 'The Teacher says, "Where is My guest room in which I may eat the Passover with My disciples?"'

15"And he himself will show you a large upper room furnished *and* ready; and prepare for us there."

16 And the disciples went out, and came to the city, and found *it* just as He had told them; and they prepared the Passover.

17 ¶ And when it was evening He *came with the twelve.

18 And as they were reclining *at the table* and eating, Jesus said, "Truly I

say to you that one of you will betray Me—one who is eating with Me."

19 They began to be grieved and to say to Him one by one, "Surely not I?"

20 And He said to them, *"It is* one of the twelve, one who dips with Me in the bowl.

21"For the Son of Man *is to* go, just as it is written of Him; but woe to that man by whom the Son of Man is betrayed! *It would have been* good for that man if he had not been born."

22 ¶ And while they were eating, He took *some* bread, and after a blessing He broke *it;* and gave *it* to them, and said, "Take *it;* this is My body."

23 And when He had taken a cup, *and* given thanks, He gave *it* to them; and they all drank from it.

24 And He said to them, "This is My blood of the covenant, which is poured out for many.

25"Truly I say to you, I shall never again drink of the fruit of the vine until that day when I drink it new in the kingdom of God."

26 ¶ And after singing a hymn, they went out to the Mount of Olives.

27 ¶ And Jesus *said to them, "You will all fall away, because it is written, 'I WILL STRIKE DOWN THE SHEPHERD, AND THE SHEEP SHALL BE SCATTERED.'

28"But after I have been raised, I will go before you to Galilee."

29 But Peter said to Him, *"Even* though all may fall away, yet I will not."

30 And Jesus *said to him, "Truly I say to you, that you yourself this very night, before a cock crows twice, shall three times deny Me."

31 But *Peter* kept saying insistently, *"Even* if I have to die with You, I will not deny You!" And they all were saying the same thing, too.

32 ¶ And they *came to a place named Gethsemane; and He *said to His disciples, "Sit here until I have prayed."

33 And He *took with Him Peter and James and John, and began to be very distressed and troubled.

34 And He *said to them, "My soul is deeply grieved to the point of death; remain here and keep watch."

35 And He went a little beyond *them,* and fell to the ground, and *began* to pray that if it were possible, the hour might pass Him by.

---

[38] The denarius was equivalent to one day's wage

36 And He was saying, "Abba! Father! All things are possible for Thee; remove this cup from Me; yet not what I will, but what Thou wilt."

37 And He *came and *found them sleeping, and *said to Peter, "Simon, are you asleep? Could you not keep watch for one hour?

38 "Keep watching and praying, that you may not come into temptation; the spirit is willing, but the flesh is weak."

39 And again He went away and prayed, saying the same words.

40 And again He came and found them sleeping, for their eyes were very heavy; and they did not know what to answer Him.

41 And He *came the third time, and *said to them, "Are you still sleeping and taking your rest? It is enough; the hour has come; behold, the Son of Man is being betrayed into the hands of sinners.

42 "Arise, let us be going; behold, the one who betrays Me is at hand!"

43 ¶ And immediately while He was still speaking, Judas, one of the twelve, *came up, accompanied by a multitude with swords and clubs, from the chief priests and the scribes and the elders.

44 Now he who was betraying Him had given them a signal, saying, "Whomever I shall kiss, He is the one; seize Him, and lead Him away under guard."

45 And after coming, he immediately went to Him, saying, "Rabbi!" and kissed Him.

46 And they laid hands on Him, and seized Him.

47 But a certain one of those who stood by drew his sword, and struck the slave of the high priest, and cut off his ear.

48 And Jesus answered and said to them, "Have you come out with swords and clubs to arrest Me, as against a robber?

49 "Every day I was with you in the temple teaching, and you did not seize Me; but *this has happened* that the Scriptures might be fulfilled."

50 And they all left Him and fled.

51 ¶ And a certain young man was following Him, wearing *nothing but* a linen sheet over *his* naked *body;* and they *seized him.

52 But he left the linen sheet behind, and escaped naked.

53 ¶ And they led Jesus away to the high priest; and all the chief priests and the elders and the scribes *gathered together.

54 And Peter had followed Him at a distance, right into the courtyard of the high priest; and he was sitting with the officers, and warming himself at the fire.

55 Now the chief priests and the whole [39]Council kept trying to obtain testimony against Jesus to put Him to death; and they were not finding any.

56 For many were giving false testimony against Him, and *yet* their testimony was not consistent.

57 And some stood up and *began* to give false testimony against Him, saying,

58 "We heard Him say, 'I will destroy this temple made with hands, and in three days I will build another made without hands.'"

59 And not even in this respect was their testimony consistent.

60 And the high priest stood up *and came* forward and questioned Jesus, saying, "Do You make no answer? What is it that these men are testifying against You?"

61 But He kept silent, and made no answer. Again the high priest was questioning Him, and saying to Him, "Are You the Christ, the Son of the Blessed *One?"*

62 And Jesus said, "I am; and you shall see THE SON OF MAN SITTING AT THE RIGHT HAND OF POWER, and COMING WITH THE CLOUDS OF HEAVEN."

63 And tearing his clothes, the high priest *said, "What further need do we have of witnesses?

64 "You have heard the blasphemy; how does it seem to you?" And they all condemned Him to be deserving of death.

65 And some began to spit at Him, and to blindfold Him, and to beat Him with their fists, and to say to Him, "Prophesy!" And the officers received Him with slaps *in the face.*

66 ¶ And as Peter was below in the courtyard, one of the servant-girls of the high priest *came,

67 and seeing Peter warming himself,

[39] Or, *Sanhedrin*

she looked at him, and *said, "You, too, were with Jesus the Nazarene."

68 But he denied *it*, saying, "I neither know nor understand what you are talking about." And he went out onto the porch.[40]

69 And the maid saw him, and began once more to say to the bystanders, "This is *one* of them!"

70 But again he was denying it. And after a little while the bystanders were again saying to Peter, "Surely you are *one* of them, for you are a Galilean too."

71 But he began to curse and swear, "I do not know this man you are talking about!"

72 And immediately a cock crowed a second time. And Peter remembered how Jesus had made the remark to him, "Before a cock crows twice, you will deny Me three times." And he began to weep.

CHAPTER 15

AND early in the morning the chief priests with the elders and scribes, and the whole [41]Council, immediately held a consultation; and binding Jesus, they led Him away, and delivered Him up to Pilate.

2 And Pilate questioned Him, "Are You the King of the Jews?" And answering He *said to him, "It is as you say."

3 And the chief priests *began* to accuse Him harshly.

4 And Pilate was questioning Him again, saying, "Do You make no answer? See how many charges they bring against You!"

5 But Jesus made no further answer; so that Pilate was amazed.

6 ¶ Now at *the* feast he used to release for them *any* one prisoner whom they requested.

7 And the man named Barabbas had been imprisoned with the insurrectionists who had committed murder in the insurrection.

8 And the multitude went up and began asking him *to do* as he had been accustomed to do for them.

9 And Pilate answered them, saying, "Do you want me to release for you the King of the Jews?"

10 For he was aware that the chief priests had delivered Him up because of envy.

11 But the chief priests stirred up the multitude *to ask* him to release Barabbas for them instead.

12 And answering again, Pilate was saying to them, "Then what shall I do with Him whom you call the King of the Jews?"

13 And they shouted back, "Crucify Him!"

14 But Pilate was saying to them, "Why, what evil has He done?" But they shouted all the more, "Crucify Him!"

15 And wishing to satisfy the multitude, Pilate released Barabbas for them, and after having Jesus scourged, he delivered *Him* to be crucified.

16 ¶ And the soldiers took Him away into the palace (that is, the Praetorium), and they *called together the whole *Roman* [42]cohort.

17 And they *dressed Him up in purple, and after weaving a crown of thorns, they put it on Him;

18 and they began to acclaim Him, "Hail, King of the Jews!"

19 And they kept beating His head with a [43]reed, and spitting at Him, and kneeling and bowing before Him.

20 And after they had mocked Him, they took the purple off Him, and put His garments on Him. And they *led Him out to crucify Him.

21 ¶ And they *pressed into service a passer-by coming from the country, Simon of Cyrene (the father of Alexander and Rufus), to bear His cross.

22 ¶ And they *brought Him to the place Golgotha, which is translated, Place of a Skull.

23 And they tried to give Him wine mixed with myrrh; but He did not take it.

24 And they *crucified Him, and *divided up His garments among themselves, casting lots for them, *to decide* what each should take.

25 And it was the [44]third hour when they crucified Him.

26 And the inscription of the charge against Him read, "THE KING OF THE JEWS."

27 And they *crucified two robbers

---

[40] Later mss. add: *and a cock crowed*   [41] Or, *Sanhedrin*   [42] Or, *battalion*   [43] Or, *staff* (made of a reed)   [44] I.e., 9 a.m.

with Him, one on His right and one on His left.

28 [45And the Scripture was fulfilled which says, "And He was numbered with transgressors."]

29 And those passing by were hurling abuse at Him, wagging their heads, and saying, "Ha! You who *are going to* destroy the temple and rebuild it in three days,

30 save Yourself, and come down from the cross!"

31 In the same way the chief priests also, along with the scribes, were mocking *Him* among themselves and saying, "He saved others; He cannot save Himself.

32 "Let *this* Christ, the King of Israel, now come down from the cross, so that we may see and believe!" And those who were crucified with Him were casting the same insult at Him.

33 ¶ And when the 46sixth hour had come, darkness fell over the whole land until the 47ninth hour.

34 And at the ninth hour Jesus cried out with a loud voice, "ELOI, ELOI, LAMA SABACHTHANI?" which is translated, "MY GOD, MY GOD, WHY HAST THOU FORSAKEN ME?"

35 And when some of the bystanders heard it, they *began* saying, "Behold, He is calling for Elijah."

36 And someone ran and filled a sponge with sour wine, put it on a reed, and gave Him a drink, saying, "Let us see whether Elijah will come to take Him down."

37 And Jesus uttered a loud cry, and breathed His last.

38 And the veil of the temple was torn in two from top to bottom.

39 And when the centurion, who was standing right in front of Him, saw the way He breathed His last, he said, "Truly this man was the Son of God!"

40 And there were also *some* women looking on from a distance, among whom *were* Mary Magdalene, and Mary the mother of James the Less and Joses, and Salome.

41 And when He was in Galilee, they used to follow Him and minister to Him; and *there were* many other women who had come up with Him to Jerusalem.

42 ¶ And when evening had already

come, because it was the preparation day, that is, the day before the Sabbath,

43 Joseph of Arimathea came, a prominent member of the Council, who himself was waiting for the kingdom of God; and he gathered up courage and went in before Pilate, and asked for the body of Jesus.

44 And Pilate wondered if He was dead by this time, and summoning the centurion, he questioned him as to whether He was already dead.

45 And ascertaining this from the centurion, he granted the body to Joseph.

46 And *Joseph* bought a linen cloth, took Him down, wrapped Him in the linen cloth, and laid Him in a tomb which had been hewn out in the rock; and he rolled a stone against the entrance of the tomb.

47 And Mary Magdalene and Mary the *mother* of Joses were looking on *to see* where He was laid.

CHAPTER 16

AND when the Sabbath was over, Mary Magdalene, and Mary the *mother* of James, and Salome, bought spices, that they might come and anoint Him.

2 And very early on the first day of the week, they *came to the tomb when the sun had risen.

3 And they were saying to one another, "Who will roll away the stone for us from the entrance of the tomb?"

4 And looking up, they *saw that the stone had been rolled away, although it was extremely large.

5 And entering the tomb, they saw a young man sitting at the right, wearing a white robe; and they were amazed.

6 And he *said to them, "Do not be amazed; you are looking for Jesus the Nazarene, who has been crucified. He has risen; He is not here; behold, *here is* the place where they laid Him.

7 "But go, tell His disciples and Peter, 'He is going before you into Galilee; there you will see Him, just as He said to you.' "

8 And they went out and fled from the tomb, for trembling and astonishment had gripped them; and they said nothing to anyone, for they were afraid.

45 Many mss. do not contain this verse
46 I.e., noon   47 I.e., 3 p.m.

9 ¶ [[48]Now after He had risen early on the first day of the week, He first appeared to Mary Magdalene, from whom He had cast out seven demons.

10 She went and reported to those who had been with Him, while they were mourning and weeping.

11 And when they heard that He was alive, and had been seen by her, they refused to believe it.

12 ¶ And after that, He appeared in a different form to two of them, while they were walking along on their way to the country.

13 And they went away and reported it to the others, but they did not believe them either.

14 ¶ And afterward He appeared to the eleven themselves as they were reclining *at the table;* and He reproached them for their unbelief and hardness of heart, because they had not believed those who had seen Him after He had risen.

15 And He said to them, "Go into all the world and preach the gospel to all creation.

16'He who has believed and has been baptized shall be saved; but he who has disbelieved shall be condemned.

17'And these signs will accompany those who have believed: in My name they will cast out demons, they will speak with new tongues;

18 they will pick up serpents, and if they drink any deadly *poison,* it shall not hurt them; they will lay hands on the sick, and they will recover."

19 ¶ So then, when the Lord Jesus had spoken to them, He was received up into heaven, and sat down at the right hand of God.

20 And they went out and preached everywhere, while the Lord worked with them, and confirmed the word by the signs that followed.]

[[49]*And they promptly reported all these instructions to Peter and his companions. And after that, Jesus Himself sent out through them from east to west the sacred and imperishable proclamation of eternal salvation.*]

---

[48] Some of the oldest mss. do not contain vv. 9–20

[49] A few later mss. and versions contain this paragraph, usually after verse 8; a few have it at the end of chapter.

THE GOSPEL ACCORDING TO

LUKE

INASMUCH as many have undertaken to compile an account of the things accomplished among us,

2 just as those who from the beginning were eyewitnesses and servants of the [1]word have handed them down to us,

3 it seemed fitting for me as well, having investigated everything carefully from the beginning, to write *it* out for you in consecutive order, most excellent Theophilus;

4 so that you might know the exact truth about the things you have been taught.

5 ¶ In the days of Herod, king of Judea, there was a certain priest named Zacharias, of the division of [2]Abijah; and he had a wife [3]from the daughters of Aaron, and her name was Elizabeth.

6 And they were both righteous in the sight of God, walking blamelessly in all the commandments and requirements of the Lord.

7 And they had no child, because Elizabeth was barren, and they were both advanced in years.

8 ¶ Now it came about, while he was performing his priestly service before God in the *appointed* order of his division,

9 according to the custom of the priestly office, he was chosen by lot to enter the temple of the Lord and burn incense.

10 And the whole multitude of the people were in prayer outside at the hour of the incense offering.

---

[1] I.e., gospel   [2] Gr., *Abia*   [3] I.e., of priestly descent

11 And an angel of the Lord appeared to him, standing to the right of the altar of incense.

12 And Zacharias was troubled when he saw *him,* and fear gripped him.

13 But the angel said to him, "Do not be afraid, Zacharias, for your petition has been heard, and your wife Elizabeth will bear you a son, and you will give him the name John.

14"And you will have joy and gladness, and many will rejoice at his birth.

15"For he will be great in the sight of the Lord, and he will drink no wine or liquor; and he will be filled with the Holy Spirit, while yet in his mother's womb.

16"And he will turn back many of the sons of Israel to the Lord their God.

17"And it is he who will go *as a forerunner* before Him in the spirit and power of Elijah, TO TURN THE HEARTS OF THE FATHERS BACK TO THE CHILDREN, and the disobedient to the attitude of the righteous; so as to make ready a people prepared for the Lord."

18 ¶ And Zacharias said to the angel, "How shall I know this *for certain?* For I am an old man, and my wife is advanced in years."

19 And the angel answered and said to him, "I am Gabriel, who stands in the presence of God; and I have been sent to speak to you, and to bring you this good news.

20"And behold, you shall be silent and unable to speak until the day when these things take place, because you did not believe my words, which shall be fulfilled in their proper time."

21 And the people were waiting for Zacharias, and were wondering at his delay in the temple.

22 But when he came out, he was unable to speak to them; and they realized that he had seen a vision in the temple; and he kept making signs to them, and remained mute.

23 And it came about, when the days of his priestly service were ended, that he went back home.

24 ¶ And after these days Elizabeth his wife became pregnant; and she kept herself in seclusion for five months, saying,

25"This is the way the Lord has dealt with me in the days when He looked *with favor* upon *me,* to take away my disgrace among men."

26 ¶ Now in the sixth month the angel Gabriel was sent from God to a city in Galilee, called Nazareth,

27 to a virgin engaged to a man whose name was Joseph, of the descendants of David; and the virgin's name was Mary.

28 And coming in, he said to her, "Hail, favored one! The Lord *is* with you."[4]

29 But she was greatly troubled at *this* statement, and kept pondering what kind of salutation this might be.

30 And the angel said to her, "Do not be afraid, Mary; for you have found favor with God.

31"And behold, you will conceive in your womb, and bear a son, and you shall name Him Jesus.

32"He will be great, and will be called the Son of the Most High; and the Lord God will give Him the throne of His father David;

33 and He will reign over the house of Jacob forever; and His kingdom will have no end."

34 And Mary said to the angel, "How can this be, since I am a virgin?"

35 And the angel answered and said to her, "The Holy Spirit will come upon you, and the power of the Most High will overshadow you; and for that reason the holy offspring shall be called the Son of God.

36"And behold, even your relative Elizabeth has also conceived a son in her old age; and she who was called barren is now in her sixth month.

37"For nothing will be impossible with God."

38 And Mary said, "Behold, the [5]bondslave of the Lord; be it done to me according to your word." And the angel departed from her.

39 ¶ Now at this time Mary arose and went with haste to the hill country, to a city of Judah,

40 and entered the house of Zacharias and greeted Elizabeth.

41 And it came about that when Elizabeth heard Mary's greeting, the baby leaped in her womb; and Elizabeth was filled with the Holy Spirit.

42 And she cried out with a loud

---

4 Later mss. add: *you are blessed among women*
5 I.e., *female slave*

voice, and said, "Blessed among women *are* you, and blessed *is* the fruit of your womb!

43"And how has it *happened* to me, that the mother of my Lord should come to me?

44"For behold, when the sound of your greeting reached my ears, the baby leaped in my womb for joy.

45"And blessed *is* she who believed that there would be a fulfillment of what had been spoken to her by the Lord."

46 And Mary said:

"My soul exalts the Lord,

47 "And my spirit has rejoiced in God my Savior.

48 "For He has had regard for the humble state of His bondslave;
For behold, from this time on all generations will count me blessed.

49 "For the Mighty One has done great things for me;
And holy is His name.

50 "AND HIS MERCY IS UPON GENERA-TION AFTER GENERATION
TOWARD THOSE WHO FEAR HIM.

51 "He has done mighty deeds with His arm;
He has scattered *those who were* proud in the thoughts of their heart.

52 "He has brought down rulers from *their* thrones,
And has exalted those who were humble.

53 "HE HAS FILLED THE HUNGRY WITH GOOD THINGS;
And sent away the rich empty-handed.

54 "He has given help to Israel His servant,
In remembrance of His mercy,

55 As He spoke to our fathers,
To Abraham and his offspring forever."

56 ¶ And Mary stayed with her about three months, and *then* returned to her home.

57 ¶ Now the time had come for Elizabeth to give birth, and she brought forth a son.

58 And her neighbors and her relatives heard that the Lord had displayed His great mercy toward her; and they were rejoicing with her.

59 And it came about that on the eighth day they came to circumcise the child, and they were going to call him Zacharias, after his father.

60 And his mother answered and said, "No indeed; but he shall be called John."

61 And they said to her, "There is no one among your relatives who is called by that name."

62 And they made signs to his father, as to what he wanted him called.

63 And he asked for a tablet, and wrote as follows, "His name is John." And they were all astonished.

64 And at once his mouth was opened and his tongue *loosed,* and he *began* to speak in praise of God.

65 And fear came on all those living around them; and all these matters were being talked about in all the hill country of Judea.

66 And all who heard them kept them in mind, saying, "What then will this child *turn out to* be?" For the hand of the Lord was certainly with him.

67 ¶ And his father Zacharias was filled with the Holy Spirit, and prophesied, saying:

68 "Blessed *be* the Lord God of Israel,
For He has visited us and accomplished redemption for His people,

69 And has raised up a horn of salvation for us
In the house of David His servant—

70 As He spoke by the mouth of His holy prophets from of old—

71 Salvation FROM OUR ENEMIES,
And FROM THE HAND OF ALL WHO HATE US;

72 To show mercy toward our fathers,
And to remember His holy covenant,

73 The oath which He swore to Abraham our father,

74 To grant us that we, being delivered from the hand of our enemies,
Might serve Him without fear,

75 In holiness and righteousness before Him all our days.

76 "And you, child, will be called the prophet of the Most High;
For you will go on BEFORE THE LORD TO PREPARE HIS WAYS;

77 To give to His people *the* knowledge of salvation
By the forgiveness of their sins,
78 Because of the tender mercy of our God,
With which the Sunrise from on high shall visit us,
79 TO SHINE UPON THOSE WHO SIT IN DARKNESS AND THE SHADOW OF DEATH,
To guide our feet into the way of peace."

80 ¶ And the child continued to grow, and to become strong in spirit, and he lived in the deserts until the day of his public appearance to Israel.

CHAPTER 2

NOW it came about in those days that a decree went out from Caesar Augustus, that a census be taken of all [6]the inhabited earth.

2 This was the first census taken while [7]Quirinius was governor of Syria.

3 And all were proceeding to register for the census, everyone to his own city.

4 And Joseph also went up from Galilee, from the city of Nazareth, to Judea, to the city of David, which is called Bethlehem, because he was of the house and family of David,

5 in order to register, along with Mary, who was engaged to him, and was with child.

6 And it came about that while they were there, the days were completed for her to give birth.

7 And she gave birth to her firstborn son; and she wrapped Him in cloths, and laid Him in a manger, because there was no room for them in the inn.

8 ¶ And in the same region there were *some* shepherds staying out in the fields, and keeping watch over their flock by night.

9 And an angel of the Lord suddenly stood before them, and the glory of the Lord shone around them; and they were terribly frightened.

10 And the angel said to them, "Do not be afraid; for behold, I bring you good news of a great joy which shall be for all the people;

11 for today in the city of David there has been born for you a Savior, who is [8]Christ the Lord.

12 "And this *will be* a sign for you: you will find a baby wrapped in cloths, and lying in a manger."

13 And suddenly there appeared with the angel a multitude of the heavenly host praising God, and saying,

14 "Glory to God in the highest,
And on earth peace among men [9]with whom He is pleased."

15 And it came about when the angels had gone away from them into heaven, that the shepherds *began* saying to one another, "Let us go straight to Bethlehem then, and see this thing that has happened which the Lord has made known to us."

16 And they came in haste and found their way to Mary and Joseph, and the baby as He lay in the manger.

17 And when they had seen this, they made known the statement which had been told them about this Child.

18 And all who heard it wondered at the things which were told them by the shepherds.

19 But Mary treasured up all these things, pondering them in her heart.

20 And the shepherds went back, glorifying and praising God for all that they had heard and seen, just as had been told them.

21 ¶ And when eight days were completed before His circumcision, His name was *then* called Jesus, the name given by the angel before He was conceived in the womb.

22 ¶ And when the days for their purification according to the law of Moses were completed, they brought Him up to Jerusalem to present Him to the Lord

23 (as it is written in the Law of the Lord, "EVERY *first-born* MALE THAT OPENS THE WOMB SHALL BE CALLED HOLY TO THE LORD"),

24 and to offer a sacrifice according to what was said in the Law of the Lord, "A PAIR OF TURTLEDOVES, OR TWO YOUNG PIGEONS."

25 And behold, there was a man in Jerusalem whose name was Simeon; and this man was righteous and devout, looking for the consolation of

---

[6] I.e., the Roman empire   [7] Gr., *Kyrenios*
[8] I.e., Messiah
[9] Lit., *of good pleasure;* or possibly, *of good will*

Israel; and the Holy Spirit was upon him.

26 And it had been revealed to him by the Holy Spirit that he would not see death before he had seen the Lord's Christ.

27 And he came in the Spirit into the temple; and when the parents brought in the child Jesus, to carry out for Him the custom of the Law,

28 then he took Him into his arms, and blessed God, and said,

29 "Now Lord, Thou dost let Thy bond-servant depart
   In peace, according to Thy word;

30 For my eyes have seen Thy salvation,

31 Which Thou hast prepared in the presence of all peoples,

32 A LIGHT OF REVELATION TO THE GENTILES,
   And the glory of Thy people Israel."

33 And His father and mother were amazed at the things which were being said about Him.

34 And Simeon blessed them, and said to Mary His mother, "Behold, this *Child* is appointed for the fall and rise of many in Israel, and for a sign to be opposed—

35 and a sword will pierce even your own soul—to the end that thoughts from many hearts may be revealed."

36 And there was a prophetess, Anna the daughter of Phanuel, of the tribe of Asher. She was advanced in years, having lived with a husband seven years after her marriage,

37 and then as a widow to the age of eighty-four. And she never left the temple, serving night and day with fastings and prayers.

38 And at that very moment she came up and *began* giving thanks to God, and continued to speak of Him to all those who were looking for the redemption of Jerusalem.

39 ¶ And when they had performed everything according to the Law of the Lord, they returned to Galilee, to their own city of Nazareth.

40 And the Child continued to grow and become strong, increasing in wisdom; and the grace of God was upon Him.

41 ¶ And His parents used to go to Jerusalem every year at the Feast of the Passover.

42 And when He became twelve, they went up *there* according to the custom of the Feast;

43 and as they were returning, after spending the full number of days, the boy Jesus stayed behind in Jerusalem. And His parents were unaware of it,

44 but supposed Him to be in the caravan, and went a day's journey; and they *began* looking for Him among their relatives and acquaintances.

45 And when they did not find Him, they returned to Jerusalem, looking for Him.

46 And it came about that after three days they found Him in the temple, sitting in the midst of the teachers, both listening to them, and asking them questions.

47 And all who heard Him were amazed at His understanding and His answers.

48 And when they saw Him, they were astonished; and His mother said to Him, "Son, why have You treated us this way? Behold, Your father and I have been anxiously looking for You."

49 And He said to them, "Why is it that you were looking for Me? Did you not know that I had to be in My Father's *house?*"

50 And they did not understand the statement which He had made to them.

51 And He went down with them, and came to Nazareth; and He continued in subjection to them; and His mother treasured all *these* things in her heart.

52 ¶ And Jesus kept increasing in wisdom and stature, and in favor with God and men.

CHAPTER 3

NOW in the fifteenth year of the reign of Tiberius Caesar, when Pontius Pilate was governor of Judea, and Herod was tetrarch of Galilee, and his brother Philip was tetrarch of the region of Ituraea and Trachonitis, and Lysanias was tetrarch of Abilene,

2 in the high priesthood of Annas and Caiaphas, the word of God came to John, the son of Zacharias, in the wilderness.

3 And he came into all the district

around the Jordan, preaching a baptism of repentance for the forgiveness of sins;

4 as it is written in the book of the words of Isaiah the prophet,

"THE VOICE OF ONE CRYING IN THE
    WILDERNESS,
'MAKE READY THE WAY OF THE
    LORD,
MAKE HIS PATHS STRAIGHT.
5 'EVERY RAVINE SHALL BE FILLED
    UP,
AND EVERY MOUNTAIN AND HILL
    SHALL BE BROUGHT LOW;
AND THE CROOKED SHALL BECOME
    STRAIGHT,
AND THE ROUGH ROADS SMOOTH;
6 AND ALL FLESH SHALL SEE THE
    SALVATION OF GOD.' "

7 ¶ He therefore *began* saying to the multitudes who were going out to be baptized by him, "You brood of vipers, who warned you to flee from the wrath to come?

8 "Therefore bring forth fruits in keeping with repentance, and do not begin to say to yourselves, 'We have Abraham for our father,' for I say to you that God is able from these stones to raise up children to Abraham.

9 "And also the axe is already laid at the root of the trees; every tree therefore that does not bear good fruit is cut down and thrown into the fire."

10 And the multitudes were questioning him, saying, "Then what shall we do?"

11 And he would answer and say to them, "Let the man who has two tunics share with him who has none; and let him who has food do likewise."

12 And *some* [10]tax-gatherers also came to be baptized, and they said to him, "Teacher, what shall we do?"

13 And he said to them, "Collect no more than what you have been ordered to."

14 And *some* [11]soldiers were questioning him, saying, "And *what about* us, what shall we do?" And he said to them, "Do not take money from anyone by force, or accuse *anyone* falsely, and be content with your wages."

15 ¶ Now while the people were in a state of expectation and all were wondering in their hearts about John, as to whether he might be the Christ,

16 John answered and said to them all, "As for me, I baptize you with water; but One is coming who is mightier than I, and I am not fit to untie the thong of His sandals; He will baptize you with the Holy Spirit and fire.

17 "And His winnowing fork is in His hand to thoroughly clear His threshing floor, and to gather the wheat into His barn; but He will burn up the chaff with unquenchable fire."

18 ¶ So with many other exhortations also he preached the gospel to the people.

19 But when Herod the tetrarch was reproved by him on account of Herodias, his brother's wife, and on account of all the wicked things which Herod had done,

20 he added this also to them all, that he locked John up in prison.

21 ¶ Now it came about when all the people were baptized, that Jesus also was baptized, and while He was praying, heaven was opened,

22 and the Holy Spirit descended upon Him in bodily form like a dove, and a voice came out of heaven, "Thou art My beloved Son, in Thee I am well-pleased."

23 ¶ And when He began His ministry, Jesus Himself was about thirty years of age, being supposedly *the* son of Joseph, the *son* of Eli,

24 the *son* of Matthat, the *son* of Levi, the *son* of Melchi, the *son* of Jannai, the *son* of Joseph,

25 the *son* of Mattathias, the *son* of Amos, the *son* of Nahum, the *son* of Hesli, the *son* of Naggai,

26 the *son* of Maath, the *son* of Mattathias, the *son* of Semein, the *son* of Josech, the *son* of Joda,

27 the *son* of Joanan, the *son* of Rhesa, the *son* of Zerubbabel, the *son* of Shealtiel, the *son* of Neri,

28 the *son* of Melchi, the *son* of Addi, the *son* of Cosam, the *son* of Elmadam, the *son* of Er,

29 the *son* of Joshua, the *son* of Eliezer, the *son* of Jorim, the *son* of Matthat, the *son* of Levi,

30 the *son* of Simeon, the *son* of Judah, the *son* of Joseph, the *son* of Jonam, the *son* of Eliakim,

31 the *son* of Melea, the *son* of Menna, the *son* of Mattatha, the *son* of Nathan, the *son* of David,

32 the *son* of Jesse, the *son* of Obed, the *son* of Boaz, the *son* of Salmon, the *son* of Nahshon,

33 the *son* of Amminadab, the *son* of Admin, the *son* of Ram, the *son* of Hezron, the *son* of Perez, the *son* of Judah,

34 the *son* of Jacob, the *son* of Isaac, the *son* of Abraham, the *son* of Terah, the *son* of Nahor,

35 the *son* of Serug, the *son* of Reu, the *son* of Peleg, the *son* of Heber, the *son* of Shelah,

36 the *son* of Cainan, the *son* of Arphaxad, the *son* of Shem, the *son* of Noah, the *son* of Lamech,

37 the *son* of Methuselah, the *son* of Enoch, the *son* of Jared, the *son* of Mahalaleel, the *son* of Cainan,

38 the *son* of Enosh, the *son* of Seth, the *son* of Adam, the *son* of God.

CHAPTER 4

AND Jesus, full of the Holy Spirit, returned from the Jordan and was led about by the Spirit in the wilderness

2 for forty days, being tempted by the devil. And He ate nothing during those days; and when they had ended, He became hungry.

3 And the devil said to Him, "If You are the Son of God, tell this stone to become bread."

4 And Jesus answered him, "It is written, 'MAN SHALL NOT LIVE ON BREAD ALONE.'"

5 And he led Him up and showed Him all the kingdoms of the world in a moment of time.

6 And the devil said to Him, "I will give You all this domain and its glory; for it has been handed over to me, and I give it to whomever I wish.

7 "Therefore if You worship before me, it shall all be Yours."

8 And Jesus answered and said to him, "It is written, 'YOU SHALL WORSHIP THE LORD YOUR GOD AND SERVE HIM ONLY.'"

9 And he led Him to Jerusalem and had Him stand on the pinnacle of the temple, and said to Him, "If You are the Son of God, throw Yourself down from here;

10 for it is written,

'HE WILL GIVE HIS ANGELS CHARGE CONCERNING YOU TO GUARD YOU,'

11 and,

'ON *their* HANDS THEY WILL BEAR YOU UP,

LEST YOU STRIKE YOUR FOOT AGAINST A STONE.'"

12 And Jesus answered and said to him, "It is said, 'YOU SHALL NOT [12]PUT THE LORD YOUR GOD TO THE TEST.'"

13 ¶ And when the devil had finished every temptation, he departed from Him until an opportune time.

14 ¶ And Jesus returned to Galilee in the power of the Spirit; and news about Him spread through all the surrounding district.

15 And He *began* teaching in their synagogues and was praised by all.

16 ¶ And He came to Nazareth, where He had been brought up; and as was His custom, He entered the synagogue on the Sabbath, and stood up to read.

17 And the book of the prophet Isaiah was handed to Him. And He opened the book, and found the place where it was written,

18 "THE SPIRIT OF THE LORD IS UPON ME,

BECAUSE HE ANOINTED ME TO PREACH THE GOSPEL TO THE POOR.

HE HAS SENT ME TO PROCLAIM RELEASE TO THE CAPTIVES,

AND RECOVERY OF SIGHT TO THE BLIND,

TO SET FREE THOSE WHO ARE DOWNTRODDEN,

19 TO PROCLAIM THE FAVORABLE YEAR OF THE LORD."

20 And He closed the book, and gave it back to the attendant, and sat down; and the eyes of all in the synagogue were fixed upon Him.

21 And He began to say to them, "Today this Scripture has been fulfilled in your hearing."

22 And all were speaking well of Him, and wondering at the gracious words which were falling from His lips; and they were saying, "Is this not Joseph's son?"

23 And He said to them, "No doubt you will quote this proverb to Me, 'Physician, heal yourself! Whatever we heard was done at Capernaum, do here in your home town as well.'"

24 And He said, "Truly I say to you,

[12]Or, tempt . . . God

no prophet is welcome in his home town.

25 "But I say to you in truth, there were many widows in Israel in the days of Elijah, when the sky was shut up for three years and six months, when a great famine came over all the land;

26 and yet Elijah was sent to none of them, but only to Zarephath, *in the land* of Sidon, to a woman who was a widow.

27 "And there were many lepers in Israel in the time of Elisha the prophet; and none of them was cleansed, but only Naaman the Syrian."

28 And all in the synagogue were filled with rage as they heard these things;

29 and they rose up and cast Him out of the city, and led Him to the brow of the hill on which their city had been built, in order to throw Him down the cliff.

30 But passing through their midst, He went His way.

31 ¶ And He came down to Capernaum, a city of Galilee. And He was teaching them on the Sabbath;

32 and they were amazed at His teaching, for His message was with authority.

33 And there was a man in the synagogue possessed by the spirit of an unclean demon, and he cried out with a loud voice,

34 "Ha! What do we have to do with You, Jesus of Nazareth? Have You come to destroy us? I know who You are—the Holy One of God!"

35 And Jesus rebuked him, saying, "Be quiet and come out of him!" And when the demon had thrown him down in *their* midst, he came out of him without doing him any harm.

36 And amazement came upon them all, and they *began* discussing with one another saying, "What is this message? For with authority and power He commands the unclean spirits, and they come out."

37 And the report about Him was getting out into every locality in the surrounding district.

38 ¶ And He arose and *left* the synagogue, and entered Simon's home.

Now Simon's mother-in-law was suffering from a high fever; and they made request of Him on her behalf.

39 And standing over her, He rebuked the fever, and it left her; and she immediately arose and waited on them.

40 ¶ And while the sun was setting, all who had any sick with various diseases brought them to Him; and laying His hands on every one of them, He was healing them.

41 And demons also were coming out of many, crying out and saying, "You are the Son of God!" And rebuking them, He would not allow them to speak, because they knew Him to be the Christ.

42 ¶ And when day came, He departed and went to a lonely place; and the multitudes were searching for Him, and came to Him, and tried to keep Him from going away from them.

43 But He said to them "I must preach the kingdom of God to the other cities also, for I was sent for this purpose."

44 ¶ And He kept on preaching in the synagogues of [13]Judea.

CHAPTER 5

Now it came about that while the multitude were pressing around Him and listening to the word of God, He was standing by the lake of Gennesaret;

2 and He saw two boats lying at the edge of the lake; but the fishermen had gotten out of them, and were washing their nets.

3 And He got into one of the boats, which was Simon's, and asked him to put out a little way from the land. And He sat down and *began* teaching the multitudes from the boat.

4 And when He had finished speaking, He said to Simon, "Put out into the deep water and let down your nets for a catch."

5 And Simon answered and said, "Master, we worked hard all night and caught nothing, but at Your bidding I will let down the nets."

6 And when they had done this, they enclosed a great quantity of fish; and their nets *began* to break;

[13] I.e., the country of the Jews (including Galilee); some mss. read *Galilee*

7 and they signaled to their partners in the other boat, for them to come and help them. And they came, and filled both of the boats, so that they began to sink.

8 But when Simon Peter saw *that,* he fell down at Jesus' feet, saying, "Depart from me, for I am a sinful man, O Lord!"

9 For amazement had seized him and all his companions because of the catch of fish which they had taken;

10 and so also James and John, sons of Zebedee, who were partners with Simon. And Jesus said to Simon, "Do not fear, from now on you will be catching men."

11 And when they had brought their boats to land, they left everything and followed Him.

12 ¶ And it came about that while He was in one of the cities, behold, *there was* a man full of leprosy; and when he saw Jesus, he fell on his face and implored Him, saying, "Lord, if You are willing, You can make me clean."

13 And He stretched out His hand, and touched him, saying, "I am willing; be cleansed." And immediately the leprosy left him.

14 And He ordered him to tell no one, "But go and show yourself to the priest, and make an offering for your cleansing, just as Moses commanded, for a testimony to them."

15 But the news about Him was spreading even farther, and great multitudes were gathering to hear *Him* and to be healed of their sicknesses.

16 But He Himself would *often* slip away to the wilderness and pray.

17 ¶ And it came about one day that He was teaching; and there were *some* Pharisees and teachers of the law sitting *there,* who had come from every village of Galilee and Judea and *from* Jerusalem; and the power of the Lord was *present* for Him to perform healing.

18 And behold, *some* men *were* carrying on a bed a man who was paralyzed; and they were trying to bring him in, and to set him down in front of Him.

19 And not finding any *way* to bring him in because of the crowd, they went up on the roof and let him down through the tiles with his stretcher,

right in the center, in front of Jesus.

20 And seeing their faith, He said, "Friend, your sins are forgiven you."

21 And the scribes and the Pharisees began to reason, saying, "Who is this *man* who speaks blasphemies? Who can forgive sins, but God alone?"

22 But Jesus, aware of their reasonings, answered and said to them, "Why are you reasoning in your hearts?

23 'Which is easier, to say, 'Your sins have been forgiven you,' or to say, 'Rise and walk'?

24 'But in order that you may know that the Son of Man has authority on earth to forgive sins,'' —He said to the paralytic—"I say to you, rise, and take up your stretcher and go home."

25 And at once he rose up before them, and took up what he had been lying on, and went home, glorifying God.

26 And they were all seized with astonishment and *began* glorifying God; and they were filled with fear, saying, "We have seen remarkable things today."

27 ¶ And after that He went out, and noticed a [14]tax-gatherer named Levi, sitting in the tax office, and He said to him, "Follow Me."

28 And he left everything behind, and rose and *began* to follow Him.

29 ¶ And Levi gave a big reception for Him in his house; and there was a great crowd of tax-gatherers and other *people* who were reclining *at the table* with them.

30 And the Pharisees and their scribes *began* grumbling at His disciples, saying, "Why do you eat and drink with the tax-gatherers and sinners?"

31 And Jesus answered and said to them, "*It is* not those who are well who need a physician, but those who are sick.

32 'I have not come to call the righteous but sinners to repentance."

33 ¶ And they said to Him, "The disciples of John often fast and offer prayers; the *disciples* of the Pharisees also do the same; but Yours eat and drink."

34 And Jesus said to them, "You cannot make the attendants of the

14 I.e., Collector of Roman taxes for profit

bridegroom fast while the bridegroom is with them, can you?

35 "But *the* days will come; and when the bridegroom is taken away from them, then they will fast in those days."

36 And He was also telling them a parable: "No one tears a piece from a new garment and puts it on an old garment; otherwise he will both tear the new, and the piece from the new will not match the old.

37 "And no one puts new wine into old wineskins; otherwise the new wine will burst the skins, and it will be spilled out, and the skins will be ruined.

38 "But new wine must be put into fresh wineskins.

39 "And no one, after drinking old *wine* wishes for new; for he says, 'The old is good *enough.*'"

CHAPTER 6

NOW it came about that on a *certain* Sabbath He was passing through *some* grainfields; and His disciples were picking and eating the heads *of grain,* rubbing them in their hands.

2 But some of the Pharisees said, "Why do you do what is not lawful on the Sabbath?"

3 And Jesus answering them said, "Have you not even read what David did when he was hungry, he and those who were with him,

4 how he entered the house of God, and took and ate the [15]consecrated bread which is not lawful for any to eat except the priests alone, and gave it to his companions?"

5 And He was saying to them, "The Son of Man is Lord of the Sabbath."

6 ¶ And it came about on another Sabbath, that He entered the synagogue and was teaching; and there was a man there whose right hand was withered.

7 And the scribes and the Pharisees were watching Him closely, *to see* if He healed on the Sabbath, in order that they might find *reason* to accuse Him.

8 But He knew what they were thinking, and He said to the man with the withered hand, "Rise and come

forward!" And he rose and came forward.

9 And Jesus said to them, "I ask you, is it lawful on the Sabbath to do good, or to do harm, to save a life, or to destroy it?"

10 And after looking around at them all, He said to him, "Stretch out your hand!" And he did *so;* and his hand was restored.

11 But they themselves were filled with rage, and discussed together what they might do to Jesus.

12 ¶ And it was at this time that He went off to the mountain to pray, and He spent the whole night in prayer to God.

13 And when day came, He called His disciples to Him; and chose twelve of them, whom He also named as apostles:

14 Simon, whom He also named Peter, and Andrew his brother; and James and John; and Philip and Bartholomew;

15 and Matthew and Thomas; James *the son* of Alphaeus, and Simon who was called the Zealot;

16 Judas *the son* of James, and Judas Iscariot, who became a traitor.

17 And He descended with them, and stood on a level place; and *there was* a great multitude of His disciples, and a great throng of people from all Judea and Jerusalem and the coastal region of Tyre and Sidon,

18 who had come to hear Him, and to be healed of their diseases; and those who were troubled with unclean spirits were being cured.

19 And all the multitude were trying to touch Him, for power was coming from Him and healing *them* all.

20 ¶ And turning His gaze on His disciples, He *began* to say, "Blessed *are* you *who are* poor, for yours is the kingdom of God.

21 "Blessed *are* you who hunger now, for you shall be satisfied. Blessed *are* you who weep now, for you shall laugh.

22 "Blessed *are* you when men hate you, and ostracize you, and cast insults at you, and spurn your name as evil, for the sake of the Son of Man.

23 "Be glad in that day, and leap *for joy,* for behold, your reward is great in heaven; for in the same way their fathers used to treat the prophets.

---

[15] Or, *showbread,* lit., *loaves of presentation*

24"But woe to you who are rich, for you are receiving your comfort in full.

25"Woe to you who are well-fed now, for you shall be hungry. Woe *to you* who laugh now, for you shall mourn and weep.

26"Woe *to you* when all men speak well of you, for in the same way their fathers used to treat the false prophets.

27 ¶"But I say to you who hear, love your enemies, do good to those who hate you,

28 bless those who curse you, pray for those who mistreat you.

29"Whoever hits you on the cheek, offer him the other also; and whoever takes away your coat, do not withhold your shirt from him either.

30"Give to everyone who asks of you, and whoever takes away what is yours, do not demand it back.

31"And just as you want people to treat you, treat them in the same way.

32"And if you love those who love you, what credit is *that* to you? For even sinners love those who love them.

33"And if you do good to those who do good to you, what credit is *that* to you? For even sinners do the same.

34"And if you lend to those from whom you expect to receive, what credit is *that* to you? Even sinners lend to sinners, in order to receive back the same *amount.*

35"But love your enemies, and do good, and lend, expecting nothing in return; and your reward will be great, and you will be sons of the Most High; for He Himself is kind to ungrateful and evil *men.*

36"Be merciful, just as your Father is merciful.

37"And do not judge and you will not be judged; and do not condemn, and you will not be condemned; pardon, and you will be pardoned;

38"Give, and it will be given to you; good measure, pressed down, shaken together, running over, they will pour into your lap. For by your standard of measure it will be measured to you in return."

39 ¶ And He also spoke a parable to them: "A blind man cannot guide a blind man, can he? Will they not both fall into a pit?

40"A pupil is not above his teacher; but everyone, after he has been fully trained, will be like his teacher.

41"And why do you look at the speck that is in your brother's eye, but do not notice the log that is in your own eye?

42"Or how can you say to your brother, 'Brother, let me take out the speck that is in your eye,' when you yourself do not see the log that is in your own eye? You hypocrite, first take the log out of your own eye, and then you will see clearly to take out the speck that is in your brother's eye.

43"For there is no good tree which produces bad fruit; nor, on the other hand, a bad tree which produces good fruit.

44"For each tree is known by its own fruit. For men do not gather figs from thorns, nor do they pick grapes from a briar bush.

45"The good man out of the good treasure of his heart brings forth what is good; and the evil *man* out of the evil *treasure* brings forth what is evil; for his mouth speaks from that which fills his heart.

46 ¶"And why do you call Me, 'Lord, Lord,' and do not do what I say?

47"Everyone who comes to Me, and hears My words, and acts upon them, I will show you whom he is like:

48 he is like a man building a house, who dug deep and laid a foundation upon the rock; and when a flood rose, the torrent burst against that house and could not shake it, because it had been well built.

49"But the one who has heard, and has not acted *accordingly,* is like a man who built a house upon the ground without any foundation; and the torrent burst against it and immediately it collapsed, and the ruin of that house was great."

CHAPTER 7

WHEN He had completed all His discourse in the hearing of the people, He went to Capernaum.

2 ¶ And a certain centurion's slave, who was highly regarded by him, was sick and about to die.

3 And when he heard about Jesus, he sent some Jewish elders asking Him to come and save the life of his slave.

4 And when they had come to Jesus, they earnestly entreated Him, saying, "He is worthy for You to grant this to him;

5 for he loves our nation, and it was he who built us our synagogue."

6 Now Jesus *started* on His way with them; and when He was already not far from the house, the centurion sent friends, saying to Him, "Lord, do not trouble Yourself further, for I am not worthy for You to come under my roof;

7 for this reason I did not even consider myself worthy to come to You, but *just* say the word, and my servant will be healed.

8 "For I, too, am a man under authority, with soldiers under me; and I say to this one, 'Go!' and he goes; and to another, 'Come!' and he comes; and to my slave, 'Do this!' and he does it."

9 Now when Jesus heard this, He marveled at him, and turned and said to the multitude that was following Him, "I say to you, not even in Israel have I found such great faith."

10 And when those who had been sent returned to the house, they found the slave in good health.

11 ¶ And it came about soon afterwards, that He went to a city called Nain; and His disciples were going along with Him, accompanied by a large multitude.

12 Now as He approached the gate of the city, behold, a dead man was being carried out, the only son of his mother, and she was a widow; and a sizeable crowd from the city was with her.

13 And when the Lord saw her, He felt compassion for her, and said to her, "Do not weep."

14 And He came up and touched the coffin; and the bearers came to a halt. And He said, "Young man, I say to you, arise!"

15 And the dead man sat up, and began to speak. And *Jesus* gave him back to his mother.

16 And fear gripped them all, and they *began* glorifying God, saying, "A great prophet has arisen among us!" and, "God has visited His people!"

17 And this report concerning Him went out all over Judea, and in all the surrounding district.

18 ¶ And the disciples of John reported to him about all these things.

19 And summoning two of his disciples, John sent them to the Lord, saying, "Are You the Expected One, or do we look for someone else?"

20 And when the men had come to Him, they said, "John the Baptist has sent us to You, saying, 'Are You the Expected One, or do we look for someone else?' "

21 At that very time He cured many *people* of diseases and afflictions and evil spirits; and He granted sight to many *who were* blind.

22 And He answered and said to them, "Go and report to John what you have seen and heard: the BLIND RECEIVE SIGHT, *the* lame walk, *the* lepers are cleansed, and *the* deaf hear, *the* dead are raised up, *the* POOR HAVE THE GOSPEL PREACHED TO THEM.

23 "And blessed is he who keeps from stumbling over Me."

24 ¶ And when the messengers of John had left, He began to speak to the multitudes about John, "What did you go out into the wilderness to look at? A reed shaken by the wind?

25 "But what did you go out to see? A man dressed in soft clothing? Behold, those who are splendidly clothed and live in luxury are *found* in royal palaces.

26 "But what did you go out to see? A prophet? Yes, I say to you, and one who is more than a prophet.

27 "This is the one about whom it is written,

'BEHOLD, I SEND MY MESSENGER
    BEFORE YOUR FACE,
  WHO WILL PREPARE YOUR WAY
    BEFORE YOU.'

28 "I say to you, among those born of women, there is no one greater than John; yet he who is least in the kingdom of God is greater than he."

29 And when all the people and the [16]tax-gatherers heard *this*, they acknowledged God's justice, having been baptized with the baptism of John.

30 But the Pharisees and the [17]lawyers rejected God's purpose for themselves, not having been baptized by John.

31 "To what then shall I compare the

[16] I.e., Collectors of Roman taxes for profit
[17] I.e., experts in the Mosaic law

men of this generation, and what are they like?

32'They are like children who sit in the market place and call to one another; and they say, 'We played the flute for you, and you did not dance; we sang a dirge, and you did not weep.'

33'For John the Baptist has come eating no bread and drinking no wine; and you say, 'He has a demon!'

34'The Son of Man has come eating and drinking; and you say, 'Behold, a gluttonous man, and a drunkard, a friend of tax-gatherers and sinners!'

35'Yet wisdom is vindicated by all her children."

36 ¶ Now one of the Pharisees was requesting Him to dine with him. And He entered the Pharisee's house, and reclined *at the table*.

37 And behold, there was a woman in the city who was a sinner; and when she learned that He was reclining *at the table* in the Pharisee's house, she brought an alabaster vial of perfume,

38 and standing behind *Him* at His feet, weeping, she began to wet His feet with her tears, and kept wiping them with the hair of her head, and kissing His feet, and anointing them with the perfume.

39 Now when the Pharisee who had invited Him saw this, he said to himself, "If this man were a prophet He would know who and what sort of person this woman is who is touching Him, that she is a sinner."

40 And Jesus answered and said to him, "Simon, I have something to say to you." And he replied, "Say it, Teacher."

41'A certain moneylender had two debtors: one owed five hundred [18]denarii, and the other fifty.

42'When they were unable to repay, he graciously forgave them both. Which of them therefore will love him more?"

43 Simon answered and said, "I suppose the one whom he forgave more." And He said to him, "You have judged correctly."

44 And turning toward the woman, He said to Simon, "Do you see this woman? I entered your house; you

[18] The denarius was equivalent to one day's wage

gave Me no water for My feet, but she has wet My feet with her tears, and wiped them with her hair.

45'You gave Me no kiss; but she, since the time I came in, has not ceased to kiss My feet.

46'You did not anoint My head with oil, but she anointed My feet with perfume.

47'For this reason I say to you, her sins, which are many, have been forgiven, for she loved much; but he who is forgiven little, loves little."

48 And He said to her, "Your sins have been forgiven."

49 And those who were reclining *at the table* with Him began to say to themselves, "Who is this *man* who even forgives sins?"

50 And He said to the woman, "Your faith has saved you; go in peace."

CHAPTER 8

AND it came about soon afterwards, that He *began* going about from one city and village to another, proclaiming and preaching the kingdom of God; and the twelve were with Him,

2 and *also* some women who had been healed of evil spirits and sicknesses: Mary who was called Magdalene, from whom seven demons had gone out,

3 and Joanna the wife of Chuza, Herod's steward, and Susanna, and many others who were contributing to their support out of their private means.

4 ¶ And when a great multitude were coming together, and those from the various cities were journeying to Him, He spoke by way of a parable:

5'The sower went out to sow his seed; and as he sowed, some fell beside the road; and it was trampled under foot, and the birds of the air ate it up.

6'And other *seed* fell on rocky *soil*, and as soon as it grew up, it withered away, because it had no moisture.

7'And other *seed* fell among the thorns; and the thorns grew up with it, and choked it out.

8'And other *seed* fell into the good soil, and grew up, and produced a crop a hundred times as great." As He said these things, He would call out, "He who has ears to hear, let him hear."

9 ¶ And His disciples *began* questioning Him as to what this parable might be.

10 And He said, "To you it has been granted to know the mysteries of the kingdom of God, but to the rest *it is* in parables, in order that SEEING THEY MAY NOT SEE, AND HEARING THEY MAY NOT UNDERSTAND.

11 "Now the parable is this: the seed is the word of God.

12 "And those beside the road are those who have heard; then the devil comes and takes away the word from their heart, so that they may not believe and be saved.

13 "And those on the rocky *soil are* those who, when they hear, receive the word with joy; and these have no *firm* root; they believe for a while, and in time of temptation fall away.

14 "And the *seed* which fell among the thorns, these are the ones who have heard, and as they go on their way they are choked with worries and riches and pleasures of *this* life, and bring no fruit to maturity.

15 "And the *seed* in the good soil, these are the ones who have heard the word in an honest and good heart, and hold it fast, and bear fruit with perseverance.

16 ¶ "Now no one after lighting a lamp covers it over with a container, or puts it under a bed; but he puts it on a lampstand, in order that those who come in may see the light.

17 "For nothing is hidden that shall not become evident, nor *anything* secret that shall not be known and come to light.

18 "Therefore take care how you listen; for whoever has, to him shall *more* be given; and whoever does not have, even what he thinks he has shall be taken away from him."

19 ¶ And His mother and brothers came to Him, and they were unable to get to Him because of the crowd.

20 And it was reported to Him, "Your mother and Your brothers are standing outside, wishing to see You."

21 But He answered and said to them, "My mother and My brothers are these who hear the word of God and do it."

22 ¶ Now it came about on one of *those* days, that He and His disciples got into a boat, and He said to them,

"Let us go over to the other side of the lake." And they launched out.

23 But as they were sailing along He fell asleep; and a fierce gale of wind descended upon the lake, and they *began* to be swamped and to be in danger.

24 And they came to Him and woke Him up, saying, "Master, Master, we are perishing!" And being aroused, He rebuked the wind and the surging waves, and they stopped, and it became calm.

25 And He said to them, "Where is your faith?" And they were fearful and amazed, saying to one another, "Who then is this, that He commands even the winds and the water, and they obey Him?"

26 ¶ And they sailed to the country of the Gerasenes, which is opposite Galilee.

27 And when He had come out onto the land, He was met by a certain man from the city who was possessed with demons; and who had not put on any clothing for a long time, and was not living in a house, but in the tombs.

28 And seeing Jesus, he cried out and fell before Him, and said in a loud voice, "What do I have to do with You, Jesus, Son of the Most High God? I beg You, do not torment me."

29 For He had been commanding the unclean spirit to come out of the man. For it had seized him many times; and he was bound with chains and shackles and kept under guard; and *yet* he would burst his fetters and be driven by the demon into the desert.

30 And Jesus asked him, "What is your name?" And he said, "Legion"; for many demons had entered him.

31 And they were entreating Him not to command them to depart into the abyss.

32 Now there was a herd of many swine feeding there on the mountain; and *the demons* entreated Him to permit them to enter the swine. And He gave them permission.

33 And the demons came out from the man and entered the swine; and the herd rushed down the steep bank into the lake, and were drowned.

34 And when the herdsmen saw what had happened, they ran away and reported it in the city and *out* in the country.

35 And *the people* went out to see what had happened; and they came to Jesus, and found the man from whom the demons had gone out, sitting down at the feet of Jesus, clothed and in his right mind; and they became frightened.

36 And those who had seen it reported to them how the man who was demon-possessed had been made well.

37 And all the people of the country of the Gerasenes and the surrounding district asked Him to depart from them; for they were gripped with great fear; and He got into a boat, and returned.

38 But the man from whom the demons had gone out was begging Him that he might accompany Him; but He sent him away, saying,

39 "Return to your house and describe what great things God has done for you." And he went away, proclaiming throughout the whole city what great things Jesus had done for him.

40 ¶ And as Jesus returned, the multitude welcomed Him, for they had all been waiting for Him.

41 And behold, there came a man named Jairus, and he was an official of the synagogue; and he fell at Jesus' feet, and *began* to entreat Him to come to his house;

42 for he had an only daughter, about twelve years old, and she was dying. But as He went, the multitudes were pressing against Him.

43 ¶ And a woman who had a hemorrhage for twelve years, [19]and could not be healed by anyone,

44 came up behind Him, and touched the fringe of His cloak; and immediately her hemorrhage stopped.

45 And Jesus said, "Who is the one who touched Me?" And while they were all denying it, Peter said, "Master, the multitudes are crowding and pressing upon You."

46 But Jesus said, "Someone did touch Me, for I was aware that power had gone out of Me."

47 And when the woman saw that she had not escaped notice, she came trembling and fell down before Him, and declared in the presence of all the people the reason why she had touched Him, and how she had been immediately healed.

48 And He said to her, "Daughter, your faith has made you well; go in peace."

49 ¶ While He was still speaking, someone *came from *the house of* the synagogue official, saying, "Your daughter has died; do not trouble the Teacher anymore."

50 But when Jesus heard *this,* He answered him, "Do not be afraid *any longer;* only believe, and she shall be made well."

51 And when He had come to the house, He did not allow anyone to enter with Him, except Peter and John and James, and the girl's father and mother.

52 Now they were all weeping and lamenting for her; but He said, "Stop weeping, for she has not died, but is asleep."

53 And they *began* laughing at Him, knowing that she had died.

54 He, however, took her by the hand and called, saying, "Child, arise!"

55 And her spirit returned, and she rose immediately; and He gave orders for *something* to be given her to eat.

56 And her parents were amazed; but He instructed them to tell no one what had happened.

CHAPTER 9

AND He called the twelve together, and gave them power and authority over all the demons, and to heal diseases.

2 And He sent them out to proclaim the kingdom of God, and to perform healing.

3 And He said to them, "Take nothing for *your* journey, neither a staff, nor a bag, nor bread, nor money; and do not *even* have two tunics apiece.

4 "And whatever house you enter, stay there, and take your leave from there.

5 "And as for those who do not receive you, as you go out from that city, shake off the dust from your feet as a testimony against them."

6 And departing, they *began* going about among the villages, preaching the gospel, and healing everywhere.

7 ¶ Now Herod the tetrarch heard of all that was happening; and he was

---

[19] Some mss. add *who had spent all her living upon physicians*

greatly perplexed, because it was said by some that John had risen from the dead,

8 and by some that Elijah had appeared, and by others, that one of the prophets of old had risen again.

9 And Herod said, "I myself had John beheaded; but who is this man about whom I hear such things?" And he kept trying to see Him.

10 ¶ And when the apostles returned, they gave an account to Him of all that they had done. And taking them with Him, He withdrew by Himself to a city called Bethsaida.

11 But the multitudes were aware of this and followed Him; and welcoming them, He *began* speaking to them about the kingdom of God and curing those who had need of healing.

12 And the day began to decline, and the twelve came and said to Him, "Send the multitude away, that they may go into the surrounding villages and countryside and find lodging and get something to eat; for here we are in a desolate place."

13 But He said to them, "You give them *something* to eat!" And they said, "We have no more than five loaves and two fish, unless perhaps we go and buy food for all these people."

14 (For there were about five thousand men.) And He said to His disciples, "Have them recline *to eat* in groups of about fifty each."

15 And they did so, and had them all recline.

16 And He took the five loaves and the two fish, and looking up to heaven, He blessed them, and broke *them*, and kept giving *them* to the disciples to set before the multitude.

17 And they all ate and were satisfied; and the broken pieces which they had left over were picked up, twelve baskets *full*.

18 ¶ And it came about that while He was praying alone, the disciples were with Him, and He questioned them, saying, "Who do the multitudes say that I am?"

19 And they answered and said, "John the Baptist, and others *say* Elijah; but others, that one of the prophets of old has risen again."

20 And He said to them, "But who do you say that I am?" And Peter answered and said, "The Christ of God."

21 But He warned them, and instructed *them* not to tell this to anyone,

22 saying, "The Son of Man must suffer many things, and be rejected by the elders and chief priests and scribes, and be killed, and be raised up on the third day."

23 And He was saying to *them* all, "If anyone wishes to come after Me, let him deny himself, and take up his cross daily, and follow Me.

24 'For whoever wishes to save his life shall lose it, but whoever loses his life for My sake, he is the one who will save it.

25 'For what is a man profited if he gains the whole world, and loses or forfeits himself?

26 'For whoever is ashamed of Me and My words, of him will the Son of Man be ashamed when He comes in His glory, and *the glory* of the Father and of the holy angels.

27 'But I say to you truthfully, there are some of those standing here who shall not taste death until they see the kingdom of God."

28 ¶ And some eight days after these sayings, it came about that He took along Peter and John and James, and went up to the mountain to pray.

29 And while He was praying, the appearance of His face became different, and His clothing *became* white *and* gleaming.

30 And behold, two men were talking with Him; and they were Moses and Elijah,

31 who, appearing in glory, were speaking of His departure which He was about to accomplish at Jerusalem.

32 Now Peter and his companions had been overcome with sleep; but when they were fully awake, they saw His glory and the two men standing with Him.

33 And it came about, as these were parting from Him, Peter said to Jesus, "Master, it is good for us to be here; and let us make three tabernacles: one for You, and one for Moses, and one for Elijah"—not realizing what he was saying.

34 And while he was saying this, a cloud formed and *began* to overshadow them; and they were afraid as they entered the cloud.

35 And a voice came out of the cloud, saying, "This is My Son, *My* Chosen One; listen to Him!"

36 And when the voice had spoken, Jesus was found alone. And they kept silent, and reported to no one in those days any of the things which they had seen.

37 ¶ And it came about on the next day, that when they had come down from the mountain, a great multitude met Him.

38 And behold, a man from the multitude shouted out, saying, "Teacher, I beg You to look at my son, for he is my only *boy,*

39 and behold, a spirit seizes him, and he suddenly screams, and it throws him into a convulsion with foaming *at the mouth,* and as it mauls him, it scarcely leaves him.

40 "And I begged Your disciples to cast it out, and they could not."

41 And Jesus answered and said, "O unbelieving and perverted generation, how long shall I be with you, and put up with you? Bring your son here."

42 And while he was still approaching, the demon dashed him *to the ground,* and threw him into a convulsion. But Jesus rebuked the unclean spirit, and healed the boy, and gave him back to his father.

43 And they were all amazed at the greatness of God.

¶ But while everyone was marveling at all that He was doing, He said to His disciples,

44 "Let these words sink into your ears; for the Son of Man is going to be delivered into the hands of men."

45 But they did not understand this statement, and it was concealed from them so that they might not perceive it; and they were afraid to ask Him about this statement.

46 ¶ And an argument arose among them as to which of them might be the greatest.

47 But Jesus, knowing what they were thinking in their heart, took a child and stood him by His side,

48 and said to them, "Whoever receives this child in My name receives Me; and whoever receives Me receives Him who sent Me; for he who is least among you, this is the one who is great."

49 ¶ And John answered and said, "Master, we saw someone casting out demons in Your name; and we tried to hinder him because he does not follow along with us."

50 But Jesus said to him, "Do not hinder *him;* for he who is not against you is for you."

51 ¶ And it came about, when the days were approaching for His ascension, that He resolutely set His face to go to Jerusalem;

52 and He sent messengers on ahead of Him. And they went, and entered a village of the Samaritans, to make arrangements for Him.

53 And they did not receive Him, because He was journeying with His face toward Jerusalem.

54 And when His disciples James and John saw *this,* they said, "Lord, do You want us to command fire to come down from heaven and consume them?"

55 But He turned and rebuked them, [and said, "You do not know what kind of spirit you are of;

56 for the Son of Man did not come to destroy men's lives, but to save them."] And they went on to another village.

57 ¶ And as they were going along the road, someone said to Him, "I will follow You wherever You go."

58 And Jesus said to him, "The foxes have holes, and the birds of the air *have* nests, but the Son of Man has nowhere to lay His head."

59 And He said to another, "Follow Me." But he said, "[20]Permit me first to go and bury my father."

60 But He said to him, "Allow the dead to bury their own dead; but as for you, go and proclaim everywhere the kingdom of God."

61 And another also said, "I will follow You, Lord; but first permit me to say good-bye to those at home."

62 But Jesus said to him, "No one, after putting his hand to the plow and looking back, is fit for the kingdom of God."

CHAPTER 10

NOW after this the Lord appointed seventy others, and sent them two and two ahead of Him to every city and

[20] Some mss. add *Lord*

place where He Himself was going to come.

2 And He was saying to them, "The harvest is plentiful, but the laborers are few; therefore beseech the Lord of the harvest to send out laborers into His harvest.

3 "Go your ways; behold, I send you out as lambs in the midst of wolves.

4 "Carry no purse, no bag, no shoes; and greet no one on the way.

5 "And whatever house you enter, first say, 'Peace *be* to this house.'

6 "And if a man of peace is there, your peace will rest upon him; but if not, it will return to you.

7 "And stay in that house, eating and drinking what they give you; for the laborer is worthy of his wages. Do not keep moving from house to house.

8 "And whatever city you enter, and they receive you, eat what is set before you;

9 and heal those in it who are sick, and say to them, 'The kingdom of God has come near to you.'

10 "But whatever city you enter and they do not receive you, go out into its streets and say,

11 'Even the dust of your city which clings to our feet, we wipe off *in protest* against you; yet be sure of this, that the kingdom of God has come near.'

12 "I say to you, it will be more tolerable in that day for Sodom, than for that city.

13 "Woe to you, Chorazin! Woe to you, Bethsaida! For if the miracles had been performed in Tyre and Sidon which occurred in you, they would have repented long ago, sitting in sackcloth and ashes.

14 "But it will be more tolerable for Tyre and Sidon in the judgment, than for you.

15 "And you, Capernaum, will not be exalted to heaven, will you? You will be brought down to Hades!

16 "The one who listens to you listens to Me, and the one who rejects you rejects Me; and he who rejects Me rejects the One who sent Me."

17 ¶ And the seventy returned with joy, saying, "Lord, even the demons are subject to us in Your name."

18 And He said to them, "I was watching Satan fall from heaven like lightning.

19 "Behold, I have given you authority to tread upon serpents and scorpions, and over all the power of the enemy, and nothing shall injure you.

20 "Nevertheless do not rejoice in this, that the spirits are subject to you, but rejoice that your names are recorded in heaven."

21 ¶ At that very time He rejoiced greatly in the Holy Spirit, and said, "I praise Thee, O Father, Lord of heaven and earth, that Thou didst hide these things from the wise and intelligent and didst reveal them to babes. Yes, Father, for thus it was well-pleasing in Thy sight.

22 "All things have been handed over to Me by My Father, and no one knows who the Son is except the Father, and who the Father is except the Son, and anyone to whom the Son wills to reveal *Him*."

23 And turning to the disciples, He said privately, "Blessed *are* the eyes which see the things you see,

24 for I say to you, that many prophets and kings wished to see the things which you see, and did not see *them*, and to hear the things which you hear, and did not hear *them*."

25 ¶ And behold, a certain lawyer stood up and put Him to the test, saying, "Teacher, what shall I do to inherit eternal life?"

26 And He said to him, "What is written in the Law? How does it read to you?"

27 And he answered and said, "YOU SHALL LOVE THE LORD YOUR GOD WITH ALL YOUR HEART, AND WITH ALL YOUR SOUL, AND WITH ALL YOUR STRENGTH, AND WITH ALL YOUR MIND; AND YOUR NEIGHBOR AS YOURSELF."

28 And He said to him, "You have answered correctly; DO THIS, AND YOU WILL LIVE."

29 But wishing to justify himself, he said to Jesus, "And who is my neighbor?"

30 Jesus replied and said, "A certain man was going down from Jerusalem to Jericho; and he fell among robbers, and they stripped him and beat him, and went off leaving him half dead.

31 "And by chance a certain priest was going down on that road, and when he saw him, he passed by on the other side.

32"And likewise a Levite also, when he came to the place and saw him, passed by on the other side.

33"But a certain Samaritan, who was on a journey, came upon him; and when he saw him, he felt compassion,

34 and came to him, and bandaged up his wounds, pouring oil and wine on *them;* and he put him on his own beast, and brought him to an inn, and took care of him.

35"And on the next day he took out two [21]denarii and gave them to the innkeeper and said, 'Take care of him; and whatever more you spend, when I return, I will repay you.'

36"Which of these three do you think proved to be a neighbor to the man who fell into the robbers' *hands?*"

37 And he said, "The one who showed mercy toward him." And Jesus said to him, "Go and do the same."

38 ¶ Now as they were traveling along, He entered a certain village; and a woman named Martha welcomed Him into her home.

39 And she had a sister called Mary, who moreover was listening to the Lord's word, seated at His feet.

40 But Martha was distracted with all her preparations; and she came up *to Him,* and said, "Lord, do You not care that my sister has left me to do all the serving alone? Then tell her to help me."

41 But the Lord answered and said to her, "Martha, Martha, you are worried and bothered about so many things;

42 but *only* a few things are necessary, really *only* one, for Mary has chosen the good part, which shall not be taken away from her."

CHAPTER 11

AND it came about that while He was praying in a certain place, after He had finished, one of His disciples said to Him, "Lord, teach us to pray just as John also taught his disciples."

2 And He said to them, "When you pray, say:
    '[22]Father, hallowed be Thy name.
    Thy kingdom come.

3 'Give us each day our daily bread.

4 'And forgive us our sins,
    For we ourselves also forgive
        everyone who is indebted to us.
    And lead us not into tempta-
        tion.'"

5 ¶ And He said to them, "Suppose one of you shall have a friend, and shall go to him at midnight, and say to him, 'Friend, lend me three loaves;

6 for a friend of mine has come to me from a journey, and I have nothing to set before him';

7 and from inside he shall answer and say, 'Do not bother me; the door has already been shut and my children and I are in bed; I cannot get up and give you *anything.*'

8"I tell you, even though he will not get up and give him *anything* because he is his friend, yet because of his persistence he will get up and give him as much as he needs.

9"And I say to you, ask, and it shall be given to you; seek, and you shall find; knock, and it shall be opened to you.

10"For everyone who asks, receives; and he who seeks, finds; and to him who knocks, it shall be opened.

11"Now suppose one of you fathers is asked by his son for a fish; he will not give him a snake instead of a fish, will he?

12"Or *if* he is asked for an egg, he will not give him a scorpion, will he?

13"If you then, being evil, know how to give good gifts to your children, how much more shall *your* heavenly Father give the Holy Spirit to those who ask Him?"

14 ¶ And He was casting out a demon, and it was dumb; and it came about that when the demon had gone out, the dumb man spoke; and the multitudes marveled.

15 But some of them said, "He casts out demons by Beelzebul, the ruler of the demons."

16 And others, to test *Him,* were demanding of Him a sign from heaven.

17 But He knew their thoughts, and said to them, "Any kingdom divided against itself is laid waste; and a house *divided* against itself falls.

18"And if Satan also is divided against himself, how shall his kingdom stand? For you say that I cast out demons by Beelzebul.

---

[21] The denarius was equivalent to one day's wage
[22] Some mss. insert phrases from Matt. 6:9-13 to make the two passages closely similar

19'And if I by Beelzebul cast out demons, by whom do your sons cast them out? Consequently they shall be your judges.

20'But if I cast out demons by the finger of God, then the kingdom of God has come upon you.

21'When a strong *man*, fully armed, guards his own homestead, his possessions are undisturbed;

22 but when someone stronger than he attacks him and overpowers him, he takes away from him all his armor on which he had relied, and distributes his plunder.

23'He who is not with Me is against Me; and he who does not gather with Me, scatters.

24'When the unclean spirit goes out of a man, it passes through waterless places seeking rest, and not finding any, it says, 'I will return to my house from which I came.'

25'And when it comes, it finds it swept and put in order.

26'Then it goes and takes *along* seven other spirits more evil than itself, and they go in and live there; and the last state of that man becomes worse than the first."

27 ¶ And it came about while He said these things, one of the women in the crowd raised her voice, and said to Him, "Blessed is the womb that bore You, and the breasts at which You nursed."

28 But He said, "On the contrary, blessed are those who hear the word of God, and observe it."

29 ¶ And as the crowds were increasing, He began to say, "This generation is a wicked generation; it seeks for a sign, and *yet* no sign shall be given to it but the sign of Jonah.

30'For just as Jonah became a sign to the Ninevites, so shall the Son of Man be to this generation.

31'The Queen of the South shall rise up with the men of this generation at the judgment and condemn them, because she came from the ends of the earth to hear the wisdom of Solomon; and behold, something greater than Solomon is here.

32'The men of Nineveh shall stand up with this generation at the judgment and condemn it, because they repented at the preaching of Jonah; and behold, something greater than Jonah is here.

33 ¶'No one, after lighting a lamp, puts it away in a cellar, nor under a peck-measure, but on the lampstand, in order that those who enter may see the light.

34'The lamp of your body is your eye; when your eye is clear, your whole body also is full of light; but when it is bad, your body also is full of darkness.

35'Then watch out that the light in you may not be darkness.

36'If therefore your whole body is full of light, with no dark part in it, it shall be wholly illumined, as when the lamp illumines you with its rays."

37 ¶ Now when He had spoken, a Pharisee *asked Him to have lunch with him; and He went in, and reclined *at the table.*

38 And when the Pharisee saw it, he was surprised that He had not first ceremonially washed before the meal.

39 But the Lord said to him, "Now you Pharisees clean the outside of the cup and of the platter; but inside of you, you are full of robbery and wickedness.

40'You foolish ones, did not He who made the outside make the inside also?

41'But give that which is within as charity, and then all things are clean for you.

42 ¶'But woe to you Pharisees! For you pay tithe of mint and rue and every *kind of* garden herb, and *yet* disregard justice and the love of God; but these are the things you should have done without neglecting the others.

43'Woe to you Pharisees! For you love the front seats in the synagogues, and the respectful greetings in the market places.

44'Woe to you! For you are like concealed tombs, and the people who walk over *them* are unaware *of it.*"

45 ¶ And one of the [23]lawyers *said to Him in reply, "Teacher, when You say this, You insult us too."

46 But He said, "Woe to you lawyers as well! For you weigh men down with burdens hard to bear, while you yourselves will not even touch the burdens with one of your fingers.

[23] I.e., experts in the Mosaic law

47"Woe to you! For you build the tombs of the prophets, and *it was* your fathers *who* killed them.

48"Consequently, you are witnesses and approve the deeds of your fathers; because it was they who killed them, and you build *their tombs.*

49"For this reason also the wisdom of God said, 'I will send to them prophets and apostles, and *some* of them they will kill and *some* they will persecute,

50 in order that the blood of all the prophets, shed since the foundation of the world, may be charged against this generation,

51 from the blood of Abel to the blood of Zechariah, who perished between the altar and the house *of God;* yes, I tell you, it shall be charged against this generation.'

52"Woe to you lawyers! For you have taken away the key of knowledge; you did not enter in yourselves, and those who were entering in you hindered."

53 ¶ And when He left there, the scribes and the Pharisees began to be very hostile and to question Him closely on many subjects,

54 plotting against Him, to catch *Him* in something He might say.

CHAPTER 12

UNDER these circumstances, after so many thousands of the multitude had gathered together that they were stepping on one another, He began saying to His disciples first *of all,* "Beware of the leaven of the Pharisees, which is hypocrisy.

2"But there is nothing covered up that will not be revealed, and hidden that will not be known.

3"Accordingly, whatever you have said in the dark shall be heard in the light, and what you have whispered in the inner rooms shall be proclaimed upon the housetops.

4"And I say to you, My friends, do not be afraid of those who kill the body, and after that have no more that they can do.

5"But I will warn you whom to fear: fear the One who after He has killed has authority to cast into hell; yes, I tell you, fear Him!

6"Are not five sparrows sold for two cents? And *yet* not one of them is forgotten before God.

7"Indeed, the very hairs of your head are all numbered. Do not fear; you are of more value than many sparrows.

8"And I say to you, everyone who confesses Me before men, the Son of Man shall confess him also before the angels of God;

9 but he who denies Me before men shall be denied before the angels of God.

10"And everyone who will speak a word against the Son of Man, it shall be forgiven him; but he who blasphemes against the Holy Spirit, it shall not be forgiven him.

11"And when they bring you before the synagogues and the rulers and the authorities, do not become anxious about how or what you should speak in your defense, or what you should say;

12 for the Holy Spirit will teach you in that very hour what you ought to say."

13 ¶ And someone in the crowd said to Him, "Teacher, tell my brother to divide the *family* inheritance with me."

14 But He said to him, "Man, who appointed Me a judge or arbiter over you?"

15 And He said to them, "Beware, and be on your guard against every form of greed; for not *even* when one has an abundance does his life consist of his possessions."

16 And He told them a parable, saying, "The land of a certain rich man was very productive.

17"And he began reasoning to himself, saying, 'What shall I do, since I have no place to store my crops?'

18"And he said, 'This is what I will do: I will tear down my barns and build larger ones, and there I will store all my grain and my goods.

19 'And I will say to my soul, "Soul, you have many goods laid up for many years *to come;* take your ease, eat, drink *and* be merry." '

20"But God said to him, 'You fool! This *very* night your soul is required of you; and *now* who will own what you have prepared?'

21"So is the man who lays up treasure for himself, and is not rich toward God."

22 ¶ And He said to His disciples, "For this reason I say to you, do not be anxious for *your* life, *as to* what you shall eat; nor for your body, *as to* what you shall put on.

23 "For life is more than food, and the body than clothing.

24 "Consider the ravens, for they neither sow nor reap; and they have no storeroom nor barn; and *yet* God feeds them; how much more valuable you are than the birds!

25 "And which of you by being anxious can add a *single* [24]cubit to his [25]life's span?

26 "If then you cannot do even a very little thing, why are you anxious about other matters?

27 "Consider the lilies, how they grow; they neither toil nor spin; but I tell you, even Solomon in all his glory did not clothe himself like one of these.

28 "But if God so arrays the grass in the field, which is *alive* today and tomorrow is thrown into the furnace, how much more *will He clothe* you, O men of little faith!

29 "And do not seek what you shall eat, and what you shall drink, and do not keep worrying.

30 "For all these things the nations of the world eagerly seek; but your Father knows that you need these things.

31 "But seek for His kingdom, and these things shall be added to you.

32 "Do not be afraid, little flock, for your Father has chosen gladly to give you the kingdom.

33 "Sell your possessions and give to charity; make yourselves purses which do not wear out, an unfailing treasure in heaven, where no thief comes near, nor moth destroys.

34 "For where your treasure is, there will your heart be also.

35 ¶ "Be dressed in readiness, and *keep* your lamps alight.

36 "And be like men who are waiting for their master when he returns from the wedding feast, so that they may immediately open *the door* to him when he comes and knocks.

37 "Blessed are those slaves whom the master shall find on the alert when he comes; truly I say to you, that he will

gird himself *to serve*, and have them recline *at the table*, and will come up and wait on them.

38 "Whether he comes in the [26]second watch, or even in the [27]third, and finds *them* so, blessed are those *slaves*.

39 "And be sure of this, that if the head of the house had known at what hour the thief was coming, he would not have allowed his house to be broken into.

40 "You too, be ready; for the Son of Man is coming at an hour that you do not expect."

41 ¶ And Peter said, "Lord, are You addressing this parable to us, or to everyone *else* as well?"

42 And the Lord said, "Who then is the faithful and sensible steward, whom his master will put in charge of his servants, to give them their rations at the proper time?

43 "Blessed is that slave whom his master finds so doing when he comes.

44 "Truly I say to you, that he will put him in charge of all his possessions.

45 "But if that slave says in his heart, 'My master will be a long time in coming,' and begins to beat the slaves, *both* men and women, and to eat and drink and get drunk;

46 the master of that slave will come on a day when he does not expect *him*, and at an hour he does not know, and will cut him in pieces, and assign him a place with the unbelievers.

47 "And that slave who knew his master's will and did not get ready or act in accord with his will, shall receive many lashes,

48 but the one who did not know *it*, and committed deeds worthy of a flogging, will receive but few. And from everyone who has been given much shall much be required; and to whom they entrusted much, of him they will ask all the more.

49 ¶ "I have come to cast fire upon the earth; and how I wish it were already kindled!

50 "But I have a baptism to undergo, and how distressed I am until it is accomplished!

51 "Do you suppose that I came to grant peace on earth? I tell you, no, but rather division;

52 for from now on five *members* in

---

[24] I.e., One cubit equals approx. 18 in.   [25] Or, *height*   [26] I.e., 9 p.m. to midnight   [27] I.e., midnight to 3 a.m.

one household will be divided, three against two, and two against three.

53"They will be divided, father against son, and son against father; mother against daughter, and daughter against mother; mother-in-law against daughter-in-law, and daughter-in-law against mother-in-law."

54 ¶ And He was also saying to the multitudes, "When you see a cloud rising in the west, immediately you say, 'A shower is coming,' and so it turns out.

55"And when *you see* a south wind blowing, you say, 'It will be a hot day,' and it turns out *that way.*

56"You hypocrites! You know how to analyze the appearance of the earth and the sky, but why do you not analyze this present time?

57"And why do you not even on your own initiative judge what is right?

58"For while you are going with your opponent to appear before the magistrate, on *your* way *there* make an effort to settle with him, in order that he may not drag you before the judge, and the judge turn you over to the constable, and the constable throw you into prison.

59"I say to you, you shall not get out of there until you have paid the very last cent."

CHAPTER 13

NOW on the same occasion there were some present who reported to Him about the Galileans, whose blood Pilate had mingled with their sacrifices.

2 And He answered and said to them, "Do you suppose that these Galileans were *greater* sinners than all *other* Galileans, because they suffered this *fate?*

3"I tell you, no, but, unless you repent, you will all likewise perish.

4"Or do you suppose that those eighteen on whom the tower in Siloam fell and killed them, were *worse* culprits than all the men who live in Jerusalem?

5"I tell you, no, but unless you repent, you will all likewise perish."

6 ¶ And He *began* telling this parable: "A certain man had a fig tree which had been planted in his vineyard; and he came looking for fruit on it, and did not find any.

7"And he said to the vineyard-keeper, 'Behold, for three years I have come looking for fruit on this fig tree without finding any. Cut it down! Why does it even use up the ground?'

8"And he answered and said to him, 'Let it alone, sir, for this year too, until I dig around it and put in fertilizer;

9 and if it bears fruit next year, *fine;* but if not, cut it down.' "

10 ¶ And He was teaching in one of the synagogues on the Sabbath.

11 And behold, there was a woman who for eighteen years had had a sickness caused by a spirit; and she was bent double, and could not straighten up at all.

12 And when Jesus saw her, He called her over and said to her, "Woman, you are freed from your sickness."

13 And He laid His hands upon her; and immediately she was made erect again, and *began* glorifying God.

14 And the synagogue official, indignant because Jesus had healed on the Sabbath, *began* saying to the multitude in response, "There are six days in which work should be done; therefore come during them and get healed, and not on the Sabbath day."

15 But the Lord answered him and said, "You hypocrites, does not each of you on the Sabbath untie his ox or his donkey from the stall, and lead him away to water *him?*

16"And this woman, a daughter of Abraham as she is, whom Satan has bound for eighteen long years, should she not have been released from this bond on the Sabbath day?"

17 And as He said this, all His opponents were being humiliated; and the entire multitude was rejoicing over all the glorious things being done by Him.

18 ¶ Therefore He was saying, "What is the kingdom of God like, and to what shall I compare it?

19"It is like a mustard seed, which a man took and threw into his own garden; and it grew and became a tree; and THE BIRDS OF THE AIR NESTED IN ITS BRANCHES."

20 ¶ And again He said, "To what shall I compare the kingdom of God?

21"It is like leaven, which a woman took and hid in three pecks of meal, until it was all leavened."

22 ¶ And He was passing through from one city and village to another, teaching, and proceeding on His way to Jerusalem.

23 And someone said to Him, "Lord, are there *just* a few who are being saved?" And He said to them,

24"Strive to enter by the narrow door; for many, I tell you, will seek to enter and will not be able.

25"Once the head of the house gets up and shuts the door, and you begin to stand outside and knock on the door, saying, 'Lord, open up to us!' then He will answer and say to you, 'I do not know where you are from.'

26"Then you will begin to say, 'We ate and drank in Your presence, and You taught in our streets';

27 and He will say, 'I tell you, I do not know where you are from; DEPART FROM ME, ALL YOU EVILDOERS.'

28"There will be weeping and gnashing of teeth there when you see Abraham and Isaac and Jacob and all the prophets in the kingdom of God, but yourselves being cast out.

29"And they will come from east and west, and from north and south, and will recline *at the table* in the kingdom of God.

30"And behold, *some* are last who will be first and *some* are first who will be last."

31 ¶ Just at that time some Pharisees came up, saying to Him, "Go away and depart from here, for Herod wants to kill You."

32 And He said to them, "Go and tell that fox, 'Behold, I cast out demons and perform cures today and tomorrow, and the third *day* I reach My goal.'

33"Nevertheless I must journey on today and tomorrow and the next *day*; for it cannot be that a prophet should perish outside of Jerusalem.

34"O Jerusalem, Jerusalem, *the city* that kills the prophets and stones those sent to her! How often I wanted to gather your children together, just as a hen *gathers* her brood under her wings, and you would not *have it!*

35"Behold, your house is left to you *desolate;* and I say to you, you shall not see Me until *the time* comes when you say, 'BLESSED IS HE WHO COMES IN THE NAME OF THE LORD!' "

CHAPTER 14

AND it came about when He went into the house of one of the leaders of the Pharisees on *the* Sabbath to eat bread, that they were watching Him closely.

2 And there, in front of Him was a certain man suffering from dropsy.

3 And Jesus answered and spoke to the lawyers and Pharisees, saying, "Is it lawful to heal on the Sabbath, or not?"

4 But they kept silent. And He took hold of him, and healed him, and sent him away.

5 And He said to them, "Which one of you shall have a son or an ox fall into a well, and will not immediately pull him out on a Sabbath day?"

6 And they could make no reply to this.

7 ¶ And He *began* speaking a parable to the invited guests when He noticed how they had been picking out the places of honor *at the table;* saying to them,

8"When you are invited by someone to a wedding feast, do not take the place of honor, lest someone more distinguished than you may have been invited by him,

9 and he who invited you both shall come and say to you, 'Give place to this man,' and then in disgrace you proceed to occupy the last place.

10"But when you are invited, go and recline at the last place, so that when the one who has invited you comes, he may say to you, 'Friend, move up higher'; then you will have honor in the sight of all who are at the table with you.

11"For everyone who exalts himself shall be humbled, and he who humbles himself shall be exalted."

12 ¶ And He also went on to say to the one who had invited Him, "When you give a luncheon or a dinner, do not invite your friends or your brothers or your relatives or rich neighbors, lest they also invite you in return, and repayment come to you.

13"But when you give a reception, invite *the* poor, *the* crippled, *the* lame, *the* blind,

14 and you will be blessed, since they do not have *the means* to repay you;

for you will be repaid at the resurrection of the righteous."

15 ¶ And when one of those who were reclining *at the table* with Him heard this, he said to Him, "Blessed is everyone who shall eat bread in the kingdom of God!"

16 But He said to him, "A certain man was giving a big dinner, and he invited many;

17 and at the dinner hour he sent his slave to say to those who had been invited, 'Come; for everything is ready now.'

18 "But they all alike began to make excuses. The first one said to him, 'I have bought a piece of land and I need to go out and look at it; please consider me excused.'

19 "And another one said, 'I have bought five yoke of oxen, and I am going to try them out; please consider me excused.'

20 "And another one said, 'I have married a wife, and for that reason I cannot come.'

21 "And the slave came *back* and reported this to his master. Then the head of the household became angry and said to his slave, 'Go out at once into the streets and lanes of the city and bring in here the poor and crippled and blind and lame.'

22 "And the slave said, 'Master, what you commanded has been done, and still there is room.'

23 "And the master said to the slave, 'Go out into the highways and along the hedges, and compel *them* to come in, that my house may be filled.

24 'For I tell you, none of those men who were invited shall taste of my dinner.' "

25 ¶ Now great multitudes were going along with Him; and He turned and said to them,

26 "If anyone comes to Me, and does not [28]hate his own father and mother and wife and children and brothers and sisters, yes, and even his own life, he cannot be My disciple.

27 "Whoever does not carry his own cross and come after Me cannot be My disciple.

28 "For which one of you, when he wants to build a tower, does not first

sit down and calculate the cost, to see if he has enough to complete it?

29 "Otherwise, when he has laid a foundation, and is not able to finish, all who observe it begin to ridicule him,

30 saying, 'This man began to build and was not able to finish.'

31 "Or what king, when he sets out to meet another king in battle, will not first sit down and take counsel whether he is strong enough with ten thousand *men* to encounter the one coming against him with twenty thousand?

32 "Or else, while the other is still far away, he sends a delegation and asks terms of peace.

33 "So therefore, no one of you can be My disciple who does not give up all his own possessions.

34 "Therefore, salt is good; but if even salt has become tasteless, with what will it be seasoned?

35 "It is useless either for the soil or for the manure pile; it is thrown out. He who has ears to hear, let him hear."

CHAPTER 15

NOW all the tax-gatherers and the sinners were coming near Him to listen to Him.

2 And both the Pharisees and the scribes *began* to grumble, saying, "This man receives sinners and eats with them."

3 ¶ And He told them this parable, saying,

4 "What man among you, if he has a hundred sheep and has lost one of them, does not leave the ninety-nine in the open pasture, and go after the one which is lost, until he finds it?

5 "And when he has found it, he lays it on his shoulders, rejoicing.

6 "And when he comes home, he calls together his friends and his neighbors, saying to them, 'Rejoice with me, for I have found my sheep which was lost!'

7 "I tell you that in the same way, there will be *more* joy in heaven over one sinner who repents, than over ninety-nine righteous persons who need no repentance.

8 ¶ "Or what woman, if she has ten silver coins and loses one coin, does not light a lamp and sweep the house and search carefully until she finds it?

[28] I.e., by comparison of his love for Me

9'And when she has found it, she calls together her friends and neighbors, saying, 'Rejoice with me, for I have found the coin which I had lost!'

10'In the same way, I tell you, there is joy in the presence of the angels of God over one sinner who repents."

11 ¶ And He said, "A certain man had two sons;

12 and the younger of them said to his father, 'Father, give me the share of the estate that falls to me.' And he divided his wealth between them.

13"And not many days later, the younger son gathered everything together and went on a journey into a distant country, and there he squandered his estate with loose living.

14"Now when he had spent everything, a severe famine occurred in that country, and he began to be in need.

15"And he went and attached himself to one of the citizens of that country, and he sent him into his fields to feed swine.

16"And he was longing to fill his stomach with the pods that the swine were eating, and no one was giving *anything* to him.

17"But when he came to his senses, he said, 'How many of my father's hired men have more than enough bread, but I am dying here with hunger!

18'I will get up and go to my father, and will say to him, "Father, I have sinned against heaven, and in your sight;

19 I am no longer worthy to be called your son; make me as one of your hired men."'

20'And he got up and came to his father. But while he was still a long way off, his father saw him, and felt compassion *for him*, and ran and embraced him, and kissed him.

21"And the son said to him, 'Father, I have sinned against heaven and in your sight; I am no longer worthy to be called your son.'

22"But the father said to his slaves, 'Quickly bring out the best robe and put it on him, and put a ring on his hand and sandals on his feet;

23 and bring the fattened calf, kill it, and let us eat and be merry;

24 for this son of mine was dead, and has come to life again; he was lost, and

has been found.' And they began to be merry.

25'Now his older son was in the field, and when he came and approached the house, he heard music and dancing.

26'And he summoned one of the servants and *began* inquiring what these things might be.

27"And he said to him, 'Your brother has come, and your father has killed the fattened calf, because he has received him back safe and sound.'

28'But he became angry, and was not willing to go in; and his father came out and *began* entreating him.

29'But he answered and said to his father, 'Look! For so many years I have been serving you, and I have never neglected a command of yours; and *yet* you have never given me a kid, that I might be merry with my friends;

30 but when this son of yours came, who has devoured your wealth with harlots, you killed the fattened calf for him.'

31"And he said to him, 'My child, you have always been with me, and all that is mine is yours.

32'But we had to be merry and rejoice, for this brother of yours was dead and *has begun* to live, and *was* lost and has been found.' "

CHAPTER 16

NOW He was also saying to the disciples, "There was a certain rich man who had a steward, and this *steward* was reported to him as squandering his possessions.

2"And he called him and said to him, 'What is this I hear about you? Give an account of your stewardship, for you can no longer be steward.'

3"And the steward said to himself, 'What shall I do, since my master is taking the stewardship away from me? I am not strong enough to dig; I am ashamed to beg.

4'I know what I shall do, so that when I am removed from the stewardship, they will receive me into their homes.'

5"And he summoned each one of his master's debtors, and he *began* saying to the first, 'How much do you owe my master?'

6"And he said, 'A hundred measures of oil.' And he said to him, 'Take your bill, and sit down quickly and write fifty.'

7"Then he said to another, 'And how much do you owe?' And he said, 'A hundred measures of wheat.' He *said to him, 'Take your bill, and write eighty.'

8"And his master praised the unrighteous steward because he had acted shrewdly; for the sons of this age are more shrewd in relation to their own kind than the sons of light.

9"And I say to you, make friends for yourselves by means of the [29]mammon of unrighteousness; that when it fails, they may receive you into the eternal dwellings.

10"He who is faithful in a very little thing is faithful also in much; and he who is unrighteous in a very little thing is unrighteous also in much.

11"If therefore you have not been faithful in the *use of* unrighteous mammon, who will entrust the true *riches* to you?

12"And if you have not been faithful in *the use of* that which is another's, who will give you that which is your own?

13"No servant can serve two masters; for either he will hate the one, and love the other, or else he will hold to one, and despise the other. You cannot serve God and mammon."

14 ¶ Now the Pharisees, who were lovers of money, were listening to all these things, and they were scoffing at Him.

15 And He said to them, "You are those who justify yourselves in the sight of men, but God knows your hearts; for that which is highly esteemed among men is detestable in the sight of God.

16"The Law and the Prophets *were proclaimed* until John; since then the gospel of the kingdom of God is preached, and everyone is forcing his way into it.

17"But it is easier for heaven and earth to pass away than for one stroke of a letter of the Law to fail.

18"Everyone who divorces his wife and marries another commits adultery; and he who marries one who is

divorced from a husband commits adultery.

19 ¶"Now there was a certain rich man, and he habitually dressed in purple and fine linen, gaily living in splendor every day.

20"And a certain poor man named Lazarus was laid at his gate, covered with sores,

21 and longing to be fed with the *crumbs* which were falling from the rich man's table; besides, even the dogs were coming and licking his sores.

22"Now it came about that the poor man died and he was carried away by the angels to Abraham's bosom; and the rich man also died and was buried.

23"And in Hades he lifted up his eyes, being in torment, and *saw Abraham far away, and Lazarus in his bosom.

24"And he cried out and said, 'Father Abraham, have mercy on me, and send Lazarus, that he may dip the tip of his finger in water and cool off my tongue; for I am in agony in this flame.'

25"But Abraham said, 'Child, remember that during your life you received your good things, and likewise Lazarus bad things; but now he is being comforted here, and you are in agony.

26 'And besides all this, between us and you there is a great chasm fixed, in order that those who wish to come over from here to you may not be able, and *that* none may cross over from there to us.'

27"And he said, 'Then I beg you, Father, that you send him to my father's house—

28 for I have five brothers—that he may warn them, lest they also come to this place of torment.'

29"But Abraham *said, 'They have Moses and the Prophets; let them hear them.'

30"But he said, 'No, Father Abraham, but if someone goes to them from the dead, they will repent!'

31"But he said to him, 'If they do not listen to Moses and the Prophets, neither will they be persuaded if someone rises from the dead.' "

CHAPTER 17

A ND He said to His disciples, "It is inevitable that stumbling blocks

[29] Or, *riches*

should come, but woe to him through whom they come!

2"It would be better for him if a millstone were hung around his neck and he were thrown into the sea, than that he should cause one of these little ones to stumble.

3"Be on your guard! If your brother sins, rebuke him; and if he repents, forgive him.

4"And if he sins against you seven times a day, and returns to you seven times, saying, 'I repent,' forgive him."

5 ¶ And the apostles said to the Lord, "Increase our faith!"

6 And the Lord said, "If you had faith like a mustard seed, you would say to this mulberry tree, 'Be uprooted and be planted in the sea'; and it would obey you.

7"But which of you, having a slave plowing or tending sheep, will say to him when he has come in from the field, 'Come immediately and sit down to eat'?

8"But will he not say to him, 'Prepare something for me to eat, and *properly* clothe yourself and serve me until I have eaten and drunk; and afterward you will eat and drink'?

9"He does not thank the slave because he did the things which were commanded, does he?

10"So you too, when you do all the things which are commanded you, say, 'We are unworthy slaves; we have done *only* that which we ought to have done.'"

11 ¶ And it came about while He was on the way to Jerusalem, that He was passing between Samaria and Galilee.

12 And as He entered a certain village, ten leprous men who stood at a distance met Him;

13 and they raised their voices, saying, "Jesus, Master, have mercy on us!"

14 And when He saw them, He said to them, "Go and show yourselves to the priests." And it came about that as they were going, they were cleansed.

15 Now one of them, when he saw that he had been healed, turned back, glorifying God with a loud voice,

16 and he fell on his face at His feet, giving thanks to Him. And he was a Samaritan.

17 And Jesus answered and said, "Were there not ten cleansed? But the nine—where are they?

18"Was no one found who turned back to give glory to God, except this foreigner?"

19 And He said to him, "Rise, and go your way; your faith [30]has made you well."

20 ¶ Now having been questioned by the Pharisees as to when the kingdom of God was coming, He answered them and said, "The kingdom of God is not coming with signs to be observed;

21 nor will they say, 'Look, here *it is!*' or, 'There *it is!*' For behold, the kingdom of God is in your midst."

22 ¶ And He said to the disciples, "The days shall come when you will long to see one of the days of the Son of Man, and you will not see it.

23"And they will say to you, 'Look there! Look here!' Do not go away, and do not run after *them.*

24"For just as the lightning, when it flashes out of one part of the sky, shines to the other part of the sky, so will the Son of Man be in His day.

25"But first He must suffer many things and be rejected by this generation.

26"And just as it happened in the days of Noah, so it shall be also in the days of the Son of Man:

27 they were eating, they were drinking, they were marrying, they were being given in marriage, until the day that Noah entered the ark, and the flood came and destroyed them all.

28"It was the same as happened in the days of Lot: they were eating, they were drinking, they were buying, they were selling, they were planting, they were building;

29 but on the day that Lot went out from Sodom it rained fire and brimstone from heaven and destroyed them all.

30"It will be just the same on the day that the Son of Man is revealed.

31"On that day, let not the one who is on the housetop and whose goods are in the house go down to take them away; and likewise let not the one who is in the field turn back.

32"Remember Lot's wife.

[30] Or, *has saved you*

33"Whoever seeks to keep his life shall lose it, and whoever loses *his life* shall preserve it.

34"I tell you, on that night there will be two men in one bed; one will be taken, and the other will be left.

35"There will be two women grinding at the same place; one will be taken, and the other will be left.

36 ["³¹Two men will be in the field; one will be taken and the other will be left."]

37 And answering they *said to Him, "Where, Lord?" And He said to them, "Where the body *is*, there also will the vultures be gathered."

CHAPTER 18

NOW He was telling them a parable to show that at all times they ought to pray and not to lose heart,

2 saying, "There was in a certain city a judge who did not fear God, and did not respect man.

3"And there was a widow in that city, and she kept coming to him, saying, 'Give me legal protection from my opponent.'

4"And for a while he was unwilling; but afterward he said to himself, 'Even though I do not fear God nor respect man,

5 yet because this widow bothers me, I will give her legal protection, lest by continually coming she wear me out.'"

6 And the Lord said, "Hear what the unrighteous judge *said;

7 now shall not God bring about justice for His elect, who cry to Him day and night, and will He delay long over them?

8"I tell you that He will bring about justice for them speedily. However, when the Son of Man comes, will He find faith on the earth?"

9 ¶ And He also told this parable to certain ones who trusted in themselves that they were righteous, and viewed others with contempt:

10"Two men went up into the temple to pray, one a Pharisee, and the other a tax-gatherer.

11"The Pharisee stood and was praying thus to himself, 'God, I thank Thee

that I am not like other people: swindlers, unjust, adulterers, or even like this tax-gatherer.

12 'I fast twice a week; I pay tithes of all that I get.'

13"But the tax-gatherer, standing some distance away, was even unwilling to lift up his eyes to heaven, but was beating his breast, saying, 'God, be merciful to me, the sinner!'

14"I tell you, this man went down to his house justified rather than the other; for everyone who exalts himself shall be humbled, but he who humbles himself shall be exalted."

15 ¶ And they were bringing even their babies to Him so that He might touch them, but when the disciples saw it, they *began* rebuking them.

16 But Jesus called for them, saying, "Permit the children to come to Me, and do not hinder them, for the kingdom of God belongs to such as these.

17"Truly I say to you, whoever does not receive the kingdom of God like a child shall not enter it *at all*."

18 ¶ And a certain ruler questioned Him, saying, "Good Teacher, what shall I do to inherit eternal life?"

19 And Jesus said to him, "Why do you call Me good? No one is good except God alone.

20"You know the commandments, 'DO NOT COMMIT ADULTERY, DO NOT MURDER, DO NOT STEAL, DO NOT BEAR FALSE WITNESS, HONOR YOUR FATHER AND MOTHER.'"

21 And he said, "All these things I have kept from *my* youth."

22 And when Jesus heard *this*, He said to him, "One thing you still lack; sell all that you possess, and distribute it to the poor, and you shall have treasure in heaven; and come, follow Me."

23 But when he had heard these things, he became very sad; for he was extremely rich.

24 And Jesus looked at him and said, "How hard it is for those who are wealthy to enter the kingdom of God!

25"For it is easier for a camel to go through the eye of a needle, than for a rich man to enter the kingdom of God."

26 And they who heard it said, "Then who can be saved?"

27 But He said, "The things impossible with men are possible with God."

³¹ Many mss. do not contain this verse

28 And Peter said, "Behold, we have left our own *homes,* and followed You."

29 And He said to them, "Truly I say to you, there is no one who has left house or wife or brothers or parents or children, for the sake of the kingdom of God,

30 who shall not receive many times as much at this time and in the age to come, eternal life."

31 ¶ And He took the twelve aside and said to them, "Behold, we are going up to Jerusalem, and all things which are written through the prophets about the Son of Man will be accomplished.

32 "For He will be delivered to the Gentiles, and will be mocked and mistreated and spit upon,

33 and after they have scourged Him, they will kill Him; and the third day He will rise again."

34 And they understood none of these things, and this saying was hidden from them, and they did not comprehend the things that were said.

35 ¶ And it came about that as He was approaching Jericho, a certain blind man was sitting by the road, begging.

36 Now hearing a multitude going by, he *began* to inquire what this might be.

37 And they told him that Jesus of Nazareth was passing by.

38 And he called out, saying, "Jesus, Son of David, have mercy on me!"

39 And those who led the way were sternly telling him to be quiet; but he kept crying out all the more, "Son of David, have mercy on me!"

40 And Jesus stopped and commanded that he be brought to Him; and when he had come near, He questioned him,

41 "What do you want Me to do for you?" And he said, "Lord, *I want* to regain my sight!"

42 And Jesus said to him, "Receive your sight; your faith has made you well."

43 And immediately he regained his sight, and *began* following Him, glorifying God; and when all the people saw it, they gave praise to God.

CHAPTER 19

AND He entered and was passing through Jericho.

2 And behold, there was a man called by the name of Zaccheus; and he was a chief tax-gatherer, and he was rich.

3 And he was trying to see who Jesus was, and he was unable because of the crowd, for he was small in stature.

4 And he ran on ahead and climbed up into a sycamore tree in order to see Him, for He was about to pass through that way.

5 And when Jesus came to the place, He looked up and said to him, "Zaccheus, hurry and come down, for today I must stay at your house."

6 And he hurried and came down, and received Him gladly.

7 And when they saw it, they all *began* to grumble, saying, "He has gone to be the guest of a man who is a sinner."

8 And Zaccheus stopped and said to the Lord, "Behold, Lord, half of my possessions I will give to the poor, and if I have defrauded anyone of anything, I will give back four times as much."

9 And Jesus said to him, "Today salvation has come to this house, because he, too, is a son of Abraham.

10 "For the Son of Man has come to seek and to save that which was lost."

11 ¶ And while they were listening to these things, He went on to tell a parable, because He was near Jerusalem, and they supposed that the kingdom of God was going to appear immediately.

12 He said therefore, "A certain nobleman went to a distant country to receive a kingdom for himself, and *then* return.

13 "And he called ten of his slaves, and gave them ten [32]minas, and said to them, 'Do business *with this* until I come *back.*'

14 "But his citizens hated him, and sent a delegation after him, saying, 'We do not want this man to reign over us.'

15 "And it came about that when he returned, after receiving the kingdom, he ordered that these slaves, to whom

[32] A mina is equal to about 100 days' wages or nearly $20

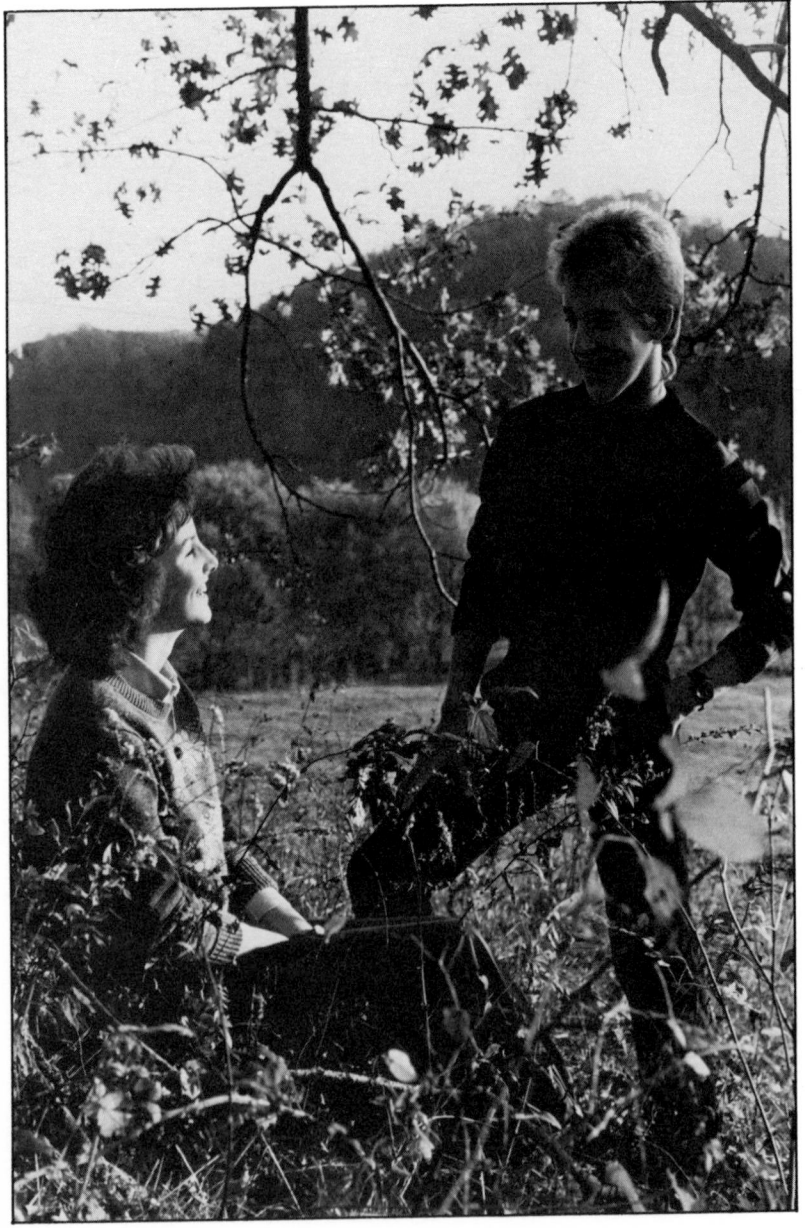

he had given the money, be called to him in order that he might know what business they had done.

16"And the first appeared, saying, 'Master, your mina has made ten minas more.'

17"And he said to him, 'Well done, good slave, because you have been faithful in a very little thing, be in authority over ten cities.'

18"And the second came, saying, 'Your mina, master, has made five minas.'

19"And he said to him also, 'And you are to be over five cities.'

20"And another came, saying, 'Master, behold your mina, which I kept put away in a handkerchief;

21 for I was afraid of you, because you are an exacting man; you take up what you did not lay down, and reap what you did not sow.'

22"He *said to him, 'By your own words I will judge you, you worthless slave. Did you know that I am an exacting man, taking up what I did not lay down, and reaping what I did not sow?

23 'Then why did you not put the money in the bank, and having come, I would have collected it with interest?'

24"And he said to the bystanders, 'Take the mina away from him, and give it to the one who has the ten minas.'

25"And they said to him, 'Master, he has ten minas *already.'

26"I tell you, that to everyone who has shall *more be given, but from the one who does not have, even what he does have shall be taken away.

27"But these enemies of mine, who did not want me to reign over them, bring them here and slay them in my presence."

28 ¶ And after He had said these things, He was going on ahead, ascending to Jerusalem.

29 ¶ And it came about that when He approached Bethphage and Bethany, near the mount that is called Olivet, He sent two of the disciples,

30 saying, "Go into the village opposite *you, in which as you enter you will find a colt tied, on which no one yet has ever sat; untie it, and bring it *here.

31"And if anyone asks you, 'Why are you untying it?' thus shall you speak, 'The Lord has need of it.'"

32 And those who were sent went away and found it just as He had told them.

33 And as they were untying the colt, its owners said to them, "Why are you untying the colt?"

34 And they said, "The Lord has need of it."

35 And they brought it to Jesus, and they threw their garments on the colt, and put Jesus *on it.

36 And as He was going, they were spreading their garments in the road.

37 And as He was now approaching, near the descent of the Mount of Olives, the whole multitude of the disciples began to praise God joyfully with a loud voice for all the miracles which they had seen,

38 saying,
> "Blessed is the King who comes
> in the name of the Lord;
> Peace in heaven and glory in the
> highest!"

39 And some of the Pharisees in the multitude said to Him, "Teacher, rebuke Your disciples."

40 And He answered and said, "I tell you, if these become silent, the stones will cry out!"

41 ¶ And when He approached, He saw the city and wept over it,

42 saying, "If you had known in this day, even you, the things which make for peace! But now they have been hidden from your eyes.

43"For the days shall come upon you when your enemies will throw up a bank before you, and surround you, and hem you in on every side,

44 and will level you to the ground and your children within you, and they will not leave in you one stone upon another, because you did not recognize the time of your visitation."

45 ¶ And He entered the temple and began to cast out those who were selling,

46 saying to them, "It is written, 'And My house shall be a house of prayer,' but you have made it a robbers' den."

47 ¶ And He was teaching daily in the temple; but the chief priests and the scribes and the leading men

among the people were trying to destroy Him,

48 and they could not find anything that they might do, for all the people were hanging upon His words.

CHAPTER 20

AND it came about on one of the days while He was teaching the people in the temple and preaching the gospel, that the chief priests and the scribes with the elders confronted *Him,*

2 and they spoke, saying to Him, "Tell us by what authority You are doing these things, or who is the one who gave You this authority?"

3 And He answered and said to them, "I shall also ask you a question, and you tell Me:

4"Was the baptism of John from heaven or from men?"

5 And they reasoned among themselves, saying, "If we say, 'From heaven,' He will say, 'Why did you not believe him?'

6"But if we say, 'From men,' all the people will stone us to death, for they are convinced that John was a prophet."

7 And they answered that they did not know where *it came* from.

8 And Jesus said to them, "Neither will I tell you by what authority I do these things."

9 ¶ And He began to tell the people this parable: "A man planted a vineyard and rented it out to vine-growers, and went on a journey for a long time.

10"And at the *harvest* time he sent a slave to the vine-growers, in order that they might give him *some* of the produce of the vineyard; but the vine-growers beat him and sent him away empty-handed.

11"And he proceeded to send another slave; and they beat him also and treated him shamefully, and sent him away empty-handed.

12"And he proceeded to send a third; and this one also they wounded and cast out.

13"And the owner of the vineyard said, 'What shall I do? I will send my beloved son; perhaps they will respect him.'

14"But when the vine-growers saw him, they reasoned with one another,

saying, 'This is the heir; let us kill him that the inheritance may be ours.'

15"And they threw him out of the vineyard and killed him. What, therefore, will the owner of the vineyard do to them?

16"He will come and destroy these vine-growers and will give the vineyard to others." And when they heard it, they said, "May it never be!"

17 But He looked at them and said, "What then is this that is written,

'THE STONE WHICH THE BUILDERS REJECTED,

THIS BECAME THE CHIEF CORNER *stone*'?

18"Everyone who falls on that stone will be broken to pieces; but on whomever it falls, it will scatter him like dust."

19 ¶ And the scribes and the chief priests tried to lay hands on Him that very hour, and they feared the people; for they understood that He spoke this parable against them.

20 And they watched Him, and sent spies who pretended to be righteous, in order that they might catch Him in some statement, so as to deliver Him up to the rule and the authority of the governor.

21 And they questioned Him, saying, "Teacher, we know that You speak and teach correctly, and You are not partial to any, but teach the way of God in truth.

22"Is it lawful for us to pay taxes to Caesar, or not?"

23 But He detected their trickery and said to them,

24"Show Me a [33]denarius. Whose likeness and inscription does it have?" And they said, "Caesar's."

25 And He said to them, "Then render to Caesar the things that are Caesar's, and to God the things that are God's."

26 And they were unable to catch Him in a saying in the presence of the people; and marveling at His answer, they became silent.

27 ¶ Now there came to Him some of the Sadducees (who say that there is no resurrection),

28 and they questioned Him, saying, "Teacher, Moses wrote for us that IF A MAN'S BROTHER DIES, having a wife,

[33] The denarius was equivalent to one day's wage

AND HE IS CHILDLESS, HIS BROTHER SHOULD TAKE THE WIFE AND RAISE UP OFFSPRING TO HIS BROTHER.

29 "Now there were seven brothers; and the first took a wife, and died childless;

30 and the second

31 and the third took her; and in the same way all seven died, leaving no children.

32 "Finally the woman died also.

33 "In the resurrection therefore, which one's wife will she be? For all seven had her as wife."

34 And Jesus said to them, "The sons of this age marry and are given in marriage,

35 but those who are considered worthy to attain to that age and the resurrection from the dead, neither marry, nor are given in marriage;

36 for neither can they die anymore, for they are like angels, and are sons of God, being sons of the resurrection.

37 "But that the dead are raised, even Moses showed, in the *passage about the burning* bush, where he calls the Lord THE GOD OF ABRAHAM, AND THE GOD OF ISAAC, AND THE GOD OF JACOB.

38 "Now He is not the God of the dead, but of the living; for all live to Him."

39 And some of the scribes answered and said, "Teacher, You have spoken well."

40 For they did not have courage to question Him any longer about anything.

41 ¶ And He said to them, "How *is it that* they say [34]the Christ is David's son?

42 "For David himself says in the book of Psalms,

'THE LORD SAID TO MY LORD,
"SIT AT MY RIGHT HAND,

43 UNTIL I MAKE THINE ENEMIES A FOOTSTOOL FOR THY FEET." '

44 "David therefore calls Him 'Lord,' and how is He his son?"

45 ¶ And while all the people were listening, He said to the disciples,

46 "Beware of the scribes, who like to walk around in long robes, and love respectful greetings in the market places, and chief seats in the synagogues, and places of honor at banquets,

[34] I.e., the Messiah

47 who devour widows' houses, and for appearance's sake offer long prayers; these will receive greater condemnation."

CHAPTER 21

AND He looked up and saw the rich putting their gifts into the treasury.

2 And He saw a certain poor widow putting in two small copper coins.

3 And He said, "Truly I say to you, this poor widow put in more than all *of them;*

4 for they all out of their surplus put into the offering; but she out of her poverty put in all that she had to live on."

5 ¶ And while some were talking about the temple, that it was adorned with beautiful stones and votive gifts, He said,

6 "*As for* these things which you are looking at, the days will come in which there will not be left one stone upon another which will not be torn down."

7 And they questioned Him, saying, "Teacher, when therefore will these things be? And what *will be* the sign when these things are about to take place?"

8 And He said, "See to it that you be not misled; for many will come in My name, saying, 'I am *He*,' and, 'The time is at hand'; do not go after them.

9 "And when you hear of wars and disturbances, do not be terrified; for these things must take place first, but the end *does* not *follow* immediately."

10 ¶ Then He continued by saying to them, "Nation will rise against nation, and kingdom against kingdom,

11 and there will be great earthquakes, and in various places plagues and famines; and there will be terrors and great signs from heaven.

12 "But before all these things, they will lay their hands on you and will persecute you, delivering you to the synagogues and prisons, bringing you before kings and governors for My name's sake.

13 "It will lead to an opportunity for your testimony.

14 "So make up your minds not to prepare beforehand to defend yourselves;

15 for I will give you utterance and

wisdom which none of your opponents will be able to resist or refute.

16"But you will be delivered up even by parents and brothers and relatives and friends, and they will put *some* of you to death,

17 and you will be hated by all on account of My name.

18"Yet not a hair of your head will perish.

19"By your endurance you will gain your lives.

20 ¶"But when you see Jerusalem surrounded by armies, then recognize that her desolation is at hand.

21"Then let those who are in Judea flee to the mountains, and let those who are in the midst of the city depart, and let not those who are in the country enter the city;

22 because these are days of vengeance, in order that all things which are written may be fulfilled.

23"Woe to those who are with child and to those who nurse babes in those days; for there will be great distress upon the land, and wrath to this people,

24 and they will fall by the edge of the sword, and will be led captive into all the nations; and Jerusalem will be trampled under foot by the Gentiles until the times of the Gentiles be fulfilled.

25 ¶"And there will be signs in sun and moon and stars, and upon the earth dismay among nations, in perplexity at the roaring of the sea and the waves,

26 men fainting from fear and the expectation of the things which are coming upon the world; for the powers of the heavens will be shaken.

27"And then they will see THE SON OF MAN COMING IN A CLOUD with power and great glory.

28"But when these things begin to take place, straighten up and lift up your heads, because your redemption is drawing near."

29 ¶ And He told them a parable: "Behold the fig tree and all the trees;

30 as soon as they put forth *leaves,* you see it and know for yourselves that summer is now near.

31"Even so you, too, when you see these things happening, recognize that the kingdom of God is near.

32"Truly I say to you, this generation will not pass away until all things take place.

33"Heaven and earth will pass away, but My words will not pass away.

34 ¶"Be on guard, that your hearts may not be weighted down with dissipation and drunkenness and the worries of life, and that day come on you suddenly like a trap;

35 for it will come upon all those who dwell on the face of all the earth.

36"But keep on the alert at all times, praying in order that you may have strength to escape all these things that are about to take place, and to stand before the Son of Man."

37 ¶ Now during the day He was teaching in the temple, but at evening He would go out and spend the night on the mount that is called Olivet.

38 And all the people would get up early in the morning *to come* to Him in the temple to listen to Him.

CHAPTER 22

NOW the Feast of Unleavened Bread, which is called the Passover, was approaching.

2 And the chief priests and the scribes were seeking how they might put Him to death; for they were afraid of the people.

3 ¶ And Satan entered into Judas who was called Iscariot, belonging to the number of the twelve.

4 And he went away and discussed with the chief priests and officers how he might betray Him to them.

5 And they were glad, and agreed to give him money.

6 And he consented, and *began* seeking a good opportunity to betray Him to them apart from the multitude.

7 ¶ Then came the *first* day of Unleavened Bread on which the Passover *lamb* had to be sacrificed.

8 And He sent Peter and John, saying, "Go and prepare the Passover for us, that we may eat it."

9 And they said to Him, "Where do You want us to prepare it?"

10 And He said to them, "Behold, when you have entered the city, a man will meet you carrying a pitcher of water; follow him into the house that he enters.

11"And you shall say to the owner of

the house, 'The Teacher says to you, "Where is the guest room in which I may eat the Passover with My disciples?" '

12"And he will show you a large, furnished, upper room; prepare it there."

13 And they departed and found *everything* just as He had told them; and they prepared the Passover.

14 ¶ And when the hour had come He reclined *at the table,* and the apostles with Him.

15 And He said to them, "I have earnestly desired to eat this Passover with you before I suffer;

16 for I say to you, I shall never again eat it until it is fulfilled in the kingdom of God."

17 And when He had taken a cup *and* given thanks, He said, "Take this and share it among yourselves;

18 for I say to you, I will not drink of the fruit of the vine from now on until the kingdom of God comes."

19 And when He had taken *some* bread *and* given thanks, He broke *it,* and gave *it* to them, saying, "This is My body [35] which is given for you; do this in remembrance of Me."

20 And in the same way *He took* the cup after they had eaten, saying, "This cup which is poured out for you is the new covenant in My blood.

21"But behold, the hand of the one betraying Me is with Me on the table.

22"For indeed, the Son of Man is going as it has been determined; but woe to that man by whom He is betrayed!"

23 And they began to discuss among themselves which one of them it might be who was going to do this thing.

24 ¶ And there arose also a dispute among them *as to* which one of them was regarded to be greatest.

25 And He said to them, "The kings of the Gentiles lord it over them; and those who have authority over them are called 'Benefactors.'

26"But not so with you, but let him who is the greatest among you become as the youngest, and the leader as the servant.

27"For who is greater, the one who reclines *at the table,* or the one who serves? Is it not the one who reclines *at the table?* But I am among you as the one who serves.

28"And you are those who have stood by Me in My trials;

29 and just as My Father has granted Me a kingdom, I grant you

30 that you may eat and drink at My table in My kingdom, and you will sit on thrones judging the twelve tribes of Israel.

31 ¶"Simon, Simon, behold, Satan has demanded *permission* to sift you like wheat;

32 but I have prayed for you, that your faith may not fail; and you, when once you have turned again, strengthen your brothers."

33 And he said to Him, "Lord, with You I am ready to go both to prison and to death!"

34 And He said, "I say to you, Peter, the cock will not crow today until you have denied three times that you know Me."

35 ¶ And He said to them, "When I sent you out without purse and bag and sandals, you did not lack anything, did you?" And they said, "No, nothing."

36 And He said to them, "But now, let him who has a purse take it along, likewise also a bag, and let him who has no sword sell his robe and buy one.

37"For I tell you, that this which is written must be fulfilled in Me, 'AND HE WAS NUMBERED WITH TRANSGRESSORS'; for that which refers to Me has *its* fulfillment."

38 And they said, "Lord, look, here are two swords." And He said to them, "It is enough."

39 ¶ And He came out and proceeded as was His custom to the Mount of Olives; and the disciples also followed Him.

40 And when He arrived at the place, He said to them, "Pray that you may not enter into temptation."

41 And He withdrew from them about a stone's throw, and He knelt down and *began* to pray,

42 saying, "Father, if Thou art willing, remove this cup from Me; yet not My will, but Thine be done."

43 Now an angel from heaven appeared to Him, strengthening Him.

---

[35] Some ancient mss. do not contain the remainder of v. 19 nor any of v. 20

44 And being in agony He was praying very fervently; and His sweat became like drops of blood, falling down upon the ground.

45 And when He rose from prayer, He came to the disciples and found them sleeping from sorrow,

46 and said to them, "Why are you sleeping? Rise and pray that you may not enter into temptation."

47 ¶ While He was still speaking, behold, a multitude *came*, and the one called Judas, one of the twelve, was preceding them; and he approached Jesus to kiss Him.

48 But Jesus said to him, "Judas, are you betraying the Son of Man with a kiss?"

49 And when those who were around Him saw what was going to happen, they said, "Lord, shall we strike with the sword?"

50 And a certain one of them struck the slave of the high priest and cut off his right ear.

51 But Jesus answered and said, "Stop! No more of this." And He touched his ear and healed him.

52 And Jesus said to the chief priests and officers of the temple and elders who had come against Him, "Have you come out with swords and clubs as against a robber?

53 "While I was with you daily in the temple, you did not lay hands on Me; but this hour and the power of darkness are yours."

54 ¶ And having arrested Him, they led Him *away*, and brought Him to the house of the high priest; but Peter was following at a distance.

55 And after they had kindled a fire in the middle of the courtyard and had sat down together, Peter was sitting among them.

56 And a certain servant-girl, seeing him as he sat in the firelight, and looking intently at him, said, "This man was with Him too."

57 But he denied *it*, saying, "Woman, I do not know Him."

58 And a little later, another saw him and said, "You are *one* of them too!" But Peter said, "Man, I am not!"

59 And after about an hour had passed, another man *began* to insist, saying, "Certainly this man also was with Him, for he is a Galilean too."

60 But Peter said, "Man, I do not know what you are talking about." And immediately, while he was still speaking, a cock crowed.

61 And the Lord turned and looked at Peter. And Peter remembered the word of the Lord, how He had told him, "Before a cock crows today, you will deny Me three times."

62 And he went out and wept bitterly.

63 ¶ And the men who were holding Jesus in custody were mocking Him, and beating Him,

64 and they blindfolded Him and were asking Him, saying, "Prophesy, who is the one who hit You?"

65 And they were saying many other things against Him, blaspheming.

66 ¶ And when it was day, the [36]Council of elders of the people assembled, both chief priests and scribes, and they led Him away to their council *chamber*, saying,

67 "If You are the Christ, tell us." But He said to them, "If I tell you, you will not believe;

68 and if I ask a question, you will not answer.

69 "But from now on THE SON OF MAN WILL BE SEATED AT THE RIGHT HAND of the power OF GOD."

70 And they all said, "Are You the Son of God, then?" And He said to them, "Yes, I am."

71 And they said, "What further need do we have of testimony? For we have heard it ourselves from His own mouth."

CHAPTER 23

THEN the whole body of them arose and brought Him before Pilate.

2 And they began to accuse Him, saying, "We found this man misleading our nation and forbidding to pay taxes to Caesar, and saying that He Himself is Christ, a King."

3 And Pilate asked Him, saying, "Are You the King of the Jews?" And He answered him and said, "*It is as you say.*"

4 And Pilate said to the chief priests and the multitudes, "I find no guilt in this man."

5 But they kept on insisting, saying, "He stirs up the people, teaching all

[36] Or, *Sanhedrin*

over Judea, starting from Galilee, even as far as this place."

6 But when Pilate heard it, he asked whether the man was a Galilean.

7 And when he learned that He belonged to Herod's jurisdiction, he sent Him to Herod, who himself also was in Jerusalem at that time.

8 ¶ Now Herod was very glad when he saw Jesus; for he had wanted to see Him for a long time, because he had been hearing about Him and was hoping to see some sign performed by Him.

9 And he questioned Him at some length; but He answered him nothing.

10 And the chief priests and the scribes were standing there, accusing Him vehemently.

11 And Herod with his soldiers, after treating Him with contempt and mocking Him, dressed Him in a gorgeous robe and sent Him back to Pilate.

12 Now Herod and Pilate became friends with one another that very day; for before they had been at enmity with each other.

13 ¶ And Pilate summoned the chief priests and the rulers and the people,

14 and said to them, "You brought this man to me as one who incites the people to rebellion, and behold, having examined Him before you, I have found no guilt in this man regarding the charges which you make against Him.

15 "No, nor has Herod, for he sent Him back to us; and behold, nothing deserving death has been done by Him.

16 "I will therefore punish Him and release Him."

17 [[37]Now he was obliged to release to them at the feast one prisoner.]

18 But they cried out all together, saying, "Away with this man, and release for us Barabbas!"

19 (He was one who had been thrown into prison for a certain insurrection made in the city, and for murder.)

20 And Pilate, wanting to release Jesus, addressed them again,

21 but they kept on calling out, saying, "Crucify, crucify Him!"

22 And he said to them the third

time, "Why, what evil has this man done? I have found in Him no guilt *demanding* death; I will therefore punish Him and release Him."

23 But they were insistent, with loud voices asking that He be crucified. And their voices *began* to prevail.

24 And Pilate pronounced sentence that their demand should be granted.

25 And he released the man they were asking for who had been thrown into prison for insurrection and murder, but he delivered Jesus to their will.

26 ¶ And when they led Him away, they laid hold of one Simon of Cyrene, coming in from the country, and placed on him the cross to carry behind Jesus.

27 ¶ And there were following Him a great multitude of the people, and of women who were mourning and lamenting Him.

28 But Jesus turning to them said, "Daughters of Jerusalem, stop weeping for Me, but weep for yourselves and for your children.

29 "For behold, the days are coming when they will say, 'Blessed are the barren, and the wombs that never bore, and the breasts that never nursed.'

30 "Then they will begin TO SAY TO THE MOUNTAINS, 'FALL ON US,' AND TO THE HILLS, 'COVER US.'

31 "For if they do these things in the green tree, what will happen in the dry?"

32 ¶ And two others also, who were criminals, were being led away to be put to death with Him.

33 ¶ And when they came to the place called The Skull, there they crucified Him and the criminals, one on the right and the other on the left.

34 But Jesus was saying, "Father, forgive them; for they do not know what they are doing." And they cast lots, dividing up His garments among themselves.

35 And the people stood by, looking on. And even the rulers were sneering at Him, saying, "He saved others; let Him save Himself if this is the Christ of God, His Chosen One."

36 And the soldiers also mocked Him, coming up to Him, offering Him sour wine,

---

[37] Many mss. do not contain this verse

37 and saying, "If You are the King of the Jews, save Yourself!"

38 Now there was also an inscription above Him, "THIS IS THE KING OF THE JEWS."

39 ¶ And one of the criminals who were hanged *there* was hurling abuse at Him, saying, "Are You not the Christ? Save Yourself and us!"

40 But the other answered, and rebuking him said, "Do you not even fear God, since you are under the same sentence of condemnation?

41 "And we indeed justly, for we are receiving what we deserve for our deeds; but this man has done nothing wrong."

42 And he was saying, "Jesus, remember me when You come in Your kingdom!"

43 And He said to him, "Truly I say to you, today you shall be with Me in Paradise."

44 ¶ And it was now about [38]the sixth hour, and darkness fell over the whole land until [39]the ninth hour,

45 the sun being obscured; and the veil of the temple was torn in two.

46 And Jesus, crying out with a loud voice, said, "Father, INTO THY HANDS I COMMIT MY SPIRIT." And having said this, He breathed His last.

47 Now when the centurion saw what had happened, he *began* praising God, saying, "Certainly this man was innocent."

48 And all the multitudes who came together for this spectacle, when they observed what had happened, *began* to return, beating their breasts.

49 And all His acquaintances and the women who accompanied Him from Galilee, were standing at a distance, seeing these things.

50 ¶ And behold, a man named Joseph, who was a member of the Council, a good and righteous man

51 (he had not consented to their plan and action), *a man* from Arimathea, a city of the Jews, who was waiting for the kingdom of God;

52 this man went to Pilate and asked for the body of Jesus.

53 And he took it down and wrapped it in a linen cloth, and laid Him in a tomb cut into the rock, where no one had ever lain.

54 And it was the preparation day, and the Sabbath was about to begin.

55 Now the women who had come with Him out of Galilee followed after, and saw the tomb and how His body was laid.

56 And they returned and prepared spices and perfumes.

¶ And on the Sabbath they rested according to the commandment.

CHAPTER 24

BUT on the first day of the week, at early dawn, they came to the tomb, bringing the spices which they had prepared.

2 And they found the stone rolled away from the tomb,

3 but when they entered, they did not find the body of the Lord Jesus.

4 And it happened that while they were perplexed about this, behold, two men suddenly stood near them in dazzling apparel;

5 and as *the women* were terrified and bowed their faces to the ground, *the men* said to them, "Why do you seek the living One among the dead?

6 "He is not here, but He has risen. Remember how He spoke to you while He was still in Galilee,

7 saying that the Son of Man must be delivered into the hands of sinful men, and be crucified, and the third day rise again."

8 And they remembered His words,

9 and returned from the tomb and reported all these things to the eleven and to all the rest.

10 Now they were Mary Magdalene and Joanna and Mary the *mother* of James; also the other women with them were telling these things to the apostles.

11 And these words appeared to them as nonsense, and they would not believe them.

12 [[40]But Peter arose and ran to the tomb; stooping and looking in, he *saw the linen wrappings only; and he went away to his home, marveling at that which had happened.]

13 ¶ And behold, two of them were going that very day to a village named Emmaus, which was [41]about seven miles from Jerusalem.

[40] Some ancient mss. do not contain v. 12
[41] I.e., 60 stadia, one stadion was about 600 feet

[38] I.e., 12 noon   [39] I.e., 3 p.m.

14 And they were conversing with each other about all these things which had taken place.

15 And it came about that while they were conversing and discussing, Jesus Himself approached, and *began* traveling with them.

16 But their eyes were prevented from recognizing Him.

17 And He said to them, "What are these words that you are exchanging with one another as you are walking?" And they stood still, looking sad.

18 And one of them, named Cleopas, answered and said to Him, "Are You the only one visiting Jerusalem and unaware of the things which have happened here in these days?"

19 And He said to them, "What things?" And they said to Him, "The things about Jesus the Nazarene, who was a prophet mighty in deed and word in the sight of God and all the people,

20 and how the chief priests and our rulers delivered Him up to the sentence of death, and crucified Him.

21 "But we were hoping that it was He who was going to redeem Israel. Indeed, besides all this, it is the third day since these things happened.

22 "But also some women among us amazed us. When they were at the tomb early in the morning,

23 and did not find His body, they came, saying that they had also seen a vision of angels, who said that He was alive.

24 "And some of those who were with us went to the tomb and found it just exactly as the women also had said; but Him they did not see."

25 And He said to them, "O foolish men and slow of heart to believe in all that the prophets have spoken!

26 "Was it not necessary for the Christ to suffer these things and to enter into His glory?"

27 And beginning with Moses and with all the prophets, He explained to them the things concerning Himself in all the Scriptures.

28 And they approached the village where they were going, and He acted as though He would go farther.

29 And they urged Him, saying, "Stay with us, for it is *getting* toward evening, and the day is now nearly

over." And He went in to stay with them.

30 And it came about that when He had reclined *at the table* with them, He took the bread and blessed *it*, and breaking *it*, He *began* giving *it* to them.

31 And their eyes were opened and they recognized Him; and He vanished from their sight.

32 And they said to one another, "Were not our hearts burning within us while He was speaking to us on the road, while He was explaining the Scriptures to us?"

33 And they arose that very hour and returned to Jerusalem, and found gathered together the eleven and those who were with them,

34 saying, "The Lord has really risen, and has appeared to Simon."

35 And they *began* to relate their experiences on the road and how He was recognized by them in the breaking of the bread.

36 ¶ And while they were telling these things, He Himself stood in their midst.[42]

37 But they were startled and frightened and thought that they were seeing a spirit.

38 And He said to them, "Why are you troubled, and why do doubts arise in your hearts?

39 "See My hands and My feet, that it is I Myself; touch Me and see, for a spirit does not have flesh and bones as you see that I have."

40 [[43]And when He had said this, He showed them His hands and His feet.]

41 And while they still could not believe *it* for joy and were marveling, He said to them, "Have you anything here to eat?"

42 And they gave Him a piece of a broiled fish;

43 and He took it and ate *it* before them.

44 ¶ Now He said to them, "These are My words which I spoke to you while I was still with you, that all things which are written about Me in the Law of Moses and the Prophets and the Psalms must be fulfilled."

45 Then He opened their minds to understand the Scriptures,

46 and He said to them, "Thus it is

---

[42] Some ancient mss. insert *And He says to them, "Peace be to you."* [43] Many mss. do not contain this verse

written, that the Christ should suffer and rise again from the dead the third day;

47 and that repentance for forgiveness of sins should be proclaimed in His name to all the nations, beginning from Jerusalem.

48 "You are witnesses of these things.

49 "And behold, I am sending forth the promise of My Father upon you; but you are to stay in the city until you are clothed with power from on high."

50 ¶ And He led them out as far as Bethany, and He lifted up His hands and blessed them.

51 And it came about that while He was blessing them, He parted from them.[44]

52 And they[45] returned to Jerusalem with great joy,

53 and were continually in the temple, praising God.

[44] Some mss. add *and was carried up into heaven*
[45] Some mss. insert *worshiped Him, and*

THE GOSPEL ACCORDING TO

JOHN

IN the beginning was the Word, and the Word was with God, and the Word was God.

2 He was in the beginning with God.

3 All things came into being by Him, and apart from Him nothing came into being that has come into being.

4 In Him was life, and the life was the light of men.

5 And the light shines in the darkness, and the darkness did not [1]comprehend it.

6 ¶ There [2]came a man, sent from God, whose name was John.

7 He came for a witness, that he might bear witness of the light, that all might believe through him.

8 He was not the light, but *came* that he might bear witness of the light.

9 ¶ There was the true light [3]which, coming into the world, enlightens every man.

10 He was in the world, and the world was made through Him, and the world did not know Him.

11 He came to His [4]own, and those who were His own did not receive Him.

12 But as many as received Him, to them He gave the right to become children of God, *even* to those who believe in His name,

13 who were born not of blood, nor of the will of the flesh, nor of the will of man, but of God.

14 ¶ And the Word became flesh, and dwelt among us, and we beheld His glory, glory as of the only begotten from the Father, full of grace and truth.

15 John *bore witness of Him, and cried out, saying, "This was He of whom I said, 'He who comes after me has a higher rank than I, for He existed before me.'"

16 For of His fulness we have all received, and grace upon grace.

17 For the Law was given through Moses; grace and truth were realized through Jesus Christ.

18 No man has seen God at any time; the only begotten [5]God, who is in the bosom of the Father, He has explained Him.

19 ¶ And this is the witness of John, when the Jews sent to him priests and Levites from Jerusalem to ask him, "Who are you?"

20 And he confessed, and did not deny, and he confessed, "I am not the Christ."

21 And they asked him, "What then? Are you Elijah?" And he *said, "I am not." "Are you the Prophet?" And he answered, "No."

22 They said then to him, "Who are you, so that we may give an answer to

[1] Or, *overpower*   [2] Or, *came into being*
[3] Or, *which enlightens every man coming into the world*
[4] Or, *own things, possessions, domain*
[5] Some later mss. read *Son*

those who sent us? What do you say about yourself?"

23 He said, "I am a VOICE OF ONE CRYING IN THE WILDERNESS, 'MAKE STRAIGHT THE WAY OF THE LORD,' as Isaiah the prophet said."

24 Now they had been sent from the Pharisees.

25 And they asked him, and said to him, "Why then are you baptizing, if you are not the Christ, nor Elijah, nor the Prophet?"

26 John answered them saying, "I baptize [6]in water, *but* among you stands One whom you do not know.

27 "*It is* He who comes after me, the thong of whose sandal I am not worthy to untie."

28 These things took place in Bethany beyond the Jordan, where John was baptizing.

29 ¶ The next day he *saw Jesus coming to him, and *said, "Behold, the Lamb of God who takes away the sin of the world!

30 "This is He on behalf of whom I said, 'After me comes a Man who has a higher rank than I, for He existed before me.'

31 "And I did not recognize Him, but in order that He might be manifested to Israel, I came baptizing [6]in water."

32 And John bore witness saying, "I have beheld the Spirit descending as a dove out of heaven, and He remained upon Him.

33 "And I did not recognize Him, but He who sent me to baptize [6]in water said to me, 'He upon whom you see the Spirit descending and remaining upon Him, this is the one who baptizes in the Holy Spirit.'

34 "And I have seen, and have borne witness that this is the Son of God."

35 ¶ Again the next day John was standing with two of his disciples,

36 and he looked upon Jesus as He walked, and *said, "Behold, the Lamb of God!"

37 And the two disciples heard him speak, and they followed Jesus.

38 And Jesus turned, and beheld them following, and *said to them, "What do you seek?" And they said to Him, "Rabbi (which translated means Teacher), where are You staying?"

39 He *said to them, "Come, and you

will see." They came therefore and saw where He was staying; and they stayed with Him that day, for it was about the [7]tenth hour.

40 One of the two who heard John *speak,* and followed Him, was Andrew, Simon Peter's brother.

41 He *found first his own brother Simon, and *said to him, "We have found the Messiah" (which translated means Christ).

42 He brought him to Jesus. Jesus looked at him, and said, "You are Simon the son of John; you shall be called Cephas" (which is translated Peter).

43 ¶ The next day He purposed to go forth into Galilee, and He *found Philip. And Jesus *said to him, "Follow Me."

44 Now Philip was from Bethsaida, of the city of Andrew and Peter.

45 Philip *found Nathanael and *said to him, "We have found Him of whom Moses in the Law and *also* the Prophets wrote, Jesus of Nazareth, the son of Joseph."

46 And Nathanael *said to him, "Can any good thing come out of Nazareth?" Philip *said to him, "Come and see."

47 Jesus saw Nathanael coming to Him, and *said of him, "Behold, an Israelite indeed, in whom is no guile!"

48 Nathanael *said to Him, "How do You know me?" Jesus answered and said to him, "Before Philip called you, when you were under the fig tree, I saw you."

49 Nathanael answered Him, "Rabbi, You are the Son of God; You are the King of Israel."

50 Jesus answered and said to him, "Because I said to you that I saw you under the fig tree, do you believe? You shall see greater things than these."

51 And He *said to him, "Truly, truly, I say to you, you shall see the heavens opened, and the angels of God ascending and descending on the Son of Man."

CHAPTER 2

AND on the third day there was a wedding in Cana of Galilee, and the mother of Jesus was there;

---

[6] The Gr. here can be translated *in, with* or *by*

[7] Perhaps 10 a.m. (Roman time)

2 and Jesus also was invited, and His disciples, to the wedding.

3 And when the wine gave out, the mother of Jesus *said to Him, "They have no wine."

4 And Jesus *said to her, "Woman, what do I have to do with you? My hour has not yet come."

5 His mother *said to the servants, "Whatever He says to you, do it."

6 Now there were six stone waterpots set there for the Jewish custom of purification, containing twenty or thirty gallons each.

7 Jesus *said to them, "Fill the waterpots with water." And they filled them up to the brim.

8 And He *said to them, "Draw some out now, and take it to the [8]headwaiter." And they took it to him.

9 And when the headwaiter tasted the water which had become wine, and did not know where it came from (but the servants who had drawn the water knew), the headwaiter *called the bridegroom,

10 and *said to him, "Every man serves the good wine first, and when men have drunk freely, then that which is poorer; you have kept the good wine until now."

11 This beginning of His signs Jesus did in Cana of Galilee, and manifested His glory, and His disciples believed in Him.

12 ¶ After this He went down to Capernaum, He and His mother, and His brothers, and His disciples; and there they stayed a few days.

13 ¶ And the Passover of the Jews was at hand, and Jesus went up to Jerusalem.

14 And He found in the temple those who were selling oxen and sheep and doves, and the moneychangers seated.

15 And He made a scourge of cords, and drove them all out of the temple, with the sheep and the oxen; and He poured out the coins of the moneychangers, and overturned their tables;

16 and to those who were selling the doves He said, "Take these things away; stop making My Father's house a house of merchandise."

17 His disciples remembered that it was written, "ZEAL FOR THY HOUSE WILL CONSUME ME."

[8] Or, steward

18 The Jews therefore answered and said to Him, "What sign do You show to us, seeing that You do these things?"

19 Jesus answered and said to them, "Destroy this temple, and in three days I will raise it up."

20 The Jews therefore said, "It took forty-six years to build this temple, and will You raise it up in three days?"

21 But He was speaking of the temple of His body.

22 When therefore He was raised from the dead, His disciples remembered that He said this; and they believed the Scripture, and the word which Jesus had spoken.

23 ¶ Now when He was in Jerusalem at the Passover, during the feast, many believed in His name, beholding His signs which He was doing.

24 But Jesus, on His part, was not entrusting Himself to them, for He knew all men,

25 and because He did not need anyone to bear witness concerning man for He Himself knew what was in man.

CHAPTER 3

NOW there was a man of the Pharisees, named Nicodemus, a ruler of the Jews;

2 this man came to Him by night, and said to Him, "Rabbi, we know that You have come from God as a teacher; for no one can do these signs that You do unless God is with him."

3 Jesus answered and said to him, "Truly, truly, I say to you, unless one is born again, he cannot see the kingdom of God."

4 Nicodemus *said to Him, "How can a man be born when he is old? He cannot enter a second time into his mother's womb and be born, can he?"

5 Jesus answered, "Truly, truly, I say to you, unless one is born of water and the Spirit, he cannot enter into the kingdom of God.

6 "That which is born of the flesh is flesh, and that which is born of the Spirit is spirit.

7 "Do not marvel that I said to you, 'You must be born again.'

8 "The wind blows where it wishes and you hear the sound of it, but do not know where it comes from and

where it is going; so is everyone who is born of the Spirit."

9 Nicodemus answered and said to Him, "How can these things be?"

10 Jesus answered and said to him, "Are you the teacher of Israel, and do not understand these things?

11"Truly, truly, I say to you, we speak that which we know, and bear witness of that which we have seen; and you do not receive our witness.

12"If I told you earthly things and you do not believe, how shall you believe if I tell you heavenly things?

13"And no one has ascended into heaven, but He who descended from heaven, *even* the Son of Man.

14"And as Moses lifted up the serpent in the wilderness, even so must the Son of Man be lifted up;

15 that whoever [9]believes may in Him have eternal life.

16 ¶ "For God so loved the world, that He gave His only begotten Son, that whoever believes in Him should not perish, but have eternal life.

17"For God did not send the Son into the world to judge the world, but that the world should be saved through Him.

18"He who believes in Him is not judged; he who does not believe has been judged already, because he has not believed in the name of the only begotten Son of God.

19"And this is the judgment, that the light is come into the world, and men loved the darkness rather than the light; for their deeds were evil.

20"For everyone who does evil hates the light, and does not come to the light, lest his deeds should be exposed.

21"But he who practices the truth comes to the light, that his deeds may be manifested as having been wrought in God."

22 ¶ After these things Jesus and His disciples came into the land of Judea, and there He was spending time with them and baptizing.

23 And John also was baptizing in Aenon near Salim, because there was much water there; and they were coming and were baptized.

24 For John had not yet been thrown into prison.

25 There arose therefore a discussion on the part of John's disciples with a Jew about purification.

26 And they came to John and said to him, "Rabbi, He who was with you beyond the Jordan, to whom you have borne witness, behold, He is baptizing, and all are coming to Him."

27 John answered and said, "A man can receive nothing, unless it has been given him from heaven.

28"You yourselves bear me witness, that I said, 'I am not the Christ,' but, 'I have been sent before Him.'

29"He who has the bride is the bridegroom; but the friend of the bridegroom, who stands and hears him, rejoices greatly because of the bridegroom's voice. And so this joy of mine has been made full.

30"He must increase, but I must decrease.

31 ¶ "He who comes from above is above all, he who is of the earth is from the earth and speaks of the earth. He who comes from heaven is above all.

32"What He has seen and heard, of that He bears witness; and no man receives His witness.

33"He who has received His witness has set his seal to *this*, that God is true.

34"For He whom God has sent speaks the words of God; for He gives the Spirit without measure.

35"The Father loves the Son, and has given all things into His hand.

36"He who believes in the Son has eternal life; but he who does not obey the Son shall not see life, but the wrath of God abides on him."

CHAPTER 4

WHEN therefore the Lord knew that the Pharisees had heard that Jesus was making and baptizing more disciples than John

2 (although Jesus Himself was not baptizing, but His disciples were),

3 He left Judea, and departed again into Galilee.

4 And He had to pass through Samaria.

5 So He *came to a city of Samaria, called Sychar, near the parcel of ground that Jacob gave to his son Joseph;

6 and Jacob's well was there. Jesus

[9] Some mss. read *believes in Him may have eternal life*

therefore, being wearied from His journey, was sitting thus by the well. It was about [10]the sixth hour.

7 There *came a woman of Samaria to draw water. Jesus *said to her, "Give Me a drink."

8 For His disciples had gone away into the city to buy food.

9 The Samaritan woman therefore *said to Him, "How is it that You, being a Jew, ask me for a drink since I am a Samaritan woman?" (For Jews have no dealings with Samaritans.)

10 Jesus answered and said to her, "If you knew the gift of God, and who it is who says to you, 'Give Me a drink,' you would have asked Him, and He would have given you living water."

11 She *said to Him, "Sir, You have nothing to draw with and the well is deep; where then do You get that living water?

12"You are not greater than our father Jacob, are You, who gave us the well, and drank of it himself, and his sons, and his cattle?"

13 Jesus answered and said to her, "Everyone who drinks of this water shall thirst again;

14 but whoever drinks of the water that I shall give him shall never thirst; but the water that I shall give him shall become in him a well of water springing up to eternal life."

15 The woman *said to Him, "Sir, give me this water, so I will not be thirsty, nor come all the way here to draw."

16 He *said to her, "Go, call your husband, and come here."

17 The woman answered and said, "I have no husband." Jesus *said to her, "You have well said, 'I have no husband';

18 for you have had five husbands, and the one whom you now have is not your husband; this you have said truly."

19 The woman *said to Him, "Sir, I perceive that You are a prophet.

20"Our fathers worshiped in this mountain, and you *people* say that in Jerusalem is the place where men ought to worship."

21 Jesus *said to her, "Woman, believe Me, an hour is coming when neither in this mountain, nor in Jerusalem, shall you worship the Father.

22"You worship that which you do not know; we worship that which we know, for salvation is from the Jews.

23"But an hour is coming, and now is, when the true worshipers shall worship the Father in spirit and truth; for such people the Father seeks to be His worshipers.

24"God is spirit, and those who worship Him must worship in spirit and truth."

25 The woman *said to Him, "I know that Messiah is coming (He who is called Christ); when that One comes, He will declare all things to us."

26 Jesus *said to her, "I who speak to you am *He*."

27 ¶ And at this point His disciples came, and they marveled that He had been speaking with a woman; yet no one said, "What do You seek?" or, "Why do You speak with her?"

28 So the woman left her waterpot, and went into the city, and *said to the men,

29"Come, see a man who told me all the things that I *have* done; this is not the Christ, is it?"

30 They went out of the city, and were coming to Him.

31 In the meanwhile the disciples were requesting Him, saying, "Rabbi, eat."

32 But He said to them, "I have food to eat that you do not know about."

33 The disciples therefore were saying to one another, "No one brought Him *anything* to eat, did he?"

34 Jesus *said to them, "My food is to do the will of Him who sent Me, and to accomplish His work.

35"Do you not say, 'There are yet four months, and *then* comes the harvest'? Behold, I say to you, lift up your eyes, and look on the fields, that they are white for harvest.

36"Already he who reaps is receiving wages, and is gathering fruit for life eternal; that he who sows and he who reaps may rejoice together.

37"For in this *case* the saying is true, 'One sows, and another reaps.'

38"I sent you to reap that for which you have not labored; others have

[10] Perhaps 6 p.m. (Roman time)

labored, and you have entered into their labor."

39 ¶ And from that city many of the Samaritans believed in Him because of the word of the woman who testified, "He told me all the things that I *have* done."

40 So when the Samaritans came to Him, they were asking Him to stay with them; and He stayed there two days.

41 And many more believed because of His word;

42 and they were saying to the woman, "It is no longer because of what you said that we believe, for we have heard for ourselves and know that this One is indeed the Savior of the world."

43 ¶ And after the two days He went forth from there into Galilee.

44 For Jesus Himself testified that a prophet has no honor in his own country.

45 So when He came to Galilee, the Galileans received Him, having seen all the things that He did in Jerusalem at the feast; for they themselves also went to the feast.

46 ¶ He came therefore again to Cana of Galilee where He had made the water wine. And there was a certain royal official, whose son was sick at Capernaum.

47 When he heard that Jesus had come out of Judea into Galilee, he went to Him, and was requesting *Him* to come down and heal his son; for he was at the point of death.

48 Jesus therefore said to him, "Unless you *people* see signs and wonders, you *simply* will not believe."

49 The royal official *said to Him, "Sir, come down before my child dies."

50 Jesus *said to him, "Go your way; your son lives." The man believed the word that Jesus spoke to him, and he started off.

51 And as he was now going down, *his* slaves met him, saying that his son was living.

52 So he inquired of them the hour when he began to get better. They said therefore to him, "Yesterday at the [11]seventh hour the fever left him."

53 So the father knew that *it was* at that hour in which Jesus said to him,

"Your son lives"; and he himself believed, and his whole household.

54 This is again a second sign that Jesus performed, when He had come out of Judea into Galilee.

CHAPTER 5

AFTER these things there was [12]a feast of the Jews, and Jesus went up to Jerusalem.

2 Now there is in Jerusalem by the sheep *gate* a pool, which is called in Hebrew Bethesda, having five porticoes.

3 In these lay a multitude of those who were sick, blind, lame, and withered, [[13]waiting for the moving of the waters;

4 for an angel of the Lord went down at certain seasons into the pool, and stirred up the water; whoever then first, after the stirring up of the water, stepped in was made well from whatever disease with which he was afflicted.]

5 And a certain man was there, who had been thirty-eight years in his sickness.

6 When Jesus saw him lying there, and knew that he had already been a long time *in that condition*, He *said to him, "Do you wish to get well?"

7 The sick man answered Him, "Sir, I have no man to put me into the pool when the water is stirred up, but while I am coming, another steps down before me."

8 Jesus *said to him, "Arise, take up your pallet, and walk."

9 And immediately the man became well, and took up his pallet and *began to walk.

¶ Now it was the Sabbath on that day.

10 Therefore the Jews were saying to him who was cured, "It is the Sabbath, and it is not permissible for you to carry your pallet."

11 But he answered them, "He who made me well was the one who said to me, 'Take up your pallet and walk.'"

12 They asked him, "Who is the man who said to you, 'Take up *your pallet*, and walk?'"

13 But he who was healed did not know who it was; for Jesus had slipped

---

[11] Perhaps 7 p.m. (Roman time)

[12] Many mss. read *the feast,* i.e., the Passover
[13] Many mss. do not contain the remainder of v. 3 nor v. 4

away while there was a crowd in *that* place.

14 Afterward Jesus *found him in the temple, and said to him, "Behold, you have become well; do not sin anymore, so that nothing worse may befall you."

15 The man went away, and told the Jews that it was Jesus who had made him well.

16 And for this reason the Jews were persecuting Jesus, because He was doing these things on the Sabbath.

17 But He answered them, "My Father is working until now, and I Myself am working."

18 For this cause therefore the Jews were seeking all the more to kill Him, because He not only was breaking the Sabbath, but also was calling God His own Father, making Himself equal with God.

19 ¶ Jesus therefore answered and was saying to them, "Truly, truly, I say to you, the Son can do nothing of Himself, unless *it is* something He sees the Father doing; for whatever *the Father* does, these things the Son also does in like manner.

20 "For the Father loves the Son, and shows Him all things that He Himself is doing; and greater works than these will He show Him, that you may marvel.

21 "For just as the Father raises the dead and gives them life, even so the Son also gives life to whom He wishes.

22 "For not even the Father judges anyone, but He has given all judgment to the Son,

23 in order that all may honor the Son, even as they honor the Father. He who does not honor the Son does not honor the Father who sent Him.

24 "Truly, truly, I say to you, he who hears My word, and believes Him who sent Me, has eternal life, and does not come into judgment, but has passed out of death into life.

25 "Truly, truly, I say to you, an hour is coming and now is, when the dead shall hear the voice of the Son of God; and those who hear shall live.

26 "For just as the Father has life in Himself, even so He gave to the Son also to have life in Himself;

27 and He gave Him authority to execute judgment, because He is *the* Son of Man.

28 "Do not marvel at this; for an hour is coming, in which all who are in the tombs shall hear His voice,

29 and shall come forth; those who did the good *deeds* to a resurrection of life, those who committed the evil *deeds* to a resurrection of judgment.

30 ¶ "I can do nothing on My own initiative. As I hear, I judge; and My judgment is just, because I do not seek My own will, but the will of Him who sent Me.

31 "If I *alone* bear witness of Myself, My testimony is not true.

32 "There is another who bears witness of Me, and I know that the testimony which He bears of Me is true.

33 "You have sent to John, and he has borne witness to the truth.

34 "But the witness which I receive is not from man, but I say these things that you may be saved.

35 "He was the lamp that was burning and was shining and you were willing to rejoice for a while in his light.

36 "But the witness which I have is greater than *that* of John; for the works which the Father has given Me to accomplish, the very works that I do, bear witness of Me, that the Father has sent Me.

37 "And the Father who sent Me, He has borne witness of Me. You have neither heard His voice at any time, nor seen His form.

38 "And you do not have His word abiding in you, for you do not believe Him whom He sent.

39 [14]"You search the Scriptures, because you think that in them you have eternal life; and it is these that bear witness of Me;

40 and you are unwilling to come to Me, that you may have life.

41 "I do not receive glory from men;

42 but I know you, that you do not have the love of God in yourselves.

43 "I have come in My Father's name, and you do not receive Me; if another shall come in his own name, you will receive him.

44 "How can you believe, when you receive glory from one another, and you do not seek the glory that is from the *one and* only God?

45 "Do not think that I will accuse you before the Father; the one who

[14] Or, (a command) *Search the Scriptures!*

accuses you is Moses, in whom you have set your hope.

46 "For if you believed Moses, you would believe Me; for he wrote of Me.

47 "But if you do not believe his writings, how will you believe My words?"

CHAPTER 6

AFTER these things Jesus went away to the other side of the Sea of Galilee (or Tiberias).

2 And a great multitude was following Him, because they were seeing the signs which He was performing on those who were sick.

3 And Jesus went up on the mountain, and there He sat with His disciples.

4 Now the Passover, the feast of the Jews, was at hand.

5 Jesus therefore lifting up His eyes, and seeing that a great multitude was coming to Him, *said to Philip, "Where are we to buy bread, that these may eat?"

6 And this He was saying to test him; for He Himself knew what He was intending to do.

7 Philip answered Him, "Two hundred [15]denarii worth of bread is not sufficient for them, for everyone to receive a little."

8 One of His disciples, Andrew, Simon Peter's brother, *said to Him,

9 "There is a lad here who has five barley loaves and two fish, but what are these for so many people?"

10 Jesus said, "Have the people sit down." Now there was much grass in the place. So the men sat down, in number about five thousand.

11 Jesus therefore took the loaves; and having given thanks, He distributed to those who were seated; likewise also of the fish as much as they wanted.

12 And when they were filled, He *said to His disciples, "Gather up the leftover fragments that nothing may be lost."

13 And so they gathered them up, and filled twelve baskets with fragments from the five barley loaves, which were left over by those who had eaten.

14 When therefore the people saw the sign which He had performed, they said, "This is of a truth the Prophet who is to come into the world."

15 ¶ Jesus therefore perceiving that they were intending to come and take Him by force, to make Him king, withdrew again to the mountain by Himself alone.

16 ¶ Now when evening came, His disciples went down to the sea,

17 and after getting into a boat, they *started to* cross the sea to Capernaum. And it had already become dark, and Jesus had not yet come to them.

18 And the sea *began* to be stirred up because a strong wind was blowing.

19 When therefore they had rowed about three or four miles, they *beheld Jesus walking on the sea and drawing near to the boat; and they were frightened.

20 But He *said to them, "It is I; do not be afraid."

21 They were willing therefore to receive Him into the boat; and immediately the boat was at the land to which they were going.

22 ¶ The next day the multitude that stood on the other side of the sea saw that there was no other small boat there, except one, and that Jesus had not entered with His disciples into the boat, but *that* His disciples had gone away alone.

23 There came other small boats from Tiberias near to the place where they ate the bread after the Lord had given thanks.

24 When the multitude therefore saw that Jesus was not there, nor His disciples, they themselves got into the small boats, and came to Capernaum, seeking Jesus.

25 And when they found Him on the other side of the sea, they said to Him, "Rabbi, when did You get here?"

26 Jesus answered them and said, "Truly, truly, I say to you, you seek Me, not because you saw signs, but because you ate of the loaves, and were filled.

27 "Do not work for the food which perishes, but for the food which endures to eternal life, which the Son of Man shall give to you, for on Him the Father, *even* God, has set His seal."

28 They said therefore to Him, "What shall we do, that we may work the works of God?"

---

[15] The denarius was equivalent to one day's wage

29 Jesus answered and said to them, "This is the work of God, that you believe in Him whom He has sent."

30 They said therefore to Him, "What then do You do for a sign, that we may see, and believe You? What work do You perform?

31 "Our fathers ate the manna in the wilderness; as it is written, 'HE GAVE THEM BREAD OUT OF HEAVEN TO EAT.' "

32 Jesus therefore said to them, "Truly, truly, I say to you, it is not Moses who has given you the bread out of heaven, but it is My Father who gives you the true bread out of heaven.

33 "For the bread of God is [16]that which comes down out of heaven, and gives life to the world."

34 They said therefore to Him, "Lord, evermore give us this bread."

35 Jesus said to them, "I am the bread of life; he who comes to Me shall not hunger, and he who believes in Me shall never thirst.

36 "But I said to you, that you have seen Me, and yet do not believe.

37 "All that the Father gives Me shall come to Me, and the one who comes to Me I will certainly not cast out.

38 "For I have come down from heaven, not to do My own will, but the will of Him who sent Me.

39 "And this is the will of Him who sent Me, that of all that He has given Me I lose nothing, but raise it up on the last day.

40 "For this is the will of My Father, that everyone who beholds the Son and believes in Him, may have eternal life; and I Myself will raise him up on the last day."

41 ¶ The Jews therefore were grumbling about Him, because He said, "I am the bread that came down out of heaven."

42 And they were saying, "Is not this Jesus, the son of Joseph, whose father and mother we know? How does He now say, 'I have come down out of heaven?'"

43 Jesus answered and said to them, "Do not grumble among yourselves.

44 "No one can come to Me, unless the Father who sent Me draws him; and I will raise him up on the last day.

45 "It is written in the prophets, 'AND THEY SHALL ALL BE TAUGHT OF GOD.' Everyone who has heard and learned from the Father, comes to Me.

46 "Not that any man has seen the Father, except the One who is from God; He has seen the Father.

47 "Truly, truly, I say to you, he who believes has eternal life.

48 "I am the bread of life.

49 "Your fathers ate the manna in the wilderness, and they died.

50 "This is the bread which comes down out of heaven, so that one may eat of it and not die.

51 "I am the living bread that came down out of heaven; if anyone eats of this bread, he shall live forever; and the bread also which I shall give for the life of the world is My flesh."

52 ¶ The Jews therefore *began* to argue with one another, saying, "How can this man give us *His* flesh to eat?"

53 Jesus therefore said to them, "Truly, truly, I say to you, unless you eat the flesh of the Son of Man and drink His blood, you have no life in yourselves.

54 "He who eats My flesh and drinks My blood has eternal life, and I will raise him up on the last day.

55 "For My flesh is true food, and My blood is true drink.

56 "He who eats My flesh and drinks My blood abides in Me, and I in him.

57 "As the living Father sent Me, and I live because of the Father, so he who eats Me, he also shall live because of Me.

58 "This is the bread which came down out of heaven; not as the fathers ate, and died, he who eats this bread shall live forever."

59 These things He said in the synagogue, as He taught in Capernaum.

60 ¶ Many therefore of His disciples, when they heard *this* said, "This is a difficult statement; who can listen to it?"

61 But Jesus, conscious that His disciples grumbled at this, said to them, "Does this cause you to stumble?

62 "*What* then if you should behold the Son of Man ascending where He was before?

63 "It is the Spirit who gives life; the flesh profits nothing; the words that I have spoken to you are spirit and are life.

[16] Or, *He who comes*

64 But there are some of you who do not believe." For Jesus knew from the beginning who they were who did not believe, and who it was that would betray Him.

65 And He was saying, "For this reason I have said to you, that no one can come to Me, unless it has been granted him from the Father."

66 ¶ As a result of this many of His disciples withdrew, and were not walking with Him anymore.

67 Jesus said therefore to the twelve, "You do not want to go away also, do you?"

68 Simon Peter answered Him, "Lord, to whom shall we go? You have words of eternal life.

69 "And we have believed and have come to know that You are the Holy One of God."

70 Jesus answered them, "Did I Myself not choose you, the twelve, and yet one of you is a devil?"

71 Now He meant Judas the son of Simon Iscariot, for he, one of the twelve, was going to betray Him.

CHAPTER 7

AND after these things Jesus was walking in Galilee; for He was unwilling to walk in Judea, because the Jews were seeking to kill Him.

2 Now the feast of the Jews, the Feast of Booths, was at hand.

3 His brothers therefore said to Him, "Depart from here, and go into Judea, that Your disciples also may behold Your works which You are doing.

4 "For no one does anything in secret, when he himself seeks to be known publicly. If You do these things, show Yourself to the world."

5 For not even His brothers were believing in Him.

6 Jesus therefore *said to them, "My time is not yet at hand, but your time is always opportune.

7 "The world cannot hate you; but it hates Me because I testify of it, that its deeds are evil.

8 "Go up to the feast yourselves; I do not go up to this feast because My time has not yet fully come."

9 And having said these things to them, He stayed in Galilee.

10 ¶ But when His brothers had gone up to the feast, then He Himself also went up, not publicly, but as it were, in secret.

11 The Jews therefore were seeking Him at the feast, and were saying, "Where is He?"

12 And there was much grumbling among the multitudes concerning Him; some were saying, "He is a good man"; others were saying, "No, on the contrary, He leads the multitude astray."

13 Yet no one was speaking openly of Him for fear of the Jews.

14 ¶ But when it was now the midst of the feast Jesus went up into the temple, and began to teach.

15 The Jews therefore were marveling, saying, "How has this man become learned, having never been educated?"

16 Jesus therefore answered them, and said, "My teaching is not Mine, but His who sent Me.

17 "If any man is willing to do His will, he shall know of the teaching, whether it is of God, or whether I speak from Myself.

18 "He who speaks from himself seeks his own glory; but He who is seeking the glory of the one who sent Him, He is true, and there is no unrighteousness in Him.

19 "Did not Moses give you the Law, and yet none of you carries out the Law? Why do you seek to kill Me?"

20 The multitude answered, "You have a demon! Who seeks to kill You?"

21 Jesus answered and said to them, "I did one deed, and you all marvel.

22 "On this account Moses has given you circumcision (not because it is from Moses, but from the fathers), and on the Sabbath you circumcise a man.

23 "If a man receives circumcision on the Sabbath that the Law of Moses may not be broken, are you angry with Me because I made an entire man well on the Sabbath?

24 "Do not judge according to appearance, but judge with righteous judgment."

25 ¶ Therefore some of the people of Jerusalem were saying, "Is this not the man whom they are seeking to kill?

26 "And look, He is speaking publicly, and they are saying nothing to Him.

The rulers do not really know that this is the Christ, do they?

27"However, we know where this man is from; but whenever the Christ may come, no one knows where He is from."

28 Jesus therefore cried out in the temple, teaching and saying, "You both know Me and know where I am from; and I have not come of Myself, but He who sent Me is true, whom you do not know.

29"I know Him; because I am from Him, and He sent Me."

30 They were seeking therefore to seize Him; and no man laid his hand on Him, because His hour had not yet come.

31 But many of the multitude believed in Him; and they were saying, "When the Christ shall come, He will not perform more signs than those which this man has, will He?"

32 The Pharisees heard the multitude muttering these things about Him; and the chief priests and the Pharisees sent officers to seize Him.

33 Jesus therefore said, "For a little while longer I am with you, then I go to Him who sent Me.

34"You shall seek Me, and shall not find Me; and where I am, you cannot come."

35 The Jews therefore said to one another, "Where does this man intend to go that we shall not find Him? He is not intending to go to the Dispersion among the Greeks, and teach the Greeks, is He?

36"What is this statement that He said, 'You will seek Me, and will not find Me; and where I am, you cannot come'?"

37 ¶ Now on the last day, the great day of the feast, Jesus stood and cried out, saying, "If any man is thirsty, let him come to Me and drink.

38"He who believes in Me, as the Scripture said, 'From his innermost being shall flow rivers of living water.'"

39 But this He spoke of the Spirit, whom those who believed in Him were to receive; for the Spirit was not yet given, because Jesus was not yet glorified.

40 Some of the multitude therefore, when they heard these words, were saying, "This certainly is the Prophet."

41 Others were saying, "This is the Christ." Still others were saying, "Surely the Christ is not going to come from Galilee, is He?

42"Has not the Scripture said that the Christ comes from the offspring of David, and from Bethlehem, the village where David was?"

43 So there arose a division in the multitude because of Him.

44 And some of them wanted to seize Him, but no one laid hands on Him.

45 ¶ The officers therefore came to the chief priests and Pharisees, and they said to them, "Why did you not bring Him?"

46 The officers answered, "Never did a man speak the way this man speaks."

47 The Pharisees therefore answered them, "You have not also been led astray, have you?

48"No one of the rulers or Pharisees has believed in Him, has he?

49"But this multitude which does not know the Law is accursed."

50 Nicodemus *said to them (he who came to Him before, being one of them),

51"Our Law does not judge a man, unless it first hears from him and knows what he is doing, does it?"

52 They answered and said to him, "You are not also from Galilee, are you? Search, and see that no prophet arises out of Galilee."

53 [17And everyone went to his home.

CHAPTER 8

BUT Jesus went to the Mount of Olives.

2 And early in the morning He came again into the temple, and all the people were coming to Him; and He sat down and began to teach them.

3 And the scribes and the Pharisees *brought a woman caught in adultery, and having set her in the midst,

4 they *said to Him, "Teacher, this woman has been caught in adultery, in the very act.

5"Now in the Law Moses commanded us to stone such women; what then do You say?"

6 And they were saying this, testing Him, in order that they might have

17 John 7:53–8:11 is not found in most of the old mss.

grounds for accusing Him. But Jesus stooped down, and with His finger wrote on the ground.

7 But when they persisted in asking Him, He straightened up, and said to them, "He who is without sin among you, let him *be the* first to throw a stone at her."

8 And again He stooped down, and wrote on the ground.

9 And when they heard it, they *began* to go out one by one, beginning with the older ones, and He was left alone, and the woman, where she was, in the midst.

10 And straightening up, Jesus said to her, "Woman, where are they? Did no one condemn you?"

11 And she said, "No one, Lord." And Jesus said, "Neither do I condemn you; go your way. From now on sin no more."]

12 ¶ Again therefore Jesus spoke to them, saying, "I am the light of the world; he who follows Me shall not walk in the darkness, but shall have the light of life."

13 The Pharisees therefore said to Him, "You are bearing witness of Yourself; Your witness is not true."

14 Jesus answered and said to them, "Even if I bear witness of Myself, My witness is true; for I know where I came from, and where I am going; but you do not know where I come from, or where I am going.

15 "You people judge according to the flesh; I am not judging anyone.

16 "But even if I do judge, My judgment is true; for I am not alone *in it,* but I and [18]He who sent Me.

17 "Even in your law it has been written, that the testimony of two men is true.

18 "I am He who bears witness of Myself, and the Father who sent Me bears witness of Me."

19 And so they were saying to Him, "Where is Your Father?" Jesus answered, "You know neither Me, nor My Father; if you knew Me, you would know My Father also."

20 These words He spoke in the treasury, as He taught in the temple; and no one seized Him, because His hour had not yet come.

21 ¶ He said therefore again to them,

"I go away, and you shall seek Me, and shall die in your sin; where I am going, you cannot come."

22 Therefore the Jews were saying, "Surely He will not kill Himself, will He, since He says, 'Where I am going, you cannot come'?"

23 And He was saying to them, "You are from below, I am from above; you are of this world, I am not of this world.

24 "I said therefore to you, that you shall die in your sins; for unless you believe that I am *He,* you shall die in your sins."

25 And so they were saying to Him, "Who are You?" Jesus said to them, "What have I been saying to you *from* the beginning?

26 "I have many things to speak and to judge concerning you, but He who sent Me is true; and the things which I heard from Him, these I speak to the world."

27 They did not realize that He had been speaking to them about the Father.

28 Jesus therefore said, "When you lift up the Son of Man, then you will know that I am *He,* and I do nothing on My own initiative, but I speak these things as the Father taught Me.

29 "And He who sent Me is with Me; He has not left Me alone, for I always do the things that are pleasing to Him."

30 As He spoke these things, many came to believe in Him.

31 ¶ Jesus therefore was saying to those Jews who had believed Him, "If you abide in My word, *then* you are truly disciples of Mine;

32 and you shall know the truth, and the truth shall make you free."

33 They answered Him, "We are Abraham's offspring, and have never yet been enslaved to anyone; how is it that You say, 'You shall become free'?"

34 Jesus answered them, "Truly, truly, I say to you, everyone who commits sin is the slave of sin.

35 "And the slave does not remain in the house forever; the son does remain forever.

36 "If therefore the Son shall make you free, you shall be free indeed.

37 "I know that you are Abraham's

[18] Many ancient mss. read *the Father who sent Me*

offspring; yet you seek to kill Me, because My word has no place in you.

38 "I speak the things which I have seen with *My* Father; therefore you also do the things which you heard from *your* father."

39 They answered and said to Him, "Abraham is our father." Jesus *said to them, "If you are Abraham's children, do the deeds of Abraham.

40 "But as it is, you are seeking to kill Me, a man who has told you the truth, which I heard from God; this Abraham did not do.

41 "You are doing the deeds of your father." They said to Him, "We were not born of fornication; we have one Father, *even* God."

42 Jesus said to them, "If God were your Father, you would love Me; for I proceeded forth and have come from God, for I have not even come on My own initiative, but He sent Me.

43 "Why do you not understand what I am saying? *It is* because you cannot hear My word.

44 "You are of *your* father the devil, and you want to do the desires of your father. He was a murderer from the beginning, and does not stand in the truth, because there is no truth in him. Whenever he speaks a lie, he speaks from his own *nature;* for he is a liar, and the father of lies.

45 "But because I speak the truth, you do not believe Me.

46 "Which one of you convicts Me of sin? If I speak truth, why do you not believe Me?

47 "He who is of God hears the words of God; for this reason you do not hear *them,* because you are not of God."

48 ¶ The Jews answered and said to Him, "Do we not say rightly that You are a Samaritan and have a demon?"

49 Jesus answered, "I do not have a demon; but I honor My Father, and you dishonor Me.

50 "But I do not seek My glory; there is One who seeks and judges.

51 "Truly, truly, I say to you, if anyone keeps My word he shall never see death."

52 The Jews said to Him, "Now we know that You have a demon. Abraham died, and the prophets *also;* and You say, 'If anyone keeps My word, he shall never taste of death.'

53 "Surely You are not greater than our father Abraham, who died? The prophets died too; whom do You make Yourself out *to be?*"

54 Jesus answered, "If I glorify Myself, My glory is nothing; it is My Father who glorifies Me, of whom you say, 'He is our God';

55 and you have not come to know Him, but I know Him; and if I say that I do not know Him, I shall be a liar like you, but I do know Him, and keep His word.

56 "Your father Abraham rejoiced to see My day, and he saw *it* and was glad."

57 The Jews therefore said to Him, "You are not yet fifty years old, and have You seen Abraham?"

58 Jesus said to them, "Truly, truly, I say to you, before Abraham was born, I am."

59 Therefore they picked up stones to throw at Him; but Jesus hid Himself, and went out of the temple.

CHAPTER 9

And as He passed by, He saw a man blind from birth.

2 And His disciples asked Him, saying, "Rabbi, who sinned, this man or his parents, that he should be born blind?"

3 Jesus answered, "*It was* neither *that* this man sinned, nor his parents; but *it was* in order that the works of God might be displayed in him.

4 "We must work the works of Him who sent Me, as long as it is day; night is coming, when no man can work.

5 "While I am in the world, I am the light of the world."

6 When He had said this, He spat on the ground, and made clay of the spittle, and applied the clay to his eyes,

7 and said to him, "Go, wash in the pool of Siloam" (which is translated, Sent). And so he went away and washed, and came *back* seeing.

8 The neighbors therefore, and those who previously saw him as a beggar, were saying, "Is not this the one who used to sit and beg?"

9 Others were saying, "This is he," *still* others were saying, "No, but he is like him." He kept saying, "I am the one."

10 Therefore they were saying to

him, "How then were your eyes opened?"

11 He answered, "The man who is called Jesus made clay, and anointed my eyes, and said to me, 'Go to Siloam, and wash'; so I went away and washed, and I received sight."

12 And they said to him, "Where is He?" He *said, "I do not know."

13 ¶ They *brought to the Pharisees him who was formerly blind.

14 Now it was a Sabbath on the day when Jesus made the clay, and opened his eyes.

15 Again, therefore, the Pharisees also were asking him how he received his sight. And he said to them, "He applied clay to my eyes, and I washed, and I see."

16 Therefore some of the Pharisees were saying, "This man is not from God, because He does not keep the Sabbath." But others were saying, "How can a man who is a sinner perform such signs?" And there was a division among them.

17 They *said therefore to the blind man again, "What do you say about Him, since He opened your eyes?" And he said, "He is a prophet."

18 The Jews therefore did not believe it of him, that he had been blind, and had received sight, until they called the parents of the very one who had received his sight,

19 and questioned them, saying, "Is this your son, who you say was born blind? Then how does he now see?"

20 His parents answered them and said, "We know that this is our son, and that he was born blind;

21 but how he now sees, we do not know; or who opened his eyes, we do not know. Ask him; he is of age, he shall speak for himself."

22 His parents said this because they were afraid of the Jews; for the Jews had already agreed, that if anyone should confess Him to be Christ, he should be put out of the synagogue.

23 For this reason his parents said, "He is of age; ask him."

24 ¶ So a second time they called the man who had been blind, and said to him, "Give glory to God; we know that this man is a sinner."

25 He therefore answered, "Whether He is a sinner, I do not know; one thing I do know, that, whereas I was blind, now I see."

26 They said therefore to him, "What did He do to you? How did He open your eyes?"

27 He answered them, "I told you already, and you did not listen; why do you want to hear it again? You do not want to become His disciples too, do you?"

28 And they reviled him, and said, "You are His disciple, but we are disciples of Moses.

29 "We know that God has spoken to Moses; but as for this man, we do not know where He is from."

30 The man answered and said to them, "Well, here is an amazing thing, that you do not know where He is from, and yet He opened my eyes.

31 "We know that God does not hear sinners; but if anyone is God-fearing, and does His will, He hears him.

32 "Since the beginning of time it has never been heard that anyone opened the eyes of a person born blind.

33 "If this man were not from God, He could do nothing."

34 They answered and said to him, "You were born entirely in sins, and are you teaching us?" And they put him out.

35 ¶ Jesus heard that they had put him out; and finding him, He said, "Do you believe in the Son of Man?"

36 He answered and said, "And who is He, Lord, that I may believe in Him?"

37 Jesus said to him, "You have both seen Him, and He is the one who is talking with you."

38 And he said, "Lord, I believe." And he worshiped Him.

39 And Jesus said, "For judgment I came into this world, that those who do not see may see; and that those who see may become blind."

40 Those of the Pharisees who were with Him heard these things, and said to Him, "We are not blind too, are we?"

41 Jesus said to them, "If you were blind, you would have no sin; but since you say, 'We see,' your sin remains.

CHAPTER 10

"TRULY, truly, I say to you, he who does not enter by the door into the fold of the sheep, but climbs up some other way, he is a thief and a robber.

2 "But he who enters by the door is a shepherd of the sheep.

3 "To him the doorkeeper opens, and the sheep hear his voice, and he calls his own sheep by name, and leads them out.

4 "When he puts forth all his own, he goes before them, and the sheep follow him because they know his voice.

5 "And a stranger they simply will not follow, but will flee from him, because they do not know the voice of strangers."

6 This figure of speech Jesus spoke to them, but they did not understand what those things were which He had been saying to them.

7 ¶ Jesus therefore said to them again, "Truly, truly, I say to you, I am the door of the sheep.

8 "All who came before Me are thieves and robbers, but the sheep did not hear them.

9 "I am the door; if anyone enters through Me, he shall be saved, and shall go in and out, and find pasture.

10 "The thief comes only to steal, and kill, and destroy; I came that they might have life, and might have *it* abundantly.

11 "I am the good shepherd; the good shepherd lays down His life for the sheep.

12 "He who is a hireling, and not a shepherd, who is not the owner of the sheep, beholds the wolf coming, and leaves the sheep, and flees, and the wolf snatches them, and scatters *them*.

13 "*He flees* because he is a hireling, and is not concerned about the sheep.

14 "I am the good shepherd; and I know My own, and My own know Me,

15 even as the Father knows Me and I know the Father; and I lay down My life for the sheep.

16 "And I have other sheep, which are not of this fold; I must bring them also, and they shall hear My voice; and they shall become one flock *with* one shepherd.

17 "For this reason the Father loves Me, because I lay down My life that I may take it again.

18 "No one [19] has taken it away from Me, but I lay it down on My own initiative. I have authority to lay it down, and I have authority to take it up again. This commandment I received from My Father."

19 ¶ There arose a division again among the Jews because of these words.

20 And many of them were saying, "He has a demon and is insane. Why do you listen to Him?"

21 Others were saying, "These are not the sayings of one demon-possessed. A demon cannot open the eyes of the blind, can he?"

22 ¶ At that time the Feast of the Dedication took place at Jerusalem;

23 it was winter, and Jesus was walking in the temple in the portico of Solomon.

24 The Jews therefore gathered around Him, and were saying to Him, "How long will You keep us in suspense? If You are the Christ, tell us plainly."

25 Jesus answered them, "I told you, and you do not believe; the works that I do in My Father's name, these bear witness of Me.

26 "But you do not believe, because you are not of My sheep.

27 "My sheep hear My voice, and I know them, and they follow Me;

28 and I give eternal life to them, and they shall never perish; and no one shall snatch them out of My hand.

29 "[20]My Father, who has given *them* to Me, is greater than all; and no one is able to snatch *them* out of the Father's hand.

30 "I and the Father are one."

31 ¶ The Jews took up stones again to stone Him.

32 Jesus answered them, "I showed you many good works from the Father; for which of them are you stoning Me?"

33 The Jews answered Him, "For a good work we do not stone You, but for blasphemy; and because You, being a man, make Yourself out *to be* God."

34 Jesus answered them, "Has it not been written in your Law, 'I SAID, YOU ARE GODS'?

35 "If he called them gods, to whom

---

[19] Many Gr. mss. read *takes*

[20] Some early mss. read *What My Father has given Me is greater than all*

the word of God came (and the Scripture cannot be broken),

36 do you say of Him, whom the Father sanctified and sent into the world, 'You are blaspheming,' because I said, 'I am the Son of God'?

37 'If I do not do the works of My Father, do not believe Me;

38 but if I do them, though you do not believe Me, believe the works, that you may know and understand that the Father is in Me, and I in the Father."

39 Therefore they were seeking again to seize Him, and He eluded their grasp.

40 ¶ And He went away again beyond the Jordan to the place where John was first baptizing, and He was staying there.

41 And many came to Him and were saying, "While John performed no sign, yet everything John said about this man was true."

42 And many believed in Him there.

CHAPTER 11

NOW a certain man was sick, Lazarus of Bethany, the village of Mary and her sister Martha.

2 And it was the Mary who anointed the Lord with ointment, and wiped His feet with her hair, whose brother Lazarus was sick.

3 The sisters therefore sent to Him, saying, "Lord, behold, he whom You love is sick."

4 But when Jesus heard it, He said, "This sickness is not unto death, but for the glory of God, that the Son of God may be glorified by it."

5 Now Jesus loved Martha, and her sister, and Lazarus.

6 When therefore He heard that he was sick, He stayed then two days longer in the place where He was.

7 Then after this He *said to the disciples, "Let us go to Judea again."

8 The disciples *said to Him, "Rabbi, the Jews were just now seeking to stone You, and are You going there again?"

9 Jesus answered, "Are there not twelve hours in the day? If anyone walks in the day, he does not stumble, because he sees the light of this world.

10 'But if anyone walks in the night, he stumbles, because the light is not in him."

11 This He said, and after that He *said to them, "Our friend Lazarus has fallen asleep; but I go, that I may awaken him out of sleep."

12 The disciples therefore said to Him, "Lord, if he has fallen asleep, he will recover."

13 Now Jesus had spoken of his death, but they thought that He was speaking of literal sleep.

14 Then Jesus therefore said to them plainly, "Lazarus is dead,

15 and I am glad for your sakes that I was not there, so that you may believe; but let us go to him."

16 Thomas therefore, who is called Didymus, said to his fellow disciples, "Let us also go, that we may die with Him."

17 ¶ So when Jesus came, He found that he had already been in the tomb four days.

18 Now Bethany was near Jerusalem, about two miles off;

19 and many of the Jews had come to Martha and Mary, to console them concerning their brother.

20 Martha therefore, when she heard that Jesus was coming, went to meet Him; but Mary still sat in the house.

21 Martha therefore said to Jesus, "Lord, if You had been here, my brother would not have died.

22 "Even now I know that whatever You ask of God, God will give You."

23 Jesus *said to her, "Your brother shall rise again."

24 Martha *said to Him, "I know that he will rise again in the resurrection on the last day."

25 Jesus said to her, "I am the resurrection and the life; he who believes in Me shall live even if he dies,

26 and everyone who lives and believes in Me shall never die. Do you believe this?"

27 She *said to Him, "Yes, Lord; I have believed that You are the Christ, the Son of God, even He who comes into the world."

28 And when she had said this, she went away, and called Mary her sister, saying secretly, "The Teacher is here, and is calling for you."

29 And when she heard it, she *arose quickly, and was coming to Him.

30 ¶ Now Jesus had not yet come into the village, but was still in the place where Martha met Him.

31 The Jews then who were with her in the house, and consoling her, when they saw that Mary rose up quickly and went out, followed her, supposing that she was going to the tomb to weep there.

32 Therefore, when Mary came where Jesus was, she saw Him, and fell at His feet, saying to Him, "Lord, if You had been here, my brother would not have died."

33 When Jesus therefore saw her weeping, and the Jews who came with her, *also* weeping, He was deeply moved in spirit, and was troubled,

34 and said, "Where have you laid him?" They *said to Him, "Lord, come and see."

35 Jesus wept.

36 And so the Jews were saying, "Behold how He loved him!"

37 But some of them said, "Could not this man, who opened the eyes of him who was blind, have kept this man also from dying?"

38 ¶ Jesus therefore again being deeply moved within, *came to the tomb. Now it was a cave, and a stone was lying against it.

39 Jesus *said, "Remove the stone." Martha, the sister of the deceased, *said to Him, "Lord, by this time there will be a stench, for he has been *dead* four days."

40 Jesus *said to her, "Did I not say to you, if you believe, you will see the glory of God?"

41 And so they removed the stone. And Jesus raised His eyes, and said, "Father, I thank Thee that Thou heardest Me.

42 "And I knew that Thou hearest Me always; but because of the people standing around I said it, that they may believe that Thou didst send Me."

43 And when He had said these things, He cried out with a loud voice, "Lazarus, come forth."

44 He who had died came forth, bound hand and foot with wrappings; and his face was wrapped around with a cloth. Jesus *said to them, "Unbind him, and let him go."

45 ¶ Many therefore of the Jews, who had come to Mary and beheld what He had done, believed in Him.

46 But some of them went away to the Pharisees, and told them the things which Jesus had done.

47 ¶ Therefore the chief priests and the Pharisees convened a council, and were saying, "What are we doing? For this man is performing many signs.

48 "If we let Him *go on* like this, all men will believe in Him, and the Romans will come and take away both our place and our nation."

49 But a certain one of them, Caiaphas, who was high priest that year, said to them, "You know nothing at all,

50 nor do you take into account that it is expedient for you that one man should die for the people, and that the whole nation should not perish."

51 Now this he did not say on his own initiative; but being high priest that year, he prophesied that Jesus was going to die for the nation,

52 and not for the nation only, but that He might also gather together into one the children of God who are scattered abroad.

53 So from that day on they planned together to kill Him.

54 ¶ Jesus therefore no longer continued to walk publicly among the Jews, but went away from there to the country near the wilderness, into a city called Ephraim; and there He stayed with the disciples.

55 Now the Passover of the Jews was at hand, and many went up to Jerusalem out of the country before the Passover, to purify themselves.

56 Therefore they were seeking for Jesus, and were saying to one another, as they stood in the temple, "What do you think; that He will not come to the feast at all?"

57 Now the chief priests and the Pharisees had given orders that if anyone knew where He was, he should report it, that they might seize Him.

CHAPTER 12

JESUS, therefore, six days before the Passover, came to Bethany where Lazarus was, whom Jesus had raised from the dead.

2 So they made Him a supper there, and Martha was serving; but Lazarus was one of those reclining *at the table* with Him.

3 Mary therefore took a pound of very costly perfume of pure nard, and anointed the feet of Jesus, and wiped His feet with her hair; and the house was filled with the fragrance of the perfume.

4 But Judas Iscariot, one of His disciples, who was intending to betray Him, *said,

5 "Why was this perfume not sold for [21]three hundred denarii, and given to poor *people*?"

6 Now he said this, not because he was concerned about the poor, but because he was a thief, and as he had the money box, he used to pilfer what was put into it.

7 Jesus therefore said, "Let her alone, in order that she may keep [22]it for the day of My burial.

8 "For the poor you always have with you, but you do not always have Me."

9 ¶ The great multitude therefore of the Jews learned that He was there; and they came, not for Jesus' sake only, but that they might also see Lazarus, whom He raised from the dead.

10 But the chief priests took counsel that they might put Lazarus to death also;

11 because on account of him many of the Jews were going away, and were believing in Jesus.

12 ¶ On the next day the great multitude who had come to the feast, when they heard that Jesus was coming to Jerusalem,

13 took the branches of the palm trees, and went out to meet Him, and *began* to cry out, "Hosanna! BLESSED IS HE WHO COMES IN THE NAME OF THE LORD, even the King of Israel."

14 And Jesus, finding a young donkey, sat on it; as it is written,

15 "FEAR NOT, DAUGHTER OF ZION; BEHOLD, YOUR KING IS COMING, SEATED ON A DONKEY'S COLT."

16 These things His disciples did not understand at the first; but when Jesus was glorified, then they remembered that these things were written of Him, and that they had done these things to Him.

17 And so the multitude who were with Him when He called Lazarus out of the tomb, and raised him from the dead, were bearing Him witness.

18 For this cause also the multitude went and met Him, because they heard that He had performed this sign.

19 The Pharisees therefore said to one another, "You see that you are not doing any good; look, the world has gone after Him."

20 ¶ Now there were certain Greeks among those who were going up to worship at the feast;

21 these therefore came to Philip, who was from Bethsaida of Galilee, and *began* to ask him, saying, "Sir, we wish to see Jesus."

22 Philip *came and *told Andrew; Andrew and Philip *came, and they *told Jesus.

23 And Jesus *answered them, saying, "The hour has come for the Son of Man to be glorified.

24 "Truly, truly, I say to you, unless a grain of wheat falls into the earth and dies, it remains by itself alone; but if it dies, it bears much fruit.

25 "He who loves his life loses it; and he who hates his life in this world shall keep it to life eternal.

26 "If anyone serves Me, let him follow Me; and where I am, there shall My servant also be; if anyone serves Me, the Father will honor him.

27 ¶ "Now My soul has become troubled; and what shall I say, 'Father, save Me from this hour'? But for this purpose I came to this hour.

28 "Father, glorify Thy name." There came therefore a voice out of heaven: "I have both glorified it, and will glorify it again."

29 The multitude therefore, who stood by and heard it, were saying that it had thundered; others were saying, "An angel has spoken to Him."

30 Jesus answered and said, "This voice has not come for My sake, but for your sakes.

31 "Now judgment is upon this world; now the ruler of this world shall be cast out.

32 "And I, if I be lifted up from the earth, will draw all men to Myself."

33 But He was saying this to indicate the kind of death by which He was to die.

34 The multitude therefore answered Him, "We have heard out of the Law

[21] Equivalent to 11 months' wages
[22] I.e., The custom of anointing for burial

that the Christ is to remain forever; and how can You say, 'The Son of Man must be lifted up'? Who is this Son of Man?"

35 Jesus therefore said to them, "For a little while longer the light is among you. Walk while you have the light, that darkness may not overtake you; he who walks in the darkness does not know where he goes.

36"While you have the light, believe in the light, in order that you may become sons of light."

¶ These things Jesus spoke, and He departed and hid Himself from them.

37 But though He had performed so many signs before them, *yet* they were not believing in Him;

38 that the word of Isaiah the prophet might be fulfilled, which he spoke, "LORD, WHO HAS BELIEVED OUR REPORT? AND TO WHOM HAS THE ARM OF THE LORD BEEN REVEALED?"

39 For this cause they could not believe, for Isaiah said again,

40"HE HAS BLINDED THEIR EYES, AND HE HARDENED THEIR HEART; LEST THEY SEE WITH THEIR EYES, AND PERCEIVE WITH THEIR HEART, AND BE CONVERTED, AND I HEAL THEM."

41 These things Isaiah said, because he saw His glory, and he spoke of Him.

42 Nevertheless many even of the rulers believed in Him, but because of the Pharisees they were not confessing *Him*, lest they should be put out of the synagogue;

43 for they loved the approval of men rather than the approval of God.

44 ¶ And Jesus cried out and said, "He who believes in Me does not believe in Me, but in Him who sent Me.

45"And he who beholds Me beholds the One who sent Me.

46"I have come *as* light into the world, that everyone who believes in Me may not remain in darkness.

47"And if anyone hears My sayings, and does not keep them, I do not judge him; for I did not come to judge the world, but to save the world.

48"He who rejects Me, and does not receive My sayings, has one who judges him; the word I spoke is what will judge him at the last day.

49"For I did not speak on My own initiative, but the Father Himself who sent Me has given Me commandment, what to say, and what to speak.

50"And I know that His commandment is eternal life; therefore the things I speak, I speak just as the Father has told Me."

CHAPTER 13

NOW before the Feast of the Passover, Jesus knowing that His hour had come that He should depart out of this world to the Father, having loved His own who were in the world, He loved them to the end.

2 And during supper, the devil having already put into the heart of Judas Iscariot, *the son* of Simon, to betray Him,

3 *Jesus,* knowing that the Father had given all things into His hands, and that He had come forth from God, and was going back to God,

4 *rose from supper, and *laid aside His garments; and taking a towel, He girded Himself about.

5 Then He *poured water into the basin, and began to wash the disciples' feet, and to wipe them with the towel with which He was girded.

6 And so He *came to Simon Peter. He *said to Him, "Lord, do You wash my feet?"

7 Jesus answered and said to him, "What I do you do not realize now, but you shall understand hereafter."

8 Peter *said to Him, "Never shall You wash my feet!" Jesus answered him, "If I do not wash you, you have no part with Me."

9 Simon Peter *said to Him, "Lord, not my feet only, but also my hands and my head."

10 Jesus *said to him, "He who has bathed needs only to wash his feet, but is completely clean; and you are clean, but not all *of you.*"

11 For He knew the one who was betraying Him; for this reason He said, "Not all of you are clean."

12 ¶ And so when He had washed their feet, and taken His garments, and reclined *at the table* again, He said to them, "Do you know what I have done to you?

13"You call Me Teacher and Lord; and you are right, for *so* I am.

14"If I then, the Lord and the Teacher, washed your feet, you also ought to wash one another's feet.

15"For I gave you an example that you also should do as I did to you.

16"Truly, truly, I say to you, a slave is not greater than his master; neither is one who is sent greater than the one who sent him.

17"If you know these things, you are blessed if you do them.

18"I do not speak of all of you. I know the ones I have chosen; but it is that the Scripture may be fulfilled, 'HE WHO EATS MY BREAD HAS LIFTED UP HIS HEEL AGAINST ME.'

19"From now on I am telling you before it comes to pass, so that when it does occur, you may believe that I am He.

20"Truly, truly, I say to you, he who receives whomever I send receives Me; and he who receives Me receives Him who sent Me."

21 ¶ When Jesus had said this, He became troubled in spirit, and testified, and said, "Truly, truly, I say to you, that one of you will betray Me."

22 The disciples began looking at one another, at a loss to know of which one He was speaking.

23 There was reclining on Jesus' breast one of His disciples, whom Jesus loved.

24 Simon Peter therefore *gestured to him, and *said to him, "Tell us who it is of whom He is speaking."

25 He, leaning back thus on Jesus' breast, *said to Him, "Lord, who is it?"

26 Jesus therefore *answered, "That is the one for whom I shall dip the morsel and give it to him." So when He had dipped the morsel, He *took and *gave it to Judas, the son of Simon Iscariot.

27 And after the morsel, Satan then entered into him. Jesus therefore *said to him, "What you do, do quickly."

28 Now no one of those reclining at the table knew for what purpose He had said this to him.

29 For some were supposing, because Judas had the money box, that Jesus was saying to him, "Buy the things we have need of for the feast"; or else, that he should give something to the poor.

30 And so after receiving the morsel he went out immediately; and it was night.

31 ¶ When therefore he had gone out, Jesus *said, "Now is the Son of Man glorified, and God is glorified in Him;

32 if God is glorified in Him, God will also glorify Him in Himself, and will glorify Him immediately.

33"Little children, I am with you a little while longer. You shall seek Me; and as I said to the Jews, I now say to you also, 'Where I am going, you cannot come.'

34"A new commandment I give to you, that you love one another, even as I have loved you, that you also love one another.

35"By this all men will know that you are My disciples, if you have love for one another."

36 ¶ Simon Peter *said to Him, "Lord, where are You going?" Jesus answered, "Where I go, you cannot follow Me now; but you shall follow later."

37 Peter *said to Him, "Lord, why can I not follow You right now? I will lay down my life for You."

38 Jesus *answered, "Will you lay down your life for Me? Truly, truly, I say to you, a cock shall not crow, until you deny Me three times.

CHAPTER 14

"LET not your heart be troubled; [23]believe in God, believe also in Me.

2"In My Father's house are many dwelling places; if it were not so, I would have told you; for I go to prepare a place for you.

3"And if I go and prepare a place for you, I will come again, and receive you to Myself; that where I am, there you may be also.

4"[24]And you know the way where I am going."

5 Thomas *said to Him, "Lord, we do not know where You are going, how do we know the way?"

6 Jesus *said to Him, "I am the way, and the truth, and the life; no one comes to the Father, but through Me.

7"If you had known Me, you would have known My Father also; from now on you know Him, and have seen Him."

8 Philip *said to Him, "Lord, show us the Father, and it is enough for us."

9 Jesus *said to him, "Have I been

[23] Or, you believe in God
[24] Many ancient authorities read And where I go you know, and the way you know

so long with you, and *yet* you have not come to know Me, Philip? He who has seen Me has seen the Father; how do you say, 'Show us the Father'?

10 "Do you not believe that I am in the Father, and the Father is in Me? The words that I say to you I do not speak on My own initiative, but the Father abiding in Me does His works.

11 "Believe Me that I am in the Father, and the Father in Me; otherwise believe on account of the works themselves.

12 "Truly, truly, I say to you, he who believes in Me, the works that I do shall he do also; and greater *works* than these shall he do; because I go to the Father.

13 "And whatever you ask in My name, that will I do, that the Father may be glorified in the Son.

14 "If you ask Me anything in My name, I will do *it.*

15 "If you love Me, you will keep My commandments.

16 "And I will ask the Father, and He will give you another Helper, that He may be with you forever;

17 *that is* the Spirit of truth, whom the world cannot receive, because it does not behold Him or know Him, *but* you know Him because He abides with you, and will be in you.

18 "I will not leave you as orphans; I will come to you.

19 "After a little while the world will behold Me no more; but you *will* behold Me; because I live, you shall live also.

20 "In that day you shall know that I am in My Father, and you in Me, and I in you.

21 "He who has My commandments and keeps them, he it is who loves Me; and he who loves Me shall be loved by My Father, and I will love him, and will disclose Myself to him."

22 Judas (not Iscariot) *said to Him, "Lord, what then has happened that You are going to disclose Yourself to us, and not to the world?"

23 Jesus answered and said to him, "If anyone loves Me, he will keep My word; and My Father will love him, and We will come to him, and make Our abode with him.

24 "He who does not love Me does not keep My words; and the word which

you hear is not Mine, but the Father's who sent Me.

25 ¶ "These things I have spoken to you, while abiding with you.

26 "But the Helper, the Holy Spirit, whom the Father will send in My name, He will teach you all things, and bring to your remembrance all that I said to you.

27 "Peace I leave with you; My peace I give to you; not as the world gives, do I give to you. Let not your heart be troubled, nor let it be fearful.

28 "You heard that I said to you, 'I go away, and I will come to you.' If you loved Me, you would have rejoiced, because I go to the Father; for the Father is greater than I.

29 "And now I have told you before it comes to pass, that when it comes to pass, you may believe.

30 "I will not speak much more with you, for the ruler of the world is coming, and he has nothing in Me;

31 but that the world may know that I love the Father, and as the Father gave Me commandment, even so I do. Arise, let us go from here.

CHAPTER 15

"I AM the true vine, and My Father is the vinedresser.

2 "Every branch in Me that does not bear fruit, He takes away; and every *branch* that bears fruit, He [25]prunes it, that it may bear more fruit.

3 "You are already clean because of the word which I have spoken to you.

4 "Abide in Me, and I in you. As the branch cannot bear fruit of itself, unless it abides in the vine, so neither *can* you, unless you abide in Me.

5 "I am the vine, you are the branches; he who abides in Me, and I in him, he bears much fruit; for apart from Me you can do nothing.

6 "If anyone does not abide in Me, he is thrown away as a branch, and dries up; and they gather them, and cast them into the fire, and they are burned.

7 "If you abide in Me, and My words abide in you, ask whatever you wish, and it shall be done for you.

8 "By this is My Father glorified, that you bear much fruit, and *so* prove to be My disciples.

[25] Lit., *cleanses*

9"Just as the Father has loved Me, I have also loved you; abide in My love.

10"If you keep My commandments, you will abide in My love; just as I have kept My Father's commandments, and abide in His love.

11"These things I have spoken to you, that My joy may be in you, and *that* your joy may be made full.

12"This is My commandment, that you love one another, just as I have loved you.

13"Greater love has no one than this, that one lay down his life for his friends.

14"You are My friends, if you do what I command you.

15"No longer do I call you slaves, for the slave does not know what his master is doing; but I have called you friends, for all things that I have heard from My Father I have made known to you.

16"You did not choose Me, but I chose you, and appointed you, that you should go and bear fruit, and *that* your fruit should remain, that whatever you ask of the Father in My name, He may give to you.

17"This I command you, that you love one another.

18"If the world hates you, you know that it has hated Me before *it hated* you.

19"If you were of the world, the world would love its own; but because you are not of the world, but I chose you out of the world, therefore the world hates you.

20"Remember the word that I said to you, 'A slave is not greater than his master.' If they persecuted Me, they will also persecute you; if they kept My word, they will keep yours also.

21"But all these things they will do to you for My name's sake, because they do not know the One who sent Me.

22"If I had not come and spoken to them, they would not have sin, but now they have no excuse for their sin.

23"He who hates Me hates My Father also.

24"If I had not done among them the works which no one else did, they would not have sin; but now they have both seen and hated Me and My Father as well.

25"But *they have done this* in order that the word may be fulfilled that is written in their Law, 'THEY HATED ME WITHOUT A CAUSE.'

26"When the Helper comes, whom I will send to you from the Father, *that is* the Spirit of truth, who proceeds from the Father, He will bear witness of Me,

27 and you *will* bear witness also, because you have been with Me from the beginning.

CHAPTER 16

"THESE things I have spoken to you, that you may be kept from stumbling.

2"They will make you outcasts from the synagogue, but an hour is coming for everyone who kills you to think that he is offering service to God.

3"And these things they will do, because they have not known the Father, or Me.

4"But these things I have spoken to you, that when their hour comes, you may remember that I told you of them. And these things I did not say to you at the beginning, because I was with you.

5"But now I am going to Him who sent Me; and none of you asks Me, 'Where are You going?'

6"But because I have said these things to you, sorrow has filled your heart.

7"But I tell you the truth, it is to your advantage that I go away; for if I do not go away, the Helper shall not come to you; but if I go, I will send Him to you.

8"And He, when He comes, will convict the world concerning sin, and righteousness, and judgment;

9 concerning sin, because they do not believe in Me;

10 and concerning righteousness, because I go to the Father, and you no longer behold Me;

11 and concerning judgment, because the ruler of this world has been judged.

12"I have many more things to say to you, but you cannot bear *them* now.

13"But when He, the Spirit of truth, comes, He will guide you into all the truth; for He will not speak on His own initiative, but whatever He hears, He will speak; and He will disclose to you what is to come.

14"He shall glorify Me; for He shall take of Mine, and shall disclose *it* to you.

15"All things that the Father has are Mine; therefore I said, that He takes of Mine, and will disclose *it* to you.

16"A little while, and you will no longer behold Me; and again a little while, and you will see Me."

17 *Some* of His disciples therefore said to one another, "What is this thing He is telling us, 'A little while, and you will not behold Me; and again a little while, and you will see Me'; and, 'because I go to the Father'?"

18 And so they were saying, "What is this that He says, 'A little while'? We do not know what He is talking about."

19 Jesus knew that they wished to question Him, and He said to them, "Are you deliberating together about this, that I said, 'A little while, and you will not behold Me, and again a little while, and you will see Me'?

20"Truly, truly, I say to you, that you will weep and lament, but the world will rejoice; you will be sorrowful, but your sorrow will be turned to joy.

21"Whenever a woman is in travail she has sorrow, because her hour has come; but when she gives birth to the child, she remembers the anguish no more, for joy that a child has been born into the world.

22"Therefore you too now have sorrow; but I will see you again, and your heart will rejoice, and no one takes your joy away from you.

23"And in that day you will ask Me no question. Truly, truly, I say to you, if you shall ask the Father for anything, He will give it to you in My name.

24"Until now you have asked for nothing in My name; ask, and you will receive, that your joy may be made full.

25 "These things I have spoken to you in figurative language; an hour is coming when I will speak no more to you in figurative language, but will tell you plainly of the Father.

26"In that day you will ask in My name, and I do not say to you that I will request the Father on your behalf;

27 for the Father Himself loves you, because you have loved Me, and have believed that I came forth from the Father.

28"I came forth from the Father, and have come into the world; I am leaving the world again, and going to the Father."

29 His disciples *said, "Lo, now You are speaking plainly, and are not using a figure of speech.

30"Now we know that You know all things, and have no need for anyone to question You; by this we believe that You came from God."

31 Jesus answered them, "Do you now believe?

32"Behold, an hour is coming, and has *already* come, for you to be scattered, each to his own *home,* and to leave Me alone; and *yet* I am not alone, because the Father is with Me.

33"These things I have spoken to you, that in Me you may have peace. In the world you have tribulation, but take courage; I have overcome the world."

CHAPTER 17

THESE things Jesus spoke; and lifting up His eyes to heaven, He said, "Father, the hour has come; glorify Thy Son, that the Son may glorify Thee,

2 even as Thou gavest Him authority over all mankind, that to all whom Thou hast given Him, He may give eternal life.

3"And this is eternal life, that they may know Thee, the only true God, and Jesus Christ whom Thou hast sent.

4"I glorified Thee on the earth, having accomplished the work which Thou hast given Me to do.

5"And now, glorify Thou Me together with Thyself, Father, with the glory which I had with Thee before the world was.

6"I manifested Thy name to the men whom Thou gavest Me out of the world; Thine they were, and Thou gavest them to Me, and they have kept Thy word.

7"Now they have come to know that everything Thou hast given Me is from Thee;

8 for the words which Thou gavest Me I have given to them; and they received *them,* and truly understood

that I came forth from Thee, and they believed that Thou didst send Me.

9"I ask on their behalf; I do not ask on behalf of the world, but of those whom Thou hast given Me; for they are Thine;

10 and all things that are Mine are Thine, and Thine are Mine; and I have been glorified in them.

11"And I am no more in the world; and *yet* they themselves are in the world, and I come to Thee. Holy Father, keep them in Thy name, *the name* which Thou hast given Me, that they may be one, even as We *are*.

12"While I was with them, I was keeping them in Thy name which Thou hast given Me; and I guarded them, and not one of them perished but the son of perdition, that the Scripture might be fulfilled.

13"But now I come to Thee; and these things I speak in the world, that they may have My joy made full in themselves.

14"I have given them Thy word; and the world has hated them, because they are not of the world, even as I am not of the world.

15"I do not ask Thee to take them out of the world, but to keep them from the evil *one*.

16"They are not of the world, even as I am not of the world.

17"Sanctify them in the truth; Thy word is truth.

18"As Thou didst send Me into the world, I also have sent them into the world.

19"And for their sakes I sanctify Myself, that they themselves also may be sanctified in truth.

20"I do not ask in behalf of these alone, but for those also who believe in Me through their word;

21 that they may all be one; even as Thou, Father, *art* in Me, and I in Thee, that they also may be in Us; that the world may believe that Thou didst send Me.

22"And the glory which Thou hast given Me I have given to them; that they may be one, just as We are one;

23 I in them, and Thou in Me, that they may be perfected in unity, that the world may know that Thou didst send Me, and didst love them, even as Thou didst love Me.

24"Father, I desire that they also, whom Thou hast given Me, be with Me where I am, in order that they may behold My glory, which Thou hast given Me; for Thou didst love Me before the foundation of the world.

25"O righteous Father, although the world has not known Thee, yet I have known Thee; and these have known that Thou didst send Me;

26 and I have made Thy name known to them, and will make it known; that the love wherewith Thou didst love Me may be in them, and I in them."

CHAPTER 18

WHEN Jesus had spoken these words, He went forth with His disciples over the ravine of the Kidron, where there was a garden, into which He Himself entered, and His disciples.

2 Now Judas also, who was betraying Him, knew the place; for Jesus had often met there with His disciples.

3 Judas then, having received the *Roman* cohort, and officers from the chief priests and the Pharisees, *came there with lanterns and torches and weapons.

4 Jesus therefore, knowing all the things that were coming upon Him, went forth, and *said to them, "Whom do you seek?"

5 They answered Him, "Jesus the Nazarene." He *said to them, "I am He." And Judas also who was betraying Him, was standing with them.

6 When therefore He said to them, "I am He," they drew back, and fell to the ground.

7 Again therefore He asked them, "Whom do you seek?" And they said, "Jesus the Nazarene."

8 Jesus answered, "I told you that I am He; if therefore you seek Me, let these go their way,"

9 that the word might be fulfilled which He spoke, "Of those whom Thou hast given Me I lost not one."

10 Simon Peter therefore having a sword, drew it, and struck the high priest's slave, and cut off his right ear; and the slave's name was Malchus.

11 Jesus therefore said to Peter, "Put the sword into the sheath; the cup which the Father has given Me, shall I not drink it?"

12 ¶ So the *Roman* cohort and the commander, and the officers of the Jews, arrested Jesus and bound Him,

13 and led Him to Annas first; for he was father-in-law of Caiaphas, who was high priest that year.

14 Now Caiaphas was the one who had advised the Jews that it was expedient for one man to die on behalf of the people.

15 ¶ And Simon Peter was following Jesus, and *so was* another disciple. Now that disciple was known to the high priest, and entered with Jesus into the court of the high priest,

16 but Peter was standing at the door outside. So the other disciple, who was known to the high priest, went out and spoke to the doorkeeper, and brought in Peter.

17 The slave-girl therefore who kept the door *said to Peter, "You are not also *one* of this man's disciples, are you?" He *said, "I am not."

18 Now the slaves and the officers were standing *there*, having made a charcoal fire, for it was cold and they were warming themselves; and Peter also was with them, standing and warming himself.

19 ¶ The high priest therefore questioned Jesus about His disciples, and about His teaching.

20 Jesus answered him, "I have spoken openly to the world; I always taught in synagogues, and in the temple, where all the Jews come together; and I spoke nothing in secret.

21 "Why do you question Me? Question those who have heard what I spoke to them; behold, these know what I said."

22 And when He had said this, one of the officers standing by gave Jesus a blow, saying, "Is that the way You answer the high priest?"

23 Jesus answered him, "If I have spoken wrongly, bear witness of the wrong; but if rightly, why do you strike Me?"

24 Annas therefore sent Him bound to Caiaphas the high priest.

25 ¶ Now Simon Peter was standing and warming himself. They said therefore to him, "You are not also *one* of His disciples, are you?" He denied *it*, and said, "I am not."

26 One of the slaves of the high priest, being a relative of the one whose ear Peter cut off, *said, "Did I not see you in the garden with Him?"

27 Peter therefore denied *it* again; and immediately a cock crowed.

28 ¶ They *led Jesus therefore from Caiaphas into the [26]Praetorium, and it was early; and they themselves did not enter into the Praetorium in order that they might not be defiled, but might eat the Passover.

29 Pilate therefore went out to them, and *said, "What accusation do you bring against this Man?"

30 They answered and said to him, "If this Man were not an evildoer, we would not have delivered Him up to you."

31 Pilate therefore said to them, "Take Him yourselves, and judge Him according to your law." The Jews said to him, "We are not permitted to put anyone to death,"

32 that the word of Jesus might be fulfilled, which He spoke, signifying by what kind of death He was about to die.

33 ¶ Pilate therefore entered again into the [26]Praetorium, and summoned Jesus, and said to Him, "Are You the King of the Jews?"

34 Jesus answered, "Are you saying this on your own initiative, or did others tell you about Me?"

35 Pilate answered, "I am not a Jew, am I? Your own nation and the chief priests delivered You up to me; what have You done?"

36 Jesus answered, "My kingdom is not of this world. If My kingdom were of this world, then My servants would be fighting, that I might not be delivered up to the Jews; but as it is, My kingdom is not [27]of this realm."

37 Pilate therefore said to Him, "So You are a king?" Jesus answered, "You say *correctly* that I am a king. For this I have been born, and for this I have come into the world, to bear witness to the truth. Everyone who is of the truth hears My voice."

38 Pilate *said to Him, "What is truth?"

¶ And when he had said this, he went out again to the Jews, and *said to them, "I find no guilt in Him.

39 "But you have a custom, that I should release someone for you at the

[26] I.e., governor's official residence [27] Lit., *from here*

Passover; do you wish then that I release for you the King of the Jews?"

40 Therefore they cried out again, saying, "Not this Man, but Barabbas." Now Barabbas was a robber.

CHAPTER 19

THEN Pilate therefore took Jesus, and scourged Him.

2 And the soldiers wove a crown of thorns and put it on His head, and arrayed Him in a purple robe;

3 and they *began* to come up to Him, and say, "Hail, King of the Jews!" and to give Him blows *in the face.*

4 And Pilate came out again, and *said to them, "Behold, I am bringing Him out to you, that you may know that I find no guilt in Him."

5 Jesus therefore came out, wearing the crown of thorns and the purple robe. And *Pilate* *said to them, "Behold, the Man!"

6 When therefore the chief priests and the officers saw Him, they cried out, saying, "Crucify, crucify!" Pilate *said to them, "Take Him yourselves, and crucify Him, for I find no guilt in Him."

7 The Jews answered him, "We have a law, and by that law He ought to die because He made Himself out *to be* the Son of God."

8 When Pilate therefore heard this statement, he was the more afraid;

9 and he entered into the [28]Praetorium again, and *said to Jesus, "Where are You from?" But Jesus gave him no answer.

10 Pilate therefore *said to Him, "You do not speak to me? Do You not know that I have authority to release You, and I have authority to crucify You?"

11 Jesus answered, "You would have no authority over Me, unless it had been given you from above; for this reason he who delivered Me up to you has *the* greater sin."

12 As a result of this Pilate made efforts to release Him, but the Jews cried out, saying, "If you release this Man, you are no friend of Caesar; everyone who makes himself out *to be* a king opposes Caesar."

13 When Pilate therefore heard these words, he brought Jesus out, and sat down on the judgment seat at a place called The Pavement, but in Hebrew, Gabbatha.

14 Now it was the day of preparation for the Passover; it was about the [29]sixth hour. And he *said to the Jews, "Behold, your King!"

15 They therefore cried out, "Away with *Him,* away with *Him,* crucify Him!" Pilate *said to them, "Shall I crucify your King?" The chief priests answered, "We have no king but Caesar."

16 So he then delivered Him to them to be crucified.

17 ¶ They took Jesus therefore, and He went out, bearing His own cross, to the place called the Place of a Skull, which is called in Hebrew, Golgotha.

18 There they crucified Him, and with Him two other men, one on either side, and Jesus in between.

19 And Pilate wrote an inscription also, and put it on the cross. And it was written, "JESUS THE NAZARENE, THE KING OF THE JEWS."

20 Therefore this inscription many of the Jews read, for the place where Jesus was crucified was near the city; and it was written in Hebrew, Latin, *and* in Greek.

21 And so the chief priests of the Jews were saying to Pilate, "Do not write, 'The King of the Jews'; but that He said, 'I am King of the Jews.'"

22 Pilate answered, "What I have written I have written."

23 ¶ The soldiers therefore, when they had crucified Jesus, took His outer garments and made four parts, a part to every soldier and *also* the [30]tunic; now the tunic was seamless, woven in one piece.

24 They said therefore to one another, "Let us not tear it, but cast lots for it, *to decide* whose it shall be"; that the Scripture might be fulfilled, "THEY DIVIDED MY OUTER GARMENTS AMONG THEM, AND FOR MY CLOTHING THEY CAST LOTS."

25 Therefore the soldiers did these things. But there were standing by the cross of Jesus His mother, and His mother's sister, Mary the *wife* of Clopas, and Mary Magdalene.

---

[28] I.e., governor's official residence
[29] Perhaps 6 a.m. (Roman time)
[30] Gr., *khiton,* the garment worn next to the skin

26 When Jesus therefore saw His mother, and the disciple whom He loved standing nearby, He *said to His mother, "Woman, behold, your son!"

27 Then He *said to the disciple, "Behold, your mother!" And from that hour the disciple took her into his own household.

28 ¶ After this, Jesus, knowing that all things had already been accomplished, in order that the Scripture might be fulfilled, *said, "I am thirsty."

29 A jar full of sour wine was standing there; so they put a sponge full of the sour wine upon a branch of hyssop, and brought it up to His mouth.

30 When Jesus therefore had received the sour wine, He said, "It is finished!" And He bowed His head, and gave up His spirit.

31 ¶ The Jews therefore, because it was the day of preparation, so that the bodies should not remain on the cross on the Sabbath (for that Sabbath was a high day), asked Pilate that their legs might be broken, and that they might be taken away.

32 The soldiers therefore came, and broke the legs of the first man, and of the other man who was crucified with Him;

33 but coming to Jesus, when they saw that He was already dead, they did not break His legs;

34 but one of the soldiers pierced His side with a spear, and immediately there came out blood and water.

35 And he who has seen has borne witness, and his witness is true; and he knows that he is telling the truth, so that you also may believe.

36 For these things came to pass, that the Scripture might be fulfilled, "NOT A BONE OF HIM SHALL BE BROKEN."

37 And again another Scripture says, "THEY SHALL LOOK ON HIM WHOM THEY PIERCED."

38 ¶ And after these things Joseph of Arimathea, being a disciple of Jesus, but a secret one, for fear of the Jews, asked Pilate that he might take away the body of Jesus; and Pilate granted permission. He came therefore, and took away His body.

39 And Nicodemus came also, who had first come to Him by night; bringing a mixture of myrrh and aloes, about a hundred pounds weight.

40 And so they took the body of Jesus, and bound it in linen wrappings with the spices, as is the burial custom of the Jews.

41 Now in the place where He was crucified there was a garden; and in the garden a new tomb, in which no one had yet been laid.

42 Therefore on account of the Jewish day of preparation, because the tomb was nearby, they laid Jesus there.

CHAPTER 20

NOW on the first day of the week Mary Magdalene *came early to the tomb, while it *was still dark, and *saw the stone already taken away from the tomb.

2 And so she *ran and *came to Simon Peter, and to the other disciple whom Jesus loved, and *said to them, "They have taken away the Lord out of the tomb, and we do not know where they have laid Him."

3 Peter therefore went forth, and the other disciple, and they were going to the tomb.

4 And the two were running together; and the other disciple ran ahead faster than Peter, and came to the tomb first;

5 and stooping and looking in, he *saw the linen wrappings lying there; but he did not go in.

6 Simon Peter therefore also *came, following him, and entered the tomb; and he *beheld the linen wrappings lying there,

7 and the face-cloth, which had been on His head, not lying with the linen wrappings, but rolled up in a place by itself.

8 So the other disciple who had first come to the tomb entered then also, and he saw and believed.

9 For as yet they did not understand the Scripture, that He must rise again from the dead.

10 So the disciples went away again to their own homes.

11 ¶ But Mary was standing outside the tomb weeping; and so, as she wept, she stooped and looked into the tomb;

12 and she *beheld two angels in white sitting, one at the head, and one at the feet, where the body of Jesus had been lying.

13 And they *said to her, "Woman, why are you weeping?" She *said to them, "Because they have taken away my Lord, and I do not know where they have laid Him."

14 When she had said this, she turned around, and *beheld Jesus standing *there,* and did not know that it was Jesus.

15 Jesus *said to her, "Woman, why are you weeping? Whom are you seeking?" Supposing Him to be the gardener, she *said to Him, "Sir, if you have carried Him away, tell me where you have laid Him, and I will take Him away."

16 Jesus *said to her, "Mary!" She *turned and *said to Him in Hebrew, "Rabboni!" (which means, Teacher).

17 Jesus *said to her, "Stop clinging to Me, for I have not yet ascended to the Father; but go to My brethren, and say to them, 'I ascend to My Father and your Father, and My God and your God.'"

18 Mary Magdalene *came, announcing to the disciples, "I have seen the Lord," and *that* He had said these things to her.

19 ¶ When therefore it was evening, on that day, the first *day* of the week, and when the doors were shut where the disciples were, for fear of the Jews, Jesus came and stood in their midst, and *said to them, "Peace *be* with you."

20 And when He had said this, He showed them both His hands and His side. The disciples therefore rejoiced when they saw the Lord.

21 Jesus therefore said to them again, "Peace *be* with you; as the Father has sent Me, I also send you."

22 And when He had said this, He breathed on them, and *said to them, "Receive the Holy Spirit.

23 "If you forgive the sins of any, *their sins* have been forgiven them; if you retain the *sins* of any, they have been retained."

24 ¶ But Thomas, one of the twelve, called Didymus, was not with them when Jesus came.

25 The other disciples therefore were saying to him, "We have seen the Lord!" But he said to them, "Unless I shall see in His hands the imprint of the nails, and put my finger into the place of the nails, and put my hand into His side, I will not believe."

26 ¶ And after eight days again His disciples were inside, and Thomas with them. Jesus *came, the doors having been shut, and stood in their midst, and said, "Peace *be* with you."

27 Then He *said to Thomas, "Reach here your finger, and see My hands; and reach here your hand, and put it into My side; and be not unbelieving, but believing."

28 Thomas answered and said to Him, "My Lord and my God!"

29 Jesus *said to him, "Because you have seen Me, have you believed? Blessed *are* they who did not see, and *yet* believed."

30 ¶ Many other signs therefore Jesus also performed in the presence of the disciples, which are not written in this book;

31 but these have been written that you may believe that Jesus is the Christ, the Son of God; and that believing you may have life in His name.

CHAPTER 21

AFTER these things Jesus manifested Himself again to the disciples at the Sea of Tiberias, and He manifested *Himself* in this way.

2 There were together Simon Peter, and Thomas called Didymus, and Nathanael of Cana in Galilee, and the *sons* of Zebedee, and two others of His disciples.

3 Simon Peter *said to them, "I am going fishing." They *said to him, "We will also come with you." They went out, and got into the boat; and that night they caught nothing.

4 But when the day was now breaking, Jesus stood on the beach; yet the disciples did not know that it was Jesus.

5 Jesus therefore *said to them, "Children, you do not have any fish, do you?" They answered Him, "No."

6 And He said to them, "Cast the net on the right-hand side of the boat, and you will find *a catch.*" They cast therefore, and then they were not able to haul it in because of the great number of fish.

7 That disciple therefore whom Jesus loved *said to Peter, "It is the Lord." And so when Simon Peter

heard that it was the Lord, he put his outer garment on (for he was stripped *for work*), and threw himself into the sea.

8 But the other disciples came in the little boat, for they were not far from the land, but about one hundred yards away, dragging the net *full* of fish.

9 And so when they got out upon the land, they *saw a charcoal fire *already* laid, and fish placed on it, and bread.

10 Jesus *said to them, "Bring some of the fish which you have now caught."

11 Simon Peter went up, and drew the net to land, full of large fish, a hundred and fifty-three; and although there were so many, the net was not torn.

12 Jesus *said to them, "Come *and* have breakfast." None of the disciples ventured to question Him, "Who are You?" knowing that it was the Lord.

13 Jesus *came and *took the bread, and *gave them, and the fish likewise.

14 This is now the third time that Jesus was manifested to the disciples, after He was raised from the dead.

15 ¶ So when they had finished breakfast, Jesus *said to Simon Peter, "Simon, *son* of John, do you love Me more than these?" He *said to Him, "Yes, Lord; You know that I love You." He *said to him, "Tend My lambs."

16 He *said to him again a second time, "Simon, *son* of John, do you love Me?" He *said to Him, "Yes, Lord; You know that I love You." He *said to him, "Shepherd My sheep."

17 He *said to him the third time, "Simon, *son* of John, do you love Me?" Peter was grieved because He said to him the third time, "Do you love Me?" And he said to Him, "Lord, You know all things; You know that I love You." Jesus *said to him, "Tend My sheep.

18"Truly, truly, I say to you, when you were younger, you used to gird yourself, and walk wherever you wished; but when you grow old, you will stretch out your hands, and someone else will gird you, and bring you where you do not wish to go."

19 Now this He said, signifying by what kind of death he would glorify God. And when He had spoken this, He *said to him, "Follow Me!"

20 Peter, turning around, *saw the disciple whom Jesus loved following *them;* the one who also had leaned back on His breast at the supper, and said, "Lord, who is the one who betrays You?"

21 Peter therefore seeing him *said to Jesus, "Lord, and what about this man?"

22 Jesus *said to him, "If I want him to remain until I come, what *is that* to you? You follow Me!"

23 This saying therefore went out among the brethren that that disciple would not die; yet Jesus did not say to him that he would not die, but *only,* "If I want him to remain until I come, what *is that* to you?"

24 ¶ This is the disciple who bears witness of these things, and wrote these things; and we know that his witness is true.

25 ¶ And there are also many other things which Jesus did, which if they *were written in detail, I suppose that even the world itself *would not contain the books which *were written.

THE ACTS

OF THE APOSTLES

THE first account I composed, Theophilus, about all that Jesus began to do and teach,

2 until the day when He was taken up, after He had by the Holy Spirit given orders to the apostles whom He had chosen.

3 To these He also presented Himself alive, after His suffering, by many convincing proofs, appearing to them over *a period of* forty days, and speaking of the things concerning the kingdom of God.

4 And gathering them together, He commanded them not to leave Jerusalem, but to wait for what the Father had promised, "Which," *He said,* "you heard of from Me;

5 for John baptized with water, but you shall be baptized with the Holy Spirit not many days from now."

6 ¶ And so when they had come together, they were asking Him, saying, "Lord, is it at this time You are restoring the kingdom to Israel?"

7 He said to them, "It is not for you to know times or epochs which the Father has fixed by His own authority;

8 but you shall receive power when the Holy Spirit has come upon you; and you shall be My witnesses both in Jerusalem, and in all Judea and Samaria, and even to the remotest part of the earth."

9 And after He had said these things, He was lifted up while they were looking on, and a cloud received Him out of their sight.

10 And as they were gazing intently into the sky while He was departing, behold, two men in white clothing stood beside them;

11 and they also said, "Men of Galilee, why do you stand looking into the sky? This Jesus, who has been taken up from you into heaven, will come in just the same way as you have watched Him go into heaven."

12 ¶ Then they returned to Jerusalem from the mount called Olivet, which is near Jerusalem, a Sabbath day's journey away.

13 And when they had entered, they went up to the upper room, where they were staying; that is, Peter and John and James and Andrew, Philip and Thomas, Bartholomew and Matthew, James *the son* of Alphaeus, and Simon the Zealot, and Judas *the son* of James.

14 These all with one mind were continually devoting themselves to prayer, along with *the* women, and Mary the mother of Jesus, and with His brothers.

15 ¶ And at this time Peter stood up in the midst of the brethren (a gathering of about one hundred and twenty persons was there together), and said,

16 "Brethren, the Scripture had to be fulfilled, which the Holy Spirit foretold by the mouth of David concerning Judas, who became a guide to those who arrested Jesus.

17 "For he was counted among us, and received his portion in this ministry."

18 (Now this man acquired a field with the price of his wickedness; and falling headlong, he burst open in the middle and all his bowels gushed out.

19 And it became known to all who were living in Jerusalem; so that in their own language that field was called Hakeldama, that is, Field of Blood.)

20 "For it is written in the book of Psalms,

'LET HIS HOMESTEAD BE MADE DESOLATE,

AND LET NO MAN DWELL IN IT';

and,

'HIS OFFICE LET ANOTHER MAN TAKE.'

21 "It is therefore necessary that of the men who have accompanied us all the time that the Lord Jesus went in and out among us—

22 beginning with the baptism of John, until the day that He was taken up from us—one of these should become a witness with us of His resurrection."

23 And they put forward two men, Joseph called Barsabbas (who was also called Justus), and Matthias.

24 And they prayed, and said, "Thou, Lord, who knowest the hearts of all men, show which one of these two Thou hast chosen

25 to occupy this ministry and apostleship from which Judas turned aside to go to his own place."

26 And they drew lots for them, and the lot fell to Matthias; and he was numbered with the eleven apostles.

CHAPTER 2

AND when the day of Pentecost had come, they were all together in one place.

2 And suddenly there came from heaven a noise like a violent, rushing wind, and it filled the whole house where they were sitting.

3 And there appeared to them tongues as of fire distributing themselves, and they rested on each one of them.

4 And they were all filled with the Holy Spirit and began to speak with other tongues, as the Spirit was giving them utterance.

5 ¶ Now there were Jews living in Jerusalem, devout men, from every nation under heaven.

6 And when this sound occurred, the multitude came together, and were bewildered, because they were each one hearing them speak in his own language.

7 And they were amazed and marveled, saying, "Why, are not all these who are speaking Galileans?

8 "And how is it that we each hear *them* in our own language to which we were born?

9 "Parthians and Medes and Elamites, and residents of Mesopotamia, Judea and Cappadocia, Pontus and Asia,

10 Phrygia and Pamphylia, Egypt and the districts of Libya around Cyrene, and visitors from Rome, both Jews and [1]proselytes,

11 Cretans and Arabs—we hear them in our *own* tongues speaking of the mighty deeds of God."

12 And they all continued in amazement and great perplexity, saying to one another, "What does this mean?"

13 But others were mocking and saying, "They are full of sweet wine."

14 ¶ But Peter, taking his stand with the eleven, raised his voice and declared to them: "Men of Judea, and all you who live in Jerusalem, let this be known to you, and give heed to my words.

15 "For these men are not drunk, as you suppose, for it is *only* the [2]third hour of the day;

16 but this is what was spoken of through the prophet Joel:

17 'AND IT SHALL BE IN THE LAST DAYS,' God says,
'THAT I WILL POUR FORTH OF MY SPIRIT UPON ALL MANKIND;
AND YOUR SONS AND YOUR DAUGHTERS SHALL PROPHESY,
AND YOUR YOUNG MEN SHALL SEE VISIONS,
AND YOUR OLD MEN SHALL DREAM DREAMS;

18 EVEN UPON MY BONDSLAVES, BOTH MEN AND WOMEN,
I WILL IN THOSE DAYS POUR FORTH OF MY SPIRIT
And they shall prophesy.

19 'AND I WILL GRANT WONDERS IN THE SKY ABOVE,
AND SIGNS ON THE EARTH BENEATH,
BLOOD, AND FIRE, AND VAPOR OF SMOKE.

20 'THE SUN SHALL BE TURNED INTO DARKNESS,
AND THE MOON INTO BLOOD,
BEFORE THE GREAT AND GLORIOUS DAY OF THE LORD SHALL COME.

21 'AND IT SHALL BE, THAT EVERYONE WHO CALLS ON THE NAME OF THE LORD SHALL BE SAVED.'

22 ¶ "Men of Israel, listen to these words: Jesus the Nazarene, a man attested to you by God with miracles and wonders and signs which God performed through Him in your midst, just as you yourselves know—

23 this *Man*, delivered up by the predetermined plan and foreknowledge of God, you nailed to a cross by the hands of godless men and put *Him* to death.

24 "And God raised Him up again, putting an end to the agony of death, since it was impossible for Him to be held in its power.

25 "For David says of Him,
'I WAS ALWAYS BEHOLDING THE LORD IN MY PRESENCE;
FOR HE IS AT MY RIGHT HAND, THAT I MAY NOT BE SHAKEN.

26 'THEREFORE MY HEART WAS GLAD AND MY TONGUE EXULTED;
MOREOVER MY FLESH ALSO WILL ABIDE IN HOPE;

---

[1] I.e., Gentile converts to Judaism   [2] I.e., 9 a.m.

27 BECAUSE THOU WILT NOT ABAN-
DON MY SOUL TO HADES,
NOR ALLOW THY HOLY ONE TO
UNDERGO DECAY.

28 'THOU HAST MADE KNOWN TO ME
THE WAYS OF LIFE;
THOU WILT MAKE ME FULL OF
GLADNESS WITH THY PRESENCE.'

29"Brethren, I may confidently say to you regarding the patriarch David that he both died and was buried, and his tomb is with us to this day.

30"And so, because he was a prophet, and knew that GOD HAD SWORN TO HIM WITH AN OATH TO SEAT *one* OF HIS DESCENDANTS UPON HIS THRONE,

31 he looked ahead and spoke of the resurrection of [3]the Christ, that HE WAS NEITHER ABANDONED TO HADES, NOR DID His flesh SUFFER DECAY.

32"This Jesus God raised up again, to which we are all witnesses.

33"Therefore having been exalted to the right hand of God, and having received from the Father the promise of the Holy Spirit, He has poured forth this which you both see and hear.

34"For it was not David who ascended into heaven, but he himself says:

'THE LORD SAID TO MY LORD,
"SIT AT MY RIGHT HAND,

35   UNTIL I MAKE THINE ENEMIES A
FOOTSTOOL FOR THY FEET." '

36"Therefore let all the house of Israel know for certain that God has made Him both Lord and Christ—this Jesus whom you crucified."

37 ¶ Now when they heard *this*, they were pierced to the heart, and said to Peter and the rest of the apostles, "Brethren, what shall we do?"

38 And Peter *said* to them, "Repent, and let each of you be baptized in the name of Jesus Christ for the forgiveness of your sins; and you shall receive the gift of the Holy Spirit.

39"For the promise is for you and your children, and for all who are far off, as many as the Lord our God shall call to Himself."

40 And with many other words he solemnly testified and kept on exhorting them, saying, "Be saved from this perverse generation!"

41 So then, those who had received his word were baptized; and there were added that day about three thousand [4]souls.

42 And they were continually devoting themselves to the apostles' teaching and to fellowship, to the breaking of bread and to prayer.

43 ¶ And everyone kept feeling a sense of awe; and many wonders and signs were taking place through the apostles[5].

44 And all those who had believed [6]were together, and had all things in common;

45 and they *began* selling their property and possessions, and were sharing them with all, as anyone might have need.

46 And day by day continuing with one mind in the temple, and breaking bread from house to house, they were taking their meals together with gladness and sincerity of heart,

47 praising God, and having favor with all the people. And the Lord was adding to their number day by day those who were being saved.

CHAPTER 3

NOW Peter and John were going up to the temple at the [7]ninth *hour,* the hour of prayer.

2 And a certain man who had been lame from his mother's womb was being carried along, whom they used to set down every day at the gate of the temple which is called Beautiful, in order to beg [8]alms of those who were entering the temple.

3 And when he saw Peter and John about to go into the temple, he *began* asking to receive alms.

4 And Peter, along with John, fixed his gaze upon him and said, "Look at us!"

5 And he *began* to give them his attention, expecting to receive something from them.

6 But Peter said, "I do not possess silver and gold, but what I do have I give to you: In the name of Jesus Christ the Nazarene—walk!"

7 And seizing him by the right hand, he raised him up; and immediately his feet and his ankles were strengthened.

[3] I.e., the Messiah

[4] I.e., persons
[5] Some ancient mss. add *in Jerusalem; and great fear was upon all*   [6] Some ancient mss. do not contain *were*
[7] I.e., 3 p.m.   [8] Or, *a gift of charity*

8 And with a leap, he stood upright and *began* to walk; and he entered the temple with them, walking and leaping and praising God.

9 And all the people saw him walking and praising God;

10 and they were taking note of him as being the one who used to sit at the Beautiful Gate of the temple to *beg* alms, and they were filled with wonder and amazement at what had happened to him.

11 ¶ And while he was clinging to Peter and John, all the people ran together to them at the so-called portico of Solomon, full of amazement.

12 But when Peter saw *this,* he replied to the people, "Men of Israel, why do you marvel at this, or why do you gaze at us, as if by our own power or piety we had made him walk?

13 "The God of Abraham, Isaac, and Jacob, the God of our fathers, has glorified His servant Jesus, *the one* whom you delivered up, and disowned in the presence of Pilate, when he had decided to release Him.

14 "But you disowned the Holy and Righteous One, and asked for a murderer to be granted to you,

15 but put to death the Prince of life, *the one* whom God raised from the dead, *a fact* to which we are witnesses.

16 "And on the basis of faith in His name, *it is* the name of Jesus which has strengthened this man whom you see and know; and the faith which *comes* through Him has given him this perfect health in the presence of you all.

17 "And now, brethren, I know that you acted in ignorance, just as your rulers did also.

18 "But the things which God announced beforehand by the mouth of all the prophets, that His Christ should suffer, He has thus fulfilled.

19 "Repent therefore and return, that your sins may be wiped away, in order that times of refreshing may come from the presence of the Lord;

20 and that He may send Jesus, the Christ appointed for you,

21 whom heaven must receive until *the* period of restoration of all things about which God spoke by the mouth of His holy prophets from ancient time.

22 "Moses said, 'THE LORD GOD SHALL RAISE UP FOR YOU A PROPHET LIKE ME FROM YOUR BRETHREN; TO HIM YOU SHALL GIVE HEED in everything He says to you.

23 'And it shall be that every soul that does not heed that prophet shall be utterly destroyed from among the people.'

24 "And likewise, all the prophets who have spoken, from Samuel and *his* successors onward, also announced these days.

25 "It is you who are the sons of the prophets, and of the covenant which God made with your fathers, saying to Abraham, 'AND IN YOUR SEED ALL THE FAMILIES OF THE EARTH SHALL BE BLESSED.'

26 "For you first, God raised up His Servant, and sent Him to bless you by turning every one *of you* from your wicked ways."

CHAPTER 4

AND as they were speaking to the people, the priests and the captain of the temple *guard,* and the Sadducees, came upon them,

2 being greatly disturbed because they were teaching the people and proclaiming in Jesus the resurrection from the dead.

3 And they laid hands on them, and put them in jail until the next day, for it was already evening.

4 But many of those who had heard the message believed; and the number of the men came to be about five thousand.

5 ¶ And it came about on the next day, that their rulers and elders and scribes were gathered together in Jerusalem;

6 and Annas the high priest *was there,* and Caiaphas and John and Alexander, and all who were of high-priestly descent.

7 And when they had placed them in the center, they *began to* inquire, "By what power, or in what name, have you done this?"

8 Then Peter, filled with the Holy Spirit, said to them, "Rulers and elders of the people,

9 if we are on trial today for a benefit done to a sick man, as to how this man has been made well,

10 let it be known to all of you, and to all the people of Israel, that by the name of Jesus Christ the Nazarene, whom you crucified, whom God raised from the dead—by this *name* this man stands here before you in good health.

11"He is the STONE WHICH WAS RE-JECTED by you, THE BUILDERS, *but* WHICH BECAME THE VERY CORNER *stone.*

12"And there is salvation in no one else; for there is no other name under heaven that has been given among men, by which we must be saved."

13 ¶ Now as they observed the confidence of Peter and John, and understood that they were uneducated and untrained men, they were marveling, and *began* to recognize them as having been with Jesus.

14 And seeing the man who had been healed standing with them, they had nothing to say in reply.

15 But when they had ordered them to go aside out of the Council, they *began* to confer with one another,

16 saying, "What shall we do with these men? For the fact that a noteworthy miracle has taken place through them is apparent to all who live in Jerusalem, and we cannot deny it.

17"But in order that it may not spread any further among the people, let us warn them to speak no more to any man in this name."

18 And when they had summoned them, they commanded them not to speak or teach at all in the name of Jesus.

19 But Peter and John answered and said to them, "Whether it is right in the sight of God to give heed to you rather than to God, you be the judge;

20 for we cannot stop speaking what we have seen and heard."

21 And when they had threatened them further, they let them go (finding no basis on which they might punish them) on account of the people, because they were all glorifying God for what had happened;

22 for the man was more than forty years old on whom this miracle of healing had been performed.

23 ¶ And when they had been released, they went to their own *companions,* and reported all that the chief priests and the elders had said to them.

24 And when they heard *this,* they lifted their voices to God with one accord and said, "O Lord, it is Thou who DIDST MAKE THE HEAVEN AND THE EARTH AND THE SEA, AND ALL THAT IS IN THEM,

25 who by the Holy Spirit, *through* the mouth of our father David Thy servant, didst say,

'WHY DID THE [9]GENTILES RAGE,
AND THE PEOPLES DEVISE FUTILE
THINGS?
26 'THE KINGS OF THE EARTH TOOK
THEIR STAND,
AND THE RULERS WERE GATHERED
TOGETHER
AGAINST THE LORD, AND AGAINST
HIS CHRIST.'

27"For truly in this city there were gathered together against Thy holy servant Jesus, whom Thou didst anoint, both Herod and Pontius Pilate, along with the Gentiles and the peoples of Israel,

28 to do whatever Thy hand and Thy purpose predestined to occur.

29"And now, Lord, take note of their threats, and grant that Thy bondservants may speak Thy word with all confidence,

30 while Thou dost extend Thy hand to heal, and signs and wonders take place through the name of Thy holy servant Jesus."

31 And when they had prayed, the place where they had gathered together was shaken, and they were all filled with the Holy Spirit, and *began* to speak the word of God with boldness.

32 ¶ And the congregation of those who believed were of one heart and soul; and not one *of them* claimed that anything belonging to him was his own; but all things were common property to them.

33 And with great power the apostles were giving witness to the resurrection of the Lord Jesus, and abundant grace was upon them all.

34 For there was not a needy person among them, for all who were owners of land or houses would sell them and bring the proceeds of the sales,

35 and lay them at the apostles' feet; and they would be distributed to each, as any had need.

[9] Or, *nations*

36 ¶ And Joseph, a Levite of Cyprian birth, who was also called Barnabas by the apostles (which translated means, Son of Encouragement),

37 and who owned a tract of land, sold it and brought the money and laid it at the apostles' feet.

CHAPTER 5

But a certain man named Ananias, with his wife Sapphira, sold a piece of property,

2 and kept back *some* of the price for himself, with his wife's full knowledge, and bringing a portion of it, he laid it at the apostles' feet.

3 But Peter said, "Ananias, why has Satan filled your heart to lie to the Holy Spirit, and to keep back *some* of the price of the land?

4"While it remained *unsold,* did it not remain your own? And after it was sold, was it not under your control? Why is it that you have conceived this deed in your heart? You have not lied to men, but to God."

5 And as he heard these words, Ananias fell down and breathed his last; and great fear came upon all who heard of it.

6 And the young men arose and covered him up, and after carrying him out, they buried him.

7 ¶ Now there elapsed an interval of about three hours, and his wife came in, not knowing what had happened.

8 And Peter responded to her, "Tell me whether you sold the land for such and such a price?" And she said, "Yes, that was the price."

9 Then Peter *said* to her, "Why is it that you have agreed together to put the Spirit of the Lord to the test? Behold, the feet of those who have buried your husband are at the door, and they shall carry you out *as well.*"

10 And she fell immediately at his feet, and breathed her last; and the young men came in and found her dead, and they carried her out and buried her beside her husband.

11 And great fear came upon the whole church, and upon all who heard of these things.

12 ¶ And at the hands of the apostles many signs and wonders were taking place among the people; and they

were all with one accord in Solomon's portico.

13 But none of the rest dared to associate with them; however, the people held them in high esteem.

14 And all the more believers in the Lord, multitudes of men and women, were constantly added to *their number*;

15 to such an extent that they even carried the sick out into the streets, and laid them on cots and pallets, so that when Peter came by, at least his shadow might fall on any one of them.

16 And also the people from the cities in the vicinity of Jerusalem were coming together, bringing people who were sick [10]or afflicted with unclean spirits; and they were all being healed.

17 ¶ But the high priest rose up, along with all his associates (that is the sect of the Sadducees), and they were filled with jealousy;

18 and they laid hands on the apostles, and put them in a public jail.

19 But an angel of the Lord during the night opened the gates of the prison, and taking them out he said,

20"Go your way, stand and speak to the people in the temple the whole message of this Life."

21 And upon hearing *this,* they entered into the temple about daybreak, and *began* to teach. Now when the high priest and his associates had come, they called the Council together, even all the Senate of the sons of Israel, and sent *orders* to the prison house for them to be brought.

22 But the officers who came did not find them in the prison; and they returned, and reported back,

23 saying, "We found the prison house locked quite securely and the guards standing at the doors; but when we had opened up, we found no one inside."

24 Now when the captain of the temple *guard* and the chief priests heard these words, they were greatly perplexed about them as to what would come of this.

25 But someone came and reported to them, "Behold, the men whom you put in prison are standing in the temple and teaching the people!"

26 Then the captain went along with

[10] Lit., *and*

the officers and *proceeded* to bring them *back* without violence (for they were afraid of the people, lest they should be stoned).

27 And when they had brought them, they stood them before the Council. And the high priest questioned them,

28 saying, "We gave you strict orders not to continue teaching in this name, and behold, you have filled Jerusalem with your teaching, and intend to bring this man's blood upon us."

29 But Peter and the apostles answered and said, "We must obey God rather than men.

30"The God of our fathers raised up Jesus, whom you had put to death by hanging Him on a cross.

31"He is the one whom God exalted to His right hand as a Prince and a Savior, to grant repentance to Israel, and forgiveness of sins.

32"And we are witnesses[11] of these things; and *so is* the Holy Spirit, whom God has given to those who obey Him."

33 ¶ But when they heard this, they were cut to the quick and were intending to slay them.

34 But a certain Pharisee named Gamaliel, a teacher of the Law, respected by all the people, stood up in the Council and gave orders to put the men outside for a short time.

35 And he said to them, "Men of Israel, take care what you propose to do with these men.

36"For some time ago Theudas rose up, claiming to be somebody; and a group of about four hundred men joined up with him. And he was slain; and all who followed him were dispersed and came to nothing.

37"After this man Judas of Galilee rose up in the days of the census, and drew away *some* people after him, he too perished, and all those who followed him were scattered.

38"And so in the present case, I say to you, stay away from these men and let them alone; for if this plan or action should be of men, it will be overthrown;

39 but if it is of God, you will not be able to overthrow them; or else you may even be found fighting against God."

40 And they took his advice; and after calling the apostles in, they flogged them and ordered them to speak no more in the name of Jesus, and *then* released them.

41 So they went on their way from the presence of the Council, rejoicing that they had been considered worthy to suffer shame for *His* name.

42 And every day, in the temple and from house to house, they kept right on teaching and preaching Jesus *as* the Christ.

CHAPTER 6

NOW at this time while the disciples were increasing *in number*, a complaint arose on the part of the [12]Hellenistic *Jews* against the *native* Hebrews, because their widows were being overlooked in the daily serving *of food*.

2 And the twelve summoned the congregation of the disciples and said, "It is not desirable for us to neglect the word of God in order to serve tables.

3"But select from among you, brethren, seven men of good reputation, full of the Spirit and of wisdom, whom we may put in charge of this task.

4"But we will devote ourselves to prayer, and to the ministry of the word."

5 And the statement found approval with the whole congregation; and they chose Stephen, a man full of faith and of the Holy Spirit, and Philip, Prochorus, Nicanor, Timon, Parmenas and Nicolas, a [13]proselyte from Antioch.

6 And these they brought before the apostles; and after praying, they laid their hands on them.

7 ¶ And the word of God kept on spreading; and the number of the disciples continued to increase greatly in Jerusalem, and a great many of the priests were becoming obedient to the faith.

8 ¶ And Stephen, full of grace and power, was performing great wonders and signs among the people.

9 But some men from what was

---

[11] Some mss. add *in Him,* or, *of Him*

[12] I.e., non-Palestinian Jews who normally spoke Greek
[13] I.e., a Gentile convert to Judaism

called the Synagogue of the Freedmen, *including* both Cyrenians and Alexandrians, and some from Cilicia and Asia, rose up and argued with Stephen.

10 And *yet* they were unable to cope with the wisdom and the Spirit with which he was speaking.

11 Then they secretly induced men to say, "We have heard him speak blasphemous words against Moses and *against* God."

12 And they stirred up the people, the elders and the scribes, and they came upon him and dragged him away, and brought him before the Council.

13 And they put forward false witnesses who said, "This man incessantly speaks against this holy place, and the Law;

14 for we have heard him say that this Nazarene, Jesus, will destroy this place and alter the customs which Moses handed down to us."

15 And fixing their gaze on him, all who were sitting in the Council saw his face like the face of an angel.

CHAPTER 7

AND the high priest said, "Are these things so?"

2 ¶ And he said, "Hear me, brethren and fathers! The God of glory appeared to our father Abraham when he was in Mesopotamia, before he lived in Haran,

3 and said to him, 'DEPART FROM YOUR COUNTRY AND YOUR RELATIVES, AND COME INTO THE LAND THAT I WILL SHOW YOU.'

4"Then he departed from the land of the Chaldeans, and settled in Haran. And from there, after his father died, *God* removed him into this country in which you are now living.

5"And He gave him no inheritance in it, not even a foot of ground; and *yet*, even when he had no child, He promised that HE WOULD GIVE IT TO HIM AS A POSSESSION, AND TO HIS OFFSPRING AFTER HIM.

6"But God spoke to this effect, that his OFFSPRING WOULD BE ALIENS IN A FOREIGN LAND, AND THAT THEY WOULD BE ENSLAVED AND MISTREATED FOR FOUR HUNDRED YEARS.

7" 'AND WHATEVER NATION TO

WHICH THEY SHALL BE IN BONDAGE I MYSELF WILL JUDGE,' said God, 'AND AFTER THAT THEY WILL COME OUT AND [14]SERVE ME IN THIS PLACE.'

8"And He gave him the covenant of circumcision; and so *Abraham* became the father of Isaac, and circumcised him on the eighth day; and Isaac *became the father of* Jacob, and Jacob *of* the twelve patriarchs.

9"And the patriarchs became jealous of Joseph and sold him into Egypt. And *yet* God was with him,

10 and rescued him from all his afflictions, and granted him favor and wisdom in the sight of Pharaoh, king of Egypt; and he made him governor over Egypt and all his household.

11"Now a famine came over all Egypt and Canaan, and great affliction *with it;* and our fathers could find no food.

12"But when Jacob heard that there was grain in Egypt, he sent our fathers *there* the first time.

13"And on the second *visit* Joseph made himself known to his brothers, and Joseph's family was disclosed to Pharaoh.

14"And Joseph sent *word* and invited Jacob his father and all his relatives to come to him, seventy-five persons *in all.*

15"And Jacob went down to Egypt and *there* passed away, he and our fathers.

16"And *from there* they were removed to Shechem, and laid in the tomb which Abraham had purchased for a sum of money from the sons of Hamor in Shechem.

17"But as the time of the promise was approaching which God had assured to Abraham, the people increased and multiplied in Egypt,

18 until THERE AROSE ANOTHER KING OVER EGYPT WHO KNEW NOTHING ABOUT JOSEPH.

19"It was he who took shrewd advantage of our race, and mistreated our fathers so that they would expose their infants and they would not survive.

20"And it was at this time that Moses was born; and he was lovely in the sight of God; and he was nurtured three months in his father's home.

21"And after he had been exposed,

[14] Or, *worship*

Pharaoh's daughter took him away, and nurtured him as her own son.

22"And Moses was educated in all the learning of the Egyptians, and he was a man of power in words and deeds.

23"But when he was approaching the age of forty, it entered his mind to visit his brethren, the sons of Israel.

24"And when he saw one *of them* being treated unjustly, he defended him and took vengeance for the oppressed by striking down the Egyptian.

25"And he supposed that his brethren understood that God was granting them deliverance through him; but they did not understand.

26"And on the following day he appeared to them as they were fighting together, and he tried to reconcile them in peace, saying, 'Men, you are brethren, why do you injure one another?'

27"But the one who was injuring his neighbor pushed him away, saying, 'WHO MADE YOU A RULER AND JUDGE OVER US?

28 'YOU DO NOT MEAN TO KILL ME AS YOU KILLED THE EGYPTIAN YESTERDAY, DO YOU?'

29"And at this remark MOSES FLED, AND BECAME AN ALIEN IN THE LAND OF MIDIAN, where he became the father of two sons.

30"And after forty years had passed, AN ANGEL APPEARED TO HIM IN THE WILDERNESS OF MOUNT Sinai, IN THE FLAME OF A BURNING THORN BUSH.

31"And when Moses saw it, he *began* to marvel at the sight; and as he approached to look *more* closely, there came the voice of the Lord:

32 'I AM THE GOD OF YOUR FATHERS, THE GOD OF ABRAHAM AND ISAAC AND JACOB.' And Moses shook with fear and would not venture to look.

33"BUT THE LORD SAID TO HIM, 'TAKE OFF THE SANDALS FROM YOUR FEET, FOR THE PLACE ON WHICH YOU ARE STANDING IS HOLY GROUND.

34 'I HAVE CERTAINLY SEEN THE OPPRESSION OF MY PEOPLE IN EGYPT, AND HAVE HEARD THEIR GROANS, AND I HAVE COME DOWN TO DELIVER THEM; COME NOW, AND I WILL SEND YOU TO EGYPT.'

35"This Moses whom they disowned, saying, 'WHO MADE YOU A RULER AND A JUDGE?' is the one whom God sent *to be* both a ruler and a deliverer with the help of the angel who appeared to him in the thorn bush.

36"This man led them out, performing wonders and signs in the land of Egypt and in the Red Sea and in the wilderness for forty years.

37"This is the Moses who said to the sons of Israel, 'GOD SHALL RAISE UP FOR YOU A PROPHET LIKE ME FROM YOUR BRETHREN.'

38"This is the one who was in the congregation in the wilderness together with the angel who was speaking to him on Mount Sinai, and *who was* with our fathers; and he received living oracles to pass on to you.

39"And our fathers were unwilling to be obedient to him, but repudiated him and in their hearts turned back to Egypt,

40 SAYING TO AARON, 'MAKE FOR US GODS WHO WILL GO BEFORE US; FOR THIS MOSES WHO LED US OUT OF THE LAND OF EGYPT—WE DO NOT KNOW WHAT HAPPENED TO HIM.'

41"And at that time they made a calf and brought a sacrifice to the idol, and were rejoicing in the works of their hands.

42"But God turned away and delivered them up to serve the host of heaven; as it is written in the book of the prophets, 'IT WAS NOT TO ME THAT YOU OFFERED VICTIMS AND SACRIFICES FORTY YEARS IN THE WILDERNESS, WAS IT, O HOUSE OF ISRAEL?

43 'YOU ALSO TOOK ALONG THE TABERNACLE OF MOLOCH AND THE STAR OF THE GOD ROMPHA, THE IMAGES WHICH YOU MADE TO WORSHIP THEM. I ALSO WILL REMOVE YOU BEYOND BABYLON.'

44"Our fathers had the tabernacle of testimony in the wilderness, just as He who spoke to Moses directed *him* to make it according to the pattern which he had seen.

45"And having received it in their turn, our fathers brought it in with Joshua upon dispossessing the nations whom God drove out before our fathers, until the time of David.

46"And *David* found favor in God's sight, and asked that he might find a dwelling place for the [15]God of Jacob.

[15] The earliest mss. read *house* instead of *God*; the Septuagint reads *God*

47"But it was Solomon who built a house for Him.

48"However, the Most High does not dwell in *houses* made by *human* hands; as the prophet says:

49 'HEAVEN IS MY THRONE,
AND EARTH IS THE FOOTSTOOL OF
MY FEET;
WHAT KIND OF HOUSE WILL YOU
BUILD FOR ME?' says the Lord;
'OR WHAT PLACE IS THERE FOR MY
REPOSE?

50 'WAS IT NOT MY HAND WHICH
MADE ALL THESE THINGS?'

51 ¶"You men who are stiff-necked and uncircumcised in heart and ears are always resisting the Holy Spirit; you are doing just as your fathers did.

52"Which one of the prophets did your fathers not persecute? And they killed those who had previously announced the coming of the Righteous One, whose betrayers and murderers you have now become;

53 you who received the law as ordained by angels, and *yet* did not keep it."

54 ¶ Now when they heard this, they were cut to the quick, and they *began* gnashing their teeth at him.

55 But being full of the Holy Spirit, he gazed intently into heaven and saw the glory of God, and Jesus standing at the right hand of God;

56 and he said, "Behold, I see the heavens opened up and the Son of Man standing at the right hand of God."

57 But they cried out with a loud voice, and covered their ears, and they rushed upon him with one impulse.

58 And when they had driven him out of the city, they *began* stoning *him,* and the witnesses laid aside their robes at the feet of a young man named Saul.

59 And they went on stoning Stephen as he called upon *the Lord* and said, "Lord Jesus, receive my spirit!"

60 And falling on his knees, he cried out with a loud voice, "Lord, do not hold this sin against them!" And having said this, he fell asleep.

CHAPTER 8

AND Saul was in hearty agreement with putting him to death.

¶ And on that day a great persecution arose against the church in Jerusalem; and they were all scattered throughout the regions of Judea and Samaria, except the apostles.

2 And *some* devout men buried Stephen, and made loud lamentation over him.

3 But Saul *began* ravaging the church, entering house after house; and dragging off men and women, he would put them in prison.

4 ¶ Therefore, those who had been scattered went about preaching the word.

5 And Philip went down to the city of Samaria and *began* proclaiming Christ to them.

6 And the multitudes with one accord were giving attention to what was said by Philip, as they heard and saw the signs which he was performing.

7 For *in the case of* many who had unclean spirits, they were coming out *of them* shouting with a loud voice; and many who had been paralyzed and lame were healed.

8 And there was much rejoicing in that city.

9 ¶ Now there was a certain man named Simon, who formerly was practicing magic in the city, and astonishing the people of Samaria, claiming to be someone great;

10 and they all, from smallest to greatest, were giving attention to him, saying, "This man is what is called the Great Power of God."

11 And they were giving him attention because he had for a long time astonished them with his magic arts.

12 But when they believed Philip preaching the good news about the kingdom of God and the name of Jesus Christ, they were being baptized, men and women alike.

13 And even Simon himself believed; and after being baptized, he continued on with Philip; and as he observed signs and great miracles taking place, he was constantly amazed.

14 ¶ Now when the apostles in Jerusalem heard that Samaria had received the word of God, they sent them Peter and John,

15 who came down and prayed for them, that they might receive the Holy Spirit.

16 For He had not yet fallen upon any of them; they had simply been baptized in the name of the Lord Jesus.

17 Then they *began* laying their hands on them, and they were receiving the Holy Spirit.

18 Now when Simon saw that the Spirit was bestowed through the laying on of the apostles' hands, he offered them money,

19 saying, "Give this authority to me as well, so that everyone on whom I lay my hands may receive the Holy Spirit."

20 But Peter said to him, "May your silver perish with you, because you thought you could obtain the gift of God with money!

21 "You have no part or portion in this matter, for your heart is not right before God.

22 "Therefore repent of this wickedness of yours, and pray the Lord that if possible, the intention of your heart may be forgiven you.

23 "For I see that you are in the gall of bitterness and in the bondage of iniquity."

24 But Simon answered and said, "Pray to the Lord for me yourselves, so that nothing of what you have said may come upon me."

25 ¶ And so, when they had solemnly testified and spoken the word of the Lord, they started back to Jerusalem, and were preaching the gospel to many villages of the Samaritans.

26 ¶ But an angel of the Lord spoke to Philip saying, "Arise and go south to the road that descends from Jerusalem to Gaza." (This is a desert *road.*)

27 And he arose and went; and behold, there was an Ethiopian eunuch, a court official of Candace, queen of the Ethiopians, who was in charge of all her treasure; and he had come to Jerusalem to worship.

28 And he was returning and sitting in his chariot, and was reading the prophet Isaiah.

29 And the Spirit said to Philip, "Go up and join this chariot."

30 And when Philip had run up, he heard him reading Isaiah the prophet, and said, "Do you understand what you are reading?"

31 And he said, "Well, how could I, unless someone guides me?" And he invited Philip to come up and sit with him.

32 Now the passage of Scripture which he was reading was this:

"HE WAS LED AS A SHEEP TO
    SLAUGHTER;
AND AS A LAMB BEFORE ITS
    SHEARER IS SILENT,
SO HE DOES NOT OPEN HIS
    MOUTH.

33 "IN HUMILIATION HIS JUDGMENT
    WAS TAKEN AWAY;
WHO SHALL RELATE HIS GENERA-
    TION?
FOR HIS LIFE IS REMOVED FROM
    THE EARTH."

34 And the eunuch answered Philip and said, "Please *tell me*, of whom does the prophet say this? Of himself, or of someone else?"

35 And Philip opened his mouth, and beginning from this Scripture he preached Jesus to him.

36 And as they went along the road they came to some water; and the eunuch *said, "Look! Water! What prevents me from being baptized?"

37 [¹⁶And Philip said, "If you believe with all your heart, you may." And he answered and said, "I believe that Jesus Christ is the Son of God."]

38 And he ordered the chariot to stop; and they both went down into the water, Philip as well as the eunuch; and he baptized him.

39 And when they came up out of the water, the Spirit of the Lord snatched Philip away; and the eunuch saw him no more, but went on his way rejoicing.

40 But Philip found himself at Azotus; and as he passed through he kept preaching the gospel to all the cities, until he came to Caesarea.

CHAPTER 9

NOW Saul, still breathing threats and murder against the disciples of the Lord, went to the high priest,

2 and asked for letters from him to the synagogues at Damascus, so that if he found any belonging to the Way, both men and women, he might bring them bound to Jerusalem.

3 And it came about that as he journeyed, he was approaching

---

¹⁶ Many mss. do not contain this verse

Damascus, and suddenly a light from heaven flashed around him;

4 and he fell to the ground, and heard a voice saying to him, "Saul, Saul, why are you persecuting Me?"

5 And he said, "Who art Thou, Lord?" And He *said*, "I am Jesus whom you are persecuting,

6 but rise, and enter the city, and it shall be told you what you must do."

7 And the men who traveled with him stood speechless, hearing the voice, but seeing no one.

8 And Saul got up from the ground, and though his eyes were open, he could see nothing; and leading him by the hand, they brought him into Damascus.

9 And he was three days without sight, and neither ate nor drank.

10 ¶ Now there was a certain disciple at Damascus, named Ananias; and the Lord said to him in a vision, "Ananias." And he said, "Behold, *here am* I, Lord."

11 And the Lord *said* to him, "Arise and go to the street called Straight, and inquire at the house of Judas for a man from Tarsus named Saul, for behold, he is praying,

12 and he has seen [17]in a vision a man named Ananias come in and lay his hands on him, so that he might regain his sight."

13 But Ananias answered, "Lord, I have heard from many about this man, how much harm he did to Thy saints at Jerusalem;

14 and here he has authority from the chief priests to bind all who call upon Thy name."

15 But the Lord said to him, "Go, for he is a chosen [18]instrument of Mine, to bear My name before the Gentiles and kings and the sons of Israel;

16 for I will show him how much he must suffer for My name's sake."

17 And Ananias departed and entered the house, and after laying his hands on him said, "Brother Saul, the Lord Jesus, who appeared to you on the road by which you were coming, has sent me so that you may regain your sight, and be filled with the Holy Spirit."

18 And immediately there fell from his eyes something like scales, and he regained his sight, and he arose and was baptized;

19 and he took food and was strengthened.

¶ Now for several days he was with the disciples who were at Damascus,

20 and immediately he *began* to proclaim Jesus in the synagogues, saying, "He is the Son of God."

21 And all those hearing him continued to be amazed, and were saying, "Is this not he who in Jerusalem destroyed those who called on this name, and *who* had come here for the purpose of bringing them bound before the chief priests?"

22 But Saul kept increasing in strength and confounding the Jews who lived at Damascus by proving that this *Jesus* is the Christ.

23 ¶ And when many days had elapsed, the Jews plotted together to do away with him,

24 but their plot became known to Saul. And they were also watching the gates day and night so that they might put him to death;

25 but his disciples took him by night, and let him down through *an opening in* the wall, lowering him in a large basket.

26 ¶ And when he had come to Jerusalem, he was trying to associate with the disciples; and they were all afraid of him, not believing that he was a disciple.

27 But Barnabas took hold of him and brought him to the apostles and described to them how he had seen the Lord on the road, and that He had talked to him, and how at Damascus he had spoken out boldly in the name of Jesus.

28 And he was with them moving about freely in Jerusalem, speaking out boldly in the name of the Lord.

29 And he was talking and arguing with the Hellenistic *Jews*; but they were attempting to put him to death.

30 But when the brethren learned *of it*, they brought him down to Caesarea and sent him away to Tarsus.

31 ¶ So the church throughout all Judea and Galilee and Samaria enjoyed peace, being built up; and, going on in the fear of the Lord and in the comfort of the Holy Spirit, it continued to increase.

[17] Some mss. do not contain *in a vision* [18] Or, *vessel*

32 ¶ Now it came about that as Peter was traveling through all *those parts,* he came down also to the saints who lived at Lydda.

33 And there he found a certain man named Aeneas, who had been bedridden eight years, for he was paralyzed.

34 And Peter said to him, "Aeneas, Jesus Christ heals you; arise, and make your bed." And immediately he arose.

35 And all who lived at Lydda and Sharon saw him, and they turned to the Lord.

36 ¶ Now in Joppa there was a certain disciple named Tabitha (which translated *in Greek* is called Dorcas); this woman was abounding with deeds of kindness and charity, which she continually did.

37 And it came about at that time that she fell sick and died; and when they had washed her body, they laid it in an upper room.

38 And since Lydda was near Joppa, the disciples, having heard that Peter was there, sent two men to him, entreating him, "Do not delay to come to us."

39 And Peter arose and went with them. And when he had come, they brought him into the upper room; and all the widows stood beside him weeping, and showing all the [19]tunics and garments that Dorcas used to make while she was with them.

40 But Peter sent them all out and knelt down and prayed, and turning to the body, he said, "Tabitha, arise." And she opened her eyes, and when she saw Peter, she sat up.

41 And he gave her his hand and raised her up; and calling the saints and widows, he presented her alive.

42 And it became known all over Joppa, and many believed in the Lord.

43 And it came about that he stayed many days in Joppa with a certain tanner, Simon.

CHAPTER 10

NOW *there was* a certain man at Caesarea named Cornelius, a centurion of what was called the Italian [20]cohort,

2 a devout man, and one who feared God with all his household, and gave many [21]alms to the *Jewish* people, and prayed to God continually.

3 About the [22]ninth hour of the day he clearly saw in a vision an angel of God who had *just* come in to him, and said to him, "Cornelius!"

4 And fixing his gaze upon him and being much alarmed, he said, "What is it, Lord?" And he said to him, "Your prayers and [23]alms have ascended as a memorial before God.

5 "And now dispatch *some* men to Joppa, and send for a man *named* Simon, who is also called Peter;

6 he is staying with a certain tanner *named* Simon, whose house is by the sea."

7 And when the angel who was speaking to him had departed, he summoned two of his servants and a devout soldier of those who were in constant attendance upon him,

8 and after he had explained everything to them, he sent them to Joppa.

9 ¶ And on the next day, as they were on their way, and approaching the city, Peter went up on the housetop about the [24]sixth hour to pray.

10 And he became hungry, and was desiring to eat; but while they were making preparations, he fell into a trance;

11 and he *beheld the sky opened up, and a certain [25]object like a great sheet coming down, lowered by four corners to the ground,

12 and there were in it all *kinds of* four-footed animals and [26]crawling creatures of the earth and birds of the air.

13 And a voice came to him, "Arise, Peter, kill and eat!"

14 But Peter said, "By no means, Lord, for I have never eaten anything unholy and unclean."

15 And again a voice *came* to him a second time, "What God has cleansed, no *longer* consider unholy."

16 And this happened three times; and immediately the object was taken up into the sky.

17 ¶ Now while Peter was greatly perplexed in mind as to what the vision which he had seen might be, behold, the men who had been sent by

[19] Or, *inner garments* [20] Or, *battalion*

[21] Or, *gifts of charity* [22] I.e., 3 p.m.
[23] Or, *deeds of charity* [24] I.e., noon
[25] Or, *vessel* [26] Or possibly, *reptiles*

Cornelius, having asked directions for Simon's house, appeared at the gate;

18 and calling out, they were asking whether Simon, who was also called Peter, was staying there.

19 And while Peter was reflecting on the vision, the Spirit said to him, "Behold, three men are looking for you.

20 "But arise, go downstairs, and accompany them without misgivings; for I have sent them Myself."

21 And Peter went down to the men and said, "Behold, I am the one you are looking for; what is the reason for which you have come?"

22 And they said, "Cornelius, a centurion, a righteous and God-fearing man well spoken of by the entire nation of the Jews, was *divinely* directed by a holy angel to send for you *to come* to his house and hear a message from you."

23 And so he invited them in and gave them lodging.

¶ And on the next day he arose and went away with them, and some of the brethren from Joppa accompanied him.

24 And on the following day he entered Caesarea. Now Cornelius was waiting for them, and had called together his relatives and close friends.

25 And when it came about that Peter entered, Cornelius met him, and fell at his feet and worshiped *him.*

26 But Peter raised him up, saying, "Stand up; I too am *just* a man."

27 And as he talked with him, he entered, and found many people assembled.

28 And he said to them, "You yourselves know how unlawful it is for a man who is a Jew to associate with a foreigner or to visit him; and *yet* God has shown me that I should not call any man unholy or unclean.

29 "That is why I came without even raising any objection when I was sent for. And so I ask for what reason you have sent for me."

30 And Cornelius said, "Four days ago to this hour, I was praying in my house during the [27]ninth hour; and behold, a man stood before me in shining garments,

31 and he *said, 'Cornelius, your

[27] I.e., 3 to 4 p.m.

prayer has been heard and your alms have been remembered before God.

32 'Send therefore to Joppa and invite Simon, who is also called Peter, to come to you; he is staying at the house of Simon *the* tanner by the sea.'

33 "And so I sent to you immediately, and you have been kind enough to come. Now then, we are all here present before God to hear all that you have been commanded by the Lord."

34 And opening his mouth, Peter said:

¶ "I most certainly understand *now* that God is not one to show partiality,

35 but in every nation the man who fears Him and does what is right, is welcome to Him.

36 "The word which He sent to the sons of Israel, preaching peace through Jesus Christ (He is Lord of all)—

37 you yourselves know the thing which took place throughout all Judea, starting from Galilee, after the baptism which John proclaimed.

38 "*You know of* Jesus of Nazareth, how God anointed Him with the Holy Spirit and with power, and *how* He went about doing good, and healing all who were oppressed by the devil; for God was with Him.

39 "And we are witnesses of all the things He did both in the land of the Jews and in Jerusalem. And they also put Him to death by hanging Him on a cross.

40 "God raised Him up on the third day, and granted that He should become visible,

41 not to all the people, but to witnesses who were chosen beforehand by God, *that is,* to us, who ate and drank with Him after He arose from the dead.

42 "And He ordered us to preach to the people, and solemnly to testify that this is the One who has been appointed by God as Judge of the living and the dead.

43 "Of Him all the prophets bear witness that through His name everyone who believes in Him receives forgiveness of sins."

44 ¶ While Peter was still speaking these words, the Holy Spirit fell upon all those who were listening to the message.

45 And all the circumcised believers who had come with Peter were amazed, because the gift of the Holy Spirit had been poured out upon the Gentiles also.

46 For they were hearing them speaking with tongues and exalting God. Then Peter answered,

47"Surely no one can refuse the water for these to be baptized who have received the Holy Spirit just as we *did,* can he?"

48 And he ordered them to be baptized in the name of Jesus Christ. Then they asked him to stay on for a few days.

CHAPTER 11

NOW the apostles and the brethren who were throughout Judea heard that the Gentiles also had received the word of God.

2 And when Peter came up to Jerusalem, those who were circumcised took issue with him,

3 saying, "You went to uncircumcised men and ate with them."

4 But Peter began *speaking* and *proceeded* to explain to them in orderly sequence, saying,

5"I was in the city of Joppa praying; and in a trance I saw a vision, a certain object coming down like a great sheet lowered by four corners from the sky; and it came right down to me,

6 and when I had fixed my gaze upon it and was observing it I saw the four-footed animals of the earth and the wild beasts and the [28]crawling creatures and the birds of the air.

7"And I also heard a voice saying to me, 'Arise, Peter; kill and eat.'

8"But I said, 'By no means, Lord, for nothing unholy or unclean has ever entered my mouth.'

9"But a voice from heaven answered a second time, 'What God has cleansed, no longer consider unholy.'

10"And this happened three times, and everything was drawn back up into the sky.

11"And behold, at that moment three men appeared before the house in which we were *staying,* having been sent to me from Caesarea.

12"And the Spirit told me to go with them without misgivings. And these six brethren also went with me, and we entered the man's house.

13"And he reported to us how he had seen the angel standing in his house, and saying, 'Send to Joppa, and have Simon, who is also called Peter, brought here;

14 and he shall speak words to you by which you will be saved, you and all your household.'

15"And as I began to speak, the Holy Spirit fell upon them, just as *He did* upon us at the beginning.

16"And I remembered the word of the Lord, how He used to say, 'John baptized with water, but you shall be baptized with the Holy Spirit.'

17"If God therefore gave to them the same gift as *He gave* to us also after believing in the Lord Jesus Christ, who was I that I could stand in God's way?"

18 And when they heard this, they quieted down, and glorified God, saying, "Well then, God has granted to the Gentiles also the repentance *that leads* to life."

19 ¶ So then those who were scattered because of the persecution that arose in connection with Stephen made their way to Phoenicia and Cyprus and Antioch, speaking the word to no one except to Jews alone.

20 But there were some of them, men of Cyprus and Cyrene, who came to Antioch and *began* speaking to the [29]Greeks also, preaching the Lord Jesus.

21 And the hand of the Lord was with them, and a large number who believed turned to the Lord.

22 And the news about them reached the ears of the church at Jerusalem, and they sent Barnabas off to Antioch.

23 Then when he had come and witnessed the grace of God, he rejoiced and *began* to encourage them all with resolute heart to remain *true* to the Lord;

24 for he was a good man, and full of the Holy Spirit and of faith. And considerable numbers were brought to the Lord.

25 And he left for Tarsus to look for Saul;

26 and when he had found him, he

---

[28] Or possibly, *reptiles*   [29] Some mss. read *Greek-speaking Jews*

brought him to Antioch. And it came about that for an entire year they met with the church, and taught considerable numbers; and the disciples were first called Christians in Antioch.

27 ¶ Now at this time some prophets came down from Jerusalem to Antioch.

28 And one of them named Agabus stood up and *began* to indicate by the Spirit that there would certainly be a great famine all over the world. And this took place in the *reign* of Claudius.

29 And in the proportion that any of the disciples had means, each of them determined to send *a contribution* for the relief of the brethren living in Judea.

30 And this they did, sending it in charge of Barnabas and Saul to the elders.

CHAPTER 12

NOW about that time Herod the king laid hands on some who belonged to the church, in order to mistreat them.

2 And he had James the brother of John put to death with a sword.

3 And when he saw that it pleased the Jews, he proceeded to arrest Peter also. Now it was during the days of Unleavened Bread.

4 And when he had seized him, he put him in prison, delivering him to four squads of soldiers to guard him, intending after the Passover to bring him out before the people.

5 So Peter was kept in the prison, but prayer for him was being made fervently by the church to God.

6 And on the very night when Herod was about to bring him forward, Peter was sleeping between two soldiers, bound with two chains; and guards in front of the door were watching over the prison.

7 And behold, an angel of the Lord suddenly appeared, and a light shone in the cell; and he struck Peter's side and roused him, saying, "Get up quickly." And his chains fell off his hands.

8 And the angel said to him, "Gird yourself and put on your sandals." And he did so. And he *said to him, "Wrap your cloak around you and follow me."

9 And he went out and continued to follow, and he did not know that what was being done by the angel was real, but thought he was seeing a vision.

10 And when they had passed the first and second guard, they came to the iron gate that leads into the city, which opened for them by itself; and they went out and went along one street; and immediately the angel departed from him.

11 And when Peter came to himself, he said, "Now I know for sure that the Lord has sent forth His angel and rescued me from the hand of Herod and from all that the Jewish people were expecting."

12 And when he realized *this,* he went to the house of Mary, the mother of John who was also called Mark, where many were gathered together and were praying.

13 And when he knocked at the door of the gate, a servant-girl named Rhoda came to answer.

14 And when she recognized Peter's voice, because of her joy she did not open the gate, but ran in and announced that Peter was standing in front of the gate.

15 And they said to her, "You are out of your mind!" But she kept insisting that it was so. And they kept saying, "It is his angel."

16 But Peter continued knocking; and when they had opened *the door,* they saw him and were amazed.

17 But motioning to them with his hand to be silent, he described to them how the Lord had led him out of the prison. And he said, "Report these things to James and the brethren." And he departed and went to another place.

18 ¶ Now when day came, there was no small disturbance among the soldiers *as to* what could have become of Peter.

19 And when Herod had searched for him and had not found him, he examined the guards and ordered that they be led away *to execution.* And he went down from Judea to Caesarea and was spending time there.

20 ¶ Now he was very angry with the people of Tyre and Sidon; and with one accord they came to him, and having won over Blastus the king's

chamberlain, they were asking for peace, because their country was fed by the king's country.

21 And on an appointed day Herod, having put on his royal apparel, took his seat on the rostrum and *began* delivering an address to them.

22 And the people kept crying out, "The voice of a god and not of a man!"

23 And immediately an angel of the Lord struck him because he did not give God the glory, and he was eaten by worms and died.

24 ¶ But the word of the Lord continued to grow and to be multiplied.

25 ¶ And Barnabas and Saul returned from Jerusalem when they had fulfilled their mission, taking along with *them* John, who was also called Mark.

CHAPTER 13

NOW there were at Antioch, in the church that was *there,* prophets and teachers: Barnabas, and Simeon who was called Niger, and Lucius of Cyrene, and Manaen who had been brought up with Herod the tetrarch, and Saul.

2 And while they were ministering to the Lord and fasting, the Holy Spirit said, "Set apart for Me Barnabas and Saul for the work to which I have called them."

3 Then, when they had fasted and prayed and laid their hands on them, they sent them away.

4 ¶ So, being sent out by the Holy Spirit, they went down to Seleucia and from there they sailed to Cyprus.

5 And when they reached Salamis, they *began* to proclaim the word of God in the synagogues of the Jews; and they also had John as their helper.

6 And when they had gone through the whole island as far as Paphos, they found a certain magician, a Jewish false prophet whose name was Bar-Jesus,

7 who was with the proconsul, Sergius Paulus, a man of intelligence. This man summoned Barnabas and Saul and sought to hear the word of God.

8 But Elymas the magician (for thus his name is translated) was opposing them, seeking to turn the proconsul away from the faith.

9 But Saul, who was also *known as* Paul, filled with the Holy Spirit, fixed his gaze upon him,

10 and said, "You who are full of all deceit and fraud, you son of the devil, you enemy of all righteousness, will you not cease to make crooked the straight ways of the Lord?

11 "And now, behold, the hand of the Lord is upon you, and you will be blind and not see the sun for a time." And immediately a mist and a darkness fell upon him, and he went about seeking those who would lead him by the hand.

12 Then the proconsul believed when he saw what had happened, being amazed at the teaching of the Lord.

13 ¶ Now Paul and his companions put out to sea from Paphos and came to Perga in Pamphylia; and John left them and returned to Jerusalem.

14 But going on from Perga, they arrived at Pisidian Antioch, and on the Sabbath day they went into the synagogue and sat down.

15 And after the reading of the Law and the Prophets the synagogue officials sent to them, saying, "Brethren, if you have any word of exhortation for the people, say it."

16 And Paul stood up, and motioning with his hand, he said,

¶ "Men of Israel, and you who fear God, listen:

17 "The God of this people Israel chose our fathers, and made the people great during their stay in the land of Egypt, and with an uplifted arm He led them out from it.

18 "And for a period of about forty years He put up with them in the wilderness.

19 "And when He had destroyed seven nations in the land of Canaan, He distributed their land as an inheritance—*all of which took* about four hundred and fifty years.

20 "And after these things He gave *them* judges until Samuel the prophet.

21 "And then they asked for a king, and God gave them Saul the son of Kish, a man of the tribe of Benjamin, for forty years.

22 "And after He had removed him, He raised up David to be their king, concerning whom He also testified and said, 'I HAVE FOUND DAVID the son of Jesse, A MAN AFTER MY HEART, who will do all My will.'

23"From the offspring of this man, according to promise, God has brought to Israel a Savior, Jesus,

24 after John had proclaimed before His coming a baptism of repentance to all the people of Israel.

25"And while John was completing his course, he kept saying, 'What do you suppose that I am? I am not *He*. But behold, one is coming after me the sandals of whose feet I am not worthy to untie.'

26"Brethren, sons of Abraham's family, and those among you who fear God, to us the word of this salvation is sent out.

27"For those who live in Jerusalem, and their rulers, recognizing neither Him nor the utterances of the prophets which are read every Sabbath, fulfilled *these* by condemning *Him*.

28"And though they found no ground for *putting Him to* death, they asked Pilate that He be executed.

29"And when they had carried out all that was written concerning Him, they took Him down from the cross and laid Him in a tomb.

30"But God raised Him from the dead;

31 and for many days He appeared to those who came up with Him from Galilee to Jerusalem, the very ones who are now His witnesses to the people.

32"And we preach to you the good news of the promise made to the fathers,

33 that God has fulfilled this *promise* to our children in that He raised up Jesus, as it is also written in the second Psalm, 'THOU ART MY SON; TODAY I HAVE BEGOTTEN THEE.'

34"*And as for the fact* that He raised Him up from the dead, no more to return to decay, He has spoken in this way: 'I WILL GIVE YOU THE HOLY *and* SURE *blessings* OF DAVID.'

35"Therefore He also says in another *Psalm*, 'THOU WILT NOT ALLOW THY HOLY ONE TO UNDERGO DECAY.'

36"For David, after he had served the purpose of God in his own generation, fell asleep, and was laid among his fathers, and underwent decay;

37 but He whom God raised did not undergo decay.

38"Therefore let it be known to you, brethren, that through Him forgiveness of sins is proclaimed to you,

39 and through Him everyone who believes is freed from all things, from which you could not be freed through the Law of Moses.

40"Take heed therefore, so that the thing spoken of in the Prophets may not come upon *you*:

41 'BEHOLD, YOU SCOFFERS, AND MAR-VEL, AND PERISH;

FOR I AM ACCOMPLISHING A WORK IN YOUR DAYS,

A WORK WHICH YOU WILL NEVER BELIEVE, THOUGH SOMEONE SHOULD DESCRIBE IT TO YOU.' "

42 ¶ And as Paul and Barnabas were going out, the people kept begging that these things might be spoken to them the next Sabbath.

43 Now when *the meeting of* the synagogue had broken up, many of the Jews and of the God-fearing proselytes followed Paul and Barnabas, who, speaking to them, were urging them to continue in the grace of God.

44 ¶ And the next Sabbath nearly the whole city assembled to hear the word of God.

45 But when the Jews saw the crowds, they were filled with jealousy, and *began* contradicting the things spoken by Paul, and were blaspheming.

46 And Paul and Barnabas spoke out boldly and said, "It was necessary that the word of God should be spoken to you first; since you repudiate it, and judge yourselves unworthy of eternal life, behold, we are turning to the Gentiles.

47"For thus the Lord has commanded us,

'I HAVE PLACED YOU AS A LIGHT FOR THE GENTILES,

THAT YOU SHOULD BRING SALVA-TION TO THE END OF THE EARTH.' "

48 And when the Gentiles heard this, they *began* rejoicing and glorifying the word of the Lord; and as many as had been appointed to eternal life believed.

49 And the word of the Lord was being spread through the whole region.

50 But the Jews aroused the devout women of prominence and the leading

men of the city, and instigated a persecution against Paul and Barnabas, and drove them out of their district.

51 But they shook off the dust of their feet *in protest* against them and went to Iconium.

52 And the disciples were continually filled with joy and with the Holy Spirit.

CHAPTER 14

AND it came about that in Iconium they entered the synagogue of the Jews together, and spoke in such a manner that a great multitude believed, both of Jews and of Greeks.

2 But the Jews who disbelieved stirred up the minds of the Gentiles, and embittered them against the brethren.

3 Therefore they spent a long time *there* speaking boldly *with reliance* upon the Lord, who was bearing witness to the word of His grace, granting that signs and wonders be done by their hands.

4 But the multitude of the city was divided; and some sided with the Jews, and some with the apostles.

5 And when an attempt was made by both the Gentiles and the Jews with their rulers, to mistreat and to stone them,

6 they became aware of it and fled to the cities of Lycaonia, Lystra and Derbe, and the surrounding region;

7 and there they continued to preach the gospel.

8 ¶ And at Lystra there was sitting a certain man, without strength in his feet, lame from his mother's womb, who had never walked.

9 This man was listening to Paul as he spoke, who, when he had fixed his gaze upon him, and had seen that he had faith to be made well,

10 said with a loud voice, "Stand upright on your feet." And he leaped up and *began* to walk.

11 And when the multitudes saw what Paul had done, they raised their voice, saying in the Lycaonian language, "The gods have become like men and have come down to us."

12 And they *began* calling Barnabas, Zeus, and Paul, Hermes, because he was the chief speaker.

13 And the priest of Zeus, whose *temple* was just outside the city, brought oxen and garlands to the gates, and wanted to offer sacrifice with the crowds.

14 But when the apostles, Barnabas and Paul, heard of it, they tore their robes and rushed out into the crowd, crying out

15 and saying, "Men, why are you doing these things? We are also men of the same nature as you, and preach the gospel to you in order that you should turn from these [30]vain things to a living God, WHO MADE THE HEAVEN AND THE EARTH AND THE SEA, AND ALL THAT IS IN THEM.

16"And in the generations gone by He permitted all the nations to go their own ways;

17 and yet He did not leave Himself without witness, in that He did good and gave you rains from heaven and fruitful seasons, satisfying your hearts with food and gladness."

18 And *even* saying these things, they with difficulty restrained the crowds from offering sacrifice to them.

19 ¶ But Jews came from Antioch and Iconium, and having won over the multitudes, they stoned Paul and dragged him out of the city, supposing him to be dead.

20 But while the disciples stood around him, he arose and entered the city. And the next day he went away with Barnabas to Derbe.

21 And after they had preached the gospel to that city and had made many disciples, they returned to Lystra and to Iconium and to Antioch,

22 strengthening the souls of the disciples, encouraging them to continue in the faith, and *saying*, "Through many tribulations we must enter the kingdom of God."

23 And when they had appointed elders for them in every church, having prayed with fasting, they commended them to the Lord in whom they had believed.

24 And they passed through Pisidia and came into Pamphylia.

25 And when they had spoken the word in Perga, they went down to Attalia;

[30] I.e., idols

26 and from there they sailed to Antioch, from which they had been commended to the grace of God for the work that they had accomplished.

27 And when they had arrived and gathered the church together, they *began* to report all things that God had done with them and how He had opened a door of faith to the Gentiles.

28 And they spent a long time with the disciples.

CHAPTER 15

AND some men came down from Judea and *began* teaching the brethren, "Unless you are circumcised according to the custom of Moses, you cannot be saved."

2 And when Paul and Barnabas had great dissension and debate with them, *the brethren* determined that Paul and Barnabas and certain others of them should go up to Jerusalem to the apostles and elders concerning this issue.

3 Therefore, being sent on their way by the church, they were passing through both Phoenicia and Samaria, describing in detail the conversion of the Gentiles, and were bringing great joy to all the brethren.

4 And when they arrived at Jerusalem, they were received by the church and the apostles and the elders, and they reported all that God had done with them.

5 But certain ones of the sect of the Pharisees who had believed, stood up, saying, "It is necessary to circumcise them, and to direct them to observe the Law of Moses."

6 ¶ And the apostles and the elders came together to look into this matter.

7 And after there had been much debate, Peter stood up and said to them, "Brethren, you know that in the early days God made a choice among you, that by my mouth the Gentiles should hear the word of the gospel and believe.

8 "And God, who knows the heart, bore witness to them, giving them the Holy Spirit, just as He also did to us;

9 and He made no distinction between us and them, cleansing their hearts by faith.

10 "Now therefore why do you put God to the test by placing upon the neck of the disciples a yoke which neither our fathers nor we have been able to bear?

11 "But we believe that we are saved through the grace of the Lord Jesus, in the same way as they also are."

12 ¶ And all the multitude kept silent, and they were listening to Barnabas and Paul as they were relating what signs and wonders God had done through them among the Gentiles.

13 And after they had stopped speaking, James answered, saying, "Brethren, listen to me.

14 "Simeon has related how God first concerned Himself about taking from among the Gentiles a people for His name.

15 "And with this the words of the Prophets agree, just as it is written,

16 'AFTER THESE THINGS I will return,
AND I WILL REBUILD THE TABERNACLE OF DAVID WHICH HAS FALLEN,
AND I WILL REBUILD ITS RUINS,
AND I WILL RESTORE IT,

17 IN ORDER THAT THE REST OF MANKIND MAY SEEK THE LORD,
AND ALL THE GENTILES WHO ARE CALLED BY MY NAME,'

18 SAYS THE LORD, WHO MAKES THESE THINGS KNOWN FROM OF OLD.

19 "Therefore it is my judgment that we do not trouble those who are turning to God from among the Gentiles,

20 but that we write to them that they abstain from things contaminated by idols and from fornication and from what is strangled and from blood.

21 "For Moses from ancient generations has in every city those who preach him, since he is read in the synagogues every Sabbath."

22 ¶ Then it seemed good to the apostles and the elders, with the whole church, to choose men from among them to send to Antioch with Paul and Barnabas—Judas called Barsabbas, and Silas, leading men among the brethren,

23 and they sent this letter by them,

"The apostles and the brethren who are elders, to the brethren in Antioch and Syria and Cilicia who are from the Gentiles, greetings.

24 "Since we have heard that some of our number to whom we gave no instruction have disturbed you with *their* words, unsettling your souls,

25 it seemed good to us, having become of one mind, to select men to send to you with our beloved Barnabas and Paul,

26 men who have risked their lives for the name of our Lord Jesus Christ.

27 "Therefore we have sent Judas and Silas, who themselves will also report the same things by word *of mouth.*

28 "For it seemed good to the Holy Spirit and to us to lay upon you no greater burden than these essentials:

29 that you abstain from things sacrificed to idols and from blood and from things strangled and from fornication; if you keep yourselves free from such things, you will do well. Farewell."

30 ¶ So, when they were sent away, they went down to Antioch; and having gathered the congregation together, they delivered the letter.

31 And when they had read it, they rejoiced because of its encouragement.

32 And Judas and Silas, also being prophets themselves, encouraged and strengthened the brethren with a lengthy message.

33 And after they had spent time *there,* they were sent away from the brethren in peace to those who had sent them out.

34 [[31]But it seemed good to Silas to remain there.]

35 But Paul and Barnabas stayed in Antioch, teaching and preaching, with many others also, the word of the Lord.

36 ¶ And after some days Paul said to Barnabas, "Let us return and visit the brethren in every city in which we proclaimed the word of the Lord, *and see* how they are."

37 And Barnabas was desirous of taking John, called Mark, along with them also.

38 But Paul kept insisting that they should not take him along who had deserted them in Pamphylia and had not gone with them to the work.

39 And there arose such a sharp disagreement that they separated from one another, and Barnabas took Mark with him and sailed away to Cyprus.

40 But Paul chose Silas and departed, being committed by the brethren to the grace of the Lord.

41 And he was traveling through Syria and Cilicia, strengthening the churches.

CHAPTER 16

AND he came also to Derbe and to Lystra. And behold, a certain disciple was there, named Timothy, the son of a Jewish woman who was a believer, but his father was a Greek,

2 and he was well spoken of by the brethren who were in Lystra and Iconium.

3 Paul wanted this man to go with him; and he took him and circumcised him because of the Jews who were in those parts, for they all knew that his father was a Greek.

4 Now while they were passing through the cities, they were delivering the decrees, which had been decided upon by the apostles and elders who were in Jerusalem, for them to observe.

5 So the churches were being strengthened in the faith, and were increasing in number daily.

6 ¶ And they passed through the Phrygian and Galatian region, having been forbidden by the Holy Spirit to speak the word in Asia;

7 and when they had come to Mysia, they were trying to go into Bithynia, and the Spirit of Jesus did not permit them;

8 and passing by Mysia, they came down to Troas.

9 And a vision appeared to Paul in the night: a certain man of Macedonia was standing and appealing to him, and saying, "Come over to Macedonia and help us."

10 And when he had seen the vision, immediately we sought to go into Macedonia, concluding that God had called us to preach the gospel to them.

11 ¶ Therefore putting out to sea from Troas, we ran a straight course

---

[31] Many mss. do not contain this verse

to Samothrace, and on the day following to Neapolis;

12 and from there to Philippi, which is a leading city of the district of Macedonia, a *Roman* colony; and we were staying in this city for some days.

13 And on the Sabbath day we went outside the gate to a riverside, where we were supposing that there would be a place of prayer; and we sat down and began speaking to the women who had assembled.

14 And a certain woman named Lydia, from the city of Thyatira, a seller of purple fabrics, a worshiper of God, was listening; and the Lord opened her heart to respond to the things spoken by Paul.

15 And when she and her household had been baptized, she urged us, saying, "If you have judged me to be faithful to the Lord, come into my house and stay." And she prevailed upon us.

16 ¶ And it happened that as we were going to the place of prayer, a certain slave-girl having a spirit of divination met us, who was bringing her masters much profit by fortune-telling.

17 Following after Paul and us, she kept crying out, saying, "These men are bond-servants of the Most High God, who are proclaiming to you the way of salvation."

18 And she continued doing this for many days. But Paul was greatly annoyed, and turned and said to the spirit, "I command you in the name of Jesus Christ to come out of her!" And it came out at that very moment.

19 ¶ But when her masters saw that their hope of profit was gone, they seized Paul and Silas and dragged them into the market place before the authorities,

20 and when they had brought them to the chief magistrates, they said, "These men are throwing our city into confusion, being Jews,

21 and are proclaiming customs which it is not lawful for us to accept or to observe, being Romans."

22 And the crowd rose up together against them, and the chief magistrates tore their robes off them, and proceeded to order *them* to be beaten with rods.

23 And when they had inflicted many blows upon them, they threw them into prison, commanding the jailer to guard them securely;

24 and he, having received such a command, threw them into the inner prison, and fastened their feet in the stocks.

25 But about midnight Paul and Silas were praying and singing hymns of praise to God, and the prisoners were listening to them;

26 and suddenly there came a great earthquake, so that the foundations of the prison house were shaken; and immediately all the doors were opened, and everyone's chains were unfastened.

27 And when the jailer had been roused out of sleep and had seen the prison doors opened, he drew his sword and was about to kill himself, supposing that the prisoners had escaped.

28 But Paul cried out with a loud voice, saying, "Do yourself no harm, for we are all here!"

29 And he called for lights and rushed in and, trembling with fear, he fell down before Paul and Silas,

30 and after he brought them out, he said, "Sirs, what must I do to be saved?"

31 And they said, "Believe in the Lord Jesus, and you shall be saved, you and your household."

32 And they spoke the word of the Lord to him together with all who were in his house.

33 And he took them that *very* hour of the night and washed their wounds, and immediately he was baptized, he and all his *household*.

34 And he brought them into his house and set food before them, and rejoiced greatly, having believed in God with his whole household.

35 ¶ Now when day came, the chief magistrates sent their policemen, saying, "Release those men."

36 And the jailer reported these words to Paul, *saying*, "The chief magistrates have sent to release you. Now therefore, come out and go in peace."

37 But Paul said to them, "They have beaten us in public without trial, men who are Romans, and have thrown us into prison; and now are they sending us away secretly? No indeed! But let

them come themselves and bring us out."

38 And the policemen reported these words to the chief magistrates. And they were afraid when they heard that they were Romans,

39 and they came and appealed to them, and when they had brought them out, they kept begging them to leave the city.

40 And they went out of the prison and entered *the house of* Lydia, and when they saw the brethren, they encouraged them and departed.

CHAPTER 17

Now when they had traveled through Amphipolis and Apollonia, they came to Thessalonica, where there was a synagogue of the Jews.

2 And according to Paul's custom, he went to them, and for three Sabbaths reasoned with them from the Scriptures,

3 explaining and giving evidence that the Christ had to suffer and rise again from the dead, and *saying,* "This Jesus whom I am proclaiming to you is the Christ."

4 And some of them were persuaded and joined Paul and Silas, along with a great multitude of the God-fearing Greeks and a number of the leading women.

5 But the Jews, becoming jealous and taking along some wicked men from the market place, formed a mob and set the city in an uproar; and coming upon the house of Jason, they were seeking to bring them out to the people.

6 And when they did not find them, they *began* dragging Jason and some brethren before the city authorities, shouting, "These men who have upset [32]the world have come here also;

7 and Jason has welcomed them, and they all act contrary to the decrees of Caesar, saying that there is another king, Jesus."

8 And they stirred up the crowd and the city authorities who heard these things.

9 And when they had received a pledge from Jason and the others, they released them.

[32] Lit., *the inhabited earth*

10 ¶ And the brethren immediately sent Paul and Silas away by night to Berea; and when they arrived, they went into the synagogue of the Jews.

11 Now these were more noble-minded than those in Thessalonica, for they received the word with great eagerness, examining the Scriptures daily, *to see* whether these things were so.

12 Many of them therefore believed, along with a number of prominent Greek women and men.

13 But when the Jews of Thessalonica found out that the word of God had been proclaimed by Paul in Berea also, they came there likewise, agitating and stirring up the crowds.

14 And then immediately the brethren sent Paul out to go as far as the sea; and Silas and Timothy remained there.

15 Now those who conducted Paul brought him as far as Athens; and receiving a command for Silas and Timothy to come to him as soon as possible, they departed.

16 ¶ Now while Paul was waiting for them at Athens, his spirit was being provoked within him as he was beholding the city full of idols.

17 So he was reasoning in the synagogue with the Jews and the God-fearing *Gentiles,* and in the market place every day with those who happened to be present.

18 And also some of the Epicurean and Stoic philosophers were conversing with him. And some were saying, "What would this idle babbler wish to say?" Others, "He seems to be a proclaimer of strange deities,"—because he was preaching Jesus and the resurrection.

19 And they took him and brought him to the Areopagus, saying, "May we know what this new teaching is which you are proclaiming?

20 "For you are bringing some strange things to our ears; we want to know therefore what these things mean."

21 (Now all the Athenians and the strangers visiting there used to spend their time in nothing other than telling or hearing something new.)

22 And Paul stood in the midst of the Areopagus and said, "Men of Athens, I observe that you are very religious in all respects.

23"For while I was passing through and examining the objects of your worship, I also found an altar with this inscription, 'TO AN UNKNOWN GOD.' What therefore you worship in ignorance, this I proclaim to you.

24"The God who made the world and all things in it, since He is Lord of heaven and earth, does not dwell in temples made with hands;

25 neither is He served by human hands, as though He needed anything, since He Himself gives to all life and breath and all things;

26 and He made from [33]one, every nation of mankind to live on all the face of the earth, having determined *their* appointed times, and the boundaries of their habitation,

27 that they should seek God, if perhaps they might grope for Him and find Him, though He is not far from each one of us;

28 for in Him we live and move and exist, as even some of your own poets have said, 'For we also are His offspring.'

29"Being then the offspring of God, we ought not to think that the Divine Nature is like gold or silver or stone, an image formed by the art and thought of man.

30"Therefore having overlooked the times of ignorance, God is now declaring to men that all everywhere should repent,

31 because He has fixed a day in which He will judge the world in righteousness through a Man whom He has appointed, having furnished proof to all men by raising Him from the dead."

32 ¶ Now when they heard of the resurrection of the dead, some *began* to sneer, but others said, "We shall hear you again concerning this."

33 So Paul went out of their midst.

34 But some men joined him and believed, among whom also were Dionysius the Areopagite and a woman named Damaris and others with them.

CHAPTER 18

AFTER these things he left Athens and went to Corinth.

2 And he found a certain Jew named Aquila, a native of Pontus,

having recently come from Italy with his wife Priscilla, because Claudius had commanded all the Jews to leave Rome. He came to them,

3 and because he was of the same trade, he stayed with them and they were working; for by trade they were tent-makers.

4 And he was reasoning in the synagogue every Sabbath and trying to persuade Jews and Greeks.

5 ¶ But when Silas and Timothy came down from Macedonia, Paul *began* devoting himself completely to the word, solemnly testifying to the Jews that Jesus was the Christ.

6 And when they resisted and blasphemed, he shook out his garments and said to them, "Your blood *be* upon your own heads! I am clean. From now on I shall go to the Gentiles."

7 And he departed from there and went to the house of a certain man named Titius Justus, a worshiper of God, whose house was next to the synagogue.

8 And Crispus, the leader of the synagogue, believed in the Lord with all his household, and many of the Corinthians when they heard were believing and being baptized.

9 And the Lord said to Paul in the night by a vision, "Do not be afraid *any longer*, but go on speaking and do not be silent;

10 for I am with you, and no man will attack you in order to harm you, for I have many people in this city."

11 And he settled *there* a year and six months, teaching the word of God among them.

12 ¶ But while Gallio was proconsul of Achaia, the Jews with one accord rose up against Paul and brought him before the judgment seat,

13 saying, "This man persuades men to worship God contrary to the law."

14 But when Paul was about to open his mouth, Gallio said to the Jews, "If it were a matter of wrong or of vicious crime, O Jews, it would be reasonable for me to put up with you;

15 but if there are questions about words and names and your own law, look after it yourselves; I am unwilling to be a judge of these matters."

16 And he drove them away from the judgment seat.

[33] Some later mss. read *one blood*

17 And they all took hold of Sosthenes, the leader of the synagogue, and *began* beating him in front of the judgment seat. And Gallio was not concerned about any of these things.

18 ¶ And Paul, having remained many days longer, took leave of the brethren and put out to sea for Syria, and with him were Priscilla and Aquila. In Cenchrea he had his hair cut, for he was keeping a vow.

19 And they came to Ephesus, and he left them there. Now he himself entered the synagogue and reasoned with the Jews.

20 And when they asked him to stay for a longer time, he did not consent,

21 but taking leave of them and saying, "I will return to you again if God wills," he set sail from Ephesus.

22 ¶ And when he had landed at Caesarea, he went up and greeted the church, and went down to Antioch.

23 And having spent some time *there,* he departed and passed successively through the Galatian region and Phrygia, strengthening all the disciples.

24 ¶ Now a certain Jew named Apollos, an Alexandrian by birth, an eloquent man, came to Ephesus; and he was mighty in the Scriptures.

25 This man had been instructed in the way of the Lord; and being fervent in spirit, he was speaking and teaching accurately the things concerning Jesus, being acquainted only with the baptism of John;

26 and he began to speak out boldly in the synagogue. But when Priscilla and Aquila heard him, they took him aside and explained to him the way of God more accurately.

27 And when he wanted to go across to Achaia, the brethren encouraged him and wrote to the disciples to welcome him; and when he had arrived, he helped greatly those who had believed through grace;

28 for he powerfully refuted the Jews in public, demonstrating by the Scriptures that Jesus was the Christ.

CHAPTER 19

AND it came about that while Apollos was at Corinth, Paul having passed through the upper country came to Ephesus, and found some disciples,

2 and he said to them, "Did you receive the Holy Spirit when you believed?" And they *said* to him, "No, we have not even heard whether there is a Holy Spirit."

3 And he said, "Into what then were you baptized?" And they said, "Into John's baptism."

4 And Paul said, "John baptized with the baptism of repentance, telling the people to believe in Him who was coming after him, that is, in Jesus."

5 And when they heard this, they were baptized in the name of the Lord Jesus.

6 And when Paul had laid his hands upon them, the Holy Spirit came on them, and they *began* speaking with tongues and prophesying.

7 And there were in all about twelve men.

8 ¶ And he entered the synagogue and continued speaking out boldly for three months, reasoning and persuading *them* about the kingdom of God.

9 But when some were becoming hardened and disobedient, speaking evil of the Way before the multitude, he withdrew from them and took away the disciples, reasoning daily in the school of Tyrannus.

10 And this took place for two years, so that all who lived in Asia heard the word of the Lord, both Jews and Greeks.

11 And God was performing extraordinary miracles by the hands of Paul,

12 so that handkerchiefs or aprons were even carried from his body to the sick, and the diseases left them and the evil spirits went out.

13 But also some of the Jewish exorcists, who went from place to place, attempted to name over those who had the evil spirits the name of the Lord Jesus, saying, "I adjure you by Jesus whom Paul preaches."

14 And seven sons of one Sceva, a Jewish chief priest, were doing this.

15 And the evil spirit answered and said to them, "I recognize Jesus, and I know about Paul, but who are you?"

16 And the man, in whom was the evil spirit, leaped on them and subdued all of them and overpowered them, so that they fled out of that house naked and wounded.

17 And this became known to all, both Jews and Greeks, who lived in

Ephesus; and fear fell upon them all and the name of the Lord Jesus was being magnified.

18 Many also of those who had believed kept coming, confessing and disclosing their practices.

19 And many of those who practiced magic brought their books together and *began* burning them in the sight of all; and they counted up the price of them and found it fifty thousand pieces of silver.

20 So the word of the Lord was growing mightily and prevailing.

21 ¶ Now after these things were finished, Paul purposed in the spirit to go to Jerusalem after he had passed through Macedonia and Achaia, saying, "After I have been there, I must also see Rome."

22 And having sent into Macedonia two of those who ministered to him, Timothy and Erastus, he himself stayed in Asia for a while.

23 ¶ And about that time there arose no small disturbance concerning the Way.

24 For a certain man named Demetrius, a silversmith, who made silver shrines of Artemis, was bringing no little business to the craftsmen;

25 these he gathered together with the workmen of similar *trades,* and said, "Men, you know that our prosperity depends upon this business.

26"And you see and hear that not only in Ephesus, but in almost all of Asia, this Paul has persuaded and turned away a considerable number of people, saying that gods made with hands are no gods *at all.*

27"And not only is there danger that this trade of ours fall into disrepute, but also that the temple of the great goddess Artemis be regarded as worthless and that she whom all of Asia and the world worship should even be dethroned from her magnificence."

28 And when they heard *this* and were filled with rage, they *began* crying out, saying, "Great is Artemis of the Ephesians!"

29 And the city was filled with the confusion, and they rushed with one accord into the theater, dragging along Gaius and Aristarchus, Paul's traveling companions from Macedonia.

30 And when Paul wanted to go into the assembly, the disciples would not let him.

31 And also some of the [34]Asiarchs who were friends of his sent to him and repeatedly urged him not to venture into the theater.

32 So then, some were shouting one thing and some another, for the assembly was in confusion, and the majority did not know for what cause they had come together.

33 And some of the crowd concluded *it was* Alexander, since the Jews had put him forward; and having motioned with his hand, Alexander was intending to make a defense to the assembly.

34 But when they recognized that he was a Jew, a *single* outcry arose from them all as they shouted for about two hours, "Great is Artemis of the Ephesians!"

35 And after quieting the multitude, the town clerk *said, "Men of Ephesus, what man is there after all who does not know that the city of the Ephesians is guardian of the temple of the great Artemis, and of the *image* which fell down from heaven?

36"Since then these are undeniable facts, you ought to keep calm and to do nothing rash.

37"For you have brought these men *here* who are neither robbers of temples nor blasphemers of our goddess.

38"So then, if Demetrius and the craftsmen who are with him have a complaint against any man, the courts are in session and proconsuls are *available;* let them bring charges against one another.

39"But if you want anything beyond this, it shall be settled in the lawful assembly.

40"For indeed we are in danger of being accused of a riot in connection with today's affair, since there is no *real* cause *for it;* and in this connection we shall be unable to account for this disorderly gathering."

41 And after saying this he dismissed the assembly.

CHAPTER 20

A ND after the uproar had ceased, Paul sent for the disciples and when he had exhorted them and taken his leave

[34] I.e., political or religious officials of the province of Asia

of them, he departed to go to Macedonia.

2 And when he had gone through those districts and had given them much exhortation, he came to Greece.

3 And *there* he spent three months, and when a plot was formed against him by the Jews as he was about to set sail for Syria, he determined to return through Macedonia.

4 And he was accompanied by Sopater of Berea, *the son* of Pyrrhus; and by Aristarchus and Secundus of the Thessalonians; and Gaius of Derbe, and Timothy; and Tychicus and Trophimus of Asia.

5 But these had gone on ahead and were waiting for us at Troas.

6 And we sailed from Philippi after the days of Unleavened Bread, and came to them at Troas within five days; and there we stayed seven days.

7 ¶ And on the first day of the week, when we were gathered together to break bread, Paul *began* talking to them, intending to depart the next day, and he prolonged his message until midnight.

8 And there were many lamps in the upper room where we were gathered together.

9 And there was a certain young man named Eutychus sitting on the window sill, sinking into a deep sleep; and as Paul kept on talking, he was overcome by sleep and fell down from the third floor, and was picked up dead.

10 But Paul went down and fell upon him and after embracing him, he said, "Do not be troubled, for his life is in him."

11 And when he had gone *back* up, and had broken the bread and eaten, he talked with them a long while, until daybreak, and so departed.

12 And they took away the boy alive, and were greatly comforted.

13 ¶ But we, going ahead to the ship, set sail for Assos, intending from there to take Paul on board; for thus he had arranged it, intending himself to go by land.

14 And when he met us at Assos, we took him on board and came to Mitylene.

15 And sailing from there, we arrived the following day opposite Chios; and the next day we crossed over to Samos; and the day following we came to Miletus.

16 For Paul had decided to sail past Ephesus in order that he might not have to spend time in Asia; for he was hurrying to be in Jerusalem, if possible, on the day of Pentecost.

17 ¶ And from Miletus he sent to Ephesus and called to him the elders of the church.

18 And when they had come to him, he said to them,

¶ "You yourselves know, from the first day that I set foot in Asia, how I was with you the whole time,

19 serving the Lord with all humility and with tears and with trials which came upon me through the plots of the Jews;

20 how I did not shrink from declaring to you anything that was profitable, and teaching you publicly and from house to house,

21 solemnly testifying to both Jews and Greeks of repentance toward God and faith in our Lord Jesus Christ.

22 "And now, behold, bound in spirit, I am on my way to Jerusalem, not knowing what will happen to me there,

23 except that the Holy Spirit solemnly testifies to me in every city, saying that bonds and afflictions await me.

24 "But I do not consider my life of any account as dear to myself, in order that I may finish my course, and the ministry which I received from the Lord Jesus, to testify solemnly of the gospel of the grace of God.

25 "And now, behold, I know that all of you, among whom I went about preaching the kingdom, will see my face no more.

26 "Therefore I testify to you this day, that I am innocent of the blood of all men.

27 "For I did not shrink from declaring to you the whole purpose of God.

28 "Be on guard for yourselves and for all the flock, among which the Holy Spirit has made you overseers, to shepherd the church of God which He purchased with His own blood.

29 "I know that after my departure savage wolves will come in among you, not sparing the flock;

30 and from among your own selves men will arise, speaking perverse

things, to draw away the disciples after them.

31"Therefore be on the alert, remembering that night and day for a period of three years I did not cease to admonish each one with tears.

32"And now I commend you to God and to the word of His grace, which is able to build *you* up and to give *you* the inheritance among all those who are sanctified.

33"I have coveted no one's silver or gold or clothes.

34"You yourselves know that these hands ministered to my *own* needs and to the men who were with me.

35"In everything I showed you that by working hard in this manner you must help the weak and remember the words of the Lord Jesus, that He Himself said, 'It is more blessed to give than to receive.'"

36 ¶ And when he had said these things, he knelt down and prayed with them all.

37 And they *began* to weep aloud and embraced Paul, and repeatedly kissed him,

38 grieving especially over the word which he had spoken, that they should see his face no more. And they were accompanying him to the ship.

CHAPTER 21

AND when it came about that we had parted from them and had set sail, we ran a straight course to Cos and the next day to Rhodes and from there to Patara;

2 and having found a ship crossing over to Phoenicia, we went aboard and set sail.

3 And when we had come in sight of Cyprus, leaving it on the left, we kept sailing to Syria and landed at Tyre; for there the ship was to unload its cargo.

4 And after looking up the disciples, we stayed there seven days; and they kept telling Paul through the Spirit not to set foot in Jerusalem.

5 And when it came about that our days there were ended, we departed and started on our journey, while they all, with wives and children, escorted us until *we were* out of the city. And after kneeling down on the beach and praying, we said farewell to one another.

6 Then we went on board the ship, and they returned home again.

7 ¶ And when we had finished the voyage from Tyre, we arrived at Ptolemais; and after greeting the brethren, we stayed with them for a day.

8 And on the next day we departed and came to Caesarea; and entering the house of Philip the evangelist, who was one of the seven, we stayed with him.

9 Now this man had four virgin daughters who were prophetesses.

10 And as we were staying there for some days, a certain prophet named Agabus came down from Judea.

11 And coming to us, he took Paul's belt and bound his own feet and hands, and said, "This is what the Holy Spirit says: 'In this way the Jews at Jerusalem will bind the man who owns this belt and deliver him into the hands of the Gentiles.'"

12 And when we had heard this, we as well as the local residents *began* begging him not to go up to Jerusalem.

13 Then Paul answered, "What are you doing, weeping and breaking my heart? For I am ready not only to be bound, but even to die at Jerusalem for the name of the Lord Jesus."

14 And since he would not be persuaded, we fell silent, remarking, "The will of the Lord be done!"

15 ¶ And after these days we got ready and started on our way up to Jerusalem.

16 And *some* of the disciples from Caesarea also came with us, taking us to Mnason of Cyprus, a disciple of long standing with whom we were to lodge.

17 ¶ And when we had come to Jerusalem, the brethren received us gladly.

18 And now the following day Paul went in with us to James, and all the elders were present.

19 And after he had greeted them, he *began* to relate one by one the things which God had done among the Gentiles through his ministry.

20 And when they heard it they *began* glorifying God; and they said to him, "You see, brother, how many thousands there are among the Jews

of those who have believed, and they are all zealous for the Law;

21 and they have been told about you, that you are teaching all the Jews who are among the Gentiles to forsake Moses, telling them not to circumcise their children nor to walk according to the customs.

22"What, then, is *to be done*? They will certainly hear that you have come.

23"Therefore do this that we tell you. We have four men who are under a vow;

24 take them and purify yourself along with them, and pay their expenses in order that they may shave their heads; and all will know that there is nothing to the things which they have been told about you, but that you yourself also walk orderly, keeping the Law.

25"But concerning the Gentiles who have believed, we wrote, having decided that they should abstain from meat sacrificed to idols and from blood and from what is strangled and from fornication."

26 Then Paul took the men, and the next day, purifying himself along with them, went into the temple, giving notice of the completion of the days of purification, until the sacrifice was offered for each one of them.

27 ¶ And when the seven days were almost over, the Jews from Asia, upon seeing him in the temple, *began* to stir up all the multitude and laid hands on him,

28 crying out, "Men of Israel, come to our aid! This is the man who preaches to all men everywhere against our people, and the Law, and this place; and besides he has even brought Greeks into the temple and has defiled this holy place."

29 For they had previously seen Trophimus the Ephesian in the city with him, and they supposed that Paul had brought him into the temple.

30 And all the city was aroused, and the people rushed together; and taking hold of Paul, they dragged him out of the temple; and immediately the doors were shut.

31 And while they were seeking to kill him, a report came up to the

[35]commander of the *Roman* cohort that all Jerusalem was in confusion.

32 And at once he took along *some* soldiers and centurions, and ran down to them; and when they saw the commander and the soldiers, they stopped beating Paul.

33 Then the commander came up and took hold of him, and ordered him to be bound with two chains; and he *began* asking who he was and what he had done.

34 But among the crowd some were shouting one thing *and* some another, and when he could not find out the facts on account of the uproar, he ordered him to be brought into the barracks.

35 And when he got to the stairs, it so happened that he was carried by the soldiers because of the violence of the mob;

36 for the multitude of the people kept following behind, crying out, "Away with him!"

37 ¶ And as Paul was about to be brought into the barracks, he said to the commander, "May I say something to you?" And he *said, "Do you know Greek?

38"Then you are not the Egyptian who some time ago stirred up a revolt and led the four thousand men of the Assassins out into the wilderness?"

39 But Paul said, "I am a Jew of Tarsus in Cilicia, a citizen of no insignificant city; and I beg you, allow me to speak to the people."

40 And when he had given him permission, Paul, standing on the stairs, motioned to the people with his hand; and when there was a great hush, he spoke to them in the Hebrew dialect, saying,

CHAPTER 22

"BRETHREN and fathers, hear my defense which I now *offer* to you."

2 ¶ And when they heard that he was addressing them in the Hebrew dialect, they became even more quiet; and he *said,

3 ¶"I am a Jew, born in Tarsus of Cilicia, but brought up in this city, educated under Gamaliel, strictly according to the law of our fathers,

[35] I.e., chiliarch, in command of one thousand troops

being zealous for God, just as you all are today.

4"And I persecuted this Way to the death, binding and putting both men and women into prisons,

5 as also the high priest and all the Council of the elders can testify. From them I also received letters to the brethren, and started off for Damascus in order to bring even those who were there to Jerusalem as prisoners to be punished.

6"And it came about that as I was on my way, approaching Damascus about noontime, a very bright light suddenly flashed from heaven all around me,

7 and I fell to the ground and heard a voice saying to me, 'Saul, Saul, why are you persecuting Me?'

8"And I answered, 'Who art Thou, Lord?' And He said to me, 'I am Jesus the Nazarene, whom you are persecuting.'

9"And those who were with me beheld the light, to be sure, but did not understand the voice of the One who was speaking to me.

10"And I said, 'What shall I do, Lord?' And the Lord said to me, 'Arise and go on into Damascus; and there you will be told of all that has been appointed for you to do.'

11"But since I could not see because of the brightness of that light, I was led by the hand by those who were with me, and came into Damascus.

12"And a certain Ananias, a man who was devout by the standard of the Law, and well spoken of by all the Jews who lived there,

13 came to me, and standing near said to me, 'Brother Saul, receive your sight!' And at that very time I looked up at him.

14"And he said, 'The God of our fathers has appointed you to know His will, and to see the Righteous One, and to hear an utterance from His mouth.

15 'For you will be a witness for Him to all men of what you have seen and heard.

16 'And now why do you delay? Arise, and be baptized, and wash away your sins, calling on His name.'

17"And it came about when I returned to Jerusalem and was praying in the temple, that I fell into a trance,

18 and I saw Him saying to me, 'Make haste, and get out of Jerusalem quickly, because they will not accept your testimony about Me.'

19"And I said, 'Lord, they themselves understand that in one synagogue after another I used to imprison and beat those who believed in Thee.

20 'And when the blood of Thy witness Stephen was being shed, I also was standing by approving, and watching out for the cloaks of those who were slaying him.'

21"And He said to me, 'Go! For I will send you far away to the Gentiles.'"

22 ¶ And they listened to him up to this statement, and *then* they raised their voices and said, "Away with such a fellow from the earth, for he should not be allowed to live!"

23 And as they were crying out and throwing off their cloaks and tossing dust into the air,

24 the [36]commander ordered him to be brought into the barracks, stating that he should be examined by scourging so that he might find out the reason why they were shouting against him that way.

25 And when they stretched him out with thongs, Paul said to the centurion who was standing by, "Is it lawful for you to scourge a man who is a Roman and uncondemned?"

26 And when the centurion heard *this*, he went to the commander and told him, saying, "What are you about to do? For this man is a Roman."

27 And the commander came and said to him, "Tell me, are you a Roman?" And he said, "Yes."

28 And the commander answered, "I acquired this citizenship with a large sum of money." And Paul said, "But I was actually born *a citizen*."

29 Therefore those who were about to examine him immediately let go of him; and the commander also was afraid when he found out that he was a Roman, and because he had put him in chains.

30 ¶ But on the next day, wishing to know for certain why he had been accused by the Jews, he released him and ordered the chief priests and all the Council to assemble, and brought Paul down and set him before them.

[36] I.e., chiliarch, in command of one thousand troops

CHAPTER 23

AND Paul, looking intently at the Council, said, "Brethren, I have lived my life with a perfectly good conscience before God up to this day."

2 And the high priest Ananias commanded those standing beside him to strike him on the mouth.

3 Then Paul said to him, "God is going to strike you, you whitewashed wall! And do you sit to try me according to the Law, and in violation of the Law order me to be struck?"

4 But the bystanders said, "Do you revile God's high priest?"

5 And Paul said, "I was not aware, brethren, that he was high priest; for it is written, 'YOU SHALL NOT SPEAK EVIL OF A RULER OF YOUR PEOPLE.' "

6 But perceiving that one part were Sadducees and the other Pharisees, Paul *began* crying out in the Council, "Brethren, I am a Pharisee, a son of Pharisees; I am on trial for the hope and resurrection of the dead!"

7 And as he said this, there arose a dissension between the Pharisees and Sadducees; and the assembly was divided.

8 For the Sadducees say that there is no resurrection, nor an angel, nor a spirit; but the Pharisees acknowledge them all.

9 And there arose a great uproar; and some of the scribes of the Pharisaic party stood up and *began* to argue heatedly, saying, "We find nothing wrong with this man; suppose a spirit or an angel has spoken to him?"

10 And as a great dissension was developing, the [37]commander was afraid Paul would be torn to pieces by them and ordered the troops to go down and take him away from them by force, and bring him into the barracks.

11 ¶ But on the night *immediately* following, the Lord stood at his side and said, "Take courage; for as you have solemnly witnessed to My cause at Jerusalem, so you must witness at Rome also."

12 ¶ And when it was day, the Jews formed a conspiracy and bound themselves under an oath, saying that they would neither eat nor drink until they had killed Paul.

13 And there were more than forty who formed this plot.

14 And they came to the chief priests and the elders, and said, "We have bound ourselves under a solemn oath to taste nothing until we have killed Paul.

15 "Now, therefore, you and the Council notify the commander to bring him down to you, as though you were going to determine his case by a more thorough investigation; and we for our part are ready to slay him before he comes near *the place*."

16 But the son of Paul's sister heard of their ambush, and he came and entered the barracks and told Paul.

17 And Paul called one of the centurions to him and said, "Lead this young man to the commander, for he has something to report to him."

18 So he took him and led him to the commander and *said, "Paul the prisoner called me to him and asked me to lead this young man to you since he has something to tell you."

19 And the commander took him by the hand and stepping aside, *began* to inquire of him privately, "What is it that you have to report to me?"

20 And he said, "The Jews have agreed to ask you to bring Paul down tomorrow to the Council, as though they were going to inquire somewhat more thoroughly about him.

21 "So do not listen to them, for more than forty of them are lying in wait for him who have bound themselves under a curse not to eat or drink until they slay him; and now they are ready and waiting for the promise from you."

22 Therefore the commander let the young man go, instructing him, "Tell no one that you have notified me of these things."

23 And he called to him two of the centurions, and said, "Get two hundred soldiers ready by [38]the third hour of the night to proceed to Caesarea, with seventy horsemen and two hundred spearmen.

24 *They were* also to provide mounts to put Paul on and bring him safely to Felix the governor.

25 And he wrote a letter having this form:

---

[37] I.e., chiliarch, in command of one thousand troops   [38] I.e., 9 p.m.

26 ¶ "Claudius Lysias, to the most excellent governor Felix, greetings.

27 "When this man was arrested by the Jews and was about to be slain by them, I came upon them with the troops and rescued him, having learned that he was a Roman.

28 "And wanting to ascertain the charge for which they were accusing him, I brought him down to their Council;

29 and I found him to be accused over questions about their Law, but under no accusation deserving death or imprisonment.

30 "And when I was informed that there would be a plot against the man, I sent him to you at once, also instructing his accusers to bring charges against him before you."

31 ¶ So the soldiers, in accordance with their orders, took Paul and brought him by night to Antipatris.

32 But the next day, leaving the horsemen to go on with him, they returned to the barracks.

33 And when these had come to Caesarea and delivered the letter to the governor, they also presented Paul to him.

34 And when he had read it, he asked from what province he was; and when he learned that he was from Cilicia,

35 he said, "I will give you a hearing after your accusers arrive also," giving orders for him to be kept in Herod's [39]Praetorium.

CHAPTER 24

AND after five days the high priest Ananias came down with some elders, with a certain attorney named Tertullus; and they brought charges to the governor against Paul.

2 And after Paul had been summoned, Tertullus began to accuse him, saying to the governor,

¶ "Since we have through you attained much peace, and since by your providence reforms are being carried out for this nation,

3 we acknowledge this in every way

and everywhere, most excellent Felix, with all thankfulness.

4 "But, that I may not weary you any further, I beg you to grant us, by your kindness, a brief hearing.

5 "For we have found this man a real pest and a fellow who stirs up dissension among all the Jews throughout [40]the world, and a ringleader of the sect of the Nazarenes.

6 "And he even tried to desecrate the temple; and then we arrested him. [[41]And we wanted to judge him according to our own Law.

7 "But Lysias the commander came along, and with much violence took him out of our hands,

8 ordering his accusers to come before you.] And by examining him yourself concerning all these matters, you will be able to ascertain the things of which we accuse him."

9 And the Jews also joined in the attack, asserting that these things were so.

10 ¶ And when the governor had nodded for him to speak, Paul responded:

¶ "Knowing that for many years you have been a judge to this nation, I cheerfully make my defense,

11 since you can take note of the fact that no more than twelve days ago I went up to Jerusalem to worship.

12 "And neither in the temple, nor in the synagogues, nor in the city itself did they find me carrying on a discussion with anyone or causing a riot.

13 "Nor can they prove to you the charges of which they now accuse me.

14 "But this I admit to you, that according to the Way which they call a sect I do serve the God of our fathers, believing everything that is in accordance with the Law, and that is written in the Prophets;

15 having a hope in God, which these men cherish themselves, that there shall certainly be a resurrection of both the righteous and the wicked.

16 "In view of this, I also do my best to maintain always a blameless conscience both before God and before men.

17 "Now after several years I came to

---

39 I.e., governor's official residence

40 Lit., the inhabited earth
41 Many mss. do not contain the remainder of v. 6, v. 7, nor the first part of v. 8

bring [42]alms to my nation and to present offerings;

18 in which they found me *occupied* in the temple, having been purified, without *any* crowd or uproar. But *there were* certain Jews from Asia—

19 who ought to have been present before you, and to make accusation, if they should have anything against me.

20 "Or else let these men themselves tell what misdeed they found when I stood before the Council,

21 other than for this one statement which I shouted out while standing among them, 'For the resurrection of the dead I am on trial before you today.' "

22 ¶ But Felix, having a more exact knowledge about the Way, put them off, saying, "When Lysias the [43]commander comes down, I will decide your case."

23 And he gave orders to the centurion for him to be kept in custody and *yet* have *some* freedom, and not to prevent any of his friends from ministering to him.

24 ¶ But some days later, Felix arrived with Drusilla, his wife who was a Jewess, and sent for Paul, and heard him *speak* about faith in Christ Jesus.

25 And as he was discussing righteousness, self-control and the judgment to come, Felix became frightened and said, "Go away for the present, and when I find time, I will summon you."

26 At the same time too, he was hoping that money would be given him by Paul; therefore he also used to send for him quite often and converse with him.

27 But after two years had passed, Felix was succeeded by Porcius Festus; and wishing to do the Jews a favor, Felix left Paul imprisoned.

CHAPTER 25

FESTUS therefore, having arrived in the province, three days later went up to Jerusalem from Caesarea.

2 And the chief priests and the leading men of the Jews brought charges against Paul; and they were urging him,

3 requesting a concession against

Paul, that he might have him brought to Jerusalem (*at the same time,* setting an ambush to kill him on the way).

4 Festus then answered that Paul was being kept in custody at Caesarea and that he himself was about to leave shortly.

5 "Therefore," he *said, "let the influential men among you go there with me, and if there is anything wrong about the man, let them prosecute him."

6 ¶ And after he had spent not more than eight or ten days among them, he went down to Caesarea; and on the next day he took his seat on the tribunal and ordered Paul to be brought.

7 And after he had arrived, the Jews who had come down from Jerusalem stood around him, bringing many and serious charges against him which they could not prove;

8 while Paul said in his own defense, "I have committed no offense either against the Law of the Jews or against the temple or against Caesar."

9 But Festus, wishing to do the Jews a favor, answered Paul and said, "Are you willing to go up to Jerusalem and stand trial before me on these *charges?*"

10 But Paul said, "I am standing before Caesar's tribunal, where I ought to be tried. I have done no wrong to *the* Jews, as you also very well know.

11 "If then I am a wrongdoer, and have committed anything worthy of death, I do not refuse to die; but if none of those things is *true* of which these men accuse me, no one can hand me over to them. I appeal to Caesar."

12 Then when Festus had conferred with his council, he answered, "You have appealed to Caesar, to Caesar you shall go."

13 ¶ Now when several days had elapsed, King Agrippa and Bernice arrived at Caesarea, and paid their respects to Festus.

14 And while they were spending many days there, Festus laid Paul's case before the king, saying, "There is a certain man left a prisoner by Felix;

15 and when I was at Jerusalem, the chief priests and the elders of the Jews brought charges against him, asking

---

[42] Or, *gifts to charity*
[43] I.e., chiliarch, in command of one thousand troops

for a sentence of condemnation upon him.

16"And I answered them that it is not the custom of the Romans to hand over any man before the accused meets his accusers face to face, and has an opportunity to make his defense against the charges.

17"And so after they had assembled here, I made no delay, but on the next day took my seat on the tribunal, and ordered the man to be brought.

18"And when the accusers stood up, they *began* bringing charges against him not of such crimes as I was expecting;

19 but they *simply* had some points of disagreement with him about their own religion and about a certain dead man, Jesus, whom Paul asserted to be alive.

20"And being at a loss how to investigate such matters, I asked whether he was willing to go to Jerusalem and there stand trial on these matters.

21"But when Paul appealed to be held in custody for [44]the Emperor's decision, I ordered him to be kept in custody until I send him to Caesar."

22 And Agrippa *said* to Festus, "I also would like to hear the man myself." "Tomorrow," he *said, "you shall hear him."

23 ¶ And so, on the next day when Agrippa had come together with Bernice, amid great pomp, and had entered the auditorium [45]accompanied by the commanders and the prominent men of the city, at the command of Festus, Paul was brought in.

24 And Festus *said, "King Agrippa, and all you gentlemen here present with us, you behold this man about whom all the people of the Jews appealed to me, both at Jerusalem and here, loudly declaring that he ought not to live any longer.

25"But I found that he had committed nothing worthy of death; and since he himself appealed to the Emperor, I decided to send him.

26"Yet I have nothing definite about him to write to my lord. Therefore I have brought him before you *all* and especially before you, King Agrippa, so that after the investigation has taken place, I may have something to write.

27"For it seems absurd to me in sending a prisoner, not to indicate also the charges against him."

CHAPTER 26

AND Agrippa said to Paul, "You are permitted to speak for yourself." Then Paul stretched out his hand and *proceeded* to make his defense:

2 ¶"In regard to all the things of which I am accused by the Jews, I consider myself fortunate, King Agrippa, that I am about to make my defense before you today;

3 especially because you are an expert in all customs and questions among *the* Jews; therefore I beg you to listen to me patiently.

4"So then, all Jews know my manner of life from my youth up, which from the beginning was spent among my *own* nation and at Jerusalem;

5 since they have known about me for a long time previously, if they are willing to testify, that I lived *as* a Pharisee according to the strictest sect of our religion.

6"And now I am standing trial for the hope of the promise made by God to our fathers;

7 *the promise* to which our twelve tribes hope to attain, as they earnestly serve *God* night and day. And for this hope, O King, I am being accused by Jews.

8"Why is it considered incredible among you *people* if God does raise the dead?

9"So then, I thought to myself that I had to do many things hostile to the name of Jesus of Nazareth.

10"And this is just what I did in Jerusalem; not only did I lock up many of the saints in prisons, having received authority from the chief priests, but also when they were being put to death I cast my vote against them.

11"And as I punished them often in all the synagogues, I tried to force them to blaspheme; and being furiously enraged at them, I kept pursuing them even to foreign cities.

12"While thus engaged as I was journeying to Damascus with the authority and commission of the chief priests,

13 at midday, O King, I saw on the

way a light from heaven, brighter than the sun, shining all around me and those who were journeying with me.

14"And when we had all fallen to the ground, I heard a voice saying to me in the Hebrew dialect, 'Saul, Saul, why are you persecuting Me? It is hard for you to kick against the goads.'

15"And I said, 'Who art Thou, Lord?' And the Lord said, 'I am Jesus whom you are persecuting.

16 'But arise, and stand on your feet; for this purpose I have appeared to you, to appoint you a minister and a witness not only to the things which you have seen, but also to the things in which I will appear to you;

17 delivering you from the *Jewish* people and from the Gentiles, to whom I am sending you,

18 to open their eyes so that they may turn from darkness to light and from the dominion of Satan to God, in order that they may receive forgiveness of sins and an inheritance among those who have been sanctified by faith in Me.'

19"Consequently, King Agrippa, I did not prove disobedient to the heavenly vision,

20 but *kept* declaring both to those of Damascus first, and *also* at Jerusalem and *then* throughout all the region of Judea, and *even* to the Gentiles, that they should repent and turn to God, performing deeds appropriate to repentance.

21"For this reason *some* Jews seized me in the temple and tried to put me to death.

22"And so, having obtained help from God, I stand to this day testifying both to small and great, stating nothing but what the Prophets and Moses said was going to take place;

23 that the Christ was to suffer, *and* that by reason of *His* resurrection from the dead He should be the first to proclaim light both to the *Jewish* people and to the Gentiles."

24 ¶ And while *Paul* was saying this in his defense, Festus *said in a loud voice, "Paul, you are out of your mind! *Your* great learning is driving you mad."

25 But Paul *said, "I am not out of my mind, most excellent Festus, but I utter words of sober truth.

26"For the king knows about these matters, and I speak to him also with confidence, since I am persuaded that none of these things escape his notice; for this has not been done in a corner.

27"King Agrippa, do you believe the Prophets? I know that you do."

28 And Agrippa *replied* to Paul, "In a short time you will persuade me to become a Christian."

29 And Paul *said,* "I would to God, that whether in a short or long time, not only you, but also all who hear me this day, might become such as I am, except for these chains."

30 ¶ And the king arose and the governor and Bernice, and those who were sitting with them,

31 and when they had drawn aside, they *began* talking to one another, saying, "This man is not doing anything worthy of death or imprisonment."

32 And Agrippa said to Festus, "This man might have been set free if he had not appealed to Caesar."

CHAPTER 27

AND when it was decided that we should sail for Italy, they proceeded to deliver Paul and some other prisoners to a centurion of the Augustan [46]cohort named Julius.

2 And embarking in an Adramyttian ship, which was about to sail to the regions along the coast of Asia, we put out to sea, accompanied by Aristarchus, a Macedonian of Thessalonica.

3 And the next day we put in at Sidon; and Julius treated Paul with consideration and allowed him to go to his friends and receive care.

4 And from there we put out to sea and sailed under the shelter of Cyprus because the winds were contrary.

5 And when we had sailed through the sea along the coast of Cilicia and Pamphylia, we landed at Myra in Lycia.

6 And there the centurion found an Alexandrian ship sailing for Italy, and he put us aboard it.

7 And when we had sailed slowly for a good many days, and with difficulty had arrived off Cnidus, since the wind did not permit us *to go farther,

[46] Or, *battalion*

we sailed under the shelter of Crete, off Salmone;

8 and with difficulty sailing past it we came to a certain place called Fair Havens, near which was the city of Lasea.

9 ¶ And when considerable time had passed and the voyage was now dangerous, since even the [47]fast was already over, Paul *began* to admonish them,

10 and said to them, "Men, I perceive that the voyage will certainly be *attended* with damage and great loss, not only of the cargo and the ship, but also of our lives."

11 But the centurion was more persuaded by the pilot and the captain of the ship, than by what was being said by Paul.

12 And because the harbor was not suitable for wintering, the majority reached a decision to put out to sea from there, if somehow they could reach Phoenix, a harbor of Crete, facing southwest and northwest, and spend the winter *there*.

13 And when a moderate south wind came up, supposing that they had gained their purpose, they weighed anchor and *began* sailing along Crete, close *inshore*.

14 But before very long there rushed down from the land a violent wind, called [48]Euraquilo;

15 and when the ship was caught *in it*, and could not face the wind, we gave way *to it*, and let ourselves be driven along.

16 And running under the shelter of a small island called Clauda, we were scarcely able to get the *ship's* boat under control.

17 And after they had hoisted it up, they used supporting cables in undergirding the ship; and fearing that they might run aground on *the shallows* of Syrtis, they let down the sea anchor, and so let themselves be driven along.

18 The next day as we were being violently storm-tossed, they began to jettison the cargo;

19 and on the third day they threw the ship's tackle overboard with their own hands.

20 And since neither sun nor stars appeared for many days, and no small storm was assailing *us*, from then on all hope of our being saved was gradually abandoned.

21 And when they had gone a long time without food, then Paul stood up in their midst and said, "Men, you ought to have followed my advice and not to have set sail from Crete, and incurred this damage and loss.

22 "And *yet* now I urge you to keep up your courage, for there shall be no loss of life among you, but *only* of the ship.

23 "For this very night an angel of the God to whom I belong and whom I serve stood before me,

24 saying, 'Do not be afraid, Paul; you must stand before Caesar; and behold, God has granted you all those who are sailing with you.'

25 "Therefore, keep up your courage, men, for I believe God, that it will turn out exactly as I have been told.

26 "But we must run aground on a certain island."

27 ¶ But when the fourteenth night had come, as we were being driven about in the Adriatic Sea, about midnight the sailors *began* to surmise that they were approaching some land.

28 And they took soundings, and found *it to be* twenty fathoms; and a little farther on they took another sounding and found *it to be* fifteen fathoms.

29 And fearing that we might run aground somewhere on the rocks, they cast four anchors from the stern and wished for daybreak.

30 And as the sailors were trying to escape from the ship, and had let down the *ship's* boat into the sea, on the pretense of intending to lay out anchors from the bow,

31 Paul said to the centurion and to the soldiers, "Unless these men remain in the ship, you yourselves cannot be saved."

32 Then the soldiers cut away the ropes of the *ship's* boat, and let it fall away.

33 And until the day was about to dawn, Paul was encouraging them all to take some food, saying, "Today is the fourteenth day that you have been constantly watching and going without eating, having taken nothing.

[47] I.e., Day of Atonement in September or October
[48] I.e., a northeaster

34"Therefore I encourage you to take some food, for this is for your preservation; for not a hair from the head of any of you shall perish."

35 And having said this, he took bread and gave thanks to God in the presence of all; and he broke it and began to eat.

36 And all of them were encouraged, and they themselves also took food.

37 And all of us in the ship were two hundred and seventy-six persons.

38 And when they had eaten enough, they *began* to lighten the ship by throwing out the wheat into the sea.

39 And when day came, they could not recognize the land; but they did observe a certain bay with a beach, and they resolved to [49]drive the ship onto it if they could.

40 And casting off the anchors, they left them in the sea while at the same time they were loosening the ropes of the rudders, and hoisting the foresail to the wind, they were heading for the beach.

41 But striking a reef where two seas met, they ran the vessel aground; and the prow stuck fast and remained immovable, but the stern *began* to be broken up by the force *of the waves.*

42 And the soldiers' plan was to kill the prisoners, that none *of them* should swim away and escape;

43 but the centurion, wanting to bring Paul safely through, kept them from their intention, and commanded that those who could swim should jump overboard first and get to land,

44 and the rest *should follow,* some on planks, and others on various things from the ship. And thus it happened that they all were brought safely to land.

CHAPTER 28

AND when they had been brought safely through, then we found out that the island was called Malta.

2 And the natives showed us extraordinary kindness; for because of the rain that had set in and because of the cold, they kindled a fire and received us all.

3 But when Paul had gathered a bundle of sticks and laid them on the

fire, a viper came out because of the heat, and fastened on his hand.

4 And when the natives saw the creature hanging from his hand, they *began* saying to one another, "Undoubtedly this man is a murderer, and though he has been saved from the sea, justice has not allowed him to live."

5 However he shook the creature off into the fire and suffered no harm.

6 But they were expecting that he was about to swell up or suddenly fall down dead. But after they had waited a long time and had seen nothing unusual happen to him, they changed their minds and *began* to say that he was a god.

7 ¶ Now in the neighborhood of that place were lands belonging to the leading man of the island, named Publius, who welcomed us and entertained us courteously three days.

8 And it came about that the father of Publius was lying *in bed* afflicted with *recurrent* fever and dysentery; and Paul went in *to see* him and after he had prayed, he laid his hands on him and healed him.

9 And after this had happened, the rest of the people on the island who had diseases were coming to him and getting cured.

10 And they also honored us with many marks of respect; and when we were setting sail, they supplied *us* with all we needed.

11 ¶ And at the end of three months we set sail on an Alexandrian ship which had wintered at the island, and which had the Twin Brothers for its figurehead.

12 And after we put in at Syracuse, we stayed there for three days.

13 And from there we sailed around and arrived at Rhegium, and a day later a south wind sprang up, and on the second day we came to Puteoli.

14 There we found *some* brethren, and were invited to stay with them for seven days; and thus we came to Rome.

15 And the brethren, when they heard about us, came from there as far as the Market of Appius and Three Inns to meet us; and when Paul saw them, he thanked God and took courage.

[49] Some ancient mss. read *bring the ship safely ashore*

16 ¶ And when we entered Rome, Paul was allowed to stay by himself, with the soldier who was guarding him.

17 ¶ And it happened that after three days he called together those who were the leading men of the Jews, and when they had come together, he *began* saying to them, "Brethren, though I had done nothing against our people, or the customs of our fathers, yet I was delivered prisoner from Jerusalem into the hands of the Romans.

18 "And when they had examined me, they were willing to release me because there was no ground for putting me to death.

19 "But when the Jews objected, I was forced to appeal to Caesar; not that I had any accusation against my nation.

20 "For this reason therefore, I requested to see you and to speak with you, for I am wearing this chain for the sake of the hope of Israel."

21 And they said to him, "We have neither received letters from Judea concerning you, nor have any of the brethren come here and reported or spoken anything bad about you.

22 "But we desire to hear from you what your views are; for concerning this sect, it is known to us that it is spoken against everywhere."

23 ¶ And when they had set a day for him, they came to him at his lodging in large numbers; and he was explaining to them by solemnly testifying about the kingdom of God, and trying to persuade them concerning Jesus, from both the Law of Moses and from the Prophets, from morning until evening.

24 And some were being persuaded by the things spoken, but others would not believe.

25 And when they did not agree with one another, they *began* leaving after Paul had spoken one *parting* word, "The Holy Spirit rightly spoke through Isaiah the prophet to your fathers,

26 saying,

'GO TO THIS PEOPLE AND SAY,
"YOU WILL KEEP ON HEARING, BUT
  WILL NOT UNDERSTAND;
AND YOU WILL KEEP ON SEEING,
  BUT WILL NOT PERCEIVE;

27 FOR THE HEART OF THIS PEOPLE
  HAS BECOME DULL,
AND WITH THEIR EARS THEY
  SCARCELY HEAR,
AND THEY HAVE CLOSED THEIR
  EYES;
LEST THEY SHOULD SEE WITH
  THEIR EYES,
AND HEAR WITH THEIR EARS,
AND UNDERSTAND WITH THEIR
  HEART AND RETURN,
AND I SHOULD HEAL THEM." '

28 "Let it be known to you therefore, that this salvation of God has been sent to the Gentiles; they will also listen."

29 [[50]And when he had spoken these words, the Jews departed, having a great dispute among themselves.]

30 ¶ And he stayed two full years in his own rented quarters, and was welcoming all who came to him,

31 preaching the kingdom of God, and teaching concerning the Lord Jesus Christ with all openness, unhindered.

[50] Many mss. do not contain this verse

ROMANS

Paul, a bond-servant of Christ Jesus, called *as* an apostle, set apart for the gospel of God,

2 which He promised beforehand through His prophets in the holy Scriptures,

3 concerning His Son, who was born of a descendant of David according to the flesh,

4 who was declared the Son of God with power [1]by the resurrection from the dead, according to the spirit of holiness, Jesus Christ our Lord,

5 through whom we have received grace and apostleship to bring about *the* obedience of faith among all the Gentiles, for His name's sake,

6 among whom you also are the called of Jesus Christ;

7 to all who are beloved of God in Rome, called *as* saints: Grace to you and peace from God our Father and the Lord Jesus Christ.

8 ¶ First, I thank my God through Jesus Christ for you all, because your faith is being proclaimed throughout the whole world.

9 For God, whom I serve in my spirit in the *preaching of the* gospel of His Son, is my witness *as to* how unceasingly I make mention of you,

10 always in my prayers making request, if perhaps now at last by the will of God I may succeed in coming to you.

11 For I long to see you in order that I may impart some spiritual gift to you, that you may be established;

12 that is, that I may be encouraged together with you *while* among you, each of us by the other's faith, both yours and mine.

13 And I do not want you to be unaware, brethren, that often I have planned to come to you (and have been prevented thus far) in order that I might obtain some fruit among you also, even as among the rest of the Gentiles.

14 I am [2]under obligation both to Greeks and to barbarians, both to the wise and to the foolish.

15 Thus, for my part, I am eager to preach the gospel to you also who are in Rome.

16 ¶ For I am not ashamed of the gospel, for it is the power of God for salvation to everyone who believes, to the Jew first and also to the Greek.

17 For in it *the* righteousness of God is revealed from faith to faith; as it is written, "But the righteous *man* shall live by faith."

18 ¶ For the wrath of God is revealed from heaven against all ungodliness and unrighteousness of men, who suppress the truth in unrighteousness,

19 because that which is known about God is evident within them; for God made it evident to them.

20 For since the creation of the world His invisible attributes, His eternal power and divine nature, have been clearly seen, being understood through what has been made, so that they are without excuse.

21 For even though they knew God, they did not [3]honor Him as God, or give thanks; but they became futile in their speculations, and their foolish heart was darkened.

22 Professing to be wise, they became fools,

23 and exchanged the glory of the incorruptible God for an image in the form of corruptible man and of birds and four-footed animals and [4]crawling creatures.

24 ¶ Therefore God gave them over in the lusts of their hearts to impurity, that their bodies might be dishonored among them.

25 For they exchanged the truth of God for a lie, and worshiped and served the creature rather than the Creator, who is blessed forever. Amen.

26 ¶ For this reason God gave them over to degrading passions; for their women exchanged the natural function for that which is unnatural,

27 and in the same way also the men abandoned the natural function of the woman and burned in their desire toward one another, men with men committing indecent acts and receiving in their own persons the due penalty of their error.

28 ¶ And just as they did not see fit to acknowledge God any longer, God

---

[1] Or, *as a result of*   [2] Lit., *debtor*   [3] Lit., *glorify*   [4] Or possibly, *reptiles*

gave them over to a depraved mind, to do those things which are not proper,

29 being filled with all unrighteousness, wickedness, greed, evil; full of envy, murder, strife, deceit, malice; *they are* gossips,

30 slanderers, haters of God, insolent, arrogant, boastful, inventors of evil, disobedient to parents,

31 without understanding, untrustworthy, unloving, unmerciful;

32 and, although they know the ordinance of God, that those who practice such things are worthy of death, they not only do the same, but also give hearty approval to those who practice them.

CHAPTER 2

THEREFORE you are without excuse, every man *of you* who passes judgment, for in that you judge another, you condemn yourself; for you who judge practice the same things.

2 And we know that the judgment of God rightly falls upon those who practice such things.

3 And do you suppose this, O man, when you pass judgment upon those who practice such things and do the same *yourself,* that you will escape the judgment of God?

4 Or do you think lightly of the riches of His kindness and forbearance and patience, not knowing that the kindness of God leads you to repentance?

5 But because of your stubbornness and unrepentant heart you are storing up wrath for yourself in the day of wrath and revelation of the righteous judgment of God,

6 who WILL RENDER TO EVERY MAN ACCORDING TO HIS DEEDS:

7 to those who by perseverance in doing good seek for glory and honor and immortality, eternal life;

8 but to those who are selfishly ambitious and do not obey the truth, but obey unrighteousness, wrath and indignation.

9 *There will be* tribulation and distress for every soul of man who does evil, of the Jew first and also of the Greek,

10 but glory and honor and peace to every man who does good, to the Jew first and also to the Greek.

11 For there is no partiality with God.

12 For all who have sinned without the Law will also perish without the Law; and all who have sinned under the Law will be judged by the Law;

13 for not the hearers of the Law are just before God, but the doers of the Law will be justified.

14 For when Gentiles who do not have the Law do instinctively the things of the Law, these, not having the Law, are a law to themselves,

15 in that they show the work of the Law written in their hearts, their conscience bearing witness, and their thoughts alternately accusing or else defending them,

16 on the day when, according to my gospel, God will judge the secrets of men through Christ Jesus.

17 ¶ But if you bear the name "Jew," and rely upon the Law, and boast in God,

18 and know *His* will, and approve the things that are essential, being instructed out of the Law,

19 and are confident that you yourself are a guide to the blind, a light to those who are in darkness,

20 a corrector of the foolish, a teacher of the immature, having in the Law the embodiment of knowledge and of the truth,

21 you, therefore, who teach another, do you not teach yourself? You who preach that one should not steal, do you steal?

22 You who say that one should not commit adultery, do you commit adultery? You who abhor idols, do you rob temples?

23 You who boast in the Law, through your breaking the Law, do you dishonor God?

24 For "THE NAME OF GOD IS BLASPHEMED AMONG THE GENTILES BECAUSE OF YOU," just as it is written.

25 For indeed circumcision is of value, if you practice the Law; but if you are a transgressor of the Law, your circumcision has become uncircumcision.

26 If therefore the uncircumcised man keeps the requirements of the Law, will not his uncircumcision be regarded as circumcision?

27 And will not he who is physically uncircumcised, if he keeps the Law,

We are all sinners

will he not judge you who though having the letter *of the Law* and circumcision are a transgressor of the Law?

28 For he is not a Jew who is one outwardly; neither is circumcision that which is outward in the flesh.

29 But he is a Jew who is one inwardly; and circumcision is that which is of the heart, by the Spirit, not by the letter; and his praise is not from men, but from God.

CHAPTER 3

THEN what advantage has the Jew? Or what is the benefit of circumcision?

2 Great in every respect. First of all, that they were entrusted with the oracles of God.

3 What then? If some did not believe, their unbelief will not nullify the faithfulness of God, will it?

4 May it never be! Rather, let God be found true, though every man *be found* a liar, as it is written,

"THAT THOU MIGHTEST BE JUSTIFIED IN THY WORDS,
AND MIGHTEST PREVAIL WHEN THOU ART JUDGED."

5 But if our unrighteousness demonstrates the righteousness of God, what shall we say? The God who inflicts wrath is not unrighteous, is He? (I am speaking in human terms.)

6 May it never be! For otherwise how will God judge the world?

7 But if through my lie the truth of God abounded to His glory, why am I also still being judged as a sinner?

8 And why not *say* (as we are slanderously reported and as some affirm that we say), "Let us do evil that good may come"? Their condemnation is just.

9 ¶ What then? Are we better than they? Not at all; for we have already charged that both Jews and Greeks are all under sin;

10 as it is written,
"THERE IS NONE RIGHTEOUS, NOT EVEN ONE;

11 THERE IS NONE WHO UNDERSTANDS,
THERE IS NONE WHO SEEKS FOR GOD;

12 ALL HAVE TURNED ASIDE, TOGETHER THEY HAVE BECOME USELESS;

THERE IS NONE WHO DOES GOOD,
THERE IS NOT EVEN ONE."

13 "THEIR THROAT IS AN OPEN GRAVE,
WITH THEIR TONGUES THEY KEEP DECEIVING,"
"THE POISON OF ASPS IS UNDER THEIR LIPS";

14 "WHOSE MOUTH IS FULL OF CURSING AND BITTERNESS";

15 "THEIR FEET ARE SWIFT TO SHED BLOOD,

16 DESTRUCTION AND MISERY ARE IN THEIR PATHS,

17 AND THE PATH OF PEACE HAVE THEY NOT KNOWN."

18 "THERE IS NO FEAR OF GOD BEFORE THEIR EYES."

19 ¶ Now we know that whatever the Law says, it speaks to those who are under the Law, that every mouth may be closed, and all the world may become accountable to God;

20 because by the works of the Law no flesh will be justified in His sight; for through the Law *comes* the knowledge of sin.

21 ¶ But now apart from the Law *the* righteousness of God has been manifested, being witnessed by the Law and the Prophets,

22 even *the* righteousness of God through faith in Jesus Christ for all those who believe; for there is no distinction;

23 for all have sinned and fall short of the glory of God,

24 being justified as a gift by His grace through the redemption which is in Christ Jesus;

25 whom God displayed publicly as a propitiation in His blood through faith. *This was* to demonstrate His righteousness, because in the forbearance of God He passed over the sins previously committed;

26 for the demonstration, *I say,* of His righteousness at the present time, that He might be just and the justifier of the one who has faith in Jesus.

27 Where then is boasting? It is excluded. By what kind of law? Of works? No, but by a law of faith.

28 For we maintain that a man is justified by faith apart from works of the Law.

29 Or is God *the God* of Jews only? Is He not *the God* of Gentiles also? Yes, of Gentiles also,

Turn to page 1122

30 since indeed God who will justify the circumcised by faith and the uncircumcised through faith is one.

31 ¶ Do we then nullify the Law through faith? May it never be! On the contrary, we establish the Law.

CHAPTER 4

WHAT then shall we say that Abraham, our forefather according to the flesh, has found?

2 For if Abraham was justified by works, he has something to boast about; but not before God.

3 For what does the Scripture say? "AND ABRAHAM BELIEVED GOD, AND IT WAS RECKONED TO HIM AS RIGHTEOUSNESS."

4 Now to the one who works, his wage is not reckoned as a favor, but as what is due.

5 But to the one who does not work, but believes in Him who justifies the ungodly, his faith is reckoned as righteousness,

6 just as David also speaks of the blessing upon the man to whom God reckons righteousness apart from works:

7 "BLESSED ARE THOSE WHOSE LAWLESS DEEDS HAVE BEEN FORGIVEN,
   AND WHOSE SINS HAVE BEEN COVERED.

8 "BLESSED IS THE MAN WHOSE SIN THE LORD WILL NOT TAKE INTO ACCOUNT."

9 Is this blessing then upon the circumcised, or upon the uncircumcised also? For we say, "FAITH WAS RECKONED TO ABRAHAM AS RIGHTEOUSNESS."

10 How then was it reckoned? While he was circumcised, or uncircumcised? Not while circumcised, but while uncircumcised;

11 and he received the sign of circumcision, a seal of the righteousness of the faith which he had while uncircumcised, that he might be the father of all who believe without being circumcised, that righteousness might be reckoned to them,

12 and the father of circumcision to those who not only are of the circumcision, but who also follow in the steps of the faith of our father Abraham which he had while uncircumcised.

13 For the promise to Abraham or to his descendants that he would be heir of the world was not through the Law, but through the righteousness of faith.

14 For if those who are of the Law are heirs, faith is made void and the promise is nullified;

15 for the Law brings about wrath, but where there is no law, neither is there violation.

16 For this reason *it is* by faith, that *it might be* in accordance with grace, in order that the promise may be certain to all the descendants, not only to those who are of the Law, but also to those who are of the faith of Abraham, who is the father of us all,

17 (as it is written, "A FATHER OF MANY NATIONS HAVE I MADE YOU") in the sight of Him whom he believed, *even* God, who gives life to the dead and calls into being that which does not exist.

18 In hope against hope he believed, in order that he might become a father of many nations, according to that which had been spoken, "SO SHALL YOUR DESCENDANTS BE."

19 And without becoming weak in faith he contemplated his own body, now as good as dead since he was about a hundred years old, and the deadness of Sarah's womb;

20 yet, with respect to the promise of God, he did not waver in unbelief, but grew strong in faith, giving glory to God,

21 and being fully assured that what He had promised, He was able also to perform.

22 Therefore also IT WAS RECKONED TO HIM AS RIGHTEOUSNESS.

23 Now not for his sake only was it written, that it was reckoned to him,

24 but for our sake also, to whom it will be reckoned, as those who believe in Him who raised Jesus our Lord from the dead,

25 *He* who was delivered up because of our transgressions, and was raised because of our justification.

CHAPTER 5

THEREFORE having been justified by faith, we have peace with God through our Lord Jesus Christ,

2 through whom also we have obtained our introduction by faith into

The payment God made for our sin.

this grace in which we stand; and we exult in hope of the glory of God.

3 And not only this, but we also exult in our tribulations, knowing that tribulation brings about perseverance;

4 and perseverance, proven character; and proven character, hope;

5 and hope does not disappoint, because the love of God has been poured out within our hearts through the Holy Spirit who was given to us.

6 For while we were still helpless, at the right time Christ died for the ungodly.

7 For one will hardly die for a righteous man; though perhaps for the good man someone would dare even to die.

8 But God demonstrates His own love toward us, in that while we were yet sinners, Christ died for us.

9 Much more then, having now been justified by His blood, we shall be saved from the wrath *of God* through Him.

10 For if while we were enemies, we were reconciled to God through the death of His Son, much more, having been reconciled, we shall be saved by His life.

11 And not only this, but we also exult in God through our Lord Jesus Christ, through whom we have now received the reconciliation.

12 ¶ Therefore, just as through one man sin entered into the world, and death through sin, and so death spread to all men, because all sinned—

13 for until the Law sin was in the world; but sin is not imputed when there is no law.

14 Nevertheless death reigned from Adam until Moses, even over those who had not sinned in the likeness of the offense of Adam, who is a [5]type of Him who was to come.

15 But the free gift is not like the transgression. For if by the transgression of the one the many died, much more did the grace of God and the gift by the grace of the one Man, Jesus Christ, abound to the many.

16 And the gift is not like *that which came* through the one who sinned; for on the one hand the judgment *arose* from one *transgression* resulting in condemnation, but on the other hand

the free gift *arose* from many transgressions resulting in justification.

17 For if by the transgression of the one, death reigned through the one, much more those who receive the abundance of grace and of the gift of righteousness will reign in life through the One, Jesus Christ.

18 So then as through one transgression there resulted condemnation to all men, even so through one act of righteousness there resulted justification of life to all men.

19 For as through the one man's disobedience the many were made sinners, even so through the obedience of the One the many will be made righteous.

20 And the Law came in that the transgression might increase; but where sin increased, grace abounded all the more,

21 that, as sin reigned in death, even so grace might reign through righteousness to eternal life through Jesus Christ our Lord.

CHAPTER 6

WHAT shall we say then? Are we to continue in sin that grace might increase?

2 May it never be! How shall we who died to sin still live in it?

3 Or do you not know that all of us who have been baptized into Christ Jesus have been baptized into His death?

4 Therefore we have been buried with Him through baptism into death, in order that as Christ was raised from the dead through the glory of the Father, so we too might walk in newness of life.

5 For if we have become united with *Him* in the likeness of His death, certainly we shall be also *in the likeness* of His resurrection,

6 knowing this, that our old self was crucified with *Him,* that our body of sin might be done away with, that we should no longer be slaves to sin;

7 for he who has died is freed from sin.

8 Now if we have died with Christ, we believe that we shall also live with Him,

9 knowing that Christ, having been raised from the dead, is never to die

[5] Or, *foreshadowing*

Turn to page 1136

again; death no longer is master over Him.

10 For the death that He died, He died to sin, once for all; but the life that He lives, He lives to God.

11 Even so consider yourselves to be dead to sin, but alive to God in Christ Jesus.

12 ¶ Therefore do not let sin reign in your mortal body that you should obey its lusts,

13 and do not go on presenting the members of your body to sin *as* instruments of unrighteousness; but present yourselves to God as those alive from the dead, and your members *as* instruments of righteousness to God.

14 For sin shall not be master over you, for you are not under law, but under grace.

15 ¶ What then? Shall we sin because we are not under law but under grace? May it never be!

16 Do you not know that when you present yourselves to someone *as* slaves for obedience, you are slaves of the one whom you obey, either of sin resulting in death, or of obedience resulting in righteousness?

17 But thanks be to God that though you were slaves of sin, you became obedient from the heart to that form of teaching to which you were committed,

18 and having been freed from sin, you became slaves of righteousness.

19 I am speaking in human terms because of the weakness of your flesh. For just as you presented your members *as* slaves to impurity and to lawlessness, resulting in *further* lawlessness, so now present your members *as* slaves to righteousness, resulting in sanctification.

20 For when you were slaves of sin, you were free in regard to righteousness.

21 Therefore what benefit were you then deriving from the things of which you are now ashamed? For the outcome of those things is death.

22 But now having been freed from sin and enslaved to God, you derive your benefit, resulting in sanctification, and the outcome, eternal life.

23 For the wages of sin is death, but the free gift of God is eternal life in Christ Jesus our Lord.

CHAPTER 7

OR do you not know, brethren (for I am speaking to those who know the law), that the law has jurisdiction over a person as long as he lives?

2 For the married woman is bound by law to her husband while he is living; but if her husband dies, she is released from the law concerning the husband.

3 So then if, while her husband is living, she is joined to another man, she shall be called an adulteress; but if her husband dies, she is free from the law, so that she is not an adulteress, though she is joined to another man.

4 Therefore, my brethren, you also were made to die to the Law through the body of Christ, that you might be joined to another, to Him who was raised from the dead, that we might bear fruit for God.

5 For while we were in the flesh, the sinful passions, which were *aroused* by the Law, were at work in the members of our body to bear fruit for death.

6 But now we have been released from the Law, having died to that by which we were bound, so that we serve in newness of the [6]Spirit and not in oldness of the letter.

7 ¶ What shall we say then? Is the Law sin? May it never be! On the contrary, I would not have come to know sin except through the Law; for I would not have known about coveting if the Law had not said, "You shall not covet."

8 But sin, taking opportunity through the commandment, produced in me coveting of every kind; for apart from the Law sin *is* dead.

9 And I was once alive apart from the Law; but when the commandment came, sin became alive, and I died;

10 and this commandment, which was to result in life, proved to result in death for me;

11 for sin, taking opportunity through the commandment, deceived me, and through it killed me.

12 So then, the Law is holy, and the commandment is holy and righteous and good.

13 Therefore did that which is good become *a cause of* death for me? May it never be! Rather it was sin, in order

[6] Or, *spirit*

Turn to page 1121

that it might be shown to be sin by effecting my death through that which is good, that through the commandment sin might become utterly sinful.

14 For we know that the Law is spiritual; but I am of flesh, sold into bondage to sin.

15 For that which I am doing, I do not understand; for I am not practicing what I *would* like to *do*, but I am doing the very thing I hate.

16 But if I do the very thing I do not wish *to do*, I agree with the Law, *confessing* that it is good.

17 So now, no longer am I the one doing it, but sin which indwells me.

18 For I know that nothing good dwells in me, that is, in my flesh; for the wishing is present in me, but the doing of the good *is* not.

19 For the good that I wish, I do not do; but I practice the very evil that I do not wish.

20 But if I am doing the very thing I do not wish, I am no longer the one doing it, but sin which dwells in me.

21 I find then the principle that evil is present in me, the one who wishes to do good.

22 For I joyfully concur with the law of God in the inner man,

23 but I see a different law in the members of my body, waging war against the law of my mind, and making me a prisoner of the law of sin which is in my members.

24 Wretched man that I am! Who will set me free from the body of this death?

25 Thanks be to God through Jesus Christ our Lord! So then, on the one hand I myself with my mind am serving the law of God, but on the other, with my flesh the law of sin.

CHAPTER 8

THERE is therefore now no condemnation for those who are in Christ Jesus.

2 For the law of the Spirit of life in Christ Jesus has set [7]you free from the law of sin and of death.

3 For what the Law could not do, weak as it was through the flesh, God *did:* sending His own Son in the likeness of sinful flesh and *as an offering* for sin, He condemned sin in the flesh,

4 in order that the requirement of the Law might be fulfilled in us, who do not walk according to the flesh, but according to the Spirit.

5 For those who are according to the flesh set their minds on the things of the flesh, but those who are according to the Spirit, the things of the Spirit.

6 For the mind set on the flesh is death, but the mind set on the Spirit is life and peace,

7 because the mind set on the flesh is hostile toward God; for it does not subject itself to the law of God, for it is not even able *to do so*;

8 and those who are in the flesh cannot please God.

9 However, you are not in the flesh but in the Spirit, if indeed the Spirit of God dwells in you. But if anyone does not have the Spirit of Christ, he does not belong to Him.

10 And if Christ is in you, though the body is dead because of sin, yet the spirit is alive because of righteousness.

11 But if the Spirit of Him who raised Jesus from the dead dwells in you, He who raised Christ Jesus from the dead will also give life to your mortal bodies [8]through His Spirit who indwells you.

12 ¶ So then, brethren, we are under obligation, not to the flesh, to live according to the flesh—

13 for if you are living according to the flesh, you must die; but if by the Spirit you are putting to death the deeds of the body, you will live.

14 For all who are being led by the Spirit of God, these are sons of God.

15 For you have not received a spirit of slavery leading to fear again, but you have received a spirit of adoption as sons by which we cry out, "Abba! Father!"

16 The Spirit Himself bears witness with our spirit that we are children of God,

17 and if children, heirs also, heirs of God and fellow heirs with Christ, if indeed we suffer with *Him* in order that we may also be glorified with *Him.*

18 ¶ For I consider that the sufferings of this present time are not worthy to be compared with the glory that is to be revealed to us.

[7] Some ancient mss. read *me*

[8] Some ancient mss. read *because of*

19 For the anxious longing of the creation waits eagerly for the revealing of the sons of God.

20 For the creation was subjected to futility, not of its own will, but because of Him who subjected it, [9]in hope

21 that the creation itself also will be set free from its slavery to corruption into the freedom of the glory of the children of God.

22 For we know that the whole creation groans and suffers the pains of childbirth together until now.

23 And not only this, but also we ourselves, having the first fruits of the Spirit, even we ourselves groan within ourselves, waiting eagerly for *our* adoption as sons, the redemption of our body.

24 For in hope we have been saved, but hope that is seen is not hope; for [10]why does one also hope for what he sees?

25 But if we hope for what we do not see, with perseverance we wait eagerly for it.

26 ¶ And in the same way the Spirit also helps our weakness; for we do not know how to pray as we should, but the Spirit Himself intercedes for *us* with groanings too deep for words;

27 and He who searches the hearts knows what the mind of the Spirit is, because He intercedes for the saints according to *the will of* God.

28 And we know that [11]God causes all things to work together for good to those who love God, to those who are called according to *His* purpose.

29 For whom He foreknew, He also predestined *to become* conformed to the image of His Son, that He might be the first-born among many brethren;

30 and whom He predestined, these He also called; and whom He called, these He also justified; and whom He justified, these He also glorified.

31 ¶ What then shall we say to these things? If God *is* for us, who *is* against us?

32 He who did not spare His own Son, but delivered Him up for us all, how will He not also with Him freely give us all things?

33 Who will bring a charge against God's elect? God is the one who justifies;

34 who is the one who condemns? Christ Jesus is He who died, yes, rather who was [12]raised, who is at the right hand of God, who also intercedes for us.

35 Who shall separate us from the love of [13]Christ? Shall tribulation, or distress, or persecution, or famine, or nakedness, or peril, or sword?

36 Just as it is written,

"For Thy sake we are being put
    to death all day long;
  We were considered as sheep
    to be slaughtered."

37 But in all these things we overwhelmingly conquer through Him who loved us.

38 For I am convinced that neither death, nor life, nor angels, nor principalities, nor things present, nor things to come, nor powers,

39 nor height, nor depth, nor any other created thing, shall be able to separate us from the love of God, which is in Christ Jesus our Lord.

CHAPTER 9

I AM telling the truth in Christ, I am not lying, my conscience bearing me witness in the Holy Spirit,

2 that I have great sorrow and unceasing grief in my heart.

3 For I could wish that I myself were accursed, *separated* from Christ for the sake of my brethren, my kinsmen according to the flesh,

4 who are Israelites, to whom belongs the adoption as sons and the glory and the covenants and the giving of the Law and the *temple* service and the promises,

5 whose are the fathers, and from whom is the Christ according to the flesh, who is over all, God blessed forever. Amen.

6 ¶ But *it is* not as though the word of God has failed. For they are not all Israel who are *descended* from Israel;

7 neither are they all children because they are Abraham's descendants, but: "Through Isaac your descendants will be named."

8 That is, it is not the children of the flesh who are children of God, but the

---

[9] Some ancient mss. read *in hope; because the creation*
[10] Some ancient mss. read *who hopes for what he sees?*
[11] Some ancient mss. read *all things work together for good*

[12] Some ancient mss. read *raised from the dead*
[13] Some ancient mss. read *God*

children of the promise are regarded as descendants.

9 For this is a word of promise: "AT THIS TIME I WILL COME, AND SARAH SHALL HAVE A SON."

10 And not only this, but there was Rebekah also, when she had conceived *twins* by one man, our father Isaac;

11 for though *the twins* were not yet born, and had not done anything good or bad, in order that God's purpose according to *His* choice might stand, not because of works, but because of Him who calls,

12 it was said to her, "THE OLDER WILL SERVE THE YOUNGER."

13 Just as it is written, "JACOB I LOVED, BUT ESAU I HATED."

14 ¶ What shall we say then? There is no injustice with God, is there? May it never be!

15 For He says to Moses, "I WILL HAVE MERCY ON WHOM I HAVE MERCY, AND I WILL HAVE COMPASSION ON WHOM I HAVE COMPASSION."

16 So then it *does* not *depend* on the man who wills or the man who runs, but on God who has mercy.

17 For the Scripture says to Pharaoh, "FOR THIS VERY PURPOSE I RAISED YOU UP, TO DEMONSTRATE MY POWER IN YOU, AND THAT MY NAME MIGHT BE PROCLAIMED THROUGHOUT THE WHOLE EARTH."

18 So then He has mercy on whom He desires, and He hardens whom He desires.

19 ¶ You will say to me then, "Why does He still find fault? For who resists His will?"

20 On the contrary, who are you, O man, who answers back to God? The thing molded will not say to the molder, "Why did you make me like this," will it?

21 Or does not the potter have a right over the clay, to make from the same lump one vessel for honorable use, and another for common use?

22 What if God, although willing to demonstrate His wrath and to make His power known, endured with much patience vessels of wrath prepared for destruction?

23 And *He did so* in order that He might make known the riches of His glory upon vessels of mercy, which He prepared beforehand for glory,

24 *even* us, whom He also called, not from among Jews only, but also from among Gentiles.

25 As He says also in Hosea,
"I WILL CALL THOSE WHO WERE
　NOT MY PEOPLE, 'MY PEOPLE,'
　AND HER WHO WAS NOT BELOVED,
　'BELOVED.' "

26 "AND IT SHALL BE THAT IN THE
　PLACE WHERE IT WAS SAID TO
　THEM, 'YOU ARE NOT MY PEOPLE,'
　THERE THEY SHALL BE CALLED
　SONS OF THE LIVING GOD."

27 And Isaiah cries out concerning Israel, "THOUGH THE NUMBER OF THE SONS OF ISRAEL BE AS THE SAND OF THE SEA, IT IS THE REMNANT THAT WILL BE SAVED;

28 FOR THE LORD WILL EXECUTE HIS WORD UPON THE EARTH, THOROUGHLY AND QUICKLY."

29 And just as Isaiah foretold,
"EXCEPT THE LORD OF SABAOTH
　HAD LEFT TO US A POSTERITY,
　WE WOULD HAVE BECOME AS
　SODOM, AND WOULD HAVE RE-
　SEMBLED GOMORRAH."

30 ¶ What shall we say then? That Gentiles, who did not pursue righteousness, attained righteousness, even the righteousness which is by faith;

31 but Israel, pursuing a law of righteousness, did not arrive at *that* law.

32 Why? Because *they* did not *pursue it* by faith, but as though *it were* by works. They stumbled over the stumbling stone,

33 just as it is written,
"BEHOLD, I LAY IN ZION A STONE
　OF STUMBLING AND A ROCK OF
　OFFENSE,
　AND HE WHO BELIEVES IN HIM
　WILL NOT BE DISAPPOINTED."

CHAPTER 10

BRETHREN, my heart's desire and my prayer to God for them is for *their* salvation.

2 For I bear them witness that they have a zeal for God, but not in accordance with knowledge.

3 For not knowing about God's righteousness, and seeking to establish their own, they did not subject themselves to the righteousness of God.

4 For Christ is the end of the law for

Confess Jesus as Lord.
Ask God to save you.

righteousness to everyone who believes.

5 For Moses writes that the man who practices the righteousness which is based on law shall live by that righteousness.

6 But the righteousness based on faith speaks thus, "DO NOT SAY IN YOUR HEART, 'WHO WILL ASCEND INTO HEAVEN?' (that is, to bring Christ down),

7 or 'WHO WILL DESCEND INTO THE ABYSS?' (that is, to bring Christ up from the dead)."

8 But what does it say? "THE WORD IS NEAR YOU, IN YOUR MOUTH AND IN YOUR HEART"—that is, the word of faith which we are preaching,

9 that if you confess with your mouth Jesus *as* Lord, and believe in your heart that God raised Him from the dead, you shall be saved;

10 for with the heart man believes, resulting in righteousness, and with the mouth he confesses, resulting in salvation.

11 For the Scripture says, "WHOEVER BELIEVES IN HIM WILL NOT BE DISAPPOINTED."

12 For there is no distinction between Jew and Greek; for the same *Lord* is Lord of all, abounding in riches for all who call upon Him;

13 for "WHOEVER WILL CALL UPON THE NAME OF THE LORD WILL BE SAVED."

14 How then shall they call upon Him in whom they have not believed? And how shall they believe in Him whom they have not heard? And how shall they hear without a preacher?

15 And how shall they preach unless they are sent? Just as it is written, "HOW BEAUTIFUL ARE THE FEET OF THOSE WHO BRING GLAD TIDINGS OF GOOD THINGS!"

16 ¶ However, they did not all heed the glad tidings; for Isaiah says, "LORD, WHO HAS BELIEVED OUR REPORT?"

17 So faith *comes* from hearing, and hearing by the word of Christ.

18 But I say, surely they have never heard, have they? Indeed they have;
"THEIR VOICE HAS GONE OUT INTO
ALL THE EARTH,
AND THEIR WORDS TO THE ENDS
OF THE WORLD."

19 But I say, surely Israel did not know, did they? At the first Moses says,
"I WILL MAKE YOU JEALOUS BY
THAT WHICH IS NOT A NATION,
BY A NATION WITHOUT UNDER-
STANDING WILL I ANGER YOU."

20 And Isaiah is very bold and says,
"I WAS FOUND BY THOSE WHO
SOUGHT ME NOT,
I BECAME MANIFEST TO THOSE
WHO DID NOT ASK FOR ME."

21 But as for Israel He says, "ALL THE DAY LONG I HAVE STRETCHED OUT MY HANDS TO A DISOBEDIENT AND OBSTINATE PEOPLE."

CHAPTER 11

I SAY then, God has not rejected His people, has He? May it never be! For I too am an Israelite, a descendant of Abraham, of the tribe of Benjamin.

2 God has not rejected His people whom He foreknew. Or do you not know what the Scripture says in *the passage about* Elijah, how he pleads with God against Israel?

3 "LORD, THEY HAVE KILLED THY PROPHETS, THEY HAVE TORN DOWN THINE ALTARS, AND I ALONE AM LEFT, AND THEY ARE SEEKING MY LIFE."

4 But what is the divine response to him? "I HAVE KEPT for Myself SEVEN THOUSAND MEN WHO HAVE NOT BOWED THE KNEE TO BAAL."

5 In the same way then, there has also come to be at the present time a remnant according to *God's* gracious choice.

6 But if it is by grace, it is no longer on the basis of works, otherwise grace is no longer grace.

7 What then? That which Israel is seeking for, it has not obtained, but those who were chosen obtained it, and the rest were hardened;

8 just as it is written,
"GOD GAVE THEM A SPIRIT OF STU-
POR,
EYES TO SEE NOT AND EARS TO
HEAR NOT,
DOWN TO THIS VERY DAY."

9 And David says,
"LET THEIR TABLE BECOME A SNARE
AND A TRAP,
AND A STUMBLING BLOCK AND A
RETRIBUTION TO THEM.

Turn to page 53.

10 "LET THEIR EYES BE DARKENED TO
SEE NOT,
AND BEND THEIR BACKS FOR-
EVER."

11 ¶ I say then, they did not stumble
so as to fall, did they? May it never be!
But by their transgression salvation
has come to the Gentiles, to make
them jealous.

12 Now if their transgression be
riches for the world and their failure
be riches for the Gentiles, how much
more will their fulfillment be!

13 But I am speaking to you who are
Gentiles. Inasmuch then as I am an
apostle of Gentiles, I magnify my ministry,

14 if somehow I might move to jealousy my fellow countrymen and save
some of them.

15 For if their rejection be the reconciliation of the world, what will
their acceptance be but life from the
dead?

16 And if the first piece *of dough* be
holy, the lump is also; and if the root
be holy, the branches are too.

17 But if some of the branches were
broken off, and you, being a wild olive,
were grafted in among them and became partaker with them of the rich
root of the olive tree,

18 do not be arrogant toward the
branches; but if you are arrogant,
remember that it is not you who supports the root, but the root *supports*
you.

19 You will say then, "Branches were
broken off so that I might be grafted
in."

20 Quite right, they were broken off
for their unbelief, but you stand by
your faith. Do not be conceited, but
fear;

21 for if God did not spare the natural branches, neither will He spare
you.

22 Behold then the kindness and severity of God; to those who fell, severity, but to you, God's kindness, if you
continue in His kindness; otherwise
you also will be cut off.

23 And they also, if they do not continue in their unbelief, will be grafted
in; for God is able to graft them in
again.

24 For if you were cut off from what
is by nature a wild olive tree, and were

grafted contrary to nature into a cultivated olive tree, how much more shall
these who are the natural *branches* be
grafted into their own olive tree?

25 ¶ For I do not want you, brethren, to be uninformed of this mystery,
lest you be wise in your own estimation, that a partial hardening has happened to Israel until the fulness of the
Gentiles has come in;

26 and thus all Israel will be saved;
just as it is written,
"THE DELIVERER WILL COME FROM
ZION,
HE WILL REMOVE UNGODLINESS
FROM JACOB."

27 "AND THIS IS MY COVENANT WITH
THEM,
WHEN I TAKE AWAY THEIR SINS."

28 From the standpoint of the gospel
they are enemies for your sake, but
from the standpoint of *God's* choice
they are beloved for the sake of the
fathers;

29 for the gifts and the calling of God
are irrevocable.

30 For just as you once were disobedient to God, but now have been
shown mercy because of their disobedience,

31 so these also now have been disobedient, in order that because of the
mercy shown to you they also may
now be shown mercy.

32 For God has shut up all in disobedience that He might show mercy to
all.

33 ¶ Oh, the depth of the riches both
of the wisdom and knowledge of God!
How unsearchable are His judgments
and unfathomable His ways!

34 For WHO HAS KNOWN THE MIND OF
THE LORD, OR WHO BECAME HIS COUN-
SELOR?

35 OR WHO HAS FIRST GIVEN TO HIM
THAT IT MIGHT BE PAID BACK TO HIM
AGAIN?

36 For from Him and through Him
and to Him are all things. To Him *be*
the glory forever. Amen.

CHAPTER 12

I URGE you therefore, brethren, by
the mercies of God, to present your
bodies a living and holy sacrifice, acceptable to God, *which is* your spiritual service of worship.

2 And do not be conformed to this

world, but be transformed by the renewing of your mind, that you may prove what the will of God is, that which is good and acceptable and perfect.

3 ¶ For through the grace given to me I say to every man among you not to think more highly of himself than he ought to think; but to think so as to have sound judgment, as God has allotted to each a measure of faith.

4 For just as we have many members in one body and all the members do not have the same function,

5 so we, who are many, are one body in Christ, and individually members one of another.

6 And since we have gifts that differ according to the grace given to us, *let each exercise them accordingly:* if prophecy, according to the proportion of his faith;

7 if service, in his serving; or he who teaches, in his teaching;

8 or he who exhorts, in his exhortation; he who gives, with [14]liberality; he who leads, with diligence; he who shows mercy, with cheerfulness.

9 ¶ Let love be without hypocrisy. Abhor what is evil; cling to what is good.

10 Be devoted to one another in brotherly love; give preference to one another in honor;

11 not lagging behind in diligence, fervent in spirit, serving the Lord;

12 rejoicing in hope, persevering in tribulation, devoted to prayer;

13 contributing to the needs of the saints, practicing hospitality.

14 Bless those who persecute [15]you; bless and curse not.

15 Rejoice with those who rejoice, and weep with those who weep.

16 Be of the same mind toward one another; do not be haughty in mind, but associate with the lowly. Do not be wise in your own estimation.

17 Never pay back evil for evil to anyone. Respect what is right in the sight of all men.

18 If possible, so far as it depends on you, be at peace with all men.

19 Never take your own revenge, beloved, but leave room for the wrath *of God,* for it is written, "VENGEANCE IS MINE, I WILL REPAY," says the Lord.

20"BUT IF YOUR ENEMY IS HUNGRY, FEED HIM, AND IF HE IS THIRSTY, GIVE HIM A DRINK; FOR IN SO DOING YOU WILL HEAP BURNING COALS UPON HIS HEAD."

21 Do not be overcome by evil, but overcome evil with good.

CHAPTER 13

LET every person be in subjection to the governing authorities. For there is no authority except from God, and those which exist are established by God.

2 Therefore he who resists authority has opposed the ordinance of God; and they who have opposed will receive condemnation upon themselves.

3 For rulers are not a cause of fear for good behavior, but for evil. Do you want to have no fear of authority? Do what is good, and you will have praise from the same;

4 for it is a minister of God to you for good. But if you do what is evil, be afraid; for it does not bear the sword for nothing; for it is a minister of God, an avenger who brings wrath upon the one who practices evil.

5 Wherefore it is necessary to be in subjection, not only because of wrath, but also for conscience' sake.

6 For because of this you also pay taxes, for *rulers* are servants of God, devoting themselves to this very thing.

7 Render to all what is due them: tax to whom tax *is due;* custom to whom custom; fear to whom fear; honor to whom honor.

8 ¶ Owe nothing to anyone except to love one another; for he who loves his neighbor has fulfilled *the* law.

9 For this, "YOU SHALL NOT COMMIT ADULTERY, YOU SHALL NOT MURDER, YOU SHALL NOT STEAL, YOU SHALL NOT COVET," and if there is any other commandment, it is summed up in this saying, "YOU SHALL LOVE YOUR NEIGHBOR AS YOURSELF."

10 Love does no wrong to a neighbor; love therefore is the fulfillment of *the* law.

11 ¶ And this *do,* knowing the time, that it is already the hour for you to awaken from sleep; for now [16]salvation is nearer to us than when we believed.

12 The night is almost gone, and the

---

[14] Or, *simplicity*   [15] Some ancient mss. do not contain *you*   [16] Or, *our salvation is nearer than when*

day is at hand. Let us therefore lay aside the deeds of darkness and put on the armor of light.

13 Let us behave properly as in the day, not in carousing and drunkenness, not in sexual promiscuity and sensuality, not in strife and jealousy.

14 But put on the Lord Jesus Christ, and make no provision for the flesh in regard to *its* lusts.

CHAPTER 14

Now accept the one who is weak in faith, *but* not for *the purpose of* passing judgment on his opinions.

2 One man has faith that he may eat all things, but he who is weak eats vegetables *only.*

3 Let not him who eats regard with contempt him who does not eat, and let not him who does not eat judge him who eats, for God has accepted him.

4 Who are you to judge the servant of another? To his own master he stands or falls; and stand he will, for the Lord is able to make him stand.

5 One man regards one day above another, another regards every day *alike.* Let each man be fully convinced in his own mind.

6 He who observes the day, observes it for the Lord, and he who eats, does so for the Lord, for he gives thanks to God; and he who eats not, for the Lord he does not eat, and gives thanks to God.

7 For not one of us lives for himself, and not one dies for himself;

8 for if we live, we live for the Lord, or if we die, we die for the Lord; therefore whether we live or die, we are the Lord's.

9 For to this end Christ died and lived *again,* that He might be Lord both of the dead and of the living.

10 But you, why do you judge your brother? Or you again, why do you regard your brother with contempt? For we shall all stand before the judgment seat of God.

11 For it is written,

"As I live, says the Lord, every knee shall bow to Me,

And every tongue shall give praise to God."

12 So then each one of us shall give account of himself to God.

13 ¶ Therefore let us not judge one another anymore, but rather determine this—not to put an obstacle or a stumbling block in a brother's way.

14 I know and am convinced in the Lord Jesus that nothing is unclean in itself; but to him who thinks anything to be unclean, to him it is unclean.

15 For if because of food your brother is hurt, you are no longer walking according to love. Do not destroy with your food him for whom Christ died.

16 Therefore do not let what is for you a good thing be spoken of as evil;

17 for the kingdom of God is not eating and drinking, but righteousness and peace and joy in the Holy Spirit.

18 For he who in this *way* serves Christ is acceptable to God and approved by men.

19 So then [17]let us pursue the things which make for peace and the building up of one another.

20 Do not tear down the work of God for the sake of food. All things indeed are clean, but they are evil for the man who eats and gives offense.

21 It is good not to eat meat or to drink wine, or *to do anything* by which your brother stumbles.

22 The faith which you have, have as your own conviction before God. Happy is he who does not condemn himself in what he approves.

23 But he who doubts is condemned if he eats, because *his eating is* not from faith; and whatever is not from faith is sin.

CHAPTER 15

Now we who are strong ought to bear the weaknesses of those without strength and not *just* please ourselves.

2 Let each of us please his neighbor for his good, to his edification.

3 For even Christ did not please Himself; but as it is written, "The reproaches of those who reproached Thee fell upon Me."

4 For whatever was written in earlier times was written for our instruction, that through perseverance and the encouragement of the Scriptures we might have hope.

5 Now may the God who gives perseverance and encouragement grant

[17] Many ancient mss. read *we pursue*

you to be of the same mind with one another according to Christ Jesus;

6 that with one accord you may with one voice glorify the God and Father of our Lord Jesus Christ.

7 ¶ Wherefore, accept one another, just as Christ also accepted us to the glory of God.

8 For I say that Christ has become a servant to the circumcision on behalf of the truth of God to confirm the promises *given* to the fathers,

9 and for the Gentiles to glorify God for His mercy; as it is written,

"THEREFORE I WILL GIVE PRAISE
   TO THEE AMONG THE GENTILES,
AND I WILL SING TO THY NAME."

10 And again he says,

"REJOICE, O GENTILES, WITH HIS
   PEOPLE."

11 And again,

"PRAISE THE LORD ALL YOU GEN-
   TILES,
AND LET ALL THE PEOPLES PRAISE
   HIM."

12 And again Isaiah says,

"THERE SHALL COME THE ROOT OF
   JESSE,
AND HE WHO ARISES TO RULE
   OVER THE GENTILES,
IN HIM SHALL THE GENTILES
   HOPE."

13 Now may the God of hope fill you with all joy and peace in believing, that you may abound in hope by the power of the Holy Spirit.

14 ¶ And concerning you, my brethren, I myself also am convinced that you yourselves are full of goodness, filled with all knowledge, and able also to admonish one another.

15 But I have written very boldly to you on some points, so as to remind you again, because of the grace that was given me from God,

16 to be a minister of Christ Jesus to the Gentiles, ministering as a priest the gospel of God, that *my* offering of the Gentiles might become acceptable, sanctified by the Holy Spirit.

17 Therefore in Christ Jesus I have found reason for boasting in things pertaining to God.

18 For I will not presume to speak of anything except what Christ has accomplished through me, resulting in the obedience of the Gentiles by word and deed,

19 in the power of signs and wonders, in the power of the Spirit; so that from Jerusalem and round about as far as Illyricum I have fully preached the gospel of Christ.

20 And thus I aspired to preach the gospel, not where Christ was *already* named, that I might not build upon another man's foundation;

21 but as it is written,

"THEY WHO HAD NO NEWS OF HIM
   SHALL SEE,
AND THEY WHO HAVE NOT HEARD
   SHALL UNDERSTAND."

22 ¶ For this reason I have often been hindered from coming to you;

23 but now, with no further place for me in these regions, and since I have had for many years a longing to come to you

24 whenever I go to Spain—for I hope to see you in passing, and to be helped on my way there by you, when I have first enjoyed your company for a while—

25 but now, I am going to Jerusalem serving the saints.

26 For Macedonia and Achaia have been pleased to make a contribution for the poor among the saints in Jerusalem.

27 Yes, they were pleased *to do so,* and they are indebted to them. For if the Gentiles have shared in their spiritual things, they are indebted to minister to them also in material things.

28 Therefore, when I have finished this, and have put my seal on this fruit of theirs, I will go on by way of you to Spain.

29 And I know that when I come to you, I will come in the fulness of the blessing of Christ.

30 ¶ Now I urge you, brethren, by our Lord Jesus Christ and by the love of the Spirit, to strive together with me in your prayers to God for me,

31 that I may be delivered from those who are disobedient in Judea, and *that* my service for Jerusalem may prove acceptable to the saints;

32 so that I may come to you in joy by the will of God and find *refreshing* rest in your company.

33 Now the God of peace be with you all. Amen.

CHAPTER 16

I COMMEND to you our sister Phoebe, who is a servant of the church which is at Cenchrea;

2 that you receive her in the Lord in a manner worthy of the saints, and that you help her in whatever matter she may have need of you; for she herself has also been a helper of many, and of myself as well.

3 ¶ Greet Prisca and Aquila, my fellow workers in Christ Jesus,

4 who for my life risked their own necks, to whom not only do I give thanks, but also all the churches of the Gentiles;

5 also *greet* the church that is in their house. Greet Epaenetus, my beloved, who is the first convert to Christ from Asia.

6 Greet Mary, who has worked hard for you.

7 Greet Andronicus and Junias, my kinsmen, and my fellow prisoners, who are outstanding among the apostles, who also were in Christ before me.

8 Greet Ampliatus, my beloved in the Lord.

9 Greet Urbanus, our fellow worker in Christ, and Stachys my beloved.

10 Greet Apelles, the approved in Christ. Greet those who are of the *household* of Aristobulus.

11 Greet Herodion, my kinsman. Greet those of the *household* of Narcissus, who are in the Lord.

12 Greet Tryphaena and Tryphosa, workers in the Lord. Greet Persis the beloved, who has worked hard in the Lord.

13 Greet Rufus, a choice man in the Lord, also his mother and mine.

14 Greet Asyncritus, Phlegon, Hermes, Patrobas, Hermas and the brethren with them.

15 Greet Philologus and Julia, Nereus and his sister, and Olympas, and all the saints who are with them.

16 Greet one another with a holy kiss. All the churches of Christ greet you.

17 ¶ Now I urge you, brethren, keep your eye on those who cause dissensions and hindrances contrary to the teaching which you learned, and turn away from them.

18 For such men are slaves, not of our Lord Christ but of their own appetites; and by their smooth and flattering speech they deceive the hearts of the unsuspecting.

19 For the report of your obedience has reached to all; therefore I am rejoicing over you, but I want you to be wise in what is good, and innocent in what is evil.

20 And the God of peace will soon crush Satan under your feet.

¶ The grace of our Lord Jesus be with you.

21 ¶ Timothy my fellow worker greets you, and *so do* Lucius and Jason and Sosipater, my kinsmen.

22 I, Tertius, who write this letter, greet you in the Lord.

23 Gaius, host to me and to the whole church, greets you. Erastus, the city treasurer greets you, and Quartus, the brother.

24 [[18]The grace of our Lord Jesus Christ be with you all. Amen.]

25 ¶ Now to Him who is able to establish you according to my gospel and the preaching of Jesus Christ, according to the revelation of the mystery which has been kept secret for long ages past,

26 but now is manifested, and by the Scriptures of the prophets, according to the commandment of the eternal God, has been made known to all the nations, *leading* to obedience of faith;

27 to the only wise God, through Jesus Christ, be the glory forever. Amen.

[18] Many mss. do not contain this verse

1 CORINTHIANS

PAUL, called *as* an apostle of Jesus Christ by the will of God, and Sosthenes our brother,

2 to the church of God which is at Corinth, to those who have been sanctified in Christ Jesus, saints by calling, with all who in every place call upon the name of our Lord Jesus Christ, their *Lord* and ours:

3 Grace to you and peace from God our Father and the Lord Jesus Christ.

4 ¶ I thank [1]my God always concerning you, for the grace of God which was given you in Christ Jesus,

5 that in everything you were enriched in Him, in all speech and all knowledge,

6 even as the testimony concerning Christ was confirmed in you,

7 so that you are not lacking in any gift, awaiting eagerly the revelation of our Lord Jesus Christ,

8 who shall also confirm you to the end, blameless in the day of our Lord Jesus Christ.

9 God is faithful, through whom you were called into fellowship with His Son, Jesus Christ our Lord.

10 ¶ Now I exhort you, brethren, by the name of our Lord Jesus Christ, that you all agree, and there be no divisions among you, but you be made complete in the same mind and in the same judgment.

11 For I have been informed concerning you, my brethren, by Chloe's *people,* that there are quarrels among you.

12 Now I mean this, that each one of you is saying, "I am of Paul," and "I of Apollos," and "I of Cephas," and "I of Christ."

13 Has Christ been divided? Paul was not crucified for you, was he? Or were you baptized in the name of Paul?

14 [2]I thank God that I baptized none of you except Crispus and Gaius,

15 that no man should say you were baptized in my name.

16 Now I did baptize also the household of Stephanas; beyond that, I do not know whether I baptized any other.

17 For Christ did not send me to baptize, but to preach the gospel, not in cleverness of speech, that the cross of Christ should not be made void.

18 ¶ For the word of the cross is to those who are perishing foolishness, but to us who are being saved it is the power of God.

19 For it is written,

"I WILL DESTROY THE WISDOM OF THE WISE,
AND THE CLEVERNESS OF THE CLEVER I WILL SET ASIDE."

20 Where is the wise man? Where is the scribe? Where is the debater of this age? Has not God made foolish the wisdom of the world?

21 For since in the wisdom of God the world through its wisdom did not *come to* know God, God was well-pleased through the foolishness of the message preached to save those who believe.

22 For indeed Jews ask for signs, and Greeks search for wisdom;

23 but we preach [3]Christ crucified, to Jews a stumbling block, and to Gentiles foolishness,

24 but to those who are the called, both Jews and Greeks, Christ the power of God and the wisdom of God.

25 Because the foolishness of God is wiser than men, and the weakness of God is stronger than men.

26 ¶ For consider your calling, brethren, that there were not many wise according to the flesh, not many mighty, not many noble;

27 but God has chosen the foolish things of the world to shame the wise, and God has chosen the weak things of the world to shame the things which are strong,

28 and the base things of the world and the despised, God has chosen, the things that are not, that He might nullify the things that are,

29 that no man should boast before God.

30 But by His doing you are in Christ Jesus, who became to us wisdom from God, and righteousness and sanctification, and redemption,

31 that, just as it is written, "LET HIM WHO BOASTS, BOAST IN THE LORD."

CHAPTER 2

AND when I came to you, brethren, I did not come with superiority of

---

1 Some ancient mss. do not contain *my*
2 Some ancient mss. read *I give thanks that*

3 I.e., Messiah

speech or of wisdom, proclaiming to you the [4]testimony of God.

2 For I determined to know nothing among you except Jesus Christ, and Him crucified.

3 And I was with you in weakness and in fear and in much trembling.

4 And my message and my preaching were not in persuasive words of wisdom, but in demonstration of the Spirit and of power,

5 that your faith should not rest on the wisdom of men, but on the power of God.

6 ¶ Yet we do speak wisdom among those who are mature; a wisdom, however, not of this age, nor of the rulers of this age, who are passing away;

7 but we speak God's wisdom in a mystery, the hidden *wisdom,* which God predestined before the ages to our glory;

8 *the wisdom* which none of the rulers of this age has understood; for if they had understood it, they would not have crucified the Lord of glory;

9 but just as it is written,

"THINGS WHICH EYE HAS NOT SEEN
   AND EAR HAS NOT HEARD,
AND *which* HAVE NOT ENTERED
   THE HEART OF MAN,
ALL THAT GOD HAS PREPARED FOR
   THOSE WHO LOVE HIM."

10 [5]For to us God revealed *them* through the Spirit; for the Spirit searches all things, even the depths of God.

11 For who among men knows the *thoughts* of a man except the spirit of the man, which is in him? Even so the *thoughts* of God no one knows except the Spirit of God.

12 Now we have received, not the spirit of the world, but the Spirit who is from God, that we might know the things freely given to us by God,

13 which things we also speak, not in words taught by human wisdom, but in those taught by the Spirit, combining spiritual *thoughts* with spiritual *words.*

14 But a natural man does not accept the things of the Spirit of God; for they are foolishness to him, and he cannot understand them, because they are spiritually appraised.

15 But he who is spiritual appraises all things, yet he himself is appraised by no man.

16 FOR WHO HAS KNOWN THE MIND OF THE LORD, THAT HE SHOULD INSTRUCT HIM? But we have the mind of Christ.

CHAPTER 3

AND I, brethren, could not speak to you as to spiritual men, but as to men of flesh, as to babes in Christ.

2 I gave you milk to drink, not solid food; for you were not yet able *to receive it.* Indeed, even now you are not yet able,

3 for you are still fleshly. For since there is jealousy and strife among you, are you not fleshly, and are you not walking like mere men?

4 For when one says, "I am of Paul," and another, "I am of Apollos," are you not *mere* men?

5 What then is Apollos? And what is Paul? Servants through whom you believed, even as the Lord gave *opportunity* to each one.

6 I planted, Apollos watered, but God was causing the growth.

7 So then neither the one who plants nor the one who waters is anything, but God who causes the growth.

8 Now he who plants and he who waters are one; but each will receive his own reward according to his own labor.

9 For we are God's fellow workers; you are God's field, God's building.

10 ¶ According to the grace of God which was given to me, as a wise master builder I laid a foundation, and another is building upon it. But let each man be careful how he builds upon it.

11 For no man can lay a foundation other than the one which is laid, which is Jesus Christ.

12 Now if any man builds upon the foundation with gold, silver, precious stones, wood, hay, straw,

13 each man's work will become evident; for the day will show it, because it is *to be* revealed with fire; and the fire itself will test the quality of each man's work.

14 If any man's work which he has built upon it remains, he shall receive a reward.

15 If any man's work is burned up,

---

[4] Some ancient mss. read *mystery*
[5] Some ancient mss. use *But*

he shall suffer loss; but he himself shall be saved, yet so as through fire.

16 ¶ Do you not know that you are a temple of God, and *that* the Spirit of God dwells in you?

17 If any man destroys the temple of God, God will destroy him, for the temple of God is holy, and that is what you are.

18 ¶ Let no man deceive himself. If any man among you thinks that he is wise in this age, let him become foolish that he may become wise.

19 For the wisdom of this world is foolishness before God. For it is written, "He is THE ONE WHO CATCHES THE WISE IN THEIR CRAFTINESS";

20 and again, "THE LORD KNOWS THE REASONINGS of the wise, THAT THEY ARE USELESS."

21 So then let no one boast in men. For all things belong to you,

22 whether Paul or Apollos or Cephas or the world or life or death or things present or things to come; all things belong to you,

23 and you belong to Christ; and Christ belongs to God.

CHAPTER 4

LET a man regard us in this manner, as servants of Christ, and stewards of the mysteries of God.

2 In this case, moreover, it is required of stewards that one be found trustworthy.

3 But to me it is a very small thing that I should be examined by you, or by *any* human court; in fact, I do not even examine myself.

4 For I am conscious of nothing against myself, yet I am not by this acquitted; but the one who examines me is the Lord.

5 Therefore do not go on passing judgment before [6]the time, *but wait* until the Lord comes who will both bring to light the things hidden in the darkness and disclose the motives of *men's* hearts; and then each man's praise will come to him from God.

6 ¶ Now these things, brethren, I have figuratively applied to myself and Apollos for your sakes, that in us you might learn not to exceed what is written, in order that no one of you

[6] I.e., the appointed time of judgment

might become arrogant in behalf of one against the other.

7 For who regards you as superior? And what do you have that you did not receive? But if you did receive it, why do you boast as if you had not received it?

8 You are already filled, you have already become rich, you have become kings without us; and *I* would indeed that you had become kings so that we also might reign with you.

9 For, I think, God has exhibited us apostles last of all, as men condemned to death; because we have become a spectacle to the world, both to angels and to men.

10 We are fools for Christ's sake, but you are prudent in Christ; we are weak, but you are strong; you are distinguished, but we are without honor.

11 To this present hour we are both hungry and thirsty, and are poorly clothed, and are roughly treated, and are homeless;

12 and we toil, working with our own hands; when we are reviled, we bless; when we are persecuted, we endure;

13 when we are slandered, we try to conciliate; we have become as the scum of the world, the dregs of all things, *even* until now.

14 ¶ I do not write these things to shame you, but to admonish you as my beloved children.

15 For if you were to have countless tutors in Christ, yet *you would* not *have* many fathers; for in Christ Jesus I became your father through the gospel.

16 I exhort you therefore, be imitators of me.

17 For this reason I have sent to you Timothy, who is my beloved and faithful child in the Lord, and he will remind you of my ways which are in Christ, just as I teach everywhere in every church.

18 Now some have become arrogant, as though I were not coming to you.

19 But I will come to you soon, if the Lord wills, and I shall find out, not the words of those who are arrogant, but their power.

20 For the kingdom of God does not consist in words, but in power.

21 What do you desire? Shall I come to you with a rod or with love and a spirit of gentleness?

CHAPTER 5

IT is actually reported that there is immorality among you, and immorality of such a kind as does not exist even among the Gentiles, that someone has his father's wife.

2 And you have become arrogant, and have not mourned instead, in order that the one who had done this deed might be removed from your midst.

3 For I, on my part, though absent in body but present in spirit, have already judged him who has so committed this, as though I were present.

4 In the name of our Lord Jesus, when you are assembled, and I with you in spirit, with the power of our Lord Jesus,

5 *I have decided* to deliver such a one to Satan for the destruction of his flesh, that his spirit may be saved in the day of the Lord [7]Jesus.

6 Your boasting is not good. Do you not know that a little leaven leavens the whole lump *of dough*?

7 Clean out the old leaven, that you may be a new lump, just as you are *in fact* unleavened. For Christ our Passover also has been sacrificed.

8 Let us therefore celebrate the feast, not with old leaven, nor with the leaven of malice and wickedness, but with the unleavened bread of sincerity and truth.

9 ¶ I wrote you in my letter not to associate with immoral people;

10 I *did* not at all *mean* with the immoral people of this world, or with the covetous and swindlers, or with idolaters; for then you would have to go out of the world.

11 But actually, I wrote to you not to associate with any so-called brother if he should be an immoral person, or covetous, or an idolater, or a reviler, or a drunkard, or a swindler—not even to eat with such a one.

12 For what have I to do with judging outsiders? Do you not judge those who are within *the church*?

13 But those who are outside, God judges. REMOVE THE WICKED MAN FROM AMONG YOURSELVES.

CHAPTER 6

DOES any one of you, when he has a case against his neighbor, dare to go to law before the unrighteous, and not before the saints?

2 Or do you not know that the saints will judge the world? And if the world is judged by you, are you not competent *to constitute* the smallest law courts?

3 Do you not know that we shall judge angels? How much more, matters of this life?

4 If then you have law courts dealing with matters of this life, do you appoint them as judges who are of no account in the church?

5 I say *this* to your shame. *Is it so, that* there is not among you one wise man who will be able to decide between his brethren,

6 but brother goes to law with brother, and that before unbelievers?

7 Actually, then, it is already a defeat for you, that you have lawsuits with one another. Why not rather be wronged? Why not rather be defrauded?

8 On the contrary, you yourselves wrong and defraud, and that *your* brethren.

9 Or do you not know that the unrighteous shall not inherit the kingdom of God? Do not be deceived; neither fornicators, nor idolaters, nor adulterers, nor [8]effeminate, nor homosexuals,

10 nor thieves, nor *the* covetous, nor drunkards, nor revilers, nor swindlers, shall inherit the kingdom of God.

11 And such were some of you; but you were washed, but you were sanctified, but you were justified in the name of the Lord Jesus Christ, and in the Spirit of our God.

12 ¶ All things are lawful for me, but not all things are profitable. All things are lawful for me, but I will not be mastered by anything.

13 Food is for the stomach, and the stomach is for food; but God will do away with both of them. Yet the body is not for immorality, but for the Lord; and the Lord is for the body.

---

[7] Some ancient mss. do not contain *Jesus*

[8] I.e., effeminate by perversion

14 Now God has not only raised the Lord, but will also raise us up through His power.

15 Do you not know that your bodies are members of Christ? Shall I then take away the members of Christ and make them members of a harlot? May it never be!

16 Or do you not know that the one who joins himself to a harlot is one body *with her*? For He says, "THE TWO WILL BECOME ONE FLESH."

17 But the one who joins himself to the Lord is one spirit *with Him*.

18 Flee immorality. Every *other* sin that a man commits is outside the body, but the immoral man sins against his own body.

19 Or do you not know that your body is a temple of the Holy Spirit who is in you, whom you have from God, and that you are not your own?

20 For you have been bought with a price: therefore glorify God in your body.

CHAPTER 7

Now concerning the things about which you wrote, it is good for a man not to touch a woman.

2 But because of immoralities, let each man have his own wife, and let each woman have her own husband.

3 Let the husband fulfill his duty to his wife, and likewise also the wife to her husband.

4 The wife does not have authority over her own body, but the husband *does*; and likewise also the husband does not have authority over his own body, but the wife *does*.

5 Stop depriving one another, except by agreement for a time that you may devote yourselves to prayer, and come together again lest Satan tempt you because of your lack of self-control.

6 But this I say by way of concession, not of command.

7 ⁹Yet I wish that all men were even as I myself am. However, each man has his own gift from God, one in this manner, and another in that.

8 ¶ But I say to the unmarried and to widows that it is good for them if they remain even as I.

9 But if they do not have self-control, let them marry; for it is better to marry than to burn.

10 But to the married I give instructions, not I, but the Lord, that the wife should not leave her husband

11 (but if she does leave, let her remain unmarried, or else be reconciled to her husband), and that the husband should not send his wife away.

12 But to the rest I say, not the Lord, that if any brother has a wife who is an unbeliever, and she consents to live with him, let him not send her away.

13 And a woman who has an unbelieving husband, and he consents to live with her, let her not send her husband away.

14 For the unbelieving husband is sanctified through his wife, and the unbelieving wife is sanctified through her believing husband; for otherwise your children are unclean, but now they are holy.

15 Yet if the unbelieving one leaves, let him leave; the brother or the sister is not under bondage in such *cases*, but God has called ¹⁰us to peace.

16 For how do you know, O wife, whether you will save your husband? Or how do you know, O husband, whether you will save your wife?

17 ¶ Only, as the Lord has assigned to each one, as God has called each, in this manner let him walk. And thus I direct in all the churches.

18 Was any man called *already* circumcised? Let him not become uncircumcised. Has anyone been called in uncircumcision? Let him not be circumcised.

19 Circumcision is nothing, and uncircumcision is nothing, but *what matters is* the keeping of the commandments of God.

20 Let each man remain in that condition in which he was called.

21 Were you called while a slave? Do not worry about it; but if you are able also to become free, rather do that.

22 For he who was called in the Lord while a slave, is the Lord's freedman; likewise he who was called while free, is Christ's slave.

23 You were bought with a price; do not become slaves of men.

⁹ Some ancient mss. read *For*   ¹⁰ Some ancient mss. read *you*

24 Brethren, let each man remain with God in that *condition* in which he was called.

25 ¶ Now concerning virgins I have no command of the Lord, but I give an opinion as one who by the mercy of the Lord is trustworthy.

26 I think then that this is good in view of the present distress, that it is good for a man to remain as he is.

27 Are you bound to a wife? Do not seek to be released. Are you released from a wife? Do not seek a wife.

28 But if you should marry, you have not sinned; and if a virgin should marry, she has not sinned. Yet such will have trouble in this life, and I am trying to spare you.

29 But this I say, brethren, the time has been shortened, so that from now on those who have wives should be as though they had none;

30 and those who weep, as though they did not weep; and those who rejoice, as though they did not rejoice; and those who buy, as though they did not possess;

31 and those who use the world, as though they did not make full use of it; for the form of this world is passing away.

32 But I want you to be free from concern. One who is unmarried is concerned about the things of the Lord, how he may please the Lord;

33 but one who is married is concerned about the things of the world, how he may please his [11]wife,

34 and *his interests* are divided. And the woman who is unmarried, and the virgin, is concerned about the things of the Lord, that she may be holy both in body and spirit; but one who is married is concerned about the things of the world, how she may please her husband.

35 And this I say for your own benefit; not to put a restraint upon you, but to promote what is seemly, and *to secure* undistracted devotion to the Lord.

36 ¶ But if any man thinks that he is acting unbecomingly toward his virgin *daughter,* if she should be of full age, and if it must be so, let him do what he wishes, he does not sin; let her marry.

37 But he who stands firm in his heart, being under no constraint, but has authority over his own will, and has decided this in his own heart, to keep his own virgin *daughter,* he will do well.

38 So then both he who gives his own virgin *daughter* in marriage does well, and he who does not give her in marriage will do better.

39 ¶ A wife is bound as long as her husband lives; but if her husband is dead, she is free to be married to whom she wishes, only in the Lord.

40 But in my opinion she is happier if she remains as she is; and I think that I also have the Spirit of God.

CHAPTER 8

Now concerning things sacrificed to idols, we know that we all have knowledge. Knowledge makes arrogant, but love edifies.

2 If anyone supposes that he knows anything, he has not yet known as he ought to know;

3 but if anyone loves God, he is known by Him.

4 Therefore concerning the eating of things sacrificed to idols, we know that [12]there is no such thing as an idol in the world, and that there is no God but one.

5 For even if there are so-called gods whether in heaven or on earth, as indeed there are many gods and many lords,

6 yet for us there is *but* one God, the Father, from whom are all things, and we *exist* for Him; and one Lord, Jesus Christ, by whom are all things, and we *exist* through Him.

7 ¶ However not all men have this knowledge; but some, being accustomed to the idol until now, eat *food* as if it were sacrificed to an idol; and their conscience being weak is defiled.

8 But food will not commend us to God; we are neither the worse if we do not eat, nor the better if we do eat.

9 But take care lest this liberty of yours somehow become a stumbling block to the weak.

10 For if someone sees you, who have knowledge, dining in an idol's temple, will not his conscience, if he is

---

[11] Some mss. read *wife. And there is a difference also between the wife and the virgin. One who is unmarried is concerned . . .*

[12] I.e., has no real existence

weak, be strengthened to eat things sacrificed to idols?

11 For through your knowledge he who is weak is ruined, the brother for whose sake Christ died.

12 And thus, by sinning against the brethren and wounding their conscience when it is weak, you sin against Christ.

13 Therefore, if food causes my brother to stumble, I will never eat meat again, that I might not cause my brother to stumble.

CHAPTER 9

Aм I not free? Am I not an apostle? Have I not seen Jesus our Lord? Are you not my work in the Lord?

2 If to others I am not an apostle, at least I am to you; for you are the seal of my apostleship in the Lord.

3 ¶ My defense to those who examine me is this:

4 Do we not have a right to eat and drink?

5 Do we not have a right to take along a believing wife, even as the rest of the apostles, and the brothers of the Lord, and Cephas?

6 Or do only Barnabas and I not have a right to refrain from working?

7 Who at any time serves as a soldier at his own expense? Who plants a vineyard, and does not eat the fruit of it? Or who tends a flock and does not use the milk of the flock?

8 I am not speaking these things according to human judgment, am I? Or does not the Law also say these things?

9 For it is written in the Law of Moses, "YOU SHALL NOT MUZZLE THE OX WHILE HE IS THRESHING." God is not concerned about oxen, is He?

10 Or is He speaking altogether for our sake? Yes, for our sake it was written, because the plowman ought to plow in hope, and the thresher *to thresh* in hope of sharing *the crops*.

11 If we sowed spiritual things in you, is it too much if we should reap material things from you?

12 If others share the right over you, do we not more? Nevertheless, we did not use this right, but we endure all things, that we may cause no hindrance to the gospel of Christ.

13 Do you not know that those who

perform sacred services eat the *food* of the temple, *and* those who attend regularly to the altar have their share with the altar?

14 So also the Lord directed those who proclaim the gospel to get their living from the gospel.

15 But I have used none of these things. And I am not writing these things that it may be done so in my case; for it would be better for me to die than have any man make my boast an empty one.

16 For if I preach the gospel, I have nothing to boast of, for I am under compulsion; for woe is me if I do not preach the gospel.

17 For if I do this voluntarily, I have a reward; but if against my will, I have a stewardship entrusted to me.

18 What then is my reward? That, when I preach the gospel, I may offer the gospel without charge, so as not to make full use of my right in the gospel.

19 ¶ For though I am free from all *men,* I have made myself a slave to all, that I might win the more.

20 And to the Jews I became as a Jew, that I might win Jews; to those who are under the Law, as under the Law, though not being myself under the Law, that I might win those who are under the Law;

21 to those who are without law, as without law, though not being without the law of God but under the law of Christ, that I might win those who are without law.

22 To the weak I became weak, that I might win the weak; I have become all things to all men, that I may by all means save some.

23 And I do all things for the sake of the gospel, that I may become a fellow partaker of it.

24 ¶ Do you not know that those who run in a race all run, but *only* one receives the prize? Run in such a way that you may win.

25 And everyone who competes in the games exercises self-control in all things. They then *do it* to receive a perishable wreath, but we an imperishable.

26 Therefore I run in such a way, as not without aim; I box in such a way, as not beating the air;

27 but I buffet my body and make it my slave, lest possibly, after I have

preached to others, I myself should be disqualified.

CHAPTER 10

FOR I do not want you to be unaware, brethren, that our fathers were all under the cloud, and all passed through the sea;

2 and all [13]were baptized into Moses in the cloud and in the sea;

3 and all ate the same spiritual food;

4 and all drank the same spiritual drink, for they were drinking from a spiritual rock which followed them; and the rock was Christ.

5 Nevertheless, with most of them God was not well-pleased; for they were laid low in the wilderness.

6 Now these things happened as examples for us, that we should not crave evil things, as they also craved.

7 And do not be idolaters, as some of them were; as it is written, "THE PEOPLE SAT DOWN TO EAT AND DRINK, AND STOOD UP TO PLAY."

8 Nor let us act immorally, as some of them did, and twenty-three thousand fell in one day.

9 Nor let us try the Lord, as some of them did, and were destroyed by the serpents.

10 Nor grumble, as some of them did, and were destroyed by the destroyer.

11 Now these things happened to them as an example, and they were written for our instruction, upon whom the ends of the ages have come.

12 Therefore let him who thinks he stands take heed lest he fall.

13 No temptation has overtaken you but such as is common to man; and God is faithful, who will not allow you to be tempted beyond what you are able, but with the temptation will provide the way of escape also, that you may be able to endure it.

14 ¶ Therefore, my beloved, flee from idolatry.

15 I speak as to wise men; you judge what I say.

16 Is not the cup of blessing which we bless a sharing in the blood of Christ? Is not the bread which we break a sharing in the body of Christ?

17 Since there is one bread, we who are many are one body; for we all partake of the one bread.

[13] Some ancient mss. read *received baptism*

18 Look at the nation Israel; are not those who eat the sacrifices sharers in the altar?

19 What do I mean then? That a thing sacrificed to idols is anything, or that an idol is anything?

20 *No,* but *I say* that the things which the Gentiles sacrifice, they sacrifice to demons, and not to God; and I do not want you to become sharers in demons.

21 You cannot drink the cup of the Lord and the cup of demons; you cannot partake of the table of the Lord and the table of demons.

22 Or do we provoke the Lord to jealousy? We are not stronger than He, are we?

23 ¶ All things are lawful, but not all things are profitable. All things are lawful, but not all things edify.

24 Let no one seek his own *good,* but that of his neighbor.

25 Eat anything that is sold in the meat market, without asking questions for conscience' sake;

26 FOR THE EARTH IS THE LORD'S, AND ALL IT CONTAINS.

27 If one of the unbelievers invites you, and you wish to go, eat anything that is set before you, without asking questions for conscience' sake.

28 But if anyone should say to you, "This is meat sacrificed to idols," do not eat *it,* for the sake of the one who informed *you,* and for conscience' sake;

29 I mean not your own conscience, but the other *man's;* for why is my freedom judged by another's conscience?

30 If I partake with thankfulness, why am I slandered concerning that for which I give thanks?

31 Whether, then, you eat or drink or whatever you do, do all to the glory of God.

32 Give no offense either to Jews or to Greeks or to the church of God;

33 just as I also please all men in all things, not seeking my own profit, but the *profit* of the many, that they may be saved.

CHAPTER 11

BE imitators of me, just as I also am of Christ.

2 ¶ Now I praise you because you

remember me in everything, and hold firmly to the traditions, just as I delivered them to you.

3 But I want you to understand that Christ is the head of every man, and the man is the head of a woman, and God is the head of Christ.

4 Every man who has *something* on his head while praying or prophesying, disgraces his head.

5 But every woman who has her head uncovered while praying or prophesying, disgraces her head; for she is one and the same with her whose head is shaved.

6 For if a woman does not cover her head, let her also have her hair cut off; but if it is disgraceful for a woman to have her hair cut off or her head shaved, let her cover her head.

7 For a man ought not to have his head covered, since he is the image and glory of God; but the woman is the glory of man.

8 For man does not originate from woman, but woman from man;

9 for indeed man was not created for the woman's sake, but woman for the man's sake.

10 Therefore the woman ought to have *a symbol of* authority on her head, because of the angels.

11 However, in the Lord, neither is woman independent of man, nor is man independent of woman.

12 For as the woman originates from the man, so also the man *has his birth* through the woman; and all things originate from God.

13 Judge for yourselves: is it proper for a woman to pray to God *with head* uncovered?

14 Does not even nature itself teach you that if a man has long hair, it is a dishonor to him,

15 but if a woman has long hair, it is a glory to her? For her hair is given to her for a covering.

16 But if one is inclined to be contentious, we have no other practice, nor have the churches of God.

17 ¶ But in giving this instruction, I do not praise you, because you come together not for the better but for the worse.

18 For, in the first place, when you come together as a church, I hear that divisions exist among you; and in part, I believe it.

19 For there must also be factions among you, in order that those who are approved may have become evident among you.

20 Therefore when you meet together, it is not to eat the Lord's Supper,

21 for in your eating each one takes his own supper first; and one is hungry and another is drunk.

22 What! Do you not have houses in which to eat and drink? Or do you despise the church of God, and shame those who have nothing? What shall I say to you? Shall I praise you? In this I will not praise you.

23 For I received from the Lord that which I also delivered to you, that the Lord Jesus in the night in which He was betrayed took bread;

24 and when He had given thanks, He broke it, and said, "This is My body, which [14]is for you; do this in remembrance of Me."

25 In the same way *He took* the cup also, after supper, saying, "This cup is the new covenant in My blood; do this, as often as you drink *it,* in remembrance of Me."

26 For as often as you eat this bread and drink the cup, you proclaim the Lord's death until He comes.

27 Therefore whoever eats the bread or drinks the cup of the Lord in an unworthy manner, shall be guilty of the body and the blood of the Lord.

28 But let a man examine himself, and so let him eat of the bread and drink of the cup.

29 For he who eats and drinks, eats and drinks judgment to himself, if he does not judge the body rightly.

30 For this reason many among you are weak and sick, and a number sleep.

31 But if we judged ourselves rightly, we should not be judged.

32 But when we are judged, we are disciplined by the Lord in order that we may not be condemned along with the world.

33 So then, my brethren, when you come together to eat, wait for one another.

34 If anyone is hungry, let him eat at

14 Some ancient mss. read *is broken*

home, so that you may not come to-gether for judgment. And the remaining matters I shall arrange when I come.

CHAPTER 12

Now concerning spiritual *gifts,* brethren, I do not want you to be unaware.

2 You know that when you were pagans, *you were* led astray to the dumb idols, however you were led.

3 Therefore I make known to you, that no one speaking by the Spirit of God says, "Jesus is accursed"; and no one can say, "Jesus is Lord," except by the Holy Spirit.

4 ¶ Now there are varieties of gifts, but the same Spirit.

5 And there are varieties of ministries, and the same Lord.

6 And there are varieties of effects, but the same God who works all things in all *persons.*

7 But to each one is given the manifestation of the Spirit for the common good.

8 For to one is given the word of wisdom through the Spirit, and to another the word of knowledge according to the same Spirit;

9 to another faith by the same Spirit, and to another gifts of healing by the one Spirit,

10 and to another the effecting of miracles, and to another prophecy, and to another the distinguishing of spirits, to another *various* kinds of tongues, and to another the interpretation of tongues.

11 But one and the same Spirit works all these things, distributing to each one individually just as He wills.

12 ¶ For even as the body is one and *yet* has many members, and all the members of the body, though they are many, are one body, so also is Christ.

13 For by one Spirit we were all baptized into one body, whether Jews or Greeks, whether slaves or free, and we were all made to drink of one Spirit.

14 For the body is not one member, but many.

15 If the foot should say, "Because I am not a hand, I am not *a part* of the body," it is not for this reason any the less *a part* of the body.

16 And if the ear should say, "Because I am not an eye, I am not *a part* of the body," it is not for this reason any the less *a part* of the body.

17 If the whole body were an eye, where would the hearing be? If the whole were hearing, where would the sense of smell be?

18 But now God has placed the members, each one of them, in the body, just as He desired.

19 And if they were all one member, where would the body be?

20 But now there are many members, but one body.

21 And the eye cannot say to the hand, "I have no need of you"; or again the head to the feet, "I have no need of you."

22 On the contrary, it is much truer that the members of the body which seem to be weaker are necessary;

23 and those *members* of the body, which we deem less honorable, on these we bestow more abundant honor, and our unseemly *members come to* have more abundant seemliness,

24 whereas our seemly *members* have no need *of it.* But God has *so* composed the body, giving more abundant honor to that *member* which lacked,

25 that there should be no division in the body, but *that* the members should have the same care for one another.

26 And if one member suffers, all the members suffer with it; if *one* member is honored, all the members rejoice with it.

27 Now you are Christ's body, and individually members of it.

28 And God has appointed in the church, first apostles, second prophets, third teachers, then miracles, then gifts of healings, helps, administrations, *various* kinds of tongues.

29 All are not apostles, are they? All are not prophets, are they? All are not teachers, are they? All are not *workers of* miracles, are they?

30 All do not have gifts of healings, do they? All do not speak with tongues, do they? All do not interpret, do they?

31 But earnestly desire the greater gifts.

¶ And I show you a still more excellent way.

CHAPTER 13

IF I speak with the tongues of men and of angels, but do not have love, I have become a noisy gong or a clanging cymbal.

2 And if I have *the gift of* prophecy, and know all mysteries and all knowledge; and if I have all faith, so as to remove mountains, but do not have love, I am nothing.

3 And if I give all my possessions to feed *the poor,* and if I deliver my body [15] to be burned, but do not have love, it profits me nothing.

4 Love is patient, love is kind, *and* is not jealous; love does not brag *and* is not arrogant,

5 does not act unbecomingly; it does not seek its own, is not provoked, does not take into account a wrong *suffered,*

6 does not rejoice in unrighteousness, but rejoices with the truth;

7 bears all things, believes all things, hopes all things, endures all things.

8 Love never fails; but if *there are gifts of* prophecy, they will be done away; if *there are* tongues, they will cease; if *there is* knowledge, it will be done away.

9 For we know in part, and we prophesy in part;

10 but when the perfect comes, the partial will be done away.

11 When I was a child, I used to speak as a child, think as a child, reason as a child; when I became a man, I did away with childish things.

12 For now we see in a mirror dimly, but then face to face; now I know in part, but then I shall know fully just as I also have been fully known.

13 But now abide faith, hope, love, these three; but the greatest of these is love.

CHAPTER 14

PURSUE love, yet desire earnestly spiritual *gifts,* but especially that you may prophesy.

2 For one who speaks in a tongue does not speak to men, but to God; for no one understands, but in *his* spirit he speaks mysteries.

3 But one who prophesies speaks to men for edification and exhortation and consolation.

4 One who speaks in a tongue edifies himself; but one who prophesies edifies the church.

5 Now I wish that you all spoke in tongues, but *even* more that you would prophesy; and greater is one who prophesies than one who speaks in tongues, unless he interprets, so that the church may receive edifying.

6 But now, brethren, if I come to you speaking in tongues, what shall I profit you, unless I speak to you either by way of revelation or of knowledge or of prophecy or of teaching?

7 Yet *even* lifeless things, either flute or harp, in producing a sound, if they do not produce a distinction in the tones, how will it be known what is played on the flute or on the harp?

8 For if the bugle produces an indistinct sound, who will prepare himself for battle?

9 So also you, unless you utter by the tongue speech that is clear, how will it be known what is spoken? For you will be speaking into the air.

10 There are, perhaps, a great many kinds of languages in the world, and no *kind* is without meaning.

11 If then I do not know the meaning of the language, I shall be to the one who speaks a barbarian, and the one who speaks will be a barbarian to me.

12 So also you, since you are zealous of spiritual *gifts,* seek to abound for the edification of the church.

13 Therefore let one who speaks in a tongue pray that he may interpret.

14 For if I pray in a tongue, my spirit prays, but my mind is unfruitful.

15 What is *the outcome* then? I shall pray with the spirit and I shall pray with the mind also; I shall sing with the spirit and I shall sing with the mind also.

16 Otherwise if you bless in the spirit *only,* how will the one who fills the place of the ungifted say the "Amen" at your giving of thanks, since he does not know what you are saying?

17 For you are giving thanks well enough, but the other man is not edified.

18 I thank God, I speak in tongues more than you all;

19 however, in the church I desire to

---

[15] Some ancient mss. read *that I may boast*

speak five words with my mind, that I may instruct others also, rather than ten thousand words in a tongue.

20 ¶ Brethren, do not be children in your thinking; yet in evil be babes, but in your thinking be mature.

21 In the Law it is written, "BY MEN OF STRANGE TONGUES AND BY THE LIPS OF STRANGERS I WILL SPEAK TO THIS PEOPLE, AND EVEN SO THEY WILL NOT LISTEN TO ME," says the Lord.

22 So then tongues are for a sign, not to those who believe, but to unbelievers; but prophecy *is for a sign*, not to unbelievers, but to those who believe.

23 If therefore the whole church should assemble together and all speak in tongues, and ungifted men or unbelievers enter, will they not say that you are mad?

24 But if all prophesy, and an unbeliever or an ungifted man enters, he is convicted by all, he is called to account by all;

25 the secrets of his heart are disclosed; and so he will fall on his face and worship God, declaring that God is certainly among you.

26 ¶ What is *the outcome* then, brethren? When you assemble, each one has a psalm, has a teaching, has a revelation, has a tongue, has an interpretation. Let all things be done for edification.

27 If anyone speaks in a tongue, *it should be* by two or at the most three, and *each* in turn, and let one interpret;

28 but if there is no interpreter, let him keep silent in the church; and let him speak to himself and to God.

29 And let two or three prophets speak, and let the others pass judgment.

30 But if a revelation is made to another who is seated, let the first keep silent.

31 For you can all prophesy one by one, so that all may learn and all may be exhorted;

32 and the spirits of prophets are subject to prophets;

33 for God is not *a God* of confusion but of peace, as in all the churches of the saints.

34 ¶ Let the women keep silent in the churches; for they are not permitted to speak, but let them subject themselves, just as the Law also says.

35 And if they desire to learn anything, let them ask their own husbands at home; for it is improper for a woman to speak in church.

36 Was it from you that the word of God *first* went forth? Or has it come to you only?

37 ¶ If anyone thinks he is a prophet or spiritual, let him recognize that the things which I write to you are the Lord's commandment.

38 But if anyone [16]does not recognize *this*, he is not recognized.

39 ¶ Therefore, my brethren, desire earnestly to prophesy, and do not forbid to speak in tongues.

40 But let all things be done properly and in an orderly manner.

CHAPTER 15

Now I make known to you, brethren, the gospel which I preached to you, which also you received, in which also you stand,

2 by which also you are saved, if you hold fast the word which I preached to you, unless you believed in vain.

3 For I delivered to you as of first importance what I also received, that Christ died for our sins according to the Scriptures,

4 and that He was buried, and that He was raised on the third day according to the Scriptures,

5 and that He appeared to Cephas, then to the twelve.

6 After that He appeared to more than five hundred brethren at one time, most of whom remain until now, but some have fallen asleep;

7 then He appeared to James, then to all the apostles;

8 and last of all, as it were to one untimely born, He appeared to me also.

9 For I am the least of the apostles, who am not fit to be called an apostle, because I persecuted the church of God.

10 But by the grace of God I am what I am, and His grace toward me did not prove vain; but I labored even more than all of them, yet not I, but the grace of God with me.

11 Whether then *it was* I or they, so we preach and so you believed.

12 ¶ Now if Christ is preached, that

---

[16] Some ancient mss. read *is ignorant, let him be ignorant*

He has been raised from the dead, how do some among you say that there is no resurrection of the dead?

13 But if there is no resurrection of the dead, not even Christ has been raised;

14 and if Christ has not been raised, then our preaching is vain, your faith also is vain.

15 Moreover we are even found *to be* false witnesses of God, because we witnessed against God that He raised [17]Christ, whom He did not raise, if in fact the dead are not raised.

16 For if the dead are not raised, not even Christ has been raised;

17 and if Christ has not been raised, your faith is worthless; you are still in your sins.

18 Then those also who have fallen asleep in Christ have perished.

19 If we have hoped in Christ in this life only, we are of all men most to be pitied.

20 ¶ But now Christ has been raised from the dead, the first fruits of those who are asleep.

21 For since by a man *came* death, by a man also *came* the resurrection of the dead.

22 For as in Adam all die, so also in Christ all shall be made alive.

23 But each in his own order: Christ the first fruits, after that those who are Christ's at His coming,

24 then *comes* the end, when He delivers up the kingdom to the God and Father, when He has abolished all rule and all authority and power.

25 For He must reign until He has put all His enemies under His feet.

26 The last enemy that will be abolished is death.

27 For HE HAS PUT ALL THINGS IN SUBJECTION UNDER HIS FEET. But when He says, "All things are put in subjection," it is evident that He is excepted who put all things in subjection to Him.

28 And when all things are subjected to Him, then the Son Himself also will be subjected to the One who subjected all things to Him, that God may be all in all.

29 ¶ Otherwise, what will those do who are baptized for the dead? If the dead are not raised at all, why then are they baptized for them?

30 Why are we also in danger every hour?

31 I protest, brethren, by the boasting in you, which I have in Christ Jesus our Lord, I die daily.

32 If from human motives I fought with wild beasts at Ephesus, what does it profit me? If the dead are not raised, LET US EAT AND DRINK, FOR TOMORROW WE DIE.

33 Do not be deceived: "Bad company corrupts good morals."

34 Become sober-minded as you ought, and stop sinning; for some have no knowledge of God. I speak *this* to your shame.

35 ¶ But someone will say, "How are the dead raised? And with what kind of body do they come?"

36 You fool! That which you sow does not come to life unless it dies;

37 and that which you sow, you do not sow the body which is to be, but a bare grain, perhaps of wheat or of something else.

38 But God gives it a body just as He wished, and to each of the seeds a body of its own.

39 All flesh is not the same flesh, but there is one *flesh* of men, and another flesh of beasts, and another flesh of birds, and another of fish.

40 There are also heavenly bodies and earthly bodies, but the glory of the heavenly is one, and the *glory* of the earthly is another.

41 There is one glory of the sun, and another glory of the moon, and another glory of the stars; for star differs from star in glory.

42 So also is the resurrection of the dead. It is sown a perishable *body*, it is raised an imperishable *body*;

43 it is sown in dishonor, it is raised in glory; it is sown in weakness, it is raised in power;

44 it is sown a natural body, it is raised a spiritual body. If there is a natural body, there is also a spiritual *body*.

45 So also it is written, "The first MAN, Adam, BECAME A LIVING SOUL." The last Adam *became* a life-giving spirit.

46 However, the spiritual is not first, but the natural; then the spiritual.

47 The first man is from the earth,

[17] I.e., the Messiah

earthy; the second man is from heaven.

48 As is the earthy, so also are those who are earthy; and as is the heavenly, so also are those who are heavenly.

49 And just as we have borne the image of the earthy, [18] we shall also bear the image of the heavenly.

50 ¶ Now I say this, brethren, that flesh and blood cannot inherit the kingdom of God; nor does the perishable inherit the imperishable.

51 Behold, I tell you a mystery; we shall not all sleep, but we shall all be changed,

52 in a moment, in the twinkling of an eye, at the last trumpet; for the trumpet will sound, and the dead will be raised imperishable, and we shall be changed.

53 For this perishable must put on the imperishable, and this mortal must put on immortality.

54 But when this perishable will have put on the imperishable, and this mortal will have put on immortality, then will come about the saying that is written, "DEATH IS SWALLOWED UP in victory.

55 "O DEATH, WHERE IS YOUR VICTORY? O DEATH, WHERE IS YOUR STING?"

56 The sting of death is sin, and the power of sin is the law;

57 but thanks be to God, who gives us the victory through our Lord Jesus Christ.

58 Therefore, my beloved brethren, be steadfast, immovable, always abounding in the work of the Lord, knowing that your toil is not *in* vain in the Lord.

CHAPTER 16

Now concerning the collection for the saints, as I directed the churches of Galatia, so do you also.

2 On the first day of every week let each one of you put aside and save, as he may prosper, that no collections be made when I come.

3 And when I arrive, whomever you may approve, I shall send them with letters to carry your gift to Jerusalem;

4 and if it is fitting for me to go also, they will go with me.

5 But I shall come to you after I go through Macedonia, for I am going through Macedonia;

[18] Some ancient mss. read *let us also*

6 and perhaps I shall stay with you, or even spend the winter, that you may send me on my way wherever I may go.

7 For I do not wish to see you now *just* in passing; for I hope to remain with you for some time, if the Lord permits.

8 But I shall remain in Ephesus until Pentecost;

9 for a wide door for effective *service* has opened to me, and there are many adversaries.

10 ¶ Now if Timothy comes, see that he is with you without cause to be afraid; for he is doing the Lord's work, as I also am.

11 Let no one therefore despise him. But send him on his way in peace, so that he may come to me; for I expect him with the brethren.

12 But concerning Apollos our brother, I encouraged him greatly to come to you with the brethren; and it was not at all *his* desire to come now, but he will come when he has opportunity.

13 ¶ Be on the alert, stand firm in the faith, act like men, be strong.

14 Let all that you do be done in love.

15 ¶ Now I urge you, brethren (you know the household of Stephanas, that they were the first fruits of Achaia, and that they have devoted themselves for ministry to the saints),

16 that you also be in subjection to such men and to everyone who helps in the work and labors.

17 And I rejoice over the coming of Stephanas and Fortunatus and Achaicus; because they have supplied what was lacking on your part.

18 For they have refreshed my spirit and yours. Therefore acknowledge such men.

19 ¶ The churches of Asia greet you. Aquila and Prisca greet you heartily in the Lord, with the church that is in their house.

20 All the brethren greet you. Greet one another with a holy kiss.

21 ¶ The greeting is in my own hand—Paul.

22 If anyone does not love the Lord, let him be accursed. Maranatha.

23 The grace of the Lord Jesus be with you.

24 My love be with you all in Christ Jesus. Amen.

CORINTHIANS

PAUL, an apostle of Christ Jesus by the will of God, and Timothy *our* brother, to the church of God which is at Corinth with all the saints who are throughout Achaia:

2 Grace to you and peace from God our Father and the Lord Jesus Christ.

3 ¶ Blessed *be* the God and Father of our Lord Jesus Christ, the Father of mercies and God of all comfort;

4 who comforts us in all our affliction so that we may be able to comfort those who are in any affliction with the comfort with which we ourselves are comforted by God.

5 For just as the sufferings of Christ are ours in abundance, so also our comfort is abundant through Christ.

6 But if we are afflicted, it is for your comfort and salvation; or if we are comforted, it is for your comfort, which is effective in the patient enduring of the same sufferings which we also suffer;

7 and our hope for you is firmly grounded, knowing that as you are sharers of our sufferings, so also you are *sharers* of our comfort.

8 For we do not want you to be unaware, brethren, of our affliction which came *to us* in Asia, that we were burdened excessively, beyond our strength, so that we despaired even of life;

9 indeed, we had the sentence of death within ourselves in order that we should not trust in ourselves, but in God who raises the dead;

10 who delivered us from so great a *peril of* death, and will deliver *us*, He on whom we have set our hope. And He will yet deliver us,

11 you also joining in helping us through your prayers, that thanks may be given by many persons on our behalf for the favor bestowed upon us through *the prayers of* many.

12 ¶ For our proud confidence is this, the testimony of our conscience, that in holiness and godly sincerity, not in fleshly wisdom but in the grace of God, we have conducted ourselves in the world, and especially toward you.

13 For we write nothing else to you than what you read and understand, and I hope you will understand until the end;

14 just as you also partially did understand us, that we are your reason to be proud as you also are ours, in the day of our Lord Jesus.

15 ¶ And in this confidence I intended at first to come to you, that you might twice receive a blessing;

16 that is, to pass your way into Macedonia, and again from Macedonia to come to you, and by you to be helped on my journey to Judea.

17 Therefore, I was not vacillating when I intended to do this, was I? Or that which I purpose, do I purpose according to the flesh, that with me there should be yes, yes and no, no *at the same time*?

18 But as God is faithful, our word to you is not yes and no.

19 For the Son of God, Christ Jesus, who was preached among you by us—by me and Silvanus and Timothy—was not yes and no, but is yes in Him.

20 For as many as may be the promises of God, in Him they are yes; wherefore also by Him is our Amen to the glory of God through us.

21 Now He who establishes us with you in Christ and anointed us is God,

22 who also sealed us and gave *us* the Spirit in our hearts as a pledge.

23 ¶ But I call God as witness to my soul, that to spare you I came no more to Corinth.

24 Not that we lord it over your faith, but are workers with you for your joy; for in your faith you are standing firm.

CHAPTER 2

BUT I determined this for my own sake, that I would not come to you in sorrow again.

2 For if I cause you sorrow, who then makes me glad but the one whom I made sorrowful?

3 And this is the very thing I wrote you, lest, when I came, I should have sorrow from those who ought to make me rejoice; having confidence in you all, that my joy would be *the joy* of you all.

4 For out of much affliction and anguish of heart I wrote to you with many tears; not that you should be

made sorrowful, but that you might know the love which I have especially for you.

5 ¶ But if any has caused sorrow, he has caused sorrow not to me, but in some degree—in order not to say too much—to all of you.

6 Sufficient for such a one is this punishment which was *inflicted by* the majority,

7 so that on the contrary you should rather forgive and comfort *him*, lest somehow such a one be overwhelmed by excessive sorrow.

8 Wherefore I urge you to reaffirm *your* love for him.

9 For to this end also I wrote that I might put you to the test, whether you are obedient in all things.

10 But whom you forgive anything, I *forgive* also; for indeed what I have forgiven, if I have forgiven anything, I *did it* for your sakes in the presence of Christ,

11 in order that no advantage be taken of us by Satan; for we are not ignorant of his schemes.

12 ¶ Now when I came to Troas for the gospel of Christ and when a door was opened for me in the Lord,

13 I had no rest for my spirit, not finding Titus my brother; but taking my leave of them, I went on to Macedonia.

14 ¶ But thanks be to God, who always leads us in His triumph in Christ, and manifests through us the sweet aroma of the knowledge of Him in every place.

15 For we are a fragrance of Christ to God among those who are being saved and among those who are perishing;

16 to the one an aroma from death to death, to the other an aroma from life to life. And who is adequate for these things?

17 For we are not like many, [1]peddling the word of God, but as from sincerity, but as from God, we speak in Christ in the sight of God.

CHAPTER 3

ARE we beginning to commend ourselves again? Or do we need, as some, letters of commendation to you or from you?

[1] Or, *corrupting*

2 You are our letter, written in our hearts, known and read by all men;

3 being manifested that you are a letter of Christ, cared for by us, written not with ink, but with the Spirit of the living God, not on tablets of stone, but on tablets of human hearts.

4 And such confidence we have through Christ toward God.

5 Not that we are adequate in ourselves to consider anything as *coming* from ourselves, but our adequacy is from God,

6 who also made us adequate *as* servants of a new covenant, not of the letter, but of the Spirit; for the letter kills, but the Spirit gives life.

7 But if the ministry of death, in letters engraved on stones, came with glory, so that the sons of Israel could not look intently at the face of Moses because of the glory of his face, fading *as* it was,

8 how shall the ministry of the Spirit fail to be even more with glory?

9 For if the ministry of condemnation has glory, much more does the ministry of righteousness abound in glory.

10 For indeed what had glory, in this case has no glory on account of the glory that surpasses *it*.

11 For if that which fades away *was* with glory, much more that which remains *is* in glory.

12 ¶ Having therefore such a hope, we use great boldness in *our* speech,

13 and *are* not as Moses, *who* used to put a veil over his face that the sons of Israel might not look intently at the end of what was fading away.

14 But their minds were hardened; for until this very day at the reading of the old covenant the same veil remains unlifted, because it is removed in Christ.

15 But to this day whenever Moses is read, a veil lies over their heart;

16 but whenever a man turns to the Lord, the veil is taken away.

17 Now the Lord is the Spirit; and where the Spirit of the Lord is, *there* is liberty.

18 But we all, with unveiled face beholding as in a mirror the glory of the Lord, are being transformed into the same image from glory to glory, just as from the Lord, the Spirit.

CHAPTER 4

THEREFORE, since we have this ministry, as we received mercy, we do not lose heart,

2 but we have renounced the things hidden because of shame, not walking in craftiness or adulterating the word of God, but by the manifestation of truth commending ourselves to every man's conscience in the sight of God.

3 And even if our gospel is veiled, it is veiled to those who are perishing,

4 in whose case the god of this world has blinded the minds of the unbelieving, that they might not see the light of the gospel of the glory of Christ, who is the image of God.

5 For we do not preach ourselves but Christ Jesus as Lord, and ourselves as your bond-servants for Jesus' sake.

6 For God, who said, "Light shall shine out of darkness," is the One who has shone in our hearts to give the light of the knowledge of the glory of God in the face of Christ.

7 ¶ But we have this treasure in earthen vessels, that the surpassing greatness of the power may be of God and not from ourselves;

8 *we are* afflicted in every way, but not crushed; perplexed, but not despairing;

9 persecuted, but not forsaken; struck down, but not destroyed;

10 always carrying about in the body the dying of Jesus, that the life of Jesus also may be manifested in our body.

11 For we who live are constantly being delivered over to death for Jesus' sake, that the life of Jesus also may be manifested in our mortal flesh.

12 So death works in us, but life in you.

13 But having the same spirit of faith, according to what is written, "I BELIEVED, THEREFORE I SPOKE," we also believe, therefore also we speak;

14 knowing that He who raised the Lord Jesus will raise us also with Jesus and will present us with you.

15 For all things *are* for your sakes, that the grace which is spreading to more and more people may cause the giving of thanks to abound to the glory of God.

16 ¶ Therefore we do not lose heart, but though our outer man is decaying, yet our inner man is being renewed day by day.

17 For momentary, light affliction is producing for us an eternal weight of glory far beyond all comparison,

18 while we look not at the things which are seen, but at the things which are not seen; for the things which are seen are temporal, but the things which are not seen are eternal.

CHAPTER 5

FOR we know that if the earthly tent which is our house is torn down, we have a building from God, a house not made with hands, eternal in the heavens.

2 For indeed in this *house* we groan, longing to be clothed with our dwelling from heaven;

3 inasmuch as we, having put it on, shall not be found naked.

4 For indeed while we are in this tent, we groan, being burdened, because we do not want to be unclothed, but to be clothed, in order that what is mortal may be swallowed up by life.

5 Now He who prepared us for this very purpose is God, who gave to us the Spirit as a pledge.

6 Therefore, being always of good courage, and knowing that while we are at home in the body we are absent from the Lord—

7 for we walk by faith, not by sight—

8 we are of good courage, I say, and prefer rather to be absent from the body and to be at home with the Lord.

9 Therefore also we have as our ambition, whether at home or absent, to be pleasing to Him.

10 For we must all appear before the judgment seat of Christ, that each one may be recompensed for his deeds in the body, according to what he has done, whether good or bad.

11 ¶ Therefore knowing the fear of the Lord, we persuade men, but we are made manifest to God; and I hope that we are made manifest also in your consciences.

12 We are not again commending ourselves to you but *are* giving you an occasion to be proud of us, that you may have *an answer* for those who take pride in appearance, and not in heart.

13 For if we are beside ourselves, it is for God; if we are of sound mind, it is for you.

14 For the love of Christ controls us, having concluded this, that one died for all, therefore all died;

15 and He died for all, that they who live should no longer live for themselves, but for Him who died and rose again on their behalf.

16 Therefore from now on we recognize no man according to the flesh; even though we have known Christ according to the flesh, yet now we know *Him thus* no longer.

17 Therefore if any man is in Christ, *he is* a new creature; the old things passed away; behold, new things have come.

18 Now all *these* things are from God, who reconciled us to Himself through Christ, and gave us the ministry of reconciliation,

19 namely, that God was in Christ reconciling the world to Himself, not counting their trespasses against them, and He has committed to us the word of reconciliation.

20 ¶ Therefore, we are ambassadors for Christ, as though God were entreating through us; we beg you on behalf of Christ, be reconciled to God.

21 He made Him who knew no sin *to be* sin on our behalf, that we might become the righteousness of God in Him.

CHAPTER 6

AND working together *with Him,* we also urge you not to receive the grace of God in vain—

2 for He says,

"AT THE ACCEPTABLE TIME I LISTENED TO YOU,

AND ON THE DAY OF SALVATION I HELPED YOU";

behold, now is "THE ACCEPTABLE TIME," behold, now is "THE DAY OF SALVATION"—

3 giving no cause for offense in anything, in order that the ministry be not discredited,

4 but in everything commending ourselves as servants of God, in much endurance, in afflictions, in hardships, in distresses,

5 in beatings, in imprisonments, in tumults, in labors, in sleeplessness, in hunger,

6 in purity, in knowledge, in patience, in kindness, in the Holy Spirit, in genuine love,

7 in the word of truth, in the power of God; by the weapons of righteousness for the right hand and the left,

8 by glory and dishonor, by evil report and good report; *regarded* as deceivers and yet true;

9 as unknown yet well-known, as dying yet behold, we live; as punished yet not put to death,

10 as sorrowful yet always rejoicing, as poor yet making many rich, as having nothing yet possessing all things.

11 ¶ Our mouth has spoken freely to you, O Corinthians, our heart is opened wide.

12 You are not restrained by us, but you are restrained in your own affections.

13 Now in a like exchange—I speak as to children—open wide *to us* also.

14 ¶ Do not be bound together with unbelievers; for what partnership have righteousness and lawlessness, or what fellowship has light with darkness?

15 Or what harmony has Christ with Belial, or what has a believer in common with an unbeliever?

16 Or what agreement has the temple of God with idols? For we are the temple of the living God; just as God said,

"I WILL DWELL IN THEM AND WALK AMONG THEM;

AND I WILL BE THEIR GOD, AND THEY SHALL BE MY PEOPLE.

17 "Therefore, COME OUT FROM THEIR MIDST AND BE SEPARATE," says the Lord.

"AND DO NOT TOUCH WHAT IS UNCLEAN;

And I will welcome you.

18 "And I will be a father to you, And you shall be sons and daughters to Me," Says the Lord Almighty.

CHAPTER 7

THEREFORE, having these promises, beloved, let us cleanse ourselves from all defilement of flesh and spirit, perfecting holiness in the fear of God.

2 ¶ Make room for us *in your*

hearts; we wronged no one, we corrupted no one, we took advantage of no one.

3 I do not speak to condemn you; for I have said before that you are in our hearts to die together and to live together.

4 Great is my confidence in you, great is my boasting on your behalf; I am filled with comfort. I am overflowing with joy in all our affliction.

5 ¶ For even when we came into Macedonia our flesh had no rest, but we were afflicted on every side: conflicts without, fears within.

6 But God, who comforts the depressed, comforted us by the coming of Titus;

7 and not only by his coming, but also by the comfort with which he was comforted in you, as he reported to us your longing, your mourning, your zeal for me; so that I rejoiced even more.

8 For though I caused you sorrow by my letter, I do not regret it; though I did regret it—*for* I see that that letter caused you sorrow, though only for a while—

9 I now rejoice, not that you were made sorrowful, but that you were made sorrowful to *the point of* repentance; for you were made sorrowful according to *the will of* God, in order that you might not suffer loss in anything through us.

10 For the sorrow that is according to *the will of* God produces a repentance without regret, *leading* to salvation; but the sorrow of the world produces death.

11 For behold what earnestness this very thing, this godly sorrow, has produced in you: what vindication of yourselves, what indignation, what fear, what longing, what zeal, what avenging of wrong! In everything you demonstrated yourselves to be innocent in the matter.

12 So although I wrote to you *it was* not for the sake of the offender, nor for the sake of the one offended, but that your earnestness on our behalf might be made known to you in the sight of God.

13 For this reason we have been comforted.

¶ And besides our comfort, we rejoiced even much more for the joy of Titus, because his spirit has been refreshed by you all.

14 For if in anything I have boasted to him about you, I was not put to shame; but as we spoke all things to you in truth, so also our boasting before Titus proved to be *the* truth.

15 And his affection abounds all the more toward you, as he remembers the obedience of you all, how you received him with fear and trembling.

16 I rejoice that in everything I have confidence in you.

CHAPTER 8

Now, brethren, we *wish to* make known to you the grace of God which has been given in the churches of Macedonia,

2 that in a great ordeal of affliction their abundance of joy and their deep poverty overflowed in the wealth of their liberality.

3 For I testify that according to their ability, and beyond their ability *they gave* of their own accord,

4 begging us with much entreaty for the favor of participation in the support of the saints,

5 and *this,* not as we had expected, but they first gave themselves to the Lord and to us by the will of God.

6 Consequently we urged Titus that as he had previously made a beginning, so he would also complete in you this gracious work as well.

7 But just as you abound in everything, in faith and utterance and knowledge and in all earnestness and in the [2]love we inspired in you, *see* that you abound in this gracious work also.

8 I am not speaking *this* as a command, but as proving through the earnestness of others the sincerity of your love also.

9 For you know the grace of our Lord Jesus Christ, that though He was rich, yet for your sake He became poor, that you through His poverty might become rich.

10 And I give *my* opinion in this matter, for this is to your advantage, who were the first to begin a year ago not only to do *this,* but also to desire *to do it.*

[2] Lit., *love from us in you;* some ancient mss. read *your love for us*

11 But now finish doing it also; that just as *there was* the readiness to desire it, so *there may be* also the completion of it by your ability.

12 For if the readiness is present, it is acceptable according to what *a man* has, not according to what he does not have.

13 For *this* is not for the ease of others *and* for your affliction, but by way of equality—

14 at this present time your abundance *being a supply* for their want, that their abundance also may become *a supply* for your want, that there may be equality;

15 as it is written, "HE WHO *gathered* MUCH DID NOT HAVE TOO MUCH, AND HE WHO *gathered* LITTLE HAD NO LACK."

16 ¶ But thanks be to God, who puts the same earnestness on your behalf in the heart of Titus.

17 For he not only accepted our appeal, but being himself very earnest, he has gone to you of his own accord.

18 And we have sent along with him the brother whose fame in *the things of* the gospel *has spread* through all the churches;

19 and not only *this*, but he has also been appointed by the churches to travel with us in this gracious work, which is being administered by us for the glory of the Lord Himself, and *to show* our readiness,

20 taking precaution that no one should discredit us in our administration of this generous gift;

21 for we have regard for what is honorable, not only in the sight of the Lord, but also in the sight of men.

22 And we have sent with them our brother, whom we have often tested and found diligent in many things, but now even more diligent, because of *his* great confidence in you.

23 As for Titus, *he is* my partner and fellow worker among you; as for our brethren, *they are* messengers of the churches, a glory to Christ.

24 Therefore openly before the churches show them the proof of your love and of our reason for boasting about you.

CHAPTER 9

FOR it is superfluous for me to write to you about this ministry to the saints;

2 for I know your readiness, of which I boast about you to the Macedonians, *namely,* that Achaia has been prepared since last year, and your zeal has stirred up most of them.

3 But I have sent the brethren, that our boasting about you may not be made empty in this case, that, as I was saying, you may be prepared;

4 lest if any Macedonians come with me and find you unprepared, we (not to speak of you) should be put to shame by this confidence.

5 So I thought it necessary to urge the brethren that they would go on ahead to you and arrange beforehand your previously promised bountiful gift, that the same might be ready as a bountiful gift, and not affected by covetousness.

6 ¶ Now this *I say,* he who sows sparingly shall also reap sparingly; and he who sows bountifully shall also reap bountifully.

7 Let each one *do* just as he has purposed in his heart; not grudgingly or under compulsion; for God loves a cheerful giver.

8 And God is able to make all grace abound to you, that always having all sufficiency in everything, you may have an abundance for every good deed;

9 as it is written,

"HE SCATTERED ABROAD, HE GAVE TO THE POOR,

HIS RIGHTEOUSNESS ABIDES FOREVER."

10 Now He who supplies seed to the sower and bread for food, will supply and multiply your seed for sowing and increase the harvest of your righteousness;

11 you will be enriched in everything for all liberality, which through us is producing thanksgiving to God.

12 For the ministry of this service is not only fully supplying the needs of the saints, but is also overflowing through many thanksgivings to God.

13 Because of the proof given by this ministry they will glorify God for *your* obedience to your confession of the gospel of Christ, and for the liberality of your contribution to them and to all,

14 while they also, by prayer on your behalf, yearn for you because of the surpassing grace of God in you.

15 Thanks be to God for His indescribable gift!

CHAPTER 10

NOW I, Paul, myself urge you by the meekness and gentleness of Christ—I who am meek when face to face with you, but bold toward you when absent!

2 I ask that when I am present I may not be bold with the confidence with which I propose to be courageous against some, who regard us as if we walked according to the flesh.

3 For though we walk in the flesh, we do not war according to the flesh,

4 for the weapons of our warfare are not of the flesh, but divinely powerful for the destruction of fortresses.

5 *We are* destroying speculations and every lofty thing raised up against the knowledge of God, and *we are* taking every thought captive to the obedience of Christ,

6 and we are ready to punish all disobedience, whenever your obedience is complete.

7 You are looking at things as they are outwardly. If anyone is confident in himself that he is Christ's, let him consider this again within himself, that just as he is Christ's, so also are we.

8 For even if I should boast somewhat further about our authority, which the Lord gave for building you up and not for destroying you, I shall not be put to shame,

9 for I do not wish to seem as if I would terrify you by my letters.

10 For they say, "His letters are weighty and strong, but his personal presence is unimpressive, and his speech contemptible."

11 Let such a person consider this, that what we are in word by letters when absent, such persons *we are* also in deed when present.

12 For we are not bold to class or compare ourselves with some of those who commend themselves; but when they measure themselves by themselves, and compare themselves with themselves, they are without understanding.

13 But we will not boast beyond *our* measure, but within the measure of the sphere which God apportioned to

us as a measure, to reach even as far as you.

14 For we are not overextending ourselves, as if we did not reach to you, for we were the first to come even as far as you in the gospel of Christ;

15 not boasting beyond *our* measure, *that is,* in other men's labors, but with the hope that as your faith grows, we shall be, within our sphere, enlarged even more by you,

16 so as to preach the gospel even to the regions beyond you, *and* not to boast in what has been accomplished in the sphere of another.

17 But HE WHO BOASTS, LET HIM BOAST IN THE LORD.

18 For not he who commends himself is approved, but whom the Lord commends.

CHAPTER 11

I WISH that you would bear with me in a little foolishness; but indeed you are bearing with me.

2 For I am jealous for you with a godly jealousy; for I betrothed you to one husband, that to Christ I might present you *as* a pure virgin.

3 But I am afraid, lest as the serpent deceived Eve by his craftiness, your minds should be led astray from the simplicity and purity *of devotion* to Christ.

4 For if one comes and preaches another Jesus whom we have not preached, or you receive a different spirit which you have not received, or a different gospel which you have not accepted, you bear *this* beautifully.

5 For I consider myself not in the least inferior to the most eminent apostles.

6 But even if I am unskilled in speech, yet I am not *so* in knowledge; in fact, in every way we have made *this* evident to you in all things.

7 Or did I commit a sin in humbling myself that you might be exalted, because I preached the gospel of God to you without charge?

8 I robbed other churches, taking wages *from them* to serve you;

9 and when I was present with you and was in need, I was not a burden to anyone; for when the brethren came from Macedonia, they fully supplied my need, and in everything I kept

myself from being a burden to you, and will continue to do so.

10 As the truth of Christ is in me, this boasting of mine will not be stopped in the regions of Achaia.

11 Why? Because I do not love you? God knows I do!

12 But what I am doing, I will continue to do, that I may cut off opportunity from those who desire an opportunity to be regarded just as we are in the matter about which they are boasting.

13 For such men are false apostles, deceitful workers, disguising themselves as apostles of Christ.

14 And no wonder, for even Satan disguises himself as an angel of light.

15 Therefore it is not surprising if his servants also disguise themselves as servants of righteousness; whose end shall be according to their deeds.

16 ¶ Again I say, let no one think me foolish; but if you do, receive me even as foolish, that I also may boast a little.

17 That which I am speaking, I am not speaking as the Lord would, but as in foolishness, in this confidence of boasting.

18 Since many boast according to the flesh, I will boast also.

19 For you, being so wise, bear with the foolish gladly.

20 For you bear with anyone if he enslaves you, if he devours you, if he takes advantage of you, if he exalts himself, if he hits you in the face.

21 To my shame I must say that we have been weak by comparison. But in whatever respect anyone else is bold (I speak in foolishness), I am just as bold myself.

22 Are they Hebrews? So am I. Are they Israelites? So am I. Are they descendants of Abraham? So am I.

23 Are they servants of Christ? (I speak as if insane) I more so; in far more labors, in far more imprisonments, beaten times without number, often in danger of death.

24 Five times I received from the Jews thirty-nine lashes.

25 Three times I was beaten with rods, once I was stoned, three times I was shipwrecked, a night and a day I have spent in the deep.

26 I have been on frequent journeys, in dangers from rivers, dangers from robbers, dangers from my countrymen, dangers from the Gentiles, dangers in the city, dangers in the wilderness, dangers on the sea, dangers among false brethren;

27 I have been in labor and hardship, through many sleepless nights, in hunger and thirst, often without food, in cold and exposure.

28 Apart from such external things, there is the daily pressure upon me of concern for all the churches.

29 Who is weak without my being weak? Who is led into sin without my intense concern?

30 If I have to boast, I will boast of what pertains to my weakness.

31 The God and Father of the Lord Jesus, He who is blessed forever, knows that I am not lying.

32 In Damascus the ethnarch under Aretas the king was guarding the city of the Damascenes in order to seize me,

33 and I was let down in a basket through a window in the wall, and so escaped his hands.

CHAPTER 12

BOASTING is necessary, though it is not profitable; but I will go on to visions and revelations of the Lord.

2 I know a man in Christ who fourteen years ago—whether in the body I do not know, or out of the body I do not know, God knows—such a man was caught up to the third heaven.

3 And I know how such a man—whether in the body or apart from the body I do not know, God knows—

4 was caught up into Paradise, and heard inexpressible words, which a man is not permitted to speak.

5 On behalf of such a man will I boast; but on my own behalf I will not boast, except in regard to my weaknesses.

6 For if I do wish to boast I shall not be foolish, for I shall be speaking the truth; but I refrain from this, so that no one may credit me with more than he sees in me or hears from me.

7 And because of the surpassing greatness of the revelations, for this reason, to keep me from exalting myself, there was given me a thorn in the flesh, a messenger of Satan to buffet me—to keep me from exalting myself !

8 Concerning this I entreated the Lord three times that it might depart from me.

9 And He has said to me, "My grace is sufficient for you, for ³power is perfected in weakness." Most gladly, therefore, I will rather boast about my weaknesses, that the power of Christ may dwell in me.

10 Therefore I am well content with weaknesses, with insults, with distresses, with persecutions, with difficulties, for Christ's sake; for when I am weak, then I am strong.

11 ¶ I have become foolish; you yourselves compelled me. Actually I should have been commended by you, for in no respect was I inferior to the most eminent apostles, even though I am a nobody.

12 The signs of a true apostle were performed among you with all perseverance, by signs and wonders and miracles.

13 For in what respect were you treated as inferior to the rest of the churches, except that I myself did not become a burden to you? Forgive me this wrong!

14 ¶ Here for this third time I am ready to come to you, and I will not be a burden to you; for I do not seek what is yours, but you; for children are not responsible to save up for *their* parents, but parents for *their* children.

15 And I will most gladly spend and be expended for your souls. If I love you the more, am I to be loved the less?

16 But be that as it may, I did not burden you myself; nevertheless, crafty fellow that I am, I took you in by deceit.

17 *Certainly* I have not taken advantage of you through any of those whom I have sent to you, have I?

18 I urged Titus *to go,* and sent the brother with him. Titus did not take any advantage of you, did he? Did we not conduct ourselves in the same spirit *and walk* in the same steps?

19 ¶ All this time you have been thinking that we are defending ourselves to you. *Actually,* it is in the sight of God that we have been speaking in Christ; and all for your upbuilding, beloved.

20 For I am afraid that perhaps when I come I may find you to be not what I wish and may be found by you to be not what you wish; that perhaps *there may be* strife, jealousy, angry tempers, disputes, slanders, gossip, arrogance, disturbances;

21 I am afraid that when I come again my God may humiliate me before you, and I may mourn over many of those who have sinned in the past and not repented of the impurity, immorality and sensuality which they have practiced.

CHAPTER 13

THIS is the third time I am coming to you. EVERY FACT IS TO BE CONFIRMED BY THE TESTIMONY OF TWO OR THREE WITNESSES.

2 I have previously said when present the second time, and though now absent I say in advance to those who have sinned in the past and to all the rest as well, that if I come again, I will not spare *anyone,*

3 since you are seeking for proof of the Christ who speaks in me, and who is not weak toward you, but mighty in you.

4 For indeed He was crucified because of weakness, yet He lives because of the power of God. For we also are weak ⁴in Him, yet we shall live with Him because of the power of God *directed* toward you.

5 Test yourselves *to see* if you are in the faith; examine yourselves! Or do you not recognize this about yourselves, that Jesus Christ is in you—unless indeed you fail the test?

6 But I trust that you will realize that we ourselves do not fail the test.

7 Now we pray to God that you do no wrong; not that we ourselves may appear approved, but that you may do what is right, even though we should appear unapproved.

8 For we can do nothing against the truth, but *only* for the truth.

9 For we rejoice when we ourselves are weak but you are strong; this we also pray for, that you be made complete.

10 For this reason I am writing these things while absent, in order that when present I may not use severity,

---

³ Later mss. read *My power*

⁴ Some early mss. read *with Him*

in accordance with the authority which the Lord gave me, for building up and not for tearing down.

11 ¶ Finally, brethren, rejoice, be made complete, be comforted, be like-minded, live in peace; and the God of love and peace shall be with you.

12 Greet one another with a holy kiss.

13 All the saints greet you.

14 ¶ The grace of the Lord Jesus Christ, and the love of God, and the fellowship of the Holy Spirit, be with you all.

THE EPISTLE OF PAUL TO THE

GALATIANS

PAUL, an apostle (not *sent* from men, nor through the agency of man, but through Jesus Christ, and God the Father, who raised Him from the dead),

2 and all the brethren who are with me, to the churches of Galatia:

3 Grace to you and peace from God our Father, and the Lord Jesus Christ,

4 who gave Himself for our sins, that He might deliver us out of this present evil age, according to the will of our God and Father,

5 to whom *be* the glory forevermore. Amen.

6 ¶ I am amazed that you are so quickly deserting Him who called you by the grace of Christ, for a different gospel;

7 which is *really* not another; only there are some who are disturbing you, and want to distort the gospel of Christ.

8 But even though we, or an angel from heaven, should preach to you a gospel contrary to that which we have preached to you, let him be accursed.

9 As we have said before, so I say again now, if any man is preaching to you a gospel contrary to that which you received, let him be accursed.

10 For am I now seeking the favor of men, or of God? Or am I striving to please men? If I were still trying to please men, I would not be a bond-servant of Christ.

11 ¶ For I would have you know, brethren, that the gospel which was preached by me is not according to man.

12 For I neither received it from man, nor was I taught it, but I received it through a revelation of Jesus Christ.

13 For you have heard of my former manner of life in Judaism, how I used to persecute the church of God beyond measure, and tried to destroy it;

14 and I was advancing in Judaism beyond many of my contemporaries among my countrymen, being more extremely zealous for my ancestral traditions.

15 But when He who had set me apart, *even* from my mother's womb, and called me through His grace, was pleased

16 to reveal His Son in me, that I might preach Him among the Gentiles, I did not immediately consult with flesh and blood,

17 nor did I go up to Jerusalem to those who were apostles before me; but I went away to Arabia, and returned once more to Damascus.

18 ¶ Then three years later I went up to Jerusalem to become acquainted with Cephas, and stayed with him fifteen days.

19 But I did not see any other of the apostles except James, the Lord's brother.

20 (Now in what I am writing to you, I assure you before God that I am not lying.)

21 Then I went into the regions of Syria and Cilicia.

22 And I was *still* unknown by sight to the churches of Judea which were in Christ;

23 but only, they kept hearing, "He who once persecuted us is now

preaching the faith which he once tried to destroy."

24 And they were glorifying God because of me.

CHAPTER 2

THEN after an interval of fourteen years I went up again to Jerusalem with Barnabas, taking Titus along also.

2 And it was because of a revelation that I went up; and I submitted to them the gospel which I preach among the Gentiles, but *I did so* in private to those who were of reputation, for fear that I might be running, or had run, in vain.

3 But not even Titus who was with me, though he was a Greek, was compelled to be circumcised.

4 But *it was* because of the false brethren who had sneaked in to spy out our liberty which we have in Christ Jesus, in order to bring us into bondage.

5 But we did not yield in subjection to them for even an hour, so that the truth of the gospel might remain with you.

6 But from those who were of high reputation (what they were makes no difference to me; God shows no partiality)—well, those who were of reputation contributed nothing to me.

7 But on the contrary, seeing that I had been entrusted with the gospel to the uncircumcised, just as Peter *had been* to the circumcised

8 (for He who effectually worked for Peter in *his* apostleship to the circumcised effectually worked for me also to the Gentiles),

9 and recognizing the grace that had been given to me, James and Cephas and John, who were reputed to be pillars, gave to me and Barnabas the right hand of fellowship, that we *might go* to the Gentiles, and they to the circumcised.

10 *They* only *asked* us to remember the poor—the very thing I also was eager to do.

11 ¶ But when Cephas came to Antioch, I opposed him to his face, because he stood condemned.

12 For prior to the coming of certain men from James, he used to eat with the Gentiles; but when they came, he

began to withdraw and hold himself aloof, fearing the party of the circumcision.

13 And the rest of the Jews joined him in hypocrisy, with the result that even Barnabas was carried away by their hypocrisy.

14 But when I saw that they were not straightforward about the truth of the gospel, I said to Cephas in the presence of all, "If you, being a Jew, live like the Gentiles and not like the Jews, how *is it that* you compel the Gentiles to live like Jews?

15 "We *are* Jews by nature, and not sinners from among the Gentiles;

16 nevertheless knowing that a man is not justified by the works of the Law but through faith in Christ Jesus, even we have believed in Christ Jesus, that we may be justified by faith in Christ, and not by the works of the Law; since by the works of the Law shall no flesh be justified.

17 "But if, while seeking to be justified in Christ, we ourselves have also been found sinners, is Christ then a minister of sin? May it never be!

18 "For if I rebuild what I have *once* destroyed, I prove myself to be a transgressor.

19 "For through the Law I died to the Law, that I might live to God.

20 "I have been crucified with Christ; and it is no longer I who live, but Christ lives in me; and the *life* which I now live in the flesh I live by faith in the Son of God, who loved me, and delivered Himself up for me.

21 "I do not nullify the grace of God; for if righteousness *comes* through the Law, then Christ died needlessly."

CHAPTER 3

YOU foolish Galatians, who has bewitched you, before whose eyes Jesus Christ was publicly portrayed *as* crucified?

2 This is the only thing I want to find out from you: did you receive the Spirit by the works of the Law, or by hearing with faith?

3 Are you so foolish? Having begun by the Spirit, are you now being perfected by the flesh?

4 Did you suffer so many things in vain—if indeed it was in vain?

5 Does He then, who provides you

with the Spirit and works miracles among you, do it by the works of the Law, or by hearing with faith?

6 Even so Abraham BELIEVED GOD, AND IT WAS RECKONED TO HIM AS RIGHTEOUSNESS.

7 Therefore, be sure that it is those who are of faith who are sons of Abraham.

8 And the Scripture, foreseeing that God would justify the Gentiles by faith, preached the gospel beforehand to Abraham, *saying*, "ALL THE NATIONS SHALL BE BLESSED IN YOU."

9 So then those who are of faith are blessed with Abraham, the believer.

10 For as many as are of the works of the Law are under a curse; for it is written, "CURSED IS EVERYONE WHO DOES NOT ABIDE BY ALL THINGS WRITTEN IN THE BOOK OF THE LAW, TO PERFORM THEM."

11 Now that no one is justified by the Law before God is evident; for, "THE RIGHTEOUS MAN SHALL LIVE BY FAITH."

12 However, the Law is not of faith; on the contrary, "HE WHO PRACTICES THEM SHALL LIVE BY THEM."

13 Christ redeemed us from the curse of the Law, having become a curse for us—for it is written, "CURSED IS EVERYONE WHO HANGS ON A TREE"—

14 in order that in Christ Jesus the blessing of Abraham might come to the Gentiles, so that we might receive the promise of the Spirit through faith.

15 ¶ Brethren, I speak in terms of human relations: even though it is *only* a man's covenant, yet when it has been ratified, no one sets it aside or adds conditions to it.

16 Now the promises were spoken to Abraham and to his seed. He does not say, "And to seeds," as *referring* to many, but *rather* to one, "And to your seed," that is, Christ.

17 What I am saying is this: the Law, which came four hundred and thirty years later, does not invalidate a covenant previously ratified by God, so as to nullify the promise.

18 For if the inheritance is based on law, it is no longer based on a promise; but God has granted it to Abraham by means of a promise.

19 Why the Law then? It was added because of transgressions, having been ordained through angels by the agency of a mediator, until the seed should come to whom the promise had been made.

20 Now a mediator is not for one *party only*; whereas God is *only* one.

21 Is the Law then contrary to the promises of God? May it never be! For if a law had been given which was able to impart life, then righteousness would indeed have been based on law.

22 But the Scripture has shut up all men under sin, that the promise by faith in Jesus Christ might be given to those who believe.

23 ¶ But before faith came, we were kept in custody under the law, being shut up to the faith which was later to be revealed.

24 Therefore the Law has become our tutor *to lead us* to Christ, that we may be justified by faith.

25 But now that faith has come, we are no longer under a tutor.

26 For you are all sons of God through faith in Christ Jesus.

27 For all of you who were baptized into Christ have clothed yourselves with Christ.

28 There is neither Jew nor Greek, there is neither slave nor free man, there is neither male nor female; for you are all one in Christ Jesus.

29 And if you belong to Christ, then you are Abraham's offspring, heirs according to promise.

CHAPTER 4

NOW I say, as long as the heir is a child, he does not differ at all from a slave although he is owner of everything,

2 but he is under guardians and managers until the date set by the father.

3 So also we, while we were children, were held in bondage under the elemental things of the world.

4 But when the fulness of the time came, God sent forth His Son, born of a woman, born under the Law,

5 in order that He might redeem those who were under the Law, that we might receive the adoption as sons.

6 And because you are sons, God has sent forth the Spirit of His Son into our hearts, crying, "Abba! Father!"

7 Therefore you are no longer a

slave, but a son; and if a son, then an heir through God.

8 ¶ However at that time, when you did not know God, you were slaves to those which by nature are no gods.

9 But now that you have come to know God, or rather to be known by God, how is it that you turn back again to the weak and worthless elemental things, to which you desire to be enslaved all over again?

10 You observe days and months and seasons and years.

11 I fear for you, that perhaps I have labored over you in vain.

12 ¶ I beg of you, brethren, become as I *am*, for I also *have become* as you *are.* You have done me no wrong;

13 but you know that it was because of a bodily illness that I preached the gospel to you the first time;

14 and that which was a trial to you in my bodily condition you did not despise or loathe, but you received me as an angel of God, as Christ Jesus *Himself.*

15 Where then is that sense of blessing you had? For I bear you witness, that if possible, you would have plucked out your eyes and given them to me.

16 Have I therefore become your enemy by telling you the truth?

17 They eagerly seek you, not commendably, but they wish to shut you out, in order that you may seek them.

18 But it is good always to be eagerly sought in a commendable manner, and not only when I am present with you.

19 My children, with whom I am again in labor until Christ is formed in you—

20 but I could wish to be present with you now and to change my tone, for I am perplexed about you.

21 ¶ Tell me, you who want to be under law, do you not listen to the law?

22 For it is written that Abraham had two sons, one by the bondwoman and one by the free woman.

23 But the son by the bondwoman was born according to the flesh, and the son by the free woman through the promise.

24 This is allegorically speaking: for these *women* are two covenants, one *proceeding* from Mount Sinai bearing

children who are to be slaves; she is Hagar.

25 Now this Hagar is Mount Sinai in Arabia, and corresponds to the present Jerusalem, for she is in slavery with her children.

26 But the Jerusalem above is free; she is our mother.

27 For it is written,

"Rejoice, barren woman who does not bear;

Break forth and shout, you who are not in labor;

For more are the children of the desolate

Than of the one who has a husband."

28 And you brethren, like Isaac, are children of promise.

29 But as at that time he who was born according to the flesh persecuted him *who was born* according to the Spirit, so it is now also.

30 But what does the Scripture say?

"Cast out the bondwoman and her son,

For the son of the bondwoman shall not be an heir with the son of the free woman."

31 So then, brethren, we are not children of a bondwoman, but of the free woman.

CHAPTER 5

It was for freedom that Christ set us free; therefore keep standing firm and do not be subject again to a yoke of slavery.

2 ¶ Behold I, Paul, say to you that if you receive circumcision, Christ will be of no benefit to you.

3 And I testify again to every man who receives circumcision, that he is under obligation to keep the whole Law.

4 You have been severed from Christ, you who are seeking to be justified by law; you have fallen from grace.

5 For we through the Spirit, by faith, are waiting for the hope of righteousness.

6 For in Christ Jesus neither circumcision nor uncircumcision means anything, but faith working through love.

7 You were running well; who hindered you from obeying the truth?

8 This persuasion *did* not *come* from Him who calls you.

9 A little leaven leavens the whole lump *of dough.*

10 I have confidence in you in the Lord, that you will adopt no other view; but the one who is disturbing you shall bear his judgment, whoever he is.

11 But I, brethren, if I still preach circumcision, why am I still persecuted? Then the stumbling block of the cross has been abolished.

12 Would that those who are troubling you would even mutilate themselves.

13 ¶ For you were called to freedom, brethren; only *do* not *turn* your freedom into an opportunity for the flesh, but through love serve one another.

14 For the whole Law is fulfilled in one word, in the *statement,* "You shall love your neighbor as yourself."

15 But if you bite and devour one another, take care lest you be consumed by one another.

16 ¶ But I say, walk by the Spirit, and you will not carry out the desire of the flesh.

17 For the flesh sets its desire against the Spirit, and the Spirit against the flesh; for these are in opposition to one another, so that you may not do the things that you please.

18 But if you are led by the Spirit, you are not under the Law.

19 Now the deeds of the flesh are evident, which are: immorality, impurity, sensuality,

20 idolatry, sorcery, enmities, strife, jealousy, outbursts of anger, disputes, dissensions, factions,

21 envying, drunkenness, carousing, and things like these, of which I forewarn you just as I have forewarned you that those who practice such things shall not inherit the kingdom of God.

22 But the fruit of the Spirit is love, joy, peace, patience, kindness, goodness, faithfulness,

23 gentleness, self-control; against such things there is no law.

24 Now those who belong to Christ Jesus have crucified the flesh with its passions and desires.

25 ¶ If we live by the Spirit, let us also walk by the Spirit.

26 Let us not become boastful, challenging one another, envying one another.

CHAPTER 6

Brethren, even if a man is caught in any trespass, you who are spiritual, restore such a one in a spirit of gentleness; *each one* looking to yourself, lest you too be tempted.

2 Bear one another's burdens, and thus fulfill the law of Christ.

3 For if anyone thinks he is something when he is nothing, he deceives himself.

4 But let each one examine his own work, and then he will have *reason for* boasting in regard to himself alone, and not in regard to another.

5 For each one shall bear his own load.

6 ¶ And let the one who is taught the word share all good things with him who teaches.

7 Do not be deceived, God is not mocked; for whatever a man sows, this he will also reap.

8 For the one who sows to his own flesh shall from the flesh reap corruption, but the one who sows to the Spirit shall from the Spirit reap eternal life.

9 And let us not lose heart in doing good, for in due time we shall reap if we do not grow weary.

10 So then, while we have opportunity, let us do good to all men, and especially to those who are of the household of the faith.

11 ¶ See with what large letters I am writing to you with my own hand.

12 Those who desire to make a good showing in the flesh try to compel you to be circumcised, simply that they may not be persecuted for the cross of Christ.

13 For those who [1]are circumcised do not even keep the Law themselves, but they desire to have you circumcised, that they may boast in your flesh.

14 But may it never be that I should boast, except in the cross of our Lord Jesus Christ, through which the world has been crucified to me, and I to the world.

[1] Some ancient mss. read *have been*

15 For neither is circumcision anything, nor uncircumcision, but a new creation.

16 And those who will walk by this rule, peace and mercy *be* upon them, and upon the Israel of God.

17 ¶ From now on let no one cause trouble for me, for I bear on my body the brand-marks of Jesus.

18 ¶ The grace of our Lord Jesus Christ be with your spirit, brethren. Amen.

THE EPISTLE OF PAUL TO THE

EPHESIANS

PAUL, an apostle of Christ Jesus by the will of God, to the saints who are ¹at Ephesus, and *who are* faithful in Christ Jesus:

2 Grace to you and peace from God our Father and the Lord Jesus Christ.

3 ¶ Blessed *be* the God and Father of our Lord Jesus Christ, who has blessed us with every spiritual blessing in the heavenly *places* in Christ,

4 just as He chose us in Him before the foundation of the world, that we should be holy and blameless before ²Him. In love

5 He predestined us to adoption as sons through Jesus Christ to Himself, according to the kind intention of His will,

6 to the praise of the glory of His grace, which He freely bestowed on us in the Beloved.

7 In Him we have redemption through His blood, the forgiveness of our trespasses, according to the riches of His grace,

8 which He lavished upon us. In all wisdom and insight

9 He made known to us the mystery of His will, according to His kind intention which He purposed in Him

10 with a view to an administration suitable to the fulness of the times, *that is*, the summing up of all things in Christ, things in the heavens and things upon the earth. In Him

11 also we have obtained an inheritance, having been predestined according to His purpose who works all things after the counsel of His will,

12 to the end that we who were the first to hope in ³Christ should be to the praise of His glory.

13 In Him, you also, after listening to the message of truth, the gospel of your salvation—having also believed, you were sealed in Him with the Holy Spirit of promise,

14 who is given as a pledge of our inheritance, with a view to the redemption of *God's own* possession, to the praise of His glory.

15 ¶ For this reason I too, having heard of the faith in the Lord Jesus which *exists* among you, and ⁴your love for all the saints,

16 do not cease giving thanks for you, while making mention *of you* in my prayers;

17 that the God of our Lord Jesus Christ, the Father of glory, may give to you a spirit of wisdom and of revelation in the knowledge of Him.

18 *I pray that* the eyes of your heart may be enlightened, so that you may know what is the hope of His calling, what are the riches of the glory of His inheritance in the saints,

19 and what is the surpassing greatness of His power toward us who believe. *These are* in accordance with the working of the strength of His might

20 which He brought about in Christ, when He raised Him from the dead, and seated Him at His right hand in the heavenly *places*,

21 far above all rule and authority and power and dominion, and every name that is named, not only in this age, but also in the one to come.

22 And He put all things in subjection under His feet, and gave Him as head over all things to the church,

---

¹ Some ancient mss. do not contain *at Ephesus*
² Or, *Him, in love.*
³ I.e., the Messiah
⁴ Many ancient mss. do not contain *your love*

23 which is His body, the fulness of Him who fills all in all.

CHAPTER 2

AND you were dead in your trespasses and sins,

2 in which you formerly walked according to the course of this world, according to the prince of the power of the air, of the spirit that is now working in the sons of disobedience.

3 Among them we too all formerly lived in the lusts of our flesh, indulging the desires of the flesh and of the mind, and were by nature children of wrath, even as the rest.

4 But God, being rich in mercy, because of His great love with which He loved us,

5 even when we were dead in our transgressions, made us alive together [5]with Christ (by grace you have been saved),

6 and raised us up with Him, and seated us with Him in the heavenly *places*, in Christ Jesus,

7 in order that in the ages to come He might show the surpassing riches of His grace in kindness toward us in Christ Jesus.

8 For by grace you have been saved through faith; and that not of yourselves, *it is* the gift of God;

9 not as a result of works, that no one should boast.

10 For we are His workmanship, created in Christ Jesus for good works, which God prepared beforehand, that we should walk in them.

11 ¶ Therefore remember, that formerly you, the Gentiles in the flesh, who are called "Uncircumcision" by the so-called "Circumcision," *which is* performed in the flesh by human hands—

12 *remember* that you were at that time separate from Christ, excluded from the commonwealth of Israel, and strangers to the covenants of promise, having no hope and without God in the world.

13 But now in Christ Jesus you who formerly were far off have been brought near by the blood of Christ.

14 For He Himself is our peace, who made both *groups into* one, and broke down the barrier of the dividing wall,

15 by abolishing in His flesh the enmity, *which is* the Law of commandments *contained* in ordinances, that in Himself He might make the two into one new man, *thus* establishing peace,

16 and might reconcile them both in one body to God through the cross, by it having put to death the enmity.

17 AND HE CAME AND PREACHED PEACE TO YOU WHO WERE FAR AWAY, AND PEACE TO THOSE WHO WERE NEAR;

18 for through Him we both have our access in one Spirit to the Father.

19 So then you are no longer strangers and aliens, but you are fellow citizens with the saints, and are of God's household,

20 having been built upon the foundation of the apostles and prophets, Christ Jesus Himself being the corner *stone*,

21 in whom the whole building, being fitted together is growing into a holy temple in the Lord;

22 in whom you also are being built together into a dwelling of God in the Spirit.

CHAPTER 3

FOR this reason I, Paul, the prisoner of Christ Jesus for the sake of you Gentiles—

2 if indeed you have heard of the stewardship of God's grace which was given to me for you;

3 that by revelation there was made known to me the mystery, as I wrote before in brief.

4 And by referring to this, when you read you can understand my insight into the mystery of Christ,

5 which in other generations was not made known to the sons of men, as it has now been revealed to His holy apostles and prophets in the Spirit;

6 *to be specific*, that the Gentiles are fellow heirs and fellow members of the body, and fellow partakers of the promise in Christ Jesus through the gospel,

7 of which I was made a minister, according to the gift of God's grace which was given to me according to the working of His power.

8 To me, the very least of all saints, this grace was given, to preach to the Gentiles the unfathomable riches of Christ,

[5] Some ancient mss. read *in Christ*

9 and to bring to light what is the administration of the mystery which for ages has been hidden in God, who created all things;

10 in order that the manifold wisdom of God might now be made known through the church to the rulers and the authorities in the heavenly *places*.

11 *This was* in accordance with the eternal purpose which He carried out in Christ Jesus our Lord,

12 in whom we have boldness and confident access through faith in Him.

13 Therefore I ask you not to lose heart at my tribulations on your behalf, for they are your glory.

14 ¶ For this reason, I bow my knees before the Father,

15 from whom every family in heaven and on earth derives its name,

16 that He would grant you, according to the riches of His glory, to be strengthened with power through His Spirit in the inner man;

17 so that Christ may dwell in your hearts through faith; *and* that you, being rooted and grounded in love,

18 may be able to comprehend with all the saints what is the breadth and length and height and depth,

19 and to know the love of Christ which surpasses knowledge, that you may be filled up to all the fulness of God.

20 ¶ Now to Him who is able to do exceeding abundantly beyond all that we ask or think, according to the power that works within us,

21 to Him *be* the glory in the church and in Christ Jesus to all generations forever and ever. Amen.

CHAPTER 4

I, THEREFORE, the prisoner of the Lord, entreat you to walk in a manner worthy of the calling with which you have been called,

2 with all humility and gentleness, with patience, showing forbearance to one another in love,

3 being diligent to preserve the unity of the Spirit in the bond of peace.

4 *There is* one body and one Spirit, just as also you were called in one hope of your calling;

5 one Lord, one faith, one baptism,

6 one God and Father of all who is over all and through all and in all.

7 But to each one of us grace was given according to the measure of Christ's gift.

8 Therefore it says,
"WHEN HE ASCENDED ON HIGH,
HE LED CAPTIVE A HOST OF CAPTIVES,
AND HE GAVE GIFTS TO MEN."

9 (Now this *expression*, "He ascended," what does it mean except that He also had descended into the lower parts of the earth?

10 He who descended is Himself also He who ascended far above all the heavens, that He might fill all things.)

11 And He gave some *as* apostles, and some *as* prophets, and some *as* evangelists, and some *as* pastors and teachers,

12 for the equipping of the saints for the work of service, to the building up of the body of Christ;

13 until we all attain to the unity of the faith, and of the knowledge of the Son of God, to a mature man, to the measure of the stature which belongs to the fulness of Christ.

14 As a result, we are no longer to be children, tossed here and there by waves, and carried about by every wind of doctrine, by the trickery of men, by craftiness in deceitful scheming;

15 but speaking the truth in love, we are to grow up in all *aspects* into Him, who is the head, *even* Christ,

16 from whom the whole body, being fitted and held together by that which every joint supplies, according to the proper working of each individual part, causes the growth of the body for the building up of itself in love.

17 ¶ This I say therefore, and affirm together with the Lord, that you walk no longer just as the Gentiles also walk, in the futility of their mind,

18 being darkened in their understanding, excluded from the life of God, because of the ignorance that is in them, because of the hardness of their heart;

19 and they, having become callous, have given themselves over to sensuality, for the practice of every kind of impurity with greediness.

20 But you did not learn Christ in this way,

21 if indeed you have heard Him and have been taught in Him, just as truth is in Jesus,

22 that, in reference to your former manner of life, you lay aside the old self, which is being corrupted in accordance with the lusts of deceit,

23 and that you be renewed in the spirit of your mind,

24 and put on the new self, which in *the likeness of* God has been created in righteousness and holiness of the truth.

25 ¶ Therefore, laying aside falsehood, SPEAK TRUTH, EACH ONE *of you,* WITH HIS NEIGHBOR, for we are members of one another.

26 BE ANGRY, AND *yet* DO NOT SIN; do not let the sun go down on your anger,

27 and do not give the devil an opportunity.

28 Let him who steals steal no longer; but rather let him labor, performing with his own hands what is good, in order that he may have *something* to share with him who has need.

29 Let no unwholesome word proceed from your mouth, but only such *a word* as is good for edification according to the need *of the moment,* that it may give grace to those who hear.

30 And do not grieve the Holy Spirit of God, by whom you were sealed for the day of redemption.

31 Let all bitterness and wrath and anger and clamor and slander be put away from you, along with all malice.

32 And be kind to one another, tender-hearted, forgiving each other, just as God in Christ also has forgiven [6]you.

CHAPTER 5

THEREFORE be imitators of God, as beloved children;

2 and walk in love, just as Christ also loved [6]you, and gave Himself up for us, an offering and a sacrifice to God as a fragrant aroma.

3 ¶ But do not let immorality or any impurity or greed even be named among you, as is proper among saints;

4 and *there must be no* filthiness and silly talk, or coarse jesting, which are not fitting, but rather giving of thanks.

[6] Some ancient mss. read *us*

5 For this you know with certainty, that no immoral or impure person or covetous man, who is an idolater, has an inheritance in the kingdom of Christ and God.

6 Let no one deceive you with empty words, for because of these things the wrath of God comes upon the sons of disobedience.

7 Therefore do not be partakers with them;

8 for you were formerly darkness, but now you are light in the Lord; walk as children of light

9 (for the fruit of the light *consists* in all goodness and righteousness and truth),

10 trying to learn what is pleasing to the Lord.

11 And do not participate in the unfruitful deeds of darkness, but instead even expose them;

12 for it is disgraceful even to speak of the things which are done by them in secret.

13 But all things become visible when they are exposed by the light, for everything that becomes visible is light.

14 For this reason it says,
"Awake, sleeper,
And arise from the dead,
And Christ will shine on you."

15 ¶ Therefore be careful how you walk, not as unwise men, but as wise,

16 making the most of your time, because the days are evil.

17 So then do not be foolish, but understand what the will of the Lord is.

18 And do not get drunk with wine, for that is dissipation, but be filled with the Spirit,

19 speaking to one another in psalms and hymns and spiritual songs, singing and making melody with your heart to the Lord;

20 always giving thanks for all things in the name of our Lord Jesus Christ to God, even the Father;

21 and be subject to one another in the fear of Christ.

22 ¶ Wives, *be subject* to your own husbands, as to the Lord.

23 For the husband is the head of the wife, as Christ also is the head of the

church, He Himself *being* the Savior of the body.

24 But as the church is subject to Christ, so also the wives *ought to be* to their husbands in everything.

25 Husbands, love your wives, just as Christ also loved the church and gave Himself up for her;

26 that He might sanctify her, having cleansed her by the washing of water with the word,

27 that He might present to Himself the church in all her glory, having no spot or wrinkle or any such thing; but that she should be holy and blameless.

28 So husbands ought also to love their own wives as their own bodies. He who loves his own wife loves himself;

29 for no one ever hated his own flesh, but nourishes and cherishes it, just as Christ also *does* the church,

30 because we are members of His body.

31 FOR THIS CAUSE A MAN SHALL LEAVE HIS FATHER AND MOTHER, AND SHALL CLEAVE TO HIS WIFE; AND THE TWO SHALL BECOME ONE FLESH.

32 This mystery is great; but I am speaking with reference to Christ and the church.

33 Nevertheless let each individual among you also love his own wife even as himself; and *let* the wife *see to it* that she respect her husband.

CHAPTER 6

CHILDREN, obey your parents in the Lord, for this is right.

2 HONOR YOUR FATHER AND MOTHER (which is the first commandment with a promise),

3 THAT IT MAY BE WELL WITH YOU, AND THAT YOU MAY LIVE LONG ON THE EARTH.

4 And, fathers, do not provoke your children to anger; but bring them up in the discipline and instruction of the Lord.

5 ¶ Slaves, be obedient to those who are your masters according to the flesh, with fear and trembling, in the sincerity of your heart, as to Christ;

6 not by way of eyeservice, as menpleasers, but as slaves of Christ, doing the will of God from the heart.

7 With good will render service, as to the Lord, and not to men,

8 knowing that whatever good thing each one does, this he will receive back from the Lord, whether slave or free.

9 And, masters, do the same things to them, and give up threatening, knowing that both their Master and yours is in heaven, and there is no partiality with Him.

10 ¶ Finally, be strong in the Lord, and in the strength of His might.

11 Put on the full armor of God, that you may be able to stand firm against the schemes of the devil.

12 For our struggle is not against flesh and blood, but against the rulers, against the powers, against the world forces of this darkness, against the spiritual *forces* of wickedness in the heavenly *places*.

13 Therefore, take up the full armor of God, that you may be able to resist in the evil day, and having done everything, to stand firm.

14 Stand firm therefore, HAVING GIRDED YOUR LOINS WITH TRUTH, and HAVING PUT ON THE BREASTPLATE OF RIGHTEOUSNESS,

15 and having shod YOUR FEET WITH THE PREPARATION OF THE GOSPEL OF PEACE;

16 in addition to all, taking up the shield of faith with which you will be able to extinguish all the flaming missiles of the evil *one*.

17 And take THE HELMET OF SALVATION, and the sword of the Spirit, which is the word of God.

18 With all prayer and petition pray at all times in the Spirit, and with this in view, be on the alert with all perseverance and petition for all the saints,

19 and *pray* on my behalf, that utterance may be given to me in the opening of my mouth, to make known with boldness the mystery of the gospel,

20 for which I am an ambassador in chains; that [7]in *proclaiming* it I may speak boldly, as I ought to speak.

21 ¶ But that you also may know about my circumstances, how I am doing, Tychicus, the beloved brother and faithful minister in the Lord, will make everything known to you.

[7] Some ancient mss. read *I may speak it boldly*

22 And I have sent him to you for this very purpose, so that you may know about us, and that he may comfort your hearts.

23 ¶ Peace be to the brethren, and

love with faith, from God the Father and the Lord Jesus Christ.

24 Grace be with all those who love our Lord Jesus Christ with *a love* incorruptible.

THE EPISTLE OF PAUL TO THE

PHILIPPIANS

PAUL and Timothy, bond-servants of Christ Jesus, to all the saints in Christ Jesus who are in Philippi, including the overseers and deacons:

2 Grace to you and peace from God our Father and the Lord Jesus Christ.

3 ¶ I thank my God in all my remembrance of you,

4 always offering prayer with joy in my every prayer for you all,

5 in view of your participation in the gospel from the first day until now.

6 *For I am* confident of this very thing, that He who began a good work in you will perfect it until the day of Christ Jesus.

7 For it is only right for me to feel this way about you all, because I have you in my heart, since both in my imprisonment and in the defense and confirmation of the gospel, you all are partakers of grace with me.

8 For God is my witness, how I long for you all with the affection of Christ Jesus.

9 And this I pray, that your love may abound still more and more in real knowledge and all discernment,

10 so that you may approve the things that are excellent, in order to be sincere and blameless until the day of Christ;

11 having been filled with the fruit of righteousness which *comes* through Jesus Christ, to the glory and praise of God.

12 ¶ Now I want you to know, brethren, that my circumstances have turned out for the greater progress of the gospel,

13 so that my imprisonment in *the cause of* Christ has become well

known throughout the whole [1]praetorian guard and to everyone else,

14 and that most of the brethren, trusting in the Lord because of my imprisonment, have far more courage to speak the word of God without fear.

15 Some, to be sure, are preaching Christ even from envy and strife, but some also from good will;

16 [2]the latter *do it* out of love, knowing that I am appointed for the defense of the gospel;

17 the former proclaim Christ out of selfish ambition, rather than from pure motives, thinking to cause me distress in my imprisonment.

18 What then? Only that in every way, whether in pretense or in truth, Christ is proclaimed; and in this I rejoice, yes, and I will rejoice.

19 For I know that this shall turn out for my deliverance through your prayers and the provision of the Spirit of Jesus Christ,

20 according to my earnest expectation and hope, that I shall not be put to shame in anything, but *that* with all boldness, Christ shall even now, as always, be exalted in my body, whether by life or by death.

21 For to me, to live is Christ, and to die is gain.

22 But if *I am* to live *on* in the flesh, this *will mean* fruitful labor for me; and I do not know which to choose.

23 But I am hard-pressed from both *directions,* having the desire to depart and be with Christ, for *that* is very much better;

24 yet to remain on in the flesh is more necessary for your sake.

25 And convinced of this, I know

[1] Or, *governor's palace*
[2] Some later mss. reverse the order of vv. 16 and 17

that I shall remain and continue with you all for your progress and joy in the faith,

26 so that your proud confidence in me may abound in Christ Jesus through my coming to you again.

27 ¶ Only conduct yourselves in a manner worthy of the gospel of Christ; so that whether I come and see you or remain absent, I may hear of you that you are standing firm in one spirit, with one mind striving together for the faith of the gospel;

28 in no way alarmed by *your* opponents—which is a sign of destruction for them, but of salvation for you, and that *too*, from God.

29 For to you it has been granted for Christ's sake, not only to believe in Him, but also to suffer for His sake,

30 experiencing the same conflict which you saw in me, and now hear *to be* in me.

CHAPTER 2

IF therefore there is any encouragement in Christ, if there is any consolation of love, if there is any fellowship of the Spirit, if any affection and compassion,

2 make my joy complete by being of the same mind, maintaining the same love, united in spirit, intent on one purpose.

3 Do nothing from selfishness or empty conceit, but with humility of mind let each of you regard one another as more important than himself;

4 do not *merely* look out for your own personal interests, but also for the interests of others.

5 Have this attitude in yourselves which was also in Christ Jesus,

6 who, although He existed in the form of God, did not regard equality with God a thing to be grasped,

7 but [3]emptied Himself, taking the form of a bond-servant, *and* being made in the likeness of men.

8 And being found in appearance as a man, He humbled Himself by becoming obedient to the point of death, even death on a cross.

9 Therefore also God highly exalted Him, and bestowed on Him the name which is above every name,

10 that at the name of Jesus EVERY KNEE SHOULD BOW, of those who are in heaven, and on earth, and under the earth,

11 and that every tongue should confess that Jesus Christ is Lord, to the glory of God the Father.

12 ¶ So then, my beloved, just as you have always obeyed, not as in my presence only, but now much more in my absence, work out your salvation with fear and trembling;

13 for it is God who is at work in you, both to will and to work for *His* good pleasure.

14 Do all things without grumbling or disputing;

15 that you may prove yourselves to be blameless and innocent, children of God above reproach in the midst of a crooked and perverse generation, among whom you appear as lights in the world,

16 holding fast the word of life, so that in the day of Christ I may have cause to glory because I did not run in vain nor toil in vain.

17 But even if I am being poured out as a drink offering upon the sacrifice and service of your faith, I rejoice and share my joy with you all.

18 And you too, *I urge you,* rejoice in the same way and share your joy with me.

19 ¶ But I hope in the Lord Jesus to send Timothy to you shortly, so that I also may be encouraged when I learn of your condition.

20 For I have no one *else* of kindred spirit who will genuinely be concerned for your welfare.

21 For they all seek after their own interests, not those of Christ Jesus.

22 But you know of his proven worth that he served with me in the furtherance of the gospel like a child *serving* his father.

23 Therefore I hope to send him immediately, as soon as I see how things go with me;

24 and I trust in the Lord that I myself also shall be coming shortly.

25 But I thought it necessary to send to you Epaphroditus, my brother and fellow worker and fellow soldier, who is also your messenger and minister to my need;

26 because he was longing [4]for you

---

[3] I.e., laid aside His privileges

[4] Some ancient mss. read *to see you all*

all and was distressed because you had heard that he was sick.

27 For indeed he was sick to the point of death, but God had mercy on him, and not on him only but also on me, lest I should have sorrow upon sorrow.

28 Therefore I have sent him all the more eagerly in order that when you see him again you may rejoice and I may be less concerned *about you.*

29 Therefore receive him in the Lord with all joy, and hold men like him in high regard;

30 because he came close to death for the work of Christ, risking his life to complete what was deficient in your service to me.

CHAPTER 3

FINALLY, my brethren, rejoice in the Lord. To write the same things *again* is no trouble to me, and it is a safeguard for you.

2 Beware of the dogs, beware of the evil workers, beware of the false circumcision;

3 for we are the *true* circumcision, who worship in the Spirit of God and glory in Christ Jesus and put no confidence in the flesh,

4 although I myself might have confidence even in the flesh. If anyone else has a mind to put confidence in the flesh, I far more:

5 circumcised the eighth day, of the nation of Israel, of the tribe of Benjamin, a Hebrew of Hebrews; as to the Law, a Pharisee;

6 as to zeal, a persecutor of the church; as to the righteousness which is in the Law, found blameless.

7 But whatever things were gain to me, those things I have counted as loss for the sake of Christ.

8 More than that, I count all things to be loss in view of the surpassing value of knowing Christ Jesus my Lord, for whom I have suffered the loss of all things, and count them but rubbish in order that I may gain Christ,

9 and may be found in Him, not having a righteousness of my own derived from *the* Law, but that which is through faith in Christ, the righteousness which *comes* from God on the basis of faith,

10 that I may know Him, and the power of His resurrection and the fellowship of His sufferings, being conformed to His death;

11 in order that I may attain to the resurrection from the dead.

12 Not that I have already obtained *it,* or have already become perfect, but I press on in order that I may lay hold of that for which also I was laid hold of by Christ Jesus.

13 Brethren, I do not regard myself as having laid hold of *it* yet; but one thing *I do:* forgetting what *lies* behind and reaching forward to what *lies* ahead,

14 I press on toward the goal for the prize of the upward call of God in Christ Jesus.

15 Let us therefore, as many as are perfect, have this attitude; and if in anything you have a different attitude, God will reveal that also to you;

16 however, let us keep living by that same *standard* to which we have attained.

17 ¶ Brethren, join in following my example, and observe those who walk according to the pattern you have in us.

18 For many walk, of whom I often told you, and now tell you even weeping, *that they are* enemies of the cross of Christ,

19 whose end is destruction, whose god is *their* appetite, and *whose* glory is in their shame, who set their minds on earthly things.

20 For our citizenship is in heaven, from which also we eagerly wait for a Savior, the Lord Jesus Christ;

21 who will transform the body of our humble state into conformity with the body of His glory, by the exertion of the power that He has even to subject all things to Himself.

CHAPTER 4

THEREFORE, my beloved brethren whom I long *to see,* my joy and crown, so stand firm in the Lord, my beloved.

2 ¶ I urge Euodia and I urge Syntyche to live in harmony in the Lord.

3 Indeed, true comrade, I ask you also to help these women who have shared my struggle in *the cause of* the gospel, together with Clement also,

and the rest of my fellow workers, whose names are in the book of life.

4 ¶ Rejoice in the Lord always; again I will say, rejoice!

5 Let your forbearing *spirit* be known to all men. The Lord is near.

6 Be anxious for nothing, but in everything by prayer and supplication with thanksgiving let your requests be made known to God.

7 And the peace of God, which surpasses all comprehension, shall guard your hearts and your minds in Christ Jesus.

8 ¶ Finally, brethren, whatever is true, whatever is honorable, whatever is right, whatever is pure, whatever is lovely, whatever is of good repute, if there is any excellence and if anything worthy of praise, let your mind dwell on these things.

9 The things you have learned and received and heard and seen in me, practice these things; and the God of peace shall be with you.

10 ¶ But I rejoiced in the Lord greatly, that now at last you have revived your concern for me; indeed, you were concerned *before*, but you lacked opportunity.

11 Not that I speak from want; for I have learned to be content in whatever circumstances I am.

12 I know how to get along with humble means, and I also know how to live in prosperity; in any and every circumstance I have learned the secret of being filled and going hungry, both of having abundance and suffering need.

13 I can do all things through Him who strengthens me.

14 Nevertheless, you have done well to share *with me* in my affliction.

15 And you yourselves also know, Philippians, that at the first preaching of the gospel, after I departed from Macedonia, no church shared with me in the matter of giving and receiving but you alone;

16 for even in Thessalonica you sent *a gift* more than once for my needs.

17 Not that I seek the gift itself, but I seek for the profit which increases to your account.

18 But I have received everything in full, and have an abundance; I am amply supplied, having received from Epaphroditus what you have sent, a fragrant aroma, an acceptable sacrifice, well-pleasing to God.

19 And my God shall supply all your needs according to His riches in glory in Christ Jesus.

20 Now to our God and Father *be* the glory forever and ever. Amen.

21 ¶ Greet every saint in Christ Jesus. The brethren who are with me greet you.

22 All the saints greet you, especially those of Caesar's household.

23 ¶ The grace of the Lord Jesus Christ be with your spirit.

COLOSSIANS

PAUL, an apostle of Jesus Christ by the will of God, and Timothy our brother,

2 to the saints and faithful brethren in Christ *who are* at Colossae: Grace to you and peace from God our Father.

3 ¶ We give thanks to God, the Father of our Lord Jesus Christ, praying always for you,

4 since we heard of your faith in Christ Jesus and the love which you have for all the saints;

5 because of the hope laid up for you in heaven, of which you previously heard in the word of truth, the gospel,

6 which has come to you, just as in all the world also it is constantly bearing fruit and increasing, even as *it has been doing* in you also since the day you heard *of it* and understood the grace of God in truth;

7 just as you learned *it* from Epaphras, our beloved fellow bond-servant, who is a faithful servant of Christ on ¹our behalf,

8 and he also informed us of your love in the Spirit.

9 ¶ For this reason also, since the day we heard *of it*, we have not ceased to pray for you and to ask that you may be filled with the knowledge of His will in all spiritual wisdom and understanding,

10 so that you may walk in a manner worthy of the Lord, to please *Him* in all respects, bearing fruit in every good work and increasing in the knowledge of God;

11 strengthened with all power, according to His glorious might, for the attaining of all steadfastness and patience; joyously

12 giving thanks to the Father, who has qualified us to share in the inheritance of the saints in light.

13 For He delivered us from the domain of darkness, and transferred us to the kingdom of His beloved Son,

14 in whom we have redemption, the forgiveness of sins.

15 And He is the image of the invisible God, the first-born of all creation.

16 For by Him all things were created, *both* in the heavens and on earth, visible and invisible, whether thrones or dominions or rulers or authorities—all things have been created by Him and for Him.

17 And He is before all things, and in Him all things hold together.

18 He is also head of the body, the church; and He is the beginning, the first-born from the dead; so that He Himself might come to have first place in everything.

19 For it was the *Father's* good pleasure for all the fulness to dwell in Him,

20 and through Him to reconcile all things to Himself, having made peace through the blood of His cross; through Him, *I say*, whether things on earth or things in heaven.

21 And although you were formerly alienated and hostile in mind, *engaged* in evil deeds,

22 yet He has now reconciled you in His fleshly body through death, in order to present you before Him holy and blameless and beyond reproach—

23 if indeed you continue in the faith firmly established and steadfast, and not moved away from the hope of the gospel that you have heard, which was proclaimed in all creation under heaven, and of which I, Paul, was made a minister.

24 ¶ Now I rejoice in my sufferings for your sake, and in my flesh I do my share on behalf of His body (which is the church) in filling up that which is lacking in Christ's afflictions.

25 Of *this church* I was made a minister according to the stewardship from God bestowed on me for your benefit, that I might fully carry out the *preaching of* the word of God,

26 *that is,* the mystery which has been hidden from the *past* ages and generations; but has now been manifested to His saints,

27 to whom God willed to make known what is the riches of the glory of this mystery among the Gentiles, which is Christ in you, the hope of glory.

28 And we proclaim Him, admonishing every man and teaching every man with all wisdom, that we may present every man complete in Christ.

29 And for this purpose also I labor,

¹ Some later mss. read *your*

striving according to His power, which mightily works within me.

CHAPTER 2

FOR I want you to know how great a struggle I have on your behalf, and for those who are at Laodicea, and for all those who have not personally seen my face,

2 that their hearts may be encouraged, having been knit together in love, and *attaining* to all the wealth that comes from the full assurance of understanding, *resulting* in a true knowledge of God's mystery, *that is,* Christ *Himself,*

3 in whom are hidden all the treasures of wisdom and knowledge.

4 I say this in order that no one may delude you with persuasive argument.

5 For even though I am absent in body, nevertheless I am with you in spirit, rejoicing to see your good discipline and the stability of your faith in Christ.

6 ¶ As you therefore have received Christ Jesus the Lord, so walk in Him,

7 having been firmly rooted *and now* being built up in Him and established ²in your faith, just as you were instructed, *and* overflowing with gratitude.

8 ¶ See to it that no one takes you captive through philosophy and empty deception, according to the tradition of men, according to the elementary principles of the world, rather than according to Christ.

9 For in Him all the fulness of Deity dwells in bodily form,

10 and in Him you have been made complete, and He is the head over all rule and authority;

11 and in Him you were also circumcised with a circumcision made without hands, in the removal of the body of the flesh by the circumcision of Christ;

12 having been buried with Him in baptism, in which you were also raised up with Him through faith in the working of God, who raised Him from the dead.

13 And when you were dead in your transgressions and the uncircumcision of your flesh, He made you alive together with Him, having forgiven us all our transgressions,

14 having canceled out the certificate of debt consisting of decrees against us *and* which was hostile to us; and He has taken it out of the way, having nailed it to the cross.

15 When He had disarmed the rulers and authorities, He made a public display of them, having triumphed over them through Him.

16 ¶ Therefore let no one act as your judge in regard to food or drink or in respect to a festival or a new moon or a Sabbath day—

17 things which are a *mere* shadow of what is to come; but the substance belongs to Christ.

18 Let no one keep defrauding you of your prize by delighting in self-abasement and the worship of the angels, taking his stand on *visions* he has seen, inflated without cause by his fleshly mind,

19 and not holding fast to the head, from whom the entire body, being supplied and held together by the joints and ligaments, grows with a growth which is from God.

20 ¶ If you have died with Christ to the elementary principles of the world, why, as if you were living in the world, do you submit yourself to decrees, such as,

21"Do not handle, do not taste, do not touch!"

22 (which all *refer to* things destined to perish with the using)—in accordance with the commandments and teachings of men?

23 These are matters which have, to be sure, the appearance of wisdom in self-made religion and self-abasement and severe treatment of the body, *but are* of no value against fleshly indulgence.

CHAPTER 3

IF then you have been raised up with Christ, keep seeking the things above, where Christ is, seated at the right hand of God.

2 Set your mind on the things above, not on the things that are on earth.

3 For you have died and your life is hidden with Christ in God.

4 When Christ, who is our life, is revealed, then you also will be revealed with Him in glory.

² Or, by

5 ¶ Therefore consider the members of your earthly body as dead to immorality, impurity, passion, evil desire, and greed, which amounts to idolatry.

6 For it is on account of these things that the wrath of God will come[3],

7 and in them you also once walked, when you were living in them.

8 But now you also, put them all aside: anger, wrath, malice, slander, *and* abusive speech from your mouth.

9 Do not lie to one another, since you laid aside the old self with its *evil* practices,

10 and have put on the new self who is being renewed to a true knowledge according to the image of the One who created him

11 —*a renewal* in which there is no *distinction between* Greek and Jew, circumcised and uncircumcised, barbarian, Scythian, slave and freeman, but Christ is all, and in all.

12 ¶ And so, as those who have been chosen of God, holy and beloved, put on a heart of compassion, kindness, humility, gentleness and patience;

13 bearing with one another, and forgiving each other, whoever has a complaint against anyone; just as the Lord forgave you, so also should you.

14 And beyond all these things *put on* love, which is the perfect bond of unity.

15 And let the peace of Christ rule in your hearts, to which indeed you were called in one body; and be thankful.

16 Let the word of [4]Christ richly dwell within you, with all wisdom teaching and admonishing one another with psalms *and* hymns *and* spiritual songs, singing with thankfulness in your hearts to God.

17 And whatever you do in word or deed, *do* all in the name of the Lord Jesus, giving thanks through Him to God the Father.

18 ¶ Wives, be subject to your husbands, as is fitting in the Lord.

19 Husbands, love your wives, and do not be embittered against them.

20 Children, be obedient to your parents in all things, for this is well-pleasing to the Lord.

21 Fathers, do not [5]exasperate your children, that they may not lose heart.

22 Slaves, in all things obey those who are your masters on earth, not with external service, as those who *merely* please men, but with sincerity of heart, fearing the Lord.

23 Whatever you do, do your work heartily, as for the Lord rather than for men;

24 knowing that from the Lord you will receive the reward of the inheritance. It is the Lord Christ whom you serve.

25 For he who does wrong will receive the consequences of the wrong which he has done, and that without partiality.

CHAPTER 4

MASTERS, grant to your slaves justice and fairness, knowing that you too have a Master in heaven.

2 ¶ Devote yourselves to prayer, keeping alert in it with *an attitude of* thanksgiving;

3 praying at the same time for us as well, that God may open up to us a door for the word, so that we may speak forth the mystery of Christ, for which I have also been imprisoned;

4 in order that I may make it clear in the way I ought to speak.

5 Conduct yourselves with wisdom toward outsiders, making the most of the opportunity.

6 Let your speech always be with grace, seasoned, *as it were,* with salt, so that you may know how you should respond to each person.

7 ¶ As to all my affairs, Tychicus, *our* beloved brother and faithful servant and fellow bond-servant in the Lord, will bring you information.

8 For I have sent him to you for this very purpose, that you may know *about* our circumstances and that he may encourage your hearts;

9 and with him Onesimus, *our* faithful and beloved brother, who is one of your *number.* They will inform you about the whole situation here.

10 ¶ Aristarchus, my fellow prisoner, sends you his greetings; and *also* Barnabas' cousin Mark (about whom you received instructions: if he comes to you, welcome him);

---

[3] Some early mss. add *upon the sons of disobedience*
[4] Some mss. read *the Lord;* others read *God*

[5] Some early mss. read *provoke to anger*

11 and *also* Jesus who is called Justus; these are the only fellow workers for the kingdom of God who are from the circumcision; and they have proved to be an encouragement to me.

12 Epaphras, who is one of your number, a bondslave of Jesus Christ, sends you his greetings, always laboring earnestly for you in his prayers, that you may stand perfect and fully assured in all the will of God.

13 For I bear him witness that he has a deep concern for you and for those who are in Laodicea and Hierapolis.

14 Luke, the beloved physician, sends you his greetings, and *also* Demas.

15 Greet the brethren who are in Laodicea and also [6]Nympha and the church that is in her house.

16 And when this letter is read among you, have it also read in the church of the Laodiceans; and you, for your part read my letter *that is coming* from Laodicea.

17 And say to Archippus, "Take heed to the ministry which you have received in the Lord, that you may fulfill it."

18 ¶ I, Paul, write this greeting with my own hand. Remember my imprisonment. Grace be with you.

[6] Or, *Nymphas* (masc.)

THE FIRST EPISTLE OF PAUL TO THE

THESSALONIANS

PAUL and Silvanus and Timothy to the church of the Thessalonians in God the Father and the Lord Jesus Christ: Grace to you and peace.

2 ¶ We give thanks to God always for all of you, making mention *of you* in our prayers;

3 constantly bearing in mind your work of faith and labor of love and steadfastness of hope in our Lord Jesus Christ in the presence of our God and Father,

4 knowing, brethren beloved by God, *His* choice of you;

5 for our gospel did not come to you in word only, but also in power and in the Holy Spirit and with full conviction; just as you know what kind of men we proved to be among you for your sake.

6 You also became imitators of us and of the Lord, having received the word in much tribulation with the joy of the Holy Spirit,

7 so that you became an example to all the believers in Macedonia and in Achaia.

8 For the word of the Lord has sounded forth from you, not only in Macedonia and Achaia, but also in every place your faith toward God has

gone forth, so that we have no need to say anything.

9 For they themselves report about us what kind of a reception we had with you, and how you turned to God from idols to serve a living and true God,

10 and to wait for His Son from heaven, whom He raised from the dead, *that is* Jesus, who delivers us from the wrath to come.

CHAPTER 2

FOR you yourselves know, brethren, that our coming to you was not in vain,

2 but after we had already suffered and been mistreated in Philippi, as you know, we had the boldness in our God to speak to you the gospel of God amid much opposition.

3 For our exhortation does not *come* from error or impurity or by way of deceit;

4 but just as we have been approved by God to be entrusted with the gospel, so we speak, not as pleasing men but God, who examines our hearts.

5 For we never came with flattering speech, as you know, nor with a pretext for greed—God is witness—

6 nor did we seek glory from men, either from you or from others, even though as apostles of Christ we might have asserted our authority.

7 But we proved to be [1]gentle among you, as a nursing *mother* tenderly cares for her own children.

8 Having thus a fond affection for you, we were well-pleased to impart to you not only the gospel of God but also our own lives, because you had become very dear to us.

9 For you recall, brethren, our labor and hardship, *how* working night and day so as not to be a burden to any of you, we proclaimed to you the gospel of God.

10 You are witnesses, and *so is* God, how devoutly and uprightly and blamelessly we behaved toward you believers;

11 just as you know how we *were* exhorting and encouraging and imploring each one of you as a father *would* his own children,

12 so that you may walk in a manner worthy of the God who calls you into His own kingdom and glory.

13 ¶ And for this reason we also constantly thank God that when you received from us the word of God's message, you accepted *it* not *as* the word of men, but *for* what it really is, the word of God, which also performs its work in you who believe.

14 For you, brethren, became imitators of the churches of God in Christ Jesus that are in Judea, for you also endured the same sufferings at the hands of your own countrymen, even as they *did* from the Jews,

15 who both killed the Lord Jesus and the prophets, and drove us out. They are not pleasing to God, but hostile to all men,

16 hindering us from speaking to the Gentiles that they might be saved; with the result that they always fill up the measure of their sins. But wrath has come upon them [2]to the utmost.

17 ¶ But we, brethren, having been bereft of you for a short while—in person, not in spirit—were all the more eager with great desire to see your face.

18 For we wanted to come to you—I, Paul, more than once—and *yet* Satan thwarted us.

19 For who is our hope or joy or crown of exultation? Is it not even you, in the presence of our Lord Jesus at His coming?

20 For you are our glory and joy.

CHAPTER 3

THEREFORE when we could endure *it* no longer, we thought it best to be left behind at Athens alone;

2 and we sent Timothy, our brother and God's fellow worker in the gospel of Christ, to strengthen and encourage you as to your faith,

3 so that no man may be disturbed by these afflictions; for you yourselves know that we have been destined for this.

4 For indeed when we were with you, we *kept* telling you in advance that we were going to suffer affliction; and so it came to pass, as you know.

5 For this reason, when I could endure *it* no longer, I also sent to find out about your faith, for fear that the tempter might have tempted you, and our labor should be in vain.

6 But now that Timothy has come to us from you, and has brought us good news of your faith and love, and that you always think kindly of us, longing to see us just as we also long to see you,

7 for this reason, brethren, in all our distress and affliction we were comforted about you through your faith;

8 for now we *really* live, if you stand firm in the Lord.

9 For what thanks can we render to God for you in return for all the joy with which we rejoice before our God on your account,

10 as we night and day keep praying most earnestly that we may see your face, and may complete what is lacking in your faith?

11 ¶ Now may our God and Father Himself and Jesus our Lord direct our way to you;

12 and may the Lord cause you to increase and abound in love for one another, and for all men, just as we also *do* for you;

13 so that He may establish your hearts unblamable in holiness before

---

[1] Some ancient mss. read *babes*   [2] Or, *forever; or, altogether*

our God and Father at the coming of our Lord Jesus with all His saints.

CHAPTER 4

FINALLY then, brethren, we request and exhort you in the Lord Jesus, that, as you received from us *instruction* as to how you ought to walk and please God (just as you actually do ³walk), that you may excel still more.

2 For you know what commandments we gave you ⁴by *the authority of the* Lord Jesus.

3 For this is the will of God, your sanctification; *that is,* that you abstain from sexual immorality;

4 that each of you know how to possess his own ⁵vessel in sanctification and honor,

5 not in lustful passion, like the Gentiles who do not know God;

6 *and* that no man transgress and defraud his brother in the matter because the Lord is *the* avenger in all these things, just as we also told you before and solemnly warned *you.*

7 For God has not called us for the purpose of impurity, but in sanctification.

8 Consequently, he who rejects *this* is not rejecting man but the God who gives His Holy Spirit to you.

9 ¶ Now as to the love of the brethren, you have no need for *anyone* to write to you, for you yourselves are taught by God to love one another;

10 for indeed you do practice it toward all the brethren who are in all Macedonia. But we urge you, brethren, to excel still more,

11 and to make it your ambition to lead a quiet life and attend to your own business and work with your hands, just as we commanded you;

12 so that you may behave properly toward outsiders and not be in any need.

13 ¶ But we do not want you to be uninformed, brethren, about those who are asleep, that you may not grieve, as do the rest who have no hope.

14 For if we believe that Jesus died and rose again, even so God will bring with Him those who have fallen asleep in Jesus.

15 For this we say to you by the word of the Lord, that we who are alive, and remain until the coming of the Lord, shall not precede those who have fallen asleep.

16 For the Lord Himself will descend from heaven with a shout, with the voice of *the* archangel, and with the trumpet of God; and the dead in Christ shall rise first.

17 Then we who are alive and remain shall be caught up together with them in the clouds to meet the Lord in the air, and thus we shall always be with the Lord.

18 Therefore comfort one another with these words.

CHAPTER 5

NOW as to the times and the epochs, brethren, you have no need of anything to be written to you.

2 For you yourselves know full well that the day of the Lord will come just like a thief in the night.

3 While they are saying, "Peace and safety!" then destruction will come upon them suddenly like birth pangs upon a woman with child; and they shall not escape.

4 But you, brethren, are not in darkness, that the day should overtake you like a thief;

5 for you are all sons of light and sons of day. We are not of night nor of darkness;

6 so then let us not sleep as others do, but let us be alert and ⁶sober.

7 For those who sleep do their sleeping at night, and those who get drunk get drunk at night.

8 But since we are of *the* day, let us be ⁶sober, having put on the breastplate of faith and love, and as a helmet, the hope of salvation.

9 For God has not destined us for wrath, but for obtaining salvation through our Lord Jesus Christ,

10 who died for us, that whether we are awake or asleep, we may live together with Him.

11 Therefore encourage one another, and build up one another, just as you also are doing.

12 ¶ But we request of you, brethren, that you appreciate those who

---

³ Or, *conduct yourselves*   ⁴ Lit., *through the Lord*
⁵ I.e., body; or possibly, *wife*

⁶ Or, *self-controlled*

diligently labor among you, and have charge over you in the Lord and give you instruction,

13 and that you esteem them very highly in love because of their work. Live in peace with one another.

14 And we urge you, brethren, admonish the unruly, encourage the fainthearted, help the weak, be patient with all men.

15 See that no one repays another with evil for evil, but always seek after that which is good for one another and for all men.

16 Rejoice always;

17 pray without ceasing;

18 in everything give thanks; for this is God's will for you in Christ Jesus.

19 Do not quench the Spirit;

20 do not despise prophetic [7]utterances.

21 But examine everything *carefully*; hold fast to that which is good;

22 abstain from every [8]form of evil.

23 ¶ Now may the God of peace Himself sanctify you entirely; and may your spirit and soul and body be preserved complete, without blame at the coming of our Lord Jesus Christ.

24 Faithful is He who calls you, and He also will bring it to pass.

25 ¶ Brethren, pray for us[9].

26 ¶ Greet all the brethren with a holy kiss.

27 I adjure you by the Lord to have this letter read to all the brethren.

28 ¶ The grace of our Lord Jesus Christ be with you.

[7] Or, *gifts*   [8] Or, *appearance*   [9] Some mss. add *also*

THE SECOND EPISTLE OF PAUL TO THE

THESSALONIANS

PAUL and Silvanus and Timothy to the church of the Thessalonians in God our Father and the Lord Jesus Christ:

2 Grace to you and peace from God the Father and the Lord Jesus Christ.

3 ¶ We ought always to give thanks to God for you, brethren, as is *only* fitting, because your faith is greatly enlarged, and the love of each one of you toward one another grows *ever* greater;

4 therefore, we ourselves speak proudly of you among the churches of God for your perseverance and faith in the midst of all your persecutions and afflictions which you endure.

5 *This is* a plain indication of God's righteous judgment so that you may be considered worthy of the kingdom of God, for which indeed you are suffering.

6 For after all it is *only* just for God to repay with affliction those who afflict you,

7 and *to give* relief to you who are afflicted and to us as well when the Lord Jesus shall be revealed from heaven with His mighty angels in flaming fire,

8 dealing out retribution to those who do not know God and to those who do not obey the gospel of our Lord Jesus.

9 And these will pay the penalty of eternal destruction, away from the presence of the Lord and from the glory of His power,

10 when He comes to be glorified in His saints on that day, and to be marveled at among all who have believed—for our testimony to you was believed.

11 To this end also we pray for you always that our God may count you worthy of your calling, and fulfill every desire for goodness and the work of faith with power;

12 in order that the name of our Lord Jesus may be glorified in you, and you in Him, according to the grace of our God and the Lord Jesus Christ.

CHAPTER 2

NOW we request you, brethren, with regard to the coming of our Lord Jesus Christ, and our gathering together to Him,

2 that you may not be quickly shaken from your composure or be

disturbed either by a spirit or a message or a letter as if from us, to the effect that the day of the Lord has come.

3 Let no one in any way deceive you, for *it will not come* unless the [1]apostasy comes first, and the man of lawlessness is revealed, the son of destruction,

4 who opposes and exalts himself above every so-called god or object of worship, so that he takes his seat in the temple of God, displaying himself as being God.

5 Do you not remember that while I was still with you, I was telling you these things?

6 And you know what restrains him now, so that in his time he may be revealed.

7 For the mystery of lawlessness is already at work; only he who now restrains *will do so* until he is taken out of the way.

8 And then that lawless one will be revealed whom the Lord will slay with the breath of His mouth and bring to an end by the appearance of His coming;

9 *that is,* the one whose coming is in accord with the activity of Satan, with all power and signs and false wonders,

10 and with all the deception of wickedness for those who perish, because they did not receive the love of the truth so as to be saved.

11 And for this reason God will send upon them a deluding influence so that they might believe what is false,

12 in order that they all may be judged who did not believe the truth, but took pleasure in wickedness.

13 ¶ But we should always give thanks to God for you, brethren beloved by the Lord, because God has chosen you [2]from the beginning for salvation through sanctification by the Spirit and faith in the truth.

14 And it was for this He called you through our gospel, that you may gain the glory of our Lord Jesus Christ.

15 So then, brethren, stand firm and hold to the traditions which you were taught, whether by word *of mouth* or by letter from us.

16 ¶ Now may our Lord Jesus Christ Himself and God our Father, who has loved us and given us eternal comfort and good hope by grace,

17 comfort and strengthen your hearts in every good work and word.

CHAPTER 3

FINALLY, brethren, pray for us that the word of the Lord may spread rapidly and be glorified, just as *it did* also with you;

2 and that we may be delivered from perverse and evil men; for not all have faith.

3 But the Lord is faithful, and He will strengthen and protect you from the evil *one.*

4 And we have confidence in the Lord concerning you, that you are doing and will *continue to* do what we command.

5 And may the Lord direct your hearts into the love of God and into the steadfastness of Christ.

6 ¶ Now we command you, brethren, in the name of our Lord Jesus Christ, that you keep aloof from every brother who leads an unruly life and not according to the tradition which you received from us.

7 For you yourselves know how you ought to follow our example, because we did not act in an undisciplined manner among you,

8 nor did we eat anyone's bread without paying for it, but with labor and hardship we *kept* working night and day so that we might not be a burden to any of you;

9 not because we do not have the right *to this,* but in order to offer ourselves as a model for you, that you might follow our example.

10 For even when we were with you, we used to give you this order: if anyone will not work, neither let him eat.

11 For we hear that some among you are leading an undisciplined life, doing no work at all, but acting like busybodies.

12 Now such persons we command and exhort in the Lord Jesus Christ to work in quiet fashion and eat their own bread.

13 But as for you, brethren, do not grow weary of doing good.

[1] Or, *falling away* from the faith
[2] Some ancient mss. read *first fruits*

14 And if anyone does not obey our instruction in this letter, take special note of that man and do not associate with him, so that he may be put to shame.

15 And *yet* do not regard him as an enemy, but admonish him as a brother.

16 ¶ Now may the Lord of peace Himself continually grant you peace in every circumstance. The Lord be with you all!

17 ¶ I, Paul, write this greeting with my own hand, and this is a distinguishing mark in every letter; this is the way I write.

18 The grace of our Lord Jesus Christ be with you all.

THE FIRST EPISTLE OF PAUL TO

TIMOTHY

PAUL, an apostle of Christ Jesus according to the commandment of God our Savior, and of Christ Jesus, *who is* our hope;

2 to Timothy, *my* true child in *the* faith: Grace, mercy *and* peace from God the Father and Christ Jesus our Lord.

3 ¶ As I urged you upon my departure for Macedonia, remain on at Ephesus, in order that you may instruct certain men not to teach strange doctrines,

4 nor to pay attention to myths and endless genealogies, which give rise to mere speculation rather than *furthering* the administration of God which is by faith.

5 But the goal of our instruction is love from a pure heart and a good conscience and a sincere faith.

6 For some men, straying from these things, have turned aside to fruitless discussion,

7 wanting to be teachers of the Law, even though they do not understand either what they are saying or the matters about which they make confident assertions.

8 But we know that the Law is good, if one uses it lawfully,

9 realizing the fact that law is not made for a righteous man, but for those who are lawless and rebellious, for the ungodly and sinners, for the unholy and profane, for those who kill their fathers or mothers, for murderers

10 and immoral men and homosexuals and kidnappers and liars and perjurers, and whatever else is contrary to sound teaching,

11 according to the glorious gospel of the blessed God, with which I have been entrusted.

12 ¶ I thank Christ Jesus our Lord, who has strengthened me, because He considered me faithful, putting me into service;

13 even though I was formerly a blasphemer and a persecutor and a violent aggressor. And yet I was shown mercy, because I acted ignorantly in unbelief;

14 and the grace of our Lord was more than abundant, with the faith and love which are *found* in Christ Jesus.

15 It is a trustworthy statement, deserving full acceptance, that Christ Jesus came into the world to save sinners, among whom I am foremost *of all.*

16 And yet for this reason I found mercy, in order that in me as the foremost, Jesus Christ might demonstrate His perfect patience, as an example for those who would believe in Him for eternal life.

17 Now to the King eternal, immortal, invisible, the only God, *be* honor and glory forever and ever. Amen.

18 ¶ This command I entrust to you, Timothy, my son, in accordance with the prophecies previously made concerning you, that by them you may fight the good fight,

19 keeping faith and a good conscience, which some have rejected and suffered shipwreck in regard to their faith.

20 Among these are Hymenaeus and Alexander, whom I have delivered over to Satan, so that they may be taught not to blaspheme.

CHAPTER 2

FIRST of all, then, I urge that entreaties *and* prayers, petitions *and* thanksgivings, be made on behalf of all men,

2 for kings and all who are in authority, in order that we may lead a tranquil and quiet life in all godliness and dignity.

3 This is good and acceptable in the sight of God our Savior,

4 who desires all men to be saved and to come to the knowledge of the truth.

5 For there is one God, *and* one mediator also between God and men, *the* man Christ Jesus,

6 who gave Himself as a ransom for all, the testimony *borne* at the proper time.

7 And for this I was appointed a preacher and an apostle (I am telling the truth, I am not lying) as a teacher of the Gentiles in faith and truth.

8 ¶ Therefore I want the men in every place to pray, lifting up holy hands, without wrath and dissension.

9 Likewise, *I want* women to adorn themselves with proper clothing, modestly and discreetly, not with braided hair and gold or pearls or costly garments;

10 but rather by means of good works, as befits women making a claim to godliness.

11 Let a woman quietly receive instruction with entire submissiveness.

12 But I do not allow a woman to teach or exercise authority over a man, but to remain quiet.

13 For it was Adam who was first created, *and* then Eve.

14 And *it was* not Adam *who* was deceived, but the woman being quite deceived, fell into transgression.

15 But *women* shall be preserved through the bearing of children if they continue in faith and love and sanctity with self-restraint.

CHAPTER 3

IT is a trustworthy statement: if any man aspires to the office of overseer, it is a fine work he desires *to do.*

2 An overseer, then, must be above reproach, the husband of one wife, temperate, prudent, respectable, hospitable, able to teach,

3 not addicted to wine or pugnacious, but gentle, uncontentious, free from the love of money.

4 *He must be* one who manages his own household well, keeping his children under control with all dignity

5 (but if a man does not know how to manage his own household, how will he take care of the church of God?);

6 *and* not a new convert, lest he become conceited and fall into the condemnation incurred by the devil.

7 And he must have a good reputation with those outside *the church,* so that he may not fall into reproach and the snare of the devil.

8 Deacons likewise *must be* men of dignity, not double-tongued, or addicted to much wine or fond of sordid gain,

9 *but* holding to the mystery of the faith with a clear conscience.

10 And let these also first be tested; then let them serve as deacons if they are beyond reproach.

11 Women *must* likewise *be* dignified, not malicious gossips, but temperate, faithful in all things.

12 Let deacons be husbands of *only* one wife, *and* good managers of *their* children and their own households.

13 For those who have served well as deacons obtain for themselves a high standing and great confidence in the faith that is in Christ Jesus.

14 ¶ I am writing these things to you, hoping to come to you before long;

15 but in case I am delayed, *I write* so that you may know how one ought to conduct himself in the household of God, which is the church of the living God, the pillar and support of the truth.

16 And by common confession great is the mystery of godliness:

> [1]He who was revealed in the flesh,
> Was vindicated in the Spirit,
> Beheld by angels,
> Proclaimed among the nations,

[1] Some later mss. read *God*

Believed on in the world,
Taken up in glory.

CHAPTER 4

BUT the Spirit explicitly says that in later times some will fall away from the faith, paying attention to deceitful spirits and doctrines of demons,

2 by means of the hypocrisy of liars seared in their own conscience as with a branding iron,

3 *men* who forbid marriage *and advocate* abstaining from foods, which God has created to be gratefully shared in by those who believe and know the truth.

4 For everything created by God is good, and nothing is to be rejected, if it is received with gratitude;

5 for it is sanctified by means of the word of God and prayer.

6 ¶ In pointing out these things to the brethren, you will be a good servant of Christ Jesus, *constantly* nourished on the words of the faith and of the sound doctrine which you have been following.

7 But have nothing to do with worldly fables fit only for old women. On the other hand, discipline yourself for the purpose of godliness;

8 for bodily discipline is only of little profit, but godliness is profitable for all things, since it holds promise for the present life and *also* for the *life* to come.

9 It is a trustworthy statement deserving full acceptance.

10 For it is for this we labor and strive, because we have fixed our hope on the living God, who is the Savior of all men, especially of believers.

11 Prescribe and teach these things.

12 Let no one look down on your youthfulness, but *rather* in speech, conduct, love, faith *and* purity, show yourself an example of those who believe.

13 Until I come, give attention to the *public* reading *of Scripture,* to exhortation and teaching.

14 Do not neglect the spiritual gift within you, which was bestowed upon you through prophetic utterance with the laying on of hands by the presbytery.

15 Take pains with these things; be absorbed in them, so that your progress may be evident to all.

16 Pay close attention to yourself and to your teaching; persevere in these things; for as you do this you will insure salvation both for yourself and for those who hear you.

CHAPTER 5

DO not sharply rebuke an older man, but *rather* appeal to *him* as a father, *to* the younger men as brothers,

2 the older women as mothers, *and* the younger women as sisters, in all purity.

3 Honor widows who are widows indeed;

4 but if any widow has children or grandchildren, let them first learn to practice piety in regard to their own family, and to make some return to their parents; for this is acceptable in the sight of God.

5 Now she who is a widow indeed, and who has been left alone has fixed her hope on God, and continues in entreaties and prayers night and day.

6 But she who gives herself to wanton pleasure is dead even while she lives.

7 Prescribe these things as well, so that they may be above reproach.

8 But if anyone does not provide for his own, and especially for those of his household, he has denied the faith, and is worse than an unbeliever.

9 Let a widow be put on the list only if she is not less than sixty years old, *having been* the wife of one man,

10 having a reputation for good works; *and* if she has brought up children, if she has shown hospitality to strangers, if she has washed the saints' feet, if she has assisted those in distress, *and* if she has devoted herself to every good work.

11 But refuse *to put* younger widows *on the list,* for when they feel sensual desires in disregard of Christ, they want to get married,

12 *thus* incurring condemnation, because they have set aside their previous pledge.

13 And at the same time they also learn *to be* idle, as they go around from house to house; and not merely idle, but also gossips and busybodies,

talking about things not proper *to mention.*

14 Therefore, I want younger *widows* to get married, bear children, keep house, *and* give the enemy no occasion for reproach;

15 for some have already turned aside to follow Satan.

16 If any woman who is a believer has *dependent* widows, let her assist them, and let not the church be burdened, so that it may assist those who are widows indeed.

17 ¶ Let the elders who rule well be considered worthy of double honor, especially those who work hard at preaching and teaching.

18 For the Scripture says, "YOU SHALL NOT MUZZLE THE OX WHILE HE IS THRESHING," and "The laborer is worthy of his wages."

19 Do not receive an accusation against an elder except on the basis of two or three witnesses.

20 Those who continue in sin, rebuke in the presence of all, so that the rest also may be fearful *of sinning.*

21 I solemnly charge you in the presence of God and of Christ Jesus and of *His* chosen angels, to maintain these *principles* without bias, doing nothing in a *spirit of* partiality.

22 Do not lay hands upon anyone *too* hastily and thus share *responsibility for* the sins of others; keep yourself free from sin.

23 No longer drink water *exclusively,* but use a little wine for the sake of your stomach and your frequent ailments.

24 The sins of some men are quite evident, going before them to judgment; for others, their *sins* follow after.

25 Likewise also, deeds that are good are quite evident, and those which are otherwise cannot be concealed.

CHAPTER 6

LET all who are under the yoke as slaves regard their own masters as worthy of all honor so that the name of God and *our* doctrine may not be spoken against.

2 And let those who have believers as their masters not be disrespectful to them because they are brethren, but let them serve them all the more, because those who partake of the benefit are believers and beloved. Teach and preach these *principles.*

3 ¶ If anyone advocates a different doctrine, and does not agree with sound words, those of our Lord Jesus Christ, and with the doctrine conforming to godliness,

4 he is conceited *and* understands nothing; but he has a morbid interest in controversial questions and disputes about words, out of which arise envy, strife, abusive language, evil suspicions,

5 and constant friction between men of depraved mind and deprived of the truth, who suppose that godliness is a means of gain.

6 But godliness *actually* is a means of great gain, when accompanied by contentment.

7 For we have brought nothing into the world, [2]so we cannot take anything out of it either.

8 And if we have food and covering, with these we shall be content.

9 But those who want to get rich fall into temptation and a snare and many foolish and harmful desires which plunge men into ruin and destruction.

10 For the love of money is a root of all sorts of evil, and some by longing for it have wandered away from the faith, and pierced themselves with many a pang.

11 ¶ But flee from these things, you man of God; and pursue righteousness, godliness, faith, love, perseverance *and* gentleness.

12 Fight the good fight of faith; take hold of the eternal life to which you were called, and you made the good confession in the presence of many witnesses.

13 I charge you in the presence of God, who gives life to all things, and of Christ Jesus, who testified the good confession before Pontius Pilate,

14 that you keep the commandment without stain or reproach until the appearing of our Lord Jesus Christ,

15 which He will bring about at the proper time—He who is the blessed and only Sovereign, the King of kings and Lord of lords;

16 who alone possesses immortality

[2] Later mss. read *it is clear that*

and dwells in unapproachable light; whom no man has seen or can see. To Him *be* honor and eternal dominion! Amen.

17 ¶ Instruct those who are rich in this present world not to be conceited or to fix their hope on the uncertainty of riches, but on God, who richly supplies us with all things to enjoy.

18 *Instruct them* to do good, to be rich in good works, to be generous and ready to share,

19 storing up for themselves the treasure of a good foundation for the future, so that they may take hold of that which is life indeed.

20 ¶ O Timothy, guard what has been entrusted to you, avoiding worldly *and* empty chatter *and* the opposing arguments of what is falsely called "knowledge"—

21 which some have professed and thus gone astray from the faith.

¶ **Grace** be with you.

THE SECOND EPISTLE OF PAUL TO

TIMOTHY

Paul, an apostle of Christ Jesus by the will of God, according to the promise of life in Christ Jesus,

2 to Timothy, my beloved son: Grace, mercy *and* peace from God the Father and Christ Jesus our Lord.

3 ¶ I thank God, whom I serve with a clear conscience the way my forefathers did, as I constantly remember you in my prayers night and day,

4 longing to see you, even as I recall your tears, so that I may be filled with joy.

5 For I am mindful of the sincere faith within you, which first dwelt in your grandmother Lois, and your mother Eunice, and I am sure that *it is* in you as well.

6 And for this reason I remind you to kindle afresh the gift of God which is in you through the laying on of my hands.

7 For God has not given us a spirit of timidity, but of power and love and discipline.

8 Therefore do not be ashamed of the testimony of our Lord, or of me His prisoner; but join with *me* in suffering for the gospel according to the power of God,

9 who has saved us, and called us with a holy calling, not according to our works, but according to His own purpose and grace which was granted us in Christ Jesus from all eternity,

10 but now has been revealed by the appearing of our Savior Christ Jesus, who abolished death, and brought life and immortality to light through the gospel,

11 for which I was appointed a preacher and an apostle and a teacher.

12 For this reason I also suffer these things, but I am not ashamed; for I know whom I have believed and I am convinced that He is able to guard what I have entrusted to Him until that day.

13 Retain the standard of sound words which you have heard from me, in the faith and love which are in Christ Jesus.

14 Guard, through the Holy Spirit who dwells in us, the treasure which has been entrusted to *you.*

15 ¶ You are aware of the fact that all who are in Asia turned away from me, among whom are Phygelus and Hermogenes.

16 The Lord grant mercy to the house of Onesiphorus for he often refreshed me, and was not ashamed of my chains;

17 but when he was in Rome, he eagerly searched for me, and found me—

18 the Lord grant to him to find mercy from the Lord on that day—and you know very well what services he rendered at Ephesus.

CHAPTER 2

You therefore, my son, be strong in the grace that is in Christ Jesus.

2 And the things which you have heard from me in the presence of many witnesses, these entrust to faithful men, who will be able to teach others also.

3 Suffer hardship with *me*, as a good soldier of Christ Jesus.

4 No soldier in active service entangles himself in the affairs of everyday life, so that he may please the one who enlisted him as a soldier.

5 And also if anyone competes as an athlete, he does not win the prize unless he competes according to the rules.

6 The hard-working farmer ought to be the first to receive his share of the crops.

7 Consider what I say, for the Lord will give you understanding in everything.

8 Remember Jesus Christ, risen from the dead, descendant of David, according to my gospel,

9 for which I suffer hardship even to imprisonment as a criminal; but the word of God is not imprisoned.

10 For this reason I endure all things for the sake of those who are chosen, that they also may obtain the salvation which is in Christ Jesus *and* with *it* eternal glory.

11 It is a trustworthy statement:
   For if we died with Him, we shall also live with Him;

12 If we endure, we shall also reign with Him;
   If we deny Him, He also will deny us;

13 If we are faithless, He remains faithful; for He cannot deny Himself.

14 ¶ Remind *them* of these things, and solemnly charge *them* in the presence of God not to wrangle about words, which is useless, *and leads* to the ruin of the hearers.

15 Be diligent to present yourself approved to God as a workman who does not need to be ashamed, handling accurately the word of truth.

16 But avoid worldly *and* empty chatter, for it will lead to further ungodliness,

17 and their talk will spread like ¹gangrene. Among them are Hymenaeus and Philetus,

18 *men* who have gone astray from the truth saying that the resurrection has already taken place, and thus they upset the faith of some.

19 Nevertheless, the firm foundation of God stands, having this seal, "The Lord knows those who are His," and, "Let everyone who names the name of the Lord abstain from wickedness."

20 Now in a large house there are not only gold and silver vessels, but also vessels of wood and of earthenware, and some to honor and some to dishonor.

21 Therefore, if a man cleanses himself from these *things*, he will be a vessel for honor, sanctified, useful to the Master, prepared for every good work.

22 Now flee from youthful lusts, and pursue righteousness, faith, love *and* peace, with those who call on the Lord from a pure heart.

23 But refuse foolish and ignorant speculations, knowing that they produce quarrels.

24 And the Lord's bond-servant must not be quarrelsome, but be kind to all, able to teach, patient when wronged,

25 with gentleness correcting those who are in opposition, if perhaps God may grant them repentance leading to the knowledge of the truth,

26 and they may come to their senses *and escape* from the snare of the devil, having been held captive by him to do his will.

CHAPTER 3

BUT realize this, that in the last days difficult times will come.

2 For men will be lovers of self, lovers of money, boastful, arrogant, revilers, disobedient to parents, ungrateful, unholy,

3 unloving, irreconcilable, malicious gossips, without self-control, brutal, haters of good,

4 treacherous, reckless, conceited, lovers of pleasure rather than lovers of God;

5 holding to a form of godliness, although they have denied its power; and avoid such men as these.

6 For among them are those who enter into households and captivate weak women weighed down with sins, led on by various impulses,

¹ Or, *cancer*

7 always learning and never able to come to the knowledge of the truth.

8 And just as Jannes and Jambres opposed Moses, so these *men* also oppose the truth, men of depraved mind, rejected as regards the faith.

9 But they will not make further progress; for their folly will be obvious to all, as also that of those *two* came to be.

10 But you followed my teaching, conduct, purpose, faith, patience, love, perseverance,

11 persecutions, *and* sufferings, such as happened to me at Antioch, at Iconium *and* at Lystra; what persecutions I endured, and out of them all the Lord delivered me!

12 And indeed, all who desire to live godly in Christ Jesus will be persecuted.

13 But evil men and impostors will proceed *from bad* to worse, deceiving and being deceived.

14 You, however, continue in the things you have learned and become convinced of, knowing from whom you have learned *them;*

15 and that from childhood you have known the sacred writings which are able to give you the wisdom that leads to salvation through faith which is in Christ Jesus.

16 [2]All Scripture is inspired by God and profitable for teaching, for reproof, for correction, for training in righteousness;

17 that the man of God may be adequate, equipped for every good work.

CHAPTER 4

I SOLEMNLY charge *you* in the presence of God and of Christ Jesus, who is to judge the living and the dead, and by His appearing and His kingdom:

2 preach the word; be ready in season *and* out of season; reprove, rebuke, exhort, with great patience and instruction.

3 For the time will come when they will not endure sound doctrine; but *wanting* to have their ears tickled, they will accumulate for themselves teachers in accordance to their own desires;

4 and will turn away their ears from the truth, and will turn aside to myths.

[2] Or possibly, *Every Scripture inspired by God is also profitable*

5 But you, be sober in all things, endure hardship, do the work of an evangelist, fulfill your ministry.

6 For I am already being poured out as a drink offering, and the time of my departure has come.

7 I have fought the good fight, I have finished the course, I have kept the faith;

8 in the future there is laid up for me the crown of righteousness, which the Lord, the righteous Judge, will award to me on that day; and not only to me, but also to all who have loved His appearing.

9 ¶ Make every effort to come to me soon;

10 for Demas, having loved this present world, has deserted me and gone to Thessalonica; Crescens *has gone* to Galatia, Titus to Dalmatia.

11 Only Luke is with me. Pick up Mark and bring him with you, for he is useful to me for service.

12 But Tychicus I have sent to Ephesus.

13 When you come bring the cloak which I left at Troas with Carpus, and the books, especially the parchments.

14 Alexander the coppersmith did me much harm; the Lord will repay him according to his deeds.

15 Be on guard against him yourself, for he vigorously opposed our teaching.

16 At my first defense no one supported me, but all deserted me; may it not be counted against them.

17 But the Lord stood with me, and strengthened me, in order that through me the proclamation might be fully accomplished, and that all the Gentiles might hear; and I was delivered out of the lion's mouth.

18 The Lord will deliver me from every evil deed, and will bring me safely to His heavenly kingdom; to Him *be* the glory forever and ever. Amen.

19 ¶ Greet Prisca and Aquila, and the household of Onesiphorus.

20 Erastus remained at Corinth, but Trophimus I left sick at Miletus.

21 Make every effort to come before winter. Eubulus greets you, also Pudens and Linus and Claudia and all the brethren.

22 ¶ The Lord be with your spirit. Grace be with you.

TITUS

PAUL, a bond-servant of God, and an apostle of Jesus Christ, for the faith of those chosen of God and the knowledge of the truth which is according to godliness,

2 in the hope of eternal life, which God, who cannot lie, promised long ages ago,

3 but at the proper time manifested, *even* His word, in the proclamation with which I was entrusted according to the commandment of God our Savior;

4 to Titus, my true child in a common faith: Grace and peace from God the Father and Christ Jesus our Savior.

5 ¶ For this reason I left you in Crete, that you might set in order what remains, and appoint elders in every city as I directed you,

6 *namely,* if any man be above reproach, the husband of one wife, having children who believe, not accused of dissipation or rebellion.

7 For the overseer must be above reproach as God's steward, not self-willed, not quick-tempered, not addicted to wine, not pugnacious, not fond of sordid gain,

8 but hospitable, loving what is good, sensible, just, devout, self-controlled,

9 holding fast the faithful word which is in accordance with the teaching, that he may be able both to exhort in sound doctrine and to refute those who contradict.

10 ¶ For there are many rebellious men, empty talkers and deceivers, especially those of the circumcision,

11 who must be silenced because they are upsetting whole families, teaching things they should not *teach,* for the sake of sordid gain.

12 One of themselves, a prophet of their own, said, "Cretans are always liars, evil beasts, lazy gluttons."

13 This testimony is true. For this cause reprove them severely that they may be sound in the faith,

14 not paying attention to Jewish myths and commandments of men who turn away from the truth.

15 To the pure, all things are pure; but to those who are defiled and unbelieving, nothing is pure, but both their mind and their conscience are defiled.

16 They profess to know God, but by *their* deeds they deny *Him,* being detestable and disobedient, and worthless for any good deed.

CHAPTER 2

BUT as for you, speak the things which are fitting for sound doctrine.

2 Older men are to be temperate, dignified, sensible, sound in faith, in love, in perseverance.

3 Older women likewise are to be reverent in their behavior, not malicious gossips, nor enslaved to much wine, teaching what is good,

4 that they may encourage the young women to love their husbands, to love their children,

5 *to be* sensible, pure, workers at home, kind, being subject to their own husbands, that the word of God may not be dishonored.

6 Likewise urge the young men to be sensible;

7 in all things show yourself to be an example of good deeds, *with* purity in doctrine, dignified,

8 sound *in* speech which is beyond reproach, in order that the opponent may be put to shame, having nothing bad to say about us.

9 *Urge* bondslaves to be subject to their own masters in everything, to be well-pleasing, not argumentative,

10 not pilfering, but showing all good faith that they may adorn the doctrine of God our Savior in every respect.

11 For the grace of God has appeared, bringing salvation to all men,

12 instructing us to deny ungodliness and worldly desires and to live sensibly, righteously and godly in the present age,

13 looking for the blessed hope and the appearing of the glory of our great God and Savior, Christ Jesus;

14 who gave Himself for us, that He might redeem us from every lawless deed and purify for Himself a people for His own possession, zealous for good deeds.

15 ¶ These things speak and exhort and reprove with all authority. Let no one disregard you.

CHAPTER 3

Remind them to be subject to rulers, to authorities, to be obedient, to be ready for every good deed,

2 to malign no one, to be uncontentious, gentle, showing every consideration for all men.

3 For we also once were foolish ourselves, disobedient, deceived, enslaved to various lusts and pleasures, spending our life in malice and envy, hateful, hating one another.

4 But when the kindness of God our Savior and *His* love for mankind appeared,

5 He saved us, not on the basis of deeds which we have done in righteousness, but according to His mercy, by the washing of regeneration and renewing by the Holy Spirit,

6 whom He poured out upon us richly through Jesus Christ our Savior,

7 that being justified by His grace we might be made heirs according to *the* hope of eternal life.

8 This is a trustworthy statement; and concerning these things I want you to speak confidently, so that those who have believed God may be careful to engage in good deeds. These things are good and profitable for men.

9 But shun foolish controversies and genealogies and strife and disputes about the Law; for they are unprofitable and worthless.

10 Reject a factious man after a first and second warning,

11 knowing that such a man is perverted and is sinning, being self-condemned.

12 ¶ When I send Artemas or Tychicus to you, make every effort to come to me at Nicopolis, for I have decided to spend the winter there.

13 Diligently help Zenas the lawyer and Apollos on their way so that nothing is lacking for them.

14 And let our *people* also learn to engage in good deeds to meet pressing needs, that they may not be unfruitful.

15 ¶ All who are with me greet you. Greet those who love us in *the* faith.

¶ Grace be with you all.

THE EPISTLE OF PAUL TO

PHILEMON

Paul, a prisoner of Christ Jesus, and Timothy our brother, to Philemon our beloved *brother* and fellow worker,

2 and to Apphia our sister, and to Archippus our fellow soldier, and to the church in your house:

3 Grace to you and peace from God our Father and the Lord Jesus Christ.

4 ¶ I thank my God always, making mention of you in my prayers,

5 because I hear of your love, and of the faith which you have toward the Lord Jesus, and toward all the saints;

6 *and I pray* that the fellowship of your faith may become effective [1]through the knowledge of every good thing which is in [2]you for Christ's sake.

7 For I have come to have much joy and comfort in your love, because the hearts of the saints have been refreshed through you, brother.

8 ¶ Therefore, though I have enough confidence in Christ to order you *to do* that which is proper,

9 yet for love's sake I rather appeal *to you*—since I am such a person as Paul, the aged, and now also a prisoner of Christ Jesus—

10 I appeal to you for my child, whom I have begotten in my imprisonment, [3]Onesimus,

11 who formerly was useless to you, but now is useful both to you and to me.

12 And I have sent him back to you in person, that is, *sending* my very heart,

13 whom I wished to keep with me, that in your behalf he might minister

---

[1] Or, *in*   [2] Some ancient mss. read *us*   [3] I.e., useful

to me in my imprisonment for the gospel;

14 but without your consent I did not want to do anything, that your goodness should not be as it were by compulsion, but of your own free will.

15 For perhaps he was for this reason parted *from you* for a while, that you should have him back forever,

16 no longer as a slave, but more than a slave, a beloved brother, especially to me, but how much more to you, both in the flesh and in the Lord.

17 If then you regard me a partner, accept him as *you would* me.

18 But if he has wronged you in any way, or owes you anything, charge that to my account;

19 I, Paul, am writing this with my own hand, I will repay it (lest I should mention to you that you owe to me even your own self as well).

20 Yes, brother, let me benefit from you in the Lord; refresh my heart in Christ.

21 ¶ Having confidence in your obedience, I write to you, since I know that you will do even more than what I say.

22 And at the same time also prepare me a lodging; for I hope that through your prayers I shall be given to you.

23 ¶ Epaphras, my fellow prisoner in Christ Jesus, greets you,

24 *as do* Mark, Aristarchus, Demas, Luke, my fellow workers.

25 ¶ The grace of the Lord Jesus Christ be with your spirit.[4]

4 Some ancient mss. add *Amen*

THE EPISTLE TO THE

HEBREWS

GOD, after He spoke long ago to the fathers in the prophets in many portions and in many ways,

2 in these last days has spoken to us in *His* Son, whom He appointed heir of all things, through whom also He made the world.

3 And He is the radiance of His glory and the exact representation of His nature, and upholds all things by the word of His power. When He had made purification of sins, He sat down at the right hand of the Majesty on high;

4 having become as much better than the angels, as He has inherited a more excellent name than they.

5 For to which of the angels did He ever say,

"THOU ART MY SON,
TODAY I HAVE BEGOTTEN THEE"?
And again,

"I WILL BE A FATHER TO HIM,
AND HE SHALL BE A SON TO ME"?

6 And when He again brings the first-born into the world, He says,

"AND LET ALL THE ANGELS OF GOD
WORSHIP HIM."

7 And of the angels He says,

"WHO MAKES HIS ANGELS WINDS,
AND HIS MINISTERS A FLAME OF
FIRE."

8 But of the Son *He says*,

"THY THRONE, O GOD, IS FOREVER
AND EVER,
AND THE RIGHTEOUS SCEPTER IS
THE SCEPTER OF [1]HIS KINGDOM.

9 "THOU HAST LOVED RIGHTEOUS-
NESS AND HATED LAWLESSNESS;
THEREFORE GOD, THY GOD, HATH
ANOINTED THEE
WITH THE OIL OF GLADNESS
ABOVE THY COMPANIONS."

10 And,

"THOU, LORD, IN THE BEGINNING
DIDST LAY THE FOUNDATION OF
THE EARTH,
AND THE HEAVENS ARE THE
WORKS OF THY HANDS;

11 THEY WILL PERISH, BUT THOU RE-
MAINEST;
AND THEY ALL WILL BECOME OLD
AS A GARMENT,

12 AND AS A MANTLE THOU WILT
ROLL THEM UP;
AS A GARMENT THEY WILL ALSO
BE CHANGED.

1 Some mss. read *Thy*

But Thou art the same,
And Thy years will not come
to an end."

13 But to which of the angels has He
ever said,

"Sit at My right hand,
Until I make Thine enemies
A footstool for Thy feet"?

14 Are they not all ministering spirits, sent out to render service for the
sake of those who will inherit salvation?

CHAPTER 2

For this reason we must pay much
closer attention to what we have
heard, lest we drift away *from it.*

2 For if the word spoken through
angels proved unalterable, and every
transgression and disobedience received a just recompense,

3 how shall we escape if we neglect
so great a salvation? After it was at
the first spoken through the Lord, it
was confirmed to us by those who
heard,

4 God also bearing witness with
them, both by signs and wonders and
by various miracles and by gifts of the
Holy Spirit according to His own will.

5 ¶ For He did not subject to angels
the world to come, concerning which
we are speaking.

6 But one has testified somewhere,
saying,

"What is man, that Thou re-
memberest him?
Or the son of man, that Thou
art concerned about him?

7 "Thou hast made him for a little while lower than the angels;
Thou hast crowned him with
glory and honor,
²And hast appointed him over
the works of Thy hands;

8 Thou hast put all things in
subjection under his feet."

For in subjecting all things to him, He
left nothing that is not subject to him.
But now we do not yet see all things
subjected to him.

9 But we do see Him who has been
made for a little while lower than the
angels, *namely,* Jesus, because of the
suffering of death crowned with glory

and honor, that by the grace of God
He might taste death for everyone.

10 For it was fitting for Him, for
whom are all things, and through
whom are all things, in bringing many
sons to glory, to perfect the author of
their salvation through sufferings.

11 For both He who sanctifies and
those who are sanctified are all from
one *Father;* for which reason He is not
ashamed to call them brethren,

12 saying,

"I will proclaim Thy name to
My brethren,
In the midst of the congrega-
tion I will sing Thy praise."

13 And again,

"I will put My trust in Him."

And again,

"Behold, I and the children
whom God has given Me."

14 Since then the children share in
flesh and blood, He Himself likewise
also partook of the same, that through
death He might render powerless him
who had the power of death, that is,
the devil;

15 and might deliver those who
through fear of death were subject to
slavery all their lives.

16 For assuredly He does not give
help to angels, but He gives help to the
descendant of Abraham.

17 Therefore, He had to be made like
His brethren in all things, that He
might become a merciful and faithful
high priest in things pertaining to God,
to make propitiation for the sins of the
people.

18 For since He Himself was tempted
in that which He has suffered, He is
able to come to the aid of those who
are tempted.

CHAPTER 3

Therefore, holy brethren, partakers of a heavenly calling, consider
Jesus, the Apostle and High Priest of
our confession.

2 He was faithful to Him who appointed Him, as Moses also was in all
His house.

3 For He has been counted worthy
of more glory than Moses, by just so
much as the builder of the house has
more honor than the house.

---

² Some ancient mss. do not contain *And . . . hands*

4 For every house is built by someone, but the builder of all things is God.

5 Now Moses was faithful in all His house as a servant, for a testimony of those things which were to be spoken later;

6 but Christ *was faithful* as a Son over His house whose house we are, if we hold fast our confidence and the boast of our hope firm until the end.

7 Therefore, just as the Holy Spirit says,

"TODAY IF YOU HEAR HIS VOICE,

8 DO NOT HARDEN YOUR HEARTS AS WHEN THEY PROVOKED ME,
AS IN THE DAY OF TRIAL IN THE WILDERNESS,

9 WHERE YOUR FATHERS TRIED *Me* BY TESTING *Me*,
AND SAW MY WORKS FOR FORTY YEARS.

10 "THEREFORE I WAS ANGRY WITH THIS GENERATION,
AND SAID, 'THEY ALWAYS GO ASTRAY IN THEIR HEART;
AND THEY DID NOT KNOW MY WAYS';

11 AS I SWORE IN MY WRATH,
'THEY SHALL NOT ENTER MY REST.' "

12 Take care, brethren, lest there should be in any one of you an evil, unbelieving heart, in falling away from the living God.

13 But encourage one another day after day, as long as it is *still* called "Today," lest any one of you be hardened by the deceitfulness of sin.

14 For we have become partakers of Christ, if we hold fast the beginning of our assurance firm until the end;

15 while it is said,

"TODAY IF YOU HEAR HIS VOICE,
DO NOT HARDEN YOUR HEARTS, AS WHEN THEY PROVOKED ME."

16 For who provoked *Him* when they had heard? Indeed, did not all those who came out of Egypt *led* by Moses?

17 And with whom was He angry for forty years? Was it not with those who sinned, whose bodies fell in the wilderness?

18 And to whom did He swear that they should not enter His rest, but to those who were disobedient?

19 And *so* we see that they were not able to enter because of unbelief.

CHAPTER 4

THEREFORE, let us fear lest, while a promise remains of entering His rest, any one of you should seem to have come short of it.

2 For indeed we have had good news preached to us, just as they also; but the word they heard did not profit them, because it was not united by faith in those who heard.

3 [3]For we who have believed enter that rest, just as He has said,

"AS I SWORE IN MY WRATH,
THEY SHALL NOT ENTER MY REST,"

although His works were finished from the foundation of the world.

4 For He has thus said somewhere concerning the seventh *day*, "AND GOD RESTED ON THE SEVENTH DAY FROM ALL HIS WORKS";

5 and again in this *passage*, "THEY SHALL NOT ENTER MY REST."

6 Since therefore it remains for some to enter it, and those who formerly had good news preached to them failed to enter because of disobedience,

7 He again fixes a certain day, "Today," saying through David after so long a time just as has been said before,

"TODAY IF YOU HEAR HIS VOICE,
DO NOT HARDEN YOUR HEARTS."

8 For if Joshua had given them rest, He would not have spoken of another day after that.

9 There remains therefore a Sabbath rest for the people of God.

10 For the one who has entered His rest has himself also rested from his works, as God did from His.

11 Let us therefore be diligent to enter that rest, lest anyone fall through *following* the same example of disobedience.

12 For the word of God is living and active and sharper than any two-edged sword, and piercing as far as the division of soul and spirit, of both joints and marrow, and able to judge the thoughts and intentions of the heart.

13 And there is no creature hidden from His sight, but all things are open and laid bare to the eyes of Him with whom we have to do.

[3] Some ancient mss. read *Therefore*

14 ¶ Since then we have a great high priest who has passed through the heavens, Jesus the Son of God, let us hold fast our confession.

15 For we do not have a high priest who cannot sympathize with our weaknesses, but one who has been tempted in all things as *we are, yet* without sin.

16 Let us therefore draw near with confidence to the throne of grace, that we may receive mercy and may find grace to help in time of need.

CHAPTER 5

FOR every high priest taken from among men is appointed on behalf of men in things pertaining to God, in order to offer both gifts and sacrifices for sins;

2 he can deal gently with the ignorant and misguided, since he himself also is beset with weakness;

3 and because of it he is obligated to offer *sacrifices* for sins, as for the people, so also for himself.

4 And no one takes the honor to himself, but *receives it* when he is called by God, even as Aaron was.

5 So also Christ did not glorify Himself so as to become a high priest, but He who said to Him,

"THOU ART MY SON,
TODAY I HAVE BEGOTTEN THEE";

6 just as He says also in another *passage,*

"THOU ART A PRIEST FOREVER
ACCORDING TO THE ORDER OF
MELCHIZEDEK."

7 In the days of His flesh, He offered up both prayers and supplications with loud crying and tears to the One able to save Him from death, and He was heard because of His piety.

8 Although He was a Son, He learned obedience from the things which He suffered.

9 And having been made perfect, He became to all those who obey Him the source of eternal salvation,

10 being designated by God as a high priest according to the order of Melchizedek.

11 ¶ Concerning ⁴him we have much to say, and *it is* hard to explain, since you have become dull of hearing.

12 For though by this time you

⁴ Or, *Him;* or, *this*

ought to be teachers, you have need again for someone to teach you the elementary principles of the oracles of God, and you have come to need milk and not solid food.

13 For everyone who partakes *only* of milk is not accustomed to the word of righteousness, for he is a babe.

14 But solid food is for the mature, who because of practice have their senses trained to discern good and evil.

CHAPTER 6

THEREFORE leaving the elementary teaching about the Christ, let us press on to maturity, not laying again a foundation of repentance from dead works and of faith toward God,

2 of instruction about washings, and laying on of hands, and the resurrection of the dead, and eternal judgment.

3 And this we shall do, if God permits.

4 For in the case of those who have once been enlightened and have tasted of the heavenly gift and have been made partakers of the Holy Spirit,

5 and have tasted the good word of God and the powers of the age to come,

6 and *then* have fallen away, it is impossible to renew them again to repentance, since they again crucify to themselves the Son of God, and put Him to open shame.

7 For ground that drinks the rain which often falls upon it and brings forth vegetation useful to those for whose sake it is also tilled, receives a blessing from God;

8 but if it yields thorns and thistles, it is worthless and close to being cursed, and it ends up being burned.

9 ¶ But, beloved, we are convinced of better things concerning you, and things that accompany salvation, though we are speaking in this way.

10 For God is not unjust so as to forget your work and the love which you have shown toward His name, in having ministered and in still ministering to the saints.

11 And we desire that each one of you show the same diligence so as to realize the full assurance of hope until the end,

12 that you may not be sluggish, but imitators of those who through faith and patience inherit the promises.

13 ¶ For when God made the promise to Abraham, since He could swear by no one greater, He swore by Himself,

14 saying, "I WILL SURELY BLESS YOU, AND I WILL SURELY MULTIPLY YOU."

15 And thus, having patiently waited, he obtained the promise.

16 For men swear by one greater *than themselves*, and with them an oath *given* as confirmation is an end of every dispute.

17 In the same way God, desiring even more to show to the heirs of the promise the unchangeableness of His purpose, interposed with an oath,

18 in order that by two unchangeable things, in which it is impossible for God to lie, we may have strong encouragement, we who have fled for refuge in laying hold of the hope set before us.

19 This hope we have as an anchor of the soul, a *hope* both sure and steadfast and one which enters within the veil,

20 where Jesus has entered as a forerunner for us, having become a high priest forever according to the order of Melchizedek.

CHAPTER 7

FOR this Melchizedek, king of Salem, priest of the Most High God, who met Abraham as he was returning from the slaughter of the kings and blessed him,

2 to whom also Abraham apportioned a tenth part of all *the spoils*, was first of all, by the translation *of his name*, king of righteousness, and then also king of Salem, which is king of peace.

3 Without father, without mother, without genealogy, having neither beginning of days nor end of life, but made like the Son of God, he abides a priest perpetually.

4 ¶ Now observe how great this man was to whom Abraham, the patriarch, gave a tenth of the choicest spoils.

5 And those indeed of the sons of Levi who receive the priest's office have commandment in the Law to collect a tenth from the people, that is,

from their brethren, although these are descended from Abraham.

6 But the one whose genealogy is not traced from them collected a tenth from Abraham, and blessed the one who had the promises.

7 But without any dispute the lesser is blessed by the greater.

8 And in this case mortal men receive tithes, but in that case one *receives them*, of whom it is witnessed that he lives on.

9 And, so to speak, through Abraham even Levi, who received tithes, paid tithes,

10 for he was still in the loins of his father when Melchizedek met him.

11 ¶ Now if perfection was through the Levitical priesthood (for on the basis of it the people received the Law), what further need *was there* for another priest to arise according to the order of Melchizedek, and not be designated according to the order of Aaron?

12 For when the priesthood is changed, of necessity there takes place a change of law also.

13 For the one concerning whom these things are spoken belongs to another tribe, from which no one has officiated at the altar.

14 For it is evident that our Lord was descended from Judah, a tribe with reference to which Moses spoke nothing concerning priests.

15 And this is clearer still, if another priest arises according to the likeness of Melchizedek,

16 who has become *such* not on the basis of a law of physical requirement, but according to the power of an indestructible life.

17 For it is witnessed *of Him*,

> "THOU ART A PRIEST FOREVER
> ACCORDING TO THE ORDER OF
> MELCHIZEDEK."

18 For, on the one hand, there is a setting aside of a former commandment because of its weakness and uselessness

19 (for the Law made nothing perfect), and on the other hand there is a bringing in of a better hope, through which we draw near to God.

20 And inasmuch as *it was* not without an oath

21 (for they indeed became priests

without an oath, but He with an oath through the One who said to Him,

"The Lord has sworn
  And will not change His mind,
  'Thou art a priest forever'");

22 so much the more also Jesus has become the guarantee of a better covenant.

23 And the *former* priests, on the one hand, existed in greater numbers, because they were prevented by death from continuing,

24 but He, on the other hand, because He abides forever, holds His priesthood permanently.

25 Hence, also, He is able to save forever those who draw near to God through Him, since He always lives to make intercession for them.

26 ¶ For it was fitting that we should have such a high priest, holy, innocent, undefiled, separated from sinners and exalted above the heavens;

27 who does not need daily, like those high priests, to offer up sacrifices, first for His own sins, and then for the *sins* of the people, because this He did once for all when He offered up Himself.

28 For the Law appoints men as high priests who are weak, but the word of the oath, which came after the Law, *appoints* a Son, made perfect forever.

CHAPTER 8

Now the main point in what has been said *is this*: we have such a high priest, who has taken His seat at the right hand of the throne of the Majesty in the heavens,

2 a minister in the sanctuary, and in the true tabernacle, which the Lord pitched, not man.

3 For every high priest is appointed to offer both gifts and sacrifices; hence it is necessary that this *high priest* also have something to offer.

4 Now if He were on earth, He would not be a priest at all, since there are those who offer the gifts according to the Law;

5 who serve a copy and shadow of the heavenly things, just as Moses was warned *by God* when he was about to erect the tabernacle; for, "See," He says, "that you make all things according to the pattern which was shown you on the mountain."

6 But now He has obtained a more excellent ministry, by as much as He is also the mediator of a better covenant, which has been enacted on better promises.

7 For if that first *covenant* had been faultless, there would have been no occasion sought for a second.

8 For finding fault with them, He says,

"Behold, days are coming, says the Lord,
  When I will effect a new covenant
  With the house of Israel and with the house of Judah;
9   Not like the covenant which I made with their fathers
  On the day when I took them by the hand
  To lead them out of the land of Egypt;
  For they did not continue in My covenant,
  And I did not care for them, says the Lord.
10 "For this is the covenant that I will make with the house of Israel
  After those days, says the Lord:
  I will put My laws into their minds,
  And I will write them upon their hearts.
  And I will be their God,
  And they shall be My people.
11 "And they shall not teach everyone his fellow citizen,
  And everyone his brother, saying, 'Know the Lord,'
  For all shall know Me,
  From the least to the greatest of them.
12 "For I will be merciful to their iniquities,
  And I will remember their sins no more."

13 When He said, "A new *covenant*," He has made the first obsolete. But whatever is becoming obsolete and growing old is ready to disappear.

CHAPTER 9

Now even the first *covenant* had regulations of divine worship and the earthly sanctuary.

2 For there was a tabernacle prepared, the outer one, in which *were* the lampstand and the table and the sacred bread; this is called the holy place.

3 And behind the second veil, there was a tabernacle which is called the Holy of Holies,

4 having a golden altar of incense and the ark of the covenant covered on all sides with gold, in which *was* a golden jar holding the manna, and Aaron's rod which budded, and the tables of the covenant.

5 And above it *were* the cherubim of glory overshadowing the mercy seat; but of these things we cannot now speak in detail.

6 Now when these things have been thus prepared, the priests are continually entering the outer tabernacle, performing the divine worship,

7 but into the second only the high priest *enters*, once a year, not without *taking* blood, which he offers for himself and for the sins of the people committed in ignorance.

8 The Holy Spirit *is* signifying this, that the way into the holy place has not yet been disclosed, while the outer tabernacle is still standing,

9 which *is* a symbol for the present time. Accordingly both gifts and sacrifices are offered which cannot make the worshiper perfect in conscience,

10 since they *relate* only to food and drink and various washings, regulations for the body imposed until a time of reformation.

11 ¶ But when Christ appeared *as* a high priest of the good things [5]to come, *He entered* through the greater and more perfect tabernacle, not made with hands, that is to say, not of this creation;

12 and not through the blood of goats and calves, but through His own blood, He entered the holy place once for all, having obtained eternal redemption.

13 For if the blood of goats and bulls and the ashes of a heifer sprinkling those who have been defiled, sanctify for the cleansing of the flesh,

14 how much more will the blood of Christ, who through the eternal Spirit offered Himself without blemish to God, cleanse your conscience from dead works to serve the living God?

15 And for this reason He is the mediator of a new covenant, in order that since a death has taken place for the redemption of the transgressions that were *committed* under the first covenant, those who have been called may receive the promise of the eternal inheritance.

16 For where a covenant is, there must of necessity be the death of the one who made it.

17 For a covenant is valid *only* when men are dead, [6]for it is never in force while the one who made it lives.

18 Therefore even the first *covenant* was not inaugurated without blood.

19 For when every commandment had been spoken by Moses to all the people according to the Law, he took the blood of the calves and the goats, with water and scarlet wool and hyssop, and sprinkled both the book itself and all the people,

20 saying, "THIS IS THE BLOOD OF THE COVENANT WHICH GOD COMMANDED YOU."

21 And in the same way he sprinkled both the tabernacle and all the vessels of the ministry with the blood.

22 And according to the Law, *one may* almost *say*, all things are cleansed with blood, and without shedding of blood there is no forgiveness.

23 ¶ Therefore it was necessary for the copies of the things in the heavens to be cleansed with these, but the heavenly things themselves with better sacrifices than these.

24 For Christ did not enter a holy place made with hands, a *mere* copy of the true one, but into heaven itself, now to appear in the presence of God for us;

25 nor was it that He should offer Himself often, as the high priest enters the holy place year by year with blood not his own.

26 Otherwise, He would have needed to suffer often since the foundation of the world; but now once at the consummation of the ages He has been manifested to put away sin by the sacrifice of Himself.

27 And inasmuch as it is appointed

---

[5] Some ancient mss. read *that have come*

[6] Some ancient mss. read *for is it then . . . lives?*

for men to die once and after this *comes* judgment,

28 so Christ also, having been offered once to bear the sins of many, shall appear a second time for salvation without *reference to* sin, to those who eagerly await Him.

CHAPTER 10

FOR the Law, since it has *only* a shadow of the good things to come *and* not the very form of things, [7]can never by the same sacrifices year by year, which they offer continually, make perfect those who draw near.

2 Otherwise, would they not have ceased to be offered, because the worshipers, having once been cleansed, would no longer have had consciousness of sins?

3 But in those *sacrifices* there is a reminder of sins year by year.

4 For it is impossible for the blood of bulls and goats to take away sins.

5 Therefore, when He comes into the world, He says,

"SACRIFICE AND OFFERING THOU
  HAST NOT DESIRED,
BUT A BODY THOU HAST PREPARED
  FOR ME;
6 IN WHOLE BURNT OFFERINGS AND
  sacrifices FOR SIN THOU HAST
  TAKEN NO PLEASURE.
7 "THEN I SAID, 'BEHOLD, I HAVE
  COME
  (IN THE ROLL OF THE BOOK IT IS
  WRITTEN OF ME)
  TO DO THY WILL, O GOD.'"

8 After saying above, "SACRIFICES AND OFFERINGS AND WHOLE BURNT OFFERINGS AND *sacrifices* FOR SIN THOU HAST NOT DESIRED, NOR HAST THOU TAKEN PLEASURE *in them*" (which are offered according to the Law),

9 then He said, "BEHOLD, I HAVE COME TO DO THY WILL." He takes away the first in order to establish the second.

10 By this will we have been sanctified through the offering of the body of Jesus Christ once for all.

11 And every priest stands daily ministering and offering time after time the same sacrifices, which can never take away sins;

12 but He, having offered one sacrifice for sins for all time, SAT DOWN AT THE RIGHT HAND OF GOD,

13 waiting from that time onward UNTIL HIS ENEMIES BE MADE A FOOTSTOOL FOR HIS FEET.

14 For by one offering He has perfected for all time those who are sanctified.

15 And the Holy Spirit also bears witness to us; for after saying,

16 "THIS IS THE COVENANT THAT I
  WILL MAKE WITH THEM
  AFTER THOSE DAYS, SAYS THE
  LORD:
  I WILL PUT MY LAWS UPON THEIR
  HEART,
  AND UPON THEIR MIND I WILL
  WRITE THEM,"

He then says,

17 "AND THEIR SINS AND THEIR LAWLESS DEEDS
  I WILL REMEMBER NO MORE."

18 Now where there is forgiveness of these things, there is no longer *any* offering for sin.

19 ¶ Since therefore, brethren, we have confidence to enter the holy place by the blood of Jesus,

20 by a new and living way which He inaugurated for us through the veil, that is, His flesh,

21 and since *we have* a great priest over the house of God,

22 let us draw near with a sincere heart in full assurance of faith, having our hearts sprinkled *clean* from an evil conscience and our bodies washed with pure water.

23 Let us hold fast the confession of our hope without wavering, for He who promised is faithful;

24 and let us consider how to stimulate one another to love and good deeds,

25 not forsaking our own assembling together, as is the habit of some, but encouraging *one another*; and all the more, as you see the day drawing near.

26 ¶ For if we go on sinning willfully after receiving the knowledge of the truth, there no longer remains a sacrifice for sins,

27 but a certain terrifying expectation of judgment, and THE FURY OF A FIRE WHICH WILL CONSUME THE ADVERSARIES.

28 Anyone who has set aside the Law of Moses dies without mercy on

[7] Some ancient mss. read *they can*

the testimony of two or three witnesses.

29 How much severer punishment do you think he will deserve who has trampled under foot the Son of God, and has regarded as unclean the blood of the covenant by which he was sanctified, and has insulted the Spirit of grace?

30 For we know Him who said, "VENGEANCE IS MINE, I WILL REPAY." And again, "THE LORD WILL JUDGE HIS PEOPLE."

31 It is a terrifying thing to fall into the hands of the living God.

32 ¶ But remember the former days, when, after being enlightened, you endured a great conflict of sufferings,

33 partly, by being made a public spectacle through reproaches and tribulations, and partly by becoming sharers with those who were so treated.

34 For you showed sympathy to the prisoners, and accepted joyfully the seizure of your property, knowing that you have for yourselves a better possession and an abiding one.

35 Therefore, do not throw away your confidence, which has a great reward.

36 For you have need of endurance, so that when you have done the will of God, you may receive what was promised.

37 FOR YET IN A VERY LITTLE WHILE,
    HE WHO IS COMING WILL COME,
    AND WILL NOT DELAY.

38 BUT MY RIGHTEOUS ONE SHALL
    LIVE BY FAITH;
    AND IF HE SHRINKS BACK, MY
    SOUL HAS NO PLEASURE IN HIM.

39 But we are not of those who shrink back to destruction, but of those who have faith to the preserving of the soul.

CHAPTER 11

NOW faith is the assurance of *things* hoped for, the conviction of things not seen.

2 For by it the men of old gained approval.

3 By faith we understand that the worlds were prepared by the word of God, so that what is seen was not made out of things which are visible.

4 By faith Abel offered to God a better sacrifice than Cain, through which he obtained the testimony that he was righteous, God testifying about his gifts, and through faith, though he is dead, he still speaks.

5 By faith Enoch was taken up so that he should not see death; AND HE WAS NOT FOUND BECAUSE GOD TOOK HIM UP; for he obtained the witness that before his being taken up he was pleasing to God.

6 And without faith it is impossible to please *Him*, for he who comes to God must believe that He is, and *that* He is a rewarder of those who seek Him.

7 By faith Noah, being warned *by God* about things not yet seen, in reverence prepared an ark for the salvation of his household, by which he condemned the world, and became an heir of the righteousness which is according to faith.

8 By faith Abraham, when he was called, obeyed by going out to a place which he was to receive for an inheritance; and he went out, not knowing where he was going.

9 By faith he lived as an alien in the land of promise, as in a foreign *land*, dwelling in tents with Isaac and Jacob, fellow heirs of the same promise;

10 for he was looking for the city which has foundations, whose architect and builder is God.

11 By faith even Sarah herself received ability to conceive, even beyond the proper time of life, since she considered Him faithful who had promised;

12 therefore, also, there was born of one man, and him as good as dead at that, *as many descendants* AS THE STARS OF HEAVEN IN NUMBER, AND INNUMERABLE AS THE SAND WHICH IS BY THE SEASHORE.

13 ¶ All these died in faith, without receiving the promises, but having seen them and having welcomed them from a distance, and having confessed that they were strangers and exiles on the earth.

14 For those who say such things make it clear that they are seeking a country of their own.

15 And indeed if they had been thinking of that *country* from which they went out, they would have had opportunity to return.

16 But as it is, they desire a better *country*, that is a heavenly one. Therefore God is not ashamed to be called their God; for He has prepared a city for them.

17 ¶ By faith Abraham, when he was tested, offered up Isaac; and he who had received the promises was offering up his only begotten *son*;

18 *it was he* to whom it was said, "IN ISAAC YOUR DESCENDANTS SHALL BE CALLED."

19 He considered that God is able to raise *men* even from the dead; from which he also received him back as a type.

20 By faith Isaac blessed Jacob and Esau, even regarding things to come.

21 By faith Jacob, as he was dying, blessed each of the sons of Joseph, and worshiped, *leaning* on the top of his staff.

22 By faith Joseph, when he was dying, made mention of the exodus of the sons of Israel, and gave orders concerning his bones.

23 By faith Moses, when he was born, was hidden for three months by his parents, because they saw he was a beautiful child; and they were not afraid of the king's edict.

24 By faith Moses, when he had grown up, refused to be called the son of Pharaoh's daughter;

25 choosing rather to endure ill-treatment with the people of God, than to enjoy the passing pleasures of sin;

26 considering the reproach of Christ greater riches than the treasures of Egypt; for he was looking to the reward.

27 By faith he left Egypt, not fearing the wrath of the king; for he endured, as seeing Him who is unseen.

28 By faith he kept the Passover and the sprinkling of the blood, so that he who destroyed the first-born might not touch them.

29 By faith they passed through the Red Sea as though *they were passing* through dry land; and the Egyptians, when they attempted it, were drowned.

30 By faith the walls of Jericho fell down, after they had been encircled for seven days.

31 By faith Rahab the harlot did not perish along with those who were disobedient, after she had welcomed the spies in peace.

32 ¶ And what more shall I say? For time will fail me if I tell of Gideon, Barak, Samson, Jephthah, of David and Samuel and the prophets,

33 who by faith conquered kingdoms, performed *acts of* righteousness, obtained promises, shut the mouths of lions,

34 quenched the power of fire, escaped the edge of the sword, from weakness were made strong, became mighty in war, put foreign armies to flight.

35 Women received *back* their dead by resurrection; and others were tortured, not accepting their release, in order that they might obtain a better resurrection;

36 and others experienced mockings and scourgings, yes, also chains and imprisonment.

37 They were stoned, they were sawn in two, [8]they were tempted, they were put to death with the sword; they went about in sheepskins, in goatskins, being destitute, afflicted, ill-treated

38 (*men* of whom the world was not worthy), wandering in deserts and mountains and caves and holes in the ground.

39 And all these, having gained approval through their faith, did not receive what was promised,

40 because God had provided something better for us, so that apart from us they should not be made perfect.

CHAPTER 12

THEREFORE, since we have so great a cloud of witnesses surrounding us, let us also lay aside every encumbrance, and the sin which so easily entangles us, and let us run with endurance the race that is set before us,

2 fixing our eyes on Jesus, the author and perfecter of faith, who for the joy set before Him endured the cross, despising the shame, and has sat down at the right hand of the throne of God.

3 For consider Him who has endured such hostility by sinners against Himself, so that you may not grow weary and lose heart.

4 You have not yet resisted to the

8 Some mss. do not contain *they were tempted*

point of shedding blood in your striving against sin;

5 and you have forgotten the exhortation which is addressed to you as sons,

"MY SON, DO NOT REGARD LIGHTLY
THE DISCIPLINE OF THE LORD,
NOR FAINT WHEN YOU ARE RE-
PROVED BY HIM;

6 FOR THOSE WHOM THE LORD
LOVES HE DISCIPLINES,
AND HE SCOURGES EVERY SON
WHOM HE RECEIVES."

7 It is for discipline that you endure; God deals with you as with sons; for what son is there whom *his* father does not discipline?

8 But if you are without discipline, of which all have become partakers, then you are illegitimate children and not sons.

9 Furthermore, we had earthly fathers to discipline us, and we respected them; shall we not much rather be subject to the Father of spirits, and live?

10 For they disciplined us for a short time as seemed best to them, but He *disciplines us* for *our* good, that we may share His holiness.

11 All discipline for the moment seems not to be joyful, but sorrowful; yet to those who have been trained by it, afterwards it yields the peaceful fruit of righteousness.

12 Therefore, strengthen the hands that are weak and the knees that are feeble,

13 and make straight paths for your feet, so that *the limb* which is lame may not be put out of joint, but rather be healed.

14 ¶ Pursue peace with all men, and the sanctification without which no one will see the Lord.

15 See to it that no one comes short of the grace of God; that no root of bitterness springing up causes trouble, and by it many be defiled;

16 that *there be* no immoral or godless person like Esau, who sold his own birthright for a *single* meal.

17 For you know that even afterwards, when he desired to inherit the blessing, he was rejected, for he found no place for repentance, though he sought for it with tears.

18 ¶ For you have not come to *a* mountain that may be touched and to a blazing fire, and to darkness and gloom and whirlwind,

19 and to the blast of a trumpet and the sound of words which *sound was such that* those who heard begged that no further word should be spoken to them.

20 For they could not bear the command, "IF EVEN A BEAST TOUCHES THE MOUNTAIN, IT WILL BE STONED."

21 And so terrible was the sight, *that* Moses said, "I AM FULL OF FEAR and trembling."

22 But you have come to Mount Zion and to the city of the living God, the heavenly Jerusalem, and to myriads of angels,

23 to the general assembly and church of the first-born who are enrolled in heaven, and to God, the Judge of all, and to the spirits of righteous men made perfect,

24 and to Jesus, the mediator of a new covenant, and to the sprinkled blood, which speaks better than *the blood* of Abel.

25 See to it that you do not refuse Him who is speaking. For if those did not escape when they refused him who warned *them* on earth, much less *shall* we *escape* who turn away from Him who *warns* from heaven.

26 And His voice shook the earth then, but now He has promised, saying, "YET ONCE MORE I WILL SHAKE NOT ONLY THE EARTH, BUT ALSO THE HEAVEN."

27 And this *expression,* "Yet once more," denotes the removing of those things which can be shaken, as of created things, in order that those things which cannot be shaken may remain.

28 Therefore, since we receive a kingdom which cannot be shaken, let us show gratitude, by which we may offer to God an acceptable service with reverence and awe;

29 for our God is a consuming fire.

CHAPTER 13

LET love of the brethren continue.

2 Do not neglect to show hospitality to strangers, for by this some have entertained angels without knowing it.

3 Remember the prisoners, as though in prison with them, and those who are ill-treated, since you yourselves also are in the body.

4 *Let* marriage *be held* in honor among all, and let the *marriage* bed *be* undefiled; for fornicators and adulterers God will judge.

5 Let your character be free from the love of money, being content with what you have; for He Himself has said, "I WILL NEVER DESERT YOU, NOR WILL I EVER FORSAKE YOU,"

6 so that we confidently say,

"THE LORD IS MY HELPER, I WILL NOT BE AFRAID.

WHAT SHALL MAN DO TO ME?"

7 ¶ Remember those who led you, who spoke the word of God to you; and considering the result of their conduct, imitate their faith.

8 Jesus Christ *is* the same yesterday and today, *yes* and forever.

9 Do not be carried away by varied and strange teachings; for it is good for the heart to be strengthened by grace, not by foods, through which those who were thus occupied were not benefited.

10 We have an altar, from which those who serve the tabernacle have no right to eat.

11 For the bodies of those animals whose blood is brought into the holy place by the high priest *as an offering* for sin, are burned outside the camp.

12 Therefore Jesus also, that He might sanctify the people through His own blood, suffered outside the gate.

13 Hence, let us go out to Him outside the camp, bearing His reproach.

14 For here we do not have a lasting city, but we are seeking *the city* which is to come.

15 Through Him then, let us continually offer up a sacrifice of praise to God, that is, the fruit of lips that give thanks to His name.

16 And do not neglect doing good and sharing; for with such sacrifices God is pleased.

17 Obey your leaders, and submit *to them*; for they keep watch over your souls, as those who will give an account. Let them do this with joy and not with grief, for this would be unprofitable for you.

18 ¶ Pray for us, for we are sure that we have a good conscience, desiring to conduct ourselves honorably in all things.

19 And I urge *you* all the more to do this, that I may be restored to you the sooner.

20 ¶ Now the God of peace, who brought up from the dead the great Shepherd of the sheep through the blood of the eternal covenant, *even* Jesus our Lord,

21 equip you in every good thing to do His will, working in us that which is pleasing in His sight, through Jesus Christ, to whom *be* the glory forever and ever. Amen.

22 ¶ But I urge you, brethren, bear with this word of exhortation, for I have written to you briefly.

23 Take notice that our brother Timothy has been released, with whom, if he comes soon, I shall see you.

24 Greet all of your leaders and all the saints. Those from Italy greet you.

25 ¶ Grace be with you all.

JAMES

JAMES, a bond-servant of God and of the Lord Jesus Christ, to the twelve tribes who are dispersed abroad, greetings.

2 ¶ Consider it all joy, my brethren, when you encounter various trials,

3 knowing that the testing of your faith produces endurance.

4 And let endurance have *its* perfect result, that you may be perfect and complete, lacking in nothing.

5 ¶ But if any of you lacks wisdom, let him ask of God, who gives to all men generously and without reproach, and it will be given to him.

6 But let him ask in faith without any doubting, for the one who doubts is like the surf of the sea driven and tossed by the wind.

7 For let not that man expect that he will receive anything from the Lord,

8 *being* a double-minded man, unstable in all his ways.

9 ¶ But let the brother of humble circumstances glory in his high position;

10 and *let* the rich man *glory* in his humiliation, because like flowering grass he will pass away.

11 For the sun rises with a scorching wind, and withers the grass; and its flower falls off, and the beauty of its appearance is destroyed; so too the rich man in the midst of his pursuits will fade away.

12 ¶ Blessed is a man who perseveres under trial; for once he has been approved, he will receive the crown of life, which *the Lord* has promised to those who love Him.

13 Let no one say when he is tempted, "I am being tempted by God"; for God cannot be tempted by evil, and He Himself does not tempt anyone.

14 But each one is tempted when he is carried away and enticed by his own lust.

15 Then when lust has conceived, it gives birth to sin; and when sin is accomplished, it brings forth death.

16 Do not be deceived, my beloved brethren.

17 Every good thing bestowed and every perfect gift is from above, coming down from the Father of lights, with whom there is no variation, or shifting shadow.

18 In the exercise of His will He brought us forth by the word of truth, so that we might be, as it were, the first fruits among His creatures.

19 ¶ [1]*This* you know, my beloved brethren. But let everyone be quick to hear, slow to speak *and* slow to anger;

20 for the anger of man does not achieve the righteousness of God.

21 Therefore putting aside all filthiness and *all* that remains of wickedness, in humility receive the word implanted, which is able to save your souls.

22 But prove yourselves doers of the word, and not merely hearers who delude themselves.

23 For if anyone is a hearer of the word and not a doer, he is like a man who looks at his natural face in a mirror;

24 for *once* he has looked at himself and gone away, he has immediately forgotten what kind of person he was.

25 But one who looks intently at the perfect law, the *law* of liberty, and abides by it, not having become a forgetful hearer but an effectual doer, this man shall be blessed in what he does.

26 If anyone thinks himself to be religious, and yet does not bridle his tongue but deceives his *own* heart, this man's religion is worthless.

27 This is pure and undefiled religion in the sight of *our* God and Father, to visit orphans and widows in their distress, *and* to keep oneself unstained by the world.

CHAPTER 2

MY brethren, do not hold your faith in our glorious Lord Jesus Christ with *an attitude of* personal favoritism.

2 For if a man comes into your assembly with a gold ring and dressed in fine clothes, and there also comes in a poor man in dirty clothes,

3 and you pay special attention to the one who is wearing the fine clothes, and say, "You sit here in a good place," and you say to the poor man, "You stand over there, or sit down by my footstool,"

[1] Or, *Know this*

4 have you not made distinctions among yourselves, and become judges with evil motives?

5 Listen, my beloved brethren: did not God choose the poor of this world *to be* rich in faith and heirs of the kingdom which He promised to those who love Him?

6 But you have dishonored the poor man. Is it not the rich who oppress you and personally drag you into court?

7 Do they not blaspheme the fair name by which you have been called?

8 If, however, you are fulfilling the royal law, according to the Scripture, "YOU SHALL LOVE YOUR NEIGHBOR AS YOURSELF," you are doing well.

9 But if you show partiality, you are committing sin *and* are convicted by the law as transgressors.

10 For whoever keeps the whole law and yet stumbles in one *point,* he has become guilty of all.

11 For He who said, "DO NOT COMMIT ADULTERY," also said, "DO NOT COMMIT MURDER." Now if you do not commit adultery, but do commit murder, you have become a transgressor of the law.

12 So speak and so act, as those who are to be judged by *the* law of liberty.

13 For judgment *will be* merciless to one who has shown no mercy; mercy triumphs over judgment.

14 ¶ What use is it, my brethren, if a man says he has faith, but he has no works? Can that faith save him?

15 If a brother or sister is without clothing and in need of daily food,

16 and one of you says to them, "Go in peace, be warmed and be filled," and yet you do not give them what is necessary for *their* body, what use is that?

17 Even so faith, if it has no works, is dead, *being* by itself.

18 But someone may *well* say, "You have faith, and I have works; show me your faith without the works, and I will show you my faith by my works."

19 You believe that [2]God is one. You do well; the demons also believe, and shudder.

20 But are you willing to recognize, you foolish fellow, that faith without works is useless?

21 Was not Abraham our father justified by works, when he offered up Isaac his son on the altar?

22 You see that faith was working with his works, and as a result of the works, faith was perfected;

23 and the Scripture was fulfilled which says, "AND ABRAHAM BELIEVED GOD, AND IT WAS RECKONED TO HIM AS RIGHTEOUSNESS," and he was called the friend of God.

24 You see that a man is justified by works, and not by faith alone.

25 And in the same way was not Rahab the harlot also justified by works, when she received the messengers and sent them out by another way?

26 For just as the body without *the* spirit is dead, so also faith without works is dead.

CHAPTER 3

LET not many *of you* become teachers, my brethren, knowing that as such we shall incur a stricter judgment.

2 For we all stumble in many *ways.* If anyone does not stumble in what he says, he is a perfect man, able to bridle the whole body as well.

3 Now if we put the bits into the horses' mouths so that they may obey us, we direct their entire body as well.

4 Behold, the ships also, though they are so great and are driven by strong winds, are still directed by a very small rudder, wherever the inclination of the pilot desires.

5 So also the tongue is a small part of the body, and *yet* it boasts of great things. Behold, how great a forest is set aflame by such a small fire!

6 And the tongue is a fire, the *very* world of iniquity; the tongue is set among our members as that which defiles the entire body, and sets on fire the course of *our* life, and is set on fire by hell.

7 For every species of beasts and birds, of reptiles and creatures of the sea, is tamed, and has been tamed by the human race.

8 But no one can tame the tongue; *it is* a restless evil *and* full of deadly poison.

9 With it we bless *our* Lord and Father; and with it we curse men, who

[2] Or, *there is one God*

have been made in the likeness of God;

10 from the same mouth come *both* blessing and cursing. My brethren, these things ought not to be this way.

11 Does a fountain send out from the same opening *both* fresh and bitter *water*?

12 Can a fig tree, my brethren, produce olives, or a vine produce figs? Neither *can* salt water produce fresh.

13 ¶ Who among you is wise and understanding? Let him show by his good behavior his deeds in the gentleness of wisdom.

14 But if you have bitter jealousy and selfish ambition in your heart, do not be arrogant and *so* lie against the truth.

15 This wisdom is not that which comes down from above, but is earthly, natural, demonic.

16 For where jealousy and selfish ambition exist, there is disorder and every evil thing.

17 But the wisdom from above is first pure, then peaceable, gentle, reasonable, full of mercy and good fruits, unwavering, without hypocrisy.

18 And the seed whose fruit is righteousness is sown in peace by those who make peace.

CHAPTER 4

WHAT is the source of quarrels and conflicts among you? Is not the source your pleasures that wage war in your members?

2 You lust and do not have; *so* you commit murder. And you are envious and cannot obtain; *so* you fight and quarrel. You do not have because you do not ask.

3 You ask and do not receive, because you ask with wrong motives, so that you may spend *it* on your pleasures.

4 You adulteresses, do you not know that friendship with the world is hostility toward God? Therefore whoever wishes to be a friend of the world makes himself an enemy of God.

5 Or do you think that the Scripture speaks to no purpose: "[3]He jealously desires the Spirit which He has made to dwell in us"?

[3] Or, *The Spirit which He has made to dwell in us jealously desires us*

6 But He gives a greater grace. Therefore *it* says, "GOD IS OPPOSED TO THE PROUD, BUT GIVES GRACE TO THE HUMBLE."

7 Submit therefore to God. Resist the devil and he will flee from you.

8 Draw near to God and He will draw near to you. Cleanse your hands, you sinners; and purify your hearts, you double-minded.

9 Be miserable and mourn and weep; let your laughter be turned into mourning, and your joy to gloom.

10 Humble yourselves in the presence of the Lord, and He will exalt you.

11 ¶ Do not speak against one another, brethren. He who speaks against a brother, or judges his brother, speaks against the law, and judges the law; but if you judge the law, you are not a doer of the law, but a judge *of it*.

12 There is *only* one Lawgiver and Judge, the One who is able to save and to destroy; but who are you who judge your neighbor?

13 ¶ Come now, you who say, "Today or tomorrow, we shall go to such and such a city, and spend a year there and engage in business and make a profit."

14 Yet you do not know what your life will be like tomorrow. You are *just* a vapor that appears for a little while and then vanishes away.

15 Instead, *you ought* to say, "If the Lord wills, we shall live and also do this or that."

16 But as it is, you boast in your arrogance; all such boasting is evil.

17 Therefore, to one who knows *the* right thing to do, and does not do it, to him it is sin.

CHAPTER 5

COME now, you rich, weep and howl for your miseries which are coming upon you.

2 Your riches have rotted and your garments have become moth-eaten.

3 Your gold and your silver have rusted; and their rust will be a witness against you and will consume your flesh like fire. It is in the last days that you have stored up your treasure!

4 Behold, the pay of the laborers who mowed your fields, *and* which has

been withheld by you, cries out
against you; and the outcry of those
who did the harvesting has reached
the ears of the Lord of Sabaoth.

5 You have lived luxuriously on the
earth and led a life of wanton pleasure;
you have fattened your hearts in a day
of slaughter.

6 You have condemned and put to
death the righteous *man;* he does not
resist you.

7 ¶ Be patient, therefore, brethren,
until the coming of the Lord. Behold,
the farmer waits for the precious produce of the soil, being patient about it,
until it gets the early and late rains.

8 You too be patient; strengthen
your hearts, for the coming of the
Lord is at hand.

9 Do not complain, brethren,
against one another, that you yourselves may not be judged; behold, the
Judge is standing right at the door.

10 As an example, brethren, of suffering and patience, take the prophets
who spoke in the name of the Lord.

11 Behold, we count those blessed
who endured. You have heard of the
endurance of Job and have seen the
outcome of the Lord's dealings, that
the Lord is full of compassion and *is*
merciful.

12 ¶ But above all, my brethren, do
not swear, either by heaven or by
earth or with any other oath; but let

your yes be yes, and your no, no; so
that you may not fall under judgment.

13 ¶ Is anyone among you suffering?
Let him pray. Is anyone cheerful? Let
him sing praises.

14 Is anyone among you sick? Let
him call for the elders of the church,
and let them pray over him, anointing
him with oil in the name of the Lord;

15 and the prayer offered in faith will
[4]restore the one who is sick, and the
Lord will raise him up, and if he has
committed sins, they will be forgiven
him.

16 Therefore, confess your sins to
one another, and pray for one another,
so that you may be healed. The effective prayer of a righteous man can
accomplish much.

17 Elijah was a man with a nature
like ours, and he prayed earnestly that
it might not rain; and it did not rain on
the earth for three years and six
months.

18 And he prayed again, and the sky
poured rain, and the earth produced
its fruit.

19 ¶ My brethren, if any among you
strays from the truth, and one turns
him back,

20 let him know that he who turns a
sinner from the error of his way will
save his soul from death, and will
cover a multitude of sins.

[4] Or, *save*

THE FIRST EPISTLE OF

PETER

PETER, an apostle of Jesus Christ, to
those who reside as aliens, scattered
throughout Pontus, Galatia, Cappadocia, Asia, and Bithynia, who are chosen

2 according to the foreknowledge of
God the Father, by the sanctifying
work of the Spirit, that you may obey
Jesus Christ and be sprinkled with His
blood: May grace and peace be yours
in fullest measure.

3 ¶ Blessed be the God and Father
of our Lord Jesus Christ, who according to His great mercy has caused us
to be born again to a living hope

through the resurrection of Jesus
Christ from the dead,

4 to *obtain* an inheritance *which is*
imperishable and undefiled and will
not fade away, reserved in heaven for
you,

5 who are protected by the power of
God through faith for a salvation
ready to be revealed in the last time.

6 In this you greatly rejoice, even
though now for a little while, if necessary, you have been distressed by various trials,

7 that the proof of your faith, *being*
more precious than gold which is perishable, even though tested by fire,

may be found to result in praise and glory and honor at the revelation of Jesus Christ;

8 and though you have not seen Him, you love Him, and though you do not see Him now, but believe in Him, you greatly rejoice with joy inexpressible and full of glory,

9 obtaining as the outcome of your faith the salvation of [1]your souls.

10 As to this salvation, the prophets who prophesied of the grace that *would come* to you made careful search and inquiry,

11 seeking to know what person or time the Spirit of Christ within them was indicating as He predicted the sufferings of Christ and the glories to follow.

12 It was revealed to them that they were not serving themselves, but you, in these things which now have been announced to you through those who preached the gospel to you by the Holy Spirit sent from heaven—things into which angels long to look.

13 ¶ Therefore, gird your minds for action, keep sober *in spirit,* fix your hope completely on the grace to be brought to you at the revelation of Jesus Christ.

14 As obedient children, do not be conformed to the former lusts *which were yours* in your ignorance,

15 but like the Holy One who called you, be holy yourselves also in all *your* behavior;

16 because it is written, "YOU SHALL BE HOLY, FOR I AM HOLY."

17 And if you address as Father the One who impartially judges according to each man's work, conduct yourselves in fear during the time of your stay *upon earth;*

18 knowing that you were not redeemed with perishable things like silver or gold from your futile way of life inherited from your forefathers,

19 but with precious blood, as of a lamb unblemished and spotless, *the blood* of Christ.

20 For He was foreknown before the foundation of the world, but has appeared in these last times for the sake of you

21 who through Him are believers in God, who raised Him from the dead

and gave Him glory, so that your faith and hope are in God.

22 ¶ Since you have in obedience to the truth purified your souls for a sincere love of the brethren, fervently love one another from [2]the heart,

23 for you have been born again not of seed which is perishable but imperishable, *that is,* through the living and abiding word of God.

24 For,

"ALL FLESH IS LIKE GRASS,
  AND ALL ITS GLORY LIKE THE
    FLOWER OF GRASS.
  THE GRASS WITHERS,
  AND THE FLOWER FALLS OFF,

25 BUT THE WORD OF THE LORD
    ABIDES FOREVER."

And this is the word which was preached to you.

CHAPTER 2

THEREFORE, putting aside all malice and all guile and hypocrisy and envy and all slander,

2 like newborn babes, long for the pure milk of the word, that by it you may grow in respect to salvation,

3 if you have tasted the kindness of the Lord.

4 And coming to Him as to a living stone, rejected by men, but choice and precious in the sight of God,

5 you also, as living stones, are being built up as a spiritual house for a holy priesthood, to offer up spiritual sacrifices acceptable to God through Jesus Christ.

6 For *this* is contained in Scripture:

"BEHOLD I LAY IN ZION A CHOICE
  STONE, A PRECIOUS CORNER
  stone,
  AND HE WHO BELIEVES IN HIM
  SHALL NOT BE DISAPPOINTED."

7 This precious value, then, is for you who believe. But for those who disbelieve,

"THE STONE WHICH THE BUILDERS
  REJECTED,
  THIS BECAME THE VERY CORNER
  stone,"

8 and,

"A STONE OF STUMBLING AND A
  ROCK OF OFFENSE";

for they stumble because they are disobedient to the word, and to this *doom* they were also appointed.

---

[1] Some ancient mss. do not contain *your*

[2] Some mss. read *a clean heart*

9 But you are A CHOSEN RACE, A royal PRIESTHOOD, A HOLY NATION, A PEOPLE FOR God's OWN POSSESSION, that you may proclaim the excellencies of Him who has called you out of darkness into His marvelous light;

10 for you once were NOT A PEOPLE, but now you are THE PEOPLE OF GOD; you had NOT RECEIVED MERCY, but now you have RECEIVED MERCY.

11 ¶ Beloved, I urge you as aliens and strangers to abstain from fleshly lusts, which wage war against the soul.

12 Keep your behavior excellent among the Gentiles, so that in the thing in which they slander you as evildoers, they may on account of your good deeds, as they observe them, glorify God in the day of ³visitation.

13 ¶ Submit yourselves for the Lord's sake to every human institution, whether to a king as the one in authority,

14 or to governors as sent by him for the punishment of evildoers and the praise of those who do right.

15 For such is the will of God that by doing right you may silence the ignorance of foolish men.

16 Act as free men, and do not use your freedom as a covering for evil, but use it as bondslaves of God.

17 Honor all men; love the brotherhood, fear God, honor the king.

18 ¶ Servants, be submissive to your masters with all respect, not only to those who are good and gentle, but also to those who are unreasonable.

19 For this finds favor, if for the sake of conscience toward God a man bears up under sorrows when suffering unjustly.

20 For what credit is there if, when you sin and are harshly treated, you endure it with patience? But if when you do what is right and suffer for it you patiently endure it, this finds favor with God.

21 For you have been called for this purpose, since Christ also suffered for you, leaving you an example for you to follow in His steps,

22 WHO COMMITTED NO SIN, NOR WAS ANY DECEIT FOUND IN HIS MOUTH;

23 and while being reviled, He did not revile in return; while suffering, He uttered no threats, but kept entrusting Himself to Him who judges righteously;

24 and He Himself bore our sins in His body on the cross, that we might die to sin and live to righteousness; for by His wounds you were healed.

25 For you were continually straying like sheep, but now you have returned to the Shepherd and Guardian of your souls.

CHAPTER 3

IN the same way, you wives, be submissive to your own husbands so that even if any of them are disobedient to the word, they may be won without a word by the behavior of their wives,

2 as they observe your chaste and respectful behavior.

3 And let not your adornment be merely external—braiding the hair, and wearing gold jewelry, or putting on dresses;

4 but let it be the hidden person of the heart, with the imperishable quality of a gentle and quiet spirit, which is precious in the sight of God.

5 For in this way in former times the holy women also, who hoped in God, used to adorn themselves, being submissive to their own husbands.

6 Thus Sarah obeyed Abraham, calling him lord, and you have become her children if you do what is right without being frightened by any fear.

7 ¶ You husbands likewise, live with your wives in an understanding way, as with a weaker vessel, since she is a woman; and grant her honor as a fellow heir of the grace of life, so that your prayers may not be hindered.

8 ¶ To sum up, let all be harmonious, sympathetic, brotherly, kindhearted, and humble in spirit;

9 not returning evil for evil, or insult for insult, but giving a blessing instead; for you were called for the very purpose that you might inherit a blessing.

10 For,

"LET HIM WHO MEANS TO LOVE
  LIFE AND SEE GOOD DAYS
REFRAIN HIS TONGUE FROM EVIL

³ I.e., Christ's coming again in judgment

AND HIS LIPS FROM SPEAKING GUILE.

11 "AND LET HIM TURN AWAY FROM EVIL AND DO GOOD;
LET HIM SEEK PEACE AND PURSUE IT.

12 "FOR THE EYES OF THE LORD ARE UPON THE RIGHTEOUS,
AND HIS EARS ATTEND TO THEIR PRAYER,
BUT THE FACE OF THE LORD IS AGAINST THOSE WHO DO EVIL."

13 ¶ And who is there to harm you if you prove zealous for what is good?

14 But even if you should suffer for the sake of righteousness, *you are* blessed. AND DO NOT FEAR THEIR IN-TIMIDATION, AND DO NOT BE TROUBLED,

15 but [4]sanctify Christ as Lord in your hearts, always *being* ready to make a defense to everyone who asks you to give an account for the hope that is in you, yet with gentleness and reverence;

16 and keep a good conscience so that in the thing in which you are slandered, those who revile your good behavior in Christ may be put to shame.

17 For it is better, if God should will it so, that you suffer for doing what is right rather than for doing what is wrong.

18 For Christ also died for sins once for all, *the* just for *the* unjust, in order that He might bring us to God, having been put to death in the flesh, but made alive in the spirit;

19 in which also He went and made proclamation to the spirits *now* in prison,

20 who once were disobedient, when the patience of God kept waiting in the days of Noah, during the construction of the ark, in which a few, that is, eight persons, were brought safely through *the* water.

21 And corresponding to that, bap-tism now saves you—not the removal of dirt from the flesh, but an appeal to God for a good conscience—through the resurrection of Jesus Christ,

22 who is at the right hand of God, having gone into heaven, after angels and authorities and powers had been subjected to Him.

CHAPTER 4

THEREFORE, since Christ has [5]suf-fered in the flesh, arm yourselves also with the same purpose, because he who has suffered in the flesh has ceased from sin,

2 so as to live the rest of the time in the flesh no longer for the lusts of men, but for the will of God.

3 For the time already past is suffi-cient *for you* to have carried out the desire of the Gentiles, having pursued a course of sensuality, lusts, drunken-ness, carousals, drinking parties and abominable idolatries.

4 And in *all* this, they are surprised that you do not run with *them* into the same excess of dissipation, and they malign *you*;

5 but they shall give account to Him who is ready to judge the living and the dead.

6 For the gospel has for this pur-pose been preached even to those who are dead, that though they are judged in the flesh as men, they may live in the spirit according to *the will of* God.

7 ¶ The end of all things is at hand; therefore, be of sound judgment and sober *spirit* for the purpose of prayer.

8 Above all, keep fervent in your love for one another, because love covers a multitude of sins.

9 Be hospitable to one another without complaint.

10 As each one has received a *special* gift, employ it in serving one another, as good stewards of the manifold grace of God.

11 Whoever speaks, *let him speak*, as it were, the utterances of God; who-ever serves, *let him do so* as by the strength which God supplies; so that in all things God may be glorified through Jesus Christ, to whom be-longs the glory and dominion forever and ever. Amen.

12 ¶ Beloved, do not be surprised at the fiery ordeal among you, which comes upon you for your testing, as though some strange thing were hap-pening to you;

13 but to the degree that you share the sufferings of Christ, keep on re-joicing; so that also at the revelation of His glory, you may rejoice with exultation.

[4] I.e., set apart

[5] I.e., suffered death

14 If you are reviled for the name of Christ, you are blessed, because the Spirit of glory and of God rests upon you.

15 By no means let any of you suffer as a murderer, or thief, or evildoer, or a troublesome meddler;

16 but if *anyone suffers* as a Christian, let him not feel ashamed, but in that name let him glorify God.

17 For *it is* time for judgment to begin with the household of God; and if *it begins* with us first, what *will be* the outcome for those who do not obey the gospel of God?

18 AND IF IT IS WITH DIFFICULTY THAT THE RIGHTEOUS IS SAVED, WHAT WILL BECOME OF THE GODLESS MAN AND THE SINNER?

19 Therefore, let those also who suffer according to the will of God entrust their souls to a faithful Creator in doing what is right.

CHAPTER 5

THEREFORE, I exhort the elders among you, as *your* fellow elder and witness of the sufferings of Christ, and a partaker also of the glory that is to be revealed,

2 shepherd the flock of God among you, exercising oversight not under compulsion, but voluntarily, according to *the will of* God; and not for sordid gain, but with eagerness;

3 nor yet as lording it over those allotted to your charge, but proving to be examples to the flock.

4 And when the Chief Shepherd appears, you will receive the unfading crown of glory.

5 You younger men, likewise, be subject to your elders; and all of you, clothe yourselves with humility toward one another, for GOD IS OPPOSED TO THE PROUD, BUT GIVES GRACE TO THE HUMBLE.

6 ¶ Humble yourselves, therefore, under the mighty hand of God, that He may exalt you at the proper time,

7 casting all your anxiety upon Him, because He cares for you.

8 Be of sober *spirit,* be on the alert. Your adversary, the devil, prowls about like a roaring lion, seeking someone to devour.

9 But resist him, firm in *your* faith, knowing that the same experiences of suffering are being accomplished by your brethren who are in the world.

10 And after you have suffered for a little while, the God of all grace, who called you to His eternal glory in Christ, will Himself perfect, confirm, strengthen *and* establish you.

11 To Him *be* dominion forever and ever. Amen.

12 ¶ Through Silvanus, our faithful brother (for so I regard *him*), I have written to you briefly, exhorting and testifying that this is the true grace of God. Stand firm in it!

13 [6]She who is in Babylon, chosen together with you, sends you greetings, and *so does* my son, Mark.

14 Greet one another with a kiss of love.

¶ Peace be to you all who are in Christ.

[6] Some mss. read *The church which*

PETER

[1]SIMON PETER, a bond-servant and apostle of Jesus Christ, to those who have received a faith of the same kind as ours, by the righteousness of our God and Savior, Jesus Christ:

2 Grace and peace be multiplied to you in the knowledge of God and of Jesus our Lord;

3 seeing that His divine power has granted to us everything pertaining to life and godliness, through the true knowledge of Him who called us by His own glory and excellence.

4 For by these He has granted to us His precious and magnificent promises, in order that by them you might become partakers of *the* divine nature, having escaped the corruption that is in the world by lust.

5 Now for this very reason also, applying all diligence, in your faith supply moral excellence, and in *your* moral excellence, knowledge;

6 and in *your* knowledge, self-control, and in *your* self-control, perseverance, and in *your* perseverance, godliness;

7 and in *your* godliness, brotherly kindness, and in *your* brotherly kindness, love.

8 For if these *qualities* are yours and are increasing, they render you neither useless nor unfruitful in the true knowledge of our Lord Jesus Christ.

9 For he who lacks these *qualities* is blind *or* short-sighted, having forgotten *his* purification from his former sins.

10 Therefore, brethren, be all the more diligent to make certain about His calling and choosing you; for as long as you practice these things, you will never stumble;

11 for in this way the entrance into the eternal kingdom of our Lord and Savior Jesus Christ will be abundantly supplied to you.

12 ¶ Therefore, I shall always be ready to remind you of these things, even though you *already* know *them*, and have been established in the truth which is present with *you*.

13 And I consider it right, as long as I am in this *earthly* dwelling, to stir you up by way of reminder,

14 knowing that the laying aside of my *earthly* dwelling is imminent, as also our Lord Jesus Christ has made clear to me.

15 And I will also be diligent that at any time after my departure you may be able to call these things to mind.

16 For we did not follow cleverly devised tales when we made known to you the power and coming of our Lord Jesus Christ, but we were eyewitnesses of His majesty.

17 For when He received honor and glory from God the Father, such an utterance as this was made to Him by the Majestic Glory, "This is My beloved Son with whom I am well-pleased"—

18 and we ourselves heard this utterance made from heaven when we were with Him on the holy mountain.

19 And *so* we have the prophetic word *made* more sure, to which you do well to pay attention as to a lamp shining in a dark place, until the day dawns and the morning star arises in your hearts.

20 But know this first of all, that no prophecy of Scripture is *a matter* of one's own interpretation,

21 for no prophecy was ever made by an act of human will, but men moved by the Holy Spirit spoke from God.

CHAPTER 2

BUT false prophets also arose among the people, just as there will also be false teachers among you, who will secretly introduce destructive heresies, even denying the Master who bought them, bringing swift destruction upon themselves.

2 And many will follow their sensuality, and because of them the way of the truth will be maligned;

3 and in *their* greed they will exploit you with false words; their judgment from long ago is not idle, and their destruction is not asleep.

4 For if God did not spare angels when they sinned, but cast them into hell and committed them to pits of darkness, reserved for judgment;

5 and did not spare the ancient world, but preserved Noah, a preacher of righteousness, with seven others,

---

[1] Most early mss. read *Simeon*

when He brought a flood upon the world of the ungodly;

6 and *if* He condemned the cities of Sodom and Gomorrah to destruction by reducing *them* to ashes, having made them an example to those who would live ungodly thereafter;

7 and *if* He rescued righteous Lot, oppressed by the sensual conduct of unprincipled men

8 (for by what he saw and heard *that* righteous man, while living among them, felt *his* righteous soul tormented day after day with *their* lawless deeds),

9 *then* the Lord knows how to rescue the godly from temptation, and to keep the unrighteous under punishment for the day of judgment,

10 and especially those who indulge the flesh in *its* corrupt desires and despise authority. Daring, self-willed, they do not tremble when they revile angelic majesties,

11 whereas angels who are greater in might and power do not bring a reviling judgment against them before the Lord.

12 But these, like unreasoning animals, born as creatures of instinct to be captured and killed, reviling where they have no knowledge, will in the destruction of those creatures also be destroyed,

13 suffering wrong as the wages of doing wrong. They count it a pleasure to revel in the daytime. They are stains and blemishes, reveling in their ²deceptions, as they carouse with you,

14 having eyes full of adultery and that never cease from sin, enticing unstable souls, having a heart trained in greed, accursed children;

15 forsaking the right way they have gone astray, having followed the way of Balaam, the *son* of Beor, who loved the wages of unrighteousness,

16 but he received a rebuke for his own transgression; *for* a dumb donkey, speaking with a voice of a man, restrained the madness of the prophet.

17 These are springs without water, and mists driven by a storm, for whom the black darkness has been reserved.

18 For speaking out arrogant *words* of vanity they entice by fleshly desires,

² Some ancient mss. read *love feasts,* (cf. Jude 12)

by sensuality, those who barely escape from the ones who live in error,

19 promising them freedom while they themselves are slaves of corruption; for by what a man is overcome, by this he is enslaved.

20 For if after they have escaped the defilements of the world by the knowledge of the Lord and Savior Jesus Christ, they are again entangled in them and are overcome, the last state has become worse for them than the first.

21 For it would be better for them not to have known the way of righteousness, than having known it, to turn away from the holy commandment delivered to them.

22 It has happened to them according to the true proverb, "A DOG RETURNS TO ITS OWN VOMIT," and, "A sow, after washing, *returns* to wallowing in the mire."

CHAPTER 3

THIS is now, beloved, the second letter I am writing to you in which I am stirring up your sincere mind by way of reminder,

2 that you should remember the words spoken beforehand by the holy prophets and the commandment of the Lord and Savior *spoken* by your apostles.

3 Know this first of all, that in the last days mockers will come with *their* mocking, following after their own lusts,

4 and saying, "Where is the promise of His coming? For *ever* since the fathers fell asleep, all continues just as it was from the beginning of creation."

5 For when they maintain this, it escapes their notice that by the word of God *the* heavens existed long ago and *the* earth was formed out of water and by water,

6 through which the world at that time was destroyed, being flooded with water.

7 But the present heavens and earth by His word are being reserved for fire, kept for the day of judgment and destruction of ungodly men.

8 ¶ But do not let this one *fact* escape your notice, beloved, that with the Lord one day is as a thousand

years, and a thousand years as one day.

9 The Lord is not slow about His promise, as some count slowness, but is patient toward you, not wishing for any to perish but for all to come to repentance.

10 But the day of the Lord will come like a thief, in which the heavens will pass away with a roar and the elements will be destroyed with intense heat, and the earth and its works will be [3]burned up.

11 Since all these things are to be destroyed in this way, what sort of people ought you to be in holy conduct and godliness,

12 looking for and hastening the coming of the day of God, on account of which the heavens will be destroyed by burning, and the elements will melt with intense heat!

13 But according to His promise we are looking for new heavens and a

[3] Some ancient mss. read *discovered*

new earth, in which righteousness dwells.

14 ¶ Therefore, beloved, since you look for these things, be diligent to be found by Him in peace, spotless and blameless,

15 and regard the patience of our Lord *to be* salvation; just as also our beloved brother Paul, according to the wisdom given him, wrote to you,

16 as also in all *his* letters, speaking in them of these things, in which are some things hard to understand, which the untaught and unstable distort, as *they do* also the rest of the Scriptures, to their own destruction.

17 You therefore, beloved, knowing this beforehand, be on your guard lest, being carried away by the error of unprincipled men, you fall from your own steadfastness,

18 but grow in the grace and knowledge of our Lord and Savior Jesus Christ. To Him *be* the glory, both now and to the day of eternity. Amen.

THE FIRST EPISTLE OF

JOHN

WHAT was from the beginning, what we have heard, what we have seen with our eyes, what we beheld and our hands handled, concerning the Word of Life—

2 and the life was manifested, and we have seen and bear witness and proclaim to you the eternal life, which was with the Father and was manifested to us—

3 what we have seen and heard we proclaim to you also, that you also may have fellowship with us; and indeed our fellowship is with the Father, and with His Son Jesus Christ.

4 And these things we write, so that our joy may be made complete.

5 ¶ And this is the message we have heard from Him and announce to you, that God is light, and in Him there is no darkness at all.

6 If we say that we have fellowship

with Him and *yet* walk in the darkness, we lie and do not practice the truth;

7 but if we walk in the light as He Himself is in the light, we have fellowship with one another, and the blood of Jesus His Son cleanses us from all sin.

8 If we say that we have no sin, we are deceiving ourselves, and the truth is not in us.

9 If we confess our sins, He is faithful and righteous to forgive us our sins and to cleanse us from all unrighteousness.

10 If we say that we have not sinned, we make Him a liar, and His word is not in us.

CHAPTER 2

MY little children, I am writing these things to you that you may not sin.

And if anyone sins, we have an [1]Advocate with the Father, Jesus Christ the righteous;

2 and He Himself is the propitiation for our sins; and not for ours only, but also for *those of* the whole world.

3 And by this we know that we have come to know Him, if we keep His commandments.

4 The one who says, "I have come to know Him," and does not keep His commandments, is a liar, and the truth is not in him;

5 but whoever keeps His word, in him the love of God has truly been perfected. By this we know that we are in Him:

6 the one who says he abides in Him ought himself to walk in the same manner as He walked.

7 ¶ Beloved, I am not writing a new commandment to you, but an old commandment which you have had from the beginning; the old commandment is the word which you have heard.

8 On the other hand, I am writing a new commandment to you, which is true in Him and in you, because the darkness is passing away, and the true light is already shining.

9 The one who says he is in the light and *yet* hates his brother is in the darkness until now.

10 The one who loves his brother abides in the light and there is no cause for stumbling in him.

11 But the one who hates his brother is in the darkness and walks in the darkness, and does not know where he is going because the darkness has blinded his eyes.

12 ¶ I am writing to you, little children, because your sins are forgiven you for His name's sake.

13 I am writing to you, fathers, because you know Him who has been from the beginning. I am writing to you, young men, because you have overcome the evil one. I have written to you, children, because you know the Father.

14 I have written to you, fathers, because you know Him who has been from the beginning. I have written to you, young men, because you are strong, and the word of God abides in you, and you have overcome the evil one.

15 Do not love the world, nor the things in the world. If anyone loves the world, the love of the Father is not in him.

16 For all that is in the world, the lust of the flesh and the lust of the eyes and the boastful pride of life, is not from the Father, but is from the world.

17 And the world is passing away, and *also* its lusts; but the one who does the will of God abides forever.

18 ¶ Children, it is the last hour; and just as you heard that antichrist is coming, even now many antichrists have arisen; from this we know that it is the last hour.

19 They went out from us, but they were not *really* of us; for if they had been of us, they would have remained with us; but *they went out,* in order that it might be shown that they all are not of us.

20 But you have an anointing from the Holy One, and you all know.

21 I have not written to you because you do not know the truth, but because you do know it, and because no lie is of the truth.

22 Who is the liar but the one who denies that Jesus is the Christ? This is the antichrist, the one who denies the Father and the Son.

23 Whoever denies the Son does not have the Father; the one who confesses the Son has the Father also.

24 As for you, let that abide in you which you heard from the beginning. If what you heard from the beginning abides in you, you also will abide in the Son and in the Father.

25 And this is the promise which He Himself made to us: eternal life.

26 These things I have written to you concerning those who are trying to deceive you.

27 And as for you, the anointing which you received from Him abides in you, and you have no need for anyone to teach you; but as His anointing teaches you about all things, and is true and is not a lie, and just as it has taught you, you abide in Him.

28 And now, little children, abide in Him, so that when He appears, we may have confidence and not shrink

[1] Gr., *Paracletos*, one called alongside to help

away from Him in shame at His coming.

29 If you know that He is righteous, you know that everyone also who practices righteousness is born of Him.

CHAPTER 3

SEE how great a love the Father has bestowed upon us, that we should be called children of God; and *such* we are. For this reason the world does not know us, because it did not know Him.

2 Beloved, now we are children of God, and it has not appeared as yet what we shall be. We know that, when He appears, we shall be like Him, because we shall see Him just as He is.

3 And everyone who has this hope *fixed* on Him purifies himself, just as He is pure.

4 Everyone who practices sin also practices lawlessness; and sin is lawlessness.

5 And you know that He appeared in order to take away sins; and in Him there is no sin.

6 No one who abides in Him sins; no one who sins has seen Him or knows Him.

7 Little children, let no one deceive you; the one who practices righteousness is righteous, just as He is righteous;

8 the one who practices sin is of the devil; for the devil has sinned from the beginning. The Son of God appeared for this purpose, that He might destroy the works of the devil.

9 No one who is born of God practices sin, because His seed abides in him; and he cannot sin, because he is born of God.

10 By this the children of God and the children of the devil are obvious: anyone who does not practice righteousness is not of God, nor the one who does not love his brother.

11 For this is the message which you have heard from the beginning, that we should love one another;

12 not as Cain, *who* was of the evil one, and slew his brother. And for what reason did he slay him? Because his deeds were evil, and his brother's were righteous.

13 ¶ Do not marvel, brethren, if the world hates you.

14 We know that we have passed out of death into life, because we love the brethren. He who does not love abides in death.

15 Everyone who hates his brother is a murderer; and you know that no murderer has eternal life abiding in him.

16 We know love by this, that He laid down His life for us; and we ought to lay down our lives for the brethren.

17 But whoever has the world's goods, and beholds his brother in need and closes his heart against him, how does the love of God abide in him?

18 Little children, let us not love with word or with tongue, but in deed and truth.

19 We shall know by this that we are of the truth, and shall assure our heart before Him,

20 in whatever our heart condemns us; for God is greater than our heart, and knows all things.

21 Beloved, if our heart does not condemn us, we have confidence before God;

22 and whatever we ask we receive from Him, because we keep His commandments and do the things that are pleasing in His sight.

23 And this is His commandment, that we believe in the name of His Son Jesus Christ, and love one another, just as He commanded us.

24 And the one who keeps His commandments abides in Him, and He in him. And we know by this that He abides in us, by the Spirit whom He has given us.

CHAPTER 4

BELOVED, do not believe every spirit, but test the spirits to see whether they are from God; because many false prophets have gone out into the world.

2 By this you know the Spirit of God: every spirit that confesses that Jesus Christ has come in the flesh is from God;

3 and every spirit that does not confess Jesus is not from God; and this is the *spirit* of the antichrist, of which you have heard that it is coming, and now it is already in the world.

4 You are from God, little children, and have overcome them; because

greater is He who is in you than he who is in the world.

5 They are from the world; therefore they speak *as* from the world, and the world listens to them.

6 We are from God; he who knows God listens to us; he who is not from God does not listen to us. By this we know the spirit of truth and the spirit of error.

7 ¶ Beloved, let us love one another, for love is from God; and everyone who loves is born of God and knows God.

8 The one who does not love does not know God, for God is love.

9 By this the love of God was manifested in us, that God has sent His only begotten Son into the world so that we might live through Him.

10 In this is love, not that we loved God, but that He loved us and sent His Son *to be* the propitiation for our sins.

11 Beloved, if God so loved us, we also ought to love one another.

12 No one has beheld God at any time; if we love one another, God abides in us, and His love is perfected in us.

13 By this we know that we abide in Him and He in us, because He has given us of His Spirit.

14 And we have beheld and bear witness that the Father has sent the Son *to be* the Savior of the world.

15 Whoever confesses that Jesus is the Son of God, God abides in him, and he in God.

16 And we have come to know and have believed the love which God has for us. God is love, and the one who abides in love abides in God, and God abides in him.

17 By this, love is perfected with us, that we may have confidence in the day of judgment; because as He is, so also are we in this world.

18 There is no fear in love; but perfect love casts out fear, because fear involves punishment, and the one who fears is not perfected in love.

19 We love, because He first loved us.

20 If someone says, "I love God," and hates his brother, he is a liar; for the one who does not love his brother whom he has seen, cannot love God whom he has not seen.

21 And this commandment we have

from Him, that the one who loves God should love his brother also.

CHAPTER 5

WHOEVER believes that Jesus is the [2]Christ is born of God; and whoever loves the Father loves the *child* born of Him.

2 By this we know that we love the children of God, when we love God and observe His commandments.

3 For this is the love of God, that we keep His commandments; and His commandments are not burdensome.

4 For whatever is born of God overcomes the world; and this is the victory that has overcome the world— our faith.

5 And who is the one who overcomes the world, but he who believes that Jesus is the Son of God?

6 This is the one who came by water and blood, Jesus Christ; not with the water only, but with the water and with the blood.

7 And it is the Spirit who bears witness, because the Spirit is the truth.

8 For there are three that bear witness, [3]the Spirit and the water and the blood; and the three are in agreement.

9 If we receive the witness of men, the witness of God is greater; for the witness of God is this, that He has borne witness concerning His Son.

10 The one who believes in the Son of God has the witness in himself; the one who does not believe God has made Him a liar, because he has not believed in the witness that God has borne concerning His Son.

11 And the witness is this, that God has given us eternal life, and this life is in His Son.

12 He who has the Son has the life; he who does not have the Son of God does not have the life.

13 ¶ These things I have written to you who believe in the name of the Son of God, in order that you may know that you have eternal life.

14 And this is the confidence which we have before Him, that, if we ask anything according to His will, He hears us.

[2] I.e., Messiah
[3] A few late mss. read *in heaven, the Father, the Word, and the Holy Spirit, and these three are one. And there are three that bear witness on earth, the Spirit*

15 And if we know that He hears us *in* whatever we ask, we know that we have the requests which we have asked from Him.

16 If anyone sees his brother committing a sin not *leading* to death, he shall ask and *God* will for him give life to those who commit sin not *leading* to death. There is a sin *leading* to death; I do not say that he should make request for this.

17 All unrighteousness is sin, and there is a sin not *leading* to death.

18 ¶ We know that no one who is born of God sins; but He who was born of God keeps him and the evil one does not touch him.

19 We know that we are of God, and the whole world lies in *the power of* the evil one.

20 And we know that the Son of God has come, and has given us understanding, in order that we might know Him who is true, and we are in Him who is true, in His Son Jesus Christ. This is the true God and eternal life.

21 Little children, guard yourselves from idols.

THE SECOND EPISTLE OF

JOHN

THE elder to the chosen lady and her children, whom I love in truth; and not only I, but also all who know the truth,

2 for the sake of the truth which abides in us and will be with us forever:

3 Grace, mercy *and* peace will be with us, from God the Father and from Jesus Christ, the Son of the Father, in truth and love.

4 ¶ I was very glad to find *some* of your children walking in truth, just as we have received commandment *to do* from the Father.

5 And now I ask you, lady, not as writing to you a new commandment, but the one which we have had from the beginning, that we love one another.

6 And this is love, that we walk according to His commandments. This is the commandment, just as you have heard from the beginning, that you should walk in it.

7 For many deceivers have gone out into the world, those who do not acknowledge Jesus Christ *as* coming in the flesh. This is the deceiver and the antichrist.

8 Watch yourselves, that you might not lose what we have accomplished, but that you may receive a full reward.

9 Anyone who goes too far and does not abide in the teaching of Christ, does not have God; the one who abides in the teaching, he has both the Father and the Son.

10 If anyone comes to you and does not bring this teaching, do not receive him into *your* house, and do not give him a greeting;

11 for the one who gives him a greeting participates in his evil deeds.

12 ¶ Having many things to write to you, I do not want to *do so* with paper and ink; but I hope to come to you and speak face to face, that your joy may be made full.

13 The children of your chosen sister greet you.

JOHN

THE elder to the beloved Gaius, whom I love in truth.

2 ¶ Beloved, I pray that in all respects you may prosper and be in good health, just as your soul prospers.

3 For I was very glad when brethren came and bore witness to your truth, *that is,* how you are walking in truth.

4 I have no greater joy than this, to hear of my children walking in the truth.

5 ¶ Beloved, you are acting faithfully in whatever you accomplish for the brethren, and especially *when they are* strangers;

6 and they bear witness to your love before the church; and you will do well to send them on their way in a manner worthy of God.

7 For they went out for the sake of the Name, accepting nothing from the Gentiles.

8 Therefore we ought to support such men, that we may be fellow workers with the truth.

9 ¶ I wrote something to the church; but Diotrephes, who loves to be first among them, does not accept what we say.

10 For this reason, if I come, I will call attention to his deeds which he does, unjustly accusing us with wicked words; and not satisfied with this, neither does he himself receive the brethren, and he forbids those who desire *to do so,* and puts *them* out of the church.

11 Beloved, do not imitate what is evil, but what is good. The one who does good is of God; the one who does evil has not seen God.

12 Demetrius has received a *good* testimony from everyone, and from the truth itself; and we also bear witness, and you know that our witness is true.

13 ¶ I had many things to write to you, but I am not willing to write *them* to you with pen and ink;

14 but I hope to see you shortly, and we shall speak face to face. Peace *be* to you. The friends greet you. Greet the friends by name.

THE EPISTLE OF

JUDE

JUDE, a bond-servant of Jesus Christ, and brother of James, to those who are the called, beloved in God the Father, and kept for Jesus Christ:

2 May mercy and peace and love be multiplied to you.

3 ¶ Beloved, while I was making every effort to write you about our common salvation, I felt the necessity to write to you appealing that you contend earnestly for the faith which was once for all delivered to the saints.

4 For certain persons have crept in unnoticed, those who were long beforehand marked out for this condemnation, ungodly persons who turn the grace of our God into licentiousness and deny our only Master and Lord, Jesus Christ.

5 ¶ Now I desire to remind you,

though you know all things once for all, that [1]the Lord, after saving a people out of the land of Egypt, subsequently destroyed those who did not believe.

6 And angels who did not keep their own domain, but abandoned their proper abode, He has kept in eternal bonds under darkness for the judgment of the great day.

7 Just as Sodom and Gomorrah and the cities around them, since they in the same way as these indulged in gross immorality and went after strange flesh, are exhibited as an example, in undergoing the punishment of eternal fire.

8 Yet in the same manner these men, also by dreaming, defile the flesh,

[1] Some ancient mss. read *Jesus*

and reject authority, and revile angelic majesties.

9 But Michael the archangel, when he disputed with the devil and argued about the body of Moses, did not dare pronounce against him a railing judgment, but said, "The Lord rebuke you."

10 But these men revile the things which they do not understand; and the things which they know by instinct, like unreasoning animals, by these things they are destroyed.

11 Woe to them! For they have gone the way of Cain, and for pay they have rushed headlong into the error of Balaam, and perished in the rebellion of Korah.

12 These men are those who are hidden reefs in your love feasts when they feast with you without fear, caring for themselves; clouds without water, carried along by winds; autumn trees without fruit, doubly dead, uprooted;

13 wild waves of the sea, casting up their own shame like foam; wandering stars, for whom the black darkness has been reserved forever.

14 And about these also Enoch, *in* the seventh *generation* from Adam, prophesied, saying, "Behold, the Lord came with many thousands of His holy ones,

15 to execute judgment upon all, and to convict all the ungodly of all their ungodly deeds which they have done in an ungodly way, and of all the harsh things which ungodly sinners have spoken against Him."

16 These are grumblers, finding fault, following after their *own* lusts; they speak arrogantly, flattering people for the sake of *gaining an* advantage.

17 ¶ But you, beloved, ought to remember the words that were spoken beforehand by the apostles of our Lord Jesus Christ,

18 that they were saying to you, "In the last time there shall be mockers, following after their own ungodly lusts."

19 These are the ones who cause divisions, worldly-minded, devoid of the Spirit.

20 But you, beloved, building yourselves up on your most holy faith; praying in the Holy Spirit;

21 keep yourselves in the love of God, waiting anxiously for the mercy of our Lord Jesus Christ to eternal life.

22 And have mercy on some, who are doubting;

23 save others, snatching them out of the fire; and on some have mercy with fear, hating even the garment polluted by the flesh.

24 ¶ Now to Him who is able to keep you from stumbling, and to make you stand in the presence of His glory blameless with great joy,

25 to the only God our Savior, through Jesus Christ our Lord, *be* glory, majesty, dominion and authority, before all time and now and forever. Amen.

THE REVELATION

TO JOHN

THE Revelation of Jesus Christ, which God gave Him to show to His bond-servants, the things which must shortly take place; and He sent and communicated *it* by His angel to His bond-servant John,

2 who bore witness to the word of God and to the testimony of Jesus Christ, *even* to all that he saw.

3 Blessed is he who reads and those who hear the words of the prophecy, and heed the things which are written in it; for the time is near.

4 ¶ John to the seven churches that are in Asia: Grace to you and peace, from Him who is and who was and who is to come; and from the seven Spirits who are before His throne;

5 and from Jesus Christ, the faithful witness, the first-born of the dead, and the ruler of the kings of the earth. To Him who loves us, and released us from our sins by His blood,

6 and He has made us *to be* a kingdom, priests to His God and Father; to Him *be* the glory and the dominion forever and ever. Amen.

7 BEHOLD, HE IS COMING WITH THE CLOUDS, and every eye will see Him, even those who pierced Him; and all the tribes of the earth will mourn over Him. Even so. Amen.

8 ¶ "I am the Alpha and the Omega," says the Lord God, "who is and who was and who is to come, the Almighty."

9 ¶ I, John, your brother and fellow partaker in the tribulation and kingdom and perseverance *which are* in Jesus, was on the island called Patmos, because of the word of God and the testimony of Jesus.

10 I was [1]in the Spirit on the Lord's day, and I heard behind me a loud voice like *the sound* of a trumpet,

11 saying, "Write in a book what you see, and send *it* to the seven churches: to Ephesus and to Smyrna and to Pergamum and to Thyatira and to Sardis and to Philadelphia and to Laodicea."

12 And I turned to see the voice that was speaking with me. And having turned I saw seven golden lampstands;

13 and in the middle of the lamp-

stands one like [2]a son of man, clothed in a robe reaching to the feet, and girded across His breast with a golden girdle.

14 And His head and His hair were white like white wool, like snow; and His eyes were like a flame of fire;

15 and His feet *were* like burnished bronze, when it has been caused to glow in a furnace, and His voice *was* like the sound of many waters.

16 And in His right hand He held seven stars; and out of His mouth came a sharp two-edged sword; and His face was like the sun shining in its strength.

17 And when I saw Him, I fell at His feet as a dead man. And He laid His right hand upon me, saying, "Do not be afraid; I am the first and the last,

18 and the living One; and I was dead, and behold, I am alive forevermore, and I have the keys of death and of Hades.

19 "Write therefore the things which you have seen, and the things which are, and the things which shall take place after these things.

20 "As for the mystery of the seven stars which you saw in My right hand, and the seven golden lampstands: the seven stars are the angels of the seven churches, and the seven lampstands are the seven churches.

CHAPTER 2

"TO the angel of the church in Ephesus write:

¶ The One who holds the seven stars in His right hand, the One who walks among the seven golden lampstands, says this:

2 'I know your deeds and your toil and perseverance, and that you cannot endure evil men, and you put to the test those who call themselves apostles, and they are not, and you found them *to be* false;

3 and you have perseverance and have endured for My name's sake, and have not grown weary.

4 'But I have *this* against you, that you have left your first love.

5 'Remember therefore from where you have fallen, and repent and do the

---

[1] Or, *in spirit*   [2] Or, *the Son of Man*

deeds you did at first; or else I am coming to you, and will remove your lampstand out of its place—unless you repent.

6'Yet this you do have, that you hate the deeds of the Nicolaitans, which I also hate.

7'He who has an ear, let him hear what the Spirit says to the churches. To him who overcomes, I will grant to eat of the tree of life, which is in the Paradise of God.'

8 ¶'And to the angel of the church in Smyrna write:

¶ The first and the last, who was dead, and has come to life, says this:

9'I know your tribulation and your poverty (but you are rich), and the blasphemy by those who say they are Jews and are not, but are a synagogue of Satan.

10'Do not fear what you are about to suffer. Behold, the devil is about to cast some of you into prison, that you may be tested, and you will have tribulation ten days. Be faithful until death, and I will give you the crown of life.

11'He who has an ear, let him hear what the Spirit says to the churches. He who overcomes shall not be hurt by the second death.'

12 ¶'And to the angel of the church in Pergamum write:

¶ The One who has the sharp two-edged sword says this:

13'I know where you dwell, where Satan's throne is; and you hold fast My name, and did not deny My faith, even in the days of Antipas, My witness, My faithful one, who was killed among you, where Satan dwells.

14'But I have a few things against you, because you have there some who hold the teaching of Balaam, who kept teaching Balak to put a stumbling block before the sons of Israel, to eat things sacrificed to idols, and to commit *acts of* immorality.

15'Thus you also have some who in the same way hold the teaching of the Nicolaitans.

16'Repent therefore; or else I am coming to you quickly, and I will make war against them with the sword of My mouth.

17'He who has an ear, let him hear what the Spirit says to the churches. To him who overcomes, to him I will give *some* of the hidden manna, and I will give him a white stone, and a new name written on the stone which no one knows but he who receives it.'

18 ¶'And to the angel of the church in Thyatira write:

¶ The Son of God, who has eyes like a flame of fire, and His feet are like burnished bronze, says this:

19'I know your deeds, and your love and faith and service and perseverance, and that your deeds of late are greater than at first.

20'But I have *this* against you, that you tolerate the woman Jezebel, who calls herself a prophetess, and she teaches and leads My bond-servants astray, so that they commit *acts of* immorality and eat things sacrificed to idols.

21'And I gave her time to repent; and she does not want to repent of her immorality.

22'Behold, I will cast her upon a bed *of sickness*, and those who commit adultery with her into great tribulation, unless they repent of [3]her deeds.

23'And I will kill her children with pestilence; and all the churches will know that I am He who searches the minds and hearts; and I will give to each one of you according to your deeds.

24'But I say to you, the rest who are in Thyatira, who do not hold this teaching, who have not known the deep things of Satan, as they call them—I place no other burden on you.

25'Nevertheless what you have, hold fast until I come.

26'And he who overcomes, and he who keeps My deeds until the end, TO HIM I WILL GIVE AUTHORITY OVER THE NATIONS;

27 AND HE SHALL RULE THEM WITH A ROD OF IRON, AS THE VESSELS OF THE POTTER ARE BROKEN TO PIECES, as I also have received *authority* from My Father;

28 and I will give him the morning star.

29'He who has an ear, let him hear what the Spirit says to the churches.'

CHAPTER 3

"AND to the angel of the church in Sardis write:

¶ He who has the seven Spirits of

---

[3] Some mss. read *their*

God, and the seven stars, says this: 'I know your deeds, that you have a name that you are alive, but you are dead.

2'Wake up, and strengthen the things that remain, which were about to die; for I have not found your deeds completed in the sight of My God.

3'Remember therefore what you have received and heard; and keep *it*, and repent. If therefore you will not wake up, I will come like a thief, and you will not know at what hour I will come upon you.

4'But you have a few people in Sardis who have not soiled their garments; and they will walk with Me in white; for they are worthy.

5'He who overcomes shall thus be clothed in white garments; and I will not erase his name from the book of life, and I will confess his name before My Father, and before His angels.

6'He who has an ear, let him hear what the Spirit says to the churches.'

7 ¶'And to the angel of the church in Philadelphia write:

¶ He who is holy, who is true, who has the key of David, who opens and no one will shut, and who shuts and no one opens, says this:

8'I know your ⁴deeds. Behold, I have put before you an open door which no one can shut, because you have a little power, and have kept My word, and have not denied My name.

9'Behold, I will cause *those* of the synagogue of Satan, who say that they are Jews, and are not, but lie—behold, I will make them to come and bow down at your feet, and to know that I have loved you.

10'Because you have kept the word of My perseverance, I also will keep you from the hour of testing, that *hour* which is about to come upon the whole world, to test those who dwell upon the earth.

11'I am coming quickly; hold fast what you have, in order that no one take your crown.

12'He who overcomes, I will make him a pillar in the temple of My God, and he will not go out from it anymore; and I will write upon him the name of My God, and the name of the city of My God, the new Jerusalem,

which comes down out of heaven from My God, and My new name.

13'He who has an ear, let him hear what the Spirit says to the churches.'

14 ¶'And to the angel of the church in Laodicea write:

¶ The Amen, the faithful and true Witness, the ⁵Beginning of the creation of God, says this:

15'I know your deeds, that you are neither cold nor hot; I would that you were cold or hot.

16'So because you are lukewarm, and neither hot nor cold, I will spit you out of My mouth.

17'Because you say, "I am rich, and have become wealthy, and have need of nothing," and you do not know that you are wretched and miserable and poor and blind and naked,

18I advise you to buy from Me gold refined by fire, that you may become rich, and white garments, that you may clothe yourself, and *that* the shame of your nakedness may not be revealed; and eye salve to anoint your eyes, that you may see.

19'Those whom I love, I reprove and discipline; be zealous therefore, and repent.

20'Behold, I stand at the door and knock; if anyone hears My voice and opens the door, I will come in to him, and will dine with him, and he with Me.

21'He who overcomes, I will grant to him to sit down with Me on My throne, as I also overcame and sat down with My Father on His throne.

22'He who has an ear, let him hear what the Spirit says to the churches.' "

CHAPTER 4

AFTER these things I looked, and behold, a door *standing* open in heaven, and the first voice which I had heard, like *the sound* of a trumpet speaking with me, said, "Come up here, and I will show you what must take place after these things."

2 Immediately I was ⁶in the Spirit; and behold, a throne was standing in heaven, and One sitting on the throne.

3 And He who was sitting *was* like a jasper stone and a sardius in appearance; and *there was* a rainbow around

---

⁴ Or, *deeds (behold . . . shut), that you*

⁵ I.e., origin or source   ⁶ Or, *in spirit*

the throne, like an emerald in appearance.

4 And around the throne *were* twenty-four thrones; and upon the thrones *I* saw twenty-four elders sitting, clothed in white garments, and golden crowns on their heads.

5 And from the throne proceed flashes of lightning and sounds and peals of thunder. And *there were* seven lamps of fire burning before the throne, which are the seven Spirits of God;

6 and before the throne *there was*, as it were, a sea of glass like crystal; and in the center and around the throne, four living creatures full of eyes in front and behind.

7 And the first creature *was* like a lion, and the second creature like a calf, and the third creature had a face like that of a man, and the fourth creature *was* like a flying eagle.

8 And the four living creatures, each one of them having six wings, are full of eyes around and within; and day and night they do not cease to say,

"Holy, holy, holy, is the Lord God, the Almighty, who was and who is and who is to come."

9 And when the living creatures give glory and honor and thanks to Him who sits on the throne, to Him who lives forever and ever,

10 the twenty-four elders will fall down before Him who sits on the throne, and will worship Him who lives forever and ever, and will cast their crowns before the throne, saying,

11 "Worthy art Thou, our Lord and our God, to receive glory and honor and power; for Thou didst create all things, and because of Thy will they existed, and were created."

CHAPTER 5

AND I saw in the right hand of Him who sat on the throne a book written inside and on the back, sealed up with seven seals.

2 And I saw a strong angel proclaiming with a loud voice, "Who is worthy to open the book and to break its seals?"

3 And no one in heaven, or on the earth, or under the earth, was able to open the book, or to look into it.

4 And I *began* to weep greatly, because no one was found worthy to open the book, or to look into it;

5 and one of the elders *said to me, "Stop weeping; behold, the Lion that is from the tribe of Judah, the Root of David, has overcome so as to open the book and its seven seals."

6 And I saw [7]between the throne (with the four living creatures) and the elders a Lamb standing, as if slain, having seven horns and seven eyes, which are the seven Spirits of God, sent out into all the earth.

7 And He came, and He took *it* out of the right hand of Him who sat on the throne.

8 And when He had taken the book, the four living creatures and the twenty-four elders fell down before the Lamb, having each one a harp, and golden bowls full of incense, which are the prayers of the saints.

9 And they *sang a new song, saying,

"Worthy art Thou to take the book, and to break its seals; for Thou wast slain, and didst purchase for God with Thy blood *men* from every tribe and tongue and people and nation.

10 "And Thou hast made them *to be* a kingdom and priests to our God; and they will reign upon the earth."

11 And I looked, and I heard the voice of many angels around the throne and the living creatures and the elders; and the number of them was myriads of myriads, and thousands of thousands,

12 saying with a loud voice,

"Worthy is the Lamb that was slain to receive power and riches and wisdom and might and honor and glory and blessing."

13 And every created thing which is in heaven and on the earth and under the earth and on the sea, and all things in them, I heard saying,

"To Him who sits on the throne, and to the Lamb, *be* blessing and honor and glory and dominion forever and ever."

14 And the four living creatures kept

---

[7] Lit., *in the middle of the throne and of the four living creatures, and in the middle of the elders*

saying, "Amen." And the elders fell down and worshiped.

CHAPTER 6

AND I saw when the Lamb broke one of the seven seals, and I heard one of the four living creatures saying as with a voice of thunder, "Come."

2 And I looked, and behold, a white horse, and he who sat on it had a bow; and a crown was given to him; and he went out conquering, and to conquer.

3 ¶ And when He broke the second seal, I heard the second living creature saying, "Come."

4 And another, a red horse, went out; and to him who sat on it, it was granted to take peace from the earth, and that *men* should slay one another; and a great sword was given to him.

5 ¶ And when He broke the third seal, I heard the third living creature saying, "Come." And I looked, and behold, a black horse; and he who sat on it had a pair of scales in his hand.

6 And I heard as it were a voice in the center of the four living creatures saying, "A [8]quart of wheat for a [9]denarius, and three quarts of barley for a denarius; and do not harm the oil and the wine."

7 ¶ And when He broke the fourth seal, I heard the voice of the fourth living creature saying, "Come."

8 And I looked, and behold, an ashen horse; and he who sat on it had the name Death; and Hades was following with him. And authority was given to them over a fourth of the earth, to kill with sword and with famine and with pestilence and by the wild beasts of the earth.

9 ¶ And when He broke the fifth seal, I saw underneath the altar the souls of those who had been slain because of the word of God, and because of the testimony which they had maintained;

10 and they cried out with a loud voice, saying, "How long, O Lord, holy and true, wilt Thou refrain from judging and avenging our blood on those who dwell on the earth?"

11 And there were given to each of them a white robe; and they were told

that they should rest for a little while longer, until *the number of* their fellow servants and their brethren who were to be killed even as they had been, should be completed also.

12 ¶ And I looked when He broke the sixth seal, and there was a great earthquake; and the sun became black as sackcloth *made* of hair, and the whole moon became like blood;

13 and the stars of the sky fell to the earth, as a fig tree casts its unripe figs when shaken by a great wind.

14 And the sky was split apart like a scroll when it is rolled up; and every mountain and island were moved out of their places.

15 And the kings of the earth and the great men and the [10]commanders and the rich and the strong and every slave and free man, hid themselves in the caves and among the rocks of the mountains;

16 and they *said to the mountains and to the rocks, "Fall on us and hide us from the presence of Him who sits on the throne, and from the wrath of the Lamb;

17 for the great day of their wrath has come; and who is able to stand?"

CHAPTER 7

AFTER this I saw four angels standing at the four corners of the earth, holding back the four winds of the earth, so that no wind should blow on the earth or on the sea or on any tree.

2 And I saw another angel ascending from the rising of the sun, having the seal of the living God; and he cried out with a loud voice to the four angels to whom it was granted to harm the earth and the sea,

3 saying, "Do not harm the earth or the sea or the trees, until we have sealed the bond-servants of our God on their foreheads."

4 And I heard the number of those who were sealed, one hundred and forty-four thousand sealed from every tribe of the sons of Israel:

5 from the tribe of Judah, twelve thousand *were* sealed, from the tribe of Reuben twelve thousand, from the tribe of Gad twelve thousand,

[8] Gr., *choenix;* i.e., a dry measure almost equal to a quart
[9] The denarius was equivalent to one day's wage

[10] I.e., chiliarchs, in command of one thousand troops

6 from the tribe of Asher twelve thousand, from the tribe of Naphtali twelve thousand, from the tribe of Manasseh twelve thousand,

7 from the tribe of Simeon twelve thousand, from the tribe of Levi twelve thousand, from the tribe of Issachar twelve thousand,

8 from the tribe of Zebulun twelve thousand, from the tribe of Joseph twelve thousand, from the tribe of Benjamin, twelve thousand *were* sealed.

9 ¶ After these things I looked, and behold, a great multitude, which no one could count, from every nation and *all* tribes and peoples and tongues, standing before the throne and before the Lamb, clothed in white robes, and palm branches *were* in their hands;

10 and they cry out with a loud voice, saying,

¶ "Salvation to our God who sits on the throne, and to the Lamb."

11 And all the angels were standing around the throne and *around* the elders and the four living creatures; and they fell on their faces before the throne and worshiped God,

12 saying,

¶ "Amen, blessing and glory and wisdom and thanksgiving and honor and power and might, *be* to our God forever and ever. Amen."

13 And one of the elders answered, saying to me, "These who are clothed in the white robes, who are they, and from where have they come?"

14 And I said to him, "My lord, you know." And he said to me, "These are the ones who come out of the great tribulation, and they have washed their robes and made them white in the blood of the Lamb.

15 "For this reason, they are before the throne of God; and they serve Him day and night in His temple; and He who sits on the throne shall spread His tabernacle over them.

16 "They shall hunger no more, neither thirst anymore; neither shall the sun beat down on them, nor any heat;

17 for the Lamb in the center of the throne shall be their shepherd, and shall guide them to springs of the water of life; and God shall wipe every tear from their eyes."

CHAPTER 8

And when He broke the seventh seal, there was silence in heaven for about half an hour.

2 And I saw the seven angels who stand before God; and seven trumpets were given to them.

3 ¶ And another angel came and stood at the altar, holding a golden censer; and much incense was given to him, that he might add it to the prayers of all the saints upon the golden altar which was before the throne.

4 And the smoke of the incense, with the prayers of the saints, went up before God out of the angel's hand.

5 And the angel took the censer; and he filled it with the fire of the altar and threw it to the earth; and there followed peals of thunder and sounds and flashes of lightning and an earthquake.

6 ¶ And the seven angels who had the seven trumpets prepared themselves to sound them.

7 ¶ And the first sounded, and there came hail and fire, mixed with blood, and they were thrown to the earth; and a third of the earth was burned up, and a third of the trees were burned up, and all the green grass was burned up.

8 ¶ And the second angel sounded, and *something* like a great mountain burning with fire was thrown into the sea; and a third of the sea became blood;

9 and a third of the creatures, which were in the sea and had life, died; and a third of the ships were destroyed.

10 ¶ And the third angel sounded, and a great star fell from heaven, burning like a torch, and it fell on a third of the rivers and on the springs of waters;

11 and the name of the star is called Wormwood; and a third of the waters became wormwood; and many men died from the waters, because they were made bitter.

12 ¶ And the fourth angel sounded, and a third of the sun and a third of the moon and a third of the stars were smitten, so that a third of them might be darkened and the day might not shine for a third of it, and the night in the same way.

13 ¶ And I looked, and I heard an eagle flying in midheaven, saying with a loud voice, "Woe, woe, woe, to those who dwell on the earth, because of the remaining blasts of the trumpet of the three angels who are about to sound!"

CHAPTER 9

AND the fifth angel sounded, and I saw a star from heaven which had fallen to the earth; and the key of the bottomless pit was given to him.

2 And he opened the bottomless pit; and smoke went up out of the pit, like the smoke of a great furnace; and the sun and the air were darkened by the smoke of the pit.

3 And out of the smoke came forth locusts upon the earth; and power was given them, as the scorpions of the earth have power.

4 And they were told that they should not hurt the grass of the earth, nor any green thing, nor any tree, but only the men who do not have the seal of God on their foreheads.

5 And they were not permitted to kill anyone, but to torment for five months; and their torment was like the torment of a scorpion when it stings a man.

6 And in those days men will seek death and will not find it; and they will long to die and death flees from them.

7 And the appearance of the locusts was like horses prepared for battle; and on their heads, as it were, crowns like gold, and their faces were like the faces of men.

8 And they had hair like the hair of women, and their teeth were like *the teeth* of lions.

9 And they had breastplates like breastplates of iron; and the sound of their wings was like the sound of chariots, of many horses rushing to battle.

10 And they have tails like scorpions, and stings; and in their tails is their power to hurt men for five months.

11 They have as king over them, the angel of the abyss; his name in Hebrew is [11]Abaddon, and in the Greek he has the name Apollyon.

12 ¶ The first woe is past; behold, two woes are still coming after these things.

13 ¶ And the sixth angel sounded, and I heard a voice from the [12]four horns of the golden altar which is before God,

14 one saying to the sixth angel who had the trumpet, "Release the four angels who are bound at the great river Euphrates."

15 And the four angels, who had been prepared for the hour and day and month and year, were released, so that they might kill a third of mankind.

16 And the number of the armies of the horsemen was two hundred million; I heard the number of them.

17 And this is how I saw in the vision the horses and those who sat on them: *the riders* had breastplates *the color* of fire and of hyacinth and of brimstone; and the heads of the horses are like the heads of lions; and out of their mouths proceed fire and smoke and brimstone.

18 A third of mankind was killed by these three plagues, by the fire and the smoke and the brimstone, which proceeded out of their mouths.

19 For the power of the horses is in their mouths and in their tails; for their tails are like serpents and have heads; and with them they do harm.

20 And the rest of mankind, who were not killed by these plagues, did not repent of the works of their hands, so as not to worship demons, and the idols of gold and of silver and of brass and of stone and of wood, which can neither see nor hear nor walk;

21 and they did not repent of their murders nor of their sorceries nor of their immorality nor of their thefts.

CHAPTER 10

AND I saw another strong angel coming down out of heaven, clothed with a cloud; and the rainbow was upon his head, and his face was like the sun, and his feet like pillars of fire;

2 and he had in his hand a little book which was open. And he placed his right foot on the sea and his left on the land;

3 and he cried out with a loud voice, as when a lion roars; and when he had cried out, the seven peals of thunder uttered their voices.

---

[11] I.e., destruction   [12] Some ancient mss. do not contain *four*

4 And when the seven peals of thunder had spoken, I was about to write; and I heard a voice from heaven saying, "Seal up the things which the seven peals of thunder have spoken, and do not write them."

5 And the angel whom I saw standing on the sea and on the land lifted up his right hand to heaven,

6 and swore by Him who lives forever and ever, WHO CREATED HEAVEN AND THE THINGS IN IT, AND THE EARTH AND THE THINGS IN IT, AND THE SEA AND THE THINGS IN IT, that there shall be delay no longer,

7 but in the days of the voice of the seventh angel, when he is about to sound, then the mystery of God is finished, as He preached to His servants the prophets.

8 And the voice which I heard from heaven, *I heard* again speaking with me, and saying, "Go, take the book which is open in the hand of the angel who stands on the sea and on the land."

9 And I went to the angel, telling him to give me the little book. And he *said to me, "Take it, and eat it; and it will make your stomach bitter, but in your mouth it will be sweet as honey."

10 And I took the little book out of the angel's hand and ate it, and it was in my mouth sweet as honey; and when I had eaten it, my stomach was made bitter.

11 And they *said to me, "You must prophesy again concerning many peoples and nations and tongues and kings."

CHAPTER 11

AND there was given me a measuring rod like a staff; and someone said, "Rise and measure the temple of God, and the altar, and those who worship in it.

2 "And leave out the court which is outside the temple, and do not measure it, for it has been given to the nations; and they will tread under foot the holy city for forty-two months.

3 "And I will grant *authority* to my two witnesses, and they will prophesy for twelve hundred and sixty days, clothed in sackcloth."

4 These are the two olive trees and the two lampstands that stand before the Lord of the earth.

5 And if anyone desires to harm them, fire proceeds out of their mouth and devours their enemies; and if anyone would desire to harm them, in this manner he must be killed.

6 These have the power to shut up the sky, in order that rain may not fall during the days of their prophesying; and they have power over the waters to turn them into blood, and to smite the earth with every plague, as often as they desire.

7 And when they have finished their testimony, the beast that comes up out of the abyss will make war with them, and overcome them and kill them.

8 And their dead [13] bodies *will lie* in the street of the great city which [14] mystically is called Sodom and Egypt, where also their Lord was crucified.

9 And those from the peoples and tribes and tongues and nations *will* look at their dead [13] bodies for three and a half days, and will not permit their dead bodies to be laid in a tomb.

10 And those who dwell on the earth *will* rejoice over them and make merry; and they will send gifts to one another, because these two prophets tormented those who dwell on the earth.

11 And after the three and a half days the breath of life from God came into them, and they stood on their feet; and great fear fell upon those who were beholding them.

12 And they heard a loud voice from heaven saying to them, "Come up here." And they went up into heaven in the cloud, and their enemies beheld them.

13 And in that hour there was a great earthquake, and a tenth of the city fell; and seven thousand people were killed in the earthquake, and the rest were terrified and gave glory to the God of heaven.

14 ¶ The second woe is past; behold, the third woe is coming quickly.

15 ¶ And the seventh angel sounded; and there arose loud voices in heaven, saying,

¶ "The kingdom of the world has

---

[13] Some ancient mss. read body   [14] Lit., *spiritually*

become *the kingdom* of our Lord, and of His [15]Christ; and He will reign forever and ever."

16 And the twenty-four elders, who sit on their thrones before God, fell on their faces and worshiped God,

17 saying,

¶ "We give Thee thanks, O Lord God, the Almighty, who art and who wast, because Thou hast taken Thy great power and hast begun to reign.

18"And the nations were enraged, and Thy wrath came, and the time *came* for the dead to be judged, and *the time* to give their reward to Thy bond-servants the prophets and to the saints and to those who fear Thy name, the small and the great, and to destroy those who destroy the earth."

19 ¶ And the temple of God which is in heaven was opened; and the ark of His covenant appeared in His temple, and there were flashes of lightning and sounds and peals of thunder and an earthquake and a great hailstorm.

CHAPTER 12

AND a great sign appeared in heaven: a woman clothed with the sun, and the moon under her feet, and on her head a crown of twelve stars;

2 and she was with child; and she *cried out, being in labor and in pain to give birth.

3 And another sign appeared in heaven: and behold, a great red dragon having seven heads and ten horns, and on his heads *were* seven diadems.

4 And his tail *swept away a third of the stars of heaven, and threw them to the earth. And the dragon stood before the woman who was about to give birth, so that when she gave birth he might devour her child.

5 And she gave birth to a son, a male *child*, who is to rule all the nations with a rod of iron; and her child was caught up to God and to His throne.

6 And the woman fled into the wilderness where she *had a place prepared by God, so that there she might be nourished for one thousand two hundred and sixty days.

7 ¶ And there was war in heaven, Michael and his angels waging war

with the dragon. And the dragon and his angels waged war,

8 and they were not strong enough, and there was no longer a place found for them in heaven.

9 And the great dragon was thrown down, the serpent of old who is called the devil and Satan, who deceives the whole world; he was thrown down to the earth, and his angels were thrown down with him.

10 And I heard a loud voice in heaven, saying,

¶ "Now the salvation, and the power, and the kingdom of our God and the authority of His Christ have come, for the accuser of our brethren has been thrown down, who accuses them before our God day and night.

11"And they overcame him because of the blood of the Lamb and because of the word of their testimony, and they did not love their life even to death.

12"For this reason, rejoice, O heavens and you who dwell in them. Woe to the earth and the sea, because the devil has come down to you, having great wrath, knowing that he has *only* a short time."

13 ¶ And when the dragon saw that he was thrown down to the earth, he persecuted the woman who gave birth to the male *child*.

14 And the two wings of the great eagle were given to the woman, in order that she might fly into the wilderness to her place, where she *was nourished for a time and times and half a time, from the presence of the serpent.

15 And the serpent poured water like a river out of his mouth after the woman, so that he might cause her to be swept away with the flood.

16 And the earth helped the woman, and the earth opened its mouth and drank up the river which the dragon poured out of his mouth.

17 And the dragon was enraged with the woman, and went off to make war with the rest of her offspring, who keep the commandments of God and hold to the testimony of Jesus.

CHAPTER 13

AND he stood on the sand of the seashore.

¶ And I saw a beast coming up out of the sea, having ten horns and seven heads, and on his horns *were* ten diadems, and on his heads *were* blasphemous names.

2 And the beast which I saw was like a leopard, and his feet were *like those* of a bear, and his mouth like the mouth of a lion. And the dragon gave him his power and his throne and great authority.

3 And *I saw* one of his heads as if it had been slain, and his fatal wound was healed. And the whole earth was amazed *and followed* after the beast;

4 and they worshiped the dragon, because he gave his authority to the beast; and they worshiped the beast, saying, "Who is like the beast, and who is able to wage war with him?"

5 And there was given to him a mouth speaking arrogant words and blasphemies; and authority to act for forty-two months was given to him.

6 And he opened his mouth in blasphemies against God, to blaspheme His name and His tabernacle, *that is,* those who dwell in heaven.

7 And it was given to him to make war with the saints and to overcome them; and authority over every tribe and people and tongue and nation was given to him.

8 And all who dwell on the earth will worship him, *everyone* whose name has not been [16]written from the foundation of the world in the book of life of the Lamb who has been slain.

9 If anyone has an ear, let him hear.

10 If anyone [17]*is destined* for captivity, to captivity he goes; if anyone kills with the sword, with the sword he must be killed. Here is the perseverance and the faith of the saints.

11 ¶ And I saw another beast coming up out of the earth; and he had two horns like a lamb, and he spoke as a dragon.

12 And he exercises all the authority of the first beast in his presence. And he makes the earth and those who dwell in it to worship the first beast, whose fatal wound was healed.

13 And he performs great signs, so that he even makes fire come down out of heaven to the earth in the presence of men.

14 And he deceives those who dwell on the earth because of the signs which it was given him to perform in the presence of the beast, telling those who dwell on the earth to make an image to the beast who *had the wound of the sword and has come to life.

15 And there was given to him to give breath to the image of the beast, that the image of the beast might even [18]speak and cause as many as do not worship the image of the beast to be killed.

16 And he causes all, the small and the great, and the rich and the poor, and the free men and the slaves, to be given a mark on their right hand, or on their forehead,

17 and *he provides* that no one should be able to buy or to sell, except the one who has the mark, *either* the name of the beast or the number of his name.

18 Here is wisdom. Let him who has understanding calculate the number of the beast, for the number is that of a man; and his number is [19]six hundred and sixty-six.

CHAPTER 14

A ND I looked, and behold, the Lamb *was* standing on Mount Zion, and with Him one hundred and forty-four thousand, having His name and the name of His Father written on their foreheads.

2 And I heard a voice from heaven, like the sound of many waters and like the sound of loud thunder, and the voice which I heard *was* like *the sound* of harpists playing on their harps.

3 And they *sang a new song before the throne and before the four living creatures and the elders; and no one could learn the song except the one hundred and forty-four thousand who had been purchased from the earth.

4 These are the ones who have not been defiled with women, for they [20]have kept themselves chaste. These *are* the ones who follow the Lamb wherever He goes. These have been

[16] Or, *written in the book . . . slain from the foundation of the world*   [17] Or, *leads into captivity*

[18] Some ancient mss. read *speak, and he will cause*   [19] Some mss. read 616   [20] Lit., *are chaste men*

purchased from among men as first fruits to God and to the Lamb.

5 And no lie was found in their mouth; they are blameless.

6 ¶ And I saw another angel flying in midheaven, having an eternal gospel to preach to those who live on the earth, and to every nation and tribe and tongue and people;

7 and he said with a loud voice, "Fear God, and give Him glory, because the hour of His judgment has come; and worship Him who made the heaven and the earth and sea and springs of waters."

8 ¶ And another angel, a second one, followed, saying, "Fallen, fallen is Babylon the great, she who has made all the nations drink of the wine of the passion of her immorality."

9 ¶ And another angel, a third one, followed them, saying with a loud voice, "If anyone worships the beast and his image, and receives a mark on his forehead or upon his hand,

10 he also will drink of the wine of the wrath of God, which is mixed in full strength in the cup of His anger; and he will be tormented with fire and brimstone in the presence of the holy angels and in the presence of the Lamb.

11 "And the smoke of their torment goes up forever and ever; and they have no rest day and night, those who worship the beast and his image, and whoever receives the mark of his name."

12 Here is the perseverance of the saints who keep the commandments of God and their faith in Jesus.

13 ¶ And I heard a voice from heaven, saying, "Write, 'Blessed are the dead who die in the Lord from now on!' " "Yes," says the Spirit, "that they may rest from their labors, for their deeds follow with them."

14 ¶ And I looked, and behold, a white cloud, and sitting on the cloud *was* one like [21]a son of man, having a golden crown on His head, and a sharp sickle in His hand.

15 And another angel came out of the temple, crying out with a loud voice to Him who sat on the cloud, "Put in your sickle and reap, because

the hour to reap has come, because the harvest of the earth is ripe."

16 And He who sat on the cloud swung His sickle over the earth; and the earth was reaped.

17 ¶ And another angel came out of the temple which is in heaven, and he also had a sharp sickle.

18 And another angel, the one who has power over fire, came out from the altar; and he called with a loud voice to him who had the sharp sickle, saying, "Put in your sharp sickle, and gather the clusters from the vine of the earth, because her grapes are ripe."

19 And the angel swung his sickle to the earth, and gathered *the clusters from* the vine of the earth, and threw them into the great wine press of the wrath of God.

20 And the wine press was trodden outside the city, and blood came out from the wine press, up to the horses' bridles, for a distance of [22]two hundred miles.

CHAPTER 15

AND I saw another sign in heaven, great and marvelous, seven angels who had seven plagues, *which are* the last, because in them the wrath of God is finished.

2 ¶ And I saw, as it were, a sea of glass mixed with fire, and those who had come off victorious from the beast and from his image and from the number of his name, standing on the sea of glass, holding harps of God.

3 And they *sang the song of Moses the bond-servant of God and the song of the Lamb, saying,

¶ "Great and marvelous are Thy works,

O Lord God, the Almighty;

Righteous and true are Thy ways,

Thou King of the [23]nations.

4 "Who will not fear, O Lord, and glorify Thy name?

For Thou alone art holy;

For ALL THE NATIONS WILL COME AND WORSHIP BEFORE THEE,

For Thy righteous acts have been revealed."

5 ¶ After these things I looked, and

[21] Or, *the Son of Man*

[22] Lit., *sixteen hundred stadia.* A stadion was about six hundred feet.   [23] Some ancient mss. read *ages*

the temple of the tabernacle of testimony in heaven was opened,

6 and the seven angels who had the seven plagues came out of the temple, clothed in [24]linen, clean *and* bright, and girded around their breasts with golden girdles.

7 And one of the four living creatures gave to the seven angels seven golden bowls full of the wrath of God, who lives forever and ever.

8 And the temple was filled with smoke from the glory of God and from His power; and no one was able to enter the temple until the seven plagues of the seven angels were finished.

CHAPTER 16

AND I heard a loud voice from the temple, saying to the seven angels, "Go and pour out the seven bowls of the wrath of God into the earth."

2 ¶ And the first *angel* went and poured out his bowl into the earth; and it became a loathsome and malignant sore upon the men who had the mark of the beast and who worshiped his image.

3 ¶ And the second *angel* poured out his bowl into the sea, and it became blood like *that* of a dead man; and every living [25]thing in the sea died.

4 ¶ And the third *angel* poured out his bowl into the rivers and the springs of waters; and [26]they became blood.

5 And I heard the angel of the waters saying, "Righteous art Thou, who art and who wast, O Holy One, because Thou didst judge these things;

6 for they poured out the blood of saints and prophets, and Thou hast given them blood to drink. They deserve it."

7 And I heard the altar saying, "Yes, O Lord God, the Almighty, true and righteous are Thy judgments."

8 ¶ And the fourth *angel* poured out his bowl upon the sun; and it was given to it to scorch men with fire.

9 And men were scorched with fierce heat; and they blasphemed the name of God who has the power over these plagues; and they did not repent, so as to give Him glory.

10 ¶ And the fifth *angel* poured out his bowl upon the throne of the beast; and his kingdom became darkened; and they gnawed their tongues because of pain,

11 and they blasphemed the God of heaven because of their pains and their sores; and they did not repent of their deeds.

12 ¶ And the sixth *angel* poured out his bowl upon the great river, the Euphrates; and its water was dried up, that the way might be prepared for the kings from the east.

13 And I saw *coming* out of the mouth of the dragon and out of the mouth of the beast and out of the mouth of the false prophet, three unclean spirits like frogs;

14 for they are spirits of demons, performing signs, which go out to the kings of the whole world, to gather them together for the war of the great day of God, the Almighty.

15 ("Behold, I am coming like a thief. Blessed is the one who stays awake and keeps his garments, lest he walk about naked and men see his shame.")

16 And they gathered them together to the place which in Hebrew is called [27]Har-Magedon.

17 ¶ And the seventh *angel* poured out his bowl upon the air; and a loud voice came out of the temple from the throne, saying, "It is done."

18 And there were flashes of lightning and sounds and peals of thunder; and there was a great earthquake, such as there had not been since man came to be upon the earth, so great an earthquake *was it, and* so mighty.

19 And the great city was split into three parts, and the cities of the nations fell. And Babylon the great was remembered before God, to give her the cup of the wine of His fierce wrath.

20 And every island fled away, and the mountains were not found.

21 And huge hailstones, about [28]one hundred pounds each, *came down from heaven upon men; and men blasphemed God because of the plague of the hail, because its plague *was extremely severe.

---

[24] Some mss. read *stone*
[25] Lit., *soul*. Some ancient mss. read *thing, the things in the sea.* [26] Some ancient mss. read *it became*

[27] Some authorities read *Armageddon*
[28] Lit., *the weight of a talent*

CHAPTER 17

AND one of the seven angels who had the seven bowls came and spoke with me, saying, "Come here, I shall show you the judgment of the great harlot who sits on many waters,

2 with whom the kings of the earth committed *acts of* immorality, and those who dwell on the earth were made drunk with the wine of her immorality."

3 And he carried me away [29]in the Spirit into a wilderness; and I saw a woman sitting on a scarlet beast, full of blasphemous names, having seven heads and ten horns.

4 And the woman was clothed in purple and scarlet, and adorned with gold and precious stones and pearls, having in her hand a gold cup full of abominations and of the unclean things of her immorality,

5 and upon her forehead a name *was* written, a mystery, "BABYLON THE GREAT, THE MOTHER OF HARLOTS AND OF THE ABOMINATIONS OF THE EARTH."

6 And I saw the woman drunk with the blood of the saints, and with the blood of the witnesses of Jesus. And when I saw her, I wondered greatly.

7 And the angel said to me, "Why do you wonder? I shall tell you the mystery of the woman and of the beast that carries her, which has the seven heads and the ten horns.

8"The beast that you saw was and is not, and is about to come up out of the abyss and [30]to go to destruction. And those who dwell on the earth will wonder, whose name has not been written in the book of life from the foundation of the world, when they see the beast, that he was and is not and will come.

9"Here is the mind which has wisdom. The seven heads are seven mountains on which the woman sits,

10 and they are seven kings; five have fallen, one is, the other has not yet come; and when he comes, he must remain a little while.

11"And the beast which was and is not, is himself also an eighth, and is *one* of the seven, and he goes to destruction.

12"And the ten horns which you saw are ten kings, who have not yet received a kingdom, but they receive authority as kings with the beast for one hour.

13"These have one purpose and they give their power and authority to the beast.

14"These will wage war against the Lamb, and the Lamb will overcome them, because He is Lord of lords and King of kings, and those who are with Him *are the* called and chosen and faithful."

15 And he *said to me, "The waters which you saw where the harlot sits, are peoples and multitudes and nations and tongues.

16"And the ten horns which you saw, and the beast, these will hate the harlot and will make her desolate and naked, and will eat her flesh and will burn her up with fire.

17"For God has put it in their hearts to execute His purpose by having a common purpose, and by giving their kingdom to the beast, until the words of God should be fulfilled.

18"And the woman whom you saw is the great city, which reigns over the kings of the earth."

CHAPTER 18

AFTER these things I saw another angel coming down from heaven, having great authority, and the earth was illumined with his glory.

2 And he cried out with a mighty voice, saying, "Fallen, fallen is Babylon the great! And she has become a dwelling place of demons and a prison of every unclean spirit, and a prison of every unclean and hateful bird.

3"For all the nations [31]have drunk of the wine of the passion of her immorality, and the kings of the earth have committed *acts of* immorality with her, and the merchants of the earth have become rich by the wealth of her sensuality."

4 ¶ And I heard another voice from heaven, saying, "Come out of her, my people, that you may not participate in her sins and that you may not receive of her plagues;

5 for her sins have piled up as high as heaven, and God has remembered her iniquities.

6"Pay her back even as she has paid, and give back *to her* double according to her deeds; in the cup which she has mixed, mix twice as much for her.

7"To the degree that she glorified herself and lived sensuously, to the same degree give her torment and mourning; for she says in her heart, 'I SIT *as* A QUEEN AND I AM NOT A WIDOW, and will never see mourning.'

8"For this reason in one day her plagues will come, pestilence and mourning and famine, and she will be burned up with fire; for the Lord God who judges her is strong.

9"And the kings of the earth, who committed *acts of* immorality and lived sensuously with her, will weep and lament over her when they see the smoke of her burning,

10 standing at a distance because of the fear of her torment, saying, 'Woe, woe, the great city, Babylon, the strong city! For in one hour your judgment has come.'

11"And the merchants of the earth weep and mourn over her, because no one buys their cargoes any more;

12 cargoes of gold and silver and precious stones and pearls and fine linen and purple and silk and scarlet, and every *kind of* citron wood and every article of ivory and every article *made* from very costly wood and bronze and iron and marble,

13 and cinnamon and spice and incense and perfume and frankincense and wine and olive oil and fine flour and wheat and cattle and sheep, and *cargoes* of horses and chariots and slaves and human lives.

14"And the fruit you long for has gone from you, and all things that were luxurious and splendid have passed away from you and *men* will no longer find them.

15"The merchants of these things, who became rich from her, will stand at a distance because of the fear of her torment, weeping and mourning,

16 saying, 'Woe, woe, the great city, she who was clothed in fine linen and purple and scarlet, and adorned with gold and precious stones and pearls;

17 for in one hour such great wealth has been laid waste!' And every shipmaster and every passenger and sailor, and as many as make their living by the sea, stood at a distance,

18 and were crying out as they saw the smoke of her burning, saying, 'What *city* is like the great city?'

19"And they threw dust on their heads and were crying out, weeping and mourning, saying, 'Woe, woe, the great city, in which all who had ships at sea became rich by her wealth, for in one hour she has been laid waste!'

20"Rejoice over her, O heaven, and you saints and apostles and prophets, because God has pronounced judgment for you against her."

21 ¶ And a strong angel took up a stone like a great millstone and threw it into the sea, saying, "Thus will Babylon, the great city, be thrown down with violence, and will not be found any longer.

22"And the sound of harpists and musicians and flute-players and trumpeters will not be heard in you any longer; and no craftsman of any craft will be found in you any longer; and the sound of a mill will not be heard in you any longer;

23 and the light of a lamp will not shine in you any longer; and the voice of the bridegroom and bride will not be heard in you any longer; for your merchants were the great men of the earth, because all the nations were deceived by your sorcery.

24"And in her was found the blood of prophets and of saints and of all who have been slain on the earth."

CHAPTER 19

AFTER these things I heard, as it were, a loud voice of a great multitude in heaven, saying,

¶ "Hallelujah! Salvation and glory and power belong to our God;

2 BECAUSE HIS JUDGMENTS ARE TRUE AND RIGHTEOUS; for He has judged the great harlot who was corrupting the earth with her immorality, and HE HAS AVENGED THE BLOOD OF HIS BOND-SERVANTS ON HER."

3 And a second time they said, "Hallelujah! HER SMOKE RISES UP FOR-EVER AND EVER."

4 And the twenty-four elders and the four living creatures fell down and worshiped God who sits on the throne saying, "Amen. Hallelujah!"

5 And a voice came from the throne, saying,

¶ "Give praise to our God, all you His bond-servants, you who fear Him, the small and the great."

6 And I heard, as it were, the voice of a great multitude and as the sound of many waters and as the sound of mighty peals of thunder, saying,

¶ "Hallelujah! For the Lord our God, the Almighty, reigns.

7"Let us rejoice and be glad and give the glory to Him, for the marriage of the Lamb has come and His bride has made herself ready."

8 And it was given to her to clothe herself in fine linen, bright *and* clean; for the fine linen is the righteous acts of the saints.

9 And he *said to me, "Write, 'Blessed are those who are invited to the marriage supper of the Lamb.' " And he *said to me, "These are true words of God."

10 And I fell at his feet to worship him. And he *said to me, "Do not do that; I am a fellow servant of yours and your brethren who hold the testimony of Jesus; worship God. For the testimony of Jesus is the spirit of prophecy."

11 ¶ And I saw heaven opened; and behold, a white horse, and He who sat upon it *is* called Faithful and True; and in righteousness He judges and wages war.

12 And His eyes *are* a flame of fire, and upon His head *are* many diadems; and He has a name written *upon Him* which no one knows except Himself.

13 And *He is* clothed with a robe dipped in blood; and His name is called The Word of God.

14 And the armies which are in heaven, clothed in fine linen, white *and* clean, were following Him on white horses.

15 And from His mouth comes a sharp sword, so that with it He may smite the nations; and He will rule them with a rod of iron; and He treads the wine press of the fierce wrath of God, the Almighty.

16 And on His robe and on His thigh He has a name written, "KING OF KINGS, AND LORD OF LORDS."

17 ¶ And I saw an angel standing in the sun; and he cried out with a loud voice, saying to all the birds which fly in midheaven, "Come, assemble for the great supper of God;

18 in order that you may eat the flesh of kings and the flesh of [32]commanders and the flesh of mighty men and the flesh of horses and of those who sit on them and the flesh of all men, both free men and slaves, and small and great."

19 ¶ And I saw the beast and the kings of the earth and their armies, assembled to make war against Him who sat upon the horse, and against His army.

20 And the beast was seized, and with him the false prophet who performed the signs in his presence, by which he deceived those who had received the mark of the beast and those who worshiped his image; these two were thrown alive into the lake of fire which burns with brimstone.

21 And the rest were killed with the sword which came from the mouth of Him who sat upon the horse, and all the birds were filled with their flesh.

CHAPTER 20

A<small>ND</small> I saw an angel coming down from heaven, having the key of the abyss and a great chain in his hand.

2 And he laid hold of the dragon, the serpent of old, who is the devil and Satan, and bound him for a thousand years,

3 and threw him into the abyss, and shut *it* and sealed *it* over him, so that he should not deceive the nations any longer, until the thousand years were completed; after these things he must be released for a short time.

4 ¶ And I saw thrones, and they sat upon them, and judgment was given to them. And I *saw* the souls of those who had been beheaded because of the testimony of Jesus and because of the word of God, and those who had not worshiped the beast or his image, and had not received the mark upon their forehead and upon their hand; and they came to life and reigned with Christ for a thousand years.

5 The rest of the dead did not come to life until the thousand years were completed. This is the first resurrection.

6 Blessed and holy is the one who

---

[32] I.e., chiliarchs, in command of one thousand troops

has a part in the first resurrection; over these the second death has no power, but they will be priests of God and of Christ and will reign with Him for a thousand years.

7 ¶ And when the thousand years are completed, Satan will be released from his prison,

8 and will come out to deceive the nations which are in the four corners of the earth, Gog and Magog, to gather them together for the war; the number of them is like the sand of the seashore.

9 And they came up on the broad plain of the earth and surrounded the camp of the saints and the beloved city, and fire came down from heaven and devoured them.

10 And the devil who deceived them was thrown into the lake of fire and brimstone, where the beast and the false prophet are also; and they will be tormented day and night forever and ever.

11 ¶ And I saw a great white throne and Him who sat upon it, from whose presence earth and heaven fled away, and no place was found for them.

12 And I saw the dead, the great and the small, standing before the throne, and books were opened; and another book was opened, which is *the book* of life; and the dead were judged from the things which were written in the books, according to their deeds.

13 And the sea gave up the dead which were in it, and death and Hades gave up the dead which were in them; and they were judged, every one *of them* according to their deeds.

14 And death and Hades were thrown into the lake of fire. This is the second death, the lake of fire.

15 And if anyone's name was not found written in the book of life, he was thrown into the lake of fire.

CHAPTER 21

AND I saw a new heaven and a new earth; for the first heaven and the first earth passed away, and there is no longer *any* sea.

2 And I saw the holy city, new Jerusalem, coming down out of heaven from God, made ready as a bride adorned for her husband.

3 And I heard a loud voice from the throne, saying, "Behold, the tabernacle of God is among men, and He shall dwell among them, and they shall be His people, and God Himself shall be among them,[33]

4 and He shall wipe away every tear from their eyes; and there shall no longer be *any* death; there shall no longer be *any* mourning, or crying, or pain; the first things have passed away."

5 And He who sits on the throne said, "Behold, I am making all things new." And He *said, "Write, for these words are faithful and true."

6 And He said to me, "It is done. I am the Alpha and the Omega, the beginning and the end. I will give to the one who thirsts from the spring of the water of life without cost.

7 "He who overcomes shall inherit these things, and I will be his God and he will be My son.

8 "But for the cowardly and unbelieving and abominable and murderers and immoral persons and sorcerers and idolaters and all liars, their part *will be* in the lake that burns with fire and brimstone, which is the second death."

9 ¶ And one of the seven angels who had the seven bowls full of the seven last plagues, came and spoke with me, saying, "Come here, I shall show you the bride, the wife of the Lamb."

10 And he carried me away [34] in the Spirit to a great and high mountain, and showed me the holy city, Jerusalem, coming down out of heaven from God,

11 having the glory of God. Her brilliance was like a very costly stone, as a stone of crystal-clear jasper.

12 It had a great and high wall, with twelve gates, and at the gates twelve angels; and names *were* written on them, which are *those* of the twelve tribes of the sons of Israel.

13 *There were* three gates on the east and three gates on the north and three gates on the south and three gates on the west.

14 And the wall of the city had twelve foundation stones, and on

---

[33] Some ancient mss. add, and be *their God*   [34] Or, *in spirit*

them *were* the twelve names of the twelve apostles of the Lamb.

15 And the one who spoke with me had a gold measuring rod to measure the city, and its gates and its wall.

16 And the city is laid out as a square, and its length is as great as the width; and he measured the city with the rod, [35]fifteen hundred miles; its length and width and height are equal.

17 And he measured its wall, [36]seventy-two yards, *according to* human measurements, which are *also* angelic *measurements.*

18 And the material of the wall was jasper; and the city was pure gold, like clear glass.

19 The foundation stones of the city wall were adorned with every kind of precious stone. The first foundation stone was jasper; the second, sapphire; the third, chalcedony; the fourth, emerald;

20 the fifth, sardonyx; the sixth, sardius; the seventh, chrysolite; the eighth, beryl; the ninth, topaz; the tenth, chrysoprase; the eleventh, jacinth; the twelfth, amethyst.

21 And the twelve gates were twelve pearls; each one of the gates was a single pearl. And the street of the city was pure gold, like transparent glass.

22 And I saw no temple in it, for the Lord God, the Almighty, and the Lamb, are its temple.

23 And the city has no need of the sun or of the moon to shine upon it, for the glory of God has illumined it, and its lamp *is* the Lamb.

24 And the nations shall walk by its light, and the kings of the earth shall bring their glory into it.

25 And in the daytime (for there shall be no night there) its gates shall never be closed;

26 and they shall bring the glory and the honor of the nations into it;

27 and nothing unclean and no one who practices abomination and lying, shall ever come into it, but only those whose names are written in the Lamb's book of life.

CHAPTER 22

AND he showed me a river of the water of life, clear as crystal, coming from the throne of God and of [37]the Lamb,

2 in the middle of its street. And on either side of the river was the tree of life, bearing twelve [38]*kinds of* fruit, yielding its fruit every month; and the leaves of the tree were for the healing of the nations.

3 And there shall no longer be any curse; and the throne of God and of the Lamb shall be in it, and His bond-servants shall serve Him;

4 and they shall see His face, and His name *shall be* on their foreheads.

5 And there shall no longer be *any* night; and they shall not have need of the light of a lamp nor the light of the sun, because the Lord God shall illumine them; and they shall reign forever and ever.

6 ¶ And he said to me, "These words are faithful and true"; and the Lord, the God of the spirits of the prophets, sent His angel to show to His bond-servants the things which must shortly take place.

7"And behold, I am coming quickly. Blessed is he who heeds the words of the prophecy of this book."

8 ¶ And I, John, am the one who heard and saw these things. And when I heard and saw, I fell down to worship at the feet of the angel who showed me these things.

9 And he *said to me, "Do not do that; I am a fellow servant of yours and of your brethren the prophets and of those who heed the words of this book; worship God."

10 ¶ And he *said to me, "Do not seal up the words of the prophecy of this book, for the time is near.

11"Let the one who does wrong, still do wrong; and let the one who is filthy, still be filthy; and let the one who is righteous, still practice righteousness; and let the one who is holy, still keep himself holy."

12"Behold, I am coming quickly, and My reward *is* with Me, to render to every man according to what he has done.

13"I am the Alpha and the Omega, the first and the last, the beginning and the end."

---

[35] Lit., *twelve thousand stadia; a stadion was about 600 ft.*
[36] Lit., *one hundred forty-four cubits*

[37] Or, *the Lamb. In the middle of its street, and on either side of the river, was* [38] Or, *crops of fruit*

14 Blessed are those who wash their robes, that they may have the right to the tree of life, and may enter by the gates into the city.

15 Outside are the dogs and the sorcerers and the immoral persons and the murderers and the idolaters, and everyone who loves and practices lying.

16 ¶"I, Jesus, have sent My angel to testify to you these things for the churches. I am the root and the offspring of David, the bright morning star."

17 ¶ And the Spirit and the bride say, "Come." And let the one who hears say, "Come." And let the one who is thirsty come; let the one who wishes take the water of life without cost.

18 ¶ I testify to everyone who hears the words of the prophecy of this book: if anyone adds to them, God shall add to him the plagues which are written in this book;

19 and if anyone takes away from the words of the book of this prophecy, God shall take away his part from the tree of life and from the holy city, which are written in this book.

20 ¶ He who testifies to these things says, "Yes, I am coming quickly." Amen. Come, Lord Jesus.

21 ¶ The grace of the Lord Jesus be with [39]all. Amen.

[39] Some ancient mss. read *the saints*

CONCORDANCE

**New American
Standard**

The New American Standard
CONCORDANCE
to the Old and New Testaments

This is a collection of some principal *key words* in Scripture. The following format is used: *Key words* are immediately followed by explanatory words or synonyms. Under each key word examples are listed with text and reference. The *key word* is abbreviated in the text to its first letter; e.g., "abide" is "*a.*" Variants add suffixes; e.g., "abides" appears as "*a-s*" and "abiding" appears as "*a-ing.*"

– A –

Abandon *leave*
not *a* His people	1 Sam 12:22
not *a* my soul to	Ps 16:10
not *a* His people	Ps 94:14
a my soul to Hades	Acts 2:27

Abase *humble*
lofty will be *a-d*	Is 10:33
a the haughtiness	Is 13:11
a-d before all	Mal 2:9

Abate *decrease*
water was *a-ed*	Gen 8:8
his vigor *a-ed*	Deut 34:7

Abba *father*
A!Father	Mark 14:36
we cry out, *A*!	Rom 8:15

Abhor *despise, detest*
associates *a* me	Job 19:19
nations will *a* him	Prov 24:24
A what is evil	Rom 12:9

Abide *remain, stay*
LORD *a-s* forever	Ps 9:7
a in the shadow	Ps 91:1
a in My word	John 8:31
a in My love	John 15:9
now *a* faith	1 Cor 13:13
God *a-s* in us	1 John 4:12

Ability *power, strength*
According to their *a*	Ezra 2:69
a for serving	Dan 1:4

Able *qualified*
a to judge	1 Kin 3:9
a from these stones	Matt 3:9
Him who is *a*	Matt 10:28
a to separate us	Rom 8:39
what you are *a*	1 Cor 10:13
a to comprehend	Eph 3:18
a to save Him	Heb 5:7
One who is *a*	James 4:12

Abode *habitation*
Our *a* with him	John 14:23
their proper *a*	Jude 6

Abolish
not come to *a*	Matt 5:17
who *a-ed* death	2 Tim 1:10

Abominable *detestable*
committed *a* deeds	Ps 14:1
unbelieving and *a*	Rev 21:8

Abomination *hated thing*
a to the Egyptians	Ex 8:26
seen their *a-s*	Deut 29:17

a to the LORD	Prov 3:32
a of desolation	Matt 24:15

Abound *excel, plentiful*
faithful man will *a*	Prov 28:20
a in hope	Rom 15:13
all grace *a*	2 Cor 9:8

Above *over*
disciple is not *a*	Matt 10:24
a every name	Phil 2:9
exalts himself *a*	2 Thess 2:4

Absent *being away*
a from the Lord	2 Cor 5:6
a from the body	2 Cor 5:8

Abstain *refrain from*
a-ing from foods	1 Tim 4:3
a from fleshly lusts	1 Pet 2:11

Abundance *plenty, surplus*
seven years of *a*	Gen 41:34
a of Thy house	Ps 36:8
a of counselors	Prov 24:6
he who loves *a*	Eccl 5:10
the *a* of grace	Rom 5:17

Abundant *enough, plenteous*
come...find *a* water	2 Chr 32:4
a in loving kindness	Ps 86:5
comfort is *a*	2 Cor 1:5

Abundantly *plenteous*
they may breed *a*	Gen 8:17
will prosper you *a*	Deut 30:9

Abuse (n) *insulting speech*
hurling *a* at Him	Matt 27:39
was hurling *a*	Luke 23:39

Abuse (v) *hurt, molest*
a-d her all night	Judg 19:25
uncircumcised...*a*	1 Chr 10:4

Abusive *filthy, vulgar*
a speech from your	Col 3:8
strife, *a* language	1 Tim 6:4

Abyss *deep, depth*
descend into the *a*	Rom 10:7
key of the *a*	Rev 20:1

Accept *receive*
a the work of	Deut 33:11
the LORD *a-ed* Job	Job 42:9
hear the word and *a*	Mark 4:20
a one another	Rom 15:7

Acceptable *pleasing*
sacrifice, *a* to God	Rom 12:1
now is the *a* time	2 Cor 6:2
to God an *a* service	Heb 12:28

Access *approach, entry*
grant you free *a*	Zech 3:7
our *a* in one Spirit	Eph 2:18

Accompany *attach to, follow*
who *a* my lord	1 Sam 25:27
that *a* salvation	Heb 6:9

Accomplish *perform, realize*
a-ed deliverance	1 Sam 11:13
shall *a* my desire	1 Kin 5:9
God...*a-es* all things	Ps 57:2
a-ed redemption	Luke 1:68
I am *a-ing* a work	Acts 13:41
man can *a* much	James 5:16

Accord *agreement, union*
voices...with one *a*	Acts 4:24
multitudes with one *a*	Acts 8:6
one *a* they came	Acts 12:20

According
Moses did; *a* to all	Ex 40:16
a to his deeds	Matt 16:27
heirs *a* to promise	Gal 3:29
a to His riches	Phil 4:19

Account (n) *reckoning*
settled *a-s* with	Matt 25:19
who will give an *a*	Heb 13:17

Account (v) *reckon*
do not *a* this sin	Num 12:11
Thou hast taken *a* of	Ps 56:8

Accurately *correctly*
teaching *a*...things	Acts 18:25
handling *a*...word	2 Tim 2:15

Accursed *damned*
be thought *a*	Is 65:20
Depart...*a* ones	Matt 25:41
let him be *a*	Gal 1:8

Accusation *charge of wrong*
find a ground of *a*	Dan 6:4
What *a* do you	John 18:29
Do not receive an *a*	1 Tim 5:19

Accuse *testify against*
a-d his brother	Deut 19:18
He was being *a-d*	Matt 27:12
a you before the	John 5:45
unjustly *a-ing* us	3 John 10

Accuser *complainant*
they act as my *a-s*	Ps 109:4
instructing his *a-s*	Acts 23:30
when the *a-s* stood	Acts 25:18
a of our brethren	Rev 12:10

Acknowledge *confess*
I *a-d* my sin	Ps 32:5

all your ways *a* Him Prov 3:6
see fit to *a* God Rom 1:28

Acquainted *become familiar*
a with all my ways Ps 139:3
a with grief Is 53:3

Acquaintance *friend*
dread to my *a-s* Ps 31:11
relatives and *a-s* Luke 2:44
And all His *a-s* Luke 23:49

Acquire *get, purchase*
a property in it Gen 34:10
a wise counsel Prov 1:5
Do not *a* gold Matt 10:9

Acquit *declare innocent*
not *a* me of my guilt Job 10:14
A me of hidden *faults* Ps 19:12

Act (n) *deed, work*
a detestable *a* Lev 20:13
every abominable *a* Deut 12:31
the *a-s* of Solomon 1 Kin 11:41

Act (v) *behave*
I *a-ed* ignorantly 1 Tim 1:13
So speak and so *a* James 2:12
are *a-ing* faithfully 3 John 5

Action *behavior, work*
a-s of a…harlot Ezek 16:30
gird your minds for *a* 1 Pet 1:13

Add
a-ing to the wrath Neh 13:18
if anyone *a-s* to them Rev 22:18

Adjure *charge solemnly*
many times…I *a* 1 Kin 22:16
I *a* you by Jesus Acts 19:13

Administration
a of the province Dan 3:12
a of the mystery Eph 3:9

Admonish *warn*
not cease to *a* each Acts 20:31
able also to *a* one Rom 15:14
a-ing one another Col 3:16
a him as a brother 2 Thess 3:15

Adoption *acceptance*
spirit of *a* as sons Rom 8:15
receive the *a* as sons Gal 4:5
predestined us to *a* Eph 1:5

Adorn *array, clothe*
as a bride *a-s* herself Is 61:10
a-ed with beautiful Luke 21:5
a-ed with gold Rev 17:4
as a bride *a-ed* Rev 21:2

Adulterer
eye of the *a* waits Job 24:15
associate with *a-s* Ps 50:18
a-s God will judge Heb 13:4

Adulteress
a shall surely be Lev 20:10
a who flatters with Prov 2:16
mouth of an *a* Prov 22:14
shall be called an *a* Rom 7:3

Adultery
shall not commit *a* Ex 20:14
worn out by *a-ies* Ezek 23:43
woman commits *a* Matt 5:32
Do not commit *a* Luke 18:20

Advance *ahead, beyond*
old, *a-d* in age Gen 24:1
have told you in *a* Matt 24:25
a-ing in Judaism Gal 1:14

Advantage *benefit, profit*
What *a* does man Eccl 1:3
a that I go away John 16:7
what *a* has the Jew Rom 3:1
no *a* be taken of us 2 Cor 2:11

Adversary *foe, opponent*
an *a* to Solomon 1 Kin 11:14
a-ies and my enemies Ps 27:2
crush his *a-ies* Ps 89:23
there are many *a-ies* 1 Cor 16:9
Your *a*, the devil 1 Pet 5:8

Adversity *distress, misfortune*
death and *a* Deut 30:15
not accept *a* Job 2:10
falls into *a* Prov 13:17

Advice *counsel*
forsook the *a* 1 Kin 12:13
a of the cunning Job 5:13
have followed my *a* Acts 27:21

Adviser *counselor*
with his *a* Ahuzzath Gen 26:26
Pharaoh's wisest *a-s* Is 19:11

Advocate *defender, witness*
my *a* is on high Job 16:19
A with the Father 1 John 2:1

Affection *devotion, love*
in your own *a-s* 2 Cor 6:12
a of Christ Jesus Phil 1:8

Afflict (v) *oppress, trouble*
a with hard labor Ex 1:11
not *a* any widow Ex 22:22
Egyptians…*a-ed* us Deut 26:6
the wicked *a* them 2 Sam 7:10
He was *a-ed* Is 63:9
were sick or *a-ed* Acts 5:16
those who *a* you 2 Thess 1:6
a-ed, ill-treated Heb 11:37

Afflicted (n) *troubled*
save an *a* people 2 Sam 22:28
to catch the *a* Ps 10:9
LORD supports the *a* Ps 147:6
days of the *a* Prov 15:15
good news to the *a* Is 61:1

Affliction *oppression*
my *a* and the toil Gen 31:42
the bread of *a* Deut 16:3
LORD saw the *a* 2 Kin 14:26
afflicted in their *a* Job 36:15
Look upon my *a* Ps 25:18
a or persecution Mark 4:17
healed of her *a* Mark 5:29
a-s await me Acts 20:23

out of much *a* 2 Cor 2:4
to suffer *a* 1 Thess 3:4

Afraid *dreading, fearful*
a because…naked Gen 3:10
a to look at God Ex 3:6
Whoever is *a* Judg 7:3
not *a* of the snow Prov 31:21
a to swear Eccl 9:2
a to take Mary Matt 1:20
were *a* of Him Mark 11:18
Do not be *a*, Mary Luke 1:30
a of those who kill Luke 12:4
a, lest the serpent 2 Cor 11:3
Do not be *a* Rev 1:17

Age *period, year*
David reached old *a* 1 Chr 23:1
either in this *a* Matt 12:32
sons of this *a* are Luke 16:8
in the *a-s* to come Eph 2:7
hidden…*past a-s* Col 1:26

Aged *old*
Wisdom is…*a* men Job 12:12
refined, *a* wine Is 25:6
Paul, the *a* Philem 9

Agony *anguish*
a has seized me 2 Sam 1:9
in *a* in this flame Luke 16:24
the *a* of death Acts 2:24

Agree *consent*
if two of you *a* Matt 18:19
did you not *a* Matt 20:13
have *a-d* together Acts 5:9
a with sound words 1 Tim 6:3

Agreement *accord*
an *a* in writing Neh 9:38
Saul was in hearty *a* Acts 8:1
three are in *a* 1 John 5:8

Air *breeze, sky*
no *a* can come Job 41:16
birds of the *a* Matt 6:26
not beating the *a* 1 Cor 9:26
power of the *a* Eph 2:2

Alabaster *whitish stone*
stones, and *a* 1 Chr 29:2
brought an *a* vial Luke 7:37

Alarm (n) *danger, warning*
shout of *a* at noon Jer 20:16
a on My…mountain Joel 2:1

Alarm (v) *frighten, warn*
he is not *a-ed* Job 40:23
interpretation *a* you Dan 4:19
thoughts *a-ed* him Dan 5:6
in no way *a-ed* by Phil 1:28

Alert (n) *watch*
be on the *a* Matt 24:42
be *a* and sober 1 Thess 5:6

Alert (v) *be watchful*
keeping *a* in it Col 4:2
let us be *a* 1 Thess 5:6

Alien *foreigner, stranger*
love for the *a* Deut 10:19

Our houses to *a-s* — Lam 5:2
no longer…*a-s* — Eph 2:19
I urge you as *a-s* — 1 Pet 2:11

Alienate *estrange*
Lest I be *a-d* — Jer 6:8
were formerly *a-d* — Col 1:21

Alive
Is your father still *a* — Gen 43:7
go down *a* to Sheol — Ps 55:15
when He was…*a* — Matt 27:63
heard…He was *a* — Mark 16:11
presented Himself *a* — Acts 1:3
all shall be made *a* — 1 Cor 15:22
made us *a* together — Eph 2:5
I am *a* forevermore — Rev 1:18

Allegiance *loyalty*
pledged *a* to King — 1 Chr 29:24
he pledged his *a* — Ezek 17:18

Alliance *agreement*
formed a marriage *a* — 1 Kin 3:1
after an *a* is made — Dan 11:23

Allied *joined*
a…by marriage — 2 Chr 18:1
throne of…*a* — Ps 94:20

Allot *apportion, divide*
a Him a portion — Is 53:12
a-ted to each…faith — Rom 12:3

Allotment *portion*
as a perpetual *a* — Num 18:19
Jacob is the *a* — Deut 32:9
set apart the…*a* — Ezek 48:20

Allow *permit*
not *a* the destroyer — Ex 12:23
a Thy Holy One — Ps 16:10
not be *a-ed* to live — Acts 22:22
a you to be tempted — 1 Cor 10:13

Almighty *all-powerful*
I am God *A* — Gen 17:1
A has afflicted me — Ruth 1:21
A was yet with me — Job 29:5
Lord God, the *A* — Rev 4:8

Almond
a and plane trees — Gen 30:37
and it bore ripe *a-s* — Num 17:8

Alms *charity*
therefore you give *a* — Matt 6:2
bring *a* to my nation — Acts 24:17

Alone
So He let him *a* — Ex 4:26
not live on bread *a* — Matt 4:4
He was praying *a* — Luke 9:18
receiving but you *a* — Phil 4:15
and not by faith *a* — James 2:24

Aloud *joyful, piercing*
read *a* from the book — Neh 13:1
Sing *a* with gladness — Jer 31:7
began to weep *a* — Acts 20:37

Altar *place of sacrifice*
Moses built an *a* — Ex 17:15
fire on the *a* — Lev 6:9
Gideon built an *a* — Judg 6:24

go to the *a* of God — Ps 43:4
offering at the *a* — Matt 5:23
a that sanctifies — Matt 23:19
we have an *a* — Heb 13:10

Always *ever, forever*
He will not *a* strive — Ps 103:9
fear of the LORD *a* — Prov 23:17
will I *a* be angry — Is 57:16
I am with you *a* — Matt 28:20
poor you *a* have — Mark 14:7
Rejoice in the Lord *a* — Phil 4:4
I shall *a* be ready — 2 Pet 1:12

Amazed *astonished, astounded*
are *a* at His rebuke — Job 26:11
heard Him were *a* — Luke 2:47
whole earth was *a* — Rev 13:3

Amazement *astonishment*
a came upon them — Luke 4:36
with wonder and *a* — Acts 3:10

Ambassador *envoy*
a-s of peace weep — Is 33:7
a-s for Christ — 2 Cor 5:20
an *a* in chains — Eph 6:20

Ambition *design, intention*
out of selfish *a* — Phil 1:17
a to lead a quiet — 1 Thess 4:11
jealousy…selfish *a* — James 3:14

Ambush (n) *cover, hiding place*
a for the city — Josh 8:2
Israel set men in *a* — Judg 20:29
Place men in *a* — Jer 51:12

Ambush (v) *lie in wait*
going to *a* the city — Josh 8:4
a the innocent — Prov 1:11
a their own lives — Prov 1:18

Amen *so be it*
the LORD forever! *A* — Ps 89:52
glory forever…*A* — Phil 4:20
A, Come, Lord Jesus — Rev 22:20

Amount *measure*
daily *a* of bricks — Ex 5:19
a of your valuation — Lev 27:23
large *a* of bronze — 1 Chr 18:8

Ancestors *forefathers*
blessings of my *a* — Gen 49:26
iniquities of their *a* — Jer 11:10

Anchor
they cast *a-s* — Acts 27:29
an *a* of the soul — Heb 6:19

Ancient *aged, old*
the records are *a* — 1 Chr 4:22
O *a* doors — Ps 24:9
the *a-s* were told — Matt 5:21
from *a* generations — Acts 15:21
not spare the *a* world — 2 Pet 2:5

Angel *divine messenger*
send His *a* before — Gen 24:7
an *a* to Jerusalem — 1 Chr 21:15
Praise Him, all His *a-s* — Ps 148:2
a of His presence — Is 63:9
give His *a-s* charge — Matt 4:6

a Gabriel was sent — Luke 1:26
they are like *a-s* — Luke 20:36
like the face of an *a* — Acts 6:15
worship of the *a-s* — Col 2:18
entertained *a-s* — Heb 13:2
a of the church — Rev 2:1

Angel of the Lord
a called to Abraham — Gen 22:15
I have seen the *a* — Judg 6:22
a destroying — 1 Chr 21:12
a commanded him — Matt 1:24
a appeared to Joseph — Matt 2:13
a…opened the gates — Acts 5:19

Anger *indignation, wrath*
My *a* will be kindled — Ex 22:24
from His burning *a* — Deut 13:17
a kills the simple — Job 5:2
not rebuke me in Thine *a* — Ps 6:1
a is but for a moment — Ps 30:5
a man *given* to *a* — Prov 22:24
a of the LORD — Is 5:25
sun go down…*a* — Eph 4:26
slow to *a* — James 1:19

Angry *enraged, indignant*
Why are you *a* — Gen 4:6
lest He become *a* — Ps 2:12
a beyond measure — Is 64:9
a with his brother — Matt 5:22
Be *a*…do not sin — Eph 4:26

Anguish *distress, pain*
My heart is in *a* — Ps 55:4
A has seized us — Jer 6:24
and *a* of heart — 2 Cor 2:4

Animal *beast, creature*
lies with an *a* — Ex 22:19
the fat of the *a* — Lev 7:25
a blemished *a* — Mal 1:14
like unreasoning *a-s* — 2 Pet 2:12

Annihilate *destroy*
to *a* all the Jews — Esth 3:13
to destroy and *a* — Dan 11:44
let it be *a-d* — Zech 11:9

Announce *proclaim*
I shall *a* My words — Jer 18:2
a-d…the Righteous — Acts 7:52

Annul *dismiss, make void*
he shall *a* her vow — Num 30:8
not *a* Thy covenant — Jer 14:21
a-s one of the least — Matt 5:19

Anoint *sprinkle oil upon*
a them and ordain — Ex 28:41
LORD *a-ed*…king — 1 Sam 15:17
a the most holy *place* — Dan 9:24
did not *a* My head — Luke 7:46
and *a-ed* my eyes — John 9:11
a-ed Him…Spirit — Acts 10:38

Anointed (adj) *consecrated*
if the *a* priest sins — Lev 4:3
a cherub who — Ezek 28:14

Anointed (n) *consecrated one*
he is the LORD's *a* — 1 Sam 24:10

against His *a*   Ps 2:2

Anointing (adj) *consecration*
spices for the *a* oil   Ex 25:6
for the LORD's *a* oil   Lev 10:7

Anointing (n) *consecration*
a shall qualify them   Ex 40:15
His *a* teaches you   1 John 2:27

Answer (n) *response*
the king sent an *a*   Ezra 4:17
amazed at…His *a-s*   Luke 2:47

Answer (v) *respond*
The LORD *a-ed* me   Ps 118:5
Jesus *a-ing* said   Matt 3:15
who *a-s* back to God   Rom 9:20

Ant *insect*
to the *a*, O sluggard   Prov 6:6
a-s are not a strong   Prov 30:25

Antelope *animal*
Like an *a* in a net   Is 51:20

Antichrist *foe of Christ*
a-s have arisen   1 John 2:18
This is the *a*   1 John 2:22
deceiver and the *a*   2 John 7

Anxiety *sorrow*
There is *a* by the sea   Jer 49:23
casting all your *a*   1 Pet 5:7

Anxious *concern, worry*
not be *a* in…drought   Jer 17:8
not be *a* for your life   Matt 6:25
not be *a* for tomorrow   Matt 6:34
a can add a *single*   Luke 12:25
Be *a* for nothing   Phil 4:6

Apart *separate*
tear their fetters *a*   Ps 2:3
a from your Father   Matt 10:29
a from Me you can   John 15:5

Apostasy *faithlessness*
Turned away in…*a*   Jer 8:5
unless the *a* comes   2 Thess 2:3

Apostle *sent with authority*
the twelve *a-s*   Matt 10:2
named as *a-s*   Luke 6:13
called *as* an *a*   Rom 1:1
fit to be called an *a*   1 Cor. 15:9
He gave some *as a-s*   Eph 4:11
a-s of the Lamb   Rev 21:14

Apostleship *office of apostle*
received grace and *a*   Rom 1:5
seal of my *a*   1 Cor 9:2

Apparel *clothing, garment*
majestic in His *a*   Is 63:1
put on his royal *a*   Acts 12:21

Appeal *ask, entreat*
standing and *a-ing*   Acts 16:9
Paul *a-ed* to be held   Acts 25:21
a to him as a father   1 Tim 5:1

Appear *become visible*
LORD *a-ed* to Abram   Gen 12:7
a-ed on the wings   2 Sam 22:11
and *a-ed* to many   Matt 27:53

who, *a-ing* in glory   Luke 9:31
a-ed to them tongues   Acts 2:3
a-ing of the glory   Titus 2:13
Chief Shepherd *a-s*   1 Pet 5:4

Appearance *countenance*
handsome in…*a*   Gen 39:6
at the outward *a*   1 Sam 16:7
judge according to *a*   John 7:24
a of His coming   2 Thess 2:8

Appease *moderate, mollify*
I will *a* him   Gen 32:20
have *a-d* My wrath   Zech 6:8

Appetite *desire, hunger*
a of the young lions   Job 38:39
man of *great a*   Prov 23:2
whose god is *their a*   Phil 3:19

Apple *fruit*
as the *a* of the eye   Ps 17:8
touches the *a* of His   Zech 2:8

Appoint *assign, commission*
I will *a* over you   Lev 26:16
who *a-ed* Moses   1 Sam 12:6
a magistrates and   Ezra 7:25
a-ed elders for them   Acts 14:23
For the Law *a-s* men   Heb 7:28

Apportion *distribute*
a the inheritance   Num 34:29
a this land   Josh 13:7

Appropriate *suitable*
blessing *a* to him   Gen 49:28
a to repentance   Acts 26:20

Approval *consent*
loved the *a* of men   John 12:43
give hearty *a* to   Rom 1:32

Approve *accept, attest*
the Lord does not *a*   Lam 3:36
standing by *a-ing*   Acts 22:20
present yourself *a-d*   2 Tim 2:15

Archangel
voice of *the a*   1 Thess 4:16
But Michael the *a*   Jude 9

Argue *dispute, question*
I will *a* my ways   Job 13:15
Pharisees…*a* with   Mark 8:11
a-ing with the…*Jews*   Acts 9:29

Argument *disagreement*
Please hear my *a*   Job 13:6
a arose among them   Luke 9:46

Arise *rise, stand*
A, walk about the   Gen 13:17
will *a* and play   Deut 31:16
arose and tore his robe   Job 1:20
when God *a-s*   Job 31:14
A, O LORD; save me   Ps 3:7
a-n anyone greater   Matt 11:11
false prophets will *a*   Matt 24:11
arose from the dead   Acts 10:41
a from the dead   Eph 5:14

Ark *chest, vessel*
into the *a* of Noah   Gen 7:9

a of the covenant   Josh 4:7
Noah entered the *a*   Matt 24:38

Arm (n) *part of body*
the everlasting *a-s*   Deut 33:27
a-s of the wicked   Ps 37:17
His holy *a* have gained   Ps 98:1
be carried in the *a-s*   Is 60:4
with an uplifted *a*   Acts 13:17

Arm (v) *mobilize*
A men from among   Num 31:3
a-ed with iron   2 Sam 23:7

Armed (adj) *mobilized*
the *a* men went   Josh 6:13
their *a* camps   1 Sam 28:1
like an *a* man   Prov 6:11

Armor *protective device*
a joint of the *a*   1 Kin 22:34
put on…*a* of light   Rom 13:12
full *a* of God   Eph 6:11

Army *host, war*
like the *a* of God   1 Chr 12:22
a ready for battle   2 Chr 26:11
officers of the *a*   Neh 2:9
exceedingly great *a*   Ezek 37:10
and against His *a*   Rev 19:19

Aroma *odor*
a soothing *a*   Gen 8:21
a from life to life   2 Cor 2:16
as a fragrant *a*   Eph 5:2

Arouse *raise, stir*
a-s for you the spirits   Is 14:9
He will *a* His zeal   Is 42:13
Jews *a-d* the devout   Acts 13:50

Arrange *set in order*
a what belongs on it   Ex 40:4
thus he had *a-d* it   Acts 20:13

Array (n) *arrangement, order*
went up in martial *a*   Ex 13:18
in battle *a*   Josh 4:12
Worship…in holy *a*   1 Chr 16:29

Array (v) *adorn, clothe*
Israel *a-ed* for battle   Judg 20:20
God so *a-s* the grass   Matt 6:30
a-ed Him in a purple   John 19:2

Arrest *restrain*
he *a-ed* Jeremiah   Jer 37:13
and clubs to *a* Me   Matt 26:55
proceeded to *a* Peter   Acts 12:3

Arrogance *pride*
Pride and *a* and   Prov 8:13
a, pride, and fury   Is 16:6
boast in your *a*   James 4:16

Arrogant *proud*
But a fool is *a*   Prov 14:16
Knowledge makes *a*   1 Cor 8:1
speaking…*a words*   2 Pet 2:18

Arrow *dart, missile*
shot an *a* past him   1 Sam 20:36
a cannot make him   Job 41:28
broke the flaming *a-s*   Ps 76:3
tongue is a deadly *a*   Jer 9:8

target for the *a*   Lam 3:12

Art *craft*
with their secret *a-s*   Ex 7:22
the perfumers' *a*   2 Chr 16:14

Article *object, vessel*
a-s of silver   Gen 24:53
of every precious *a*   Hos 13:15
every *a* of ivory   Rev 18:12

Ascend *go up*
If I *a* to heaven   Ps 139:8
Who has *a-ed* into   Prov 30:4
has *a-ed* into heaven   John 3:13
a-ed to the Father   John 20:17

Ascent *hill, rise*
by the *a* of Heres   Judg 8:13
a of the...Olives   2 Sam 15:30

Ascribe *attribute*
A to the LORD   1 Chr 16:28
a righteousness to   Job 36:3

Ash
but dust and *a-es*   Gen 18:27
a-es were poured   1 Kin 13:5
proverbs of *a-es*   Job 13:12
roll in *a-es*   Jer 6:26
sackcloth and *a-es*   Luke 10:13
a-es of a heifer   Heb 9:13

Ashamed *embarrassed*
and were not *a*   Gen 2:25
a when He comes   Luke 9:26
not *a* of the gospel   Rom 1:16
God is not *a*   Heb 11:16
let him not feel *a*   1 Pet 4:16

Ask *appeal, beg, inquire*
whatever you *a*   Ruth 3:11
A a sign for yourself   Is 7:11
A rain...the LORD   Zech 10:1
A, and it shall be   Matt 7:7
a...believing   Matt 21:22
Jews *a* for signs   1 Cor 1:22
let him *a* of God   James 1:5

Asleep *death, rest*
they fall *a*   Ps 90:5
not died, but is *a*   Matt 9:24
Lazarus...fallen *a*   John 11:11
fallen *a* in Jesus   1 Thess 4:14

Assail *attack*
will you *a* a man   Ps 62:3
storm was *a-ing us*   Acts 27:20

Assemble *gather*
a all the congregation   Lev 8:3
David *a-ed* all Israel   1 Chr 13:5
A...the mountains   Amos 3:9
whole city *a-ed* to   Acts 13:44

Assembly *congregation*
the people of the *a*   Lev 16:33
Or calls an *a*   Job 11:10
a of the righteous   Ps 1:5
proclaim a solemn *a*   Joel 2:15
I delight in...*a-ies*   Amos 5:21
the *a* was divided   Acts 23:7
comes into your *a*   James 2:2

Associate (n) *colleague*
All my *a-s* abhor me   Job 19:19
high priest and...*a-s*   Acts 5:21

Associate (v) *identify with*
not *a* with a man   Prov 22:24
but *a* with the lowly   Rom 12:16
not *a* with him   2 Thess 3:14

Assurance *confirmation*
a of understanding   Col 2:2
full *a* of faith   Heb 10:22
a of *things* hoped for   Heb 11:1

Assure *confirm*
I *a* you before God   Gal 1:20
shall *a* our heart   1 John 3:19

Astonished *amazed*
a at His teaching   Matt 22:33
were utterly *a*   Mark 7:37

Astounded *astonished*
prophets will be *a*   Jer 4:9
were completely *a*   Mark 5:24

Astray *erring, wandering*
like sheep have gone *a*   Is 53:6
led my people *a*   Jer 23:32
a from the faith   1 Tim 6:21
go *a* in their heart   Heb 3:10

Atonement *expiation*
make *a* for him   Lev 4:35
how can I make *a*   2 Sam 21:3

Attack (n) *assault*
king ready for the *a*   Job 15:24
joined in the *a*   Acts 24:9

Attack (v) *assault, fall upon*
adversary who *a-s*   Num 10:9
and *a-ed* the camp   Judg 8:11
no man will *a* you   Acts 18:10

Attain *acquire*
I cannot *a* to it   Ps 139:6
a to the resurrection   Phil 3:11

Attend *pay attention to*
a to your priesthood   Num 18:7
who *a* regularly   1 Cor 9:13
ears *a* to their prayer   1 Pet 3:12

Attendant *helper, servant*
the *a* of Moses   Num 11:28
a-s of...bridegroom   Mark 2:19

Attention *heed, regard*
no *a* to false words   Ex 5:9
pays *a* to falsehood   Prov 29:12

Attire *covering, dress*
in his military *a*   2 Sam 20:8
Him in holy *a*   2 Chr 20:21

Attitude *frame of mind*
Have this *a* in   Phil 2:5
have a different *a*   Phil 3:15

Author *source*
a of their salvation   Heb 2:10
a...perfecter of faith   Heb 12:2

Authority *power, right*
submit...to her *a*   Gen 16:9

Who gave Him *a*   Job 34:13
entrust him with your *a*   Is 22:21
a on earth to forgive   Matt 9:6
All *a*...given to Me   Matt 28:18
Son of Man has *a*   Luke 5:24
no *a* except from God   Rom 13:1

Avenge *revenge*
Shall I not *a* Myself   Jer 5:9
a-ing our blood   Rev 6:10

Avenger *revenger*
lest the *a* of blood   Deut 19:6
Lord is *the a*   1 Thess 4:6

Avoid *refuse*
A it, do not pass by   Prov 4:15
a-ing...chatter   1 Tim 6:20

Await *wait*
afflictions *a* me   Acts 20:23
who eagerly *a* Him   Heb 9:28

Awake *be attentive, watch*
awoke from his sleep   Gen 28:16
A, *a*, put on strength   Is 51:9
A, drunkards...weep   Joel 1:5
that I may *a-n* him   John 11:11

Aware *know, understand*
Will you not be *a*   Is 43:19
I was *a* that power   Luke 8:46

Awe *fear, reverence*
stand in *a* of Him   Ps 33:8
in *a* of My name   Mal 2:5

Awesome *fearful*
How *a* is this place   Gen 28:17
great and *a* God   Neh 1:5
a day of the LORD   Joel 2:31

Axe *cutting tool*
hammer nor *a*   1 Kin 6:7
a is already laid   Luke 3:9

– B –

Babes *infants*
From the mouth of...*b*   Ps 8:2
woe...who nurse *b*   Matt 24:19
like newborn *b*   1 Pet 2:2

Baby *infant*
b leaped...womb   Luke 1:41
b as He lay   Luke 2:16

Back *part of body*
turned his *b* to leave   1 Sam 10:9
my sins behind Thy *b*   Is 38:17

Bad *evil, wrong*
basket had very *b* figs   Jer 24:2
if your eye is *b*   Matt 6:23
B company   1 Cor 15:33

Bag *sack*
fill their *b-s*   Gen 42:25
silver in two *b-s*   2 Kin 5:23
b of...weights   Mic 6:11
Carry no purse, no *b*   Luke 10:4

Baggage *bags, supplies*
stayed with the *b*   1 Sam 25:13
prepare...yourself *b*   Ezek 12:4

Bake *cook*
b-d unleavened bread Gen 19:3
they b-d the dough Ex 12:39
grain offering b-d Lev 2:4
taste of cakes b-d Num 11:8

Baker *cook*
b for the king Gen 40:1
from the b-s' street Jer 37:21

Balance *scale*
shall have just b-s Lev 19:36
False b is an Prov 11:1

Bald *hairless*
every head is b Jer 48:37
head was made b Ezek 29:18

Baldhead *hairless*
mocked him...you b 2 Kin 2:23

Balm *aromatic ointment*
b and myrrh Gen 37:25
no b in Gilead Jer 8:22
Bring b for her pain Jer 51:8

Balsam *aromatic gum*
tops of the b trees 2 Sam 5:24
like a bed of b Song 5:13

Ban *set apart to God*
city...under the b Josh 6:17
who violated the b 1 Chr 2:7

Band *bond or group*
skillfully woven b Ex 28:8
b-s of the yoke Is 58:6

Banish *exile*
assemble the b-ed Is 11:12
I shall b them Ezek 4:13

Bank *slope*
b of the Nile Gen 41:3
b of the river Ezek 47:7

Banner *flag, standard*
b to those who fear Ps 60:4
b over me is love Song 2:4

Banquet *dinner, feast*
b lasting seven days Esth 1:5
lavish b for all Is 25:6
Herod...gave a b Mark 6:21

Baptism *symbolic washing*
b of repentance Mark 1:4
with the b of John Luke 7:29
through b into death Rom 6:4
one faith, one b Eph 4:5
buried with Him in b Col 2:12

Baptize *symbolic washing*
Jesus also was b-d Luke 3:21
sent me to b in water John 1:33
b-ing more disciples John 4:1
each of you be b-d Acts 2:38
John b-d with the Acts 19:4
b-d into Jesus Christ Rom 6:3
b-d into one body 1 Cor 12:13

Bar *metal or block*
b-s of your yoke Lev 26:13
earth with its b-s Jon 2:6

Barbarian *non-Hellenic*
obligation...to b-s Rom 1:14
b, Scythian, slave Col 3:11

Bare (adj) *barren, uncovered*
to cover *their b* flesh Ex 28:42
were naked and b Ezek 16:7

Bare (v) *expose, uncover*
b-d His holy arm Is 52:10
opened and laid b Heb 4:13

Barefoot *without sandals*
priests walk b Job 12:19
gone naked and b Is 20:3

Barley *grain*
land of wheat and b Deut 8:8
has five b loaves John 6:9

Barn *farm building*
seed still in the b Hag 2:19
nor gather into b-s Matt 6:26
tear down my b-s Luke 12:18

Barren *childless, sterile*
Sarai was b Gen 11:30
wrongs the b woman Job 24:21
Blessed are the b Luke 23:29

Base *dishonorable*
a b thought Deut 15:9
b things of...world 1 Cor 1:28

Basin *bowl, vessel*
blood...in the b Ex 12:22
a *sacrificial b* Zech 9:15

Basket *container*
b of summer fruit Amos 8:1
seven large b-s full Mark 8:8
let down in a b 2 Cor 11:33

Bath *measure of capacity*
two thousand b-s 1 Kin 7:26
only one b of *wine* Is 5:10

Bathe *wash*
b his body in water Num 19:7
B-d in milk Song 5:12

Battle (n) *conflict, war*
b is the LORD's 1 Sam 17:47
scents the b from afar Job 39:25
another king in b Luke 14:31
horses prepared for b Rev 9:7

Battle (v) *fight*
b against the sons Judg 20:14
about to go to b 1 Chr 12:19

Beach *coast*
Jesus stood on the b John 21:4
down on the b Acts 21:5

Beam *log*
one was felling a b 2 Kin 6:5
b-s of His...chambers Ps 104:3

Bear (n) *animal*
b robbed of...cubs Prov 17:12
resembling a b Dan 7:5

Bear (v) *sustain*
bore you on eagles' Ex 19:4
LORD...b-s our Ps 68:19

b their iniquities Is 53:11
she will b a Son Matt 1:21
John *bore* witness John 1:15
it b-s much fruit John 12:24
b-ing His own cross John 19:17
b fruit for God Rom 7:4
b the image of 1 Cor 15:49
b the sins of many Heb 9:28

Beard *whiskers*
infection...on the b Lev 13:29
until your b-s grow 1 Chr 19:5

Bearer *carrier*
the b-s of the ark 2 Sam 6:13
b of good news Is 40:9

Beast *animal, creature*
God formed every b Gen 2:19
b-s of the fields Lev 26:22
b of the forest Ps 50:10
mark of the b Rev 16:2

Beat *hit, strike*
b-ing a Hebrew Ex 2:11
B your plowshares Joel 3:10
b Him with their Matt 26:67
b-ing his breast Luke 18:13
b-en us in public Acts 16:37
b-en with rods 2 Cor 11:25

Beautiful *lovely, pleasing*
daughters...were b Gen 6:2
Rachel was b Gen 29:17
Most b among women Song 1:8
Your b sheep Jer 13:20
How b are the feet Rom 10:15

Beauty
behold the b of the Ps 27:4
b is vain Prov 31:30

Bed *pallet*
My b will comfort me Job 7:13
remember...on my b Ps 63:6
take up your b Matt 9:6

Beforehand *prior*
do not be anxious b Mark 13:11
prepared b for glory Rom 9:23

Beg *appeal, ask*
b You to look at Luke 9:38
I am ashamed to b Luke 16:3

Beget *bring into being, sire*
Rock who *begot* Deut 32:18
whom you shall b 2 Kin 20:18
I have *begotten* Thee Ps 2:7
have *begotten* Thee Acts 13:33

Beginning *origin, starting*
In the b God created Gen 1:1
The b of the gospel Mark 1:1
In the b was the Word John 1:1
He is the b Col 1:18
the b and the end Rev 21:6

Begotten (adj) *born one*
b from the Father John 1:14
gave His only b Son John 3:16
sent His only b Son 1 John 4:9

Behalf *sake of*
atonement on his *b*   Lev 5:6
I ask on their *b*   John 17:9
be sin on our *b*   2 Cor 5:21

Behave *act*
b properly as in   Rom 13:13
blamelessly we *b-d* 1 Thess 2:10

Behavior *conduct*
instruction in wise *b*   Prov 1:3
holy...in all *your b*   1 Pet 1:15

Beheaded *cut off*
John in the prison Matt 14:10
John, whom I *b*   Mark 6:16

Behold *look, see*
we *beheld* His glory   John 1:14
b the Son of Man   John 6:62
may *b* My glory   John 17:24
B, I stand at the door   Rev 3:20

Being *existence, life*
became a living *b*   Gen 2:7
wisdom in the...*b*   Job 38:36
truth in the...*b*   Ps 51:6

Believe *have faith, trust*
did not *b* in God   Ps 78:22
b that I am able   Matt 9:28
repent and *b*   Mark 1:15
whoever *b-s* in Him   John 3:16
men will *b* in Him   John 11:48
b in the light   John 12:36
B in the Lord Jesus   Acts 16:31
Abraham *b-d* God   Rom 4:3
how shall they *b*   Rom 10:14
whom I have *b-d*   2 Tim 1:12
demons also *b*   James 2:19

Believers *faithful ones*
example to all the *b* 1 Thess 1:7
toward you *b*   1 Thess 2:10

Belly *stomach*
On your *b*...you go   Gen 3:14
b of the sea monster Matt 12:40

Beloved *dearly loved*
gives to His *b* even   Ps 127:2
This is My *b* Son   Matt 3:17
stand firm...my *b*   Phil 4:1
Luke, the *b* physician Col 4:14
slave, a *b* brother   Philem 16
This is My *b* Son   2 Pet 1:17

Belt *waistband*
leather *b* about his   Matt 3:4
no money in their *b*   Mark 6:8

Benefit *blessing, profit*
forget none of His *b-s* Ps 103:2
His *b-s* toward me   Ps 116:12

Bereave *deprive, make sad*
be *b* of you both   Gen 27:45
I will *b* them   Jer 15:7

Beseech *ask earnestly*
LORD, I *b* Thee   Ps 116:4
b the Lord of the   Luke 10:2

Bestowed *granted*
the Spirit was *b*   Acts 8:18
which He freely *b*   Eph 1:6
b on Him the name   Phil 2:9
love the Father has *b* 1 John 3:1

Betray *break faith, disloyal*
do not *b* the fugitive   Is 16:3
how to *b* Him   Mark 14:11
one...will *b* Me   Mark 14:18

Betroth *promise to wed*
I will *b* you to Me   Hos 2:19
Mary had been *b-ed* Matt 1:18

Beware *be careful, watch*
B of the scribes   Mark 12:38
B of the leaven   Luke 12:1

Beyond *over and above*
it was *b* measure   Gen 41:49
tempted *b* what   1 Cor 10:13
b all that we ask   Eph 3:20

Big *large*
on the *b* toes   Ex 29:20
gave a *b* reception   Luke 5:29

Bind *fasten, secure*
bound his son Isaac   Gen 22:9
b them as a sign   Deut 6:8
b up the brokenhearted Is 61:1
shall *b* on earth   Matt 16:19
bound...a thousand   Rev 20:2

Bird *fowl*
let *b-s* fly above   Gen 1:20
b-s of the heavens   Ps 8:8
snare of a *b* catcher   Hos 9:8

Birth *act of being born*
A time to give *b*   Ecc 3:2
b of Jesus Christ   Matt 1:18
a man blind from *b*   John 9:1

Birthday *day of birth*
was Pharaoh's *b*   Gen 40:20
his *b*...banquet   Mark 6:21

Birthright *first-born rights*
sell me your *b*   Gen 25:31
sold his own *b*   Heb 12:16

Bite
serpent *bit* any man   Num 21:9
if you *b*...one another Gal 5:15

Bitter *painful, unpleasant*
b with hard labor   Ex 1:14
b speech *as* their arrow Ps 64:3
Strong drink is *b*   Is 24:9
fresh and *b* water   James 3:11

Bitterness *unpleasantness*
the *b* of my soul   Job 10:1
full of cursing and *b*   Rom 3:14
no root of *b*   Heb 12:15

Black *dark*
darkness and *b* gloom   Job 3:5
behold, a *b* horse   Rev 6:5

Blame *fault, responsibility*
let me bear the *b*   Gen 43:9
bear the *b*...forever Gen 44:32

Blameless *faultless*
show Thyself *b*   2 Sam 22:26
His way is *b*   Ps 18:30
a *b* conscience   Acts 24:16
in the Law, found *b*   Phil 3:6
b with great joy   Jude 24

Blaspheme *curse*
name is continually *b-d* Is 52:5
b-s...Holy Spirit   Mark 3:29
force them to *b*   Acts 26:11
name of God is *b-d*   Rom 2:24
taught not to *b*   1 Tim 1:20

Blasphemy *cursing, profanity*
b against the Spirit   Matt 12:31
man...speaks *b-ies*   Luke 5:21
stone You...for *b*   John 10:33

Blast *burst*
b with the ram's horn   Josh 6:5
a trumpet *b* of war   Jer 49:2

Blazing *burning*
LORD...a *b-ing* fire   Ex 3:2
and to a *b* fire   Heb 12:18

Blemish *imperfection, spot*
there is no *b* in you   Song 4:7
Himself without *b*   Heb 9:14

Bless (v) *bestow favor or praise*
God *b-ed* the...day   Gen 2:3
will *b* His people   Ps 29:11
B the LORD   Ps 103:2
who *b-es* his friend   Prov 27:14
b-ed of My Father   Matt 25:34
He *b-ed* *the food*   Mark 6:41
while He was *b-ing* Luke 24:51
we *b* our Lord   James 3:9

Blessed (adj) *favored, happy*
b be God Most High Gen 14:20
B be the name of   Job 1:21
b...who finds   Prov 3:13
B are the poor in   Matt 5:3
B is the...kingdom Mark 11:10
more *b* to give   Acts 20:35

Blessing (n) *God's favor*
you shall be a *b*   Gen 12:2
a *b* and a curse   Deut 11:26
showers of *b*   Ezek 34:26
pour out for you a *b*   Mal 3:10
cup of *b* which we 1 Cor 10:16

Blind (adj) *sightless*
To open *b* eyes   Is 42:7
b man was sitting Luke 18:35
I was *b*, now I see   John 9:25

Blind (n) *without sight*
I was eyes to the *b*   Job 29:15
a guide to the *b*   Rom 2:19

Blind (v) *make sightless*
b-s the clear-sighted   Ex 23:8
has *b-ed* the minds   2 Cor 4:4

Blindness *sightlessness*
madness and with *b* Deut 28:28
struck them with *b*   2 Kin 6:18

Blood

b shall be a sign	Ex 12:13
land is filled with *b*	Ezek 9:9
covenant in My *b*	Luke 22:20
sweat…drops of *b*	Luke 22:44
drinks My *b* abides	John 6:56
the moon into *b*	Acts 2:20
justified by His *b*	Rom 5:9
redemption…His *b*	Eph 1:7
b, as of a lamb	1 Pet 1:19
b of the saints	Rev 17:6

Bloodguiltiness

b is upon them	Lev 20:11
Deliver me from *b*	Ps 51:14

bloodshed *killing, murder*

abhors the man of *b*	Ps 5:6
the *b* of Jerusalem	Is 4:4
b follows *b*	Hos 4:2

Blossom *bloom*

the almost tree *b-s*	Eccl 12:5
arrogance has *b-ed*	Ezek 7:10

Blot *erase*

I will *b* out man	Gen 6:7
b out their name	Deut 9:14
b out all my iniquities	Ps 51:9

Blow *forcible stroke*

gave Jesus a *b*	John 18:22
inflicted many *b-s*	Acts 16:23

Boast (n) *bragging*

soul shall make its *b*	Ps 34:2
the *b* of our hope	Heb 3:6

Boast (v) *brag, glory*

b in the LORD	Ps 34:2
not *b* about tomorrow	Prov 27:1
who *b* in the Law	Rom 2:23
it *b-s* of great things	James 3:5

Boastful *proud*

b shall not stand	Ps 5:5
b pride of life	1 John 2:16

Boasting *bragging*

Where then is *b*	Rom 3:27
all such *b* is evil	James 4:16

Boat *watercraft*

slip by like reed *b-s*	Job 9:26
left the *b* and their	Matt 4:22
filled both of the *b-s*	Luke 5:7

Body *corpse, flesh*

b cleaves to the earth	Ps 44:25
perfume upon My *b*	Matt 26:12
this is My *b*	Mark 14:22
did not find His *b*	Luke 24:23
redemption of our *b*	Rom 8:23
present your *b-ies*	Rom 12:1
b is a temple	1 Cor 6:19
you are Christ's *b*	1 Cor 12:27
absent from the *b*	2 Cor 5:8
one *b* and one Spirit	Eph 4:4
transform the *b*	Phil 3:21
bore…sins in His *b*	1 Pet 2:24

Boil (n) *sore, swelling*

when…has a *b*	Lev 13:18
smote Job with sore *b-s*	Job 2:7

Boil (v) *cook, heat*

fire causes water to *b*	Is 64:2
b the guilt offering	Ezek 46:20

Boisterous *clamorous, loud*

woman of folly is *b*	Prov 9:13
will drink, *and* be *b*	Zech 9:15

Bold *brave, fearless*

man…*b* face	Prov 21:29
I may not be *b*	2 Cor 10:2

Boldness *confidence*

word of God with *b*	Acts 4:31
with *b* the mystery	Eph 6:19

Bond *band, restraint*

neither *b* nor free	2 Kin 14:26
with *b-s* of love	Hos 11:4
in the *b* of peace	Eph 4:3

Bondage *servitude, slavery*

Israel sighed…*b*	Ex 2:23
sold into *b* to sin	Rom 7:14

Bond-servant *servant, slave*

Paul, a *b* of Christ	Rom 1:1
ourselves as your *b-s*	2 Cor 4:5
b of God…apostle	Titus 1:1

Bondslave *servant, slave*

a *b* of Jesus Christ	Col 4:12
use it as *b-s* of God	1 Pet 2:16

Bone

now *b* of my *b-s*	Gen 2:23
rottenness in his *b-s*	Prov 12:4
can these *b-s* live	Ezek 37:3
dead men's *b-s*	Matt 23:27

Book *scroll*

blot…from Thy *b*	Ex 32:32
found the *b* of the	2 Kin 22:8
names are in the *b*	Phil 4:3
Lamb's *b* of life	Rev 21:27

Booths *shelters*

b for his livestock	Gen 33:17
in *b* during the feast	Neh 8:14

Booty *loot, plunder*

Swift is the *b*	Is 8:1
have his *own* life as *b*	Jer 38:2

Border *boundary*

enlarge your *b-s*	Ex 34:24
God extends your *b*	Ps 147:14
peace in your *b-s*	Ps 147:14

Born *brought into life*

man is *b* for trouble	Job 5:7
child will be *b* to us	Is 9:6
b King of the Jews	Matt 2:2
those *b* of women	Luke 7:28
b not of blood	John 1:13
unless one is *b* again	John 3:3
to one untimely *b*	1 Cor 15:8
love is *b* of God	1 John 4:7

Borrow *use temporarily*

if a man *b-s* anything	Ex 22:14

Bosom *breast*

take fire in his *b*	Prov 6:27
the *b* of the Father	John 1:18

Bother *pester*

you *b* the woman	Matt 26:10
this widow *b-s* me	Luke 18:5

Bottomless *without bottom*

key of the *b* pit	Rev 9:1
he opened the *b* pit	Rev 9:2

Bough *branch*

Joseph is a fruitful *b*	Gen 49:22
cedars…with its *b's*	Ps 80:10

Bound (adj) *fastened, tied*

Foolishness is *b* up	Prov 22:15
A wife is *b* as long	1 Cor 7:39

Bound (n) *boundary, limit*

set *b-s* for the people	Ex 19:12
b-s…the mountain	Ex 19:23

Boundary *border, limit*

b-s…the mountain	Ex 19:23

Boundary *border, limit*

b-ies of the peoples	Deut 32:8
the *b-ies* of the earth	Ps 74:17
the *b* of the widow	Prov 15:25

Bounty *generous gift*

to his royal *b*	1 Kin 10:13
over the *b* of the LORD	Jer 31:12

Bow (n) *rainbow*

set My *b* in the cloud	Gen 9:13

Bow (n) *shooting device*

his *b* remained firm	Gen 49:24
not trust in my *b*	Ps 44:6

Bow (v) *bend, worship*

nations *b* down to	Gen 27:29
My soul is *b-ed* down	Ps 57:6
B Thy heavens, O	Ps 144:5
every knee shall *b*	Rom 14:11

Bowels *entrails, innards*

a disease of your *b*	2 Chr 21:15
b gushed out	Acts 1:18

Bowl *dish, jug*

golden *b* is crushed	Eccl 12:6
dips with Me in…*b*	Mark 14:20

Box *container*

b with the golden	1 Sam 6:11
Judas had the…*b*	John 13:29

Boy *child, lad*

she left the *b*	Gen 21:15
Traded a *b* for a harlot	Joel 3:3

Branch *bough*

David a righteous *B*	Jer 23:5
beautiful *b-es* and	Ezek 31:3
b-es of the palm	John 12:13
you are the *b-es*	John 15:5

Breach *break*

For every *b* of trust	Ex 22:9
closed up the *b*	1 Kin 11:27
Heal its *b-s*	Ps 60:2

Bread *food*
eat unleavened *b*   Ex 12:20
He will bless your *b*   Ex 23:25
not live by *b* alone   Deut 8:3
b of heaven   Ps 105:40
Cast your *b*…waters   Eccl 11:1
not live on *b* alone   Matt 4:4
Give us…daily *b*   Matt 6:11
I am the *b* of life   John 6:35

Break *divide, shatter*
never *b* My covenant   Judg 2:1
reed He will not *b*   Is 42:3
B…fallow ground   Hos 10:12
she *broke* the vial   Mark 14:3
their nets *began* to *b*   Luke 5:6
did not *b* His legs   John 19:33

Breast *bosom*
upon my mother's *b-s*   Ps 22:9
b-s…never nursed   Luke 23:29
reclining on Jesus' *b*   John 13:23

Breastpiece *breast covering*
a *b* and an ephod   Ex 28:4
they bound the *b*   Ex 39:21

Breastplate *breast armor*
righteousness like a *b*   Is 59:17
b of faith and love   1 Thess 5:8

Breath *air, spirit, wind*
the *b* of life   Gen 2:7
man is a mere *b*   Ps 39:11
give *b* to the image   Rev 13:15

Breathe *inhale and exhale*
Abraham *b-d* his last   Gen 25:8
b on these slain   Ezek 37:9
He *b-d* on them   John 20:22

Brethren *brothers*
beating…his *b*   Ex 2:11
His *b* Will return   Mic 5:3
sinning against…*b*   1 Cor 8:12
Peace be to the *b*   Eph 6:23
the love of the *b*   1 Thess 4:9
our lives for the *b*   1 John 3:16
accuser of our *b*   Rev 12:10

Briar *thistle, thorn*
land will be *b-s*   Is 7:24
grapes from a *b* bush   Luke 6:44

Bribe *illegal gift*
nor take a *b*   Deut 10:17
who hates *b-s* will   Prov 15:27
Everyone love a *b*   Is 1:23

Brick *clay block*
they used *b* for stone   Gen 11:3
deliver…quota of *b-s*   Ex 5:18

Bride *newlywed*
as a *b* adorns herself   Is 61:10
the voice of the *b*   Jer 7:34
He who has the *b*   John 3:29
b…of the Lamb   Rev 21:9

Bridegroom *newlywed*
As a *b* decks himself   Is 61:10
voice of the *b*   Jer 7:34
out to meet the *b*   Matt 25:1

Bridle (n) *head harness*
My *b* in your lips   2 Kin 19:28
a *b* for the donkey   Prov 26:3

Bridle (v) *control*
not *b* his tongue   James 1:26
man, able to *b*   James 3:2

Bright *shining*
b in the skies   Job 37:21
B eyes gladden   Prov 15:30
the *b* morning star   Rev 22:16

Brimstone *sulfur*
b and fire from   Gen 19:24
rained fire and *b*   Luke 17:29
lake of fire and *b*   Rev 20:10

Bring *carry, lead*
shall *b* forth children   Gen 3:16
b two of every kind   Gen 6:19
Kings will *b* gifts   Ps 68:29
B the whole tithe   Mal 3:10
brought forth a son   Luke 1:57
I *b* you good news   Luke 2:10
b-ing salvation   Titus 2:11

Broad *wide*
into a *b* place   2 Sam 22:20
way is *b* that leads to   Matt 7:13

Broken *crushed, separated*
My spirit is *b*   Job 17:1
they have *b* Thy law   Ps 119:126
silver cord is *b*   Eccl 12:6
bind up the *b*   Ezek 34:16
Not a bone…*b*   John 19:36

Brokenhearted *grieving*
He heals the *b*   Ps 147:3
sent me to bind…*b*   Is 61:1

Brother *male relative*
Am I my *b-'s*   Gen 4:9
b-s may redeem   Lev 25:48
b is born for   Prov 17:17
closer than a *b*   Prov 18:24
reconciled to your *b*   Matt 5:24
not forgive his *b*   Matt 18:35
My *b* and sister   Mark 3:35
left…wife or *b-s*   Luke 18:29
b shall rise again   John 11:23
my *b* to stumble   1 Cor 8:13
yet hates his *b*   1 John 2:9

Brotherhood
love the *b*, fear God   1 Pet 2:17

Bruise (n) *wound*
for wound, *b* for *b*   Ex 21:25
the *b* He has inflicted   Is 30:26

Bruise (v) *batter, crush*
b him on the heel   Gen 3:15
b-s me with a tempest   Job 9:17

Brutal *fierce, vicious*
hand of *b* men   Ezek 21:31
b, haters of good   2 Tim 3:3

Buffet *beat*
I *b* my body   1 Cor 9:27
Satan to *b* me   2 Cor 12:7

Build *construct, form*
let us *b*…a city   Gen 11:4
built high places   2 Chr 33:19
Unless the Lord *b-s*   Ps 127:1
a time to *b* up   Eccl 3:3
built his house upon   Matt 7:24
I will *b* My church   Matt 16:18
able to *b* you up   Acts 20:32

Builder *fashioner, maker*
the *b-s* rejected   Matt 21:42
architect and *b* is   Heb 11:10

Building *structure*
reconstructing this *b*   Ezra 5:4
what wonderful *b-s*   Mark 13:1
you are…God's *b*   1 Cor 3:9
whole *b*, being fitted   Eph 2:21

Bulb *part of plant*
a *b* and a flower   Ex 25:33
b-s and their branches   Ex 25:36

Bull *animal*
b of the sin offering   Lev 4:20
blood of *b-s* and   Heb 10:4

Bundle *package*
the *b* of the living   1 Sam 25:29
in *b-s* to burn   Matt 13:30

Burden (n) *load, weight*
b-s of the Egyptians   Ex 6:6
who daily bears our *b*   Ps 68:19
Bear one another's *b's*   Gal 6:2

Burden (v) *weight down*
were *b-ed* excessively   2 Cor 1:8
the church be *b-ed*   1 Tim 5:16

Burial *interment*
give me a *b* site   Gen 23:4
prepare Me for *b*   Matt 26:12

Burn *consume, kindle*
bush was *b-ing*   Ex 3:2
Moses' anger *b-ed*   Ex 32:19
jealousy *b* like fire   Ps 79:5
not to *b* the scroll   Jer 36:25
b-ed in their desire   Rom 1:27
my body to be *b-ed*   1 Cor 13:3
works will be *b-ed*   2 Pet 3:10

Burning
Thy *b* anger   Ex 15:7
b anger of the Lord   Zeph 2:2

Burnished *polished*
gleamed like *b* bronze   Ezek 1:7
feet…like *b* bronze   Rev 1:15

Burst *break*
b his fetters   Luke 8:29
he *b* open   Acts 1:18

Bury *place in earth*
b-ied at…old age   Gen 15:15
go and *b* my father   Matt 8:21
dead to *b* their own   Matt 8:22
b-ied…in baptism   Col 2:12

Bush *shrub*
the *b* was burning   Ex 3:2
like a *b* in the desert   Jer 17:6

Business *occupation, work*
another to his *b* Matt 22:5
engage in *b* James 4:13

Busybodies *meddlers*
no work…like *b* 2 Thess 3:11
gossips and *b* 1 Tim 5:13

Butter
smoother than *b* Ps 55:21
milk produces *b* Prov 30:33

Buyer *purchaser*
the *b* like the seller Is 24:2
Let not the *b* rejoice Ezek 7:12

Bystanders *onlookers*
b…said to Peter Matt 26:73

Byword *contemptible*
b among all peoples 1 Kin 9:7
b among the nations Ps 44:14

– C –

Cake *type of bread*
and make bread *c-s* Gen 18:6
took one unleavened *c* Lev 8:26

Calamity *adversity, trouble*
day of my *c* 2 Sam 22:19
palate discern *c-ies* Job 6:30
stumble in *time of c* Prov 24:16
relents concerning *c* Jon 4:2

Calculate *count*
c the cost Luke 14:28

Calf *animal*
into a molten *c* Ex 32:4
skip about like *c-ves* Mal 4:2

Call *address, summon, name*
Go *c-ed* the light day Gen 1:5
c upon the name Gen 4:26
c upon the Lord Ps 18:3
those who *c* evil good Is 5:20
You shall *c* Me Jer 3:19
who is *c-ed* Christ Matt 1:16
to *c* the righteous Matt 9:13
c-s his own sheep John 10:3
God has not *c-ed* 1 Thess 4:7

Calling *summoning*
the *c* of assemblies Is 1:13
For consider your *c* 1 Cor 1:26
with a holy *c* 2 Tim 1:9

Calm *still*
sea may become *c* Jon 1:11
ought to keep *c* Acts 19:36

Camp (n) *lodging area*
This is God's *c* Gen 32:2
the *c* of the saints Rev 20:9

Camp (v) *settle*
you shall *c* in front Ex 14:2
Israel *c-ed* at Gilgal Josh 5:10
c around My house Zech 9:8

Captain *leader*
c of the bodyguard Gen 39:1
the *c* of the ship Acts 27:11

Captive *prisoner*
first-born of the *c* Ex 12:29
restores His *c* people Ps 14:7
release to the *c-s* Luke 4:18
having been held *c* 2 Tim 2:26

Captivity *imprisonment*
restore you from *c* Deut 30:3
had come from the *c* Ezra 8:35
destined for *c* Rev 13:10

Capture *seize, take*
c-d all his cities Deut 2:34
Can anyone *c* him Job 40:24

Care (n) *concern*
put him in my *c* Gen 42:37
friends and receive *c* Acts 27:3
c for one another 1 Cor 12:25

Care (v) *have concern for*
No one *c-s* for…soul Ps 142:4
and took *c* of him Luke 10:34
take *c* of the church 1 Tim 3:5
He *c-s* for you 1 Pet 5:7

Careful *watchful, on guard*
c to observe all Deut 6:25
be *c* not to drink Judg 13:4
be *c* how you walk Eph 5:15

Careless *thoughtless*
a fool is…*c* Prov 14:16
that every *c* word Matt 12:36

Carpenter *craftsman*
this the *c-'s* son Matt 13:55
c, the son of Mary Mark 6:3

Carry *bear*
Lord…*c-ied* you Deut 1:31
Spirit…will *c* you 1 Kin 18:12
our sorrows He *c-ied* Is 53:4
C no purse, no bag Luke 10:4
the cross to *c* Luke 23:26

Cast *throw*
Joshua *c* lots for Josh 18:10
Do not *c* me away Ps 51:11
will *c* out demons Mark 16:17
c Him out of…city Luke 4:29
clothing they *c* lots John 19:24
c-ing all your anxiety 1 Pet 5:7
c their crowns before Rev 4:10

Catch *seize, trap*
shall *c* his wife Judg 21:21
c…with her eyelids Prov 6:25
caught in My snare Ezek 12:13
unable to *c* Him Luke 20:26
caught in adultery John 8:3
if a man is *caught* Gal 6:1

Cattle *domestic animals*
the first-born of *c* Ex 12:29
c on a thousand hills Ps 50:10

Cause (n) *purpose, reason*
the *c* of the just Ex 23:8
hate me without a *c* Ps 69:4
c a man shall leave Matt 19:5

Cause (v) *make*
I *c* My name to be Ex 20:24
c Israel to inherit Deut 1:38
c His face to shine Ps 67:1
who *c* dissensions Rom 16:17

Cave *shelter*
escaped to the *c* 1 Sam 22:1
by fifties in a *c* 1 Kin 18:4
hid…in the *c-s* Rev 6:15

Cease *stop*
He makes wars to *c* Ps 46:9
c-d to kiss My feet Luke 7:45
tongues, they will *c* 1 Cor 13:8
pray without *c-ing* 1 Thess 5:17

Cedar *tree, wood*
with the *c* wood Lev 14:6
all the *c-s* of Lebanon Is 2:13

Celebrate *rejoice*
may *c* a feast to Me Ex 5:1
C the Passover 2 Kin 23:21
all Israel were *c-ing* 1 Chr 13:8

Censer *incense container*
his *c* in his hand Ezek 8:11
angel took the *c* Rev 8:5

Census *population roll*
number of the *c* 1 Chr 21:5
c which…David 2 Chr 2:17
the first *c* taken Luke 2:2
in the days of the *c* Acts 5:37

Cent *money*
paid up the last *c* Matt 5:26
amount to a *c* Mark 12:42

Centurion *captain*
Jesus said to the *c* Matt 8:13
gave orders to the *c* Acts 24:23

Certainty *sureness*
know with *c* that Josh 23:13
you know with *c* Eph 5:5

Certificate *permit, record*
a *c* of divorce Deut 24:1
c of debt Col 2:14

Chaff *husk*
make the hills like *c* Is 41:15
burn up the *c* Matt 3:12

Chain *band*
he drew *c-s* of gold 1 Kin 6:21
was bound with *c-s* Luke 8:29
c-s fell off his hands Acts 12:7
great *c* in his hand Rev 20:1

Chamber *room*
entered his *c* Gen 43:30
in his cool roof *c* Judg 3:20
bridegroom…his *c* Ps 19:5
c-s in the heavens Amos 9:6

Champion *fighter*
c, the Philistine 1 Sam 17:23
like a dread *c* Jer 20:11

Change (n) *alteration*
had a *c* of heart Ex 14:5
two *c-s* of clothes 2 Kin 5:23

a *c* of law　　　　　　　Heb 7:12

Change (v) *alter, transform*
and *c-d* my wages　　　Gen 31:7
Ethiopian *c* his skin　　Jer 13:23
LORD *c-d* His mind　　Amos 7:6
shall all be *c-d*　　1 Cor 15:51

Channel *furrow*
c-s of water appeared　Ps 18:15
heart is *like c-s*　　　Prov 21:1

Chant *sing*
David *c-ed*...this　　2 Sam 1:17
daughters...shall *c*　Ezek 32:16

Character
and proven *c*, hope　　Rom 5:4
Let your *c* be free　　Heb 13:5

Charge (n) *responsibility*
under Joseph's *c*　　Gen 39:23
c of his household　Matt 24:45

Charge (n) *accusation*
bring *c-s* against　　Acts 19:38
c against God's elect　Rom 8:33

Charge (n) *cost*
gospel without a *c*　　1 Cor 9:18

Charge (v) *command*
I *c-d* your judges　　Deut 1:16
I solemnly *c* you　　1 Tim 5:21

Charge (v) *exact a price*
c that to my account　Philem 18

Chariot *wagon*
Some *boast* in *c-s*　　Ps 20:7
Thy *c-s* of salvation　Hab 3:8
and sitting in his *c*　Acts 8:28

Charity *alms*
and give to *c*　　Luke 12:33
deeds of...*c*　　Acts 9:36

Chase *drive, pursue*
will *c* your enemies　Lev 26:7
be *c-d* like chaff　　Is 17:13

Chaste *pure*
c...behavior　　1 Pet 3:2
kept themselves *c*　　Rev 14:4

Chasten *discipline*
Man is also *c-ed*　　Job 33:19
c-ed every morning　Ps 73:14

Chastise *punish*
Thou hast *c-d* me　　Jer 31:18
I will *c* all of them　Hos 5:2

Chatter *babbling*
avoid...empty *c*　　2 Tim 2:16

Cheat *deceive*
c with...scales　　Amos 8:5

Cheek *part of face*
slapped me on the *c*　Job 16:10
hits you on the *c*　Luke 6:29

Cheerful
and be *c*　　Job 9:27
God loves a *c* giver　2 Cor 9:7
Is anyone *c*　　James 5:13

Cherish *love*
or the wife you *c*　　Deut 13:6
c-s it, just as Christ　Eph 5:29

Cherub *celestial being*
He rode on a *c*　　2 Sam 22:11
c stretched out his　Ezek 10:7

Cherubim *plural of Cherub*
c had *their* wings　　Ex 37:9
c appeared to have　Ezek 10:8

Chest *box*
the priest took a *c*　2 Kin 12:9
levies...into the *c*　2 Chr 24:10

Chew *eat*
which *c* the cud　　Lev 11:4

Chief *head, prominent*
c-s of the sons of　　Gen 36:15
of the thirty *c* men　2 Sam 23:13
C Shepherd appears　1 Pet 5:4

Child
c grew...weaned　　Gen 21:8
Train up a *c* in　　Prov 22:6
c will be born to us　Is 9:6
with *c* by the Holy　Matt 1:18
take the *C* and His　Matt 2:13
a woman with *c*　1 Thess 15:3

Childbirth
multiply...pain in *c*　Gen 3:16
pains of *c* come　　Hos 13:13

Childless
I am *c*, and the heir　Gen 15:2
c among women　1 Sam 15:33

Children
pain...bring forth *c*　Gen 3:16
compassion on *his c*　Ps 103:13
c rise up end bless　Prov 31:28
slew all the male *c*　Matt 2:16
and become like *c*　Matt 18:3
if *c*, heirs　　Rom 8:17
C, obey your parents　Eph 6:1
My little *c*　　1 John 2:1

Choice *option or best*
c men of Israel　　2 Sam 10:9
God's gracious *c*　Rom 11:5

Choir *chorus*
c proceeded to the　Neh 12:38
two *c-s* took their　Neh 12:40

Choke *stifle*
riches *c* the word　Matt 13:22
thorns...*c-d* it　　Mark 4:7

Choose *select, take*
whom the LORD *c-s*　Num 16:7
refuse evil and *c* good　Is 7:15
not God *c* the poor　James 2:5

Chose *selected*
Lot *c* for himself　　Gen 13:11
God has *c-n* you　　Deut 7:6
when I *c* Israel　　Ezek 20:5
has *c-n* the weak　1 Cor 1:27
He *c* us in Him　　Eph 1:4

Chosen *elected, selected*
Moses His *c* one　　Ps 106:23
Israel My *c* one　　Is 45:4
c of God, holy and　Col 3:12
you are a *c* race　1 Pet 2:9

Christ *Messiah*
birth of Jesus *C* was　Matt 1:18
both Lord and *C*　　Acts 2:36
are one body in *C*　Rom 12:5
ambassadors for *C*　2 Cor 5:20
faith in *C* Jesus　　Gal 2:16
sons through Jesus *C*　Eph 1:5
to live is *C*　　Phil 1:21
dead in *C* shall　1 Thess 4:16
C...high priest　　Heb 9:11
Advocate...Jesus *C*　1 John 2:1

Christian *follower of Christ*
first called *C-s* in　Acts 11:26
me to beome a *C*　Acts 26:28
suffers as a *C*　　1 Pet 4:16

Church *a called out assembly*
I will build my *c*　Matt 16:18
c-es of the Gentiles　Rom 16:4
together as a *c*　1 Cor 11:18
Christ...head of the *c* Eph 5:23
c of the living God　1 Tim 3:15

Cinnamon *spice*
and of fragrant *c*　　Ex 30:23
and *c* and spice　　Rev 18:13

Circle *area*
He has inscribed a *c*　Job 26:10
did not sit in the *c*　Jer 15:17

Circuit *course*
on the *c* to Bethel　1 Sam 7:16
its *c* to the other end　Ps 19:6

Circulate *spread*
people *c-ing*　　1 Sam 2:24
to *c* a proclamation　2 Chr 30:5

Circumcise *be pure or cut off*
every male...be *c-d*　Gen 17:10
C then your heart　Deut 10:16
C yourselves to...LORD Jer 4:4
came to *c* the child　Luke 1:59

Circumcision *act of purity*
c is...of the heart　　Rom 2:29
if you receive *c*　　Gal 5:2
we are the *true c*　Phil 3:3
those of the *c*　　Titus 1:10

Circumstance *condition*
peace in every *c*　2 Thess 3:16
of humble *c-s*　　James 1:9

Cistern *reservoir*
water from your...*c*　Prov 5:15
prophet from the *c*　Jer 38:10

Citadel *fortress*
c of the king's　　1 Kin 16:18
c-s of Jerusalem　　Amos 2:5
tramples on our *c-s*　Mic 5:5

Citizen *resident*
your fellow *c-s*　　Ezek 33:12

c-s hated him — Luke 19:14
c of no insignificant — Acts 21:39

City
Build…a c — Gen 11:4
die in my own c — 2 Sam 19:37
LORD guards the c — Ps 127:1
a c called Nazareth — Matt 2:23
into the holy c — Matt 4:5
He has prepared a c — Heb 11:16
I saw the holy c — Rev 21:2

Claim demand
Do not c honor in — Prov 25:6
c-ing to be someone — Acts 8:9

Clan family, tribe
and by your c-s — 1 Sam 10:19
I will make the c-s — Zech 12:6

Clap applaud
c-s his hands among — Job 34:37
trees…will c — Is 55:12

Clay
Father, We are the c — Is 64:8
c in the potter's hand — Jer 18:6

Clean cleansed, washed
animals that are not c — Gen 7:2
pronounce him c — Lev 13:28
Create in me a c heart — Ps 51:10
You can make me c — Matt 8:2
c because of the word — John 15:3

Cleanse purify, wash
c the house of the — 2 Chr 29:15
the lepers are c-d — Matt 11:5
let us c ourselves — 2 Cor 7:1
blood…c-s us — 1 John 1:7

Clear make free or plain
C the way for the LORD — Is 40:3
Christ had made c — 2 Pet 1:14

Cleave cling, divide
shall c to his wife — Gen 2:24
c to Thy testimonies — Ps 119:31
shall c to his wife — Eph 5:31

Cleft crevice
in the c of the rock — Judg 15:8
who live in the c-s — Obad 3

Clever smart
c in their own sight — Is 5:21

Cliff crag
nest is set in the c — Num 24:21
c-s are a refuge — Ps 104:18

Climb ascend
I will c the palm tree — Song 7:8
c-ed…a sycamore — Luke 19:4

Cling cleave
c to the LORD — Josh 23:8
c to what is good — Rom 12:9

Cloak coat, mantle
neither bread nor c — Is 3:7
fringe of His c — Matt 9:20

Close shut, stop
floodgates…were c-d — Gen 8:2
have c-d their eyes — Acts 28:27

c-s his heart — 1 John 3:17

Cloth fabric
is wrapped in a c — 1 Sam 21:9
in the linen c — Mark 15:46

Clothe array, dress
C me with skin — Job 10:11
naked…you c-d Me — Matt 25:36
c-d with power from — Luke 24:49
c…with humility — 1 Pet 5:5

Clothes garments
c of her captivity — Deut 21:13
changed his c — 2 Sam 12:20
And tearing his c — Mark 14:63

Clothing clothes, raiment
the body than c — Matt 6:25
in sheep's c — Matt 7:15
His c became white — Luke 9:29

Cloud mist
My bow in the c — Gen 9:13
in a pillar of c — Ex 13:21
c for a covering — Ps 105:39
voice came out…c — Mark 9:7
a c with power — Luke 21:27

Club weapon
C's are…as stubble — Job 41:29
with swords and c-s — Matt 26:47

Coat charcoal
walk on hot c-s — Prov 6:28
heap burning c-s — Rom 12:20

Coat cloak
with his c torn — 2 Sam 15:32
have your c also — Matt 5:40

Coffin bier
in a c in Egypt — Gen 50:26
and touched the c — Luke 7:14

Coin money
Show Me the c — Matt 22:19
woman…loses one c — Luke 15:8

Cold cool
Like the c of snow — Prov 25:13
cup of c water — Matt 10:42
neither c nor hot — Rev 3:15

Collapse fall
grass c-s into the flame — Is 5:24
pathways will c — Ezek 38:20
ancient hills c-d — Hab 3:6

Collect exact, take
c-ed his strength — Gen 48:2
cistern c-ing water — Lev 11:36
c captives like sand — Hab 1:9
C no more than — Luke 3:13
c-ed a tenth from — Heb 7:6

Collection acquisition
let your c of idols — Is 57:13
no c-s be made — 1 Cor 16:2

Colt foal
Even on a c — Zech 9:9
and a c with her — Matt 21:2
on a donkey's c — John 12:15

Come
C, let us worship — Ps 95:6
your king is c-ing — Zech 9:9
Thy kingdom c — Matt 6:10
Son of Man c-ing — Luke 21:27
His judgment has c — Rev 14:7

Comfort (n) consolation
c in my affliction — Ps 119:50
he will give you c — Prov 29:17
c of the Holy Spirit — Acts 9:31
and God of all c — 2 Cor 1:3

Comforter consoler
Sorry c-s are you all — Job 16:2
c-s, but I found none — Ps 69:20
She has no c — Lam 1:9
Where will I seek c-s — Nah 3:7

Coming (n) arrival
the day of His c — Mal 3:2
sign of Your c — Matt 24:3
Christ's at His c — 1 Cor 15:23
promise of His c — 2 Pet 3:4

Command (n) order
the c of the LORD — Lev 24:12
no c of the Lord — 1 Cor 7:25

Command (v) declare, order
may c his children — Gen 18:19
bring all that I c — Deut 12:11
c that these stones — Matt 4:3

Commandment instruction
the Ten C-s — Ex 34:28
c of the LORD is pure — Ps 19:8
which is the great c — Matt 22:36
A new c I give — John 13:34
c-s of God — Rev 14:12

Commend praise, present
I c you to God — Acts 20:32
to c ourselves again — 2 Cor 3:1

Commission appoint
c him in their sight — Num 27:19
king has c-ed me — 1 Sam 21:2

Commit entrust, practice
shall not c adultery — Ex 20:14
I c my spirit — Ps 31:5
Do not c adultery — Luke 18:20
I c My spirit — Luke 23:46
who c-ted no sin — 1 Pet 2:22

Common ordinary, shared
anyone of…c people — Lev 4:27
had all things in c — Acts 2:44
about our c salvation — Jude 3

Commotion disturbance
the noise of this c — 1 Sam 4:14
great c out of the — Jer 10:22

Companion comrade, friend
brought thirty c-s — Judg 14:11
c of fools will suffer — Prov 13:20
your c and your wife — Mal 2:14

Company assembly, group
c of the godless — Job 15:34
Bad c corrupts — 1 Cor 15:33

Compare *contrast, liken*
none to *c* with Thee Ps 40:5
c the kingdom of Luke 13:20

Compassion *concern, love*
in Thy great *c* Neh 9:19
have *c* on the poor Ps 72:13
He felt *c* for them Matt 9:36
put on a heart of *c* Col 3:12
Lord is full of *c* James 5:11

Compassionate *loving*
c, Slow to anger Neh 9:17
a gracious and *c* God Jon 4:2

Compel *force, press*
c them to come in Luke 14:23
c...to be circumcised Gal 6:12

Compete *strive*
can you *c* with horses Jer 12:5
c-s as an athlete 2 Tim 2:5

Complain *murmur*
c in the bitterness Job 7:11
Do not *c*, brethren James 5:9

Complaint *grumbling*
couch will ease my *c* Job 7:13
hospitable...without *c* 1 Pet 4:9

Complete (adj) *full, total*
a sabbath of *c* rest Ex 35:2
you have been made *c* Col 2:10
joy may be made *c* 1 John 1:4

Complete (v) *finish, fulfill*
God *c-ed* His work Gen 2:2
your days are *c* 2 Sam 7:12

Compose *write*
The first account I *c-d* Acts 1:1

Compose *make calm*
c-d and quieted my Ps 131:2
I *c* my soul Is 38:13

Comprehend *understand*
and they did not *c* Luke 18:34
darkness did not *c* John 1:5

Compulsion *coercion*
as it were by *c* Philem 14
not under *c*, but 1 Pet 5:2

Conceal *cover, hide*
man *c-s* knowledge Prov 12:23
was *c-ed* from them Luke 9:45

Conceit *pride*
selfishness or empty *c* Phil 2:3
c-ed, lovers of 2 Tim 3:4

Conceive *become pregnant*
Sarah *c-ed* and bore a Gen 21:2
sin my mother *c-d* me Ps 51:5
when lust has *c-d* James 1:15

Concern *have care*
the Lord was *c-ed* Ex 4:31
is married is *c-ed* 1 Cor 7:33

Condemn *discredit, judge*
my mouth will *c* me Job 9:20
will *c* Him to death Mark 10:33
you *c* yourself Rom 2:1

our heart *c-s* us 1 John 3:20

Condemnation *judgment*
receive greater *c* Mark 12:40
Their *c* is just Rom 3:8
c upon themselves Rom 13:2

Condition *state*
c-s were good in 2 Chr 12:12
or adds *c-s* to it Gal 3:15

Conduct (n) *behavior*
turn...*from his c* Job 33:17
holy *c* and godliness 2 Pet 3:11

Conduct (v) *behave*
c...same spirit 2 Cor 12:18
c yourselves in fear 1 Pet 1:17

Confess *acknowledge*
c my transgressions Ps 32:5
c-ing their sins Mark 1:5
c with your mouth Rom 10:9
If we *c* our sins 1 John 1:9

Confession *admission*
your *c* of the gospel 2 Cor 9:13
the *c* of our hope Heb 10:23

Confidence *boldness, trust*
What is this *c* 2 Kin 18:19
LORD will be your *c* Prov 3:26
c in me may abound Phil 1:26
no *c* in the flesh Phil 3:3

Confine *imprison, limit*
he does not *c* it Ex 21:29
c-d in the court Jer 33:1

Confinement *imprisonment*
he put me in Gen 41:10

Confirm *establish, strengthen*
LORD *c* His word 1 Sam 1:23
c the work of our Ps 90:17
c-ed...by the signs Mark 16:20

Confirmation *verification*
and *c* of the gospel Phil 1:7

Conflict *contention*
in *c* with the LORD Jer 50:24
experiencing...*c* Phil 1:30

Conformed *being like*
c...image of His Son Rom 8:29
being *c* to His death Phil 3:10

Confound *confuse*
LORD *c-ed* them Josh 10:10
c-ing the Jews Acts 9:22

Confront *challenge, face*
Days of affliction *c* Job 30:27
the elders *c-ed Him* Luke 20:1

Confuse *perplex*
c their language Gen 11:7

Confusion *disorder*
into great *c* Deut 7:23
not *a* God of *c* 1 Cor 14:33

Congregation *assembly*
all the *c* of Israel Ex 12:3
Bless God in the *c-s* Ps 68:26
the *c* of the disciples Acts 6:2

Conquer *be victorious*
but could not *c* it Is 7:1
c through Him Rom 8:37

Conscience *moral obligation*
their *c* being weak is 1 Cor 8:7
faith with a clear *c* 1 Tim 3:9
keep a good *c* 1 Pet 3:16

Consecrate *sanctify*
sons of Israel *c* Ex 28:38
C yourselves Lev 11:44
c-s his house as holy Lev 27:14
have *c-d* this house 1 Kin 9:3

Consecrated *sanctified*
touch any *c* thing Lev 12:4
there is *c* bread 1 Sam 21:4
ate the *c* bread Matt 12:4

Consent *agree*
entice you, Do not *c* Prov 1:10
c-s to live with him 1 Cor 7:12

Consider *observe, think*
C my groaning Ps 5:1
c the work of His hands Is 5:12
C the ravens, for Luke 12:24
c your calling 1 Cor 1:26
c-ed...God is able Heb 11:19

Consist *composed of*
life *c* of his Luke 12:15
does not *c* in words 1 Cor 4:20

Consolation *comfort*
Thy *c-s* delight my Ps 94:19
is any *c* of love Phil 2:1

Console *soothe*
servants to *c* him 2 Sam 10:2
c them concerning John 11:19

Conspiracy *plot, scheme*
the *c* was strong 2 Sam 15:12
from the *c-ies* of man Ps 31:20

Conspire *plot against*
have *c-d* against me 1 Sam 22:8
c-d against my 2 Kin 10:9
c together against Ps 83:3
Amos...*c-d* against Amos 7:10

Construct *build*
c a sanctuary for Me Ex 25:8

Construction *structure*
c of the sanctuary Ex 36:3
the *c* of the ark 1 Pet 3:20

Consult *confer*
c-ed with the elders 1 Kin 12:6
not...*c* with fesh Gal 1:16

Consume *destroy, devour*
the bush was not *c-d* Ex 3:2
great fire will *c* us Deut 5:25
dost *c* as a moth Ps 39:11
c-s his own flesh Eccl 4:5
c your flesh like fire James 5:3

Consuming (adj) *destroying*
the flame of a *c* fire Is 29:6
our God is a *c* fire Heb 12:29

Contain *hold*
c the burnt offering 2 Chr 7:7
not c the books John 21:25
is c-ed in Scripture 1 Pet 2:6

Contempt *scorn*
With pride and c Ps 31:18
your brother with c Rom 14:10

Contend *strive*
c with the Almighty Job 40:2
Who will c with Me Is 50:8
c...for the faith Jude 3

Content *satisfied*
Nor will he be c Prov 6:35
c with your wages Luke 3:14
learned to be c Phil 4:11

Contention *strife*
puts an end to c-s Prov 18:18
Strife exists and c Hab 1:3

Contentious *quarrelsome*
with a c woman Prov 25:24
inclined to be c 1 Cor 11:16

Continue *persevere, persist*
My covenant may c Mal 2:4
Are we to c in sin Rom 6:1

Contrary *against*
c to the command Num 24:13
c to the teaching Rom 16:17
c to sound teaching 1 Tim 1:10

Contribute *give*
c-ing to their support Luke 8:3
c-ing to...the saints Rom 12:13

Contribution *gift, offering*
to raise a c for Me Ex 25:2
a c for the poor Rom 15:26
liberality of your c 2 Cor 9:13

Contrite *sorrowful*
broken and a c heart Ps 51:17

Control (n) *order, rule*
was it not under...c Acts 5:4
your lack of self-c 1 Cor 7:5

Control (v) *rule, subdue*
he c-ed himself and Gen 43:31
Joseph could not c Gen 45:1

Controversy *dispute*
LORD has a c with the Jer 25:31
shun foolish c-ies Titus 3:9

Converse *discuss*
they were c-ing Luke 24:15
Stoic...were c-ing Acts 17:18

Conversion *change*
c of the Gentiles Acts 15:3

Converted *changed*
sinners will be c Ps 51:13
unless you are c Matt 18:3

Convict *condemn, judge*
one of you c-s Me John 8:46
to c all the ungodly Jude 15

Convinced *persuaded*
c that neither death Rom 8:38

c of better things Heb 6:9

Cool *cold*
in the c of the day Gen 3:8
who has a c spirit Prov 17:27

Copy *facsimile*
c of...law of Moses Josh 8:32
mere c of the true Heb 9:24

Cord *band, rope*
c-s of affliction Job 36:8
silver c is broken Eccl 12:6
a scourge of c-s John 2:15

Corner *angle, intersection*
the chief c stone Ps 118:22
the chief c stone Mark 12:10

Cornerstone *support stone*
who laid its c Job 38:6
the c of her tribes Is 19:13
costly c for the Is 28:16
From them...the c Zech 10:4

Corpse *dead body*
made unclean by a c Lev 22:4
a mass of c-s Nah 3:3

Correct *reprove*
c him with the rod 2 Sam 7:14
C me, O LORD Jer 10:24
gentleness c-ing 2 Tim 2:25

Correction *improvement*
refused to take c Jer 5:3
for reproof, for c 2 Tim 3:16

Corrupt (adj) *evil, rotten*
the earth was c Gen 6:11
They are c Ps 14:1

Corrupt (v) *make evil*
a bribe c-s the heart Eccl 7:7
Bad company c-s 1 Cor 15:33

Corruption *decay, evil*
their c is in them Lev 22:25
c that is in the world 2 Pet 1:4
slaves of c 2 Pet 2:19

Cost *expense, price*
let the c be paid Ezra 6:4
calculate the c Luke 14:28

Costly *expensive*
gold, silver, c stones Dan 11:38
vial of...c perfume Mark 14:3

Council *assembly*
the c of the holy ones Ps 89:7
to their c chamber Luke 22:6
conferred with his c Acts 25:12

Counsel (n) *advice, opinion*
I shall give you c Ex 18:19
To Him belong c Job 12:13
not walk in the c Ps 1:1
chief priests took c John 12:10

Counsel (v) *advise*
I c that all Israel 2 Sam 17:11
c you with My eye Ps 32:8

Counselor *adviser*
Wonderful C, Mighty Is 9:6

who became His c Rom 11:34

Count *consider, number*
could not be c-ed 1 Kin 8:5
my prayer be c-ed Ps 141:2
I c all...loss Phil 3:8

Countenance *appearance*
LORD lift up His c Num 6:26
light of Thy c Ps 4:6

Country *land, region*
Go forth from your c Gen 12:1
go out into the c Song 7:11
they are seeking a c Heb 11:14

Courage *heart, valor*
and do not lose c 2 Chr 15:7
with justice and c Mic 3:8
Take c, it is I Matt 14:27
we are of good c 2 Cor 5:8

Courageous *brave*
Be strong and c Deut 31:6
I purpose to be c 2 Cor 10:2

Course *area, extent, way*
I have finished the c 2 Tim 4:7
the c of our life James 3:6

Court *area, hall, tribunal*
a day in Thy c-s Ps 84:10
c of the LORD's house Jer 26:2
drag you into c James 2:6

Courtyard *compound*
a well in his c 2 Sam 17:18
c of the high priest Matt 26:58
Peter...in the c Mark 14:66

Covenant *agreement*
establish My c Gen 6:18
for an everlasting c Gen 17:13
ark of the c Num 10:33
book of the c 2 Kin 23:2
Remember His c 1 Chr 16:15
I will make a new c Jer 31:31
the blood of My c Zech 9:11
cup...is the new c Luke 22:20
this is My c with Rom 11:27
servants of a new c 2 Cor 3:6
blood of the...c Heb 13:20

Cover (v) *hide, protect*
and c up his blood Gen 37:26
Whose sin is c-ed Ps 32:1
love c-s all Prov 10:12
to the hills, C us Luke 23:30
love c-s a multitude 1 Pet 4:8

Covering *canopy*
a cloud for a c Ps 105:39
sackcloth their c Is 50:3
freedom as a c 1 Pet 2:16

Covet *crave, desire*
not c your neighbor's Ex 20:17
You shall not c Deut 5:21
c-ed no one's silver Acts 20:33

Covetous *desirous*
the c and swindlers 1 Cor 5:10

Craftiness *shrewd*
not walking in *c*   2 Cor 4:2
by *c* in deceitful   Eph 4:14

Crave *covet, desire*
day long he is *c-ing*   Prov 21:26
should not *c* evil   1 Cor 10:6

Crawling *creeping*
beasts and the *c*   Acts 11:6
and *c* creatures   Rom 1:23

Create *form, make*
c-ed the heavens   Gen 1:1
C in me a clean   Ps 51:10
c new heavens   Is 65:17
c-d...for good works   Eph 2:10
Thou didst *c* all   Rev 4:11

Creation
beginning of *c*   Mark 10:6
whole *c* groans   Rom 8:22

Creator *Maker*
Remember...your *C*   Eccl 12:1
The *C* of Israel   Is 43:15
rather than the *C*   Rom 1:25

Creature *created being*
every living *c* that   Gen 1:21
and crawling *c-s*   Rom 1:23
in Christ...new *c*   2 Cor 5:17

Creditor *lender*
not to act as a *c* to   Ex 22:25
Let the *c* seize all   Ps 109:11

Creeping *crawling*
cattle and *c* things   Gen 1:24
c locust has eaten   Joel 1:4

Crime *vice*
be a lustful *c*   Job 31:11
not of such *c-s*   Acts 25:18

Criminal *lawbreaker*
crucified...the *c-s*   Luke 23:33
imprisonment as a *c*   2 Tim 2:9

Crimson *deep red*
purple, *c* and violet   2 Chr 2:7
like *c*...be like wool   Is 1:18

Crippled *lame*
a son *c* in his feet   2 Sam 4:4
bring...*c* and blind   Luke 14:21

Crooked *evil, twisted*
and *c* generation   Deut 32:5
to their *c* ways   Ps 125:5
make the straight   Acts 13:10
c and perverse   Phil 2:15

Crop *yield of produce*
old things from the *c*   Lev 25:22
c-s to the grasshopper   Ps 78:46
c began to sprout   Amos 7:1
share of the *c-s*   2 Tim 2:6

Cross (n) *execution device*
take his *c* and   Matt 10:38
to bear His *c*   Mark 15:21
take up his *c* daily   Luke 9:23
standing by the *c*   John 19:25
hanging Him on a *c*   Acts 5:30

word of the *c* is   1 Cor 1:18
boast, except in the *c*   Gal 6:14
even death on a *c*   Phil 2:8
endured the *c*   Heb 12:2

Cross (v) *pass over*
you *c* the Jordan   Deut 12:10
c-ing over to   Acts 21:2

Crouch *bow, stoop*
sin is *c-ing* at the   Gen 4:7
Nothing...but to *c*   Is 10:4

Crowd *multitude*
because of the *c*   Mark 2:4
they stirred up the *c*   Acts 17:8

Crown (n) *royal emblem or top*
he set the royal *c*   Esth 2:17
gray head is a *c*   Prov 16:31
a *c* of thorns   Matt 27:29
receive the *c* of life   James 1:12
golden *c* on His head Rev 14:14

Crown (v) *to place crown on*
c him with glory   Ps 8:5
c-ed him with glory   Heb 2:7

Crucify *execution on cross*
scourge and *c* Him   Matt 20:19
c your King   John 19:15
preach Christ *c-ied*   1 Cor 1:23
not have *c-ied* the   1 Cor 2:8
c-ied with Christ   Gal 2:20
their Lord was *c-ied*   Rev 11:8

Cruel *fierce, harsh*
their...*c* bondage   Ex 6:9
c and have no mercy   Jer 6:23
people has become *c*   Lam 4:3

Crumbs *morsels*
dogs feed on the *c*   Matt 15:27
on the children's *c*   Mark 7:28

Crush *demolish, destroy*
a foot may *c* them   Job 39:15
c-ed for our iniquities   Is 53:5
who *c* the needy   Amos 4:1

Cry (n) *scream, sob*
great and bitter *c*   Gen 27:34
Hear my *c*, O God   Ps 61:1
the *c* of Jerusalem   Jer 14:2
Jesus uttered a...*c* Mark 15:37

Cry (v)
do not *c* for help   Job 36:13
His elect, who *c*   Luke 18:7
stones will *c* out   Luke 19:40

Crystal *glass*
awesome gleam of *c*   Ezek 1:22
sea of glass like *c*   Rev 4:6
water...clear as *c*   Rev 22:1

Cultivate *till*
no man to *c* the   Gen 2:5
Eden to *c* it   Gen 2:15
and *c* vineyards   Deut 28:39
and *c* faithfulness   Ps 37:3

Cunning *crafty*
he is very *c*   1 Sam 23:22

advice of the *c*   Job 5:13

Cup *container*
My *c* overflows   Ps 23:5
a *c* of consolation   Jer 16:7
c of cold water   Matt 10:42
let this *c* pass   Matt 26:39
gives you a *c* of   Mark 9:41
c...new covenant   Luke 22:20
c of blessing   1 Cor 10:16
c full of abominations Rev 17:4

Cupbearer *royal official*
c spoke to Pharaoh   Gen 41:9
c to the king   Neh 1:11

Cure *become well*
c him of his leprosy   2 Kin 5:3
that...time He *c-d*   Luke 7:21

Curse (n) *condemning oath*
upon myself a *c*   Gen 27:12
c to My chosen ones   Is 65:15
will be no more *c*   Zech 14:11
become a *c* for us   Gal 3:13

Curse (v) *verbally condemn*
You shall not *c* God   Ex 22:28
c-d the...anointed 2 Sam 19:21
bless and *c* not   Rom 12:14
with it we *c* men   James 3:9

Cursed (adj) *under a curse*
C be Canaan   Gen 9:25
C...who trusts   Jer 17:5
C...who hangs   Gal 3:13

Curtain *covering, drape*
heaven like a tent *c*   Ps 104:2
c-s of your dwellings   Is 54:2

Custody *prison, protection*
they put him in *c*   Num 15:34
holding Jesus in *c*   Luke 22:63

Custom *manner or tax*
it became a *c* in   Judg 11:39
burial *c* of the Jews John 19:40
c-s of our fathers   Acts 28:17
whom tax is *due; c*   Rom 13:7

Cut *destroy, divide*
did not *c* the birds   Gen 15:10
c off from the earth   Ex 9:15
LORD *c* off...lips   Ps 12:3
tongue will be *c*   Prov 10:31
and *c* off his ear   Matt 26:51
were *c* to the quick   Acts 7:54
you...will be *c* off   Rom 11:22

Cymbal *musical instrument*
castanets and *c-s*   2 Sam 6:5
loud-sounding *c-s*   1 Chr 15:16
with loud *c-s*   Ps 150:5
or a clanging *c*   1 Cor 13:1

– D –

Damage (n) *destruction*
any *d* may be found   2 Kin 12:5
incurred this *d* and   Acts 27:21

Damage (v) *destroy, hurt*
enemy has *d-d* Ps 74:3
Lest anyone *d* it Is 27:3

Dance (n) *rhythmic movement*
timbrels…with *d-ing* Ex 15:20
shall rejoice in the *d* Jer 31:13

Dance (v) *move rhythmically*
David was *d-ing* 2 Sam 6:14
and a time to *d* Eccl 3:4

Danger *peril*
not only is there a *d* Acts 19:27
often in *d* of death 2 Cor 11:23

Dare *presume, risk*
who would *d* to risk Jer 30:21
d from that day Matt 22:46

Dark *dim, shadow*
d places of the land Ps 74:20
live in a *d* land Is 9:2
shining in a *d* place 2 Pet 1:19

Darken *obscure*
the land was *d-ed* Ex 10:15
the stars are *d-ed* Eccl 12:2
their eyes be *d-ed* Rom 11:10

Darkness *gloom, shadow*
blind…gropes in *d* Deut 28:29
are silenced in *d* 1 Sam 2:9
that stalks in *d* Ps 91:6
those who dwelt in *d* Ps 107:10
people who walk in *d* Is 9:2
light will rise in *d* Is 58:10
into the outer *d* Matt 22:13
those who sit in *d* Luke 1:79
men loved the *d* John 3:19
has light with *d* 2 Cor 6:14
unfruitful deeds of *d* Eph 5:11
Him there is no *d* 1 John 1:5

Daughter
d-s were born to them Gen 6:1
inheritance to his *d* Num 27:8
destruction of the *d* Is 22:4
the *d* of my people Jer 9:1
mother against *d* Luke 12:53

Dawn (n) *daylight*
rise before *d* and Ps 119:147
As the *d* is spread Joel 2:2

Dawn (v) *become light*
when morning *d-s* Ps 46:5
a light *d-ed* Matt 4:16
d toward the first Matt 28:1
until the day *d-s* 2 Pet 1:19

Day *light*
called the light *d* Gen 1:5
d…LORD has made Ps 118:24
d-s of your youth Eccl 12:1
d of the LORD is near Is 13:6
the *d* of His coming Mal 3:2
Give us this *d* Matt 6:11
judge…the last *d* John 12:48
the *d* of salvation 2 Cor 6:2
perfect it until the *d* Phil 1:6
d of the Lord 1 Thess 5:2

d is as a thousand 2 Pet 3:8

Deacons *officer, server*
overseers and *d* Phil 1:1
D likewise *must be* 1 Tim 3:8
Let *d* be husbands 1 Tim 3:12

Dead *without life*
you are a *d* man Gen 20:3
forgotten as a *d* man Ps 31:12
d do not praise Ps 115:17
Your *d* will live Is 26:19
not weep for the *d* Jer 22:10
rising from the *d* Mark 9:10
resurrection of the *d* Acts 23:6
d in your trespasses Eph 2:1
living and the *d* 2 Tim 4:1
to those who are *d* 1 Pet 4:6
was *d*…I am alive Rev 1:18

Deaf *without hearing*
not curse a *d* man Lev 19:14
the *d* shall hear Is 29:18
the *d* to hear Mark 7:37
d and dumb spirit Mark 9:25

Deal *allot, barter, treat*
let us *d* wisely Ex 1:10
nor *d* falsely Lev 19:11
who *d* treacherously Ps 25:3
who *d* faithfully Prov 12:22
has *d-t* with me Luke 1:25

Dealings *actions, relations*
no *d* with anyone Judg 18:7
no *d* with Samaritans John 4:9

Dear *beloved*
Is Ephraim My *d* son Jer 31:20
my life…as *d* to Acts 20:24
had become very *d* 1 Thess 2:8

Death *without life*
d encompassed me 2 Sam 22:5
d for his own sin 2 Chr 25:4
the shadow of *d* Ps 23:4
escapes from *d* Ps 68:20
d of His godly ones Ps 116:15
He will swallow up *d* Is 25:8
d is better to me Jon 4:3
let him be put to *d* Matt 15:4
shall not taste *d* Matt 16:28
to the point of *d* Mark 14:34
passed out of *d* John 5:24
he shall never see *d* John 8:51
the agony of *d* Acts 2:24
d by hanging Him Acts 10:39
wages of sin is *d* Rom 6:23
the law of sin and *d* Rom 8:2
proclaim…*d* 1 Cor 11:26
even *d* on a cross Phil 2:8
He might taste *d* Heb 2:9
passed out of *d* 1 John 3:14
Be faithful until *d* Rev 2:10

Debate *dispute*
d-d…themselves Mark 1:27
had been much *d* Acts 15:7

Debt *obligation*
and pay your *d* 2 Kin 4:7
forgive us our *d-s* Matt 6:12

Debtor *borrower*
forgiven our *d-s* Matt 6:12
had two *d-s* Luke 7:41

Decay *corruption*
own eyes see his *d* Job 21:20
did not undergo *d* Acts 13:37

Deceased *dead*
wife of the *d* shall Deut 25:5
the widow of the *d* Ruth 4:5
the name of the *d* Ruth 4:10
the sister of the *d* John 11:39

Deceit *falsehood, deception*
full of curses and *d* Ps 10:7
D is in the heart Prov 12:20
Offspring of *d* Is 57:4
houses are full of *d* Jer 5:27
d, sensuality, envy Mark 7:22
the lusts of *d* Eph 4:22

Deceitful *false*
From a *d* tongue Ps 120:2
the wicked are *d* Prov 12:5
The heart is more *d* Jer 17:9

Deceive *cheat, mislead*
have you *d-d* me Gen 29:25
d-s his companion Lev 6:2
Do not *d* me 2 Kin 4:28
Do not *d* yourselves Jer 37:9
they keep *d-ing* Rom 3:13
Let no one *d* you Eph 5:6

Deceiver *liar*
as a *d* in his sight Gen 27:12
d and the antichrist 2 John 7

Deception *falsehood*
the hills are a *d* Jer 3:23
reveling in their *d-s* 2 Pet 2:13

Deceptive *misleading*
wicked *d* wages Prov 11:18
Do not trust in *d* words Jer 7:4

Decision *judgment, resolution*
d is from the LORD Prov 16:33
My *d* is to gather Zeph 3:8

Declare *explain, proclaim*
d Thy faithfulness Ps 30:9
d Thy lovingkindness Ps 92:2
d-s the LORD Amos 4:11
He will *d* all things John 4:25

Decline *decrease*
our days have *d-d* Ps 90:9
for the day *d-s* Jer 6:4

Decrease *abate, subside*
water *d-d* steadily Gen 8:5
increase…I must *d* John 3:30

Decree (n) *judgment, order*
and *d* of the king   Esth 2:8
only one *d* for you   Dan 2:9
to the *d-s* of Caesar   Acts 17:7
Decree (v) *decide, determine*
been *d-d* against her   Esth 2:1
And rulers *d* justice   Prov 8:15
Dedicate *consecrate, devote*
D yourselves today   Ex 32:29
David…*d-d* these   1 Chr 18:11
d-ing it to Him   2 Chr 2:4
Dedication *consecration*
the *d* of the altar   2 Chr 7:9
d of the wall   Neh 12:27
d of the image   Dan 3:2
Deed *action* or *document*
What is this *d*   Gen 44:15
for our evil *d-s*   Ezra 9:13
abominable *d-s*   Ps 14:1
their *d-s* were evil   John 3:19
for every good *d*   Titus 3:1
Deep (adj) *far ranging*
d sleep falls on men   Job 4:13
casts into a *d* sleep   Prov 19:15
into *d* darkness   Jer 13:16
Deep (n) *abyss, depth*
fountains of the…*d*   Gen 7:11
surface of the *d* is   Job 38:30
D calls to *d*   Ps 42:7
His wonders in the *d* Ps 107:24
Deer *animal*
besides *d*, gazelles   1 Kin 4:23
d pants for the water   Ps 42:1
lame will leap like a *d*   Is 35:6
Defeat *conquer, overthrow*
d-ed…and pursued   Gen 14:15
able to *d* them   Num 22:6
sons of Israel *d-ed*   Josh 12:7
d the Arameans   2 Kin 13:17
d-ed the Philistines   1 Chr 18:1
d-ed the entire army   Jer 37:10
Defect (n) *blemish, spot*
one ram without *d*   Num 6:14
if it has any *d*   Deut 15:21
in whom was no *d*   Dan 1:4
Defect (v) *rebel, disobey*
d to his master   1 Chr 12:19
many *d-ed* to him   2 Chr 15:9
Defend *protect*
LORD of hosts will *d* Zech 9:15
or else *d-ing* them   Rom 2:15
are *d-ing* ourselves   2 Cor 12:19
Defense *protection*
Thou hast been a *d*   Is 25:4
the *d*…of the gospel   Phil 1:7
Defile *pollute, profane*
d-d the high places   2 Kin 23:8
your hands are *d-d*   Is 59:3
those *d* the man   Matt 15:18
is what *d-s* the man   Mark 7:20
d-s the entire body   James 3:6
Defilement *filth*
her *interest*, for *d*   Ezek 22:3
from all *d* of flesh   2 Cor 7:1

Defraud *deprive, wrong*
To *d* a man   Lam 3:36
Do not *d*   Mark 10:19
no one keep *d-ing*   Col 2:18
Delay *hinder, linger, stall*
Do not *d* me   Gen 24:56
shall not *d* to pay   Deut 23:21
bridegroom…*d-ing*   Matt 25:5
now why do you *d*   Acts 22:16
Delight (n) *pleasure*
I have no *d* in you   2 Sam 15:26
his *d* is in the law   Ps 1:2
d in the sons of   Prov 8:31
a just weight is His *d*   Prov 11:1
I took great *d*   Song 2:3
My *d* is in her   Is 62:4
Delight (v) *desire*
d in the Almighty   Job 22:26
not *d* in sacrifice   Ps 51:16
d in my ways   Prov 23:26
I *d* in loyalty   Hos 6:6
Delightful *pleasant*
to find *d* words   Eccl 12:10
and how *d* you are   Song 7:6
Deliver *give, rescue, save*
come down to *d* them   Ex 3:8
can this one *d*   1 Sam 10:27
He will *d* you   Job 5:19
d-ed my soul from   Ps 56:13
none who can *d*   Is 43:13
d us from evil   Matt 6:13
d-ed over to death   2 Cor 4:11
d-ed to the saints   Jude 3
Deliverance *salvation*
given this great *d*   Judg 15:8
with songs of *d*   Ps 32:7
a God of *d-s*   Ps 68:20
Deliverer *savior*
the LORD raised up a *d* Judg 3:9
my fortress and my *d*   Ps 18:2
D…from Zion   Rom 11:26
Delude *lead astray*
they have *d-d* you   Is 47:10
who *d* themselves   James 1:22
Demand *order, require*
but I *d* one thing   2 Sam 3:13
d-ing of Him a sign   Luke 11:16
Demolish *destroy*
d all…high places   Num 33:52
to *d* its strongholds   Is 23:11
Demon *devil*
sacrificed to *d-s*   Deut 32:17
after the *d* was cast   Matt 9:33
d-s also believe   James 2:19
Demoniacs *possessed ones*
d, epileptics   Matt 4:24
the *incident* of the *d*   Matt 8:33
Demon-possessed
many who were *d*   Matt 8:16
to the *d* man   Mark 5:16

sayings of one *d*   John 10:21
Demonstrate *show*
God *d-s* His own love   Rom 5:8
to *d* His wrath   Rom 9:22
d His patience   1 Tim 1:16
Demonstration *a showing*
in *d* of the Spirit   1 Cor 2:4
Den *abode*
remains in its *d*   Job 37:8
From the *d-s* of lions   Song 4:8
the viper's *d*   Is 11:8
east into the lions' *d*   Dan 6:7
it a robbers' *d*   Mark 11:17
Denounce *accuse, slander*
And come, *d* Israel   Num 23:7
let us *d* him   Jer 20:10
Deny *conceal, refuse*
lest you *d* your God   Josh 24:27
and *d-ing* the LORD   Is 59:13
whoever shall *d* Me   Matt 10:33
has *d-ied* the faith   1 Tim 5:8
d-ies the Son   1 John 2:23
Depart *leave*
sword…never *d*   2 Sam 12:10
to *d* from evil is   Job 28:28
his folly will not *d*   Prov 27:22
I never knew you; *d*   Matt 7:23
D from your country   Acts 7:3
d and be with Christ   Phil 1:23
Departure *death* or *leaving*
speaking of His *d*   Luke 9:31
time of my *d* has   2 Tim 4:6
Depend *rely, rest*
d-ed on the weapons   Is 22:8
d the whole Law   Matt 22:40
Depose *release*
d you from your office   Is 22:19
d-d from his royal   Dan 5:20
Deposit (n) *security*
in regard to a *d*   Lev 6:2
d which was entrusted   Lev 6:4
Deposit (v) *place, put*
d them in the tent   Num 17:4
d it in your town   Deut 14:28
d…in the temple   Ezra 5:15
had *d-ed* the scroll   Jer 36:20
Depraved *degenerate*
over to a *d* mind   Rom 1:28
men of *d* mind   2 Tim 3:8
Deprive *take away*
d the needy of justice   Is 10:2
d-ing one another   1 Cor 7:5
Depth *abyss, deep*
down to the *d-s*   Ps 107:26
drowned in the *d*   Matt 18:6
it had no *d* of soil   Mark 4:5
nor height, nor *d*   Rom 8:39
Descend *go down*
His glory will not *d*   Ps 49:17
shall *d* to Hades   Matt 11:23

d o the abyss Rom 10:7

Descendant *seed, offspring*
your *d-s* I will give Gen 12:7
shall your *d-s* be Rom 4:18
d of Abraham Heb 2:16

Descent *hill or heritage*
the *d* of the Mount Luke 19:37
were of high-priestly *d* Acts 4:6

Describe *explain*
you shall *d* the land Josh 18:6
who had seen it *d-d* Mark 5:16

Desecrate *defile*
d the sanctuary Dan 11:31
tried to *d* the temple Acts 24:6

Desert (n) *wilderness*
better to live in a *d* Prov 21:19
in the *d* a highway Is 40:3
like a bush in the *d* Jer 17:6
he lived in the *d-s* Luke 1:80

Desert (v) *abandon, forsake*
who had *d-ed* them Acts 15:38
so quickly *d-ing* Him Gal 1:6
I will never *d* you Heb 13:5

Deserters *changers of loyalty*
d who had deserted 2 Kin 25:11
d who had gone over Jer 39:9

Deserve *earn, merit*
him as he *d-ed* Judg 9:16
He is *d-ing* of death Matt 26:66
receiving what we *d* Luke 23:41

Design *creation, plan*
d-s for work in gold Ex 31:4
makers of *d-s* Ex 35:35
All their deadly *d-s* Jer 18:23

Designate *appoint*
one whom I *d* to 1 Sam 16:3
being *d-d* by God Heb 5:10

Desirable *attractive*
the tree was *d* Gen 3:6
more *d* than gold Ps 19:10
every kind of *d* object Nah 2:9

Desire (n) *appetite, craving*
poor from *their d* Job 31:16
the *d-s* of your heart Ps 37:4
d of the righteous Prov 10:24
d of your eyes Ezek 24:16
d-s of the flesh Eph 2:3
d to depart and be Phil 1:23

Desire (v) *crave, wish*
your heart *d-s* Deut 14:26
Thou dost *d* truth Ps 51:6
all that my eyes *d-d* Eccl 2:10
d the greater gifts 1 Cor 12:31
d a better *country* Heb 11:16

Desolate *lonely, waste*
sons of the *d* one Is 54:1
d wilderness behind Joel 2:3
loaves in a *d* place Matt 15:33
children of the *d* Gal 4:27

Desolation *ruin, waste*
a heap forever, a *d* Josh 8:28
D is left in the city Is 24:12
an everlasting *d* Ezek 35:9
the abomination of *d* Dan 11:31
her *d* is at hand Luke 21:20

Despair (n) *grief*
my soul is in *d* Ps 42:6
Why are you in *d* Ps 43:5

Despair (v) *grieve*
Saul then will *d* 1 Sam 27:1
we *d-ed* even of life 2 Cor 1:8

Despise *reject, scorn*
d-d his birthright Gen 25:34
not *d* the discipline Job 5:17
Fools *d* wisdom and Prov 1:7
not *d* one of these Matt 18:10
hold to one, and *d* Luke 16:13

Despoil *injure, lay waste*
d-ed all the cities 2 Chr 14:14
the wicked who *d* me Ps 17:9
plundered and *d-ed* Is 42:22

Destine *appoint*
d you for the sword Is 65:12
things *d-d* to perish Col 2:22

Destitute *deprived, in need*
prayer of the *d* Ps 102:17
being *d*, afflicted Heb 11:37

Destroy *abolish, ruin, waste*
to *d* all flesh Gen 6:17
lest I *d* you 1 Sam 15:6
seek my life to *d* it Ps 40:14
moth and rust *d* Matt 6:19
who is able to *d* Matt 10:28
You come to *d* us Mark 1:24
d the temple and Mark 15:29
D this temple, and John 2:19
to save and to *d* James 4:12
d the works of the 1 John 3:8

Destroyer *devastator*
d of our country Judg 16:24
d comes upon him Job 15:21
I shall set apart *d-s* Jer 22:7

Destruction *calamity, ruin*
God apportion *d* Job 21:17
Your tongue devises *d* Ps 52:2
Pride *goes* before *d* Prov 16:18
called the City of *D* Is 19:18
broad that leads to *d* Matt 7:13
whose end is *d* Phil 3:19
d will come 1 Thess 5:3

Determine *decide*
his days are *d-d* Job 14:5
d-d their appointed Acts 17:26
d-d to know nothing 1 Cor 2:2

Detest *despise, loathe*
carcasses you shall *d* Lev 11:11
I *d* his citadels Amos 6:8

Detestable *abominable*
not eat any *d* thing Deut 14:3
swine's flesh, *d* Is 66:17

remove all its *d* Ezek 11:18

Devastate *destroy, lay waste*
d-d the nations 2 Kin 19:17
the LORD...*d-s* it Is 24:1

Devastation *destruction*
d of the afflicted Ps 12:5
d in their citadels Amos 3:10

Device *plan, scheme*
By their own *d-s* Ps 5:10
a man of evil *d-s* Prov 14:17
in their *d-s* you walk Mic 6:16

Devil *demon, Satan*
tempted by the *d* Matt 4:1
you son of the *d* Acts 13:10
serpent...the *d* Rev 12:9
d...into the lake Rev 20:10

Devise *design, scheme, plot*
d-ing a vain thing Ps 2:1
d-s evil continually Prov 6:14
He *d-s* wicked schemes Is 32:7
d futile things Acts 4:25

Devote *commit, dedicate*
shall *d* to the LORD Ex 13:12
d-ing...to prayer Acts 1:14
D yourselves to prayer Col 4:2

Devoted *set apart (to God)*
d to destruction 1 Sam 15:21
d thing in Israel Ezek 44:29

Devotion *consecration*
his deeds of *d* 2 Chr 32:32
the *d* of your youth Jer 2:2

Devour *consume, swallow*
wild beast *d-ed* him Gen 37:20
is *d-ed* by disease Job 18:13
To *d* the afflicted Prov 30:14
d widows' houses Mark 12:40
bite...*d* one another Gal 5:15

Devout *God-fearing*
d men are taken away Is 57:1
was righteous and *d* Luke 2:25
d men, from every Acts 2:5

Dew *drops of moisture*
d fell on the camp Num 11:9
d on the fleece only Judg 6:37
neither *d* nor rain 1 Kin 17:1
Like a cloud of *d* Is 18:4
drenched with the *d* Dan 4:15

Dialect *language*
in the Hebrew *d* Acts 21:40
the Hebrew *d* Acts 22:2

Die *decease, expire*
you shall surely *d* Gen 2:17
Curse God and *d* Job 2:9
even wise men *d* Ps 49:10
soul who sins will *d* Ezek 18:4
to *d* with You Matt 26:35
grain of wheat...*d-s* John 12:24
d-d for the ungodly Rom 5:6
we who *d-d* to sin Rom 6:2
I *d* daily 1 Cor 15:31

I *d-d* to the Law   Gal 2:19
to *d* is gain   Phil 1:21
to *d* once and after   Heb 9:27
who *d* in the Lord   Rev 14:13

Difficult *hard*
too *d* for the LORD   Gen 18:14
speech or *d* language   Ezek 3:5
last days *d* times   2 Tim 3:1

Dig *excavate, till*
opens a pit, or *d-s*   Ex 21:33
they *d* into houses   Job 24:16
dug a wine press   Matt 21:33

Dignity *majesty*
What honor or *d* has   Esth 6:3
must be men of *d*   1 Tim 3:8

Diligence *effort*
Watch…with all *d*   Prov 4:23
show the same *d*   Heb 6:11

Diligent *persistent*
hand of the *d* makes   Prov 10:4
d to present   2 Tim 2:15
d to enter that rest   Heb 4:11

Dim *cloudy, dark*
eye was not *d*   Deut 34:7
windows grow *d*   Eccl 12:3

Diminish *dwindle, reduce*
d their inheritance   Num 26:54
are *d-ed* and bowed   Ps 107:39

Dine *eat*
men are to *d* with   Gen 43:16
came and were *d-ing*   Matt 9:10

Dinner *meal*
I have prepared…*d*   Matt 22:4
because of…*d*   Mark 6:26
was giving a big *d*   Luke 14:16

Dip *plunge*
d-ped…seven times   2 Kin 5:14
d-ped…with Me   Matt 26:23
robe *d-ped* in blood   Rev 19:13

Direct *arrange, guide, order*
LORD *d-s* his steps   Prov 16:9
had *d-ed* the Spirit   Is 40:13
walks to *d* his steps   Jer 10:23
d their entire body   James 3:3

Direction *path* or *order*
which turned every *d*   Gen 3:24
of their four *d-s*   Ezek 1:17

Dirge *lament*
for you as a *d*   Amos 5:1
we sang a *d*   Luke 7:32

Disappear *vanish*
For the faithful *d*   Ps 12:1
old is ready to *d*   Heb 8:13

Disappoint *frustrate*
and were not *d-ed*   Ps 22:5
hope does not *d*   Rom 5:5

Disaster *calamity*
d was close to them   Judg 20:34

because of all its *d-s*   Jer 19:8

Disbelieve *doubt*
for those who *d*   1 Pet 2:7

Discern *understand, recognize*
would *d*…future   Deut 32:29
not *d* its appearance   Job 4:16
O fools, *d* wisdom   Prov 8:5

Discernment *judgment*
blessed be your *d*   1 Sam 25:33
knowledge and all *d*   Phil 1:9

Discharge *emission*
a *d* from his body   Lev 15:2
everyone having a *d*   Num 5:2
the *d* of your blood   Ezek 32:6

Disciple *student, learner*
to listen as a *d*   Is 50:4
His twelve *d-s*   Matt 10:1
d is not above his   Matt 10:24
make *d-s* of all   Matt 28:19
Your *d-s* do not fast   Mark 2:18
he cannot be My *d*   Luke 14:26
His *d-s* withdrew   John 6:66
was the *d-s* feet   John 13:5
d-s were first called   Acts 11:26

Discipline (n) *chastisement*
the *d* of the LORD   Deut 11:2
The rod of *d*   Prov 22:15
to see your good *d*   Col 2:5

Discipline (v) *chastise*
as a man *d-s* his son   Deut 8:5
d-d by the Lord   1 Cor 11:32
father does not *d*   Heb 12:7

Disclose *reveal*
without *d-ing* it to   1 Sam 20:2
d the motives of   1 Cor 4:5
secrets…are *d-d*   1 Cor 14:25

Discourage *dishearten*
people of the land *d-d*   Ezra 4:4
d-d with the work   Neh 6:9

Discover *find, uncover*
d the depths of God   Job 11:7
shamed…he is *d-ed*   Jer 2:26

Discretion *understanding*
LORD give you *d*   1 Chr 22:12
woman who lacks *d*   Prov 11:22

Discuss *converse, reason*
d matters of justice   Jer 12:1
d among themselves   Matt 16:7
d-ed together what   Luke 6:11

Disease *sickness*
none of the *d-s* on you   Ex 15:26
harmful *d-s* of Egypt   Deut 7:15
d-d in his feet   2 Chr 16:12
d-d…not healed   Ezek 34:4
heals all your *d-s*   Ps 103:3
various *d-s* and pains   Matt 4:24
power…to heal *d-s*   Luke 9:1

Disgrace *reproach, shame*
a *d* to us   Gen 34:14
sin is a *d* to   Prov 14:34

and bear your *d*   Ezek 16:52

Disgraceful *shameful*
d thing in Israel   Gen 34:7
d for a woman to   1 Cor 11:6

Disguise *pretend*
Arise now, and *d*   1 Kin 14:2
he *d-s* his face   Job 24:15

Disheartened *discouraged*
not be *d* or crushed   Is 42:4

Dishonest *untruthful*
those who hate *d* gain   Ex 18:21
cheat with *d* scales   Amos 8:5

Dishonor (n) *disgrace, shame*
to see the king's *d*   Ezra 4:14
man conceals *d*   Prov 12:16

Dishonor (v) *disgrace, shame*
who *d-s* his father   Deut 27:16
and you *d* Me   John 8:49
do you *d* God   Rom 2:23

Dismay *be troubled, fear*
d-ed at his presence   Gen 45:3
d-ed and…afraid   1 Sam 17:11
lest I *d* you   Jer 1:17

Dismiss *release, send away*
d-ed the people   Josh 24:28
he *d-ed* the assembly   Acts 19:41

Disobedience *rebellion*
the one man's *d*   Rom 5:19
d received a just   Heb 2:2

Disobedient *rebellious*
d and rebelled   Neh 9:26
d to parents   Rom 1:30

Disperse *spread*
d them in Jacob   Gen 49:7
d them among the   Ezek 20:23

Display *declare, show*
to *d* her beauty   Esth 1:11
works of God…*d-ed*   John 9:3

Displease *annoy, trouble*
d-ing in the sight   1 Sam 8:6
d-ing in His sight   Is 59:15

Dispossess *remove*
d-ed the Amorites   Num 21:32
Esau *d-ed* them   Deut 2:12
He will assuredly *d*   Josh 3:10
d-ing the nations   Acts 7:45

Dispute (n) *controversy*
When they have a *d*   Ex 18:16
a great *d* among   Acts 28:29

Dispute (v) *contend, debate*
with Israel he will *d*   Mic 6:2
he *d-d* with the devil   Jude 9

Dissension *division*
great *d* and debate   Acts 15:2
without wrath and *d*   1 Tim 2:8

Dissipation *intemperance*
wine, for that is *d*   Eph 5:18
not accused of *d*   Titus 1:6

Dissolve *melt*
dost *d* me in a storm   Job 30:22
And the hills *d*   Nah 1:5

Distance *far away*
sister stood at a *d*   Ex 2:4
following…at a *d*   Matt 26:58

Distinction *difference*
the LORD makes a *d*   Ex 11:7
have made no *d*   Ezek 22:26
he made no *d*   Acts 15:9
for there is no *d*   Rom 3:22

Distinguish *discern*
I *d* between good   2 Sam 19:35
d-ing of spirits   1 Cor 12:10

Distinguishing
became your *d* mark Ezek 27:7
this is a *d* mark   2 Thess 3:17

Distort *pervert*
my garment is *d-ed*   Job 30:18
d the gospel of Christ   Gal 1:7

Distress *adversity, trouble*
day of my *d*   Gen 35:3
When you are in *d*   Deut 4:30
I am in great *d*   2 Sam 24:14
d upon the land   Luke 21:23
d for every soul   Rom 2:9
widows in their *d*   James 1:27

Distribute *apportion*
to *d* their kinsmen   Neh 13:13
d it to the poor   Luke 18:22

District *area, province*
the *d* of Jerusalem   Neh 3:12
d around the Jordan   Matt 3:5
d of Galilee   Mark 1:28
the *d-s* of Libya   Acts 2:10

Disturb *annoy, bother*
no one *d* his bones   2 Kin 23:18
being greatly *d-ed*   Acts 4:2

Disturbance *turmoil*
to cause a *d* in it   Neh 4:8
d among the soldiers Acts 12:18

Divide *apportion, separate*
D the living child   1 Kin 3:25
He will *d* the booty   Is 53:12
d-d his wealth   Luke 15:12

Divination *witchcraft*
nor practice *d* or   Lev 19:26
witchcraft, used *d*   2 Chr 33:6
false vision, *d*   Jer 14:14
falsehood and lying *d* Ezek 13:6
a spirit of *d* met us   Acts 16:16

Divine (adj) *pertaining to deity*
in whom…*d* spirit   Gen 41:38
power and *d* nature   Rom 1:20
is the *d* response   Rom 11:4

Divine (v) *practice divination*
they *d* lies for you   Ezek 21:29
prophets *d* for money   Mic 3:11

Division *dissention, segment*
d between My people   Ex 8:23

no *d-s* among you   1 Cor 1:10
d of soul and spirit   Heb 4:12

Divorce (n) *separation*
a certificate of *d*   Deut 24:1
given her a writ of *d*   Jer 3:8
For I hate *d*   Mal 2:16

Divorce (v) *separate*
husband *d-s* his wife   Jer 3:1
man to *d* his wife   Matt 19:3
Whoever *d-s* his   Mark 10:11

Divorced *separated*
marries a *d* woman   Matt 5:32
marries…who is *d* Luke 16:18

Doctrine *teaching*
every wind of *d*   Eph 4:14
to teach strange *d-s*   1 Tim 1:3
to exhort in sound *d*   Titus 1:9

Doer *workman*
d-s of the Law will   Rom 2:13
d-s of the word   James 1:22
not a *d* of the law   James 4:11

Domain *estate*
give You all this *d*   Luke 4:6
the *d* of darkness   Col 1:13
keep their own *d*   Jude 6

Dominion *authority, rule*
Thine is the *d*   1 Chr 29:11
places of His *d*   Ps 103:22
and power and *d*   Eph 1:21
thrones or *d-s* or   Col 1:16

Door *entrance, opening*
crouching at the *d*   Gen 4:7
shut your *d*, pray   Matt 6:6
I am the *d*   John 10:9
right at the *d*   James 5:9
I stand at the *d*   Rev 3:20

Doorway *entrance, opening*
the *d* of the tent   Judg 4:20
d-s and doorposts   1 Kin 7:5
at my neighbor's *d*   Job 31:9
chamber with its *d* Ezek 40:38

Doubt (n) *unbelief*
life shall hang in *d*   Deut 28:66
why do *d-s* arise   Luke 24:38

Doubt (v) *disbelieve*
why did you *d*   Matt 14:31
not *d* in his heart   Mark 11:23
who *d-s* is like the   James 1:6

Dove *bird*
he sent out a *d*   Gen 8:8
had wings like a *d*   Ps 55:6
eyes are *like d-s*   Song 1:15
descending as a *d*   Matt 3:16
descending as a *d*   John 1:32
selling the *d-s*   John 2:16

Downfall *collapse*
became the *d* of   2 Chr 28:23
noise of their *d*   Jer 49:21

Drag *draw, pull*
grasshopper *d-s*   Eccl 12:5
d you into court   James 2:6

Drain *empty*
blood is to be *d-ed*   Lev 1:15
drink it and *d* it   Ezek 23:34

Draw *haul, pull*
but are *d-n* away   Deut 30:17
d near to my soul   Ps 69:18
d all men to Myself   John 12:32
D near to God   James 4:8

Dread (n) *fear*
in *d* night and day   Deut 28:66
d comes like a storm   Prov 1:27
they are in great *d*   Ps 14:5

Dread (v) *fear*
Whom shall I *d*   Ps 27:1
are *d-ed* and feared   Hab 1:7

Dream (n) *vision*
had a *d*, and behold   Gen 28:12
flies away like a *d*   Job 20:8
visions and *d-s*   Dan 1:7
to Joseph in a *d*   Matt 2:13

Dream (v) *see a vision*
like those who *d*   Ps 126:1
Your old men will *d*   Joel 2:28

Dreamer *visionary*
Here comes this *d*   Gen 37:19
your diviners, your *d-s* Jer 27:9

Dress (n) *clothing*
have taken off my *d*   Song 5:3
d was of fine linen   Ezek 16:3

Dress (v) *array, clothe*
D-ed as a harlot   Prov 7:10
d-ed Him…purple Mark 15:17

Drink (n) *refreshment*
gave the lad a *d*   Gen 21:19
thirsty…gave me *d* Matt 25:35
My blood is true *d*   John 6:55
thirsty, give him a *d* Rom 12:20

Drink (v)
Do not *d* wine   Lev 10:9
they all *drank* from Mark 14:23
ground that *d-s* the   Heb 6:7

Drive *chase, defeat*
and *drove* them away   Ex 2:17
d hard all your workers Is 58:3
drove them all out   John 2:15

Drop (n) *drip*
the *d-s* of water   Job 36:27
like *d-s* of blood   Luke 22:44

Drop (v) *fall*
olives shall *d* off   Deut 28:40
d off his unripe grape Job 15:33

Dross *metallic waste*
of the earth *like d*   Ps 119:119
Israel has become *d* Ezek 22:18

Drought *dryness*
Like heat in *d*   Is 25:5
I called for a *d*   Hag 1:11

Drowned *sank*
d in the Red Sea   Ex 15:4
were *d* in the sea   Mark 5:13

Drunk *intoxicated*
d, but not with wine   Is 29:9
not get *d* with wine   Eph 5:18

Drunkard *intoxicated person*
a glutton and a *d*   Deut 21:20
a reviler, or a *d*   1 Cor 5:11

Drunken *intoxicated*
stagger like a *d* man   Job 12:25

Drunkenness *intoxicated*
weighted down...*d* Luke 21:34
in carousing and *d*   Rom 13:13

Dry (adj) *parched, scorched*
let the *d* land appear   Gen 1:9
O *d* bones, hear   Ezek 37:4

Dry (v) *scorch, wither*
My strength is *dried*   Ps 22:15
I *d* up the sea   Is 50:2
dries up...rivers   Nah 1:4

Due (adj) *proper, right*
In *d* time their foot   Deut 32:35
d penalty of their   Rom 1:27

Due (n) *what is owed*
as *their d* forever   Lev 7:34
Indeed it is Thy *d*   Jer 10:7

Dull *heavy, stupid*
eyes are *d* from wine Gen 49:12
peple...become *d*   Matt 13:15
become *d* of hearing   Heb 5:11

Dumb *silent*
behold, a *d* man   Matt 9:32
and the *d* to speak   Mark 7:37

Dung *waste*
sweeps away *d*   1 Kin 14:10
give you cow's *d*   Ezek 4:15

Dungeon *prison*
put me into the *d*   Gen 40:15
captive...in the *d*   Ex 12:29
prisoners from the *d*   Is 42:7
Jeremiah...into the *d* Jer 37:16

Dust *dirt, earth*
formed man of *d*   Gen 2:7
And *d* shall you eat   Gen 3:14
repent in *d* and ashes   Job 42:6
You who lie in the *d*   Is 26:19
the *d* of your city   Luke 10:11
d on their heads   Rev 18:19

Duty *responsibility*
perform your *d*   Gen 38:8
his *d* to his wife   1 Cor 7:3

Dwell *abide, live*
d on Thy holy will   Ps 15:1
I will *d* in the house   Ps 23:6
d among the wise   Prov 15:31
of God *d-s* in you   1 Cor 3:16
Christ may *d* in your   Eph 3:17
mind *d* on these things   Phil 4:8

Dwelling *habitation*
earth shall be your *d* Gen 27:39
place for Thy *d*   1 Kin 8:13
might find a *d* place   Acts 7:46

– E –

Eagle *bird*
bore you on *e-s'* wings   Ex 19:4
the *e* swoops down   Deut 28:49
swifter than *e-s*   2 Sam 1:23
with wings like *e-s*   Is 40:31
the face of an *e*   Ezek 1:10
was like a flying *e*   Rev 4:7

Ear *hearing*
heard with our *e-s*   2 Sam 7:22
and incline your *e*   Ps 45:10
He whose *e* listens   Prov 15:31
let your *e* receive   Jer 9:20
and cut off his *e*   Matt 26:51
fingers into his *e-s*   Mark 7:33
if the *e* should say   1 Cor 12:16
He who has an *e*   Rev 2:7

Early *beforetime, soon*
they arose *e* and   Gen 26:31
Let us rise *e*   Song 7:12
e on the first day   Mark 16:2
at the tomb *e*   Luke 24:22

Earnings *gain, wages*
her *e* she plants   Prov 31:16

Earring *ornament*
brought...*e-s*   Ex 35:22
Like an *e* of gold   Prov 25:12

Earth *land, world*
God created the...*e*   Gen 1:1
the *e* is the LORD'S   Ex 9:29
way of all the *e*   Josh 23:14
foundation of the *e*   Job 38:4
the shields of the *e*   Ps 47:9
He established the *e*   Ps 104:5
the *e* remains forever   Eccl 1:4
the vault of the *e*   Is 40:22
the ends of the *e*   Is 45:22
the *e* is My footstool   Is 66:1
make the *e* dark   Amos 8:9
shall inherit the *e*   Matt 5:5
you shall bind on *e* Matt 16:19
glorified...on the *e*   John 17:4
heavens and a new *e*   2 Pet 3:13
e and heaven fled   Rev 20:11

Earthquake *temblor*
LORD *was* not...*e*   1 Kin 19:11
be famines and *e-s*   Matt 24:7
will be great *e-s*   Luke 21:11

Earthy *mortal*
those who are *e*   1 Cor 15:48

Ease *free from difficulty, pain*
at *e* and satisfied   Job 21:23
women who are at *e*   Is 32:9

East *direction of compass*
men of the *e*   Job 1:3
offspring from the *e*   Is 43:5
saw His star in the *e*   Matt 2:2
kings from the *e*   Rev 16:12

Easy *without difficulty*
My yoke is *e*, and   Matt 11:30

Eat *consume, dine, feast*
they *ate* every plant   Ex 10:15
e and be satisfied   Ps 22:26
will *e* curds and honey   Is 7:15
e this scroll   Ezek 3:1
what you shall *e*   Matt 6:25
e with unwashed   Matt 15:20
Take, *e;* this is My   Matt 26:26
sinners and *e-s* with   Luke 15:2
He took it and *ate*   Luke 24:43
Peter, kill and *e*   Acts 10:13
ate...spiritual food   1 Cor 10:3

Edict *decree*
the king's *e-s*   Ezra 8:36
king's command and *e* Esth 9:1

Edification *building up*
his good, to his *e*   Rom 15:2
speaks to men for *e*   1 Cor 14:3
all things...for *e*   1 Cor 14:26

Edify *build up*
but love *e-ies*   1 Cor 8:1
not all things *e*   1 Cor 10:23

Educated *taught*
be *e* three years   Dan 1:5
e under Gamaliel   Acts 22:3

Elder *aged, older*
words of her *e* son   Gen 27:42
sits among the *e-s*   Prov 31:23
tradition of the *e-s*   Matt 15:2
chief priests and *e-s* Matt 27:12
Council of *e-s* of   Luke 22:66
e-s of the church   Acts 20:17
I saw twenty-four *e*   Rev 4:4

Elect *chosen*
sake of the *e*   Matt 24:22
to lead the *e* astray Mark 13:22
justice for His *e*   Luke 18:7
against God's *e*   Rom 8:33

Elementary *basic*
e principles of the   Col 2:8
e teaching about the   Heb 6:1

Elements *physical matter*
e will be destroyed   2 Pet 3:10
the *e* will melt with   2 Pet 3:12

Embarrassed *ashamed*
e to lift up my face   Ezra 9:6
diviners will be *e*   Mic 3:7

Embittered *resentful*
e them against the   Acts 14:2

Embrace *clasp, hug*
Esau ran...and *e-d*   Gen 33:4
A time to *e*   Eccl 3:5

Eminent *renowned*
the most *e* apostles   2 Cor 11:5
inferior to...*e*   2 Cor 12:11

Empowered *authorized*
e him to eat from   Eccl 5:19

Empty (adj) *containing nothing*
Now the pit was *e*   Gen 37:24

sent widows away *e* Job 22:9
deceive you with *e* Eph 5:6

Empty (v) *remove contents*
e-ing their sacks Gen 42:35
they *e* the house Lev 14:36
but *e-ied* Himself Phil 2:7

Encamp *abide, lodge*
the tabernacle *e-s* Num 1:51
a host *e* against me Ps 27:3

Encircle *go around*
entirely *e-ing* the sea 2 Chr 4:3
cords…have *e-d* me Ps 119:61

Encompass *surround*
waves of death *e* 2 Sam 22:5
e-ed…with bitterness Lam 3:5

Encourage *strengthen*
e-d him in God 1 Sam 23:16
e one another 1 Thess 5:11
e the young women Titus 2:4

Encouragement *support*
I arose to be an *e* Dan 11:1
God who gives…*e* Rom 15:5
is any *e* in Christ Phil 2:1

End (n) *extremity, goal, result*
e of all flesh has Gen 6:13
beginning to *e* 1 Sam 3:12
wicked come to an *e* Ps 7:9
no *e* to all his labor Eccl 4:8
The *e* is coming Ezek 7:2
to the *e* of the age Matt 28:20
kingdom…no *e* Luke 1:33
He loved…to the *e* John 13:1
beginning and the *e* Rev 21:6

End (v) *complete, stop*
border *e-ed* at the sea Josh 15:4
e-s up being burned Heb 6:8

Endless *limitless*
writing…is *e* Eccl 12:12
and *e* genealogies 1 Tim 1:4

Endow *provide a gift*
God has *e-ed* me Gen 30:20
e-ed with discretion 2 Chr 2:12
To *e* those who love Prov 8:21
e-ed with salvation Zech 9:9

Endurance *patience*
have need of *e* Heb 10:36
let us run with *e* Heb 12:1
of the *e* of Job James 5:11

Endure *persevere*
will be able to *e* Ex 18:23
May his name *e* Ps 72:17
Can your heart *e* Ezek 22:14
e-s to the end Mark 13:13
e-s all things 1 Cor 13:7
blessed who *e-s* James 5:11

Enemy *foe*
delivered your *e-ies* Gen 14:20
a man finds his *e* 1 Sam 24:19
presence of my *e-ies* Ps 23:5
kisses of an *e* Prov 27:6

love your *e-ies,* Matt 5:44
e is hungry, feed Rom 12:20
an *e* of God James 4:4

Engage *be involved, betroth*
e-d in their work 1 Chr 9:33
e-d to…Joseph Luke 1:27
to *e* in good deeds Titus 3:8

Engrave *inscribe*
e the two stones Ex 28:11
e an inscription Zech 3:9

Engulf *overwhelm, swallow*
water…to *e* them Deut 11:4
She has been *e-ed* Jer 51:42

Enlarge *extend, increase*
May God *e* Japheth Gen 9:27
Sheol has *e-d* its Is 5:14

Enlighten *illumine*
e-ing the eyes Ps 19:8
who have…been *e-ed* Heb 6:4

Enmity *hostility*
e Between you and Gen 3:15
had everlasting *e* Ezek 35:5
at *e* with each other Luke 23:12

Enrage *anger*
jealousy *e-s* a man Prov 6:34
became very *e-d* Matt 2:16

Enrich *make wealthy*
king will *e* the 1 Sam 17:25
Thou dost greatly *e* Ps 65:9
You *e-ed* the kings Ezek 27:33

Enrolled *recorded*
were *e* by genealogy 1 Chr 7:9
e in heaven Heb 12:23

Enslave *subjugate*
you have been *e-d* Is 14:3
e-d to various lusts Titus 3:3

Ensnare *catch*
An evil man is *e-d* Prov 12:13

Entangle *ensnare*
sin which…*e-s* us Heb 12:1

Enter *go in*
you shall *e* the ark Gen 6:18
E His gates with Ps 100:4
E the rock and hide Is 2:10
Spirit *e-ed* me and Ezek 2:2
not *e* the kingdom Matt 5:20
E by the narrow gate Matt 7:13
afraid as they *e-ed* Luke 9:34
e into the kingdom John 3:5
not *e* by the door John 10:1

Entice *deceive, seduce*
E your husband Judg 14:15
if sinners *e* you Prov 1:10
e-d by his own lust James 1:14

Entrance *doorway*
cloud…at the *e* Ex 33:10
stone against the *e* Matt 27:60

Entreat *appeal, ask*
Moses *e-ed* the LORD Ex 32:11

Please *e* the LORD 1 Kin 13:6
demons *began* to *e* Matt 8:31
they were *e-ing* Him Luke 8:31
I *e-ed* the Lord 2 Cor 12:8

Entrust *assign, commit*
security *e-ed to him* Lev 6:2
to whom they *e-ed* Luke 12:48

Envious *covetous*
e of the arrogant Ps 73:3
is your eye *e* Matt 20:15
And you are *e* James 4:2

Envoy *agent, messenger*
e-s of the rulers 2 Chr 32:31
faithful *e brings* Prov 13:17
sent your *e-s* a great Is 57:9
His *e-s* to Egypt Ezek 17:15

Envy (n) *jealousy*
full of *e*, murder Rom 1:29
out of which arise *e* 1 Tim 6:4

Epochs *ages, seasons*
the times and the *e* Dan 2:21
to know times or *e* Acts 1:7

Equal *same*
a man my *e* Ps 55:13
That I should be *his e* Is 40:25
Himself *e* with God John 5:18

Equip *furnish, provide*
e-ped for…work 2 Tim 3:17
e you in every good Heb 13:21

Equipment *implements*
the *e* for the service Ex 39:40
e for his chariots 1 Sam 8:12
e of a foolish Zech 11:15

Equity *equality, fairness*
eyes look with *e* Ps 17:2
justice and *e* Prov 1:3

Error *mistake, sin*
can discern *his e-s* Ps 19:12
e against the LORD Is 32:6
the spirit of *e* 1 John 4:6

Escape (n) *deliverance, refuge*
there will be no *e* Job 11:20
provide…*e* 1 Cor 10:13

Escape (v) *elude*
slave who has *e-d* Deut 23:15
Our soul has *e-d* Ps 124:7
tells lies will not *e* Prov 19:5
nothing at all *e-s* Joel 2:3
had not *e-d* notice Luke 8:47
how shall we *e* if Heb 2:3

Establish *confirm, found*
I will *e* my covenant Gen 17:19
dost *e* the mountains Ps 65:6
e-ed in lovingkindness Is 16:5
we *e* the Law Rom 3:31
e-ed in the truth 2 Pet 1:12

Estate *domain* or *standard*
us in our low *e* Ps 136:23
squandered his *e* Luke 15:13

Esteem (n) *honor*
held them in high *e*   Acts 5:13

Esteem (v) *have high regard*
e-d Him stricken   Is 53:4
e them...in love   1 Thess 5:13

Estranged *separated*
e from my brothers   Ps 69:8

Eternal *everlasting*
E Father, Prince of   Is 9:6
An *e* decree   Jer 5:22
cast into the *e* fire   Matt 18:8
to inherit *e* life   Luke 10:25
gift of God is *e* life   Rom 6:23
Now to the King *e*   1 Tim 1:17
source of *e* salvation   Heb 5:9
kept us in *e* bonds   Jude 6

Eternity *perpetuity*
set *e* in their heart   Eccl 3:11
to the day of *e*   2 Pet 3:18

Eunuch *chamberlain, official*
Neither let the *e* say   Is 56:3
made *e-s* by men   Matt 19:12
an Ethiopian *e*   Acts 8:27

Evening *dusk, darkness*
as the *e* offering   Ps 141:2
when *e* had come   Matt 8:16

Event *happening*
the *e-s* of the war   2 Sam 11:18
e became sin to the   1 Kin 13:34
recorded these *e-s*   Esth 9:20
time for every *e*   Eccl 3:1

Everlasting *eternal*
LORD, the *E* God   Gen 21:33
are the *e* arms   Deut 33:27
lovingkindness is *e*   Ps 106:1
E God, the LORD   Is 40:28
loved you with an *e*   Jer 31:3

Evidence *facts, testimony*
the *e* of witnesses   Num 35:30
not able to give *e*   Ezra 2:59

Evident *obvious, plain*
the tares became *e*   Matt 13:26
work will become *e*   1 Cor 3:13
Law before God is *e*   Gal 3:11

Evil *bad, wicked, wrong*
man's heart is *e*   Gen 8:21
I fear no *e*   Ps 23:4
repay me *e* for good   Ps 35:12
turn away from *e*   Prov 3:7
taken away from *e*   Is 57:1
committed two *e-s*   Jer 2:13
deliver us from *e*   Matt 6:13
Never...*e* for *e*   Rom 12:17
love of money is...*e*   1 Tim 6:10
tongue...restless *e*   James 3:8

Evildoer *wicked one*
LORD repay the *e*   2 Sam 3:39
e listens to wicked   Prov 17:4
depart...you *e-s*   Luke 13:27
punishment of *e-s*   1 Pet 2:14

Exact (adj) *certain, correct*
e amount of money   Esth 4:7
know the *e* truth   Luke 1:4

Exact (v) *collect*
let him *e* a fifth   Gen 41:34
He *e-ed* the silver   2 Kin 23:25
e a tribute of grain   Amos 5:11

Exalt *extol, honor, lift*
He is highly *e-ed*   Ex 15:1
He is *e-ed* in power   Job 37:23
let us *e* His name   Ps 34:3
E that which is low   Ezek 21:26
e-ed to...right hand   Acts 2:33
be *e-ed* in my body   Phil 1:20
He will *e* you   James 4:10

Examine *investigate, search*
E me, O LORD,   Ps 26:2
e-ing the Scriptures   Acts 17:11
a man *e* himself   1 Cor 11:28

Example *model, pattern*
the *e* of his father   2 Chr 17:3
I gave you an *e*   John 13:15
e of disobedience   Heb 4:11
made them an *e*   2 Pet 2:6

Excellence *perfection*
greatness of Thine *e*   Ex 15:7
if there is any *e*   Phil 4:8

Excellent *outstanding*
e wife is the crown   Prov 12:4
He has done *e* things   Is 12:5
a still more *e* way   1 Cor 12:31
a more *e* name   Heb 1:4

Excess *too much*
he...had no *e*   Ex 16:18
same *e* of dissipation   1 Pet 4:4

Exchange *trade, transfer*
they *e-d* their glory   Ps 106:20
e-d the truth of God   Rom 1:25

Exclude *refuse to admit*
e-d from...assembly   Ezra 10:8
e-d all foreigners   Neh 13:3
e you for My name's   Is 66:5
e-d from the life of   Eph 4:18

Excuse *justification*
began to make *e-s*   Luke 14:18
they are without *e*   Rom 1:20

Execute *carry out*
e vengeance on the   Ps 149:7
Lord will *e* His word   Rom 9:28
e judgment upon all   Jude 15

Exercise *perform*
e-s lovingkindness   Jer 9:24
e authority over   Matt 20:25

Exhausted *used up, wearied*
too *e* to follow   1 Sam 30:21
Their strength is *e*   Jer 51:30

Exhort *admonish, urge*
and kept on *e-ing*   Acts 2:40
e in sound doctrine   Titus 1:9
e-ing and testifying   1 Pet 5:12

Exhortation *urging*
given them much *e*   Acts 20:2
this word of *e*   Heb 13:22

Exile *banishment* or *capture*
Israel away into *e*   2 Kin 17:6
captivity of the *e-s*   Neh 7:6
Israel went into *e*   Ezek 39:23

Exist *be, live, occur*
Strife *e-s* and   Hab 1:3
live and move and *e*   Acts 17:28

Expanse *firmament, vastness*
e of the heavens   Gen 1:20
in His mighty *e*   Ps 150:1

Expect *await*
never *e-ed* to see   Gen 48:11
which we did not *e*   Is 64:3

Expectation *anticipation*
to my earnest *e*   Phil 1:20
e of the wicked   Prov 10:28

Expected *awaited*
Are You the *E* One   Matt 11:3
Are You the *E* One   Luke 7:20

Experience *undergo*
people *e* hardship   Ps 60:3
e-d mockings and   Heb 11:36

Expert *very skillful*
an *e* in warfare   2 Sam 17:8
an *e* in all customs   Acts 26:3

Explain *make clear*
he did not *e* to her   2 Chr 9:2
E the parable to us   Matt 15:15
e-ed to him the way   Acts 18:26

Expose *disclose, reveal*
will *e* your sins   Lam 4:22
deeds should be *e-d*   John 3:20
e-d by the light   Eph 5:13

Extend *enlarge, stretch out*
e-ed lovingkindness   Ezra 7:28
boundary shall *e*   Ezek 47:17

Extent *amount* or *degree*
the *e* of my days   Ps 39:4
such an *e* that Jesus   Mark 1:45

Exterminate *destroy*
planned to *e* us   2 Sam 21:5
He will *e* its sinners   Is 13:9

External *outward*
not with *e* service   Col 3:22
adornment be...*e*   1 Pet 3:3

Extinguish *put out*
not *e* the lamp of   2 Sam 21:17
when *I e* you   Ezek 32:7

Extol *praise*
I will *e* Thee, O LORD   Ps 30:1
We will *e* your love   Song 1:4

Extortion *stealing*
practicing...*e*   Jer 22:17
practiced *e*, robbed   Ezek 18:18

Extraordinary *exceptional*
His *e* work   Is 28:21

e miracles by Acts 19:11

Exult *rejoice*
Let the field *e* 1 Chr 16:32
let them *e* before God Ps 68:3
I will *e* in the LORD Hab 3:18

Exultation *jubilation*
e like the nations Hos 9:1
may rejoice with *e* 1 Pet 4:13

Eye *sight*
e for *e*, tooth for Ex 21:24
his *e* was not dim Deut 34:7
e-s of LORD move 2 Chr 16:9
Haughty *e-s*, a lying Prov 6:17
e is not satisfied Eccl 1:8
To open blind *e-s* Is 42:7
have *e-s* to see but Ezek 12:2
e for an *e*, and a Matt 5:38
lamp…is your *e* Luke 11:34
which *e* has not seen 1 Cor 2:9
e-s full of adultery 2 Pet 2:14
His *e-s are* a flame Rev 19:12

Eyewitnesses *observers*
e…of the word Luke 1:2

– F –

Face *countenance*
sweat of your *f* Gen 3:19
speak to Moses *f* to *f* Ex 33:11
make His *f* shine Num 6:25
hide Thy *f* from me Ps 13:1
they spat in His *f* Matt 26:67
like the *f* of an angel Acts 6:15
His *f* was like the sun Rev 1:16

Fact *truth*
f may be confirmed Matt 18:16
are undeniable *f-s* Acts 19:36

Factions *divisions*
be *f* among you 1 Cor 11:19

Fade *wither*
it *f-s*, and withers Ps 90:6
will not *f* away 1 Pet 1:4

Fail *be spent or fall short*
He will not *f* you Deut 4:31
my strength *f-s* me Ps 38:10
faith may not *f* Luke 22:32
Love never *f-s* 1 Cor 13:8

Faint *languish, swoon*
made my heart *f* Job 23:16
grow *f* before Me Is 57:16
f when…reproved Heb 12:5

Fainthearted *weak*
Do not be *f* Deut 20:3
encourage the *f* 1 Thess 5:14

Faith *believe, trust*
Will you have *f* Job 39:12
will live by his *f* Hab 2:4
f as a mustard seed Matt 17:20
Increase our *f* Luke 17:5
man full of *f* Acts 6:5
justified by *f* Rom 5:1

if I have all *f* 1 Cor 13:2
we walk by *f* 2 Cor 5:7
live by *f* in the Son Gal 2:20
saved through *f* Eph 2:8
one Lord, one *f* Eph 4:5
breastplate of *f* 1 Thess 5:8
fall away from the *f* 1 Tim 4:1
sound in the *f* Titus 1:13
full assurance of *f* Heb 10:22
perfecter of *f* Heb 12:2
prayer offered in *f* James 5:15
the *f* of the saints Rev 13:10

Faithful *loyal, trustworthy*
f God, who keeps Deut 7:9
LORD preserves the *f* Ps 31:23
the LORD who is *f* Is 49:7
God is *f* 1 Cor 1:9
He considered me *f* 1 Tim 1:12
Be *f* until death Rev 2:10
called *F* and True Rev 19:11

Faithfulness *loyalty*
kindness and *f* Gen 47:29
A God of *f* Deut 32:4
f to all generations Ps 100:5
and mercy and *f* Matt 23:23

Faithless *unbelieving*
what *f* Israel did Jer 3:6
If we are *f* 2 Tim 2:13

Fall *descend or fail*
deep sleep to *f* upon Gen 2:21
I am ready to *f* Ps 38:17
wicked will *f* Prov 11:5
whether a tree *f-s* Eccl 11:3
f down and worship Dan 3:5
appointed for the *f* Luke 2:34
house *divided…f-s* Luke 11:17
sinned and *f* short Rom 3:23
have *f-en* asleep 1 Cor 15:6
f-en from grace Gal 5:4
rocks, *F* on us Rev 6:16

False *deceitful, dishonest*
not bear a *f* report Ex 23:1
f witness will not go Prov 19:5
F and foolish visions Lam 2:14
not bear *f* witness Matt 19:18
men are *f* apostles 2 Cor 11:13
and the *f* prophet Rev 20:10

Falsehood *deception*
delight in *f* Ps 62:4
trusted in *f* Jer 13:25
laying aside *f* Eph 4:25

Fame *greatness*
heard of Thy *f* Num 14:15
the *f* of Solomon 1 Kin 10:1
f in the things of 2 Cor 8:18

Family *household, relatives*
all the *f-ies* of Gen 12:3
my *f* is the least Judg 6:15
f-ies of the earth Amos 3:2
every *f* in heaven Eph 3:15

Famine *shortage of food*
seven years of *f* Gen 41:27

keep them alive in *f* Ps 33:19
f and pestilence Jer 14:12
f-s and earthquakes Matt 24:7
Now a *f* came Acts 7:11

Famous *well-known*
men of valor, *f* men 1 Chr 5:24

Far *distant*
Be not *f* from me Ps 22:11
As *f* as the east Ps 103:12
a God *f* off Jer 23:23
glory *f* beyond all 2 Cor 4:17
f above all rule Eph 1:21

Fashion *create, form*
f-ed into a woman Gen 2:22
f us in the womb Job 31:15
f a graven image Is 44:9

Fast (n) *food abstinence*
Proclaim a *f* 1 Kin 21:9
Consecrate a *f* Joel 1:14

Fast (v) *abstain from food*
and David *f-ed* 2 Sam 12:16
you *f* for contention Is 58:4
whenever you *f* Matt 6:16
disciples do not *f* Mark 2:18
had *f-ed* and prayed Acts 13:3

Fasting *food abstinence*
weak from *f* Ps 109:24
by prayer and *f* Matt 17:21
Pharisees were *f* Mark 2:18

Fat *animal fat or obese*
f of the land Gen 45:18
Go, eat of the *f* Neh 8:10

Fate *destiny*
appalled at his *f* Job 18:20
one *f* for all men Eccl 9:3

Father *God or parent*
f of a multitude Gen 17:4
Honor your *f* Ex 20:12
who strikes his *f* Ex 21:15
son makes a *f* glad Prov 10:1
Eternal *F*, Prince of Is 9:6
F who sees in secret Matt 6:4
Our *F* who art in Matt 6:9
F, forgive them Luke 23:34
begotten from the *F* John 1:14
F…bears witness John 8:18
I and the *F* are one John 10:30
ask the *F* for John 16:23
God and *F* of all Eph 4:6

Father-in-Law
she sent to her *f* Gen 38:25
his *f*, the girl's Judg 19:4

Fatherless *orphan*
father of the *f* Ps 68:5
f and the widow Ezek 22:7

Fatness *abundance*
f of the earth Gen 27:28
satisfied as with…*f* Ps 63:5

Fault *error, offense*
found no *f* in him — 1 Sam 29:3
does He still find *f* — Rom 9:19

Favor *kind regard*
Noah found *f* — Gen 6:8
show no *f* to them — Deut 7:2
surround him with *f* — Ps 5:12
found *f* with God — Luke 1:30
in *f* with God and — Luke 2:52
seeking the *f* of men — Gal 1:10

Fear (n) *awe, dread, reverence*
f of the LORD is clean — Ps 19:9
afraid of sudden *f* — Prov 3:25
they cried out for *f* — Matt 14:26
guards shook for *f* — Matt 28:4
men fainting from *f* — Luke 21:26
for *f* of the Jews — John 7:13
no *f* of God before — Rom 3:18
through *f* of death — Heb 2:15
love casts out *f* — 1 John 4:18

Fear (v) *be afraid, revere*
may learn to *f* me — Deut 4:10
not *f* other gods — 2 Kin 17:37
Whom shall I *f* — Ps 27:1
who *f-s* the LORD — Prov 31:30
Rather, *f* God — Eccl 5:7
Take courage, *f* not — Is 35:4
shall *f* and tremble — Jer 33:9
do not *f* them — Matt 10:26
who did not *f* God — Luke 18:2

Fearful *terrifying*
it is a *f* thing — Ex 34:10
may be *f* of sinning — 1 Tim 5:20

Feast *celebration*
a *f* to the LORD — Ex 12:14
refuse of your *f-s* — Mal 2:3
a wedding *f* — Matt 22:2
celebrate the *f* — 1 Cor 5:8

Feeble *weak*
when the flock was *f* — Gen 30:42
strengthen the *f* — Is 35:3

Feed *eat, supply*
fed you with manna — Deut 8:3
F me with the food — Prov 30:8
f you on knowledge — Jer 3:15
I will *f* My flock — Ezek 34:15
hungry, and *f* You — Matt 25:37
enemy is hungry, *f* — Rom 12:20

Feel *sense, touch*
Isaac...*felt* him and — Gen 27:22
He *felt* compassion — Matt 9:36
Jesus *felt* a love for — Mark 10:21

Fell *collapse, come upon*
wall *f* down flat — Josh 6:20
the lot *f* on Jonah — Jon 1:7
He *f* asleep — Luke 8:23
he *f* to the ground — Acts 9:4
Holy Spirit *f* upon — Acts 10:44

Fellow *companion*
your *f* exiles — Ezek 11:15
beat his *f* slaves — Matt 24:49

f heirs with Christ — Rom 8:17
f citizens with the — Eph 2:19
I am a *f* servant of — Rev 22:9

Fellowship *companionship*
sweet *f* together — Ps 55:14
right hand of *f* — Gal 2:9
f of His sufferings — Phil 3:10
f is with the Father — 1 John 1:3

Female *girl, woman*
and *f* He created — Gen 1:27
neither male nor *f* — Gal 3:28

Fervent *ardent*
being *f* in Spirit — Acts 18:25
keep *f* in your love — 1 Pet 4:8

Festival *celebration*
I reject your *f-s* — Amos 5:21
turn your *f-s* into — Amos 8:10

Fetters *chains*
they are bound in *f* — Job 36:8
tear their *f* apart — Ps 2:3

Fever *inflammation*
bones burn with *f* — Job 30:30
He rebuked the *f* — Luke 4:39
the *f* left him — John 4:52

Field *productive land*
glean in another *f* — Ruth 2:8
Zion...plowed *as a f* — Jer 26:18
the lilies of the *f* — Matt 6:28
the *f* is the world — Matt 13:38
Two men...in the *f* — Luke 17:36
F of Blood — Acts 1:19

Fierce *violent*
anger, for it is *f* — Gen 49:7
see a *f* people — Is 33:19
f wrath of God — Rev 19:15

Fierceness *intensity*
f of His anger — Josh 7:26

Fiery *burning*
LORD sent *f* serpents — Num 21:6
His arrows *f* shafts — Ps 7:13

Fig *fruit*
they sewed *f* leaves — Gen 3:7
But the *f* tree said — Judg 9:11
a piece of *f* cake — 1 Sam 30:12
nor *f-s* from thistles — Matt 7:16
the *f* tree withered — Matt 21:19
f-s from thorns — Luke 6:44
under the *f* tree — John 1:48
Can a *f* tree — James 3:12

Fight *struggle*
LORD will *f* for you — Ex 14:14
fought for Israel — Josh 10:14
and *f* our battles — 1 Sam 8:20
f-ing against God — Acts 5:39
fought the good *f* — 2 Tim 4:7

Figure *shape, type*
f-s resembling four — Ezek 1:5
using a *f* of speech — John 16:29

Fill (n) *satisfaction*
eat your *f* — Lev 25:19

its *f* of their blood — Jer 46:10

Fill (v) *make full*
and *f* the earth — Gen 1:28
Can you *f* his skin — Job 41:7
God of hope *f* you — Rom 15:13

Filthy *offensive*
like a *f* garment — Is 64:6
clothed...*f* garments — Zech 3:3

Filthiness *disgustingly foul*
your *f* is lewdness — Ezek 24:13
putting aside all *f* — James 1:21

Find *discover, uncover*
sin will *f* you out — Num 32:23
that you may *f* rest — Ruth 1:9
f gladness and joy — Is 35:10
f rest for your souls — Matt 11:29
f-ing one pearl — Matt 13:46
f a colt tied — Mark 11:2
seek, and you shall *f* — Luke 11:9
was *found* worthy — Rev 5:4

Finger *part of hand*
the *f* of God — Ex 8:19
tip of his *f* in water — Luke 16:24
Reach here your *f* — John 20:27

Finish *complete*
Moses *f-ed* the work — Ex 40:33
It is *f-ed* — John 19:30
I may *f* my course — Acts 20:24

Fire *burning* or *flame*
bush...burning with *f* — Ex 3:2
pillar of *f* by night — Ex 13:21
f of the LORD fell — 1 Kin 18:38
jealousy burn like *f* — Ps 79:5
unquenchable *f* — Matt 3:12
tongues as of *f* — Acts 2:3
lake that burns with *f* — Rev 21:8

Firm *establish, steadfast*
f on dry ground — Josh 3:17
stand *f* in the faith — 1 Cor 16:13
f foundation of God — 2 Tim 2:19
hope *f* until the end — Heb 3:6

First *number*
f fruits of your labors — Ex 23:16
seek *f* His kingdom — Matt 6:33
f take the log out — Matt 7:5
f called Christians — Acts 11:26
to the Jew *f* — Rom 2:10
He *f* loved us — 1 John 4:19
left your *f* love — Rev 2:4

First-born *oldest*
I am Esau your *f* — Gen 27:19
LORD killed every *f* — Ex 13:15
church of the *f* — Heb 12:23
f of the dead — Rev 1:5

Fish
rule over the *f* — Gen 1:26
Their *f* stink — Is 50:2
a great *f* to swallow — Jon 1:17
loaves and two *f* — Matt 14:17

Fishermen *fishers*
for they were *f* — Matt 4:18

FISHERMEN (Continued)

the *f* had gotten out — Luke 5:2

Fishers *fishermen*
make you *f* of men — Matt 4:19
become *f* of men — Mark 1:17

Fit *be suitable, worthy*
f for the kingdom — Luke 9:62
f to be…apostle — 1 Cor 15:9
f-ting in the Lord — Col 3:18

Fix *make firm, secure*
f-ing…eyes on Jesus — Heb 12:2
f your hope — 1 Pet 1:13

Flame *fire*
ascended in the *f* — Judg 13:20
f of the LORD — Song 8:6
his Holy One a *f* — Is 10:17
eyes *are* a *f* of fire — Rev 19:12

Flaming *burning*
the *f* sword — Gen 3:24
eyes were like *f* — Dan 10:6

Flash *reflect, sparkle*
why do your eyes *f* — Job 15:12
light suddenly *f-ed* — Acts 22:6

Flatter
f with their tongue — Ps 5:9
adulteress who *f-s* — Prov 2:16

Flee *escape, run away*
F as a bird — Ps 11:1
f from Thy presence — Ps 139:7
rulers have *fled* — Is 22:3
f to Egypt — Matt 2:13
fled from the tomb — Mark 16:8
f from idolatry — 1 Cor 10:14
f from youthful lusts — 2 Tim 2:22

Flesh *body, meat*
shall become one *f* — Gen 2:24
All *f* is grass — Is 40:6
the *f* is weak — Matt 26:41
the Word became *f* — John 1:14
who eats My *f* — John 6:56
thorn in the *f* — 2 Cor 12:7
desires of the *f* — Eph 2:3

Fleshly *carnal*
not in *f* wisdom — 2 Cor 1:12
abstain from *f* lusts — 1 Pet 2:11

Flight *departure*
F will perish from — Amos 2:14
f may not be in — Matt 24:20
foreign armies to *f* — Heb 11:34

Flock *goats, sheep*
a keeper of *f-s* — Gen 4:2
He will tend His *f* — Is 40:11
scattered My *f* — Jer 23:2
shall become one *f* — John 10:16

Flood *overflowing of water*
f came upon the earth — Gen 7:17
the *f-s* came — Matt 7:25

Floor *ground*
threshing *f* of Atad — Gen 50:11
go down to the…*f* — Ruth 3:3
the *f*…with gold — 1 Kin 6:30

---

f-s…full of grain — Joel 2:24
His threshing *f* — Matt 3:12
fell…from the third *f* — Acts 20:9

Flourish *blossom, thrive*
may the righteous *f* — Ps 72:7
your bones shall *f* — Is 66:14

Flow *pour forth*
f-ing with milk and — Ex 3:8
eyelids *f* with water — Jer 9:18
f…living waters — John 7:38

flower *blossom*
As a *f* of the field — Ps 103:15
glory like the *f* — 1 Pet 1:24

Flute *musical instrument*
tambourine, *f*, and — 1 Sam 10:5
playing on *f-s* — 1 Kin 1:40
the *f* or on the harp — 1 Cor 14:7
musicians…*f* — Rev 18:22

Fly *soar*
a raven, and it *flew* — Gen 8:7
As sparks *f* upward — Job 5:7
glory will *f* away — Hos 9:11
the birds which *f* — Rev 19:17

Foe *enemy*
before your *f-s* — 1 Chr 21:12
iniquity of my *f-s* — Ps 49:5
avenge…His *f-s* — Jer 46:10

Follow *imitate, pursue*
not *f* other gods — Deut 6:14
bloodshed *f-s* — Hos 4:2
He said to them, *F* — Matt 4:19
left…and *f-ed* — Matt 4:20
his cross, and *f* Me — Matt 16:24
and they *f* Me — John 10:27
f-ing after…lusts — Jude 16

Followers *disciples*
His *f*…*began* asking — Mark 4:10

Folly *foolishness*
this act of *f* — Judg 19:23
devising of *f* is sin — Prov 24:9

Food *bread, meat*
tree was good for *f* — Gen 3:6
it is deceptive *f* — Prov 23:3
life more than *f* — Matt 6:25
f is to do the will — John 4:34
milk…not solid *f* — 1 Cor 3:2

Fool *unwise person*
The *f* has said in his — Ps 14:1
too high for a *f* — Prov 24:7
shall say, You *f* — Matt 5:22
f-s for Christ's sake — 1 Cor 4:10

Foolish *silly, unwise*
O *f* and unwise — Deut 32:6
False and *f* visions — Lam 2:14
f took their lamps — Matt 25:3
let him become *f* — 1 Cor 3:18
You *f* Galatians — Gal 3:1

Foolishness *folly*
mouth is speaking *f* — Is 9:17
f of God is wiser — 1 Cor 1:25

Foot *part of body*
lamp to my *feet* — Ps 119:105
feet of the afflicted — Is 26:6
dust of your *feet* — Matt 10:14
f causes you to — Mark 9:45
kissing His *feet* — Luke 7:38
anointed the *feet* — John 12:3

Footsteps *path*
mae His *f* into a way — Ps 85:13
f of thine anointed — Ps 89:51
my *f* in Thy word — Ps 119:133

Forbearance *restraint*
in the *f* of God — Rom 3:25
showing *f* to one — Eph 4:2

Forbid *prohibit*
f-ding to pay taxes — Luke 23:2
do not *f* to speak — 1 Cor 14:39

Force (n) *power, strength*
with a heavy *f* — Num 20:20
use *f* against you — Neh 13:21
with *f* and with — Ezek 34:4

Force (v) *compel*
man *f-d* to labor — Job 7:1
f you to go one mile — Matt 5:41
f them to blaspheme — Acts 26:11

Forefather *ancestor*
iniquity of their *f-s* — Lev 26:40
Abraham, our *f* — Rom 4:1
the way my *f-s* did — 2 Tim 1:3

Forehead *brow*
on his bald *f* — Lev 13:42
stone…into his *f* — 1 Sam 17:49
put a mark on the *f-s* — Ezek 9:4
seal of God on their *f-s* — Rev 9:4
upon her *f* a name — Rev 17:5

Foreign *alien, strange*
Put away the *f* gods — Gen 35:2
sell her to a *f* people — Ex 21:8
married *f* women — Ezra 10:2
f armies to flight — Heb 11:34

Foreigner *alien, stranger*
sell it to a *f* — Deut 14:21
since I am a *f* — Ruth 2:10
a *f* in their sight — Job 19:15

Foreknew *know beforehand*
whom He *f*, He — Rom 8:29
people whom He *f* — Rom 11:2

Foreknowledge
plan and *f* of God — Acts 2:23
f of God the Father — 1 Pet 1:2

Forest *woods*
f devoured more — 2 Sam 18:8
the *f* of Lebanon — 1 Kin 7:2
f will sing for joy — 1 Chr 16:33
every beast of the *f* — Ps 50:10
the glory of his *f* — Is 10:18
beasts in the *f*, Come — Is 56:9

a *f* is set aflame | James 3:5

Foretold *predicted*
the Holy Spirit *f* | Acts 1:16
just as Isaiah *f* | Rom 9:29

Forever *always, eternal*
eat, and live *f* | Gen 3:22
the LORD abides *f* | Ps 9:7
riches are not *f* | Prov 27:24
One Who lives *f* | Is 57:15
able to save *f* | Heb 7:25
they shall reign *f* | Rev 22:5

Forfeit *lose*
f-s his own life | Prov 20:2
and *f-s* his soul | Matt 16:26

Forget *forsake, neglect*
lest you *f* the LORD | Deut 6:12
nations who *f* God | Ps 9:17
they *f-got* His deeds | Ps 78:11
do not *f* my teaching | Prov 3:1
f-ing what *lies* behind | Phil 3:13

Forgive *pardon*
f the transgression | Gen 50:17
f our sins | Ps 79:9
f us our debts | Matt 6:12
f-gave him the debt | Matt 18:27
can *f* sins but God | Mark 2:7
he who is *f-n* little | Luke 7:47
Father, *f* them | Luke 23:34
whom you *f* | 2 Cor 2:10
righteous to *f* us | 1 John 1:9

Forgiveness *pardon*
a God of *f* | Neh 9:17
repentance for *f* | Luke 24:47
receives *f* of sins | Acts 10:43
f of our trespasses | Eph 1:7
the *f* of sins | Col 1:14
there is no *f* | Heb 9:22

Form (n) *appearance, shape*
the *f* of the LORD | Num 12:8
like the *f* of a man | Is 44:13
bodily *f* like a dove | Luke 3:22
existed in the *f* of God | Phil 2:6

Form (v) *fashion, shape*
f-ed man of dust | Gen 2:7
f my inward parts | Ps 139:13
who *f-s* mountains | Amos 4:13
Christ is *f-ed* in you | Gal 4:19

Formation *mark*
in *f* against | 1 Chr 19:17
battle *f* in the | 2 Chr 14:10

Formless *without form*
earth was *f* and void | Gen 1:2

Fornication
f-s, thefts, false | Matt 15:19
were not born of *f* | John 8:41

Fornicators ·
neither *f*, nor | 1 Cor 6:9
f…God will judge | Heb 13:4

Forsake
Then he *f-sook* God | Deut 32:15

not fail you or *f* you | Josh 1:5
God has not *f-n* us | Ezra 9:9
not *f* your mother's | Prov 1:8
f the idols of Egypt | Ezek 20:8
hast Thou *f-n* Me | Matt 27:46

Fortifications *stronghold*
the unassailable *f* | Is 25:12
your *f* are fig trees | Nah 3:12

Fortified *walled*
live in the *f* cities | Num 32:17
strike every *f* city | 2 Kin 3:19

Fortress *stronghold*
my rock and my *f* | Ps 18:2
My refuge and my *f* | Ps 91:2
wealth is his *f* | Prov 10:15

Fortune *one's lot*
f-s of My people | Hos 6:11
restore their *f* | Zeph 2:7

Foul *putrid, rotten*
Nile will become *f* | Ex 7:18
f with your feet | Ezek 34:19

Foundation *establishment*
the *f* of His throne | Ps 97:2
an everlasting *f* | Prov 10:25
a *f* upon the rock | Luke 6:48
the firm *f* of God | 2 Tim 2:19
didst lay the *f* | Heb 1:10

Founded *established*
f it upon the seas | Ps 24:2
f upon the rock | Matt 7:25

Fountain *spring, well*
is the *f* of life | Ps 36:9
The *f* of wisdom | Prov 18:4
f of living waters | Jer 2:13

Fragments *pieces*
forth His ice as *f* | Ps 147:17
Gather up the…*f* | John 6:12

Fragrance *pleasant aroma*
oils have a pleasing *f* | Song 1:3
we are a *f* of Christ | 2 Cor 2:15

Frame *structure*
f-s of the tabernacle | Num 3:36
My *f* was not hidden | Ps 139:15

Frankincense *spice*
spices with pure *f* | Ex 30:34
and *f* and myrrh | Matt 2:11

Free *at liberty*
she is not to go *f* | Ex 21:7
let the oppressed go *f* | Is 58:6
who has died is *f-d* | Rom 6:7
the *f* gift of God | Rom 6:23
f from the law | Rom 8:2
Christ set us *f* | Gal 5:1

Freedom *liberty*
proclaim…*f* to | Is 61:1
you were called to *f* | Gal 5:13
do not use your *f* as | 1 Pet 2:16

Fresh *new, recently prepared*
f water from your | Prov 5:15

new wine into *f* | Mark 2:22
f and bitter *water* | James 3:11

Friend *companion, comrade*
my familiar *f* | Ps 55:13
A *f* loves at all | Prov 17:17
who blesses his *f* | Prov 27:14
f of tax-gatherers | Matt 11:19
f of the bridegroom | John 3:29
his life for his *f-s* | John 15:13

Friendship
the *f* of God | Job 29:4
f with the world | James 4:4

Frighten *terrify*
to *f* them away | Deut 28:26
I was *f-ed* and fell | Dan 8:17
Him and were *f-ed* | Mark 6:50

Fruit *growth, produce*
the *f* of the womb | Gen 30:2
offering of first *f-s* | Lev 2:12
its *f* in its season | Ps 1:3
eat its choice *f-s* | Song 4:16
bad tree bears bad *f* | Matt 7:17
bear *f* of the Spirit | Gal 5:22
f in every good work | Col 1:10

Fruitful *productive*
be *f* and multiply | Gen 9:7
gather a *f* harvest | Ps 107:37
f labor for me | Phil 1:22

Frustrate *counteract*
to *f* their counsel | Ezra 4:5
He *f-s* the plotting | Job 5:12
plans are *f-d* | Prov 15:22

Fuel *that which burns*
people are like *f* | Is 9:19
You will be *f* | Ezek 21:32

Fugitive *one who flees*
do not betray the *f* | Is 16:3
gather the *f-s* | Jer 49:5

Fulfill *complete*
to *f* the word | 2 Chr 36:21
May the Lord *f* all | Ps 20:5
to *f* the vision | Dan 11:14
to abolish, but to *f* | Matt 5:17
The time is *f-ed* | Mark 1:15
Scripture…be *f-ed* | John 13:18
husband *f* his duty | 1 Cor 7:3
f the law of Christ | Gal 6:2
f your ministry | 2 Tim 4:5

Fulfillment *completion*
the *f* of every vision | Ezek 12:23
f of *the* law | Rom 13:10

Full *complete, whole*
I went out *f* | Ruth 1:21
The earth is *f* of | Ps 33:5
twelve *f* baskets | Matt 14:20
f of dead…bones | Matt 23:27
also is *f* of light | Luke 11:34
f of grace and truth | John 1:14
f of the Spirit | Acts 6:3
f armor of God | Eph 6:11
f of compassion | James 5:11

Fulness *completeness*
f of the time came   Gal 4:4
all the f of God   Eph 3:19
f to dwell in Him   Col 1:19
the f of Deity dwells   Col 2:9

Furious *angry*
Pharaoh was f   Gen 41:10
king became...f   Dan 2:12

Furnish *supply*
shall f him liberally   Deut 15:14
upper room f-ed   Mark 14:15

Fury *anger*
terrify them in His f   Ps 2:5
the f of a fire   Heb 10:27

Futile *useless, vain*
go after f things   1 Sam 12:21
devise f things   Acts 4:25

Future *that which is ahead*
no f for the evil   Prov 24:20
foundation for the f   1 Tim 6:19

– G –

Gaiety *cheerfulness*
g...is banished   Is 24:11
an end to all her g   Hos 2:11

Gain (n) *profit, increase*
hate dishonest g   Ex 18:21
who rejects unjust g   Is 33:15
greedy for g   Jer 6:13
to die is g   Phil 1:21
fond of sordid g   1 Tim 3:8

Gain (v) *acquire*
have g-ed the victory   Ps 98:1
he will g knowledge   Prov 19:25
g-s the whole world   Matt 16:26
that I may g Christ   Phil 3:8

Gall *bitter herb, bitterness*
drink...with g   Matt 27:34
the g of bitterness   Acts 8:23

Garden *planted area*
God walking in the g   Gen 3:8
from the g of Eden   Gen 3:23
tabernacle like a g   Lam 2:6
in the g with Him   John 18:26
the g a new tomb   John 19:41

Garment *clothing, dress*
in g-s of fine linen   Gen 41:42
divide my g-s among   Ps 22:18
g of camel's hair   Matt 3:4
g as white as snow   Matt 28:3
dividing up His g-s   Luke 23:34
become old as a g   Heb 1:11
clothed in white g-s   Rev 3:5

Garrison *defense*
g of the Philistines   1 Sam 13:4
the g...trembled   1 Sam 14:15
set g-s in the land   2 Chr 17:2

Gate *entry way*
is the g of heaven   Gen 28:17
g-s with thanksgiving   Ps 100:4

justice in the g   Amos 5:15
Enter...narrow g   Matt 7:13
g-s of Hades shall   Matt 16:18

Gatekeepers *guards*
g for the camp   1 Chr 9:18
divisions of the g   1 Chr 26:12
The sons of the g   Ezra 2:42
g, and the singers   Neh 10:39

Gateway *entrance*
the g of the court   Ex 40:8
the g of the peoples   Ezek 26:2

Gather *assemble, collect*
g-ed to his people   Gen 25:8
g stubble for straw   Ex 5:12
g all nations and   Is 66:18
hens g-s her chicks   Matt 23:37
elders...were g-ed   Matt 26:3
g...His elect   Mark 13:27

Gaze (n) *view, glance*
let your g be fixed   Prov 4:25
I lifted my g and   Dan 8:3

Gaze (v) *look, stare*
man...g-ing at her   Gen 24:21
and g after Moses   Ex 33:8
g-ing...into the sky   Acts 1:10

Genealogy *family record*
found the book of...g   Neh 7:5
g of Jesus Christ   Matt 1:1
whose g is not traced   Heb 7:6

Generation *age, period*
this evil g   Deut 1:35
the righteous g   Ps 14:5
salvation to all g-s   Is 51:8
this g seek for a sign   Mark 8:12
and perverse g   Phil 2:15

Generous *bountiful*
g will be blessed   Prov 22:9
because I am g   Matt 20:15

Gentiles *foreigners, non-Jews*
Galilee of the G   Matt 4:15
revelation to the G   Luke 2:32
Why did the G rage   Acts 4:25
preach...among the G   3 John 7

Gentle *compassionate, mild*
g answer turns away   Prov 15:1
Blessed are the g   Matt 5:5
a g and quiet spirit   1 Pet 3:4

Gentleness *kindness*
and a spirit of g   1 Cor 4:21
and g of Christ   2 Cor 10:1
g, self-control   Gal 5:23

Ghost *spirit*
resort to idols and g-s   Is 19:3
saying, It is a g   Matt 14:26
it was a g   Mark 6:49

Giant
were born to the g   2 Sam 21:22
from the g-s   1 Chr 20:6

Gift *present*
children are a g   Ps 127:3

g of the Holy Spirit   Acts 2:38
impart...spiritual g   Rom 1:11
g of God is eternal   Rom 6:23
perfect g is from   James 1:17

Gird *bind*
g up your loins like   Job 38:3
g-s herself with   Prov 31:17
g-ed...with truth   Eph 6:14

Girl *maiden*
the g and consult   Gen 24:57
the g has not died   Matt 9:24

Give *bestow, yield*
g light on the earth   Gen 1:17
gave me from...tree   Gen 3:12
I will g you rest   Ex 33:14
G ear to my prayer   Ps 17:1
a son will be g-n   Is 9:6
gave birth to a Son   Matt 1:25
G us this day   Matt 6:11
g you the keys   Matt 16:19
what shall a man g   Mark 8:37
gave His only...Son   John 3:16
not as the world g-s   John 14:27
gave up His spirit   John 19:30
g-n among men   Acts 4:12
more blessed to g   Acts 20:35
always g-ing thanks   Eph 5:20
who gave Himself   1 Tim 2:6
g-n us eternal life   1 John 5:11

Glad *pleased*
g in his heart   Ex 4:14
joy and a g heart   Deut 28:47
Be g in the LORD   Ps 32:11
Rejoice, and be g   Matt 5:12
Be g in that day   Luke 6:23
who bring g tidings   Rom 10:15

Gladness *joy*
celebrate...with g   Neh 12:27
Serve the LORD with g   Ps 100:2
g and sincerity of   Acts 2:46

Glass *crystal*
or g cannot equal   Job 28:17
sea of g like crystal   Rev 4:6

Gleam *brilliance*
awesome g of crystal   Ezek 1:22
g of a Tarshish stone   Ezek 10:9
g of polished bronze   Dan 10:6

Glean *gather, pick*
Nor shall you g   Lev 19:10
she g-ed in the field   Ruth 2:17
g-ing ears of grain   Is 17:5

Gloom *darkness*
cloud and thick g   Deut 4:11
darkness and g and   Heb 12:18
and your joy to g   James 4:9

Glorify *honor, worship*
g Thy name forever   Ps 86:12
g your Father   Matt 5:16
Father, g Thy name   John 12:28
were all g-ing God   Acts 4:21
Gentiles to g God   Rom 15:9

Glorious *exalted, great*
g name be blessed   Neh 9:5
g gospel of…God   1 Tim 1:11

Glory (n) *honor, splendor*
show me Thy g   Ex 33:18
Tell of His g   1 Chr 16:24
King of g may come   Ps 24:7
exchanged their g   Ps 106:20
earth is full of His g   Is 6:3
Solomon in all his g   Matt 6:29
G…in the highest   Luke 2:14
do not seek My g   John 8:50
short of the g of God   Rom 3:23
body of His g   Phil 3:21
crowned Him with g   Heb 2:7

Glory (v) *exalt*
and g in thy praise   1 Chr 16:35
G in His holy name   Ps 105:3
in Him they will g   Jer 4:2

Glutton *excessive eater*
g…come to poverty   Prov 23:21
a companion of g-s   Prov 28:7
evil beasts, lazy g-s   Titus 1:12

Gnash *grind*
He will g his teeth   Ps 112:10
g-ing their teeth   Acts 7:54

Go *move, proceed*
Let My people g   Ex 7:16
you g, I will g   Ruth 1:16
g one mile, g…two   Matt 5:41
G into all…world   Mark 16:15
I g to prepare a   John 14:2

Goads *inducements*
kick against the g   Acts 26:14

Goal *end, object*
press on toward the g   Phil 3:14
g…is love   1 Tim 1:5

God *Deity, Eternal One*
In the beginning G   Gen 1:1
G formed man of dust   Gen 2:7
G is my…fortress   2 Sam 22:33
G of my salvation   Ps 18:46
In G…I put my trust   Ps 56:4
Search me, O G   Ps 139:23
I am G and not man   Hos 11:9
Will a man rob G   Mal 3:8
they shall see G   Matt 5:8
kingdom of G is at   Mark 1:15
My G, why hast   Mark 15:34
the Word was G   John 1:1
No man has seen G   John 1:18
the Lamb of G   John 1:29
G so loved the world   John 3:16
G is spirit   John 4:24
obey G rather than   Acts 5:29
judgment of G   Rom 2:2
bear fruit for G   Rom 7:4
are a temple of G   1 Cor 3:16
full armor of G   Eph 6:11
is inspired by G   2 Tim 3:16

G is love   1 John 4:8

Godless *pagan, without God*
hope of the g will   Job 8:13
g man destroys his   Prov 11:9
hands of g men   Acts 2:23

Godliness *holiness*
in all g and dignity   1 Tim 2:2
the mystery of g   1 Tim 3:16
to a form of g   2 Tim 3:5

Godly *holy*
keeps…His g ones   1 Sam 2:9
not forsake His g ones   Ps 37:28
to live g in Christ   2 Tim 3:12
rescue the g from   2 Pet 2:9

God(s) *false deity, idols*
no other g-s before Me   Ex 20:3
bowed…to other g-s   Jer 22:9
no other g who is   Dan 3:29
The voice of a g   Acts 12:22
the g of this world   2 Cor 4:4

Gold *precious metal*
mercy seat of pure g   Ex 25:17
more desirable than g   Ps 19:10
refine them like g   Mal 3:3
Do not acquire g   Matt 10:9
coveted no…g   Acts 20:33
city was pure g   Rev 21:18

Good *complete, right*
God saw that it was g   Gen 1:18
Do not withhold g   Prov 3:27
joyful heart is g   Prov 17:22
Seek g and not evil   Amos 5:14
how to give g gifts   Matt 7:11
Well done, g and   Matt 25:23
the g shepherd   John 10:11
nothing g…in me   Rom 7:18
work together for g   Rom 8:28
overcome evil…g   Rom 12:21
is of g repute   Phil 4:8
Fight the g fight   1 Tim 6:12
tasted the g word   Heb 6:5

Goodness *excellence, value*
My g pass before you   Ex 33:19
Surely g…will follow   Ps 23:6
kindness, g   Gal 5:22

Goods *possessions, supplies*
the g for yourself   Gen 14:21
have acquired…g   Ezek 38:12

Gospel *good news*
proclaiming the g of   Matt 4:23
preach the g to all   Mark 16:15
not ashamed of the g   Rom 1:16
distort the g of Christ   Gal 1:7
g of your salvation   Eph 1:13
defense of the g   Phil 1:16
the hope of the g   Col 1:23

Gossip *babbler*
associate with a g   Prov 20:19
g-s and busybodies   1 Tim 5:13

Govern *rule*
light to g the day   Gen 1:16

Government *authority, rule*
g…on His shoulders   Is 9:6
be no end to…His g   Is 9:7

Governor *ruler*
not offer it to your g   Mal 1:8
brought before g-s   Matt 10:18
g was quite amazed   Matt 27:14
Pilate was g of Judea   Luke 3:1
g over Egypt   Acts 7:10

Grace *benevolence, favor*
g to the afflicted   Prov 3:4
full of g and truth   John 1:14
g of our Lord Jesus   Rom 16:20
My g is sufficient   2 Cor 12:9
justified by His g   Titus 3:7
to the throne of g   Heb 4:16

Gracious *kind*
God be g to you   Gen 43:29
g to whom I will be   Ex 33:19
Be g to me, O LORD   Ps 6:2
g to a poor man   Prov 19:17

Graft *insert, join*
I might be g-ed in   Rom 11:19
g-ed into their own   Rom 11:24

Grain
Joseph stored up g   Gen 41:49
then the mature g   Mark 4:28
g of wheat falls   John 12:24

Grant *give, provide*
g this people favor   Ex 3:21
g us Thy salvation   Ps 85:7
G that we may sit   Mark 10:37
Father has g-ed Me   Luke 22:29

Grasp *hold, seize*
hands g the spindle   Prov 31:19
a thing to be g-ed   Phil 2:6

Grass *vegetation*
his days are like g   Ps 103:15
g withers, the flower   Is 40:7
All flesh is like g   1 Pet 1:24

Gratitude *thankfulness*
overflowing with g   Col 2:7
let us show g   Heb 12:28

Grave *sepulchre, tomb*
throat is an open g   Ps 5:9
made the g secure   Matt 27:66

Graven *sculptured*
make…a g image   Deut 4:23
praise to g images   Is 42:8

Great *big, excellent, grand*
make you a g nation   Gen 12:2
lovingkindness is g   Ps 57:10
your iniquity is g   Jer 30:15
g day of the LORD   Zeph 1:14
reward is g in   Luke 6:23
because of His g love   Eph 2:4
so g a salvation   Heb 2:3
so g a cloud of   Heb 12:1

a *g* white throne   Rev 20:11

Greatest *most important*
who is the *g* among   Luke 22:26
g of these is love   1 Cor 13:13

Greatness *magnitude*
Thine…is the *g*   1 Chr 29:11
g of Thy compassion   Ps 51:1
the *g* of His strength Is 63:1
surpassing *g* of His   Eph 1:19

Greed *excessive desire*
every form of *g*   Luke 12:15
a pretext for *g*   1 Thess 2:5

Greedy *craving*
had *g* desires   Num 11:4
Everyone is *g* for   Jer 6:13

Greet *hail, welcome*
g no one on the way   Luke 10:4
G one another with   1 Pet 5:14

Grief *heartache, sorrow*
weeps because of *g*   Ps 119:28
foolish son is a *g*   Prov 17:25
acquainted with *g*   Is 53:3

Grieve *distress, sorrow*
was *g-d* in his heart   Gen 6:6
g-d His Holy Spirit   Is 63:10
Peter was *g-d*   John 21:17
not *g* the Holy Spirit Eph 4:30

Grind *crush, press*
g-ing…the poor   Is 3:15
and *g-s* his teeth   Mark 9:18

Groan *cry, moan*
wounded will *g*   Jer 51:52
whole creation *g-s*   Rom 8:22

Groaning *crying*
God heard their *g*   Ex 2:24
O Lord, Consider my *g* Ps 5:1
g-s too deep for   Rom 8:26

Grope *move about blindly*
They *g* in darkness   Job 12:25
g like…blind men   Is 59:10

Ground *earth, land, soil*
Cursed is the *g*   Gen 3:17
crossed on dry *g*   Josh 3:17
talent in the *g*   Matt 25:25
finger wrote on the *g* John 8:6
standing is holy *g*   Acts 7:33

Grounded *established*
hope…is firmly *g*   2 Cor 1:7
rooted and *g* in love Eph 3:17

Grow *develop, increase*
You are *g-n* fat   Deut 32:15
my spirit *g-s* faint   Ps 77:3
lilies of the field *g* Matt 6:28
love will *g* cold   Matt 24:12
grew strong in faith Rom 4:20
not *g* weary of   2 Thess 3:13
g in the grace   2 Pet 3:18

Growth *increase*
God who causes the *g* 1 Cor 3:7

Grudge *hostile feeling*
Esau bore a *g*   Gen 27:41
nor bear any *g*   Lev 19:18

Grumble *complain*
the congregation *g*   Num 14:36
scribes *began* to *g* Luke 15:2
g among yourselves   John 6:43

Grumbling *complaint*
He hears your *g-s*   Ex 16:7
Do all…without *g*   Phil 2:14

Guard (n) *keeper*
be a *g* for them   Ezek 38:7
g-s shook for fear   Matt 28:4

Guard (v) *keep watch*
g-ed the threshold   2 Kin 12:9
Discretion will *g* you Prov 2:11
shall *g* your hearts   Phil 4:7

Guardian *overseer*
g-s of *the children* 2 Kin 10:1
under *g-s* and   Gal 4:2
G of your souls   1 Pet 2:25

Guest *visitor*
to the invited *g-s*   Luke 14:7
g of a…sinner   Luke 19:7

Guidance *counsel*
make war by wise *g*   Prov 20:18

Guide (n) *advisor, director*
Woe to…blind *g-s*   Matt 23:16
are a *g* to the blind Rom 2:19

Guide (v) *direct, lead*
He *g-s* me in the paths Ps 23:3
g us until death   Ps 48:14
g you into…truth   John 16:13

Guile *deceit*
in whom is no *g*   John 1:47
lips from speaking *g* 1 Pet 3:10

Guilt *offence*
be free from *g*   Num 5:31
charge me with a *g*   2 Sam 3:8
land is full of *g*   Jer 51:5
must bear their *g*   Hos 10:2

Guilty *charged or condemned*
as one who is *g*   2 Sam 14:13
g of an eternal sin   Mark 3:29

Gushed *burst, flowed*
so that waters *g* out Ps 78:20
all his bowels *g* out Acts 1:18

– H –

Habitation *abode, dwelling*
from Thy holy *h*   Deut 26:15
a rock of *h*   Ps 71:3
live in a peaceful *h* Is 32:18
laid waste his *h*   Jer 10:25

Hades *hell, place of dead*
shall descend to *H*   Matt 11:23
in *H* he lifted up   Luk 16:23
abandoned to *H*   Rev 1:18

Hail (n) *pieces of ice*
rained *h* on the land Ex 9:23
storehouses of the *h* Job 38:22
gave them *h* for rain Ps 105:32
plague of the *h*   Rev 16:21

Hail (v) *greeting*
H, Rabbi   Matt 26:49
H, King of…Jews   Matt 27:29

Hair
gray *h*…to Sheol   Gen 42:38
locks of his *h* and   Judg 16:14
garment of camel's *h* Matt 3:4
h-s…all numbered   Matt 10:30
His feet with her *h*   John 11:2

Hall *corridor*
h of pillars   1 Kin 7:6
h of judgment   1 Kin 7:7
wedding *h* has   Matt 22:10

Hallelujah *praise Yahweh*
H! Salvation and   Rev 19:1
H! Her smoke rises   Rev 19:3

Hallowed *consecrated, holy*
H be Thy name   Matt 6:9

Hand *part of body*
for tooth, *h* for *h*   Deut 19:21
They pierced my *h-s* Ps 22:16
buries his *h*   Prov 19:24
clay in the potter's *h* Jer 18:6
the right *h* of God   Mark 16:19
into Thy *h-s* I   Luke 23:46
reach here your *h*   John 20:27
not made with *h-s*   2 Cor 5:1
lifting up holy *h-s*   1 Tim 2:8

Handmaid *servant, slave*
save the son of Thy *h* Ps 86:16
the son of Thy *h*   Ps 116:16
her *h-s* are moaning   Nah 2:7

Handsome *attractive*
a choice and *h* man   1 Sam 9:2
ruddy, with a *h*   1 Sam 17:42

Hang *attach, suspend*
h you on a tree   Gen 40:19
h-ing in an oak   2 Sam 18:9
they *h-ed* Haman   Esth 7:10
he…*h-ed* himself   Matt 27:5
who *h-s* on a tree   Gal 3:13

Happiness *joy*
give *h* to his wife   Deut 24:5
I have forgotten *h*   Lam 3:17

Happy *blessed, joyful*
Leah said, *H* am I   Gen 30:13
h…who keeps the   Prov 29:18

Hard *difficult, firm*
bitter with *h* labor   Ex 1:14
made our yoke *h*   2 Chr 10:4
h for a rich man   Matt 19:23
worked *h* all night   Luke 5:5

Harden *make hard, callous*
h Pharaoh's heart   Ex 7:3
who *h-s* his neck   Prov 29:1
Do not *h* your hearts Heb 3:15

Hardness *callousness*
Because of your *h*   Matt 19:8
grieved at their *h*   Mark 3:5

Hardship *difficulty*
people experience *h*   Ps 60:3
our labor and *h*   1 Thess 2:9

Harlot *prostitute*
the hire of a *h*   Deut 23:18
Dressed as a *h*   Prov 7:10
also played the *h*   Ezek 16:26
to a *h* is one body   1 Cor 6:16
Mother of *H-s*   Rev 17:5

Harlotry *prostitution*
profaned by *h*   Lev 21:7
children of *h*   Hos 1:2
spirit of *h*   Hos 5:4

Harm (n) *evil, hurt*
h to this people   Ex 5:22
Do not devise *h*   Prov 3:29
the fire without *h*   Dan 3:25
did me much *h*   2 Tim 4:14

Harm (v) *damage, hurt*
David seeks to *h*   1 Sam 24:9
planning to *h* me   Neh 6:2
in order to *h* you   Acts 18:10
is there to *h* you   1 Pet 3:13

Harmony *agreement*
what *h* has Christ   2 Cor 6:15
live in *h* in the   Phil 4:2

Harp *musical instrument*
my *h* is turned to   Job 30:31
praises...with a *h*   Ps 33:2
Awake, *h* and lyre   Ps 57:8
gaiety of the *h* ceases   Is 24:8
having each one a *h*   Rev 5:8
holding *h-s* of God   Rev 15:2

Harsh *difficult, hard*
man was *h* and evil   1 Sam 25:3
h word stirs up anger   Prov 15:1

Harvest *reap and gather*
Seedtime and *h*   Gen 8:22
you reap your *h*   Deut 24:19
like rain in *h*   Prov 26:1
time of *h* will come   Jer 51:33
Lord of the *h*   Matt 9:38
fields...white for *h*   John 4:35

Hasten *accelerate*
H to me, O God   Ps 70:5
they *h* to shed blood   Prov 1:16
h-ing...day of God   2 Pet 3:12

Hate *despise, loathe*
you *h* discipline   Ps 50:17
I *h* every false way   Ps 119:104
fools *h* knowledge   Prov 1:22
a time to *h*   Eccl 3:8
For I *h* divorce   Mal 2:16
you will be *h-d*   Luke 21:17
he who *h-s* his life   John 12:25
the very thing I *h*   Rom 7:15
yet *h-s* his brother   1 John 2:9

Haters *those who hate*
slanderers, *h* of God   Rom 1:30

Hatred *hate, ill will*
h for my love   Ps 109:5
H stirs up strife   Prov 10:12

Haughty *proud*
nor my eyes *h*   Ps 131:1
H eyes, a lying   Prov 6:17
Proud, *H*, Scoffer   Prov 21:24

Haven *harbor, shelter*
be a *h* for ships   Gen 49:13
to their desired *h*   Ps 107:30

Head *chief* or *part of body*
anointed my *h* with oil   Ps 23:5
gray *h* is a crown   Prov 16:31
coals on his *h*   Prov 25:22
had four *h-s*   Dan 7:6
an oath by your *h*   Matt 5:36
nowhere to lay His *h*   Matt 8:20
h of John the Baptist   Matt 14:8
crown...on His *h*   John 19:2
husband is the *h*   Eph 5:23

Headlong *headfirst*
He rushes *h* at Him   Job 15:26
falling *h*, he burst   Acts 1:18
h into the error   Jude 11

Heal *make well, restore*
will *h* their land   2 Chr 7:14
h-s the brokenhearted   Ps 147:3
a time to *h*   Eccl 3:3
H me, O Lord   Jer 17:14
will *h* their apostasy   Hos 14:4
H the sick, raise   Matt 10:8
Physician, *h* yourself   Luke 4:23

Healing *health, wholeness*
be *h* to your body   Prov 3:8
sorrow is beyond *h*   Jer 8:18
h every kind of   Matt 4:23
gifts of *h*   1 Cor 12:9
h of the nations   Rev 22:2

Health *soundness, wholeness*
no *h* in my bones   Ps 38:3
and be in good *h*   3 John 2

Heap (n) *mound, pile*
made a refuse *h*   Ezra 6:11
needy from the ash *h*   Ps 113:7
altars are...*h-s*   Hos 12:11

Heap (v) *pile up, place*
h misfortunes on   Deut 32:23
H on the wood   Ezek 24:10

Hear *listen*
God *h-d* their groaning   Ex 2:24
H, O Israel   Deut 6:4
Will God *h* his cry   Job 27:9
h Thy lovingkindness   Ps 143:8
to *h*, let him *h*   Matt 11:5
does not *h* sinners   John 9:31
sheep *h* My voice   John 10:27
anyone *h-s* My voice   Rev 3:20

Hearing *listening*
in the Lord's *h*   1 Sam 8:21

fulfilled in your *h*   Luke 4:21
become dull of *h*   Heb 5:11

Heart *mind* or *seat of emotions*
I will harden his *h*   Ex 4:21
fool has said in his *h*   Ps 14:1
meditation of my *h*   Ps 19:14
in me a clean *h*   Ps 51:10
and a contrite *h*   Ps 51:17
Deceit is in the *h*   Prov 12:20
A joyful *h* is good   Prov 17:22
bribe corrupts the *h*   Eccl 7:7
uncircumcised in *h*   Ezek 44:7
are the pure in *h*   Matt 5:8
and humble in *h*   Matt 11:29
pierced to the *h*   Acts 2:37
who searches the *h-s*   Rom 8:27
not lose *h* in doing   Gal 6:9
melody with your *h*   Eph 5:19
intentions of the *h*   Heb 4:12

Heat *hotness, warmth*
the *h* of the day   Gen 18:1
hidden from its *h*   Ps 19:6
scorching *h* of the   Matt 20:12
with intense *h*   2 Pet 3:10

Heaven *place of God* or *sky*
God created the *h-s*   Gen 1:1
shut up the *h-s*   Deut 11:17
fire came...from *h*   2 Kin 1:14
I consider Thy *h-s*   Ps 8:3
lights in the *h-s*   Ezek 32:8
kingdom of *h* is at   Matt 3:2
reward in *h* is great   Matt 5:12
Father who art in *h*   Matt 6:9
shall be loosed in *h*   Matt 16:19
no...name under *h*   Acts 4:12
citizenship is in *h*   Phil 3:20
new *h* and a new   Rev 12:1

Heavenly *related to God*
h Father is perfect   Matt 5:48
h host praising God   Luke 2:13
Him in the *h* places   Eph 2:6

Heavy *burdensome, hard to lift*
Moses' hands were *h*   Ex 17:12
h drinkers of wine   Prov 23:20
eyes were very *h*   Mark 14:40

Hedge *border or protection*
Thou not made a *h*   Job 1:10
as a *h* of thorns   Prov 15:19
along the *h-s*, and   Luke 14:23

Heel *back of foot*
bruise him on the *h*   Gen 3:15
on to Esau's *h*   Gen 25:26
his *h* against Me   John 13:18

Height *elevation, heaven, sky*
from His holy *h*   Ps 102:19
ascend above the *h-s*   Is 14:14
nor *h*, nor depth   Rom 8:39

Heir *person who inherits*
in my house is my *h*   Gen 15:3
an *h* through God   Gal 4:7
h-s of the kingdom   James 2:5

Hell *place of dead*
go into the fiery *h*	Matt 5:22
soul and body in *h*	Matt 10:28
to be cast into *h*	Mark 9:47
set on fire by *h*	James 3:6
cast them into *h*	2 Pet 2:4

Helmet *headpiece*
h of salvation	Is 59:17
take the *h* of	Eph 6:17

Help (n) *assistance, relief*
He is our *h* and our	Ps 33:20
present *h* in trouble	Ps 46:1
I cried for *h*	Jon 2:2

Help (v) *aid, assist*
whence shall my *h*	Ps 121:1
I will *h* you	Is 41:13
Lord, *h* me	Matt 15:25
h my unbelief	Mark 9:24
must *h* the weak	Acts 20:35

Helper *one who assists*
h of the orphan	Ps 10:14
Behold, God is my *h*	Ps 54:4
H, the Holy Spirit	John 14:26

Helpless *weak*
who considers the *h*	Ps 41:1
while we were still *h*	Rom 5:6

Herb *dried plant*
bread and bitter *h-s*	Ex 12:8
fade like the green *h*	Ps 37:2
h-s of…mountains	Prov 27:25
sweet-scented *h-s*	Song 5:13

Herd *cattle, flock*
first-born of your *h*	Deut 12:6
h, or flock taste a	Jon 3:7
h of many swine	Matt 8:30

Herdsmen *keepers of flocks*
h of Abram's	Gen 13:7
between my *h* and	Gen 13:8
the *h* ran away	Matt 8:33

Heritage *what is inherited*
my *h* is beautiful	Ps 16:6
their land as a *h*	Ps 136:21

Hide *conceal, cover*
man and his wife hid	Gen 3:8
h me in Sheol	Job 14:13
H me in the shadow	Ps 17:8
Do not *h* Thy face	Ps 27:9
hid your talent	Matt 25:25
nothing is *h-den*	Mark 4:22
Jesus *hid* himself	John 8:59

Hidden (adj) *concealed*
Acquit me of *h* faults	Ps 19:12
h snares for my feet	Jer 18:22

Hiding Place
Clouds are a *h*	Job 22:14
Thou art my *h*	Ps 32:7

High *elevated or heavenly*
h above all nations	Deut 26:19
h as the heavens	Job 11:8
set him *securely* on *h*	Ps 91:14

the *h* priest	Matt 26:57
Son of the Most *H*	Mark 5:7
He ascended on *h*	Eph 4:8

Highway *road*
along the king's *h*	Num 20:17
h from Egypt to	Is 19:23
the *H* of Holiness	Is 35:8
a *h* for our God	Is 40:3
Go out into the *h-s*	Luke 14:23

Hill *mountain*
the *h* of God	1 Sam 10:5
to Thy holy *h*	Ps 43:3
cattle…thousand *h-s*	Ps 50:10
city set on a *h*	Matt 5:14
the brow of the *h*	Luke 4:29

Hinder *delay, impede, restrain*
do not *h* them	Matt 19:14
prayers…not be *h-ed*	1 Pet 3:7

Hire (n) *wages*
it came for its *h*	Ex 22:15
the *h* of a harlot	Deut 23:18

Hire (v) *engage for labor*
he who *h-s* a fool	Prov 26:10
to *h* laborers for	Matt 20:1

Hired (adj) *employed*
as a *h* man, as if	Lev 25:40
as one of your *h*	Luke 15:19

Hireling *employee*
because he is a *h*	John 10:13

Hiss *to show dislike*
h him from his place	Job 27:23
object of…*h-ing*	Jer 18:16
They *h* and shake	Lam 2:15
h And wave his hand	Zeph 2:15

Hold *grasp, retain*
h fast to Him	Deut 11:22
Take *h* of instruction	Prov 4:13
h to one and despise	Matt 6:24
h fast the word	1 Cor 15:2
h of the eternal	1 Tim 6:12

Hole *opening*
the *h* of the cobra	Is 11:8
a *h* in the wall	Ezek 8:7
a purse with *h-s*	Hag 1:6
foxes have *h-s*	Matt 8:20

Holiday *period of leisure*
a feast and a *h*	Esth 8:17
a *h* for rejoicing	Esth 9:19
mourning into a *h*	Esth 9:22

Holiness *sacredness*
majestic in *h*	Ex 15:11
the Highway of *H*	Is 35:8
may share His *h*	Heb 12:10

Holy *sacred, sanctified*
standing is *h* ground	Ex 3:5
sabbath…keep it *h*	Ex 20:8
you are a *h* people	Deut 7:6
h like the LORD	1 Sam 2:2
His *h* dwelling	2 Chr 30:27
Jerusalem, the *h* city	Neh 11:1
bless His *h* name	Ps 145:21

the *H* One of Israel	Is 30:15
the *H* One of God	Luke 4:34
lifting up *h* hands	1 Tim 2:8
with a *h* calling	2 Tim 1:9
I saw the *h* city	Rev 21:2

Homage *act of reverence*
did *h* to the LORD	1 Chr 29:20
did *h* to Daniel	Dan 2:46

Home *place of dwelling*
free at *h* one year	Deut 24:5
to his eternal *h*	Eccl 12:5
let him eat at *h*	1 Cor 11:34
at *h* with the Lord	2 Cor 5:8

Homestead *family dwelling*
h forlorn and forsaken	Is 27:10
guards his own *h*	Luke 11:21
h be made desolate	Acts 1:20

Honest *respectable, truthful*
we are *h* men	Gen 42:11
an *h* and good heart	Luke 8:15

Honey *sweetness*
with milk and *h*	Ex 3:8
swarm of bees and *h*	Judg 14:8
is sweeter than *h*	Judg 14:18
sweet as *h* in my	Ezek 3:3
locusts and wild *h*	Matt 3:4

Honor (n) *glory, great respect*
both riches and *h*	1 Kin 3:13
wise will inherit *h*	Prov 3:35
is not without *h*	Matt 13:57
marriage *be held* in *h*	Heb 13:4

Honor (v) *show respect*
H your father	Ex 20:12
A son *h-s his* father	Mal 1:6
h-s Me with…lips	Matt 15:8
fear God, *h* the king	1 Pet 2:17

Honorable *respectable*
the elder and *h* man	Is 9:15
one vessel for *h* use	Rom 9:21
whatever is *h*	Phil 4:8

Hook *fastener*
into pruning *h-s*	Is 2:4
My *h* in your nose	Is 37:29
h-s into your jaws	Ezek 38:4

Hope (n) *expectation*
h of the afflicted	Ps 9:18
My *h* is in Thee	Ps 39:7
Thou art my *h*	Ps 71:5
the *h* of Israel	Jer 17:13
our *h* has perished	Ezek 37:11
on trial for the *h*	Acts 23:6
h does not disappoint	Rom 5:5
rejoicing in *h*	Rom 12:12
may the God of *h*	Rom 15:13
now abide faith, *h*	1 Cor 13:13
the *h* of His calling	Eph 1:18
the *h* of the gospel	Col 1:23
the *h* of glory	Col 1:27
the *h* of salvation	1 Thess 5:8
h of eternal life	Titus 3:7
to a living *h*	1 Pet 1:3

h that is in you — 1 Pet 3:15

Hope (v) *expect with confidence*
I will *h* in Him — Job 13:15
We *h* for justice — Is 59:11
Gentiles will *h* — Matt 12:21
I *h* in the Lord Jesus — Phil 2:19
I *h* to come to you — 2 John 12

Horn
h-s of the altar — Ex 29:12
h of my salvation — 2 Sam 22:3
it had ten *h-s* — Dan 7:7

Horror *terror*
h overwhelms me — Is 21:4
clothed with *h* — Ezek 7:27

Horsemen *cavalry, horse rider*
Pharaoh, his *h* and — Ex 14:9
chariots and *h* — 1 Kin 10:26
h riding on — Ezek 23:12
H charging, Swords — Nah 3:3
armies of the *h* — Rev 9:16

Hosanna *acclamation of praise*
H to the Son — Matt 21:9
H in the highest — Mark 11:10
H! Blessed is He — John 12:13

Hospitable *friendly*
h, able to teach — 1 Tim 3:2
h to one another — 1 Pet 4:9

Hospitality *open to guests*
practicing *h* — Rom 12:13
show *h* to strangers — Heb 13:2

Host *army, multitude*
all the *h* of heaven — Deut 4:19
of the heavenly *h* — Luke 2:13

Hostile *antagonistic*
h to…Jesus — Acts 26:9
h to all men — 1 Thess 2:15

Hot *very warm, violent*
when the sun grew *h* — Ex 16:21
My heart was *h* within — Ps 39:3
neither cold nor *h* — Rev 3:15

Hour *time*
healed that *very h* — Matt 8:13
the *h* is at hand — Matt 26:45
Save Me from this *h* John 12:27
the *h* has come — John 17:1
the *h* of testing — Rev 3:10

House *home or temple*
passed over the *h-s* — Ex 12:27
consecrates his *h* — Lev 27:14
me and my *h* — Josh 24:15
Set your *h* in order — 2 Kin 20:1
LORD builds the *h* — Ps 127:1
in My *h* of prayer — Is 56:7
O *h* of Israel — Jer 18:6
his *h* upon the rock — Matt 7:24
devour widows' *h-s* Mark 12:40
In My Father's *h* — John 14:2

Household *family, home*
herds and a great *h* — Gen 26:14
each one with his *h* — Ex 1:1

like a head of a *h* — Matt 13:52
manages his own *h* — 1 Tim 3:4

Human *mankind, person*
the life of any *h* — Lev 24:17
they had *h* form — Ezek 1:5
tablets of *h* hearts — 2 Cor 3:3

Humble (adj) *gentle, modest*
Moses was very *h* — Num 12:3
h will inherit — Ps 37:11
gentle and *h* in — Matt 11:29
grace to the *h* — James 4:6

Humble (v) *modest*
refuse to *h* yourself — Ex 10:3
He might *h* you — Deut 8:2
H yourselves — 1 Pet 5:6

Humiliate *embarrass*
h-d who seek my hurt Ps 71:24
Neither feel *h-d* — Is 54:4
His…*h-d* — Luke 13:17

Humiliation *embarrassment*
go away together in *h* Is 45:16
let our *h* cover us — Jer 3:25

Humility *self-abasement*
with *h* of mind — Phil 2:3
clothe…with *h* — 1 Pet 5:5

Hundred *number or many*
Adam had lived one *h* Gen 5:3
h of you will chase — Lev 26:8
captains of *h-s* — Num 31:14
h pieces of money Josh 24:32
went out by *h-s* — 2 Sam 18:14
in companies of *h-s* Mark 6:40

Hunger *craving, starvation*
in *h*, in thirst — Deut 28:48
man will suffer *h* — Prov 19:15
h is not satisfied — Is 29:8
sleeplessness, in *h* — 2 Cor 6:5

Hunger (v) *crave, need food*
are those who *h* — Matt 5:6
to Me shall not *h* — John 6:35

Hungry *empty, needing food*
people are *h* and — 2 Sam 17:29
If your enemy is *h* Prov 25:21
He then became *h* — Matt 4:2
For I was *h* — Matt 25:35
if your enemy is *h* — Rom 12:20

Hunt *pursue, seek*
to *h* for game — Gen 27:5
h-s a partridge — 1 Sam 26:20
evil *h* the violent — Ps 140:11
H-ed me down like Lam 3:52
companions *h-ed* for Mark 1:36

Hurt (n) *damage, harm, wound*
Who delight in my *h* Ps 70:2
your brother is *h* — Rom 14:15

Hurt (v) *cause pain, wound*
will not *h* or destroy — Is 11:9
their power to *h* men Rev 9:10

Husband *family head, spouse*
honor to their *h-s* — Esth 1:20

crown of her *h* — Prov 12:4
divorces her *h* and Mark 10:12
if her *h* dies — Rom 7:2
have her own *h* — 1 Cor 7:2
h is the head of — Eph 5:23
H-s, love your wives Eph 5:25

Hymn *song of praise*
h-s of thanksgiving Neh 12:46
after singing a *h* — Matt 26:30
singing *h-s* of praise Acts 16:25
psalms and *h-s* and — Eph 5:19

Hypocrisy *pretense*
full of *h* and — Matt 23:28
without *h* — James 3:17

Hypocrite *a pretender*
as the *h-s* do — Matt 6:2
and Pharisees, *h-s* Matt 23:13

– I –

Idle *unemployed, uninvolved*
i man will suffer — Prov 19:15
been standing here *i* Matt 20:6

Idol *false deity, image*
not make…an *i* — Ex 20:4
the gods…are *i-s* — Ps 96:5
abstain from…*i-s* Acts 15:20
guard…from *i-s* — 1 John 5:21

Idolator *idol worshiper*
covetous, or an *i* — 1 Cor 5:11
sorcerers and *i* — Rev 21:8

Idolatry *idol worship*
flee from *i* — 1 Cor 10:14
i, sorcery, enmities Gal 5:20

Ignorance *lack of knowledge*
you worship in *i* — Acts 17:23
i that is in them — Eph 4:18

Ignorant *without knowledge*
I was senseless and *i* Ps 73:22
not *i* of his schemes 2 Cor 2:11

Ill *unhealthy, sick*
woman who is *i* — Lev 15:33
healed many…*i* — Mark 1:34

Illegitimate *bastard*
No one of *i* birth — Deut 23:2
you are *i* children — Heb 12:8

Illness *infirmity, sickness*
sick with the *i* — 2 Kin 13:14
because of a bodily *i* Gal 4:13

Illumine *light up*
God *i-s* my darkness Ps 18:28
God shall *i* them — Rev 22:5

Image *copy, likeness*
make man in Our *i* Gen 1:26
worshiped a molten *i* Ps 106:19
made an *i* of gold — Dan 3:1
i of the invisible — Col 1:15
the *i* of the beast — Rev 13:15

Imitators *followers*
be *i* of me — 1 Cor 4:16
be *i* of God — Eph 5:1

Immoral *lewd, unchaste*
the *i* man sins   1 Cor 6:18
i or godless person   Heb 12:16

Immorality *immoral acts*
no *i* in your midst   Lev 20:14
Flee *i*   1 Cor 6:18
the wine of her *i*   Rev 17:2

Immortality *everlasting life*
must put on *i*   1 Cor 15:53
alone possesses *i*   1 Tim 6:16

Impatient *restless*
the people became *i*   Num 21:4
my soul was *i* with   Zech 11:8

Imperishable *indestructible*
wreath, but we an *i*   1 Cor 9:25
will be raised *i*   1 Cor 15:52

Implore *ask, beseech*
I *i* you, give glory   Josh 7:19
I *i* You by God   Mark 5:7

Impose *force upon*
i-d hard labor on us   Deut 26:6
i-d until a time of   Heb 9:10

Impossible *cannot be done*
nothing…will be *i*   Gen 11:6
With men this is *i*   Matt 19:26
without faith it is *i*   Heb 11:6

Imprison *jail, restrict*
i his princes at will   Ps 105:22
not *i* their survivors   Obad 14

Imprisonment *confinement*
in *i-s*, in tumults   2 Cor 6:5
Remember my *i*   Col 4:18

Impure *unclean*
her *i* discharge   Lev 15:25
eating…with *i* hands   Mark 7:2

Impurity *uncleanness*
as slaves to *i*   Rom 6:19
of *i* with greediness   Eph 4:19

Incense *fragrant substance*
burn fragrant *i* on   Ex 30:7
i on the high places   2 Kin 14:4
i before the LORD   1 Chr 23:13
golden altar of *i*   Heb 9:4

Incite *stir up*
i-d David against   2 Sam 24:1
who *i-s* the people   Luke 23:14

Incline *bend, lean*
i your hearts to   Josh 24:23
I Thine ear, O LORD   Is 37:17

Income *wages*
i of the wicked   Prov 10:16
i with injustice   Prov 16:8
abundance *with its i*   Eccl 5:10

Incorruptible *not impure*
glory of the *i* God   Rom 1:23
Christ with *a love i*   Eph 6:24

Increase (n) *multiplication*
the *i* of your house   1 Sam 2:33
the LORD give you *i*   Ps 115:14

Increase (v) *multiply*
If riches *i*, do not   Ps 62:10
i-ing in wisdom   Luke 2:52
Lord cause…to *i*   1 Thess 3:12

Incurable *fatal, without cure*
with an *i* sickness   2 Chr 21:18
Your wound is *i*   Jer 30:12

Indignant *be angry*
i toward His enemies   Is 66:14
the ten became *i*   Matt 20:24

Indignation *anger*
God who has *i*   Ps 7:11
Pour out Thine *i*   Ps 69:24

Indwells *inhabits*
but sin which *i* me   Rom 7:17
His Spirit who *i* you   Rom 8:11

Infection *disease*
an *i* of leprosy   Lev 13:2

Inferior *lower in status*
I am not *i* to you   Job 12:3
i against the honorable   Is 3:5
i to…apostles   2 Cor 12:11

Infinite *unlimited*
His understanding is *i*   Ps 147:5

Inflict *strike, impose*
i all these curses   Deut 30:7
i-ed many blows   Acts 16:23

Inhabit *dwell*
no one would *i*   Job 15:28
build houses and *i*   Is 65:22

Inherit *receive a legacy*
shall *i* it forever   Ex 32:13
wise will *i* honor   Prov 3:35
gentle…*i* the earth   Matt 5:5
not *i* the kingdom   1 Cor 6:9

Inheritance *bequest, legacy*
the LORD is his *i*   Deut 10:9
the nations as Thine *i*   Ps 2:8
man leaves an *i*   Prov 13:22
Thine *i* a reproach   Joel 2:17
A man and his *i*   Mic 2:2
we…obtained an *i*   Eph 1:11

Iniquity *injustice, wickedness*
the *i* of the fathers   Deut 5:9
blot out all my *i-ies*   Ps 51:9
the workers of *i*   Is 31:2
the bondage of *i*   Acts 8:23
the *very* world of *i*   James 3:6

Injure *harm, wrong*
who seek to *i* me   Ps 38:12
do you *i* one another   Acts 7:26

Injury *wound*
there is no *further i*   Ex 21:22
because of my *i*   Jer 10:19

Injustice *inequity, unfairness*
there *i* on my tongue   Job 6:30
is no *i* with God   Rom 9:14

Inn *lodge for travelers*
no room…in the *i*   Luke 2:7
brought him to…*i*   Luke 10:34

Innocence *blamelessness*
wash my hands in *i*   Ps 26:6
be incapable of *i*   Hos 8:5

Innocent *blameless*
do not kill the *i*   Ex 23:7
the blood of the *i*   Deut 19:13
the *i* mock them   Job 22:19
that shed *i* blood   Prov 6:17
betraying *i* blood   Matt 27:4
holy, *i*, undefiled   Heb 7:26

Inquire *ask, seek*
to *i* of the LORD   Gen 25:22
you come to *i* of Me   Ezek 20:3
i-d of them the hour   John 4:52

Insane *mad*
a demon and is *i*   John 10:20
I speak as if *i*   2 Cor 11:23

Inscribe *carve, write*
i it on a scroll   Is 30:8
i it on tablets   Hab 2:2

Inscription *writing*
could not read the *i*   Dan 5:8
Pilate wrote an *i*   John 19:19
i, To An Unknown   Acts 17:23

Insight *discernment*
according to his *i*   Prov 12:8
not gained any *i*   Mark 6:52
In all wisdom and *i*   Eph 1:8

Insignificant *unimportant*
was *i* in Thine eyes   2 Sam 7:19
citizen of no *i* city   Acts 21:39

Inspired *stimulated*
the love we *i* in you   2 Cor 8:7
All Scripture is *i*   2 Tim 3:16

Instinct *natural tendency*
as creatures of *i*   2 Pet 2:12
they know by *i*   Jude 10

Instruct *teach*
Thy good Spirit to *i*   Neh 9:20
i-ed out of the Law   Rom 2:18
may *i* certain men   1 Tim 1:3

Instruction *teaching*
Get wisdom and *i*   Ps 23:23
i-s to His twelve   Matt 11:1
written for our *i*   Rom 15:4
i of the Lord   Eph 6:4

Insult (n) *affront, indignity*
casting the same *i*   Matt 27:44
evil, or *i* for *i*   1 Pet 3:9

Insult (v) *treat with scorn*
to *i* the LORD   2 Chr 32:17
i-ed the Spirit of   Heb 10:29

Integrity *honesty*
dealt in truth and *i*   Judg 9:19
holds fast his *i*   Job 2:3
have walked in my *i*   Ps 26:1

Intelligence *mental ability*
He deprives of *i*   Job 12:24
Paulus, a man of *i*   Acts 13:7

Intelligent *bright, smart*
was *i* and beautiful 1 Sam 25:3
from *the* wise and *i* Matt 11:25

Intend *purpose*
I *i* to build a house 1 Kin 5:5
i to make My people Jer 23:27

Intention *aim, goal*
the *i-s* of the heart 1 Chr 29:18
kind *i* of His will Eph 1:5

Intercede *plead, mediate*
i-d for the people Num 21:7
who can *i* for him 1 Sam 2:25
do not *i* with Me Jer 7:16

Interest *concern or usury*
not charge him *i* Ex 22:25
i to a foreigner Deut 23:20
his money at *i* Ps 15:5
mind on God's *i-s* Matt 16:23

Intermarry
And *i* with us Gen 34:9
i with the peoples Ezra 9:14

Interpret *explain, translate*
no one who could *i* Gen 41:8
He *i* the message Is 28:9
pray that he may *i* 1 Cor 14:13

Interpretation *explain*
the dream and its *i* Judg 7:15
make its *i* known Dan 5:16
of one's own *i* 2 Pet 1:20

Intimate *close*
my *i* friends have Job 19:14
i with the upright Prov 3:32

Invalidate *nullify*
i-d the word of God Matt 15:6
does not *i* a covenant Gal 3:17

Investigate *examine*
the judges shall *i* Deut 19:18
the plot was *i-d* Esth 2:23
i, and to seek wisdom Eccl 7:25
having *i-d* everything Luke 1:3

Invisible *unseen*
image of the *i* God Col 1:15
visible and *i* Col 1:16

Invite *request*
i-d us to impoverish Judg 14:15
did not *i* Me in Matt 25:43
i the poor Luke 14:13

Iron *metal*
was an *i* bedstead Deut 3:11
whose stones are *i* Deut 8:9
had *i* chariots Judg 1:19
made the *i* float 2 Kin 6:6
break them…rod of *i* Ps 2:9
from the *i* furnace Jer 11:4
as strong as *i* Dan 2:40
rule…rod of *i* Rev 19:15

Isolate *set apart*
priest shall *i* him Lev 13:4
i him for seven days Lev 13:21
fortified city is *i-d* Is 27:10

Issue (n) *outflow, out go*
first *i* of the womb Num 3:12
concerning this *i* Acts 15:2

Issue (v) *go forth, put forth*
shall *i* from you 2 Kin 20:18
i-d a proclamation Dan 5:29

Ivory *elephant tusk*
a great throne of *i* 1 Kin 10:18
silver, *i* and apes 2 Chr 9:21
Out of *i* palaces Ps 45:8
every article of *i* Rev 18:12

– J –

Jail *place of confinement*
put him into the *j* Gen 39:20
in *j* in the house Jer 37:15

Jailer *warden*
sight of the chief *j* Gen 39:21
the *j* to guard them Acts 16:23

Jar *container, jug*
and a *j* of honey 1 Kin 14:3
Bring me a new *j* 2 Kin 2:20
potter's earthenware *j* Jer 19:1
j full of sour wine John 19:29

Jaw *part of face*
j-s of the wicked Job 29:17
j teeth *like* knives Prov 30:14

Jealous *envious, zealous*
brothers were *j* of Gen 37:11
He is a *j* God Josh 24:19
j and avenging God Nah 1:2
j for Jerusalem Zech 1:14
I will make you *j* Rom 10:19
love is kind…not *j* 1 Cor 13:4

Join *bring together, couple*
j field to field Is 5:8
God…*j-ed* together Matt 19:6
j…me in suffering 2 Tim 1:8

Joint *juncture*
bones are out of *j* Ps 22:14
both *j-s* and marrow Heb 4:12

Journey *traveling, trip*
Let us take our *j* Gen 33:12
a bag for *your j* Matt 10:10
Sabbath day's *j* away Acts 1:12

Journeyed *traveled*
about as they *j* east Gen 11:2
the sons of Israel *j* Num 22:1

Joy *delight, happiness*
raise sounds of *j* 1 Chr 15:16
see His face with *j* Job 33:26
Restore to me the *j* Ps 51:12
Everlasting *j* will be Is 61:7
with great *j* Matt 2:10
enter into the *j* Matt 25:21
j in heaven over one Luke 15:7
j in the Holy Spirit Rom 14:17
love, *j*, peace Gal 5:22
make my *j* complete Phil 2:2

Joyful *feeling gladness*
be altogether *j* Deut 16:15
shall reap with *j* Ps 126:5
j heart is good Prov 17:22

Joyfully *full of joy, happy*
Shout *j* to God, all Ps 66:1
to praise God *j* Luke 19:37

Jubilant *elated*
Is this your *j* city Is 23:7
they may become *j* Jer 51:39

Judge (n) *leader*
J of all the earth Gen 18:25
For God Himself is *j* Ps 50:6
one Lawgiver and *J* James 4:12

Judge (v) *pass judgment*
LORD *j* between you Gen 16:5
Moses sat to *j* the Ex 18:13
coming to *j* the earth Ps 98:9
He will *j* the poor Is 11:4
not *j* lest you be *j-d* Matt 7:1
not come to *j* the John 12:47
adulterers God will *j* Heb 13:4

Judgment *condemnation*
I will execute *j-s* Ex 12:12
let *j* be executed Ezra 7:26
in the day of *j* Matt 10:15
My *j* is just John 5:30
after this *comes j* Heb 9:27
not fall under *j* James 5:12
j of the great day Jude 6
His *j-s* are true Rev 19:2

Jump *leap*
legs with which to *j* Lev 11:21
if a fox should *j* Neh 4:3

Just *fair, right*
shall have *j* balances Lev 19:36
He is *j* and endowed Zech 9:9
My judgment is *j* John 5:30

Justice *fairness, righteousness*
shall not distort *j* Deut 16:19
j to the afflicted Job 36:6
Righteousness and *j* Ps 89:14
j is turned back Is 59:14
let *j* roll down Amos 5:24
acknowledged…*j* Luke 7:29

Justification *vindication*
because of our *j* Rom 4:25
j of life to all men Rom 5:18

Justify *declare guiltless*
they *j* the righteous Deut 25:1
he *j-ied* himself Job 32:2
wishing to *j* himself Luke 10:29
seeking to be *j-ied* Gal 2:17

– K –

Keep *hold, guide, preserve*
love Me and *k* My Ex 20:6
shall *k* your sabbath Lev 23:32
to *k* the Passover Matt 26:18
he will *k* My word John 14:23

k yourself free   1 Tim 5:22

Keeper *guard, protector*
Am I my brother's *k*   Gen 4:9
The LORD is your *k*   Ps 121:5

Key *unlocking tool*
k-s of the kingdom   Matt 16:19
k-s of death and of   Rev 1:18
k of the bottomless pit   Rev 9:1

Kill *take life*
for Cain *k-ed* him   Gen 4:25
who *k-s* a man shall   Lev 24:21
Am I God, to *k*   2 Kin 5:7
he *k-s* the innocent   Ps 10:8
A time to *k*   Eccl 3:3
unable to *k* the   Matt 10:28
Arise, Peter, *k* and   Acts 10:13
who *k* their fathers   1 Tim 1:9

Kind (adj) *good, tender*
be *k* to this people   2 Chr 10:7
He Himself is *k*   Luke 6:35
love is *k*   1 Cor 13:4
be *k* to one another   Eph 4:32

Kind (n) *group, variety*
fruit after their *k*   Gen 1:11
all *k-s* of evil   Matt 5:11
every *k* of impurity   Eph 4:19

Kindle *cause to burn*
anger…was *k-d*   Num 11:10
man to *k* strife   Prov 26:21
k-d a fire in Zion   Lam 4:11

Kindness *tenderness*
to love *k*, And to   Mic 6:8
with deeds of *k*   Acts 9:36
joy, peace, patience, *k*   Gal 5:22
godliness, brotherly *k*   2 Pet 1:7

Kindred *relatives*
her people or her *k*   Esth 2:10
no one…of *k* spirit   Phil 2:20

King *monarch, regent*
no *k* in Israel   Judg 17:6
anointed David *k*   2 Sam 5:3
The LORD is *K* forever   Ps 10:16
Who is the *k* of glory   Ps 24:8
O *K* of the nations   Jer 10:7
born *K* of the Jews   Matt 2:2
Are You the *K* of   Matt 27:11
your *K* is coming   John 12:15
no *k* but Caesar   John 19:15
K of *k-s* and Lord   1 Tim 6:15

Kingdom *domain, monarchy*
to Me a *k* of priests   Ex 19:6
will establish his *k*   1 Chr 28:7
the *k* is the LORD's   Ps 22:28
an everlasting *k*   Ps 145:13
k of heaven is at   Matt 3:2
Thy *k* come   Matt 6:10
keys of the *k*   Matt 16:19
in My Father's *k*   Matt 26:29
to give you the *k*   Luke 12:32
preaching the *k*   Acts 28:31
to His heavenly *k*   2 Tim 4:18

heirs of the *k*   James 2:5

Kinsman *relative*
of my master's *k*   Gen 24:48
he took his *k-men*   Gen 31:23
a man has no *k*   Lev 25:26
Naomi had a *k* of her   Ruth 2:1
k-men stand afar off   Ps 38:11
Herodion, my *k*   Rom 16:11

Kiss (n) *expression of affection*
threw a *k* from my   Job 31:27
You gave Me no *k*   Luke 7:45
with a holy *k*   Rom 16:16
with a *k* of love   1 Pet 5:14

Kiss (v) *expression of affection*
come close and *k*   Gen 27:26
not…to *k* my feet   Luke 7:45

Knead *work dough, clay*
took flour, *k-ed* it   1 Sam 28:24
the women *k* dough   Jer 7:18

Knee *part of body*
strengthened feeble *k-s*   Job 4:4
every *k* shall bow   Rom 14:11

Kneel *bend, rest on knee*
made the camels *k*   Gen 24:11
k before the LORD   Ps 95:6
He *knelt* down   Luke 22:41

Knife *cutting instrument*
k to slay his son   Gen 22:10
with a scribes *k*   Jer 36:23

Knit *joined together*
Jonathan was *k* to   1 Sam 18:1
his thighs are *k*   Job 40:17
k together in love   Col 2:2

Knock *smite, strike*
k, and it shall be   Matt 7:7
stand outside and *k*   Luke 13:25
at the door and *k*   Rev 3:20

Know *experience, understand*
k that my Redeemer   Job 19:25
He *k-s* the secrets   Ps 44:21
k that I am God   Ps 46:10
made *k-n* His salvation   Ps 98:2
Try me and *k* my   Ps 139:23
k…by their fruits   Matt 7:20
I never *knew* you   Matt 7:23
you shall *k* the truth   John 8:32
and *k* all mysteries   1 Cor 13:2
who *knew* no sin   2 Cor 5:21
value of *k-ing* Christ   Phil 3:8
I *k* your deeds   Rev 2:2

Knowledge *information*
tree of the *k* of   Gen 2:9
LORD is a God of *k*   1 Sam 2:3
k is too wonderful   Ps 139:6
fools hate *k*   Prov 1:22
k increases power   Prov 24:5
accordance with *k*   Rom 10:2
k, it will be done   1 Cor 13:8
have no *k* of God   1 Cor 15:34
treasures of *k*   Col 2:3

– L –

Labor (n) *work* or *childbirth*
fruits of your *l-s*   Ex 23:16
return for their *l*   Eccl 4:9
like a woman in *l*   Is 42:14
in *l* and hardship   2 Cor 11:27
faith and *l* of love   1 Thess 1:3

Labor (v) *toil, work*
Six days you shall *l*   Ex 20:9
l in vain who build   Ps 127:1

Laborer *workman*
l-s for his vineyard   Matt 20:1
l-s into His harvest   Luke 10:2
l is worthy of his   Luke 10:7

Lack (n) *deficiency, need*
for *l* of instruction   Prov 5:23
l of self-control   1 Cor 7:5

Lack (v) *be deficient, need*
shall not *l* anything   Deut 8:9
One thing you *l*   Mark 10:21
if any…*l-s* wisdom   James 1:5

Lad *boy*
God heard the *l*   Gen 21:17
the *l* is not *with us*   Gen 44:31
the *l* was dead   2 Kin 4:32
a *l* here who has five   John 6:9

Lake *pool, water*
standing by the *l*   Luke 5:1
into the *l* of fire   Rev 20:10

Lamb *young sheep*
l for the burnt   Gen 22:7
l without defect   Lev 14:10
l…led to slaughter   Is 53:7
send you out as *l-s*   Luke 10:3
the *L* of God   John 1:29
Worthy is the *L* of   Rev 5:12

Lame *crippled, disabled*
was *l* in both feet   2 Sam 9:13
feet to the *l*   Job 29:15
Then the *l* will leap   Is 35:6
the l walk   Matt 11:5
l from his mother's   Acts 14:8

Lament (v) *mourn, wail*
house of Israel *l-ed*   1 Sam 7:2
her gates will *l*   Is 3:26
fishermen will *l*   Is 19:8
And I over you   Ezek 27:32
weep and *l* over her   Rev 18:9

Lamp *light*
Thou art my *l*   1 Sam 22:29
l-s of pure gold   2 Chr 4:20
Thy word is a *l*   Ps 119:105
l of the body is   Matt 6:22
l shining in a dark   2 Pet 1:19
seven *l-s* of fire   Rev 4:5

Lampstand *candlestick*
l of pure gold   Ex 25:31
puts it on a *l*   Luke 8:16
will remove your *l*   Rev 2:5

Land *country, earth*
let the dry *l* appear Gen 1:9
l flowing with milk Deut 6:3
in to possess the *l* Josh 1:11
will heal their *l* 2 Chr 7:14
will inherit the *l* Ps 37:11
dry and weary *l* Ps 63:1
again to this *l* Jer 24:6
smite the *l* with a Mal 4:6
owned a tract of *l* Acts 4:37

Language *speech, word*
in figurative *l* John 16:25
speak in his own *l* Acts 2:6
many kinds of *l*-s 1 Cor 14:10

Languish *faint*
My soul *l-es* for Ps 119:81
never *l* again Jer 31:12

Large *big, great, huge*
a *l* upper room Mark 14:15
a *l* multitude Luke 7:11

Last *final, utmost*
breathed his *l* Gen 25:8
first will be *l* Matt 19:30
The *l* Adam 1 Cor 15:45
at the *l* trumpet 1 Cor 15:52
in these *l* days Heb 1:2
it is the *l* hour 1 John 2:18
the first and the *l* Rev 1:17

Laugh *be amused, mock*
Why did Sarah *l* Gen 18:13
l at your calamity Prov 1:26
weep, and a time to *l* Eccl 3:4

Laughingstock *derision*
l among the peoples Ps 44:14
I have become a *l* Lam 3:14

Laughter *amusement*
God has made *l* for Gen 21:6
Even in *l* the heart Prov 14:13

Law *scripture, statute*
tablets with the *l* Ex 24:12
Moses wrote this *l* Deut 31:9
l...is perfect Ps 19:7
I delight in Thy *l* Ps 119:70
by a *l* of faith Rom 3:27
L brings...wrath Rom 4:15
not under *l* Rom 6:14
Is the *L* sin Rom 7:7
thus fulfill the *l* Gal 6:2
L...nothing perfect Heb 7:19

Lawful *legal, right*
Is it *l* to heal Matt 12:10
All things are *l* 1 Cor 6:12

Lawgiver *lawmaker*
The LORD is our *l* Is 33:22
one *L* and Judge James 4:12

Lawless *illegal, without law*
l one will be 2 Thess 2:8
from every *l* deed Titus 2:14

Lawyer *interpreter of law*
a *l*, asked Him *a* Matt 22:35
Woe to you *l-s* Luke 11:52

Lay *place, put*
l My hand on Egypt Ex 7:4
l up...treasures Matt 6:20
l-s down His life John 10:11
l I down My life John 10:15
have you *laid* Him John 11:34

Lazy *idle, slothful*
Because they are *l* Ex 5:8
beasts, *l* gluttons Titus 1:12

Lead (v) *direct, guide*
God *led* the people Ex 13:18
l-s me beside quiet Ps 23:2
L me in Thy truth Ps 25:5
little boy will *l* Is 11:6
not *l* us into Matt 6:13
and *l-s* them out John 10:3
led by the Spirit Rom 8:14
l-s to salvation 2 Tim 3:15

Leader *director, guide*
Let us appoint a *l* Num 14:4
one *l* of every tribe Num 34:18
l over My people 1 Kin 14:7
the *l* as the servant Luke 22:26
Obey your *l-s* Heb 13:17

Leaf *foliage*
sewed fig *l-ves* Gen 3:7
sound of a driven *l* Lev 26:36
its *l* does not wither Ps 1:3
puts forth its *l-ves* Matt 24:32

Lean (v) *incline, rest*
may *l* against them Judg 16:26
l on the God of Is 48:2

Leap *jump, spring*
l-ing and dancing 2 Sam 6:16
baby *l-ed* in her Luke 1:41
and *l* for joy Luke 6:23

Learn *get knowledge*
l to fear the LORD Deut 31:13
l Thy statutes Ps 119:71
will they *l* war Is 2:4
l from Me Matt 11:29
l-ed to be content Phil 4:11

Learning (n) *knowledge*
increase *his l* Prov 9:9
great *l* is driving Acts 26:24

Least *insignificant*
greatest to the *l* 2 Chr 34:30
l in the kingdom Matt 5:19
l of the apostles 1 Cor 15:9

Leave *abandon, depart*
shall *l* his father Gen 2:24
l the ninety-nine Matt 18:12
Peace I *l* with you John 14:27

Leaven *yeast*
not be baked with *l* Lev 6:17
heaven is like *l* Matt 13:33
little *l* leavens the 1 Cor 5:6

Legal *lawful*
has a *l* matter Ex 24:14
Give me *l* protection Luke 18:3

Legion *division, group*
twelve *l-s* of angels Matt 26:53
My name is *L* Mark 5:9

Lend *loan*
l-ing them money Neh 5:10
l, expecting nothing Luke 6:35

Lender *loaner*
becomes the *l-'s* slave Prov 22:7
l like the borrower Is 24:2

Length
the *l* of the ark Gen 6:15
breadth and *l* and Eph 3:18

Leper *one having leprosy*
King Uzziah...a *l* 2 Chr 26:21
a *l* came to Him Matt 8:2
cleanse *the l-s* Matt 10:8

Leprosy *infectious disease*
of *l* on the skin Lev 13:2
mark of *l* on a Lev 14:34
an infection of *l* Deut 24:8
cure him of his *l* 2 Kin 5:3
his *l* was cleansed Matt 8:3

Let *allow, permit*
L there be light Gen 1:3
L My people go Ex 5:1
L not your heart be John 14:1

Letter *epistle or symbol*
a *l* sent to Solomon 2 Chr 2:11
smallest *l* or stroke Matt 5:18
You are our *l* 2 Cor 3:2
l caused you sorrow 2 Cor 7:8
large *l-s* I am writing Gal 6:11

Level *flat, plain*
path of the righteous *l* Is 26:7
stood on a *l* place Luke 6:17

Levy (v) *impose a tax*
l a tax for the LORD Num 31:28
l-ied forced laborers 1 Kin 9:21

Lewdness *lascivious, lust*
land...full of *l* Lev 19:29
not commit this *l* Ezek 16:43
I will uncover her *l* Hos 2:10

Liar *one telling lies*
who...prove me a *l* Job 24:25
a poor man than a *l* Prov 19:22
hypocrisy of *l-s* 1 Tim 4:2
we make Him a *l* 1 John 1:10

Liberty *freedom*
I will walk at *l* Ps 119:45
proclaim *l* to captives Is 61:1
the *law* of *l* James 1:25

Lick *lap up*
dogs shall *l* up 1 Kin 21:19
his enemies *l* the dust Ps 72:9

Lie (n) *false statement*
tells *l-s* will perish Prov 19:9
the father of *l-s* John 8:44
truth of God for a *l* Rom 1:25

Lie (v) *make false statement*
nor *l* to one another Lev 19:11

l to the Holy Spirit   Acts 5:3
not *l* to one another   Col 3:9

Lie (v) *recline*
when you *l* down   Deut 11:19
Saul *lay* sleeping   1 Sam 26:7
makes his *l* down   Ps 23:2
lying in a manger   Luke 2:12

Life *living or salvation*
the breath of *l*   Gen 2:7
my *l* is *but* breath   Job 7:7
the springs of *l*   Prov 4:23
to everlasting *l*   Dan 12:2
take my *l* from me   Jon 4:3
anxious for your *l*   Matt 6:25
loses his *l* for My   Matt 16:25
His *l* a ransom for   Matt 20:28
to inherit eternal *l*   Mark 10:17
but have eternal *l*   John 3:16
out of death into *l*   John 5:24
lay down his *l* for   John 15:13
walk in newness of *l*   Rom 6:4
the Spirit gives *l*   2 Cor 3:6
receive…crown of *l*   James 1:12
lay down our *lives*   1 John 3:16

Lifeblood
I will require your *l*   Gen 9:5
l of the innocent   Jer 2:34

Lifetime *length of life*
His favor is for a *l*   Ps 30:5
my *l* of futility   Ecc 7:15

Lift *exalt, raise*
l up your eyes and   Gen 13:14
l up your voice   Job 38:34
I Will *l* up my eyes   Ps 121:1
Son of Man be *l-ed*   John 3:14
He was *l-ed* up   Acts 1:9

Light *brightness, lamp*
Let there be *l*   Gen 1:3
l of the wicked   Job 18:5
LORD is my *l*   Ps 27:1
And a *l* to my path   Ps 119:105
your *l* has come   Is 60:1
the *l* of the world   Matt 5:14
I am the *l*   John 8:12
walk as children of *l*   Eph 5:8
if we walk in the *l*   1 John 1:7

Lightning *flash of light in sky*
thunder and *l* flashes   Ex 19:16
He spreads His *l*   Job 36:30
makes *l* for the rain   Jer 10:13
l…from the east   Matt 24:27
appearance…like *l*   Matt 28:3

Likeness *similarity*
an idol, or any *l*   Ex 20:4
made in the *l* of men   Phil 2:7

Lily *flower*
The *l* of the valleys   Song 2:1
blossom like the *l*   Hos 14:5
l-ies of the field   Matt 6:28

Limit *end, extent*
there is no *l*   1 Chr 22:16

no l to windy words   Job 16:3

Line *boundary* or *cord*
draw your *border l*   Num 34:7
ran from…battle *l*   1 Sam 4:12
a *l* into the Nile   Is 19:8
plumb *l* in the hand   Zech 4:10

Lips *part of mouth*
My *l* will praise   Ps 63:3
With her flattering *l*   Prov 7:21
a man of unclean *l*   Is 6:5

Listen *hear, heed*
Pharaoh will not *l*   Ex 7:4
l to His voice   Deut 4:30
L to your father   Prov 23:22
draw near to *l*   Eccl 5:1
care what you *l* to   Mark 4:24
My son…*l* to Him   Luke 9:35

Little *small quantity*
a *l* lower than God   Ps 8:5
O men of *l* faith   Matt 6:30
forgiven *l*, loves *l*   Luke 7:47
l children, abide   1 John 2:28

Live (v) *reside or be alive*
does not *l* by bread   Deut 8:3
my Redeemer *l-s*   Job 19:25
Let my soul *l*   Ps 119:175
can these bones *l*   Ezek 37:3
not *l* on bread alone   Matt 4:4
l even if he dies   John 11:25
shall *l* by faith   Rom 1:17
no longer I who *l*   Gal 2:20
to *l* is Christ   Phil 1:21

Living (adj) *alive*
became a *l* being   Gen 2:7
Son of the *l* God   Matt 16:16
given you *l* water   John 4:10
became a *l* soul   1 Cor 15:45
temple of the *l* God   2 Cor 6:16
word of God is *l*   Heb 4:12

Living (n) *what is alive*
land of the *l*   Job 28:13
God…of the *l*   Matt 22:32
judge the *l* and the   1 Pet 4:5

Load *burden*
in all their *l-s*   Num 4:27
I alone bear the *l*   Deut 1:12
My *l* is light   Matt 11:30

Loaf *portion of bread*
gave him a *l* of bread   Jer 37:21
shall ask him for a *l*   Matt 7:9
five *l-ves* and two   Matt 14:17

Loan *something lent*
your neighbor a *l*   Deut 24:10
rich with *l-s*   Hab 2:6

Loathe *despise, detest*
I *l-d* that generation   Ps 95:10
sated man *l-s* money   Prov 27:7
I *l* the arrogance of   Amos 6:8

Lock (n) *tuft of hair*
seven *l-s* of my hair   Judg 16:13
a *l* of my head   Ezek 8:3

Lock (v) *secure, shut*
l the door behind   2 Sam 13:17
l up…the saints   Acts 26:10

Lodge *dwell, spend the night*
you *l*, I will *l*   Ruth 1:16
l in the wilderness   Ps 55:7

Lodging (adj) *dwelling*
fodder at the *l* place   Gen 42:27
prepare for me a *l*   Philem 22

Loftiness *elevated, haughty*
l of man will be   Is 2:11
l of your dwelling   Obad 3

Lofty *grand, high*
built Thee a *l* house   1 Kin 8:13
high and *l* mountain   Is 57:7

Loins *lower back*
Gird up your *l*   2 Kin 4:29
having girded your *l*   Eph 6:14

Lonely *alone, isolated*
I am *l* and afflicted   Ps 25:16
to a *l* place and rest   Mark 6:31

Long (adj) *extended*
there was a *l* war   2 Sam 3:1
you make *l* prayers   Matt 23:14

Long (v) *desire, want*
Who *l* for death   Job 3:21
my soul *l-s* for Thee   Is 26:9
I *l* to see you   Rom 1:11
l for the pure milk   1 Pet 2:2

Look *see, stare*
afraid to *l* at God   Ex 3:6
L upon my affliction   Ps 25:18
not *l* on the wine   Prov 23:31
l to the Holy One   Is 17:7
L at the birds of   Matt 6:26
plow and *l-ing* back   Luke 9:62
l on the fields   John 4:35
l-ing for…heavens   2 Pet 3:13

Loose *release*
hast *l-d* my bonds   Ps 116:16
l on earth shall be   Matt 16:19

Lord *human master, ruler*
Hear us, my *l*   Gen 23:6
Moses, my *l*   Num 11:28
counsel of my *l*   Ezra 10:3
l-s of the nations   Is 16:8
his *l* commanded   Matt 18:25
write to my *l*   Acts 25:26

Lose *mislay, suffer loss*
do not *l* courage   2 Chr 15:7
lost their confidence   Neh 6:16
his life shall *l* it   Matt 10:39
not *l* his reward   Mark 9:41

Loss *damage, what is lost*
might not suffer *l*   Dan 6:2
might not suffer *l*   2 Cor 7:9
all things to be *l*   Phil 3:8

Lost (adj) *missing, ruined*
like a *l* sheep   Ps 119:176
have become *l* sheep   Jer 50:6

Lost (n) *without God*
I will seek the *l* Ezek 34:16
sent only to the *l* Matt 15:24

Lot *portion or decision process*
one *l* for the LORD Lev 16:8
your *l* with us Prov 1:14
tear it, but cast *l-s* John 19:24
l fell to Matthias Acts 1:26

Loud *great, noisy*
very *l* trumpet sound Ex 19:16
Jesus cried…*l* voice Matt 27:50

Love (n) *compassion, devotion*
l covers all Prov 10:12
l will grow cold Matt 24:12
abide in My *l* John 15:10
separate us from…*l* Rom 8:39
l edifies 1 Cor 8:1
l is kind 1 Cor 13:4
Pursue *l* 1 Cor 14:1
fruit…is *l* Gal 5:22
speaking…truth in *l* Eph 4:15
l of money is a root 1 Tim 6:10
God is *l* 1 John 4:16
have left your first *l* Rev 2:4

Love (v)
who *l* Me and keep My Ex 20:6
l your neighbor as Lev 19:18
l the LORD your God Deut 6:5
I *l* Thy testimonies Ps 119:119
A time to *l* Eccl 3:8
Hate evil, *l* good Amos 5:15
l your enemies Matt 5:44
you *l* one another John 13:34
Husbands, *l*…wives Eph 5:25
not *l* the world 1 John 2:15

Lovers *those who desire, love*
I called to my *l* Lam 1:19
l of pleasure…*l* of 2 Tim 3:4

Lovingkindness *compassion*
His *l* is upon Israel Ezra 3:11
sing of the *l* of the Ps 89:1
By *l* and truth Prov 16:6

Lowly *humble, little*
He regards the *l* Ps 138:6
associate with the *l* Rom 12:16

Loyalty *faithfulness*
proclaims his own *l* Prov 20:6
l delight in *l* Hos 6:6

Lust *sexual desire*
from youthful *l-s* 2 Tim 2:22
l of the eyes 1 John 2:16

Luxury *extravagance*
L is not fitting for Prov 19:10
clothed and live in *l* Luke 7:25

Lying (adj) *false*
with a *l* tongue Ps 109:2
hatred *has l* lips Prov 10:18

– M –

Mad *insane*
makes a wise man *m* Eccl 7:7
nations are going *m* Jer 51:7

Madman *insane person*
behaving as a *m* 1 Sam 21:14
m who prophesies Jer 29:26

Magic *sorcery*
practicing *m* Acts 8:9
who practiced *m* Acts 19:19

Magician *sorcerer, wizard*
called for…*m-s* Gen 41:8
the *m-s* of Egypt Ex 7:11
of any *m*, conjurer or Dan 2:10
found a certain *m* Acts 13:6

Magnify *extol, praise*
name…be *m-ied* 2 Sam 7:26
O *m* the LORD Ps 34:3
hast *m-ied* Thy word Ps 138:2

Maid
gave my *m* to my Gen 30:18
way of a man…a *m* Prov 30:19

Maidservant *female slave*
do…to your *m* Deut 15:17
give Thy *m* a son 1 Sam 1:11
Let your *m* speak 2 Sam 14:12
while your *m* slept 1 Kin 3:20

Majestic *dignified, grand*
with His *m* voice Job 37:4
How *m* is Thy name Ps 8:1
m is His work Ps 111:3

Majesty *grandeur*
He is clothed with *m* Ps 93:1
The *m* of our God Is 35:2

Make *cause, create, do*
Let Us *m* man in Gen 1:26
M me know Thy ways Ps 25:4
m you fishers of Matt 4:19

Maker *creator*
kneel before…our *M* Ps 95:6
M of heaven and Ps 115:15

Male
m and female He Gen 1:27
likeness of *m* or Deut 4:16
neither *m* nor female Gal 3:28

Malice *evil, mischief*
perceived their *m* Matt 22:18
putting aside all *m* 1 Pet 2:1

Malicious *harmful, spiteful*
to be a *m* witness Ex 23:1
m gossips, without 2 Tim 3:3

Mammon *wealth*
serve God and *m* Matt 6:24
m…unrighteousness Luke 16:9

Man *male*
formed *m* of dust Gen 2:7
m is born for trouble Job 5:7
m is a mere breath Ps 39:11

Will a *m* rob God Mal 3:8
fishers of *men* Mark 1:17
rich *m* to enter Mark 10:25
what is a *m* profited Luke 9:25
a *m*, sent from God John 1:6
through one *m* sin Rom 5:12
I became a *m* 1 Cor 13:11

Manger
spend…at your *m* Job 39:9
the *m* is clean Prov 14:4
laid Him in a *m* Luke 2:7

Manifest *reveal*
became *m* to those Rom 10:20
made *m* to God 2 Cor 5:11

Manifold *many and varied*
m wisdom of God Eph 3:10

Mankind *the human race*
All *m* is stupid Jer 51:17
His love for *m* Titus 3:4

Manner *way*
spoke in such a *m* Acts 14:1
walk in a *m* worthy Eph 4:1

Manslayer
for the *m* to flee to Num 35:6
m might flee there Deut 4:42
the *m* who kills any Josh 20:3

Mantle *cloak, garment*
threw his *m* on him 1 Kin 19:19
the *m* of Elijah 2 Kin 2:13
as a *m* Thou wilt roll Heb 1:12

Mark *sign, spot*
m on the foreheads Ezek 9:4
m of the beast Rev 19:20

Market *selling or trading place*
was the *m* of nations Is 23:3
coastlands…*m* Ezek 27:15
idle in the *m* place Matt 20:3
sold in the meat *m* 1 Cor 10:25

Marriage *wedlock*
a *m* alliance with 1 Kin 3:1
nor are given in *m* Matt 22:30
m be held in honor Heb 13:4

Marry *join in wedlock*
m-ies a divorced Matt 5:32
better not to *m* Matt 19:10
better to *m* than to 1 Cor 7:9

Marvel *be amazed, wonder*
multitude *m-ed* Matt 15:31
m at the sight Acts 7:31

Marvelous *extraordinary*
It is *m* in our eyes Ps 118:23
into His *m* light 1 Pet 2:9
m are Thy works Rev 15:3

Master *lord, ruler*
can serve two *m-s* Matt 6:24
death no longer is *m* Rom 6:9
sin shall not be *m* Rom 6:14
a *M* in heaven Col 4:1

Mature *full grown or stable*
then the *m* grain Mark 4:28

those who are *m* 1 Cor 2:6
food is for the *m* Heb 5:14

Meal *prepared food*
a *m* for enjoyment Eccl 10:19
not even eat a *m* Mark 3:20
washed before…*m* Luke 11:38
m-s together with Acts 2:46
for a *single m* Heb 12:16

Meaningless *senseless*
with *m* arguments Is 29:21
not use *m* repetition Matt 6:7

Measure (n) *amount*
a full and just *m* Deut 25:15
good *m*, pressed Luke 6:38
m of Christ's gift Eph 4:7

Measure (v) *determine extent*
m their former work Is 65:7
shall be *m-ed* to you Mark 4:24

Measuring *standard*
justice the *m* line Is 28:17
given me a *m* rod Rev 11:1

Meat *flesh, food*
you may eat *m* Deut 12:20
rained *m* upon them Ps 78:27
good not to eat *m* Rom 14:21
I will never eat *m* 1 Cor 8:13

Mediator *intermediary*
agency of a *m* Gal 3:19
Jesus…*m* of a new Heb 12:24

Meditate *ponder*
His law he *m-s* day Ps 1:2
M in your heart Ps 4:4

Meditation *deep reflection*
m be pleasing to Ps 104:34
my *m* all the day Ps 119:97

Meekness *gentleness*
cause of truth and *m* Ps 45:4
m and…of Christ 2 Cor 10:1

Meet *encounter*
Esau ran to *m* him Gen 33:4
Prepare to *m*…God Amos 4:12
m-s his accusers Acts 25:16
m…in the air 1 Thess 4:17

Meeting *assembly*
house of *m* for all Job 30:23
midst of Thy *m* place Ps 74:4

Melt *dissolve*
people *m* with fear Josh 14:8
mountains *m-ed* like Ps 97:5

Member *part of the whole*
m-s of…household Matt 10:25
if one *m* suffers 1 Cor 12:26
m-s of His body Eph 5:30

Memorial *commemoration*
in a book as a *m* Ex 17:14
ascended as a *m* Acts 10:4

Memory *remembrance*
M of him perishes Job 18:17
m of the righteous Prov 10:7

Merchant *buyer/seller*
m-s procured *them* 1 Kin 10:28
m of the peoples Ezek 27:3
A *m*, in whose hands Hos 12:7
m seeking…pearls Matt 13:45
m-s of the earth Rev 18:3

Merciful *compassionate*
God *m* and gracious Ps 86:15
Blessed are the *m* Matt 5:7
as your Father is *m* Luke 6:36

Mercy *compassion*
m to *the* poor Dan 4:27
they shall receive *m* Matt 5:7
the *m-ies* of God Rom 12:1

Merry *joyful, lively*
wine makes life *m* Eccl 10:19
drink *and* be *m* Luke 12:19

Message *communication*
m and my preaching 1 Cor 2:4
the *m* of truth Eph 1:13
m we have heard 1 John 1:5

Messenger *one sent*
My *m* whom I send Is 42:19
send My *m* before Matt 11:10
m of Satan 2 Cor 12:7

Middle *midst*
the *m* of the garden Gen 3:3
m of the lampstands Rev 1:13

Midst *middle, within*
God is in the *m* Ps 46:5
in the *m* of the fire Dan 3:25
I am in their *m* Matt 18:20

Might *strength*
and with all your *m* Deut 6:5
Not by *m* nor by Zech 4:6
strength of His *m* Eph 1:19

Mighty *powerful*
a *m* hunter before Gen 10:9
m men of valor 1 Chr 12:8
The LORD *m* in battle Ps 24:8
m in the Scriptures Acts 18:24
the *m* hand of God 1 Pet 5:6

Mile *distance, measurement*
one *m*, go with him Matt 5:41
m-s from Jerusalem Luke 24:13

Milk
land flowing with *m* Ex 3:8
m to drink, not 1 Cor 3:2
pure *m* of the word 1 Pet 2:2

Millstone *grinding stone*
upper *m* in pledge Deut 24:6
woman threw…*m* Judg 9:53
m be hung around Matt 18:6
stone like a great *m* Rev 18:21

Mind *memory, thought*
I test the *m* Jer 17:10
He opened…*m-s* Luke 24:45
with one *m* in the Acts 2:46
m set on the flesh Rom 8:7
the *m* of Christ 1 Cor 2:16

with humility of *m* Phil 2:3

Mindful *aware*
Lord be *m* of me Ps 40:17
LORD has been *m* Ps 115:12

Minister (n) *one who serves*
spoken of *as m-s* Is 61:6
a *m* of Christ Jesus Rom 15:16
I was made a *m* Eph 3:7
a *m* in the sanctuary Heb 8:2

Minister (v) *give help, serve*
to *m* as priest to Me Ex 28:1
not stand to *m* 1 Kin 8:11
angels were *m-ing* Mark 1:13

Ministry *service*
He began His *m* Luke 3:23
m of the Spirit 2 Cor 3:8
m of reconciliation 2 Cor 5:18
a more excellent *m* Heb 8:6

Miracle *supernatural event*
Work a *m* Ex 7:9
He could do no *m* Mark 6:5
this *m* of healing Acts 4:22
works *m-s* among you Gal 3:5

Mirror *image reflector*
see in a *m* dimly 1 Cor 13:12

Miserable *unhappy*
loathe this *m* food Num 21:5
Be *m* and mourn James 4:9

Misery *sorrow, suffering*
conscious of my *m* Job 10:15
Destruction and *m* Rom 3:16

Misfortune *adversity*
M will not come Jer 5:12
The day of his *m* Obad 12

Mislead *lead astray*
m-led My people Ezek 13:10
that no one *m-s* you Mark 13:5

Mistreat *treat badly, wrong*
not *m*…the stranger Jer 22:3
mocked and *m-ed* Luke 18:32

Mistress *woman in charge*
m of the house 1 Kin 17:17
the *m* of sorceries Nah 3:4

Mock *ridicule, scorn*
Fools *m* at sin Prov 14:9
God is not *m-ed* Gal 6:7

Mockery *object of ridicule*
a *m* of the Egyptians Ex 10:2
a *m* of justice Prov 19:28

Molten *cast metal*
made it into a *m* calf Ex 32:4
make…no *m* in gods Ex 34:17
destroy…*m* images Num 33:52
capitals of *m* bronze 1 Kin 7:16
his *m* images are Jer 10:14

Money *currency*
not sell her for *m* Deut 21:14
loves *m* will not be Eccl 5:10
no *m* in their belt Mark 6:8

love of *m* is a root   1 Tim 6:10

Moneychangers
the tables of the *m*   Matt 21:12
coins of the *m*   John 2:15

Monster *enormous animal*
created…sea *m-s*   Gen 1:21
sea, or the sea *m*   Job 7:12
sea *m-s* in the waters   Ps 74:13
belly of the sea *m*   Matt 12:40

Moon
the *m* stopped   Josh 10:13
m and stars to rule   Ps 136:9
the *m* into blood   Joel 2:31

Morning *dawn*
Rise early in the *m*   Ex 8:20
the *m* stars sang   Job 38:7
the bright *m* star   Rev 22:16

Morsel *piece of bread*
have eaten my *m*   Job 31:17
Better is a dry *m*   Prov 17:1
after the *m*, Satan   John 13:27

Mortal *what eventually dies*
not trust…In *m* man   Ps 146:3
in our *m* flesh   2 Cor 4:11

Mother
m of all *the* living   Gen 3:20
a grief to his *m*   Prov 10:1
Who is My *m*   Matt 12:48
Honor your…*m*   Matt 19:19
Behold, your *m*   John 19:27

Motives *attitudes, intentions*
LORD weighs the *m*   Prov 16:2
than from pure *m*   Phil 1:17
ask with wrong *m*   James 4:3

Mount (v) *climb up*
to *m* his chariot   2 Chr 10:18
m up *with* wings   Is 40:31

Mountain
from His holy *m*   Ps 3:4
lovely on the *m-s*   Is 52:7
the *m* will move   Zech 14:4
faith…remove *m-s*   1 Cor 13:2

Mourn *grieve, lament*
A time to *m*   Eccl 3:4
comfort all who *m*   Is 61:2
Blessed…who *m*   Matt 5:4
Be miserable and *m*   James 4:9

Mouth
m condemns you   Job 15:6
the words of my *m*   Ps 19:14
confess with your *m*   Rom 10:9

Move *change position, stir*
Spirit of God…*m-ing*   Gen 1:2
I shall not be *m-d*   Ps 10:6
m-d…compassion   Mark 1:41
in Him we live…*m*   Acts 17:28

Multiply *increase*
Be fruitful and *m*   Gen 1:22
He *m-ies* lies and   Hos 12:1

Multitude *crowd*
father of a *m* of   Gen 17:4
Him a great *m*   Luke 23:27
cover a *m* of sins   James 5:20

Murder *premeditated killing*
You shall not *m*   Ex 20:13
full of envy, *m*   Rom 1:29

Music *harmony, melody*
instruments of *m*   1 Chr 15:16
m to the LORD   2 Chr 7:6

Mustard *type of plant*
kingdom…like a *m*   Matt 13:31
faith as a *m* seed   Matt 17:20

Mystery *hidden truth, secret*
no *m* baffles you   Dan 4:9
the *m* of the gospel   Eph 6:19
the *m* of the faith   1 Tim 3:9

Myths *fables*
to pay attention to *m*   1 Tim 1:4
will turn aside to *m*   2 Tim 4:4
attention to Jewish *m*   Titus 1:14

– N –

Nailed (v) *attached, pinned*
you *n* to a cross   Acts 2:23
n it to the cross   Col 2:14

Naive *simple, not suspicious*
prudence to the *n*   Prov 1:4
the *n* becomes wise   Prov 21:11

Naked *unclothed*
n and…not ashamed   Gen 2:25
n…you clothed Me   Matt 25:36

Name *designation, title*
takes His *n* in vain   Ex 20:7
blot out his *n*   Deut 29:20
praises to Thy *n*   Ps 18:49
Hallowed be Thy *n*   Matt 6:9
such child in My *n*   Matt 18:5
will come in My *n*   Luke 21:8
baptized in the *n*   Acts 2:38
of faith in His *n*   Acts 3:16
other *n* under heaven   Acts 4:12

Narrow *limited*
Enter by the *n* gate   Matt 7:13

Nation *government, people*
makes you a great *n*   Gen 12:2
priests and a holy *n*   Ex 19:6
glory among the *n-s*   Is 66:19
n should not perish   John 11:50
men, from every *n*   Acts 2:5

Native *indigenous*
or a *n* of the land   Ex 12:19
the *n-s* showed us   Acts 28:2

Natural *normal*
died a *n* death   Ezek 44:31
is sown a *n* body   1 Cor 15:44

Nature *essence*
of the same *n* as you   Acts 14:15
of *the* divine *n*   2 Pet 1:4

Neck *part of body*
yoke on your *n*   Deut 28:48
stiffened their *n-s*   Jer 17:23

Need *necessity, obligation*
sufficient for his *n*   Deut 15:8
n-s of the saints   2 Cor 9:12
supply all your *n-s*   Phil 4:19

Needle
the eye of a *n*   Matt 19:24
n than for a rich   Mark 10:25

Needy *destitute, poor*
a father to the *n*   Job 29:16
the LORD hears the *n*   Ps 69:33

Neglect *disregard, ignore*
You *n-ed* the Rock   Deut 32:18
n so great a salvation   Heb 2:3
do no *n* doing good   Heb 13:16

Neighbor *one living nearby*
shall love your *n*   Lev 19:18
love your *n*, and   Matt 5:43
And who is my *n*   Luke 10:29
love your *n* as   Gal 5:14

Nest
n among the stars   Obad 4
birds…*have n-s*   Matt 8:20

Net *snare*
a *n* for my steps   Ps 57:6
casting a *n* into   Matt 4:18
n full of fish   John 21:8

New *fresh, recent*
nothing *n* under the   Eccl 1:9
a *n* spirit within   Ezek 11:19
n wine into old   Mark 2:22
A *n* commandment   John 13:34
he is a *n* creature   2 Cor 5:17
making all things *n*   Rev 21:5

Newness *freshness*
walk in *n* of life   Rom 6:4
in *n* of the Spirit   Rom 7:6

News *report, tidings*
a day of good *n*   2 Kin 7:9
the *n* about Jesus   Matt 14:1
n of a great joy   Luke 2:10

Night *darkness*
darkness He called *n*   Gen 1:5
meditate…day and *n*   Josh 1:8
The terror by *n*   Ps 91:5
over their flocks by *n*   Luke 2:8
a thief in the *n*   1 Thess 5:2

Noble *lofty, renown*
king's most *n* princes   Esth 6:9
speak *n* things   Prov 8:6
all the *n-s* of Judah   Jer 39:6

Nobleman *of high rank*
the house of a *n*   Job 21:28
a certain *n* went   Luke 19:12

Noise *loud sound*
Egypt *is but* a big *n*   Jer 46:17
from heaven a *n*   Acts 2:2

Nonsense *foolishness*
a fool speaks *n* Is 32:6
appeared…as *n* Luke 24:11

Notice *attention*
take *n* of me Ruth 2:10
not *n* the log Matt 7:3

Nourish *feed, sustain*
n-s and cherishes it Eph 5:29
constantly *n-ed* on 1 Tim 4:6
she might be *n-ed* Rev 12:6

Nullify *annul, make void*
LORD *n-ies* counsel Ps 33:10
unbelief will not *n* Rom 3:3
the promise is *n-ied* Rom 4:14
n the grace of God Gal 2:21

Number (n) *group, total*
the *n* of the stars Ps 147:4
increasing in *n* daily Acts 16:5

Number (v) *count, enumerate*
Thou dost *n* my steps Job 14:16
hairs…all *n-ed* Matt 10:30

– O –

Oath *declaration, vow*
free from the *o* Josh 2:20
make no *o* at all Matt 5:34
priests without an *o* Heb 7:21

Obedience *submission*
the *o* of the peoples Gen 49:10
the *o* of the One Rom 5:19
in *o* to the truth 1 Pet 1:22

Obedient *willing to obey*
we will be *o* Ex 24:7
o from the heart Rom 6:17

Obey *follow commands, orders*
o My voice and keep Ex 19:5
to *o* is better than 1 Sam 15:22
and the sea *o* Him Matt 8:27
o your parents Eph 6:1
O your leaders Heb 13:17

Object
an *o* of loathing to Ps 88:8
god or *o* of worship 2 Thess 2:4

Obligation *duty*
o toward the LORD Num 32:22
under *o*, not to the Rom 8:12

Observe *keep or notice*
o all My statutes Lev 19:37
O how the lilies Matt 6:28
o-ing the traditions Mark 7:3

Obstacle *hindrance*
Remove *every o* out of Is 57:14
an *o* or stumbling Rom 14:13

Obstinate
you are an *o* people Ex 33:3
disobedient and *o* Rom 10:21

Obtain *get possession of*
o children through Gen 16:2
may *o* eternal life Matt 19:16
o the gift of God Acts 8:20

Occur *happen, take place*
this sign shall *o* Ex 8:23
lest a riot be *o* Matt 26:5
predestined to *o* Acts 4:28

Offend *insult or violate*
I will not *o* anymore Job 34:31
Pharisees were *o-ed* Matt 15:12

Offense *anger or transgression*
of the *o* of Adam Rom 5:14
and a rock of *o* 1 Pet 2:8

Offer (v) *give, present*
O to God a sacrifice Ps 50:14
my mouth *o-s* praises Ps 63:5
o both gifts and Heb 5:1
o-ed Himself Heb 9:14

Offering (n) *contribution*
freewill *o* to the LORD Ex 35:29
o of first fruits Lev 2:12
presenting your *o* Matt 5:23

Office *function or position*
wield the staff of *o* Judg 5:14
priests in their *o-s* 2 Chr 35:2

Official *one in authority*
o-s in the palace 2 Kin 20:18
o of the synagogue Luke 8:41

Offspring *descendants*
o in place of Abel Gen 4:25
you are Abraham's *o* Gal 3:29
and the *o* of David Rev 22:16

Oil
anointed my head…*o* Ps 23:5
prudent took *o* in Matt 25:4
not anoint…with *o* Luke 7:46

Ointment *salve*
a jar of *o* Job 41:31
anointed…with *o* John 11:2

Old *aged, obsolete*
honor of *o* men Prov 20:29
o men will dream Joel 2:28
o self was crucified Rom 6:6
o things passed away 2 Cor 5:17
men of *o* gained Heb 11:2

Olive *tree or fruit*
land of *o* oil and Deut 8:8
children like *o* plants Ps 128:3

One *single unit*
shall become *o* flesh Gen 2:24
God, the LORD is *o* Deut 6:4
His chosen *o-s* Ps 105:6
joy…over *o* sinner Luke 15:7
they may all be *o* John 17:21
o body in Christ Rom 12:5
o died for all 2 Cor 5:14
o Lord, *o* faith Eph 4:5
husband of *o* wife 1 Tim 3:2

Open (adj) *not shut, exposed*
throat is an *o* grave Ps 5:9
before you an *o* door Rev 3:8

Open (v) *expose, free, unfasten*
eyes will be *o-ed* Gen 3:5
O LORD, *o* my lips Ps 51:15

O my eyes, that I Ps 119:18
knock…shall be *o-ed* Matt 7:7
and *o-s* the door Rev 3:20

Opponent *adversary*
friends…with your *o* Matt 5:25
protection from my *o* Luke 18:3

Opportunity *occasion*
o to betray Him Matt 26:16
an *o* for the flesh Gal 5:13

Oppose *contend, resist*
o the Prince of Dan 8:25
also *o* the truth 2 Tim 3:8

Opposition *hostility*
you…know My *o* Num 14:34
these are in *o* Gal 5:17

Oppress (v) *trouble, tyrannize*
Egyptians are *o-ing* Ex 3:9
woman *o-ed* in 1 Sam 1:15
rich who *o* you James 2:6

Oppressed (n) *afflicted*
justice for the *o* Ps 146:7
vengeance for the *o* Acts 7:24

Oppression *affliction*
Do not trust in *o* Ps 62:10
o makes a…man mad Eccl 7:7
and water of *o* Is 30:20
o of My people Acts 7:34

Ordain *invest, set apart*
anoint…and *o* them Ex 28:41
o-ed His covenant Ps 111:19

Ordeal *difficulty, trial*
great *o* of affliction 2 Cor 8:2
at the fiery *o* 1 Pet 4:12

Order (n) *arrangement*
Set your house in *o* 2 Kin 20:1
fixed *o* of the moon Jer 31:35
the *o* of Melchizedek Heb 5:6

Order (v) *command or request*
I will *o* my prayer Ps 5:3
confidence…to *o* you Philem 8

Ordinance *statute*
o of the Passover Ex 12:43
o-s of the heavens Job 38:33

Ordination
Aaron's ram of *o* Ex 29:26
period of your *o* Lev 8:33

Origin *beginning, source*
of Jewish *o* Esth 6:13
o is from antiquity Is 23:7
Your *o* and your Ezek 16:3

Ornament *decoration*
put off your *o-s* Ex 33:5
o of fine gold Prov 25:12

Orphan *fatherless child*
justice for the *o* Deut 10:18
helper of the *o* Ps 10:14

Outburst *sudden release*
great *o* of anger Deut 29:24
jealousy, *o-s* of anger Gal 5:20

Outcast *rejected*
the *o-s* of Israel — Ps 147:2
called you an *o* Jer 30:17

Outcry *strong cry* or *protest*
no *o* in our streets Ps 144:14
o is heard among the Jer 50:46
a *single o* arose Acts 19:34

Outward *external*
the *o* appearance 1 Sam 16:7
is *o* in the flesh Rom 2:28

Overcome *conquer, master*
man *o* with wine Jer 23:9
o evil with good Rom 12:21
who *o-s* shall inherit Rev 21:7

Overflow *flood, inundate*
My cup *o-s* Ps 23:5
o-ing with gratitude Col 2:7

Overlaid *decorate, spread*
o…with gold 1 Kin 6:28
vessel *o* with silver Prov 26:23
o with gold…silver Hab 2:19

Overlook *ignore* or *view*
o a transgression Prov 19:11
widows were…*o-ed* Acts 6:1

Overpower *subdue*
deceive you and *o* you Obad 7
Hades shall not *o* Matt 16:18
attacks him and *o-s* Luke 11:22

Overseer *director, leader*
o in the house of Jer 29:26
the office of *o* 1 Tim 3:1

Overshadow *engulf, obscure*
Most High…*o* you Luke 1:35
o-ing the mercy seat Heb 9:5

Oversight *supervision*
o of the house of 2 Kin 12:11
exercising *o* not 1 Pet 5:2

Overwhelm *crush, overcome*
darkness will *o* me Ps 139:11
o-ed by…sorrow 2 Cor 2:7

Owe *be indebted*
O nothing to anyone Rom 13:8
that you *o* to me Philem 19

Own (adj) *belonging to*
man in His *o* image Gen 1:27
calls his *o* sheep John 10:3

Own (n) *belonging to*
He came to His *o* John 1:11
provide for his *o* 1 Tim 5:8

Owner *possessor*
restitution to its *o* Ex 22:12
when the *o*…comes Matt 21:40
who were *o-s* of land Acts 4:34

– P –

Pain *discomfort, hurt*
multiply Your *p* Gen 3:16
rest from your *p* Is 14:3
Your *p* is incurable Jer 30:15
suffering great *p* Matt 8:6

Painful *hurting*
p are honest words Job 6:25
the bread of *p* labors Ps 127:2

Pallet *bed, mat*
they let down the *p* Mark 2:4
take up your *p* and Mark 2:9

Panic *fear*
P seized them there Ps 48:6
P and pitfall have Lam 3:47
great *p*…will fall Zech 14:13

Pant *breathe rapidly*
deer *p-s* for the water Ps 42:1
my soul *p-s* for Thee Ps 42:1

Parable *story for illustration*
speak a *p* to Ezek 17:2
p of the sower Matt 13:18
spoke by way of a *p* Luke 8:4

Pardon *forgive, release*
he will not *p* your Ex 23:21
May the…Lord *p* 2 Chr 30:18
He will abundantly *p* Is 55:7

Parents *father and mother*
rise up against *p* Matt 10:21
children, obey your *p* Eph 6:1

Part *portion*
God…have no *p* in 2 Chr 19:7
prophesy in *p* 1 Cor 13:9
now I know in *p* 1 Cor 13:12
tongue is a small *p* James 3:5

Partakers *participators*
become *p* of Christ Heb 3:14
p of the Holy Spirit Heb 6:4

Partial *favoring*
you shall not be *p* Deut 16:19
You are not *p* Matt 22:16

Partiality *favoritism*
p is not good Prov 28:21
God shows no *p* Gal 2:6

Participate *take part*
not *p*…deeds of Eph 5:11
not *p* in her sins Rev 18:4

Partner *comrade*
is a *p* with a thief Prov 29:24
been *p-s* with them Matt 23:30
regard me as a *p* Philem 17

Pass *proceed*
Lord will *p* over the Ex 12:23
words shall not *p* Matt 24:35
this cup *p* from Me Matt 26:39
old things *p-ed* away 2 Cor 5:17

Passion *desire, lust*
flesh with its *p-s* Gal 5:24
dead to…*p* Col 3:5
not in lustful *p* 1 Thess 4:5

Pastors *shepherds of people*
and some *as p* Eph 4:11

Pasture (n) *grazing field*
lie down in green *p-s* Ps 23:2
sheep of Thy *p* Ps 79:13

Patch *mending cloth*
p of unshrunk cloth Matt 9:16
p pulls away from it Mark 2:21

Path *way*
snake in the *p* Gen 49:17
a light to my *p* Ps 119:105
Make His *p-s* straight Matt 3:3

Patience *endurance*
love, joy, peace, *p* Gal 5:22
endure it with *p* 1 Pet 2:20

Patient *bearing, enduring*
Love is *p*, love is 1 Cor 13:4
Lord…is *p* toward 2 Pet 3:9

Patriarch *father of clan*
regarding the *p* David Acts 2:29
the twelve *p-s* Acts 7:8
Abraham, the *p*, gave Heb 7:4

Pattern *model, plan*
fixed *p-s* of heaven Jer 33:25

Pay *give what is due*
p Thee my vows Ps 66:13
never *p* back evil Rom 12:17
p the penalty 2 Thess 1:9

Peace *calmness, tranquility*
grant *p* in the land Lev 26:6
Seek *p*, and pursue Ps 34:14
a time for *p* Eccl 3:8
Prince of *P* Is 9:6
P I leave with you John 14:27
we have *p* with God Rom 5:1
He Himself is our *p* Eph 2:14
gospel of *p* Eph 6:15
p through the blood Col 1:20

Pearl *precious gem*
p-s before swine Matt 7:6
one *p* of great value Matt 13:46

Penalty *punishment*
will bear the *p* Ezek 23:49
pay the *p* of eternal 2 Thess 1:9

People *group, nation*
Let My *p* go Ex 5:1
You are an obstinate *p* Ex 33:5
Lord loves His *p* 2 Chr 2:11
We are His *p* Ps 100:3
p are unrestrained Prov 29:18
do *p* say that I am Mark 8:27
they feared the *p* Luke 20:19
not rejected His *p* Rom 11:2
every tribe and *p* Rev 13:7

Perceive *be aware, discern*
listening, but do not *p* Is 6:9
p with their heart John 12:40

Perdition *damnation*
the son of *p* John 17:12

Perfect (adj) *flawless*
His work is *p* Deut 32:4
law of the Lord is *p* Ps 19:7
be *p* and complete James 1:4
p love casts out 1 John 4:18

Perfect (v) *complete*
is *p-ed* in weakness   2 Cor 12:9
love is *p-ed* with us   1 John 4:17

Perform *carry out*
I will *p* miracles   Ex 34:10
p a miracle in My   Mark 9:39
John *p-ed* no sign   John 10:41

Perfume *fragrant oil*
instead of sweet *p*   Is 3:24
p upon My body   Matt 26:12
prepared...*p*   Luke 23:56

Perish *be destroyed*
we *p*, we are dying   Num 17:12
if I *p*, I *p*   Esth 4:16
the wicked will *p*   Ps 1:6
little ones *p*   Matt 18:14
p by the sword   Matt 26:52
p, but have eternal   John 3:16

Permanent *lasting*
it is a *p* ordinance   Lev 6:18
p home for the ark   1 Chr 28:2

Permission *consent*
He gave them *p*   Mark 5:13
he had given him *p*   Acts 21:40

Permit *allow*
p the children   Mark 10:14
if the Lord *p-s*   1 Cor 16:7

Perpetual *lasting*
as a *p* covenant   Ex 31:16
for a *p* priesthood   Ex 40:15

Persecute *afflict, oppress*
has *p-d* my soul   Ps 143:3
p you in this city   Matt 10:23
used to *p* the church   Gal 1:13

Persecution *oppression*
p arose against the   Acts 8:1
a *p* against Paul   Acts 13:50

Perseverance *persistence*
by *p* in doing good   Rom 2:7
p of the saints   Rev 14:12

Person *human being*
If a *p* sins   Lev 4:2
p be in subjection   Rom 13:1

Persuade *convince, prevail on*
trying to *p* Jews and   Acts 18:4
you will *p* me   Acts 26:28

Persuasive *convincing*
p words of wisdom   1 Cor 2:4
delude you with *p*   Col 2:4

Perverse *corrupt*
a *p* and crooked   Deut 32:5
mind will utter *p*   Prov 23:33

Pervert *distort, misdirect*
not *p* the justice   Ex 23:6
have *p-ed* their way   Jer 3:21

Petition *request, supplication*
God...grant your *p*   1 Sam 1:17
p to any god or man   Dan 6:7
p-s...be made   1 Tim 2:1

Pestilence *epidemic, plague*
Lord sent a *p*   2 Sam 24:15
sword, famine, and *p*   Jer 27:13

Physician
all worthless *p-s*   Job 13:4
P, heal yourself   Luke 4:23
Luke, the beloved *p*   Col 4:14

Piece *part, portion*
thirty *p-s* of silver   Matt 27:3
woven in one *p*   John 19:23

Pierce *penetrate*
They *p-d* my hands   Ps 22:16
sword will *p*...soul   Luke 2:35
p-d His side   John 19:34

Piety *reverence*
learn to practice *p*   1 Tim 5:4
because of His *p*   Heb 5:7

Pillar *column or memorial*
became a *p* of salt   Gen 19:26
p of fire by night   Ex 13:21
feet like *p-s* of fire   Rev 10:1

Pilot *steersman*
sailors, and your *p-s*   Ezek 27:27
the *p* and...captain   Acts 27:11
inclination of the *p*   James 3:4

Pinnacle *highest point*
had Him...on the *p*   Matt 4:5
p of the temple   Luke 4:9

Pit *deep hole, dungeon*
redeems...from the *p*   Ps 103:4
to *p-s* of darkness   2 Pet 2:4
the bottomless *p*   Rev 9:1

Pitch (v) *set up*
he will *p* the tents   Dan 11:45
tabernacle...Lord *p-ed*   Heb 8:2

Pity (n) *sympathy*
shall not show *p*   Deut 19:21
I will not show *p*   Jer 13:14

Pity (v) *have compassion*
she had *p* on him   Ex 2:6
P me, *p* me, O you   Job 19:21
most to be *p-ied*   1 Cor 15:19

Place *area, space*
God is a dwelling *p*   Deut 33:27
a *p* for My people   1 Chr 17:9
Thou art my hiding *p*   Ps 32:7
I go to prepare a *p*   John 14:2

Plague *contagious disease*
no *p* will befall you   Ex 12:13
p of the hail   Rev 16:21

Plan *design, scheme*
P-s formed long ago   Is 25:1
follow our own *p-s*   Jer 18:12

Plant (v) *put into soil*
p...trees for food   Lev 19:23
A time to *p*   Eccl 3:2
I *p-ed*, Apollos   1 Cor 3:6

Play *take part*
who *p* the lyre   Gen 4:21
man who can *p*   1 Sam 16:17

not *p* the harlot   Hos 3:3

Plead *appeal, beseech*
p-ed with the Lord   Deut 3:23
P for the widow   Is 1:17

Pleasant *pleasing*
P words are a   Prov 16:24
Speak to us *p* words   Is 30:10

Please *satisfy*
how he may *p* his   1 Cor 7:33
striving to *p* men   Gal 1:10
impossible to *p*   Heb 11:6

Pleasing *agreeable*
tree that is *p*   Gen 2:9
meditation be *p*   Ps 104:34
not as *p* men but   1 Thess 2:4
p in His sight   1 John 3:22

Pleasure *gratification*
p in His people   Ps 149:4
work for *His* good *p*   Phil 2:13
passing *p-s* of sin   Heb 11:25

Pledge *promise*
cloak as a *p*   Ex 22:26
the Spirit as a *p*   2 Cor 5:5
p of our inheritance   Eph 1:14

Plentiful *abundant*
shed abroad a *p* rain   Ps 68:9
harvest is *p*   Matt 9:37

Plot *plan, scheme*
wicked *p-s* against   Ps 37:12
you have *p-ted* evil   Prov 30:32
Jews *p-ted* together   Acts 9:23

Plow *dig the soil*
sluggard does not *p*   Prov 20:4
his hand to the *p*   Luke 9:62

Plunder (v) *rob*
will *p* the Egyptians   Ex 3:22
stouthearted were *p-ed*   Ps 76:5
he will *p* his house   Matt 12:29

Point *particular time*
obedient to the *p* of   Phil 2:8
to the *p* of shedding   Heb 12:4

Poison *lethal substance*
given us *p-ed* water   Jer 8:14
turned justice into *p*   Amos 6:12

Pollute *contaminate*
blood *p-s* the land   Num 35:33
earth is also *p-d*   Is 24:5

Ponder *think deeply*
not *p* the path of life   Prov 5:6
Or *p* things...past   Is 43:18

Pool *pond*
rock into a *p*   Ps 114:8
in the *p* of Siloam   John 9:7

Poor *impoverished, needy*
lest you become *p*   Prov 20:13
are the *p* in spirit   Matt 5:3
a *p* widow came   Mark 12:42
sake He became *p*   2 Cor 8:9

Portion *part, share*
double *p* of...spirit	2 Kin 2:9
The LORD is my *p*	Ps 119:57
joy over their *p*	Is 61:7

Possess *control, take*
are to *p* their land	Lev 20:24
go in and *p* the land	Deut 1:8
sell all you *p*	Mark 10:21
do not *p* silver and	Acts 3:6

Possession *ownership*
for an everlasting *p*	Gen 17:8
full of Thy *p-s*	Ps 104:24
charge of all his *p-s*	Matt 24:47
selling their...*p-s*	Acts 2:45

Possible *can be done*
| all things are *p* | Matt 19:26 |
| *p* with God | Luke 18:27 |

Pot *container, vessel*
death in the *p*	2 Kin 4:40
refining *p* is for	Prov 17:3
I see a boiling *p*	Jer 1:13

Potter *one who molds clay*
| clay say to the *p* | Is 45:9 |
| as it pleased the *p* | Jer 18:4 |

Pour *cause to flow*
p me out like milk	Job 10:10
I *p* out my soul	Ps 42:4
P out Thy wrath	Jer 10:25
p-ed it upon His	Matt 26:7

Poverty *destitution, want*
| through His *p* might | 2 Cor 8:9 |

Power *authority, strength*
to show you My *p*	Ex 9:16
the *p* of His works	Ps 111:6
p of the tongue	Prov 18:21
the *p* of the sword	Jer 18:21
Thine is...the *p*	Matt 6:13
you shall receive *p*	Acts 1:8
the *p* of our Lord	1 Cor 5:4
prince of the *p* of	Eph 2:2
by the word of His *p*	Heb 1:3
quenched the *p* of	Heb 11:34

Powerless *without strength*
| *p* before this great | 2 Chr 20:12 |
| He might render *p* | Heb 2:14 |

Practice (v) *engage in*
He who *p-s* deceit	Ps 101:7
Who *p* righteousness	Ps 106:3
learn to *p* piety	1 Tim 5:4

Praise (n) *acclamation, honor*
offering of *p*	Lev 19:24
sing *p-s* to Him	1 Chr 16:9
sound His *p* abroad	Ps 66:8
anything worthy of *p*	Phil 4:8
Give *p* to our God	Rev 19:5

Praise (v) *extol, glorify*
I will *p* Him	Ex 15:2
heavens will *p* Thy	Ps 89:5
P Him with trumpet	Ps 150:3
heavenly host *p-ing*	Luke 2:13
leaping and *p-ing* God	Acts 3:8

Pray *ask, worship*
Abraham *p-ed* to	Gen 20:17
For to Thee do I *p*	Ps 5:2
p for...persecute	Matt 5:44
by Himself to *p*	Matt 14:23
p and ask, believe	Mark 11:24
Lord, teach us to *p*	Luke 11:1
they ought to *p*	Luke 18:1
p-ed with fasting	Acts 14:23
p without ceasing	1 Thess 5:17

Prayer
I have heard your *p*	2 Chr 7:12
LORD receives my *p*	Ps 6:9
Give ear to my *p*	Ps 55:1
you make long *p-s*	Matt 23:14
whole night in *p*	Luke 6:12
everything by *p*	Phil 4:6
p-s of the saints	Rev 5:8

Preach *exhort, proclaim*
as you go, *p*	Matt 10:7
p-ing...repentance	Mark 1:4
p the gospel to all	Mark 16:15
p...the good news	Acts 13:32
p Christ crucified	1 Cor 1:23
p the word	2 Tim 4:2

Preacher *one who proclaims*
| hear without a *p* | Rom 10:14 |
| Noah, a *p* of | 2 Pet 2:5 |

Precepts *commandments*
| All His *p* are sure | Ps 111:7 |
| meditate on Thy *p* | Ps 119:15 |

Precious *beloved or costly*
P in the sight of	Ps 116:15
more *p* than jewels	Prov 3:15
more *p* than gold	1 Pet 1:7

Predestined *foreordained*
| foreknew, He also *p* | Rom 8:29 |
| *p* us to adoption | Eph 1:5 |

Preparation *readiness*
| Jewish day of *p* | John 19:42 |
| *p* of the gospel of | Eph 6:15 |

Prepare *make ready*
p a savory dish	Gen 27:4
p a table before me	Ps 23:5
will *p* Your way	Matt 11:10
to *p* Me for burial	Matt 26:12
p-d spices and	Luke 23:56
I go to *p* a place	John 14:2

Presence *appearance*
in the *p* of my enemies	Ps 23:5
tremble at Thy *p*	Is 64:2
the *p* of the Lamb	Rev 14:10

Present (v) *give, offer*
p Him to the Lord	Luke 2:22
p yourselves to God	Rom 6:13
p your bodies a	Rom 12:1

Preserve *protect*
no son to *p* my	2 Sam 18:18
P me, O God	Ps 16:1
LORD *p-s* the simple	Ps 116:6
p the unity of the	Eph 4:3

Press *compel, force*
| measure, *p-ed* down | Luke 6:38 |
| I *p* on toward...goal | Phil 3:14 |

Pretend *deceive, feign*
| *p* to be a mourner | 2 Sam 14:2 |
| *p* to be another | 1 Kin 14:5 |

Prevail *exist or triumph*
water *p-ed*	Gen 7:18
not by might...man *p*	1 Sam 2:9
Iniquities *p* against me	Ps 65:3
overcome me and *p-ed*	Jer 20:7

Prey *what is hunted*
| birds of *p* came | Gen 15:11 |
| lion tearing the *p* | Ezek 22:25 |

Price *cost, value*
shall increase its *p*	Lev 25:16
their redemption *p*	Num 18:16
it is the *p* of blood	Matt 27:6
bought with a *p*	1 Cor 7:23

Pride *exaggerated self-esteem*
| *P* goes before | Prov 16:18 |
| envy, slander; *p* | Mark 7:22 |

Priest *intermediary*
a kingdom of *p-s*	Ex 19:6
p...make atonement	Lev 4:31
Thou art a *p* forever	Ps 110:4
have a great high *p*	Heb 4:14
Thou art a *p* forever	Heb 5:6

Priesthood *office of priest*
| for a perpetual *p* | Ex 40:15 |
| royal *p*, a holy nation | 1 Pet 2:9 |

Prime *fully mature period*
| die in the *p* of life | 1 Sam 2:33 |

Prince *ruler*
Who made you a *p*	Ex 2:14
contempt upon *p-s*	Ps 107:40
Do not trust in *p-s*	Ps 146:3
Father, *P* of Peace	Is 9:6
p of...the air	Eph 2:2

Prison *jail*
Put this man in *p*	1 Kin 22:27
my soul out of *p*	Ps 142:7
I was in *p*, and	Matt 25:36
spirits *now* in *p*	1 Pet 3:19

Prisoner *one who is confined*
| sets the *p-s* free | Ps 146:7 |
| *p* of the law of sin | Rom 7:23 |

Private *not public*
| reprove him in *p* | Matt 18:15 |
| but I did so in *p* | Gal 2:2 |

Prize *reward*
| one receives the *p* | 1 Cor 9:24 |
| *p* of the upward call | Phil 3:14 |

Proceed *go forth*
| *p-s* out of the mouth | Matt 4:4 |
| *p-s* from...Father | John 15:26 |

Proclaim *announce, declare*
p...name of the LORD	Ex 33:19
p liberty to captives	Is 61:1
he *began* to *p* Jesus	Acts 9:20

faith is being *p-ed*   Rom 1:8

Produce (v) *bring forth*
cannot *p* bad fruit   Matt 7:18

Profane *defile, desecrate*
p My holy name   Lev 20:3
to *p* the covenant   Mal 2:10

Profess *confess, declare*
P-ing to be wise   Rom 1:22
They *p* to know God   Titus 1:16

Profit (v) *reap an advantage*
what does it *p* a   Mark 8:36
it *p-s* me nothing   1 Cor 13:3

Profitable *useful*
not all things are *p*   1 Cor 6:12
p for teaching   2 Tim 3:16

Promise (n) *agreement, pledge*
p of the Holy Spirit   Acts 2:33
the *p* made by God   Acts 26:6
children of the *p*   Rom 9:8
heirs of the *p*   Heb 6:17
the *p* of His coming   2 Pet 3:4

Pronounce *declare officially*
shall *p* him clean   Lev 13:23
God…*p-d* judgment   Rev 18:20

Proof *evidence*
furnished *p* to all   Acts 17:31
p of the Christ   2 Cor 13:3

Proper *suitable*
is it *p* for a woman   1 Cor 11:13
as is *p* among saints   Eph 5:3

Property *goods or land*
acquire *p* in it   Gen 34:10
who owned much *p*   Matt 19:22
things…common *p*   Acts 4:32

Prophecy *proclamation*
p…fulfilled   Matt 13:14
have *the gift of p*   1 Cor 13:2

Prophesy *predict, proclaim*
he never *p-ies* good   2 Chr 18:7
sons and…will *p*   Joel 2:28
P to us…Christ   Matt 26:68

Prophet *spokesman for God*
a *p* or a dreamer   Deut 13:1
I will raise up a *p*   Deut 18:18
vision of…the *p*   2 Chr 32:32
written by the *p*   Matt 2:5
persecuted the *p-s*   Matt 5:12
Beware…false *p-s*   Matt 7:15
the *p* Jesus   Matt 21:11
p of the Most High   Luke 1:76
great *p* has arisen   Luke 7:16
Are you the *P*   John 1:21
and some *as p-s*   Eph 4:11

Prophetic *predictive*
not…*p* utterances   1 Thess 5:20
p word…sure   2 Pet 1:19

Propitiation *atonement*
a *p* in His blood   Rom 3:25
p for the sins   Heb 2:17
p for our sins   1 John 4:10

Proselyte *convert*
both Jews and *p-s*   Acts 2:10
God-fearing *p-s*   Acts 13:43

Prosper *flourish, succeed*
I will surely *p* you   Gen 32:12
His ways *p* at all   Ps 10:5
they *p* who love you   Ps 122:6

Prosperity *success, wealth*
soul will abide in *p*   Ps 25:13

Prosperous *successful*
exceedingly *p*   Gen 30:43
make your way *p*   Josh 1:8

Prostitute *harlot*
Where…temple *p*   Gen 38:21
an adulterer and a *p*   Is 57:3

Protect *guard, shield*
The LORD will *p* him   Ps 41:2
He will…*p* you   2 Thess 3:3

Protection *safe-keeping*
For wisdom is *p*   Eccl 7:12
p from the storm   Is 4:6

Proud *exaggerated self-esteem*
heart becomes *p*   Deut 8:14
eyes and a *p* heart   Prov 21:4
opposed to the *p*   James 4:6

Prove *establish, test*
you be *p-d* a liar   Prov 30:6
p to be My disciples   John 15:8
p yourselves doers   James 1:22

Proverb *adage, short saying*
become…a *p*   Deut 28:37
spoke 3,000 *p-s*   1 Kin 4:32
Israel…become a *p*   1 Kin 9:7
To understand a *p*   Prov 1:6
quote this *p* to Me   Luke 4:23
to the true *p*   2 Pet 2:22

Provide *furnish, supply*
p for…redemption   Lev 25:24
p…way of escape   1 Cor 10:13
not *p* for his own   1 Tim 5:8
God had *p-d*   Heb 11:40

Province *district or territory*
rulers of the *p-s*   2 Kin 20:17
holiday for the *p-s*   Esth 2:18
whole *p* of Babylon   Dan 2:48
arrived in the *p*   Acts 25:1

Provision *supply*
bread of their *p* was   Josh 9:5
no *p* for the flesh   Rom 13:14

Provoke *evoke, excite*
images to *p* Me   1 Kin 14:9
love…is not *p-d*   1 Cor 13:5
not *p* your children   Eph 6:4

Prudent *careful, wise*
a *p* man conceals   Prov 12:16
the *p* took oil in   Matt 25:4

Psalms *sacred songs*
shout…with *p*   Ps 95:2
speaking…in *p*   Eph 5:19

Public *open*
of his *p* appearance   Luke 1:80
made a *p* display   Col 2:15

Punish *chastise, penalize*
p them for their sin   Ex 32:34
will *p* your iniquity   Lam 4:22
I *p-ed* them often   Acts 26:11

Punishment *penalty*
My *p* is too great   Gen 4:13
fear involves *p*   1 John 4:18

Purchase *buy*
p-d with…blood   Acts 20:28
p for God with Thy   Rev 5:9

Pure *genuine, undefiled*
My teaching is *p*   Job 11:4
As *p* as the sun   Song 6:10
Blessed are the *p* in   Matt 5:8
love from a *p* heart   1 Tim 1:5
p milk of the word   1 Pet 2:2

Purge *remove*
p…evil from among   Deut 13:5
Many will be *p-d*   Dan 12:10

Purification *cleansing*
Jewish custom of *p*   John 2:6
He…made *p* of sins   Heb 1:3

Purify *make clean*
P me with hyssop   Ps 51:7
p…a people   Titus 2:14
p your hearts   James 4:8

Purpose *intention, reason*
rejected God's *p*   Luke 7:30
for this *p* I have   Acts 26:16
according to *His p*   Rom 8:28

Purse *bag, pouch*
gold from the *p*   Is 46:6
Carry no *p*, no bag   Luke 10:4

Pursue *chase, follow*
p the manslayer   Deut 19:6
Seek peace, and *p* it   Ps 34:14
may *p* strong drink   Is 5:11
p righteousness   2 Tim 2:22

Put *place*
He *p* a new song   Ps 40:3
p on the new self   Eph 4:24
P on the full armor   Eph 6:11

– Q –

Quake *shake, tremble*
The mountains *q-d*   Judg 5:5
q at Thy presence   Is 64:1

Quality *character*
test the *q* of each   1 Cor 3:13
imperishable *q* of a   1 Pet 3:4

Quantity *amount*
large *q-ies* of cedar   1 Chr 22:4
a great *q* of fish   Luke 5:6

Quarrel (n) *altercation*
So abandon the *q*   Prov 17:14
are *q-s* among you   1 Cor 1:11

Quarrel (v) *contend, fight*
did not *q* over it   Gen 26:22
Why do you *q* with me   Ex 17:2
any fool will *q*   Prov 20:3
those who *q* with you   Is 41:12

Quench *extinguish*
donkeys *q* their thirst Ps 104:11
waters cannot *q* love   Song 8:7
not *q* the Spirit   1 Thess 5:19
q-d...power of fire   Heb 11:34

Question (n) *inquiry, problem*
Jesus asked...a *q*   Matt 22:41
in controversial *q-s*   1 Tim 6:4

Question (v) *ask*
He *began to q* them   Mark 9:33
Q those who have   John 18:21

Quick (adj) *rapid*
is *q*-tempered exalts Prov 14:29
q to hear, slow to   James 1:19

Quick (n) *deepest feelings*
cut to the *q* and   Acts 5:33
were cut to the *q*   Acts 7:54

Quiet (adj) *calm, still*
knew no *q* within   Job 20:20
me beside *q* waters   Ps 23:2
gentle and *q* spirit   1 Pet 3:4

Quiet (v) *become calm, still*
and *q-ed* my soul   Ps 131:2
Be *q*, and come out   Mark 1:25

– R –

Race (n) *nation, people*
r has intermingled   Ezra 9:2
advantage of our *r*   Acts 7:19
you are a chosen *r*   1 Pet 2:9

Race (n) *competition of speed*
r is not to...swift   Eccl 9:11
r...set before us   Heb 12:1

Radiance *brightness*
a *r* around Him   Ezek 1:27
r of His glory   Heb 1:3

Radiant *shining brightly*
you will see and be *r*   Is 60:5
His garments...*r*   Mark 9:3

Rage (v) *be very angry*
r-s against the LORD Prov 19:3
foolish man...*r-s*   Prov 29:9
Why...Gentiles *r*   Acts 4:25

Rain (n)
God had not sent *r*   Gen 2:5
r fell upon the earth   Gen 7:12
LORD sent...*r*   1 Sam 12:18
the mountain *r-s*   Job 24:8
anger a flooding *r*   Ezek 13:13
r on *the* righteous   Matt 5:45

Rain (v) *fall down, pour*
r bread from heaven   Ex 16:4
it *r-ed* fire and   Luke 17:29

Rainbow *colored arc in the sky*
appearance of the *r*   Ezek 1:28
a *r* around the throne   Rev 4:3

Raise *elevate, lift*
r up a prophet   Deut 18:18
r up shepherds over   Jer 23:4
Heal...*r the* dead   Matt 10:8
He will be *r-d* up   Matt 20:19
three days I will *r*   John 2:19
Jesus God *r-d* up   Acts 2:32

Raisin *dried grapes*
clusters of *r-s*   2 Sam 16:1
Sustain me with *r*   Song 2:5
and love *r* cakes   Hos 3:1

Rank *position*
men of *r* are a lie   Ps 62:9
He...has a higher *r* Josh 1:15
a Man...higher *r*   John 1:30

Ransom (n) *payment*
not take *r* for   Num 35:31
His life a *r* for   Matt 20:28
gave Himself as a *r*   1 Tim 2:6

Ransom (v) *redeem*
Thou hast *r-ed* me   Ps 31:5
I will *r* them from   Hos 13:14

Ravage *devastate*
famine will *r* the   Gen 41:30
mice that *r* the land   1 Sam 6:5
r-ing the church   Acts 8:3

Ravenous *wildly hungry*
inwardly are *r* wolves Matt 7:15

Read
r from the scroll   Jer 36:6
Moses is *read*   2 Cor 3:15
Blessed is he who *r-s*   Rev 1:3

Ready *equipped, prepared*
and *r* to forgive   Ps 86:5
Make *r* the way   Matt 3:3
be *r* in season   2 Tim 4:2

Realize *achieve* or *understand*
r-d through Jesus   John 1:17
to *r*...assurance   Heb 6:11

Reap *cut, gather*
they *r* the whirlwind   Hos 8:7
neither sow nor *r*   Luke 12:24
r eternal life   Gal 6:8

Reason (n) *explanation*
this *r* the Father   John 10:17
For this *r*, rejoice   Rev 12:12

Reason (v) *analyze, argue*
upright would *r* with   Job 23:7
let us *r* together   Is 1:18
as a child, *r* as a   1 Cor 13:11

Rebellion *insurrection*
he has counseled *r*   Deut 13:5
I know your *r*   Deut 31:27
r is as the sin of   1 Sam 15:23
my *r* and my sin   Job 13:23
children of *r*   Is 57:4

Rebellious *defiant*
r against the LORD   Deut 9:7
r generation   Ps 78:8
stubborn and *r* heart   Jer 5:23
there are many *r*   Titus 1:10

Rebuild *restore*
let us *r* the wall   Neh 2:17
r it in three days   Matt 26:61

Rebuke (n) *reprimand*
amazed at His *r*   Job 26:11
the poor hears no *r*   Prov 13:8

Rebuke (v) *scold*
r the arrogant   Ps 119:21
LORD *r* you, Satan   Zech 3:2
r-d the winds   Matt 8:26
He *r-d* the fever   Luke 4:39
reprove, *r*, exhort   2 Tim 4:2

Receive *encounter, take*
freely you *r-d*   Matt 10:8
the blind *r* sight   Matt 11:5
This man *r-s* sinners Luke 15:2
r you to Myself   John 14:3
R the Holy Spirit   John 20:22
you shall *r* power   Acts 1:8
r the crown of life   James 1:12

Reckoned *accounted for*
r it to him as   Gen 15:6
his wage is not *r*   Rom 4:4

Recline *lean, lie down*
r on beds of ivory   Amos 6:4
r on the grass   Matt 14:19
r at the table in   Luke 13:29
r-ing on Jesus'   John 13:23

Recognize *be aware, know*
he did not *r* him   Gen 27:23
Saul *r-d* David's   1 Sam 26:17
r that He is near   Matt 24:33
I did not *r* Him   John 1:31

Recompense (n) *reward*
the *r* of the wicked   Ps 91:8
r to the proud   Ps 94:2
received a just *r*   Heb 2:2

Recompense (v) *compensate*
LORD has *r-d* me   2 Sam 22:25
He will *r* the evil   Ps 54:5
But if you do *r* Me   Joel 3:4

Reconcile *bring together*
be *r-d* to God   2 Cor 5:20
r all...to Himself   Col 1:20

Reconciliation
now received the *r*   Rom 5:11
the ministry of *r*   2 Cor 5:18

Record (n) *document, register*
the *r-s* are ancient   1 Chr 4:22
r-s of the kings   2 Chr 33:18
discover in...*r* books Ezra 4:15
I found the...*r*   Neh 7:5

Recover *reclaim, regain*
you not *r* them   Judg 11:26
and they will *r*   Mark 16:18

Redeem *buy back*
family may *r* him Lev 25:49
I will *r* it Ruth 4:4
He will *r* Israel Ps 130:8
He might *r* those Gal 4:5

Redeemer *one who buys back*
that my *R* lives Job 19:25
my rock and my *R* Ps 19:14

Redemption *deliverance*
have my right of *r* Ruth 4:6
r is drawing near Luke 21:28
r of our body Rom 8:23
r through His blood Eph 1:7
in whom we have *r* Col 1:14
obtained eternal *r* Heb 9:12

Refine *purify*
r-d seven times Ps 12:6
r them like gold Mal 3:3
gold *r-d* by fire Rev 3:18

Refrain *abstain*
to *r* from working 1 Cor 9:6
r from judging Rev 6:10

Refresh *renew, replenish*
you may *r* yourselves Gen 18:5
times of *r-ing* may Acts 3:19

Refuge *protection, shelter*
in whom I take *r* 2 Sam 22:3
God is our *r* Ps 46:1
who have fled for *r* Heb 6:18

Refuse (n) *waste*
be made a *r* heap Ezra 6:11
its waters toss up *r* Is 57:20

Refuse (v) *decline*
hands *r* to work Prov 21:25
they *r* to know Me Jer 9:6
can *r* the water Acts 10:47
not *r* Him who is Heb 12:25

Refute *confute*
R me if you can Job 33:5
to *r* those who Titus 1:9

Regain *recover*
r-ed their sight Matt 20:34
he might *r* his sight Acts 9:12

Regard (n) *respect*
LORD had *r* for Abel Gen 4:4
r for the humble Luke 1:48

Regard (v) *esteem, respect*
If I *r* wickedness Ps 66:18
highly *r-ed* by him Luke 7:2
you *r* one another Phil 2:3

Regeneration *renewal*
r when the Son Matt 19:28
the washing of *r* Titus 3:5

Region *area*
r of the Jordan Josh 22:10
the *r-s* of Galilee Matt 2:22
to the *r* of Judea Mark 10:1
same *r*...shepherds Luke 2:8

Register *enroll, record*
to *r* for the census Luke 2:3

Reign *rule*
LORD shall *r* forever Ex 15:18
The LORD *r-s* Ps 93:1
will *r* righteously Is 32:1
He must *r* until 1 Cor 15:25
He will *r* forever Rev 11:15

Reject *decline, refuse*
will *r* you forever 1 Chr 28:9
not *r* the discipline Prov 3:11
have *r-ed* knowledge Hos 4:6
they *r-ed* the law Amos 2:4
the builders *r-ed* Matt 21:42
He who *r-s* Me John 12:48

Rejoice *be glad*
R, O nations Deut 32:43
let the earth *r* 1 Chr 16:31
my soul shall *r* Ps 35:9
r and be glad Ps 118:24
r-d exceedingly Matt 2:10
r at his birth Luke 1:14
multitude was *r-ing* Luke 13:17
r-ing in hope Rom 12:12
yet always *r-ing* 2 Cor 6:10
R in the Lord Phil 4:4
r, O heavens Rev 12:12

Relative *kinsman*
The man is our *r* Ruth 2:20
among his *own r-s* Mark 6:4

Release (n) *liberation*
a *r* through the land Lev 25:10
r to the captives Luke 4:18

Release (v) *set free*
he *r-d* Barabbas Matt 27:26
efforts to *r* Him John 19:12
R the four angels Rev 9:14

Relief *lessening of burden*
r and deliverance Esth 4:14
my *prayer for r* Lam 3:56

Rely *depend, trust*
r-ied on the LORD 2 Chr 16:8
who...*r* on horses Is 31:1
r on his God Is 50:10
You *r* on your sword Ezek 33:26
r upon the Law Rom 2:17

Remain *abide, be left*
While the earth *r-s* Gen 8:22
not *r* in the darkness John 12:46
not *r* on the cross John 19:31
gospel might *r* Gal 2:5

Remember *recall, recollect*
God *r-ed* Noah Gen 8:1
R the sabbath day Ex 20:8
R also your Creator Eccl 12:1
Peter *r-ed* the word Matt 26:75
R Lot's wife Luke 17:32
to *r* the poor Gal 2:10

Remembrance *memory*
Thy *r*, O LORD Ps 135:13
Put Me in *r* Is 43:26
in *r* of Me 1 Cor 11:25

Remnant *remaining part*
preserve for you a *r* Gen 45:7
prayer for the *r* 2 Kin 19:4
A *r* will return Is 10:21
a *r* of the Spirit Mal 2:15

Remove *take away* or *off*
r your sandals Ex 3:5
He *r-d* the high 2 Kin 18:4
r this cup from Me Luke 22:42
as to *r* mountains 1 Cor 13:2

Rend *tear*
r the heavens Is 64:1
r their garments Jer 36:24

Render *inflict, repay*
I will *r* vengeance Deut 32:41
r to Caesar the Matt 22:21

Renew *make new, revive*
r a steadfast spirit Ps 51:10
R our days as of old Lam 5:21

Renown *fame*
men of *r* Gen 6:4
a people, for *r* Jer 13:11
shame into...and *r* Zeph 3:19

Repair *restore*
r of the house of 1 Chr 26:27
r-ing...foundations Ezra 4:12
r of the walls Neh 4:7

Repay *pay back*
LORD *r* the evildoer 2 Sam 3:39
r their iniquity Jer 16:18
He will fully *r* Jer 51:56
in secret will *r* Matt 6:4

Repent *change mind*
that He should *r* Num 23:19
have refused to *r* Jer 5:3
R, for the kingdom Matt 3:2
r and believe Mark 1:15
R,...be baptized Acts 2:38
r and turn to God Acts 26:20

Repentance *penitence*
with water for *r* Matt 3:11
r for forgiveness Luke 24:47
r from dead works Heb 6:1

Report *account, statement*
not bear a false *r* Ex 23:1
r concerning Him Luke 7:17

Representation *likeness*
exact *r* of His nature Heb 1:3

Reproach (n) *dishonor*
taken away my *r* Gen 30:23
I have become a *r* Ps 31:11
the *r* of Christ Heb 11:26

Reproach (v) *accuse, rebuke*
to *r* the living God 2 Kin 19:4
enemies have *r-ed* me Ps 102:8

Reproof *correction, rebuke*
spurned all my *r* Prov 1:30
who hates *r* will Prov 15:10
for teaching, for *r* 2 Tim 3:16

Reprove *correct, rebuke*
r your neighbor — Lev 19:17
LORD loves He *r-s* — Prov 3:12
r him in private — Matt 18:15
whom I love, I r — Rev 3:19

Reputation *character*
seven men of good r — Acts 6:3
a r for good works — 1 Tim 5:10

Request *desire, petition*
the r of his lips — Ps 21:2
r-s be made known to — Phil 4:6

Require *demand, insist*
r your lifeblood — Gen 9:5
God r from you — Deut 10:12
r-d of stewards — 1 Cor 4:2

Requirement *necessity*
r-s of the Lord — Luke 1:6
r of the Law — Rom 8:4

Rescue *deliver, redeem*
O LORD, r my soul — Ps 6:4
He delivers and *r-s* — Dan 6:27

Reserve *retain, store up*
r-d a blessing for — Gen 27:36
lips may r knowledge — Prov 5:2

Reside *dwell, live*
a son of man r in it — Jer 49:18
those who r as aliens — 1 Pet 1:1

Resist *oppose, withstand*
none…able to r — Luke 21:15
R the devil — James 4:7

Respect (n) *regard*
no r for the old — Deut 28:50
where is My r — Mal 1:6
please *Him* in…*r-s* — Col 1:10
to your masters…r — 1 Pet 2:18

Respect (v) *esteem*
They will r my son — Matt 21:37
R what is right — Rom 12:17

Respond *answer, reply*
He will r to them — Is 19:22
how you should r — Col 4:6

Rest (n) *remainder*
the r of the exiles — Ezra 6:16
the r of your days — Prov 19:20
I will slay the r — Amos 9:1

Rest (n) *tranquility*
r from our work — Gen 5:29
God gives you r — Josh 1:13
Return to your r — Ps 116:7
I will give you r — Matt 11:28
no r for my spirit — 2 Cor 2:13
not enter My r — Heb 3:11

Rest (v) *place on, refresh*
Spirit *r-ed* upon — Num 11:25
R in the LORD — Ps 37:7
government will r on — Is 9:6
r from their labors — Rev 14:13

Restitution *reparation*
owner…make r — Ex 21:34

r for the lamb — 2 Sam 12:6

Restore *reestablish, replace*
He *r-s* my soul — Ps 23:3
R to me the joy — Ps 51:12
the LORD *r-s* Zion — Is 52:8
his hand was *r-d* — Mark 3:5

Restrain *hold back*
who can r Him — Job 11:10
Wilt Thou r Thyself — Is 64:12
R your voice from — Jer 31:16

Result (n) *consequence, effect*
not as a r of works — Eph 2:9
have *its* perfect r — James 1:4

Resurrection
r of the righteous — Luke 14:14
r of judgment — John 5:29
r of the dead — Acts 24:21
if there is no r — 1 Cor 15:13
power of His r — Phil 3:10
hope through the r — 1 Pet 1:3

Retribution *punishment*
days of r have come — Hos 9:7
dealing out r to — 2 Thess 1:8

Return *go back, turn back*
to dust you shall r — Gen 3:19
a remnant…will r — Is 10:22
Repent… and r — Acts 3:19

Reveal *expose, make known*
will r his iniquity — Job 20:27
r this mystery — Dan 2:47
r them to babes — Matt 11:25
blood did not r *this* — Matt 16:17
glory…to be *r-ed* — Rom 8:18
r-ed with fire — 1 Cor 3:13
to r His Son in me — Gal 1:16

Revelation *divine disclosure*
the r ended — Dan 7:28
r to the Gentiles — Luke 2:32
the r of the mystery — Rom 16:25
through a r of Jesus — Gal 1:12
The R of Jesus — Rev 1:1

Revenge *vengeance*
take our r on him — Jer 20:10
Never take…r — Rom 12:19

Reverence *respect, awe*
you do away with r — Job 15:4
bow in r for Thee — Ps 5:7

Revile *use abusive language*
Do you r God's high — Acts 23:4
r-d for the name of — 1 Pet 4:14

Revive *bring back to life*
let your heart r — Ps 69:32
r us again — Ps 85:6

Revolt *rebellion*
incited r within it — Ezra 4:15
stirred up a r — Acts 21:38

Reward *prize*
r for the righteous — Ps 58:11
The r of humility — Prov 22:4
His r is with Him — Is 62:11

your r in heaven — Matt 5:12
not lose his r — Matt 10:42
receive a full r — 2 John 8

Rich (adj) *wealthy*
makes poor…r — 1 Sam 2:7
not a r man boast — Jer 9:23
a certain r man — Luke 16:1
r in good works — 1 Tim 6:18

Riches *wealth*
R do not profit — Prov 11:4
deceitfulness of r — Matt 13:22
abounding in r — Rom 10:12
r of His grace — Eph 1:7
r of Christ — Eph 3:8
uncertainty of r — 1 Tim 6:17

Riddle *puzzle*
propound a r — Judg 14:12
my r on the harp — Ps 49:4
wise and their *r-s* — Prov 1:6
propound a r — Ezek 17:2

Right (adj) *correct or direction*
r in his own eyes — Judg 17:6
r eye makes you — Matt 5:29
Sit at My r hand — Matt 22:44
whatever is r — Phil 4:8

Right (n) *due, prerogative*
r of redemption — Lev 25:32
the *r-s* of the poor — Prov 29:7
my r in the gospel — 1 Cor 9:18

Righteous (adj) *virtuous*
Noah was a r man — Gen 6:9
You are more r — 1 Sam 24:17
God is a r judge — Ps 7:11
LORD our God is r — Dan 9:14
none r, not even — Rom 3:10
prayer of a r man — James 5:16

Righteous (n) *moral one*
LORD tests the r — Ps 11:5
the paths of the r — Prov 2:20
joy for the r — Prov 21:15
way of the r is — Is 26:7
r into eternal life — Matt 25:46

Righteousness
reckoned it…as r — Gen 15:6
in the paths of r — Ps 23:3
declare his r — Ps 97:6
His r endures forever — Ps 111:3
The LORD our r — Jer 23:6
and thirst for r — Matt 5:6
kingdom and His r — Matt 6:33
breastplate of r — Eph 6:14
the crown of r — 2 Tim 4:8
suffer for…r — 1 Pet 3:14

Riot *tumult, uprising*
lest a r occur — Matt 26:5
a r was starting — Matt 27:24
accused of a r — Acts 19:40

Ripe *fully developed*
old man of r age — Gen 35:29
the harvest is r — Joel 3:13

Rise *go up, issue forth*
mist used to r from | Gen 2:6
witnesses r up | Ps 35:11
children r up | Prov 31:28
nation will r | Matt 24:7
R and walk | Luke 5:23
R and pray | Luke 22:46

River
r flowed out of Eden | Gen 2:10
r of Thy delights | Ps 36:8
the r-s of Babylon | Ps 137:1
r-s in the desert | Is 43:20
peace…like a r | Is 66:12
r-s of living water | John 7:38

Roar (n) *loud deep sound*
the sound of the r | 1 Kin 18:41
young lions' r | Zech 11:3

Roar (v) *utter a deep sound*
Let the sea r | Ps 96:11
LORD will r from | Jer 25:30

Rob *steal*
Will a man r God | Mal 3:8
do you r temples | Rom 2:22

Robber *thief*
become a den of r-s | Jer 7:11
crucified two r-s | Mark 15:27
he fell among r-s | Luke 10:30

Robe *cloak, garment*
cut off…Saul's r | 1 Sam 24:4
justice was like a r | Job 29:14
r of righteousness | Is 61:10
put a scarlet r on | Matt 27:28
walk…in long r-s | Mark 12:38
wearing a white r | Mark 16:5
bring…the best r | Luke 15:22
washed their r-s | Rev 7:14
a r dipped in blood | Rev 19:13

Rock *stone*
the cleft of the r | Ex 33:22
R of his salvation | Deut 32:15
LORD is my r | 2 Sam 22:2
r and my Redeemer | Ps 19:14
set my feet upon a r | Ps 40:2
an everlasting R | Is 26:4
his house upon the r | Matt 7:24
upon this r I will | Matt 16:18
a r of offense | Rom 9:33

Rod *staff, stick*
break them with a r | Ps 2:9
Thy r and Thy staff | Ps 23:4
The r of discipline | Prov 22:15

Roll *move*
let justice r down | Amos 5:24
r-ed away the stone | Matt 28:2

Roof
brought…to the r | Josh 2:6
r…woman bathing | 2 Sam 11:2
removed from r above | Mark 2:4
r and let him down | Luke 5:19

Room *chamber*
the ark with r-s | Gen 6:14

go into your inner r | Matt 6:6
a large upper r | Mark 14:15
no r for them in | Luke 2:7
r for the wrath | Rom 12:19

Root (n) *source*
the r of Jesse | Is 11:10
of money is a r | 1 Tim 6:10
the R of David | Rev 5:5

Rot *decay*
their flesh will r | Zech 14:12
riches have r-ted | James 5:2

Rough *jagged, uneven*
r ground become a | Is 40:4
the r places smooth | Is 45:2

Royal *kingly*
a certain r official | John 4:46
fulfilling the r law | James 2:8
a r priesthood | 1 Pet 2:9

Ruin (n) *destruction*
be a r forever | Deut 13:16
the perpetual r-s | Ps 74:3
Jerusalem in r-s | Ps 79:1
rebuild its r-s | Acts 15:16

Rule (n) *authority, government*
to establish his r | 1 Chr 18:3
will walk by this r | Gal 6:16
according to the r-s | 2 Tim 2:5

Rule (v) *govern*
r over the fish | Gen 1:26
r-s over the nations | Ps 22:28
The sun to r by day | Ps 136:8
r over the Gentiles | Rom 15:12
peace of Christ r | Col 3:15

Ruler *king, monarch*
Joseph was the r | Gen 42:6
nor curse a r | Ex 22:28
no chief…or r | Prov 6:7
your r-s have fled | Is 22:3
Most High God is r | Dan 4:32
come forth a R | Matt 2:6
r of the demons | Matt 9:34
r-s of the Gentiles | Mark 10:42
the r of this world | John 12:31
Who made you a r | Acts 7:27
be subject to r-s | Titus 3:1

Rumor *gossip, hearsay*
wars and r-s of wars | Matt 24:6

Run *move rapidly*
their feet r to evil | Prov 1:16
r and not get tired | Is 40:31
disciple ran ahead | John 20:4
who r in a race | 1 Cor 9:24

Rush *move quicky*
r-es headlong at Him | Job 15:26
herd r-ed down the | Matt 8:32

Rust *corrosion*
in which there is r | Ezek 24:6
moth and r destroy | Matt 6:19

Ruthless *cruel*
Reprove the r | Is 1:17
song of the r is | Is 25:5

most r of the | Ezek 28:7

– S –

Sabbath *day of rest*
Remember the s day | Ex 20:8
Observe the s day | Deut 5:12
new moon nor s | 2 Kin 4:23
is Lord of the S | Matt 12:8
S was made for man | Mark 2:27
a S day's journey | Acts 1:12
are read every S | Acts 13:27

Sacred *consecrated, holy*
perform s services | 1 Cor 9:13
table and the s bread | Heb 9:2

Sacrifice (n) *offering of a life*
a Passover s to | Ex 12:27
The s of the wicked | Prov 15:8
compassion…not s | Matt 9:13
a living and holy s | Rom 12:1
an acceptable s | Phil 4:18
offer up spiritual s-s | 1 Pet 2:5

Sacrifice (v) *offer a life*
we may s to the LORD | Ex 5:3
they s-d to the LORD | Judg 2:5
they s to demons | 1 Cor 10:20

Sad *sorrowful, unhappy*
people heard s word | Ex 33:4
Why is your face s | Neh 2:2

Safe *free from danger*
houses are s from fear | Job 21:9
runs into it and is s | Prov 18:10
back s and sound | Luke 15:27

Saints *ones faithful to God*
s of the Highest | Dan 7:22
s…fallen asleep | Matt 27:52
intercedes for the s | Rom 8:27
citizens with the s | Eph 2:19
perseverance of the s | Rev 14:12

Salt *preservative*
became a pillar of s | Gen 19:26
and sowed it with s | Judg 9:45
the s of the earth | Matt 5:13

Salvation *deliverance*
For Thy s I wait | Gen 49:18
S belongs to the LORD | Ps 3:8
my light and my s | Ps 27:1
lift up the cup of s | Ps 116:13
My s shall be forever | Is 51:6
S is from the LORD | Jon 2:9
s in no one else | Acts 4:12
power of God for s | Rom 1:16
now is the day of s | 2 Cor 6:2
take the helmet of s | Eph 6:17
work out your s with | Phil 2:12
neglect so great a s | Heb 2:3
S to our God who | Rev 7:10

Sanctification *holiness*
resulting in s | Rom 6:22
righteousness and s | 1 Cor 1:30
s by the Spirit | 2 Thess 2:13

Sanctify *set apart to God*
S to Me every   Ex 13:2
They will *s* My name   Is 29:23
will *s* the Holy One   Is 29:23
s-ied by the...Spirit Rom 15:16
s Christ as Lord   1 Pet 3:15

Sanctuary *place of worship*
revere My *s*   Lev 19:30
into the *s* of God   Ps 73:17
Praise God in His *s*   Ps 150:1
a minister in the *s*   Heb 8:2

Sand
descendants as the *s*   Gen 32:12
treasures of the *s*   Deut 33:19
built...upon the *s*   Matt 7:26
innumerable as the *s*   Heb 11:12

Satisfy *be content*
eat and not be *s-ied*   Lev 26:26
to *s* the multitude   Mark 15:15

Save *deliver, rescue*
s-d by the LORD   Deut 33:29
He will *s* you   Prov 20:22
s you from afar   Jer 30:10
will *s* His people   Matt 1:21
Son...has come to *s*   Matt 18:11
faith has *s-d* you   Luke 7:50
be *s-d* by His life   Rom 5:10
Jesus came...to *s*   1 Tim 1:15
One who is able to *s*   James 4:12

Savior *one who saves*
forgot God their *S*   Ps 106:21
no *s* besides Me   Is 43:11
S, who is Christ   Luke 2:11
the *S* of the world   John 4:42
S of all men   1 Tim 4:10
kingdom of our...*S*   2 Pet 1:11

Say *pronounce, speak*
not *s* in your heart   Deut 9:4
Do not *s* to your   Prov 3:28
Many will *s* to Me   Matt 7:22
If we *s*...no sin   1 John 1:8

Sayings *statements*
utter dark *s* of old   Ps 78:2
s of the wise   Prov 24:23

Scale *for measuring weight*
with accurate *s-s*   Job 31:6
false *s* is not good   Prov 20:23
with dishonest *s-s*   Amos 8:5

Scatter *spread, sprinkle*
s among the nations   Lev 26:33
storm will *s* them   Is 41:16
s him like dust   Matt 21:44

Scepter *symbol of authority*
s shall not depart   Gen 49:10
s...rise from Israel   Num 24:17
A *s* of uprightness   Ps 45:6
The *s* of rulers   Is 14:5
s of His kingdom   Heb 1:8

Scheme *plan, plot*
s...he had devised   Esth 9:25
s brings him down   Job 18:7

carries out wicked *s-s* Ps 37:7
ignorant of his *s-s*   2 Cor 2:11
the *s-s* of the devil   Eph 6:11

Scoff *mock, sneer*
s at all the nations   Ps 59:8
were *s-ing* at Him   Luke 16:14

Scoffer *mocker*
sit in the seat of *s-s* Ps 1:1
Behold, you *s-s*   Acts 13:41

Scorn *treat with contempt*
s-ed...his salvation   Deut 32:15

Scourge (n) *whip*
the *s* of the tongue   Job 5:21
made a *s* of cords   John 2:15

Scourge (v) *flog, whip*
having Jesus *s-d*   Matt 27:26
lawful for you to *s*   Acts 22:25

Scribe *copier, writer*
lying pen of the *s-s*   Jer 8:8
chief priests and *s-s* Matt 2:4
Where is the *s*   1 Cor 1:20

Scripture
S has been fulfilled   Luke 4:21
You search the *S-s*   John 5:39
S cannot be broken   John 10:35
what does the *S* say   Rom 4:3
S is inspired by God   2 Tim 3:16

Scroll *parchment*
these curses on a *s*   Num 5:23
Take a *s* and write   Jer 36:2
eat this *s*, and go   Ezek 3:1
like a *s*...rolled   Rev 6:14

Sea *body of salt water*
to the *s* in ships   Ps 107:23
rebukes the *s* and   Nah 1:4
walking on the *s*   Matt 14:26
s of glass like crystal Rev 4:6

Search *examine, inquire*
LORD *s-es* all hearts   1 Chr 28:9
S me, O God, and   Ps 139:23
s for the Child   Matt 2:13
You *s* the Scriptures   John 5:39

Season *time of year*
rains in their *s*   Lev 26:4
in *s* and out of *s*   2 Tim 4:2

Seat (n) *chair, stool*
sit in the *s* of scoffers Ps 1:1
before...judgment *s*   Rom 14:10

Seat (v) *sit*
s-ed at His feet   Luke 10:39
s-ed at the right hand Col 3:1

Secret *what is hidden*
sets *it* up in *s*   Deut 27:15
the *s-s* of the heart   Ps 44:21
have not spoken in *s*   Is 45:19
alms may be in *s*   Matt 6:4
Father who sees in *s*   Matt 6:4

Secure *safe, stable*
overthrows the *s*   Job 12:19

s in the mountain   Amos 6:1

Security *certainty, safety*
Israel dwells in *s*   Deut 33:28
will lie down in *s*   Is 14:30

Seduce *entice, persuade*
if a man *s-s* a virgin Ex 22:16
s you from LORD   Deut 13:10
s them to do evil   2 Kin 21:9
lips she *s-s* him   Prov 7:21

See *look, perceive*
No eye will *s* me   Job 24:15
s the works of God   Ps 66:5
the blind shall *s*   Is 29:18
s your good works   Matt 5:16
s the Son of Man   Matt 16:28
No man has *s-n* God   John 1:18
you will *s* Me   John 16:16
s in a mirror dimly   1 Cor 13:12

Seed *descendant* or *plant*
establish your *s*   Ps 89:4
O *s* of Abraham   Ps 105:6
like a mustard *s*   Matt 13:31
His *s* abides in him   1 John 3:9

Seek *pursue, search for*
and *s* My face   2 Chr 7:14
s me will find me   Prov 8:17
s wisdom and an   Eccl 7:25
times to *s* the LORD   Hos 10:12
s first His kingdom   Matt 6:33
s for a sign   Mark 8:12
s-ing the things above Col 3:1

Seize *grasp, take*
mother shall *s* him   Deut 21:19
seeking...to *s* Him   John 7:30

Self-control
your lack of *s*   1 Cor 7:5
gentleness, *s*   Gal 5:23

Selfish *self-centered*
s ambition in your   James 3:14

Sell *barter, trade*
s me your birthright   Gen 25:31
sold all that he had   Matt 13:46
sold into bondage   Rom 7:14

Send *convey, dispatch*
s rain on the earth   Gen 7:4
Whom shall I *s*   Is 6:8
He has *sent* Me   Luke 4:18
God *sent* forth His Son Gal 4:4

Sensuality
deceit, *s*, envy   Mark 7:22
promiscuity and *s*   Rom 13:13

Sentence *judgment*
escape the *s* of hell   Matt 23:33
to the *s* of death   Luke 24:20

Separate *divide, set apart*
God *s-d* the light   Gen 1:4
let no man *s*   Matt 19:6
Who shall *s* us from   Rom 8:35

Separation *division, isolation*
his *s* he is holy   Num 6:8

have made a *s*   Is 59:2

Servant *helper, slave*
s-s of a new covenant   2 Cor 3:6
s of Christ Jesus   1 Tim 4:6

Serve *help, work for*
shall *s* the LORD   Ex 23:25
s-d as priests   1 Chr 24:2
s God and mammon   Matt 6:24
If anyone *s-s* Me   John 12:26
through love *s* one   Gal 5:13

Service *ministry, work*
s of righteousness   Is 32:17
s with reverence   Heb 12:28

Settled *arranged* or *inhabited*
cloud *s* over the   Num 9:18
word is *s* in heaven   Ps 119:89
s in the lawful   Acts 19:39

Sew *fasten, join*
s-ed fig leaves together   Gen 3:7
s-ed sackcloth over   Job 16:15
a time to *s* together   Eccl 3:7
women *s magic*   Ezek 13:18

Sexual
not in *s* promiscuity   Rom 13:13
from *s* immorality   1 Thess 4:3

Shackles *fetters*
will tear off your *s*   Nah 1:13
s broken in pieces   Mark 5:4
with chains and *s*   Luke 8:29

Shade *protection*
cover him with *s*   Job 40:22
lived under its *s*   Ezek 31:6
over Jonah to be a *s*   Jon 4:6

Shadow *image of shade*
the *s* of Thy wings   Ps 17:8
his *s* might fall on   Acts 5:15

Shake *quiver, tremble*
made all my bones *s*   Job 4:14
peace will not be *s-n*   Is 54:10
s off the dust   Matt 10:14

Shame *disgrace, dishonor*
wicked be put to *s*   Ps 31:17
wise men are put to *s*   Jer 8:9
worthy to suffer *s*   Acts 5:41
glory is in their *s*   Phil 3:19

Share (n) *portion*
them take their *s*   Gen 14:24
give me the *s*   Luke 15:12
I do my *s*   Col 1:24

Share (v) *partake, participate*
s in the inheritance   Prov 17:2
s all good things   Gal 6:6
s the sufferings of   1 Pet 4:13

Sharp *cutting*
S...two-edged sword   Prov 5:4

Shatter *break, burst*
the mighty are *s-ed*   1 Sam 2:4
s the doors of bronze   Is 45:2

Shed *pour out*
Whoever *s-s* man's   Gen 9:6
hasten to *s* blood   Prov 1:16
swift to *s* blood   Rom 3:15

Sheep *animal*
not be like *s*   Num 27:17
s of His pasture   Ps 100:3
All of us like *s*   Is 53:6
lost *s* of...Israel   Matt 10:6
s from the goats   Matt 25:32
my *s* which was lost   Luke 15:6
His life for the *s*   John 10:11
s hear My voice   John 10:27
Tend My *s*   John 21:17
Shepherd of the *s*   Heb 13:20

Shelter *cover, refuge*
under the *s* of my   Gen 19:8
in the *s* of Thy wings   Ps 61:4
a *s* from the storm   Is 32:2

Shepherd (n)
sheep...have no *s*   Num 27:17
The LORD is my *s*   Ps 23:1
for lack of a *s*   Ezek 34:5
raise up a *s*   Zech 11:16
sheep without a *s*   Matt 9:36
I am the good *s*   John 10:11
the great *S*   Heb 13:20
the Chief *S*   1 Pet 5:4

Shield *protection*
He is a *s* to all   2 Sam 22:31
My *s* is with God   Ps 7:10
the *s* of faith   Eph 6:16

Shine *be radiant, glow*
his face *shone*   Ex 34:29
His face *s* on you   Num 6:25
Thy face to *s* upon us   Ps 80:3
s-s in the darkness   John 1:5

Ship *boat*
a haven for *s-s*   Gen 49:13
like merchant *s-s*   Prov 31:14
to the sea in *s-s*   Ps 107:23
escape from the *s*   Acts 27:30

Shoot *new growth*
like a tender *s*   Is 53:2
His *s-s* will sprout   Hos 14:6

Short *lacking*
Is My hand so *s*   Is 50:2
days shall be cut *s*   Matt 24:22

Shout *cry out loudly*
s with a great *s*   Josh 6:5
s for joy   Ps 35:27

Show *manifest, reveal*
s me Thy glory   Ex 33:18
s Thy lovingkindness   Ps 17:7
S us the Father   John 14:9

Shower *abundant flow*
Like *s-s* that water   Ps 72:6
be *s-s* of blessing   Ezek 34:26

Shrewd *cunning*
frustrates...the *s*   Job 5:12
be *s* as serpents   Matt 10:16

Shrine *object of worship*
built yourself a *s*   Ezek 16:24
tear down your *s-s*   Ezek 16:39
who made silver *s-s*   Acts 19:24

Shut *close*
s the lions' mouths   Dan 6:22
s your door, pray   Matt 6:6

Sick *unwell*
s with a fever   Mark 1:30
Lazarus was *s*   John 11:2

Sickness *illness*
authority over...*s*   Matt 10:1
s is not unto death   John 11:4

Sight *perception, vision*
acceptable in Thy *s*   Ps 19:14
precious in My *s*   Is 43:4
blind receive *s*   Matt 11:5
by faith, not by *s*   2 Cor 5:7

Sign *indication* or *wonder*
s of the covenant   Gen 9:12
this shall be the *s*   Ex 3:12
Ask a *s* for yourself   Is 7:11
an everlasting *s*   Is 55:13
s of Your coming   Matt 24:3
s of circumcision   Rom 4:11
Jews ask for *s-s*   1 Cor 1:22

Silence *quietness*
My soul *waits* in *s*   Ps 62:1
s the ignorance   1 Pet 2:15

Silent *quiet*
A time to be *s*   Eccl 3:7
But Jesus kept *s*   Matt 26:63

Silver *precious metal*
rich in...*s*   Gen 13:2
took no plunder in *s*   Judg 5:19
as *s* is refined   Ps 66:10
in settings of *s*   Prov 25:11
s has become dross   Is 1:22
The *s* is Mine   Hag 2:8
not acquire...*s*   Matt 10:9
thirty pieces of *s*   Matt 26:15

Simple *innocent* or *humble*
making wise the *s*   Ps 19:7
LORD preserves the *s*   Ps 116:6

Sin (n) *transgression*
atonement for your *s*   Ex 32:30
purification from *s*   Num 19:9
Fools mock at *s*   Prov 14:9
bore the *s* of many   Is 53:12
an eternal *s*   Mark 3:29
forgive us our *s-s*   Luke 11:4
takes away the *s*   John 1:29
wages of *s* is death   Rom 6:23
died for our *s-s*   1 Cor 15:3
confess your *s-s*   James 5:16
a multitude of *s-s*   James 5:20
s is lawlessness   1 John 3:4

Sin (v) *transgress*
s against the LORD   1 Sam 14:34
Job did not *s*   Job 1:22

Sin _Continued_

s against Thee | Ps 119:11
s no more | John 8:11
all have **s-ned** | Rom 3:23

Sincere _without deceit_
be s and blameless | Phil 1:10

Sinful _wicked_
a brood of s men | Num 32:14
s generation | Mark 8:38
I am a s man | Luke 5:8
likeness of s flesh | Rom 8:3

Sing
s to the LORD | Ex 15:1
I will s praises | 2 Sam 22:50
morning stars **sang** | Job 38:7
birds will s | Zeph 2:14
sang a new song | Rev 5:9

Sink _descend, fall_
do not let me s | Ps 69:14
so shall Babylon s | Jer 51:64

Sinner _wrongdoer_
He instructs s-s | Ps 25:8
a friend of...s-s | Matt 11:19
one s who repents | Luke 15:7
while we were yet s-s | Rom 5:8

Sit _recline, rest_
Nor s in the seat | Ps 1:1
S at My right hand | Ps 110:1
who s in darkness | Luke 1:79

Skill _proficiency_
filled them with s | Ex 35:35
the heavens with s | Ps 136:5
word of s-ed men | Jer 10:9
s-ed in destruction | Ezek 21:31

Sky _heavens_
the s grew black | 1 Kin 18:45
witness in the s | Ps 89:37
for the s is red | Matt 16:2
appear in the s | Matt 24:30
s was shut up | Luke 4:25
s was split apart | Rev 6:14

Slaughter (n) _brutal killing_
lamb led to the s | Jer 11:19
as a sheep to s | Acts 8:32
in a day of s | James 5:5

Slave _bondservant_
The Hebrew s | Gen 39:17
sold in a s sale | Lev 25:42
Is Israel a s | Jer 2:14
s above his master | Matt 10:24
shall be s of all | Mark 10:44
is the s of sin | John 8:34
neither s nor free | Gal 3:28
as s-s of Christ | Eph 6:6

Slavery _servitude_
from the house of s | Ex 13:3
a spirit of s | Rom 8:15
to a yoke of s | Gal 5:1

Slay _destroy, kill_
knife to s his son | Gen 22:10
Though He s me | Job 13:15
Lamb that was **slain** | Rev 5:12

Sleep (n) _rest_
caused a deep s | Gen 2:21
a spirit of deep s | Is 29:10
overcome by s | Acts 20:9

Sleep (v) _slumber_
why dost Thou s | Ps 44:23
found them s-ing | Matt 26:43
we shall not all s | 1 Cor 15:51

Slow _not quick_
I am s of speech | Ex 4:10
gracious, S to anger | Ps 103:8
Lord is not s | 2 Pet 3:9

Sluggard _lazy one_
to the ant, O s | Prov 6:6
s buries his hand | Prov 26:15

Slumber _sleep_
s in their beds | Job 33:15
Dreamers...love to s | Is 56:10

Small _little_
s among the nations | Jer 49:15
For the gate is s | Matt 7:14
tongue is a s part | James 3:5

Smile _grin_
I s-d on them | Job 29:24
that I may s again | Ps 39:13

Smite _hit, strike_
s...with frogs | Ex 8:2
righteous s me | Ps 141:5
s the earth | Rev 11:6

Smoke _mist, vapor_
Sinai was all in s | Ex 19:18
like s they vanish | Ps 37:20
s rises up forever | Rev 19:3

Smooth _no roughness_
I am a s man | Gen 27:11
Make s...a highway | Is 40:3
the rough roads s | Luke 3:5

Snake _serpent_
a s bites him | Amos 5:19
s instead of a fish | Luke 11:11

Snare _trap_
gods shall be a s | Judg 2:3
s-s of death | 2 Sam 22:6
laid a s for me | Ps 119:110
his lips are the s | Prov 18:7
caught in My s | Ezek 12:13
table become a s | Rom 11:9
s of the devil | 1 Tim 3:7

Snow _ice flakes_
be whiter than s | Ps 51:7
Like s in summer | Prov 26:1
as white as s | Matt 28:3

Sober _serious, temperate_
words of s truth | Acts 26:25
Be of s spirit | 1 Pet 5:8

Soft _kind_
s tongue breaks | Prov 25:15

Soil _earth, ground_
first fruits of your s | Ex 23:19

fell into the good s | Mark 4:8
produce of the s | James 5:7

Sojourn _visit temporarily_
S in this land | Gen 26:3
s...land of Moab | Ruth 1:25

Sojourner
s in a foreign land | Ex 2:22
oppressed the s | Ezek 22:29

Soldier _military man_
s-s took Him away | Mark 15:16
a devout s | Acts 10:7
good s of Christ | 2 Tim 2:3

Solemn _deeply earnest, serious_
sabbath of s rest | Lev 16:31
bound...a s oath | Acts 23:14

Son _male descendant_
Take...your only s | Gen 22:2
O Absalom, my s | 2 Sam 18:33
Thou art My S | Ps 2:7
wise s makes a | Prov 10:1
Discipline your s | Prov 19:18
My beloved S | Matt 3:17
the carpenter's s | Matt 13:55
I am the S of God | Matt 27:43
her first-born s | Luke 2:7
only begotten S | John 3:16
S also gives life | John 5:21
sending His own S | Rom 8:3
image of His S | Rom 8:29
if a s, then an heir | Gal 4:7
abide in the S | 1 John 2:24

Song _melody, music_
LORD is my...s | Ex 15:2
Sing to Him a new s | Ps 33:3
A s of my beloved | Is 5:1
hymns...spiritual s-s | Eph 5:19

Sorcery _witchcraft_
practiced s | 2 Chr 33:6
idolatry, s, enmities | Gal 5:20
deceived by your s | Rev 18:23

Sordid _filthy_
fond of s gain | 1 Tim 3:8
the sake of s gain | Titus 1:11
not for s gain | 1 Pet 5:2

Sorrow _grief, sadness_
life is spent with s | Ps 31:10
man of s-s | Is 53:3
s...turned to joy | John 16:20
if I cause you s | 2 Cor 2:2

Soul _life, spirit_
humble your s-s | Lev 16:29
poured out my s | 1 Sam 1:15
He restores my s | Ps 23:3
unable to kill the s | Matt 10:28
exchange for his s | Matt 16:26
s exalts the Lord | Luke 1:46
your s is required | Luke 12:20
war against the s | 1 Pet 2:11

Sound (adj) *accurate, stable*
give you s teaching   Prov 4:2
the s doctrine   1 Tim 4:6
Sound (n) *noise*
s of Thee in...garden   Gen 3:10
s of war in the camp   Ex 32:17
s of a great army   2 Kin 7:6
s of many waters   Ezek 43:2
Sovereignty *authority*
His s rules over all   Ps 103:19
s will be uprooted   Dan 11:4
Sow *plant, spread*
who s in tears   Ps 126:5
they s the wind   Hos 8:7
s good seed   Matt 13:27
whatever a man s-s   Gal 6:7
Sower *planter*
seed to the s   Is 55:10
s went out to sow   Matt 13:3
s sows the word   Mark 4:14
Spare *save or be lenient*
who s-s his rod   Prov 13:24
not s His own Son   Rom 8:32
Speak *proclaim, tell*
God s-s with man   Deut 5:24
and a time to s   Eccl 3:7
the dumb to s   Mark 7:37
Never did a man s   John 7:46
s with other tongues   Acts 2:4
If I s with tongues   1 Cor 13:1
Speech *message, word*
I am slow of s   Ex 4:10
in cleverness of s   1 Cor 1:17
Spin *make thread*
nor do they s   Matt 6:28
neither toil nor s   Luke 12:27
Spirit
God sent an evil s   Judg 9:23
My s is broken   Job 17:1
my s grows faint   Ps 77:3
a haughty s before   Prov 16:18
his s was troubled   Dan 2:1
are the poor in s   Matt 5:3
yielded up His s   Matt 27:50
S like a dove   Mark 1:10
born of...the S   John 3:5
worship in s and   John 4:24
gave up His s   John 19:30
Jesus, receive my s   Acts 7:59
power of the S   Rom 15:19
taught by the S   1 Cor 2:13
pray with the s   1 Cor 14:15
walk by the S   Gal 5:16
fruit of the S is love   Gal 5:22
be filled with the S   Eph 5:18
sword of the S   Eph 6:17
not quench the S   1 Thess 5:19
Spirit of God
the S was moving   Gen 1:2
a vision by the S   Ezek 11:24
S descending as a   Matt 3:16
being led by the S   Rom 8:14
Spiritual *of the spirit*
the Law is s   Rom 7:14

s service of worship   Rom 12:1
raised a s body   1 Cor 15:44
hymns and s songs   Eph 5:19
Split *divide*
He s the rock   Is 48:21
sky was s apart   Rev 6:14
Spoil *booty, pillage*
he divides the s   Gen 49:27
the s of the cities   Deut 2:35
Spot *speck*
the leopard his s-s   Jer 13:23
no s or wrinkle   Eph 5:27
Spotless *no defects*
unblemished and s   1 Pet 1:19
s and blameless   2 Pet 3:14
Spread *stretch out*
He s His wings   Deut 32:11
death s to all men   Rom 5:12
Spring (n) *water source*
went down to the s   Gen 24:16
twelve s-s of water   Ex 15:27
stop all s-s of water   2 Kin 3:19
s-s of the...fixed   Prov 8:28
the s-s of salvation   Is 12:3
s of the water of life   Rev 21:6
Spring (v) *jump, leap*
S up, O well   Num 21:17
s-ing up to eternal   John 4:14
Sprinkle *scatter*
take its blood and s   Ex 29:16
s some of the blood   Lev 4:6
s it seven times   Lev 4:17
s some of the oil   Lev 14:16
Spy *investigate*
to s out Jericho   Josh 6:25
s out our liberty   Gal 2:4
Staff *rod*
Thy s, they comfort   Ps 23:4
a mere s; no bread   Mark 6:8
Stain *blemish*
s of your iniquity   Jer 2:22
without s or   1 Tim 6:14
Stand *maintain position*
s before the LORD   Deut 10:8
word of our God s-s   Is 40:8
do you s looking   Acts 1:11
s by your faith   Rom 11:20
s firm in the faith   1 Cor 16:13
I s at the door   Rev 3:20
Star *heavenly body*
He made the s-s   Gen 1:16
s of the morning   Is 14:12
His s in the east   Matt 2:2
bright morning s   Rev 22:16
Stature *height*
was growing in s   1 Sam 2:26
in wisdom and s   Luke 2:52
he was small in s   Luke 19:3
measure of the s   Eph 4:13
Statute *law, rule*
keep My s-s   Lev 18:5
Teach me Thy s-s   Ps 119:26

Steadfast *established, firm*
be s and not fear   Job 11:15
be s, immovable   1 Cor 15:58
Steal *rob, take*
You shall not s   Ex 20:15
thieves break in...s   Matt 6:19
Steps *distance or movements*
dost number my s   Job 14:16
His s do not slip   Ps 37:31
follow in His s   1 Pet 2:21
Steward *supervisor*
and sensible s   Luke 12:42
s-s of the mysteries   1 Cor 4:1
Stewardship *responsibility*
account of your s   Luke 16:2
s of God's grace   Eph 3:2
Still *motionless or quiet*
O sun, stand s   Josh 10:12
sea, Hush, be s   Mark 4:39
Sting *pain*
where is your s   1 Cor 15:55
s of death is sin   1 Cor 15:56
Stir *agitate*
word s-s up anger   Prov 15:1
s-red up the water   John 5:4
Stone (n) *rock*
two s tablets   Ex 34:1
do these s-s mean   Josh 4:6
foot against a s   Ps 91:12
in Zion a s   Is 28:16
foot against a s   Matt 4:6
will give him a s   Matt 7:9
rolled away the s   Matt 28:2
first to throw a s   John 8:7
as to a living s   1 Pet 2:4
A s of stumbling   1 Pet 2:8
Stop *cease*
put a s to sacrifice   Dan 9:27
s sinning   1 Cor 15:34
Store *accumulate*
s up the grain   Gen 41:35
s-d up your treasure   James 5:3
Storehouse *storage place*
s-s of the snow   Job 38:22
wind from His s-s   Jer 10:13
tithe into the s   Mal 3:10
Storm *tempest, whirlwind*
A refuge from the s   Is 25:4
a great s on the sea   Jon 1:4
Straight *direct*
Make Thy way s   Ps 5:8
Make His paths s   Matt 3:3
Strange *foreign*
no s god among you   Ps 81:9
to teach s doctrines   1 Tim 1:3
Stranger *alien, sojourner*
s-s in the land   Gen 22:21
shall not wrong a s   Ex 22:21
LORD protects the s-s   Ps 146:9
I was a s   Matt 25:35

Straw *stalk of grain*
s to make brick Ex 5:7
wood, hay, s 1 Cor 3:12

Stray *wander*
s-s from the truth James 5:19
s-ing like sheep 1 Pet 2:25

Stream *current, flow*
planted by s-s of water Ps 1:3
like a rushing s Is 59:19

Strength *force, power*
The LORD is my s Ex 15:2
My s is dried up Ps 22:15
The LORD is my s Ps 28:7
s of my salvation Ps 140:7
s to the weary Is 40:29
with all your s Mark 12:30
sun shining in its s Rev 1:16

Strengthen *make strong*
please s me Judg 16:28
s your brothers Luke 22:32
s-ed in the faith Acts 16:5
Him who s-s me Phil 4:3
s your hearts 2 Thess 2:17

Stretch *extend*
I will s out My hand Ex 3:20
S-ing out heaven Ps 104:2

Strife *discord, quarrel*
the s of tongues Ps 31:20
Hatred stirs up s Prov 10:12
and s among you 1 Cor 3:3

Strike *hit*
you shall s the rock Ex 17:6
you s your foot Ps 91:12
He will s the earth Is 11:4
S the Shepherd Zech 13:7

Strive *contend, struggle*
will not always s Ps 103:9
s-ing to please men Gal 1:10
we labor and s 1 Tim 4:10

Strong *powerful, steadfast*
very s west wind Ex 10:19
Israel became s Judg 1:28
LORD s and mighty Ps 24:8
love is as s as death Song 8:6
grew s in faith Rom 4:20
act like men, be s 1 Cor 16:13
be s in the Lord Eph 6:10

Stronghold *fortress, refuge*
David lived in the s 2 Sam 5:9
s and my refuge 2 Sam 22:3
s for the oppressed Ps 9:9
For God is my s Ps 59:9
my salvation, My s Ps 62:2
a s to the upright Prov 10:29

Struggle (n) *conflict*
our s is not against Eph 6:12
have shared my s Phil 4:3

Stubble *short stumps*
gather s for straw Ex 5:12
fire consumes s Is 5:24

give birth to s Is 33:11
house of Esau…s Obad 18

Stubborn *obstinate*
Pharaoh's heart is s Ex 7:14
you are a s people Deut 9:6

Stumble *fall, trip*
foot will not s Prov 3:23
eye makes you s Matt 5:29
a stone of s-ing Rom 9:33

Stumbling Block *obstacle*
You are a s to Me Matt 16:23
to Jews a s 1 Cor 1:23
s of the cross Gal 5:11

Stupid *foolish, senseless*
I am more s than Prov 30:2
are altogether s Jer 10:8

Subdue *conquer, overcome*
fill the earth, and s Gen 1:28
s nations before him Is 45:1

Subject (adj) *under authority*
s to forced labor Judg 1:30
s to…husbands Titus 2:5
be s to the Father Heb 12:9

Subjection *under authority*
He continued in s Luke 2:51
all things in s 1 Cor 15:27

Submissive *yielding*
Servants, be s 1 Pet 2:18
s to…husbands 1 Pet 3:5

Submit *yield to*
Foreigners s to me Ps 18:44
S therefore to God James 4:7

Substitute
s darkness for light Is 5:20
s bitter for sweet Is 5:20

Suddenly *abruptly*
lest he come s Mark 13:36
s…from heaven Acts 2:2

Suffer *experience pain*
Son of Man must s Mark 8:31
s and rise again Luke 24:46
we s with *Him* Rom 8:17
if one member s-s 1 Cor 12:26
Christ also s-ed 1 Pet 2:21

Sufferings *distress*
s of this present Rom 8:18
sharers of our s 2 Cor 1:7
fellowship of His s Phil 3:10
rejoice in my s Col 1:24
share the s of Christ 1 Pet 4:13

Sufficient *enough*
s for its redemption Lev 25:26
My grace is s 2 Cor 12:9

Summon *call, gather*
s all the prophets 2 Kin 10:19
He s-ed the twelve Matt 6:7

Sun *heavenly body*
the s stood still Josh 10:13
God is a s Ps 84:11

s to rule by day Ps 136:8
new under the s Eccl 1:9
clothed with the s Rev 12:1

Sunrise *appearance of sun*
toward the s Num 3:38
Jordan toward the s Josh 1:15

Supper *meal*
made Him a s John 12:2
eat the Lord's S 1 Cor 11:20
marriage s of the Rev 19:9
the great s of God Rev 19:17

Supplication *petition*
s of Thy people 1 Kin 8:52
LORD has heard my s Ps 6:9
by prayer and s Phil 4:6

Supply *provide*
my God shall s Phil 4:19
s moral excellence 2 Pet 1:5

Support (n) *strength*
gave Him strong s 1 Chr 11:10
worthy of his s Matt 10:10

Sure *secure, true*
testimony…is s Ps 19:7
His precepts are s Ps 111:7

Surety *liable, security*
I myself will be s Gen 43:9
s for a stranger Prov 11:15

Surface *exterior*
s of the deep Gen 1:2
water was on the s Gen 8:9

Surpass *excel*
s-ing riches of His Eph 2:7

Surround *encircle*
s me with songs Ps 32:7
witnesses s-ing us Heb 12:1

Survive *outlive*
household will s Jer 38:17
how can we s Ezek 33:10

Sustain *provide for*
land could not s Gen 13:6
He will s you Ps 55:22

Swallow (v) *take in*
he will s up death Is 25:8
s-ed up in victory 1 Cor 15:54

Swear *take oath, vow*
s by the LORD Gen 24:3
not s falsely Lev 19:12
s by My name Jer 12:16
brethren do not s James 5:12

Sweat *perspiration*
s of your face Gen 3:19
s…like drops of Luke 22:44

Sweet *fresh, pleasant*
waters became s Ex 15:25
s are Thy words Ps 119:103
Stolen water is s Prov 9:17

Swift *fast, rapid*
race is not to the s Eccl 9:11
s to shed blood Rom 3:15

Swine *pig*
your pearls before *s*   Matt 7:6
Send us into the *s*   Mark 5:12

Sword *weapon with blade*
your *s* you shall   Gen 27:40
s devour forever   2 Sam 2:26
fell on his *s*   1 Chr 10:5
as a two-edged *s*   Prov 5:4
s against nation   Is 2:4
s-s into plowshares   Mic 4:3
perish by the *s*   Matt 26:52
s of the Spirit   Eph 6:17

Sympathy *mutual feeling*
I looked for *s*   Ps 69:20
s to the prisoners   Heb 10:34

Synagogue *assembly*
pray in the *s-s*   Matt 6:5
taught in *s-s*   John 18:20
reasoning in the *s*   Acts 17:17

– T –

Table *furniture*
dost prepare a *t*   Ps 23:5
drink at My *t*   Luke 22:30
t of the Lord   1 Cor 10:21

Tablet *writing surface*
t-s of the testimony   Ex 31:18
the *t* of their heart   Jer 17:1

Take *get, grasp*
T My yoke upon   Matt 11:29
T, eat; this is My   Matt 26:26
t-s away the sin   John 1:29

Talk (n) *conversation, speech*
argue with useless *t*   Job 15:3

Talk (v) *converse, speak*
lips *t* of trouble   Prov 24:2
who *t* about you   Ezek 33:30

Tall *high*
cut…its *t* cedars   2 Kin 19:23
a nation *t* and smooth   Is 18:2
grew up, became *t*   Ezek 16:7

Tares *weeds*
t…among the wheat   Matt 13:25
gather up the *t*   Matt 13:30
parable of the *t*   Matt 13:36

Taste *test flavor*
O *t* and see   Ps 34:8
shall not *t* death   Matt 16:28

Taunt *object of ridicule*
a *t* among all   Deut 28:37
I have become their *t*   Job 30:9

Tax *charge, tribute*
sitting in the *t* office   Matt 9:9
t to whom *t* is due   Rom 13:7

Tax-gatherer *tax collector*
t-s do the same   Matt 5:46
Matthew the *t*   Matt 10:3
he was a chief *t*   Luke 19:2

Teach *instruct*
T me Thy paths   Ps 25:4
He *began* to *t* them   Matt 5:2
t-ing…in parables   Mark 4:2

Teacher *instructor*
not above his *t*   Matt 10:24
the *t* of Israel   John 3:10
call me *T* and Lord   John 13:13
as pastors and *t-s*   Eph 4:11

Teaching (n) *instruction*
amazed at His *t*   Matt 7:8
contrary to sound *t*   1 Tim 1:10

Tear *crying*
sow in *t-s* shall reap   Ps 126:5
eyes a fountain of *t-s*   Jer 9:1
His feet with her *t-s*   Luke 7:38

Tell *relate, speak*
T of His glory   1 Chr 16:24
t-s lies will perish   Prov 19:9
t you the mystery   Rev 17:7

Temper *anger*
always loses his *t*   Prov 29:11
the ruler's *t* rises   Eccl 10:4

Tempest *storm*
bruises me with a *t*   Job 9:17
stormy wind *and t*   Ps 55:8
t of destruction   Is 28:2
on the day of *t*   Amos 1:14

Temple *structure for worship*
LORD is in His holy *t*   Ps 11:4
meditate in His *t*   Ps 27:4
pinnacle of the *t*   Matt 4:5
will destroy this *t*   Mark 14:58
are a *t* of God   1 Cor 3:16
t of the Holy Spirit   1 Cor 6:19

Tempt *test, try*
t-ed by Satan   Mark 1:13
lest Satan *t* you   1 Cor 7:5

Temptation *testing, trial*
not lead us into *t*   Matt 6:13
not enter into *t*   Matt 26:41

Tend *take care of*
He will *t* His flock   Is 40:11
T My sheep   John 21:17

Tender *gentle, young*
t and choice calf   Gen 18:7
your heart was *t*   2 Kin 22:19
like a *t* shoot   Is 53:2
t mercy of our God   Luke 1:78

Tent *mobile shelter*
Abram moved his *t*   Gen 13:18
man, living in *t-s*   Gen 25:27
your *t-s*, O Israel   1 Kin 12:16
t-s of the destroyers   Job 12:6
dwell in Thy *t* forever   Ps 61:4
grumbled in their *t-s*   Ps 106:25
Like a shepherd's *t*   Is 38:12

Terrible *dreadful*
t day of the LORD   Mal 4:5

Terrify *frighten*
t-ied by the sword   1 Chr 21:30

t me by visions   Job 7:14
t them with Thy storm   Ps 83:15
t you by my letters   2 Cor 10:9

Territory *country, land*
smite your whole *t*   Ex 8:2
God enlarges your *t*   Deut 19:8
t of…inheritance   Josh 19:10
will possess the *t*   Obad 19

Terror *intense fear*
t-s of Sheol came   Ps 116:3
t-s and great signs   Luke 21:11

Test (n) *trial*
put God to the *t*   Ps 78:18
you fail the *t*   2 Cor 13:5

Test (v) *try*
God *t-ed* Abraham   Gen 22:1
she came to *t* him   1 Kin 10:1
word of God is *t-ed*   Prov 30:5
t the spirits to see   1 John 4:1

Testify *give witness*
nor shall you *t*   Ex 23:2
sins *t* against us   Is 59:12

Testimony *witness*
two tablets of the *t*   Ex 31:18
t of the LORD is sure   Ps 19:7
t against Jesus   Matt 26:59
ashamed of the *t*   2 Tim 1:8
This *t* is true   Titus 1:13

Thank (v) *express gratitude*
song I shall *t* Him   Ps 28:7
I *t* God always   1 Cor 1:4

Thanks (n) *gratitude*
give *t* to the LORD   1 Chr 16:7
It is good to give *t*   Ps 92:1
But *t* be to God   Rom 6:17
always to give *t*   2 Thess 1:3

Thanksgiving *gratitude*
with the voice of *t*   Ps 26:7
His presence with *t*   Ps 95:2

Thief *robber*
partner with a *t*   Prov 29:24
a *t* in the night   1 Thess 5:2

Think *ponder, reflect*
t as a child   1 Cor 13:11
t-s he is something   Gal 6:3

Thirst (n) *craving, dryness*
not hunger or *t*   Is 49:10
Me shall never *t*   John 6:35

Thirsty *lacking water*
dry and *t* land   Ezek 19:13
If any man is *t*   John 7:37

Thorn *sharp point*
have reaped *t-s*   Jer 12:13
fell among the *t-s*   Matt 13:7
a crown of *t-s*   Matt 27:29
t in the flesh   2 Cor 12:7

Thought *concept, idea*
t-s are not your *t-s*   Is 55:8
heart come evil *t-s*   Matt 15:19

Lord, *t* us to pray   Luke 11:1
Spirit will *t* you   Luke 12:12
t strange doctrines   1 Tim 1:3

Throat *part of neck*
t is an open grave Ps 5:9

Throne *seat of sovereign*
LORD's *t* is in heaven Ps 11:4
Thy *t* is established Ps 93:2
to the *t* of grace Heb 4:16
a great white *t* Rev 20:11

Thrust *cast, push*
He shall *t* them out Josh 23:5
Nor to *t* aside Prov 18:5

Thunder (n)
LORD sent *t* and hail Ex 9:23
sound of loud *t* Rev 14:2

Tidings *information, news*
not fear evil *t* Ps 112:7
glad *t* of good Rom 10:15

Time *day, period, season*
in *t-s* of trouble Ps 9:9
signs of the *t-s* Matt 16:3
deny Me three *t-s* Luke 22:61
My *t* is not yet John 7:6
is the acceptable *t* 2 Cor 6:2

Tired *weary*
I am *t* of living Gen 27:46
run and not get *t* Is 40:31

Tithe (n) *tenth*
a *t* of the *t* Num 18:26
the *t* of your grain Deut 12:17
t into the storehouse Mal 3:10

Toil (n) *labor, work*
the *t* of our hands Gen 5:29
t is not in vain 1 Cor 15:58

Tomb *grave, sepulchre*
from womb to *t* Job 10:19
laid Him in a *t* Mark 15:46
outside the *t* John 20:11

Tomorrow *future time*
for *t* we may die Is 22:13
not be anxious for *t* Matt 6:34

Tongue *speech, talk*
flatter with their *t* Ps 5:9
a lying *t* Prov 6:17
t is a deadly arrow Jer 9:8
cool off my *t* Luke 16:24
no one...tame the *t* James 3:8

Tongue *language*
speak with new *t-s* Mark 16:17
speak with other *t-s* Acts 2:4
t-s of men...angels 1 Cor 13:1
if I pray in a *t* 1 Cor 14:14
every tribe and *t* Rev 5:9

Tooth
eye for eye, *t* for *t* Ex 21:24
and a *t* for a *t* Matt 5:38

Torment (n) *pain, torture*
this place of *t* Luke 16:28
the fear of her *t* Rev 18:15

Touch *feel, handle*
not eat...or *t* it Gen 3:3
not *t* My anointed Ps 105:15

T nothing unclean Is 52:11
not to *t* a woman 1 Cor 7:1

Tower *fortress structure*
t whose top *will reach* Gen 11:4
Count her *t-s* Ps 48:12
name...strong *t* Prov 18:10
and built a *t* Matt 21:33

Tradition *custom*
sake of your *t* Matt 15:3
hold...to the *t-s* 1 Cor 11:2

Train *guide, instruct*
T up a child Prov 22:6
t-ed to discern good Heb 5:14

Trample *crush, hurt*
let him *t* my life Ps 7:5
didst *t* the nations Hab 3:12

Transform *change*
t-ed into the same 2 Cor 3:18
who will *t* the body Phil 3:21

Transgress *break, overstep*
you *t* the covenant Josh 23:16
disciples *t* the Matt 15:2

Transgression *trespass, sin*
I know my *t-s* Ps 51:3
love covers all *t-s* Prov 10:12
dead in our *t-s* Eph 2:5

Translated
t and read before me Ezra 4:18
Immanuel...*t* means Matt 1:23
Golgotha, which is *t* Mark 15:22
Messiah...*t* means John 1:41

Trap (v) *catch*
they might *t* Him Matt 22:15

Treasure (n) *valuable thing*
the LORD is his *t* Is 33:6
opening their *t-s* Matt 2:11
for where your *t* is Matt 6:21
have *t* in heaven Matt 19:21
t in earthen vessels 2 Cor 4:7

Treaty *agreement, contract*
Let there be a *t* 1 Kin 15:19
go, break your *t* 2 Chr 16:3

Tree *woody plant*
t of life Gen 2:9
hang him on a *t* Deut 21:22
t firmly planted Ps 1:3
she is a *t* of life Prov 3:18
like a *t* planted by Jer 17:8
good *t* bears good Matt 7:17
eat of the *t* of life Rev 2:7

Tremble *shake*
T before Him 1 Chr 16:30
T, and do not sin Ps 4:4
make the heavens *t* Is 13:13

Trembling (n) *fear, reverence*
rejoice with *t* Ps 2:11
with fear and *t* Phil 2:12

Trespass *fault, sin*
caught in any *t* Gal 6:1

dead in your *t-es* Eph 2:1

Trial *testing*
if we are on *t* today Acts 4:9
perseveres under *t* James 1:12

Tribe *common ancestry*
twelve *t-s* of Israel Gen 49:28
a man of each *t* Num 1:4
men from every *t* Rev 5:9

Tribulation *affliction*
world you have *t* John 16:33
out of the great *t* Rev 7:14

Triumph *victory*
the righteous *t* Prov 28:12
His *t* in Christ 2 Cor 2:14
mercy *t-s* over James 2:13

Trouble (n) *affliction*
forget all my *t* Gen 41:51
man is born for *t* Job 5:7
very present help in *t* Ps 46:1
day has enough *t* Matt 6:34

True *actual, real, reliable*
gets a *t* reward Prov 11:18
There was the *t* light John 1:9
let God be found *t* Rom 3:4
This testimony is *t* Titus 1:13
faithful and *t* Witness Rev 3:14

Trumpet *wind instrument*
t-s of rams' horns Josh 6:6
Praise Him with *t* Ps 150:3
at the last *t* 1 Cor 15:52
voice like...a *t* Rev 1:10

Trust (n) *confidence, hope*
In God... put my *t* Ps 56:11
put My *t* in Him Heb 2:13

Trust (v) *commit to*
t in the LORD Ps 4:5
Than to *t* in man Ps 118:8
not *t* in ourselves 2 Cor 1:9

Trustworthy *reliable*
who can find a *t* Prov 20:6
It is a *t* statement 1 Tim 3:1

Truth *genuineness, honesty*
speaks *t* in his heart Ps 15:2
Thy word is *t* Ps 119:160
full of grace and *t* John 1:14
the way, and the *t* John 14:6
t of the gospel Gal 2:5
the word of *t* 2 Tim 2:15

Tumult *disturbance*
t of the peoples Ps 65:7
t of waters Jer 51:16

Turmoil *tumult*
ill repute, full of *t* Ezek 22:5

Turn *change or move*
T from you evil 2 Kin 17:13
t-ed to his own way Is 53:6
t from darkness to Acts 26:18
t away from evil 1 Pet 3:11

Tutor *teacher*
Law...become our *t* Gal 3:24

Twelve *number*
t tribes of Israel Gen 49:28
summoned His *t* Matt 10:1
t legions of angels Matt 26:53
when He became *t* Luke 2:42
a crown of *t* stars Rev 12:1

– U –

Ugly *unsightly*
u and gaunt cows Gen 41:4
seven lean…*u* cows Gen 41:27

Unbelief *lack of faith*
wondered at their *u* Mark 6:6
help my *u* Mark 9:24
continue in their *u* Rom 11:23

Unbeliever *non-believer*
a place with the *u-s* Luke 12:46
wife who is an *u* 1 Cor 7:12
worse than an *u* 1 Tim 5:8

Unbelieving *doubting*
O *u* generation Mark 9:19
u husband is 1 Cor 7:14
evil, *u* heart Heb 3:12

Uncircumcised
But an *u* male Gen 17:14
the nations are *u* Jer 9:26
the gospel to the *u* Gal 2:7

Uncircumcision
has become *u* Rom 2:25
who are called *U* Eph 2:11
the *u* of your flesh Col 2:13

Unclean *not clean* or *not holy*
touches any *u* thing Lev 5:2
man of *u* lips Is 6:5
u spirits entered Mark 5:13

Undefiled *uncorrupted*
holy, innocent, *u* Heb 7:26
marriage bed be *u* Heb 13:4
imperishable and *u* 1 Pet 1:4

Undergo *experience*
Holy One to *u* decay Ps 16:10
should not *u* decay Ps 49:9
did not *u* decay Acts 13:37

Understand *comprehend*
do not *u* justice Prov 28:5
Hear, and *u* Matt 15:10
to *u* the Scriptures Luke 24:45
Why do you not *u* John 8:43
things hard to *u* 2 Pet 3:16

Unfaithful
u to her husband Num 5:27
u to our God Ezra 10:2

Unfaithfulness *faithless*
u…they committed Lev 26:40
the *u* of the exiles Ezra 9:4

Unfathomable
How…*u* His ways Rom 11:33
u riches of Christ Eph 3:8

Unfruitful *not productive*
the land is *u* 2 Kin 2:19

u deeds of darkness Eph 5:11

Ungodly *sinful, wicked*
Christ died for the *u* Rom 5:6
their own *u* lusts Jude 18

United *joined, union*
become *u* with *Him* Rom 6:5
love, *u* in spirit Phil 2:2

Unity *united, union*
dwell together in *u* Ps 133:1
perfected in *u* John 17:23
all attain to the *u* Eph 4:13
perfect bond of *u* Col 3:14

Unjust *unfair*
For God is not *u* Heb 6:10
the just for *the u* 1 Pet 3:18

Unknown *not known*
To An *U* God Acts 17:23
as *u* yet well-known 2 Cor 6:9

Unleavened *non-fermented*
you shall eat *u* bread Ex 12:15
day of *U* Bread Matt 26:17

Unmarried *single*
I say to the *u* 1 Cor 7:8
let her remain *u* 1 Cor 7:11

Unprincipled *unscrupulous*
conduct of *u* men 2 Pet 2:7
error of *u* men 2 Pet 3:17

Unprofitable *without value*
u and worthless Titus 3:9
grief…*u* for you Heb 13:17

Unpunished *not punished*
shall go *u* Ex 21:19
not let him go *u* 1 Kin 2:9

Unquenchable
burn…with *u* fire Matt 3:12
into the *u* fire Mark 9:43

Unrestrained *uncontrolled*
the people are *u* Prov 29:18
with *u* persecution Is 14:6

Unrighteous *evil, wicked*
u man his thoughts Is 55:7
u shall not inherit 1 Cor 6:9
u under punishment 2 Pet 2:9

Unrighteousness *evil*
not rejoice in *u* 1 Cor 13:6
cleanse us from all *u* 1 John 1:9

Unsearchable *inscrutable*
His greatness is *u* Ps 145:3
u are His judgments Rom 11:33

Unstable *unreliable*
Her ways are *u* Prov 5:6
enticing *u* souls 2 Pet 2:14

Unwilling *reluctant*
u to move the ark 2 Sam 6:10
u to be obedient Acts 7:39

Unworthy *not deserving*
We are *u* slaves Luke 17:10
u of eternal life Acts 13:46

Upright *honest, just*
the death of the *u* Num 23:10
led you in *u* paths Prov 4:11
God made men *u* Eccl 7:29

Urge *entreat*
not *u* me to leave Ruth 1:16
I *u* you therefore Rom 12:1

Use *utilization*
for common *u* Ezek 48:15
for honorable *u* Rom 9:21
not make full *u* of 1 Cor 7:31

Useful *beneficial*
man be *u* to himself Job 22:2
u to me for service 2 Tim 4:11

Useless *worthless*
they have become *u* Rom 3:12
without works is *u* James 2:20

Utter *express*
Let my lips *u* praise Ps 119:171
u words of…truth Acts 26:25

Utterance *expression*
was giving them *u* Acts 2:4
in faith and *u* 2 Cor 8:7

– V –

Vain *empty* or *profane*
name of…God in *v* Ex 20:7
our preaching is *v* 1 Cor 15:14

Valiant *brave, strong*
these…*v* warriors Judge 20:46
be a *v* man for me 1 Sam 18:17
even all the *v* men 1 Chr 28:1
He drags off the *v* Job 24:22

Valley *ravine*
v of the shadow of Ps 23:4
The lily of the *v-s* Song 2:1
the *v* of decision Joel 3:14

Value *worth*
you are of more *v* Matt 10:31
pearl of great *v* Matt 13:46

Vanish *disappear*
When a cloud *v-s* Job 7:9
sky will *v* like smoke Is 51:6
v-ed from…sight Luke 24:31

Vanity *futility, pride*
will reap *v* Prov 22:8
V of *v-ies!* All is *v* Eccl 1:2

Vapor *smoke*
Is a fleeting *v* Prov 21:6
You are *just* a *v* James 4:14

Various *different*
v diseases and pains Matt 4:24
distressed by *v* trials 1 Pet 1:6

Vegetation *plant life*
earth brought forth *v* Gen 1:12
ate up all *v* Ps 105:35
wither all their *v* Is 42:15

Veil *cover, curtain*
v of the sanctuary Lev 4:6

v of the temple	Matt 27:51
enters within the *v*	Heb 6:19

Vengeance *revenge*
not take *v*	Lev 19:18
V is Mine	Deut 32:35
V is Mine, I will	Heb 10:30

Vessel *utensil*
Go, borrow *v-s*	2 Kin 4:3
I am like a broken *v*	Ps 31:12
v-s of wrath	Rom 9:22
treasure in…*v-s*	2 Cor 4:7
be a *v* for honor	2 Tim 2:21
as with a weaker *v*	1 Pet 3:7
v-s of the potter	Rev. 2:27

Victory *triumph*
Lord brought…*v*	2 Sam 23:10
the glory and the *v*	1 Chr 29:11
leads justice to *v*	Matt 12:20
swallowed up in *v*	1 Cor 15:54

Vigor *vitality*
nor his *v* abated	Deut 34:7
his youthful *v*	Job 20:11

Village *small town*
land of unwalled *v-s*	Ezek 38:11
Go into the *v*	Matt 21:2
entered a certain *v*	Luke 10:38

Vindicate *justify*
will *v* His people	Deut 32:36
V the weak	Ps 82:3
wisdom is *v-d* by	Matt 11:19

Vine *stem of plant*
trees said to the *v*	Judg 9:12
every man…his *v*	1 Kin 4:25
like a fruitful *v*	Ps 128:3
the *v-s* in blossom	Song 2:13
mother was like a *v*	Ezek 19:10
Israel is a luxuriant *v*	Hos 10:1
The *v* dries up	Joel 1:12
fruit of the *v*	Matt 26:29
I am the true *v*	John 15:1

Vinegar *sour liquid*
he shall drink no *v*	Num 6:3
bread in the *v*	Ruth 2:14
gave me *v* to drink	Ps 69:21
Like *v* to the teeth	Prov 10:26

Vineyard *grapevines*
shelter in a *v*	Is 1:8
ruined My *v*	Jer 12:10
laborers for his *v*	Matt 20:1
Who plants a *v*	1 Cor 9:7

Violate *assault or break*
shall not *v* his word	Num 30:2
do not *v* me	2 Sam 13:12

Violence *destructive action*
implements of *v*	Gen 49:5
drink the wine of *v*	Prov 4:17
He had done no *v*	Is 53:9

Virgin *unmarried maiden*
very beautiful, a *v*	Gen 24:16
the *v* shall rejoice	Jer 31:13
v shall be with child	Matt 1:23

kept her a *v*	Matt 1:25
if a *v* should marry	1 Cor 7:28

Visible *manifest, seen*
things which are *v*	Heb 11:3

Vision *dream, foresight*
to Abram in a *v*	Gen 15:1
there is no *v*	Prov 29:18
I saw *v-s* of God	Ezek 1:22
young men…see *v-s*	Joel 2:28

Visit *come or go to see*
Thou dost *v* the earth	Ps 65:9
For He has *v-ed* us	Luke 1:68
v orphans…widows	James 1:27

Voice *sound, speech*
have obeyed My *v*	Gen 22:18
listen to His *v*	Deut 4:30
Thou wilt hear my *v*	Ps 5:3
v of the turtledove	Song 2:12
A *v* is calling	Is 40:3
v came from heaven	Dan 4:31
v of one crying in	Luke 3:4
v of the Son of God	John 5:25
v of *the* archangel	1 Thess 4:16
anyone hears My *v*	Rev 3:20

Void *empty, invalid*
was formless and *v*	Gen 1:2
faith is made *v*	Rom 4:14
cross…be made *v*	1 Cor 1:17

Vow *solemn promise*
Jacob made a *v*	Gen 28:20
I shall pay my *v-s*	Ps 22:25
not make false *v-s*	Matt 5:33
he was keeping a *v*	Acts 18:18

– W –

Wage *salary*
w is not reckoned	Rom 4:4
the *w-s* of sin	Rom 6:23
worthy of his *w-s*	1 Tim 5:18

Wail *lament, mourn*
w with a broken spirit	Is 65:14
I must lament and *w*	Mic 1:8
weeping and *w-ing*	Mark 5:38

Wait *expect*
For Thee I *w*	Ps 25:5
who *w* for the Lord	Is 40:31
creation *w-s* eagerly	Rom 8:19

Walk *follow, go along*
w-ing in the garden	Gen 3:8
w in My statutes	Lev 26:3
I will *w* at liberty	Ps 119:45
w in the light	Is 2:5
w and not…weary	Is 40:31
Rise, and *w*	Matt 9:5
w in newness of life	Rom 6:4
we *w* by faith	2 Cor 5:7
w in love	Eph 5:2
w as children of light	Eph 5:8

Wall *structure*
So we built the *w*	Neh 4:6

w-s of Jerusalem	Jer 39:8
built a siege *w*	Jer 52:4
you whitewashed *w*	Acts 23:3

Wander *roam*
w in the wilderness	Num 32:13
people *w* like sheep	Zech 10:2

Wanderer *roamer*
a *w* on the earth	Gen 4:12
an exile and a *w*	Is 49:21

War *battle, conflict*
when they see *w*	Ex 13:17
land…rest from *w*	Josh 11:23
the weapons of *w*	Ps 76:3
A time for *w*	Eccl 3:18
w against the law	Rom 7:23
w in your members	James 4:1
w against the soul	1 Pet 2:11

Warn *give notice*
w the people	Ex 19:21
w-ed…in a dream	Matt 2:12
w you whom to fear	Luke 12:5

Warrior *soldier*
The Lord is a *w*	Ex 15:3
O valiant *w*	Judg 6:12
w from his youth	1 Sam 17:33
w-s will flee naked	Amos 2:16

Wash *bathe, clean*
w in the Jordan	2 Kin 5:10
not *w* their hands	Matt 15:2
w the disciples' feet	John 13:5
w away your sins	Acts 22:16
who *w* their robes	Rev 22:14

Waste (n) *wilderness*
land was laid *w*	Ex 8:24
lay *w* the mountains	Is 42:15
laid *w* like a desert	Jer 9:12

Waste (v) *destroy, use up*
perfume been *w-d*	Mark 14:4

Waste Place *barren*
w-s of the wealthy	Is 5:17
Seek Me in a *w*	Is 45:19
like the ancient *w-s*	Ezek 26:20
w-s will be rebuilt	Ezek 36:10

Watch (n) *guard*
at the morning *w*	Ex 14:24
keep *w* with Me	Matt 26:38
w over their flock	Luke 2:8

Watch (v) *observe*
Lord *w* between you	Gen 31:49
W over your heart	Prov 4:23
w…for the Lord	Mic 7:7

Watchman *one who guards*
w keeps awake in vain	Ps 127:1
w-men for…morning	Ps 130:6
W, how far gone is	Is 21:11
I set *w-men* over you	Jer 6:17
Ephraim was a *w*	Hos 9:8

Water (n) *flood, liquid*
flood of *w* came	Gen 7:6
poured out like *w*	Ps 22:14

beside quiet *w-s*	Ps 23:2	widows could not *w*	Ps 78:64	have his own *w*	1 Cor 7:2
bread on the...*w-s*	Eccl 11:1	*w* day and night	Jer 9:1	husband of one *w*	1 Tim 3:2
come to the *w-s*	Is 55:1	*w-ing* and gnashing	Matt 13:42	*w-ves*, be submissive	1 Pet 3:1
fountain of living *w-s*	Jer 2:13	*w* for youselves	Luke 23:28	**Wilderness** *barren area*	
baptize you with *w*	Matt 3:11	Jesus *wept*	John 11:35	journey into the *w*	Ex 5:3
a cup of cold *w*	Matt 10:42	**Weight** *heaviness*		forty years in the *w*	Deut 29:5
walked on the *w*	Matt 14:29	a full and just *w*	Deut 25:15	roadway in the *w*	Is 43:19
one is born of *w*	John 3:5	eternal *w* of glory	2 Cor 4:17	preaching in the *w*	Matt 3:1
given you living *w*	John 4:10	**Welcome** *gladly receive*		manna in the *w*	John 6:31
of *w* with the word	Eph 5:26	no prophet is *w*	Luke 4:24	**Will** *attitude, purpose*	
by *w* and blood	1 John 5:6	multitude *w-d* Him	Luke 8:40	Thy *w* be done	Matt 6:10
Waves *billows*		who fears Him...*w*	Acts 10:35	the *w* of My Father	Matt 7:21
w of death	2 Sam 22:5	she...*w-d* the spies	Heb 11:31	not My *w*, but	Luke 22:42
Thy *w* have rolled	Ps 42:7	**Well** *water shaft*		who resists His *w*	Rom 9:19
w were breaking	Mark 4:37	sat down by a *w*	Ex 2:15	what the *w* of God	Rom 12:2
Way *manner or path*		*w* of Bethlehem	1 Chr 11:17	knowledge of His *w*	Col 1:9
all His *w-s* are just	Deut 32:4	Jacob's *w* was there	John 4:6	an act of human *w*	2 Pet 1:21
joy of His *w*	Job 8:19	**Well-pleased** *satisfied*		**Win** *succeed*	
Commit your *w* to	Ps 37:5	in whom I am *w*	Matt 3:17	will *w* him over	Matt 28:14
is the *w* of death	Prov 14:12	God was not *w*	1 Cor 10:5	*won* without a word	1 Pet 3:1
w of the wicked	Jer 12:1	**Wheat** *grain*		**Wind**	
Make ready the *w*	Matt 3:3	to sift you like *w*	Luke 22:31	will inherit *w*	Prov 11:29
teach...*w* of God	Mark 12:14	unless a grain of *w*	John 12:24	they sow the *w*	Hos 8:7
I am the *w*	John 14:6	**Whirlwind**		*w* and the sea obey	Mark 4:41
the *w* of salvation	Acts 16:17	take...Elijah by a *w*	2 Kin 2:1	He rebuked the *w*	Luke 8:24
the *w* of escape	1 Cor 10:13	comes on like a *w*	Prov 1:27	every *w* of doctrine	Eph 4:14
new and living *w*	Heb 10:20	chariots like a *w*	Jer 4:13	**Window** *opening*	
Weak *feeble*		they reap the *w*	Hos 8:7	enter through the *w-s*	Joel 2:9
Rescue the *w*	Ps 82:4	**Whisper** *talk quietly*		open...*w-s* of heaven	Mal 3:10
but the flesh is *w*	Matt 26:41	who hate me *w*	Ps 41:7	sitting on the *w* sill	Acts 20:9
Weakness *fault*		*w* a prayer	Is 26:16	basket through a *w*	2 Cor 11:33
Spirit...helps our *w*	Rom 8:26	your speech shall *w*	Is 29:4	**Wine** *strong drink*	
w of God is stronger	1 Cor 1:25	**Whitewashed** *wall covering*		Do not drink *w*	Lev 10:9
it is sown in *w*	1 Cor 15:43	like *w* tombs	Matt 23:27	*W* is a mocker	Prov 20:1
Wealth *riches*		you *w* wall	Acts 23:3	new *w* into old	Matt 9:17
a man of great *w*	Ruth 2:1	**Whole** *entire*		gave Him *w* to	Matt 27:34
who trust in their *w*	Ps 49:6	water the *w* surface	Gen 2:6	full of sweet *w*	Acts 2:13
a *w* of salvation	Is 33:6	leavens the *w* lump	1 Cor 5:6	not addicted to *w*	1 Tim 3:3
the *w* of all nations	Hag 2:7	keeps the *w* law	James 2:10	**Wings**	
rich by her *w*	Rev 18:19	**Wicked** *evil, ungodly*		He spread His *w*	Deut 32:11
Weapon *armament*		condemn the *w*	Deut 25:1	*with w* like eagles	Is 40:31
girded on his *w-s*	Deut 1:41	counsel of the *w*	Ps 1:1	healing in its *w*	Mal 4:2
flee from the iron *w*	Job 20:24	devises *w* plans	Prov 6:18	**Wipe** *pass over, rub*	
turn back the *w-s*	Jer 21:4	no peace for the *w*	Is 48:22	GOD will *w* tears	Is 25:8
w-s of righteousness	2 Cor 6:7	**Wickedness** *evil*		*w-d* His feet	John 11:2
Weary *tired*		if I regard *w*	Ps 66:18	*w* away every tear	Rev 21:4
the *w* are at rest	Job 3:17	inclines toward *w*	Is 32:6	**Wisdom** *discernment*	
and not become *w*	Is 40:31	*w* of My people	Jer 7:12	the spirit of *w*	Ex 28:3
all who are *w*	Matt 11:28	repent of this *w*	Acts 8:22	the beginning of *w*	Ps 111:10
Weave *interlace*		**Widow** *husband dead*		Fools despise *w*	Prov 1:7
Thou didst *w* me	Ps 139:13	not afflict any *w*	Ex 22:22	any of you lacks *w*	James 1:5
w the spider's web	Is 59:5	Plead for the *w*	Is 1:17	**Wise** *judicious, prudent*	
after *w-ing* a crown	Matt 27:29	*w* put in more	Mark 12:43	making *w* the simple	Ps 19:7
Wedding *marriage*		visit orphans...*w-s*	James 1:27	the words of the *w*	Prov 22:17
had no *w* songs	Ps 78:63	**Wife** *married woman*		He is not a *w* son	Hos 13:13
come to the *w* feast	Matt 22:4	cleave to his *w*	Gen 2:24	**Wither** *dry up*	
Week *period of time*		shall not covet...*w*	Ex 20:17	its leaf does not *w*	Ps 1:3
first *day* of the *w*	Matt 28:1	*w* of your youth	Prov 5:18	*w*...like the grass	Ps 37:2
I fast twice a *w*	Luke 18:12	An excellent *w*	Prov 31:10	earth mourns *and w-s*	Is 24:4
Weep *cry, sorrow*		who divorces his *w*	Matt 5:32	the leaf shall *w*	Jer 8:13
My eye *w-s* to God	Job 16:20			with a *w-ed* hand	Mark 3:1

the fig tree *w-ed*   Mark 11:20

Witness (n) *testimony*
my *w* is in heaven   Job 16:19
a *w* to the LORD   Is 19:20
w to all the nations   Matt 24:14
He came for a *w*   John 1:7
My *w* is true   John 8:14
For God is my *w*   Phil 1:8
Christ, the faithful *w*   Rev 1:5

Witness (v) *testify*
not bear false *w*   Ex 20:16
John bore *w*   John 1:32
bear *w* of Me   John 15:26
Spirit...bears *w*   Rom 8:16

Wolf *animal*
w will dwell with   Is 11:6
the midst of *w-ves*   Matt 10:16
w snatches them   John 10:12

Woman *female, lady*
she shall be called *W*   Gen 2:23
a *w* of excellence   Ruth 3:11
Man...born of *w*   Job 14:1
gracious *w* attains   Prov 11:16
a contentious *w*   Prov 25:24
like a *w* in labor   Is 42:14
w-en...grinding   Matt 24:41
not to touch a *w*   1 Cor 7:1
w is the glory of   1 Cor 11:7
w to speak in   1 Cor 14:35
His Son, born of a *w*   Gal 4:4
w clothed with...sun   Rev 12:1

Womb
nations...in your *w*   Gen 25:28
LORD...closed her *w*   1 Sam 1:5
from *w* to tomb   Job 10:19
baby leaped in...*w*   Luke 1:41

Wonder *marvel, sign*
consider the *w-s* of   Job 37:14
tell of all Thy *w-s*   Ps 9:1
His *w-s* in the deep   Ps 107:24
w-s in the sky   Joel 2:30
were filled with *w*   Acts 3:10

Wonderful *marvelous*
His *w* deeds   1 Chr 16:12
name will be called *W*   Is 9:6

Wood *cut tree*
ark of gopher *w*   Gen 6:14
other gods, *w* and   Deut 28:36
children gather *w*   Jer 7:18
stones, *w*, hay   1 Cor 3:12

Wool *cloth or hair*
of *w* and linen   Deut 22:11
put a fleece of *w* on   Judg 6:37
They will be like *w*   Is 1:18
hair...like pure *w*   Dan 7:9
white like white *w*   Rev 1:14

Word *message, speech*
to the *w* of Moses   Lev 10:7
declare to you the *w*   Deut 5:5
Joshua wrote...*w-s*   Josh 24:26
proclaim the *w* of   1 Sam 9:27

Thy *w*...confirmed   2 Chr 6:17
w-s of my mouth   Ps 19:14
Thy *w* is a lamp   Ps 119:105
harsh *w* stirs up   Prov 15:1
w of God is tested   Prov 30:5
despised the *w*   Is 5:24
w-s of a sealed book   Is 29:11
speak My *w* in truth   Jer 23:28
conceal these *w-s*   Dan 12:4
these *w-s* of Mine   Matt 7:24
sower sows the *w*   Mark 4:14
the *W* was God   John 1:1
the *W* became flesh   John 1:14
w-s of eternal life   John 6:68
abide in My *w*   John 8:31
glorifying the *w*   Acts 13:48
too deep for *w-s*   Rom 8:26
hearing by the *w*   Rom 10:17
the *w* of the cross   1 Cor 1:18
fulfilled in one *w*   Gal 5:14
no unwholesome *w*   Eph 4:29
sanctified by...*w*   1 Tim 4:5
the *w* of truth   2 Tim 2:15
the faithful *w*   Titus 1:9
w of God is living   Heb 4:12
doers of the *w*   James 1:22
pure milk of the *w*   1 Pet 2:2
the *W* of Life   1 John 1:1
The *W* of God   Rev 19:13

Work (n) *act, deed, labor*
God completed His *w*   Gen 2:2
You shall *w* six days   Ez 34:21
His *w* is perfect   Deut 32:4
the *w* of His hands   Ps 19:1
see the *w-s* of God   Ps 66:5
let Him hasten His *w*   Is 5:19
see your good *w-s*   Matt 5:16
the *w-s* of Christ   Matt 11:2
the *w* of the Law   Rom 2:15
faith apart from *w-s*   Rom 3:28
not...a result of *w-s*   Eph 2:9
for the *w* of service   Eph 4:12
began a good *w*   Phil 1:6
fruit in good *w*   Col 1:10
rich in good *w-s*   1 Tim 6:18
faith without *w-s*   James 2:20

Work (v) *perform, produce*
those who *w* iniquity   Ps 28:3
w together for good   Rom 8:28
So death *w-s* in us   2 Cor 4:12
w out your salvation   Phil 2:12

Worker *laborer*
O *w* of deceit   Ps 52:2
w-s of iniquity   Prov 10:29
w is worthy of his   Matt 10:10
God's fellow *w-s*   1 Cor 3:9
beware...evil *w-s*   Phil 3:2
pure, *w-s* at home   Titus 2:5

Workman *craftsman*
a skillful *w*   Ex 38:23
approved...as a *w*   2 Tim 2:15

World *earth, humanity*
He will judge the *w*   Ps 9:8
the light of the *w*   Matt 5:14
the field is the *w*   Matt 13:38
Go into all the *w*   Mark 16:15
gains the whole *w*   Luke 9:25
God so loved the *w*   John 3:16
Savior of the *w*   John 4:42
the light of the *w*   John 8:12
overcome the *w*   John 16:33
sin entered...the *w*   Rom 5:12
reconciling the *w*   2 Cor 5:19
Do not love the *w*   1 John 2:15

Worldly *earthly*
w fables fit only   1 Tim 4:7
avoid *w*...chatter   2 Tim 2:16

Worm *creeping animal*
But I am a *w*   Ps 22:6
w-s are your covering   Is 14:11
God appointed a *w*   Jon 4:7
their *w* does not die   Mark 9:48
he was eaten by *w-s*   Acts 12:23

Worship *bow, revere*
you shall *w* Him   Deut 6:13
W the LORD   Ps 2:11
in vain do they *w*   Matt 15:9
w in spirit and truth   John 4:24
w in the Spirit   Phil 3:3

Worthless *useless*
all *w* physicians   Job 13:4
your *w* offerings   Is 1:13
your faith is *w*   1 Cor 15:17
man's religion is *w*   James 1:26

Worthy *having merit*
sin *w* of death   Deut 21:22
is not *w* of Me   Matt 10:37
is *w* of his wages   Luke 10:7
w of the gospel   Phil 1:27
W is the Lamb   Rev 5:12

wound *injury*
My *w* is incurable   Job 34:6
binds up their *w-s*   Ps 147:3
fatal *w* was healed   Rev 13:3

Wrath *anger, indignation*
and in great *w*   Deut 29:28
Pour out Thy *w*   Ps 79:6
turn away *w*   Prov 15:1
from the *w* to come   Matt 3:7
w of God abides   John 3:36
children of *w*   Eph 2:3
the *w* of the Lamb   Rev 6:16

Wretched *miserable*
in to this *w* place   Num 20:5
W man that I am   Rom 7:24

Write *enscribe*
W them on a tablet   Prov 3:3
w a certificate   Mark 10:4
with His finger *wrote*   John 8:6
W in a book   Rev 1:11

Written *enscribed*
w in the law   2 Chr 23:18
w by the prophet   Matt 2:5
about whom it is *w*   Matt 11:10
w in the Lamb's   Rev 21:27

Wrong *do evil, harm*
not *w* one another   Lev 25:14
Love does no *w*   Rom 13:10

Wrought *accomplished*
He *w* wonders   Ps 78:12
been *w* in God   John 3:21

– Y –

Year *period, time*
atonement…every *y* Lev 16:34
favorable *y* of the Lord Is 61:2
y of the Lord   Luke 4:19
sacrifices *y* by *y*   Heb 10:1
y-s as one day   2 Pet 3:8

Yearns *deeply moved*
my flesh *y* for Thee   Ps 63:1
My heart *y* for him   Jer 31:20

Yesterday *past*
thousand years…*y*   Ps 90:4
same *y* and today   Heb 13:8

Yield *produce*
y-ed up *His* spirit   Matt 27:50
not *y* in subjection   Gal 2:5

Yoke *wooden bar*
break his *y* from   Gen 27:40
iron *y* on…neck   Deut 28:48
made our *y* hard   1 Kin 12:4
the *y* of their burden   Is 9:4
Take My *y* upon   Matt 11:29
to a *y* of slavery   Gal 5:1

Young *early age, youth*
he sent *y* men   Ex 24:5
glory of *y* men is   Prov 20:29

like a *y* lion   Hos 5:14
y men…visions   Acts 2:17

Youth *young*
evil from his *y*   Gen 8:21
the sins of my *y*   Ps 25:7
your *y* is renewed   Ps 103:5
the wife of your *y*   Prov 5:18
life from my *y* up   Acts 26:4

– Z –

Zeal *fervor, passion*
my *z* for the Lord   2 Kin 10:16
z has consumed me Ps 119:139
have a *z* for God   Rom 10:2

Zealous *fervent*
z for the Lord   1 Kin 19:10
z for good deeds   Titus 2:14
be *z*…and repent   Rev 3:19

Bible Content Helps

Bible Content Helps

Summaries of Bible Books

Memorize and review the names of the books of the Bible in order. Ask a friend to test you on what you've memorized. Then you'll be able to find any book of the Bible that you want to find in a matter of seconds. Next, you will want to study the following summaries of the contents and teachings of each of the Bible books. You may also want to memorize these summaries so that you may have an understanding of the basic contents and teachings of the Bible. Then, as you study a particular Bible passage, you will be able to place it in its larger context and make it a part of the teaching of the entire book.

Old Testament

GENESIS Genesis means birth or beginning. The book of Genesis begins with God's creation of the world and of the human creature in His own image. It shows how humans chose to follow their selfish desires rather than to follow God's leadership and directions. As a result, God punished them by sending the flood, but He also gave them the grace of saving Noah and his family and making a covenant of promise with Noah. After the tower of Babel showed the continued disobedience of the human creatures, God scattered them over the face of the earth. But God did not give up. He called Abraham to be the patriarch or father of a new nation in a new land promised by God. God honored Abraham's faith and made a covenant with him to bless him and give him the land. Abraham was called to be a blessing to the nations. Isaac, his son, and Jacob, his grandson, carried on the covenant tradition. Finally, Joseph was set out for dead by his eleven brothers, but he escaped into Egypt. There through God's leadership he came into a position of leadership in the Egyptian government and saved the nation and his own family from famine and starvation.

EXODUS Exodus means the going out. This refers to the children of Israel going out from Egypt under the leadership of Moses to escape the persecution of the Egyptian pharaoh. Israel followed God's instructions in celebrating the first Passover festival just before God led them across the Red Sea and drowned pharaoh's army in the waters of the Red Sea. Then God led them through the wilderness, where the children of Israel murmured against Moses and against God. God led them to Mount Sinai and gave them the Ten Commandments and the rest of the Law. Here Israel turned to worship the golden calf. Moses in his anger threw down the law tablets and had to go back up the mountain and receive them again. Israel then carried out God's directions to build a tabernacle in which to worship.

LEVITICUS Leviticus and Levite are derived from Levi the name of one of the twelve sons of Jacob. The tribe of Levi became the priestly tribe which had charge of the rites and ceremonies in the worship sacrifices. The Levites also were teachers, teaching the Law of Moses to Israel. The book of Leviticus gives directions to the priests on how to carry out each of the rituals and also calls upon God's people to be a holy people as God is holy.

NUMBERS The book of Numbers records two numberings or censuses of the children of Israel. It describes the sending out of the spies and the refusal of the children of Israel to enter the Promised Land under God's leadership because they feared the giants in the land. As a result, they wandered forty years in the terrible wilderness. Numbers shows both how Israel murmured and disobeyed God and how they were able to conquer the territory east of the Jordan river. Here Moses and Aaron both disobeyed God and were denied the right to enter the Promised Land.

DEUTERONOMY Deuteronomy means second law. Moses repeated and expanded the laws he had given the children of Israel to remind them of the way God wanted them to live in the Promised Land. He told them they must serve one God at the one place He would choose in the one land He had given them with the one book of the law that was being given to them. Moses warned them of the curses that would come upon them should they refuse to follow the law and gave them the blessings they would receive when they followed God's law. He made a final blessing upon the tribes of Israel and then installed Joshua as his successor. The final chapter records Moses' death.

JOSHUA The book of Joshua is named after one of the two spies who encouraged Israel to enter the Promised Land before they refused to do so. Joshua was the successor of Moses and led the Israelites across the Jordan to conquer the land. He divided the land by lot among the tribes of Israel and then instructed the children of Israel on God's expectations of His people living in the land. In the final chapter we read of the covenant Joshua renewed between Israel and God. Then we read of Joshua's death.

JUDGES Judges describes the history of Israel from the death of Joshua to the time of Samuel. Israel repeatedly disobeyed God who gave them over to foreign nations to discipline them. When Israel cried for help, God sent judges or deliverers who saved them from the foreign nations and led them back to serve God. Thus Judges shows us the importance of proper leadership for God's people.

RUTH The book of Ruth is a love story set in the time of the judges. It gives a remarkable picture of the life and customs of that early day. It shows how a foreign woman became a heroine in Israel by showing devotion to her bereaved mother-in-law. Ruth was rewarded by marriage to Boaz, and they became the great-grandparents of David. Thus the foreign woman, Ruth, became an ancestress of Jesus Christ.

1-2 SAMUEL 1-2 Samuel form one book in the Hebrew Bible. The book relates the closing days of the judges when God ruled as king over Israel. It also shows Samuel's anointing of first Saul and then David to be the king over God's people.

This came about because Israel rejected God as their king and desired a king like the other nations. Saul was a man of goodly appearance and a skillful warrior but was not a man after God's own heart. David was anointed as Saul's successor. The book of 1 Samuel shows much of the conflict between Saul and David, whereas the book of 2 Samuel shows how David gained the territory of the Promised Land for Israel but had rebellion and heartache from his own sons.

1-2 KINGS These two books are one in the Hebrew Bible. They show how Solomon succeeded his father David as king and gained wisdom and wealth. They also show Solomon's sins in bringing foreign wives with their foreign religions into the kingdom. Eventually this led to the split of the kingdom under his son Rehoboam. The family of David ruled only Judah, whereas Jeroboam took the northern tribes to form the kingdom of Israel. The book of Kings shows how prophets tried to lead the kings to follow God, but the kings tried to make "wise political decisions" and began accepting foreign worship. Elijah and Elisha play a prominent role in the book. Finally in 722 BC, God let Asyria conquer the northern kingdom and carry it away captive. Then in 587, God let the Babylonians destroy Jerusalem and carry the southern kingdom captive. This was all because Israel refused to listen to her prophets or to God's law.

1-2 CHRONICLES 1-2 Chronicles form the last book of the Hebrew Bible. They use the books of Kings as source material to describe the great worship activities of David in his kingship. They show how the prophets and the Levites tried to give leadership to the southern Kingdom. Chronicles basically ignores the northern kingdom except wherein it related to the history of Judah. The worship at the Temple plays a central role in the book of Chronicles which ends with Israel in Captivity in Babylon in 538 BC receiving word that Cyrus, king of Persia, has allowed them to return to the land of Judah and rebuild the Temple there.

EZRA Ezra continues the story of Chronicles and shows how Israel overcame opposition to rebuild the Temple, which was rededicated in 515 B.C. Over fifty years later Ezra led others back to Jerusalem from Babylon and read to them the Law of Moses. He showed them how to reform their social life to conform with God's law.

NEHEMIAH Nehemiah was a contemporary of Ezra and led the children of Israel to rebuild the walls defending the city of Jerusalem. A great political leader, Nehemiah was also a great man of prayer. He and Ezra led Israel to renew the covenant with God.

ESTHER Esther records how God used a dedicated woman to deliver the Jews from Persian treachery. Modern Jews read the book in their synagogues at the feast of Purim in commemoration of this deliverance. The book furnishes a good example of the providence of God—that is, God seeing what is going to take place and arranging matters for his people so that his children are taken care of or saved from harm.

JOB Job lived in the period of the patriarchs and was a righteous man who pleased God. Then Satan challenged God and claimed Job was righteous only because of what he received. God allowed Satan to take away Job's family and his wealth. Job himself was plunged into great physical suffering. Still he did not lose his faith and trust in God. The major portion of the book of Job reports a dialogue between Job and each of three friends who try to get him to admit his sin and repent. Job continues to seek an audience with God so that an umpire or judge can decide the case between him and God. After a fourth friend added his wisdom, God appeared to Job and taught him that his greatest need was trust in God not the assurance of justice in this life or vendication before some heavenly court.

PSALMS The book of Psalms was the hymnbook of the Hebrew people. The book is composed of 150 different songs used in the worship and teaching of Israel. The Psalms are of different types. Some praise God. Others express thanksgiving, confession, or lamentation and complaint about the present condition of life. Several are wisdom psalms teaching truths learned from life. From the book of Psalms we learn how to praise God and how to pray to him in the various situations of life.

PROVERBS A proverb is a short sentence conveying a moral truth in a concise and pointed form. Israel shared the method of teaching in proverbs with her neighbors in the Near East. Most of the proverbs are ascribed to king Solomon, and the essential message is that wisdom begins with the fear of God. Here we see the practical everyday philosophy of life taught by the Hebrew scholars and men of God.

ECCLESIASTES Ecclesiastes means "preacher or speaker." The book preserves an old man's teaching about the emptiness of life based simply on earthly existence. The word "vanity" occurs many times as a refrain in the book. It describes all earthly treasures and activities as transitory, passing away quickly and not bringing lasting value or meaning. The last chapter is very frequently quoted. Symbolic references to parts of the human body describe the human decline in old age. Ecclesiastes thus forms a check on people who are too optimistic about life and prepares the way for the Christian hope in the resurrection as giving eternal meaning to human life.

SONG OF SOLOMON This book is also known as the Song of Songs or the Canticles. It is a collection of love poetry showing the wonder of a deep, pure love between man and woman. It describes the beauty and sacredness of such devotion and love.

ISAIAH Isaiah is the first of the prophetic books. It was written in a time when prosperity was vanishing. During Isaiah's ministry Israel, the northern kingdom, was taken into captivity. The people were irreligious, corrupt, and debased. The prophet predicted the captivity of both Israel and Judah. He also prophesied God's deliverance from captivity and the coming of a Messianic king to lead God's people. In chapters 9, 11, and 53 will be found wonderful descriptions of the Messiah and his kingdom. These were fulfilled in the life, death, and resurrection of Jesus Christ. The book of Isaiah is more widely quoted in the New Testament than any other Old Testament book.

Basically, the book describes three major time periods in the history of God's people. Chapters 1-39 describe Judah in the time between 740 and 700 BC. Chapters 40-55 describe the plight of the Jewish exiles and their hope for the return and leadership by the Suffering Servant. Chapters 56-66 describe the period of the rebuilding of the second Temple. God had prophetic words for his people during each of these crisis situations.

JEREMIAH Jeremiah lived in a sad period in the history of the Hebrews. In his day, the people of the southern kingdom, or Judah, were car-

ried by Nebuchadnezzar into captivity in Babylon, though Jeremiah himself escaped into Egypt. Jeremiah wrote with authority not only of the certainty of the judgment of God upon a sinful people but also of the greatness of His love. The personal laments of Jeremiah show how a prophet argued with God about the task God had given him. Chapter 31 points to God's new covenant to be made with his people. This new covenant was fulfilled in the work of Jesus.

LAMENTATIONS Lamentations represents a series of poems expressing the grief of the people of Jerusalem at the destruction of their city in 587 BC. The book has been called "the funeral dirge over Jerusalem."

EZEKIEL Ezekiel was a priest carried captive by the Babylonians in 597 BC. He used exotic visions and symbolic acts to describe God's justice in destroying His city and to describe the hope of the resurrection of the dead nation. Ezekiel emphasized the individual responsibility of the sinner before God. He gave a hope of return to Jerusalem and specific instructions for rebuilding the city of Jerusalem around a new Temple.

DANIEL Daniel is the Old Testament representative of apocalyptic literature. This literature is written in symbolic language to encourage and comfort a people suffering extreme persecution. The first six chapters of Daniel are stories about Daniel and his three young friends in Babylonian captivity. They show how even persons in such dire circumstances can stand up and give testimony for God. The apocalyptic visions in chapters 7-12 describe the downfall of the great kingdoms of the world and God's victory over these kingdoms. These chapters are difficult to interpret and have led to several different interpretations by students of the Bible.

HOSEA Hosea preached to the northern kingdom of Israel in the middle of the eighth century BC. The first three chapters give an account of his troubles with his unfaithful wife, Gomer. They are intended to picture Israel's sins and God's unfailing love for even the sinful people. The remainder of the book contains pronouncements of judgment upon the people for their idolatry and sins, balanced with pictures of God's unceasing love which cannot give up on His beloved people.

JOEL The book of Joel describes a great calamity caused by an army of locusts. Joel said this was God's judgment upon the nation calling the people to repent and obey their God. In the second part of the book God responds to the people's prayers, promising judgment upon the wicked nations and deliverance for the faithful people. Joel 2:28 describes the coming of the Spirit of God and is used in the New Testament to interpret the day of Pentecost (see Acts 2:16-17).

AMOS Amos is the earliest of the prophets whose sermons were preserved in prophetic books. The author was a southerner who preached in the northern kingdom about 760 BC. The author prophesied that God loves mercy and not mere formal sacrifices. He taught that Israel's future greatness was not to be secured through power and wealth, but through justice and judgment.

OBADIAH Obadiah lived in Jerusalem about 586 BC. He was God's messenger announcing doom on the Edomites, the descendants of Esau, who had gloried over Judah's downfall. He prophesied a future when God's kingdom would again rule over all the lands formerly under David's control. His book shows us how God deals with those people who persecute His people.

JONAH The book of Jonah is unique among the prophetic books. It does not contain sermons of a great prophet. Instead, it tells a story about a disobedient prophet. Jonah is an example of how blind nationalism can blind God's people to His universal purpose. It is the great missionary book of the Old Testament.

MICAH Micah lived about the same time as Isaiah in the last half of the eighth century BC. Like Isaiah he preached against the sins of his time and especially against oppression of the poor by the rich. He prophesied the destruction of both Israel and Judah just before judgment fell on Israel. He pointed to the birth of the Messiah in Bethlehem (5:2) and to a future kingdom of peace (4:1-5).

NAHUM The book prophesies the destruction of Nineveh and is in two major divisions. The first section presents God the jealous judge, while the second shows God's judgment upon the wicked capital city of Assyria. The book has sometimes been called a hymn of hate against God's enemies.

HABAKKUK Habakkuk prophesied in Judah during the reign of Jehoiakim (609-598 BC). Habakkuk wrote of the wickedness of Judah and of its impending overthrow by the Babylonians. He described the sinfulness of the Babylonian conquerors and prophesied their ultimate downfall. The book shows the prophet's struggle with the question, "Why do the wicked prosper?" He waited until God showed him that the righteous shall live by his faith (2:4).

ZEPHANIAH Zephaniah lived in the time of Jeremiah and Habakkuk just before the fall of Judah and its capital, Jerusalem. Zephaniah prophesied against the sins of the people of his time. He promised judgment upon Judah and the surrounding nations, but he also promised blessings for a restored Jerusalem. Zephaniah looked forward to the day when a righteous remnant would be blessed by God in the promised land.

HAGGAI The book of Haggai contains four prophesies, all dealing with the rebuilding of the Temple under Zerubbabel. God raised up Haggai along with His younger compatriot, Zechariah, to stir up the people to rebuild His house. Haggai saw an important role to be played by Zerubbabel, the governor, and Joshua, the high priest.

ZECHARIAH The book of Zechariah has two major parts. Chapters 1-8 are in the form of night visions dealing with the restoration of the Temple and the work of Zerubbabel, the governor, and Joshua, the high priest. Chapters 9-14 point to the time of the Messiah when the Prince of Peace, the shepherd of God's people, will gather the scattered Israelites and again show that He and He alone controls history. Thus the book points to the final victory of God and His people over the evil powers of this world.

MALACHI Malachi lived about 450 BC, after the Temple had been rebuilt and worship restored. He found the people to be sliding back into their old habits, seeking personal wealth and prestige rather than trying to please God. He rebuked them for their spiritual condition and called them to bring their tithes and offerings into God's storehouse. He talked of the day when God would send Elijah the prophet to institute His great day of judgment and of victory. The New Testament sees John the Baptist fulfilling this promise.

New Testament

MATTHEW A disciple of Jesus wrote the first Gospel. It is written for Jews and is divided into five sections of teachings of Christ followed by His works. It is sometimes called The gospel of the Kingdom. It begins with the genealogy of Jesus the son of David and quotes frequently from Old Testament Scripture showing Jesus is the promised Messiah. Apparently Matthew used Mark's Gospel in composing his own. He concluded his Gospel with the Great Commission of Christ for his disciples to go into all the world and preach the gospel to all the nations.

MARK Mark's Gospel is considered by most Bible students to be the first gospel to be written. It was probably written to the church in Rome. Mark appears to have been a young disciple and friend of the apostle Peter from whom he got much of his information. Mark showed how the great miraculous works of Christ prove him to be the Son of God. Mark concentrated mainly on Christ's work, giving only a few of His teachings.

LUKE The Gospel of Luke used Mark, as well as other sources, to describe the meaning of Christ's ministry for Gentiles. Luke wrote both the Gospel and the book of Acts to show how the Christian message became a message for all peoples throughout the world of his day. The church led by God's Spirit was the only true continuation and fulfillment of God's work and purpose for Israel. Luke emphasized especially Jesus' kindness in helping outcasts who were not ordinarily accepted in the Jewish religion.

JOHN John, the youngest of the twelve apostles, wrote his Gospel sometime after the others had been written. John used very simple language to deal with the deepest questions of life. He portrayed Jesus as the only begotten Son of God. He emphasized Christ's unity with the Father and His desire for unity among His own disciples and followers. He showed how God loved the world and gave Himself for the sins of the world.

ACTS Luke wrote Acts as a continuation of his Gospel to show how the Great Commission of Christ was carried out in the early church. The record covers the first thirty years of history of the Christian church. It includes an account of the organization and early history of the church. It shows how at Pentecost God empowered the church with the Holy Spirit. It traces the spread of the gospel from Jerusalem through Judea into Samaria and unto the uttermost parts of the world. It shows how Paul and Barnabas began the missionary activities of the church. It concludes with Paul in Rome preaching the gospel without hindrance. The book shows the church that Christ continues his work through the believers under the direction of the Holy Spirit.

ROMANS Paul had founded the churches in Asia Minor and in Greece and was looking forward to going to Rome to preach the gospel there. First, he was assembling a collection of gifts to help the poverty-stricken church in Jerusalem. He was in Corinth in about AD 58 waiting to go to Jerusalem and then to Rome, when he wrote the book of Romans. The book serves as his introduction of his own message to the church at Rome. The book of Romans is considered by many to be Paul's most important theological work. Its major theme is to show that *all* persons, Jew or Gentile, are justified in Christ through faith and not through works. It seems a controversy had arisen between the Jewish and Gentile Christians as to

whether the Jews were to have preeminence over Gentiles in the church. Paul showed that "all have sinned" so that none could have preference in God's eyes over any other people. God loves people of all origins and calls people everywhere to salvation through Jesus Christ. From the twelfth chapter onwards, Paul makes a stirring call to the believers to present themselves as living sacrifices for Christ.

1 CORINTHIANS The first epistle to the Corinthians was written from Ephesus about a year after Paul established the church at Corinth or about 55 AD. Corinth was a cosmopolitan city in an age when moral restraints sat very lightly on people. Naturally, the church had difficulty in becoming established and keeping itself pure amid such surroundings. Paul's purpose in writing the letter appears to have been two-fold: to direct the church away from the error and disorder that had evidenced itself and to answer specific questions submitted to him by members of the church. The Greeks had had much difficulty with Paul's doctrine of resurrection, so Paul wrote about it in chapter 15. In chapter 13, Paul showed that love is the supreme virtue in all of life and called on the Corinthians to exercise love rather than bickering and disputes.

2 CORINTHIANS The second letter to the Corinthians was written a few months after the first to which it is a sequel. From Titus, Paul had learned that his first letter had borne fruit. Many of the church people at Corinth had repented. He also learned that Judaizers had come preaching a false gospel denouncing Paul's authority. Thus the second letter to Corinth was written to express pleasure at the reported repentance and to warn against false teachers. In it Paul showed his own authority as an apostle of Jesus Christ.

GALATIANS The apostle Paul visited Galatia on his first missionary journey and established a church there. Some years later word came to him that Judaizers had infiltrated the Galatian church. The people had been led away from true Christianity by accepting Jewish rites and ceremonies as a substitute for the religion Paul had taught them. Paul recognized the situation as a crisis in the Galatian church and wrote accordingly. His emphasis was upon the fundamental Christian doctrine of justification by faith. Galatians is a good place to begin learning how Paul dealt with crisis situations in the churches and what Paul taught as the heart of the Christian gospel.

EPHESIANS Some people have called this the crown of Paul's writings. It is Paul's discussion of the nature and meaning of the church. He centered on Christ and the church as the united body of Christ. He showed that in Jesus Christ we understand the mystery of existence through all the ages. The epistle was apparently written while Paul was in Rome about AD 62 or 63.

PHILIPPIANS The church at Philippi was the first church to be organized in Europe (see Acts 16:8-40). Paul was in prison, probably in Rome, when he wrote this letter of joy. The epistle deals with personal conduct much more than with theology. Its major theme is that of the joy we have in Christ. The second chapter of Philippians is one of the great writings about the work of Jesus Christ humbling himself to die for us.

COLOSSIANS Colosse was a small town near Ephesus in Asia Minor. Here, too, false teachers had come into the church and tried to show a superior knowledge to the people. They had defined certain practices and rituals which

they thought the Christians needed to practice to be saved. Paul wrote this letter also from prison about the same time he wrote Ephesians. The two letters have many similarities. Paul tried to show the meaning of Jesus Christ in the history of the cosmos. He showed that Christ is above all and that real joy is gained only by living the Christian life. Again Paul underlined the central importance of Christian love.

1 THESSALONIANS The letter to the church at Thessalonica, established on Paul's second missionary journey, was the first of Paul's letters. He wrote it about AD 51. Paul wrote to a church under persecution from the Jews and tried to give them assurance of the hope they had in Jesus Christ. Thus, he dealt with the second coming of Christ. Paul also had to deal with attacks made against his own ministry and to defend himself as a rightful teacher sent by God.

2 THESSALONIANS This letter was sent from Corinth a few months after the writing of 1 Thessalonians. Misunderstandings in reference to the first letter and the teaching on the second coming made it necessary for Paul to write this second letter to the Thessalonians. Paul warned the church not to be idle while they waited for the second coming but to work like he was working.

1-2 TIMOTHY These letters were written to the young pastor Timothy to give him guidance in dealing with the church. Timothy, the son of a Greek father and Jewish mother, had been converted under Paul's ministry and subsequently became a missionary companion of the great apostle. He was pastor of the church at Ephesus. Paul wrote as a spiritual father to the young pastor, instructing him in matters of doctrine and life. He particularly showed him the need for leadership in the church and for proper worship. He showed how the church was to deal with those in need. He warned against false teachers particularly those who tried to make a profit for themselves out of their religion.

TITUS The epistle to Titus like those to Timothy was a pastoral epistle written for a young pastor. Titus was a Gentile. He had become pastor of the church at Crete, where he faced a difficult situation. The church had been in a state of disorder. Heresy or false teaching was evident in the church. Paul wrote to encourage and counsel Titus. The letter to Titus deals with the officials or officers of the church, with how a pastor deals with various age groups in the church, and with the ethical expectations God has of the people He has saved by grace.

PHILEMON This is the shortest of Paul's letters and is very private in nature. Onesimus, a slave, had belonged to Philemon, a rich member of the church at Colosse. Onesimus had stolen money from his master and run away to Rome. There he had been converted under the ministry of Paul. Paul asked that Philemon forgive the crime and receive Onesimus back as a brother in Christ. Thus Paul showed in a specific example how reconciliation should take place between Christians.

HEBREWS This letter was written to a group of Jewish Christians probably about 64 AD. The Jewish Christians were being persecuted, and many were considering going back to Judaism and forsaking Christianity. To point out the superiority of the Christian religion and to encourage the Christians to remain faithful, the writer wrote this letter. He emphatically pointed out that Christ is greater than the prophets, angels, and all human leaders. God had spoken through each of these, but now he spoke through Jesus Christ, his Son. Jesus fulfilled all of the offices and sacrificial rites of the Jewish religion. Chapter 11 is one of the great chapters of the Bible, listing the heroes of faith.

JAMES James is the first of the so-called catholic or general epistles. This means that the letter was written to the Christians in general rather than to a particular church or individual. The letter is concerned with very practical, everyday Christian life. Morals and ethics are the center of its purpose. It shows that faith must express itself in ethical living. The writer of the letter is usually considered to be James, the half brother of Jesus.

1 PETER 1 Peter was sent to Christians in Asia Minor. It is an exhortation to them to stand fast under the persecutions they were suffering. The writer is the apostle Peter, who probably wrote around 64 AD. He called upon his readers to rejoice in Christ and be faithful to him even in the midst of persecution.

2 PETER Peter's second letter was written to encourage Christians in the face of false teachers. Peter showed that Christ is truly the fulfillment of the Old Testament prophecies and that he will come again. Christians must be patient and faithful while waiting for the second coming. They must be assured that false teachers will be judged. They will face punishment for their greed, immorality, and false doctrine.

1 JOHN 1 John is a warm and affectionate writing concerning the love of God and the response of brotherly love which God expects. The letter seeks to deepen the spiritual life of its audience and to correct various teachings of false teachers. It assures Christians that they can see in the love in their life the assurance of God's working in their lives.

2 JOHN

This brief letter is a companion to 1 John written to one specific church calling upon them to reject false teachers and to remain fast in the doctrine of Christ.

3 JOHN

This short letter is addressed to a Christian individual named Gaius. John commended Gaius for his humble service to Christian travelers and church members. He warned him about the false teaching and practice of Diotrephes, who refused to show hospitality to Christian travelers.

JUDE

The general epistle of Jude is a plea to Christians to remain constant in faith and life. It points to the penalties of immorality and closes with a benediction reminding that Christ can keep the believer from yielding to the temptations of life. Jude, a half brother of Jesus, wrote the epistle about AD 80. He sought to warn against false teachers who were immoral and greedy.

REVELATION

Revelation, like Daniel in the Old Testament, is an apocalyptic writing, using symbolic language to discuss the hope of Christians in a time of persecution and to point them to God's ultimate victory. Bible students have developed many theories about how to interpret the book. Its basic purpose remains clear: To reveal Jesus Christ as the Lord who is triumphant over evil. The book was written by John in his old age while im-

prisoned on the island of Patmos about AD 95. The book brings comfort and hope to every generation of Christians in their suffering.

Important Bible Dates

David as king	ca. 1000
Temple begun	967
Israel, Judah split	931
Asa, King of Judah	911-870
Omri of Israel	885-874
Ahab of Israel	874-853
Jehoshaphat of Judah	873-848
Jehoram of Judah	853-841
Jehu of Israel	841-814
Amaziah of Judah	796-767
Jeroboam II of Israel	793-753
Uzziah of Judah	792-740
Pekah of Israel	752-732
Ahaz of Judah	735-716
Hoshea of Israel	732-722
End of Israel	722/721
Hezekiah	716-687
Manasseh	697-643
Josiah	641-609
Jehoiakim	609-598
First exiles to Babylon	598/597
Zedekiah	597-586
Jerusalem Destroyed	587/586
Cyrus of Persia	559-530
Return from Exile	538
Darius of Persia	522-486
Temple work begun	520
Temple Dedicated	515
Xerxes I	486-465
Nehemiah	445-432
Alexander defeats Persia at Issus	333
Maccabeans	175-63
Temple Rededicated	165
Herod the Great	37-4
Jesus' Ministry	ca. 30-33AD
Temple Destroyed	70AD

The Gospels Paralleled

Ministry of Jesus Events	Places	Matthew	Mark	Luke	John
Luke's Prologue				1:1-4	
Pre-existence and Genealogies		1:1-17		3:23-38	1:1-18
Birth of John the Baptist foretold	Jerusalem			1:5-23	
Annunciation to Mary	Nazareth			1:24-38	
Songs of Elizabeth and Mary	Judea			1:39-56	
Birth of John the Baptist	Judea			1:57-80	
Birth of Jesus	Bethlehem	1:18-25		2:1-21	
Presentation in the Temple at	Jerusalem			2:22-39	
Visit of the Magi	Bethlehem	2:1-12			
Flight into Egypt		2:13-23			
Childhood and youth	Nazareth	2:23		2:39-52	
First Passover he attended	Jerusalem			2:41-50	

SPECIAL PREPARATIONS

Ministry of John the Baptist	Wilderness of Judea	3:1-12	1:1-8	3:1-18	1:19-28
Baptism of Jesus	Jordan	3:13-17	1:9-11	3:21-22	1:29-34
Temptation of Jesus	Wilderness of Judea	4:1-11	1:12,13	4:1-13	

JUDEAN MINISTRY

First disciples won	Bethabara				1:35-51
First miracle: Wedding at Cana	Cana				2:1-12
First cleansing of the Temple	Jerusalem				2:13-25
First recorded discourse: Nicodemus	Jerusalem				3:1-21
First ministry in Judea begun	Judea				3:22-36
First converts in Samaria: Jacob's Well	Sychar				4:1-42
Healing of the nobleman's son	Capernaum				4:43-54

	MATTHEW	MARK	LUKE	JOHN
THE GREAT GALILEAN MINISTRY				
Passover				5:1
Imprisonment of John the Baptist	Macherus	14:3-5	6:17-18	3:19-20
Beginning of Great Galilean Ministry	Galilee	4:12	1:14, 15	4:14, 15
Rejection at Nazareth	Nazareth			4:16-30
Takes up residence at Capernaum	Capernaum	4:13-17		4:31
Calls first disciples to follow Him	Capernaum	4:18-22	1:16-20	5:1-11
Cure of demoniac in Synagogue	Capernaum		1:21-28	4:31-37
Many miracles of healing	Capernaum Galilee	4:23-25 8:14-17	1:29-39	4:38-44
Cure of a leper	Galilee	8:1-4	1:40-45	5:12-16
Healing a paralytic	Capernaum	9:1-8	2:1-12	5:17-26
Call of Matthew; His feast	Capernaum	9:9-17	2:13-22	5:27-39
Healing at Pool of Bethsaida	Jerusalem			5:2-47
Man with withered hand	Capernaum	12:1-14	2:23-3:6	6:1-11
Christ Heals Multitudes		12:15-21	3:7-12	6:17-19
Appointing of the twelve Apostles	Horns of Hattin	10:1-4	3:13-19	6:12-16
The Sermon on the Mount	Horns of Hattin	Chs. 5-7		6:20-49
Healing of the Centurion's servant	Capernaum	8:5-13		7:1-10
Raising of the widow's son	Nain			7:11-17
John the Baptist sends messengers to Jesus	Galilee	11:2-19		7:18-35
Warnings and Invitations		11:20-30		
Anointing of Jesus by the penitent woman				7:36-50
Another tour of Galilee	Galilee			8:1-3
Demon Controversy	Capernaum	12:22-45	3:20-30	11:14-36
Visit of his mother and brethren	Capernaum	12:46-50	3:31-35	8:19-21
Eight parables by the seaside	Capernaum	13:1-53	4:1-34	8:4-18
Stilling of the tempest	Sea of Galilee	8:18-27	4:35-41	8:22-25
Restoration of the demoniac	Gergesa	8:28-34	5:1-20	8:26-39
Jairus' daughter raised; Woman cured	Capernaum	9:18-26	5:21-43	8:40-56
Cure of two blind and one dumb	Capernaum	9:27-34		

	MATTHEW	MARK	LUKE	JOHN
GREAT DEEDS AMID GREAT OPPOSITION				
Rejection at Nazareth	Nazareth 13:54-58	6:1-6	(4:16-30)	
The twelve sent out to preach	Galilee 9:35-11:1	6:6-13	9:1-6	
Death of John the Baptist	Macherus 14:1-12	6:14-29	9:7-9	
Feeding of the 5000	Bethsaida 14:13-21	6:30-46	9:10-17	6:1-15
Jesus walks on the water	Sea of Galilee 14:22-33	6:47-52		6:16-21
Heals many sick	Gennesaret 14:34-36	6:53-56		
Discourse on the Bread of Life	Capernaum			6:22-71
Eating with unwashed hands	Capernaum 15:1-20	7:1-23		
Heals daughter of Syrophenician woman	Phoenicia 15:21-28	7:24-30		
Miracles of healing in Decapolis	Decapolis 15:29-31	7:31-37		
Feeding the 4000	Decapolis 15:32-39	8:1-10		
Demand for a sign from heaven	Capernaum 16:1-12	8:11-21		
Blind man healed	Bethsaida	8:22-26		
Peter's great confession of faith	Near Caesarea-Philippi 16:13-20	8:27-30	9:18-21	
Jesus for the first time foretells his death	Near Caesarea-Philippi 16:21-28	8:31-9:1	9:22-27	
The Transfiguration	Near Caesarea-Philippi 17:1-13	9:2-13	9:28-36	
Healing of the demoniac boy	Near Caesarea-Philippi 17:14-21	9:14-29	9:37-43	
Jesus again foretells his death	Galilee 17:22,23	9:30-32	9:43-45	
Temple Tax	17:24-27			
Jesus and the children	Capernaum 18:1-14	9:33-50	9:46-50	
Unmerciful servant	Capernaum 18:15-35			
YEAR OF DEVELOPMENT				
At the Feast of Tabernacles	Jerusalem			7:1 to 10:21
The Water of Life	Jerusalem			7:37-39
Officers sent to arrest him	Jerusalem			7:44-53
Discourse on light and freedom	Jerusalem			8:12-59
Healing of man born blind	Jerusalem			9:1-41
The Good Shepherd	Jerusalem			10:1-21
Returns to Galilee; final departure	19:1	10:1	9:51	

	MATTHEW	MARK	LUKE	JOHN
Repulsed by the Samaritans	Samaria		9:51-62	
The mission of the Seventy	Perea		10:1-24	
Parable of the Good Samaritan	Perea		10:25-37	
Discourse on prayer	Perea		11:1-13	
Answers attack of Pharisees	Perea		11:14-54	
The Rich Fool; the Watchful Servant	Perea		12:1-59	
Discourses: Galileans slain by Pilate; Healing on Sabbath; Parables of mustard seed and leaven; the narrow door; lament over Jerusalem			13:1-35	
Jesus the guest of Mary and Martha	Bethany		10:38-42	
Feast of Dedication; Discourses	Jerusalem			10:22-39

CULMINATION OF MIRACLES AND TEACHING

	MATTHEW	MARK	LUKE	JOHN
Jesus retires beyond Jordan	Perea			10:40-42
Dines with a Pharisee	Perea		14:1-14	
Parable of the Great Supper	Perea		14:15-24	
Counting the cost of discipleship	Perea		14:25-35	
Parables of lost sheep and lost coin	Perea		15:1-10	
Parable of prodigal son	Perea		15:11-32	
Parable of the unjust steward	Perea		16:1-13	
Parable of the rich man and Lazarus	Perea		16:14-31	
Teachings on forgiveness	Perea		17:1-10	
Raising of Lazarus	Bethany			11:1-46
Retreat to Ephraim	Ephraim			11:47-57
The healing of the ten lepers	Samaria		17:11-19	
On the coming of the kingdom	Perea		17:20-37	
Parable of the importunate widow	Perea		18:1-8	
Parable of the Pharisee and publican	Perea		18:9-14	
Discourse about divorce	Perea	19:2-12	10:2-12	
Christ blesses little children	Perea	19:13-15	10:13-16	18:15-17
The rich young man	Perea	19:16-30	10:17-31	18:18-30
The laborers in the vineyard	Perea	20:1-16		
Jesus again predicts his death	Perea	20:17-19	10:32-34	18:31-34

		MATTHEW	MARK	LUKE	JOHN
Ambitious request of					
James and John	Perea	20:20-28	10:35-45		
Healing two blind men					
(one being Bartimeus)	Jericho	20:29-34	10:46-52	18:35-43	
Visit to Zaccheus the					
publican	Jericho			19:1-10	
Parable of the minas	Jericho			19:11-28	

THE LAST WEEK—MARCH 31 TO APRIL 7

Jesus arrives at Bethany	Bethany				12:1
Anointing by Mary	Bethany	26:6-13	14:3-9		12:2-11
Triumphal Entry; Visit					
to Temple; Return					
to Bethany	Jerusalem	21:1-11	11:1-11	19:29-44	12:12-19
Cursing of barren	Mt. of				
fig tree	Olives	21:18-19	11:12-14		
Cleansing of the Temple				19:45-48	
and return to Bethany	Jerusalem	21:12-17	11:15-19	21:37, 38	

THE LAST DAY OF PUBLIC TEACHING

The fig tree withered;	Mt. of				
Lesson on faith	Olives	21:20-22	11:20-26		
Christ's authority					
challenged	The Temple	21:23-27	11:27-33	20:1-8	
Three parables of					
warning:					
The Two Sons	The Temple	21:28-32			
The Wicked					
Vine-growers	The Temple	21:33-46	12:1-12	20:9-19	
Marriage of the king's					
son	The Temple	22:1-14			
Three Questions by					
Jewish rulers	The Temple	22:15-40	12:13-34	20:20-40	
Christ's unanswerable					
question	The Temple	22:41-46	12:35-37	20:41-44	
Woes against Scribes					
and Pharisees	The Temple	23:1-36	12:38-40	20:45-47	
Lamentation over					
Jerusalem	The Temple	23:37-39			
The Widow's two coins	The Temple		12:41-44	21:1-4	
Greeks seeking Jesus	The Temple				12:20-36
Prophecy of the end of	Mt. of				
the age	Olives	24:1-51	13:1-37	21:5-36	
Parable of the ten	Mt. of				
virgins	Olives	25:1-13			
Parable of the talents	Mt. of				
	Olives	25:14-30			
The last judgment	Mt. of				
	Olives	25:31-46			
Conspiracy between the		26:1-5	14:1, 2	22:1-6	12:36b-50
rulers and Judas	Jerusalem	26:14-16	14:10-11		

THE LAST DAY WITH HIS DISCIPLES

Preparation for the Passover	Jerusalem	26:17-20	14:12-17	22:7-14	
Strife for precedence	Jerusalem			22:24-30	

		MATTHEW	MARK	LUKE	JOHN
Jesus washes the disciples' feet	Jerusalem				13:1-20
The last supper	Jerusalem			22:15-18	
Jesus declares the betrayer; Judas goes out	Jerusalem	26:21-25	14:18-21	22:21-23	13:21-35
Institution of the Lord's Supper	Jerusalem	26:26-30	14:22-25	22:19, 20	1 Cor. 11
Jesus foretells the fall of Peter	Jerusalem			22:31-38	13:36-38
Christ's farewell Discourses	Jerusalem				Chs. 14-16
Prayer of Jesus for the disciples	Jerusalem				17:1-26
Jesus goes forth; Peter's confidence	Jerusalem	26:30-35	14:26-31	22:39	18:1-3
The Agony in the Garden of Gethsemane	Mt. of Olives	26:36-46	14:32-42	22:40-46	

THE LAST DAY

		MATTHEW	MARK	LUKE	JOHN
Betrayal by Judas		26:47-50	14:43-45	22:47, 48	18:4-9
The arrest		26:50-56	14:46-52	22:49-53	18:10-12

THE JEWISH TRIAL

		MATTHEW	MARK	LUKE	JOHN
The trial before Annas	Jerusalem				18:13-15
Before Caiaphas	Jerusalem	26:57, 58	14:53,54	22:54, 55	18:19-24
Before the Sanhedrin	Jerusalem	26:59-66	14:55-64		
Denials by Peter	Jerusalem	26:69-75	14:66-72	22:56-62	18:15-27
Mockery by enemies	Jerusalem	26:67, 68	14:65	22:63-65	
Legal meeting of Sanhedrin; Jesus condemned for blasphemy	Jerusalem	27:1, 2	15:1	22:66-71	
Death of Judas	Jerusalem	27:3-10		Acts 1:18, 19	

THE ROMAN TRIAL

		MATTHEW	MARK	LUKE	JOHN
Jesus before Pilate	Jerusalem	27:11-14	15:2-5	23:1-5	18:28-38
Jesus sent to Herod	Jerusalem			23:6-12	
Pilate seeks to release Jesus; people demand Barabbas	Jerusalem	27:15-23	15:6-14	23:13-23	18:38-40
Jesus condemned, scourged and mocked	Jerusalem	27:26-30	15:15-19	23:24, 25	19:1-3
Other attempts by Pilate to release Jesus	Jerusalem	27:24, 25			19:4-16

THE CRUCIFIXION

		MATTHEW	MARK	LUKE	JOHN
Jesus led away to be crucified	Jerusalem	27:31-38	15:20-28	23:26-32	19:16-18
The superscription	Jerusalem	27:37	15:26	23:38	19:19-22
First word from the cross: *"Father forgive them"*	Jerusalem			23:33, 34	

		MATTHEW	MARK	LUKE	JOHN
Soldiers cast lots for garments	Jerusalem	27:35, 36	15:24	23:34	19:23,24
Jews mock at Jesus on the cross	Jerusalem	27:39-44	15:29-32	23:35-37	
Second word from the cross: to the penitent thief	Jerusalem			23:39-43	
Third word: "Woman behold your son"	Jerusalem				19:25-27
Darkness covers the land	Jerusalem	27:45	15:33	23:44, 45	
Fourth word: Cry of distress to God	Jerusalem	27:46, 47	15:34,35		
Fifth word: "I am thirsty"	Jerusalem	27:48, 49	15:36		19:28, 29
Sixth word: "It is finished"	Jerusalem				19:30
Seventh word: "Into thy hands"	Jerusalem			23:46	
Jesus dies; Veil rent; Earthquake	Jerusalem	27:50-56	15:37-41	23:45-49	19:30
Jesus is pierced in the side	Jerusalem				19:31-37
The burial	Jerusalem	27:57-61	15:42-47	23:50-56	19:38-42

THREE DAYS IN THE TOMB

		MATTHEW	MARK	LUKE	JOHN
The watch at the tomb	Jerusalem	27:62-66			

RESURRECTION APPEARANCES

		MATTHEW	MARK	LUKE	JOHN
The morning of the resurrection	Jerusalem	28:2-4			
Women come to the tomb	Jerusalem	28:1	16:1-4	24:1, 2	20:1
Mary Magdalene calls Peter and John	Jerusalem				20:2
The women at the tomb	Jerusalem	28:5-8	16:5-8	24:3-8	
Peter and John at the tomb	Jerusalem			24:12	20:3-10
Jesus appears to Mary Magdalene	Jerusalem		16:9-11		20:11-18
Jesus appears to the women	Jerusalem	28:9,10		24:9-11	
The guards report to the priests	Jerusalem	28:11-15			
The walk to Emmaus	Emmaus		16:12,13	24:13-35	
Jesus appears to Peter	Jerusalem	1 Cor. 15:5		24:34	
Jesus appears to the Apostles except Thomas	Jerusalem	1 Cor. 15:5	16:14	24:36-48	20:19-23

		MATTHEW	MARK	LUKE	JOHN
Jesus appears to all the Apostles including Thomas	Jerusalem				20:24-29
Jesus appears to seven in Galilee	Sea of Galilee				21:1-23
Appears to over 500 at once	Sea of Galilee	28:16-20	16:15-18		1 Cor. 15:6
Jesus appears to James	Sea of Galilee				1 Cor. 15:7
Jesus appears to the Apostles	Jerusalem			24:49	Acts 1:1-18
Jesus ascends to heaven	Bethany Mt. of Olives		16:19	24:50-53	Acts 1:9-12
The conclusions of Mark and John			16:20		20:30, 31 21:24, 25

BIRTH OF THE CHURCH

Holy Spirit given at Pentecost	Jerusalem			Acts 2:1-11	
Jesus appears to Paul	Damascus			Acts 22:6-16	
Jesus appears to John	Patmos				Rev. 1:9-20

Where to Find Help

Where to Find Help

In this section of *Disciple Youth Bible,* you will find Scripture references to help you find answers to searching questions in the area of basic beliefs, special concerns, and life planning. When you have a problem or need, locate the section of related Scriptures and use the references and statements as a guide for study. For an in-depth approach to the study, follow suggestions in "How to Study the Bible," pages 16a-18a. Memorize verses that have been especially helpful to you, following the plan described in "How to Memorize Scripture," pages 18a-22a.

Basic Beliefs

Bible

The Bible is God's inspired Word.	2 Timothy 3:16-17, *page 1183*
God spoke directly to his prophets.	Exodus 24:12, *page 82*
The Holy Spirit inspired the people who wrote the Bible.	2 Peter 1:20-21, *page 1206*
The Bible records God's revelation of Himself.	Hebrews 1:1-2, *page 1186*
The authority of the Bible is seen in Jesus.	Colossians 1:15, *page 1169*
	Matthew 5:17, *page 956*
All Scripture is a witness to Jesus.	Luke 24:44, *page 1049*
	John 5:39-40, *page 1056*
The Bible is given to help us believe.	John 20:31, *page 1077*
The Bible tells us how to live.	Joshua 1:8, *pages 222-23*
	Psalm 19:7, *page 555*
Our faith grows through Bible study.	Romans 10:17, *page 1126*
Jesus taught from the Old Testament.	Luke 4:16-21, *page 1017*
God's Word is central for the church.	Colossians 3:16, *page 1171*

God

God always has been and always will be.	Genesis 1:1, *page 1*
	Psalm 90:2, *page 601*
	Isaiah 57:15, *page 737*
God created the world.	Genesis 1:1, *page 1*
	Proverbs 3:19, *page 638*
	John 1:3, *page 1050*
	Colossians 1:16-17, *page 1169*
	Hebrews 1:2, *page 1186*
We can count on God never to change.	Deuteronomy 7:9, *page 191*
	1 Corinthians 1:9, *page 1132*
	James 1:17, *page 1198*
God is always present everywhere.	Psalm 139:7-12, *pages 630-31*
	Matthew 28:20*b*
God is near His people.	Psalm 145:18, *page 634*
God is greater than all we can imagine.	Romans 11:33-36, *page 1127*
God knows everything.	Matthew 6:8, *page 958*
God demands first place.	Deuteronomy 5:7-10, *page 189*
God is holy.	Isaiah 6:1-5, *page 686*
	Leviticus 11:44, *page 114*
	Psalm 29:2, *page 561*
God is the source of truth.	John 17:17, *page 1073*
	John 14:6, *page 1069*
God is love.	1 John 4:7-11, *page 1211*
God is Trinity; the Father has revealed Himself through Jesus the Son and continues to reveal Himself to people through the Holy Spirit; three in one.	1 Corinthians 8:6, *page 1137*
	John 8:26, *page 1061*
	John 14:26, *page 1070*
	Matthew 28:19, *page 988*
Loving God is loving people.	1 John 4:20, *page 1211*

Jesus

Jesus Christ always existed as God.	John 1:1-2, *page 1050*
Jesus came to earth as God the Son.	John 1:14-18, *page 1050*
	Colossians 2:9, *page 1170*
	Philippians 2:6-8, *page 1166*
Jesus came to earth as God's Word to a sinful world.	John 1:1, *page 1050*
	2 Corinthians 5:19, *page 1149*
Jesus made God visible.	Colossians 1:15, *page 1169*
	John 14:9, *pages 1069-70*
Jesus came as the Messiah, the Promised One.	Matthew 16:13-16, *page 971*
Jesus' birth was a human birth.	Luke 2:7, *page 1014*
Jesus grew physically, mentally, socially, and spiritually.	Luke 2:52, *page 1015*
Though human, Jesus did not sin.	Hebrews 4:15, *page 1189*
Jesus taught Christians how to live.	Matthew 5:1-12, *page 956*
Jesus cared about people.	John 4:46-54, *page 1055*
	Matthew 9:22-25, *page 961*
Jesus called disciples and instructed them to carry on His work.	Matthew 4:18-22, *page 956*
	Matthew 28:18-20, *page 988*
Jesus chose to do God's will.	Luke 22:39-44, *pages 1045-46*
	John 15:10, *page 1071*
Jesus died for the sins of humanity.	John 10:11, *page 1064*
	Hebrews 9:26-28, *pages 1192-93*
Jesus was raised from the dead.	1 Corinthians 15:3-4, *page 1143*
	Mark 16:6, *page 1010*
Jesus lives within believers.	John 15:4, *page 1070*
Jesus will come to earth again.	John 14:3, *page 1069*
	Matthew 16:27, *page 971*

Holy Spirit

God the Holy Spirit took part in the creation of the world.	Genesis 1:2, *page 1*
The Holy Spirit was present at Jesus' baptism.	Matthew 3:16, *page 955*
The Holy Spirit is with us.	John 14:16-17,26, *page 1070*
	John 16:7-15, *pages 1071-72*
The Holy Spirit . . .	
comforts	John 14:16-18, 26, *page 1070*
testifies	John 15:26, *page 1071*
convicts	John 16:8, *page 1071*
guides	John 16:13, *page 1071*
helps	Acts 1:8, *page 1079*
grieves	Ephesians 4:30, *page 1163*
The Holy Spirit is God . . .	
present everywhere	Psalm 139:7-8, *pages 630-31*
all-knowing	1 Corinthians 2:10, *page 1133*
all-powerful	1 Corinthians 12:11, *page 1141*
The Holy Spirit does God's work.	John 3:5; 16:8, *pages 1052 and 1071*
	Romans 8:11, *page 1123*

The Holy Spirit gives personal power to
witness.   Acts 1:8, *page 1079*
The Holy Spirit gives boldness in witness-
ing..   Acts 4:8-13, *pages 1082-83*
The Holy Spirit is our divine Counselor.   John 14:1 to 16:33, *pages 1069-72*
The Holy Spirit takes up permanent resi-
dence within us.   Ephesians 1:13, *page 1160*
The Holy Spirit is our teacher.   John 14:26, *page 1070*
The Holy Spirit is our instructor to com-
plete the training Christ began.   John 16:12-15, *pages 1071-72*
The Holy Spirit within the believer bears
fruit.   Galatians 5:22, *page 1159*
The Holy Spirit guarantees our salvation.   Ephesians 1:13-14, *page 1160*

Humanity
God created people in his image.   Genesis 1:26-27, *page 1*
                                                  Genesis 9:6, *page 8*
God made human beings responsible care-   Genesis 1:28-29, *pages 1-2*
takers of his creation.   Psalm 8:5-8, *page 549*
                                                  Hebrews 2:7, *page 1187*
Adam and Eve disobeyed God.   Genesis 3:1-24, *pages 3-4*
A person is spirit, soul, and body.   1 Thessalonians 5:23, *page 1175*
                                                  Genesis 2:7, *page 2*
All people have sinned.   Romans 3:23, *page 1119*
                                                  Romans 7:14-17, *page 1123*
God created humans male and female.   Mark 10:6, *page 1001*
                                                  Genesis 1:27, *page 1*

Church
Christ loved the church.   Ephesians 5:25, *page 1164*
Christ is the foundation of the church.   1 Corinthians 3:11, *page 1133*
The church has a mission.   Matthew 28:18-20, *page 988*
                                                  Ephesians 3:10-11, *page 1162*
                                                  1 Peter 2:4-10, *pages 1202-3*
The church is a fellowship, a community of
God's people.   Hebrews 10:25, *page 1193*
The church gathers to worship, learn, and
pray.   Acts 2:42, *page 1081*
The church gives evidence of God's love.   John 13:35, *page 1069*
The local church is a democratic body . . .
    selecting deacons   Acts 6:1-6, *page 1085*
    administering the ordinances   Acts 2:41-42, *page 1081*
    approving evangelistic work   Acts 11:1-18, *page 1093*
    sending missionaries   Acts 13:1 to 14:28, *pages 1095-98*
    administering church discipline   1 Corinthians 5:1-7, *page 1135*

Sin
Sin is disobeying God.   1 John 3:4, *page 1210*
Sin entered the world through Adam: grace
and life came through Christ.   Romans 5:12-17, *page 1121*
Sin brings death.   Ephesians 2:1-7, *page 1161*
                                                  Romans 6:23, *page 1122*

Through Christ's death, we have opportunity for new life.	2 Corinthians 5:21, *page 1149*
We must confess our sin, repent, and trust Christ to forgive us.	Matthew 10:32, *page 963*
	Acts 16:31, *page 1100*
	Romans 10:9-11, *page 1126*
	1 John 1:9, *page 1208*
	1 John 4:15, *page 1211*

Salvation

Salvation is an event and a process that makes us whole spiritually.	Romans 1:16, *page 1117*
	Philippians 2:12, *page 1166*
	Titus 2:11, *page 1184*
Salvation is God's gift.	John 3:16, *page 1053*
	Ephesians 2:8-10, *page 1161*
Salvation begins when a person repents and professes faith in Christ.	Romans 10:9-10, *page 1126*
The believer becomes a new creation.	2 Corinthians 5:17 *page 1149*
The Holy Spirit within helps the individual develop and grow.	Colossians 1:8-10, *page 1169*
	2 Peter 3:18, *page 1208*
We can know we are saved.	1 John 5:9-10, *page 1211*
The saved are to serve.	Romans 14:16-18, *page 1129*
	Ephesians 2:10, *page 1161*

Second Coming

Jesus will return.	Matthew 16:27, *page 971*
	John 5:25-29; 14:2, *pages 1056 and 1069*
Jesus warned against false signs of his return.	Matthew 24:4-7; 23:31, *pages 980-81*
We prepare for His return by living according to Christ's teachings.	Titus 2:11-13, *page 1184*
The Christian can look forward to Jesus' second coming.	Hebrews 9:28, *page 1193*
At the end the saved will be with God in heaven, and the lost will be with the devil in hell.	Revelation 20:10; 22:5, *pages 1230-31*

Special Concerns

Anger

Sometimes, there are just causes for our anger.	Mark 10:14, *page 1001*
	John 2:13-17, *page 1052*
	Ephesians 4:26, *page 1163*
At times, Jesus was angry.	Mark 3:5, *page 991*
Try not to become angry.	Colossians 3:8, *page 1171*
	Psalm 37:8, *page 556*
	James 1:19-20, *page 1198*
Don't look for things to make you angry.	Ecclesiastes 7:9, *page 670*
	Proverbs 14:17, 29, *page 648*
Work through anger.	Ephesians 4:26-27, *page 1163*
You can express your anger to God in prayer.	Psalm 137, *page 630*
	Psalm 28, *pages 560-561*

Authority

People questioned Jesus' authority. — Matthew 21:23-27, *page 976*

Near the end of His life Jesus declared His authority. — Matthew 28:18, *page 988*

Jesus taught with authority. — Mark 1:22-27, *page 989*

God is our highest authority. — Acts 5:29, *page 1085*

Respect civil authorities. — Romans 13:1-7, *page 1128*
1 Peter 2:13-17, *page 1203*

Pray for leaders. — 1 Timothy 2:1-2, *page 1178*

Death and Eternal Life

God intends for us to live fully. — John 8:51, *page 1062*
John 10:10, *page 1064*

We live eternally through faith in Christ. — John 3:15, *page 1053*

Living abundantly involves giving oneself in service. — Romans 12:1-2, *pages 1127-28*

Faithfulness to God will be rewarded. — Revelation 2:10b, *page 1216*
2 Timothy 4:7-8, *page 1183*

A Christian can face death courageously. — John 14:1-3, *page 1069*
Deuteronomy 31:6, *page 216*

God comforts us in pain and sorrow. — Psalm 91:1-4, *page 602*

Because Jesus overcame death, Christians have eternal life. — 1 Corinthians 15:20-22, *page 1144*
2 Corinthians 5:1-5, *page 1148*

Future life with God gives us hope. — Revelation 21:1-4, *page 1230*

Comfort is assured for those who mourn. — Psalm 34:18a, *page 564*
Matthew 5:4, *page 956*

Disappointment

Jesus doesn't want us to be troubled. — John 14:1, *page 1069*

God gives us help in times of trouble. — Psalm 40:1-3, *page 569*
Psalm 34:17-19, *page 564*

Things will get better. — 2 Corinthians 4:17, *page 1148*

Troubles make us more dependent on God. — 2 Corinthians 12:7-10, *pages 1153-54*

God walks with us, no matter what the circumstances we face. — Psalm 23:1-6, *page 558*

God gives us peace. — Isaiah 26:3, *page 703*
John 14:27, *page 1070*

God works for our good as we trust in Him. — Romans 8:28, *page 1124*

Persevere, in spite of disappointment. — 2 Timothy 3:14-15, *page 1183*

Ecology

God created a good world and put humanity in charge of His creation. — Genesis 1:1-31, *page 1*

We are caretakers of the land. — Genesis 2:4-9, *page 2*
Exodus 23:10-11, *pages 80-81*
Leviticus 25:1-5, *pages 130-31*

God has provided for the needs of every creature He created. — Psalm 104:1-35, *pages 609-10*

We need to recognize and accept our responsibility for the earth. — Genesis 1:26-28, *page 1*

Family

God's ways are to be taught in the family.

Deuteronomy 6:4-7, *page 190*
Proverbs 4:1-4, *page 639*

Parents' teachings are implanted in their children.

Proverbs 22:6, *page 656*

Parents should teach children God's Word.

2 Timothy 3:15, *page 1183*

Fellow Christians can be like family.

Mark 3:31-35, *page 992*

We have instructions for family relationships.

Ephesians 6:1-4, *page 1164*
Colossians 3:18-21, *page 1171*

Respect parents.

Exodus 20:12, *pages 77-78*
Ephesians 6:1-3, *page 1164*

Parents should discipline children.

Proverbs 13:24, *page 648*

Family loyalty is cherished.

Ruth 1:16-18, *page 277*

Children take care of aging parents.

Proverbs 23:22, *page 657*

Forgiveness

We can worship God more effectively when we are at peace with other people.

Matthew 5:23-24, *page 957*

God forgives us as we forgive other people.

Matthew 6:14-15, *page 958*
Matthew 18:21-3, *page 973*

There should be no limit to our forgiveness.

Luke 17:3-4, *page 1038*

Cultivate a kind, forgiving spirit.

Ephesians 4:31-32, *page 1163*

God faithfully forgives us.

1 John 1:9, *page 1208*

We need to accept God's forgiveness.

Isaiah 1:18, *page 681*

Honesty

Honesty involves more than telling the truth.

Isaiah 33:15-16, *page 711*
Matthew 23:25-28, *page 979*
Hebrews 13:18, *page 1197*

Promote honesty.

2 Corinthians 8:21, *page 1151*
1 Corinthians 13:6, *page 1142*

Do honest acts.

2 Corinthians 13:7, *page 1154*

Think honest thoughts.

Philippians 4:8, *page 1168*
Psalm 51:6, *page 576*

Tell the truth.

1 Peter 2:12, *page 1203*
Proverbs 12:17, 19, 22, *page 647*
John 8:31-32, 44, *pages 1061-62*
Ephesians 4:25, *page 1163*

Serve God sincerely.

Joshua 24:14, *page 248*
1 Samuel 12:24, *page 291*
Romans 12:1-2, *pages 1127-28*

Truth endures.

Psalm 117:2, *page 618*

Jesus guides us to truth.

John 14:6, *page 1069*
John 16:13, *page 1071*

Illness

Paul told how he was strengthened through physical affliction.

2 Corinthians 12:7-10, *pages 1153-54*

Christians pray for persons who are sick.

James 5:14-15, *page 1201*

God will stand by those who have helped others.

Psalm 41:1-3, *page 570*

God will answer our prayers for healing according to His will.

Matthew 8:1-3, *page 959*

Justice

All people are worthy and should be treated fairly.

James 2:1-13, *pages 1198-99*
Proverbs 24:23, *pages 658-59*
Zechariah 7:9-10, *page 940*
Psalm 82:3, *page 596*

God expects His people to work for justice.

Amos 5:12, 24, *page 913*
Micah 6:8, *page 924*

Judgment of evil is necessary.

Deuteronomy 25:1-4, *page 209*
Ezra 7:26, *page 484*
Amos 5:15, *page 913*

Do not judge people by their appearance.

John 7:24, *page 1059*
James 2:1-4, *pages 1198-1199*

God praises a just person.

Ezekiel 18:5-9, *page 839*
2 Samuel 8:15, *page 323*

Loneliness

God is with us in our loneliness.
God will remain with us.

Psalm 4:8, *page 547*
Isaiah 54:10, *page 735*
John 14:18, *page 1070*

Pray to God for help.
At times, being alone brings rest and peace.
Nothing can separate us from God's love.

Psalm 25:16-21, *page 559*
Mark 6:30-32, *page 996*
Romans 8:37-39, *page 1124*

Peace

The Holy Spirit gives peace.
Seek peace.

Galatians 5:22, *page 1159*
Psalm 34:14, *page 564*
Hebrews 12:14, *page 1196*
1 Peter 3:11, *page 1204*
Romans 14:19, *page 1129*
1 Thessalonians 5:13, *page 1175*

The prophets said the Messiah would bring justice and peace.
The Messiah is the Prince of Peace.
Jesus blessed peacemakers.
God's enemies oppose peace.
Return good for evil.

Isaiah 2:4, *page 682*
Micah 4:3-4, *pages 922-23*
Isaiah 9:6, *page 688*
Matthew 5:9, *page 956*
Psalm 120:7, *page 625*
Matthew 5:39-41, *page 957*
Romans 12:18-21, *page 1128*

Jesus came to guide us to peace.

Luke 1:79, *page 1014*
John 16:33, *page 1072*

Those who take up arms must pay the consequences.
Live in peace.
Peace is the goal for God's world.

Matthew 26:52, *page 984*
Romans 12:18, *page 1128*
Psalm 72:7, *page 588*
Isaiah 32:17, *page 710*

Relationships

Patience and forgiveness are essential in building relationships.
Colossians 3:12-13, *page 1171*

Jealousy hurts the one who is jealous.
Proverbs 6:34, *pages 641-42*
James 3:14-16, *page 1200*

Be willing to admit fault.
James 5:16, *page 1201*

Self-esteem helps a person love others.
Mark 12:31, *page 1005*

Every person has value in God's sight.
Romans 12:3-5, *page 1128*

A friend continues to be loving.
Proverbs 17:17, *page 652*

Don't try to impress other people.
Philippians 2:3-4, *page 1166*

People are known by the company they keep.
Proverbs 13:20, *page 648*

Friends help each other.
Proverbs 27:10, *page 661*

Paul described the characteristics of love.
1 Corinthians 13:1-13, *page 1142*

Loving other people is one way of loving God.
1 John 4:9-21, *page 1211*

Self-esteem

You are created in God's image.
Genesis 1:26-27, *page 1*

You are God's highest creation.
Psalm 8:3-8, *page 549*

You have a special combination of gifts and abilities.
1 Corinthians 12:4-11, *page 1141*

God made you and cares about you.
Psalm 139:13-18, *page 631*

You can grow and develop.
2 Peter 1:5-6, *page 1206*

Christ is present in a Christian's life.
Romans 12:1-2, *pages 1127-28*
Galatians 2:20, *page 1156*

Give yourself in service as Christ did.
Philippians 2:5-8, *page 1166*

Temptation

Be careful not to give in to temptation.
Matthew 26:41, *page 984*
Luke 22:40, *page 1045*

Pray that you will not be tempted.
Luke 11:4, *page 1029*

Do not tempt others to do wrong.
Romans 14:13-15,21, *page 1129*

God gives Christians the strength to withstand temptations.
1 Corinthians 10:13,28-32, *page 1139*
James 1:2-4,12-16, *page 1198*

Jesus was tempted, and he understands.
Hebrews 4:15, *page 1189*

Jesus taught against adultery and lust.
Matthew 5:27-28, *page 957*

Paul instructed Christians to be pure.
1 Corinthians 6:9-20, *pages 1135-36*

Homosexuality was condemned in the Bible.
Leviticus 18:22, *page 123*
Leviticus 20:13, *page 125*
Romans 1:22-32, *page 1117*

Avoid the appearance of evil.
1 Corinthians 10:23-33, *page 1139*
1 Thessalonians 5:22, *page 1175*

Don't eat or drink anything that harms your body or ability to think.
Leviticus 10:8-10, *page 112*
Ephesians 5:18, *page 1163*
Numbers 6:2-3, *page 143*
Proverbs 23:29-35, *pages 657-58*

Worry

Trusting in God brings peace of mind.
Isaiah 26:3-4, *page 703*
Philippians 4:6-8, *page 1168*

Don't worry about the future.
Matthew 6:34, *page 958*
Luke 12:22-28, *page 1032*

Be thankful for what you have.	Philippians 4:11-13, *page 1168*
	1 Timothy 6:6-8, *page 1180*
God knows you and will take care of you.	Matthew 10:26-31, *page 963*
	Psalm 112:7-8, *page 617*
	Hebrews 13:6, *page 1197*
	1 Peter 5:7, *page 1205*
God gives strength and courage.	Isaiah 41:10, *page 719*
	Psalm 32:7, *page 563*
	Romans 8:31-32, *page 1124*

Life Planning

Calling

All Christians are called to share the gospel.	Acts 1:8, *page 1079*
	1 Peter 2:9, *page 1203*
God guides our lives.	Psalm 16:7-8, *pages 552-53*
	Psalm 25:8-10, *page 559*
Obey God's will.	James 1:22-25, *page 1198*
	Hebrews 11:8, *page 1194*
You are chosen.	1 Peter 2:9-10, *page 1203*
	John 15:16, *page 1071*
Christians of all races are called to serve God.	
	Colossians 3:11-12, *page 1171*

Career

Some people are called to church-related careers.	Romans 1:1, *page 1117*
We should work where we feel God has called us.	1 Corinthians 7:20-24, *pages 1136-37*
There are different kinds of church-related careers.	1 Corinthians 12:28-30, *page 1141*
	Ephesians 4:11-12, *page 1162*
Behave in keeping with your calling.	Ephesians 4:1-3, *page 1162*
	1 Thessalonians 2:10-12, *page 1173*
	2 Thessalonians 1:11, *page 1175*

Gifts

People have different gifts for doing God's work.	1 Corinthians 12:4-10, *page 1141*
	Ephesians 4:11-12, *page 1162*
Use your gifts in ministry.	1 Peter 4:10-11, *page 1204*
Give yourself and your gifts to God in service.	Romans 12:1-2, *pages 1127-28*

God's Will

Give yourself to God.	Romans 12:1-2, *pages 1127-28*
God will bless you and faithfully keep you.	1 Thessalonians 5:23-24, *page 1175*
Seek God's leadership in your life.	Isaiah 2:3, *page 682*
	Proverbs 3:6, *page 638*
As we obey God's law, we live according to His will.	
	Micah 6:8, *page 924*

Though sometimes things do not happen like we want them to, God works things together for our good.

Romans 8:28-30, *page 1124*

In times of trouble, God gives us strength and peace.

Psalm 46:1, *page 573*
Isaiah 2:3-4, *page 682*

God provides what we need.

Matthew 6:25-34, *page 958*
Luke 12:22-31, *page 1032*

Marriage

God made men and women companions.

Genesis 2:18-24, *page 2*

God reserved full sexual expression for marriage.

Exodus 20:14, *page 78*
1 Corinthians 7:3-5, *page 1136*

God intended children for married couples.

Jeremiah 29:6, *page 782*

Though divorce is not what God intended, the Bible recognizes some reasons for divorce.

Matthew 19:3-12, *pages 973-74*
1 Corinthians 7:10-11,15-16, *page 1136*
Deuteronomy 24:1-4, *page 208*

Widows and widowers may marry again.

Romans 7:1-3, *page 1122*

Some people should not marry.

1 Corinthians 7:6-9, *page 1136*
1 Corinthians 7:32-38, *page 1137*

Paul encouraged parents to stay married.

1 Corinthians 7:12-14, *page 1136*

Husband and wives should love each other as Christ loved the church.

Ephesians 5:21-22, 25-28, *pages 1163-64*

Inner beauty is desired.

1 Peter 3:1-7, *page 1203*

Money Management

Give God a tithe (tenth) of your income.

Leviticus 27:30-32, *page 135*
Proverbs 3:9-10, *page 638*
Malachi 3:8-10, *page 948*
Matthew 23:23, *page 979*

Give regularly as God prospers you.

1 Corinthians 16:1-2, *page 1145*

God expects us to be faithful stewards (caretakers) of what He has given us.

Luke 16:10, *page 1037*
1 Corinthians 4:1-2, *page 1134*

Love of money gets us into trouble.

1 Timothy 6:6-10, *page 1180*

Material things are not as important as faith in God.

Luke 12:16-21, *page 1031*
2 Corinthians 8:7-9, 13-15, *pages 1150-51*
Ecclesiastes 5:10, *page 669*
Proverbs 3:5-6, *page 638*
2 Corinthians 9:6-11, *page 1151*

God likes for His people to give cheerfully and blesses the cheerful giver.

God will supply our needs.

Philippians 4:12-13,19, *page 1168*

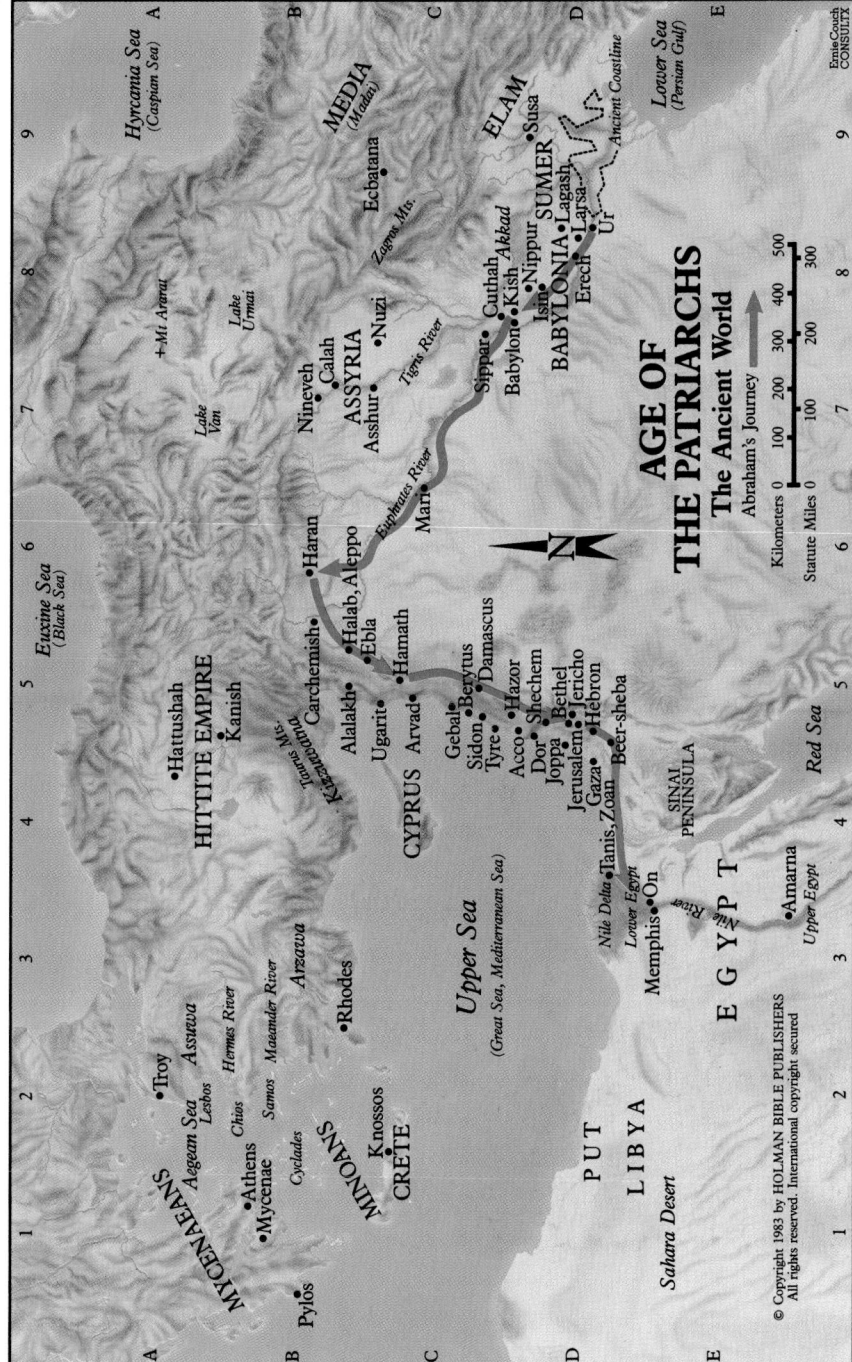

AGE OF
THE PATRIARCHS
The Ancient World

Abraham's Journey

Kilometers 0   100   200   300   400   500
Statute Miles 0   100   200   300

Ernie Couch
CONSULIX

A **B** **C** **D** **E**

Hyrcania Sea
(Caspian Sea)

MEDIA
(Madai)

ELAM

Lower Sea
(Persian Gulf)

Ancient Coastline

Susa
Ecbatana

Zagros Mts.

SUMER
Cuthah Akkad Nippur Lagash
Sippar Kish Isin Erech
Babylon Ur
BABYLONIA Larsa

+Mt Ararat

Lake Urmai

Lake Van

Nineveh
Calah
ASSYRIA
Asshur Nuzi

Tigris River

Euphrates River

Euxine Sea
(Black Sea)

Haran
Mari

HITTITE EMPIRE

Hattushah
Kanish

Taurus Mts.

Kizzuwatna

Carchemish
Halab, Aleppo
Ebla
Hamath
Alalakh
Ugarit
Arvad

CYPRUS

Gebal
Berytus
Sidon Damascus
Tyre Hazor
Acco Shechem
Dor Bethel
Joppa Jericho
Jerusalem Hebron
Gaza Beer-sheba

Troy
Assuwa
Lesbos
Aegean Sea
Hermes River
Chios
Samos Maeander River
Arzawa
Rhodes

MYCENAEANS
Athens
Mycenae
Cyclades
Pylos
Knossos
MINOANS
CRETE

Upper Sea
(Great Sea, Mediterranean Sea)

SINAI
PENINSULA

Red Sea

Nile Delta
Tanis, Zoan
Lower Egypt
Memphis On

EGYPT

Amarna
Upper Egypt

Nile River

PUT
LIBYA
Sahara Desert

N

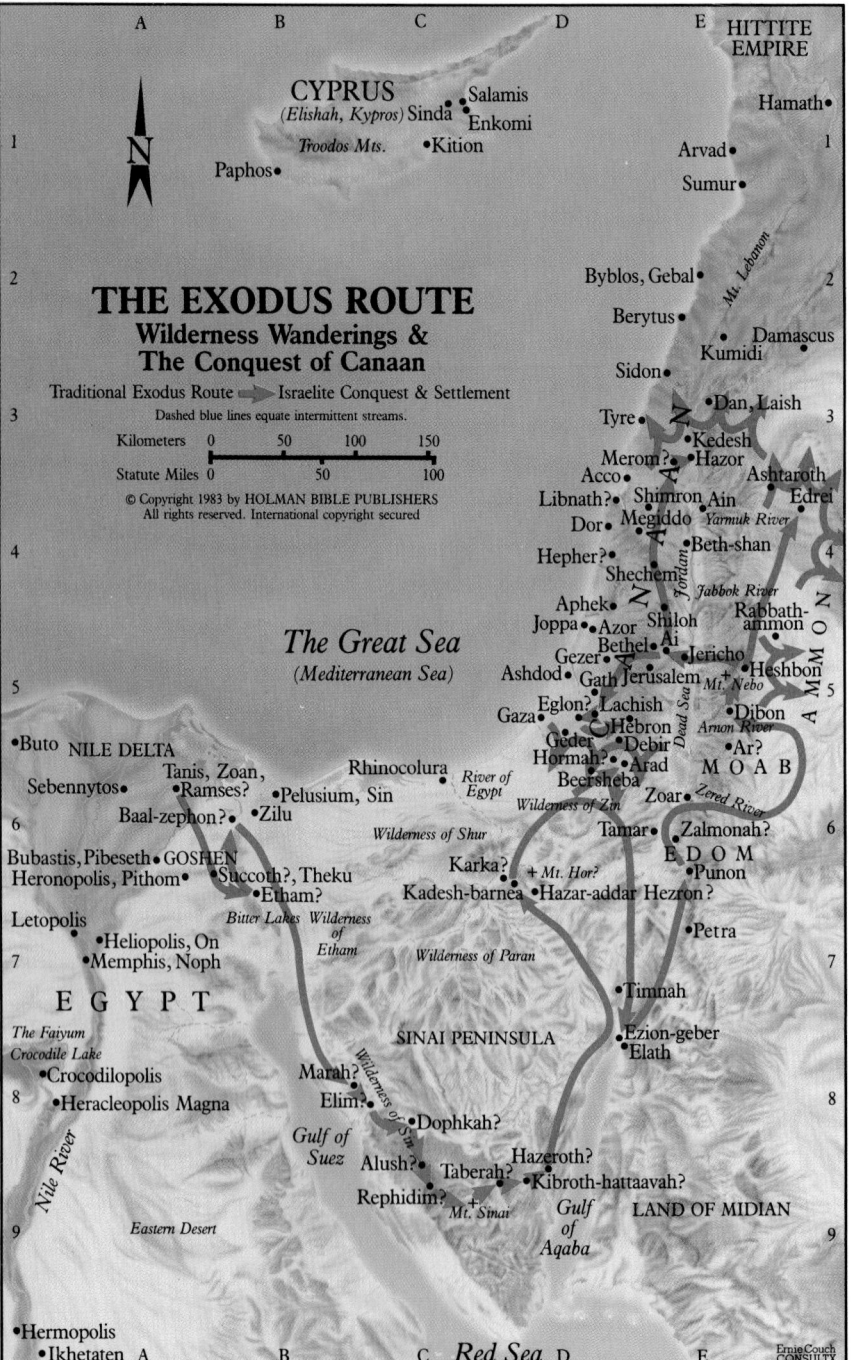

THE EXODUS ROUTE
Wilderness Wanderings &
The Conquest of Canaan

Traditional Exodus Route ➡ Israelite Conquest & Settlement

Dashed blue lines equate intermittent streams.

Kilometers 0   50   100   150

Statute Miles 0   50   100

© Copyright 1983 by HOLMAN BIBLE PUBLISHERS
All rights reserved. International copyright secured

Map grid labels: A B C D E (top and bottom); 1 2 3 4 5 6 7 8 9 (sides)

HITTITE EMPIRE

CYPRUS
(Elishah, Kypros) Sinda
Troodos Mts.
Paphos•
Salamis•
•Enkomi
•Kition

Hamath•
Arvad•
Sumur•

Byblos, Gebal•
Berytus•
Sidon•
Tyre•
Damascus•
Kumidi•
Mt. Lebanon
•Dan, Laish
•Kedesh
Merom?• •Hazor
Acco• Ashtaroth
Libnath?• Shimron Ain Edrei
Dor• Megiddo Yarmuk River
•Beth-shan
Hepher?•
Shechem•
Aphek•
Joppa • •Azor Shiloh
Bethel •Ai Rabbath-ammon
Gezer• •Jericho
Ashdod• Gath Jerusalem Mt. Nebo Heshbon
Eglon?•Lachish •Dibon
Gaza• Arnon River
Geder Hebron Debir •Ar?
Hormah?• •Arad M O A B
Beersheba Zoar•
Zered River

THE EXODUS ROUTE

The Great Sea
(Mediterranean Sea)

AMMON

Kedesh

Jordan River
Jabbok River

Dead Sea

Tamar• Zalmonah?•
E D O M
•Punon
Karka?•
+ Mt. Hor?
Kadesh-barnea •Hazar-addar Hezron?
•Petra
Wilderness of Shur
Wilderness of Zin
Wilderness of Paran

•Buto NILE DELTA
Rhinocolura•
River of Egypt
Sebennytos•
Tanis, Zoan,
•Ramses?
•Pelusium, Sin
Baal-zephon?• •Zilu
Bubastis, Pibeseth• GOSHEN
Heronopolis, Pithom•
Succoth?, Theku
•Etham?
Bitter Lakes Wilderness of Etham
Letopolis•
•Heliopolis, On
•Memphis, Noph

E G Y P T

The Faiyum
Crocodile Lake
•Crocodilopolis
•Heracleopolis Magna

Marah?•
Wilderness of Sin
Elim?•
•Dophkah?
Gulf of Suez
Alush? •Taberah?
Rephidim?•
+ Mt. Sinai

Hazeroth?•
•Kibroth-hattaavah?

SINAI PENINSULA

•Timnah
•Ezion-geber
•Elath

Gulf of Aqaba

LAND OF MIDIAN

Nile River
Eastern Desert

•Hermopolis
•Ikhetaten

Red Sea

ErnieCouch
CONSULTX

THE TWELVE TRIBES IN CANAAN
c. 1200 - 1020 B.C.
The Twelve Tribes (DAN)
The Empire of David and Solomon
c. 1000 - 925 B.C.
Extent of Empire ▪▪▪▪▪▪

Dashed blue lines equate intermittent streams.

Kilometers 0   10   20   30   40
Statute Miles 0   10   20   30

N

The Great Sea
(Mediterranean Sea)

Sidon
SIDONIANS
Mt. Lebanon
Leontes River
Mt. Hermon
PHOENICIA
Tyre
DAN
Dan (Laish)
Kedesh
Merom?
ASHER
NAPHTALI
Hazor
Acco
Chinnereth
Mt. Carmel
Sea of Chinnereth
Yarmuk River
Libnath? Achshaph?
Shimron
ZEBULUN
Ain?
Jokneam
Mt. Tabor
Dor
Ophrah?
Megiddo
ISSACHAR
Taanach + Mt. Gilboa Beth-shean
Gina
Pehel
Migdal?
Dothan
MANASSEH
Hepher?
Jordan River
MANASSEH
Tirzah
Succoth
Jabbok River
Shechem
GAD
Gath-rimmon? Aphek
Tappuah
Adam
Jogbehah
Joppa
Azor
Shiloh
EPHRAIM
Jazer?
Bethel
AMMON
Gibeon Ai
Gilgal
Heshbon
DAN
Chephirah Jericho
Pisgah
Gezer
BENJAMIN Beth-jeshimoth
Mt. Nebo
Timnah
Jerusalem,
Jebus
PHILISTINES
Ashdod
Beth-shemesh
Medeba
Gath
Bethlehem
REUBEN
Ashkelon
Zippor
Adullam
Kedemoth?
Libnah? Gedor
Wilderness of Judah
Ataroth
Lachish
JUDAH
Dibon
Gaza
Eglon?
Hebron
Salt Sea
(Dead Sea)
Aroer
Sharuhen?
Arnon River
Deir el-Balah
En-gedi
Ziklag?
Yurza?
Gerar
Anab
Debir
Ar?
Raphia
MOAB
Ader
Beer-sheba Hormah? Arad
SIMEON
River of Egypt
W. al' Arish
Zoar
Zered River
Wilderness of Zin
EDOM

Ernie Couch
CONSULTX

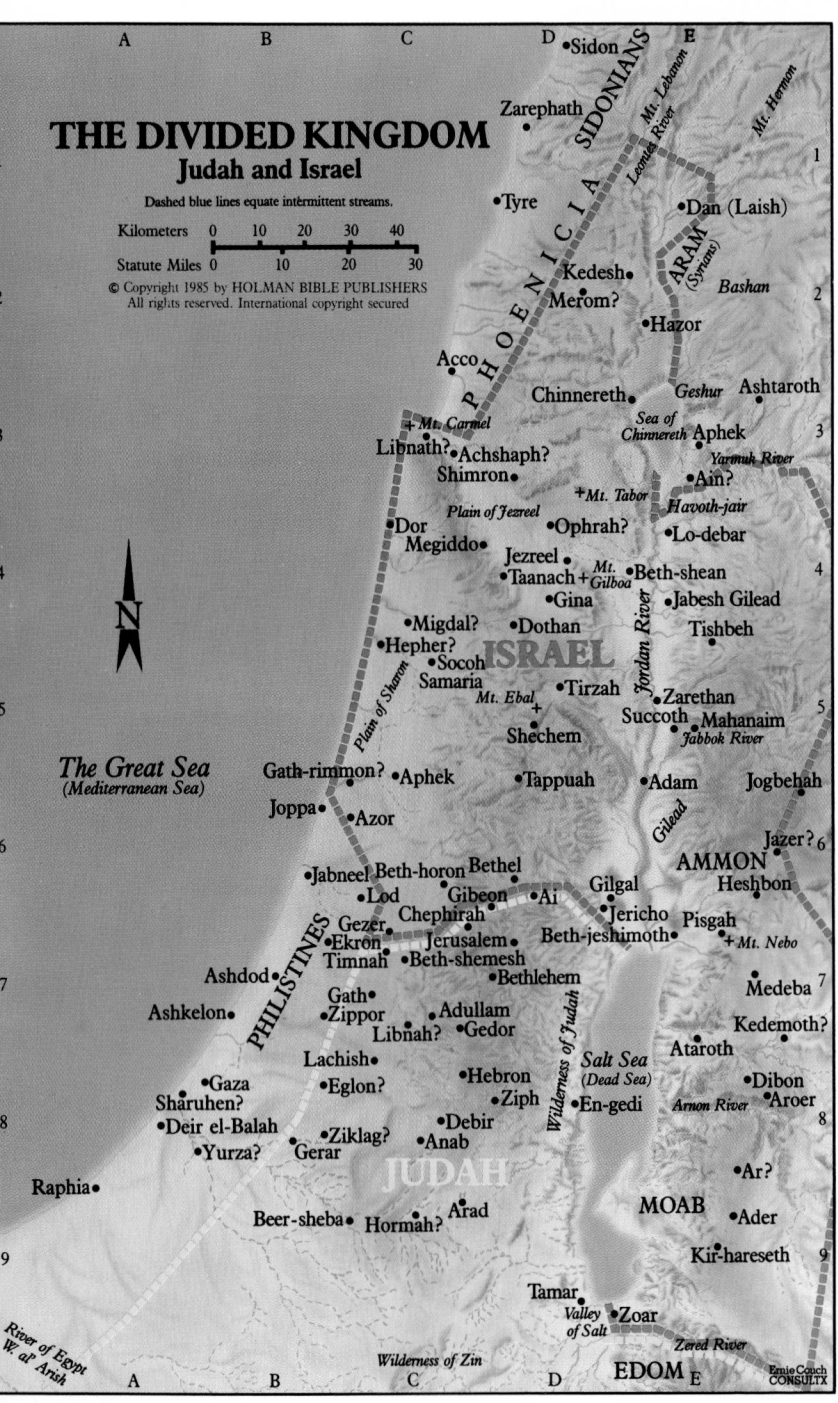

THE DIVIDED KINGDOM
Judah and Israel

Dashed blue lines equate intermittent streams.

Kilometers 0 10 20 30 40

Statute Miles 0 10 20 30

© Copyright 1985 by HOLMAN BIBLE PUBLISHERS
All rights reserved. International copyright secured

Sidon

SIDONIANS

Zarephath

Mt. Lebanon

Leontes River

Mt. Hermon

Tyre

Dan (Laish)

Kedesh

ARAM (Syrians)

Merom?

Bashan

Hazor

Acco

PHOENICIA

Chinnereth

Geshur

Ashtaroth

Mt. Carmel

Sea of Chinnereth

Aphek

Libnath?

Achshaph?

Yarmuk River

Shimron

Ain?

Plain of Jezreel

Mt. Tabor

Havoth-jair

Dor

Ophrah?

Lo-debar

Megiddo

Jezreel

Mt. Gilboa

Beth-shean

Taanach

Gina

Jabesh Gilead

Dothan

Tishbeh

Migdal?

Jordan River

Hepher?

ISRAEL

Socoh

Samaria

Tirzah

Zarethan

Mt. Ebal

Succoth

Mahanaim

Shechem

Jabbok River

Plain of Sharon

Gath-rimmon?

Aphek

Tappuah

Adam

Jogbehah

Joppa

Azor

Gilead

Jazer?

Jabneel

Beth-horon

Bethel

AMMON

Lod

Gibeon

Ai

Gilgal

Heshbon

Chephirah

Jericho

Pisgah

Gezer

Jerusalem

Beth-jeshimoth

Ekron

Mt. Nebo

Timnah

Beth-shemesh

Ashdod

Bethlehem

Medeba

PHILISTINES

Gath

Ashkelon

Zippor

Adullam

Kedemoth?

Libnah?

Gedor

Lachish

Hebron

Ataroth

Gaza

Eglon

Ziph

Salt Sea (Dead Sea)

Dibon

Sharuhen?

Debir

En-gedi

Aroer

Deir el-Balah

Anab

Arnon River

Ziklag?

Yurza?

Gerar

JUDAH

Ar?

Raphia

Beer-sheba

Hormah?

Arad

MOAB

Ader

Kir-hareseth

The Great Sea
(Mediterranean Sea)

N

Tamar

Valley of Salt

Zoar

Wilderness of Judah

Zered River

River of Egypt
W. at Arish

Wilderness of Zin

EDOM

Ernie Couch
CONSULTX

PALESTINE IN THE TIME OF JESUS

Dashed blue lines equate intermittent streams.

Kilometers 0   10   20   30   40
Statute Miles 0   10   20   30

© Copyright 1983 by HOLMAN BIBLE PUBLISHERS
All rights reserved. International copyright secured

N

SYRIA

ABILENE

PHOENICIA
Mt. Lebanon
Leontes River
Mt. Hermon

•Sidon

•Tyre

Caesarea Philippi

Cadasa•

•Ecdippa   •Thella
          Sepph• •Jamnith
Ptolemais,   •Sogane
Acco•   GALILEE   •Chorazin
          Gennesaret •Bethsaida?
          • •Capernaum
Cana• Magdala Sea of   •Gergesa
          Galilee   Yarmuk River
Sepphoris• Tiberias Hippus• •Abila
          Ammathus
          •Nazareth •Philoteria
          Japhia•   •Gadara
                •Nain

•Dora

Capercotnei,
Kefar Otnay   Scythopolis•   •Pella
Caesarea•   •Narbata   DECAPOLIS
Strato's Tower   Ginae•
                              •Agrippina?
          SAMARIA •Aenon?   Gerasa•
          •Samaria   •Ragaba
          •Sychar Amathus• Jabbok River
          Shechem

The Great Sea
(Mediterranean Sea)

Apollonia•
          •Antipatris Acrabeta• •Coreae
Joppa•   •Tower of Aphek •Alexandrium •Zia
          Gerasa• Phasaelis• •Gadora
Adida•   •Thamna Archelais• PEREA
Lydda,• Lod   Gophna• •Ephraim •Philadelphia
          •Sappho Rama• •Neara •Bethennabris
Jamnia• Emmaus,•Gabaon •Jericho Abila, Abel
          Nicopolis Mt. of Olives •Livias, Julias,
          Emmaus,•   Beth-ramatha
          Jerusalem•† •Qumran
          Ramat Rahel• Bethany• Essene community
Bethletepha• Bethlehem• Hyrcania•   •Medeba
          JUDEA   •Herodium
•Ascalon   Baaras•
          •Betogabris Tekoa• •Machaerus
Beror Hayil• •Belzedek?   Callirrhoe•
•Antheldon   •Dibon
•Gaza   •Adora Hebron•
          En-gedi• Arnon River

•Raphia   IDUMEA   Masada•
          •Arad   Areopolis•
Beer-sheba•   NABATAEANS
          Malatha En Boqeq•
          Charachmoba•

•Elusa

•Zoar

Zered River

ErnieCouch
CONSULTX

Lake Asphaltitis
(Dead Sea, Salt Sea)

Jordan River

Plain of Sharon

THE MINISTRY OF JESUS

Early Period

Kilometers 0 5 10 15
Statute Miles 0 5 10

Galilean Tours

Kilometers 0 5 10 15
Statute Miles 0 5 10

Later Journeys

Dashed blue lines equate intermittent streams.

Kilometers 0 10 20 30 40
Statute Miles 0 5 10 15 20 25

Ernie Couch
CONSULTX

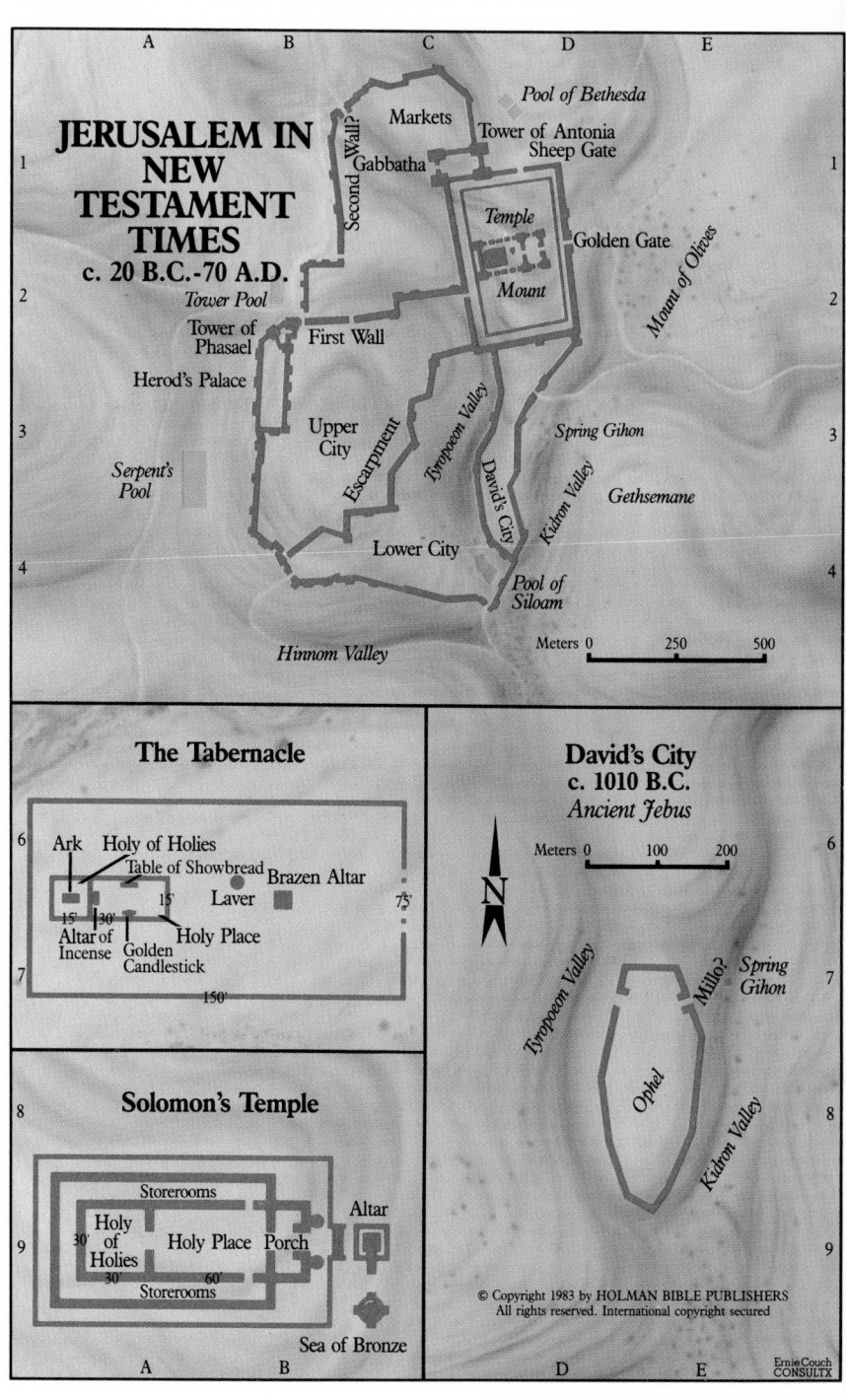

JERUSALEM IN NEW TESTAMENT TIMES
c. 20 B.C.-70 A.D.

Pool of Bethesda
Markets
Second Wall?
Gabbatha
Tower of Antonia
Sheep Gate
Temple
Mount
Golden Gate
Mount of Olives
Tower Pool
Tower of Phasael
First Wall
Herod's Palace
Upper City
Escarpment
Tyropoeon Valley
David's City
Spring Gihon
Kidron Valley
Gethsemane
Serpent's Pool
Lower City
Pool of Siloam
Hinnom Valley

Meters 0   250   500

The Tabernacle

Ark
Holy of Holies
Table of Showbread
Brazen Altar
Laver
75'
15'   30'   15'
Altar of Incense
Golden Candlestick
Holy Place
150'

Solomon's Temple

Storerooms
Holy of Holies
Holy Place
Porch
Altar
30'   30'
60'
Storerooms
Sea of Bronze

David's City
c. 1010 B.C.
Ancient Jebus

Meters 0   100   200

N

Tyropoeon Valley
Millo?
Spring Gihon
Ophel
Kidron Valley

© Copyright 1983 by HOLMAN BIBLE PUBLISHERS
All rights reserved. International copyright secured

Ernie Couch
CONSULTX

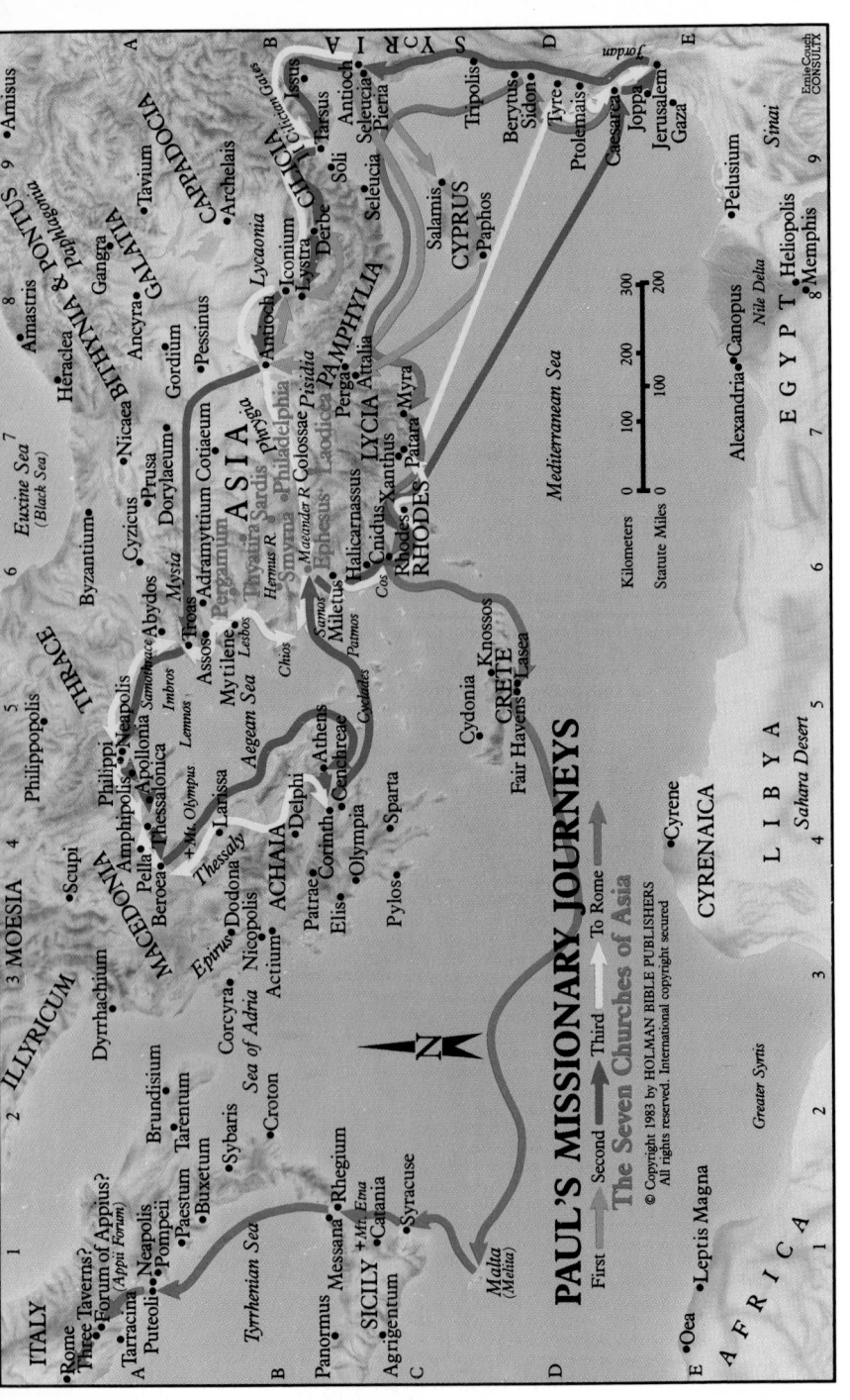

PAUL'S MISSIONARY JOURNEYS

First — Second — Third — To Rome
The Seven Churches of Asia

© Copyright 1983 by HOLMAN BIBLE PUBLISHERS
All rights reserved. International copyright secured

Kilometers 0 100 200 300
Statute Miles 0 100 200

Mediterranean Sea